Rotary

This dictionary is presented to:

Adela Leighem Riv

with compliments of the

Rotary Club of
Dodge City

www.rotary5680.org

The Four Way Test is a Code of Ethics of Rotarians
1. Is it the truth?
2. Is it fair to all concerned?
3. Will it build goodwill and better friendships?
4. Will it be beneficial to all concerned?

www.usadictionaryproject.org

SCHOLASTIC

Children's
Dictionary

SCHOLASTIC

Children's
Dictionary

SCHOLASTIC

Dictionary Staff

LEXICOGRAPHY TEAM
Chief Lexicographer: Orin Hargraves
Managing Editor and Pronunciation Adviser: Constance Baboukis
Etymologist: Martha Mayou
Editor and Contributing Writer: Johanna Baboukis
Editors: Daniel Barron, Victoria Neufeldt, Marina Padakis, Deborah M. Posner, Katherine C. Sietsema, Sue Ellen Thompson, Katy M. Isaacs
Assistant Editors: Carl Burnett, Tyler Cassidy-Heacock, Rebecca Shapiro, Jane Solomon

Editor in Chief: Donnali Fifield
Consulting Editors: Jane Sunderland, Amy C. Shields, Jacob Field, Ph.D.
Research Coordinator: Betty J. Sun
Copyeditors: Helen Mules, Erica Rose
Contributing Writers: Chrissa Banner, Will Hector

Designer/Art Director: Carol Farrar Norton
Production Designer: Al Morrow
Picture Manager: Christine Vincent
Picture Researchers: Susannah Jayes, Sharon Southren

SPECIAL THANKS TO
Ellen Dupont, Toucan Books
Agnès Tabah, Esq.
Mapping Specialists, Inc.
Stephen Perkins, Jason Bush, Allan Orsnes, IDM USA, LLC

PRODUCED BY POTOMAC GLOBAL MEDIA, LLC
Kevin Mulroy, Publisher

Photo and illustration credits appear on pages 878-879

Library of Congress Cataloging-in-Publication Data

Title: Scholastic children's dictionary. Description: New York, NY : Scholastic Inc., [2019] |

Audience: Ages 8-12. Identifiers: LCCN 2018040909 | ISBN 9781338230062 (paper over board hardcover: alk. paper)

Subjects: LCSH: English language—Dictionaries, Juvenile. Classification: LCC PE1628.5 .S3 2019 |

DDC 423—dc23 LC record available at https://catalog.loc.gov/vwebv/search?searchCode=LCCN&searchArg=2018040909&searchType=1&permalink=y

10 9 8 7 6 5 4 3   21 22 23 24 25

Printed in China   38

First edition, September 2019

Advisory Board

GENERAL CONSULTANT
Joe A. Hairston, Ph.D., Superintendent, Baltimore County Public Schools

LANGUAGE ARTS ADVISER
Susan B. Neuman, Ed.D., Professor in Educational Studies, School of Education, University of Michigan

SCIENCE ADVISER
Brian Greene, Ph.D., Professor of Physics and Mathematics, Columbia University

MATHEMATICS ADVISER
Maria Hernandez, M.S., teaches mathematics at the North Carolina School of Science and Mathematics and has helped develop a high school math curriculum. She also leads teacher workshops that focus on real-world applications of math and the use of technology in the classroom.

TECHNOLOGY ADVISER
Grace Aquino, B.A., is a technology columnist who writes for *Bloomberg News*, *Wired*, *Popular Science*, *PC World*, and *Laptop*.

TEACHER ADVISERS
Dana Darby Johnson, B.A., is a language arts teacher and lexicographer in Santa Fe, New Mexico, who has taught elementary, middle, and high school English and Spanish.

Susan Lipman, B.S., M.E., is a reading and special education specialist who has taught elementary and middle school English in independent and public schools in Montgomery County, Maryland.

Adriane Collett, B.A., is an elementary school teacher in Chatham, New Jersey. In collaboration with her third-grade class, she tested and contributed to word banks for the *Oxford American Writer's Thesaurus*.

LIBRARY ADVISERS
Susan Viola, B.A., M.S.L.S., specializes in children's literature and school library media. She has worked as a literature consultant for the Discovery Channel and for Addison-Wesley Longman.

Karen Stern, M.L.I.S., is a librarian and lexicographer in the Boston area with special training in children's literature and media collections, young adult literature, and digital information services.

Kristi Jemtegaard is the youth services coordinator for the Arlington Public Library in Virginia. She teaches children's and adolescent literature and has served on both the Caldecott and the Newbery committees.

BOOKSELLER ADVISERS
Terri Schmitz, The Children's Bookshop, Brookline, Massachusetts

Dara LaPorte, Politics & Prose Bookstore, Washington, DC

Sara Yu, Bank Street Bookstore, New York, New York

Contents

Overview

A dictionary is a reference book that gives all kinds of information about words. This dictionary is your guidebook to the English language. You can refer to it to find out what a word means, check its spelling or pronunciation, or figure out how to use it in a sentence. Synonym boxes suggest similar words to help you add variety to your writing and your speech. On the next three pages, we've highlighted some of the other features of this book.

"About this letter" boxes appear on the opening page of each new letter. In each one, you will find a fact about that letter or a spelling tip for words containing that letter's sound.

Tabs help you quickly locate the section of the alphabet that you are looking for.

Entries are listed in alphabetical order. Many words have several different meanings and uses that are listed under different numbers within the entry. Some entries have illustrations or photographs.

Language tips appear throughout this dictionary. Word History boxes describe the interesting origins of the words highlighted in the boxes. Prefix, Suffix, Synonym, and Language Note boxes give you extra information about the usage of a word or word part.

Main entry words are set in red type and jut out from the meanings. The dictionary was designed this way to make it easy for you to find the words you look up.

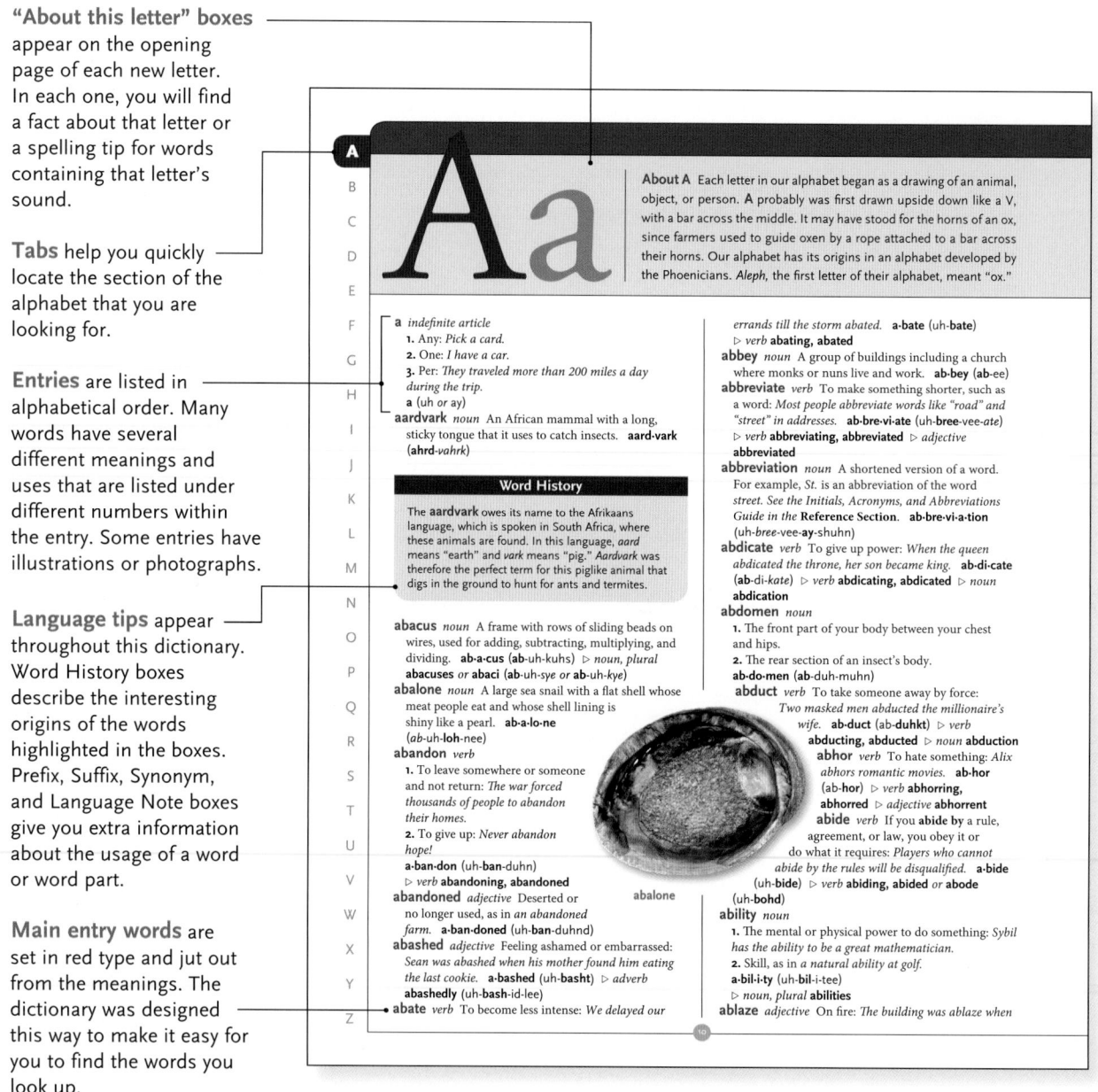

About A Each letter in our alphabet began as a drawing of an animal, object, or person. A probably was first drawn upside down like a V, with a bar across the middle. It may have stood for the horns of an ox, since farmers used to guide oxen by a rope attached to a bar across their horns. Our alphabet has its origins in an alphabet developed by the Phoenicians. *Aleph,* the first letter of their alphabet, meant "ox."

a *indefinite article*
1. Any: *Pick a card.*
2. One: *I have a car.*
3. Per: *They traveled more than 200 miles a day during the trip.*
a (uh *or* ay)
aardvark *noun* An African mammal with a long, sticky tongue that it uses to catch insects. **aard·vark** (**ahrd**-*vahrk*)

Word History

The **aardvark** owes its name to the Afrikaans language, which is spoken in South Africa, where these animals are found. In this language, *aard* means "earth" and *vark* means "pig." *Aardvark* was therefore the perfect term for this piglike animal that digs in the ground to hunt for ants and termites.

abacus *noun* A frame with rows of sliding beads on wires, used for adding, subtracting, multiplying, and dividing. **ab·a·cus** (**ab**-uh-kuhs) ▷ *noun, plural* **abacuses** *or* **abaci** (**ab**-uh-sye *or* **ab**-uh-kye)
abalone *noun* A large sea snail with a flat shell whose meat people eat and whose shell lining is shiny like a pearl. **ab·a·lo·ne** (ab-uh-**loh**-nee)
abandon *verb*
1. To leave somewhere or someone and not return: *The war forced thousands of people to abandon their homes.*
2. To give up: *Never abandon hope!*
a·ban·don (uh-**ban**-duhn) ▷ *verb* **abandoning, abandoned**
abandoned *adjective* Deserted or no longer used, as in *an abandoned farm.* **a·ban·doned** (uh-**ban**-duhnd)
abashed *adjective* Feeling ashamed or embarrassed: *Sean was abashed when his mother found him eating the last cookie.* **a·bashed** (uh-**basht**) ▷ *adverb* **abashedly** (uh-**bash**-id-lee)
abate *verb* To become less intense: *We delayed our*

abalone

errands till the storm abated.* **a·bate** (uh-**bate**) ▷ *verb* **abating, abated**
abbey *noun* A group of buildings including a church where monks or nuns live and work. **ab·bey** (**ab**-ee)
abbreviate *verb* To make something shorter, such as a word: *Most people abbreviate words like "road" and "street" in addresses.* **ab·bre·vi·ate** (uh-**bree**-vee-ate) ▷ *verb* **abbreviating, abbreviated** ▷ *adjective* **abbreviated**
abbreviation *noun* A shortened version of a word. For example, *St.* is an abbreviation of the word *street. See the Initials, Acronyms, and Abbreviations Guide in the Reference Section.* **ab·bre·vi·a·tion** (uh-bree-vee-**ay**-shuhn)
abdicate *verb* To give up power: *When the queen abdicated the throne, her son became king.* **ab·di·cate** (**ab**-di-kate) ▷ *verb* **abdicating, abdicated** ▷ *noun* **abdication**
abdomen *noun*
1. The front part of your body between your chest and hips.
2. The rear section of an insect's body.
ab·do·men (**ab**-duh-muhn)
abduct *verb* To take someone away by force: *Two masked men abducted the millionaire's wife.* **ab·duct** (ab-**duhkt**) ▷ *verb* **abducting, abducted** ▷ *noun* **abduction**
abhor *verb* To hate something: *Alix abhors romantic movies.* **ab·hor** (ab-**hor**) ▷ *verb* **abhorring, abhorred** ▷ *adjective* **abhorrent**
abide *verb* If you **abide by** a rule, agreement, or law, you obey it or do what it requires: *Players who cannot abide by the rules will be disqualified.* **a·bide** (uh-**bide**) ▷ *verb* **abiding, abided** *or* **abode** (uh-**bohd**)
ability *noun*
1. The mental or physical power to do something: *Sybil has the ability to be a great mathematician.*
2. Skill, as in *a natural ability at golf.*
a·bil·i·ty (uh-**bil**-i-tee) ▷ *noun, plural* **abilities**
ablaze *adjective* On fire: *The building was ablaze when*

Dictionary Entries Close Up

Numbers appear at the beginning of each meaning when a word has more than one meaning. The most frequently used meanings generally appear first.

Pronunciations, given in parentheses, let you know how the entry words should sound. The Pronunciation Guide on page 9 explains which letters represent each sound. If the pronunciation of a word changes depending on its meaning, the appropriate pronunciation appears with the appropriate meaning.

Part of speech labels usually appear on the first lines of entries. However, if a word's part of speech changes from one meaning to the next, the part of speech label starts each new meaning. When a meaning shows the word as part of a common phrase, which is known as an idiom, no part of speech is given.

Usage labels tell you that a meaning of a word is informal or slang. Informal words are used in everyday speech but not usually in formal speech or in writing. Many slang terms or meanings are very popular only for a short period of time. Like informal words, they are not appropriate in formal writing such as term papers and essays.

satellite *noun*
1. A spacecraft that is sent into orbit around the earth, the moon, or another heavenly body.
2. A moon or other heavenly body that travels in an orbit around a larger heavenly body.
See **moon.**
sat·el·lite (**sat**-uh-*lite*)

attribute
1. (**at**-ruh-*byoot*) *noun* A quality or characteristic that belongs to or describes a person or thing: *Kindness is her greatest attribute.*
2. (uh-**trib**-yoot) *verb* When you **attribute** something to someone, you give him or her credit for it: *The author attributed her success to her ninth-grade English teacher.*
▷ *verb* **attributing, attributed**
at·trib·ute

rap
1. *verb* To hit something with a quick, sharp blow: *Bettina rapped on the window.* ▷ *noun* **rap**
2. *noun* A type of popular music in which the words are spoken rhythmically to a musical background. ▷ *noun* **rapper** ▷ *verb* **rap**
3. *verb* (*slang*) To talk: *The boys rapped for hours.*
rap (rap)
Rap sounds like **wrap.** ▷ *verb* **rapping, rapped**

Cross-references tell you where to turn in the dictionary for more information about the main entry word.

Definitions tell the meanings of words. When the main entry word is used within the definition, it is printed in **boldface**.

Sample sentences appear in italics after some of the meanings. These sentences illustrate how a word is used by showing it in context.

Syllable breaks are indicated by small dots. Entries made up of two separate words or two words and a hyphen are not broken into syllables. To find their syllable breaks, look up each part of the term separately. For example, to find the syllable breaks for *solar energy*, look up *solar* and *energy*.

Homophones, words that sound alike but have different spellings and meanings, are listed at or near the end of a definition.

Related words and word forms appear at the end of an entry or at the end of a meaning. This dictionary also lists irregular plural forms for noun entries, *-er* and *-est* forms for adjectives, and irregular, *-ing,* and *-ed* forms for verbs.

Illustrations and Special Features

Guide words tell you the first and last main entry words that appear on a page.

of something, such as a vehicle, room, or building. Abbreviated as **CAD**.

computer graphics *noun, plural* The pictures or images that can be made on a computer.

comrade *noun* A good friend or a colleague. **com·rade** (**kahm**-rad) ▷ *noun* **comradeship**

concave *adjective* Curved inward, like the inside of a bowl. **con·cave** (kahn-**kave** or kahng-**kave**)

conceal *verb* To hide something: *The stolen jewels were concealed in a secret drawer.* **con·ceal** (kuhn-**seel**) ▷ *verb* **concealing, concealed** ▷ *noun* **concealment**

concede *verb*
1. To admit something is true after denying it first.
2. To admit defeat in a competition or election.
3. To give something up: *The defeated kingdom was forced to concede some territory.*
con·cede (kuhn-**seed**)
▷ *verb* **conceding, conceded**

conceited *adjective* Overly proud of yourself and

what you can do. **con·ceit·ed** (kuhn-**see**-tid)
▷ *noun* **conceit**

conceive *verb*
1. To come up with an idea: *Lee conceived the plan of collecting newspapers for recycling.*
2. To become pregnant.
con·ceive (kuhn-**seev**)
▷ *verb* **conceiving, conceived**

concentrate *verb*
1. To give all of your thought and attention to something: *Beverly concentrated on learning her lines for the play.*
2. To come together in one place: *The insects concentrate in areas where they find the best nectar sources.*
3. To make a liquid thicker and stronger by removing water from it.
con·cen·trate (**kahn**-suhn-*trate*)
▷ *verb* **concentrating, concentrated** ▷ *noun* **concentrate** ▷ *noun* **concentration** ▷ *adjective* **concentrated**

Special features, in boxes with captions and labeled images, cover a topic in more depth.

Computers

A computer is a system of electronic components that work together to store, retrieve, and process data. The physical components are called hardware. The programs, or instructions telling the computer what to do, are known as software.

The first automatic computing engine was designed by an English mathematician, Charles Babbage, in the 1830s. Since then, computers have become much faster and smaller. The internet now connects millions of computers in a worldwide network.

Modern computers do far more than mathematical calculations. ...eir users to keep ...rol machinery, ...mation, and play ...computer graphics ...ple can draw ...gn objects, and create ... films and television.

tablet computer

laptop computer

touch pad

monitor

wireless mouse

desktop computer

keyboard

helmet

visor

earphones

camera

radio microphone

spacesuit controls

oxygen tank

underwear

astronaut

Labeled illustrations provide you with more details about the topics defined in main entries.

There are no strange symbols in this dictionary's pronunciation system. Instead, letters and letter combinations are used to stand for different sounds. To make our system as clear as possible, we have included more than one way to pronounce some sounds. These alternatives are indented, below. For example, the *ay* sound is given the pronunciation symbol (ay), as in **pay** or **rain**. Sometimes, when the word ends with a consonant followed by a silent *e*, the a-*consonant*-e spelling is used for the pronunciation, as in **made** or **ate**.

Pronunciations are not listed for some entries that consist of two or more words, such as **acid rain**, or words that are hyphenated, such as **mix-up**. The pronunciations for those words are found at the entries for the individual words. The pronunciations for **acid rain**, for example, appear at the entries for **acid** and **rain**, and the pronunciations for the words in **mix-up** are given at **mix** and **up**.

Many words contain two or more syllables. In most cases, those words have one syllable that receives a stronger stress than any other syllable. This accented syllable is marked in boldface letters, as in (**ak**-shuhn) for the word **action**. Some words also have a syllable with a lighter stress. This secondary, lighter-accented syllable is marked in italics, as in (**buht**-ur-*milk*) for **buttermilk**.

The symbol (uh) is used both for the accented vowel in the word **cup** (kuhp) and for many unaccented vowels in words, as in (uh-**bout**) for the word **about**. Here are the letters and letter combinations that stand for each sound in this dictionary.

Vowels

a	at, dash, hammer
ah	honor, father, drama, rock
ahr	art, dark, far
air	air, care
aw	autumn, caught, raw
ay	ail, rain, pay
	(a-*consonant*-e) made, ate
e	egg, men, insect
ee	each, beet, me
eer	ear, here, career
eye	item, iron
	(i-*consonant*-e) file, ripe
	(*consonant*-ye) rye, lie, my
i	it, still
oh	over, coat, foe, dough
	(o-*consonant*-e) code, stone
oi	oil, coin, toy
oo	pool, rude
oor	poor, tour, rural
or	orbit, corn, more
ou	ouch, house, cow
u	put, book
uh	sun, about, comma, camel, lesson, circus
ur	earn, dirt, worker, fur
yoo	music, few, beauty, cue

Consonants

b	bad, rabbit, sob
ch	chip, nature, ditch
d	dip, ladder, red
f	fun, offer, laugh
g	get, tiger, beg
h	ham, who
j	jam, giant, page, edge
k	keep, car, ache, sack
l	lap, salt, tell
m	man, common, lamb, condemn
n	now, annoy, ten, gnat, know
ng	hanger, wink, song
p	pan, upper, sip
r	rib, arrow, pour
s	set, castle, yes, pass
sh	ship, gracious, nation, rash
t	tub, battle, rat
th	thin, method, bath
TH	this, mother, bathe
v	van, over, hive
w	well, aware, whale, awhile
y	yell, canyon
z	zip, dazzle, has, those
zh	measure, occasion, azure

Aa

About A Each letter in our alphabet began as a drawing of an animal, object, or person. **A** probably was first drawn upside down like a V, with a bar across the middle. It may have stood for the horns of an ox, since farmers used to guide oxen by a rope attached to a bar across their horns. Our alphabet has its origins in an alphabet developed by the Phoenicians. *Aleph*, the first letter of their alphabet, meant "ox."

a *indefinite article*
1. Any: *Pick a card.*
2. One: *I have a car.*
3. Per: *They traveled more than 200 miles a day during the trip.*
a (uh *or* ay)

aardvark *noun* An African mammal with a long, sticky tongue that it uses to catch insects. **aard·vark** (**ahrd**-*vahrk*)

Word History

The **aardvark** owes its name to the Afrikaans language, which is spoken in South Africa, where these animals are found. In this language, *aard* means "earth" and *vark* means "pig." *Aardvark* was therefore the perfect term for this piglike animal that digs in the ground to hunt for ants and termites.

---

abacus *noun* A frame with rows of sliding beads on wires, used for adding, subtracting, multiplying, and dividing. **ab·a·cus** (**ab**-uh-kuhs) ▷ *noun, plural* **abacuses** *or* **abaci** (**ab**-uh-*sye or* **ab**-uh-*kye*)

abalone *noun* A large sea snail with a flat shell whose meat people eat and whose shell lining is shiny like a pearl. **ab·a·lo·ne** (*ab*-uh-**loh**-nee)

abandon *verb*
1. To leave somewhere or someone and not return: *The war forced thousands of people to abandon their homes.*
2. To give up: *Never abandon hope!*
a·ban·don (uh-**ban**-duhn)
▷ *verb* **abandoning, abandoned**

abandoned *adjective* Deserted or no longer used, as in *an abandoned farm.* **a·ban·doned** (uh-**ban**-duhnd)

abashed *adjective* Feeling ashamed or embarrassed: *Sean was abashed when his mother found him eating the last cookie.* **a·bashed** (uh-**basht**) ▷ *adverb* **abashedly** (uh-**bash**-id-lee)

abate *verb* To become less intense: *We delayed our errands till the storm abated.* **a·bate** (uh-**bate**)
▷ *verb* **abating, abated**

abbey *noun* A group of buildings including a church where monks or nuns live and work. **ab·bey** (**ab**-ee)

abbreviate *verb* To make something shorter, such as a word: *Most people abbreviate words like "road" and "street" in addresses.* **ab·bre·vi·ate** (uh-**bree**-vee-*ate*) ▷ *verb* **abbreviating, abbreviated** ▷ *adjective* **abbreviated**

abbreviation *noun* A shortened version of a word. For example, *St.* is an abbreviation of the word *street. See the Initials, Acronyms, and Abbreviations Guide in the* **Reference Section**. **ab·bre·vi·a·tion** (uh-*bree*-vee-**ay**-shuhn)

abdicate *verb* To give up power: *When the queen abdicated the throne, her son became king.* **ab·di·cate** (**ab**-di-*kate*) ▷ *verb* **abdicating, abdicated** ▷ *noun* **abdication**

abdomen *noun*
1. The front part of your body between your chest and hips.
2. The rear section of an insect's body.
ab·do·men (**ab**-duh-muhn)

abduct *verb* To take someone away by force: *Two masked men abducted the millionaire's wife.* **ab·duct** (ab-**duhkt**) ▷ *verb* **abducting, abducted** ▷ *noun* **abduction**

abhor *verb* To hate something: *Alix abhors romantic movies.* **ab·hor** (ab-**hor**) ▷ *verb* **abhorring, abhorred** ▷ *adjective* **abhorrent**

abide *verb* If you **abide by** a rule, agreement, or law, you obey it or do what it requires: *Players who cannot abide by the rules will be disqualified.* **a·bide** (uh-**bide**) ▷ *verb* **abiding, abided** *or* **abode** (uh-**bohd**)

ability *noun*
1. The mental or physical power to do something: *Sybil has the ability to be a great mathematician.*
2. Skill, as in *a natural ability at golf.*
a·bil·i·ty (uh-**bil**-i-tee)
▷ *noun, plural* **abilities**

ablaze *adjective* On fire: *The building was ablaze when*

abalone

the firefighters arrived. **a·blaze** (uh-**blaze**)

able *adjective*

  1. If you are **able** to do something, you can do it.

  2. Skillful or talented: *We picked the most able players for the team.*

  a·ble (**ay**-buhl)

  ▷ *adjective* **abler, ablest** ▷ *adverb* **ably**

Suffix

The suffix **-able** turns a root word into an adjective by adding one of the following meanings to the root word:

  1. Capable of or able to, as in *a breakable toy* (capable of breaking).

  2. Likely to, as in *an agreeable kid* (likely to agree).

  3. Worthy of or deserving, as in *a lovable kitten* (worthy of love).

abnormal *adjective* Not normal, in a way that may cause problems. **ab·nor·mal** (ab-**nor**-muhl) ▷ *noun* **abnormality** (*ab*-nor-**mal**-i-tee)

aboard *adverb* On or onto a train, ship, or aircraft: *Climb aboard!* **a·board** (uh-**bord**) ▷ *preposition* **aboard**

abode *noun*

  1. Someone's home: *His new abode is a small house on the edge of town.*

  2. The **right of abode** is the legal right to live in a particular place, especially a country that you were not born in.

  a·bode (uh-**bohd**)

abolish *verb* To put an end to something officially: *The 13th Amendment to the US Constitution abolished slavery.* **a·bol·ish** (uh-**bah**-lish) ▷ *verb* **abolishes, abolishing, abolished** ▷ *noun* **abolition**

abolitionist *noun* Someone who worked to abolish slavery before the Civil War. **a·bo·li·tion·ist** (*ab*-uh-**lish**-uh-nist)

abominable *adjective* Unpleasant or horrible, as in *an abominable mess.* **a·bom·i·na·ble** (uh-**bah**-muh-nuh-buhl) ▷ *adverb* **abominably**

abomination *noun*

  1. A person, thing, or action that makes you feel disgusted: *In my opinion, it is an abomination that people in the world are still starving.*

  2. A feeling of disgust and hatred: *They regarded the blatant cheating with abomination.*

  a·bom·i·na·tion (uh-*bah*-muh-**nay**-shuhn)

Aborigine *noun*

  1. One of the native peoples of Australia who have lived there since before the Europeans arrived. The name of these people is capitalized.

  2. **aborigine** The native people of a place, such as the

Inuit and Native Americans in North America. **ab·o·rig·i·ne** (*ab*-uh-**rij**-uh-nee) ▷ *adjective* **aboriginal** (*ab*-uh-**rij**-uh-nuhl)

abort *verb* To stop something from happening in the early stages: *The pilot aborted the takeoff because of bad weather.* **a·bort** (uh-**bort**) ▷ *verb* **aborting, aborted** ▷ *adjective* **abortive**

abortion *noun* A medical procedure in which a fetus is removed from a pregnant woman before it is developed enough to live. **a·bor·tion** (uh-**bor**-shuhn)

abound *verb* To have or contain large amounts of something: *The prairie abounds with native grasses and wildflowers.* **a·bound** (uh-**bound**) ▷ *verb* **abounding, abounded**

about

  1. *preposition* On a particular subject: *I'm reading a book about the Etruscans.*

  2. *adverb* Almost; approximately: *Althea is probably about 14 now.*

  3. *adjective* Moving around: *After a week in bed with the flu, Matthew was finally up and about.*

  a·bout (uh-**bout**)

Aborigines

above

  1. *adverb* In a higher place, as in *the sun above.*

  2. *preposition* Higher up than or over something: *The balloons were flying high above us.*

  3. *preposition* More than or better than, as in *above average.*

  a·bove (uh-**buhv**)

aboveboard *adjective* If an action is **aboveboard**, it is completely honest and legal: *The city council's handling of the scandal was open and aboveboard.* **a·bove·board** (uh-**buhv**-bord)

abrasive *adjective*

1. Rough and coarse: *Sandpaper has an abrasive surface.*

2. Rude and often offensive to others: *Roger has an abrasive way of speaking.*
ab·ra·sive (uh-**bray**-siv)

abreast *adverb* Side by side: *The soldiers marched two abreast.* **a·breast** (uh-**brest**)

abridged *adjective* Shortened by leaving parts out, as in *an abridged dictionary.* **a·bridged** (uh-**brijd**)
▷ *verb* **abridge**

abroad *adverb* In or to another country. In the United States, the word **abroad** usually means "overseas": *I'm going to study abroad next year.* **a·broad** (uh-**brawd**)

abrupt *adjective*

1. Sudden and unexpected: *The rain put an abrupt stop to the picnic.*

2. Quick, short, and rude, as in *an abrupt answer.*
a·brupt (uh-**bruhpt**)
▷ *adverb* **abruptly**

abscess *noun* A painful infected area full of a yellow substance called pus. **ab·scess** (**ab**-ses) ▷ *noun, plural* **abscesses**

abscond *verb* To go away suddenly and hide somewhere, often after stealing something: *After stealing the jewels, he absconded to Brazil.* **ab·scond** (ab-**skahnd**) ▷ *verb* **absconding, absconded**

absence *noun* The state of not being somewhere or of not existing: *Everyone noted her absence from the wedding.* **ab·sence** (**ab**-suhns)

absent *adjective* Not present: *Mary was absent for the math test.* **ab·sent** (**ab**-suhnt) ▷ *noun* **absentee** ▷ *noun* **absenteeism**

absent-minded *adjective* Not able to remember or notice things very well. **absent-mind·ed** (**mine**-did) ▷ *adverb* **absent-mindedly**

absolute *adjective*

1. Certain and without any doubt: *I am sure that what he says is the absolute truth.*

2. Complete, without any limit: *The king had absolute control over his people.*
ab·so·lute (**ab**-suh-*loot*)

absolutely *adverb* Fully and completely; without qualification or limit: *I'm absolutely sure the biology test is next Tuesday.* **ab·so·lute·ly** (*ab*-suh-**loot**-lee)

absolve *verb* To officially remove the blame or responsibility for something bad from someone. **ab·solve** (ab-**zahlv**) ▷ *verb* **absolving, absolved** ▷ *noun* **absolution** (*ab*-suh-**loo**-shuhn)

absorb *verb*

1. To soak up liquid: *He used a towel to absorb the water.*

2. To take in or learn information: *While studying Arabic, Vanessa absorbed the history of the Middle East.*

3. To get all of someone's attention: *That new novel has completely absorbed him.*
ab·sorb (ab-**zorb**)
▷ *verb* **absorbing, absorbed**

absorbent *adjective* Something that soaks up liquid, such as a washcloth, towel, or sponge, is **absorbent.** **ab·sorb·ent** (ab-**zor**-buhnt)

absorption *noun* The process of soaking up liquid, heat, or light. **ab·sorp·tion** (ab-**zorp**-shuhn)

abstain *verb*

1. To stop yourself from doing something that you might normally do: *Some people abstain from eating meat because of their love for animals.*

2. To not participate in something such as a vote or a discussion.
ab·stain (ab-**stayn**)
▷ *verb* **abstaining, abstained** ▷ *noun* **abstention**

abstract *adjective*

1. Based on ideas rather than things that you can touch and see: *Her abstract paintings were colorful but didn't remind you of anything.*

2. Hard to understand: *Your explanation of atoms and electrons is too abstract for me.*
ab·stract (**ab**-strakt *or* ab-**strakt**)

absurd *adjective* Silly; ridiculous: *Wearing a bathing suit in snowy weather is absurd.* **ab·surd** (ab-**surd** *or* ab-**zurd**) ▷ *noun* **absurdity** ▷ *adverb* **absurdly**

abundant *adjective* Widely available or present in great quantity. **a·bun·dant** (uh-**buhn**-duhnt) ▷ *noun* **abundance** ▷ *adverb* **abundantly**

abuse

1. (uh-**byoos**) *noun* Rude and offensive speech: *The abuse from her boss drove Kate to quit her job.*

2. (uh-**byooz**) *verb* To treat a person or animal cruelly: *The animal shelter treats dogs and cats that have been abused.* ▷ *verb* **abusing, abused** ▷ *noun* **abuser**

3. (uh-**byoos**) *noun* Wrong or harmful use of something or treatment of someone, as in *drug abuse* or *child abuse.* ▷ *verb* **abuse** (uh-**byooz**) ▷ *adjective* **abusive** (uh-**byoo**-siv)
a·buse

abuzz *adjective* Filled with a humming or buzzing sound: *The auditorium was abuzz with excitement as the audience waited for the musical to start.* **a·buzz** (uh-**buhz**)

abyss *noun*

1. A very deep hole that seems to have no bottom.

2. A situation that gets worse and worse: *They are*

entering into an abyss of constant fighting and accusations.
a·byss (uh-**bis**)
▷ *noun, plural* **abysses**

Word History

When we want to "undo" the meaning of a word, we add the prefix *un-* to it: The word *untie* is the opposite of *tie*, for example. The people in ancient Greece could also change the meaning of a word to its opposite: They used the prefix *a-*, meaning "not." You can see it in the word **abyss**, which has the meaning of "bottomless": Greek speakers formed *abyssos* from *a-* and the word *byssos*, meaning "bottom of the sea." Naturally, we know that any deep hole in the sea is not truly "bottomless." Now the word *abyss* can refer to a very deep hole anywhere, not just in the sea.

acacia *noun* A small tree or shrub that has feathery leaves and pleasant-smelling white or yellow flowers and grows in warm parts of the world. **a·ca·cia** (uh-**kay**-shuh)

academic
1. *adjective* Of or having to do with study and learning: *His academic background is in the classics.* ▷ *adverb* **academically**
2. *noun* Someone who teaches in a university or college or someone who does research.
ac·a·dem·ic (*ak*-uh-**dem**-ik)

academy *noun*
1. A private junior high, middle school, or high school.
2. A school that teaches special subjects, as in *a military academy.*
a·cad·e·my (uh-**kad**-uh-mee)
▷ *noun, plural* **academies**

Word History

Today, people all over the world still study the writings of Plato, a philosopher who lived in ancient Greece. The park where he taught his students was called the *Akademeia,* and from this name we get the word **academy**.

acai *noun* A kind of palm tree that grows in Central and South America. Its purple berries are thought to contain healthful substances. **a·ca·i** (*ah*-sah-**ee**)

acacia

accelerate *verb* To get faster and faster: *The car accelerated down the steep hill.* **ac·cel·er·ate** (ak-**sel**-uh-*rate*) ▷ *verb* **accelerating, accelerated** ▷ *noun* **acceleration**

accent *noun*
1. The way that you pronounce sounds and put them together: *Diego speaks with a Spanish accent.* ▷ *verb* **accent**
2. A mark placed over or on a letter that changes its usual sound: *English sometimes uses accents on words borrowed from French, such as in "fiancé."*
ac·cent (**ak**-sent)

accentuate *verb* To emphasize something, or make it stand out: *Mascara accentuates eyelashes.*
ac·cen·tu·ate (ak-**sen**-choo-*ate*) ▷ *verb* **accentuating, accentuated**

accept *verb*
1. To take or say yes to something that is offered: *Pauline accepted her friend's invitation.*
2. To agree that something is correct, satisfactory, or enough: *Manny hasn't accepted that our idea is the best solution.*
ac·cept (ak-**sept**)
▷ *verb* **accepting, accepted**

acceptable *adjective*
1. Good enough; satisfactory: *Most people find 2 percent milk an acceptable alternative to whole milk.*
2. Within limits that are normal or that people can accept: *This sort of behavior is not acceptable on the school grounds.*
ac·cept·able (ak-**sep**-tuh-buhl)

acceptance *noun* The act or fact of accepting something: *Newly coined tech words, like the verbs "blog" and "tweet," have gained widespread acceptance very quickly.* **ac·cept·ance** (ak-**sep**-tuhns)

access
1. *noun* A way to enter, or an approach to a place: *Only people with passes are allowed access to the beach.* ▷ *noun, plural* **accesses**
2. *verb* To get information from a computer: *Orlando accessed the database.* ▷ *verb* **accesses, accessing, accessed**
ac·cess (**ak**-ses)

accessible *adjective*
1. Able to be accessed or reached, especially to people with disabilities: *The ramp makes this building accessible to people in wheelchairs.*
2. If someone is **accessible**, they are easy to talk to or get in contact with.
ac·ces·si·ble (ak-**ses**-uh-buhl)

accessory *noun*
1. An extra, optional part for something, as in *computer accessories.*
2. A small item that you wear with your clothes, such as a belt, gloves, or a scarf: *That red hat is a perfect accessory for my new coat.*
3. An **accessory** to a crime is someone who helps another person commit it.
ac·ces·so·ry (ak-**ses**-ur-ee)
▷ *noun, plural* **accessories**

accident *noun*
1. An unfortunate and unplanned event: *At least no one was hurt in the automobile accident.*
2. Lack of intention; chance: *We met in the park by accident.*
ac·ci·dent (**ak**-si-duhnt)

accidental *adjective* Happening by accident; not planned or expected: *Many important advances in science were based on accidental discoveries.* **ac·ci·den·tal** (*ak*-si-**den**-tuhl)

accidentally *adverb* Not on purpose; without meaning to: *She accidentally spilled the milk.* **ac·ci·den·tal·ly** (*ak*-si-**dent**-lee)

acclaim *noun* Praise: *The students received much acclaim for their performance.* **ac·claim** (uh-**klaym**)
▷ *verb* **acclaim**

accommodate *verb*
1. To help out or reply to a request: *We try to accommodate people on special diets.*
2. To provide with a place to stay: *The hotel has just enough rooms to accommodate our group.*
ac·com·mo·date (uh-**kah**-muh-date)
▷ *verb* **accommodating, accommodated**

accommodation *noun*
1. The act of accommodating someone, or a thing that you do to make things easier: *As required by law, the schools are making an accommodation for their students who are disabled or have medical conditions.*
2. Accommodations is a somewhat formal word for places to stay while you are traveling: *What sort of accommodations are there on the island?*
ac·com·mo·da·tion (uh-*kah*-muh-**day**-shuhn)

accompany *verb*
1. To go somewhere with someone: *The teacher accompanied him to the principal's office.*
2. To play along with a singer on a musical instrument: *Sarah will be accompanied by Josh on the piano.*
ac·com·pa·ny (uh-**kuhm**-puh-nee)
▷ *verb* **accompanies, accompanying, accompanied**
▷ *noun* **accompaniment** ▷ *noun* **accompanist**

accomplice *noun* Someone who helps another person commit a crime. **ac·com·plice** (uh-**kahm**-plis)

accomplish *verb* To do or complete something successfully: *Meredith accomplished her goal of getting straight As.* **ac·com·plish** (uh-**kahm**-plish) ▷ *verb* **accomplishes, accomplishing, accomplished** ▷ *noun* **accomplishment**

accomplished *adjective* Skillful, as in *an accomplished musician.* **ac·com·plished** (uh-**kom**-plisht)

accord *noun*
1. A signed agreement between countries about the way they will deal with something that concerns them: *In order to stop the war, the two countries must reach an accord.*
2. If you do something **of your own accord**, you do it without being asked.
ac·cord (uh-**kord**)

accordingly *adverb* In a way that is suitable, appropriate, or fitting: *They told us it was a formal dinner, so I dressed accordingly and put on a jacket and tie.* **ac·cord·ing·ly** (uh-**kor**-ding-lee)

according to *preposition*
1. As someone has said or written: *According to the schedule, a bus stops here every half hour.*
2. In a way that corresponds to something: *Babysitters are usually paid according to the number of hours they work.*
ac·cord·ing to (uh-**kor**-ding)

accordion

accordion *noun* A keyboard wind instrument that you hold to your chest and squeeze while pressing keys and buttons. **ac·cor·di·on** (uh-**kor**-dee-uhn)

accost *verb* To start talking to someone in a threatening or hostile way: *A beggar accosted me on the street.* **ac·cost** (uh-**kawst**) ▷ *verb* **accosting, accosted**

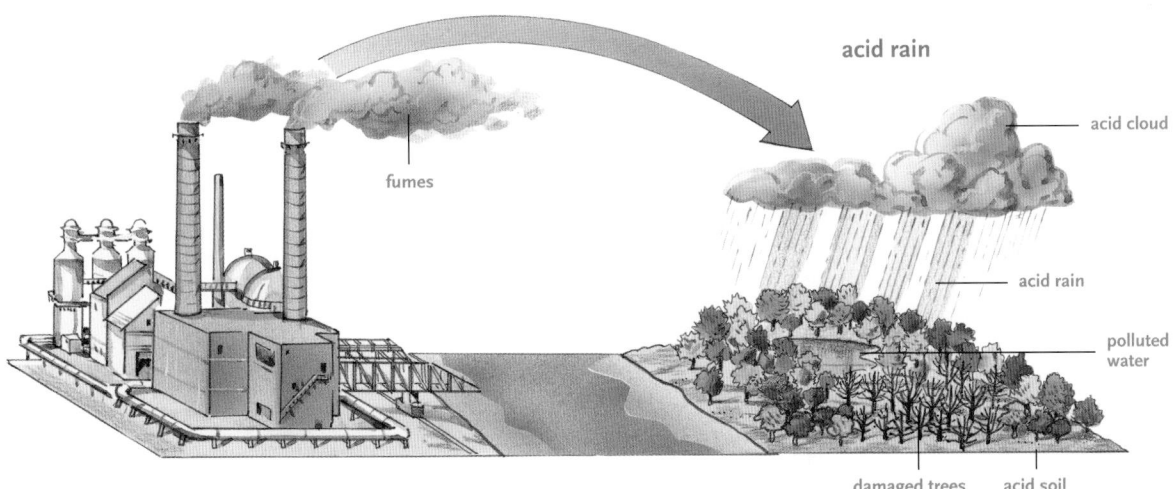

acid rain

fumes

acid cloud

acid rain

polluted water

damaged trees   acid soil

account
> **1.** *noun* A description of something that has happened, as in *an account of the accident.*
> **2.** *noun* An arrangement to keep money in a bank, as in *a checking account* or *a savings account.*
> **3. accounts** *noun, plural* A record of money earned and spent: *Jennifer kept careful accounts of the club's expenses.*
> **4.** *verb* If you **account for** something, you explain it: *How do you account for the missing cookies?* ▷ *verb* **accounting, accounted** ▷ *adjective* **accountable**
> **ac·count** (uh-**kount**)

accountant *noun* Someone whose job is keeping accounts for a company or business. **ac·count·ant** (uh-**koun**-tuhnt) ▷ *noun* **accounting**

accumulate *verb* To collect things or let them pile up: *My sister accumulated so many stuffed animals that they covered her bed.* **ac·cu·mu·late** (uh-**kyoo**-myuh-*late*) ▷ *verb* **accumulating, accumulated**

accumulation *noun*
> **1.** The process of something getting bigger or thicker, little by little: *Rock candy is formed by the accumulation of sugar crystals on a stick.*
> **2.** An amount of something that has slowly increased: *There's an accumulation of mold on the basement walls.*
> **ac·cum·u·la·tion** (uh-*kyoo*-myuh-**lay**-shuhn)

accuracy *noun* The quality of being correct and exact: *For scientists, accuracy is extremely important.* **ac·cu·ra·cy** (**ak**-yur-uh-see)

accurate *adjective* Correct in details; exact, as in *an accurate description.* **ac·cu·rate** (**ak**-yuh-rit)

accurately *adverb* Correctly with respect to quantity, size, or amount: *If you don't measure the space accurately, the shelves you are building may not fit.* **ac·cu·rate·ly** (**ak**-yur-it-lee)

accuse *verb* To say that someone has done something wrong: *The teacher accused Dawn of cheating on the math test.* **ac·cuse** (uh-**kyooz**) ▷ *verb* **accusing, accused** ▷ *noun* **accusation** (ak-yuh-**zay**-shuhn) ▷ *noun* **accuser**

accustomed *adjective*
> **1.** Usual and familiar: *Denise took her accustomed place at the table.*
> **2.** When you are **accustomed to** something, you are used to it.
> **ac·cus·tomed** (uh-**kus**-tuhmd)

ace *noun*
> **1.** A playing card with only one symbol on it. In most card games, the ace has the highest value.
> **2.** Someone who is an expert at something, as in *a tennis ace.*
> **ace** (ays)

ache *noun* A dull pain that doesn't go away: *Richard had an ache in his legs after running the marathon.* **ache** (ake) ▷ *verb* **ache**

achieve *verb* To do something successfully after making an effort: *Sophia worked hard to achieve her ambition of becoming an astronaut.* **a·chieve** (uh-**cheev**) ▷ *verb* **achieving, achieved** ▷ *noun* **achievement** ▷ *noun* **achiever**

acid
> **1.** *noun* A substance with a sour taste that will react with a base to form a salt. Acids turn blue litmus paper red. Strong acids can burn your skin.
> **2.** *adjective* Sour, or bitter.
> **ac·id** (**as**-id)
> ▷ *adjective* **acidic** (uh-**sid**-ik)

acid rain *noun* Rain that is polluted by chemicals in the air, damaging lakes, forests, and buildings.

acknowledge *verb*

1. To accept the truth about something: *We all acknowledged that we needed to work harder.*
2. To show that you have noticed or recognized something or someone: *Terri waved to acknowledge that she had seen me.*
3. To let the sender know that you have received something: *He sent me a note to acknowledge the package I mailed him.*
ac·knowl·edge (ak-**nah**-lij) ▷ *verb* **acknowledging, acknowledged** ▷ *noun* **acknowledgment**

acne *noun* A skin condition that causes inflammation and pimples on the face, back, or chest. **ac·ne** (**ak**-nee)

acorn *noun* The seed of an oak tree. **a·corn** (**ay**-korn)

acoustic

1. *adjective* Of or having to do with sound or hearing.
2. acoustics *noun, plural* The qualities of a place that affect how sound is heard in it: *The gym has terrible acoustics for a piano recital.*
a·cou·stic (uh-**koo**-stik)

acquaintance *noun* Someone you have met but do not know very well. **ac·quain·tance** (uh-**kwayn**-tuhns)

acquire *verb*

1. To get something so that you own it or have it: *Josie acquired a car when she turned 17.*
2. If something is an **acquired taste**, you don't like it at first but learn to like it: *For some people, olives are an acquired taste.*
ac·quire (uh-**kwire**) ▷ *verb* **acquiring, acquired**

acquit *verb* To find someone not guilty of a crime: *The jury acquitted the defendant for lack of evidence.* **ac·quit** (uh-**kwit**) ▷ *verb* **acquitting, acquitted** ▷ *noun* **acquittal**

acre *noun* A measurement of area equal to 43,560 square feet. An acre is almost the size of a standard football field. **a·cre** (**ay**-kur) ▷ *noun* **acreage**

acrobat *noun* A person who performs exciting gymnastic acts that require great skill. Acrobats often work at circuses. **ac·ro·bat** (**ak**-ruh-bat)

acronym *noun* A word made from the first or first few letters of the words in a phrase. Radar, for example, is short for *radio detection and ranging.* See the *Initials, Acronyms, and Abbreviations Guide* in the

acrobat

Reference Section. **ac·ro·nym** (**ak**-ruh-nim)

across *preposition*

1. From one side of something to the other: *The cat ran across the room.*
2. On the other side of something: *Her house is across from mine.*
a·cross (uh-**kraws**)

acrylic *noun* A chemical substance used to make fibers and paints: *My sports clothes are made of lightweight acrylic.* **a·cryl·ic** (uh-**kril**-ik)

act

1. *verb* To do something for a reason, or in a particular way: *He acted as if he owned the place.*
2. *verb* To perform in a play, movie, or other form of entertainment: *Jesse loves to act in school plays.*
3. *verb* To have an effect: *This medicine acts by stopping pain signals from reaching the brain.*
4. *noun* A short performance, as in *a circus act.*
5. *noun* Behavior that is intended to fool someone: *She said she missed him and started to cry, but I think it was an act.*
6. *noun* One of the parts of a play: *The third act of the play was the shortest.*
7. *noun* A bill that has been passed by Congress. If signed by the president, it becomes law.
act (akt) ▷ *verb* **acting, acted**

action *noun*

1. Something that you do: *Sonia's quick action prevented a forest fire.*
2. Things happening in general: *This new movie doesn't have much of a plot, but it has lots of car chases and action.*
3. When you **take action**, you act to achieve some result.
ac·tion (**ak**-shuhn)

activate *verb* To turn on, or to cause to work: *The smoke from the oven activated the fire alarm.* **ac·ti·vate** (**ak**-tuh-*vate*) ▷ *verb* **activating, activated** ▷ *noun* **activator**

active *adjective*

1. Energetic and busy, as in *an active social life.*
2. The subject of an **active** verb does an action, while the subject of a passive verb has something done to it: *The verb in the sentence "Joe pitched the ball" is active, because the subject, "Joe," is performing the action.* See **passive.**
ac·tive (**ak**-tiv)

activist *noun* Someone who supports a cause and believes in taking action to change things, as in *a*

political activist or *an environmental activist.*
ac·tiv·ist (ak-tuh-vist) ▷ *noun* **activism**

activity *noun*
1. Things happening or people doing things: *After dark there is not much activity downtown.*
2. Something that you do for pleasure, as in *a rainy-day activity.*
ac·tiv·i·ty (ak-**tiv**-i-tee)
▷ *noun, plural* **activities**

actor *noun* Someone whose job is to perform, as in the theater, movies, or television. **ac·tor** (**ak**-tur)

actress *noun* A girl or a woman whose job is to perform, as in the theater, movies, or television. **ac·tress** (**ak**-tris) ▷ *noun, plural* **actresses**

actual *adjective* Real, existing, or true: *A fire drill prepares you for an actual fire.* **ac·tu·al** (**ak**-choo-uhl)
▷ *adverb* **actually**

acupuncture *noun* A way of treating illness or pain by sticking needles in different parts of the body. **ac·u·punc·ture** (**ak**-yoo-*pungk*-chur)

acute *adjective*
1. Strong and severe, as in *an acute pain.*
2. Able to detect things easily and accurately, as in *an acute sense of hearing.* ▷ *noun* **acuteness** ▷ *adverb* **acutely**
3. An **acute** angle is an angle of less than 90 degrees.
a·cute (uh-**kyoot**)
▷ *adjective* **acuter, acutest**

A.D. An abbreviation of the Latin phrase *Anno Domini*, which means "in the year of the Lord." *A.D.* shows that a date comes after the birth of Jesus.

ad *noun* Short for **advertisement** or **advertising**, as in *an ad agency.* **ad** (ad)

adage *noun* An old saying that people generally believe is true: *"Time heals all wounds" is an example of an adage.* **ad·age** (**ad**-ij)

adamant *adjective* Strongly determined; not willing to change your mind or plan: *Rachel is adamant that all she wants for her birthday is a trip to the beach.* **ad·a·mant** (**ad**-uh-muhnt) ▷ *adverb* **adamantly**

adapt *verb*
1. To make something work in a different way or for a different purpose: *Construction workers are adapting the building for wheelchair access.*
2. To change because you are in a different situation: *It took us a while to adapt to the new schedule.*
a·dapt (uh-**dapt**)
▷ *verb* **adapting, adapted** ▷ *adjective* **adaptable**

adaptation *noun*
1. The act of adjusting, such as changing something from one form to another: *The film adaptation of my favorite book comes out this summer.*
2. A change that a living thing goes through so it fits in better with its environment: *A turtle's hard shell is an adaptation that protects it from predators.*
ad·ap·ta·tion (*ad*-ap-**tay**-shuhn)

adapter or **adaptor** *noun* A device that connects two parts that are of slightly different shapes or sizes: *We needed an adapter to hook up the CD player to the old stereo.* **a·dapt·er** or **a·dap·tor** (uh-**dap**-tur)

add *verb*
1. To find the sum of two or more numbers: *She added up the price of all her groceries.*
2. To put or mix one thing with another: *Add the eggs to the flour.*
add (ad)
▷ *verb* **adding, added**

ADD *noun* A condition in which a person has trouble keeping still and concentrating. ADD is short for *attention deficit disorder.*

addend *noun* Any number that is added to another to form a sum: *In the equation 6 + 4 = 10, the addends are 6 and 4.* **ad·dend** (**ad**-end)

adder *noun*
1. A North American snake that hisses and swells up its head when annoyed.
2. A small, poisonous European snake. Sometimes also called a **viper**.
ad·der (**ad**-ur)

addict *noun* A person who cannot give up doing or using something, as in *a drug addict.* **ad·dict** (**ad**-ikt)
▷ *noun* **addiction** ▷ *adjective* **addicted**

addictive *adjective* An **addictive** substance or activity makes you think you need it, even though it is harmful: *Nicotine is addictive.* **ad·dic·tive** (uh-**dik**-tiv)

addition *noun*
1. In math, **addition** is the adding together of two or more numbers to come up with a sum.
2. A part of a building that is added on to the original: *Our home is so much bigger now with the new addition.*
3. Anything or anyone new: *We have a new addition to our family.*
ad·di·tion (uh-**dish**-uhn)

additional *adjective* Extra, or more, as in *additional research.* **ad·di·tion·al** (uh-**dish**-uh-nuhl)

adder

additive *noun* Something added to a substance, especially food: *The additives in American cheese keep it from spoiling.* **ad·di·tive** (ad-i-tiv)

address

1. (uh-**dres** *or* ad-res) *noun* Information such as the street, city, and state of a business or residence: *My home address is 1011 Maple Avenue.* ▷ *noun, plural* **addresses**

2. address book (uh-**dres** *or* ad-res) *noun* A book in which you keep addresses, or a place on a computer where email addresses and other information are stored.

3. (uh-**dres**) *verb* To write an address on a letter, card, or package: *Remember to address the envelope.* ▷ *noun* **addressee** (ad-res-ee)

4. (uh-**dres**) *verb* To give a speech to: *The governor addressed the conference on regional issues.* ▷ *noun* **address**

5. (uh-**dres**) *verb* When you **address** a problem, you tackle it or deal with it.

ad·dress

▷ *verb* **addresses, addressing, addressed**

adenoid *noun* A spongy lump of flesh at the back of your nose that can become swollen, making it hard to breathe. **ad·e·noid** (ad-uh-*noid*)

adept *adjective* Able to do something well: *My dad is quite adept at cooking.* **a·dept** (uh-**dept**)

adequate *adjective* Just enough, or good enough: *Public schools need adequate funding to provide art classes.* **ad·e·quate** (ad-i-kwit) ▷ *adverb* **adequately**

ADHD *noun* A set of behaviors including restlessness, too much activity, and poor concentration that may interfere with learning. ADHD is short for *attention deficit hyperactivity disorder.*

adhere *verb*

1. To stick very tightly to something: *This glue adheres permanently.*

2. To stick with an idea or plan: *If we adhere to the schedule, we'll finish on time.*

ad·here (ad-**heer**)

▷ *verb* **adhering, adhered**

adhesive *noun* A substance, such as glue, that makes things stick together. **ad·he·sive** (ad-**hee**-siv)

▷ *adjective* **adhesive**

adios *interjection* The Spanish word for "good-bye." **a·di·os** (*ah*-dee-**ohs**)

adjacent *adjective* Close or next to something. If two things are **adjacent**, they are next to each other: *My family's store is adjacent to our house.* **ad·ja·cent** (uh-**jay**-suhnt)

adjective *noun* A word that describes a noun or pronoun. For example, in the phrase "the red house," the adjective *red* tells you how the house looks. *See the Grammar Guide in the* **Reference Section**. **ad·jec·tive** (aj-ik-tiv)

adjoin *verb* To be next to or in contact with: *The door leads to the garage, which adjoins the house.* **ad·join** (uh-**join**) ▷ *verb* **adjoining, adjoined**

adjourn *verb* To close or end something, especially a court session or government meeting: *After several hours of testimony, court adjourned for the day.* **ad·journ** (uh-**jurn**) ▷ *verb* **adjourning, adjourned**

adjust *verb*

1. To move or change something slightly: *Evan adjusted the picture on the wall.* ▷ *adjective* **adjustable**

2. To get used to something new and different: *I'm adjusting to my new school very quickly.*

ad·just (uh-**juhst**)

▷ *verb* **adjusting, adjusted**

adjustment *noun*

1. The act or process of changing something slightly to make it work better: *Garrett made an adjustment to the brakes so he could control his bike better.*

2. A small change to improve something: *The piano tuner had to make several adjustments to the piano before it could be played.*

ad·just·ment (uh-**juhst**-muhnt)

ad-lib *verb* To do something, especially speak in front of people, without preparing for it: *Some comedians like to ad-lib onstage.* **ad-lib** (ad lib)

▷ *verb* **ad-libbing, ad-libbed** ▷ *adjective, adverb* **ad-lib**

administer *verb*

1. To manage something so that it runs smoothly: *Pat administers the English department at the high school.* ▷ *noun* **administrator** (ad-**min**-i-*stray*-tur)

2. To give something to someone in an official or controlled way: *Only a doctor can administer the injection.*

ad·min·is·ter (ad-**min**-i-stur)

▷ *verb* **administering, administered**

administration *noun*

1. The activity of managing all the details of something, such as a business or project: *The Internal Revenue Service is in charge of the administration and collection of federal income taxes.*

2. The department or the people whose job it is to manage and supervise an organization.

3. The government of a president, including the president's cabinet and advisers. The word *administration* also means the time that a particular president is in office, as in *the Reagan administration.* **ad·min·is·tra·tion** (ad-*min*-i-stray-shuhn)

admirable *adjective* Deserving praise or admiration, as in *an admirable performance.* **ad·mi·ra·ble** (**ad**-mur-uh-buhl)

admiral *noun* A high-ranking officer in a country's navy or coast guard. **ad·mi·ral** (**ad**-mur-uhl)

admire *verb*
1. To like and respect someone: *I admire my teacher.*
2. To look at something with enjoyment: *Anna admired the painting.*
ad·mire (ad-**mire**)
▷ *verb* **admiring, admired** ▷ *noun* **admiration**

admission *noun*
1. The act of allowing someone into a place, as in *admission to college.*
2. The price of getting into a place: *Admission to the museum is $5.*
3. An act of telling the truth about something you did or something that happened.
4. admissions *noun, plural* A department that decides and deals with who gets admitted to a place.
ad·mis·sion (ad-**mish**-uhn)

admit *verb*
1. To say that you did something bad: *Sonia admitted that she had taken the bracelet.*
2. To agree or accept that something is true: *We have to admit that our chances of success are not that good.*
3. To allow someone or something to enter: *Jay admitted me to his secret hiding place.*
ad·mit (ad-**mit**)
▷ *verb* **admitting, admitted** ▷ *noun* **admittance**

admonish *verb* To scold someone sternly for his or her faults or mistakes. **ad·mon·ish** (ad-**mah**-nish)
▷ *verb* **admonishes, admonishing, admonished**
▷ *noun* **admonishment**

adobe

adobe
1. *noun* Bricks made of clay mixed with straw and dried in the sun.
2. *adjective* Made from adobe, as in *an adobe wall.*
a·do·be (uh-**doh**-bee)

Word History

Adobe is a Spanish word for a popular building material in Mexico and the southwestern United States with a long history that began in Egypt. The ancient Egyptians were the first to build with bricks made of straw and dried mud. The Arabic word for these bricks, pronounced "at-toob," made its way to Europe. Spanish explorers brought a version of the word to the New World, and it was taken into English.

adolescent *noun* A young person who is more grown-up than a child but is not yet an adult; a teenager. **ad·o·les·cent** (*ad*-uh-**les**-uhnt) ▷ *noun* **adolescence** ▷ *adjective* **adolescent**

adopt *verb*
1. To take a person or animal into your family.
▷ *adjective* **adopted**
2. To accept a new way of doing things: *The mayor adopted a tough approach to crime.*
a·dopt (uh-**dahpt**)
▷ *verb* **adopting, adopted** ▷ *noun* **adoption**

adorable *adjective* Sweet, cute, and lovable: *What an adorable kitten!* **a·dor·a·ble** (uh-**dor**-uh-buhl)

adore *verb*
1. To be very fond of someone or something: *I adore ice cream.*
2. To be devoted to the point of worshiping someone or something.
a·dore (uh-**dor**)
▷ *verb* **adoring, adored** ▷ *noun* **adoration** (*ad*-uh-**ray**-shuhn)

adorn *verb* To decorate something: *We adorned the parade floats with roses, carnations, and lilies.* **a·dorn** (uh-**dorn**)

adrenaline *noun* A chemical that your body produces when you need more energy or when you sense danger: *Adrenaline flooded through Marcus when he realized that he had overslept and was late for the race.* **ad·ren·a·line** (uh-**dren**-uh-lin)

Word History

The chemical that we know as **adrenaline** was named after the kidneys. The word is based on the prefix *ad-*, meaning "toward," and the Latin word *renes*, meaning "kidneys," so the term means "near the kidneys." People chose this name for *adrenaline* because it is produced by the adrenal glands, which are organs near the kidneys.

adrift *adverb* Drifting or floating freely through water or air: *He set his toy boat adrift in the river and it got away.* **a·drift** (uh-**drift**) ▷ *adjective* **adrift**

adult *noun* A fully grown person or animal. **a·dult** (uh-**duhlt** *or* **ad**-uhlt) ▷ *noun* **adulthood** ▷ *adjective* **adult**

advance

1. *verb* To move forward: *The explorers advanced farther into the mountains.*

2. *verb* To make progress: *Jill is really optimistic about advancing as a singer.* ▷ *noun* **advancement**

3. *adjective* Happening before something else, as in *advance warning.*

4. *verb* To lend money: *My mom advanced me $5 on my allowance.* ▷ *noun* **advance**

5. *noun* A movement forward in a military situation.

ad·vance (uhd-**vans**)

▷ *verb* **advancing, advanced**

advanced *adjective*

1. At a higher or more developed level: *The disease is very difficult to cure in its advanced stages.*

2. More difficult or demanding: *Do you think you can handle the advanced math class?*

ad·vanced (uhd-**vanst**)

advantage

1. *noun* Something that helps you or puts you ahead: *Her knowledge of the area gave her a real advantage.* ▷ *adjective* **advantageous** (*ad*-vuhn-**tay**-juhs)

2. If you **take advantage of** someone, you use him or her for your own benefit.

3. If you **take advantage of** something, you find a use for it that benefits you.

ad·van·tage (uhd-**van**-tij)

advent *noun*

1. The beginning of something new or important, as in *the advent of the information age.*

2. Advent The period leading up to Christmas in the Christian calendar.

ad·vent (**ad**-vent)

adventure *noun* An exciting or dangerous experience: *Trying to get home during the ice storm turned out to be quite an adventure.* **ad·ven·ture** (uhd-**ven**-chur) ▷ *adjective* **adventurous**

adverb *noun* A word usually used to describe a verb, adjective, or other adverb. Adverbs indicate how, when, where, how often, or how much something happens. For example, in the sentence "He walks quickly," the adverb *quickly* tells you how he walks. *See the Grammar Guide in the* **Reference Section**. **ad·verb** (**ad**-*vurb*)

adversary *noun* An opponent or enemy: *They are political adversaries but friends in personal life.* **ad·ver·sar·y** (**ad**-vur-*ser*-ee) ▷ *noun, plural* **adversaries**

homemade advertisement

adverse *adjective* Unfavorable, negative, or causing a problem: *Does the medication have any adverse side effects?* **ad·verse** (ad-**vurs**) ▷ *adverb* **adversely**

adversity *noun* A difficult situation that lasts for a long time: *Immigrant families often have to overcome adversity to succeed.* **ad·ver·si·ty** (ad-**vur**-si-tee) ▷ *noun, plural* **adversities**

advertise *verb* To give information about something that you want to promote or sell: *Bob used handouts to advertise his show.* **ad·ver·tise** (**ad**-vur-*tize*) ▷ *verb* **advertising, advertised** ▷ *noun* **advertiser**

advertisement *noun* A broadcast or published notice that calls attention to something, such as a product or an event. **ad·ver·tise·ment** (*ad*-vur-**tize**-muhnt *or* ad-**vur**-tiz-muhnt)

advertising *noun*

1. The activity or industry that brings products and services to people's attention.

2. Advertisements of all kinds, considered together: *This magazine has so much advertising that it's hard to tell an article from an ad.*

ad·ver·tis·ing (**ad**-vur-*tye*-zing)

advice *noun* A suggestion about what someone should do: *Grace gave me some useful advice about netbooks.* **ad·vice** (uhd-**vise**)

advisable *adjective* Sensible, wise, and worth doing. **ad·vis·a·ble** (uhd-**vye**-zuh-buhl) ▷ *adverb* **advisably**

advise *verb* To give someone information or suggestions: *My doctor advised me to rest for a few days.* **ad·vise** (uhd-**vize**) ▷ *verb* **advising, advised** ▷ *noun* **adviser** *or* **advisor** ▷ *adjective* **advisory**

advocate
1. (**ad**-vuh-*kate*) *verb* To support or call for an idea or a plan: *The group is advocating for an end to the war.*
▷ *verb* **advocating, advocated**
2. (**ad**-vuh-kit) *noun* A person who supports an idea or plan, as in *a women's rights advocate.*
ad·vo·cate

aerial
1. *noun* An antenna that receives television or radio signals.
2. *adjective* Happening in the air, as in *aerial skiing.*
aer·i·al (**air**-ee-uhl)

Language Note

Aero- is a type of combining form, a word part that combines with other words or word parts to form new terms. *Aero-* means "air" or "atmosphere." *Aerospace* is the earth's atmosphere and outer space. *Aerobics* are exercises that cause your breathing (or intake of air) and heart rate to increase temporarily.

aerobics *noun, plural* Energetic exercises that strengthen the heart and improve breathing. Aerobics are often done with music playing. **aer·o·bics** (air-**oh**-biks) ▷ *adjective* **aerobic**

aerodynamic *adjective* Designed to move through the air very easily and quickly. **aer·o·dy·nam·ic** (*air*-oh-dye-**nam**-ik)

aeronautic or **aeronautical** *adjective* Of or having to do with the design and building of aircraft. **aer·o·nau·tic** (*air*-uh-**naw**-tik) or **aer·o·nau·ti·cal** (*air*-uh-**naw**-tik-uhl)

aerosol *noun*
1. A mass of tiny particles mixed in air or another gas: *Smoke is a natural aerosol.*
2. A product, such as a deodorant or insecticide, that is sold in a spray can.
aer·o·sol (**air**-uh-*sawl*)
▷ *adjective* **aerosol**

aerospace
1. *noun* The earth's atmosphere and all the space beyond it.
2. *adjective* Of or having to do with the science and technology of jet flight or space travel: *Claude's mom works in the aerospace industry.*
aer·o·space (**air**-oh-*spase*)

affair
1. *noun* A happening or event: *We hired a caterer to provide food for the whole affair.*

2. affairs *noun, plural* Matters connected with private or public life, as in *personal affairs* or *business affairs.*
af·fair (uh-**fair**)

affect *verb* To influence or change someone or something: *The drug affects different people in different ways.* **af·fect** (uh-**fekt**) ▷ *verb* **affecting, affected**

affected *adjective* Unnatural and not sincere: *Jemma's affected voice makes her sound like she's always acting.* **af·fect·ed** (uh-**fek**-tid)

affection *noun* Love for someone or something familiar to you: *I have a lot of affection for my puppy.* **af·fec·tion** (uh-**fek**-shuhn)

affectionate *adjective* Loving, as in *an affectionate hug.* **af·fec·tion·ate** (uh-**fek**-shuh-nit) ▷ *adverb* **affectionately**

affiliate *verb* To join or connect closely with something: *Our softball team is affiliated with the county league.* **af·fil·i·ate** (uh-**fil**-ee-*ate*) ▷ *verb* **affiliating, affiliated** ▷ *noun* **affiliate** (uh-**fil**-ee-it)

affirmative *adjective* Giving the answer "yes," or stating that something is true, as in *an affirmative reply.* **af·firm·a·tive** (uh-**fur**-muh-tiv)

affirmative action *noun* A program that promotes increased opportunities for minorities and women in order to make up for past discrimination.

afflict *verb* To cause to suffer from a disease, or to cause distress: *Rabies can afflict people if they are bitten by bats or other animals that carry the disease.* **af·flict** (uh-**flikt**) ▷ *verb* **afflicting, afflicted**

affliction *noun* Something that causes suffering: *Chicken pox used to be one of the most common afflictions of childhood.* **af·flic·tion** (uh-**flik**-shuhn)

affluent *adjective* Having lots of money; wealthy.

afghan

af·flu·ent (**af**-loo-uhnt) ▷ *noun* **affluence**

afford *verb*
1. To have enough money to buy something.
2. To have enough time or ability to do something: *Can we afford to stop by the library so I can return these books?*
af·ford (uh-**ford**)
▷ *verb* **affording, afforded**

afghan *noun* A crocheted or knitted blanket. **af·ghan** (**af**-gan)

afloat *adjective*
1. Floating on water: *Move your arms and legs to stay afloat.*
2. If a business, plan, or program **stays afloat** or if someone **keeps it afloat,** it keeps going and does not fail.
a·float (uh-**floht**)

afraid *adjective*
1. Frightened; full of fear: *I'm afraid of the dark.*
2. If you begin or end a sentence with **I'm afraid**, you show that you are sorry that what you are saying is true: *I'm afraid I'm too tired to come visit you.*
a·fraid (uh-**frayd**)

Synonyms

Afraid means feeling great fear of something. It may be happening right now: *I'm afraid the wind is going to blow the roof off the house.* It may be something in the future that you're always worried about: *I'm afraid to sleep without the hall light on.* The word *afraid* is not used before nouns.

- -

■ **Frightened** means very afraid and is used before nouns or after the verb *be*: *The frightened children waited for their teacher. The passengers were frightened when the bus stalled on the railroad tracks.*

■ **Scared** is used when something causes someone to be frightened or afraid: *The horror movie scared some of the little kids.*

■ **Terrified** means really scared, to the point where you have trouble even breathing normally or thinking straight: *When the earthquake struck, people in the street were terrified.*

Africa *noun* The world's second-largest continent, after Asia. It lies in the Eastern Hemisphere and is bordered by the Atlantic Ocean, the Indian Ocean, and the Mediterranean Sea. **Af·ri·ca** (af-ri-kuh)
▷ *adjective* **African**

African American *noun* Someone who was born in the United States or who became a US citizen and can trace his or her ancestors back to Africa. **Af·ri·can American** (af-ri-kuhn) ▷ *adjective* **African American**

Afro *noun* A hairstyle with tight curls in a full, rounded shape. **Af·ro** (af-roh)

aft *adverb* Toward the back of a ship or an aircraft. **aft** (aft)

after *preposition*   Afro
1. Later than, as in *after dinner.*
2. Following behind: *The marching band passed by after the parade float.*
3. Trying to catch someone or something: *The dog chased after the ball.*
af·ter (af-tur)

aftercare *noun*
1. Care for children after school during the hours before their parents come home from work.

2. Care for a person after a difficult event in his or her life, such as being in the hospital or being in prison.
af·ter·care (af-tur-*kair*)

aftermath *noun* The situation after a bad thing happens: *In the aftermath of the storm, thousands of people needed emergency services.* **af·ter·math** (af-tur-*math*)

Word History

Disasters like hurricanes or earthquakes are devastating events, and 17th-century English speakers thought that a disaster or other bad event in people's lives was like a mower cutting everything down. **Aftermath** first meant "the crop that comes up after mowing," referring to a crop that grows after the first crop has been harvested. People then applied the term *aftermath* to the situation after a bad thing happens. The Old English noun *math* was an old word that meant "a mowing." The verb *mow* is related to this noun.

afternoon *noun* The time of day between noon and evening. **af·ter·noon** (*af*-tur-**noon**)

aftershock *noun* A relatively small earthquake that comes soon after a stronger earthquake in the same general location. **af·ter·shock** (**af**-tur-*shahk*)

afterward *or* **afterwards** *adverb* Later: *We watched a movie, and afterward we played cards.* **af·ter·ward** (af-tur-wurd) *or* **af·ter·wards** (af-tur-wurdz)

again *adverb* One more time: *The Ravens won again last night.* **a·gain** (uh-**gen**)

against *preposition*
1. Next to and touching: *Lean against me if you get tired.*
2. Competing with: *We've won every time we've gone up against them.*
3. Directed at or toward: *What are the charges against him?*
4. Opposed to: *The school board is against changing the dress code.*
a·gainst (uh-**genst**)

age
1. *noun* The length of time that someone has lived or that something has existed: *Mrs. Elkins lived to the age of 97.*
2. *noun* A period of time in history, as in *the Bronze Age.*
3. *verb* To become or seem older: *The president has aged since the election.* ▷ *verb* **aging** *or* **ageing, aged**

4. When you **come of age**, you become an adult in the eyes of the law.
age (ayj)

aged *adjective*
1. (ayjd) Being a particular number of years old: *The track meet is for students aged 14 and over.*
2. (**ay**-jid) Very old: *He lives with his aged father.*
3. the aged (**ay**-jid) *noun, plural* Old people in general.
aged

agency *noun* An office, business, or government department that provides a service to the public: *We're trying to figure out which federal agency deals with this issue.* **a·gen·cy** (**ay**-juhn-see) ▷ *noun, plural* **agencies**

agenda *noun*
1. A list of things that need to be done or discussed.
2. The real reasons that someone wants to do something, which may be secret or hidden: *He joined the company with a hidden agenda of taking it over.* **a·gen·da** (uh-**jen**-duh)

agent *noun*
1. Someone who arranges things for other people, as in *a real estate agent.*
2. A spy: *No one on the street knew that their quiet neighbor was a secret agent.* **a·gent** (**ay**-juhnt)

aggravate *verb*
1. To make something even worse: *He aggravated his cold by swimming in the lake.*
2. To annoy or bother: *My older sister claims that I never stop aggravating her.* **ag·gra·vate** (**ag**-ruh-*vate*)
▷ *verb* **aggravating, aggravated** ▷ *noun* **aggravation**
▷ *adjective* **aggravating**

aggregate *adjective* Formed by adding together different things or amounts: *The aggregate demand for new cars and appliances has dropped off in recent months.* **ag·gre·gate** (**ag**-ri-git)

aggression *noun* Violent or threatening behavior: *The dog's aggression frightened her.* **ag·gres·sion** (uh-**gresh**-uhn)

aggressive *adjective* Pushy and always ready to attack: *Her aggressive manner made it hard to like her.* **ag·gres·sive** (uh-**gres**-iv) ▷ *adverb* **aggressively**

agile *adjective*
1. Able to move fast and easily.
2. Able to think quickly and accurately.
ag·ile (**aj**-il *or* **aj**-ile)
▷ *noun* **agility** (uh-**jil**-i-tee)

agile

agitate *verb*
1. To make someone nervous and upset: *She became more agitated as the wasp flew nearer.* ▷ *noun* **agitation** ▷ *adjective* **agitated**
2. To stir or shake up: *Washing machines clean by agitating clothes.*
ag·i·tate (**aj**-i-*tate*)
▷ *verb* **agitating, agitated**

agnostic *noun* Someone who believes that it is impossible to know if God exists. **ag·nos·tic** (ag-**nah**-stik) ▷ *adjective* **agnostic**

ago *adverb* Before now, or in the past, as in *five months ago.* **a·go** (uh-**goh**)

agony *noun* Severe pain or suffering: *As his knee twisted under him, Brent screamed in agony.* **ag·o·ny** (**ag**-uh-nee) ▷ *noun, plural* **agonies** ▷ *adjective* **agonizing**

agree *verb*
1. To say yes to something: *I agreed to his proposal.*
2. To share the same opinion: *Lately it seems like we can't agree on movies at all.*
3. To be suitable or acceptable to someone.
a·gree (uh-**gree**)
▷ *verb* **agreeing, agreed**

agreeable *adjective*
1. Pleasing or likable: *Ken is an agreeable person.*
2. Willing or ready to say yes: *We'll eat early if everyone is agreeable.*
a·gree·a·ble (uh-**gree**-uh-buhl)

agreement *noun*
1. If you are **in agreement** with someone, you think the same way about a particular topic.
2. A formal understanding between two sides: *The workers and owners signed an agreement on salary levels.*
a·gree·ment (uh-**gree**-muhnt)

agriculture *noun* The raising of crops and animals; farming. **ag·ri·cul·ture** (**ag**-ri-*kuhl*-chur)
▷ *adjective* **agricultural**

aground *adverb* Stuck on the bottom in shallow water: *The ship ran aground at low tide.* **a·ground** (uh-**ground**)

ahead *adverb*
1. In front: *She is ahead of me in line.*
2. Before: *Can you get there ahead of us and give us a call?*
3. Further on in time or space: *You need to plan ahead.*
a·head (uh-**hed**)

ahoy *interjection* An exclamation used by sailors to call other ships or attract attention: *"Ahoy!" yelled the captain from the deck of the ship.* **a·hoy** (uh-**hoi**)

B
C
D
E
F
G
H
I
J
K
L
M
N
O
P
Q
R
S
T
U
V
W
X
Y
Z

aircraft

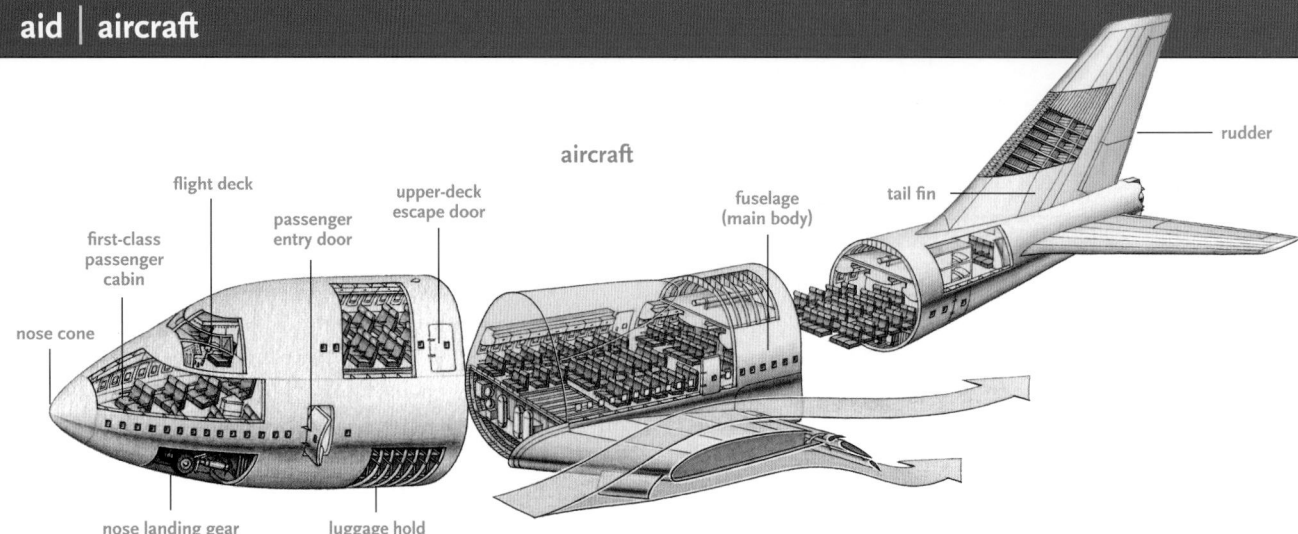

- rudder
- tail fin
- fuselage (main body)
- flight deck
- passenger entry door
- upper-deck escape door
- first-class passenger cabin
- nose cone
- nose landing gear
- luggage hold

aid

1. *verb* To help someone: *Relief agencies aided the earthquake victims.* ▷ *verb* **aiding, aided**

2. *noun* An object or action that helps someone do something: *It's a very hard concept to understand without the use of visual aids.*

3. *noun* Money or equipment for people in need, as in *foreign aid.*
aid (ayd)

aide *noun* A person who works along with others to help them do their jobs: *Kevin worked as a nurse's aide.* **aide** (ayd)

AIDS *noun* An often fatal illness that attacks the immune system, which protects the body against disease. AIDS is short for *acquired immune deficiency syndrome.* **AIDS** (aydz)

aikido *noun* A Japanese art of self-defense in which you use wrist, joint, and elbow grips to stop or throw your opponent. **ai·ki·do** (eye-**kee**-doh)

ail *verb*

1. To give pain or trouble to: *You need to see a doctor and find out what's ailing you.*

2. To have poor health: *His father has been ailing for a long time.*
ail (ayl)
▷ *verb* **ailing, ailed**

aileron *noun* A movable piece on an aircraft wing that pilots control. **ai·le·ron** (**ay**-luh-*rahn*)

ailment *noun* An illness, especially one that isn't serious. **ail·ment** (**ayl**-muhnt)

aim *verb*

1. To hit, throw, or shoot something in a particular direction: *Aim the bow carefully and then let the arrow fly.*

2. To plan or do something with a particular audience in mind: *The movie is aimed at the teenage market.*

3. To intend or hope to achieve something: *I aim to start my own business.*
aim (aym)
▷ *verb* **aiming, aimed** ▷ *noun* **aim**

aimless *adjective* Without direction or purpose: *I spent an aimless couple of hours wandering around downtown.* **aim·less** (**aym**-lis) ▷ *adverb* **aimlessly**

ain't *contraction* (*slang*) A short form of *am not, is not, are not, has not,* or *have not.* **ain't** (aynt)

Language Note

Although **ain't** sometimes is used in casual speech and song lyrics, it is not considered proper English. *Ain't* should not be used in formal speech or writing.

air

1. *noun* The mixture of gases around the earth that you need in order to breathe.

2. *verb* To express publicly: *People aired their opinions at the city council meeting.*

3. *verb* To let air into a room: *I opened the window and aired the room.*

4. *noun* An appearance, or a manner: *There's an air of royalty about her.*
air (air)
Air sounds like **heir**. ▷ *verb* **airing, aired**

air bag *noun* A bag in motor vehicles that automatically inflates during an accident to protect a driver or passenger.

airball *or* **air ball** *noun* A basketball shot that misses the basket: *He shot an airball three-pointer and then the coach swapped him out.* **air·ball** (**air**-bawl)

air-conditioning *noun* A system for keeping the air inside a building or vehicle cool, dry, and clean.

aircraft *noun* A vehicle that can fly. **air·craft** (**air**-kraft) ▷ *noun, plural* **aircraft**

aircraft carrier *noun* A warship with a large, flat deck where aircraft take off and land. **aircraft car·ri·er** (**kar**-ee-ur)

air force *noun* The part of a country's military that attacks and defends mainly with aircraft.

airline *noun* A company that carries passengers and freight by air in exchange for money. **air·line** (**air**-*line*)

airmail *noun* Letters and packages that are carried by aircraft, or the service that does this. **air·mail** (**air**-*mayl*)

air marshal *noun* A government security officer who wears ordinary clothes and flies on airplanes along with regular passengers.

airplane *noun* A vehicle with wings and an engine that flies through the air. **air·plane** (**air**-*playn*)

airport *noun* A place where aircraft take off and land, with buildings for passengers, businesses, freight, and other services. **air·port** (**air**-*port*)

air pressure *noun* The density or weight of the air, which is greater near the earth than it is high up: *The change in air pressure in the plane made the passengers' ears pop.*

airship *noun* An inflated frame shaped like a sausage with engines and a passenger compartment hanging underneath it. Blimps and zeppelins are airships. **air·ship** (**air**-*ship*)

airsick *adjective* Feeling sick to your stomach or dizzy from flying in a plane. **air·sick** (**air**-*sik*)

airtight *adjective* Not allowing air in or out, as in *an airtight container.* **air·tight** (**air**-*tite*)

airy *adjective* Full of fresh air. **air·y** (**air**-ee) ▷ *adjective* **airier, airiest** ▷ *adverb* **airily**

aisle *noun*
1. The passage that runs between the rows of seats in a room or large area, as in a theater, house of worship, or aircraft.
2. The passage between shelves in a store or supermarket, or the line of shelves: *Which aisle is peanut butter in?*
aisle (ile)
Aisle sounds like **isle** or **I'll**.

ajar *adjective* If a door is **ajar**, it is open or partly open. **a·jar** (uh-**jahr**) ▷ *adverb* **ajar**

akimbo *adjective* If you have your arms **akimbo**, your hands or knuckles are on your hips and your elbows are turned outward: *He stood with arms akimbo.* **a·kim·bo** (uh-**kim**-boh) ▷ *adverb* **akimbo**

albatross

Word History

About 800 years ago, *in kene bowe* was the English phrase for "in a sharp bend." People mispronounced the phrase and ran the words together, but the meaning stuck. Today, when you stand with arms **akimbo**, your hands are on your hips and your elbows are "in a sharp bend" outward.

---

akin *adjective*
1. Belonging to the same family: *Lions are akin to tigers and leopards.*
2. Similar: *This herb has a flavor akin to licorice.*
a·kin (uh-**kin**)

alabaster
1. *noun* A smooth, white kind of stone, often used for sculpture.
2. *adjective* Smooth, pale, and almost see-through, as in *alabaster skin.*
a·la·bas·ter (al-uh-*bas*-tur)

alarm
1. *noun* A mechanical, electric, or digital device with a bell, buzzer, or siren that wakes people or warns them of danger: *I set my alarm to wake me up at seven o'clock every morning.*
2. *noun* Fear that something bad will happen: *The plane's sudden descent gave everyone on board reason for alarm.*
3. *verb* To make someone afraid that something bad might happen: *The bank's announcement alarmed its customers.* ▷ *verb* **alarming, alarmed** ▷ *adjective* **alarming** ▷ *adverb* **alarmingly**
a·larm (uh-**lahrm**)

alas *interjection* Unfortunately, or sadly: *I ran to catch my train, but, alas, I was too late.* **a·las** (uh-**las**)

albatross *noun*
1. A large seabird with webbed feet and long wings that can fly for a long time.
2. If something is an **albatross around your neck**, it is a burden.
al·ba·tross (al-buh-*traws*)
▷ *noun, plural* **albatrosses**

Word History

In "The Rime of the Ancient Mariner," a poem written by the English poet Samuel Taylor Coleridge in 1798, the captain of a ship shoots an albatross with a crossbow. Believing that the killing will bring them bad luck, his angry shipmates make him wear the bird around his neck as punishment. The phrase **albatross around your neck** still means a "burden."

albino *noun* A person or animal born with the absence of pigment. This condition makes hair and skin very pale or white, and sometimes makes eyes pink. **al·bi·no** (al-**bye**-noh)

album *noun*
1. A book in which you keep things you collect.
2. A collection of music on a CD, tape, or record.
al·bum (**al**-buhm)

alchemist *noun* A medieval scientist who tried to turn lead or other metals into gold, find a cure for disease, or extend life forever: *Alchemists developed practices that laid the foundations for modern chemistry and modern medicine.* **al·che·mist** (**al**-kuh-mist) ▷ *noun* **alchemy** (**al**-kuh-mee)

alcohol *noun*
1. A colorless liquid found in drinks such as wine, whiskey, and beer that can make people drunk.
2. A drink that contains this liquid: *How much alcohol had they drunk?*
3. A liquid used in making medicines, chemicals, and fuels.
al·co·hol (**al**-kuh-*hawl*)

alcoholic
1. *adjective* Containing alcohol.
2. *noun* A person who is unable to stop the habit of drinking too much alcohol, even though it has very bad effects. ▷ *noun* **alcoholism**
al·co·hol·ic (*al*-kuh-**haw**-lik)

alcove *noun* A smaller part of a room that is separated from the main area: *He keeps all his books in an alcove off the living room.* **al·cove** (**al**-kove)

alder *noun* A tree or bush with rough bark and jagged leaves that grows in cool, moist places. **al·der** (**awl**-dur)

ale *noun* An alcoholic drink that is similar to beer but has a more bitter taste. **ale** (ayl)

alert
1. *adjective* Paying attention to what is around you and ready to act: *A good lifeguard must be constantly alert.*
2. *verb* To warn someone of possible danger: *My neighbor alerted me to the break-ins on our block.* ▷ *verb* **alerting, alerted**
3. *noun* A warning of possible danger, as in *a winter weather alert.*
a·lert (uh-**lurt**)

alfalfa *noun* A plant related to clover that is used mostly to feed farm animals. **al·fal·fa** (al-**fal**-fuh)

algae *noun, plural* Small plants without roots or stems that grow mainly in water: *We saw green and purple algae wash up on the beach.* **al·gae** (**al**-jee)

algebra *noun* A type of mathematics in which symbols and letters are used to represent numbers. **al·ge·bra** (**al**-juh-bruh)

Word History

A mathematician named al-Khwarizmi lived in the city of Baghdad in the ninth century. Now part of the country of Iraq, Baghdad was an important center of Islamic scientific thought. Al-Khwarizmi wrote a famous book on algebra, and our word **algebra** comes from a Latin translation of that book. In Arabic, *al-jebr* meant "the reunion of broken parts," from the words *al*, meaning "the," and *jabara*, meaning "to bring together again." *Al-jebr* was also a term for "bonesetting," or pushing the parts of a broken bone back into place. Two other English words that come from Arabic are *zero* and *zenith*.

alias *noun* A false name, especially one used by a criminal. **a·li·as** (**ay**-lee-uhs) ▷ *noun, plural* **aliases**

alibi *noun* A claim that a person accused of a crime was somewhere else when the crime was committed: *Her alibi was questioned in court.* **al·i·bi** (**al**-uh-*bye*)

alien
1. *noun* A being from another planet: *I love science fiction movies in which aliens attack the earth.*
2. *noun* A foreigner: *Aliens cannot hold certain government jobs.*
3. *adjective* Different and strange: *Their table manners were completely alien to us.*
a·li·en (**ay**-lee-uhn or **ayl**-yuhn)

align *verb* To put things in a straight line: *Use this command to align the text with the graphic.* **a·lign** (uh-**line**) ▷ *verb* **aligning, aligned**

alignment *noun*
1. Arrangement in a straight line or an orderly way: *Several of his ribs were out of alignment after the accident.*
2. The way that text, columns, or data are arranged: *Use Control + R for right alignment of the text.*
a·lign·ment (uh-**line**-muhnt)

alike
1. *adjective* Looking or acting the same: *The identical twins were alike in every way.*
2. *adverb* In a similar way: *I'm glad to see that we think alike on that issue.*
a·like (uh-**like**)

alimentary canal *noun* The path that food follows as it is digested by the body. It includes the esophagus, stomach, small intestine, and large intestine. **al·i·men·ta·ry canal** (*al*-uh-**men**-tur-ee)

alive *adjective*
1. Living; not dead: *You must water the plants to keep them alive.*
2. Energetic or active: *Myra's eyes were alive with excitement.*
a·live (uh-**live**)

alkali *noun* A strong base, such as lye or ammonia, that dissolves in water and reacts with an acid to form a salt. Strong alkalis can burn your skin. **al·ka·li** (**al**-kuh-*lye*) ▷ *adjective* **alkaline** (**al**-kuh-*line*)

all
1. *adjective* **All** of a group or thing is the whole of it: *All the candy was gone in 30 seconds.*
2. *pronoun* Everyone: *All must pay taxes on time.*
3. *adverb* Completely: *When you are all dressed, we can leave.*
4. *adverb* For each side: *The score was four all after nine innings.*
5. *noun* Everything: *Is this all you want me to do?*
all (awl)
All sounds like **awl**.

Allah *noun* The Muslim name for God. **Al·lah** (**ah**-luh *or* ah-**lah**)

allegation *noun* A claim without any proof that someone has done something wrong or that something illegal has happened: *She hired a defense attorney to fight the allegation that she had committed fraud.* **al·le·ga·tion** (*al*-i-**gay**-shuhn)

allege *verb* To say that something is true without offering proof: *The news story alleged that the official had taken a bribe.* **al·lege** (uh-**lej**) ▷ *verb* **alleging, alleged**

alleged *adjective* Said to be true or to have happened, but without proof: *Some police officers are investigating the alleged burglary.* **al·leged** (uh-**lejd** *or* uh-**lej**-id) ▷ *adverb* **allegedly**

allegiance *noun* Loyal support for someone or something. **al·le·giance** (uh-**lee**-juhns)

allergen *noun* A substance that causes an allergic reaction in someone: *Our cafeteria has a menu that*

avoids peanuts and other common allergens. **al·ler·gen** (**al**-ur-juhn)

allergen

allergic *adjective* If you are **allergic** to a substance, it causes you to sneeze, develop a rash, or have another unpleasant reaction. **al·ler·gic** (uh-**lur**-jik) ▷ *noun* **allergy** (**al**-ur-jee)

alley *noun* A narrow passageway between or behind buildings or backyards. **al·ley** (**al**-ee) ▷ *noun, plural* **alleys**

alliance *noun* An agreement to work together for some result: *The countries formed an alliance during the war.* **al·li·ance** (uh-**lye**-uhns)

allied *adjective*
1. Working together, or on the same side: *The allied troops forced the enemy back across the border.*
2. Similar or related: *Her courses are in biology, chemistry, and other allied subjects.*
al·lied (**al**-ide)

alligator *noun* A large reptile with strong jaws and very sharp teeth, related to the crocodile. Alligators live in parts of North America and China. **al·li·ga·tor** (**al**-i-*gay*-tur)

Word History

Spanish explorers had never seen an **alligator** before they came to the New World. When they encountered one, they thought it looked like a very large lizard. They called it *el lagarto,* Spanish for "the lizard." Later, when English settlers heard *el lagarto* spoken fast, they spelled it the way they heard it, naming the animal an alligator.

alliteration *noun* Repetition of the same sound at the beginning of a group of words, such as in the sentence "Fred is the first to finish five files." **al·lit·er·a·tion** (uh-*lit*-uh-**ray**-shuhn) ▷ *adjective* **alliterative**

allocate *verb* To set something aside for a particular purpose: *The company has allocated about $15,000 to the new project.* **al·lo·cate** (**al**-uh-*kate*) ▷ *verb* **allocating, allocated** ▷ *noun* **allocation**

alligator

allot *verb*

1. To give out something in equal shares or parts: *The teacher allotted two crayons to each child.*

2. To set aside for a particular purpose: *The teacher allotted 20 minutes for the test.* **al·lot** (uh-**laht**)

▷ *verb* **allotting, allotted**

▷ *noun* **allotment**

allow *verb*

1. To let someone have or do something: *My mom allows me to stay up until ten o'clock.*

2. To make something possible: *The new schedule allows more time for athletics and music.* **al·low** (uh-**lou**)

▷ *verb* **allowing, allowed**

allowance *noun*

1. Money given to someone regularly, especially from parents to a child.

2. A change that you make for a particular reason: *Make some allowance for the fact that not all guests have cars.* **al·low·ance** (uh-**lou**-uhns)

alloy *noun* A metal made from mixing other metals, or mixing a metal with an element that is not a metal. **al·loy** (**al**-oi)

all right

1. *adjective* Good enough or acceptable, but not very good: *The band was all right, but I have heard better ones.*

2. *adjective* Not hurt or sick: *After getting plenty of rest, she is feeling all right again.*

3. *interjection* Yes; I agree or I will.

all-star *adjective* Made up of the best people in a particular sport or skill: *The play has an all-star cast.* ▷ *noun* **all-star**

allude *verb* To hint at or mention briefly: *Brenda alluded to an argument she had with her brother.* **al·lude** (uh-**lood**) ▷ *verb* **alluding, alluded**

ally *noun* A person or country that is on the same side as another during a war or disagreement: *The United States and the United Kingdom are longtime allies.* **al·ly** (**al**-eye) ▷ *noun, plural* **allies**

almanac *noun* A book published once a year with facts and statistics about a variety of subjects. **al·ma·nac** (**awl**-muh-*nak*)

aloe plant

almighty *adjective*

1. Thought to have total or great power, as in *the almighty dollar.*

2. *(informal)* Very large or great: *We heard an almighty bang, and then were told to evacuate the building.*

3. the Almighty God. **al·might·y** (awl-**mye**-tee)

almond *noun* An oval-shaped nut that is used in cooking or baking or eaten alone. **al·mond** (**ah**-muhnd or **al**-muhnd)

almost *adverb* Very nearly: *I almost forgot to bring my homework to school.* **al·most** (**awl**-mohst)

aloe *noun* A plant whose gel can be used to help heal burns and cuts. **al·oe** (**al**-oh)

aloft *adjective* High up in the air: *The plane was aloft moments after speeding down the runway.* **a·loft** (uh-**lawft**) ▷ *adverb* **aloft**

aloha *interjection* In Hawaiian, a term used to say hello or good-bye. **a·lo·ha** (uh-**loh**-hah)

Language Note

Aloha is the Hawaiian word for "love," so when Hawaiians use the word *aloha* to greet someone or say good-bye, they are also wishing the person love. Hawaii's nickname is the Aloha State.

---

alone *adjective* Without anyone or anything else: *Ed stayed home alone. You can't succeed just by luck alone.* **a·lone** (uh-**lone**) ▷ *adverb* **alone**

along

1. *preposition* Following the length or direction of: *I walked along the avenue.*

2. *adverb* Forward; in the same direction: *The police came and moved people along.*

3. *adverb* With someone else; as a companion: *Can I come along for the ride?*

4. all along All the time: *I knew all along that Jonah would come back.* **a·long** (uh-**lawng**)

alongside

1. *adverb* Near to the side: *We waited on the dock while the ship came alongside.*

2. *preposition* Parallel to: *The two boys ran alongside each other.* **a·long·side** (uh-**lawng**-side)

aloof

1. *adverb* When you remain **aloof** from someone or something, you keep yourself apart and don't get involved: *Akimi always seems to remain aloof from her classmates.*

2. *adjective* Not friendly or talkative: *His aloof manner made Mr. Harding unpopular.*

a·loof (uh-**loof**)

aloud *adverb* So that other people can hear: *Do we have to read our reports aloud to the class?* **a·loud** (uh-**loud**)

alpaca *noun* A South American animal, related to the camel and the llama, that produces long, silky wool. **al·pac·a** (al-**pak**-uh)

alpacas

alphabet *noun* All the letters of a language arranged in order. **al·pha·bet** (**al**-fuh-*bet*) ▷ *adjective* **alphabetical**

alphabetize *verb* To arrange things so that they follow the order of the letters of the alphabet: *The entries in this dictionary are alphabetized.* **al·pha·bet·ize** (**al**-fuh-buh-*tize*) ▷ *verb* **alphabetizing, alphabetized**

already *adverb* Before now, or before a certain time in the past: *He had read that book already. They'd already finished eating when I got there.* **al·read·y** (awl-**red**-ee)

also *adverb* As well; in addition: *She left her business card and also a phone number where she'll be today.* **al·so** (**awl**-soh)

altar *noun* A large table in a house of worship, used for religious ceremonies. **al·tar** (**awl**-tur) **Altar** sounds like **alter**.

alter *verb* To change: *We altered the dining room to use part of it as an office.* **al·ter** (**awl**-tur) **Alter** sounds like **altar**. ▷ *verb* **altering, altered**

alteration *noun* The act or process of changing something, or a change made: *We asked the architect to make alterations to the house's design so that we could have a bigger kitchen.* **al·ter·a·tion** (*awl*-tuh-**ray**-shuhn)

altercation *noun* A fight, often including loud and noisy arguing: *The altercation between the fans of the two rival teams lasted several minutes, but no one was hurt.* **al·ter·ca·tion** (*awl*-tur-**kay**-shuhn)

alternate

1. (**awl**-tur-nit) *adjective* Every other one: *We have gym only on alternate days.*

2. (**awl**-tur-*nate*) *verb* To take turns: *We alternate who goes first when we play cards.* ▷ *verb* **alternating, alternated**

al·ter·nate

alternative

1. *noun* A choice that is not the usual one: *Her parents are looking for an eco-friendly alternative to gasoline.*

2. *adjective* Different from the usual thing or kind, as in *alternative medicine.*

al·ter·na·tive (awl-**tur**-nuh-tiv)

alternative energy *noun* Energy from natural sources that are renewable and don't harm the environment, such as the sun, ocean waves, and wind.

alternatively *adverb* As an alternative: *Walk to school; alternatively, you could take the bus.* **al·ter·na·tive·ly** (awl-**tur**-nuh-tiv-lee)

although *conjunction*

1. In spite of the fact that: *Although it's cold, we are having a good time playing outdoors.*

2. But: *The house has only a few rooms, although it seems much bigger.*

al·though (*awl*-**THoh**)

altimeter *noun* An instrument that measures how high something is above the ground. **al·tim·e·ter** (al-**tim**-i-tur)

altitude *noun* The height of something above the ground or above sea level: *The small plane flew at an average altitude of 2,000 feet.* **al·ti·tude** (**al**-ti-*tood*)

altar

alto *noun*
1. A singing voice that is higher than a tenor but lower than a soprano.
2. A person with an alto voice.
al·to (**al**-toh)

altogether *adverb*
1. With everything or everyone counted: *At the meet, our school won 17 ribbons altogether.*
2. Completely, or entirely: *What he showed us was altogether different from what we expected.*
3. On the whole; in general: *Altogether, we were glad we went.*
al·to·geth·er (*awl*-tuh-**geTH**-ur)

aluminum *noun* A light, silver-colored metal: *We put the aluminum cans in the recycling bin behind our house.* **a·lu·mi·num** (uh-**loo**-mi-nuhm)

always *adverb*
1. All the time or very many times.
2. Since the beginning and up until now: *We've always lived in small towns.*
al·ways (**awl**-*wayz*)

Alzheimer's disease *noun* A disease that damages brain cells, making it hard to remember even simple things, to speak, and eventually to move. **Alz·hei·mer's disease** (**awlts**-hye-murz)

a.m. An abbreviation of the Latin phrase *ante meridiem*, which means "before noon."

am *verb* The first-person singular present tense of *be. Am* is used only with the pronoun *I.* **am** (am)

amateur *noun* Someone who does some activity for pleasure rather than for money: *The choir includes professional singers and amateurs.* **am·a·teur** (**am**-uh-chur *or* **am**-uh-tur) ▷ *adjective* **amateur**

amaze *verb* To make someone extremely surprised: *They were amazed at how well she could ride a horse.* **a·maze** (uh-**maze**) ▷ *verb* **amazing, amazed** ▷ *noun* **amazement**

amazing *adjective* Extremely impressive and perhaps difficult to believe: *After having a serious bout of the flu, she's made an amazing recovery and will be able to sing in the show tonight.* **a·maz·ing** (uh-**may**-zing) ▷ *adverb* **amazingly**

ambassador *noun* The top person sent by a government to represent it in another country: *My uncle became the US ambassador to Ethiopia.* **am·bas·sa·dor** (am-**bas**-uh-dur)

amber *noun*
1. A yellowish-brown substance formed from fossilized tree sap.
2. A yellowish-brown color.

am·ber (**am**-bur)
▷ *adjective* **amber**

AMBER alert *noun*
A public notice or media broadcast that tells people about a missing child.

ambidextrous *adjective* Able to use both hands equally well, especially for writing. **am·bi·dex·trous** (*am*-bi-**dek**-struhs)

amber

> **Word History**
>
> In Latin, *ambi-* means "both" and *dexter* means "right-handed." So if you are **ambidextrous**, it is as if you had two right hands. Since most people can use one hand better than the other (and for many people it is the right hand), *ambidextrous* means you are able to use both hands equally well. The word *dexterity*, which means "skill in using your hands," comes from the same Latin root.

ambiguous *adjective* Having two possible meanings: *His answer was ambiguous—it was hard to tell if he meant yes or no.* **am·big·u·ous** (am-**big**-yoo-uhs)
▷ *noun* **ambiguity** (*am*-bi-**gyoo**-i-tee)
▷ *adverb* **ambiguously**

ambition *noun*
1. Something that you want to do in the future: *My greatest ambition is to be president.*
2. A strong wish to be successful: *It takes hard work and ambition to succeed in the music industry.*
am·bi·tion (am-**bish**-uhn)

ambitious *adjective*
1. Having a strong desire and will to succeed: *Her colleagues describe her as ambitious and even ruthless.*
2. Requiring a lot of money, effort, or resources: *The company undertook the ambitious project of building the city's tallest skyscraper.*
am·bi·tious (am-**bish**-uhs)

ambivalent *adjective* Having two different opinions about something at the same time: *I felt ambivalent about going on vacation because I had to leave my dog in a kennel.* **am·biv·a·lent** (am-**biv**-uh-luhnt)
▷ *noun* **ambivalence**

amble *verb* To walk slowly because you are not in a hurry. **am·ble** (**am**-buhl) ▷ *verb* **ambling, ambled**

ambulance *noun* A vehicle that takes ill or injured people to a hospital. **am·bu·lance** (**am**-byuh-luhns)

ambush *verb* To attack someone from a hiding place: *The soldiers were ambushed on a quiet road.* **am·bush** (**am**-*bush*) ▷ *verb* **ambushes, ambushing, ambushed** ▷ *noun* **ambush**

ameba *See* **amoeba.**

amen *interjection*

1. People say **amen** after a prayer to mean "May it be so."

2. **Amen** also shows agreement with a statement: *"That's enough for today—let's stop and have dinner." "Amen to that!"*

a·men (ay-**men** *or* ah-**men**)

amend

1. *verb* To change a legal document or a law: *I need to amend the contract before I sign it.* ▷ *verb* **amending, amended**

2. *noun, plural* When you make **amends**, you do something to make up for a wrong or a mistake.

a·mend (uh-**mend**)

amendment *noun* A change that is made to a law or a legal document: *The first ten amendments to the Constitution are known as the Bill of Rights.* **a·mend·ment** (uh-**mend**-muhnt)

American

1. *adjective* Of or having to do with the United States, as in *the American government.*

2. *adjective* Of or having to do with North, Central, or South America, as in *the American continents.*

3. *noun* Someone born or living in the United States.

4. *noun* Someone born or living in North, Central, or South America.

A·mer·i·can (uh-**mer**-i-kuhn)

American English *noun* The variety of English that Americans speak and that is most common in the United States: *"Biscuit" has a different meaning in American English than it does to a British person.*

American Indian *noun* A member of any of the original people of North, Central, or South America. American Indians are sometimes called **Native Americans**. ▷ *adjective* **American Indian**

amethyst *noun* A type of quartz crystal that is usually purple and often is used in jewelry. **am·e·thyst** (**am**-uh-thist)

amethyst

amiable *adjective* Friendly and easygoing: *Sue's amiable boss was pleasant even when things went wrong.* **a·mi·a·ble** (ay-mee-uh-buhl)

amid *preposition* In the middle of or surrounded by: *The senator could be seen amid a large group of reporters.* **a·mid** (uh-**mid**)

amigo *noun* The Spanish word for "male friend." The Spanish word for "female friend" is *amiga* (uh-**mee**-guh). **a·mi·go** (uh-**mee**-goh)

Amish

1. *noun, plural* The members of a strict Christian group who live mostly in Pennsylvania and Ohio: *The Amish live without cars or electricity.*

2. *adjective* Of or having to do with the Amish.

A·mish (**ah**-mish)

amiss

1. *adverb* In the wrong way, or in an inappropriate or unexpected direction: *We were nervous that something would go amiss in the performance, but it was fine.*

2. *adjective* Incorrect, faulty, or imperfect: *Something is seriously amiss with his explanation—it doesn't make sense!*

a·miss (uh-**mis**)

ammonia *noun* A chemical with a strong smell. It dissolves in water and is used in some cleaning products. **am·mo·nia** (uh-**mohn**-yuh)

ammunition *noun*

1. Things such as bullets or shells that can be fired from weapons: *The soldiers ran out of ammunition for their rifles.*

2. Information that you can use to support or oppose something: *The news story gave him ammunition to argue against building the highway.*

am·mu·ni·tion (am-yuh-**nish**-uhn)

amnesia *noun* A partial or total loss of memory that can be temporary or permanent. **am·ne·sia** (am-**nee**-zhuh)

amnesty *noun* An official decision to release prisoners and pardon crimes or mistakes: *The government granted amnesty to all war protesters.* **am·nes·ty** (**am**-ni-stee) ▷ *noun, plural* **amnesties**

amoeba *or* **ameba** *noun* A microscopic creature made of only one cell that is able to move through fluid. **a·moe·ba** *or* **a·me·ba** (uh-**mee**-buh) ▷ *noun, plural* **amoebas** *or* **amoebae** (uh-**mee**-bee)

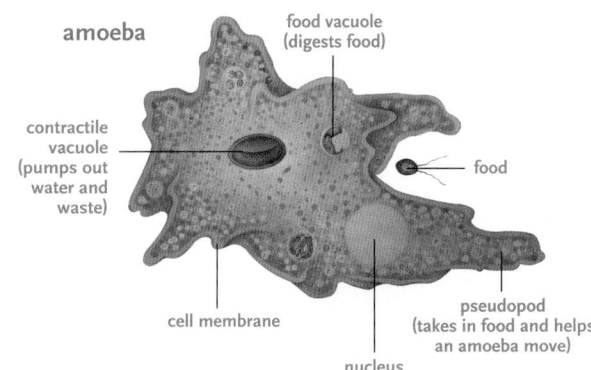

amoeba

food vacuole (digests food)

contractile vacuole (pumps out water and waste)

food

cell membrane

nucleus

pseudopod (takes in food and helps an amoeba move)

B
C
D
E
F
G
H
I
J
K
L
M
N
O
P
Q
R
S
T
U
V
W
X
Y
Z

amok *or* **amuck**

1. *adverb* In a way that is uncontrollable and violent.

2. *idiom* When people **run amok**, they behave wildly or violently: *The peaceful protest turned into a riot as some people began to vandalize cars and run amok.*

a·mok *or* **a·muck** (uh-**muhk**)

among *preposition*

1. In the middle of, or surrounded by: *Kerry felt safe because she was among friends.*

2. Giving some to each person or thing: *Her mother baked a big chocolate cake and divided it among the five of us.*

3. Included as part of a certain group: *These pieces are among the most popular for piano that Beethoven wrote.*

a·mong (uh-**muhng**)

amount

1. *noun* A quantity of something: *The amount of snow this winter was several inches more than usual.*

2. *verb* To add up to a certain figure or quantity: *The cost of the damage amounted to several hundred dollars.* ▷ *verb* **amounting, amounted**

a·mount (uh-**mount**)

amp *noun*

1. A unit used to measure the strength of an electrical current, short for *ampere* (**am**-peer).

2. Short for **amplifier**.

amp (amp)

ampersand *noun* A symbol (&) that stands for the word *and*: *Lisette worked for a law firm called Callahan & Smithson.* **am·per·sand** (**am**-pur-*sand*)

ampersand

amphibian *noun*

1. A cold-blooded animal with a backbone that lives in water and breathes with gills when young. As an adult, it develops lungs and lives on land. Frogs, toads, and salamanders are amphibians.

2. A vehicle that can travel on land and in water.

am·phib·i·an (am-**fib**-ee-uhn)

▷ *adjective* **amphibious**

Amphibians

Found everywhere but Antarctica and Greenland, amphibians include more than 6,000 species. Frogs and toads are the most common type. They usually live in wet places such as marshes. Newts, salamanders, and caecilians—wormlike creatures that burrow in the ground—also need damp environments to survive.

salamander

caecilian

tree frog

red-eyed tree frog

poison dart frog

toad

amphitheater *noun* A large building or area with rows of seats in a high circle around a central place like a stage. In ancient Rome, amphitheaters were used for public entertainment. **am·phi·the·a·ter** (am-fi-*thee*-uh-tur)

ample *adjective*
1. More than enough: *There is an ample supply of cupcakes for the party.* ▷ *adverb* **amply** (**am**-plee)
2. Large: *The car has an ample trunk.* **am·ple** (**am**-puhl)
▷ *adjective* **ampler, amplest**

amplifier *noun* A piece of equipment that makes sound louder. **am·pli·fi·er** (am-pluh-*fye*-ur)

amplify *verb* To make something louder or stronger: *He amplified his voice with a microphone.* **am·pli·fy** (am-pli-*fye*) ▷ *verb* **amplifies, amplifying, amplified** ▷ *noun* **amplification**

amputate *verb* To cut off someone's limb, such as an arm, leg, or finger, usually because it is damaged or diseased. **am·pu·tate** (**am**-pyuh-*tate*) ▷ *verb* **amputating, amputated** ▷ *noun* **amputation**

amulet *noun* A small object, such as a charm or necklace, worn in the belief that it will protect the wearer from evil things or people: *Archaeologists found many jade amulets in the king's tomb.* **am·u·let** (**am**-yuh-lit)

amuse *verb*
1. To make someone laugh or smile: *Your jokes amuse me.* ▷ *adjective* **amusing**
2. To prevent someone from being bored in an enjoyable way: *Brook's new video game amused him for hours.*
a·muse (uh-**myooz**)
▷ *verb* **amusing, amused** ▷ *noun* **amusement**

amusement park *noun* A place where people pay to go on rides, play games of skill, and enjoy other forms of entertainment.

an *indefinite article* A form of *a* used before a word that is pronounced with a vowel as its first sound, as in *an onion* or *an herb.* **an** (uhn *or* an)

anaconda *noun* A large, nonpoisonous South American snake that wraps itself tightly around its prey to kill it. **an·a·con·da** (an-uh-**kahn**-duh)

anagram *noun* A word or phrase made by rearranging the letters in another word or phrase: *"Editor" is an anagram of "rioted."* **an·a·gram** (**an**-uh-*gram*)

analog *adjective*
1. Using moving parts to show a continuous change in information, as in *an analog clock.*
2. Measuring or representing data with continuous changes in physical properties rather than with numbers, as is the case for something that is digital:

Analog technology

Big Ben, a tower at the northern end of the Houses of Parliament in London, has a clock dial on each of its four sides. The largest four-faced chiming clock in the world, it celebrated its 150th anniversary in 2009. It is an analog clock, so it uses hour and minute hands to show the time. A digital clock uses only numbers to indicate the time.

analog

digital

An analog speedometer tells you a car's speed by measuring how fast the wheels rotate.
an·a·log (**an**-uh-*lawg*)

analysis *noun* The process or result of analyzing something, as in *a scientific analysis* or *a financial analysis.* **a·nal·y·sis** (uh-**nal**-i-sis) ▷ *noun, plural* **analyses**

analyze *verb* To examine something carefully in order to understand it: *The panel analyzed the latest developments in the war.* **an·a·lyze** (**an**-uh-*lize*) ▷ *verb* **analyzing, analyzed** ▷ *adjective* **analytical** (an-uh-**lit**-i-kuhl)

anatomy *noun*
1. The structure of a living thing, such as an animal or insect.
2. The scientific study of the structure of living things. **a·nat·o·my** (uh-**nat**-uh-mee)
▷ *noun, plural* **anatomies** ▷ *adjective* **anatomical** (an-uh-**tah**-mi-kuhl)

ancestor *noun* A member of your family who lived long ago, usually before your grandparents: *One of my ancestors was President Grover Cleveland.* **an·ces·tor** (**an**-ses-tur) ▷ *adjective* **ancestral**

B
C
D
E
F
G
H
I
J
K
L
M
N
O
P
Q
R
S
T
U
V
W
X
Y
Z

ancestry *noun* Your ancestors, or some aspect of them: *Do you have any Scandinavian ancestry?* **an·ces·try (an**-ses-tree)

anchor
1. *noun* A heavy metal object that is lowered from a ship or boat when it stops, to keep it from drifting.
2. *noun* The main person on camera during a TV news show.
3. *verb* To keep a boat in place by dropping an anchor. ▷ *verb* **anchoring, anchored**
an·chor (ang-kur)

anchovy *noun* A small, edible fish that is often salted and canned. **an·cho·vy (an**-*choh*-vee)
▷ *noun, plural* **anchovies**

ancient *adjective*
1. Very old: *Our textbooks are ancient.*
2. Belonging to a period long ago, as in *an ancient monument* or *ancient Egypt.*
an·cient (ayn-shuhnt)

and *conjunction*
1. As well as: *The dog jumped up and barked.*
2. Added to, or plus: *Five and one make six.*
3. As a result: *My mom got a new job, and we had to move.*
and (and *or* uhnd)

android *noun* A robot that is designed to act and look like a human being. **an·droid (an**-droid)

anecdote *noun* A short, often funny story about an experience: *Maria had an anecdote about running into an old friend.* **an·ec·dote (an**-ik-*dote*)
▷ *adjective* **anecdotal**

anemic *adjective* If you are **anemic**, you feel weak and become easily tired because your body isn't producing enough red blood cells. **a·ne·mic (uh-nee**-mik) ▷ *noun* **anemia**

anemometer *noun* A scientific instrument used to measure the wind's speed. **an·e·mom·et·er** (*an*-i-**mah**-mi-tur)

Angora rabbit

anemone *noun*
1. A small plant with purple, red, white, or pink flowers.
2. Short for **sea anemone**.
a·nem·o·ne (uh-**nem**-uh-nee)

anesthesiologist *noun* A physician who specializes in giving people drugs or gas to prevent pain during operations. **an·es·the·si·ol·o·gist** (*an*-is-*thee*-zee-**ah**-luh-jist)

anesthetic *noun* A drug or a gas given to people to prevent or lessen pain: *My dentist used a local anesthetic when he filled my cavity.* **an·es·thet·ic** (*an*-is-**thet**-ik)

anew *adverb* Again, or once more, as in *to start anew.* **a·new** (uh-**noo**)

angel *noun*
1. In religion, a messenger of God. Most pictures of angels show them with wings.
2. A very kind, gentle person.
an·gel (ayn-juhl)
▷ *adjective* **angelic** (an-**jel**-ik)

anger *noun* The strong feeling of being very annoyed or hostile toward someone: *Her anger with Jim increased as he became more quarrelsome.* **an·ger (ang**-gur)

angle *noun*
1. The area formed by two lines that start at the same point and go in different directions. Angles are measured in degrees.
2. A way of looking at or dealing with something: *Let's approach this from another angle.*
3. If something is **at an angle**, it is sloping.
an·gle (ang-guhl)

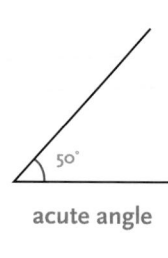

50°

acute angle

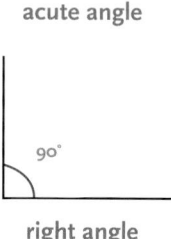

90°

right angle

angora *noun*
1. Fluffy fiber or yarn made from the hair of Angora rabbits.
2. A long-haired variety of rabbit, goat, or cat. The name for the breed of these animals is capitalized.
an·go·ra (ang-**gor**-uh)

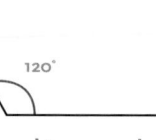

120°

obtuse angle

angry *adjective* Feeling or showing annoyance or bad feelings toward someone or something: *Everyone was surprised by Rebecca's angry outburst.* **an·gry (ang**-gree) ▷ *adjective* **angrier, angriest** ▷ *adverb* **angrily**

anguish *noun* A strong feeling of pain or distress:

The lack of news about their relatives caused the families terrible anguish. **an·guish** (**ang**-gwish) ▷ *adjective* **anguished**

angular *adjective* Having straight lines and sharp turns or corners: *Jamie has angular features and a tall build.* **an·gu·lar** (**ang**-gyuh-lur)

animal *noun* Any living creature that can move around and that eats other organisms to survive. Humans are animals, too, but usually when people refer to animals they mean pigs, donkeys, elephants, or other such beings. **an·i·mal** (**an**-uh-muhl)

animal rights *noun* The idea that animals should be treated with kindness and respect, and that they should not suffer because of things that humans want.

animated *adjective*
1. Lively, as in *an animated conversation.* ▷ *adverb* **animatedly**
2. Made by projecting a series of slightly different images very quickly, one after the other, so that the characters in the images seem to move. ▷ *verb* **animate** ▷ *noun* **animator**
an·i·mat·ed (**an**-uh-*may*-tid)

animation *noun* The activity of making movies by using drawings, pictures, or computer graphics. **an·i·ma·tion** (*an*-uh-**may**-shuhn)

anime *noun* Japanese animation for film, television, and video. **an·i·me** (**an**-uh-*may*)

animosity *noun* A strong dislike for someone: *The animosity between them grew when they became political rivals.* **an·i·mos·i·ty** (*an*-uh-**mah**-si-tee)

ankle *noun* The joint that connects your foot to your leg: *I twisted my ankle while running down the stairs.* **an·kle** (**ang**-kuhl)

annex
1. (**an**-eks *or* an-**eks**) *verb* To take control of a country or territory by force. ▷ *verb* **annexes, annexing, annexed** ▷ *noun* **annexation**
2. (**an**-eks) *noun* A smaller building that is connected to or located near a main building. **an·nex**

annihilate *verb* To destroy something completely: *Doctors use radiation to annihilate cancer cells.* **an·ni·hi·late** (uh-**nye**-uh-*late*) ▷ *verb* **annihilating, annihilated** ▷ *noun* **annihilation**

anniversary *noun* A date that people remember each year because of an important event that happened

anime

on that date in an earlier year, as in *a wedding anniversary.* **an·ni·ver·sa·ry** (an-uh-**vur**-sur-ee) ▷ *noun, plural* **anniversaries**

annotate *verb* To add notes to a text or picture in order to explain it better: *Annotate the article and bring it to class for discussion tomorrow.* **an·no·tate** (**an**-uh-*tate*) ▷ *verb* **annotating, annotated** ▷ *noun* **annotation** ▷ *adjective* **annotated**

announce *verb* To say something officially or publicly: *Abe announced his retirement.* **an·nounce** (uh-**nouns**) ▷ *verb* **announcing, announced**

announcement *noun*
1. A public statement that gives new information about something: *Did you hear the announcement that tonight's game was canceled?*
2. The act of announcing something: *We were all waiting excitedly for the announcement of the winner.*
an·nounce·ment (uh-**nouns**-muhnt)

announcer *noun*
1. Someone who introduces programs on television or radio.
2. Someone who describes the action during a sports event.
an·nounc·er (uh-**noun**-sur)

annoy *verb* To make someone lose patience or feel angry: *It really annoys me when a car alarm rings for half an hour.* **an·noy** (uh-**noi**) ▷ *verb* **annoying, annoyed** ▷ *noun* **annoyance** ▷ *adjective* **annoying** ▷ *adverb* **annoyingly**

annual
1. *adjective* Happening once every year or over a period of one year, as in *the annual Labor Day parade* or *an annual magazine subscription.* ▷ *adverb* **annually**
2. *noun* A book published once a year; a yearbook.
3. *noun* A plant that lives for only one year: *Marigolds and petunias are annuals.*
an·nu·al (**an**-yoo-uhl)

anoint *verb* To honor someone during a religious ceremony by dabbing oil on his or her head. **a·noint** (uh-**noint**) ▷ *verb* **anointing, anointed**

anomaly *noun* Something that is strange, different, or unexpected: *Usually she's a very calm dog, so her loud barking today was an anomaly.* **a·nom·a·ly** (uh-**nah**-muh-lee)

anon *adjective* *(old-fashioned)* Soon. This word is found mainly in old poems: *Anon I woke, but in one corner of my soul I stayed asleep.* **a·non** (uh-**nahn**)

anonymous *adjective* Written, done, or given by a person whose name is not known or made public, as in *an anonymous letter.* **a·non·y·mous** (uh-**nah**-nuh-muhs) ▷ *noun* **anonymity** (*an*-uh-**nim**-i-tee) ▷ *adverb* **anonymously**

anorexia *noun* A mental illness that makes people think they are too fat when in fact they are dangerously thin because they won't eat enough. **an·o·rex·i·a** (*an*-uh-**rek**-see-uh)
▷ *adjective* **anorexic** (*an*-uh-**rek**-sik)

another
1. *adjective* One more of the same kind of thing: *Take another apple.*
2. *pronoun* A different one, or one more: *Art owns one home on the beach and another in the mountains.*
an·oth·er (uh-**nuhTH**-ur)

answer
1. *verb* To say or write something as a reply, as in *to answer a question.* ▷ *noun* **answer**
2. *noun* The solution to a problem: *Taking a nap is the answer if you are feeling tired.*
3. answer for *verb* To be responsible for something: *Should parents answer for their children's vandalism?*
an·swer (**an**-sur)
▷ *verb* **answering, answered**

ant *noun* A small but very strong insect that lives in a large group called a colony. **ant** (ant)

antacid *noun* A medicine that works by reducing the amount of acid in your stomach: *Baking soda is an effective antacid.* **ant·ac·id** (ant-**as**-id)

antagonize *verb* To make someone oppose you or be angry with you: *Cassie was punished for antagonizing her little sister.* **an·tag·o·nize** (an-**tag**-uh-*nize*) ▷ *verb* **antagonizing, antagonized** ▷ *noun* **antagonism** ▷ *noun* **antagonist**

Antarctic *noun* The area around the South Pole. **Ant·arc·tic** (ant-**ahrk**-tik) ▷ *adjective* **Antarctic**

Antarctica *noun* The continent around the South Pole. Antarctica and its surrounding waters are part of the Antarctic. **Ant·arc·ti·ca** (ant-**ahrk**-ti-kuh)

anteater *noun* A mammal with a long, sticky tongue that it uses to search for ants and other small insects. Anteaters are found in Central and South America. **ant·eat·er** (**ant**-*ee*-tur)

antecedent *noun* The word or phrase that a pronoun refers to. For example, in the sentence "Ramón cooked the burger and then ate it," the antecedent of the pronoun *it* is "the burger." **an·te·ced·ent** (*an*-ti-**see**-duhnt)

antelope *noun* An animal that looks like a deer and runs very fast. Antelopes have long horns without branches and are found in Africa and parts of Asia. **an·te·lope** (**an**-tuh-*lope*)

antenna *noun*
1. A feeler on the head of an insect.
2. A device that receives radio and television signals:

Antarctic

Adjust the antenna to get rid of the static on the radio. **an·ten·na** (an-**ten**-uh)
▷ *noun, plural* **antennas** or **antennae** (an-**ten**-ee)

anthem *noun* A religious or national song, or a song that expresses the ideas of a particular group. **an·them** (**an**-thuhm)

anther *noun* The part of a flower at the tip of the stamen that contains its pollen. **an·ther** (**an**-thur)

anthology *noun* A book that contains articles, poems, or stories by different writers: *I just finished reading an anthology of modern poetry.* **an·thol·o·gy** (an-**thah**-luh-jee) ▷ *noun, plural* **anthologies**

anthropology *noun* The study of the beliefs and ways of life of different peoples and cultures. **an·thro·pol·o·gy** (*an*-thruh-**pah**-luh-jee) ▷ *noun* **anthropologist**

Prefix

The prefix **anti-** adds one of these meanings to a root word:

1. Against, as in *antisocial* (against society) or *antiwar* (against war).

2. Preventing or working against, as in *antiperspirant* (something that works against perspiration) or *antiseptic* (something that works against germs).

When a word begins with a capital letter, the prefix *anti-* is added with a hyphen, as in *anti-Nazi* or *anti-American.*

antibiotic *noun* A drug that kills bacteria and is used to treat infections and diseases. **an·ti·bi·ot·ic** (*an*-ti-bye-**ah**-tik)

antibody *noun* A protein that your blood makes to stop an infection that has entered your body. **an·ti·bod·y** (**an**-ti-*bah*-dee) ▷ *noun, plural* **antibodies**

anticipate *verb* To expect something to happen and be prepared for it: *Anticipating bad weather this weekend, we rescheduled the meeting.* **an·tic·i·pate**

(an-**tis**-uh-*pate*) ▷ *verb* **anticipating, anticipated** ▷ *noun* **anticipation**

anticlimax *noun* An event that you expect will be exciting, interesting, or important but then isn't: *After the fun of getting ready, the party was an anticlimax.* **an·ti·cli·max** (an-ti-**klye**-maks) ▷ *noun, plural* **anticlimaxes**

antidote *noun* Something that stops a poison from working: *Common herbs can be used as antidotes for some poisons.* **an·ti·dote** (**an**-ti-dote)

antifreeze *noun* A chemical mixture that is added to liquid to stop it from freezing. **an·ti·freeze** (**an**-tee-*freez*)

antiperspirant *noun* A substance that you put on your skin to stop you from sweating too much. **an·ti·per·spi·rant** (*an*-ti-**pur**-spur-uhnt)

antique
1. *noun* An object that is old and considered valuable because it is rare or beautiful: *The tea set she inherited from her grandma was an antique.*
2. *adjective* Very old, as in *antique jewelry.*
an·tique (an-**teek**)

antiseptic *noun* A substance that kills germs and prevents infection by stopping the growth of germs. **an·ti·sep·tic** (*an*-ti-**sep**-tik)

antisocial *adjective*
1. An **antisocial** person does not enjoy being with others.
2. Antisocial behavior upsets or harms other people.
an·ti·so·cial (*an*-ti-**soh**-shuhl)

antivirus *adjective* Designed to protect computers from viruses: *Which antivirus software do you use?* **an·ti·vi·rus** (*an*-ti-**vye**-ruhs)

antler *noun* One of the two large, branching, bony structures on the head of a deer, moose, or elk. **ant·ler** (**ant**-lur)

antler

Word History

When the Romans watched a stag, or male deer, bending his head to drink water, they noticed that his antler looked like a branch in front of his eyes. So they named it *ramum ante ocularis,* the "branch before the eyes." The Latin *ante ocularis* developed into the French *antoillier,* which became **antler** later on in English.

antonym *noun* A word, often an adjective, that means the opposite of another word. *Hot* and *cold* are antonyms; so are *weak* and *strong, up* and *down,* and *over* and *under.* **an·to·nym** (**an**-tuh-*nim*)

anxiety *noun* A feeling of worry or fear: *Max wondered if his anxiety about the test would affect his score.* **anx·i·e·ty** (ang-**zye**-i-tee) ▷ *noun, plural* **anxieties**

anxious *adjective*
1. Worried: *We got more anxious as the day wore on with no news.* ▷ *adverb* **anxiously**
2. Very eager to do something: *They're all anxious to go camping this weekend.*
anx·ious (**angk**-shuhs)

any
1. *adjective* One or more: *Do you have any brothers or sisters?*
2. *adjective* Every: *Any teacher would be proud to have you as a student.*
3. *pronoun* A way of suggesting people or things without naming them: *She'd gladly team up with any of them for the debate.*
4. *adverb* At all: *Do you feel any better?*
an·y (**en**-ee)

anybody *pronoun* Any person: *Anybody who buys a ticket could win the raffle.* **an·y·bod·y** (**en**-ee-*bah*-dee)

anyhow *adverb* In any case: *I didn't want to come anyhow.* **an·y·how** (**en**-ee-*hou*)

anymore *adverb*
1. Now, or from now on: *I won't bother you anymore.*
2. You use **anymore** to talk about differences between now and the past: *They don't make that kind of candy anymore.*
an·y·more (**en**-ee-**mor**)

anyone *pronoun* Any person: *Does anyone know if it's supposed to rain today?* **an·y·one** (**en**-ee-*wuhn*)

anyplace *adverb* Anywhere: *Your glasses could be anyplace.* **an·y·place** (**en**-ee-*plase*)

anything
1. *pronoun* Any thing or item of any kind: *Morgan likes to collect anything that has a Civil War theme.*
2. *adverb* At all: *You aren't anything like your brother.*
an·y·thing (**en**-ee-*thing*)

anytime *adverb* At any hour or date, or whenever: *Since my parents own a pizza parlor, I can eat pizza anytime I want.* **an·y·time** (**en**-ee-*time*)

anyway *adverb*
1. In any case: *I didn't want to go to the supermarket today anyway.*
2. (*informal*) People sometimes use **anyway** at the beginning of a sentence to change the subject, or return to an earlier subject.
an·y·way (**en**-ee-*way*)

anywhere *adverb* In or to any place: *Della has the skills to get a job anywhere.* **an·y·where** (**en**-ee-*wair*)

aorta *noun* The main tube that carries blood away from the heart to the rest of the body, except the lungs. **a·or·ta** (ay-**or**-tuh)

Apache *noun* A member of a group of Native Americans who live primarily in the southwestern United States. **A·pach·e** (uh-**pach**-ee) ▷ *noun, plural* **Apache** or **Apaches**

apart *adverb*
1. Separated in time or space: *Our trains arrived 20 minutes apart.*
2. Apart is used with verbs to say that something that was once a single thing is now divided or broken: *The violent winds tore the barn apart.* **a·part** (uh-**pahrt**)

ape: chimpanzee

apartment *noun* A set of rooms to live in, usually rented and on one floor of a building. **a·part·ment** (uh-**pahrt**-muhnt)

apathetic *adjective* Not having or showing much interest in something. **ap·a·thet·ic** (*ap*-uh-**thet**-ik)

apathy *noun* Lack of interest or concern: *The mayor tried to rouse the town's citizens from their apathy and get them motivated to participate in community affairs.* **ap·a·thy** (**ap**-uh-thee)

apatosaurus *noun* A huge, plant-eating dinosaur with a small head, a long neck and tail, and four thick legs. Formerly called a **brontosaurus**. **a·pat·o·saur·us** (uh-*pat*-uh-**sor**-uhs)

ape
1. *noun* A large animal related to monkeys and humans: *Gorillas, gibbons, orangutans, and chimpanzees are types of apes.*
2. *verb* To copy the way someone behaves or speaks: *He aped Jennifer behind her back.* ▷ *verb* **aping, aped**
ape (ape)

apex *noun* The highest point of something, as in *the apex of a mountain.* **a·pex** (**ay**-peks) ▷ *noun, plural* **apexes**

aphid *noun* A tiny insect that feeds by sucking the juices from plants. **a·phid** (**ay**-fid)

apiece *adverb* Each: *The apples are 50 cents apiece.* **a·piece** (uh-**pees**)

apnea *noun* The stopping of your breath when it's not on purpose. When babies do this, it is called **infant apnea**. When adults do it in their sleep, it is called **sleep apnea**. **ap·nea** (**ap**-nee-uh)

apologize *verb* To say that you are sorry about something: *Did you apologize for speaking so rudely?* **a·pol·o·gize** (uh-**pah**-luh-*jize*) ▷ *verb* **apologizing, apologized** ▷ *adjective* **apologetic** (uh-*pah*-luh-**jet**-ik)

apology *noun* Words that express that you are sorry for something you did: *He made an apology for his behavior at dinner.* **apol·o·gy** (uh-**pah**-luh-jee)

apostle *noun*
1. A close follower of another person or cause.
2. In Christianity, one of the 12 men chosen by Jesus to spread his teaching, plus Saint Paul. **a·pos·tle** (uh-**pah**-suhl)

apostrophe *noun*
1. A punctuation mark (') that is used with the letter *s* to show ownership, as in *Gene's book.*
2. The punctuation mark used to show that letters have been left out, as in the word *didn't.* **a·pos·tro·phe** (uh-**pah**-struh-fee)

apothecary *noun*
1. An old word for a person who is trained to prepare and sell drugs and other medicines; a pharmacist: *Before dispensing*

apatosaurus

the medication, the apothecary explained its possible side effects.

2. A drugstore or pharmacy. People used to go to the apothecary to get medicines, often made from herbs. The word is now old-fashioned: *The apothecary shelves were crowded with jars of herbs and powders.*
a·poth·e·car·y (uh-**pah**-thuh-*ker*-ee)

app *noun (informal)* A computer application: *I need an app that will remember all my usernames and passwords.* **app** (ap)

appall *verb* To cause a strong feeling of shock, horror, or disbelief: *I was appalled by the violence in these video games.* **ap·pall** (uh-**pawl**) ▷ *verb* **appalling, appalled**

appalling *adjective* Horrifying and shocking: *After the food fight, the cafeteria was an appalling sight.* **ap·pall·ing** (uh-**paw**-ling) ▷ *adverb* **appallingly**

apparatus *noun*
1. Equipment used for performing sports, especially gymnastics.
2. Equipment or machines needed to do a job or experiment.
ap·pa·rat·us (*ap*-uh-**rat**-uhs)
▷ *noun, plural* **apparatus** *or* **apparatuses**

apparel *noun* Clothing: *This store sells women's apparel.* **ap·par·el** (uh-**par**-uhl)

apparent *adjective*
1. Obvious or clear, so anyone can see or understand: *Bernardo's skills as a woodworker were apparent in the cabinet he built.*
2. Seeming to be real or true: *Cleo's apparent concern is really just an act.*
ap·par·ent (uh-**par**-uhnt)

apparently *adverb*
1. According to what seems true or obvious, or judging by what is known: *There were apparently several attempted break-ins at the factory, but the one last night was the first that succeeded.*
2. You can begin a sentence with **apparently** as a way of showing that you have come to a conclusion about something from facts that imply it: *Apparently the bus driver thought everyone was on the bus, because he just drove off and left us!*
ap·par·ent·ly (uh-**par**-uhnt-lee)

appeal
1. *verb* To ask for something that is badly needed: *We appealed to the doctor for help.*
2. *noun* A request for something needed, especially for donations: *The Red Cross has made an urgent appeal for type A blood.*
3. *verb* To apply to a higher court for a change in

a legal decision: *The lawyer appealed his client's conviction on robbery charges.*
4. *noun* A request for a change in a legal decision.
5. *noun* A quality that people find attractive: *Skiing has a lot of appeal for active, outdoor types.*
6. If something **appeals to** you, you like it or find it interesting.
ap·peal (uh-**peel**)
▷ *verb* **appealing, appealed**

appear *verb*
1. To come into view: *Suddenly, gray clouds appeared and then it rained.*
2. To seem: *Marian appears to be enjoying herself.*
ap·pear (uh-**peer**)
▷ *verb* **appearing, appeared**

appearance *noun*
1. An act of appearing: *Look for Jupiter's appearance in the western sky after sunset.*
2. The way something or someone looks: *Dwayne's outward appearance is very athletic.*
ap·pear·ance (uh-**peer**-uhns)

appease *verb*
1. To make someone content or calm: *Father was really angry, and nothing we could say would appease him.*
2. To give someone what is needed, or to satisfy someone: *The Democrats hope these compromises will appease the bill's critics.*
ap·pease (uh-**peez**)
▷ *verb* **appeasing, appeased**

appendicitis *noun* An infection of the appendix. Surgery to remove the organ is the most common treatment. **ap·pen·di·ci·tis** (uh-*pen*-di-**sye**-tis)

appendix *noun*
1. A small, closed tube attached to the large intestine: *Anna had to go to the hospital when her appendix burst.*
2. A section at the end of a book with extra information: *The appendix of this dictionary includes a grammar guide.*
ap·pen·dix (uh-**pen**-diks)
▷ *noun, plural* **appendixes** *or* **appendices**
(uh-**pen**-di-seez)

appetite *noun*
1. Desire for food: *My cat has a very large appetite.*
2. Great ability to do something enthusiastically: *Heather has a real appetite for going ocean fishing.*
ap·pe·tite (**ap**-uh-*tite*)

appetizer *noun* A small portion of food eaten before a meal or at the start of a meal: *We had shrimp cocktail for an appetizer.* **ap·pe·tiz·er** (**ap**-uh-*tye*-zur)

appetizing *adjective* **Appetizing** foods or smells make you want to eat. **ap·pe·tiz·ing** (**ap**-uh-*tye*-zing)

applaud *verb* To show that you like something, usually by clapping your hands: *They applauded when the governor said there would be no new taxes.* **ap·plaud** (uh-**plawd**) ▷ *verb* **applauding, applauded** ▷ *noun* **applause**

applauding

apple *noun* A round, usually crisp fruit with a thin skin that is either red, green, or yellow when ripe. **ap·ple** (**ap**-uhl)

appliance *noun* A machine that does a particular job, such as a dryer, toaster, or blender: *He went to buy a microwave and other kitchen appliances.* **ap·pli·ance** (uh-**plye**-uhns)

applicable *adjective* Relevant or appropriate; able to be applied: *Many of the questions on the form were not applicable to me.* **ap·pli·ca·ble** (**ap**-li-kuh-buhl)

applicant *noun* Someone who applies for something, such as a job, a loan, or entrance to a school: *There were 200 applicants for the three job openings.* **ap·pli·cant** (**ap**-li-kuhnt)

application *noun*
1. A written request for something, as in *a college application.*
2. The act of applying something, or of applying for something: *An application of a second coat of paint will make the color brighter. To get into the program, you need to fill out an online application.*
3. A way of using something: *There are many different applications for the skills we learn in math.*
4. A computer program that performs a certain task: *Most computers have applications for word processing, web browsing, and email.* **ap·pli·ca·tion** (*ap*-li-**kay**-shuhn)

apply *verb*
1. To bring something into direct contact with something else, as in *to apply makeup.*
2. To ask for something officially, as in *to apply for a loan.*
3. To be relevant: *The school's dress code applies to all the students.*
4. To use something for a purpose: *You can also apply this memory technique to learning foreign languages.*
5. If you **apply yourself** to something, you work hard at it.
ap·ply (uh-**plye**)
▷ *verb* **applies, applying, applied**

appoint *verb*
1. To choose someone for a job or position: *Libby was the first woman appointed to be a judge in this county.*
2. To arrange something officially: *We need to appoint a time for the conference.*
ap·point (uh-**point**)
▷ *verb* **appointing, appointed**

appointment *noun*
1. The act of naming or choosing someone for a job: *The mayor announced the appointment of the new school superintendent.*
2. The job itself: *Nadia was thrilled to receive the appointment as company vice president.*
3. An arrangement to meet someone at a certain time, as in *a dental appointment.*
ap·point·ment (uh-**point**-muhnt)

appraise *verb* To decide on the value of something by having an expert inspect it: *I want a highly respected jeweler to appraise my grandfather's gold pocket watch.* **ap·praise** (uh-**praze**) ▷ *verb* **appraising, appraised**

appreciate *verb*
1. To enjoy or value somebody or something: *I appreciate it when you remember to clean up after yourself.* ▷ *adjective* **appreciative** (uh-**pree**-shee-uh-tiv) ▷ *adverb* **appreciatively**
2. To understand something: *I appreciate the reasoning behind your argument.*
3. To increase in worth: *Property values nearly always appreciate.*
ap·pre·ci·ate (uh-**pree**-shee-*ate*)
▷ *verb* **appreciating, appreciated** ▷ *noun* **appreciation**

apprehend *verb*
1. To capture and arrest someone: *Thanks to a tip, the police apprehended the bank robber.*
2. To understand, or to capture the meaning of something: *I couldn't apprehend what he meant by that strange gesture.*
ap·pre·hend (*ap*-ri-**hend**)
▷ *verb* **apprehending, apprehended**

apprehensive *adjective* Worried and slightly afraid that something bad will happen: *Darla was apprehensive about speaking in front of so many people.* **ap·pre·hen·sive** (*ap*-ri-**hen**-siv) ▷ *noun* **apprehension** ▷ *adverb* **apprehensively**

apprentice

apprentice *noun* Someone who learns a skill by working with an expert, as in *a carpenter's apprentice.* **ap·pren·tice** (uh-**pren**-tis) ▷ *noun* **apprenticeship**

approach *verb*
1. To move nearer: *A big storm is approaching.*
2. To go to a person with a question or request: *Why don't you approach your boss and ask for a raise?*
3. To begin to deal with something: *Let's approach the problem step by step.*
4. To come closer in time: *The holidays are approaching.*
ap·proach (uh-**prohch**)
▷ *verb* **approaches, approaching, approached**
▷ *noun* **approach**

approachable *adjective* Friendly and easy to talk to. **ap·proach·a·ble** (uh-**proh**-chuh-buhl)

appropriate
1. (uh-**proh**-pree-it) *adjective* Suitable, or right, as in *appropriate clothing.*
▷ *adverb* **appropriately**
2. (uh-**proh**-pree-ate) *verb* To take something unfairly: *Helen appropriated my favorite book and never gave it back.* ▷ *verb* **appropriating, appropriated**
ap·pro·pri·ate

approve *verb*
1. To have a good opinion about a person or thing: *Older people sometimes do not approve of younger people's lifestyles.*
2. To officially accept a plan or an idea: *Congress approved the transportation bill.*
ap·prove (uh-**proov**)
▷ *verb* **approving, approved** ▷ *noun* **approval**

approximate
1. (uh-**prahk**-suh-mit) *adjective* Close to or nearly

accurate: *I can give you an approximate figure for how much the trip will cost.* ▷ *adverb* **approximately**
2. (uh-**prahk**-suh-mayt) *verb* To form an estimate of something: *The detective was able to use the footprint to approximate the suspect's height.* ▷ *noun* **approximation** (uh-*prahk*-suh-**may**-shuhn)
ap·prox·i·mate

apricot *noun* A small, soft fruit similar to a peach. **a·pri·cot** (**ay**-pri-*kaht* or **ap**-ri-*kaht*)

Word History

The Latin name for **apricot** was *praecoquum,* meaning "early ripener," because the Romans thought of apricots as early-ripening apples. In Arabic, the term became *al-burquq,* which meant "the apricot." Speakers of other languages thought that *al-,* meaning "the," was part of the fruit's name. English speakers used to call them *abrecocks,* but after other changes to the word, we now know them as *apricots.*

April *noun* The fourth month on the calendar, after March and before May. April has 30 days. **A·pril** (**ay**-pruhl)

April Fools' Day April 1, a day when it is customary to play practical jokes on people.

apron *noun*
1. An article of clothing that you wear to protect your clothes when you are cooking or taking part in a messy activity: *She wears an apron when she bakes so she won't get flour on her clothes.*
2. The part of a stage in front of the curtain.
a·pron (**ay**-pruhn)

apt *adjective*
1. Suitable for what is happening, as in *an apt reply.*
2. Quick to learn things, as in *an apt student.*
3. If you are **apt** to do something, you are likely to do it: *He's apt to return tomorrow.*
apt (apt)

aptitude *noun* A natural ability to learn quickly or do something well, as in *an aptitude for drawing.* **ap·ti·tude** (**ap**-ti-*tood*)

apricots

aquarium *noun*
1. A glass tank in which you can keep fish.
2. A place set up for visitors to see different kinds of ocean creatures, such as dolphins, seals, and sharks.
a·quar·i·um (uh-**kwair**-ee-uhm)
▷ *noun, plural* **aquariums** *or* **aquaria** (uh-**kwair**-ee-uh)

aquatic *adjective*
1. Living or growing in water, as in *aquatic plants*.
2. Performed in or on water: *Synchronized swimming is an aquatic sport.*
a·quat·ic (uh-**kwat**-ik *or* uh-**kwah**-tik)

aqueduct *noun* A man-made channel for carrying water over valleys and rivers. In Europe, many aqueducts were built in Roman times and are still standing. **aq·ue·duct** (**ak**-wuh-*duhkt*)

Arabic *noun* A language spoken by many people in the Middle East and North Africa. **Ar·a·bic** (**ar**-uh-bik) ▷ *adjective* **Arabic**

Arabic numerals *noun, plural* The figures 0, 1, 2, 3, 4, 5, 6, 7, 8, and 9 that we use today. These numerals were first taught to Europeans by Arab scholars.

arable *adjective* **Arable** land is suitable for farming. **ar·a·ble** (**ar**-uh-buhl)

arachnid *noun* One of various wingless, eight-legged creatures with a body divided into two parts. Spiders, scorpions, mites, and ticks are arachnids. **a·rach·nid** (uh-**rak**-nid) ▷ *adjective* **arachnid**

arbitrary *adjective* Based on personal feelings or opinions rather than on reason or logic, as in *an arbitrary decision.* **ar·bi·trar·y** (**ahr**-bi-*trer*-ee)

arbitrate *verb* To help two opposing sides reach an agreement about something they are arguing about: *It's the counselor's job to arbitrate disputes between students.* **ar·bi·trate** (**ahr**-bi-*trate*) ▷ *verb* **arbitrating, arbitrated** ▷ *noun* **arbitration** ▷ *noun* **arbitrator**

arbor *noun*
1. A small place that is surrounded and shaded by trees, shrubs, and vines, as in *a garden arbor*.
2. **Arbor Day** is a day in spring that is set aside for planting trees. The actual date varies.
ar·bor (**ahr**-bur)

arc *noun*
1. Part of a curve: *I saw the arc of a rainbow in the sky.*
2. In math, an **arc** is a curved line between two points, usually part of a circle.
arc (ahrk)
Arc sounds like **ark**.

arcade *noun*
1. A row of arches supported by columns, in a building or standing freely as a separate structure.
2. A business with machines for amusement, such as pinball games, which you pay to use.
ar·cade (ahr-**kade**)

arch
1. *noun* A curved shape over an opening. The structure of an arch often helps support the weight of a building, wall, or bridge: *The windows of the church have pointed Gothic arches.*
2. *verb* To curve: *I had to arch my neck to see the*

arch

screen. ▷ *verb* **arches, arching, arched** ▷ *adjective* **arched**
arch (ahrch)

archaeology *or* **archeology** *noun* The study of the distant past, which often involves digging up old buildings, objects, and bones and examining them carefully. **ar·chae·ol·o·gy** *or* **ar·che·ol·o·gy** (*ahr*-kee-**ah**-luh-jee) ▷ *noun* **archaeologist** ▷ *adjective* **archaeological** (*ahr*-kee-uh-**lah**-ji-kuhl)

archaic *adjective* From the past and not used anymore, as in *archaic customs*. **ar·cha·ic** (ahr-**kay**-ik)

archbishop *noun* A bishop of the highest rank in some Christian denominations. **arch·bish·op** (ahrch-**bish**-uhp)

archeology *See* **archaeology.**

archery *noun* The sport using a bow and arrow: *To do well in archery, you need good eyesight and a steady aim.* **arch·er·y** (**ahr**-chur-ee) ▷ *noun* **archer**

archipelago *noun* A group of islands. **ar·chi·pel·a·go** (*ahr*-kuh-**pel**-uh-*goh*)

archipelago

architect *noun* Someone who designs buildings and supervises the way they are built. **ar·chi·tect** (**ahr**-ki-*tekt*)

architecture *noun*
1. The activity of designing and drawing plans for buildings.
2. A style of building, as in *Roman architecture*.
▷ *adjective* **architectural**
ar·chi·tec·ture (**ahr**-ki-*tek*-chur)

archive
1. *noun* A collection of related documents or other things that is stored in a library or other public place: *We found an early picture of the courthouse in the archives.* ▷ *adjective* **archival**
2. *verb* To put a document, object, or computer file into an archive: *I archived the website on a CD.*
ar·chive (**ahr**-kive)

archrival *noun* Your **archrival** is your main rival, and the one you most want to defeat: *The Army and Navy football teams have been archrivals for years.* **arch·ri·val** (**ahrch**-rye-vuhl)

arctic
1. *adjective* Extremely cold and wintry: *This week we are going to have blizzards and arctic temperatures.*
2. **the Arctic** *noun* The area around the North Pole.
▷ *adjective* **Arctic**
arc·tic (**ahrk**-tik)

ardent *adjective* Feeling or showing very strong emotions, as in *an ardent supporter of animal rights.* **ar·dent** (**ahr**-duhnt) ▷ *adverb* **ardently**

arduous *adjective* Very difficult and requiring a lot of effort, as in *an arduous climb.* **ar·du·ous** (**ahr**-joo-uhs)

area *noun*
1. The amount of surface within a given boundary, measured in square units: *The playground has an area of about 20,000 square feet.*
2. A part of a place, as in *a wealthy area of town.*
3. A subject or activity: *He reads everything in the area of sports.*
ar·e·a (**air**-ee-uh)

area code *noun* A three-digit number that indicates a telephone service area, such as "206" for Seattle.

arena *noun* A large area or building that is used for sports or entertainment. **a·re·na** (uh-**ree**-nuh)

aren't *contraction* A short form of *are not*: *You aren't going to like this.* **aren't** (ahrnt or **ahr**-uhnt)

argue *verb*
1. To give your opinion about something: *Hafez argued that the school could do more to be environmentally friendly.*

2. To disagree in talking about or discussing something: *I argued with my father about staying out late.*
ar·gue (**ahr**-gyoo)
▷ *verb* **arguing, argued**

Architecture

Imhotep, who lived nearly 5,000 years ago, is the first known architect. He designed a pyramid-shaped tomb for the pharaoh Zoser. During the Middle Ages, architects in Europe developed the Gothic style, erecting cathedrals with buttresses and high steeples. In other parts of the world, too, the most important structures were religious. Today, significant buildings are often devoted to entertainment or commerce.

pagoda (Summer Palace, Beijing, China)

skyscraper (Empire State Building, New York City)

Gothic cathedral (Salisbury Cathedral, England)

pyramids (Giza, Egypt)

mosque (Blue Mosque, Istanbul, Turkey)

argument *noun*

1. A set of reasons that supports an idea or opinion: *The librarian made a convincing argument that the new books were a great investment.*

2. A verbal disagreement, especially a loud or angry one: *We heard an argument going on in the next room.*

ar·gu·ment (**ahr**-gyuh-muhnt)

▷ *adjective* **argumentative** (ar-gyuh-**men**-tuh-tiv)

arid *adjective* Extremely dry because of a lack of rain. **ar·id** (**ar**-id)

arise *verb*

1. To get up from bed or from lying down.

2. To come into being; start existing: *A problem arose.*

a·rise (uh-**rize**)

▷ *verb* **arising, arose** (uh-**rohz**), **arisen** (uh-**riz**-uhn)

aristocracy *noun* The group of people in a society who carry titles, or the most wealthy and prestigious group. **ar·is·toc·ra·cy** (ar-i-**stah**-kruh-see)

aristocrat *noun* A member of a group of people thought to be the best in some way, usually based on their social class. **a·ris·to·crat** (uh-**ris**-tuh-*krat*)

▷ *adjective* **aristocratic**

arithmetic *noun* The science of numbers and computation. Addition, subtraction, multiplication, and division are the four basic operations of arithmetic. **a·rith·me·tic** (uh-**rith**-muh-tik)

ark *noun*

1. In the Bible, a boat built by Noah to carry his family and two of every kind of animal during the Great Flood.

2. In a synagogue, the cabinet in which the Torah scrolls are kept.

ark (ahrk)

Ark sounds like **arc**.

ark

arm

1. *noun* The part of your body between your shoulder and your hand.

2. *noun* The part of an armchair or sofa where you rest your arms.

3. *verb* To supply a person or group with weapons.

▷ *verb* **arming, armed**

4. arms *noun, plural* Weapons, especially guns.

arm (ahrm)

armada *noun* A large group of warships. **ar·ma·da** (ahr-**mah**-duh)

armadillo *noun* A mammal covered by hard, bony plates that is found in warm parts of North and South America. **ar·ma·dil·lo** (ahr-muh-**dil**-oh) ▷ *noun, plural* **armadillos**

Word History

Like the alligator, the **armadillo** was a creature the Spanish explorers of North America had never seen before. Since they had no name for this bony, armor-covered mammal, they called it an *armadillo*, Spanish for the "little armored one." Many words with the root *arma-* or *arm-*, such as *armada*, *armor*, and *army*, come from the Latin word for "weapons," *arma*.

armaments *noun, plural* Weapons and other equipment used for fighting wars. **ar·ma·ments** (**ahr**-muh-muhnts)

armchair *noun* A comfortable chair with flat rests on each side for the arms. **arm·chair** (**ahrm**-*chair*)

armed forces *noun, plural* All of the branches of a country's military. In the United States, the armed forces include the Army, Navy, Air Force, Marine Corps, and Coast Guard.

armistice *noun* A temporary agreement to stop a war: *Both sides stopped shooting during the armistice.* **ar·mis·tice** (**ahr**-mi-stis)

armor *noun*

1. Metal protection worn by soldiers in battle.

2. Strong metal protection for tanks and other military vehicles.

3. Protective scales, spines, or shells that cover some animals and plants.

ar·mor (**ahr**-mur)

armory *noun* A place where weapons are stored or soldiers are trained. **ar·mor·y** (ahr-mur-ee) ▷ *noun, plural* **armories**

armpit *noun* The area under your arm where it joins your shoulder. **arm·pit** (ahrm-*pit*)

army *noun* A military group trained mainly to fight on land: *Young Israeli citizens are required to join the army.* **ar·my** (ahr-mee) ▷ *noun, plural* **armies**

aroma *noun* A smell that is usually pleasant: *The cookies baking in the oven had a delicious aroma.* **a·ro·ma** (uh-roh-muh) ▷ *adjective* **aromatic** (ar-uh-mat-ik)

around
1. *preposition* Surrounding: *He put the belt around his waist.*
2. *preposition* Close to some number, time, or quantity: *I'll pick you up around 4 p.m.*
3. *preposition* On the other side of something: *They were waiting for me around the corner.*
4. *adverb* In many different places or parts of a place: *Nell is traveling around Europe.*
5. *adverb* In a circle: *We went around and around the park but couldn't find them.*
6. *adverb* More or less: *Around 40 people came to the party.*
a·round (uh-round)

arouse *verb*
1. To stir up a feeling: *His talk on dinosaurs aroused my interest.*
2. To awaken from sleep: *We were aroused from bed by the sound of sirens.*
a·rouse (uh-rouz)
▷ *verb* **arousing, aroused** ▷ *noun* **arousal**

arrange *verb*
1. To make plans or prepare for something to happen: *Let's arrange a surprise party for Mom.*
2. To place things so that they are in order or look attractive, as in *to arrange flowers.*
3. To change a piece of music slightly, so that it can be played on different instruments.
4. In an **arranged marriage**, parents agree on a husband or wife for their son or daughter.
ar·range (uh-raynj)
▷ *verb* **arranging, arranged**

arrangement *noun*
1. A plan for something to happen: *Shawna made all the arrangements for the birthday luncheon.*
2. The way that something is arranged or set out, as in *a flower arrangement.*
3. A particular way for a piece of music to be sung or performed: *The choir sang Peter Wilhousky's arrangement of the "Battle Hymn of the Republic."*
ar·range·ment (uh-raynj-muhnt)

array *noun*
1. A large number of things: *Aggie was excited by the array of delicious foods.*
2. An orderly arrangement: *The soldiers marched in battle array.*
ar·ray (uh-ray)
▷ *verb* **array**

arrest *verb*
1. To stop and hold someone by the power of law: *The police arrested the thief.*
2. To stop something from developing or happening anymore, as in *to arrest the spread of the flu.*
ar·rest (uh-rest)
▷ *verb* **arresting, arrested** ▷ *noun* **arrest**

arrival *noun*
1. The act of getting to a place: *She eagerly awaited his arrival at the airport.*
2. Someone or something that has gotten to a place: *The museum's newest arrival is a 500-year-old skeleton of a horse.*
ar·ri·val (uh-rye-vuhl)

arrive *verb*
1. To reach a place: *They arrived in Kansas last week.*
2. People say that an event or date **arrives** when they have been looking forward to it or dreading it: *Halloween has finally arrived.*
ar·rive (uh-rive)
▷ *verb* **arriving, arrived**

Word History

After a long journey, we **arrive** at our destination. The word *arrive* used to refer to traveling by boat, however, because it originally meant "come to the shore." In ancient times, many people traveled by boat, because planes, trains, and cars had not been invented yet. Latin speakers formed the verb *adripare*, meaning "come to the shore," by combining their words for "to," *ad*, and "shore," *ripa*. Eventually they began to pronounce *adripare* as *arripare*. *Arripare* became *ariver* in French, giving us the word *arrive*.

arrogant *adjective* Acting as if you are more important and smarter than other people: *After he won the prize, he became arrogant and bossy.* **ar·ro·gant** (ar-uh-guhnt) ▷ *noun* **arrogance** ▷ *adverb* **arrogantly**

arrow *noun*
1. A stick with a sharp point shot from a bow: *The arrow hit the edge of the target.*
2. A sign (→) showing a direction, as on maps and road signs.
ar·row (ar-oh)

arrowhead *noun* The sharp tip of an arrow, made of metal or (long ago) of stone. **ar·row·head** (**ar**-oh-*hed*)

arrowhead

arsenal *noun* A place where weapons and ammunition are made or stored. **ar·se·nal** (**ahr**-suh-nuhl)

arsenic *noun* An extremely poisonous chemical element that occurs naturally, usually as a gray-white crystal. **ar·se·nic** (**ahr**-suh-nik)

arson *noun* The crime of setting fire to property with the intention of destroying it. **ar·son** (**ahr**-suhn) ▷ *noun* **arsonist**

art
  1. *noun* The activity of creating something beautiful for others to enjoy, such as a painting, sculpture, piece of music, or poem.
  2. *noun* Things that are created by this activity, as in *19th-century art.*
  3. *noun* Something that requires practiced skill, as in *the art of French cuisine.*
  4. the arts *noun, plural* Making, showing, and performing works of art.
  art (ahrt)

artery *noun* One of the tubes that carries blood from your heart to all the rest of your body. **ar·ter·y** (**ahr**-tur-ee) ▷ *noun, plural* **arteries**

arthritis *noun* A disease in which joints become swollen and painful. **ar·thri·tis** (ahr-**thrye**-tis) ▷ *adjective* **arthritic** (ahr-**thrit**-ik)

arthropod *noun* An animal without a backbone that has a hard outer skeleton and three or more pairs of legs that can bend. Insects, spiders, lobsters, and shrimp are all arthropods. **ar·thro·pod** (**ahr**-thruh-*pahd*)

artichoke *noun* A tall plant in the thistle family, with large, prickly flower heads that are cooked and eaten as a vegetable. **ar·ti·choke** (**ahr**-ti-*chohk*)

artichoke

article *noun*
  1. An object, as in *an article of clothing.*
  2. A piece of writing published in a newspaper, in a magazine, or online.
  3. A word, such as *a, an,* or *the,* that goes in front of a noun.
  ar·ti·cle (**ahr**-ti-kuhl)

articulate
  1. (ahr-**tik**-yuh-lit) *adjective* Able to express yourself clearly in words.

Art

Humans have created art since prehistoric people made cave paintings using pigments and charcoal. Ancient Egyptians decorated their pyramids with images of pharaohs and animal gods, while Renaissance artists used sculpture and oil paints to depict people realistically. Artists today are expanding the boundaries of art, adding collage, photography, and performance to their traditional tools: pencils, paints, and clay.

colored pencils

paintbrushes

oil paints

  2. (ahr-**tik**-yuh-*late*) *verb* To pronounce or say something in a particular way, especially in a clear way: *She has difficulty articulating the letter "r" properly.* ▷ *verb* **articulating, articulated** **ar·tic·u·late** ▷ *adverb* **articulately** (ahr-**tik**-yuh-lit-lee)

artifact *noun* An object made or changed by human beings, especially a tool or weapon used in the past: *We saw wooden bowls, leather pouches, and other artifacts at the museum.* **ar·ti·fact** (**ahr**-tuh-*fakt*)

artificial *adjective*

1. Made by people rather than existing in nature, as in *artificial flowers.*

2. Not sincere; pretended: *Their friendliness seems artificial to me.*

ar·ti·fi·cial (ahr-tuh-**fish**-uhl)

▷ *adverb* **artificially**

artificial intelligence *noun* The science of making computers do things that previously needed human intelligence, such as understanding language. Abbreviated as *AI.*

artificial respiration *noun* A method of helping someone start to breathe after the person's breathing has stopped. It is done by forcing air into and out of the lungs.

artillery *noun*

1. Large, powerful guns that are mounted on wheels or tracks.

2. The part of an army that uses these weapons.

ar·til·ler·y (ahr-**til**-ur-ee)

artisan *noun* Someone who is skilled at working with his or her hands at a particular craft. Wood-carvers and cheese makers are artisans. **ar·ti·san** (**ahr**-ti-zuhn)

artist *noun* Someone very skilled at painting, making things, or performing in the arts. **art·ist** (**ahr**-tist)

▷ *adjective* **artistic** ▷ *adverb* **artistically**

artistic *adjective*

1. Showing or having creative skill: *He painted a colorful dragon on the back of his T-shirt, showing real artistic flair.*

2. Of, having to do with, or responsible for the creative aspects of something: *The DVD includes an interview with the film's artistic director.*

ar·tis·tic (ahr-**tis**-tik)

▷ *adverb* **artistically**

as

1. *conjunction* In comparison with: *Are you as good a basketball player as Angela is?*

2. *adverb* To the same degree: *I like my answer better because yours is not as good.*

3. *conjunction* In the same way that: *Raise your hand as I do.*

4. *conjunction* While or when: *Todd petted the cat as she lay on his lap.*

5. *conjunction* Since or because: *As you seemed to enjoy the roller coaster, we should go on it again.*

6. *preposition* In the manner of, or in the role of: *As your mother, I know what's best for you.*

as (az *or* uhz)

ASAP *adverb* A short way of saying *as soon as possible*: *Please sign up for the field trip ASAP so we know how many cars we will need.* **ASAP** (**ay**-sap)

asbestos *noun* A grayish mineral whose fibers can be woven into a fireproof fabric. Asbestos is rarely used today because breathing its fibers causes serious illness. **as·bes·tos** (as-**bes**-tuhs)

ascend *verb* To move or go up: *The plane took off and began to ascend.* **as·cend** (uh-**send**) ▷ *verb* **ascending, ascended** ▷ *noun* **ascent**

ascribe *verb*

1. To say that one thing belongs to or is a quality of another: *Many different meanings can be ascribed to the word "pitch."*

2. If you **ascribe** something to a person or group, you are saying that they created it or are responsible for it: *This music is traditionally ascribed to Bach, but it is now believed that one of Bach's students wrote it.*

as·cribe (uh-**skribe**)

▷ *verb* **ascribing, ascribed**

ash *noun*

1. The powder that remains after something has burned.

2. A kind of tree with long, thin leaves that fall off every year.

ash (ash)

▷ *noun, plural* **ashes**

ash tree

B
C
D
E
F
G
H
I
J
K
L
M
N
O
P
Q
R
S
T
U
V
W
X
Y
Z

ashamed *adjective* Feeling embarrassed and guilty. **a·shamed** (uh-**shaymd**)

ashore *adverb* On or to the shore or land: *The strong tide washed the raft ashore.* **a·shore** (uh-**shor**)

Asia *noun* The world's largest continent. Part of the Eurasian landmass, it lies east of Europe and is bordered by the Pacific, Arctic, and Indian Oceans. **A·sia** (**ay**-zhuh) ▷ *adjective* **Asian**

Asian American *noun* Someone who was born in the United States or became a US citizen and can trace his or her ancestors back to Asia. **A·sian American** (**ay**-zhuhn) ▷ *adjective* **Asian American**

aside

1. *adverb* To one side, or out of the way: *Elena put her drawing aside.*

2. *noun* A remark made quietly so only certain people can hear it. **a·side** (uh-**side**)

ask *verb*

1. To make a request of someone: *Yoshiko asked her sister to turn down the radio.*

2. To put a question to someone when you want information: *Ask that man what time it is, please.*

3. To invite someone to do something: *Martin asked Brenda to go to the movies.*

4. To want a certain amount in order to sell something: *How much are they asking for that antique dresser?* **ask** (ask)

▷ *verb* **asking, asked**

askew *adverb* Crooked or out of line: *The fall knocked her helmet askew, but she was OK otherwise.* **a·skew** (uh-**skyu**)

askew

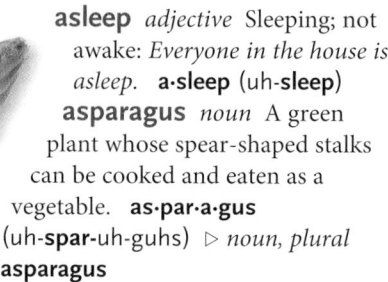

asparagus

asleep *adjective* Sleeping; not awake: *Everyone in the house is asleep.* **a·sleep** (uh-**sleep**)

asparagus *noun* A green plant whose spear-shaped stalks can be cooked and eaten as a vegetable. **as·par·a·gus** (uh-**spar**-uh-guhs) ▷ *noun, plural* **asparagus**

aspect *noun* A feature or characteristic of something: *What aspects of the field trip did you find most interesting?* **as·pect** (**as**-pekt)

aspen *noun* A kind of poplar tree with white bark that grows typically in mountain areas. **as·pen** (**as**-puhn)

asphalt *noun* A black, tarlike substance that is mixed with sand and gravel and then rolled flat to make roads. **as·phalt** (**as**-fawlt)

asphyxiate *verb* To kill or attempt to kill people or animals by making them unable to breathe. **as·phyx·i·ate** (as-**fik**-see-*ate*) ▷ *verb* **asphyxiating, asphyxiated** ▷ *noun* **asphyxiation**

aspiration *noun* A desire to achieve something in the future: *Jewelle's aspiration is to become a famous actress.* **as·pi·ra·tion** (*as*-puh-**ray**-shuhn) ▷ *verb* **aspire** (uh-**spire**)

aspirin *noun* A drug that relieves pain and reduces fever. **as·pi·rin** (**as**-pur-in)

ass *noun*

1. A donkey.

2. *(informal)* A silly or stupid person. Many people consider this word offensive. **ass** (as)

▷ *noun, plural* **asses**

assassinate *verb* To murder someone who is well-known or important: *The terrorists planned to assassinate the president.* **as·sas·si·nate** (uh-**sas**-uh-*nate*) ▷ *verb* **assassinating, assassinated** ▷ *noun* **assassin** ▷ *noun* **assassination**

assault *verb* To attack someone or something violently. **as·sault** (uh-**sawlt**) ▷ *verb* **assaulting, assaulted** ▷ *noun* **assault**

assemble *verb*

1. To gather in one place: *The whole school assembled in the gym.*

2. To put together the parts of something, as in *to assemble a desk.* **as·sem·ble** (uh-**sem**-buhl)

▷ *verb* **assembling, assembled**

assembly *noun*

1. A meeting of lots of people: *The principal spoke at the school assembly.*

2. In some states, the **assembly** is one of the two lawmaking bodies that voters in the state elect.

3. assembly line An arrangement of machines and workers in a factory, in which a product passes from one person or machine to the next, with each performing a small, separate task, until it is completely assembled.

as·sem·bly (uh-**sem**-blee)

assent *verb* To agree to something: *You can be on the show only if you assent to be videotaped.* **as·sent** (uh-**sent**) ▷ *verb* **assenting, assented** ▷ *noun* **assent**

assert *verb*

1. To state something in a forceful or emphatic way, as in *to assert your innocence.*

2. If you **assert yourself**, you behave confidently and express yourself easily.

as·sert (uh-**surt**)

▷ *verb* **asserting, asserted**

assertive *adjective* Able to behave confidently and express yourself positively. **as·ser·tive** (uh-**sur**-tiv) ▷ *noun* **assertiveness** ▷ *adverb* **assertively**

assess *verb* To judge the value or qualities of something: *The teacher used the test to assess the progress of his students.* **as·sess** (uh-**ses**) ▷ *verb* **assesses, assessing, assessed** ▷ *noun* **assessor**

assessment *noun* The act or process of determining value or significance: *State officials are visiting the flood site to make an assessment of the damage.*

as·sess·ment (uh-**ses**-muhnt)

asset *noun*

1. A valuable thing that a person or business owns: *The company sold most of its assets to pay the debt.*

2. Someone who is helpful or useful: *Dr. Lawrence is a great asset to our community.*

as·set (**as**-et)

assign *verb*

1. To give someone a job to do: *Ms. Popovich assigned us two chapters to read this weekend.*

2. To set apart for a specific purpose: *The camp director assigned the cabin to the youngest campers.*

as·sign (uh-**sine**)

assignment *noun* A specific job that is given to somebody: *Did you finish the homework assignment yet?* **as·sign·ment** (uh-**sine**-muhnt)

assist

1. *verb* To help someone: *These loans will assist farmers who have had a difficult year because of the drought.* ▷ *verb* **assisting, assisted**

assembly line

2. *noun* An **assist** in sports is an act of one player helping another, especially to score.

as·sist (uh-**sist**)

assistance *noun* Help that makes things easier for someone. **as·sist·ance** (uh-**sis**-tuhns)

assistant *noun* Someone who helps another to do something. **as·sist·ant** (uh-**sis**-tuhnt)

assisted living *noun* Housing for older people that provides the help they need to do things.

associate

1. (uh-**soh**-see-*ayt*) *verb* To form a connection between things in your mind: *What flavors do you associate with Mexican food?*

2. (uh-**soh**-see-*ayt*) *verb* To form a relationship or spend time with someone: *My parents associate with a lot of artists.*

3. (uh-**soh**-see-it) *adjective* Having responsibility at a lower level: *The associate editors report to the senior editor.*

4. (uh-**soh**-see-it) *noun* Someone who works for a company: *An associate will be with you in a moment.*

as·so·ci·ate

▷ *verb* **associating, associated**

association *noun*

1. A group of people who are organized to do something.

2. The condition of being connected with someone or something: *His association with known criminals made him a suspect in the robbery.*

3. A connection that you make in your mind between thoughts and feelings and a person or thing: *Ocean Beach has many pleasant associations for me.*

as·so·ci·a·tion (uh-*soh*-see-**ay**-shuhn)

assortment *noun* A mixture of different things: *The bakery offers an assortment of pies.* **as·sort·ment** (uh-**sort**-muhnt) ▷ *adjective* **assorted**

assume *verb*

1. To suppose that something is true, without knowing for sure: *We assumed that the information on the form was correct.*

2. If you **assume** responsibility for something, you agree to do it or take care of it.

3. An **assumed name** is a false name.
as·sume (uh-**soom**)
▷ *verb* **assuming, assumed**

assumption *noun* A thing that you assume: *We planned to go to an outdoor concert, based on the assumption that it wouldn't rain tonight, but it's starting to pour.* **as·sump·tion** (uh-**suhmp**-shuhn)

assurance *noun* A firm promise to do something: *He gave her his assurance that he would arrive on time.* **as·sur·ance** (uh-**shoor**-uhns)

assure *verb*

1. To say or promise something with confidence that it is true or that it will happen: *When I ran for club president, Estelle assured me of her vote.*

2. To make something certain: *Their victory last night assured them a place in the playoffs.*
as·sure (uh-**shoor**)
▷ *verb* **assuring, assured**

aster *noun* A plant with flowers that have white, pink, yellow, or purple petals around a yellow center. Some asters look like daisies. **as·ter** (**as**-tur)

asterisk *noun* The mark (*) used in printing and writing to tell readers to look elsewhere on the page for more information. **as·ter·isk** (**as**-tuh-*risk*)

asteroid *noun* A small rocky object that travels around the sun. **as·ter·oid** (**as**-tuh-*roid*)

asteroid

asthma *noun* A lung disease that causes coughing and difficulty in breathing. **asth·ma** (**az**-muh)
▷ *noun* **asthmatic** (*az*-**mat**-ik) ▷ *adjective* **asthmatic**

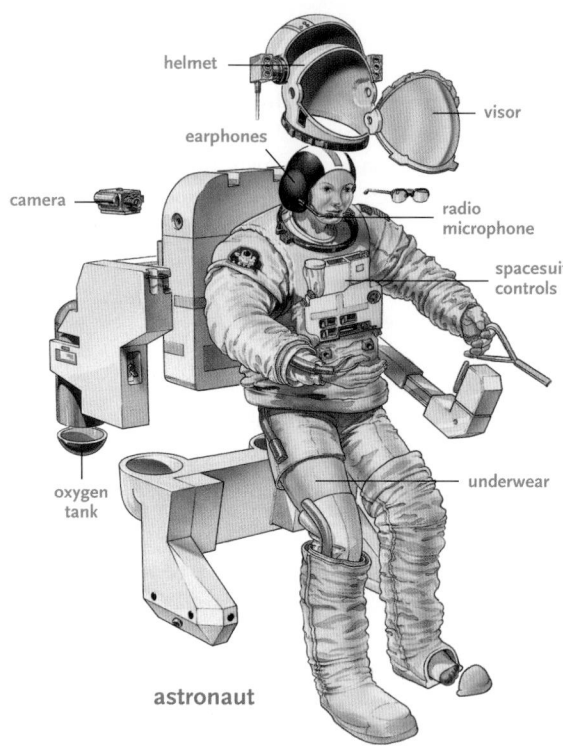

helmet

visor

earphones

camera

radio microphone

spacesuit controls

oxygen tank

underwear

astronaut

astonish *verb* To surprise someone very much: *Kelly astonished me with her kindness.* **as·ton·ish** (uh-**stah**-nish) ▷ *verb* **astonishes, astonishing, astonished** ▷ *noun* **astonishment** ▷ *adjective* **astonishing** ▷ *adverb* **astonishingly**

astound *verb* To amaze or astonish someone: *Dad astounded us by bringing home a puppy.* **as·tound** (uh-**stound**) ▷ *verb* **astounding, astounded**

astray *adverb*

1. If something has gone **astray**, it has been lost.

2. If someone **leads** you **astray**, he or she encourages you to do something wrong or gives you incorrect information.
a·stray (uh-**stray**)

astride *preposition* With a leg on either side of something: *In the story, the hero rides astride a majestic white horse.* **a·stride** (uh-**stride**)

astronaut *noun* Someone who travels in a spacecraft. **as·tro·naut** (**as**-truh-*nawt*)

Language Note

Both **astro-** and **naut** are combining forms. (See *aero-* for more on this type of vocabulary builder.) In Greek, *astro-* means "star" and *naut* means "sailor." An astronaut "sails" among the stars. *Astronomy* and *nautical* also use these combining forms.

astronomical *adjective*
1. Of or having to do with astronomy.
2. Very large or very high, as in *an astronomical salary.*
as·tro·nom·i·cal (*as*-truh-**nah**-mi-kuhl)
▷ *adverb* **astronomically**

astronomy *noun* The study of stars, planets, and space. **as·tron·o·my** (uh-**strah**-nuh-mee) ▷ *noun* **astronomer**

astute *adjective* Having or showing an ability to understand clearly and quickly. **as·tute** (uh-**stoot**)

asunder *adverb* If something is **torn asunder**, it is broken into pieces or separated. **a·sun·der** (uh-**suhn**-dur)

asylum *noun*
1. Protection given to someone who has left a dangerous place.
2. *(old-fashioned)* A hospital for people who are mentally ill and cannot live independently.
a·sy·lum (uh-**sye**-luhm)

asymmetrical *adjective* Not the same on one half as on the other: *Most people's faces are slightly asymmetrical.* **a·sym·met·ri·cal** (*ay*-si-**met**-ri-kuhl)

at *preposition*
1. In a place or position: *We were at the movies.*
2. Describing a time: *We'll meet at noon.*
3. In the direction of: *Look at all those books!*
4. In a state or condition of: *The two countries were at war.*

5. For the amount or price of: *The store sells apples at $1 per pound.*
6. The **at sign** is a symbol (@) that means "at" and is used in email addresses.
at (at)

ate *verb* The past tense of **eat**. **ate** (ayt)

atheist *noun* Someone who does not believe that there is a God. **a·the·ist** (**ay**-thee-ist) ▷ *noun* **atheism**

athlete *noun* Someone who is trained in or very good at sports and physical exercise. **ath·lete** (**ath**-leet) ▷ *adjective* **athletic** (**ath**-let-ik)

athlete's foot *noun* An itchy rash caused by a fungus that can develop on your feet and between your toes.

athletics *noun, plural* Sports and physical exercise. **ath·let·ics** (ath-**let**-iks) ▷ *adjective* **athletic**

Atlantic Ocean *noun* The world's second-largest ocean, after the Pacific Ocean. It stretches between the continents of North and South America and the continents of Europe and Africa. **At·lan·tic Ocean** (uht-**lan**-tik)

atlas *noun* A book of maps: *I checked the atlas for the location of Vienna.* **at·las** (**at**-luhs)

Word History

In Greek mythology, Atlas was a giant who was punished for taking part in a revolt against the gods. As his punishment, he was forced to stand on a mountain, holding the heavens apart from the earth. Pioneer mapmaker Gerardus Mercator used a drawing of Atlas holding a globe for the cover of a book of maps he published in the 1500s. So many other mapmakers copied his cover idea that a collection of maps became known as an **atlas**.

ATM *noun* A machine linked to a bank that lets you put money into your account or take it out without actually going into the bank. ATM is short for *automatic teller machine* or *automated teller machine.*

atmosphere *noun*
1. The mixture of gases that surrounds a planet: *The earth's atmosphere is mostly made up of nitrogen and oxygen.*
2. The air in a particular place: *We love the cool, refreshing atmosphere of the mountains.*
3. The mood or feeling that you get in a place or situation: *The old mansion had a creepy atmosphere.*
at·mos·phere (**at**-muhs-*feer*)
▷ *adjective* **atmospheric**

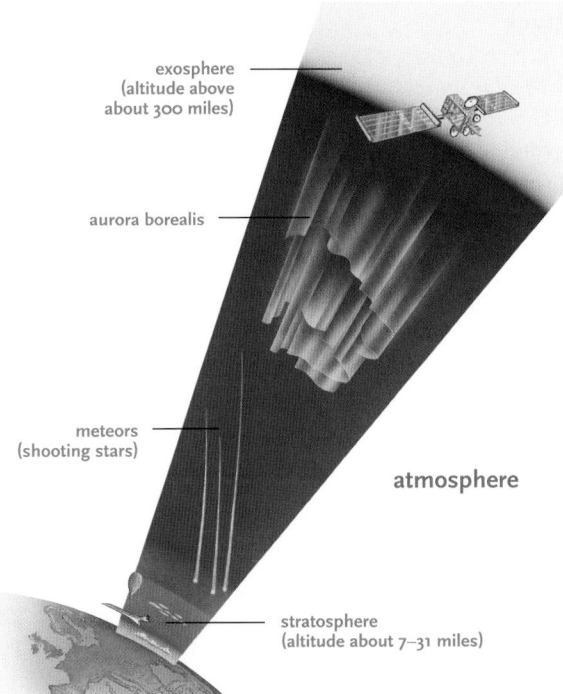

exosphere
(altitude above
about 300 miles)

aurora borealis

meteors
(shooting stars)

atmosphere

stratosphere
(altitude about 7–31 miles)

atoll *noun* One or more coral islands that form a ring around a lagoon. **at·oll** (**at**-awl)

atom *noun* The tiniest part of an element that has all the properties of that element. All the matter in the universe is made up of atoms. **at·om** (**at**-uhm)

atomic *adjective*

1. Of or having to do with atoms, as in *atomic research.*

2. Using the power created when atoms are split: *The submarine is powered by atomic energy.*

a·tom·ic (uh-**tah**-mik)

atomic bomb *noun* A very powerful bomb that explodes with great force, heat, and bright light. The explosion results from the energy that is released by splitting atoms.

atomic energy *noun* The energy released when atoms are split apart or forced together. Also called **nuclear energy**.

atomic number *noun* The number of protons in the nucleus of an atom of a chemical element, which helps determine the element's properties and its place in the periodic table.

atone *verb* To do something that makes up for a mistake you have made or a bad thing you have done: *Troy wants to atone for his bad behavior at the party.* **a·tone** (uh-**tone**) ▷ *verb* **atoning, atoned**

at-risk *adjective* Someone who is **at-risk** is in danger of getting into serious trouble, such as being part of a gang: *The program offers special counseling to at-risk students to keep them in school.*

atomic bomb

atoll

atrium *noun*

1. Either of two sections of the heart that receive blood from the veins.

2. An open area inside a building.

a·tri·um (**ay**-tree-uhm)

▷ *noun, plural* **atriums** or **atria** (**ay**-tree-uh)

atrocious *adjective* Very cruel or terrible, as in *an atrocious crime.* **a·tro·cious** (uh-**troh**-shuhs)

attach *verb*

1. To join or fix one thing to another: *Write his address on the label and attach it to the box.*

2. If you **attach** a file to an email, you send that file along with the email.

3. If you are **attached to** someone, you are very fond of that person.

at·tach (uh-**tach**)

▷ *verb* **attaches, attaching, attached** ▷ *noun* **attachment**

attack

1. *verb* To use violence against someone or something: *The dog attacks strangers who enter the yard.*

2. *verb* To criticize someone strongly: *The commercials attacked the candidate's stand on health care reform.*

3. *noun* A sudden onset of illness, as in *a bad attack of asthma.*

at·tack (uh-**tak**)

▷ *verb* **attacking, attacked** ▷ *noun* **attack**

▷ *noun* **attacker**

attain *verb*

1. To achieve or get something: *She was the first in her family to attain a college degree.*

2. To reach a certain age, size, or amount: *The study found that animals at high elevations attained a greater body size.*

at·tain (uh-**tayn**)

▷ *verb* **attaining, attained** ▷ *adjective* **attainable**

attempt *verb* To try to do something: *I attempted to swim across the big lake.* **at·tempt** (uh-**tempt**)

▷ *verb* **attempting, attempted** ▷ *noun* **attempt**

attend *verb*
1. To be present in a place or at an event: *She attends a school 20 miles from her home.*
2. To listen or pay attention.
3. attend to To deal with something: *I'll attend to that when I come back from vacation.*
at·tend (uh-**tend**)
▷ *verb* **attending, attended**

attendance *noun*
1. The number of people who attend an event: *The attendance at the band concert was much greater than expected.*
2. The act or state of attending, especially regularly, as in *church attendance.*
at·tend·ance (uh-**ten**-duhns)

attendant *noun* Someone who takes care of a person or place, as in *a parking lot attendant.* **at·ten·dant** (uh-**ten**-duhnt)

attention *noun*
1. Concentration on one thing, as in *attention to detail.*
2. If you **pay attention**, you concentrate on one thing.
3. If something **needs attention**, it needs someone to do something to it.
4. When soldiers **stand at attention**, they stand straight with their feet together and their arms by their sides.
at·ten·tion (uh-**ten**-shuhn)

attentive *adjective* Alert and paying close attention to something or someone: *The class is least attentive just before and just after lunch.* **at·ten·tive** (uh-**ten**-tiv)
▷ *adverb* **attentively**

attest *verb*
1. To declare that something is true: *My father can attest to all the work I put into this project.*
2. To be proof of something: *This wonderful performance attests to your talent as a musician.*
at·test (uh-**test**)
▷ *verb* **attesting, attested**

attic *noun* A space in a building just under the roof. **at·tic** (**at**-ik)

attire *noun* Clothing: *We wore formal attire to the wedding.* **at·tire** (uh-**tire**) ▷ *verb* **attire**

attitude *noun*
1. Your opinions and feelings about someone or something that affect how you behave: *Theo is cheerful and has a good attitude toward everybody.*
2. The position in which you are standing or sitting.
at·ti·tude (**at**-i-*tood*)

attorney *noun* A lawyer: *The attorney argued her case before the court.* **at·tor·ney** (uh-**tur**-nee)

attract *verb*
1. To get your interest: *Video games always attract my attention.*
2. If a person **attracts** you, you like him or her.
3. To cause something to move closer or touch: *In science class, we used magnets to attract bits of iron.*
at·tract (uh-**trakt**)
▷ *verb* **attracting, attracted**

attraction *noun*
1. The power of attracting something: *The rise and fall of the ocean's tides are mainly caused by the gravitational attraction of the moon on the earth.*
2. A person or thing that attracts people's attention, admiration, or interest: *Our town's attractions include an amusement park, a zoo, and a planetarium.*
at·trac·tion (uh-**trak**-shuhn)

attractive *adjective*
1. Enjoyable to look at or experience: *Nora has a very attractive smile.*
2. Interesting or exciting, as in *an attractive idea.*
at·trac·tive (uh-**trak**-tiv)
▷ *noun* **attractiveness** ▷ *adverb* **attractively**

attribute
1. (**at**-ruh-*byoot*) *noun* A quality or characteristic that belongs to or describes a person or thing: *Kindness is her greatest attribute.*
2. (uh-**trib**-yoot) *verb* When you **attribute** something to someone, you give him or her credit for it: *The author attributed her success to her ninth-grade English teacher.* ▷ *verb* **attributing, attributed**
at·trib·ute

ATV *noun* A vehicle with three or more large wheels, ridden like a motorcycle, that can travel over rough ground. ATV is short for *all-terrain vehicle.*

auburn *noun* A reddish-brown color. **au·burn** (**aw**-burn) ▷ *adjective* **auburn**

auction *noun* A sale where items are sold to those who offer the most money. **auc·tion** (**awk**-shuhn)
▷ *noun* **auctioneer** (*awk*-shuh-**neer**)

audacity *noun*
1. Extreme, reckless, or foolish boldness: *I can't believe you had the audacity to argue with our teacher.*
2. Shameless behavior that offends someone: *Even though she bumped into me, she had the audacity to say that it was my fault.*
au·dac·i·ty (aw-**das**-i-tee)

ATV

audible *adjective* Loud enough to be heard: *Galina thought she was whispering, but her words were audible across the room.* **au·di·ble** (**aw**-duh-buhl)

audience *noun*

1. The people who watch or listen to a performance, speech, or movie.

2. A formal meeting with an important or powerful person, as in *an audience with the queen.*
au·di·ence (**aw**-dee-uhns)

audio

1. *adjective* Of or having to do with how sound is heard, recorded, and played back: *I listened to the audio file after I downloaded it to my computer.*

2. *noun* Sound, especially the sound portion of a film or television program.
au·di·o (**aw**-dee-*oh*)

audiobook *noun* A sound recording of a book being read aloud that can be listened to on a CD, audiotape, or computer. **aud·i·o·book** (**aw**-dee-oh-*buk*)

audiotape *noun* Magnetic tape that records sound: *The library has audiotapes of all the mayor's speeches.* **au·di·o·tape** (**aw**-dee-oh-*tape*)

audiovisual *adjective* Of or having to do with both sound and images, as in *audiovisual aids for the classroom.* **au·di·o·vis·u·al** (*aw*-dee-oh-**vizh**-oo-uhl)

audition *noun* A short performance by an actor, singer, musician, or dancer to see whether he or she is suitable for a part in a play, concert, or other performance: *Her audition for the role of Juliet went well.* **au·di·tion** (aw-**dish**-uhn)
▷ *verb* **audition**

auditorium *noun* A building or large room where people gather for meetings, plays, concerts, or other events. **au·di·to·ri·um** (*aw*-di-**tor**-ee-uhm)

augment *verb* You **augment** something when you add to it or make it larger: *She augmented her allowance with the money she earned delivering newspapers.* **aug·ment** (awg-**ment**) ▷ *verb* **augmenting, augmented**

August *noun* The eighth month on the calendar, after July and before September. August has 31 days. **Au·gust** (**aw**-guhst)

Word History

August is named after the first emperor of ancient Rome, Augustus Caesar. Originally, the month of August was supposed to have only 30 days, but Augustus Caesar protested. July, named after his uncle, Julius Caesar, had 31 days, and Augustus thought his month should be just as long. To please the emperor, calendar makers stole one day from February to give August 31 days in all.

aurora borealis

aunt *noun* The sister of your father or mother, or the wife of your uncle. **aunt** (ant *or* ahnt)

au pair *noun* A young person, usually from a foreign country, who lives with a family and helps with housework and child care in return for room and board. **au pair** (**oh** pair)

aurora borealis *noun* Colorful bands of flashing lights that sometimes can be seen at night, especially near the Arctic Circle. Also called the **northern lights**. **au·ro·ra bo·re·al·is** (uh-**ror**-uh *bor*-ee-**al**-is)

austere *adjective* Severe or cold in manner or appearance: *The austere room had only a lamp, a table, and four wooden chairs.* **aus·tere** (aw-**steer**)

austerity *noun* A way of living without extras or comforts: *He liked the austerity of the monk's cell.* **aus·ter·i·ty** (aw-**ster**-i-tee) ▷ *noun, plural* **austerities**

authentic *adjective* Real, or genuine: *This is an authentic Greek vase.* **au·then·tic** (aw-**then**-tik)

author *noun* The writer of a book, story, play, or article. **au·thor** (**aw**-thur) ▷ *noun* **authorship**

authoritative *adjective*

1. Official, or coming from someone who has the power to give orders: *His teacher spoke in an authoritative manner.*

2. Expert: *They believed the story because it came from an authoritative source.*
au·thor·i·ta·tive (uh-**thor**-i-*tay*-tiv)

authority *noun*

1. The power to do something officially or to tell other people what to do: *The federal agency has the authority to regulate milk prices.*

2. An organization with power in a certain area: *The Transportation Authority is adding new bus routes.*

3. Someone who knows a lot about a particular subject: *Jodi is an authority on butterflies.* **au·thor·i·ty** (uh-**thor**-i-tee) ▷ *noun, plural* **authorities**

authorize *verb* To give official permission for something to happen: *The school did not authorize students to leave the building during lunch.* **au·thor·ize** (**aw**-thuh-*rize*) ▷ *verb* **authorizing, authorized** ▷ *noun* **authorization**

autism *noun* A condition that causes someone to have trouble learning, communicating, and forming relationships with people. **au·tism** (**aw**-tiz-uhm) ▷ *adjective* **autistic** (aw-**tis**-tik)

auto *noun* Short for **automobile. au·to** (**aw**-toh)

autobiography *noun* A book in which the author tells the story of his or her life. **au·to·bi·og·ra·phy** (*aw*-toh-bye-**ah**-gruh-fee) ▷ *noun, plural* **autobiographies** ▷ *adjective* **autobiographical** (*aw*-toh-bye-uh-**graf**-i-kuhl)

autograph *noun* A person's handwritten signature, as in *a star's autograph.* **au·to·graph** (**aw**-tuh-*graf*)

automatic *adjective*
1. Able to operate without direct control, as in *an automatic sprinkler system.*
2. Done without your thinking about it: *When she asked if I could help, my automatic response was yes.*
au·to·mat·ic (*aw*-tuh-**mat**-ik) ▷ *adverb* **automatically**

automation *noun* The use of machines rather than people to do jobs, especially in factories. **au·to·ma·tion** (*aw*-tuh-**may**-shuhn) ▷ *verb* **automate**

automobile *noun* A car, SUV, or pickup. **au·to·mo·bile** (**aw**-tuh-muh-*beel*)

autonomy *noun*
1. The right or condition of people being able to choose their government: *Under the new regime, the country's citizens have the autonomy to elect their own local leaders.*
2. The state of being independent or self-governing.
au·ton·o·my (aw-**tah**-nuh-mee) ▷ *adjective* **autonomous** (aw-**tah**-nuh-muhs)

autopsy *noun* An examination performed on a dead person to find the cause of death. **au·top·sy** (**aw**-*tahp*-see) ▷ *noun, plural* **autopsies**

autumn *noun* The season between summer and winter, from late September to late December in the

autumn foliage

Northern Hemisphere. Also called **fall. au·tumn** (**aw**-tuhm) ▷ *adjective* **autumnal** (aw-**tuhm**-nuhl)

auxiliary *adjective* Helping, or giving extra support: *An auxiliary verb is a verb that helps to complete the meaning of the main verb.* **aux·il·ia·ry** (awg-**zil**-yur-ee) ▷ *noun* **auxiliary**

available *adjective*
1. Ready to be used or bought: *The new toys will be available in stores next week.*
2. Not busy, and therefore free to participate in something: *Are you available to work today?*
a·vail·a·ble (uh-**vay**-luh-buhl) ▷ *noun* **availability**

avalanche *noun* A large mass of snow, ice, or earth that suddenly falls down the side of a mountain: *The weight of the snowmobile triggered an avalanche.* **av·a·lanche** (**av**-uh-*lanch*)

avatar *noun*
1. A person who is an example of an idea: *The media calls her an avatar of traditional family values.*
2. In computer games, an **avatar** is a character that represents the person playing: *In this game, avatars change in appearance after every encounter with each other.*
3. In online social networking, your **avatar** is the image or photo you use to identify yourself.
av·a·tar (**av**-uh-*tahr*)

avenge *verb* To take revenge for: *The Raiders are hoping to avenge their loss next week.* **a·venge** (uh-**venj**) ▷ *verb* **avenging, avenged** ▷ *noun* **avenger**

avalanche

avenue *noun* A wide road in a town or city: *There are new shops on both sides of the avenue.* **av·e·nue** (**av**-uh-*noo*)

average

1. *noun* A number that you get by adding a group of numbers together and then dividing the sum by the number of figures you have added: *The average of 2, 5, and 14 is 7.* ▷ *verb* **average**

2. *adjective* Usual, or ordinary: *Rasheed is of average height.*
av·er·age (**av**-ur-ij)

avert *verb* To turn away from something or avoid it: *Make sure to avert your eyes from the sun during an eclipse.* **a·vert** (uh-**vurt**) ▷ *verb* **averting, averted** ▷ *noun* **aversion** (uh-**vur**-zhuhn)

aviation *noun* The practice and science of building and flying aircraft. **a·vi·a·tion** (*ay*-vee-**ay**-shuhn) ▷ *noun* **aviator**

Word History

When you travel in an airplane, you are truly flying like a "bird." When the Wright brothers invented the airplane at the beginning of the 20th century, the word **aviation**, meaning the science of flying aircraft, had already been in existence for 25 years. Balloons were already used for flying: Manned balloon rides had been taking place since the 18th century. People chose the term *aviation* because by flying, they were imitating birds: *Aviation* is based on the Latin word for "bird," *avis.* You can see the same root in the word *aviary*, which refers to an enclosed area for birds, such as at a zoo.

---

avid *adjective* Very eager or committed: *She's an avid golfer.* **av·id** (**av**-id) ▷ *adverb* **avidly**

avocado *noun* A green or black pear-shaped fruit with a tough skin and a creamy, light green pulp. **av·o·ca·do** (*av*-uh-**kah**-doh) ▷ *noun, plural* **avocados** or **avocadoes**

Word History

The word **avocado** traces its history to *ahuacatl*, a word in the Nahuatl language of Mexico. Spanish speakers borrowed the word, pronouncing it as *aguacate.* Since another Spanish word, *avocado*, meaning "lawyer," sounded very similar, they came to use *avocado* for the fruit as well. The word entered the English language in the 1600s.

---

avoid *verb*

1. To stay away from a person or place: *Julio tried to avoid Jackie after their argument.*

2. To try to prevent something from happening:

How can we avoid another mishap like this?
a·void (uh-**void**)
▷ *verb* **avoiding, avoided** ▷ *noun* **avoidance**
▷ *adjective* **avoidable**

await *verb* To wait for or expect someone or something: *I eagerly awaited the last day of school.* **a·wait** (uh-**wayt**) ▷ *verb* **awaiting, awaited**

awake

1. *adjective* Not asleep: *The baby is wide awake.*

2. *verb* To wake up: *Farmers awake before dawn in the summer.* ▷ *verb* **awaking, awoke** (uh-**wohk**), **awoken** (uh-**woh**-kuhn) ▷ *noun* **awakening**
a·wake (uh-**wake**)

award *verb*

1. To give someone something valuable as a reward or honor, as in *to award a prize.*

2. To give someone something because of the decision of a court: *In 2005, a court awarded him $360,000 in damages.*
a·ward (uh-**word**)
▷ *verb* **awarding, awarded** ▷ *noun* **award**

aware *adjective* If you are **aware** of something, you notice it and are conscious of it: *Are you aware that you can apply for a scholarship?*
a·ware (uh-**wair**)

awareness *noun* The condition or fact of being aware: *The ad campaign is meant to increase the public's awareness of the dangers of obesity.* **a·ware·ness** (uh-**wair**-nis)

away

1. *adverb* Moving from a place, person, or thing: *Toshi went away to New Zealand.*

2. *adverb* Distant from a place: *The airport is about 15 miles away.*

3. *adverb* Not at home, or not present: *I'm away from the phone right now, so please leave a message.*

4. *adverb* In a secure place: *She unlocked the safe and put her jewels away.*

5. *adjective* An **away** game in sports is one you play at your opponent's home field or court.
a·way (uh-**way**)

awe *noun* A feeling of admiration and respect, sometimes mixed with a little fear: *Nikki is in awe of her drama teacher.* **awe** (aw)

awesome *adjective*

1. Causing you to feel awe: *Parenthood is an awesome responsibility.*

avocado

2. (*informal*) Very good, as in *a totally awesome performance*.
awe·some (**aw**-*suhm*)

awful

1. *adjective* Terrible or horrible: *Failing that test was awful!*
2. *adverb, adjective* (*informal*) **Awful** is sometimes used before nouns and adjectives with a negative meaning to make them more intense: *He spends an awful lot of time on the phone. You're awful close to flunking this subject.*
aw·ful (**aw**-fuhl)
▷ *adverb* **awfully**

Synonyms

Awful is a word used very often to describe anything or anyone that is unpleasant, unlikable, or nasty. Besides those words, there are some other words you can use to describe things, situations, or people that you dislike. Sometimes, of course, the word *awful* fits: *The radio reception in my area is just awful.*

■ **Terrible** can mean very unpleasant, damaging, or having serious results: *The storm last week was terrible. The gymnast broke her leg during a terrible fall off the balance beam.*

■ **Dreadful** means really bad or dangerous: *She had a dreadful case of pneumonia.*

■ **Horrible** can describe something so awful that you can hardly stand to look at it or be around it: *The hero of the story was turned into a horrible monster by an evil witch.*

■ **Ghastly** can mean so bad that you can hardly face up to the situation: *It was ghastly for the little girl to be lost all night on the mountain.*

awhile *adverb* For a short time: *We waited awhile, but Tariq never arrived.* **a·while** (uh-**wile**)

awkward *adjective*

1. Difficult or embarrassing: *In an awkward moment, Jorge forgot my name.*
2. Not able to relax and talk to people easily: *Edward feels awkward during class discussions.*
3. Not graceful or smooth; clumsy: *I'm pretty awkward when it comes to ice-skating.*
awk·ward (**awk**-wurd)
▷ *noun* **awkwardness**
▷ *adverb* **awkwardly**

awl *noun* A sharp metal tool for making holes in

leather or wood. **awl** (awl) **Awl** sounds like **all**.

awning *noun* A piece of cloth, metal, or wood that is fastened to the top of a window or to the front roof of a building to shade it from sun and help keep out rain. **aw·ning** (**aw**-ning)

awry *adverb* In an unexpected or undesirable direction: *The movie is about an experiment that goes awry and releases mutant insects.* **a·wry** (uh-**rye**)

ax *or* **axe**

1. *noun* A tool with a sharp blade on the end of a handle, used for chopping wood. ▷ *noun, plural* **axes**
2. *verb* To bring something to an end: *The company axed more than 600 jobs.* ▷ *verb* **axes, axing, axed**
ax *or* **axe** (aks)

axis *noun*

1. An imaginary line through the middle of an object, around which that object spins, as in *the earth's axis*.
2. A line at the side or the bottom of a graph.
ax·is (**ak**-sis)
▷ *noun, plural* **axes** (**ak**-seez)

axle *noun* A rod in the center of a wheel, around which the wheel turns. **ax·le** (**ak**-suhl)

Word History

An **axle** for a wheel used to be called an *axle-tree*. English speakers borrowed this term from the Old Norse word *öxul-tré*, meaning "axle-log," because axles were made out of wood. *Öxul-tré* was a combination of *öxull*, meaning "axle," and *tré*, meaning "log" or "tree." Eventually, speakers left out *tree* in the word *axle-tree*, leaving only *axle*. The word *axis*, referring to the imaginary line around which a planet revolves, is related to *axle*.

aye *noun* A vote of "yes": *The proposal was approved, with 54 ayes and 33 nays.* **aye** (eye)
▷ *interjection* **aye**

azalea *noun* A shrub with funnel-shaped pink, orange, or white flowers and dark green leaves. **a·za·lea** (uh-**zayl**-yuh)

Aztec *noun* A member of a Mexican Indian people who built a great civilization before the conquest of Mexico by Cortés in the 16th century. **Az·tec** (**az**-tek) ▷ *adjective* **Aztec**

azure *noun* A bright blue color, like the color of the sky on a sunny day. **az·ure** (**azh**-ur)
▷ *adjective* **azure**

Aztec mask

Bb

About B Words that begin with a *bye* sound are spelled *bi* or *by*. Examples: bike, bind, bypass, bystander. Some words include the letter **B**, but it is silent, which means you don't pronounce it. This usually occurs when the letter comes after an *m* or before a *t*. Examples: comb, doubt, subtle. The first and second letters of the Greek alphabet, *alpha* and *beta,* became our *a* and *b*. Together, their names are the source for the word *alphabet*.

babble *verb*
1. To talk quickly and excitedly but without making any sense: *Bob tends to babble when he gets nervous.*
2. To make a low, murmuring sound: *We could hear the brook babbling outside our window.*
bab·ble (**bab**-uhl)
▷ *verb* **babbling, babbled**

babe *noun* A baby. **babe** (babe)

baboon *noun* A large African or Asian monkey with a long snout and large teeth. **ba·boon** (ba-**boon**)

baby
1. *noun* An infant or very young child or animal.
2. *noun* Someone who acts like a very young child: *Don't be a baby when the doctor gives you that shot.*
3. *verb* To fuss over or treat someone like an infant: *My mother babies me every time I get a sore throat.*
▷ *verb* **babying, babied**
ba·by (**bay**-bee)
▷ *noun, plural* **babies** ▷ *adjective* **babyish**

baboon

baby boom *noun* An increase in the number of babies born in a nation. The term is often used to refer to the generation of people born in the United States between 1946 and 1964. ▷ *noun* **baby boomer**

babysitter *noun* Someone who takes care of children when their parents aren't home. **ba·by·sit·ter** (**bay**-bee-sit-ur) ▷ *verb* **babysit**

baby tooth *noun* A first tooth in infants and baby mammals. Baby teeth fall out and are replaced by permanent teeth. ▷ *noun, plural* **baby teeth**

bachelor *noun* A man who has never been married. **bach·e·lor** (**bach**-uh-lur)

back
1. *noun* The rear part of your body between your neck and the end of your spine.

2. *noun* The part or area farthest from the front, as in *the back of the room.* ▷ *adjective* **back**
3. *adverb* In, to, or toward a place from which someone or something came: *Why did she come back after being away for so long?*
4. *verb* To give financial or other support to someone or something: *We all back the mayor's reelection.* ▷ *noun* **backer**
5. back down *verb* To stop arguing for something: *I backed down because George was getting really angry.*
6. back out *verb* To withdraw from or change your mind about doing something you had promised to do: *He had to back out of the dinner invitation because he had to work late.*
7. back up *verb* To make a copy of a computer file, or of all your computer files: *Before you close the program, it will prompt you to back up your files.*
back (bak)
▷ *verb* **backing, backed**

backboard *noun* The upright board behind a basketball hoop. **back·board** (**bak**-bord)

backbone *noun* A set of connected bones that run down the middle of the back. The backbone is also called the **spine** and the **spinal column**. **back·bone** (**bak**-bohn)

backfire *verb*
1. If an action **backfires,** it leads to the opposite of what you wanted or expected: *My plan to throw my mom a surprise party backfired when she saw the invitation.*
2. If a car **backfires,** there is a small explosion of unburned fuel that causes a loud bang in the exhaust pipe.
back·fire (**bak**-*fire*)
▷ *verb* **backfiring, backfired**

background *noun*
1. The part of a picture or scene that lies behind the main figures: *The portrait of George Washington has an American flag in the background.*
2. A person's past experience: *We check the background of everyone we hire.*
3. Information that explains something: *What's the background of this kidnapping?*

back·ground (**bak**-*ground*)
▷ *adjective* **background**

backhand *noun* A stroke in tennis, badminton, and other racket sports that you play with your arm across your body and the back of your hand facing outward. **back·hand** (**bak**-*hand*)

backhoe *noun* A digging machine that has a bucket with teeth. **back·hoe** (**bak**-*hoh*)

backpack
1. *noun* A bag that you carry on your back, which holds your supplies when you are hiking or camping.
2. *verb* To go on a long walk or hike carrying a backpack: *We went backpacking in a state forest preserve last weekend.* ▷ *verb* **backpacking, backpacked**
back·pack (**bak**-*pak*)

backslash *noun* A character (\) that computers use to separate data and to perform some commands. **back·slash** (**bak**-*slash*)

backstory *noun* Information from the past about a person, thing, or character: *The third chapter of the novel explains Rachel's backstory—she has American parents but grew up in Argentina.* **back·sto·ry** (**bak**-*stor*-ee)

backstroke *noun* A style of swimming in which you lie on your back and lift your arms, one at a time, in a backward circular movement while kicking your feet. **back·stroke** (**bak**-*stroke*)

backup *noun*
1. An exact copy of a computer file that can be used if something happens to the original one.
2. The job of making a copy of all the files on a computer or server: *The school runs a backup of its computers every night.*
back·up (**bak**-*uhp*)

backward *or* **backwards**
1. *adverb* In the reverse direction: *Eric stepped backward.*
2. *adverb* In a way that is opposite to the normal or usual way: *Carina learned how to skate backwards.*
3. *adjective* Lagging behind: *That part of the state is so backward that most of the children have never seen a dentist.*
back·ward (**bak**-wurd) *or* **back·wards** (**bak**-wurdz)

backyard *noun* An open area behind a house. **back·yard** (**bak**-yahrd)

bacon *noun* Smoked or salted meat from the back or sides of a pig. **ba·con** (**bay**-kuhn)

bacteria *noun, plural* Microscopic, single-celled living things that exist everywhere and that can either be useful or harmful. **bac·te·ri·a** (bak-**teer**-ee-uh)
▷ *noun, singular* **bacterium** (bak-**teer**-ee-uhm)

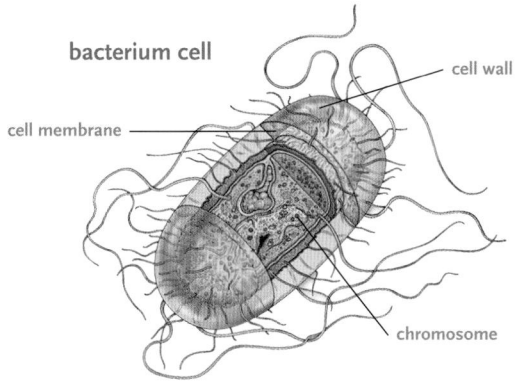

bacterium cell
cell membrane
cell wall
chromosome

bad *adjective*
1. Unwelcome or unpleasant, as in *bad news.*
2. Serious or severe, as in *a bad storm.*
3. Rotten or spoiled, as in *bad meat.*
4. Wicked or evil, as in *a bad person.*
5. Sorry: *I feel bad that you didn't enjoy the film.*
bad (bad)
▷ *adjective* **worse, worst**

Synonyms

Bad, like **awful**, can describe anything that is not good. Food, ideas, the weather—almost anything you can imagine or have an opinion about—can be bad or awful: *It was a bad idea to leave my bicycle unlocked while I returned the library book. I thought that was a bad movie. We were caught in an awful storm on the way home from school.*

– –

■ **Naughty** refers to some action or activity that is bad and a bit mischievous. Naughty usually describes the disobedient actions of young children: *My little sister was being very naughty when she pulled the kitten's tail.*

■ **Serious** can describe something bad enough to have very unpleasant effects or results: *A serious disagreement led to the end of their friendship.*

■ **Poor** can mean "inferior" or "lacking in quality": *My eyesight is so poor that I need to wear glasses all the time.*

■ **Wrong** means "incorrect" or "not good in a moral sense": *She gave a wrong answer. It is wrong to take something that does not belong to you.*

■ **Rotten** and **spoiled** describe something that has changed from good to bad and often refers to food: *The apples were so old that they had become rotten.*

bade *verb* A past tense of **bid** (sense 2 only). **bade** (bad *or* bayd)

badge *noun* A small, flat object that you pin to your clothes to show who you are or what you do, as in *a policeman's badge.* **badge** (baj)

badger
> **1.** *noun* A mammal with gray fur and a black-and-white head that lives in a burrow and feeds at night.
> **2.** *verb* To pester someone: *Karen kept badgering me to print her document.* ▷ *verb* **badgering, badgered**
> **badg·er** (**baj**-ur)

badly *adverb*
> **1.** Very much; intensely: *How badly do you need the money?*
> **2.** Not well, or not skillfully: *Mr. Isaacs plays the piano badly.*
> **bad·ly** (**bad**-lee)

badminton *noun* A game in which players use light, long-handled rackets to hit a shuttlecock back and forth over a high, narrow net. **bad·min·ton** (**bad**-*min*-tuhn)

badmouth *verb* To say negative things about someone or something: *Everyone's been badmouthing the movie, but I thought it was pretty good.* **bad·mouth** (**bad**-*mouth*) ▷ *verb* **badmouthing, badmouthed**

bae *noun* (*slang*) A boyfriend or girlfriend. Bae is short for **babe.** **bae** (bay)

baffle *verb* To make someone feel puzzled or confused: *Your actions baffle me.* **baf·fle** (**baf**-uhl) ▷ *verb* **baffling, baffled** ▷ *adjective* **baffling**

bag
> **1.** *noun* A flexible container with an opening at the top, used for carrying things.
> **2.** *verb* To put something in a bag or sack: *The boy who bagged our groceries was a neighbor.* ▷ *verb* **bagging, bagged**
> **bag** (bag)

bagel *noun* A chewy kind of bread that is shaped like a doughnut. **ba·gel** (**bay**-guhl)

Word History

The **bagel** is named for its shape. In the Middle Ages, German speakers called the bread roll a *bouc,* meaning "ring." In Yiddish, a Jewish-German language, the word became *beygel,* and then entered English.

baggage *noun* Travelers' suitcases, bags, and trunks. **bag·gage** (**bag**-ij)

baggy *adjective* Hanging loosely, as in *baggy pants.* **bag·gy** (**bag**-ee) ▷ *adjective* **baggier, baggiest**

bagpipes *noun, plural* A musical instrument popular in Scotland with a flexible bag that you blow into through a mouthpiece. **bag·pipes** (**bag**-*pipes*)

bail *noun* Money paid to a court for the release of someone accused of a crime, with the promise that he or she will show up for the trial: *Keith was released on bail.* **bail** (bayl)

bailiff *noun* An official in a court of law who maintains order in the court. **bail·iff** (**bay**-lif)

bail out *verb*
> **1.** To jump out of an aircraft in an emergency, using a parachute.
> **2.** To scoop water out of a boat.
> **3.** If you **bail** someone **out,** you pay that person's bail or help him or her out of a difficult situation: *If we ran out of money, we knew our parents would bail us out.* ▷ *verb* **bailing out, bailed out**

bait *noun* A small amount of food put on a hook or in a trap to attract a fish or other animal. **bait** (bayt)

bake *verb*
> **1.** To cook food, especially bread or cake, with dry heat in an oven: *Kyle baked a cake for dessert.* ▷ *noun* **baker** ▷ *noun* **bakery** (**bay**-kur-ee)
> **2.** To heat something in order to make it hard: *Bake the clay pot in a kiln before glazing it.*
> **3.** To be or become very hot: *While everyone else found a place in the shade, we were baking.*
> **bake** (bayk)
> ▷ *verb* **baking, baked**

baking powder *noun* A white powder used in baking to make dough or batter rise.

baking soda *noun* A white powder used to make dough rise, or to soothe an upset stomach. Also called **sodium bicarbonate.**

balance
> **1.** *noun* Your **balance** is your ability to remain steady and upright: *She lost her balance when the bus started moving.*
> **2.** *verb* If you **balance** something, you keep it steady: *The waiter balanced a large tray stacked with dishes.* ▷ *verb* **balancing, balanced**
> **3.** *noun* A device used for weighing things.
> **4.** *noun* Remainder: *After a sunny morning, the balance of the day was cloudy.*
> **bal·ance** (**bal**-uhns)

bagpipes

balanced diet *noun* A diet that contains the proper kinds and amounts of food to keep you healthy.

balcony *noun*
1. A platform surrounded by a railing or low wall on the outside of a building, usually above street level.
2. An upstairs seating area in a theater or auditorium that projects over the main floor.
bal·co·ny (**bal**-kuh-nee)

bald *adjective*
1. Having little or no hair on the head. ▷ *noun* **baldness** ▷ *adjective* **balding**
2. Without any natural covering: *The lawn was bald where the trash barrels had covered it.*
bald (bawld)
▷ *adjective* **balder, baldest**

bald eagle *noun* An eagle with a brown body and a white head that appears bald from a distance. The bald eagle is the national symbol of the United States.

bale
1. *noun* A large bundle of things, such as straw or hay, that is tied tightly together.
2. *verb* To put hay or some other substance into a tightly packed bundle: *We've got to bale all the hay before it rains again.* ▷ *verb* **baling, baled**
bale (bale)

balk *verb* To stop and refuse to go on or be involved in something: *The others balked when Lee suggested stealing some apples.* **balk** (bawk) ▷ *verb* **balking, balked**

ball *noun*
1. A round object that is hit, thrown, or kicked in games.
2. Something that has been squeezed or formed into a round shape, as in *a ball of dough.*
3. A formal gathering where people come to dance.
4. In baseball, a pitch that a batter does not swing at and that does not cross home plate between the batter's shoulders and knees.
5. (*informal*) If you are **on the ball,** you are quick at understanding things.
6. If you **have a ball,** you have a very good time: *It was supposed to be a punishment, but we were having a ball.*
ball (bawl)
Ball sounds like **bawl**.

ballad *noun* A poem that tells a story and is meant to be sung. **bal·lad** (**bal**-uhd)

ballast *noun* Heavy material, such as water or sand, that is carried in the bottom of a ship or hot-air balloon to make it more stable. **bal·last** (**bal**-uhst)

ball bearings *noun, plural* Small metal balls, usually in a ring-shaped track, that keep machine parts moving smoothly against each other.

ballerina *noun* A female ballet dancer. **bal·le·ri·na** (*bal*-uh-**ree**-nuh)

ballet *noun*
1. A style of dance that uses precise, graceful movements.
2. A theatrical performance that uses dance, music, costumes, and scenery, often to tell a story.
bal·let (**bal**-ay *or* ba-**lay**)

ballistics *noun, plural* The study of how things like bullets and missiles fly through the air. **bal·lis·tics** (buh-**lis**-tiks)

balloon *noun*
1. A thin rubber bag filled with air and used as a toy or decoration.
2. A **hot-air balloon** is an aircraft consisting of a very large bag filled with hot air or gas, with a basket for carrying passengers and equipment.
bal·loon (buh-**loon**)

ballerina

Word History
Balloons come in all sizes, but according to the name, every **balloon** is large. French speakers added the ending *-on,* meaning "large," to their word for "ball," *balle.* In this way, they created the word *ballon,* referring to a large inflated ball.

ballot *noun*
1. A way of voting secretly, using a machine or slips of paper.
2. **ballot box** A box with a long, narrow hole in the top for collecting votes.
bal·lot (**bal**-uht)

Word History
Modern voters cast **ballots** by marking their votes on paper, but "casting a ballot" once referred to throwing a small ball into a box. The winner was the candidate whose box contained the most balls. In Italian, *ballotta* means "little ball," and this word is the source of the English word *ballot.*

ballpark *noun*
1. A place where people play or watch a ball game, especially baseball.
2. A **ballpark figure** is a number or amount that is partly a guess because there is not enough information available: *They gave a ballpark figure of $50 million for the cost of the new building.*
ball·park (**bawl**-pahrk)

ballpoint *noun* A pen with a tiny ball for its point that transfers ink to a writing surface. **ball·point** (**bawl**-*point*)

ballroom *noun* A large room where parties and dances are held. **ball·room** (**bawl**-*room*)

balsa *noun* A lightweight tropical wood used for making model airplanes. **bal·sa** (**bawl**-suh)

balsam fir *noun* A type of fragrant evergreen tree. **bal·sam fir** (**bawl**-suhm)

bamboo *noun* A tropical plant with a hollow, woody stem, often used for making fishing poles and furniture. **bam·boo** (bam-**boo**)

banana tree

Word History

The **bamboo** plant is the main food of the giant panda. These large bearlike animals, which live in central China, like to eat bamboo shoots, the new parts of the plant that are just beginning to grow. The origins of the plant name *bamboo* are not very clear. The name may go back to the word *bambu* in Malay, a southeast Asian language, or to the word *banbu* in Kannada, a language of southern India, both meaning "bamboo." Most bamboo plants grow in Asia, but a few species are native to the United States.

ban *verb* To officially forbid something or prevent someone from doing something: *Swimming was banned because of the pollution.* **ban** (ban) ▷ *verb* **banning, banned** ▷ *noun* **ban**

banana *noun* A long, curved, tropical fruit with a thick yellow skin. **ba·nan·a** (buh-**nan**-uh)

banana split *noun* A dessert of ice cream served on two halves of a banana with nuts, syrup, and other flavorings on top.

band
1. *noun* A thin strip of flexible material, such as rubber or plastic, that holds one or a number of things together: *Metal bands kept the stacks of bricks from falling over.*
2. *noun* A group of musicians who perform together: *I play guitar in a band.*
3. *noun* A group of people with a common purpose, as in *a band of robbers.*
4. *noun* A stripe of color or material: *The bird has a band of blue on its wings.*
5. *verb* When people **band** together, they form a group to achieve a common purpose. ▷ *verb* **banding, banded band** (band)

bandage *noun* A piece of cloth or material that protects an injured part of the body while it heals. **band·age** (**ban**-dij) ▷ *verb* **bandage**

bandanna *noun* A large, brightly colored square of fabric, usually worn around the head or neck. **ban·dan·na** (ban-**dan**-uh)

bandit *noun* An outlaw, usually a member of a gang, who robs people at gunpoint. **ban·dit** (**ban**-dit)

bandwidth *noun* The amount of data that can move at one time on a computer network: *The company is expanding quickly and will soon need to add more bandwidth to its network.* **band·width** (**band**-*width*)

bang
1. *noun* A sharp, loud noise.
2. *verb* To hit forcefully and noisily: *The musician banged the cymbals together.* ▷ *verb* **banging, banged bang** (bang)

bangle *noun* A rigid band of metal or plastic, worn as jewelry around the wrist or ankle. **bang·le** (**bang**-guhl)

bangs *noun, plural* Hair that is cut short and often straight across a person's forehead. **bangs** (bangz)

banish *verb* To force someone to leave a place and never return: *He was banished from the playground after his third fight.* **ban·ish** (**ban**-ish) ▷ *verb* **banishing, banished** ▷ *noun* **banishment**

banister *noun* A handrail, usually supported by upright posts, that runs along the side of a stairway. **ban·is·ter** (**ban**-is-tur)

banjo *noun* A musical instrument with a round body, a long neck, and four or five strings that are plucked or strummed. **ban·jo** (**ban**-joh) ▷ *noun, plural* **banjos** or **banjoes**

bank
1. *noun* A place where money is kept for saving and lending purposes. ▷ *verb* **bank**
2. *noun* The sloping land along the sides of a river or a canal: *The banks of the river were steep.*
3. *noun* A supply of something for future use, as in *a blood bank.*
4. *verb* If you **bank on** something, you are counting on it: *I'm banking*

banjo

on the weather being good tomorrow. ▷ verb **banking, banked**
bank (bangk)

Word History

In medieval Italy, moneylenders worked on narrow benches. The French borrowed the Italian word for bench, *banca,* and changed it to *banque.* This form was the source of the English word **bank**, as in *savings bank.*

banker *noun* Someone who has an important job in a bank or owns a bank. **bank·er** (**bang**-kur)

bankroll *verb* To supply with the money to do something: *Her wealthy aunt is going to bankroll her internet start-up.* **bank·roll** (**bangk**-*rohl*) ▷ verb **bankrolling, bankrolled**

bankrupt
1. *adjective* If people or companies are **bankrupt,** they no longer have enough money to pay their debts: *The shop went bankrupt and had to close.*
2. *verb* To take or require all of a person's money: *Mr. Sanchez was afraid that the hospital bills would bankrupt him.* ▷ verb **bankrupting, bankrupted**
bank·rupt (**bangk**-*ruhpt*)
▷ noun **bankruptcy**

banner *noun*
1. A long piece of material with writing, pictures, or designs on it, hung from a pole or displayed at sporting events or parades.
2. banner ad An advertisement across the top, bottom, or side of a webpage: *A flashing banner ad appeared when I clicked on the site.*
ban·ner (**ban**-ur)

banquet *noun* A formal meal for a large number of people, usually in honor of someone or something: *The team captains were asked to speak at the sports banquet.* **ban·quet** (**bang**-kwit)

banter *verb* To tease someone in a friendly way: *The Democrats and Republicans bantered before the opening session of Congress.* **ban·ter** (**ban**-tur) ▷ verb **bantering, bantered** ▷ noun **banter**

baptize *verb* To pour water on someone's head or to immerse someone in water, as a sign that he or she has become a Christian. **bap·tize** (**bap**-tize) ▷ verb **baptizing, baptized** ▷ noun **baptism** (**bap**-*tiz*-uhm)

bar
1. *noun* A long, straight piece of

something rigid, as in *an iron bar.*
2. *noun* A block of something hard, as in *a bar of soap.*
3. *noun* A place where people can buy drinks, especially alcoholic drinks.
4. *noun* In music, the same thing as a **measure**.
5. *verb* To block someone, or to keep someone out: *The police barred the reporters from the courtroom.* ▷ verb **barring, barred**
bar (bahr)

barb *noun* A sharp point that sticks out and backward, as on a hook or arrowhead. **barb** (bahrb) ▷ adjective **barbed**

barbarian *noun* Someone who is considered wild and uncivilized. **bar·bar·i·an** (bahr-**bair**-ee-uhn)

barbaric *adjective* Very cruel or primitive: *The animals were kept in barbaric conditions.* **bar·bar·ic** (bahr-**bar**-ik)

barbecue *noun*
1. An outdoor grill for cooking meat and other food. ▷ verb **barbecue**
2. An outdoor meal or party in which food is grilled over an open fire.
bar·be·cue (**bahr**-buh-*kyoo*)

barbed wire *noun* Twisted strands of wire with small, sharp spikes, used for fences. **barbed wire** (barbd)

barber *noun* Someone who cuts hair for men and boys, and trims or shaves beards. **bar·ber** (**bahr**-bur)

bar code *noun* A band of thick and thin lines printed on items sold in stores. When read electronically, the bar code gives the price and other information about the product: *The bar code for this dictionary is on the back cover.*

bare
1. *adjective* Wearing no clothes, or not covered: *Although it was cold, Tim went out with a bare head.*
2. *adjective* Empty or unfurnished: *The newly painted walls were bare.*
3. *verb* To expose or reveal something: *Alison was willing to bare all her secrets.* ▷ verb **baring, bared**
4. *adjective* Basic: *All we wanted were the bare facts, with no apologies.*
bare (bair)
Bare sounds like **bear.** ▷ adjective **barer, barest**

barefaced *adjective* Bold or shameless, as in *a barefaced lie.* **bare·faced** (**bair**-*fayst*)

barefoot *adjective* Without shoes or socks. **bare·foot** (**bair**-*fut*) ▷ adverb **barefoot**

barely *adverb* Hardly, or almost not: *The room was so hot, we could barely breathe.* **bare·ly** (**bair**-lee)

barbecue

barf *verb* (informal) To vomit: *I almost barfed when the plane suddenly lost altitude in the storm.* **barf** (bahrf) ▷ *verb* **barfing, barfed** ▷ *noun* **barf**

bargain
1. *noun* Something offered or bought for a lower than usual price: *Those beach towels were a real bargain.*
2. *verb* When you **bargain** with someone, you discuss the price of something or the terms of an agreement: *We bargained for a better deal on the car rental.*
▷ *verb* **bargaining, bargained**
bar·gain (**bahr**-guhn)

barge
1. *noun* A long, flat-bottomed boat that is often towed or pushed by another boat.
2. *verb* If you **barge** into a room, you enter it rudely or abruptly: *My little sister always barges into my room without knocking.* ▷ *verb* **barging, barged**
barge (bahrj)

bar graph *noun* A chart that compares information by showing it as rectangular bars of varying length.

baritone *noun*
1. The second-lowest male singing voice, higher than a bass voice but lower than a tenor voice. ▷ *adjective* **baritone**
2. A singer with such a voice.
bar·i·tone (**bar**-i-*tone*)

barium *noun* A silver-colored chemical element used in paints, ceramics, and medical imaging. **bar·i·um** (**bair**-ee-uhm)

bark
1. *verb* When a dog **barks,** it makes a sudden, harsh sound in its throat. ▷ *noun* **bark**
2. *noun* The tough outer covering on the stems of shrubs, trees, and other plants.
3. *verb* To speak sharply or abruptly: *The construction boss continually barked orders at the workers.*
bark (bahrk)
▷ *verb* **barking, barked**

Word History

The noun **bark** refers to two different things, and each meaning has its own history. The sound a dog makes comes from an Old English word for that sound, *beorcan.* The Scandinavians gave us the other definition, from the word *borkr,* which means "tree skin."

barley *noun* A cereal plant whose grains are used for food, especially for farm animals. Barley is also used to make beer. **bar·ley** (**bahr**-lee)

bar mitzvah *noun* A ceremony and celebration that takes place on or close to a Jewish boy's 13th birthday, after which he takes on the role of an adult in his religion. **bar mitz·vah** (*bahr* **mits**-vuh)

barn *noun* A large farm building where crops, animals, and equipment are kept. **barn** (bahrn)

barnacle *noun* A small shellfish that attaches itself firmly to underwater surfaces, such as rocks and the hulls of boats. **bar·na·cle** (**bahr**-nuh-kuhl)

barnyard *noun* The area near a barn, usually surrounded by a fence. **barn·yard** (**bahrn**-*yahrd*)

barometer *noun* An instrument that measures changes in air pressure and is used to forecast the weather. **ba·rom·e·ter** (buh-**rah**-mi-tur)

baron *noun*
1. A nobleman of the lowest rank.
2. Someone who has a lot of power and influence in a certain area: *Her father was a Texas oil baron.*
bar·on (**bar**-uhn)
▷ *adjective* **baronial** (buh-**roh**-nee-uhl)

baroness *noun* A noblewoman of the lowest rank. **bar·on·ess** (**bar**-uh-nis) ▷ *noun, plural* **baronesses**

barracks *noun, plural* A large building or group of buildings where soldiers are housed. **bar·racks** (**bar**-uhks)

barracuda

barracuda *noun* A fish with a long, narrow body and many sharp teeth. **bar·ra·cu·da** (*bar*-uh-**koo**-duh)

barrage *noun*
1. Concentrated firing from guns or other weapons.
2. A huge outpouring of something, as in *a barrage of protest.*
bar·rage (buh-**rahzh**)

barrel *noun*
1. A large container that bulges out in the middle and has a flat top and bottom.
2. A tube-shaped part of something, as in *the barrel of a gun.*
3. If someone has you **over a barrel,** he or she has put you in a difficult position: *The rising cost of fuel has the company over a barrel.*
bar·rel (**bar**-uhl)

barren *adjective*
1. Unable to produce crops, as in *barren land.*
2. Bleak, lifeless, or without interest: *His life as a prisoner was barren and lonely.*
bar·ren (**bar**-uhn)

barrette *noun* A plastic or metal clip used to hold the hair in place. **bar·rette** (buh-**ret**)

barricade

1. *noun* A barrier to stop people from getting past a certain point.

2. *verb* If people **barricade** themselves in a place, they put up obstacles to stop other people from getting to them: *We barricaded ourselves in the bedroom until the fight was over.* ▷ *verb* **barricading, barricaded**
bar·ri·cade (bar-i-*kade*)

barrier *noun*

1. A structure, such as a wall or a fence, that prevents people or things from going past it: *I had to ride my bike around the barrier in the road.*

2. Anything that makes communication or progress difficult, as in *a language barrier.*
bar·ri·er (bar-ee-ur)

barring *preposition* Except for; apart from: *Barring a major traffic tie-up, we should be there by noon.* bar·ring (bahr-ing)

barrio *noun* A neighborhood where Spanish is the main language. Barrio means "neighborhood" in Spanish. bar·ri·o (bar-ee-*oh*)

barrow *noun* A mound of earth or stones placed over a grave in ancient times. bar·row (bar-oh)

barter *verb* To do business by exchanging products or services, rather than paying for them: *My uncle bartered some accounting work for a new lawn mower.* bar·ter (bahr-tur) ▷ *verb* **bartering, bartered** ▷ *noun* **barter**

base

1. *noun* The lowest or supporting part of something, as in *the base of a lamp.*

2. *verb* To use something as the foundation for something else: *The movie was based on the life of a famous French singer.* ▷ *verb* **basing, based**

3. *noun* The headquarters or main place for something, as in *a base of operations.*

4. *noun* In baseball, a **base** is one of the four corners of the diamond to which you must run in order to score.

5. *noun* In chemistry, a **base** is a substance that will react with an acid to form a salt: *The addition of a base will turn red litmus paper blue.*

6. *noun* In mathematics, a **base** is the number on which a counting system is built: *Ten is the base of the decimal system.*

7. *adjective* Selfish or without moral standards, as in *base instincts.* ▷ *adjective* **baser, basest**
base (base)

baseball *noun*

1. A game played on a large, grassy field with a bat and ball and two teams of nine players each.

2. The ball used in this game.
base·ball (base-*bawl*)

Baseball

Baseball is played on a diamond-shaped field with four bases. Two teams, with nine players each, take turns batting (hitting the ball) and fielding (pitching and catching). Each complete turn is called an inning. A point, known as a run in baseball, is scored each time a batter runs around the bases and crosses home plate. The team with the most runs at the end of nine innings wins the game.

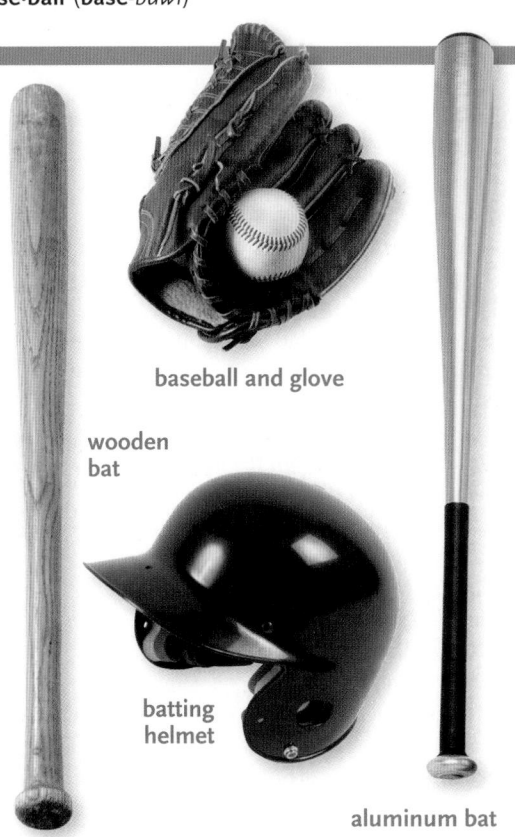

baseball and glove

wooden bat

batting helmet

aluminum bat

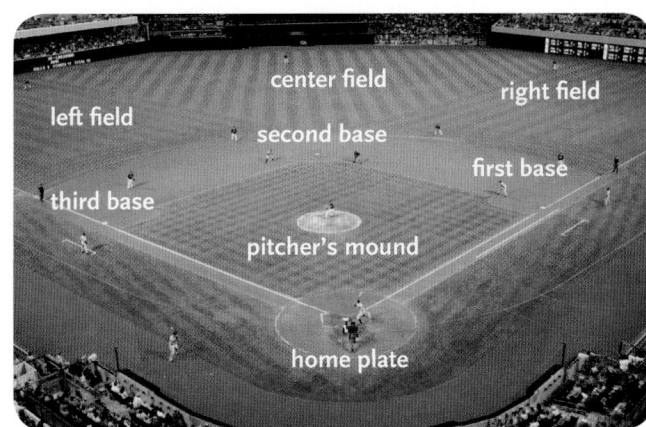

center field

right field

left field

second base

first base

third base

pitcher's mound

home plate

baseball diamond

basement *noun* The lowest room or area in a building, usually below ground level. **base·ment** (**base**-muhnt)

bash

1. *verb* To hit something hard or strike it with a heavy blow: *Dawn accidentally bashed her head against the wall.* ▷ *verb* **bashes, bashing, bashed**

2. *noun* (informal) A very large party: *The seniors had a big bash at the end of the school year.* **bash** (bash)

bashful *adjective* If you are **bashful,** you are shy and easily embarrassed: *I was too bashful to ask her if she wanted to go to the dance.* **bash·ful** (**bash**-fuhl) ▷ *adverb* **bashfully**

basic

1. *adjective* Essential and fundamental: *You need to learn basic math skills before you can do algebra.*

2. the basics *noun, plural* If you know **the basics,** you know the most important elements of something: *I couldn't begin to play the piano until I had learned the basics.* **ba·sic** (**bay**-sik)

BASIC *noun* A computer programming language that is easy to learn. BASIC is short for *beginner's all-purpose symbolic instruction code.* **BA·SIC** (**bay**-sik)

basically *adverb* In most or all important ways: *A red flag warning from the National Weather Service basically means that all the conditions are ripe for a forest fire.* **ba·si·cal·ly** (**bay**-sik-lee)

basin *noun*

1. A round container that is wider than it is deep, usually used for holding liquids: *Soak your sore feet in a basin of warm water.*

2. An area of land drained by a river system, as in *the Amazon basin.* **ba·sin** (**bay**-suhn)

basis *noun* The underlying support for something, as in *the basis of an argument.* **ba·sis** (**bay**-sis)

bask *verb*

1. To lie or sit in the sun for pleasure: *Three turtles basked on the bank of the river.*

2. If you **bask in** something, you take pleasure in it: *She basked in the glory of winning the race.* **bask** (bask) ▷ *verb* **basking, basked**

basket *noun*

1. A container, often with handles, made of woven material.

2. The goal or the act of scoring in basketball: *She made a basket in the first few seconds of the game.* **bas·ket** (**bas**-kit)

basketball

basketball *noun*

1. A game played by two teams of five players each who try to score points by throwing a ball through a hoop with a hanging net. The hoops are attached to backboards at each end of the court.

2. The large, round ball used in this game. **bas·ket·ball** (**bas**-kit-*bawl*)

bass *noun*

1. (base) The lowest male singing voice. ▷ *adjective* **bass**

2. (base) A singer with such a voice.

3. (base) A musical instrument, especially a double bass or bass guitar, that produces very low tones.

4. (bas) Any of several freshwater or saltwater fish. **bass** ▷ *noun, plural* **bass** *or* **basses**

bass drum *noun* A very large drum that makes a deep, loud noise. **bass drum**

bassoon *noun* A wind instrument with keys, holes, and a small curved reed. The bassoon makes a very deep sound. **bas·soon** (buh-**soon**)

baste *verb*

1. To spoon juices from the pan over food while it is cooking in an oven: *Baste the turkey to keep it from drying out.*

2. To sew something with loose stitches to hold it in place temporarily. **baste** (bayst) ▷ *verb* **basting, basted**

bat

bat

1. *noun* A small, flying mammal with leathery wings that feeds at night and finds its way around by listening for the echoes of its own squeaking cry.

2. *noun* A piece of wood or aluminum used for hitting the ball in baseball and softball.

3. *verb* To take a turn at hitting the ball in baseball or softball: *James was batting when the rain started.* ▷ *verb* **batting, batted** **bat** (bat)

batch *noun* A group of things that are made at one time, as in *a batch of brownies*. **batch** (bach)
▷ *noun, plural* **batches**

bath *noun*
1. The act of washing in a container of water.
2. The water or the tub used in bathing: *I got into a steaming hot bath to help me relax.*
3. A bathroom: *The house has two baths.*
bath (bath)

bathe *verb*
1. To take a bath: *She bathes every day.*
2. To give someone a bath, as in *to bathe a baby*.
bathe (bayTH)
▷ *verb* **bathing, bathed** ▷ *noun* **bather**

bathrobe *noun* A long, loose piece of clothing that people wear after bathing or while relaxing. **bath·robe** (**bath**-*robe*)

bathroom *noun* A room that contains a sink and a toilet and often a bathtub or a shower. **bath·room** (**bath**-*room*)

bathtub *noun* A large, open container for water in which you sit and wash your whole body. **bath·tub** (**bath**-*tuhb*)

batik *noun* A method of printing colored designs on fabric by using wax to cover the parts that will not be dyed. **ba·tik** (buh-**teek**)

bat mitzvah *noun* A ceremony and celebration that takes place on or close to a Jewish girl's 12th birthday, after which she can take part in her religion as an adult. Also known as *bas mitzvah* (*bahs* **mits**-vuh). **bat mitz·vah** (*baht* **mits**-vuh)

baton *noun*
1. A thin stick used by a conductor to direct an orchestra or band.
2. A stick that is twirled by a person in a parade.
3. A short stick that one runner passes to the next in a relay race.
ba·ton (buh-**tahn**)

battalion *noun* A large unit of soldiers. **bat·tal·ion** (buh-**tal**-yuhn)

batter
1. *verb* To injure someone by hitting him or her over and over: *The thugs battered the old man after taking his money.* ▷ *verb* **battering, battered** ▷ *noun* **battering** ▷ *adjective* **battered**
2. *noun* A mixture consisting mainly of milk, eggs, and flour used to make pancakes or baked goods or to form a coating over food that is going to be fried: *If the batter is too thick, add more milk.*
3. *noun* The player whose turn it is to bat in baseball or softball.
bat·ter (**bat**-ur)

battering ram *noun* A heavy wooden beam used in the past as a weapon to break down walls or gates.

battery *noun*
1. A container filled with chemicals that produces electrical power.
2. A large number or series of something, as in *a battery of tests*.
bat·ter·y (**bat**-ur-ee)
▷ *noun, plural* **batteries**

battle *noun*
1. A fight between two armies, ships, or aircraft.
2. A long struggle or competition: *We have a constant battle about whose turn it is to babysit.*
bat·tle (**bat**-uhl)
▷ *verb* **battle**

battleground *noun* A field or an area where a battle is fought. **bat·tle·ground** (**bat**-uhl-*ground*)

battlement *noun* A low wall at the top of a fort or castle with openings for soldiers to shoot through: *Archers were shooting from the battlements of the castle.* **bat·tle·ment** (**bat**-uhl-muhnt)

battleship *noun* A heavily armed warship. **bat·tle·ship** (**bat**-uhl-*ship*)

bawl *verb*
1. To wail or cry loudly.
2. To shout in an angry voice: *"Get that dog out of my yard!" bawled Mrs. Diaz.*
3. When you **bawl** someone **out**, you scold him or her.
bawl (bawl)
Bawl sounds like **ball**. ▷ *verb* **bawling, bawled**

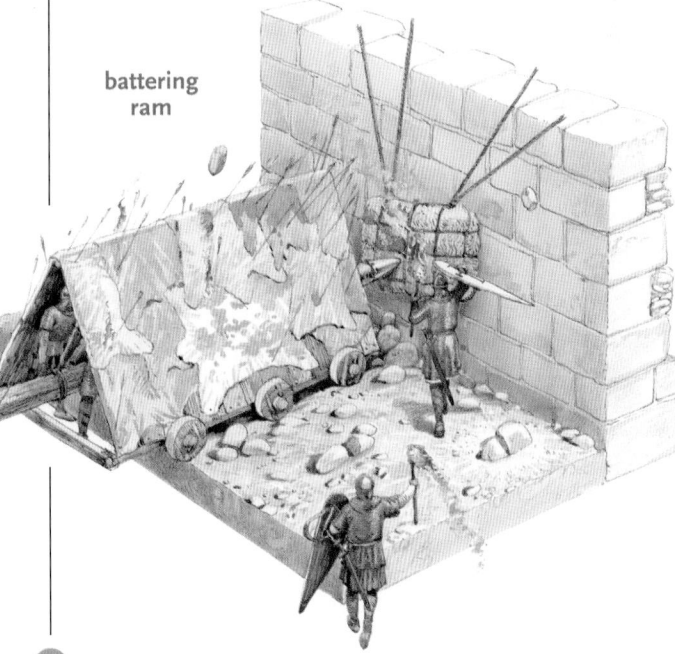

battering ram

bay *noun*

1. A portion of the ocean that is partly enclosed by land.

2. If you keep someone or something **at bay,** you prevent someone or something from coming near or having an effect: *I managed to keep my mother's curiosity at bay.*

3. bay window A window that is built out from the wall of a house or other building.

bay (bay)

bayonet *noun* A long blade that can be fastened to the end of a rifle and used as a weapon. **bay·o·net** (**bay**-uh-*net*)

bayou *noun* A stream that runs slowly through a swamp and leads to or from a lake or river. Bayous are most common in Texas, Louisiana, and Mississippi. **bay·ou** (**bye**-oo)

Word History

In the 18th century, French speakers in Louisiana learned the word *bayuk* from a Native American people, the Choctaw. The Choctaw word *bayuk* meant "a river forming part of a delta." The French speakers borrowed the term as **bayou**, but the term now refers to a stream running through a swamp that leads to or from a lake or river.

bazaar *noun*

1. A fair or sale at which things are sold to raise money for charity.

2. A street market, especially one found in a Middle Eastern country.

ba·zaar (buh-**zahr**)

B.C. An abbreviation for "before Christ," used after a date to show that it comes before the birth of Jesus: *He lived during the second century B.C.*

be *verb*

1. To exist: *There is time left to play.*

2. To happen: *The start of our vacation was last week.*

3. To come or go: *I've been to the store many times today.*

4. To stay or continue: *They've been in class for over an hour.*

5. Be can connect the subject of a sentence to a noun, adjective, pronoun, or prepositional phrase: *Roses are beautiful. The cat is on the couch.*

6. Be can support the main verb in a sentence: *We are eating dinner together tonight.*

be (bee)

Be sounds like **bee.**

Language Note

Be is a word that takes different forms, depending upon the tense and the person to whom it refers.

	First Person	Second Person	Third Person
Present Tense			
Singular	am	are	is
Plural	are	are	are
Present Participle	being	being	being
Past Tense			
Singular	was	were	was
Plural	were	were	were
Past Participle	been	been	been

beach *noun* A strip of sand or gravel at the edge of a body of water. **beach** (beech) **Beach** sounds like **beech.** ▷ *noun, plural* **beaches**

beacon *noun* A light or fire used as a signal or for guidance: *The lighthouse was a beacon that could be seen for miles.* **bea·con** (**bee**-kuhn)

bead *noun*

1. A small piece of glass, wood, or other material that can be threaded on a string to make a necklace or to decorate something.

2. A drop of liquid on the surface of something: *There were beads of water on the table.*

bead (beed)

beagle *noun* A medium-sized dog with short legs, long ears, and a smooth coat. Beagles are often kept as pets or used as hunting dogs. **bea·gle** (**bee**-guhl)

beak *noun* The horny, pointed jaw of a bird. **beak** (beek)

beaker *noun* A plastic or glass jar with a spout for pouring, used in a laboratory. **beak·er** (**bee**-kur)

beam

1. *noun* A ray or band of light from a flashlight, a car headlight, or the sun.

2. *noun* A long, thick piece of wood, concrete, or metal used as a support in a building: *The roof beams were ten inches wide.*

3. *verb* To smile broadly: *Greg beamed when he saw the A on his report.* ▷ *verb* **beaming, beamed**
beam (beem)

beagle

beaver dam

entrance

moat

outer walls

dam

lodge

bean

1. *noun* The seed or pod of various climbing plants that can be eaten or used to make a drink, as in *coffee beans*.

2. *verb* To hit someone on the head with something you throw, such as a baseball: *A fan got beaned by a foul ball.* ▷ *verb* **beaning, beaned**
bean (been)

bear

1. *verb* To carry someone or something or to hold someone or something up: *We weren't sure the ice would bear our weight.*

2. *verb* To produce fruit, flowers, or leaves: *This shrub bears blossoms in June.*

3. *verb* To accept or put up with someone or something: *Some people can't bear loud music.* ▷ *adjective* **bearable**

4. *verb* If you **bear** a resemblance to someone, you look somewhat like the person.

5. *noun* A large, heavy mammal with thick, shaggy fur and a short tail that lives typically in forests.
bear (bair)
Bear sounds like **bare**. ▷ *verb* **bearing, bore** (bor), **borne** (born)

beard *noun* The hair on a man's chin and lower cheeks. **beard** (beerd) ▷ *adjective* **bearded**

bearing *noun*

1. The way someone stands, moves, or behaves: *That man has the bearing of an athlete.*

2. A connection to something else: *The weather will have no bearing on our plans.*

3. In machinery, a part that allows moving parts to work with as little friction as possible: *The bearings around the axle were completely worn away.*

4. *noun, plural* Your **bearings** are your sense of direction in relation to where things are: *The hikers lost their bearings and spent hours walking in circles.*
bear·ing (**bair**-ing)

beast *noun*

1. An animal, especially one that is dangerous or that

walks on four feet: *The jungle was filled with beasts the explorers had never seen before.*

2. A cruel or wicked person.
beast (beest)
▷ *noun* **beastliness** ▷ *adjective* **beastly**

beat

1. *verb* To hit someone or something over and over again: *That bully beats up at least one kid a week.* ▷ *noun* **beating**

2. *verb* To defeat someone or something: *We refused to let the other team beat us.*

3. *noun* The regular rhythm of something, such as your heart: *This song has a great beat for dancing.*

4. *verb* In cooking, if you **beat** something, you stir it quickly with a machine, spoon, or fork: *Beat the eggs and add them to the flour mixture.*

5. *noun* A regular route, as in *a police officer's beat*.
beat (beet)
Beat sounds like **beet**. ▷ *verb* **beating, beat, beaten** (**bee**-tuhn)

beautiful *adjective* Very pleasing to the senses, as in *beautiful music*. **beau·ti·ful** (**byoo**-ti-ful) ▷ *verb* **beautify** (**byoo**-ti-*fye*) ▷ *adverb* **beautifully**

beauty *noun*

1. The quality of being very attractive and pleasing to people: *He is learning to appreciate the beauty of orchestral music.*

2. A person, usually a woman, who is considered beautiful.
beau·ty (**byoo**-tee)
▷ *noun, plural* **beauties**

beaver *noun*

1. A rodent with a wide, flat tail and strong teeth that gnaws down trees and uses them to create dams and lodges in which it lives and protects its young.

2. Someone who is an **eager beaver** works very hard and is quick to volunteer.
bea·ver (**bee**-vur)

because *conjunction* Since; for the reason that: *We're here because we want to help you.* **be·cause** (bi-**kawz** or bi-**kuhz**)

beckon *verb* To make a sign to someone, encouraging that person to come or to follow: *Sally beckoned me with her finger, and I immediately ran to her side.* **beck·on** (**bek**-uhn) ▷ *verb* **beckoning, beckoned**

become *verb*
1. To develop into or come to be: *She became the team's most valuable player.*
2. To suit, or to look good on: *That haircut becomes you.* **be·come** (bi-**kuhm**) ▷ *verb* **becoming, became** (bi-**kaym**)

becoming *adjective* Flattering or attractive: *She wore a really becoming dress that her mother made.* **be·com·ing** (bi-**kuhm**-ing)

bed *noun*
1. A piece of furniture or a place for lying down and sleeping: *Jason made a bed out of leaves and was asleep in five minutes.* ▷ *verb* **bed**
2. A piece of land where flowers are planted, as in *a bed of lilies.*
3. The bottom of a body of water, as in *a lake bed.* **bed** (bed)

Word History

Our beds today are a lot more comfortable than when the word **bed** came into use. The word goes back to the root *bhedh,* meaning "to dig." In the old Germanic languages, which became English, German, and Swedish, the word was *bedde* or *betti,* which meant both "a garden plot" and "a sleeping place." This suggests that early people slept in "beds" dug out of the ground.

bedbug *noun* A kind of insect that lives in mattresses and bites people when they sleep, causing painful swelling and itching. **bed·bug** (**bed**-buhg)

bedding *noun* Sheets, blankets, comforters, quilts, and other such items for beds: *The store's bedding department has a wide choice of bedspreads.* **bed·ding** (**bed**-ing)

bedraggled *adjective* Wet, limp, or soiled; messy: *Caught in a rainstorm, the bedraggled hikers finally got home.* **be·drag·gled** (bi-**drag**-uhld)

bedridden *adjective* Unable to get out of bed, usually because of illness: *My grandmother was bedridden for the last two years of her life.* **bed·rid·den** (**bed**-rid-uhn)

bedrock *noun* The solid layer of rock under the soil. **bed·rock** (**bed**-rahk)

bedroom *noun* A room that has a bed and is used for sleeping. **bed·room** (**bed**-room)

bedspread *noun* A decorative quilt or other cover for a bed. **bed·spread** (**bed**-spred)

bee *noun*
1. An insect with four wings that collects pollen. Some types of bees make honey, and some bees sting.
2. A group competition or work activity, as in *a spelling bee.*
bee (bee)
Bee sounds like **be.**

beech *noun* A tree with smooth, gray bark and small nuts that are eaten as food. **beech** (beech) **Beech** sounds like **beach.** ▷ *noun, plural* **beeches**

beef *noun* The meat from a steer, bull, ox, or cow: *He cooked the beef with onions.* **beef** (beef)

beehive *noun* A nest or house for a swarm of bees. **bee·hive** (**bee**-hive)

beeline *noun* The most direct route: *Adam made a beeline for the dessert table.* **bee·line** (**bee**-line)

been *verb* The past participle of **be.** **been** (bin)

beep *noun* A short, high sound, as made by a horn or machine: *The cell phone beeps when there is a message.* **beep** (beep) ▷ *noun* **beeper** ▷ *verb* **beep** ▷ *adjective* **beeping**

beer *noun* An alcoholic drink made from malt and flavored with hops and other ingredients. **beer** (beer)

beeswax *noun* A waxy substance produced and used by bees to make their honeycombs. **bees·wax** (**beez**-waks)

beet *noun* A dark red root vegetable. **beet** (beet)
Beet sounds like **beat.**

beetle *noun* An insect with two pairs of wings. A pair of hard wings in front protects a pair of soft flying wings, which are folded underneath. **bee·tle** (**bee**-tuhl)

befall *verb* To happen to someone: *He wondered what fate would befall him if he opened the door to the abandoned house.* **be·fall** (bi-**fawl**) ▷ *verb* **befalling, befell, befallen**

beetle

before
1. *preposition* Sooner, or earlier than: *Please get back before six.*
2. *preposition* In front of: *The criminal stood before the judge.*
3. *adverb* Earlier: *If you've been here before, why don't you know your way around?*

4. *conjunction* Rather than: *I would starve before I would eat at that restaurant.* **be·fore** (bi-**for**)

beforehand *adverb* Ahead of time: *If you decide to come over, let me know beforehand.* **be·fore·hand** (bi-**for**-hand)

befriend *verb* To make friends with someone: *She finds it easy to befriend people.* **be·friend** (bi-**frend**) ▷ *verb* **befriending, befriended**

beg *verb*
1. To ask someone in the street for food or money.
2. To ask in a pleading way: *She begged me to stop calling her by her nickname.*
beg (beg)
▷ *verb* **begging, begged**

beggar *noun* Someone who lives by asking others for food and money. **beg·gar** (**beg**-ur)

begin *verb* To start or to take the first step in doing something: *We began our report on the rivers of France by showing a large map.* **be·gin** (bi-**gin**)
▷ *verb* **beginning, began** (bi-**gan**), **begun** (bi-**guhn**)
▷ *noun* **beginner**

beginning *noun* The time or occasion when something starts; the first or earliest part of something: *I forgot the lyrics to that song—how does the beginning go again?* **be·gin·ning** (bi-**gin**-ing)

begonia *noun* A tropical plant with white, yellow, red, or pink flowers. **be·go·ni·a** (bi-**gohn**-yuh)

behalf *noun* If you do something **on behalf** of someone else, you are acting in their interests or as their representative: *The vice president, on behalf of her boss, thanked everyone for coming.* **be·half** (bi-**haf**)

behave *verb*
1. To act in a polite or proper way: *I wish my little brother would learn to behave himself.*
2. To act in a particular way: *She behaved as if she were our mother, not our older sister.*
be·have (bi-**hayv**)
▷ *verb* **behaving, behaved**

behavior *noun*
1. The way someone acts, either typically or in a particular situation: *The man's neighbors reported his strange behavior to the police.*
2. The way that a machine, software program, or piece of equipment operates: *When you see this sort of unstable behavior in your computer, you should reboot.*
be·hav·ior (bi-**hayv**-yur)

behead *verb* To chop off someone's head. **be·head** (bi-**hed**) ▷ *verb* **beheading, beheaded**

beheld *verb* The past tense and the past participle of **behold**. **be·held** (bi-**held**)

behind
1. *preposition* Toward the back of something or on the opposite side: *Look behind that drawer if you want to find your missing sock.*
2. *preposition* In a lesser position, or farther back than: *He finished the race behind his younger brother.*
3. *preposition* Later than: *He had fallen behind schedule but wouldn't stop working.*
4. *preposition* In support of: *My friends were behind me all the way when I tried out for the team.*
5. *adverb* Slow or late in getting something done: *She is so far behind; she'll never catch up.*
be·hind (bi-**hinde**)

behold *verb* To look at something with great interest, or to see: *The sun setting over the ocean is a beautiful sight to behold.* **be·hold** (bi-**hohld**)
▷ *verb* **beholding, beheld**

beige *noun* A pale grayish-brown color. **beige** (bayzh)

belfry

being *noun*
1. The state of existing.
2. A person or creature that is alive: *Kindness to our fellow beings always pays off.*
be·ing (**bee**-ing)

belabor *verb* To spend too much time and effort explaining something: *We knew Mr. Readle was belaboring the topic of being tardy because we were late.* **be·la·bor** (bi-**lay**-bur) ▷ *verb* **belaboring, belabored**

belated *adjective* Delayed, or late, as in *a belated birthday card.* **be·lat·ed** (bi-**lay**-tid) ▷ *adverb* **belatedly**

belch *verb*
1. To burp or let gas from your stomach out through your mouth: *He belched loudly after drinking a can of soda.* ▷ *noun* **belch**
2. To send out smoke or flames in an explosive way: *The volcano belched ashes and lava.*
belch (belch)
▷ *verb* **belches, belching, belched**

belfry *noun* The tower, or the room in a tower, where a large bell is hung. **bel·fry** (**bel**-free) ▷ *noun, plural* **belfries**

a
b
c
d
e
f
g
h
i
j
k
l
m
n
o
p
q
r
s
t
u
v
w
x
y
z

belief *noun*

1. Something that someone believes is true: *She stated her belief that Twitter could change the world.*

2. One of a number of ideas that together form someone's religion: *Their beliefs don't allow them to take part in politics.*

be·lief (bi-**leef**)

believe *verb*

1. To accept as true or real: *Tina believed her cousin's story.* ▷ *adjective* **believable**

2. To have faith in someone or something; to support: *I know it sounds lame, but I believe in the power of love.*

be·lieve (bi-**leev**)

▷ *verb* **believing, believed** ▷ *noun* **believer**

bell *noun*

1. An instrument that is designed to make a ringing sound when it is struck.

2. *(informal)* If something **rings a bell,** it sounds familiar.

3. Something that is shaped like a bell, especially the part of a musical instrument where the sound comes out.

bell (bel)

belligerent *adjective*

1. Eager to fight, or hostile: *Sam's belligerent attitude cost him his place on the team.*

2. Warlike, as in *belligerent nations.*

bel·lig·er·ent (buh-**lij**-ur-uhnt)

▷ *adverb* **belligerently**

bellow

1. *verb* To shout or make a deep roaring sound: *He bellowed in pain.* ▷ *verb* **bellowing, bellowed** ▷ *noun* **bellow**

2. bellows *noun, plural* A device whose sides are squeezed to pump air into something, such as a fire.

bel·low (**bel**-oh)

belly *noun*

1. The stomach, or the part of the body below the ribs.

2. belly flop A dive in which the front of your body lands flat against the water.

bel·ly (**bel**-ee)

▷ *noun, plural* **bellies**

belly button *noun* A hollow or raised dimple in the center of your stomach where your umbilical cord was attached to your mother before you were born; your navel.

belong *verb*

1. If something **belongs** to you, it is your property: *Does this notebook belong to you?* ▷ *noun, plural* **belongings**

2. To be a member of a group or club: *I belong to the French club that meets after school.*

3. To be in the proper place or position: *The silverware belongs in the wooden chest on the shelf.*

be·long (bi-**lawng**)

▷ *verb* **belonging, belonged**

beloved

1. *adjective* Greatly loved or dear to someone's heart: *I was so sad when my beloved dog died.*

2. *noun* Someone who is greatly loved: *I wrote a letter to my beloved.*

be·lov·ed (bi-**luhv**-id)

below

1. *preposition* Beneath or in a lower position than: *The sun is below the horizon.*

2. *adverb* Toward or in a lower place: *If you look below, you'll see why the bridge is shaking.*

be·low (bi-**loh**)

belt

1. *noun* A long, narrow piece of leather or other material that you wear around your waist to support clothing, tools, or weapons.

2. *noun* A continuous band of rubber used for moving things along or for transferring motion from one part

belt

of a machine to another: *The fan belt broke, and the cider press came to a halt.*

3. *verb (informal)* To hit someone or something very hard.

4. *verb* If you **belt** something **out,** you play or sing it very loudly: *The opera star belted out the national anthem before the game.*

5. *noun* An area known for a particular thing, as in *the corn belt.*

belt (belt)

▷ *verb* **belting, belted**

bench *noun*

1. A long, narrow seat for more than one person, usually made of wood or plastic.

2. A table in a workshop or laboratory, as in *a carpenter's bench.*

3. The place where a judge sits in a court of law. Judges ask lawyers to "approach the bench" to discuss issues in private during a trial.

bench (bench)

benchmark *noun* A standard that is used to measure, compare, or evaluate things: *Benchmarks for manufacturing that were set before 2005 need to be* *updated.* **bench·mark** (**bench**-*mahrk*)

bend *verb*

1. If you **bend** or **bend over,** you lean forward from the waist or curve your body downward: *I bent over to pick up the quarter I dropped.*

2. If something **bends,** it turns in a curved or angled direction: *When the trail bends to the right, you'll be almost to the top.* ▷ *noun* **bend**

3. To give something that was straight a curved or angled shape: *Bend your arm.* **bend** (bend)

▷ *verb* **bending, bent** (bent)

beneath *preposition*

1. Of a lower status than, or not worthy of: *Don't apologize; it's beneath your dignity.*

2. Underneath or hidden by: *We found the missing book beneath a pile of papers.* **be·neath** (bi-**neeth**)

▷ *adverb* **beneath**

beneficial *adjective* Good for someone or something, as in *a beneficial program.* **ben·e·fi·cial** (*ben*-uh-**fish**-uhl) ▷ *adverb* **beneficially**

benefit

1. *verb* If you **benefit** from something, you receive something that helps you or gives you an advantage: *I've really benefited from the after-school tutoring I'm getting in math.* ▷ *verb* **benefiting, benefited** ▷ *noun* **benefit**

2. *noun* An event whose purpose is to raise money for a cause, charity, or cultural organization.

3. *noun* An advantage or valuable thing that comes with a job in addition to the pay: *Besides my salary, I have lots of employee benefits, such as health insurance and three weeks' paid vacation.*

4. benefits *noun, plural* Money that people may receive in special circumstances, as in *unemployment benefits.* **ben·e·fit** (**ben**-uh-fit)

benevolent *adjective* Known for doing good; well-meaning: *They lived in a benevolent community where everyone looked out for each other.* **be·nev·o·lent** (buh-**nev**-uh-luhnt) ▷ *noun* **benevolence** ▷ *adverb* **benevolently**

benign *adjective* Not dangerous to your health; harmless: *The lump on my mother's leg was benign.* **be·nign** (bi-**nine**)

bent *adjective*

1. Crooked or curved: *The bent key would not fit in the lock.*

2. If you're **bent on** doing something, you are determined to do it: *Doug was bent on going home.* **bent** (bent)

beret

bequeath *verb* To pass something on to someone, or to leave something to somebody in your will: *My uncle bequeathed a farm to my parents.* **be·queath** (bi-**kweeth**) ▷ *verb* **bequeathing, bequeathed** ▷ *noun* **bequest** (bi-**kwest**)

bereaved *adjective* A **bereaved** person feels sad because someone very close to him or her has died. **be·reaved** (bi-**reevd**) ▷ *noun* **bereavement**

beret *noun* A round, flat cap made of felt, wool, or some other soft material. **be·ret** (buh-**ray**)

berry *noun* A small, fleshy fruit that grows on bushes or trees. **ber·ry** (**ber**-ee) **Berry** sounds like **bury.** ▷ *noun, plural* **berries**

berserk *adjective* Violently destructive or out of control: *Jasper goes berserk when he doesn't get his way.* **ber·serk** (bur-**zurk** or bur-**surk**)

Word History

Ancient armies of Norsemen from Scandinavia fought ferociously. These warriors were clothed in bear skins instead of armor. Because of this, they were called berserks or berserkers, a word formed from the old Icelandic words *ber,* meaning "bear," and *serkr,* meaning "coat." Today, saying that someone has gone **berserk** means that the person is violently out of control like the ferocious Norsemen of long ago.

berth

1. *noun* A built-in bed or bunk on a ship or train.

2. *noun* A place in a harbor where a ship is tied up or anchored: *The ocean liner was berthed in lower Manhattan.*

3. *verb* To tie up to a dock or a pier. ▷ *verb* **berthing, berthed**

berth (burth)

Berth sounds like **birth.**

beseech *verb* To ask someone in a very serious way; to beg: *He beseeched the judge to allow his son to go free.* **be·seech** (bi-**seech**) ▷ *verb* **beseeching, besought** (bi-**sawt**), **beseeched**

beset *verb* To attack or trouble someone: *I was beset by difficulties.* **be·set** (bi-**set**) ▷ *verb* **besetting, beset**

beside *preposition*

1. Next to or at the side of someone or something: *Walk beside me.*

2. Apart from: *Your excuse is beside the point.*

3. If you are **beside yourself,** you are extremely worried, angry, or excited. **be·side** (bi-**side**)

besides

1. *preposition* In addition to, or other than: *Who, besides Marian, will ever know the truth?*

2. *adverb* Also, or furthermore: *I have no intention of calling him, and besides, I haven't got his number.*

be·sides (bi-**sidez**)

besiege *verb*

1. To surround with armed forces: *By the next day, the enemy had besieged the American base.*

2. To crowd around: *Screaming fans besieged the rock star.*

be·siege (bi-**seej**)

▷ *verb* **besieging, besieged**

best

1. *adjective* Better than everyone or everything else in some way: *The restaurant serves the best tacos in town.*

2. *verb* To do better than someone else: *Carl bested me again in the 500-meter race.* ▷ *verb* **besting, bested**

3. *adverb* More than any or all others: *I like the blue car best.*

4. *noun* A thing or person that is better than all others: *Thanks, Tim. You're the best!*

5. *phrase* When you **do your best,** you make a very great effort to do something as well as you possibly can.

best (best)

best man *noun* A brother or close male friend of a bridegroom, whose duties at the wedding include keeping the rings safe and making a toast. **best man** (**best man**)

bestow *verb* To give someone a gift or a prize: *The gym teacher bestowed the blue ribbon on the winner.* **be·stow** (bi-**stoh**) ▷ *verb* **bestowing, bestowed**

bet *verb*

1. To risk a sum of money on the outcome of something that is hard to predict, such as a race or a game: *My uncle lost a lot of money when he bet on his friend's horse.* ▷ *noun* **bet** ▷ *noun* **betting**

2. If you **bet** someone that he or she can't do something, you challenge him or her to try it: *I bet you can't run a mile without collapsing.*

3. *(informal)* If you **bet** that someone will do something, you are confident that he or she will do it: *I bet Jonathan will get an A on that test.*

bet (bet)

▷ *verb* **betting, bet**

beverage

betray *verb*

1. To be disloyal to someone or something: *Nancy's best friend betrayed her by telling everyone her secret.* ▷ *noun* **betrayal**

2. If you **betray** your feelings, you reveal them without meaning to do so.

be·tray (bi-**tray**)

▷ *verb* **betraying, betrayed**

better

1. *adjective* More suitable or satisfactory, as in *a better job.*

2. *adjective* Recovering from illness or injury: *Jenny is much better today.*

3. better off *adjective* Having more money or being in a more favorable position: *We are better off eating healthier snacks.*

4. *adverb* In a more complete, effective, or satisfactory way: *The new car runs better than the old one.*

5. *verb* To improve something: *Moving to a new community has really bettered our lives.* ▷ *verb* **bettering, bettered**

bet·ter (**bet**-ur)

between *preposition*

1. If something is **between** two things, it is in the place that separates them: *The car is parked between two trucks.*

2. From one to another: *The airfare between Chicago and Miami was a bargain.*

3. Somewhere in the period separating two points in time: *We should arrive between eight and nine o'clock tomorrow night.*

4. By comparing: *Please choose between the boots and the sneakers.*

be·tween (bi-**tween**)

beverage *noun* A drink, especially other than water. **bev·er·age** (**bev**-rij)

beware *verb* To be careful about or to guard against: *They were warned to beware of the dog in the yard next door.* **be·ware** (bi-**wair**)

bewilder *verb* To confuse someone: *The instructions to the game completely bewilder me.* **be·wil·der** (bi-**wil**-dur) ▷ *verb* **bewildering, bewildered** ▷ *noun* **bewilderment** ▷ *adjective* **bewildered**

bewitch *verb* To cast a spell on someone. **be·witch** (bi-**wich**) ▷ *verb* **bewitching, bewitched**

beyond *preposition*

1. On the far side of or past something: *The dogs couldn't get beyond the chain-link fence.* ▷ *adverb* **beyond**

2. If something is **beyond** you, it is outside your

experience or understanding: *How you can live in such a messy room is beyond me.*
be·yond (bee-**ahnd**)

Prefix

The prefix **bi-** adds one of the following meanings to a root word:

1. Twice every, as in *bimonthly* (twice every month).
2. Having two, as in *bicuspid* (a tooth having two points).

bias
1. *noun* A tendency to favor or oppose a particular group or person; prejudice, as in *a racial bias.*
2. *verb* To influence someone in favor or against a group or individual: *The constant news coverage biased the jury against the defendants.* ▷ *verb* **biasing, biased**
bi·as (**bye**-uhs)

biased *adjective* Prejudiced, or favoring one person or point of view more than another: *The newspaper is strongly biased toward the right.* **bi·ased** (**bye**-uhst)

Bible *noun*
1. The sacred book of the Christian religion that contains the Old and New Testaments.
2. The sacred book in the Jewish religion, consisting of the Old Testament.
Bi·ble (**bye**-buhl)

biblical *adjective* Of, from, or having to do with the Bible, as in *a biblical scholar.* **bib·li·cal** (**bib**-li-kuhl)

bibliography *noun* A list of books and articles on a subject, especially one in the back of a book. **bib·li·og·ra·phy** (*bib*-lee-**ah**-gruh-fee) ▷ *noun, plural* **bibliographies** ▷ *adjective* **bibliographical** (*bib*-lee-uh-**graf**-i-kuhl)

biceps *noun, plural* The large muscle on the front of your arm between your shoulder and inner elbow. **bi·ceps** (**bye**-seps)

bicker *verb* To argue about small things: *My brother and I bicker over almost everything.* **bick·er** (**bik**-ur) ▷ *verb* **bickering, bickered**

bicoastal *adjective* Living and working on both the East and West Coasts of the United States. **bi·coast·al** (bye-**koh**-stuhl)

bicuspid *noun* A tooth with two points located just beside the front sets of upper and lower teeth. **bi·cus·pid** (bye-**kuhs**-pid)

bicycle *noun* A light-framed vehicle with two wheels, handlebars for steering and braking, and pedals that you push with your feet: *The bicycle is the most common form of transportation in some countries.* **bi·cy·cle** (**bye**-si-kuhl) ▷ *verb* **bicycle**

bid¹
1. *verb* To offer a certain amount of money for something, as at an auction: *We bid $50 for the trunk.* ▷ *verb* **bidding, bid** ▷ *noun* **bidder**
2. *noun* An effort to win or achieve something, as in *a bid for reelection.*
bid (bid)

bid² *verb*
1. To order someone to do something: *The teacher bid the class to be quiet.*
2. To express something, as in *to bid farewell.*
bid (bid)
▷ *verb* **bidding, bid** *or* **bade, bidden** *or* **bid**

bidden *verb* A past participle of **bid** (sense 2 only). **bid·den** (**bid**-uhn)

bide *verb* To wait for the right moment: *I will have to bide my time until I ask for a higher weekly allowance.* **bide** (bide) ▷ *verb* **biding, bided**

biennial
1. *adjective* Happening or celebrated every two years, as in *a biennial conference.*
2. *noun* A plant that lives for two growing seasons.
bi·en·ni·al (bye-**en**-ee-uhl)

bifocals *noun, plural* Glasses or lenses that have two sections, for seeing up close and farther away. **bi·fo·cals** (bye-*foh*-kuhlz)

big *adjective*
1. Large in size: *What a big car!*
2. Of great importance: *I couldn't wait to hear the big news.*
big (big)
▷ *adjective* **bigger, biggest**

Synonyms

Big can describe things, people, ideas, or anything else that has great size or importance: *An elephant is a big animal. Choosing a career is a big decision.*

- -

▪ **Large** is often used in place of *big* and refers to anything greater than normal size or quantity: *My mom runs a large business with a lot of employees.*

▪ **Immense** describes something so big that you can hardly measure or comprehend it: *An immense snowstorm blanketed several states with deep snow.*

▪ **Enormous**, like *immense*, means extremely big or large: *He gave me an enormous hug.*

▪ **Huge** means very large in scope or a very large amount: *My parents took me out for a huge meal at my favorite restaurant.*

▪ **Vast** means extending for great distances: *The farmer grew vast fields of corn.*

Big Bang theory

Big Bang *noun* An explosion of dense matter more than 13 billion years ago that most scientists believe was the beginning of the universe: *The idea that the universe started with an explosion is called the Big Bang theory.*

Big Crunch *noun* A theory about the ending of the universe, in which the universe collapses upon itself and winds up as a single black hole.

big data *or* **Big Data** *noun* Very large amounts of information that is collected by computers or sensors and that can only be analyzed by big, modern computers: *Many companies now use big data to decide how to develop new products.*

bighorn *noun* A type of wild sheep with large, curved horns, found in the Rocky Mountains and other mountain ranges in western North America. **big·horn** (**big**-*horn*)

bigot *noun* Someone who has strong opinions and prejudices, especially against people of other races, nationalities, or religions. **big·ot** (**big**-uht) ▷ *noun* **bigotry** ▷ *adjective* **bigoted**

bike
1. *noun* A bicycle, motorcycle, or motorbike.
2. *verb* To ride a bicycle, motorcycle, or motorbike: *Malcolm and I biked to the mall.* ▷ *verb* **biking, biked** ▷ *noun* **biker**
bike (bike)

bikini *noun* A very small, close-fitting, two-piece bathing suit worn by women and girls. **bi·ki·ni** (bi-**kee**-nee)

bile *noun* A greenish-yellow fluid that is made by the liver. It is stored in the gallbladder and helps you digest your food. **bile** (bile)

bilingual *adjective*
1. Able to speak two languages well: *They are bilingual in French and English.*
2. Dealing with two languages: *My school has a bilingual program for Spanish speakers.*
bi·lin·gual (bye-**ling**-gwuhl)

bill
1. *noun* A document that tells you how much money you owe for certain goods or services: *I receive my phone bill online every month.*
2. *noun* A written plan for a new law, to be debated and passed by a body of legislators: *A new election reform bill goes before the Senate next week.*
3. *noun* The beak or jaws of a bird.
4. *noun* A piece of paper money, as in *a dollar bill.*
5. *verb* To send someone a bill to be paid: *The company never billed me for the repairs.* ▷ *verb* **billing, billed**
bill (bil)

billboard *noun* A large outdoor sign used to advertise products or services. **bill·board** (**bil**-*bord*)

billfold *noun* A small folding wallet for paper money. **bill·fold** (**bil**-*fohld*)

billiards *noun, plural* A game in which you use a stick, called a cue, to hit balls around a rectangular, cloth-covered table. **bil·liards** (**bil**-yurdz)

billion
1. *noun* One thousand times one million, written numerically as 1,000,000,000.
2. *noun* A very large amount, as in *billions of dollars.*
3. *adjective* Equal to a very large amount: *I have a billion questions about your trip.*
bil·lion (**bil**-yuhn)

billionaire *noun* A person whose money and property are worth a billion dollars or more. **bil·lion·aire** (*bil*-yuh-**nair**)

Bill of Rights *noun* The first ten amendments to the US Constitution, which define the rights that protect every American.

billow
1. *verb* To bulge or swell out, especially when pushed by the wind: *The sheets billowed on the clothesline.*
2. *verb* If smoke or fog **billows,** it rolls or rises up like a huge wave.
3. *noun* A large wave or swell of water.
bil·low (**bil**-oh)
▷ *verb* **billowing, billowed**

bin *noun* A large covered container or box for storing things, as in *a trash bin.* **bin** (bin)

binary *adjective*
1. Having two parts or based on two things, as in a *binary star system.*
2. In mathematics, the **binary** number system uses only two digits, 1 and 0.
3. In computers, **binary** refers to files and codes that convert all numbers and letters into strings of

1s and 0s: *The data is stored in binary format, but the program displays it so you can read it.* **bi·na·ry** (**bye**-nur-ee *or* **bye**-*ner*-ee)

bind *verb*

1. To secure something by tying it up: *Bind the newspapers with string for recycling.*

2. To enclose something by wrapping a piece of material around it, as in *to bind a wound.*

3. If you **bind** a book, you fasten its pages together between covers. ▷ *noun* **binding**

4. To oblige: *This contract binds you to do the job.* **bind** (binde)

▷ *verb* **binding, bound** (bound)

▷ *adjective* **binding**

binder *noun* A detachable cover used for holding papers: *She organized all her notes in a three-ring binder.* **bind·er** (**bine**-dur)

binge

1. *verb* To overdo an activity such as eating or drinking: *She felt sick after bingeing on pizza.* ▷ *verb* **bingeing** or **binging, binged**

2. *noun* A period of overdoing something; a spree, as in *a shopping binge.* **binge** (binj)

binge-watch *verb* To watch many programs one after the other on television or online, such as all of the episodes of a series: *We spent the weekend binge-watching old Disney movies on Netflix.* **binge-watch** (**binj**-*wahch*) ▷ *verb* **binge-watching, binge-watched**

bingo *noun* A game of chance in which the players have cards with numbered squares on them, and they cross out the numbers that are drawn at random and announced by a caller. **bin·go** (**bing**-goh)

binoculars *noun, plural* A device that you look through with both eyes to make things that are far away seem larger and nearer. **bin·oc·u·lars** (buh-**nah**-kyuh-lurz)

biodegradable *adjective* Able to be broken down by natural processes: *It's OK to throw out apple cores; they're biodegradable.* **bi·o·de·grad·a·ble** (bye-oh-di-**gray**-duh-buhl)

biodiversity *noun* The condition of nature in which a wide variety of species live in a single area. **bi·o·di·ver·si·ty** (*bye*-oh-duh-**vur**-si-tee)

biofuel *noun* A fuel that is made from renewable materials such as plants or animal waste. **bi·o·fu·el** (**bye**-oh-*fyoo*-uhl)

biography *noun* A book that tells the life story of someone other than the author. **bi·og·ra·phy** (bye-**ah**-gruh-fee) ▷ *noun, plural* **biographies** ▷ *noun* **biographer** ▷ *adjective* **biographical** (bye-uh-**graf**-i-kuhl)

biology *noun* The study of life and of all living things. **bi·ol·o·gy** (bye-**ah**-luh-jee) ▷ *noun* **biologist** ▷ *adjective* **biological** (bye-uh-**lah**-ji-kuhl) ▷ *adverb* **biologically**

biomass *noun* The amount or weight of living matter in a certain area or volume of a habitat: *Bacteria make up much of the earth's biomass.* **bi·o·mass** (**bye**-oh-*mas*)

biplane

bionic *adjective* Of or having to do with electronic or mechanical parts that replace a part of the body or extend its natural capabilities: *She was trained to control the movements of her bionic arm with her thoughts.* **bi·on·ic** (bye-**ah**-nik)

biotechnology *noun* The use of biological materials and processes in industry. **bi·o·tech·nol·o·gy** (*bye*-oh-tek-**nah**-luh-jee)

biplane *noun* An airplane with a double set of wings, one above and one below the body of the plane. **bi·plane** (**bye**-*plane*)

bipolar *adjective*

1. Of or having to do with bipolar disorder: *Prescription medication is one of the treatments for people who are bipolar.*

2. Having two different poles, as in *bipolar cells.*

3. Of, concerning, or occurring at both the North Pole and the South Pole, as in *bipolar species of birds.*

4. Having different or opposing views, opinions, or moods: *The Cold War had a bipolar nature, pitting Western democracies against communist countries.*

bi·po·lar (bye-**poh**-lur)

▷ *noun* **bipolarity** (*bye*-puh-**lar**-i-tee)

birch *noun* A type of tree with hard wood and smooth bark that peels off easily in long strips. **birch** (burch)

bird *noun* A warm-blooded animal with feathers, two legs and wings, and a beak. **bird** (burd)

Word History

Occasionally speakers can switch the sounds in a word so that it comes to have a new pronunciation and spelling. This happened with the word **bird**. *Bird* used to rhyme with *mid*, because in Old English, this word was spelled "brid." At that time, it meant only "a young bird" or "a chicken." The common name for a bird until about 1600 was *fugol*. *Fugol* survives today as the word *fowl*, but the word *bird* has mainly replaced it as the name for these feathered animals.

bird flu *noun* A kind of flu that kills birds and that can also spread to people: *The outbreak of bird flu has medical authorities very worried.*

birth *noun*
1. The act or process of being born: *I was there at my dog's birth.*
2. The starting point of something, as in *the birth of television.*
3. When a woman or female animal **gives birth,** she has a baby.
birth (burth)

Birth sounds like **berth**.

birthday *noun* The day that someone was born, or the anniversary of that date in the years that follow, often marked by a celebration. **birth·day** (**burth**-*day*)

birthmark *noun* A mark on the skin that was there from birth. **birth·mark** (**burth**-*mahrk*)

birth mother *noun* The biological mother of a person. Used in reference to adoption, the term means the woman who actually gave birth to a child, as opposed to the woman who adopts and raises that child.

birthplace *noun* The place where someone was born, or where something began: *Springfield, Massachusetts, is the birthplace of basketball.* **birth·place** (**burth**-*plase*)

birthright *noun* A right or privilege that someone has because of being born into a specific family or group. **birth·right** (**burth**-*rite*)

biscuit *noun* A small, round kind of bread, made from dough that is rolled out and cut into circles or dropped from a spoon. **bis·cuit** (**bis**-kit)

bisect *verb* To cut or divide into two equal parts: *We learned how to bisect an angle in math.* **bi·sect** (**bye**-*sekt*) ▷ *verb* **bisecting, bisected** ▷ *noun* **bisection**

Birds

Birds are found all over the world. There are more than 9,000 species. Most can fly, but some are flightless. Their beaks are adapted to the different kinds of food they eat. Birds sing to communicate with other birds. All birds lay eggs, and care for their babies when they hatch. Some kinds of birds migrate to warmer climates in the winter.

penguin

owl

blue jay

hatchlings being fed

toucan

bishop *noun*
1. A senior member of the Christian clergy, who is in charge of all the churches in an area. This church district is called a **diocese**.
2. In chess, a piece that can move across the board in a diagonal direction.
bish·op (**bish**-uhp)

bison *noun* A large animal with a big, shaggy head, a humped back, and short horns, found in western North America; a buffalo. **bi·son** (**bye**-suhn)
▷ *noun, plural* **bison**

bit *noun*
1. A small portion or amount of something, as in *a bit of food*.
2. A unit of information that can be stored in a computer's memory.
3. A metal mouthpiece that is attached to the reins and used to control a horse.
4. The pointed part of a drill.
bit (bit)

Bitcoin *noun* A kind of money that you can only use online or with an app, and that doesn't belong to any country: *More and more countries are allowing people to use Bitcoin as an alternative currency.* **Bit·coin** (**bit**-*koin*)

bite *verb*
1. To cut into something with your teeth: *I couldn't wait to bite into that watermelon.*
2. If an insect or snake **bites** you, it makes a wound in your skin with its stinger or its teeth.
3. If a fish **bites,** it takes the bait at the end of a fishing line into its mouth.
bite (bite)
Bite sounds like **byte**. ▷ *verb* **biting, bit** (bit), **bitten** (**bit**-uhn) ▷ *noun* **bite**

bitten *verb* The past participle of **bite**. **bit·ten** (**bit**-uhn)

bitter *adjective*
1. Tasting sharp, not sweet: *Mustard is too bitter for my taste.*
2. If you feel **bitter,** you are angry or resentful because you don't think you've been treated fairly: *She is still bitter about losing the contest.*
3. Extremely cold: *A bitter wind swept in from the north.*
bit·ter (**bit**-ur)
▷ *adjective* **bitterest** ▷ *noun* **bitterness**

bivalve *noun* A mollusk that lives inside two shells that close together. Bivalves include oysters, mussels, scallops, and clams. **bi·valve** (**bye**-*valv*)

bizarre *adjective* Very strange or odd: *I had a bizarre dream in which I lived on a spaceship.* **bi·zarre** (bi-**zahr**)

Bitcoin

This digital currency network allows its users to make payments and transfer funds to each other directly, without a central bank or government. Using a method of encryption called cryptography, it protects the privacy of transactions and confirms that they are accurate. The software for Bitcoin was released in 2008 by a mysterious individual or group of programmers under the pseudonym Satoshi Nakamoto.

Bitcoin

black *noun* A color that is completely dark, like that of coal or of the sky at night. **black** (blak)
▷ *adjective* **black**

blackberry *noun* A small, juicy, black fruit that grows on a prickly, climbing shrub. **black·ber·ry** (**blak**-*ber*-ee) ▷ *noun, plural* **blackberries**

blackbird *noun* One of a large number of birds with black feathers. Crows and grackles are types of blackbirds. **black·bird** (**blak**-*burd*)

blackboard *noun* A hard, smooth surface, often made of slate, that people write on with chalk. **black·board** (**blak**-*bord*)

blacken *verb* To make black or become black: *The soldiers blackened their faces so they could not be seen in the dark.* **black·en** (**blak**-uhn) ▷ *verb* **blackening, blackened**

black eye *noun* A bruise on the skin around the eye, caused by broken blood vessels.

Blackfoot *noun* A member of a group of Native Americans who live mainly in Montana and the Canadian province of Alberta. **Black·foot** (**blak**-*fut*) ▷ *noun, plural* **Blackfoot** *or* **Blackfeet**

black hole *noun* An area in space where a star has collapsed and where gravity is so strong that nothing can escape, not even light.

blackmail

1. *noun* The crime of demanding money from someone in exchange for not revealing information that might threaten or embarrass the person.
2. *verb* When you **blackmail** someone, you threaten or pressure the person to do something he or she doesn't want to do: *Renata blackmailed Wallace into voting for her.* ▷ *verb* **blackmailing, blackmailed** **black·mail** (**blak**-*mayl*)

blackout *noun*

1. A period of unconsciousness: *The doctors didn't know what was causing her blackouts.*
2. If a town or city has a **blackout,** the lights go off because the electricity has failed: *There was a blackout during the storm.* **black·out** (**blak**-*out*)
▷ *verb* **black out**

blacksmith *noun* Someone who makes things by heating and bending iron. **black·smith** (**blak**-*smith*)

blacktop *noun* The hard black surface that covers roads and other paved areas; asphalt: *The blacktop in the parking lot is great for roller-skating.* **black·top** (**blak**-*tahp*)

black widow *noun* A spider with a poisonous bite. The female black widow has a shiny black body and a red hourglass shape on the underside of its abdomen.

bladder *noun* The organ where urine is stored before your body gets rid of it. **blad·der** (**blad**-ur)

blade *noun*

1. The flat, sharp-edged part of a tool or utensil, such as a knife, sword, or dagger.
2. The flat, wide part of an oar or propeller that pushes against the water.
3. A long, narrow leaf of a plant such as grass or wheat.
4. The metal runner on an ice skate.
blade (blade)

blame *verb* To feel or say that something is someone's fault: *Don't blame yourself for things you didn't do.* **blame** (blame) ▷ *verb* **blaming, blamed** ▷ *noun* **blame**

bland *adjective* Without much flavor: *I thought the spaghetti sauce was bland.* **bland** (bland)
▷ *adjective* **blander, blandest**

blank

1. *adjective* Bare, empty, or with nothing written on it, as in *a blank sheet of paper.* ▷ *adjective* **blanker, blankest**
2. *noun* An empty line or space: *Fill in the blanks.*

3. *noun* A cartridge for a gun that contains gunpowder but no bullet, used for training.
4. If you **go blank,** you suddenly cannot think of something: *I went blank and couldn't remember the words to the song.*
blank (blangk)

blanket *noun*

1. A covering for a bed.
2. A thick layer of something: *All we could see out the window was a blanket of wildflowers.*
blan·ket (**blang**-kit)
▷ *verb* **blanket**

blare *verb* To make a very loud, harsh sound: *My neighbor's TV is constantly blaring.* **blare** (blair)
▷ *verb* **blaring, blared**

blasphemy *noun* The act of speaking in a disrespectful way about God or holy things. **blas·phe·my** (**blas**-fuh-mee) ▷ *verb* **blaspheme** (**blas**-feem)
▷ *adjective* **blasphemous** (**blas**-fuh-muhs)

blast

1. *noun* An explosion or sudden, loud noise, as in *a bomb blast.*
2. *noun* A strong gust of air: *The blast of the fan blew the papers off the table.*
3. *verb* To blow up with explosives: *The dynamite blasted the building into a pile of dust.*
4. *verb* When a rocket **blasts off,** it is launched.
blast (blast)
▷ *verb* **blasting, blasted**

blastoff *noun* The launching into space of a rocket, missile, or spaceship. **blast·off** (**blast**-*awf*)

blatant *adjective* Open, obvious, and without shame: *The excuse he gave me was a blatant lie.* **bla·tant** (**blay**-tuhnt) ▷ *adverb* **blatantly**

blaze

1. *verb* To burn fiercely or shine brightly.
2. *noun* A large or fiercely burning fire.
3. *verb* If you **blaze a trail,** you mark out a path or set an example: *I would never have gone to college if my sister hadn't blazed a trail for me.*
blaze (blayz)
▷ *verb* **blazing, blazed**

blazer *noun* A solid color sports jacket, especially one with metal buttons. **blaz·er** (**blay**-zur)

bleach

1. *noun* A chemical that takes color, dirt, and stains out of materials.
2. *verb* To make something cleaner or lighter in color by using a bleach or the sun: *She bleached the stains out of her white shirt.* ▷ *verb* **bleaching, bleached** **bleach** (bleech)

blazer

bleachers

bleachers *noun, plural* Raised seats or benches arranged in rows. Bleachers are usually found in stadiums or along a parade route. **bleach·ers** (**blee**-churz)

bleak *adjective*
1. Cold, miserable, and exposed to the weather, as in *a bleak landscape.*
2. Unlikely to have a positive outcome: *The economic forecast is really bleak.* **bleak** (bleek)
▷ *adjective* **bleaker, bleakest**

bleat *noun* The cry of a sheep or a goat. **bleat** (bleet)
▷ *verb* **bleat**

bleed *verb*
1. To lose blood as a result of illness or injury: *Sarah was bleeding from the cut on her arm.*
2. If your heart **bleeds** for someone, you feel sorrow or pity for the person. **bleed** (bleed)
▷ *verb* **bleeding, bled** (bled) ▷ *adjective* **bleeding**

bleep *verb* To make a short, high-pitched sound like that of an electronic device: *The alarm clock bleeped, waking me up.* **bleep** (bleep) ▷ *verb* **bleeping, bleeped** ▷ *noun* **bleep**

blemish *noun* A mark or spot that makes something less than perfect; a flaw. **blem·ish** (**blem**-ish)
▷ *verb* **blemish**

blend *verb* To mix two or more things together so that they combine: *Blend the butter and sugar together with a wooden spoon.* **blend** (blend)
▷ *verb* **blending, blended** ▷ *noun* **blend**

blended family *noun* A family in which not all of the children have the same two parents: *They were single parents when they met, and now that they are married, they have a blended family of seven children.*

blender *noun* A small appliance that grinds and mixes food. **blend·er** (**blen**-dur)

bless *verb*
1. To make holy: *The priest blessed our new home.*
2. To ask God to protect someone or something.
3. Bless you! is what you say when a person has just sneezed, or if you want to thank someone.
bless (bles)
▷ *verb* **blesses, blessing, blessed** ▷ *noun* **blessing**

blew *verb* The past tense of **blow**. **blew** (bloo)
Blew sounds like **blue**.

blight *noun*
1. A disease that destroys plants: *Only two potato fields survived the blight.*
2. Something that can hurt or destroy the health or beauty of something: *The dilapidated house was a blight on the neighborhood.*
blight (blite)

blimp *noun* An airship, or dirigible, whose body does not have a rigid frame. **blimp** (blimp)

blind
1. *adjective* Not able to see. ▷ *noun* **blindness**
2. *adjective* A **blind** corner is so sharp that it is impossible to see around.
3. *noun* A covering for a window that can be pulled down to keep out the light: *You should lower your blinds for some privacy.*
4. A driver's **blind spot** is an area that cannot be seen in either the side or rearview mirrors.
5. *verb* To cause to lose judgment: *Donna's strong feelings for Marcus blinded her to his faults.*
▷ *verb* **blinding, blinded**
blind (blinde)

blindfold
1. *verb* To cover someone's eyes with a strip of material so that he or she cannot see.
▷ *verb* **blindfolding, blindfolded**
2. *noun* A scarf or other material that is tied around the head to cover the eyes and keep the wearer from seeing.
blind·fold (**blinde**-*fohld*)

blink *verb*
1. To close and open your eyes very quickly: *I tend to blink a lot when my eyes are tired.*
2. To flash on and off: *The light blinked all night.*
blink (blingk)
▷ *verb* **blinking, blinked** ▷ *noun* **blink**

bliss *noun* A state of perfect happiness: *It was bliss to be on vacation at last.* **bliss** (blis)
▷ *adjective* **blissful** ▷ *adverb* **blissfully**

blister *noun* A small, fluid-filled bubble on the skin, caused by something burning or rubbing against it: *She got painful blisters from her new shoes.* **blis·ter** (**blis**-tur) ▷ *verb* **blister**

blizzard *noun* A severe snowstorm with strong winds. **bliz·zard** (**bliz**-urd)

bloated *adjective* Swollen with fluid or gas, often as a result of overeating: *I always feel bloated after Thanksgiving dinner.* **bloat·ed** (**bloh**-tid)

blob *noun* A small lump of something soft, wet, or thick: *You spilled a blob of paint right there by the door.* **blob** (blahb)

block

1. *noun* A piece of something solid with flat sides, as in *a block of cement.*

2. *verb* To prevent movement or progress: *The police blocked the road near the accident.* ▷ *verb* **blocking, blocked** ▷ *noun* **block**

3. *noun* The distance or area from one street to another: *Bobbie lived only three blocks from school.*

4. *noun* The area or section in a city surrounded by four streets.

block (blahk)

blockade *noun* The closing off of an area to keep people or supplies from going in or out: *There was a blockade that kept ships from delivering food.* **block·ade** (blah-**kade**)

blog

1. *noun* A webpage or website to which new messages are added easily. Blogs usually discuss a single subject or issue, and they may be written by a single person, like a diary, or as a discussion by many people.

2. *verb* To add new entries to a blog: *I blog whenever I read an interesting news story on science.* ▷ *verb* **blogging, blogged** ▷ *noun* **blogger**

blog (blawg *or* blahg)

Word History

Blog is short for *weblog,* and is usually written by one person, who then posts it on the internet. Often, it is in a style similar to a diary but is available for everyone to read. Some blogs are written by several people. Like a ship's log kept by a captain, a blog gets updated with new writing, sometimes daily.

blond *adjective* Having golden or pale yellow hair. When the word is spelled *blonde,* with an *e* at the end, it usually refers to a girl or woman with such hair. **blond** (blahnd) ▷ *noun* **blond, blonde**

blood *noun* The red fluid that your heart pumps through your veins and arteries: *It was only a small cut, but there was blood all over the sink.* **blood** (bluhd)

blood bank *noun* A place where blood is donated and stored. Hospitals use this stored blood to replace blood lost by someone during an operation or in an accident.

blizzard

bloodhound *noun* A large dog with a wrinkled face, drooping ears, and a very good sense of smell. **blood·hound** (**bluhd**-*hound*)

bloodshed *noun* The injury or killing of human beings, particularly as a result of a battle or war: *There was no way to resolve the crisis without bloodshed.* **blood·shed** (**bluhd**-*shed*)

bloodshot *adjective* **Bloodshot** eyes are red and irritated. **blood·shot** (**bluhd**-*shaht*)

bloodstream *noun* The blood circulating through the body: *Aspirin won't work until it gets into your bloodstream.* **blood·stream** (**bluhd**-*streem*)

bloodthirsty *adjective* Someone who is **bloodthirsty** is eager for or takes pleasure in violence or killing. **blood·thirst·y** (**bluhd**-*thur*-stee)

blood vessel *noun* Any of the tubes in your body through which your blood flows.

bloody *adjective*

1. Full of blood, or covered with blood: *The bandage soon became bloody.*

2. Violent, or showing blood: *That horror film was too bloody for me.*

blood·y (**bluhd**-ee)

▷ *adjective* **bloodier, bloodiest**

bloom

1. *noun* A flower: *There wasn't a single bloom left on the lilies.*

2. *verb* To produce flowers or to be in flower: *The garden usually bloomed in early May.*

3. *verb* To flourish: *Her career as an artist has really bloomed.*

bloom (bloom)

▷ *verb* **blooming, bloomed** ▷ *adjective* **blooming**

blossom
1. *noun* A flower on a fruit tree or other plant, as in *apple blossoms.*
2. *verb* To grow or to develop: *Tina has blossomed into a beautiful young woman.* ▷ *verb* **blossoming, blossomed**
blos·som (blah-suhm)

blot
1. *noun* A mark or stain, such as one made by ink or paint.
2. *verb* To dry by soaking up excess liquid: *She blotted her lips with a tissue.* ▷ *verb* **blotting, blotted**
blot (blaht)

blotch *noun* A stain or a large, irregular mark on the skin: *The red blotches on her cheeks are from too much sun.* **blotch** (blahch) ▷ *noun, plural* **blotches**
▷ *adjective* **blotchy**

blotter *noun* A pad or piece of thick paper that absorbs extra ink. **blot·ter (blah-**tur)

blouse *noun* A loose-fitting shirt worn by women and girls that covers the area from the neck to the waist, or just below. **blouse** (blous)

blow
1. *verb* To force air out of your mouth through your lips: *She blew on her hot chocolate to cool it down.*
2. *verb* To move in the wind or be carried as if by the wind: *Our tent blew away while we were sleeping.*
3. *noun* A sudden and forceful stroke with your hand or a weapon: *The boxer suffered many blows to the ribs.*
4. *noun* A shock or a disappointment: *Not getting the job was a blow to Greg's confidence.*
5. blow up *verb* To explode something or to destroy it with an explosion.
6. blow up *verb* To lose your temper: *My father blew up when he found out I'd been watching TV all night.*
blow (bloh)
▷ *verb* **blowing, blew** (bloo), **blown** (blohn)

blowhole *noun*
1. A nostril on the top of the head through which a whale, dolphin, or porpoise can breathe. Some whales have two blowholes; others have only one.
2. A hole in the ice through which seals and whales breathe.
blow·hole (bloh-hohl)

blowtorch *noun* A small torch with an intense flame that is used to melt metal or take off paint: *The welder used a blowtorch to solder the joints of the copper pipe.* **blow·torch (bloh-**torch)
▷ *noun, plural* **blowtorches**

blubber
1. *noun* The layer of fat under the skin of a whale, seal, or other large marine mammal.
2. *verb* To sob loudly: *Katie blubbered through the*

blowtorch

whole movie. ▷ *verb* **blubbering, blubbered**
blub·ber (bluhb-ur)

blue
1. *noun* The color of the ocean or the sky on a sunny day. ▷ *adjective* **blue**
2. *adjective* Sad, gloomy, or depressed: *Winter makes me blue.* ▷ *adjective* **bluer, bluest**
3. If something comes to you **out of the blue**, it comes from a source or at a time when you didn't expect it: *Help arrived out of the blue.*
blue (bloo)
Blue sounds like **blew**.

blueberry *noun* The sweet, dark blue fruit of a bush common in the northeastern United States. **blue·ber·ry (bloo-**ber-ee) ▷ *noun, plural* **blueberries**

bluebird *noun* A small songbird that has blue feathers on its back and wings. **blue·bird (bloo-**burd)

bluefish *noun* A silver-blue ocean fish. **blue·fish (bloo-**fish) ▷ *noun, plural* **bluefish** or **bluefishes**

bluegrass *noun*
1. A grass with a slightly blue tinge, used for lawns and for cattle and horse feed.
2. A type of country music, typically played on banjos and guitars.
blue·grass (bloo-gras)

blue jay *noun* A fairly large, blue-and-white bird, related to crows, with a crest of feathers on its head. **blue jay** (jay)

blueprint *noun* A model or detailed plan of action: *The town's recycling program was a blueprint for the entire state.* **blue·print (bloo**-print)

blues *noun, plural*
1. A type of music first sung by African Americans, with songs about difficulties in life and love.
2. Low spirits: *Since her best friend moved, Orlene has had the blues.*
blues (blooz)

blue whale *noun* A bluish-gray whale that is the largest living animal.

bluff
1. *verb* To try to mislead someone by appearing more confident than you really are: *Sarah said she wasn't afraid, but we all knew she was bluffing.*
▷ *verb* **bluffing, bluffed**
2. *noun* A statement or action that is intended to mislead someone.
3. *noun* A cliff or other mountain with a very steep face.
4. If you **call** someone's **bluff,** you challenge the person to do something he or she has boasted about or threatened to do.
bluff (bluhf)

blunder
1. *noun* A stupid or careless mistake: *My worst blunder was getting lost on the way home.*
2. *verb* To make a stupid mistake: *He blundered by spelling my name wrong.*
3. *verb* To move in a confused or clumsy way: *The troops blundered their way through the dense fog.*
blun·der (bluhn-dur)
▷ *verb* **blundering, blundered**

blunt
1. *adjective* Having a dull edge or point, as in *a blunt instrument.*
2. *verb* To make or become less sharp. ▷ *verb* **blunting, blunted**
3. *adjective* Abrupt and honest in what you say: *Her blunt criticism is helpful, even if it hurts.*
▷ *adjective* **blunter, bluntest** ▷ *noun* **bluntness**
▷ *adverb* **bluntly**
blunt (bluhnt)

blur
1. *verb* To make something less clear or unclear: *The fog blurred the outline of the houses up on the hill.* ▷ *verb* **blurring, blurred**
2. *noun* Something that can't be seen or remembered clearly: *I wish I could remember what happened that day, but it's all a blur.* ▷ *adjective* **blurred**
blur (blur)

blurb *noun* A short written piece that promotes a book, a movie, or a product: *James read blurbs about several new computers.* **blurb** (blurb)

Word History

In the early 20th century, the American humor writer Gelett Burgess added a picture of a beautiful young woman to a short, boastful text he wrote promoting one of his books and named her Miss Belinda Blurb. He then put them on the jacket of the book. Although he meant it as a joke, **blurb** soon came to mean a short publicity notice for a book, movie, or product.

blurt *verb* If you **blurt** something out, you say it suddenly and without thinking about its effect: *I blurted out the truth without thinking about how the rest of the family would feel.* **blurt** (blurt)
▷ *verb* **blurting, blurted**

blush *verb* To become red in the face because you are shy, embarrassed, or ashamed: *Sarah blushes whenever she gives a wrong answer.* **blush** (bluhsh)
▷ *verb* **blushes, blushing, blushed** ▷ *noun* **blush**

bluster *verb*
1. To blow in violent gusts: *The wind blustered all day, stripping the trees of their leaves.* ▷ *adjective* **blustery**
2. To act or speak in a bullying, overconfident way: *He can bluster his way through any meeting.*
blus·ter (bluhs-tur)
▷ *verb* **blustering, blustered**
▷ *noun* **bluster**

Blvd. Short for **boulevard.**

BMI *noun* A measure of whether you have too much fat. Your BMI is your weight in kilograms divided by the square of your height in meters. BMI is short for *body mass index:* *You are considered overweight if your BMI is 25 or higher.*

boa constrictor

boa constrictor *noun* A large, nonpoisonous tropical snake that kills its prey by coiling around it and squeezing. **bo·a con·stric·tor (boh**-uh kuhn-*strik*-tur)

boar *noun*
1. A male pig.
2. A type of wild pig with tusks.
boar (bor)
Boar sounds like **bore.**

board

1. *noun* A long, flat piece of wood, used for building or making things.

2. *noun* A specially marked square or rectangle on which a game is played: *Set up the board, and I'll play you a game of chess.*

3. *verb* To get on or enter a ship, aircraft, or other vehicle: *Her parents waved to her as they boarded the cruise ship.* ▷ *verb* **boarding, boarded**

4. *noun* The **board** of a company or organization is the group of people who control it: *Let's run the idea past the members of the board to see what they think.*

5. *noun* Meals provided to paying guests: *The college fee includes room and board.*
board (bord)

board

boarder *noun* A person who pays to live in a house and receive meals there. **board·er** (**bor**-dur)

boarding *noun* The sport of riding a skateboard or snowboard: *We did our homework and then went boarding.* **board·ing** (**bor**-ding)

boarding school *noun* A school that students may live in during the school year.

boast *verb*

1. To brag about something in order to impress people: *Mariah boasted about her achievements but didn't tell us what they were.*

2. If a place **boasts** something, it has something that others would like to have: *New Orleans boasts many fine restaurants.*
boast (bohst)
▷ *verb* **boasting, boasted** ▷ *noun* **boast**
▷ *adjective* **boastful** ▷ *adverb* **boastfully**

boat *noun* A vessel that travels on water and is used to carry people and goods: *Canoes, yachts, and barges are types of boats.* **boat** (boht) ▷ *verb* **boat**

boathouse *noun* A building where small boats are sheltered or stored. **boat·house** (**boht**-hous)

boat people *noun, plural* People who are forced to leave their country in boats because of the poverty or difficult conditions there: *I had no idea that her parents were Vietnamese boat people.*

bob

1. *verb* To keep moving up and down quickly: *A piece of driftwood bobbed on the water.* ▷ *verb* **bobbing, bobbed**

2. *noun* A short hairstyle where all the hair is the same length. ▷ *verb* **bob**
bob (bahb)

bobbin *noun* A spool inside a sewing machine or on a loom that holds the thread. **bob·bin** (**bah**-bin)

bobby pin *noun* A flat hairpin that keeps hair in place. **bob·by pin** (**bah**-bee)

bobcat *noun* A small, wild cat with reddish-brown fur, black spots, and a short tail. A bobcat is a type of lynx. **bob·cat** (**bahb**-kat)

bobolink *noun* A North and South American songbird with black, white, and yellow feathers. **bob·o·link** (**bah**-buh-*link*)

bobsled *noun* A long sled with a steering wheel and brakes, used for racing down a steep, icy run. **bob·sled** (**bahb**-sled) ▷ *verb* **bobsled**

bobwhite *noun* A common North American quail with a reddish-brown body and white, black, and tan markings. A bobwhite's call sounds like its name. **bob·white** (**bahb**-wite) ▷ *noun, plural* **bobwhite** *or* **bobwhites**

bode *verb* To be a sign of something: *The wet weather did not bode well for our hike.* **bode** (bode) ▷ *verb* **boding, boded**

boarding

body *noun*
1. All the physical parts of a person or an animal, as in *the human body.*
2. The main or central part of something: *The body of the car had extensive damage.*
3. Someone who has died; a corpse: *The firefighters found the body in the basement of the burned-out building.*
4. A group of people working together, as in *the student body.*
5. A mass of matter, as in *a heavenly body.*
bod·y (**bah**-dee)

bodyguard *noun* A man or woman who protects someone, especially a famous or important person: *If you wanted to shake hands with the president, you had to get past his bodyguards.* **bod·y·guard** (**bah**-dee-*gahrd*)

bog
1. *noun* An area of soft, wet land. ▷ *adjective* **boggy**
2. *verb* If you are **bogged down,** you are stuck and can't make any progress: *We were so bogged down in details that we couldn't make a decision.* ▷ *verb* **bogging, bogged**
bog (bahg)

bogeyman *noun* An imaginary, scary man who is sometimes used to frighten children. **bo·gey·man** (**bu**-gee-*man*) ▷ *noun, plural* **bogeymen**

bogus *adjective* Fake or not true: *I was late for school, but the reasons I gave to the teacher were bogus.* **bo·gus** (**boh**-guhs)

Word History

It would be rather disappointing to discover that some of your money was fake, and you would not be able to buy anything with it. One of the first meanings of the word **bogus** was "counterfeit money." Machines for making counterfeit coins were discovered in Ohio in the early 19th century, and, naturally, the police took them away since making fake money is illegal. People called the machine a *bogus,* and later also used the term for the money, giving us *bogus* as an adjective meaning "false."

boil
1. *verb* To heat a liquid to the point where it bubbles and gives off steam: *Dad boiled some water for tea.*
▷ *noun* **boil** ▷ *adjective* **boiling**
2. *verb* To cook or clean something in boiling water: *Be sure to boil my egg for only three minutes.*
3. *noun* A painful swelling on or under the skin.
boil (boil)
▷ *verb* **boiling, boiled**

boiler *noun* A device that heats water for a house or for use in a heating system. **boil·er** (**boi**-lur)

boiling point *noun*
1. The temperature at which a liquid turns to a gas. The boiling point of water is 212 degrees Fahrenheit or 100 degrees Celsius.
2. When you reach your **boiling point,** you are about to lose your temper.

boisterous *adjective* Noisy and high-spirited: *The fans cheered and grew boisterous.* **bois·ter·ous** (**boi**-stur-uhs) ▷ *noun* **boisterousness** ▷ *adverb* **boisterously**

bold *adjective*
1. Having or showing confidence and courage: *Claude was bold enough to dive from the cliffs.* ▷ *noun* **boldness**
2. Bold colors stand out because they are bright and clear.
bold (bohld)
▷ *adjective* **bolder, boldest** ▷ *adverb* **boldly**

boll weevil *noun* A beetle that lays eggs in cotton plants. **boll wee·vil** (**bohl wee**-vuhl)

bolster
1. *verb* To support or give a boost to someone or something: *Your phone call has bolstered my courage.* ▷ *verb* **bolstering, bolstered**
2. *noun* A long, narrow pillow or cushion.
bol·ster (**bohl**-stur)

bolt
1. *noun* A metal pin or bar that slides into place and fastens a door or window: *The door bolt was so rusted it wouldn't move.* ▷ *verb* **bolt**
2. *noun* A metal pin that screws into a nut to fasten things together.
3. *verb* To run away or move suddenly: *The deer bolted as soon as they saw us.*
4. *verb* If you **bolt your food,** you eat it very quickly.
5. *noun* A flash of lightning or crack of thunder.
6. *noun* A roll of something, such as cloth.
bolt (bohlt)
▷ *verb* **bolting, bolted**

bomb
1. *noun* A container filled with explosives, designed to destroy someone or something, as in *a nuclear bomb.*
2. *verb* To attack someone or something with bombs: *We bombed the enemy until they had no choice but to surrender.* ▷ *verb* **bombing, bombed**
bomb (bahm)

bombard *verb*
1. To attack a place with bombs, missiles, or gunfire.

2. To overwhelm someone with questions, information, or complaints: *When they asked for feedback, the town officials were bombarded with comments.*
bom·bard (bahm-**bahrd**)
▷ *verb* **bombarding, bombarded** ▷ *noun* **bombardment**

bomber *noun*
1. A large airplane that drops bombs on targets.
2. Someone who sets off bombs.
bomb·er (**bah**-mur)

bombshell *noun*
1. A bomb.
2. An event that is very surprising, usually not in a good way.
bomb·shell (bahm-*shel*)

bona fide *adjective*
1. Genuine or sincere, as in *a bona fide friendship.*
2. In good faith, or without fraud, as in *a bona fide agreement.*
bo·na fide (boh-nuh *fide*)

bond
1. *noun* A close connection with or strong feeling for someone, as in *the mother-daughter bond* or *the bonds of friendship.*
2. *verb* When you **bond** two things, you make them stick together: *I used glue to bond the airplane model to the base.* ▷ *verb* **bonding, bonded** ▷ *noun* **bond**
3. *noun* A document that allows companies or governments to raise money. People buy the bonds and are later paid back, with interest added.
bond (bahnd)

bondage *noun* The condition of being under the control of someone or something when it is against your will: *Slaves escaped bondage with the help of the abolitionists who set up the Underground Railroad.* **bond·age** (**bahn**-dij)

bone *noun* The hard, whitish tissue that makes up the skeleton of a person or an animal: *The paleontologist found a dinosaur bone.* **bone** (bohn)

bonfire *noun* A large outdoor fire, typically used to celebrate something, to burn trash, or to send a signal. **bon·fire** (bahn-*fire*)

bongo drum *noun* Either of a pair of small connected drums, held between the knees and struck with the fingers. **bon·go drum** (**bahng**-goh)

bonnet *noun* A baby's or woman's hat, usually one with a brim and strings that tie under the chin. **bon·net** (**bah**-nit)

bonsai *noun* A miniature tree or shrub that is grown in a pot and shaped by pruning. **bon·sai** (**bahn**-sye) ▷ *noun, plural* **bonsai**

bonus *noun*
1. An extra reward or benefit: *Joe's boss gave him a bonus for completing the project ahead of schedule.*
2. Something that is unexpected but welcome: *Having a doctor move in next door was a real bonus.*
bo·nus (**boh**-nuhs)
▷ *noun, plural* **bonuses** ▷ *adjective* **bonus**

bony *adjective*
1. Extremely thin or full of bones: *She stuck her bony hand out and tapped my shoulder.*
2. Made of bone: *The skeleton is a bony structure.*
bon·y (**boh**-nee)

boo
1. *interjection* A word used to surprise or startle someone, or to express dislike or disapproval.
2. *verb* To express dislike or disapproval by saying boo. ▷ *verb* **boos, booing, booed**
boo (boo)

booby trap *noun*
1. A harmless-looking object with a hidden device that explodes when someone or something touches it.
2. A situation that tricks you or catches you by surprise when you're not paying attention: *The thieves thought they were breaking into an empty house, but they walked right into a booby trap.*
boo·by trap (**boo**-bee)
▷ *verb* **booby-trap**

boo-hoo *interjection* A word that you use in a jokey way to show that you are sad or upset about something. It is an imitation of crying: *Oh, boo-hoo! Mom says we have to leave the party early.* **boo-hoo** (**boo**-hoo) ▷ *verb* **boo-hoo, boo-hooing, boo-hooed**

book
1. *noun* A set of pages that are fastened along one side and put between two covers.
2. *verb* To arrange for something ahead of time: *We've booked a bicycle tour of France.* ▷ *verb* **booking, booked** ▷ *noun* **booking**
book (buk)

bonsai

bookkeeper *noun* Someone who keeps financial records for a business or an organization. **book·keep·er (buk-**_kee_-pur) ▷ *noun* **bookkeeping**

booklet *noun* A small, thin book with a soft cover. **book·let (buk**-lit)

bookmark

1. *noun* A piece of ribbon, paper, or other material used to mark a place in a book.

2. *noun* The address of a webpage that you have saved in your browser.

3. *verb* To save the address of a webpage by using the "Favorites" or "Bookmarks" feature in your browser. ▷ *verb* **bookmarking, bookmarked**

book·mark (buk-_mahrk_)

bookmobile *noun* A van or truck that is used as a small, mobile library. **book·mo·bile (buk**-muh-_beel_)

bookworm *noun* Someone who loves books and spends a lot of time reading. **book·worm (buk**-_wurm_)

boom

1. *noun* A very loud, deep sound, as in *a sonic boom.*

2. *verb* To speak in a loud, deep voice, as in *to boom out orders.* ▷ *verb* **booming, boomed**

3. *noun* A period of rapid growth or expansion, as in *a building boom.*

4. If you **lower the boom** on someone, you punish the person.

boom (boom)

boomerang *noun* A curved stick made so that after it is thrown, it will return to the thrower. It was originally used as a weapon by the Aborigines of Australia. **boo·mer·ang (boo**-muh-_rang_)

boomerang

Word History

In 1788, the British began settling in Sydney, Australia, at Port Jackson, one of the world's best natural harbors. When the British encountered the native people, the Aborigines, they learned some of the Aborigines' words. One word was *wo-mur-rang,* the name of a type of throwing stick, and English speakers adopted the word as **boomerang.** The Aborigines used both returning and non-returning types of throwing sticks, but only the returning types are called boomerangs.

boor *noun* A person with bad manners and no consideration for others. **boor** (boor) ▷ *adjective* **boorish**

boost

1. *verb* To lift someone or something by pushing from below: *My brother boosted me up so I could see in the window.*

2. *verb* To increase or encourage something, as in *to boost profits.*

3. *noun* If something gives you a **boost,** it cheers you up or makes you feel better: *Winning the photography contest gave me a real boost.*

boost (boost)

▷ *noun* **boost** ▷ *verb* **boosting, boosted**

booster *noun*

1. A rocket that helps a spacecraft get off the ground.

2. A person or thing that is encouraging or that makes something better: *The company picnic was a real morale booster.*

3. A **booster shot** is an additional injection of a drug that makes the first dose more effective.

boost·er (boo-stur)

boot

1. *noun* A heavy, protective shoe that covers your foot and ankle and sometimes your lower leg, as in *sturdy hiking boots.*

2. *verb* When you **boot up** a computer, you turn it on so that it can start working.

3. *verb* To kick something hard, especially the ball in football.

boot (boot)

▷ *verb* **booting, booted**

Word History

The expression "to **boot** up" a computer is short for "use a *bootstrap* routine," a small program that loads the computer operating system. Computer programmers named the bootstrap routine from the expression *to pull oneself up by one's bootstraps,* meaning "to improve your life without help from others." They felt that this was what the computer was doing when it ran one program to load and run another.

booth *noun*

1. A temporary display area that is used to sell or show a product, as in *a booth at a fair.*

2. A restaurant dining area consisting of two benches with a table in between them.

3. A small enclosed place, as in *a voting booth, a ticket booth,* or *a telephone booth.*

booth (booth)

booty *noun* Valuable objects that are taken away by force, as by an army after a battle. **boo·ty (boo**-tee)

border

1. *noun* The dividing line between two countries or regions, as in *a tightly controlled border.*

2. *verb* If two countries **border** each other, they share a common boundary. ▷ *verb* **bordering, bordered**

3. *noun* A decorative band or design around the edge of something: *Joan drew a black border around the photo.*
bor·der (**bor**-dur)

bore
1. *verb* To make someone feel dull and weary: *All this talk about stamp collecting bored me.* ▷ *noun* **bore**
2. *verb* To make a hole in something with a drill or similar tool: *He had to bore through wood and plaster before he could hang the mirror.*
3. *noun* The hollow part of a gun barrel.
bore (bor)
Bore sounds like **boar**. ▷ *verb* **boring, bored**

bored *adjective* Not interested in what you are doing, or not having anything interesting to do: *Tim often gets into mischief when he is bored.* **bored** (bord)

boredom *noun* The state or experience of being bored. **bore·dom** (**bor**-duhm)

boring *adjective* Not at all interesting or engaging, as in *a boring movie.* **bor·ing** (**bor**-ing)

born *adjective*
1. Brought into life: *Jade was born in 2001.*
2. Naturally gifted at something: *He's a born entertainer.*
born (born)
Born sounds like **borne**.

borne *verb* The past participle of **bear**. **borne** (born)
Borne sounds like **born**.

borough *noun*
1. In some states, a town or area that has its own local government.
2. One of the five political divisions of New York City.
bor·ough (**bur**-oh)
Borough sounds like **burro** and **burrow**.

borrow *verb* To use something that belongs to someone else, with the understanding that you will return it as soon as you're done with it: *May I borrow your headphones?* **bor·row** (**bor**-oh) ▷ *verb* **borrowing, borrowed**

bosom
1. *noun* The front part of a person's chest.
2. *adjective* Close and dear, as in *bosom buddies.*
bos·om (**buz**-uhm *or* **boo**-zuhm)

boss
1. *noun* Someone who is in charge of a company's employees or who has control or authority: *You'd better get Terry's permission; he's the boss.* ▷ *noun, plural* **bosses** ▷ *verb* **boss**

bored

2. boss around *verb* To give orders to someone: *I'm tired of him bossing me around!* ▷ *verb* **bosses, bossing, bossed**
boss (baws)

bossy *adjective* A **bossy** person likes to give orders. **bos·sy** (**baw**-see) ▷ *adjective* **bossier, bossiest** ▷ *noun* **bossiness**

bot *noun*
1. Short for **robot**.
2. A computer program that runs continuously on the internet, doing a repetitive job such as crawling the web to get information for a search engine. While many bots are useful, some can be dangerous, such as ones used by hackers to steal passwords and credit card numbers.
bot (baht)

botany *noun* The scientific study of plant life. **bot·a·ny** (**bah**-tuh-nee) ▷ *noun* **botanist** ▷ *adjective* **botanical** (buh-**tan**-i-kuhl)

botch
1. *verb* To do something badly or clumsily: *The plumber botched the faucet repair and water is spraying everywhere.* ▷ *verb* **botching, botched**
2. *noun* Something that is a mess because it was done badly or clumsily: *We didn't bake the cupcakes long enough and made a complete botch of them.*
botch (bahch)

both
1. *pronoun* Two things or people: *You should both come in now.*
2. *adjective* Referring to the one and the other: *Use both your eyes.*
3. *conjunction* Equally, or as well: *The movie was both scary and funny.*
both (bohth)

bother
1. *verb* If something **bothers** you, it disturbs or annoys you: *It bothers me when people say my name wrong.*
2. *noun* Something that annoys you.
3. *verb* To take the trouble to do something: *Don't bother with the dishes—we'll do them later.*
both·er (bah-**THur**)
▷ *verb* **bothering, bothered**

botnet *noun* A group of computers that have been infected with malware and that work together to do something bad, like infecting even more computers or causing a system crash. **bot·net** (**baht**-*net*)

Botox *noun* A trademark for an injected drug that relaxes muscles and makes wrinkles appear to be less deep. **Bo·tox** (**boh**-tahks)

bottle

1. *noun* A glass or plastic container with a narrow neck and mouth and no handle.

2. *verb* To put in a bottle.

3. *verb* If you **bottle up** something, you hold it in: *It's not healthy to bottle up your feelings.* **bot·tle** (**bah**-tuhl) ▷ *verb* **bottling, bottled**

bottleneck *noun* A narrow section of road where traffic often backs up: *The worst bottleneck is where Route 50 joins the thruway.* **bot·tle·neck** (**bah**-tuhl-*nek*)

bottom *noun*

1. The lowest or deepest part of something, as in *the bottom of a well.* ▷ *adjective* **bottom**

2. A person's buttocks.

3. The most basic part of something: *We need get to the bottom of this problem.* **bot·tom** (**bah**-tuhm)

bough *noun* A tree branch, especially a large one. **bough** (bou)

bought *verb* The past tense and the past participle of **buy**. **bought** (bawt)

boulder *noun* A large, rounded rock. **boul·der** (**bohl**-dur)

boulevard *noun* A wide city street that often has grass, trees, or flowers planted down the middle or along either side. **bou·le·vard** (**bul**-uh-*vahrd*)

bounce

1. *verb* To move quickly in the opposite direction after hitting something: *The ball bounced off the wall and hit someone.* ▷ *noun* **bounce**

2. If you **bounce a check,** you don't have enough money in your bank account to cover it.

3. *noun* If someone has lots of **bounce,** he or she is very energetic and cheerful. ▷ *adjective* **bouncy** **bounce** (bouns) ▷ *verb* **bouncing, bounced**

bound

1. *verb* To walk or run with leaps and jumps: *My dog bounded toward me, wagging his tail with joy.* ▷ *verb* **bounding, bounded** ▷ *noun* **bound**

2. *adjective* If something is **bound** to happen, it will certainly or almost certainly take place.

3. Someone or something that is **out of bounds** is beyond the boundaries or limits that have been set. In sports, **out of bounds** means out of the field of play. **bound** (bound)

bouquet

boundary *noun* The line, fence, or other object that separates one area from another. **bound·a·ry** (**boun**-dur-ee) ▷ *noun, plural* **boundaries**

bountiful *adjective* More than enough; generous; plentiful: *We had a bountiful feast on Thanksgiving.* **boun·ti·ful** (**boun**-ti-fuhl)

bounty *noun*

1. Something that is given or that exists in generous amounts: *We enjoyed the bounty of apples from the orchard.*

2. A reward offered for the capture of a criminal or a harmful animal: *The sheriff offered a bounty of $100 to anyone who killed the wolf.* **boun·ty** (**boun**-tee)

bouquet *noun* A bunch of picked or cut flowers. **bou·quet** (boh-**kay** or boo-**kay**)

bout *noun*

1. An attack or a spell: *I was out of school for a week with a bout of the flu.*

2. An athletic match or contest: *Last night, I watched a wrestling bout on television.* **bout** (bout)

boutique *noun* A small shop that sells fashionable clothes or other specialty items. **bou·tique** (boo-**teek**)

bow

1. (bou) *verb* To bend the head or upper body as a sign of respect, greeting, or shame, or to accept applause: *At the end of the concert, the conductor bowed as he received a standing ovation.* ▷ *verb* **bowing, bowed** ▷ *noun* **bow**

2. (boh) *noun* A knot with two loops and two ends.

3. (bou) *noun* The front section of a ship or boat: *Let's go sit in the bow, where we can feel the wind.*

violin bow

4. (boh) *noun* A long, flat piece of wood with horsehair stretched between the ends, used for playing instruments like the violin or the cello.

5. (boh) *noun* A curved, flexible piece of wood with a string stretched between the two ends, used for shooting arrows: *The archer drew his bow and fixed his eyes on the target.* **bow**

bowels *noun, plural* Intestines.
bow·els (**bou**-uhlz)

bowl

1. *noun* A round, open dish for food or liquid: *I ate my cereal from a plastic bowl.*

2. *verb* When you **bowl,** you roll a heavy ball down an alley to knock over wooden pins. ▷ *noun* **bowler**

3. When something **bowls you over,** it greatly surprises you: *Ted was bowled over by his teammates' performance.*
bowl (bohl)
▷ *verb* **bowling, bowled**

bowlegged *adjective* If someone is **bowlegged,** he or she has legs that are curved outward so that the knees do not touch when the ankles are together. **bow·leg·ged** (**boh**-*leg*-id)

bowling *noun*

1. A game played indoors by rolling a heavy ball down an alley at ten wooden pins, or similar games using fewer pins or wider pins.

2. lawn bowling A game played mainly outdoors by rolling a small ball down a lawn, then rolling heavy balls toward it, trying to get them as close as possible to the small ball. In Britain, this game is known as *bowls.*
bowl·ing (**boh**-ling)

bowling alley *noun* A building where people go to bowl.

bow tie *noun* A necktie in the shape of a bow, often worn on formal occasions. **bow tie** (boh)

box

1. *noun* A container with a flat bottom and sides. ▷ *noun, plural* **boxes** ▷ *verb* **box**

2. *verb* To fight someone with your fists. ▷ *noun* **boxer** ▷ *noun* **boxing**

3. *verb* If you **box** someone or something **in,** you create a situation where escape is impossible: *We finally captured the rat after boxing it into a corner.*
box (bahks)
▷ *verb* **boxes, boxing, boxed**

bow tie

boxcar *noun* An enclosed railroad car with sliding doors to load and unload freight. **box·car** (**bahks**-*kahr*)

boxer shorts *noun, plural* Loose shorts worn by men or boys as underwear. Also known as **boxers.** **box·er shorts** (**bahk**-sur *shorts*)

box office *noun* The ticket office at a theater. It is also a term used to describe how successful a play or movie is: *The movie had big-name stars, but it didn't do well at the box office.*

boy *noun* A male child or young person. **boy** (boi) ▷ *adjective* **boyish**

boycott

1. *verb* To refuse to buy something or do business with someone as a punishment or protest: *They disagreed with the store owner's political views and decided to boycott his store.* ▷ *verb* **boycotting, boycotted**

2. *noun* Refusal to do business as a punishment or protest: *The Birmingham bus boycott helped end racial segregation.*
boy·cott (**boi**-kaht)

boyfriend *noun*

1. The man or boy with whom someone is having a romantic relationship.

2. A male friend.
boy·friend (**boi**-*frend*)

boyhood *noun* The time during which someone is a boy: *He spent his boyhood in Ohio.* **boy·hood** (**boi**-*hud*)

bra *noun* A women's undergarment that covers and supports the breasts. Bra is short for *brassiere.* **bra** (brah)

brace

1. *noun* An object fastened to another object to support it. ▷ *verb* **brace**

2. braces *noun, plural* A device worn inside your mouth, with wires attached to your teeth to straighten them.

3. *verb* If you **brace yourself,** you prepare yourself for an attack or a shock: *When the doctor called, Juan and his wife braced themselves for bad news.* ▷ *verb* **bracing, braced**
brace (brase)

bracelet *noun* A band or chain worn around the arm or wrist: *They made every patient wear an identification bracelet.* **brace·let** (**brase**-lit)

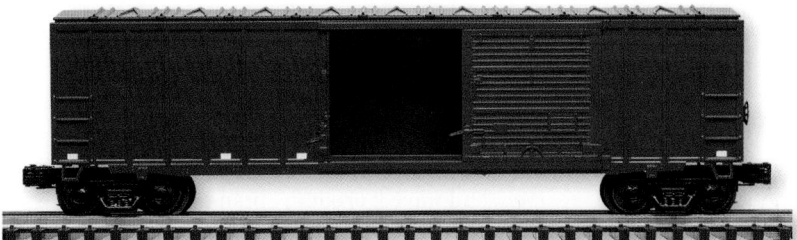

boxcar

a
b
c
d
e
f
g
h
i
j
k
l
m
n
o
p
q
r
s
t
u
v
w
x
y
z

bracket *noun*
1. A rigid support that is attached to a wall and used to hold up a shelf or cupboard.
2. A grouping of similar people or things: *These sneakers aren't exactly in my price bracket.*
3. *noun, plural* **Brackets** are the two symbols [ ] that are used to separate some material from the main written text. ▷ *verb* **bracket**
brack·et (**brak**-it)

brag *verb* To talk in a boastful way: *The boys were always bragging that they were the best soccer players around.* **brag** (brag) ▷ *verb* **bragging, bragged**

braid *noun* A length of hair or other material that has been divided into three or more parts and woven together. **braid** (brayd) ▷ *verb* **braid**

Braille *noun* A system of writing and printing for blind people that uses raised dots for letters and numbers: *Each of the elevator's buttons has a Braille number to indicate the floor.* **Braille** (brayl)

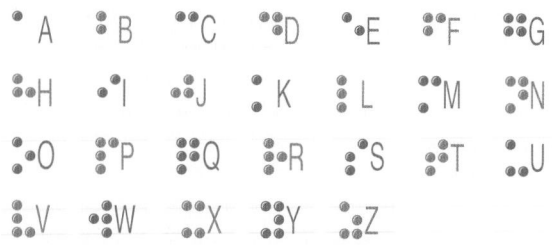

the Braille alphabet

brain *noun*
1. The organ inside your skull that controls your body's activities as well as your thoughts, memories, and emotions.
2. Your mind or the power of your intelligence.
brain (brayn)

brainchild *noun* An invention or an idea, especially an important or clever one that becomes successful: *The technology used in modern drones is actually the*

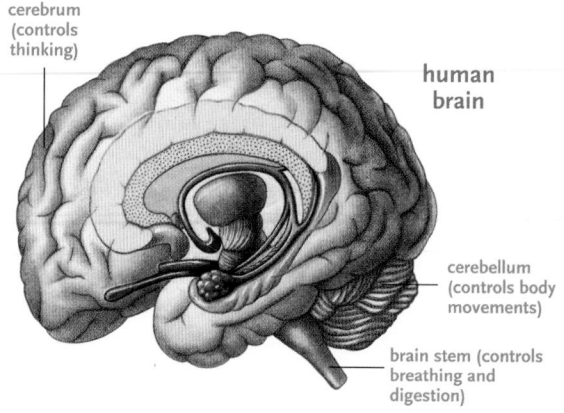

cerebrum (controls thinking)

human brain

cerebellum (controls body movements)

brain stem (controls breathing and digestion)

brainchild of Nikola Tesla, who patented a device for radio-controlled vehicles. **brain·child** (**brayn**-*childe*)

brainstorm
1. *verb* When people **brainstorm,** they get together to come up with ideas or a solution to a problem. ▷ *verb* **brainstorming, brainstormed** ▷ *noun* **brainstorming**
2. *noun* A great idea that comes to you all of a sudden: *I had a brainstorm about how to finish the project.*
brain·storm (**brayn**-*storm*)

brainwash *verb* To force someone to accept or believe something by using various forms of mental pressure. **brain·wash** (**brayn**-*wahsh*) ▷ *verb* **brainwashes, brainwashing, brainwashed** ▷ *noun* **brainwashing**

brainy *adjective* (*informal*) Very intelligent. **brain·y** (**bray**-nee) ▷ *adjective* **brainier, brainiest**

brake
1. *noun* A device to slow down or stop a vehicle.
2. *verb* To slow down or stop a vehicle by using a brake. ▷ *verb* **braking, braked**
brake (brake)
Brake sounds like **break**.

bran *noun* The outer covering of wheat or other grains that is sifted out when flour is made. Bran is used in baked goods and cereals, as in *bran muffins.* **bran** (bran)

branch
1. *noun* A part of a tree that grows out of the main trunk or a bough.
2. *verb* To divide into two or more parts that go in different directions: *His house is near where the river branches.* ▷ *noun* **branch**
3. *noun* A **branch** of a company or organization is one of its stores or offices in a particular area: *The Colorado branch of our store has done well this year.*
4. *verb* If you **branch out,** you start doing something new.
branch (branch)
▷ *noun, plural* **branches** ▷ *verb* **branches, branching, branched**

brand
1. *noun* A name that identifies a product or the company that makes it, as in *a brand of shampoo.*
2. *verb* To burn a mark on the skin of cattle and other animals to show who owns them. ▷ *noun* **brand**
3. *verb* To call by a shameful name: *The politician was branded a liar.*
brand (brand)
▷ *verb* **branding, branded**

brandish *verb* To hold up something, such as a weapon, and wave it around. **bran·dish** (**bran**-dish) ▷ *verb* **brandishes, brandishing, brandished**

brand-new *adjective* Never used before; completely new, or recently purchased: *His skates are brand-new.* **brand-new** (bran-noo)

Word History

The word **brand-new** is a reminder of the time when all metal tools were made by a blacksmith working with fire and an anvil, which is an iron block. *Brand* is an Old English word meaning a "piece of burning wood," so something that is *brand-new* is like a metal tool that a blacksmith has just made: It is as hot as a log that has just been taken off the fire.

brandy *noun* A strong alcoholic drink made from wine or fruit juice. **brand·y** (bran-dee)

brash *adjective*
1. Disrespectful in a loud way that people notice: *The new principal will not tolerate rude or brash behavior.*
2. Overly hasty or without thinking ahead, as in *a brash decision.*
3. Unattractively showy or overly bright: *The show's brash colors and bright lights made it difficult to watch.* **brash** (brash)
▷ *adjective* **brasher, brashest** ▷ *noun* **brashness**
▷ *adverb* **brashly**

brass
1. *noun* A shiny yellow metal made from copper and zinc.
2. *adjective* The **brass** section of an orchestra is composed of musical instruments that are made of brass, such as the trumpet and the trombone. **brass** (bras)

brat *noun* An unpleasant or spoiled child who misbehaves. **brat** (brat)

brat

bratwurst *noun* A kind of pork sausage that is often fried or grilled. Also known as **brats**: *Bratwurst, corn, and coleslaw are the perfect picnic foods.* **brat·wurst** (braht-*wurst*)

brava *interjection* A way to say "Well done!" to a woman or group of women. **bra·va** (brah-vah)

bravado *noun* If you are full of **bravado,** you try to impress someone by pretending to be braver or more confident than you really are: *Danielle could see how scared Rob was, despite his bravado.* **bra·va·do** (bruh-**vah**-doh)

brave
1. *adjective* If you are **brave,** you have courage and are willing to face danger, difficulty, or pain: *You were brave to tell him to stop picking on Joe.* ▷ *adjective* **braver, bravest** ▷ *noun* **bravery** ▷ *adverb* **bravely**
2. *verb* If you **brave** something, you face it with courage and determination: *Firefighters brave danger each time they enter a burning building.* ▷ *verb* **braving, braved**
3. *noun* In history, a Native American warrior. **brave** (brave)

Synonyms

Brave describes someone who is unafraid to face danger: *The brave woman leaped into the water to save the drowning boy.*

- -

■ **Courageous** refers to a person who faces danger repeatedly or for an extended time: *The courageous rescue workers searched the collapsed building despite the risks.*

■ **Bold** refers to someone or something that is fearless and daring: *It was a bold move for Dorothy to speak to the Wizard of Oz.*

■ **Fearless** describes someone who takes great risks in dangerous situations: *The fearless performer walked on the tightrope high above the floor of the circus tent.*

■ **Heroic** refers to people or actions that are inspiring to others because they are so courageous: *The sergeant received many medals for his heroic deeds during the war.*

■ **Valiant** describes someone with great courage or something requiring great courage: *It took a valiant effort to carry the injured hiker down the mountain.*

bravo *interjection* Well done! **bra·vo** (brah-voh or brah-**voh**)

brawl *noun* A rough or noisy fight: *The boys got into quite a brawl over which team had the ball.* **brawl** (brawl) ▷ *verb* **brawl**

bray *verb*
1. When a donkey **brays,** it makes a loud, harsh cry. ▷ *noun* **bray**
2. When a person **brays,** he or she speaks or laughs in a way that sounds like a donkey. **bray** (bray)
▷ *verb* **braying, brayed**

brazen *adjective*

1. Bold, self-assured, and shameless: *His brazen boasting made him unpopular at work.* ▷ *adverb* **brazenly**

2. Sounding harsh or loud. **braz·en** (**bray**-zuhn)

breach

1. *verb* To break through something; to make a hole in something: *The waves breached the sea wall, and water poured into the streets.* ▷ *verb* **breaches, breaching, breached**

2. *noun* A failure to live up to a law or promise, as in *a breach of contract.*

3. *noun* A break in a relationship: *Joel and Anthony never mended the breach in their friendship.* **breach** (breech)

▷ *noun, plural* **breaches**

bread *noun*

1. A food made from flour, water, and yeast, shaped into loaves and baked.

2. *(slang)* Money. **bread** (bred)

breadth *noun*

1. The distance or measurement from one side of something to the other, as in *length, breadth, and height.*

2. Wide range or scope: *Johanna's breadth of knowledge about gardening is amazing.* **breadth** (bredth)

breadwinner *noun* Someone whose earnings are the main source of support for a family or household. **bread·win·ner** (**bred**-*win*-ur)

break

1. *verb* To cause something to crack, snap off, or separate into pieces: *Elephants can break rocks just by stepping on them.* ▷ *noun* **break** ▷ *noun* **breakage** ▷ *adjective* **breakable** ▷ *adjective* **broken**

2. *verb* To damage something so that it doesn't work: *We broke the lawn mower by running over a rock.*

3. *noun* A short rest, pause, or vacation: *Write another paragraph and then take a break.*

4. *verb* To stop, as in *to break a bad habit.*

5. *verb* To do better than, as in *to break a record.*

6. *verb* If someone **breaks** the rules, the person fails to obey them: *George broke one of the most important rules of rafting: Never panic.*

7. break in *verb* To force your way into a building.

8. break out *verb* To start suddenly: *By the end of the month, war broke out.* **break** (brayk)

breaker

Break sounds like **brake**.

▷ *verb* **breaking, broke** (brohk), **broken** (**brohk**-in)

breakdown *noun*

1. If your car has a **breakdown,** it stops moving because something has gone wrong with it.

2. A sudden collapse in someone's health, as in *a nervous breakdown.*

3. A case of something failing or falling apart, as in *a communications breakdown.* **break·down** (**brayk**-doun)

breaker *noun* A big sea wave that breaks into foam when it reaches the shore. **break·er** (**bray**-kur)

breakfast *noun* The first meal of the day, or a meal eaten in the morning. **break·fast** (**brek**-fuhst)

break-in *noun* The act of forcibly entering a building or house in order to steal things: *There was a series of break-ins in the neighborhood.*

breakthrough *noun* A successful, often sudden development that makes progress possible: *The doctors had just about given up on finding a cure for the disease when they had a breakthrough.* **break·through** (**brayk**-*throo*) ▷ *adjective* **breakthrough**

breakwater *noun* A barrier that protects a harbor or beach from the force of waves. **break·wa·ter** (**brayk**-*waw*-tur)

breast *noun*

1. One of the glands in a female mammal that can produce milk to feed her young.

2. The chest of a person or an animal: *The bird had black wings and a red breast.* **breast** (brest)

breaststroke *noun* A style of swimming facedown in which you stretch your arms out in front of your head and then sweep them back to your sides while kicking your legs like a frog. **breast·stroke** (**brest**-*stroke*)

breath *noun*

1. The air that you take into and send out of your lungs: *Take a deep breath before you begin.*

2. If you are **out of breath,** you are having trouble breathing or are gasping for air.

3. When you say something **under your breath,** you say it in a very quiet voice. **breath** (breth)

breathe *verb*

1. To take air into and send it out of your lungs: *With so much smoke in the air, it was difficult to breathe.*

2. To whisper: *Don't breathe a word to anyone.* **breathe** (breeTH)

▷ *verb* **breathing, breathed**

breather *noun* A short pause or rest: *After I dusted, I took a breather before doing the vacuuming.* **breath·er** (**bree**-THur)

breathless *adjective*
1. Out of breath.
2. If you are **breathless,** you are experiencing a strong feeling: *We were breathless with excitement when the curtain went up.*
breath·less (**breth**-lis)

breathtaking *adjective* Very beautiful, impressive, or awe-inspiring: *The view of the sunset from the Grand Canyon is breathtaking.* **breath·tak·ing** (**breth**-*tay*-king) ▷ *adverb* **breathtakingly**

breed
1. *verb* To keep animals or plants under controlled conditions so they produce more and better quality offspring: *She was breeding a new kind of rose.* ▷ *noun* **breeder**
2. *verb* When animals **breed,** they mate and give birth to their young.
3. *noun* A particular type of plant or animal, as in *a friendly breed of dog.*
breed (breed)
▷ *verb* **breeding, bred** (bred)

breeze
1. *noun* A light wind. ▷ *adjective* **breezy**
2. *verb* To move quickly and easily: *Once we passed the city, the traffic breezed along.* ▷ *verb* **breezing, breezed**
breeze (breez)

brew *verb*
1. To make tea or coffee by mixing it with hot water.
2. To make beer.
3. To start developing: *There's a storm brewing off the coast.*
brew (broo)
▷ *verb* **brewing, brewed** ▷ *noun* **brew**

brewery *noun* A place where beer is made. **brew·er·y** (**broo**-ur-ee) ▷ *noun, plural* **breweries**

Brexit *noun* The process of the United Kingdom leaving the European Union. Brexit happened because of a special referendum in 2016 when a slim majority voted in favor of it. **Brex·it** (**breg**-zit)

briar *See* **brier.** **bri·ar** (**brye**-ur)

bribe
1. *noun* Money or a gift that you offer someone to persuade the person to do what you want him or her to do: *Candy was the only bribe that my little sister would accept.*
2. *verb* To persuade someone to do something by offering them money or a gift: *According to a news story I read, he tried to bribe one of the jurors.* ▷ *verb* **bribing, bribed** ▷ *noun* **bribery**
bribe (bribe)

brick *noun* A block of clay, baked in the sun or in a kiln and used for building. **brick** (brik)

bride *noun* A woman on her wedding day or one who has just gotten married. **bride** (bride) ▷ *adjective* **bridal**

bridegroom *noun* A man on his wedding day or one who has just gotten married. **bride·groom** (**bride**-groom)

bridesmaid *noun* A female relative or close friend of a bride, who helps the bride get ready for the wedding and who assists at the ceremony. **brides·maid** (**bridez**-*mayd*)

bridge
1. *noun* A structure built over a river, railroad, or road that allows people or vehicles to cross to the other side. ▷ *verb* **bridge**
2. *noun* A card game in which a deck of cards is divided evenly among the four players.
3. *noun* The bony part of your nose between your eyes.
4. If something **bridges a gap,** it makes the difference between two groups or things seem less important: *It's important that we bridge the gap between the freshman and senior classes.* ▷ *verb* **bridging, bridged**
bridge (brij)

bridge

bridle *noun* A harness that fits around a horse's head and is used to guide or control the horse. **bri·dle** (**brye**-duhl) ▷ *verb* **bridle**

brief

1. *adjective* Lasting only a little while, as in *a brief stop.*

2. *adjective* Using as few words as possible: *Please try to make your speech brief.*

3. *verb* To give information, instructions, or advice that will prepare someone: *The sales manager briefed her staff on the new products.* ▷ *verb* **briefing, briefed**

4. *noun* An outline of the main information and arguments of a legal case.

brief (breef)

▷ *adjective* **briefer, briefest** ▷ *adverb* **briefly**

briefcase *noun* A flat, rectangular bag with a handle, used for carrying books and papers. **brief·case** (**breef**-*kase*)

brier *noun* A prickly twig, or the shrub that it grows on: *Roses are briers.* **bri·er** (**brye**-ur)

brig *noun*

1. A military prison, usually on a ship: *The sailor was thrown in the brig.*

2. A sailing ship with two masts and square sails.

brig (brig)

brigade *noun*

1. A unit of an army, larger than a battalion but smaller than a division.

2. A group of workers organized for a special purpose: *We quickly formed a bucket brigade to put out the fire.*

bri·gade (bri-**gayd**)

bright *adjective*

1. Giving out or reflecting a large amount of light, as in *a bright star.* ▷ *adverb* **brightly**

2. A **bright** color is bold and vivid, as in *bright orange.*

3. Smart: *Professor Stark called Dan his brightest student in years.*

bright (brite)

▷ *adjective* **brighter, brightest** ▷ *noun* **brightness**

brighten *verb* To make something brighter or to become brighter: *Their faces brightened up when Grandma walked in.* **bright·en** (**brye**-tuhn) ▷ *verb* **brightening, brightened**

brilliant *adjective*

1. Full of light or shining brightly, as in *brilliant sunshine.*

2. Very smart, as in *a brilliant thinker.*

3. Splendid, or terrific, as in *a brilliant performance.*

bril·liant (**bril**-yuhnt)

▷ *noun* **brilliance** ▷ *adverb* **brilliantly**

brim *noun*

1. The edge of a hat that sticks out over the face and neck of the person wearing it.

2. The edge of a cup or glass: *The glass is filled to the brim.*

brim (brim)

brine *noun* Seawater, or water that is very salty: *Pickles are usually stored in brine.* **brine** (brine)

bring *verb*

1. To take someone or something with you: *Bring your own lunch.*

2. To cause something to happen: *Clouds often bring rain.*

3. To sell for: *My coin collection should bring a good price.*

4. If a company **brings out** a product, it introduces the product and starts selling it.

5. bring up To raise a child: *Tina was brought up mostly by her grandmother.*

bring (bring)

▷ *verb* **bringing, brought** (brawt)

brink *noun*

1. The edge of something, before it drops off steeply or meets the water: *We found her standing on the brink of a rocky ledge.*

2. on the brink The point at which something is about to begin: *The United States was on the brink of war.*

brink (bringk)

brisk *adjective*

1. Quick and lively, as in *a brisk pace.*

2. If the wind or weather is **brisk,** it is chilly but refreshing.

brisk (brisk)

▷ *adjective* **brisker, briskest** ▷ *adverb* **briskly**

bristle

1. *noun* A stiff, animal or man-made hair, used to make a brush.

2. *verb* To show anger: *I bristled when Nick asked me to leave the room.* ▷ *verb* **bristling, bristled**

▷ *adjective* **bristly**

bris·tle (**bris**-uhl)

British English *noun* The form of English used by the people in Great Britain: *British English is different in many ways from the English spoken in the United States or Canada.* **Brit·ish Eng·lish** (**brit**-ish **ing**-glish)

brittle *adjective* Likely to snap off, crack, or break: *There was a brittle layer of ice on the pond.* **brit·tle** (**brit**-uhl) ▷ *adjective* **brittler, brittlest**

bro *noun* *(informal)* A boy or man, especially one who spends time with other males doing things they enjoy: *I was on a surfing trip in Mexico with some bros when I broke my leg.* **bro** (broh) ▷ *noun, plural* **bros**

broach *verb* When you **broach** a subject, you bring it up for discussion. **broach** (brohch) ▷ *verb* **broaches, broaching, broached**

broad *adjective*
1. Wider than usual from side to side: *They live on a broad, tree-lined street.*
2. Including many things: *The company sells a broad range of laptop computers.*
3. Without a lot of detail, as in *a broad outline.*
broad (brawd)
▷ *adjective* **broader, broadest** ▷ *adverb* **broadly**

broadband *noun* A fast internet connection over a cable modem or a telephone line, as in *a broadband provider.* **broad·band** (brawd-*band*)

broadcast
1. *verb* To send out a radio or television program to its audience. ▷ *verb* **broadcasting, broadcasted** ▷ *noun* **broadcaster** ▷ *noun* **broadcasting**
2. *noun* A radio or television program: *Don't miss tonight's broadcast of the election debates.*
broad·cast (brawd-*kast*)

broaden *verb* To make something broader or more tolerant: *The principal broadened the rules*

Bronze Age

Bronze is a metal made by combining copper and tin. Its use probably first occurred in the Middle East around 3500 B.C. Bronze is stronger than copper alone. Its invention allowed people to produce better tools and weapons. After the discovery of how to make iron, around 1200 B.C., iron replaced bronze for most purposes. The transition from bronze to iron began in western Asia and Egypt.

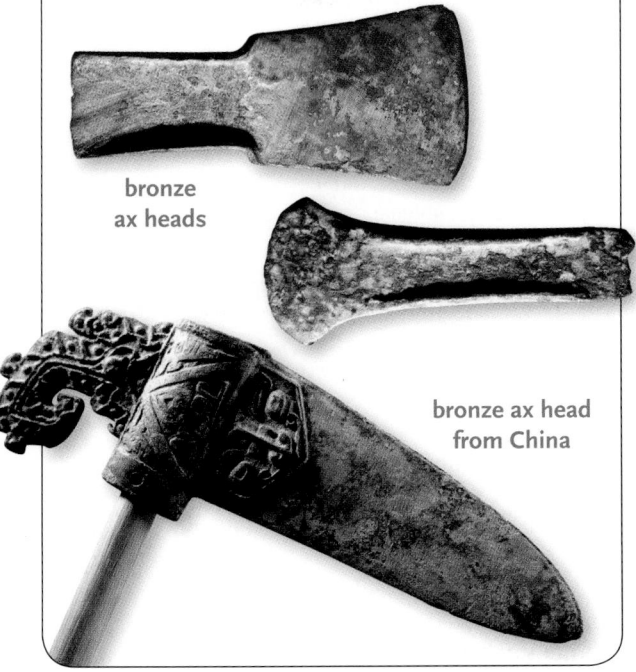

bronze
ax heads

bronze ax head
from China

of the dress code slightly. **broad·en** (braw-duhn)
▷ *verb* **broadening, broadened**

broad-minded *adjective* If you are **broad-minded,** you are open to new ideas and other people's views. **broad-mind·ed** (**mine**-did)

brocade *noun* Fabric woven with a raised pattern. **bro·cade** (broh-**kayd**)

broccoli *noun* A vegetable with many clusters of green flower buds on thick stalks. **broc·co·li** (**brah**-kuh-lee)

brochure *noun* A booklet with pictures that advertises or gives information about something: *When you go to the museum, will you pick up a brochure for me?* **bro·chure** (broh-**shoor**)

broil *verb*
1. To cook by exposing food directly to the source of heat from above.
2. To be or make very hot: *We were broiling in the sun.*
broil (broil)
▷ *verb* **broiling, broiled**

broiler *noun* The part of an oven that heats food from above. **broil·er** (**broi**-lur)

broke *adjective* (*informal*) Having no money: *I wanted to go to the movies, but I was broke.* **broke** (broke)

broken
1. *verb* The past participle of **break.**
2. *adjective* In pieces; not whole: *Be careful of the broken glass on the floor.*
3. *adjective* Not working: *The radio part still works, but the CD player is broken.*
brok·en (**broh**-kuhn)

bronchial tubes *noun, plural* Tubes in your lungs that air passes through when you breathe. **bron·chi·al tubes** (**brahng**-kee-uhl)

bronchitis *noun* A disease of the bronchial tubes inside your lungs. **bron·chi·tis** (brahng-**kye**-tis)

bronco *noun* A wild horse found in the western United States. **bron·co** (**brahng**-koh) ▷ *noun, plural* **broncos**

brontosaurus *noun* See **apatosaurus.** **bron·to·saur·us** (*brahn*-tuh-**sor**-uhs)

bronze
1. *noun* A yellowish-brown metal that is a mixture of copper and tin.
2. *noun* A yellowish-brown color.
3. *adjective* Being yellowish brown in color.
4. *verb* If you **bronze** yourself, you get a dark suntan. ▷ *verb* **bronzing, bronzed**
bronze (brahnz)

Bronze Age *noun* A period of history, before the introduction of iron, when bronze was commonly used to make tools and weapons. This period occurred at different times in different parts of the world.

brooch *noun* A large, decorative pin that you wear at or near your neck: *My grandmother never went anywhere without her butterfly brooch.* **brooch** (brohch *or* brooch)

brood
1. *verb* To worry or think deeply about something: *Juan was brooding about his grades.* ▷ *verb* **brooding, brooded**
2. *noun* A group of young birds who all hatched at the same time.
3. *noun* (*informal*) All the children in one family: *Mrs. Selden was out shopping with her brood.*
brood (brood)

brook *noun* A small stream; a creek. **brook** (bruk)

broom *noun* A long-handled brush, used for sweeping floors. **broom** (broom)

broth *noun* The liquid that remains after meat or vegetables have been cooked in water. **broth** (brawth)

brother *noun* A boy or man who has the same parents as another person. **broth·er** (bruhTH-ur) ▷ *adjective* **brotherly**

brotherhood *noun*
1. Warm feelings and goodwill among people.
2. A group that works or lives together in a brotherly way.
broth·er·hood (bruhTH-ur-*hud*)

brother-in-law *noun* Someone's **brother-in-law** is the brother of his or her spouse or the husband of his or her sister. ▷ *noun, plural* **brothers-in-law**

brought *verb* The past tense and the past participle of **bring**. **brought** (brawt)

brow *noun*
1. A person's forehead: *He was bleeding from a deep cut on his brow.*
2. The upper part of a steep place, as in *the brow of a hill.*
brow (brou)

brown
1. *noun* The color of chocolate, leather, or coffee. ▷ *adjective* **brown**
2. *verb* To make something brown, especially by cooking it: *Brown the chopped meat in a pan.* ▷ *verb* **browning, browned**
brown (broun)

brownie *noun* A square piece of a heavy, rich chocolate cake. **brown·ie** (brou-nee)

brownout *noun* A partial loss of electrical power that causes the lights to dim: *When we all turned on our air conditioners, it caused a brownout.* **brown·out** (broun-*out*)

browse *verb*
1. To look at something in a casual way: *I browsed through a few of the books on the shelf.*
2. To eat by nibbling on twigs, leaves, or shoots: *The deer browsed on the fresh buds.*
3. To spend time looking at different things that interest you on the internet.
browse (brouz)
▷ *verb* **browsing, browsed**

browser *noun*
1. A computer program that lets you find and look through webpages or other data: *Which browser do you use most?*
2. An animal that eats by browsing.
brows·er (brou-zur)

bruise *noun* A discolored area that appears when blood vessels burst underneath your skin, usually because you have fallen or been hit by something. **bruise** (brooz) ▷ *verb* **bruise** ▷ *adjective* **bruised**

brunch *noun* A late-morning meal that combines breakfast and lunch, typically eaten on a weekend. **brunch** (bruhnch)

brunette *adjective* Having brown or black hair. **bru·nette** (broo-net) ▷ *noun* **brunette**

brush
1. *noun* An object with bristles fastened to a handle, used for scrubbing, sweeping, painting, or smoothing hair.
2. *verb* To clean, groom, or apply with a brush.
3. *verb* To touch something lightly or gently: *The runner brushed his opponent as he passed him.*
4. *noun* An area of land where small trees and shrubs grow.
brush (bruhsh)
▷ *noun, plural* **brushes**
▷ *verb* **brushes, brushing, brushed**

Brussels sprout *noun*
A vegetable that looks like a small head of cabbage.
Brus·sels sprout (bruhs-uhlz *sprout*)
▷ *noun, plural* **Brussels sprouts**

Brussels sprouts

brutal *adjective* Extremely cruel or violent: *The final battle of the war was a brutal one.* **bru·tal** (broo-tuhl) ▷ *noun* **brutality** (broo-tal-i-tee) ▷ *adverb* **brutally**

brute
1. *noun* A savage or violent person or animal: *That dog of theirs is a real brute.*
2. *adjective* Involving physical strength rather than intelligence, as in *brute force.*
brute (broot)

BTW *adverb* The short form of *by the way* that people use in texts and emails, to introduce something that is slightly related to what they said before: *I will be late getting home. BTW, there are good leftovers in the fridge.*

bubble
1. *noun* One of the tiny balls of gas that rise to the surface of boiling water, soda, or other fizzy drinks.
2. *noun* A thin film of liquid surrounding a ball of air or some other gas, as in *blowing bubbles.*
3. *noun* A **bubble** in a market is a situation where the price of something becomes higher than its actual worth: *During the housing bubble, the cost of a home more than doubled.*
4. *verb* To form or produce bubbles: *Soup bubbled on the stove.* ▷ *verb* **bubbling, bubbled**
bub·ble (**buhb**-uhl)

bubbly *adjective*
1. If a liquid is **bubbly,** it is full of bubbles.
2. If a person is **bubbly,** he or she is very cheerful and talkative.
bub·bly (**buhb**-lee)

buccaneer *noun* A pirate, especially one who attacked Spanish ships in the Caribbean in the 17th century. **buc·ca·neer** (*buhk*-uh-**neer**)

Word History

In the Caribbean and West Indies, people prepared meat by drying and smoking it on a wooden barbecue placed over a fire. French speakers adopted the native people's word for this kind of barbecue and spelled it as "boucan," and from this word we get the term **buccaneer**. In French, a *boucanier* referred to a person who smoked meat on a *boucan*. This name was given to French hunters in that region, some of whom were also pirates.

buck
1. *noun* A male deer, antelope, or rabbit.
2. *verb* If a horse **bucks,** it jumps in the air with its back arched.
3. If you **pass the buck,** you shift the responsibility for something to someone else.
4. *noun* (*slang*) A dollar.
5. *verb* To stubbornly resist something or go against it, as in *to buck family tradition.*
buck (buhk)
▷ *verb* **bucking, bucked**

bucket *noun* A plastic, wooden, or metal container with a handle, used for carrying liquids or other things. **buck·et** (**buhk**-it)

buckle
1. *noun* A flat frame with a pin, used to fasten shoes, belts, or straps. ▷ *verb* **buckle**
2. *verb* To collapse under pressure: *I tried to run away, but my legs buckled.*
3. **buckle down** *verb* To work very hard.
buck·le (**buhk**-uhl)
▷ *verb* **buckling, buckled**

buckskin *noun* A strong, soft material made from the skin of a deer or sheep. **buck·skin** (**buhk**-*skin*)

buckwheat *noun* A plant with small seeds, used as cattle feed or made into flour. **buck·wheat** (**buhk**-*weet*)

Word History

Sometimes when words are borrowed from other languages, only one part of the word is translated. For example, **buckwheat** has its origins in the old Dutch noun *boecweite*, a compound of *boeke*, meaning "beech," and *weite*, meaning "wheat." The plant received this name because its seeds look like the nuts of the beech tree. In English, *boec-* did not get translated as "beech," but *weite* became "wheat."

bud *noun* A small knob on a plant that grows into a leaf, shoot, or flower. **bud** (buhd) ▷ *verb* **bud**

Buddha *noun*
1. The man whose teachings are the basis of Buddhism. He lived in India around 500 B.C.
2. A statue or picture of Buddha.
Bud·dha (**boo**-duh)

Buddhism *noun* A way of life based on the teachings of Buddha. Buddhists believe that wanting things is the cause of most suffering, and that we are born again after we die. **Bud·dhism** (**boo**-*diz*-uhm) ▷ *noun* **Buddhist** ▷ *adjective* **Buddhist**

statue of Buddha

budding *adjective* In the early stages of maturity, or gaining skill: *She is a budding artist.* **bud·ding** (**buhd**-ing)

buddy *noun* A close friend; a pal: *He and his uncle were real buddies.* **bud·dy** (**buhd**-ee) ▷ *noun, plural* **buddies**

budge *verb*
1. To make or cause a slight movement: *I tried to lie down on the sofa, but my dog wouldn't budge.*
2. To give in or change your opinion: *Judith tried every argument she could think of, but her mother wouldn't budge.*
budge (buhj)
▷ *verb* **budging, budged**

budget

1. *noun* A plan for how much money you will earn and spend during a particular period of time: *She presented a detailed budget for the coming year.*
▷ *adjective* **budgetary**
2. *verb* If you **budget** your money, you plan how you will spend it: *Bruce budgeted $30 a month for movie tickets.* ▷ *verb* **budgeting, budgeted**
budg·et (**buhj**-it)

buffalo: American bison

Word History

The British official who was responsible for planning government spending carried his papers in a leather bag called a **budget**. In the 18th century, the English began to use the word for his bag to mean the spending plan itself. The English word *budget* comes from the French word *bougette*, meaning "little leather bag."

---

buff

1. *noun* A yellowish-beige color. ▷ *adjective* **buff**
2. *noun* (*informal*) Someone who is very interested in a subject and knows a lot about it, as in *a railroad buff.*
3. *verb* To polish something: *He buffed his car every Saturday.* ▷ *verb* **buffing, buffed**
buff (buhf)

buffalo *noun*

1. A type of wild ox with horns that curve backward, found in Europe, Africa, and Asia.
2. An American bison.
buf·fa·lo (**buhf**-uh-*loh*)
▷ *noun, plural* **buffaloes** *or* **buffalos** *or* **buffalo**

buffer *noun*

1. Something that softens a blow or forms a protective barrier: *The padding on the outfield wall serves as a buffer when players run into it.*
2. Someone who keeps opposing groups or individuals from harming each other or coming into direct contact: *Sadie had to act as the buffer between her parents during the divorce.*
buff·er (**buhf**-ur)
▷ *verb* **buffer**

buffet

1. (**buhf**-it) *verb* To strike repeatedly: *The wind buffeted the trees.* ▷ *verb* **buffeting, buffeted**
2. (buh-**fay**) *noun* A meal in which people serve themselves from a table on which many different foods are laid out: *Amy had three kinds of cake at the all-you-can-eat buffet.*
3. (buh-**fay**) *noun* A piece of furniture with a flat top for serving food and drawers for storing dishes and silverware.
buf·fet

bug

1. *noun* A small insect.
2. *noun* An illness caused by a germ, as in *a flu bug.*
3. *noun* An error in a computer program or system: *I wouldn't buy that software until they've worked the bugs out.*
4. *verb* To hide microphones in a place in order to hear what people are saying: *We were afraid to talk, thinking that the room was bugged.* ▷ *noun* **bug**
5. *verb* (*informal*) If people or things **bug** you, they bother or annoy you.
bug (buhg)
▷ *verb* **bugging, bugged**

buggy *noun*

1. A light carriage with two wheels pulled by a horse.
2. A baby carriage.
bug·gy (**buhg**-ee)
▷ *noun, plural* **buggies**

bugle *noun*
A musical instrument shaped like a trumpet but without valves. Bugles are often used in the army to send signals to the troops. **bu·gle** (**byoo**-guhl) ▷ *noun* **bugler**

build

1. *verb* To make something by putting parts or materials together: *You can build a house out of recycled plastic.*
2. *noun* The way a person's body is put together: *Theo has the build of a football player.*
3. build up *verb* To gradually increase or develop: *He built up his leg muscles with special exercises.*
build (bild)
▷ *verb* **building, built** (bilt)

building *noun*
A structure with walls and a roof, such as a house or a factory: *Her apartment building is near the ocean.* **build·ing** (**bil**-ding)

built-in *adjective*
Built as a permanent part of something, as in *built-in shelves.*

bulb *noun*

1. The underground, onion-shaped part of some plants that stores food from which the plants grow: *Tulips, lilies, and garlic are among the plants that grow from bulbs.*
2. The part of an electric light that glows when switched on: *I knocked the lamp over and broke the bulb.*
bulb (buhlb)

bulge *verb* To swell or stick out: *His eyes were bulging with fear.* **bulge** (buhlj) ▷ *verb* **bulging, bulged** ▷ *noun* **bulge**

bulk *noun*
1. Large size: *We were surprised by the bulk of the dresser.*
2. The **bulk** of something is the greater part of it: *I've already moved the bulk of my things into the new apartment.*
3. When you buy something **in bulk,** you buy it in large quantities, usually for a lower price.
bulk (buhlk)

bulky *adjective*
1. Large and awkward to handle, as in *a bulky package.*
2. Taking up a lot of space, as in *a bulky sweater.*
bulk·y (**buhl**-kee)
▷ *adjective* **bulkier, bulkiest**

bull *noun*
1. An adult male of the cattle family.
2. An adult male of a large species of animals, such as elephants, seals, moose, or whales.
bull (bul)

bulldog *noun* A strong dog with a round head, powerful jaws, and short legs. **bull·dog** (**bul**-*dawg*)

bulldozer *noun* A powerful tractor with a broad, curved blade in the front, used for clearing ground. **bull·doz·er** (**bul**-*doh*-zur)

bullet *noun*
1. A metal object fired from a gun, usually shaped like a pointed cylinder or ball.
2. A dot or symbol that is printed before items in a list so that they stand out. ▷ *adjective* **bulleted**
bul·let (**bul**-it)

bulletin *noun* An official statement or brief news summary, broadcast on television or the radio. **bul·le·tin** (**bul**-i-tin)

bulletin board *noun*
1. A place on a wall where people can put signs and notices that they want others to see.
2. A place on the internet where anyone, or members of an organization, can put notices for others to see.

bullfight *noun* A public entertainment in which people fight against bulls, popular in Spain, Portugal, and parts of Latin America. **bull·fight** (**bul**-*fite*) ▷ *noun* **bullfighter**

bullfrog *noun* A large frog with a deep croak. **bull·frog** (**bul**-*frawg*)

bull's-eye *noun* The center of a target that is usually round and is used for archery or darts.

bully *verb*
1. To frighten or pick on people who are smaller or weaker than you are: *The brothers were accused of bullying a classmate.*
2. If you **bully** someone **into** something, you make him or her do it by using force or threats: *He bullied the other man into giving him a loan.*
bul·ly (**bul**-ee)
▷ *verb* **bullies, bullying, bullied** ▷ *noun* **bully**

bumblebee *noun* A large, hairy bee with yellow and black stripes that hums when it flies. **bum·ble·bee** (**buhm**-buhl-*bee*)

bump
1. *verb* To knock or run into something: *I bumped into the tree.* ▷ *noun* **bump**
2. *noun* A light blow or collision.
3. *noun* A round lump or swelling on the skin, as in *a nasty bump on the head.*
4. *verb* If you **bump into** someone, you meet the person by chance.
5. *verb* To move or travel in a jolting way: *The cart bumped along the dirt road.*
bump (buhmp)
▷ *verb* **bumping, bumped**

bumper
1. *noun* The horizontal bar or projecting piece on the front or back of a vehicle that helps protect it in an accident.
2. *adjective* Very large: *The gardener had a bumper crop of corn this year.*
bump·er (**buhm**-pur)

bumpy *adjective* Very uneven or full of bumps, as in *a bumpy road.* **bump·y** (**buhm**-pee)
▷ *adjective* **bumpier, bumpiest**

bun *noun*
1. A round bread roll, as in *sesame-seed hamburger buns.*
2. A tight, round knot of hair worn at the back of the head.
bun (buhn)

bulldozer

bunch *noun* A group of people or things of the same kind: *Noel picked a bunch of flowers for his wife.* **bunch** (buhnch) ▷ *noun, plural* **bunches**

bundle *verb*
1. To tie, wrap, or gather things together. ▷ *noun* **bundle**
2. To push or carry someone in a forceful way: *We bundled the children off to the movies.*
3. To sell or deliver software programs together rather than separately: *New laptops often come bundled with trial versions of popular programs.*
bun·dle (**buhn**-duhl)
▷ *verb* **bundling, bundled**

bungalow *noun* A small house, usually with only one floor. **bun·ga·low** (**buhng**-guh-*loh*)

Word History

When the British colonized India, they referred to the unfamiliar single-story houses they found there as *bangla*. They got the name from a Hindi word that originally meant "belonging to Bengal." Hindi speakers had named the **bungalows** after the Bengal region of India, where that type of house is common. When things are named for the place they come from, we call the word a *toponym*.

bungee *noun* An elastic cord with hooks at either end, used to hold things in place. **bun·gee** (**buhn**-jee)

bungle *verb* To do something badly or clumsily, resulting in failure or the wrong outcome: *Because the electrician bungled the repair job, all the lights went out.* **bun·gle** (**buhng**-guhl) ▷ *verb* **bungling, bungled**

bunk
1. *noun* A narrow bed built into or against a wall.
2. bunk bed *noun* A piece of furniture consisting of two beds, one stacked on top of another.
3. *verb* To sleep in a bed or spend the night: *Tony bunked with his cousins last night.* ▷ *verb* **bunking, bunked**
bunk (buhngk)

bunker *noun*
1. An underground shelter, especially during wartime.
2. A sand trap on a golf course.
bun·ker (**buhng**-kur)

bunny *noun* (*informal*) A rabbit. **bun·ny** (**buhn**-ee) ▷ *noun, plural* **bunnies**

Bunsen burner *noun* A device used in laboratories that burns gas to provide a small, hot flame. **Bun·sen burner** (**buhn**-suhn)

bunt *verb* To tap a baseball lightly with a bat, so that the ball doesn't go very far. **bunt** (buhnt) ▷ *verb* **bunting, bunted**

bunting *noun*
1. A light cloth used for making flags.
2. Decorations made of the same fabric and colors as the American flag.
bun·ting (**buhn**-ting)

buoy *noun* A floating marker, often with a bell or a light, that warns boats of underwater dangers or shows them where to go. **buoy** (**boo**-ee *or* boi)

buoyant *adjective*
1. Able to float or stay afloat. ▷ *noun* **buoyancy**
2. Cheerful and lighthearted, as in *a buoyant personality.*
buoy·ant (**boi**-uhnt *or* **boo**-yuhnt)
▷ *adverb* **buoyantly**

burden
1. *noun* A heavy load that has to be carried: *I'm sure that backpack is quite a burden.*
2. *verb* To load or overload someone: *We burdened Tony with the suitcases.* ▷ *verb* **burdening, burdened**
3. *noun* A serious task or responsibility: *The prosecutor has the burden of proving a defendant's guilt.*
4. *noun* A source of great worry: *Caring for a sick child turned out to be a terrible burden.*
bur·den (**bur**-duhn)
▷ *adjective* **burdensome**

bureau *noun*
1. A chest of drawers; a dresser.
2. An office or business that provides a specific service or kind of information, as in *a travel bureau.*
bu·reau (**byoor**-oh)

burger *noun* A sandwich consisting of a flat, round piece of beef or other food on a bun. Burger is short for **hamburger.** **burg·er** (**bur**-gur)

burglar *noun* Someone who breaks into a building and steals something: *Last month, a burglar robbed several homes in the neighborhood.* **bur·glar** (**bur**-glur) ▷ *noun* **burglary**

burial *noun* The placing of a dead body in the earth or sea. **bur·i·al** (**ber**-ee-uhl)

burlap *noun* A tough, coarse material used to make strong bags. **bur·lap** (bur-*lap*)

burly *adjective* Husky; strong and with large muscles: *The burly teenager was able to subdue the criminal until the police arrived.* **bur·ly** (bur-lee) ▷ *adjective* **burlier, burliest**

burn
1. *verb* To hurt or damage someone or something by means of heat, a chemical, or radiation: *It smells like Sam burned the toast again.*
2. *noun* An injury or mark caused by burning: *There was a cigarette burn in her new sweater.*
3. *verb* To feel very hot: *Erica is burning with fever.*
4. *verb* To feel strong emotion: *I burned with anger when I found out what Jackie did.*
5. *verb* If you **burn** a CD or DVD on your computer, you put data such as music or video on it.
burn (burn)
▷ *verb* **burning, burned** *or* **burnt** (burnt)

burner *noun*
1. The area on top of a stove where a flame or heat is used to cook things: *The water didn't boil because the burner wasn't working.*
2. A device on a computer that can write data onto CDs or DVDs: *She's got a really old computer that doesn't have a CD burner.*
burn·er (bur-nur)

burning *adjective* On fire: *Four people rushed out of the burning building just before it exploded.*
burn·ing (**bur**-ning)

burnt
1. *verb* A past tense and past participle of **burn**.
2. *adjective* Cooked too much, or damaged by fire.
burnt (burnt)

burp *verb* To make a noise as you release gases that have been forced up from your stomach out through your throat. **burp** (burp) ▷ *verb* **burping, burped** ▷ *noun* **burp**

burqa *noun* A garment worn by some Muslim women that completely covers the head, body, arms, and legs. **bur·qa** (bur-kuh)

burr *or* **bur** *noun*
1. A prickly pod that sticks to the clothing of people or the fur of animals.
2. The bush that produces these pods.
burr (bur)

burro *noun* A small donkey. **bur·ro** (bur-oh) **Burro** sounds like **borough** and **burrow**. ▷ *noun, plural* **burros**

burrow
1. *noun* A tunnel or hole in the ground made or used as a home by a rabbit or other animal.
2. *verb* To dig or live in such a tunnel or hole: *These animals burrow deep into the ground to stay warm.*
▷ *verb* **burrowing, burrowed**
bur·row (bur-oh)
Burrow sounds like **borough** and **burro**.

burst
1. *verb* To break apart suddenly and violently: *The plastic bag burst, and garbage spilled all over the ground.*
2. *noun* A sudden, brief outbreak of something, such as gunfire or applause.
3. *verb* To suddenly begin doing something: *Teresa burst into tears.*
4. *verb* To be very full: *The suitcase is bursting with clothes.*
burst (burst)
▷ *verb* **bursting, burst**

bury *verb*
1. To put a dead body in a grave or tomb.
2. To hide something underground or at the bottom of something: *I buried the letters in my dresser drawer.*
bur·y (ber-ee)
Bury sounds like **berry**. ▷ *verb* **buries, burying, buried**

bus
1. *noun* A large vehicle for carrying passengers, usually along a specific route. ▷ *noun, plural* **buses**
2. *verb* To take people somewhere by bus: *Eighty percent of our school's students are bussed.* ▷ *verb* **busing** *or* **bussing, bused** *or* **bussed**
bus (buhs)

bush *noun*
1. A shrub with many branches.
2. If you **beat around the bush,** you talk a lot but don't come to the point.
bush (bush)
▷ *noun, plural* **bushes**

bushel *noun* A unit of dry measure that tells how much a container holds. A bushel equals 32 quarts. **bush·el** (bush-uhl)

bushy *adjective* Thick and spreading, as in *a bushy beard.* **bush·y** (bush-ee) ▷ *adjective* **bushier, bushiest**

business *noun*
1. Commercial activity: *My parents do a lot of business with local builders.*
2. A person's job or profession: *My uncle is in the advertising business.*
3. A commercial organization: *She ran a travel business.*
4. If something is **none of your business,** it should not concern you.
busi·ness (**biz**-nis)
▷ *noun, plural* **businesses**

Butterflies

Butterflies can be distinguished by their size and by the color, pattern, and shape of their wings. There are four stages in the life cycle of a butterfly. First, the adult female lays an egg. The egg hatches into a larva, or caterpillar. The larva eats leaves and grows quickly. It then enters a resting state and is called a pupa, or chrysalis. The caterpillar emerges from the pupa state as an adult butterfly.

Morpho peleides

swallowtail

anise swallowtail after leaving chrysalis

monarch larva and butterfly

Priamus poseidon

business card *noun* A small card printed with a person's name, job, and company: *Her business card had her email address and other contact information.*

businesslike *adjective* Practical and unemotional: *Her businesslike manner reassures customers.* **busi·ness·like** (**biz**-nis-*like*)

bust
1. *noun* A sculpture of a person's head, neck, and shoulders.
2. *verb (informal)* To smash or break something.
▷ *verb* **busting, busted** *or* **bust** ▷ *adjective* **busted**
bust (buhst)

bustle *verb* To rush about or move energetically.
bus·tle (**buhs**-uhl) ▷ *verb* **bustling, bustled**
▷ *noun* **bustle**

busy *adjective*
1. Having a lot to do: *I was busy setting up for the debate.* ▷ *verb* **busy** ▷ *adverb* **busily**
2. If a place is **busy**, it is full of people and activity.
3. In use: *Your phone has been busy all morning.*
bus·y (**biz**-ee)
▷ *adjective* **busier, busiest**

busybody *noun* Someone who likes to know other people's business: *She won an Oscar for her role as a small-town busybody.* **bus·y·bod·y** (**biz**-ee-*bah*-dee)

▷ *noun, plural* **busybodies**

but
1. *conjunction* On the other hand: *He may be large, but he's not strong.*
2. *preposition* Other than: *There is no road to riches but through hard work.*
3. *preposition* With the exception of: *We've chosen everyone but him.*
4. *adverb* Only, or just: *The train left but a minute ago.*
but (buht)
But sounds like **butt**.

butcher *noun* Someone who cuts up and sells meat. **butch·er** (**buch**-ur)

butler *noun* The chief male servant in a house.
but·ler (**buht**-lur)

butt
1. *noun* A common and informal word for **buttocks**.
2. *noun* Someone who is teased or made fun of by other people: *She was the butt of everyone's jokes.*
3. *verb* To hit someone or something with the head or horns: *He butted the soccer ball halfway down the field.* ▷ *verb* **butting, butted**
4. *noun* The thicker end, as in *a rifle butt.*
butt (buht)
Butt sounds like **but**.

butte *noun* A hill or mountain with steep sides and a flat top that stands by itself, mostly found in the western United States. **butte** (byoot)

butter *noun* A yellowish fatty substance made by churning cream, used in cooking and to flavor food. **but·ter** (buht-ur)

buttercup *noun* A plant with bright yellow cup-shaped flowers. **but·ter·cup** (buht-ur-*kuhp*)

butterfly *noun*
1. An insect with a thin body and large, often colorful wings.
2. If you **have butterflies,** you are feeling very nervous. **but·ter·fly** (buht-ur-*flye*)
▷ *noun, plural* **butterflies**

buttermilk *noun* The sour liquid left over after butter has been churned from cream. **but·ter·milk** (buht-ur-*milk*)

butterscotch *noun* A flavor or candy made by mixing brown sugar, butter, and vanilla extract. **but·ter·scotch** (buht-ur-*skahch*)

buttocks *noun, plural* The fleshy part of your body that you sit on. **but·tocks** (buht-uhks)

button *noun*
1. A disc-shaped fastener that is used to join two parts of a piece of clothing. ▷ *verb* **button**
2. A small knob that you turn or press to control a machine, such as a TV or radio: *Holly pressed buttons at random until the computer turned on.* **but·ton** (buht-uhn)

buttonhole *noun* The small hole that you push a button through in order to close a garment. **but·ton·hole** (buht-uhn-*hole*)

buttress
1. *noun* A structure built against a wall to help support it.
2. *verb* To give support or make stronger: *Her argument is buttressed by the results of the experiment.*
▷ *verb* **buttresses, buttressing, buttressed**
but·tress (buht-ris)

buy
1. *verb* To get something in exchange for money. ▷ *verb* **buying, bought** (bawt)
2. *noun* A bargain: *The shirt was a good buy.*
buy (bye)
Buy sounds like **by.**

buyer *noun* Someone who buys, or who is interested in buying something: *There are three potential buyers for the failing business.* **buy·er** (bye-ur)

buzz *verb* To make a vibrating sound like that of a bee or a wasp. **buzz** (buhz) ▷ *verb* **buzzes,** buzzing, buzzed ▷ *noun* **buzz** ▷ *noun* **buzzer**

buzzard *noun* A large bird of prey, similar to a vulture, with a hooked beak and long, sharp claws. **buz·zard** (buhz-urd)

by
1. *preposition* Next to, or beside, as in *a phone by the door.*
2. *adverb* Near, or close at hand: *They just stood by and laughed.*
3. *preposition* Through the work of: *His portrait was painted by my father.*
4. *preposition* Through the means of: *We went home by bus.*
5. *preposition* Beyond, or past: *They drove by the accident.*
6. *adverb* Past: *Time goes by slowly.*
7. **by and by** *adverb* After a while; soon: *We'll do the work by and by.*
by (bye)
By sounds like **buy.**

bygone *adjective* Past or former: *Grandma had memories of bygone days.* **by·gone** (bye-*gawn*)

bypass
1. *noun* A highway that goes around an urban area rather than through the middle of it. ▷ *noun, plural* **bypasses**
2. *verb* To avoid something by using a different route: *He bypassed the heavy traffic on the highway by going on some side roads.* ▷ *verb* **bypasses, bypassing, bypassed** ▷ *adjective* **bypass**
by·pass (bye-*pas*)

by-product *noun* Something that is left over after you make or do something: *Sawdust is a by-product of sawing lumber.*

bystander *noun* Someone who is at a place where something happens to someone else; a spectator: *She was a bystander when the accident occurred.* **by·stand·er** (bye-*stan*-dur)

byte *noun* A unit of information stored in a computer. **byte** (bite)
Byte sounds like **bite.**

Byzantine *adjective*
1. Of or having to do with the ancient city of Byzantium (bi-**zan**-tee-uhm), where Istanbul, Turkey, is now located.
2. In the style of art or architecture popular in the Byzantine Empire. Byzantine buildings of the fifth and sixth centuries have large domes, rounded arches, and a lot of surface decoration, especially colored-glass mosaics.
Byz·an·tine (biz-uhn-*teen*)

buttress

About C The letter **C** is usually pronounced with a *k* sound when the letter is followed by *a, o,* or *u,* and most consonants. Examples: cat, cot, cut, clap. The letter *c* can also sound like the letter *s,* when it is followed by *e, i,* or *y.* Examples: cell, cite, cycle. When it makes the *s* sound, we call it a "soft c." *C* was a *g* in the Phoenician alphabet. The Romans made the two letters separate to represent different sounds.

c. Short for **cup** or the plural form *cups.*

cab *noun*
  1. A car that takes people from one place to another in exchange for money; a taxi.
  2. The driver's area of a large truck or machine, such as a bulldozer.
  cab (kab)

cabbage *noun* A large vegetable with green or purple leaves shaped into a round head. **cab·bage** (**kab**-ij)

cabin *noun*
  1. A small, simple house, often built of wood.
  2. A private room for passengers or members of the crew to sleep in on a ship.
  3. A section of an airplane for the passengers, crew, or cargo, as in *a first-class cabin.*
  cab·in (**kab**-in)

cabinet *noun*
  1. A piece of furniture with shelves or drawers.
  2. A group of advisers for the head of a government.
  cab·i·net (**kab**-uh-nit)

cable *noun*
  1. A thick rope made of wire.
  2. An insulated bundle of wires used for carrying electricity or communication signals, such as television.
  3. cable car A vehicle pulled by a moving cable, used for carrying people along city streets or up mountains.
  4. cable modem A modem that uses your cable television connection to provide high-speed access to the internet.
  ca·ble (**kay**-buhl)

caboose *noun* The last car on a freight train, occupied by the crew. **ca·boose** (kuh-**boos**)

cacao *noun* An evergreen tree found in warm climates that produces a seed from which cocoa and chocolate are made. **ca·ca·o** (kuh-**kou**)

cache
  1. *noun* A hidden stash of supplies or treasure, as in *a squirrel's cache of nuts* or a *pirate's cache of gold.*
  2. *noun* The place where such a hidden stash is kept: *The smugglers stored the contraband in an underground cache.*
  3. *noun* A kind of computer memory that improves a computer's performance by storing information so that it can be accessed quickly: *Your browser's cache keeps copies of the pictures and other data from the webpages you visit, allowing your computer to load those pages faster the next time you visit.*
  4. *verb* To hide or store something in a cache: *Many animals cache food for the winter.* ▷ *verb* **caching, cached**
  cache (kash)

cackle *verb*
  1. To give a loud, clucking cry, like a hen or a goose.
  2. To laugh in a sharp, loud way: *We cackled all through the movie.*
  cack·le (**kak**-uhl)
  ▷ *verb* **cackling, cackled** ▷ *noun* **cackle**

cacophony *noun* A harsh, unpleasant mixture of sounds. **ca·coph·o·ny** (kuh-**kah**-fuh-*nee*)
  ▷ *noun, plural* **cacophonies** ▷ *adjective* **cacophonous**

cactus

cactus *noun* A plant with a thick stem and sharp spikes in place of leaves, which grows in hot, dry areas. **cac·tus** (**kak**-tuhs)
  ▷ *noun, plural* **cacti** (**kak**-tye) or **cactuses**

CAD Short for **computer-aided design**. **CAD** (kad)

cadet *noun* A young person who is training to become a member of the armed forces or a police force. **ca·det** (kuh-**det**)

café *noun* A small restaurant that serves light meals and drinks. **ca·fé** (ka-**fay**)

cafeteria *noun*
  1. A self-service restaurant.
  2. A room in a school or business where meals are served and eaten.
  caf·e·te·ri·a (*kaf*-uh-**teer**-ee-uh)

caffeine *noun* A chemical found in tea, coffee, and some soft drinks that acts as a stimulant. **caf·feine** (ka-**feen** *or* **kaf**-een)

caftan *noun* An ankle-length, loose piece of clothing with long sleeves, often worn in the Middle East. **caf·tan** (**kaf**-tan)

cage
1. *noun* A container in which something can be kept, made of wires or bars.
2. *verb* To put something, especially an animal, in a cage: *The lion escaped from the zoo but was finally caught and has now been caged.* ▷ *verb* **caging, caged**
cage (kayj)

cagey *adjective* Cautious and reluctant to give away information: *Detective Kingston was a cagey and experienced police officer.* **ca·gey** (**kay**-jee)

cajole *verb* To persuade someone to do something by flattering or coaxing the person: *Don't think you can cajole me into taking you to dinner.* **ca·jole** (kuh-**johl**) ▷ *verb* **cajoling, cajoled**

Cajun
1. *noun* A descendant of the French-speaking people who left eastern Canada for Louisiana in the 1700s.
2. *adjective* Of or having to do with a style of spicy cooking invented by the Cajuns, as in *Cajun rice.*
Ca·jun (**kay**-juhn)

Word History

Acadia was the name of a French colony in North America, on land that is now in eastern Canada. In the early 1700s, the British took control of the area, and in 1755 they forced many French-speaking Acadians to leave. Many Acadians ended up settling in Louisiana. People sometimes ran some of the sounds of the word *Acadian* together, pronouncing it as **Cajun**, and *Cajun* became a separate word.

cake
1. *noun* A sweet food made by combining flour, butter, eggs, sugar, and other ingredients, and then baking this mixture.
2. *noun* A shaped mass of something, as in *a cake of soap.*
3. *verb* To dry or harden into a solid mass: *The wet sand caked on our legs.* ▷ *verb* **caking, caked** ▷ *adjective* **caked**
cake (kake)

calf

calamity *noun* A terrible disaster. **ca·lam·i·ty** (kuh-**lam**-i-tee) ▷ *noun, plural* **calamities** ▷ *adjective* **calamitous**

calcium *noun* A silver-white chemical element found in teeth and bones, which is necessary for many chemical processes in the human body. **cal·ci·um** (**kal**-see-uhm)

calculate *verb* To figure out by using mathematics: *Martin calculated the distance between the two towns.* **cal·cu·late** (**kal**-kyuh-*late*) ▷ *verb* **calculating, calculated**

calculating *adjective* Acting in a scheming way to get what you want. **cal·cu·lat·ing** (**kal**-kyuh-*lay*-ting)

calculation *noun*
1. The process of finding a number or amount using math: *According to our calculations, this work should cost no more than $5,000.*
2. An assessment of a course of action with respect to risks, cost, outcome, or other factors.
cal·cu·la·tion (*kal*-kyuh-**lay**-shuhn)

calculator *noun* An electronic machine used for figuring out math problems: *I added the numbers with my pocket calculator.* **cal·cu·la·tor** (**kal**-kyuh-*lay*-tur)

calendar *noun*
1. A chart showing all the days, weeks, and months in a year.
2. A system of measuring time over a period of a year, as in *the Jewish calendar* or *the school calendar.*
cal·en·dar (**kal**-uhn-dur)

calf *noun*
1. The young of several large species of animals, such as cows, seals, elephants, giraffes, or whales.
2. The fleshy part at the back of your leg, below your knee.
calf (kaf)
▷ *noun, plural* **calves**

calico
1. *noun* Cotton cloth printed with a colorful pattern, as in *a dress made of calico.* ▷ *noun, plural* **calicoes** *or* **calicos** ▷ *adjective* **calico**
2. *adjective* Having spotted colors, as in *a calico cat.*
cal·i·co (**kal**-i-*koh*)

calico cat

a
b
c
d
e
f
g
h
i
j
k
l
m
n
o
p
q
r
s
t
u
v
w
x
y
z

call *verb*

1. To give someone or something a name: *I'm going to call my new puppy Rex.*

2. To shout something out, especially someone's name: *Victoria's parents called for her to come in for dinner.*

3. To telephone someone. ▷ *noun* **caller**

4. call on To visit a person.

5. call off To cancel: *The tennis match was called off due to rain.*

6. call for To make necessary or to demand: *This emergency calls for quick action.*

7. call collect To reverse telephone charges from the person who is making the call to the person who is receiving it.

call (kawl)

▷ *verb* **calling, called** ▷ *noun* **call**

calligraphy *noun* Decorative handwriting: *Jessica used a special pen to do the calligraphy for her wedding invitations.* **cal·lig·ra·phy** (kuh-**lig**-ruh-fee)

calling *noun* Your **calling** is the job, profession, or other important thing that you want to do in your life: *Marco found his calling as a maker of violins.* **call·ing** (**kawl**-ing)

call number *noun* A sequence of numbers and letters that identifies the location of an item in a collection, especially a library.

callous *adjective* Having no tender feelings; cruel. **cal·lous** (**kal**-uhs) ▷ *noun* **callousness** ▷ *adverb* **callously**

calm

1. *adjective* Peaceful and not troubled. ▷ *adjective* **calmer, calmest** ▷ *noun* **calmness** ▷ *adverb* **calmly**

2. *verb* To soothe or to quiet: *The music calmed her nerves.* ▷ *verb* **calming, calmed**

Bactrian camel

dromedary or Arabian camel

3. *noun* Peacefulness; lack of trouble or violence.

4. *noun* A lack of wind or motion.

calm (kahm)

calorie *noun* A measurement of the amount of energy contained in food. **cal·o·rie** (**kal**-ur-ee)

calves *noun, plural* The plural of **calf**. **calves** (kavz)

cam *noun* A video camera connected to the internet that records what is happening somewhere, as in a traffic cam or a helmet cam. **cam** (kam)

camcorder *noun* A small video camera that also records sound. **cam·cord·er** (**kam**-kor-dur)

camel *noun* A mammal with one or two humps on its back. It can survive for long periods of time without food or water, which makes it useful for carrying people and goods across the desert: *Bactrian camels have two humps, while dromedaries, or Arabian camels, have only one hump.* **cam·el** (**kam**-uhl)

Camembert *noun* A soft cheese from France with a white rind and a yellowish inside. **Cam·em·bert** (**kam**-uhm-*bair*)

cameo *noun*

1. A piece of jewelry with a raised portrait carved on it.

2. A small character part in a play or a movie, usually played by a famous actor or actress.

cam·e·o (**kam**-ee-*oh*)

camera *noun* A device for capturing images through a lens and storing them digitally or on film. **cam·er·a** (**kam**-ur-uh)

camouflage

1. *noun* A disguise or a natural coloring that allows animals, people, or objects to hide by making them look like their surroundings.

2. *verb* To disguise something so that it blends in with its surroundings: *We tried to camouflage ourselves by stuffing leaves and branches in our hats.* ▷ *verb* **camouflaging, camouflaged** **cam·ou·flage** (**kam**-uh-*flahzh*)

Word History

In sieges, soldiers on both sides would dig underground passageways and place bombs in walls made out of earth. The French name for one of these bombs was *camouflet*. Since the devices were "hidden" in walls, the word **camouflage**, which French speakers formed from the name for the bomb, meant "disguising." English speakers first used the word *camouflage* only when they were talking about warfare, but now it has a broader meaning. For example, we call the colors and patterns of animals *camouflage*, because they help "hide" the animals from predators.

camp

1. *noun* A place where people stay in tents or cabins, usually as part of a vacation: *We set up camp on the north side of the lake.*

2. *noun* A place or a program devoted to a particular recreational activity, as in *basketball camp* or *Boy Scout camp*.

3. *noun* A place where people stay in an emergency because their homes are destroyed or not safe: *Government officials visited several refugee camps in the area.*

4. *verb* To live or stay in a camp.
▷ *verb* **camping, camped** ▷ *noun* **camping**
camp (kamp)

campaign *noun* Organized action in order to achieve a particular goal, as in *an election campaign*. **cam·paign** (kam-**payn**)
▷ *verb* **campaign**

camper *noun*

1. A person who stays or vacations at a camp.

2. A large motor vehicle in which you can sleep and cook meals when camping. **camp·er** (**kam**-pur)

campfire *noun* A fire lit at the site of a camp for warmth and for cooking. **camp·fire** (**kamp**-*fire*)

campus *noun* The land and buildings of a school, college, or university: *Brad preferred to get around campus by skateboard.* **camp·us** (**kam**-puhs)
▷ *noun, plural* **campuses**

can¹ *verb*

1. To be able to: *Janet can swim across the lake.*

2. *(informal)* To be allowed to do something: *You can go to the movies if you like.*
can (kan)
▷ *verb* **could** (kud)

can²

1. *noun* A metal container with the shape of a cylinder, used mainly for storing food.

2. *verb* To put into a jar or can; to preserve, as in *to can tomatoes.* ▷ *verb* **canning, canned** ▷ *adjective* **canned**

3. can of worms An awkward or difficult situation: *Mentioning the mayor's new plan right now would open a real can of worms.*
can (kan)

canal *noun*

1. A channel that is dug across land so that boats or ships can travel between two bodies of water, or so that water can flow from one place to another.

2. A tube in a plant or animal, through which food, fluid, or air can travel.
ca·nal (kuh-**nal**)

canary *noun* A bright yellow bird noted for its singing ability. **ca·nar·y** (kuh-**nair**-ee) ▷ *noun, plural* **canaries**

cancel *verb*

1. To decide or announce that a planned event is not going to happen: *Gerald is going to cancel the picnic if it rains.*

2. To stop an action on a computer if you don't want to complete it. Usually you do this by clicking on a **cancel button**: *The only choices in the dialog box are "OK" and "Cancel."*

3. To mark a postage stamp with a postmark so that it cannot be used again.

4. cancel out To have one action stop the effect of another action: *Mom decided that Jack's honesty canceled out his lateness, so she didn't punish him.*
can·cel (**kan**-suhl)
▷ *verb* **canceling, canceled** ▷ *noun* **cancellation**

cancer *noun* A serious disease in which some cells in the body grow faster than normal cells and destroy healthy organs and tissues. **can·cer** (**kan**-sur) ▷ *adjective* **cancerous**

candelabra or **candelabrum** *noun* A candle holder with holes for two or more candles: *An ornate silver candelabra adorned the table.* **can·de·la·bra** (*kan*-duh-**lah**-bruh) or **can·de·la·brum** (*kan*-duh-**lah**-bruhm)

candid *adjective* Speaking openly and honestly: *If you want my candid opinion, I think you look silly in that hat.* **can·did** (**kan**-did) ▷ *noun* **candor** ▷ *adverb* **candidly**

candidate *noun* A person who is applying for a job or running in an election. **can·di·date** (**kan**-di-*date*) ▷ *noun* **candidacy**

candelabra

Word History

Candidate comes from the Latin word *candidatus*, meaning "clothed in white." *Candidatus* comes from the Latin word *candidus*, meaning "white." In ancient Rome, candidates wore bleached white togas to the public forum as a symbol of political purity.

candle *noun* A stick of wax with a wick strung through it that you burn to produce light. **can·dle** (**kan**-duhl) ▷ *noun* **candlelight**

candlestick *noun* A holder for a candle or candles. **can·dle·stick** (**kan**-duhl-*stik*)

candy

1. *noun* Food made with sugar or syrup and often chocolate, nuts, or other flavorings. ▷ *noun, plural* **candies**

2. *verb* To coat with sugar, as in *to candy yams.* ▷ *verb* **candies, candying, candied** ▷ *adjective* **candied**

can·dy (**kan**-dee)

Word History

The word **candy** came into English by way of French and Italian from the Arabic *qandi*. The word had its origins in India, however, where it meant "sugar." The first meaning of *candy* in English was of candy made from pure sugar, and in the term *sugar candy*, it still has that sense.

cane

1. *noun* The woody, sometimes hollow, stem of a plant such as bamboo or sugarcane.

2. *noun* A plant or grass with this kind of woody, jointed stem.

3. *noun* A stick, especially one used for assistance in walking or for beating someone.

4. *verb* To make or repair furniture with cane. ▷ *verb* **caning, caned**

cane (kane)

canine

1. *adjective* Of or having to do with dogs. ▷ *noun* **canine**

2. *noun* One of the pointed teeth on each side of your upper and lower jaws. People have four canines.

ca·nine (**kay**-nine)

cannabis *noun* The scientific name for the hemp or marijuana plant. **Cannabis** is used when people talk about the uses of the plant to make drugs and medicines, or about whether it should be legal: *In some states, the use of cannabis for medical reasons is legal.* **can·na·bis** (**kan**-uh-bis)

cannibal *noun* A person who eats human flesh. **can·ni·bal** (**kan**-uh-buhl) ▷ *noun* **cannibalism**

cannon *noun* A heavy gun, usually mounted on wheels, that fires large metal balls. **can·non** (**kan**-uhn)

cannot *verb* To be unable to do something: *They cannot come to our party.* **can·not** (**kan**-aht or ka-**naht**)

canoe *noun* A narrow boat with pointed ends that you move through the water with paddles. **ca·noe** (kuh-**noo**)

canopy *noun*

1. A piece of cloth or other material suspended as a cover, shade, or decoration, especially over an entrance, a bed, or a throne.

2. A hanging shelter or cover: *We sat in the garden under a canopy of green branches.*

3. A cover over an airplane or helicopter cockpit.

4. The upper level of a rain forest, consisting mostly of branches, vines, and leaves.

can·o·py (**kan**-uh-pee) ▷ *noun, plural* **canopies**

can't *contraction* A short form of *can not* or *cannot.* **can't** (kant)

cantaloupe *noun* A melon with a rough skin and sweet, juicy, orange fruit. **can·ta·loupe** (**kan**-tuh-*lope*)

canteen *noun*

1. A small portable metal container for holding water or other liquids.

2. The area in a factory, school, or office where people can take breaks and eat simple meals: *I'll just get my lunch out of the vending machines in the canteen.*

can·teen (kan-**teen**)

canter *verb* To run at a speed between a trot and a gallop on a horse. **can·ter** (**kan**-tur) ▷ *verb* **cantering, cantered** ▷ *noun* **canter**

cantor *noun* An official who sings and leads prayers in a synagogue. **can·tor** (**kan**-tur)

canvas *noun*

1. A type of coarse, strong cloth used to make tents, sails, and clothing.

2. A piece of canvas stretched over a wooden frame for painting on, or the painting itself: *She paints about a dozen canvases a year.*

can·vas (**kan**-vuhs) ▷ *noun, plural* **canvases**

canvass *verb* To go around among a group of people, asking for their opinions or votes: *Why not canvass the class and see how many prefer the later date?* **can·vass** (**kan**-vuhs) ▷ *verb* **canvasses, canvassing, canvassed** ▷ *noun* **canvasser**

canyon *noun* A deep, narrow river valley with steep sides. **can·yon** (**kan**-yuhn)

cap *noun*

1. A soft, flat hat without a brim, sometimes with a visor in the front.

2. The cover of a bottle or a pen. ▷ *verb* **cap**

3. A small amount of explosive on a piece of paper that makes a bang when struck, often used in toy guns.

4. *(informal)* A capital letter: *Put the title of your essay in all caps.*

cap (kap)

cantaloupes

capability *noun* The power or ability to do something: *Vivian has the capability of becoming a great pianist.* **ca·pa·bil·i·ty** (*kay*-puh-**bil**-i-tee) ▷ *noun, plural* **capabilities**

capable *adjective*
1. Able to do something: *Stephanie is capable of winning the competition.*
2. Adept and skillful: *Katie is a capable babysitter.*
ca·pa·ble (**kay**-puh-buhl)
▷ *adverb* **capably**

capacity *noun*
1. The amount or number that something can hold: *The concert hall has a total capacity of about 1,200 seats.*
2. The ability to do a particular thing: *Steve has the capacity to understand people's feelings.*
3. A role or job: *In Linda's capacity as president, she has the final say.*
ca·pac·i·ty (kuh-**pas**-i-tee)
▷ *noun, plural* **capacities**

cape *noun*
1. A sleeveless coat that you wear over your shoulders and wrap around your body.
2. A piece of land that sticks out into the sea, as in *Cape May, New Jersey.*
cape (kape)

caper
1. *noun* A trick or prank.
2. *noun* (*slang*) A criminal act, as in *a bank caper.*
3. *verb* To skip or dance around playfully. ▷ *verb* **capering, capered**
ca·per (**kay**-pur)

capillary *noun* One of many small tubes in your body that transfers blood between the arteries and the veins. **cap·il·lar·y** (**kap**-uh-*ler*-ee) ▷ *noun, plural* **capillaries**

capital *noun*
1. A letter with the form A, B, C, D, E, rather than a, b, c, d, e, and so on: *You begin a sentence with a capital.*
2. The city in a country or state where the government is based: *Washington, DC, is the capital of the United States.*
3. An amount of money used to start a business.
cap·i·tal (**kap**-i-tuhl)
Capital sounds like **capitol**.

capitalism *noun* A way of organizing a country's economy so that most of the land, houses, factories, and other property belong to individuals and private companies rather than to the government. **cap·i·tal·ism** (**kap**-i-tuh-*liz*-uhm)

capitalist
1. *noun* Someone who supports capitalism and uses their wealth to invest.
2. *adjective* Of or having to do with capitalism, as in *capitalist economies.*
cap·i·tal·ist (**kap**-i-tuh-list)

capitalize *verb*
1. To put a capital letter at the beginning of a word or sentence.
2. To write or print in capital letters.
3. To benefit by taking advantage of something: *He capitalized on his popularity as an athlete by opening his own restaurant.*
cap·i·tal·ize (**kap**-i-tuh-*lize*)
▷ *verb* **capitalizing, capitalized** ▷ *noun* **capitalization** (*kap*-i-tuhl-i-**zay**-shuhn)

capital punishment *noun* Punishment that causes death, carried out by a government.

capitol *noun*
1. The building where state lawmakers meet.
2. Capitol The building in Washington, DC, where the US Congress meets.
cap·i·tol (**kap**-i-tuhl)
Capitol sounds like **capital**.

United States Capitol

capsize *verb* To turn over in the water: *Our raft capsized in the rough waves.* **cap·size** (**kap**-size)
▷ *verb* **capsizing, capsized**

capsule *noun*
1. A small container made of gelatin that holds one dose of medicine for a person to swallow.
2. The part of a spacecraft in which the crew travels.
cap·sule (**kap**-suhl)

captain *noun*
1. The person in charge of a ship or an aircraft.
2. The leader of a team.
3. A police or military officer at a certain level of authority.
cap·tain (**kap**-tuhn)
▷ *verb* **captain**

caption *noun* A short title or description appearing with an illustration. **cap·tion** (**kap**-shuhn)

captivate *verb* To attract and hold someone's attention: *Kim captivated us with her singing.* **cap·ti·vate** (**kap**-tuh-*vate*) ▷ *verb* **captivating, captivated**

captive
1. *noun* A person who has been taken prisoner, or an animal that has been caught.
2. *adjective* Confined to a place and not able to escape: *She was held captive in a jungle for more than five years.*
cap·tive (**kap**-tiv)

captivity *noun* The condition of being held or trapped by people: *Is the captivity of zoo animals cruel?* **cap·tiv·i·ty** (kap-**tiv**-i-tee)

captor *noun* A person who has captured another person or an animal or thing: *Subdued by a tranquilizer, the tiger was no longer a threat to its captors.* **cap·tor** (**kap**-tur)

capture *verb*
1. To take a person, an animal, or a place by force.
2. To attract and hold: *The book captured my attention.*
cap·ture (**kap**-chur)
▷ *verb* **capturing, captured** ▷ *noun* **capture**

car *noun*
1. A motor vehicle that has four wheels and two or four doors, designed to carry a driver and passengers; an automobile.
2. A vehicle on wheels that carries passengers and freight, such as a unit of a train.
3. The part of an elevator that carries people or freight.
car (kahr)

caramel *noun*
1. Sugar or syrup heated until it turns brown, used as a flavoring or coloring for food or drinks.
2. Candy made from sugar and butter.
3. A light brown color.
car·a·mel (**kar**-uh-muhl *or* **kahr**-muhl)
▷ *adjective* **caramel**

carat *noun* A unit for measuring the weight of gemstones. **car·at** (**kar**-uht) **Carat** sounds like **carrot**.

caravan *noun* A group of people using animals or vehicles to travel together. **car·a·van** (**kar**-uh-van)

carbohydrate *noun* One of the substances in foods such as bread, rice, and potatoes that give you energy. Carbohydrates are made up of carbon, hydrogen, and oxygen and are produced by plants. **car·bo·hy·drate** (*kahr*-buh-**hye**-drate)

male cardinal

carbon *noun*
1. A chemical element found in coal and diamonds and in all plants and animals.
2. carbon di·ox·ide (dye-**ahk**-side) A gas that is a mixture of carbon and oxygen, with no color or odor. People and animals breathe this gas out, while plants absorb it during the day.
3. carbon emissions *noun, plural* Carbon dioxide that goes into the air from the burning of fossil fuels and forests, as well as other human activities.
4. carbon mon·ox·ide (muh-**nahk**-side) A poisonous gas produced by the engines of vehicles and other things that burn carbon-based fuels.
5. carbon footprint A measure of the amount of carbon dioxide produced by a person, object, or organization and released into the atmosphere.
car·bon (**kahr**-buhn)

carbs *noun, plural (informal)* Carbohydrates or foods that contain them: *Marathon runners often load up on carbs before a race.* **carbs** (kahrbz)

carburetor *noun* The part of an engine where air and gasoline mix. **car·bu·re·tor** (**kahr**-buh-*ray*-tur)

carcass *noun* The dead body of an animal. **car·cass** (**kar**-kuhs) ▷ *noun, plural* **carcasses**

card *noun*
1. A folded, decorated piece of stiff paper sent on special occasions, as in *a get-well card.*
2. One of a set of rectangular pieces of stiff paper, used in games.
3. A small, rectangular piece of plastic with electronic coding that allows you to do certain things, such as get cash from an ATM, make a telephone call, or open a locked door, as in *a credit card.*
card (kahrd)

cardamom *noun* An aromatic seed used as a spice, especially in South Asian cooking: *Mom made hot cider spiced with cinnamon, cardamom, and cloves.* **car·da·mom** (**kahr**-duh-muhm)

cardboard *noun* Thick, stiff paper used for making boxes and other things. **card·board** (**kahrd**-bord)

cardiac *adjective* Of or having to do with the heart. **car·di·ac** (**kahr**-dee-*ak*)

cardinal
1. *noun* A songbird with black coloring around the beak and a crest of feathers on its head. The male is bright red.
2. *noun* One of the officials in the Roman Catholic Church, ranking just below the pope.
3. *adjective* Most important, as in *a cardinal rule.*
car·di·nal (**kahr**-duh-nuhl)

cardinal number *noun* A number, such as one, two, three, or four, used to show the amount of something. *See the Numbers Table in the* **Reference Section**.

care
1. *verb* To feel interest or concern about something.
2. *verb* To want or to be willing: *Would you care to come to the play with us?*
3. *noun* Concern or attention, as in *to work with care.*
4. *noun* Supervision and protection: *The baby is in the care of her aunt.*
5. take care of To do what is needed to keep someone safe, well, happy, or comfortable: *Our neighbor takes care of us when our parents go out.*
6. take care of To solve a problem or deal with a situation: *I'll take care of the broken lamp tomorrow.*
7. *noun* A worry or a fear about something: *As the rain clouds lifted, Brian forgot all his cares.*
care (kair)
▷ *verb* **caring, cared** ▷ *adjective* **caring**

career *noun* The work or the series of jobs that a person has. **ca·reer** (kuh-**reer**)

carefree *adjective* Having no worries or responsibilities. **care·free** (kair-*free*)

careful *adjective*
1. Cautious; paying close attention so as not to take risks.
2. Thoughtful and attentive: *Bonnie gave careful consideration to the idea of quitting her job.*
care·ful (**kair**-fuhl)
▷ *noun* **carefulness**

Synonyms

Careful means paying close attention when you are doing something, so that you avoid mistakes or injuries: *I was careful when I walked across the icy street.*

- -

■ **Painstaking** means taking great care while you are doing something: *Scientists conduct painstaking research to make sure their findings are accurate.*

■ **Thorough** means doing something completely without missing anything: *After the smoke cleared, the firefighters made a thorough search of the house to make sure nothing was left burning.*

■ **Exact** means doing something correctly and carefully, with much attention to detail: *The carpenter made exact measurements of the space where the bookcase will go.*

■ **Accurate** means truthful and exact, without any mistake: *The police spoke to everyone in the building to get an accurate description of the intruder.*

carefully *adverb*
1. In a way that shows close attention or concern: *If you listen carefully, you'll be able to hear the baby chicks in the nest.*
2. In a way that shows great care or caution: *Handle those teacups carefully—they belonged to your great-grandmother!*
care·ful·ly (**kair**-fuh-lee)

caregiver

caregiver *noun* Someone who takes care of children, old people, or sick people. **care·giv·er** (**kair**-*giv*-ur)

careless *adjective* Not paying attention, and making mistakes as a result: *Erik is careless about washing the dishes.* **care·less** (**kair**-lis) ▷ *noun* **carelessness** ▷ *adverb* **carelessly**

caress *verb* To stroke gently. **ca·ress** (kuh-**res**) ▷ *verb* **caresses, caressing, caressed** ▷ *noun* **caress**

caretaker *noun* A person whose job is to take care of a building, property, animals, or other people. **care·tak·er** (**kair**-*tay*-kur)

cargo *noun* Freight that is carried by a ship, plane, train, truck, or other vehicle: *The freighter was bound for Europe with a cargo of electronics.* **car·go** (**kahr**-goh) ▷ *noun, plural* **cargoes**

Word History

The ancient Romans had a wagon with two wheels that they used to carry loads. They called it a *carrus.* Later, Latin speakers formed the verb "to load," *carricare,* from *carrus.* Eventually, the noun **cargo,** meaning a "load that has to be carried," developed in Spanish from *carricare.* We use *cargo* in a similar way, referring to freight that is carried by a vehicle, although usually not in a wagon anymore.

Caribbean *noun* The sea near the Atlantic Ocean, between North and South America. The Caribbean contains many small islands. **Ca·rib·be·an** (kuh-**rib**-ee-uhn or kar-uh-**bee**-uhn) ▷ *adjective* **Caribbean**

caribou *noun* A large North American mammal of the deer family. Caribou are related to reindeer. **car·i·bou** (**kar**-uh-*boo*) ▷ *noun, plural* **caribou** *or* **caribous**

caricature *noun* An exaggerated drawing or verbal description of someone: *The newspaper ran an unflattering caricature of the president.* **car·i·ca·ture** (**kar**-i-kuh-*choor*)

carjack *verb* To steal a car by threatening to harm the driver. **car·jack** (**kahr**-*jak*) ▷ *verb* **carjacking, carjacked** ▷ *noun* **carjacking**

carnage *noun*
1. The violent killing of a large number of people at the same time: *The political tension in that region is likely to end in carnage.*
2. A lot of bodies of people that have died violently: *The FBI sent some of its agents to investigate the carnage from the bombing and examine it for clues.*
car·nage (**kahr**-nij)

carnation *noun* A fragrant flower, usually pink, white, or red. **car·na·tion** (kahr-**nay**-shuhn)

carnival *noun* A public celebration, often with rides, games, and parades. **car·ni·val** (**kahr**-nuh-vuhl)

carnivore *noun* An animal that eats meat. **car·ni·vore** (**kahr**-nuh-*vor*)

carnivorous *adjective* Having meat as a regular part of the diet. Wolves, lions, dogs, and most people are carnivorous. **car·niv·o·rous** (kahr-**niv**-ur-uhs)

carnival

carob *noun*
1. An evergreen tree whose beans are used to make a flavoring that tastes something like chocolate.
2. Brown powder from carob beans, used as a food or flavoring.
car·ob (**kar**-uhb)

carol *noun* A joyful song, especially one that people sing at Christmas. **car·ol** (**kar**-uhl) ▷ *verb* **carol**

carousel *noun*
1. A merry-go-round: *One of the highlights of our trip to Washington, DC, was riding the carousel on the Mall.*
2. Something that revolves like a merry-go-round, as in *a luggage carousel.*
car·ou·sel (*kar*-uh-**sel**)

carp
1. *noun* A large fish that lives in freshwater and is used as food. ▷ *noun, plural* **carp** *or* **carps**

2. *verb* To find fault with someone or something: *Instead of carping about the mess in the kitchen, let's just clean it up.* ▷ *verb* **carping, carped** **carp** (kahrp)

carpenter *noun* A person who works with wood or builds and repairs the wooden parts of buildings. **car·pen·ter** (**kahr**-puhn-tur) ▷ *noun* **carpentry**

carpet *noun*
1. A thick floor covering made of a woven fabric.
2. A thick layer of something, as in *a carpet of pine needles.*
car·pet (**kahr**-pit)
▷ *verb* **carpet**

car pool *noun*
1. A system in which a group of people travel together, often taking turns driving their own cars.
2. A group of people involved in such a system.
▷ *verb* **car-pool**

carriage *noun*
1. A vehicle with wheels, sometimes pulled by horses.
2. Your posture; the way you stand, sit, and walk.
car·riage (**kar**-ij)

carrier *noun*
1. Someone or something that carries: *You can be a carrier of some diseases without being sick.*
2. A company whose business is to transport people or things: *We use a local carrier for our deliveries.*
3. A company that provides telephone and other communications services: *I'm thinking about switching carriers for my cell phone.*
car·ri·er (**kar**-ee-ur)

carrot *noun*
1. An orange root eaten as a vegetable.
2. An offer of something nice in order to persuade someone to do something.
car·rot (**kar**-uht)
Carrot sounds like **carat**.

carry *verb*
1. To move something from one place to another: *Please carry this box inside.*
2. To travel for some distance: *Sound really carries in this huge lobby.*
3. To offer something for sale: *The store carries my favorite brand of jeans.*
4. To be infected with a disease that can be transmitted to others: *Dirty water can carry many kinds of illnesses.*

5. To continue or to extend: *You carried your complaining a bit too far.*

6. carry a tune To be able to sing reasonably well.

7. be carried away or **get carried away** To become too enthusiastic about something: *Dave got so carried away with his baking that he made 12 dozen cookies.*

8. carry on To continue to do something: *Dad carried on mowing the lawn until well after dark.*

9. carry on To behave in an exaggerated or inappropriate way: *Please stop carrying on about the baseball you lost.*

10. carry out To put a plan or an idea into practice: *The students carried out a well-planned prank.*
car·ry (**kar**-ee)
▷ *verb* **carries, carrying, carried**

carry-on *noun* A bag or suitcase that you keep with you on an airplane instead of checking it. **carry-on**

cart
1. *noun* A small wagon with two or four wheels, often pulled by an animal.
2. *noun* A light wagon that is pushed by someone and used to carry heavy items such as groceries.
3. *verb* To carry something with effort: *Kevin carts a huge pile of books around all day.* ▷ *verb* **carting, carted**
cart (kahrt)

cartilage *noun* A strong, elastic tissue that forms the outer ear and nose of humans and mammals, and lines the bones at the joints. **car·ti·lage** (**kahr**-tuh-lij)

cartography *noun* The science of making maps. **car·tog·ra·phy** (kahr-**tah**-gruh-fee) ▷ *noun* **cartographer**

carton *noun* A cardboard or plastic box or container used for holding or shipping goods. **car·ton** (**kahr**-tuhn)

cartoon *noun*
1. A short film using animation rather than real people or objects.
2. A humorous or exaggerated drawing.
car·toon (kahr-**toon**)
▷ *noun* **cartoonist**

cartridge *noun*
1. A container that holds a bullet or shot and the explosive for firing it.
2. A small container that holds something and that is designed to be inserted into something else, as in *an ink cartridge.*
car·tridge (**kahr**-trij)

cartwheel

cartwheel *noun* A circular, sideways handspring with arms and legs extended. **cart·wheel** (**kahrt**-*weel*)

carve *verb*
1. To cut meat into slices for eating: *Who's good at carving a turkey?*
2. To cut a piece of wood, stone, or other hard substance into a particular shape: *All of the lodge's oak trim was carved by hand.*
carve (kahrv)
▷ *verb* **carving, carved**
▷ *noun* **carver** ▷ *noun* **carving**

cascade
1. *noun* A waterfall.
2. *noun* Anything arranged in a downward pattern, or falling in a downward pattern, as in *a cascade of falling papers.*
3. *verb* To fall like water over rocks. ▷ *verb* **cascading, cascaded**
cas·cade (kas-**kade**)

case *noun*
1. An instance or example of something: *This is a case of simple carelessness.*
2. A trial in a court of law: *The lawyer decided to take on the case free of charge.*
3. A crime that the police are investigating: *The detectives are working on the kidnapping case.*
4. An occurrence of an illness, as in *a bad case of chicken pox.*
5. A set of circumstances: *I don't know quite what to do in your case.*
6. A box or container that holds something, as in *a camera case.*
7. in any case No matter what happens: *We will have to repaint the living room in any case.*
8. just in case In the event that something happens or that something is needed: *Take a warm sweatshirt, just in case.*
case (kase)

case sensitive *adjective* Working only when you type it using the correct combination of capital and lowercase letters: *All the passwords for this computer program are case sensitive.*

cash
1. *noun* Money in the form of bills and coins.
2. *verb* To exchange something, like a check, for money.
3. cash in *verb* To take advantage of something: *Bella cashed in on her good looks by becoming a model.*
cash (kash)
▷ *verb* **cashes, cashing, cashed**

a
b
c
d
e
f
g
h
i
j
k
l
m
n
o
p
q
r
s
t
u
v
w
x
y
z

cashew *noun* A nut that is shaped like a bean. Cashews grow on evergreen trees in tropical countries. **cash·ew** (**kash**-oo)

Word History

In the Tupi language of Brazil, *acaju* meant the tree that the **cashew** nut grows on. When the Portuguese colonized Brazil beginning in the 1500s, they borrowed this word along with other words for native plants and animals.

cashier *noun* A person who takes in or pays out money in a store or bank. **cash·ier** (ka-**sheer**)

cash machine *noun* Another name for an **ATM**.

cash register *noun* A machine used in stores that has a drawer for money and that keeps an account of each purchase.

casino *noun* A public building or room that is used for gambling, as in *the casinos of Las Vegas*. **ca·si·no** (kuh-**see**-noh)

cask *noun* A large, wooden barrel, usually used to make and store wine. **cask** (kask)

casket *noun* A wooden or metal container into which a dead person is placed for burial; a coffin. **cas·ket** (**kas**-kit)

casserole *noun*
1. A glass or ceramic dish with a lid that is used for cooking and serving.
2. Food that is cooked in such a dish: *Here's a recipe for a healthy vegetarian casserole.*
cas·se·role (**kas**-uh-*role*)

cast
1. *noun* The actors in a play, movie, or television program: *The film flopped despite its all-star cast.*
2. *noun* A hard covering that holds a broken bone in place while it heals.
3. *verb* To throw, as in *to cast a fishing line* or *to cast a shadow*. ▷ *noun* **cast**
4. cast a ballot *verb* To vote.
5. *verb* To form something by pouring soft or molten material into a mold: *The sculptor cast the statue in bronze.* ▷ *verb* **casting, cast**
cast (kast)

castanets *noun, plural* A percussion instrument consisting of two shell-shaped pieces of wood, ivory, or plastic, joined by a cord, that are clapped together with the fingers: *Castanets are traditionally used by dancers in Spain.* **cas·ta·nets** (*kas*-tuh-**nets**)

castaway *noun* A person who has been shipwrecked in an isolated place. **cast·a·way** (**kas**-tuh-*way*)

cast iron *noun* A hard and brittle form of iron made by melting iron with other metals. The mixture is poured into a mold to make something.

castle *noun*
1. A large building protected by thick walls and often a moat. Most castles were built in the Middle Ages.
2. A piece used in chess, also called a rook, that moves around the board in horizontal or vertical lines.
cas·tle (**kas**-uhl)

casual *adjective*
1. Informal, as in *casual dress*.
2. Happening by chance, as in *a casual meeting*.
3. Relaxed and unworried: *There was a casual atmosphere at the party.*
cas·u·al (**kazh**-oo-uhl)
▷ *adverb* **casually**

casualty *noun* A person who is injured or killed in an accident, a natural disaster, or a war. **cas·u·al·ty** (**kazh**-oo-uhl-tee) ▷ *noun, plural* **casualties**

cat *noun*
1. A small, furry animal with sharp claws and whiskers, often kept as a pet.
2. Any member of the cat family, including lions, tigers, and cheetahs.
3. let the cat out of the bag To tell a secret by mistake.
cat (kat)

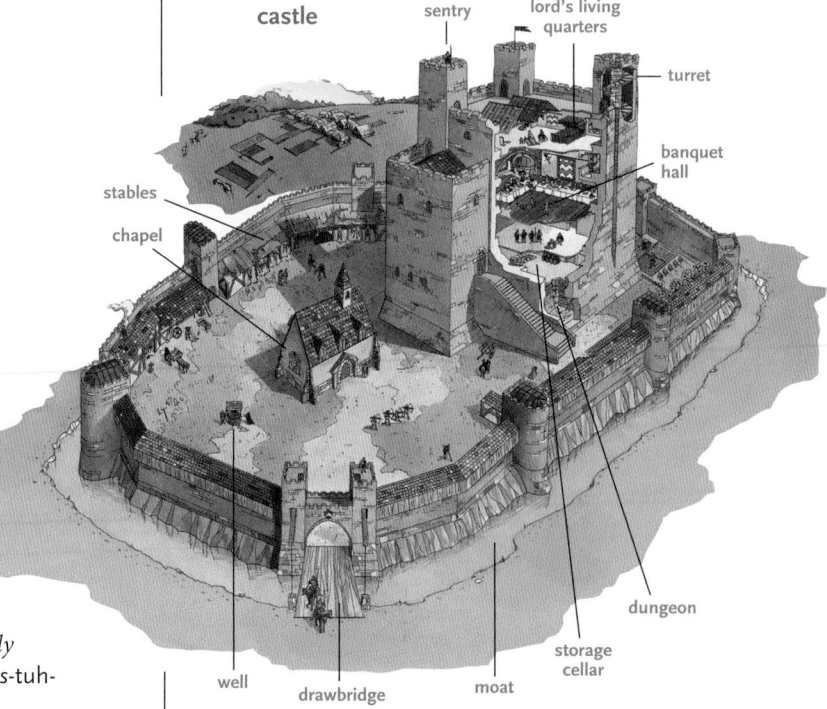

castle — sentry — lord's living quarters — turret — banquet hall — stables — chapel — dungeon — storage cellar — well — drawbridge — moat

catamaran

catalog *or* **catalogue** *noun*
1. A book or magazine listing things you can buy from a company or the works of art in an exhibition, often including pictures and descriptions.
2. An alphabetical list of all the books in a library.
cat·a·log *or* **cat·a·logue** (**kat**-uh-*lawg*)
▷ *verb* **catalog** *or* **catalogue**

catalyst *noun*
1. A substance that causes or speeds up a chemical reaction.
2. A person or thing that causes something to happen.
cat·a·lyst (**kat**-uh-list)

catamaran *noun* A boat with two hulls that are joined together. **cat·a·ma·ran** (*kat*-uh-muh-**ran**)

catapult
1. *noun* A device used to launch airplanes from the deck of a ship.
2. *noun* A weapon, similar to a large slingshot, used in the past for firing rocks or other objects over castle walls.
3. *verb* To cause someone to suddenly move ahead of many others: *His hard work and ability to soak up information catapulted him to the head of the class.*
▷ *verb* **catapulting, catapulted**
cat·a·pult (**kat**-uh-*puhlt*)

cataract *noun*
1. A cloudy film that sometimes grows on the lens of a person's eye, causing blindness or partial blindness.
2. A steep waterfall.
cat·a·ract (**kat**-uh-*rakt*)

catastrophe *noun* A terrible and sudden disaster.
ca·tas·tro·phe (kuh-**tas**-truh-fee) ▷ *adjective*
catastrophic (*kat*-uh-**strah**-fik)

catbird *noun* A gray songbird with a call that sounds like a cat meowing. **cat·bird** (**kat**-*burd*)

catch
1. *verb* To seize something moving through the air, as in *to catch a ball.* ▷ *noun* **catch**
2. *verb* To get something or someone you are chasing: *Joe caught the dog as it tried to run away.*
3. *verb* To arrive at a bus, train, or other kind of transportation in time to get on.
4. *verb* To see someone doing something: *Mom caught Mandy taking cookies from the box.*
5. *verb* To become sick with a particular disease: *Paula caught a cold from her brother.*
6. *verb* To become stuck or trapped: *My sleeve caught on the corner of the desk.*
7. *noun* A fastening on a door, box, piece of jewelry, or other object that needs to be held shut.
8. *noun* A game in which two or more people throw a ball to one another.
9. *noun* A hidden problem or disadvantage: *This offer sounds too good to be true—what's the catch?*
10. *verb* To attend or to watch: *I want to catch the ball game on TV tonight.*
11. *verb* To hear and understand: *I didn't catch what she said as she raced out the door.*
12. catch up with *verb* To reach a person or thing after a chase: *I finally caught up with Brian at the corner.*
13. catch up on *verb* To complete work that should have been done earlier: *If I catch up on my homework tonight, I'll be able to go out tomorrow.*
14. catch on *verb* To become very popular.
15. catch on *verb* To understand: *Andy finally caught on that we were teasing him.*
catch (kach)
▷ *verb* **catches, catching, caught** (kawt) ▷ *noun, plural* **catches**

catcher *noun* A person who catches; the baseball player behind home plate who catches the balls thrown by the pitcher. **catch·er** (**kach**-ur)

categorical *adjective* Completely clear: *Brandon made a categorical statement that he had never set foot in the store.* **cat·e·gor·i·cal** (*kat*-uh-**gor**-i-kuhl) ▷ *adverb* **categorically**

category *noun* A group of people or things that has certain characteristics in common: *Connor was the fastest runner in the 8- to 12-year-old category.* **cat·e·go·ry** (**kat**-uh-gor-ee) ▷ *noun, plural* **categories**

cater *verb*
1. To provide food for a party or other social occasion: *Shawn and Linda had their wedding catered by their favorite restaurant.*
▷ *noun* **caterer** ▷ *noun* **catering**
2. To provide people with the things they need or want, especially if it involves special requests: *This store caters to experienced mountain climbers.*
ca·ter (**kay**-tur)
▷ *verb* **catering, catered**

caterpillar *noun* A larva that changes into a butterfly or moth. It looks like a worm and is sometimes hairy: *A caterpillar breathes through tiny holes on the sides of its body.* **cat·er·pil·lar** (**kat**-ur-pil-ur)

catfish *noun* A freshwater fish with long feelers around its mouth that look like cat whiskers. **cat·fish** (**kat**-fish)

cathedral *noun* A large and important church, with a bishop or an archbishop as its main priest. **ca·the·dral** (kuh-**thee**-druhl)

Catholic *noun* A member of the Roman Catholic Church. **Cath·o·lic** (**kath**-uh-lik)
▷ *noun* **Catholicism** (kuh-**thah**-luh-siz-uhm)
▷ *adjective* **Catholic**

catnip *noun* A small flowering mint that is particularly attractive to cats: *Spike purred loudly as he rolled around in a patch of catnip.* **cat·nip** (**kat**-nip)

CAT scan *noun* An image made by computer from a series of X-rays, resulting in a single three-dimensional image. CAT is short for *computerized axial tomography.*

catsup See **ketchup**. **cat·sup** (**kat**-suhp *or* **kech**-uhp)

cattail *noun* A tall, thin plant with long, brown, furry pods at the top and narrow leaves. Cattails grow in large groups in marshes. **cat·tail** (**kat**-tayl)

cattle *noun, plural* Cows, bulls, and steers that are raised for food or for their hides. **cat·tle** (**kat**-uhl)

catwalk *noun*
1. A narrow elevated walkway, such as along a bridge or above a stage: *The catwalks on a ship are high above the ship's decks.*
2. A long, narrow platform that models walk along to display clothes during a fashion show. Also called a **runway**. **cat·walk** (**kat**-wawk)

Caucasian *noun* A member of a race of peoples with light or tan skin. Caucasians may come from Europe, the Americas, northern Africa, India, and other regions. **Cau·ca·sian** (kaw-**kay**-zhuhn)
▷ *adjective* **Caucasian**

cauldron *noun* A large metal pot, used for cooking over an open fire. **caul·dron** (**kawl**-druhn)

cauliflower *noun* A vegetable with a large, rounded, white head surrounded by leaves. **cau·li·flow·er** (**kaw**-li-flou-ur)

caulk
1. *noun* A waterproof paste that is applied to a hole or a gap, such as the edges of a bathtub, to close it and make it watertight: *I used caulk to seal the cracks in the window frame.*
2. *verb* To apply a waterproof material to something in order to prevent water from leaking in or out: *We took the sailboat out of the water to caulk the leaks.*
▷ *verb* **caulking, caulked**
caulk (kawk)

cause
1. *verb* To make something happen: *Be careful, or you'll cause an accident!* ▷ *verb* **causing, caused**
2. *noun* The reason that something happens: *Police are still investigating the cause of the explosion.*
3. *noun* A principle or a goal to which people commit themselves and for which they work.
cause (kawz)

caution
1. *noun* Carefulness or watchfulness: *Exercise caution when crossing the street.*
2. *verb* To warn about something or someone: *Mom cautioned us not to hitchhike.* ▷ *verb* **cautioning, cautioned**
cau·tion (**kaw**-shuhn)

cautious *adjective* Acting carefully to avoid mistakes or danger: *He is always cautious when he crosses the street.* **cau·tious** (**kaw**-shuhs) ▷ *adverb* **cautiously**

cavalry *noun*
1. In earlier times, the part of an army that fought on horseback.
2. In modern times, soldiers who fight in armored vehicles.
cav·al·ry (**kav**-uhl-ree)
▷ *noun, plural* **cavalries**

caterpillar

cave
1. *noun* A large opening underground, in a hillside, or in a cliff.
2. **cave in** *verb* To fall down suddenly: *The roof caved in from the heavy snow.* ▷ *verb* **caving, caved** **cave** (kave)

cavern *noun* A large cave, or a room in a cave. **cav·ern** (**kav**-ern) ▷ *adjective* **cavernous**

caviar *noun* The eggs of a sturgeon (a kind of fish), eaten as a delicacy: *It was a very elegant banquet, with champagne and caviar.* **cav·i·ar** (**kav**-ee-*ahr*)

cavity *noun*
1. An empty space in something solid.
2. A hole in a tooth, caused by decay.
cav·i·ty (**kav**-i-tee)
▷ *noun, plural* **cavities**

CD *noun* Short for **compact disk**.

CD-ROM *noun* A compact disk that stores text, music, video clips, and other information that can be read by a computer. CD-ROM is short for *compact disk read-only memory.* **CD-ROM** (**see** *dee* **rahm**) ▷ *noun, plural* **CD-ROMs**

cease *verb* To stop. **cease** (sees) ▷ *verb* **ceasing, ceased**

cease-fire *noun* A temporary pause during a war, usually to allow peace talks to take place.

cedar *noun* A type of evergreen tree with hard wood and leaves shaped like needles. The fragrant wood is used for furniture and moth-repellent linings. **ce·dar** (**see**-dur) ▷ *adjective* **cedar**

ceiling *noun*
1. The overhead surface of a room.
2. The highest level that something can reach, as in *a wage ceiling.*
ceil·ing (**see**-ling)

cello

Word History

Ceiling comes from the word *ceil,* a verb meaning "to build an overhead surface." If the ceiling of a room was made of oak boards, for example, people would describe the room as being "ceiled with oak." At first, *ceiling* referred to the action of making an overhead surface for a room. Later, English speakers started using *ceiling* to mean the surface itself. The Latin word *caelum,* meaning "heaven," may be the source of the word *ceil.* If so, *ceiling* is related to the English word *celestial.*

celebrate *verb* To do something special to mark a happy occasion. **cel·e·brate** (**sel**-uh-*brate*) ▷ *verb* **celebrating, celebrated** ▷ *adjective* **celebratory** (**sel**-uh-bruh-*tor*-ee)

celebration *noun* A joyous ceremony or gathering, usually to mark a major event: *We held a huge celebration on the last day of school.* **cel·e·bra·tion** (*sel*-uh-**bray**-shuhn)

celebrity *noun* A famous person. **ce·leb·ri·ty** (suh-**leb**-ri-tee) ▷ *noun, plural* **celebrities**

celery *noun* A vegetable with crisp white or green stalks, often eaten raw in salads or cooked in soups and stews. **cel·e·ry** (**sel**-ur-ee)

celestial *adjective* Of or having to do with the sky or the heavens. **ce·les·tial** (suh-**les**-chuhl) ▷ *adverb* **celestially**

cell *noun*
1. A small room in a place such as a prison or monastery, where people stay.
2. The smallest unit of an animal or a plant.
3. A box in a spreadsheet in which an item of data can be entered.
cell (sel)
Cell sounds like **sell**.

cellar *noun* A room below ground level in a house, often used for storage. **cel·lar** (**sel**-ur)

cello *noun* A large stringed instrument that rests on the floor. It is played with a bow like a violin but is held between the knees. **cel·lo** (**chel**-oh)

cell phone *noun* A portable telephone that often has features like a camera and internet access. A cell phone uses signals sent over radio channels: *If I'm not at home, you can call me on my cell phone.* **cell phone** (**sel** *fone*)

Word History

With a **cell phone**, you can make and receive calls over a large area. Instead of only a single antenna, there are many antenna "cells" located throughout the area to send and receive the signals. The stations were named *cells* because they work together in a system, like cells in our bodies, to create a communication network.

cellular *adjective*
1. Made of or having to do with cells, as in *cellular damage.*
2. Of or having to do with cell phones and their technology, as in *cellular service.*
cel·lu·lar (**sel**-yuh-lur)

a
b
c
d
e
f
g
h
i
j
k
l
m
n
o
p
q
r
s
t
u
v
w
x
y
z

cellulose *noun* The substance from which the cell walls of plants, and plant fibers, are made. Cellulose is used to make paper, cloth, and plastics. **cel·lu·lose** (**sel**-yuh-*lohs*)

Celsius *adjective* A measurement of temperature using a scale on which water boils at 100 degrees and freezes at 0 degrees. It is also called **centigrade**. **Cel·si·us** (**sel**-see-uhs)

cement *noun*
1. A gray powder made from crushed limestone that is used in building and that becomes hard when you mix it with water and let it dry. Cement is used to make concrete.
2. A substance that joins two things together: *Use rubber cement to seal the edges.*
ce·ment (suh-**ment**)
▷ *verb* **cement**

cemetery *noun* A place where dead people are buried. **cem·e·ter·y** (**sem**-i-*ter*-ee) ▷ *noun, plural* **cemeteries**

cemetery

censor
1. *verb* To remove parts of a book, movie, or other work that are thought to be unacceptable or offensive. ▷ *verb* **censoring, censored** ▷ *noun* **censorship**
2. *noun* A person whose job is to examine books, movies, or other works for objectionable parts before they are published or released.
cen·sor (**sen**-sur)

census *noun* An official count of all the people living in a country or district. **cen·sus** (**sen**-suhs)

cent *noun* A unit of money in the United States, Canada, Australia, many parts of Europe, and New Zealand. One hundred cents are equal to one dollar or one euro. **cent** (sent) **Cent** sounds like **scent** and **sent**.

centaur *noun* A creature in Greek and Roman mythology that has the body and legs of a horse but the chest, arms, and head of a man. **cen·taur** (**sen**-tor)

centaur

centennial *noun* The 100th-year celebration of an event. **cen·ten·ni·al** (sen-**ten**-ee-uhl)
▷ *adjective* **centennial**

center
1. *noun* The middle of something: *The bowling ball rolled right down the center of the lane.*
2. *noun* A place devoted to a particular activity, as in *an arts center.*
3. *verb* To concentrate on something: *The campaign centers on the treatment of recent immigrants.*
4. *verb* To put something in the center: *The mirror was centered on the wall between the two lamps.*
5. *verb* To put printed text in the middle of a line so that there is equal blank space to the left and to the right of it: *Center your name under the title of your essay.*
6. center of gravity *noun* The point on an object at which half of its weight is on one side and half on the other.
cen·ter (**sen**-tur)
▷ *verb* **centering, centered**

centigrade *adjective* See **Celsius**. **cen·ti·grade** (**sen**-ti-*grade*)

centiliter *noun* A unit for measuring liquids in the metric system equal to 1/100 of a liter, or about 0.338 fluid ounces. **cen·ti·li·ter** (**sen**-tuh-*lee*-tur)

centimeter *noun* A unit of length in the metric system. A centimeter is equal to 1/100 of a meter, or about four-tenths of an inch; 2.54 centimeters equals one inch. **cen·ti·me·ter** (**sen**-tuh-*mee*-tur)

centipede *noun* A small creature with a very long, segmented body and one pair of legs per segment. **cen·ti·pede** (**sen**-ti-*peed*)

central *adjective*
1. In the middle: *They warmed themselves around the cabin's central wood stove.*
2. Most important, as in *the central issue.*
cen·tral (**sen**-truhl)
▷ *adverb* **centrally**

Central America *noun* The central region of the Americas, connecting North America and South America. Central America includes all the countries from Belize south to Panama.

Central American

1. *adjective* From Central America or having to do with Central America.

2. *noun* Someone who was born in Central America or whose parents come from there.

central heating *noun* A system for heating a building by heating water or air in one place and sending it through pipes or vents through the entire building.

centrifugal *adjective* Moving or tending to move away from the center. **cen·tri·fu·gal** (sen-**trif**-yuh-guhl)

centripetal *adjective* Moving or tending to move toward the center. **cen·trip·e·tal** (sen-**trip**-i-tuhl)

century *noun* A period of 100 years. **cen·tu·ry** (**sen**-chur-ee) ▷ *noun, plural* **centuries**

cephalopod *noun* A sea creature that has tentacles attached to its head, such as an octopus or a squid. **ceph·a·lo·pod** (**sef**-uh-luh-*pahd*)

ceramics

1. *noun* The art of making objects out of clay.

2. *noun, plural* Objects made of clay. ▷ *adjective* **ceramic**

ce·ram·ics (suh-**ram**-iks)

cereal *noun*

1. A grain crop grown for food, such as wheat, corn, rice, oats, and barley.

2. A breakfast food made from grain, often eaten with milk.

ce·re·al (**seer**-ee-uhl)

Cereal sounds like **serial**.

ceremony

ceremony *noun* A formal sequence of events to mark an important occasion, as in *an inauguration ceremony.* **cer·e·mo·ny** (**ser**-uh-*moh*-nee) ▷ *noun, plural* **ceremonies** ▷ *adjective* **ceremonial** ▷ *adverb* **ceremonially**

certain *adjective*

1. Sure, having no doubt: *Ray was certain he had mailed the letter.*

2. Particular and usually known, but not specifically named: *Maintaining a healthy diet reduces the risk of certain cancers.*

cer·tain (**sur**-tuhn)

certainly

1. *adverb* You can use **certainly** with a verb when you want to emphasize your belief in the truth of what you are saying: *We certainly don't need any more rain this week—we've had five inches already!*

2. *interjection* You can say **certainly** or **certainly not** as an emphatic way of saying yes or no, or to show that you strongly agree or disagree with what someone has said. These two words are often used in sentences that end with an exclamation mark: *"Can we have a party while you're away this weekend?" "Certainly not!"*

cer·tain·ly (**sur**-tuhn-lee)

certainty *noun*

1. The state or quality of being completely certain: *We know with certainty that the earth is round.*

2. A statement or fact about which there is no doubt: *According to the newspaper, it is a certainty that the government will appeal the case.*

cer·tain·ty (**sur**-tuhn-tee) ▷ *noun, plural* **certainties**

certificate *noun* A piece of paper that officially states that something is a fact: *A birth certificate states when and where you were born.* **cer·tif·i·cate** (sur-**tif**-uh-kit)

certify *verb* To state officially that something is true, correct, or genuine: *The election results have been certified by independent observers.* **cer·ti·fy** (**sur**-tuh-fye) ▷ *verb* **certifying, certified**

chafe *verb*

1. To make something raw or sore by rubbing: *The elastic chafed her wrists.*

2. To be annoyed or irritated: *We chafed at her constant instructions to be quiet.*

chafe (chafe) ▷ *verb* **chafing, chafed**

Word History

If the collar of a jacket is chafing someone's neck, for example, it is "making it warm" by rubbing it repeatedly. The Latin word *calefacere*, meaning "to make warm," is the source of the English word **chafe**. Latin speakers formed *calefacere* from *calere*, meaning "to be warm," and *facere*, meaning "to make." The English word *chauffeur*, referring to a person who is hired to drive a car, also comes from *calefacere*. Originally, chauffeurs kept the furnace of a locomotive going by supplying it with fuel.

a b c d e f g h i j k l m n o p q r s t u v w x y z

chagrin

1. *noun* A feeling of embarrassment or humiliation: *To his chagrin, Noah had to apologize to his whole class.*

2. *adjective* Feeling strong embarrassment or humiliation: *She was usually the top scorer and felt deeply chagrined when she failed to shoot even one basket.*

cha·grin (shuh-**grin**)

▷ *adjective* **chagrined**

chain

1. *noun* A flexible series of metal rings, called links, joined together.

2. *noun* A series of similar or connected items, as in *a chain of events.*

3. chain store *noun* A group of stores that is owned by the same company and sells similar products.

4. *verb* To attach with a chain: *She chains her bike to the fence when she's not using it.* ▷ *verb* **chaining, chained**

chain (chayn)

chair

1. *noun* A piece of furniture that you sit on, with a seat, legs, and a back.

2. *noun* A chairman or a chairwoman.

3. *verb* To be in charge of a meeting: *It was Laura's turn to chair the club's monthly meeting.* ▷ *verb* **chairing, chaired**

chair (chair)

chairman *noun* A person who is in charge of a committee, a company, or a department in a school. The term usually applies to a man but can sometimes refer to a woman. **chair·man** (**chair**-muhn) ▷ *noun, plural* **chairmen**

chairperson *noun* A chairman or a chairwoman. **chair·per·son** (**chair**-*pur*-suhn)

chairwoman *noun* A woman who is in charge of a committee, a company, or a department in a school. **chair·woman** (**chair**-*wum*-uhn) ▷ *noun, plural* **chairwomen**

chalet *noun* A wooden house with a sloping roof and overhanging eaves, especially in mountainous areas of Europe. **cha·let** (sha-**lay**)

chalk *noun*

1. A soft, white rock, made from the remains of ancient sea creatures.

2. A stick of this material, sometimes colored, used for writing or drawing.

chalk (chawk)

▷ *verb* **chalk**

chalkboard *noun* Another name for a **blackboard**. **chalk·board** (**chawk**-*bord*)

challenge

1. *noun* Something difficult that requires extra work or effort to do: *Building the new picnic table was a challenge for the boys.* ▷ *adjective* **challenging**

2. *verb* To invite someone to compete or to try to do something: *Wayne challenged me to a chess match.*

3. *verb* To question whether something is right or not: *The professor challenged the statements in the article.*

chal·lenge (**chal**-inj)

▷ *noun* **challenge** ▷ *verb* **challenging, challenged**

chamber *noun*

1. A room, especially a bedroom.

2. A division of a legislative body: *The upper chamber of the United States' legislature is called the Senate.*

3. An enclosed space in a machine or an animal's body, as in *the four chambers of the human heart.*

4. chamber music Classical music for a small number of instruments.

cham·ber (**chaym**-bur)

chameleon *noun* A lizard that can change color, sometimes matching its surroundings. **cha·me·le·on** (kuh-**meel**-yuhn)

Word History

Animals were often named after other creatures. For instance, the seahorse owes its name to its resemblance to a horse. There is also the sea lion, though this creature does not look much like a lion. The **chameleon** is among this group, with the original animal's name hidden in the word: The word *chameleon* means "ground-lion." Greek speakers put the two words *chamai,* meaning "on the ground," and *leon,* meaning "lion," together to make this name.

chameleon

champagne *noun* A white wine made in Champagne, France, with small bubbles, often drunk at a celebration. **cham·pagne** (sham-**pane**)

champion

1. *noun* The winner of a competition.

2. *noun* A person who stands up for another person or an idea: *The senator is a great champion of equal rights.*

3. *verb* To support a cause. ▷ *verb* **championing, championed** **cham·pi·on** (**cham**-pee-uhn)

championship *noun* A contest or final game of a series that determines which team or player will be the overall winner. **cham·pi·on·ship** (**cham**-pee-uhn-*ship*)

chance *noun*

1. The possibility of something happening: *There's a 50 percent chance of rain this afternoon.*

2. An opportunity to do something: *Gary has a chance to travel to Europe.*

3. take a chance To try something even though it is risky.

4. by chance In an accidental or unplanned way: *We met Meredith in the library by chance.* **chance** (chans)

chandelier *noun* A light fixture that hangs from the ceiling and is usually lit by many small lights. **chan·de·lier** (*shan*-duh-**leer**)

chandelier

change

1. *verb* To become different or to make different: *We changed the furniture in the living room.* ▷ *noun* **change**

2. *verb* To put on different clothes: *I have to go and change for the party.*

3. *noun* The money you receive back if you pay more than something costs.

4. *noun* Coins rather than bills: *I have a dollar's worth of change in my pocket.*

5. *verb* To exchange: *Do you mind changing seats so I can sit with my friend?* **change** (chaynj) ▷ *verb* **changing, changed**

channel *noun*

1. A narrow stretch of water between two areas of land.

2. A television or radio station: *The story was on all the news channels at once.* **chan·nel** (**chan**-uhl)

channel surf *verb* To change television channels quickly in order to find something interesting: *I was channel surfing when I came across a program about dinosaurs.* ▷ *verb* **channel surfing, channel surfed**

chant *verb*

1. To say or sing a phrase repeatedly.

2. To sing, especially certain kinds of religious music. **chant** (chant) ▷ *verb* **chanting, chanted** ▷ *noun* **chant**

chaos *noun* Complete and usually noisy disorder: *Chaos broke out after the home team won the championship.* **cha·os** (**kay**-ahs) ▷ *adjective* **chaotic** (kay-**ah**-tik) ▷ *adverb* **chaotically**

chap

1. *verb* To make something, especially skin, so rough or dry that it cracks: *The hot sun chapped her lips.* ▷ *verb* **chapping, chapped** ▷ *adjective* **chapped**

2. *noun* A man or boy; a fellow: *Who's that chap in the yellow shirt?* **chap** (chap)

chapel *noun*

1. A small church.

2. A small, separate section of a large church or synagogue.

3. A place in a college, prison, or other institution where religious services are held. **chap·el** (**chap**-uhl)

chaperone *or* **chaperon** *noun* An adult who protects the safety of young people at an event such as a dance or a class trip and who makes sure they behave well. **chap·er·one** *or* **chap·er·on** (**shap**-uh-*rohn*) ▷ *verb* **chaperone, chaperon**

chaplain *noun* A priest, minister, or rabbi who works in the military, or in a school or prison. A chaplain leads religious services and counsels people. **chap·lain** (**chap**-lin)

chaps *noun, plural* Leather coverings that fit over jeans and protect the legs of people riding on horseback. **chaps** (chaps)

chapter *noun*

1. A section of a book.

2. A branch of an organization: *Sonja is a member of the local chapter of the National Organization for Women.* **chap·ter** (**chap**-tur)

character *noun*

1. The sort of person you are, or the qualities that make you that person.

2. One of the people in a story, book, play, movie, or television program.

3. A letter or symbol used in printing or on computers. All the letters of the alphabet are characters.

4. An unusual or amusing person: *Eddie is a real character with those funny stories of his.* **char·ac·ter** (**kar**-ik-tur)

characteristic

1. *noun* A typical feature or quality: *Curly hair is a characteristic of our family.*

2. *adjective* Typical: *Fred's homework shows his characteristic neatness.* ▷ *adverb* **characteristically**

char·ac·ter·is·tic (kar-ik-tuh-**ris**-tik)

characterize *verb*

1. To describe or identify the important qualities of someone or something: *How would you characterize the hero of this book?*

2. To be a feature that identifies something: *The disease is characterized by a rapidly developing fever and a rash.*

char·ac·ter·ize (kar-ik-tuh-**rize**)

▷ *verb* **characterizing, characterized**

charcoal

charcoal *noun* A substance made from incompletely burned wood. Charcoal is used in drawing pencils and as barbecue fuel. **char·coal** (**char**-kohl)

charcoal

charge

1. *verb* To demand a particular price for something: *They charge about 30 bucks for an oil change.*

2. *noun* The cost or price: *There is a $1 charge for extra pepperoni.*

3. *verb* To attack in a rush: *The soldiers charged the fort.*

4. *noun* An attack.

5. *verb* To put off paying for something by using a credit card or signing an agreement: *We charged the dinner on Felix's credit card.*

6. *verb* To accuse: *Jana's boss charged her with spending too much time on the telephone.*

7. *noun* An accusation or statement of blame, as in *a charge of armed robbery.*

8. *verb* To pass an electric current through a battery so that it stores electricity.

9. in charge In a position of leadership or control: *Rebecca is in charge of computer supplies for the office.* **charge** (chahrj)

▷ *verb* **charging, charged**

chariot *noun* A small vehicle pulled by a horse, used in ancient times in battles or for racing. **char·i·ot** (**char**-ee-uht)

charisma *noun* A powerful personal appeal that attracts a great number of people, as in *the charisma of a popular politician.* **cha·ris·ma** (kuh-**riz**-muh)

▷ *adjective* **charismatic** (kar-iz-**mat**-ik)

charity *noun*

1. An organization that raises money to help people in need or some other worthy cause.

2. Money or other help that is given to people in need: *My grandpa was poor but didn't like to accept charity.*

3. Kindness toward others: *Most religions teach people to act with charity toward their neighbors.*

char·i·ty (**char**-i-tee)

▷ *noun, plural* **charities** ▷ *adjective* **charitable**

charm

1. *noun* Pleasing and attractive appearance and behavior. ▷ *noun* **charmer**

2. *verb* To please someone and make the person like you. ▷ *verb* **charming, charmed**

3. *noun* A small object that is believed to bring good luck.

charm (chahrm)

charming *adjective* Attractive, full of charm, or delightful. **charm·ing** (**chahr**-ming)

chart

1. *noun* A table, graph, or diagram that presents information.

chariots

2. *noun* A map of the stars or the oceans.

3. *verb* To record or present information in the form of a chart. ▷ *verb* **charting, charted**
chart (chahrt)

charter

1. *noun* A formal document that states the rights or duties of a group of people, or that creates an institution such as a company or a university.

2. *verb* To rent a form of transportation for private use: *The club chartered a plane to visit the remote island.* ▷ *verb* **chartering, chartered**
char·ter (chahr-tur)

charter school *noun* A school that receives some money from the government but that operates independently of other public schools: *My sister attends a charter school that specializes in the arts.*

chartreuse *noun* A yellowish-green color.
char·treuse (shahr-**troos**) ▷ *adjective* **chartreuse**

chase *verb* To run after someone or something in order to catch them or scare them away.
chase (chase) ▷ *verb* **chasing, chased** ▷ *noun* **chase**

chasm *noun* A deep crack in the earth or in some other surface. **chasm** (**kaz**-uhm)

chassis *noun* The frame of a vehicle, on which the body is assembled. **chas·sis** (**chas**-ee *or* **shas**-ee) ▷ *noun, plural* **chassis**

chat *verb*

1. To talk in a friendly and informal way, usually about subjects that are not very serious.

2. To communicate with others in a chat room.
chat (chat)
▷ *verb* **chatting, chatted** ▷ *noun* **chat**

château *noun* A castle or large country house in France. **châ·teau** (sha-**toh**) ▷ *noun, plural* **châteaux** (sha-**toh** *or* sha-**tohz**)

chat room *noun* An internet site or a website in which people can type messages back and forth.

chatter *verb*

1. To talk continuously about unimportant things. ▷ *noun* **chatter**

2. To knock together because you are cold; said of your teeth.
chat·ter (**chat**-ur)
▷ *verb* **chattering, chattered**

chauffeur *noun* A person who is hired to drive a car for somebody else. **chauf·feur** (**shoh**-fur) ▷ *verb* **chauffeur**

chauvinist *noun* A person who is overly proud of his

château

or her nationality, gender, ethnic background, or other personal characteristic. **chau·vin·ist** (**shoh**-vuh-nist) ▷ *noun* **chauvinism** ▷ *adjective* **chauvinistic**

cheap *adjective*

1. Not costing or worth very much. ▷ *noun* **cheapness** ▷ *adverb* **cheaply**

2. Unkind and mean: *Hiding Spencer's jacket was a cheap trick.*

3. Not willing to spend very much money: *We made our own costumes because Dad is too cheap to buy all of them.*
cheap (cheep)
▷ *adjective* **cheaper, cheapest**

cheat

1. *verb* To get something in a dishonest way: *Universities often expel students caught cheating on exams.* ▷ *verb* **cheating, cheated**

2. *noun* A person who acts dishonestly.
cheat (cheet)

check

1. *verb* To look at something in order to find out its condition.

2. *verb* To stop something from moving or growing: *The mother tried to check her children's tendency to be late.*

3. *verb* To leave an item you own, such as a coat or a suitcase, in the care of someone else for a short time: *The line for people with bags to check was a lot longer.*

4. *noun* A pattern of squares of different colors. ▷ *adjective* **checked**

5. *noun* A printed piece of paper on which someone writes to tell the bank to pay a specific amount of money from his or her account to another person or to a company.

6. *noun* A mark (✓) used to show that a thing has been looked at or verified. ▷ *verb* **check**

7. check in *verb* To register for a hotel room, a meeting, or some other facility or activity.

8. check out *verb* To pay your bill at a hotel or motel before leaving.

9. *verb* To remove items officially from their proper location: *Penny checked out six books from the library.*

10. check out *verb* To investigate something: *Let's check out that new store on Main Street.*
check (chek)
▷ *verb* **checking, checked**

checkers *noun* A game for two people with 12 round pieces each, played on a board marked with squares of alternating colors. **check·ers** (**chek**-urz)

checkout *noun* The place in a store where you pay for your purchases. **check·out** (**chek**-*out*)

checkup *noun* A thorough medical or dental examination. **check·up** (**chek**-*uhp*)

cheek *noun* Either side of your face below your eyes. **cheek** (cheek)

cheer

1. *verb* To praise or encourage with shouts: *The crowd cheered wildly when the magician came onstage.*

2. *noun* A shout of encouragement.

3. cheer up *verb* To begin to feel better after being sad or worried.

4. *noun* Happiness; good spirits: *Everyone at the holiday celebration was full of cheer.*

5. be of good cheer To be happy.

cheer (cheer)

▷ *verb* **cheering, cheered**

cheerful *adjective* Visibly happy. **cheer·ful** (**cheer**-fuhl) ▷ *noun* **cheerfulness** ▷ *adverb* **cheerfully**

cheese *noun* A food made from the curds of milk. **cheese** (cheez)

cheeseburger *noun* A hamburger with cheese melted on top of the meat. **cheese·bur·ger** (**cheez**-*bur*-gur)

cheetah *noun* A wild cat with a spotted coat that is found in Africa and southern Asia. Cheetahs are the fastest-running animals on land. **chee·tah** (**chee**-tuh)

chef *noun* The chief cook in a restaurant. **chef** (shef)

chef's hat *noun* A white hat that fits close around the head and is puffy at the top, worn by chefs.

chemical

1. *noun* A substance used in or made by chemistry, as in *household chemicals.*

2. *adjective* Of or having to do with chemistry or chemicals, as in *a chemical burn.* ▷ *adverb* **chemically**

3. chemical symbol *noun* A one- to three-letter abbreviation that is used to identify one of the elements: *The chemical symbol for gold is Au.* **chem·i·cal** (**kem**-i-kuhl)

chemist *noun* A person trained in chemistry. **chem·ist** (**kem**-ist)

chemistry *noun* The scientific study of substances, what they are composed of, and how they react with each other. **chem·is·try** (**kem**-i-stree)

chemotherapy *noun* The use of chemicals to kill diseased cells in cancer patients. **che·mo·ther·a·py** (*kee*-moh-**ther**-uh-pee) ▷ *noun* **chemotherapist**

cherish *verb*

1. To protect and care for someone or something lovingly.

cheetah

2. To value or hold dear: *My mom cherishes the time she gets to spend with her friends.*

cher·ish (**cher**-ish)

▷ *verb* **cherishes, cherishing, cherished**

Cherokee *noun* A member of a group of Native Americans who live primarily in Oklahoma and North Carolina. **Cher·o·kee** (**cher**-uh-kee) ▷ *noun, plural* **Cherokee** or **Cherokees**

cherry *noun*

1. A small, sweet, red fruit with a pit inside.

2. A tree that produces cherries.

cher·ry (**cher**-ee)

▷ *noun, plural* **cherries** ▷ *adjective* **cherry**

cherry

chess *noun* A game for two people with 16 pieces each, played on a board marked with squares of alternating colors. **chess** (ches)

Word History

Saying "check" in **chess** led to the English name for this game. A player says "check" when making a move that exposes the other player's king to an attack. This move was called *eschec* in Old French, and its plural was spelled "eschés," meaning "moves of check." French speakers soon began using *eschés* as the name of the game itself, and the term passed into English as *ches*. The French word *eschec* went back to the word for "king" in Persian, *shah*, referring to the king piece in chess.

chest *noun*

1. The front part of your body between your neck and belly.

2. A large, strong box for storage or shipping.

chest (chest)

a
b
c
d
e
f
g
h
i
j
k
l
m
n
o
p
q
r
s
t
u
v
w
x
y
z

chestnut *noun*
1. A large, reddish-brown nut.
2. A tree that produces chestnuts.
3. A reddish-brown color.
chest·nut (**ches**-*nuht*)
▷ *adjective* **chestnut**

chest of drawers *noun* A piece of furniture with drawers, usually used for storing clothes.
▷ *noun, plural* **chests of drawers**

chew *verb* To grind food between your teeth. **chew** (choo) ▷ *verb* **chewing, chewed**

chewing gum *noun* A sweet, flavored substance that you chew for a long time but do not swallow.

Cheyenne *noun* A member of a group of Native Americans who live primarily in Montana and Oklahoma. **Chey·enne** (shye-**en**) ▷ *noun, plural* **Cheyenne** *or* **Cheyennes**

Chicana *noun*
1. An American girl or woman born of Mexican parents; a Mexican American.
2. A Mexican woman living and working in the United States.
Chi·ca·na (chi-**kah**-nuh)
▷ *noun, plural* **Chicanas**

Chicano *noun*
1. An American boy or man born of Mexican parents; a Mexican American.
2. A Mexican man living and working in the United States.
Chi·ca·no (chi-**kah**-noh)
▷ *noun, plural* **Chicanos**

chick *noun* A very young bird, especially a very young chicken, or a small lobster. **chick** (chik)

chickadee *noun* A kind of small bird with a black head and throat, gray wings, and a white belly. The call of the chickadee sounds like its name. **chick·a·dee** (**chik**-uh-*dee*)

chicken *noun*
1. A common type of fowl that is raised on farms for its meat and eggs.
2. The meat from this bird, used as food, as in *fried chicken*.
3. *(slang)* A person who is too scared to do something.
chick·en (**chik**-uhn)

chicken pox *noun* A common, contagious disease, especially among children, that causes red, itchy spots on the skin. **chicken pox** (pahks)

chickpea *noun* The edible seed of a plant originally grown in Asia. Also called a **garbanzo**. **chick·pea** (**chick**-*pee*)

chide *verb* To scold or to find fault with someone: *My mother chided me for playing in the dirt.* **chide** (chide) ▷ *verb* **chiding, chided**

chief
1. *noun* The leader of a group, as in *a chief of police*.
2. *adjective* Main, or most important: *A teacher's chief objective is to educate students.*
chief (cheef)

chiefly *adverb* Mainly or mostly: *He can sing in a variety of styles, but he is chiefly a jazz performer.* **chief·ly** (**cheef**-lee)

chieftain *noun* The chief or leader of a tribe, clan, or community. **chief·tain** (**cheef**-tuhn)

chigger *noun* A tiny insect that feeds on skin cells, causing a rash and severe itching. **chig·ger** (**chig**-ur)

chihuahua *noun* A breed of small, short-haired dog, originally from Mexico. **chi·hua·hua** (chi-**wah**-wuh)

child *noun*
1. A young boy or girl.
2. A son or daughter: *The McKinleys have one child.*
child (childe)
▷ *noun, plural* **children** (**chil**-drin)

childbirth *noun* The act or process of giving birth to a baby: *A midwife assisted her during childbirth.* **child·birth** (**childe**-*burth*)

childhood *noun* The time when you are a child: *Childhood is a time for learning and growing.* **child·hood** (**childe**-hud)

childish *adjective* Immature and silly, as in *childish behavior.* **child·ish** (**chile**-dish) ▷ *noun* **childishness** ▷ *adverb* **childishly**

chili *noun*
1. A kind of pepper with green or red skin that is used to make food spicy.
2. A spicy food made with chilies, and often with beans and meat.
chil·i (**chil**-ee)
▷ *noun, plural* **chilies**

chill
1. *verb* To make someone or something cold: *If we chill the water, we won't need to use ice.*
2. *noun* A slight coldness: *The chill in the air reminded us that summer was over.* ▷ *adjective* **chilly**
3. *noun* A shiver you feel in your body, often related to cold or fear: *I felt a chill go up my spine.* ▷ *adjective* **chilling**
4. *adjective* Cool or cold: *A chill wind made us huddle together.* ▷ *adjective* **chillier, chilliest**
5. **chill** *or* **chill out** *verb (slang)* To relax or stop worrying: *Chill out—we can handle this problem easily.*
chill (chil)
▷ *verb* **chilling, chilled**

chime *verb* To make a ringing sound, like a bell or a clock. **chime** (chime) ▷ *verb* **chiming, chimed** ▷ *noun* **chime**

chimney *noun* An upright pipe or channel that carries smoke away from a fire, usually out of a building. **chim·ney** (**chim**-nee)

chimpanzee *noun* A small ape with dark fur that comes from Africa. Chimpanzees are the closest genetic relative of humans. Also known as a *chimp*. **chim·pan·zee** (*chim*-pan-**zee** or chim-**pan**-zee)

Word History

Chimpanzees are among the few animals that make tools. To find food, for example, they chew or strip off the bark from twigs, then use them to poke termite mounds, eating the termites that cling to the twigs. In the 18th century, when people in England saw a chimpanzee for the first time, they were amazed by the animal's intelligence. One London publication described it as "a most surprising Creature," and one of the country's top naturalists called it "the nearest to the Human Species of any Creature." The term **chimpanzee** comes from *chimpenzi*, the animal's name in the Bantu language of Africa.

chin *noun* The part of your face below your mouth, formed by the point of the lower jaw. **chin** (chin)

china *noun*
1. A very thin, delicate ceramic material.
2. Cups, plates, and dishes made of china: *Tyler carefully washed and dried the china and put it away.* **chi·na** (**chye**-nuh)

chinchilla *noun* A small South American rodent with very soft fur. **chin·chil·la** (chin-**chil**-uh)

chink *noun* A small crack or opening: *We could see flames through a chink in the old wall.* **chink** (chingk)

chip
1. *noun* A small piece of something that is cut or broken off.
2. *verb* To break a small piece off something: *He chipped a tooth while eating a hard nut.*
3. **have a chip on your shoulder** To feel angry because you think you have been treated unfairly.
4. **chip in** *verb* To add your money to other people's money to make a purchase together.
5. *noun* A very thin piece of food

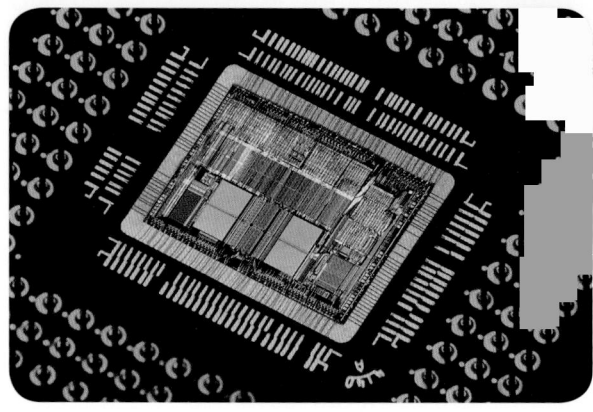

microchip

cooked in oil until it is crisp: *I had potato chips with my burger.*
6. *noun* Short for **microchip**. **chip** (chip) ▷ *verb* **chipping, chipped**

chipmunk *noun* A small animal related to the squirrel that has brown fur and dark stripes on its back and tail. **chip·munk** (**chip**-*muhnk*)

Chippewa See **Ojibwa**. **Chip·pe·wa** (**chip**-uh-*wah*)

chiropractor *noun* A person who treats back pain and other illnesses by adjusting the spine. **chi·ro·prac·tor** (**kye**-ruh-*prak*-tur)

chirp
1. *noun* A high-pitched sound made by some birds and insects: *I sat outside and listened to the chirp of the crickets.*
2. *verb* To make such a sound: *My alarm clock chirps every morning at seven.* ▷ *verb* **chirping, chirped** **chirp** (churp)

chisel
1. *noun* A tool with a broad, sharp end used to cut or shape wood, stone, or metal.
2. *verb* To cut something carefully and form it into a desired shape: *The sculptor chiseled the marble into a graceful statue.* ▷ *verb* **chiseling, chiseled** **chis·el** (**chiz**-uhl)

chivalry *noun*
1. Courteous and helpful behavior, especially by a man toward a woman.
2. A code of noble and polite behavior that was expected of a medieval knight. **chiv·al·ry** (**shiv**-uhl-ree) ▷ *adjective* **chivalrous**

chlorinate *verb* To add chlorine to water in order to kill germs. **chlo·ri·nate** (**klor**-i-*nate*) ▷ *verb* **chlorinating, chlorinated**

chinchilla

chlorine *noun* A chemical element that is a poisonous gas with a strong smell. It is added to water in very small amounts to keep it free from bacteria. **chlo·rine** (**klor**-een)

chlorophyll *noun* The green substance in plants that uses light to manufacture food from carbon dioxide and water. **chlo·ro·phyll** (**klor**-uh-fil)

chocolate
1. *noun* A food made from roasting and grinding the beans that grow on the tropical cacao tree.
2. *adjective* Being made from or having the flavor of chocolate, as in *chocolate cake*.
choc·o·late (**chaw**-kuh-lit *or* **chawk**-lit)
▷ *adjective* **chocolatey**

Word History

The Aztec ruler Montezuma of Mexico often drank a bitter beverage. It was made from cocoa beans, mashed up to make a powder and mixed with water, corn, and spice. This drink was called *xocoatl* by the Aztecs, meaning "bitter water." The words *xococ,* meaning "bitter," and *atl,* meaning "water," were the sources for this name. The Spanish conquerors took the name of the drink as **chocolate** and added ingredients such as sugar, cinnamon, and vanilla, so that it was no longer bitter. Now we use the word *chocolate* for the food and add the adjective *hot* when we mean the drink.

Choctaw *noun* A member of a group of Native Americans who live primarily in Oklahoma, Mississippi, and Louisiana. **Choc·taw** (**chahk**-taw)
▷ *noun, plural* **Choctaw** *or* **Choctaws**

choice
1. *noun* The thing or person that has been selected: *Vinh was a good choice as class president.*
2. *noun* A group or range of things from which you can choose: *The university offers a wide choice of classes.*
3. *noun* The chance to choose: *I have the choice of taking Spanish or French at school next year.*
4. *adjective* Of very good quality, as in *choice foods.*
choice (chois)

choir *noun* A group of people who sing together, especially in a church. **choir** (kwire)

choke *verb*
1. To have great difficulty breathing because something is blocking your breathing passages or because of lack of air.
2. To cause someone to stop breathing by squeezing his or her neck.
3. To block something: *The streets were choked with traffic.*
4. choke back To hide a feeling or refuse to express it: *Her father choked back his anger.*
choke (choke)
▷ *verb* **choking, choked**

cholera *noun* A dangerous disease that causes severe vomiting and diarrhea, usually due to contaminated water. **chol·e·ra** (**kah**-lur-uh)

cholesterol *noun* A fatty substance that humans and animals need to digest food and produce certain vitamins and hormones. Too much cholesterol in the blood can increase the possibility of heart disease. **cho·les·ter·ol** (kuh-**les**-tuh-*rawl*)

choose *verb*
1. To pick out one person or thing from several possibilities: *Oliver was chosen for the job out of 20 candidates.*
2. To decide to do something: *He chose to study medicine.*
choose (chooz)
▷ *verb* **choosing, chose** (chohz), **chosen** (**choh**-zuhn)

choosy *adjective*
1. Careful and selective about making choices, as in *a choosy shopper.*
2. Overly particular and finicky, as in *a choosy eater.*
choos·y (**choo**-zee)
▷ *adjective* **choosier, choosiest**

chop
1. *verb* To cut by striking repeatedly with a knife or an ax. ▷ *verb* **chopping, chopped** ▷ *noun* **chop**
2. *noun* A small piece of lamb, veal, or pork with a rib or other bone attached.
chop (chahp)

choppy *adjective* Quite rough or uneven, as in *a choppy sea.* **chop·py** (**chah**-pee) ▷ *adjective* **choppier, choppiest**

chopsticks *noun, plural* A pair of thin, tapered sticks for handling food, used primarily by people in East Asian countries. **chop·sticks** (**chahp**-stiks)

choral *adjective* Sung by a choir, or having to do with a choir, as in *choral music.* **cho·ral** (**kor**-uhl)
Choral sounds like **coral.**

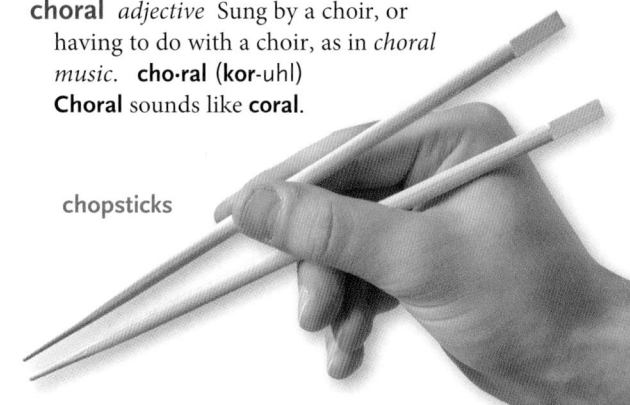
chopsticks

chord *noun* Two or more musical notes played at the same time. **chord** (kord) **Chord** sounds like **cord**.

chore *noun* A job that has to be done regularly, and that is usually considered unpleasant or tedious: *Every Saturday, we dust the living room and do other light chores.* **chore** (chor)

choreographer *noun* A person who arranges steps and movements for a ballet or other forms of dance. **cho·re·og·ra·pher** (*kor*-ee-**ah**-gruh-fur) ▷ *noun* **choreography** ▷ *verb* **choreograph** (**kor**-ee-uh-*graf*)

chorus *noun*
1. The part of a song that is repeated after each verse.
2. A large group of people who sing or recite together.
cho·rus (**kor**-uhs)
▷ *noun, plural* **choruses**

chose *verb* The past tense of **choose**. **chose** (chohz)

chosen *verb* The past participle of **choose**. **chos·en** (**choh**-zuhn)

chowder *noun* A thick soup made with clams or fish and vegetables. **chow·der** (**chou**-dur)

Christ *noun* Jesus, the person whom Christians worship as the son of God. **Christ** (kriste)

Christianity *noun* The religion based on the life and teachings of Jesus. **Chris·ti·an·i·ty** (*kris*-chee-**an**-i-tee) ▷ *noun* **Christian** ▷ *adjective* **Christian**

Christmas *noun* The Christian festival on December 25 that celebrates the birth of Jesus. **Christ·mas** (**kris**-muhs) ▷ *noun, plural* **Christmases** ▷ *adjective* **Christmas**

chrome *noun* A shiny silver metal that is used as a protective covering or for decoration. **chrome** (krohm)

chromosome *noun* The structure inside the nucleus of a cell that carries the genes that give living things their individual characteristics. **chro·mo·some** (**kroh**-muh-*sohm*)

chronic *adjective* Lasting for a long time or returning periodically: *My grandfather has chronic bronchitis.* **chron·ic** (**krah**-nik) ▷ *adverb* **chronically**

chronicle *verb* To record historical events in a factual and detailed way. **chron·i·cle** (**krah**-ni-kuhl) ▷ *verb* **chronicling, chronicled** ▷ *noun* **chronicle**

chronological *adjective* Arranged in the order in which things occurred. **chron·o·log·i·cal** (*krah*-nuh-**lah**-ji-kuhl) ▷ *noun* **chronology** (kruh-**nah**-luh-jee) ▷ *adverb* **chronologically**

chrysalis *noun* A butterfly or moth in a quiet stage of development between a caterpillar and an adult. It spends this stage inside a hard outer shell. **chrys·a·lis** (**kris**-uh-lis) ▷ *noun, plural* **chrysalises**

chorus

chrysanthemum *noun* A flower of various shapes and colors that has many petals. **chry·san·the·mum** (kruh-**san**-thuh-muhm)

chubby *adjective* Slightly fat or plump. **chub·by** (**chuhb**-ee) ▷ *adjective* **chubbier, chubbiest**

chuckle *verb* To laugh quietly or inwardly. **chuck·le** (**chuhk**-uhl) ▷ *verb* **chuckling, chuckled** ▷ *noun* **chuckle**

chuckwagon *noun* A covered wagon or truck that serves as a portable kitchen. **chuck·wag·on** (**chuhk**-*wag*-uhn)

chug *verb*
1. To make a series of muffled explosive sounds while moving along: *The boat chugged upstream.*
2. *(informal)* To drink a large quantity at once without stopping: *He chugged a whole can of soda pop.*
chug (chuhg)
▷ *verb* **chugging, chugged**

chum *noun* A friend, buddy, or pal. **chum** (chuhm)

chunk *noun* A thick, solid piece of something, as in *floating chunks of ice.* **chunk** (chuhngk)

chunky *adjective*
1. Full of chunks or pieces: *He likes smooth peanut butter; I like it chunky.*
2. Short and solid in build; stocky.
chunk·y (**chuhng**-kee)
▷ *adjective* **chunkier, chunkiest**

church *noun*
1. A building used by Christians for worship.
2. A group of Christians who share similar beliefs: *They belong to a local Catholic church.*
3. Christian religious services: *Her family goes to church every week.*
church (church)
▷ *noun, plural* **churches**

churn
1. *noun* A machine or device in which cream is made into butter.

2. *verb* To form butter by stirring cream.

3. *verb* To move a substance around roughly: *The cars parking in the field churned up the ground.*

4. If your stomach **churns,** you feel very upset or a little sick.

churn (churn)

▷ *verb* **churning, churned**

chute *noun* A narrow, tilted passage for sending things like garbage, laundry, grain, or coal to a lower level. **chute** (shoot) **Chute** sounds like **shoot**.

Suffix

The suffix **-cide** forms words that can mean someone or something is going to die (or already did). Common examples include *homicide, herbicide, pesticide,* and *genocide.* Some exceptions are *decide* and *coincide.* They come from a different source.

cider *noun* A beverage made by pressing apples.
ci·der (**sye**-dur)

cigar *noun* A cylinder of rolled-up tobacco leaves that people smoke. **ci·gar** (si-**gahr**)

cigarette *noun* A thin roll of finely chopped tobacco covered with paper that people smoke. **cig·a·rette** (*sig*-uh-**ret**)

cinder *noun* A small piece of wood or coal that has been partly burned. **cin·der** (**sin**-dur)

cinema *noun*
1. A movie theater.
2. The movie industry.
cin·e·ma (**sin**-uh-muh)
▷ *adjective* **cinematic**

cinnamon *noun* A reddish-brown spice that comes from the inner bark of a tropical tree. **cin·na·mon** (**sin**-uh-muhn)

circa *preposition* The Latin word for "around," indicating that something, especially a date, is not known exactly. Abbreviated as *c.* or *ca.*: *My estimate is that he was born circa 1730.* **cir·ca** (**sur**-kuh)

circle
1. *noun* A flat, perfectly round shape: *The diameter of a circle is twice as long as its radius.*
▷ *adjective* **circular** (**sur**-kyuh-lur)
2. go around in circles To do something over and over again

without accomplishing anything.

3. *verb* To run or form a circle around something: *The runners circled the track several times.* ▷ *verb* **circling, circled**

4. *noun* A group of people who all know each other: *After Carmen moved, she missed her old circle of friends.*

cir·cle (**sur**-kuhl)

circuit *noun*
1. A route or trip with several stops that ends in the place where it began: *We made a circuit of Yellowstone Park and saw some fantastic sights.*
2. A complete path for an electrical current.
3. An area that is under the authority of a particular court: *A judge for the local circuit reviewed the case.*
cir·cuit (**sur**-kit)

circuit board *noun* A piece of plastic that has electrical circuits printed onto it in the form of small metal strips.

circuit breaker *noun* A safety device that switches the electricity off when there is too much current in the system.

circulate *verb*
1. To move in a circle or pattern: *The ventilation system circulates air throughout the building.*
2. To follow a course from place to place or person to person: *She circulated at the party and talked to every person there.*
cir·cu·late (**sur**-kyuh-*late*)
▷ *verb* **circulating, circulated**

circulation *noun*
1. The movement of blood in blood vessels through the body.
▷ *adjective* **circulatory** (**sur**-kyuh-luh-*tor*-ee)
2. The number of copies of a newspaper, magazine, or other publication that are bought in a day, week, month, or year.
cir·cu·la·tion (*sur*-kyuh-**lay**-shuhn)

circulatory system *noun* The group of organs that pump blood through the body: *The circulatory system includes the heart, veins, and arteries.*

circumference *noun*
1. The outer edge of a circle or the length of this edge.
2. The distance around something: *We walked around the whole circumference of the ranch.*
cir·cum·fer·ence (sur-**kuhm**-fur-uhns)

vein

heart

artery

human circulatory system

circumstances *noun, plural* The facts or conditions that are connected to an event or period of time: *The pioneers lived in very challenging circumstances.* **cir·cum·stanc·es** (**sur**-kuhm-*stan*-sez)

circumstantial *adjective* Of or having to do with circumstances that suggest that someone is guilty but without any means of proving it: *The DA built a strong circumstantial case against the defendant.* **cir·cum·stan·tial** (*sur*-kuhm-**stan**-shuhl)

circus *noun*
1. A traveling show in which clowns, acrobats, trained animals, and other entertainers perform.
2. A noisy and confused situation: *The entrance to the rock concert was a real circus.*
cir·cus (**sur**-kuhs)
▷ *noun, plural* **circuses**

cistern *noun* A reservoir or tank for storing water. **cis·tern** (**sis**-turn)

citadel *noun* A fortress that is built to protect a town. It usually overlooks the town and often includes a castle that is fortified against attack: *The knights fought bravely to defend their citadel.* **cit·a·del** (**sit**-uh-del)

cite *verb*
1. To quote from a written work: *Carrie cited a paragraph from his book in her research project.*
2. To give someone a commendation or medal: *He was cited for bravery after he rescued the baby from the pool.*
3. To summon someone to appear in court: *The driver was cited for driving without a license.*
4. To use a thing or an event as proof of an argument: *He cited a number of essays that supported his beliefs.*
cite (site)
Cite sounds like **site** and **sight**.
▷ *verb* **citing, cited**

citizen *noun*
1. A person who has full rights in a particular country, such as the right to live there, to work there, and to vote in the country's elections.
2. A resident of a particular town or city: *My friend Marie is a citizen of Geneva.*
cit·i·zen (**sit**-i-zuhn)

citizenship *noun* The condition of being a citizen of a certain country. **cit·i·zen·ship** (**sit**-i-zuhn-*ship*)

citrus fruit *noun* An acidic, juicy fruit such as an orange, a lemon, or a grapefruit. **cit·rus fruit** (**sit**-ruhs)

city *noun* A very large or important town. **cit·y** (**sit**-ee) ▷ *noun, plural* **cities**

Word History

City comes to us from the older French word *cité*. Its Latin root is *civitas,* meaning "an organized community." You can see this same Latin root in the words *civilian* and *civilization*.

civic *adjective* Of or having to do with a city or the people who live in it, as in *civic organizations*. **civ·ic** (**siv**-ik)

civics *noun* The study of the way government works, and of how to be a good citizen of a community or country. **civ·ics** (**siv**-iks)

civil
1. *adjective* Of or having to do with the government or people of a country, rather than its military forces or religion, as in *civil aviation*.
2. *adjective* Polite. ▷ *noun* **civility** (suh-**vil**-i-tee)
3. civil rights *noun, plural* The individual rights that all members of a democratic society have to freedom and equal treatment under the law.
4. civil servant *noun* A person who works for the government.
civ·il (**siv**-uhl)

civilian *noun* A person who is not a member of the armed forces or a police force. **ci·vil·ian** (suh-**vil**-yuhn)

civilization *noun*
1. An advanced stage of human organization, technology, and culture.
2. A developed and organized society, as in *the ancient civilizations of the Middle East.*
civ·i·li·za·tion (*siv*-uh-li-**zay**-shuhn)

civilize *verb*
1. To improve a person's manners and education.
2. To bring a society to a level of development that is considered higher or better.
civ·i·lize (**siv**-uh-*lize*)
▷ *verb* **civilizing, civilized** ▷ *adjective* **civilized**

citrus fruit

civil war *noun*

1. A war between different groups within the same country.

2. Civil War The war in the United States between the Confederacy, or Southern states, and the Union, or Northern states, that lasted from 1861 to 1865.

cl Short for **centiliter** or the plural form *centiliters*.

clad *adjective* Dressed in a particular way: *She was clad only in a light jacket and caught a cold.* **clad** (klad)

claim *verb*

1. To demand something because you think that it belongs to you or that you have a right to it: *My sister claims credit for persuading Mom to take us to the circus.*

2. To say that something is true: *José claims he can beat me at checkers.*

claim (klaym)

▷ *verb* **claiming, claimed** ▷ *noun* **claim**

clam

1. *noun* A shellfish, often used as food, that has two tightly closed shells, which are hinged together.

2. clam up *verb (informal)* To refuse to speak: *The suspect clammed up as soon as the police started interrogating him.* ▷ *verb* **clamming, clammed**

clam (klam)

clamber *verb* To climb or move quickly and awkwardly: *The hikers clambered up the rocky cliff.*

clam·ber (**klam**-bur) ▷ *verb* **clambering, clambered**

clammy *adjective* Unpleasantly damp, sticky, and chilly, as in *a clammy raincoat.* **clam·my** (**klam**-ee) ▷ *adjective* **clammier, clammiest**

clamor

1. *verb* To demand something noisily: *All the toddlers were clamoring for attention.* ▷ *verb* **clamoring, clamored**

2. *noun* A disturbance caused by a large group of people making noise or demanding something.

clam·or (**klam**-ur)

clamp

1. *noun* A tool or instrument for holding things firmly in place.

2. *verb* To fasten something with a clamp: *The surgeon clamped the blood vessel during the operation.*

3. clamp down *verb* To try to stop something or control it more tightly: *The police have clamped down on late-night parties.*

clamp (klamp)

▷ *verb* **clamping, clamped**

Civil War

Eleven Southern states left the Union in 1861 to protect their right to keep slaves. After four years of war, the Confederacy surrendered on April 9, 1865. President Abraham Lincoln worked hard to hold the Union together and to end slavery. He succeeded, but he was assassinated only five days after the war's end. The Civil War was the bloodiest in American history. About 620,000 soldiers died in the conflict.

Union Army leader General Ulysses S. Grant

the Battle of Cold Harbor, 1864, between the Union Army (in blue) and the Confederate Army

Confederate Army leader General Robert E. Lee

a b **c** d e f g h i j k l m n o p q r s t u v w x y z

clan *noun* A large group of families descended from a common ancestor. **clan** (klan)

clap
1. *verb* To strike your hands together to show that you have enjoyed something, to keep time to music, or to get someone's attention.
▷ *verb* **clapping, clapped** ▷ *noun* **clap**
2. *noun* A loud bang of thunder.
clap (klap)

clapper *noun* The part inside a bell that makes the bell ring by striking its sides.
clap·per (**klap**-ur)

clarify *verb* To explain something; to make something clear. **clar·i·fy** (**klar**-uh-*fye*)
▷ *verb* **clarifies, clarifying, clarified**
▷ *noun* **clarification**

clarinet *noun* A long, hollow woodwind instrument. A clarinet is played by blowing into a mouthpiece and pressing keys or covering holes with the fingers to change the pitch. **clar·i·net** (*klar*-uh-**net**)

clarity *noun* The quality of being clear, or easy to understand: *Add more explanations to your essay to give it greater clarity.* **clar·i·ty** (**klar**-i-tee)

clash *verb*
1. To fight or argue vehemently.
2. To not match or go together well, as in *colors that clash.*
3. To make a loud ringing noise by striking two objects against each other.
clash (klash)
▷ *verb* **clashes, clashing, clashed**
▷ *noun* **clash**

clasp
1. *verb* To hold tightly: *The children clasped hands and started across the street.* ▷ *verb* **clasping, clasped**
2. *noun* A small fastener: *Irene couldn't close her necklace because the clasp was broken.*
clasp (klasp)

class *noun*
1. A group of students who are taught together, as in *a fifth-grade class.*
2. A group of people or things that are similar, as in *a class of automobiles.*
3. A group of people in society with a similar way of life or range of income, as in *the middle class.*
4. In taxonomy, a **class** is a group of related plants and animals that is larger than an order but smaller than a phylum.
5. *(informal)* Attractiveness and style in appearance or behavior: *That outfit has class.*
class (klas)
▷ *noun, plural* **classes**

classic
1. *adjective* Very well liked or of very good quality, and therefore likely to remain popular for a long time, as in *a classic suit* or *a classic movie.*
2. *adjective* Typical: *This computer virus is a classic example of a worm.*
3. *noun* An outstanding example of its kind: *The novel "Huckleberry Finn" is a favorite classic.*
4. **classics** *noun, plural* The languages and literature of ancient Greece and Rome.
clas·sic (**klas**-ik)

classical *adjective*
1. In the style of ancient Greece or Rome, as in *classical architecture.*
2. Traditional or accepted: *Biology and chemistry are classical subjects for people who want to study medicine.*
3. **Classical** music is serious music in the European tradition, such as opera, chamber music, and music for large orchestras.
clas·si·cal (**klas**-i-kuhl)

classified *adjective*
1. Declared secret by the government or other authority, as in *classified documents.*
2. A **classified** ad in a newspaper is a small ad for a job, a service, an item for sale, or other similar transactions, organized in sections according to category.
clas·si·fied (**klas**-uh-*fide*)

classify *verb* To put things into groups according to the characteristics they have in common. **clas·si·fy** (**klas**-uh-*fye*) ▷ *verb* **classifies, classifying, classified** ▷ *noun* **classification**

classmate *noun* A person who is in the same class as another person. **class·mate** (**klas**-*mate*)

classroom *noun* A room in a school in which classes take place. **class·room** (**klas**-*room*)

clatter *verb* To fall or bang together noisily. **clat·ter** (**klat**-ur) ▷ *verb* **clattering, clattered** ▷ *noun* **clatter**

clause *noun*
1. A group of words that contains a subject and a predicate and forms a sentence or one part of a sentence: *The sentence "She ran away when she saw the fire" is made up of two clauses: "She ran away" and "when she saw the fire."*
2. One section of a formal legal document.
clause (klawz)

clarinet

claustrophobia *noun* Extreme fear of being in small, enclosed places. **claus·tro·pho·bi·a** (*klaws*-truh-**foh**-bee-uh) ▷ *adjective* **claustrophobic**

claw
1. *noun* A hard, sharp nail on the foot of an animal or a bird.
2. *verb* To scratch with nails or claws: *The lion clawed at the bars of the cage.* ▷ *verb* **clawing, clawed**
claw (klaw)

Word History

In Old English, the same word had different forms depending on how you used it in a sentence. Our modern word **claw** is an example. In a sentence in which the claw was the subject, the form of the word was *clea.* So you would say that an animal's *clea* was sharp, for example. But you would use the form *clawe* if the claw was not the subject. For instance, you would say that an animal had hurt its *clawe,* since the word *animal* is the subject. After a while, people just used the word *clawe,* later spelled "claw."

clay *noun* A kind of earth that can be shaped when wet and baked to make bricks, pottery, or figures. **clay** (klay)

clean
1. *adjective* Not dirty, messy, or marked up. ▷ *noun* **cleanness** ▷ *adverb* **cleanly**
2. *adjective* Fair, or obeying the rules: *Both candidates ran clean campaigns.*
3. *adjective* Not rude or offensive, as in *clean language.*
4. keep your nose clean To stay out of trouble.
5. *verb* To remove the dirt from something. ▷ *verb* **cleaning, cleaned** ▷ *noun* **cleaner**
clean (kleen)
▷ *adjective* **cleaner, cleanest**

cleaning *noun* An act or instance of removing the dirt, grime, or dust from something: *The car, including the fan under the hood, will need a good cleaning.* **clean·ing** (**klee**-ning)

cleanliness *noun* Cleanness, especially of a person's body and surroundings: *Cleanliness is important for good health.* **clean·li·ness** (**klen**-lee-nis)

cleanse *verb* To make something thoroughly clean or pure. **cleanse** (klenz) ▷ *verb* **cleansing, cleansed**

cleanser *noun* A powder or liquid used to clean or scrub things. **cleans·er** (**klen**-zur)

clear
1. *adjective* Easy to see through.
2. *adjective* Colorless, as in *a clear liquid.*
3. *verb* To make or become bright: *The weather cleared.*
4. *adjective* Bright; not dark or cloudy, as in *clear skies.*
5. *adjective* Easy to understand, as in *clear instructions.*
6. *adjective* Free of obstructions, as in *a clear path.*
7. *adjective* Free of appointments or commitments, as in *a clear calendar.*
8. *verb* To remove things that are covering or blocking a place: *Clear the table.*
9. *verb* To jump over something without touching it: *The runners cleared all the hurdles.*
10. *verb* To declare that someone is not guilty of a crime: *The jury cleared her of all charges.*
11. *adjective* Free from worry or guilt, as in *a clear conscience.*
12. *adverb* In a clear way; distinctly: *Say it loud and clear.*
clear (kleer)
▷ *verb* **clearing, cleared** ▷ *noun* **clearness**
▷ *adjective* **clearer, clearest**

clearance *noun*
1. The act of clearing.
2. The sale of merchandise at a low price to get rid of it quickly, usually in order to make room for newer items: *I bought this blouse on clearance at the department store.*
3. Permission to do something.
4. The space needed so that an object can move freely without touching something else: *I couldn't drive my truck into the tunnel because there was not enough clearance between the top of my truck and the roof of the tunnel.*
clear·ance (**kleer**-uhns)

clearing *noun* An open area in a forest. **clear·ing** (**kleer**-ing)

clearly *adverb*
1. In a way that is clear: *I can't hear you very clearly; we must have a bad phone connection.*
2. Obviously and without a doubt: *If we have one more rainstorm, the river is clearly going to overflow.*
clear·ly (**kleer**-lee)

clef *noun* A symbol written at the beginning of a line of music to show the pitch of the notes, as in *bass clef* or *treble clef.* **clef** (klef)

cleft *noun*
1. A split or division: *Moss grew in a cleft in the rock.*
2. An indentation similar to a dimple: *Uncle Max has a cleft in his chin.*
cleft (kleft)

treble clef

clench *verb* To close or hold something tightly. **clench** (klench) ▷ *verb* **clenches, clenching, clenched**

clergy *noun* A group of people trained to lead religious groups, such as priests, ministers, and rabbis. **cler·gy** (**klur**-jee) ▷ *noun, plural* **clergies**

clerical *adjective*
1. Of or having to do with the clergy.
2. Of or having to do with office work, especially routine work such as filing. **cler·i·cal** (**kler**-i-kuhl)

clerk *noun*
1. A salesperson in a store.
2. A person who keeps records in an office, a bank, or a law court. **clerk** (klurk)

clever *adjective*
1. Able to learn, understand, and do things quickly and easily: *Ann is a clever math student.*
2. Ingenious; well thought out, as in *a clever plan.* **clev·er** (**klev**-ur)
▷ *adjective* **cleverer, cleverest** ▷ *noun* **cleverness** ▷ *adverb* **cleverly**

cliché *noun* An idea or a phrase that is used often but that doesn't have very much meaning: *"If you know what I mean" is a cliché.* **cli·ché** (klee-**shay**)

click *verb*
1. To make a short, sharp sound. ▷ *noun* **click**
2. *(informal)* To become suddenly clear: *The meaning of Julie's statement finally clicked.*
3. To instruct a computer to do something by pressing the mouse button when the cursor is over or pointing to the desired choice: *Clicking the link will take you to my website.* **click** (klik)
▷ *verb* **clicking, clicked**

clickbait *noun* A picture or headline on the internet that is designed to be attractive or interesting so you will click on it: *This site is nothing but clickbait and ads for stuff I don't even understand.* **click·bait** (**klik**-*bayt*)

client *noun*
1. A customer of a professional person or company: *The offices have several rooms where attorneys can consult with their clients.*
2. A computer that can exchange data with a server. **cli·ent** (**klye**-uhnt)

cliff *noun* A high, steep rock face: *From the cliff, we could see the valley below.* **cliff** (klif)

cliff-hanger *noun*
1. A story, movie, or television program presented in several parts that is exciting because each part ends at a moment of suspense.
2. A suspenseful situation: *The soccer game was a cliff-hanger right up to the final minute.*

climate *noun*
1. The weather typical of a place over a long period of time, as in *a rainy climate.* ▷ *adjective* **climatic** (klye-**mat**-ik)
2. The general situation, mood, or public opinion at a particular time, as in *a positive climate for change.* **cli·mate** (**klye**-mit)

climate change *noun* Global warming and other changes in the weather and weather patterns that are happening because of human activity.

climax *noun* The most exciting or important part of a story or an event, usually happening near the end. **cli·max** (**klye**-maks) ▷ *noun, plural* **climaxes**

climb
1. *verb* To move upward, usually with effort. ▷ *noun* **climber**
2. *noun* The process of moving upward, or an upward slope: *It was a rough climb to the top of the hill.*
3. *verb* To go in various directions using your hands to support and help you: *We climbed down the tree.* **climb** (klime)
▷ *verb* **climbing, climbed**

clinch *verb* To settle a matter definitely: *We already liked the house, but seeing the swimming pool clinched the deal.* **clinch** (klinch) ▷ *verb* **clinches, clinching, clinched**

cliffs

cling *verb* To stick to or hold on to something or someone very tightly: *The climber clung tightly to the steep rock face.* **cling** (kling) ▷ *verb* **clinging, clung** (kluhng)

clinic *noun*
1. A hospital department or other place where people receive medical treatment or advice, as in *a walk-in clinic.*
2. A class or session for teaching some specific skill or information, as in *a soccer clinic.*
clin·ic (**klin**-ik)

Word History

A **clinic** used to be known as the place with "beds." The ancient Greek word *klinikos* meant "having to do with beds," and Greek speakers formed it from their word for "bed," *kline.*

clip
1. *verb* To fasten things together with a small, tight fastener.
2. *noun* A small fastener.
3. *verb* To trim something, as in *to clip your nails.*
4. *noun* A short piece of a movie or television program shown by itself.
5. *noun* A rapid pace: *We paddled down the river at a good clip.*
clip (klip)
▷ *verb* **clipping, clipped**

clip art *noun* Simple images or pictures that are stored on a computer or online for use in illustrating a document.

clipboard *noun*
1. A thin board with a clip at the top for holding papers and writing on them.
2. A place on your computer where you can store text or pictures temporarily: *Select the paragraph and press Control + C to copy it to the clipboard.*
clip·board (**klip**-bord)

clipper *noun*
1. A tool that clips something, such as hedges or fingernails.
2. A fast-sailing ship with three masts, built in the United States in the 1800s and used to carry cargo.
clip·per (**klip**-ur)

clipping *noun* Something clipped or cut from something else, as in *a magazine clipping* or *grass clippings.* **clip·ping** (**klip**-ing)

clique *noun* A small group of friends who do not easily allow others to join them. **clique** (kleek *or* klik) ▷ *adjective* **cliquish**

cloak *noun* A loose, sleeveless coat that fastens at the neck and is wrapped around your body. **cloak** (klohk)

cloakroom *noun* A room where you can hang coats and store umbrellas, hats, and bags. **cloak·room** (**klohk**-room)

clobber *verb*
1. To hit hard: *Graham was almost clobbered by a brick that fell off a building.*
2. To defeat someone by a large margin: *The Montpelier team clobbered us 14–6 in the final game of the tournament.*
clob·ber (**klah**-bur)
▷ *verb* **clobbering, clobbered**

clock
1. *noun* An instrument that tells the time.
2. *verb* To measure the time or speed of something, as in *to clock a race.* ▷ *verb* **clocking, clocked**
clock (klahk)

Word History

Early bells were made for ringing by hand. They were made out of hammered iron sheets that were fastened together, so a bell had four sides like the cowbells we use today. When someone rang it, the clapper made a rattling sound rather than the ringing one that comes from a modern bell. If you struck this bell with a hammer once an hour, you would be measuring time, and the first **clocks** were instruments of this kind. In naming them, people tried to imitate the sharp, rattling sound of the hammer stroke.

clockwise *adverb* In the direction in which the hands of a clock move: *Turn the lid of the jar clockwise to tighten it.* **clock·wise** (**klahk**-*wize*) ▷ *adjective* **clockwise**

clockwise

clockwork *noun*
1. A mechanism with gears, springs, and wheels that makes things such as clocks and toys work. ▷ *adjective* **clockwork**
2. **like clockwork** Smoothly and without problems.
clock·work (**klahk**-*wurk*)

clod *noun*
1. A lump of earth or clay.
2. A dull or awkward person.
clod (klahd)

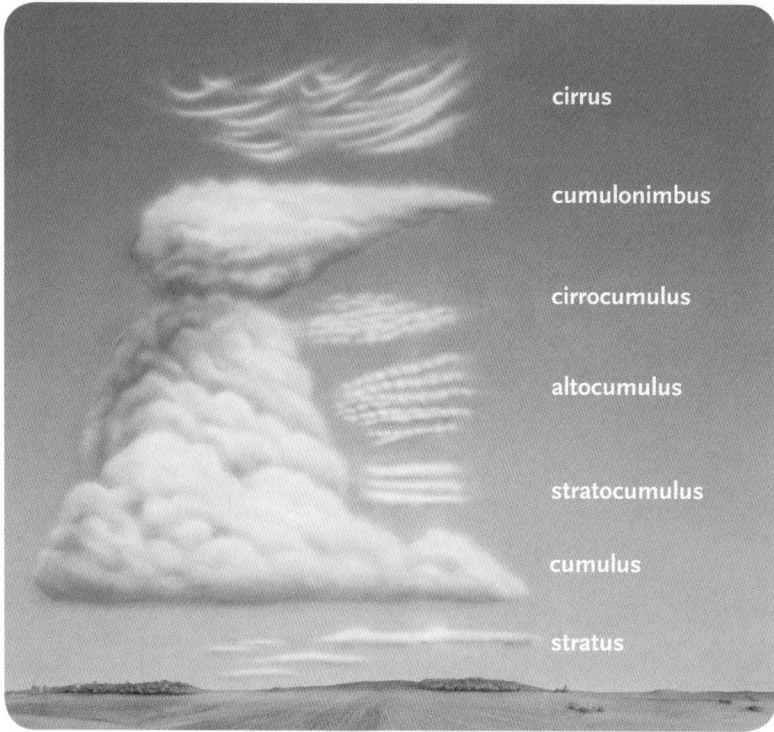

Clouds

cirrus

cumulonimbus

cirrocumulus

altocumulus

stratocumulus

cumulus

stratus

Clouds are collections of water droplets or ice crystals that usually form high in the sky. When the crystals or droplets become large enough, they fall as rain, snow, hail, or sleet.

There are three main forms of clouds. Cumulus clouds are fluffy with flat bases. Large ones can produce thunderstorms. Stratus clouds are flat, and sometimes mean wet weather. Cirrus clouds are wispy. Isolated cirrus clouds indicate stable, clear weather, but an increasing number of such clouds may be a sign of an approaching storm.

The name of a cloud can have a prefix that designates the cloud's altitude. *Cirro-* is for a high cloud. The prefix *alto-* is for a cloud at a middle elevation, and *strato-* is for a low cloud.

clog
1. *verb* To fill up or block something with foreign matter: *The gutters were clogged with trash.* ▷ *verb* **clogging, clogged**
2. *noun* A sturdy, round-toed shoe.
clog (klahg)

clone *verb* To grow an identical plant or animal from the cells of another plant or animal: *Scientists have managed to clone sheep and other mammals.* **clone** (klohn) ▷ *verb* **cloning, cloned** ▷ *noun* **clone**

close
1. (klohz) *verb* To shut something that is open: *Please close the window.*
2. (klohz) *verb* To bring something to an end: *The police have closed the investigation.*
3. (klohz) *verb* To stop running a computer program: *Save all of your work and close the program, then shut down the computer.*
4. (klohz) *noun* The end of something: *Swimming lessons are available till the close of the season.*
5. (klohs) *adverb* Near: *The dog came close to the children.*
6. (klohs) *adjective* Only a short distance away: *Their hotel is close to the shore.*
7. (klohs) *adjective* Careful: *Hal keeps a close eye on all his pets.* ▷ *adverb* **closely**

8. (klohs) *adjective* Almost even: *The race was close, but Jeremy won.*
close
▷ *verb* **closing, closed** ▷ *adverb* **closer, closest** ▷ *adjective* **closer, closest**

close call *noun* A narrow escape from danger or trouble. **close call** (klohs)

closed *adjective*
1. Not open for business: *The store was closed by the time we got there.*
2. Not welcoming to newcomers or strangers, as in *a closed society.*
closed (klohzd)

closed-circuit television *noun* A television system that shows images on a limited number of television screens.

closet *noun* A small room used for storing things. **clos·et** (**klah**-zit)

close-up *noun* A very detailed look at something, especially a camera shot taken at close range: *The scene opens with a close-up of a cowboy's hands pulling on his horse's reins.* **close-up** (**klohs**-up) ▷ *adjective* **close-up**

clot *noun* A mass of liquid that has become thicker and more solid, as in *a blood clot.* **clot** (klaht) ▷ *verb* **clot, clotting, clotted**

cloth *noun*
1. A material that is made from weaving or knitting threads, used to make clothing and many other things.
2. A small piece of this material used for a particular purpose, as in *a dusting cloth.*
cloth (klawth)

clothe *verb* To dress or provide with clothing: *Money that you donate will help feed and clothe refugees.* **clothe** (klohTH) ▷ *verb* **clothing, clothed**

clothes *noun, plural* Things that you wear, such as shirts, pants, and dresses. **clothes** (klohz)

clothespin *noun* A wooden or plastic clip used to hold clothes on a line while they dry. **clothes·pin** (klohz-*pin*)

clothing *noun* Garments worn to cover the body; clothes. **cloth·ing** (kloh-THing)

cloud
1. *noun* A visible white or gray mass of tiny water drops or ice particles suspended in the air: *Clouds formed near the horizon, obscuring the setting sun.*
2. *noun* A mass of smoke or dust.
3. **cloud over** *verb* To become covered with clouds; to become less clear or less bright: *The sky clouded over and rain began to fall.* ▷ *verb* **clouding, clouded**
cloud (kloud)

cloudy *adjective*
1. Covered with clouds.
2. Not clear: *The water looked cloudy, so it did not seem safe to drink.*
cloud·y (klou-dee)
▷ *adjective* **cloudier, cloudiest**

clove *noun*
1. The dried flower bud of a tropical tree, used whole or ground up as a spice in cooking.
2. One of the sections of a bulb of garlic.
clove (klove)

clover *noun* A small plant with white or pink flowers and three-part leaves. **clo·ver** (kloh-vur)

clown
1. *noun* A performer with a painted face and funny clothes, who tries

clown

to make people laugh.
2. *noun* A person who does silly things on purpose.
3. *verb* To do silly things in order to make people laugh or to cause disruption: *The teacher told the class to stop clowning around and sit down.*
▷ *verb* **clowning, clowned**
clown (kloun)

club *noun*
1. A group or organization devoted to a particular interest or activity.
2. The place where a group meets to share a common interest.
3. A stick with a metal or wooden head used for playing golf.
4. A thick, heavy stick, especially when used as a weapon. ▷ *verb* **club**
5. **clubs** *noun, plural* One of the four suits in a deck of cards, with a black symbol having three leaves.
club (kluhb)

clue *noun* An object or a piece of information that helps you answer a question or solve a mystery.
clue (kloo)

clump
1. *noun* A group of trees, plants, dirt, or other material, as in *a clump of hair.*
2. *verb* To walk slowly, heavily, and noisily: *Kumar clumped through the house in his ski boots.* ▷ *verb* **clumping, clumped** ▷ *noun* **clump**
clump (kluhmp)

clumsy *adjective* Careless and awkward: *Grace felt particularly clumsy after dropping an entire stack of dishes.* **clum·sy** (kluhm-zee) ▷ *adjective* **clumsier, clumsiest** ▷ *noun* **clumsiness** ▷ *adverb* **clumsily**

clung *verb* The past tense and the past participle of **cling**. **clung** (kluhng)

cluster *verb* To form a group close together: *The fans clustered around the famous actor.* **clus·ter** (kluhs-tur) ▷ *verb* **clustering, clustered** ▷ *noun* **cluster**

clutch
1. *verb* To grip something tightly: *They left the store, clutching several shopping bags.* ▷ *verb* **clutches, clutching, clutched** ▷ *noun* **clutch**
2. *noun* The pedal or lever of some motor vehicles that you press to change gears.
clutch (kluhch)

clutter *verb* To make a place messy by filling it up with a jumble of things: *The field was cluttered with empty cans and bottles.* **clut·ter** (kluht-ur) ▷ *verb* **cluttering, cluttered** ▷ *noun* **clutter**

cm Short for **centimeter** or the plural form *centimeters.*

Co. Short for **company**.

Prefix

The prefix **co-** adds one of the following meanings to a root word:

1. Together with, as in *coexist* (to exist together with).
2. Joint, as in *coauthor* (a joint author).
3. To the same degree, as in *coequal* (equal to the same degree).

coach

1. *verb* To train someone in a sport, a skill, or a subject: *My brother coaches our school basketball team.* ▷ *verb* **coaches, coaching, coached** ▷ *noun* **coach**
2. *noun* A large carriage pulled by horses.
3. *noun* A section of passenger seats on a bus, a train, or an airplane that is less expensive than first class.
4. *noun* A bus or a railroad passenger car. ▷ *noun, plural* **coaches**
coach (kohch)

Word History

Before cars and planes, the fastest way around was by **coach**—either pulled by horses or powered by steam. The word comes from Kocs, the name of a village in Hungary where such carriages originated. Some language specialists believe that the word has come to mean "tutor" or "trainer" because a coach is an instructor who brings his or her pupils along in their studies in the fastest way possible.

coal *noun*
1. A black mineral formed from the remains of ancient plants. Coal is mined underground and burned as a fuel.
2. A small piece of coal.
3. A piece of burned or slightly burning wood: *We toasted marshmallows over the coals of the campfire.*
coal (kohl)

coalition *noun* A group formed for a common purpose, as in *a coalition of student activists.* **co·a·li·tion** (koh-uh-**lish**-uhn)

coarse *adjective*
1. Having a rough surface or texture.
2. Rude and offensive, as in *coarse behavior.*
3. Having large particles, as in *coarse salt.*
coarse (kors)
Coarse sounds like **course.** ▷ *adjective* **coarser, coarsest** ▷ *noun* **coarseness** ▷ *adverb* **coarsely**

coast
1. *noun* Land that lies along the sea. ▷ *adjective* **coastal**
2. **the coast is clear** It is safe to act without being

seen or caught: *The lookout told the thieves that the coast was clear.*
3. *verb* To move along in a car or other vehicle without using any power, or to move on a bicycle or skates without exerting any effort.
4. *verb* To complete a task without much effort: *Sam coasted through the math exam.*
coast (kohst)
▷ *verb* **coasting, coasted**

coast guard *noun* The branch of a nation's armed forces that watches the sea for ships in danger and protects the coastline.

coastline *noun* The place where the land and the ocean meet; the outline of the coast. **coast·line** (**kohst**-line)

coat
1. *noun* A piece of clothing that you wear on your body over other clothes to keep you warm.
2. *noun* An animal's covering of hair or fur.
3. *noun* A thin layer: *There was a coat of ice on the trees.*
4. *verb* To cover with a thin layer of something: *The tools were thinly coated with oil.* ▷ *verb* **coating, coated**
coat (koht)

coating *noun* A layer that is covering something, as in *a coating of dust.* **coat·ing** (**koh**-ting)

coat of arms *noun* A design on a shield that identifies a noble family or person, a city, or an organization. ▷ *noun, plural* **coats of arms**

coax *verb* To persuade someone to do something, gradually or by flattery: *We've coaxed Jacqui to come with us to the movie.* **coax** (kohks) ▷ *verb* **coaxes, coaxing, coaxed** ▷ *adjective* **coaxing** ▷ *adverb* **coaxingly**

cob *noun* The center part of an ear of corn on which the kernels grow. **cob** (kahb)

cobalt *noun*
1. A silver-white metallic element used to make alloys and paints.
2. A deep blue color.
co·balt (**koh**-bawlt)
▷ *adjective* **cobalt**

cobbler *noun*
1. A person who makes or repairs shoes.
2. A dessert made of fruit, with a top crust.
cob·bler (**kah**-blur)

cobblestone *noun* A flat, round rock used in construction or formerly to pave roads. **cob·ble·stone** (**kah**-buhl-stone) ▷ *adjective* **cobblestoned**

cobra *noun* A large, poisonous snake that can raise its head and spread its skin so that its head and neck look like a hood. **co·bra** (**koh**-bruh)

cobweb *noun* A spider's web, especially one that is old and covered with dust. **cob·web** (**kahb**-web)

cocaine *noun* A powerful, addictive drug that is sold illegally in the form of a white powder or rock crystals. **co·caine** (koh-**kayn**)

cock
1. *noun* An adult male chicken.
2. *noun* A male bird of certain kinds.
3. *verb* To turn up to one side: *When she heard her name, Princess cocked her head.* ▷ *verb* **cocking, cocked**
cock (kahk)

cockatoo *noun* A white parrot with a crest of feathers, found in Asia and Australia. **cock·a·too** (**kah**-kuh-*too*)

cocker spaniel

cocker spaniel *noun* A popular breed of small dog, with a long, silky coat and long ears. **cock·er span·iel** (**kah**-kur **span**-yuhl)

cockpit *noun* The control area in the front of a plane, boat, or spacecraft where the pilot and sometimes the crew sits. **cock·pit** (**kahk**-*pit*)

cockroach *noun* A brown or black insect that lives in warm, dark places and is a household pest. **cock·roach** (**kahk**-*rohch*)

cocktail *noun*
1. A drink, usually alcoholic, made by mixing several different kinds of liquids together.
2. Seafood or fruit served at the start of a meal, as in *a shrimp cocktail.*
cock·tail (**kahk**-*tayl*)

cocky *adjective (informal)* Self-confident to the point of being unpleasant: *Hannah was acting cocky, bragging about her perfect report card.* **cock·y** (**kah**-kee) ▷ *adjective* **cockier, cockiest**

cocoa *noun*
1. A chocolate powder made from roasted and ground cacao seeds.
2. A hot drink made with cocoa powder, sugar, and milk or water.
co·coa (**koh**-koh)

coconut *noun* A very large nut with a hard, hairy shell and white insides that can be eaten. Coconuts grow on a kind of palm tree. **co·co·nut** (**koh**-kuh-nuht)

Word History

In Portuguese, an ugly mask used for frightening children was called a *coco*. The **coconut** was named after these masks, because the three holes at the bottom of the shell looked like a scary face.

cocoon *noun* A covering made from silky threads produced by the larvae of some insects and by certain other small animals to protect themselves or their eggs. **co·coon** (kuh-**koon**)

cod *noun* A fish that is found in the northern Atlantic Ocean, used for food. **cod** (kahd) ▷ *noun, plural* **cod**

coddle *verb*
1. To treat someone too gently, as if they are a baby or a little child: *The mayor accused the courts of coddling criminals and making it easy for them to avoid jail.*
2. If you **coddle** an egg, you cook it very slowly and gently in hot water that is not boiling.
cod·dle (**kahd**-uhl) ▷ *verb* **coddling, coddled**

code *noun*
1. A system of words, letters, symbols, or numbers used instead of ordinary words to send messages or to store information, as in *a secret code.* ▷ *verb* **code** ▷ *adjective* **coded**
2. A set of rules or standards, as in *a building code.*
3. The instructions of a computer program, written in a programming language.
code (kode)

coeducational *adjective* A **coeducational** school teaches both boys and girls. A **coeducational** dormitory has rooms for both males and females. Often shortened to *coed.* **co·ed·u·ca·tion·al** (*koh*-ej-uh-**kay**-shuhn-uhl)

coerce *verb* To persuade someone to do something by using threats or force: *Several people said they were coerced into signing the document.* **co·erce** (koh-**urs**) ▷ *verb* **coercing, coerced** ▷ *noun* **coercion** (koh-**ur**-shuhn)

coffee *noun*
1. A drink made from the roasted and ground beans of the coffee shrub.
2. Ground coffee beans.
cof·fee (**kaw**-fee)

Word History

The plant that **coffee** is made from is an evergreen shrub that grew naturally in Africa, probably in Ethiopia. In the 15th century, people brought the plant to Arabia. The Arabic term *qahwah* referred to the drink made from the plant's beans, and speakers of Turkish adopted the word as *kahveh*. The name eventually entered English as *coffe*, but today we spell it "coffee."

a
b
c
d
e
f
g
h
i
j
k
l
m
n
o
p
q
r
s
t
u
v
w
x
y
z

coffin *noun* A box into which a dead person is placed for burial. **cof·fin** (**kaw**-fin)

cog *noun* One of the teeth on the edge of a wheel or bar that makes machinery run. **cog** (kahg)

cogs

coherent *adjective*
1. Logical and consistent, as in *a coherent line of reasoning.*
2. United; acting together to form a whole, as in *a coherent group of workers.*
co·her·ent (koh-**heer**-uhnt)

coil
1. *verb* To wind something into a series of loops: *Coil up the hose when you're through watering.*
2. *verb* To wind or wrap around something: *The snake was coiled around the branch.*
3. *noun* A loop or series of loops.
coil (koil)
▷ *verb* **coiling, coiled**

coin
1. *noun* A small piece of metal stamped with a design and used as money.
2. *verb* To invent a new word or phrase, or a new meaning of an old word or phrase: *Yogi Berra coined the phrase "It ain't over till it's over."* ▷ *verb* **coining, coined** ▷ *noun* **coinage**
coin (koin)

Word History

The object for stamping coins with a design eventually gave the **coin** its name. The French name for the stamp was *coin,* which meant "wedge," because the stamp had the shape of a wedge—thin at one end and thick at the other. English speakers adopted the word *coin* in the Middle Ages, but soon transferred the word from the stamp to the thing that was stamped: our modern *coin.*

coincide *verb* To happen at the same time: *My birthday coincides with Labor Day this year.*
co·in·cide (*koh*-in-**side**) ▷ *verb* **coinciding, coincided**

coincidence *noun* A surprising or remarkable event that seems to happen by chance: *By a strange coincidence, Joey knocked on my door just when I was calling him on the phone.* **co·in·ci·dence** (koh-**in**-si-duhns) ▷ *adjective* **coincidental** (koh-*in*-si-**den**-tuhl) ▷ *adverb* **coincidentally**

colander *noun* A bowl-shaped utensil with holes, used for draining liquid from foods. **col·an·der** (**kah**-luhn-dur)

cold
1. *adjective* At a low temperature. ▷ *noun* **cold**
2. *adjective* Unfriendly, as in *a cold stare.* ▷ *noun* **coldness** ▷ *adverb* **coldly** ▷ *adjective* **colder, coldest**
3. *noun* A common mild illness that causes sneezes, a sore throat, a stuffy nose, and sometimes a cough and a mild fever.
cold (kohld)

Synonyms

Cold describes anything that is not as warm as you expect it to be or that is not as warm as your body temperature: *It seemed warm in the sun and cold in the shade.*

- -

■ **Chilly** means cold enough to be unpleasant: *She wrapped her coat tightly around her in the chilly evening air.*

■ **Icy** means covered with ice, or extremely cold to the touch: *During the snowstorm, the windshield became icy.* Icy can also refer to an attitude that is distant and hostile: *He looked at his enemy with an icy stare.*

■ **Freezing** means so cold that you are really uncomfortable: *With the heat turned down, we were freezing when we got up this morning.*

■ **Frozen,** in its original sense, means at or below the freezing point of 32 degrees Fahrenheit, as in *frozen yogurt.* In another sense it means uncomfortably cold: *My hands are frozen.*

cold-blooded *adjective*
1. Having a body temperature that changes according to the temperature of the surroundings, like reptiles or fish.
2. Done deliberately and cruelly, as in *a cold-blooded murder.*
cold-blood·ed (**bluhd**-id)

coleslaw *noun* A salad made of shredded cabbage mixed with other ingredients. **cole·slaw** (**kohl**-*slaw*)

coliseum *noun* A large stadium or auditorium for sports or other events. **col·i·se·um** (*kah*-li-see-uhm)

collaborate *verb* To work together to do something. **col·lab·o·rate** (kuh-**lab**-uh-*rate*) ▷ *verb* **collaborating, collaborated** ▷ *noun* **collaboration** ▷ *noun* **collaborator**

collage *noun* A piece of art made by gluing different things onto a surface, such as pieces of cloth or tissue onto cardboard. **col·lage** (kuh-**lahzh**)

collapse *verb*
1. To fall down suddenly: *The apartment building collapsed after the earthquake.*
2. To fail suddenly and completely: *The bank collapsed shortly after the scandal was reported.*

col·lapse (kuh-**laps**)
▷ *verb* **collapsing, collapsed** ▷ *noun* **collapse**

collapsible *adjective* Capable of being folded into a small space: *They escaped from the sinking ship in a collapsible boat.* **col·laps·i·ble** (kuh-**lap**-suh-buhl)

collar
1. *noun* The part of a piece of clothing, such as a shirt, blouse, or coat, that goes around your neck and is usually folded down.
2. *noun* A thin band of leather or other material worn around an animal's neck.
3. *verb* To catch someone, usually because the person is in trouble: *The police officer collared the pickpocket.* ▷ *verb* **collaring, collared**
col·lar (**kah**-lur)

collards *noun, plural* The green leaves of a vegetable related to cabbage, popular in the southern United States. **col·lards** (**kah**-lurdz)

colleague *noun* A person who works with you. **col·league** (**kah**-leeg)

collect *verb*
1. To gather things together: *Collect your bags and wait for us outside.*
2. To assemble a group of similar objects in an organized way, often as a hobby: *Mark collects baseball cards.*
3. To receive money that someone owes you: *Many businesses are having a hard time collecting their debts.*
col·lect (kuh-**lekt**)
▷ *verb* **collecting, collected**

collection *noun*
1. A group of similar things gathered on purpose, as in *a coin collection.*
2. take up a collection To gather money for a specific purpose.
col·lec·tion (kuh-**lek**-shuhn)

collective *adjective* Shared by everyone in a group: *All of the students, teachers, and staff at the school have a collective responsibility for the school's success.* **col·lec·tive** (kuh-**lek**-tiv)

college *noun* A place of higher learning where students can continue to study after they have finished high school. **col·lege** (**kah**-lij)

collide *verb* To crash together forcefully, often at high speed. **col·lide** (kuh-**lide**) ▷ *verb* **colliding, collided**

collie *noun* A breed of large dog with a long nose, a narrow head, and a thick coat. **col·lie** (**kah**-lee)

collision *noun* A sudden and violent striking together of two objects: *She swerved at the last minute to avoid a collision with a deer.* **col·li·sion** (kuh-**lizh**-uhn)

cologne *noun* A perfumed liquid used for grooming. It is named after the German city of Cologne, where it was first produced: *My father's favorite cologne has a citrus scent.* **co·logne** (kuh-**lohn**)

colon *noun*
1. The punctuation mark (:) used to introduce a list of things or a statement that will explain the preceding statement.
2. The main part of your large intestine, where partially digested food is broken down by bacteria and water is removed from it.
co·lon (**koh**-luhn)

colonel *noun* An officer in the Army, Air Force, or Marine Corps ranking below a general. **colo·nel** (**kur**-nuhl) **Colonel** sounds like **kernel**.

colonist *noun* A person who lives in a colony or who helps to establish a colony: *English colonists founded Jamestown, Virginia, in 1607.* **col·o·nist** (**kah**-luh-nist)

colonize *verb* To establish a new colony in a place. **col·o·nize** (**kah**-luh-*nize*) ▷ *verb* **colonizing, colonized**

colony *noun*
1. A group of people who leave their country to settle in a new area.
2. A territory that has been settled by people from another country and is controlled by that country.
3. A large group of animals that live together, as in *a colony of prairie dogs.*
col·o·ny (**kah**-luh-nee)
▷ *noun, plural* **colonies** ▷ *adjective* **colonial** (kuh-**loh**-nee-uhl)

color
1. *noun* A property of an object that reflects light of a certain wavelength. The eye perceives such light as being red, blue, yellow, or some other color. ▷ *adjective* **colorful** ▷ *adjective* **colorless**
2. *verb* To draw, paint, or turn something from one color to another: *Timmy colored the drawing of the flower red.* ▷ *verb* **coloring, colored**
3. *noun* The appearance of a person's skin: *You have good color since you returned from the beach.*
col·or (**kuhl**-ur)

color-blind *adjective* Unable to tell certain colors apart: *Some people who are color-blind can't distinguish red from green.* ▷ *noun* **color-blindness**

coloring *noun*
1. The way in which something is colored.
2. Something used to color something else.
col·or·ing (**kuhl**-ur-ing)

colossal *adjective* Extremely large, as in *a colossal mistake.* **co·los·sal** (kuh-**lah**-suhl)

red
green
color-blindness test

a
b
c
d
e
f
g
h
i
j
k
l
m
n
o
p
q
r
s
t
u
v
w
x
y
z

colt *noun* A young horse, donkey, or zebra, especially the male of such animals. **colt** (kohlt)

columbine *noun* A tall flower with long, narrow petals, often in two colors. **col·um·bine** (**kah**-luhm-*bine*)

Columbus Day *noun* A holiday celebrating Christopher Columbus's arrival in North America in 1492, observed on the second Monday in October. **Co·lum·bus Day** (kuh-**luhm**-buhs)

column *noun*
1. A pillar that helps support a building or statue.
2. A series of numbers or words arranged vertically: *This dictionary is printed with two columns per page.*
3. A piece of writing by the same author, or on the same subject, that appears regularly in a printed periodical or on a website. ▷ *noun* **columnist** (**kah**-luhm-nist) **col·umn** (**kah**-luhm)

coma *noun* A state of deep unconsciousness, usually caused by injury or illness. **co·ma** (**koh**-muh)

comb
1. *noun* A flat piece of metal or plastic with a row of long, thin teeth, used for making your hair smooth and neat.
2. *verb* To use a comb to arrange your hair.
3. *verb* To search a place systematically: *The searchers combed the forest looking for the missing man.*
4. *noun* The brightly colored crest on the head of a rooster or a related bird.
comb (kohm)
▷ *verb* **combing, combed**

combat
1. (**kahm**-bat) *noun* Fighting between people or armies: *The two wrestlers were engaged in fierce combat.*
2. (kahm-**bat**) *verb* To fight against something in order to destroy it or prevent it: *Everyone can help combat crime by reporting suspicious activity to the police.* ▷ *verb* **combating, combated** *or* **combatting, combatted**
com·bat

combination *noun*
1. The act of combining two or more things, or the state of being so combined: *Doctors have found that the two drugs work better in combination.*
2. Two or more things put together to act or be used as one.

com·bi·na·tion (*kahm*-buh-**nay**-shuhn)

combine *verb* To put two or more things together. **com·bine** (kuhm-**bine**) ▷ *verb* **combining, combined**

combining form *noun* A group of letters with a particular meaning that can be added to the beginning or end of a word or another combining form to make a new word. Combining forms are often used to form technical and scientific words. *Duo-, maxi-,* and *-fication* are examples of combining forms.

comb-over *noun* A men's hairstyle in which hair is combed over from the side of the head to cover a bald area.

Christopher Columbus

combustible *adjective* Capable of catching fire: *This mixture of chemicals is highly combustible and must be handled carefully.* **com·bus·ti·ble** (kuhm-**buhs**-tuh-buhl)

combustion *noun* The process of burning. **com·bus·tion** (kuhm-**bus**-chuhn)

come *verb*
1. To move toward a place where the person who is speaking or writing is already located: *The puppy came right into our classroom.*
2. To arrive: *The mail comes every day at noon.*
3. come from To be born or grow up in a particular place: *Caroline comes from Chicago.*
4. come about To happen: *How did this ridiculous situation come about?*
5. come across To find by chance: *While I was hiking, I came across a stray dog.*
6. come down with To become sick with a particular illness: *The whole family came down with the flu in the same week.*
7. come into To inherit something, such as money or property: *When the king died, the prince came into a huge fortune.*
8. come to To become conscious again: *When Nick came to, he was lying in a grassy field.*
come (kuhm)
▷ *verb* **coming, came** (kame), **come**

comeback *noun*
1. A return to success or fame after failure or after being absent from people's notice: *The singer hopes that her new album will be the beginning of a comeback.*
2. A reply that is effective, clever, or memorable: *The president's spokesman didn't have a comeback to the reports that the figures were not accurate.*
come·back (**kuhm**-*bak*)

comet

comedian *noun* An entertainer who tries to make people laugh by telling jokes and funny stories. **co·me·di·an** (kuh-**mee**-dee-uhn)

comedy *noun*
1. A funny movie or play.
2. Actions or events that make people laugh. **com·e·dy** (**kah**-mi-dee)
▷ *noun, plural* **comedies**

comet *noun* A bright heavenly body with a long tail of light. A comet travels around the sun in a long, slow path. **com·et** (**kah**-mit)

Word History

Comet comes from a Greek word meaning "long-haired star," because the tail of the comet looks like flowing hair.

comfort
1. *verb* To calm or reassure someone: *Lisa comforted the crying baby.* ▷ *verb* **comforting, comforted** ▷ *adjective* **comforting** ▷ *adverb* **comfortingly**
2. *noun* The feeling of being at ease, without pain, unpleasantness, or worry.
3. *noun* Something that makes your life more pleasant and enjoyable, as in *the comforts of home.* **com·fort** (**kuhm**-furt)

comfortable *adjective*
1. Relaxed in your body or your mind; free from pain or worry.
2. Allowing you to relax and feel pleasure; offering comfort, as in *a comfortable bed.* **com·fort·a·ble** (**kuhm**-fur-tuh-buhl)
▷ *adverb* **comfortably**

comforter *noun* A thick, warm covering for a bed, filled with feathers or fibers. **com·fort·er** (**kuhm**-fur-tur)

comic
1. *noun* A person who tells jokes and funny stories.
2. *adjective* Funny or amusing.
3. **the comics** *noun, plural* A group of comic strips. **com·ic** (**kah**-mik)

comical *adjective* Causing amusement or laughter; funny. **com·i·cal** (**kah**-mi-kuhl) ▷ *adverb* **comically**

comic book *noun* A booklet with stories told in cartoons.

comic strip *noun* A story told in a sequence of panels or cartoons, found in a newspaper or comic book.

coming *adjective* Getting closer in time; about to happen: *What are your plans for the coming weekend?* **com·ing** (**kuhm**-ing)

comma *noun* The punctuation mark (,) used for separating parts of a sentence, words in a list, or groups of three digits in large numbers. **com·ma** (**kah**-muh)

command
1. *verb* To order someone to do something.
2. *verb* To have authority over a group of people, especially in the armed forces: *The general commanded a force of thousands of troops.*
3. *noun* A word or phrase that you type to tell a computer program what to do: *It's a very simple program; there are only half a dozen commands.*
4. *noun* Your knowledge of a subject and your skill in using it: *Teresa has a good command of German.* **com·mand** (kuh-**mand**)
▷ *verb* **commanding, commanded** ▷ *noun* **command**

commander *noun* Someone who has official command over a uniformed force. Both police and military leaders can be called commanders. **com·mand·er** (kuh-**man**-dur)

commandment *noun* A law or rule, especially one that is considered to come from a divine being. **com·mand·ment** (kuh-**mand**-muhnt)

commemorate *verb* To honor and remember an important person or event: *The town commemorated the anniversary of its founding with a parade.* **com·mem·o·rate** (kuh-**mem**-uh-*rate*)
▷ *verb* **commemorating, commemorated** ▷ *noun* **commemoration** ▷ *adjective* **commemorative**

commence *verb* To begin. **com·mence** (kuh-**mens**)
▷ *verb* **commencing, commenced**

commencement *noun*
1. The start or beginning of something.
2. Graduation day, or a graduation ceremony. **com·mence·ment** (kuh-**mens**-muhnt)

commend *verb* To praise someone formally or officially: *The mayor commended us for our clean-up campaign.* **com·mend** (kuh-**mend**) ▷ *verb* **commending, commended** ▷ *noun* **commendation** (*kah*-muhn-**day**-shuhn) ▷ *adjective* **commendable**

comment
1. *noun* A remark or note that expresses your opinion or gives an explanation.
2. *verb* To give an explanation or an opinion about something. ▷ *verb* **commenting, commented** **com·ment** (**kah**-ment)

commentary *noun*

1. A description of and comments about an event, as in *sports commentary.* ▷ *noun* **commentator**

2. Something that serves as an example or an illustration: *The team's failure to win a game is a sad commentary on its lack of practice.*

com·men·tar·y (**kah**-muhn-*ter*-ee)

▷ *noun, plural* **commentaries**

commerce *noun* The buying and selling of things, especially in large amounts. **com·merce** (**kah**-murs)

commercial

1. *adjective* Of or having to do with buying and selling things, as in *commercial real estate.*

2. *noun* A television or radio advertisement.

3. *adjective* Of or having to do with making money, as in *a commercial idea.*

com·mer·cial (kuh-**mur**-shuhl)

commercialize *verb* To organize, change, or use something in order to make money: *Researchers are looking for a way to commercialize the new invention.* **com·mer·cial·ize** (kuh-**mur**-shuh-*lize*)

▷ *verb* **commercializing, commercialized** ▷ *noun* **commercialization** (kuh-*mur*-shuh-luh-**zay**-shuhn)

commission

1. *noun* A group of people who meet to solve a particular problem or do certain tasks.

2. *noun* An offer of money to do creative work, such as writing music or designing a building.

3. *noun* A written order giving someone rank in the armed services: *After leaving West Point, he received a commission in the Army.*

4. *noun* The act of doing some undesirable thing: *How can we help prevent the commission of violent crimes?*

5. *noun* Working order or condition: *When I have a cold, I'm totally out of commission.*

6. *verb* To give someone the authority to do something: *An architect was commissioned to design a new room for the house.*

7. *verb* To put a ship into service.

com·mis·sion (kuh-**mish**-uhn)

▷ *verb* **commissioning, commissioned**

commit *verb*

1. To do something wrong or illegal, as in *to commit a crime.*

2. To promise to do a specific thing or to support a specific cause.

com·mit (kuh-**mit**)

▷ *verb* **committing, committed** ▷ *adjective* **committed**

commitment *noun*

1. The state or fact of being committed or pledged to something: *Sandy made a commitment that he would be on time for practice from now on.*

2. An engagement or appointment that prevents you from doing something else: *We had to reschedule because Julie had a previous commitment.*

com·mit·ment (kuh-**mit**-muhnt)

committee *noun* A group of people chosen to discuss a particular issue and make decisions or take action for a larger group. **com·mit·tee** (kuh-**mit**-ee)

commodity *noun*

1. A raw material or an agricultural product that is bought and sold.

2. A useful or valuable thing: *Time is a precious commodity.*

com·mod·i·ty (kuh-**mah**-di-tee)

▷ *noun, plural* **commodities**

common

1. *adjective* Existing in large numbers, as in *the common housefly.*

2. *adjective* Found or occurring often, as in *a common misunderstanding.*

3. *adjective* Ordinary, usual, not special, as in *a common procedure.*

4. *adjective* Not refined or cultured; crude or vulgar.

5. *adjective* Shared by two or more people or things: *France and Germany have a common border.*

6. *noun* An area of public land that people can use.

7. *phrase* If two or more people share something, they have it **in common**: *Mark and I have an interest in science fiction in common.*

com·mon (**kah**-muhn)

▷ *adjective* **commoner, commonest** ▷ *adverb* **commonly**

common denominator *noun*

1. A denominator shared by several fractions. In the fractions ¼ and ¾, the common denominator is the number 4.

2. A trait or belief held in common by many people: *Freedom of speech is the common denominator in most democracies.*

common noun *noun* A noun that refers to a class of people, places, or things and is generally not spelled with a capital letter. The words *boy* and *island* are common nouns in the sentence "The boy lives on an island." *See* **proper noun.**

commonplace *adjective* Ordinary, easy to find, or not new: *Computers are commonplace in most offices today.* **com·mon·place** (**kah**-muhn-*plase*)

common sense *noun* The ability to think clearly and make good decisions.

commonwealth *noun*

1. A nation or state that is governed by the people who live there.

2. The people who live in and make up a nation.

com·mon·wealth (**kah**-muhn-*welth*)

commotion *noun* A confused and noisy disturbance. **com·mo·tion** (kuh-**moh**-shuhn)

communal *adjective* Shared by a number of people, as in *a communal kitchen.* **com·mu·nal** (kuh-**myoo**-nuhl) ▷ *adverb* **communally**

communicable *adjective* Easily passed from one person to another: *The common cold is a communicable disease.* **com·mu·ni·ca·ble** (kuh-**myoo**-ni-kuh-buhl)

communicate *verb* To share information, ideas, or feelings with another person through language, eye contact, or gestures: *Deaf people can communicate using sign language.* **com·mu·ni·cate** (kuh-**myoo**-ni-*kate*) ▷ *verb* **communicating, communicated** ▷ *adjective* **communicative** (kuh-**myoo**-ni-kuh-tiv)

communication *noun*
1. The activity of communicating: *The internet is a powerful means of communication.*
2. Something that is communicated; a message: *We have received no communications from them for five months.*
com·mu·ni·ca·tion (kuh-*myoo*-ni-**kay**-shuhn)

Communion *noun* A Christian church service in which people eat bread and drink wine or grape juice to remember the last meal of Jesus. **Com·mun·ion** (kuh-**myoon**-yuhn)

communism *noun* A way of organizing the economy of a country so that all the land, property, businesses, and resources belong to the government or community, and the profits are shared by all. **com·mun·ism** (**kahm**-yuh-*niz*-uhm) ▷ *noun* **communist** ▷ *adjective* **communist**

community *noun*
1. A place and the people who live in it: *Jon's mom is a well-known figure in our community.*
2. A group of people who all have something in common, as in *the local Hispanic community.*
com·mu·ni·ty (kuh-**myoo**-ni-tee) ▷ *noun, plural* **communities**

community college *noun* A college that has programs of study lasting two years or less, and that usually does not have dormitories where students live.

commute *verb* To travel some distance each day to work or school: *Students who commute may find it hard to participate in social activities on campus.* **com·mute** (kuh-**myoot**) ▷ *verb* **commuting, commuted**

commuter *noun* A person who travels some distance to work or school each day, usually by car, bus, or train. **com·mut·er** (kuh-**myoo**-tur) ▷ *verb* **commute**

compact
1. (kahm-**pakt** *or* **kahm**-pakt) *adjective* Designed to take up very little space, as in *a compact car.*
2. (kahm-**pakt** *or* **kahm**-pakt) *adjective* Grouped closely together, as in *a compact group of stores.* ▷ *noun* **compactness**
3. (**kahm**-pakt) *noun* A small, flat case containing face powder and a mirror.
4. (**kahm**-pakt) *noun* An agreement between people or groups.
5. (kuhm-**pakt**) *verb* To press or crush something to make it take up less space: *The garbage truck compacts the garbage as it is loaded.* ▷ *verb* **compacting, compacted**
com·pact

compact disk *noun* A disk with music, data, or other information stored on it that can be read by using a laser beam; a CD.

companion *noun* A person who is with you, or with whom you spend time with: *We were traveling companions for a month and I got to know her pretty well.* **com·pan·ion** (kuhm-**pan**-yuhn) ▷ *noun* **companionship**

company *noun*
1. An organization that produces or sells products or services.
2. A visiting person or group of people: *Mom invited company for dinner.*
3. An army unit under the command of a captain.
4. A group of performers, as in *a ballet company* or *a theater company.*
5. Companionship: *I was grateful for my cousin's company last week.*
com·pa·ny (**kuhm**-puh-nee) ▷ *noun, plural* **companies**

commuters

comparable *adjective* Similar enough to be compared: *Would you say this book is comparable to Harry Potter?* **com·pa·ra·ble** (**kahm**-pur-uh-buhl)

comparative *adjective*
1. Judged in relation to similar things: *Her paintings have been a comparative success.* ▷ *adverb* **comparatively**
2. Comparative forms of adjectives and adverbs are used when you compare two things or actions. For example, the comparative form of the adjective *young* is *younger,* and the comparative form of the adverb *slowly* is *more slowly.* **com·par·a·tive** (kuhm-**par**-uh-tiv) ▷ *noun* **comparative**

compare *verb*
1. To judge one thing in relation to another in order to see the similarities and differences: *When you compare these two bicycles, you'll see that one has more extra features than the other.*
2. To be like or as good as something or somebody else: *As a violinist, he compares with the best professional performers.* **com·pare** (kuhm-**pair**) ▷ *verb* **comparing, compared**

comparison *noun* The activity or result of comparing: *Before he buys a car, my father always does a thorough comparison of all the models available.* **com·par·i·son** (kuhm-**par**-i-suhn)

compartment *noun* A separate part of a container, where certain things can be kept apart from others, as in *a luggage compartment.* **com·part·ment** (kuhm-**pahrt**-muhnt)

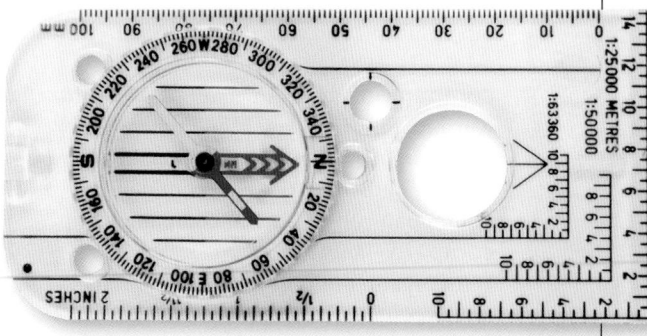
compass

compass *noun*
1. An instrument with a magnetic pointer that always points north, used for finding directions: *I used a compass to find my way out of the woods.*
2. An instrument with two legs connected by a movable joint, used for drawing circles and arcs. **com·pass** (**kuhm**-puhs)

▷ *noun, plural* **compasses**

compassion *noun* A feeling of sympathy for and a desire to help someone who is suffering. **com·pas·sion** (kuhm-**pash**-uhn) ▷ *adjective* **compassionate** ▷ *adverb* **compassionately**

compatible *adjective* Able to get along well or to be used together. **com·pat·i·ble** (kuhm-**pat**-uh-buhl) ▷ *noun* **compatibility**

compel *verb* To force someone to do something. **com·pel** (kuhm-**pel**) ▷ *verb* **compelling, compelled**

compensate *verb*
1. To repay or make up for something: *We have extra school days at the end of the year to compensate for snow days.*
2. To pay: *The study found that men and women were not compensated equally for the same work.* **com·pen·sate** (**kahm**-puhn-*sate*) ▷ *verb* **compensating, compensated**

compensation *noun* Money given to someone for work, for something they have given up, or for some loss or injury they have suffered. **com·pen·sa·tion** (*kahm*-puhn-**say**-shuhn)

compete *verb* To try hard to outdo others at a task, race, or contest: *I want to compete in a marathon someday.* **com·pete** (kuhm-**peet**) ▷ *verb* **competing, competed**

competence *noun* The state or fact of being competent to do something: *The judge handled the case with great competence.* **com·pe·tence** (**kahm**-pi-tuhns)

competent *adjective* Able to do something well: *There is a shortage of competent teachers for the blind and visually impaired.* **com·pe·tent** (**kahm**-puh-tuhnt) ▷ *adverb* **competently**

competition *noun*
1. A situation in which two or more people are trying to obtain something of which there is only a limited amount: *The competition for work time in the computer lab was stiff.*
2. A contest of some kind, as in *a swimming competition* or *a dance competition.* **com·pe·ti·tion** (*kahm*-puh-**tish**-uhn)

competitive *adjective*
1. Having to do with a situation where the participants are trying to win a contest or obtain something, as in *competitive sports.*
2. Very eager to win, succeed, or excel: *The two brothers are very close in age and have always been competitive.*
3. Similar to, or better than, others of the same kind: *This store offers very competitive prices.* **com·pet·i·tive** (kuhm-**pet**-i-tiv)

competitor *noun* Someone who competes, especially an athlete. **com·pet·i·tor** (kuhm-**pet**-i-tur)

compile *verb* To bring together many pieces of information into one larger unit: *I compiled a list of the top colleges in my area.* **com·pile** (kuhm-**pile**) ▷ *verb* **compiling, compiled** ▷ *noun* **compilation** (*kahm*-puh-**lay**-shun)

complacent *adjective* Overly satisfied or happy with your situation in life, so that you feel no need to change or improve it. **com·pla·cent** (kuhm-**play**-suhnt)

complain *verb*
1. To express dissatisfaction about something: *Bev always complains about the heat in the summer.*
2. To report, or to make an accusation: *We complained to the police about the noisy party.* **com·plain** (kuhm-**playn**)
▷ *verb* **complaining, complained**

complaint *noun*
1. A statement expressing dissatisfaction about something.
2. A cause for complaining, such as an illness: *Arthritis is a common complaint in Miguel's family.*
3. A formal charge against someone: *She filed a complaint against them for trespassing.* **com·plaint** (kuhm-**playnt**)

complement
1. *noun* Something that completes something else or makes a thing whole or better: *Dessert is the perfect complement to a good meal.*
2. *verb* To complete or enhance something: *Carola's new hat complements her outfit beautifully.* ▷ *verb* **complementing, complemented** **com·ple·ment** (**kahm**-pluh-muhnt)

complete
1. *adjective* Having all the parts that are needed or wanted, as in *a complete sewing kit.*
2. *verb* To finish something. ▷ *verb* **completing, completed**
3. *adjective* Total: *The meal was a complete disaster.* **com·plete** (kuhm-**pleet**)

completely *adverb*
1. Totally and fully; in every way: *These cherries taste completely different from the ones we had yesterday.*
2. People often use **completely** to emphasize the truth of what they are saying, or to emphasize their strong feeling about it: *We were completely lost and*

competitor

didn't even have a cell phone with us. **com·plete·ly** (kuhm-**pleet**-lee)

completion *noun* The act of completing something or the state of being complete: *After the completion of the highway, traffic moved much faster.* **com·ple·tion** (kuhm-**plee**-shuhn)

complex
1. (kuhm-**pleks** *or* kahm-pleks) *adjective* Very complicated, as in *complex instructions.* ▷ *noun* **complexity**
2. (kuhm-**pleks** *or* kahm-pleks) *adjective* Having a large number of parts: *A computer is a complex mechanism.*
3. (**kahm**-pleks) *noun* A set of strong feelings that causes you anxiety.
4. (**kahm**-pleks) *noun* A group of buildings that are near each other and are used for similar purposes, as in *a sports complex.* **com·plex**
▷ *noun, plural* **complexes**

complexion *noun* The color and look of the skin, especially the skin on your face. **com·plex·ion** (kuhm-**plek**-shuhn)

complicate *verb* To make something more difficult by introducing new elements: *Let's not complicate things by trying to do too much at once.* **com·pli·cate** (**kahm**-pli-kate) ▷ *verb* **complicating, complicated** ▷ *noun* **complication** (*kahm*-pli-*kay*-shuhn)

complicated *adjective* Difficult to use or understand because of having many different parts or ideas: *Getting permission to visit this factory is a complicated process.* **com·pli·cat·ed** (**kahm**-pli-*kay*-tid)

compliment
1. (**kahm**-pluh-muhnt) *noun* A remark or action that shows you appreciate something: *I received a lot of compliments for my coconut cookies.*
2. (**kahm**-pluh-*ment*) *verb* To make a remark or do something to show appreciation: *Everyone complimented Mrs. Bezon on her students' behavior.*
▷ *verb* **complimenting, complimented** **com·pli·ment**

complimentary *adjective*
1. Full of praise or giving praise: *The visitors were very complimentary about our concert.*
2. Costing nothing, especially when given as a gift, as in *complimentary tickets.* **com·pli·men·ta·ry** (*kahm*-pluh-**men**-tur-ee)

a
b
c
d
e
f
g
h
i
j
k
l
m
n
o
p
q
r
s
t
u
v
w
x
y
z

comply *verb* To act in agreement with rules or requests: *All students must comply with the school dress code.* **com·ply** (kuhm-**plye**) ▷ *verb* **complies, complying, complied**

component *noun* A part of a larger whole, especially a machine or a system. **com·po·nent** (kuhm-**poh**-nuhnt)

compose *verb* To write or create something, such as a piece of music, a story, or a poem. **com·pose** (kuhm-**poze**) ▷ *verb* **composing, composed**

composed *adjective* Made of certain things: *Steel is composed mainly of iron and carbon.* **com·posed** (kuhm-**pohzd**)

composer *noun* Someone who writes or composes something, especially music. **com·pos·er** (kuhm-**poh**-zur)

composite *adjective* Made up of many parts from different sources: *The police used a composite sketch to catch the burglar.* **com·pos·ite** (kuhm-**pah**-zit)

composition *noun*
1. The combining of parts to form a whole: *The composition of the painting was very balanced.*
2. What something is made of: *Today we learned about the composition of the moon.*
3. Something that is created, especially a written or musical work: *My composition on Benjamin Franklin is due tomorrow.*
com·po·si·tion (kahm-puh-**zish**-uhn)

compost *noun* A mixture of organic material, such as rotted leaves, vegetables, or manure, that is added to soil to make it more productive. **com·post** (**kahm**-pohst)

compound
1. (**kahm**-*pound*) *noun* An area of land, usually fenced in and containing one or more buildings.
2. (**kahm**-*pound*) *noun* Something formed by combining two or more parts: *The unpleasant odor was a compound of gasoline and garbage.*
3. (**kahm**-*pound*) *noun* A substance, such as salt or water, made from two or more chemical elements.
4. (**kahm**-*pound*) *adjective* Having two or more parts: *"Rowboat" is a compound word.*
5. (kahm-**pound**) *verb* To add to, or to make more complicated, as in *to compound the problem.*
▷ *verb* **compounding, compounded**
com·pound

comprehend *verb* To understand fully: *The scale of that disaster is hard to comprehend.* **com·pre·hend** (*kahm*-pri-**hend**) ▷ *verb* **comprehending, comprehended**

comprehension *noun* Understanding, or the power to understand. **com·pre·hen·sion** (*kahm*-pri-**hen**-shuhn)

comprehensive *adjective* Complete and inclusive, as in *a comprehensive set of instructions.* **com·pre·hen·sive** (*kahm*-pri-**hen**-siv) ▷ *adverb* **comprehensively**

compress *verb*
1. To press or flatten something in order to fit it into a smaller space.
2. To make a computer file smaller so that it is easier to store or send: *Compress the files in the folder to zip it, then attach it to the email.*
com·press (kuhm-**pres**)
▷ *verb* **compresses, compressing, compressed**
▷ *noun* **compression**

comprise *verb* To include or to contain: *The class comprises 25 students.* **com·prise** (kuhm-**prize**) ▷ *verb* **comprising, comprised**

compromise
1. *verb* To agree to accept something that is not entirely what you wanted, in order to satisfy some of the requests of other people. ▷ *verb* **compromising, compromised**
2. *noun* An agreement that is reached after people with opposing views each give up some of their demands: *Senators from both parties announced a compromise that will allow the bill to pass.*
com·pro·mise (**kahm**-pruh-*mize*)

compulsory *adjective* Required by a rule or a law: *Wearing a seat belt is compulsory in every state.* **com·pul·so·ry** (kuhm-**puhl**-sur-ee)

compute *verb* To find an answer by using mathematics; to calculate. **com·pute** (kuhm-**pyoot**) ▷ *verb* **computing, computed** ▷ *noun* **computation**

computer *noun* An electronic machine that can store and retrieve large amounts of information, do very quick and complicated calculations, and perform many other tasks. **com·put·er** (kuhm-**pyoo**-tur) ▷ *noun* **computing**

computer-aided design *noun* The process of creating plans and drawings on a computer to develop the design

computer-aided design

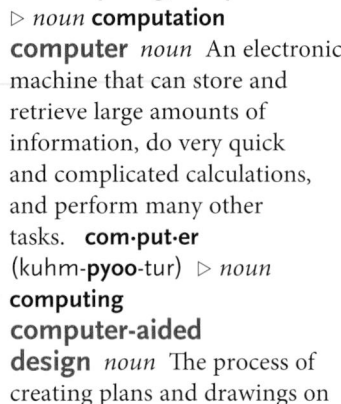

of something, such as a vehicle, room, or building. Abbreviated as **CAD**.

computer graphics *noun, plural* The pictures or images that can be made on a computer.

comrade *noun* A good friend or a colleague. **com·rade** (**kahm**-rad) ▷ *noun* **comradeship**

concave *adjective* Curved inward, like the inside of a bowl. **con·cave** (kahn-**kave** *or* kahng-**kave**)

conceal *verb* To hide something: *The stolen jewels were concealed in a secret drawer.* **con·ceal** (kuhn-**seel**) ▷ *verb* **concealing, concealed** ▷ *noun* **concealment**

concede *verb*
1. To admit something is true after denying it first.
2. To admit defeat in a competition or election.
3. To give something up: *The defeated kingdom was forced to concede some territory.*
con·cede (kuhn-**seed**)
▷ *verb* **conceding, conceded**

conceited *adjective* Overly proud of yourself and what you can do. **con·ceit·ed** (kuhn-**see**-tid) ▷ *noun* **conceit**

conceive *verb*
1. To come up with an idea: *Lee conceived the plan of collecting newspapers for recycling.*
2. To become pregnant.
con·ceive (kuhn-**seev**)
▷ *verb* **conceiving, conceived**

concentrate *verb*
1. To give all of your thought and attention to something: *Beverly concentrated on learning her lines for the play.*
2. To come together in one place: *The insects concentrate in areas where they find the best nectar sources.*
3. To make a liquid thicker and stronger by removing water from it.
con·cen·trate (**kahn**-suhn-*trate*)
▷ *verb* **concentrating, concentrated** ▷ *noun* **concentrate** ▷ *noun* **concentration** ▷ *adjective* **concentrated**

Computers

A computer is a system of electronic components that work together to store, retrieve, and process data. The physical components are called hardware. The programs, or instructions telling the computer what to do, are known as software.

The first automatic computing engine was designed by an English mathematician, Charles Babbage, in the 1830s. Since then, computers have become much faster and smaller. The internet now connects millions of computers in a worldwide network.

Modern computers do far more than mathematical calculations. They allow their users to keep records, control machinery, transmit information, and play games. With computer graphics programs, people can draw pictures, design objects, and create animation for films and television.

tablet computer

laptop computer

touch pad

monitor

wireless mouse

desktop computer

keyboard

concentric *adjective* Having their centers at the same point, as in *concentric circles.* **con·cen·tric** (kuhn-**sen**-trik)

concentric circles

concept *noun* An abstract or general idea: *The concept of democracy has developed over centuries.* **con·cept** (**kahn**-sept)

conception *noun*
1. A general idea, or the way in which something is understood: *Jeanne's conception of the situation was overly optimistic.*
2. The process of becoming pregnant. **con·cep·tion** (kuhn-**sep**-shuhn)

concern *verb*
1. To involve someone, or to be of interest or importance to someone: *The new schedule concerns everyone who rides this bus.*
2. To be about a certain topic or idea: *This report concerns the company's budget for next year.*
3. To worry: *Your health concerns all of us.* **con·cern** (kuhn-**surn**)
▷ *verb* **concerning, concerned** ▷ *noun* **concern**

concerned *adjective* Worried or anxious about something: *I'm concerned about those broken windows in the garage.* **con·cerned** (kuhn-**surnd**)

concerning *preposition* Having to do with; about: *The call was concerning our lost dog.* **con·cern·ing** (kuhn-**sur**-ning)

concert *noun* A performance by musicians. **con·cert** (**kahn**-surt)

concerto *noun* A piece of music, usually fairly long, for one or more solo instruments playing with an orchestra. **con·cer·to** (kuhn-**chair**-toh) ▷ *noun, plural* **concertos** *or* **concerti** (kuhn-**chair**-tee)

concession *noun*
1. Something that is allowed or agreed, as a result of special conditions or a special request: *As a concession, parking was permitted in the field during the outdoor concert.*
2. Permission to sell something granted by a governing body to the seller.
3. A **concession stand** is a small business in a building or stadium where food and drinks are sold. **con·ces·sion** (kuhn-**sesh**-uhn)

conch *noun*
1. A marine animal that lives in a large spiral shell.
2. The shell of this animal. **conch** (kahngk *or* kahnch)

conch shell

concise *adjective* Giving a lot of information clearly in a few words. **con·cise** (kuhn-**sise**) ▷ *adverb* **concisely**

conclude *verb*
1. To arrive at a decision or realization based on the facts that you have: *When I saw that all the cars were gone, I concluded that I would have to walk.*
2. To finish or end something: *We concluded the meeting after discussing the report.* **con·clude** (kuhn-**klood**) ▷ *verb* **concluding, concluded**

conclusion *noun*
1. The end or last part of an event or process: *There will be a question-and-answer session at the conclusion of the talk.*
2. A judgment or decision that you make after thinking about it: *Have you come to any conclusion about whether he's telling the truth?*
3. The last part of a text, especially one that repeats the main points: *In her conclusion, she listed the reasons why the study was flawed.* **con·clu·sion** (kuhn-**kloo**-zhuhn)

conclusive *adjective* Proving something or contributing strongly to the proof of something: *There's no conclusive evidence that the chemicals in these bottles are harmful.* **con·clu·sive** (kuhn-**kloo**-siv) ▷ *adverb* **conclusively**

concoct *verb*
1. To make something by combining several ingredients: *Jamie concocted a smoothie out of her favorite fruits and vegetables.* ▷ *noun* **concoction**
2. To invent something, such as a story, a plan, or an excuse. **con·coct** (kahn-**kahkt** *or* kuhn-**kahkt**) ▷ *verb* **concocting, concocted**

concord *noun*
1. A state of harmony and peace, especially between two people or groups.
2. A treaty or an agreement. **con·cord** (**kahn**-kord)

concrete
1. *noun* A building material made from a mixture of sand, gravel, cement, and water, which becomes very hard when it dries.
2. *adjective* Physically real, not abstract: *Bricks, steel girders, and wooden beams are concrete objects.* **con·crete** (**kahn**-kreet *or* kahn-**kreet**)

concur *verb* To agree: *We all concur that the performance date must be changed.* **con·cur** (kuhn-**kur**) ▷ *verb* **concurring, concurred**

concussion *noun* An injury to the brain caused by a heavy blow to the head. **con·cus·sion** (kuhn-**kuhsh**-uhn) ▷ *adjective* **concussed**

condemn *verb*

1. To disapprove strongly of something: *Senators from both parties condemned the report.*
▷ *noun* **condemnation** (*kahn*-dem-**nay**-shuhn)
2. To sentence someone to a particular punishment: *The judge condemned the thief to many years in prison.*
3. To state that something is unsafe: *The city condemned the old building.*
con·demn (kuhn-**dem**)
▷ *verb* **condemning, condemned**

condensation *noun*

1. The act or process of condensing something.
2. Something that has been condensed: *Ivan read the condensation of the novel.*
3. The changing of a gas or vapor into its liquid form: *Drops of water formed on the windows due to condensation.*
con·den·sa·tion (*kahn*-den-**say**-shuhn)

condense *verb*

1. To turn from a gas into a liquid, usually as a result of cooling.
2. To make a piece of writing shorter by removing parts of it: *The author struggled to condense his novel into a movie screenplay.*
3. To make something thicker by boiling away liquid.
con·dense (kuhn-**dens**)
▷ *verb* **condensing, condensed**
▷ *adjective* **condensed**

condescend *verb* To behave in a way that shows you think you are better than others: *She finally condescended to join us, but she kept on listening to her music and wouldn't take off her headphones.* **con·de·scend** (*kahn*-di-**send**)
▷ *verb* **condescending, condescended**
▷ *noun* **condescension** (*kahn*-di-**sen**-shuhn)

condescending *adjective* Showing an attitude that gives people the idea that you think you are better than them: *The choir conductor's condescending tone made all the singers uncomfortable.* **con·de·scend·ing** (*kahn*-duh-**sen**-ding)

condition

1. *noun* The general state of a person, animal, or thing: *The house was in terrible condition.*
2. *noun* General health or physical fitness: *Runners try to stay in good condition.*
3. *verb* To get into good health: *Physical exercise conditions your body.*
4. *noun* A medical problem that lasts for a long time, as in *a lung condition.*
5. *noun* Something that must occur before another thing can occur: *She spoke on the condition that she would not be identified.*
6. *verb* To train a person or animal to think or behave in a certain way, sometimes unintentionally: *The cat was conditioned to expect food when it heard the can opener.* ▷ *noun* **conditioning**
con·di·tion (kuhn-**dish**-uhn)
▷ *verb* **conditioning, conditioned**

conditional *adjective* Requiring something else to happen first: *Getting into college is conditional on maintaining good grades.* **con·di·tion·al** (kuhn-**dish**-uh-nuhl) ▷ *adverb* **conditionally**

conditioner *noun* A liquid that you put on your hair after washing it to improve its appearance and condition. **con·di·tion·er** (kuhn-**dish**-uh-nur)

condolence *noun* An expression of sympathy, especially when someone has just died: *You have my condolences for the loss of your grandfather.* **con·do·lence** (kuhn-**doh**-luhns)

condominium *noun* An apartment house or other development in which each unit is owned by the person who lives in it. Also known as a *condo.* **con·do·min·i·um** (*kahn*-duh-**min**-ee-uhm)

condor *noun* A type of very large vulture that lives in North or South America. **con·dor** (**kahn**-dur)

condor

conduct

1. (kuhn-**duhkt**) *verb* To organize and carry out an activity or a process: *The detectives conducted a thorough search of the building.*
2. (kuhn-**duhkt**) *verb* To direct a group of musicians as they sing or play.
3. (kuhn-**duhkt**) *verb* To lead someone on a particular route: *The guide conducted us through the museum.*
4. (kuhn-**duhkt**) *verb* To allow heat, electricity, or sound to pass through: *Copper and aluminum conduct electricity.*
5. (**kahn**-duhkt) *noun* Behavior: *The fan was thrown out of the stadium for his rowdy conduct.*
con·duct
▷ *verb* **conducting, conducted**

conductor *noun*

1. A person who directs the playing or singing of a group of musicians.

2. A person who collects fares or tickets on a train.

3. A substance that allows heat, electricity, or sound to travel through it: *Gold is an excellent conductor of electricity.*

con·duc·tor (kuhn-**duhk**-tur)

cone *noun*

1. An object or a shape with a round base and a point at the other end. ▷ *adjective* **conical** (**kah**-ni-kuhl)

2. The hard, woody fruit of an evergreen tree.

cone (kohn)

confederacy *noun*

1. A union of states, provinces, tribes, towns, or people with a common goal.

2. the Confederacy The group of 11 states that declared independence from the rest of the United States just before the Civil War.

con·fed·er·a·cy (kuhn-**fed**-ur-uh-see)

▷ *noun, plural* **confederacies**

confederate

1. *adjective* Belonging to a confederacy or union.

2. Confederate *adjective* Of or having to do with the Confederacy before and during the Civil War.

3. *noun* A person who bands together with others for a common purpose.

con·fed·er·ate (kuhn-**fed**-ur-it)

confederation *noun* A union of several groups, such as labor unions, political parties, or countries.

con·fed·er·a·tion (kuhn-*fed*-uh-**ray**-shun)

confer *verb*

1. To give someone something, such as a gift, an honor, or a reward: *The high school conferred a diploma on each of its graduates.*

2. To hold a meeting with someone; to seek someone's advice: *School officials conferred with the mayor's office about the homecoming parade.*

con·fer (kuhn-**fur**)

▷ *verb* **conferring, conferred**

conference *noun* A formal meeting for discussion: *Our city will host a conference on global warming later this year.* **con·fer·ence** (**kahn**-fur-uhns)

confess *verb* To admit that you have done something wrong: *No one has yet confessed to the vandalism.*

con·fess (kuhn-**fes**) ▷ *verb* **confesses, confessing, confessed** ▷ *noun* **confession**

confetti *noun* Small pieces of colored paper that are thrown at parades, carnivals, and other celebrations. **con·fet·ti** (kuhn-**fet**-ee)

confide *verb* To tell someone a secret: *I can always confide in my sister.* **con·fide** (kuhn-**fide**) ▷ *verb* **confiding, confided**

confetti

confidence *noun*

1. The feeling that something or someone is good and can be trusted: *Although his car was old, he had confidence that it could make the long trip.*

2. A belief that you have the necessary ability to succeed. **con·fi·dence** (**kahn**-fi-duhns)

confident *adjective*

1. Self-assured; having a strong belief in your own abilities: *Tawanda is a confident skier.*

2. Certain that things will happen in the way you expect: *I am confident that I will pass the test.*

con·fi·dent (**kahn**-fi-duhnt)

▷ *adverb* **confidently**

confidential *adjective* Secret, as in *confidential government information.* **con·fi·den·tial** (*kahn*-fi-**den**-shuhl) ▷ *adverb* **confidentially**

confine *verb*

1. To keep within certain bounds; to limit: *He confined his remarks to the subject at hand.*

2. To shut or keep in or prevent from leaving a place: *The prisoner was confined to her cell.*

con·fine (kuhn-**fine**)

▷ *verb* **confining, confined** ▷ *noun* **confinement**

confirm *verb*

1. To say that something is definitely true or will definitely happen, when it was previously just a rumor or a possibility: *Can you confirm that you're coming to my birthday party?*

2. To accept a person as a full member of a church or synagogue in a special ceremony.

con·firm (kuhn-**furm**)

▷ *verb* **confirming, confirmed** ▷ *noun* **confirmation**

confiscate *verb* To take something away as a punishment or because the item is not permitted: *The teacher confiscated the students' comic books.* **con·fis·cate** (**kahn**-fi-skate) ▷ *verb* **confiscating, confiscated** ▷ *noun* **confiscation**

conflict

1. (**kahn**-flikt) *noun* A serious and usually lengthy disagreement: *Bryce and I put our conflicts behind us and became friends again.*

2. (kahn-flikt) *noun* A war or some other period of fighting.

3. (kuhn-flikt) *verb* To clash or to disagree: *Sometimes one person's rights conflict with someone else's.* ▷ *verb* **conflicting, conflicted**
con·flict

conform *verb*
1. To think or behave in the same way as everyone else. ▷ *noun* **conformist** ▷ *noun* **conformity**
2. To follow a rule, a law, or an expectation: *All construction must conform to the city's building code.*
con·form (kuhn-**form**)
▷ *verb* **conforming, conformed**

confront *verb*
1. To meet or face someone in a hostile way: *The man confronted his accusers.*
2. To deal with something directly: *The mayor confronted the protesters and asked for a meeting.*
con·front (kuhn-**fruhnt**)
▷ *verb* **confronting, confronted**

confrontation *noun* A hostile meeting between enemies or opposing sides: *He had a terrible confrontation with his boss and resigned soon after.* **con·fron·ta·tion** (*kahn*-fruhn-**tay**-shuhn)

confuse *verb*
1. To make someone uncertain or puzzled: *The instruction manual confused us, but we eventually figured out what to do.*
2. To mistake one thing for another: *I confused cornstarch with powdered sugar and ruined the recipe.*
3. To make something more complicated: *Dale's comments only confused the issue further.*
con·fuse (kuhn-**fyooz**)
▷ *verb* **confusing, confused** ▷ *adjective* **confusing**
▷ *adjective* **confused**

confusion *noun*
1. The mental state of being completely uncertain as to what is right or wrong, or what is true or false: *Her confusion was understandable—she'd just been knocked out by the baseball.*
2. A condition in which there is no order or regularity: *After the tornado hit, confusion reigned throughout the city.*
con·fu·sion (kuhn-**fyoo**-zhuhn)

congeal *verb* To go from a liquid or semiliquid state to a thick or solid one. **con·geal** (kuhn-**jeel**)
▷ *verb* **congealing, congealed**

congested *adjective* So blocked up or full that it is impossible to move, as in *congested traffic.* **con·ges·ted** (kuhn-**jes**-tid) ▷ *noun* **congestion**

congratulate *verb* To offer good wishes to someone when something good has happened or when the person has done something special: *Myra's friends congratulated her on the birth of her first child.* **con·grat·u·late** (kuhn-**grach**-uh-*late*)
▷ *verb* **congratulating, congratulated** ▷ *noun, plural* **congratulations**

congregate *verb* To gather together for a common activity: *The athletes congregated for the track meet.* **con·gre·gate** (**kahng**-gri-*gate*) ▷ *verb* **congregating, congregated**

Word History

Congregate comes from the Latin verb *congregare*, meaning "to flock together," as animals or birds do. It is applied to people who come together for a purpose. The same Latin root is found in the word *segregate*, which means "to go from the flock," or "to separate."

---

congregation *noun* A group of people asembled for religious worship. **con·gre·ga·tion** (*kahng*-gri-**gay**-shuhn)

Congress *noun* The lawmaking body of the United States, made up of the Senate and the House of Representatives. **Con·gress** (**kahng**-gris) ▷ *adjective* **congressional** (kuhn-**gresh**-uh-nuhl)

Congress

The United States Congress consists of two houses. In the House of Representatives, the states are represented according to their population. In the Senate, each state is represented by two senators. Any new federal law must be approved by both houses. Then the president must sign it before it can become law. This system, called checks and balances, means that no one branch of government can have too much power.

United States Congress

congruent *adjective* Equal in shape and size, as in *congruent triangles.* **con·gru·ent** (kuhn-**groo**-uhnt *or* **kahng**-groo-uhnt)

conifer *noun* An evergreen tree that produces its seeds in cones. **con·i·fer** (**kah**-nuh-fur *or* **koh**-nuh-fur) ▷ *adjective* **coniferous** (kuh-**nif**-ur-uhs)

conjunction *noun* A word that connects words or phrases within a sentence. The words *and, but,* and *if* are all conjunctions. **con·junc·tion** (kuhn-**juhngk**-shuhn)

conjure *verb*

1. To perform a magic trick: *The magician conjured a rabbit out of his tall black hat.*

2. To create, as if by magic: *She conjured up a delicious dinner from leftovers.*

3. To bring to mind: *The word "autumn" conjures up brilliant reds and yellows, and the smell of hot apple cider.*

con·jure (**kahn**-jur)

▷ *verb* **conjuring, conjured**

conjurer *or* **conjuror** *noun* A person who performs magic tricks to entertain people. **con·jur·er** *or* **con·ju·ror** (**kahn**-jur-ur) ▷ *noun* **conjuring**

Word History

When you take an oath, you are making a serious, formal promise, which we sometimes call "swearing." *Conjuring* used to mean that you were making someone "swear" to do something. The Latin verb meaning "to swear," *jurare,* lies behind this word. Many people in the Middle Ages believed in supernatural beings, and they began to use the word *conjure* to mean "force a spirit to do something by using a magic spell." We now think of a **conjurer** only as someone who does magic tricks.

connect *verb* To join together. **con·nect** (kuh-**nekt**) ▷ *verb* **connecting, connected**

connection *noun*

1. A link between things, such as objects, people, or ideas: *Studying history allows you to understand the connections between past events.*

2. A train, plane, or bus that you take in order to continue on a trip you have already begun on another train, plane, or bus: *My first flight was so late that I missed my connection to London.*

3. connections *noun, plural* People you know, especially people who might be useful to you in your career: *He has connections to all of the most important people in Hollywood.*

con·nec·tion (kuh-**nek**-shuhn)

connoisseur *noun* A person who knows a lot about a subject, particularly how to recognize good quality

conjurer

in objects connected with that subject. **con·nois·seur** (*kah*-nuh-**sur**)

conquer *verb*

1. To defeat and take control of an enemy or a territory.

2. To overcome a problem or a weakness: *Marcie finally conquered her fear of the dark.*

con·quer (**kahng**-kur)

▷ *verb* **conquering, conquered** ▷ *noun* **conqueror**

conquest *noun*

1. Something that is won, such as land, treasure, or buildings.

2. The act of conquering.

con·quest (**kahn**-kwest)

conscience *noun* Your moral sense that acts as a guide to help you tell right from wrong. **con·science** (**kahn**-shuhns)

conscientious *adjective*

1. Doing things thoroughly and well. ▷ *adverb* **conscientiously**

2. A **conscientious objector** is a person who refuses to serve in the armed forces because he or she believes that it is wrong to fight and kill.

con·sci·en·tious (*kahn*-shee-**en**-shuhs)

conscious *adjective*

1. Awake and able to think and perceive: *Charlie was still conscious even after hitting his head in the accident.*

2. Aware of something: *Vera suddenly became conscious of the fact that her water bottle was leaking.*

3. Deliberate: *Bill is making a conscious effort to keep his room neater.*

con·scious (**kahn**-shuhs)

▷ *adverb* **consciously**

consciousness *noun*

1. Awareness of something: *Jenny is always late and has no consciousness of time.*

2. The faculty of mind that makes it possible for you to be aware and process input from your five senses. **con·scious·ness (kahn**-shuhs-nis)

consecutive *adjective* One right after the other: *Marcia was absent four consecutive days.* **con·sec·u·tive (kuhn-sek**-yuh-tiv) ▷ *adverb* **consecutively**

consensus *noun* An agreement among all the people in a discussion or meeting: *We reached a consensus on the date of the play.* **con·sen·sus** (kuhn-**sen**-suhs)

consent
1. *verb* To agree to something. ▷ *verb* **consenting, consented**
2. *noun* Official agreement that something can happen: *You need your parents' consent to go on the field trip.* **con·sent** (kuhn-**sent**)

consequence *noun* The result of an action, a condition, or a decision: *Being careless can sometimes have serious consequences.* **con·se·quence (kahn**-si-*kwens*) ▷ *adjective* **consequent**

consequently *adverb* As a result; because of that: *Mr. Sowles was wearing a seat belt and consequently had only minor injuries.* **con·se·quent·ly (kahn**-si-kwuhnt-lee)

conservation *noun* The protection of valuable things, especially forests, wildlife, natural resources, or artistic or historic objects. **con·ser·va·tion** (*kahn*-sur-**vay**-shuhn) ▷ *noun* **conservationist**

conservative
1. *adjective* Moderate, cautious, and traditional: *Perry is a very conservative dresser.* ▷ *adverb* **conservatively**
2. *adjective* In your political views, favoring smaller government and businesses, and being opposed to large social welfare programs.
3. *noun* A candidate or office holder who supports conservative political ideas.
4. *noun* A person who opposes big changes and believes in traditional ways of doing things. **con·serv·a·tive** (kuhn-**sur**-vuh-tiv)

conserve *verb* To save something from loss, decay, or waste; to preserve: *To conserve energy, we turn out the lights when we leave a room.* **con·serve** (kuhn-**surv**) ▷ *verb* **conserving, conserved**

consider *verb*
1. To think about something carefully, usually before making a decision or taking action: *Julio didn't consider the effect his actions would have on his family.*
2. To believe something: *Shelley considers soccer practice the most important part of her day.*
3. To take something into account: *We must consider everyone's point of view.* **con·sid·er** (kuhn-**sid**-ur) ▷ *verb* **considering, considered**

considerable *adjective* Fairly large, as in *a considerable amount of rain.* **con·sid·er·a·ble** (kuhn-**sid**-ur-uh-buhl)

considerably *adverb* More than a little; to a noticeable degree or extent: *It's considerably colder than it was yesterday.* **con·sid·er·a·bly** (kuhn-**sid**-ur-uh-blee)

considerate *adjective* Careful and concerned for other people's needs and feelings: *Derek is considerate of his classmates.* **con·sid·er·ate** (kuhn-**sid**-ur-it) ▷ *adverb* **considerately**

consideration *noun*
1. Care and concern for other people's needs and feelings: *I was impressed with how much consideration she showed her grandfather.*
2. Careful thought before making a decision: *After much consideration, I decided to stop taking piano lessons.*
3. Something that needs to be taken into account when making a decision: *Safety should be a consideration when we plan the playground.* **con·sid·er·a·tion** (kuhn-**sid**-uh-**ray**-shuhn)

consist *verb* To be made up of certain elements: *The team consists of five boys and five girls.* **con·sist** (kuhn-**sist**) ▷ *verb* **consisting, consisted**

consistent *adjective*
1. Always behaving in the same way or according to the same principles.
2. In agreement with something: *Fred's dislike of sweets is consistent with his belief in the importance of a healthy diet.* **con·sis·tent** (kuhn-**sis**-tuhnt) ▷ *noun* **consistency** ▷ *adverb* **consistently**

console
1. (kuhn-**sole**) *verb* To comfort someone who is sad or disappointed. ▷ *verb* **consoling, consoled** ▷ *noun* **consolation** (*kahn*-suh-**lay**-shun)
2. (**kahn**-sole) *noun* A cabinet for something electronic, such as a television or radio, designed to stand on the floor. **con·sole**

consolidate *verb* To bring several different parts together into one: *We consolidated our two reports.* **con·sol·i·date** (kuhn-**sah**-li-*date*) ▷ *verb* **consolidating, consolidated** ▷ *noun* **consolidation**

consonant *noun* A speech sound or letter that is not a vowel. Letters such as *b, m, r,* and *k* represent consonants. **con·so·nant** (**kahn**-suh-nuhnt)

conspicuous *adjective* Easy to see or notice, as in *a conspicuous birthmark.* **con·spic·u·ous** (kuhn-**spik**-yoo-uhs) ▷ *adverb* **conspicuously**

a
b
c
d
e
f
g
h
i
j
k
l
m
n
o
p
q
r
s
t
u
v
w
x
y
z

conspiracy *noun* A secret plan made by two or more people to do something illegal or harmful. **con·spir·a·cy** (kuhn-**spir**-uh-see) ▷ *noun, plural* **conspiracies** ▷ *noun* **conspirator** ▷ *verb* **conspire** (kuhn-**spire**) ▷ *adjective* **conspiratorial** (kuhn-*spir*-uh-**tor**-ee-uhl)

constable *noun* A police officer, especially in a rural area of Great Britain. **con·sta·ble** (**kahn**-stuh-buhl)

constant *adjective*
1. Never stopping, as in *constant activity*.
2. Staying the same over a period of time, as in *a constant beat* or *a constant temperature*.
con·stant (**kahn**-stuhnt)

constantly *adverb* All the time; without stopping: *She's constantly tweeting—she tweets about every single thing she does.* **con·stant·ly** (**kahn**-stuhnt-lee)

constellation *noun* A group of stars that forms a shape or figure and usually has a name, as in *the constellation Orion*. **con·stel·la·tion** (*kahn*-stuh-**lay**-shuhn)

Word History

The word **constellation** is based on the Latin words *con-*, meaning "together," and *stella*, meaning "star." A well-known group of stars is the Big Dipper, but it is not considered to be a constellation by itself. The Big Dipper is part of the Great Bear constellation. Ancient cultures had many legends about the animals and people that the constellations were supposed to represent. But now astronomers know that in any constellation, the stars are at different distances away from us. The stars only appear to us to be "together."

constituent *noun* A voter represented by an elected official: *The senator went home to speak to his constituents.* **con·stit·u·ent** (kuhn-**stich**-oo-uhnt)

constitute *verb*
1. To form or to compose; to make up: *Minorities now constitute about 43 percent of all Americans under 20.*
2. To set up or form legally, as in *to constitute a set of laws.*
con·sti·tute (**kahn**-sti-*toot*)
▷ *verb* **constituting, constituted**

constitution *noun*
1. The basic laws of a country that state the rights of the people and the powers of the government.
2. the Constitution The written document containing the governmental principles by which the United States is governed. It went into effect in 1789.
3. Your general physical condition, as in *a strong constitution.*
con·sti·tu·tion (*kahn*-sti-**too**-shuhn)

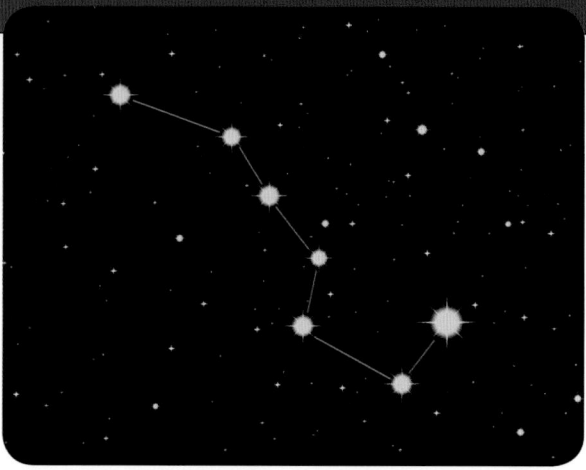

constellation: the Big Dipper

constitutional *adjective*
1. Of or having to do with a constitution, as in *a constitutional provision.*
2. Consistent with what is written in a constitution: *In the United States, it is constitutional for the government to hold a census every ten years.*
con·sti·tu·tion·al (*kahn*-sti-**too**-shuh-nuhl)

constraint *noun* Something that limits your actions. **con·straint** (kuhn-**straynt**) ▷ *verb* **constrain**

constrict *verb* To slow or stop a natural flow by making a passage narrower; to squeeze. **con·strict** (kuhn-**strikt**) ▷ *verb* **constricting, constricted**

construct *verb* To make or build something: *They've almost finished constructing the new hospital.* **con·struct** (kuhn-**struhkt**) ▷ *verb* **constructing, constructed**

construction *noun*
1. The act or process of building or constructing something: *The construction of the sports complex is expected to take nine months.*
2. The industry or job of building: *Her dad works in construction.*
con·struc·tion (kuhn-**struhk**-shuhn)

constructive *adjective* Helpful, useful, and positive, as in *constructive advice*. **con·struc·tive** (kuhn-**struhk**-tiv) ▷ *adverb* **constructively**

consul *noun* A person appointed by the government of a country to live and work in another country. A consul's job is to protect fellow citizens who are working or traveling in the foreign country. **con·sul** (**kahn**-suhl)

consult *verb*
1. To check with someone for advice: *If you need help with your taxes, you should consult an accountant.*
2. To use something as a source of information: *Philip consulted his encyclopedia to learn more about tigers.*
con·sult (kuhn-**suhlt**)
▷ *verb* **consulting, consulted**

consultant *noun* An expert in a particular field who is hired by others to give advice: *The firm has hired a computer consultant.* **con·sul·tant** (kuhn-**suhl**-tuhnt)

consultation *noun* The action of formally discussing something, or an instance of doing this: *I had a consultation with the school counselor about how to get financial aid for college.* **con·sul·ta·tion** (*kahn*-suhl-**tay**-shuhn)

consume *verb*
1. To eat or drink something: *We consumed a gallon of ice cream.*
2. To use something up: *School consumes most of my time.*
3. To destroy something: *The fire consumed the old barn.*
con·sume (kuhn-**soom**)
▷ *verb* **consuming, consumed**

consumer *noun* A person who buys and uses products and services. **con·sum·er** (kuhn-**soo**-mur)

consumption *noun* The act of consuming, using, or eating something: *We are trying to reduce our consumption of fossil fuels.* **con·sump·tion** (kuhn-**suhmp**-shuhn)

contact
1. *noun* The state or action of physically touching someone or something.
2. *noun* The state or action of communicating or meeting with someone: *Ginny is in contact with a musician in New York.*
3. *verb* To communicate with someone: *You can contact me by phone or email.*
▷ *verb* **contacting, contacted**
con·tact (**kahn**-takt)

contact lens *noun* A small plastic lens that you wear on your eyeball to improve your vision. ▷ *noun, plural* **contact lenses**

contagion *noun*
1. The spreading of a disease through contact with an infected person or animal.
2. The rapid spreading of an emotion: *The program led to a contagion of enthusiasm about family history in the area.*
con·ta·gion (kuhn-**tay**-juhn)

contagious *adjective* Spread by direct or indirect contact with an infected person or animal: *Tuberculosis is a contagious disease.* **con·ta·gious** (kuhn-**tay**-juhs)

contain *verb*
1. To hold or include something: *This kit contains everything you need to get started.*

2. To control an emotion: *I tried to contain my tears.*
con·tain (kuhn-**tayn**)
▷ *verb* **containing, contained**

container *noun* An object, such as a box, jar, or barrel, that is used to hold something. **con·tain·er** (kuhn-**tay**-ner)

contaminated *adjective* Containing harmful or undesirable substances, as in *contaminated drinking water.* **con·tam·i·nat·ed** (kuhn-**tam**-uh-*nay*-tid)
▷ *noun* **contamination** ▷ *verb* **contaminate**

contemplate *verb*
1. To think about something: *Nancy contemplated jumping into the water.*
2. To look thoughtfully at something: *Laura contemplated the flowers in the garden.*
con·tem·plate (**kahn**-tuhm-*plate*)
▷ *verb* **contemplating, contemplated** ▷ *noun* **contemplation**

contemporary
1. *adjective* Belonging or occurring in the present; modern.
2. *adjective* Happening or existing at about the same time: *The recently discovered ruins are contemporary with the Roman Empire.*
3. *noun* A person of about the same age as you.
▷ *noun, plural* **contemporaries**
con·tem·po·rar·y (kuhn-**tem**-puh-*rer*-ee)

contempt *noun* The belief that something is worthless and deserves no respect. **con·tempt** (kuhn-**tempt**) ▷ *adjective* **contemptuous** (kuhn-**temp**-choo-uhs) ▷ *adverb* **contemptuously**

contend *verb*
1. To compete for a specific goal or prize: *The two teams contended for the league championship.* ▷ *noun* **contender**
2. To claim: *She contends that it was my fault we missed the flight.*
3. To deal with or put up with: *We contended with dreadful weather to get here.*
con·tend (kuhn-**tend**)
▷ *verb* **contending, contended**

content
1. *adjective* Peacefully happy. ▷ *noun* **content** ▷ *noun* **contentment** ▷ *adjective* **contented** ▷ *adverb* **contentedly**
2. content oneself *verb* To be satisfied with something. ▷ *verb* **contenting, contented**
con·tent (kuhn-**tent**)

contents *noun, plural* The things that are inside something or that compose it: *The label lists the contents and nutritional information.* **con·tents** (**kahn**-tents)

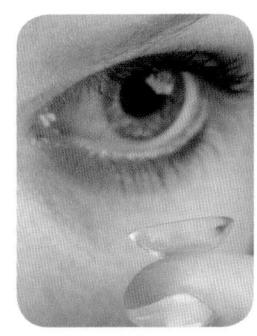
contact lens

contest
1. (**kahn**-test) *noun* A competition: *Wrestling is a contest of strength.*
2. (kuhn-**test**) *verb* To compete for something.
3. (kuhn-**test**) *verb* To dispute a decision or a result: *Tony contested the results of the race.*
con·test
▷ *verb* **contesting, contested**

contestant *noun* A participant in a competition: *A panel of chefs judged the contestants in the cooking competition.* **con·test·ant** (kuhn-**tes**-tuhnt)

context *noun*
1. The language around a word or phrase that affects or helps you understand its meaning.
2. **in context** Taking into account all the things that affect something: *This chapter looks at the Civil War in context.*
con·text (**kahn**-*tekst*)

continent *noun*
1. One of the seven large landmasses of the earth. They are Asia, Africa, Europe, North America, South America, Australia, and Antarctica.
2. **the Continent** The mainland of Europe.
con·ti·nent (**kahn**-tuh-nuhnt)
▷ *adjective* **continental**

continental shelf *noun* A comparatively shallow, gently sloping area of the seafloor near a coastline.

continual *adjective*
1. Happening repeatedly; frequent: *Your continual complaining is not helping to change my mind!*

2. Happening without a pause; continuous.
con·tin·u·al (kuhn-**tin**-yoo-uhl)

continually *adverb* Repeatedly; again and again: *The information on the website is updated continually.* **con·tin·u·al·ly** (kuhn-**tin**-yoo-uh-lee)

continue *verb* To keep on doing something: *We'll continue working until we've finished our report.* **con·tin·ue** (kuhn-**tin**-yoo) ▷ *verb* **continuing, continued** ▷ *noun* **continuation**

continuous *adjective* Present or happening all the time and not stopping, as in *a continuous noise.* **con·tin·u·ous** (kuhn-**tin**-yoo-uhs) ▷ *adverb* **continuously**

contour *noun* The outline of an object.
con·tour (**kahn**-toor)

contraband *noun* Things that are brought illegally from one place to another: *Customs officers sometimes check passengers' bags for contraband.* **con·tra·band** (**kahn**-truh-*band*) ▷ *adjective* **contraband**

contract
1. (**kahn**-trakt) *noun* A legal agreement between people or companies stating what each of them has agreed to do and any amounts of money involved, as in *a real estate contract.*
2. (kuhn-**trakt**) *verb* To become smaller: *The pupils of people's eyes contract in bright light.*
3. (kuhn-**trakt**) *verb* To catch a disease: *He contracted the flu.*
con·tract
▷ *verb* **contracting, contracted**

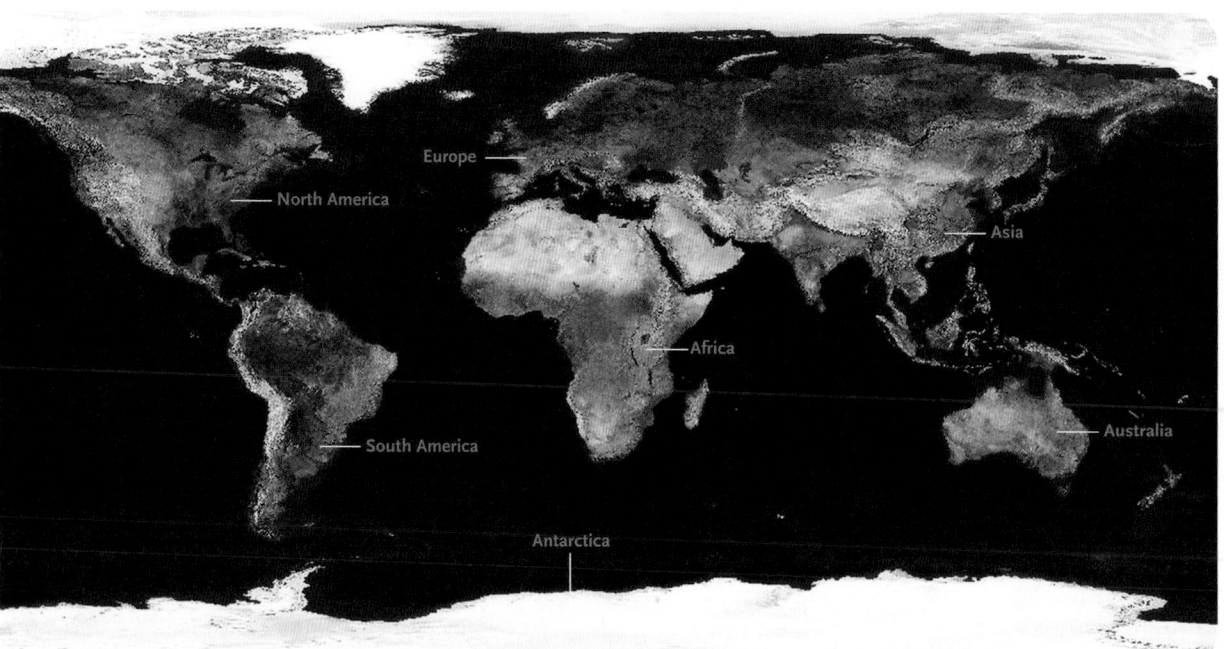

Europe
North America
Asia
Africa
South America
Australia
Antarctica

continents

aircraft control panel

contraction *noun*
1. A shortening or shrinking of something: *There has been a sharp contraction in grain exports this year.*
2. A shortening of a muscle in order to cause a part of the body to move: *Contractions of the leg muscles allow us to walk.*
3. Two words combined with an apostrophe, such as *can't, wouldn't, I'd, won't.*
con·trac·tion (kuhn-**trak**-shuhn)

contractor *noun* A person who agrees to do a particular job for a certain price, especially in the building industry, as in *a plumbing contractor.* **con·trac·tor** (**kahn**-*trak*-tur)

contradict *verb* To say the opposite of what has already been said. **con·tra·dict** (*kahn*-truh-**dikt**)
▷ *verb* **contradicting, contradicted**

contradiction *noun* A combination of statements or conditions that are opposed to each other, or the act of making a statement that opposes another: *She saw no contradiction between her faith and her work as a scientist.* **con·tra·dic·tion** (*kahn*-truh-**dik**-shuhn)

contradictory *adjective* Opposite, contrary, or not consistent. **con·tra·dic·tor·y** (*kahn*-truh-**dik**-tur-ee)

contraption *noun* A strange or complicated device or machine. **con·trap·tion** (kuhn-**trap**-shuhn)

contrary *adjective*
1. (**kahn**-trer-ee) Opposite: *John and Denise have contrary views on politics; he is liberal, while she is conservative.* ▷ *noun* **contrary**
2. (kuhn-**trair**-ee) Deliberately stubborn and difficult: *Jim is the most contrary boy I've ever met.*
con·trar·y

contrast *verb*
1. To differ greatly: *The report contrasted strongly with what we saw.*
2. To point out the differences between things: *Contrast this rock sample with that one.*
con·trast (kuhn-**trast**)

▷ *verb* **contrasting, contrasted** ▷ *noun* **contrast** (**kahn**-trast)

contribute *verb*
1. To give help or money in order to accomplish a specific goal: *Molly's parents contribute thousands of dollars to charity.*
2. To help to bring about: *The artwork on the walls contributes to the cheerful feeling in the room.*
3. To write for a publication: *Would you like to contribute an article to our online newsletter?*
con·tri·bute (kuhn-**trib**-yoot)
▷ *verb* **contributing, contributed** ▷ *noun* **contributor**

contribution *noun* The act of giving or contributing something, or the thing given: *We did a mural on the town's history, and Adrian's contribution was to paint a picture of the town's founder.* **con·tri·bu·tion** (*kahn*-truh-**byoo**-shuhn)

contrive *verb*
1. To make something happen by using skill and cleverness: *The criminals contrived to kidnap someone.*
2. To make something up: *The boys contrived a story to explain their lateness.*
con·trive (kuhn-**trive**)
▷ *verb* **contriving, contrived**

control
1. *verb* To make something or someone act in a particular way: *Frederick controls his horse expertly.*
▷ *noun* **control**
2. *noun* Power or authority over people or a situation.
3. controls *noun, plural* The levers, switches, and other devices that make a machine work.
4. *verb* To hold back: *Please control your anger.*
con·trol (kuhn-**trohl**)
▷ *verb* **controlling, controlled**

control panel *noun*
1. The part of an aircraft or machine where all the controls are.
2. The place on a computer where you can change settings that affect the way the computer operates.

controversial *adjective* Causing a great deal of disagreement. **con·tro·ver·sial** (*kahn*-truh-**vur**-shuhl)

controversy *noun* An argument in which people express strongly opposing views about something: *Women can now vote, but women's suffrage was a matter of great controversy in the 19th century.* **con·tro·ver·sy** (**kahn**-truh-*vur*-see)
▷ *noun, plural* **controversies**

convalescence *noun* The time during which a person is recovering from an illness, an injury, or an operation. **con·va·les·cence** (*kahn*-vuh-**les**-uhns)
▷ *verb* **convalesce**

a b c d e f g h i j k l m n o p q r s t u v w x y z

convalescent
1. *noun* A person who is recovering from an illness, an injury, or an operation.
2. *adjective* Of or having to do with a person recovering from an illness, injury, or operation, or with a period of convalescence.
con·va·les·cent (*kahn*-vuh-**les**-uhnt)

convection *noun* The circulation of heat through liquids and gases. **con·vec·tion** (kuhn-**vek**-shuhn)

convene *verb* To gather together: *The meeting convened at eight o'clock.* **con·vene** (kuhn-**veen**)
▷ *verb* **convening, convened**

convenience *noun*
1. Something that makes a job or a situation easier and more pleasant: *The cottage has been equipped with all the modern conveniences.*
2. **convenience food** Food that is quick and easy to prepare, such as a frozen dinner.
con·ven·ience (kuhn-**veen**-yuhns)

convenient *adjective* Useful, or easy to use: *The bus is very convenient for me, since it stops right near my house.* **con·ven·ient** (kuhn-**veen**-yuhnt)
▷ *adverb* **conveniently**

convent *noun* A building occupied by nuns.
con·vent (**kahn**-vent)

convention *noun*
1. A formal gathering of people who have the same profession or interests: *Jack went off to a convention of stamp collectors.*
2. A customary or accepted way to behave.
con·ven·tion (kuhn-**ven**-shuhn)

conventional *adjective*
1. Usual, accepted, or traditional, as in *conventional methods of controlling weeds.*
2. Preferring the traditional way of doing things, as in *a conventional person.*
con·ven·tion·al (kuhn-**ven**-shuh-nuhl)
▷ *adverb* **conventionally**

conversation *noun* The act of talking with another person for a while. **con·ver·sa·tion** (*kahn*-vur-**say**-shuhn)

converse
1. *verb* (kahn-**vurs**) To talk with someone.
▷ *verb* **conversing, conversed**
2. *noun* (**kahn**-vurs) Something that is the reverse or opposite of something else. ▷ *adverb*
conversely
con·verse

convert
1. (kuhn-**vurt**) *verb* To turn something into something else: *We've converted our extra bedroom into an*

office. ▷ *verb* **converting, converted**
2. (**kahn**-vurt) *noun* A person who has changed his or her religion or other beliefs: *Which religion is attracting the most converts today?*
con·vert
▷ *noun* **conversion** (kuhn-**vur**-zhuhn)

convertible
1. *adjective* Able to be changed into something else: *Our convertible couch becomes a bed at night.*
2. *noun* A car with a top that can be put down.
con·vert·i·ble (kuhn-**vur**-tuh-buhl)

convex *adjective* Curved outward, like the outside of a bowl. **con·vex** (**kahn**-veks *or* kahn-**veks**)

convey *verb*
1. To carry or take from one place to another: *Taxis conveyed the visitors to the auditorium.*
2. To tell or to communicate: *Would you mind conveying a message to your aunt for me?*
con·vey (kuhn-**vay**)
▷ *verb* **conveying, conveyed**

convict
1. (kuhn-**vikt**) *verb* To declare that someone is guilty of a crime: *The suspect was convicted of breaking and entering.* ▷ *verb* **convicting, convicted**
2. (**kahn**-vikt) *noun* A person who is in prison because he or she has committed a crime.
con·vict

conviction *noun*
1. A strong belief or opinion, as in *moral convictions.*
2. A formal declaration that a person has committed a crime.
con·vic·tion (kuhn-**vik**-shuhn)

convince *verb* To persuade someone to do or believe something: *We convinced Hal that he should try out for the play.* **con·vince** (kuhn-**vins**) ▷ *verb* **convincing, convinced**

convincing *adjective* Having qualities that make you want to believe something or change your mind about something: *At the meeting, he made several convincing arguments for why the old gym should be converted into a library.* **con·vinc·ing** (kuhn-**vin**-sing)
▷ *adverb* **convincingly**

convertible

convoy *noun* A group of vehicles or ships that travel together for convenience or safety. **con·voy** (**kahn**-voi)

convulsion *noun* An involuntary jerking movement of the muscles or the whole body, sometimes causing the person to fall or to lose consciousness. **con·vul·sion** (kuhn-**vuhl**-shuhn)

cook
1. *verb* To prepare and heat food for eating. ▷ *verb* **cooking, cooked** ▷ *noun* **cooking**
2. *noun* A person whose job is to prepare food. **cook** (kuk)

cookbook *noun* A book filled with recipes, cooking directions, and information about food. **cook·book** (**kuk**-*buk*)

cookie *noun*
1. A small, sweet, usually flat cake.
2. A small file that is stored on your computer by a website so that when you visit the site again it will remember some things about you, such as the pages you visited: *Most cookies expire after a certain amount of time.* **cook·ie** (**kuk**-ee)

cool
1. *adjective* Somewhat cold. ▷ *noun* **coolness**
2. *verb* To reduce the temperature of something. ▷ *verb* **cooling, cooled**
3. *adjective* Unfriendly or unenthusiastic: *Chico met my news with a cool stare.* ▷ *adverb* **coolly**
4. *adjective* (*informal*) Attractive, impressive, or fashionable. **cool** (kool) ▷ *adjective* **cooler, coolest**

co-op *noun* A store, society, or building in which members own shares. Co-op is short for **cooperative**. **co-op** (**koh**-*ahp*)

coop
1. *noun* A small building or pen used to house chickens or other small animals.
2. *verb* **coop up** To confine in a small space: *We've been cooped up in the house all day because of the rain.* ▷ *verb* **cooping, cooped** **coop** (koop)

cooperate *verb* To work together toward the same goal. **co·op·er·ate** (koh-**ah**-puh-*rate*) ▷ *verb* **cooperating, cooperated**

cooperation *noun* The activity of working together to achieve something: *Thanks to everyone's cooperation, the neighborhood fair this weekend was a great success.* **co·op·er·a·tion** (koh-*ah*-puh-**ray**-shuhn)

cooperative
1. *adjective* Willing to work with other people, as in *a cooperative student.* ▷ *noun* **cooperativeness**
2. *noun* A business owned by all the people who work in it, and who share the responsibilities and the profits. **co·op·er·a·tive** (koh-**ah**-pur-uh-tiv)

coordinate
1. (koh-**or**-duh-*nate*) *verb* To organize activities or people so that they function smoothly together: *Julie was in charge of coordinating all of the museum's volunteers.* ▷ *verb* **coordinating, coordinated** ▷ *noun* **coordination** ▷ *noun* **coordinator**
2. (koh-**or**-duh-*nit*) *noun* One of a set of numbers used to show the position of a point on a line, graph, or map. **co·or·di·nate**

copperhead

coordinated *adjective* Able to make your arms and legs work well together; graceful. **co·or·di·nat·ed** (koh-**or**-duh-*nay*-tid)

cope *verb* To deal with something effectively: *Peter's family is coping well with the flood damage.* **cope** (kope) ▷ *verb* **coping, coped**

copier *noun* A machine that copies printed material. **cop·i·er** (**kah**-pee-ur)

copilot *noun* The assistant pilot of an airplane. **co·pi·lot** (**koh**-*pye*-luht)

copper *noun*
1. A reddish-brown metal that conducts heat and electricity well.
2. A reddish-brown color. **cop·per** (**kah**-pur) ▷ *adjective* **copper** ▷ *adjective* **coppery**

copperhead *noun* A poisonous snake with a light brown body and dark brown markings. Copperheads are found in the eastern part of the United States. **cop·per·head** (**kah**-pur-*hed*)

copy
1. *verb* To do or say the same as another person: *Erin worked hard to copy her older brother's success.*
2. *noun* Something that looks, sounds, or acts exactly the same as the original. ▷ *noun, plural* **copies**
3. *verb* To make a similar or identical version of something. **cop·y** (**kah**-pee) ▷ *verb* **copies, copying, copied**

copyright *noun* The legal right to control the use of something created, such as a song or book. **cop·y·right** (**kah**-pee-*rite*)

coral *noun*
1. A substance found underwater, made up of the skeletons of tiny sea creatures.
2. A pink-red color.
cor·al (**kor**-uhl)
Coral sounds like **choral**.

coral reef *noun* A reef made of coral and other materials that have solidified into rock.

cord *noun*
1. A string or rope.
2. A covered wire that connects an electrical appliance to an outlet.
3. A pile of cut wood four feet wide, four feet high, and eight feet long.
cord (kord)
Cord sounds like **chord**.

cordial *adjective* Friendly and cheerful, as in *a cordial visit.* **cor·dial** (**kor**-juhl) ▷ *adverb* **cordially**

corduroy *noun* A heavy cotton material with a ribbed pattern. **cor·du·roy** (**kor**-duh-*roi*)

core *noun*
1. The hard center part of a fruit, such as an apple or pear, which often contains seeds. ▷ *verb* **core**
2. The intensely hot, most inner part of the earth.
3. The most important part of something: *The core of the project was to build a new bridge.*
4. The place in a nuclear reactor where fission occurs.
core (kor)
Core sounds like **corps**.

cork *noun* Soft bark used to make mats, stoppers for bottles, wall covering, and other objects. **cork** (kork) ▷ *verb* **cork**

corks

corkscrew
1. *noun* A tool for pulling corks out of bottles.
2. *adjective* Turning in circles or spirals, as in *corkscrew pasta.*
cork·screw (**kork**-*skroo*)

cormorant *noun* A large diving bird with a long neck, a hooked bill, and mainly dark feathers. **cor·mor·ant** (**kor**-mur-uhnt)

corn *noun*
1. A plant that produces its seeds in rows on the ears of the plant, grown for many consumer and industrial uses: *This year, we planted 30 acres of corn.*
2. The sweet yellow or white seeds of one variety of this plant, eaten as a vegetable.

3. A small, painful patch of thick, hard skin on your foot.
corn (korn)

cornea *noun* The transparent outer layer of the eyeball. The cornea covers the iris and pupil. **cor·ne·a** (**kor**-nee-uh)

corner
1. *noun* The place where two or more sides or edges of something meet: *June swept the cobwebs out of the corners of the room.* ▷ *adjective* **corner**
2. *noun* The place where two streets intersect.
3. just around the corner Very close by.
4. just around the corner Expected to happen very soon: *Christmas is just around the corner.*
5. *verb* To get a person or an animal into a situation or position that is a trap: *The cat cornered a mouse and was about to eat it.*
6. corner the market To control the supply or the price of a particular thing: *The company is attempting to corner the market on frozen orange juice.*
cor·ner (**kor**-nur)
▷ *verb* **cornering, cornered**

cornet *noun* A brass musical instrument that is similar to but shorter than a trumpet. **cor·net** (kor-**net**)

cornmeal *noun* Ground dried corn. **corn·meal** (**korn**-*meel*)

cornrow *noun* A flat braid of hair arranged close to the scalp: *She wore her hair in cornrows.* **corn·row** (**korn**-*roh*) ▷ *verb* **cornrow**

cornstarch *noun* Flour made from the starchy part of corn kernels, used to thicken sauces.

corner

corn·starch (**korn**-*stahrch*)

coronary
1. *adjective* Of or having to do with the heart, as in *coronary disease.*
2. *noun* A heart attack. ▷ *noun, plural* **coronaries**
cor·o·nar·y (**kor**-uh-*ner*-ee)

coronation *noun* The ceremony in which a king, queen, or other ruler is crowned. **cor·o·na·tion** (*kor*-uh-**nay**-shun)

coroner *noun* An official who investigates sudden, violent, or unnatural deaths. **cor·o·ner** (**kor**-uh-nur)

corporal *noun* A soldier who ranks below a sergeant. **cor·po·ral** (**kor**-pur-uhl)

corporal punishment *noun* Physical punishment, such as spanking.

corporation *noun* A group of people who are allowed by law to run a company, college, or town as a single person. Like an individual, a corporation can enter into contracts and buy and sell property. **cor·po·ra·tion** (kor-puh-**ray**-shuhn)

corps *noun*
1. A group of people acting together or doing the same thing.
2. A company of military officers and enlisted personnel.
corps (kor)
Corps sounds like **core**. ▷ *noun, plural* **corps** (korz)

corpse *noun* A dead body, especially of a human. **corpse** (korps)

corpuscle *noun* A red or white blood cell. **cor·pus·cle** (**kor**-*puhs*-uhl)

corral
1. *noun* A fenced area that holds horses, cattle, or other animals.
2. *verb* To gather people, animals, or things in an enclosed area: *Mom corralled the whole family in the kitchen.* ▷ *verb* **corralling, corralled**
cor·ral (kuh-**ral**)

correct
1. *adjective* True, right, or having no errors, as in *the correct answer.* ▷ *adverb* **correctly**
2. *verb* To put an error right: *Please correct the spelling in your essay.* ▷ *verb* **correcting, corrected**
cor·rect (kuh-**rekt**)

correction *noun* The act of making something correct, or a statement, number, or piece of information that does this: *The publisher promised to make several corrections before the book goes into a second printing.* **cor·rec·tion** (kuh-**rek**-shuhn)

correspond *verb*
1. To write letters or emails to someone.
2. To match in some way: *Your skills correspond to our needs.*
cor·re·spond (kor-uh-**spahnd**)
▷ *verb* **corresponding, corresponded**

correspondence *noun*
1. Letters or other communications between people, or the activity of exchanging messages: *The book is about the private correspondence of Abraham Lincoln.*
2. Similarity in particular points: *Each caption in an illustrated book has to have a direct correspondence with the picture it accompanies.*
cor·re·spond·ence (kor-uh-**spahn**-duhns)

correspondent *noun*
1. A person who reports for television, radio, or a printed publication about a particular subject or place, as in *a war correspondent.*
2. A person who writes letters, especially to the same recipient on a regular basis.
cor·res·pond·ent (kor-uh-**spahn**-duhnt)

corresponding *adjective* Similar with respect to form, position, scale, or change: *When the economy gets worse, there is a corresponding rise in poverty.* **cor·re·spond·ing** (kor-uh-**spahn**-ding)

corridor *noun* A long hallway or passage in a building or train. **cor·ri·dor** (**kor**-i-dur)

corrode *verb* To destroy or eat away at something little by little: *The salty water had corroded the pipes so badly that they had to be replaced.* **cor·rode** (kuh-**rode**) ▷ *verb* **corroding, corroded** ▷ *noun* **corrosion** ▷ *adjective* **corrosive**

corrugated *adjective* Shaped into ridges or ripples, as in *corrugated cardboard.* **cor·ru·gated** (**kor**-uh-*gay*-tid)

corrupt
1. *verb* To make someone dishonest or immoral: *The power that comes with political office often corrupts politicians.* ▷ *verb* **corrupting, corrupted** ▷ *adjective* **corrupt**
2. *adjective* Containing errors that make a thing unreliable or useless, as in *corrupt computer files.* ▷ *verb* **corrupt**
cor·rupt (kuh-**ruhpt**)

corruption *noun*
1. Dishonesty and cheating by public officials.
2. The condition of behaving improperly and being corrupt: *The preacher gave a sermon on how to avoid moral corruption.*
3. The state of being spoiled and corrupted: *The scratches on the CD resulted in the corruption of all its data.*
cor·rup·tion (kuh-**ruhp**-shuhn)

corsage *noun* A small bouquet worn on clothing or fastened to the wrist. **cor·sage** (kor-**sahzh**)

cosmetic
1. **cosmetics** *noun, plural* Beauty products; makeup.
2. *adjective* Of or having to do with the way a person or thing looks, as in *cosmetic changes* or *cosmetic surgery.*
cos·met·ic (kahz-**met**-ik)

Word History

What's *cosmic* about lipstick? A lot, as it turns out. The ancient Greek word *kosmos* meant "order," and the Greeks thought that well-arranged things were beautiful. A later Greek word, *kosmetikos*, meant "skilled in decorating." The English word **cosmetic** carries on this meaning; *cosmic* is from the same root.

a
b
c
d
e
f
g
h
i
j
k
l
m
n
o
p
q
r
s
t
u
v
w
x
y
z

cosmic *adjective* Of or having to do with the universe apart from the earth, as in *cosmic matter*. **cos·mic** (**kahz**-mik) ▷ *adverb* **cosmically**

cosmos *noun* The universe. **cos·mos** (**kahz**-mohs)

cosplay *noun* The activity of dressing up as a character from a book, show, or movie and acting like that character: *Jacob found a lightsaber at a garage sale that he could use in cosplay.* **cos·play** (**kaws**-play) ▷ *verb* **cosplay**

cost
1. *verb* To have a price; to be worth a certain amount: *Each book costs two dollars.*
2. *verb* To cause the loss of something: *Ron's speeding cost him his driver's license.*
3. **cost of living** *noun* The amount of money you need to spend on necessary items, such as food, housing, and clothing: *The cost of living is usually higher in a city than in the country.*
cost (kawst) ▷ *verb* **costing, cost** ▷ *noun* **cost**

co-star *noun* A famous performer who appears in a movie, play, or television show with another performer who is equally famous. ▷ *verb* **co-star**

costly *adjective*
1. Expensive, as in *costly jewels.*
2. Causing a loss or disadvantage, as in *a costly mistake.*
cost·ly (**kawst**-lee) ▷ *adjective* **costlier, costliest**

costume *noun*
1. Clothes worn by actors or people dressing in disguise.
2. Clothes worn by people at a particular time or in a particular place: *A kimono is a traditional Japanese costume.*
cos·tume (**kahs**-toom)

cot *noun* A small, narrow bed that can be folded up and put away. **cot** (kaht)

cottage *noun* A small house, especially in a beach or country setting. **cot·tage** (**kah**-tij)

cottage cheese *noun* Soft, white cheese made from curdled milk.

cotton *noun*
1. A plant that produces seed pods containing fluffy white fibers.
2. The cloth made from such fibers.
cot·ton (**kah**-tuhn)

cotton ▷ *adjective* **cotton**

cougar

cottonmouth *noun* A poisonous snake that lives near water and in swamps in the southeastern part of the United States. It is also called a **water moccasin**. **cot·ton·mouth** (**kah**-tuhn-*mouth*)

cottontail *noun* A rabbit with a short, fluffy, white tail. **cot·ton·tail** (**kah**-tuhn-*tayl*)

cottonwood *noun* A kind of poplar tree with seeds covered with whitish hairs that look like cotton. **cot·ton·wood** (**kah**-tuhn-*wud*)

couch *noun*
1. A long, cushioned piece of furniture that two or more people can sit on at the same time. ▷ *noun, plural* **couches**
2. **couch potato** *(informal)* A person who spends a lot of time watching television rather than being active.
couch (kouch)

cougar *noun* A member of the cat family with a small head, long legs, and a strong body. Cougars live in the mountains of North and South America; also called **mountain lion**, **panther**, or **puma**. **cou·gar** (**koo**-gur)

cough
1. *verb* To force air out of your lungs with a sudden sharp sound. ▷ *verb* **coughing, coughed** ▷ *noun* **cough**
2. *noun* An illness or condition that makes you cough. **cough** (kawf)

could *verb* Past tense of **can**. **could** (kud)

couldn't *contraction* A short form of *could not*: *Jesse couldn't write his report until he went to the library and did some research.* **could·n't** (**kud**-uhnt)

council *noun* A group of people chosen to run a town, a county, or an organization, as in *the city council*. **coun·cil** (**koun**-suhl) **Council** sounds like **counsel**.

counsel
1. *verb* To give people advice about problems: *My mom counseled me on how to study for the test.* ▷ *verb* **counseling, counseled**
2. *noun* Advice.
coun·sel (**koun**-suhl)
Counsel sounds like **council**. ▷ *noun* **counseling**

counselor *noun*
1. Someone trained to help with problems or give advice: *He felt better after seeing the school counselor.*
2. A lawyer.
coun·sel·or (**koun**-suh-lur)

count *verb*
1. To say numbers in order. ▷ *noun* **counting**
2. To figure out how many there are of something: *Molly counted five trucks in front of the building.* ▷ *noun* **count**
3. To be worth something: *In our family, everyone's opinion counts.*
4. count on To rely on something or someone: *Reporters count on the research service to give them good information.*
5. To consider: *We count ourselves lucky to have survived the earthquake.*
count (kount)
▷ *verb* **counting, counted**

countdown *noun* A backward counting from a certain number down to zero, to mark the moment when something happens, as in *a missile launch countdown.* **count·down** (**kount**-*doun*)

counter
1. *noun* A long, flat surface, usually used for work or display, as in *a kitchen counter.*
2. *noun* A small piece of wood or plastic used in some games or to do math.
3. *adjective* Opposite: *Your opinion is counter to mine.* ▷ *adverb* **counter**
coun·ter (**koun**-tur)

Prefix

The prefix **counter-** adds one of the following meanings to a root word:

1. Against, as in *counteract* (act against someone or something).
2. The opposite of, as in *counterclockwise* (the opposite of clockwise).

---

counteract *verb* To act against something in order to reduce its effect: *Resting in the shade will counteract the effects of too much sun.* **coun·ter·act** (*koun*-tur-**akt**) ▷ *verb* **counteracting, counteracted**

counterclockwise *adverb* In a direction opposite to the way the hands of a clock move: *A hurricane is a severe tropical storm that spins counterclockwise.* **coun·ter·clock·wise** (*koun*-tur-**klahk**-*wize*) ▷ *adjective* **counterclockwise**

countryside

counterclockwise

counterfeit *adjective* Fake, but looking almost exactly like the real thing, as in *counterfeit money.* **coun·ter·feit** (**koun**-tur-fit) ▷ *noun* **counterfeit** ▷ *verb* **counterfeit**

counterpart *noun*
1. A person or thing whose position or function is similar in some way to that of another: *This computer is much faster than its counterpart in the other classroom.*
2. One of two parts that complete each other.
coun·ter·part (**koun**-tur-*pahrt*)

countless *adjective* Too many to count: *We had countless arguments about who should go first.* **count·less** (**kount**-lis)

country *noun*
1. A part of the world with its own territory and government.
2. Land away from towns or cities, containing farmland, forests, or other land that has not been built on and where few people live. ▷ *adjective* **country**
3. The people of a nation: *He asked the country's forgiveness.*
coun·try (**kuhn**-tree)
▷ *noun, plural* **countries**

countryman *noun* Someone from your own country: *The league's only Chinese team member had a rare chance to play in front of an audience of his countrymen.* **coun·try·man** (**kuhn**-tree-muhn) ▷ *noun, plural* **countrymen**

countryside *noun* Land outside of towns or cities, with few inhabitants or buildings. **coun·try·side** (**kuhn**-tree-*side*)

county *noun* A division of a state with its own local government. **coun·ty** (**koun**-tee) ▷ *noun, plural* **counties** ▷ *adjective* **county**

coup *noun*
1. An achievement that comes suddenly and unexpectedly.
2. The sudden overthrow of a government.
coup (koo)

couple *noun*
1. Two of the same kind of thing.
2. Two people paired together.
cou·ple (**kuhp**-uhl)

coupon *noun*

1. A small piece of paper, sometimes cut out of a newspaper or magazine, that gives you a discount on something.

2. A small form that you fill out and mail to get information about something or to order merchandise.

cou·pon (**koo**-pahn)

courage *noun* Bravery; the ability to do something that scares you. **cour·age** (**kur**-ij) ▷ *adjective* **courageous** (kuh-**ray**-juhs) ▷ *adverb* **courageously**

Word History

The word **courage** is related to *cordial,* meaning "friendly." This word comes from the Latin term *cor,* meaning "heart." A *cor* could mean either a person's heart, or the part of a person that feels emotion. Latin speakers added an ending to *cor,* creating the word *coraticum. Coraticum* became *corage* in Old French, meaning "heart," the part that feels emotion. English speakers began using *courage* to mean "bravery," because of its earlier senses of "heart" and "purpose."

courier *noun* A person or a service that carries messages or packages for somebody else. **cour·i·er** (**kur**-ee-ur *or* **koor**-ee-ur)

course *noun*

1. A part of a meal served by itself: *The main course was a pasta dish.*

2. A series of lessons or classes.

3. An area where certain sports are played, as in *a golf course.*

4. A route: *The ship followed a straight course from Florida to Bermuda.*

course (kors)

Course sounds like **coarse.**

court

1. *noun* A place where legal cases are heard and decided.

2. *noun* An area where certain sports are played, as in *a squash court* or *a tennis court.*

3. *noun* An open space closed in by walls or buildings.

4. *verb* To try to win the love of someone, especially so as to marry.

5. *verb* To try to attract: *Politicians court voters at election time.*

6. *verb* To risk misfortune by behaving carelessly: *Don't court disaster.*

court (kort)

▷ *verb* **courting, courted**

courteous *adjective* Polite, respectful, and considerate. **cour·te·ous** (**kur**-tee-uhs) ▷ *noun* **courteousness** ▷ *adverb* **courteously**

courtesy *noun*

1. Well-mannered behavior: *He showed her the greatest courtesy on their date.*

2. A thoughtful act; a favor: *We offer free delivery as a courtesy to our customers.* ▷ *noun, plural* **courtesies** **cour·te·sy** (**kur**-ti-see)

courthouse *noun* A building where trials and government business are conducted. **court·house** (**kort**-hous)

court-martial *noun* A court in which military trials are held, using military law. ▷ *noun, plural* **courts-martial** ▷ *verb* **court-martial**

courtship *noun* Attempts by one person to win the love and affection of another, usually with the intention of marrying. **court·ship** (**kort**-ship)

courtyard *noun* An open area surrounded by walls or buildings; a court. **court·yard** (**kort**-*yahrd*)

couscous *noun* A dish made from tiny grains of pasta. **cous·cous** (**koos**-*koos*)

cousin *noun* A child of your uncle or aunt. **cous·in** (**kuhz**-in)

cove *noun* A small, sheltered inlet along a coast. **cove** (kove)

covenant *noun* A formal and often legal agreement to do or to avoid a certain thing: *To keep the neighborhood residential, we have a covenant that prohibits businesses from operating here.* **cov·e·nant** (**kuhv**-uh-nuhnt)

cover *verb*

1. To put something on top of or in front of something else: *Laine covered her bed with a bright quilt.* ▷ *noun* **cover**

2. To teach or study a particular topic: *In this course, we will cover fish, frogs, and lizards.*

3. To travel a certain distance: *The cyclists covered ten miles this afternoon.*

4. To extend or apply over a certain area: *This delivery service covers the entire county.*

5. To provide compensation for a loss: *Our insurance covers fire, flood, and theft.* **cov·er** (**kuhv**-ur) ▷ *verb* **covering, covered** ▷ *noun* **coverage**

covered wagon *noun* A large wooden wagon with a canvas cover spread over metal hoops, used by American pioneers crossing the country during the nation's westward expansion.

coverup *noun* An attempt to prevent people from finding out about

covered wagon

something bad, especially a crime: *The Army denies that there was any coverup concerning the soldier's death.* **cov·er·up** (**kuhv**-ur-*uhp*)

covert *adjective* Secret: *The government agent was on a covert mission in enemy territory.* **co·vert** (**koh**-vurt) ▷ *adverb* **covertly**

covet *verb* To want something very much even though it may belong to someone else. **cov·et** (**kuhv**-it) ▷ *verb* **coveting, coveted**

cow *noun*
1. An adult female farm animal, raised especially for her milk.
2. An adult female of some other large mammals, including elk, seals, and whales.
3. **till the cows come home** (*informal*) For a very long time: *Those two could sit and trade tall tales till the cows come home.*
cow (kou)

coward *noun* A person who lacks the courage to face dangerous or unpleasant situations. **cow·ard** (**kou**-urd)

cowardice *noun* Lack of bravery. **cow·ard·ice** (**kou**-ur-dis)

cowardly *adjective* Having or showing a lack of courage that also suggests weakness: *Coming up and hitting him from behind was a cowardly thing to do.* **cow·ard·ly** (**kow**-urd-lee)

cowboy *noun* A man or boy who herds and takes care of cattle. **cow·boy** (**kou**-*boi*)

cowgirl *noun* A woman or girl who herds and takes care of cattle. **cow·girl** (**kou**-*gurl*)

cowhand *noun* A person who works on a ranch. **cow·hand** (**kou**-*hand*)

cowhide *noun* The skin of a cow, used to make leather goods. **cow·hide** (**kou**-*hide*)

coworker *noun* A person who works with another; a colleague: *He sent an email to his coworkers about the staff meeting.* **co·work·er** (**kou**-*wur*-kur)

coyote *noun* An animal that looks like a small wolf and is native to the western United States. **coy·o·te** (kye-**oh**-tee *or* **kye**-oht) ▷ *noun, plural* **coyote** *or* **coyotes**

cozy *adjective* Comfortable, snug, and warm: *Our country cottage was small but cozy.* **co·zy** (**koh**-zee) ▷ *adjective* **cozier, coziest** ▷ *noun* **coziness** ▷ *adverb* **cozily**

CPR *noun* A method of reviving a victim of a heart attack or suffocation using mouth-to-mouth breathing and rhythmic compressing of the chest. CPR is short for *cardiopulmonary resuscitation.*

CPU *noun* The part of a computer that processes commands and manages the programs that are running. CPU is short for *central processing unit.*

crab *noun* A creature that lives in water and has a hard shell, eight legs, and two claws. Some kinds of crabs can be eaten. **crab** (krab)

crab apple *noun* A small, sour apple used to make jelly.

crabby *adjective* Grouchy or irritable. **crab·by** (**krab**-ee) ▷ *adjective* **crabbier, crabbiest** ▷ *noun* **crabbiness** ▷ *adverb* **crabbily**

crack
1. *verb* To break or split without completely separating, often with a loud, sharp noise: *The vase cracked when she dropped it.* ▷ *noun* **crack**
2. *verb* To solve a puzzle: *The detectives finally cracked the case.*
3. *noun* A break or a narrow opening: *We opened the window a crack.*
4. *noun* (*informal*) A nasty or sarcastic remark.
5. *noun* (*slang*) A form of the drug cocaine.
6. **take a crack at** (*informal*) To try to do something: *I'll be glad to take a crack at repairing your bike.*
crack (krak)
▷ *verb* **cracking, cracked**

cracker *noun* A thin, crisp biscuit or wafer. **crack·er** (**krak**-ur)

crackle *verb* To make a lot of quick, sharp sounds: *The dry twigs crackled underfoot.* **crack·le** (**krak**-uhl) ▷ *verb* **crackling, crackled** ▷ *noun* **crackle**

cradle
1. *noun* A small bed for a young baby, usually on rockers.
2. *verb* To hold something or someone in or as if in a cradle: *Veronica cradled the vase carefully in her arms.* ▷ *verb* **cradling, cradled**
3. *noun* The place where something starts, as in *the cradle of democracy.*
cra·dle (**kray**-duhl)

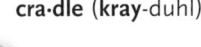

crab

craft *noun*

1. Skillful work involving making things with your hands: *Knitting is a craft that requires attention and patience.* ▷ *verb* **craft**

2. A boat, ship, spaceship, or plane.
craft (kraft)

craftsmanship *noun* Skill in making or doing something, especially with your hands.
crafts·man·ship (**krafts**-muhn-*ship*)

crafty *adjective* Good at tricking people. **craft·y** (**kraf**-tee) ▷ *adjective* **craftier, craftiest** ▷ *adverb* **craftily**

crag *noun* A steep, rough cliff or rock face. **crag** (krag) ▷ *adjective* **craggy**

cram *verb*

1. To force things into a small or crowded space: *Stan crammed all his clean shirts into a drawer.*

2. To study very hard over a short period of time, as in *to cram for an exam.*
cram (kram)
▷ *verb* **cramming, crammed**

cramp

1. *noun* A painful muscle contraction, often caused by strain or fatigue.

2. cramp your style *verb* (*informal*) To keep you from expressing yourself freely: *The school dress code really cramps my style.* ▷ *verb* **cramping, cramped**

3. cramps *noun, plural* Sharp pains in your abdomen.
cramp (kramp)

cramped *adjective* Too small or crowded to hold the people or things that need to fit: *With four of us on board, the boat's cabin was rather cramped.* **cramped** (krampt)

cranberry *noun* A small, red, sour berry that grows on low bushes in bogs and in swamps. **cran·ber·ry** (**kran**-*ber*-ee)

crane

1. *noun* A large wading bird with long legs and a long neck and bill.

2. *noun* A machine with a long arm used to lift and move heavy objects.

3. *verb* To stretch your neck so that you can see over or around something better: *Martha had to crane to one side to see around the man in front of her.* ▷ *verb* **craning, craned**
crane (krane)

crank

1. *noun* A handle that is attached at a right angle to a shaft and is turned to make a machine work.

2. *verb* To start something, or make something run, by turning a crank. ▷ *verb* **cranking, cranked**

3. *noun* (*informal*) Someone with strange ideas: *A*

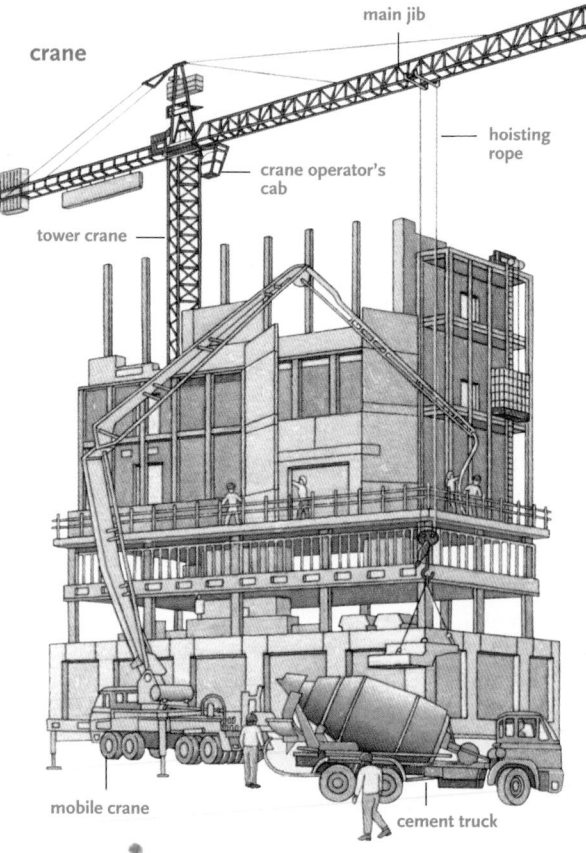

crane

main jib

crane operator's cab

hoisting rope

tower crane

mobile crane

cement truck

crank called the radio station at least once a day. ▷ *adjective* **crank**
crank (krangk)

cranky *adjective* Acting in an annoyed way; grouchy: *The baby gets cranky before her nap.*
crank·y (**krang**-kee) ▷ *adjective* **crankier, crankiest**

crappy *noun*

1. (*slang*) Not good at all; of poor quality: *With those crappy shoes it's no wonder your feet got wet!*

2. Unpleasant and not at all enjoyable, as in *a crappy mood* or *crappy weather.*
crap·py (**krap**-ee)

crash

1. *verb* To make a loud, smashing noise.

2. *verb* To collide violently with another object.

3. *noun* A violent collision, especially an accident involving a vehicle: *A crash on the interstate is causing traffic jams.* ▷ *noun, plural* **crashes**

4. *verb* To fail completely: *My computer crashed.*
crash (krash)
▷ *verb* **crashes, crashing, crashed**

crate *noun* A large wooden or plastic box used for transporting and storing things, as in *a crate of apples.* **crate** (krate) ▷ *verb* **crate**

crater *noun*
1. The mouth of a volcano or geyser.
2. A large hole in the ground caused by something falling or exploding, such as a meteorite or a bomb. **cra·ter** (**kray**-tur)

crave *verb* To want something very much: *Bernie always craved ice cream after dinner.* **crave** (krave) ▷ *verb* **craving, craved** ▷ *noun* **craving**

crawdad *or* **crawfish** *noun* (*informal*) Other names for **crayfish.** **craw·dad** (**kraw**-dad) *or* **craw·fish** (**kraw**-fish)

crawl
1. *verb* To move on your hands and knees.
2. *verb* To move slowly: *Traffic crawled during the morning rush hour.*
3. *noun* A style of swimming facedown in which you alternate your arm strokes while kicking your legs rapidly. **crawl** (krawl) ▷ *verb* **crawling, crawled** ▷ *noun* **crawl**

crayfish *noun* A small animal related to the lobster that lives in freshwater and is used for food. **cray·fish** (**kray**-*fish*) ▷ *noun, plural* **crayfish** *or* **crayfishes**

crayon
1. *noun* A stick of colored wax used for drawing and coloring.
2. *verb* To draw or color with a crayon. ▷ *verb* **crayoning, crayoned** **cray·on** (**kray**-uhn *or* **kray**-ahn)

craze *noun* A very popular fashion or pastime that usually does not stay popular very long: *Squeezing lots of people into telephone booths was a craze in the 1950s.* **craze** (kraze)

crazy *adjective*
1. Insane or foolish.
2. (*informal*) Extremely enthusiastic: *Laurie is crazy about horses.* **cra·zy** (**kray**-zee) ▷ *adjective* **crazier, craziest** ▷ *noun* **craziness** ▷ *adverb* **crazily**

crater

creak *verb* To make a high-pitched squeaking noise when something is moved or weight is put on it: *The floors of the old house creak loudly.* **creak** (kreek) **Creak** sounds like **creek.** ▷ *verb* **creaking, creaked** ▷ *noun* **creak** ▷ *adjective* **creaky** ▷ *adverb* **creakily**

cream *noun*
1. A thick, fatty liquid found in whole milk: *Butter is made by churning cream.*
2. A thick, smooth liquid that you put on your skin to soften and protect it, as in *face cream.*
3. A yellow-white color, or the color of cream. ▷ *adjective* **cream**
4. The best part, as in *the cream of the crop.* **cream** (kreem) ▷ *noun* **creaminess** ▷ *adjective* **creamy**

cream cheese *noun* A soft white cheese that is spread on bread or used to make dip or cheesecake.

crease *verb* To make folds or lines in something, especially fabric or paper. **crease** (krees) ▷ *verb* **creasing, creased** ▷ *noun* **crease**

create *verb*
1. To make something new: *Rachel created a website for her mom's company.*
2. To make something happen as a result of an action or a situation: *Jeremy's absence created difficulties for the rest of the team.* **cre·ate** (kree-**ate**) ▷ *verb* **creating, created**

creation *noun*
1. Something that has been made or invented, especially something that shows artistic talent: *All sorts of student creations are on sale at the art fair.*
2. The act of making something: *The scientist gave a talk about the creation of the new cell technology.* **cre·a·tion** (kree-**ay**-shuhn)

creative *adjective* Skillful at using your imagination and thinking of new ideas. **cre·a·tive** (kree-**ay**-tiv) ▷ *noun* **creativity** ▷ *adverb* **creatively**

creator *noun* A person who creates something: *Millions of Americans are now content creators, meaning that they are contributing material, like an image or a video clip, that appears on a website.* **cre·a·tor** (kree-**ay**-tur)

creature *noun* A living being, human or animal. **crea·ture** (**kree**-chur)

credentials *noun, plural* Written proof of someone's background, experience, or certification, such as a diploma or certificate: *What credentials are required for teaching in this state?* **cre·den·tials** (kri-**den**-shuhlz)

credible *adjective* Believable, as in *a credible witness.* **cred·i·ble** (**kred**-uh-buhl) ▷ *noun* **credibility**

credit *noun*

1. The balance in your favor in an account: *I have a credit of $36 at the store because I returned a blouse that I bought.*

2. Public acknowledgment or praise: *The boss gave a great deal of credit to his staff for their help.*

3. on credit To be paid for later, as in *buying a car on credit.*

4. credits *noun, plural* A list of names at the end of a movie or television program that tells you who made it. ▷ *verb* **credit** **cred·it** (**kred**-it)

credit card *noun* A small, plastic card used in stores and restaurants to purchase products and services on credit.

creditor *noun* A person or company to whom another person or company owes money: *There was a meeting of all the company's creditors when it went bankrupt.* **cred·i·tor** (**kred**-i-tur)

creed *noun* A system of beliefs; a guiding belief. **creed** (kreed)

creek *noun* A stream, usually one that is smaller than a river. **creek** (kreek) **Creek** sounds like **creak.**

creep

1. *verb* To move very slowly and carefully so as not to make noise: *Sophie crept up and surprised her dad.* ▷ *noun* **creep**

2. *verb* To move slowly because of an obstruction: *The traffic crept along in the fog.*

3. *noun* (*slang*) An unpleasant person.

4. give you the creeps (*informal*) To be unpleasant and frightening: *Horror movies give me the creeps.* **creep** (kreep)

▷ *verb* **creeping, crept** (krept) ▷ *adjective* **creepy**

cremate *verb* To burn a dead body to ashes. **cre·mate** (**kree**-mate) ▷ *verb* **cremating, cremated** ▷ *noun* **cremation**

Creole

1. *noun* Someone of mixed European and African descent born in the West Indies or South America.

2. *noun* Someone of French or Spanish descent living in Louisiana or Texas.

3. *noun* The languages based on French that are spoken in Louisiana and Haiti.

4. creole or **Creole** *adjective* Prepared with a spicy sauce of tomatoes, peppers, and okra. The word usually comes after a noun rather than before it, as in *shrimp creole.* **Cre·ole** (**kree**-ohl)

crepe *noun* A very thin pancake that is sometimes rolled up around a filling. **crepe** (krape)

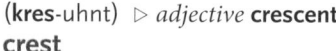

crescent

crepe paper *noun* A thin paper with a wrinkled texture, often used in party decorations.

crescent *noun* A curved shape similar to that of the moon when it is just a sliver in the sky. **cres·cent** (**kres**-uhnt) ▷ *adjective* **crescent**

crest

1. *noun* The top of something, especially a mountain, a hill, or a wave.

2. *noun* A tuft of feathers on the top of a bird's head. ▷ *adjective* **crested**

3. *verb* To reach the highest point: *The river crested and overflowed its banks during the huge storm.* ▷ *verb* **cresting, crested**

4. *noun* Part of a coat of arms.

crest (krest)

crevice *noun* A narrow opening in something, such as a rock. **crev·ice** (**krev**-is)

crew *noun* A team of people who work together on a ship, an aircraft, or a specific job, as in *a cleanup crew.* **crew** (kroo)

crib *noun*

1. A small bed for a baby, usually with bars on the sides.

2. A small farm building in which grain is stored.

crib (krib)

cricket *noun*

1. A jumping insect that makes a high-pitched chirping sound.

2. An outdoor game played by two teams of 11 players with smooth, flat bats and a small, hard ball.

crick·et (**krik**-it)

crime *noun* An act that is against the law. **crime** (krime)

criminal

1. *noun* A person who commits a crime.

2. *adjective* Of or having to do with crime, as in *a criminal record.* ▷ *adverb* **criminally**

crim·i·nal (**krim**-uh-nuhl)

cricket

crimson
   1. *noun* A dark red color.
   2. *adjective* Being a dark red in color, as in *crimson blossoms.*
   crim·son (**krim**-zuhn)

cringe *verb* To shrink back and cower out of fear, surprise, or disgust: *I cringed when I saw the teacher look in my direction, and wished I had read the chapter.* **cringe** (krinj) ▷ *verb* **cringing, cringed**

cripple
   1. *noun* A handicapped person who cannot function normally. Most people find this word offensive.
   2. *verb* To injure someone in a way that causes a serious handicap.
   3. *verb* To stop someone or something from moving or working properly, or to cause severe damage: *The whole state was crippled by the hurricane.*
   crip·ple (**krip**-uhl)
   ▷ *verb* **crippling, crippled** ▷ *adjective* **crippled**

crisis *noun* A time of severe difficulty or danger: *The uncontrolled fire has created a crisis for local residents and authorities.* **cri·sis** (**krye**-sis) ▷ *noun, plural* **crises** (**krye**-seez)

crisp *adjective*
   1. Firm, dry, and easily broken, as in *a crisp slice of bacon.* ▷ *adjective* **crispy**
   2. Pleasantly cool and fresh, as in *a crisp autumn day.*
   crisp (krisp)
   ▷ *adjective* **crisper, crispest** ▷ *adverb* **crisply**

crisscross *verb* To form or move in a pattern of intersecting lines: *The party streamers crisscrossed the ceiling.* **criss·cross** (**kris**-kraws) ▷ *verb* **crisscrossing, crisscrossed** ▷ *noun* **crisscross** ▷ *adjective* **crisscross**

criterion *noun* A fact or quality that you use as a standard when you judge something. Note that *criterion* is used less often than the plural form of the word, *criteria*: *What are the criteria for getting on the honor roll?* **cri·te·ri·on** (krye-**teer**-ee-uhn) ▷ *noun, plural* **criteria**

critic *noun*
   1. A person who finds something wrong with people or things: *He is a critic of the government.*
   2. A person whose job is to judge and write about books, movies, plays, or restaurants.
   crit·ic (**krit**-ik)

critical *adjective*
   1. Expressing a negative opinion or finding fault: *Ben's critical remarks about the game upset the players.*
   2. Dangerous or serious, as in *a critical procedure.*
   crit·i·cal (**krit**-i-kuhl)
   ▷ *adverb* **critically**

criticism *noun*
   1. A critical comment or complaint about something.
   2. The activity of evaluating books, movies, performances, or works of art.
   crit·i·cism (**krit**-i-*siz*-uhm)

criticize *verb*
   1. To tell someone what he or she has done wrong, often in a hostile or impatient way.
   2. To evaluate something, such as a book, movie, play, or television program.
   crit·i·cize (**krit**-i-*size*)
   ▷ *verb* **criticizing, criticized**

croak *verb*
   1. To make a deep, hoarse sound like a frog.
   2. To speak with a deep, hoarse voice. ▷ *adjective* **croaky**
   3. *(slang)* To die.
   croak (krohk)
   ▷ *verb* **croaking, croaked** ▷ *noun* **croak**

crochet *verb* To make patterned cloth from thread or yarn using a hooked needle. **cro·chet** (kroh-**shay**) ▷ *verb* **crocheting, crocheted** ▷ *noun* **crocheting**

crocodile *noun* A large reptile with a long body, short legs, and strong jaws. Crocodiles live in water and are related to alligators. **croc·o·dile** (**krah**-kuh-*dile*)

Word History

Crocodile comes from the Greek word *krokodilos*, meaning "lizard," because the animal looks like a very large lizard.

---

crocus *noun* A small plant with purple, yellow, or white flowers and thin leaves like blades of grass. Most crocuses bloom early in the spring. **cro·cus** (**kroh**-kuhs) ▷ *noun, plural* **crocuses**

croissant *noun* A flaky roll that is shaped like a crescent moon. **crois·sant** (kruh-**sahnt**)

crook *noun*
   1. A bent or curved part of something, as in *the crook of your arm.* ▷ *verb* **crook**
   2. A criminal or a dishonest person.
   3. A long, hooked staff used by shepherds.
   crook (kruk)

crooked *adjective*
1. Not straight, as in *a crooked line*.
2. Dishonest or illegal, as in *a crooked plan*.
crook·ed (**kruk**-id)

crop
1. *noun* A plant grown for food for people or animals: *Potatoes and barley are the main crops in this area*.
2. *noun* The amount of food produced in a single harvest, as in *a big tomato crop*.
3. *verb* To eat the top part of grass while grazing: *The sheep cropped the grass on the prairie*.
4. *verb* To cut off or remove the edges from something, as in *to crop a photograph*.
5. *noun* The pouch in a bird's throat where food is stored or prepared for digestion.
crop (krahp)
▷ *verb* **cropping, cropped**

croquet *noun* An outdoor game played by hitting wooden balls with mallets through wire hoops that are stuck into the ground. cro·quet (kroh-**kay**)

crore *noun* A word used in India and surrounding countries to represent the number ten million in quantities of money, as in *25 crore rupees*. **crore** (kror)

cross
1. *verb* To travel from one side of something to the other: *We crossed the street*.
2. *verb* To reach from one side to the other: *The bridge crossed a wide river*.
3. *adjective* Annoyed or irritable.
4. *noun* A shape made up of two intersecting lines, such as the x or the plus sign (+).
5. *noun* An upright post with a horizontal bar that crosses it, or a pendant shaped this way. The cross is the symbol of Christianity.
6. *verb* To draw a line through, as in *to cross your t's*.
7. *verb* To intersect: *Elm Street crosses Broadway*.
8. *verb* To oppose someone, or to obstruct someone's plans.
cross (kraws)
▷ *verb* **crosses, crossing, crossed** ▷ *noun, plural* **crosses**

crossbow *noun* A weapon with a bow mounted across a piece of wood. Crossbows were used in the Middle Ages. cross·bow (**kraws**-boh)

cross-country *adjective* Run through the countryside instead of on a track, as in *a cross-country race*.

cross-examine *verb* To question a witness in a court case who has already been questioned by the lawyers on the other side: *The lawyer cross-examined the prosecution's star witness about what he had seen*. ▷ *verb* **cross-examining, cross-examined** ▷ *noun* **cross-examination**

cross-eyed *adjective* Having eyes that turn inward, toward each other, so that they are difficult to focus and the person cannot see clearly.

cross-reference *noun* A mention in one part of a book that tells you where to find more information on the same subject in another part. A cross-reference can be in the index or in the text of the book.

crossroads *noun*
1. A place where two or more roads meet.
2. A point where an important decision must be made: *She has reached a crossroads in her career plans*.
cross·roads (**kraws**-rohdz)
▷ *noun, plural* **crossroads**

cross section *noun*
1. A diagram that shows the inside of something, as if it had been cut through.
2. A selection of different types of people or things, as in *a cross section of the community*.
▷ *adjective* **cross-sectional**

crosswalk *noun* A place where pedestrians can safely cross a street, often marked with painted lines. cross·walk (**kraws**-wawk)

crossword puzzle *noun* A puzzle in which you answer clues in order to fill blank squares with words, writing one letter in each square. cross·word puzzle (**kraws**-wurd)

crotch *noun* The area of the body where your legs meet. **crotch** (krahtch)

crouch *verb* To bend your legs and lower your body: *The catcher crouched behind home plate*. crouch (krouch) ▷ *verb* **crouches, crouching, crouched** ▷ *noun* **crouch**

crow
1. *noun* A large black bird with a loud, rough voice.
2. *verb* To make a loud, crying noise like a rooster.
▷ *noun* **crow**
3. *verb* To brag in a satisfied way about something: *Ricky crowed about the As on his report card*.
crow (kroh)
▷ *verb* **crowing, crowed**

crowbar *noun* A heavy steel or iron bar with a flat end that can be used to lift heavy things or to pry something open. **crow·bar** (**kroh**-bahr)

crowd
1. *noun* A large number of people gathered together.
▷ *adjective* **crowded**
2. *verb* To not give someone else enough room: *The other people crowded me so much, I couldn't reach the counter*. ▷ *verb* **crowding, crowded**
crowd (kroud)

crowdsource *verb* To use the internet in order to get people to do something such as work, supply information, or contribute money to a person or cause: *The researchers decided to crowdsource when they realized they could not afford to pay observers.* **crowd·source** (**kroud**-*sors*) ▷ *verb* **crowdsourcing, crowdsourced** ▷ *noun* **crowdsourcing**

crown

1. *noun* A headdress worn by a king, a queen, or another ruler, made from gold or silver and jewels.

2. *verb* To put someone into a position of authority or honor by placing a crown on his or her head.

3. *noun* The top part of something: *The ball hit him on the crown of his head.*

4. *verb* To declare someone to be the winner: *Sonya was crowned the champion of the race.*

5. *noun* A wreath or headdress given to the winner of a competition.

crown (kroun)

▷ *noun* **crowning** ▷ *verb* **crowning, crowned**

crow's nest *noun* A small platform used for a lookout, found on top of the mast of a sailing ship.

crucial *adjective* Decisive; extremely important for the success of something: *The congresswoman's support was crucial to the passage of the bill.* **cru·cial** (**kroo**-shuhl) ▷ *adverb* **crucially**

crude *adjective*

1. Rough, not refined or finished: *The crude material irritated my skin.*

2. Rude and in poor taste, as in *a crude remark.*

crude (krood)

▷ *adjective* **cruder, crudest**

▷ *noun* **crudity** ▷ *adverb* **crudely**

cruel *adjective*

1. Deliberately causing pain to others, or happy to see them suffer.

2. Hurtful or humiliating, as in *a cruel joke.*

cru·el (**kroo**-uhl)

▷ *adjective* **crueler, cruelest** ▷ *noun* **cruelty** ▷ *adverb* **cruelly**

cruise

1. *noun* A vacation on a ship that docks at several places. ▷ *verb* **cruise**

2. *verb* To travel smoothly and easily: *We cruised down the highway.* ▷ *verb* **cruising, cruised**

cruise (krooz)

crumb *noun* A tiny piece of bread or other baked

crown

food, as in *cracker crumbs.* **crumb** (kruhm)

crumble *verb* To break into tiny pieces: *Andy crumbled the cookie onto his plate.* **crum·ble** (**kruhm**-buhl) ▷ *verb* **crumbling, crumbled** ▷ *adjective* **crumbly**

crumple *verb*

1. To crush something, usually paper or fabric, into wrinkles and folds: *Rose crumpled the newspaper and threw it away.*

2. To collapse into bent pieces: *Buildings crumpled at the earthquake's epicenter.*

crum·ple (**kruhm**-puhl)

▷ *verb* **crumpling, crumpled** ▷ *adjective* **crumpled**

crunch *verb* To crush or chew something noisily: *Ali crunched through the fallen leaves.* **crunch** (kruhnch) ▷ *verb* **crunches, crunching, crunched** ▷ *noun* **crunch** ▷ *adjective* **crunchy**

crusade *noun*

1. A battle or fight for which someone feels a great deal of emotion: *He was on a crusade against crime in the neighborhood.*

2. Crusade One of the battles fought in the 11th, 12th, and 13th centuries by European Christians attempting to capture biblical lands from Muslims. **cru·sade** (kroo-**sade**)

crusader *noun*

1. A person who works very hard to bring change to a social or political situation: *She is a crusader for the rights of illegal immigrants.*

2. One of the soldiers or knights who took part in the Crusades of the 11th, 12th, and 13th centuries. **cru·sad·er** (kroo-**say**-dur)

crush

1. *verb* To damage or destroy something by pressing it under a heavy weight: *The flowers were crushed under our feet.*

2. *noun* Strong romantic feelings toward someone, usually lasting only for a short time.

3. *noun* A person that you have such feelings about.

4. *verb* To bring a sudden end to something: *My hopes were crushed when I didn't make the team.*

crush (kruhsh)

▷ *verb* **crushes, crushing, crushed**

crust *noun*

1. The crisp, outer layer of bread or pastry. ▷ *adjective* **crusty**

2. The hard outer layer of the earth.

crust (kruhst)

crustacean *noun* A sea creature that has an outer skeleton, such as a crab, lobster, or shrimp. **crus·ta·cean** (kruh-**stay**-shuhn)

crutch *noun* A long stick with a padded top, used to help support someone with a leg or foot injury. **crutch** (kruhch) ▷ *noun, plural* **crutches**

cry *verb*
1. To produce tears because of strong feelings: *The sad movie made us cry.*
2. To shout: *They were thrilled to hear the conductor cry, "All aboard!"*
cry (krye)
▷ *verb* **cries, crying, cried** ▷ *noun* **cry**

cryptic *adjective* Not clear or easy to understand, mysterious: *Her cryptic comments were meant to keep us guessing.* **cryp·tic** (**krip**-tik)

crystal *noun*
1. A clear or nearly clear mineral or rock with many flat faces, such as quartz.
2. A substance that forms a pattern of many flat surfaces when it becomes a solid. Salt and snowflakes are crystals.
3. Glass of superior quality, used to make fine things, such as drinking glasses or vases.
crys·tal (**kris**-tuhl)
▷ *adjective* **crystal** ▷ *adjective* **crystalline** (**kris**-tuh-lin)

crystallize *verb*
1. To form crystals.
2. To take form: *After several minutes of thought, a plan began to crystallize in her mind.*
crys·tal·lize (**kris**-tuh-*lize*)
▷ *verb* **crystallizing, crystallized**

CSA *noun* A system that allows people to buy fruit, vegetables, and farm products directly from gardeners and farmers. CSAs usually operate during the growing season. CSA is short for *Community Supported Agriculture.*

cub *noun* A young animal, such as a lion, wolf, or bear, as in *a newborn bear cub.* **cub** (kuhb)

cube
1. *noun* A three-dimensional shape with six square faces. Dice are cubes. ▷ *adjective* **cubic**
2. *verb* To multiply a number by itself twice. The number 4 cubed is 4 x 4 x 4. It is written 4^3. ▷ *verb* **cubing, cubed**
cube (kyoob)

Word History

The ancient Greeks played games with two types of dice: four-sided and six-sided. The six-sided die, like the ones in common use today, was called a *kybos*, and from this term we get the English word **cube**.

CSA (Community Supported Agriculture)

Members of CSAs buy "shares" in a farm's harvest. In return, they receive a box of local, seasonal produce, either picked up or delivered, usually weekly. Farms may also offer other foods and products, such as meat, bread, flowers, or other farm products. Farmers benefit from by receiving income to prepare for the growing season and finding consumers before they are busy in the fields. CSAs were first organized in the United States in the 1980s, based on models that began in Japan and Europe in the 1960s.

CSA

cubic *adjective*
1. In the form of a cube.
2. Of or relating to a measure of volume that is calculated by multiplying a unit of length by itself twice, as in *cubic centimeters.*
cu·bic (**kyoo**-bik)

cubicle *noun* A small office or area surrounded by partitions. **cu·bi·cle** (**kyoo**-bi-kuhl)

cubit *noun* An ancient form of measurement based on the length of the forearm, measured from the elbow to the tip of the middle finger. **cu·bit** (**kyoo**-bit)

cuckoo
1. *noun* A bird with a distinct call and a long tail. Some cuckoos lay their eggs in other birds' nests. ▷ *noun, plural* **cuckoos**
2. *adjective* (*informal*) Silly, or acting in a scatterbrained manner.
cuck·oo (**koo**-koo)

cucumber *noun* A long, crisp, green vegetable with a soft center filled with seeds. **cu·cum·ber** (**kyoo**-*kuhm*-bur)

cud *noun* Food that some animals, such as cows and sheep, bring up from the first part of their stomachs to chew again. **cud** (kuhd)

cuddle *verb* To hold someone or something closely and lovingly in your arms. **cud·dle** (**kudh**-uhl) ▷ *verb* **cuddling, cuddled** ▷ *noun* **cuddle**

cue *noun*
1. The signal to say lines or perform an action in a play: *Walk onstage when you hear your cue.*
2. Any signal to do something: *My whistle will be your cue to start shouting.*
3. A long stick used to hit the ball in billiards and pool.
cue (kyoo)
Cue sounds like **queue**. ▷ *verb* **cue**

cuff *noun*
1. The band or folded part of the sleeve of a shirt or blouse that goes around your wrist.
2. The folded part at the bottom of a pant leg.
3. **off the cuff** Without preparation, as in *giving a speech off the cuff.*
cuff (kuhf)

cuisine *noun* A style or manner of cooking or presenting food. **cui·sine** (kwi-**zeen**)

cul-de-sac *noun* A road that is closed at one end.
cul-de-sac (**kuhl**-duh-**sak**)

culminate *verb* To reach the highest or final point: *The athlete's career culminated in winning an Olympic gold medal.* **cul·mi·nate** (**kuhl**-muh-*nate*) ▷ *verb* **culminating, culminated** ▷ *noun* **culmination**

culprit *noun* A person who is guilty of doing something wrong or of committing a crime. **cul·prit** (**kuhl**-prit)

cult *noun*
1. A particular form of religious worship, especially one that people who don't share its beliefs think is strange or allows no freedom.
2. A strong, almost religious devotion to a person, thing, idea, or way of life, as in *a cult of sun lovers.*
3. **cult hero** A person who is very popular with a small group of followers.
cult (kuhlt)

cultivate *verb*
1. To grow crops on land.
2. To develop by studying: *Doug wants to cultivate an appreciation for opera.*
cul·ti·vate (**kuhl**-tuh-*vate*)
▷ *verb* **cultivating, cultivated** ▷ *noun* **cultivation**

culture *noun*
1. An appreciation for the arts, such as music, literature, and painting.
2. An artificial growth of cells or tissue in a laboratory: *These cell cultures are mostly from mice and are being used in genetic experiments.*
3. The ideas, customs, traditions, and way of life of a group of people: *We're studying some of the musical instruments used in Asian cultures.*
cul·ture (**kuhl**-chur)
▷ *adjective* **cultural**

cultured *adjective* Well-educated or refined.
cul·tured (**kuhl**-churd)

cumbersome *adjective* Heavy or bulky and difficult to move around: *The couch is too cumbersome to move out of the room.* **cum·ber·some** (**kum**-bur-suhm)

cunning *adjective* Having or showing the ability to trick people. **cun·ning** (**kuhn**-ing) ▷ *noun* **cunning** ▷ *adverb* **cunningly**

cup *noun*
1. A small container for holding liquids, often with a handle.
2. A unit of measurement equal to eight fluid ounces: *Add one cup of sugar to the batter.*
3. Any ornament shaped like a cup: *I won a silver cup as first prize.*
cup (kuhp)

cupboard *noun* A cabinet or closet for storing things, such as dishes or food. **cup·board** (**kuhb**-urd)

cupcake *noun* A small, round cake with frosting, for one person to eat. **cup·cake** (**kuhp**-*kake*)

cupcake

cupful *noun*
1. The amount a cup can hold.
2. An amount equal to eight fluid ounces; half a pint.
cup·ful (**kuhp**-*ful*)

curable *adjective* Able to be cured with proper medical treatment: *Many infections are curable with antibiotics.* **cur·a·ble** (**kyoor**-uh-buhl)

curator *noun* A person who is in charge of a collection of art or an exhibit in a museum. **cu·ra·tor** (**kyoor**-ay-tur *or* kyoo-**ray**-tur)

curb
1. *noun* A raised border along the edge of a paved street.
2. *verb* To control or hold back something: *I curbed my impulse to scream in the movie theater.* ▷ *verb* **curbing, curbed**
curb (kurb)

curd *noun* The solid part of milk that is sour or separated, often used to make cheese. **curd** (kurd)

curdle *verb* To separate into curds or lumps, either because a food has gone sour or because something has been added to it. **cur·dle** (**kur**-duhl) ▷ *verb* **curdling, curdled** ▷ *adjective* **curdled**

cure
1. *verb* To make someone better when he or she has been sick. ▷ *verb* **curing, cured**
2. *noun* A drug or some other kind of treatment that ends an illness in a sick person.
cure (kyoor)

curfew *noun* A rule or an order that prevents people from traveling around freely, especially after dark. **cur·few (kur-**fyoo)

Word History

Curfew comes from the medieval law that hearth fires had to be put out at a specific hour at night, probably to lessen the risk of a general fire in the town. In French, the term was *couvre-feu,* a combination of *couvrir,* "to cover," and *feu,* "fire."

curious *adjective*
1. Eager to know or learn about something.
2. Unusual or remarkable, as in *a curious coincidence.*
cu·ri·ous (kyoor-ee-uhs)
▷ *noun* **curiosity** (kyoor-ee-**ah**-si-tee) ▷ *adverb* **curiously**

curl
1. *noun* A coiled lock of hair.
2. *verb* To move, or to make something move, in a spiral or curved direction. ▷ *verb* **curling, curled**
curl (kurl)

curly *adjective* Having curls; twisted. **cur·ly (kur-**lee) ▷ *adjective* **curlier, curliest**

currant *noun*
1. A small dried berry used in cooking and baking.
2. A small sour berry, used in making jelly.
cur·rant (kur-uhnt)
Currant sounds like **current**.

currency *noun* The form of money used in a country: *We paid for the flight in British currency.* **cur·ren·cy (kur-**uhn-see) ▷ *noun, plural* **currencies**

current
1. *noun* The movement of water in a definite direction in a river or an ocean, or the movement of electricity through a cable or wire.
2. *adjective* Happening now, as in *current events.*
▷ *adverb* **currently**
cur·rent (kur-uhnt)
Current sounds like **currant**.

curriculum *noun* An organized program of study in a school or college, as in *the science curriculum.* **cur·ric·u·lum** (kuh-**rik**-yuh-luhm)
▷ *noun, plural* **curricula** (kuh-**rik**-yuh-luh)

curry *noun*
1. A powder with a hot, spicy taste, made from various spices.
2. A dish made with curry and meat, fish, or vegetables.
cur·ry (kur-ee)
▷ *noun, plural* **curries** ▷ *adjective* **curried**

curse
1. *noun* A spell intended to harm someone by calling on evil spirits or other such powers. ▷ *verb* **curse**

2. *verb* To use offensive language. ▷ *verb* **cursing, cursed**
curse (kurs)

cursor *noun* A small indicator on a computer screen that shows where the computer's next action will take place. **cur·sor (kur-**sur)

curt *adjective* Short and abrupt; delivered in a rude manner, as in *a curt answer.* **curt** (kurt) ▷ *adjective* **curter, curtest**

curtain *noun* A piece of fabric that can be pulled across a window, a stage, or a similar opening to cover it. **cur·tain (kur-**tuhn)

curtsy *verb* To bend slightly at the knees, with one foot in front of the other. Women and girls sometimes curtsy to show respect or to acknowledge applause. **curt·sy (kurt-**see) ▷ *verb* **curtsies, curtsying, curtsied** ▷ *noun* **curtsy**

curve
1. *verb* To bend or turn continuously: *The road curved toward the forest.* ▷ *verb* **curving, curved**
2. *noun* A continuous bend in something.
3. **curve ball** *noun* A baseball or softball pitch that spins away from a straight path as it approaches the batter.
curve (kurv)
▷ *adjective* **curved** ▷ *adjective* **curvy**

cushion
1. *noun* A pillow used to make furniture more comfortable to sit or lie on.
2. *verb* To soften the effect of something: *The pile of leaves cushioned her fall.* ▷ *verb* **cushioning, cushioned** ▷ *noun* **cushion**
cush·ion (kush-uhn)

custard *noun* A sweet, thick dessert made from milk, eggs, sugar, and sometimes other flavorings. **cus·tard (kuhs-**turd)

custodian *noun*
1. A person who has responsibility for something valuable, such as a museum collection or a set of standards and ideals: *The courts are the custodians of the law.*
2. A person whose job is to clean and maintain a building or institution, as in *a school custodian.*
cus·to·di·an (kuhs-**toh**-dee-uhn)

custody *noun*
1. The legal right to supervise and take care of a child.
2. Police supervision: *The suspect was taken into custody after a short struggle.*
cus·to·dy (kuhs-tuh-dee)
▷ *adjective* **custodial** (kuhs-**toh**-dee-uhl)

custom *noun*
1. A tradition in a culture or society: *Playing tricks on one another is a custom on April Fools' Day.*

2. Something that you do regularly, as in *a holiday custom*.

3. customs *noun, plural* A place at a country's borders, ports, or airports where officials may ask questions and check your luggage to make sure that you are not bringing in anything illegal. **cus·tom** (**kuhs**-tuhm)

customary *adjective* Happening regularly by habit or custom; usual: *It's customary for me to sleep late on Saturday.* **cus·tom·ar·y** (**kus**-tuh-*mer*-ee)

customer *noun* A person who buys things from a particular store or business: *Many customers wanted to buy that book.* **cus·tom·er** (**kuhs**-tuh-mur)

customize *verb* To change something to suit an individual's needs or preferences, as in *to customize a loan.* **cus·tom·ize** (**kuhs**-tuh-*mize*) ▷ *verb* **customizing, customized**

cut

1. *verb* To use a sharp instrument, such as scissors or a knife, to separate something into smaller pieces, to remove part of it, or to change its shape.

2. *verb* To reduce something: *The government is cutting taxes.*

3. *noun* A skin wound caused by a sharp object.

4. *verb* To shorten or trim, as in *to cut the grass.*

5. *verb* To stop or interrupt: *The storm cut our power.*

6. cut off *verb* To isolate a person or thing from others.

7. cut down *verb* To have or use something less often, as in *to cut down on desserts.*

8. cut back *verb* To reduce the amount of money you spend, or the amount of something that you use. ▷ *noun* **cutback**

9. cut and paste *verb* To move words or images from one place to another on a computer. **cut** (kuht) ▷ *verb* **cutting, cut** ▷ *noun* **cut**

cute *adjective* Charming, pretty, or attractive. **cute** (kyoot) ▷ *adjective* **cuter, cutest**

cuticle *noun* The tough layer of skin around the edges of a fingernail or a toenail. **cu·ti·cle** (**kyoo**-ti-kuhl)

cutting

1. *noun* A small part of a plant taken off to put in the ground and grow a new plant: *The new cuttings are growing well.*

2. *adjective* Mean and hurtful, as in *a cutting comment.*

cut·ting (**kuht**-ing)

cyberspace *noun* The world of communication and interaction represented by the internet: *If you didn't receive my email, perhaps it got lost in cyberspace.* **cy·ber·space** (**sye**-bur-*spase*)

cycle

1. *verb* To ride a bicycle. ▷ *verb* **cycling, cycled** ▷ *noun* **cyclist**

2. *noun* A bicycle.

3. *noun* A series of events that are repeated in the same order, as in *a washing machine cycle.* **cy·cle** (**sye**-kuhl)

cyclone *noun* A storm with very strong, destructive winds that rotate. **cy·clone** (**sye**-klone)

cyclone

cylinder *noun*

1. A shape with flat, circular ends and sides shaped like the outside of a tube: *Paper towels are wrapped around cardboard cylinders.* ▷ *adjective* **cylindrical** (suh-**lin**-dri-kuhl)

2. A chamber in an engine that is shaped like a tube. **cyl·in·der** (**sil**-uhn-dur)

cymbal *noun* A musical instrument made of brass and shaped like a plate. It is played by striking it with a stick or another cymbal. **cym·bal** (**sim**-buhl) **Cymbal** sounds like **symbol**.

cynical *adjective* Believing that the worst will always happen and that people are basically selfish and dishonest: *Sharon is so cynical about politicians that she refuses to vote.* **cyn·i·cal** (**sin**-i-kuhl) ▷ *noun* **cynic** ▷ *noun* **cynicism** (**sin**-i-*siz*-uhm) ▷ *adverb* **cynically**

cypress *noun* An evergreen tree with small, dark green leaves that resemble scales. **cy·press** (**sye**-pruhs) ▷ *noun, plural* **cypresses**

cyst *noun* A small sac of tissue inside the body that fills with some substance, such as air, fluid, or pus. **cyst** (sist)

cytoplasm *noun* The contents of a living cell, except for the nucleus. **cy·to·plasm** (**sye**-tuh-*plaz*-uhm)

czar *or* **tsar** *noun* An emperor of Russia before the revolution of 1917. **czar** *or* **tsar** (zahr)

czarina *or* **tsarina** *noun* A former empress of Russia or wife of a czar. **cza·ri·na** *or* **tsa·ri·na** (zah-**ree**-nuh)

Dd

dab

1. *verb* To touch something lightly and quickly: *She dabbed her eyes with a handkerchief.*
2. *verb* To apply: *Anna dabbed some cream on her face.*
3. *noun* A little bit, as in *a dab of mustard.*
dab (dab)
▷ *verb* **dabbing, dabbed**

dabble *verb*

1. If you **dabble** in something, you do not do it very seriously or very thoroughly. ▷ *noun* **dabbler**
2. To dip something playfully in and out of water: *The children dabbled their feet in the pool.*
dab·ble (**dab**-uhl)
▷ *verb* **dabbling, dabbled**

dachshund *noun* A breed of dog with a long body, brownish fur, very short legs, and drooping ears. **dachs·hund** (**dahks**-*hunt*)

dad *or* **daddy** *noun* (*informal*) Father. **dad** (dad) *or* **dad·dy** (**dad**-ee)

daddy-longlegs *noun* An animal that looks like a spider but has a small, rounded body and very long, spindly legs. **daddy-long·legs** (**lawng**-*legz*) ▷ *noun, plural* **daddy-longlegs**

daffodils

daffodil *noun* A plant that has yellow or white bell-like flowers and long, narrow leaves. **daf·fo·dil** (**daf**-uh-dil)

dagger *noun* A short, pointed weapon that is used for stabbing. **dag·ger** (**dag**-ur)

daily *adjective* Produced or happening every day, or every working day, as in *a daily news show.* **dai·ly** (**day**-lee) ▷ *noun* **daily** ▷ *adverb* **daily**

dainty *adjective* Attractively delicate: *The tablecloth had a dainty design around the edges.* **dain·ty** (**dayn**-tee) ▷ *adjective* **daintier, daintiest** ▷ *noun* **daintiness** ▷ *adverb* **daintily**

dairy

1. *noun* A business that buys milk from farmers and sells milk and other products made from it. ▷ *noun, plural* **dairies**
2. *adjective* Of or having to do with milk and milk cows: *Dairy farmers are concerned that the new rules will hurt their business.*
dair·y (**dair**-ee)

daisy *noun* A flower with white, pink, or yellow petals and a yellow center. **dai·sy** (**day**-zee) ▷ *noun, plural* **daisies**

dale *noun* A valley: *Our hike took us over hill and dale.* **dale** (dayl)

dalmatian *noun* A breed of large dog with a white coat and black or brown spots. **dal·ma·tian** (dal-**may**-shuhn)

dam *noun* A barrier across a stream or river that holds back water. **dam** (dam)

damage

1. *verb* To harm or spoil something: *The fire damaged the museum.* ▷ *verb* **damaging, damaged** ▷ *adjective* **damaging**
2. *noun* The harm caused by something: *County officials are assessing the storm's damage.*
3. damages *noun, plural* Money awarded to individuals by a court to try to make up for an injury or a loss that they have suffered: *The jury awarded the accident victims $12 million in damages.*
dam·age (**dam**-ij)

damp *adjective* Slightly wet, or moist: *Halloween was a damp and chilly day.* **damp** (damp) ▷ *adjective* **damper, dampest** ▷ *noun* **dampness**

dampen *verb*

1. To make something moist or slightly wet: *The nurse dampened a cloth and wiped the patient's forehead.*
2. To make dull or depressed: *The sad news dampened our spirits.*
damp·en (**dam**-puhn)
▷ *verb* **dampening, dampened**

damsel *noun* A young woman. This word is now used mainly in stories, or in a joking way. **dam·sel** (**dam**-zuhl)

dance

1. *verb* To move in time to music: *The girls and boys danced at the party.* ▷ *verb* **dancing, danced**

2. *noun* An event where people dance.

3. *noun* A particular set of steps, such as a waltz or a square dance. ▷ *noun* **dancing**
dance (dans)

dancer *noun* Someone who knows how to dance, or who dances as a job: *I didn't know Margie was such a great dancer.* **danc·er** (**dan**-sur)

dandelion *noun* A plant with bright yellow flowers, often found growing in lawns. **dan·de·li·on** (**dan**-duh-*lye*-uhn)

dandruff *noun* Small flakes of dead skin from the scalp, sometimes found in hair or seen on people's clothes. **dan·druff** (**dan**-druhf)

dandy

1. *noun* A man who pays too much attention to his appearance or clothing. ▷ *noun, plural* **dandies**

dappled horse

2. *adjective* Great, or fine: *My mom just bought a dandy new car.* ▷ *adjective* **dandier, dandiest**
dan·dy (**dan**-dee)

danger *noun*

1. A strong possibility that something bad or harmful may happen: *Her carelessness has put us all in danger.*

2. Something that may cause harm or injury: *Icy roads are a danger to drivers.*
dan·ger (**dayn**-jur)

dangerous *adjective* Likely to cause harm or injury; not safe; risky: *The roads will be dangerous till the snowplows have finished.* **dan·ger·ous** (**dayn**-jur-uhs) ▷ *adverb* **dangerously**

dangle *verb* To swing or hang down loosely: *The rope dangled from the tree branch.* **dan·gle** (**dang**-guhl) ▷ *verb* **dangling, dangled**

dank *adjective* Unpleasantly damp and smelly, as in *a dank cellar.* **dank** (dangk) ▷ *adjective* **danker, dankest**

dappled *adjective* Marked with areas of light and dark, as in *a dappled kitten.* **dap·pled** (**dap**-uhld)

Dance

Dances can serve religious purposes, as in the traditional dances of Native Americans. Dancing can also be for enjoyment. In Europe, lively folk dances, which started in villages in the 1300s, developed into ballroom dancing in the royal courts. These dances were more formal and quieter, and had precise steps.

Waltzes became popular in the 1800s. In the 20th century, music such as jazz, disco, and hip-hop inspired new types of dances. These popular dances are for everyone. Other forms of dance, such as ballet, are done by performers as entertainment.

hip-hop
tango
Indian dance
modern dance

dare

1. *verb* To challenge someone to do something that involves a risk: *My sister dared me to ski down the steepest slope.*

2. *verb* To be brave enough to do something: *I wanted to see what was inside the room, but I didn't dare go in.*

3. *noun* A challenge to someone to do something risky: *The boys said that they had gone into the cave on a dare.*
dare (dair)
▷ *verb* **daring, dared**

daredevil
noun Someone who enjoys doing risky things: *My brother is a daredevil on his bicycle.* **dare·dev·il** (**dair**-*dev*-uhl)

daring
adjective Involving some risk and requiring courage: *The prisoners made a daring escape in broad daylight, disguised as guards.* **dar·ing** (**dair**-ing) ▷ *adverb* **daringly**

dark

1. *adjective* Without any or very much light, as in *a dark forest.*

2. *adjective* Containing more black than white, as in *dark red.*

3. *noun* The time of day when sunlight ends: *I don't want you out after dark without reflective clothing.*

4. *noun* Lack or absence of light: *We got lost in the dark.*

5. *adjective* Bad, or evil, as in *a dark secret.*

6. *adjective* Gloomy, or dismal: *After the war, there were many dark days for the townspeople.*
dark (dahrk)
▷ *adjective* **darker, darkest**

Synonyms

Dark means having very little light: *It was too dark in the basement to find the toolbox.*

- -

■ **Dim** means darkened enough to make it difficult to see things clearly, or to make out exactly what you are seeing: *In the dim light of his closet, Bobby thought he saw a monster.*

■ **Shadowy** means darkened by shadows, so that what you see is not clear: *We could just make out the thief's shadowy form in the moonlight.*

■ **Gloomy** means dark and unpleasant, especially describing people, things, or conditions that make you sad: *The gloomy weather caused our usually happy spirits to fall.*

■ **Murky** means very dark or dim, especially when caused by something thick, smoky, or foggy: *The water of the lake was murky because of the muddy bottom.*

darken
verb To make or become darker: *I pulled down the shade to darken the room.* **dark·en** (**dahr**-kuhn) ▷ *verb* **darkening, darkened** ▷ *adjective* **darkened**

darkness
noun Lack of light; the state of being dark. **dark·ness** (**dahrk**-nis)

darkroom
noun A room with all the light blocked out and with special equipment for developing photographs. **dark·room** (**dahrk**-*room*)

darling

1. *noun* Someone who is dearly loved.

2. *adjective* Loved very much, as in *my darling daughter.*

3. *adjective* Charming, or adorable, as in *a darling kitten.*
dar·ling (**dahr**-ling)

darn
verb To mend a hole in a piece of cloth by sewing back and forth across it: *Joe darned the hole in his sock.* **darn** (dahrn) ▷ *verb* **darning, darned** ▷ *noun* **darning**

dart

1. *noun* A pointed object like a small arrow that you throw in the game of darts.

2. darts *noun* A game in which players score by throwing darts at a target that usually has concentric circles and a bull's-eye in the center.

3. *verb* To move suddenly and quickly: *The cat darted out into the traffic.* ▷ *verb* **darting, darted**
dart (dahrt)

dash

1. *noun* A very small amount of something: *Add a dash of salt.*

2. *noun* A horizontal line (—) used as a punctuation mark, usually to show a pause in a sentence: *The whale was huge—and it was only a baby.*

3. *verb* To move quickly, usually over a short distance: *I dashed to the phone.*

4. *noun* A short race, as in *a 50-yard dash.*

5. *verb* To destroy or bring an end to: *Kelli's broken leg dashed her plans of going skiing.*
dash (dash)
▷ *noun, plural* **dashes** ▷ *verb* **dashes, dashing, dashed**

dashboard
noun

1. The instrument panel of a car or truck, where the gauges and warning lights are located: *Check the gas gauge on the dashboard.*

2. A window on a computer screen that provides information about a program that is currently running.
dash·board (**dash**-bord)

data
noun Information collected in a place so that something can be done with it: *The research team studied the data.* **da·ta** (**day**-tuh)

daredevil

Language Note

Data is used with both singular and plural verbs. With a singular verb, it means "information": *The data was put into the computer.* However, it was originally a plural noun and was used with a plural verb. It is still used that way to mean "facts": *The data were incorrect.*

database *noun* A set of related information that is organized and stored in a computer, as in *a database of addresses.* **da·ta·base** (**day**-tuh-*base*)

dataset or **data set** *noun* A collection of related pieces of information that can be searched and manipulated using a computer: *The scientists analyzed a ten-year dataset of satellite observations to test their hypothesis.* **da·ta·set** (**day**-tuh-*set*)

date
1. *noun* A particular day: *Today's date is June 25.*
2. *noun* An appointment to meet someone, especially for romance: *They made a date to go to the movies.*
3. *verb* To go out with someone on a date: *Barbie and Ken have been dating for years.*
4. *verb* If something **dates** from a certain time, it was made then: *This vase dates from 1854.*
5. *verb* To accurately determine the time that something was made or first existed: *Archaeologists date the fortifications to the early 14th century.*
6. *noun* A small brown fruit from a palm tree with a long, thin pit.
7. *adjective* If something is **up-to-date**, it is modern or has the latest features or information: *He installed new tech features throughout his house and made it very up-to-date.*
8. *adjective* If something is **out of date**, it is old-fashioned and dated, or lacks modern features or information: *The furniture in the house was from the 1960s and looked out of date.*
date (date)
▷ *verb* **dating, dated**

dated *adjective* Old-fashioned or lacking modern features or information, as in *dated clothes* or *a dated software program.* **dat·ed** (**day**-tid)

daughter *noun* Someone's female child: *My daughter was born in February.* **daugh·ter** (**daw**-tur)

daughter-in-law *noun* The wife of someone's son.
▷ *noun, plural* **daughters-in-law**

daunt *verb* To make someone feel frightened or discouraged: *I am daunted by the size of that hill.* **daunt** (dawnt) ▷ *verb* **daunting, daunted**

dawdle *verb* To do something slowly, or to waste time: *Jenny dawdled over her breakfast.* **daw·dle** (**daw**-duhl)
▷ *verb* **dawdling, dawdled** ▷ *noun* **dawdler**

dawn
1. *noun* The beginning of the day when light first appears in the sky.
2. *noun* The start of a new period of time, as in *the dawn of the information age.*
3. *verb* If something **dawns** on you, you start to understand it: *It finally dawned on me that Jane was really smart.* ▷ *verb* **dawning, dawned**
dawn (dawn)

day *noun*
1. A 24-hour period, especially as measured from midnight to midnight: *A week has seven days.*
2. The period of light between sunrise and sunset: *What are you going to do with your day?*
3. The part of the day spent at work, as in *an eight-hour day.*
4. A certain period of time: *In the 1920s, bobbed hair was the fashion of the day.*
day (day)

daybreak

daybreak *noun* Dawn, or the time when the first rays of sunlight appear. **day·break** (**day**-*brayk*)

day care *noun* Care given by adults to young children away from their homes during the day.
▷ *adjective* **day-care**

daydream
1. *noun* A pleasant dream you have while you are awake: *In her daydream, Iris saw herself at the beach.*
2. *verb* To let your mind wander and imagine things: *Ron daydreams whenever he listens to that music.*
▷ *verb* **daydreaming, daydreamed** ▷ *noun* **daydreamer**
day·dream (**day**-*dreem*)

daylight *noun*
1. The light of the sun during daytime hours: *We rushed to finish our hike while it was still daylight.*
2. If something happens **in broad daylight**, it is not secret or hidden: *The wealthy businessman was kidnapped in broad daylight by masked men.*
day·light (**day**-*lite*)

daytime *noun* The hours of daylight, from dawn till dusk. **day·time** (**day**-*time*)

daze

1. *noun* A condition in which you are not able to think clearly: *He was wandering around in a daze when a policeman stopped to help him.*

2. *verb* To confuse or bewilder someone: *Getting hit by the snowball dazed me.* ▷ *verb* **dazing, dazed** **daze** (dayz)

dazzle *verb*

1. To blind someone for a moment with a bright light: *The spotlight dazzled Willie.*

2. To amaze and impress someone: *Hiroko dazzled the crowd with her singing.*

daz·zle (**daz**-uhl)

▷ *verb* **dazzling, dazzled** ▷ *adjective* **dazzling**

Prefix

The prefix **de-** adds one of these meanings to a root word:

1. Take away or remove, as in *defrost* (take away frost) or *detach* (remove something).

2. Undo or do the opposite of, as in *decode* (undo a code) or *desegregate* (undo segregation).

deacon *noun* In the Christian church, a person who helps a minister or preacher. **dea·con** (**dee**-kuhn)

dead

1. *adjective* Not alive.

2. *adjective* Without activity or excitement: *This town is dead after 6 p.m.*

3. *adverb* Completely, as in *dead tired.*

4. the dead *noun, plural* All those who are no longer alive: *We said a prayer for the dead at the cemetery.*

dead (ded)

deaden *verb* To weaken or make less sharp: *Some people pat cold tea on sunburned skin to deaden the pain.* **dead·en** (**ded**-uhn) ▷ *verb* **deadening, deadened**

dead end sign

dead end

1. *noun* A street that ends without a place to enter another street.

2. dead-end *adjective* Leading to nothing better: *George is worried that he has a dead-end job.*

deadline *noun* A time when something must be finished: *The deadline for the assignment is Monday.* **dead·line** (**ded**-*line*)

deadlock *noun* A situation where two sides cannot

agree: *The players and team owner arrived at a deadlock.* **dead·lock** (**ded**-*lahk*)

deadly *adjective*

1. Capable of killing, as in *a deadly explosion.*

2. Aiming to kill or destroy someone, as in *deadly enemies.*

dead·ly (**ded**-lee)

▷ *adjective* **deadlier, deadliest**

deaf *adjective*

1. Unable to hear. ▷ *adjective* **deafer, deafest**

2. If you are **deaf to** something, you are not willing to consider or accept it: *He was deaf to my pleas.*

deaf (def)

▷ *noun* **deafness**

deafening *adjective* Very loud, as in *a deafening roar.* **deaf·en·ing** (**def**-uh-ning) ▷ *adverb* **deafeningly**

deal

1. *verb* To do business: *That store deals in baseball cards.*

2. *noun* An agreement: *Yoko made a deal with her brother.*

3. *verb* To give or to deliver, as in *to deal the cards* or *to deal a blow.*

4. *verb* When a text **deals with** a subject, it is about that subject: *The book deals with the most recent political developments in Afghanistan.*

5. *verb* When you **deal with** something, you take some sort of action about it: *The parents dealt with the situation by forming a neighborhood watch group.*

deal (deel)

▷ *verb* **dealing, dealt** (delt)

dealer *noun*

1. Someone who buys and sells things: *My uncle is an antiques dealer.*

2. Someone who gives out cards during a card game.

deal·er (**dee**-lur)

dealt *verb* The past tense and past participle of **deal**. **dealt** (delt)

dear

1. *adjective* Much loved, as in *a dear friend.*

2. *noun* A kind or sweet person: *You are a dear to help me out.*

3. *adjective* You use **dear** at the beginning of a letter, as in *Dear Sir.*

dear (deer)

Dear sounds like **deer**.

▷ *adjective* **dearer, dearest**

dearly *adverb* Very much: *We loved her dearly and will miss her every day.* **dear·ly** (**deer**-lee)

death *noun*

1. The end of life: *His death came after a long illness.*

2. The destruction or end of something, as in *the death of the Roman Empire.*
death (deth)

deathly *adjective* Reminding you of death or of something dead: *Carl's face turned deathly white.*
death·ly (**deth**-lee)

death trap *noun* A situation, place, or vehicle that is very dangerous: *The old car was a death trap.*
death trap (**deth** trap)

debate
1. *noun* A discussion in which people express different opinions: *The candidates held a debate before the election.*
2. *verb* To discuss or think about something from different points of view: *Her relatives debated where to go for their picnic.* ▷ *verb* **debating, debated**
▷ *adjective* **debatable**
de·bate (di-**bate**)

debit
1. *noun* A record of money that is taken out of an account.
2. *verb* To remove money from an account: *Did you authorize the company to debit your account for that much?* ▷ *verb* **debiting, debited**
deb·it (**deb**-it)

debit card *noun* A plastic card that is connected to a bank account and that can be used to pay for things, just like a check or cash.

debris *noun* The pieces of something that has been broken or destroyed: *The debris from the plane crash was all over the field.* **de·bris** (duh-**bree**)

debt *noun*
1. Money or something else that someone owes: *I will pay all my debts this month.*
2. The condition of owing money or something else to someone: *Carl was $50,000 in debt to the bank.*
debt (det)

Word History

If you ever forget the silent *b* when you spell **debt**, you can blame the language experts of the 16th century. *Debt* comes from the French word *dette*, but those experts thought it came from the Latin *debitum*. They chose "debt" as the official spelling, with the *b* from Latin, even though people continued to leave it out when they said the word.

debtor *noun* Someone who owes money: *Credit counseling helps debtors manage their debts.* **debt·or** (**det**-ur)

debut
1. *noun* A first public appearance or performance, as in *a singing debut.*

2. *verb* To perform something for the first time: *The dance company will debut the new ballet tonight.*
▷ *verb* **debuting, debuted**
de·but (day-**byoo** or **day**-byoo)

decade *noun* A period of ten years. **dec·ade** (**dek**-ayd)

decal *noun* A picture or label on specially treated paper that can be transferred to glass, metal, or other hard surfaces: *Kyle's suitcase is covered with decals from every state he's visited.* **de·cal** (**dee**-kal)

decathlon *noun* A track-and-field contest made up of ten athletic events. **de·cath·lon** (di-**kath**-lahn)

decay
1. *verb* To rot or break down.
2. *verb* To decline in quality: *The signal decays with increasing distance from the transmission tower.*
3. *noun* The breaking down of plant or animal matter by natural causes, as in *tooth decay.*
4. *noun* A decline in quality.
de·cay (di-**kay**)
▷ *verb* **decaying, decayed**

deceased *adjective* Dead: *The library is named after our deceased mayor.* **de·ceased** (di-**seest**)

deceit *noun* The act of lying to or deceiving someone. **de·ceit** (di-**seet**)

deceitful *adjective* Intentionally deceiving or misleading: *The deceitful store clerk gave her the wrong change and pocketed the rest of the money.* **de·ceit·ful** (di-**seet**-fuhl) ▷ *adverb* **deceitfully**

deceive *verb* To trick someone into believing something that is not true: *Armies have used false signals throughout history to deceive their enemies.* **de·ceive** (di-**seev**) ▷ *verb* **deceiving, deceived**

December *noun* The 12th month on the calendar. December follows November and has 31 days. **De·cem·ber** (di-**sem**-bur)

Word History

Since **December** comes from the Latin word *decem*, meaning "ten," you might expect it to be the tenth month of the year. That was the case 2,000 years ago. Then the Romans introduced a new calendar, adding more months to their old calendar. That's how December, the "tenth month," became the 12th.

decent *adjective*
1. Acceptable or satisfactory, as in *decent shape.*
2. Respectful and proper, as in *decent language.*
3. Thoughtful or kind: *It was decent of them to walk the girls home.*
de·cent (**dee**-suhnt)
▷ *noun* **decency** ▷ *adverb* **decently**

a
b
c
d
e
f
g
h
i
j
k
l
m
n
o
p
q
r
s
t
u
v
w
x
y
z

deception *noun* Something that makes people believe what is not true; a lie: *His deception made us take a wrong turn.* **de·cep·tion** (di-**sep**-shuhn)

deceptive *adjective* Misleading, or not telling the true situation: *Her smile was deceptive.* **de·cep·tive** (di-**sep**-tiv) ▷ *adverb* **deceptively**

decibel *noun* A unit for measuring the loudness of sounds: *An alarm clock produces a sound of about 80 decibels.* **dec·i·bel** (**des**-uh-buhl)

decide *verb*
1. To make up your mind: *They decided to stay.*
2. To settle something that has more than one possible result: *The proposal to increase the sales tax was decided by a voter referendum.*
de·cide (di-**side**)
▷ *verb* **deciding, decided**

deciduous *adjective* Shedding all leaves every year in the fall: *Beeches and maples are deciduous trees.* **de·cid·u·ous** (di-**sij**-oo-uhs)

decimal
1. *adjective* Using the number 10 as a base.
2. *noun* A number that is written with a decimal point, such as 0.75, 5.56, and 92.50.
dec·i·mal (**des**-uh-muhl)

decimal point *noun* A period used in a number to show that all the numbers to its right are less than 1. The number 3.14 combines the whole number 3 and the fraction .14, or 14 hundredths.

decipher *verb* To figure out something that is written in code or is hard to understand: *I can't decipher these instructions.* **de·ci·pher** (di-**sye**-fur) ▷ *verb* **deciphering, deciphered** ▷ *adjective* **decipherable**

Word History

When Arabic numerals were introduced into Europe in the 12th century, they seemed like secret signs to people. The zero seemed especially mysterious, since before this there was no mathematical symbol meaning "nothing." So the new word meaning "zero," *cipher*, also came to mean "a secret way of writing." Discovering what a *cipher* meant was to **decipher** it. English speakers formed the word *decipher* from the prefix *de-*, meaning "to undo," and the word *cipher*. The Arabic word *cifr*, meaning "zero," was the source of *cipher*.

decision *noun*
1. The act of making up your mind about something: *I have to make a decision about where to spend my vacation.*
2. The result of making up your mind; a conclusion: *The president's decision could affect a whole generation of children.*
de·ci·sion (di-**sizh**-uhn)

deck

decisive *adjective*
1. Able to make choices quickly and easily.
2. Causing a certain result: *Someone needs to take decisive action here.*
3. Not leaving any doubt about the result: *We scored a decisive victory that put us into the playoffs.*
de·ci·sive (di-**sye**-siv)
▷ *adverb* **decisively**

deck *noun*
1. The floor of a boat or ship.
2. A platform with railings on the outside of a building: *We ate lunch out on the deck.*
3. A full set of playing cards.
deck (dek)

declaration *noun* The act of announcing something, or the announcement made, as in *a declaration of war.* **dec·la·ra·tion** (dek-luh-**ray**-shuhn)

Declaration of Independence *noun* A document declaring the freedom of the 13 American colonies from British rule. It was adopted on July 4, 1776.

signing the Declaration of Independence

declare *verb*
1. To say something firmly: *Liz declared that she was ready to leave and wasn't going to wait for him any longer.*
2. To announce something formally or officially: *The governor declared a state of emergency after the quake.*
de·clare (di-**klair**)
▷ *verb* **declaring, declared**

decline *verb*
1. To refuse something, especially in a way that is polite, as in *to decline an invitation.*
2. To get worse, smaller, or lower: *The number of visitors to the resort has declined in the past year.*
3. To bend or slope downward: *The road declines and ends at the dock.*
de·cline (di-**kline**)
▷ *verb* **declining, declined** ▷ *noun* **decline**

decode *verb* To change information into a form that is easier to understand: *The detective decoded the message.* **de·code** (dee-**kode**) ▷ *verb* **decoding, decoded** ▷ *noun* **decoder**

decompose *verb* To rot or decay: *The leaves were left on the ground all winter and were decomposing.* **de·com·pose** (*dee*-kuhm-**poze**) ▷ *verb* **decomposing, decomposed** ▷ *noun* **decomposition**

decongestant *noun* A drug or treatment that makes it easier for you to breathe when you have a cold or infection. **de·con·ges·tant** (*dee*-kuhn-**jes**-tuhnt) ▷ *noun* **decongestion** ▷ *verb* **decongest**

decorate *verb*
1. To add color, design, or other features that improve the appearance of something: *Let's decorate the Christmas tree.* ▷ *noun* **decorator** ▷ *adjective* **decorative** (**dek**-ur-uh-tiv)
2. To give a medal or badge to someone: *She was decorated for her bravery in the war.*
dec·o·rate (**dek**-uh-*rate*)
▷ *verb* **decorating, decorated** ▷ *noun* **decorating**

decoration *noun*
1. Something that makes an object or a place more attractive: *I thought the bedroom needed more decoration.*
2. The act of decorating something.
3. A badge or pin given to someone for achievement, especially in the military.
dec·o·ra·tion (*dek*-uh-**ray**-shuhn)

decorator *noun* Someone whose job is to decorate the inside of buildings. **dec·o·ra·tor** (**dek**-uh-*ray*-tur)

decoupage *noun* The art of decorating a surface by pasting on pieces of paper and then covering the whole object with layers of varnish. **de·cou·page** (*day*-koo-**pahzh**)

decoy *noun*
1. A carved model of a bird used by hunters to attract real birds.
2. Someone who lures a person into a trap or draws attention away from something.
de·coy (**dee**-koi)

Word History

The word **decoy** has always been a hunting word, but at first it referred to a pond surrounded by nets set up as a trap for wild birds. It later meant a wild bird trained to stay in an area as a lure for other birds, and the current meanings for the word grew out of this sense. *Decoy* probably derives from the Dutch *de kooi*, meaning "the cage."

decrease
1. (di-**krees**) *verb* To become less, smaller, or fewer: *If I sit down, the pain decreases.* ▷ *verb* **decreasing, decreased** ▷ *adjective* **decreasing** ▷ *adverb* **decreasingly**
2. (**dee**-krees) *noun* A loss, or the amount by which something gets less or smaller, as in *a decrease in your allowance.*
de·crease

decree
1. *verb* To give an order officially: *The governor decreed a new state holiday.* ▷ *verb* **decreeing, decreed**
2. *noun* An official decision or order, as in *a divorce decree.*
de·cree (di-**kree**)

decrepit *adjective* Weakened by old age or too much use, as in *a decrepit building.* **de·crep·it** (di-**krep**-it)

dedicate *verb*
1. If you are **dedicated** to something or if you **dedicate** yourself to something, you give a lot of time and energy to it: *He is completely dedicated to his work.*
2. To put someone's name in or on something, usually to say thanks or show appreciation: *The new reading room is dedicated to one of the university's founders.*
3. To set aside an amount of money for a particular purpose: *The senator wanted to dedicate $1 billion over ten years to rebuild the coastline.*
ded·i·cate (**ded**-i-*kate*)
▷ *verb* **dedicating, dedicated**

dedication *noun*
1. Devotion or concentration of effort: *They worked with much dedication.*
2. The inscription written in a book.
3. The opening of a place such as a new bridge or hospital, with a special ceremony.
ded·i·ca·tion (*ded*-i-**kay**-shun)

a b c d e f g h i j k l m n o p q r s t u v w x y z

deduce *verb* To figure something out from the amount of information that you have: *Mohammed deduced the solution to the mystery.* **de·duce** (di-**doos**) ▷ *verb* **deducing, deduced**

deduct *verb* To take away or subtract: *Lizzie deducted the cost of the skates from the total bill.* **de·duct** (di-**duhkt**) ▷ *verb* **deducting, deducted** ▷ *adjective* **deductible**

deduction *noun*
1. An amount that is taken away or subtracted: *The deduction on all items was 50 percent off the original price.*
2. Something that is figured out from a little information, as in *a logical deduction.* **de·duc·tion** (di-**duhk**-shuhn)

deed *noun*
1. Something that is done, as in *a good deed.*
2. A legal document that shows who owns property. **deed** (deed)

deem *verb* To have an opinion or to think about something in a particular way: *Many countries deem it necessary to restrict the ownership of firearms.* **deem** (deem) ▷ *verb* **deeming, deemed**

deep *adjective*
1. Going down a long way, as in *a deep canyon.*
2. Very intense and strong, as in *deep emotions.*
3. Low in pitch, as in *a deep voice.*
4. Not easy to understand: *That lecture was too deep for me.* **deep** (deep) ▷ *adjective* **deeper, deepest** ▷ *noun* **deep** ▷ *adverb* **deeply**

deepen *verb*
1. To become deeper: *They climbed onto the roof as the floodwaters deepened.*
2. To become larger, more important, or more intense: *The report deepened our understanding of the situation.* **deep·en** (**dee**-puhn) ▷ *verb* **deepening, deepened**

deep-sea *adjective* Living or happening far under the ocean: *Deep-sea divers worked to secure the cables to the ocean floor.*

deer *noun* An animal with hoofs that runs very fast and eats plants. Male deer grow bony, branching antlers. **deer** (deer) **Deer** sounds like **dear**. ▷ *noun, plural* **deer**

deface *verb* To spoil the way something looks by writing on it or scratching it: *A group of vandals went around town defacing the posters for the new movie.* **de·face** (di-**fase**) ▷ *verb* **defacing, defaced**

default
1. *noun* A setting or option that will be effective if you don't specifically choose one in a computer program: *I changed the default for the paper size from letter to legal, which is bigger.*
2. *adjective* Standard; in effect unless you choose something else: *The default font is Times Roman, but there are hundreds of others you can use.*
3. *verb* To use a standard setting that has already been chosen: *The measurement defaults to inches, but you can choose centimeters if you want.*
4. *verb* To fail to pay back a loan, as in *to default on a mortgage.* **de·fault** (di-**fawlt**) ▷ *verb* **defaulting, defaulted**

defeat
1. *verb* To beat someone in a war or a competition: *The Allies defeated Germany in World War II.* ▷ *verb* **defeating, defeated**
2. *noun* An instance of losing something such as a competition, an election, or a war: *Our baseball team suffered its first defeat last night.* **de·feat** (di-**feet**)

defect
1. (**dee**-fekt *or* di-**fekt**) *noun* A fault or weakness that makes something less valuable or useful. ▷ *adjective* **defective**
2. (di-**fekt**) *verb* To leave your country or political party and go to another, as in *to defect from the Republican Party to the Democratic Party.* ▷ *verb* **defecting, defected** ▷ *noun* **defector** ▷ *noun* **defection** **de·fect**

defend *verb*
1. To protect from harm: *The bear defended her cubs.*
2. To give the reasons for something or for your support of someone: *The*

deer

country had to defend its position on human rights.
3. To try to stop points being scored in a game with opposing sides or teams: *The goalkeeper defended the goal well.*
de·fend (di-**fend**)
▷ *verb* **defending, defended** ▷ *noun* **defender**

defendant *noun* The person in a court case who has been accused or who is being sued: *After the jury found the defendant not guilty, she was released.* **de·fend·ant** (di-**fen**-duhnt)

defense *noun*
1. (di-**fens**) The ability to protect from harm or attack, or something that does this: *The gang was not able to penetrate the building's defenses.*
2. (di-**fens**) The accused person or party in a trial, or the lawyer who represents the accused person or party.
3. (di-**fens**) An explanation that supports someone or some action: *Several people spoke in her defense, but she was still expelled.*
4. (di-**fens** *or* **dee**-fens) In sports, the **defense** is the side that doesn't have the ball, and tries to prevent the other team from scoring: *The game's outcome will be decided by the Ravens' defense.*
de·fense

defensive *adjective*
1. Serving to defend yourself or others, as in *a defensive action* or *defensive plans.*
2. If you are **defensive** or **on the defensive**, you act as if you are being attacked or criticized.
de·fen·sive (di-**fen**-siv)
▷ *noun* **defensiveness** ▷ *adverb* **defensively**

defer *verb*
1. To postpone until later: *The field trip will be deferred for a few more weeks.*
2. To give in to another's wishes or opinions: *Maria deferred to her older sister.*
de·fer (di-**fur**)
▷ *verb* **deferring, deferred** ▷ *noun* **deferment**

defiant *adjective* Refusing to obey, or showing an attitude of opposition: *He gave a defiant speech in which he made no concessions.* **de·fi·ant** (di-**fye**-uhnt) ▷ *noun* **defiance** ▷ *adverb* **defiantly**

deficient *adjective* Lacking something necessary: *Their food is deficient in nutrients.* **de·fi·cient** (di-**fish**-uhnt) ▷ *noun* **deficiency**

deficit *noun*
1. A situation where more money has been spent than has come in: *The expenses of the war caused a deficit in the budget.*
2. A situation where there is less of something than normal: *Farmers are coping with a serious rainfall deficit this year.*
def·i·cit (**def**-i-sit)

deforestation

define *verb*
1. To explain the meaning of something: *A dictionary defines words.*
2. To describe something exactly and in detail: *The handbook defines your rights and responsibilities.*
de·fine (di-**fine**)
▷ *verb* **defining, defined** ▷ *noun* **definer**

definite *adjective*
1. Certain: *Is there a definite date for the concert?*
2. Easy to see or understand: *Her answer was clear and definite—"No," she said, "I didn't like that movie."*
def·i·nite (**def**-uh-nit)

definite article *noun* The term for the word *the*. A definite article is used before a noun when the noun refers to something specific.

definitely *adverb* Without any doubt; with certainty: *I see only one duck on the pond, but there were definitely three of them just a minute ago.* **def·i·nite·ly** (**def**-uh-nit-lee)

definition *noun* An explanation of the meaning of a word or phrase: *Ellen gave a clear definition of the new word.* **def·i·ni·tion** (*def*-uh-**nish**-uhn)

deflate *verb*
1. To let the air out of something.
2. To reduce in size or importance: *Weeks of bad reviews had deflated the actor's self-confidence.*
de·flate (di-**flate**)
▷ *verb* **deflating, deflated** ▷ *noun* **deflation**

deflect *verb* To make something go in a different direction: *He missed the goal because the goalie deflected the ball with his head.* **de·flect** (di-**flekt**)
▷ *verb* **deflecting, deflected** ▷ *noun* **deflection**

deforest *verb* To remove or cut down forests.
de·for·est (dee-**for**-ist) ▷ *verb* **deforesting, deforested** ▷ *noun* **deforestation**

deformed *adjective* Twisted, bent, or disfigured.
de·formed (di-**formd**) ▷ *noun* **deformity**
▷ *verb* **deform**

defraud *verb* To cheat someone out of something that belongs to him or her, such as money or property: *The two business partners were scheming to defraud a Utah company of millions of dollars.* **de·fraud** (di-**frawd**) ▷ *verb* **defrauding, defrauded**

defrost *verb*
1. To completely thaw out an item that is frozen, as in *to defrost a steak.*
2. To remove ice from something, such as a refrigerator or freezer. **de·frost** (di-**frawst**) ▷ *verb* **defrosting, defrosted**

deft *adjective* Skillful, quick, and effective, as in *deft piano playing.* **deft** (deft) ▷ *adjective* **defter, deftest** ▷ *noun* **deftness** ▷ *adverb* **deftly**

defuse *verb*
1. To make a bomb safe so that it cannot explode.
2. To make a situation calmer: *Zoe's quiet words defused the argument.* **de·fuse** (dee-**fyooz**) ▷ *verb* **defusing, defused**

defy *verb*
1. To refuse to obey a person, order, rule, or law: *Martin Luther King Jr. and his companions defied racist laws.*
2. To challenge or dare someone to do something: *I defy you to swim across the lake.* **de·fy** (di-**fye**) ▷ *verb* **defies, defying, defied**

degenerate *verb* To become worse or inferior in quality: *After a few minutes, our discussion degenerated into an argument.* **de·gen·er·ate** (di-**gen**-uh-*rate*) ▷ *verb* **degenerating, degenerated**

degrading *adjective* Making you lose your self-respect or dignity. **de·grad·ing** (di-**gray**-ding) ▷ *noun* **degradation** (*deg*-ruh-**day**-shuhn) ▷ *verb* **degrade**

degree *noun*
1. A step in a series.
2. A unit for measuring temperature. The symbol for a degree is °, as in *85° Fahrenheit.*
3. A unit for measuring arcs and angles: *A right angle contains 90 degrees.*
4. A title given by a college or university, as in *a degree in medicine.* **de·gree** (di-**gree**)

dehydrated *adjective*
1. With all the water removed: *We carried dehydrated food in pouches on our camping trip.*
2. Lacking enough water in your body for normal functioning: *The baby was severely dehydrated and had*

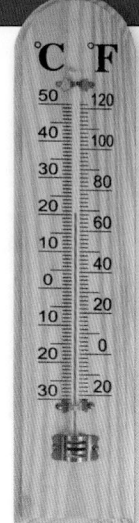

degrees

to be taken to the hospital. **de·hy·drat·ed** (dee-**hye**-dray-tid) ▷ *noun* **dehydration** ▷ *verb* **dehydrate**

deity *noun*
1. A god or a goddess.
2. the Deity God. **de·i·ty** (**dee**-i-tee) ▷ *noun, plural* **deities**

dejected *adjective* Sad and depressed: *Miko felt dejected when she failed the test.* **de·ject·ed** (di-**jek**-tid) ▷ *noun* **dejection** ▷ *adverb* **dejectedly**

delay *verb*
1. To make someone or something late: *The traffic jam delayed the bus.*
2. To postpone until later, as in *to delay going to bed.* **de·lay** (di-**lay**) ▷ *verb* **delaying, delayed** ▷ *noun* **delay**

delegate
1. (**del**-i-*gate*) *verb* To give someone responsibility to do something: *Joey delegated some of his chores to his brother.* ▷ *verb* **delegating, delegated**
2. (**del**-i-git) *noun* Someone who represents other people at a meeting or in a legislature: *She is going to the political convention as a delegate for Missouri.* **del·e·gate**

delegation *noun* A group of people who represent an organization or a government at meetings: *The US delegation was the first to arrive at the peace talks.* **del·e·ga·tion** (*del*-i-**gay**-shuhn)

delete *verb* To remove something from a text or from a computer storage area: *Delete the last two sentences from the paragraph.* **de·lete** (di-**leet**) ▷ *verb* **deleting, deleted** ▷ *noun* **deletion**

deli *noun* Short for **delicatessen**. **del·i** (**del**-ee)

deliberate
1. (di-**lib**-ur-it) *adjective* Done on purpose; intentional.
2. (di-**lib**-ur-it) *adjective* Careful and slow: *She walked with deliberate steps on the icy sidewalk.*
3. (di-**lib**-uh-*rate*) *verb* To consider something carefully: *Dad deliberated before punishing me.* ▷ *verb* **deliberating, deliberated** ▷ *noun* **deliberation** **de·lib·er·ate**

deliberately *adverb* On purpose; with a specific intention: *Terri deliberately hid the book from her brother.* **de·lib·er·ate·ly** (di-**lib**-ur-it-lee)

delicate *adjective*
1. Very pleasant to the senses, as in *a delicate flavor.*
2. Finely made or sensitive, as in *a delicate instrument.*
3. Not very strong and likely to become ill: *He has been very delicate since his gallbladder operation.* **del·i·cate** (**del**-i-kit) ▷ *adverb* **delicately**

delicatessen *noun* A store that sells prepared foods, such as salads and sliced meats. **del·i·ca·tes·sen** (*del*-i-kuh-**tes**-uhn)

delicious *adjective* Tasting or smelling very good: *That apple pie was delicious!* **de·li·cious** (di-**lish**-uhs) ▷ *adverb* **deliciously**

delight
1. *noun* Great pleasure: *The trip was a delight.* ▷ *adjective* **delightful** ▷ *adverb* **delightfully**
2. *verb* To please someone very much: *The birthday gift delighted Sandy.* ▷ *verb* **delighting, delighted**
de·light (di-**lite**)

delighted *adjective* Feeling very happy because of something that has happened: *My cousin came to visit me from Canada, and I was delighted to see her again.* **de·light·ed** (di-**lye**-tid)

delinquent
1. *noun* A person who is often in trouble with the law, as in *a juvenile delinquent.* ▷ *adjective* **delinquent**
2. *adjective* Overdue for payment, as in *a delinquent account.* ▷ *noun* **delinquency**
de·lin·quent (di-**ling**-kwuhnt)

delirious *adjective* Unable to think straight because of either a high fever or extreme happiness. **de·lir·i·ous** (di-**leer**-ee-uhs) ▷ *adverb* **deliriously**

delirium *noun* A state of mental confusion caused by high fever, shock, or poison: *In his delirium, he began to move restlessly and mutter nonsense.* **de·lir·i·um** (di-**leer**-ee-uhm)

deliver *verb*
1. To take something to someone: *A messenger was sent to deliver the package.*
2. To say or state, usually in a formal way: *The teacher delivered an exciting talk.*
3. To help a baby to be born.
4. To free someone from something bad: *Deliver us from evil.*
de·liv·er (di-**liv**-ur)
▷ *verb* **delivering, delivered** ▷ *noun* **deliverance**

delivery *noun*
1. The act of handing over something that is expected or has been ordered: *When do you expect the delivery of the package?*
2. The gestures, tone, and behavior of someone speaking before people: *She needs to work on her delivery a bit, but her subject is fascinating.*
3. The act of bringing a baby out of his or her mother's womb, as in *a difficult delivery.*
de·liv·er·y (di-**liv**-ur-ee)
▷ *noun, plural* **deliveries**

delta *noun* An area of land shaped like a triangle where a river enters the sea. **del·ta** (**del**-tuh)

deluge
1. *noun* Heavy rain, often causing flooding.
2. *verb* To cover a place in water: *The hurricane deluged the city.*
3. *verb* To send or give large amounts of something: *The station has been deluged with requests to rebroadcast the program.* ▷ *noun* **deluge**
del·uge (**del**-yooj)
▷ *verb* **deluging, deluged**

delusion *noun* A false idea or a hallucination: *He has a delusion that he is the richest person in the world.* **de·lu·sion** (di-**loo**-zhuhn) ▷ *verb* **delude**

deluxe *adjective* Of the best quality, or having extra, expensive features: *Whenever they travel, they stay only in deluxe hotels.* **de·luxe** (di-**luhks**)

delve *verb* If you **delve** into something, you find out everything about it that you can by studying or asking questions, as in *to delve into a problem.* **delve** (delv) ▷ *verb* **delved, delving**

demand
1. *verb* To ask for something firmly because you think it is right, as in *to demand civil rights.*
2. *verb* To require: *Having a successful business demands a lot of hard work.*
3. *noun* An official or urgent request: *The kidnappers so far have made no demands.*
4. *noun* Desire to buy or use something, as in *a demand for gas.*
de·mand (di-**mand**)
▷ *verb* **demanding, demanded**

demanding *adjective* Requiring a lot of time, attention, or effort: *Cecilia's job was very demanding.* **de·mand·ing** (di-**man**-ding)

demeanor *noun* The way you behave: *His calm demeanor made it easy to talk to him.* **de·mea·nor** (di-**mee**-nur)

demented *adjective*
1. Suffering from dementia: *He became demented as a result of the repeated blows to his head when he was a boxer.*
2. Acting in a crazy way because of anger, excitement, or distress: *Cory was so furious that he threw a chair and started shouting like a demented lunatic.*
de·ment·ed (di-**men**-tid)
▷ *adverb* **dementedly**

dementia *noun* A mental illness, caused by a brain disease or injury, that makes people lose the ability to think clearly and often leads to personality changes: *Alzheimer's disease is the leading cause of dementia among the elderly.* **de·men·tia** (di-**men**-shuh)

a
b
c
d
e
f
g
h
i
j
k
l
m
n
o
p
q
r
s
t
u
v
w
x
y
z

demise *noun*

1. Death: *The beloved leader's sudden demise left the nation in a state of shock and sorrow.*

2. The ending of something: *Laptops and tablets may be hastening the demise of the desktop computer.*

de·mise (di-**mize**)

demo *noun (informal)*

1. A recording made to introduce a new performer or piece of music.

2. Something that shows you how another thing will work: *Click here for a demo of the software's capabilities.*

dem·o (**dem**-oh)

democracy *noun*

1. A form of government in which the people choose their leaders in elections.

2. A country that has this kind of government: *The leaders of 34 democracies attended the economic conference.*

de·moc·ra·cy (di-**mah**-kruh-see)

▷ *noun, plural* **democracies**

democrat *noun*

1. Someone who agrees with the system of democracy.

2. Democrat A member of the Democratic Party.

dem·o·crat (**dem**-uh-*krat*)

democratic *adjective*

1. Having to do with or in favor of democracy.

2. Democratic Belonging to or connected with the Democratic Party.

dem·o·crat·ic (*dem*-uh-**krat**-ik)

▷ *adverb* **democratically**

Democratic Party *noun* One of the two main political parties in the United States. The other is the **Republican Party**.

demolish *verb* To knock down or destroy something: *The bomb demolished the town.*

de·mol·ish (di-**mah**-lish) ▷ *verb* **demolishes, demolishing, demolished** ▷ *noun* **demolition** (*dem*-uh-**lish**-uhn)

demon *noun* A devil or an evil spirit. This word is sometimes used in a positive way to describe someone who seems to have magical ability because he or she works very hard. **de·mon** (**dee**-muhn) ▷ *adjective* **demonic** (di-**mah**-nik)

demonstrate *verb*

1. To show how to do something or use something: *In his presentation, Mark demonstrated how to use a GPS.*

2. To show something clearly: *The damage from the storm demonstrates how rough the weather can be at this time of year.*

3. To join together with other people to protest something: *The students demonstrated against the budget cuts to the library.*

dem·on·strate (**dem**-uhn-*strate*)

▷ *verb* **demonstrating, demonstrated**

demonstration *noun*

1. The act or process of showing how something works: *Can you give us a demonstration of the new software?*

2. A public protest, as in *an antiwar demonstration.*

dem·on·stra·tion (*dem*-uhn-**stray**-shuhn)

demonstrative

1. *adjective* Showing and expressing feelings freely: *The audience hated the speech and was quite demonstrative about it.*

2. *noun* A word that tells you which one or ones. The pronouns *this, that, these,* and *those* are the main demonstratives in English.

dem·on·stra·tive (duh-**mahn**-struh-tiv)

demonym *noun* A name for a person who comes from a particular place: *Coloradan is the usual demonym for someone from Colorado.* **dem·o·nym** (**dem**-uh-nim)

demote *verb*

1. To decrease someone's rank or position: *The sergeant was demoted to corporal.*

2. To put a student in a lower grade: *After failing all his courses, Tom was demoted.*

de·mote (di-**moht**)

▷ *verb* **demoting, demoted** ▷ *noun* **demotion** (di-**moh**-shuhn)

den *noun*

1. The home of a wild animal, such as a lion.

2. A comfortable room where you can work or play: *We watched television in the den.*

den (den)

denial *noun*

1. The act of saying that something is not true or valid: *The actor's lawyer issued a denial of the charges against his client.*

2. If someone is **in denial**, he or she refuses to believe something that is true.

de·ni·al (di-**nye**-uhl)

denim *noun* Strong cotton material used to make jeans and other articles of clothing. **den·im** (**den**-uhm)

▷ *adjective* **denim**

denomination *noun*

1. An organized religion: *All the main Protestant denominations have churches in our town.*

2. A value or unit in a system of measurement: *Nearly all countries issue currency in denominations that are multiples of ten.*

de·nom·i·na·tion (di-*nah*-muh-**nay**-shuhn)

denominator *noun* The number in a fraction that is under the line and that shows how many equal parts the whole number can be divided into: *In the fraction ¾, 4 is the denominator.* **de·nom·i·na·tor** (di-**nah**-muh-*nay*-tur)

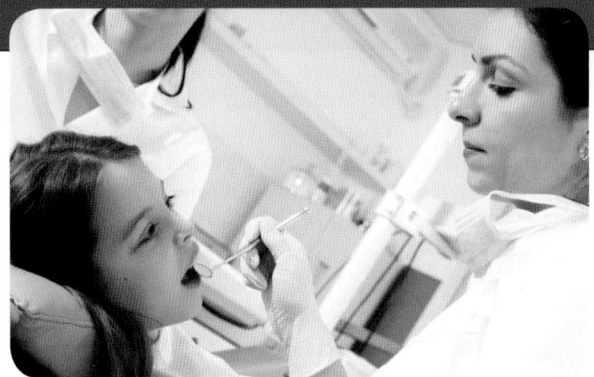

dentist

denote *verb*
1. To show or be a sign of something: *The stars on the flag of the United States denote the 50 states.*
2. To mean: *The word "bird" denotes a creature with two legs, wings, feathers, and a beak.*
de·note (di-**note**)
▷ *verb* **denoting, denoted** ▷ *noun* **denotation**

denounce *verb* To say in public that something is wrong or that someone has done something wrong: *The newspaper editorial denounced the mayor's lapse of judgment.* **de·nounce** (di-**nouns**) ▷ *verb* **denouncing, denounced**

dense *adjective*
1. Crowded or thick, as in *dense fog.*
2. *(informal)* Slow to understand; stupid: *Josie was dense when it came to arithmetic.*
dense (dens)
▷ *adjective* **denser, densest** ▷ *noun* **denseness**
▷ *adverb* **densely**

density *noun*
1. A measure of how heavy or light an object is for its size. Density is measured by dividing an object's mass by its volume.
2. The amount of something per unit: *Population density is greater within the city limits.*
den·si·ty (**den**-si-tee)

dent *verb* To damage something by bashing it in: *Lester dented his new car.* **dent** (dent) ▷ *verb* **denting, dented** ▷ *noun* **dent**

dental *adjective* Of or having to do with your teeth, as in *dental hygiene.* **den·tal** (**den**-tuhl)

dental floss *See* **floss.**

dentist *noun* A doctor who is qualified to examine, clean, and treat teeth. **den·tist** (**den**-tist) ▷ *noun* **dentistry**

Word History

Dentist, the English word for "tooth doctor," comes from *dent*, the French word for "tooth."

dentures *noun, plural* A set of false teeth. **den·tures** (**den**-churz)

deny *verb*
1. To say that something is not true: *Do you deny that you were there that night?*
2. To refuse to allow something: *The bank denied his request for a mortgage.*
de·ny (di-**nye**)
▷ *verb* **denies, denying, denied**

deodorant *noun* A substance used to cover up or get rid of unpleasant smells. **de·o·dor·ant** (dee-**oh**-dur-uhnt)

depart *verb*
1. To leave, especially to go on a trip: *We will depart for New York early tomorrow.*
2. To change a course of action: *Departing from the script, the actor ad-libbed a couple of lines.*
de·part (di-**pahrt**)
▷ *verb* **departing, departed**

department *noun* A part of a place like a store, hospital, or university that has a particular function or purpose, as in *a shoe department.* **de·part·ment** (di-**pahrt**-muhnt) ▷ *adjective* **departmental**

department store *noun* A large store with sections for the different kinds of goods sold.

departure *noun*
1. The act of leaving a place: *The plane's departure was right on time.*
2. A change in the way that something is usually done: *Christmas dinner was a real departure this year—we ate in a Chinese restaurant!*
de·par·ture (di-**pahr**-chur)

depend *verb*
1. To rely on someone or something: *I depend on my father for advice.* ▷ *adjective* **dependable**
2. If a thing **depends on** something else, it is determined or influenced by it: *Whether we go to Kansas will depend on the cost of the plane fare.*
de·pend (di-**pend**)
▷ *verb* **depending, depended** ▷ *noun* **dependence**

dependent
1. *noun* A person who is taken care of and supported by someone else: *My parents have four dependents: me, my brother, and my two sisters.*
2. *adjective* Depending on or controlled by something or someone else: *Tomorrow's schedule will be dependent on weather conditions.*
3. A **dependent clause** is a part of a sentence that cannot stand on its own: *In the sentence "He will take his coat when he goes," the dependent clause is "when he goes."* See **independent clause.**
de·pend·ent (di-**pen**-duhnt)

depict *verb* To show something using pictures or language: *She was depicted in the article as being a very responsible mother.* **de·pict** (di-**pikt**) ▷ *verb* **depicting, depicted**

deplete *verb* To empty, or to use up: *The long strike depleted our savings.* **de·plete** (di-**pleet**) ▷ *verb* **depleting, depleted** ▷ *noun* **depletion** (di-**plee**-shuhn)

deplorable *adjective* Very bad, as in *deplorable conditions.* **de·plor·a·ble** (di-**plor**-uh-buhl) ▷ *verb* **deplore** ▷ *adverb* **deplorably**

deploy *verb*
1. To use something or put it into action: *The pilot deployed the plane's landing gear.*
2. To send troops or weapons: *The National Guard deployed troops to help with the cleanup after the flood.* **de·ploy** (di-**ploi**)
▷ *verb* **deploying, deployed** ▷ *noun* **deployment**

deport *verb* To send someone back to his or her own country: *Because he was convicted of a serious crime, immigration officials are making plans to deport him.* **de·port** (di-**port**) ▷ *verb* **deporting, deported** ▷ *noun* **deportation** (*dee*-por-**tay**-shuhn)

depose *verb* To remove a ruler from office, usually by force. **de·pose** (di-**poze**) ▷ *verb* **deposing, deposed**

deposit
1. *noun* Money given as a first payment or as a promise to buy or take part in something: *We paid a small deposit for the new refrigerator.*
2. *noun* A natural layer of rock, sand, or minerals.
3. *verb* To place, or to lay down: *She deposited her bags in the trunk of the car.*
4. *verb* To put money into a bank account. **de·pos·it** (di-**pah**-zit)
▷ *verb* **depositing, deposited**

depot *noun* A bus or railroad station. **de·pot** (**dee**-poh)

depreciate *verb* To lose value: *Cars depreciate as they get older.* **de·pre·ci·ate** (di-**pree**-shee-*ate*) ▷ *verb* **depreciating, depreciated** ▷ *noun* **depreciation**

depressed *adjective* Sad and unhappy with life. **de·pressed** (di-**prest**) ▷ *adjective* **depressing** ▷ *verb* **depress**

depression *noun*
1. Unhappiness that doesn't go away.
2. A medical condition in which you feel unhappy or hopeless and can't concentrate or sleep well.
3. A time when the economy of a country is shrinking and many people lose their jobs.
4. A hollow or concave place: *Juanita's body made a depression in the sand.*
de·pres·sion (di-**presh**-uhn)

derby

deprive *verb* To take a thing away from someone, or prevent him or her from having it: *Opponents claim the new law will deprive them of choice in education.* **de·prive** (di-**prive**)
▷ *verb* **depriving, deprived** ▷ *noun* **deprivation** (*dep*-ruh-**vay**-shuhn)
▷ *adjective* **deprived**

depth *noun*
1. Deepness, or a measurement of how deep something is: *The depth of the pool at the shallow end is three feet.*
2. Something done **in depth** is very thorough: *The book analyzed the presidential election in depth.*
3. If you are **out of your depth**, something is too complex for you to understand it fully: *I felt out of my depth in the advanced math class.*
depth (depth)

deputy *noun* Someone who helps or acts for somebody else, as in *a sheriff's deputy.* **dep·u·ty** (**dep**-yuh-tee)
▷ *noun, plural* **deputies** ▷ *verb* **deputize**

deranged *adjective* Insane: *The criminal was deranged.* **de·ranged** (di-**raynjd**)

derby *noun*
1. A stiff hat with a narrow brim and a round top.
2. A race or contest, especially one involving horses: *The Kentucky Derby takes place the first Saturday in May.*
der·by (**dur**-bee)
▷ *noun, plural* **derbies**

derelict
1. *adjective* Neglected and falling apart: *The house was in a derelict state.*
2. *noun* A wandering, homeless person.
der·e·lict (**der**-uh-likt)

derive *verb*
1. To take or receive something from another thing, as in *to derive satisfaction from a job.*
2. If a word is **derived** from another word, it has developed from it: *The word "pyramid" is derived from the Greek words for "fire" and "middle."*
de·rive (di-**rive**)
▷ *verb* **deriving, derived** ▷ *noun* **derivation** (*der*-i-**vay**-shuhn)

derogatory *adjective* Making something or someone seem worse or inferior: *She made a derogatory comment about my new shoes.* **de·rog·a·to·ry** (di-**rah**-guh-*tor*-ee) ▷ *adverb* **derogatorily** (di-*rah*-guh-**tor**-uh-lee)

derrick *noun*
1. A tall crane with a long, movable arm that can raise or lower heavy objects.

2. A tall framework that holds the machines used to drill oil wells.
der·rick (**der**-ik)

descend *verb*

1. To go down to a lower level: *To get downstairs, you will need to descend the staircase.*

2. If you are **descended** from someone, that person is one of your ancestors: *He is descended from a famous artist.*

de·scend (di-**send**)

▷ *verb* **descending, descended** ▷ *noun* **descent**

descendant *noun* Your **descendants** are your children, their children, and so on into the future.   **de·scend·ant** (di-**sen**-duhnt)

describe *verb* To tell about something so that your listener gets an understanding of it: *Several witnesses described the robber as tall and bearded.*   **de·scribe** (di-**skribe**) ▷ *verb* **describing, described** ▷ *adjective* **descriptive** (di-**skrip**-tiv)

description *noun* A written or spoken statement that tells about someone or something: *Paul gave me a very precise description of his new car.*   **de·scrip·tion** (di-**skrip**-shuhn)

desegregate *verb* To do away with the practice of separating people of different races in schools, restaurants, and other public places.   **de·seg·re·gate** (dee-**seg**-ruh-*gate*) ▷ *verb* **desegregating, desegregated** ▷ *noun* **desegregation**

desert

1. (di-**zurt**) *verb* To go away from a person, place, or thing for good, or to run away from the army: *The cat deserted her kittens.* ▷ *verb* **deserting, deserted** ▷ *noun* **deserter** ▷ *noun* **desertion**

2. (**dez**-urt) *noun* A dry area where hardly any plants grow because there is so little rain. ▷ *adjective* **desert**
de·sert

Deserts

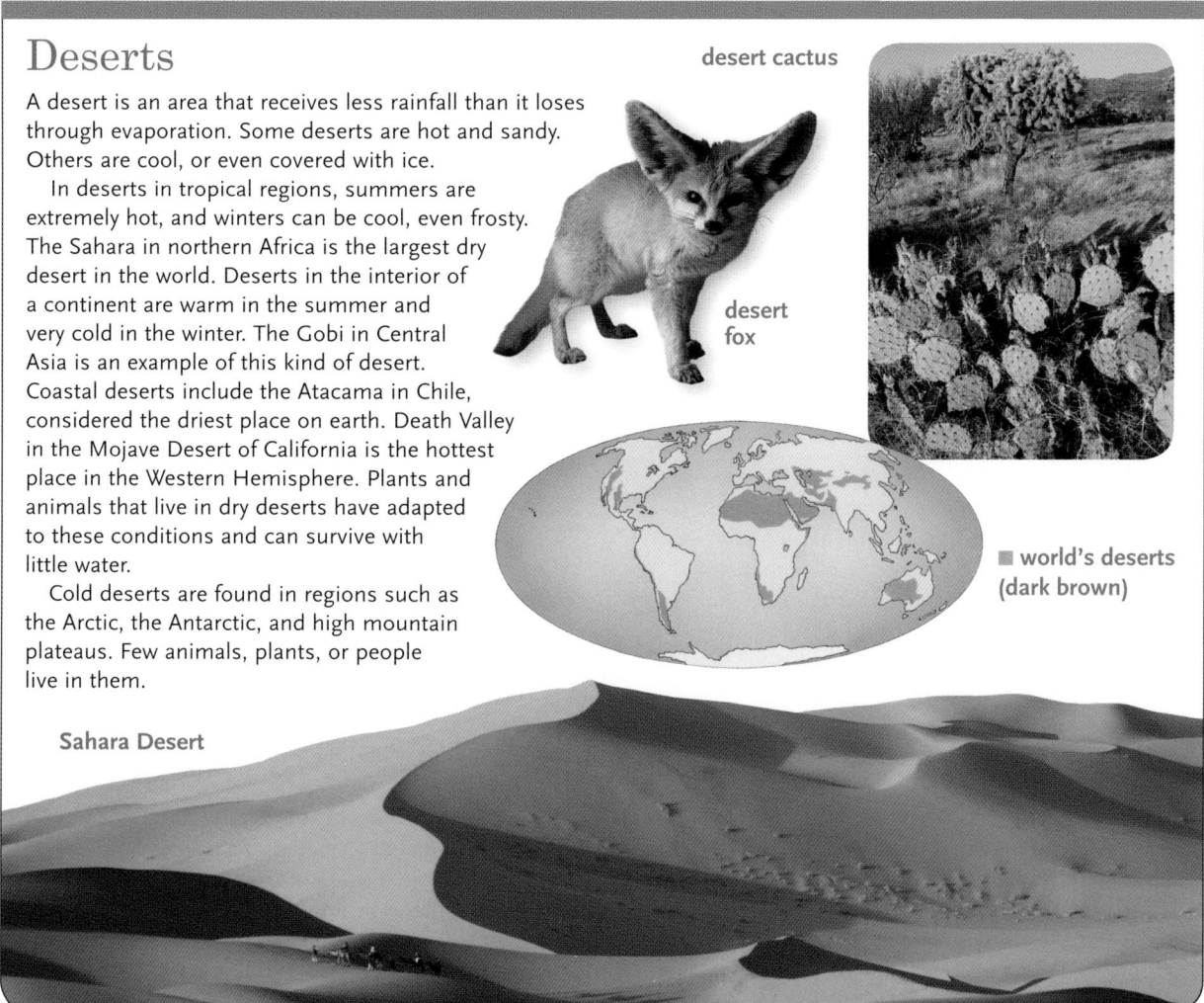

desert cactus

A desert is an area that receives less rainfall than it loses through evaporation. Some deserts are hot and sandy. Others are cool, or even covered with ice.

In deserts in tropical regions, summers are extremely hot, and winters can be cool, even frosty. The Sahara in northern Africa is the largest dry desert in the world. Deserts in the interior of a continent are warm in the summer and very cold in the winter. The Gobi in Central Asia is an example of this kind of desert. Coastal deserts include the Atacama in Chile, considered the driest place on earth. Death Valley in the Mojave Desert of California is the hottest place in the Western Hemisphere. Plants and animals that live in dry deserts have adapted to these conditions and can survive with little water.

Cold deserts are found in regions such as the Arctic, the Antarctic, and high mountain plateaus. Few animals, plants, or people live in them.

desert fox

■ world's deserts (dark brown)

Sahara Desert

deserted *adjective* Empty of people; without anyone around: *After school starts, the beaches are usually deserted.* **de·sert·ed** (di-**zur**-tid)

deserve *verb* To earn something because of something you have done: *Angelica deserves praise for her volunteer work.* **de·serve** (di-**zurv**) ▷ *verb* **deserving, deserved** ▷ *adjective* **deserving**

design
1. *verb* To draw a plan for something that can be made: *The architect designed a new house.* ▷ *verb* **designing, designed**
2. *noun* The shape or style of something: *The floor design had diamonds and squares.*
de·sign (di-**zine**)

designate *verb*
1. To name or mark something: *Maps of the United States often use a star to designate a state capital.*
2. To call or name something: *People sometimes designate New York City by its nickname, the Big Apple.*
3. To choose someone for an office or duty: *Shawna was designated captain of the soccer team.*
des·ig·nate (**dez**-ig-*nate*)
▷ *verb* **designating, designated** ▷ *noun* **designation**

designated driver *noun* A person who has agreed not to drink alcohol so that he or she can drive for others who are drinking.

designated hitter *noun* In baseball, a player who is named at the start of the game to bat in the pitcher's place without causing the pitcher to be taken out of the game.

designer *noun* Someone who designs something, especially as a job: *The dress is by a local fashion designer, who is known for her colorful, geometric patterns.* **de·sign·er** (di-**zye**-nur)

desirable *adjective* Pleasing and worth having: *Which smartphone do you think has the most desirable features?* **de·sir·a·ble** (di-**zire**-uh-buhl)

desire *noun* A strong feeling of needing to do or have something: *Clifford had a burning desire to run in the marathon.* **de·sire** (di-**zire**) ▷ *verb* **desire**

desk *noun* A piece of furniture with a flat top where you sit and do work. **desk** (desk)

desktop *noun*
1. The surface on the top of a desk where you do work.
2. An image on a computer screen showing icons of files and programs in the computer.
desk·top (**desk**-*tahp*)
▷ *adjective* **desktop**

desktop publishing *noun* The process of writing, editing, and designing pages on a computer to publish in print or electronic form.

desolate *adjective*
1. Empty of people, as in *a desolate landscape.*
2. Extremely sad and lonely: *Carly felt desolate when Andy snubbed her.*
des·o·late (**des**-uh-lit)
▷ *noun* **desolation** ▷ *adverb* **desolately**

despair
1. *verb* To lose hope that something will happen: *Sam despaired of finding us in the crowd.* ▷ *verb* **despairing, despaired**
2. *noun* Extreme sadness after something terrible has happened: *Losing his dog threw Mike into despair.*
de·spair (di-**spair**)
▷ *adjective* **despairing** ▷ *adverb* **despairingly**

desperado *noun* A bold, reckless criminal; a bandit. **des·per·a·do** (*des*-puh-**rah**-doh) ▷ *noun, plural* **desperadoes** or **desperados**

desperate *adjective*
1. Willing to do anything to change a situation: *Lee was desperate to get away from the fight.* ▷ *noun* **desperation** (*des*-puh-**ray**-shuhn)
2. Dangerous but done only because there is no other choice: *They made one last desperate attempt to save the people in the water.*
des·per·ate (**des**-pur-it)
▷ *adverb* **desperately**

despise *verb* To dislike and disrespect someone or something very strongly. **de·spise** (di-**spize**)
▷ *verb* **despising, despised** ▷ *adjective* **despicable** (di-**spik**-uh-buhl)

despite *preposition* In spite of: *We enjoyed the hike, despite the chilly wind.* **de·spite** (di-**spite**)

dessert *noun* A sweet food, such as ice cream, fruit, or cake, usually served at the end of a meal. **des·sert** (di-**zurt**)

destination *noun* The place that a person or vehicle is traveling to: *The plane's destination was Miami.* **des·ti·na·tion** (*des*-tuh-**nay**-shuhn)

destined *adjective*
1. Having a certain fate: *Carolyn is destined to become a great teacher.*
2. Bound for a certain place, as in *a cruise ship destined for the Caribbean.*
des·tined (**des**-tuhnd)

destiny *noun*
1. The future events in your life, as determined by something that happened earlier: *Her sensational audition changed her destiny and made her a star.*
2. A force that is believed to control the future and the course of people's lives; fate.
des·ti·ny (**des**-tuh-nee)
▷ *noun, plural* **destinies**

destroyer

destitute *adjective* Lacking food, shelter, and clothing. **des·ti·tute** (**des**-ti-*toot*) ▷ *noun* **destitution**

destroy *verb* To ruin something completely so that nothing usable is left: *Insects destroyed all my tomatoes.* **de·stroy** (di-**stroi**) ▷ *verb* **destroying, destroyed**

destroyer *noun* A very fast warship that uses guns, missiles, and torpedoes to protect other ships from submarines. **de·stroy·er** (di-**stroi**-ur)

destruction *noun* The act of destroying something: *The riot caused enormous destruction.* **de·struc·tion** (di-**struhk**-shuhn)

destructive *adjective* Causing damage and harm: *The storm had destructive winds.* **de·struc·tive** (di-**struhk**-tiv) ▷ *adverb* **destructively**

detach *verb* To separate one thing from another: *We detached the trailer from our car.* **de·tach** (di-**tach**) ▷ *verb* **detaches, detaching, detached** ▷ *adjective* **detachable**

detached *adjective*
1. Able to stand back from a situation and not get too involved in it. ▷ *noun* **detachment**
2. Separate and not connected to something else: *Our detached garage is about 25 feet from our house.*
de·tached (di-**tacht**)

detail *noun*
1. A small part of a whole item, as in *a detail of a painting*.
2. The treatment of something item by item: *Jeb's stories are full of detail.* ▷ *adjective* **detailed**
3. **details** *noun, plural* Items of specific information: *She said the principal was resigning but didn't provide any details.* ▷ *verb* **detail**
de·tail (di-**tayl** *or* **dee**-tayl)

detain *verb* To hold somebody back when he or she wants to go: *The police arrested him, then detained him at the local jail.* **de·tain** (di-**tayn**) ▷ *verb* **detaining, detained**

detect *verb* To notice or discover something: *I detected a strange smell in the house.* **de·tect** (di-**tekt**) ▷ *verb* **detecting, detected** ▷ *noun* **detection** ▷ *adjective* **detectable**

detective *noun* Someone who investigates crimes, usually for or with the police: *The police sent a detective to investigate the robbery.* **de·tec·tive** (di-**tek**-tiv)

detector *noun* A machine used to reveal the presence of something, such as smoke, metal, or radioactivity: *The county building code requires smoke detectors on every floor.* **de·tec·tor** (di-**tek**-tur)

detention *noun*
1. A punishment in which a student has to stay after school or has to report early to school.
2. The state of being forced to stay in a place, usually by authorities: *The new facility was built for the detention of illegal aliens.*
de·ten·tion (di-**ten**-shuhn)

deter *verb* To prevent or discourage something: *The snow deterred us from going to the play.* **de·ter** (di-**tur**) ▷ *verb* **deterring, deterred**

detergent *noun* A substance similar to soap for cleaning things. **de·ter·gent** (di-**tur**-juhnt)

deteriorate *verb* To get worse: *The weather deteriorated throughout the day.* **de·te·ri·o·rate** (di-**teer**-ee-uh-**rate**) ▷ *verb* **deteriorating, deteriorated** ▷ *noun* **deterioration**

determination *noun*
1. A strong will to do something: *I'm impressed by their determination to win the game.*
2. The act of deciding or determining something: *The jury discussed the evidence and came to the determination that the defendant was guilty.*
de·ter·mi·na·tion (di-*tur*-muh-**nay**-shuhn)

determine *verb*
1. To have an effect on: *The war determined their fate.*
2. To make a discovery or to find out: *I determined that the witness was lying.*
3. If you **determine** the solution to a problem, you are able to settle or resolve it.
4. If you **determine** a date or time, you decide it after considering everything necessary: *The legislature will determine the date for the public hearings.*
de·ter·mine (di-**tur**-min) ▷ *verb* **determining, determined**

determined *adjective* Having or showing a strong intention to do something: *They made a determined effort to hold back the river.* **de·ter·mined** (di-**tur**-mind) ▷ *adverb* **determinedly**

detergent

deterrent *noun* A thing that stops something else from happening: *Insect repellent is a good deterrent against mosquito bites.* **de·ter·rent** (di-**tur**-uhnt)

detest *verb* To dislike very much: *I detest her constant interruptions and demands.* **de·test** (di-**test**) ▷ *verb* **detesting, detested** ▷ *adjective* **detestable**

detonate *verb* To set off an explosion: *This switch will detonate a blast that will cause the tunnel to collapse.* **det·o·nate** (**det**-uh-*nate*) ▷ *verb* **detonating, detonated** ▷ *noun* **detonator**

detour *noun* A different, usually longer way to go somewhere when the direct route is closed or blocked: *The detour added an hour to our trip.* **de·tour** (**dee**-toor)

detract *verb* To reduce the enjoyment or value of something: *The outdoor concert was good, except that the noise from the plane detracted from it.* **de·tract** (di-**trakt**) ▷ *verb* **detracting, detracted**

detrimental *adjective* Harmful: *Eating too much candy is detrimental to your teeth.* **det·ri·men·tal** (*det*-ri-**men**-tuhl) ▷ *noun* **detriment**

devalue *verb* To reduce the value of something, especially a currency. **de·val·ue** (dee-**val**-yoo) ▷ *verb* **devaluing, devalued** ▷ *noun* **devaluation**

devastate *noun*
1. To damage severely or destroy: *The earthquake has devastated the island.* ▷ *noun* **devastation**
2. To upset extremely: *I was devastated when I heard about their car wreck.*
dev·as·tate (**dev**-uh-*stayt*)
▷ *adjective* **devastating**

develop *verb*
1. To grow in a natural way to a more mature or advanced state: *The boys' friendship developed slowly.*
2. To make something grow in this way: *The writer developed his short story into a novel.*
3. To treat film with chemicals in order to bring out the photos that have been taken on the film, or to make prints of photos taken with a digital camera.
de·vel·op (di-**vel**-uhp)
▷ *verb* **developing, developed** ▷ *noun* **developer**

developing country *noun* A country in which most people are poor and there is not yet much industry.

development *noun*
1. The natural and expected growth or change in something, as in *economic development* or *industrial development.*
2. The appearance of something that wasn't there before: *She hasn't felt well lately, but her sudden spell of nausea is a startling new development.*
3. Something that happens in a process and that is seen as a change in that process: *What are the new developments today in the World Cup?*

4. An area of land that has been modified for a particular use, as in *a housing development.*
de·vel·op·ment (di-**vel**-uhp-muhnt)

deviate *verb* To do something differently from the usual way: *The mail carrier deviated from her usual route.* **de·vi·ate** (**dee**-vee-*ate*) ▷ *verb* **deviating, deviated** ▷ *noun* **deviation**

device *noun*
1. A piece of equipment that does a particular job: *The computer is a device with many functions.*
2. If you are **left to your own devices**, you can do what you want.
de·vice (di-**vise**)

devil *noun*
1. the devil In many religions, the primary spirit of evil. The word is often capitalized.
2. A person who is full of mischief or is wicked: *My devil of a little brother took my baseball glove.*
dev·il (**dev**-uhl)
▷ *adjective* **devilish**

devious *adjective* Misleading or not direct in communicating the real reasons for something: *This is a devious plot to put the two countries at war again.* **de·vi·ous** (**dee**-vee-uhs) ▷ *noun* **deviousness** ▷ *adverb* **deviously**

devil

devise *verb* To think of a way to do or create something, as in *to devise a new invention.* **de·vise** (di-**vize**) ▷ *verb* **devising, devised**

devoid *adjective* Lacking something that you would expect to be present: *His apology was devoid of any sign of remorse.* **de·void** (di-**void**)

devote *verb* To give your time, effort, or attention to some purpose: *He devoted his life to helping the poor.* **de·vote** (di-**voht**) ▷ *verb* **devoting, devoted**

devoted *adjective* Having or showing strong feelings of loyalty and love: *Devoted fans began to gather in the street outside the singer's home.* **de·vot·ed** (di-**voh**-tid) ▷ *noun* **devotion** ▷ *adverb* **devotedly**

devour *verb* To eat something quickly and hungrily: *Geena devoured her lunch.* **de·vour** (di-**vour**) ▷ *verb* **devouring, devoured**

devout *adjective* Deeply religious, as in *devout churchgoers.* **de·vout** (di-**vout**) ▷ *noun* **devoutness** ▷ *adverb* **devoutly**

dew *noun* Moisture in the form of small drops that collects overnight on cool surfaces outside. **dew** (doo) ▷ *adjective* **dewy**

dewlap *noun* The loose skin that hangs under an animal's chin or neck. **dew·lap** (**doo**-lap)

dexterity *noun* Skill in using your hands or in thinking or speaking: *Knitting requires great dexterity.* **dex·ter·i·ty** (dek-**ster**-i-tee) ▷ *adjective* **dexterous** (**dek**-struhs)

diabetes *noun* A disease in which there is too much sugar in the blood. **di·a·be·tes** (dye-uh-**bee**-tis *or* dye-uh-**bee**-teez) ▷ *adjective* **diabetic** (dye-uh-**bet**-ik)

diabolical *or* **diabolic** *adjective*
1. Wicked and evil, as in *a diabolical plan.*
2. Of or having to do with the devil.
di·a·bol·i·cal (dye-uh-**bah**-li-kuhl) *or* **di·a·bol·ic** (dye-uh-**bah**-lik) ▷ *adverb* **diabolically**

diagnose *verb* To determine what disease a patient has or what the cause of a problem is: *The mechanic diagnosed that the car had a dead battery.* **di·ag·nose** (dye-uhg-**nohs**) ▷ *verb* **diagnosing, diagnosed** ▷ *noun* **diagnosis**

diagonal *adjective* Joining opposite corners of a square or rectangle: *Draw a diagonal line from the upper left to the bottom right.* **di·ag·o·nal** (dye-**ag**-uh-nuhl) ▷ *noun* **diagonal** ▷ *adverb* **diagonally**

diagram *noun* A drawing or plan that explains something with the use of arrows, colors, shapes, and other things: *Jeff built the model rocket by following the diagram.* **di·a·gram** (**dye**-uh-*gram*) ▷ *adjective* **diagrammatic**

dial
1. *noun* The face on a clock, gauge, or other measuring instrument.
2. *noun* A disk on certain devices, such as a radio, that is moved to operate the device.
3. *verb* To enter a phone number by pushing buttons or, on older phones, by turning a dial, as in *to dial a number.* ▷ *verb* **dialing, dialed**
4. dial tone *noun* The sound that you hear when you first pick up the receiver of a phone. This sound tells you that the phone is working.
di·al (**dye**-uhl)

dialect *noun* A way a language is spoken in a particular place or among a particular group of people, as in *a regional dialect.* **di·a·lect** (**dye**-uh-*lekt*)

dialog box *noun* A window on a computer screen that requires you to input text or make a choice.

dialogue *or* **dialog** *noun* Conversation, especially in a play, movie, television program, or book: *The movie's dialogue was awfully silly.* **di·a·logue** *or* **di·a·log** (**dye**-uh-*lawg*)

diamond

diameter *noun*
1. A straight line through the center of a circle, connecting opposite sides.
2. The length of this line.
di·am·e·ter (dye-**am**-i-tur)

diamond *noun*
1. A clear, precious stone that is a form of carbon, and is the hardest known mineral.
2. A shape with four equal sides, resting on one of its points.
3. diamonds *noun, plural* One of the four suits in a deck of cards.
4. The area of a baseball field enclosed by first, second, and third base, and home plate.
dia·mond (**dye**-muhnd *or* **dye**-uh-muhnd)

diaper *noun* A piece of soft, absorbent clothing worn as underwear by babies and young children. **di·a·per** (**dye**-pur *or* **dye**-uh-pur)

diaphragm *noun* The wall of muscle in your lower chest that draws air into and pushes air out of your lungs. **di·a·phragm** (**dye**-uh-*fram*)

diarrhea *noun* A condition in which normally solid waste from your body becomes liquid. **di·ar·rhe·a** (dye-uh-**ree**-uh)

diary *noun* A book in which people write down things that happen every day, or at regular intervals: *Greg wrote down the day's events in his diary.* **di·a·ry** (**dye**-ur-ee) ▷ *noun, plural* **diaries**

dice
1. *noun, plural* Cubes with a different number of dots on each face, used in games. The singular of *dice* is *die,* although some people use *dice* as the singular.
2. *verb* To cut something into small cubes, as in *to dice onions.* ▷ *verb* **dicing, diced** ▷ *adjective* **diced**
dice (dise)

dice

dictate *verb*
1. To say something so that someone can write down what you say: *The supervisor dictated a long letter to her assistant.* ▷ *noun* **dictation** (dik-**tay**-shuhn)
2. To order something with authority: *His boss dictated when he could go on vacation.*
dic·tate (**dik**-tate) ▷ *verb* **dictating, dictated**

dictator *noun* A ruler who has complete control of a country, often by force. **dic·ta·tor** (**dik**-tay-tur) ▷ *noun* **dictatorship**

a b c d e f g h i j k l m n o p q r s t u v w x y z

dictatorial *adjective*

1. Of or having to do with a dictator, as in *dictatorial powers.*

2. Extremely bossy: *My older sister's dictatorial manner was driving us all crazy.*
dic·ta·to·rial (*dik*-tuh-**tor**-ee-uhl)

dictionary *noun* A book such as this one that lists words in a language in alphabetical order and explains what they mean. **dic·tion·ar·y** (**dik**-shuh-*ner*-ee)
▷ *noun, plural* **dictionaries**

didn't *contraction* A short form of *did not: I didn't go to the park.* **did·n't** (**did**-uhnt)

die

1. *verb* To come to the end of life: *The sound of the train's whistle died in the distance.*

2. *verb* To come to an end because nothing supports continuing: *Their hopes have died.*

3. *verb* If you are **dying** to do something, you really want to do it.

4. *noun* The singular form of the word **dice.**
die (dye)

Die sounds like **dye.** ▷ *verb* **dying, died**

diesel *noun* A fuel used in diesel engines that is heavier than gasoline: *Around here, diesel is always more expensive than gas.* **die·sel** (**dee**-zuhl)

Word History

Diesel engines owe their name to their inventor, Dr. Rudolf Diesel. This engineer developed his heavy-duty engine in Germany from 1892 through 1897 and spent the rest of his life perfecting it.

diesel engine *noun* A type of engine that works using heat produced by compressing air. By contrast, a gasoline engine uses an electric spark to start the burning process.

diet

1. *noun* The food you usually or typically eat.
▷ *adjective* **dietary** (**dye**-i-*ter*-ee)

2. *noun* A planned way of eating, usually for losing weight, as in *a low-fat diet.*

3. *verb* To eat less according to a plan in order to lose weight: *I will need to diet if I'm going to fit into that suit.* ▷ *verb* **dieting, dieted** ▷ *noun* **dieter**
di·et (**dye**-it)

differ *verb*

1. To be unlike something or someone else: *I didn't expect the looks of the two brothers to differ so much.*

2. To disagree about something: *We're friends, but we differ on politics.*
dif·fer (**dif**-ur)
▷ *verb* **differing, differed**

difference *noun*

1. A way in which one thing is not like another: *Is there a difference between violet and purple?*

2. The amount left after you subtract one number from another: *The difference between 55 and 20 is 35.*
dif·fer·ence (**dif**-ur-uhns *or* **dif**-ruhns)

different *adjective* Not the same: *Jill thinks we should go, but I have a different opinion.* **dif·fer·ent** (**dif**-ur-uhnt *or* **dif**-ruhnt)

differently *adverb* Not in the same way: *The girls complained that the librarian treated them differently from the boys.* **dif·fer·ent·ly** (**dif**-ur-uhnt-lee *or* **dif**-ruhnt-lee)

difficult *adjective*

1. Not easy, as in *a difficult book.*

2. Not easy to get along with: *She says that all of her in-laws are difficult.*
dif·fi·cult (**dif**-i-*kuhlt*)

difficulty *noun* A problem that prevents or slows down progress: *There were many difficulties to resolve before we could get started.* **dif·fi·cul·ty** (**dif**-i-*kuhl*-tee) ▷ *noun, plural* **difficulties**

dig

1. *verb* To break up or move earth.

2. *verb* To look very hard for information: *Dig up all the facts.*

3. *noun* A push or a poke, as in *a dig in the ribs.*

4. *noun* A critical and thoughtless remark: *That was a nasty dig.*

5. *noun* An archaeological excavation.
dig (dig)
▷ *verb* **digging, dug** (duhg)

digest

1. (dye-**jest** *or* di-**jest**) *verb* To break down food in the organs of digestion so that it can be absorbed into the blood and used by the body: *Milk is easy for babies to digest.* ▷ *verb* **digesting, digested**

2. (**dye**-jest) *noun* A shortened form of a book or other written work, or a collection of such shortened forms: *I read a digest of that article.*
di·gest

digestion *noun* The process of breaking down food and separating from it the things that the body needs. **di·ges·tion** (dye-**jes**-chuhn *or* di-**jes**-chuhn)
▷ *adjective* **digestive**

digit *noun*

1. Any one of the numerals from 1 to 9, and sometimes 0: *There are seven digits in my phone number.*

2. A finger or toe: *Some birds have three digits on their claws.*
dig·it (**dij**-it)

digital *adjective*
1. Represented in or by numerals: *The system receives digital data from Mars and converts it into sound.*
2. Using the binary number system for recording text, images, or sound in a form that can be used on a computer: *With a digital camera, you can put your own pictures on the web.*
dig·it·al (**dij**-i-tuhl)

Word History

Digital is one of the many English words that go back to the name for a body part. *Digitus* was the Latin word for "finger," and we still sometimes refer to fingers or toes as digits. The Arabic numerals for 1 to 9 are called digits because people counted on their fingers. Anything that we call digital, such as a digital display, received the name because it uses digits, or numerals. Computers, digital cameras, and many other electronic devices operate using the digits 1 and 0. We may type on a computer keyboard with our fingers, but otherwise the word *digital* doesn't have much to do with fingers anymore.

digital rights *noun, plural* The rights of artists, musicians, writers, and others to protect the things that they create and put on the internet or on other electronic media.

digitize *verb* To convert or change data or graphic images to digital form, usable by a computer: *The company is digitizing its music collection for internet*

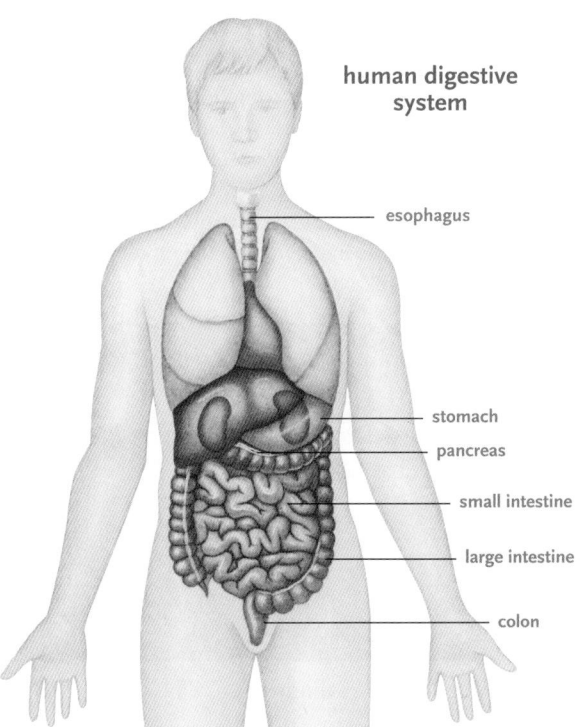

human digestive system

esophagus

stomach
pancreas
small intestine
large intestine
colon

distribution. **dig·i·tize** (**dij**-i-*tize*) ▷ *verb* **digitizing, digitized**

dignified *adjective* Calm and serious in a way that deserves respect: *The tennis player accepted defeat in a dignified manner.* **dig·ni·fied** (**dig**-nuh-*fide*)

dignity *noun* The quality or manner that makes a person worthy of honor or respect. **dig·ni·ty** (**dig**-ni-tee)

dike *noun* A high wall or dam that is built to hold back water and prevent flooding. **dike** (dike)

dilapidated *adjective* Shabby and falling apart, as in *a dilapidated old barn.* **di·lap·i·dat·ed** (duh-**lap**-i-*day*-tid) ▷ *noun* **dilapidation**

dilemma *noun* A situation in which any possible choice has some disadvantages: *The dilemma for the school board is whether to cut sports programs or lay off teachers.* **di·lem·ma** (duh-**lem**-uh)

diligence *noun* A constant and sincere effort to do what is necessary to accomplish something, usually with careful attention to details: *Marquita worked with diligence to prepare for her college entrance exams.* **dil·i·gence** (**dil**-i-juhns)

diligent *adjective* Working hard and carefully: *Maria was diligent about doing her homework before watching television.* **dil·i·gent** (**dil**-i-juhnt) ▷ *adverb* **diligently**

dilute *verb* To make something weaker by adding water or some other liquid to it: *Dilute the vinegar with two parts of water.* **di·lute** (duh-**loot** *or* dye-**loot**) ▷ *verb* **diluting, diluted** ▷ *noun* **dilution**

dim
1. *adjective* Somewhat dark, as in *a dim corner of the room.*
2. *adjective* Formless, or hard to see: *When I turned the corner, I could see the dim outline of a building in the fog.*
3. *verb* To make less bright: *The teacher dimmed the lights so he could show the movie.* ▷ *verb* **dimming, dimmed**
dim (dim)

dime *noun* A small coin of the United States and Canada that is worth ten cents: *The parking meter only takes dimes and quarters.* **dime** (dime)

dimension *noun* Any of the three measures of an object: length, width, or height: *The dimensions of the table are three feet by four feet by two feet.* **di·men·sion** (duh-**men**-shuhn) ▷ *adjective* **dimensional**

diminish *verb* To make or become smaller or weaker: *The long drought diminished our water supply.* **di·min·ish** (duh-**min**-ish) ▷ *verb* **diminishes, diminishing, diminished**

a b c **d** e f g h i j k l m n o p q r s t u v w x y z

diminutive

1. *adjective* Tiny, or very small: *Although she is a diminutive woman, her strong singing voice can fill an auditorium.*

2. *noun* A word that indicates a smaller version of something: *"Booklet" is a diminutive of "book," using the suffix "-let."*

di·min·u·tive (duh-**min**-yuh-tiv)

dimple *noun* A small hollow in a person's cheek or chin. **dim·ple** (**dim**-puhl)
▷ *adjective* **dimpled**

dimple

din *noun* A great deal of noise: *We could not hear each other over the din of the crowd.* **din** (din)

dine *verb* To have a meal, especially dinner, in a formal way: *We dined by candlelight.* **dine** (dine)
▷ *verb* **dining, dined**

diner *noun*

1. A person eating in a public place like a restaurant or hotel.

2. A restaurant where people sit at a long counter or in booths.

din·er (**dye**-nur)

dinghy *noun* A small rowboat. **din·ghy** (**ding**-ee)
▷ *noun, plural* **dinghies**

dingy *adjective* Dull and dirty, as in *a dingy room.*
din·gy (**din**-jee) ▷ *adjective* **dingier, dingiest**

dining room *noun* A room where meals are served at a table: *Our cousins met us for lunch in the hotel dining room.*

dinner *noun*

1. The main meal of the day.

2. A formal banquet: *The president gave a dinner for the queen of England.*

din·ner (**din**-ur)

dinosaur *noun* A kind of large reptile that lived in prehistoric times. **di·no·saur** (**dye**-nuh-*sor*)

diocese *noun* A church district under the authority of a bishop. **di·o·cese** (**dye**-uh-sis *or* **dye**-uh-*seez*)
▷ *noun, plural* **dioceses**

dip

1. *verb* To put something briefly into a liquid: *Dip your foot in the water to see how cold it is.*

2. *verb* To slope downward: *The road ahead dipped sharply.* ▷ *noun* **dip**

3. *noun* If you **take a dip**, you go for a short swim.

4. *noun* A thick sauce into which you dip foods such as raw vegetables and chips.

dip (dip)
▷ *verb* **dipping, dipped**

diploma *noun* A certificate from a school showing that you have finished a course of study. **di·plo·ma** (duh-**ploh**-muh)

diplomat *noun* Someone who officially represents his or her country's government in a foreign country as a job: *She is a diplomat in the American Embassy in France.* **dip·lo·mat** (**dip**-luh-*mat*)

diplomatic *adjective*

1. Of or having to do with being a diplomat: *She hopes to get a place in the diplomatic service after college.*

2. Tactful and good at dealing with people: *Fred's diplomatic explanation settled the argument.*

dip·lo·mat·ic (*dip*-luh-**mat**-ik)
▷ *noun* **diplomacy** (duh-**ploh**-muh-see)

dipper *noun* A cup with a long handle used to scoop liquid out of a large container: *The Big Dipper is a constellation whose stars form the shape of a dipper.* **dip·per** (**dip**-ur)

dire *adjective* Dreadful or urgent, as in *dire need.* **dire** (dire) ▷ *adjective* **direr, direst**

direct

1. *adjective* Moving or laid out in a straight line: *The arrow traveled in a direct path.*

2. *verb* To supervise people, especially in a play, movie, or television program: *Jennifer directed her classmates in the school play.*

3. *verb* To tell someone the way to reach a place: *I asked him to direct me to the nearest police station.*

4. *adjective* Communicating straight to the point; frank: *Eve has a direct way of speaking.*

di·rect (duh-**rekt**)
▷ *verb* **directing, directed**

direction *noun*

1. The line that someone or something is moving on or pointing toward: *We traveled in the direction of the lake.*

2. Guidance or supervision: *Luís learned to ski under the direction of a famous pro.*

3. **directions** *noun, plural* Instructions, especially for getting to a place, as in *driving directions.*

di·rec·tion (duh-**rek**-shuhn)

dinghy

Dinosaurs

parasaurolophus

stegosaurus

velociraptor

triceratops

brachiosaur

tyrannosaur

The word *dinosaur* comes from Greek words meaning "fearfully great lizard." These reptiles lived during the Mesozoic era (about 250–65 million years ago), divided into three periods: the Triassic, Jurassic, and Cretaceous. There were two main types of dinosaurs, the Saurischia, with lizardlike hips, and the Ornithischia, with birdlike hips.

Meat-eating saurischians walked upright on their hind legs. The most famous is the tyrannosaur, whose name means "tyrant lizard." Plant-eating saurischians walked on all four legs. One such dinosaur was the brachiosaur; another was the apatosaurus, formerly known as the brontosaurus.

The ornithischians ate plants. Some looked like birds but were often huge. Others, such as the stegosaurus and the triceratops, had bony plates or horns.

No one knows why the dinosaurs became extinct. Perhaps climate change destroyed their food and habitat. Maybe a giant meteorite crashed into the earth, creating dust that blocked the sunlight. Or an exploding star might have released deadly radiation. But these are all theories, and we may never know for certain.

directive *noun* An order from an authority: *Last week, the Environmental Protection Agency issued new directives about insecticides.* **di·rec·tive** (duh-**rek**-tiv)

directly *adverb* Immediately and straight through, without changing direction or stopping: *I think you should take this matter directly to the principal.* **di·rect·ly** (duh-**rekt**-lee)

director *noun*
1. Someone who directs a play, a movie, or a radio or television program, as in *a film director.*
2. One of a group of people responsible for the important decisions of a company: *The plan was approved by the company's directors.* **di·rec·tor** (duh-**rek**-tur)

directory *noun*
1. A book that gives addresses, phone numbers, or other information in alphabetical order, as in *a telephone directory.*
2. A named area of disk memory that can hold a number of computer files; a folder. **di·rec·to·ry** (duh-**rek**-tur-ee)
▷ *noun, plural* **directories**

dirigible *noun* An aircraft that is shaped like a fat cigar, filled with a gas that makes it rise, and powered by a motor. **di·ri·gi·ble** (**dir**-i-juh-buhl)

dirge *noun* A poem or song that is very sad, especially one that is part of a funeral. **dirge** (durj)

dirt *noun*
1. Earth or soil: *The car left tracks in the dirt.*
2. Mud, dust, and other unclean substances: *My brother paid me $5 to wash the dirt off his car.* **dirt** (durt)

dirty *adjective*
1. Not clean.
2. Unfair or dishonest, as in *dirty politics*.
3. Showing hostile feelings toward someone, as in *dirty looks*.
dir·ty (**dur**-tee)
▷ *adjective* **dirtier, dirtiest**

Synonyms

Dirty means not clean. It can refer to people or things: *We all got really dirty when we played soccer on the muddy field. Dirty clothes go in a pile near the washing machine.*

- -

■ **Filthy** is a much stronger word that means dirty to the extreme: *When we moved into the apartment, it was so filthy that we didn't know where to begin cleaning it.*

■ **Foul** describes something that not only is dirty but also smells that way: *The refrigerator was foul with the smell of spoiled milk.*

■ **Smudged** means smeared or a little bit dirty: *Her arm was smudged with charcoal after she cleaned the barbecue grill.*

■ **Soiled** means stained or dirty. It especially refers to clothing: *He changed the baby's soiled diaper.*

dis *verb* (slang) To show disrespect for someone: *I didn't mean to dis you when I said you couldn't dance.* **dis** (dis) ▷ *verb* **disses, dissing, dissed**

Prefix

The prefix **dis-** adds one of these meanings to a root word:

1. Not or opposite, as in *disagree* (to not agree) or *disinfect* (to do the opposite of infect).
2. Lack of, as in *disbelief* (lack of belief) or *disrespect* (lack of respect).

disability *noun*
1. Something that prevents someone from being able to move easily, or from being able to act or think in ways typically expected of a person: *She's in a special class for children with learning disabilities.*
2. The lack of an ability to do something.
dis·a·bil·i·ty (*dis*-uh-**bil**-i-tee)
disable *verb* To take away the ability to do something: *The thief disabled the alarm.* **dis·a·ble** (dis-**ay**-buhl)
▷ *verb* **disabling, disabled**
disabled *adjective* Not able to do the things that most people can do, usually because of an illness or injury or from a condition present from birth. **dis·a·bled** (dis-**ay**-buhld)

disadvantage *noun*
1. Something that makes success more difficult: *Being heavy is a disadvantage for a dancer.*
2. **at a disadvantage** Less likely to succeed: *The lawyer was at a huge disadvantage when her witness disappeared.*
dis·ad·van·tage (*dis*-uhd-**van**-tij)
disadvantaged *adjective* Poor and lacking many opportunities: *He overcame all the challenges of his disadvantaged background.* **dis·ad·van·taged** (*dis*-uhd-**van**-tijd)
disagree *verb*
1. To have a different opinion: *They disagreed about the cause of the problem, but they agreed on the solution.*
2. To cause discomfort after being eaten: *Peppers disagree with me.*
dis·a·gree (*dis*-uh-**gree**)
▷ *verb* **disagreeing, disagreed**
disagreement *noun*
1. A difference of opinion with someone, especially when it causes unpleasant feelings: *We had a disagreement over whether we should cut down the tree.*
2. The fact of not being in agreement: *The sentence has a plural subject but a singular verb, so there is a disagreement in number between the subject and the verb.*
dis·a·gree·ment (*dis*-uh-**gree**-muhnt)
disappear *verb* To go out of sight: *The car sped off and disappeared around the corner.* **dis·ap·pear** (*dis*-uh-**peer**) ▷ *verb* **disappearing, disappeared** ▷ *noun* **disappearance**
disappoint *verb* To let someone down by not doing what he or she expected: *George's grades will disappoint his parents.* **dis·ap·point** (*dis*-uh-**point**) ▷ *verb* **disappointing, disappointed** ▷ *adjective* **disappointed** ▷ *adjective* **disappointing**
disappointment *noun*
1. A person or thing that disappoints you: *Geoff said the new puzzle he got was a disappointment.*
2. Unhappiness or discouragement that you feel when you get a bad result or when something turns out worse than you expected: *To my disappointment, I did very poorly on the exam.*
dis·ap·point·ment (*dis*-uh-**point**-muhnt)
disapprove *verb* To think that a particular action or behavior is bad: *The poll found that 46 percent of voters disapproved of the proposed law.* **dis·ap·prove** (*dis*-uh-**proov**) ▷ *verb* **disapproving, disapproved** ▷ *noun* **disapproval**
disarm *verb*
1. To take weapons away from somebody: *The police officer disarmed the suspect.*

2. To give up weapons: *Neither militia will agree to disarm until the other one does.* ▷ *noun* **disarmament** (dis-**ahr**-muh-muhnt)

3. To win over: *Rebecca disarmed me with her directness.*

dis·arm (dis-**ahrm**)

▷ *verb* **disarming, disarmed** ▷ *adjective* **disarming**

disaster *noun*

1. An event that causes great damage, loss, or suffering, such as a flood or a plane crash.

2. A result or outcome in which everything goes wrong: *Thanksgiving dinner was a complete disaster—the turkey ended up on the kitchen floor.*

dis·as·ter (di-**zas**-tur)

▷ *adjective* **disastrous** ▷ *adverb* **disastrously**

Word History

The original meaning of **disaster** was "unlucky position of a star or planet." The word goes back to the Latin *dis-*, a prefix meaning "bad," and *astrum*, meaning "star." In earlier times, people thought that when planets and stars were in certain places in the sky, this caused bad luck.

disbelief *noun* Refusal to believe something: *I reacted with total disbelief when she told me about the accident.* **dis·be·lief** (*dis*-bi-**leef**)

disbelieve *verb* To think that something is not true. **dis·be·lieve** (*dis*-bi-**leev**) ▷ *verb* **disbelieving, disbelieved**

disc *noun* Another spelling of **disk**. **disc** (disk)

discard *verb* To throw something away: *Peter discarded all his old toys.* **dis·card** (dis-**kahrd**) ▷ *verb* **discarding, discarded**

disc jockey

discharge *verb*

1. To tell someone officially that he or she can go or leave: *The doctor has discharged her from the hospital.*

2. To release a substance into the open: *The dairy was forbidden from discharging wastewater into the stream.*

dis·charge (dis-**chahrj**)

▷ *verb* **discharging, discharged** ▷ *noun* **discharge** (**dis**-*chahrj*)

disciple *noun* Someone who follows the teachings of a leader, as in *a disciple of the Buddha.* **dis·ci·ple** (di-**sye**-puhl)

discipline *noun*

1. Control over your own or someone else's behavior: *My aunt thinks my brother is too wild and needs more discipline.* ▷ *verb* **discipline** ▷ *adjective* **disciplinary**

2. An area of study: *Science and history are both disciplines.*

dis·ci·pline (**dis**-uh-plin)

disc jockey *noun* Someone who plays music on the radio or at a party or club. Abbreviated as *DJ.*

disclose *verb* To reveal something: *The police did not disclose the contents of the note found in the car.* **dis·close** (dis-**klohz**) ▷ *verb* **disclosing, disclosed** ▷ *noun* **disclosure** (dis-**kloh**-zhur)

disco

1. *noun* A club where music is played for dancing. ▷ *noun, plural* **discos**

2. *adjective* A type of music played at clubs.

dis·co (**dis**-koh)

discomfort *noun* A feeling of pain or uneasiness that keeps you from relaxing: *The dentist said I might feel some discomfort when I got home.* **dis·com·fort** (dis-**kuhm**-furt)

disconnect *verb* To separate things that are joined or break a connection: *Carol disconnected the printer from the computer.* **dis·con·nect** (*dis*-kuh-**nekt**) ▷ *verb* **disconnecting, disconnected** ▷ *noun* **disconnection**

discontented *adjective* Not satisfied: *Elizabeth was discontented with her boring part-time job.* **dis·con·tent·ed** (*dis*-kuhn-**ten**-tid) ▷ *noun* **discontent** ▷ *adverb* **discontentedly**

discontinue *verb* To stop doing or providing something: *We discontinued the newspaper delivery while we were away.* **dis·con·tin·ue** (*dis*-kuhn-**tin**-yoo) ▷ *verb* **discontinuing, discontinued**

discord *noun* Disagreement or conflict, especially in a group: *The arrival of my new stepmother led to discord in the family.* **dis·cord** (**dis**-kord) ▷ *adjective* **discordant** (dis-**kord**-uhnt)

discount

1. *noun* A reduction in price, as in *a 15 percent discount.*

2. *noun* A **discount store** sells things at reduced prices.

3. *verb* To reduce the price of something: *They discounted the tools by 20 percent because some were damaged in shipping.* ▷ *verb* **discounting, discounted**
dis·count (**dis**-kount)

discourage
verb To try to persuade someone not to do something: *My parents discouraged me from hanging out with older kids.* **dis·cour·age** (dis-**kur**-ij) ▷ *verb* **discouraging, discouraged** ▷ *noun* **discouragement**

discouraged
adjective Feeling less confident or enthusiastic because of some setback: *Jon was discouraged after failing the driving test.* **dis·cour·aged** (dis-**kur**-ijd)

discourse
noun Communication in words between people or groups: *The group is campaigning to make child labor a topic of public discourse.* **dis·course** (**dis**-kors)

discover
verb

1. To find something: *We discovered the treasure as we were exploring the attic.*

2. To become aware of or learn something: *Kieran discovered that Larry had been cheating on the test.*

dis·cov·er (dis-**kuhv**-ur)
▷ *verb* **discovering, discovered** ▷ *noun* **discoverer**

discovery
noun

1. The act of discovering something: *The discovery of silver and gold plays a large part in Colorado's history.*

2. A thing that has been discovered: *Was the transistor the most important discovery of the 20th century?*

dis·cov·er·y (dis-**kuhv**-ur-ee)
▷ *noun, plural* **discoveries**

discreet
adjective Careful to avoid hurting or upsetting others, especially by revealing a secret: *I'm telling you this because I can count on you to be discreet.* **dis·creet** (dis-**kreet**) **Discreet** sounds like **discrete.** ▷ *adverb* **discreetly**

discrete
adjective Separate and distinct: *The mansion had been divided into several discrete apartments.* **discrete** (dis-**kreet**) **Discrete** sounds like **discreet.**

discretion
noun

1. Sensitivity and good judgment about matters that might upset, offend, injure, or embarrass someone: *When you're on the web, use discretion if you share information about yourself.*

2. Freedom to decide what to do: *The company allows*

discus thrower

its employees to arrange their work schedules at their own discretion.
dis·cre·tion (dis-**kresh**-uhn)

discriminate
verb

1. To treat someone unfairly while you treat someone else better. ▷ *adjective* **discriminatory**

2. To recognize differences between types of things: *How do you discriminate between a friendly stranger and a threatening one?*

dis·crim·i·nate (dis-**krim**-uh-*nate*)
▷ *verb* **discriminating, discriminated** ▷ *adjective* **discriminating**

discrimination
noun

1. Prejudice or unfair behavior to others based on differences in such things as age, race, or gender: *Discrimination because of race is illegal in the United States.*

2. The ability to recognize small differences, especially in the quality of things: *He is selective about his clothes and shops with discrimination.*

dis·crim·i·na·tion (dis-**krim**-i-**nay**-shuhn)

discus
noun A large, heavy disk that is thrown in a track-and-field event. **dis·cus** (**dis**-kuhs) ▷ *noun, plural* **discuses**

discuss
verb To talk about something in order to understand it better or to reach a decision about it, as in *to discuss a problem.* **dis·cuss** (dis-**kuhs**)
▷ *verb* **discusses, discussing, discussed**

discussion
noun A conversation with a purpose, in which different opinions are expressed: *After the slideshow, we had a discussion about cultural differences.* **dis·cus·sion** (dis-**kuhsh**-uhn)

disease
noun

1. A specific illness: *Tuberculosis is a lung disease.*

2. Sickness in general: *Disease is present throughout the camp.*

dis·ease (di-**zeez**)
▷ *adjective* **diseased**

disembark *verb* To leave a ship or an airplane: *We disembarked from the cruise ship in the late afternoon.* **dis·em·bark** (*dis*-em-**bahrk**) ▷ *verb* **disembarking, disembarked** ▷ *noun* **disembarkation** (dis-*em*-bahr-**kay**-shuhn)

disfigure *verb* To spoil the way something looks: *The accident disfigured him.* **dis·fig·ure** (dis-**fig**-yur) ▷ *verb* **disfiguring, disfigured** ▷ *noun* **disfigurement** ▷ *adjective* **disfigured**

disgrace
1. *noun* Something that causes shame or disapproval. ▷ *adjective* **disgraceful**
2. *verb* To cause shame or dishonor to yourself or your family. ▷ *verb* **disgracing, disgraced**
dis·grace (dis-**grase**)

disgruntled *adjective* Unhappy or dissatisfied, as in *disgruntled employees.* **dis·grun·tled** (dis-**gruhn**-tuhld)

disguise
1. *verb* To hide something, especially by changing the way it appears: *As a joke, Steve disguised his voice and pretended to be a newspaper reporter.* ▷ *verb* **disguising, disguised**
2. *noun* A way of dressing or behaving that hides your identity or your intentions: *The witness testified in disguise for her own safety.*
dis·guise (dis-**gize**)

disgust
1. *verb* To make someone feel very strong dislike and disapproval: *It disgusts me when I see people mistreat their pets.* ▷ *verb* **disgusting, disgusted**
2. *noun* A strong feeling of dislike or disapproval, sometimes combined with anger: *She reacted with disgust when she saw the slug.*
dis·gust (dis-**guhst**)

disgusting *adjective* Very unpleasant and offensive: *The room had a disgusting smell.* **dis·gust·ing** (dis-**guhs**-ting) ▷ *adverb* **disgustingly**

dish
1. *noun* A container, such as a plate or bowl, used for serving food.
2. *noun* Food made in a certain way, as in *a spicy beef dish.*
3. *verb* If you **dish up** food, you put or serve it in a dish. ▷ *verb* **dishes, dishing, dished**
dish (dish)
▷ *noun, plural* **dishes**

disheveled *adjective* Very messy: *Hector's clothes were always disheveled.* **di·shev·eled** (di-**shev**-uhld)

dishonest *adjective* Not honest or truthful: *It is*

dishonest to cheat. **dis·hon·est** (dis-**ah**-nist) ▷ *adverb* **dishonestly**

dishonesty *noun* The quality or trait of not being honest and truthful: *She was disciplined by the teacher for her dishonesty.* **dis·hon·est·y** (dis-**ah**-nis-tee)

dishonor *verb* To bring shame or disgrace upon yourself or others: *The editorial said that the governor had dishonored his office and those who elected him.* **dis·hon·or** (dis-**ah**-nur) ▷ *verb* **dishonoring, dishonored** ▷ *noun* **dishonor** ▷ *adjective* **dishonorable**

dishwasher *noun*
1. A machine for washing dishes.
2. Someone whose job is to wash dishes.
dish·wash·er (**dish**-*wah*-shur)

disillusion *verb* To take away someone's mistaken ideas or unrealistic hopes: *I hate to disillusion you, but an elf is a creature in fairy tales.* **dis·il·lu·sion** (*dis*-i-**loo**-zhuhn) ▷ *verb* **disillusioning, disillusioned** ▷ *noun* **disillusionment**

disinfectant *noun* A chemical used to kill germs, as on a cut or on a household surface. **dis·in·fect·ant** (*dis*-in-**fek**-tuhnt) ▷ *verb* **disinfect**

disintegrate *verb*
1. To break into small pieces: *The walnut shell disintegrated when I hit it with a hammer.*
2. To fall apart: *They could not solve their problems, so their friendship eventually disintegrated.*
dis·in·te·grate (dis-**in**-tuh-*grate*) ▷ *verb* **disintegrating, disintegrated** ▷ *noun* **disintegration**

disinterested *adjective* Having no personal feelings for either side of a contest or an argument: *He moderated the debate in a fair and disinterested manner.* **dis·in·ter·est·ed** (dis-**in**-tuh-*res*-tid *or* dis-**in**-tri-stid)

disk *or* **disc** *noun*
1. A flat, circular object: *A Frisbee is a disk.*
2. A circular object that can store information usable by a computer, as in *a hard disk.*
disk *or* **disc** (disk)

disk drive *noun* The part of a computer that reads information from, or saves information onto, a disk.

dislike *verb* To have a feeling of displeasure about someone or something: *I dislike the hot sun.* **dis·like** (dis-**like**) ▷ *verb* **disliking, disliked** ▷ *noun* **dislike**

dislocate *verb* To move something out of its usual place, as in *to dislocate a shoulder.* **dis·lo·cate** (dis-**loh**-kate *or* **dis**-loh-*kate*) ▷ *verb* **dislocating, dislocated** ▷ *noun* **dislocation** ▷ *adjective* **dislocated**

disk drive

a
b
c
d
e
f
g
h
i
j
k
l
m
n
o
p
q
r
s
t
u
v
w
x
y
z

dislodge *verb* To force something out of position: *She used a shovel to dislodge the boulder.* **dis·lodge** (dis-**lahj**) ▷ *verb* **dislodging, dislodged**

disloyal *adjective* Hurting someone whom you should support; not loyal: *The company accused the strikers of being disloyal.* **dis·loy·al** (dis-**loi**-uhl)

dismal *adjective*
1. Gloomy, sad, or dreary.
2. Extremely bad; failed: *It was the most dismal performance of the national anthem that I've ever heard.*
dis·mal (**diz**-muhl)

dismayed *adjective* Concerned or worried about something: *She said she was dismayed by her students' lack of interest in history.* **dis·mayed** (dis-**mayd**) ▷ *noun* **dismay**

dismiss *verb*
1. To allow someone to leave: *My mathematics teacher dismissed me from class because I said I wasn't feeling well.*
2. To fire someone from a job: *The airline dismissed 500 workers.*
3. To put something out of your mind: *I'd like to travel abroad, but it's so expensive that I've had to dismiss the idea.*
dis·miss (dis-**mis**)
▷ *verb* **dismisses, dismissing, dismissed**

dismissal *noun*
1. The act of letting someone leave, or officially making them leave: *We have early dismissal today because of the snow.*
2. A **dismissal** by a judge or court is a decision not to consider a case anymore.
dis·mis·sal (dis-**mis**-uhl)

dismount *verb* To get off of a horse, vehicle, or apparatus: *Arnold dismounted from the parallel bars and the crowd applauded wildly.* **dis·mount** (dis-**mount**) ▷ *verb* **dismounting, dismounted** ▷ *noun* **dismount**

disobedience *noun* Failure to obey: *Denise's reckless disobedience shocked and saddened her father.* **dis·o·be·di·ence** (*dis*-uh-**bee**-dee-uhns)

disobedient *adjective* Failing or refusing to obey. **dis·o·be·di·ent** (*dis*-uh-**bee**-dee-uhnt) ▷ *adverb* **disobediently**

disobey *verb* To go against the rules or someone's wishes: *The soldier was punished for disobeying an order.* **dis·o·bey** (*dis*-uh-**bay**)

▷ *verb* **disobeying, disobeyed**

disorder *noun*
1. Lack of order: *Alex's room was in complete disorder, with books and clothes all over the floor.*
2. A physical or mental illness: *Our cat has a muscle disorder.*
dis·or·der (dis-**or**-dur)

disorderly *adjective*
1. Messy and disorganized, as in *a disorderly room.*
2. Uncontrolled and possibly violent, as in *a disorderly crowd.*
dis·or·der·ly (dis-**or**-dur-lee)
▷ *noun* **disorderliness**

disorganized *adjective* Not properly planned, controlled, or in order, as in *a disorganized office.* **dis·or·gan·i·zed** (dis-**or**-guh-*nized*) ▷ *noun* **disorganization**

disorient *verb*
1. To cause someone to become lost: *The city's winding little streets usually disorient tourists.*
2. To confuse someone: *The strange new surroundings disoriented the child.*
dis·o·ri·ent (dis-**or**-ee-uhnt)
▷ *verb* **disorienting, disoriented** ▷ *adjective* **disoriented**

disown *verb*
1. To refuse to accept someone as your relative any longer: *His parents disowned him after he stole from them.*
2. If you **disown** a statement or a responsibility, you are saying that you have nothing to do with it.
dis·own (dis-**ohn**)
▷ *verb* **disowning, disowned**

dispatch
1. *noun* A message or a report, as in *a news dispatch.* ▷ *noun, plural* **dispatches**
2. *verb* To send something or somebody off: *We dispatched a messenger to their office.* ▷ *verb* **dispatches, dispatching, dispatched**
dis·patch (dis-**pach**)

dispel *verb* To put an end to something, as in *to dispel a rumor.* **dis·pel** (dis-**pel**) ▷ *verb* **dispelling, dispelled**

dispense *verb* To give something out: *Grandpa is always ready to dispense advice.* **dis·pense** (dis-**pens**) ▷ *verb* **dispensing, dispensed**

dispenser *noun* A device or machine that gives out one thing or a small amount at a time, as in *a soap dispenser.* **dis·pens·er** (dis-**pen**-sur)

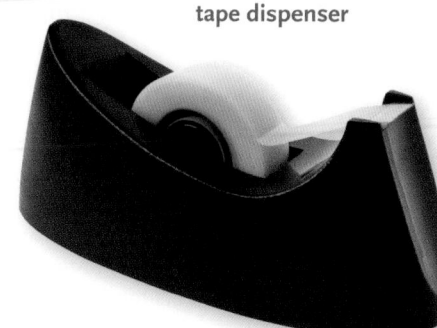
tape dispenser

window display

disperse *verb* To scatter or move in different directions: *The police dispersed the crowd.* **dis·perse** (dis-**purs**) ▷ *verb* **dispersing, dispersed** ▷ *noun* **dispersal**

displace *verb*
1. To move someone or something from its usual place: *The hurricane displaced many people.*
2. To take the place of something or somebody else: *They want to use wind power to displace the use of coal.*
dis·place (dis-**plase**)
▷ *verb* **displacing, displaced**
▷ *noun* **displacement**

display
1. *verb* To show something: *You displayed real courage when you spoke up against his mistreatment of his dog.* ▷ *verb* **displaying, displayed**
2. *noun* A public show or exhibition: *The library had a display of rare manuscripts.*
3. *noun* A screen or panel on electronic equipment that shows information: *My new TV has a flat-panel display.*
dis·play (dis-**play**)

displease *verb* If you **displease** someone, you annoy the person or cause him or her to be dissatisfied: *Loud music displeases my parents.*
dis·please (dis-**pleez**) ▷ *verb* **displeasing, displeased** ▷ *noun* **displeasure** (dis-**plezh**-ur)
▷ *adjective* **displeased**

disposable *adjective* Made to be thrown away after use, as in *disposable diapers.* **dis·pos·a·ble** (dis-**poh**-zuh-buhl)

disposal *noun*
1. The act of throwing away or recycling something: *Campers are responsible for the proper disposal of their trash.*
2. A **garbage disposal** is a small machine under a sink that grinds up leftover food and sends it into the sewer system.
dis·pos·al (dis-**poh**-zuhl)

dispose *verb*
1. If you **dispose of** something, you get rid of it or throw it away: *Dispose of any waste in the trash cans before leaving the campground.*
2. If you are **disposed to** do something, or **disposed toward** something, you are willing to do it: *Anthony and Sylvia are favorably disposed to being part of our new project.*
dis·pose (dis-**poze**)
▷ *verb* **disposing, disposed**

disposition *noun*
1. A person's general attitude or mood: *Julie has a pleasant disposition.*
2. The act of disposing of something, as in *the disposition of toxic waste.*
dis·po·si·tion (dis-puh-**zish**-uhn)

disprove *verb* To show that something cannot be true: *Bill used the results of his experiment to disprove Tom's theory.* **dis·prove** (dis-**proov**) ▷ *verb* **disproving, disproved**

dispute
1. *noun* A disagreement about an issue: *The dispute began over who owned the property.*
2. *verb* To say that you think something said or written is not true or accurate. ▷ *verb* **disputing, disputed**
dis·pute (dis-**pyoot**)

disqualify *verb* To say that someone cannot take part in an activity, often because the person has broken a rule: *Ed was disqualified from the three-legged race because it was for a younger age group.* **dis·qual·i·fy** (dis-**kwah**-luh-*fye*)
▷ *verb* **disqualifies, disqualifying, disqualified**
▷ *noun* **disqualification**

disregard *verb* To ignore someone or something: *Please disregard the announcement about the change in schedule.* **dis·re·gard** (*dis*-ri-**gahrd**) ▷ *verb* **disregarding, disregarded** ▷ *noun* **disregard**

disreputable *adjective* Having or deserving a bad reputation. **dis·rep·u·ta·ble** (dis-**rep**-yuh-tuh-buhl)
▷ *noun* **disrepute** (*dis*-ri-**pyoot**)

disrespect *noun* A lack of respect, or rudeness: *Talking while someone else is talking shows disrespect.* **dis·res·pect** (*dis*-ri-**spekt**) ▷ *adjective* **disrespectful** ▷ *adverb* **disrespectfully**

disrupt *verb* To disturb or interrupt something that is happening: *He kept disrupting the movie by talking loudly to his friends.* **dis·rupt** (dis-**ruhpt**) ▷ *verb* **disrupting, disrupted** ▷ *noun* **disruption**

disruptive *adjective*
1. Disturbing the usual order or progress of something in an undesirable way: *She was reprimanded for her disruptive behavior.*
2. If a business or technology is **disruptive**, it introduces a new way of doing something that threatens the old way of doing it.
dis·rup·tive (dis-**ruhp**-tiv)

dissatisfied *adjective* Unhappy or discontented. **dis·sat·is·fied** (dis-**sat**-is-*fide*) ▷ *noun* **dissatisfaction** (dis-*sat*-is-**fak**-shuhn) ▷ *verb* **dissatisfy**

dissect *verb*
1. To cut apart an animal or a human body so as to examine it.
2. To examine and analyze something very carefully, as in *to dissect an argument.*
dis·sect (di-**sekt**)
▷ *verb* **dissecting, dissected** ▷ *noun* **dissection**

dissent
1. *verb* To disagree with an idea or opinion: *A few parents dissented with the proposed change to the school's curriculum.* ▷ *verb* **dissenting, dissented**
2. *noun* Disagreement with an opinion or idea: *There was dissent among the union's members over the new contract.* ▷ *noun* **dissension** (di-**sen**-shuhn)
dis·sent (di-**sent**)

dissolve *verb*
1. To seem to disappear when mixed with liquid: *Ink dissolves in water.*
2. To end something officially: *The company's owners have dissolved their business partnership.*
dis·solve (di-**zahlv**)
▷ *verb* **dissolving, dissolved** ▷ *noun* **dissolution** (dis-uh-**loo**-shuhn)

distance *noun*
1. The space between two places, as in *a short distance from home.*
2. A distant place or area: *In the distance we could see headlights approaching.*
3. If you **keep your distance** from somebody, you keep away from the person.
dis·tance (**dis**-tuhns)

distant *adjective*
1. Not close in space or time, as in *a distant land* or *the distant future.*

disruptive

2. Not closely related, as in *a distant cousin.*
3. Not warm or friendly: *She sometimes has a distant attitude toward her friends.*
dis·tant (**dis**-tuhnt)

distaste *noun* A feeling of not liking: *I have a distaste for violent movies.* **dis·taste** (dis-**tayst**)

distasteful *adjective* Unpleasant or not to a person's taste; offensive: *I find that remark distasteful.* **dis·taste·ful** (dis-**tayst**-fuhl)

distill *verb* To purify a liquid by boiling it, collecting the steam, and then letting it cool until it takes a liquid form again, as in *to distill water.* **dis·till** (di-**stil**) ▷ *verb* **distilling, distilled** ▷ *noun* **distillation** (dis-tuh-**lay**-shuhn) ▷ *noun* **distiller** ▷ *adjective* **distilled**

distinct *adjective*
1. Very clear and easy to notice: *Charlie has a distinct way of walking.* ▷ *adverb* **distinctly**
2. Different in an obvious way: *A zebra's stripes make it distinct from a horse.*
dis·tinct (di-**stingkt**)

distinction *noun*
1. A difference: *There's a very faint distinction between the two flavors.*
2. Excellence, as in *an actor of distinction.*
3. Something that makes an object or a person unusual or different: *Gloria has the distinction of being the best player on the soccer team.*
dis·tinc·tion (di-**stingk**-shuhn)

distinctive *adjective* Making a person or thing different from all others: *Carrie has a very distinctive taste in clothes.* **dis·tinc·tive** (di-**stingk**-tiv)

distinguish *verb*
1. To recognize the difference between things: *Sometimes it's hard to distinguish one type of*

mushroom from another.

2. To see or hear clearly: *We were able to distinguish their faces in the crowd.*
dis·tin·guish (di-**sting**-gwish)
▷ *verb* **distinguishes, distinguishing, distinguished**
▷ *adjective* **distinguishable**

distinguished *adjective*
Well-known or honored for important achievements: *The distinguished guests include the governor and two of the state's congressmen.* **dis·tin·guished** (di-**sting**-gwisht)

distort *verb*
1. To twist out of the normal shape.
2. To lie about something in order to mislead someone: *The magazine article distorted the real story about the politician.*
dis·tort (di-**stort**)
▷ *verb* **distorting, distorted** ▷ *noun* **distortion** (di-**stor**-shuhn) ▷ *adjective* **distorted**

distract *verb* To weaken your concentration on what you are doing: *Television distracts me when I'm studying.* **dis·tract** (di-**strakt**) ▷ *verb* **distracting, distracted** ▷ *noun* **distraction**

distress *noun*
1. A feeling of emotional pain or sadness: *The news of your accident caused me great distress.*
▷ *verb* **distress** ▷ *adjective* **distressed** ▷ *adjective* **distressing**
2. in distress In need of help: *The ship was in distress.*
dis·tress (di-**stres**)

distribute *verb* To give things out to a number of people, or at different places: *The letter carrier distributes the mail for our building at around noon.* **dis·trib·ute** (di-**strib**-yoot) ▷ *verb* **distributing, distributed**

distorted

distribution *noun*
1. The activity of delivering things to people or places: *What company handles the distribution of this product?*
2. The way that something is found or arranged within an area: *They are mapping the distribution of low-income housing in the state.*
dis·tri·bu·tion (*dis*-truh-**byoo**-shuhn)

distributor *noun*
1. A company that buys products from one company and arranges for other

companies to sell them.
2. The part of a car engine that sends electricity from the ignition system to the spark plugs.
dis·trib·u·tor (di-**strib**-yuh-tur)

district *noun*
1. An area or a region, as in *an urban district.*
2. district attorney *noun* An elected official who represents a state government in court and who has the power to bring government cases to court. Abbreviated as *DA.*
dis·trict (**dis**-trikt)

distrust *verb* To think that someone or something is false and cannot be relied on: *If you distrust the media, why are you so sure this story is true?*
dis·trust (dis-**truhst**) ▷ *verb* **distrusting, distrusted** ▷ *noun* **distrust** ▷ *adjective* **distrustful** ▷ *adverb* **distrustfully**

disturb *verb*
1. To bother someone who is busy or doing something quiet: *Don't disturb the baby when she's sleeping.*
2. To worry or upset someone.
3. To change the way that something is arranged: *Do not disturb anything in the room or you'll get in big trouble.*
dis·turb (di-**sturb**)
▷ *verb* **disturbing, disturbed** ▷ *adjective* **disturbing**

disturbance *noun* An action or event that upsets a calm and orderly situation: *The police responded to a disturbance in the 800 block of Elm Avenue.*
dis·turb·ance (di-**sturb**-buhns)

ditch
1. *noun* A long, narrow trench that drains water away or that carries water to fields. ▷ *noun, plural* **ditches**
2. *verb* To land an aircraft on water in an emergency.
3. *verb (slang)* To suddenly leave or stop seeing someone, as in *to ditch a job* or *to ditch a boyfriend.*
ditch (dich)
▷ *verb* **ditches, ditching, ditched**

ditto
1. *adverb* As indicated before; similarly: *The house was locked up tight. Ditto the garage.*
2. *noun* **Ditto** marks (") are used in lists to show that what is written above is repeated on the line with the marks.
▷ *noun, plural* **dittos**
dit·to (**dit**-oh)

diva *noun*

1. A woman who is a famous concert singer or opera star: *The opera singer Maria Callas was one of the most celebrated divas of the 20th century.*

2. *(informal)* A woman who acts like a star and is demanding and spoiled; a prima donna: *She is a complete diva—when she doesn't get what she wants, she throws a fit.*

di·va (**dee**-vuh)

Word History

The word **diva** can be traced to the Latin word *diva*, meaning "goddess." Speakers of Italian used the word *diva* to mean not only a goddess but any fine lady. In English, writers who wrote about theater and opera in the late 19th century borrowed the word to refer to the main female performer. By the late 20th century, diva took on the additional meanings of a spoiled or temperamental person, or of a famous female performer.

dive *verb*

1. To go headfirst into water with your arms out in front of you.

2. To drop down suddenly: *The pelican dived into the sea.*

dive (dive)

▷ *verb* **diving, dived** *or* **dove** (dohv) ▷ *noun* **dive**

diver *noun*

1. Someone who dives underwater, especially in a competition.

2. Someone who uses special equipment to swim or explore underwater.

div·er (**dye**-vur)

diverse *adjective* Having many different types or kinds; varied: *Helen enjoys reading a diverse assortment of books.* **di·verse** (di-**vurs** *or* dye-**vurs**) ▷ *verb* **diversify** (di-**vur**-si-fye)

diversion *noun* Something that is amusing and takes your mind away from work: *Dad's favorite diversion is riding his bicycle.* **di·ver·sion** (di-**vur**-zhuhn)

diversity *noun* A variety: *The people in the room represented a diversity of backgrounds and experiences.* **di·ver·si·ty** (di-**vur**-si-tee)

divert *verb*

1. To change the course or direction that something is moving in: *The*

diver

engineers will attempt to divert the river to prevent flooding.

2. To take someone's attention away from something.

di·vert (di-**vurt** *or* dye-**vurt**)

▷ *verb* **diverting, diverted** ▷ *adjective* **diverting**

divide *verb*

1. To separate into parts: *George divided the blocks into two piles.*

2. If you **divide** one number by another, you figure out how many times the second number will go into the first: *When you divide 120 by 10, you get 12.*

3. To share something by giving everyone a portion: *Elaine divided the cookies among the four of us.*

4. To split into opposing groups: *The judges were divided in their choice for the winner.*

di·vide (di-**vide**)

▷ *verb* **dividing, divided**

dividend *noun*

1. In a division problem, the number that is divided: *In the problem 12 ÷ 3, the dividend is 12.*

2. A share of the money earned by an investment or a business.

div·i·dend (**div**-i-*dend*)

divider *noun* A thing that makes a boundary or separation between two things: *Sophia has a three-ring binder with dividers in different colors for each subject she is taking this year.* **di·vid·er** (di-**vye**-dur)

divine

1. *adjective* Having to do with God or from God, as in *divine worship* or *divine love.*

2. *verb* To discover something by intuition or guessing, as in *to divine the truth.* ▷ *verb* **divining, divined**

3. *adjective* Wonderful: *Our dinner was divine.*

di·vine (di-**vine**)

diving board *noun* A plank that sticks out over a swimming pool, allowing people to jump or dive into the water.

divisible *adjective* Able to be divided: *Nine is evenly divisible only by itself, 3, and 1.* **di·vis·i·ble** (di-**viz**-uh-buhl)

division *noun*

1. The operation of dividing one number by another, as in *long division.*

2. One of the parts into which something has been divided: *The divisions of the academic year are called quarters or semesters, depending on the school.*

3. A part of an organization that does some things independently: *She* *works in the research division of a chemical company.*

4. Part of an army made up of several regiments.

5. The action of dividing: *Cell division is the main way that living things grow.*
di·vi·sion (di-**vizh**-uhn)

divisor *noun* In a division problem, the number that you divide by: *In the problem 12 ÷ 3, the divisor is 3.* **di·vi·sor** (di-**vye**-zur)

divorce

1. *noun* The official ending of a marriage by a court. ▷ *verb* **divorce**

2. *verb* To separate completely: *The mayor has divorced herself from the controversy.* ▷ *verb* **divorcing, divorced** ▷ *adjective* **divorced**
di·vorce (di-**vors**)

divulge *verb* To reveal information that was secret or unknown: *The author divulged the identity of the murderer in the last chapter.* **di·vulge** (di-**vuhlj**) ▷ *verb* **divulging, divulged**

dizzy *adjective*

1. If you are **dizzy**, you feel very unsteady on your feet, and your head seems to be turning: *The roller coaster made us all dizzy.*

2. Bewildered and confused: *Having so many choices made me feel dizzy.*
diz·zy (**diz**-ee)
▷ *adjective* **dizzier, dizziest** ▷ *adjective* **dizzying**
▷ *noun* **dizziness**

DJ *noun* Short for **disc jockey**.

DNA *noun* The molecule that carries our genes, found inside the nucleus of cells. DNA is short for *deoxyribonucleic acid: The police identified the suspect through a test of his DNA.*

DNS *noun* The system that translates the addresses of websites into numbers that computers use. This system keeps track of all the addresses on the internet. DNS is short for *domain name server.*

do *verb*

1. To perform an action: *Tommy is doing his chores.*

2. To complete or deal with: *Please do your homework!*

3. To be acceptable: *It's a small house, but it will do.*

4. To get along: *I'm doing well in school.*

5. To behave or act in a certain way: *Do as you're told.*

6. To create or perform: *You did a great presentation.*

7. To bring about a result: *Yelling will do nothing to change my mind.*
do (doo)
▷ *verb* **does** (duhz), **doing, did** (did), **done** (duhn)

DNA strand

Doberman pinscher *noun* A breed of dog with a long head; a large, muscular body; and a short, black or brown coat. **Do·ber·man pin·scher** (**doh**-bur-muhn **pin**-chur)

docile *adjective* Calm and easy to manage or train, as in *a docile pet.*
doc·ile (**dah**-suhl)

dock

1. *noun* A platform that sticks out over the water so boats and ships can stop beside it.

2. *noun* A part of a building with large doors where trucks load and unload.

3. *verb* To stop at a dock: *The ship docked in New Jersey before going to Baltimore.* ▷ *verb* **docked, docking**
dock (dahk)

doctor *noun*

1. Someone who is trained and licensed to treat illnesses. Abbreviated as *Dr.: Fortunately, there was a doctor nearby when Dad became ill.*

2. Someone who has the highest academic degree given by a college or university.
doc·tor (**dahk**-tur)

doctrine *noun* A belief or teaching of a religion, political party, or other group, as in *the doctrine of the Republican Party.* **doc·trine** (**dahk**-trin)

document *noun*

1. A piece of paper containing official information: *You can use your passport as a document to identify yourself.*

2. A computer file containing information that can be viewed on the screen or printed, as in *a word processing document.*
doc·u·ment (**dahk**-yuh-muhnt)
▷ *verb* **document** (**dahk**-yuh-*ment*)

documentary *noun* A movie or television program about real people and events, as in *a science documentary.* **doc·u·men·ta·ry** (*dahk*-yuh-**men**-tur-ee)
▷ *noun, plural* **documentaries**

documentation *noun*

1. The documents you use to present official and identifying information about yourself, such as a passport, birth certificate, or driver's license.

2. The act of providing such documents.

3. The printed information that explains how something works, such as a computer, a computer program, or an appliance: *The documentation was very clear, and I had no problem setting up the system.*
doc·u·men·ta·tion (*dahk*-yuh-men-**tay**-shuhn)

dodecahedron *noun* A solid shape with 12 faces. **do·dec·a·he·dron** (doh-*dek*-uh-**hee**-druhn)

a
b
c
d
e
f
g
h
i
j
k
l
m
n
o
p
q
r
s
t
u
v
w
x
y
z

dodge *verb*
1. To avoid something or somebody by moving quickly, as in *to dodge a thrown ball.*
2. To avoid something in a clever or dishonest way: *Trina dodged his question by pretending not to hear it.* **dodge** (dahj)
▷ *verb* **dodging, dodged** ▷ *noun* **dodge**

dodgeball *noun* A team game in which players on the defending team are out if they get hit by a ball thrown by the other team. **dodge·ball** (**dahj**-*bawl*)

dodo *noun*
1. An extinct bird that had a large body and wings so small it was unable to fly. Dodos lived on the island of Mauritius in the Indian Ocean.
2. *(slang)* A stupid person.
do·do (**doh**-doh)
▷ *noun, plural* **dodos** or **dodoes**

doe *noun* A female deer or the female of various other mammals where the male is called a buck, for example, kangaroos and rabbits. **doe** (doh) **Doe** sounds like **dough**.

does *verb* The third-person singular present tense form of **do**. **does** (duhz)

doesn't *contraction* A short form of *does not*: *My mother doesn't like me to chew gum.* **does·n't** (**duhz**-uhnt)

dog
1. *noun* A domestic mammal with four legs that is often kept as a pet or as a work animal. Dogs are related to wolves, coyotes, and foxes.
2. *verb* To follow someone closely: *The child dogged his babysitter all morning.* ▷ *verb* **dogging, dogged**
dog (dawg *or* dahg)

Word History

Dog is a word original to English, rather than coming from another language. At first, the word *hund,* later spelled "hound," was used to refer to all breeds of dogs, and *dogge* referred only to one large, powerful breed. Over time, however, *dog* came to mean all breeds, and *hound* started to apply only to hunting dogs.

dogma *noun* Ideas that a religion or group expects you to believe without questioning: *She did not accept her church's dogma that prophets are free of error.* **dog·ma** (**dawg**-muh)

dogmatic *adjective* If you are **dogmatic**, you insist very strongly that you are right about things. **dog·mat·ic** (dawg-**mat**-ik)

dog paddle *noun* A swimming stroke in which your arms and legs move the same way that a dog's limbs move when it is swimming. ▷ *verb* **dog-paddle**

dogwood *noun* A tree or shrub that has small, green flowers surrounded by pink or white leaves that look like petals. **dog·wood** (**dawg**-*wud*)

doily *noun* A small piece of lace or cut paper placed under a plate or other item as a decoration or on furniture to protect it. **doi·ly** (**doi**-lee) ▷ *noun, plural* **doilies**

do-it-yourself *adjective* Of or having to do with home improvements, repairs, or projects that you do yourself. Abbreviated as *DIY.*

dole *verb* If you **dole out** something, such as food or money, you give it out in small quantities: *Mom doled out cookies after lunch.* **dole** (dohl) ▷ *verb* **doling, doled**

doll *noun* A small model of a human used as a child's toy. **doll** (dahl)

dollar *noun* The main unit of money in the United States, Canada, Australia, and New Zealand. **dol·lar** (**dah**-lur)

dollhouse *noun* A small toy house. **doll·house** (**dahl**-*hous*)

dolphin *noun* An intelligent water mammal with a long snout. Dolphins are related to whales but are smaller. **dol·phin** (**dahl**-fin)

Dolphins

Most dolphin species live in the ocean, but some are freshwater animals. They are playful and intelligent creatures. Unlike most wild animals, they voluntarily associate with humans. They are easily trained, and often perform at aquariums. Dolphins, too, like bats, make sounds and use the echoes to navigate and to find food.

Dolphins are related to whales and porpoises. They are much smaller than whales. Porpoises are usually smaller than dolphins and have shorter snouts and differently shaped teeth.

domain *noun*
1. A region or place controlled by a government or person: *Dad's workshop is his private domain.*
2. A part of the internet where all the sites have the same letters after the period in their address. For example, the domain for all US government sites is ".gov."
3. **domain name** A general address on the World Wide Web, such as scholastic.com or whitehouse.gov.
do·main (doh-**mayn**)

dome *noun* A roof shaped like half of a sphere. **dome** (dohm)

domestic *adjective*
1. Of or having to do with the home, as in *domestic work.*
2. Of, having to do with, or within your own country, as in *domestic commerce.*
3. **Domestic animals** are animals that have been tamed. People use them as a source of food or as work animals, or keep them as pets.
do·mes·tic (duh-**mes**-tik)

domesticate *verb* To tame an animal so it can live with or be used by people, as in *to domesticate a horse.* **do·mes·ti·cate** (duh-**mes**-ti-*kate*) ▷ *verb* **domesticating, domesticated** ▷ *adjective* **domesticated**

dominant *adjective* Most influential or powerful: *Our country plays a dominant role in the world's economy.* **dom·i·nant** (**dah**-muh-nuhnt)

dominate *verb*
1. To control, or to rule: *The king dominated a huge territory.* ▷ *noun* **domination**
2. To be the main feature of something: *The scandal has dominated the news this week.* **dom·i·nate** (**dah**-muh-*nate*) ▷ *verb* **dominating, dominated**

dominion *noun*
1. A large area of land controlled by a single ruler or government: *Canada was once a British dominion.*
2. Power to rule over something: *The captain has dominion over his ship.* **do·min·ion** (duh-**min**-yuhn)

domino *noun*
1. A small rectangular tile that is divided into two halves that are blank or contain dots.
2. **dominoes** *noun, plural* A game played with a number of these tiles.
dom·i·no (**dah**-muh-*noh*)

dominoes

don *verb* If you **don** clothing, you put it on: *She donned a jacket because the weather had turned chilly.* **don** (dahn) ▷ *verb* **donning, donned**

donate *verb* To give something to a charity or cause: *I'm donating money to the homeless shelter.* **do·nate** (**doh**-nate) ▷ *verb* **donating, donated**

donation *noun* A gift, usually of money, to an organization, such as a charity: *The animal shelter was happy to receive my donation of $50.* **do·na·tion** (doh-**nay**-shuhn)

done *verb* The past participle of **do**. **done** (duhn)

donkey *noun* A mammal with long ears that is sometimes used as a work animal. Donkeys are related to horses but are smaller. **don·key** (**dahng**-kee)

donor *noun*
1. Someone who gives something, usually to an organization or a charity: *The food at the shelter comes from various donors.*
2. Someone who agrees to give his or her body, or a part of it, to medical science to help sick people: *I volunteered to be a blood donor.* **do·nor** (**doh**-nur)

don't *contraction* A short form of *do not*: *I don't know what my parents are getting me for my birthday.* **don't** (dohnt)

donut See **doughnut.**

doodle *verb* To draw absent-mindedly while you are listening or thinking. **doo·dle** (doo-duhl) ▷ *verb* **doodling, doodled** ▷ *noun* **doodle**

doom *noun* A terrible situation that cannot be escaped, especially one that involves death or destruction: *The farmers in our state are facing doom if the drought continues.* **doom** (doom) ▷ *verb* **doom** ▷ *adjective* **doomed**

door *noun*
1. A tall, flat panel that opens and closes at the entrance or exit of a building or room.
2. A house or a building: *Muriel lives two doors away from me.*
door (dor)

doorbell *noun* A bell or buzzer outside a door that is rung by someone who wants the door to be opened. **door·bell** (**dor**-*bel*)

doorman

doorknob *noun* A handle that you turn to open a door. **door·knob** (**dor**-*nahb*)

doorman *noun* A man who works at the door of a large building to provide security and to help visitors: *I'll leave my keys with the doorman, and he'll give them to you.* **door·man** (**dor**-*man*) ▷ *noun, plural* **doormen**

doorstep *noun* A step or steps on the outside doorway of a building. **door·step** (**dor**-*step*)

doorway *noun* The space between two rooms, or between the inside and outside of a building, that can be closed by a door. **door·way** (**dor**-*way*)

dope
1. *noun* (*informal*) A stupid person.
2. *noun* (*informal*) An illegal or addictive drug.
3. *adjective* (*informal*) Very good: *We looked at some really dope skateboards.*
dope (dohp)

dormant *adjective*
1. A **dormant** animal is one that is hibernating.
2. A **dormant** volcano is not doing anything now but could erupt again.
3. A **dormant** plant or seed is alive but not growing.
dor·mant (**dor**-muhnt)

dormitory *noun* A building with many separate sleeping rooms, as in *a college dormitory.* **dor·mi·to·ry** (**dor**-mi-*tor*-ee) ▷ *noun, plural* **dormitories**

dose *noun*
1. An amount of a medicine or chemical that is used or taken at one time: *The bottle says to give the dog one dose three times a day.*
2. A small amount, especially of something unpleasant, as in *a dose of punishment.*
dose (dohs)

dot
1. *noun* A small, round point.
2. *verb* To write a dot over a letter that requires one.
3. *verb* To be here and there around an area: *Trees dotted the hills.*
dot (daht) ▷ *verb* **dotting, dotted**

dot-com *noun* A company that does business mainly online, especially one whose website has ".com" at the end of the address: *Amazon and Google are dot-coms.* **dot-com** (**daht**-*kahm*)

dote *verb* To pay a lot of attention to, or to show a lot of fondness for, someone: *She doted on her granddaughter.* **dote** (doht) ▷ *verb* **doting, doted**

double
1. *adjective* Twice the amount, the number, or the strength: *Sally made a double batch of brownies.*
2. *adverb* Twice as much: *It cost us double what it should have.*
3. *verb* To make something twice as big: *We doubled the size of the pile of leaves in just one hour.*
4. *noun* A person who looks just like you.
5. *noun* A hit in baseball that allows the player to get to second base.
6. **doubles** *noun, plural* Team play with two players on each side.
7. *verb* To bend or fold in two.
8. *verb* To serve more than one purpose: *The dining room table doubles as a desk.*
dou·ble (**duhb**-uhl) ▷ *verb* **doubling, doubled**

double bass *noun* The largest string instrument in the violin family. You play it by standing next to it and plucking the strings or using a bow.

double-click *verb* To quickly click twice on a mouse button in order to make something happen on a computer: *Double-click on the icon to open it.*

double-cross *verb* To tell someone you will do one thing, knowing that you are really going to do something else. ▷ *verb* **double-crosses, double-crossing, double-crossed** ▷ *noun* **double cross**

double-header *noun* Two baseball games played one right after the other. **double-head·er** (**hed**-ur) ▷ *noun, plural* **double-headers**

doubt
1. *noun* The state or quality of being uncertain: *Wayne*

was in doubt about the date of the party.
2. *verb* To be uncertain about something: *I doubt we will reach home before dark.* ▷ *verb* **doubting, doubted**
doubt (dout)

doubtful *adjective*
1. Full of doubts: *They are doubtful about whether they'll attend the wedding.*
2. Uncertain and unlikely: *It's doubtful whether enough people will sign up for the trip.* ▷ *adverb* **doubtfully**
doubt·ful (**dout**-ful)

kneading dough

dough *noun*
1. A thick mixture of mainly flour and water, used to make bread, cookies, and other foods.
2. *(slang)* Money.
dough (doh)
Dough sounds like **doe**.

doughnut *or* **donut** *noun* A cake fried in oil. A doughnut is round and usually has a hole in the middle. **dough·nut** *or* **do·nut** (**doh**-nuht)

dove *noun* A plump bird that makes a cooing sound. Doves are often used as a symbol of peace. **dove** (duhv)

down
1. *preposition* In a direction lower or farther away, as in *down the ladder* or *down the road.*
2. *preposition* From a higher to a lower place: *We raced down the mountain.*
▷ *adjective* **downward** (**doun**-wurd)
▷ *adverb* **downward** *or* **downwards**
3. *adverb* To a lower place or condition: *Push the button down.*
4. *noun* In football, one of a series of four attempts to advance the ball ten yards.

dove

5. *noun* The soft feathers of a bird. ▷ *adjective* **downy**
6. *adjective (informal)* Sad or depressed: *What are you so down about?*
down (doun)

downcast *adjective* Very sad. **down·cast** (**doun**-kast)

downfall *noun*
1. A sudden negative change in position or reputation: *Analysts agree that greed and poor planning caused the bank's downfall.*
2. Something that causes a downfall: *Her inability to get organized was her downfall.*
down·fall (**doun**-fawl)

downgrade
1. *verb* To reduce the value, rank, status, or level of importance of someone or something: *The weather bureau has downgraded the hurricane to a tropical storm.* ▷ *verb* **downgrading, downgraded**
2. *noun* The descending slope of a road: *The sign indicated a steep downgrade ahead, so Mom shifted into second gear.*
3. *noun* A change to a lower or worse condition: *The company's credit suffered a downgrade when the story came out.*
down·grade (**doun**-grayd)

downhill
1. (**down**-hil) *adverb* From the higher to the lower part of a slope or hill: *I got up to 30 miles an hour coasting downhill on my bike.*
2. (**down**-hil) *adverb* From a better to a worse position or situation: *Gina's health has really gone downhill in the last six months.*
3. (**down**-hil) *adjective* Going downward or getting worse: *The stockmarket's downhill slide alarmed investors.*
down·hill

download *verb* To transfer information from a larger to a smaller computer, or from an internet location to your own computer: *I will download some pictures to add to my report.* **down·load** (**doun**-lohd)
▷ *verb* **downloading, downloaded**

downpour *noun* A very heavy rain. **down·pour** (**doun**-por)

downright
1. *adjective (informal)* Total, or complete: *It's a downright shame that you have to leave so soon.*
2. *adverb* Absolutely, or completely: *Your reasons for not going to the concert with us are downright silly.*
down·right (**doun**-rite)

a
b
c
d
e
f
g
h
i
j
k
l
m
n
o
p
q
r
s
t
u
v
w
x
y
z

downs *noun, plural* An area of rolling hills, especially in England. **downs** (dounz)

downside *noun* Something bad about a situation, especially one that is good in other ways: *Her life as a movie star is glamorous, but the downside is that she is always being stalked by photographers.* **down·side** (doun-*side*)

downsize *verb* To reduce the size of something, such as the scale of an automobile or the number of employees in a company: *Many people lost their jobs when the factory had to downsize.* **down·size** (**doun**-*size*) ▷ *verb* **downsizing, downsized**

downstairs
1. (**doun**-stairz) *adverb* Down the stairs or to a lower floor: *The ball bounced downstairs.*
2. (**doun**-*stairz*) *adjective* On a lower level of a house: *Jasper is in the downstairs playroom.*
▷ *noun* **downstairs**
down·stairs

downstream *adverb* In the direction of the flowing current in a river or stream: *We stopped rowing and let the boat float downstream.* **down·stream** (**doun**-streem) ▷ *adjective* **downstream**

Down syndrome *noun* A genetic condition in which a person is born with learning disabilities and with eyes that appear to slant, a broad skull, and shorter fingers than normal. Also called *Down's syndrome.*

downtime *noun* A time when a machine or computer is not running, or when a person is not working: *Dad likes to spend his downtime on weekends with the family.* **down·time** (**doun**-*time*)

downtown *adverb* To or in a city's main business district: *My mom took us downtown to our favorite restaurant.* **down·town** (**doun**-toun) ▷ *adjective* **downtown** ▷ *noun* **downtown**

downwind *adverb, adjective* In the direction in which the wind is blowing: *The wolves were traveling downwind of the elk and caught their scent very quickly.* **down·wind** (**doun**-wind)

dowry *noun* Money or property that a woman's family supplies to a man or his family in some cultures when the woman marries him. **dow·ry** (**dou**-ree) ▷ *noun, plural* **dowries**

doze *verb* To sleep lightly or take a brief, unintentional nap: *I dozed off a few times during the lecture.* **doze** (dohz) ▷ *verb* **dozing, dozed** ▷ *noun* **doze**

doze

dozen *noun* A group of 12: *Gary brought a dozen doughnuts.* **doz·en** (**duhz**-uhn)

dpi *noun* A measure of the sharpness of an image on a scanner or printer based on the number of dots per inch. The higher the dpi, the sharper the image. Dpi is short for *dots per inch.*

Dr. Short for **Doctor**.

drab *adjective* Plain and uninteresting to look at, as in *a drab shirt.* **drab** (drab) ▷ *noun* **drabness**

draft
1. *noun* A flow of air, especially a cold one: *The draft from the window is making me cold.* ▷ *adjective* **drafty**
2. *verb* To write a first rough copy of a document: *The memo was drafted by one of the senator's staffers.*
3. *noun* A first version of a document, or one that is not final.
4. *verb* To make someone join the armed forces: *He was drafted in 1967 and served in Vietnam.*
5. *noun* The **draft** was the system that required young men in the United States to serve in the armed forces. It ended in 1973, but it can be resumed if there is a need.
6. *adjective* Drawn out of a barrel or keg, as in *draft beer.*
draft (draft)
▷ *verb* **drafting, drafted**

drag
1. *verb* To pull something along the ground: *Shirley dragged her backpack behind her.*
2. *verb* To move along the ground or floor: *Her shoelace was dragging and she tripped on it.*
3. *verb* To move something from one place to another on a computer, using the mouse: *I dragged the files to a new folder on my hard drive.*
4. *verb* If an activity or event **drags**, it seems to go slowly: *The concert really dragged.*
5. *noun* A person or an activity that is a **drag** is boring or not much fun. *I thought Martha was a real drag last night.*
6. *noun* A force that slows down the forward motion of a vehicle, boat, or aircraft.
7. *noun* If someone is **in drag**, they are wearing clothes that are typically worn by a person of the opposite sex.
8. *noun* (*informal*) A boring activity or event: *The movie was such a drag that we walked out.*
drag (drag)
▷ *verb* **dragging, dragged**

drag and drop *verb* A method of moving text or an image on a computer by selecting it and holding down

Chinese dragon

the mouse button while you move the cursor to a new position. When you release the button, the moved material will be inserted in the new place.

dragon *noun* An imaginary monster that breathes fire: *Dragons are considered good luck in China.* **drag·on** (**drag**-uhn)

dragonfly *noun* A large insect with two sets of wings and a long, slender body. **drag·on·fly** (**drag**-uhn-*flye*)

drain
1. *verb* To remove the liquid from something: *Drain the water from the spaghetti.*
2. *noun* An opening leading to a pipe or channel that takes away liquid.
3. *verb* To tire, or to use up: *Building the new house drained our savings.*
drain (drayn)
▷ *verb* **draining, drained**

drainage *noun* The act or process of removing liquid from an area: *Engineers are working to improve the town's storm drainage.* **drain·age** (**dray**-nij)

drained *adjective* If you feel **drained**, you have no energy left. **drained** (draynd)

drama *noun*
1. A play that is serious rather than funny.
2. The subject or practice of acting: *She studies drama at the city's fine arts high school.*
3. Something that causes people to experience strong, usually unpleasant feelings: *His rowdy behavior at the wedding caused a big family drama.* **dra·ma** (**drah**-muh)

dramatic *adjective*
1. Of or having to do with acting and the theater.
2. Exciting in the way that a movie or a play can be: *People were able to watch the dramatic rescue live on TV.*
3. Very noticeable: *In the past year, gold has shown a dramatic increase in value.*
4. Expressing or showing more feeling than is really necessary: *No one was hurt in the accident, so there's no need to get dramatic about it!*
dra·mat·ic (druh-**mat**-ik)
▷ *adverb* **dramatically**

dramatist *noun* Someone who writes plays. **dram·a·tist** (**dram**-uh-tist)

dramatize *verb*
1. To adapt a story into a play.
2. To make an event seem more exciting than it really was: *Alice dramatizes every little thing that happens to her.*
dram·a·tize (**dram**-uh-*tize*)
▷ *verb* **dramatizing, dramatized**

drank *verb* The past tense of **drink**. **drank** (drank)

drape
1. *noun* A piece of material placed across a window or stage to cover it: *We have drapes in the den.*
▷ *noun* **drapery**
2. *verb* To cover with a loosely hanging cloth: *I draped a sweater over my shoulders.* ▷ *verb* **draping, draped**
drape (drape)

drastic *adjective* Serious and likely to have important or long-lasting effects, as in *a drastic problem*. **dras·tic** (**dras**-tik)
▷ *adverb* **drastically**

draw
1. *verb* To make a picture with something you write with, such as a pencil, pen, or crayon.
2. *verb* To pull something: *The cart was drawn by a donkey.*
3. *verb* To attract, as in *to draw a crowd*.
4. *verb* To figure out by using your power of reason, as in *to draw conclusions*.
5. *verb* To inhale, as in *to draw a deep breath*.
6. *noun* An equal score for both teams at the end of a competition.
draw (draw)
▷ *verb* **drawing, drew** (droo), **drawn** (drawn)

drawback *noun* A problem or disadvantage: *Does the proposal have any drawbacks that you are aware of?* **draw·back** (**draw**-bak)

drawbridge *noun* A bridge that can be raised or moved to let boats pass underneath. **draw·bridge** (**draw**-brij)

drawer *noun* A storage compartment that slides out of a piece of furniture. **draw·er** (dror)

dragonfly

drawing *noun* A picture made by hand, such as with pen, pencil, crayons, or chalk: *The architectural drawings that accompanied the article were very detailed.* **draw·ing** (**draw**-ing)

drawl

1. *verb* To speak in a slow manner, stretching out the vowel sounds: *To be funny, Tyler drawled his answer and winked as he spoke.* ▷ *verb* **drawling, drawled**

2. *noun* A slow manner of speaking: *Cindy's Southern drawl brought back memories of my vacation in Georgia.* **drawl** (drawl)

drawstring *noun* A string or cord that closes or tightens a bag or piece of clothing when you pull the ends: *I like these pants because they have a drawstring around the waist.* **draw·string** (**draw**-string)

dread *verb* To be afraid of something you expect in the near future. People often use the word *dread* for things they do not actually fear, but do not look forward to: *I dread listening to Uncle Harry's dumb jokes at Thanksgiving.* **dread** (dred) ▷ *verb* **dreading, dreaded** ▷ *noun* **dread** ▷ *adjective* **dreaded**

dreadful *adjective*

1. Very frightening; awful, as in *a dreadful storm.*
2. Very bad, as in *a dreadful movie.*
dread·ful (**dred**-fuhl)
▷ *adverb* **dreadfully**

dreadlocks *noun, plural* A hairstyle in which the hair is grown long and worn in thick, ropelike strands. **dread·locks** (**dred**-*lahks*)

dreadlocks

Word History

People who were part of the Rastafarian movement in Jamaica in the mid-20th century felt that there were things wrong with society, and they wore their hair in **dreadlocks** as one way of setting themselves apart from it. Letting their hair grow in dreadlocks also seemed more natural to them than combing and straightening it. The word *dreadlocks* entered the English language in the 1960s. *Dread* meant "fear," and *locks* meant "hair." *Dread* perhaps referred to dread of the Lord, or to the dread that others would feel when they saw Rastafarians wearing dreadlocks.

dream

1. *verb* To imagine events while you are asleep.
2. *noun* An experience while you are asleep that feels like it is happening in real life.
3. *verb* To have a strong wish for something in the future: *Kayla dreams of becoming an astronaut.*
4. *noun* Something you hope for in the future: *My dream is to get a job as a chef.*
dream (dreem)
▷ *verb* **dreaming, dreamed** or **dreamt** (dremt)
▷ *noun* **dreamer**

dreamy *adjective* Vague or soft, as in *dreamy music.* **dream·y** (**dree**-mee) ▷ *adjective* **dreamier, dreamiest** ▷ *adverb* **dreamily**

dreary *adjective* Dull, unattractive, or sad, as in *dreary weather.* **drear·y** (**dreer**-ee) ▷ *adjective* **drearier, dreariest** ▷ *adverb* **drearily**

dredge *verb* To scrape the bottom of a body of water to make it deeper or to find or catch something: *They are dredging the river to reduce flooding.* **dredge** (drej) ▷ *verb* **dredging, dredged**

dregs *noun, plural* The solid bits that drop to the bottom of some liquids, such as coffee. **dregs** (dregz)

drench *verb* To make someone or something completely wet: *We got drenched walking home in the rain.* **drench** (drench) ▷ *verb* **drenches, drenching, drenched**

Word History

The words **drench** and **drink** look somewhat alike, but it's not immediately clear how they are related. *Drench* means to make something thoroughly wet. Usually people who get caught in a rainstorm come home and say, "I'm drenched!" To drench someone originally meant to make that person drink, and this old meaning of the word *drench* still survives in the sense of forcing an animal to drink medicine. But soon people began using the term to mean "to cover with water," and our meaning grew out of that.

dress

1. *verb* To put clothes on.
2. *noun* A piece of women's clothing that covers the body from the shoulders to the legs. ▷ *noun, plural* **dresses**
3. *noun* Clothes in general, as in *fancy dress.*
4. *verb* If you **dress** a salad, you mix a sauce into it in order to add flavor.
5. *verb* If you **dress** a wound or injury, you put

an ointment on it and bandage it. **dress** (dres)
▷ verb **dresses, dressing, dressed**

dresser noun A piece of furniture with drawers, used for storing clothes. **dress·er** (**dres**-ur)

dressing noun
1. A type of sauce for salads.
2. A mixture used to stuff a chicken or turkey before it is roasted.
3. A covering for a wound. **dress·ing** (**dres**-ing)

dressing table noun A piece of bedroom furniture with a mirror and drawers.

dress rehearsal noun The last rehearsal of a play or concert, performed as if an audience were present.

dribble

dribble verb
1. To let liquid trickle from your mouth: *Saliva dribbled down the baby's chin.*
2. To drop liquid in small amounts: *Carefully dribble wax along the seam in order to seal it.*
3. To bounce a basketball while walking or running, keeping it under your control. **drib·ble** (**drib**-uhl)
▷ verb **dribbling, dribbled**

drier adjective The comparative of **dry**. **dri·er** (**drye**-ur)

driest adjective The superlative of **dry**. **dri·est** (**drye**-ist)

drift
1. verb To move in the same direction as water or wind.
2. verb To move or act without any sense of purpose: *After he lost his job, Don drifted for a couple of months.* ▷ noun **drifter**
3. noun A pile of sand or snow created by the wind.
4. (informal) If you **get someone's drift**, you understand what the person is saying. **drift** (drift)
▷ verb **drifting, drifted**

driftwood noun Wood that floats ashore or is floating on water. **drift·wood** (**drift**-wud)

drill
1. noun A rotating tool used for making holes.
2. verb To use a drill: *Brenda drilled holes in the wall to hang the shelves.*
3. verb To teach someone how to do something by having the person do it over and over again: *The*

sergeant drilled the soldiers on how to march.
▷ noun **drill**

drill (dril)
▷ verb **drilling, drilled**

drink
1. noun A liquid that you swallow.
2. noun An alcoholic liquid: *Dad called to say he was going out for a drink with his boss.* ▷ noun **drinker**
3. verb To swallow liquid: *Do you drink water with your meals?*
4. verb To drink alcoholic beverages, or to have the habit of doing this: *Never drink and drive.*

drink (dringk)
▷ verb **drinking, drank** (drangk), **drunk** (druhngk)

drip
1. verb To fall in drops, or to make liquid fall in drops. ▷ verb **dripping, dripped** ▷ noun **drip**
2. noun (informal) A boring person.

drip (drip)

drippings noun, plural Fat and juice that comes from meat while it is cooking: *I used the drippings from the turkey for the gravy.* **drip·pings** (**drip**-ingz)

drive
1. verb To operate and control a vehicle. ▷ noun **driving**
2. verb To take someone somewhere in a vehicle: *She drove Lou to the mall to do some shopping.* ▷ noun **drive**
3. verb To hit something hard and far: *Jerry drove the golf ball over the hill.*
4. verb To force someone into a desperate state: *Losing his home to fire drove him to despair.*
5. noun A computer device that can read and sometimes write to some form of storage media: *I back up my files on a separate hard drive.*
6. noun A road, especially one that is scenic and often winding.
7. noun Energy and determination: *He undertook the project with a lot of drive.*
8. noun An organized campaign to do something: *The Boy Scouts have organized a drive to collect old newspapers.*

drive (drive)
▷ verb **driving, drove, driven** (**driv**-uhn)

drive-in adjective Designed so that customers may be served or entertained in their cars, as in *a drive-in movie theater.* ▷ noun **drive-in**

drivel noun Nonsense, in speech or writing. **driv·el** (**driv**-uhl)

drone

driver *noun*
   1. Someone who drives a vehicle: *The bus driver was texting on his cell phone when the accident occurred.*
   2. A computer program that controls the way a connected device works: *You probably need to update your printer driver.*
   driv·er (**drye**-vur)

drive-through *or* **drive-thru**
   1. *adjective* Offering services to people while they are still in their cars, as in *a drive-through pharmacy.*
   2. *noun* A window, as at a restaurant or bank, that can be used by the driver of a car: *You can make a deposit at the bank's drive-through.*

driveway *noun* A private road that leads from the street to a house or garage. **drive·way** (**drive**-*way*)

drizzle *noun* Light rain. **driz·zle** (**driz**-uhl) ▷ *verb* **drizzle**

dromedary *noun* A camel with one hump, found in the Middle East and northern Africa. It is also known as an *Arabian camel.* **drom·e·dar·y** (**drah**-mi-*der*-ee) ▷ *noun, plural* **dromedaries**

drone
   1. *verb* To make a low, dull, steady humming or buzzing sound, like the noise an engine makes: *Police helicopters droned overhead.*
   2. *verb* To talk in a dull, monotonous way: *Sam droned on about his skill at racquetball.*
   3. *noun* An aircraft without a pilot that is controlled remotely: *The government used drones to take videos of damage from the recent floods.*
   4. *noun* A male insect, such as a bee, whose function is to mate with the queen.
   drone (drohn)

▷ *verb* **droning, droned**

drool *verb*
   1. To let saliva trickle from your mouth.
   2. drool over To think that someone or something is very attractive and desirable.
   drool (drool)
   ▷ *verb* **drooling, drooled**

droop *verb*
   1. To hang downward; sag. ▷ *adjective* **drooping**
   2. To run out of energy and feel very tired.
   droop (droop)
   ▷ *verb* **drooping, drooped**

drop
   1. *verb* To let something fall: *She dropped her bag on the table.*
   2. *verb* To fall down or move to a lower place: *We dropped behind the fence so they wouldn't see us.*
   3. *noun* The distance from a higher to a lower place: *There's a 100-foot drop from the top of the cliff to the sea.*
   4. *noun* A small quantity of liquid, as in *a drop of milk.*
   5. *noun* Any small amount, as in *a drop of kindness.*
   6. A **drop in the bucket** is a very small amount.
   7. *noun* A small piece of candy or medication for the throat, as in *lemon drops* or *cough drops.*
   8. *verb* To leave out: *You drop the letter "e" when you add "ing" to the word "write."*
   9. *verb* To stop using someone or something, or to stop doing something: *He has decided to drop working on the night shift.*
   10. If you **drop the ball,** you fail to do what is expected of you.
   11. drop by *verb* To pay a short visit: *Let's drop by Grandma's house.*
   12. drop off *verb* To deliver: *I will drop off the present*

drool

drum set

ride cymbal

crash cymbal

medium tom

high tom

hi-hat cymbal

floor tom

snare drum

bass drum

drown (droun)
▷ *verb* **drowning, drowned**

drowsy *adjective* Not fully awake; sleepy: *You certainly shouldn't drive if you feel drowsy.* **drow·sy** (**drou**-zee) ▷ *adjective* **drowsier, drowsiest** ▷ *noun* **drowsiness** ▷ *verb* **drowse** ▷ *adverb* **drowsily**

drudgery *noun* Difficult, boring, or unpleasant work, as in *household drudgery.* **drudg·er·y** (**druhj**-ur-ee)

drug
1. *noun* A substance, either natural or synthetic, used to treat an illness.
2. *noun* A chemical substance that people take because they like its effect on them. Drugs are dangerous and usually cause addiction.
3. *verb* To make someone unconscious by giving him or her a drug. ▷ *verb* **drugging, drugged** ▷ *adjective* **drugged**
4. **drug addict** *noun* Someone who cannot give up using drugs.
drug (druhg)

drugstore *noun* A store that contains a pharmacy and also sells other medicines, cosmetics, and personal items. **drug·store** (**druhg**-stor)

drum
1. *noun* A percussion instrument shaped like a cylinder with one closed end that makes a noise when you hit it with your hands or drumsticks.
2. *noun* A container shaped like a drum: *Oil is stored in drums.*
3. *verb* To play a drum or other surface with drumsticks or with your fingers: *Growing impatient, Clive began to drum his fingers on the table.*
▷ *verb* **drumming, drummed** ▷ *noun* **drummer**
drum (druhm)

Word History

A **drum** doesn't sound much like a trumpet, but the history of the word *drum* involves this other instrument. English speakers most likely took the term *drum* from the Old German word *trumme*, also meaning "drum," though it's unclear why the two words begin with different sounds. *Trumme* meant "trumpet" originally, and people perhaps invented the word by imitating the sound of a loud, booming instrument.

on my way home from the store.
13. **drop out** *verb* To stop taking part in something: *Bruce dropped out of basketball because it took too much time.*
drop (drahp)
▷ *verb* **dropping, dropped**

dropout *noun* Someone who has left a school or course before finishing, especially high school: *It's hard to make a living when you're a high school dropout.* **drop·out** (**drahp**-out)

drought *noun* A long period without rain. Droughts damage crops and cause the soil to dry out. **drought** (drout)

drove
1. *noun* A large herd of animals being moved as a group: *Rangers moved a drove of mountain goats to the western end of the park.*
2. *noun* A large crowd of people: *Fans showed up in droves.*
3. *verb* The past tense of **drive**.
drove (drove)

drown *verb*
1. To die from a lack of air when under water or another liquid.
2. **drown out** To make a louder noise than something else: *The noise of the air-conditioning drowned out the TV.*

drumstick *noun*
1. A stick used to hit a drum.
2. The leg portion of a chicken or turkey.
drum·stick (**druhm**-stik)

a b c **d** e f g h i j k l m n o p q r s t u v w x y z

drunk

1. *adjective* If people are **drunk**, they have had too much alcohol to drink and cannot control their actions or emotions.
2. *noun* A person who often gets drunk; a drunkard. ▷ *adjective* **drunken**
3. *verb* The past participle of **drink**.
drunk (druhngk)

drunkard *noun* Someone who drinks too much alcohol or who is often drunk. **drunk·ard** (druhng-kurd)

dry

1. *verb* To remove the moisture from something: *You can dry the clothes by hanging them on the clothesline.* ▷ *verb* **dries, drying, dried**
2. *adjective* Not wet.
3. *adjective* Lacking rain, as in *a dry climate.*
4. *adjective* Lacking features that are interesting; dull.
dry (drye)
▷ *adjective* **drier, driest** ▷ *adverb* **drily**

dry cell *noun* A small electric battery that contains no liquid. Most common sizes of batteries for toys and appliances are dry cells.

dry cleaning *noun* A method of cleaning clothes with liquid chemicals that remove stains. Dry cleaning is used for fabrics and materials that would be damaged by soap and water. ▷ *noun* **dry cleaner** ▷ *verb* **dry-clean**

dryer *noun* A machine that dries something: *We just bought a new clothes dryer.* **dry·er** (drye-ur)

dry goods *noun, plural* Fabrics, clothing, and related materials, such as threads and ribbons.

DSL *noun* A fast form of internet connection that uses a special telephone line. DSL is short for *digital subscriber line.*

dual *adjective*
1. Combining two things or aspects in one: *I have dual citizenship because my parents are American, but I was born in England.*
2. Made up of two parts or pieces: *Dual airbags are now standard on many cars.*
du·al (doo-uhl)
Dual sounds like **duel**.

dubious *adjective* Having or showing doubts. **du·bi·ous** (doo-bee-uhs) ▷ *adverb* **dubiously**

duchess *noun* The wife or widow of a duke,

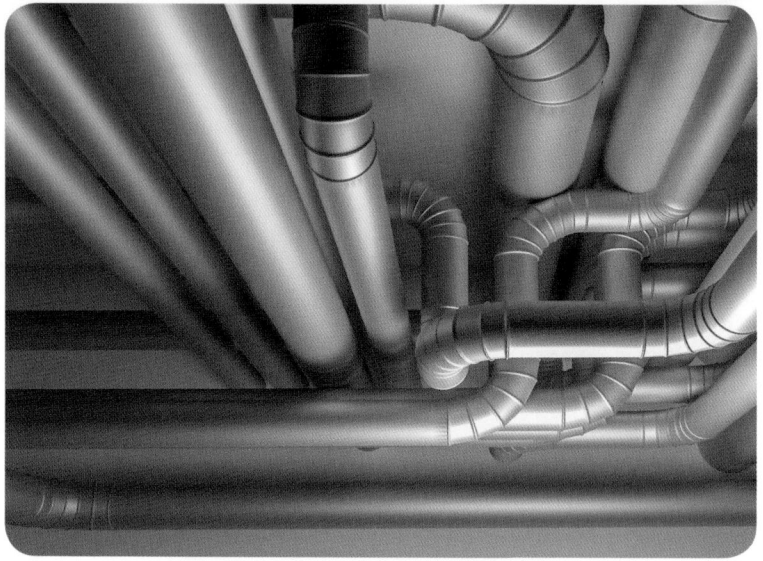

ducts

or a woman with the rank that is equal to that of a duke. **du·chess** (duhch-is)

duck

1. *noun* A bird with webbed feet that swims and feeds in water.
2. *verb* To bend low to avoid something: *We had to duck to get into the cave.*
3. *verb* To avoid or to evade: *The celebrity ducked the newspaper reporters.*
duck (duhk)
▷ *verb* **ducking, ducked**

duckling *noun* A young duck. **duck·ling** (duhk-ling)

duct *noun* A tube that carries air or liquid from one place to another. **duct** (duhkt)

dud *noun*
1. A bomb or firework that does not explode as expected.
2. A dull and unsuccessful entertainment or event: *The sequel was a real dud.*
dud (duhd)
▷ *adjective* **dud**

dude *noun*
1. A person from a town or city who has little or no experience on a Western ranch.
2. *(informal)* A man or boy.
dude (dood)

due
1. *adjective* Expected to arrive or happen: *The train is due at six o'clock.*
2. *adjective* Owed, as in *the amount due.*
3. *adjective* Suitable or appropriate: *After years of being ignored, her book is now receiving due attention.*

duckling

dugout

4. *preposition* **due to** Because of: *We're hurrying to finish the school paper due to the deadline.*
5. *adverb* **Due** south (or north, east, or west) means exactly in that compass direction: *This road runs due south until it reaches US highway 160.*
due (doo)
▷ *adverb* **duly** (**doo**-lee) *duly elected officers*

duel *noun* A fight between two people using swords or guns, fought according to strict rules. **du·el** (**doo**-uhl) **Duel** sounds like **dual**.

duet *noun* A piece of music for two singers or performers, or the performers themselves. **du·et** (doo-**et**)

duffel bag *noun* A bag made from strong cloth in the shape of a cylinder, often used by soldiers or campers. **duf·fel bag** (**duhf**-uhl)

dug *verb* The past tense and past participle of **dig**. **dug** (duhg)

dugout *noun*
1. A long, low shelter where baseball players sit when they are not at bat or in the field.
2. A rough shelter dug out of the ground or in the side of a hill.
3. A canoe made from the outer portion of a large log.
dug·out (**duhg**-out)

duke *noun* A nobleman. In Britain, a duke holds the rank just below that of a prince. **duke** (dook)

dull *adjective*
1. Not bright; dim: *The lamp shed a dull light.*
2. Not perceptive or intelligent.
3. Boring: *After the fourth episode, the show became dull and I stopped watching it.*

4. Not shiny, as in *a dull finish.*
5. Not sharp, as in *a dull blade.*
6. Slow or sluggish.
dull (duhl)
▷ *adjective* **duller, dullest** ▷ *verb* **dull**
▷ *adverb* **dully**

dumb *adjective*
1. *(informal)* Stupid. ▷ *adjective* **dumber, dumbest**
2. Unable to speak. This word is now considered offensive by many people. The preferred term is *speech impaired.*
dumb (duhm)

dumbbell *noun*
1. A short bar with heavy weights at each end, used to exercise and strengthen the muscles.
2. *(slang)* A stupid person.
dumb·bell (**duhm**-bel)

dumbfounded *adjective* So amazed that you cannot speak: *I was completely dumbfounded when I discovered that she couldn't swim.* **dumb·found·ed** (**duhm**-foun-did)

Word History

A description of a person as *dumb* used to mean that he or she couldn't speak. English speakers created *dumbfounded* by adding part of another word to *dumb. Confound* is a verb meaning "to confuse." People took the ending *-found* from *confound* and added it to *dumb*, making the word *dumbfound. Dumbfound* means to astonish someone so much that you leave the person speechless, but it is rare, and usually only its past participle **dumbfounded** is used.

dummy *noun*
1. A model of a person or object made for some practical purpose.
2. *(informal)* A stupid person.
dum·my (**duhm**-ee)
▷ *noun, plural* **dummies**

dumbbells

dump
1. *verb* To put something down thoughtlessly or roughly: *Keith dumped his bag on the floor.*
2. *noun (informal)* A place where garbage and other unwanted things are left; a landfill.
3. *verb (informal)* To end a relationship with someone: *Jeremy dumped Peg last weekend.*
dump (duhmp)
▷ *verb* **dumping, dumped**

dumpster

dumpling *noun* Dough that has been boiled, fried, or steamed, sometimes with meat, vegetables, or fruit wrapped inside. **dump·ling (duhmp**-ling)

dumpster *noun* A large metal container in which people can dump trash or items from trash cans. Dumpsters are designed so that they can be lifted and emptied or moved by garbage trucks. **dump·ster (duhmp**-stur)

dune *noun* A sand hill formed by wind or tides. **dune** (doon)

dungeon *noun* An underground prison. **dun·geon (duhn**-juhn)

dunk *verb*

1. To dip something into liquid: *I like to dunk cookies in milk.*

2. To push someone underwater in a playful way: *We tried to dunk each other in the pool.*

3. To jump and force a basketball down through the basket.

dunk (duhngk)

▷ *verb* **dunking, dunked**

Word History

The Pennsylvania Dutch are a people who came to America from Germany and Switzerland around the 17th century and settled in the colony of Pennsylvania. A common sports term derives from Pennsylvania Dutch, which is based on German. The word *dunke*, meaning "to dip," passed into English as **dunk**. We still use this word to refer to "dipping" bread or cookies into drinks, but *dunking* a basketball is a much bigger action.

dupe

1. *verb* To fool or trick someone in a way that makes them look foolish: *The caller duped me into believing I had won a new TV.* ▷ *verb* **duping, duped**

2. *noun* A person who is easily fooled or tricked.

dupe (doop)

Synonyms

Dupe To dupe someone is to fool or trick them in a way that makes them look foolish: *I was duped by a guy pretending to be a policeman.*

- -

■ **Fool** means to make someone believe something that is not true: *You fooled me; I thought that was your real hair!*

■ **Deceive** means to make someone believe something that is untrue by lying or giving a false impression: *Sam tried to deceive his mother about the tidiness of his room.*

■ **Trick** means to deceive someone by doing something clever: *The app tricks users into downloading a file that contains a virus.*

■ **Hoodwink** means to deceive someone and cause them to believe or do something foolish: *The commercial seems designed to hoodwink consumers into buying expensive insurance that they don't need.*

duplicate

1. (**doo**-pli-*kate*) *verb* To make an exact copy of something. ▷ *verb* **duplicating, duplicated** ▷ *noun* **duplication** ▷ *noun* **duplicator**

2. (**doo**-pli-kit) *noun* An exact copy of something, especially one that is not needed: *We went through the address list to eliminate the duplicates.* **du·pli·cate**

durable *adjective* Tough and lasting for a long time, as in *a durable roof.* **du·ra·ble (door**-uh-buhl) ▷ *noun* **durability (door**-uh-**bil**-i-tee)

duration *noun* The period of time that something lasts: *I sat next to my dad for the duration of our trip.* **du·ra·tion** (du-**ray**-shuhn)

during *preposition* Within a particular time: *The gym is open during the day.* **dur·ing (door**-ing)

dusk *noun* The time of day after sunset when it starts getting dark. **dusk** (duhsk)

dust

1. *noun* Tiny particles of something like dirt or fluff that gather on surfaces or in the air.

2. *verb* To remove these particles from surfaces: *We need to dust the living room before the guests arrive.* ▷ *verb* **dusting, dusted** ▷ *noun* **duster**

dust (duhst)

dustpan

dustpan *noun* A small tray with a handle that you use with a broom to pick up dust and dirt from the floor. **dust·pan (duhst**-pan)

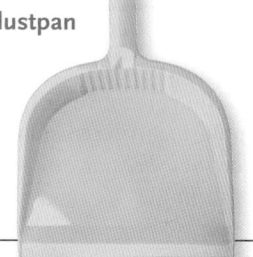

dusty *adjective* Full of or covered with dust: *We found an old dictionary on a dusty shelf.* **dust·y** (**duhs**-tee)

dutiful *adjective* Obedient and careful to do what you are supposed to do, as in *a dutiful child.* **du·ti·ful** (**doo**-ti-fuhl)
▷ *adverb* **dutifully**

duty *noun*
1. A thing a person must do or ought to do: *It is your duty to make sure the flag is folded properly.*
2. A tax charged on imported products.
3. If you are **on duty**, you are at work or responsible for something.
du·ty (**doo**-tee)
▷ *noun, plural* **duties**

DVD *noun* A disk the size of a compact disk but that can hold much more information. A DVD can contain computer data or recordings of movies or music. DVD is short for *digital versatile disk* or *digital video disk.*

DVR *noun* A device that receives a video broadcast signal and stores it digitally on a hard drive so that the broadcast can be watched later. DVR is short for *digital video recorder.*

dwarf
1. *noun* A person, animal, or plant that is smaller than normal. ▷ *noun, plural* **dwarfs** *or* **dwarves** (dworvz) ▷ *adjective* **dwarf**
2. *verb* To make something else seem small: *The giant sequoias dwarfed the trees around them.*
▷ *verb* **dwarfing, dwarfed**
dwarf (dworf)

dwarf planet *noun* A round heavenly body that orbits the sun or another star. A dwarf planet is smaller than a planet: *Pluto is now classified as a dwarf planet.*

dwell *verb* To live in a place. **dwell** (dwel)
▷ *verb* **dwelling, dwelt** (dwelt) *or* **dwelled**

dwelling *noun* The place where someone lives, such as a house or an apartment: *The street was lined with small dwellings.* **dwell·ing** (**dwel**-ing)

dwindle *verb* To become smaller or less till very few or little is left: *Our supply of food is dwindling.*
dwin·dle (**dwin**-duhl) ▷ *verb* **dwindling, dwindled**

dye
1. *noun* A substance used to change the color of something.
2. *verb* To change the color of something, especially fabric, by soaking it in dye. ▷ *verb* **dying, dyed**
▷ *adjective* **dyed**
dye (dye)
Dye sounds like **die**.

dusty

dynamic *adjective*
1. If someone is **dynamic**, he or she is very energetic and good at getting things done.
2. If a situation is **dynamic**, it is constantly changing because there are many things that influence it: *Her work as a daily news reporter is fast-paced and dynamic.*
dy·nam·ic (dye-**nam**-ik)
▷ *noun* **dynamism** (**dye**-nuh-*miz*-uhm)

dynamite *noun* A very powerful explosive. **dy·na·mite** (**dye**-nuh-*mite*)

dynamo *noun*
1. A machine for converting the power of a turning wheel into electricity; a generator.
2. A forceful person who works very hard.
dy·na·mo (**dye**-nuh-*moh*)
▷ *noun, plural* **dynamos**

dynasty *noun*
1. A series of rulers belonging to the same family, as in *the Ming Dynasty.*
2. A group, family, or team that succeeds for a long time: *Some say that the Cowboys of the early 1990s were the last great football dynasty.*
dy·nas·ty (**dye**-nuh-stee)
▷ *noun, plural* **dynasties**

dyslexia *noun* A condition that makes it difficult to read, write, and distinguish letters properly or in the correct order. **dys·lex·i·a** (dis-**lek**-see-uh)
▷ *adjective* **dyslexic** (dis-**lek**-sik)

dye for Easter eggs

E e

About E The vowel **E** is the most commonly used letter in the English language. In order of use, *e* is followed by *t*, and then by *a*. English vowels have at least two sounds. The *e* can be pronounced as a short *e*, as in the words *elm* and *end*. The long *e* sound says its name in words such as *equal* and *eat*. Some technology words begin with an *e-* or an *e*, which stands for *electronic*. Examples: e-book, e-commerce, and email, or e-mail.

each
1. *adjective* Every one of two or more people or things: *The building has an emergency exit on each floor.*
2. *pronoun* Every person or thing: *We each have our own bike.*
3. *adverb* Apiece; for each one: *You can have two cookies each.*
each (eech)

eager *adjective* Having or showing a lot of interest and excitement: *Katie was eager to get into the pool.* **ea·ger** (**ee**-gur)
▷ *noun* **eagerness** ▷ *adverb* **eagerly**

eagle *noun* A large bird of prey that can see very well and eats small birds and animals. **ea·gle** (**ee**-guhl)

eagle

ear *noun*
1. The organ on either side of the head that we use to hear with.
2. The part of some plants on which grain or seeds grow, as in *an ear of corn.*
ear (eer)

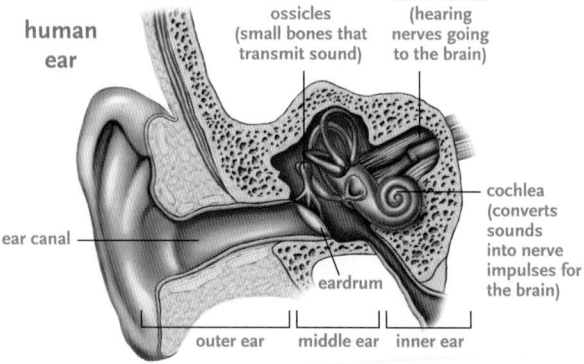

human ear

- aural nerves (hearing nerves going to the brain)
- ossicles (small bones that transmit sound)
- ear canal
- cochlea (converts sounds into nerve impulses for the brain)
- eardrum
- outer ear
- middle ear
- inner ear

earache *noun* A pain inside the ear. **ear·ache** (**eer**-ake)

eardrum *noun* A thin piece of skin inside the ear that vibrates when sound hits it, which makes us able to hear. **ear·drum** (**eer**-druhm)

earlobe *noun* The soft, fleshy part at the bottom of your ear. **ear·lobe** (**eer**-lohb)

early
1. *adverb* At or near the beginning: *The package should get here early next week.*
2. *adjective* Before the usual time: *We are planning to have an early lunch.*
3. *adjective* Near the beginning of a period of time, as in *the early 1990s.*
ear·ly (**ur**-lee)
▷ *adjective* **earlier, earliest**

earmark
1. *verb* To decide that money will be used for a particular purpose: *The mayor earmarked $10,000 to rebuild the playground.* ▷ *verb* **earmarking, earmarked**
2. *noun* A quality that is typical of something and that helps you to identify it: *The story has a hero and all the other earmarks of an epic.*
3. *noun* An amount of money that has been set aside for a purpose, as in *an earmark for a hospital.*
ear·mark (**eer**-mahrk)

Word History

The term **earmark** dates from the 16th century in England. English farmers earmarked their animals by cutting a special sign on their ears to identify them in case the herd was stolen. Today, when you earmark something, you indicate how you want it to be used.

earmuffs *noun, plural* Thick pads attached to a band, which cover the ears to keep them warm in cold weather. **ear·muffs** (**eer**-muhfs)

earn *verb*
1. To get money by doing work: *Jade earns $5 an hour babysitting.* ▷ *noun* **earner**
2. To get something that you deserve: *She earns her good grades by studying hard.*
earn (urn)
Earn sounds like **urn**. ▷ *verb* **earning, earned**

earnest *adjective* Honest and serious: *The team made an earnest effort to get into the playoffs.* **ear·nest** (**ur**-nist) ▷ *adverb* **earnestly**

earnings *noun, plural* Money that is paid for work: *Her earnings from her new job are much better.* **earn·ings** (**ur**-ningz)

earphone *noun* Either of a pair of small speakers that are worn on or in the ears. **ear·phone** (**eer**-fohn)

earring *noun* A piece of jewelry worn on or through the ear: *The pirate wore gold earrings.* **ear·ring** (**eer**-ing)

earth *noun*
1. The planet that we live on. The earth is the third planet from the sun, between Venus and Mars. The name of the planet is sometimes capitalized.
2. Soil: *Be sure to water the earth after you plant the seeds.*
3. The ground: *The earth shook when the bomb went off.*
4. **down to earth** Realistic, practical, and easy to deal with: *He is surprisingly down to earth, considering how famous he is.* **earth** (urth)
▷ *adjective* **earthly**

earthen *adjective* Made of earth: *An earthen dam is made of solidly packed earth.* **earth·en** (**ur**-thuhn)

earthquake *noun* A sudden, violent shaking of the earth that may damage buildings and cause injuries. **earth·quake** (**urth**-kwayk)

earthworm *noun* A worm that lives in the ground and eats the nutrients in soil: *Earthworms do not have eyes or legs.* **earth·worm** (**urth**-wurm)

ease
1. *noun* Freedom from hard work, pain, or discomfort: *After she retired from her job, she led a life of ease.*
2. *noun* A state of feeling relaxed: *The friendly teacher put the new students at ease.*
3. *verb* To make something less difficult: *This medicine should ease your sore throat.*
4. *verb* To lessen, as in *to ease someone's pain.*
5. *verb* To move something slowly and carefully into a tight space, as in *to ease a car into a parking space.* **ease** (eez)
▷ *verb* **easing, eased**

easel *noun* A folding stand with a small shelf that can hold something up, such as a painting or sign. **ea·sel** (**ee**-zuhl)

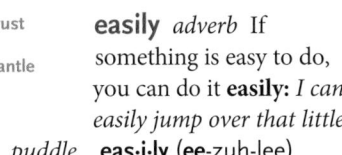

crust
mantle
outer core
inner core

the earth

Word History

The words *easel*, *sketch*, and *landscape* are painting terms that have come into English from the Netherlands, a country of great painters such as Rembrandt. **Easel** has its origins in the Dutch word *ezel*, which meant "donkey" and later also came to mean "easel," since the shape of an easel reminded people of a donkey. An easel holds up a painter's canvas, so it carries a load, like a donkey does.

easily *adverb* If something is easy to do, you can do it **easily**: *I can easily jump over that little puddle.* **eas·i·ly** (**ee**-zuh-lee)

east
1. *noun* One of the four main points of the compass: *The sun rises in the east.* ▷ *adverb* **east**
2. **East** *noun* Any area or region lying in this direction. ▷ *adjective* **Eastern**
3. **the East** *noun* In the United States, the states lying along the Atlantic coast.
4. **the East** *noun* A name sometimes used to mean the countries of Asia, such as Japan, China, and Korea.
5. *adjective* Having to do with or existing in the east, as in *the east side of town.* The adjective is capitalized if it is used to designate a specific place, as in *the East Coast.* ▷ *adjective* **eastern** **east** (eest)

Easter *noun* The holiday on which Christians celebrate that Jesus rose from the dead, according to Christian belief. **Eas·ter** (**ee**-stur)

Easter egg *noun* A hard-boiled egg that is colored or decorated, or a candy egg that looks like this.

Eastern Hemisphere *noun* The half of the world east of the Atlantic Ocean. It includes Europe, Africa, Asia, and Australia, and surrounding waters.

Eastern Orthodox *adjective* Belonging to or having to do with a group of churches that goes back to the beginning of Christianity.

eastward *adverb* To or toward the east: *The morning sun shone in our faces as we drove eastward.* **east·ward** (**eest**-wurd) ▷ *adjective* **eastward**

easy *adjective*
1. Not requiring much effort, ability, or training: *This game is easy to play.* ▷ *noun* **easiness**
2. Not stressful or difficult, as in *an easy life.*
3. Not strict or hard to please, as in *an easy teacher.* **eas·y** (**ee**-zee)
▷ *adjective* **easier, easiest**

eat *verb*
1. To put food in your mouth, then chew and swallow it: *Ben eats a lot of junk food.*
2. To have a meal: *Tonight, we are going to eat dinner early.*
3. **eat away** To destroy slowly: *The waves are eating away the sand dunes.*
4. **eat up** To use all of something: *The videos eat up a lot of memory on my computer.* **eat** (eet)
▷ *verb* **eating, ate** (ayt), **eaten** (**ee**-tin)

a b c d **e** f g h i j k l m n o p q r s t u v w x y z

eaves *noun, plural* The edges of a roof that hang over the side of a building. **eaves** (eevz)

eavesdrop *verb* To listen to a conversation secretly: *Don't eavesdrop on your sister while she's on the phone.* **eaves·drop** (**eevz**-*drahp*) ▷ *verb* **eavesdropping, eavesdropped** ▷ *noun* **eavesdropper**

Word History

Long ago in England, a house could not legally be closer than two feet from the edge of the property, because the edges of the roof, called *eaves*, dripped rainwater that could damage a neighbor's land. The area where the water dripped was known as an *eavesdrip*, and someone standing there was close enough to hear the conversations inside the house. A small change in the word, from *-drip* to *-drop*, led to the verb **eavesdrop**, meaning to listen in secret to a private conversation.

ebb *verb*
1. When the tide **ebbs**, it goes down and back out to sea. ▷ *noun* **ebb**
2. To fade or to get weaker: *Her energy started to ebb halfway through the race.*
ebb (eb)
▷ *verb* **ebbing, ebbed**

ebony *noun*
1. A very hard, black wood, or the African tree that it comes from: *The black piano keys are made of ebony.*
2. A deep black color.
eb·on·y (**eb**-uh-nee)
▷ *adjective* **ebony**

e-book *noun* An electronic book that can be read on a computer or on a special device. **e-book** (**ee**-*buk*)

eccentric
1. *adjective* Unusual or strange, but in a harmless or amusing way: *The eccentric millionaire left his entire fortune to his dog.* ▷ *adverb* **eccentrically**
2. *noun* Someone with strange or unusual habits: *In the movie, he plays an eccentric who lives in an attic and keeps a pet raccoon.*
ec·cen·tric (ek-**sen**-trik)

echinoderm *noun* A sea creature that has five similar body parts and rough or pointy skin, such as a starfish or sea urchin. **e·chi·no·derm** (i-**kye**-nuh-*durm*)

echo *verb*
1. When a sound **echoes**, it repeats because sound waves bounce back from a hard surface: *The announcer's voice echoed through the stadium.*
2. When you **echo** what another person says, you repeat what he or she said, sometimes to show that

echinoderm: starfish

you agree: *The captain of the team echoed the coach's instructions.*
ech·o (**ek**-oh)
▷ *verb* **echoes, echoing, echoed** ▷ *noun* **echo**

eclectic *adjective* Having or showing a wide variety: *New York City has an eclectic mix of restaurants.* **e·clec·tic** (i-**klek**-tik)

eclipse
1. **eclipse of the moon** *noun* A time when the earth comes between the sun and the moon so that all or part of the moon's light is blocked.
2. **eclipse of the sun** *noun* A time when the moon comes between the sun and the earth so that all or part of the sun's light is blocked.
3. *verb* To become better, more well-known, or more important than someone else: *He eclipsed everyone else in the film with his moving performance.* ▷ *verb* **eclipsing, eclipsed**
e·clipse (i-**klips**)

eco-friendly *adjective* Not harmful to the environment; nonpolluting: *I'd rather buy products that have eco-friendly packaging.* **e·co-friend·ly** (**ee**-koh-*frend*-lee *or* **ek**-oh-*frend*-lee)

ecology *noun* The scientific study of the relationships between living things and their environment. **e·col·o·gy** (i-**kah**-luh-jee) ▷ *noun* **ecologist** ▷ *adjective* **ecological** (ee-kuh-**lah**-ji-kuhl) ▷ *adverb* **ecologically**

e-commerce *noun* The activity of buying and selling on the internet: *E-commerce is changing the way people shop.* **e-com·merce** (**ee**-*kah*-murs)

economic *adjective* Of or having to do with economics or the economy: *The economic forecast is good.* **e·co·nom·ic** (ee-kuh-**nah**-mik *or* ek-uh-**nah**-mik)

economical *adjective* Not wasteful or expensive: *We are installing an economical heating system to lower our gas bill.* **e·co·nom·i·cal** (ee-kuh-**nah**-mi-kuhl *or* ek-uh-**nah**-mi-kuhl) ▷ *adverb* **economically**

economics *noun* The study of the way that money, resources, and services are used in a society. **e·co·nom·ics** (*ee*-kuh-**nah**-miks or *ek*-uh-**nah**-miks)

economist *noun* A person who is trained in economics: *The bank employed two economists to provide them with forecasts.* **e·con·o·mist** (i-**kah**-nuh-mist)

economize *verb* To cut down on spending in order to save money: *We had to economize after Mom lost her job.* **e·con·o·mize** (i-**kah**-nuh-*mize*)
▷ *verb* **economizing, economized**

economy *noun*
1. The system of buying, selling, making things, and managing money in a place: *The governor has a plan to improve the state's troubled economy.*
2. The careful use of money and other things to cut down on waste, as in *to practice economy.* **e·con·o·my** (i-**kah**-nuh-mee)
▷ *noun, plural* **economies**

ecosystem *noun* All the living things in a place and their relation to their environment: *The ocean's ecosystem includes fish, marine birds and mammals, and plants such as kelp.* **e·co·sys·tem** (*ee*-koh-*sis*-tuhm or **ek**-oh-*sis*-tuhm)

ecstasy *noun* A feeling of great joy. **ec·sta·sy** (**ek**-stuh-see) ▷ *noun, plural* **ecstasies**

ecstatic *adjective* Feeling or expressing extreme joy: *Meryl was ecstatic about going on vacation.* **ec·stat·ic** (ek-**stat**-ik) ▷ *adverb* **ecstatically**

eczema *noun* A medical condition that makes the skin dry, rough, and itchy. **ec·ze·ma** (**ek**-suh-muh or eg-**zee**-muh)

Suffix

The suffix **-ed** makes one of these changes to a root word:
1. Forms the past tense and past participle of regular verbs, as in *shouted, sprinted, planted.*
2. Turns a noun into an adjective, as in *talented, bearded.*

eddy *noun* A current in water or air that makes it move in a circle. **ed·dy** (**ed**-ee) ▷ *noun, plural* **eddies** ▷ *verb* **eddy** ▷ *adjective* **eddying**

edge
1. *noun* The part of an object or area that is farthest from the center: *Push your glass away from the edge of the table.*
2. *verb* To move very carefully and slowly: *She edged away from the barking dog.* ▷ *verb* **edging, edged**
3. *noun* The sharp side of a cutting tool, as in *the knife's edge.*
4. *noun* An advantage: *Fast runners will have an edge in this race.*

eddy

5. If you are **on edge**, you feel anxious. ▷ *adjective* **edgy**
edge (ej)

edgewise *adverb*
1. With the edge first: *The mail carrier slid the magazine edgewise through the slot.*
2. If you cannot **get a word in edgewise** in a discussion, you do not get a chance to speak because others are talking a lot.
edge·wise (**ej**-*wize*)

edible *adjective* Able to be eaten: *Check to make sure this berry is edible.* **ed·i·ble** (**ed**-uh-buhl)

edit *verb*
1. To correct a piece of writing and shorten it if it is too long: *Chris had to edit the story before it could be printed.*
2. To prepare video or film for viewing: *Marcus edited all the tapes into a one-hour show.*
ed·it (**ed**-it)
▷ *verb* **editing, edited**

edition *noun*
1. The form or version of a book or newspaper that is printed at a particular time, as in *a hardcover edition.*
2. The number of copies of a newspaper, book, or magazine that are printed at the same time.
e·di·tion (i-**dish**-uhn)

editor *noun*
1. Someone whose job is to edit writing before it is published, and sometimes to choose which books will be published.
2. The person who is in charge of a newspaper or a magazine.
3. A computer program for editing documents. *See* **text editor**.
ed·i·tor (**ed**-i-tur)

editorial

1. *adjective* Of or having to do with putting together a publication, as in *an editorial assistant.*

2. *noun* An article that gives the opinion of the writer or of a newspaper, rather than just reporting facts in the news: *The paper published an editorial today criticizing the governor's speech.*
ed·i·to·ri·al (*ed*-i-**tor**-ee-uhl)

educate *verb*

1. To give someone knowledge or a skill through teaching: *The workshops educate teenagers about the dangers of drug use.*

2. To arrange for someone's education: *My parents want me to be educated at a private school.*
ed·u·cate (**ej**-uh-*kate*)
▷ *verb* **educating, educated** ▷ *noun* **educator**

educated *adjective* Having finished a course of education, especially at a high school, college, or another place of higher learning: *She has a diploma from the University of Maryland and is the most educated member of her family.* **ed·u·cat·ed** (**ej**-uh-*kay*-tid)

education *noun*

1. The process of teaching and learning.

2. The knowledge, skills, and abilities that you learn from school, college, or some other experience: *At camp I received an education in outdoor survival skills.*
ed·u·ca·tion (*ej*-uh-**kay**-shuhn)

educational *adjective*

1. Of or having to do with education, as in *educational objectives.*

2. Providing an education: *I thought our class trip to Washington, DC, was very educational—we learned a lot about the government.*
ed·u·ca·tion·al (*ej*-uh-**kay**-shuh-nuhl)

eel *noun* A long, slippery, snakelike fish. **eel** (eel)

eerie *adjective* Strange and spooky, as in *an eerie sound.* **ee·rie** (**eer**-ee) ▷ *adjective* **eerier, eeriest** ▷ *adverb* **eerily**

eel

Word History

The word **eerie** has switched directions: It used to describe people who were "fearful," but now it has to do with something so "strange" that it scares people. You can see the old meaning of *eerie*, "afraid," in this sentence written in the 1800s: "The watchdog's howling makes the nightly wanderer eerie." The word *eerie* has its origins in the old word *argh,* which could mean either "fearful" or "lazy."

effect

1. *noun* Something that happens because of something else; a result: *What are the environmental effects of acid rain?*

2. *noun* Influence or power to make something happen: *The praise she gave her puppy had a great effect on its behavior.*

3. *noun* When something **goes into effect**, it starts to happen: *The new tax laws go into effect today.*

4. *verb* To cause or bring about, as in *to effect a change.* ▷ *verb* **effecting, effected**
ef·fect (i-**fekt**)

effective *adjective*

1. Having the intended effect: *She took some aspirin for her headache, but it wasn't very effective.*

2. Skillful and able to get things done: *James is an effective manager who always helps his team meet project deadlines.*

3. In force: *The law becomes effective next week.*
ef·fec·tive (i-**fek**-tiv)

effectively *adverb*

1. In a way that produces a good result: *My dog has arthritis, and I'm trying to find out if there are ways to treat it effectively.*

2. For all practical purposes; in effect: *The trade sanctions imposed on the country effectively ended its ability to market its goods abroad.*
ef·fec·tive·ly (i-**fek**-tiv-lee)

effectiveness *noun* The quality or state of being effective: *The trial studied the effectiveness of several popular diet plans.* **ef·fec·tive·ness** (i-**fek**-tiv-nis)

effeminate *adjective* Behaving, looking, or talking like a woman. This word applies to men and is considered insulting. **ef·fem·i·nate** (i-**fem**-uh-nit)

effervescent *adjective*

1. Full of bubbles, as in *an effervescent drink.*

2. Very lively and cheerful: *People are attracted to his warm smile and effervescent personality.*
ef·fer·ves·cent (*ef*-ur-**ves**-uhnt)
▷ *noun* **effervescence**

efficiency *noun*

1. The quality of working or operating well, quickly, and without waste: *Our new car runs on less gas and has better energy efficiency.*

2. An **efficiency** or **efficiency apartment** is an apartment of only one room where the occupant lives, eats, and sleeps.
ef·fi·cien·cy (i-**fish**-uhn-see)
▷ *noun, plural* **efficiencies**

efficient *adjective* Working very well and not wasting time or energy: *We need to find a more efficient way to communicate with all the students at once.* **ef·fi·cient**

(i-**fish**-uhnt) ▷ *adverb* **efficiently**

effort *noun* The activity of trying hard to achieve something: *He really needs to make an effort to get better grades.* **ef·fort** (**ef**-urt)

effortless *adjective* Something that is **effortless** is easy to do: *He walked with a smooth, effortless stride.* **ef·fort·less** (**ef**-urt-lis) ▷ *adverb* **effortlessly**

e.g. The initials of the Latin phrase *exempli gratia*, which means "for example." **e.g.** (**ee jee**)

egg
1. *noun* An oval or round object that contains a baby bird, reptile, fish, or insect. It is produced by the females of these species to protect their young as they develop: *An egg can be covered by either a shell or a membrane.*
2. *noun* A chicken's egg, used as food: *Could you pick up a dozen eggs on the way home?*
3. *noun* A cell created inside the female body that grows into a new individual if it is fertilized.
4. *verb* To urge or challenge someone to do something. ▷ *verb* **egging, egged**
egg (eg)

eggnog *noun* A sweet, thick drink made with eggs and milk, usually flavored with nutmeg. **egg·nog** (**eg**-*nahg*)

eggplant *noun* A purple vegetable with white flesh and tiny seeds inside. **egg·plant** (**eg**-*plant*)

ego *noun*
1. The sense of yourself as a person separate from others.
2. A sense of self-importance: *The mayor sure has a big ego—he tried to name the new park after himself.*
e·go (**ee**-goh)

egocentric *adjective* Being a lot more interested in yourself than you are in others. **e·go·cen·tric** (*ee*-goh-**sen**-trik) ▷ *noun* **egocentricity** (*ee*-goh-sen-**tris**-i-tee)

egret *noun* A tall white bird with long legs that lives near water. **e·gret** (**ee**-grit)

Egyptian
1. *noun* A person who lived in ancient Egypt.
2. *noun* A person who was born or is living in modern Egypt.
3. *adjective* Of or having to do with the people or culture of ancient or modern Egypt, as in *the Egyptian pharaohs.*
E·gyp·tian (i-**jip**-shuhn)

eider *noun* A large, northern sea duck. The males are mainly black and white, and the females are brown: *A female eider duck has very soft down, which she plucks to line her nest.* **ei·der** (**eye**-dur)

either
1. *conjunction* **Either** can be used to indicate a choice:

He can either stay here or go home.
2. *pronoun* One of two: *You can take either the train or the bus.*
3. *adverb* Also, or similarly: *I'm not going to the party either.*
4. *adjective* One or the other of two, as in *either glove.*
5. *adjective* Each of two: *Maya and Sam sat on either side of the car.*
ei·ther (**ee**-THur or **eye**-THur)

eject *verb*
1. To push or force something out: *To eject the CD, push this button.*
2. To force someone to leave: *The coach ejected him from the team for always being late.*
3. To leave the cockpit of a fighter plane quickly, using a special mechanism: *The fighter pilot ejected from the plane before it crashed.*
e·ject (i-**jekt**)
▷ *verb* **ejecting, ejected**

eke *verb* To barely manage to do something: *They eked out a living by selling vegetables at the roadside.* **eke** (eek) ▷ *verb* **eking, eked**

elaborate
1. (i-**lab**-ur-it) *adjective* Complex and detailed, as in *an elaborate plan.* ▷ *adverb* **elaborately**
2. (i-**lab**-uh-*rate*) *verb* To give more details about something: *The professor elaborated on his ideas about evolution.* ▷ *verb* **elaborating, elaborated**
e·lab·o·rate

elapse *verb* To pass, usually used in reference to time: *Many years had elapsed since he last saw her.* **e·lapse** (i-**laps**) ▷ *verb* **elapsing, elapsed**

elastic
1. *noun* A type of rubber that returns to its original shape after you stretch it.
2. *adjective* Able to stretch and then return to its original shape: *I prefer pants with an elastic waist.*
e·las·tic (i-**las**-tik)
▷ *noun* **elasticity** (i-las-**tis**-i-tee)

elated *adjective* Very excited and happy: *Julia was elated about her promotion.* **e·lat·ed** (i-**lay**-tid)
▷ *noun* **elation**

elbow *noun* The joint that connects the upper arm to the lower arm. **el·bow** (**el**-boh)

elder
1. *adjective* Older: *Grandma had two elder brothers.*
2. *noun* An old person, especially one who is respected or is an authority: *The tribal elders suggested a different solution to the problem.*
3. *noun* When a father and son share the same name and both of them are well-known, the father is often called **the Elder**.
eld·er (**el**-dur)

eggplant

elderly

1. *adjective* Old. The word *elderly* is usually considered a polite way of saying "old": *An elderly man won the dance contest.*

2. *noun* Old people in general; senior citizens: *Caring for China's elderly will become more and more expensive as their numbers increase.*

eld·er·ly (**el**-dur-lee)

eldest *adjective* The oldest in a group, as in *my eldest son.* **eld·est** (**el**-dist)

elect *verb* To choose someone by voting for him or her: *They elected the governor for a second term.* **e·lect** (i-**lekt**) ▷ *verb* **electing, elected**

election *noun* The act or process of choosing someone or deciding something by voting: *She won the election by only 15 votes.* **e·lec·tion** (i-**lek**-shuhn)

elective *adjective* If something is **elective**, you are free to choose whether or not to do it. For example, an elective class is a class that you are not required to take in order to complete your grade. **e·lec·tive** (i-**lek**-tiv) ▷ *noun* **elective**

electric *adjective*

1. Supplied by or having to do with electricity, as in *an electric heater.* ▷ *adjective* **electrical**

2. Extremely exciting and stimulating: *The music was so rousing that there was an electric atmosphere in the concert hall.*

e·lec·tric (i-**lek**-trik)

electric eel *noun* A long, snakelike fish that can give off electric shocks to protect itself and stun its prey.

electrician *noun* Someone who installs electrical systems and fixes electrical equipment. **e·lec·tri·cian** (i-lek-**trish**-uhn)

electricity *noun*

1. A form of energy caused by the motion of electrons and protons.

2. Electrical power that is generated in special, large

Word History

In ancient times, a Greek philosopher named Thales noticed that rubbing amber—a dark yellow substance from pine trees—caused it to attract other materials such as bits of straw or splinters of wood. In the 16th century, the English scientist William Gilbert experimented with amber, too. When he wrote about his experiments, he used the word **electricity** to describe what was happening. The root of *electricity* is the Latin word *electrum*, which came from the Greek word *elektron*, meaning "amber." The root lives on in the words *electron, electronic,* and many other English words beginning with the prefix *electro-*.

plants and distributed to all parts of a country through wires.

e·lec·tric·i·ty (i-lek-**tris**-i-tee)

electrocute *verb* To injure or kill with a severe electric shock. **e·lec·tro·cute** (i-lek-truh-*kyoot*) ▷ *verb* **electrocuting, electrocuted** ▷ *noun* **electrocution**

electrode *noun* A point through which an electric current can flow into or out of a device or substance. **e·lec·trode** (i-**lek**-trode)

electrolyte *noun* A substance that electricity can travel through. **e·lec·tro·lyte** (i-**lek**-truh-*lite*)

electromagnet *noun* A magnet that is formed when electricity flows through a coil of wire. **e·lec·tro·mag·net** (i-*lek*-troh-**mag**-nit) ▷ *adjective* **electromagnetic**

electron *noun* A tiny particle that moves around the nucleus of an atom. Electrons carry a negative electrical charge. **e·lec·tron** (i-**lek**-trahn)

electronic *adjective* Powered or achieved by very small amounts of electricity: *The city has set up electronic voting machines for the election.* **e·lec·tron·ic** (i-lek-**trah**-nik) ▷ *adverb* **electronically**

electronics *noun*

1. The scientific study of the behavior of electrons.

2. Electronic equipment: *Sales of household electronics are way up this year.*

e·lec·tron·ics (i-lek-**trah**-niks)

elegance *noun* The quality of being graceful or stylish in appearance or manner: *The elegance of their mountain cabin surprised us, as we were expecting it to be rustic.* **el·e·gance** (**el**-uh-guhns)

elegant *adjective* Graceful and pleasing to look at, as in *an elegant dinner party.* **el·e·gant** (**el**-uh-guhnt) ▷ *adverb* **elegantly**

elegy *noun* A poem or speech in memory of someone who has died. An elegy is often reflective and sad. **el·e·gy** (**el**-uh-jee) ▷ *noun, plural* **elegies**

element *noun*

1. One of the simple, basic parts of something: *Good computer skills are an important element of the job.*

2. A substance that cannot be divided up into simpler substances: *Hydrogen is the lightest and simplest element.*

3. the elements *noun, plural* The weather: *A tent will help protect you from the elements.*

el·e·ment (**el**-uh-muhnt)

elementary *adjective* Simple or basic, but still important, as in *elementary algebra.* **el·e·men·ta·ry** (el-uh-**men**-tur-ee)

elementary school *noun* A school that children attend, usually from kindergarten through fifth or sixth grade.

elephant *noun* A large, gray animal with a long trunk and ivory tusks. Elephants are mammals and are native to Africa or Asia. **el·e·phant** (**el**-uh-fuhnt)

elevate *verb*
1. To raise something up: *The doctor told her to rest and elevate her sprained ankle.*
2. To give someone a more important position: *Frank was elevated to manager last week.* **el·e·vate** (el-uh-*vate*)
▷ *verb* **elevating, elevated** ▷ *adjective* **elevated**

elevation *noun*
1. A place that is higher than the surrounding land.
2. A move to a more important position: *We congratulated Deena on her elevation to head chef.*
3. The height above sea level: *The elevation of this hill is 400 feet.* **el·e·va·tion** (*el*-uh-**vay**-shuhn)

Elephants

There are two species of elephant: African and Asian (also known as Indian). Elephants are the largest land animals in the world, and they can eat hundreds of pounds of plant material each day. The elephant uses its long trunk for breathing, smelling, feeding, drinking, lifting, and trumpeting. Its tusks are extremely long ivory teeth that grow throughout its life. Females and calves live in herds led by an older female. Adult males visit these herds but live separately.

African elephant

Asian elephant

elevator *noun*
1. A large box that carries people or things up and down between different floors of a building.
2. A very large, hollow building used for storing crops after they are harvested, as in *a grain elevator.* **el·e·va·tor** (el-uh-*vay*-tur)

elf *noun* A small, imaginary person with pointed ears and magical powers. Elves are usually mischievous characters in fairy tales. **elf** (elf) ▷ *noun, plural* **elves** (elvz) ▷ *adjective* **elfin** (el-fin)

eligible *adjective*
1. Having the right abilities or qualifications for something: *She will be eligible to vote at 18.*
2. Suitable for someone to marry, as in *an eligible bachelor.* **el·i·gi·ble** (el-i-juh-buhl)
▷ *noun* **eligibility**

eliminate *verb*
1. To leave out, or to get rid of, as in *to eliminate a problem.*
2. To remove from a competition by a defeat: *Our team was eliminated from the playoffs.* **e·lim·i·nate** (i-**lim**-uh-*nate*)
▷ *verb* **eliminating, eliminated** ▷ *noun* **elimination**

elite
1. *noun* A group of people who have more advantages and privileges than other people.
2. *adjective* Designed for very rich or important people, or made up of them: *She attended an elite private school in New England.* **e·lite** (i-**leet** *or* ay-**leet**)
▷ *noun* **elitism**

elixir *noun*
1. In alchemy, a substance that was thought to be able to change metals into gold or extend life forever.
2. A potion believed to bring about a magical or mysterious result.
3. A medical potion with the ability to cure.
4. Something that is considered able to cure everything. Also known as a **cure-all:** *Money makes life easier, but it isn't an elixir that solves all problems.* **e·lix·ir** (i-**lik**-sur)

elk *noun* A type of large deer that lives in the Rocky Mountains and in parts of Asia. **elk** (elk)

ellipse *noun* A flat oval shape. **el·lipse** (i-**lips**) ▷ *adjective* **elliptical** (i-**lip**-ti-kuhl)

elm *noun* A tall shade tree with spreading branches, or the wood that comes from it. **elm** (elm)

El Niño *noun* Warm water temperatures, currents, and wind conditions in the Pacific Ocean that affect weather conditions over much of the earth: *An El Niño can bring additional rain to parts of North and South America, but drought to Indonesia, Australia, and parts of Africa.* **El Ni·ño** (el **neen**-yoh)

Word History

El Niño is Spanish for "the Child." This name refers to the infant Jesus, because El Niño weather conditions usually occur around Christmas.

elongate *verb* To make something longer or more stretched out. **e·lon·gate** (i-**lawng**-gate) ▷ *verb* **elongating, elongated**

elope *verb* To run away and get married secretly. **e·lope** (i-**lope**) ▷ *verb* **eloping, eloped** ▷ *noun* **elopement**

eloquent *adjective* Using language in a graceful way that persuades people: *Her eloquent speech resulted in large donations to the charity.* **el·o·quent** (**el**-uh-kwuhnt) ▷ *noun* **eloquence** ▷ *adverb* **eloquently**

else *adverb*
1. Another, or a different place, person, or thing: *I may travel to Oregon, or I could decide to go somewhere else.*
2. More: *After serving me dessert, the waiter asked me if I wanted anything else.*
else (els)

elsewhere *adverb* Somewhere different: *After Nino's Restaurant closed, we had to go elsewhere for pizza.* **else·where** (**els**-wair)

elude *verb* To escape or get away from someone: *The criminals eluded the police for weeks before getting caught.* **e·lude** (i-**lood**) ▷ *verb* **eluding, eluded**

elusive *adjective*
1. Very hard to find or capture: *Very few photos exist of the elusive giant squid.*
2. Difficult to understand: *Most people find black holes a rather elusive concept.*
e·lu·sive (i-**loo**-siv)
▷ *noun* **elusiveness** ▷ *adverb* **elusively**

elves *noun, plural* The plural of **elf**. **elves** (elvz)

email *or* **e-mail**
1. Electronic messages that are sent through a computer network or over the internet. Short for *electronic mail.*
2. A single message sent in this way: *I got an email from her yesterday.*
e·mail *or* **e-mail** (**ee**-mayl)
▷ *verb* **email** ▷ *adjective* **email**

address line
additional addresses
subject line
message area

email

emancipate *verb* To free a person or group from slavery or control: *American slaves were emancipated in 1862.* **e·man·ci·pate** (i-**man**-suh-pate) ▷ *verb* **emancipating, emancipated** ▷ *noun* **emancipation**

embalm *verb* To treat a dead body with substances that will keep it from decaying for a long time: *Scientists still study the methods that ancient Egyptians used to embalm bodies.* **em·balm** (em-**bahm**) ▷ *verb* **embalming, embalmed**

embankment *noun*
1. A high wall at the sides of a river that keeps it from flooding.
2. A long piece of raised earth built to support railroad tracks or a road.
em·bank·ment (em-**bangk**-muhnt)

embargo
1. *noun* An official order that forbids something from happening, as in *a trade embargo.* ▷ *noun, plural* **embargoes**
2. *verb* To forbid that a particular thing be imported or exported: *China temporarily embargoed grain shipments from the United States.* ▷ *verb* **embargoes, embargoing, embargoed**
em·bar·go (em-**bahr**-goh)

Word History

The word **embargo** is from the days when the main way of traveling the world was by ship. During a war between two countries, there would be an embargo on ships from one country leaving or entering ports of the other country. The Spanish word *embargo* goes back to words meaning "bar" and "in," because people imagined that "bars" were keeping ships "inside" a port by blocking their way out.

embark *verb*
1. To get on a ship or an airplane that is ready to travel.

2. To start something that is new or difficult: *My grandmother is embarking on a huge new puzzle.* **em·bark** (em-**bahrk**) ▷ *verb* **embarking, embarked**

embarrass *verb* To make someone feel ashamed and uncomfortable: *Terrence's rudeness to the hotel clerk embarrassed his wife.* **em·bar·rass** (em-**bar**-uhs) ▷ *verb* **embarrasses, embarrassing, embarrassed** ▷ *adjective* **embarrassing** ▷ *adjective* **embarrassed**

embarrassment *noun*
1. The feeling of being ashamed: *The scandal has caused the star athlete a lot of embarrassment.*
2. Someone or something that causes people to feel ashamed: *This movie is so bad that it's an embarrassment to everyone involved in making it.* **em·bar·rass·ment** (em-**bar**-uhs-muhnt)

embassy *noun* The official place in a foreign country where an ambassador works: *The US Embassy in France is in Paris.* **em·bas·sy** (**em**-buh-see) ▷ *noun, plural* **embassies**

embed *verb* To **embed** something is to put it inside something else so that it cannot be easily removed: *The splinter was embedded deep in his finger.* **em·bed** (em-**bed**) ▷ *verb* **embedding, embedded**

embers *noun, plural* The hot, glowing pieces of a fire after the flames are gone. **em·bers** (**em**-burz)

embezzle *verb* To secretly steal money from the place you work for: *She was arrested for embezzling nearly half a million dollars from her company.* **em·bez·zle** (em-**bez**-uhl) ▷ *verb* **embezzling, embezzled** ▷ *noun* **embezzler** ▷ *noun* **embezzlement**

emblem *noun* A symbol or a sign that represents something: *The bald eagle is an emblem of the United States.* **em·blem** (**em**-bluhm)

embody *verb* To give a solid form to an idea or feeling: *The new arts museum embodied the town's hopes of attracting more tourists.* **em·bod·y** (em-**bah**-dee) ▷ *verb* **embodying, embodied**

emboss *verb* To create raised lettering or designs on a flat surface: *The stationery was embossed with the hotel's name.* **em·boss** (em-**baws**) ▷ *verb* **embosses, embossing, embossed**

embrace *verb*
1. To hug: *We embraced before he left.* ▷ *noun* **embrace**
2. To start doing something eagerly, or to think of something in a very positive way: *Alicia embraced the chance to do volunteer work.*

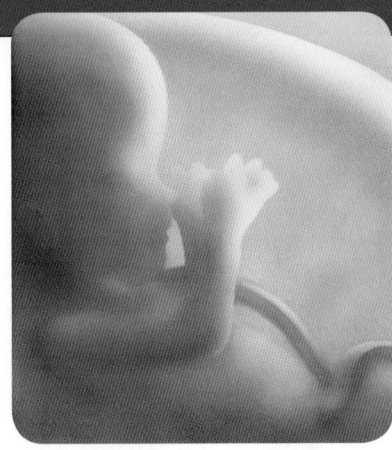

human embryo

3. To include: *The book embraces different points of view.* **em·brace** (em-**brase**) ▷ *verb* **embracing, embraced**

embroider *verb* To sew a picture or a design onto cloth, using different colors of thread or yarn. **em·broi·der** (em-**broi**-dur) ▷ *verb* **embroidering, embroidered** ▷ *noun* **embroiderer** ▷ *noun* **embroidery**

embryo *noun* A baby, animal, or plant in the very early stages of development before birth. **em·bry·o** (**em**-bree-*oh*) ▷ *noun, plural* **embryos**

embryonic *adjective* Made from or using embryos, as in *embryonic stem cell research.* **em·bry·on·ic** (em-bree-**ah**-nik)

emerald
1. *noun* A bright green gem, as in *an emerald ring.*
2. *noun* A bright green color.
3. *adjective* Being bright green in color. **em·er·ald** (**em**-ur-uhld)

emerge *verb*
1. To come out from a place where you are hidden: *Several deer emerged from the edge of the forest.*
2. To become apparent or publicly known: *During the trial, new evidence emerged that cleared the defendant.* **e·merge** (i-**murj**) ▷ *verb* **emerging, emerged** ▷ *noun* **emergence**

emergency *noun* A sudden and dangerous situation that requires immediate action. **e·mer·gen·cy** (i-**mur**-juhn-see) ▷ *noun, plural* **emergencies**

emigrate *verb* To leave your home country to live in another country, as in *to emigrate for economic opportunities.* **em·i·grate** (**em**-i-*grate*) ▷ *verb* **emigrating, emigrated** ▷ *noun* **emigrant** (**em**-i-gruhnt) ▷ *noun* **emigration**

eminent *adjective* Well-known and highly respected, as in *an eminent scientist.* **em·i·nent** (**em**-uh-nuhnt) ▷ *noun* **eminence** ▷ *adverb* **eminently**

emissary *noun* An **emissary** is a person who is sent to do a special job as a representative for someone: *The government sent an emissary to attend the peace talks.* **em·is·sar·y** (**em**-i-ser-ee) ▷ *noun, plural* **emissaries**

emission *noun*
1. The release of something, especially chemicals, into the atmosphere.
2. emissions *noun, plural* Substances released into the atmosphere. **e·mis·sion** (i-**mish**-uhn)

a
b
c
d
e
f
g
h
i
j
k
l
m
n
o
p
q
r
s
t
u
v
w
x
y
z

emit *verb* To produce or send out something such as heat, light, signals, or sound: *The volcano emitted gases and smoke into the air.* **e·mit** (i-**mit**)
▷ *verb* **emitting, emitted**

emoji *noun* A small picture or symbol that can be used in place of words to express a word, feeling, or idea: *He only used emoji in his text, but I think he said he won first prize.* **e·mo·ji** (i-**moh**-jee) ▷ *noun, plural* **emoji** or **emojis**

Word History

Emoji is a Japanese word formed from the words *e* for "picture" and *moji* for "letter" or "character." Japanese speakers in the early 1900s may have devised the word to be similar to the English word *pictograph,* a picture used as a symbol. English speakers in the late 20th century then borrowed the Japanese word with the modern meaning of pictures used in electronic communication. Even though the word *emoji* looks similar to *emoticon,* the two words were formed separately.

emoticon *noun* A small image of a face expressing some emotion, that you type in email and texting to communicate a feeling or attitude, like :-) or :-(. Computers sometimes turn these characters into faces or other images. **e·mo·ti·con** (i-**moh**-ti-*kahn*)

emotion *noun* A feeling, such as happiness, love, or anger: *She had mixed emotions about her parents' divorce.* **e·mo·tion** (i-**moh**-shuhn)

emotional *adjective*
1. Of or having to do with your feelings, as in *emotional issues.*
2. Showing or expressing strong feelings: *Paul made an emotional speech at the funeral.*
e·mo·tion·al (i-**moh**-shuh-nuhl)
▷ *adverb* **emotionally**

emperor *noun* The male ruler of an empire.
em·per·or (**em**-pur-ur)

emphasis *noun* Importance given to something: *I'd like you to put a greater emphasis on your schoolwork this year.* **em·pha·sis** (**em**-fuh-sis)
▷ *noun, plural* **emphases** (**em**-fuh-*seez*)

emphasize *verb* To make something stand out or draw attention to it because you think it is important or true: *The coach emphasized the importance of arriving on time to practice.*
em·pha·size (**em**-fuh-*size*) ▷ *verb* **emphasizing, emphasized**

emphatic *adjective* Forceful and strong so that people pay attention: *Mrs. Brown was emphatic that the rules should be followed.* **em·phat·ic** (em-**fat**-ik)

Roman emperor Constantine the Great

empire *noun*
1. A group of countries or states that have the same ruler, as in *the Roman Empire.*
2. A country that is ruled over by an emperor or empress: *Puyi became the last emperor of the Chinese empire in 1908.*
3. A large group of companies that is controlled by one person or organization, as in *a software empire.*
em·pire (**em**-pire)

empirical *adjective* Based on experience and on things that you can test using experiments: *What is the empirical evidence for the safety of this device?* **em·pir·i·cal** (em-**peer**-i-kuhl)

employ *verb*
1. To pay someone to do work: *The shoe factory on the edge of town employs about 40 people.*
2. To use something: *Potters employ several different techniques to produce glazes.*
em·ploy (em-**ploi**)
▷ *verb* **employing, employed**

employed *adjective* Having a job: *As the economy improved, jobs became more plentiful, and the number of employed people rose.* **em·ployed** (em-**ploid**)

employee *noun* A person who is paid to work for another person or business: *How many employees does the restaurant have?* **em·ploy·ee** (em-**ploi**-ee)

employer *noun* A person or company that employs people: *His employer owns several restaurants.*
em·ploy·er (em-**ploy**-ur)

employment *noun*
1. The work someone does for salary or wages: *She graduated from college and is now seeking employment.*
2. The condition of having a job or providing a job: *The tire factory is the biggest source of employment in our town.*
em·ploy·ment (em-**ploy**-munt)

empower *verb* To give someone power, authority, or ability that they did not have before: *The new program empowers women in poor countries to start their own businesses.* **em·pow·er** (em-**pou**-ur) ▷ *verb* **empowering, empowered**

empress *noun* The female ruler of an empire, or the wife of an emperor. **em·press** (**em**-pris)

empty

1. *adjective* With nothing inside, as in *an empty gas tank.*

2. *adjective* Not being used or enjoyed by people: *The house has been empty for ten years.*

3. *verb* To take everything out of a container: *Eva emptied her pockets onto the table.* ▷ *verb* **empties, emptying, emptied**

4. *noun* An empty bottle or can: *Toss the empties into the recycling bin.* ▷ *noun, plural* **empties**

5. *adjective* Without meaning or value, as in *an empty threat.*

emp·ty (**emp**-tee)

▷ *adjective* **emptier, emptiest** ▷ *noun* **emptiness**

emu *noun* A large bird from Australia that does not fly but can run very fast. **e·mu** (**ee**-myoo)

emulate *verb*

1. To try to be like someone or something you admire: *He tried to emulate his big brother's confident way of speaking.*

2. When a computer program **emulates** another, it acts in the same way.

em·u·late (**em**-yuh-*layt*)

▷ *verb* **emulating, emulated**

▷ *noun* **emulation**

(em-yuh-**lay**-shuhn)

emulsion *noun* A mixture of two liquids in which the particles of one liquid mix with the other liquid but do not dissolve. This occurs, for example, when mixing oil and vinegar. **e·mul·sion** (i-**muhl**-shuhn)

enable *verb* To allow or make it possible for someone to do something: *Microscopes enable us to see tiny things, such as cells.* **en·a·ble** (en-**ay**-buhl) ▷ *verb* **enabling, enabled** ▷ *noun* **enabler**

enamel *noun*

1. A shiny substance made from melted glass that is used to coat and protect different materials.

2. The hard, white surface of your teeth.

3. Paint that dries to a hard, shiny surface.

e·nam·el (i-**nam**-uhl)

▷ *verb* **enamel** ▷ *adjective* **enameled**

emu

Suffix

The suffix **-ence** adds one of these meanings to a root word:

1. A state or quality of being, as in *independence* (the state of being independent).

2. The act of being, as in *absence* (the act of being absent).

enchant *verb* To delight or charm someone: *We were enchanted by the tales of his travels in Africa.* **en·chant** (en-**chant**) ▷ *verb* **enchanting, enchanted**

enchanted *adjective* Magical, or under a magic spell, as in *an enchanted castle.* **en·chant·ed** (en-**chan**-tid)

enchanting *adjective* Delightful and charming: *Karen sang an enchanting song.* **en·chant·ing** (en-**chan**-ting) ▷ *adverb* **enchantingly**

enchantment *noun*

1. Something that causes you to feel charmed and delighted: *Greece in the springtime is pure enchantment.*

2. The state of being enchanted: *I was under such a spell of enchantment while reading the book that I didn't notice how many hours had passed.*

en·chant·ment (en-**chant**-muhnt)

enclose *verb*

1. To put a fence or a wall around something: *The yard was enclosed by a fence.*

2. To put something in with a letter or a package that you are sending: *Grandma mailed me a birthday card and enclosed a $5 bill in the envelope.*

en·close (en-**kloze**)

▷ *verb* **enclosing, enclosed** ▷ *adjective* **enclosed**

enclosure *noun*

1. An area surrounded by a barrier such as a fence or walls.

2. Something that is put in with a letter or a package: *The enclosure that came in the box contained additional instructions.*

en·clo·sure (en-**kloh**-zhur)

encompass *verb*

1. To include something: *Our history class will encompass the Civil War period.*

2. To form a circle around something: *A moat encompassed the castle.*

en·com·pass (en-**kuhm**-puhs)

▷ *verb* **encompasses, encompassing, encompassed**

endangered species: Siberian tiger

encore

1. *noun* A small, extra performance after an event because the audience is still clapping enthusiastically: *There was so much applause that the band came out for an encore.*

2. *interjection* Again, please!
en·core (**ahng**-kor *or* **ahn**-kor)

encounter

1. *noun* An unexpected or difficult situation or meeting: *She had an unpleasant encounter with one of her neighbors last week.*

2. *verb* To meet someone or experience something without expecting to, especially someone or something difficult, as in *to encounter problems.*
▷ *verb* **encountering, encountered**
en·coun·ter (en-**koun**-tur)

encourage
verb To give someone confidence, usually by using praise and support: *Coach Rodriguez encouraged us to do our best.* **en·cour·age** (en-**kur**-ij) ▷ *verb* **encouraging, encouraged** ▷ *adjective* **encouraging** ▷ *adverb* **encouragingly**

encouragement
noun The act of encouraging someone, or the state of being encouraged: *Maia is a talented musician, but she needs lots of encouragement.* **en·cour·age·ment** (en-**kur**-ij-muhnt)

encrypt
verb To write a message in a code so that others won't understand it unless they know the code: *My mom has a program that encrypts the files on her computer.* **en·crypt** (en-**kript**) ▷ *verb* **encrypting, encrypted** ▷ *noun* **encryption** (en-**krip**-shuhn)

encyclopedia
noun A book or set of books with very detailed information, usually arranged in alphabetical order: *I want a baseball encyclopedia so I can look up pitching statistics.* **en·cy·clo·pe·di·a** (en-sye-kloh-**pee**-dee-uh) ▷ *adjective* **encyclopedic**

end

1. *noun* The last part or final point of something:

The baseball season is over at the end of September.

2. *noun* A point that is farthest from the middle of an object or place: *My house is at the end of the street.*

3. *verb* To finish: *Her birthday party ended at about six o'clock.* ▷ *verb* **ending, ended**
end (end)

Synonyms

End means to stop what you are doing because you have finished it: *The gymnast ended her routine with a triple somersault.* The word *end* also refers to anything that is all done, as in *the end of the day, the end of a book,* or *the end of a long journey.*

- -

■ **Finish** means to bring something to an end, especially after a good deal of time or effort: *After a month of work, I finally finished my science project.*

■ **Complete** means to finish down to the last detail: *The workers will complete construction of the movie theater in time for the opening on Friday.*

■ **Conclude** means to bring to an end in a particular way or with a particular action: *The mayor concluded her speech with a promise to create new jobs.*

■ **Terminate** means to bring something to an end, sometimes before it is finished and often when things have been going badly in some way: *We terminated our trip when we all came down with the flu.*

■ **Halt** means to stop marching or traveling: *The police halted traffic while the president's car made its way down Pennsylvania Avenue toward the White House.*

endanger
verb To put someone or something in a dangerous situation: *Cutting down the trees will endanger the area's wildlife.* **en·dan·ger** (en-**dayn**-jur) ▷ *verb* **endangering, endangered** ▷ *adjective* **endangered**

endangered species
noun A plant or animal that is in danger of becoming extinct, usually because of human activity: *The Siberian tiger is an endangered species because of poaching and habitat loss.*

endeavor

1. *verb* To try very hard to do something: *I will endeavor to get this done on time.* ▷ *verb* **endeavoring, endeavored**

2. *noun* A serious attempt or effort: *We supported her endeavor to run a marathon.*
en·deav·or (en-**dev**-ur)

ending
noun The final part of something, especially of a story, movie, or book. **end·ing** (**en**-ding)

endless
adjective Having no end or seeming to have no end: *Her boring speech seemed endless.* **end·less** (**end**-lis) ▷ *adverb* **endlessly**

endorphin *noun* A substance created by the brain that reduces pain and causes pleasant feelings. **en·dor·phin** (en-**dor**-fin)

endorse *verb*
1. To support or approve of someone or something: *Our local newspaper is endorsing his candidacy for mayor.*
2. To sign your name on the reverse side of a document, especially a check: *Endorse the back of the check before you cash it.*
en·dorse (en-**dors**)
▷ *verb* **endorsing, endorsed** ▷ *noun* **endorsement**

endow *verb*
1. If you are **endowed** with a gift or a talent, you have it naturally: *All of their children seem endowed with great athletic ability.*
2. To give money or property: *The university was endowed by a wealthy graduate.*
en·dow (en-**dou**)
▷ *verb* **endowing, endowed**

endowment *noun* The money and investments that a big institution like a university owns and earns money on. **en·dow·ment** (en-**dou**-muhnt)

endurance *noun* The ability to do something difficult for a long time: *Although she's a fast runner, she doesn't have the endurance for a long race.* **en·dur·ance** (en-**door**-uhns)

endure *verb*
1. To put up with something difficult or painful: *We endured a lot of rain and mosquitoes on our camping trip.*
2. To last for a long time: *The cold weather endured well into the spring.*
en·dure (en-**door**)
▷ *verb* **enduring, endured** ▷ *adjective* **enduring**

end zone *noun* The part of a football field at each end, in front of the goalpost. The end zone is ten yards deep. *See* **football.**

enemy *noun*
1. Someone who hates another person and wants to hurt him or her.
2. The country or army that your country is fighting against in a war.
en·e·my (**en**-uh-mee)
▷ *noun, plural* **enemies**

Word History

The word **enemy** has a lot in common with its opposite, *friend*. It comes from the Latin root *amicus*, which means "friend." The word for "enemy" in Latin was *inimicus*, combining the prefix *in-*, meaning "not," and *amicus*. *Enemy* is a good example of how a negative prefix can reverse the meaning of a word.

energetic *adjective* Strong, active, and full of energy, as in *an energetic workout.* **en·er·get·ic** (*en*-ur-**jet**-ik)
▷ *adverb* **energetically**

energy *noun*
1. The ability or strength to do things without getting tired: *Do you have enough energy for a hike?*
2. Power from coal, electricity, or other sources that makes machines work and produces heat: *Our electrical energy comes from the power plant nearby.*
3. The ability of something to do work. Energy is a concept in physics and is measured in **joules**.
en·er·gy (**en**-ur-jee)

Word History

In physics, **energy** is the capacity of something to do work. Thomas Young, an English physicist, was the first to use the word *energy* with this meaning, in 1807. The meaning in physics led to another sense: the force that drives machines to work and create heat. The word *energy* goes back to the ancient Greek term *energeia*. The physicist and philosopher Aristotle used *energeia* to mean "an action." It was based on the prefix *en-*, meaning "in," and the word *ergon*, meaning "work."

enforce *verb* To make sure that a law or rule is obeyed: *Police officers enforce the traffic laws by using radar traps.* **en·force** (en-**fors**) ▷ *verb* **enforcing, enforced** ▷ *noun* **enforcement**

engage *verb*
1. To hire someone to do a job: *The company has engaged a team of consultants for the project.*
2. To attract something, as in *to engage somebody's attention.*
en·gage (en-**gayj**)
▷ *verb* **engaging, engaged**

engaged *adjective*
1. If two people are **engaged**, they are going to get married: *My sister is engaged to a policeman.*
2. Busy doing something: *Xavier is engaged in a biology research project.*
en·gaged (en-**gayjd**)

engagement *noun*
1. The period between a proposal of marriage and the wedding ceremony: *Marcy and Tom's engagement was announced in the paper this weekend.*
2. The act of engaging a person or group in something: *Over the years, the organization has increased its engagement with the environmental movement.*
3. An appointment or date that carries responsibilities: *The opera star has engagements in Europe throughout the fall, then she will perform in the United States.*
en·gage·ment (en-**gayj**-muhnt)

engine

engine *noun*
1. A machine that makes something move by using gasoline, steam, or another energy source.
2. The front part of a train that pulls the cars; a locomotive.
en·gine (**en**-jin)

Word History

The ancient Romans thought that people had natural talents and abilities. Their word for "talent," *ingenium*, was based on *gen-*, a root meaning "born." *Gen-* came from the verb *gignere*, meaning "bring forth a child." Latin speakers formed the word *ingenium* by combining the prefix *in-*, meaning "in," and the root *gen-*. So *ingenium* referred to talent that someone was born with. The term developed into *engin* in Old French, meaning "skill." Later, French speakers began using *engin* to mean "a machine created by skill." The word entered English in the 14th century, and **engine** now refers either to a machine that can make something move or to a locomotive, the part of a train that pulls the train's cars along a track.

engineer
1. *noun* Someone who is specially trained to design and build machines or large structures such as bridges and roads, as in *an electrical engineer.*
▷ *noun* **engineering**
2. *verb* To plan or do something in a clever way: *Marisol's friends are engineering a surprise birthday party for her.* ▷ *verb* **engineering, engineered**
en·gi·neer (*en*-juh-**neer**)

English
1. *noun* The main language spoken in the United States, Canada, Great Britain, Australia, New Zealand, and many other countries.
2. *adjective* Of or having to do with the English language.
3. *adjective* From England, or having to do with England.
Eng·lish (**ing**-glish)

Word History

The **English** language was named after a tribe called the Angles. The Angles were among several tribes who invaded England in the fifth century, introducing the English language into the area. The original home of the Angles was probably a region in northern Germany and southern Denmark. The Old English name for an Angle was *Engle*. We pronounce the beginning of the word *English* as "ing," but it was pronounced "eng" in the Middle Ages. This change also happened with other words, such as *wing* and *string*.

engrave *verb* To cut a design or writing into a metal or other hard surface: *I had my initials engraved on the locket.* **en·grave** (en-**grave**)
▷ *verb* **engraving, engraved** ▷ *noun* **engraver**
▷ *noun* **engraving** ▷ *adjective* **engraved**

engrossed *adjective* Giving all of your attention to something: *She was so engrossed in her book that she didn't hear the doorbell.* **en·grossed** (en-**grohst**)
▷ *adjective* **engrossing**

engulf *verb* To cover up or completely surround someone or something: *Flames engulfed the building in a matter of minutes.* **en·gulf** (en-**guhlf**)
▷ *verb* **engulfing, engulfed**

enhance *verb* To make something bigger, better, or more attractive: *Adding herbs really enhances the flavor of the stew.* **en·hance** (en-**hans**) ▷ *verb* **enhancing, enhanced**
▷ *noun* **enhancement**

enigma *noun* A mystery or something that is hard to understand: *The dog's disappearance is still an enigma to us.* **e·nig·ma** (i-**nig**-muh) ▷ *adjective* **enigmatic** (*en*-ig-**mat**-ik)

enjoy *verb*
1. To get pleasure or satisfaction from doing something: *Lou enjoys meeting new people.*
2. To get a benefit from something: *The town enjoys sunshine all year long.*
en·joy (en-**joi**)
▷ *verb* **enjoying, enjoyed** ▷ *noun* **enjoyment**
▷ *adjective* **enjoyable** ▷ *adverb* **enjoyably**

enlarge *verb* To make bigger: *There are new plans to enlarge the stadium.* **en·large** (en-**lahrj**)
▷ *verb* **enlarging, enlarged** ▷ *noun* **enlarger**

enlargement *noun*
1. The act of making something bigger: *Smoking can cause the enlargement of the pores on your face.*
2. A bigger version of something: *Let's have enlargements made of the wedding photos.*
en·large·ment (en-**lahrj**-muhnt)

enlighten *verb* To teach or explain something to someone: *Our doctor enlightened us about the need for a healthy diet.* **en·light·en** (en-**lye**-tuhn) ▷ *verb* **enlightening, enlightened** ▷ *noun* **enlightenment**

enlist *verb*
1. To join or get someone to join the army, navy, or one of the other armed forces: *Darren decided to enlist in the United States Navy.*
2. To get someone's help: *They enlisted me to help serve the food at the family reunion.* **en·list** (en-**list**) ▷ *verb* **enlisting, enlisted**

enormous *adjective* Extremely big: *Have you seen their house? It's enormous.* **e·nor·mous** (i-**nor**-muhs) ▷ *noun* **enormousness** ▷ *adverb* **enormously**

enough
1. *adjective* As much as you need or is necessary: *There were enough apples to feed everyone in our group.* ▷ *adverb* **enough**
2. *pronoun* An amount equal to as much as is needed or necessary: *I have enough to do to keep me busy.* **e·nough** (i-**nuhf**)

enrage *verb* To make someone very angry: *His neighbor's rudeness enraged Mr. Phillips.* **en·rage** (en-**rayj**) ▷ *verb* **enraging, enraged**

enrich *verb*
1. To improve something by adding good things to it: *The orange juice is enriched with extra vitamin C.*
2. To make richer: *The crooked mayor enriched himself at the city's expense.*
3. To fertilize: *Compost enriches the soil and makes your plants grow better.* **en·rich** (en-**rich**) ▷ *verb* **enriches, enriching, enriched** ▷ *noun* **enrichment** ▷ *adjective* **enriching** ▷ *adjective* **enriched**

enroll *verb* To register as a student or a member of something: *Kenny's mother enrolled him in kindergarten today.* **en·roll** (en-**rohl**) ▷ *verb* **enrolling, enrolled** ▷ *noun* **enrollment**

en route *adverb* On the way: *Many people claim that Washington slept here en route to Philadelphia.* **en route** (ahn **root**) ▷ *adjective* **en route**

ensemble *noun* A group of musicians, actors, or dancers who usually perform together. **en·sem·ble** (ahn-**sahm**-buhl)

ensue *verb* To happen next, usually as a result of something: *She pulled the fire alarm and chaos ensued.* **en·sue** (en-**soo**) ▷ *verb* **ensuing, ensued** ▷ *adjective* **ensuing**

ensure *verb* To make sure that something happens: *Please ensure that you have sealed the jar tightly.* **en·sure** (en-**shoor**) ▷ *verb* **ensuring, ensured**

entail *verb* To involve or require something, especially something difficult or complicated: *The job entails long hours and hard work.* **en·tail** (en-**tayl**) ▷ *verb* **entailing, entailed**

ensemble

a
b
c
d
e
f
g
h
i
j
k
l
m
n
o
p
q
r
s
t
u
v
w
x
y
z

entangle *verb*

1. To catch or trap something, especially accidentally: *They are redesigning the nets so that sea turtles won't get entangled in them.*

2. To involve someone in a difficult situation: *She was entangled in a dangerous scheme.*

en·tan·gle (en-**tang**-guhl)

▷ *verb* **entangling, entangled** ▷ *noun* **entanglement**

enter

1. *verb* To go or come into a place.

2. *verb* To sign up for a competition or a race: *Kim entered the science fair.*

3. *verb* To type information into a computer or write it in a book: *Linda entered all the figures into the database.*

4. *noun* The large key at the far right-hand side of the middle row of a keyboard that you hit to end a line or to move to another place on your screen.

en·ter (**en**-tur)

▷ *verb* **entering, entered**

enterprise *noun*

1. A plan that has several steps leading to a result, especially the making of money: *They're involved in a research enterprise.*

2. A business.

3. The activity of starting businesses and developing an economy: *The government has announced new plans to encourage enterprise in the area.*

en·ter·prise (**en**-tur-*prize*)

enterprising *adjective* Having or showing a lot of good ideas for solving problems or making money: *An enterprising reporter found the information by looking at court records.* **en·ter·pris·ing** (**en**-tur-*prize*-ing)

entertain *verb*

1. To amuse someone in an enjoyable way. ▷ *noun* **entertainer** ▷ *adjective* **entertaining**

2. To invite people to your home for a party, a visit, or a meal, as in *to entertain friends.*

en·ter·tain (*en*-tur-**tayn**)

▷ *verb* **entertaining, entertained**

entertainment *noun*

1. The activity or industry of making people laugh and enjoy themselves: *There was a clown at the party for entertainment.*

2. A thing that provides entertainment: *The event will feature a buffet and musical entertainments* by the show's cast.

en·ter·tain·ment (*en*-tur-**tayn**-muhnt)

enthrall *verb* To excite or charm someone: *The band has enthralled audiences in every city on the tour.* **en·thrall** (en-**thrawl**) ▷ *verb* **enthralling, enthralled**

enthusiasm *noun* Great eagerness or interest: *Tony's speech filled his supporters with enthusiasm.* **en·thu·si·asm** (en-**thoo**-zee-*az*-uhm)

enthusiastic *adjective* Having or showing feelings of excitement and interest about something: *Jessica is enthusiastic about painting.* **en·thu·si·as·tic** (en-*thoo*-zee-**as**-tik) ▷ *noun* **enthusiast** ▷ *adverb* **enthusiastically**

entice *verb* To persuade someone to do something: *How can we entice our customers to spend more?* **en·tice** (en-**tise**) ▷ *verb* **enticing, enticed** ▷ *noun* **enticement** ▷ *adjective* **enticing**

entire *adjective* Whole: *The entire family gets together about once a year.* **en·tire** (en-**tire**)

entirely *adverb* Completely, wholly, or fully: *Brenda told us what happened, but then we heard an entirely different version of it from one of her relatives.* **en·tire·ly** (en-**tire**-lee)

entrance

entitle *verb*

1. To give a right or a privilege to someone: *My library card entitles me to borrow books as well as CDs and DVDs.* ▷ *noun* **entitlement**

2. To give a name to a book or other work: *He entitled his essay "Lost in the Mountains."*

en·ti·tle (en-**tye**-tuhl)

▷ *verb* **entitling, entitled**

entity *noun* Something that exists by itself, apart from other things: *The two distant stars merged to form a single entity.* **en·ti·ty** (**en**-ti-tee) ▷ *noun, plural* **entities**

entrance

1. (**en**-truhns) *noun* The way into a place, as in *the main entrance.*

2. (en-**trans**) *verb* To fill someone with feelings of pleasure. ▷ *verb* **entrancing, entranced** ▷ *adjective* **entrancing**

en·trance

entrap *verb* To trick someone, especially into doing something wrong or admitting they did something wrong. **en·trap** (en-**trap**) ▷ *verb* **entrapping, entrapped**

entrepreneur *noun* Someone who starts businesses and finds new ways to make money. **en·tre·pre·neur** (*ahn*-truh-pruh-**nur**) ▷ *adjective* **entrepreneurial**

entrust *verb*

1. To give someone responsibility for doing something: *This task is too important to entrust to someone I don't know very well.*

2. To give something valuable or important to someone who will take care of it for you: *I entrusted my dogs to my neighbor while I was away.*

en·trust (en-**truhst**)

▷ *verb* **entrusting, entrusted**

entry *noun*

1. A way into a place.

2. Something such as a picture or story that you enter in a competition: *Marcel's entry in the pie contest won a blue ribbon.*

3. A piece of information in a dictionary, diary, computer program, or other work: *I added several entries to the database.*

en·try (**en**-tree)

▷ *noun, plural* **entries**

enunciate *verb* To speak or pronounce words: *A TV news anchor learns to enunciate clearly.* **e·nun·ci·ate** (i-**nuhn**-see-*ate*) ▷ *verb* **enunciating, enunciated** ▷ *noun* **enunciation**

envelop *verb* To completely cover or surround something: *The top of the mountain was enveloped in clouds.* **en·vel·op** (en-**vel**-uhp) ▷ *verb* **enveloping, enveloped**

envelope *noun* A paper or plastic container for anything flat, like a card or folded papers. **en·ve·lope** (**en**-vuh-*lope* or **ahn**-vuh-*lope*)

enviable *adjective* Making you wish that you had something; desirable: *Martha has an enviable job with the company.* **en·vi·a·ble** (**en**-vee-uh-buhl)

envious *adjective* Wishing you could have something that someone else has: *He was envious of Fred's new bicycle.* **en·vi·ous** (**en**-vee-uhs) ▷ *adverb* **enviously**

environment *noun*

1. All the things that are part of your life and have an effect on it, such as your family and your school, the place where you live, and the events that happen to you: *The aftercare teachers created a lively environment for their students.*

2. The natural surroundings of living things, such as the air, land, or sea: *Hotter temperatures are affecting the environment of Arctic creatures.*

3. The situation or set of circumstances that affects how something happens: *Students find it impossible to study in such a noisy environment.*

en·vi·ron·ment (en-**vye**-ruhn-muhnt)

envelope

▷ *noun* **environmentalist** ▷ *adjective* **environmental** ▷ *adverb* **environmentally**

environmentally friendly *adjective*

1. Made of substances that do not damage or pollute the natural environment, as in *environmentally friendly food containers.*

2. Done in a way that does not damage or pollute the natural environment, as in *environmentally friendly manufacturing.*

envision *verb* To imagine something for the future, especially something pleasant, as in *to envision a life of prosperity.* **en·vi·sion** (en-**vizh**-uhn) ▷ *verb* **envisioning, envisioned**

envy *verb* To wish that you could have something that someone else has, or could do something that someone else has done: *Peter envied his sister's success in the chess competition.* **en·vy** (**en**-vee) ▷ *verb* **envies, envying, envied** ▷ *noun* **envy**

enzyme *noun* A protein produced by a plant or animal that causes chemical reactions to occur inside: *Food is broken down by the activity of stomach enzymes.* **en·zyme** (**en**-zime)

eon *noun* A very long period of time: *The universe has existed for eons.* **e·on** (**ee**-ahn)

epic

1. *noun* A long story, poem, or movie about heroic adventures and great battles that happened in the past, or in some imaginary place.

2. *adjective* Ambitious or impressive, as in *an epic ocean voyage.*

3. *adjective* Very large: *The spaceship was of epic proportions.*

ep·ic (**ep**-ik)

epicenter *noun* The area directly above where an earthquake occurs. Often, the people who live at or near the epicenter are in the greatest danger during an earthquake. **ep·i·cen·ter** (**ep**-i-*sen*-tur)

epidemic *noun* An infectious disease present in a large number of people at the same time, as in *a flu epidemic.* **ep·i·dem·ic** (**ep**-i-**dem**-ik)

epigram *noun* A short, witty saying. **ep·i·gram** (**ep**-i-*gram*) ▷ *adjective* **epigrammatic**

epilepsy *noun* A disease of the brain that may cause a person to have sudden blackouts or to lose control of his or her movements. **ep·i·lep·sy** (**ep**-uh-*lep*-see) ▷ *noun* **epileptic** (*ep*-uh-**lep**-tik) ▷ *adjective* **epileptic**

a
b
c
d
e
f
g
h
i
j
k
l
m
n
o
p
q
r
s
t
u
v
w
x
y
z

epilogue *noun* A short speech or piece of writing at the end of a play, story, or poem. **ep·i·logue** (ep-uh-*lawg*)

EpiPen *noun* A trademark for a medical device that is used to help someone who is having a very serious allergic reaction. **Epi·Pen** (ep-ee-*pen*)

episode *noun*
1. One of the programs in a television series.
2. An event in your life that is unusual or remarkable: *Lately, I've been experiencing some episodes of dizziness.* **ep·i·sode** (ep-i-*sode*)

epitaph *noun* Something written on a person's gravestone about him or her. **ep·i·taph** (ep-i-*taf*)

epoch *noun* A period of important events in history: *The second part of the 20th century is sometimes described as the epoch of space travel.* **e·poch** (ep-uhk)

eponym *noun* A name for something that is based on a person's name: *The word "zinnia" is an eponym— the flower was named after the 18th-century German botanist Johann G. Zinn.* **ep·o·nym** (ep-uh-nim)

equal
1. *adjective* The same as something else in size, value, or amount: *Two pints are equal to one quart.* ▷ *adverb* **equally**
2. *adjective* The same for each member of a group, as in *equal housing opportunities.*
3. *noun* A person of equal ability or position, or a thing of equal quality, as in *a jury of your equals.*
4. *verb* To do or be the same as something else in amount, score, or quantity: *Sheryl needs a 96 to equal the top score.* ▷ *verb* **equaling, equaled** **e·qual** (ee-kwuhl)

equality *noun* The right of everyone to be treated the same, with no one getting special advantages, as in *gender equality.* **e·qual·i·ty** (i-kwah-li-tee)

equate *verb* To say or to consider that two things are the same: *It sounds like you're equating success with happiness.* **e·quate** (ee-kwayt) ▷ *verb* **equating, equated**

equation *noun* A mathematical statement in which one set of numbers or values is equal to another. For example, 5 x 4 = 20 is an equation. **e·qua·tion** (i-kway-zhuhn)

equator *noun* An imaginary line around the middle of the earth that is an equal distance from the North and South Poles. **e·qua·tor** (i-kway-tur) ▷ *adjective* **equatorial** (ee-kwuh-tor-ee-uhl)

equestrian
1. *adjective* Of or having to do with horseback riding, as in *an equestrian event.*

2. *noun* Someone who rides a horse as a hobby or to compete in events. **e·ques·tri·an** (i-kwes-tree-uhn)

equilateral *adjective* Having sides of equal length: *The three angles and sides of an equilateral triangle are all equal.* **e·qui·lat·er·al** (ee-kwuh-**lat**-ur-uhl)

equilibrium *noun*
1. The ability to keep from falling over: *It is difficult to keep your equilibrium while standing on one foot.*
2. A state in which everything is balanced, in a place or in your mind: *I think a weekend away will help restore our equilibrium.* **e·qui·lib·ri·um** (ee-kwuh-**lib**-ree-uhm)

equinox *noun* One of the two days each year, in March and in September, when day and night last exactly the same length of time all over the world. **e·qui·nox** (ee-kwuh-*nahks*) ▷ *noun, plural* **equinoxes**

equator

equip *verb* To provide with the things that are needed: *Our classroom is equipped with chairs, desks, a chalkboard, and books.* **e·quip** (i-kwip) ▷ *verb* **equipping, equipped**

equipment *noun* The tools, machines, or products needed for a particular purpose, as in *camping equipment.* **e·quip·ment** (i-**kwip**-muhnt)

equities *noun, plural* Shares of stock issued by publicly traded companies. **eq·ui·ties** (ek-wi-teez)

equity *noun* Equal treatment for everyone in a situation: *The new law is intended to promote pay equity for women, so that they can earn just as much as men if they are equally qualified for a job.* **eq·ui·ty** (ek-wi-tee)

equivalent
1. *adjective* The same in amount, value, or importance: *If you don't have butter, use an equivalent amount of margarine.*
2. *noun* A thing that is equal to or can be used in place of another thing: *A mile is the equivalent of 5,280 feet.* **e·quiv·a·lent** (i-**kwiv**-uh-luhnt) ▷ *noun* **equivalence**

Suffix

There are two suffixes **-er** in English. The first adds one of the following meanings to a root word:

1. One who, as in *baker* (one who bakes).

2. A person who lives in or comes from a place, as in *islander, mainlander.*

The second **-er** suffix adds the meaning "more" to a root adjective or adverb, as in *warmer* (more warm), *thinner* (more thin), *slower* (more slow).

ermine

era *noun* A long period of time in history that has some consistent feature: *The era of print news seems to be coming to an end.* **e·ra** (**er**-uh *or* **eer**-uh)

eradicate *verb* To get rid of something completely, especially something bad such as disease, crime, or poverty: *Eradicating malaria is a huge challenge in many countries.* **e·rad·i·cate** (i-**rad**-i-*kate*)
▷ *verb* **eradicating, eradicated** ▷ *noun* **eradication**
▷ *noun* **eradicator**

erase *verb*
1. To remove writing with an eraser: *Will someone please erase the blackboard?*
2. To delete something stored in a computer or recorded on a tape: *He worried that he had accidentally erased his homework from his laptop.*
3. To get rid of completely: *Erase that thought from your mind.*
e·rase (i-**rase**)
▷ *verb* **erasing, erased** ▷ *noun* **erasure** (i-**ray**-shur)

eraser *noun* Something used for removing pencil marks from paper, or chalk marks from a surface such as a blackboard. **e·ras·er** (i-**ray**-sur)

e-reader *noun* An electronic device that stores and enables you to read e-books. **e-read·er** (**ee**-*ree*-dur)

erect
1. *adjective* Standing up straight. ▷ *adverb* **erectly**
2. *verb* To put up a building or other structure: *The synagogue was erected in the 19th century.* ▷ *verb* **erecting, erected**
e·rect (i-**rekt**)

ermine *noun* A kind of weasel. Its brown fur turns white in winter. **er·mine** (**ur**-min)

erode *verb*
1. To wear away gradually by water or wind.
2. To become weaker or less powerful: *After three successive losses, the team's confidence began to erode.*
e·rode (i-**rode**)
▷ *verb* **eroding, eroded**

erosion *noun* The wearing away of something by water or wind, as in *soil erosion.* **e·ro·sion** (i-**roh**-zhuhn)

errand *noun* A small job that involves going somewhere to take or get something: *She ran an errand for her mother.* **er·rand** (**er**-uhnd)

erratic *adjective* Not following a regular or normal pattern, as in *erratic behavior.* **er·rat·ic** (i-**rat**-ik)
▷ *adverb* **erratically**

error *noun* A mistake: *There were no errors on Stephen's test.* **er·ror** (**er**-ur)

erupt *verb*
1. When a volcano **erupts**, it suddenly and violently throws out lava, hot ashes, and steam.
2. To happen suddenly: *A brawl erupted between some unruly fans at the football game.*
3. To suddenly get very angry.
e·rupt (i-**ruhpt**)
▷ *verb* **erupting, erupted** ▷ *noun* **eruption**

Word History

When a volcano erupts, it is "bursting out." The English word **erupt** comes from the Latin verb *erumpere,* meaning "to burst out." Its past participle was *eruptus,* and this was the source of our word *erupt.* Latin speakers formed *erumpere* from the prefix *e-,* meaning "out," and the verb *rumpere,* meaning "to break." In English, the verbs *rupture,* meaning "to break open," and *interrupt,* meaning "to break between," also come from the Latin word *rumpere.*

escalator *noun* A staircase that moves up or down. **es·ca·la·tor** (**es**-kuh-*lay*-tur)

escape
1. *verb* To get out of a place where you have been kept against your will, as in *to escape from prison.*
2. *verb* To avoid something: *We escaped the summer heat by going up to the mountains.*
3. *verb* To leak out: *Some water was escaping from the radiator.*
4. *noun* The act of getting out of a place, especially suddenly or when there is danger.
5. *noun* A way of escaping: *The bridge was their only means of escape after the earthquake.*
es·cape (i-**skape**)
▷ *verb* **escaping, escaped**

escort *verb* To go with or follow someone, especially for protection, as in *a police escort.* **es·cort** (i-**skort**)
▷ *verb* **escorting, escorted** ▷ *noun* **escort** (**es**-kort)

Eskimo *noun* A historical term for an Inuit. Eskimo is not used officially and many of the Inuit do not like this old-fashioned word. **Es·ki·mo** (**es**-kuh-*moh*)
▷ *noun, plural* **Eskimo** *or* **Eskimos**

esophagus *noun* The tube that carries food from the throat to the stomach. **e·soph·a·gus** (i-**sah**-fuh-guhs)

especially *adverb*
1. More so; particularly: *He excels at several sports, but is especially good at football.*
2. To a great degree; very or very much: *I don't especially enjoy getting up early.*
es·pe·cial·ly (i-**spesh**-uh-lee)

espionage *noun* The act of spying, or the work of a spy for a government or organization. **es·pi·o·nage** (**es**-pee-uh-*nahzh*)

essay *noun* A short piece of writing on a particular subject: *Annalaura wrote an essay about architecture.* **es·say** (**es**-ay)

essence *noun* The most important quality of something that makes it what it is: *The essence of friendship is loyalty.* **es·sence** (**es**-uhns)

essential
1. *adjective* Necessary or very important: *Reading the introduction is essential to understanding the main themes of the book.*
2. *noun* Something that you consider necessary and that you cannot do without: *I carry only essentials when I travel.*
es·sen·tial (i-**sen**-shuhl)

essentially *adverb* In all important respects; in every way that matters: *The Braille system, which uses raised dots for letters, has remained essentially unchanged since it was developed in the 1820s.* **es·sen·tial·ly** (uh-**sen**-shuh-lee)

Suffix

The suffix **-est** means "most" when added to a root adjective or adverb, as in *hottest* (most hot), *biggest* (most big), *slowest* (most slow).

Sometimes the final consonant in the root word is doubled before the -est suffix is added. Always look up the word if you're not sure how to spell it.

establish *verb*
1. To start up something that will last for some time: *The debating club was established last year.*
2. To determine that something is true or correct: *We counted the tree's rings to establish how old the tree was.*
es·tab·lish (i-**stab**-lish)
▷ *verb* **establishes, establishing, established**

establishment *noun*
1. The process or act of establishing something: *The US Geological Survey has collected data on rivers and other bodies of water since its establishment in 1879.*
2. A business or store: *A hotel is an establishment that provides paid lodging on a short-term basis.* **es·tab·lish·ment** (i-**stab**-lish-muhnt)

estate *noun*
1. A large area of land, usually with a house on it.
2. All the money, property, and other things that someone leaves behind when he or she dies: *Grandpa's estate includes his antique cars.* **es·tate** (i-**state**)

esteem *noun* A feeling of respect and admiration for someone: *The election result reflects the high esteem that the governor earned in her first term.* **es·teem** (i-**steem**) ▷ *verb* **esteem** ▷ *adjective* **esteemed**

estimate
1. (**es**-tuh-mit) *noun* A rough guess or calculation about an amount, distance, cost, or other quantity, as in *an estimate of the room's length.*
2. (**es**-tuh-*mate*) *verb* To calculate something such as a value, amount, or distance in a way that is not exact: *Leon estimated the distance to the road as about 70 feet.* ▷ *verb* **estimating, estimated** ▷ *noun* **estimator** ▷ *noun* **estimation**
es·ti·mate

estimated *adjective* Guessed at, often because exact measurement or calculation is not possible: *The bridge is being built now, and the estimated date for its completion is next March.* **es·ti·mat·ed** (**es**-tuh-*may*-tid)

estrogen *noun* A hormone found in the human body, especially in females, that produces typically female physical and sexual characteristics. **es·tro·gen** (**es**-truh-juhn)

estuary *noun* The wide part of a river, where it joins the ocean: *New York is at the estuary of the Hudson River.* **es·tu·ar·y** (**es**-choo-er-ee) ▷ *noun, plural* **estuaries**

ETA *noun* The time that someone is expected to arrive somewhere. ETA is short for *estimated time of arrival.*

etc. An abbreviation of the Latin phrase *et cetera,* which means "and the rest." *Etc.* is used at the end of a list to mean that other, similar items could be added: *The artist gathered her brushes, paints, canvases, etc.* **etc.** (*et* **set**-ur-uh)

etch *verb* To cut a design on metal or glass, using a sharp object or acid: *The store name was etched into the window.* **etch** (ech) ▷ *verb* **etches, etching, etched** ▷ *adjective* **etched**

etching *noun* A picture or print that is made from an etched plate: *The museum has a collection of etchings of the town's earliest buildings.* **etching** (**ech**-ing)

eternal *adjective* Lasting or staying the same forever. **e·ter·nal** (i-**tur**-nuhl) ▷ *adverb* **eternally**

koala in a eucalyptus tree

eternity *noun*
 1. All of time, without beginning or end.
 2. A seemingly endless amount of time: *Jean waited an eternity for the bus.*
 e·ter·ni·ty (i-**tur**-ni-tee)
 ▷ *noun, plural* **eternities**

ethical *adjective* Something that is **ethical** is good and honest: *They decided that it would not be ethical to accept such a big gift from the customer.* **eth·i·cal** (**eth**-i-kuhl)

ethnic *adjective* Of or having to do with a group of people sharing the same national origins, language, or culture: *The United States is home to many ethnic groups.* **eth·nic** (**eth**-nik) ▷ *adverb* **ethnically**

ethnic cleansing *noun* The killing or removal of a particular ethnic group by a government or by another ethnic group: *The government of that nation has launched a new round of ethnic cleansing.*

etiquette *noun* Rules of polite behavior that most people in a society are aware of: *It is proper etiquette to put your napkin on your lap when eating.* **et·i·quette** (**et**-i-kit)

Etruscan *adjective* Of or having to do with an ancient civilization in an area that later became part of Italy. **E·trus·can** (i-**truhs**-kuhn)

etymology *noun* The history of a word, including its earlier forms and meanings: *Each Word History in this dictionary gives a brief etymology of the highlighted word.* **et·y·mol·o·gy** (*et*-uh-**mah**-luh-jee) ▷ *noun, plural* **etymologies**

eucalyptus *noun* An evergreen tree originally from Australia that is now grown in many places: *Koala bears feed on eucalyptus leaves.* **eu·ca·lyp·tus** (*yoo*-kuh-**lip**-tuhs) ▷ *noun, plural* **eucalyptuses** *or* **eucalypti** (*yoo*-kuh-**lip**-tye)

Eurasia *noun* The landmass consisting of the continents of Europe and Asia. It is located in the Eastern and Northern Hemispheres. **Eur·a·sia** (*yoor*-**ay**-zhuh) ▷ *adjective* **Eurasian**

euro *noun* The main unit of money in many of the countries in the European Union: *My parents gave me 50 euros to spend in France.* **eu·ro** (**yoor**-oh)

Europe *noun* The continent on the western side of the Eurasian landmass. It lies west of Asia and is surrounded by the Arctic Ocean, the Mediterranean Sea, and the Atlantic Ocean. **Eu·rope** (**yoor**-uhp)

European
 1. *adjective* From Europe or having to do with Europe.
 2. *noun* Someone who was born in Europe or whose parents come from there.
 Eu·ro·pe·an (*yoor*-uh-**pee**-uhn)

European Union *noun* A group of 27 European countries that have joined together to encourage economic and political cooperation. The European Union is continuing to expand. Abbreviated as *EU*.

euthanasia *noun* The ending of a life to save an animal or a person from horrible suffering. Opinions vary widely on whether euthanasia should be legal for people. **eu·tha·na·sia** (*yoo*-thuh-**nay**-zhuh)

Etruscan sculpture

evacuate *verb* To move away from an area or building because it is dangerous there: *Everyone safely evacuated the burning building.* **e·vac·u·ate** (i-**vak**-yoo-*ate*) ▷ *verb* **evacuating, evacuated** ▷ *noun* **evacuation**

evade *verb*
1. To avoid someone or something unpleasant: *They evaded capture by hiding in a cave.*
2. To avoid answering or giving information: *Ramona keeps evading my questions.*
e·vade (i-**vade**)
▷ *verb* **evading, evaded**

evaluate *verb* To decide the value of something by thinking carefully about it: *Mary agreed only after evaluating the situation.* **e·val·u·ate** (i-**val**-yoo-*ate*)
▷ *verb* **evaluating, evaluated** ▷ *noun* **evaluator**

evaluation *noun* The process of forming an idea of the value or qualities of something: *An inspector carried out an evaluation of the town's supply of drinking water.* **e·val·u·a·tion** (i-*val*-yoo-**ay**-shuhn)

evangelical *adjective* An **evangelical** Christian is very enthusiastic about his or her religious beliefs and wants others to be as well. **e·van·gel·i·cal** (*ee*-van-**jel**-i-kuhl) ▷ *noun* **evangelism** (*ee*-**van**-juh-*liz*-uhm) ▷ *noun* **evangelist** (*ee*-**van**-juh-list)

evaporate *verb*
1. To change into a vapor or gas: *All the puddles had evaporated by the next day.*
2. To become less and then disappear completely: *The gladiator's bravado evaporated when he saw how tall and strong his opponent was.*
e·vap·o·rate (i-**vap**-uh-*rate*)
▷ *verb* **evaporating, evaporated** ▷ *noun* **evaporation**

evasion *noun*
1. The activity of avoiding something unpleasant.
2. Something that you do or say as a way of avoiding what you should do or say: *His answers were full of evasions, so I think he's hiding something.*
e·va·sion (i-**vay**-zhuhn)

evasive *adjective* Intending or intended to avoid something unpleasant. **e·va·sive** (i-**vay**-siv)

eve *noun* The evening or day before an important or special day, as in *Christmas Eve.* **eve** (eev)

even
1. *adjective* Staying about the same, as in *an even speed* or *an even temperature.*
2. *adjective* Equal in amount, size, score, or other quantity, as in *an even length.*
3. *adjective* Flat and level, as in *a smooth, even surface.*
4. *verb* To make something smooth, level, or equal: *A gentle tug will even out the rug.* ▷ *verb* **evening**

(*ee*-vuh-ning), **evened**
5. *adverb* Surprisingly or unexpectedly: *Even George liked the cake.*
6. even if *adverb* Whether or not: *I'm going to get this job done today, even if I have to work until late tonight.*
e·ven (**ee**-vuhn)
▷ *adverb* **evenly**

evening *noun* The time of day between late afternoon and night. **eve·ning** (**eev**-ning)

even number *noun* A number that can be divided exactly by 2 without leaving a remainder: *Twelve and 36 are even numbers.*

event *noun*
1. Something that happens, especially something that is planned, interesting, or important: *The town's 100th anniversary was marked by a parade and other events.* ▷ *adjective* **eventful**
2. A contest in a sports competition, as in *a pole-vaulting event.*
e·vent (i-**vent**)

eventual *adjective* Final, or happening at the end: *His constant pranks led to his eventual suspension from school.* **e·ven·tu·al** (i-**ven**-choo-uhl)

eventually *adverb*
1. Finally or after a long time: *Eventually the baby fell asleep.*
2. At some indefinite time in the future: *You will have to organize your grandparents' book collection eventually.*
e·ven·tu·al·ly (i-**ven**-choo-uh-lee)

ever *adverb*
1. At any time: *I doubt I'll ever try an extreme sport.*
2. All the time or continually, as in *ever changing.*
3. Ever is sometimes used to give emphasis: *Boy, is it ever cold outside!*
ev·er (**ev**-ur)

everglade *noun* An area of swampy land with tall grasses and many swamps. **ev·er·glade** (**ev**-ur-*glade*)

everglade

Evolution

Evolution is the development of the characteristics of animals or plants over many generations. Fossils provide evidence of life on earth changing over millions of years. The theory of how and why living things change is called natural selection, and was developed by the 19th-century naturalist Charles Darwin. According to his theory, organisms will survive and reproduce if they have traits that are helpful in their environment. An example of one of these traits, or adaptations, is the long neck of the giraffe, which allows it to eat from treetops.

Charles Darwin

giraffe, adapted for browsing on the leaves of trees

evergreen *noun* A bush or tree that has green leaves throughout the year. **ev·er·green** (**ev**-ur-*green*)
▷ *adjective* **evergreen**

everlasting *adjective* Lasting forever or for a very long time. **ev·er·last·ing** (*ev*-ur-**las**-ting)

every *adjective* Each of the people or things in a group or all the parts of something: *She was out sick every day this week.* **eve·ry** (**ev**-ree)

everybody *pronoun* Each and every person: *Everybody is going to the pool today.* **eve·ry·bod·y** (**ev**-ree-*bah*-dee or **ev**-ree-*buhd*-ee)

everyday *adjective*
1. Happening every day, as in *everyday events.*
2. All right for ordinary, daily use, as in *everyday clothes.*
eve·ry·day (**ev**-ree-*day*)

everyone *pronoun* Every person; everybody: *Everyone is asleep.* **eve·ry·one** (**ev**-ree-*wuhn*)

everyplace *adverb* (*informal*) Another word for **everywhere**. **eve·ry·place** (**ev**-ree-*plase*)

everything *pronoun*
1. Each and every thing: *They enjoyed everything at the amusement park.*
2. A very important thing: *Love is everything to me.*
eve·ry·thing (**ev**-ree-*thing*)

everywhere *adverb* In all places: *There were traffic jams everywhere after the parade.* **eve·ry·where** (**ev**-ree-*wair*)

evict *verb* To force someone to move out of a place: *They were evicted from their apartment for not paying the rent.* **e·vict** (i-**vikt**) ▷ *verb* **evicting, evicted** ▷ *noun* **eviction**

evidence *noun* Information and facts that help prove something is true or not true: *There was plenty of evidence that he was the thief.* **ev·i·dence** (**ev**-i-duhns)

evident *adjective* Easy to see or understand; obvious: *It is evident that you don't believe what I'm saying.* **ev·i·dent** (**ev**-i-duhnt)

evidently *adverb* In a way that is clear and obvious, especially if it was not clear before: *If he finished high school 15 years ago, he is evidently a lot older than he looks.* **ev·i·dent·ly** (**ev**-i-duhnt-lee)

evil *adjective* Cruel and immoral. **e·vil** (**ee**-vuhl)
▷ *noun* **evil**

evolution *noun*
1. The gradual change of living things that takes place very slowly from generation to generation, as in *the evolution of marsupials.*
2. Gradual change or development into another form: *The class watched the insect's evolution—from an egg to a caterpillar, then to a butterfly.*
ev·o·lu·tion (*ev*-uh-**loo**-shuhn)
▷ *adjective* **evolutionary**

evolve *verb*
1. To change slowly and naturally over time: *Dogs and wolves evolved from a common ancestor.*
2. To develop and change as a result of many small steps: *Her interest in working outdoors gradually evolved into her decision to study landscape gardening.*
e·volve (i-**vahlv**)
▷ *verb* **evolving, evolved**

ewe *noun* A female sheep. **ewe** (yoo) **Ewe** sounds like **you** and **yew**.

ex *noun* A person who used to have a particular position, especially a former husband or wife: *She is on good terms with her ex.* **ex** (eks) ▷ *noun, plural* **exes**

Prefix

The prefix **ex-** adds the meaning "former" when added to a root word, as in *ex-senator*. It is always followed by a hyphen.

a
b
c
d
e
f
g
h
i
j
k
l
m
n
o
p
q
r
s
t
u
v
w
x
y
z

exact *adjective*

1. Correct, complete, and accurate: *The cashier handed me exact change.*

2. Exact is sometimes used for emphasis: *We arrived at the hotel at the exact same time.* **ex·act** (ig-**zakt**)

▷ *noun* **exactness**

exactly *adverb* Accurately in every detail; precisely: *No one knows exactly how the dog ended up on the roof.* **ex·actl·y** (ig-**zakt**-lee)

exaggerate *verb* To make something seem bigger, better, more important, or more extreme than it really is: *Ted exaggerated his abilities at tennis.* **ex·ag·ger·ate** (ig-**zaj**-uh-*rate*) ▷ *verb* **exaggerating, exaggerated** ▷ *adjective* **exaggerated**

exaggeration *noun* The act of exaggerating something, or a statement that does this: *He says he can jump so well that he could leap over the canyon—what an exaggeration!* **ex·ag·ger·a·tion** (ig-*zaj*-uh-**ray**-shuhn)

examination *noun*

1. An official test of your knowledge of a subject. Often shortened to *exam.*

2. A careful check, especially of your body by a doctor, as in *a physical examination.* **ex·am·i·na·tion** (ig-*zam*-uh-**nay**-shuhn)

examine *verb*

1. To look carefully at something in order to learn about it: *The scientist examined the cells with a microscope.*

2. To check a person's body to discover if anything is not healthy or normal about it: *The doctor examined her and said she had tonsillitis.* **ex·am·ine** (ig-**zam**-in)

▷ *verb* **examining, examined** ▷ *noun* **examiner**

example *noun*

1. Someone or something that shows what a whole group is like: *The whale is an example of a mammal.*

2. A way of behaving that others should copy: *Sandra's polite manner sets a good example for the rest of the class.*

3. A question or a problem, given with its answer: *Use the example on the board to help you with your homework.*

4. You use **for example** to help explain what you are saying or to show that it is true: *Some animals—cats, for example—have excellent night vision.*

5. If you **make an example** of someone, you punish him or her as a way to warn others not to do the same thing. **ex·am·ple** (ig-**zam**-puhl)

excavate

exasperate *verb* To make someone very annoyed. **ex·as·per·ate** (ig-**zas**-puh-*rate*) ▷ *verb* **exasperating, exasperated** ▷ *noun* **exasperation** ▷ *adjective* **exasperating** ▷ *adjective* **exasperated**

excavate *verb* To dig a large hole in the earth to search for something buried, as in archaeological research, or to prepare the ground for the construction of a building. **ex·ca·vate** (**ek**-skuh-*vate*) ▷ *verb* **excavating, excavated** ▷ *noun* **excavation** ▷ *noun* **excavator**

exceed *verb*

1. To be bigger or better than something else: *My grades this year exceeded my parents' expectations.*

2. To do or be more than is allowed or expected: *He received a ticket for exceeding the speed limit.* **ex·ceed** (ik-**seed**)

▷ *verb* **exceeding, exceeded**

excel *verb* To do something extremely well: *To excel in a tough job, you need to be dedicated.* **ex·cel** (ik-**sel**) ▷ *verb* **excelling, excelled**

excellence *noun* The quality or state of being extremely good or superior, as in *academic excellence.* **ex·cel·lence** (**ek**-suh-luhns)

excellent *adjective* Very good: *The boys did an excellent job of cleaning up the playground.* **ex·cel·lent** (**ek**-suh-luhnt) ▷ *adverb* **excellently**

except

1. *preposition* Apart from; not including: *Everyone except Jamie stayed at the hotel.*

2. *conjunction* However; but for the fact that: *I would have bought it, except I didn't have enough money.* **ex·cept** (ik-**sept**)

exception *noun*
1. Something that is different or not included: *Julian dislikes yellow vegetables, with the exception of squash.*
2. If you **make an exception**, you do not include something or you do something in a different way than usual: *Because you were sick, I'll make an exception and give you an extra day for the assignment.*
ex·cep·tion (ik-**sep**-shuhn)

exceptional *adjective*
1. Unusual or rare: *Bella displays an exceptional aptitude for mathematics.*
2. Very good: *The steak at that restaurant is exceptional.*
ex·cep·tion·al (ik-**sep**-shuh-nuhl)

excerpt *noun* A short piece taken from a longer piece of writing, music, or film: *The author read us an excerpt from her new book.* **ex·cerpt** (**ek**-surpt)
▷ *verb* **excerpt** (ik-**surpt**)

excess
1. *noun* A larger amount than is needed or wanted: *When the water overflowed, I used a sponge to soak up the excess.*
2. *adjective* Extra; more than is needed or wanted: *The excess money in the gym fund was transferred to the music department.*
3. in excess of More than an amount: *He earns in excess of $100,000 a year.*
4. *noun* If you do something **to excess**, you do it too much.
ex·cess (**ek**-ses *or* ik-**ses**)
▷ *noun, plural* **excesses**

excessive *adjective* More than necessary: *Mike spends an excessive amount of time playing games online.* **ex·ces·sive** (ik-**ses**-iv) ▷ *adverb* **excessively**

exchange
1. *verb* To give one thing and receive a similar thing back: *Sally and I exchange birthday gifts every year.*
▷ *verb* **exchanging, exchanged**
▷ *noun* **exchange**
2. *noun* A place where people meet to buy and sell such things as stocks or merchandise, as in *a stock exchange.*
3. exchange rate *noun* A comparison of the worth of money in different countries. You use the exchange rate to calculate how much money you will get when you exchange one country's money for another.
ex·change (eks-**chaynj**)

excessive buying

excite *verb* To make someone feel eager and interested. **ex·cite** (ik-**site**) ▷ *verb* **exciting, excited**

excited *adjective* Eagerly interested and stimulated: *We were excited about going on the field trip.* **ex·cit·ed** (ik-**sye**-tid)

excitement *noun* A state or condition of being excited: *All the excitement of the party had left her thrilled but a little tired.* **ex·cite·ment** (ik-**site**-muhnt)

exciting *adjective* Causing eager enthusiasm and interest about something: *The game was exciting right up until the last minute.* **ex·cit·ing** (ik-**sye**-ting)

exclaim *verb* To say something suddenly or with force, especially because you are surprised or excited: *"You won? You are so lucky!" exclaimed Teresa.* **ex·claim** (ik-**sklaym**) ▷ *verb* **exclaiming, exclaimed** ▷ *noun* **exclamation** (ek-skluh-**may**-shuhn)

exclamation point *noun* The punctuation mark (!) used after a sentence or word to show surprise, excitement, or another strong feeling. It is also known as an *exclamation mark.*

exclude *verb*
1. To keep someone from joining or taking part in something: *Don't exclude your little sister from the game.* ▷ *noun* **exclusion**
2. To leave out or not consider something: *The judge ruled to exclude part of the evidence.* ▷ *preposition* **excluding** **ex·clude** (ik-**sklood**) ▷ *verb* **excluding, excluded**

exclamation point

exclusive
1. *adjective* Available or offered only to one person, or to a special group: *The network's exclusive interview with the winner will be broadcast tonight.*
2. *adjective* Complete or whole: *You have my exclusive attention.*
3. *noun* A story that appears in one place only, as in *a magazine exclusive.* **ex·clu·sive** (ik-**skloo**-siv)

exclusively *adverb* Only; in a way that excludes all others: *He used to be a studio photographer, but now he's focusing exclusively on making videos.* **ex·clu·sive·ly** (ik-**skloo**-siv-lee)

excrete *verb* To get rid of waste matter or other substances from the body: *You excrete a lot of sweat during a long race.* **ex·crete** (ik-**skreet**) ▷ *verb* **excreting, excreted** ▷ *noun* **excretion** ▷ *adjective* **excretory** (**ek**-skruh-*tor*-ee)

excruciating *adjective* Very painful, as in *an excruciating headache.* **ex·cru·ci·a·ting** (ik-**skroo**-shee-*ay*-ting) ▷ *adverb* **excruciatingly**

excursion *noun*
1. A short trip for pleasure, often to an interesting place.
2. An **excursion fare**, on a plane, train, or other form of passenger transportation, is cheaper than the standard fare.
ex·cur·sion (ik-**skur**-zhuhn)

excuse
1. (ik-**skyoos**) *noun* A reason you give to explain a mistake or why you have done something wrong.
2. (ik-**skyoos**) *noun* A false reason someone gives for not doing something: *Monica hadn't sprained her ankle, but she used it as an excuse to get out of running laps.*
3. (ik-**skyooz**) *verb* To allow someone not to do something: *Our gym teacher excused Kristy from class because she wasn't feeling well.*
4. (ik-**skyooz**) *verb* To forgive someone who has done something wrong or offensive. ▷ *adjective* **excusable**
ex·cuse
▷ *verb* **excusing, excused**

execute *verb*
1. To do something that you have planned: *The company executed a plan to increase its sales.*
2. To kill someone to punish him or her for a crime.
ex·e·cute (**ek**-suh-*kyoot*)
▷ *verb* **executing, executed**

execution *noun*
1. The way that something is carried out, done, or performed: *The players' poor execution of the coach's strategy cost them the game.*
2. The killing of a person who has been condemned to death, usually for a crime.
ex·e·cu·tion (*ek*-suh-**kyoo**-shuhn)

executive
1. *noun* Someone who has one of the highest jobs in a company or organization. ▷ *adjective* **executive**
2. *adjective* Of or having to do with the branch of government that carries out the laws of the United States or any state: *The president represents the executive branch of government.*
ex·ec·u·tive (ig-**zek**-yuh-tiv)

exempt
1. *adjective* Excused from having to do something that others have to do: *Some of the school's athletes are exempt from physical education classes.*

exercise

2. *verb* To officially excuse someone, or leave something out of a rule or law. ▷ *verb* **exempting, exempted**
ex·empt (ig-**zempt**)
▷ *noun* **exemption**

exercise
1. *noun* Physical activity that you do to stay strong and healthy: *Jorge is doing exercises that will strengthen his biceps and his back.*
2. *verb* To do physical activities, such as sports, in order to stay strong and healthy.
3. *noun* Something that you do in order to practice a skill, as in *writing exercises.*
4. *verb* To put something, such as a skill or right, into practice: *Every eligible citizen can exercise his or her right to vote.*
ex·er·cise (**ek**-sur-*size*)
▷ *verb* **exercising, exercised**

exert *verb*
1. To make an effort to do something: *Philip had to exert himself to get his book report done on time.*
2. To use power or control to make something happen: *The hospital is exerting pressure on doctors to keep more thorough records.*
ex·ert (ig-**zurt**)
▷ *verb* **exerting, exerted** ▷ *noun* **exertion**

exhale *verb* To breathe out of your mouth or nose. **ex·hale** (eks-**hale**) ▷ *verb* **exhaling, exhaled** ▷ *noun* **exhalation**

exhaust

1. *verb* To make someone feel very tired: *Latisha was exhausted after running to catch the dog.* ▷ *adjective* **exhausting** ▷ *adjective* **exhausted**

2. *verb* To use up all of something, as in *to exhaust natural resources.*

3. *noun* The gases or steam produced by the engine of a motor vehicle, as in *car exhaust.*

4. *noun* The pipe on a motor vehicle that releases waste gases.

ex·haust (ig-**zawst**)

▷ *verb* **exhausting, exhausted**

exhaustion *noun* The state of being extremely tired and unable to continue: *She was working three jobs until the physical exhaustion wore her out.* **ex·haus·tion** (ig-**zaws**-chuhn)

exhibit *verb* To show a thing or a group of things to the public: *They will exhibit the paintings next week.* **ex·hib·it** (ig-**zib**-it) ▷ *verb* **exhibiting, exhibited** ▷ *noun* **exhibit** ▷ *noun* **exhibitor**

exhibition *noun* A public display of things that interest people, as in *a museum exhibition on Egyptian mummies.* **ex·hi·bi·tion** (ek-suh-**bish**-uhn)

exhilarating *adjective* Very exciting and enjoyable, as in *an exhilarating ride on the roller coaster.* **ex·hil·a·rat·ing** (ig-**zil**-uh-*ray*-ting) ▷ *noun* **exhilaration** ▷ *verb* **exhilarate**

exile

1. *verb* To send someone away from his or her own country, usually for political reasons: *The king was exiled from his homeland for 20 years.* ▷ *verb* **exiling, exiled**

2. *noun* A person who has been sent away from his or her country.

3. *noun* A situation in which you are forbidden to live in your own country: *After 12 years in exile, the prince returned to the island of his birth.*

ex·ile (**eg**-zile *or* **ek**-sile)

exist *verb*

1. To be real or alive: *Do unicorns really exist?*

2. To have barely enough food to stay alive: *They existed on nuts and berries until they were rescued.*

ex·ist (ig-**zist**)

▷ *verb* **existing, existed**

existence *noun*

1. The fact or state of being real or alive: *Do you know of the existence of any other paintings by him?*

2. The condition of continuing to be alive: *The fish's existence depends on the health of the algae that they feed on.*

ex·ist·ence (ig-**zis**-tuhns)

exit

1. *verb* To leave or go out of a place: *You can exit at the front or back of the theater.* ▷ *verb* **exiting, exited**

2. *noun* The way out of a place, such as a door.

3. *noun* The act of going away or leaving: *She made a quick exit to avoid the crowds.*

ex·it (**eg**-zit *or* **ek**-sit)

exodus *noun* A departure of a large number of people at one time: *After the big game, there was a mass exodus.* **ex·o·dus** (**ek**-suh-duhs)

Word History

The Book of **Exodus** in the Bible tells the story of the Israelites leaving Egypt because they wanted to be free from slavery. The Greek word *exodos* meant "going out," from *ex-*, a prefix meaning "out," and *hodos*, a root meaning "road." You can see the same Greek root in the words *period* and *episode*.

exorbitant *adjective* Much more or higher than necessary: *The fruits and vegetables are excellent at that market, but the prices are exorbitant.* **ex·or·bi·tant** (ig-**zor**-buh-tuhnt) ▷ *adverb* **exorbitantly**

exotic *adjective*

1. Unusual and fascinating, as in *an exotic flavor.*

2. From a faraway country, as in *an exotic bird.*

ex·o·tic (ig-**zah**-tik)

Word History

Anything that is **exotic** must not be from "here," because the word *exotic* goes back to the Greek term for "outside." Speakers of ancient Greek formed *exotikos* from the word *exo*, meaning "outside." The English word *exodus* is related to *exotic.*

expand *verb* To become larger: *Rice expands when it's cooked.* **ex·pand** (ik-**spand**) ▷ *verb* **expanding, expanded** ▷ *adjective* **expandable**

expanse *noun* A large, open area: *To reach the foothills, we had to cross a broad expanse of prairie.* **ex·panse** (ik-**spans**)

expansion *noun* The act or process of expanding or being expanded: *The mayor pushed for the expansion of the city's borders.* **ex·pan·sion** (ik-**span**-shuhn)

expect *verb*

1. To wait for someone or something to arrive: *We're expecting a package tomorrow.*

2. To think that something should happen: *Our teacher expects us to behave properly.*

3. If a woman is **expecting**, she is going to have a baby.

ex·pect (ik-**spekt**)

▷ *verb* **expecting, expected**

a
b
c
d
e
f
g
h
i
j
k
l
m
n
o
p
q
r
s
t
u
v
w
x
y
z

expectation *noun* A strong belief that something will happen or be true: *He is the best chess player in the group, so my expectation is that he will win the tournament.* **ex·pec·ta·tion** (*ek*-spek-**tay**-shuhn)

expedition *noun*
1. A long trip made for a specific purpose, such as for exploration.
2. A short trip to do something you enjoy, as in *a fishing expedition.*
ex·pe·di·tion (*ek*-spuh-**dish**-uhn)

expel *verb*
1. To make someone leave a school or organization, usually because of poor behavior.
2. To send or push something out: *I expelled the water from my snorkel by blowing into the mouthpiece.*
ex·pel (ik-**spel**)
▷ *verb* **expelling, expelled** ▷ *noun* **expulsion** (ik-**spuhl**-shuhn)

expenditure *noun*
1. The spending or using up of time or money for a purpose.
2. The total amount of money that a person, company, or government spends.
ex·pend·i·ture (ik-**spen**-di-chur)

expense *noun* Money for a particular job or task, as in *business expenses.* **ex·pense** (ik-**spens**)

expensive *adjective* Costing a lot of money.
ex·pen·sive (ik-**spen**-siv) ▷ *adverb* **expensively**

experience
1. *noun* Something that happens to you: *Going camping in the snow was quite an experience.*
2. *verb* If you **experience** something, it happens to you: *She experienced great joy at being back in her homeland.* ▷ *verb* **experiencing, experienced**
3. *noun* The knowledge and skills that you gain by doing a job or activity: *Do you have any experience in using computers?*
▷ *adjective* **experienced**
ex·pe·ri·ence (ik-**speer**-ee-uhns)

experiment
1. *noun* A test to try out a theory or to see the effect of something.
2. *verb* To scientifically test or try something in order to learn something particular: *Scientists were experimenting with mice when they discovered the phenomenon.*
3. *verb* To try something new to find out what it is like: *We've been experimenting with different kinds of*

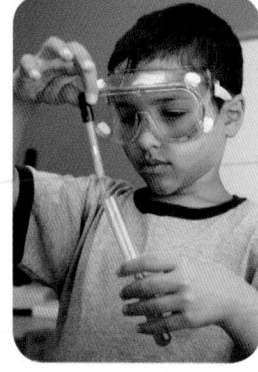
experiment

peanut butter in the recipe.
ex·per·i·ment (ik-**sper**-uh-ment)
▷ *verb* **experimenting, experimented**

experimental *adjective* Not yet tested thoroughly or proven. **ex·per·i·men·tal** (ik-*sper*-uh-**men**-tuhl)

expert *noun* Someone who has a special skill or knows a lot about a particular subject: *She is an expert on modern art.* **ex·pert** (ek-spurt) ▷ *adjective* **expert** (ek-**spurt** or ek-spurt)

expertise *noun* Expert skill or knowledge about something: *Pole-vaulting requires enormous technical expertise as well as confidence and strong nerves.* **ex·per·tise** (ek-spur-**teez**)

expire *verb*
1. When something **expires**, it reaches the end of the time when it can be legally or properly used: *My driver's license expires next month.* ▷ *noun* **expiration** (*ek*-spuh-**ray**-shuhn)
2. To die.
ex·pire (ik-**spire**)
▷ *verb* **expiring, expired**

explain *verb*
1. To make something easier to understand.
▷ *adjective* **explanatory** (ik-**splan**-uh-*tor*-ee)
2. To give or be a reason for something: *I had to explain why I had missed class.*
ex·plain (ik-**splayn**)
▷ *verb* **explaining, explained**

explanation *noun* A statement or fact that explains or provides the reason for something: *Lori's explanation for why she was late didn't satisfy the teacher.* **ex·pla·na·tion** (*ek*-spluh-**nay**-shuhn)

explicit *adjective*
1. Very clearly stated: *The instructor gave the pilots explicit instructions on how to open their parachutes.*
2. Containing sex, violence, bad language, or other material that many people do not like to see.
ex·plic·it (ik-**splis**-it)

explode *verb*
1. To burst into pieces with a loud noise and great force.
2. To get very loud and angry suddenly: *He exploded with rage when the waiter gave him the wrong drink.*
3. To prove an idea or opinion false: *This article explodes the image people have of the actor.*
ex·plode (ik-**splode**)
▷ *verb* **exploding, exploded**

exploit
1. (**ek**-sploit) *noun* A brave or exciting action.
2. (ek-**sploit**) *verb* To treat someone unfairly for your own advantage: *The company was fined for exploiting illegal immigrants.*
3. (ek-**sploit**) *verb* To use something for your own advantage: *We are exploiting all available resources to*

explosion

get the fire under control.

ex·ploit

▷ *verb* **exploiting, exploited** ▷ *noun* **exploitation**

exploration *noun* The act of studying an unknown thing or place. **ex·plo·ra·tion** (*ek*-spluh-**ray**-shuhn)

explore *verb*

1. To travel and look around in order to discover things. ▷ *noun* **explorer**

2. To think carefully about something: *Before buying a car, Hal did a lot of research online and explored his options.*

ex·plore (ik-**splor**)

▷ *verb* **exploring, explored** ▷ *adjective* **exploratory**

explosion *noun*

1. A sudden and loud burst of energy.

2. A sudden increase in the number or amount of something, as in *a population explosion.*

ex·plo·sion (ik-**sploh**-zhuhn)

explosive

1. *noun* Something that can blow up, as in *powerful explosives.*

2. *adjective* Able to cause an explosion. ▷ *adverb* **explosively**

3. *adjective* If a situation is **explosive**, it is likely to make people angry or violent.

ex·plo·sive (ik-**sploh**-siv)

exponent *noun* A number placed next to and above another to show how many times that number is to be multiplied by itself: *In 4^3, 3 is the exponent.* **ex·po·nent** (ik-**spoh**-nuhnt)

export

1. (ek-**sport** *or* **ek**-sport) *verb* To send products to another country to sell them there: *Mexico exports*

mangoes and oranges to the United States.

2. (ek-**sport** *or* **ek**-sport) *verb* To create a copy of a computer file in a different format so you can use it with another program: *After you scan the photos, you can export them as JPEGs.*

3. (**ek**-sport) *noun* The act of selling something to another country, or a product sold this way: *One of our major exports is soybeans.* ▷ *noun* **exporter**

ex·port

▷ *verb* **exporting, exported**

expose *verb*

1. To uncover something so it can be seen.

2. To reveal a secret about someone or something: *The scandal was exposed on the news last night.*

3. To let light fall on photographic film.

4. To leave in the open, without protection: *When the tent blew away, we were exposed to the full force of the storm.*

5. To put someone in danger: *The fumes from the oil refinery exposed the people in the town to harmful chemicals.*

6. To let someone experience something: *Serena's parents want to expose her to classical music.*

ex·pose (ik-**spoze**)

▷ *verb* **exposing, exposed**

exposé *noun* An article that investigates and exposes a serious problem: *The newspaper published an exposé last year on the filthy conditions at the meatpacking plant.* **ex·po·sé** (*ek*-spuh-**zay**)

exposure *noun*

1. The act of coming into contact with something harmful: *Chronic exposure to low levels of radiation can cause cancer.*

2. The act of coming into contact with something: *The three-month study program gives students exposure to another language and culture.*

3. The harmful effect of severe weather on someone's body: *The mountain climbers suffered from frostbite and exposure.*

4. A piece of film that produces a photo when it is exposed to light: *This film has 24 exposures per roll.*

5. The length of time that the shutter is open when you take a picture.

ex·po·sure (ik-**spoh**-zhur)

express

1. *verb* To show what you feel or think with words, writing, or actions: *I find it hard sometimes to express my emotions.* ▷ *verb* **expresses, expressing, expressed**

2. *noun* A fast train or bus that does not stop in many places. ▷ *noun, plural* **expresses**

3. *adjective* Faster than usual, as in *express service.*

ex·press (ik-**spres**)

expression *noun*
1. A phrase that has a particular meaning, as in *the expression "break a leg."*
2. The look on someone's face that shows what he or she is feeling or thinking, as in *an angry expression.*
3. A way of showing your feelings, as in *an expression of our concern.*
ex·pres·sion (ik-**spresh**-uhn)

expressive *adjective* Full of meaning or feeling: *The mime's expressive eyes allowed him to communicate sadness without using words.* **ex·pres·sive** (ik-**spres**-iv) ▷ *adverb* **expressively**

expressway *noun* A wide highway without traffic lights or stop signs that you can only get onto and get off at certain places. **ex·press·way** (ik-**spres**-*way*)

exquisite *adjective* Very beautiful and finely done, as in *exquisite jewelry.* **ex·quis·ite** (ek-**skwiz**-it *or* **ek**-skwi-zit) ▷ *adverb* **exquisitely**

extend *verb*
1. To make something longer or larger: *The frog extended its tongue, catching the beetle.*
2. To stretch out, or go as far as: *Our yard extends to the lake.*
3. To offer, as in *to extend a warm welcome.*
ex·tend (ik-**stend**)
▷ *verb* **extending, extended**

extension *noun*
1. The increasing of something in time or space, as in *an extension on a class assignment.*
2. A new part added to an existing building.
3. An extra telephone added to an existing phone line.
4. See **file extension.**
ex·ten·sion (ik-**sten**-shuhn)

extensive *adjective*
1. Covering a wide area: *The storms brought extensive flooding to the northern part of the state.*
2. Containing or including a lot of things, as in *an extensive menu.*
ex·ten·sive (ik-**sten**-siv)

extent *noun* How large, serious, or important something is: *We still don't know the extent of the flooding.* **ex·tent** (ik-**stent**)

exterior *noun* The outer part of something, especially a building: *What color are you going to use for the exterior?* **ex·te·ri·or** (ek-**steer**-ee-ur) ▷ *adjective* **exterior**

exterminate *verb* To kill large numbers of something, especially insects or animals. **ex·ter·mi·nate** (ik-**stur**-muh-nate) ▷ *verb* **exterminating, exterminated** ▷ *noun* **extermination** ▷ *noun* **exterminator**

external *adjective* On the outside of something: *The external part of the shell is shiny.* **ex·ter·nal** (ek-**stur**-nuhl) ▷ *adverb* **externally**

expressway

extinct *adjective*
1. No longer found alive; known about only through fossils or history: *The woolly mammoth became extinct at the end of the Ice Age.* ▷ *noun* **extinction**
2. If a volcano is **extinct**, it does not erupt anymore.
ex·tinct (ik-**stingkt**)

extinguish *verb*
1. To make a fire stop burning. ▷ *noun* **extinguisher**
2. To cause the end or death of something, as in *to extinguish hope.*
ex·tin·guish (ik-**sting**-gwish)
▷ *verb* **extinguishes, extinguishing, extinguished**

extra
1. *adjective* More than the usual or normal amount, as in *an extra helping of potatoes.*
2. *adverb* Extremely, or more than usual, as in *extra large.*
3. *noun* Something that is added to the usual or the normal: *The extras on the new car included an alarm system and air-conditioning.*
ex·tra (**ek**-struh)

extract
1. (ek-**strakt**) *verb* To remove or pull something out: *The dentist extracted her wisdom teeth.* ▷ *verb* **extracting, extracted** ▷ *noun* **extraction**
2. (**ek**-strakt) *noun* A short piece taken from a book, speech, song, or other work.
ex·tract

extraordinary *adjective* Very unusual or impressive, as in *an extraordinary tale.* **ex·traor·di·nar·y** (ek-**stror**-duh-*ner*-ee) ▷ *adverb* **extraordinarily**

extraterrestrial
1. *adjective* Coming from a place beyond the earth, or beyond our solar system: *The topic of the conference was the search for extraterrestrial life.*
2. *noun* A being from outer space.
ex·tra·ter·res·tri·al (*ek*-struh-tuh-**res**-tree-uhl)

extravagant *adjective* Very wasteful of money or resources, as in *a movie star's extravagant lifestyle.* **ex·trav·a·gant** (ik-**strav**-uh-guhnt) ▷ *adverb* **extravagantly**

Word History

The *extra-* in **extravagant** is the same as our word *extra,* meaning "more than the usual amount." In Latin, the prefix *extra-* meant "outside," and *vagari* was the word for "wander." So an *extravagant* person several centuries ago was someone who wandered around outside. For example, a military officer who was supposed to move around constantly, because he had to check on soldiers in different locations, was called *extravagant.* Soon people began to connect the word with the idea of going out of bounds, and it came to have the sense of "doing what you are not supposed to do." So they referred to someone who was spending too much money as *extravagant.*

extreme
   1. *adjective* Very great, as in *extreme temperatures.*
   2. *adjective* Farthest from the center, as in *a neighborhood at the extreme edge of town.*
   3. *noun* Either of two opposites, as in *extremes of love and hate.*
   4. *adjective* Exciting and very dangerous, as in *extreme sports.*
   ex·treme (ik-**streem**)

extremely *adverb* To a high or extreme degree; very: *It's extremely important that you carry out the steps in the exact order listed.* **ex·treme·ly** (ik-**streem**-lee)

extremist
   1. *noun* A person who has extreme views, usually about religion or politics: *The party's leaders worry that if it becomes dominated by extremists, it will lose more moderate followers.*
   2. *adjective* Of or having to do with extremists, as in *extremist groups.*
   ex·trem·ist (ik-**stree**-mist)

extremity *noun*
   1. The extreme point or end of something.
   2. **extremities** Your hands and feet: *Frostbite usually attacks your extremities first.*
   ex·trem·i·ty (ik-**strem**-i-tee)
   ▷ *noun, plural* **extremities**

extrovert *noun* Someone who enjoys being with other people and is confident and talkative. **ex·tro·vert** (**ek**-struh-*vurt*) ▷ *adjective* **extrovert** ▷ *adjective* **extroverted**

exuberant *adjective* Very cheerful and bubbly, as in *an exuberant mood.* **ex·u·ber·ant** (ig-**zoo**-bur-uhnt) ▷ *noun* **exuberance** ▷ *adverb* **exuberantly**

eye
   1. *noun* Either of the pair of organs that you use to see with.

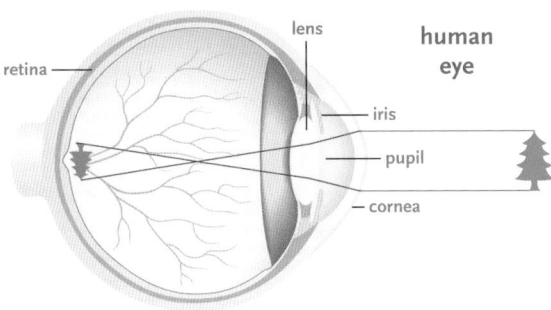

human eye

lens
retina
iris
pupil
cornea

   2. *noun* The small hole on one end of a needle.
   3. *noun* The calm, clear area at the center of a hurricane.
   4. If you **have an eye for something**, you are able to assess its value accurately: *Sue has an eye for bargains.*
   5. *verb* To look at someone or something in a close or careful way: *Rob eyed his opponent suspiciously.* ▷ *verb* **eyeing, eyed**
   eye (eye)

eyeball
   1. *noun* The round part of the eye that is found in nearly all animals with backbones.
   2. *verb* To take a close look at something: *The baseball player eyeballed the distance to the back fence before he hit the ball.* ▷ *verb* **eyeballing, eyeballed**
   eye·ball (**eye**-*bawl*)

eyebrow *noun* The line of hair that grows at the base of your forehead, above each of your eyes. **eye·brow** (**eye**-*brou*)

eyeglasses

eyeglasses *noun, plural* A pair of lenses in a frame that helps a person see better. Also called **glasses**. **eye·glass·es** (**eye**-*glas*-iz)

eyelash *noun* One of the short, curved hairs that grows on the edge of an eyelid. **eye·lash** (**eye**-*lash*) ▷ *noun, plural* **eyelashes**

eyelid *noun* One of the folds of skin that covers the eye when it is closed. **eye·lid** (**eye**-*lid*)

eyesight *noun* The ability to see: *Maria's eyesight improved with glasses.* **eye·sight** (**eye**-*site*)

eyesore *noun* Something that is ugly and out of place: *That old shed is a real eyesore in the yard.* **eye·sore** (**eye**-*sor*)

eyewall *noun* The ring of enormous thunderstorms that surrounds the eye of a hurricane or cyclone: *The winds and rain became even worse as the eyewall passed over us.* **eye·wall** (**eye**-*wawl*)

eyewitness *noun* Someone who has seen something happen and can describe it, as in *an eyewitness to an accident.* **eye·wit·ness** (**eye**-*wit*-nis) ▷ *noun, plural* **eyewitnesses**

Ff

About F Originally, the shape of the letter **F** was an Egyptian hieroglyph for a horned viper. Some words that begin with an *f* sound are spelled *ph*. Examples: phonograph, phosphorescence, photo, phrase, physician. These words, and the letter combination *ph*, came from the Greeks. The letter *f* can sound like the letter *v*, as in the word *of*. Some words spelled *-augh* or *-ough*, such as *laugh* and *rough*, are pronounced with an *f* sound.

fable *noun*
1. A story that teaches a lesson. Fables often have animal characters that talk and act like people.
2. A lie or an untrue story.
fa·ble (**fay**-buhl)

fabric *noun* Cloth or material: *The fabric of her shirt is silky.* **fab·ric** (**fab**-rik)

fabulous *adjective*
1. Wonderful or marvelous. ▷ *adverb* **fabulously**
2. Amazing or hard to believe: *I wrote a story about dragons and other fabulous creatures.*
fab·u·lous (**fab**-yuh-luhs)

facade *noun*
1. The front of a building.
2. A person's **facade** is the way he or she wants to be seen or thought of: *Jaime kept up a brave facade, but he was really scared.*
fa·cade (fuh-**sahd**)

facade

face
1. *noun* The front part of your head, from your forehead to your chin.
2. *noun* An expression or look on the face: *The clown made a silly face.*
3. *noun* The front, outer, or upper surface of something, as in *a rock face* or *a watch face*.
4. *verb* To look toward something: *Our house faces the woods.* ▷ *adjective* **facing**
5. *verb* To deal with something boldly or bravely: *Maria faced her accusers.*
face (fase)
▷ *verb* **facing, faced**

facebook *verb* To bring attention to something by writing about it on the social networking site Facebook: *Megan facebooked a link for the upcoming school fair.* **face·book** (**fase**-buk) ▷ *verb* **facebooking, facebooked**

Language Note

Technology is introducing many new words into the language. Names for such companies as Facebook and the search engine Google are being turned into verbs, usually in a lowercase style. The word *google* was first included in an English dictionary in 2006. Using the verb **facebook** is even more recent. Facebook was founded in 2004, and is six years younger than Google. Words that did not exist even a decade ago are rapidly entering English and other languages around the world, spread through the internet. But some companies that own the trademark for these words object to their use.

facepalm *noun* A gesture in which you bring the palm of your hand to your face. You might do this when you have made a silly mistake or done something clumsy that makes you feel embarrassed or ashamed. **face·palm** (**fase**-pahm)

facet *noun*
1. A flat, polished surface of a cut gem.
2. A part or side of something: *Blake is a new father and is enjoying this new facet of his life.*
fac·et (**fas**-it)

facial
1. *adjective* Of or having to do with the face: *The clown's facial expressions were very silly.*
2. *noun* A relaxing treatment that cleanses and tones the skin of your face.
fa·cial (**fay**-shuhl)

facilitate *verb* To make something easier: *A computer can facilitate the task of writing a report.* **fa·cil·i·tate** (fuh-**sil**-i-tate) ▷ *verb* **facilitating, facilitated** ▷ *noun* **facilitator**

facility *noun*
1. The ability to do something easily or skillfully: *Lena has a great facility for math.*
2. A place or building for a particular activity, as in *an ice-skating facility* or *a hospital facility*.
fa·cil·i·ty (fuh-**sil**-i-tee) ▷ *noun, plural* **facilities**

facsimile *noun*
1. A reproduction or exact copy of something written or of a work of art: *The museum sells facsimiles of its*

most popular paintings.
2. *See* **fax.**
fac·sim·i·le (fak-**sim**-uh-lee)

fact *noun*
1. A piece of information that is known to be true, as in *a scientific fact.*
2. in fact Actually or really: *I thought he was coming with us, but in fact he chose to stay home.*
fact (fakt)

factor *noun*
1. Something that helps produce a result: *Her quick response time was the principal factor why she did so well on the quiz show.*
2. A whole number that can be divided into a larger number without a remainder: *The numbers 1, 2, 3, 4, 6, and 12 are factors of 12.*
fac·tor (**fak**-tur)

automobile factory

factory *noun* A building where products, such as cars or chemicals, are made in large numbers, often using machines. Also called a **plant.** **fac·to·ry** (**fak**-tur-ee)
▷ *noun, plural* **factories**

factual *adjective* If something is **factual,** it is real or true; it contains a fact: *The government has issued a factual report on global warming.* **fac·tu·al** (**fak**-choo-uhl) ▷ *adverb* **factually**

faculty *noun*
1. The teachers and professors at a school, college, or university, or a group of them, as in *the history faculty.*
2. One of the powers of the body or mind, such as memory, reason, sight, or speech.
3. A unique talent or ability: *She has a faculty for making friends easily.*
fac·ul·ty (**fak**-uhl-tee)
▷ *noun, plural* **faculties**

fad *noun* Something that is very popular for a short time. **fad** (fad)

fade *verb*
1. To lose color and become paler: *My red shirt has faded because I've washed it so many times.*
2. To lose freshness and strength: *The flowers in the vase are beginning to fade.*
3. To disappear slowly or become weaker: *The cheers finally faded away.*
fade (fade)
▷ *verb* **fading, faded**

Fahrenheit *adjective* Based on the measurement of temperature using a scale in which water boils at 212 degrees and freezes at 32 degrees. **Fahr·en·heit** (**far**-uhn-*hite*)

fail *verb*
1. If you **fail** to do something, you do not do it: *Jimmy failed to clean his room.*
2. If you **fail** a test, you do not pass it.
3. If you **fail** someone, you do not do what is expected of you: *Georgia failed her teammates when she didn't show up for the game.*
4. To break down or stop working: *Fortunately, no one was hurt when the brakes in the car failed.*
5. To lose power or strength: *My grandfather's hearing is failing.*
6. To go bankrupt: *Many businesses fail due to lack of proper planning.*
7. without fail Surely, certainly, or every single time: *Grandma calls us every Sunday without fail.*
fail (fayl)
▷ *verb* **failing, failed**

failure *noun*
1. Someone or something that is not successful.
2. Lack of favorable results: *Despite all her hard work, her new business venture ended in failure.*
3. A weakening or loss of ability, as in *heart failure.*
4. The fact that you did not do something you were supposed to do: *Toshi got fired because of his failure to show up on time for his job.*
fail·ure (**fayl**-yur)

faint
1. *adjective* Not clear or strong, as in *a faint voice.*
2. *adjective* Dizzy and weak: *I felt faint after climbing four flights of stairs.*
3. *verb* To suddenly lose consciousness for a short time: *Charles fainted when he saw the crash.* ▷ *verb* **fainting, fainted** ▷ *noun* **faint**
4. *adjective* Weak or feeble; small: *There is a faint chance of rain tomorrow.*
faint (faynt)
Faint sounds like **feint**. ▷ *noun* **faintness** ▷ *adjective* **fainter, faintest** ▷ *adverb* **faintly**

faint-hearted *adjective* Timid or scared; not confident. **faint-heart-ed** (hahr-tid)

fair

1. *adjective* Reasonable and just, as in *fair laws.* ▷ *noun* **fairness**

2. *adjective* **Fair** hair is light colored.

3. *adjective* Neither good nor bad: *Greg is only a fair student.*

4. *adjective* **Fair** weather is clear and sunny.

5. *adjective* Having a pleasing appearance, as in *a fair princess.*

6. *noun* An outdoor show of farm products and animals, often with entertainment, food, and rides.

7. *adverb* By the rules: *Play fair!* ▷ *adverb* **fairer, fairest**

fair (fair)

Fair sounds like **fare**. ▷ *adjective* **fairer, fairest**

fairground *noun* A large outdoor area where fairs are held. **fair-ground** (fair-*ground*)

fairly *adverb*

1. Quite; somewhat: *Even though his closet is fairly large, it isn't big enough to hold all his clothes.*

2. In a way that is reasonable and just: *We have to play fairly, or they won't play with us.*

fair-ly (fair-lee)

fairy *noun* An imaginary creature with magical abilities that looks like a tiny person with wings, found in fairy tales. **fair-y** (fair-ee) ▷ *noun, plural* **fairies**

fairy tale *noun*

1. A children's story about magical beings such as fairies, giants, and witches. Some fairy tales, such as "Cinderella," are many hundreds of years old.

2. A made-up story, usually meant to deceive: *His account of his adventures in Australia was just a fairy tale—he never even went there.*

fairy tale

faith *noun*

1. Confidence in someone or something: *My teacher has faith in my ability to understand complicated math problems.*

2. Belief in God, or in a system or religion.

3. A religion: *People of all faiths are welcome here.*

faith (fayth)

faithful *adjective* Loyal and worthy of trust: *Amrita's faithful dog barked at* anyone who came near her. **faith-ful** (fayth-fuhl) ▷ *noun* **faithfulness** ▷ *adverb* **faithfully**

fake

1. *verb* To pretend that something is genuine: *Sabrina faked a headache to avoid taking the test.*

2. *verb* To make a copy of something and pretend that it is the real thing: *John faked his mother's signature on the note from school.* ▷ *noun* **faker** ▷ *adjective* **fake**

3. *noun* Someone or something that is not what it seems to be: *This is not a real diamond, but it's a good fake.*

fake (fake)

▷ *verb* **faking, faked**

fake news *noun* Information that is not true, presented as if it were true and important: *The social media companies are under pressure to prevent fake news from appearing on legitimate websites.*

falcon *noun* A bird that hunts small birds and animals and has long wings and hooked claws. **fal-con** (fawl-kuhn *or* fal-kuhn)

fall

1. *verb* To drop from a higher place to a lower place: *Some snow is falling.*

2. *verb* To lessen or become lower: *The house's value has fallen significantly in the past year.*

3. *verb* To become: *When the principal entered the room, all the students fell silent.*

4. *verb* To happen or take place: *Thanksgiving always falls on a Thursday.*

5. *noun* The season between summer and winter, when it gets colder, the sun sets earlier, and the leaves turn color and then fall from the trees. Also called **autumn**.

6. *verb* To be defeated, captured, or overthrown: *The town fell to the enemy after a long battle.*

7. *verb* If two people **fall out**, they argue and stop getting along well.

8. *verb* If something **falls through**, it doesn't happen: *Our plans for the picnic fell through because of the rain.* ▷ *noun* **fall**

fall (fawl)

▷ *verb* **falling, fell, fallen**

fallen *verb* The past participle of **fall**. **fall-en** (faw-luhn)

fallout *noun*

1. Radioactive dust from a nuclear explosion.

2. The result of an action: *He made risky financial decisions, and the fallout was that he lost his home.*

fall-out (fawl-*out*)

falcon

fallow *adjective* Land that is **fallow** has not been planted with crops and is being allowed to rest, so that its nutrients can be restored. **fal·low** (**fal**-oh)

false *adjective*
1. Not true or correct: *The false data led her to make a bad decision.* ▷ *adverb* **falsely**
2. Not loyal: *Liars make false friends.*
3. Not real, as in *false fingernails.*
false (fawls)

falsehood *noun* A lie. **false·hood** (**fawls**-hud)

falsetto
1. *noun* A way of singing for a man that is very high and sounds like a woman's voice.
2. *noun* A male singer who uses this style of singing.
3. *adjective* Of or having to do with a falsetto.
4. *adverb* In a falsetto: *Tony started singing falsetto, surprising the other band members.*
fal·set·to (fawl-**set**-oh)

falter *verb*
1. To act or move in an unsteady way: *Pedro faltered as he tried to learn the dance step.*
2. To pause while speaking because you are unsure or confused: *Audrey faltered as she recited the poem because she couldn't remember the next line.*
fal·ter (**fawl**-tur)
▷ *verb* **faltering, faltered**

fame *noun* The condition of being well-known: *The young actor longed for fame.* **fame** (fame) ▷ *adjective* **famed**

familiar *adjective*
1. Well-known, common, or easily recognized, as in *a familiar tune.*
2. Knowing something well: *Clarisse and I are familiar with the rules of checkers.*
3. Friendly: *We are on familiar terms with our neighbors.*
fa·mil·iar (fuh-**mil**-yur)

family *noun*
1. A group of people related to each other, especially parents or guardians and their children.
2. A group of living things that are related to each other: *Donkeys and mules are members of the horse family.*
3. **family room** A room in a house that is used for relaxing, playing, and watching television: *We played games in the family room until the rain stopped.*
fam·i·ly (**fam**-uh-lee)
▷ *noun, plural* **families**

family name *noun* The part of your name that you share with any brothers and sisters and that is the same as one of your parents', usually your father.

family tree *noun* A diagram that shows how all the members of a family are related, going back many generations.

famine *noun* A serious lack of food in a geographic area. **fam·ine** (**fam**-in)

famished *adjective* Very hungry: *I was famished by the time I got to the picnic.* **fam·ished** (**fam**-isht)

famous *adjective* Very well-known to many people. **fa·mous** (**fay**-muhs)

fan *noun*
1. A person who is very interested in or enthusiastic about something, as in *a soccer fan* or *a music fan.*
2. A wooden or cardboard object that you use to wave air onto yourself in order to keep cool.
3. A machine that blows air around a room in order to cool it.
fan (fan)
▷ *verb* **fan**

Word History

When someone loves a sport or other entertainment a lot, he or she is a **fan**. The word *fan* is a shortened form of *fanatic*, which comes from the Latin word *fanaticus*, meaning "wildly excited." *Fanatic* now means having an intense feeling for something.

fanatic *noun* Someone who is very and sometimes overly enthusiastic about a belief, a cause, or an interest, as in *a sports fanatic* or *a religious fanatic.* **fa·nat·ic** (fuh-**nat**-ik) ▷ *adjective* **fanatical** ▷ *adverb* **fanatically**

fancy
1. *adjective* Decorated; not plain or ordinary: *Alberto eyed the fancy chocolates.* ▷ *adjective* **fancier, fanciest**
2. *noun* Imagination: *Ogres and trolls are creatures of fancy.*
3. *noun* A great liking: *My aunt has a fancy for big hats.*
4. *verb* To imagine: *He fancied himself a great baseball player.* ▷ *verb* **fancies, fancying, fancied**
fan·cy (**fan**-see)
▷ *noun, plural* **fancies**

fang *noun* An animal's long, pointed tooth. **fang** (fang)

fanny pack *noun* A small bag on a belt. It is worn around the waist and used to carry personal items. **fan·ny pack** (**fan**-ee)

fan

fantasize *verb* To imagine that something that is not real is happening: *I fantasized that I was the queen of England.* **fan·ta·size** (**fan**-tuh-*size*)
▷ *verb* **fantasizing, fantasized**

fantastic *adjective*
1. Very strange and unbelievable: *She told the most fantastic tale of being captured by aliens.*
2. Terrific or wonderful: *Frances told me she had a fantastic time in Mexico.*
fan·tas·tic (fan-**tas**-tik)
▷ *adverb* **fantastically**

fantasy *noun*
1. Something you imagine happening that is not realistic or likely to occur: *Ellen's favorite fantasy was to perform on stage before the president.*
2. A story with magical or strange characters, places, or events.
fan·ta·sy (**fan**-tuh-see or **fan**-tuh-zee)
▷ *noun, plural* **fantasies**

FAQ *noun* A file, document, or webpage that contains answers to questions people commonly ask. FAQ is short for *frequently asked questions: The FAQ on the website explains how to use the product.* **FAQ** (fak)
▷ *noun, plural* **FAQs**

far
1. *adverb* A great distance: *We rode our bikes far today.*
2. *adverb* Very much: *I'm enjoying this summer camp far more than the one I went to last year.*
3. *adjective* Distant or not near: *Jasper swam to the far side of the lake.*
far (fahr)
▷ *adjective, adverb* **farther, farthest** or **further, furthest**

faraway *adjective*
1. Distant or remote: *As a young boy, Christopher Columbus dreamed of visiting faraway lands.*
2. Dreamy or lost in thought: *I could tell she wasn't listening to me because she had a faraway look in her eyes.*
far·a·way (**fahr**-uh-*way*)

farce *noun* A ridiculous situation: *The losing candidate complained that the election was a farce.* **farce** (fahrs)

fare
1. *noun* The cost of a ticket to travel on a plane, bus, or other vehicle.
2. *noun* A particular kind of available foods: *The restaurant serves simple vegetarian fare.*
3. *verb* To get along: *How did you fare on your test?*
▷ *verb* **faring, fared**
fare (fair)
Fare sounds like **fair**.

Far East *noun* The countries in eastern Asia, such as China, Japan, and Korea.

dairy farm

farewell
1. *interjection* Good-bye and good luck: *Farewell, Hector! Have a good trip!*
2. *noun* A statement of good wishes for a journey: *We wished him farewell at the airport.*
3. *adjective* Last or final, as in *a farewell speech.*
fare·well (*fair*-**wel**)

far-fetched *adjective* Difficult to believe; not likely: *He gave a far-fetched excuse about why he didn't have his report ready.*

farm
1. *verb* To grow crops and raise animals: *My grandparents farmed 60 acres of land.* ▷ *verb* **farming, farmed** ▷ *noun* **farmer** ▷ *noun* **farming**
2. *noun* An area of land used for growing crops or raising animals, usually with a house and other buildings. ▷ *adjective* **farm**
farm (fahrm)

farmyard *noun* The open space enclosed by farm buildings, or the land around the farm buildings, especially the barnyard. **farm·yard** (**fahrm**-*yahrd*)

Farsi *noun* Another name for **Persian**. **Far·si** (**fahr**-see)

farsighted *adjective*
1. Able to see things in the distance more clearly than things that are close.
2. Able to imagine and plan for the future: *Melanie was farsighted enough to open a savings account so she could start putting money aside for a car.*
far·sight·ed (**fahr**-**sye**-tid)

farther
1. *adjective, adverb* A comparative of **far**. *Further* is a more common comparative of *far* than the word *farther*, but you can use *farther* when you are talking about physical distances.
2. *adverb* At greater distance than something else: *As part of my exercise program, I tried to walk farther each day.*
3. *adjective* More distant or remote: *The spacecraft is now in the farther reaches of the solar system.*
far·ther (**fahr**-THur)

farthest *adjective, adverb* A superlative of **far**. You use *farthest* to indicate what is most distant or remote, as in *the farthest corner of the basement.* **far·thest** (**fahr**-THist)

fascinate *verb* To attract and hold the attention of: *My cat sat at the window, fascinated by the bird outside.* **fas·ci·nate** (**fas**-uh-nate) ▷ *verb* **fascinating, fascinated** ▷ *noun* **fascination**

fascism *noun* A form of government in which a dictator and the dictator's political party have complete power over a country. **fas·cism** (**fash**-iz-uhm) ▷ *noun* **fascist**

fashion
1. *noun* A style or a piece of clothing that is popular at a certain time: *The latest fashions all look like they were designed for tall, skinny people.*
2. *noun* A way of doing things: *During the fire drill, we left the building in an orderly fashion.*
3. *verb* To make or shape something: *Dad fashioned a bird out of folded paper.* ▷ *verb* **fashioning, fashioned** **fash·ion** (**fash**-uhn)

fashionable *adjective* Liked and admired by many people at a particular time; in fashion: *Very tall hairdos and wigs were fashionable in 18th-century Europe.* **fash·ion·a·ble** (**fash**-uh-nuh-buhl) ▷ *adverb* **fashionably**

fast
1. *adjective* Moving quickly; rapid. ▷ *adverb* **fast**
2. *verb* To stop eating all food or particular foods for a time: *People sometimes fast because of their religion.* ▷ *verb* **fasting, fasted** ▷ *noun* **fast**

Synonyms

Fast means moving in a hurry and can be used as an adjective or an adverb. Adjective: *She's a fast runner.* Adverb: *She runs fast.* The examples below show synonyms that are adjectives.

- -

■ **Speedy** means having great quickness: *He's a speedy runner.* It also can mean happening faster than usual, as in *a speedy trial.*

■ **Hasty** means speedy, but implies carelessness: *My hasty decision did not allow me to weigh all the possibilities.*

■ **Rapid** means moving forward quickly: *I am making rapid progress in learning Spanish.*

■ **Quick** means very fast, and often refers to mental abilities: *Kia has a quick mind and comes up with good solutions to problems.*

■ **Swift** means quick to respond and often refers to physical speed: *Ben's swift action saved the dog from being hit by a car.*

---

3. *adjective* If a dye or color is **fast,** it will not fade when you wash the material.
4. *adjective* Ahead of the real time: *I set my alarm clock to be ten minutes fast.*
fast (fast)
▷ *adjective* **faster, fastest**

fasten *verb* To tie, attach, or close firmly: *Please fasten your seat belt before the plane takes off.* **fas·ten** (**fas**-uhn) ▷ *verb* **fastening, fastened** ▷ *noun* **fastening**

fastener *noun* An object such as a button, buckle, or clip that is used to hold something together: *Please help me close the fastener on this necklace.* **fas·ten·er** (**fas**-uh-nur)

fast food *noun* Food such as hamburgers, fried chicken, and pizza that is prepared and served quickly by restaurants: *Too much fast food in your diet can lead to health problems.*

fast track *noun* A way of doing something that gets results or success faster than the usual way: *This new technology will put our company on the fast track.*

fat
1. *adjective* Heavy or plump; weighing much more than normal. ▷ *noun* **fatness** ▷ *verb* **fatten**
2. *noun* An oily substance found in the body tissues of animals and some plants. Fats are found in foods such as meat, milk, cheese, nuts, and avocados. ▷ *adjective* **fatty**
3. *adjective* Thick and heavy, as in *a fat instruction manual.*
fat (fat)
▷ *adjective* **fatter, fattest**

fatal *adjective*
1. Causing or leading to death, as in *a fatal illness.* ▷ *adverb* **fatally**
2. Likely to have very bad or harmful results, as in *a fatal mistake.*
fa·tal (**fay**-tuhl)

fatality *noun* A death that results from an accident, disaster, war, or other violent cause. **fa·tal·i·ty** (fay-**tal**-i-tee) ▷ *noun, plural* **fatalities**

fast food

fate *noun*

1. A force that some believe controls events and people's lives: *The daredevil was sure that fate was on his side.*

2. Destiny: *It was fate that they should meet and fall in love.*

fate (fate)

fateful *adjective* Having a strong and usually bad effect on future events: *The cyclist made a fateful choice when he decided not to wear his helmet.* **fate·ful** (**fate**-fuhl) ▷ *adverb* **fatefully**

father *noun*

1. A male parent. ▷ *noun* **fatherhood** ▷ *adjective* **fatherly**

2. A priest.

fa·ther (**fah**-THur)

father-in-law *noun* Your **father-in-law** is the father of your wife or husband. ▷ *noun, plural* **fathers-in-law**

Father's Day *noun* A holiday that honors fathers, celebrated on the third Sunday in June.

fathom

1. *noun* A unit for measuring how deep the water is. One fathom equals six feet.

2. *verb* To be unable to understand something: *I can't fathom how the contestant could miss such an easy question.* ▷ *verb* **fathoming, fathomed**

fath·om (**faTH**-uhm)

Word History

If you stretch out your arms to the side and measure the length from your fingertips on one hand to your fingertips on the other hand, you will get an idea of how the word **fathom** got its meaning. The Old English word *faethm* meant "the length of the outstretched arms," estimated at six feet for an adult male. Later, people used this term mainly when they were measuring the depth of water. The word now carries both a meaning of depth and of embracing something. If you go deeply into something and fathom it, you have studied it so thoroughly that you understand it—you have wrapped your arms around it.

fatigue *noun* The feeling of being very tired or weary. **fa·tigue** (fuh-**teeg**) ▷ *verb* **fatigue**

faucet *noun* A device with a valve used to turn the flow of a liquid on or off. **fau·cet** (**faw**-sit)

fault

1. *noun* If something is your **fault,** you caused it to happen: *It was Ken's fault that they were late.*

2. *noun* Something wrong that keeps another thing from working well: *The car broke down because of a fault in the engine.*

3. *noun* A weakness in a person's character: *His greatest fault is laziness.*

4. *verb* To criticize or find problems with something or someone: *I faulted him for lying.* ▷ *verb* **faulting, faulted**

5. *noun* A large break in the earth's surface that can cause an earthquake, as in *the San Andreas Fault in California.*

fault (fawlt)

fauna *noun* The animals of a particular area or region: *The local fauna includes groundhogs, foxes, skunks, possums, and deer.* **fau·na** (**faw**-nuh)

favor

1. *noun* Something helpful or nice that you do for someone else: *Ronaldo lent me his bike as a favor.*

2. *verb* To prefer someone or something more than others; to have as a favorite: *Grandma always favored Aunt Rose—she spoiled her but was strict with all of the other children.*

3. *verb* To look like or be like someone from an earlier generation in your family: *Hank favors his grandfather.*

4. *noun* A small gift: *All the children at her party received crayons, coloring books, and other favors.*

5. If you are **in favor of** something, you approve of it and think it is good.

fa·vor (**fay**-vur)

▷ *verb* **favoring, favored**

favorable *adjective*

1. Helpful: *The favorable winds helped our sailboat get to shore quickly.*

earthquake fault

2. Approving, as in *a favorable review.*
3. Pleasing, as in *a favorable impression.*
fa·vor·a·ble (**fay**-vur-uh-buhl)

favorite
1. *noun* The person or thing that you like more than all the others: *Of all the big cats at the zoo, my favorite was the lion.*
2. *noun* The person, team, or animal that most people think will win a race: *The Chiefs are the favorite to win the semifinal.*
3. *adjective* Referring to the person or thing that you like more than all the others: *Regine's favorite color is blue.*
fa·vor·ite (**fay**-vur-it)

fawn *noun*
1. A deer less than a year old.
2. A light brown color. ▷ *adjective* **fawn**
fawn (fawn)

fax *noun* A copy of a document printed on a special machine, generated by an electrical signal sent on a telephone line. Fax is short for **facsimile**. **fax** (faks) ▷ *noun, plural* **faxes** ▷ *verb* **fax**

fax machine

fear
1. *noun* The feeling you have when you are afraid that something dangerous or bad will happen: *I felt fear when I saw the snake.* ▷ *adjective* **fearful**
2. *verb* To be afraid of someone or something: *Timmy feared the park bullies.*
3. *verb* To be worried about something: *Dad feared he would lose his job.*
fear (feer)
▷ *verb* **fearing, feared**

fearless *adjective* Not afraid, even when there is danger; very brave, as in *a fearless soldier.* **fear·less** (**feer**-lis) ▷ *adverb* **fearlessly**

fearsome *adjective* Very scary, as in *a fearsome creature.* **fear·some** (**feer**-suhm)

feasible *adjective* Able to be achieved successfully: *Getting to the top of the mountain is feasible despite the cold weather today.* **fea·si·ble** (**fee**-zuh-buhl) ▷ *noun* **feasibility** ▷ *adverb* **feasibly**

feast *noun* A large, special meal, usually for a lot of people on a holiday or other occasion: *The Thanksgiving feast included turkey, yams, and cranberry sauce.* **feast** (feest) ▷ *verb* **feast**

feat *noun* An achievement that shows great courage, strength, or skill: *Walking a tightrope is a tremendous feat.* **feat** (feet)

feather *noun* One of the light, soft parts that cover a bird's body. **feath·er** (**feTH**-ur) ▷ *adjective* **feathered** ▷ *adjective* **feathery**

feature *noun*
1. A particular part or quality of something: *My cell phone has some exciting new features.* ▷ *verb* **feature**
2. The different parts of a person's face: *His most striking feature is his large nose.*
3. A full-length movie.
4. A newspaper or magazine article, or a part of a TV show, that presents a particular subject.
fea·ture (**fee**-chur)

February *noun* The second month on the calendar, after January and before March. February has 28 days except in a leap year, when it has 29. **Feb·ru·ar·y** (**feb**-roo-*er*-ee *or* **feb**-yoo-*er*-ee)

Word History

The month of **February** gets its name from the Latin word for a feast of purification, *februa,* held every year on February 15 in ancient Rome.

fed *verb* The past tense and past participle of **feed**. **fed** (fed)

federal *adjective* In a country with a **federal** government, such as the United States, several states are united under and controlled by one central power or authority. However, each state also has its own government and can make its own laws. **fed·er·al** (**fed**-ur-uhl)

federation *noun* A union of states, nations, or other groups joined together by an agreement, as in *the Russian Federation.* **fed·er·a·tion** (*fed*-uh-**ray**-shuhn)

fed up *adjective* (*informal*) If you are **fed up,** you are annoyed, bored, or disgusted about something.

fee *noun* The amount of money that is charged for a service, as in *an airline baggage fee.* **fee** (fee)

feeble *adjective* Weak; not strong enough: *She tried to read by the feeble light of the candle.* **fee·ble** (**fee**-buhl) ▷ *adjective* **feebler, feeblest**

feed
1. *verb* To give food to a person or an animal.
2. *verb* When animals **feed,** they eat.
3. *noun* Food for animals.
4. *noun* An electronic signal or program that is sent to a receiving station or computer, such as information sent by a news organization to its subscribers, as in *a news feed.*
5. *verb* To supply, or to put in: *We fed two quarters into the parking meter.*
feed (feed)
▷ *verb* **feeding, fed** (fed)

feedback *noun*

1. Written or spoken reactions to something that you are doing: *I received some good feedback from my classmates on my book report.*

2. The sharp, loud noise made when a sound produced by an amplifier goes through it again: *The feedback from the amp made such a horrible squeal that everybody cringed.*
feed·back (**feed**-*bak*)

feel *verb*

1. To touch something or to experience something touching you: *The sun felt warm on my back.* ▷ *noun* **feel**

2. To have a certain emotion or sensation: *I feel sorry for the people who lost their homes in the twister.*

3. To think or to have an idea about something: *Tyrone felt that his plan was better than Steve's.*

4. To have some quality that you can notice by touching: *This towel still feels damp.*
feel (feel) ▷ *verb* **feeling, felt**

feeling *noun*

1. A thought or emotion: *I have a bad feeling about this test.*

2. feelings *noun, plural* Your inner self; your emotions: *His comment really hurt my feelings.*
feel·ing (**fee**-ling)

feet *noun, plural* The plural of **foot**. **feet** (feet)

feign *verb* To pretend in order to fool someone: *Lars feigned a headache so he could leave the party early.* **feign** (fayn) ▷ *verb* **feigning, feigned**

feint *noun* A blow or movement meant to take attention away from the real point of attack: *Some of the troops made a feint on one side of the island, causing a distraction while the main army invaded from the other side.* **feint** (faynt) **Feint** sounds like **faint**. ▷ *verb* **feint**

feisty *adjective*

1. Easily angered or likely to quarrel: *The feisty coach argued with the referee about his decision.*

2. Very lively or frisky, as in *a feisty puppy*.
feist·y (**fye**-stee)

feline

1. *adjective* Of or having to do with cats, as in *feline leukemia*.

2. *noun* Any animal of the cat family.

3. *adjective* Like a cat: *The dancer moved with feline grace.*
fe·line (**fee**-line)

fell *verb*

1. To cut something down on purpose: *The lumberjacks felled the giant oak tree.*

2. To cause someone or something to fall: *In the Bible,*

feline

David felled Goliath with a slingshot.

3. The past tense of **fall**.
fell (fel)
▷ *verb* **felling, felled**

fellow

1. *noun* A man or a boy: *I asked the fellow next to me if he knew what time it was.*

2. *adjective* Being in the same group, category, or situation, as in *fellow classmates*. ▷ *noun* **fellow**
fel·low (**fel**-oh)

fellowship *noun*

1. A group of people sharing an interest: *There is a youth fellowship meeting in our church each week.*

2. A friendly feeling among people who share an interest or do something together: *I have enjoyed the fellowship of my classmates.*
fel·low·ship (**fel**-oh-*ship*)

felon *noun* A person who has committed a serious crime, such as murder or burglary. **fel·on** (**fel**-uhn) ▷ *noun* **felony** (**fel**-uh-nee)

felt *noun*

1. A thick cloth made of wool or other fibers that are pressed and shrunk together in layers.

2. *verb* The past tense and past participle of **feel**.
felt (felt)

female *noun* A person or an animal of the sex that can give birth to young or lay eggs: *Females slightly outnumber males in the population.* **fe·male** (**fee**-male) ▷ *adjective* **female**

Word History

The word **female** comes to us from the French *femelle*, from the Latin word *femella*, "girl." The form of the English word shifted from *femelle* to *female* under the influence of the English word *male*, so that now the words for the genders seem as though they have the same root.

feminine *adjective*

1. Of or having to do with women.

2. Having qualities that are supposed to be typical of women.
fem·i·nine (**fem**-uh-nin)
▷ *noun* **femininity**

feminist *noun* Someone who believes strongly that women are equal to men and should have the same rights and opportunities. **fem·i·nist** (**fem**-uh-nist) ▷ *noun* **feminism** ▷ *adjective* **feminist**

fence

1. *noun* A structure, often made of wood or wire, used to surround, protect, or mark off an area.
▷ *verb* **fence**

2. *verb* To fight with special swords called foils, which are long and very thin, as a sport. ▷ *verb* **fencing, fenced** ▷ *noun* **fencer**

3. If you are **on the fence,** you are undecided about which side you are on: *Latoya was on the fence about whose project to vote for.*

4. *noun* A person who knowingly sells or receives stolen goods.
fence (fens)

fencing *noun*
1. The sport of fighting with long, thin swords called foils.
2. Fences, or the material used to make them.
fenc·ing (**fen**-sing)

fend *verb*
1. If you **fend for** yourself, you take care of yourself.
2. When you **fend off** someone who is attacking you, you defend yourself and hold off the attack.
fend (fend)
▷ *verb* **fending, fended**

fender *noun* A cover over the wheel of a car or bicycle that protects the wheel against damage and reduces splashing. **fend·er** (**fen**-dur)

ferment *verb* When a liquid **ferments,** the sugars in the liquid turn into alcohol. **fer·ment** (fur-**ment**) ▷ *verb* **fermenting, fermented** ▷ *noun* **fermentation**

fern *noun* A plant that has feathery leaves, or fronds, and no flowers. Ferns usually grow in damp places and reproduce by spores instead of seeds. **fern** (furn)

ferocious *adjective* Very dangerous, violent, and savage, as in *a ferocious lion.* **fe·ro·cious** (fuh-**roh**-shuhs) ▷ *noun* **ferocity** (fuh-**rah**-si-tee) ▷ *adverb* **ferociously**

ferret
1. *noun* A long, thin animal that is related to the weasel and is sometimes kept as a pet.
2. *verb* To search: *He ferreted through his drawer and found his other sock.*
▷ *verb* **ferreting, ferreted**
fer·ret (**fer**-it)

Ferris wheel *noun* A large, spinning wheel with seats hung on its side, used as a ride in a carnival or amusement park. **Fer·ris wheel** (**fer**-is)

ferry
1. *noun* A boat that regularly carries people across a body of water such as a river,

lake, or bay: *We took a ferry to the island.* ▷ *noun, plural* **ferries**
2. *verb* To carry people or things from one place to another: *My mother ferries us to and from school each day.* ▷ *verb* **ferries, ferrying, ferried**
fer·ry (**fer**-ee)

fertile *adjective*
1. Land that is **fertile** is good for growing crops and plants: *We were lucky to live on a farm that had such fertile soil.*
2. Able to have babies.
3. Having a lot of ideas, as in *a fertile imagination.*
fer·tile (**fur**-tuhl)
▷ *noun* **fertility**

fertilize *verb*
1. To put an organic or synthetic substance into the soil to make it richer so that plants grow better: *Autumn is the best time to fertilize the lawn for the following year.* ▷ *noun* **fertilizer**
2. To begin reproduction in an animal or a plant by causing a sperm cell to join with an egg cell or pollen to come into contact with the reproductive part of the animal or plant.
fer·ti·lize (**fur**-tuh-*lize*)
▷ *verb* **fertilizing, fertilized** ▷ *noun* **fertilization**

fervent *adjective* Showing strong or intense feeling: *Susan B. Anthony was a fervent feminist.* **fer·vent** (**fur**-vuhnt) ▷ *adverb* **fervently**

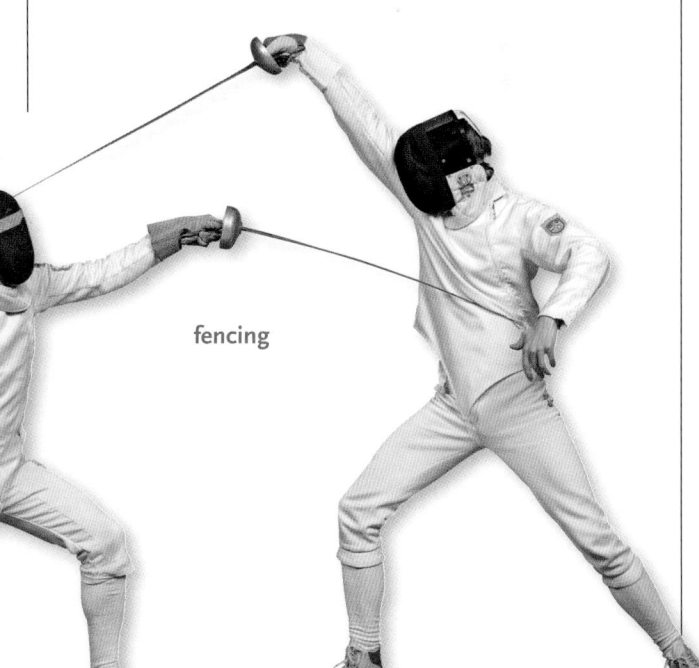
fencing

festival *noun*
1. A celebration or holiday, as in *a spring festival* or *a religious festival.*
2. An organized program of cultural, artistic, or musical events, often held every year around the same time: *My parents saw many plays at the Shakespeare festival.*
fes·ti·val (**fes**-tuh-vuhl)

festive *adjective* Cheerful and lively, as in *festive music.* **fes·tive** (**fes**-tiv)

festivity *noun* A celebration or an activity that is part of a celebration: *Naomi was allowed to join the festivities after she finished her chores.* **fes·tiv·i·ty** (fes-**tiv**-i-tee) ▷ *noun, plural* **festivities**

fetal *adjective* Of or pertaining to a fetus (a baby or animal before it is born): *A fetal heartbeat is usually detectable by the tenth week of pregnancy.* **fe·tal** (**fee**-tuhl)

fetch *verb*
1. To go after and bring back something or somebody: *Caitlin has gone to fetch Grandma.*
2. To sell for a particular price: *Her diamond ring fetched a good price.*
fetch (fech) ▷ *verb* **fetches, fetching, fetched**

fetching *adjective* Charming or attractive: *Sameera looked very fetching with her new hairdo.* **fetch·ing** (**fech**-ing)

fettuccine *or* **fettuccini** *noun* Pasta in narrow strips shaped like ribbons. **fet·tuc·ci·ne** *or* **fet·tuc·ci·ni** (*fet*-uh-**chee**-nee)

fetus *noun* A baby or an animal in the mother's body before birth, at a later stage of development. **fe·tus** (**fee**-tuhs)

feud *noun* An angry argument between two people or families that lasts for a long time, sometimes for many generations: *The feud between my uncles has ruined many family reunions.* **feud** (fyood) ▷ *verb* **feud**

feudalism *noun* The medieval system in which a lord gave people land and protection. In return, they had to work and fight for him. **feu·dal·ism** (**fyoo**-duh-*liz*-uhm) ▷ *adjective* **feudal**

fever *noun*
1. A body temperature that is higher than normal. Most people have a fever if their temperature is more than 98.6 degrees Fahrenheit: *My sister had a sore throat and a fever of 101 degrees.*
2. Great excitement or activity: *Everyone is caught up in the fever of the championship tournament.*
fe·ver (**fee**-vur) ▷ *adjective* **feverish** ▷ *adverb* **feverishly**

few *adjective* Not many: *Few people realize how much the new stadium will cost.* **few** (fyoo) ▷ *adjective* **fewer, fewest** ▷ *noun* **few**

fiancé *noun* A man who is engaged to be married. **fi·an·cé** (*fee*-ahn-**say** *or* fee-**ahn**-say)

fiancée *noun* A woman who is engaged to be married. **fi·an·cée** (*fee*-ahn-**say** *or* fee-**ahn**-say)

fib *verb* To tell a small lie. **fib** (fib) ▷ *verb* **fibbing, fibbed** ▷ *noun* **fib** ▷ *noun* **fibber**

fiber *noun*
1. A thin strand of material such as cotton, wool, hemp, or nylon: *The comforter is stuffed with polyester fibers.*
2. A part of fruits, vegetables, and grains that passes through the body but is not digested. Fiber helps food move through the intestines: *It's important to have enough fiber in your diet.*
fi·ber (**fye**-bur) ▷ *adjective* **fibrous** (**fye**-bruhs)

fiberglass *noun* A strong insulating material made from very fine glass fibers, used in buildings, cars, boats, and many other things. **fi·ber·glass** (**fye**-bur-*glas*)

fickle *adjective* Changing very often, or inconsistent, as in *fickle weather* or *a fickle friend.* **fick·le** (**fik**-uhl) ▷ *noun* **fickleness**

fiction *noun*
1. Stories about characters and events that are not real: *My brother likes to read about sports, but I prefer fiction.*
2. Something that is made up: *When Timmy talks about his weekends, it's hard to tell fact from fiction.*
fic·tion (**fik**-shuhn) ▷ *adjective* **fictional**

fiddle
1. *noun* (informal) A violin. ▷ *noun* **fiddler**
2. *verb* To touch or play nervously with something, as in *to fiddle with a pencil.*
3. *verb* To waste: *Oscar fiddled the whole morning away doing nothing.*
fid·dle (**fid**-uhl) ▷ *verb* **fiddling, fiddled**

fidget *verb* To keep moving because you are restless, bored, or nervous: *Barney sat fidgeting in his seat after he finished the test.* **fidg·et** (**fij**-it) ▷ *verb* **fidgeting, fidgeted** ▷ *adjective* **fidgety**

fiddle and bow

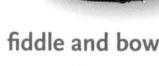

field

1. *noun* A piece of open land, sometimes used for growing crops, grazing animals, or playing sports.
2. *noun* A space in a spreadsheet or database where you can enter a particular kind of data: *You have to enter the state abbreviation and the ZIP code in different fields.*
3. *noun* An area of interest, study, or occupation: *His field is American history.*
4. *verb* In baseball, to catch or stop a ball that has been hit: *Byron was able to field the ball, so the batter was called out.* ▷ *verb* **fielding, fielded**
field (feeld)

fielder *noun* A baseball player who is not batting and has a position on the field. **field·er** (**feel**-dur)

field goal *noun*

1. In football, a play in which the ball is kicked from the field, scoring three points.
2. In basketball, a basket made when the ball is in play, scoring two or three points.

field hockey *noun* A team game played on a rectangular field using curved sticks and a small ball. Players attempt to hit the ball along the ground and into the other team's goal.

field trip *noun* A group trip to a place where you can see things and learn: *Our class went on a field trip to the science museum.*

fiend *noun*

1. An evil spirit.
2. An evil or cruel person.
fiend (feend)
▷ *adjective* **fiendish** ▷ *adverb* **fiendishly**

Word History

The word **fiend** comes from a root word meaning "hate" or "foe." In Old English it could refer to an enemy or the devil. Today it refers to a devilish spirit or an evil person.

fierce *adjective*
1. Violent or dangerous: *Many animals become fierce when they are trapped.*
2. Very strong or extreme: *The fierce wind blew down many trees.*
fierce (feers)
▷ *adjective* **fiercer, fiercest** ▷ *noun* **fierceness**
▷ *adverb* **fiercely**

fiery *adjective*
1. Like fire; very hot or glowing: *The oven was fiery hot.*

2. Very emotional and spirited, as in *a fiery speech.*
fier·y (**fire**-ee or **fye**-ur-ee)
▷ *adjective* **fierier, fieriest**

fiesta *noun* A religious festival or other public holiday, especially in Latin America and Spain.
fi·es·ta (fee-**es**-tuh)

fife *noun* A small instrument, similar to a flute, that has a high pitch. **fife** (fife)

fig *noun* A small, sweet fruit with tiny seeds, eaten fresh or dried. **fig** (fig)

fig

fight

1. *noun* A battle in which each side tries to hurt the other: *A fight broke out when the visiting team's fans stormed onto the field.* ▷ *verb* **fight**
2. *verb* To have an argument or a quarrel: *I don't like to fight with my parents.* ▷ *verb* **fighting, fought** (fawt) ▷ *noun* **fight**
3. *noun* A hard struggle to gain a goal, as in *the fight against disease.* ▷ *noun* **fighter**
fight (fite)

figure

1. *noun* A symbol that represents a number, such as 1, 2, 3, and so on.
2. figures *noun, plural* Arithmetic: *She's very good at figures.*
3. *noun* An amount given in numbers, as in *population figures.*
4. *noun* A shape or an outline: *We saw a shadowy figure in the doorway.*
5. *noun* A person's shape: *Suki has a slim figure.*
6. *noun* A well-known person, as in *a public figure.*
7. figure out *verb* To come to understand something: *He figured out the answer by asking good questions.*
▷ *verb* **figuring, figured**
fig·ure (**fig**-yur)

field hockey

figurehead *noun*

1. Someone who holds an important position or office but has no real power: *The king or queen is a figurehead in most democracies.*

2. A carved statue found on the bow of a ship.

fig·ure·head (**fig**-yur-*hed*)

figure of speech *noun* An expression, such as a simile, in which words are used in a poetic way. Authors often use figures of speech to make their writing more colorful. For example, the phrase "as strong as an ox" is a figure of speech that means someone is very strong. ▷ *noun, plural* **figures of speech**

filament *noun* A very fine wire or thread. In a lightbulb, the filament is a fine thread of tungsten that glows and produces light. **fil·a·ment** (**fil**-uh-muhnt)

file

1. *noun* A folder or binder for papers or documents: *Last year's grades are all in this file.*

2. *verb* To put papers or documents in a file, in some particular order: *Please file these records in alphabetical order.* ▷ *verb* **filing, filed**

3. *noun* A tool used to make something smoother, as in *a nail file* or *a carpenter's file.* ▷ *verb* **file**

4. *noun* A collection of information stored on a computer and given a name that identifies it: *Can I delete all these files from the hard drive?*

5. in single file A line of people one behind the other: *We marched in single file.*

file (file)

file extension *noun* The letters that come after the period in the name of a computer file that indicate what kind of file it is, or which program can open it. For example, an ".exe" file extension indicates that a file is a program.

filename *noun* The name of a computer file. **file·name** (**file**-naym)

fill *verb*

1. To make or become full: *I hope Mom fills the swimming pool today.*

2. To take up the whole space of: *The crowd filled the gym.*

3. To stop or plug up, as in *to fill a hole.*

4. If you **fill in** or **fill out** a form, you put information wherever it is required.

5. If you **fill in** for someone, you do that person's job while he or she is away.

fill (fil)

▷ *verb* **filling, filled**

fillet

1. *noun* A piece of meat or fish with the bones removed.

2. *verb* To remove the bones from a piece of fish or meat.

fil·let (fi-**lay** *or* fil-ay)

▷ *verb* **filleting** (fi-**lay**-ing), **filleted** (fi-**layd**)

filling *noun*

1. Material that a dentist puts into holes in your teeth to prevent more decay.

2. The substance that is used to repair the holes or cracks in something, such as a piece of wood or other material.

3. The food inside a sandwich, pie, or cake.

fill·ing (**fil**-ing)

filly *noun* A young female horse. **fil·ly** (**fil**-ee) ▷ *noun, plural* **fillies**

film

1. *noun* A thin layer of something, as in *a film of dust.*

2. *noun* A roll of thin plastic that you put in a camera so you can take photographs or motion pictures. The film reacts to the light and allows the images on the film to appear when the film is developed.

3. *verb* To record something with a film or video camera: *They filmed the spelling bee.*

▷ *verb* **filming, filmed**

4. *noun* A movie: *I've watched my favorite film at least 35 times.*

film (film)

filter

1. *noun* A device that cleans liquids or gases as they pass through it.

2. *verb* To put something through a filter: *Filter that water before you drink it.*

3. *verb* To go through very slowly or sparsely: *Sunlight filtered through the clouds.*

fil·ter (**fil**-tur)

▷ *verb* **filtering, filtered**

filth *noun*

1. Dirt: *The filth in the house was intolerable.*

2. Foul or obscene language or images.

filth (filth)

▷ *noun* **filthiness** ▷ *adjective* **filthy**

fin *noun*

1. A part on the body of a fish shaped like a flap that is used for moving and steering through the water.

fins

finch

2. A small, flat structure on an airplane or boat, used to help with steering.

3. One of two long, flat attachments worn on the feet to help you swim underwater. Also called a **flipper**.
fin (fin)

final

1. *adjective* Last: *This is your final chance.*

2. *adjective* Not to be changed or discussed: *His decision was final.*

3. *noun* The last and usually most important examination in a school subject: *The score I get on my final is worth half my grade.*

4. *noun* The last and final round, game, or match in a series to determine who is the absolute winner: *Our team played well all season but lost in the finals.*
fi·nal (**fye**-nuhl)

finale *noun* The last part of a show or piece of music. **fi·na·le** (fuh-**nal**-ee *or* fuh-**nah**-lee)

finalist *noun* Someone who has reached the last part of a competition: *Vera is a finalist in the chess tournament.* **fi·nal·ist** (**fye**-nuh-list)

finally *adverb*

1. After many attempts: *I finally got my driver's license.*

2. Eventually; at last: *School was finally over for the year.*
fi·nal·ly (**fye**-nuh-lee)

finance

1. *noun* The management and use of money by businesses, banks, and governments. ▷ *adjective* **financial** ▷ *adverb* **financially**

2. *verb* To provide money for something: *The government will finance the new library.* ▷ *verb* **financing, financed**

3. finances *noun, plural* The total amount of money that an individual, a company, or a government has: *The city is trying to improve its finances.*
fi·nance (fuh-**nans** *or* **fye**-nans)

finch *noun* A small songbird with a strong, thick bill used for cracking seeds. **finch** (finch) ▷ *noun, plural* **finches**

find

1. *verb* To come across something by chance: *I found a penny on my way to school today.*

2. *verb* To come to and state a decision: *The jury found the defendant not guilty.*

3. *noun* An important or valuable discovery: *The discovery of the king's tomb was a great archaeological find.*

4. find out *verb* To learn about something or someone: *I found out from Peggy that he skipped school today.*
find (finde)
▷ *verb* **finding, found** (found)

finding *noun* One of the results of an investigation or a study: *The findings show that too much sugar isn't healthy.* **find·ing** (**fine**-ding)

fine

1. *adjective* Very well or healthy: *"I'm fine, thanks."*

2. *adjective* Very good or excellent, as in *a fine musician.*

3. *adjective* Not cloudy or rainy, as in *fine weather.*

4. *adjective* Thin or delicate, as in *fine hair* or *fine satin.*

5. *noun* A sum of money to be paid as a punishment for doing something wrong: *After receiving a parking ticket, Lauren paid the fine.* ▷ *verb* **fine**
fine (fine)
▷ *adjective* **finer, finest** ▷ *noun* **fineness**

finger

1. *noun* One of the long parts of your hands that you can move. Our hands have five fingers each, enabling us to pick up and hold things.

2. *verb* To touch something lightly with your fingers: *He was nervously fingering some coins in his pocket as we talked.*

3. *verb* To blame or accuse someone of something: *They fingered him as the main conspirator in the plot.*
fin·ger (**fing**-gur)
▷ *verb* **fingering, fingered**

fingernail *noun* The hard protective layer at the upper tip of each finger that grows and requires regular trimming. **fin·ger·nail** (**fing**-gur-*nayl*)

fingerprint *noun* The print made by the pattern of curved ridges on the tips of your fingers: *I wiped my fingerprints off the bathroom mirror.* **fin·ger·print** (**fing**-gur-*print*)

fingerprint

a b c d e **f** g h i j k l m n o p q r s t u v w x y z

finicky *adjective* Fussy, especially about food: *Cats are known to be finicky eaters.* **fin·ick·y** (**fin**-i-kee)

finish
1. *verb* To end or complete something: *I'm not allowed to watch television until I finish my homework.*
2. *noun* The end of something, such as a race: *The horses Bright Beauty and Happy Dancer were nose to nose going into the finish.*
3. *verb* To use the last of something: *I finished the milk, then threw away the container.*
4. *noun* A coating on a surface such as metal or wood: *The floor has a shiny finish.* ▷ *verb* **finish**
fin·ish (**fin**-ish)
▷ *verb* **finishing, finished**

finite *adjective* Having an end: *The lifetime of a person is finite.* **fi·nite** (**fye**-nite)

fiord *noun* See **fjord. fiord** (fyord)

fir *noun* An evergreen tree with needlelike leaves and upright cones. **fir** (fur) **Fir** sounds like **fur.**

fire
1. *noun* Flames, heat, and light produced by burning.
2. *verb* To shoot a gun or other weapon. ▷ *noun* **fire**
3. *noun* Strong emotion: *The preacher's sermon was full of fire.*
4. *verb* To dismiss someone from his or her job: *Pete was fired from his job because he always showed up late for work.*
fire (fire)
▷ *verb* **firing, fired**

firearm *noun* A weapon that shoots bullets. Rifles, pistols, and shotguns are firearms: *The police officer carried a loaded firearm.* **fire·arm** (**fire**-ahrm)

firecracker *noun* A paper tube containing gunpowder and a fuse. Firecrackers make loud popping noises when they explode. **fire·crack·er** (**fire**-krak-ur)

fire engine *noun* A large truck that carries powerful pumps, hoses, ladders, and firefighters to a fire.

fire escape *noun* A set of metal stairs on the outside of a building, designed to allow people to escape in case of fire: *We quickly left the building by using the fire escape.*

fire extinguisher *noun* A portable metal container that holds chemicals and sometimes water, used to put out a fire.

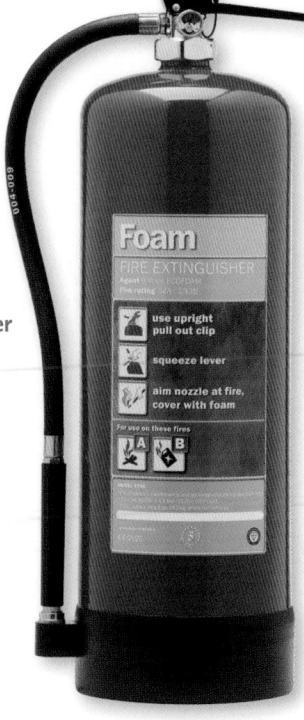

fire extinguisher

firefighter *noun* Someone who is trained to put out fires: *Charlene wants to be a firefighter.* **fire·fight·er** (**fire**-fye-tur)

firefly *noun* A small beetle that flies at night and gives off flashes of green light from its abdomen. Also called a **lightning bug. fire·fly** (**fire**-flye) ▷ *noun, plural* **fireflies**

firehouse *noun* A building where fire engines are kept and where firefighters wait until they are called to put out a fire. Also called a **fire station. fire·house** (**fire**-hous)

fireman *noun* A male firefighter. **fire·man** (**fire**-muhn) ▷ *noun, plural* **firemen**

fireplace *noun* A structure, usually made of brick or stone, in which a fire can burn safely: *Our ski cabin has a fireplace.* **fire·place** (**fire**-plase)

fireproof *adjective* Made from a material that has been chemically treated so that it will not burn. **fire·proof** (**fire**-proof)

fire station *noun* Another term for **firehouse.**

firewall *noun*
1. A wall in a building that is designed to keep a fire from spreading.
2. Software designed to control access to a computer in order to protect it from outside attacks.
fire·wall (**fire**-wawl)

firewood *noun* Logs or other pieces of wood that are burned as fuel. **fire·wood** (**fire**-wud)

fireworks *noun, plural* Devices that make very loud noises and colorful lights when they are burned or exploded. **fire·works** (**fire**-wurks)

firm
1. *adjective* Strong and solid, as in *a firm mattress.*
2. *adjective* Definite and not easily changed, as in *a firm belief.*
3. *adjective* Steady, as in *a firm voice.*
4. *noun* A business or a company.
firm (furm)
▷ *adjective* **firmer, firmest** ▷ *adverb* **firmly**

first
1. *adjective* Before every other: *Sparky is the first name we thought of for our dog.*
2. *adjective* Earliest in time: *This is the first day of vacation.*
3. *noun* Someone or something that acts or happens before any other: *She was the first in her family to graduate from college.*
4. *adverb* Before something else; earliest of all: *Bridget usually gets home from school first.*

5. *adjective* Best, or most important, as in *the first violinist in an orchestra.*
first (furst)

first aid *noun* Emergency care given to an injured or sick person before he or she is examined by a doctor: *The paramedics gave the crash victim first aid while the ambulance sped to the hospital.*

first class

1. *noun* The most expensive level of service offered to travelers on trains, ships, and airplanes: *We were rewarded for our patience with two seats in first class.*

2. *noun* The standard level of mail service used for letters, postcards, and bills.

3. first-class *adjective* Being of the highest quality, as in *a first-class hotel.*

4. first-class *adverb* Traveling by means of the most expensive level of service, as in *flying first-class.*

firsthand *adjective* Direct from the original source: *Ian gave a firsthand account of the accident.* **first·hand** (**furst**-hand) ▷ *adverb* **firsthand**

first lady *noun* The wife of the head of a country, state, province, or city. This term is often capitalized: *The reporters at the White House all stood up when the president and the First Lady entered the room.*

first-rate *adjective* Excellent: *This diner makes first-rate sandwiches.*

first responder *noun* Someone whose job is to respond first in an emergency, such as a police officer, firefighter, or paramedic. **first re·spond·er** (ri-**spahn**-dur)

First World problem *noun* A personal problem that only occurs in developed and wealthy countries. People often use this term to talk about things that people complain about but that really don't matter very much: *Their First World problem is that their swimming pool is so big, it takes a long time to heat up.*

fish

1. *noun* A cold-blooded animal that lives in water and has scales, fins, and gills. ▷ *noun, plural* **fish** or **fishes**

2. *verb* To try to catch fish. ▷ *noun* **fishing**

3. *verb* When a person **fishes** for information, he or she is trying to find something out in a sly or indirect way: *Brianna was fishing for clues about her birthday gift.*

fishhook

fist

fish (fish)
▷ *verb* **fishes, fishing, fished**

fisherman *noun* A person who catches fish to earn a living or for sport. **fish·er·man** (**fish**-ur-muhn) ▷ *noun, plural* **fishermen**

fishery *noun*

1. A place where fish are bred commercially.

2. A place where fish are caught.
fish·er·y (**fish**-ur-ee)
▷ *noun, plural* **fisheries**

fishhook *noun* A small hook with a barb, used for catching fish. **fish·hook** (**fish**-*huk*)

fishing rod *noun* A long, flexible pole used with a hook, line, and reel to catch fish.

fishy *adjective*

1. Having a strong smell or taste of fish: *Last night's dinner left a fishy odor all over the house.*

2. *(informal)* Unlikely, doubtful, or suspicious, as in *a fishy excuse.*
fish·y (**fish**-ee)
▷ *adjective* **fishier, fishiest**

fission *noun*

1. The act of splitting into parts, as in *cell fission.*

2. nuclear fission *noun* The splitting of the nucleus of an atom, which creates energy.
fis·sion (**fish**-uhn)

fist *noun* A tightly closed hand: *The boxer's gloves protected his large fists.* **fist** (fist)

fit

1. *verb* To be the right shape or size to cover something: *Carmen's school uniform fits her well.*

2. *verb* To be the right shape or size to contain something: *We won't all fit in this elevator.*

3. *verb* To be right for, as in *fit for a king.*

4. *adjective* Strong and healthy, as in *a fit athlete.*

5. *noun* A sudden attack of something that cannot be controlled, as in *a fit of laughter.*

6. *adjective* Good enough, as in *fit to eat.*
fit (fit)
▷ *verb* **fitting, fitted** or **fit** ▷ *adjective* **fitter, fittest**

fitness *noun* Your **fitness** is how healthy and strong you are. You can improve your fitness by exercising and eating healthy foods. **fit·ness** (**fit**-nis)

fitting

1. *adjective* Suitable or proper: *Is it fitting to wear shorts to church?*

2. *noun* A small metal or plastic part that connects things, as in *pipe fittings.*
fit·ting (**fit**-ing)

fix

1. *verb* To repair something, as in *to fix a bike.*

2. *verb* To arrange or tidy something, as in *to fix your hair.*

3. *verb* To get something ready to eat, as in *to fix lunch.*

4. *verb* To place or fasten firmly, as in *to fix the poles for a tent in the ground.*

5. in a fix In a difficult situation or in trouble: *Marilyn was in a fix when her car broke down.*
fix (fiks)
▷ *verb* **fixes, fixing, fixed** ▷ *noun, plural* **fixes**

fixture *noun* Something that is fixed firmly and permanently in place, especially in a house or building, as in *porcelain fixtures in a bathroom.* **fix·ture** (fiks-chur)

fizz

1. *verb* To make bubbles and a hissing noise. ▷ *verb* **fizzes, fizzing, fizzed**

2. *noun* A lot of tiny, hissing bubbles: *I like a lot of fizz in my soda.* ▷ *adjective* **fizzy**
fizz (fiz)

fizzle *verb*

1. To make a hissing or sputtering sound.

2. *(informal)* To fail or die out, especially after a good start: *All our plans fizzled out.*
fiz·zle (fiz-uhl)
▷ *verb* **fizzling, fizzled**

fjord *noun* A long, narrow inlet of the ocean between high cliffs. **fjord** (fyord)

flab *noun* Extra fat on your body. **flab** (flab) ▷ *noun* **flabbiness** ▷ *adjective* **flabby**

flag

1. *noun* A square or rectangular piece of cloth with a pattern on it that is a symbol of a country or an organization.

2. *verb* To stop, or to signal: *We flagged down the police officer.* ▷ *verb* **flagging, flagged**
flag (flag)

Flag Day *noun* A holiday that celebrates the day in 1777 when the Stars and Stripes became the official flag of the United States. It is observed on June 14.

flagpole *noun* A tall pole made of wood or metal for raising and flying a flag. **flag·pole** (flag-pole)

flair *noun* A natural ability or skill: *Marina has a flair for learning languages.* **flair** (flair) **Flair** sounds like **flare**.

flak *noun*

1. Shots fired against an aircraft.

2. *(informal)* Criticism and negative reactions: *The mayor's idea received a lot of flak from the media.*
flak (flak)

flake

1. *noun* A small, flat piece of something, as in *flakes of snow* or *flakes of paint.* ▷ *adjective* **flaky**

2. *verb* To peel off in small, flat pieces: *The old paint flaked off the wall.* ▷ *verb* **flaking, flaked**
flake (flake)

flamboyant *adjective* Brightly colored or showy, as in *a flamboyant shirt.* **flam·boy·ant** (flam-**boi**-uhnt)

flame *noun* The light given off by a fire: *We roasted marshmallows over the flame.* **flame** (flame)
▷ *adjective* **flaming**

flamingo *noun* A pink bird with a long neck, long legs, and webbed feet. **fla·min·go** (fluh-**ming**-goh)
▷ *noun, plural* **flamingos** or **flamingoes**

flammable *adjective* Quick to catch fire and burn: *These dried leaves are highly flammable.* **flam·ma·ble** (**flam**-uh-buhl)

flank

1. *noun* The side of an animal, between its ribs and hips.

2. *noun* The far left or right side of something such as a group of soldiers, a fort, or a naval fleet: *The enemy troops crept up on our left flank.*

3. *verb* To guard or be at the side of something or someone: *The Secret Service flanked the president as he stepped off the plane.* ▷ *verb* **flanking, flanked**
flank (flangk)

flannel *noun* A soft, woven cloth, usually made of cotton or wool. **flan·nel** (**flan**-uhl)

flap

1. *verb* To move up and down: *The baby bird sat in the nest flapping its wings.*

2. *verb* To swing loosely and make a noise: *The flag flapped in the wind.*

3. *noun* A part of something that hangs on the side or edge, as in *the flap of a purse.*

4. *noun* A movable part on an airplane wing, used to control the plane's rise and fall.
flap (flap)
▷ *verb* **flapping, flapped**

flapjack *noun* A pancake. **flap·jack** (**flap**-jak)

flare

1. *verb* To burn with a sudden, very bright light.

2. *verb* To break out in sudden or violent feeling: *Tempers flared during the argument.*

3. flare out *verb* To spread out in a bell shape at the bottom: *Her skirt flares out just above her knees.*

4. flare up *verb* To suddenly become stronger and

flamingo

more intense or violent: *It had become less windy, but then the storm flared up again.*

5. *noun* A stick that produces a flame or bright light to warn people of something: *The climbers were found when one of the helicopters spotted a flare on the mountainside.*
flare (flair)
Flare sounds like **flair**. ▷ *verb* **flaring, flared**

flash
1. *noun* A short burst of light, as in *a flash of lightning.*
2. *noun* A very brief period of time: *He was there in a flash.*
3. *verb* To move rapidly: *A car flashed by.*
▷ *verb* **flashes, flashing, flashed**
4. *noun* A sudden outburst, as in *a flash of anger.*
5. news flash *noun* A brief report of very recent or important news.
flash (flash)
▷ *noun, plural* **flashes**

flashback *noun*
1. A scene in a movie or a story that tells you something that happened in the past: *The last part of the movie was a flashback to the hero's childhood.*
2. A sudden memory of something that happened and was forgotten.
flash·back (**flash**-*bak*)

flash drive *noun* A form of computer memory that has no moving parts and is small enough to carry in your pocket.

flashlight *noun* A portable light that is powered by a battery: *Let's make sure the flashlight has fresh batteries before we leave on our camping trip.* **flash·light** (**flash**-*lite*)

flashy *adjective* Very bright and attracting attention, as in *a flashy tie.* **flash·y** (**flash**-ee)
▷ *adjective* **flashier, flashiest**

flask *noun*
1. A small, flat bottle made to be carried in the pocket.
2. A bottle with a narrow neck used in science laboratories.
flask (flask)

flat
1. *adjective* Smooth and even, as in *flat land.*
2. *adjective* Not very deep or thick; shallow: *She tried to guess what was in the large, flat box under*

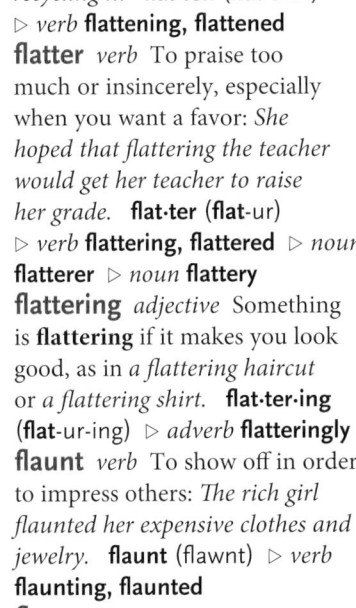

flash drive

the Christmas tree.
3. *adjective* Absolute, as in *a flat denial.*
4. *adjective* Containing no air, as in *a flat tire.*
5. *adjective* Dull or lifeless, as in *a flat performance.*
6. *adjective* Lower than the correct or usual pitch: *The soprano sounded a little flat.*
7. *adverb* Fully stretched out or spread out against a surface: *He was lying flat on his back.*
8. *noun* In music, a **flat** is a note that is one half step lower in pitch than the usual note.
9. *noun* A written sign in sheet music that shows that the next note is a flat.
flat (flat)
▷ *adjective* **flatter, flattest** ▷ *noun* **flat**

flatbed *noun* A truck with a large, flat cargo area in the back, designed to carry a heavy load, like a car. **flat·bed** (**flat**-*bed*)

flatfish *noun* A fish with a flat body and both eyes on its upper side, such as halibut, sole, or flounder. **flat·fish** (**flat**-*fish*)
▷ *noun, plural* **flatfish** or **flatfishes**

flatten *verb* To make something flat or almost flat by pressing on it: *I flattened the milk carton before recycling it.* **flat·ten** (**flat**-uhn)
▷ *verb* **flattening, flattened**

flatter *verb* To praise too much or insincerely, especially when you want a favor: *She hoped that flattering the teacher would get her teacher to raise her grade.* **flat·ter** (**flat**-ur)
▷ *verb* **flattering, flattered** ▷ *noun* **flatterer** ▷ *noun* **flattery**

flattering *adjective* Something is **flattering** if it makes you look good, as in *a flattering haircut* or *a flattering shirt.* **flat·ter·ing** (**flat**-ur-ing) ▷ *adverb* **flatteringly**

flaunt *verb* To show off in order to impress others: *The rich girl flaunted her expensive clothes and jewelry.* **flaunt** (flawnt) ▷ *verb* **flaunting, flaunted**

flavor
1. *noun* Taste: *The flavor of this apple is more sweet than tart.* ▷ *adjective* **flavored** ▷ *adjective* **flavorless**
2. *verb* To add taste to food during its preparation: *Mom flavored the soup with herbs and spices.* ▷ *verb* **flavoring, flavored** ▷ *noun* **flavoring**
fla·vor (**flay**-vur)

flatbed

flaw *noun* A weakness: *The investigation conducted by the hospital found serious flaws in the patient's treatment.* **flaw** (flaw) ▷ *adjective* **flawed** ▷ *adjective* **flawless**

flax *noun*
1. A plant with blue flowers that produces oil and fiber.
2. The fiber of the flax plant, which can be woven into thread that is used to make linen.
flax (flaks)

flea *noun*
1. A small, wingless insect that lives on the blood of people and other animals.
2. **flea market** An indoor or outdoor market selling secondhand items and used clothing.
flea (flee)
Flea sounds like **flee.**

fled *verb* The past tense and past participle of **flee.** **fled** (fled)

flee *verb* To run away, especially from danger: *Nicholas wanted to flee, but instead he froze in panic.* **flee** (flee) **Flee** sounds like **flea.** ▷ *verb* **fleeing, fled** (fled)

fleece
1. *noun* The woolly coat of a sheep. ▷ *adjective* **fleecy**
2. *verb* To swindle someone out of his or her money or possessions, especially by doing it in a tricky way: *The company fleeced them by adding some hidden charges to their bill.* ▷ *verb* **fleecing, fleeced**
fleece (flees)

fleek *adjective* (*informal*) If something is **on fleek** it is well done, attractive, and admirable: *We practiced all afternoon to make sure our presentation would be on fleek.* **fleek** (fleek)

fleet
1. *noun* A group of warships under one command.
2. *noun* A number of ships, planes, or cars that form a group, as in *a fleet of taxis.*
3. *adjective* Swift or fast.
fleet (fleet)

fleeting *adjective* Not lasting long, as in *a fleeting glimpse.* **fleet·ing** (**flee**-ting) ▷ *adverb* **fleetingly**

flesh *noun*
1. The soft part of your body that covers your bones. Flesh is made up of fat and muscle.
2. The meat of an animal.
3. The parts of a fruit or vegetable that people eat, as in *the flesh of a ripe peach.*
flesh (flesh)

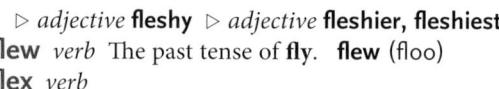

flexible

▷ *adjective* **fleshy** ▷ *adjective* **fleshier, fleshiest**

flew *verb* The past tense of **fly.** **flew** (floo)

flex *verb*
1. To tighten a muscle, as in *to flex your biceps.*
2. To bend or stretch something, as in *to flex your toes.*
flex (fleks)
▷ *verb* **flexes, flexing, flexed**

flexible *adjective*
1. Able to bend: *Rubber is flexible.*
2. Able to change: *Francesca has a flexible work schedule and can leave early if she needs to.*
flex·i·ble (**flek**-suh-buhl)
▷ *noun* **flexibility** ▷ *adverb* **flexibly**

flick
1. *noun* A light, quick movement, as in *a flick of the wrist.*
2. *verb* To touch something with a quick, snapping movement: *Paula flicked the towel at her sister.* ▷ *verb* **flicking, flicked**
flick (flik)

flicker *verb* To burn or shine unsteadily: *The candle flickered in the breeze.* **flick·er** (**flik**-ur) ▷ *verb* **flickering, flickered** ▷ *noun* **flicker**

flier *or* **flyer** *noun*
1. Someone who flies, such as an airplane pilot.
2. A paper advertisement sent or given to people: *We made a flier to let people know about our school concert.*
fli·er *or* **fly·er** (**flye**-ur)

flea

flight *noun*
1. The act or manner of flying, or the ability to fly, as in *the graceful flight of a swallow.*
2. An airplane journey: *Our flight takes us across four states.*
3. A set of stairs or steps between floors or landings of a building: *Her apartment is three flights up.*
4. When a person **takes flight,** he or she runs away.
5. When a bird **takes flight,** it flies up from the ground or a tree.
flight (flite)

flight attendant *noun* Someone who helps passengers and serves food and drinks on an airplane.

flimsy *adjective* Easy to tear or break, as in *flimsy cotton* or *flimsy construction.* **flim·sy** (**flim**-zee) ▷ *adjective* **flimsier, flimsiest** ▷ *noun* **flimsiness** ▷ *adverb* **flimsily**

flinch *verb* To draw back with a quick, sudden movement from a source of pain or fear: *Carmela flinched at the sight of the long needle in the nurse's hand.* **flinch** (flinch) ▷ *verb* **flinches, flinching, flinched** ▷ *noun* **flinch**

fling *verb* To throw something with force or violence: *Vince flung the towel onto the floor.* **fling** (fling) ▷ *verb* **flinging, flung** (fluhng)

flint *noun* A very hard kind of rock that makes sparks when steel is struck against it. In prehistoric times, flint was used to make tools and weapons. **flint** (flint)

flip
1. *verb* To toss or fling something: *We flipped a coin to see whose turn it was.*
2. *verb* To turn something over: *The cook flipped the burgers without even looking at them.*
3. *noun* A somersault.
4. *verb* (*informal*) If someone **flips** or **flips out,** he or she suddenly becomes extremely angry.
flip (flip)
▷ *verb* **flipping, flipped**

flipper *noun*
1. One of the broad, flat limbs that sea mammals such as seals, whales, and dolphins use when they swim.
2. One of the two long, flat rubber attachments that you wear on your feet to help you swim. Also called a **fin**.
flip·per (**flip**-ur)

flood

flirt *verb*
1. To show romantic interest in someone, but in a casual way. ▷ *noun* **flirt**
2. To consider an idea, but not seriously: *We flirted with the idea of going to Spain for Easter.*
flirt (flurt)
▷ *verb* **flirting, flirted**

float
1. *verb* To rest or move on a liquid or in the air, as in *to float on a raft* or *to float on a breeze.*
2. *verb* To move without effort: *The skater floated past us on the ice.*
3. *noun* A small floating object attached to the end of a fishing line that holds the line up.
4. *noun* A decorated truck or platform that forms part of a parade.
float (floht)
▷ *verb* **floating, floated**

flock
1. *noun* A group of animals of one kind that live, travel, or feed together, as in *a flock of birds.*
2. *verb* To come together in a large group: *The singer's fans flocked to see her when she arrived in Los Angeles.* ▷ *verb* **flocking, flocked**
flock (flahk)

floe *noun* A large sheet or block of floating ice in a sea, lake, or river. **floe** (floh)

flog *verb* To beat with a whip or a stick. **flog** (flahg) ▷ *verb* **flogging, flogged** ▷ *noun* **flogging**

flood *verb*
1. To overflow with water beyond its normal limits: *Fortunately, no one was hurt when the river flooded.*
2. To come in large amounts: *The kitchen was flooded with sunlight.*
flood (fluhd)
▷ *verb* **flooding, flooded** ▷ *noun* **flood**

floodlight *noun* An outside lamp that produces a broad and very bright beam of light. **flood·light** (**fluhd**-*lite*)

floor
1. *noun* The flat surface that you walk or stand on inside a building. ▷ *noun* **flooring**
2. *noun* A story in a building: *We live on the third floor.*
3. *verb* (*informal*) To surprise: *Maria was floored by the news.* ▷ *verb* **flooring, floored**
floor (flor)

flop *verb*
1. To fall or drop heavily: *Nikki flopped into a chair.*
2. To flap or move about: *The kite flopped about in the breeze.* ▷ *adjective* **floppy, floppier, floppiest**
3. (*informal*) To fail: *The play flopped.* ▷ *noun* **flop**
flop (flahp)
▷ *verb* **flopping, flopped**

flora *noun* All the plants of a particular area as a group, as in *desert flora*. **flo·ra (flor**-uh)

floral *adjective* Of, having to do with, or showing flowers, as in *a floral arrangement* or *a floral couch*. **flo·ral (flor**-uhl)

florist *noun* Someone who sells flowers and plants. **flo·rist (flor**-ist)

floss

1. *noun* A thin strand of thread used to clean between the teeth. Also called **dental floss**.
2. *verb* To clean your teeth using dental floss: *I always floss just before I go to bed.* ▷ *verb* **flossing, flossed**
floss (flaws *or* flahs)

FLOTUS *noun* A name for the president's wife. FLOTUS is short for *First Lady of the United States*. **FLOTUS (floh**-tuhs)

flounder

1. *verb* To have difficulty moving through snow, mud, or water.
2. *verb* To have trouble doing something: *Bill is floundering with his science project.*
3. *noun* A flat ocean fish used for food.
floun·der (floun-dur)
▷ *verb* **floundering, floundered**

flour *noun* Ground wheat or other grain that you use for baking or frying. **flour** (flour) ▷ *adjective* **floury**

flourish *verb*

1. To grow well: *Our garden is flourishing.*
2. To develop and succeed: *Damien's new business began to flourish.*
3. To wave something around, especially to show it off: *Jan flourished her medal.*
flour·ish (flur-ish)
▷ *verb* **flourishes, flourishing, flourished** ▷ *noun* **flourish**

flout *verb* To break rules on purpose: *He flouted the law by not wearing his seat belt.* **flout** (flout) ▷ *verb* **flouting, flouted**

flow *verb* To move smoothly, like water: *The traffic flowed easily on the parkway.* **flow** (floh) ▷ *verb* **flowing, flowed** ▷ *noun* **flow**

flower

1. *noun* The colorful blossoms of a plant that produces seeds or fruit.
2. *noun* A plant that is grown for its flowers.
3. *verb* To produce flowers: *My magnolia tree has begun to flower.* ▷ *verb* **flowering, flowered**
flow·er (flou-ur)

flown *verb* The past participle of **fly**. **flown** (flohn)

flu *noun* An illness, caused by a virus, that is like a bad cold, with fever and muscle pains. Flu is short for **influenza**. **flu** (floo)

Flowers

Flowers begin as buds, which swell and open as the petals and other structures inside them grow. A typical flower has four main parts: the sepals, petals, pistils, and stamens. The sepals form the calyx, and the petals form the corolla. The pistil is made up of the ovary, stigma, and style. Each stamen consists of a filament and an anther. When pollen is transferred from the anther to the stigma, pollination occurs. This allows the flower to be fertilized and produce seeds.

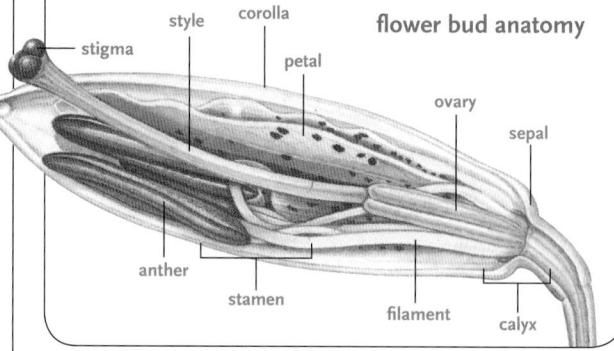

flower bud anatomy

style, corolla, stigma, petal, ovary, sepal, anther, stamen, filament, calyx

fluctuate *verb* To change back and forth or up and down: *The price of gas continues to fluctuate.* **fluc·tu·ate (fluhk**-choo-ate) ▷ *verb* **fluctuating, fluctuated** ▷ *noun* **fluctuation**

flue *noun* A hollow part or passage, such as the pipe inside a chimney that carries smoke away from a fire. **flue** (floo)

fluent *adjective* Able to speak easily and well, especially in another language: *John is fluent in Spanish.* **flu·ent (floo**-uhnt) ▷ *noun* **fluency (floo**-uhn-see) ▷ *adverb* **fluently**

fluff

1. *noun* A light, soft, tiny mass of material, as from wool or cotton.
2. *verb* To shake something out, as a bird does its feathers, or to plump something up, such as a pillow.
3. *verb* To make a mistake in speaking or reading something: *He fluffed his lines in the play.*
fluff (fluhf)
▷ *verb* **fluffing, fluffed**

fluffy *adjective*

1. Light and airy, as in *a fluffy pillow*.
2. Covered with soft, fine hair or feathers, as in *a fluffy rabbit*.
fluff·y (fluhf-ee)
▷ *adjective* **fluffier, fluffiest**

fly-fishing

fluid
1. *noun* A substance that can flow, such as a liquid or a gas: *Water, oil, and nitrogen are fluids.*
2. *adjective* Flowing: *The dancer took fluid steps.*
flu·id (floo-id)
▷ *noun* **fluidity** (floo-**id**-i-tee)

fluke *noun*
1. An accident, especially a lucky accident: *It was a fluke to run into Akeelah at the fair.*
2. Part of the tail of a sea creature such as a whale or dolphin.
fluke (flook)

flung *verb* The past tense and past
participle of *fling.* **flung** (fluhng)

flunk *verb*
1. Another word for fail, used especially for not passing a test or not moving on to the next year in school: *I can't believe I flunked!*
2. flunk out To leave school with failing grades.
flunk (fluhngk)
▷ *verb* **flunking, flunked**

fluorescent *adjective*
1. Giving out a bright light by using a certain type of energy, such as ultraviolet light or X-rays, as in *fluorescent lighting.* ▷ *noun* **fluorescence**
2. A **fluorescent** color seems to glow when you shine a light on it.
fluo·res·cent (flu-**res**-uhnt)

fluoridate *verb* To add fluoride in order to fight
tooth decay: *The city plans to fluoridate its water supply.* **fluor·i·date** (**flor**-i-*date*) ▷ *verb* **fluoridating, fluoridated**

fluoride *noun* A chemical compound put in toothpaste
and added to the public water supply to prevent tooth decay. **fluor·ide** (**flor**-ide)

flurry *noun*
1. A confusion or a commotion, as in *a flurry of activity.*
2. A brief snow shower: *The forecast calls for light flurries.*
flur·ry (**flur**-ee)
▷ *noun, plural* **flurries**

flush
1. *verb* To turn red or to blush: *I flushed with embarrassment.*
2. *verb* To flood something with water in order to clean or empty it: *Always flush the toilet after use.*
▷ *noun* **flush**
3. *adjective* Exactly even: *The door was flush with the wall.*
flush (fluhsh)
▷ *verb* **flushes, flushing, flushed**

flushed *adjective* A **flushed** face has turned red, as
with embarrassment or anger. **flushed** (fluhsht)
▷ *noun* **flush**

fluster *verb* To confuse or disturb someone: *Using
the cell phone still flusters my grandmother.* **flus·ter** (**fluhs**-tur) ▷ *verb* **flustering, flustered**

flute *noun* A long, cylindrical wind instrument played
by blowing air across a hole at one end and fingering keys to change notes. **flute** (floot)

flutter
1. *verb* To wave back and forth rapidly: *The bird fluttered its wings.* ▷ *verb* **fluttering, fluttered**
2. *noun* When you are in a **flutter,** you are excited and nervous.
3. *noun* A quick, beating sensation or movement: *She felt a flutter in her stomach at the thought of going onstage.*
flut·ter (**fluht**-ur)

fishing fly

fly
1. *verb* To travel through the air.
2. *noun* An insect with two wings.
3. *noun* The opening at the top of a pair of pants where they fasten.
4. *verb* To move or pass quickly: *The hours flew by.*
5. *noun* A fishhook used for fishing.
6. *noun* A baseball hit high in the air: *Vida's pop fly was caught by the shortstop.*
fly (flye)
▷ *noun, plural* **flies** ▷ *verb* **flies, flying, flew** (floo), **flown** (flohn)

flycatcher *noun* A kind of songbird that feeds on
insects caught in the air. **fly·catch·er** (**flye**-kach-ur)

flyer *noun* Another spelling of **flier.** **fly·er** (**flye**-ur)

fly-fishing *noun* A type of fishing using fake flies
attached to a fishhook and made from such materials as feathers, bits of fur, thread, and plastic.

flying fish *noun* A type of fish with large fins that spread open like wings, allowing it to jump out of the water and glide in the air for a short time.

flying saucer *noun* A spacecraft that some people believe has come from another planet, shaped like a saucer.

foal
1. *noun* A young horse, mule, donkey, or zebra.
2. *verb* To give birth to a young horse, mule, donkey, or zebra. ▷ *verb* **foaling, foaled**
foal (fohl)

foam
1. *noun* A mass of small bubbles: *The foam in my glass of soda tickles my nose when I drink.*
2. *verb* To make bubbles: *The soapy water foams when I splash in it.* ▷ *verb* **foaming, foamed**
foam (fohm)

foam rubber *noun* A light spongy material, used for mattresses and pillows and to make certain toys.

focus
1. *noun* The point where rays of light meet after being bent by a lens. ▷ *verb* **focus**
2. *verb* To adjust your eyes or the lens of a camera to see something clearly: *The camera lens focuses automatically on some big object in front of it.*
3. *verb* To concentrate on something or somebody, as in *to focus on a task.*
4. *noun* The center of activity, interest, or attention, as in *the focus of an investigation.*
fo·cus (**foh**-kuhs)
▷ *noun, plural* **focuses** or **foci** (**foh**-sye) ▷ *verb* **focuses, focusing, focused** ▷ *adjective* **focal**

focus group *noun* A group of people who are assembled to test a new product or service, or to share their experiences about something they all own or have done. Focus groups are a way for companies to improve their products and services by listening to what people think.

fodder *noun* Food for cattle and horses. **fod·der** (**fah**-dur)

foe *noun* An opponent or enemy. **foe** (foh)

fog *noun*
1. A cloud of mist near the ground: *The fog rolls in almost every night.*
2. A state of confusion or unclear thinking, as in *a fog of misery* or *a fog of grief.*
fog (fahg *or* fawg)
▷ *verb* **fog, fogging, fogged** ▷ *adjective* **foggy, foggier, foggiest**

foghorn *noun* A very loud, deep horn used to warn ships in foggy weather that the coast is near. **fog·horn** (**fahg**-horn)

flying fish

foil
1. *noun* Very thin, silvery sheets of metal, as in *aluminum foil.*
2. *verb* To prevent someone from doing something, as in *to foil a robbery.* ▷ *verb* **foiling, foiled**
3. *noun* A long, thin sword used in fencing.
foil (foil)

fold
1. *verb* To bend something over on itself: *Josh folded the blanket at the foot of the bed.*
2. *noun* A line or crease made by folding.
3. *verb* To bring together, or to bend close to the body, as in *to fold one's arms.*
4. *noun* A small, enclosed area for sheep.
5. *verb* If a company **folds,** it goes out of business.
fold (fohld)
▷ *verb* **folding, folded**

folder *noun*
1. A cardboard holder to keep papers in: *My folders are in alphabetical order.*
2. A named area of disk memory that can hold a number of computer files; a directory: *Copy the whole folder to your flash drive so you'll have a backup.*
fold·er (**fohl**-dur)

foliage *noun* Leaves of a plant or tree: *The bush's foliage looks almost purple.* **fo·li·age** (**foh**-lee-ij)

folk
1. *noun* People: *Do you know the folks in this neighborhood?* ▷ *noun, plural* **folk** *or* **folks**
2. **folks** *noun, plural* Family members, especially parents: *These are my folks.*
3. *adjective* Traditional and belonging to the common people in a region, as in *folk dancing.*
folk (fohk)

folk dance *noun* A kind of dance that is native to a particular area or group.

folklore *noun* The stories, customs, and beliefs of the common people that are handed down from one generation to the next. **folk·lore** (**fohk**-*lor*)

folk music *noun* Traditional music of an area that is often handed down from one generation to the next.

folk singer *noun* Someone who sings folk music.

folk song *noun* A traditional song with music and words, usually with a simple melody.

folktale *noun* A story that is passed down orally from one generation to the next: *Grandma said that she heard the folktale from her grandmother.* **folk·tale** (**fohk**-*tale*)

follow *verb*
1. To go after someone or something: *Jose climbed up the tree, and Sandy followed.*
2. To come after something: *Wednesday follows Tuesday.*
3. To go behind someone: *Follow my car, and I'll lead you there.*
4. To obey, as in *to follow orders* or *to follow directions.*
5. To imitate or copy, as in *to follow the latest fashions.*
6. If you **follow up** on something, you return to something that you started. **fol·low** (**fah**-loh)
▷ *verb* **following, followed**

follower *noun* A **follower** follows someone or something: *The TV preacher has thousands of devoted followers.* **fol·low·er** (**fah**-loh-ur)

following
1. *preposition* Next, after, or coming after: *Following the ceremony, dessert will be served.*
2. *adjective* Next in time or order of occurrence, as in *the following day.*
3. *noun* A group of supporters or admirers: *That singer has a big following.* **fol·low·ing** (**fah**-loh-ing)

folly *noun* Foolishness: *It's folly to think you can go out in this weather.* **fol·ly** (**fah**-lee) ▷ *noun, plural* **follies**

fond *adjective*
1. Liking someone or something very much: *Nicky is fond of chocolate cake.*
2. A **fond memory** or a **fond hope** is a memory or hope that you care for very much. **fond** (fahnd)
▷ *adjective* **fonder, fondest** ▷ *noun* **fondness**
▷ *adverb* **fondly**

fondue *noun*
1. A dish made of melted cheese that is served hot and eaten by dipping pieces of bread into it: *Fondues are very popular in Switzerland.*
2. A dish in which people dip pieces of meat or vegetables into a hot oil, or pieces of fruit into a heated chocolate sauce, as in *a beef fondue* or *a chocolate fondue.* **fon·due** (**fahn**-doo)

font *noun*
1. A bowl or other large container used in a church to hold the water for baptisms.
2. A style of type: *Which font did you use for the headings in your report?* **font** (fahnt)

serif font

sans serif font

food *noun* Substances that living things eat to stay alive and grow. **food** (food)

food chain *noun* An ordered arrangement of animals and plants in which each feeds on the one below it in the chain.

food court *noun* The area in a shopping mall or other place where there are food sellers and tables.

food processor *noun* A machine that cuts up, purees, or liquefies food.

food web *noun* The complex network of related food chains within an ecosystem.

fool
1. *noun* A person who lacks good sense.
2. *verb* To trick or cheat someone: *He fooled me into giving him some money.* ▷ *verb* **fooling, fooled** **fool** (fool)

foolish *adjective* Not showing good sense; not wise. **fool·ish** (**foo**-lish) ▷ *noun* **foolishness**

foolproof *adjective* Something that is **foolproof** is so simple to use or so well planned that anyone can use it or do it without failing: *The burglars thought their plan was foolproof.* **fool·proof** (**fool**-proof)

fondue

a
b
c
d
e
f
g
h
i
j
k
l
m
n
o
p
q
r
s
t
u
v
w
x
y
z

foot *noun*

1. The part of your body at the end of your leg. It includes your ankle and your toes.

2. The bottom or lowest part of something, as in *the foot of a table* or *at the foot of the hills.*

3. A unit of length that equals 12 inches: *I am five feet nine inches tall.*

4. If you **put your foot down,** you insist on something and act firmly.

5. If you **put your foot in your mouth,** you say something that hurts or upsets someone and you get embarrassed.
foot (fut)

▷ *noun, plural* **feet** (feet)

football *noun*

1. A game played by two teams of 11 players each on a long field with goals at each end. Each team tries to score points by getting the ball across the opponent's goal line.

2. The ball used in this game.
foot·ball (**fut**-*bawl*)

foothill *noun* A low hill at the base of a mountain or mountain range. **foot·hill** (**fut**-*hil*)

footing *noun*

1. A secure place on which to stand: *Be careful! The footing is slippery after it rains.*

2. In architecture, the **footing** of a building is the bottom of its foundation, next to the earth.

3. If you **lose your footing,** you are no longer standing firmly.
foot·ing (**fut**-ing)

footlights *noun, plural* Lights arranged along the front floor of a stage that allow the audience to see the actors. **foot·lights** (**fut**-*lites*)

footnote *noun* A note at the bottom of a page that explains something in the text: *According to the footnote, the author got this information from an eyewitness.* **foot·note** (**fut**-*note*)

footprint *noun*

1. A mark made by a foot or shoe.

2. The shape and the amount of space that something takes up on the floor, ground, or some other surface: *My printer has a small footprint.*

3. Something that is left behind by an activity, especially an amount of pollution or damage to the environment: *The company is trying to lessen*

Football

Football is played on a large field between two teams of 11 players each. Offense players score points by carrying, kicking, or passing (throwing) the ball past the opposing team's goal line. Defense players can block the ball, sometimes by tackling (knocking down) the person carrying the ball. Possession of the ball switches between the teams during the game. A touchdown, worth six points, is scored when a player runs or passes the ball across the goal line.

helmet — shoulder pads

cleats

football uniform

football

goalpost
goal line
yardage marker
sideline

football field

fording a stream

the footprint of drilling activities.
foot·print (**fut**-*print*)

footstep *noun*
1. The act of placing the foot on the ground or floor.
2. The sound that the foot makes when it hits the ground or floor: *I heard footsteps on the stairs and thought it must be Lena.*
foot·step (**fut**-*step*)

for
1. *preposition* Intended to be used on or with: *These markers are for posters.*
2. *preposition* Meeting the needs of; in order to benefit: *I take vitamins for my health.*
3. *preposition* Over the time or distance of: *We marched for miles.*
4. *preposition* Due to; because of: *She has to travel for her job.*
5. *preposition* In honor of, or on behalf of: *He picked the flowers for me.*
6. *preposition* Worth the amount of: *I bought a pack of gum for 50 cents.*
7. *preposition* Intended to be given or sent to: *This is for you.*
8. *preposition* In place of: *In the recipe, we substituted honey for sugar.*
9. *conjunction* Because: *We took a cab, for we had to hurry.*
for (for)

forage
1. *noun* Hay, grain, and other food for horses, cattle, and similar animals.
2. *verb* To go in search of food: *The bear foraged for plants and berries.* ▷ *verb* **foraging, foraged**
for·age (**for**-ij)

forbade *verb* The past tense of **forbid**. **for·bade** (fur-**bad**)

forbid *verb* To order someone not to do something: *Mom and Dad forbid us to go to the park after dark.* **for·bid** (fur-**bid**) ▷ *verb* **forbidding, forbade, forbidden**

forbidden
1. *verb* The past participle of **forbid**.
2. *adjective* Not allowed to be done or used: *She hesitated before going into the forbidden room.*
for·bid·den (fur-**bid**-uhn)

forbidding *adjective* Looking unfriendly or dangerous: *At night, the alley was forbidding.*
for·bid·ding (fur-**bid**-ing) ▷ *adverb* **forbiddingly**

force
1. *noun* Strength or power: *The batter hit the ball with great force.* ▷ *adjective* **forceful** ▷ *adverb* **forcefully**
2. *verb* To make someone do something: *Pat's mother used to force her to do her homework, but now Pat does it on her own.* ▷ *verb* **forcing, forced**
3. *noun* In physics, a **force** is any action that produces, stops, or changes the shape or the movement of an object.
4. *noun* A group of people who work together, as in *a sales force.*
force (fors)

forceps *noun, plural* Tongs used for grasping, holding, or pulling, especially by dentists or surgeons. **for·ceps** (**for**-seps)

ford
1. *noun* A shallow part of a stream or river where you can cross.
2. *verb* To cross at a ford. ▷ *verb* **fording, forded**
ford (ford)

Prefix

The prefix **fore-** adds one of the following meanings to a root word:
1. Before or ahead of time, as in *forecast* (tell what will happen before it actually does).
2. The front or in front of, as in *forearm* (the front of your arm).

forearm *noun* The part of your arm from your wrist to your elbow. **fore·arm** (**for**-ahrm)

forecast *verb* To tell what you believe will happen in the future: *The TV station is forecasting snow for the weekend.* **fore·cast** (**for**-kast) ▷ *verb* **forecasting, forecast** *or* **forecasted** ▷ *noun* **forecast** ▷ *noun* **forecaster**

forefather *noun* An ancestor: *George said his forefathers came from Russia.* **fore·fa·ther** (**for**-*fah*-THur)

forefinger *noun* The finger used for pointing; the index finger. **fore·fin·ger** (**for**-*fing*-gur)

forefinger

foregone *adjective* Decided in advance, as in *a foregone conclusion.* **fore·gone** (**for**-*gawn*)

foreground *noun* The part of a picture that is or seems to be nearest to the person looking at it: *In the painting's foreground, two children are playing, while in the background, some adults are watching them from a porch.* **fore·ground** (**for**-*ground*)

forehead *noun* The top part of your face above your eyes. **fore·head** (**for**-id *or* **for**-*hed*)

foreign *adjective*
1. Of, having to do with, or coming from another country: *We like to visit foreign countries and experience other cultures.*
2. Unfamiliar and strange: *All the food they served was foreign to us and a little scary.*
for·eign (**for**-uhn)

foreigner *noun* A person who is staying or living in a country that is not his or her own country; an alien: *Because he was a foreigner, he couldn't vote.* **for·eign·er** (**for**-uh-nur)

foreman *noun*
1. Someone, usually in a factory, who is in charge of a group of workers.
2. The lead man or woman on a jury.
fore·man (**for**-muhn)
▷ *noun, plural* **foremen**

foremost *adjective* First in rank, position, or importance: *Dr. Lyons is the foremost heart surgeon at the hospital.* **fore·most** (**for**-*mohst*)

forensic *adjective* Using science and technology to investigate evidence and establish facts for use in a court of law. A forensic laboratory looks at clues such as fingerprints, DNA, and blood spatters. **fo·ren·sic** (fuh-**ren**-sik)

foreperson *noun* A foreman or a forewoman. **fore·per·son** (**for**-*pur*-suhn)

forerunner *noun*
1. Someone who has come before, such as an ancestor or a predecessor.
2. Something that has come before and led to something else: *The papyrus of the ancient Egyptians is the forerunner of paper.*
3. A sign of something to come: *Crocuses pushing up through the snow are forerunners of spring.*
fore·run·ner (**for**-*ruhn*-ur)

foresee *verb* To expect or know beforehand: *Do you foresee any problems with the way we've arranged the chairs?* **fore·see** (for-**see**) ▷ *verb* **foreseeing, foresaw, foreseen** ▷ *adjective* **foreseeable**

foreshadow *verb* To give an indication that something is going to happen, often something bad: *Her frequent fainting spells foreshadowed a heart problem that developed when she was older.* **fore·shad·ow** (for-**shad**-oh) ▷ *verb* **foreshadowing, foreshadowed**

foresight *noun* The ability to see into or plan for the future: *Teresa had the foresight to save money for college.* **fore·sight** (**for**-*site*)

forest *noun* A large area thickly covered with full-grown trees and plants. **for·est** (**for**-ist) ▷ *adjective* **forested**

forest ranger *noun* Someone whose job is to manage and protect a forest.

forest ranger

foretell *verb* To forecast or predict something: *The prophet foretold the destruction of the city.* **fore·tell** (for-**tel**) ▷ *verb* **foretelling, foretold**

forever *adverb*
1. For all time: *No one can expect to live forever.*
2. Always or continually: *My brother is forever talking about sports.*
for·ev·er (fur-**ev**-ur)

forewoman *noun*
1. A woman who leads a group of people who work together.
2. The lead woman on a jury.
fore·wom·an (**for**-*wum*-an)
▷ *noun, plural* **forewomen**

forfeit
1. *noun* A penalty for something not done or badly done.
2. *verb* To give up the right to something: *The wrestler had to forfeit the match because he failed to show up.*
▷ *verb* **forfeiting, forfeited** ▷ *noun* **forfeiture** (**for**-fi-chur)
for·feit (**for**-fit)

forgave *verb* The past tense of **forgive**. **for·gave** (fur-**gave**)

forge
1. *verb* To make a copy of something, such as money or a person's signature; to counterfeit: *It is a crime to forge someone's signature on a check.* ▷ *noun* **forger**
2. *verb* If you **forge ahead,** you move forward steadily or continue to make progress: *They forged ahead through the deepening snow.*
3. *verb* To make or form something slowly and steadily, such as a friendship or an agreement: *The senators forged an agreement.*
4. *noun* A blacksmith's shop or the furnace in a blacksmith's shop.
forge (forj)
▷ *verb* **forging, forged**

forgery *noun* Something that has been forged; an illegal copy: *The art experts said that the painting was a forgery.* **for·ger·y** (**for**-jur-ee)

forget *verb* If you **forget** something, you fail to remember it: *I forgot to take out the garbage before I went to school.* **for·get** (fur-**get**) ▷ *verb* **forgetting, forgot, forgotten**

forgetful *adjective* Having a habit of forgetting things: *Because she was forgetful, she aways carried a list of things she had to do.* **for·get·ful** (fur-**get**-fuhl) ▷ *noun* **forgetfulness**

forget-me-not *noun* A plant with clusters of small, blue flowers, often used as a symbol of friendship.

forgive *verb* To stop being angry with someone, or to stop blaming the person for something: *Rita forgave me for coming late to her birthday party.* **for·give** (fur-**giv**) ▷ *verb* **forgiving, forgave, forgiven** ▷ *noun* **forgiveness** ▷ *adjective* **forgiving**

fork
1. *noun* A kitchen tool with prongs used for eating.
2. *noun* A farm tool with prongs used for lifting hay.
3. *noun* A place where something, such as a road, river, or tree, branches into two or more directions: *We're going fishing on the small island that lies at the fork of the river.* ▷ *verb* **fork** ▷ *adjective* **forked**
4. *verb* If you **fork out** or **fork over** money, you give it even though you don't want to: *The company forked out thousands of dollars to repair the damage.* ▷ *verb* **forking, forked**
fork (fork)

forklift *noun* A vehicle with two long horizontal bars at the front, used for lifting and carrying large loads. **fork·lift** (**fork**-lift)

forklift

forlorn *adjective*
1. Sad and lonely.
2. A **forlorn** attempt or hope is one that has little chance of success, or of coming true.
for·lorn (for-**lorn**)
▷ *adverb* **forlornly**

form
1. *noun* Type or kind: *Democracy is the best form of government.*
2. *noun* Shape: *The cloud had the form of a whale.* ▷ *adjective* **formless**
3. *verb* To make up or create something: *The lines formed a large square.*
4. *noun* A printed document with a list of questions and spaces for answers to be filled in: *Sandy had to fill out lots of forms to get a driver's license.*
5. *verb* To make or to organize: *We formed a club.*
6. *noun* In grammar, one of the ways a word appears, depending on how it is used. For example, the word *children* is the plural form of the word *child.*
form (form)
▷ *verb* **forming, formed**

formal *adjective*
1. Dressy and not casual, as in *formal attire.* ▷ *noun* **formal**
2. Official: *We're waiting for a formal letter of approval from the bank.*
for·mal (**for**-muhl)
▷ *adverb* **formally**

format
1. *noun* The appearance, shape, or style of something: *After the blog was redesigned, it had a much livelier format.*
2. *verb* To prepare a computer disk for use by erasing anything that may be on it. ▷ *verb* **formatting, formatted**
for·mat (**for**-mat)

forget-me-not

formation *noun*

1. The process of something coming into existence, as in *the formation of a coral reef.*

2. A pattern or a shape, as in *a cloud formation.*

3. The way in which the members of a group are arranged: *The tanks rolled in battle formation.*

for·ma·tion (for-**may**-shuhn)

former

1. *noun* The first of two things that have been mentioned: *I like both kittens and puppies, but I prefer the former.*

2. *adjective* Previous or earlier, as in *my former school* or *my former home.*

for·mer (**for**-mur)

formerly *adverb* In the past, or at an earlier time: *She is now an engineer, but she formerly worked as a medical technician.* **for·mer·ly** (**for**-mur-lee)

formidable *adjective* Frightening and awesome, as in *a formidable opponent.* **for·mi·da·ble** (**for**-mi-duh-buhl) ▷ *adverb* **formidably**

formula *noun*

1. A scientific or mathematical rule or principle that is written with numbers and symbols.

2. A suggested series of actions: *He taught me his formula for mastering golf.*

3. A mixture with several ingredients, or the recipe that you use to make one: *Chinese medicine uses ancient formulas developed over thousands of years.*

4. A liquid substitute for mother's milk: *Heat the baby's formula.*

for·mu·la (**for**-myuh-luh)

▷ *noun, plural* **formulas** or **formulae** (**for**-myuh-lee)

formulate *verb* To work out an idea and then state it clearly: *We need to formulate a strategy that will enable us to win.* **for·mu·late** (**for**-myuh-*late*) ▷ *verb* **formulating, formulated**

forsake *verb* To give up, leave, or abandon: *Don't forsake your old friends when you move.* **for·sake** (for-**sake**) ▷ *verb* **forsaking, forsook** (for-**suk**), **forsaken**

forsaken *adjective* Abandoned or left, as in *a forsaken building.* **for·sak·en** (for-**say**-kuhn)

forsythia *noun* A bush with bright yellow flowers that blooms in spring. **for·syth·i·a** (for-**sith**-ee-uh)

fort *noun*

1. A structure that is built to survive enemy attacks.

2. If you **hold the fort,** you take care of things for someone who is away.

fort (fort)

forth *adverb*

1. Forward, or onward: *The army marched forth.*

2. Out from hiding: *She burst forth from behind a tree.*

fortress

3. Away, or abroad: *Their journey forth was a long time overdue.*

forth (forth)

forthcoming *adjective*

1. Coming soon: *I am eager to vote in the forthcoming election.*

2. If someone is not very **forthcoming,** he or she talks very little, or does not tell the entire truth.

forth·com·ing (forth-*kuhm*-ing)

fortify *verb*

1. To build walls for protection from attack: *The Roman soldiers fortified their camp with a rampart.* ▷ *noun* **fortification**

2. If you **fortify** yourself, you make yourself feel better and stronger: *We drank some cocoa to fortify ourselves against the cold.*

3. To improve or to enrich: *Cereals are often fortified with vitamins.*

for·ti·fy (**for**-tuh-*fye*)

▷ *verb* **fortifies, fortifying, fortified**

fortress *noun* A place such as a castle that is fortified against attack. **for·tress** (**for**-tris) ▷ *noun, plural* **fortresses**

fortunate *adjective* Lucky: *It was fortunate that we were able to find you in that crowd!* **for·tu·nate** (**for**-chuh-nit) ▷ *adverb* **fortunately**

fortune *noun*

1. Fate or destiny: *The psychic told my fortune by looking into her crystal ball.*

2. Chance or good luck: *I had the good fortune to find a summer job.*

3. A large amount of money: *That gold necklace must have cost her a fortune.*

for·tune (**for**-chuhn)

Word History

Fortune comes from the Latin word *fortuna,* meaning "fate" or "luck." The same Latin word in its plural form, *fortunae,* means "possessions" or "goods," and hence the English word *fortune,* today, also means "riches."

forum *noun*

1. The town square of an ancient Roman city.

2. A public discussion of an issue: *We attended a forum on city planning.*

fo·rum (**for**-uhm)

forward

1. *also* **forwards** *adverb* To or toward the front, or ahead: *Guillermo strode forward briskly, hoping his nervousness didn't show.* ▷ *adjective* **forward**

2. *adverb* If you **look forward** to something, you are eager to do it or experience it: *Henry is looking forward to summer vacation.*

3. *adjective* Bold or rude: *He has a forward way of talking.*

4. *noun* A player in basketball, hockey, or soccer who plays in an attacking position and tries to score goals.

5. *verb* To send something to a different person or address after it has been received, as in *to forward an email.* ▷ *verb* **forwarding, forwarded**

for·ward (**for**-wurd)

fossil *noun* A bone, shell, or other trace of an animal or plant from millions of years ago, preserved as rock. **fos·sil** (**fah**-suhl) ▷ *verb* **fossilize** ▷ *adjective* **fossilized**

fossil

fossil fuel *noun* Coal, oil, or natural gas, formed from the remains of prehistoric plants and animals: *The engines of most automobiles run on fossil fuel.*

foster *verb*

1. To bring up a child who is not your own, without adopting that child. ▷ *adjective* **foster**

2. To help the growth and development of something, as in *to foster cooperation between nations.*

fos·ter (**faws**-tur)

▷ *verb* **fostering, fostered**

fought *verb* The past tense and past participle of **fight.** **fought** (fawt)

foul

1. *adjective* Filthy and disgusting: *The sewer had a foul smell.* ▷ *noun* **foulness** ▷ *adverb* **foully**

2. *verb* To pollute: *Chemical waste fouled the water system.* ▷ *verb* **fouling, fouled**

3. *adjective* **Foul** weather is rainy, stormy, and unpleasant.

4. *noun* Something done in a sport that is against the rules. ▷ *verb* **foul**

foul (foul)

Foul sounds like **fowl.** ▷ *adjective* **fouler, foulest**

foul line *noun*

1. In baseball, either of the two lines drawn from home plate to first and third bases. A ball hit outside of the foul lines is a *foul ball.*

2. In basketball, the line on either side of the court from which a player shoots a penalty shot.

found *verb*

1. The past tense and past participle of **find.**

2. To establish something, such as a school, a business, or an organization: *The museum was founded in 1862.* ▷ *verb* **founding, founded** ▷ *noun* **founder**

found (found)

foundation *noun*

1. A solid structure on which a building is constructed.

2. The basis of something: *That rumor has no foundation in fact.*

3. An organization that gives money to worthwhile causes.

foun·da·tion (foun-**day**-shuhn)

foundry *noun* A factory for melting and shaping metal. **found·ry** (**foun**-dree) ▷ *noun, plural* **foundries**

fountain *noun*

1. A controlled stream or jet of water used for drinking or for decoration.

2. A rich or abundant source: *My reading teacher is a fountain of knowledge.*

foun·tain (**foun**-tuhn)

fountain pen *noun* A pen with a point that is supplied with liquid ink from a container inside the pen.

Fourth of July *noun* A holiday that celebrates the signing of the Declaration of Independence on July 4, 1776. Also called **Independence Day.**

fowl *noun* A bird, such as a chicken, turkey, or duck, often raised for its eggs or its meat. **fowl** (foul) **Fowl** sounds like **foul.** ▷ *noun, plural* **fowl** or **fowls**

fox *noun* A wild animal related to the dog, with thick fur, a pointed nose and ears, and a bushy tail. **fox** (fahks) ▷ *noun, plural* **foxes**

foxhound *noun* A breed of dog of medium size that is trained to hunt foxes. **fox·hound** (**fahks**-*hound*)

foyer *noun* An entrance hall, especially of a theater, an apartment building, or a hotel. **foy·er** (**foi**-ur *or* foi-**ay**)

Word History

In ancient Rome, cooking was done over a fire, so every kitchen had a *focus,* the Latin word for "hearth." The Old French word *foier,* later spelled **foyer,** also meant "hearth." In France, a room with a fireplace was probably a good place to get warm and rest, and *foyer* evolved to mean "a room for resting." In English the meaning has changed to "entrance hall."

fractal *noun* A shape, often drawn on a computer, that repeats itself in a pattern over and over again. **frac·tal** (**frak**-tuhl)

Word History

If a cup falls to the floor and breaks, the pieces are of different sizes. When the mathematician Benoit Mandelbrot invented the word **fractal,** he based it on the Latin word *fractus,* meaning "broken," because he was thinking of the different-sized fragments created by something breaking.

fraction *noun*
1. A part of a whole number. For example, ¼, ½, and ¾ are all fractions.
2. A part of a whole.
3. A small amount: *The furniture was on sale at a fraction of its original cost.*
frac·tion (**frak**-shuhn)
▷ *adjective* **fractional** ▷ *adverb* **fractionally**

fracture *verb* To crack or break something, such as a bone or a tooth. **frac·ture** (**frak**-chur) ▷ *verb* **fracturing, fractured** ▷ *noun* **fracture**

fragile *adjective* Easily broken, as in *a fragile vase.* **frag·ile** (**fraj**-uhl)

fragment *noun* A small piece or a part that is broken off: *The museum displays some fragments of very old Native American pottery.* **frag·ment** (**frag**-muhnt) ▷ *verb* **fragment** (frag-**ment**)

fragrant *adjective* Having a sweet smell, as in *a fragrant lilac bush.* **fra·grant** (**fray**-gruhnt) ▷ *noun* **fragrance**

frail *adjective* Weak. **frail** (frayl) ▷ *adjective* **frailer, frailest** ▷ *noun* **frailty**

frame
1. *noun* A basic structure that provides the support for a building, as in *the steel frame of a skyscraper.*
2. *noun* A border that surrounds and holds something, as in *a digital photo frame.* ▷ *verb* **frame**
3. *noun* A **frame** on a webpage is a separate, self-contained area that works independently of the rest of the page.
4. *noun* The way in which a person's body is built: *That football player has a large frame.*
5. *verb* (*informal*) To make an innocent person seem guilty by providing false information or evidence: *Joseph insisted that he had been framed for the crime.* ▷ *verb* **framing, framed**
frame (frame)

framework *noun* A structure that gives shape or support to something. **frame·work** (**frame**-wurk)

franc *noun* The main unit of money in Switzerland, many African countries, and formerly in France and Belgium. **franc** (frangk) **Franc** sounds like **frank.**

French franc

franchise
1. *noun* The right to vote.
2. *noun* Permission given by a company to sell its services or distribute its products in a certain area.
3. *noun* A single location of a chain store or restaurant.
4. *verb* To give the right to someone to sell a product or service in a certain area. ▷ *verb* **franchising, franchised** ▷ *noun* **franchiser** ▷ *noun* **franchisee** (*fran*-chye-**zee**)
fran·chise (**fran**-chize)

frank *adjective* Honest in saying what you think or feel: *She made some frank comments about my paper.* **frank** (frangk) **Frank** sounds like **franc.** ▷ *adjective* **franker, frankest** ▷ *noun* **frankness** ▷ *adverb* **frankly**

Frankenfood *noun* (*informal*) Food made from genetically modified crops. **Fran·ken·food** (**frang**-kuhn-*food*)

frankfurter *noun* A hot dog or small smoked sausage made of beef, pork, chicken, or other meat. **frank·fur·ter** (**frangk**-fur-tur)

frantic *adjective* Having or showing extreme worry or fear: *We made a frantic attempt to finish the project on time.* **fran·tic** (**fran**-tik) ▷ *adverb* **frantically**

fraud *noun*
1. Dishonest behavior and tricks that are intended to deceive people or get money from them. ▷ *adjective* **fraudulent** (**fraw**-juh-luhnt) ▷ *adverb* **fraudulently**
2. If someone is a **fraud,** the person pretends to be something he or she is not.
fraud (frawd)

fray
1. *verb* To unravel: *Stan sewed elbow patches on his jacket where the fabric had frayed.* ▷ *verb* **fraying, frayed**

2. *noun* A noisy argument or fight.
fray (fray)

freak

1. *noun* A person, an animal, or a plant that has not developed normally.
2. *adjective* Very odd or unusual, as in *a freak storm.*
3. *noun* (*informal*) A person who is very enthusiastic about or devoted to something, as in *an exercise freak.* ▷ *adjective* **freakish** ▷ *adjective* **freaky**
freak (freek)

freckle *noun* A small, light brown spot on the skin. **freck·le** (**frek**-uhl) ▷ *adjective* **freckled** ▷ *adjective* **freckly**

free

1. *adjective* If something is **free,** you can use it or enjoy it without having to pay for it, as in *a free concert.*
2. *adjective* If people or animals are **free,** they can do what they like without being stopped or controlled: *My cat is free to go outside during the day.* ▷ *adverb* **freely**
3. *verb* To let a person or animal go from a prison or cage. ▷ *verb* **freeing, freed**
4. *adjective* Not held back, as in *a free and open discussion.*
5. *adjective* Not busy: *We could go skating tomorrow—I'll be free all afternoon.*
6. *adjective* Not affected by something, as in *free of disease.*
▷ *adjective* **freer, freest**
free (free)

freebie *noun* Something that is given for free: *I got some balloons and other freebies at the fair.* **free·bie** (**free**-bee)

freedom *noun* The right or power to do and say what you like: *He had the freedom to choose what kind of job he wanted to do.* **free·dom** (**free**-duhm)

freelance *adjective* If you are a **freelance** worker, you get paid for each individual job you do, instead of earning a salary like an employee: *Annika works as a freelance illustrator.* **free·lance** (**free**-*lans*) ▷ *noun* **freelancer** ▷ *noun* **freelance**

free-range *adjective* **Free-range** animals are not kept indoors in cages, pens, or stalls. They are free to feed and move around outside.

freeware *noun* Software that doesn't cost anything and that you usually download from the internet. **free·ware** (**free**-*wair*)

freeway *noun* A wide highway that you can travel on without paying tolls. **free·way** (**free**-*way*)

freckles

French horn

freeze *verb*

1. To become solid or turn into ice at a very low temperature: *Milk freezes at a lower temperature than water.*
▷ *adjective* **freezing**
2. To make or become very cold: *As the temperature dropped, we started to freeze and decided to leave the stadium.*
3. To suddenly stop moving because you are very afraid: *She froze when she heard the noise in the bushes.*
4. If your computer **freezes** or **freezes up,** it stops responding, usually because a program has caused it to stop.
5. To be damaged or killed from the cold: *The orange crop froze last winter. He froze to death.*
6. To keep from rising: *The government plans to freeze food prices.*
freeze (freez)
▷ *verb* **freezing, froze** (frohz), **frozen**

freezer *noun* An appliance or part of a refrigerator that freezes food quickly and keeps it from spoiling. **freez·er** (**free**-zur)

freezing point *noun* The temperature at which a liquid turns solid or freezes. The freezing point of water is 32 degrees Fahrenheit, or 0 degrees Celsius.

freight *noun* Goods that are carried by trains, ships, planes, or trucks. **freight** (frayt)

freighter *noun* A ship or plane that carries cargo. **freight·er** (**fray**-tur)

French fries *noun, plural* Strips of potato that are fried in deep fat or oil. **French fries** (**french**)

French horn *noun* A brass instrument made of a coiled tube that opens outward into a bell shape at the end. The French horn's musical range is below the trumpet's and above the tuba's.

frenzy *noun* If you are in a **frenzy,** you are wildly excited or frantic about something: *The media frenzy over the celebrity's death lasted for weeks.* **fren·zy** (**fren**-zee) ▷ *noun, plural* **frenzies** ▷ *adjective* **frenzied**

frequency *noun*
1. If something happens with **frequency,** it happens often.
2. The number of times that something happens: *The amount of crime in the area is increasing, especially the frequency of theft.*
3. The number of cycles per second of a radio wave.
4. The numbers that identify where on the dial a radio station can be found: *What frequency does WITF broadcast on?*
5. The number of vibrations per second in a light wave.
fre·quen·cy (**free**-kwuhn-see)
▷ *noun, plural* **frequencies**

frequent
1. (**free**-kwuhnt) *adjective* Happening often: *We were frequent visitors to the library.* ▷ *adverb* **frequently**
2. (free-**kwent**) *verb* To visit somewhere often or regularly: *Jim and his friend Luis frequent the video arcade, much to their mothers' dismay.*
▷ *verb* **frequenting, frequented**
fre·quent

fresco *noun* A painting made on the damp plaster of a wall or ceiling. **fres·co** (**fres**-koh) ▷ *noun, plural* **frescoes** or **frescos**

fresh *adjective*
1. Clean or new, as in *a fresh piece of paper.* ▷ *adverb* **freshly**
2. Recently harvested, as in *fresh vegetables.*
3. Cool or refreshing, as in *fresh mountain air.*
4. Not salty, as in *fresh spring water.*
5. Rude: *Wade gets into trouble at school because he makes so many fresh remarks to the teacher.*
fresh (fresh)
▷ *adjective* **fresher, freshest**

freshen *verb* To make something fresh, or fresher than it was before: *I slipped a mint into my mouth to freshen my breath.* **fresh·en** (**fresh**-uhn) ▷ *verb* **freshening, freshened**

freshman *noun* Someone in the first year of high school or college. **fresh·man** (**fresh**-muhn) ▷ *noun, plural* **freshmen**

freshwater *adjective* Of or having to do with or living in water that does not contain salt, as in *freshwater turtles.* **fresh·wa·ter** (**fresh**-*waw*-tur) ▷ *noun* **freshwater**

fret
1. *verb* To worry, get upset, or complain: *The baby fretted for 20 minutes before she finally fell asleep.*
▷ *verb* **fretting, fretted** ▷ *noun* **fretfulness**
▷ *adjective* **fretful** ▷ *adverb* **fretfully**
2. *noun* One of the bars or ridges on the neck of a stringed musical instrument, such as a guitar.
fret (fret)

friction *noun*
1. The rubbing of one object against another: *Friction causes heat.*
2. The force that slows down objects when they rub against each other.
3. Disagreement or anger: *There was much friction between the two political parties.*
fric·tion (**frik**-shuhn)

Friday *noun* The sixth day of the week, after Thursday and before Saturday. **Fri·day** (**frye**-*day* or **frye**-dee)

Word History

Long ago, when England was pagan, the English named the sixth day of the week after Frigga, queen of the gods. "Frigga's day" became **Friday**.

fridge *noun* Short for **refrigerator.** **fridge** (frij)

friend
1. *noun* Someone you like and know well. ▷ *noun* **friendship**
2. *noun* Someone who supports a group or cause: *He is a friend to animals and often volunteers at the local shelter.*
3. *noun* A contact on a social networking site: *How can he have 650 friends when he just signed up on the site last week?*
4. *verb* To add someone to your list of friends on a social networking site: *I saw that my old Sunday school teacher was on Facebook, so I friended him.*
▷ *verb* **friending, friended**
friend (frend)

friendly *adjective*
1. Warm, kind, or helpful; acting like a friend, as in *friendly advice.*
2. Not angry or hostile, as in *friendly relations between nations.*
friend·ly (**frend**-lee)
▷ *adjective* **friendlier, friendliest** ▷ *noun* **friendliness**

Language Note

The adjective **friendly** is added after a hyphen to nouns in order to form adjectives that mean one of the following things:

1. Making it easy or welcoming for someone, as in *family-friendly* and *consumer-friendly.*
2. Not causing any harm to someone or something, as in *environment-friendly* and *market-friendly.*

fries *noun, plural* A short form of **French fries**. **fries** (frize)

fright *noun* A sudden, intense feeling of fear or alarm: *It gave me a fright when he jumped out of the bushes.* **fright** (frite)

frighten *verb*

1. To make someone afraid: *Eva hoped to frighten her friends with her scary Halloween costume.* ▷ *adjective* **frightening**

2. If you **frighten** someone **off**, you make that person too afraid to get involved or to stay nearby: *Lester was so loud, he frightened off the quieter members of the class.* **fright·en** (**frye**-tuhn)
▷ *verb* **frightening, frightened**

frightful *adjective* Terrifying, horrifying, or shocking: *The children created a frightful mess in the kitchen when they tried to bake a cake on their own.* **fright·ful** (**frite**-fuhl) ▷ *adverb* **frightfully**

frigid *adjective*

1. Extremely cold: *My mom says we're in for a frigid winter this year.*

2. Stiff and formal; unfriendly: *Our waiter's frigid manner made us all wish we'd gone to another restaurant.* **frig·id** (**frij**-id)

frill *noun* A ruffled, gathered, or pleated edge or border: *I wore a blue silk blouse with a frill around the neck.* **frill** (fril) ▷ *adjective* **frilly**

fringe

1. *noun* A border of cords or threads attached to something: *The pillow has a silk fringe.*

2. *noun* Something that resembles a border or edging: *She put a fringe of parsley leaves on top of the salad.*

3. *verb* To form an edge or a border: *Tulips and daffodils fringed the path.* ▷ *verb* **fringing, fringed** **fringe** (frinj)

Frisbee *noun* A trademark for a plastic disk tossed from person to person in various outdoor games. **Fris·bee** (**friz**-bee)

frisk *verb*

1. To search someone for something hidden, especially weapons or drugs: *The smuggler was caught when he was frisked by the security guards at the airport.*

2. To move in a lively and playful way: *It's fun to watch the kittens frisk about the house.* **frisk** (frisk)
▷ *verb* **frisking, frisked**

frisky *adjective* Playful and full of energy. **frisk·y** (**fris**-kee) ▷ *adverb* **friskily**

Frisbee

fritter

1. *verb* To use up in a careless, wasteful way: *They frittered away their whole day.* ▷ *verb* **frittering, frittered**

2. *noun* A small fried cake containing corn, clams, fruit, or other ingredients. **frit·ter** (**frit**-ur)

frivolous *adjective*

1. Silly or without any real purpose: *Isabella's hat is frivolous—it doesn't even protect her from the sun.*

2. Not important; trivial: *His frivolous lawsuit was bogging down the court.* **friv·o·lous** (**friv**-uh-luhs)
▷ *adverb* **frivolously**

frog *noun* A small amphibian with webbed feet and long hind legs that allow it to jump far. Frogs live in or near water. **frog** (frawg *or* frahg)

frolic *verb* To behave playfully and happily: *Our new puppies are frolicking in the backyard.* **frol·ic** (**frah**-lik) ▷ *verb* **frolicking, frolicked** ▷ *noun* **frolic**

Frogs

Frogs are born from eggs (spawn) released by a female, often into water, and fertilized by a male. Each egg hatches a tadpole, a fishlike creature with gills and a long tail. As it grows, its tail shrinks and legs develop. The gills gradually disappear and lungs develop so it will be able to breathe on land. Frogs and toads are both amphibians, but the toad has thicker skin and secretes a poison stored behind its eyes when it is attacked.

young tadpole

mature tadpole

frog

from *preposition*

1. Starting at or in: *The hurricane came from the south.*

2. In relative distance to: *The garage is not far from the house.*

3. In contrast to: *I can't tell him apart from his twin brother.*

4. Out of: *The first little pig's house was made from straw.*

5. Because of: *I became sick from food poisoning.*

6. At: *I got this sundae from the ice-cream shop.*

from (fruhm *or* frahm)

frond *noun* A large leaf with many divisions, such as a fern or palm leaf. **frond** (frahnd)

front *noun*

1. The part of something that comes first, as in *the front of the line.*

2. The forward-facing part of someone or something: *I will meet you at the front of the building at four o'clock.*

3. The area where two armies meet and fight.

4. The forward edge of a mass of air, as in *a cold front.*

5. If you **put up a front,** you try to fool people by behaving in a certain way: *Deborah was scared to death, but she put up a brave front.*

front (fruhnt)

▷ *adjective* **front**

frontier *noun*

1. The far edge of a country, where few people live.

2. The border separating two countries.

3. A subject or an area of study that is just beginning to be understood, as in *the frontiers of medicine.*

fron·tier (fruhn-**teer**)

frost

1. *noun* A fine layer of powdery ice that forms on things when the temperature goes below freezing.

2. frost up *verb* To get covered with frost: *The windshield quickly frosted up.*

3. *noun* A period of cold weather when the temperature falls below the freezing point: *We're expecting the first frost of the season tonight.*

4. *verb* To put frosting on, as in *to frost a cake.*

frost (frawst)

▷ *verb* **frosting, frosted**

frostbite *noun* A condition that occurs when extremely cold temperatures damage parts of a person's body, such as fingers, toes, ears, or nose. **frost·bite** (**frawst**-bite) ▷ *adjective* **frostbitten**

frosting *noun* Icing used to decorate cakes and pastries. **frost·ing** (**fraw**-sting)

frosty *adjective*

1. Covered with powdery ice.

2. Cold enough to form frost, as in *frosty temperatures.*

3. Not at all friendly: *We got a much frostier welcome than we expected at the wedding reception.*

frost·y (**fraw**-stee)

▷ *adjective* **frostier, frostiest** ▷ *noun* **frostiness**
▷ *adverb* **frostily**

froth *noun* A mass of small bubbles that forms in or on a liquid. **froth** (frawth) ▷ *verb* **froth** ▷ *adjective* **frothy**

frown *verb*

1. To have an angry or annoyed look on your face: *Ashley frowned when she heard that they had left without her.* ▷ *noun* **frown**

2. If you **frown on** something, you disapprove of it: *My gym teacher really frowns on tardiness.*

frown (froun)

▷ *verb* **frowning, frowned**

frozen *adjective*

1. Forming into ice or turned into ice because of extremely low temperatures, as in *a frozen pond* or *a frozen tundra.*

2. Extremely cold: *Our hands and feet were frozen.*

3. Chilled until hard, then stored in a freezer, as in *frozen food.*

4. Plugged up with ice, as in *frozen pipes.*

5. Too frightened to move, as in *frozen with terror.*

fro·zen (**froh**-zuhn)

frugal *adjective* Not wasteful; using money wisely, as in *a frugal shopper.* **fru·gal** (**froo**-guhl) ▷ *noun* **frugality** (froo-**gal**-i-tee) ▷ *adverb* **frugally**

fruit *noun*

1. The fleshy, juicy product of a plant that contains one or more seeds and is usually edible: *Melons and grapes are fruit.* ▷ *adjective* **fruity**

2. The part of a flowering plant that contains seeds: *The fruit of a magnolia is enclosed in a hard red case.*

3. The result or outcome: *This mural is the fruit of the whole group's efforts.*

fruit (froot)

▷ *noun, plural* **fruit** *or* **fruits**

fruitful *adjective* Producing results, as in *a fruitful discussion.* **fruit·ful** (**froot**-fuhl) ▷ *noun* **fruitfulness** ▷ *adverb* **fruitfully**

frown

fruitless *adjective* Unproductive or unsuccessful: *His efforts to stop the fire were fruitless.* **fruit·less** (**froot**-lis) ▷ *adverb* **fruitlessly**

frustrate *verb*

1. To prevent something from happening or from being successful: *The blaring noise from next door frustrated his attempt to go to sleep.*

2. To make someone feel helpless or discouraged: *I became really frustrated when my computer kept shutting down.* ▷ *noun* **frustration**

frus·trate (**fruhs**-trate)

▷ *verb* **frustrating, frustrated** ▷ *adjective* **frustrated** ▷ *adjective* **frustrating**

fry *verb* To cook food in hot fat or oil. **fry** (frye)

▷ *verb* **fries, frying, fried** ▷ *adjective* **fried**

ft. Short for **foot** or the plural form *feet.*

fudge

1. *noun* A sweet, rich candy made with butter, sugar, milk, and usually chocolate.

2. *verb* To cheat or be dishonest about something: *He paid less tax than he should have because he fudged the numbers on his income taxes.* ▷ *verb* **fudging, fudged**

fudge (fuhj)

fuel *noun*

1. *noun* Something that is used as a source of heat or energy, such as coal, wood, gasoline, or natural gas: *My car uses diesel fuel.*

2. *verb* To supply the power for something: *Will hydrogen fuel the cars of the future?*

3. *verb* To cause something to become bigger or more widely known or believed: *Quinn's behavior is fueling rumors that he plans to leave his job soon.*

fu·el (**fyoo**-uhl)

▷ *verb* **fueling, fueled**

fugitive *noun* Someone who is running away, especially from the police, as in *a fugitive from justice.* **fu·gi·tive** (**fyoo**-ji-tiv) ▷ *adjective* **fugitive**

Suffix

The suffix **-ful** adds one of the following meanings to a root word:

1. Full of, as in *careful* (full of care) and *shameful* (full of shame).

2. Able to, as in *harmful* (able to harm).

3. As much as will fill, as in *cupful* (as much as will fill a cup).

fulcrum *noun* The point on which a lever rests or turns. For example, the support on which a seesaw balances acts as a fulcrum. **ful·crum** (**ful**-kruhm) ▷ *noun, plural* **fulcrums** or **fulcra** (**ful**-kruh)

fulfill *verb*

1. To perform or to do what is needed: *The company has not fulfilled its promise to supply dependable electricity.*

2. To satisfy or measure up to something: *She was able to fulfill all of the requirements to graduate.*

ful·fill (ful-**fil**)

▷ *verb* **fulfilling, fulfilled** ▷ *noun* **fulfillment**

full *adjective*

1. With no empty space left inside: *Barbara's piggy bank was completely full of coins.*

2. Not leaving anything out: *I gave the principal a full explanation of why I missed class.* ▷ *adverb* **fully**

3. Having a large number: *Our house was full of guests.*

4. Not hungry anymore; having eaten enough: *If everyone's full, I'll just put away this pie.*

full (ful)

▷ *adjective* **fuller, fullest**

full moon *noun* The phase of the moon when it is a full circle in the sky.

full-time *adjective* If you have a **full-time** job, the job takes up most of your day. You usually work five days a week for seven or eight hours a day.

fumble *verb*

1. To look for something in a clumsy way: *I fumbled around for my keys.*

2. To drop something or to handle it clumsily.

3. To lose control of a football or a baseball after you have touched it: *The lineman jumped on the football after the quarterback fumbled the snap.*

fum·ble (**fuhm**-buhl)

▷ *verb* **fumbling, fumbled** ▷ *noun* **fumble**

fume

1. *fumes noun, plural* Unpleasant or harmful gas, smoke, or vapor: *The car emitted smelly fumes.*

2. *verb* To feel anger, frustration, or resentment: *By the time I got home, it was way past my curfew and my parents were fuming.* ▷ *verb* **fuming, fumed**

fume (fyoom)

fun *noun* A good time, or something that provides enjoyment. **fun** (fuhn)

function

1. *verb* If something **functions**, it works properly: *The school's speaker system was fixed and is fully functioning again.* ▷ *verb* **functioning, functioned**

2. *noun* A role, job, or activity that is someone's or something's purpose: *Her chief function is to provide the company with legal advice.*

3. *noun* A formal social gathering, such as a wedding: *We were busy all weekend with graduation functions.*

4. *noun* One of the things that a computer program can do: *That function is not available when you are in Page View mode.*

func·tion (**fuhngk**-shuhn)

functional *adjective* If something is **functional**, it works well or is designed to be practical and useful. **func·tion·al** (**fuhngk**-shuh-nuhl)

function key *noun* Any of the keys on the top row of a computer keyboard, numbered F1 to F12, that have different jobs in different programs.

fund

1. *noun* Money kept for a special purpose, as in *a college fund.*

2. *noun* A supply: *This book has a fund of information on Olympic athletes.*

3. funds *noun, plural* Money that is ready to use: *The school lacks the funds to buy new books.*

4. *verb* To provide the money for something to happen: *The scholarship program is funded mainly by donations.* ▷ *verb* **funding, funded**
fund (fuhnd)

fundamental *adjective*

1. Basic and indispensable: *To play chess well, it is essential to learn the fundamental rules of the game.*

2. Very important; major: *The two senators have a fundamental difference of opinion on the war.*
fun·da·men·tal (**fuhn**-duh-**men**-tuhl)
▷ *noun, plural* **fundamentals** ▷ *adverb* **fundamentally**

funeral *noun* The memorial ceremony that is held shortly after someone has died and that includes the person's burial or cremation. **fu·ner·al** (**fyoo**-nur-uhl)

fungus *noun* A plantlike organism that has no leaves, flowers, roots, or chlorophyll and grows on other plants or decaying matter. Some fungi can be poisonous: *Mushrooms, molds, and toadstools are all types of fungi.* **fun·gus** (**fuhn**-guhs) ▷ *noun, plural* **fungi** (**fuhn**-jye *or* **fuhng**-gye)

fungus

funnel

1. *noun* An open cone that narrows to a tube, used for pouring something into a container that has a narrow neck.

2. *noun* A smokestack on a ship or locomotive.

3. *verb* To pour something through a funnel. ▷ *verb* **funneling, funneled**
fun·nel (**fuhn**-uhl)

funny *adjective*

1. Amusing or humorous, as in *a funny joke.*

2. Peculiar: *What's that funny smell coming from the basement?*
fun·ny (**fuhn**-ee)
▷ *adjective* **funnier, funniest** ▷ *adverb* **funnily**

Synonyms

Funny describes something that causes you or other people to laugh. People, things, ideas, or situations can be funny: *Doug is a funny guy. A funny thing happened on my way to class.*

- -

■ **Hilarious** describes a situation so funny that people laugh almost out of control: *I thought that the movie was hilarious.*

■ **Comical** refers to a funny person or situation: *The circus clowns offered us one comical treat after another.*

■ **Witty** can refer to something funny or amusing through the clever use of words: *The speaker's witty remarks kept the audience listening and laughing.*

■ **Silly** describes something foolish or lacking sense: *It was silly to eat a piece of pizza just 20 minutes before dinner.*

■ **Laughable** describes something that turns out to be funny or causes laughter, though it was meant to be serious: *Her attempts to give the cat a bath in the tub were laughable.*

---

fur *noun* The coat of thick, soft hair on the skin of an animal. **fur** (fur) **Fur** sounds like **fir**.
▷ *adjective* **furry**

furious *adjective*

1. Full of anger: *I was furious when my brother yelled at my best friend.*

2. Fierce or violent, as in *a furious storm.*
fu·ri·ous (**fyoor**-ee-uhs)
▷ *adverb* **furiously**

furlough *noun*

1. Time off from duty for military people.

2. Time off from work for a government employee when there is a budget problem.
fur·lough (**fur**-loh)

Word History

In the 1600s, English speakers must have encountered some Dutch soldiers, because around this time they began to use the Dutch military term *verlof*, which meant "time off from duty." Soon people stopped saying the *f* sound at the end of the word and wrote *-gh* instead, giving us **furlough**. The Dutch word came from *ver-*, a prefix meaning "completely," and *-lof*, a root meaning "permission."

---

furnace *noun* A large, enclosed metal chamber in which fuel is burned to produce heat. Furnaces are used to heat buildings and to melt metals, glass, and other materials. **fur·nace** (**fur**-nis)

furniture

furnish *verb*
1. To equip a room or a house with furniture.
▷ *noun, plural* **furnishings**
2. To supply, provide, or equip someone with something: *The captain of the boat furnished life jackets to all of the passengers.*
fur·nish (**fur**-nish)
▷ *verb* **furnishes, furnishing, furnished**

furniture *noun* The large, movable things in a room or office that make it a place to live or work, such as chairs, tables, desks, and beds. **fur·ni·ture** (**fur**-ni-chur)

furry *adjective* Something that is **furry** has a lot of fur, as in *a furry kitten.* **fur·ry** (**fur**-ee)

further
1. *adjective or adverb* A comparative of **far**.
2. *adverb* To a greater degree or extent: *We read no further.*
3. *adverb* At a greater distance; farther: *I don't feel like I can drive any further tonight.*
4. *adjective* Additional, as in *further information.*
5. *adjective* More distant or remote, as in *the further shore.*
6. *verb* To help advance or go forward: *Hard work will further your career.* ▷ *verb* **furthering, furthered**
fur·ther (**fur**-THur)

furthermore *adverb* In addition; besides: *We can't come tomorrow night; furthermore, we'll be gone all week.* **fur·ther·more** (**fur**-THur-*mor*)

furthest *adjective, adverb* A superlative of **far** and another form of **farthest**. **fur·thest** (**fur**-THist)

furtive *adjective* Sly or sneaky, as in *a furtive glance.* **fur·tive** (**fur**-tiv) ▷ *noun* **furtiveness** ▷ *adverb* **furtively**

fury *noun*
1. Extreme anger, rage, or violence: *He reacted with fury to the news of her elopement.*
2. A dangerous or violent force: *We were surprised by the fury of the storm.*
fu·ry (**fyoor**-ee)
▷ *noun, plural* **furies**

fuse
1. *noun* A safety device in electrical equipment that cuts off the power if something goes wrong.
2. *verb* To melt two pieces of something, such as metal or plastic, together by heating them. ▷ *verb* **fusing, fused**
3. *noun* A cord that burns slowly and then causes a bomb or firework to explode.
fuse (fyooz)

fuselage *noun* The main body of an aircraft where the passengers, crew, and cargo are carried. **fu·se·lage** (**fyoo**-suh-*lahzh*)

fusion *noun* The joining together of two different things by blending or melting: *Their music was a fusion of jazz and pop.* **fu·sion** (**fyoo**-zhuhn)

fuss
1. *verb* To be in a state of nervous, worried, or useless activity: *She fusses over her baby every time he coughs or sneezes.* ▷ *verb* **fusses, fussing, fussed**
2. *noun* A flurry of needless activity or excitement: *He makes such a fuss when his parents come to visit.*
▷ *noun, plural* **fusses**
fuss (fuhs)

fussy *adjective*
1. Overly concerned with small details.
2. If you are a **fussy** eater, there are many foods that you don't like or won't eat.
fuss·y (**fuhs**-ee)
▷ *adjective* **fussier, fussiest**

futile *adjective* If an action is **futile,** it has no useful outcome: *It started to rain, and we made a futile attempt to stay dry.* **fu·tile** (**fyoo**-tuhl) ▷ *noun* **futility** (fyoo-**til**-i-tee)

futon *noun* A hard mattress that is filled with cotton or similar material and does not contain springs. **fu·ton** (**foo**-tahn)

future *noun* The time yet to come: *We expect to save more money in the future.* **fu·ture** (**fyoo**-chur)
▷ *adjective* **future**

future tense *noun* A form of a verb using "will," "be going to," or "shall" to indicate future time. The sentences "I will mow the lawn tomorrow," "She is going to travel to the East Coast," and "We shall obey the rules" are examples of the future tense.

fuzz *noun* A coating of short, soft hair or fibers, as in *peach fuzz.* **fuzz** (fuhz)

fuzzy *adjective*
1. Like fuzz, or covered with fuzz, as in *a fuzzy sweater.*
2. Not clear or distinct, as in *a fuzzy idea.*
fuzz·y (**fuhz**-ee)
▷ *adjective* **fuzzier, fuzziest**

FYI *adverb* A short way of saying *for your information,* used in emails and texts.

Gg

About G Some words with the letter **G** are pronounced with a "hard" *g* sound. Examples: gate, green, go. When the letter *g* is before an *e, i,* or *y,* it is often pronounced with a *j* sound, or what is called a "soft" *g* sound. Examples: gene, giraffe, gym. The letter's name in the Phoenician alphabet was *gimel,* which meant "camel." The Greeks changed it to *gamma* when they borrowed the Phoenician alphabet.

g Short for **gram** or the plural form *grams.*

gab *verb (slang)* To chat or to gossip: *They like to gab about celebrities.* **gab** (gab)

gable *noun* The triangular part of the outside wall of a building between the eaves and the ridge of the roof. **ga·ble** (**gay**-buhl)

gadget *noun* A small tool that does a particular job: *I have a gadget for opening jars.* **gad·get** (**gaj**-it)

gag
1. *verb* To tie a piece of cloth around someone's mouth to stop the person from talking or crying out: *The hostages were gagged so they couldn't call for help.*
2. *noun* Something put over the mouth to stop someone from making a noise.
3. *verb* If you **gag**, you feel as though you are about to choke or throw up.
4. *noun (informal)* A joke: *Dave switched the salt and sugar as a gag.*
gag (gag)
▷ *verb* **gagging, gagged**

gain
1. *verb* To get or win something: *He is still hoping to gain his party's nomination.*
2. *verb* To increase the amount of something: *Eating too many cookies will make you gain weight.*
3. *noun* A profit, or an increase: *The family invested all of their gains back into the company.*
4. *verb* If you **gain on** someone, you start to catch up with the person.
gain (gayn)
▷ *verb* **gaining, gained**

gait *noun* A way of walking: *His gait changed from a slow walk to a jog.* **gait** (gayt) **Gait** sounds like **gate**.

gal. Short for **gallon** or the plural form *gallons.*

gala *noun* A special event that usually includes food, entertainment, and important guests. **ga·la** (**gay**-luh *or* **gal**-uh) ▷ *adjective* **gala**

galaxy *noun* A very large group of stars and planets. **gal·ax·y** (**gal**-uhk-see) ▷ *noun, plural* **galaxies** ▷ *adjective* **galactic** (guh-**lak**-tik)

gale *noun*
1. A very strong wind: *A gale blew the ship off course.*

galaxy

2. A noisy outburst, as in *gales of laughter.*
gale (gale)

gallant *adjective*
1. Brave and selfless: *She made a gallant effort to defend her sister's behavior.*
2. Courteous and attentive, especially to women.
gal·lant (**gal**-uhnt)
▷ *adverb* **gallantly**

gallbladder *noun* The organ in your body that stores a liquid called bile, or gall, that helps you digest food. **gall·blad·der** (**gawl**-*blad*-ur)

galleon *noun* A sailing ship with three masts used in the 15th to early 18th centuries for trading and warfare. **gal·le·on** (**gal**-ee-uhn)

gallery *noun*
1. A place where paintings, sculpture, and other works of art are exhibited and sometimes sold.
2. An upstairs seating area or balcony, especially in large halls and theaters.
gal·ler·y (**gal**-ur-ee)
▷ *noun, plural* **galleries**

galley *noun*
1. The kitchen on a boat or an airplane.
2. A long, flat boat with many oars, used in ancient times.
gal·ley (**gal**-ee)
▷ *noun, plural* **galleys**

gallon *noun* A liquid measure equal to four quarts. **gal·lon** (**gal**-uhn)

gallop *verb* When a horse **gallops**, it runs as fast as it can with all four feet off the ground at once: *The horse started galloping the minute the barn came into view.* **gal·lop** (**gal**-uhp) ▷ *verb* **galloping, galloped** ▷ *noun* **gallop**

gallows *noun* A wooden frame with two standing posts and a beam from which a noose is suspended, once used for hanging criminals. **gal·lows** (**gal**-ohz)

galore *adjective* In large numbers: *There were games and prizes galore at the county fair.* **ga·lore** (guh-**lor**)

galoshes *noun, plural* Waterproof shoes that fit over ordinary shoes and protect them from rain and snow. **ga·losh·es** (guh-**lah**-shiz)

galvanize *verb*
1. To coat steel or iron with zinc to keep it from rusting.
2. To strongly encourage and bring about action, support, or change: *We are working hard to galvanize support for a new community center.*
gal·va·nize (**gal**-vuh-*nize*)
▷ *verb* **galvanizing, galvanized**

gamble *verb*
1. To bet money on the outcome of a race, game, or contest.
2. To take a risk or behave recklessly: *He gambled with his health every time he lit a cigarette.*
gam·ble (**gam**-buhl)
▷ *verb* **gambling, gambled** ▷ *noun* **gambler**

gambling *noun* The activity of betting money on cards, races, or the outcome of future events. **gam·bling** (**gam**-bling)

game
1. *noun* An activity with rules that can be played by one or more people, as in *a game of tennis.*
2. *noun* Wild animals that are hunted for sport or for food: *Rabbits, pheasants, grouse, and venison are types of game.*
3. *adjective* Eager and willing to do something: *She is always game when it comes to trying new recipes.*
▷ *adverb* **gamely**
game (game)

Word History

It is a joy to play games, and an early meaning of the word **game** in English was "joy." This word, though, was originally a combination of the prefix *ga-*, meaning "together," and the word *man*. So the word *game* meant "men together." Of course, now everyone can play games, not just men. The Swedish word *gamman*, meaning "joyfully," is related to *game*.

gamer *noun* Someone who plays video games or who plays games online. **gam·er** (**gay**-mur)

gaming *noun*
1. The activity of playing video games or playing games online.
2. The activity or business of gambling: *The state legislature might expand legalized gaming.*
gam·ing (**gay**-ming)

gander *noun*
1. A male goose.
2. (*informal*) If you **take a gander** at something, you look or glance at it.
gan·der (**gan**-dur)

gang
1. *noun* A group of people who spend a lot of time together: *Their gang liked to hang out at the mall.*
2. *noun* An organized group of criminals or young people involved in crime: *The gang was responsible for several acts of vandalism.*
3. *noun* A group of people organized to do physical work: *A gang from the local prison was repairing the road.*
4. *verb* If several people **gang up** on you, they all turn against you. ▷ *verb* **ganging, ganged**
gang (gang)

gangplank

gangplank *noun* A movable bridge or wooden ramp used for walking onto and off a ship or boat. **gang·plank** (**gang**-*plangk*)

gangrene *noun* A dangerous condition in which your skin or organs decay, usually because the blood supply has been cut off to a part of the body. **gan·grene** (**gang**-green)

gangster *noun* A member of an organized group of criminals. **gang·ster** (**gang**-stur)

gangway
1. (**gang**-*way*) *noun* A passageway on a ship or walkway between buildings: *Wooden gangways connected the trailers to the main building.*
2. (**gang**-*way*) *noun* A gangplank.
3. (**gang**-way) *interjection* A word used to tell people that they need to get out of the way: *As he passed by me, he shouted, "Gangway!"*
gang·way

gap *noun*

1. A space between things: *There is a small gap between her two front teeth.*

2. Something that is missing: *There are big gaps in this file and the text doesn't make sense.*

3. A difference between people or things: *This program bridges the gap between children of different backgrounds.*

gap (gap)

gape

1. *verb* To open your mouth wide and stare in surprise: *We gaped in amazement when we saw the giant swordfish.*

2. *verb* To open widely: *After the earthquake, a jagged hole gaped in the middle of the street.*

3. *noun* A large opening: *Through the gape of his shirt, I could see his sunburn.*

4. *noun* The part of a beak that opens.

gape (gape)

▷ *verb* **gaping, gaped**

garage *noun*

1. A building used for storing vehicles.

2. A place where cars and other vehicles are repaired: *Pam's car was towed to the garage after it broke down.*

ga·rage (guh-**rahzh** or guh-**rahj**)

garbage *noun*

1. Food or things thrown away: *The garbage is collected on Mondays and Thursdays.*

2. Something considered worthless or meaningless: *All the information they gave us turned out to be garbage.*

gar·bage (**gahr**-bij)

garbanzo *noun* See **chickpea**. **gar·ban·zo** (gahr-**bahn**-zoh) ▷ *noun, plural* **garbanzos**

garbled *adjective* **Garbled** language or speech is mixed up and does not make sense: *He couldn't understand the garbled message on the answering machine.* **gar·bled** (**gahr**-buhld)

garden

1. *noun* A piece of land, often near a house, where flowers, vegetables, herbs, and shrubs are planted.

2. *verb* To grow or take care of plants in a garden: *He likes to garden and can grow his own vegetables.*

gar·den (**gahr**-duhn)

▷ *noun* **gardener** ▷ *noun* **gardening**

gardenia *noun* A tropical evergreen tree or bush with fragrant, usually white flowers. **gar·de·nia** (gahr-**deen**-yuh)

gargle *verb* To breathe out with liquid in your mouth while your head is held back, usually to clean or treat your throat: *Gargling with salty water can help a sore throat.* **gar·gle** (**gahr**-guhl) ▷ *verb* **gargling, gargled**

gargoyles at Notre Dame Cathedral in Paris

gargoyle *noun* A grotesque animal head or figure carved out of stone and used to carry rainwater away from the wall of a building: *Winged gargoyles jutted out from the roof of the Gothic church.* **gar·goyle** (**gahr**-goil)

Word History

The **gargoyle** was named for its function of carrying rainwater away from the wall of a building. The word *gargouille* in French meant "throat." French speakers began using *gargouille* as a name for these carved figures because they acted as "throats" for the water passing through their mouths. A related English word is *gargle*. Gargling is helpful for treating your throat.

garish *adjective* Too brightly colored and overly decorated; flashy: *The house was painted a garish purple.* **gar·ish** (**gair**-ish) ▷ *adverb* **garishly**

garland *noun* A wreath of flowers and leaves, often worn on the head as a mark of honor: *The winner of the marathon wears a garland of laurel.* **gar·land** (**gahr**-luhnd)

garlic *noun*

1. A strong-smelling plant related to an onion.

2. The strong-tasting bulb of the garlic plant, used in cooking to add flavor and in home remedies.

gar·lic (**gahr**-lik)

garment *noun* A piece of clothing. **gar·ment** (**gahr**-muhnt)

garnet *noun* A dark red stone worn as jewelry or used in industry. **gar·net** (**gahr**-nit)

garnish *verb* To decorate food that is going to be served: *The chef garnished the fish with lemon wedges.* **gar·nish** (**gahr**-nish) ▷ *verb* **garnishing, garnished** ▷ *noun* **garnish**

garrison *noun*
  1. A group of soldiers assigned to defend a town.
  2. The building occupied by these soldiers.
  gar·ri·son (**gar**-i-suhn)
  ▷ *verb* **garrison**

garter *noun* An elastic band that people wear to keep a piece of clothing, such as a stocking or sock, from sliding down. **gar·ter** (**gahr**-tur)

garter snake *noun* A small, harmless snake with yellow stripes on its back.

gas *noun*
  1. A substance, such as air, that will spread to fill any space that contains it: *Carbon monoxide is a poisonous gas.*
  2. A liquid fuel used in many vehicles. Gas is short for **gasoline**: *The price of gas went up right before I had to drive to Alaska.*
  3. A type of fuel, such as natural gas, that is used as a fuel for heating or cooking: *We converted our oil-burning furnace to one that burns gas.*
  4. The accelerator pedal on a motor vehicle: *You'd better step on the gas if you want to get there on time.*
  5. A gaseous substance produced in your intestines when you eat food, or the discomfort it sometimes causes: *Beans often cause gas.*
  6. *(informal)* If someone or something is **a gas**, it is entertaining or amusing: *Watching our parents put on a talent show was a gas.*
  gas (gas)

gash
  1. *noun* A long, deep cut, as in *a gash on the forehead.*
  2. *verb* To make a deep cut in something: *The skate blade gashed the car's leather seat.* ▷ *verb* **gashing, gashed**
  gash (gash)

gasoline *noun* A liquid fuel made from oil, which is used in many vehicles. Also called **gas**. **gas·o·line** (**gas**-uh-*leen*)

gasp *verb*
  1. To breathe in suddenly because you are surprised, are in pain, or have exercised heavily: *When she reached the top of the hill, Laura stopped and gasped for air.* ▷ *noun* **gasp**
  2. To speak while out of breath: *"Help!" the boy gasped as he waved to the firefighter.*
  gasp (gasp)
  ▷ *verb* **gasping, gasped**

gas station *noun* A place that sells gasoline, oil, and other things needed to keep motor vehicles running.

gastric *adjective* Of or having to do with the stomach, as in *gastric juices.* **gas·tric** (**gas**-trik)

gastropod *noun* An animal that slides on a long foot that also contains its mouth parts, such as a slug or a snail. **gas·tro·pod** (**gas**-truh-*pahd*)

gate *noun*
  1. A frame on hinges in an outdoor wall or fence, that opens like a door.
  2. The number of people paying to see a game, a sporting event, or a performance, such as a concert: *The gate didn't generate enough money to pay for the golf tournament.*
  gate (gayt)
  Gate sounds like **gait**.

gateway *noun*
  1. An opening through which you can enter by a gate.
  2. A way to get something you want: *Learning is a gateway to fulfillment and happiness.*
  3. A place where people enter a country: *Miami is a major gateway to the United States.*
  gate·way (**gate**-*way*)

gather *verb*
  1. To collect things into one place: *We gathered acorns from the oak trees in the yard.*
  2. To come together in a group: *A large crowd gathered to watch the space shuttle launch.*
  3. To learn something by listening or watching: *I gather you're going home for Thanksgiving.*
  4. To gain little by little: *The tornado gathered force as it approached.*
  5. To attract or accumulate: *Knickknacks gathered dust on every tabletop.*
  6. To draw toward yourself: *She gathered the weeping children in her arms.*
  gath·er (**gaTH**-ur)
  ▷ *verb* **gathering, gathered**

gaudy *adjective* If someone's clothing is **gaudy**, it is too brightly colored and fancy. If someone's jewelry is **gaudy**, it is too large and showy. **gaud·y** (**gaw**-dee) ▷ *adjective* **gaudier, gaudiest**

gauge
  1. *verb* To judge something or make a guess about it: *I was able to gauge her reaction from her nervous smile.*
  2. *verb* To measure the amount or level of something: *This device is used to gauge the amount of moisture in the soil.*
  3. *noun* An instrument for measuring something, as in *a pressure gauge.*
  4. *noun* A set measurement, such as the distance between two rails of a railroad track.
  gauge (gayj)
  ▷ *verb* **gauging, gauged**

gaunt *adjective* Very thin and bony: *Mr. Lopez has lost so much weight that he looks gaunt.* **gaunt** (gawnt)

gauntlet *noun*
1. A long, protective glove, worn in the past by soldiers to prevent injury from weapons.
2. If you **throw down the gauntlet**, you challenge someone to do something. If you **take up the gauntlet**, you accept a challenge that someone has made.
gaunt·let (**gawnt**-lit)

gauze *noun* A thin woven cloth used as a bandage: *My mother wrapped my bloody knee in gauze.* **gauze** (gawz)

gave *verb* The past tense of **give**. **gave** (gayv)

gavel *noun* A small, wooden hammer that is used to signal the beginning of a meeting or to call for quiet. A gavel is used by an auctioneer or a judge. **gav·el** (**gav**-uhl)

gay *adjective*
1. A **gay** person is attracted to people of the same sex.
2. Lighthearted and lively: *The birthday party was a gay occasion for everyone.*
3. Decorated with bright colors: *Gay banners fluttered in the breeze.*
gay (gay)
▷ *adjective* **gayer, gayest** ▷ *adverb* **gaily**

gaze *verb* To look at something steadily: *We gazed in wonder as the sun rose.* **gaze** (gayz) ▷ *verb* **gazing, gazed** ▷ *noun* **gaze**

gazelle *noun* A graceful, fast-running antelope found in Africa and Asia. **ga·zelle** (guh-**zel**)

gear
1. **gears** *noun, plural* A set of wheels with teeth that fit together to control the flow of energy and movement in a machine.
2. *noun* Equipment or clothing, as in *hiking gear.*
3. *verb* To make suitable: *The lecture was geared to eight-year-olds.*
4. *verb* If you **gear up** for something, you get ready for it: *The class is gearing up for a field trip on Friday.*
gear (geer)
▷ *verb* **gearing, geared**

gecko *noun* A kind of small, harmless lizard often found in houses in warm countries. **geck·o** (**gek**-oh)
▷ *noun, plural* **geckos** or **geckoes**

geek out *verb* (*informal*) To take part in an activity very enthusiastically that only a few people enjoy: *The girls geeked out all afternoon, sharing Harry Potter trivia.* ▷ *verb* **geeking out, geeked out**

geese *noun, plural* The plural of **goose**. **geese** (gees)

Geiger counter *noun* An instrument that finds and measures radioactivity. **Gei·ger counter** (**gye**-gur)

gel *noun* A substance between a liquid and a solid, as in *hair gel.* **gel** (jel)

gavel

gelatin *noun* A clear substance with thickening properties used in making glue and such desserts as Jell-O and marshmallows. Gelatin is made from animal bones and other tissues. **gel·a·tin** (**jel**-uh-tin)

gem *noun*
1. A precious stone that is cut for use in jewelry.
2. A person, place, or thing that you think is very valuable: *Her new movie is a gem that you won't want to miss.*
gem (jem)

gemstone *noun* A material, usually a mineral, that can be used to make jewelry once it is cut and polished. Sapphires, garnets, and amethysts are examples of gemstones. **gem·stone** (**jem**-*stohn*)

gender *noun*
1. The male or female sex: *The classes used to be divided by gender, but now boys and girls study together.*
2. A category of nouns. In English we show the gender of a noun mainly by the kind of pronoun that can refer to it. Feminine nouns such as *girl* use *she,* masculine nouns such as *boy* use *he,* neuter nouns such as *table* use *it,* and plural nouns such as *children* use *they.*
gen·der (**jen**-dur)

gene *noun* One of the parts that make up chromosomes. Genes are passed from parents to children and determine how you look and the way you grow: *She inherited genes for blue eyes from both her parents.* **gene** (jeen)

genealogy *noun*
1. The study of family history over many generations.
▷ *noun* **genealogist**
2. The history of a family: *The genealogy of our family is recorded in a family tree.*
ge·ne·al·o·gy (*jee*-nee-**al**-uh-jee)
▷ *noun, plural* **genealogies**

genera *noun, plural* A plural of **genus**. **gen·er·a** (**jen**-ur-uh)

general
1. *adjective* Of or having to do with everybody or everything: *I've noticed a general improvement in the class's work.*
2. *adjective* Not detailed or specialized: *The professor gave a general overview of the course.*
3. *adjective* Not very specific or definite: *Witnesses could give only a general description of the man.*
4. *noun* A very high-ranking officer in the army, air force, or marines: *My dad is a four-star general.*
gen·er·al (**jen**-ur-uhl)

generalize *verb*
1. To make a statement that applies to everyone or everything: *When it comes to people's taste in music, it's hard to generalize.*

2. To discuss something in a vague or general way: *I can only generalize because I don't know the specifics of the case.*
gen·er·al·ize (jen-ur-uh-*lize*)
▷ *verb* **generalizing, generalized** ▷ *noun* **generalization**

generally *adverb* Usually; under most circumstances or in most cases: *Squirrels generally don't make good pets.* **gen·er·al·ly** (jen-ur-uh-lee)

generate *verb* To create or produce something: *Dan generated a lot of comments when he grew a beard.* **gen·er·ate** (jen-uh-*rate*) ▷ *verb* **generating, generated**

generation *noun*
1. All the people born around the same time, as in *the younger generation.*
2. The average amount of time between the birth of parents and that of their children. A generation is 25 to 30 years.
3. The descendants from a shared ancestor.
4. The process of bringing something into being, as in *generation of electricity.*
gen·er·a·tion (jen-uh-**ray**-shuhn)

generator *noun* A machine that produces electricity by turning a magnet inside a coil of wire: *They bought a generator after living through many power failures.* **gen·er·a·tor** (jen-uh-*ray*-tur)

generic *adjective*
1. Of or having to do with a whole group or class of something: *The word "folktale" is a generic term that applies to myths, legends, and fairy tales.*
2. Not sold under a trademark and available from different companies, as in *a generic drug.*
ge·ner·ic (juh-**ner**-ik)

generosity *noun* The quality of or an act of being generous and giving: *The minister is admired for his generosity and kindness.* **gen·er·os·i·ty** (jen-uh-**rah**-si-tee)

generous *adjective*
1. Willing and happy to give to and share with others.
2. Larger than expected or larger than usual: *A generous gift from Josh's family paid for the whole party.*
gen·er·ous (jen-ur-uhs)
▷ *adverb* **generously**

genetic *adjective* Controlled by or having to do with genes and heredity: *Eye color is a genetic trait.* **ge·net·ic** (juh-**net**-ik) ▷ *adverb* **genetically**

genetically modified *adjective* Containing genes that have been changed in order to produce a desirable quality: *All of the farmers in this area now grow genetically modified corn and soybeans.*

genetics *noun* The study of how personal characteristics are passed from one generation to the next through genes: *How tall you are is largely a matter of genetics.* **ge·net·ics** (juh-**net**-iks)

genial *adjective* Friendly and welcoming, as in *a genial conversation.* **ge·nial** (**jeen**-yuhl) ▷ *noun* **geniality** (*jee*-nee-**al**-i-tee) ▷ *adverb* **genially**

genie *noun* A magical spirit who grants the wishes of the person who summons it: *I love that story about the genie who lives in a bottle.* **ge·nie** (**jee**-nee)

genius *noun*
1. A highly intelligent or talented person.
2. An exceptional or natural ability: *She had a genius for making children happy.*
gen·ius (**jeen**-yuhs)
▷ *noun, plural* **geniuses**

Genealogy

People study family history, or genealogy, for many reasons. They may want to learn about their ancestors or trace family medical history. Some are proud to descend from royalty, their country's settlers, or people who survived difficult times. Family history is also an important part of some religions. Amateur genealogists now have access to many historical records on the internet, making genealogy a popular hobby. Other sources for research include library collections, oral interviews, and genetic analysis, because DNA contains information passed down from a person's ancestors. Some family histories have been recorded for long periods. The family tree of Chinese philosopher Confucius has been maintained for more than 2,500 years.

Word History

Today, a **genius** is a gifted person with an unusual intelligence or talent. The word *genius* in Latin originally referred to a protecting spirit. The ancient Romans believed that when a person was born, a spirit (genius) was born, too, to stay with and guard that person always.

genocide *noun* The killing of a group of people on purpose because of their national origin, language, religion, culture, or race. **gen·o·cide** (**jen**-uh-*side*) ▷ *adjective* **genocidal** (*jen*-uh-**sye**-duhl)

genome *noun* A full set of chromosomes in an organism. **ge·nome** (**jee**-nohm)

genre *noun* A particular kind of creative work. For example, science fiction and fantasy are two genres of story writing. **gen·re** (**zhahn**-ruh)

genteel *adjective* Extremely polite and careful in your behavior: *She had a very genteel way of getting people to cooperate.* **gen·teel** (jen-**teel**) ▷ *noun* **gentility** (jen-**til**-i-tee)

gentile *or* **Gentile** *noun* A person who is not Jewish. **gen·tile** *or* **Gen·tile** (**jen**-tile)

gentle *adjective*
1. Not rough: *Hannah was very gentle when she was petting the kitten.*
2. Kind and sensitive to people: *The librarian has a gentle manner, and the children like her.*
3. Not steep or extreme, as in *a gentle incline.*
gen·tle (**jen**-tuhl)
▷ *adjective* **gentler, gentlest** ▷ *noun* **gentleness**
▷ *adverb* **gently**

gentleman *noun*
1. A polite term for a man: *"Ladies and gentlemen," the announcer began.*
2. A man with good manners who treats other people well: *Alexander is a gentleman; he holds the door for others and is polite.*
3. A man who belongs to a high social class.
gen·tle·man (**jen**-tuhl-muhn)
▷ *noun, plural* **gentlemen** ▷ *adjective* **gentlemanly**

gentrification *noun* The rebuilding of old city neighborhoods to attract people with more money: *Not everyone in the old part of the city was in favor of gentrification.* **gen·tri·fi·ca·tion** (*jen*-truh-fi-**kay**-shuhn) ▷ *verb* **gentrify**

genuine *adjective*
1. Real and not fake, as in *a genuine pearl.*
2. Honest and sincere: *Her affection for her stepchildren is genuine.*
gen·u·ine (**jen**-yoo-in)

genuinely *adverb*
1. Truly; really: *Going to the prom is genuinely important to me.*
2. Sincerely: *She was genuinely sorry that she had hurt his feelings.*
gen·u·ine·ly (**jen**-yoo-in-lee)

genus *noun* In taxonomy, a **genus** is a group of related plants or animals that is larger than a species but smaller than a family. Dogs and wolves, for example, belong to the genus *Canis.* **ge·nus**

(**jee**-nuhs) ▷ *noun, plural* **genera** (**jen**-ur-uh) *or* **genuses**

geocaching *noun* The hobby or activity of looking for a hidden object after you get clues about its latitude and longitude that you find online. **geo·cach·ing** (**jee**-oh-*kash*-ing)

geodesic *adjective* Of or having to do with the geometry of curved surfaces, as in *a geodesic dome.* **ge·o·des·ic** (*jee*-uh-**des**-ik)

geography *noun*
1. The study of the earth's physical features and the relationships that living things have with the parts of the earth where they are found.
2. The physical features of a place or an area: *The geography of the Grand Canyon is truly awe-inspiring.*
ge·og·ra·phy (jee-**ah**-gruh-fee)
▷ *noun, plural* **geographies** ▷ *noun* **geographer**
▷ *adjective* **geographical** (*jee*-uh-**graf**-i-kuhl)

Geocaching

Players in this real-world treasure hunt use GPS (Global Positioning System) devices to find containers known as caches. Other members of the geocaching community hide them in outdoor locations all around the world. The cache includes a notebook for the finder to sign, and may include items, known as trinkets, which the finder can trade for other trinkets. Geocaching got started in 2000 when GPS technology improved and a GPS enthusiast named Dave Ulmer tested its accuracy by hiding a container and sharing its navigational coordinates on the internet.

Geography

Geography is the study of the earth's physical features—the land, climate, and soils—and people's relationship to them. In the 1400s, Christopher Columbus and other explorers began charting areas that had not been previously mapped. By the early 1800s, all the continents had been sighted. Today, geographers can collect data using computers and satellites. Technology helps them gather information more accurately than through exploration alone.

geology *noun* The study of the earth's physical structure, especially its layers of soil and rock. **ge·ol·o·gy** (jee-**ah**-luh-jee) ▷ *noun* **geologist** ▷ *adjective* **geological** (*jee*-uh-**lah**-ji-kuhl)

geometric *adjective*
1. Of or having to do with geometry: *The numbers are increasing in a geometric sequence.*
2. Having a regular shape on the outside: *Squares, circles, triangles, rectangles, and spheres all have geometric forms.*
3. A **geometric** design is one that uses simple lines, circles, or squares to form a pattern: *She wore a brightly colored scarf with a geometric design in red, orange, and black.* **ge·o·met·ric** (*jee*-uh-**met**-rik)

geometry *noun* The branch of mathematics that deals with points, lines, angles, shapes, and solids. **ge·om·e·try** (jee-**ah**-muh-tree)

geothermal *adjective* Of or having to do with the heat inside the earth and its commercial use, as in *geothermal steam* or *geothermal electricity.* **ge·o·ther·mal** (*jee*-oh-**thur**-muhl)

geranium *noun* A common house or garden plant with thick stems and clusters of red, pink, or white flowers. **ge·ra·ni·um** (juh-**ray**-nee-uhm) ▷ *noun, plural* **geraniums**

gerbil *noun* A mouselike rodent with long hind legs and a tufted tail, often kept as a pet. **ger·bil** (**jur**-buhl)

geriatrics *noun, plural* The study of the health and care of very old people. **ger·i·at·rics** (*jer*-ee-**at**-riks) ▷ *adjective* **geriatric**

germ *noun*
1. A tiny living organism that can cause disease: *You should wash your hands often to avoid spreading germs.*
2. The very beginning of something, as in *the germ of an idea.* **germ** (jurm)

Germanic
1. *noun* A language that scholars believe was the parent of modern English, German, Dutch, and other related languages.
2. *adjective* Of or having to do with Germans, Germany, or languages related to German, as in *Germanic customs.* **Ger·man·ic** (juhr-**man**-ik)

German measles *noun* A contagious illness that gives you a rash and a slight fever. **Ger·man measles** (**jur**-muhn)

German shepherd *noun* A breed of large dog with pointed ears, a narrow nose, and black, brown, or gray fur. German shepherds are often used for police work and as guide dogs for blind people.

germinate *verb*
1. When seeds or beans **germinate**, they start to put out shoots: *The seeds germinated quickly in the rich soil.*
2. To come into being and develop: *The idea of studying in Russia germinated in my head last year.* **ger·mi·nate** (**jur**-muh-*nate*) ▷ *verb* **germinating, germinated** ▷ *noun* **germination**

gesture
1. *verb* To move a part of the body in order to communicate a feeling or an intention: *He gestured to me to move aside so they could pass.* ▷ *verb* **gesturing, gestured** ▷ *noun* **gesture**
2. *noun* An action that shows a feeling.
3. *noun* Something that is done for show, even though it is unlikely to have any effect: *Offering a tax rebate was a gesture to increase support before the election.* **ges·ture** (**jes**-chur)

geranium

a b c d e f g h i j k l m n o p q r s t u v w x y z

get *verb*

1. To obtain something or begin to have it in your possession: *I'm going to the store to get some milk.*

2. To capture: *The police got the intruder as he was running from the scene of the crime.*

3. To become: *As the tree got bigger, it cast a shadow on the nearby house.*

4. To arrive somewhere: *We got home a little after midnight.*

5. To be present and affected by something that happens: *We got two inches of rain last night.*

6. To become sick with something: *I could tell that Andy was getting a cold by how much he was sneezing.*

7. *(informal)* To fully understand something: *Dad showed Mariel how to set the burglar alarm, but I don't think she got it.*

8. get away with To escape blame or punishment: *Everyone knew John had broken the window, but somehow he got away with it.*

9. get by To manage with very little money: *Somehow we'll get by.*

10. get over To recover from something: *She missed her dog, but eventually she got over it.*

11. get to To annoy or upset: *Don't let Susan's constant whining get to you.*

get (get)

▷ *verb* **getting, got** (gaht), **got** *or* **gotten** (gah-tuhn)

Synonyms

Get is the general word that means to come to have something: *For my birthday, I hope to get a new bike. If you don't take care of yourself, you'll get a cold.*

■ **Obtain** means to get something, usually after some effort: *The concert was sold out, but we were finally able to obtain tickets.*

■ **Acquire** also is used when there is effort involved in getting something: *Tracy plans to acquire as many souvenirs of her vacation as she can.*

■ **Receive** is used when you get something from someone else: *I think I will receive at least three CDs for my birthday.*

■ **Gain** means to get something, usually as the result of cleverness or hard work: *My uncle has gained a fortune by investing carefully in real estate.*

■ **Win** means to get something in spite of obstacles or competition: *The politician needs 1,000 more votes to win the election.*

geyser *noun* An underground hot spring that shoots boiling water and steam into the air: *Old Faithful is the most famous geyser in Yellowstone National Park.* **gey·ser** (**gye**-zur)

ghastly *adjective*

1. Horrible, as in *a ghastly crime.*

2. *(informal)* Very bad or unpleasant, as in *a ghastly party.*

3. If you feel or look **ghastly**, you feel or look very ill. **ghast·ly** (**gast**-lee)

▷ *adjective* **ghastlier, ghastliest**

ghetto *noun* A usually poor neighborhood in a city where people of the same race, religion, or ethnic background live. **ghet·to** (**get**-oh) ▷ *noun, plural* **ghettos** *or* **ghettoes**

ghost

1. *noun* The spirit of a dead person that haunts a place or is visible to the living: *"You look as if you've just seen a ghost!" my mother exclaimed.*

2. *noun* A faint trace: *A ghost of a smile flitted across her face.*

3. *verb* To suddenly avoid someone and stop communicating with them: *Meredith ghosted me after we had an argument.*

4. *verb* To leave a place quietly, without saying good-bye to anyone: *We ate and then ghosted when there was no more dessert.*

ghost (gohst)

▷ *verb* **ghosting, ghosted**

Word History

The soul of a dead person has been known as a **ghost** for many centuries, but at first people never saw *ghosts*. The modern meaning of "the spirit of a dead person that haunts a place or is visible" dates from a later period. The Old English word was *gast*, but later people began to pronounce the *a* as an *o*. They also wrote the word with *gh-* at the beginning, giving us *ghost*. Another early meaning was simply "soul." This sense survives only in the expression *to give up the ghost*, meaning "to die."

ghostly *adjective* Like a ghost, as in *a ghostly figure.* **ghost·ly** (**gohst**-lee)

ghost town *noun* A deserted town with few or no people living there.

GI *noun*

1. An American soldier.

2. GI Bill A set of laws that give benefits to people who have served in the military: *She's going to college on the GI Bill.*

giant

1. *noun* In folktales and fairy tales, a **giant** is a mythical being of superhuman size.

2. *adjective* Very large, as in *giant size.* **gi·ant** (**jye**-uhnt)

gibberish *noun* Speech or writing that makes no

sense: *He was so nervous that what came out of his mouth was pure gibberish.* **gib·ber·ish** (jib-ur-ish)

gibbon *noun* A kind of small ape that lives in trees in Southeast Asia. **gib·bon** (gib-uhn)

giddy *adjective*

1. Feeling dizzy and unsteady from being unwell: *John felt a little giddy after climbing the big hill too quickly.*

2. Feeling excited: *Mary was giddy with anticipation as she waited for the party to begin.* **gid·dy** (gid-ee)
▷ *adjective* **giddier, giddiest**
▷ *noun* **giddiness** ▷ *adverb* **giddily**

GIF *noun* A common format for image files. GIF stands for *graphics interchange format.* **GIF** (jif or gif)

gift *noun*

1. A present: *Her birthday gift from Kevin was a puppet.*

2. A natural ability or special talent: *Samantha has a gift for writing poetry.* **gift** (gift)

gifted *adjective* Having a special, natural ability to do something: *Jill's piano teacher says that she's particularly gifted.* **gift·ed** (gif-tid)

gig *noun* (*informal*)

1. A job for a musician or band playing jazz or popular music: *The band managed to get several gigs in local nightclubs.*

2. A temporary job: *She had a gig teaching art for a while.*

3. Short for **gigabyte.** **gig** (gig)

gigabyte *noun* A unit for measuring the amount of data in a computer memory or file. A **gigabyte** is about one billion bytes. **gig·a·byte** (gig-uh-*bite*)

gigahertz *noun* A measure of frequency equal to one billion cycles per second. **Gigahertz** are used to measure the speed of some computers, and also the frequency of some radio broadcasts. **gi·ga·hertz** (**gig**-uh-*hurts*) ▷ *noun, plural* **gigahertz or gigahertzes**

gigantic *adjective* Huge in size or extent, as in *gigantic dinosaurs.* **gi·gan·tic** (jye-**gan**-tik)

giggle *verb* To laugh in a nervous or silly way. **gig·gle** (gig-uhl) ▷ *verb* **giggling, giggled** ▷ *noun* **giggle** ▷ *adjective* **giggly**

gild

1. *verb* To coat something with a thin layer

ginger

of gold: *She gilded the mirror frame.* ▷ *verb* **gilding, gilded**

2. gilded *adjective* Very wealthy or privileged: *His gilded youth did not prepare him for life's hardships.* **gild** (gild)

gill *noun* Either of the pair of organs near a fish's mouth through which it breathes by extracting oxygen from water. **gill** (gil)

gilt *adjective* Decorated with a thin coating of gold or gold paint. **gilt** (gilt) **Gilt** sounds like **guilt.**

gimmick *noun* A clever gadget, trick, or idea that gets people's attention: *The company gave away pens as a sales gimmick.* **gim·mick** (**gim**-ik)

ginger *noun*

1. A fragrant plant root that gives a spicy flavor to food and drink: *Ginger is supposed to soothe an upset stomach.*

2. A light reddish-yellow or reddish-brown color. **gin·ger** (**jin**-jur) ▷ *adjective* **ginger** ▷ *adjective* **gingery**

gingerbread *noun* A brown cake or cookie flavored with ginger and other spices. **gin·ger·bread** (**jin**-jur-*bred*)

gingerly *adverb* In a cautious or careful way: *The new mother picked up her baby and placed him gingerly in his crib.* **gin·ger·ly** (**jin**-jur-lee)

gingham *noun* Lightweight cotton cloth with a checked pattern: *My grandmother washed the gingham curtains in her kitchen every month.* **ging·ham** (**ging**-uhm)

ginkgo *noun* A tree with leaves shaped like fans, originally from China but now grown in many places. **gink·go** (**ging**-koh) ▷ *noun, plural* **ginkgos**

Word History

The **ginkgo** is one of the oldest trees still living, older than mankind or even the dinosaurs. We will never know what early humans called the ginkgo because our knowledge of language does not go back that far, but we do know that the English word *ginkgo* is based on the Chinese name for the tree, *yinhsing*, meaning "silver apricot."

ginkgo

giraffe *noun* A large African mammal with a very long neck and legs and dark brown patches on its coat. The giraffe is the tallest animal in the world. **gi·raffe** (juh-**raf**)

girder *noun* A large, heavy beam made of steel or concrete, used in construction. **gird·er** (**gur**-dur)

a b c d e f g h i j k l m n o p q r s t u v w x y z

girl *noun* A female child or young woman. **girl** (gurl)

Word History

Once, long ago, a boy could be a **girl**. We commonly think of a girl as a female child, but between the 13th and 15th centuries the word *gurle* or *gerle* in Middle English meant a child of either sex. By the 16th century, though, the word became spelled "girl" and it always meant a female child.

girlfriend *noun*
1. The girl or woman with whom someone is having a romantic relationship.
2. A female friend: *Beth likes to go out and have fun with her girlfriends.*
girl·friend (**gurl**-frend)

girlhood *noun* The time during which someone is a girl: *She spent her girlhood in Indiana.* **girl·hood** (**gurl**-hud)

girlish *adjective* Like a girl or like what girls usually do, as in *girlish laughter.* **girl·ish** (**gur**-lish)

girth *noun* A measure around something: *The girth of that redwood tree is about 40 feet.* **girth** (gurth)

gist *noun* The main point or general meaning of something: *What was the gist of her speech?* **gist** (jist)

give *verb*
1. To hand something to another person: *Please give me the key and I'll unlock the door.*
2. To pay: *He gave her $20 in cash.*
3. To supply: *The new lamp gave us more light.*
4. To offer: *We gave thanks that the rain finally stopped.*
5. To cause to happen: *The blizzard gave the students an unexpected vacation.*
6. give in To stop fighting or arguing with someone: *John gave in once he saw there was no hope of winning.*
7. give rise to To be the cause or source of: *All that stress gave rise to more health problems.*
8. give up To stop trying.
9. give up on To lose faith in: *Ruth gave up on asking Jack to dance.*
give (gɪv)
▷ *verb* **giving, gave** (gayv), **given** (**giv**-uhn)

gizzard *noun*
1. A pouch in the stomach of many birds and reptiles that grinds food, using pebbles or grit that the bird or reptile has swallowed.
2. A similar organ in the gut of some insects, mollusks, fish, crustaceans, and other invertebrates that serves the same purpose, often lined with small teeth to help grind the food.
giz·zard (**giz**-urd)

glacier *noun* A slow-moving mass of ice found in mountain valleys or polar regions. A glacier is formed when snow falls and does not melt because the temperature remains below freezing. **gla·cier** (**glay**-shur)

glad *adjective* Pleased or happy: *"I'm so glad you could come!" she said, grabbing my hand.* **glad** (glad)
▷ *adjective* **gladder, gladdest** ▷ *noun* **gladness**
▷ *verb* **gladden** ▷ *adverb* **gladly**

glade *noun* An open, grassy space in the middle of a forest or wooded area. **glade** (glade)

gladiator *noun* A man in ancient Rome who fought other men or wild animals, often to the death, in order to provide entertainment. Some gladiators were

Glaciers

A glacier develops when layers of snow build up over many years and compress into an enormous mass of ice. When the ice is thick and heavy enough to flow slowly downhill, it is called a glacier.

As a glacier moves, it can carve away the land beneath it. The pressure of the ice, as well as the grinding action of the sediment that becomes part of the glacier, is powerful enough to crush rocks.

An icecap is a glacier that covers a high mountain plateau. Icecaps that cover vast areas of land are called ice sheets. There are two continental ice sheets: one that covers more than 80 percent of Greenland, and one that covers about 98 percent of Antarctica.

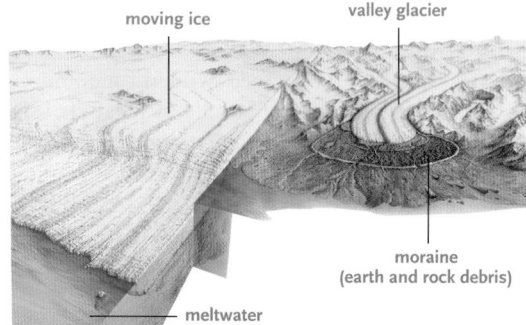

moving ice · valley glacier · moraine (earth and rock debris) · meltwater

professional fighters, but others were slaves, criminals, or captives from other countries. **glad·i·a·tor** (**glad**-ee-*ay*-tur)

gladiolus *noun* A popular plant for bouquets, with long sword-shaped leaves, and brightly colored flowers arranged in a row on a long stem. **glad·i·o·lus** (*glad*-ee-**oh**-luhs) ▷ *noun, plural* **gladioli** (*glad*-ee-**oh**-lye)

glamorous *adjective* Attractive and exciting, as in *a glamorous job.* **glam·or·ous** (**glam**-ur-uhs)

glamour *or* **glamor** *noun* An exciting or fascinating quality that makes people or things attractive: *She had always longed for the glamour of Hollywood.* **glam·our** *or* **glam·or** (**glam**-ur)

glance *verb*
1. To look at something quickly: *Connie glanced at her watch before hurrying off to her next class.* ▷ *noun* **glance**
2. To hit something and bounce off at an angle: *The baseball glanced off the top of Roger's mitt.* **glance** (glans) ▷ *verb* **glancing, glanced** ▷ *adjective* **glancing**

gland *noun* An organ in the body that produces or releases natural chemicals: *Your salivary glands are located near your mouth and throat.* **gland** (gland) ▷ *adjective* **glandular** (**glan**-juh-lur)

glare
1. *noun* Very bright light that makes it hard for you to see: *I couldn't see the stop sign because of the glare on the windshield.* ▷ *verb* **glare**
2. *verb* To look at someone in an angry way: *I asked a question, and he just glared at me.* ▷ *verb* **glaring, glared** ▷ *noun* **glare** **glare** (glair)

glaring *adjective*
1. Very bright and gaudy, as in *glaring colors.*
2. Very obvious, as in *a glaring error.* **glar·ing** (**glair**-ing) ▷ *adverb* **glaringly**

glass *noun*
1. A transparent material made from melted sand, used in windows, bottles, and lenses.
2. A container for drinking, made from glass or plastic: *There was plenty to drink, but we ran out of glasses.* **glass** (glas) ▷ *noun, plural* **glasses**

glasses *noun, plural* Lenses set in frames that rest on a person's nose and ears, worn to correct eyesight. Also called **eyeglasses.** **glass·es** (**glas**-iz)

glaze
1. *noun* A thin coat of liquid that is applied to pottery before it is fired to give it a shiny, colorful finish.

2. *noun* A liquid used to form a coating on food: *We were served chicken with a teriyaki glaze.*
3. *noun* A thin coating of something: *After the storm, the roads had a glaze of ice.*
4. *verb* To put glass into a window.
5. *verb* If you are bored or tired, your eyes may **glaze over**, taking on a fixed and vacant appearance: *The lecture was interesting for the first hour, but afterward my eyes started to glaze over.* **glaze** (glayz) ▷ *verb* **glazing, glazed** ▷ *adjective* **glazed**

gleam
1. *verb* To shine: *Her face gleamed with happiness.* ▷ *verb* **gleaming, gleamed** ▷ *noun* **gleam**
2. *noun* A brief or faint light or sign of emotion: *His frightened expression gave way to a gleam of hope.* **gleam** (gleem)

glee *noun* Great enjoyment or excitement: *The children laughed with glee at the clown.* **glee** (glee) ▷ *adjective* **gleeful** ▷ *adverb* **gleefully**

glen *noun* A narrow or small valley. **glen** (glen)

glide *verb*
1. To move smoothly and without effort: *Some gulls glided by our ferry.*
2. To fly without power, as in a glider. **glide** (glide) ▷ *verb* **gliding, glided** ▷ *noun* **glide**

glider *noun* A very light aircraft designed to fly without engine power. **glid·er** (**glye**-dur)

glimmer
1. *verb* To shine faintly or for brief periods: *Stars glimmered in the sky.* ▷ *verb* **glimmering, glimmered** ▷ *noun* **glimmer**
2. *noun* A trace, as in *a glimmer of hope.* **glim·mer** (**glim**-ur)

glimpse *verb* To see something very briefly: *I barely glimpsed the president through the crowd.* **glimpse** (glimps) ▷ *verb* **glimpsing, glimpsed** ▷ *noun* **glimpse**

glint
1. *verb* To reflect light in small flashes: *We could see moonlight glinting off the snow.* ▷ *verb* **glinting, glinted**
2. *noun* A hint of emotion, especially in a person's eyes: *There was a glint of amusement in her eyes.* **glint** (glint)

glisten
1. *verb* To shine and sparkle: *Snow glistened under the streetlights.* ▷ *verb* **glistening, glistened**
2. *noun* A sparkling light reflected off a moist surface: *Jenna could see the glisten of tears on his cheeks.* **glis·ten** (**glis**-uhn)

glitch *noun* (*informal*) Any sudden thing that goes wrong or causes a problem, usually with machinery, as in *a computer glitch.* **glitch** (glich)

glitter *verb* To shine with many small flashes of reflected light: *The diamond ring glittered on her finger.* **glit·ter** (glit-ur) ▷ *verb* **glittering, glittered**

gloat *verb* To take satisfaction or delight in your own success or someone else's misfortune: *I had to gloat a little after the principal praised my science project.* **gloat** (gloht) ▷ *verb* **gloating, gloated**

global *adjective* Of or having to do with the whole world, or globe. **glob·al** (gloh-buhl) ▷ *adverb* **globally**

global warming *noun* A gradual rise in the temperature of the earth's atmosphere, caused by human activities that pollute.

globe *noun*
1. The world: *The internet makes it a great deal easier for people around the globe to communicate with each other.*
2. A round model of the world used for study or decoration: *We found New Zealand on the globe.*
3. A ball-shaped object: *A crystal globe on the desk captured the sun's rays as they streamed through the window.*
globe (glohb)
▷ *adjective* **globular** (glah-byuh-lur)

glockenspiel *noun* A musical instrument consisting of a frame with tuned metal bars. The bars are struck with small hammers to sound different notes. **glock·en·spiel** (glah-kuhn-*speel*)

gloom *noun*
1. A sense of hopelessness and depression.
2. Shade or darkness: *Daylight could not pierce the forest's gloom.*
gloom (gloom)

gloomy *adjective*
1. Overcast or dimly lit, as in *a gloomy dungeon*.
2. Feeling or expressing sadness and pessimism.
gloom·y (gloo-mee)
▷ *adjective* **gloomier, gloomiest**

glorify *verb*
1. To praise or treat as very important or splendid: *At graduation, the principal glorified the students' accomplishments.*
2. To honor or promote the glory of: *This hymn glorifies God.*
glo·ri·fy (glor-uh-*fye*)
▷ *verb* **glorifies, glorifying, glorified**

glory *noun*
1. Great fame or honor, as in *the glory of victory*.
2. Something that brings honor or praise: *The soldier's*

globe

bravery during the battle won him glory.
3. Splendor or magnificence, as in *the glory of a sunrise.*
glo·ry (glor-ee)
▷ *noun, plural* **glories** ▷ *adjective* **glorious**

gloss *noun* A shine on a surface: *The table had been polished to a high gloss.* **gloss** (glaws *or* glahs) ▷ *noun, plural* **glosses** ▷ *adjective* **glossy**

glossary *noun* A list of technical or specialized words and phrases along with their definitions. **glos·sa·ry** (glah-sur-ee) ▷ *noun, plural* **glossaries**

glove *noun*
1. A warm or protective hand covering that has separate parts for the thumb and each finger.
2. A padded leather covering for the hand, worn by players of sports such as boxing and baseball.
3. If something **fits like a glove**, it fits exactly.
glove (gluhv)

glow
1. *verb* To give off a steady, low light, because of heat or chemical activity: *The embers glowed faintly as the fire burned out.*
2. *noun* A steady light: *The glow of sunrise turned the treetops to gold.*
3. *verb* To show a color suggesting warmth or good health: *The cold air made Maya's cheeks glow when she went outside.*
4. *noun* A bright, warm, or healthy color: *There was a glow on her cheeks.*
5. *verb* To show a warm feeling: *He glowed with contentment.*
glow (gloh)
▷ *verb* **glowing, glowed** ▷ *adjective* **glowing**

glower *verb* To stare angrily: *Ted glowered at the driver who bumped into his car.* **glow·er** (glou-ur) ▷ *verb* **glowering, glowered** ▷ *noun* **glower**

glowworm *noun* The larva of a firefly, or a wingless female firefly that glows to attract males. **glow·worm** (gloh-*wurm*)

glucose *noun*
1. A naturally produced sugar in plants and in the blood of animals. It is a source of energy for living things.
2. A syrup made from cornstarch and widely used in the food industry.
glu·cose (gloo-kose)

glue
1. *noun* A substance used to make materials or objects stick together tightly.
2. *verb* To stick things together with or as if with glue:

Heather glued the model airplane parts together.
3. *verb (informal)* If you are **glued to** something, you are not leaving or letting your attention stray from it: *We were glued to our seats throughout the entire speech.*
glue (gloo)
▷ *verb* **gluing, glued**

glum *adjective* Looking or feeling unhappy: *The captain of the losing team had a glum expression on his face.* **glum** (gluhm) ▷ *adjective* **glummer, glummest**
▷ *adverb* **glumly**

glut *noun* An overabundant supply, as in *a glut of houses on the market.* **glut** (gluht)

glutton *noun*
1. A person who is greedy, especially for food.
2. A person who is always eager for something difficult or unpleasant: *Some people are just gluttons for punishment.*
glut·ton (**gluht**-uhn)
▷ *noun* **gluttony** ▷ *adjective* **gluttonous**

GMO *noun* A plant or animal that has been developed by changing its genetic makeup. Most GMOs that people talk about are ingredients in food and some people think they can be harmful. GMO is short for *genetically modified organism.*

gnarled *adjective* Twisted and knobby, especially with age, as in *a gnarled oak tree.* **gnarled** (nahrld)

gnash *verb* To grind together in anger or grief: *There's no point gnashing your teeth over a situation you cannot change.* **gnash** (nash) ▷ *verb* **gnashes, gnashing, gnashed**

gnat *noun* A small, winged, biting insect similar to a mosquito. **gnat** (nat)

gnaw *verb*
1. To bite or nibble persistently: *You could tell from the marks on the chair leg that a dog had gnawed it.*
2. If something **gnaws at** you, it is a source of distress or anxiety.
gnaw (naw)
▷ *verb* **gnawing, gnawed**

gnome *noun*
1. In folktales and fairy tales, **gnomes** are dwarflike old men believed to live underground and guard the earth's treasure.
2. A garden statue that looks like an old man with a beard and a pointy hat.
gnome (nome)

gnu *noun* A kind of antelope found in Africa that

hockey goalie

has a head like an ox, a short mane, curved horns, and a long tail. **gnu** (noo) **Gnu** sounds like **new**.
▷ *noun, plural* **gnus** *or* **gnu**

go
1. *verb* To move away from or closer to a place: *After school I'll go straight home.*
2. *verb* To function properly: *No matter what he did, the car just wouldn't go.*
3. *verb* To pass: *Spring has gone.*
4. *verb* To have a certain place: *That picture goes on the kitchen wall.*
5. *verb* If you are **going to** do something, you intend to do it in the future: *I'm going to get a job.*
6. *verb* To be suitable: *Pie and ice cream go well together.*
7. *verb* To turn out: *How did the exam go?*
8. *adjective* Ready to happen: *All systems are go for the space shuttle launch.*
go (goh)
▷ *verb* **goes, going, went** (went), **gone** (gawn)

goad *verb* To tease or urge someone into doing something: *Hillary tried to goad Ben into climbing the fence, but he wouldn't do it.* **goad** (gohd)
▷ *verb* **goading, goaded**

goal
1. *noun* An area or a frame with a net that is the target of scoring in a game: *The soccer players stopped the ball just short of the goal.*
2. *noun* The act of sending a ball or puck into or past a goal and scoring because of this: *There were no goals in the first half of the match.*
3. *verb* To send a ball or puck into or through a goal: *Carmela goaled to make it 16–6 at halftime.* ▷ *verb* **goaling, goaled**
4. *noun* Something that you aim to do: *Shelly's goal is to go to medical school.*
goal (gohl)

goalie *noun* Someone who guards the goal in soccer or hockey to prevent the other team from scoring. **goal·ie** (**goh**-lee)

goalkeeper *noun* A goalie. **goal·keep·er** (**gohl**-*kee*-pur)

goat *noun*
1. An animal with a beard and horns that curve backward, often raised on farms for its milk.
2. If someone **gets your goat**, he or she has succeeded in annoying you.
goat (goht)

goatee *noun* A small beard around the mouth and chin, pointed like that of a goat. **goa·tee** (goh-**tee**)

gobble *verb*

1. To eat food in a hurry: *She gobbled her dinner and ran out the door.*

2. To make the sound a turkey makes. **gob·ble** (**gah**-buhl)

▷ *verb* **gobbling, gobbled**

goblet *noun* A tall drinking glass with a stem and a base. **gob·let** (**gah**-blit)

goblin *noun* In fairy tales, **goblins** are small, ugly creatures who like to cause trouble. **gob·lin** (**gah**-blin)

God *noun*

1. The creator and ruler of the universe in Christianity and other religions.

2. god A superhuman being who is worshiped.

3. god A much-loved, admired, or influential person: *The soccer player was a god to his fans.* **God** (gahd)

goddess *noun*

1. A female god.

2. A woman who is much loved or greatly admired, especially for her beauty: *She was a goddess in the eyes of her many male admirers.* **god·dess** (**gah**-dis)

godparent *noun* In the Christian religion, someone who promises to oversee a child's religious education when the child is baptized. **god·par·ent** (**gahd**-*pair*-uhnt)

goes *verb* The third-person singular present form of **go**. **goes** (gohz)

goggles *noun, plural* Protective glasses that fit tightly around your eyes, as in *skiing goggles.* **gog·gles** (**gah**-guhlz)

go-kart *or* **go-cart** *noun* A small racing vehicle that is low on the ground and built without doors or a roof. **go-kart** *or* **go-cart** (**goh**-*kahrt*)

gold *noun*

1. A chemical element that is a precious metal used in jewelry and to guarantee the value of a country's currency.

2. A deep yellow or yellow-brown color. **gold** (gohld)

▷ *adjective* **gold** ▷ *adjective* **golden**

goldenrod *noun* A tall, wild plant with short spikes of small, yellow flowers. Goldenrods bloom in the late summer and fall. **gold·en·rod** (**gohl**-duhn-*rahd*)

goldfinch *noun* A small bird that looks very much like a canary. The male goldfinch is yellow with black markings. **gold·finch** (**gohld**-*finch*) ▷ *noun, plural* **goldfinches**

goldfish *noun* A reddish-golden fish often seen in ponds and kept in aquariums. **gold·fish** (**gohld**-*fish*) ▷ *noun, plural* **goldfish** *or* **goldfishes**

goldfish

golf *noun* A game in which players use clubs to hit a small white ball around a special grassy course and into a series of holes. A golf course has either 9 or 18 holes. **golf** (gahlf) ▷ *noun* **golfer** ▷ *noun* **golfing** ▷ *verb* **golf**

gondola *noun*

1. A light, flat-bottomed rowboat with high, pointed ends. Gondolas are used to transport people and goods through the canals of Venice, Italy.

2. A railroad freight car with low sides and no roof.

3. A cabin or enclosure for passengers on a ski lift or under a hot-air balloon or blimp. **gon·do·la** (**gahn**-duh-luh)

gondolier

gondolier *noun* A person who rows and steers a gondola to transport people or goods through a canal. **gon·do·lier** (*gahn*-duh-**leer**)

gone *verb* The past participle of **go**. **gone** (gawn)

gong *noun* A metal disk that, when hit with a hammer, makes a resonant sound: *The gong signaled that it was time for dinner.* **gong** (gahng *or* gawng)

good *adjective*

1. Well-behaved: *Blackie is such a good dog—he never begs at the table.*

2. Pleasant or agreeable: *I know we'll have a good time at the movies.*

3. Suitable for or beneficial to: *Herbal tea with honey is good for a sore throat.*

4. Of high quality, as in *a good piece of furniture.*

5. Full: *We waited a good 20 minutes before anyone showed up.*

6. Clever or skillful, as in *a good hitter.*

7. Kind or helpful, as in *good to animals.*

8. If you **make good** at something, you are doing well at it: *Veronica made good on her promise to visit her grandmother every week.*

good (gud)
▷ *adjective* **better, best** ▷ *noun* **good**

Synonyms

Good is the opposite of *bad* in most of its meanings. Sometimes *good* is just the right word: *The man did a good deed when he returned the lost dog to its owner. She is a good friend.* Other times you can find more colorful words to describe things that are "good."

- -

▪ **Enjoyable** can describe something good that is extremely pleasant: *We had an enjoyable time when we visited our cousins.*

▪ **Excellent** describes something of very good quality, with no faults or mistakes: *That was an excellent meal.*

▪ **Capable** can describe a person who is good at doing something: *He's a capable chess player.*

▪ **Well-behaved** describes a person who has good manners: *Ms. Stuart's well-behaved students were rewarded with a trip to the museum.*

▪ **Tasty** means full of good flavor: *For Mother's Day, Brian and Emma served their mom a tasty breakfast of pancakes and fruit.*

good-bye or **good-by** *interjection* A word of farewell said when leaving or ending a conversation: *She hung up on me without even saying good-bye.* **good-bye** or **good-by** (gud-bye)

Good Friday *noun* A date commemorated by Christian religions as the day Jesus died on the cross; the Friday before Easter.

good-natured *adjective* Pleasant and generally warm and kind: *Judy and Anne are having a good-natured competition to see who can read the most books this summer.* **good-na·tured** (**nay**-churd)

goodness *noun* Generosity or kindness: *Maude gave me her coat out of the goodness of her heart.* **good·ness** (gud-nis)

goods *noun, plural* Things that are sold or things that someone owns, as in *household goods.* **goods** (gudz)

goodwill *noun*
1. A kindly feeling of support and cooperation: *The solution depends upon the goodwill of all nations.*

2. The value a business has because of a good relationship with its customers. **good·will** (gud-wil)

gooey *adjective* (*informal*) Soft and sticky, as in *gooey brownies.* **goo·ey** (goo-ee) ▷ *adjective* **gooier, gooiest** ▷ *noun* **gooeyness**

goofy *adjective* (*informal*) Ridiculous and absurd, but usually in a funny and likable way: *The baby laughed at all the goofy faces and sounds we made.* **goof·y** (goo-fee) ▷ *adjective* **goofier, goofiest** ▷ *noun* **goofiness** ▷ *adverb* **goofily** (goo-fuh-lee)

google *verb* To search for information about someone or something on the internet, using the Google search engine or some other online search service. **goo·gle** (goo-guhl) ▷ *verb* **googling, googled**

goose *noun* A large waterbird with a long neck, short legs, and webbed feet. **goose** (goos) ▷ *noun, plural* **geese** (gees)

goose bumps *noun, plural* When you are cold or frightened, you can sometimes get **goose bumps**. Tiny bumps appear on your skin, and the hairs on your skin stand up: *Hearing the scary story gave them goose bumps.*

gopher *noun* A small, furry animal related to the squirrel. Gophers live underground. **go·pher** (goh-fur)

gore
1. *noun* Clotted blood or blood that has been shed as a result of violence: *Those Halloween movies are nothing but an excuse to show lots of gore.* ▷ *adjective* **gory**
2. *verb* If you are **gored** by an animal, you are pierced by its horns or tusks. ▷ *verb* **goring, gored**
gore (gor)

gorge
1. *noun* A deep valley or ravine.
2. *verb* To eat greedily or stuff yourself with food: *They gorged on popcorn and candy.* ▷ *verb* **gorging, gorged**
gorge (gorj)

gorgeous *adjective* Very attractive or beautiful: *The bride was as gorgeous as her dress.* **gor·geous** (gor-juhs)

gorilla *noun* A dark, broad-shouldered ape with a large head and a short neck, found in Africa. **go·ril·la** (guh-ril-uh) **Gorilla** sounds like **guerrilla**.

Word History

Sometime around the fifth century B.C., an explorer from Carthage named Hanno wrote about his visit to the western coast of Africa, where he saw some wild and hairy creatures he had never seen before. His guides said the creatures were called *gorillas,* so the word **gorilla** may be from an African language. We don't know what Hanno saw; he may have seen gorillas or some other kind of ape.

gosling *noun* A young goose. **gos·ling** (**gahz**-ling)

gospel *noun*
1. The teachings of Jesus.
2. **Gospel** One of the first four books in the New Testament of the Bible, which tell the story of Jesus's life and teachings.
3. Something that is absolutely true or accepted as truth: *Everything the cult leader said was considered gospel by his followers.*
gos·pel (**gahs**-puhl)

gossamer
1. *noun* A very delicate film spun by a spider; a cobweb: *Gossamer stretched from the chandelier to the corner of the room.*
2. *adjective* Fine, delicate, or insubstantial: *She wore a white dress with a gossamer veil.*
gos·sa·mer (**gah**-suh-mur)

gossip *noun*
1. Idle talk about other people's personal business.
2. A person who likes to talk about other people's personal business.
gos·sip (**gah**-sip)
▷ *verb* **gossip**

got *verb* The past tense of **get**. The word *got* is also used as the past participle of the verb *get* in some meanings. **got** (gaht)

Goth
1. *noun* A member of the Germanic tribes that invaded the Roman Empire between the third and fifth centuries A.D.
2. **goth** *noun* A young person who dresses in black, has piercings, and wears a lot of shiny jewelry: *She hangs out with other goths at the mall on Saturdays.*
3. **goth** *adjective* Belonging to a style of music or fashion that goths like: *We're checking out the goth stuff in this new store.*
Goth (gahth)

Gothic *adjective*
1. Of or having to do with the style of art or architecture used in Europe between the 12th and 16th centuries: *Gothic buildings are known for their pointed arches and stained-glass windows.*
2. **Gothic** stories and fiction are often set in the past and are full of scary things.
Goth·ic (**gah**-thik)

gotten *verb* A past participle of **get**. The word **gotten** is used as the past participle in sentences where the verb *get* means "become" or "obtain." **got·ten** (**gah**-tuhn)

Gouda *noun* A mild, yellow cheese made in the Netherlands. **Gou·da** (**goo**-duh)

gouge
1. *noun* A tool used to make deep impressions in wood or other hard materials.
2. *noun* A deep cut caused by such a tool or other object.
3. *verb* To cut something deeply with or as if with a sharp tool: *We had to gouge a hole in the wall to get inside.*
4. *verb* To cheat or steal from someone: *The company was accused of gouging its customers.*
gouge (gouj)
▷ *verb* **gouging, gouged**

gourd

gourd *noun* A hard-skinned fruit that grows on a vine, similar to a squash or pumpkin. **gourd** (gord)

gourmet
1. *noun* An expert on food and wine, or someone who appreciates them: *The chef and cookbook author Julia Child was a famous gourmet.*
2. *adjective* Of or having to do with good food, as in *a gourmet kitchen.*
gour·met (goor-**may**)

govern *verb*
1. To control or exercise authority over a country, organization, or group: *The president said that she would govern fairly and openly.*
2. To control, influence, or regulate: *She was incapable of governing her own emotions.*
gov·ern (**guhv**-urn)
▷ *verb* **governing, governed**

government *noun*
1. The system by which a country, state, or organization is governed: *Most of the state's problems could be traced to poor government.*
2. The group of people who govern a country or state: *She works for the federal government.*
gov·ern·ment (**guhv**-urn-muhnt or **guhv**-ur-muhnt)
▷ *adjective* **governmental**

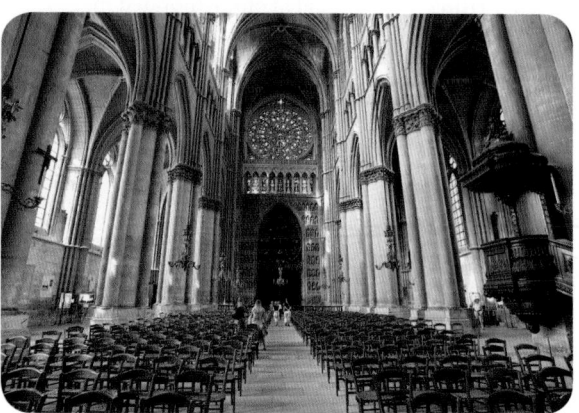

Gothic cathedral

governor *noun*
1. The highest elected official of a US state, as in *the governor of New Jersey.*
2. An official appointed to govern a colony or territory.
3. A person in charge of a certain type of organization or institution, such as a bank.
gov·er·nor (**guhv**-ur-nur)

gown *noun*
1. A long dress worn on special or formal occasions, as in *a wedding gown.*
2. A loose robe worn by judges, by surgeons and patients, and by students at their graduation ceremonies: *The senior class wore red caps and gowns.*
gown (goun)

GPS *noun* A system of satellites and devices that people use to find out where they are, or to get directions to a place. GPS is short for *Global Positioning System.*

grab *verb*
1. To take hold of something suddenly: *I grabbed the rail of the boat to steady myself.*
2. To obtain something hastily or when the opportunity arises: *You'd better grab a seat before the lights go out.*
grab (grab)
▷ *verb* **grabbing, grabbed**

GPS

In 1973, the Department of Defense developed the Global Positioning System, or GPS, to help the military keep track of its planes, ships, and vehicles around the world. Today, people use a GPS device as a navigation tool to map their position while they are driving or hiking, among many other useful applications. The device pinpoints a location by receiving radio signals from satellites that orbit the earth.

touch screen display · destination

current speed · estimated arrival time

grace *noun*
1. Movement that shows smoothness and elegance: *She danced across the room with grace.*
▷ *adjective* **graceful** ▷ *adverb* **gracefully**
2. Pleasant and polite behavior: *He was offended by the question but responded with grace.* ▷ *adjective* **gracious** (**gray**-shuhs) ▷ *adverb* **graciously**
3. A short prayer or blessing before a meal: *We bowed our heads and said grace before dinner.*
grace (grase)

grackle *noun* A type of blackbird that has shiny black feathers and a long tail. **grack·le** (**grak**-uhl)

grade
1. *noun* A letter or number rating the quality of work done in school. ▷ *verb* **grade**
2. *noun* Quality: *The house was built with the highest grade of lumber.*
3. *noun* A class or year in a school, or the students in it: *Mindy is in the fourth grade.*
4. *verb* To even out or make level, as in *to grade an unpaved road.* ▷ *verb* **grading, graded**
5. *noun* The amount that a road slants up or down, as in *a steep grade.*
grade (grade)

gradual *adjective* Happening slowly and steadily, as in *a gradual improvement.* **grad·u·al** (**graj**-oo-uhl) ▷ *adverb* **gradually**

graduate
1. (**graj**-oo-it) *noun* Someone who has finished the course requirements of a school and has received a diploma: *You must be a college graduate to apply for the job.*
2. (**graj**-oo-ate) *verb* To finish the course requirements of a school and receive a diploma: *Carolyn graduated from cooking school and started work as a chef.*
3. (**graj**-oo-ate) *verb* To move up to a higher level: *Within a year she had graduated to performing solo.*
grad·u·ate
▷ *verb* **graduating, graduated**

graduation *noun*
1. The successful completion of the highest grade in a school, or of a degree program in a college.
2. A ceremony in which graduating students receive their diplomas or degrees.
grad·u·a·tion (graj-oo-**ay**-shuhn)

graffiti *noun, plural* Drawings or words people put on surfaces, such as walls, buses, and subway cars, that are not supposed to be there: *The side of the bridge was covered with grafitti.* **graf·fi·ti** (gruh-**fee**-tee)

a
b
c
d
e
f
g
h
i
j
k
l
m
n
o
p
q
r
s
t
u
v
w
x
y
z

graft

1. *noun* The taking of money dishonestly, especially in politics or government.

2. *noun* Bribery or money that is taken dishonestly.

3. *verb* To perform an operation that removes a patch of skin to help repair an injury to another part of the body: *The surgeon had to graft skin from Marie's hip to her burned leg.*

4. *verb* To insert a shoot from one plant into the trunk or stem of another so that they grow together. ▷ *noun* **graft**

graft (graft)

▷ *verb* **grafting, grafted**

graham cracker *noun* A sweet cracker made with whole wheat flour. **gra·ham cracker** (gram)

grain *noun*

1. A very small piece of something, as in *a grain of salt.*

2. Cereal plants in general. Grains include such cereals as barley, oats, wheat, and rye.

3. The seed or fruit of a cereal plant.

grain (grayn)

gram *noun* A metric unit of measurement or weight that is equal to one thousandth of a kilogram: *A nickel weighs about five grams.* **gram** (gram)

grammar *noun* The rules that tell you how to speak and write correctly: *The students learned about adverbs in their grammar lesson.* **gram·mar** (gram-ur)

grammar school *noun* Another name for an **elementary school**.

grammatical *adjective* Correct according to the rules of a language: *Your sentence is not grammatical because the subject doesn't agree with the verb.* **gram·mat·i·cal** (gruh-**mat**-i-kuhl)

grand *adjective*

1. Large and admirable, as in *a grand hotel.*

2. Important or dignified, as in *a grand lady.*

3. Wonderful or very enjoyable: *We had a grand time at the festival.*

4. Complete or added up: *The trip cost a grand total of $2,300.*

grand (grand)

▷ *adjective* **grander, grandest** ▷ *adverb* **grandly**

grandchild *noun* The child of someone's son or daughter. **grand·child** (**grand**-*childe*)

▷ *noun, plural* **grandchildren**

granddaughter *noun* Someone's **granddaughter** is the daughter of that person's child. **grand·daugh·ter** (**gran**-*daw*-tur)

grandfather *noun* The father of your mother or father. **grand·fa·ther** (**grand**-*fah*-THur)

grandfather clock *noun* A clock built into the top of a tall, narrow, usually wooden cabinet.

grand jury *noun* A group of people who meet to decide if there is enough evidence to try someone for a crime. ▷ *noun, plural* **grand juries**

grandmother *noun* The mother of your mother or father. **grand·moth·er** (**grand**-*muhTH*-ur)

grandparent *noun* The parent of your mother or father. **grand·pa·rent** (**grand**-*pair*-uhnt)

grandson *noun* Someone's **grandson** is the son of that person's child. **grand·son** (**grand**-*suhn*)

grandstand *noun* The main area at an arena or stadium with seats for spectators. **grand·stand** (**grand**-*stand*)

granite *noun* A hard, gray rock used in construction: *Anna's mother chose granite for the new kitchen counter.* **gran·ite** (**gran**-it)

granola *noun* A food made with grains, nuts, and dried fruit and often eaten as a breakfast cereal. **gra·no·la** (gruh-**noh**-luh)

grant

1. *verb* To agree to give or allow something: *The prisoners were eventually granted their freedom.*

2. *noun* An amount of money given by an organization or government for a particular purpose: *The museum applied for a grant from the National Endowment for the Arts, so it could buy more sculptures.*

3. *verb* To admit or agree that something is true: *He's smarter than he looks, I'll grant you that.*

4. If you **take** someone or something **for granted**, you fail to appreciate it because it is too familiar.

grant (grant)

▷ *verb* **granting, granted**

grape *noun* A juicy, smooth-skinned berry that grows on a vine and can be eaten fresh, dried to make raisins, or crushed to make wine. **grape** (grape)

grapefruit *noun* A large, round citrus fruit with a yellow or pink rind and pulp, and a rather bitter taste. **grape·fruit** (**grape**-*froot*)

grapevine *noun*

1. A vine on which grapes grow.

2. If you receive information **through the**

grandfather clock

grapevine, you hear it unofficially or as a rumor. **grape·vine** (**grape**-*vine*)

Suffix

The suffix **-graph** adds one of these meanings to a root word:

1. Something that can transmit writing or an image, as in *telegraph* and *seismograph*.
2. Something that is the result of having been recorded, as in *photograph*.

---

graph
1. *noun* A diagram that shows the relationship between numbers or amounts. Common graphs use bars, lines, or parts of a circle to display data.
2. *verb* To trace or represent on a graph: *Once a month they would meet to graph the progress of their investments.* ▷ *verb* **graphing, graphed**
graph (graf)

graphic *adjective*
1. Giving a very realistic picture with explicit detail: *Her description of the accident could not have been more graphic.*
2. Of or having to do with the visual arts, especially involving drawing, lettering, or engraving: *He studied graphic design at the art school.*
3. Of or having to do with handwriting, as in *graphic symbols.*
graph·ic (**graf**-ik)

graphics *noun, plural* Images such as drawings, maps, or graphs: *The graphics helped explain the financial information.* **graph·ics** (**graf**-iks)

graphite *noun* A common black or gray mineral used as lead in pencils. **graph·ite** (**graf**-ite)

grapple *verb*
1. To engage in a close physical struggle that doesn't involve weapons: *The two boys grappled with each other on the playground.*
2. To try to figure out or deal with something: *Sonya grappled with the math problem and finally solved it.*
grap·ple (**grap**-uhl)
▷ *verb* **grappling, grappled**

grasp *verb*
1. To seize something or someone and hold it firmly: *Tom reached out his hand, but his brother couldn't quite grasp it.*
2. To fully understand something: *I couldn't really grasp what the teacher was saying.*
grasp (grasp)
▷ *verb* **grasping, grasped** ▷ *noun* **grasp**

grass *noun*
1. Any of several plants whose leaves are long, thin blades, such as grains, bamboo, and sugarcane.
2. An area of these plants growing wild, planted as a crop, or used for a lawn: *The club was surrounded by lush grass.*
grass (gras)
▷ *noun, plural* **grasses** ▷ *adjective* **grassy**

grasshopper *noun* An insect that eats plants and has long rear legs adapted for leaping. **grass·hop·per** (**gras**-hah-pur)

grassland *noun* A large, open area of grass, often used as pasture for animals. **grass·land** (**gras**-land)

grate
1. *verb* To shred food by rubbing it back and forth on a device covered with sharp-edged holes: *She grated carrots for the salad.*
2. *verb* If something **grates on** you, it has an annoying or irritating effect: *The music in the doctor's office grated on her nerves.*
3. *noun* A framework of bars or wires that covers or protects something.
grate (grayt)
Grate sounds like **great**. ▷ *verb* **grating, grated**

grateful *adjective* If you are **grateful** for someone or something, you are thankful and appreciative. **grate·ful** (**grate**-fuhl) ▷ *adverb* **gratefully**

grater *noun* A tool that has a flat surface with holes with sharp, raised edges for grating food such as cheese and vegetables. **grat·er** (**gray**-tur)

gratify *verb* To give pleasure to someone by fulfilling his or her needs or desires: *The students gratified their teacher by working hard.* **grat·i·fy** (**grat**-uh-*fye*) ▷ *verb* **gratifies, gratifying, gratified** ▷ *noun* **gratification**

gratitude *noun* A feeling of being grateful or thankful. **grat·i·tude** (**grat**-i-*tood*)

grave
1. *noun* A hole in the ground in which someone is buried or going to be buried.
2. *adjective* Very serious or alarming, as in *grave danger.* ▷ *adjective* **graver, gravest** ▷ *adverb* **gravely**
grave (grave)

gravel *noun* A loose mixture of small stones used on paths and roads: *Their house is at the end of a long gravel driveway.* **grav·el** (**grav**-uhl)

grasshopper

a b c d e f **g** h i j k l m n o p q r s t u v w x y z

gravestone *noun* A piece of carved stone that marks someone's grave. **grave·stone** (grave-*stone*)

graveyard *noun* A cemetery, especially a small one next to a church. **grave·yard** (grave-*yahrd*)

gravity *noun*
1. The force that pulls things toward the center of the earth and keeps them from floating away: *The astronauts had a hard time getting used to the lack of gravity in space.*
2. Extreme importance or seriousness: *The doctors told us of the gravity of Lynn's condition.*
grav·i·ty (grav-i-tee)

gravy *noun*
1. A flavored sauce served with meat and usually made by adding flour and seasoning to the fat and juices of cooked meat: *My aunt's gravy is the best part of Thanksgiving dinner.*
2. Something unearned or unexpected: *The bonus she received for her work, on top of her regular salary, was pure gravy.*
gra·vy (gray-vee)
▷ *noun, plural* **gravies**

gray *noun* A color between black and white, such as the color of ashes or of an overcast sky. **gray** (gray) ▷ *adjective* **gray**

graze *verb*
1. To feed on grass that is growing in a field: *The sheep graze high in the mountains in summer.*
2. To scrape or break the skin: *The bullet grazed the officer's leg.* ▷ *noun* **graze**
3. To touch just barely: *The pitch grazed the batter's shirt.*
graze (graze)
▷ *verb* **grazing, grazed**

grease *noun*
1. A thick, oily substance, used to keep the parts of something moving smoothly against each other: *A little grease will fix that door hinge.*
2. An oily substance found in animal fat, used in cooking: *There was grease splattered all over the stove.*
grease (grees)
▷ *verb* **grease** ▷ *adjective* **greasy**

great *adjective*
1. Very large: *A great moon was shining down on us.* ▷ *adverb* **greatly**
2. Of more than average ability or quality: *The South African leader Nelson Mandela is considered a great man.* ▷ *noun* **greatness**
3. Very good or excellent: *The kids had a great time*

grazing cattle

at the amusement park.
great (grayt)
Great sounds like **grate.** ▷ *adjective* **greater, greatest**

Great Dane *noun* A very large, powerful dog with a short coat and long legs. **Great Dane** (dane)

great-grandchild *noun* The son or daughter of someone's grandchild. **great-grand·child** (grayt-grand-*childe*)

great-grandfather *noun* The grandfather of your mother or father. **great-grand·fa·ther** (grayt-grand-*fah*-THur)

great-grandmother *noun* The grandmother of your mother or father. **great-grand·moth·er** (grayt-grand-*muhTH*-ur)

great-grandparent *noun* The father or mother of one of your grandparents.

Great Lakes *noun, plural* A group of five freshwater lakes between the United States and Canada. The Great Lakes are made up of Lake Superior, Lake Huron, Lake Ontario, Lake Michigan, and Lake Erie.

greatly *adverb* Very much: *They were greatly relieved that the program had gone so well after all.* **great·ly** (grayt-lee)

greed *noun* Extreme selfishness; wanting everything for yourself: *Greed drove them to take risks with other people's money.* **greed** (greed)

greedy *adjective* Having a strong or selfish desire for something. **greed·y** (gree-dee) ▷ *adjective* **greedier, greediest** ▷ *adverb* **greedily**

Greek *adjective*
1. Of, from, or having to do with modern Greece.
2. Of, from, or having to do with the ancient civilization or the language from the area where modern Greece is today: *Our high school offers a class in Greek mythology.*
Greek (greek)

green
1. *noun* A color like that of grass: *The green of the Irish countryside made a big impression on us.* ▷ *adjective* **green**
2. *adjective* Not ripe, as in *a green banana.*
3. *noun* An area of grass for public use, especially in the center of a town: *The festival was held on the village green.*
4. *noun* An area of very short grass surrounding the hole on a golf course.
5. greens *noun, plural* Green leaves or stems used as food, as in *salad greens.*
6. *adjective* Having little experience: *The rookie police*

gridlock

officers are still green and need a lot more training.
▷ *adjective* **greener, greenest**

7. *adjective* Supporting or concerned with the protection of the environment. The word is sometimes capitalized, as in *supporting the Green Party.*
green (green)

green bean *noun* A kind of bean that is grown for its long green pods, which are eaten with the seeds inside, while they are still small and soft.

green card *noun* A permit or identification card that allows someone who is not a citizen to live and work in the United States.

greenhouse *noun* An enclosed structure for plants that has controlled lighting and heat so that the plants can grow even when it's cold. **green·house** (**green**-*hous*)

greenhouse effect *noun* The warming of the lower layers of the earth's atmosphere, caused by carbon dioxide and other gases that prevent the sun's heat from escaping.

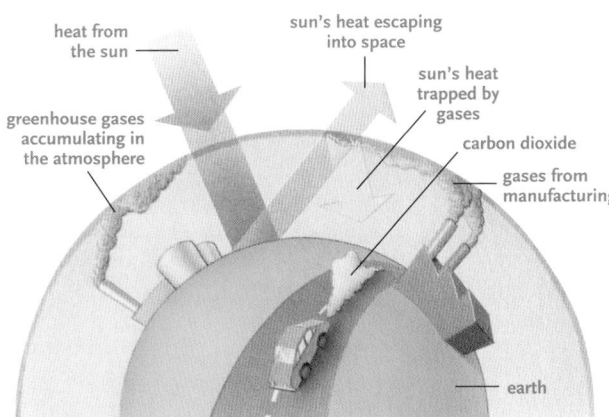

heat from the sun

sun's heat escaping into space

sun's heat trapped by gases

greenhouse gases accumulating in the atmosphere

carbon dioxide

gases from manufacturing

earth

greenhouse effect

greenhouse gases *noun, plural* Gases such as carbon dioxide and methane that contribute to the greenhouse effect.

green thumb *noun* A talent for making plants grow: *You don't need a green thumb to grow big, juicy tomatoes.*

greet *verb*
1. To give a sign of recognition or welcome when you meet someone: *The train conductor greets me every day.* ▷ *noun* **greeting** ▷ *noun* **greeter**
2. To acknowledge or respond to something in a particular way: *The crowd greeted the news with a shout of joy.*
greet (greet)
▷ *verb* **greeting, greeted**

grenade *noun* A small bomb that is thrown by hand or launched mechanically: *A soldier tossed a grenade at the tank.* **gre·nade** (gruh-**nade**)

grew *verb* The past tense of **grow**. **grew** (groo)

greyhound *noun* A thin dog with a smooth coat that can run very fast. Greyhounds are often used for racing. **grey·hound** (**gray**-*hound*)

grid *noun*
1. A network of uniformly spaced vertical and horizontal lines that forms a regular pattern of squares.
2. A network of cables and wires for supplying electricity.
grid (grid)

griddle *noun*
1. A large, flat, heated surface used for cooking.
2. A flat pan with a handle, used for frying food.
grid·dle (**grid**-*uhl*)

gridiron *noun* A playing field marked with evenly spaced parallel lines for football. **grid·i·ron** (**grid**-*eye*-urn)

gridlock *noun* A severe traffic jam that results in blocking many intersections in a grid of streets so that vehicles cannot move in any direction: *The accident during rush hour created gridlock.* **grid·lock** (**grid**-*lahk*)

grief *noun* A feeling of great sadness or deep distress: *She was overcome with grief after her dog was hit by a car.* **grief** (greef)

grievance *noun* If you have a **grievance**, you feel angry or annoyed enough about something that you complain about it or want to complain about it: *Her main grievance was the constant foot traffic across her lawn.* **griev·ance** (**gree**-*vuhns*)

grieve *verb* To feel intense sorrow, usually because someone you love has died or gone away: *The child grieved after his bunny ran away.* **grieve** (greev)
▷ *verb* **grieving, grieved**

grill

1. *noun* An outdoor cooking device consisting of a metal framework on which food is suspended over a source of intense heat: *Let's cook some burgers on the grill tonight.*

2. *verb* To cook food on a grill: *If you grill vegetables, they have more flavor.*

3. *verb (informal)* To question someone aggressively: *The defense lawyer grilled the witness about the details of the robbery.*

grill (gril)

▷ *verb* **grilling, grilled**

grim *adjective* Very serious or forbidding: *I could tell from the grim look on her face that we were in trouble.* **grim** (grim) ▷ *adjective* **grimmer, grimmest** ▷ *adverb* **grimly**

Word History

A thousand years ago, a *grimm* animal was a fierce, savage beast, so it was not only people who could be *grimm*. This Old English word could also mean "very angry." Related words such as the German adjective *grimmig*, meaning "very angry," still have this sense. The word **grim** retains some idea of being "angry" or "fierce," but today we use it to mean something that is very stern and intimidating.

grimace *noun* A facial expression that usually expresses a negative reaction: *A grimace spread across Calvin's face when the bully entered the cafeteria.* **gri·mace** (**grim**-is or gri-**mase**) ▷ *verb* **grimace**

grime *noun* Dirt or soot that accumulates on a surface: *The factory windows were covered with grime.* **grime** (grime) ▷ *adjective* **grimy**

grin *verb* To smile broadly in amusement or pleasure: *The surprise party made him grin all day.* **grin** (grin) ▷ *verb* **grinning, grinned** ▷ *noun* **grin**

grind

1. *verb* To crush something into small pieces or into a powder: *Every morning I grind the beans so the coffee tastes fresh.*

2. *verb* To sharpen a blade on a rough, hard surface.

3. If you **grind your teeth**, you rub them together, sometimes making a noise.

4. *noun* A period of very hard work or study: *It was a grind studying for the final exam.*

grind (grinde)

▷ *verb* **grinding, ground** (ground)

grindstone *noun*

1. A rotating stone used to sharpen or shape something.

2. If you **keep your nose to the grindstone**, you do not let anything distract you from your work.

grind·stone (**grinde**-*stone*)

grip

1. *verb* To keep a tight hold on something: *She gripped my shoulders and shook me.*

2. *noun* A hold on something: *She tightened her grip on the handlebars.*

3. *verb* If something **grips** you, it holds your attention or interest.

4. *noun (informal)* An understanding: *This week we're trying to get a grip on plate tectonics.*

grip (grip)

▷ *adjective* **gripping** ▷ *verb* **gripping, gripped**

gripe

1. *verb* To complain and express dissatisfaction: *Mom rarely griped about anything, but after the eighth day of nonstop rain, even she started complaining.* ▷ *verb* **griping, griped**

2. *noun* A complaint: *I hate having to listen to her gripes about her older sister.*

gripe (gripe)

gristle *noun* A tough, inedible substance found in meat. Gristle is cartilage tissue. **gris·tle** (**gris**-uhl)

grit

1. *noun* Fine particles of sand or stone: *My mountain bike was covered in dirt and grit after the trail ride.* ▷ *adjective* **gritty**

2. *noun* The ability to keep on doing something even though it is very difficult.

3. *verb* To grind your teeth together: *She gritted her teeth every time he yelled at her.* ▷ *verb* **gritting, gritted**

grit (grit)

grits *noun, plural* Coarsely ground grain, especially white corn, boiled and eaten as a cereal or side dish. **grits** (grits)

grizzly bear *noun* A large brown or gray bear found in the Northwest and in Alaska. Grizzly bears are often very aggressive. **griz·zly bear** (**griz**-lee)

grizzly bear

groan *verb* To make a long, low sound because you are suffering or unhappy: *Brian groaned when he saw his report card.* **groan** (grohn) ▷ *verb* **groaning, groaned** ▷ *noun* **groan**

grocery
1. *noun* A store that sells food and household goods. Also called a *grocery store.*
2. **groceries** *noun, plural* Food and household goods that you buy in a grocery store: *Monday was the day they shopped for groceries.*
gro·cer·y (**groh**-sur-ee)

groggy *adjective* Sleepy or dazed and unsteady: *That cold medicine sure made me feel groggy.* **grog·gy** (**grah**-gee) ▷ *adjective* **groggier, groggiest**

groin *noun* The front of your body where your legs meet. **groin** (groin)

groom
1. *noun* A man who is about to get married or has just gotten married.
2. *verb* To take care of your appearance and your clothing: *He groomed himself well each morning.*
3. *noun* Someone who takes care of horses.
4. *verb* To brush and clean an animal: *Marilyn loves to groom her pony.*
5. *verb* To teach or prepare someone to take over a job: *Matthew was grooming his daughter to take his place as president of the company.*
groom (groom)
▷ *verb* **grooming, groomed** ▷ *noun* **grooming**

groove *noun*
1. A long, narrow cut in the surface of something hard: *The door slides along a groove in the floor.*
2. A habitual or routine way of doing something: *She was working for hours and fell into a comfortable groove.*
groove (groov)

grope *verb*
1. To search for something with your hands that you cannot see: *Sophia groped in the dark for a candle.*
2. To look for or think about in an uncertain way: *The speaker had to grope for an answer to the question.*
grope (grope)
▷ *verb* **groping, groped**

gross
1. *adjective* Very large, as in *a gross error.*
2. *adjective* Very rude and improper, as in *gross behavior.*
3. *adjective* Unpleasantly big and ugly or capable of making you feel that way: *Eating too much always makes me feel gross.*
4. *noun* A group of 12 dozen (or 144) things, as in *a gross of pens.*
5. *adjective* The **gross** amount is the total amount earned, before subtracting taxes or anything else.
gross (grohs)
▷ *adjective* **grosser, grossest** ▷ *adverb* **grossly**

grotesque *adjective* Very strange or ugly: *The monster had a grotesque smile.* **gro·tesque** (groh-**tesk**) ▷ *adverb* **grotesquely**

grotto *noun* A small cave, or a structure built to look like one. **grot·to** (**grah**-toh) ▷ *noun, plural* **grottoes** *or* **grottos**

grouch *noun* Someone who is in a bad mood: *A famous grouch on TV lives in a trash can.* **grouch** (grouch) ▷ *noun, plural* **grouches**

grouchy *adjective* Mean, nasty, or grumpy: *Scrooge was a grouchy old man who hated Christmas.* **grouch·y** (**grou**-chee)

ground
1. *noun* The earth's surface: *The gardener put some flower bulbs in the ground.*
2. *noun* Land used for a certain activity, as in *a parade ground.*
3. *noun* A wire that will carry an electric current into the ground or to a place where it won't be dangerous.
4. *verb* To restrict the activity of someone or something: *The storm was so fierce that they grounded our flight. His dad grounded him for breaking curfew.* ▷ *verb* **grounding, grounded**
5. **ground ball** *noun* In baseball, a ball hit along the ground by a batter.
6. See also **grounds.**
ground (ground)

groundbreaking
1. *adjective* New, important, and unlike what has been done before: *This groundbreaking technology will allow rural communities to have much faster internet connections at lower cost.*
2. *noun* The activity of starting a new building by digging, often done as a ceremony at the very beginning.
ground·break·ing (**ground**-bray-king)

grounded *adjective*
1. If an aircraft is **grounded**, it cannot fly.
2. If an electrical appliance is **grounded**, it is connected directly to the earth and is safe to use.
ground·ed (**groun**-did)

groundhog *noun* A small, furry, burrowing animal with large front teeth. Also called a **woodchuck**. **ground·hog** (**ground**-hawg)

Groundhog Day *noun* According to legend, people can predict when spring will arrive by watching the behavior of a groundhog on **Groundhog Day**, February 2. If it comes out of its burrow and sees its shadow, there will be six more weeks of winter. If it does not see its shadow, spring will come early.

grounds *noun, plural*
1. The land surrounding a large building or a group of buildings: *The grounds of the hospital were beautifully landscaped.*
2. A reason for doing or thinking something: *They didn't listen to him because he had no grounds for his complaint.*
3. The particles of coffee that remain after the coffee is brewed: *I'm saving the grounds to use them for compost.*
grounds (groundz)

groundwater *noun* Water far below the ground that can be used for drinking and other purposes when wells are dug into it. **ground·wa·ter** (**ground**-*waw*-tur)

group
1. *noun* A number of people or things that go together or have something in common: *The government published a list of healthy food groups.*
2. *verb* To put people or things together or to place in a group: *The students were grouped by their grade level at the assembly.* ▷ *verb* **grouping, grouped**
3. *noun* A number of people who gather together or share a common purpose, as in *a musical group.*
group (groop)

grouse
1. *noun* A small, plump game bird.
2. *verb* To complain about something: *Judy groused constantly about having to babysit her brother.*
▷ *verb* **grousing, groused**
grouse (grous)

grove *noun* A group of trees growing or planted near each other, as in *an olive grove.* **grove** (grove)

grovel *verb* To behave in a very humble way toward a person of much greater rank, such as a king, or because you want someone to forgive you or give you something: *I had to grovel before my dad would let me go to the party.* **grov·el** (**gruhv**-uhl *or* **grah**-vuhl)
▷ *verb* **groveling, groveled**

grow *verb*
1. To increase in size, develop, or change physically: *Jethro grew five inches last year.*
2. To plant and care for something so that it gets bigger: *She grows many different kinds of roses in the garden.*
3. To gradually become: *The longer we waited, the more nervous we grew.*
4. If something **grows on** you, it gradually becomes more acceptable or appealing: *I didn't like his new haircut at first, but it's starting to grow on me.*
grow (groh)
▷ *verb* **growing, grew, grown**

grouse

growl *verb* To show anger by making a low, deep sound. **growl** (groul) ▷ *verb* **growling, growled** ▷ *noun* **growl**

grown *verb* The past participle of **grow**. **grown** (grohn)

grown-up *noun* An adult. ▷ *adjective* **grown-up**

growth *noun*
1. The process of increasing in size, value, or maturity: *Her growth as a concert pianist is reflected in the ambitious pieces she is now choosing to play.*
2. A tumor or abnormal lump of body tissue: *Eric had a benign growth removed from his wrist.*
growth (grohth)

grub *noun*
1. The wormlike larva of some insects.
2. *(slang)* Food: *Where can I get some grub around here?*
grub (gruhb)

grudge *noun* A long-lasting feeling of resentment toward someone who has hurt or insulted you: *Jane held a grudge against her brother for teasing her when they were children.* **grudge** (gruhj)

grueling *adjective* Very tiring or demanding: *The lead runner kept up a grueling pace.* **gru·el·ing** (**groo**-uh-ling)

gruesome *adjective* Very unpleasant, disgusting, or horrible, as in *a gruesome attack.* **grue·some** (**groo**-suhm)

gruff *adjective* Abrupt, rough, or unfriendly: *"Don't bother me now!" was the gruff reply.* **gruff** (gruhf) ▷ *adjective* **gruffer, gruffest** ▷ *adverb* **gruffly**

grumble *verb* To complain about something in a grouchy but not very loud or angry way: *She grumbles every day about doing the dishes.* **grum·ble** (**gruhm**-buhl) ▷ *verb* **grumbling, grumbled**

grumpy *adjective* Easily irritated; grouchy: *Christopher is always a little grumpy before breakfast.* **grump·y**

(**gruhm**-pee) ▷ *adjective* **grumpier,**
grumpiest ▷ *adverb* **grumpily**

grunt *verb* To make a low, gruff sound
like a pig, especially to express effort or
agreement: *The two men grunted as they*
dragged the boat into the back of their
truck. **grunt** (gruhnt) ▷ *verb* **grunting,**
grunted ▷ *noun* **grunt**

guacamole *noun* A dip made of
avocado, onions, lime juice, and
seasonings. **gua·ca·mo·le**
(*gwah*-kuh-**moh**-lee)

guarantee *noun*
1. A promise made by manufacturers
that if their product breaks within a
certain time, or is defective, they will
repair or replace it.
2. A promise that something will be done or
will happen: *Because of heavy traffic, there's*
no guarantee that they will arrive on time.
guar·an·tee (*gar*-uhn-**tee**)
▷ *verb* **guarantee**

guard
1. *verb* To protect someone from harm: *The*
Secret Service guards the US president at all
times.
2. *verb* To watch over someone so that he
or she can't escape: *It is always important*
to guard prisoners on the way to court.
3. *noun* Someone whose job it is to protect a person
or control access to a place: *He got a job as a guard*
at the jewelry store.
4. *noun* A football player whose job is often to
protect the quarterback or tackle the opposition's
quarterback.
5. *noun* A basketball player whose job is often to
initiate plays.
6. *noun* A device worn by a person or placed on
something to prevent injury or damage: *"Don't forget*
your shin guards," my mother called down the stairs.
7. *verb* If you **guard against** something, you
take steps to keep it from happening: *I*
guarded against getting the flu by washing
my hands several times a day.
guard (gahrd)
▷ *verb* **guarding, guarded**

guardian *noun*
1. Someone who is not a child's parent
but who is legally responsible for him
or her.
2. Someone who defends or protects
something: *Our new dog was already acting*
like the guardian of the house.

guard

guacamole

guard·i·an (gahr-dee-uhn)
▷ *adjective* **guardian**

guava *noun* A tropical fruit with pink flesh and
a very sweet taste. **gua·va** (**gwah**-vuh)

guerrilla *noun* A member of a small group
of fighters or soldiers that often launches
surprise attacks against an official army: *The*
guerrillas escaped into the jungle, pursued by
the army. **guer·ril·la** (guh-**ril**-uh) Guerrilla
sounds like **gorilla.** ▷ *adjective* **guerrilla**

guess *verb*
1. To give an answer without being sure
that you're right: *I'd guess there are about*
100 people here. ▷ *noun* **guess**
2. To suppose or believe something: *I*
guess I can do it.
guess (ges)
▷ *verb* **guesses, guessing, guessed**

guest *noun*
1. Someone who has been invited to visit or to
stay in another person's home: *My parents love*
to have guests visit in the summer.
2. Someone who pays to stay in a hotel, a motel,
or an inn.
guest (gest)

guidance *noun*
1. Advice or counsel, especially about a
student's future plans, as in *career guidance.*
2. Direction or supervision: *Tony wanted*
some guidance from his coach on how to be a better
fielder.
guid·ance (**gye**-duhns)

guide *verb* To help someone, usually by showing the
way or by providing advice or instruction: *My new*
job is to guide visitors through the museum's exhibits
on ancient Egypt. **guide** (gide) ▷ *verb* **guiding,**
guided ▷ *noun* **guide**

guidebook *noun* A book containing information
about a place, for use by tourists and
visitors. **guide·book** (**gide**-buk)

guide dog *noun* A dog trained to lead a
visually impaired person.

guideline *noun* A rule or suggestion
that tells how something should be or
will be done: *The American Academy*
of Pediatrics has issued new guidelines
to help parents deal with head
lice. **guide·line** (**gide**-line)

guide word *noun* One of the
words at the top of a page in a
dictionary or encyclopedia that show
the part of the alphabet included on
that page.

a
b
c
d
e
f
g
h
i
j
k
l
m
n
o
p
q
r
s
t
u
v
w
x
y
z

guild *noun* A group or organization of people who do the same kind of work or have the same interests. **guild** (gild)

guile *noun* Clever but dishonest or misleading behavior: *His success as a salesperson was based on personal charm and a bit of guile.* **guile** (gile)

guillotine *noun* A large machine with a sharp blade that slides down a frame, used to cut off the heads of criminals. **guil·lo·tine** (**gil**-uh-*teen* or **gee**-uh-*teen*)

guilt *noun*
1. The state of being responsible for having committed a crime or for having done something wrong: *The trial was meant to determine her guilt or innocence.*
2. A feeling of shame or remorse for having done something wrong or for having failed to do something: *After taking money from her mother's purse, she was overcome by guilt.* **guilt** (gilt)

Guilt sounds like **gilt**.

guilty *adjective*
1. If you are **guilty**, you are responsible for committing a crime or doing something wrong: *He pleaded guilty and was sentenced to prison.*
2. If you feel **guilty**, you are ashamed or filled with regret because you know that you've done something wrong. **guilt·y** (**gil**-tee) ▷ *adjective* **guiltier, guiltiest** ▷ *adverb* **guiltily**

guinea pig *noun*
1. A small, stout rodent with short ears and legs, a smooth coat, and no visible tail. Guinea pigs are often kept as pets or used in laboratory research.
2. A person who is used in an experiment: *I didn't want to try his new yogurt concoction, but I finally agreed to be his guinea pig.* **guin·ea pig** (**gin**-ee)

guitar *noun* A musical instrument with six or twelve strings on a long neck. **gui·tar** (gi-**tahr**)

gulch *noun* A valley that often fills with water when it rains. **gulch** (guhlch) ▷ *noun, plural* **gulches**

gulf *noun*
1. An area of the sea that is partly surrounded by land, as in *the Gulf of Mexico.*
2. A difference between two people or situations: *The gulf between those who still had jobs and the unemployed was growing wider.* **gulf** (guhlf)

Gulf of Mexico *noun* A large gulf of the Atlantic Ocean. It is bordered by the United States to the north and the eastern coast of Mexico to the south. **Gulf of Mex·i·co** (**mek**-si-*koh*)

gull *noun* Short for **seagull**. **gull** (guhl)

gullible *adjective* If you are **gullible**, it's easy to fool you because you believe anything you are told. **gul·li·ble** (**guhl**-uh-buhl) ▷ *noun* **gullibility**

gully *noun* A long, narrow ditch created by running water. **gul·ly** (**guhl**-ee) ▷ *noun, plural* **gullies**

gulp
1. *verb* To swallow food or drink quickly in large mouthfuls: *I was so thirsty that I gulped water straight from the hose.* ▷ *verb* **gulping, gulped**
2. *noun* A mouthful of something that is swallowed: *He took a large gulp of milk.* **gulp** (guhlp)

gum *noun*
1. Your **gums** are the areas of firm, pink flesh around the roots of your teeth in your upper and lower jaws.
2. A thick, sticky substance produced by various plants.
3. Glue made from such a substance and used to stick paper and other materials together.
4. A sweet substance used for chewing. Also called **chewing gum**: *My teacher doesn't allow gum in the classroom.* **gum** (guhm)

gumdrop *noun* A small, chewy candy covered with sugar. **gum·drop** (**guhm**-*drahp*)

gun
1. *noun* A weapon that uses explosive force to fire bullets through a long metal tube.
2. **gun down** *verb* To shoot someone deliberately with a gun: *The police gunned down the robbers as they tried to escape.*
3. *verb* To speed up something quickly, as in *to gun an engine.* **gun** (guhn) ▷ *verb* **gunning, gunned**

guitar

Word History

The word **gun** comes from the term *Lady Gunilda,* a huge crossbow that shot large ammunition in the 14th century. Later, the word *gun* was used for cannons as well as for hand-carried firearms.

gunpowder *noun* A powder that explodes easily. Gunpowder is used in bullets, in fireworks, and in blasting. **gun·pow·der** (**guhn**-*pou*-dur)

guppy *noun* A tiny freshwater fish popular in home aquariums. **gup·py** (**guhp**-ee) ▷ *noun, plural* **guppies**

gurgle *verb*

1. When water **gurgles**, it makes a hollow, bubbling sound, like water being poured out of a bottle.

2. To make a sound like gurgling water: *My stomach started gurgling as soon as I drank the soda.* **gur·gle** (**gur**-guhl) ▷ *verb* **gurgling, gurgled** ▷ *noun* **gurgle**

guru *noun*

1. A spiritual leader or guide in the Hindu religion.

2. A person who has special knowledge and who is looked up to by many people: *He is a famous financial guru.* **gu·ru** (**goo**-roo)

gush *verb*

1. When liquid **gushes**, it flows quickly in a sudden stream: *The water gushed from the broken faucet.* ▷ *noun* **gush**

2. A person who **gushes** speaks or writes with exaggerated enthusiasm: *She gushed over my new dress, even though it was just a plain jumper.* **gush** (guhsh) ▷ *verb* **gushes, gushing, gushed** ▷ *adjective* **gushing**

gust *noun* A brief, strong rush of wind or sudden burst of something: *Her joke was greeted with gusts of laughter.* **gust** (guhst) ▷ *adjective* **gusty**

gusto *noun* If you do something with **gusto**, you do it with energy and enthusiasm. **gus·to** (**guhs**-toh)

gut

1. *noun* The stomach or intestines of a person or animal: *I woke up in the middle of the night with a pain in my gut.*

2. guts *noun, plural* The internal organs of a person or animal. This sense of the word is usually used when referring to the organs after they have been exposed or removed from the body: *The hunters removed the deer's guts to make it easier to carry out of the woods.*

3. guts *noun, plural (informal)* Personal courage and determination: *It takes guts to travel around the world alone.*

4. *verb* To remove the guts from an animal, usually before cooking: *He is learning how to fish, including how to gut and clean what he catches.*

5. *verb* To destroy the inside of a building: *The old church was gutted to make apartments.* **gut** (guht) ▷ *verb* **gutting, gutted**

guppies

gutter

1. *noun* A shallow trough or channel through which rain is carried away from a road or the roof of a building: *Leaves had clogged up the gutters, and water was pouring into the basement.*

2. *verb* To burn low or begin to flicker: *The flame of the candle was guttering and nearly out.*

3. *verb* To make channels or gutters in something: *The tornado guttered the road.* **gut·ter** (**guht**-ur) ▷ *verb* **guttering, guttered**

guy *noun (informal)* A man or a boy. **guy** (gye)

guzzle *verb* To drink something in a noisy or greedy manner: *He limped off the field and started guzzling water.* **guz·zle** (**guhz**-uhl) ▷ *verb* **guzzling, guzzled**

gym *noun*

1. A large room or building with special equipment for exercising and playing games. Gym is short for **gymnasium**.

2. A class or course in physical education. **gym** (jim)

gymnasium *noun* A gym. **gym·na·si·um** (jim-**nay**-zee-uhm)

gymnast *noun* Someone who practices gymnastics. **gym·nast** (**jim**-nast)

gymnastics *noun* Physical exercises, often performed on special equipment such as ropes or parallel bars, that involve flexibility, strength, balance, and coordination. **gym·nas·tics** (jim-**nas**-tiks) ▷ *adjective* **gymnastic**

gypsy *noun*

1. Someone who moves around a lot or has an unconventional lifestyle: *She tried to settle down, but she was a gypsy at heart.*

2. Gypsy A term formerly used for one of the Romany people. It is now considered offensive. *See* **Rom**. **gypsy** (**jip**-see) ▷ *noun, plural* **gypsies**

gyrate *verb*

1. To move in a circle or spiral.

2. To dance by rotating the hips: *Everyone was up on the stage, gyrating to the music.* **gy·rate** (**jye**-rate) ▷ *verb* **gyrating, gyrated**

gyroscope *noun* A device consisting of a wheel or disk that spins rapidly around an axis that can be tilted in any direction. Gyroscopes are used to provide stability on ships and airplanes. **gy·ro·scope** (**jye**-ruh-skope)

Hh

About H The sound of **H** at the beginning of a word is usually an unvoiced sound. The sound doesn't vibrate when you put your fingers on your vocal cords as you say it. Examples: hat, hip. Some words that begin with an *h* sound are spelled *wh*. Examples: who, whole. The Greeks borrowed the letter from the Phoenicians, and it then came into the Latin alphabet through the Etruscans.

ha *interjection*
> **1.** A word used to express joy, surprise, or triumph.
> **2.** A word used to express laughter.
> **ha** (hah)

habit *noun*
> **1.** An activity or behavior that you do regularly, often without thinking about it, as in *good eating habits*.
> **2.** Special clothing for a particular activity, or for members of a religious order, as in *a nun's habit*.
> **hab·it** (**hab**-it)

habitable *adjective* Safe and good enough for people to live in. **hab·it·a·ble** (**hab**-i-tuh-buhl)

habitat *noun* The place where an animal or a plant is usually found is its **habitat**: *The Rocky Mountains are the habitat of the bighorn sheep.* **hab·i·tat** (**hab**-i-*tat*)

habitual *adjective*
> **1.** Behaving from habit, as in *a habitual smoker*.
> **2.** Done over and over again: *His habitual lying has cost him several friends.*
> **3.** Regular or usual: *Kelly's father took his habitual seat at the head of the table.*
> **ha·bit·u·al** (huh-**bich**-oo-uhl)

habitually *adverb* Usually or regularly: *Dan is habitually late.* **ha·bit·u·al·ly** (huh-**bich**-oo-uh-lee)

hacienda *noun* A large ranch or estate found in the southwestern part of the United States or in Spanish-speaking countries. **ha·ci·en·da** (*hah*-see-**en**-duh)

hack
> **1.** *verb* To cut something roughly or violently, as in *to hack weeds*.
> **2.** *verb* If you **hack** into a computer system, you secretly change it or get information from it without permission.
> **3.** *noun* A loud, dry cough.
> **4.** *verb* To cough loudly.
> **hack** (hak)
> ▷ *verb* **hacking, hacked**

hacker *noun* Someone who has a special skill for getting into a computer system without permission. **hack·er** (**hak**-ur)

hadn't *contraction* A short form of *had not*: *They hadn't gotten very far before the police caught up with them.* **had·n't** (**had**-uhnt)

haggard *adjective* Someone who is **haggard** looks sick and thin, usually because the person is tired, worried, or in pain. **hag·gard** (**hag**-urd)

haggle *verb* To argue with someone, usually in order to agree on the price of something: *We haggled with the merchant over the price of the rug.* **hag·gle** (**hag**-uhl) ▷ *verb* **haggling, haggled**

haiku *noun* A short Japanese poem in three lines containing a total of 17 syllables. **hai·ku** (**hye**-*koo*)

hail
> **1.** *verb* When it **hails**, small balls of ice fall from the sky.

hairpin curve

> **2.** *verb* To get someone's attention, especially by calling out or making a signal, as in *to hail a cab*.
> **3.** *noun* Small balls of ice that fall from the sky.
> **hail** (hayl)
> ▷ *verb* **hailing, hailed**

hair *noun* The mass of thin, soft strands that grow from your head or body or from the body of an animal. **hair** (hair) **Hair** sounds like **hare**.

haircut *noun* The act of someone cutting and styling your hair: *I try to get a haircut every two months.* **hair·cut** (**hair**-*kuht*)

hairdo *noun* The way a person's hair is styled or arranged. Also called a *hairstyle*. **hair·do** (**hair**-*doo*)

hairdresser *noun* Someone whose job is to cut and style people's hair. **hair·dress·er** (**hair**-*dres*-ur)

hairpin
> **1.** *noun* A piece of bent wire with sides that press together to hold hair in place.
> **2.** *adjective* Shaped like a hairpin, as in *a hairpin curve*.
> **hair·pin** (**hair**-*pin*)

hair-raising *adjective* Extremely exciting or frightening: *The roller-coaster ride was a hair-raising experience.*

hairstyle *noun* A way of combing or styling your hair: *You could tell it was an old movie by the hairstyles of the women.* **hair·style** (**hair**-*stile*)

hairy *adjective*
1. Having a lot of hair.
2. *(slang)* Frightening and dangerous: *Things got a little hairy when we were climbing back down the mountain.*
hair·y (**hair**-ee)
▷ *adjective* **hairier, hairiest**

half
1. *noun* One of the two equal parts that something can be divided into: *Rebecca gave half of her bagel to Kevin.* ▷ *adjective* **half**
2. *adverb* Not completely: *The turkey was only half cooked.*
3. *noun* One of two equal lengths of time played in a game: *Jerry scored a goal late in the first half.*
half (haf)
▷ *noun, plural* **halves** (havz)

half brother *noun* A brother who shares only one parent with someone else.

halfhearted *adjective* Without much enthusiasm or interest: *Chris made only a halfhearted attempt to study before the test.* **half·heart·ed** (**haf**-hahr-tid)
▷ *adverb* **halfheartedly**

half-mast *noun* The position halfway between the top and bottom of a flagpole or mast. Flags are flown at this position as a sign of respect for a person who has just died.

half sister *noun* A sister who shares only one parent with someone else.

halftime *noun* A short break in the middle of a game such as football, basketball, hockey, or soccer. **half·time** (**haf**-*time*)

halfway
1. *adjective* Half the distance from one point to another, as in *the halfway point in a race.*
2. *adjective* Not thorough or complete, as in *a halfway effort.*
3. *adverb* To or at half the distance: *We ran halfway down the street.*
half·way (**haf**-*way*)

halibut *noun* A type of fish found in both the Atlantic and Pacific Oceans and used as food. **hal·i·but** (**hal**-uh-buht) ▷ *noun, plural* **halibut** or **halibuts**

hall *noun*
1. A long, narrow passage that goes to other rooms: *There are three bedrooms off the hall.*
2. An area of a house just inside the entrance: *Leave your umbrellas in the hall by the front door!*
3. A large room or building used for public events such as meetings: *We went to the concert hall to hear some live music.*
hall (hawl)

Hall sounds like **haul**.

hallmark *noun* A feature or characteristic that people use to distinguish something: *The band's newest single has all the hallmarks of a pop hit.* **hall·mark** (**hawl**-*mahrk*)

hallelujah *interjection* A word used to express joy, praise, or thanks, especially to God. **hal·le·lu·jah** (*hal*-uh-**loo**-yuh)

hallowed *adjective* Sacred or holy. **hal·lowed** (**hal**-ohd) ▷ *verb* **hallow**

Halloween *noun* The evening of October 31, once thought to be the night witches and ghosts came out and haunted people. On Halloween, children dress up in costumes and go out to trick-or-treat. **Hal·low·een** (*hal*-uh-**ween**)

Word History

About 500 years ago, the English phrase *All Hallow Even* referred to the evening before All Hallows Day. The word *hallows* meant "holy people" or "saints." Over time, people left out the word *All* when they talked about this night, and they ran the words *Hallow* and *Even* together, giving us **Halloween**.

hallucinate *verb* To see or hear something or someone that is not really there. **hal·lu·ci·nate** (huh-**loo**-suh-*nate*) ▷ *verb* **hallucinating, hallucinated** ▷ *noun* **hallucination**

halo *noun*
1. A ring of light around an object: *The moon sometimes has a halo around it.*
2. A circle of light shown in pictures around the heads of angels and sacred people.
ha·lo (**hay**-loh)

halo

halogen

1. *noun* Any of a group of five chemically related elements: fluorine, chlorine, bromine, iodine, and astatine. These elements react readily with most metals, combining with them to form salts.
2. *adjective* Containing or using a halogen, as in *a halogen lamp* or *a halogen lightbulb*.
hal·o·gen (**hal**-uh-juhn)

halt

1. *noun* A brief or temporary stop: *The driver came to a halt at the stoplight.*
2. *verb* To stop or cause someone or something to stop. ▷ *verb* **halting, halted**
halt (hawlt)

halter

halter *noun*

1. A rope or strap used to lead or tie an animal such as a horse. A halter fits over the animal's nose and behind its ears.
2. A woman's top with a band that ties behind the neck, leaving the back and shoulders bare.
hal·ter (**hawl**-tur)

halve *verb*

1. To divide or cut something into two equal parts: *Ron halved the banana so he could share it with me.*
2. To reduce something by half: *By cutting down on our energy consumption, we have nearly halved our electric bill.*
halve (hav)
Halve sounds like **have**. ▷ *verb* **halving, halved**

ham *noun*
The meat from the top part of a pig's hind leg that has been salted and sometimes smoked.
ham (ham)

hamburger *noun*

1. A round, flat piece of chopped beef that is cooked and usually served on a bun.
2. Ground beef.
ham·burg·er (**ham**-*bur*-gur)

Word History

Hamburg is a city in northern Germany. In the 19th century, a food called Hamburger steak, which was made out of cooked beef, became popular in the United States. German immigrants probably introduced this dish to America. The name *Hamburger steak* meant "steak from the city of Hamburg," though the reason for this name is unknown. Soon the word *steak* was dropped, and we no longer write the word **hamburger** with a capital letter, either.

hamlet *noun* A very small village. **ham·let** (**ham**-lit)

hammer

1. *noun* A tool with a handle and a heavy metal head, used especially for hitting nails. ▷ *verb* **hammer**
2. *verb* To hit something very hard: *Peyton hammered on the door.* ▷ *verb* **hammering, hammered**
ham·mer (**ham**-ur)

hammock *noun* A piece of strong net or cloth that is hung up by each end and used as a bed or as a place to relax. **ham·mock** (**ham**-uhk)

hamper

1. *noun* A large box or basket used for carrying food or for storing dirty clothing, as in *a picnic hamper* or *a laundry hamper*.
2. *verb* To make it difficult for something to succeed, or for someone to do something: *The heavy snow hampered the rescue effort.* ▷ *verb* **hampering, hampered**
ham·per (**ham**-pur)

hamster *noun* A small furry animal that is kept as a pet. **ham·ster** (**ham**-stur)

Word History

Would a **hamster** be as cute if it were called a *chomestoru*? That was an old Russian name for the animal. But the name is even older than that, perhaps more than 2,000 years old. It derives from an ancient Persian word. We don't know what the people of Persia (now Iran) called hamsters, but they called a cruel person a *hamaestar*, which we know is related to the word for "hamster" in their language. We think differently of hamsters today, and love them as pets.

hamster

hand

1. *noun* The part of your body on the end of your arm. The hand includes your wrist, palm, fingers, and thumb.
2. *verb* To give or pass something to someone: *Hand me a sheet of paper, please.* ▷ *verb* **handing, handed**
3. *noun* A set of cards that you hold during a card game: *Mark could not believe the great hand he was dealt.*

4. *noun* One of the parts of a clock that points to the numbers, as in *the hour hand.*

5. *noun* A worker or a work crew, as in *a hired hand* or *all hands on deck.*

6. *noun* A round of applause: *Let's give our next guest a big hand.*

7. If you **give** or **lend a hand** to someone, you help the person: *Can you give me a hand with this box?*

8. If something is **on hand**, it is nearby and handy to use: *We always have a first aid kit on hand in case someone gets hurt.*

9. If something is **out of hand**, it is not under control: *Things got really out of hand when the fans started fighting in the stands.*

10. If you **have your hands full** with something, you are very busy with it.

11. If you **wash your hands of** something, you refuse to have anything more to do with it.

12. If you are **in good hands**, you are well taken care of.

13. If you **hand** something **in**, you give it to someone, as in *to hand in homework.*

14. If something is made **by hand**, a person has done it with his or her hands rather than with a machine.

15. If people or things work **hand in hand**, they are cooperating to achieve something: *Working hand in hand, the various law enforcement agencies put an end to the crime ring.*
hand (hand)

handbag *noun* A bag or purse in which a woman carries her wallet and other small things. **hand·bag** (**hand**-*bag*)

handball *noun*

1. A game played in a large room or outdoors in which two or four players take turns hitting a small, hard rubber ball against a wall with their hands.

2. The rubber ball used for playing handball.
hand·ball (**hand**-*bawl*)

handbook *noun* A book containing useful information or instructions, as in *a handbook on birds.* **hand·book** (**hand**-*buk*)

handcuffs *noun, plural* Metal rings joined by a chain that are put around a prisoner's wrists to keep him or her from escaping. **hand·cuffs** (**hand**-*kuhfs*)
▷ *verb* **handcuff**

handful *noun*

1. The amount of something that can be held in a hand: *Naomi ate a handful of gumdrops.*

2. A small number of things or people: *Only a handful of people were at practice today.*

3. *(informal)* If someone is a **handful**, he or she is difficult to control: *When Melinda is tired, she gets cranky and becomes a real handful.*
hand·ful (**hand**-ful)

handgun *noun* A gun that can be held and fired with one hand; a pistol. **hand·gun** (**hand**-*guhn*)

handicap

1. *noun* A physical or mental limitation. The word *disability* is now the preferred term to describe the inability to do some things, such as walk or see.
▷ *adjective* **handicapped**

2. *noun* A situation or condition that makes it difficult for you to do something: *A sore throat is a handicap when you try to sing.*

3. *noun* A disadvantage given in a sport, such as golf, to the stronger players in order to make the competition more equal.

4. *verb* To make more difficult: *A strong wind handicapped the firefighters' efforts.* ▷ *verb* **handicapping, handicapped** ▷ *noun* **handicapper**
hand·i·cap (**han**-dee-*kap*)

handicraft *noun* A skill, such as sewing or pottery, that involves using your hands to make things. **hand·i·craft** (**han**-dee-*kraft*)

handkerchief *noun* A small square of cloth that you use for wiping your face, hands, or nose. **hand·ker·chief** (**hang**-kur-chif)

handle

1. *noun* The part of an object that you use to hold, carry, move, or open that object, as in *the handle of a pan.*

2. *verb* To pick up, touch, or feel something with your hands, as in *to handle china with care.*

3. *verb* To deal with someone or something, such as a situation, in a successful way: *Tom is very good at handling difficult customers.*
han·dle (**han**-duhl)
▷ *verb* **handling, handled**

handlebars *noun, plural* The bar at the front of a bicycle or motorcycle that you use for steering.
han·dle·bars (**han**-duhl-*bahrz*)

handbag

a b c d e f g **h** i j k l m n o p q r s t u v w x y z

handmade *adjective* Made by hand, not by a machine, as in *a handmade sweater.* **hand·made (hand-made)**

hand-me-down *noun* An article of clothing or another item that belongs to someone and is passed along for use by another person: *She doesn't like having to wear her sister's hand-me-downs.* ▷ *noun, plural* **hand-me-downs**

handout *noun*
1. Money, food, or clothing that is given to a needy person: *The beggar asked me for a handout.*
2. An informative pamphlet or leaflet that is given out for free at an event such as a meeting or lecture, or during a class. **hand·out (hand-out)**

handrail *noun* A narrow rail that can be held for support, usually used on stairways. **hand·rail (hand-rayl)**

handshake *noun* A way of greeting or saying good-bye to someone by shaking the person's hand. **hand·shake (hand-shake)**

handstand

handsome *adjective*
1. Attractive in appearance, used especially to describe a man.
2. Generous, as in *a handsome contribution.* **hand·some (han-suhm)**

handspring *noun* A gymnastic movement in which you spring forward or backward onto both hands, then flip all the way over to land back on your feet. **hand·spring (hand-spring)**

handstand *noun* When you do a **handstand**, you balance on your hands and put your feet in the air. **hand·stand (hand-stand)**

handwriting *noun*
1. The way the letters and words look when you write: *Her handwriting is much bigger than mine.*
2. Writing done by a person, not a machine: *The wedding invitations were addressed in the bride's handwriting.* **hand·writ·ing (hand-rye-ting)** ▷ *adjective* **handwritten**

handy *adjective*
1. Useful, convenient, and easy to use: *A small iron is a handy thing to take on vacation.*
2. Skillful, especially with your hands: *Suzie is handy with all kinds of tools.*

3. Near to someone or something: *I keep a pad of paper handy so I can write notes.* **hand·y (han-dee)** ▷ *adjective* **handier, handiest**

hang
1. *verb* To put an object on a thing, such as a hook or rod, that holds it up: *The towels hang on a rack in the bathroom.*
2. *verb* To kill someone by putting a rope around the person's neck and then letting the person's body drop: *The murderer was hanged at midnight.*
3. hang up *verb* To end a phone conversation by putting down the receiver or by turning off the phone.
4. hang out *verb* (informal) To spend a lot of time in a place, as in *to hang out at the mall.* ▷ *noun* **hangout**
5. If you **get the hang of** something, you learn how to do it and become comfortable doing it: *It took me a while to get the hang of my new computer.* **hang (hang)** ▷ *verb* **hanging, hung** (huhng) *or* **hanged**

hangar *noun* A large building in which planes are kept and repaired. **han·gar (hang-ur) Hangar** sounds like **hanger.**

hanger *noun* A frame used for hanging clothes that is made of wood, metal, or plastic and has a hook. **hang·er (hang-ur) Hanger** sounds like **hangar.**

hang glider *noun* A small aircraft like a giant kite, which you control through the motions of your body and that you hang from in order to fly. ▷ *noun* **hang gliding**

hangover *noun* A headache, nausea, and other unpleasant feelings caused by drinking too much alcohol. **hang·over (hang-oh-vur)**

hangry *adjective* (informal) A little bit angry because you are so hungry. **han·gry (hang-gree)**

hang-up *noun* (informal) If you have a **hang-up** about something, it bothers you: *Ellis has a hang-up about being short.*

hanker *verb* To want something very much: *Denise is hankering for a hamburger.* **han·ker (hang-kur)** ▷ *verb* **hankering, hankered** ▷ *noun* **hankering**

Hanukkah *noun* An eight-day Jewish holiday, also called the Feast or Festival of Lights, that usually falls in December. During this celebration, Jews light a menorah, a special candleholder with eight branches. **Ha·nuk·kah** (**hah**-nuh-kuh)

haphazard *adjective* Without any plan or organization: *Instead of being in alphabetical order, the company's records were filed in a haphazard manner.* **hap·haz·ard** (*hap*-**haz**-urd) ▷ *adverb* **haphazardly**

hapless *adjective* Unlucky or unfortunate: *The hapless Red Sox lost their ninth game in a row.* **hap·less** (**hap**-lis) ▷ *adverb* **haplessly** ▷ *noun* **haplessness**

happen *verb*
1. To occur or to take place: *A lot has happened since you left.*
2. If you **happen** to do something, you do it by chance: *I happened to find just the right book in the library.*
hap·pen (**hap**-uhn)
▷ *verb* **happening, happened**

happiness *noun* The state or feeling of being happy, especially over a period of time: *Lita likes her new school and has found happiness there.* **hap·pi·ness** (**hap**-ee-nis)

happy *adjective*
1. Feeling or showing pleasure or enjoyment.
2. Fortunate or lucky: *By a happy chance, my car broke down right in front of a garage.*
hap·py (**hap**-ee)
▷ *adjective* **happier, happiest** ▷ *adverb* **happily**

Synonyms

Happy describes a general feeling of well-being. If you are happy, you may feel good about something you have done or seen or something that happened to you: *When I woke up, the sun was shining, which made me happy.*

- -

■ **Glad** describes your good feelings about something specific, such as an occasion or event: *I'm glad you can make it to my party.*

■ **Pleased** means that you have good feelings about the way something has turned out: *I was pleased that Mr. Tanaka liked my idea for having a talent show.*

■ **Delighted** describes extreme pleasure about something: *We all were delighted to hear that Ginny will play the lead in the school play.*

■ **Joyful** describes something that shows or causes joy: *The room was filled with the joyful sounds of children playing.*

■ **Joyous** is very close in meaning to *joyful*, but it usually refers to the event that causes joy: *It was a joyous occasion for the whole family when my cousin graduated from college.*

happy-go-lucky *adjective* A person who is **happy-go-lucky** is carefree and does not have many worries or troubles.

harass *verb* To bother or annoy someone again and again: *The bully harassed everyone who walked by.* **har·ass** (huh-**ras** *or* **har**-uhs) ▷ *verb* **harasses, harassing, harassed** ▷ *noun* **harassment**

harbor
1. *noun* An area of calm water near land where ships can safely dock or put down their anchors, often to unload cargo.
2. *verb* To keep bad thoughts in your mind for a long time, as in *to harbor a grudge.*
3. *verb* To hide someone, as in *to harbor a fugitive.*
har·bor (**hahr**-bur)
▷ *verb* **harboring, harbored**

hard
1. *adjective* Firm and stiff, as in *a hard mattress.*
2. *adjective* Difficult to do or understand, as in *a hard test.*
3. *adjective* Strong and forceful, as in *a hard hitter.*
4. *adjective* Strong and powerful enough to cause addiction, as in *hard drugs.*
5. *adjective* Energetic, as in *a hard worker.*
6. *adverb* Energetically, as in *to work hard.*
7. *adjective* Difficult and severe, as in *a hard winter.*
hard (hahrd)
▷ *adjective* **harder, hardest** ▷ *noun* **hardness**

Synonyms

Hard is the opposite of *easy* and describes something that requires work or effort: *The homework was so hard that Ellen spent all evening on it.*

- -

■ **Difficult** means that extra effort and perhaps some skills are needed to do something because there are obstacles in the way: *It was difficult to communicate with the visitors because they understood only a few words of English.*

■ **Arduous** refers to something that requires continued extra effort: *The arduous journey through the ice and snow took the travelers more than a week.*

■ **Oppressive** describes something that is very difficult to bear because of harsh or extreme conditions: *The heat in the factory was so oppressive that some people became ill.*

■ **Exhausting** refers to something that requires hard work and makes you tired: *Johnny found an hour of babysitting more exhausting than three hours of playing basketball.*

a b c d e f g **h** i j k l m n o p q r s t u v w x y z

hard-boiled *adjective*

1. Cooked by boiling until solid, as in *a hard-boiled egg.*

2. Tough and not sympathetic, as in *a hard-boiled detective.*

hard copy *noun* A printed copy of a document created by a computer.

hard drive or **hard disk** *noun* A device fixed inside a computer containing a disk that can store large amounts of data. A hard drive connected to the outside of a computer is known as an *external hard drive.*

harden *verb*

1. To become firm or stiff, or to make something firm or stiff: *The ice cream hardened once I put it in the freezer.*

2. To make or become tough and less sensitive to others: *Prison hardened him.*

hard·en (**hahr**-duhn)

▷ *verb* **hardening, hardened** ▷ *adjective* **hardened**

hardly *adverb*

1. Barely or only just: *The room was so crowded we could hardly move.*

2. Surely not: *We can hardly have a picnic today—the grass is all soggy from the rain.*

hard·ly (**hahrd**-lee)

hardship *noun* Something that makes life difficult, such as not having enough money or food, as in *the hardship of failing health.* **hard·ship** (**hahrd**-ship)

hardware *noun*

1. Tools and other equipment that are used especially in the house or yard.

2. Computer equipment, such as a printer, a monitor, or a keyboard: *I installed a scanner and plan to connect other hardware to my new computer.*

hard·ware (**hahrd**-*wair*)

hardwired *adjective*

1. Doing something in a particular way or by instinct, without having to learn it: *Researchers say that birds are hardwired to fear the color red.*

2. Operating with or involving connections using wires or hardware: *The building has smoke alarms that are hardwired into its electrical system.*

hard·wired (**hahrd**-wired)

hardwood *noun* Very strong, heavy wood from trees such as oak, maple, beech, and mahogany. **hard·wood** (**hahrd**-*wud*)

hardy *adjective* Strong and healthy and able to survive in very difficult conditions. **har·dy** (**hahr**-dee) ▷ *adjective* **hardier, hardiest**

hare *noun* A mammal that runs very fast and is like a large rabbit but with longer ears and strong hind legs. **hare** (hair) **Hare** sounds like **hair.**

harm *verb* To hurt, injure, or damage someone or something: *No one was harmed in the accident.* **harm** (hahrm) ▷ *verb* **harming, harmed** ▷ *noun* **harm** ▷ *adjective* **harmful**

harmless *adjective* Not able or likely to cause injury or damage, as in *a harmless joke.* **harm·less** (**hahrm**-lis) ▷ *noun* **harmlessness** ▷ *adverb* **harmlessly**

harmonica *noun* A small musical instrument that you play by blowing out and breathing in through the mouthpiece. **har·mon·i·ca** (hahr-**mah**-ni-kuh)

harmonica

harmonize *verb*

1. To sing or play musical notes that sound pleasing together.

2. To go together in a pleasing or agreeable way: *The colors of the couch and chairs harmonize nicely.*

har·mo·nize (**hahr**-muh-*nize*)

▷ *verb* **harmonizing, harmonized**

harmony *noun*

1. A situation in which people work or live together in a peaceful way: *The two groups are learning to live in harmony.*

2. A pleasing combination or arrangement: *We want the house to be in harmony with its surroundings.*

3. A set of musical notes played at the same time that are part of a chord and that sound pleasing together.

har·mo·ny (**hahr**-muh-nee)

▷ *noun, plural* **harmonies** ▷ *adjective* **harmonious** (hahr-**moh**-nee-uhs)

Word History

What makes your favorite song sound good to you? The ancient Greeks thought that the notes of a song were like joints in the body that fit together well. Your shoulder joint, for example, is where your arm connects to your body. A beautiful piece of music has notes that "fit together" well, so the Greeks based the word *harmonia* on *harmos*, a word meaning "joint." From *harmonia* we get the word **harmony.**

harness

1. *noun* A set of leather straps and metal pieces that connect a horse or another animal to a plow, cart, or wagon.
2. *noun* A set of straps used to connect you to something and keep you safe, as in *a parachute harness.*
3. *verb* To control something and use it for a particular purpose: *Scientists are working on a better way to harness wind power.* ▷ *verb* **harnesses, harnessing, harnessed**
har·ness (**hahr**-nis)
▷ *noun, plural* **harnesses**

harp

1. *noun* A large, triangular musical instrument with strings. It is played by plucking the strings with your fingers. ▷ *noun* **harpist**
2. *verb* If you **harp on** something, you keep talking about it in a way that is annoying: *Stop harping on that one silly mistake she made.* ▷ *verb* **harping, harped**
harp (hahrp)

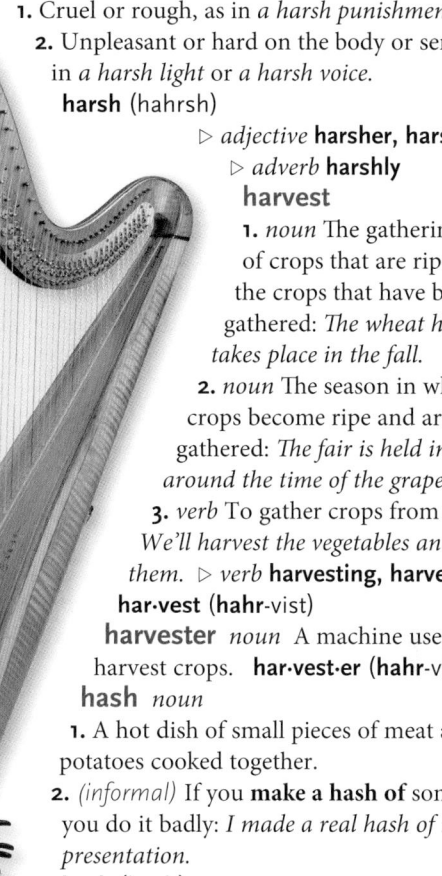

harp

harpoon

1. *noun* A long spear with an attached rope that can be thrown or shot out of a special gun. It is usually used for hunting large fish or whales.
2. *verb* To hit or kill with a harpoon, as in *to harpoon a whale.* ▷ *verb* **harpooning, harpooned**
har·poon (hahr-**poon**)

Word History

A **harpoon** has one or more sharp projections bent backward so that it will not come out of its target easily. English speakers adopted the word *harpoon* from *harpon,* a French word that referred to a metal bar with bent ends, used for holding stone blocks together in the wall of a building. So the bent parts of this tool, like a harpoon, helped in capturing or clamping things. *Harpon* was based on the French word *harpe,* meaning a "clamp."

harpsichord *noun* A keyboard instrument that looks like a small piano. A harpsichord has wire strings that are plucked rather than being struck like the strings in a piano. **harp·si·chord** (**hahrp**-si-*kord*)

harsh *adjective*

1. Cruel or rough, as in *a harsh punishment.*
2. Unpleasant or hard on the body or senses, as in *a harsh light* or *a harsh voice.*
harsh (hahrsh)
▷ *adjective* **harsher, harshest**
▷ *adverb* **harshly**

harvest

1. *noun* The gathering of crops that are ripe, or the crops that have been gathered: *The wheat harvest takes place in the fall.*
2. *noun* The season in which crops become ripe and are gathered: *The fair is held in October, around the time of the grape harvest.*
3. *verb* To gather crops from a field: *We'll harvest the vegetables and sell them.* ▷ *verb* **harvesting, harvested**
har·vest (**hahr**-vist)

harvester *noun* A machine used to harvest crops. **har·vest·er** (**hahr**-vi-stur)

hash *noun*

1. A hot dish of small pieces of meat and potatoes cooked together.
2. *(informal)* If you **make a hash of** something, you do it badly: *I made a real hash of my presentation.*
hash (hash)
▷ *noun, plural* **hashes**

hash sign *noun* The symbol #. Its uses include indicating weight in pounds, as in 5# potatoes, and introducing a hashtag, as in #photooftheday.

hashtag *noun* A word or phrase introduced by a hash sign that is used to label a tweet, an image, or a status update. Hashtags make it easier for people to find some things online. **hash·tag** (**hash**-tag)

hasn't *contraction* A short form of *has not*: *Simon hasn't arrived yet.* **has·n't** (**haz**-uhnt)

hassle

1. *verb (informal)* If someone **hassles** you, the person keeps bothering you about something: *Dad hassles me every day about my haircut.* ▷ *verb* **hassling, hassled**
2. *noun (informal)* Something that is annoying and causes problems: *The traffic jam made it a real hassle to drive to school.*
has·sle (**has**-uhl)

haste *noun* Speed in doing something, especially because you do not have enough time: *We had to hurry for school so we ate breakfast in great haste.* **haste** (hayst)

hasten *verb*

1. To move quickly.

2. To make someone or something move or happen faster: *Lots of tender, loving care hastened Grandpa's recovery from the operation.*

3. To be quick to do or say something: *She hastened to apologize.*

has·ten (**hay**-suhn)

▷ *verb* **hastening, hastened**

hasty *adjective* Done too quickly, especially with bad results, as in *a hasty choice.* **has·ty** (**hay**-stee)

▷ *adjective* **hastier, hastiest** ▷ *adverb* **hastily**

hat *noun* A piece of clothing that you wear on your head. **hat** (hat)

hatch

1. *verb* When an egg **hatches**, it breaks open and a baby bird or reptile comes out of it.

2. *verb* To think of a plan, usually in secret: *The prisoners hatched a plot to escape.*

3. *noun* An opening in a floor, deck, wall, or ceiling, or the door that covers it: *The sailor opened the hatch to the lower deck of the ship.* ▷ *noun, plural* **hatches** **hatch** (hach)

▷ *verb* **hatches, hatching, hatched**

hatchback *noun* A car with a large back door that opens upward. **hatch·back** (**hach**-bak)

hatchet *noun* A small ax with a short handle. **hatch·et** (**hach**-it)

hate *verb* To strongly dislike someone or something: *She hates cleaning her room.* **hate** (hate) ▷ *verb* **hating, hated** ▷ *noun* **hate**

hateful *adjective* Very bad and unkind, as in *a hateful remark.* **hate·ful** (**hate**-fuhl) ▷ *adverb* **hatefully**

hatred *noun* Intense dislike; the feeling of someone who hates: *She gave him a look of pure hatred.* **hat·red** (**hay**-trid)

haughty *adjective* If you are **haughty**, you are very proud and think you are better or smarter than other people: *Anne's haughty attitude annoyed her friends.* **haugh·ty** (**haw**-tee) ▷ *adjective* **haughtier, haughtiest** ▷ *noun* **haughtiness** ▷ *adverb* **haughtily**

haul

1. *verb* To pull or drag something with a lot of effort or difficulty: *Mia hauled her suitcase into the house.*

2. *verb* To transport with a vehicle, as in *to haul grain to the mill.*

hatchet

3. *noun* A large amount of something that has been caught or captured: *The fishing boat returned with a big haul of tuna.*

4. *noun* The distance someone travels or over which something is transported: *It's a long haul from New York to Tokyo.*

haul (hawl)

Haul sounds like **hall**. ▷ *verb* **hauling, hauled**

haunch *noun* The hip, buttock, and upper thigh of an animal or a person: *The bear sat up on its haunches.* **haunch** (hawnch) ▷ *noun, plural* **haunches**

haunt

1. *verb* If a ghost **haunts** a place, it appears there often: *The ship was said to be haunted by the ghost of an old pirate.* ▷ *adjective* **haunted**

2. *verb* If something **haunts** you, it upsets you and you are unable to forget it: *Jack continues to be haunted by the memory of seeing his house burn down.* ▷ *adjective* **haunting**

3. *noun* A place someone often visits: *You can usually find him at his favorite haunt—the library.*

haunt (hawnt)

▷ *verb* **haunting, haunted**

have *verb*

1. To own or possess something: *Maria has a new computer.*

2. To hold something: *He had a book in his hand.*

3. To experience something: *Everyone had a good time.*

4. To receive or get something: *Waiter, may I have the check, please?*

5. To need or be obliged to do: *I have to study for the math test.*

6. To contain or consist of: *The cookies have chocolate chips in them.*

7. To be the parent or parents of: *My cousin has two children.*

8. To be sick with something: *Martha has the flu.*

9. To arrange for: *Let's have the painters come at the end of the week.*

have (hav)

Have sounds like **halve**. ▷ *verb* **has** (haz), **having, had** (had)

haven *noun* A safe place for animals or people: *The wildlife refuge is a haven for storks.* **ha·ven** (**hay**-vuhn)

haven't *contraction* A short form of *have not*: *I haven't seen my jacket anywhere.* **have·n't** (**hav**-uhnt)

havoc *noun* Great destruction or confusion: *The hurricane caused a lot of havoc.* **hav·oc** (**hav**-uhk)

hawk

1. *noun* A large bird with a hooked beak and sharp

hayloft

claws that eats small animals and other birds.

2. *verb* To sell something, especially by offering goods in the street or some other public place and shouting to draw attention to them: *Some vendors are hawking hot dogs and soft drinks in the baseball stadium.* ▷ *verb* **hawking, hawked**

hawk (hawk)

hay *noun* Long grass that is dried and used as food for farm animals. **hay** (hay) **Hay** sounds like **hey**.

hay fever *noun* A sickness like a cold that affects your eyes, nose, and throat. It is an allergy caused by breathing in pollen from plants.

hayloft *noun* A platform high above the floor of a barn, where hay is stored. **hay·loft** (**hay**-*lawft*)

haystack *noun* A big, firm pile of hay. **hay·stack** (**hay**-*stak*)

haywire *adjective*

1. Out of order or not working properly: *We were watching TV when the picture went haywire.*

2. Wild or out of control: *When Dara hit the winning home run, the crowd went haywire.*

hay·wire (**hay**-*wire*)

hazard

1. *noun* Something that is dangerous or likely to cause problems: *The stack of newspapers was a fire hazard.*

2. *verb* To make a guess or suggestion, even though you know it might be wrong, as in *to hazard a guess.*

▷ *verb* **hazarding, hazarded**

haz·ard (**haz**-urd)

Word History

When you throw the dice in a board game, the biggest **hazard** is that you won't get the numbers you want! But there used to be a popular dice game called hazard, in which players would bet money. Winning or losing a lot of money would depend on a single throw of the dice, so when people thought of the game, they thought of "risk" or "danger." Its name may be based on *az-zahr* in Arabic, meaning "the die"; a die is one of the dice.

hazardous *adjective* Dangerous or risky: *Smoking is hazardous to your health.* **haz·ard·ous** (**haz**-ur-duhs)

hazardous waste *noun* Dangerous materials that should not be thrown away without some sort of protective covering.

haze *noun* Smoke, dust, or moisture in the air that prevents you from seeing very far. **haze** (haze)

hazel *noun*

1. A small tree or shrub that produces light brown nuts; a hazelnut tree.

2. A green-brown color.

ha·zel (**hay**-zuhl)

▷ *adjective* **hazel**

hazy *adjective*

1. Unclear because of smoke, dust, or moisture, as in *a hazy sky.*

2. If you have a **hazy** memory of something, the details are unclear in your mind.

haz·y (**hay**-zee)

▷ *adjective* **hazier, haziest** ▷ *adverb* **hazily**

H-bomb *See* **hydrogen bomb.**

he *pronoun*

1. The male person or animal mentioned before: *I asked my brother to rake the leaves, but he forgot to do it.*

2. Any person: *He who hesitates is lost.*

he (hee)

head

1. *noun* The top part of your body where your brain, eyes, ears, nose, and mouth are.

2. *noun* The person who leads an organization or group of people, as in *the head of a company.* ▷ *adjective* **head**

3. *noun* The top or front of something, as in *the head of the line* or *the head of a pin.*

4. *verb* To lead: *Admiral Peary headed an expedition to the North Pole.*

5. *verb* To move in the direction of something: *We headed toward the door.*

6. *noun* A single person or animal: *The admission fee is $15 a head.*

7. heads *noun* The main side of a coin, which usually shows a head or a face.

8. *noun* A cluster of leaves or flowers, as in *a head of lettuce.*

9. If something **goes to your head**, it makes you dizzy.

10. If a compliment **goes to your head**, it makes you think you are better than other people.

11. If you **keep a cool head** in an emergency, you remain calm and relaxed.

head (hed)

▷ *verb* **heading, headed**

headache *noun* An ache or pain in your head: *The bright sun gave me a headache.* **head·ache** (**hed**-*ake*)

headband *noun* A strip of cloth or plastic worn around the head to soak up sweat or keep hair out of the face. **head·band** (**hed**-*band*)

headdress *noun* A covering for the head, usually worn as a decoration on special occasions. **head·dress** (**hed**-*dres*) ▷ *noun, plural* **headdresses**

headfirst *adverb* With the head first, or leading with the head: *She dove into the pool headfirst.* **head·first** (**hed**-*furst*)

headhunter *noun* Someone whose job is to find the best people for important jobs and introduce them to employers. **head·hunt·er** (**hed**-*huhn*-tuhr)

heading *noun* Words written as a title at the top of a page or over a section of writing in a magazine, newspaper, or book. **head·ing** (**hed**-ing)

headlight *noun* A bright light on the front of a vehicle that allows the driver to see ahead in the dark. **head·light** (**hed**-*lite*)

headlight

headline *noun* The title of a newspaper, magazine, or web article, appearing in large, usually bold type: *The main headline in today's paper was "Major Snowstorm Predicted for the Midwest."* **head·line** (**hed**-*line*) ▷ *verb* **headline**

headlong *adverb*
1. With the head first: *She plunged headlong into the water.*
2. Without thinking about what you are doing: *Cynthia rushed headlong into the street.*
head·long (**hed**-*lawng*)

headmaster *noun* A man who is in charge of a private school. **head·mas·ter** (**hed**-*mas*-tur)

headmistress *noun* A woman who is in charge of a private school. **head·mis·tress** (**hed**-*mis*-tris) ▷ *noun, plural* **headmistresses**

head-on *adjective*
1. With the head or front end first: *Our car was in a head-on collision with a truck.*
2. In direct opposition, as in *a head-on confrontation.*
▷ *adverb* **head-on**

headphones *noun, plural* Small speakers that you wear in or over your ears to listen to music or other audio. **head·phones** (**hed**-*fohnz*)

headquarters *noun* The main building or office of a company or organization. Abbreviated as *HQ.* **head·quar·ters** (**hed**-*kwor*-turz)

head start *noun* An advantage, usually in a race when one runner is allowed to start first: *We gave Thomas a head start because he is younger and smaller than the rest of us.*

headstrong *adjective* Determined to do what you want and not listen to advice, as in *a headstrong child.* **head·strong** (**hed**-*strawng*)

headway *noun* Progress or forward movement: *We can't make much headway in this blizzard.* **head·way** (**hed**-*way*)

heal *verb*
1. To get better: *Jake's cut finger healed quickly.*
2. To cure someone or make the person healthy: *She used herbs to heal the sick.* ▷ *noun* **healer** ▷ *noun* **healing**
heal (heel)
Heal sounds like **heel**. ▷ *verb* **healing, healed**

health *noun*
1. The state of being free from disease: *I was ill last week, but now I'm better and have my health again.*
2. The condition of your body or mind: *The doctor said I was in excellent health.*
3. The condition of something such as a business or organization: *The company's employees are starting to worry about the health of the firm.*
health (helth)

health food *noun* Food that is considered to be healthy because it is grown in a natural way and does not contain anything artificial.

healthy *adjective*
1. If you are **healthy**, you are strong and not likely to become sick, as in *a healthy baby.*
2. Something that is **healthy** is good for the health of your body, as in *a healthy snack.*
3. Successful and working effectively, as in *a healthy economy.*
health·y (**hel**-thee) ▷ *adjective* **healthier, healthiest** ▷ *adverb* **healthily**

headphones

heap

1. *noun* A large, messy pile of things: *There's a heap of junk in the basement.*

2. *verb* To pile things on top of each other. ▷ *verb* **heaping, heaped**

3. *noun (informal)* A lot of something: *He made heaps of money in the stock market.*
heap (heep)

hear *verb*

1. To take in sounds through your ears: *We can hear the fireworks from our porch.*

2. To get news: *I heard on the radio that it's going to snow tonight.*

3. To listen to: *Have you ever heard Mariah sing?*
hear (heer)

Hear sounds like **here.** ▷ *verb* **hearing, heard** (hurd)

hearing *noun*

1. The ability to hear: *Bats have excellent hearing.*

2. An opportunity for an accused person in a court case to tell their version of what happened: *The police declared her a fugitive when she didn't show up for her court hearing.*

3. An opportunity to state an idea and have it be heard and respected: *I was grateful to my teacher because he gave my opinions a fair hearing.*
hear·ing (**heer**-ing)

hearing aid *noun* A small device worn behind one or both ears that helps a person hear better.

hearsay *noun* Something you have heard from someone else but have not seen or experienced yourself; a rumor. **hear·say** (**heer**-*say*)

hearse *noun* A car that carries a coffin to a funeral and burial. **hearse** (hurs)

heart *noun*

1. The organ in your chest that pumps blood all through your body.

2. The part of you that feels emotion: *Jody has a kind heart.*

3. Love and caring: *The story is about how the prince won the young woman's heart.*

4. Courage or hope: *Don't lose heart when things go wrong.*

5. The center or most important part of something: *We need to get to the heart of the matter.*

6. If you learn something **by heart**, you have memorized it and know it very well: *He recited the poem by heart.*

7. hearts *noun, plural* One of the four suits in a deck of cards, having a red symbol shaped like a heart, as in *the ace of hearts.*

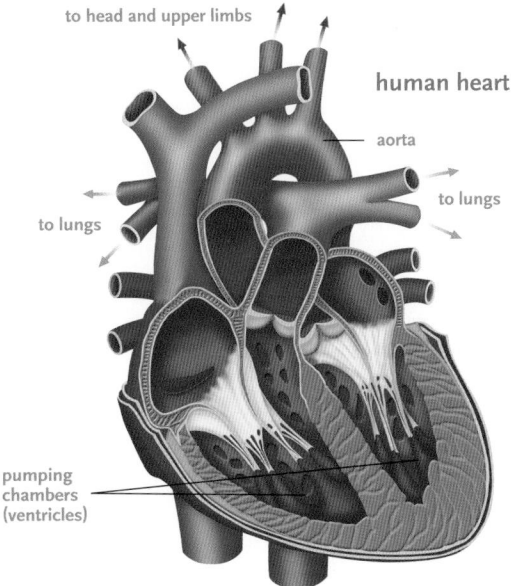

to head and upper limbs

human heart

aorta

to lungs

to lungs

pumping
chambers
(ventricles)

hearing aid

8. If you **take something to heart**, you think about it seriously.
heart (hahrt)

heart attack *noun* If someone has a **heart attack**, the person's heart suddenly stops pumping blood properly to the rest of the body. This can cause death in the most serious cases.

heartbeat *noun* One complete pumping movement of the heart. **heart·beat** (**hahrt**-*beet*)

heartbroken *adjective* Extremely sad: *Evan was heartbroken when his dog died.* **heart·bro·ken** (**hahrt**-*broh*-kuhn)

hearth *noun* The floor in front of or inside a fireplace. **hearth** (hahrth)

heartless *adjective* Cruel and feeling no sympathy for other people. **heart·less** (**hahrt**-lis) ▷ *noun* **heartlessness** ▷ *adverb* **heartlessly**

hearty *adjective*

1. Friendly and enthusiastic: *The team received a hearty welcome home after winning the state championship.* ▷ *adverb* **heartily**

2. Large and filling, as in *a hearty meal.*

3. If you have a **hearty** appetite, you are able to eat a lot of food.
heart·y (**hahr**-tee)
▷ *adjective* **heartier, heartiest** ▷ *noun* **heartiness**

heat

1. *noun* The quality of being very warm, as in *the heat of the sun.*

2. *noun* Hot weather: *We went inside to escape the heat.*

3. *noun* The level of temperature, such as on a stove or in a building: *Please turn the heat up.*

4. *verb* To cause something to become hot or warm: *Jason will heat up some soup for dinner.* ▷ *verb* **heating, heated**

5. *noun* An early round in a race: *Linda won the first heat in the 100-meter dash.*

6. *noun* Strong emotions, such as anger or excitement: *He spoke with passion and great heat.* ▷ *adjective* **heated** ▷ *adverb* **heatedly**

7. *noun* In physics, energy that comes from the motion of molecules passing from one substance to another, which increases temperature.

8. heat wave *noun* A long period of unusually hot weather.

heat (heet)

heater *noun* A device that produces heat, such as a radiator or a furnace. **heat·er** (**hee**-tur)

heath *noun* An area of open land that is covered with grass and small, wild plants. **heath** (heeth)

heathen *noun*

1. Someone who does not believe in one of the major religions.

2. (*informal*) Someone who is not civilized or educated.

hea·then (**hee**-THuhn)

heather *noun* A small bush with pink, purple, or white flowers. **heath·er** (**heTH**-ur)

heave

1. *verb* To lift, pull, push, or throw something heavy using a lot of effort: *Ben heaved the suitcase up the stairs.*

2. *verb* To go up and down with regular movements: *As Clark ran up the steep hill, his chest heaved because he was breathing so hard.*

3. *noun* A strong push, pull, throw, or lift.

heave (heev)

▷ *verb* **heaving, heaved**

heaven *noun*

1. The home of God, according to Christianity and some other religions. It is thought to be a glorious place where good people go after they die.

2. A wonderful situation or place: *It was heaven being in the mountains for a week.*

3. the heavens *noun, plural* The sky.

heav·en (**hev**-uhn)

heavenly *adjective*

1. Of or having to do with heaven, as in *heavenly creatures.*

2. Of or having to do with the sky or outer space, as in *heavenly bodies.*

3. Delightful or wonderful: *This cake is heavenly.*

heav·en·ly (**hev**-uhn-lee)

heavy *adjective*

1. Weighing a lot; hard to move or lift, as in *a heavy box.*

2. Larger, stronger, or more than usual, as in *heavy snow* or *heavy traffic.*

3. Needing a lot of effort or physical strength, as in *heavy exercise.*

4. Making you feel very full, as in *a heavy meal.*

5. Serious, difficult, or hard to understand: *I wanted to see a comedy—nothing too heavy.*

heav·y (**hev**-ee)

▷ *adjective* **heavier, heaviest** ▷ *noun* **heaviness**

▷ *adverb* **heavily**

heavy metal *noun* A type of rock-and-roll music with a strong beat and very loud electric guitars.

Hebrew

1. *noun* The language of the ancient Hebrews, used today as a language of prayer. Hebrew is also the language spoken by the people who live in Israel.

2. *noun* A member of or descendant from one of the Jewish tribes of ancient times.

3. *adjective* Of or having to do with the Hebrews or their language.

He·brew (**hee**-broo)

Hebrew letters

heckle *verb* To interrupt a speaker or a performer in a rude way by making loud comments. **heck·le** (**hek**-uhl) ▷ *verb* **heckling, heckled** ▷ *noun* **heckler**

hectare *noun* A unit of area in the metric system. One hectare is equal to 10,000 square meters, or about 2.5 acres. **hect·are** (**hek**-tair)

hectic *adjective* Very busy and filled with activity and excitement, as in *a hectic schedule.* **hec·tic** (**hek**-tik) ▷ *adverb* **hectically**

hedge

1. *noun* A row of bushes or small trees that are planted very close to each other, usually used as a border

around yards or fields, as in *a hedge of yews.*
2. *verb* To avoid giving a direct answer: *Quit hedging and answer the question.* ▷ *verb* **hedging, hedged**
hedge (hej)

hedgehog *noun* A small, insect-eating mammal with a pointed nose and spines on its back. It rolls into a ball to protect itself when it is frightened: *Hedgehogs are found in Europe but not in the Americas.* **hedge·hog** (**hej**-hawg *or* **hej**-hahg)

heed *verb* To pay close attention to someone or something, as in *to heed a doctor's advice.* **heed** (heed) ▷ *verb* **heeding, heeded** ▷ *noun* **heed**

heel *noun*
1. The back part of your foot.
2. The part of a shoe or sock that covers the back of your foot.
3. The part on the bottom of a shoe or boot that raises the back: *She was looking for shoes with high heels.*
4. If you **kick up your heels**, you are having a very good time.
heel (heel)
Heel sounds like **heal**.

hefty *adjective* (informal)
1. Someone who is **hefty** is large, heavy, or strong.
2. A **hefty** amount of something, such as money, is very large, as in *a hefty raise.*
hef·ty (**hef**-tee)
▷ *adjective* **heftier, heftiest** ▷ *noun* **heftiness**
▷ *adverb* **heftily**

heifer *noun* A young cow that has not yet had a baby. **heif·er** (**hef**-ur)

height *noun*
1. A measurement of how tall someone or something is: *The height of the wall is nine feet.*
2. A measurement of how high above the ground something is: *The plane was flying at a height of 26,000 feet.*
3. The most important or peak point of something, as in *the height of luxury* or *the height of summer.*
height (hite)

heighten *verb* To increase something or make it stronger: *The governor hopes to heighten awareness of the disease.* **height·en** (**hye**-tuhn) ▷ *verb* **heightening, heightened**

Heimlich maneuver *noun* A way of helping someone who is choking by putting your arms around the person from behind, below the ribs, and squeezing in order to force food out of the person's throat: *He performed the Heimlich maneuver on her, and a piece of sandwich came flying out of her mouth.* **Heim·lich maneuver** (**hime**-lik)

Word History

The approved way of helping someone who was choking used to be to hit the person sharply on the back. But an American surgeon named Henry J. Heimlich noticed that this method did not work very well in some cases, so in the 1970s he invented the technique that is named after him, the **Heimlich maneuver.**

heir *noun* Someone who receives someone else's money, property, or title when that person dies, as in *the heir to a fortune.* **heir** (air) **Heir** sounds like **air.**

heiress *noun* A girl or woman who receives someone else's money, property, or title when that person dies. **heir·ess** (**air**-uhs) ▷ *noun, plural* **heiresses**

heirloom *noun* Something valuable, such as an antique, that is passed from one generation of a family to the next. **heir·loom** (**air**-*loom*)

helicopter *noun* An aircraft with large, rotating blades on top and no wings. A helicopter can fly straight up and down and does so for takeoff and landing, requiring little space. **hel·i·cop·ter** (**hel**-i-*kahp*-tur)

Word History

The French word *hélicoptère* was borrowed into English as **helicopter.** The French word comes from the Greek *heliko,* a form of the Greek noun *helix,* which means "spiral," and *pteron,* which means "wing."

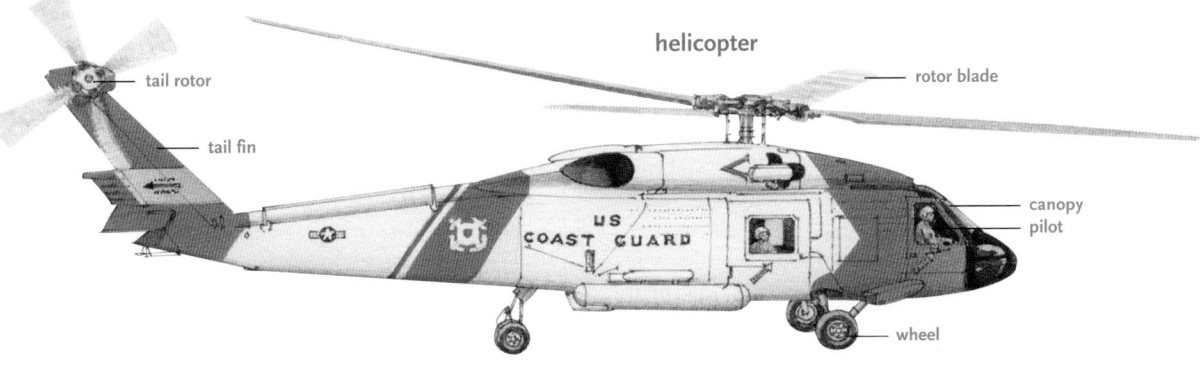

helicopter

tail rotor
tail fin
rotor blade
canopy
pilot
wheel

US COAST GUARD

a b c d e f g h i j k l m n o p q r s t u v w x y z

helium *noun* A light, colorless gas that does not burn. It is used to fill airships and balloons. **he·li·um** (**hee**-lee-uhm)

hell *noun* A very hot, miserable place where evil people go when they die in order to be punished, according to some Christian and other religious groups. **hell** (hel) ▷ *adjective* **hellish**

hello *interjection* A word you say to greet a person you meet or speak to on the telephone. **hel·lo** (he-**loh** *or* huh-**loh**)

helm *noun*
1. The wheel or handle used to steer a boat or ship.
2. Someone who is **at the helm** is in charge of something: *He is at the helm of a major company.* **helm** (helm)

helmet *noun* A hard hat that covers and protects your head, as in *a bike helmet.* **hel·met** (**hel**-mit)

help
1. *verb* To make it possible or easier for another person to do something: *Let me help you carry those boxes.*
2. *noun* Something you do that makes it possible or easier for another person to do something: *I could use some help moving this table and these chairs.*
3. *verb* To make a situation better: *The medicine helped his cough.*
4. *verb* If you **help yourself**, you take something you want, such as food or drink, often without asking for permission: *I helped myself to the cake in the fridge.*
5. *verb* If you **can't help** something, you can't avoid it or stop doing it: *I couldn't help laughing.* **help** (help) ▷ *verb* **helping, helped**

helper *noun* A person or thing that helps someone: *I'm going to need some helpers in the garden this weekend.* **help·er** (**hel**-pur)

helpful *adjective*
1. Willing to help, as in *a helpful teacher.*
2. Able to make a situation better or easier, as in *a helpful suggestion.* **help·ful** (**help**-fuhl) ▷ *noun* **helpfulness** ▷ *adverb* **helpfully**

helping *noun* An amount of food that is put on a person's plate, as in *a helping of mashed potatoes.* **help·ing** (**hel**-ping)

helping verb *noun* A verb, such as *may* or a form of *be, do,* or *have,* that is used together with another verb to complete the meaning of that verb, as in "may travel" or "is married." A helping verb is also called an *auxiliary verb.*

helpless *adjective* If you are **helpless**, you cannot take care of yourself, as in *a helpless baby.* **help·less** (**help**-lis) ▷ *noun* **helplessness** ▷ *adverb* **helplessly**

hem
1. *noun* An edge of material that has been folded over and sewn down. ▷ *verb* **hem**
2. *verb* If you are **hemmed in**, you are surrounded and cannot move or get out. ▷ *verb* **hemming, hemmed** **hem** (hem)

hemisphere *noun* One half of a round object, especially of the earth, as in *the Western Hemisphere.* **hem·i·sphere** (**hem**-i-sfeer)

hemlock *noun*
1. A very poisonous plant of the carrot family, or the poison made from this plant.
2. A tree similar to the pine that has green leaves throughout the year. **hem·lock** (**hem**-lahk)

hemoglobin *noun* A substance in your red blood cells that carries oxygen to all parts of your body. **he·mo·glo·bin** (**hee**-muh-*gloh*-bin)

hemophilia *noun* A serious disease in which a person bleeds too much from cuts or bruises. **he·mo·phil·i·a** (*hee*-muh-**fil**-ee-uh)

hemorrhage *noun* A serious medical condition in which a person bleeds a lot and cannot stop it, as in *a brain hemorrhage.* **hem·or·rhage** (**hem**-ur-ij)

hemp *noun* A plant that is used to make rope and cloth. **hemp** (hemp)

hen *noun*
1. An adult female bird.
2. A female bird raised for its eggs and meat. **hen** (hen)

hence *adverb* As a result, for this reason: *The prickly pear is a cactus with sharp spines, hence the name.* **hence** (hense)

hepatitis *noun* Inflammation of the liver. There are different kinds of hepatitis that result from different causes, and all of them require medical treatment: *He contracted hepatitis A from contaminated food while he was traveling and got very sick.* **hep·a·ti·tis** (*hep*-uh-**tye**-tis)

heptathlon *noun* An athletic competition, usually for women, made up of seven events. **hep·tath·lon** (hep-**tath**-luhn)

helmet

herd of cattle

her

1. *pronoun* The form of the word *she* used as a grammatical object: *I saw her yesterday.*

2. *adjective* Belonging to or related to a girl or woman: *Her voice is beautiful.*

her (hur)

herald

1. *noun* A person in the past who carried messages and made announcements on behalf of a ruler: *The king sent his herald to make a royal proclamation.*

2. *verb* To signal the approach of something: *Crocuses herald the arrival of spring.* ▷ *verb* **heralding, heralded her·ald** (**her**-uhld)

heraldry *noun* The study of the history of families and their symbols, such as their coats of arms. **her·ald·ry** (**her**-uhl-dree)

herb *noun* A plant or part of a plant that is used in cooking or medicine. **herb** (urb) ▷ *noun* **herbalist** ▷ *adjective* **herbal**

herbivore *noun* An animal that only eats plants: *Cows, horses, sheep, and rabbits are examples of herbivores.* **her·bi·vore** (**hur**-buh-*vor*) ▷ *adjective* **herbivorous** (hur-**biv**-ur-uhs)

herd

1. *noun* A large number of animals that stay together or move together, as in *a herd of cattle.*

2. *verb* To move people or animals together in a group, as in *to herd sheep.* ▷ *verb* **herding, herded** ▷ *noun* **herder**

herd (hurd)

here

1. *adverb* At or in this place: *Put the bag here.*

2. *adverb* At this point or time: *Here the music becomes softer.*

3. *interjection* A word used to answer a roll call: *Here!*

4. *noun* This place: *The boundary is from here to that tree.*

here (heer)

Here sounds like **hear**.

hereafter *adverb* From now on. **here·af·ter** (*heer*-**af**-tur)

hereby *adverb* By means of or as a result of these words or this statement: *Lindsay said, "I hereby resign," and then she packed her belongings and left the company.* **here·by** (**heer**-*bye* or heer-**bye**)

hereditary *adjective* Passed from parent to child before the child is born, as in *hereditary traits.* **he·red·i·tar·y** (huh-**red**-i-*ter*-ee)

heredity *noun*

1. The process of passing physical and mental qualities from a parent to a child before the child is born: *Hair loss is determined by heredity.*

2. All of the qualities that are passed on in this way. **he·red·i·ty** (huh-**red**-i-tee)

heretic *noun* Someone whose views are thought to be wrong or evil by a particular religion or by people in authority. **her·e·tic** (**her**-uh-tik) ▷ *noun* **heresy** (**her**-i-see) ▷ *adjective* **heretical** (huh-**ret**-i-kuhl)

heritage *noun* Traditions and beliefs that a country or society considers an important part of its history: *Museums help to preserve our cultural heritage.* **her·i·tage** (**her**-i-tij)

hermit *noun* Someone who prefers to live alone and stay away from other people. **her·mit** (**hur**-mit)

hero *noun*

1. A person who is admired for doing something brave or good, as in *a war hero.*

2. The main character in a book, play, movie, or any kind of story: *Harry Potter is the hero of a popular series of books.*

3. **hero** or **hero sandwich** Another word for a **submarine sandwich**.

he·ro (**heer**-oh)

▷ *noun* **heroism**

heroic *adjective*

1. Very brave and admired by many people, as in *a heroic police officer.*

2. Involving the actions of heroes, as in *heroic exploits.*

he·ro·ic (hi-**roh**-ik)

▷ *adverb* **heroically**

heroin *noun* A powerful and illegal drug that can cause addiction. **her·o·in** (**her**-oh-in) **Heroin** sounds like **heroine**.

heroine *noun*

1. A girl or woman who is admired for doing something brave or good.

2. The main female character in a book, play, movie, or any kind of story: *The heroine of the story finally finds the lost treasure.*

her·o·ine (**her**-oh-in)

Heroine sounds like **heroin**.

heron *noun* A bird with a long, thin beak and long legs that lives near water. **her·on** (**her**-uhn)

herpes *noun* A disease, caused by a virus, resulting in painful blisters. **her·pes** (**hur**-peez)

herring *noun* A fish that swims in the northern Atlantic and Pacific Oceans and is used for food. **her·ring** (**her**-ing)

heron

hers *pronoun* The thing or things belonging to or related to a girl or woman: *That pen is hers.* **hers** (hurz)

herself *pronoun* Her and no one else: *Emily hurt herself when she fell off her bike.* **her·self** (hur-**self**)

hertz *noun* A unit for measuring the frequency of vibrations and waves, equal to one cycle per second. Abbreviated as *Hz*. **hertz** (hurts) ▷ *noun, plural* **hertz** or **hertzes**

hesitate *verb* To pause before saying or doing something, especially because you feel nervous or unsure: *Hillary stood on the diving board and hesitated about jumping.* **hes·i·tate** (**hez**-i-*tate*) ▷ *verb* **hesitating, hesitated** ▷ *noun* **hesitation** ▷ *adjective* **hesitant**

hexagon *noun* A shape with six straight sides. **hex·a·gon** (**hek**-suh-*gahn*) ▷ *adjective* **hexagonal** (hek-**sag**-uh-nuhl)

hey *interjection* A word used to get someone's attention or to show surprise or joy. **hey** (hay) **Hey** sounds like **hay**.

heyday *noun* The time when someone or something was most successful or popular: *In his heyday, he always had plenty of money.* **hey·day** (**hay**-*day*)

hi *interjection* A word used as a greeting; hello. **hi** (hye) **Hi** sounds like **high**.

hibernate *verb* When animals **hibernate**, they sleep for the entire winter. This protects them and helps them survive when the temperatures are cold and food is hard to find: *Bears, frogs, and groundhogs are some of the animals that hibernate.* **hi·ber·nate** (**hye**-bur-*nate*) ▷ *verb* **hibernating, hibernated** ▷ *noun* **hibernation**

Word History

The English word **hibernate** comes from the Latin word *hibernus*, meaning "wintry." Winter is the time when certain kinds of animals hibernate.

hiccup *noun*
1. A sound in your throat caused by a sudden movement in your chest that you cannot control. Hiccups are usually caused by drinking or eating too quickly.
2. **hiccups** *noun, plural* The condition of having a series of these for a period of time. Sometimes also known as *the hiccups*.
hic·cup (**hik**-uhp)

hickory *noun* A tall tree with hard wood and a nut that you can eat. **hick·o·ry** (**hik**-ur-ee) ▷ *noun, plural* **hickories** ▷ *adjective* **hickory**

Word History

Native Americans made a drink from the pressed nuts of the **hickory** tree. The tree was unknown to the early explorers of the New World, so they didn't have a word for it. The English speakers took the Native American name for the drink, *pocohiquara*, and used it to refer to the tree, shortening the name to *hickory*.

hidden
1. *verb* The past participle of **hide**.
2. *adjective* Not in view; not obvious or known about: *Using a hidden camera, the TV news producer helped expose the company's unsafe working conditions.*
hid·den (**hid**-uhn)

hide
1. *verb* To put something in a place where it cannot be seen: *I hid the money in a box under the bed.*
2. *verb* To go to a place where you cannot be seen: *Tanya hid up in the attic.*
3. *verb* To keep something secret, such as a feeling: *Maria tried to hide her fear.*
4. *noun* The skin of an animal that is used to make leather, as in *deer hide*.
5. If something stays **in hiding**, it remains out of sight.
hide (hide)
▷ *verb* **hiding, hid** (hid), **hidden** (**hid**-uhn)

hide-and-seek *noun* A game in which people hide while one person looks for them.

hideous *adjective* Very ugly or horrible, as in *a hideous crime*. **hid·e·ous** (**hid**-ee-uhs) ▷ *noun* **hideousness** ▷ *adverb* **hideously**

hideout *noun* A place where someone can hide, especially a criminal trying to escape from the police. **hide·out** (**hide**-*out*)

hierarchy *noun* An arrangement in which people or things have different ranks or levels of importance, as in *the hierarchy of a company*. **hi·er·ar·chy** (**hye**-ur-*ahr*-kee) ▷ *adjective* **hierarchical** (*hye*-ur-**ahr**-ki-kuhl)

hieroglyphics *noun, plural* A system of writing used by ancient Egyptians, made up of pictures and symbols that stand for words. **hier·o·glyph·ics** (*hire*-uh-**glif**-iks)

high *adjective*
1. Something that is **high** is a long way above the ground, as in *a high ceiling*. ▷ *adverb* **high**
2. Measuring a particular distance from top to bottom: *The wall was 15 feet high.*
3. More or better than the normal level, amount,

Hieroglyphics

The ancient Egyptians developed their system of writing, known as hieroglyphics, probably around 3000 B.C. Its pictographs, or symbols in the form of pictures, could represent both an object and a sound. Hieroglyphics were used on sacred monuments and texts, while an almost identical form, called hieratics, was used to record information in everyday life. Only scribes knew how to write, and they held a high position in Egyptian society. The name of a pharaoh inscribed in an oval plaque is called a cartouche.

or quality, as in *high prices* or *high standards*.
▷ *noun* **high** ▷ *adverb* **highly**
high (hye)
High sounds like **hi**. ▷ *adjective* **higher, highest**

high-definition *adjective* Using new technology that creates very clear and detailed images. Often shortened to *high-def*, as in *high-def TV*.

higher education *noun* Education at a college or university.

high jump *noun* A track-and-field event in which athletes must jump over a bar without knocking it down. The bar is raised higher each time they successfully jump over it.

highland *noun* An area of land with mountains or hills. **high·land** (**hye**-luhnd) ▷ *adjective* **highland**

highlight
1. *verb* To make something easy to notice: *This summary highlights the important parts of the story.*
2. *noun* The most interesting or important part of something, as in *the highlight of our trip*.
3. *verb* To mark text using a pen with brightly colored ink that you can see through: *Highlight the verb in each sentence.*
4. *verb* To select text or an image on a computer monitor in order to do something with it: *Highlight the paragraph you want to move and drag it to the new location.*
5. highlights *noun, plural* Areas of a light color in hair: *Jen put blond highlights in her hair.*
high·light (**hye**-*lite*)
▷ *verb* **highlighting, highlighted**

highlighter *noun* A special pen with brightly colored ink that you can see through, used to mark important text. **high·light·er** (**hye**-*lye*-tur)

high-profile *adjective* Receiving a lot of attention from the news media because of interest or importance: *She got rich representing professional athletes in high-profile criminal cases.*

high-rise *noun* A tall building. High-rises are found mostly in cities. ▷ *adjective* **high-rise**

high school *noun* A school that usually includes grades nine through twelve or ten through twelve.
▷ *adjective* **high-school** ▷ *noun* **high schooler**

high seas *noun, plural* The parts of an ocean or a sea that are not controlled by any country: *Navy ships patrol the high seas.*

high-strung *adjective* Very nervous or easily excited.

high-tech *adjective* Using the most modern technology, as in *a high-tech computer program*.
high-tech (tek) ▷ *noun* **high tech**

high tide *noun* The time at which the water level in an ocean, a gulf, or a bay is at its highest point.

a b c d e f g **h** i j k l m n o p q r s t u v w x y z

highway *noun* A large public road that connects cities or towns. **high·way** (**hye**-*way*)

hijack *verb* If someone **hijacks** a vehicle, such as a plane, the person takes illegal control of it and forces its pilot or driver to go somewhere. **hi·jack** (**hye**-*jak*) ▷ *verb* **hijacking, hijacked** ▷ *noun* **hijacker** ▷ *noun* **hijacking**

hike *noun* A long walk, especially in the country or the mountains: *Tomorrow we'll take a long hike in the woods.* **hike** (hike) ▷ *noun* **hiker** ▷ *noun* **hiking** ▷ *verb* **hike**

hilarious *adjective* Very funny. **hi·lar·i·ous** (hi-**lair**-ee-uhs) ▷ *noun* **hilarity**

hill *noun* A raised area of land that is not as high as a mountain. **hill** (hil) ▷ *adjective* **hilly**

hillside *noun* The sloping side of a hill. **hill·side** (**hil**-*side*)

hilltop *noun* The highest part of a hill. **hill·top** (**hil**-*tahp*)

hilt *noun*
1. The handle of a sword or knife.
2. to the hilt As much as possible; completely: *Businesses have been borrowing money to the hilt.* **hilt** (hilt)

him *pronoun* The form of the word *he* used as a grammatical object. **him** (him) **Him** sounds like **hymn**.

himself *pronoun* Him and no one else: *Justin often talks to himself.* **him·self** (him-**self**)

hind *adjective* At the back or rear: *The horse kicked up its hind legs.* **hind** (hinde)

hinder *verb* To make it more difficult for something to happen or succeed: *The storm hindered our progress across town.* **hin·der** (**hin**-dur) ▷ *verb* **hindering, hindered**

Hindu god statue

Hinduism *noun* A religion and philosophy practiced mainly in India. Hindus worship many gods and believe in reincarnation. **Hin·du·ism** (**hin**-doo-iz-uhm) ▷ *noun* **Hindu** ▷ *adjective* **Hindu**

hinge
1. *noun* A metal joint on a door, gate, or lid that allows it to open and close easily. ▷ *adjective* **hinged**
2. *verb* To depend on something completely: *My final grade hinges on this test.* ▷ *verb* **hinging, hinged**
hinge (hinj)

hint *noun*
1. A helpful piece of information that makes it easier for you to do something or guess an answer: *His accent gave me a hint that he was from Maine.* ▷ *verb* **hint**
2. A very small amount of something: *I thought I saw a hint of a smile.*
hint (hint)

hip *noun* The part of your body below your waist that sticks out on either side, right above the top of your leg. **hip** (hip)

hip-hop *noun* A style of dancing, art, music, and dress that began in cities. Hip-hop includes rap music, break dancing, and graffiti art.

hippie *noun* A young person, especially one in the 1960s, who rejected traditional values. Hippies often had long hair, wore bright clothes, and were against war and violence. **hip·pie** (**hip**-ee)

hippopotamus *noun* A large African mammal with thick gray skin, a big head and mouth, and short legs. Hippopotamuses eat plants and live in or near water. The animal is also known as a *hippo.* **hip·po·pot·a·mus** (*hip*-uh-**pah**-tuh-muhs) ▷ *noun, plural* **hippopotamuses** *or* **hippopotami** (*hip*-uh-**pah**-tuh-*mye*)

Word History

If you were the first person ever to see a **hippopotamus**, what would you call it? The ancient Greeks called it a *hippopotamos,* meaning "a river horse," because it lives near water and has four legs like a horse. They created the name by combining their words for horse, *hippos,* and river, *potamos.* In English, the second part of the word became spelled with the letter *u.*

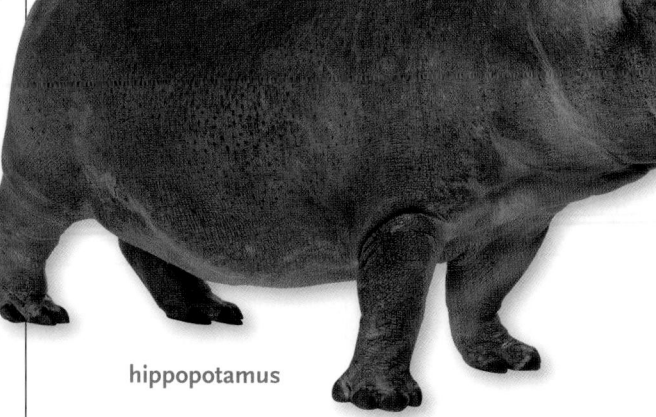
hippopotamus

hire *verb* To give someone a job. **hire** (hire) ▷ *verb* **hiring, hired**

his

1. *adjective* Belonging to or related to a boy or man: *He let me borrow his car.*

2. *pronoun* The thing or things belonging to or related to him: *That book is his.*

his (hiz)

Hispanic *adjective* Coming from or related to countries where Spanish is spoken, as in *the Hispanic community.* **His·pan·ic** (hi-**span**-ik) ▷ *noun* **Hispanic**

hiss *verb* To make a sound like a long *s*, especially to show that you do not like something or someone: *The audience hissed as the speaker reached the stage.* **hiss** (his) ▷ *verb* **hisses, hissing, hissed** ▷ *noun* **hiss**

historian *noun* Someone who writes about or knows about history, as in *a famous Civil War historian.* **his·to·ri·an** (his-**tor**-ee-uhn)

historic *adjective* If an event is **historic**, it was important in the past and will be remembered in the future, as in *the historic signing of the Declaration of Independence.* **his·tor·ic** (hi-**stor**-ik)

historical *adjective* Of or having to do with people or events of the past, as in *a historical moment.* **his·tor·ic·al** (hi-**stor**-i-kuhl) ▷ *adverb* **historically**

history *noun*

1. The study of things that happened in the past.

2. A description of things that happened in the past: *I'm reading a history of medicine.*

his·to·ry (**his**-tur-ee)

▷ *noun, plural* **histories**

hit

1. *verb* To strike something with your hand or with an object such as a bat or a hammer, as in *to hit a ball* or *to hit a nail.* ▷ *noun* **hitter**

2. *verb* To fall or crash into something with force: *The shoe hit the floor with a thud.*

3. *verb* To have a strong, often harmful effect on someone or something: *Florida was hit by a hurricane last week.*

4. *noun* Something, such as a song or play, that is popular or successful: *Her new movie was a hit with audiences.*

5. *noun* A result from a search that you do on the internet: *I typed in my uncle's name and got thousands of hits about his new book.*

6. *noun* A play in baseball, in which a batter hits the ball and is able to reach a base safely.

7. *verb (informal)* If you **hit it off** with someone, you get along well with the person: *Owen and I*

hitchhike

hit it off right away.

hit (hit)

▷ *verb* **hitting, hit**

hitch

1. *verb* To connect one thing to another using something such as a rope, as in *to hitch a horse to a wagon.*

2. *verb (informal)* To hitchhike: *We hitched a ride to Memphis.*

3. *noun* A problem or difficulty: *The restaurant opened without a hitch.* ▷ *noun, plural* **hitches**

4. *(slang)* If you **get hitched**, you get married.

hitch (hich)

▷ *verb* **hitches, hitching, hitched**

hitchhike *verb* To travel by getting rides in other people's vehicles, often by standing on the side of the road and holding out your thumb to get someone to stop: *He hitchhiked from Boston to San Francisco.* **hitch·hike** (**hich**-hike) ▷ *verb* **hitchhiking, hitchhiked** ▷ *noun* **hitchhiker**

hither

1. *adverb (old-fashioned)* Here. This word is now used mainly in a literary way: *Come hither!*

2. hither and thither *idiom* Here and there; going in various directions in a random way: *They ran hither and thither looking for the lost puppy.*

3. hither and yon *idiom* From here to over there, to some distant place: *We traveled hither and yon across the country.*

hith·er (**hiTH**-ur)

HIV *noun*

1. A virus that can develop into AIDS. HIV is short for *human immunodeficiency virus.*

2. If someone is **HIV positive**, the person has the HIV virus and his or her immune system is weakened. People who are HIV positive can develop AIDS.

a b c d e f g h i j k l m n o p q r s t u v w x y z

hive *noun*
1. Short for **beehive**.
2. **hives** *noun, plural* An allergic reaction of the skin, producing a rash that itches or burns: *I used to get hives from strawberries.*
hive (hive)

HMO *noun* An organization that provides all the health care for its members who make a regular payment to it. HMO is short for *health maintenance organization.*

hoard *verb*
1. To collect and store things, sometimes secretly: *Squirrels hoard nuts for the winter.*
2. To buy up a lot of supplies because you think they will be gone soon, as in *to hoard food for an emergency.*
hoard (hord)
Hoard sounds like **horde**. ▷ *verb* **hoarding, hoarded** ▷ *noun* **hoard** ▷ *noun* **hoarder**

hoarse *adjective* A **hoarse** voice is rough and sounds croaky, often because of a sore throat. **hoarse** (hors) **Hoarse** sounds like **horse**.

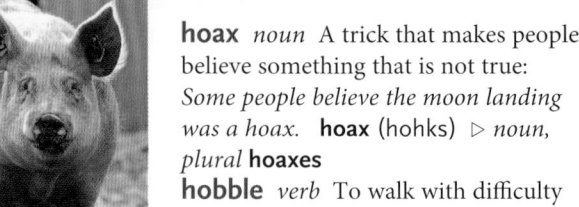

hog

hoax *noun* A trick that makes people believe something that is not true: *Some people believe the moon landing was a hoax.* **hoax** (hohks) ▷ *noun, plural* **hoaxes**

hobble *verb* To walk with difficulty because you are injured or weak. **hob·ble** (hah-buhl) ▷ *verb* **hobbling, hobbled**

hobby *noun* Something that you enjoy doing when you have free time: *Teresa's hobby is coin collecting.* **hob·by** (hah-bee) ▷ *noun, plural* **hobbies**

hockey See **ice hockey, field hockey**. **hock·ey** (hah-kee)

Hodgkin's lymphoma *noun* A disease in which the lymph glands, spleen, and liver gradually become larger. **Hodg·kin's lym·pho·ma** (hahj-kinz lim-**foh**-muh)

hoe *noun* A gardening tool with a long handle and flat blade, used to turn over soil and remove weeds. **hoe** (hoh) ▷ *verb* **hoe**

hog
1. *noun* A fully grown pig.
2. *noun* (informal) A selfish person who takes or uses more than his or her fair share of something, as in *a road hog.*
3. *verb* (informal) To take or use more than one's fair share of something, as in *to hog the couch.* ▷ *verb* **hogging, hogged**
hog (hawg *or* hahg)

hogan *noun* A Navajo house made with logs and branches and covered with soil. **ho·gan** (**hoh**-gahn)

hoist
1. *verb* To lift something heavy, usually with rope or a piece of equipment: *The crane hoisted the cars off the ship.* ▷ *verb* **hoisting, hoisted**
2. *noun* A piece of equipment used for lifting heavy things.
hoist (hoist)

hold
1. *verb* To have something in your hand, hands, or arms: *He was holding a suitcase.*
2. *verb* To contain or have enough room for something: *The stadium holds 70,000 people.*
3. *verb* To support the weight of something or someone: *How much weight can that bridge hold?*
4. *verb* To cause something to happen, as in *to hold a meeting* or *to hold a party.*
5. *verb* To have a particular position or job, as in *to hold the position of governor.*
6. *verb* To have an opinion or belief: *Americans hold many different religious beliefs.*

beekeeper inspecting a hive

7. *verb* To keep control of something or someone, for example by defending something that is being attacked, as in *to hold a fort*.

8. *noun* The part of a ship where goods are stored: *Barrels of fish were stored in the hold*.

9. If you **hold something against** someone, you have a bad opinion of that person because of something he or she did in the past: *She was rude to him once, and he still holds it against her*.

10. hold off *verb* To delay doing something, especially because you are waiting for something else to happen or finish: *Hold off cleaning the room until we're done painting*.

11. hold on *verb* To succeed in doing something, even though it is difficult to do: *We managed to hold on and win the game 6–5*.

12. If you ask someone to **hold on**, you ask the person to wait briefly: *Hold on, I'll be ready to go in a minute*.

13. If you **hold out** in a difficult situation, you continue with what you are doing: *We'll have to hold out until help arrives*.

14. hold up *verb* To rob with a weapon: *Three men held up a bank today*.

15. If you **hold up** someone or something, you delay the person or thing: *Traffic held up the parade*.
hold (hohld)
▷ *verb* **holding, held** (held)

holder *noun*
1. An object that holds something: *This car doesn't have very good cup holders*.
2. A person who holds or owns something: *He is the world-record holder in the 200-meter butterfly*.
hold·er (**hohl**-dur)

holding *noun*
1. A penalty in various sports in which one player illegally obstructs another.
2. holdings *noun, plural* Things that a company or a person owns, especially investments or real estate: *The banana company has substantial land holdings in Honduras*.
hold·ing (**hohl**-ding)

holdup *noun*
1. A robbery by someone who has a weapon.
2. A delay in activity: *The accident caused a holdup on the freeway*.
hold·up (**hohld**-*uhp*)

holly

hole *noun*
1. A hollow place or an opening in something solid: *The dog dug a hole under the fence*.
2. A weakness or flaw: *His argument was full of holes*.
3. A small animal's home, as in *a rabbit hole*.
4. (*informal*) A small, dark, unpleasant place.
hole (hole)
Hole sounds like **whole**.

holiday *noun*
1. A day when most people do not work or go to school, and many businesses are closed, especially because of a religious or national celebration.
2. A vacation, as in *a beach holiday*.
hol·i·day (**hah**-li-*day*)

holistic *adjective* Considering the whole of something rather than its individual parts. Holistic medicine deals with the whole patient, meaning the patient's mind and body, not just the place where the patient feels the injury or pain. **ho·lis·tic** (hoh-**lis**-tik)

hollow
1. *adjective* If something is **hollow**, it is empty inside, as in *a hollow tube*. ▷ *noun* **hollow**
2. hollow out *verb* If you **hollow** something **out**, you take its inside parts out: *Greg hollowed out the pumpkin and carved a face in it*. ▷ *verb* **hollowing, hollowed**
hol·low (**hah**-loh)

holly *noun* A tree or bush with red berries and leaves with sharp points. **Holly** is often used as a decoration at Christmas. **hol·ly** (**hah**-lee)

hollyhock *noun* A tall garden plant grown for its large, brightly colored flowers. **hol·ly·hock** (**hah**-lee-*hahk*)

holocaust *noun*
1. Total destruction and great loss of life, especially by fire, as in *a nuclear holocaust*.
2. the Holocaust The killing of millions of European Jews and others by the Nazis during World War II.
ho·lo·caust (**hah**-luh-*kawst*)

hologram *noun* An image made by laser beams that looks as if it has depth and is three-dimensional. **ho·lo·gram** (**hah**-luh-gram) ▷ *noun* **holography** (huh-**lah**-gruh-fee)

holster *noun* A holder for a gun worn on a belt. **hol·ster** (**hohl**-stur)

holy *adjective* Related to or belonging to God or a higher being. **ho·ly** (**hoh**-lee) **Holy** sounds like **wholly**. ▷ *adjective* **holier, holiest**

Holy Communion *noun* A Christian ceremony in which people eat bread and sip wine or grape juice to remind them of the body and blood of Jesus.

home *noun*

1. Your **home** is where you live, belong, or come from. ▷ *adverb* **home**

2. A place where you are likely to find something: *Philadelphia is the home of the cheesesteak sandwich.*

3. A place where sick, old, or homeless people can receive proper care, as in *a nursing home.*

4. A place in some sports or games, such as baseball, where players must go in order to score a point.

5. If you feel **at home**, you feel comfortable and relaxed with a particular person or in a particular place: *I've always felt at home in London.*
home (home)

homeland *noun* The country or region that you or your family comes from: *My great-grandparents left their homeland of Ireland to come to the United States many years ago.* **home·land** (**home**-*land*)

Homeland Security *noun* The federal government department that is responsible for protecting the United States from attacks and danger.

homeless

1. *adjective* Without a permanent home or place to sleep: *We volunteer at a shelter for homeless women.*

2. **the homeless** *noun, plural* People who have no permanent home or place to sleep: *Our spaghetti dinner raised $400 to feed the homeless.*
home·less (**home**-lis)

homely *adjective*

1. Not attractive; plain.

2. Simple and not fancy.
home·ly (**home**-lee)
▷ *adjective* **homelier, homeliest**

homemade *adjective* Made at home or by hand, as in *homemade soup.* **home·made** (**home**-made)

homemaker *noun* Someone who takes care of a house and family. **home·mak·er** (**home**-*may*-kur)
▷ *noun* **homemaking** ▷ *adjective* **homemaking**

homepage *noun*

1. The main page of a website. It usually has links to other webpages or websites.

2. The first page that appears when you open a web browser to go online. It is typically of a website that you use often.
home·page (**home**-*payj*)

homeless people

home plate *noun* In baseball, the base next to which a batter stands to hit the ball. The batter must run to all the bases and touch home plate to score a run.

homeroom *noun* A classroom in which students meet with a teacher before classes begin. **home·room** (**home**-*room*)

home run *noun* In baseball, a hit that allows the batter to run all the way around the bases and score a run.

homeschool *verb* To educate someone at home rather than at a school: *I was homeschooled for two years.* **home·school** (**home**-*skool*)
▷ *verb* **homeschooling, homeschooled** ▷ *noun* **homeschooler**

homesick *adjective* If you are **homesick**, you miss your home, family, and friends when you are away: *Gina got very homesick at camp.* **home·sick** (**home**-*sik*)

homespun *adjective*

1. Plain and simple, as in *homespun humor.*

2. Made at home, especially fabric, as in *homespun cloth.*
home·spun (**home**-*spuhn*)

homestead *noun*

1. A house, especially a farmhouse, with its buildings and land.

2. In the American West, a piece of land measuring 160 acres (65 hectares) given to a settler by the US government. The settler was required to build a house and farm the land.
home·stead (**home**-sted)
▷ *noun* **homesteader** ▷ *verb* **homestead**

homeward

1. *adverb* In the direction of home: *After a long day, the travelers finally turned homeward.*

2. *adjective* Going in the direction of home, as in *a homeward flight.*
home·ward (**hohm**-wurd)

homework *noun* Schoolwork that is to be done at home. **home·work** (**home**-*wurk*)

homicide *noun* The crime of killing someone; murder. **ho·mi·cide** (**hah**-mi-*side*)
▷ *adjective* **homicidal**

homogenize *verb* To mix milk so that the cream in it is spread evenly and does not rise to the top. **ho·mog·e·nize** (huh-**mah**-juh-*nize*) ▷ *verb* **homogenizing, homogenized** ▷ *noun* **homogenization**

homograph *noun* One of two or more words that have the same spelling but different meanings and sometimes different pronunciations. For example, the noun *wind*, meaning "a current of air," and the verb *wind*, meaning "to wrap around," are homographs that aren't pronounced the same. **hom·o·graph** (**hah**-muh-*graf*)

homonym *noun* One of two or more words that have the same pronunciation and spelling but different meanings, such as the noun *watch* and the verb *watch*. **hom·o·nym** (**hah**-muh-nim)

homophone *noun* One of two or more words that have the same pronunciation but different spellings and different meanings, such as the words *to, too,* and *two*. **hom·o·phone** (**hah**-muh-*fone*)

honcho *noun* (*informal*) A leader, boss, or other important person: *The company is still searching for a new head honcho.* **hon·cho** (**hahn**-choh) ▷ *noun, plural* **honchos**

Word History

American soldiers learned the word **honcho** when they were stationed in Japan after World War II. In Japanese, the word was *hancho,* and it meant "group leader."

honest *adjective*
1. Truthful and never stealing or cheating, as in *an honest man.*
2. Done without lying or cheating: *I'm just trying to make an honest living.*
hon·est (**ah**-nist)

honestly *adverb*
1. In an honest and truthful way: *When he asked me if I broke the window, I answered honestly and told him yes.*
2. People use **honestly** to emphasize that they are telling the truth: *Honestly, when you walked into the room I had no idea who you were!*
hon·est·ly (**ah**-nist-lee)

honesty *noun* The quality or trait of being honest and truthful: *Karen's friends appreciate her honesty and sense of fairness.* **hon·est·y** (**ah**-nis-tee)

honey *noun* A sweet, sticky substance that is made by bees and eaten as food. **hon·ey** (**huhn**-ee)

honeycomb *noun* A wax structure made by bees to store honey and pollen, and to raise young bees. A honeycomb is made up of many rows of cells with six sides. **hon·ey·comb** (**huhn**-ee-*kohm*)

honeymoon *noun* A trip that a bride and groom take together after their wedding: *They are going to the Bahamas for their honeymoon.* **hon·ey·moon** (**huhn**-ee-*moon*)

honeysuckle *noun* A climbing plant with white, red, or yellow flowers that have a pleasant smell. **hon·ey·suck·le** (**huhn**-ee-*suhk*-uhl)

honeysuckle

honk
1. *noun* The sound a car horn makes.
2. *noun* The sound a goose makes.
3. *verb* To make the sound of a goose or a car horn: *The car honked at the dog in the road.* ▷ *verb* **honking, honked**
honk (hahngk *or* hawngk)

honor
1. *noun* A person's good reputation and the respect that a person gets from other people: *He was willing to fight to protect his honor.*
2. *verb* To praise someone or give him or her an award: *The principal honored students for their achievements.* ▷ *noun* **honor**
3. *verb* To do what you have promised to do, as in *to honor an agreement.*
4. *noun* A special privilege: *"It's an honor to be here today,"* said the mayor as he began his speech.
hon·or (**ah**-nur)
▷ *verb* **honoring, honored**

honorable *adjective*
1. Deserving respect and praise, as in *an honorable profession.*
2. An **honorable** person is honest and has good moral character.
hon·or·a·ble (**ah**-nur-uh-buhl)

honorary *adjective* Given as an honor without the usual requirements or duties: *The university gave the governor an honorary degree.* **hon·or·ar·y** (**ah**-nuh-*rer*-ee)

honeycomb

hood *noun*
1. A part attached to the top of a coat or jacket that goes over your head. ▷ *adjective* **hooded**
2. The cover for a car's engine, usually found in the front of a car.
hood (hud)

a b c d e f g h i j k l m n o p q r s t u v w x y z

hoodlum *noun*

1. A violent criminal.

2. A young adult who is rough, mean, or violent. **hood·lum** (**hood**-luhm)

hoodwink *verb* To make someone believe something that isn't true: *That email scam hoodwinked me into donating to a fake charity.* **hood·wink** (**hud**-*wingk*)

▷ *verb* **hoodwinking, hoodwinked**

hoof *noun*

1. The hard part that covers the foot of an animal such as a horse or deer.

2. The entire foot of an animal such as a horse or deer. **hoof** (huf *or* hoof)

▷ *noun, plural* **hoofs** *or* **hooves**

▷ *adjective* **hoofed** *or* **hooved**

hook *noun*

1. A curved piece of metal or plastic used for hanging things: *Hang your coat on the hook.*

2. A fishhook.

3. A punch in boxing made when the elbow is bent, as in *a left hook.* **hook** (huk)

▷ *verb* **hook**

hooked *adjective*

1. Curved or shaped like a hook, as in *a hooked claw.*

2. If you are **hooked on** something, you are very interested in it and want to do it as much as possible: *She's hooked on surfing.* **hooked** (hukt)

hooligan *noun* A noisy, violent person, especially a young man, who causes trouble. **hoo·li·gan** (**hoo**-luh-guhn) ▷ *noun* **hooliganism**

hoop *noun*

1. A large ring made of a material such as metal or plastic, as in *the hoops of a barrel.* ▷ *adjective* **hooped**

2. A ring with a net attached, used as a goal in basketball.

3. hoops *noun, plural* (informal) Basketball: *Let's play some hoops!* **hoop** (hoop *or* hup)

hoot *verb*

1. To make a sound like an owl.

2. To show dislike or disapproval by shouting loudly: *We hooted at the player who struck out.* **hoot** (hoot)

▷ *verb* **hooting, hooted** ▷ *noun* **hoot**

hop

1. *verb* To jump on one foot.

2. *verb* To move with short jumps or leaps: *Birds hop around.*

3. *verb* To jump over something, as in *to hop a fence.*

Hopi girl

4. hops *noun, plural* The seed cases of hop plants, which are dried and used to make beer. **hop** (hahp)

▷ *verb* **hopping, hopped** ▷ *noun* **hop**

hope

1. *verb* To wish for something to happen and believe that it is possible: *I hope to visit New York this summer.* ▷ *verb* **hoping, hoped**

2. *noun* A feeling of wishing for something to happen and confidence that it will happen, as in *the hope of a good job.*

3. *noun* Something that you wish for: *We talked about all of our hopes and dreams.* **hope** (hope)

hopeful *adjective*

1. Believing that what you wish for will happen: *She felt very hopeful about the test.*

2. Making you feel that what you wish for will happen, as in *a hopeful sign.* **hope·ful** (**hope**-ful)

▷ *noun* **hopefulness**

hopefully *adverb*

1. Used to say what you hope will happen: *Hopefully, the game will start on time.*

2. In a hopeful way: *"Can you give me a ride into town?"* she asked hopefully. **hope·ful·ly** (**hope**-fuh-lee)

hopeless *adjective*

1. Not likely to happen or be successful, as in *a hopeless situation.*

2. Bad at doing something: *I'm a hopeless cook, but I'll try to make us some supper.* **hope·less** (**hope**-lis)

▷ *noun* **hopelessness** ▷ *adverb* **hopelessly**

Hopi *noun* A member of a group of Native Americans who live primarily in northeastern Arizona. **Ho·pi** (**hoh**-pee) ▷ *noun, plural* **Hopi** *or* **Hopis**

hopscotch *noun* A game in which players throw a stone or other object into a pattern of numbered shapes drawn on the ground. The players hop into the shapes in a certain order and try to pick up the stone. **hop·scotch** (**hahp**-skahch)

Word History

Children have been playing **hopscotch** since at least the 1600s. To play it, you hop over "scotches," which are lines made in the dirt. Maybe you have not heard the word *scotch* before, but it still survives in the term *hopscotch.* An old name for the game was "scotch-hoppers."

horde *noun* A large, noisy crowd of people, animals, or insects, as in *a horde of wasps*. **horde** (hord) **Horde** sounds like **hoard**.

horizon *noun*
1. The line where the earth or ocean seems to meet the sky: *There was a line of hills on the horizon.*
2. The limit of your experience, knowledge, or interests: *Traveling has really expanded my horizons.*
ho·ri·**zon** (huh-**rye**-zuhn)

horizontal *adjective* Straight and level; parallel to the ground, as in *a horizontal bar*. **hor·i·zon·tal** (hor-i-**zahn**-tuhl) ▷ *adverb* **horizontally**

hormone *noun* Your **hormones** are chemical substances made by your body that affect the way your body grows, develops, and functions. **hor·mone** (**hor**-mone) ▷ *adjective* **hormonal**

horn *noun*
1. A hard, pointed growth on the heads of some animals, such as goats and sheep. ▷ *adjective* **horned**
2. A device that gives a signal by making a loud sound, as in *a car horn*.
3. A brass musical instrument that you blow into, as in *a French horn*.
horn (horn)

hornet *noun* A large wasp with a painful sting that lives in a large group and builds a large nest. **hor·net** (**hor**-nit)

horoscope *noun* A diagram of the stars and planets on the day when you were born, used by astrologers to talk about your personality and predict events in your future. **hor·o·scope** (**hor**-uh-skope)

horrible *adjective*
1. Shocking or frightening, as in *a horrible crime*.
2. Very bad or unpleasant, as in *a horrible cold*.
hor·ri·ble (**hor**-uh-buhl)
▷ *adverb* **horribly**

horrid *adjective* Nasty or shocking. **hor·rid** (**hor**-id)

horrific *adjective* Shocking or frightening, as in *a horrific accident*. **hor·rif·ic** (hor-**if**-ik)

horrify *verb* If something **horrifies** you, it shocks, frightens, or disgusts you. **hor·ri·fy** (**hor**-uh-fye) ▷ *verb* **horrifies, horrifying, horrified** ▷ *adjective* **horrifying**

horror
1. *noun* A feeling of fear, terror, or shock.
2. *noun* Something that brings on such a feeling: *The family was touched by the horror of war.*
3. *adjective* Frightening or terrifying, as in *a horror story*.
hor·ror (**hor**-ur)

hornet

horse
1. *noun* A large, strong animal with four legs that people ride or use to pull things, such as carts or plows.
2. *noun* A piece of gymnastics equipment that you jump over.
3. *verb* If you **horse around**, you play in a rough and noisy way. ▷ *verb* **horsing, horsed**
horse (hors)
Horse sounds like **hoarse**.

horseback
1. *noun* The back of a horse.
2. *adverb* On the back of a horse: *They rode horseback into the mountains.*
horse·back (**hors**-bak)

horsefly *noun* A large fly. The female bites and sucks the blood of humans, horses, cattle, and other animals. **horse·fly** (**hors**-flye) ▷ *noun, plural* **horseflies**

horseplay *noun* Rough, noisy, and playful behavior, especially by children. **horse·play** (**hors**-play)

horsepower *noun* A unit for measuring the power of an engine, as in *a 300-horsepower engine*. **horse·pow·er** (**hors**-pou-ur)

horse

a b c d e f g h i j k l m n o p q r s t u v w x y z

horseradish *noun* A plant with a hard white root that is used to make a sauce with a very strong taste, usually eaten with meat. **horse·rad·ish** (**hors**-*rad*-ish)

horseshoe *noun*
1. A piece of metal shaped like a U and nailed to the bottom of a horse's hoof to protect it.
2. horseshoes *noun, plural* A game in which horseshoes are thrown around a metal stake.
horse·shoe (**hors**-*shoo*)

horseshoe

horticulture *noun* The science of growing flowers, fruits, and vegetables. **hor·ti·cul·ture** (**hor**-ti-*kuhl*-chur) ▷ *adjective* **horticultural**

hose
1. *noun* A long rubber or plastic tube that liquids or gases can flow through.
2. *noun* Stockings or socks.
3. *verb* To wash or water something with a hose: *Will you hose the soap off the car?* ▷ *verb* **hosing, hosed hose** (hohz)

hosiery *noun* Stockings and socks. **ho·sier·y** (**hoh**-zhur-ee)

hospice *noun* A place that provides care for people who are dying and comfort for their families. **hos·pice** (**hahs**-pis)

hospitable *adjective* Friendly, welcoming, and generous to visitors or strangers, as in *a hospitable city.* **hos·pi·ta·ble** (**hah**-spi-tuh-buhl)

hospital *noun* A place where sick or injured people receive medical treatment and are taken care of. **hos·pi·tal** (**hah**-spi-tuhl)

hospitality *noun* A generous and friendly way of treating guests, so that they feel comfortable and at home. **hos·pi·tal·i·ty** (*hah*-spi-**tal**-i-tee) ▷ *noun, plural* **hospitalities**

hospitalize *verb* To keep a person in a hospital for medical treatment. **hos·pi·tal·ize** (**hah**-spi-tuh-*lize*) ▷ *verb* **hospitalizing, hospitalized** ▷ *noun* **hospitalization**

host *noun*
1. A person who entertains guests: *Our host served delicious food.*
2. A large number of people or things: *He can speak on a host of topics.*
3. A person who is in charge of a TV show, especially one that includes music or conversation with celebrities: *She is the host of a popular game show.*
4. An animal or plant from which a parasite gets nutrition. **host** (hohst) ▷ *verb* **host**

hostage *noun* Someone who is kept prisoner by a person who demands something, such as money, before the captured person is released. **hos·tage** (**hah**-stij)

hostel *noun* A building with cheap, basic rooms where people can stay overnight. Hostels are used especially by young people who are traveling. **hos·tel** (**hah**-stuhl) **Hostel** sounds like **hostile**.

hostess *noun*
1. A woman who entertains guests.
2. A woman who greets people in a restaurant. **host·ess** (**hoh**-stis) ▷ *noun, plural* **hostesses**

hostile *adjective* Angry and aggressive, as in *a hostile audience.* **hos·tile** (**hah**-stuhl) **Hostile** sounds like **hostel**.

hostility *noun* Strong feelings against someone or something. **hos·til·i·ty** (*hah*-**stil**-i-tee) ▷ *noun, plural* **hostilities**

hot *adjective*
1. Having a high temperature, as in *a hot soup.*
2. Very spicy and strong in taste, as in *hot Mexican food.*
3. Showing anger very easily, as in *a hot temper.*
4. *(informal)* New, exciting, and popular, as in *a hot new singer.*
hot (haht) ▷ *adjective* **hotter, hottest**

hot-air balloon *See* **balloon.**

hot dog *noun* A long sausage usually eaten in a bun.

hotel *noun* A place where you pay to stay overnight when you are traveling. Many hotels serve meals. **ho·tel** (hoh-**tel**)

hot spot *noun*
1. A place, such as a restaurant, club, or resort, that is popular and attracts a lot of people, as in *a downtown hot spot.*

hot dog

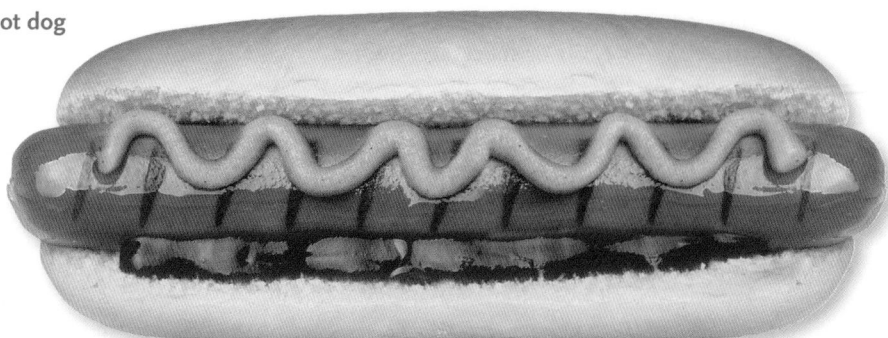

2. A place where there is a lot of trouble happening, as in *hot spots in the Middle East.*

3. A place where there is a wireless signal available so you can use the internet: *The coffee shop has free hot spots.*

hot spring *noun* A source of hot water that flows naturally from the ground.

hound

1. *noun* A kind of dog with a very good sense of smell that has been bred to hunt, as in *a basset hound.*

2. *verb* To keep chasing or bothering somebody: *George keeps hounding me about the money I owe him.* ▷ *verb* **hounding, hounded**
hound (hound)

Word History

There used to be many more *hounds* than *dogs.* The usual word for "dog" in Old English was *hund,* an earlier form of our word **hound**. *Hound* still means a dog today, but has come to refer only to dogs that have been bred for hunting. The German word *hund* is related to *hound* and is still the main word Germans use for "dog." The English word *dog* appeared in Old English also, spelled as *docga,* but it was not a common word then.

hour *noun*

1. A unit of time equal to 60 minutes. There are 24 hours in a day: *The TV program lasts one hour.*

2. A fixed period of time when a particular activity happens: *The building is open during regular office hours.*
hour (our)
▷ *adverb* **hourly**

hourglass *noun* An instrument for measuring time. It is made of two glass bulbs joined in the middle by a narrow glass tube. A quantity of sand falls from the upper bulb into the lower one in exactly one hour. **hour·glass** (**our**-*glas*)

house

1. (hous) *noun* A building made for people to live in: *A neat row of houses lined the road.*

2. (hous) *noun* All the people who live in a house: *The alarm woke up the whole house.*

3. (hous) *noun* A large building used for a particular purpose, as in *an opera house.*

4. (hous) *noun* A group of people who meet to make the laws of a country. In the United States, the houses are the Senate

and the House of Representatives: *The bill was passed by both houses of Congress.*

5. (hous) *noun* If something in a restaurant is **on the house**, you do not have to pay for it.

6. (houz) *verb* If you **house** someone, you provide the person with a place to stay or live. ▷ *verb* **housing, housed**
house

houseboat *noun* A boat that you can live on, with places for cooking and sleeping. **house·boat** (**hous**-*boht*)

housefly *noun* A common fly found in most parts of the world, which lives in or around people's houses. **house·fly** (**hous**-*flye*) ▷ *noun, plural* **houseflies**

household

1. *noun* All the people who live in a house: *Most of the households on our street are families with children.*

2. *adjective* Of or having to do with a house or a family, as in *household expenses.*
house·hold (**hous**-*hohld*)

House of Representatives *noun* One of the two houses of the US Congress. In this body, members are elected for two-year terms, and the number of members from each state is based on population.

house-sit *verb* To live in or take care of a home while the owners or regular residents are away: *Joe will house-sit for the neighbors when they go on vacation.* ▷ *verb* **house-sitting, house-sat** ▷ *noun* **house sitter**

housewife *noun* A married woman who spends her time managing her household, for example, by cooking, cleaning, and taking care of her children. **house·wife** (**hous**-*wife*)

housework *noun* Work done to keep a house neat and clean: *I want to finish the housework before Grandma arrives.* **house·work** (**hous**-*wurk*)

housing *noun*

1. Buildings or other shelters where people live, as in *student housing.*

2. A frame or cover that protects a machine's moving parts: *The jeweler took the watch out of its housing so he could repair it.*
hous·ing (**hou**-*zing*)

hovel *noun* A small house, hut, or room that is dirty and in bad condition, especially one that a very poor person lives in. **hov·el** (**huhv**-uhl or **hah**-vuhl)

hourglass

hover *verb*

1. To remain in one place in the air: *A helicopter hovered overhead.*

2. To stay attentively nearby: *She hovered over her sick child.*

3. To wait nearby, especially because you do not know what to do: *Joe hovered by the door for almost 20 minutes.*

hov·er (**huhv**-ur)

▷ *verb* **hovering, hovered**

how *adverb*

1. In what way, or by what means: *How do you carve a turkey?*

2. In what condition: *How are you?*

3. To what extent, amount, or degree: *How long is this play?*

4. For what reason, or why: *How did you happen to walk by at just the right time?*

how (hou)

however

1. *conjunction* In spite of that: *It's very cold; however, we still plan to go.*

2. *adverb* In whatever way: *I promise to pay for the damages, however much it costs.*

how·ev·er (hou-**ev**-ur)

howl *verb*

1. To make a loud noise that sounds like a dog or a wolf: *She howled when I stepped on her foot.*

2. To yell out with laughter, anger, or excitement: *We howled at Gina's joke.*

3. If the wind **howls**, it makes a loud, sad noise.

howl (houl)

▷ *verb* **howling, howled** ▷ *noun* **howl**

HTML *noun* The set of computer codes that is used to make basic webpages. HTML is short for *hypertext markup language.*

HTTP *noun* The set of rules that controls how data travels over the internet. HTTP is short for *hypertext transfer protocol.*

HTTPS *noun* A secure form of HTTP that is used, for example, when you buy something online, so that no one can steal information about you. IITTPS is short for *hypertext transfer protocol secure.*

hub *noun*

1. The center part of a wheel.

2. The center or most important part of an activity or organization: *Hollywood is the hub of the film industry.*

hub (huhb)

Hubble Space Telescope *noun* A large telescope that travels around the earth. It was launched by a space shuttle in 1990. It is named in honor of US astronomer Edwin Powell Hubble (1889–1953). **Hub·ble Space Tel·e·scope** (**huhb**-uhl **spays** *tel*-uh-skohp)

huckleberry *noun* A shiny, dark blue or black berry that is similar to a blueberry and grows on a shrub. The name *huckleberry* can mean both the berry and the shrub. **huck·le·ber·ry** (**huhk**-uhl-*ber*-ee) ▷ *noun, plural* **huckleberries**

huckleberries

huddle

1. *verb* To come together closely in a group: *We huddled around the fire to keep warm.* ▷ *verb* **huddling, huddled** ▷ *noun* **huddle**

2. *noun* A grouping of players in football who gather to prepare for the next play: *The team formed a huddle.* ▷ *verb* **huddle**

hud·dle (**huhd**-uhl)

hue *noun* A color, or a type of a color. **hue** (hyoo)

huff *noun* If you are **in a huff**, you are in a bad mood because someone upset or annoyed you. **huff** (huhf)

Hubble Space Telescope

NASA's giant space telescope—about the size of a school bus—orbits earth above the atmosphere, which blocks and distorts light from space. Hubble can take higher quality pictures of the universe than telescopes on our planet. It has photographed galaxies, black holes, stars, and comets. It helped to determine the age of the universe.

hull

hug *verb* To put your arms around someone or something in a caring or loving way: *Marta hugged her sister.* **hug** (huhg) ▷ *verb* **hugging, hugged** ▷ *noun* **hug**

huge *adjective* Extremely large, as in *a huge crowd.* **huge** (hyooj) ▷ *adjective* **huger, hugest**

hula *or* **hula-hula** *noun*
1. A Hawaiian dance with undulating hip movements and flowing hand gestures that imitate natural phenomena, such as the waves of the sea, or that recall Hawaiian historical or mythological subjects, often accompanied by chants and rhythmic drumming. Other forms of hula are also performed in Tahiti, Fiji, and other parts of Polynesia.
2. hula skirt A long grass skirt worn by a hula dancer: *The dancers had jasmine leis around their necks and wore hula skirts.*
hu·la (**hoo**-luh)

hulk *noun*
1. The remains of a wrecked ship or vehicle.
2. A large, heavy person.
hulk (huhlk)
▷ *adjective* **hulking**

hull
1. *noun* The frame or body of a boat or ship.
2. *noun* The outer covering of certain fruits, seeds, or nuts.
3. *verb* To remove the outer skin of a seed or nut.
▷ *verb* **hulling, hulled**
hull (huhl)

hum
1. *verb* To sing a tune with your mouth closed: *Janet hummed as she worked.*
2. *verb* To make a steady buzzing sound: *The bees hummed outside the window.*
3. *noun* A steady buzzing sound, as in *the hum of a car's engine.*
hum (huhm)

▷ *verb* **humming, hummed**

human
1. *noun* A person. ▷ *adjective* **human**
2. *adjective* Typical and understandable: *It was only human to take the money.*
3. human rights *noun, plural* Everyone's right to justice, fair treatment, and free speech.
hu·man (**hyoo**-muhn)

human being *noun* A person.

humane *adjective* Someone or something that is **humane** is kind and not cruel to people or animals. **hu·mane** (hyoo-**mane**) ▷ *adverb* **humanely**

humanitarian *adjective* Of or having to do with helping people and improving their lives, as in *humanitarian assistance.* **hu·man·i·tar·i·an** (hyoo-*man*-i-**ter**-ee-uhn)

humanity *noun*
1. All people.
2. Kindness and sympathy toward other people.
3. the humanities *noun, plural* Subjects outside the sciences, such as literature, history, and art.
hu·man·i·ty (hyoo-**man**-i-tee)

humble *adjective*
1. Not thinking you are better or more important than other people: *Ivan is a shy and humble man.*
2. Having a low social position: *Stephen comes from a humble background.*
hum·ble (**huhm**-buhl)
▷ *adjective* **humbler, humblest** ▷ *adverb* **humbly**

humdrum *adjective* Dull and ordinary, as in *a humdrum life.* **hum·drum** (**huhm**-*druhm*)

humid *adjective* **Humid** weather is moist and usually very warm, in a way that is uncomfortable. **hu·mid** (**hyoo**-mid)

humidity *noun* The amount of moisture in the air: *Washington, DC, has a high level of humidity in the summer.* **hu·mid·i·ty** (hyoo-**mid**-i-tee)

hula dancers

humiliate *verb* To make someone look or feel foolish or embarrassed: *She took every opportunity to humiliate him in front of others.* **hu·mil·i·ate** (hyoo-**mil**-ee-*ate*) ▷ *verb* **humiliating, humiliated** ▷ *noun* **humiliation**

humility *noun* If you show **humility**, you do not think you are better or more important than others, and you recognize your own faults. **hu·mil·i·ty** (hyoo-**mil**-i-tee)

hummingbird *noun* A very small, brightly colored bird that moves its wings very quickly and makes a humming sound. **hum·ming·bird** (**huhm**-ing-*burd*)

hummus *noun* A dip or sandwich spread made of chickpeas and sesame paste. **hum·mus** (**huhm**-uhs)

humongous *adjective* (*informal*) Very large: *It was a humongous plate of food, but he ate it all.* **hu·mon·gous** (hyoo-**muhng**-guhs)

humor

1. *noun* The quality of something that makes it funny or amusing: *There was no humor in the story.*

2. *noun* If you have a **sense of humor**, you are quick to laugh or to make others laugh.

3. *noun* Mood or state of mind, as in *a good humor.*

4. *verb* To agree with someone or do what the person wants so the person does not become upset: *Lenny humored his brother to avoid an argument.* ▷ *verb* **humoring, humored** **hu·mor** (**hyoo**-mur)

Word History

In the Middle Ages, the word **humor** meant any of the four liquids believed to determine the state of a person's body and health. Today, the word refers to somebody's state of mind. You can be in a good humor or a bad humor, but we no longer attribute these moods to the four liquids in a person's body.

humorous *adjective* Amusing or funny, as in *a humorous story.* **hu·mor·ous** (**hyoo**-mur-uhs)

hump *noun* A large lump that sticks out or up from something: *Camels have either one or two humps.* **hump** (huhmp) ▷ *adjective* **humped**

humpback *noun*

1. A humped or severely crooked back. Both *humpback* and another word for this condition, *hunchback,* are now considered offensive. Use the medical term *kyphosis* instead.

2. A person who has a hump on their back; a hunchback. The preferred term is *a person with kyphosis.*

3. Short for **humpback whale**. **hump·back** (**huhmp**-*bak*)

humus *noun* Rich, dark soil made from decaying plant and animal matter. **hu·mus** (**hyoo**-muhs)

Hummingbirds

Hummingbirds are very small birds named for the hum of their rapid wing beats. They can flap their wings as fast as 80 times per second, hover in the air, and even fly backward. Hummingbirds have long, thin beaks and tongues that allow them to drink great quantities of nectar. They also eat insects and spiders. Many have shimmering feathers in brilliant colors. Hummingbirds are native to the Americas.

hunch

1. *verb* To sit or stand with your head lowered into your shoulders and your body leaning forward so that your back is curved: *Hassan hunched over his homework.* ▷ *verb* **hunches, hunching, hunched**

2. *noun* An idea that is based on a feeling you have and not backed by facts or information: *I have a hunch that the test will be on Thursday.* ▷ *noun, plural* **hunches** **hunch** (huhnch)

hundred

1. *noun* The number that is equal to 10 times 10, written numerically as 100.

2. *adjective* Of or having to do with the number 100. **hun·dred** (**huhn**-drid)

hunger *noun*

1. The state of not having enough food to eat for a long time, especially when it causes sickness or death.

2. The feeling of wanting to eat: *I had a sudden hunger for pizza.*

3. The feeling of wanting something very much, as in *the hunger for knowledge.* **hun·ger** (**hung**-ger)

hungry *adjective*

1. Wanting to eat food: *I'm hungry for ice cream.*

2. Wanting something very much: *The team was hungry for a win.*
hun·gry (**huhng**-gree)
▷ *adjective* **hungrier, hungriest** ▷ *adverb* **hungrily**

hunk *noun* A large piece of something, such as bread, cheese, or meat. **hunk** (huhngk)

hunt *verb*
1. To chase and kill wild animals for food or sport.
2. To try to find something: *I spent an hour hunting for my glasses.*
hunt (huhnt)
▷ *verb* **hunting, hunted** ▷ *noun* **hunt** ▷ *noun* **hunting**

hunter *noun*
1. Someone who hunts.
2. A horse or a dog that you use to help during hunting.
hunt·er (**huhn**-tur)

hurdle
1. *noun* A small barrier, like a fence, that you jump over in a race. ▷ *noun* **hurdler**
2. *verb* To jump over something while you are running. ▷ *verb* **hurdling, hurdled**
3. *noun* A problem that you need to deal with to achieve something: *The biggest hurdle was getting our teacher's permission.*
hur·dle (**hur**-duhl)

hurl *verb* To throw something with great effort: *Craig hurled a stone into the lake.* **hurl** (hurl) ▷ *verb* **hurling, hurled**

hurray *interjection* A word used when people cheer. Also spelled as *hooray* (huh-**ray**) and *hurrah* (huh-**rah**). **hur·ray** (huh-**ray**)

hurricane *noun* A violent storm with heavy rain and high winds: *We are all waiting to see if the hurricane will hit land.* **hur·ri·cane** (**hur**-i-kane)

hurdle

Word History

"Furricanes" could have ended up as our name for *hurricanes*, but things turned out differently. The source of *hurricane* was a word in the language of the Carib people. These people of South America and the West Indies probably called a hurricane either a *huracan* or a *furacan*. English speakers then learned the word both ways, through the Spanish *huracán* and the Portuguese *furacão*, and at first they wrote the word several different ways: *furicane, haurachana, harrycain,* and so on. The spelling **hurricane** finally won out, though.

---

hurry
1. *verb* To move or do things quickly, especially because you do not have much time: *Jackie hurried through her homework.* ▷ *verb* **hurries, hurrying, hurried**

2. When you are **in a hurry**, you do things very quickly because you do not have much time.
▷ *adjective* **hurried**
hur·ry (**hur**-ee)

hurt *verb*
1. To cause physical or emotional pain: *He fell down and hurt his arm. She hurt him with her insulting remarks.* ▷ *adjective* **hurtful**
2. To feel pain: *My head hurts.*
3. To cause problems or difficulty: *If you don't do your homework, you're only hurting yourself.*
hurt (hurt)
▷ *verb* **hurting, hurt**

hurtle *verb* To move with force at great speed, as in *an asteroid hurtling through space.* **hur·tle** (**hur**-tuhl)
▷ *verb* **hurtling, hurtled**

Word History

The word *hurt* used to mean "to strike or hit," and **hurtle** comes from this old meaning. English speakers added the suffix *-le* to *hurt*, forming *hurtle*. Usually the suffix meant "doing an action again and again," but here it just added the idea of force. So *hurtle* first meant "to strike something forcefully," as in this sentence from a 19th-century writer: "The horse was not sure-footed and hurtled his rider against a tree." The word has kept its "forcefulness," but now it refers to moving at great speed.

husband *noun* A male partner in a marriage, or any married man. **hus·band** (**huhz**-buhnd)

hush

1. *noun* A sudden period of silence, especially after a period of noise: *A hush fell over the crowd.* ▷ *noun, plural* **hushes** ▷ *verb* **hush**

2. *interjection* Used to tell someone to be quiet: *Hush! I can't hear what she's saying!*

3. **hush up** *verb* To keep something secret, especially something that is embarrassing, as in *to hush up a scandal.* ▷ *verb* **hushes, hushing, hushed**

4. **hush-hush** *adjective (informal)* Very secret: *We've been trying to keep the news hush-hush.*
hush (huhsh)

husk *noun* The outer covering of seeds and some types of grains and fruits. **husk** (huhsk)

husky

1. *adjective* A **husky** voice sounds low and rough.

2. *adjective* Large and powerful, used especially to describe men or boys.

3. *noun* A strong dog with a thick coat, bred to pull sleds in the snow. ▷ *noun, plural* **huskies**
husk·y (**huhs**-kee)
▷ *adjective* **huskier, huskiest** ▷ *noun* **huskiness**

huskies

hustle *verb*

1. To push or move someone roughly in order to make the person move quickly: *Police arrested the thief and hustled him into a car.*

2. To work quickly and energetically: *Andy hustled to finish the job by noon.*
hus·tle (**huhs**-uhl)
▷ *verb* **hustling, hustled** ▷ *noun* **hustler**

hut *noun* A small, very simple house. **hut** (huht)

hydrant

hutch *noun*

1. A cage used to hold rabbits or other small pets.

2. A piece of furniture with shelves on top to hold dishes.
hutch (huhch)
▷ *noun, plural* **hutches**

hyacinth *noun* A plant with small, pleasant-smelling blue, white, or pink flowers that grow closely together. **hy·a·cinth** (**hye**-uh-*sinth*)

hybrid *noun*

1. A plant or an animal, such as a mule, that has parents of two different types or species.

2. Something that is made by combining two or more things: *The band's music is a hybrid of jazz, blues, and soul.*
hy·brid (**hye**-brid)
▷ *adjective* **hybrid**

hydrant *noun* A large pipe in the street that supplies water to use against fires and in other emergencies. **hy·drant** (**hye**-druhnt)

hydraulic *adjective* **Hydraulic** machines work on power created by liquid moving through pipes under pressure: *Most large trucks and buses have hydraulic brakes.* **hy·drau·lic** (hye-**draw**-lik) ▷ *noun* **hydraulics**

Word History

The English word **hydraulic** first referred to an ancient musical instrument, a water organ with rows of pipes. In this instrument, water was used to compress the air in the pipes, creating sounds. The Greek name for it was *hydraulikon organon*, meaning "hydraulic organ." *Hydraulikon* was based on the prefix *hydr-*, which meant "water," and the word for "pipe," *aulos*. Soon English speakers began using *hydraulic* as an adjective to describe a machine-powered liquid forced through tubes.

hydroelectric *adjective* Using the power of water to produce electricity. Hydroelectric power plants are often built at dams. **hy·dro·e·lec·tric** (*hye*-droh-i-**lek**-trik)

hydroelectricity *noun* Electricity made from the power of running water. **hy·dro·e·lec·tric·i·ty** (*hye*-droh-i-lek-**tris**-i-tee)

hydrogen *noun* A gas with no smell or color that is lighter than air and catches fire easily. Hydrogen mixed with oxygen makes water. **hy·dro·gen** (**hye**-druh-juhn)

hydrogen bomb *noun* An extremely powerful nuclear bomb. Its tremendous force comes from the energy that is released when hydrogen atoms combine to form helium atoms. Also called an **H-bomb**.

hyena *noun* A wild animal that looks somewhat like a dog. It eats meat and makes a sound similar to a laugh. **hy·e·na** (hye-**ee**-nuh)

hygiene *noun* Keeping yourself and the things around you clean, in order to stay healthy: *Brushing your teeth after every meal is an example of good hygiene.* **hy·giene** (**hye**-jeen) ▷ *adjective* **hygienic** (hye-**jen**-ik) ▷ *adverb* **hygienically**

hygienist *noun* Someone trained to help people stay healthy and clean: *My dental hygienist cleaned my teeth and showed me how to brush my teeth better.* **hy·gien·ist** (hye-**jee**-nist)

hymn *noun* A song that praises God. **hymn** (him) **Hymn** sounds like **him**.

hymnal *noun* A book of religious songs used in religious services. **hym·nal** (**him**-nuhl)

hype *noun* Claims that make something seem very important or exciting in order to get people interested: *There's a lot of hype about the new science fiction movie.* **hype** (hipe) ▷ *verb* **hype**

hyperactive *adjective* If someone, especially a child, is **hyperactive**, the person has difficulty sitting quietly or keeping still. **hy·per·ac·tive** (hye-pur-**ak**-tiv) ▷ *noun* **hyperactivity**

hyperlink
1. *noun* A piece of text on a webpage that is linked to another webpage, so that when you click on it you go to the second webpage.
2. *verb* To link one webpage to another by using a hyperlink: *People's names in the story were hyperlinked to their biographies on another site.* ▷ *verb* **hyperlinking, hyperlinked** **hy·per·link** (**hye**-pur-*lingk*)

hyphen *noun* The punctuation mark (-) used in a word made of two or more parts or words. Words such as half-mast, middle-aged, and part-time use hyphens. **hy·phen** (**hye**-fuhn) ▷ *noun* **hyphenation** ▷ *verb* **hyphenate**

hypnosis *noun* A state in which a person appears to be sleeping but can still see and hear and respond to suggestions and questions. **hyp·no·sis** (hip-**noh**-sis)

hypnotize *verb* To put someone into a state in which the person appears to be asleep but is still able to respond to suggestions and questions. **hyp·no·tize** (**hip**-nuh-*tize*) ▷ *verb* **hypnotizing, hypnotized** ▷ *noun* **hypnotism** (**hip**-nuh-*tiz*-uhm) ▷ *noun* **hypnotist**

hypochondriac *noun* Someone who continually thinks that he or she is sick even when healthy. **hy·po·chon·dri·ac** (*hye*-puh-**kahn**-dree-ak) ▷ *noun* **hypochondria**

hypocrite *noun* Someone who pretends or claims to have certain beliefs or feelings that he or she does not really have. **hyp·o·crite** (**hip**-uh-krit) ▷ *noun* **hypocrisy** (hi-**pah**-kri-see)

hypocritical *adjective* Pretending or claiming to have certain beliefs or values when this is not true: *They claim they care about the environment, but they are being hypocritical—they never recycle.* **hyp·o·crit·i·cal** (hip-uh-**krit**-i-kuhl) ▷ *adverb* **hypocritically**

hypodermic
1. *noun* A hollow needle used for giving medicine through the skin. Also known as a **hypodermic needle**.
2. *noun* An injection given by means of this needle. Also known as a **hypodermic injection**.
3. *adjective* Of or having to do with an injection through the skin, as in *a hypodermic syringe*.
4. *adjective* Of or having to do with the area right under the skin. **hy·po·der·mic** (*hye*-puh-**dur**-mik) ▷ *adverb* **hypodermically**

hypotenuse *noun* The side opposite the right angle in a right triangle. **hy·pot·e·nuse** (hye-**pah**-tuh-*noos*)

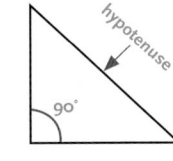

hypotenuse

Word History

In a right triangle, the **hypotenuse** is the side opposite the right angle. Speakers of ancient Greek thought of the hypotenuse as "stretching under" the right angle, so they named it *hypoteinousa*, meaning "stretching under." *Hypoteinousa* was based on the words *hypo*, meaning "under," and *teinein*, meaning "to stretch."

hypothermia *noun* If someone is suffering from **hypothermia**, the person's body temperature has become dangerously low. **hy·po·ther·mi·a** (hye-puh-**thur**-mee-uh)

hypothesis *noun* An idea that could explain how something works but that has to be tested through experiments to be proven right. **hy·poth·e·sis** (hye-**pah**-thi-sis) ▷ *noun, plural* **hypotheses**

hysteria *noun* Wild, uncontrolled feeling and expression in a person or group: *The rock band's arrival was greeted with hysteria.* **hys·ter·i·a** (hi-**ster**-ee-uh)

hysterical *adjective* Someone who is **hysterical** laughs or cries in an uncontrolled way because he or she is very excited, frightened, or angry: *The comedian was so funny that the whole audience was hysterical with laughter.* **hys·ter·i·cal** (hi-**ster**-i-kuhl) ▷ *adverb* **hysterically**

a b c d e f g h i j k l m n o p q r s t u v w x y z

Ii

About I The letter **I** looks like something close at hand: the shape of a finger. The earliest version of the letter was a symbol in the Phoenician alphabet that meant a hand. It later took a zigzag form, and became further simplified when the Greeks turned it into a vertical line. *I* is not just a letter but also a word we use when we talk about ourselves. We capitalize it to show that we mean the word *I*. In the 11th century, people began dotting their *i*'s to make words that had the letter easier to read.

I *pronoun* The person who is speaking or writing: *Joey and I will be home before dark.* **I** (eye)

Suffix

The suffix **-ic** or **-ical** turns a root word into an adjective by adding one of the following meanings:

1. Of or having to do with, as in *historic, historical* (having to do with history).
2. Like, as in *metallic* (like metal).
3. Made of or with, as in *alcoholic* (made with alcohol).

ice

1. *noun* Frozen water: *Ice forms on the pond in the winter.*
2. *verb* To turn into ice: *The juice iced up because the refrigerator was too cold.*
3. *verb* To cool with ice: *We iced the fish so it wouldn't spoil.*
4. *noun* A frozen dessert made from fruit juice and sweetened water.
5. *verb* To cover a cake or cupcake with icing.
6. **break the ice** To say or do something to relieve tension or help people get acquainted.
ice (ise)
▷ *verb* **icing, iced**

ice-skating

ICE *noun* The US government agency that is responsible for enforcing laws about border control, customs, trade, and immigration. ICE is short for *Immigration and Customs Enforcement.* **ICE** (ise)

Ice Age or **ice age** *noun* A period of time in history, many centuries ago, when a large part of the earth was covered with ice.

iceberg *noun* A large mass of ice that has broken off from a glacier and is floating in the sea: *The ship hit an iceberg and sank.* **ice·berg** (ise-*burg*)

icebox *noun*
1. A box or chest kept cool with blocks of ice.
2. A refrigerator.
ice·box (ise-*bahks*)
▷ *noun, plural* **iceboxes**

icebreaker *noun*
1. A ship designed to break through the ice in frozen waters so that other ships can pass through.
2. An event or comment that relieves the tension at a social gathering: *Tina's joke was a real icebreaker—it got everyone talking.*
ice·break·er (ise-*bray*-kur)

icecap *noun* A very thick layer of ice that covers an area of land and may get bigger or smaller as the climate cools or warms, as in *Greenland's icecap.* **ice·cap** (ise-*kap*)

ice cream *noun* A frozen dessert made from milk or cream, various flavors, and sweeteners.

ice hockey *noun* A team game played on ice with sticks and a flat disk called a puck that skaters try to hit into their opponents' net to make a goal.

ice skate *noun* A shoe or boot with a metal blade attached to the sole, used for gliding on ice.
▷ *verb* **ice-skate, ice-skating, ice-skated** ▷ *noun* **ice-skater** ▷ *noun* **ice-skating**

icicle *noun* A vertical ice formation caused by water that freezes as it drips: *Icicles hung from the roof.* **i·ci·cle** (eye-si-kuhl)

icing *noun* A sweet layer of creamy mixture used to decorate cakes or cookies, as in *chocolate icing.* Also called **frosting.** **ic·ing** (eye-sing)

icon *noun*
1. A graphic symbol on the desktop of a computer screen representing a program, function, or file.
2. A picture of a holy figure that is present in Christian churches and homes for veneration, especially those of the Eastern Orthodox faith.
i·con (eye-kahn)
▷ *adjective* **iconic**

icy *adjective*
1. Extremely cold, or covered with ice, as in *icy roads.*
2. Very unfriendly, as in *an icy stare.*
i·cy (eye-see)
▷ *adjective* **icier, iciest**

ID Short for **identification:** *You must show your ID to get into the stadium.*

I'd *contraction* A short form of *I had* or *I would*: *I'd go with you if I weren't so busy.* **I'd** (ide)

idea *noun*
1. A thought, a plan, or an opinion: *Latoya's idea was to go to the movies and then eat.*
2. An aim or purpose: *The idea of the club is to give students a place to go after school.*
i·de·a (eye-**dee**-uh)

ideal
1. *adjective* The best or most suitable: *Tulips make ideal spring flower arrangements.*
2. *noun* Someone or something considered perfect: *When it comes to vacations, my ideal is going to the beach.*
3. *noun* A standard of excellence: *Freedom is an American ideal.*
i·de·al (eye-**dee**-uhl)

idealist *noun* A person who believes in the highest ideals, even if they seem unrealistic. **i·de·al·ist** (eye-**dee**-uh-list) ▷ *noun* **idealism** (eye-**dee**-uh-*liz*-uhm)

idealistic *adjective* Believing that ideals are more important than practical matters: *The candidate for governor has idealistic plans for improving public services, but hasn't said how he will get the funds for them.* **i·de·al·is·tic** (eye-*dee*-uh-**lis**-tik)

identical *adjective* Exactly the same, as in *identical twins.* **i·den·ti·cal** (eye-**den**-ti-kuhl) ▷ *adverb* **identically**

identification *noun* A document or other item that proves who you are: *Travelers use passports for identification to enter a country.* **i·den·ti·fi·ca·tion** (eye-*den*-tuh-fi-**kay**-shuhn)

identify *verb* To recognize or tell what something is or who someone is: *Can you identify this strange insect?* **i·den·ti·fy** (eye-**den**-tuh-*fye*) ▷ *verb* **identifies, identifying, identified**

identity *noun* Who or what you are: *Amy had to prove her identity to claim the package.* **i·den·ti·ty** (eye-**den**-ti-tee) ▷ *noun, plural* **identities**

identical twins

identity theft *noun* The crime of pretending that you are another person so that you can spend that person's money or use his or her credit.

ideology *noun* A system of ideas that something is based on, such as a political party, economy, or society, as in *a religious ideology.* **i·de·ol·o·gy** (*eye*-dee-**ah**-luh-jee) ▷ *noun, plural* **ideologies**

idiom *noun* A commonly used expression whose meaning is not obvious, or not what you would expect. For example, if a homework assignment is "a piece of cake," it is easy. *See the Idioms Guide in the* **Reference Section**. **id·i·om** (**id**-ee-uhm) ▷ *adjective* **idiomatic** (*id*-ee-uh-**mat**-ik)

idiot *noun* A stupid or foolish person. **id·i·ot** (**id**-ee-uht) ▷ *adjective* **idiotic** (*id*-ee-**ah**-tik) ▷ *adverb* **idiotically**

Word History

It was not an insult to call someone an **idiot** in ancient Greece. The word was *idiotes,* and it simply meant "ordinary person." If you did not have any special knowledge, you were an *idiotes.* Now we think of an *idiot* as not having much knowledge at all.

idle
1. *adjective* Not busy, or not working; lazy: *During their summer break, Jess and her friends are spending their idle time reading and playing cards.* ▷ *verb* **idle**
2. *adjective* Not active, or not in use, as in *an idle computer.*
3. *verb* To run slowly without being connected to the transmission: *The engine was idling as we waited for him to arrive.* ▷ *verb* **idling, idled**
i·dle (**eye**-duhl)
Idle sounds like **idol.** ▷ *adjective* **idler, idlest** ▷ *adverb* **idly** ▷ *noun* **idleness** ▷ *noun* **idler**

idol *noun*
1. An image or object that is worshiped.
2. A popular person admired and loved for his or her accomplishments.
i·dol (**eye**-duhl)
Idol sounds like **idle.**

i.e. An abbreviation of the Latin phrase *id est,* which means "that is." It is used to show that what follows is a fuller explanation of something: *The scientific name for an animal, i.e., the name scientists use to classify an animal, always has two parts: the genus and the species names.*

if *conjunction* In the event that something else happens first: *We will arrive by noon if we walk quickly.* **if** (if)

igloo *noun* The traditional house of the Inuit people, made in the shape of a dome out of sod, stone, blocks of ice, or hard snow. **ig·loo** (**ig**-loo)

igneous *adjective*
1. Of or having to do with fire or the intense heat of a volcano, as in *igneous minerals.*
2. Of or having to do with rock that is produced by great heat or by a volcano. Obsidian, pumice, and hardened lava are examples of igneous rocks. **ig·ne·ous** (**ig**-nee-uhs)

ignite *verb* To set fire to something, or to catch fire: *The charcoal ignited quickly.* **ig·nite** (ig-**nite**) ▷ *verb* **igniting, ignited**

Word History

The words **igneous** and **ignite** both go back to the same Latin word, *ignis,* meaning "fire." *Igneous* refers to the "fire," or heat, produced by substances inside the earth, such as the magma of a volcano. The verb *ignite* means to set fire to something, or to catch fire. A car's ignition switch must ignite, or "fire up," the engine to start the car.

ignition *noun*
1. The activation of a machine by means of an electrical spark: *The ignition died and the car wouldn't start.*
2. The firing or blasting off of a rocket. **ig·ni·tion** (ig-**nish**-uhn)

ignorance *noun* The state or condition of not knowing something: *His ignorance about how to survive in the wild nearly cost him his life.* **ig·no·rance** (**ig**-nur-uhns)

ignorant *adjective*
1. Not aware of something: *Without clear instructions, I remained ignorant of what I was supposed to do.*
2. Uneducated, or lacking knowledge in general. **ig·no·rant** (**ig**-nur-uhnt) ▷ *adverb* **ignorantly**

ignore *verb* To pay no attention to something, as in *to ignore a traffic light.* **ig·nore** (ig-**nor**) ▷ *verb* **ignoring, ignored**

iguana *noun* A large tropical American lizard that can grow to more than five feet in length. **i·gua·na** (i-**gwah**-uh)

I'll *contraction* A short form of *I will* or *I shall*: *I'll be downstairs in a moment.* **I'll** (ile) **I'll** sounds like **aisle** and **isle**.

ill *adjective*
1. Sick; not enjoying good health: *Carla was too ill to go to the show.*
2. Bad, or negative: *This medicine has several ill* effects, including drowsiness. **ill** (il) ▷ *adverb* **ill**

illegal *adjective* Against the law: *False advertising is illegal.* **il·le·gal** (i-**lee**-guhl) ▷ *adverb* **illegally**

illegible *adjective* Difficult or impossible to read: *Brenda's science notes are illegible.* **il·leg·i·ble** (i-**lej**-uh-buhl)

illiterate *adjective* Unable to read or write. **il·lit·er·ate** (i-**lit**-ur-it) ▷ *noun* **illiteracy**

illness *noun* The condition of not being in good health; sickness: *He missed a week of work due to illness.* **ill·ness** (**il**-nis) ▷ *noun, plural* **illnesses**

illogical *adjective* Making no sense. **il·log·i·cal** (i-**lah**-ji-kuhl) ▷ *adverb* **illogically**

illuminate *verb*
1. To bring light to or on something; to light up something, such as a building: *The skyscraper is illuminated at night.*
2. To make something easier to understand: *These pictures in the product manual help illuminate how to assemble the toy.*
▷ *adjective* **illuminating**
3. To decorate a text with pictures and other artwork. This was often done in the Middle Ages. **il·lu·mi·nate** (i-**loo**-muh-*nate*)
▷ *verb* **illuminating, illuminated**
▷ *noun* **illumination** ▷ *adjective* **illuminated**

illuminated manuscript

Iguanas

The iguana lives primarily in tropical areas of the Americas. Like other lizards, it occasionally sheds its skin. It has a row of spines down its back. A male iguana extends its dewlap, the flap of skin below its neck, to appear bigger when fighting predators or to attract a female. Iguanas use their excellent vision to navigate and to find food, mainly plants and fruit.

iguana

illusion *noun*
1. Something you see that does not really exist: *The oasis in the desert was an illusion.*
2. A false idea: *Mahmoud was under the illusion that the train would arrive before noon.*
il·lu·sion (i-**loo**-zhuhn)
▷ *adjective* **illusory** (i-**loo**-sur-ee)

illustrate *verb*
1. To add visual images to text: *Zara works closely with the author when she illustrates a book.* ▷ *adjective* **illustrated**
2. To make clear or explain by using examples or comparisons: *The teacher illustrated how the heart works by comparing it with a pump.*
il·lus·trate (**il**-uh-*strate*)
▷ *verb* **illustrating, illustrated** ▷ *noun* **illustrator**

illustration *noun*
1. A picture in a book, magazine, or other publication or document: *The colorful illustrations made the story more interesting.*
2. An example: *A triangle is an illustration of a geometric shape.*
il·lus·tra·tion (*il*-uh-**stray**-shuhn)
▷ *adjective* **illustrative** (i-**luhs**-truh-tiv)

illustrious *adjective* Famous because of doing something very well or making something important: *He had an illustrious career as a federal judge.* **il·lus·tri·ous** (i-**luhs**-tree-uhs)

ill will *noun* Unfriendly feeling or hatred: *We've had our disagreements, but I hope you feel no ill will toward me.*

Prefix

The prefix **im-** or **in-** changes a root word by adding one of these meanings:

1. Not, as in *immature* (not mature), *imperfect* (not perfect), or *incapable* (not capable).
2. A lack of, as in *inefficiency* (a lack of efficiency).
3. In or into, as in *imperil* (to place in peril) or *inborn* (to be born in).

I'm *contraction* A short form of *I am.* **I'm** (ime)

IM *verb* To send messages back and forth over the internet using an instant messaging computer program. IM is short for **instant message**: *Diane likes to IM her friends after school.* ▷ *verb* **IMing, IMed** *or* **IM'd** ▷ *noun* **IM** ▷ *noun* **IMing**

image *noun*
1. An idea of how something looks: *A beach with palm*

imitate

trees and white sand is my image of a perfect tropical resort.
2. A representation of something: *We enjoy illustrated books because they have lots of images.*
3. The way a person appears to other people: *Toshiro has an athletic, energetic image.*
4. A person or thing that closely resembles another: *Ella is the image of her mother.*
5. A picture formed in a lens or mirror.
im·age (**im**-ij)

imagery *noun* Language that describes how something looks: *The poet uses the imagery of a flower to describe a beautiful girl.* **im·age·ry** (**im**-ij-ree)

imaginary *adjective* Existing in the imagination and not the real world: *Young children often have imaginary friends.* **i·mag·i·nar·y** (i-**maj**-uh-*ner*-ee)

imagination *noun*
1. The ability to form pictures in your mind of things that are not present or real, or to create new images or ideas: *It took great imagination to write that science fiction story.*
2. The part of your mind that imagines things, as in *a vivid imagination.*
i·mag·i·na·tion (i-*maj*-uh-**nay**-shuhn)

imaginative *adjective*
1. Creative or having great imagination, as in *an imaginative child.*
2. Showing imagination: *Ike told an imaginative story about a boy who grew to be ten feet tall.*
i·mag·i·na·tive (i-**maj**-uh-nuh-tiv)
▷ *adverb* **imaginatively**

imagine *verb*
1. To form an image of something in your mind: *Imagine a castle on a mountain.*
2. To believe that something exists when it does not: *Jules imagined that he saw a monster in the shadows.*
im·ag·ine (i-**maj**-in)
▷ *verb* **imagining, imagined**

imitate *verb* To copy or mimic someone or something: *Beth imitated a chattering squirrel.*
im·i·tate (**im**-i-*tate*) ▷ *verb* **imitating, imitated**

imitation
1. *noun* The act of imitating somebody or something: *They all laughed at his imitation of a robot.*
2. *noun* A copy; something that is not real: *That's not a real emerald; it's an imitation.*
3. *adjective* Made to be like something else: *The countertop was imitation marble.*
im·i·ta·tion (*im*-i-**tay**-shuhn)

immaculate *adjective* Very clean or neat, as in *an immaculate kitchen.* **im·mac·u·late** (i-**mak**-yuh-lit)
▷ *adverb* **immaculately**

immature *adjective*
1. Not fully developed.
2. Behaving in a silly, childish way.
im·ma·ture (*im*-uh-**choor** or *im*-uh-**toor**)
▷ *noun* **immaturity** ▷ *adverb* **immaturely**

immeasurable *adjective* Too great or vast to be measured. **im·mea·sur·a·ble** (i-**mezh**-ur-uh-buhl)
▷ *adverb* **immeasurably**

immediate *adjective*
1. Happening or done at once, as in *an immediate reply.*
2. Close or near: *The park is in the immediate vicinity of the train terminal.*
im·me·di·ate (i-**mee**-dee-it)

immediately *adverb*
1. Right away: *Come here immediately!*
2. Closely, or next: *She was immediately behind me in line.*
im·me·di·ate·ly (i-**mee**-dee-it-lee)

immense *adjective* Extremely large: *An immense puddle blocked the whole sidewalk.* **im·mense** (i-**mens**) ▷ *noun* **immensity** ▷ *adverb* **immensely**

immerse *verb*
1. To cover someone or something with a liquid: *The pasta was immersed in tomato sauce.*
2. In some religions, to baptize someone by placing the person completely underwater for a moment.
3. To be totally absorbed in something: *Benito was so immersed in his book that he didn't hear the bell.*
im·merse (i-**murs**)
▷ *verb* **immersing, immersed** ▷ *noun* **immersion** (i-**mur**-zhuhn)

immigrant *noun* Someone who moves from one country to another and settles there, as in *German immigrants.* **im·mi·grant** (**im**-i-gruhnt) ▷ *noun*

immigrants

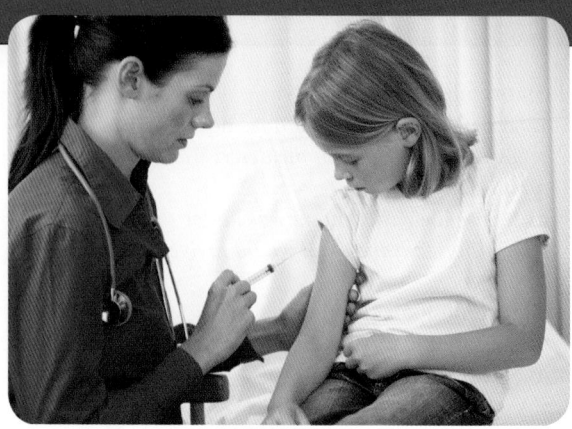

immunize

immigration (*im*-i-**gray**-shuhn) ▷ *verb* **immigrate**

imminent *adjective* About to happen, as in *imminent danger.* **im·mi·nent** (**im**-uh-nuhnt)
▷ *adverb* **imminently**

immobilize *verb* To prevent something or someone from moving: *Raina's broken leg had to be immobilized for six weeks.* **im·mo·bi·lize** (i-**moh**-buh-*lize*) ▷ *verb* **immobilizing, immobilized**

immoral *adjective* Bad, or without a sense of right and wrong: *The criminal's immoral acts landed him in jail.* **im·mor·al** (i-**mor**-uhl) ▷ *adverb* **immorally**

immorality *noun* Immoral actions, or the condition of being without morals: *Lincoln often spoke and wrote about the basic immorality of slavery.* **im·mor·al·i·ty** (*im*-uh-**ral**-i-tee)

immortal
1. *adjective* Living or lasting forever.
2. *adjective* Famous or remembered forever: *Shakespeare wrote a number of immortal works, such as "Romeo and Juliet."*
3. *noun* Someone or something that lives or is famous forever. ▷ *noun* **immortality** (*im*-or-**tal**-i-tee)
im·mor·tal (i-**mor**-tuhl)

immune *adjective*
1. If you are **immune** to a disease, you don't get sick from it: *This vaccine will make you immune to measles.*
2. Protected from physical or emotional harm: *The stubborn politician seemed immune to criticism.*
im·mune (i-**myoon**)
▷ *noun* **immunity**

immune system *noun* The system that protects your body against disease and infection. It includes white blood cells and antibodies.

immunize *verb* To make someone immune to a disease: *It is important to immunize babies against dangerous diseases.* **im·mu·nize** (**im**-yuh-*nize*)
▷ *verb* **immunizing, immunized**
▷ *noun* **immunization**

imp *noun*
1. A small demon who is full of mischief.
2. A cute child who is full of mischief.
imp (imp)

impact *noun*
1. The forceful striking of one thing against another: *The asteroid crashed into the moon, and its impact left a wide crater.*
2. A strong impression someone or something has made on a person: *His speech had a great impact on me.*
im·pact (**im**-pakt)

impair *verb* To damage something or make it less effective: *Alcohol impairs a driver's ability to drive safely.* **im·pair** (im-**pair**) ▷ *verb* **impairing, impaired** ▷ *noun* **impairment**

impala *noun* A small African antelope with curved horns and a reddish-brown coat, which can leap great distances. **im·pal·a** (im-**pal**-uh) ▷ *noun, plural* **impala** or **impalas**

impartial *adjective* Treating all persons or points of view equally: *Baseball games require an impartial umpire.* **im·par·tial** (im-**pahr**-shuhl) ▷ *adverb* **impartially**

impassable *adjective* Not providing any way through: *These mountain roads become impassable in winter.* **im·pass·a·ble** (im-**pas**-uh-buhl)

impatient *adjective*
1. In a hurry and unwilling to wait: *The impatient visitor banged on the door.*
2. Easily annoyed: *My grandfather gets impatient if there's a line at the store.*
im·pa·tient (im-**pay**-shuhnt) ▷ *noun* **impatience** ▷ *adverb* **impatiently**

impeach *verb* To bring formal charges against a public official for misconduct. An official can be impeached for committing a crime and be removed from office. **im·peach** (im-**peech**) ▷ *verb* **impeaches, impeaching, impeached** ▷ *noun* **impeachment**

impede *verb* To slow something down or stop it from making progress: *The building's construction was impeded by the storm.* **im·pede** (im-**peed**) ▷ *verb* **impedes, impeding, impeded**

imperative *adjective*
1. Extremely important: *It is imperative that you stay off your sprained ankle for a week.*
2. Expressing a command, an order, or a request, as in *an imperative sentence.*
im·per·a·tive (im-**per**-uh-tiv) ▷ *noun* **imperative**

imperfect *adjective* Faulty or not perfect. **im·per·fect** (im-**pur**-fikt) ▷ *noun* **imperfection** ▷ *adverb* **imperfectly**

imperial *adjective*
1. Of or having to do with an empire, as in *imperial Rome.*
2. Of or having to do with an emperor or empress, as in *the imperial palace.*
im·pe·ri·al (im-**peer**-ee-uhl)

impersonal *adjective*
1. Lacking in feeling: *The detective asked his questions in a frosty, impersonal manner.*
2. Having a style that is not emotional or meant to have personality, as in *a dry and impersonal government report.*
im·per·son·al (im-**pur**-suh-nuhl) ▷ *adverb* **impersonally**

impersonate *verb* To pretend to be someone else: *Carlos impersonated the mayor.* **im·per·son·ate** (im-**pur**-suh-*nate*) ▷ *verb* **impersonating, impersonated** ▷ *noun* **impersonation** ▷ *noun* **impersonator**

impertinent *adjective* Disrespectful and not courteous, as in *impertinent behavior.* **im·per·ti·nent** (im-**pur**-tuh-nuhnt) ▷ *noun* **impertinence** ▷ *adverb* **impertinently**

impetuous *adjective* Done quickly and without thinking first. **im·pet·u·ous** (im-**pech**-oo-uhs) ▷ *adverb* **impetuously**

implant *verb*
1. To establish or instill firmly and deeply: *He has implanted his love of music in all his children.*
2. To put an organ or a device into the body by surgery, as in *to implant a liver.*
im·plant (im-**plant**) ▷ *verb* **implanting, implanted** ▷ *noun* **implant** (**im**-*plant*)

impala

implement

1. (**im**-pluh-muhnt) *noun* A tool or a utensil: *Garden implements are kept in the shed.*

2. (**im**-pluh-*ment*) *verb* To put a plan or an idea into action: *The government implemented its emergency relief plan by sending food and water to the area hit by the hurricane.* ▷ *verb* **implementing, implemented** ▷ *noun* **implementation**
im·ple·ment

implication *noun*

1. The meaning or significance of something: *We had no way of knowing the implications of our decision to move to the city.*

2. Something suggested but not said directly: *When Harry asked what time it was, the implication was that he wanted to leave.*
im·pli·ca·tion (*im*-pli-**kay**-shuhn)

implicit *adjective* Known or understood without being talked about: *It was implicit in his statement that he believes all the students are innocent.* **im·pli·cit** (im-**plis**-it) ▷ *adverb* **implicitly**

imply *verb* To suggest or mean something without stating it directly: *The look on Von's face implied that he was sorry.* **im·ply** (im-**plye**) ▷ *verb* **implies, implying, implied**

impolite *adjective* Not courteous; inconsiderate: *It is impolite to cut in line.* **im·po·lite** (*im*-puh-**lite**) ▷ *adverb* **impolitely**

import *verb*

1. To bring into a place or country from somewhere else: *Russia imports a lot of grain.*

2. To transfer data into a file or document: *You can import the spreadsheet directly into the database.*
im·port (**im**-port *or* im-**port**)
▷ *verb* **importing, imported** ▷ *noun* **import** (**im**-port)
▷ *noun* **importer**

importance *noun* The quality of being important: *White House officials understand the importance of communicating with the media.* **im·por·tance** (im-**por**-tuhns)

important *adjective*

1. Having great significance or impact, as in *an important discovery.* ▷ *adverb* **importantly**

2. Powerful, or necessary in a particular situation: *A good electrician is important when you're building a house.*
im·por·tant (im-**por**-tuhnt)

importantly *adverb* People use **importantly**, usually with the word *more* or *most*, to give emphasis to part of what they are saying: *She is smart, pretty, and fun to be with, but most importantly, she's a real friend.* **im·por·tant·ly** (im-**por**-tuhnt-lee)

impose *verb*

1. To force to accept by legal means, as in *to impose taxes* or *to impose a prison sentence.*

2. To take advantage of someone or make unfair demands: *I won't impose on you by staying for dinner.*
im·pose (im-**poze**)
▷ *verb* **imposing, imposed** ▷ *noun* **imposition** (*im*-puh-**zish**-uhn)

impossible *adjective* Not able to happen or exist. **im·pos·si·ble** (im-**pah**-suh-buhl) ▷ *noun* **impossibility** (im-*pah*-suh-**bil**-i-tee) ▷ *adverb* **impossibly**

impostor *noun* A person who tries to fool others by pretending to be someone else: *The man says he is Elvis, but he is obviously an impostor.* **im·pos·tor** (im-**pah**-stur)

Word History

Originally, an **impostor** was simply someone who tried to cheat people by tricking them into believing something that wasn't true. The Latin verb *imponere*, which meant "to put on," is the source of our word *impostor.* An *impostor* tried to make people accept a false story, or "put" it "on" them. The past participle of *imponere* was *impositus,* and *impostor* came from that. Today, the English word *impostor* still refers to someone who deceives others, but the meaning has narrowed to mean a person who pretends to be somebody else.

impractical *adjective* Not useful or sensible, as in *an impractical idea.* **im·prac·ti·cal** (im-**prak**-ti-kuhl)

impress *verb*

1. To make someone feel admiration or respect: *Charlie's work impressed his teacher.*

2. To make something very clear to someone: *Our leader impressed on us the need to stay together.*

3. To have an effect on someone's mind: *The destruction caused by the fire impressed Jake so much that he decided to be a firefighter.*

4. To make a mark on something, using pressure: *The potter impressed a design on the side of the cup.*
im·press (im-**pres**)
▷ *verb* **impresses, impressing, impressed**

impression *noun*

1. An idea or a feeling based on something you saw, read, or heard: *I had the impression that Barbara didn't want to come along.*

2. An imitation of someone or something: *Simon did his impression of a barking dog.*

3. A strong effect: *Her excellent work made a good impression on the boss.*

4. A mark made by pressing or stamping something

into a surface or substance: *The sharp tool left an impression on the leather.*
im·pres·sion (im-**presh**-uhn)

impressionable *adjective* Easily influenced.
im·pres·sion·a·ble (im-**presh**-uh-nuh-buhl)

impressive *adjective* Creating a strong and good impression: *Nan gave an impressive performance at the tennis tournament.* **im·press·ive** (im-**pres**-iv)

imprint

1. (**im**-*print*) *noun* A mark made by pressing or stamping something on a surface: *His sneakers made imprints in the sand.* ▷ *verb* **imprint** (im-**print**)

2. (**im**-*print*) *noun* A strong influence or effect: *Immigrants from many countries have made a strong imprint on American life.*

3. (im-**print**) *verb* To fix firmly in the mind or memory. ▷ *verb* **imprinting, imprinted**
im·print

imprison *verb*

1. To put someone into prison: *The thief was imprisoned for two years.*

2. To confine to a particular place: *I felt imprisoned in my tiny new office.*
im·pris·on (im-**priz**-uhn)
▷ *verb* **imprisoning, imprisoned**
▷ *noun* **imprisonment**

improper *adjective*

1. Wrong, as in *an improper response.*

2. Showing bad manners or bad taste: *It is improper to burp at the table.*

3. An **improper fraction** is a fraction whose numerator is greater than its denominator, as in $^4/_3$ or $^{15}/_{13}$.
im·prop·er (im-**prah**-pur)
▷ *adverb* **improperly**

improve *verb* To get better or to make better: *Doug's grades have improved this year.* **im·prove** (im-**proov**) ▷ *verb* **improving, improved**
▷ *adjective* **improved**

improvement *noun*

1. Something that makes a person or thing better: *The new windows have better insulation and look more stylish— they are a big improvement over the old windows.*

2. The process of getting better: *After resting in bed for three days, Stanley started to feel better and began to show some improvement.*
im·prove·ment
(im-**proov**-muhnt)

imprisoned

improvise *verb*

1. To create or achieve something with whatever is available: *We improvised some curtains by using a couple of patterned sheets.*

2. To make something up on short notice: *The band improvised some background music while waiting for the singer to come onstage.*
im·pro·vise (**im**-pruh-*vize*)
▷ *verb* **improvising, improvised**
▷ *noun* **improvisation** (im-*prah*-vuh-**zay**-shuhn)
▷ *noun* **improviser**

imprudent *adjective* Lacking in good judgment; unwise: *It was imprudent to schedule the trip without confirming that everyone was free to travel on those dates.* **im·pru·dent** (im-**proo**-duhnt)

impudent *adjective* Bold and disrespectful, as in *an impudent joke.* **im·pu·dent** (**im**-pyuh-duhnt)
▷ *noun* **impudence** ▷ *adverb* **impudently**

impulse *noun*

1. A sudden urge to do something: *I had a wild impulse to buy the computer.*

2. A sudden push or thrust.

3. A pulse of energy, as in *an electrical impulse.*
im·pulse (**im**-puhls)

impulsive *adjective* Acting on impulse, or done on impulse, as in *an impulsive person.* **im·pul·sive** (im-**puhl**-siv)
▷ *adverb* **impulsively**

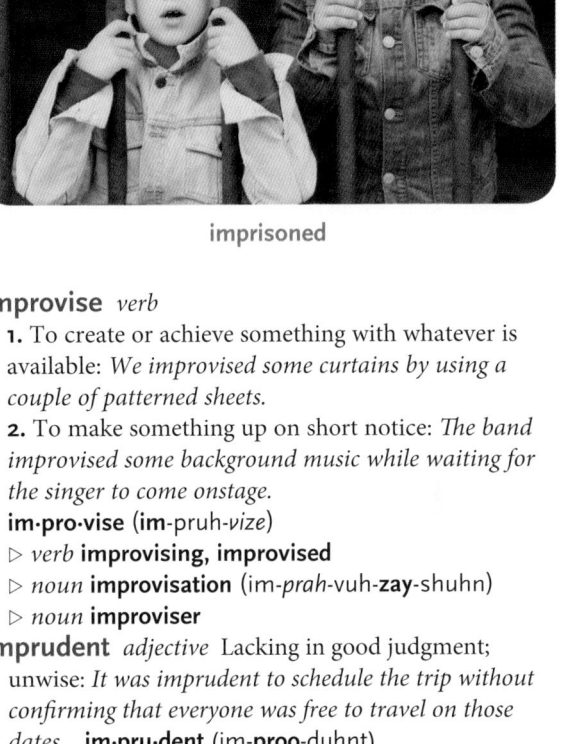
impudent behavior

impure *adjective*

1. Unclean or contaminated, as in *impure water.*

2. Mixed with foreign substances, as in *an impure metal.*
im·pure (im-**pyoor**)
▷ *adverb* **impurely**

a
b
c
d
e
f
g
h
i
j
k
l
m
n
o
p
q
r
s
t
u
v
w
x
y
z

in

  1. *preposition* Inside an enclosed space: *Your socks are in the top drawer.*

  2. *preposition* Into: *Let's put it in the house.*

  3. *preposition* During, as in *in the autumn.*

  4. *adverb* In or into some condition, relation, or place, as in *to join in* or *to fall in.*

  5. *adverb* Inside a certain place: *The rain is keeping us in today.*

  in (in)

  In sounds like **inn.**

in. Short for **inch** or the plural form *inches.*

inability *noun* Lack of power or ability: *Marisol's inability to arrive on time made us all late.* **in·a·bil·i·ty** (*in*-uh-**bil**-i-tee)

inaccessible *adjective* Not reachable; not able to be accessed, reached, or contacted: *The monastery is in a nearly inaccessible area high in the mountains.* **in·ac·ces·si·ble** (*in*-uhk-**ses**-uh-buhl)

inaccurate *adjective*

  1. Not precise or correct.

  2. Off the mark; not on target.

  in·ac·cu·rate (in-**ak**-yur-it)

  ▷ *noun* **inaccuracy** (in-**ak**-yur-uh-see)

  ▷ *adverb* **inaccurately**

inadequate *adjective* Not enough or not good enough: *That jacket is inadequate for snowy weather.* **in·ad·e·quate** (in-**ad**-i-kwit) ▷ *adverb* **inadequately**

inanimate *adjective* Something that has no life is **inanimate.** Rocks and buildings are inanimate objects. **in·an·i·mate** (in-**an**-uh-mit)

inappropriate *adjective* Unsuitable for the situation: *That outfit is inappropriate for school.* **in·ap·pro·pri·ate** (*in*-uh-**proh**-pree-it) ▷ *adverb* **inappropriately**

inarticulate *adjective* Unable to express yourself clearly in speech or writing. **in·ar·tic·u·late** (*in*-ahr-**tik**-yuh-lit)

inaudible *adjective* Impossible to hear. **in·au·di·ble** (in-**aw**-duh-buhl) ▷ *noun* **inaudibility** ▷ *adverb* **inaudibly**

inaugurate *verb*

  1. To swear a public official into office with a formal ceremony, as in *to inaugurate a president.*

  2. To open formally, or to begin to use publicly, as in *to inaugurate a new plan.*

  in·au·gu·rate (in-**aw**-gyuh-*rate*)

  ▷ *verb* **inaugurating, inaugurated**

inauguration *noun* The ceremony of swearing in a public official. **in·au·gu·ra·tion** (in-*aw*-gyuh-**ray**-shuhn)

Word History

Before a government official could take office in ancient Rome, people wanted to see whether the gods thought this was a good idea. So special priests called *augurs* would look at how birds were flying in the air, and find clues about whether the gods approved. The word **inauguration** has its roots in this Roman practice of predicting the future, known as *augury.*

---

inborn *adjective* Existing from birth and natural to a person: *Janine has an inborn sense of style.* **in·born** (**in**-*born*)

inbound *adjective* Moving or traveling toward a particular place: *Inbound traffic to Kansas City was really heavy because we got there just at the morning rush hour.* **in·bound** (**in**-*bound*)

inbox *noun*

  1. A tray on a desk or table for mail and other paperwork that needs to be done.

  2. In a computer mail system, the folder that contains all the emails that have come in.

  in·box (**in**-*bahks*)

  ▷ *noun, plural* **inboxes**

incandescent *adjective*

  1. Glowing with light as a result of being heated, as in *an incandescent bulb.*

  2. Radiant or brightly shining, as in *an incandescent smile.*

  in·can·des·cent (*in*-kuhn-**des**-uhnt)

incapable *adjective* Unable to do something: *My brother is incapable of writing neatly.* **in·ca·pa·ble** (in-**kay**-puh-buhl)

incarcerate *verb* To put in prison as punishment for a crime: *He was incarcerated for ten years on a charge of felony arson.* **in·car·cer·ate** (in-**kahr**-suh-*rate*) ▷ *verb* **incarcerating, incarcerated**

incense

  1. (**in**-sens) *noun* A substance that is burned to produce a pleasant smell.

  2. (in-**sens**) *verb* To make very angry: *The governor's speech about budget cuts incensed the state employees.* ▷ *verb* **incensing, incensed** **in·cense**

incentive *noun* Inspiration to do something: *The chance to win a prize gave the Girl Scout troops the incentive to sell more cookies.* **in·cen·tive** (in-**sen**-tiv)

inch

  1. *noun* A unit of length equal to $\frac{1}{12}$ of a foot. The diameter of a quarter measures about an inch.

  2. *noun* A very small distance: *We couldn't budge the boulder an inch.*

incinerator

3. *verb* To move very slowly: *Miriam inched her way through the crowd.* ▷ *verb* **inches, inching, inched inch** (inch)
▷ *noun, plural* **inches**

inchworm *noun* A caterpillar that moves by arching and stretching its body. **inch·worm** (**inch**-*wurm*)

incident *noun* Something that happens; an event, as in *an unfortunate incident.* **in·ci·dent** (**in**-si-duhnt)

incidentally *adverb* A word used to add a remark unrelated to the original subject: *We're leaving tomorrow, and, incidentally, I can't find my toothbrush.* **in·ci·den·tal·ly** (in-si-**dent**-uh-lee)

incinerator *noun* A furnace for burning garbage and other waste materials. **in·cin·er·a·tor** (in-**sin**-uh-*ray*-tur)

incision *noun* A precise cut made by a knife or blade: *The surgeon made an incision in order to take out my appendix.* **in·ci·sion** (in-**sizh**-uhn)

incisor *noun* A kind of tooth in the front of the mouth that is used for cutting. Humans have four upper incisors and four lower incisors. **in·ci·sor** (in-**sye**-zur)

incite *verb* To stir up feelings that make someone do something violent or foolish. **in·cite** (in-**site**)
▷ *verb* **inciting, incited**

incline *verb* To lean or slant. **in·cline** (in-**kline**)
▷ *verb* **inclining, inclined**
▷ *noun* **incline** (**in**-kline)

inclined *adjective*
1. Leaning or slanting.
2. Liking or tending to do

inchworm

something: *I'm inclined to fall asleep when it's hot.*
in·clined (in-**klinde**)
▷ *noun* **inclination** (in-kluh-**nay**-shuhn)

include *verb* To contain something or someone as part of a whole: *The cost of the meal includes dessert.* **in·clude** (in-**klood**) ▷ *verb* **including, included**

inclusion *noun* The act of including somebody or something: *The inclusion of good maps made the history book very useful.* **in·clu·sion** (in-**kloo**-zhuhn)

inclusive *adjective*
1. Covering everything: *The workweek is Monday to Friday, inclusive.*
2. Welcoming to everyone: *The country has an open and inclusive immigration policy.* ▷ *noun* **inclusiveness in·clu·sive** (in-**kloo**-siv)

incoherent *adjective* Not clear or logical; difficult to understand: *There was an incoherent message on my answering machine.* **in·co·her·ent** (in-koh-**heer**-uhnt) ▷ *adverb* **incoherently**

income *noun* The money that a person earns or receives, especially from working: *Both of her parents earn a good income.* **in·come** (**in**-kuhm)

income tax *noun* A payment made to the government based on the amount of money a person earns. ▷ *noun, plural* **income taxes**

incompatible *adjective*
1. Unable to get along: *Hilary's friends are incompatible with her brother's buddies.*
2. Unable to work together or to be used together: *This printer is incompatible with our computer.* **in·com·pat·i·ble** (in-kuhm-**pat**-uh-buhl)
▷ *noun* **incompatibility**

incompetent *adjective* Unable to do something successfully. **in·com·pe·tent** (in-**kahm**-pi-tuhnt) ▷ *noun* **incompetence** ▷ *adverb* **incompetently**

incomplete *adjective* Not having all the necessary parts; not finished or complete: *The new deck is still incomplete.* **in·com·plete** (in-kuhm-**pleet**) ▷ *adverb* **incompletely**

incomprehensible *adjective* Impossible to understand: *This portion of the novel is incomprehensible.* **in·com·pre·hen·si·ble** (in-kahm-pri-**hen**-suh-buhl)

inconceivable *adjective* Not believable: *It is inconceivable that your dog ate your homework again.* **in·con·ceiv·a·ble** (in-kuhn-**see**-vuh-buhl)
▷ *adverb* **inconceivably**

inconclusive *adjective* Unclear or uncertain, as in *inconclusive data.* **in·con·clu·sive** (in-kuhn-**kloo**-siv)
▷ *adverb* **inconclusively**

inconsiderate *adjective* Not caring about other people's needs or feelings. **in·con·sid·er·ate** (*in*-kuhn-**sid**-ur-it) ▷ *adverb* **inconsiderately**

inconspicuous *adjective* Not easy to see; not attracting attention: *Conrad felt uneasy and bashful at the party, so he stayed in a corner and tried to look inconspicuous.* **in·con·spic·u·ous** (*in*-kuhn-**spik**-yoo-uhs) ▷ *adverb* **inconspicuously**

inconvenience
1. *noun* Trouble or difficulty.
2. *noun* Something that causes trouble or difficulty: *Walking the two miles to school is a real inconvenience.*
3. *verb* To cause trouble or difficulty: *I don't want to inconvenience you by visiting at a bad time.* ▷ *verb* **inconveniencing, inconvenienced** **in·con·ven·ience** (*in*-kuhn-**veen**-yuhns)

inconvenient *adjective* Causing difficulty or discomfort: *This closet is in an inconvenient place.* **in·con·ven·ient** (*in*-kuhn-**veen**-yuhnt) ▷ *adverb* **inconveniently**

incorporate *verb*
1. To include something as part of another thing: *We've incorporated a new dance number into our performance.*
2. To make or become a corporation. **in·cor·po·rate** (in-**kor**-puh-*rate*) ▷ *verb* **incorporating, incorporated** ▷ *noun* **incorporation** ▷ *adjective* **incorporated**

incorrect *adjective* Wrong. **in·cor·rect** (*in*-kuh-**rekt**) ▷ *adverb* **incorrectly**

incorrigible *adjective* Not able to be corrected or made better, as in *an incorrigible problem* or *an incorrigible liar.* **in·cor·ri·gi·ble** (in-**kor**-i-juh-buhl)

increase *verb* To become larger: *The number of students in the school increases every year.* **in·crease** (in-**krees**) ▷ *verb* **increasing, increased** ▷ *noun* **increase** (**in**-krees) ▷ *adverb* **increasingly**

incredible *adjective* Unbelievable or amazing: *He spent an incredible amount of money to build that place.* **in·cred·i·ble** (in-**kred**-uh-buhl) ▷ *adverb* **incredibly**

incredulous *adjective* Unable to believe something or accept that something is true: *When I heard that my favorite teacher was retiring, I was incredulous.* **in·cred·u·lous** (in-**krej**-uh-luhs) ▷ *adverb* **incredulously**

incriminate *verb* To provide evidence that someone is guilty of something: *The man incriminated his friend in the robbery.* **in·crim·i·nate** (in-**krim**-uh-*nate*) ▷ *verb* **incriminating, incriminated** ▷ *noun* **incrimination**

incubate *verb*
1. To keep eggs warm before they hatch.
2. To keep a premature or sick baby safe and warm in a specially heated apparatus.
3. To nurture, or to allow to develop, as in *to incubate an idea.* **in·cu·bate** (**ing**-kyuh-*bate*) ▷ *verb* **incubating, incubated** ▷ *noun* **incubation**

incubator *noun*
1. A heated container in which premature or sick babies are kept safe and warm.
2. A container that keeps eggs warm until they hatch. **in·cu·ba·tor** (**ing**-kyuh-*bay*-tur)

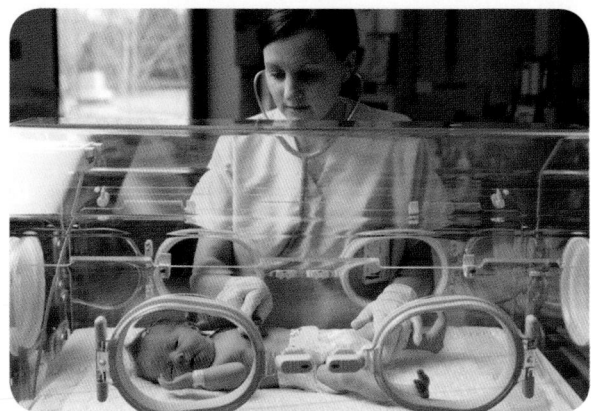

incubator

incur *verb* To make something happen, especially something that is not good: *She was careful not to incur unnecessary expenses.* **in·cur** (in-**kur**) ▷ *verb* **incurring, incurred**

incurable *adjective* Unable to be made well or healthy: *The doctor said that the patient's disease was incurable.* **in·cur·a·ble** (in-**kyoor**-uh-buhl)

indebted *adjective*
1. You can be **indebted** to someone for a favor that person did for you: *I am indebted to Pablo for his help.*
2. A person who owes money to a bank is **indebted** to the bank. **in·debt·ed** (in-**det**-id) ▷ *noun* **indebtedness**

indecent *adjective* Inappropriate or obscene, as in *indecent language.* **in·de·cent** (in-**dee**-suhnt) ▷ *noun* **indecency** ▷ *adverb* **indecently**

indeed *adverb* Truly: *We are indeed lucky to be in good health.* **in·deed** (in-**deed**)

indefinite
1. *adjective* Unclear or uncertain, as in *an indefinite amount of time.* ▷ *adverb* **indefinitely**
2. **indefinite article** *noun* The grammatical term for *a* or *an*, used before a noun when it refers to something

general or not specific, as in *a baseball* or *an orange.* **in·def·i·nite** (in-**def**-uh-nit)

indent *verb* To start a line of writing or typing farther from the margin: *Always indent the beginning of a new paragraph.* **in·dent** (in-**dent**) ▷ *verb* **indenting, indented** ▷ *noun* **indent** (**in**-dent) ▷ *noun* **indentation** (in-den-**tay**-shuhn)

independence *noun* Freedom; the condition of being independent. **in·de·pen·dence** (in-di-**pen**-duhns)

Independence Day *noun* A US holiday, celebrated on July 4th, to commemorate the signing of the Declaration of Independence in 1776. Also called the **Fourth of July.**

independent

1. *adjective* Not controlled or affected by other people or things: *The colonists wanted to be independent of England.*

2. *adjective* Not wanting or needing much help from other people: *Although Rob is blind, he tries to be as independent as possible.*

3. independent clause *noun* A sentence that can stand alone and be grammatical: *The sentence "He likes to swim" is an example of an independent clause. See* **dependent clause.**

in·de·pend·ent (in-di-**pen**-duhnt)

independently *adverb*

1. With no outside control or interference: *If my friends like a TV show, I'll take a look at it but then make up my mind independently about whether to watch it.*

2. If one thing works, acts, or operates **independently of** another, neither one influences the other: *Like public schools, charter schools are publicly funded and free, but they operate independently of local school districts.*

in·de·pen·dent·ly (in-di-**pen**-duhnt-lee)

indestructible *adjective* Unable to be destroyed. **in·de·struc·ti·ble** (in-di-**struhk**-tuh-buhl) ▷ *adverb* **indestructibly**

index

1. *noun* An alphabetical list showing where to find things in a book: *In most books, the index is at the back.* ▷ *noun, plural* **indexes** or **indices** (**in**-di-*seez*)

2. *verb* To supply with an index: *It helps readers if a book has been indexed.*

3. *verb* To arrange in the form of an index: *The* program automatically extracts all the words in a document and indexes them. ▷ *noun* **indexer** **in·dex** (**in**-deks)

▷ *verb* **indexes, indexing, indexed**

index finger *noun* The finger next to the thumb, used for pointing.

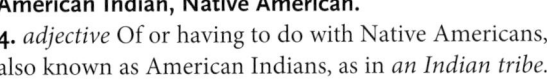
index finger

Indian

1. *noun* A person from India.

2. *adjective* Of or having to do with India, its people, or its culture.

3. *noun* A Native American. *See* **American Indian, Native American.**

4. *adjective* Of or having to do with Native Americans, also known as American Indians, as in *an Indian tribe.* **In·di·an** (**in**-dee-uhn)

Indian Ocean *noun* The third-largest ocean in the world. It is bordered by Africa to the west, India to the north, and Indochina and Australia to the east.

Independence Day

indicate *verb*

1. To show something: *The number of new jobs indicates that the economy is beginning to recover.* ▷ *adjective* **indicative** (in-**dik**-uh-tiv)

2. To point out something: *A road sign indicates the route to the beach.* **in·di·cate** (**in**-di-*kate*)

▷ *verb* **indicating, indicated**

indication *noun* Something that indicates or points out: *A fever is an indication of infection.* **in·di·ca·tion** (in-di-**kay**-shuhn)

indicator *noun* Something that shows or points out something else: *The turn indicator shows which way a car is about to turn.* **in·di·ca·tor** (**in**-di-*kay*-tur)

indict *verb* To officially charge someone with a crime: *The man was indicted for murder.* **in·dict** (in-**dite**) ▷ *verb* **indicting, indicted** ▷ *noun* **indictment**

indifferent *adjective* Not caring much about something: *Valerie felt indifferent about the movie and was surprised that everyone else liked it so much.* **in·dif·fer·ent** (in-**dif**-ur-uhnt) ▷ *noun* **indifference** ▷ *adverb* **indifferently**

indigestion *noun* Discomfort in the stomach because of difficulty digesting food. **in·di·ges·tion** (in-di-**jes**-chuhn)

indignant *adjective* Annoyed about something that seems unfair: *Adamo was indignant when he was accused of cheating.* **in·dig·nant** (in-**dig**-nuhnt) ▷ *noun* **indignation** (in-dig-**nay**-shuhn) ▷ *adverb* **indignantly**

indigo *noun*
1. A plant with dark purple berries from which a dark blue dye can be made.
2. A dark violet-blue color or dye.
in·di·go (**in**-di-*goh*)
▷ *noun, plural* **indigos** *or* **indigoes**

indirect *adjective*
1. Not in a straight line, as in *an indirect path.*
2. Not directly connected: *Making new friends is an indirect benefit of joining the drama club.*
3. Not to the point: *Yusuf answered my question in an indirect way.*
4. indirect object Someone or something that is affected by the action of a verb in a sentence, but is not the direct object. For example, in the sentence "Josh threw me the ball," the word *ball* is the direct object and *me* is the indirect object.
in·di·rect (*in*-duh-**rekt**)
▷ *adverb* **indirectly**

indiscriminate *adjective* Not carefully chosen or thought out: *The indiscriminate use of these herbicides has made some weeds resistant to them.* **in·dis·crim·i·nate** (*in*-dis-**krim**-uh-nit)

indispensable *adjective* Absolutely necessary. **in·dis·pen·sa·ble** (*in*-di-**spen**-suh-buhl) ▷ *adverb* **indispensably**

individual
1. *adjective* Single and separate: *The individual pieces fit together to form a cube.*
2. *noun* A person, as in *a tall individual.*
3. *adjective* Unusual or different: *Jenna has a very individual dancing style.*
in·di·vid·u·al (*in*-di-**vij**-oo-uhl)

individuality *noun* The qualities that set a person apart from all others. **in·di·vid·u·al·i·ty** (*in*-di-*vij*-oo-**al**-i-tee)

individually *adverb* Separately or one at a time: *The director of the play thanked each cast member individually.* **in·di·vid·u·al·ly** (*in*-di-**vij**-oo-uh-lee)

indivisible *adjective* Unable to be divided or broken into pieces. **in·di·vis·i·ble** (*in*-di-**viz**-uh-buhl) ▷ *adverb* **indivisibly**

indoor *adjective* Used, done, or built inside: *An indoor mall is a nice place to shop on a hot day.* **in·door** (**in**-*dor*)

indoors *adverb* Inside a building: *We played indoors because of the rain.* **in·doors** (**in**-dorz)

induce *verb*
1. To persuade someone to do something: *May I*

indigo

induce you to buy something at our bake sale?
2. To cause something to happen: *With certain kinds of poisons, you can get rid of the poison by drinking an antidote that induces vomiting.*
in·duce (in-**doos**)
▷ *verb* **inducing, induced**

indulge *verb*
1. To give in to a person's wishes: *Gustav's grandparents indulge him by buying him anything he wants.* ▷ *adjective* **indulgent**
2. If you **indulge in** something, you take pleasure in it.
in·dulge (in-**duhlj**)
▷ *verb* **indulging, indulged** ▷ *noun* **indulgence**

industrial *adjective*
1. Of or having to do with factories and making things in large quantities: *The manufacturing plants in the city's industrial zone are busy around the clock.*
2. Having an economy that is based on factories and making things, as in *an industrial society.*
in·dus·tri·al (in-**duhs**-tree-uhl)
▷ *adverb* **industrially**

industry *noun*
1. Manufacturing companies and other businesses, taken together: *Our town needs more industry.*
2. A single branch of business or trade, as in *the tourist industry.*
3. Hard work or effort: *Thanks to Dana's industry, the project was completed on time.* ▷ *adjective* **industrious** (in-**duhs**-tree-uhs)
in·dus·try (**in**-duh-stree)
▷ *noun, plural* **industries**

inefficient *adjective* Ineffective and wasteful: *It is inefficient to write your essay by hand if you can key it into your computer.* **in·ef·fi·cient** (*in*-uh-**fish**-uhnt) ▷ *noun* **inefficiency** ▷ *adverb* **inefficiently**

inequality *noun* Differences that seem unfair between people or things: *Inequality of incomes means that some people are much richer than others.* **in·e·qual·i·ty** (*in*-i-**kwah**-li-tee) ▷ *noun, plural* **inequalities**

inert *adjective*
1. Not moving.
2. Not reacting easily with other chemicals or substances.
in·ert (i-**nurt**)

inertia *noun*
1. Unwillingness to move or act because of laziness or tiredness.
2. A physical property of objects that means they stay

at rest or keep moving in the same way unless an outside force acts on them. **in·er·tia** (i-**nur**-shuh)

inevitable *adjective* Certain to happen: *The end of our vacation was inevitable.* **in·ev·i·ta·ble** (i-**nev**-i-tuh-buhl) ▷ *noun* **inevitability** ▷ *adverb* **inevitably**

inexcusable *adjective* So bad that it cannot be excused: *Sebastian's rudeness to his elderly aunt was inexcusable and angered his parents.* **in·ex·cus·a·ble** (*in*-ik-**skyoo**-zuh-buhl)

inexpensive *adjective* Not costing a lot of money. **in·ex·pen·sive** (*in*-ik-**spen**-siv) ▷ *adverb* **inexpensively**

inexperienced *adjective* Having little practice in doing something: *He is a new and inexperienced lawyer.* **in·ex·pe·ri·enced** (*in*-ik-**speer**-ee-uhnst)

inexplicable *adjective* Impossible to explain. **in·ex·pli·ca·ble** (*in*-ik-**splik**-uh-buhl *or* in-**ek**-spli-kuh-buhl) ▷ *adverb* **inexplicably**

infallible *adjective* Not capable of making mistakes or of being wrong: *DNA testing for this condition is not infallible.* **in·fal·li·ble** (in-**fal**-uh-buhl) ▷ *noun* **infallibility** (in-*fal*-uh-**bil**-i-tee)

infamous *adjective* Having a very bad reputation: *Jesse James was an infamous outlaw.* **in·fa·mous** (**in**-fuh-muhs)

infant *noun* A newborn child. Babies are considered infants until the time they can walk. **in·fant** (**in**-fuhnt) ▷ *noun* **infancy** (**in**-fuhn-see) ▷ *adjective* **infant**

infantry *noun* The foot soldiers of an army: *At the outbreak of World War II, my grandfather joined the infantry.* **in·fan·try** (**in**-fuhn-tree)

Word History

The **infantry** of an army is composed of foot soldiers. This part of an army was named for the youth of the soldiers, because the word *infantry* is based on the Latin word for "child," *infant-*. In Latin, *in-* meant "not," and *fant-* was the present participle of the verb "speak," *fari*. So *infant-* meant "not speaking." The word became *infante* in Italian, meaning "a youth." From *infante*, Italian speakers created the word *infanteria*, meaning "foot soldiers." *Infanteria* became the English word *infantry*.

infatuated *adjective* So strongly attracted to someone that you can no longer think sensibly about that person: *Polly is infatuated with the movie star.* **in·fat·u·at·ed** (in-**fach**-oo-*ay*-tid) ▷ *noun* **infatuation**

infect *verb* To cause disease or contaminate by

inferno

introducing germs or viruses: *Some mosquitoes carry malaria and can infect people when they bite.* **in·fect** (in-**fekt**) ▷ *verb* **infecting, infected** ▷ *adjective* **infected**

infection *noun* An illness caused by bacteria or viruses: *The infection was treated with an antibiotic.* **in·fec·tion** (in-**fek**-shuhn)

infectious *adjective*
1. Spread from one person to another by bacteria or viruses in the air or on objects, as in *an infectious disease*.
2. Easily passed from one person to another, as in *an infectious mood*.
in·fec·tious (in-**fek**-shuhs)

infer *verb* To draw a conclusion after considering all the facts: *We inferred from Beth's silence that she did not agree with our decision.* **in·fer** (in-**fur**) ▷ *verb* **inferring, inferred** ▷ *noun* **inference** (**in**-fur-uhns)

inferior *adjective* Not as good; lower in quality: *I traded my inferior backpack for a better one.* **in·fe·ri·or** (in-**feer**-ee-ur) ▷ *noun* **inferiority** (in-*feer*-ee-**or**-i-tee)

inferno *noun*
1. A huge, destructive fire: *Within minutes the whole building was a blazing inferno.*
2. A condition or place that is like hell, especially with a raging fire or with a lot of human suffering and death, as in *the inferno of the Holocaust* or *the inferno of a nuclear attack*.
in·fer·no (in-**fur**-noh)

infertile *adjective*
1. Unsuitable for growing crops and plants, as in *infertile land*.
2. Unable to have offspring, as in *an infertile cow*.
in·fer·tile (in-**fur**-tuhl) ▷ *noun* **infertility** (*in*-fur-**til**-i-tee)

a b c d e f g h **i** j k l m n o p q r s t u v w x y z

infest *verb* To be present in large numbers in a way that causes harm or disease: *The mattress was infested with bedbugs and we had to throw it out.* **in·fest** (in-**fest**) ▷ *verb* **infesting, infested** ▷ *noun* **infestation** (in-fes-**tay**-shuhn)

infested *adjective* Full of harmful animals or insects: *The kitchen is infested with ants.* **in·fes·ted** (in-**fes**-tid)

infield *noun* In baseball, the area enclosed by home plate and the bases, or the group of players at first base, second base, shortstop, and third base. **in·field** (in-*feeld*) ▷ *noun* **infielder**

infield

infinite *adjective*
1. Without end, as in *infinite choices.*
2. Too large to be measured or counted: *I bet there are an infinite number of stars.*
in·fi·nite (in-**fuh**-nit)
▷ *noun* **infinity** (in-**fin**-i-tee) ▷ *adverb* **infinitely**

infinitive *noun* The basic form of a verb, often preceded by *to*, for example, *to run, to be, to write.* **in·fin·i·tive** (in-**fin**-i-tiv)

infirm *adjective* Weak or ill: *The elderly woman was blind and infirm.* **in·firm** (in-**furm**) ▷ *noun* **infirmity** (in-**fur**-mi-tee)

infirmary *noun* A place where sick people are cared for, as in *a school infirmary.* **in·fir·ma·ry** (in-**fur**-mur-ee)

inflame *verb*
1. To make hot, red, or swollen, usually as the result of an infection or injury.
2. To stir up or excite the emotions of a person or group: *The speaker inflamed the crowd's hatred.*
in·flame (in-**flame**)
▷ *verb* **inflaming, inflamed**

inflammable *adjective* Able to catch fire easily. **in·flam·ma·ble** (in-**flam**-uh-buhl)

---

inflammation *noun* Redness, swelling, heat, and pain, usually caused by an infection or injury. **in·flam·ma·tion** (in-fluh-**may**-shuhn)

inflatable *adjective* Able to be expanded by filling with air. **in·flat·a·ble** (in-**flay**-tuh-buhl) ▷ *noun* **inflatable**

inflate *verb*
1. To make something expand by blowing or pumping air into it: *Aziz used a pump to inflate his bike tires.*
2. To increase or improve, sometimes deceptively: *The success of George's store inflated his hopes of becoming rich.*
in·flate (in-**flate**)
▷ *verb* **inflating, inflated**

inflation *noun*
1. A general increase in prices. ▷ *adjective* **inflationary** (in-**flay**-shuh-*ner*-ee)
2. The process of making something expand by blowing air into it.
in·fla·tion (in-**flay**-shuhn)

inflect *verb* To change the form of a word according to the job it is doing in a sentence. **in·flect** (in-**flekt**) ▷ *verb* **inflecting, inflected**

inflection *noun* A slightly changed form of a word that affects some aspect of its meaning. For example, *striking, struck,* and *stricken* are inflections of the verb *strike.* **in·flec·tion** (in-**flek**-shuhn)

inflexible *adjective*
1. Unable to bend, as in *an inflexible material.*
2. Unable to change; rigid, as in *inflexible rules.*
in·flex·i·ble (in-**flek**-suh-buhl)
▷ *noun* **inflexibility** (in-*flek*-suh-**bil**-i-tee) ▷ *adverb* **inflexibly**

inflict *verb* To harm someone or something: *She twisted his arm to inflict pain.* **in·flict** (in-**flikt**) ▷ *verb* **inflicting, inflicted** ▷ *noun* **infliction**

influence *verb* To have an effect on someone or something: *My mother often influences my decisions.* **in·flu·ence** (**in**-floo-uhns) ▷ *verb* **influencing, influenced** ▷ *noun* **influence**

influential *adjective* Having the power to change or affect someone or something, as in *an influential senator.* **in·flu·en·tial** (*in*-floo-**en**-shuhl)

influenza *noun* An illness caused by a virus. *See* **flu.** in·flu·en·za (*in*-floo-**en**-zuh)

influx *noun* A movement inward of something, especially a large amount or number: *Authorities are struggling to deal with the massive influx of refugees.* in·flux (**in**-*fluhks*)

infomercial *noun* A program-length TV commercial with detailed information about a service or product. in·fo·mer·cial (*in*-foh-**mur**-shuhl)

inform *verb*
1. To tell someone something: *Liam informed me that he was accepted into medical school.*
2. To give information to the police about a criminal: *After he was caught, the thief informed on his accomplices.*
in·form (in-**form**)
▷ *verb* **informing, informed** ▷ *noun* **informer**
▷ *noun* **informant**

informal *adjective*
1. Relaxed and casual, as in *an informal outfit.*
▷ *noun* **informality** (*in*-for-**mal**-i-tee)
2. Unofficial: *The police made an informal investigation but didn't arrest anyone.*
3. Informal language is used in everyday speech but not usually in formal speaking or in writing. For example, saying that Ivy is "gonna have a cow" is an informal way of saying that she is "going to be very upset."
in·for·mal (in-**for**-muhl)
▷ *adverb* **informally**

information *noun* Facts and knowledge you get from exploring something, or that you learn by listening: *Before I went to San Francisco, I looked up information about it online.* in·for·ma·tion (*in*-fur-**may**-shuhn)

information technology *noun* The use of computers and other electronic equipment to find, create, store, or communicate information. Abbreviated as *IT.*

informative *adjective* Providing useful information: *My guidebook to Paris is very informative.* in·for·ma·tive (in-**for**-muh-tiv)

infrared
1. *adjective* Of or having to do with a type of energy that produces heat and has radiation wavelengths that are longer than visible light waves but shorter than radio waves, as in *infrared rays.*
2. *adjective* Using or able to detect infrared light, as in *an infrared camera.*
3. *noun* Infrared radiation. Also known as **infrared light**.
in·fra·red (*in*-fruh-**red**)

infrastructure *noun* The structures and services that a population depends on because everyone uses them, such as roads, bridges, railroads, drinking water, schools, internet, and commercial transportation: *Critics say that the new budget doesn't have enough money to maintain the city's infrastructure.* in·fra·struc·ture (**in**-fruh-*struhk*-chur)

infrequent *adjective* Not happening very often. in·fre·quent (in-**free**-kwuhnt) ▷ *adverb* **infrequently**

infuriate *verb* To make someone extremely angry. in·fu·ri·ate (in-**fyoor**-ee-*ate*) ▷ *verb* **infuriating, infuriated** ▷ *adjective* **infuriating** ▷ *adverb* **infuriatingly**

inflate

Suffix

The suffix **-ing** has important jobs in English. You use it to form the present participles of verbs to indicate that something is continuing to happen, as in *going, seeing,* and *falling.* They are made by adding *-ing* to the verbs *go, see,* and *fall.*

1. You can also use the *-ing* form of a verb as a noun when you are discussing the activity meant by the verb. In the sentence "Swimming is as much fun as diving," the nouns *swimming* and *diving* describe two types of actions.

2. The *-ing* form of a verb is also useful as an adjective. For example, in *a developing story,* the adjective tells you that the story is developing right now. The meaning of the adjective is closely related to the meaning of the verb.

---

ingenious *adjective* Inventive and original, as in *an ingenious solution.* in·gen·ious (in-**jeen**-yuhs) ▷ *adverb* **ingeniously**

ingenuity *noun* The ability to be inventive and original, especially in order to solve a problem: *Lesley used her ingenuity to repair the broken toy.* in·ge·nu·i·ty (*in*-juh-**noo**-i-tee)

ingot *noun* A mass of metal that has been shaped into a block or bar. **in·got** (**ing**-guht)

ingredient *noun* An item used to make something, as in *an ingredient in a recipe.* **in·gre·di·ent** (in-**gree**-dee-uhnt)

inhabit *verb* To live in a place: *Some robins inhabit the tree by my window.* **in·hab·it** (in-**hab**-it) ▷ *verb* **inhabiting, inhabited**

inhabitant *noun* Someone who lives in a particular place: *The Canadian province of Ontario has more than 13 million inhabitants.* **in·hab·i·tant** (in-**hab**-i-tuhnt)

inhale *verb* To breathe in: *After being cooped up all day, it feels great to go outside and inhale the fresh air.* **in·hale** (in-**hayl**) ▷ *verb* **inhaling, inhaled** ▷ *noun* **inhalation** (*in*-huh-**lay**-shuhn)

inhaler *noun* A small device for inhaling medicine through your mouth: *Sean uses an inhaler for his asthma.* **in·hal·er** (in-**hay**-lur)

inherent *adjective* Existing as a natural and characteristic part of something: *Toxic chemicals present an inherent danger to human health.* **in·her·ent** (in-**heer**-uhnt *or* in-**her**-uhnt) ▷ *adverb* **inherently**

inherit *verb*
1. To receive money, property, or a title from someone who has died: *We inherited my great-aunt's china when she died.*
2. To receive a particular characteristic from one of your parents: *I inherited my hazel eyes from my father.* **in·her·it** (in-**her**-it) ▷ *verb* **inheriting, inherited**

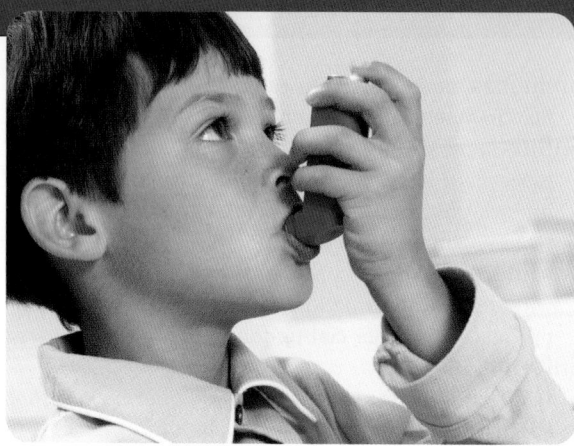
inhaler

Word History

In the 17th century and earlier, you could **inherit** someone. This meant that you made a will leaving all your possessions to a single person named as your heir. You can still see this old meaning in the word *disinherit.* But the word *inherit* now only has the sense of "receiving" something from someone who has died, or "receiving" a characteristic from your parents. So the meaning is almost the opposite of the original one. The Latin word for "heir," *heres*, was the source of the English word *inherit.*

inheritance *noun*
1. The money and property that someone inherits, usually from parents or grandparents: *They spent all of their inheritance on a beach condo.*
2. The action of inheriting: *The rules and customs of inheritance differ greatly from one culture to another.* **in·her·it·ance** (in-**her**-i-tuhns)

inhibit *verb*
1. To stop the progress or development of something, or to stop something from happening: *This soap has special ingredients that inhibit or kill off germs.*
2. To make someone feel too embarrassed or shy to do something: *Fear of making mistakes can inhibit people from trying new things.* **in·hib·it** (in-**hib**-it) ▷ *verb* **inhibiting, inhibited** ▷ *adjective* **inhibited**

inhibition *noun*
1. A feeling of embarrassment or shyness that stops you from doing something. The word is often used in the plural: *Don't let your inhibitions keep you from getting out on the dance floor and having a great time.*
2. The act or process of stopping the progress or development of something: *The drug seems to help in the inhibition of cancer cells, keeping them from dividing.* **in·hi·bi·tion** (*in*-hi-**bish**-uhn)

inhuman *adjective* Lacking human qualities like sympathy or mercy; cruel, as in *inhuman treatment.* **in·hu·man** (in-**hyoo**-muhn) ▷ *noun* **inhumanity** (*in*-hyoo-**man**-i-tee) ▷ *adverb* **inhumanly**

initial
1. *noun* The first letter of a name or word.
2. *adjective* First, as in *an initial impression* or *an initial step.* ▷ *adverb* **initially**
3. *verb* To write your initials on; *Dr. Morris initialed the prescription.* ▷ *verb* **initialing, initialed** **in·i·tial** (i-**nish**-uhl)

initiate *verb*
1. To introduce or start something new: *I initiated a discussion on today's topic.*
2. To bring someone into a club or group, often with a ceremony: *Cory was initiated into the National Honor Society last week.* **i·ni·ti·ate** (i-**nish**-ee-*ate*) ▷ *verb* **initiating, initiated** ▷ *noun* **initiation**

initiative *noun* The ability to take action without being told what to do: *Jeff took the initiative in* *organizing the picnic.* **in·i·tia·tive** (i-**nish**-uh-tiv)

inject *verb*

1. To put medicine or nourishment into someone's body through a needle: *The nurse injected Petra with the flu vaccine.*

2. To add something needed: *The speaker's jokes injected a little humor into a tense situation.* **in·ject** (in-**jekt**)

▷ *verb* **injecting, injected**

injection *noun*

1. The introduction of medicine into the body through a thin needle; a shot: *The doctor gave me a malaria injection before my trip to Africa.*

2. The act of adding something needed: *Her speech was a morale booster and gave all of us an injection of enthusiasm.*

in·jec·tion (in-**jek**-shuhn)

injure *verb* To hurt or harm yourself or someone else: *Bev injured herself when she fell off her bicycle.* **in·jure** (in-**jur**) ▷ *verb* **injuring, injured**

injury *noun* Damage or harm: *Because of her injury, Nicolette couldn't play volleyball.* **in·ju·ry** (in-**jur**-ee) ▷ *noun, plural* **injuries** ▷ *adjective* **injurious** (in-**joor**-ee-uhs)

injustice *noun*

1. Unfairness or lack of justice, as in *the injustice of racial discrimination.*

2. An unfair situation or action: *You did me an injustice when you punished me for something I didn't do.* **in·jus·tice** (in-**juhs**-tis)

ink *noun* A colored liquid used for writing and printing. **ink** (ingk) ▷ *adjective* **inky**

inkjet *adjective* Of or having to do with a kind of printer that forms words and images by shooting tiny drops of ink onto paper. **ink·jet** (**ingk**-*jet*)

inland *adjective* Located away from the sea: *The inland states are very warm in summer.* **in·land** (**in**-luhnd) ▷ *adverb* **inland**

in-law *noun* A person who is related to someone because of a marriage, not because they both share the same ancestor. Usually when people refer to their in-laws, they mean their husband's or wife's parents: *We have the in-laws visiting all next week.*

inlet *noun* A narrow body of water that leads inland from a larger body of water, such as an ocean. **in·let** (**in**-let)

in-line skate *noun* A skate whose wheels are in a straight line.

inmate *noun* A person in prison or a hospital. **in·mate** (**in**-mate)

in-line skate

inn *noun* A small hotel that often includes a restaurant: *We stayed at an inn on Cape Cod.* **inn** (in) **Inn** sounds like **in**.

inner *adjective*

1. Inside, or near the center: *The inner part of the earth's core is extremely hot.*

2. Inside a person's own mind or self: *Elsa rarely shares her inner thoughts.* **in·ner** (**in**-ur)

inning *noun* A part of a baseball game in which each team gets a turn at bat: *No runs were scored during the first four innings of Friday's game.* **in·ning** (**in**-ing)

innocent *adjective*

1. Not guilty: *He was accused of stealing the watch but was able to prove that he was innocent.*

2. Not knowing much about the world; not sophisticated: *The boy was just four years old and was still very innocent and naive.*

3. Not knowing about something or not being involved in something: *Tanya was innocent of the gang's plans.* **in·no·cent** (**in**-uh-suhnt)

▷ *noun* **innocence** ▷ *adverb* **innocently**

Word History

The history of the word *innocent* tells us that an **innocent** person is "not harming" anyone. The Latin verb *nocere* meant "to harm." Its present participle was *nocent-*, meaning "harming." Latin speakers formed the word *innocent-* by adding the prefix *in-*, meaning "not," to the word *nocent-*. The original English meaning of *innocent* was "pure," and it could even mean "holy." But now we use this word when someone is not guilty of something or did not know about something.

innovation *noun* A new idea or invention: *The company's innovation is a more efficient lawn mower.* **in·no·va·tion** (*in*-uh-**vay**-shuhn) ▷ *verb* **innovate** ▷ *adjective* **innovative**

innovator *noun* Someone who has a talent for thinking of new ideas or new ways of doing things: *She was given an award for being an innovator in genetic research.* **in·no·va·tor** (**in**-uh-*vay*-tur)

inoculate *verb* To inject a weakened form of a disease into someone's body so that the person becomes protected against it: *The child was inoculated against mumps.* See also **vaccinate**. **in·oc·u·late** (i-**nah**-kyuh-*late*)

▷ *verb* **inoculating, inoculated** ▷ *noun* **inoculation**

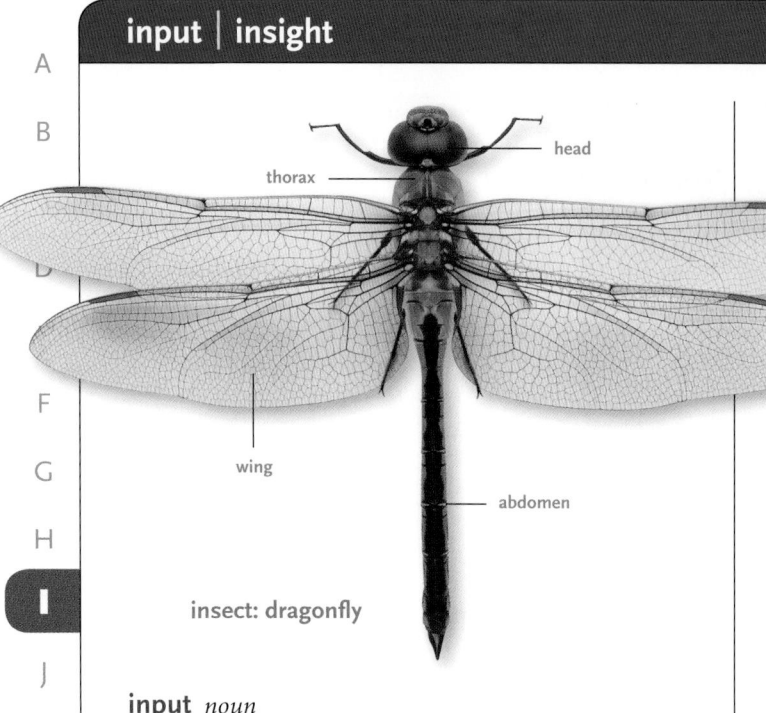

head

thorax

wing

abdomen

insect: dragonfly

input *noun*
1. Advice or information offered by a person: *Kara's input helped us solve the problem faster.*
2. Information fed into a computer. ▷ *verb* **input**
3. Something that is put in, such as energy to be used by a machine.
in·put (**in**-*put*)

inquire *verb* To ask about someone or something: *Monica inquired about the cost of a new car.* **in·quire** (in-**kwire**) ▷ *verb* **inquiring, inquired** ▷ *adjective* **inquiring** ▷ *adverb* **inquiringly**

inquiry *noun*
1. An official attempt to discover the facts about something: *The inquiry into the plane crash has gone on for months.*
2. A request for information: *How may I direct your inquiry?*
in·quir·y (in-**kwye**-ree *or* **in**-kwur-ee)
▷ *noun, plural* **inquiries**

inquisitive *adjective* Curious or asking a lot of questions: *What an inquisitive mind you have!*
in·quis·i·tive (in-**kwiz**-i-tiv) ▷ *noun* **inquisitiveness**
▷ *adverb* **inquisitively**

insane *adjective*
1. Mentally ill.
2. Very foolish: *What an insane idea!*
in·sane (in-**sane**)
▷ *noun* **insanity** (in-**san**-i-tee) ▷ *adverb* **insanely**

inscribe *verb*
1. To write, carve, or engrave letters on a surface.
2. To write a special message in a book: *I inscribed a dedication in the book of poems I gave Nate.*
in·scribe (in-**skribe**)
▷ *verb* **inscribing, inscribed** ▷ *adjective* **inscribed**

inscription *noun* A specially written message, usually to identify an object or a person, as in *an inscription on a gravestone.* **in·scrip·tion** (in-**skrip**-shuhn)

insect *noun* A small animal with three pairs of legs, one or two pairs of wings, and three main parts to its body. Insects have hard outer skeletons and do not have backbones. **in·sect** (**in**-sekt)

insecticide *noun* A chemical used to kill insects: *The farmer sprayed the fields with insecticides.* **in·sec·ti·cide** (in-**sek**-tuh-*side*)

insecure *adjective*
1. Unsafe, or not providing any security: *The lock on the front door is very insecure.*
2. Anxious and uncertain: *Paula felt very insecure on her first day at her new school.*
in·se·cure (*in*-si-**kyoor**)
▷ *noun* **insecurity** ▷ *adverb* **insecurely**

insensitive *adjective* Thoughtless and unconcerned about other people's feelings: *Ivan made an insensitive comment about Jim's stutter.*
in·sen·si·tive (in-**sen**-si-tiv) ▷ *noun* **insensitivity**
▷ *adverb* **insensitively**

inseparable *adjective* Not able to be separated; always found together: *The two became inseparable after they met at summer camp last year.* **in·sep·a·ra·ble** (in-**sep**-ur-uh-buhl)

insert
1. *verb* (in-**surt**) To put something inside something else: *Insert this key into the lock.* ▷ *verb* **inserting, inserted** ▷ *noun* **insertion**
2. *noun* (**in**-surt) Something extra that is put inside something else: *The Sunday newspaper has inserts with store coupons.*
in·sert

inside
1. *noun* (**in**-side) The interior of something: *Our house looks bigger on the inside.* ▷ *adjective* **inside** (**in**-side *or* in-**side**)
2. *preposition* (in-**side**) In less than: *You should be able to finish your homework inside an hour.*
3. *preposition* (in-**side**) Within: *Put the letter inside the envelope.*
4. *adverb* (in-**side**) Into an enclosed space, such as a house: *They went inside the movie theater.*
in·side

insight *noun* The ability to understand something that is not obvious: *The writer's descriptions of the characters showed a lot of insight into people.*
in·sight (**in**-site)

insignia *noun* A badge, emblem, or design that shows someone's rank or membership in an organization: *Justin wore the Marine Corps insignia with pride.* **in·sig·ni·a** (in-**sig**-nee-uh)

insignia

insignificant *adjective* Small and unimportant: *The old church looks insignificant next to the skyscraper.* **in·sig·nif·i·cant** (in-sig-**nif**-i-kuhnt) ▷ *noun* **insignificance** ▷ *adverb* **insignificantly**

insincere *adjective* Not genuine or honest. **in·sin·cere** (in-sin-**seer**) ▷ *noun* **insincerity** (in-sin-**ser**-i-tee) ▷ *adverb* **insincerely**

insist *verb* To demand something and refuse to accept a negative reply: *Fleur insisted on wearing her party dress to school.* **in·sist** (in-**sist**) ▷ *verb* **insisting, insisted** ▷ *noun* **insistence** ▷ *adjective* **insistent**

insomnia *noun* Difficulty falling asleep or staying asleep. **in·som·ni·a** (in-**sahm**-nee-uh) ▷ *noun* **insomniac** (in-**sahm**-nee-*ak*)

inspect *verb* To examine something carefully: *Carol inspected the table before agreeing to buy it.* **in·spect** (in-**spekt**) ▷ *verb* **inspecting, inspected**

inspection *noun* A careful look at something or someone; an examination: *The inspection of the fire scene took several days.* **in·spec·tion** (in-**spek**-shuhn)

inspector *noun*
1. A person who checks or examines things, as in *a restaurant inspector.*
2. A high-ranking detective, as in *a homicide inspector.*
in·spec·tor (in-**spek**-tur)

inspiration *noun*
1. The act of inspiring someone, or the feeling of being inspired: *Reading Emily Dickinson's poetry gave me the inspiration to write.*
2. Something that inspires someone, such as a person, an event, or an idea: *Martina said the inspiration for her wanting to ride horses professionally is her sister, who is a jockey.*
in·spi·ra·tion (in-spuh-**ray**-shuhn) ▷ *adjective* **inspirational** (in-spuh-**ray**-shuh-nuhl)

inspire *verb*
1. To fill someone with an emotion, an idea, or an attitude: *Maggie's optimism about the project inspired confidence in her fellow workers.*
2. To influence and encourage someone to achieve or do something: *My trip to Mexico inspired me to study Spanish.*

in·spire (in-**spire**)
▷ *verb* **inspiring, inspired** ▷ *adjective* **inspiring**

Word History

An early meaning of **inspire** was "breathe into," and this is the sense of the Latin verb *inspirare*. Latin speakers formed *inspirare* from the words *in*, meaning "into," and *spirare*, meaning "to breathe." When we use the word *inspire* today, we are thinking of feelings rather than breathing. If a great person *inspires* you, it means that you are filled with a feeling, attitude, or belief, because the person has "breathed into" you by his or her impressive deeds.

install *verb*
1. To put something into a place where it can be used: *We had a new oven installed in our kitchen.*
2. To put a program or part of a program on a computer's hard drive: *You'll need to install the updates before the program's new features will work.*
in·stall (in-**stawl**)
▷ *verb* **installing, installed**

installation *noun* The act or process of installing something: *The installation of the new software will take only a few minutes.* **in·stal·la·tion** (in-stuh-**lay**-shuhn)

installment *noun*
1. One of a series of regular payments over a period of time for a purchased object.
2. One part of a story that is printed or shown in separate parts: *The movie will be shown on television in two installments.*
in·stall·ment (in-**stawl**-muhnt)

instance *noun*
1. An example: *We saw several instances of unsafe stair rails on our tour of the building.*
2. for instance As an example: *Her interests include the sciences—for instance, biology and physics.*
in·stance (in-**stuhns**)

instant
1. *adjective* Happening right away, as in *instant results.*
2. *noun* A moment: *The cat disappeared in an instant.* ▷ *adjective* **instantaneous** (in-stuhn-**tay**-nee-uhs) ▷ *adverb* **instantaneously**
3. *adjective* Already mixed and prepared, needing only quick preparation, as in *instant pudding.*
in·stant (in-**stuhnt**)

instantly *adverb* Right away; without any delay: *Her remarks were unfair and made me instantly furious.* **in·stant·ly** (in-**stuhnt**-lee)

instant message *verb* To send a message over the internet using an instant messaging computer program. ▷ *noun* **instant message**

instant messaging *noun* The use of a computer program that allows people to email messages back and forth very quickly over the internet. **instant mes·sag·ing** (**mes**-i-jing)

instead *adverb* In place of another person or thing: *We were out of cookies, so Bill had sherbet instead.* **in·stead** (in-**sted**)

instigate *verb* To start something, especially something that leads to trouble: *The accident instigated a huge traffic jam.* **in·sti·gate** (**in**-sti-*gate*) ▷ *noun* **instigator**

instill *verb* To put into a person's mind slowly, over a period of time: *The teacher instilled a sense of pride in his students.* **in·still** (in-**stil**) ▷ *verb* **instilling, instilled**

instinct *noun*
1. Behavior that is natural rather than learned: *Birds build their nests by instinct.* ▷ *adjective* **instinctual** (in-**stingk**-choo-uhl)
2. Knowledge that comes without thinking or studying: *My instincts tell me that he is hiding something.*
in·stinct (**in**-stingkt)
▷ *adjective* **instinctive** ▷ *adverb* **instinctively**

institute
1. *noun* A society or organization with a particular goal, as in *an institute of marine studies.*
2. *verb* To begin or establish something: *The school nurse instituted a flu vaccination program.* ▷ *verb* **instituting, instituted**
in·sti·tute (**in**-sti-*toot*)

institution *noun*
1. A large organization where people live or work together, as in *an institution of learning.* ▷ *adjective* **institutional**
2. A custom or tradition: *Sunday dinner is an institution in our house.*
in·sti·tu·tion (in-sti-**too**-shuhn)

instruct *verb*
1. To teach a subject or a skill, as in *to instruct mathematics.* ▷ *noun* **instructor**
2. To give instructions: *The chief instructed the new firefighters on how to connect a hose.*
in·struct (in-**struhkt**)
▷ *verb* **instructing, instructed**

instruction *noun*
1. The act of teaching or giving lessons: *We would not have been able to sing so well without our choir director's instruction.*
2. instructions *noun, plural* Directions on how to do something, or orders on what to do, as in *to give instructions* or *to follow instructions.*
in·struc·tion (in-**struhk**-shuhn)

instruction

instrument *noun*
1. An object that is used to make music.
▷ *adjective* **instrumental** (*in*-struh-**men**-tuhl) ▷ *noun* **instrumentalist**
2. A tool designed to do a specific thing, especially something difficult or delicate, as in *laboratory instruments.*
in·stru·ment (**in**-struh-muhnt)

insufficient *adjective* Not enough or inadequate: *The amount of food was insufficient to feed all the people who showed up.* **in·suf·fi·cient** (*in*-suh-**fish**-uhnt) ▷ *adverb* **insufficiently**

insulate *verb* To cover something with material in order to stop heat, electricity, or sound from escaping: *We insulated all the pipes in the basement.* **in·su·late** (**in**-suh-*late*) ▷ *verb* **insulating, insulated** ▷ *noun* **insulation** ▷ *noun* **insulator** ▷ *adjective* **insulating**

insulin *noun* A hormone produced in the pancreas that regulates the level of sugar in the blood. People who have diabetes do not produce enough of this hormone and may need to receive it through injections. **in·su·lin** (**in**-suh-lin)

musical instruments

insult *verb* To say or do something disrespectful and upsetting to somebody: *Jeremy insulted his friend by calling him a liar.* **in·sult** (in-**suhlt**) ▷ *verb* **insulting, insulted** ▷ *noun* **insult** (**in**-suhlt) ▷ *adjective* **insulting**

insurance *noun* An arrangement in which someone pays money to a company that agrees to pay the person a certain amount in the event of sickness, fire, accident, or other loss, as in *car insurance.* **in·sur·ance** (in-**shoor**-uhns)

insure *verb* To buy insurance on something, as in *to insure a house.* **in·sure** (in-**shoor**) ▷ *verb* **insuring, insured** ▷ *adjective* **insured**

intact *adjective* Not broken or damaged; complete: *The new trees were still intact after the storm.* **in·tact** (in-**takt**)

intake *noun*
1. The amount of something taken in: *Runners often increase their intake of carbohydrates before a race.*
2. The act of taking something in, as in *an intake of food.*
in·take (**in**-*take*)

intangible *adjective*
1. Not able to be grasped or touched: *There are many intangible benefits to living in a good neighborhood.*
2. Not very clear or definite: *The principal's intangible argument left everyone confused.*
in·tan·gi·ble (in-**tan**-juh-buhl) ▷ *noun* **intangibility** (in-*tan*-juh-**bil**-uh-tee) ▷ *adverb* **intangibly**

integer *noun* A whole number, either positive or negative. Examples of integers include –3, –2, –1, 0, 1, 2, and 3. **in·te·ger** (**in**-ti-jur)

integrate *verb*
1. To combine several things or people into one: *Mr. Platt integrated all of the students' ideas into the story.*
2. To include people of all races.
in·te·grate (**in**-ti-*grate*) ▷ *verb* **integrating, integrated**

integrated *adjective*
1. Not separated by race; open to or used by all sorts of people, as in *an integrated neighborhood.*
2. Combining different elements to work together effectively: *The math curriculum follows the integrated approach used in Japan and other countries.*
in·te·grat·ed (**in**-tuh-*gray*-tid)

integration *noun* The act or practice of making facilities or an organization open to people of all races and ethnic groups. **in·te·gra·tion** (in-ti-**gray**-shuhn)

integrity *noun* The quality of being honest and having high moral principles: *We chose our doctor for her compassion and integrity.* **in·teg·ri·ty** (in-**teg**-ri-tee)

intellect *noun* The power of the mind to think, reason, understand, and learn: *Albert Einstein was a genius who was known for his great intellect.* **in·tel·lect** (**in**-tuh-*lekt*)

intellectual
1. *adjective* Involving thought and reason: *Solving mysteries is an intellectual challenge.* ▷ *adverb* **intellectually**
2. *noun* A person with a highly developed intellect.
in·tel·lec·tu·al (*in*-tuh-**lek**-choo-uhl)

intelligence *noun*
1. The fact or state of being intelligent: *Nico's intelligence was evident from the many ideas he brought up during our conversation.*
2. Information about what is happening or is going to happen, especially when obtained by spying.
in·tel·li·gence (in-**tel**-i-juhns)

intelligent *adjective* Quick to understand, think, and learn. **in·tel·li·gent** (in-**tel**-i-juhnt) ▷ *adverb* **intelligently**

intelligible *adjective* Able to be understood. **in·tel·li·gi·ble** (in-**tel**-i-juh-buhl) ▷ *adverb* **intelligibly**

intend *verb*
1. To mean to do something: *I intend to go hiking today.*
2. Designed for a particular purpose: *This cake is intended for your birthday.*
in·tend (in-**tend**) ▷ *verb* **intending, intended**

intense *adjective*
1. Very strong, as in *intense cold* or *intense competition.*
2. Showing strong feelings about something: *When Jayne concentrates, she gets an intense look on her face.*
in·tense (in-**tens**) ▷ *adverb* **intensely**

intensify *verb* To make something stronger or more powerful: *The bank intensified its security after the break-in.* **in·ten·si·fy** (in-**ten**-suh-*fye*) ▷ *verb* **intensifies, intensifying, intensified**

intensity *noun* The quality of being intense: *The intensity of the battle scenes made it difficult for us to watch the movie.* **in·ten·si·ty** (in-**ten**-si-tee)

intensive *adjective*
1. Characterized by a lot of effort or hard work: *After seven years of intensive training and study, she was ready to start practicing as a lawyer.*
2. An **intensive** adverb, such as the word *very,* is used to give emphasis to adjectives and other adverbs.
in·ten·sive (in-**ten**-siv) ▷ *noun* **intensiveness** ▷ *adverb* **intensively**

intent
> **1.** *adjective* Determined to do something: *Bruno is intent on finishing this job.*
> **2.** *noun* A plan or a purpose: *Ralph's intent was to ask Kayla out to dinner.* ▷ *adverb* **intently**
> **in·tent** (in-**tent**)

intention *noun* Something that you mean to do: *It's my intention to clean up the yard before the party.* **in·ten·tion** (in-**ten**-shuhn)

intentional *adjective* Done on purpose; deliberate: *The omission of their names was not intentional; it was a careless mistake.* **in·ten·tion·al** (in-**ten**-shuh-nuhl) ▷ *adverb* **intentionally**

interact *verb* When you play a game or talk with people, you are **interacting** with them: *Elissa is shy and is finding it hard to interact with the other children.* **in·ter·act** (*in*-tur-**akt**) ▷ *verb* **interacting, interacted** ▷ *noun* **interaction**

interactive *adjective*
> **1.** Working together or influencing each other.
> **2.** Allowing the users of a computer program to make choices in order to control or change features of the program, as in *an interactive video game.* **in·ter·ac·tive** (*in*-tur-**ak**-tiv)

intercept *verb* To prevent someone or something from moving from one place to another, as in *to intercept a pass in football.* **in·ter·cept** (*in*-tur-**sept**) ▷ *verb* **intercepting, intercepted** ▷ *noun* **interception**

interchangeable *adjective* Easily switched with someone or something else: *Socks are interchangeable because each sock can go on either foot.* **in·ter·change·a·ble** (*in*-tur-**chayn**-juh-buhl) ▷ *adverb* **interchangeably**

intercom *noun* A system that uses a microphone and speaker through which a person can listen and talk to someone in another location. Intercom is short for *intercommunication system.* **in·ter·com** (**in**-tur-*kahm*)

interest
> **1.** *verb* To attract a person's curiosity or attention. ▷ *verb* **interesting, interested**
> **2.** *noun* A feeling of curiosity or concern, as in *an interest in sports.*
> **3.** *noun* The power to cause curiosity or concern: *Music is of great interest to me.*
> **4.** *noun* A legal share, as in a business: *Chef Enrico has sold his interest in his first restaurant.*
> **5.** *noun* A fee paid for borrowing money, usually a percentage of the amount borrowed: *I took out a loan with a low rate of interest.*
> **6.** *noun* Money paid to you by a bank for keeping your savings there: *My little brother was thrilled to*

intercom

see that he'd earned $2 in interest from his savings account.
> **7.** If it is **in your interest** to do something, it will benefit you in some way.
> **in·ter·est** (**in**-trist)
> ▷ *adjective* **interested** ▷ *adjective* **interesting**

interface *noun* The point at which two different things meet: *A keyboard is one type of interface between a computer and its user.* **in·ter·face** (**in**-tur-*fase*) ▷ *verb* **interface**

interfere *verb*
> **1.** To become involved in a situation or activity without being asked to do so.
> **2.** To hinder: *The noise interfered with my work.*
> **in·ter·fere** (*in*-tur-**feer**)
> ▷ *verb* **interfering, interfered** ▷ *adjective* **interfering**

interference *noun*
> **1.** An unwelcome involvement in the affairs of others: *Pat got annoyed at Gunther's constant interference with her work.*
> **2.** Interruption in a broadcast or an electronic signal so that you cannot see or hear the program or the message properly.
> **3.** In sports, the illegal obstruction of an opponent: *The referee called a penalty for pass interference.*
> **in·ter·fer·ence** (*in*-tur-**feer**-uhns)

interior *noun* The inside of something: *They are painting the interior of the school this summer.* **in·te·ri·or** (in-**teer**-ee-ur) ▷ *adjective* **interior**

interjection *noun* A word spoken suddenly and used to express surprise, pain, delight, or some other emotion. An interjection is often used with an exclamation point: *"Hello!" and "Ouch!" are examples of interjections.* **in·ter·jec·tion** (*in*-tur-**jek**-shuhn)

intermediate *adjective* Between two things, or in the middle of a series of things: *I am in the intermediate swimming class.* **in·ter·me·di·ate** (*in*-tur-**mee**-dee-*it*)

intermission *noun* A short break in a performance: *We bought candy during the play's intermission.* **in·ter·mis·sion** (*in*-tur-**mish**-uhn)

intermittent *adjective* Stopping and starting, not continuous, as in *an intermittent snowfall.* **in·ter·mit·tent** (*in*-tur-**mit**-uhnt) ▷ *adverb* **intermittently**

intern *noun*
1. Someone who is learning a skill or job by working with an expert in that field.

Internet

The internet consists of thousands of connected computer networks. In the 1960s, the US military developed a system that linked networks many miles apart. As more computers around the world connected to it, what came to be known as the internet grew. In the 1990s, computers became more affordable and the number of people accessing the internet increased dramatically.

The English computer scientist Tim Berners-Lee invented the World Wide Web in 1989. It allows computers to access documents written in HTML (hypertext markup language), each with a unique address on the web, called a URL, or uniform resource locator. An example of a URL is http://www.loc.gov/families, the resource site for kids at the Library of Congress.

Communicating by email is the most popular activity on the internet. People navigate the web using search engines, entering keywords to find sites, images, media files, and other resources.

intersection

2. A newly graduated doctor of medicine who is working at a hospital to get practical experience. **in·tern** (**in**-turn)
▷ *noun* **internship** ▷ *verb* **intern**

internal *adjective*
1. On the inside of someone or something, as in *internal bleeding.* ▷ *adverb* **internally**
2. Of or having to do with matters inside a country or an organization, as in *internal affairs.* **in·ter·nal** (in-**tur**-nuhl)

international *adjective* Involving more than one country, as in *international banking.* **in·ter·na·tion·al** (*in*-tur-**nash**-uh-nuhl) ▷ *adverb* **internationally**

internet *noun* The electronic network that allows millions of computers around the world to connect together: *We can access the internet on the school's computers.* **In·ter·net** (**in**-tur-*net*)

interpret *verb*
1. To translate a conversation between people who speak different languages. ▷ *noun* **interpreter**
2. To figure out what something means: *I interpreted his lateness as a sign that he didn't really want to attend the meeting.* **in·ter·pret** (in-**tur**-prit)
▷ *verb* **interpreting, interpreted**

interpretation *noun* An explanation of the meaning of something: *This essay discusses my interpretation of the sonnet.* **in·ter·pre·ta·tion** (in-*tur*-pri-**tay**-shuhn)

interrogate *verb* To question someone in detail, usually in connection with a crime: *The police interrogated the suspect for hours.* **in·ter·ro·gate** (in-**ter**-uh-*gate*) ▷ *verb* **interrogating, interrogated**
▷ *noun* **interrogation**

a b c d e f g h i j k l m n o p q r s t u v w x y z

A B C D E F G H I J K L M N O P Q R S T U V W X Y Z

interrupt *verb*

1. To stop or hinder for a short time: *The TV program was interrupted by a weather report.*

2. To start talking while someone else is talking: *I asked Saul to stop interrupting me when I talk.* in·ter·rupt (*in*-tuh-**ruhpt**)

▷ *verb* **interrupting, interrupted** ▷ *noun* **interruption** ▷ *adjective* **interruptive**

intersect *verb* To meet or cross something: *Route 44 intersects Route 2 at Davidsonville.* in·ter·sect (*in*-tur-**sekt**) ▷ *verb* **intersecting, intersected**

intersection *noun* The point at which two things meet and cross each other: *My house is near the intersection of Colby and Wood Streets.* in·ter·sec·tion (*in*-tur-**sek**-shuhn *or* *in*-tur-*sek*-shuhn)

interstate *adjective* Connecting, between, or having to do with two or more states, as in *an interstate highway.* in·ter·state (*in*-tur-**state**)

interval *noun* A time between two events, or a space between two objects. in·ter·val (*in*-tur-vuhl)

intervene *verb*

1. To get involved in a situation in order to change it: *The police stood ready to intervene if the protest turned violent.*

2. To occur between two other events: *The holidays intervened between the regular basketball season and the playoffs.*

in·ter·vene (*in*-tur-**veen**)

▷ *verb* **intervening, intervened**

intervention *noun* The act of becoming involved in something that is happening in a way that stops it or changes its course: *A fight broke out at school, and without our teacher's intervention, somebody might have gotten seriously hurt.* in·ter·ven·tion (*in*-tur-**ven**-shuhn)

interview *noun* A meeting at which someone is asked questions, as in *a job interview* or *a radio interview.* in·ter·view (**in**-tur-*vyoo*)

▷ *verb* **interview**

intestine *noun* A long tube in the body extending below the stomach that digests food and absorbs liquids and salts. It consists of the **small intestine** and the **large intestine**. in·tes·tine (in-**tes**-tin)

Word History

The **intestine** received its name from its location. Since it is "inside" the body, English speakers named it "the thing that is inside." The Latin word *intestinus* means simply "internal" or "inside," and this was the source of the English word *intestine*.

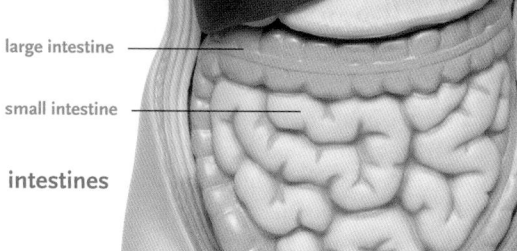

large intestine

small intestine

intestines

intimate *adjective* Very closely acquainted or connected, as in *intimate friends.* in·ti·mate (**in**-tuh-mit) ▷ *noun* **intimacy** (**in**-tuh-muh-see) ▷ *adverb* **intimately**

intimidate *verb* To frighten someone, especially in order to make him or her do something: *The bully intimidated Hugo into giving him the money.* in·tim·i·date (in-**tim**-i-*date*) ▷ *verb* **intimidating, intimidated** ▷ *noun* **intimidation** ▷ *adjective* **intimidating**

into *preposition*

1. To the inside of: *She went into the tent.*

2. To the occupation of: *She went into biology.*

3. To the condition or form of: *The cat got into trouble.*

4. To the subject or situation of: *The police are looking into the burglary.*

5. Against: *Her car bumped into ours.*

6. Toward: *The kite flew into the wind.*

7. *(informal)* Extremely interested in: *Ben is into surfing.* in·to (**in**-too *or* **in**-tuh)

intolerable *adjective* Impossible to endure: *The noise from the lawn mower is intolerable.* in·tol·er·a·ble (in-**tah**-lur-uh-buhl) ▷ *adverb* **intolerably**

intolerant *adjective* Unable or unwilling to accept another kind of person, idea, or behavior. in·tol·er·ant (in-**tah**-lur-uhnt) ▷ *noun* **intolerance** ▷ *adverb* **intolerantly**

intoxicate *verb*

1. To make drunk, especially with alcohol.

2. To excite or to make enthusiastic, as in *an intoxicating aroma.*

in·tox·i·cate (in-**tahk**-si-*kate*)

▷ *verb* **intoxicating, intoxicated** ▷ *noun* **intoxication**

intransitive *adjective* If a verb is **intransitive**, it does not need an object in order to complete its meaning. For example, in the sentences "Where are we going to sleep?" and "It's raining," the verbs *sleep* and *rain* are intransitive. in·tran·si·tive (in-**tran**-suh-tiv) *See* **transitive.**

intrepid *adjective* Very brave, especially when exploring something unknown. **in·trep·id** (in-**trep**-id)

intricate *adjective* Complicated or containing many small parts or details, as in *an intricate design*. **in·tri·cate** (in-tri-kit) ▷ *noun* **intricacy** ▷ *adverb* **intricately**

intrigue
1. (in-**treeg**) *verb* To be very interesting or fascinating to someone: *I'm intrigued by the idea of space travel.* ▷ *verb* **intriguing, intrigued** ▷ *adjective* **intriguing**
2. (**in**-treeg *or* in-**treeg**) *noun* A secret plot or scheme. ▷ *verb* **intrigue** (in-**treeg**)
in·trigue

introduce *verb*
1. To bring in something new: *The library is introducing a new procedure for checking out books.*
2. To tell someone your name the first time you meet: *We introduced ourselves to our new neighbors.*
3. To start: *She introduced the report with a series of statistics.*
in·tro·duce (*in*-truh-**doos**) ▷ *verb* **introducing, introduced**

introduction *noun*
1. A person's first experience of something: *Mona's introduction to sailing took place on Lake Erie.*
2. The presentation of one person to another: *I finally got an introduction to Emilio's parents.*
3. The opening section of a book, speech, or other presentation: *The novel begins with a long introduction.*
in·tro·duc·tion (*in*-truh-**duhk**-shuhn) ▷ *adjective* **introductory** (*in*-truh-**duhk**-tur-ee)

introvert *noun* A shy person who does not share his or her thoughts or feelings easily. **in·tro·vert** (*in*-truh-*vurt*) ▷ *adjective* **introverted**

intrude *verb* To go into a place or get involved in a situation where you are not wanted. **in·trude** (in-**trood**) ▷ *verb* **intruding, intruded** ▷ *noun* **intruder** ▷ *noun* **intrusion** (in-**troo**-zhuhn) ▷ *adjective* **intrusive** (in-**troo**-siv)

intuition *noun* An understanding of something that is based on feelings rather than reason or logic: *My intuition tells me that you are unhappy about something.* **in·tu·i·tion** (*in*-too-**ish**-uhn) ▷ *verb* **intuit** (**in**-too-it)

intuitive *adjective* Able to know or understand something by intuition: *My mother is an intuitive person who always seems to know what I'm thinking.* **in·tu·i·tive** (in-**too**-i-tiv)

Inuit *noun* A native person of the Arctic. The Inuit live today mainly in Alaska, Canada, and Greenland. The Inuit used to be called **Eskimos**. **In·u·it** (**in**-oo-it *or* **in**-yoo-it) ▷ *noun, plural* **Inuit** *or* **Inuits** ▷ *adjective* **Inuit**

inundate *verb*
1. To flood: *The town often gets inundated by the river during the rainy season.*
2. To bring so much of something that it is hard or impossible to deal with: *After the hurricane, the government's relief agency was inundated with requests for help.*
in·un·date (**in**-uhn-*date*) ▷ *verb* **inundating, inundated** ▷ *noun* **inundation**

invade *verb*
1. To enter a place or situation in large numbers, usually with a negative effect: *Ants invaded our picnic.*
2. To send armed forces into a place in order to occupy or control it: *The soldiers invaded the island.*
in·vade (in-**vade**) ▷ *verb* **invading, invaded** ▷ *noun* **invader**

invalid
1. (**in**-vuh-lid) *noun* A person whose movements and activities are limited because he or she is seriously ill.
2. (in-**val**-id) *adjective* Unable to be used because it is no longer legal or in effect, as in *an invalid driver's license.*
in·va·lid

invaluable *adjective* Indispensible, necessary, or precious. **in·val·u·a·ble** (in-**val**-yuh-buhl) ▷ *adverb* **invaluably**

invasion *noun*
1. The act of intruding: *Secretly reading someone else's emails is an invasion of privacy.*
2. The act of invading by a military force: *Napoleon's disastrous invasion of Russia led to the collapse of his army.*
in·va·sion (in-**vay**-zhuhn)

Inuit family in traditional clothes

invent *verb*
1. To think up and create something new: *Alexander Bain invented the fax machine in the early 1840s.* ▷ *noun* **inventor**
2. To make something up, especially with the idea of deceiving someone: *Shelly invented a ridiculous excuse to get out of mowing the lawn.*
in·vent (in-**vent**)
▷ *verb* **inventing, invented**

invention *noun* Some useful thing that is newly designed or created: *Alexander Graham Bell's invention of the telephone allowed people to communicate over wide distances.* **in·ven·tion** (in-**ven**-chuhn)

inventive *adjective* Good at thinking up new ideas or ways of doing things; creative. **in·ven·tive** (in-**ven**-tiv)

inventory
1. *noun* A complete list of items someone owns.
2. *noun* All the items on hand for sale in a store: *The local hardware store has a small inventory.*
3. *verb* To count and list the items someone owns, or the items available for sale in a store. ▷ *verb* **inventories, inventorying, inventoried** **in·ven·to·ry** (in-vuhn-*tor*-ee)
▷ *noun, plural* **inventories**

invert *verb*
1. To turn something upside down: *If you invert a 6, it looks like a 9.*
2. To reverse the order of something: *If you invert the letters of the word "stop," you get "pots."*
in·vert (in-**vurt**)
▷ *verb* **inverting, inverted**

invertebrate *noun* An animal without a backbone: *Octopuses, earthworms, and snails are examples of invertebrates.* **in·ver·te·brate** (in-**vur**-tuh-brit)
▷ *adjective* **invertebrate**

invest *verb*
1. To give or lend money to something, such as a company, with the intention of getting more money back later: *We invested in a new ice-cream franchise.* ▷ *noun* **investor**
2. To devote time or effort to something: *Maria has invested a lot of work in remodeling her house.*
in·vest (in-**vest**)
▷ *verb* **investing, invested**

invertebrate: octopus

investigate *verb* To gather information about something: *I suspected that Keiko was keeping a secret and decided to investigate.* **in·ves·ti·gate** (in-**ves**-ti-*gate*) ▷ *verb* **investigating, investigated** ▷ *noun* **investigator** ▷ *adjective* **investigative**

investigation *noun* The act or process of looking into how something works or why something happened: *The investigation of the rocket's failure began this week.* **in·ves·ti·ga·tion** (in-*ves*-ti-**gay**-shuhn)

investment *noun*
1. An activity that involves giving money, time, or effort in the hope of getting something back: *After spending months setting up his shop, Albert has a real investment in making a success of his new business.*
2. Something in which someone has invested money, time, or effort: *She has a large financial investment in the new e-book company.*
3. Something in which someone may invest, or has invested: *The mine is said to be a good investment.*
in·vest·ment (in-**vest**-mint)

invincible *adjective* Impossible to defeat. **in·vin·ci·ble** (in-**vin**-suh-buhl) ▷ *adverb* **invincibly**

invisible *adjective* Impossible to see: *Although germs are invisible, they're still all around us.* **in·vis·i·ble** (in-**viz**-uh-buhl) ▷ *noun* **invisibility** (in-*viz*-uh-**bil**-i-tee) ▷ *adverb* **invisibly**

invite *verb* To ask someone to do something or to go somewhere, usually enjoyable: *I will invite Fletcher to join us for dinner.* **in·vite** (in-**vite**) ▷ *verb* **inviting, invited** ▷ *noun* **invitation** (in-vi-**tay**-shuhn)

invoice *noun* An itemized bill for goods shipped to a customer or for work done or to be done for a customer. **in·voice** (**in**-vois) ▷ *verb* **invoice**

involuntary *adjective*
1. Not done willingly or by choice: *The suspect claimed that his confession was involuntary.*
2. Done without a person's control: *Breathing is an involuntary act.*
in·vol·un·tar·y (in-**vah**-luhn-*ter*-ee)

involve *verb* To include something: *The project involves library research.* **in·volve** (in-**vahlv**) ▷ *verb* **involving, involved** ▷ *noun* **involvement**

iron
spearheads

Iron Age

The Iron Age is defined by the shift from tools made of bronze and copper to those made of iron, which produced sharper edges. Many iron tools were used by the Romans, who also developed iron nails. This period follows the Bronze Age, which came after the Stone Age, and is the last of the three ages categorizing prehistoric societies. It spanned from about 1200 B.C. to A.D. 400, but these dates vary widely by region.

involved *adjective*
1. Taking part in something: *I am involved in planning the picnic.*
2. Complicated, as in *an involved story.*
in·volved (in-**vahlvd**)

inward *adverb* Toward the inside: *The door opens inward.* **in·ward** (**in**-wurd) ▷ *adjective* **inward**

Suffix

The suffix **-ion** turns a root word into a noun by adding one of these meanings:

1. The act of, as in *participation* (the act of participating).
2. A state of being, as in *confusion* (the state of being confused).

iodine *noun*
1. A chemical element found in seaweed and saltwater that is used in medicine and photography.
2. A brown medicine containing iodine and alcohol that is used to kill germs on wounds.
i·o·dine (**eye**-uh-dine)

ion *noun* An electrically charged atomic particle. Ions are either positive or negative. **i·on** (**eye**-uhn or **eye**-ahn)

iota *noun* The smallest amount of something. The word is rarely used in the plural and often appears in phrases with a negative and emphatic meaning, such as *not one iota*: *"The school has not changed one iota since I left—everything looks exactly the same,"* said Mabel. **i·o·ta** (eye-**oh**-tuh)

IPO *noun* The selling of shares of stock in a company when it goes from being a privately owned company to a publicly owned company. IPO is short for *initial public offering.*

IQ *noun* A number that represents a measure of someone's intelligence. IQ is short for *intelligence quotient.*

irate *adjective* Extremely angry or annoyed: *Dad was irate when I damaged the car.* **i·rate** (eye-**rate**) ▷ *adverb* **irately**

iris *noun*
1. The round, colored part of the eye around the pupil.
2. A plant with long, thin leaves and large flowers in a variety of colors that blooms in the spring.
i·ris (**eye**-ris)

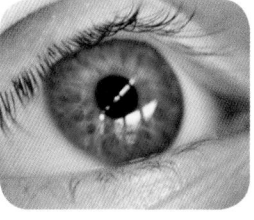

iris

Irish setter *noun* A large hunting dog with a silky, red coat. These dogs originally were bred in Ireland. **I·rish set·ter** (**eye**-rish **set**-ur)

iron
1. *noun* A strong, hard metal that is magnetic and that is used to make a great variety of things. It is also found in some foods as well as in the body's red blood cells: *The old house is surrounded by a high iron fence.* ▷ *adjective* **iron**
2. *noun* An electrical appliance with a handle and a heated surface, used to smooth wrinkles out of clothing. ▷ *verb* **iron**
3. iron out *verb* To solve a problem or arrange details: *We've finally gotten our vacation schedule ironed out.* ▷ *verb* **ironing, ironed**
i·ron (**eye**-urn)

Iron Age *noun* A period of history when iron was commonly used to make tools and weapons. This period occurred at different times in different parts of the world.

a b c d e f g h i j k l m n o p q r s t u v w x y z

ironic *adjective*
1. Happening in the opposite way to what is expected: *It was ironic that the librarian returned her books late.*
2. Slightly sarcastic: *The giant Christmas tree failed to light up, drawing ironic comments from the crowd.*
i·ron·ic (eye-**rah**-nik)
▷ *adverb* **ironically**

irony *noun* A way of speaking or writing that means the opposite of what the words say, especially when it is meant humorously, such as saying "Beautiful weather, isn't it?" when it is raining. **i·ro·ny** (**eye**-ruh-nee)

Iroquois *noun* A member of a confederation of Native American tribes originally of New York. **I·ro·quois** (**eer**-uh-*kwoi*) ▷ *noun, plural* **Iroquois**

irrational *adjective* Not logical or reasonable: *A phobia is an irrational fear of something.* **ir·ra·tio·nal** (i-**rash**-uh-nuhl) ▷ *adverb* **irrationally**

irregular *adjective*
1. Not standard in shape, timing, size, or arrangement, as in *an irregular ferry service.*
2. Contrary to the normal rules or pattern: *The company's irregular accounting practices led to bankruptcy.* ▷ *noun* **irregularity** (i-reg-yuh-**lar**-i-tee)
3. An **irregular** verb is one whose main parts are not formed according to a regular pattern. For example, the verb *sink* is irregular because its past tense is *sank* rather than *sinked.*
ir·reg·u·lar (i-**reg**-yuh-lur)
▷ *adverb* **irregularly**

irrelevant *adjective* Having nothing to do with a particular subject: *His questions were completely irrelevant to the discussion.* **ir·rel·e·vant** (i-**rel**-uh-vuhnt) ▷ *noun* **irrelevance** ▷ *adverb* **irrelevantly**

irresistible *adjective* Impossible to resist: *The irresistible force of the river carried away trees and rocks.* **ir·re·sist·i·ble** (ir-i-**zis**-tuh-buhl) ▷ *adverb* **irresistibly**

irresponsible *adjective* Careless and lacking a sense of responsibility: *It was irresponsible to leave the children alone in the house.* **ir·re·spon·si·ble** (ir-i-**spahn**-suh-buhl) ▷ *noun* **irresponsibility** ▷ *adverb* **irresponsibly**

irreversible *adjective* Unable to be changed or undone: *The president's decision to go to war was irreversible.* **ir·re·vers·i·ble** (ir-uh-**ver**-suh-buhl)

irrigate *verb* To supply water to crops by artificial means, such as channels and pipes: *The farmer irrigated his fields.* **ir·ri·gate** (**ir**-uh-*gate*)
▷ *verb* **irrigating, irrigated** ▷ *noun* **irrigation**

irritable *adjective* Grumpy and quick to be annoyed: *If he doesn't get enough sleep, he's very irritable.* **ir·ri·ta·ble** (**ir**-i-tuh-buhl) ▷ *adverb* **irritably**

irritate *verb*
1. To annoy or make angry.
2. To make sore or sensitive: *Dylan coughed so much, he irritated his throat.*
ir·ri·tate (**ir**-i-*tate*)
▷ *verb* **irritating, irritated** ▷ *noun* **irritation**
▷ *adjective* **irritating** ▷ *adverb* **irritatingly**

is *verb* The third-person present singular form of **be**. **is** (iz)

ISIS *noun* A terrorist organization that wants to establish a country in the Middle East that is governed by their rules. ISIS is short for *Islamic State in Iraq and Syria.* **ISIS** (**eye**-sis)

Islam *noun* The religion based on the teachings of Muhammad. Muslims believe that Allah is the only God and that Muhammad is Allah's prophet. The religion is based on prayer, fasting, charity, and pilgrimage, as taught through the Koran. **Is·lam** (is-**lahm** *or* iz-**lahm**)

Islamic *adjective* Of or having to do with Islam. **Is·lam·ic** (is-**lahm**-ik *or* iz-**lahm**-ik)

island *noun* A piece of land completely surrounded by water: *Manhattan is an island bordered on the east by the East River and on the west by the Hudson River.* **is·land** (**eye**-luhnd)

Word History

The word **island** has a strange pronunciation: Why is the letter s silent? Until the 17th century, the word was spelled *iland*. But there was an unrelated word, *isle*, in English. People connected the two words and started to spell *iland* as *island*, but kept on pronouncing it the same way as before. *Iland* came from Old English *ig*, meaning "island," and the word *land*. So *island* really means "island-land."

islander *noun* A person who comes from or lives on an island. **is·land·er** (**eye**-luhn-dur)

isle *noun* An island, especially a small one. **isle** (ile) **Isle** sounds like **aisle** and **I'll**.

islet *noun* A very small island. **is·let** (**eye**-lit)

isn't *contraction* A short form of *is not*: *Anastasia isn't going to school today.* **is·n't** (**iz**-uhnt)

isolate *verb*
1. To keep something or someone alone or separate: *Annie had to be isolated from the rest of her family while she had the swine flu.*
2. To identify something so as to deal with it separately: *The mechanic checked our car and eventually was able to isolate the problem as a leak in its fuel system.*
i·so·late (**eye**-suh-*late*)
▷ *verb* **isolating, isolated**

isthmus

isolated *adjective*
1. Far separated from other people or things: *He left his successful career for life in an isolated monastery.*
2. If someone feels **isolated**, they feel lonely and not connected with other people.
i·so·lated (**eye**-suh-*lay*-tid)

isolation *noun*
1. The state of being completely apart from other things or people: *He was highly contagious and had to be kept in complete isolation at the hospital.*
2. The act or process of isolating something: *Scientists in the lab are working on the isolation of proteins from milk.*
i·so·la·tion (*eye*-suh-**lay**-shuhn)

isosceles *adjective* An **isosceles** triangle has two equal sides. **i·sos·ce·les** (eye-**sah**-suh-*leez*)

ISP *noun* A company that provides people with access to the internet in exchange for a monthly fee. ISP is short for *internet service provider*.

issue
1. *noun* The main topic for debate or decision: *What issues will be covered at the meeting?*
2. *noun* An edition of a newspaper, magazine, or other periodical.
3. *noun* A problem or difficulty: *Janice has issues with spiders.*
4. *verb* To provide or distribute, as in *to issue supplies*.
5. *verb* To come out of: *Muffled cries issued from the locked closet.*
is·sue (**ish**-oo)
▷ *verb* **issuing, issued**

isthmus *noun* A narrow strip of land that lies between two bodies of water and connects two larger landmasses: *Panama is an isthmus that links North and South America.* **isth·mus** (**is**-muhs)

it
1. *pronoun* An object or situation mentioned earlier or later: *You can't see it, but there's a squirrel on the other side of that tree.*
2. *pronoun* The subject of some verbs that shows an action or condition: *It is snowing. It is hot today.*
3. *noun* The player in a game who performs the main action, such as trying to find others in hide-and-seek.

it (it)

italics *noun* A slanting form of print used to emphasize certain words or to show that they are special in some way: *The sentence you are reading is in italics.* **i·tal·ics** (i-**tal**-iks) ▷ *verb* **italicize** (i-**tal**-i-*size*) ▷ *adjective* **italic**

itch *verb* To experience an uncomfortable tickling sensation on the skin that makes the person want to scratch it. **itch** (ich) ▷ *verb* **itches, itching, itched** ▷ *noun* **itch** ▷ *adjective* **itchy**

it'd *contraction* A short form of *it had* or *it would*. **it'd** (**it**-uhd)

item *noun* One of a list or collection of things, as in *an item of jewelry*. **i·tem** (**eye**-tuhm)

itemize *verb* To list the individual units or parts of something: *The archaeologist itemized the artifacts that she found at the dig site.* **i·tem·ize** (**eye**-tuh-*mize*) ▷ *verb* **itemizing, itemized** ▷ *adjective* **itemized**

itinerant *adjective* Traveling from place to place, usually to find or do work: *Many small towns in the West used to depend on itinerant judges who went from town to town, trying cases.* **i·tin·er·ant** (eye-**tin**-ur-uhnt)

itinerary *noun* A plan for a trip, as in *a tour itinerary*. **i·tin·er·ar·y** (eye-**tin**-uh-*rer*-ee) ▷ *noun, plural* **itineraries**

it'll *contraction* A short form of *it will*. **it'll** (**it**-uhl)

it's *contraction* A short form of *it is* or *it has*: *It's been a few days since I talked to Holly.* **it's** (its)

its *adjective* Belonging to or related to something: *The puppy chased its tail.* **its** (its)

itself *pronoun*
1. It and nothing else: *This program will install by itself.*
2. Used when the subject of a verb is also the object: *The cat launched itself off the porch and up the tree.*
it·self (it-**self**)

Suffix

The suffix **-ive** turns a root word into an adjective by adding the following meaning to the root word: Tending to do something, as in *active* (tending to act), *possessive* (tending to possess), *corrective* (tending to correct).

I've *contraction* A short form of *I have*: *I've got to hurry or I'll miss my lesson.* **I've** (ive)

ivory *noun*
1. A hard, whitish substance that forms the tusks of mammals, especially elephants.
2. A creamy white color.
i·vo·ry (**eye**-vur-ee)
▷ *adjective* **ivory**

ivy *noun* An evergreen climbing or trailing plant with pointed leaves. **i·vy** (**eye**-vee)

a
b
c
d
e
f
g
h
i
j
k
l
m
n
o
p
q
r
s
t
u
v
w
x
y
z

J j

jab

1. *verb* To poke someone or something quickly with a pointed object: *The nurse jabbed me in the arm with a needle.* ▷ *verb* **jabbing, jabbed**

2. *noun* A short, quick punch: *The boxer hit his opponent with a jab from the left.*
jab (jab)

jabber *verb* To talk quickly in an unclear or confused way that is hard to understand: *Stan's jabbering distracted Anouk from her homework.* **jab·ber** (**jab**-ur) ▷ *verb* **jabbering, jabbered** ▷ *noun* **jabber**

jack *noun*

1. A device for raising a heavy vehicle off the ground: *We lifted the car with a jack to put on a new tire.* ▷ *verb* **jack**

2. A playing card with a picture of a soldier or servant, with a value of ten, as in *a jack of hearts.*

3. A small metal piece with six points used in the game of jacks.

4. A hole or set of holes arranged in a particular way that a plug fits into; a socket: *There aren't any phone jacks in that room.*

5. jacks A game played with jacks and a rubber ball.
jack (jak)

jackal *noun* A long-legged wild dog, found in Africa and southern Asia, that feeds off dead animals. **jack·al** (**jak**-uhl)

jacket *noun*

1. A short coat, as in *a denim jacket.*

2. An outer covering, as for a book.
jack·et (**jak**-it)

jackhammer *noun* A machine that uses compressed air to drill through rock, concrete, and similar hard materials. **jack·ham·mer** (**jak**-*ham*-ur)

jack-in-the-box *noun* A toy box with a clown's head that pops out when the lid is opened. ▷ *noun, plural* **jack-in-the-boxes**

jackknife

1. *noun* A knife with a blade that folds into a handle.

jackknife

2. *noun* A type of dive that involves bending at the waist in the air, then straightening out before entering the water headfirst.

3. *verb* To bend or fold in like a jackknife: *There were delays when a truck jackknifed in the snow.* ▷ *verb* **jackknifing, jackknifed**
jack·knife (**jak**-*nife*) ▷ *noun, plural* **jackknives**

jack-o'-lantern *noun* A hollowed-out pumpkin with a face carved into it and a candle inside, used at Halloween. **jack-o'-lan·tern** (**jak**-uh-*lan*-turn)

jackpot *noun* The top prize in a game or contest: *Donna's parents won the jackpot in the state lottery.* **jack·pot** (**jak**-*paht*)

jack-o'-lantern

jackrabbit *noun* A large hare, common in the western part of the United States. The jackrabbit has very long ears and strong back legs for leaping. **jack·rab·bit** (**jak**-*rab*-it)

Jacuzzi *noun* A trademark for a large hot tub with a system of underwater jets that massage the body. **Ja·cuz·zi** (ja-**koo**-zee)

jade *noun*

1. A hard, blue-green stone used for making ornaments and jewelry.

2. A light bluish-green color.
jade (jade) ▷ *adjective* **jade**

jagged *adjective* With sharp, uneven points sticking out, as in *a jagged edge.* **jag·ged** (**jag**-id)

jaguar *noun* A large wildcat with a yellowish-brown coat and black spots, found in the southwestern United States, Mexico, and South and Central America. **jag·uar** (**jag**-wahr)

jail
1. *noun* A building for keeping people who are awaiting trial or who have been found guilty of minor crimes. ▷ *noun* **jailer**
2. *verb* To put someone in jail: *After being convicted of theft, he was jailed for two years.* ▷ *verb* **jailing, jailed**
jail (jayl)

jam
1. *noun* A sweet, thick food made from boiled fruit and sugar, as in *apricot jam.*
2. *noun* A situation in which things or people are stuck, as in *a traffic jam.*
3. *verb* To pack or press something tightly into a space: *I tried to jam enough clothes for two weeks into one suitcase.*
4. *noun* (informal) An awkward, difficult position to be in: *Jeff was in a terrible jam—he'd locked his keys inside his car.*
5. *verb* To become stuck and not work: *The key jammed in the lock.*
6. *verb* To bruise or crush by squeezing: *I jammed my finger in the door.*
7. *(informal)* When musicians have a **jam session**, they play together without following written notes: *My friends came by and we jammed in the basement all night.* ▷ *verb* **jam**
jam (jam)
▷ *verb* **jamming, jammed**

jangle *verb* To make a ringing, metallic sound: *Alina's bracelets jangled on her wrist.* **jan·gle** (jang-guhl)
▷ *verb* **jangling, jangled**

janitor *noun* Someone who maintains a building. **jan·i·tor** (jan-i-tur)

January *noun* The first month on the calendar. January is followed by February and has 31 days. **Jan·u·ar·y** (jan-yoo-er-ee)

Word History

Is there such a thing as a "month with two faces"? The Roman god Janus was often shown with two heads, looking in opposite directions, since he was the protector of gates and doors. His month, **January**, "looks two ways," back to the last year and ahead to the new one.

jar
1. *noun* A container with a wide mouth, as in *a jelly jar.*
2. *verb* To send a painful shock through a part of the body: *I jarred my back when I fell.*
3. *verb* If something **jars** you, it has a surprising, unpleasant effect: *The noise of the accident jarred me out of my sleep.*
4. *verb* If something **jars** with the facts, it conflicts with them: *We got caught when my version of the story jarred with hers.*
jar (jahr)
▷ *verb* **jarring, jarred**

jargon *noun* Words or expressions used only by a particular group of people, as in *medical jargon.* **jar·gon** (jahr-guhn)

jaundice *noun* A medical condition that turns the skin or the whites of the eyes a yellowish color. **jaun·dice** (jawn-dis)

jaunt *noun* A short trip for pleasure: *Leigh suggested a jaunt to the park for a picnic.* **jaunt** (jawnt)

jaunty *adjective* Having or expressing a lively and self-confident manner, as in *a jaunty walk.* **jaun·ty** (jawn-tee) ▷ *adjective* **jauntier, jauntiest** ▷ *adverb* **jauntily**

javelin *noun* A long metal spear that is thrown for distance in a track-and-field event. **jave·lin** (jav-uh-lin)

jaw
1. *noun* Either of the two bones that frame your mouth and hold your teeth in place.
2. *noun* The lower part of your face, just above your neck: *She clenched her jaw anxiously.*
3. **jaws** *noun, plural* The parts of a tool that close to grip an object, as in *the jaws of a clamp.*
jaw (jaw)

jay *noun* A bold, noisy bird that is related to crows. North America has several kinds of jays, including the common **blue jay**. **jay** (jay)

jaywalk *verb* To cross a street illegally, against the traffic light or not at a crosswalk. **jay·walk** (jay-*wawk*) ▷ *verb* **jaywalking, jaywalked** ▷ *noun* **jaywalker**

jazz *noun* A type of music that was started by African Americans at the turn of the 20th century. It has a strong rhythm and does not follow written notes: *Duke Ellington was one of the pioneers of jazz.* **jazz** (jaz) ▷ *adjective* **jazzy**

jazz musician

jealous *adjective*

1. Feeling envious of what someone else possesses or has achieved: *I'm very jealous of Christo's amazing drum playing.*

2. Afraid that a person you love cares more for someone else than for you: *Mark got jealous when Anita started seeing Mateo every day.*

jeal·ous (**jel**-uhs)

▷ *noun* **jealousy** ▷ *adverb* **jealously**

jeans *noun, plural* Pants for casual wear made of denim or similar strong cloth. **jeans** (jeenz)

Word History

Jeans are a common garment today. The word probably comes from the name of the fabric used to make them, *jean fustian.* The word *jean* is from Gene, the Middle English form of Genoa, a city in Italy where such fabric was made, and *fustian* refers to a heavy cotton cloth. Now when we speak of jeans, we mean the pants and not the cloth that they are made from.

Jeep *noun* A trademark for a small, powerful vehicle with four-wheel drive. **Jeep** (jeep)

jeer *verb* To make loud, mocking remarks about someone: *The audience jeered at the singer when he showed up an hour late.* **jeer** (jeer) ▷ *verb* **jeering, jeered** ▷ *noun* **jeer** ▷ *adverb* **jeeringly**

Jehovah *noun* A Hebrew name for God, used in the Old Testament. **Je·ho·vah** (juh-**hoh**-vuh)

jell *verb*

1. To change from a liquid to a somewhat solid form like jelly.

2. To become more certain: *Our plans for the weekend haven't jelled yet.*

jell (jel)

Jell sounds like **gel.** ▷ *verb* **jelling, jelled**

Jell-O *noun* A trademark for a dessert made with gelatin and a flavoring, which is boiled and then allowed to set. **Jell-O** (**jel**-oh)

jelly *noun* A sweet, clear food that is soft, somewhat solid, and made from boiled fruit and sugar, as in *grape jelly.* **jel·ly** (**jel**-ee) ▷ *noun, plural* **jellies**

jellyfish *noun* A sea creature with a soft, almost transparent body, and long, trailing tentacles that sometimes can sting. **jel·ly·fish** (**jel**-ee-*fish*) ▷ *noun, plural* **jellyfish** *or* **jellyfishes**

jeopardy *noun* Danger of loss, harm, or failure: *The recent cutbacks put Paul's job in jeopardy.* **jeop·ard·y** (**jep**-ur-dee) ▷ *verb* **jeopardize**

jerk

1. *verb* To move or pull someone or something very suddenly and sharply: *She jerked her hand away from the hot pan.*

2. *verb* If someone **jerks** you **around,** he or she treats you in an unfair or dishonest way: *My father thought that the used car dealer was jerking him around.*

3. *noun* A sudden, sharp movement: *The old car moved forward with a jerk.*

4. *noun* An annoyingly stupid or foolish person.

▷ *adjective* **jerky** ▷ *adverb* **jerkily**

jerk (jurk)

▷ *verb* **jerking, jerked**

jersey *noun*

1. A knitted material used for clothing.

2. A knitted pullover top worn by athletes, such as football or hockey players, as part of their uniform.

jer·sey (**jur**-zee)

▷ *noun, plural* **jerseys**

jest *noun* Something said in a mocking or amusing tone. **jest** (jest) ▷ *verb* **jest**

Jellyfish

There are about 200 known species of jellyfish. They are related to corals and sea anemones, and live in coastal waters. The body of a jellyfish is a bell-shaped bag formed from two layers of cells separated by a jellylike substance, with a mouth surrounded by hanging tentacles. Jellyfish are carried along by ocean currents, but they can contract their muscles to expel water and change their direction and depth.

jester *noun* A professional joker or entertainer in medieval courts. **jest·er** (**jes**-tur)

Jesus *noun* A Jewish religious teacher who lived in Palestine around 2,000 years ago. His teachings became the basis of Christianity. Also called *Jesus Christ. See* **Christ**. **Je·sus** (**jee**-zuhs)

jet
1. *noun* A stream of liquid or gas forced through a small opening with great pressure: *He accidentally shook the bottle and out came a jet of soda as he opened it.*
2. *noun* An aircraft powered by one or more jet engines: *The jet took off noisily.*
3. *verb* To travel by jet: *They jetted off to South America that night.* ▷ *verb* **jetting, jetted**
jet (jet)

jet engine *noun* An engine that is powered by a stream of gases made by burning a mixture of fuel and air inside the engine itself.

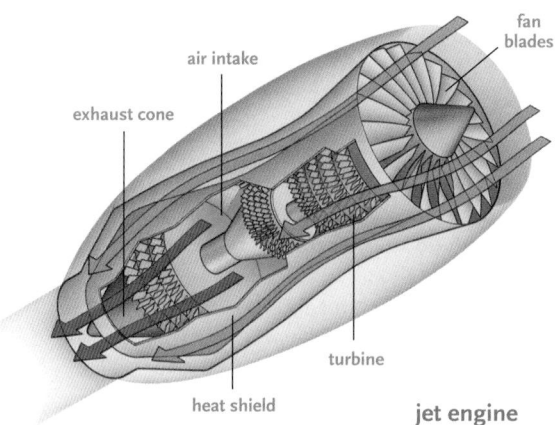

fan blades
air intake
exhaust cone
turbine
heat shield
jet engine

jet lag *noun* Extreme tiredness felt by someone who has taken a long flight across several time zones: *My uncle suffered from jet lag after he returned from his trip to China.*

jet propulsion *noun* A way of moving an aircraft in one direction by using a stream of hot gas propelled in the opposite direction.

jet stream *noun* A very strong current of wind, usually found between four and nine miles above the earth's surface. Jet streams usually move west to east at speeds reaching more than 200 miles per hour.

jettison *verb* To abandon or get rid of something you no longer need: *When we moved, we jettisoned all the old stuff that was stored in the attic.* **jet·ti·son** (**jet**-i-suhn) ▷ *verb* **jettisoning, jettisoned**

jetty *noun* A structure projecting out into the sea to protect a waterfront area from the waves. **jet·ty** (**jet**-ee) ▷ *noun, plural* **jetties**

Jew *noun*
1. Someone who is descended from the ancient Hebrew tribes of Israel.
2. Someone whose religion is Judaism.
Jew (joo)

jewel *noun*
1. A precious stone, usually cut into a shape with many flat sides or facets, worn as an ornament.
2. A person or thing that is greatly admired or valued: *The etching is the jewel of his art collection.*
jew·el (**joo**-uhl)

Word History

An old history book tells the story of how Richard the Lionhearted gave a **jewel** to another king. It turns out, though, that this "jewel" was a sword. This is an old meaning of *jewel*: "something valuable." English speakers adopted the word from *joel*, an Old French term for an ornament, but we don't know much more about the word's history. It could have meant "something pleasant" and come from the Latin word *jocus*, the source for the English word *joke*. The idea of a jest or a game gave to *jewel* a sense of being a trifle, a little plaything.

jeweler *noun* A person who designs, makes, repairs, or sells jewelry. **jew·el·er** (**joo**-uh-lur)

jewelry *noun* Personal ornaments, such as rings, bracelets, and necklaces, often made of gold and gems, as in *antique jewelry.* **jew·el·ry** (**joo**-uhl-ree)

Jewish *adjective* Of or having to do with Jews, their religion, or their culture, as in *a Jewish bakery.* **Jew·ish** (**joo**-ish)

jib *noun*
1. The arm of a mechanical crane that can move up, down, and sideways.
2. A triangular sail that is set in front of the mast and attached to the bow of a boat or ship.
jib (jib)

jiffy *noun* A very short time; a moment: *I'll be with you in a jiffy.* **jif·fy** (**jif**-ee) ▷ *noun, plural* **jiffies**

jig *noun*
1. A fast, lively dance, or the music played during this dance. ▷ *verb* **jig**
2. *(informal)* If **the jig is up**, the trick you are playing or the secret you are keeping is over because someone has caught on to you.
jig (jig)

jigsaw *noun* An electric saw with a very narrow blade for cutting curves and patterns in wood. **jig·saw** (**jig**-saw)

jigsaw puzzle *noun* A wooden or cardboard puzzle made up of many small, interlocking pieces of a picture that have to be fitted together.

jingle *noun*

1. A light ringing sound made from small bells or from metal objects hitting each other, as in *the jingle of keys.* ▷ *verb* **jingle**

2. A simple, upbeat tune or song used to advertise a product: *He wrote a jingle for the new soda ad.*
jin·gle (**jing**-guhl)

jinx

1. *noun* A person or thing believed to bring bad luck: *My red shirt seems to be a jinx—every time I wear it, I get into trouble.*

2. *verb* To seem to bring bad luck. ▷ *verb* **jinxing, jinxed**
jinx (jingks)

job *noun*

1. Work to be done: *My job is to set the table for dinner.*

2. A paid position of employment: *Amina is looking for a job in publishing.*
job (jahb)

jock *noun* (*informal*) A male athlete, especially one who is not very interested in other things: *Ian is a real jock—all he wants to do is play sports.* **jock** (jahk)

jockey

1. *noun* A professional rider in a horse race. ▷ *verb* **jockey**

2. *verb* If you **jockey for** something, you try every possible way to gain or achieve it: *The two teams jockeyed for the lead.* ▷ *verb* **jockeying, jockeyed**
jock·ey (**jah**-kee)

jog *verb*

1. To run at a slow, steady pace, especially for exercise: *Faith went for a jog despite the rain and wind.* ▷ *noun* **jog** ▷ *noun* **jogger** ▷ *noun* **jogging**

2. To shake or to push: *Someone jogged my elbow.*

3. If something **jogs your memory**, it causes you to suddenly remember something.
jog (jahg)
▷ *verb* **jogging, jogged**

join *verb*

1. To secure or link two things together: *The artist joined the sections of the collage with glue.* ▷ *noun* **join**

2. To come into the company of something or someone: *I joined them for breakfast.*

3. To become a member of a group or an employee of an organization, as in *to join a club.*

4. If you **join up**, you become a member of the armed forces.
join (join)
▷ *verb* **joining, joined**

jockeys

joint

1. *noun* A connection between two bones of a skeleton: *The knee is a troublesome joint for many runners.*

2. *noun* A place where two or more things meet or come together: *The joint of this chair is loose.*
▷ *adjective* **jointed**

3. *adjective* Done or shared by two or more people, as in *a joint project.* ▷ *adverb* **jointly**

4. *noun* (*informal*) A cheap, often unattractive place to eat, drink, or spend the night, as in *a beer joint.*
joint (joint)

joke *verb* To amuse people with funny stories or remarks; to play tricks on people: *Uncle Richie always jokes with the kids.* **joke** (joke) ▷ *verb* **joking, joked** ▷ *noun* **joke**

jolly *adjective* Cheerful and in good humor; high-spirited: *He's a jolly old man who reminds me of Santa Claus.* **jol·ly** (**jah**-lee) ▷ *adjective* **jollier, jolliest**

jolt

1. *verb* To move with sudden, rough jerks: *The train's sudden stop jolted us awake.* ▷ *verb* **jolting, jolted** ▷ *noun* **jolt**

2. *noun* A sudden surprise or shock: *The news of his death gave me quite a jolt.*
jolt (johlt)

jonquil *noun* A plant that grows from a bulb and has long, narrow leaves and fragrant white or yellow flowers. The jonquil is a kind of daffodil. **jon·quil** (**jahn**-kwil)

jonquil

jostle *verb* To bump or push roughly: *I hate getting jostled by the crowds when I go Christmas shopping.* **jos·tle** (**jah**-suhl) ▷ *verb* **jostling, jostled**

jot *verb* To write something quickly: *I jotted down the address while talking on the phone.* **jot** (jaht) ▷ *verb* **jotting, jotted**

joule *noun* A unit for measuring work or energy. **joule** (jool)

journal *noun*
 1. A diary in which you regularly write down your thoughts and experiences.
 2. A magazine or newspaper that deals with a particular subject.
 jour·nal (**jur**-nuhl)

journalism *noun* The work of gathering and reporting news for newspapers, magazines, and other media. **jour·na·lism** (**jur**-nuh-*liz*-uhm)

journalist *noun* Someone who writes for newspapers, magazines, and other media. **jour·nal·ist** (**jur**-nuh-list) ▷ *adjective* **journalistic**

journey *noun* A long trip, as in *an overseas journey.* **jour·ney** (**jur**-nee) ▷ *verb* **journey**

joust
 1. *noun* A competition between two knights on horseback with lances.
 2. *verb* To compete closely: *Everyone enjoyed watching the two debate teams joust with each other.* ▷ *verb* **jousting, jousted**
 joust (joust)

jovial *adjective* Someone who is **jovial** is cheerful and friendly. **jo·vi·al** (**joh**-vee-uhl) ▷ *noun* **joviality** (*joh*-vee-**al**-i-tee) ▷ *adverb* **jovially**

jowl *noun* A layer of loose flesh that hangs down around the throat or lower jaw. **jowl** (joul)

joy *noun*
 1. A feeling of great delight or happiness: *Sari was full of joy when her cat returned home.*
 2. A person or thing that brings great happiness to someone: *Walking through the woods was a real joy.*
 joy (joi)
 ▷ *adjective* **joyous**

joyful *adjective* Feeling or causing great happiness. **joy·ful** (**joi**-fuhl) ▷ *noun* **joyfulness** ▷ *adverb* **joyfully**

joystick *noun* A lever that can be moved in several directions, used to control an aircraft or the movement of an image in a computer game. **joy·stick** (**joi**-stik)

JPEG *noun* A common format for image files. JPEG is short for *Joint Photographic Experts Group.* **JPEG** (**jay**-peg)

Jr. The abbreviation for *Junior: Martin Luther King Jr. was a famous civil rights leader.* See **Junior. Jr.** (**joon**-yur)

jubilant *adjective* Filled with or expressing great happiness or triumph: *Our school was jubilant when our team won.* **ju·bi·lant** (**joo**-buh-luhnt) ▷ *noun* **jubilation** (*joo*-buh-**lay**-shuhn) ▷ *adverb* **jubilantly**

jubilee *noun* The celebration of an important event, such as a 25th or 50th anniversary. **ju·bi·lee** (**joo**-buh-*lee*)

Judaism *noun* The religion of the Jewish people, based on a belief in one God and the teachings of the Torah, the first five books of the Old Testament. **Ju·da·ism** (**joo**-dee-*iz*-uhm)

judge
 1. *noun* The person in charge in a court of law who decides the matters brought to the court: *The judge called for order at the start of the hearing.* ▷ *verb* **judge**
 2. *verb* To decide the results of a competition: *My friend Jeanne has been asked to judge the film competition.* ▷ *noun* **judge**
 3. *verb* To form an opinion or come to a conclusion about something or someone: *I don't believe in judging people by the way they look.*
 judge (juhj)
 ▷ *verb* **judging, judged**

judgment *or* **judgement** *noun*
 1. An opinion or conclusion about someone or something: *I think your judgment of the situation is right.*
 2. A decision made by a judge or a court of law: *He faced a judgment of one year of community service.*
 3. The ability to decide or form opinions wisely: *They showed good judgment in deciding not to drink and drive.*
 judg·ment *or* **judge·ment** (**juhj**-muhnt)

judicial *adjective* Of or having to do with a court of law or a judge, as in *the judicial system.* **ju·di·cial** (joo-**dish**-uhl) ▷ *adverb* **judicially**

judicious *adjective* Showing good sense or judgment, as in *a judicious choice.* **ju·di·cious** (joo-**dish**-uhs) ▷ *adverb* **judiciously**

judo *noun* An Asian martial art in which two people try to throw each other off balance by using quick, controlled movements. **ju·do** (**joo**-doh)

jug *noun* A container with a narrow neck and a small handle. **jug** (juhg)

juggernaut *noun* A very powerful force that can destroy anything in its path. **jug·ger·naut** (**juhg**-ur-*nawt*)

Word History

In a Hindu religious festival, worshipers would pull a large cart with an image of their god Krishna. Legend has it that worshipers long ago had thrown themselves under the wheels of the cart. The cart kept going, crushing them to death. Krishna was called *Jagannath,* meaning "lord of the world," in the Hindi language, but English speakers use the word **juggernaut** to mean a powerful force that can destroy anything in its path.

juggle *verb* To keep objects such as balls or clubs up in the air by catching them and then quickly tossing them up again, over and over. Jugglers usually juggle three or more objects at a time. **jug·gle** (**juhg**-uhl)
▷ *verb* **juggling, juggled**
▷ *noun* **juggler**

juice *noun* A liquid derived from fruit, vegetables, or meat, that is often made into a drink or sauce, as in *cranberry juice*. **juice** (joos) ▷ *adjective* **juicy**

jukebox *noun* A machine that, when you put coins in it, automatically plays a piece of music you have selected. **juke·box** (**jook**-bahks) ▷ *noun*, plural **jukeboxes**

jukebox

July *noun* The seventh month on the calendar, after June and before August. July has 31 days. **Ju·ly** (ju-**lye**)

Word History

The ancient Romans named most of their months for gods. **July**, however, was kept for the great general and statesman of Rome, Julius Caesar, whose birthday falls in July. The English spelling was at first "Julie" and then "July."

jumble *verb* To mix things up so that they are messy or confused: *The cat jumped on the desk and jumbled all the papers.* **jum·ble** (**juhm**-buhl) ▷ *verb* **jumbling, jumbled** ▷ *noun* **jumble**

jumbo
1. *adjective* Very large, as in *jumbo shrimp*.
2. jumbo jet *noun* A very large jet airplane, such as the wide-body Boeing 747.
jum·bo (**juhm**-boh)

jump
1. *verb* To push off with your legs and feet and move through or into the air: *I can reach the top shelf if I jump.*
2. *noun* The distance covered by a jump, as in *a jump across the brook.*
3. *verb* To move or get up suddenly, as in *to jump in surprise.*
4. *noun* A sudden rise or increase, as in *a jump in prices.*
5. If you **jump on** someone, you attack or criticize the person: *I didn't expect Ward to jump on me the minute I opened my mouth.*
6. If you **jump at** an offer or an opportunity, you accept it eagerly: *She jumped at the chance to try out for the school play.*
jump (juhmp)
▷ *verb* **jumping, jumped**

Synonyms

Jump means to propel yourself into or through the air, using the power of your feet and legs. You can jump down from a height, or straight up, or in any direction: *In the movie, the sheriff jumped onto the stagecoach as it passed under the bridge.*

- -

■ **Leap** means to jump quickly or in a dramatic way: *Lucia leaped into the air when Valerie's pet hamster crawled up her leg.*

■ **Spring** means to jump up suddenly as if there were springs underneath you: *My puppy springs up and runs into the kitchen whenever he hears me pour food in his bowl.*

■ **Vault** means to jump up and over something, using your hands or a pole: *Shelly vaulted over the fence to get to her neighbor's yard.*

■ **Hurdle** means to jump up and over something, especially while running: *The horse and rider hurdled the last brick wall and finished the race in record time.*

jumper *noun* A dress without sleeves or a collar, usually worn over a blouse or sweater: *Abby's favorite winter outfit is a corduroy jumper.* **jum·per** (**juhm**-pur)

jump rope *noun*
1. A rope that you swing over your head and under your feet as a game or exercise.
2. A game in which this rope is used.

junction *noun* A place where two or more roads or railroad lines meet: *Ride one mile to the junction of Bay Street and Alden Avenue, then turn right.* **junc·tion** (**juhngk**-shuhn)

June *noun* The sixth month on the calendar, after May and before July. June has 30 days. **June** (joon)

Word History

There are two theories as to the origin of the word **June**. Many scholars point to the Latin name Junius, the name of a powerful Roman family. Other scholars, however, believe that the ancient Romans named this month for Juno, the goddess who protected women.

jungle *noun* A forest in tropical geographic areas that is thickly covered with trees, vines, and bushes: *The Peruvian jungle is full of unique plants.* **jun·gle** (**juhng**-guhl)

Word History

Jungle goes back to the ancient Indian word *jangala*, which meant a dry land without plants. Later, the word came to mean any kind of uncultivated land. When the English occupied India, the word passed into English, where it came to mean land overgrown with vegetation, or the vegetation itself.

junior
1. *adjective* **Junior** is used after the name of a son who has the same name as his father. It is often abbreviated as **Jr.** and means "the younger of two," as in *John Smith, Jr.*
2. *adjective* Lower in rank or position, as in *a junior counselor.*
3. *adjective* For younger people, as in *junior tennis.*
4. *noun* A third-year high school or college student.
jun·ior (**joon**-yur)

junior high school *noun* A school between elementary school and high school. It usually includes the seventh and eighth grades and sometimes includes the ninth grade.

juniper *noun* An evergreen bush or tree similar to a pine. It bears purple fruit that look like berries. **ju·ni·per** (**joo**-nuh-pur)

junk *noun*
1. Old metal, wood, rags, or other items that are thrown away: *He makes art out of junk he finds on the street.*
2. Something that has no value or use: *She sat around all evening watching junk on TV.*
3. A flat-bottomed boat with square sails, used in China and the East Indies.
junk (juhngk)

junk food *noun* Food with very little nutritional value that is prepared and packaged ahead of time, such as potato chips, candy, and cookies: *I've decided to give up junk food and eat better.*

junk mail *noun* Advertisements and catalogs that are sent to you without your asking for them.

junkyard *noun* An area used to collect, store, and sometimes sell discarded materials, such as old or wrecked cars. **junk·yard** (**juhngk**-yahrd)

Jupiter *noun* The fifth planet from the sun. Jupiter is the largest planet in our solar system. **Ju·pi·ter** (**joo**-pi-tur)

Jupiter

juror *noun* A member of a jury. **ju·ror** (**joor**-ur)

jury *noun* A group of people, usually 12 in number, who listen to the facts at a trial and decide whether the accused person is innocent or guilty: *In her closing statement, the lawyer appealed directly to the jury.* **ju·ry** (**joor**-ee) ▷ *noun, plural* **juries**

just
1. *adjective* Based on or acting according to what is fair, as in *a just verdict.* ▷ *adverb* **justly**
2. *adverb* Exactly: *That cantaloupe weighs just two pounds.*
3. *adverb* A short while ago: *Hillary just left for school.*
4. *adverb* Barely or by a small amount: *We just made the train.*
5. *adverb* Nothing more than: *It's just a small scratch.*
just (juhst)

justice *noun*
1. Fair and impartial behavior or treatment: *The soldiers' mission was to bring about peace and justice.*
2. A country's system for carrying out laws and punishing those who break them: *The sheriff was determined to bring the thieves to justice.*
3. A judge.
4. **justice of the peace** Someone who hears cases in a local court of law and performs marriages.
jus·tice (**juhs**-tis)

justify *verb*
1. To explain your actions to try to prove that they are right: *He justified spending so much on clothes by saying he needed them for work.*
2. To arrange text so that the left and right margins are in a straight line.
jus·ti·fy (**juhs**-tuh-*fye*)
▷ *verb* **justifies, justifying, justified**
▷ *noun* **justification** (**juhs**-tuh-fi-**kay**-shuhn)

jut *verb* To stick out: *The mountain peak jutted into the sky.* **jut** (juht) ▷ *verb* **jutting, jutted**

jute *noun* A strong fiber that is used to make rope and a coarse material called burlap. Jute comes from a plant that grows in tropical Asia. **jute** (joot)

juvenile
1. *noun* A person who is legally below the age at which he or she can be treated as an adult for a crime.
2. *adjective* Of or for young people, as in *juvenile literature.*
3. *adjective* Childish or immature, as in *juvenile behavior.*
ju·ve·nile (**joo**-vuh-nuhl)

a
b
c
d
e
f
g
h
i
j
k
l
m
n
o
p
q
r
s
t
u
v
w
x
y
z

Kk

About K Words that begin with a **K** sound are spelled with a *k* or a *c*. Examples: kabob, keen, capital, coin. Words ending with a consonant and a *k* sound are usually spelled with a *k*, as in *milk*. The *k* can also be silent, often when it comes before *n*, as in *knowledge*. *K* is the 11th letter in the alphabet, the same position it had in the earliest forms of the alphabet more than 3,000 years ago.

kabob *or* **kebab** *noun* Small pieces of meat or vegetables that have been roasted or grilled on a skewer. **ka·bob** *or* **ke·bab** (kuh-**bahb**)

Kabuki *noun* A type of Japanese drama traditionally performed by men in elaborate costumes. **Ka·bu·ki** (kuh-**boo**-kee)

kaleidoscope *noun*
1. A tube containing mirrors and pieces of colored glass that you twist or turn as you look into it to see an endless variety of patterns.
2. A changing pattern or sequence: *She showed me scarves in a kaleidoscope of colors.* **ka·lei·do·scope** (kuh-**lye**-duh-*skope*)
▷ *adjective* **kaleidoscopic** (kuh-*lye*-duh-**skah**-pik)

kangaroo *noun* An Australian marsupial with short front legs and long, powerful hind legs that are used for leaping—its principal means of moving. The female carries her young in a pouch. The kangaroo is a national symbol of Australia. **kan·ga·roo** (*kang*-guh-**roo**)

karaoke *noun* A form of entertainment that originated in Japan in which people sing the words of popular songs to recorded background music. **kar·a·o·ke** (*kar*-ee-**oh**-kee)

karate *noun* An Asian martial art of self-defense in which people fight each other using controlled kicks and punches. **ka·ra·te** (kuh-**rah**-tee)

Word History

Karate is a Japanese word meaning "empty hand." In the martial art of karate, your hands are empty because you don't hold a weapon. Instead, you use your hands, feet, and other parts of your body to defeat an opponent.

karma *noun*
1. The force or effect from the good or bad things that someone does. The idea of karma is that when you do bad things, eventually you will get a bad result, even if that doesn't happen right away. The same rule applies when you do good things.
2. **good karma** *or* **bad karma** (*informal*) In popular culture, the effect of a person's actions, with good or bad things happening to them depending on the good or bad things they have done: *I'll give you a ride to the airport; I need some good karma.* **kar·ma** (**kahr**-muh)
▷ *adjective* **karmic**

Word History

Hinduism and Buddhism share the idea of **karma**. The word comes from an ancient language of India called Sanskrit and it originally meant "action." English speakers were traveling to and trading with India in the early 19th century when they began to use the word. Sometimes speakers of one language take a word from another language without changing the spelling or meaning. Words taken like this are called loanwords.

Katrina *or* **Hurricane Katrina** *noun* A hurricane that formed in the Gulf of Mexico in the summer of 2005 and came ashore near New Orleans. It was at the time the costliest natural disaster in the history of the United States. **Ka·tri·na** (kuh-**tree**-nuh)

katydid *noun* A large, green insect that is related to the grasshopper. The noise that the male makes when it rubs its front wings together sounds like its name. **ka·ty·did** (**kay**-tee-*did*)

kayak *noun* A covered, narrow boat with a small opening in the top in which you sit and paddle. Kayaks were first used by the Inuit. **kay·ak** (**kye**-ak)

KB Short for **kilobyte** or the plural form *kilobytes*: *Each of the files I'll send you is about 30 KB.*

keel
1. *noun* The structure along the bottom of a boat or ship that keeps it stable and upright.
2. **keel over** *verb* (*informal*) To fall over or collapse:

kangaroo

A B C D E F G H I J **K** L M N O P Q R S T U V W X Y Z

398

He keeled over in the hot sun. ▷ *verb* **keeling, keeled**
keel (keel)

keen *adjective*

1. Very sharp, as in *a keen blade.*
2. Highly developed, as in *keen eyesight.*
3. Quick or alert, as in *a keen mind.*
4. Interested in or enthusiastic about: *I am keen on sports.*

keen (keen)

▷ *adjective* **keener, keenest**

keep *verb*

1. To have something and not give it up: *Let's keep this candy for ourselves.*
2. To remain in the same condition, as in *to keep quiet.*
3. To continue an activity: *He kept waving his arms and calling to me.*
4. To store: *We'll keep the new car in the garage.*
5. To hold back or to stop: *The blizzard kept us from going outside.*
6. To carry out or to fulfill, as in *to keep a promise.*

keep (keep)

▷ *verb* **keeping, kept** (kept)

keeper *noun* Someone who manages or takes care of someone or something, as in *a keeper of a lighthouse.* **keep·er** (**kee**-pur)

keg *noun* A small barrel, especially one that holds less than 16 gallons. **keg** (keg)

kelp *noun* A large, edible, brown seaweed, also used to produce iodine, fertilizer, and other products. **kelp** (kelp) ▷ *noun, plural* **kelp**

kennel *noun*

1. A shelter where dogs and cats are kept.
2. A place where dogs and cats are raised and trained or cared for when their owners are away: *We'll have to send the cat to a kennel before we go on vacation.* **ken·nel** (**ken**-uhl)

Word History

A **kennel** houses both cats and dogs. Can you guess which type of animal is the source for the word? The root of *kennel* turns out to be the Latin word for "dog," *canis*, which you can also see in the word *canine*.

kept *verb* The past tense and the past participle of **keep**. **kept** (kept)

kerchief *noun* A piece of cloth, usually square, worn around the head or neck. **ker·chief** (**kur**-chif)

kernel *noun*

1. A grain or seed of corn, wheat, or other cereal plant, as in *a kernel of corn.*
2. The soft part inside the shell of a nut that is good to eat.
3. The central or most important part of something, as in *a kernel of truth.*

ker·nel (**kur**-nuhl)

Kernel sounds like **colonel**.

kerosene *noun* A colorless liquid fuel that is made from petroleum. **ker·o·sene** (**ker**-uh-*seen*)

ketchup *noun* A thick, red sauce made with tomatoes, onions, salt, sugar, and spices. **ketch·up** (**kech**-uhp)

Word History

Some people write **ketchup** and others write **catsup**. Both forms of this word may come from the Chinese term *ke-tsiap*, the name of a pickled fish sauce.

kettle *noun* A metal pot mainly used for boiling liquids. **ket·tle** (**ket**-uhl)

kettledrum *noun* A large drum with a metal body shaped like a bowl that makes a deep, booming sound. **ket·tle·drum** (**ket**-uhl-*druhm*)

kettledrum

key

1. *noun* A piece of metal shaped to fit into a lock to open it or to start an engine: *I left the house key in my other jacket, and now I'm locked out!*
2. *noun* Something that provides a solution or an explanation, as in *the key to the mystery.*
3. *noun* One of many buttons on a panel that is used to operate a computer or typewriter.
4. *noun* One of the black or white bars that you press when you play an organ or a piano.
5. *adjective* Very important, as in *a key decision.*
6. *noun* A list or chart that explains the symbols on a map: *The key shows that the parts in green are forests.*
7. *noun* A group of musical notes based around one particular note, as in *a sonata in the key of D.*

key (kee)

Key sounds like **quay**.

keyboard *noun*

1. The set of keys on a computer, typewriter, or musical instrument, as in *the keyboard of a PC* or *the keyboard of an organ.*
2. An **electronic keyboard** is an electric musical instrument that has keys like a piano and buttons that you control to change the sound in some way. **key·board** (**kee**-*bord*)

keyboard shortcut *noun* A combination of two or three keys that you can press on a computer keyboard to do something that would take longer if you used the mouse: *Control + V is a keyboard shortcut that allows you to paste text or an image.*

keyhole *noun* The hole in a lock where a key fits. **key·hole** (**kee**-*hole*)

keypad *noun* A small panel of keys or buttons used for operating an electronic machine such as a calculator. **key·pad** (**kee**-*pad*)

keystone *noun*
1. A wedge-shaped piece at the top of an arch that keeps the other pieces in place.
2. Something necessary or very important that other things depend on: *Her self-confidence has been the keystone of her success.*
key·stone (**kee**-*stone*)

keystroke *noun* The action of hitting a key on a computer or typewriter keyboard. **key·stroke** (**kee**-*strohk*)

keyword *noun* A word that can be used to find a particular book, website, or computer file: *I typed "kangaroo" as a keyword on the search engine and got a lot of hits for websites about kangaroos.* **key·word** (**kee**-*wurd*)

kg Short for **kilogram** or the plural form *kilograms.*

khaki *noun*
1. A dull, brownish-yellow color.
2. A strong cotton cloth of this color, often used for soldiers' uniforms.
kha·ki (**kak**-ee *or* **kah**-kee)
▷ *adjective* **khaki**

kibbutz *noun* A farming settlement in Israel where people live and work together. **kib·butz** (ki-**buts**) ▷ *noun, plural* **kibbutzim** (ki-*but*-**seem**)

kick
1. *verb* To strike something with your foot: *Lulu kicked my ankle under the table to get my attention.* ▷ *verb* **kicking, kicked** ▷ *noun* **kick**
2. *noun* (*informal*) A feeling of excitement or pleasure: *My dad gets a kick out of watching me play the tuba.*
kick (kik)

kickoff *noun*
1. A kick of the ball that starts the action in a football or soccer game.
2. The start of something, as in *the kickoff of a fund-raising campaign.*
kick·off (**kik**-*awf*)

kid
1. *noun* (*informal*) A child.
2. *noun* A young goat.
3. *verb* To make fun of or tease someone: *Are you kidding me?* ▷ *verb* **kidding, kidded**
kid (kid)

kidnap *verb* The illegal activity of capturing someone and keeping the person as a prisoner, as in *to kidnap a businessman for ransom.* **kid·nap** (**kid**-nap) ▷ *verb* **kidnapping** *or* **kidnaping, kidnapped** *or* **kidnaped** ▷ *noun* **kidnapper** *or* **kidnaper**

kidney *noun* One of a pair of organs in your body that clean your blood by filtering out waste matter and turning it into urine. **kid·ney** (**kid**-nee)

kidney bean *noun* A bean plant with kidney-shaped seeds. Many of the beans we eat are different kinds of kidney beans.

kidney bean

kill *verb*
1. To cause the death of a person, animal, or other living thing: *I've tried to grow orchids, but I always seem to kill them.* ▷ *noun* **killer**
2. To end or to destroy: *Failing the test killed my chances of getting an A in English.*
3. To hurt very much: *My back is killing me.*
kill (kil)
▷ *verb* **killing, killed**

killdeer *noun* A bird that is a kind of plover, with a high, piercing call and a white breast with two black bands. **kill·deer** (**kil**-*deer*) ▷ *noun, plural* **killdeers** *or* **killdeer**

kiln *noun* A very hot oven used to bake or dry bricks, pottery, or other objects made of clay. **kiln** (kil *or* kiln)

kilo *noun* Short for **kilogram**: *They bought two kilos of potatoes.* **ki·lo** (**kee**-loh *or* **kil**-oh) ▷ *noun, plural* **kilos**

kilobyte *noun* A unit for measuring the amount of data in a computer memory or file. A kilobyte is equal to 1,024 bytes. **kil·o·byte** (**kil**-uh-*bite*)

kilogram *noun* A unit of mass or weight in the metric system equal to 1,000 grams, or 2.2 pounds. **kil·o·gram** (**kil**-uh-*gram*)

kilohertz *noun* A unit for measuring the frequency of radio waves. One kilohertz is equal to 1,000 vibrations per second. **kil·o·hertz** (**kil**-uh-*hurts*) ▷ *noun, plural* **kilohertz** *or* **kilohertzes**

kilojoule *noun* A unit for measuring energy or work. One kilojoule is equal to 1,000 joules. **kil·o·joule** (**kil**-uh-*jool*)

kiloliter *noun* A unit for measuring liquids in the metric system equal to 1,000 liters, or about 264 gallons. **kil·o·li·ter** (**kil**-uh-*lee*-tur)

kilometer *noun* A unit of length in the metric system equal to 1,000 meters, or about 0.6 miles. **ki·lo·me·ter** (ki-**lah**-mi-tur)

kilowatt *noun* A unit for measuring electrical power. One kilowatt equals 1,000 watts. **kil·o·watt** (**kil**-uh-*waht*)

kilt *noun* A pleated, knee-length plaid skirt, often worn by Scottish men as part of their traditional costume. **kilt** (kilt)

kilter *noun* The usual or proper state of something; now usually used only in the phrases **out of kilter** or **off kilter**: *The delay threw their plans out of kilter.* **kil·ter** (kil-tur)

kimono *noun* A long, loose robe with wide sleeves and a sash, traditionally worn by women in Japan. **ki·mo·no** (ki-**moh**-nuh)

kin *noun* Your family and relatives: *It's good to be home among my kin.* **kin** (kin)

kind

1. *adjective* Having or showing a caring and generous nature, as in *a kind teacher.* ▷ *adjective* **kinder, kindest** ▷ *noun* **kindness** ▷ *adverb* **kindly**

2. *noun* A group of the same or similar people or things: *The beagle is one kind of dog.*

3. *noun* A type or sort: *That's the kind of book that makes me laugh.*

4. If something is **one of a kind**, there is no other like it: *That sister of yours, she's one of a kind.* **kind** (kinde)

kindergarten *noun* A class for children ages four to six that is usually attended before entering first grade. **kin·der·gar·ten** (**kin**-dur-*gahr*-tuhn)

kimonos

Word History

Kindergarten is the German word for "children's garden." The first kindergarten was opened in Germany in 1837 by the educator Friedrich Wilhelm August Froebel. Froebel, who had a strict and unhappy childhood, spent his life opening schools where children could play and explore.

kindhearted *adjective* Having or showing a friendly, helpful, and generous nature: *Their kindhearted neighbor offered to look after their cat while they were away.* **kind·heart·ed** (kinde-*hahr*-tid) ▷ *adverb* **kindheartedly**

kindle *verb*

1. To set on fire: *We used dry twigs and matches to kindle our campfire.*

2. To stir up or to excite: *Watching my father draw every evening kindled my interest in art.* **kin·dle** (kin-duhl) ▷ *verb* **kindling, kindled**

kindling *noun* Small pieces of wood or twigs used to start a fire: *I gathered kindling for a campfire.* **kin·dling** (kind-ling)

kindly

1. *adjective* Kind, as in *a kindly old gentleman.*

2. *adverb* In a kind way: *She kindly patted the crying boy on the shoulder.*

3. *adverb* If you **take kindly** to something, you accept it willingly: *He did not take kindly to criticism.* **kind·ly** (kinde-lee)

kindness *noun* The quality of being friendly, helpful, and generous: *They thanked him for his kindness in helping them with their luggage.* **kind·ness** (kinde-nis) ▷ *noun, plural* **kindnesses**

kinetic *adjective* Of or having to do with motion, as in *kinetic energy.* **ki·net·ic** (ki-**net**-ik) ▷ *adverb* **kinetically**

king *noun*

1. A male ruler of a country, especially one who comes from a royal family, as in *the king of the Netherlands.*

2. A playing card with a picture of a king on it, as in *the king of spades.*

3. The most important piece in a game of chess. **king** (king)

kingdom *noun*

1. A country that is ruled by a king or queen, as in *the kingdom of Sweden.*

2. An area that is associated with or under the control of a person or thing: *Marco considered his room his own little kingdom.*

3. One of the main groups into which all living things are divided, such as the animal kingdom and the plant kingdom. **king·dom** (king-duhm)

kingfisher *noun* A colorful bird with a long, sharp beak that lives near water and dives for fish. **king·fish·er** (king-*fish*-ur)

kink *noun*

1. A tight curl or twist in a rope, wire, hose, chain, or hair: *Darren smoothed the kinks out of the hose as he coiled it.* ▷ *adjective* **kinky**

2. A painful or stiff feeling, as in *a kink in the neck.*

3. An imperfection or obstacle that is likely to cause problems: *The storm put a kink in our flight plans.* **kink** (kingk)

a b c d e f g h i j **k** l m n o p q r s t u v w x y z

kinship *noun*
1. A family relationship.
2. Any close connection: *Juan felt a kinship with Meg because they were both new at the school.*
kin·ship (**kin**-ship)

kiosk *noun* A small structure with one or more open sides, often used as a stand for selling newspapers. **ki·osk** (**kee**-ahsk)

kiss *verb* To touch someone with your lips as a greeting or sign of love or affection. **kiss** (kis)
▷ *verb* **kisses, kissing, kissed** ▷ *noun* **kiss**

kit *noun*
1. A set of parts needed to put something together, as in *a model race car kit.*
2. A set of tools and materials for a certain purpose, as in *a sewing kit* or *a first aid kit.*
kit (kit)

kitchen *noun* A room or area where food is prepared and cooked: *Demi went straight to the kitchen for a snack.* **kitch·en** (**kich**-uhn)

kite *noun* A light frame covered with paper or other material that is attached to a long piece of string and flown in the wind. **kite** (kite)

kitten *noun* A young cat. **kit·ten** (**kit**-uhn)

kitty *noun*
1. A kitten: *Janie called out, "Here, kitty, kitty."*
2. A fund of money, to which everyone in a group contributes, that is used to buy something: *We all put a dollar in the kitty to pay for refreshments.*
kit·ty (**kit**-ee)
▷ *noun, plural* **kitties**

kiwi *noun*
1. A bird from New Zealand that cannot fly, with a down-curved bill and hair-like feathers.
2. A small, round fruit with fuzzy brown skin and green flesh. Kiwis are grown in New Zealand. Also called *kiwifruit.*
ki·wi (**kee**-wee)

kl Short for **kiloliter** or the plural form *kiloliters.*

Kleenex *noun* A trademark for a soft tissue paper that can be used as a handkerchief. **Klee·nex** (**klee**-neks)

kleptomania *noun* A mental disorder that makes someone feel the need to steal things: *She was diagnosed with kleptomania after being caught shoplifting several times.* **klep·to·ma·ni·a** (*klep*-tuh-**may**-nee-uh) ▷ *noun* **kleptomaniac**

klutz *noun* (*slang*) A clumsy person. **klutz** (kluhts)

km Short for **kilometer** or the plural form *kilometers.*

knack *noun* A skill or natural ability: *Greg has a knack for math.* **knack** (nak)

knapsack *noun* A canvas or leather bag used to carry books or supplies on your back. **knap·sack** (**nap**-sak)

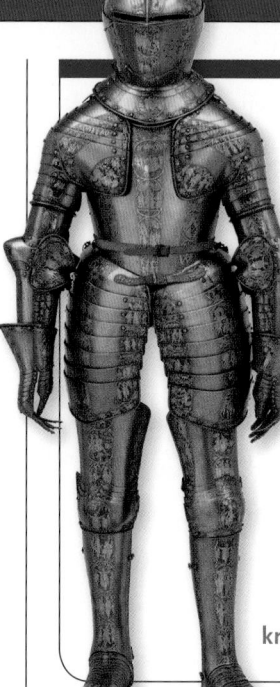

Knights

Knights fought on horseback and were the highest warrior class in medieval Europe. They followed a code called chivalry, pledging to be loyal to the king, to serve the church, to be courteous to women, and to protect the weak. In the 12th century, knights wore armor made of chain mail, small iron rings woven together to form protective tunics. Later, they wore heavy metal plates and helmets with visors.

knight's suit of armor

knead *verb* To press, fold, and stretch dough with your hands to make it smooth. **knead** (need) **Knead** sounds like **need**. ▷ *verb* **kneading, kneaded**

knee *noun* The joint between your thigh and lower leg, which bends when you walk. **knee** (nee)

kneecap *noun* The round bone at the front of the knee. **knee·cap** (**nee**-kap)

kneel *verb* To support your weight on one or both knees: *She knelt down to get the spoon that fell under the table.* **kneel** (neel) ▷ *verb* **kneeling, kneeled** or **knelt** (nelt)

knew *verb* The past tense of **know**. **knew** (noo) **Knew** sounds like **new** and **gnu**.

knickknack *noun* A small object used as a decoration: *Dusting all my mother's knickknacks is quite a chore.* **knick·knack** (**nik**-*nak*)

knife
1. *noun* A tool with a handle and a sharp blade for cutting things, as in *a steak knife.* ▷ *noun, plural* **knives**
2. *verb* To stab or wound someone with a knife. ▷ *verb* **knifing, knifed**
knife (nife)

knight *noun*
1. In the Middle Ages, a **knight** was a soldier who wore armor and fought on horseback.
2. In Great Britain, a man who is rewarded for service to his country and can use the title "Sir." ▷ *noun* **knighthood** ▷ *verb* **knight**
3. In the game of chess, a piece with a horse's head that can make an L-shaped move.
knight (nite)
Knight sounds like **night**.

knit *verb*

1. To make fabric out of yarn using a pair of pointed needles to create rows of interconnected loops: *For Christmas, Stephanie knitted a pair of socks for everyone in the family.* ▷ *noun* **knitting**

2. When a broken bone **knits**, it grows together again during healing.

knit (nit)

▷ *verb* **knitting, knitted** *or* **knit**

knives *noun, plural* The plural of **knife**. **knives** (nivez)

knob *noun*

1. A ball-shaped handle on a drawer or door, as in *a glass knob.*

2. A round button used to control a radio, television, or other device.

3. A roundish lump: *The trunk of the tree was covered with knobs.* ▷ *adjective* **knobby**

knob (nahb)

knock *verb*

1. To strike something or someone forcefully, as in *to knock on a door.* ▷ *noun* **knock**

2. To hit and cause to fall: *The car skidded and knocked over a telephone pole.*

3. To criticize harshly: *Critics knocked the new movie.*

4. knock out To cause someone to lose consciousness: *One of the other swimmers hit Eric and knocked him out.*

knock (nahk)

▷ *verb* **knocking, knocked**

knocker *noun* A hinged, metal object fastened to a door that can be used to knock on the door loudly. **knock·er** (**nah**-kur)

knoll *noun* A small hill. **knoll** (nohl)

knot

1. *noun* A fastening made by tying one or more pieces of string or rope, as in *a shoelace knot.*

2. *verb* To make a knot in: *Ellie pulled the canoe up to the dock and knotted the rope securely.* ▷ *verb* **knotting, knotted**

3. *noun* A round, hard spot in a piece of wood where a branch grew out of the trunk.

4. *noun* A unit for measuring the speed of a ship or an aircraft, equal to 6,076 feet per hour.

knot (naht)

Knot sounds like **not**.

knotty *adjective*

1. Having many knots, as in *knotty pine.*

2. Difficult to understand or solve, as in *a knotty problem.*

knot·ty (**nah**-tee)

▷ *adjective* **knottier, knottiest**

knot

know *verb* To be aware of or familiar with someone or something: *The vet knows how to help my dog get better.* **know** (noh) **Know** sounds like **no**. ▷ *verb* **knowing, knew** (noo), **known** (nohn)

know-how *noun* The knowledge and skill needed to complete a task or job correctly: *With my ideas and Nicole's know-how, we're a perfect team.*

knowledge *noun*

1. Understanding and information that someone gets by study and experience: *The quiz tested our knowledge.*

2. Awareness of a fact or situation: *The knowledge that he would be punished stopped the boy from misbehaving.*

know·ledge (**nah**-lij)

knowledgeable *adjective* Well informed: *Chico is very knowledgeable about sailing.* **knowl·edge·a·ble** (**nah**-li-juh-buhl)

known *verb* The past participle of **know**. **known** (nohn)

knuckle *noun* One of the joints in a finger. **knuck·le** (**nuhk**-uhl)

koala *noun* An Australian animal with thick gray fur that looks like a teddy bear and eats eucalyptus leaves. **ko·a·la** (koh-**ah**-luh)

kook *noun* (*slang*) Someone who acts in a silly or strange way or who has crazy ideas: *They thought he was a kook because he wore sandals even when it snowed.* **kook** (kook) ▷ *adjective* **kooky**

kookaburra *noun* An Australian bird in the kingfisher family, whose loud, cackling call sounds like someone laughing. **kook·a·bur·ra** (kuk-uh-*bur*-uh)

Koran *or* **Qur'an** *noun* The holy book of the Muslim religion. **Ko·ran** *or* **Qu·r'an** (kuh-**rahn** *or* kuh-**ran**)

kosher *adjective* Prepared according to the laws of the Jewish religion: *Daniel's mother serves only kosher meals.* **ko·sher** (**koh**-shur)

Ku Klux Klan *noun* A secret organization in the United States dedicated to the idea that white people are better than people of other races. This group, often abbreviated as the **KKK**, has committed acts of violence to achieve its goals of white supremacy. The group is also sometimes known as the **Klan**. **Ku Klux Klan** (koo *kluks* klan)

kung fu *noun* One of the Chinese martial arts in which a person uses punches, kicks, and blocks for self-defense. Kung fu is similar to karate. **kung fu** (**kuhng foo**)

Kwanzaa *noun* An African American holiday started in the mid-1960s, based on a traditional African harvest festival. Kwanzaa, meaning "first fruits" in Swahili, is celebrated for seven days beginning on December 26 and ending on New Year's Day, January 1. Each day is devoted to a different principle, such as faith, creativity, unity, and purpose. **Kwan·zaa** (**kwahn**-zuh)

a
b
c
d
e
f
g
h
i
j
k
l
m
n
o
p
q
r
s
t
u
v
w
x
y
z

About L The original shape of the letter **L** was a crook—a long, curved stick shepherds use to steer their flock. The Phoenician letter developed from the Egyptian hieroglyph for a resting lion. *L* is sometimes silent when it is used before a *d, f, k, m,* or *v.* Examples: could, half, talk, calm, salve. Pronouncing the letter can be difficult for users of other languages. In some words of Spanish origin such as *quesadilla* and *tortilla,* the double *l* sounds like a *y.*

l Short for **liter** or the plural form *liters.*

lab *noun*
1. Short for **laboratory.**
2. Lab Short for **Labrador retriever.**
lab (lab)

label
1. *noun* A small piece of paper or other material that is attached to something and identifies its owner, use, or contents: *The label says this shirt must be washed in cold water.*
2. *noun* A descriptive word or phrase, as in *the label "City of Brotherly Love" for Philadelphia.*
3. *verb* To attach a label to something: *We labeled each item for the yard sale with a price.* ▷ *verb* **labeling, labeled**
la·bel (**lay**-buhl)

labor
1. *verb* To work hard, either physically or mentally: *Nick labored all weekend on his term paper.* ▷ *verb* **laboring, labored** ▷ *noun* **labor** ▷ *noun* **laborer**
2. *noun* The process of giving birth to a child.
3. *noun* Workers as a group, especially those who do physical work: *Labor and management agreed on a new contract.*
la·bor (**lay**-bur)

laboratory *noun* A room or building that has special equipment for people to use in scientific experiments, as in *a biology laboratory.* **lab·o·ra·tor·y** (**lab**-ruh-*tor*-ee) ▷ *noun, plural* **laboratories**

Word History

A laboratory is a place where people "work." Latin speakers formed the word *laboratorium* from their verb meaning "to work," *laborare. Laborare* was based on the word for "work," *labor.* The English word **laboratory** originally referred to a building for doing chemistry experiments, and later the term began to apply to a place for experiments in any scientific field.

Labor Day *noun* A legal holiday in the United States to honor people who work. It is celebrated on the first Monday in September.

lace

laborious *adjective* Requiring a lot of very difficult and often tedious work, and taking a long time: *Counting every one of the 600,000 votes by hand was a laborious task.* **la·bo·ri·ous** (luh-**bor**-ee-uhs) ▷ *noun* **laboriousness** ▷ *adverb* **laboriously**

labor union *noun* An organized group of workers set up to help improve working conditions and pay.

Labrador retriever or **Labrador** *noun* A breed of dog with a thick tail and a short, dense coat that is black, yellow, or dark brown. It is a type of retriever and is often used as a guide dog. Often shortened to **Lab. Lab·ra·dor re·triev·er** (**lab**-ruh-*dor* ri-**tree**-vur) or **Lab·ra·dor**

labyrinth *noun*
1. A specially designed maze that you walk through to try to find the middle. A common type of labyrinth has paths that are separated from one another by high bushes or hedges.
2. A place that is full of confusing paths and roads that are difficult to find your way around: *The ancient part of the city is a labyrinth of crisscrossing cobblestoned streets without a sign anywhere to help you get your bearings.*
3. A system or process that is confusing and takes a lot of effort to use or understand: *Court cases can drag on for years in the labyrinth of the legal system.*
lab·y·rinth (**lab**-uh-rinth)
▷ *adjective* **labyrinthine** (*lab*-uh-**rin**-thin)

lace
1. *noun* A fine, patterned cloth with large spaces between the threads, used mainly for decoration. ▷ *adjective* **lacy**
2. *noun* A long piece of thin string, cord, or leather used to tie shoes.
3. *verb* To fasten a shoe or piece of clothing with a lace, as in *to lace up skates.* ▷ *verb* **lacing, laced**
lace (lase)

lack
1. *verb* To be without or not to have enough

of something: *The research facility lacks advanced medical equipment.* ▷ *verb* **lacking, lacked**

2. *noun* The complete absence or a shortage of something, as in *a lack of rain.*

3. *noun* Something that is needed or is missing: *The most serious lack in his diet is protein.* **lack** (lak)

lacking *adjective* Not having something that is considered important or essential: *The park is beautiful but is sorely lacking in tourist facilities.* **lack·ing (lak-ing)**

lacrosse *noun* A ball game for two teams in which each player uses a long-handled stick with a net on the end to run with the ball, pass it, and try to throw it in the other team's goal. **la·crosse (luh-kraws)**

lad *noun* A boy or a young man. **lad** (lad)

ladder *noun* A structure made of metal, rope, or wood that is used to climb up and down. **lad·der (lad-ur)**

ladle *noun* A large, long-handled spoon with a deep bowl, used for serving soups and other liquids. **la·dle (lay-duhl)** ▷ *verb* **ladle**

lady *noun*

1. A woman.

2. A girl or woman who has good manners: *All the young girls behaved like ladies at the mother-daughter tea.*

3. Lady In Great Britain, a title used by a woman who has been rewarded for serving her country or who is married to a man who has the title "Sir." **la·dy (lay-dee)**

▷ *noun, plural* **ladies**

ladybug *noun* A small, round beetle with a red or orange back and black spots. **la·dy·bug (lay-dee-*buhg*)**

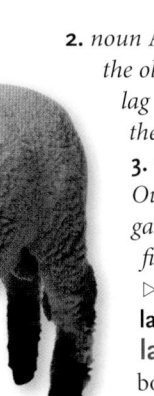
lamb

Word History

Not all **ladybugs** are female. This insect got its name not because of gender, but because of religion. The ladybug honors Mary, the mother of Jesus, who is referred to as "Our Lady" in Christianity. According to one legend, the colorful beetles received this tribute because they helped farmers by feeding on harmful insects.

lag

1. *verb* To move so slowly that you fall behind the others: *The slower joggers lagged behind and soon were out of sight.*

2. *noun* A delay: *After we turned on the old TV set, there was a slight lag before a picture appeared on the screen.*

3. *verb* To drop, or to lessen: *Our interest in the football game lagged after a scoreless first half.* ▷ *noun* **lag** ▷ *verb* **lagging, lagged** **lag** (lag)

lagoon *noun* A shallow body of water separated from the sea by a reef. **la·goon (luh-goon)**

laid *verb* The past tense and the past participle of **lay**. **laid** (layd)

lain *verb* The past participle of **lie**. **lain** (layn)

lair *noun* A wild animal's resting place or den. **lair** (lair)

lake *noun* A large body of water surrounded by land. Most lakes contain freshwater rather than saltwater. **lake** (lake)

lakh *noun* A word used in India and surrounding countries to represent the number one hundred thousand in quantities of money, as in *20 lakhs of rupees.* **lakh** (lak)

lamb *noun*

1. A young sheep.

2. The flesh of a young sheep, eaten for food. **lamb** (lam)

lame *adjective*

1. Someone who is **lame** is having trouble walking due to illness or injury to the foot or leg. ▷ *noun* **lameness**

2. *(informal)* Unsatisfactory or unconvincing, as in *a lame reason.* **lame** (laym) ▷ *adverb* **lamely**

lament

1. *verb* To express great sadness or regret about something, as in *to lament a lost opportunity.* ▷ *verb* **lamenting, lamented**

2. *noun* A song or poem expressing deep sadness, especially about someone's death. **la·ment (luh-ment)**

lamp *noun* A gas, oil, or electric device that gives off light, as in *a desk lamp.* **lamp** (lamp)

lance

1. *noun* A long spear with a pointed metal tip, used in the past by soldiers fighting on horseback.

2. *verb* To cut open with a sharp knife: *The doctor lanced the boil.* ▷ *verb* **lancing, lanced** **lance** (lans)

land

1. *noun* The part of the earth's surface that is solid ground: *I loved the cruise but was happy to be back on land.*

2. *noun* Earth or soil: *The pioneers looked for good land to farm.*

3. *verb* To arrive on the ground after being in the air or on the water: *The balloon landed near the ground crew.*

4. *noun* A country: *Canada is a vast land.*

5. *verb* To get or achieve something you want: *I've landed a full-time job in sports management.*

6. *verb* To cause you to end up somewhere: *His rude behavior landed him in trouble.*

land (land)

▷ *verb* **landing, landed**

landfall *noun*

1. The act of arriving on land after being on a boat.

2. The time when a hurricane over the ocean hits land: *Forecasters say the storm will make landfall in Florida by Monday.*

land·fall (**land**-*fawl*)

landfill *noun*

1. Garbage that is stacked and covered with earth.

2. **landfill site** A large area where garbage is buried, as in *a city's landfill site.*

land·fill (**land**-*fil*)

landing *noun*

1. The act of coming to land or coming ashore after a flight or voyage, as in *a rough landing.*

2. The place on a dock or pier where boats load and unload: *Nate steered the boat away from the landing.*

3. A level area of floor at the top of or partway up a staircase: *Hannah waited on the landing for me to come up the stairs.*

4. **landing strip** A level area of ground used by aircraft for taking off and landing.

land·ing (**lan**-ding)

landlady *noun* A woman who owns and rents out an apartment, a room, a house, or other property. **land·la·dy** (**land**-*lay*-dee) ▷ *noun, plural* **landladies**

landlocked *adjective* A country that does not have any border on the sea is called **landlocked**: *Paraguay is a landlocked country in South America.* **land·locked** (**land**-lahkt)

landlord *noun* A man who owns and rents out an apartment, a room, a house, or other property. **land·lord** (**land**-*lord*)

landmark *noun*

1. An object in a landscape that stands out: *The statue of the general is our town's main landmark.*

2. An important event: *The invention of the silicon*

landslide

chip is a landmark in the history of technology.

3. A building or place selected and pointed out as important, as in *a historical landmark.*

land·mark (**land**-*mahrk*)

landscape *noun*

1. A large area of land that can be seen in a single view: *Dad took photos of the Maine landscape.*

2. A painting, drawing, or photograph that shows such a stretch of land.

3. **landscape gardening** Laying out trees, shrubs, and gardens in an attractive way.

land·scape (**land**-*skape*)

landslide *noun*

1. A mass of earth and rocks that suddenly slides down a mountain or a hill: *The heavy rain caused a landslide.*

2. An overwhelming majority of votes in an election: *The president won by a landslide.*

land·slide (**land**-*slide*)

lane *noun*

1. A narrow road or a passageway between walls, fences, or hedges.

2. A strip of road that has been marked out as wide enough for a single line of vehicles: *I followed Bernardo's car, staying in the same lane.*

3. One of a series of parallel courses into which a running track or swimming pool is divided: *Maura was the only swimmer in her lane.*

4. A narrow wooden path on which bowling balls are rolled.

lane (lane)

language *noun*

1. The use of words to communicate thoughts and

feelings: *He is able to use simple language to explain complex ideas.*

2. Speech used by one country or group of people, as in *the Spanish language.*

3. The communication of thoughts and ideas by using signs, symbols, or movements, as in *body language.* **lan·guage** (**lang**-gwij)

language arts *noun, plural* Reading, composition, grammar, and spelling, taught as a single subject in school.

lanky *adjective* Someone who is **lanky** is tall and thin in an awkward way. **lank·y** (**lang**-kee)
▷ *adjective* **lankier, lankiest**

lantern *noun* A kind of lamp with a metal frame and glass sides. Lanterns can also be made out of paper. **lan·tern** (**lan**-turn)

Word History

The word **lantern** comes from the Greek word *lampein,* meaning "to shine." Lantern is an example of an ancient word for a thing that is still used but has changed in some way. In olden times, lanterns held candles or burning oil. Today, most lanterns are powered by electricity.

lap

1. *noun* The flat area between your waist and knees when you are sitting down: *I held my baby cousin Kara on my lap.*

2. *noun* One complete trip around something, such as a racetrack: *Sol ran four laps around the track.*

3. *verb* To lie partly upon or over something else; to overlap: *The insect's wings lap over each other.*

4. *verb* When water **laps** against something, it washes up against it with a gentle rippling sound.

5. *verb* When an animal **laps up** a drink, it takes the liquid into its mouth with rapid motions of its tongue.

lap (lap)
▷ *verb* **lapping, lapped**

lapel *noun* The part of a coat or jacket collar that folds back over against the front opening: *Brent wore a pin on the lapel of his jacket.* **la·pel** (luh-**pel**)

lapse

1. *noun* A brief failure, as in *a lapse of memory.*
▷ *verb* **lapse**

2. *noun* The time that passes between two events: *After a lapse of several weeks, work resumed on the construction project.*

3. *verb* To drop or fall off little by little: *The story was so boring that our interest began to lapse.*

4. *verb* To come to an end: *Our magazine subscription lapsed last month.*

lantern

lapse (laps)
▷ *verb* **lapsing, lapsed**

laptop *noun* A portable computer that is small and light enough to use while traveling: *My laptop holds the same amount of data as a big desktop computer.* **lap·top** (**lap**-tahp)

larceny *noun* The crime of taking something that belongs to someone else and intending to keep it. **lar·ce·ny** (**lahr**-suh-nee) ▷ *noun, plural* **larcenies** ▷ *adjective* **larcenous**

lard *noun* A solid, white grease made from the melted-down fat of pigs and hogs, used in cooking. **lard** (lahrd)

large

1. *adjective* Great in size or amount, as in *a large pile of leaves.* ▷ *adjective* **larger, largest**

2. at large Escaped and not yet captured; free: *The convict broke out of prison and is now at large.*

large (lahrj)

large intestine *noun* The thick, lower end of the digestive system, containing the appendix, colon, and rectum.

largely *adverb* To a great degree, or in general: *Rosie's story is largely untrue.* **large·ly** (**lahrj**-lee)

lariat *noun* A lasso. **lar·i·at** (**lar**-ee-uht)

lark *noun*

1. A small, brown bird that sings as it flies.

2. A harmless prank or playful adventure: *As a lark, we played on the beach during the snowstorm.* **lark** (lahrk)

larkspur *noun* A tall plant that has long stalks of blue, purple, or white flowers. **lark·spur** (**lahrk**-spur)

lariat

a b c d e f g h i j k l m n o p q r s t u v w x y z

larva *noun* An insect at the stage of development between an egg and a pupa, when it looks like a worm. A caterpillar is the larva of a moth or a butterfly. **lar·va** (**lahr**-vuh) ▷ *noun, plural* **larvae** (**lahr**-vee)

Word History

The term **larva** goes back to the Latin word for "mask," *larva*, because people thought that the adult stage of the animal was disguised while it was a larva.

laryngitis *noun* An infection of the larynx that makes it difficult to talk. **lar·yn·gi·tis** (*lar*-in-**jye**-tis)

larynx *noun* An organ in your throat that holds your vocal cords and makes it possible for you to speak. **lar·ynx** (**lar**-ingks) ▷ *noun, plural* **larynges** or **larynxes**

lasagna *noun* An Italian dish made with layers of wide noodles, chopped meat or vegetables, tomato sauce, and cheese. **la·sa·gna** (luh-**zahn**-yuh)

laser *noun*
1. A device that produces a very narrow, intense beam of light that can be used for surgery, for cutting things, and for reading CDs. Laser is short for *light amplification by stimulated emission of radiation*.
2. laser beam The concentrated beam of light that a laser produces: *Laser beams are used to cut gems.* **la·ser** (**lay**-zur)

laser

laser printer *noun* A computer printer that reproduces high-quality images using a laser.

lash
1. *noun* An eyelash.
2. *noun* A blow with a whip or stick. ▷ *verb* **lash**
3. *verb* To fasten something securely using rope or cord: *Lewis lashed the boxes together in the back of his truck.*
4. *verb* To whip back and forth: *The lion grew angry and lashed its tail from side to side.*
5. lash out *verb* To hit or to speak out against someone suddenly and angrily: *Philippa lashed out at*

Janet, yelling that Janet had hurt her feelings. **lash** (lash)
▷ *verb* **lashes, lashing, lashed** ▷ *noun, plural* **lashes**

lass *noun* A girl or a young woman. **lass** (las)
▷ *noun, plural* **lasses**

lasso
1. *noun* A length of rope with a large loop at one end that can be used to catch wild horses or cattle. Also called a **lariat**. ▷ *noun, plural* **lassos** or **lassoes**
2. *verb* To catch or stop something by throwing a lasso around it: *It wasn't easy to lasso the runaway horse.* ▷ *verb* **lassoing, lassoed**
las·so (**las**-oh *or* la-**soo**)

Word History

The **lasso**, a length of rope with a loop at one end for catching an animal, was invented by Native Americans, but the name is from Spanish. The Spanish word *lazo*, meaning "lasso," is related to the English word *lace*, a type of material with a pattern of small holes. Other Spanish words that English speakers have adopted include *sombrero, tortilla,* and *rodeo*.

last
1. *adjective* Being or coming after all others: *My parents were the last ones to leave the meeting.*
▷ *adverb* **lastly**
2. *adjective* Being the only one left: *He ate the last piece of meat.*
3. *adjective* Just passed; most recent: *The last time I checked, she was still running a fever.*
4. *noun* A person or thing that is last: *I was the last to get picked for the dodgeball team.*
5. *verb* To exist or to go on or for a certain length of time: *The school day seemed to last forever.*
6. *verb* To stay in good condition: *My sneakers lasted for a year.*
last (last)
▷ *verb* **lasting, lasted**

lasting *adjective* Continuing or remaining for a long time, as in *a lasting impression.* **last·ing** (**las**-ting)

last name *noun* Your family name, or surname. In English-speaking countries, it usually comes after your given names, which means your first name and any middle names you may have.

latch
1. *noun* A bar that fits into a notch, used to close a door or gate. ▷ *noun, plural* **latches** ▷ *verb* **latch**
2. latch on *verb* To become very attached to someone or something: *They latched on to the idea of building a series of windmills.* ▷ *verb* **latches, latching, latched**
latch (lach)

latchkey *noun*
1. The key that opens an outside door.
2. Latchkey children are alone at home after school because their parents are working.
latch·key (**lach**-*kee*)

late *adjective*
1. Arriving, acting, or happening after the correct or usual time: *We were late for Martha's dinner party.* ▷ *noun* **lateness** ▷ *adverb* **late**
2. Toward the end of a period of time, as in *the late Middle Ages*.
3. No longer living, as in *the late President Gerald Ford*.
late (late)
▷ *adjective* **later, latest**

lately *adverb* Not long ago; recently: *Lately, the mail carrier has been coming earlier than she used to.* **late·ly** (**late**-lee)

latent *adjective* Present but not active or visible yet: *Kathy has a latent talent for music; she only needs more training to develop it.* **la·tent** (**lay**-tuhnt)

later *adjective* Following in time or space: *We can go on the noon bus or take the later bus, which leaves at three.* **lat·er** (**lay**-tur)

lateral *adjective* On, at, from, or to the side: *The quarterback threw a lateral pass.* **lat·er·al** (**lat**-ur-uhl)

latex *noun*
1. A milky liquid that comes from certain plants. This natural liquid is used to make rubber.
2. A similar liquid that is produced artificially and is used to make rubber, paints, and chewing gum.
la·tex (**lay**-teks)
▷ *noun, plural* **latexes**

lather *noun* A thick, creamy foam formed when soap is mixed with water, as in *shaving lather*. **lath·er** (**laTH**-ur) ▷ *verb* **lather**

Latin *noun* The language of ancient Rome. **Lat·in** (**lat**-in)

Latina *noun*
1. A woman or girl who was born in or lives in Latin America.
2. A woman or girl born in Latin America who lives in the United States.
La·ti·na (lah-**tee**-nuh *or* luh-**tee**-nuh)
▷ *adjective* **Latina**

Latin America *noun* All of the Americas found south of the United States, including Mexico as well as the countries of Central America and South America. **Latin A·mer·i·ca** (uh-**mer**-i-kuh)

launch

Latin American *adjective* Of or having to do with the people, cultures, and countries of Mexico, Central America, and South America. ▷ *noun* **Latin American**

Latino *noun*
1. A person who was born in or lives in Latin America.
2. A person born in Latin America who lives in the United States.
La·ti·no (lah-**tee**-noh *or* luh-**tee**-noh)
▷ *adjective* **Latino**

latitude *noun* The distance north or south of the equator, measured in degrees: *Chicago is at a latitude of about 42 degrees north.* **lat·i·tude** (**lat**-i-*tood*) ▷ *adjective* **latitudinal** (*lat*-i-**too**-duh-nuhl)

latter
1. *noun* The second of two persons or things just mentioned: *If I had to choose between poached or scrambled eggs, I'd choose the latter.*
2. *adjective* Nearer the end than the beginning, as in *the latter part of the century*.
lat·ter (**lat**-ur)

laugh *verb* When you **laugh**, you make sounds and move your face and body in a way that shows you think something is funny, as in *to laugh at a joke*. **laugh** (laf) ▷ *verb* **laughing, laughed** ▷ *noun* **laugh**

laughable *adjective* If something is **laughable**, it is ridiculous and people don't take it seriously. **laugh·a·ble** (**laf**-uh-buhl)

laughter *noun* The action or sound of people laughing: *We could hear laughter from behind the closed door.* **laugh·ter** (**laf**-tur)

launch
1. *verb* To set a boat or ship afloat, especially if it has just been built: *It's a good day to launch the boat because the water is calm.*
2. *verb* To send a rocket or missile into space, as in *to launch a space shuttle*.
3. *verb* To get something started or to introduce something new, as in *to launch a political campaign*.
4. *noun* A type of boat that is often used for sightseeing. ▷ *noun, plural* **launches**
5. launching pad *or* **launch pad** *noun* The platform from which a rocket or missile is sent into space.
launch (lawnch)
▷ *verb* **launches, launching, launched**
▷ *noun* **launch**

a b c d e f g h i j k l m n o p q r s t u v w x y z

launder *verb* To wash and iron clothes, as in *to launder work clothes.* **laun·der** (**lawn**-dur) ▷ *verb* **laundering, laundered**

laundry *noun*
1. Clothes, towels, sheets, and other such items that need to be washed or are being washed: *My chore this week is to do the family's laundry.*
2. A room or an area for doing the wash. **laun·dry** (**lawn**-dree) ▷ *noun, plural* **laundries**

laurel *noun*
1. An evergreen shrub or tree with dark green, shiny leaves and black berries.
2. **laurels** The leaves of this tree, especially when woven into a wreath and given to the winner of a race or contest to wear as a crown.
3. If you **rest on your laurels**, you are satisfied with what you have already achieved and you no longer strive to do better. **lau·rel** (**lor**-uhl)

lava *noun*
1. The hot, liquid rock that pours out of a volcano when it erupts.
2. The rock formed when this liquid has cooled and hardened. **la·va** (**lah**-vuh *or* **lav**-uh)

lavatory *noun* A bathroom. **lav·a·to·ry** (**lav**-uh-*tor*-ee) ▷ *noun, plural* **lavatories**

lavender *noun*
1. A plant with fragrant bluish-purple flowers and narrow leaves.
2. A pale bluish-purple color. **lav·en·der** (**lav**-uhn-dur) ▷ *adjective* **lavender**

lavish
1. *adjective* Extravagant, generous, or luxurious, as in *a lavish meal.* ▷ *adverb* **lavishly**
2. *verb* To give large amounts of something to someone: *My grandmother lavished attention on all of her grandchildren.* ▷ *verb* **lavishes, lavishing, lavished** **lav·ish** (**lav**-ish)

law *noun*
1. A rule established and enforced by a government: *The state passed a law that protects certain animals from being hunted.*

2. A statement in science or math about what always happens whenever certain events take place, as in *the law of gravity.*
3. The profession and work of a lawyer, as in *a career in law.* **law** (law)

law-abiding *adjective* If you are **law-abiding**, you respect and obey the laws of society, as in *a dutiful, law-abiding citizen.*

lawful *adjective* Following or allowed by the law, as in *a lawful agreement.* **law·ful** (**law**-fuhl) ▷ *noun* **lawfulness** ▷ *adverb* **lawfully**

lawn *noun* An area of mown grass around a house. **lawn** (lawn)

lawn mower *noun* A machine with a rotating blade that cuts grass.

lawsuit *noun* A legal action or case brought against a person or a group in a court of law: *Her lawsuit was reviewed by the Supreme Court.* **law·suit** (**law**-soot)

lawyer *noun* A person who has studied the law and is trained to advise people and represent them in court, as in *a divorce lawyer.* **law·yer** (**law**-yur *or* **loi**-ur)

lax *adjective* Not strict or careful enough, as in *lax management.* **lax** (laks) ▷ *noun* **laxity** ▷ *noun* **laxness** ▷ *adverb* **laxly**

laxative *noun* A substance that people drink or take as a pill to help move waste from their bowels. **lax·a·tive** (**lak**-suh-tiv)

lay *verb*
1. The past tense of **lie**.
2. To put something down or to place it somewhere: *You can lay the book on the table.*
3. To produce an egg or eggs.
4. If a person has been **laid off**, he or she has been dismissed from a job: *The employees were temporarily laid off when there was no work at the factory.*
5. If you are **laid up**, you are in bed with an injury or illness. **lay** (lay)

Lay sounds like **lei**. ▷ *verb* **laying, laid** (layd)

layer *noun* A thickness or coating of something, as in *a layer of dust.* **lay·er** (**lay**-ur) ▷ *verb* **layer** ▷ *adjective* **layered**

layoff *noun* A period in which employees are dismissed from their jobs because there is not enough work for them to do or enough money to

laundry

lava

pay them: *The company was forced to consider layoffs in order to cut costs.* **lay·off** (**lay**-*awf*)

layup *noun* In basketball, a shot made with one hand from under the basket or from one side of the basket: *Johnson scored with an easy layup.* **lay·up** (**lay**-uhp)

laziness *noun* Lazy behavior, or the trait of being lazy: *Gayle needs to back up her computer, but hasn't done it yet because of laziness.* **la·zi·ness** (**lay**-zee-nis)

lazy *adjective* If you are **lazy**, you are unwilling to work or be active. **la·zy** (**lay**-zee) ▷ *adjective* **lazier, laziest** ▷ *verb* **laze** ▷ *adverb* **lazily**

lb. An abbreviation for a pound, as in *one lb. of potatoes* or *five lbs. of carrots.* The abbreviation is pronounced like the word. *See* **pound.**

LCD *noun* Short for **liquid crystal display**.

lead

1. (leed) *verb* To show the way by going first: *Gary led his friends to the treasure chest he had found.*

2. (leed) *verb* To guide or direct, as in *to lead a discussion.*

3. (leed) *noun* A person's position at the front: *Olga took the lead in the race.*

4. (leed) *noun* A piece of helpful advice or information: *I got several good leads on how to research job opportunities.*

5. (leed) *noun* The main actor or role in a play or movie: *Janet was chosen as the lead in the school play.*

6. (led) *noun* A heavy, soft, bluish-gray metal.

7. (led) *noun* The black or gray material used in pencils; graphite.

8. (leed) *noun* A leash.

lead

▷ *verb* **leading, led** (led)

leader *noun* Someone who leads, governs, or has authority over others: *The pope is the leader of the Roman Catholic Church.* **lead·er** (**lee**-dur)

leadership *noun* The ability to lead people and the skills associated with this: *Under Marla's leadership, the club has grown and added many new members.* **lea·der·ship** (**lee**-dur-*ship*)

leading *adjective* Most important, successful, or best: *They are staying at the leading hotel in the city.* **lead·ing** (**lee**-ding)

leaf

1. *noun* A flat and usually green structure attached to a stem and growing from a branch of a tree or plant. ▷ *adjective* **leafy**

2. *noun* A single sheet of paper, especially as part of a book.

3. *verb* To turn pages and glance at them quickly: *Waiting in the dentist's office, Rose leafed through a magazine.* ▷ *verb* **leafing, leafed**

4. *noun* A flat, removable part of a table that can

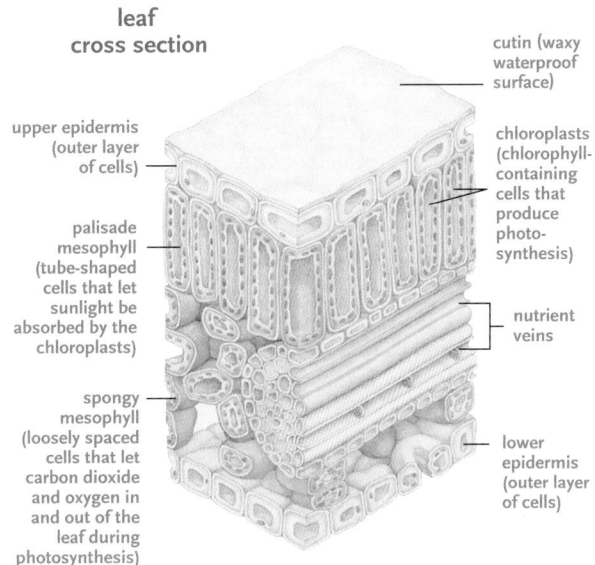

leaf
cross section

upper epidermis (outer layer of cells)

palisade mesophyll (tube-shaped cells that let sunlight be absorbed by the chloroplasts)

spongy mesophyll (loosely spaced cells that let carbon dioxide and oxygen in and out of the leaf during photosynthesis)

cutin (waxy waterproof surface)

chloroplasts (chlorophyll-containing cells that produce photosynthesis)

nutrient veins

lower epidermis (outer layer of cells)

expand its surface: *Before the dinner party we added two extra leaves to the table.*

leaf (leef)

▷ *noun, plural* **leaves**

leaflet *noun*

1. A single sheet of paper giving information or advertising something: *After our dog was lost, we passed out leaflets with his photo and our cell number.*

2. A small or young leaf.

leaf·let (**leef**-lit)

league *noun*

1. A group of people with a common interest or activity, such as a group of sports teams or a political organization, as in *a bowling league.*

2. A measure of distance equal to about three miles.

league (leeg)

leak *verb*

1. If a container **leaks**, it allows whatever it was holding to escape from it: *Check that the pail doesn't leak before you fill it with water.* ▷ *adjective* **leaky**

2. If a liquid or gas **leaks**, it escapes or enters accidentally through a hole or crack: *We have an alarm that will tell us if the furnace leaks carbon monoxide.*

3. To allow a secret to become known: *Someone leaked to the principal that the whole team was planning to cut class.*

leak (leek)

Leak sounds like **leek**. ▷ *verb* **leaking, leaked** ▷ *noun* **leak**

lean

1. *verb* To stand at a slant or bend from an upright position: *You'll find the broom leaning against the back door.*

2. *verb* To rest part of your weight on something: *Floyd leaned against the railing.*

3. *verb* To rely on for help: *I lean on my dad whenever I have a problem.*

4. *adjective* Someone who is **lean** is slender and muscular, with no excess fat.

5. *adjective* If meat is **lean**, it contains very little fat.
lean (leen)
▷ *verb* **leaning, leaned** ▷ *noun* **lean**
▷ *adjective* **leaner, leanest**

leap *verb*

1. To jump up or across something: *My dogs leap all over anyone who comes in the door.*

2. If you **leap at** something, you accept it eagerly: *He leapt at the chance to try out for the school play.*
leap (leep)
▷ *verb* **leaping, leaped** *or* **leapt** (lept) ▷ *noun* **leap**

leapfrog *noun*
A game in which one player bends over and another jumps over his or her back, using the hands for support. **leap·frog** (**leep**-*frawg*)
▷ *verb* **leapfrog**

leap year *noun*
A year that has 366 days. An extra day is added at the end of February every four years to make up for the difference between the calendar year and the solar year: *The year 2020 is a leap year.*

learn *verb*

1. To gain knowledge, understanding, or a skill: *I learned how to ride a bicycle by myself.*

2. To memorize: *We each learned a poem that we could recite.*

3. To become aware of something, as in *to learn a secret.*
learn (lurn)
▷ *verb* **learning, learned**

learned *adjective*
Having or showing a lot of knowledge or education, as in *a learned scholar.* **learn·ed** (**lur**-nid)

learner *noun*
Someone who is learning something: *The company offers tutoring for struggling math and English learners.* **learn·er** (**lur**-nur)

learning disabled *adjective*
Having difficulty in learning a basic skill, such as reading, because of a physical condition, such as dyslexia. Abbreviated as *LD.*
▷ *noun* **learning disability**

lease *noun*
An agreement that a landlord and tenant sign when renting an apartment, a house, or other property: *Lakshmi signed a two-year lease for her apartment.* **lease** (lees) ▷ *verb* **lease**

leash *noun*
A strap, cord, or chain that you use to hold and control an animal. **leash** (leesh) ▷ *noun, plural* **leashes**

least

1. *noun* The smallest in size, amount, or importance: *Being late is the least of our worries.* ▷ *adjective* **least**

2. *adverb* In the smallest degree; less than anything else: *Soccer was her least favorite sport.*

3. **at least** Not less or fewer than: *We need at least another week to finish the project.*
least (leest)

leather *noun*
Animal skin that has been treated with chemicals so it can be used to make things like shoes and handbags. **leath·er** (**leTH**-ur) ▷ *adjective* **leathery**

leave

1. *verb* To go away from someone or something, as in *to leave home.*

2. *verb* To allow someone or something to remain: *Please leave me some dessert.*

3. *verb* To give property to someone through a will, after death: *My grandmother left her estate to my father.*

4. *verb* To quit: *Joanne will leave her job when she finds a better one.*

5. *noun* Time away from work, as in *maternity leave.*

6. *verb* To have remaining: *Subtracting 10 from 24 leaves 14.*
leave (leev)
▷ *verb* **leaving, left** (left)

leaves *noun, plural*
The plural of **leaf**. **leaves** (leevz)

lecture *noun*

1. A talk prepared ahead of time and given to a class or an audience: *We went to a fascinating lecture on how bees communicate.* ▷ *noun* **lecturer**

2. A scolding that lasts a long time: *The last thing I need is one of my dad's lectures.*
lec·ture (**lek**-chur)
▷ *verb* **lecture**

leash

led *verb*
The past tense and the past participle of **lead**. **led** (led)

ledge *noun*

1. A narrow surface that sticks out like a shelf, as in *a window ledge.*

2. Something that looks like a shelf on the side of a mountain or a cliff.
ledge (lej)

leeks

lee *adjective* Being on the side of something, such as a ship or mountain, that is away from the wind; shelter: *We waited on the lee side of the hill until the storm blew over.* **lee** (lee) ▷ *noun* **lee**

leech *noun*
1. A worm that lives in water or wet earth and survives by sucking blood from animals. In the past, doctors often used leeches to take blood from patients.
2. A person who clings to others, hoping to get something from them: *I heard Jim shout to Gus, "Find your own friends and don't be such a leech!"* **leech** (leech)
▷ *noun, plural* **leeches**

leek *noun* A vegetable with a slender white bulb and green, overlapping leaves. Leeks taste like mild onions. **leek** (leek) **Leek** sounds like **leak**.

leer *noun* A sly or evil grin, as in *a fiendish leer.* **leer** (leer) ▷ *verb* **leer**

left *noun*
1. The side you begin to read from in a line of English writing; the side on which the heart is located in the human body: *Statistically, more people write with their right hand than with their left.* ▷ *adjective* **left** ▷ *adverb* **left**
2. In politics, people **on the left** have liberal, progressive views about society and government. **left** (left)

left-handed *adjective*
1. If you are **left-handed**, you write with your left hand and use it more easily than your right hand.
2. If you receive a **left-handed compliment**, you are not sure if it really is a compliment because it seems to you that it could be insincere.
▷ *noun* **left-hander**

leftovers *noun, plural* Food that was not eaten at one meal and can be used for another meal. **left·o·vers** (**left**-oh-vurz)

leg *noun*
1. One of the lower limbs of your body, between your hip and your foot.
2. The part of a pair of stockings or pants that covers your leg.
3. The supporting part of a chair, table, or other piece of furniture.
4. A stage in a journey or race: *The longest leg of our trip is between Chicago and San Francisco.*
5. Either of two sides of a triangle besides the base.
6. *(informal)* If you **pull** someone's **leg**, you tease the person by telling him or her something untrue.
7. If something is **on its last legs**, it is about to collapse or die: *Becky's rusty car is on its last legs.*
leg (leg)

legacy *noun*
1. Money or property that someone has left you in his or her will: *My legacy from my grandfather was a collection of antique fishing poles.*
2. Something handed down from one generation to another.
leg·a·cy (**leg**-uh-see)
▷ *noun, plural* **legacies**

legal *adjective*
1. Of or having to do with the law or required by law: *He had to meet the legal requirements for citizenship.*
2. Allowed by law: *If a company sends you something you didn't order, it's legal for you to keep it.*
le·gal (**lee**-guhl)
▷ *verb* **legalize** ▷ *adverb* **legally**

legend *noun*
1. A story handed down from earlier times. Legends are often based on fact, but they are not entirely true.
2. Someone who is famous or well-known for something: *She was a legend in the art world.*
3. The words written beneath or beside a map or chart to explain it.
leg·end (**lej**-uhnd)

legendary *adjective*
1. Very well known, usually because of some remarkable event or action, as in *a legendary war hero.*
2. Based on or known about through legends: *I'm reading about the exploits of the legendary Hercules.*
leg·end·ar·y (**lej**-uhn-der-ee)

leggings *noun, plural* Leg coverings that fit like tights. **leg·gings** (**leg**-ingz)

legible *adjective* If handwriting or print is **legible**, it is clear enough to be read easily. **leg·i·ble** (**lej**-uh-buhl)
▷ *noun* **legibility** ▷ *adverb* **legibly**

legion

1. *noun* A unit in the Roman army consisting of 3,000 to 6,000 soldiers.
2. *noun* A large group of soldiers or former soldiers: *The American Legion is the largest veterans organization in the United States.*
3. *adjective* Great in number: *Harry's flaws were legion, but we all loved him anyway.*
le·gion (**lee**-juhn)

legislation *noun* Laws that have been proposed or made: *The Senate is considering new health care legislation.* **leg·is·la·tion** (*lej*-is-**lay**-shuhn) ▷ *noun* **legislator** ▷ *verb* **legislate**

legislature *noun* A group of people who have the power to make or change laws for a country or state: *The legislature decided to put off the vote until after the holiday.* **leg·is·la·ture** (**lej**-is-*lay*-chur)

legitimate *adjective*
1. In keeping with the law or rules, as in *a legitimate election* or *a legitimate government.*
2. Reasonable or justified, as in *a legitimate complaint.*
le·git·i·mate (luh-**jit**-uh-mit)
▷ *adverb* **legitimately**

legume *noun* A plant with seeds that grow in pods. Peas, beans, lentils, and peanuts are legumes.
le·gume (**leg**-yoom)

lei *noun* A necklace of leaves or flowers, often given as a gift of welcome in Hawaii. **lei** (lay) **Lei** sounds like **lay.**

leisure
1. *noun* Free time in which you can relax and enjoy yourself.
2. *adjective* Relaxed and enjoyable, as in *leisure activities.*
leis·ure (**lee**-zhur *or* **lezh**-ur)

leisurely *adjective* Not hurried or not rushed, as in *a leisurely stroll.* **lei·sure·ly** (**lee**-zhur-lee *or* **lezh**-ur-lee)

lemon *noun*
1. A yellow citrus fruit with a thick skin and a sour taste.
2. Something that is defective.
lem·on (**lem**-uhn)

lemonade *noun* A drink made from lemon juice, water, and sugar. **lem·on·ade** (*lem*-uh-**nade**)

lentils

lemur *noun* An animal with large eyes, soft fur, and a long tail. Most lemurs are nocturnal and live in trees, and they are mainly found on the island of Madagascar. **le·mur** (**lee**-mur)

lend *verb* To let someone have something that you expect to get back: *Felicia looked so cold that I decided to lend her my jacket.* **lend** (lend) ▷ *verb* **lending, lent** (lent)

length *noun*
1. The measurement of something from end to end. *See the Measurements Tables in the* **Reference Section.**
2. The amount or extent of something from beginning to end, as in *the length of a vacation* or *the length of a book.* ▷ *adjective* **lengthy**
3. A piece of something, as in *a length of rope.*
length (lengkth)

lengthen *verb* To make or become longer: *The tailor lengthened the sleeves of my coat.* **length·en** (**lengk**-thuhn) ▷ *verb* **lengthening, lengthened**

lengthwise *adverb* In the direction of the length: *Cut the bread in half lengthwise.* **length·wise** (**lengkth**-*wize*) ▷ *adjective* **lengthwise**

lenient *adjective* Not harsh or strict, as in *lenient rules.* **le·ni·ent** (**lee**-nee-uhnt) ▷ *adverb* **leniently**

lens *noun*
1. A piece of glass or plastic with one or both sides curved that brings together or spreads rays of light as they pass through, making things look larger or clearer.
2. The clear part of your eye that focuses light on the retina.
lens (lenz)
▷ *noun, plural* **lenses**

Lent *noun* The 40 days before Easter, not including Sundays. During this period, some Christian denominations expect their members to pray and cut back on luxuries: *Megan decided to give up chocolate for Lent.* **Lent** (lent)

lentil *noun* The flat, round seed of a plant related to beans and peas. Lentils are often cooked in soups and stews. **len·til** (**len**-tuhl)

leopard *noun* A large wildcat with a light brown, spotted coat, found in Africa, India, and eastern Asia. **leop·ard** (**lep**-urd)

magnifying lens

leotard *noun* A tight-fitting one-piece garment worn for dancing, gymnastics, and exercise. **le·o·tard** (**lee**-uh-*tahrd*)

Word History

In a popular 19th-century song, the lyrics speak of a "daring young man on the flying trapeze," who flies "through the air with the greatest of ease." The song was written about Jules Léotard, a French acrobat who amazed audiences with his fearless trapeze act. He invented a tight suit to wear while performing, and people later named it a **leotard** after him.

leprechaun *noun* A playful and annoying elf in Irish folklore who promises gold or other treasure if you can catch him. **lep·re·chaun** (**lep**-ri-*kahn*)

Suffix

The suffix **-less** adds one of these meanings to a root word:

1. Without, as in *doubtless* (without doubt) or *effortless* (without effort).
2. Unable to be, as in *countless* (unable to be counted).

less
1. *adjective* Smaller in quantity; not as much of something: *A CD has less space than a DVD.* ▷ *adverb* **less**
2. *adjective* Made up of a smaller number than wanted, needed, or expected: *I have less homework than I thought I would have.*
3. *preposition* Minus: *My bike was cheap because I bought it at the sale price less a $15 discount from a gift coupon.*
less (les)

lessen *verb* To decrease or diminish: *The medicine helped lessen her headache.* **les·sen** (**les**-uhn) **Lessen** sounds like **lesson**. ▷ *verb* **lessening, lessened**

lesser *adjective* Smaller or less important: *They decided to work on the lesser problem first.* **less·er** (**les**-ur)

lesson *noun*
1. An assignment or exercise: *Finish your math lesson before you go out.*
2. What students are taught during one class or period of instruction: *Monday's lesson will be on the proper use of commas.*
3. An experience from which you learn something important: *Getting the facts wrong for my paper taught me a lesson about checking what I write.*
les·son (**les**-uhn)
Lesson sounds like **lessen**.

let *verb*
1. To allow or give permission for something: *My mother let me go over to my friend's house after dinner.*
2. To allow to pass or go: *Let the cat out.*
3. To rent out a house or an apartment: *We are letting a house in Italy for the year.*
4. If you are **let down** by someone, you are disappointed because the person did not help or support you as promised.
let (let)
▷ *verb* **letting, let**

lethal *adjective* Very harmful or deadly, as in *a lethal poison.* **le·thal** (**lee**-thuhl) ▷ *adverb* **lethally**

let's *contraction* A short form of *let us*: *Let's go to the movies tonight.* **let's** (lets)

letter *noun*
1. A mark that is part of an alphabet. A letter stands for a sound or sounds and is used in writing, as in *the letter B.* ▷ *verb* **letter**
2. A written or printed message, especially one sent by mail: *I received an airmail letter from my grandfather, who lives in England.*
let·ter (**let**-ur)

letter carrier *noun* See **mail carrier.**

lettering *noun* Letters that have been drawn, painted, or printed on something, such as a sign or a greeting card. **let·ter·ing** (**let**-ur-ing)

lettuce *noun* A green plant with leaves that can be eaten, used in salads. **let·tuce** (**let**-is)

leukemia *noun* A serious disease of the bone marrow, which produces too many white blood cells. **leu·ke·mi·a** (loo-**kee**-mee-uh)

levee *noun*
1. A bank built up near a river to prevent flooding.
2. A place for boats or ships to land.
lev·ee (**lev**-ee)
Levee sounds like **levy.**

levee

level

1. *adjective* Flat and even, as in *a level surface.*

2. *adjective* At the same height: *We trimmed the bushes to make them level with each other.*

3. *noun* A floor or story of a structure: *Our car is parked on the upper level.*

4. *noun* A height or depth, as in *sea level.*

5. *noun* A position or rank in a series: *My mom has risen to the level of company vice president.*

6. *verb* To flatten: *The tornado leveled every building on the street.*

7. *verb* If something **levels off**, it becomes more stable or consistent: *Unemployment eventually leveled off, but it was still high.*

8. *noun* A carpentry tool used to show if a surface is flat and even.
lev·el (**lev**-uhl)
▷ *verb* **leveling, leveled**

lever *noun*

1. A bar resting on a pivot, used to lift an object placed on one end by pushing down on the other end: *They had to use a lever to lift the stove in order to clean under it.* ▷ *verb* **lever**

2. A bar or a handle that you use to work or control a machine: *The scientist had the monkeys press a lever to release a treat.*
lev·er (**lev**-ur *or* **lee**-vur)

leverage *noun*

1. The amount of influence you need to make someone do something or make something happen: *The employees didn't have enough leverage to negotiate a good contract, so they hired a prominent lawyer.*

2. The power needed to lift an object using a lever: *We'll need more leverage to move those big pieces of concrete.*
lev·er·age (**lev**-ur-ij)

levitate *verb*

1. To rise in the air and float, seeming to defy gravity.

2. To cause to rise in the air and float.
lev·i·tate (**lev**-i-*tate*)
▷ *noun* **levitation**

levy

1. *verb* To impose or collect by lawful actions or by force: *The government levied a tax on gasoline.*
▷ *verb* **levies, levying, levied**

2. *noun* A tax. ▷ *noun, plural* **levies**
lev·y (**lev**-ee)
Levy sounds like **levee**.

carpenter's level

lexicographer *noun* Someone whose job is to research and write the entries for a dictionary. **lex·i·cog·ra·pher** (*lek*-si-**kah**-gruh-fur)

lexicography *noun* The work of researching and writing the entries for dictionaries. **lex·i·cog·ra·phy** (*lek*-si-**kah**-gruh-fee)

liability *noun*

1. Responsibility: *The owner's liability for repairs was explained in the contract.*

2. Somebody or something that causes problems or holds a person back: *She loved that big house, but its size became a liability for her.*
li·a·bil·i·ty (*lye*-uh-**bil**-i-tee)
▷ *noun, plural* **liabilities**

liable *adjective*

1. Likely to do something: *Our yard is liable to flood if we get too much rain.*

2. Legally required or responsible: *Because Jack's car ran into my car, he is liable for the damages to it.*
li·a·ble (**lye**-uh-buhl)

liar *noun* A person who tells lies: *Once I knew he was a liar, it became difficult to believe anything he said.* **li·ar** (**lye**-ur)

liberal *adjective*

1. Given or used in generous amounts, as in *a liberal donation.*

2. Plentiful or large, as in *a liberal helping of food.*

3. Broad-minded and tolerant of opinions and ideas that are different from your own: *My mother is not very liberal about dating.*

4. In favor of political change and reform, as in *a liberal Democrat.* See also **left**.
lib·er·al (**lib**-ur-uhl)
▷ *noun* **liberal** ▷ *noun* **liberalism**

liberate *verb* To set free or release from captivity: *The police broke in and liberated the hostages.*
lib·er·ate (**lib**-uh-*rate*) ▷ *verb* **liberating, liberated**
▷ *noun* **liberator**

liberated *adjective* Someone who is **liberated** has been set free or feels free, especially from rules about acceptable behavior. **lib·er·at·ed** (**lib**-uh-*ray*-tid)

liberation *noun* The act of freeing someone or something from imprisonment, slavery, or oppression: *Each year, the former colony marks its date of liberation with fireworks and celebrations.* **lib·er·a·tion** (*lib*-uh-**ray**-shuhn)

liberty *noun* Freedom. **lib·er·ty** (**lib**-ur-tee) ▷ *noun, plural* **liberties**

librarian *noun* A person who works in a library, especially one who is trained in managing a library. **li·brar·i·an** (lye-**brair**-ee-uhn)

library *noun* A place where books, magazines, newspapers, tapes, CDs, and DVDs are kept for reading or borrowing. **li·brar·y** (**lye**-brer-ee) ▷ *noun, plural* **libraries**

lice *noun, plural* Small, wingless insects that attach themselves to animals or people, often in their hair. Lice is the plural form of **louse**. **lice** (lise)

license
1. *noun* A document that officially grants permission for you to own, use, or do something, as in *a fishing license* or *a driver's license*.
2. *verb* If someone is **licensed** to do something, such as practice medicine, he or she is authorized to do it: *My sister is licensed to practice law in Indiana.* ▷ *verb* **licensing, licensed**
li·cense (**lye**-suhns)

lichee *noun* An alternative spelling for **lychee**. **li·chee** (**lee**-chee)

lichen *noun* A flat, spongelike growth on rocks, walls, and trees that consists of algae and fungi growing close together. **li·chen** (**lye**-kuhn)

lick *verb*
1. To pass your tongue over or along something: *My cat licks her paws after she eats.* ▷ *noun* **lick**
2. To pass over something lightly, like a tongue: *Flames licked the pile of twigs.*
3. (*informal*) To defeat: *We licked their team last week.* ▷ *noun* **licking**
lick (lik)
▷ *verb* **licking, licked**

lichen

licorice *noun*
1. A plant with a sweet, edible root that is used to flavor medicine and candy.
2. A candy flavored with licorice.
lic·o·rice (**lik**-ur-ish *or* **lik**-ur-is)

Word History

Licorice is a delicious type of candy, but the licorice herb that the candy is made from is also useful in medicine. Doctors have used licorice to treat sores in the walls of people's stomachs, for example. The Greek name for the plant, *glykyrrhiza*, meant "sweet root." Greek speakers formed it from the words for "sweet," *glykys*, and "root," *rhiza*. For some reason, after the word made its way to Latin, speakers stopped saying the letter *g* at the beginning, and the word ended up as *liquiritia*, giving us *licorice* in English.

lid *noun*
1. A removable top or a hinged cover, as in *a lid on a jar.*
2. An eyelid.
lid (lid)

lie¹ *verb*
1. To get into or be in a flat, horizontal position: *I decided to lie down for a nap.*
2. To be situated somewhere: *The cottage lies just over that hill.*
3. To stay in a certain place or condition, as in *to lie hidden.*
lie (lye)
Lie sounds like **lye**. ▷ *verb* **lying, lay** (lay), **lain** (layn)

lie²
1. *verb* To deliberately say something that is not true: *He said he got to school on time, but he lied.* ▷ *verb* **lying, lied**
2. *noun* A statement that is deliberately false: *She told me that she liked my shoes, but it was a lie.*
lie (lye)
Lie sounds like **lye**.

lieutenant *noun* An officer of low rank in the armed forces. **lieu·ten·ant** (loo-**ten**-uhnt)

life *noun*
1. The quality that makes it possible for people and things to grow, breathe, and reproduce, and that separates people, animals, and plants from things that are not alive: *It was exciting to see the calf being born and to experience the miracle of life.*
2. The period of time from your birth until your death.
3. A living person: *No lives were lost in the crash.*
4. Living things: *There was little plant life out in the desert.*
5. An energetic feeling, as in *full of life.*
life (life)
▷ *noun, plural* **lives** (livez)

a b c d e f g h i j k **l** m n o p q r s t u v w x y z

lifeboat *noun* A strong boat, usually carried on a larger ship, that is used in case of emergencies. **life·boat** (**life**-*boht*)

life cycle *noun* The series of changes each living thing goes through from birth to death.

lifeguard *noun* An expert swimmer who is trained to rescue other swimmers when they are in danger at a beach or swimming pool. **life·guard** (**life**-*gahrd*)

life jacket *noun* A life preserver that looks like a sleeveless jacket or vest and that keeps you afloat in the water.

lifeless *adjective*
1. Dead or without life, as in *a lifeless body* or *a lifeless planet.*
2. Boring or dull, as in *a lifeless party.*
life·less (**life**-*lis*)
▷ *noun* **lifelessness** ▷ *adverb* **lifelessly**

lifelike *adjective* Looking alive or real, as in *a lifelike drawing.* **life·like** (**life**-*like*)

lifelong *adjective* Lasting for a lifetime, as in *lifelong friends.* **life·long** (**life**-*lawng*)

life preserver *noun* A belt, vest, or ring designed to keep a person afloat in water. **life pre·serv·er** (pri-**zur**-ver)

lifesaving *adjective* Saving a person from serious harm or death, as in *a lifesaving medical treatment.* **life·sav·ing** (**life**-*say*-ving)

life span *noun* The period of time a person, an animal, a plant, or an object is expected to live or last: *A fly has a short life span.* ▷ *noun, plural* **life spans**

lifestyle *noun* The way someone lives, as in *a rural lifestyle* or *an athletic lifestyle.* **life·style** (**life**-*stile*)

lifetime *noun* The period of time that a person lives or an object lasts: *The comet won't be visible again for another 75 years, so it's probably my only chance to see it during my lifetime.* **life·time** (**life**-*time*)

lift
1. *verb* To raise something or someone to a higher position or level, as in *to lift a box* or *to lift weights.*
2. *verb* To rise into the air: *The kite slowly lifted as the wind picked up.* ▷ *noun* **lift**
3. *verb* To rise and disappear: *The fog lifted.*
4. *noun* A ride in a vehicle given to someone going in the same direction: *My mom gave me a lift to school on her way to work this morning.*

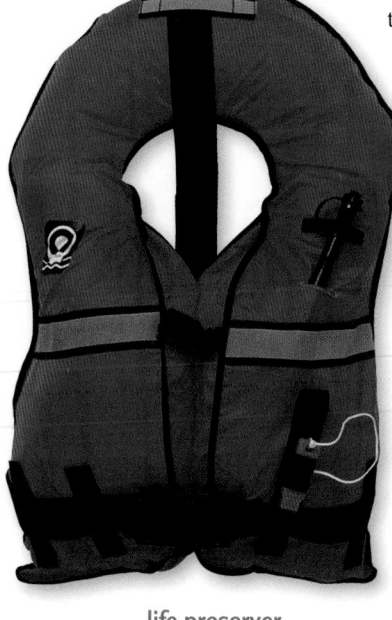

life preserver

5. *noun* A happy feeling: *Her compliment gave me a lift.*
lift (lift)
▷ *verb* **lifting, lifted**

liftoff *noun* The movement of a rocket or spacecraft as it rises from its launching pad: *Just before liftoff, the rocket's engines made a huge roaring sound.* **lift·off** (**lift**-*awf*)

ligament *noun* A tough band of tissue that connects bones and holds some organs in place. **lig·a·ment** (**lig**-uh-muhnt)

light
1. *verb* To set on fire: *We lit a campfire to toast marshmallows.* ▷ *noun* **light**
2. *verb* To fill with light or cause something to give off light: *Gabe turned on the lamp to light the room.*
3. *noun* Brightness or illumination: *The light from the window woke me up this morning.*
4. *adjective* Pale in color, as in *light green.*
5. *noun* Something that gives off light, such as a flashlight or lamp: *In December we have to turn the lights on early in the evening.*
6. *adjective* Gentle or having little impact, as in *a light rain.*
7. *adjective* Not having much weight; not strongly made: *The antique dishes are delicate and light.* ▷ *noun* **lightness**
8. *adjective* Moving easily or gracefully: *The dancer was light on his feet.*
9. *adjective* Not serious, as in *a light novel.*
10. *adjective* Low in calories or fat, as in *a diet of light foods.*
11. *verb* If you **shed light on** or **throw light on** something, you make it clear: *This article sheds some light on why the mayor had to resign.*
light (lite)
▷ *verb* **lighting, lighted** *or* **lit** (lit) ▷ *adjective* **lighter, lightest**

lightbulb *noun*
1. An electric bulb, usually round, that produces light when the filament inside it is heated by an electric current when the bulb is switched on. Also known as an **incandescent bulb**.
2. An electric bulb, sold in a variety of shapes, that produces light when the fluorescent coating inside it is stimulated by an electric current when the bulb is switched on. Also known as a **fluorescent bulb**.
light·bulb (**lite**-*buhlb*)

lighten *verb*
1. To make brighter or lighter: *The new wallpaper really lightens the room.*
2. To make or become lighter in color: *Spending the summer in the sun lightened Alan's hair.*
3. To make or become lighter in weight or quantity, as in *to lighten a load* or *to lighten a task.*
4. To make or become more cheerful: *A visit from Aunt Agatha always lightens my mood.*
light·en (**lye**-tuhn)
▷ *verb* **lightening, lightened**

lighthearted *adjective* Funny and not very serious; cheerful: *The movie takes a lighthearted look at recent fashion trends.* **light·heart·ed** (**lite**-*hahr*-tid)

lighthouse *noun* A tower set in or near the sea with a flashing light at the top that helps ships avoid danger. **light·house** (**lite**-*hous*)

lightning *noun* A flash of light in the sky when electricity moves between clouds or between a cloud and the ground: *Thunder and lightning scare my little brother.* **light·ning** (**lite**-ning)

lightning bug *noun* See **firefly**.

lightsaber *noun* An imaginary weapon, used in the Star Wars movies, that is a sword with a blade consisting of a laser. **light·sa·ber** (**lite**-*say*-bur)

lightweight
1. *adjective* Not weighing very much, as in *a lightweight jacket.*
2. *adjective* Not serious; not having much influence, as in *a lightweight talk show.*
3. *noun* Someone who is not that important, influential, or smart: *The actor is considered a lightweight by film critics.*
light·weight (**lite**-*wayt*)

light-year *noun*
1. The distance that light travels in one year.
2. A very long way: *I'm getting better, but I'm light-years away from being a competitive gymnast.*

likable *adjective* Easy to like. **lik·a·ble** (**lye**-kuh-buhl)

Suffix

The suffix **-like** adds the following meaning to a root word: Similar to or resembling, as in *lifelike* (similar to life) or *childlike* (resembling a child).

like
1. *verb* To find someone or something pleasant or enjoyable: *I really like going to the movies.*
2. *verb* To wish for or want something: *I'd like a glass*

lighthouse

of juice, please.
3. *preposition* Similar to or resembling closely: *My computer is like the one Simon has.*
4. *preposition* Typical or characteristic of: *It isn't like Alina to be late for a party.*
5. *preposition* Such as; as for example: *I do well in subjects like reading and language arts.*
6. *adjective* Similar or equal, as in *a like amount.*
7. *conjunction* (*informal*) As if: *He looked like he might be sick.*
like (like)
▷ *verb* **liking, liked**

likely *adjective* Probable or to be expected: *It is likely to be a perfect day for skiing.* **like·ly** (**like**-lee) ▷ *adjective* **likelier, likeliest** ▷ *noun* **likelihood**

liken *verb* To compare one thing or person to another: *They likened the thrill of riding the roller coaster to being six years old again.* **lik·en** (**lye**-kuhn)
▷ *verb* **likening, likened**

likeness *noun*
1. A strong similarity or resemblance: *Ellena bears a striking likeness to her aunt.*
2. A picture or portrait: *That painting is a very good likeness of my grandfather.*
like·ness (**like**-nis)
▷ *noun, plural* **likenesses**

likewise *adverb* Also, or in a similar way: *Andrea went to bed early and Lia did likewise.* **like·wise** (**like**-*wize*)

liking *noun*
1. Enjoyment of something or someone: *He had a great liking for the outdoors and spent most of his vacations hiking.*
2. If you **take a liking** to someone, it means you are beginning to like that person: *I took a liking to her when I got to know her better.*
lik·ing (**lye**-king)

lilac *noun*
1. A shrub or tree with large clusters of fragrant purple, pink, or white flowers.
2. A pale purple color.
li·lac (**lye**-lak *or* **lye**-lahk)

Word History

Plants can be named after the color of their flowers. The **lilac** shrub, for example, gets its name from an old word meaning "blue." The word was *nilak*, in the language spoken in Persia, now called Iran. Some people there started saying *lilak* instead of *nilak*, though. *Lilak* led to *lilac*, the English name for the shrub.

a b c d e f g h i j k l m n o p q r s t u v w x y z

lily *noun* Any of several plants that grow from bulbs and have flowers that are shaped like trumpets. **lil·y (lil**-ee) ▷ *noun, plural* **lilies**

lily of the valley *noun* A plant of the lily family with broad leaves and a stem covered with small, white flowers shaped like bells. ▷ *noun, plural* **lilies of the valley**

lima bean *noun* A flat, light green, edible bean, or the plant it grows on. **li·ma bean (lye**-muh)

limb *noun*
1. A part of a body used in moving or grasping. Arms, legs, wings, and flippers are limbs.
2. A large tree branch: *A huge limb broke off the maple tree during the storm.*
limb (lim)

limber
1. *adjective* Bending or moving easily.
2. *verb* When you **limber up**, you warm up your muscles before exercising or beginning an activity. ▷ *verb* **limbering, limbered**
lim·ber (lim-bur)

lime *noun*
1. A small, round citrus fruit with a green rind and sour taste.
2. A white substance obtained by burning limestone, shells, and similar materials, used to make cement and as a fertilizer.
lime (lime)

limelight *noun* If you are **in the limelight**, you are the focus of everyone's attention. **lime·light (lime**-*lite*)

limerick *noun* A funny poem made up of five lines that rhyme in a set pattern. **lim·er·ick (lim**-ur-ik)

limestone *noun* A hard rock used in building and in making lime and cement. Limestone is formed from the remains of shells or coral. **lime·stone (lime**-*stohn*)

limit
1. *noun* A point beyond which someone or something cannot or should not go, as in *the speed limit.* ▷ *adjective* **limitless** ▷ *adverb* **limitlessly**
2. *verb* To set a limit on someone or something: *I've limited myself to one can of soda a day.* ▷ *verb* **limiting, limited**
3. limits *noun, plural* Boundaries, as in *the city limits.*
lim·it (lim-it)

limitation *noun*
1. A fact, rule, or situation that limits something: *The players' major limitation was their lack of experience.*

limes

2. The act of limiting something: *If you think you can't do math, you could be putting a limitation on yourself that will keep you from being good at it.* **lim·i·ta·tion (lim**-i-**tay**-shuhn)

limited *adjective* Small or restricted in size, amount, or ability, as in *limited shelf space.* **lim·it·ed (lim**-i-tid)

limousine *noun* An automobile that is bigger and more luxurious than a regular car. Limousines are often driven by a chauffeur. The word is sometimes shortened as *limo* (**lim**-oh). **lim·ou·sine (lim**-uh-*zeen*)

limp
1. *verb* To walk with difficulty, placing more weight on one leg than the other, usually because of an injury. ▷ *verb* **limping, limped** ▷ *noun* **limp**
2. *adjective* Lacking strength, spirit, or firmness, as in *a limp handshake.* ▷ *adjective* **limper, limpest** ▷ *adverb* **limply**
limp (limp)

Lincoln's Birthday *noun* A holiday on February 12 when some states celebrate the birth of Abraham Lincoln (1809–1865), 16th president of the United States. The holiday is observed in some states on Presidents' Day, the third Monday in February. **Lin·coln's Birthday (ling**-kuhnz)

line
1. *noun* A long, thin mark made by a pen, pencil, or other tool: *She used a ruler to draw a straight line.*
2. *noun* A row or series of people or things, as in *a long line for tickets.*
3. *noun* A long, thin rope, string, or cord, as in *a fishing line.*
4. *noun* A boundary, as in *the state line.*
5. *noun* A short letter: *Drop us a line when you get there.*
6. *noun* A wire or set of wires that carries electricity or connects points in a telephone system: *He ordered an additional phone line for his business.*
7. *noun* A transportation system that runs on a specific route: *We need a new bus line in our neighborhood.*
8. lines *noun, plural* Words that you speak in a play: *Don't forget your lines.*
9. *noun* In mathematics, a set of points extending in a straight path without end in either direction.
10. *verb* To cover the inside surface of something: *She lined the jacket with fleece so that it would be warm.*
11. *noun* An attitude toward something: *He takes a*

very hard line on team members who misbehave.
12. line up *verb* To form a straight line: *Cars lined up at the gas station.*
line (line)
▷ *verb* **lining, lined**

linear *adjective*
1. Using or having to do with lines, as in *a linear drawing.*
2. Of or having to do with length. Feet, miles, centimeters, and kilometers are linear measures.
lin·e·ar (**lin**-ee-ur)

linebacker *noun* A football player who stands in the second line of defense to tackle players on the other team who try to run down the field or make short passes. The linebackers stand behind the linemen, the first line of defense, who are at the line of scrimmage. **line·back·er** (line-*bak*-ur)

lineman *noun*
1. A person whose work is installing or repairing electric power lines or telephone lines.
2. A football player who is part of the forward line of a team. A lineman blocks or tackles players of the other team in a game.
line·man (**line**-muhn)
▷ *noun, plural* **linemen**

linen *noun*
1. Cloth woven from fibers of the flax plant.
2. Household items, such as tablecloths and sheets, that were once made of linen.
lin·en (**lin**-uhn)

lineup *noun*
1. A group of people who are going to do the same thing, one after the other: *I didn't see your name in the lineup of speakers.*
2. A schedule of activities or programs, as in *NBC's primetime lineup.*
3. A group of people lined up by police so that a witness to a crime can look at them and say which one may be guilty.
line·up (**line**-*uhp*)

linger *verb* To be slow in leaving or to continue to stay: *Some of the guests lingered at the party.* **lin·ger** (**ling**-gur) ▷ *verb* **lingering, lingered** ▷ *adjective* **lingering**

linguine *noun* Pasta cut into long, thin strips.
lin·gui·ne (ling-**gwee**-nee)

linguist *noun* Someone who studies the structure and nature of languages or speaks them well. **lin·guist** (**ling**-gwist) ▷ *noun* **linguistics** (ling-**gwis**-tiks)

lining *noun* The layer or coating that covers the inside of something, as in *the lining of a stomach* or *the lining of a coat.* **lin·ing** (**lye**-ning)

lioness

link
1. *noun* One of the rings or loops that make up a chain.
2. *noun* A connection or relationship between people or things.
3. *noun* A connection between one webpage or website and another; a hyperlink: *His homepage has links to his blog and to his slideshow on his trip to Venice.*
4. *verb* To connect or become connected. ▷ *verb* **linking, linked**
link (lingk)

linking verb *noun* A verb that does not show action. Its function is to link the subject of a sentence to what is said about the subject. For example, the verb *be* is a linking verb, as in the sentence "Paul is happy."

linoleum *noun* A material with a strong, shiny surface and a canvas or cloth back. Linoleum is used as a floor covering, most commonly in kitchens. **li·no·le·um** (luh-**noh**-lee-uhm)

lint *noun* Very small bits of thread or fluff from cloth. **lint** (lint)

lion *noun* A large, light brown wildcat found in sub-Saharan Africa and India. Male lions have manes. **li·on** (**lye**-uhn)

lioness *noun* A female lion. **li·on·ess** (**lye**-uh-nis)
▷ *noun, plural* **lionesses**

lip *noun*
1. Your **lips** are the two fleshy parts that form the edges of your mouth and that help to form speech sounds.
2. The edge or rim of something, especially of a pitcher, cup, bowl, or other container.
3. *(slang)* Disrespectful talk: *"Don't give me any lip,"* *my mother warned.*
lip (lip)

lip-read *verb* To understand what someone is saying by watching his or her lip movements. **lip-read** (lip-*reed*) ▷ *verb* **lip-reading, lip-read** (red) ▷ *noun* **lipreading**

lipstick *noun* A small, crayonlike stick used to color the lips. **lip·stick** (**lip**-*stik*)

a b c d e f g h i j k l m n o p q r s t u v w x y z

liquefy *verb* To make something solid into a liquid: *She liquefied fruit to add to the punch.* **liq·ue·fy** (lik-wuh-*fye*) ▷ *verb* **liquefies, liquefying, liquefied**

liquid *noun* A substance that flows readily and can be poured: *Most children study the properties of solids and liquids in elementary school.* **liq·uid** (lik-wid) ▷ *adjective* **liquid**

liquid crystal display *noun* A way of showing numbers and letters on clocks, calculators, and digital watches by putting a liquid between layers of plastic or glass and then passing an electric current through it. Abbreviated as **LCD**.

liquor *noun* A strong alcoholic drink, such as vodka, whiskey, or rum. **liq·uor** (lik-ur)

lisp *noun* A speech defect in which the letter *s* is pronounced like *th*. **lisp** (lisp) ▷ *verb* **lisp**

list
1. *noun* A series of names or items, often written in a particular order, as in *a shopping list*.
2. *verb* To put into a list, as in *to list chores*.
3. *verb* To lean to one side: *The damaged ship was listing as it entered the harbor.* **list** (list) ▷ *verb* **listing, listed**

listen *verb* To make a conscious effort to hear something: *Kevin likes to listen to music while he works.* **lis·ten** (lis-uhn) ▷ *verb* **listening, listened** ▷ *noun* **listener**

listicle *noun* An article, especially one on a website, that consists of a numbered list of short paragraphs. **lis·ti·cle** (lis-ti-kuhl)

listless *adjective* Showing no interest in or enthusiasm about anything; lacking energy: *I felt too tired and listless to go on the hike.* **list·less** (list-lis)

lit *verb* The past tense and the past participle of **light**. **lit** (lit)

liter *noun* A unit of measurement in the metric system. A liter is equal to about 1.1 quarts. **li·ter** (lee-tur)

literacy *noun* The ability to read and write, as in *a high rate of literacy*. **lit·er·a·cy** (lit-ur-uh-see)

literal *adjective*
1. Following the original text exactly: *This translation of the poem is loose and not very literal.*
2. True to the facts and not exaggerated; actual: *How can she claim to give us a literal description of the place when she's never even been there?* **lit·er·al** (lit-ur-uhl)

literally *adverb*
1. Word for word: *I translated the story from Spanish into English literally.*
2. Actually: *I woke up so late that there was literally no way I could catch the plane.*
3. If you **take** something **literally**, you believe it without questioning it at all. **lit·er·al·ly** (lit-ur-uh-lee)

literate *adjective*
1. Able to read and write.
2. Highly educated. **lit·er·ate** (lit-ur-it)

literature *noun* Written works that have lasting value or interest. Literature includes novels, plays, short stories, essays, and poems. **lit·er·a·ture** (lit-ur-uh-chur) ▷ *adjective* **literary** (lit-uh-*rer*-ee)

litmus paper *noun* Paper soaked in a dye that changes from red to blue in a base solution and from blue to red in an acid solution. **lit·mus paper** (lit-muhs)

litter *noun*
1. Bits or scraps of paper or other garbage scattered around carelessly. ▷ *verb* **litter**
2. A number of baby animals that are born at the same time to the same mother: *My cat had a litter of five kittens.*
3. A stretcher for carrying a sick or wounded person. **lit·ter** (lit-ur)

little
1. *adjective* Small in size or amount, as in *a little tree.* ▷ *adjective* **littler, littlest**

Literature

Literature includes works of imagination, called fiction, and factual writing on subjects such as history, called nonfiction. Epic poems were the earliest type of literature. These long poems about heroes were recited by a musician or a poet. Few people knew how to read. After the invention of the printing press by the German craftsman and printer Johannes Gutenberg in the 1400s, books became widely available, and literacy increased.

2. *noun* A small quantity or amount of something: *Save a little for me.*
3. *adjective* Not much: *There is little time left to make changes.* ▷ *adjective* **less** (les), **least** (leest)
lit·tle (**lit**-uhl)

Synonyms

Little is the opposite of big and has to do with size more than importance: *It's hard to imagine your parents as little children.*

- -

■ **Small** also means little, but it refers to something's number, capacity, or value, as in *a small audience, a small pitcher,* or *a small raise in pay.*

■ **Minute** describes something that is extremely small: *Even a minute amount of poison can be fatal.*

■ **Miniature** refers to something that has been scaled down to a very small size: *Every detail of the model airplane is authentic, right down to the miniature pilot sitting in the cockpit.*

■ **Diminutive** describes something that is unusually or abnormally small: *We were surprised that such a large woman would have such diminutive hands.*

■ **Tiny** is an informal way of saying that something is minute, which means that it is extremely small: *The spot of ink on the sweater is so tiny that you can hardly see it.*

live
1. (liv) *verb* To remain alive: *My grandfather lived to be 90.*
2. (live) *adjective* Living: *There was a tank full of live lobsters at the grocery store.*
3. (liv) *verb* To make your home in a particular place: *We lived in Germany for three years.*
4. (liv) *verb* To support yourself: *He lives on a small salary.*
5. (live) *adjective* Broadcast while actually being performed; not recorded, as in *a live performance* or *a live broadcast.*
6. (live) *adjective* Burning, as in *live coals.*
7. (live) *adjective* If an electrical wire or device is **live**, it is connected to a source of electricity and can give you a shock.
8. (live) *adjective* Not yet exploded, as in *a live bomb.*
9. If you **live and let live**, you are tolerant and able to accept or respect the behavior, customs, beliefs, or opinions of others.
10. If you can **live with** a difficult situation, you can put up with it or bear it.
live
▷ *verb* **living, lived**
livelihood *noun* The way that you earn money in order to live: *When he got sick, he lost his livelihood as*

well as his health. **live·li·hood** (**live**-lee-*hud*)
lively *adjective*
1. Full of life and energy, as in *a lively dance step.*
2. Bright: *Red is a lively color.*
3. Exciting, as in *a lively debate.*
4. Creative, as in *a lively imagination.*
live·ly (**live**-lee)
▷ *adjective* **livelier, liveliest** ▷ *noun* **liveliness**
liver *noun*
1. The organ in a human or animal body that cleans the blood and produces bile, which helps digest food.
2. A food prepared from the liver of a calf, pig, or other animal.
liv·er (**liv**-ur)
lives
1. (livez) *noun, plural* The plural of **life**.
2. (livz) *verb* The third person singular present form of **live**.
lives
livestock *noun* Sheep, horses, cows, pigs, or other animals that are kept or raised on a farm or ranch. They are used to do work, to provide a profit from the sale of their fur or meat, or to provide pleasure, such as horseback riding. **live·stock** (**live**-*stahk*)

livestock

living
1. *adjective* Alive now; not dead: *All of their grandparents are still living.*
2. *noun* A way of earning an income: *She makes a living taking care of other people's kids.*
3. *adjective* Still active or in use: *Spanish is a living language.*
liv·ing (**liv**-ing)
living room *noun* A room in a house intended for social and leisure activities.

lizard *noun* A reptile with a scaly body, four legs, and a long tail. **liz·ard** (**liz**-urd)

llama *noun* A large South American mammal raised for its wool and used to carry loads. The llama is related to the camel. **lla·ma** (**lah**-muh)

load

1. *noun* Something heavy or bulky that is being carried or is about to be carried: *The truck carried a heavy load of wood in the back.*

2. *noun* The amount carried at one time: *We need four loads of dirt for the yard.*

3. *verb* To put things on or into a carrier: *We loaded the wheelbarrow with bricks.*

4. *verb* To insert something into a device, such as a gun or a camera, so that it works: *I loaded the software on my new computer.*

5. *noun, plural (informal)* If you have **loads** of something, you have a great number or amount of it: *We've got loads of Christmas presents to open this year.* **load** (lohd)

▷ *verb* **loading, loaded**

loaf

1. *noun* Bread baked in one piece, as in *a whole wheat loaf.*

2. *noun* Food in the shape of a rectangular loaf of bread, as in *a meat loaf.*

3. *verb* To spend time doing little or nothing.

▷ *verb* **loafing, loafed**
loaf (lohf)

▷ *noun, plural* **loaves** (lohvz)

loafer *noun*

1. Someone who lounges around and doesn't do much.

2. Loafer A trademark for a flat, casual shoe.
loaf·er (**loh**-fur)

loan

1. *noun* The act of lending something to someone.

2. *noun* Something borrowed, especially money: *The books were a loan from my neighbor.*

3. *verb* To lend something to someone, as in *to loan money.*

▷ *verb* **loaning, loaned**
loan (lohn)

Loan sounds like **lone**.

loathe *verb* To feel great dislike or disgust for someone or something.
loathe (lohTH) ▷ *verb* **loathing, loathed**
▷ *noun* **loathing**

loathsome *adjective* Causing hatred or disgust, as in *a loathsome*

lobby

disease. **loath·some** (**lohTH**-suhm)

lob *verb* To throw or hit something, especially a ball, in a high arc. **lob** (lahb) ▷ *verb* **lobbing, lobbed** ▷ *noun* **lob**

lobby

1. *noun* A hall or room at the entrance to a building: *We waited for our friends in the lobby of the theater.*

2. *noun* A group of people who try to influence politicians on a specific issue.

3. *verb* To work to influence someone about something, especially about a specific political issue: *My cousin lobbies for an environmental group.* ▷ *verb* **lobbying, lobbied**
lob·by (**lah**-bee)

▷ *noun, plural* **lobbies**

lobbyist *noun* A person who works on behalf of a particular group to persuade members of the government to act or vote in support of that group's interests. **lob·by·ist** (**lah**-bee-ist)

lobster *noun* A sea creature used for food, with a hard shell and five pairs of legs. The front pair of legs are large, heavy claws. **lob·ster** (**lahb**-stur)

lobster

local

1. *adjective* Of or having to do with the area in which you live, as in *a local library.* ▷ *adverb* **locally**

2. *noun* A train, subway, or bus that makes all the stops on a route. ▷ *adjective* **local**

3. *adjective* Affecting only a part of the body, as in *a local anesthetic.*
lo·cal (**loh**-kuhl)

locality *noun* A district, an area, or a neighborhood: *This locality is known for its excellent Indian restaurants.* **lo·cal·i·ty** (loh-**kal**-i-tee) ▷ *noun, plural* **localities**

locate *verb*
1. To find out the exact place or position of something: *The town was so small it was difficult to locate on a map.*
2. To put or place somewhere: *The company located its fifth store in a popular mall.*
3. To settle in a particular place: *My family has located in Texas.*
lo·cate (**loh**-kate)
▷ *verb* **locating, located**

location *noun*
1. A place or position: *I found the location of the stadium on the map.*
2. If a movie is made **on location**, it is filmed in the type of place where the story is set, not in the studio: *Many fantasy epics are filmed on location in New Zealand because of the wild landscape there.*
lo·ca·tion (loh-**kay**-shuhn)

lock
1. *verb* To fasten or secure something with or as if with a lock: *I make sure to lock all the doors whenever I leave home.*
2. *noun* A device for keeping a door or container fastened that you can open and shut with a key.
3. *verb* To join or link together: *We locked arms and formed a circle.*
4. *noun* A section of a canal with gates at each end, used for raising and lowering boats by changing the water level.
5. *noun* A tuft of hair, as in *long, thick locks.*
lock (lahk)
▷ *verb* **locking, locked**

lockdown *noun* A time when people have to stay locked inside classrooms or other rooms because there might be a danger if they go out. **lock·down** (**lahk**-doun)

locker *noun* A small chest or closet, especially at a school or gym, that can be locked and where you can store your belongings. **lock·er** (**lah**-kur)

locket *noun* A piece of jewelry worn on a chain around the neck that often contains a photograph, lock of hair, or other memento. **lock·et** (**lah**-kit)

lockjaw *noun* See **tetanus**. **lock·jaw** (**lahk**-*jaw*)

locksmith *noun* Someone who makes and repairs locks and also makes keys. **lock·smith** (**lahk**-*smith*)

locomotion *noun* The act of moving from one place to another, or the ability to do so. **lo·co·mo·tion** (*loh*-kuh-**moh**-shuhn)

locomotive

locomotive *noun* An engine used to push or pull railroad cars. **lo·co·mo·tive** (*loh*-kuh-**moh**-tiv)

locust *noun* A type of grasshopper that moves in huge swarms and destroys crops and vegetation. **lo·cust** (**loh**-kuhst)

lodestone *noun* A stone with iron in it that acts as a magnet. **lode·stone** (**lohd**-*stone*)

Word History

The magnetic properties of a **lodestone** made it useful as a compass. Sailors used the stone to help them navigate. The word *lode* in *lodestone* means "way." So the rock's name means "way stone," because the lodestone showed sailors the way.

lodge
1. *noun* A small house, cottage, or cabin, often used for a short stay, as in *a ski lodge.*
2. *verb* If you **lodge** with someone, you live in the person's house and usually pay rent.
3. *verb* If something **lodges** somewhere, it comes to rest there and becomes firmly fixed: *The cap of the shampoo bottle got lodged in the bathtub drain.*
4. *noun* The den of a beaver.
5. *verb* To bring to the attention of someone in charge, as in *to lodge a complaint.*
lodge (lahj)
▷ *verb* **lodging, lodged**

lodger *noun* Somebody who rents a room in someone else's house. **lodg·er** (**lah**-jur) ▷ *noun* **lodgings**

loft *noun*
1. A room or space under the roof of a building.
2. An upper story in a business building used as a place to live in or as an artist's studio.
loft (lawft)

a b c d e f g h i j k l m n o p q r s t u v w x y z

lofty *adjective*
1. Very tall and impressive, as in *a lofty skyscraper.*
2. Aloof and proud, as in *a lofty manner.*
loft·y (**lawf**-tee)
▷ *adjective* **loftier, loftiest**

log
1. *noun* A part of a tree that has fallen or been cut off: *The lumberjack cut down the tree and sawed it into logs.*
2. *noun* A written record, kept by the captain, of a ship's speed, progress, and what happens on its voyage: *A lot of what we know about whaling comes from reading old ships' logs.*
3. *noun* A written record of the progress of something, such as a trip or an experiment, as in *a log of an expedition to the Antarctic.*
4. *verb* To cut down trees: *The owner had logged his property, and now there were only a few trees left.*
5. *verb* To keep a record of something: *Make sure you log all the phone calls you make and receive.*
6. *verb* When you **log on** or **log in** to a computer, you take whatever steps are required to begin using it, such as entering a username or a password: *If I don't use my computer for a while, I have to log on again.*
7. *verb* When you **log off** or **log out**, you go through the steps required to finish using a computer.
log (lawg *or* lahg)
▷ *verb* **logging, logged** ▷ *noun* **logger**

logic *noun*
1. Good or valid thinking or reasoning, as in *a well-written essay with solid logic.*
2. The study of the rules for correct reasoning.
3. A particular way of thinking: *I couldn't see the logic in going on vacation right after Christmas.*
log·ic (**lah**-jik)

logical *adjective* Easy to figure out and consistent with logic; sensible: *There has to be a logical reason why she never showed up.* **log·i·cal** (**lah**-ji-kuhl)
▷ *adverb* **logically**

login *or* **logon** *noun*
1. An act of logging in to a network, website, computer, or online account: *The software keeps track of your logins.*
2. A username: *Don't share your login and password with anyone.*
log·in (**lawg**-in) *or* **log·on** (**lawg**-awn)

logo *noun* A distinctive symbol or trademark that identifies a particular company or organization: *The logo of the Olympics is five linked rings.* **lo·go** (**loh**-goh)

loin
1. **loins** *noun, plural* In people or animals, the part of the sides and back of the body between the ribs and the hip.
2. *noun* A cut of meat from this part of an animal.
loin (loin)

loiter *verb* To stand around aimlessly or move slowly with many stops: *The policeman accused him of loitering when he was just waiting for a ride home.* **loi·ter** (**loi**-ter) ▷ *verb* **loitering, loitered**
▷ *noun* **loiterer**

lollipop *noun* A piece of hard candy on a stick.
lol·li·pop (**lah**-lee-*pahp*)

lone *adjective*
1. Alone or solitary: *The lone hawk sat on a high branch.*
2. Only or single, as in *the lone survivor of a plane crash.*
lone (lohn)
Lone sounds like **loan.**

lonely *adjective*
1. If you are **lonely,** you miss the company of other people. ▷ *noun* **loneliness**
2. Remote and standing apart from others like it, as in *a lonely cabin.*
lone·ly (**lone**-lee)
▷ *adjective* **lonelier, loneliest**

lonesome *adjective*
1. If you are **lonesome,** you are sad because you feel alone: *Al felt lonesome while his best friend was away.*
2. Not often visited or used by people, as in *a lonesome road.*
lone·some (**lone**-suhm)

long
1. *adjective* Of greater than usual length, height, distance, or time, as in *a long trip.*
2. *adjective* Measured from end to end: *The driveway was about a mile long.*
3. *adjective* Lasting a long time: *The concert was unusually long.*
4. *adverb* For a long time: *The plane is long overdue.*
5. *adverb* Throughout the length or duration of, as in *all week long.*
6. *noun* A long time: *He was not gone for long.*
7. *verb* To wish for something or to want someone or something very much: *Hans longed to beat his older brother in chess.* ▷ *verb* **longing, longed** ▷ *noun* **longing**
long (lawng)
▷ *adjective* **longer, longest**

lollipop

longevity *noun*

1. The long span of a person's life: *She was nearly 95 years old, and she attributed her longevity to regular exercise.*

2. The length of life: *The medical researchers were studying ways to prolong human longevity.*

3. The length of time that something lasts or exists: *The show was on television for more than 20 years—its longevity was thanks to its popular cast and its hilarious scripts.*

lon·gev·i·ty (lahn-**jev**-uh-tee)

longitude *noun* The distance east or west, measured in degrees, of an imaginary line that runs through Greenwich, England. On a map or globe, lines of longitude are drawn from the North Pole to the South Pole. **lon·gi·tude** (**lahn**-ji-*tood*) ▷ *adjective* **longitudinal** (*lahn*-ji-**too**-duh-nuhl)

long-standing *adjective* Established long ago and therefore accepted or usual: *We have a long-standing commitment to ensuring that no one in our community goes hungry.*

long-term *adjective* Having to do with or extending over a long period of time, as in *long-term goals.*

long-winded *adjective* Speaking or writing at great length, often in a boring way: *He gave a long-winded speech about the economy.* **long-wind·ed** (**win**-did)

look

1. *verb* To use your eyes to see someone or something: *I'm looking at the birds up in the tree.*

2. *verb* To turn your eyes or attention: *Look at the camera.*

3. *noun* A glance or facial expression that reveals how you are feeling or what you are thinking, as in *a worried look.*

4. *verb* To seem or appear to be: *It looks like it's going to be another hot, humid summer.*

5. *noun* Appearance, style, or fashion: *Dylan's haircut has given him a whole new look.*

6. *verb* To face in a certain direction: *The hotel looks out over the beach.*

7. *verb* If you **look after** someone or something, you take care of or watch over him, her, or it.

8. *verb* If you **look down on** someone, you think you are superior to the person.

9. *verb* If you **look forward to** something, you can't wait for it to happen: *Miranda looked forward to her 12th birthday.*

10. *verb* If you **look** something **up**, you search for information about it in a book or other reference: *It's so easy to look up facts on the internet.*

11. *verb* If you **look up to** a person, you respect him or her.

look (luk)

▷ *verb* **looking, looked**

lookout *noun* Someone who keeps watch for danger or trouble: *The soldiers posted a lookout outside the fort.* **look·out** (**luk**-*out*)

loom

1. *verb* To take shape or come into view in a threatening way: *A ghostlike ship loomed out of the mist.*

2. *verb* To be about to happen: *No one knew there was a financial crisis looming.*

3. *noun* A machine or device used for weaving cloth.

loom (loom)

▷ *verb* **looming, loomed**

loon *noun* A large diving bird with webbed feet, short legs, and a speckled back. The cry of the loon sounds like wild laughter. **loon** (loon)

loop *noun* The shape formed when a piece of string, rope, or some other flexible material bends around and crosses itself. **loop** (loop)

▷ *verb* **loop**

loose *adjective*

1. Not fastened or attached firmly: *The car wouldn't start because of a loose wire.*

2. Free: *The dog was loose in the street.*

3. Not fitting tightly or closely, as in *a loose jacket.*

4. Not held together or attached in one place, as in *loose notebook paper.*

5. Not placed or packed tightly together, as in *loose gravel* or *a loose weave.*

loose (loos)

▷ *adjective* **looser, loosest** ▷ *adverb* **loosely**

loose-leaf *adjective* Holding or made to hold pages that have holes and are easily removed, as in *a loose-leaf notebook.*

loosen *verb*

1. To make something loose, as in *to loosen a screw.*

2. To set free: *We loosened the dog from the leash.*

3. If you **loosen up**, you relax, talk more freely, or warm up for an activity: *Fifteen minutes in a hot tub should loosen up your leg muscles.*

loos·en (**loo**-suhn)

▷ *verb* **loosening, loosened**

loot

1. *verb* To steal from shops or homes during a riot, war, natural disaster, or other crisis: *After the hurricane, people began looting the stores downtown.* ▷ *verb* **looting, looted** ▷ *noun* **looter**

2. *noun* Items that have been stolen or taken by force: *The robbers spread their loot out on the floor.*

loot (loot)

Loot sounds like **lute.**

lopsided *adjective* Unbalanced, with one side heavier, larger, or higher than the other: *Jeannie braided her own hair this morning, and her pigtails are lopsided.* **lop·sid·ed (lahp-sye-did)**

lord *noun*
1. A person who has great power or authority over others. In the Middle Ages, a lord lived in a castle and had many people under his rule. ▷ *adjective* **lordly**
2. Lord A name for God.
3. Lord In Great Britain, a title for a man of noble birth. Some British men earn this title as a reward for service to their country.
lord (lord)

lose *verb*
1. If you **lose** something, you no longer have it: *I lost my hat in the park.*
2. To fail to keep or hold on to something: *Don't lose your temper.*
3. To fail to win something, such as a contest, election, or argument, as in *to lose a game.* ▷ *noun* **loser**
4. To waste or fail to take advantage of something: *We'll lose time if we don't take the shortcut.*
lose (looz)
▷ *verb* **losing, lost** (lawst)

loss *noun*
1. The act or an instance of losing something, as in *the loss of a race* or *a loss of memory.*
2. The person, thing, or amount that is lost: *We all suffered great losses when a tornado hit our town.*
loss (laws)
▷ *noun, plural* **losses**

lot
1. *noun* A great number or amount of something: *A lot of apples rolled off the pile.*
2. *noun* A piece of land, as in *a vacant lot.*
3. a lot or **lots** *adverb* Much: *He feels a lot worse today.*
4. *noun* A group of objects or people: *This kitten is the cutest of the lot.*
lot (laht)

lotion *noun* A thin cream that is used to clean, soften, or heal the skin. **lo·tion (loh-shuhn)**

lottery *noun* A way of raising money in which people buy numbered tickets in the hope of winning a prize if their number is drawn. **lot·ter·y (lah-tur-ee)** ▷ *noun, plural* **lotteries**

lotus *noun* A water plant with large flowers that float on the surface. The flowers are usually pink or white. **lo·tus (loh-tuhs)** ▷ *noun, plural* **lotuses**

loud *adjective*
1. Producing a very intense sound, as in *a loud horn.* ▷ *adverb* **loud** ▷ *adverb* **loudly**
2. Bright and colorful but in poor taste, as in *a loud tie.*

Lotus

The lotus is an aquatic plant resembling a water lily, with flowers that are usually white or pink, but that can sometimes be other colors. In ancient Egypt, the lotus was a sacred symbol of creation and rebirth. In Hinduism, the lotus often symbolizes divine beauty, and in Buddhism it represents purity and enlightenment. The word *lotus* is also the name of a shrub whose fruit was important in Greek mythology.

loud (loud)
▷ *adjective* **louder, loudest**

loudspeaker *noun* A machine that turns electrical signals into sounds that are loud enough to be heard in a large room or area. **loud·speak·er (loud-spee-kur)**

lounge
1. *verb* To stand, sit, or lie in a lazy or relaxed way: *Instead of doing our homework, we lounged on the porch.* ▷ *verb* **lounging, lounged**
2. *noun* A room in a hotel or airport where people can sit and relax.
lounge (lounj)

louse *noun* A small, wingless insect that lives on people or animals and sucks their blood. **louse** (lous) ▷ *noun, plural* **lice** (lise)

louse

lousy *adjective*
1. (*informal*) Really bad; terrible: *The job was OK, but the pay was lousy.*
2. (*informal*) Unpleasant, immoral, or dishonest: *That lousy swindler never paid me for my bike.*
3. Infested with lice, as in *a lousy bundle of old clothes.*
lous·y (lou-zee)
▷ *adjective* **lousier, lousiest** ▷ *adverb* **lousily**
▷ *noun* **lousiness**

Word History

Even if people know the original meaning of **lousy**, "infested with lice," they probably aren't thinking of lice when they use this word to mean "terrible." *Lousy* comes from the word *louse*, an insect that can live on people or animals. If something was full of lice, people thought it was dirty, and lousy came to mean something that was very nasty.

lovable *adjective* Easy to love, as in *a lovable kitten.* **lov·a·ble (luhv**-uh-buhl**)** ▷ *adverb* **lovably**

love

1. *verb* To feel a deep affection for or strong attachment to someone or something: *Alec loves his new computer.* ▷ *verb* **loving, loved**

2. *noun* A strong liking for something, as in *a love of music.*

3. If you are **in love** with someone, you are fond of him or her in a tender, passionate way. **love (**luhv**)**

lovely *adjective*

1. If someone is **lovely**, the person has pleasing looks or has inner qualities that inspire love, affection, or admiration. The word is more often used for girls and women than for boys and men: *I think Michael's daughters are lovely.* ▷ *noun* **loveliness**

2. Enjoyable or delightful: *We had a lovely time at the party.* **love·ly (luhv**-lee**)** ▷ *adjective* **lovelier, loveliest**

lover *noun*

1. Someone who loves something, as in *a music lover* or *a cat lover.*

2. Someone involved in a romantic relationship. **lov·er (luhv**-ur**)**

loving *adjective* Having or showing a lot of love and affection, as in *a loving mother.* **lov·ing (luhv**-ing**)**

low *adjective*

1. Not high or tall, as in *a low branch.*

2. Below the usual level: *The reservoir was low during the drought.*

3. Below average, as in *a low grade.*

4. A **low** sound is not very loud or intense.

5. Not having enough: *We were low on gas.*

6. If someone feels **low**, the person is depressed and has no energy. **low (**loh**)** ▷ *adjective* **lower, lowest**

lower

1. *verb* To move or bring something down, as in *to lower a flag.*

2. *adjective* Not as high in position, authority, or importance, as in *a lower court.*

3. *verb* To make or become less: *The store lowered its prices.*

4. *verb* To make less loud: *Please lower your voice.* **lower (**loh**-**ur**)** ▷ *verb* **lowering, lowered**

lowercase *adjective* Using letters that are not capitals: *Except for the first "e," this entire sentence is in lowercase letters.* **low·er·case (**loh**-ur-**kase**)** ▷ *noun* **lowercase** ▷ *verb* **lowercase**

capital   lowercase

low tide *noun* The time at which the water level in an ocean, a gulf, or a bay is at its lowest point.

loyal *adjective* Firm in supporting and being faithful to one's country, family, friends, or beliefs: *He is a loyal supporter of the high school swim team.* **loy·al (**loi**-uhl)** ▷ *adverb* **loyally**

Word History

Would you be **loyal** if a law made you do it? We think of loyalty as meaning "faithfulness" rather than having the sense of a legal duty, but that was not always so. The word *loyal* goes back to the Latin adjective *legalis*, meaning "having to do with the law." *Legalis* evolved into the Old French term *loial*, which could mean either "legal" or "faithful." "Legal" was an early meaning of the English word *loyal* also.

loyalty *noun* The quality of being loyal and faithful: *They have been friends forever and feel great loyalty toward each other.* **loy·al·ty (**loi**-uhl-tee)** ▷ *noun, plural* **loyalties**

lubricate *verb* To add a substance such as oil or grease to make something move or operate more smoothly: *Once I lubricated the chain on my bike, it stopped squeaking.* **lu·bri·cate (**loo**-bri-***kate***)** ▷ *verb* **lubricating, lubricated** ▷ *noun* **lubricant (**loo**-bri-kuhnt)** ▷ *noun* **lubrication**

luck *noun*

1. The chance occurrence of good or bad events: *Winning this game is just a matter of luck.*

2. Good fortune or success: *We wished them good luck on their journey.* **luck (**luhk**)**

lucky *adjective*

1. Having good luck or happening as a result of good luck, as in *a lucky girl* or *a lucky break.* ▷ *adverb* **luckily**

2. A **lucky** number or charm is one that you think will bring you good luck. **luck·y (luhk**-ee**)** ▷ *adjective* **luckier, luckiest**

lug *verb* To carry something with great difficulty or effort: *He lugged the suitcases out to the car.* **lug** (luhg) ▷ *verb* **lugging, lugged**

luggage *noun* Suitcases and bags that travelers fill with their belongings: *The elevator was so full of their luggage that they had to take the stairs.* **lug·gage** (**luhg**-ij)

Word History

All suitcases are called **luggage**, even light ones that you can carry easily. The term *luggage*, though, comes from a word meaning "carry something with great difficulty," *lug*. English speakers added the noun suffix *-age* to this verb, creating *luggage*. The first meaning of *luggage* was "extremely heavy suitcases." It could also refer to the baggage of an army. Now *luggage* simply means the bags that are taken on a trip, although weary travelers still have to *lug* their *luggage*.

lukewarm *adjective*
1. Barely or only slightly warm, as in *lukewarm water.*
2. Not very enthusiastic, as in *a lukewarm response.* **luke·warm** (**look**-*worm*)

lull
1. *verb* To soothe someone or send him or her to sleep: *The sound of the brook lulled us to sleep every night.* ▷ *verb* **lulling, lulled**
2. *noun* A short pause or period of calm: *The soldiers took advantage of the brief lull in the fighting to reload their weapons.* **lull** (luhl)

lullaby *noun* A soothing song sung to help a baby fall asleep. **lul·la·by** (**luhl**-uh-*bye*) ▷ *noun, plural* **lullabies**

lumberjack

lumber
1. *noun* Wood or timber that has been sawed into planks or boards: *After we build the deck, we can store the leftover lumber in the garage.*
2. *verb* To move in a slow, heavy, clumsy way: *Several hippopotamuses lumbered into view.* ▷ *verb* **lumbering, lumbered** **lum·ber** (**luhm**-bur)

lumberjack *noun* Someone whose job is to cut down trees and get the logs to a sawmill. **lum·ber·jack** (**luhm**-bur-*jak*)

luminous *adjective* Shining or giving off light, especially in the dark, as in *a luminous clock dial.* **lu·mi·nous** (**loo**-muh-nuhs) ▷ *adverb* **luminously**

lump
1. *noun* A shapeless piece of something, as in *a lump of dirt.*
2. *noun* A swelling or a bump: *There was a lump on her shin where she'd fallen.*
3. *verb* To pull or bring together: *We lumped our savings to buy the radio.*
4. *adjective* Whole, as in *a lump sum.*
5. *verb* To form lumps: *The potter lumped together some clay, then shaped it into a bowl.* **lump** (luhmp) ▷ *verb* **lumping, lumped**

lunar *adjective* Of or having to do with the moon or resembling the moon, as in *a lunar landscape.* **lu·nar** (**loo**-nur)

lunatic *noun* Someone who is insane or who behaves wildly and foolishly. **lu·na·tic** (**loo**-nuh-tik) ▷ *adjective* **lunatic**

Word History

The moon seems to change shape throughout the month, and we call these changing shapes the moon's "phases." In ancient times, people believed that the moon's phases could control human behavior. *Luna* was the word for "moon" in Latin, so a person who acted insane sometimes was called a *lunaticus*. The word entered English as **lunatic**. We don't connect people's moods with the moon much anymore, although the idea that somebody can act a little crazy during a full moon is still found in movies and popular culture.

lunch *noun* A meal eaten in the middle of the day, after breakfast and before dinner. **lunch** (luhnch) ▷ *noun, plural* **lunches** ▷ *verb* **lunch**

luncheon *noun* A lunch, especially a large, formal one: *My parents' club is holding a charity luncheon next week.* **lunch·eon** (**luhn**-chuhn)

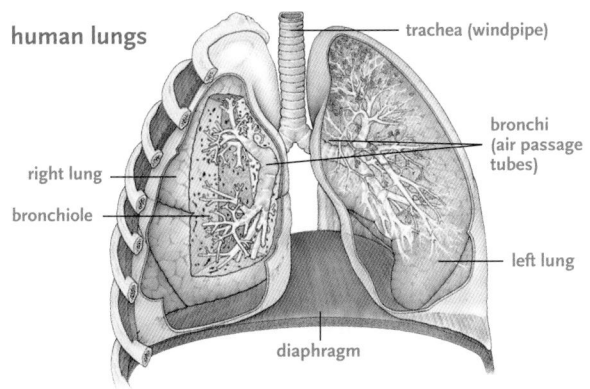

human lungs

trachea (windpipe)

bronchi (air passage tubes)

right lung

left lung

bronchiole

diaphragm

lung *noun* One of a pair of baglike organs inside your chest that fill with air when you breathe. The lungs supply the blood with oxygen and rid the blood of carbon dioxide. **lung** (luhng)

lunge *verb* To leap or plunge forward suddenly: *I lunged to catch the dish before it fell.* **lunge** (luhnj)
▷ *verb* **lunging, lunged** ▷ *noun* **lunge**

lurch
1. *verb* To stagger or move forward in a sudden, unsteady way: *My father slammed on the brakes, and the car lurched to a halt.* ▷ *verb* **lurches, lurching, lurched** ▷ *noun* **lurch**
2. If you **leave** someone **in the lurch**, you leave the person in a difficult situation, needing help. **lurch** (lurch)

lure
1. *verb* To attract or tempt someone or something: *I lured the raccoon into the trap and released it far away from my house.* ▷ *verb* **luring, lured**
2. *noun* Something that has a strong power to attract, as in *the lure of wealth.*
lure (loor)

lurk *verb*
1. To lie hidden, especially for an evil purpose: *The thief lurked in the darkness.*
2. To view but not participate in online social networks, as in *to lurk in a web forum.*
lurk (lurk)
▷ *verb* **lurking, lurked**

lush *adjective* Growing thickly or in abundance, as in *a lush lawn.* **lush** (luhsh) ▷ *adjective* **lusher, lushest**

lute *noun* A stringed instrument with a body shaped like a pear, played by plucking the strings. **lute** (loot) **Lute** sounds like **loot**.

luxury *noun*
1. Something expensive that is nice to have but that you do not really need: *My parents permit themselves the luxury of eating out once a week.*

▷ *adjective* **luxury**
2. If you live **in luxury**, you live a very comfortable life, surrounded by expensive and beautiful things.
lux·u·ry (**luhk**-shur-ee *or* **luhg**-zhur-ee)
▷ *adjective* **luxurious** (luhg-**zhoor**-ee-uhs)

lychee *or* **litchi** *or* **lichee** *noun*
1. A small, oval fruit covered by a hard, reddish rind, with a large seed inside that is surrounded by sweet, whitish flesh.
2. The tree that produces this fruit.
ly·chee (**lye**-chee)

lye *noun* A strong substance used in making soap and detergents. Lye is made by soaking wood ashes in water. **lye** (lye) **Lye** sounds like **lie**.

Lyme disease *noun* A bacterial disease transmitted by the bite of a tick. If it is not treated early, it can lead to joint pain, arthritis, and heart and nerve problems. **Lyme disease** (lime)

lymph *noun* A clear liquid that carries nutrients and white blood cells throughout the body while cleansing waste. **lymph** (limf)

lynx *noun* A wildcat with long legs, a short tail, light brown or orange fur, and tufts of hair on its ears. **lynx** (lingks) ▷ *noun, plural* **lynx** *or* **lynxes**

lyre *noun* A small, stringed, harplike instrument played mostly in ancient Egypt, Israel, and Greece. **lyre** (lire)

lyric
1. **lyrics** *noun, plural* The words of a song: *Stefania knows the lyrics to the entire musical.*
2. *noun* A short poem expressing the writer's feelings or mood: *In our poetry class, we read a number of lyrics by living American poets.*
lyr·ic (**lir**-ik)

Word History

The *lyrics* of a song owe their name to an ancient Greek musical instrument, the lyre. The lyre had seven strings, and was played by plucking. Greek speakers formed the adjective *lyrikos* from their name for the instrument, *lyra*. *Lyrikos* meant "singing to the lyre," and poetry that was *lyrikos* was meant to be sung while a lyre was played. In English, the plural of **lyric** came to refer to the words to a song, even though a lyre is not the instrument used anymore.

lyrical *adjective*
1. Expressing a strong, personal emotion, especially in a way that suggests a song, as in *a passionate, lyrical poem.*
2. Like a song, or fit for singing, as in *the lyrical sounds of a nightingale.*
lyr·i·cal (**lir**-i-kuhl) chee)

a
b
c
d
e
f
g
h
i
j
k
l
m
n
o
p
q
r
s
t
u
v
w
x
y
z

Mm

About M The letter **M** may have its origins in an Egyptian hieroglyph for "water." The Phoenicians gave it the *m* sound, since their word for "water" was *mem*. In the consonant pairs -*mn* or -*mb* at the end of a word, only the *m* is pronounced. Examples: hymn, lamb.

m Short for **meter** or the plural form *meters*.

ma'am *noun* A polite or respectful way of addressing a woman. Ma'am is short for **madam**. **ma'am** (mam)

macabre *adjective* Terrifying and gruesome, as in *a macabre crime*. **ma·ca·bre** (muh-**kahb** *or* muh-**kah**-bruh)

macaron *noun* A kind of cookie, often brightly colored, that has two puffy soft round pieces with creamy filling between them. **ma·ca·ron** (*mah*-kuh-**rahn**)

macaroni *noun* Pasta in the shape of curved, hollow tubes. **mac·a·ro·ni** (*mak*-uh-**roh**-nee)

macaroon *noun* A soft cookie made mainly from coconut, sugar, and egg whites. **mac·a·roon** (*mak*-uh-**roon**

Mach *noun* A unit for measuring speed, often used for aircraft. Mach 1 is the speed of sound, 761 miles per hour at sea level. **Mach** (mahk)

machete *noun* A long, heavy knife with a broad blade, used as a tool and weapon. **ma·chet·e** (muh-**shet**-ee)

machine *noun*
1. A piece of equipment whose different pieces work together to do a job, often using electricity or an engine.
2. A simple device that makes it easier to move something. Levers, screws, and pulleys are simple machines.
3. **machine gun** An automatic gun that can fire bullets very quickly one after another.
ma·chine (muh-**sheen**)

machinery *noun* The parts of a machine, or a group of machines that do the same work or related kinds of work. **ma·chin·er·y** (muh-**shee**-nur-ee)

machinist *noun* A person who runs machines that make tools and parts. **ma·chin·ist** (muh-**shee**-nist)

mackerel *noun* A shiny saltwater fish that can be used as food. **mack·er·el** (mak-ur-uhl) ▷ *noun, plural* **mackerel** *or* **mackerels**

mackerel

macro *noun* A short computer program that performs a number of instructions with a single command. **mac·ro** (**mak**-roh)

mad *adjective*
1. Very angry: *Don't be mad at me.*
2. Insane; mentally ill. ▷ *noun* **madness**
3. Extremely foolish or crazy: *Jeannie has a mad plan to run away to New York.*
4. **be mad about** (*informal*) To like someone or something very much: *Everyone is mad about the cute new girl at school.*
mad (mad)
▷ *adjective* **madder, maddest** ▷ *adverb* **madly**

Synonyms

Mad is used to describe someone who is very angry about something: *Bobby was mad that we didn't wait for him after school.* The adjectives that follow are similar to *mad*, but they describe feelings or actions of different origins or degrees.

- -

■ **Angry**, like *mad*, can be used to describe someone who feels upset about something and shows it: *I was so angry at Camila for breaking my bike that I yelled at her.*

■ **Indignant** describes a person who is angry because he or she feels that something is unfair: *Brian was indignant that his little brother got a bigger slice of cake.*

■ **Irate** often refers to someone who does something about his or her anger: *The irate customer demanded her money back because the television set did not work.*

■ **Enraged** describes someone who is filled with rage, usually as a result of being annoyed or provoked: *The louder our neighbors play their music, the more enraged my mother becomes.*

■ **Furious** describes someone who is full of intense anger, or fury, to the point of losing control: *Mr. Thompkins was so furious when his car was broken into that he made himself sick.*

madam *noun* A polite or respectful way of addressing a woman, used in formal speech and writing: *Please step this way, madam.* **mad·am** (**mad**-uhm)

made *verb* The past tense and the past participle of **make**. **made** (made) **Made** sounds like **maid**.

maestro *noun* Someone with great skill and talent, especially a conductor of an orchestra or a composer of classical music. **maes·tro** (**mye**-stroh)

Mafia *noun*
1. the Mafia A secret crime organization in the United States, Italy, and other countries, originally established on the island of Sicily in southern Italy.
2. Any secret crime organization that is like the Mafia: *The Japanese Mafia is called the Yakuza.*
3. Any group of people who share the same interests or backgrounds. The word is often used negatively, to imply that the group is working in a secret, organized, and sinister way. This sense of the word is usually lowercase: *He is an extremist who believes that every journalist is part of a corrupt mafia that twists the truth.*
Ma·fi·a (**mah**-fee-uh)

magazine *noun*
1. A monthly or weekly publication that can contain stories, articles, photographs, advertisements, and other material.
2. The part of a gun that holds the bullets.
mag·a·zine (**mag**-uh-*zeen*)

Word History

The word **magazine** comes from the Arabic word *makhzan*, meaning "storehouse." A magazine could be thought of as a storehouse of information.

magenta *noun* A deep purplish red color.
ma·gen·ta (muh-**jen**-tuh) ▷ *adjective* **magenta**

maggot *noun* The larva of certain flies. It looks like a small worm and often feeds on rotting animal flesh. **mag·got** (**mag**-uht)

Magi *noun, plural* In the New Testament, the three kings who visited the baby Jesus, bringing gifts. **Ma·gi** (**may**-*jye*)

magic *noun*
1. The power or forces that some people believe can make impossible things happen. ▷ *adjective* **magical** ▷ *adverb* **magically**
2. Tricks done to entertain people, such as pulling a rabbit out of a hat or making something disappear.
mag·ic (**maj**-ik)
▷ *adjective* **magic**

magician *noun*
1. Someone who is thought to have the ability to perform magic and make impossible things happen: *The magician in the story I'm reading can change his shape, taking the form of a bird or a tiger.*
2. An entertainer who performs tricks before an

Magi

audience: *He was a successful magician, and his best-loved trick was to make a person levitate then disappear.*
ma·gi·cian (muh-**jish**-uhn)

magistrate *noun* A government official who can act as a judge in a court. **mag·is·trate** (**maj**-i-*strate*)

maglev *noun* Short for *magnetic levitation*, a system of high-speed train transportation in which the train uses powerful magnets to float above its track. **mag·lev** (**mag**-*lev*)

magma *noun* Melted rock found beneath the earth's surface that becomes lava when it flows out of volcanoes. **mag·ma** (**mag**-muh)

magnesium *noun* A light, silver-white metal that burns with a bright white light. **mag·ne·si·um** (mag-**nee**-zee-uhm)

magnet *noun* A piece of metal that attracts iron or steel. Magnets have two ends, or poles, called north and south. **mag·net** (**mag**-nit) ▷ *noun* **magnetism** (**mag**-ni-*tiz*-uhm)

magnetic *adjective*
1. Acting like or including a magnet, as in *a magnetic picture frame.*
2. Very attractive or exciting, as in *a magnetic personality.*
mag·net·ic (mag-**net**-ik)

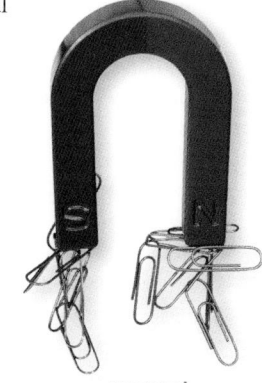

magnet

magnetic field *noun* The area around a magnet or electric current that has the power to attract other metals, usually iron or steel.

magnetic tape *noun* A thin ribbon of plastic coated with a magnetic material on which sound, images, and other information can be recorded or stored.

a b c d e f g h i j k l m n o p q r s t u v w x y z

magnetize *verb* To make something magnetic, either by exposing it to an electric current or by attaching a magnet to it. **mag·net·ize** (**mag**-nuh-*tize*) ▷ *verb* **magnetizing, magnetized** ▷ *noun* **magnetization**

magnificent *adjective* Extremely beautiful, good, or big: *The king lived in a magnificent palace.* **mag·nif·i·cent** (mag-**nif**-i-suhnt) ▷ *noun* **magnificence** ▷ *adverb* **magnificently**

magnify
1. *verb* To make something appear larger so that it is easier to see, usually using a lens or mirror: *The encyclopedia is easier to read if you magnify the pages.* ▷ *noun* **magnification** ▷ *adjective* **magnified**
2. *verb* To make something seem bigger, more important, or more effective: *The brightness of the room was magnified by the mirrors that covered the walls.*
3. **magnifying glass** *noun* A glass lens that makes things look bigger, used for looking at very small objects.
mag·ni·fy (**mag**-nuh-fye) ▷ *verb* **magnifies, magnifying, magnified**

magnitude *noun* The size or importance of something. **mag·ni·tude** (**mag**-ni-*tood*)

magnolia *noun* A tree or tall shrub that has large, fragrant, white, pink, purple, or yellow flowers. **mag·no·li·a** (mag-**nohl**-yuh)

magpie *noun* A noisy, black-and-white bird with a long tail that is related to crows. **mag·pie** (**mag**-*pye*)

mahogany *noun*
1. A tropical tree with hard, dark, reddish-brown wood, or the wood from this tree.
2. A dark, reddish-brown color.
ma·hog·a·ny (muh-**hah**-guh-nee) ▷ *noun, plural* **mahoganies**

maid *noun*
1. A woman who is paid to clean a house or hotel rooms.
2. **maid of honor** An unmarried woman who is the bride's chief attendant at a wedding.
maid (mayd)
Maid sounds like **made**.

maiden *noun*
1. A young, unmarried woman.
2. **maiden voyage** or **maiden flight** The first trip made by a particular ship or plane.
maid·en (**may**-duhn)

maiden name *noun* The last name that a married woman used before she was married. Some women continue to use their maiden names after they marry.

magnolia blossom

mail *noun*
1. Letters and packages sent through a public postal system. ▷ *verb* **mail**
2. **mail order** A way to buy things in which you order and pay for the item and it is mailed to you.
mail (mayl)
Mail sounds like **male**.

Word History

Today we think of **mail** as being the letters and packages delivered to us, but originally the word referred to the bag the mail was delivered in. The word comes from the Old French word *male*, which referred to a leather sack.

mailbox *noun*
1. A large, public box that you put letters and packages in so they can be picked up by a mail carrier.
2. A box for letters and packages that are delivered to a home or business.
mail·box (mayl-*bahks*) ▷ *noun, plural* **mailboxes**

mail carrier *noun* A person who delivers mail to a house or business. Also called a **letter carrier**.

mailman *noun* A male mail carrier. **mail·man** (**mayl**-*man*) ▷ *noun, plural* **mailmen**

maim *verb* To injure a part of the body so it is permanently damaged: *Jason's right hand was maimed in a motorcycle accident.* **maim** (maym) ▷ *verb* **maiming, maimed**

main
1. *adjective* Largest, or most important, as in *the main reason.*
2. *noun* A large pipe that supplies water or gas to a building, or removes waste.
main (mayn)
Main sounds like **mane**.

mainframe *noun* A large and very powerful computer that can help to run smaller computers. **main·frame** (**mayn**-*frame*)

mainland *noun* The largest part of a country, territory, or continent rather than its islands or peninsulas. **main·land** (**mayn**-luhnd)

mainly *adverb* For the most part: *Our town is mainly on the south side of the river.* **main·ly** (**mayn**-lee)

mainstay *noun* A person or thing that is the most basic or important part of something: *Rice is the mainstay of our diet.* **main·stay** (**mayn**-stay)

mainstream

1. *noun* People, ideas, or activities that are thought to be normal or typical: *The candidate's beliefs are well within the mainstream of US politics.*

2. *verb* To place a child with disabilities in a regular classroom. ▷ *verb* **mainstreaming, mainstreamed** **main·stream** (**mayn**-streem)

maintain *verb*

1. To keep something in good condition: *The building is so clean, I can tell the landlord maintains it well.*

2. To state your opinion strongly: *The suspect maintains that he is innocent.*

3. To make an effort to keep something at the same level or rate, as in *maintaining an A average.*

4. To provide support for somebody: *He maintained his kids after the divorce.*

main·tain (mayn-**tayn**)

▷ *verb* **maintaining, maintained**

maintenance *noun*

1. The process of keeping something in good condition by checking and repairing it.

2. Money that helps to take care of someone: *Both parents contribute to the maintenance of the children.*

main·te·nance (**mayn**-tuh-nuhns)

maize *noun* Corn. **maize** (maze) **Maize** sounds like **maze.**

majestic *adjective*

1. Having the appearance or qualities of a powerful ruler: *The senator looked majestic as she swept into the Capitol.*

2. Having a lot of power or beauty: *The ocean is majestic during a storm.*

ma·jes·tic (muh-**jes**-tik)

▷ *adverb* **majestically**

majesty *noun*

1. Impressiveness or dignity: *The queen walks with majesty.*

2. His Majesty or **Her Majesty** A formal title for a king or queen.

maj·es·ty (**maj**-i-stee)

major

1. *adjective* Larger, more serious, or more important: *The US is a major participant in the United Nations.*

2. *noun* The main subject studied by a student at a college or university, as in *an English major.*

3. *noun* An officer in the army and other branches of the armed forces who ranks above a captain.

4. *adjective* A **major** scale in music has a half step between the third and fourth and the seventh and eighth notes.

ma·jor (**may**-jur)

majorette *noun* A girl or woman who twirls a baton in a marching band. **ma·jor·ette** (*may*-juh-**ret**)

majority *noun*

1. More than half the people or things in a group.

2. The number of votes by which someone wins an election.

ma·jor·i·ty (muh-**jor**-i-tee)

▷ *noun, plural* **majorities**

make

1. *verb* To build, create, produce, or say something: *We helped Dad make dinner.*

2. *verb* To do a specific action: *Ari made two trips to the store.*

3. *verb* To cause something to happen: *Flowers make me sneeze.*

4. *verb* To add up to: *Four and five make nine.*

5. *verb* To earn: *My sister makes money by delivering newspapers.*

6. *noun* A particular brand or type of product: *This make of car has become very popular.*

7. *verb* To turn out to be: *Anna will make a good teacher.*

8. *verb* To cause to become: *Your letters always make me happy.*

9. *verb* To get on a team: *Juan has a good chance of making the soccer team.*

10. make believe *verb* To pretend or imagine: *Let's make believe we're on a spaceship to Venus.*

11. make out *verb* To be able to see something: *You can just make out the Empire State Building on the horizon.*

12. make up *verb* To become friends again after a fight.

13. make up *verb* To do something later because you could not do it at the original time, as in *to make up a test.*

make (make)

▷ *verb* **making, made** (mayd)

make-believe

1. *noun* Playful pretending or imagination: *That fairy tale is only make-believe.*

2. *adjective* Imaginary, or not real: *She has a make-believe friend.*

makeshift *adjective* Made from things that are available to use for a short time: *I held my book up as a makeshift umbrella.* **make·shift** (**make**-shift)

makeup *noun*

1. A substance applied to the face to change or improve its appearance, used mainly by women.

2. The way something is put together: *The makeup of the class is half girls and half boys.*

make·up (**make**-uhp)

majorette

a b c d e f g h i j k l **m** n o p q r s t u v w x y z

malaria *noun* A serious disease that people get from a particular kind of mosquito. Symptoms include chills, fever, and sweating. **ma·lar·i·a** (muh-**lair**-ee-uh)

male *noun* A person or animal of the sex that cannot lay eggs or give birth to babies. **male** (mayl) **Male** sounds like **mail**. ▷ *adjective* **male**

malfunction
1. *noun* A situation in which part of a machine or process stops working correctly: *There was a malfunction in one of the plane's engines, so we had to land.*
2. *verb* To function badly or improperly: *I downloaded a program that had a virus, and now my computer is malfunctioning.* ▷ *verb* **malfunctioning, malfunctioned**
mal·func·tion (mal-**fungk**-shuhn)

malice *noun* A desire to hurt or embarrass someone: *It was an accident—she did not trip Layla out of malice.* **mal·ice** (**mal**-is)

malicious *adjective* Intended to hurt or embarrass someone, as in *malicious rumors*. **ma·li·cious** (muh-**lish**-uhs) ▷ *adverb* **maliciously**

malign
1. *verb* To say hurtful or untrue things about someone: *Some people malign the principal by saying he's unfair.* ▷ *verb* **maligning, maligned**
2. *adjective* Evil or intended to cause harm, as in *a malign influence*.
ma·lign (muh-**line**)

malignancy *noun* A cancerous tumor. **ma·lig·nan·cy** (muh-**lig**-nuhn-see) ▷ *noun, plural* **malignancies**

malignant *adjective* Dangerous because it cannot be controlled, and usually causes death: *Cancers that affect the pancreas are particularly malignant.* **ma·lig·nant** (muh-**lig**-nuhnt) ▷ *adverb* **malignantly**

mall *noun* A large, enclosed shopping center. **mall** (mawl) **Mall** sounds like **maul**.

mallard *noun* A common wild duck. The male has a green head, a white band around the neck, and a dark body. **mal·lard** (**mal**-urd)

malleable *adjective*
1. Soft and easily formed into different shapes.
2. Easily controlled or influenced by other people, as in *malleable public opinion*.
mal·le·a·ble (**mal**-ee-uh-buhl)

mallet *noun* A wooden hammer with a heavy round head. **mal·let** (**mal**-it)

malnutrition *noun* Sickness or weakness caused by not eating enough food, or by eating food that is not good for you. **mal·nu·tri·tion** (mal-noo-**trish**-uhn)

malt *noun* Grain, usually barley, that has been soaked and dried. It is often used to make alcoholic drinks. **malt** (mawlt) ▷ *adjective* **malted**

malted milk *noun* A milk shake flavored with malt.

maltreat *verb* To be cruel to a person or an animal: *Rescue organizations take good care of maltreated pets.* **mal·treat** (mal-**treet**) ▷ *verb* **maltreating, maltreated** ▷ *noun* **maltreatment**

malware *noun* Software that is intended to harm or create problems. Malware gets onto computers through an internet connection or email attachment. **mal·ware** (**mal**-*wair*)

mammal *noun* A warm-blooded animal that has hair or fur and usually gives birth to live babies. Female mammals produce milk to feed their young: *People, cows, and whales are all mammals.* **mam·mal** (**mam**-uhl)

mammoth
1. *noun* An animal that looked like a large elephant, with long, curved tusks and shaggy hair. Mammoths lived during the Ice Age and are now extinct.
2. *adjective* Huge or taking a lot of effort: *Building a skyscraper is a mammoth job.*
mam·moth (**mam**-uhth)

man
1. *noun* An adult male human being. ▷ *noun* **manliness** ▷ *adjective* **manly**
2. *noun* Humans in general: *Man shares the common needs of food, shelter, and sleep.*
3. *noun* A piece used in games such as chess and checkers.
4. *verb* To work with a piece of equipment: *The sailors*

mallet

manatee

manned the pumps to remove the water from the hold. ▷ *verb* **manning, manned**
man (man)
▷ *noun, plural* **men** (men)

manage *verb*
1. To be in charge of a store, business, or process: *Lola manages the children's department at this store.*
2. To succeed in doing something that is difficult: *Joe managed to get to work in the snowstorm.*
man·age (**man**-ij)
▷ *verb* **managing, managed**

management *noun*
1. The act of controlling or dealing with people, animals, or things: *The local deer population has exploded, and its management has become quite difficult.*
2. The people who run a business or an organization: *There had been a change in management at the restaurant.*
man·age·ment (**man**-ij-muhnt)

manager *noun* Someone in charge of a store, a business, or a process, or in charge of a group of people at work. **man·a·ger** (**man**-i-jur) ▷ *adjective* **managerial** (man-i-**jeer**-ee-uhl)

manatee *noun* A large, plant-eating ocean mammal with flippers and a flat tail that lives in warm coastal waters and rivers. **man·a·tee** (**man**-uh-tee)

Word History

The **manatee** was called "a fish of the sea" in one early description, but we know now that these plant-eating creatures are ocean mammals. In the 16th century, Spanish speakers learned the name *manátí* from the Caribs, a native people in South America and the West Indies. The word became *manatí* in Spanish, and we now spell it *manatee* in English.

man bun *noun* A hairstyle for men with long hair, where the hair is gathered in a tight knot at the back of the head.

mandarin *noun*
1. A high official in ancient China.
2. Mandarin The official language of the People's Republic of China.
3. A small, sweet orange with a thin rind that is easy to peel. It is also called a **mandarin orange**.
man·da·rin (**man**-dur-in)

Word History

The **mandarin** orange is named after officials in ancient China who wore yellow robes, because the fruit has a similar color. The word itself is not Chinese, though. It goes back to *mantri*, a word in an old language of India, meaning "a person who gives advice."

mandate *noun* A task or policy that an elected official has to carry out: *The president received a clear mandate to balance the budget.* **man·date** (**man**-date)
▷ *verb* **mandate**

mandatory *adjective* Necessary or required, usually because of a rule or law, as in *a mandatory inspection.* **man·da·to·ry** (**man**-duh-*tor*-ee)

mandolin *noun* A small, stringed, pear-shaped musical instrument. **man·do·lin** (**man**-duh-lin)

Word History

Our English word **mandolin** refers to a small guitar-like instrument. The name in Italian, *mandolino*, originally meant "a small *mandola*." A *mandola* was a larger instrument that people played in the 17th century, but a smaller version of it, which had been developed in the Italian city of Naples, became more popular.

mane *noun* The long, thick hair on the head and neck of lions, horses, and some other animals. **mane** (mayn) **Mane** sounds like **main**.

maneuver
1. *noun* A difficult movement that requires planning and skill: *The movers got the couch onto the truck with a series of clever maneuvers.*
2. *verb* To move something carefully: *I maneuvered the car into a tight parking space.* ▷ *verb* **maneuvering, maneuvered**
3. maneuvers *noun, plural* Training exercises for battle that involve a large number of soldiers, tanks, and other equipment.
ma·neu·ver (muh-**noo**-vur)

manga *noun* A kind of Japanese comic that often has stories with a science fiction theme. **man·ga** (**mahng**-guh)

Word History

The Japanese word **manga** means "pictures without purpose." In the early 19th century, the *manga* style began with the work of Katsushika Hokusai, a Japanese artist. He referred to his drawings as *manga* to show that he didn't spend much time planning them. Speakers of Japanese formed *manga* from the word parts *man-*, meaning "without purpose," and *-ga*, meaning "picture." In Japanese, the word came to mean "comic" or "cartoon," and it entered English in the 1950s.

manger *noun* A large, open box that holds food for cattle and horses. **man·ger** (**mayn**-jur)

mangle *verb* To spoil or destroy something by cutting, tearing, or crushing it: *Many buildings were mangled in the earthquake.* **man·gle** (**mang**-guhl) ▷ *verb* **mangling, mangled** ▷ *adjective* **mangled**

mango *noun* A tropical fruit with a large seed and sweet orange flesh. **man·go** (**mang**-goh) ▷ *noun, plural* **mangoes** or **mangos**

manhole *noun* A covered hole in the street that leads to sewers or underground pipes or wires. **man·hole** (**man**-hole)

manhood *noun*
1. The time or state of being a man instead of a boy.
2. Men as a group: *The editorial about lazy husbands seemed an insult to all manhood.*
man·hood (**man**-hud)

maniac *noun*
1. A person who is crazy or acts in a dangerous or violent way. ▷ *adjective* **maniacal** (muh-**nye**-uh-kuhl)
2. A person who is very enthusiastic about something, as in *a football maniac.*
ma·ni·ac (**may**-nee-*ak*)

manicure *noun* The cleaning, shaping, and polishing of the fingernails. **man·i·cure** (**man**-i-*kyoor*) ▷ *verb* **manicure**

manipulate *verb*
1. To use or control a person or an event for your own benefit: *He manipulated his mother into buying him a new laptop.* ▷ *adjective* **manipulative**
2. To handle or control something skillfully: *Ella manipulated the plane's controls like an expert.*
ma·nip·u·late (muh-**nip**-yuh-*late*)

mango

▷ *verb* **manipulating, manipulated** ▷ *noun* **manipulation**

mankind *noun* The human race, or human beings as a group. **man·kind** (man-*kinde*)

man-made *adjective* Made by people, not produced naturally: *Cotton is often more comfortable than man-made fabrics.*

mannequin *noun* A life-size model of a human being, used especially to display clothing for sale in a store. **man·ne·quin** (**man**-i-kin)

manner *noun*
1. The way in which something is done: *Leslie does her chores in a cheerful manner.*
2. The way in which a person behaves around other people: *Lenny walks with a really confident manner.*
3. Kind: *We saw all manner of birds at the zoo.*
4. manners *noun, plural* Polite behavior: *It is good manners to thank your host.*
man·ner (**man**-ur)
Manner sounds like **manor**.

mannerism *noun* A small gesture or other movement that a person has a habit of making, usually without thinking. **man·ner·ism** (**man**-uh-*riz*-uhm)

manor *noun*
1. A lord's estate in the Middle Ages.
2. A mansion.
man·or (**man**-ur)
Manor sounds like **manner**.

mansion *noun* A very large and impressive house. **man·sion** (**man**-shuhn)

manslaughter *noun* The crime of killing someone without intending to do it. **man·slaught·er** (**man**-*slaw*-tur)

mantel *noun* A wooden or stone shelf above a fireplace. **man·tel** (**man**-tuhl)
Mantel sounds like **mantle**.

mantle *noun*
1. A loose cloak without sleeves.
2. Something that covers or hides like a mantle: *The trees were covered by a mantle of snow.*
3. The part of the earth between the crust and the core.
man·tle (**man**-tuhl)
Mantle sounds like **mantel**.

manual
1. *adjective* Operated or done with your hands rather than with electricity or machines, as in *manual calculations.* ▷ *adverb* **manually**
2. *noun* A book of instructions that tells you how to do something or operate a machine.
3. manual labor *noun* Hard work that uses your

hands or your strength.
man·u·al (**man**-yoo-uhl)

manufacture *verb*

1. To make something, often with machines: *Pencils are manufactured in factories by big machines.*
▷ *noun* **manufacturer**
2. To make something up, usually a story or an explanation: *Instead of telling the truth about why he was late, Simon manufactured a silly excuse.*
man·u·fac·ture (*man*-yuh-**fak**-chur)
▷ *verb* **manufacturing, manufactured**

manufactured *adjective* Made by people or in

a factory, rather than occurring naturally: *China and India both export huge quantities of manufactured goods to Africa.* **man·u·fac·tured** (*man*-yuh-**fak**-churd)

manufacturing

1. *noun* The activity or industry of making something on a large scale using special equipment or machinery: *In Detroit, auto manufacturing is a way of life.*
2. *adjective* Of or having to do with the large-scale production of something: *I've heard that the new manufacturing company in town is hiring more people.*
man·u·fac·tur·ing (*man*-yuh-**fak**-chur-ing)

manure *noun* Animal waste that is used as fertilizer.

ma·nure (muh-**noor**)

manuscript *noun* An original handwritten or typed

document, especially the content of a book before it is printed. **man·u·script** (**man**-yuh-*skript*)

many

1. *adjective* A lot of: *A clock has many parts.*
▷ *adjective* **more, most**
2. *noun* A large number of people or things: *Many were late for the party because of the snowstorm.*
man·y (**men**-ee)

map

1. *noun* A drawing of an area, showing natural features, roads, towns, and other important objects.
2. *verb* To make a map of a place.
3. **map out** *verb* To plan something carefully, as in *to map out a campaign.*
map (map)
▷ *verb* **mapping, mapped**

maple *noun* A tree that has large, pointed leaves and

hard wood. Some maples produce sap that is used to make maple syrup. **ma·ple** (**may**-puhl)

mar *verb* To damage or spoil something: *Their

vacation was marred by bad weather.* **mar** (mahr)
▷ *verb* **marring, marred**

marathon *noun*

1. A running race that is 26 miles and 385 yards long.

playing marbles

2. Any task or competition that is tiring and takes a long time, as in *a dance marathon.*
mar·a·thon (**mar**-uh-*thahn*)

marble *noun*

1. A type of hard stone used to make buildings, sculptures, and fixtures for kitchens and bathrooms. Marble is usually white but can have different colors or streaks of color.
2. A small, hard glass ball used in children's games.
3. **marbles** A game in which these balls are rolled on the ground.
mar·ble (**mahr**-buhl)

march

1. *verb* To walk with even steps, often in a group.
2. *noun* A piece of music with a strong beat, intended to accompany marching.
3. *verb* To walk somewhere quickly and in a determined way: *Mom marched down to the store to return the defective toy.*
4. *noun* A large, organized group of people walking together to protest or support something: *The march for civil rights had thousands of participants.*
march (mahrch)
▷ *verb* **marches, marching, marched** ▷ *noun, plural* **marches**

March *noun* The third month on the calendar, after

February and before April. March has 31 days.
March (mahrch)

Word History

The Roman new year at one time began with the month of **March**. The beginning of the year, the Romans felt, was a good time to wage war, so they named this first month after Mars, the god of war. Later, March became the third month, as it is today.

mare *noun* The female of certain animals, such as the

horse, donkey, and zebra. **mare** (mair)

margarine *noun* A yellow spread similar to butter, that is usually made from vegetable oil. **mar·ga·rine** (**mahr**-jur-in)

margin *noun*
1. The blank space that runs around the outer edges of a page.
2. An amount, especially of time, in addition to what is needed: *When traffic is heavy, allow a margin of 30 minutes for driving to school.*
3. An amount by which something wins or falls short, especially in a contest or vote: *The new law passed by a very narrow margin.* **mar·gin** (**mahr**-jin)

marginal *adjective*
1. Written in the margin of a page, as in *marginal notes.*
2. Small or not very important, as in *a marginal difference.*
3. Barely good enough to be acceptable, as in *marginal grades.* **mar·gin·al** (**mahr**-juh-nuhl)

marigold *noun* A garden plant that has orange, yellow, or red flowers. **mar·i·gold** (**mar**-ri-gohld)

marigold

marijuana *noun* A drug made from the dried leaves and buds of the hemp plant. **mar·i·juan·a** (*mar*-uh-**wah**-nuh)

marimba *noun* A kind of xylophone, originally from Africa, that has wooden bars with gourds attached to make the sound louder. **ma·rim·ba** (muh-**rim**-buh)

marina *noun* A special harbor for small private boats. **ma·ri·na** (muh-**ree**-nuh)

marinara *adjective* Made with tomatoes, as in *marinara sauce.* The term *marinara* comes from an Italian word that means "in sailor style." **mar·i·na·ra** (*mar*-uh-**nar**-uh)

marine
1. *adjective* Of or having to do with the ocean, as in *marine biology.*
2. *adjective* Of or having to do with ships or navigation, as in *a marine museum.*
3. **Marine** *noun* A member of the US Marine Corps. **ma·rine** (muh-**reen**)

Marine Corps *noun* One of the armed forces of the United States. Marines are trained to fight on both land and water.

marionette *noun* A puppet, usually made of wood, that you move by pulling strings or wires attached to parts of its body. **mar·i·o·nette** (*mar*-ee-uh-**net**)

maritime *adjective*
1. Of or having to do with the sea, ships, or navigation: *Maritime travel is difficult if you get seasick.*
2. Of, relating to, or near the sea: *A whale is a maritime mammal.* **mar·i·time** (**mar**-i-*time*)

mark
1. *noun* A small, visible blemish usually caused by damage: *This shirt has a pen mark on it.*
2. *noun* A written sign or symbol, as in *a question mark.*
3. *noun* A line or an object that shows the position of something: *Put your foot on the mark before the race begins.*
4. *noun* A grade on a piece of schoolwork. ▷ *verb* **mark**
5. *verb* To show clearly where something is or was: *The signs marked the way to the private beach.* ▷ *verb* **marking, marked**
6. *noun* Something that shows clearly: *A mark of good manners is saying "please."*
7. **make your mark** *phrase* To have an impressive and lasting effect in a particular field: *Bruce hopes to make his mark in the political world.* **mark** (mahrk)

marked *adjective*
1. Having one or more visible marks: *Have you noticed the beautifully marked foliage on that bush?*
2. Very noticeable: *There has been a marked increase in car thefts.* **marked** (mahrkt)

marker *noun*
1. A pen that has a wide tip, usually made of felt: *We used markers to make posters for our bake sale.*
2. A sign that something is present or happening: *This protein is a marker of heart disease risk.*
3. An object such as a stone or sign that tells people something important about a place.
4. A small object used in a game to show a player's position: *Roll the dice and move your marker.* **mark·er** (**mahr**-kur)

market
1. *noun* A place where people buy and sell food or other goods.
2. *noun* A store where specific kinds of goods are sold, as in *a fish market.*
3. *noun* The amount of demand for something, as in *a large market for video games.*
4. *verb* To offer for sale: *The farmers' market their*

lambs in the spring.

5. *verb* To advertise or promote something so people will want to buy it: *The new brand of sneakers was marketed chiefly to teenagers.*

6. on the market Available for people to buy, as in *new toys on the market before Christmas.*
mar·ket (mahr-kit)
▷ *verb* **marketing, marketed**

marketing *noun* The act of promoting and selling products or services: *Good marketing made the new hair salon very successful.* **mar·ket·ing (mahr**-ki-ting)

marketplace *noun*
1. A place, such as a town square, where many individual sellers offer their goods for sale.
2. Business and trade in general or as a whole: *The success of her new invention will be decided in the marketplace.*
mar·ket·place (mahr-kit-*plase*)

market research *noun* The process of collecting information about the products that customers buy and new products that they might want.

marksman *noun* A person who is an expert at shooting a gun. **marks·man (mahrks**-muhn)
▷ *noun, plural* **marksmen**

marmalade *noun* A jam made from the peel and juice of oranges or other citrus fruits. **mar·ma·lade (mahr**-muh-*lade*)

maroon
1. *noun* A dark reddish-brown color. ▷ *adjective* **maroon**
2. *verb* To leave someone in a place that is difficult to escape from. ▷ *verb* **marooning, marooned**
ma·roon (muh-**roon**)

marquee *noun* A cover over a theater entrance that displays the name of the current play or movie. **mar·quee (mahr**-**kee**)

marriage *noun*
1. The state of being married, or the relationship between two spouses.
2. The act of marrying someone, or the wedding ceremony: *He wrote his own vows for the marriage.*
mar·riage (mar-ij)

married *adjective* Having a husband or wife.
mar·ried (mar-eed)

marrow *noun*
1. The soft substance inside bones that produces blood cells and platelets. It is also called **bone marrow**.
2. The basic and most important part of something; the core: *It was easy to grasp the marrow of his*

argument, because his essay was clear and well structured.
mar·row (mar-oh)

marry *verb*
1. To legally become someone's husband or wife in a formal ceremony.
2. To perform a marriage ceremony: *A judge will marry Ted and Maria next week.*
mar·ry (mar-ee)
▷ *verb* **marries, marrying, married**

Mars *noun* The fourth planet in distance from the sun, between the earth and Jupiter. Mars is the seventh-largest planet in our solar system. **Mars** (mahrz)

marsh *noun* An area of wet, muddy land. **marsh** (mahrsh) ▷ *adjective* **marshy**

Mars

marshal
1. *noun* A police officer who is responsible for a particular area.
2. *noun* An officer in the fire department.
3. *noun* A person who helps organize a public event such as a parade.
4. *verb* To bring together a group of people or things and arrange them for a purpose: *The committee marshaled its resources and put everyone to work.*
▷ *verb* **marshaling, marshaled**
marshal (mahr-shuhl)
Marshal sounds like **martial**.

marshmallow *noun* A soft, white, spongy candy. **marsh·mal·low (mahrsh**-*mel*-oh)

marsupial *noun* Any of a large group of animals that includes the kangaroo, the koala, and the opossum. Female marsupials carry their babies in pouches on their abdomens.
mar·su·pi·al (mahr-**soo**-pee-uhl)

marsupial

martial
1. *adjective* Of or having to do with war or soldiers: *The veterans gave a martial air to the parade.*
2. martial art *noun* A style of fighting or self-defense that comes mostly from Asia. Judo and karate are martial arts.
3. martial law *noun* Rule by the army in time of war or disaster.
mar·tial (mahr-shuhl)
Martial sounds like **marshal**.

a b c d e f g h i j k l **m** n o p q r s t u v w x y z

Martian

1. *adjective* Of, similar to, or having to do with the planet Mars or one of its supposed inhabitants. This word is often capitalized: *The Mars rover beamed back images of the Martian landscape.*

2. *noun* One of the supposed inhabitants of the planet Mars. This word is often capitalized.
Mar·tian (**mahr**-shuhn)

martin *noun* A bird related to swallows that eats insects while flying. **mar·tin** (**mahr**-tin)

Martin Luther King Jr. Day *noun* A national holiday that honors the birth of Dr. Martin Luther King Jr., the African American civil rights leader who was assassinated in 1968. It is celebrated on the third Monday of January. **Martin Lu·ther King Jr. Day** (**loo**-thur)

martyr *noun* A person who is killed or made to suffer because of his or her beliefs. **mar·tyr** (**mahr**-tur)
▷ *noun* **martyrdom** (**mahr**-tur-duhm)

marvel *verb* To be filled with surprise, admiration, or wonder: *We marveled at the beauty of the lakes.* **mar·vel** (**mahr**-vuhl) ▷ *verb* **marveling, marveled** ▷ *noun* **marvel**

marvelous *adjective*

1. Causing surprise, wonder, or admiration: *The movie had several marvelous plot twists.*

2. Very good or outstanding: *What a marvelous dinner we had last night!*
mar·vel·ous (**mahr**-vuh-luhs)
▷ *adverb* **marvelously**

mascara *noun* Makeup put on eyelashes to darken them and make them look thicker and longer. **mas·car·a** (mas-**kar**-uh)

mascot *noun* An animal or symbol that is supposed to bring good luck, especially an animal that represents a sports team. **mas·cot** (**mas**-kaht)

Word History

When a team wins, is it the magic of its **mascot**? *Mascoto* meant "a magic spell" in a language in southern France; *mascoto* was from the word *masco*, meaning "witch." Later, a French music composer wrote a work called *La Mascotte* about a young woman who brought good luck to a home. So the word *mascot* ended up meaning "something that brings good luck."

masculine *adjective*

1. Of or having to do with men: *His deep, masculine voice filled the room.*

2. Having qualities that are supposed to be

Martin Luther King Jr.

typical of men.
mas·cu·line (**mas**-kyuh-lin)
▷ *noun* **masculinity** (*mas*-kyuh-**lin**-i-tee)

mash *verb* To crush something into a soft mass: *Please mash the potatoes as soon as they are boiled.* **mash** (mash) ▷ *verb* **mashes, mashing, mashed** ▷ *noun* **mash**

mask

1. *noun* A covering for the face to hide, protect, or disguise it: *My werewolf mask really frightened Mom.* ▷ *adjective* **masked**

2. *verb* To hide or disguise something: *A smile masked his grief.* ▷ *verb* **masking, masked** ▷ *noun* **mask**
mask (mask)

mason *noun* A person who makes or builds with stone, cement, or bricks. **ma·son** (**may**-suhn)

mascot

masonry *noun* Part of a building or wall that is made of stone, cement, or bricks. **ma·son·ry** (**may**-suhn-ree)

masquerade

1. *noun* A party or other event at which all the people dress up in costumes.

2. *verb* To dress up in order to disguise yourself at a party or other event.

3. *verb* To pretend to be something you are not: *He masqueraded as a doctor for years before he was found out and arrested.*
mas·quer·ade (mas-kuh-**rade**)
▷ *verb* **masquerading, masqueraded**

mass *noun*

1. A large amount of something, as in *a mass of snow.*

2. A large number of people or things

grouped together in a messy way: *A mass of students blocked the doorway.* ▷ *verb* **mass** ▷ *adjective* **mass**

3. In science, the amount of physical matter that an object contains: *Mass is measured in grams or ounces.*

4. the masses *noun, plural* The ordinary people in a society: *This program attempts to make classical music appealing to the masses.*
mass (mas)

Mass *noun* The main religious service in the Roman Catholic Church and some other churches. **Mass** (mas)

massacre *noun* The violent killing of a large number of people at the same time, often in battle. **mas·sa·cre** (**mas**-uh-kur) ▷ *verb* **massacre**

massage *verb* To rub someone's body with the hands in order to loosen the muscles, relieve pain, or help the person relax. **mas·sage** (muh-**sahzh**) ▷ *verb* **massaging, massaged** ▷ *noun* **massage**

massive *adjective* Large in size or amount: *Thirty people sat around the massive table.* **mas·sive** (**mas**-iv) ▷ *adverb* **massively**

mass media *noun, plural* Forms of communication, such as television, radio, newspapers, and the internet, that reach a large number of people.

mass production *noun* The method of making large amounts of identical things with machines in a factory. ▷ *verb* **mass-produce**

mass transit *noun* A system of subways, buses, and trains that transport large numbers of people into and around major cities.

mast *noun* A tall, upright pole on a boat or ship that holds up one or more sails. **mast** (mast)

master
1. *noun* A person with power, rule, or authority over another: *The dog came when his master whistled.*
2. *noun* An expert: *O. Henry was a master of the short story.*
3. *verb* To become very good at something, as in *to master a skill.*
4. *verb* To have control over something, as in *to master a fear.*
5. *adjective* Most important or largest, as in *the master bedroom.*
mas·ter (**mas**-tur)
▷ *verb* **mastering, mastered**

mastermind
1. *verb* To plan and control a complicated or difficult activity: *The thieves masterminded a plan to steal priceless art from the museum.* ▷ *verb* **masterminding, masterminded**
2. *noun* The main person who plans and controls an activity, often a harmful or illegal one.
mas·ter·mind (**mas**-tur-*minde*)

masterpiece *noun*
1. An extremely good piece of work, especially in the areas of art, literature, or music.
2. A person's greatest achievement: *This play is Shakespeare's masterpiece.*
mas·ter·piece (**mas**-tur-*pees*)

mastery *noun* When you have become very good at something, you have **mastery** of it, as in *the young violinist's mastery of her instrument.* **mas·ter·y** (**mas**-tur-ee) ▷ *noun, plural* **masteries**

mat *noun*
1. A thick pad of material used to cover and protect a floor, a table, or some other surface: *Put a mat under that hot pot.*
2. A large, thick floor pad used to protect wrestlers, gymnasts, and other athletes.
3. A thick, tangled mass, especially of hair. ▷ *verb* **mat**
mat (mat)
Mat sounds like **matte**.

matador

matador *noun* A person who fights bulls. **mat·a·dor** (**mat**-uh-*dor*)

match
1. *noun* A small, thin piece of wood or cardboard with a chemical tip that produces a flame when you strike it.
2. *noun* Someone or something that is similar to or goes well with another: *These shoes are a good match for your dress.*
3. *verb* To go well with: *Green shoes will not match that suit.*
4. *noun* Someone or something that is equal to another: *You are no match for our chess champion.*
5. *verb* To equal: *She will match all the donations, dollar for dollar.*
6. *noun* A game or a sporting competition, as in *a tennis match.*
7. *verb* To put into competition: *Today's game matches two powerful college teams.*
match (mach)
▷ *verb* **matches, matching, matched** ▷ *noun, plural* **matches**

mate

1. *noun* One of a pair: *Can you find the mate to this sock?*

2. *noun* A husband or a wife.

3. *noun* The male or female partner of a pair of animals.

4. *verb* To join together to produce babies. ▷ *verb* **mating, mated** ▷ *noun* **mating**
mate (mate)

material

1. *noun* Cloth or fabric.

2. *noun* Things you need for a particular project or activity, as in *materials for finger painting.*

3. *adjective* Of or having to do with possessions or money rather than ideas or values, as in *material wealth.*

4. *adjective* Of or having to do with the body: *Good food and warm clothes are material needs.*
ma·te·ri·al (muh-**teer**-ee-uhl)

materialistic *adjective* Too concerned or impressed with money and possessions. **ma·te·ri·al·is·tic** (muh-*teer*-ee-uh-**lis**-tik) ▷ *noun* **materialism**

materialize *verb* To appear or to happen: *The cats always materialize when I open a can of food.* **ma·te·ri·al·ize** (muh-**teer**-ee-uh-*lize*) ▷ *verb* **materializing, materialized**

maternal *adjective* Of or typical of a mother, as in *maternal love.* **ma·ter·nal** (muh-**tur**-nuhl)

maternity *noun*

1. Motherhood.

2. maternity leave Time off from a job for a woman to give birth and take care of her baby.
ma·ter·ni·ty (muh-**tur**-ni-tee)

math *noun* Short for **mathematics**. **math** (math)

mathematician *noun* An expert in mathematics. **math·e·ma·ti·cian** (*math*-uh-muh-**tish**-uhn)

mathematics *noun* The study of numbers, quantities, shapes, and measurements and how they relate to each other. **math·e·mat·ics** (*math*-uh-**mat**-iks) ▷ *adjective* **mathematical**

matinee *noun* An afternoon performance of a play or showing of a movie. **mat·i·nee** (*mat*-uh-**nay**)

Word History

For the people in the big cities of France, a **matinee** meant "a performance in the morning or afternoon"; the time period of a *matinée* could be as late as 6 or 7 p.m., even though *matinée* developed from the Old French word *matin*, meaning "morning."

matrimony *noun* Marriage, as in *joined in matrimony.* **mat·ri·mo·ny** (**mat**-ruh-*moh*-nee) ▷ *adjective* **matrimonial** (*mat*-ruh-**moh**-nee-uhl)

matrix *noun* An arrangement of numbers or other items in columns and rows. A chart showing the standings of major league baseball teams is a type of matrix. **ma·trix** (**may**-triks) ▷ *noun, plural* **matrices** (**may**-tri-*seez*)

matron *noun*

1. An older woman who is married or widowed.

2. matron of honor A married woman who is a bride's most important attendant in her wedding.
ma·tron (**may**-truhn)

matte *adjective* Dull rather than shiny, as in *a matte finish.* **matte** (mat) **Matte** sounds like **mat**.

matter

1. *noun* Something that has weight and takes up space, such as a solid, liquid, or gas.

2. *noun* Content or material, as in *vegetable matter* or *reading matter.*

3. *noun* Something that you talk about or are interested in, as in *a legal matter.*

4. *noun* A situation, event, or task that you have to deal with: *We need to settle this matter before we leave on vacation.*

5. *verb* To be important: *Does it really matter whether you ride in the front or the back?* ▷ *verb* **mattering, mattered**
mat·ter (**mat**-ur)

mattress *noun* A large, soft, thick pad that you put on a bed to make it comfortable to sleep on. **mat·tress** (**mat**-ris) ▷ *noun, plural* **mattresses**

mature *adjective*

1. Adult or fully grown, as in *a mature audience.*

2. Ripe or completely developed, as in *mature cheese.*

3. Behaving in a sensible, responsible way: *We expect you to behave in a mature way in the museum.*
ma·ture (muh-**choor** or muh-**toor**) ▷ *adverb* **maturely** ▷ *verb* **mature**

maturity *noun* The state of being fully mature, ripe, or developed: *Girls typically reach maturity sooner than boys.* **ma·tur·i·ty** (muh-**choor**-i-tee)

maul *verb* To attack and damage or injure someone or something: *One of the rangers was mauled by a bear.* **maul** (mawl) **Maul** sounds like **mall**. ▷ *verb* **mauling, mauled**

mausoleum *noun* A building that contains a tomb or tombs. **mau·so·le·um** (*maw*-suh-**lee**-uhm or *maw*-zuh-**lee**-uhm)

mauve *noun* A light purple color. **mauve** (mohv) ▷ *adjective* **mauve**

maverick *noun* A person who does not follow rules, and does not think or behave in the same way as other people. **mav·er·ick** (**mav**-ur-ik)

max. Short for **maximum**.

maximize *verb*
1. To make something as large or as important as possible, as in *cutting costs to maximize profits.*
2. To make a window on a computer desktop fill the entire screen.
max·i·mize (**mak**-suh-*mize*)
▷ *verb* **maximizing, maximized**

maximum *noun* The largest amount possible: *Two hours is the maximum allowed for the test.* **max·i·mum** (**mak**-suh-muhm) ▷ *adjective* **maximum**

may *verb* A helping verb that is used in the following ways:
1. To say that something is possible or true: *I may have to leave tomorrow.*
2. To ask for or give permission: *May I drive your car? Yes, you may.*
3. To say you hope or wish for something: *May you live long and prosper!*
may (may)

May *noun* The fifth month on the calendar, after April and before June. May has 31 days. **May** (may)

Word History

Planting a garden in **May** seems especially appropriate because the ancient Romans named the month in honor of the earth goddess, Maia.

Maya *noun* A member of a group of Native American tribes who live in southern Mexico and Central America. The Maya flourished until about A.D. 1000. They were conquered by the Spanish during the 16th century. **Ma·ya** (**mye**-uh) ▷ *noun, plural* **Maya** *or* **Mayas** ▷ *adjective* **Mayan** (**mye**-uhn)

maybe *adverb* Used to say that you are uncertain or you do not know if something is true: *Maybe I spoke too soon when I said this play was boring.* **may·be** (**may**-bee)

Mayday *noun* **Mayday** is a word used all over the world to ask for help or rescue. **May·day** (**may**-*day*)

Word History

When pilots or ships' captains call for help, they say **Mayday** three times: "Mayday, Mayday, Mayday." Rescuers can easily hear and understand this as a distress call, even when the radio reception is not very good. English speakers wrote the French words *m'aider*, meaning "help me," the way they sounded to them: Mayday. *M'aider* was based on the French phrase *venez m'aider*, meaning "come help me."

mayhem *noun* Confused or violent disorder: *There was mayhem at the gate when the flight was canceled.* **may·hem** (**may**-hem)

mayonnaise *noun* A thick white sauce made from egg yolks, oil, and vinegar or lemon juice. **may·on·naise** (**may**-uh-*naze*)

mayor *noun* A person who is elected to be the leader of a town or city government. **may·or** (**may**-ur)

Word History

In the Middle Ages, the city of London in England was the first to have a **mayor**. English speakers adopted *mayor* from the French term *maire*, the title for the main official of a town. The French word *maire* came from an adjective in Latin, *major*, meaning "greater." So the original meaning of *mayor* was "the greater one," or the person who is more important than others.

maze *noun* A complicated system of paths or passages, used as a puzzle or as a way of keeping people away from something: *I could barely find my way through the maze of aisles at the new grocery store.* **maze** (maze) **Maze** sounds like **maize**.

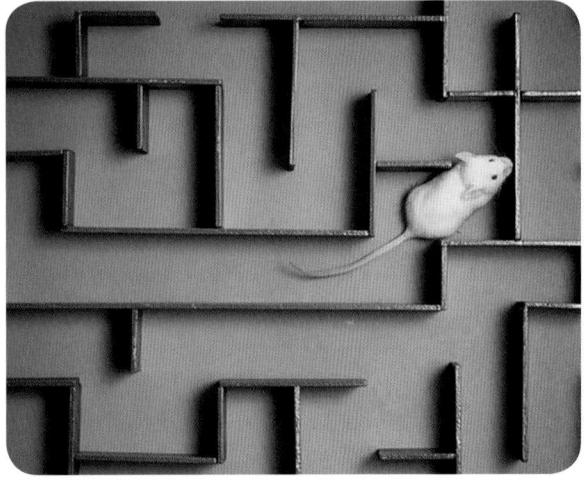

maze

MB Short for **megabyte**.

MD Short for the Latin words *medicinae doctor*, which mean "teacher of medicine." This abbreviation is used after a doctor's name, as in *Samuel Fleury, MD.*

me *pronoun* The form of the pronoun *I* used as the object of a verb or a preposition: *Give the book to me.* **me** (mee)

meadow *noun* A grassy field, especially one used for grazing or for harvesting hay. **mead·ow** (**med**-oh)

meadowlark *noun* A songbird with a pointed bill and a yellow chest with a black crescent across it. **mead·ow·lark** (**med**-oh-*lahrk*)

meager *adjective* Very small, or not enough, as in *a meager meal of bread and milk.* **mea·ger** (**mee**-gur)

meal *noun*

1. Food that you eat at a regular time each day. Breakfast, lunch, and dinner are **meals**.

2. Grain that has been crushed into tiny pieces: *This bread is made with wheat flour and cornmeal.*

meal (meel)

mean

1. *verb* To try to express or refer to something: *I don't understand what Steve means.*

2. *verb* To do something deliberately: *I didn't mean to hurt you.*

3. *verb* To be defined as: *The word "thin" means "skinny."*

4. *verb* To matter or be important: *Your friendship means a lot to me.*

5. *adjective* Unkind or cruel: *Those mean kids are always teasing me.* ▷ *noun* **meanness**

6. *noun* In mathematics, another word for **average**.

7. *adjective (slang)* Very skillful or excellent: *Greg grills a mean steak.*

mean (meen)

▷ *verb* **meaning, meant** (ment) ▷ *adjective* **meaner, meanest**

meander *verb* To follow a route that has a lot of bends. **me·an·der** (mee-an-dur) ▷ *verb* **meandering, meandered**

meaning *noun*

1. The idea that someone or something is trying to express or refer to: *We discussed the meaning of the poem.*

2. The importance or significance of something: *What is the meaning of these delays when we have work to do?* **mean·ing** (**mee**-ning)

meaningful *adjective* Having meaning, significance, or value; not trivial: *After years of running a tanning salon, she felt a need for more meaningful work.* **mean·ing·ful** (**mee**-ning-fuhl)

meant *verb* The past tense and the past participle of **mean**. **meant** (ment)

meantime *noun* The time between two events: *Ian will be home soon—in the meantime, let's rake the lawn so he can mow it.* **mean·time** (**meen**-time)

meanwhile *adverb*

1. In or during the time between: *Our next practice is on Saturday; meanwhile, you should work on catching and batting.*

2. At the same time: *Mom went out to do errands; meanwhile, I watched my little brothers.* **mean·while** (**meen**-*wile*)

measles *noun, plural* An infectious disease caused by a virus that produces fever and a red rash. **mea·sles** (**mee**-zuhlz)

measly *adjective (informal)* Small in size or number; not enough, as in *a measly sandwich for dinner.* **mea·sly** (**meez**-lee) ▷ *adjective* **measlier, measliest**

measure

1. *verb* To find out the size or weight of something: *Make sure to measure the wood before you cut it.*

2. *verb* To have a particular size, length, or amount: *The frame measures 5 by 7 inches.*

3. *noun* A unit of measurement: *Pounds and ounces are measures of weight.*

4. *noun* An action that has a particular purpose: *The police took severe measures to prevent rioting.*

5. *noun* The strength or amount of something, as in *a measure of success.*

6. *noun* A bar of music: *The flutes come in on the third measure.* **meas·ure** (**mezh**-ur)

▷ *verb* **measuring, measured**

measurement *noun*

1. The act or process of measuring, as in *measurement of land.*

2. The size, weight, or amount of something that has been measured, as in *an accurate measurement.*

3. A system of measuring, such as the metric system. *See the Measurements Tables in the **Reference Section**.*

4. measurements *noun, plural* All the measured dimensions of an object, taken together: *The measurements of the crate are 36 inches by 24 inches by 18 inches.*

5. Measures of various parts of your body, used as a guide to what size clothing to buy. **meas·ure·ment** (**mezh**-ur-muhnt)

meat *noun*

1. The flesh of an animal that is eaten as food: *He's a vegetarian and doesn't eat meat.*

2. The edible part of a fruit or nut.

3. The most important part of something, as in *the meat of a discussion.* **meat** (meet)

Meat sounds like **meet**. ▷ *adjective* **meaty**

measure

mechanic

mechanic *noun* A person who repairs machinery, especially engines: *My mechanic said we need a new transmission.* **me·chan·ic** (muh-**kan**-ik)

mechanical *adjective*
1. Of or having to do with machines or engines, as in *mechanical problems.*
2. Operated by a machine, as in *a mechanical toy.*
3. Done without thinking: *She has done it so many times that it's become mechanical.*
me·chan·i·cal (muh-**kan**-i-kuhl)
▷ *adverb* **mechanically**

mechanics *noun*
1. The science that deals with motion and forces.
2. The operating parts of something, as in *the mechanics of an engine.*
me·chan·ics (muh-**kan**-iks)

mechanism *noun* A system of parts working together inside a machine. **mech·a·nism** (**mek**-uh-*niz*-uhm)

medal *noun* A piece of metal with a special shape or design that is given to someone as an award or for a special event. **med·al** (**med**-uhl) **Medal** sounds like **meddle**.

meddle *verb* To get involved in someone else's personal business: *Aunt Bea should not meddle—it's not any of her business.* **med·dle** (**med**-uhl) **Meddle** sounds like **medal**. ▷ *verb* **meddling, meddled** ▷ *noun* **meddler**

meddlesome *adjective* Inclined to interfere in other people's business. **med·dle·some** (**med**-uhl-suhm)

media *noun, plural*
1. A plural of **medium**.
2. Ways of communicating with large numbers of people, considered as a group: *The news media quickly picked up the story of the president's illness.*

3. Substances used to create a work of art: *The sculpture uses clay, paint, and other media.*
me·di·a (**mee**-dee-uh)

median *noun*
1. The middle number, or the average of the two middle numbers, in a series of numbers listed from smallest to largest: *In the set 5, 10, 15, the median is 10. In the set 2, 4, 6, 8, the median is the average of 4 + 6, or 5.*
2. A narrow strip of land that separates the opposite sides of a large road.
me·di·an (**mee**-dee-uhn)
▷ *adjective* **median**

medic *noun* A person who is trained to give medical treatment in an emergency or in the military. **med·ic** (**med**-ik)

Medicaid *noun* A US government system that provides medical care for people who cannot afford it. **Med·i·caid** (**med**-i-kayd)

medical *adjective* Of or having to do with doctors or medicine, as in *medical care.* **med·i·cal** (**med**-i-kuhl)
▷ *adverb* **medically**

Medicare *noun* A US government system that provides medical care to people over the age of 65. **Med·i·care** (**med**-i-kair)

medication *noun* A substance used for treating an injury or illness. **med·i·ca·tion** (*med*-i-**kay**-shuhn)

medicinal *adjective* Of or having the curing properties of a medicine: *Some herbs have medicinal value.* **me·dic·i·nal** (muh-**dis**-uh-nuhl)

medicine *noun*
1. A substance such as a drug that is used to treat an illness.
2. The study and treatment of diseases and injuries.
med·i·cine (**med**-i-sin)

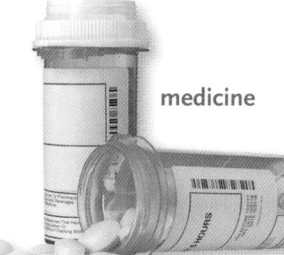

medicine

medieval *adjective* Of or having to do with the Middle Ages, the period of history between approximately A.D. 1000 and 1450. **me·di·e·val** (mee-**dee**-vuhl *or* *med*-ee-**ee**-vuhl)

mediocre *adjective* Of only average quality; not very good, as in *a mediocre performance.* **me·di·o·cre** (*me*-dee-**oh**-kur)

mediocrity *noun* A condition or quality that is only average and not very good: *Despite years of practice, she never rose above mediocrity as a violinist.* **me·di·oc·ri·ty** (*mee*-dee-**ah**-kri-tee)

meditate *verb*

1. To think deeply and quietly as a way of relaxing your mind and body: *I feel much less tense after I meditate.*

2. To think about something in a very focused way: *I meditated on what to say before starting the letter.* **med·i·tate** (med-i-*tate*)

▷ *verb* **meditating, meditated**

meditation *noun*

1. The act of thinking deeply and quietly: *Meditation and exercise are Zack's cures for stress.*

2. Serious thoughts on a subject that are put into a speech or essay, as in *a brief meditation on friendship.* **med·i·ta·tion** (*med*-i-*tay*-shuhn)

Mediterranean Sea *noun* An inland sea connected to the Atlantic Ocean. It is bordered by Africa to the south and Europe to the north. **Med·i·ter·ra·ne·an Sea** (*med*-i-tuh-**ray**-nee-uhn)

medium

1. *adjective* Average or middle in size: *Alison ordered a sandwich and a medium soda.*

2. *noun* The substance that something lives or grows in: *Water is the medium for whales and fish.*

3. *noun* A way of communicating information to large numbers of people: *Radio is a less popular medium than TV.*

4. *noun* Something that is used for a particular purpose: *Metal is a medium for electrical currents.*

5. *noun* A substance used to create a work of art: *This painter's favorite medium is watercolors.*

6. *noun* A person who claims to communicate with spirits of dead people. **me·di·um** (**mee**-dee-uhm)

▷ *noun, plural* **mediums** (for all senses) *or* **media** (**mee**-dee-uh) (for senses 3 and 5)

medley *noun*

1. A musical piece that consists of parts of different songs: *The group performed a medley of carols.*

2. A mixture or assortment of things: *The chicken was served with a medley of vegetables.* **med·ley** (**med**-lee)

meek *adjective* Quiet, gentle, and eager to please, as in *a meek servant.* **meek** (meek)

▷ *adjective* **meeker, meekest** ▷ *adverb* **meekly**

meet

1. *verb* To come together with someone or something: *We will meet tomorrow at three.*

2. *verb* To join: *The rivers meet at the foot of the mountain.*

3. *verb* To see or be introduced to for the first time: *Have you met Ian?*

4. *verb* To go to a place and wait for someone to arrive: *I'll meet your train tomorrow night.*

5. *verb* To fulfill or to be equal to; satisfy: *His performance did not meet my expectations.*

6. *noun* A sports competition, as in *a track meet.* **meet** (meet)

Meet sounds like **meat**. ▷ *verb* **meeting, met** (met)

meeting *noun* A scheduled event in which people meet to discuss or decide something. **meet·ing** (**mee**-ting)

meg *noun* Short for **megabyte**. **meg** (meg)

megabyte *noun* A unit measuring computer memory or file size. A megabyte is about one million bytes. Abbreviated as *MB*. **meg·a·byte** (**meg**-uh-*bite*)

megahertz *noun* A unit used to measure the frequency of radio waves and the speed of computer processors. It is equal to one million hertz. Abbreviated as *MHz*. **meg·a·hertz** (**meg**-uh-*hurts*)

▷ *noun, plural* **megahertz** *or* **megahertzes**

megaphone *noun* A device used to make the voice louder, sometimes shaped like a cone: *The organizers used megaphones to be heard over the crowd.* **meg·a·phone** (**meg**-uh-*fone*)

megapixel *noun* A unit used to tell how precise an image is, or how much space a digital camera can use to store a photograph. It is equal to one million pixels. **meg·a·pix·el** (**meg**-uh-*pik*-suhl)

melancholy *adjective* Sad or depressed, as in *a melancholy mood.* **mel·an·cho·ly** (**mel**-uhn-*kah*-lee)

▷ *noun* **melancholy** ▷ *adjective* **melancholic**

mellow

1. *adjective* Soft, rich, and soothing, as in *mellow music* or *mellow lighting.*

2. *verb* To become gentler and more relaxed. ▷ *verb* **mellowing, mellowed**

3. *adjective* Soft, smooth, and fully ripe, as in *a mellow peach.* ▷ *adjective* **mellower, mellowest** **mel·low** (**mel**-oh)

melodious *adjective* Pleasant to hear, like a melody, as in *a pleasant, melodious voice.* **me·lo·di·ous** (muh-**loh**-dee-uhs) ▷ *noun* **melodiousness** ▷ *adverb* **melodiously**

melodramatic *adjective* Too dramatic or emotional, as in *a melodramatic soap opera.* **mel·o·dra·mat·ic** (*mel*-uh-druh-**mat**-ik) ▷ *noun* **melodrama** (**mel**-uh-*drah*-muh)

melody *noun* An arrangement of musical notes that makes a tune: *Sopranos usually sing the melody.* **mel·o·dy** (**mel**-uh-dee)

▷ *noun, plural* **melodies**

megaphone

▷ *adjective* **melodic** (muh-**lah**-dik)

melon *noun* A large, round, juicy fruit with a hard skin. Melons grow on vines.   **mel·on** (**mel**-uhn)

melt *verb*
1. To change something from a solid to a liquid by heating it.
2. To dissolve in liquid: *Sugar melts in water.*
3. To fade away or disappear: *The crowd melted away at the end of the concert.*
4. If something **melts your heart**, or if your heart melts, you become more gentle and understanding.
melt (melt)
▷ *verb* **melting, melted**

meltdown *noun*
1. The melting of the core of a nuclear reactor, which allows dangerous radiation to escape into the atmosphere.
2. Loss of emotional control because you are tired or stressed: *Jamie had a meltdown in the candy aisle.*
melt·down (**melt**-*doun*)

member *noun*
1. A person, animal, or thing that belongs to a group: *I am a member of the local gym.*
2. A part of the body, especially an arm or a leg.
mem·ber (**mem**-bur)

membership *noun*
1. The state of being a member of something, as in *a club membership.*
2. All the members of a club or other group: *The membership voted for a new chairperson.*
mem·ber·ship (**mem**-bur-*ship*)

membrane *noun*
1. A very thin layer of tissue that lines or covers certain organs or cells.
2. A thin layer of plastic or other material that protects something.
mem·brane (**mem**-brane)

meme *noun* A funny picture on the internet that spreads around quickly when people copy it, sometimes making small changes.   **meme** (meem)

Word History

You may already know a cousin of **meme,** *mime,* which comes from a Greek word that means "imitate." The British scientist Richard Dawkins invented the word *meme* to stand for an idea, image, or behavior that spreads very quickly throughout a culture. He was influenced by the Greek origin noted above, but he also wanted a short, easy-to-pronounce word that was similar to *gene,* and he noted that *meme* also makes one think of *memory,* and perhaps the French word *même,* which means "same."

memento *noun* A small item you keep to remind you of a person or place: *My shell collection is a memento of our trip to the beach.*   **me·men·to** (muh-**men**-toh)

memo *noun* Short for **memorandum**: *I sent a memo out to cancel the meeting.*   **mem·o** (**mem**-oh)

memorable *adjective* Worth remembering, or easy to remember because of some special feature, as in *a movie full of memorable characters.*   **mem·o·ra·ble** (**mem**-ur-uh-buhl)
▷ *adverb* **memorably**

memorandum *noun*
1. A short written reminder.
2. A short letter written to people who work in the same organization.
mem·o·ran·dum (*mem*-uh-**ran**-duhm)
▷ *noun, plural* **memorandums** *or* **memoranda** (*mem*-uh-**ran**-duh)

memorial
1. *noun* Something that is built, such as a statue or monument, or done to help people remember a person or an event.
2. *adjective* Done to help people remember a person or event, as in *a memorial service.*
me·mo·ri·al (muh-**mor**-ee-uhl)

Memorial Day *noun* A holiday celebrated on the last Monday of May to honor Americans who have died in wars.

memorize *verb* To commit something to memory; to learn something by heart: *Please memorize the poem for the assembly program.*   **mem·o·rize** (**mem**-uh-*rize*) ▷ *verb* **memorizing, memorized**

memory *noun*
1. The ability to remember things: *My memory for details is terrible.*
2. A thought of something that you remember from the past: *I have happy memories of my last birthday party.*
3. Honor and respect for people or events from the past: *This statue was built in memory of the founders.*
4. The part of a computer in which instructions and information are stored.
mem·o·ry (**mem**-ur-ee)
▷ *noun, plural* **memories**

memory foam *noun* A kind of foam that takes the shape of something that touches it but returns to its original shape when the touching stops.

men *noun, plural* The plural of **man**.   **men** (men)

menace *noun* Something that is dangerous or can cause harm: *That dog is a menace to the whole neighborhood.*   **men·ace** (**men**-is) ▷ *adjective* **menacing**

mend

1. *verb* To fix or repair something, especially clothing, as in *to mend a sock.* ▷ *verb* **mending, mended**

2. *noun* If someone or something is **on the mend**, they are getting better after injury or illness.
mend (mend)

menorah *noun* A special holder for seven or nine candles. Menorahs for nine candles are used during Hanukkah, the Jewish Festival of Lights. **me·no·rah** (muh-**nor**-uh)

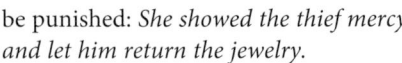
menorah

mental *adjective* Having to do with or done in the mind, as in *mental illness* or *a mental picture.* **men·tal** (**men**-tuhl) ▷ *adverb* **mentally**

mention *verb* To give a small bit of information about something: *The mayor did not mention the election in his speech.* **men·tion** (**men**-shuhn) ▷ *verb* **mentioning, mentioned** ▷ *noun* **mention**

menu *noun*

1. A list of foods available in a restaurant.

2. A list of choices you can click on in a computer program.
men·u (**men**-yoo)

menu bar *noun* A bar across the top of a computer display that contains the titles of menus.

meow *verb* To make the crying sound a cat makes. **me·ow** (mee-**ou**) ▷ *verb* **meowing, meowed** ▷ *noun* **meow**

mercenary

1. *noun* A soldier who is hired to serve in a foreign army. ▷ *noun, plural* **mercenaries**

2. *adjective* Interested only in getting or making money.
mer·ce·nar·y (**mur**-suh-**ner**-ee)

merchandise *noun* Goods that are bought or sold; things for sale, as in *new merchandise on display.* **mer·chan·dise** (**mur**-chuhn-*dize* or **mur**-chuhn-*dise*)

merchant *noun*

1. A person who sells goods to make money, especially in a store.

2. A country's **merchant marine** is made up of crews and ships that carry goods for trade.
mer·chant (**mur**-chuhnt)

mercury *noun* A silvery metal that is poisonous and liquid at room temperature. Mercury was once commonly used in thermometers and barometers. **mer·cu·ry** (**mur**-kyur-ee)

Mercury *noun* The smallest planet in our solar system and the closest planet to the sun. **Mer·cu·ry** (**mur**-kyur-ee)

mercy *noun*

1. Compassion or forgiveness for someone who should be punished: *She showed the thief mercy and let him return the jewelry.*

2. Something to be thankful for because it stops something unpleasant: *Your donation was a real mercy in such a bad situation.*
mer·cy (**mur**-see)
▷ *noun, plural* **mercies** ▷ *adjective* **merciful** ▷ *adverb* **mercifully**

mere *adjective* Nothing more than; unimportant: *He missed the train by a mere minute.* **mere** (meer) ▷ *adjective* **merest**

merely *adverb* Only or just: *I didn't kick the cat— I merely nudged it to get it out the door.* **mere·ly** (**meer**-lee)

merge *verb* To join together into one: *Traffic is slow because it merges into one lane ahead.* **merge** (murj) ▷ *verb* **merging, merged**

merger *noun* The act of joining two businesses, teams, or other units into one. **merg·er** (**mur**-jur)

meridian *noun* An imaginary circle on the earth's surface that passes through the North and South Poles. Meridians are used to show locations of places on earth. **me·rid·i·an** (muh-**rid**-ee-uhn)

meringue *noun* A mixture of sugar and egg whites that is beaten until it is white and fluffy, then baked as a topping for a pie or other dessert, as in *a lemon meringue pie.* **me·ringue** (muh-**rang**)

merit

1. *noun* If something has **merit**, it is valuable or praiseworthy: *My story won the prize for literary merit.*

2. *noun* A good point or feature: *The plan for the new park has many merits, but also has some serious downsides.*

3. *verb* To deserve praise or attention: *My idea merits more consideration.* ▷ *verb* **meriting, merited**

4. merits *noun, plural* The actual facts of a matter: *The judge will decide the case on its merits.*
mer·it (**mer**-it)

mermaid *noun* An imaginary sea creature with a woman's head and upper body, and a fish's tail instead of legs. **mer·maid** (**mur**-mayd)

Word History

Sailors sometimes imagined seeing women swimming in the sea, and called them **mermaids**. *Mermaid* is a combination of two old words, *mere* and *maid*. *Mere* is rare now, but was then a common word for "sea." Today, a *maid* is a woman who cleans, but it once meant any young woman. We now use different words for "woman" and "sea," but the term *mermaid* lives on. Some people think that the sailors were actually seeing manatees.

merry *adjective* Lively and cheerful, as in *a merry tune.* **mer·ry** (**mer**-ee) ▷ *adjective* **merrier, merriest**

merry-go-round *noun* A revolving ride at amusement parks and fairs with seats that look like horses or other animals. Also called a **carousel. mer·ry-go-round** (**mer**-ee-goh-*round*)

mesa *noun* A large hill with steep sides and a flat top. **me·sa** (**may**-suh)

Word History

Spanish explorers encountered many **mesas** in the American Southwest. They named these geographical features with the Spanish word for "table."

mesh
1. *noun* A woven material made of threads or wires with open spaces between them. ▷ *noun, plural* **meshes**
2. *verb* To fit together or closely match: *Our ideas finally meshed.* ▷ *verb* **meshes, meshing, meshed** **mesh** (mesh)

Mesopotamia *noun* An ancient region between the Tigris and Euphrates Rivers that was the site of the Babylonian empire and other early civilizations. Much of it is now part of modern-day Iraq. **Mes·o·po·ta·mi·a** (*mes*-uh-puh-**tay**-mee-uh)

Mesopotamian
1. *noun* A person who lived in ancient Mesopotamia.
2. *adjective* Of or having to do with the people or culture of ancient Mesopotamia, as in *Mesopotamian astronomy.*
Mes·o·po·ta·mi·an (*mes*-uh-puh-**tay**-mee-uhn)

mess
1. *noun* Something that is dirty or untidy: *Dad made such a mess in the kitchen.*
2. *noun* A situation that is full of problems: *The new bus schedule is a mess.*

mesa

Mesopotamia

The name of this ancient territory in the eastern Mediterranean region means "between the rivers" in Greek. It was part of the Fertile Crescent, an area of land shaped like a crescent moon, with rich soil and plenty of water. Its people created farming, writing, mathematics, astronomy, and the wheel. The Sumer people first formed cities there around 5000 B.C., with other people settling there even earlier.

a relief from a Mesopotamian palace

3. **mess up** *verb* To make something dirty or untidy, or to make something go wrong: *My younger cousins messed up my room.* ▷ *verb* **messes, messing, messed**
4. **mess hall** *noun* A room or building in a military unit or a camp where meals are served and eaten. **mess** (mes) ▷ *noun, plural* **messes**

message *noun*
1. A piece of information sent to or left for someone: *Did she leave a message when she called?*
2. The meaning or lesson of something: *The message of the movie was that it's always better to tell the truth.*
mes·sage (**mes**-ij)

messenger *noun* A person who delivers messages and documents. **mes·sen·ger** (**mes**-uhn-jur)

messy *adjective* Not neat or tidy; not arranged or orderly: *There was a messy pile of papers and books on the table.* **mess·y** (**mes**-ee) ▷ *adjective* **messier, messiest** ▷ *adverb* **messily**

met *verb* The past tense and the past participle of **meet. met** (met)

metabolism *noun* The process in our bodies that changes the food we eat into the energy we need to breathe, digest, and grow. **me·tab·o·lism** (muh-**tab**-uh-*liz*-uhm)

metal *noun* A solid material such as iron or silver that is usually hard and shiny. Many metals are good conductors of heat and electricity. **met·al** (**met**-uhl)

metallic *adjective*
1. Made of metal or partly of metal.
2. Seeming like metal: *The lake had a metallic sheen in the moonlight.*
me·tal·lic (adjective)

metamorphic *adjective*
1. Of or having to do with metamorphosis, as in *the metamorphic process that turns limestone into marble.*
2. Of or having to do with rock whose structure has been changed by pressure, heat, or water, making it a different type of rock. A metamorphic rock is usually harder and more compact than its original form and has a higher amount of crystal. Marble, slate, and gneiss are examples of metamorphic rocks.
met·a·mor·phic (*met*-uh-**mor**-fik)
▷ *adverb* **metamorphically**

metamorphosis *noun*
1. A series of changes some animals, such as caterpillars, go through as they develop into adults.
2. A complete or great change in appearance or form; a transformation.
met·a·mor·pho·sis (*met*-uh-**mor**-fuh-sis)
▷ *noun, plural* **metamorphoses**
(*met*-uh-**mor**-fuh-*seez*)

metaphor *noun* A word or phrase you use to compare something to something different that has a similar feature, for example, "That performer is a shining star" or "That cat is a lightning bolt when she's scared." **met·a·phor** (**met**-uh-*for*) ▷ *adjective* **metaphorical**

meteor *noun* A piece of rock or metal from space that speeds into the earth's atmosphere and forms a streak of light as it burns and falls to the earth. **me·te·or** (**mee**-tee-ur)

Word History

The word **meteor** comes from the Greek word *meteoron*, meaning "something high in the air," because meteors are seen as streaks of light high in the air.

meteorite *noun* A piece of rock from space that falls to the earth. **me·te·or·ite** (**mee**-tee-uh-*rite*)

meteorologist *noun* An expert in the study of the earth's atmosphere. **me·te·o·rol·o·gist** (*mee*-tee-uh-**rah**-luh-jist)

meteorology *noun* The study of the earth's atmosphere, especially in relation to climate and weather. **me·te·or·ol·o·gy** (*mee*-tee-uh-**rah**-luh-jee) ▷ *adjective* **meteorological** (*mee*-tee-ur-uh-**lah**-ji-kuhl)

meter *noun*
1. The basic unit of length in the metric system equal to 39.37 inches, or a little more than 3 feet.
2. A device that measures the amount or speed of something, especially the amount of something that has been used, as in *a gas meter* or *a parking meter.* ▷ *verb* **meter**
3. The pattern of rhythm in a line of poetry formed by stressing some syllables and not others.
me·ter (**mee**-tur)

methane *noun* A colorless, odorless gas that burns easily and is used for fuel. **meth·ane** (**meth**-ane)

method *noun* A particular way of doing something. **meth·od** (**meth**-uhd)

methodical *adjective* Done in a careful or logical way, as in *a methodical search.* **me·thod·i·cal** (muh-**thah**-di-kuhl) ▷ *adverb* **methodically**

meticulous *adjective* Very careful and thorough; paying great attention to detail. **me·tic·u·lous** (muh-**tik**-yuh-luhs) ▷ *adverb* **meticulously**

metric *adjective* Of or having to do with a measuring system based on the meter and related units. **met·ric** (**met**-rik)

metric system *noun* A system of measurement based on the meter. In the metric system, the meter is the basic unit of length, the gram is the basic unit of mass or weight, and the liter is the basic unit of liquid volume.

metronome *noun* A device that makes a regular beat to help musicians play at the correct speed. **met·ro·nome** (**met**-ruh-*nome*)

metropolitan *adjective* Of or having to do with a large city, and sometimes its surrounding area, as in *the New York metropolitan area.* **met·ro·pol·i·tan** (*met*-ruh-**pah**-li-tuhn)

metronome

mg Short for **milligram** or the plural form *milligrams.*

MHz Short for **megahertz.**

mi. Short for **mile** or the plural form *miles.*

mic drop *noun* (*informal*) The act of dropping or tossing aside a microphone after you have used it to say or sing something very impressive. People sometimes use **mic drop** to say that a remark was impressive, even if the person saying it wasn't using a microphone. **mic drop** (**mike** *drahp*)

mice *noun, plural* The plural of **mouse.** **mice** (mise)

microaggression *noun* A statement or action that insults a member of a minority group in a subtle way. **mi·cro·ag·gres·sion** (*mye*-kroh-uh-**gresh**-uhn)

microbe *noun* An extremely small living thing, especially one that causes disease. **mi·crobe** (**mye**-krobe)

microchip *noun* A very thin piece of silicon that contains electronic circuits, used in computers and other electronic equipment. Often shortened as **chip**. **mi·cro·chip** (**mye**-kroh-*chip*)

Micronesia *noun* A group of thousands of small islands in the western Pacific Ocean, northeast of Australia and New Guinea. It includes the Federated States of Micronesia, Guam, Kiribati, the Marshall Islands, Nauru, and the Northern Mariana Islands. **Mi·cro·ne·sia** (*mye*-kruh-**nee**-zhuh) ▷ *adjective* **Micronesian**

microorganism *noun* A living thing that is so small it can be seen only with a microscope, such as a bacterium or virus. **mi·cro·or·gan·ism** (*mye*-kroh-**or**-guh-*niz*-uhm)

microphone *noun* An instrument that is used to record sound or make sound louder. **mi·cro·phone** (**mye**-kruh-*fone*)

microprocessor *noun* A computer chip that controls the functions of an electronic device. Microprocessors are often used to program small devices like appliances. **mi·cro·pro·ces·sor** (**mye**-kroh-*prah*-ses-ur)

microscope *noun* An instrument that makes very small things look larger so that they can be seen and studied. **mi·cro·scope** (**mye**-kruh-*skope*)

microscopic *adjective* Extremely small. **mi·cro·scop·ic** (*mye*-kruh-**skah**-pik) ▷ *adverb* **microscopically**

microwave *noun*
1. An electromagnetic wave that can pass through solid objects. Microwaves are used in radar to send messages over long distances, and to cook food in microwave ovens.
2. microwave oven An oven that cooks food very quickly by sending microwaves into it. Microwaves cook the food from the inside by making the moisture in the food vibrate and heat up. **mi·cro·wave** (**mye**-kroh-*wave*)

mid
1. *adjective* In the middle of something. *Mid* is often used in combination with another word. *Mid-January* means "in the middle of January."
2. *preposition* In the middle. This use of mid is found mainly in old songs and poems: *Mid the snows of*

microscope

winter, the house stood snug and warm. **mid** (mid)

midday *noun* Noon, or the middle part of the day. **mid·day** (**mid**-*day*) ▷ *adjective* **midday**

middle
1. *adjective* Halfway between two things, sides, or points: *I am the middle sister.* ▷ *noun* **middle**
2. in the middle Involved in doing something: *Pete called when I was in the middle of doing my homework.* **mid·dle** (**mid**-uhl)

middle-aged *adjective* A person who is **middle-aged** is between about 45 and 65 years old. **middle-aged** (ayjd)

Middle Ages *noun* The period of European history from approximately A.D. 1000 to 1450.

middle class *noun* The social class that is neither rich nor poor. It falls between the upper class and lower class. ▷ *adjective* **middle-class**

Middle East *noun* A region that is part of Africa and Asia that is made up of Egypt, Iran, Iraq, Israel, Saudi Arabia, Syria, Turkey, and other nearby countries. ▷ *adjective* **Middle Eastern**

Middle English *noun* The English language that was spoken from around A.D. 1100 to 1475.

middle school *noun* A school between elementary school and high school. It usually includes the seventh and eighth grades and sometimes the fifth and sixth grades.

midnight *noun* Twelve o'clock at night. **mid·night** (**mid**-*nite*) ▷ *adjective* **midnight**

midst *noun* The middle part: *They were in the midst of an argument when their mother came in.* **midst** (midst)

midway
1. (**mid**-*way*) *adverb and adjective* Halfway: *The school is located midway between the park and the highway.*
2. (**mid**-*way*) *noun* An area of a carnival or fair in which games, rides, and other amusements are located. **mid·way**

Midwest *noun* The north-central region of the United States, roughly between the Ohio River in the East and the Rocky Mountains in the West. **Mid·west** (**mid**-west) ▷ *adjective* **Midwestern**

midwife *noun* A person who is trained to help women give birth. **mid·wife** (**mid**-*wife*) ▷ *noun, plural* **midwives** ▷ *noun* **midwifery** (mid-**wif**-ur-ee)

a b c d e f g h i j k l **m** n o p q r s t u v w x y z

might

1. *noun* Strength or power: *It took all my might to move the couch.*

2. *verb* The past tense of **may**: *We asked if we might go to the movies tonight.*

might (mite)

Might sounds like **mite**.

mighty *adjective* Powerful: *Alexander the Great was a mighty king of ancient times.* **might·y** (**mye**-tee)
▷ *adjective* **mightier, mightiest** ▷ *adverb* **mightily** (**mye**-tuh-lee)

migraine *noun* A very bad kind of headache that can make you sick. **mi·graine** (**mye**-grane)

migrant

1. *noun* A person or thing that moves from one area or country to another.

2. *adjective* Of or having to do with someone who moves around to do work in different seasons, as in *a migrant farm worker.*

mi·grant (**mye**-gruhnt)

migrate *verb*

1. To move from one country or area to another: *My ancestors migrated from France to America.*

2. To move to another area or climate at a particular time of year: *This type of bird migrates south in the winter.*

mi·grate (**mye**-grate)
▷ *verb* **migrating, migrated** ▷ *adjective* **migratory** (**mye**-gruh-*tor*-ee)

migration *noun* Movement of people or animals from one region or habitat to another: *Geese fill the sky during their fall migration.* **mi·gra·tion** (mye-**gray**-shuhn)

mild *adjective*

1. Moderate, not harsh, as in *a mild climate.*

2. Gentle and not easily provoked: *He has a mild temper and rarely starts an argument.*

mild (milde)
▷ *adjective* **milder, mildest** ▷ *noun* **mildness** ▷ *adverb* **mildly**

mildew *noun* A white, powdery fungus that can grow on damp cloth, paper, food, and other substances. **mil·dew** (**mil**-doo) ▷ *verb* **mildew** ▷ *adjective* **mildewed** ▷ *adjective* **mildewy**

mile *noun* A unit of length equal to 5,280 feet. It takes about 20 minutes to walk one mile. **mile** (mile)

mileage *noun*

1. The total distance traveled or measured

mileage

in miles: *We put a lot of mileage on the car in the summer.*

2. The average number of miles a vehicle travels on a gallon of fuel: *You can get better mileage if you drive at a slower speed.*

mile·age (**mye**-lij)

milestone *noun*

1. A marker on the side of a road that shows the distance to other points.

2. An important event or development: *Learning to walk is a milestone in a baby's development.*

mile·stone (**mile**-*stone*)

militant *adjective* Very aggressive or willing to use force to support a cause you believe in, as in *a militant crusader for animal rights.* **mil·i·tant** (**mil**-i-tuhnt)
▷ *noun* **militancy** (**mil**-i-tuhn-see) ▷ *adverb* **militantly**

military

1. *adjective* Of or having to do with soldiers, the armed forces, or war, as in *military training.*

2. *noun* The armed forces of a country, such as the army or navy.

mil·i·tar·y (**mil**-i-*ter*-ee)

militia *noun* A group of people who are trained to fight but are not professional soldiers. **mi·li·tia** (muh-**lish**-uh)

milk

1. *noun* The white fluid produced by female mammals to feed their young.

2. *noun* This fluid from cows, which many people drink. ▷ *adjective* **milky** (**mil**-kee)

3. *verb* To take milk from a cow or other animal. ▷ *verb* **milking, milked**

4. *noun* A white liquid that is made in plants, as in *coconut milk.*

milk (milk)

Milky Way *noun* The galaxy that includes the earth and our solar system. The Milky Way is made up of more than 100 billion stars and can be seen as a white streak in the night sky.

milk

mill

1. *noun* A building that contains machinery for grinding grain into flour: *We buy cornmeal straight from the mill.*

2. *noun* A factory that produces fabrics, paper, steel, or other processed materials: *That funny smell is from the paper mill across the river.*

3. *noun* A small machine used for grinding something into powder, as in *a coffee mill.*

4. *verb* To make grain into flour by crushing it: *The wheat will be sent to Springfield to be milled.*

5. mill around *verb* If lots of people **mill around**, they move around within an area: *He tried to find his mother in the crowd of people milling around the auditorium.*

mill (mil)

▷ *verb* **milling, milled**

millennium *noun* A time period of a thousand years. **mil·len·ni·um** (muh-**len**-ee-uhm) ▷ *noun, plural* **millenniums** or **millennia** (muh-**len**-ee-uh) ▷ *adjective* **millennial**

millet *noun* Small, edible seeds from a grass similar to wheat. **mil·let** (**mil**-it)

milligram *noun* A metric measure equal to 1/1000 of a gram. **mil·li·gram** (**mil**-i-*gram*)

milliliter *noun* A unit for measuring liquids in the metric system equal to 1/1000 of a liter, or about .034 fluid ounces. **mil·li·li·ter** (**mil**-uh-*lee*-tur)

millimeter *noun* A metric measure equal to 1/1000 of a meter. **mil·li·me·ter** (**mil**-uh-*mee*-tur)

million

1. *noun* A thousand thousands, written numerically as 1,000,000.

2. *noun* A very large amount, as in *millions of stars.*

3. *adjective* Equal to a very large amount: *I have a million things to get done today.*

mil·lion (**mil**-yuhn)

millionaire *noun* A person whose money and property are worth a million dollars or more; a rich person. **mil·lion·aire** (*mil*-yuh-**nair**)

mime *noun*

1. Acting that uses movements and facial expressions instead of words.

2. A performer who acts without words: *The mime's silly gestures made us laugh.*

mime (mime)

▷ *verb* **mime**

mimic *verb* To imitate someone else, especially to make fun of the person: *Kyle loves to mimic his teacher's squeaky voice.* **mim·ic** (**mim**-ik) ▷ *verb* **mimicking, mimicked** ▷ *noun* **mimic**

min. Short for **minimum**. Also short for **minute** or the plural form *minutes.*

minaret *noun* The tall, slim tower of a mosque, from which Muslims are called to prayer. **min·a·ret** (*min*-uh-**ret**)

Word History

A **minaret** is the tall tower of a mosque, from which Muslims are called to prayer five times a day. The person who does the calling is known as a *muezzin.* The Arabic word *manara* could mean either "minaret" or "lighthouse." Speakers of Arabic formed *manara* from the word *nara*, meaning "to shine." The English name of this tower has a final *-t* because the Arabic word *manara* had another form, *manarat. Manarat* ended up as the English word *minaret.*

mince *verb* To cut into tiny pieces: *Mince one onion and add it to the mixture.* **mince** (mins) ▷ *verb* **mincing, minced**

mincemeat *noun* A sweet mixture of finely chopped dried fruit, spices, and other ingredients, used in pies. **mince·meat** (**mins**-*meet*)

mind

1. *noun* The part of you that thinks, feels, and remembers.

2. *verb* To take care of something or someone: *I will mind the neighbor's dog while he is away.*

3. *verb* To care about or to be annoyed by something: *I don't mind the noise if it doesn't last very long.*

4. *verb* To be reluctant or unwilling to do something: *Would you mind driving me to the store?*

5. *noun* An opinion or thoughts about something: *Andrew spoke his mind about the new dress code.*

6. *noun* Thoughts or attention: *I can't keep my mind on my work.*

7. *noun* Memory: *The meeting just slipped my mind.*

mind (minde)

▷ *verb* **minding, minded**

mine

1. *pronoun* The one or ones belonging to me: *That coat is mine.*

2. *verb* To dig up minerals that are in the ground: *They used to mine coal from these mountains.* ▷ *verb* **mining, mined** ▷ *noun* **mine** ▷ *noun* **miner**

3. *noun* A bomb placed underground or underwater: *Some land mines remained buried after the war ended.*

4. *noun* A good source of something: *The dictionary is a mine of information.*

mine (mine)

minaret

a
b
c
d
e
f
g
h
i
j
k
l
m
n
o
p
q
r
s
t
u
v
w
x
y
z

mineral

1. *noun* A solid substance found in the earth that does not come from an animal or plant: *Your body needs vitamins and minerals to stay healthy.*
2. *adjective* Of or having to do with minerals: *He handed her a bottle of mineral water.*
min·er·al (**min**-ur-uhl)

Word History

Minerals can be found in many different places on earth. They can form in an exploding volcano or in caves, for example. Originally, any substance that people could get by mining was called a mineral, but scientists now use the term to refer to a natural substance that is not an animal or a plant. The Latin word *mina*, referring to a "mine," was the source of the English word *mineral*.

mingle
verb To combine things or people: *The guests mingled easily at the party.* **min·gle** (**ming**-guhl)
▷ *verb* **mingling, mingled**

miniature

1. *adjective* Much smaller than usual, as in *a miniature poodle.*
2. *noun* Something that is much smaller than normal, especially a copy, model, or picture: *My aunt likes to paint miniatures in her spare time.*
min·i·a·ture (**min**-ee-uh-chur)

Word History

The Italian word *miniatura* referred at first to a small picture in a book. Painters made these pictures as decorations for the first letter of a chapter. Since these paintings were small, the first meaning of **miniature** in English was "a small representation of something larger." Speakers later began using *miniature* as an adjective to mean "much smaller than the usual size." The Latin name of the mineral cinnabar, *minium*, was the source of this word, because painters used cinnabar as a pigment for making red paint.

minimal
adjective As little as possible in amount or degree: *He put forth a minimal effort to study.* **min·i·mal** (**min**-uh-muhl)

minimize
verb
1. To reduce something as much as possible, as in *to minimize our grocery costs.*
2. To remove a window from the display on a computer screen.
3. To make something seem less important or significant than it really is: *Stories about skydiving often minimize how dangerous it is.*

Minerals

Minerals are natural substances with a crystal structure. They exist in rocks and in the ground, and on some other planets. A mineral can be a single element, such as gold, or be made up of two or more elements, such as quartz. A mineral is called an ore if it is mined for the materials it contains, usually metals. A gem is a mineral that is considered beautiful or rare.

malachite

gold

pyrite

azurite

sulfur

rose quartz

min·i·mize (**min**-uh-*mize*)
▷ *verb* **minimizing, minimized**

minimum
noun The least amount or the smallest number possible: *We need a minimum of eight people to get a group discount.* **min·i·mum** (**min**-uh-muhm)
▷ *adjective* **minimum**

minion
noun A follower of an important person, who does whatever the important person tells him or her to do, as in *the king's minions.* **min·ion** (**min**-yuhn)

miniseries
noun A television production of a drama presented in separate parts, usually three to six. **min·i·ser·ies** (**min**-ee-*seer*-eez)

miniskirt
noun A very short skirt. **min·i·skirt** (**min**-ee-*skurt*)

minister

1. *noun* A person who leads religious ceremonies in a church, especially a Protestant church.
2. *noun* In certain countries, the head of a government department, as in *foreign minister.*
3. *verb* To take care of or serve someone: *This group of*

volunteers ministers to the needs of homeless people.
▷ *verb* **ministering, ministered**
min·is·ter (**min**-i-stur)

ministry *noun*
1. The work and duties of a member of the clergy; religious service: *Anthony decided to enter the ministry after college.*
2. In some countries, a government department, as in *Ministry of Health.*
min·is·try (**min**-i-stree)
▷ *adjective* **ministerial** (min-i-**steer**-ee-uhl)

mink *noun*
1. A small animal with dark brown, soft fur, often raised for its fur.
2. A coat made from this animal's fur.
mink (mingk)
▷ *noun, plural* **mink** or **minks** ▷ *adjective* **mink**

minnow *noun* A small freshwater fish, often used as bait. **min·now** (**min**-oh)

minor
1. *adjective* Not very serious or important, as in *a minor problem.*
2. *noun* A person who is under the legal adult age.
3. *adjective* A **minor** scale in music has a half step between the second and third and the fifth and sixth notes.
mi·nor (**mye**-nur)

minority *noun*
1. Less than half of a group: *A minority of the senators voted for the new law.*
2. A group of people of a particular race, ethnic group, or religion living among a larger group of a different race, ethnic group, or religion.
mi·nor·i·ty (muh-**nor**-i-tee)
▷ *noun, plural* **minorities**

minstrel *noun* A musician or reciter of poems in medieval times. **min·strel** (**min**-struhl)

mint *noun*
1. The leaves of a plant that have a strong scent and are used for flavoring.
2. A candy flavored with mint.
3. A place where coins are made. ▷ *verb* **mint**
4. (*informal*) A very large amount of money: *That house must have cost a mint.*
mint (mint)

minuend *noun* The number from which another number is subtracted. In the problem 60 – 40, 60 is the minuend. **min·u·end** (**min**-yoo-*end*)

mink

minus
1. *adjective* A **minus** sign (–) is used in a subtraction problem: *5 minus 3 equals 2, or 5 – 3 = 2.* ▷ *noun* **minus**
2. *preposition* Without: *Scott will be minus a bike while it gets fixed.*
3. *adjective* Less than zero: *We expect a temperature of minus five tomorrow.*
4. *adjective* Lower than, as in *an A minus.*
5. *noun* A disadvantage: *We have to consider the pluses and minuses of the plan.* ▷ *noun, plural* **minuses**
mi·nus (**mye**-nuhs)

minute
1. (**min**-it) *noun* A unit of time equal to 60 seconds.
2. (**min**-it) *noun* A very short time: *It will only take a minute to make a sandwich.*
3. (mye-**noot**) *adjective* Extremely small: *The garden has bugs so minute they are hard to see.* ▷ *adjective* **minuter, minutest** ▷ *adverb* **minutely**
4. minutes (**min**-its) *noun, plural* A written record of what happened in a meeting.
min·ute

minuteman *noun* A volunteer soldier in the American Revolutionary War who was ready to fight at a minute's notice. **min·ute·man** (**min**-it-*man*)
▷ *noun, plural* **minutemen**

miracle *noun*
1. An amazing act or event that has no obvious explanation.
2. An extraordinary and lucky event: *It was a miracle that no one was hurt.*
mir·a·cle (**mir**-uh-kuhl)

miraculous *adjective* By a miracle or like a miracle, as in *a miraculous escape.* **mi·rac·u·lous** (mi-**rak**-yuh-luhs) ▷ *adverb* **miraculously**

mirage *noun* Something that you think you see that is not really there, especially water. Mirages are caused by the bending of light rays by hot air. **mi·rage** (muh-**rahzh**)

Miranda
1. Miranda rights *noun, plural* The legal rights that protect a person when he or she is arrested by the police.
2. Miranda warnings *noun, plural* The things that a police officer must tell a person who is being arrested, so that the person will know what his or her rights are.
Mi·ran·da (muh-**ran**-duh)

mirror

1. *noun* A metal or glass surface that reflects a clear image of the things in front of it.

2. *noun* Something that clearly shows what another thing is like: *This story is a mirror of life in Poland during the Holocaust.*

3. *verb* To clearly show what another thing is like: *The expression on Kayla's face mirrored my feelings exactly.* ▷ *verb* **mirroring, mirrored**
mir·ror (**mir**-ur)

mirth *noun* A feeling of great amusement and joy, usually with laughter, as in *the mirth of the holiday season.* **mirth** (murth)

Prefix

The prefix **mis-** adds the following meanings to a root word: Bad, wrongly, or badly, as in *misconduct* (bad conduct), *mispronounce* (to pronounce wrongly), or *misbehave* (to behave badly).

misbehave *verb* To behave badly. **mis·be·have** (*mis*-bi-**hayv**) ▷ *verb* **misbehaving, misbehaved** ▷ *noun* **misbehavior**

miscalculate *verb* To estimate something incorrectly, or to misjudge a situation: *I miscalculated how much pizza we would need.* **mis·cal·cu·late** (mis-**kal**-kyuh-*late*) ▷ *verb* **miscalculating, miscalculated** ▷ *noun* **miscalculation**

miscarriage *noun*

1. A pregnant woman's sudden and unexpected loss of a fetus that cannot survive. ▷ *verb* **miscarry**

2. miscarriage of justice Failure of the legal system to make a good decision, especially when an innocent person is convicted of a crime.
mis·car·riage (mis-**kar**-ij *or* mis-*kar*-ij)

miscellaneous *adjective* Of varied kinds, or from different sources, as in *miscellaneous tools.*
mis·cel·la·ne·ous (*mis*-uh-*lay*-nee-uhs) ▷ *noun* **miscellany** (**mis**-uh-*lay*-nee)

mischief *noun* Playful behavior that may cause annoyance or harm to others: *Please try not to get into any mischief at Grandma's house.* **mis·chief** (**mis**-chif)

mischievous *adjective*

1. Tending to get in trouble and create mischief: *He's a mischievous boy who plays jokes on everyone.*

2. Expressing a sense of mischief: *Kara shot me a mischievous grin.*
mis·chie·vous (**mis**-chuh-vuhs) ▷ *adverb* **mischievously**

misconduct *noun* Unacceptable or dishonest behavior, especially by a professional person. **mis·con·duct** (mis-**kahn**-duhkt)

miscount *verb* To count something wrongly. **mis·count** (mis-**kount**) ▷ *verb* **miscounting, miscounted** ▷ *noun* **miscount** (**mis**-*kount*)

misdemeanor *noun* A crime, such as vandalism or trespassing, that is less serious than a felony: *Jordan was charged with a misdemeanor and fined $200.* **mis·de·mean·or** (*mis*-di-**mee**-nur)

miser *noun* A very stingy person who spends as little money as possible. **mi·ser** (**mye**-zur) ▷ *noun* **miserliness** ▷ *adjective* **miserly**

miserable *adjective*

1. Very unhappy: *I was miserable after my dog died.*

2. Depressing or uncomfortable, as in *a miserable day* or *miserable weather.*
mis·er·a·ble (**miz**-ur-uh-buhl) ▷ *adverb* **miserably**

misery *noun* Great suffering, because of poverty, pain, or sorrow: *The misery after the earthquake was heartbreaking.* **mis·er·y** (**miz**-ur-ee) ▷ *noun, plural* **miseries**

misfortune *noun*

1. An unlucky event or accident that causes trouble or disappointment: *The tornado was a great misfortune for the town.*

2. Bad luck: *She had the misfortune of losing two grandparents at a young age.*
mis·for·tune (mis-**for**-chuhn)

misgivings *noun, plural* Worries or doubts: *We had misgivings about driving during the storm.* **mis·giv·ings** (mis-**giv**-ingz)

misguided *adjective* Wrong because you have not understood or judged something correctly: *The misguided tourists thought the church was a castle.* **mis·guid·ed** (mis-**gye**-did) ▷ *adverb* **misguidedly**

mishap *noun* A small or unlucky accident: *My latest mishap was falling off my bike.* **mis·hap** (**mis**-*hap*)

mislay *verb* To lose something because you cannot remember where you put it: *Juanita mislaid her keys.* **mis·lay** (mis-**lay**) ▷ *verb* **mislaying, mislaid**

mislead *verb* To give someone the wrong idea or inaccurate information about something, usually on purpose: *He misled them into thinking they needed to pay extra fees.* **mis·lead** (mis-**leed**) ▷ *verb* **misleading, misled** (mis-**led**) ▷ *adjective* **misleading** ▷ *adverb* **misleadingly**

misplace *verb* To forget where you have put something: *Mom is always misplacing her glasses.* **mis·place** (mis-**plays**) ▷ *verb* **misplacing, misplaced** ▷ *noun* **misplacement**

misprint *noun* A mistake in printed text, such as in a book or newspaper. **mis·print** (**mis**-print) ▷ *verb* **misprint** (*mis*-**print**)

mispronounce *verb* To say a word the wrong way. **mis·pro·nounce** (*mis*-pruh-**nouns**) ▷ *verb* **mispronouncing, mispronounced** ▷ *noun* **mispronunciation** (*mis*-pruh-*nuhn*-see-**ay**-shuhn)

miss
1. *verb* To fail to hit or reach something: *The batter missed the pitch.* ▷ *noun* **miss**
2. *verb* To fail to catch, see, meet, or do something: *I missed the bus because I woke up late.*
3. *verb* To fail to attend or be present for: *I missed last week's meeting.*
4. *verb* To feel sad because you cannot see someone or do something you like: *Gail misses her brother.*
5. *verb* To avoid or to escape: *I just missed being out in the storm.*
6. To notice the absence of something: *Beth will never miss these shoes.*
7. Miss *noun* A title given to a girl or an unmarried woman. It is written before a name, as in *Miss Sanchez.*
miss (mis) ▷ *verb* **misses, missing, missed** ▷ *noun, plural* **misses** *or* **Misses**

misshapen *adjective* Twisted or bent; not having the usual shape: *Her first pottery project was a misshapen vase.* **mis·shap·en** (mis-**shay**-puhn)

missile *noun* A weapon that is aimed at a target, as in *a nuclear missile.* **mis·sile** (**mis**-uhl)

missing *adjective*
1. Not found or included, as in *missing pages.*
2. Not at home or in the usual place, as in *a missing dog.*
missing (**mis**-ing)

missiles

mission *noun*
1. An important job or task: *The charity's mission is to help people in need.*
2. A group of people who travel to do an important job: *A rescue mission was sent to help the flood victims.*
3. A church or other place where missionaries live and work.
mis·sion (**mish**-uhn)

missionary *noun* Someone who is sent to a foreign country to teach about religion and do good works. **mis·sion·ar·y** (**mish**-uh-*ner*-ee) ▷ *noun, plural* **missionaries**

Mississippi River *noun* The longest river system in the United States. It flows from northern Minnesota to the southeastern coast of Louisiana, where it empties into the Gulf of Mexico. **Mis·sis·sip·pi River** (*mis*-i-**sip**-ee)

misspell *verb* To spell something incorrectly. **mis·spell** (mis-**spel**) ▷ *verb* **misspelling, misspelled** ▷ *noun* **misspelling**

mist *noun* A cloud of tiny water droplets that hangs low in the air, like fog: *We had to drive slowly through the mist.* **mist** (mist) ▷ *verb* **mist** ▷ *adjective* **misty**

mistake
1. *noun* An error, a misunderstanding, or a misjudgment: *I made a lot of mistakes on the test and had to retake it.*
2. *verb* To believe that a person or thing is a different person or thing: *The dog mistook my slipper for a chew toy.* ▷ *verb* **mistaking, mistook, mistaken**
mis·take (mi-**stake**)

mistaken
1. *verb* The past participle of **mistake**.
2. *adjective* Based on an error or misunderstanding: *The police realized it was a case of mistaken identity and released the man.*
3. *adjective* Wrong in opinion or judgment: *I was mistaken in thinking that the money was missing.*
mis·tak·en (mi-**stay**-kuhn) ▷ *adverb* **mistakenly**

mister *noun* A title for a man. It is written **Mister** or **Mr.** before a name. **mis·ter** (**mis**-tur)

mistletoe *noun* A plant with thick leaves and white berries that grows on trees. Mistletoe is often used as a Christmas decoration. **mis·tle·toe** (**mis**-uhl-*toh*)

mistook *verb* The past tense of **mistake**. **mis·took** (mi-**stuk**)

mistreat *verb* To treat cruelly, unfairly, or unkindly, as in *to mistreat an animal.* **mis·treat** (mis-**treet**) ▷ *verb* **mistreating, mistreated** ▷ *noun* **mistreatment**

mistletoe

a b c d e f g h i j k l **m** n o p q r s t u v w x y z

mistress *noun* A woman with power or responsibility over something: *She is the mistress of her own happiness.* **mis·tress** (**mis**-tris) ▷ *noun, plural* **mistresses**

mistrust *verb* To be suspicious of someone; to have no confidence in someone: *I started to mistrust her after she had lied to me about the money.* **mis·trust** (mis-**truhst**) ▷ *verb* **mistrusting, mistrusted** ▷ *noun* **mistrust**

misunderstand *verb* To not understand something, or understand it incorrectly: *I misunderstood her instructions.* **mis·un·der·stand** (*mis*-uhn-dur-**stand**) ▷ *verb* **misunderstanding, misunderstood**

misunderstanding *noun*
1. A situation in which something is not understood correctly: *Because of a misunderstanding, I was the only one who came.*
2. A disagreement between people.
mis·un·der·stand·ing (*mis*-uhn-dur-**stan**-ding)

misuse *verb* To use something the wrong way or for the wrong purpose, as in *to misuse funds.* **mis·use** (mis-**yooz**) ▷ *verb* **misusing, misused** ▷ *noun* **misuse** (mis-**yoos**)

mite *noun*
1. A tiny animal with eight legs that is like a spider. Mites mostly live on plants and animals.
2. A small person or animal: *He was just a mite when he was young.*
3. A small amount of anything.
mite (mite)
Mite sounds like **might**.

mitt *noun*
1. A padded leather glove worn to catch a baseball.
2. (*informal*) Someone's hand: *Get your mitts off me!*
mitt (mit)

mitten *noun* A warm covering for the hand with one part for the thumb and another for the rest of the fingers. **mit·ten** (**mit**-uhn)

mix
1. *verb* To combine different things into one mass or substance: *Sarah mixed all the ingredients in a bowl.*
2. mix up *verb* To confuse someone: *Tim's instructions always mix me up.* ▷ *adjective* **mixed-up**
3. *noun* A combination of people, things, or qualities: *The library has a good mix of fiction and nonfiction.*
4. *noun* A prepared combination of ingredients for making a certain kind of food, as in *a cake mix.*
5. *noun* A version of a recording that is different in some ways from the original one, as in *a dance mix.*
mix (miks)
▷ *verb* **mixes, mixing, mixed**

mixed number *noun* A number made up of a whole number and a fraction, such as 6½.

mixture *noun* A combination of different things mixed together, as in *a spice mixture.* **mix·ture** (**miks**-chur)

mix-up *noun* A situation that is confused because a mistake has been made: *We were late to the restaurant because there was a mix-up over the reservation.* ▷ *noun, plural* **mix-ups**

ml Short for **milliliter** or the plural form *milliliters.*

mm Short for **millimeter** or the plural form *millimeters.*

moan *verb*
1. To make a long, low sound, because of sadness or pain.
2. To complain in a sad way: *"I don't want to go," Isabelle moaned.*
moan (mohn)
▷ *verb* **moaning, moaned** ▷ *noun* **moan**

moat *noun* A deep, wide ditch dug around a castle, fort, or town and filled with water to prevent enemy attacks. **moat** (moht)

mob
1. *noun* A crowd of people, especially one that is violent and may cause trouble, as in *an angry mob.*
2. *noun* Any large crowd, as in *a mob of excited teenagers.*
3. the Mob *noun* Another name for the **Mafia**.
4. *verb* To gather around in a crowd: *Fans mobbed the movie star.* ▷ *verb* **mobbing, mobbed**
mob (mahb)

mobile
1. (**moh**-buhl) *adjective* Able to move or be moved easily, as in *a mobile launch pad.*
2. (**moh**-beel) *noun* A decoration made of several items hanging from wires or threads that are balanced at different heights.
mo·bile

mobile home *noun* A small building on wheels that people can live in. **mo·bile home** (**moh**-buhl)

mobile phone *noun* A cell phone. **mo·bile phone** (**moh**-buhl)

mobility *noun*
1. The ability to move freely and easily: *Mobility was a problem after Mitch broke his leg.*
2. The ability to move from one social or economic class to another, as in *upward mobility.*
mo·bil·i·ty (moh-**bil**-i-tee)

mobilize *verb*
1. To assemble armed forces to be ready to fight, or to be assembled in this way: *After declaring war, the government mobilized the army.*
2. To organize something so that it can be used

effectively to accomplish something: *The financial crisis led the country's leader to mobilize political support for banking reform.*
mo·bil·ize (**moh**-buh-*lize*)
▷ *verb* **mobilizing, mobilized**

moccasin *noun* A flat, soft leather shoe or slipper.   **moc·ca·sin** (**mah**-kuh-sin)

Word History

English speakers heard and adopted the Native American term for a kind of soft leather shoe, first calling it a *mockasin*. Today, Native Americans are still making **moccasins**, which are often decorated with beads or porcupine quills in colorful designs.

moccasins

mock
1. *verb* To tease or laugh at someone in a mean way, especially by imitating him or her: *She mocked me for my bad pronunciation.*   ▷ *verb* **mocking, mocked**
2. *adjective* Imitation; not real, as in *a mock trial.*
mock (mahk)

mockery *noun* The act of imitating or making fun of someone or something: *Dan's mockery of her speech was really cruel.*   **mock·er·y** (**mah**-kur-ee)

mockingbird *noun* A gray-and-white songbird that imitates the calls of other birds.   **mock·ing·bird** (**mah**-king-*burd*)

mode *noun*
1. A particular way of doing something: *The bus is a cheaper mode of transportation than the train.*
2. In mathematics, the number that appears most often in a set: *In the set 3, 3, 3, 4, 4, 5, 6, 7, the mode is 3.*
mode (mohd)

model
1. *adjective* Identical but smaller, as in *a model train.*
2. *noun* A thing someone builds as an example of something larger, to see how it will work or look.
3. *adjective* Perfect or ideal, as in *a model student.*
4. *noun* A person who poses for an artist or a photographer or who wears clothing to show it to people who might want to buy it. ▷ *noun* **modeling** ▷ *verb* **model**
5. *noun* A thing or person who is a good example of something: *Katie is the model of a good student.*
6. *noun* A particular type or design of a product: *This model of camera is the easiest to use.*
mod·el (**mah**-duhl)

modem *noun* An electronic device that allows computers to exchange data, especially over a telephone line.   **mo·dem** (**moh**-duhm)

moderate
1. (**mah**-dur-it) *adjective* Not excessive or extreme, as in *moderate success.* ▷ *adverb* **moderately**
2. (**mah**-duh-*rate*) *verb* To make or become less severe or extreme: *I moderated my criticisms with some compliments.* ▷ *noun* **moderation**
3. (**mah**-dur-it) *noun* A person with opinions that are not extreme.
4. (**mah**-duh-*rate*) *verb* To lead or be in charge of a meeting, a debate, or a discussion. ▷ *noun* **moderator**
mod·er·ate
▷ *verb* **moderating, moderated**

modern *adjective*
1. Of or having to do with the present or recent times, as in *modern life.*
2. New, or having the latest technology, as in *modern computer systems.*
mod·ern (**mah**-durn)

modernize *verb* To make something more up-to-date: *We modernized the kitchen with new appliances.*   **mod·ern·ize** (**mah**-dur-*nize*) ▷ *verb* **modernizing, modernized** ▷ *noun* **modernization**

modest *adjective*
1. Not talking very much about your abilities, possessions, or achievements. ▷ *noun* **modesty**
2. Not large, showy, or expensive, as in *a modest house.*
3. Shy about showing your body: *Claire is way too modest to wear a skirt that short.*
mod·est (**mah**-dist)
▷ *adverb* **modestly**

modification *noun* A change or adjustment: *With a few modifications, my grandmother's dress will be the perfect costume for my character in the play.*   **mod·i·fi·ca·tion** (*mah*-duh-fi-**kay**-shuhn)

modifier *noun* A word that limits the meaning of another word or phrase. In the sentence "I tripped over the sleeping dog," the word *sleeping* is a modifier of the word *dog.*   **mod·i·fi·er** (**mah**-duh-*fye*-ur)

modify *verb*
1. To change something slightly in order to meet a specific need: *You can modify that recipe to make it vegetarian.*
2. To restrict the meaning of a word or phrase: *Adjectives can modify nouns.*
mod·i·fy (**mah**-duh-*fye*)
▷ *verb* **modifies, modifying, modified** ▷ *noun* **modifier**

module *noun* A separate unit that can be joined to others to make things such as machines and buildings, as in *a space module.*   **mod·ule** (**mah**-jool)

Mohammed *noun* See **Muhammad**. **Mo·ham·med** (muh-**ham**-uhd *or* muh-**hah**-muhd)

Mohawk *noun* A member of a group of Native Americans who live primarily near the Mohawk River in New York. The Mohawk are part of the Iroquois Confederation. **Mo·hawk** (**moh**-hawk) ▷ *noun,* plural **Mohawk** or **Mohawks**

Mohegan *or* **Mohican** *noun* A member of a group of Native Americans who originally lived in southeastern Connecticut. **Mo·he·gan** (moh-**hee**-guhn) or **Mo·hi·can** (moh-**hee**-kuhn) ▷ *noun,* plural **Mohegan, Mohegans** or **Mohican, Mohicans**

moist *adjective* Slightly wet: *The soil is still moist after yesterday's rain.* **moist** (moist) ▷ *adjective* **moister, moistest** ▷ *noun* **moisture** (**mois**-chur) ▷ *verb* **moisten** (**moi**-suhn)

molar *noun* One of the wide, flat teeth at the back of the mouth used for crushing and chewing food. **mo·lar** (**moh**-lur)

molasses *noun* A thick, dark, sweet syrup made when sugarcane is processed into sugar. **mo·las·ses** (muh-**las**-iz)

Word History

Molasses owes its name to the Latin word for "honey," even though it is not made from honey. When the Portuguese came to the New World and colonized the islands in the Caribbean Sea, where sugarcane is grown, they called the syrup made from sugarcane *melaço*. *Melaço* has its origins in the Latin word *mel*, meaning "honey."

mold
1. *noun* A kind of fungus that grows on old food or things that are warm and moist. ▷ *noun* **moldiness** ▷ *adjective* **moldy**
2. *verb* To shape a substance into a particular form: *Molly molded the clay into a cup.* ▷ *verb* **molding, molded**
3. *noun* A container in a particular shape that you can pour liquid into so that it sets in that shape, as in *a heart-shaped mold.* **mold** (mohld)

molding *noun* A strip of wood or other material around the edges of windows or doorways: *We are replacing all the molding around the doors.* **mold·ing** (**mohl**-ding)

mole *noun*
1. A small, furry mammal that burrows and lives underground.
2. A small, slightly raised dark spot on the skin. **mole** (mohl)

mole

molecule *noun* The smallest unit that a chemical compound can be divided into that still displays all of its chemical properties. A molecule is made up of more than one atom. **mol·e·cule** (**mah**-luh-*kyool*) ▷ *adjective* **molecular** (muh-**lek**-yuh-lur)

mollusk *noun* An animal with a soft body, no spine, and usually a hard shell that lives in water or a damp habitat: *Snails and oysters are mollusks.* **mol·lusk** (**mah**-luhsk)

molt *verb* To lose old fur, feathers, shell, or skin so that new ones can grow: *After the snakes molted, we found their skins in the woodpile.* **molt** (mohlt) ▷ *verb* **molting, molted**

Word History

A *molting* bird would probably not appreciate being called a *mutant*. Yet these two words, **molt** and *mutant*, are related. Both go back to the Latin verb meaning "to change," *mutare*. A bird losing all its feathers has certainly undergone a "change," and the different characteristics of a mutant come from a "change" in its parents' genes. The "l" is a surprise guest in the word *molt*, though. It appeared because English speakers were used to such words as *fault*, with *-lt* at the end, and they ended up saying *molt* the same way.

molten *adjective* Melted at a high temperature, usually describing metal or rock, as in *molten lava.* **mol·ten** (**mohl**-tuhn)

mom *noun* (*informal*) Mother. **mom** (mahm)

moment *noun*
1. A short time: *The sun appeared for a moment before the clouds covered it again.*
2. **at this moment** Right now. **mo·ment** (**moh**-muhnt)

momentary *adjective* Lasting only a moment: *In the momentary flash of lightning, she saw the tree clearly.* **mo·men·tar·y** (**moh**-muhn-*ter*-ee) ▷ *adverb* **momentarily** (*moh*-muhn-**ter**-uh-lee)

momentum *noun* Force or speed that something gains when it is moving: *My bike gained momentum as it sped down the hill.* **mo·men·tum** (moh-**men**-tuhm)

monarch *noun*
1. A person who rules a country, such as a king or queen.
2. A large orange-and-black butterfly.
mon·arch (**mah**-nurk)

monarchy *noun*
1. A government in which the head of state is a king or queen.
2. A country with this type of government.
mon·arch·y (**mah**-nur-kee) ▷ *noun, plural* **monarchies**

monastery *noun* A building or group of buildings where monks or nuns live and work. **mon·as·ter·y** (**mah**-nuh-*ster*-ee) ▷ *noun, plural* **monasteries** ▷ *adjective* **monastic** (muh-**nas**-tik)

Monday *noun* The second day of the week, after Sunday and before Tuesday. **Mon·day** (**muhn**-day or **muhn**-dee)

Word History

The Romans were honoring the moon when they named **Monday**. In mythology, the moon was the wife of the sun. Since the sun has his day of the week, Sunday, the moon deserved her own day, too. "Moon day" was *lunae dies* in Latin. In Old English the translation became "moon's day," and that gradually became *Monday* in modern English.

monetary *adjective* Of or having to do with money: *That necklace has no monetary value.* **mon·e·tar·y** (**mah**-ni-*ter*-ee)

money *noun* The coins and bills that people use to buy things; what you earn when you work. **mon·ey** (**muhn**-ee) ▷ *noun, plural* **moneys** or **monies**

mongoose *noun* An animal with a slender body, a long tail, and brown or black fur. Mongooses are known for killing poisonous snakes and rats. **mon·goose** (**mahn**-goos) ▷ *noun, plural* **mongooses**

mongrel *noun* A dog or other animal that is a mixture of different breeds. **mon·grel** (**mahng**-gruhl)

monitor
1. *noun* A student who is given a special job to do in the classroom, as in *a line monitor*.
2. *verb* To regularly check something over a period of time. ▷ *verb* **monitoring, monitored**

3. *noun* A person or a device that keeps track of or checks on people, machines, or a situation.
4. *noun* The visual display screen of a computer.
5. *noun* A television screen in a studio that shows or selects what is being recorded or transmitted.
mon·i·tor (**mah**-ni-tur)

monk *noun* A man who lives apart from society in a religious community according to strict rules. **monk** (muhngk)

monkey
1. *noun* An animal related to an ape, usually with a long tail.
2. *verb* To play in a silly or naughty way: *Stop monkeying around with your salad and eat it.* ▷ *verb* **monkeying, monkeyed**
mon·key (**muhng**-kee)

monkey wrench *noun* A tool that adjusts to fit different sizes of nuts and bolts.

monkey wrench

monogram *noun* A design made from two or more letters, usually someone's initials, often embroidered onto clothing or stamped onto paper. **mon·o·gram** (**mah**-nuh-*gram*) ▷ *verb* **monogram, monogramming, mongrammed** ▷ *adjective* **monogrammed**

monolingual *adjective* Speaking or using only one language: *Unlike Europeans, most Americans are monolingual.* **mon·o·lin·gual** (**mah**-nuh-**ling**-gwuhl)

monologue *noun* A long speech made by one person, usually in a play or movie. **mon·o·logue** (**mah**-nuh-*lawg*)

mononucleosis *noun* An infectious illness that gives you a sore throat, swollen glands, and a high temperature, and makes you weak for weeks or months. Also known as *mono*. **mon·o·nu·cle·o·sis** (*mah*-nuh-*noo*-klee-**oh**-sis)

monopolize *verb* To control or keep the largest part of something for yourself so it isn't shared, as in *to monopolize a conversation*. **mo·nop·o·lize** (muh-**nah**-puh-*lize*) ▷ *verb* **monopolizing, monopolized**

monopoly *noun*
1. The complete possession or control of the supply of a product or service: *The companies combined to create a monopoly in the toy industry.* ▷ *adjective* **monopolistic** (muh-*nah*-puh-**lis**-tik)
2. A group or company that has such control.
mo·nop·o·ly (muh-**nah**-puh-lee) ▷ *noun, plural* **monopolies**

monorail *noun*

1. A railroad that runs on one rail, usually high above the ground, with the train hanging from it or balanced on it.

2. A railroad track that has only one rail.

mon·o·rail (**mah**-nuh-*rayl*)

monotonous *adjective* Repetitive and boring, as in *a monotonous task*. **mo·not·o·nous** (muh-**nah**-tuh-nuhs) ▷ *noun* **monotony** ▷ *adverb* **monotonously**

monsoon *noun*

1. Very strong winds that occur in different parts of the world. In summer the winds blow from the ocean, causing heavy rains; in winter they blow toward the ocean, creating hot, dry weather.

2. The rainy summer season brought on by the monsoon.

mon·soon (mahn-**soon**)

monster

1. *noun* A large, ugly, frightening creature, usually imaginary: *The shadow looked like a giant monster.*

2. *noun* A very evil or cruel person: *The newspaper called the murderer a monster.*

3. *adjective* Huge, as in *a monster truck*.

mon·ster (**mahn**-stur)

monstrosity *noun* Something huge, frightening, ugly, or offensive: *The new shopping center is a monstrosity.* **mon·stros·i·ty** (mahn-**strah**-si-tee)

monstrous *adjective*

1. Ugly or frightening, as in *a monstrous troll*.

2. Very large.

3. Evil and shocking, as in *a monstrous killing*.

mon·strous (**mahn**-struhs)

▷ *adverb* **monstrously**

month *noun* One of the 12 parts that make up a year. **month** (muhnth) ▷ *adjective* **monthly** ▷ *adverb* **monthly**

monument *noun*

1. A statue, building, or other structure that reminds people of an event or a person, as in *a historical monument*.

2. An example of important work or a great achievement: *Einstein's theory of relativity was a monument in physics.*

mon·u·ment (**mahn**-yuh-muhnt)

monumental *adjective* Extremely important or having a lot of influence, as in *a monumental task* or *monumental significance*. **mon·u·men·tal** (mahn-yuh-**men**-tuhl) ▷ *adverb* **monumentally**

mood *noun* The way that you are feeling at a particular time; your emotional state: *I'm in a bad mood today.* **mood** (mood)

moody *adjective*

1. Upset or unhappy: *He seemed moody and wouldn't*

monsoon

join the conversation. ▷ *adverb* **moodily**

2. Having moods or feelings that change often. **mood·y** (**moo**-dee)

▷ *adjective* **moodier, moodiest** ▷ *noun* **moodiness**

moon *noun*

1. The natural satellite that moves around the earth once each month and is visible because it reflects light from the sun.

2. A natural satellite of another planet: *Astronomers keep discovering more moons around Jupiter.*

moon (moon)

moonlight

1. *noun* The light of the moon. ▷ *adjective* **moonlit**

2. *verb (informal)* To hold a second job that is usually done secretly. ▷ *verb* **moonlighting, moonlighted**

moon·light (**moon**-*lite*)

moor

1. *verb* To tie up a boat to land, to a pier, or to an anchor. ▷ *verb* **mooring, moored** ▷ *noun, plural* **moorings**

2. *noun* In the British Isles, a high, open area that is not used for farming.

moor (moor)

moose *noun* A large animal in the deer family that lives in the cold forests of North America, Europe, and Asia. **moose** (moos) **Moose** sounds like **mousse.** ▷ *noun, plural* **moose**

Word History

The **moose** got its name from Native Americans. In one Native American language of the eastern United States, the word *mus* means "he strips off the bark," because a moose strips off and eats the bark of trees. Many English words for plants and animals have come from Native American languages.

mop

1. *noun* A long stick with a sponge or cloth strips at one end, used to clean floors.

2. *verb* To clean a floor or soak up liquid with a mop, towel, or sponge: *We had to mop the floor after juice spilled everywhere.* ▷ *verb* **mopping, mopped**

3. *noun* A thick, tangled mass, as in *a mop of hair.* **mop** (mahp)

mope *verb* To feel depressed and sorry for yourself. **mope** (mope) ▷ *verb* **moping, moped**

moped *noun* A heavy bicycle with a motor. **mo·ped** (**moh**-*ped*)

Word History

In a book called *Through the Looking-Glass*, Humpty Dumpty explains to a girl named Alice that a word can be like a suitcase, with "two meanings packed up into one word." **Moped** is a word like this. It is a combination of the beginning sounds from two Swedish words: *motor*, meaning "motor," and *pedaler*, meaning "pedals," because a *moped* has both a *motor* and *pedals*.

moral

1. *adjective* Concerned with right and wrong behavior: *Deciding how to act in this situation is a moral judgment.*

2. *adjective* Fair and honest: *A moral person would never lie or cheat.*

3. morals *noun, plural* Beliefs about what is right and acceptable.

4. *noun* The lesson taught by a story or an experience. **mor·al** (**mor**-uhl) ▷ *adverb* **morally**

morale *noun* The mood or spirit of a person or group: *The campers' morale was low after the third day of rain.* **mo·rale** (muh-**ral**)

morality *noun* Principles about what is right and wrong that guide your actions: *His sense of morality would not allow him to accept money for helping the lost visitors.* **mo·ral·i·ty** (muh-**ral**-i-tee)

morbid *adjective* Unusually interested in death and unpleasant things. **mor·bid** (**mor**-bid) ▷ *adverb* **morbidly**

more

1. *adjective* Greater in number, size, amount, or degree: *Jessie did more studying than anyone else.*

2. *adjective* Additional: *I added more sugar to the batter.*

3. *adverb* To a larger extent or degree: *I like broccoli more than carrots.*

4. *adverb* In addition or again: *He came in for lunch, then went out to play more.*

5. *noun* An extra amount: *I would like more cake.*

6. *pronoun* A greater number: *More are coming than we expected.*

7. more or less Nearly or approximately: *I'm more or less ready to go.* **more** (mor)

moreover *adverb* In addition to or supporting what has already been said: *"I'm sorry I was rude," she apologized, "and moreover, I promise that it won't happen again."* **more·o·ver** (mor-**oh**-vur)

Mormon *noun* A member of the Church of Jesus Christ of Latter-day Saints, a religion founded in 1830 by Joseph Smith in Fayette, New York. **Mor·mon** (**mor**-muhn)

morning *noun* The early part of a day between midnight and noon or sunrise and noon. **morn·ing** (**mor**-ning) **Morning** sounds like **mourning**.

morning glory *noun* A climbing vine with trumpet-shaped flowers that open early in the morning and close in the afternoon. ▷ *noun, plural* **morning glories**

moron *noun* *(informal)* A very stupid person. This word is usually used as an insult: *He said I was a moron because I forgot my keys.* **mo·ron** (**mor**-ahn)

morose *adjective* Depressed and not talking very much: *Tad has been morose since he left the baseball team.* **mo·rose** (muh-**rohs**) ▷ *adverb* **morosely**

morph *verb* To change smoothly from one shape to another or into something different, especially as done by computer animation: *Suddenly, the girl morphed into an ugly witch.* **morph** (morf) ▷ *verb* **morphing, morphed**

morphine *noun* A drug used to make people calm and to help relieve severe pain. It is highly addictive and legal only for medical use. **mor·phine** (**mor**-feen)

Morse code *noun* A communication system that uses light or sound in patterns of dots and dashes to represent letters and numbers. **Morse code** (mors)

morsel *noun* A small piece of something, especially food, as in *a morsel of cheese* or *a morsel of gossip.* **mor·sel** (**mor**-suhl)

mortal

1. *adjective* Not able to live forever.

2. *adjective* Causing death or likely to cause death, as in *a mortal injury.* ▷ *adverb* **mortally**

3. *adjective* Lasting until death, as in *mortal enemies.*

4. *adjective* Very intense or extreme, as in *a mortal fear of spiders.*

5. *noun* A human being. **mor·tal** (**mor**-tuhl)

mortality *noun*

1. The state of being human and not living forever.

2. The rate at which people die of a particular cause: *Mortality from cancer has decreased over the last century.* **mor·tal·i·ty** (mor-**tal**-i-tee)

mortar *noun*
1. A mixture of lime, sand, water, and cement that is used to hold bricks and stones together.
2. A heavy, hard bowl, used with a pestle for crushing things into powder or paste, especially in cooking and pharmacy.
3. A heavy gun that fires shells or rockets high in the air. **mor·tar** (**mor**-tur)

mortgage *noun* A loan from a bank used to buy a house or other property. **mort·gage** (**mor**-gij) ▷ *verb* **mortgage**

mortuary *noun* A room or building where dead bodies are kept until they are buried or cremated. **mor·tu·ar·y** (**mor**-choo-er-ee) ▷ *noun, plural* **mortuaries**

mosaic *noun* A pattern or picture made up of small pieces of colored stone, tile, or glass. **mo·sa·ic** (moh-**zay**-ik)

Moses *noun* A prophet in the Old Testament who led the ancient Jews out of Egypt. **Mo·ses** (**moh**-zis or **moh**-ziz)

mosey *verb* (*informal*) To walk slowly or aimlessly: *We moseyed around the lobby, waiting for the movie to begin.* **mo·sey** (**moh**-zee) ▷ *verb* **moseying, moseyed**

moshing *noun* The activity of swaying, dancing, and flinging yourself around to loud music while banging into other people at a concert. **mosh·ing** (**mah**-shing) ▷ *verb* **mosh** (mahsh)

mosh pit *noun* The place in front of the stage at a concert where people mosh.

Moslem *noun* See **Muslim**. **Mos·lem** (**mahz**-lim)

mosque *noun* A building where Muslims worship. **mosque** (mahsk)

mosquito *noun* A small insect that bites animals and humans and sucks their blood. Female mosquitoes can spread diseases such as malaria and yellow fever. **mos·qui·to** (muh-**skee**-toh) ▷ *noun, plural* **mosquitoes** *or* **mosquitos**

Word History

The Latin word for a "fly," *musca*, gave us our name for the **mosquito**. *Musca* developed into *mosca* in Spanish, also meaning "fly." From this word, Spanish speakers formed the term *mosquito*, which originally meant "little fly." We now use this word to refer to a small insect that bites animals and humans, sucking their blood and often spreading disease.

moss *noun* A small, fuzzy, green plant that grows on damp soil, rocks, and tree trunks. Mosses do not have roots, flowers, or fruit, and reproduce from spores. **moss** (maws) ▷ *noun, plural* **mosses** ▷ *adjective* **mossy**

most
1. *adjective* Largest in number, amount, or degree: *Which candidate got the most votes?*
2. *adjective* The majority of: *Most people prefer sun to rain.*
3. *noun* The largest number, amount, or degree: *Two miles is the most I can run.*
4. *adverb* Very; completely: *Skiing most certainly is not easy.*
5. *adverb* To the largest degree or extent: *He is the most awful singer I have ever heard.* **most** (mohst)

mostly *adverb* Usually or mainly: *The houses on this street are mostly empty.* **most·ly** (**mohst**-lee)

motel *noun* A small hotel on a main road that provides parking next to the rooms. **mo·tel** (moh-**tel**)

moth *noun* An insect similar to a butterfly with a thicker body, a dull color, and feathery antennae. **moth** (mawth)

mother
1. *noun* A female parent of a child or animal. ▷ *noun* **motherhood** ▷ *verb* **mother**
2. *adjective* Native, as in *mother country*. **moth·er** (**muhTH**-ur)

motherboard

motherboard *noun* The main circuit board in a computer, which usually holds the computer's main processor and memory. **moth·er·board** (**muhTH**-ur-bord)

mother-in-law *noun* Your **mother-in-law** is the mother of your wife or husband. ▷ *noun, plural* **mothers-in-law**

motherly *adjective* Of, like, or typical of a mother: *She was full of motherly advice for me.* **moth·er·ly** (muhTH-ur-lee)

Mother's Day *noun* A special day for honoring mothers, celebrated on the second Sunday in May.

motion
1. *noun* The act or process of moving or the way something moves: *The dancers moved in a circular motion.*
2. *verb* To use a movement to communicate something: *The teacher motioned to Deirdre to sit down.* ▷ *verb* **motioning, motioned**
3. *noun* A formal suggestion or proposal made at a meeting or in a court of law.
mo·tion (**moh**-shuhn)

motionless *adjective* Not moving; still: *The fox crouched motionless, waiting for the chicken to come closer.* **mo·tion·less** (**moh**-shun-lis) ▷ *adverb* **motionlessly**

motion picture *noun* A formal term for **movie**.

motivate *verb* To encourage someone to do something or want to do something: *Our teacher is good at motivating us to do better.* **mo·ti·vate** (**moh**-tuh-*vate*) ▷ *verb* **motivating, motivated** ▷ *adjective* **motivated**

motivation *noun*
1. Desire to accomplish something: *The team lacked motivation and kept losing.*
2. A reason for doing something: *Earning more money was Jack's motivation for doing extra chores.* **mo·ti·va·tion** (*moh*-tuh-**vay**-shuhn)

motive *noun* A reason for doing something: *Meg's motive for practicing was her desire to win.* **mo·tive** (**moh**-tiv)

motocross *noun* A motorcycle race over rough ground. **mo·to·cross** (**moh**-tuh-*kraws*)

motor
1. *noun* A machine that provides the power to make something run or move.
2. *adjective* Of or having to do with a motor or something run by a motor, as in *motor vehicles* or *motor oil.* **mo·tor** (**moh**-tur)

motorbike *noun*
1. A bicycle that has a small motor.
2. A small or light motorcycle. **mo·tor·bike** (**moh**-tur-*bike*)

motorcade *noun* A group of cars traveling together, often to transport an important person. **mo·tor·cade** (**moh**-tur-*kade*)

motorcycle *noun* A road vehicle with two wheels and an engine. **mo·tor·cy·cle** (**moh**-tur-*sye*-kuhl)

motorist *noun* A person who drives a car or travels by car. **mo·tor·ist** (**moh**-tur-ist)

mottled *adjective* Covered with shapes of different colors in an irregular pattern: *The female mallard has a mottled brown body.* **mot·tled** (**mah**-tuhld)

motto *noun* A short sentence that states someone's beliefs, or is used as a rule for behavior: *My motto is "Honesty is the best policy."* **mot·to** (**mah**-toh) ▷ *noun, plural* **mottoes** *or* **mottos**

mound *noun*
1. A hill or a pile of something, as in *a mound of earth.* ▷ *verb* **mound**
2. A small hill for the pitcher in the middle of a baseball diamond.
mound (mound)

mount
1. *verb* To get on or to climb up, as in *to mount a horse* or *to mount the steps.*
2. *verb* To increase gradually: *Our anxiety mounted as the storm grew stronger.*
3. *verb* To put in place for display or to be examined: *We mounted the photos in silver frames.*
4. *verb* To place on a raised support: *The torches were mounted on tall poles.*
5. *noun* A horse or other animal you ride on.
6. *noun* Mountain. This word is used in place names, as in *Mount Kilimanjaro.*
mount (mount) ▷ *verb* **mounting, mounted**

mountain *noun*
1. A very large and high hill.
2. A large amount or number of something, as in *a mountain of homework.*
moun·tain (**moun**-tuhn)

mountain bike *noun* A strong bicycle with many gears, wide tires, and heavy treads designed for riding on rough ground.

mountaineer *noun* A person who climbs mountains for fun. **moun·tain·eer** (moun-tuh-**neer**) ▷ *noun* **mountaineering**

mountain lion *noun* A large, powerful wildcat that lives in the mountains of North, Central, and South America. The mountain lion is also known as a **cougar**, **puma**, or **panther**.

mountain bike

a b c d e f g h i j k l **m** n o p q r s t u v w x y z

mourn *verb* To feel and show you are sad for a death or for some other kind of loss: *Crowds gathered to mourn the opera singer's death.* **mourn** (morn)
▷ *verb* **mourning, mourned** ▷ *noun* **mourner**

mournful *adjective* Feeling, showing, or filled with grief, as in *a mournful look on her face.* **mourn·ful** (**morn**-fuhl) ▷ *adverb* **mournfully**

mourning *noun* Sadness because someone has died: *They didn't go to the party because they were still in mourning for their father.* **mourn·ing** (**mor**-ning)
Mourning sounds like **morning**.

mouse *noun*
1. A small, furry mammal with a pointed nose, small ears, and a long tail.
2. A small handheld device that you use to move the cursor on your computer screen.
mouse (mous)
▷ *noun, plural* **mice** (mise)

mousse *noun*
1. A cold dessert containing beaten egg whites and cream. Mousse is like a light and fluffy pudding.
2. A foamy substance that you use to style your hair.
mousse (moos)
Mousse sounds like **moose**.

moustache *noun See* **mustache**. **mous·tache** (muh-**stash** *or* **muhs**-tash)

mousy *adjective*
1. Dull light brown, usually used to describe hair.
2. Timid and shy; not having a strong personality: *I was a mousy child who preferred reading to sports.*
mous·y (**mou**-see)
▷ *noun* **mousiness** ▷ *adverb* **mousily**

mouth
1. (mouth) *noun* The opening in the face and the area inside the head through which people and animals eat, speak, and breathe.
2. (mouth) *noun* An opening or entrance to something, as in *the mouth of a jar* or *the mouth of a cave.*
3. (mouth) *noun* The part of a river where it joins the ocean or other large body of water.
4. (mouTH) *verb* To move your lips as if you are talking without making any sound. ▷ *verb* **mouthing, mouthed**
mouth

mouth organ *noun See* **harmonica**.

mouthpiece *noun*
1. The part of a telephone that you speak into.
2. The part of a musical instrument that you put in or near your mouth.
3. A person who speaks for an individual or a group: *We chose our most outspoken member to be the club's mouthpiece.*
mouth·piece (**mouth**-pees)

move
1. *verb* To change your place or position: *Ayumi moved to the back row.*
2. *verb* To change the place you live or work: *We are moving to Connecticut.*
3. *noun* A step or a movement: *The runner made a quick move to gain the lead.*
4. *verb* To cause someone to have strong feelings: *We were all moved by her speech.*
5. *verb* To put or keep in motion: *Cars are moved by an engine.*
6. *verb* To cause to do something: *What moved you to give him all that money?*
7. *verb* To formally make a proposal at a meeting: *I move that the budget be passed as it stands.*
8. *noun* The act or process of changing your home or job: *Tanisha is looking foward to her move to California.*
9. *noun* An action planned to achieve something: *My boss still hasn't made a move to promote me.*
10. *noun* A person's turn to change the position of a playing piece in games such as chess or checkers.
move (moov)
▷ *verb* **moving, moved** ▷ *adjective* **movable** *or* **moveable**

movement *noun*
1. The act of moving, or moving something, from one place to another: *They watched the enemy's movements carefully to avoid attack.*
2. The act of moving a part of the body: *The song was accompanied by wild hand movements.*
3. A group of people working together to promote a cause, as in *a movement for peace.*
4. One of the main sections of a long piece of classical music.
move·ment (**moov**-muhnt)

movie *noun*
1. Moving pictures, usually with sound, that tell a story, shown on a screen.
2. **movies** *noun, plural* The industry or profession of making or starring in motion pictures.
mov·ie (**moo**-vee)

moving *adjective*
1. In motion or capable of changing position: *It's more difficult to hit a moving target than a stationary one.*
2. Of or having to do with changing where you live, as in *a moving van.*
3. Triggering deep emotion or sympathy, as in *a very moving story.*
mov·ing (**moo**-ving)

mow *verb* To cut grass or other long plants, such as grain or hay. **mow** (moh) ▷ *verb* **mowing, mowed, mown** (mohn) ▷ *noun* **mower**

Movies

Movies, one of the most popular forms of entertainment today, have their roots in the photographic technology of the 19th century. Hollywood, California, became the center of the film industry in the early 1900s; and in 1927, the movie *The Jazz Singer* brought speech and singing to the silent movie era. Now special effects create new illusions in cinema, and digital recording (digital cinematography) provides an alternative to film.

movie poster for *The Jazz Singer*

cameraperson

MP3 *noun* A type of computer file that records sound. MP3 files can be played by a computer program or a device known as an *MP3 player*.

MPEG *noun* The standard electronic format for storing video in a compact space. MPEG is short for *Moving Picture Experts Group*. **MPEG** (**em**-*peg*)

mph or **m.p.h.** Short for *miles per hour*: *The speed limit on this highway is 65 mph.*

Mr. *noun* A title put in front of a man's name, as in *Mr. Stephen Jones*. **Mr.** (**mis**-ter)

Mrs. *noun* A title put in front of a married woman's name, as in *Mrs. Linda Collins*. **Mrs.** (**mis**-iz)

Ms. *noun* A title put in front of a woman's name whether she is married or unmarried, as in *Ms. Catherine Snow*. **Ms.** (miz)

much
1. *adjective* Large in amount or degree: *I have too much work to do.*
2. *adverb* Very: "*Were you annoyed by the noise?*" "*Not much.*"
3. *noun* A large amount or degree of something: *She doesn't eat very much.*
much (muhch)

mucilage *noun* A liquid glue. **mu·ci·lage** (**myoo**-suh-lij)

muck *noun* Anything that is thick and dirty, wet, sticky, or slimy, especially mud or manure. **muck** (muhk)

mucus *noun* A thick slimy liquid that coats and protects the inside of your mouth, nose, throat, and other breathing passages. **mu·cus** (**myoo**-kuhs) ▷ *adjective* **mucous** (**myoo**-kuhs)

mud *noun*
1. Wet earth that is sticky and soft.
2. **your name is mud** You are in trouble or disgrace with someone: *If you forget to bring back that library book, your name will be mud.*
mud (muhd)

muddle
1. *verb* To mix things up or put them in the wrong order: *She dropped the manuscript and the pages got all muddled up.*
2. *noun* A mess or a state of confusion: *We missed our plane and now our plans are all in a muddle.*
mud·dle (**muhd**-uhl) ▷ *adjective* **muddled**

muddy
1. *adjective* Covered with wet, soft dirt. ▷ *adjective* **muddier, muddiest**
2. *verb* To make something unclear by adding something: *Don't muddy the argument by bringing up something new.* ▷ *verb* **muddies, muddying, muddied**
mud·dy (**muhd**-ee)

muffin *noun* A small cake or bread baked in a pan with multiple cups. **muf·fin** (**muhf**-in)

muffle *verb* To make a sound quieter or less clear: *The carpet muffled our footsteps.* **muf·fle** (**muhf**-uhl) ▷ *verb* **muffling, muffled**

muffler *noun*
1. A device on a vehicle that reduces engine noise.
2. A warm scarf.
muf·fler (**muhf**-lur)

mug
1. *noun* A cup with a handle.
2. *verb* (*informal*) To attack someone violently in public and try to steal the person's money. ▷ *verb* **mugging, mugged** ▷ *noun* **mugger**
mug (muhg)

muggy *adjective* Warm and damp, as in *muggy weather*. **mug·gy** (**muhg**-ee) ▷ *adjective* **muggier, muggiest** ▷ *noun* **mugginess**

Muhammad *noun* The founder of the Islamic religion. Muslims believe that Muhammad is God's last and most important prophet. Also spelled **Mohammed**. **Mu·ham·mad** (muh-**ham**-uhd or muh-**hah**-muhd)

a
b
c
d
e
f
g
h
i
j
k
l
m
n
o
p
q
r
s
t
u
v
w
x
y
z

mulberry *noun*
1. A tree that produces dark purple berries. Mulberry leaves are sometimes used as food for silkworms.
2. The edible berry produced by this tree.
3. A dark red or purple color.
mul·ber·ry (muhl-*ber*-ee)

mule *noun* An animal whose parents are a female horse and a male donkey. **mule** (myool)

multicultural *adjective* Involving or made up of people from different countries or cultures, as in *a multicultural society*. **mul·ti·cul·tur·al** (*muhl*-ti-**kuhl**-chur-uhl) ▷ *adverb* **multiculturally**

multilingual *adjective* Using or able to speak several different languages, as in *a multilingual translator*. **mul·ti·lin·gual** (*muhl*-ti-**ling**-gwuhl)

multimedia *adjective* Using several different media at the same time, such as text, sound, and video. **mul·ti·me·di·a** (*muhl*-ti-**mee**-dee-uh) ▷ *noun* **multimedia**

multinational *adjective* Involving or operating in more than one country. **mul·ti·na·tion·al** (*muhl*-ti-**nash**-uh-nuhl) ▷ *noun* **multinational**

multiplayer
1. *adjective* Involving or requiring many players, especially in an online game: *The game is a team-based multiplayer action game based on a popular fantasy series.*
2. *noun* A multiplayer game: *They're developing a new multiplayer aimed at the young teen market.*
mul·ti·play·er (*muhl*-tee-*play*-ur)

multiple
1. *adjective* Involving many people or things: *There are multiple problems with her plan.*
2. *noun* A number that can be exactly divided by a smaller number: *Some multiples of 3 are 9, 33, and 51.*
3. *adjective* A **multiple-choice** test gives you several answers to choose from for each question.
mul·ti·ple (**muhl**-tuh-puhl)

multiple sclerosis *noun* A serious disease that damages small areas of the brain and spinal cord. It causes numbness, paralysis, and other problems in the nervous system. **multiple scle·ro·sis** (skluh-**roh**-sis)

multiplicand *noun* A number that is to be multiplied by another number. In the problem 2 × 8, 8 is the multiplicand. **mul·ti·pli·cand** (*muhl*-tuh-pli-**kand**)

multiplication
1. In math, the multiplying of numbers.
2. A **multiplication table** is a list of all the multiples of the numbers from one to twelve.
3. Growth in the number or amount of something.
mul·ti·pli·ca·tion (*noun*)

multiplier *noun* The number by which you multiply another. In the problem 2 × 8, 2 is the multiplier. **mul·ti·pli·er** (mul-tuh-*plye*-ur)

multiply *verb*
1. To add a number to itself a particular number of times: *If you multiply 3 by 4, you get 12.*
2. To increase or make something increase: *The papers on my desk keep multiplying.*
mul·ti·ply (**muhl**-tuh-*plye*)
▷ *verb* **multiplies, multiplying, multiplied**

multiracial *adjective* Made up of people of different races, as in *a multiracial neighborhood*. **mul·ti·ra·cial** (*muhl*-ti-**ray**-shuhl) ▷ *adverb* **multiracially**

multitask *verb* To do two or more things at the same time. **mul·ti·task** (*muhl*-tee-*task*)

multitude *noun*
1. A large number of people; a crowd.
2. A large or varied number of things: *The camp offers a multitude of sports and activities.*
mul·ti·tude (**muhl**-ti-*tood*)

multivitamin *noun* A pill that contains several different vitamins. **mul·ti·vi·ta·min** (*muhl*-ti-**vye**-tuh-min)

mumble *verb* To speak quietly in an unclear way: *I can't understand you when you mumble.* **mum·ble** (**muhm**-buhl) ▷ *verb* **mumbling, mumbled**

mummy *noun* A dead body that has been preserved with special chemicals and wrapped in cloth. Sometimes bodies that have been preserved accidentally, by ice or natural chemicals, are also called mummies. **mum·my** (**muhm**-ee) ▷ *noun, plural* **mummies** ▷ *verb* **mummify** (**muhm**-uh-*fye*) ▷ *adjective* **mummified**

mumps *noun, plural* An infectious illness caused by a virus that causes painful swelling of the glands around your face. **mumps** (muhmps)

munch *verb* To eat in a noisy way, especially something crunchy: *She munched on an apple.* **munch** (muhnch) ▷ *verb* **munches, munching, munched**

mundane *adjective* Ordinary and everyday: *He lived a mundane life of working, eating, and sleeping.* **mun·dane** (muhn-**dane**)

municipal *adjective* Of or having to do with a city or town and its services: *The city's municipal workers went on strike to get better pay and benefits.* **mu·nic·i·pal** (myoo-**nis**-uh-puhl)

mural *noun* A large painting done on a wall: *The city commissioned a mural for the train station.* **mu·ral** (**myoor**-uhl)

murder *verb* To kill someone deliberately. **mur·der** (**mur**-dur) ▷ *verb* **murdering, murdered** ▷ *noun* **murder** ▷ *noun* **murderer**

murky *adjective* Dark, cloudy, or dirty: *The boat sank into the murky waters of the river.* **murk·y** (**mur**-kee)
▷ *adjective* **murkier, murkiest**

murmur
1. *verb* To say something very quietly: *She spoke in a murmur so the others wouldn't hear.*
2. *verb* To make a low, continuous sound: *The leaves murmured in the breeze.*
3. *noun* Quiet, unclear speech or other sound, as in *the murmur of waves on the lake.*
4. *noun* An abnormal sound made by your heart that is sometimes a sign of disease or damage.
mur·mur (**mur**-mur)
▷ *verb* **murmuring, murmured**

muscle
1. *noun* A type of tissue in the body that can contract to produce movement. Your muscles are attached to your skeleton and pull on your bones to make them move.
2. *noun* Strength or power: *You need some muscle to be a linebacker.*
3. *verb* To accomplish something with strength: *The kids muscled the bookcase into place.* ▷ *verb* **muscling, muscled**
mus·cle (**muhs**-uhl)
Muscle sounds like **mussel**.

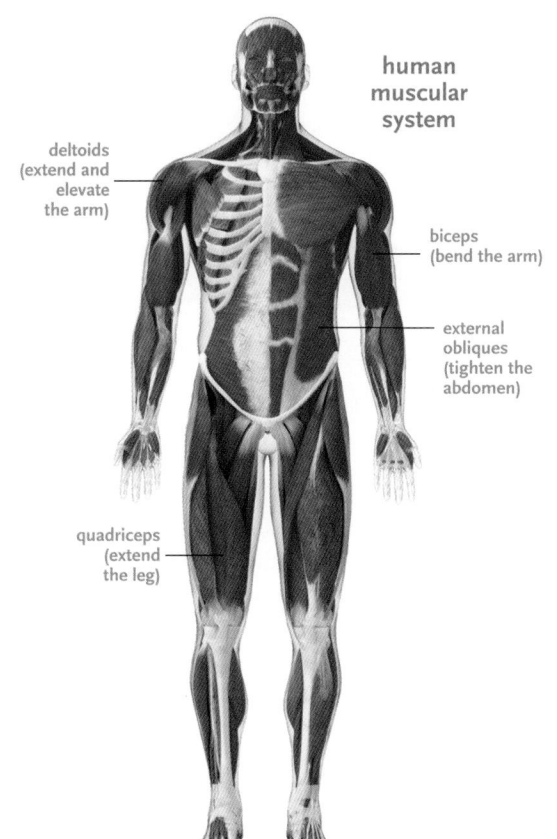

human muscular system

deltoids (extend and elevate the arm)

biceps (bend the arm)

external obliques (tighten the abdomen)

quadriceps (extend the leg)

muscular *adjective*
1. Having strong muscles: *He was muscular from years of hard physical labor.*
2. Involving a muscle or muscles, as in *a muscular contraction.*
mus·cu·lar (**muhs**-kyuh-lur)

muse *verb*
1. To think carefully or to reflect on something: *I like to muse on the events of the day and write in my journal.*
2. *noun* A person or thing, either real or imaginary, that serves as an inspiration to an artist: *The woman in the portrait was the painter's muse.*
muse (myooz)
▷ *verb* **musing, mused** ▷ *noun* **musing**

museum *noun* A place where interesting and valuable objects of art, history, or science are preserved and displayed. **mu·se·um** (myoo-**zee**-uhm)

mush *noun*
1. A thick cereal made of cornmeal boiled in water or milk.
2. A thick, soft mixture or mass: *The vegetables were overcooked and had turned to mush.* ▷ *adjective* **mushy**
mush (muhsh)

mushroom
1. *noun* A small fungus that has a short stem and a top shaped like an umbrella. Many mushrooms can be eaten, but some are poisonous.
2. *verb* To grow or spread rapidly: *We expect the business to mushroom in the coming year.* ▷ *verb* **mushrooming, mushroomed**
mush·room (**muhsh**-room)

a b c d e f g h i j k l **m** n o p q r s t u v w x y z

music *noun*
1. Sounds that are arranged in a way that is pleasant to hear, produced by voices or instruments.
2. Symbols that represent such sounds: *This page of music is easy to read.*
mu·sic (**myoo**-zik)

musical
1. *adjective* Fond of or skilled in music.
2. *adjective* Of or having to do with music, as in *musical talent.*
3. *noun* A play or movie that includes a lot of singing and dancing.
4. *adjective* Resembling music: *She speaks with a soft, musical voice.*
mu·si·cal (**myoo**-zi-kuhl)
▷ *adverb* **musically**

musical instrument *noun* An instrument for playing music, as in *a stringed musical instrument.*

musician *noun* A person who plays, sings, or writes music. **mu·si·cian** (myoo-**zish**-uhn)

musk *noun* A substance with a strong smell that is used in perfume, medicine, and soap. Musk is produced by some male deer. **musk** (muhsk)

musket *noun* A type of long gun that was used by soldiers before the rifle was invented. **mus·ket** (**muhs**-kit)

musketeer *noun* A soldier who carried a musket. **mus·ket·eer** (*muhs*-ki-**teer**)

muskrat *noun* A small rodent with webbed hind feet, a flat tail, and thick, brown fur. Muskrats live in and around water. **musk·rat** (**muhsk**-*rat*) ▷ *noun, plural* **muskrat** *or* **muskrats**

Muslim *or* **Moslem** *noun* A person whose religion is Islam. **Mus·lim** (**muhz**-lim *or* **muz**-lim) *or* **Mos·lem** (**mahz**-lim) ▷ *adjective* **Muslim** *or* **Moslem**

muslin *noun* A thin cotton cloth used to make sheets, curtains, and clothing. **mus·lin** (**muhz**-lin)

mussel *noun* A type of shellfish that has a black shell and can be eaten. **mus·sel** (**muhs**-uhl) **Mussel** sounds like **muscle.**

must
1. *verb* To have to do something: *I must get to the store before it closes.*
2. *verb* To say something is likely or certain to happen: *You must be thirsty after running home.*
3. *verb* To recommend or insist on something: *We must get together soon.*
4. *noun* Something that you need or should have: *Sturdy boots are a must for hiking.*
must (muhst)

mustache *or* **moustache** *noun* Hair that grows on a man's upper lip. **mus·tache** *or* **mous·tache** (muh-**stash** *or* **muhs**-tash)

Music

Cultures around the world have created music throughout history. Elements such as melody, harmony, and rhythm are combined to make music, which can be written using a system called notation. Classical music, which developed from medieval religious music, includes symphonies and operas. Composers expressed their feelings through music in the 1800s and experimented with clashing harmonies in the 1900s. Jazz, rock, and rap are popular styles of contemporary music.

gospel

rock

jazz

country

classical

mustang *noun* A small wild horse found mostly on the western plains of the United States. **mus·tang** (**muhs**-tang)

mustard *noun*
1. A leafy plant related to cabbage that is eaten as a vegetable in many parts of the world.
2. A yellowish, spicy paste made from the seeds of the mustard plant.
mus·tard (**muhs**-turd)

muster *verb*
1. To gather in a group, especially to prepare for a battle: *The army mustered 10,000 troops.*
2. To collect or summon: *Jackie mustered up all her courage and jumped into the freezing lake.*

3. pass muster To be adequate or acceptable: *My outfits have to pass muster with my mother before I can leave the house.*
mus·ter (**muhs**-tur)
▷ *verb* **mustering, mustered**

mustn't *contraction* A short form of *must not*.
must·n't (**muhs**-uhnt)

musty *adjective* Smelling of dampness or decay because there is no fresh air.　**must·y** (**muhs**-tee)
▷ *adjective* **mustier, mustiest** ▷ *noun* **mustiness**

mutant *noun* A living thing that is different from others of its kind because of a change in its genes: *The blue lobster is a mutant.*　**mu·tant** (**myoo**-tuhnt)

mutate *verb* (of DNA) To change in a way that results in different qualities or characteristics in an organism: *The virus mutates so fast that researchers have not been able to develop a vaccine for it.*　**mu·tate** (**myoo**-tate) ▷ *verb* **mutating, mutated** ▷ *noun* **mutation** (myoo-**tay**-shuhn)

mute
1. *adjective* Not speaking; silent: *She was mute with worry.* ▷ *adverb* **mutely**
2. *noun* A person who cannot speak.
3. *noun* A device that can be put on a musical instrument to soften its sounds. ▷ *verb* **mute**
mute (myoot)

muted *adjective*
1. Muffled or softened, as in *muted speech.*
2. Quieter or less brilliant, as in *muted colors.*
mut·ed (**myoo**-tid)

mutilate *verb* To injure or damage something or someone by disfiguring it: *Her arm was badly mutilated in the accident.*　**mu·ti·late** (**myoo**-tuh-*late*)
▷ *verb* **mutilating, mutilated** ▷ *noun* **mutilation**

mutiny *noun* A revolt against or refusal to obey authority, especially in the military: *The captain's cruelty provoked a mutiny on the ship.*　**mu·ti·ny** (**myoo**-tuh-nee) ▷ *noun, plural* **mutinies** ▷ *noun* **mutineer** (*myoo*-tuh-**neer**) ▷ *verb* **mutiny**
▷ *adjective* **mutinous** (**myoo**-tuh-nuhs)

mutt *noun* A dog that comes from several breeds; a mongrel.　**mutt** (muht)

mutter *verb* To speak in a quiet voice with the mouth almost closed, especially because you are annoyed.
mut·ter (**muht**-ur) ▷ *verb* **muttering, muttered**
▷ *noun* **mutter**

mutton *noun* The flesh of a sheep, eaten for food.
mut·ton (**muht**-uhn)

mutual *adjective* Shared or experienced by all the people involved, as in *mutual respect.*　**mu·tu·al** (**myoo**-choo-uhl) ▷ *adverb* **mutually**

muzzle *noun*
1. An animal's nose and mouth.

2. A cover you put over an animal's mouth to keep it from biting. ▷ *verb* **muzzle**
3. The open end of a gun barrel where bullets come out.
muz·zle (**muhz**-uhl)

MVP *noun* A short way of saying *most valuable player*. Being an MVP is sometimes an award or recognition in a game, tournament, or season.

my *adjective* Belonging to or having to do with me: *My homework is done.*　**my** (mye)

mynah or **myna** *noun* A dark brown Asian bird that can imitate the human voice.　**my·nah** or **my·na** (**mye**-nuh)

myriad *noun* An extremely large or uncountable number: *A myriad of stars sparkled in the sky.*　**my·ri·ad** (**mir**-ee-uhd) ▷ *adjective* **myriad**

mynah

myself *pronoun* Me and no one else: *I did all the chores by myself.*　**my·self** (**mye**-self)

mysterious *adjective* Very hard to explain or understand, as in *a mysterious occurrence*
mys·te·ri·ous (mis-**teer**-ee-uhs) ▷ *adverb* **mysteriously**

mystery *noun*
1. Something that is hard to explain or understand: *It is a mystery to me how they could have fired him.*
2. A story containing strange events or crimes that have to be solved.
mys·ter·y (**mis**-tur-ee)
▷ *noun, plural* **mysteries**

mystify *verb* To confuse someone completely: *We were mystified about the dog's disappearance.*
mys·ti·fy (**mis**-tuh-*fye*) ▷ *verb* **mystifies, mystifying, mystified** ▷ *noun* **mystification** (*mis*-tuh-fi-**kay**-shuhn)

myth *noun*
1. An old story that expresses the beliefs or history of a group of people or explains some natural event.
2. A belief held by many people that is false or does not exist: *It is a myth that touching a toad will give you warts.*
myth (mith)

mythical *adjective*
1. Found in or having to do with myths: *The mermaid is a mythical creature.*
2. Imaginary or untrue, as in *a mythical trip to Mars.*
myth·i·cal (**mith**-i-kuhl)

mythology *noun* A group of myths, especially ones that belong to a particular culture or religion.　**my·thol·o·gy** (mi-**thah**-luh-jee)
▷ *adjective* **mythological** (*mith*-uh-**lah**-ji-kuhl)

a b c d e f g h i j k l **m** n o p q r s t u v w x y z

Nn

nag

1. *verb* To keep asking someone to do something or complaining to someone in a way that is annoying: *My parents sometimes nag me about my messy room.* ▷ *verb* **nagging, nagged**

2. *noun* A horse, especially one that is old or worn-out.

nag (nag)

nail *noun*

1. A small, thin, pointed piece of metal that you force into wood with a hammer. ▷ *verb* **nail**

2. The thin, hard layer that grows on the tips of your fingers and toes.

nail (nayl)

nail

naive *or* **naïve** *adjective* Not having much experience of life or very much knowledge, and believing or trusting people too much. **na·ive** *or* **na·ïve** (nah-**eev**) ▷ *noun* **naiveté** *or* **naïveté** (nah-*eev*-**tay**) ▷ *adverb* **naively**

naked *adjective*

1. Not wearing any clothes. ▷ *noun* **nakedness** ▷ *adverb* **nakedly**

2. Bare, or without what usually covers it, as in *a naked lightbulb hanging from the ceiling.*

3. Expressed in a strong way, as in *the naked truth.*

4. Without the help of an instrument like a telescope or microscope: *It's hard to see the Milky Way with the naked eye.*

na·ked (**nay**-kid)

name

1. *noun* A word that you call a person, an animal, a place, or a thing: *What is her name?* ▷ *verb* **name**

2. *noun* A bad or mean word or phrase that you call a person: *He is not your friend if he is calling you names.*

3. *noun* The reputation or opinion that others have of someone or something: *Jaden's outbursts have given him a bad name.*

4. *verb* To say the name of someone or something: *Name your favorite animal.*

5. *verb* To choose someone for a position or job: *The coach named a new team captain.*

name (name)

▷ *verb* **naming, named**

namely *adverb* You use **namely** to let a listener or reader know that you are going to explain more or give details about something: *The letter confirmed his secret suspicion—namely, that his sister had married.* **name·ly** (**name**-lee)

nanny *noun*

1. A woman who takes care of young children as a job, especially in the children's home.

2. **nanny goat** A female goat.

nan·ny (**nan**-ee)

▷ *noun, plural* **nannies**

Prefix

The prefix **nano-** is used today to form many new words. *Nano-* at the beginning of a word tells you that it is about something that is so small that it has to be measured in units that are a billionth of the size of more ordinary units, as in *nanometer* and *nanosecond*. Special microscopes and other equipment are needed to deal with *nanoscale* objects.

---

nanotechnology *noun* Technology that attempts to harness extremely small things such as atoms and molecules. **nan·o·tech·nol·o·gy** (nan-oh-tek-**nah**-luh-jee)

nap *verb* To sleep for a short time, especially during the day: *The baby needs to nap in the afternoon.* **nap** (nap) ▷ *verb* **napping, napped** ▷ *noun* **nap**

nape *noun* The back part of your neck. **nape** (nape)

napkin *noun* A small piece of paper or cloth used to clean your hands and mouth while eating, as in *a linen napkin.* **nap·kin** (**nap**-kin)

narcissus *noun* A spring plant that has yellow or white flowers and long, thin leaves. The daffodil is a kind of narcissus. **nar·cis·sus** (nahr-**sis**-uhs) ▷ *noun, plural* **narcissuses** *or* **narcissus**

narcotic *noun* A strong drug that relieves pain or helps you relax or sleep better. **nar·cot·ic** (nahr-**kah**-tik) ▷ *adjective* **narcotic**

narrate *verb* To tell a story or speak the words in a program or documentary: *The audiobook was*

narrated by the author. **nar·rate**
(**nar**-ate) ▷ *verb* **narrating, narrated**
▷ *noun* **narration**

narrative

1. *noun* A story, or a description of events.
2. *adjective* Telling a story or describing something, as in *a narrative poem.*
nar·ra·tive (**nar**-uh-tiv)

narrator *noun* A person who tells a story. A narrator can be someone telling a story to another person, or it can be the character in a book who tells the story, as he or she experienced it or heard about it. **nar·ra·tor** (**nar**-ay-tur)

narrow *adjective*

1. Measuring a short distance from one side to the other, as in *a narrow path.* ▷ *verb* **narrow**
2. Limited, or small in amount: *The store sells only a narrow range of brands.*
3. If you have a **narrow** escape, you almost do not avoid something.
4. If you are **narrow-minded**, you do not want to listen to or understand new or different ideas or opinions.
nar·row (**nar**-oh)
▷ *adjective* **narrower, narrowest** ▷ *noun* **narrowness**
▷ *adverb* **narrowly**

nasal *adjective*

1. Of or having to do with the nose, as in *a nasal spray.*
2. Sounding as if produced through the nose instead of the mouth. *M, n,* and *ng* are nasal sounds.
na·sal (**nay**-zuhl)

nasturtium *noun* A plant with yellow, red, or orange flowers that can be eaten. **nas·tur·tium**
(nuh-**stur**-shuhm)

nasty *adjective*

1. Unkind or mean, as in *nasty comments.* ▷ *adverb* **nastily**
2. Bad or unpleasant, as in *a nasty storm.*
3. Dangerous or severe, as in *a nasty accident.*
nas·ty (**nas**-tee)
▷ *adjective* **nastier, nastiest** ▷ *noun* **nastiness**

nation *noun*

1. A country whose people share a language, culture, and history, and have the same government.
2. All the people in a certain country: *It seems like the entire nation watches the Super Bowl.*
3. A group of people who share a culture, language, or ancestry, as in *the Navajo nation.*
na·tion (**nay**-shuhn)

national *adjective* Of, having to do with, or shared by a whole nation, as in *a national anthem.* **na·tion·al**
(**nash**-uh-nuhl) ▷ *adverb* **nationally**

nasturtiums

National Guard *noun* A volunteer military organization with units in each state that are commanded by the governor.

nationalist *noun* Someone who is very proud of his or her country, or who wants it to be independent. **na·tion·al·ist**
(**nash**-uh-nuh-list) ▷ *noun* **nationalism**

nationality *noun*

1. The legal right to be a citizen of a certain country.
2. A group of people with the same language, culture, and history: *New York City is an area with many nationalities.*
na·tion·al·i·ty (*nash*-uh-**nal**-i-tee)
▷ *noun, plural* **nationalities**

national park *noun* A large section of land that is protected by the government for people to visit.

native

1. *noun* A person who was born in or lives in a particular country or place, as in *a native of Rome.*
2. *noun* An animal or a plant that lives or grows naturally in a certain place.
3. *adjective* Connected to the place where you were born or lived during the early part of your life: *Greek is my mother's native language.*
na·tive (**nay**-tiv)

National Parks

The US National Park System includes more than 390 national parks, monuments, and preserves. Grand Canyon National Park is known for its 277-mile-long gorge, reaching more than a mile deep. Yellowstone, the world's first national park, opened in 1872 and has many geysers, including Old Faithful. Yosemite National Park is famous for its granite cliffs, waterfalls, and plant and animal diversity.

Grand Canyon National Park

a b c d e f g h i j k l m **n** o p q r s t u v w x y z

Native American *noun* One of the peoples who originally lived in North, Central, or South America, or a descendant of these peoples. Native Americans are sometimes called **American Indians**. ▷ *adjective* **Native American**

Language Note

Many people now use **Native American** instead of *Indian* or *American Indian* to correct a mistake Christopher Columbus made when he named the peoples he found living in the New World. He thought he had reached the Indies, a region in Southeast Asia that includes India. The phrase *Native American* distinguishes the people who were originally living in North, Central, and South America from those who inhabited the Asian country of India. Although the words *Indian* and *American Indian* aren't old-fashioned or offensive to many Native Americans, *Native American* is used to show ethnic pride and is becoming the more commonly accepted term.

Nativity *noun* A display or scene that shows the story and place of the birth of Jesus. **Na·tiv·i·ty** (nuh-**tiv**-i-tee)

NATO *noun* An organization of countries that have agreed to give each other military help. This group includes the United States, Canada, and some countries in Europe. NATO stands for *North Atlantic Treaty Organization*. **NATO** (**nay**-toh)

natural
1. *adjective* Found in or made by nature instead of people, as in *a room with a lot of natural light.*
2. *adjective* Normal or as you would expect: *It's only natural to be tired after working all day.*
3. *adjective* Present or developing in a person from birth: *She is a natural entertainer.*
4. *adjective* Lifelike or closely following nature: *The fruit in the painting looks really natural.*
5. *adjective* Relaxed; not pretending to be different: *She spoke in a sincere and natural manner.*
6. *noun* A person who has a special talent or ability: *Marina is a natural with languages.*
7. *adjective* In music, a **natural** note is one that is not flat or sharp.
8. *adjective* In a musical score, a **natural** sign shows that the next note is natural.
nat·u·ral (**nach**-ur-uhl)

natural gas *noun* A gas that is found under the ground or the ocean. It mostly consists of methane and is used for fuel.

natural history *noun* The study of plants and animals and the places they come from.

naturalist *noun* Someone who studies plants, animals, and other living things. **na·tu·ral·ist** (**nach**-ur-uh-list)

naturalize *verb* To make someone a citizen of a country where they were not born. **nat·u·ral·ize** (**nach**-ur-uh-*lize*) ▷ *verb* **naturalizing, naturalized** ▷ *noun* **naturalization**

naturally *adverb*
1. In a natural way: *He did not seem at all nervous and spoke very naturally.*
2. Of course: *Naturally, she took the shortest route.*
nat·u·ral·ly (**nach**-ur-uh-lee)

natural resource *noun* A material produced by the earth that is necessary or useful to people. Forests, water, oil, and minerals are some natural resources.

nature *noun*
1. Things in the world, such as animals, plants, and the weather, that are not made by people.
2. The qualities or character of a person or thing: *Stories of a romantic nature don't interest me.*
na·ture (**nay**-chur)

naught *noun* Nothing: *All our efforts came to naught.* **naught** (nawt)

naughty *adjective* Badly behaved and disobedient, as in *a naughty little boy.* **naught·y** (**naw**-tee) ▷ *adjective* **naughtier, naughtiest** ▷ *noun* **naughtiness** ▷ *adverb* **naughtily**

nausea *noun* A feeling of wanting to throw up. **nau·se·a** (**naw**-zee-uh *or* **naw**-zhuh) ▷ *adjective* **nauseous** (**naw**-shuhs) ▷ *adjective* **nauseated** (**naw**-zee-*ay*-tid)

nautical
1. *adjective* Of or having to do with ships or sailing, as in *a nautical chart.*
2. nautical mile *noun* A unit that measures distance in the sea or in the air. One nautical mile equals 6,076 feet.
nau·ti·cal (**naw**-ti-kuhl)

Navajo *or* **Navaho** *noun* A member of the second-largest group of Native Americans. The Navajo live primarily in New Mexico, Arizona, and Utah. **Nav·a·jo** *or* **Nav·a·ho** (**nav**-uh-hoh) ▷ *noun, plural* **Navajo, Navajos** *or* **Navaho, Navahos**

naval *adjective* Of or having to do with the navy of a country. **na·val** (**nay**-vuhl) **Naval** sounds like **navel**.

navel *noun* The small, round hollow or raised part in the middle of your stomach where your umbilical cord used to be attached. **na·vel** (**nay**-vuhl) **Navel** sounds like **naval**.

navigate *verb*
1. To find where you are and where you need to go when you travel in a ship, an aircraft, or other vehicle.
2. To sail along or across: *We navigated the rapids in a kayak.*
nav·i·gate (**nav**-i-*gate*)

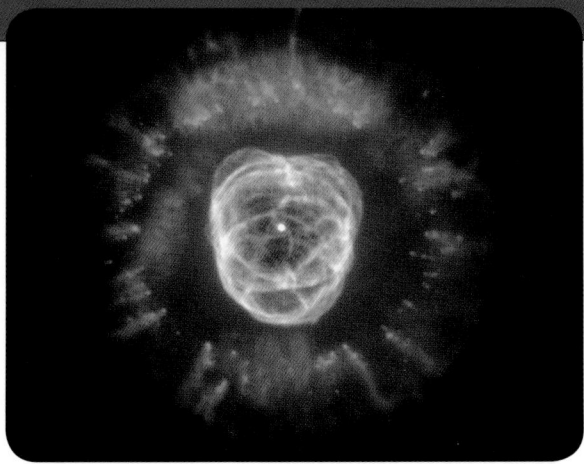

nebula

▷ *verb* **navigating, navigated** ▷ *noun* **navigation**
▷ *noun* **navigator**

navy *noun* The part of a country's military that fights at sea, including ships, aircraft, weapons, land bases, and people. **na·vy** (**nay**-vee) ▷ *noun, plural* **navies**

navy blue *noun* A dark blue color. ▷ *adjective* **navy blue**

nay *noun* A word used to say no when you are voting: *There were 65 ayes and 32 nays.* **nay** (nay) **Nay** sounds like **neigh**.

Nazi *noun*
1. A member of the political group that ruled Germany from 1933 to 1945. Led by Adolf Hitler, the Nazis killed millions of Jews, Roma, and others before and during World War II. ▷ *noun* **Nazism** (**naht**-siz-uhm)
2. nazi or **Nazi** A person who uses his or her power in a cruel way or is violently racist.
Na·zi (**naht**-see)
▷ *adjective* **Nazi** or **nazi**

near
1. *preposition* A short distance to: *Brian lives near me.*
2. *adverb* Close, or a short distance away: *Don't come near.* ▷ *adjective* **near**
3. *verb* To get closer to something: *The ship neared the shore.* ▷ *verb* **nearing, neared**
4. *adjective* Close to being something: *We had a near escape from a crash.*
5. *adjective* Closely related or similar: *My aunt is my nearest relative.*
near (neer)
▷ *noun* **nearness** ▷ *adjective, adverb* **nearer, nearest**

nearby *adjective* A short distance away, as in *a nearby street.* **near·by** (**neer-bye**) ▷ *adverb* **nearby**

nearly *adverb* Almost or not completely: *He nearly died in the accident.* **near·ly** (**neer**-lee)

nearsighted *adjective* Able to see objects clearly only if they are close to you. **near·sight·ed** (**neer**-*sye*-tid)

neat *adjective*
1. Not messy: *Mom keeps the house really neat.*
▷ *noun* **neatness**
2. Good or excellent: *It was neat how she could do a back handspring.*
neat (neet)
▷ *adjective* **neater, neatest** ▷ *adverb* **neatly**

nebula *noun* A bright area made of stars or gas and dust that can be seen in the night sky. **neb·u·la** (**neb**-yuh-luh) ▷ *noun, plural* **nebulae** (**neb**-yuh-*lee*) or **nebulas**

necessarily **not necessarily** Possibly but not always true: *That highway is not necessarily the fastest route home.* **nec·es·sar·i·ly** (*nes*-uh-**ser**-uh-lee)

necessary *adjective* If something is **necessary**, you need to do it or it needs to happen. **nec·es·sar·y** (**nes**-uh-*ser*-ee)

necessity *noun*
1. The fact that something needs to happen or be done, as in *a necessity for more food.*
2. Necessities are the things you must have and cannot live without, such as food and shelter.
ne·ces·si·ty (nuh-**ses**-i-tee)

neck *noun*
1. The part of your body between your head and your shoulders.
2. The part of a piece of clothing that goes around your neck.
3. A long, narrow part of something, as in *the neck of a bottle.*
neck (nek)

necklace *noun* A piece of jewelry you wear on your neck, as in *a bead necklace.* **neck·lace** (**nek**-lis)

necktie *noun* A long, narrow piece of cloth that wraps around the neck and hangs down in front. **neck·tie** (**nek**-*tye*)

nectar *noun* A sweet liquid from flowers that bees gather and make into honey. **nec·tar** (**nek**-tur)

nectarine *noun* A fruit like a peach but without fuzz on its skin. **nec·tar·ine** (**nek**-tuh-**reen**)

need
1. *verb* To require something because it is important or necessary: *The baby needs food every two hours.*
2. *noun* Something that you must have to survive, as in *basic needs like food and shelter.*
3. *verb* Used to show that you should or have to do something: *I need to finish my homework.*
4. *noun* Something that is necessary or required: *There is no need for you two to argue.*
5. *noun* A situation of not having enough money or food: *The soup kitchen feeds people in need.*
need (need)
Need sounds like **knead**. ▷ *verb* **needing, needed**

a
b
c
d
e
f
g
h
i
j
k
l
m
n
o
p
q
r
s
t
u
v
w
x
y
z

needle
> **1.** *noun* A small, thin piece of metal with a sharp point and a hole for thread, used for sewing.
> **2.** *noun* A long, thin piece of metal or plastic with a pointed end, used for knitting.
> **3.** *noun* A very thin, hollow piece of metal with a sharp point that is used for putting a drug into your body or taking blood.
> **4.** *noun* A pointer on a scientific instrument that shows a measurement or direction.
> **5.** *noun* A thin, pointy leaf on a pine tree.
> **6.** *verb* (*informal*) To annoy someone on purpose: *The other kids needled him about his new haircut.* ▷ *verb* **needling, needled**
> **nee·dle** (**nee**-duhl)

needle

needless *adjective* Not necessary, because it could have been avoided, as in *needless traffic accidents.* **need·less** (**need**-lis) ▷ *adverb* **needlessly**

needlework *noun* Something that is sewn or made with a needle, such as embroidery or needlepoint. **nee·dle·work** (**need**-uhl-*wurk*)

needn't *contraction* A short form of *need not*: *She needn't worry about the weather; it's supposed to be sunny all day.* **need·n't** (**need**-uhnt)

needy *adjective* Not having enough money, food, or clothes, as in *help for the needy refugees.* **need·y** (**nee**-dee) ▷ *adjective* **needier, neediest**

negative
> **1.** *adjective* Showing only the bad side of someone or something: *The article about the president was very negative.* ▷ *adverb* **negatively**
> **2.** *adjective* Damaging or bad: *Eating junk food can have a negative effect on your health.*
> **3.** *adjective* Giving no as an answer: *I asked Sophie to help me, but she gave me a negative reply.*
> **4.** *noun* Photographic film that has been developed. A negative shows light areas dark and dark areas light.
> **5.** *adjective* Less than zero in number: *Negative five plus seven equals two.*
> **6.** *adjective* Producing one of two opposite kinds of electricity.
> **7.** *adjective* Not showing that something, such as a disease, is present: *The drug tests were negative.*
> **neg·a·tive** (**neg**-uh-tiv)

neglect
> **1.** *verb* To not take care of or not pay attention to someone or something: *That plant will die if you neglect it.* ▷ *adjective* **neglectful**
> **2.** *verb* To fail or forget to do something: *She neglected to turn off the stove.*
> **3.** *noun* The failure to take care of or pay attention

to something or someone: *The yard was suffering from neglect.*
> **neg·lect** (ni-**glekt**)
> ▷ *verb* **neglecting, neglected**

negligent *adjective* Not caring or paying attention to someone or something, especially when this causes serious problems: *The driver went through the light and was found to be negligent.* **neg·li·gent** (**neg**-li-juhnt) ▷ *noun* **negligence**

negotiate *verb* To try to reach an agreement by discussing something or making a bargain: *The workers tried to negotiate with the company for better benefits.* **ne·go·ti·ate** (ni-**goh**-shee-*ate*) ▷ *verb* **negotiating, negotiated** ▷ *noun* **negotiation** ▷ *noun* **negotiator**

neigh *noun* The sound made by a horse. **neigh** (nay) **Neigh** sounds like **nay**. ▷ *verb* **neigh**

neighbor *noun*
> **1.** Someone who lives next to you or nearby.
> **2.** A person, place, or thing that is located near another: *Spain and Portugal are neighbors.*
> **3.** Any other person: *Love your neighbor.*
> **neigh·bor** (**nay**-bur)

neighborhood *noun*
> **1.** The people who live in a particular area, especially near your house: *The whole neighborhood came to our party.*
> **2.** In a city or town, a small area or section where people live, as in *an Irish American neighborhood.*
> **neigh·bor·hood** (**nay**-bur-*hud*)

neighborly *adjective* Friendly, welcoming, and helpful. **neigh·bor·ly** (**nay**-bur-lee)

neither
> **1.** *adjective* Not either: *Neither one of my parents is home.*
> **2.** *pronoun* Not one or the other of two things: *Both Chad and Ella cheated; neither ended up winning.*
> **3.** *conjunction* Nor: *My brother doesn't like broccoli, and neither do I.*
> **4.** *conjunction* Used with the conjunction *nor* to show something negative about two things or people: *Neither Josie nor Tommy is going to the game.*
> **nei·ther** (**nee**-THur or **nye**-THur)

nemesis *noun* An opponent whom you constantly struggle to defeat, often without success: *The Medford team was our nemesis—we had only beaten them once in ten seasons.* **nem·e·sis** (**nem**-uh-sis)

neon *noun* A gas that glows brightly when electricity is passed through it, used in lights and signs. **ne·on** (**nee**-ahn)

nephew *noun* The son of your brother or sister. **neph·ew** (**nef**-yoo)

Neptune *noun* The eighth planet in distance from the sun. Neptune is the fourth-largest planet in our solar system. **Nep·tune** (**nep**-toon)

nest

nerd *noun* *(slang)* A person who is very smart, but considered unfashionable or awkward, as in *a science nerd.* **nerd** (nurd) ▷ *adjective* **nerdy**

nerve *noun*
1. A **nerve** is one of the threads that sends messages between your brain and other parts of your body so you can move and feel.
2. Courage to do something difficult or dangerous: *I didn't have the nerve to go on the roller coaster.*
3. *(informal)* The quality of being bold or rude: *You've got a lot of nerve, taking my bike without asking!*
4. nerves *noun, plural* *(informal)* Feelings of being frightened or worried.
nerve (nurv)

nervous *adjective*
1. Anxious or worried about something: *I am nervous about tomorrow's test.*
2. Easily upset or tense and often worried: *His nervous mother wouldn't allow him to play on the jungle gym.*
3. Of or having to do with the nerves, as in *nervous energy.*
nerv·ous (**nur**-vuhs)
▷ *noun* **nervousness** ▷ *adverb* **nervously**

nervous system *noun* A system in the body that includes the brain, spinal cord, and nerves. In humans and animals, the nervous system controls all the feelings and actions of the body.

Suffix

The suffix **-ness** adds the following meaning to a root word: Quality or state, as in *goodness* (the quality of being good) and *happiness* (the state of being happy).

nest
1. *noun* A place built by birds and other small creatures to live in and take care of their young.
2. *verb* To make or settle in a nest or home: *Birds have nested in that tree.* ▷ *verb* **nesting, nested**
3. *noun* A comfortable place or shelter.
nest (nest)

nestle *verb* To sit or lie down in a safe and comfortable place. **nes·tle** (**nes**-uhl) ▷ *verb* **nestling, nestled**

net
1. *noun* Material made from a grid of threads or ropes with small spaces in between.
2. *noun* A bag made of this material used to catch something, such as fish or butterflies.
3. *noun* A **net amount** of money is the amount that remains after taking out taxes and expenses.
4. *noun* The **net weight** of something is its weight without its container or wrapping.
5. *noun* The **Net** is short for the **internet**.
6. *verb* To catch something in a net: *We netted five salmon on our fishing trip.*
7. *verb* To gain an amount of money as profit: *We netted more than $50 selling lemonade.*
net (net)
▷ *verb* **netting, netted**

netbook *noun* A small laptop computer that can access the internet and does most other tasks that an ordinary laptop can do, but that usually does not have as much memory as an ordinary laptop. **net·book** (**net**-buk)

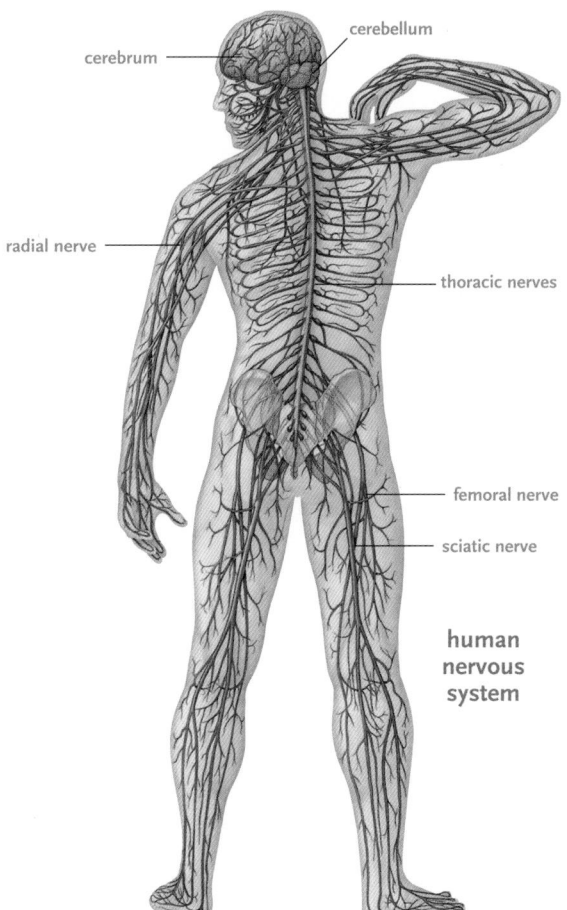

cerebellum
cerebrum
radial nerve
thoracic nerves
femoral nerve
sciatic nerve

human
nervous
system

a b c d e f g h i j k l m **n** o p q r s t u v w x y z

net neutrality *noun* A way of operating the internet so that everyone who uses it to exchange information has the same rights, and no one has the ability to block or slow down another website or company.

nettle *noun* A weed with sharp, pointed leaves, covered with hairs that sting you if you touch them. **net·tle** (**net**-uhl)

network

1. *noun* A large number of lines that cross over each other or are connected to each other, as in *a network of railroad tracks*.

2. *noun* A group of televison or radio stations in different places that broadcast the same programs at the same time.

3. *verb* To connect computers and other equipment to each other so that they can work together and share information.

4. *noun* A group of connected computers or communications equipment.

5. *noun* A group of people who share professional or social information with each other. ▷ *noun* **networking**

6. *verb* To meet and talk with people in order to get and give helpful information.

net·work (**net**-*wurk*)

▷ *verb* **networking, networked**

neurology *noun* The branch of medicine that studies and treats the nervous system, especially the diseases that affect it. **neu·rol·o·gy** (nu-**rah**-luh-jee)

▷ *adjective* **neurological** (*nur*-uh-**lah**-ji-kuhl)

neuron *noun* A cell that carries information between the brain and other parts of the body; a nerve cell. **neu·ron** (**noor**-ahn)

neuroscience *noun* The science that deals with the brain, the nervous system, and how they work. **neu·ro·sci·ence** (*noor*-oh-**sye**-uhns)

▷ *noun* **neuroscientist**

neurotoxin *noun* A toxic or poisonous substance that affects the nervous system. **neu·ro·tox·in** (**noor**-oh-*tahk*-sin)

neuter

1. *adjective* Neither masculine nor feminine.

2. *adjective* In some languages, nouns, pronouns, verbs, and adjectives that are neither masculine nor feminine in gender are **neuter**. In English, the pronoun *it* refers to neuter nouns, such as *table*.

3. *verb* To make an animal unable to produce young: *All pets that come from the shelter have already been*

neutered. ▷ *verb* **neutering, neutered**

neu·ter (**noo**-tur)

neutral

1. *adjective* Not supporting or agreeing with either side of a disagreement or competition, such as a war or a sports event: *Mom usually stays neutral when my sister and I argue.* ▷ *noun* **neutrality** (noo-**tral**-i-tee)

▷ *adverb* **neutrally**

2. *adjective* **Neutral** colors are pale and not colorful, such as beige and gray.

3. *adjective* In chemistry, a **neutral** substance is neither an acid nor a base.

4. *noun* When a car is in **neutral**, the gears cannot give power to the wheels.

neu·tral (**noo**-truhl)

neutralize *verb* To stop something from working or having an effect: *Mouthwash can neutralize bad breath.* **neu·tral·ize** (**noo**-truh-*lize*) ▷ *verb* **neutralizing, neutralized**

neutron *noun* One of the extremely small parts that form the nucleus of an atom. The neutron has no electrical charge. **neu·tron** (**noo**-trahn)

never *adverb* Not at any time or not ever: *I have never been to Japan.* **nev·er** (**nev**-ur)

nevertheless *adverb* In spite of something you have just mentioned: *She didn't study very much but she got good grades nevertheless.* **nev·er·the·less** (*nev*-ur-THuh-**les**)

new *adjective*

1. Just begun, made, or thought of: *Have you heard their new album?*

2. Already existing but seen or known for the first time: *Scientists have discovered a new planet.*

3. Unfamiliar or strange: *The teacher saw many new faces in his class.*

4. Not yet used to or experienced at: *Marla is new to skiing.*

5. Recently arrived or established in a place, position, relationship, or role: *Please try to make the new student feel welcome.*

6. Not worn or used, as in *new shoes*.

7. Repeating or beginning again, as in *a new decade*.

8. Taking the place of a previous one: *Our new babysitter is more fun than our old one.*

new (noo)

New sounds like **gnu** and **knew**.

▷ *adjective* **newer, newest**

newbie *noun* A beginner at an activity, especially in using computers or the internet. **new·bie** (**noo**-bee)

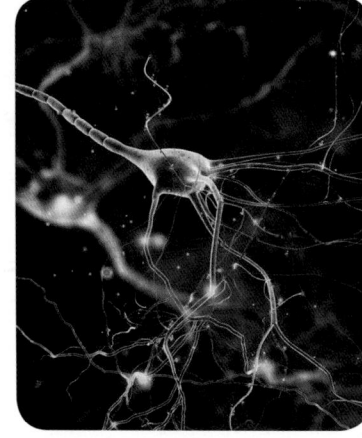

neuron

newborn *adjective* Recently born, as in *a newborn puppy.* **new·born** (**noo**-*born*) ▷ *noun* **newborn**

newcomer *noun* Someone who has just arrived in a place or started a new activity. **new·com·er** (**noo**-*kuhm*-ur)

New England *noun* A region of the northeastern United States made up of six states: Maine, New Hampshire, Vermont, Massachusetts, Rhode Island, and Connecticut. **New Eng·land** (**ing**-gluhnd) ▷ *noun* **New Englander**

newly *adverb* Recently, as in *a newly redecorated room.* **new·ly** (**noo**-lee)

new moon *noun*
The phase of the moon when it is completely dark or just after this, when it is a very thin crescent.

news *noun*
1. New information or facts about something that has happened recently: *Did you hear the news about the fire?*
2. A broadcast or story of new information about subjects that interest people.
news (nooz)

newscast *noun* A television or radio broadcast that presents the news. **news·cast** (**nooz**-kast) ▷ *noun* **newscaster**

newspaper *noun* Large, printed sheets of paper folded together that contain news reports, articles, letters, and photographs. Newspapers are usually published daily. **news·pa·per** (**nooz**-pay-pur)

newsstand *noun* A kiosk, booth, or stall where newspapers, magazines, and sometimes snacks and tobacco are sold. **news·stand** (**nooz**-stand)

newt *noun* A small salamander with short legs and a long tail that lives on land and in water. **newt** (noot)

New Testament *noun* The second section of the Christian Bible that deals with the life and teachings of Jesus Christ and his followers.

newton *noun* A unit used in physics to measure force. **new·ton** (**noo**-tuhn)

New World *noun* North and South America. European explorers used this term to compare them to Europe and places east of Europe.

New Year's Day *noun* January 1, a holiday celebrating the first day of the new year.

next
1. *adjective* Coming right after this one or the previous one, as in *the next train to Boston.*
2. *adjective* Nearest or closest: *I live on the next block.*
3. *adverb* After something else: *The bus dropped us off next.*
next (nekst)

newt

next door *adverb* In or at the nearest house, building, or room: *Grandma lives next door to us.* ▷ *adjective* **next-door**

Nez Percé *noun* A member of a group of Native Americans who live primarily in Idaho, and also in Washington and Oregon. French explorers called them Nez Percé, or "pierced nose," in error. **Nez Percé** (**nez purs**) ▷ *noun, plural* **Nez Percé** *or* **Nez Percés**

nibble *verb* To eat something by taking small bites. **nib·ble** (**nib**-uhl) ▷ *verb* **nibbling, nibbled** ▷ *noun* **nibble**

nice *adjective*
1. Pleasant or enjoyable, as in *nice weather for a picnic.*
2. Kind or friendly: *Be nice to your sister!*
3. Polite: *It isn't nice to stick out your tongue.*
4. Of good quality, as in *a nice dress.*
nice (nise)
▷ *adjective* **nicer, nicest**

Synonyms

Nice is a word used to describe someone you like or something that makes you feel good: *We had a nice time at the picnic.* The word *nice* is often used when a more specific term would be better. Here are some synonyms to help you say exactly what you mean:

- -

■ **Pleasing** and **pleasant** both mean that something is agreeable and gives pleasure to someone: *Jazz often has a pleasing effect. We love to be outdoors when there is pleasant weather.*

■ **Delightful** means that something or someone is highly pleasing: *What a delightful little girl!*

■ **Wonderful** means that something or someone is terrific or nice to an unusual degree: *Jack is the most wonderful friend you could have.*

■ **Fantastic** also describes something that is much better than just nice: *Between going to the ball game and having pizza for dinner, I had a fantastic day.*

niche *noun*
1. A place, job, or situation that suits someone very well: *Rob found his niche in computer programming.*
2. A hollow place in a wall that is often used to display a statue.
niche (nich)

nick
1. *noun* A small cut or chip on the surface or edge of something. ▷ *verb* **nick**
2. If something happens **in the nick of time**, it happens at the last moment or just in time before something bad could happen.
nick (nik)

a b c d e f g h i j k l m n o p q r s t u v w x y z

nickel *noun*

1. A hard, silver-gray metal that is added to alloys to make them strong.

2. A coin of the United States and Canada equal to five cents.

nick·el (**nik**-uhl)

nickname *noun*

1. A name for a person that friends use instead of the person's real name.

2. A familiar or shortened form of a name: *Kate is a nickname for Katherine.*

nick·name (**nik**-*name*)

▷ *verb* **nickname**

nicotine *noun* A poisonous substance in tobacco that causes people to become addicted to it. **nic·o·tine** (**nik**-uh-*teen*)

niece *noun* The daughter of your brother or sister. **niece** (nees)

night *noun* The dark time between days; the time between sunset and sunrise. **night** (nite) **Night** sounds like **knight**.

nightfall *noun* The time of day when it begins to get dark. **night·fall** (**nite**-*fawl*)

nightgown *noun* A long, loose dress that is worn in bed. Often shortened to **nightie**. **night·gown** (**nite**-*goun*)

nightingale *noun* A small brown-and-white bird. The male is known for its beautiful song. **night·in·gale** (**nye**-tin-*gale*)

nightly *adverb* Done or happening every night: *Sally calls her mother nightly.* **night·ly** (**nite**-lee)

▷ *adjective* **nightly**

nightmare *noun*

1. A frightening or unpleasant dream.

2. A difficult or frightening experience: *Parking at the mall was a nightmare.*

night·mare (**nite**-*mair*)

nighttime *noun* The time between days when it is dark, from sunset until sunrise. **night·time** (**nite**-*time*)

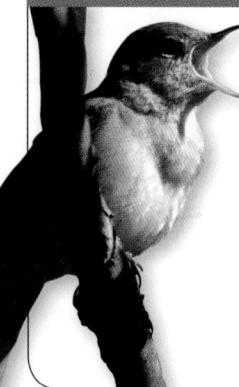

Nightingales

The nightingale is a small brown-and-white bird native to Europe and southwest Asia. It migrates to Africa in the winter. The nightingale gets its name because the male bird often sings at night, as well as during the day. Its distinctive song has inspired numerous poems, stories, and folk songs.

nimble *adjective* Able to move quickly and easily. **nim·ble** (**nim**-buhl) ▷ *adjective* **nimbler, nimblest** ▷ *adverb* **nimbly** (**nim**-blee)

ninja *noun* A person who is very skilled in Japanese martial arts, especially one hired as a spy or to kill someone. **nin·ja** (**nin**-juh) ▷ *noun, plural* **ninjas** or **ninja**

Word History

Ninjas were spies in Japan who were trained in the arts of war. Since what they did was supposed to be secret, they would wear black when working at night, or white if they went out in the snow. Ninjas were also experts at using disguises to get into an enemy castle or camp. The Japanese term *ninja* was based on the word parts *nin-*, meaning "doing quietly," and *-ja*, "person," a fitting description for a person whose work can't be seen.

nip *verb*

1. To bite or pinch quickly but not hard: *The kitten nipped my ankle.*

2. To sting or damage with cold: *The freezing air nipped my ears.*

nip (nip)

▷ *verb* **nipping, nipped** ▷ *adjective* **nippy** ▷ *noun* **nip**

nipple *noun*

1. The raised part of a breast that in females contains ducts for milk.

2. A small rubber cap with a hole, attached to the top of a baby's bottle.

nip·ple (**nip**-uhl)

nitrogen *noun* A colorless, odorless gas that makes up about four-fifths of the earth's atmosphere. **ni·tro·gen** (**nye**-truh-juhn)

nits *noun, plural* Eggs laid by lice. **nits** (nits)

no

1. *adverb* Used as a negative response to a question. *"Have you been to San Francisco?" "No, I haven't."*

2. *adverb* Not: *The newborn puppy was no larger than her hand*

3. *interjection* A word used to show surprise or disbelief: *No! I don't believe it!*

4. *adjective* Not any; not one: *There is no cake left.*

5. *adjective* Not a: *That jerk is no friend of mine.*

6. *noun* A word used to show that you do not agree: *Dad's suggestion was met with a chorus of noes.*

7. *noun* A vote of no or a voter who votes no.

no (noh)

No sounds like **know**. ▷ *noun, plural* **noes**

noble *adjective*

1. Having admirable qualities, such as courage, honesty, and generosity. ▷ *adverb* **nobly**

2. Belonging to a family that is of a very high social class. ▷ *noun* **noble** ▷ *noun* **nobleman** ▷ *noun* **noblewoman**

3. Impressive or magnificent in size or quality, as in *a noble bald eagle.*

no·ble (**noh**-buhl)
▷ *adjective* **nobler, noblest**
▷ *noun* **nobility** (noh-**bil**-i-tee)

nobody

1. *pronoun* No one: *I rang the bell, but nobody answered the door.*

2. *noun* Someone who is not thought to be important: *They treated me like I was a nobody.* ▷ *noun, plural* **nobodies**

no·bod·y (**noh**-*bah*-dee or **noh**-buh-dee)

nocturnal *adjective*

1. Happening at night, as in *nocturnal sleep.* ▷ *adverb* **nocturnally**

2. A **nocturnal** animal is active at night.

noc·tur·nal (nahk-**tur**-nuhl)

nod *verb*

1. To move your head up and down, to show that you agree or understand.

2. To let your head fall forward when you are falling asleep sitting up.

3. To indicate or say something by nodding: *She nodded at the speaker to get started.*

4. To bend or to sway: *The flowers nodded in the breeze.*

nod (nahd)
▷ *verb* **nodding, nodded** ▷ *noun* **nod**

noise *noun* A sound or sounds, especially loud or disturbing ones: *A lot of noise was coming from the playground.* **noise** (noiz)

nomad

noisy *adjective* Loud: *The party was noisy and crowded.* **nois·y** (**noi**-zee) ▷ *adjective* **noisier, noisiest** ▷ *adverb* **noisily** ▷ *noun* **noisiness**

nomad *noun*

1. A member of a community that travels from place to place instead of living in the same place all the time.

2. A person who wanders from place to place.

no·mad (**noh**-mad)
▷ *adjective* **nomadic** (noh-**mad**-ik)

nominate *verb* To suggest that someone would be a good person to do an important job or to receive an honor: *I nominated Cesar for chairman.* **nom·i·nate** (**nah**-muh-nate) ▷ *verb* **nominating, nominated** ▷ *noun* **nomination**

nominee *noun* Someone who is suggested to run in an election, to fill a job, or to receive an honor. **nom·i·nee** (*nah*-muh-**nee**)

Prefix

The prefix **non-** adds one of the following meanings to a root word:

1. Not, as in *nontoxic* (not toxic).

2. Not having or without, as in *nonsense* (not having sense) and *nonfat* (without fat).

If the root word is a proper noun, *non-* is added with a hyphen, as in *non-Catholic* (not Catholic).

none *pronoun*

1. Not one of a group of people or things: *A lot of people accepted the invitation to the party, but none of them came.*

2. Not any or no part: *None of the pumpkin pie was left.*

none (nuhn)
None sounds like **nun.**

nonetheless *adverb* Despite that: *He didn't play very well; nonetheless, he still made the team.* **none·the·less** (nuhn-THuh-**les**)

nonfiction *noun* Writing about real things, people, and events. **non·fic·tion** (nahn-**fik**-shuhn)

nonsense *noun*

1. Ideas or statements that are silly, untrue, or make no sense.

2. Behavior that is silly or annoying.

non·sense (**nahn**-*sens*)
▷ *adjective* **nonsensical**

nonstop *adjective* Without any pauses or stops, as in *a nonstop flight.* **non·stop** (**nahn**-stahp) ▷ *adverb* **nonstop**

noodle *noun* A flat strip of dried dough, usually made from flour, water, and eggs. **noo·dle** (**noo**-duhl)

nook *noun*
1. A corner or section of a room: *We ate in the breakfast nook.*
2. A small, private area or place: *We had lunch in a shady nook by the lake.* **nook** (nuk)

noon *noun* Twelve o'clock in the middle of the day. **noon** (noon)

no one *pronoun* Not anyone; not a single person: *There was no one on the train.*

noose *noun* A large loop tied in a piece of rope that closes up tightly when the rope is pulled. **noose** (noos)

nope *noun* (*informal*) No. **nope** (nohp)

nor *conjunction* And not. Often used together with *neither* to show something negative about two things or people: *Neither Judy nor Katie was able to go.* **nor** (nor)

norm *noun* An accepted standard or the usual thing: *In some corporations, it is the norm for men to wear a suit and tie.* **norm** (norm)

normal
1. *adjective* Usual or typical: *The normal time for my soccer practice is 4 p.m.*
2. *adjective* Healthy: *He has normal blood pressure.*
3. *noun* What you would expect: *My dentist appointment took longer than normal.* ▷ *noun* **normality** (nor-**mal**-i-tee) ▷ *noun* **normalcy** (**nor**-muhl-see) **nor·mal** (**nor**-muhl)

normally *adverb* Under typical conditions: *Normally I wouldn't be up this early.* **nor·mal·ly** (**nor**-muh-lee)

north
1. *noun* One of the four main points of the compass. North is the direction to your left when you face the sunrise. ▷ *adverb* **north**
2. **North** *noun* Any area or region lying in this direction.
3. **the North** *noun* In the United States, the region that is north of Maryland, the Ohio River, and Missouri, especially the states that fought against the Confederacy in the Civil War.
4. *adjective* In or having to do with the north, as in *the north shore of the lake.* ▷ *adjective* **northern** (**nor**-THuhrn) **north** (north)

North America *noun* The continent in the Western Hemisphere that includes the United States, Canada, Mexico, and Central America. **North A·mer·ic·a** (uh-**mer**-i-kuh)

North American
1. *adjective* From North America or having to do with North America.

2. *noun* Someone who was born in North America or whose parents come from there.

Northern Hemisphere *noun* The half of the earth that is north of the equator.

northern lights *noun, plural* Bright, colorful streaks of light that appear in the night sky in the far north. The northern lights are also called the **aurora borealis**.

North Pole *noun* The most northern point on earth, located at the top of the earth's axis.

North Star *noun* A bright star that is located directly over the North Pole.

northward *adverb* To or toward the north: *It got colder as we drove northward.* **north·ward** (**north**-wurd) ▷ *adjective* **northward**

noose

nose
1. *noun* The part of your face above your mouth that you use to smell and breathe.
2. *noun* The pointed front part of planes and some other aircraft.
3. *verb* To move forward slowly and carefully: *The taxi nosed its way through the rush hour traffic.* ▷ *verb* **nosing, nosed** **nose** (nohz)

nosebleed *noun* Bleeding in or from the nose. **nose·bleed** (**nohz**-bleed)

nostalgia *noun* A feeling of longing for good times in the past and wishing things hadn't changed. **nos·tal·gia** (nah-**stal**-juh)

nostalgic *adjective* Feeling sad when thinking about good times in the past and how things have changed since then. **nos·tal·gic** (nah-**stal**-jik) ▷ *adverb* **nostalgically**

nostril *noun* One of the two openings in your nose that you breathe and smell through. **nos·tril** (**nah**-struhl)

Word History

The beginning of the word **nostril** looks like the word *nose*, and sure enough, it really *is* the word *nose*. In Old English, *nose* was spelled *nosu*, and people combined it with the word *thyrel*, meaning "hole." The result was *nosthyrl*, meaning "nose hole." Later, people started pronouncing the letters *th* as *t*, giving us *nostril*.

---

nosy *adjective* Someone who is **nosy** is too interested in other people's business, especially things that do not concern them. **nos·y** (**noh**-zee) ▷ *adjective* **nosier, nosiest** ▷ *adverb* **nosily** (**noh**-zuh-lee)

not *adverb* At no time or in no way. The word *not* is used to make a statement negative: *You may not come in. It did not rain.* **not** (naht) **Not** sounds like **knot**.

notable
1. *adjective* Important, remarkable, or deserving to be noticed.
2. *noun* An important or famous person.
no·ta·ble (**noh**-tuh-buhl)

notably *adverb* In a noticeable way: *When the teacher took attendance, Will was notably absent.* **no·ta·bly** (**noh**-tuh-blee)

notation *noun*
1. A system of signs or symbols used to represent information, especially in music, math, or science.
2. A short note: *She made notations in the margins.*
no·ta·tion (noh-**tay**-shuhn)

notch *noun*
1. A V-shaped cut or nick. ▷ *verb* **notch**
2. A level or degree on a scale: *Jude did such a good job that she moved up a notch in her boss's estimation.*
notch (nahch)
▷ *noun, plural* **notches**

note
1. *noun* A short message or letter: *Dad left a note saying there was leftover pizza in the fridge.*
2. *noun* A word, phrase, or short sentence you write down to help you remember something: *I took notes in class.*
3. *noun* A short comment in a book or article that gives more information: *There is a note about the author at the end of the essay.*
4. *noun* A quality in someone's voice or in music that suggests a feeling or mood: *There was a note of sadness in his voice.*
5. *noun* A piece of paper money, as in *a bank note.*
6. *noun* A musical sound, or the symbol that represents it.
7. *verb* To notice or pay attention to something: *Drew noted that Zac was not back yet.*
8. *verb* To write something down so you do not forget it: *I noted your information in my address book.*
9. *verb* To mention something important: *Mr. Brill noted that the school doors would be locked on Saturday.*
note (note)
▷ *verb* **noting, noted**

notebook *noun*
1. A small book of blank or lined pages used for writing.
2. A small computer that is easy to carry.
note·book (**note**-buk)

noted *adjective* Famous or distinguished: *The city invited a noted singer to open the Fourth of July celebration.* **not·ed** (**noh**-tid)

notepad *noun* A pad of paper for writing notes on.
note·pad (**note**-pad)

nothing
1. *pronoun* Not anything: *There was nothing in the bag.*
2. *pronoun* Not anything important or interesting: *I did nothing all weekend.*
3. *noun* Zero, as in *a score of five to nothing.*
noth·ing (**nuhth**-ing)

notice
1. *verb* To see or become aware of something: *Did you notice what color she was wearing?* ▷ *verb* **noticing, noticed** ▷ *adjective* **noticeable** ▷ *adverb* **noticeably**
2. *noun* Attention or knowledge: *They escaped notice by crawling through the bushes.*
3. *noun* A printed paper giving information, especially one that is in a public place.
4. *noun* A warning or an announcement: *The tornado hit without any notice.*
5. If someone **gives notice**, the person tells his or her employer that he or she will be leaving that job soon.
no·tice (**noh**-tis)

notify *verb* To tell someone about something officially or formally. **no·ti·fy** (**noh**-tuh-*fye*) ▷ *verb* **notifies, notifying, notified** ▷ *noun* **notification**

notion *noun*
1. An idea or something you believe: *I don't have any notion why he would leave so quickly.*
2. A sudden desire to do something: *I had a notion to go on a picnic.*
no·tion (**noh**-shun)

notorious *adjective* Widely known for being bad or doing something bad: *The neighbors are notorious for their loud parties.* **no·to·ri·ous** (noh-**tor**-ee-uhs)

noun *noun* A word that names a person, place, or thing. The words *cat, Miami,* and *goodness* are all nouns. **noun** (noun)

nourish *verb* To keep a person or an animal strong and healthy by feeding them. **nour·ish** (**nur**-ish) ▷ *verb* **nourishes, nourishing, nourished** ▷ *noun* **nourishment** ▷ *adjective* **nourishing**

novel
1. *noun* A book that tells a made-up story about people and events. ▷ *noun* **novelist**
2. *adjective* New and different, as in *a novel idea.*
nov·el (**nah**-vuhl)

notebooks

a b c d e f g h i j k l m **n** o p q r s t u v w x y z

novelty *noun* Something new, different, and interesting: *Computers were a novelty in the 1970s.*
nov·el·ty (**nah**-vuhl-tee) ▷ *noun, plural* **novelties**
▷ *adjective* **novelty**

November *noun* The 11th month on the calendar, after October and before December. November has 30 days. **No·vem·ber** (noh-**vem**-bur)

Word History

November got its name from the Latin word *novem*, meaning "nine." November might seem like an odd name for the 11th month of the year. November started out as the ninth month, but then the ancient Romans changed their calendar. They decided to keep some of the old names, even though the months' positions on the calendar had changed.

novice *noun*
1. A beginner or someone who is not very experienced in a job or activity: *Ginny is a novice with the sewing machine.*
2. A beginner in a religious community who is training to become a monk or a nun.
nov·ice (**nah**-vis)

now
1. *adverb* At the present time: *I'd rather not discuss this now.*
2. *adverb* Right away; from this moment on: *Please take care of it now.*
3. *adverb* In the recent past: *He arrived just now.*
4. *noun* The present time: *Now is the time to make a decision.*
5. *conjunction* Since: *Things aren't the same now that you're gone.*
now (nou)

nowadays *adverb* At the present time, as compared to the past: *Kids don't play as much outside nowadays.*
now·a·days (**nou**-uh-*days*)

nowhere
1. *adverb* Not in or to any place: *There was nowhere to hide.*
2. *noun* An unknown or unimportant place or state of being: *That storm just came out of nowhere!*
no·where (noh-*wair*)

nozzle *noun* A short tube or opening on a hose or pipe that controls the flow of liquid, gas, or air. **noz·zle** (**nah**-zuhl)

nuclear
1. *adjective* Of or having to do with the nucleus of an atom or cell.
2. *adjective* Of or having to do with the energy created by splitting atoms.
3. nuclear energy *noun* Energy created by splitting atoms.
4. nuclear power *noun* Power created by splitting atoms.
5. nuclear reactor *noun* A large device in a power station that produces nuclear power.
6. nuclear weapon *noun* A weapon that uses the power created by splitting atoms.
nu·cle·ar (**noo**-klee-ur)

nucleus *noun*
1. A central part around which other things are grouped or located: *The nucleus of the city was the financial district.*
2. The central part of an atom that is made up of neutrons and protons.
3. The central part of a cell that contains the chromosomes.
nu·cle·us (**noo**-klee-uhs)
▷ *noun, plural* **nuclei** (**noo**-klee-*eye*)

nude
1. *adjective* Not wearing any clothes. ▷ *noun* **nudist**
▷ *noun* **nudity** (**noo**-di-tee)
2. *noun* A naked human figure in a work of art, such as a sculpture or painting.
nude (nood)

nudge *verb* To push someone or something gently, especially with the elbow. **nudge** (nuhj) ▷ *verb*
nudging, nudged ▷ *noun* **nudge**

nugget *noun*
1. A small lump of something, especially precious metal, as in *a nugget of gold.*
2. A small bit of something, as in *a nugget of wisdom.*
nug·get (**nuhg**-it)

nuisance *noun* Someone or something that is annoying and causes problems: *The barking dogs next door are a real nuisance.* **nui·sance** (**noo**-suhns)

numb *adjective*
1. Not able to feel anything: *My ears are numb with cold.*
2. Stunned; not able to react: *Jennifer went numb when she was told about the accident.*
numb (nuhm)
▷ *noun* **numbness** ▷ *verb* **numb**

number
1. *noun* A word or symbol used for counting and for adding and subtracting; a numeral. *See the Numbers Table in the* **Reference Section**.
2. *verb* To give a number to something in a set or list: *The pages were numbered from 1 to 40.*
3. *verb* To make up a particular number: *The fans in the stadium numbered more than 10,000.*
4. *noun* A number that is used to identify someone or something, as in *a cell phone number.*
5. *noun* A large amount or group: *A number of sandwiches were on the menu.*
num·ber (**nuhm**-bur)
▷ *verb* **numbering, numbered**

numeral *noun* A sign or symbol that represents a number, such as 8 or VIII. **nu·mer·al** (**noo**-mur-uhl)

numerator *noun* In fractions, the **numerator** is the number above the line. The numerator shows how many parts of the denominator are taken: *In the fraction ⅖, the numerator is 2.* **nu·mer·a·tor** (noo-muh-**ray**-tur)

numerical *adjective* Relating to or expressed with numbers, as in *listed in numerical order.* **nu·mer·i·cal** (noo-**mer**-i-kuhl) ▷ *adverb* **numerically**

numeric keypad *noun* The small keypad on the right side of most computer keyboards that consists mainly of number keys.

numerous *adjective* Many, or made up of a large number: *Evan owns numerous video games.* **nu·mer·ous** (**noo**-mur-uhs)

nun *noun* A woman who lives in a religious community of women and has devoted her life to God. **nun** (nuhn) **Nun** sounds like **none**.

nurse
1. *noun* Someone whose job is taking care of people who are sick or injured, usually in a hospital.
2. *verb* To take care of someone who is sick or injured: *We nursed my grandmother back to health.*
3. *verb* To feed a baby milk from a breast.
4. *verb* To treat with care or attention, as in *to nurse a plant.*
nurse (nurs) ▷ *verb* **nursing, nursed**

nursery *noun*
1. A baby's bedroom.
2. A place that sells trees, plants, and seeds.
3. **nursery rhyme** A short poem, especially for very young children.
4. **nursery school** A school for children aged three to five years old, before they go to kindergarten.
nurs·er·y (**nur**-sur-ee) ▷ *noun, plural* **nurseries**

nursing home *noun* A place where old or disabled people live and are cared for, because they cannot take care of themselves.

nurture *verb* To protect and take care of something or someone while they are growing, especially a child: *Jay's kindergarten teacher really nurtured her students.* **nur·ture** (**nur**-chur) ▷ *verb* **nurturing, nurtured**

nut *noun*
1. A small fruit or seed from a tree, with a hard shell and softer parts inside.

nutcracker

2. The inside part of a nut that can be eaten.
3. A small piece of metal with a hole in the middle that screws on to a bolt and holds it in place.
4. A strange or silly person: *Stop acting like a nut!*
5. Someone who is very enthusiastic about something, as in *a rock climbing nut.*
nut (nuht) ▷ *adjective* **nutty**

nutcracker *noun* A tool for cracking nuts open. **nut·crack·er** (**nuht**-krak-ur)

nuthatch *noun* A small bird that eats insects and can climb down trees headfirst. **nut·hatch** (**nuht**-hach)

nutmeg *noun* A spice used in cooking that is made from the ground-up seeds of a tropical tree. **nut·meg** (**nuht**-meg)

nutrient *noun* A substance such as a protein, a mineral, or a vitamin that is needed by people, animals, and plants to stay strong and healthy. **nu·tri·ent** (**noo**-tree-uhnt)

nutrition *noun*
1. Something that nourishes: *Look for information about nutrition on the label.*
2. The process by which the body changes food into living tissues.
nu·tri·tion (noo-**trish**-uhn) ▷ *adjective* **nutritional**

nutritious *adjective* Containing substances that help you stay healthy and strong, as in *a nutritious breakfast.* **nu·tri·tious** (noo-**trish**-uhs) ▷ *adverb* **nutritiously**

nuzzle *verb*
1. To rub or touch with the nose or mouth as an animal does: *The horse nuzzled my neck.*
2. To lie very close to someone or something.
nuz·zle (**nuhz**-uhl) ▷ *verb* **nuzzling, nuzzled**

nylon *noun*
1. A strong artificial fiber used to make things such as clothing, carpets, and rope.
2. **nylons** *noun, plural* Women's stockings made from nylon.
ny·lon (**nye**-lahn)

nymph *noun*
1. In ancient Greek and Roman stories, a beautiful female spirit or goddess who lived in a forest, a meadow, a mountain, or a stream.
2. A young form of an insect, such as a grasshopper, that changes into an adult by shedding its skin many times.
nymph (nimf)

Oo

About O The shape of the letter **O** probably started as a drawing of a human eye, with a center dot for the pupil. In the Phoenician alphabet, the letter had become a circle and no longer had the dot. The Greeks made the letter a vowel to represent the *o* sound. In English, the vowel can be long, as in *home*, or short, as in *shop*, and it can produce different sounds if it is paired with other vowels.

oak *noun* A tree that produces acorns and a very hard wood used in building houses and making furniture. **oak** (ohk)

oak

oar *noun* A long, usually wooden pole with a flat blade at one end, used for rowing or steering a boat. **oar** (or) **Oar** sounds like **or** and **ore**.

oasis *noun* A place in a desert where water can be found above the ground and where plants and trees can grow. **o·a·sis** (oh-**ay**-sis) ▷ *noun, plural* **oases** (oh-**ay**-seez)

oat *noun* The grain from a kind of grass plant used as food for humans and animals. **oat** (oht)

oath *noun* A solemn, formal promise or declaration: *The witness took an oath to tell the truth in court.* **oath** (ohth)

oatmeal *noun*
1. Meal made from oats that have been ground or rolled flat.
2. A hot cereal made from oats.
oat·meal (oht-*meel*)

Obamacare *noun* The US health care system that started with the Affordable Care Act in 2010. It is nicknamed Obamacare after then president Barack Obama. **Oba·ma·care** (oh-**bah**-muh-*kair*)

obedient *adjective* If you are **obedient**, you do what you are told, or are willing to follow orders. **o·be·di·ent** (oh-**bee**-dee-uhnt) ▷ *noun* **obedience** ▷ *adverb* **obediently**

obese *adjective* Extremely fat, in a way that is not healthy. **o·bese** (oh-**bees**) ▷ *noun* **obesity** (oh-**bee**-si-tee)

obey *verb*
1. To do what you are told to do: *Kayla always obeys her father.*
2. To carry out or to follow orders or instructions, as in *to obey the law.*
o·bey (oh-**bay**)
▷ *verb* **obeying, obeyed**

object
1. (**ahb**-jikt) *noun* A thing that takes up space and can be seen or touched: *Several objects were on display.*
2. (**ahb**-jikt) *noun* A person or thing that someone pays attention to, discusses, or thinks about: *His new painting was the object of much criticism.*
3. (**ahb**-jikt) *noun* Something that you are trying to achieve: *The object of the game is to get as many runs as possible.*
4. (**ahb**-jikt) *noun* The **object** or **direct object** of a verb is the noun or pronoun that is affected by the action of the verb. In the sentence "Billy hit the ball," the noun *ball* is the object of the verb *hit*. The **indirect object** of a verb is the noun or pronoun that the action is done for or to. In "Mona gave her an apple," *her* is the indirect object.
5. (uhb-**jekt**) *verb* If you **object** to something, you don't like it or don't agree with it: *Charlie objected to his early curfew.* ▷ *verb* **objecting, objected** ▷ *noun* **objector**
ob·ject

objection *noun* An expression or a feeling of not liking or not approving of something: *His objection was that it was too late to do anything.* **ob·jec·tion** (uhb-**jek**-shuhn)

objectionable *adjective* Unpleasant or offensive to others, as in *objectionable song lyrics.* **ob·jec·tion·a·ble** (uhb-**jek**-shuh-nuh-buhl)

objective
1. *noun* A goal or something you are trying to achieve: *Our objective is to upgrade all the computers.*
2. *adjective* Based on or influenced by facts, instead of opinions or feelings; fair: *Judges must try to be objective.* ▷ *noun* **objectivity** (ahb-juhk-**tiv**-i-tee)

▷ *adverb* **objectively**
ob·jec·tive (uhb-**jek**-tiv)

obligate *verb* To force someone do something because of a law, contract, or promise: *The player's contract obligates him to stay on the team for two years.* **ob·li·gate** (**ahb**-li-*gate*) ▷ *verb* **obligating, obligated**

obligation *noun* Something you have to do because it is your duty or you have promised: *All workers have the obligation to pay taxes.* **ob·li·ga·tion** (*ahb*-li-**gay**-shuhn) ▷ *adjective* **obligatory** (uh-**blig**-uh-*tor*-ee)

oblige *verb*
1. If you are **obliged** to do something, you must do it because it is a law or responsibility: *I felt obliged to replace the window I broke.*
2. To do something to help or please someone by doing a favor: *Our neighbor obliged us by driving us home when our car broke down.*
o·blige (uh-**blije**)
▷ *verb* **obliging, obliged** ▷ *adjective* **obliging**
▷ *adverb* **obligingly**

obliterate *verb* To destroy or cover something completely, so that nothing remains or can be seen. **o·blit·er·ate** (uh-**blit**-uh-*rate*) ▷ *verb* **obliterating, obliterated**

oblong *adjective* Having a shape that is longer than it is wide: *Cucumbers have an oblong shape.* **ob·long** (**ahb**-*lawng*) ▷ *noun* **oblong**

obnoxious *adjective* Very unpleasant or annoying in a way that offends people, as in *an obnoxious comedian.* **ob·nox·ious** (uhb-**nahk**-shuhs) ▷ *adverb* **obnoxiously**

oboe *noun* A long, thin woodwind instrument with a double-reed mouthpiece. An oboe makes a high, sweet sound. **o·boe** (**oh**-boh) ▷ *noun* **oboist** (**oh**-boh-ist)

obscene *adjective* Offensive or vulgar, as in *obscene language* or *obscene gestures.* **ob·scene** (ahb-**seen**) ▷ *noun* **obscenity** (ahb-**sen**-i-tee) ▷ *adverb* **obscenely**

obscure
1. *adjective* Not well known, or not yet discovered: *She is doing research on obscure medieval music.* ▷ *noun* **obscurity**
2. *adjective* Difficult to understand: *Calculus is usually too obscure for sixth graders to grasp.*
3. *verb* To hide from view: *The snow obscured our footprints.* ▷ *verb* **obscuring, obscured**
ob·scure (ahb-**skyoor**)

observant *adjective*
1. Able to pay close attention and notice things quickly.
2. Adhering strictly to the rules of a religion.
ob·serv·ant (uhb-**zur**-vuhnt)

observation *noun*
1. The act of watching someone or something carefully, especially to learn something: *The suspect is under observation by the FBI.*
2. Something that you have noticed by watching carefully: *We made observations about fish on our field trip to the aquarium.*
3. A remark: *Mrs. Lowry made an observation about his bad behavior.*
ob·ser·va·tion (*ahb*-zur-**vay**-shuhn)

observatory *noun* A special building that has telescopes or other instruments for studying the stars and the weather: *Scientists discovered a new moon from the observatory.* **ob·serv·a·to·ry** (uhb-**zur**-vuh-*tor*-ee) ▷ *noun, plural* **observatories**

observatory

observe *verb*
1. To watch someone or something closely, especially to learn something: *We observed the birds in our yard.*
2. To notice someone or something: *I observed that the butterfly had spots on its wings.*
3. To make a comment: *Mom observed that it was getting late and that we should come inside.*
4. To follow or to obey: *If you do not observe the speed limit, you may get a ticket.*
5. To celebrate: *Martin Luther King Jr. Day is observed on the third Monday of January.*
ob·serve (uhb-**zurv**)
▷ *verb* **observing, observed** ▷ *noun* **observer**
▷ *noun* **observance**

obsess *verb* If something **obsesses** you, you are constantly talking or thinking about it: *She is obsessed with that actor.* **ob·sess** (uhb-**ses**)
▷ *verb* **obsesses, obsessing, obsessed** ▷ *noun* **obsession** ▷ *adjective* **obsessive**

obsolete *adjective* Out-of-date; no longer made or used because something new has been invented: *My old computer is now obsolete.* **ob·so·lete** (*ahb*-suh-**leet**)

obstacle *noun* Something that makes it difficult to do or achieve something: *The traffic was an obstacle to arriving on time.* **ob·sta·cle** (**ahb**-stuh-kuhl)

obstinate *adjective* If someone is **obstinate**, the person is stubborn and refuses to change his or her mind or behavior. **ob·sti·nate** (**ahb**-stuh-nit) ▷ *noun* **obstinacy** ▷ *adverb* **obstinately**

oboe

a
b
c
d
e
f
g
h
i
j
k
l
m
n
o
p
q
r
s
t
u
v
w
x
y
z

Oceans

Oceans support thousands of species of animals and plants. A tiny organism called plankton is one of the most common, and many sea animals feed on it. Some plankton are like plants on land: They use chlorophyll to create food and produce oxygen through photosynthesis. More than 70 percent of the world's surface is covered by ocean and sea waters. Waves, currents, and tides keep these waters in constant motion. The two largest oceans are the Pacific and the Atlantic.

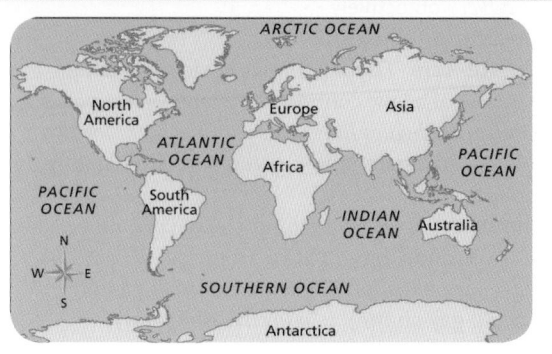

obstruct *verb*

1. To block a road or passage: *The snow drifts obstructed the driveway.*

2. To get in the way of: *The standing fans were obstructing our view of the field.*

3. To slow down the progress of something or prevent it from happening: *The protesters attempted to obstruct the destruction of the forest.*

ob·struct (uhb-**struhkt**)

▷ *verb* **obstructing, obstructed** ▷ *noun* **obstruction**
▷ *adjective* **obstructive**

obtain *verb* To get something, especially after making an effort: *Julio obtained the information from the internet.* **obtain** (uhb-**tayn**) ▷ *verb* **obtaining, obtained**

obtuse *adjective*

1. If someone is **obtuse**, he or she is slow or not willing to understand something: *I'm not trying to be obtuse—I really don't understand the equation.*

2. An **obtuse** angle is more than 90 degrees and less than 180 degrees.

ob·tuse (uhb-**toos**)

obvious *adjective* If something is **obvious**, you can see or understand it easily: *It was obvious that Chelsea was unhappy.* **ob·vi·ous** (**ahb**-vee-uhs) ▷ *adverb* **obviously**

occasion *noun*

1. A time when something takes place: *I have met Ramón on several occasions.*

2. A special event or celebration: *The birth of a baby is a happy occasion.*

oc·ca·sion (uh-**kay**-zhuhn)

occasional *adjective* Happening sometimes but not often: *We made occasional trips to the beach over the course of the summer.* **oc·ca·sion·al** (uh-**kay** zhuh-nuhl) ▷ *adverb* **occasionally**

occupant *noun* A person who occupies a place: *The occupants of the apartment building were given a month to leave.* **oc·cu·pant** (**ahk**-yuh-puhnt)

occupation *noun*

1. A job or profession: *His occupation was physical*

therapist, but skiing was his passion. ▷ *adjective* **occupational**

2. The invasion and control of a country or an area by a foreign army: *The enemy's occupation of the village lasted two years.*

oc·cu·pa·tion (*ahk*-yuh-**pay**-shuhn)

occupy *verb*

1. To live or work in a place: *Two companies occupy this office.* ▷ *noun* **occupier**

2. To fill or use a space or an amount of time: *Soccer occupies all of my free time.*

3. If an army **occupies** a country or an area, it enters and takes control of it by force.

4. To fill up time or keep yourself busy: *The children were occupied all evening by the jigsaw puzzle.*

oc·cu·py (**ahk**-yuh-*pye*)

▷ *verb* **occupies, occupying, occupied**

occur *verb*

1. To take place; to happen.

2. If something **occurs to you**, it comes into your mind suddenly.

oc·cur (uh-**kur**)

▷ *verb* **occurring, occurred**

occurrence *noun* Something that happens: *Bad air quality is a common occurrence here in the summer.* **oc·cur·rence** (uh-**kur**-uhns)

ocean *noun*

1. The mass of saltwater that covers about 71 percent of the earth's surface.

2. One of the five main parts of this mass of water.

o·cean (**oh**-shuhn)

oceanography *noun* The scientific study of the ocean and the plants and animals that live in it. **o·cean·og·ra·phy** (*oh*-shuh-**nah**-gruh-fee) ▷ *noun* **oceanographer**

ocelot *noun* A wildcat with spotted fur. The ocelot lives in the southwestern United States, Central America, and parts of South America. **oce·lot** (**ah**-suh-*laht*)

o'clock *adverb* Used to say what hour it is: *It's five o'clock.* **o'clock** (uh-**klahk**)

octagon *noun* A flat shape with eight sides and eight angles. **oc·ta·gon** (**ahk**-tuh-*gahn*) ▷ *adjective* **octagonal** (ahk-**tag**-uh-nuhl)

octagon

octahedron *noun* A solid shape with eight surfaces that are usually triangles. **oc·ta·he·dron** (*ahk*-tuh-**hee**-druhn)

octave *noun* The eight-note difference on a musical scale between two notes with the same name. **oc·tave** (**ahk**-tiv)

October *noun* The tenth month on the calendar, after September and before November. October has 31 days. **Oc·to·ber** (ahk-**toh**-bur)

Word History

October is another month whose name is misleading. October was the eighth month on the ancient Roman calendar, getting its name from *octo*, which is Latin for "eight." When the Romans adopted a new calendar, October became the tenth month.

octopus *noun* A sea creature with a soft body and eight long arms, or tentacles, with suckers that it uses to move along the ocean bottom and catch its prey. **oc·to·pus** (**ahk**-tuh-pus) ▷ *noun, plural* **octopuses** or **octopi** (**ahk**-tuh-*pye*)

Word History

When the Greeks gave the **octopus** its name, they called it *oktopous*, or "the creature with eight feet." They might more properly have called it *oktobrach*, or "the creature with eight arms."

odd *adjective*
1. Strange, unusual, or hard to explain: *The car was making an odd noise, and I discovered it had a flat tire.* ▷ *adjective* **odder, oddest** ▷ *adverb* **oddly**
2. An **odd** number cannot be divided evenly by two; it will always have a remainder of one: *Five and 17 are odd numbers.*
3. Not with the pair or set that something matches or belongs to, as in *an odd mitten.*
4. Not frequent or regular: *I only make the odd mistake on my quizzes.*
odd (ahd)

oddity *noun* A person or thing that seems unusual or strange: *The platypus is an oddity in the animal kingdom.* **odd·i·ty** (**ah**-di-tee)

odds *noun, plural* The chances that something is likely to happen: *The odds are high that we will not win today.* **odds** (ahdz)

odds and ends *noun, plural*
1. Small items that are not part of a set, as in *a drawer full of odds and ends.*
2. Small jobs to be done: *I have some odds and ends to do this weekend.*

ode *noun* A long poem that praises a person or thing or celebrates an event. **ode** (ohd)

odor *noun* A smell, especially a bad one. **o·dor** (**oh**-dur)

of *preposition*
1. Belonging to: *She is a friend of mine.*
2. Made with, as in *a ring of silver.*
3. Named or called, as in *the city of Atlanta.*
4. Containing or holding, as in *a glass of milk.*
5. Before or until: *It is ten minutes of six.*
6. About or concerning: *I thought of you yesterday.*
of (uhv *or* ahv)

off
1. *preposition* Away from: *Please get your feet off the couch.*
2. *adverb* Away from a place: *They went off down the street.*
3. *adverb* Not turned on or not operating: *Frank turned off the lights.*
4. *adverb* In the future: *Our vacation is just a week off.*
5. *adjective* Not at work: *Mom is off for a week.*
6. *adjective* Not as good as usual: *His game was off after the injury.*
7. *adjective* Not correct: *His time estimate was off by several hours.*
off (awf)

offend *verb* To make someone feel upset or angry: *He offended me with his critical comments.* **of·fend** (uh-**fend**) ▷ *verb* **offending, offended**

offender *noun* A criminal or someone who commits an offense. **of·fend·er** (uh-**fen**-dur)

offense
1. (uh-**fens**) *noun* Something that breaks a law or rule; a crime.
2. (uh-**fens**) If you **cause offense**, you hurt or insult someone: *I'm sorry—I didn't mean to cause offense when I laughed.*
3. (uh-**fens**) If you **take offense**, you feel hurt or insulted by something that someone has done or said: *Grandma takes offense at bad language.*
4. (**aw**-fens) *noun* In sports, the team or part of a team that is attacking or trying to score.
of·fense

a
b
c
d
e
f
g
h
i
j
k
l
m
n
o
p
q
r
s
t
u
v
w
x
y
z

offensive

1. *adjective* Causing upset or hurt feelings, as in *offensive language.*

2. *adjective* Unpleasant or disgusting, as in *an offensive smell.*

3. *noun* An attack, especially by armed forces.

4. *adjective* Aggressive or attacking: *The soldiers had no choice but to take offensive action.*

of·fen·sive (uh-**fen**-siv)

offer *verb*

1. To present something to someone that he or she might want, or to make something available: *Can I offer you a cup of coffee?*

2. To express that you are willing to do something: *I offered to help her with her homework.*

3. To suggest something: *They offered no explanation for their behavior.*

of·fer (**aw**-fur)

▷ *verb* **offering, offered** ▷ *noun* **offer**

offhand *adjective* Showing little thought, interest, or preparation, as in *an offhand comment.* **off·hand** (**awf**-hand) ▷ *adverb* **offhand**

office *noun*

1. A room or building in which people work at desks or business is conducted.

2. An important position of authority or power: *She is running for the office of mayor.*

3. The people who work in an office: *Most of the office came in late today.*

of·fice (**aw**-fis)

officer *noun*

1. Someone who is in charge or holds a position of authority, especially in the armed forces or the police.

2. Someone who has a responsible position in a club or similar group.

of·fi·cer (**aw**-fi-sur)

official

1. *adjective* Of or having to do with someone in a position of authority: *There will be an official investigation into the cause of the fire.* ▷ *adverb* **officially**

2. *noun* Someone who is in an important position or public office, as in *a government official.*

3. *noun* In sports, the person who enforces the rules of the game, such as the referee or umpire.

of·fi·cial (uh-**fish**-uhl)

officer

offline

1. *adjective* Not controlled by or directly connected to a computer or the internet: *All of these documents are stored in an offline archive.*

2. *adverb* While not connected to a computer or the internet: *You can download the files and then work on them offline.*

off·line (**awf**-line)

off-putting *adjective* Annoying or disturbing, in a way that makes you dislike something: *Her constant chatting is really off-putting.*

offset *verb* To cancel out, or to make up for: *You can offset your carbon footprint by recycling.* **off·set** (**awf**-set) ▷ *verb* **offsetting, offset**

offshoot *noun*

1. A new stem that grows from the main stem of a plant.

2. Something that develops or grows from something else: *The café is an offshoot of the restaurant next door.*

off·shoot (**awf**-shoot)

offside *adjective* In football, soccer, or hockey, in an illegal position ahead of the ball or puck. **off·side** (**awf**-side)

offspring *noun* The young of an animal or a human being. **off·spring** (**awf**-spring) ▷ *noun, plural* **offspring**

often *adverb* Frequently: *We often go to the movies.* **of·ten** (**aw**-fuhn)

ogre *noun*

1. A cruel giant or monster in stories, that eats human beings.

2. A person who is cruel or scary: *Jessica used to think her neighbor was an ogre, but he is just grumpy.*

o·gre (**oh**-gur)

oh *interjection* A word used to express emotion such as surprise, disappointment, fear, or pain. **oh** (oh) **Oh** sounds like **owe**.

ohm *noun* A unit for measuring resistance to the flow of electricity through a substance. **ohm** (ohm)

oil

1. *noun* A thick, greasy liquid that burns easily and does not mix with water. ▷ *adjective* **oily**

2. *verb* To smear, polish, or put oil on something: *You should oil your bike before you put it away.* ▷ *verb* **oiling, oiled**

3. *noun* A paint that is used by an artist and contains oil.

oil (oil)

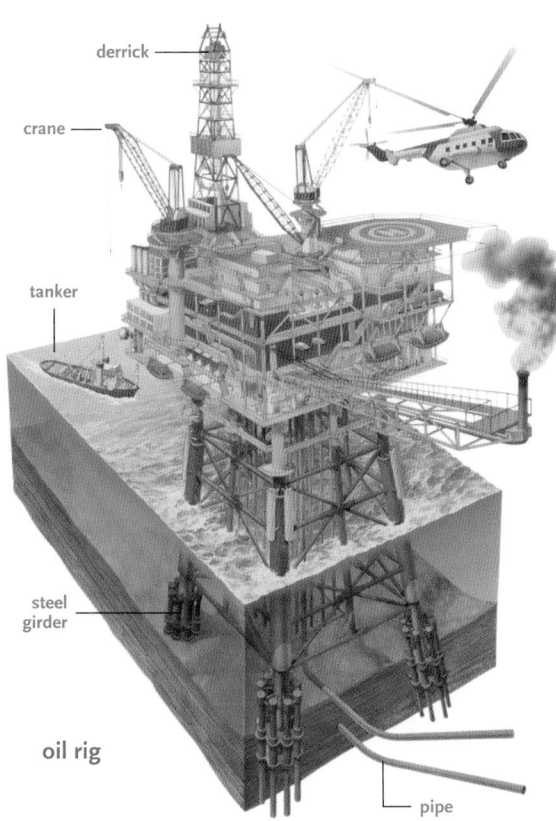

oil rig

oil rig *noun* A large platform that is built above the sea as a base for drilling for oil under the ocean floor.

ointment *noun* A thick, oily substance used to heal or protect the skin. **oint·ment** (**oint**-muhnt)

Ojibwa *noun* A member of a group of Native Americans who settled near the western Great Lakes in the United States and Canada. The Ojibwa are also called the **Chippewa**. **O·jib·wa** (oh-**jib**-way) ▷ *noun, plural* **Ojibwa** *or* **Ojibwas**

OK *or* **okay**

1. *adjective* All right; acceptable but not very good: *My day was OK, but could have been better.*

2. *verb* If you **OK** something, you agree to it or allow it to happen. ▷ *verb* **OKing, OKed**

3. *noun* Permission or approval: *I hope Dad will give his OK to our trip.*

OK *or* **o·kay** (oh-**kay**)

okra

okra *noun* A tall plant whose long seedpods are eaten as a vegetable. **ok·ra** (**oh**-kruh)

old *adjective*

1. Having lived for a long time.

2. Existing or used for a long time, as in *an old chair.*

3. Of a particular age: *He is 12 years old.*

4. Worn out by a lot of use: *We need to throw out that old rug.*

5. Former, or from a time past: *I miss my old school.*

old (ohld)

▷ *adjective* **older, oldest**

Synonyms

Old means not young or new and can refer to people, animals, things, or ideas: *The old car rattled down the street.*

- -

■ **Elderly** refers to people who are old: *My elderly great-grandfather is 90.*

■ **Antique** refers to objects that are old and usually have retained or increased their value over time: *My grandparents have a lot of antique furniture.*

■ **Ancient** describes something that occurred in or survived from the distant past: *We are studying the ancient civilizations of Greece and Rome.*

■ **Obsolete** describes an object or a practice that is out-of-date and has been replaced by something more modern: *My computer is only four years old, but it's already obsolete.*

olden days *noun, plural* A time long ago: *In the olden days, people rode in carriages pulled by horses.* **old·en days** (**ohl**-duhn)

Old English *noun* The English language that was spoken before the 12th century.

old-fashioned *adjective*

1. Outdated or no longer fashionable: *That hairstyle looks really old-fashioned.*

2. Attached to or keeping the ways, ideas, or customs of an earlier time, as in *old-fashioned values.*

old-fash·ioned (**fash**-uhnd)

Old Testament *noun* A collection of writings that makes up the Jewish Bible and the first part of the Christian Bible.

Old World *noun* Europe, Asia, and Africa. They are called by this name usually in comparison with North and South America, known as the New World.

olive *noun* The small, black or green fruit of a Mediterranean evergreen tree. Olives are eaten whole or crushed for their oil. **ol·ive** (**ah**-liv)

olive oil *noun* A yellow or green oil that is made by crushing olives. It is used for cooking and as a salad dressing.

Olympic Games *noun, plural* A competition for athletes from all over the world. The Olympic Games are held every two years, alternating summer and winter sports. Also called the *Olympics*. **O·lym·pic Games** (uh-**lim**-pik)

omelet *or* **omelette** *noun* Beaten eggs that have been cooked in a pan, filled with cheese, vegetables, or meat, and folded over. **om·e·let** *or* **om·e·lette** (**ahm**-lit *or* **ah**-muh-lit)

omen *noun* A sign or warning about your luck in the future: *Seeing a black cat was thought to be a bad omen.* **o·men** (**oh**-muhn)

OMG *noun* A short way of saying *oh my god,* usually as an expression of surprise. People use OMG because it is short and also because they can avoid saying *god,* which some people may find offensive when it is used informally.

ominous *adjective* Threatening or making you feel that something bad is going to happen, as in *an ominous black cloud* or *an ominous silence.* **om·i·nous** (**ah**-muh-nuhs) ▷ *adverb* **ominously**

omit *verb* To leave something out or fail to do something: *I omitted Nate's name from the list by mistake.* **omit** (oh-**mit**) ▷ *verb* **omitting, omitted** ▷ *noun* **omission** (oh-**mish**-uhn)

omnivore *noun* An animal or person that eats both plants and meat. Pigs and chickens are omnivores. **om·ni·vore** (**ahm**-nuh-*vor*) ▷ *adjective* **omnivorous** (ahm-**niv**-ur-uhs)

on
1. *preposition* Over and supported by: *The book is on the shelf.*
2. *preposition* Next to and touching: *Pin the poster on the wall.*
3. *preposition* During a day or date: *There is no practice on Saturday.*
4. *preposition* In the direction of: *The sugar is in the cabinet on your left.*
5. *preposition* In a state of: *The store is on fire!*
6. *preposition* Using: *I go to school on the bus.*
7. *preposition* About: *I'm looking for a book on bears.*
8. *adverb* In contact with or covering something: *Put on your shoes.*
9. *adverb* Into use: *Please turn the computer on.*
10. *adverb* Forward in time or space: *Read on for the exciting conclusion!*
11. *adjective* In operation: *Is the oven still on?*
on (awn *or* ahn)

once
1. *adverb* For one time only: *I've only had the flu once.*
2. *adverb* In the past; formerly: *This part of the peninsula was once underwater.*
3. *conjunction* As soon as something has happened: *You'll feel better once you get some sleep.*
4. **at once** *adverb* Immediately or at the same time: *They all tried to speak at once.*
once (wuhns)

oncoming *adjective* Coming nearer or toward you, as in *an oncoming truck.* **on·com·ing** (**awn**-*kuhm*-ing)

one
1. *noun* See the Numbers Table in the **Reference Section**.
2. *noun* A single thing: *One slice is enough.*
3. *adjective* Single or alone: *We only need one car.*
4. *adjective* Some: *One day I'll be rich and famous.*
5. *pronoun* A certain person or thing: *I can't find one of my gloves.*
6. *pronoun* Any person: *One should be able to see how serious this is.*
one (wuhn)
One sounds like **won**.

one-sided *adjective*
1. Showing only one side of a situation, or favoring one side: *The newspaper has been accused of one-sided reporting.*
2. Not equal or balanced: *The game was very one-sided; we lost 9 to 1.*
one-sid·ed (**sye**-did)

Olympic Games

The modern Olympic Games were first held in 1896, inspired by athletic competitions that occurred in ancient Greece. Amateur athletes from many countries compete for medals. The Summer Games include sports such as track and field, and they alternate every two years with the Winter Games, which include skiing and ice-skating.

one-way *adjective* Allowing travel in only one direction, as in *a one-way street* or *a one-way ticket.*

ongoing *adjective* If something is **ongoing**, it is still in progress or developing: *The ongoing rivalry between my brothers creates a lot of trouble at home.* **on·go·ing** (**awn**-goh-ing)

onion *noun* A round vegetable with many layers that is known for its strong smell and taste. **on·ion** (**uhn**-yuhn)

Word History

The word **onion** comes from the Latin word *unio*, which means "oneness" or "union." If you cut an onion in half, you'll find out why. This vegetable is a "union" of many different layers. Throughout history, the onion has been a symbol of strength. Civil War general Ulysses S. Grant once refused to move his troops until he received a shipment of onions to keep his soldiers strong.

online *adjective* Connected to or controlled by a central computer or a system of computers and modems, as in *an online database.* **on·line** (**awn**-line) ▷ *adverb* **online**

only
1. *adverb* No one or nothing except; just: *There are only a few people who can do that job.*
2. *adjective* Alone of its or their kind: *I was the only one waiting there when the doors opened.*
3. *conjunction* Except that: *I would have been here on time, only I ran into traffic.*
4. *noun* An **only child** is one who has no brothers or sisters.
on·ly (**ohn**-lee)

onomatopoeia *noun* The use of a word that sounds like the thing or action it describes: *"Buzz" and "sizzle" are examples of onomatopoeia.* **on·o·mat·o·poe·ia** (ah-nuh-*mat*-uh-**pee**-uh) ▷ *adjective* **onomatopoeic** (ah-nuh-*mat*-uh-**pee**-ik) *or* **onomatopoetic** (ah-nuh-*mat*-uh-poh-**et**-ik)

onset *noun* The beginning or start of something: *Bears start hibernating at the onset of winter.* **on·set** (**awn**-set)

onto *preposition* To a place or position on or upon: *She stepped up onto the bus.* **on·to** (**awn**-too *or* **awn**-tuh)

onward *or* **onwards** *adverb* Ahead or in a forward direction, as in *from 2009 onward.* **on·ward** (**awn**-wurd) *or* **on·wards** (**awn**-wurdz) ▷ *adjective* **onward**

ooze
1. *verb* To flow or seep out slowly: *Chocolate sauce oozed out from under the lid.* ▷ *verb* **oozing, oozed**
2. *noun* Very soft mud, usually found underwater in a pond or stream.
ooze (ooz)

opal *noun* A precious stone that shows different colors when you move it in the light. **o·pal** (**oh**-puhl)

opaque *adjective* Not clear enough to let light through; not transparent: *The window was opaque with paint.* **o·paque** (oh-**pake**)

open
1. *adjective* Not shut, closed, or fastened, as in *an open window* or *an open carton of milk.* ▷ *verb* **open**
2. *adjective* Exposed; not covered or protected, as in *open country.*
3. *adjective* If a company or store is **open**, people are working there and you can do business: *The supermarket is open until 10 p.m. every night.*
4. *adjective* If you are **open** about something, you are willing to talk about it honestly. ▷ *noun* **openness** ▷ *adverb* **openly**
5. *adjective* Not limited or restricted to only a few, as in *an open meeting of the board.*
6. *adjective* If a computer file is **open**, this usually means that it can be worked on, read from, or written to.
7. *verb* To start or begin something: *The movie opens with a huge battle scene.*
8. *noun* If you have an **open mind**, you are willing to listen to new ideas and arguments.
9. *verb* To begin working hours: *The store opens at nine o'clock.*
o·pen (**oh**-puhn)
▷ *verb* **opening, opened**

opening
1. *noun* A hole, gap, or space in something: *We crept through a small opening in the fence.*
2. *adjective* Coming at the beginning; initial: *The opening scene is the best one in the whole play.*
3. *noun* A job that is available: *We have an opening in the shoe department.*
4. *noun* The first time a play is performed.
o·pen·ing (**oh**-puh-ning)

open-minded *adjective* Willing to listen to new or different ideas about something. ▷ *noun* **open-mindedness**

opera *noun* A play in which all or most of the words are sung and there is an orchestra. **op·er·a** (**ah**-pur-uh) ▷ *adjective* **operatic** (ah-puh-**rat**-ik)

onions

operate *verb*

1. To work in a particular way: *My new lawn mower operates on electricity.*

2. To make something work or to put something in action: *Can you operate a motorcycle?*

3. To repair or remove something from someone's body; to perform surgery, as in *to operate on a heart.*
op·er·ate (**ah**-puh-*rate*)
▷ *verb* **operating, operated**

operating system *noun* The software in a computer that supports all the programs that run on it. Abbreviated as *OS.*

operation *noun*

1. The act of cutting open someone's body to remove or repair a damaged or diseased part.

2. A well-organized plan, project, or event that involves a lot of people, as in *a rescue operation.*

3. in operation Working or functioning: *There are very few sawmills still in operation.*
op·er·a·tion (*ah*-puh-**ray**-shuhn)
▷ *adjective* **operational**

operator *noun*

1. Someone whose job is to help people make telephone calls.

2. Someone who works a machine or device, as in *a computer operator.*
op·er·a·tor (**ah**-puh-**ray**-tur)

ophthalmologist *noun* A medical doctor who studies and treats diseases of the eye. **oph·thal·mol·o·gist** (*ahf*-thuhl-**mah**-luh-jist) ▷ *noun* **ophthalmology**

opinion *noun*

1. Your personal feelings about someone or something: *What's your opinion of the new coach?*

2. The beliefs or views of people in general, as in *public opinion.*

3. The judgment of an expert, as in *a professional opinion.*

4. opinion poll A survey of what people think about something, made by asking questions to a selected group of people.
o·pin·ion (uh-**pin**-yuhn)

opioid *noun* A kind of drug made from poppy plants that reduces pain and is often addictive. **o·pi·oid** (**oh**-pee-*oid*)

opossum *noun* A gray, furry animal with a hairless tail that lives mostly in trees and carries its young in a pouch. If it is threatened, the opossum lies still and pretends to be dead. It is also called a **possum. o·pos·sum** (uh-**pah**-suhm)

opponent *noun* The person or team you play or compete against in a fight, contest, debate, or election. **op·po·nent** (uh-**poh**-nuhnt)

opportunity *noun* A chance or a good time to do

opossum

something: *A rainy day is the perfect opportunity to catch up on my reading.* **op·por·tu·ni·ty** (*ah*-pur-**too**-ni-tee) ▷ *noun, plural* **opportunities**

oppose *verb* To disagree with someone or something; to try to prevent or to resist: *The protesters opposed the city's plan to tear down the building.* **op·pose** (uh-**poze**) ▷ *verb* **opposing, opposed**

opposite

1. *preposition* Across from or facing: *My friend and I sat opposite each other on the bus.*

2. *adjective* Located or facing directly across: *Her building was on the opposite side of the river.*

3. *adjective* Facing or moving in the other direction: *When my cat sees a dog, she runs in the opposite direction.*

4. *adjective* Different in every way: *I thought she would agree with me, but she had the opposite opinion.*

5. *noun* A person, thing, or idea that is completely different from another: *The sisters are total opposites.*
op·po·site (**ah**-puh-zit *or* **ah**-puh-sit)

opposition *noun*

1. Resistance to or disagreement with someone or something: *She made her opposition to the new housing development very clear.*

2. The person or team that you play against in a game or competition.
op·po·si·tion (*ah*-puh-**zish**-uhn)

oppress *verb*

1. To use power or authority in a cruel and unfair way: *The country was oppressed by a cruel dictator.*
▷ *noun* **oppression** ▷ *noun* **oppressor**

2. If something **oppresses** you, it makes you feel worried or anxious because you cannot stop thinking about it.
op·press (uh-**pres**)
▷ *verb* **oppresses, oppressing, oppressed** ▷ *adjective* **oppressive**

opt *verb*

1. To choose or decide something: *Bruce opted to ride his bike rather than walk.*

2. If you **opt out** of something, you choose not to participate in it: *I opted out of the school play because I was too busy.*
opt (ahpt)
▷ *verb* **opting, opted**

optical
1. *adjective* Of or having to do with eyes or eyesight, as in *optical eyeglass lenses.*
2. *adjective* Designed to help eyesight: *Microscopes and telescopes are optical instruments.*
3. optical illusion *noun* Something that tricks your eye by seeming to be what it is not.
op·ti·cal (**ahp**-ti-kuhl)

optician *noun* Someone who examines your eyes, and makes or sells glasses and contact lenses. **op·ti·cian** (ahp-**tish**-uhn)

optimistic *adjective* People who are **optimistic** believe that things will usually turn out well or for the best. **op·ti·mis·tic** (*ahp*-tuh-**mis**-tik) ▷ *noun* **optimism** ▷ *noun* **optimist**

option *noun* A choice: *You have two options—you can walk or take the bus.* **op·tion** (**ahp**-shuhn)

optional *adjective* If something is **optional**, you can choose whether or not you want to do it: *Music classes are optional in our school.* **op·tion·al** (**ahp**-shuh-nuhl) ▷ *adverb* **optionally**

optometrist *noun* A person who is licensed to test your vision and prescribe glasses or contact lenses. **op·tom·e·trist** (ahp-**tah**-muh-trist)

Suffix

The suffix **-or** adds the following meaning when added to a root word: One who, as in *actor* (one who acts) and *conductor* (one who conducts).

or *conjunction*
1. A word used to show choices or alternatives: *Should I stay or should I go?*
2. A word used to introduce words or phrases that have the same meaning: *He is studying astronomy, or the science of the stars and planets.*
3. A word used with *either* or *whether* to show choices: *You can wear either the blue shirt or the red one.*
or (or)
Or sounds like **oar** and **ore**.

oral *adjective*
1. Spoken instead of written, as in *an oral report.*
2. Of or having to do with your mouth, as in *oral hygiene.*
o·ral (**or**-uhl)
▷ *adverb* **orally**

orange *noun*
1. A color between red and yellow, or the color of

Orangutans

The orangutan, an endangered species, lives in the rain forests of southeast Asia. Its survival is threatened as its habitat is being destroyed. The orangutan mostly dwells in trees, and its name means "man of the forest." Among the most intelligent primates, it can use objects, such as sticks, as tools.

a pumpkin. ▷ *adjective* **orange**
2. A round citrus fruit with a thick, reddish-yellow skin and a juicy inside that is divided in sections. **or·ange** (**or**-inj)

orangutan *noun* A large ape of Southeast Asia with long, reddish-brown hair and long, strong arms. **o·rang·u·tan** (uh-**rang**-uh-*tan*)

orbit
1. *noun* The curved path followed by a moon, planet, or satellite as it circles a planet or the sun. ▷ *adjective* **orbital**
2. *verb* To travel in a circular path around something, especially a planet or the sun. ▷ *verb* **orbiting, orbited**
or·bit (**or**-bit)

orchard *noun* An area of land where fruit or nut trees are grown. **or·chard** (**or**-churd)

Word History

Orchard originally meant "garden." It is a combination of the Latin word *hortus*, meaning "garden," and the Old English word *geard*, meaning "yard." The word *yard* also comes from *geard*.

Orchestra diagram labels: bass drum, gong, cymbals, triangle, timpani, trombones, French horns, flutes and clarinets, tuba, orchestra, harp, bassoons, oboes, violas, trumpets, double basses, violins, conductor, cellos

orchestra *noun* An often large group of musicians who play a variety of musical instruments together. **or·ches·tra** (**or**-kuh-struh) ▷ *adjective* **orchestral** (or-**kes**-truhl)

orchid *noun* A plant known for its colorful flowers with unusual shapes. There are many varieties of orchids, especially in tropical areas. **or·chid** (**or**-kid)

ordain *verb*
1. To make someone a priest or rabbi. ▷ *noun* **ordination** (or-duh-**nay**-shuhn)
2. To order by law: *The state ordains that all children must attend school.*
or·dain (or-**dane**)
▷ *verb* **ordaining, ordained**

ordeal *noun* A long and very difficult or unpleasant experience: *Getting lost in the storm was quite an ordeal.* **or·deal** (or-**deel**)

order
1. *verb* To instruct or command someone to do something: *Cara's mom ordered her to take out the trash.* ▷ *noun* **order**
2. *verb* To ask for something to be served or supplied, as in *to order a pizza* or *to order a book online.*
3. *noun* An arrangement, as in *alphabetical order* or *chronological order.*
4. *noun* A state in which everything is neatly arranged: *An outline gets your ideas in order before you write.*
5. *noun* A state in which everyone or everything is calm and obeys the rules: *We need order in this classroom.*
6. *noun* Written instructions to pay money to someone, as in *a money order.*
7. *noun* A group of people living in a religious community, as in *an order of nuns.*
8. *noun* A group of related plants or animals that is bigger than a family but smaller than a class.
9. If you put things **in order**, you arrange them so that everything is in the right sequence or position.
10. If something is **out of order**, it is not working properly or not working at all: *The telephone was out of order so we couldn't call.*
11. If a person is **out of order**, he or she is not behaving properly.
or·der (**or**-dur)
▷ *verb* **ordering, ordered**

orderly
1. *adjective* Arranged in a neat and careful way: *The corn was planted in orderly rows.* ▷ *noun* **orderliness**
2. *adjective* Behaving well, as in *an orderly crowd.*
3. *noun* A person who cleans and does other jobs in a hospital.
or·der·ly (**or**-dur-lee)

ordinal number *noun* A number that shows the position of something in a series, such as first, second, or third. *See the Numbers Table in the* **Reference Section**. **or·di·nal number** (**or**-duh-nuhl)

ordinance *noun* A law or regulation, especially one for a town or city. **or·di·nance** (**or**-duh-nuhns)

ordinary *adjective*
1. Not different or unusual in any way: *We didn't do anything special—it was just an ordinary evening at home.* ▷ *adverb* **ordinarily** (or-duh-**nair**-uh-lee)

2. Not having features that are interesting or unusual: *For such a fancy restaurant, it was a pretty ordinary meal.*
or·di·nar·y (or-duh-*ner*-ee)

ore *noun* A rock or earth that contains a metal or valuable mineral, as in *iron ore.* **ore** (or) **Ore** sounds like **oar** and **or.**

organ *noun*
1. A musical instrument that looks like a piano, with one or more keyboards. Some organs have rows of pipes that make sounds when air passes through them. ▷ *noun* **organist**
2. A part of the body, such as the heart or the kidneys, that has a certain purpose.
or·gan (or-guhn)

organic *adjective*
1. Grown without artificial chemicals or fertilizers, as in *organic vegetables.* ▷ *adverb* **organically**
2. From or produced by living things: *You can enrich the soil with compost and other organic matter.*
or·gan·ic (or-**gan**-ik)

organism *noun* A living thing, such as a plant or animal: *Bacteria are organisms.* **or·gan·ism** (**or**-guh-*niz*-uhm)

organization *noun*
1. A number of people joined together for a particular purpose: *Our organization helps the homeless.*
2. The act or process of planning and running something: *The organization of the carnival was left up to us.*
3. The way in which the parts of something are planned or arranged: *The candidate has suggested changes for the organization of the state government.*
or·gan·i·za·tion (or-guh-ni-**zay**-shuhn)

organize *verb*
1. To prepare for and run an event or activity: *A group of parents organized a graduation party.* ▷ *noun* **organizer**
2. To arrange the parts of something in a particular order or structure: *My little brother likes to organize his toys according to color.*
or·gan·ize (or-guh-*nize*)
▷ *verb* **organizing, organized**

Orient *noun* The countries of the Far East, especially Japan and China. **O·ri·ent** (**or**-ee-uhnt) ▷ *adjective* **Oriental** (or-ee-**en**-tuhl)

orientation *noun*
1. The position of something or the direction something faces, especially in relation to the compass: *We built our house with an east-west orientation to get maximum sunlight.*
2. Someone's feelings or beliefs about a particular issue: *What is her political orientation?*

3. A set of activities that get you ready to take part in something new: *Freshman orientation takes place on the first two days of school.*
or·i·en·ta·tion (or-ee-uhn-**tay**-shuhn)

orienteering *noun* A race in which players use maps and compasses to find their way across rough country. **o·ri·en·teer·ing** (or-ee-uhn-**teer**-ing)

origami *noun* The Japanese art of folding paper into decorative shapes. **o·ri·ga·mi** (or-i-**gah**-mee)

origin *noun*
1. The point where something starts, or the cause of something: *No one knows the origin of that myth.*
2. A person's family background: *The Wong family is of Chinese origin.*
or·i·gin (**or**-i-jin)

original
1. *adjective* First, earliest, or existing from the beginning: *The house has all of its original features.*
2. *adjective* New or interesting: *She was full of original ideas for raising money.* ▷ *noun* **originality** (uh-*rij*-uh-**nal**-i-tee)
3. *noun* A work of art or a piece of writing that is not a copy. ▷ *adjective* **original**
o·rig·i·nal (uh-**rij**-uh-nuhl)

originally *adverb* At the beginning; at first: *The building originally had three floors. The fourth floor was added later.* **o·rig·i·nal·ly** (uh-**rij**-uh-nuh-lee)

originate *verb* To happen or to begin in a particular place or situation: *Where did the word "cookie" originate?* **o·rig·i·nate** (uh-**rij**-uh-*nate*) ▷ *verb* **originating, originated** ▷ *noun* **origination**

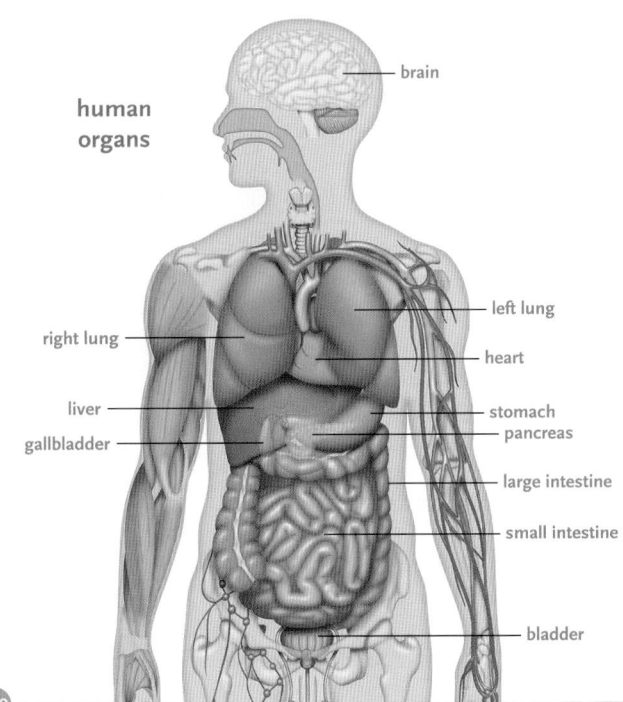

human organs

brain · left lung · right lung · heart · liver · stomach · gallbladder · pancreas · large intestine · small intestine · bladder

a b c d e f g h i j k l m n **o** p q r s t u v w x y z

oriole *noun* Any of a group of songbirds in which the male has bright orange or yellow markings. **o·ri·ole** (**or**-ee-*ohl*)

ornament *noun* A small object that is used for decoration, as in *a Christmas tree ornament.* **or·na·ment** (**or**-nuh-muhnt) ▷ *adjective* **ornamental**

ornate *adjective* Covered with a lot of decorations, as in *an ornate headdress.* **or·nate** (or-**nayt**) ▷ *adverb* **ornately**

orphan *noun* A child whose parents are not alive. **or·phan** (**or**-fuhn) ▷ *adjective* **orphaned**

orphanage *noun* A place where orphans live and are cared for. **or·phan·age** (**or**-fuh-nij)

orthodontist *noun* A dentist who straightens crooked teeth and corrects jaw and bite problems. **or·tho·don·tist** (or-thuh-**dahn**-tist)

orthodox *adjective*
1. A religion is described as **orthodox** if it has very traditional and established teachings.
2. Orthodox views and beliefs are ones that are generally accepted or approved. **or·tho·dox** (**or**-thuh-*dahks*) ▷ *noun* **orthodoxy**

orthopedic *adjective* Of or having to do with the branch of medicine that deals with bones and joints. **or·tho·pe·dic** (*or*-thuh-**pee**-dik) ▷ *noun* **orthopedics**

osmosis *noun*
1. The process in which a more concentrated solution passes through a membrane into a less concentrated one, until the concentrations on both sides are equal.
2. The process of absorbing ideas, attitudes, or information gradually: *While living in France, Sally learned to speak French by osmosis.* **os·mo·sis** (ahz-**moh**-sis or ahs-**moh**-sis)

ostrich *noun* A large African bird with a long neck that can run very fast but cannot fly. The ostrich is the largest living bird and can weigh up to 300 pounds. **os·trich** (**aws**-trich) ▷ *noun, plural* **ostriches**

ostrich

other
1. *adjective* Different; not the same: *Don't you have this in some other color?* ▷ *pronoun* **other**
2. *adjective* Remaining: *Tell her personally and email the other people.*
3. *adjective* More or extra: *There are other coats in the closet.* ▷ *pronoun* **other**
4. *adjective* In the recent past: *It snowed the other day.*
5. others *pronoun* The rest, or in addition to those already mentioned: *Part of the team is here, but where are the others?* **oth·er** (**uhTH**-ur)

otherwise
1. *conjunction* Or else: *I'll have to borrow some money; otherwise, I won't be able to buy that bike.*
2. *adverb* In a different way: *A few of the kids were out of tune, but otherwise it was a good concert.* **oth·er·wise** (**uhTH**-ur-*wize*)

otter *noun* A fish-eating mammal with webbed feet and a long tail that lives partly in water and partly on land. Otters are related to weasels and minks. **ot·ter** (**ah**-tur)

ouch *interjection* A cry of sudden pain: *"Ouch! Don't pinch me!"* **ouch** (ouch)

ought *verb* A helping verb used in the following ways:
1. To show something you must do: *You ought to obey the rules.*
2. To show what you expect or think will happen: *This coat is my size, so it ought to fit.*
3. To give advice: *You ought to eat your vegetables.* **ought** (awt)

ounce *noun*
1. A unit of weight equal to ¹⁄₁₆ of a pound. A mouse weighs about one ounce. *See the Measurements Table in the* **Reference Section**.
2. A **fluid ounce** is a unit used in liquid measurement. There are 16 fluid ounces in a pint and 32 fluid ounces in a quart.
3. A small amount: *Gina never makes an ounce of effort.* **ounce** (ouns)

our *adjective* Belonging to or connected with us: *The party is at our house.* **our** (our *or* ahr)

ours *pronoun* The one or ones belonging to or connected with us: *That house is ours.* **ours** (ourz *or* ahrz)

ourselves *pronoun* Us and no one else: *We can get ourselves there, but the others will have to get a ride.* **our·selves** (our-**selvz**)

Suffix

The suffix **-ous** adds the following meaning when added to a root word: Full of, as in *joyous* (full of joy) and *dangerous* (full of danger).

oust *verb* To force someone out of a place, a job, or a position of power: *Kyle was ousted as class treasurer.* **oust** (oust) ▷ *verb* **ousting, ousted**

out

1. *adverb* Away from the inside or middle of a place or thing: *I went out to play.*

2. *adverb* Away from home or work: *We're going out for lunch.*

3. *adverb* Into the open, or into the public: *Is his new album out yet?*

4. *adverb* No longer on fire or lit: *By the time we returned, the fire was out.*

5. *adverb, adjective* Removed from a game or contest: *The Vikings are now out of the playoffs.*

6. *adverb* Aloud or forcefully: *We were encouraged to speak out and make our opinions known.*

7. *adjective* In baseball, no longer a batter or base runner: *Three strikes and you're out.* ▷ *noun* **out**
out (out)

outage *noun* A time when a service such as electricity or the internet fails and is not available: *Our house was freezing this morning because of a power outage last night.* **out·age** (**ou**-tij)

outbox *noun*

1. A box where you place letters that are ready to mail or go to another office.

2. A place on a computer where email can wait until you send it.
out·box (**out**-*bahks*)

outbreak *noun* The sudden start of something unpleasant: *There was an outbreak of flu in our school last winter.* **out·break** (**out**-*brake*)

outburst *noun* A sudden release of emotion or violence, as in *an outburst of tears.* **out·burst** (**out**-*burst*)

outcast *noun* Someone who has been rejected by other people: *New students often feel like outcasts.* **out·cast** (**out**-*kast*)

outcome *noun* The result of an action or an event: *We are waiting to hear about the outcome of the election.* **out·come** (**out**-*kuhm*)

outcry *noun* Protests or complaints from many people: *There was a public outcry when the school was closed.* **out·cry** (**out**-*krye*) ▷ *noun, plural* **outcries**

outdated *adjective* Old-fashioned: *Grandma's hairstyle is really outdated.* **out·dat·ed** (**out**-**day**-tid)

outdo *verb* To go beyond or do better than someone else can: *When it comes to the high jump, no one can outdo Drew.* **out·do** (**out**-**doo**) ▷ *verb* **outdoes, outdoing, outdid, outdone**

outdoors *adverb* In or into the open air; outside, as in *to play outdoors.* **out·doors** (**out**-**dorz**) ▷ *noun* **outdoors** ▷ *adjective* **outdoor**

outer *adjective* Farthest from the center or middle; on the outside: *The outer layer of the jacket was waterproof.* **out·er** (**ou**-tur)

outer space *noun* The universe beyond the earth's atmosphere.

outfield *noun*

1. The part of a baseball field beyond the infield and inside the foul lines.

2. The group of baseball players assigned to this area when not at bat.
out·field (**out**-*feeld*)

outfit

1. *noun* Pieces of clothing that are worn together, as in *a skating outfit.*

2. *noun* A group of people who work together or form a team, as in *a computer repair outfit.*

3. *verb* To obtain all the equipment you need to do something: *We need to outfit ourselves with camping equipment.* ▷ *verb* **outfitting, outfitted**
out·fit (**out**-fit)

outgoing *adjective* Someone who is **outgoing** is very warm, friendly, and confident. **out·go·ing** (**out**-*goh*-ing)

outgrow *verb*

1. To grow too big for something: *I outgrew my sneakers.*

2. To lose interest in someone or something as you grow older: *I am starting to outgrow playing with dolls.*
out·grow (**out**-**groh**) ▷ *verb* **outgrowing, outgrew, outgrown**

outing *noun* A short trip for pleasure or education: *The class had an outing to the museum last week.* **out·ing** (**ou**-ting)

outlaw

1. *noun* A criminal, especially one who is hiding from the police.

2. *verb* To make something illegal: *The town outlawed smoking in restaurants.* ▷ *verb* **outlawing, outlawed**
out·law (**out**-*law*)

outlet *noun*

1. A place where electronics and appliances can be plugged in and connected to electricity.

2. A pipe or hole that can release liquid or gas.

3. A store where a company's goods can be bought for lower prices.

4. A way of expressing your talents, energy, or feelings: *Becoming an artist is a good outlet for Ramsay's gift for drawing.*
out·let (**out**-let)

outlet

outline *noun*
1. A line that shows the outer edges of something: *In the dark, we could only see the outline of the house.*
2. A brief description of the main points; a summary: *The assignment was to write an outline of the book's plot.*
out·line (**out**-line)
▷ *verb* **outline**

outlook *noun*
1. Your general attitude toward life and the world around you: *Even in difficult times, my parents maintain a positive outlook.*
2. Something that is likely to happen: *The outlook for the weekend is beautiful and sunny.*
out·look (**out**-luk)

outnumber *verb* To be greater in number than: *Girls outnumber boys in the freshman class.*
out·num·ber (**out**-**nuhm**-bur) ▷ *verb* **outnumbering, outnumbered**

outpatient *noun* Someone who is treated in a hospital or clinic but does not stay the night. **out·pa·tient** (**out**-*pay*-shuhnt)

outpost *noun*
1. A military camp set up away from the main camp, used to keep watch on the enemy.
2. A town or buildings in a remote area: *The company established outposts far from the city.*
out·post (**out**-pohst)

output *noun*
1. The amount of something that a person, machine, or company makes or produces: *This copy machine is known for its fast, high-quality output.*
2. The information a computer produces: *My computer's output is really slow because I'm running several programs.*
out·put (**out**-put)
▷ *verb* **output**

outrage *noun*
1. A strong feeling of anger or shock: *Protesters expressed outrage about the company's chemical dumping.*
2. An act that is very violent, cruel, or extremely offensive, as in *the outrages of animal cruelty.*
out·rage (**out**-rayj)

outrageous *adjective* Very shocking or unacceptable: *We would love to shop at that store but their prices are outrageous.* **out·ra·geous** (**out**-**ray**-juhs) ▷ *adverb* **outrageously**

outright
1. *adjective* Complete and total, as in *an outright lie.*
2. *adverb* Immediately: *They were killed outright in the plane crash.*
out·right (**out**-rite)

outset *noun* The start or the beginning: *The project was difficult from the outset.* **out·set** (**out**-set)

outside
1. (**out**-side) *adverb* In or into the open air; outdoors: *The children played outside all morning.*
2. (**out**-side) *noun* The outer surface or side: *The outside of the building was covered with ivy.*
▷ *adjective* **outside**
3. (**out**-side) *preposition* Away from, or not in a certain place: *My aunt lives just outside Chicago.*
out·side

outskirts *noun, plural* The outer edges of a city or town: *Most of the poor families lived on the outskirts of town.* **out·skirts** (**out**-skurts)

outsource *verb*
1. To get products or services from an outside company or source: *The county outsourced tax collection to a private company.*
2. To move a job to a place where workers are cheaper: *Many customer service jobs have been outsourced to India.*
out·source (**out**-sors)
▷ *verb* **outsourcing, outsourced**

outspoken *adjective* Very honest and direct, especially when criticizing someone or something: *She is an outspoken critic of the new recycling policies.* **out·spo·ken** (**out**-**spoh**-kuhn)

outstanding *adjective*
1. Extremely good or better than others of its kind, as in *an outstanding performance.*
2. Not yet paid or collected, as in *an outstanding payment.*
out·stand·ing (**out**-**stan**-ding)

outward *or* **outwards**
1. *adjective* Showing the way things seem rather than how they really are; on the surface: *His outward calm masked how angry he was.* ▷ *adverb* **outwardly**
2. *adverb* Away from a place, especially one that will be returned to: *Car doors always open outward.*
▷ *adjective* **outward**
out·ward (**out**-wurd) *or* **out·wards** (**out**-wurdz)

outweigh *verb*
1. To be more important or more valuable than something else: *She thought the future benefits outweighed the risks, so she went ahead with her plans.*
2. To weigh more than something or somebody else.
out·weigh (**out**-way)
▷ *verb* **outweighing, outweighed**

outwit *verb* To fool or get an advantage over someone by being more clever: *The kids always outwit the parents on this program.* **out·wit** (**out**-wit)
▷ *verb* **outwitting, outwitted**

overcast

oval *noun* Something that has the shape of an egg, as in *an oval-shaped face.*
o·val (**oh**-vuhl) ▷ *adjective* **oval**

ovary *noun*
1. The part of a flowering plant that produces seeds.
2. One of a pair of female organs that produce eggs.
o·va·ry (**oh**-vur-ee)
▷ *noun, plural* **ovaries**

ovation *noun* A loud and enthusiastic outburst of clapping: *The singers received a standing ovation.*
o·va·tion (oh-**vay**-shuhn)

oven *noun* The part of a stove in which you can bake or roast food. **ov·en** (**uhv**-uhn)

over
1. *preposition* In a position higher than but not touching something: *We hung the chandelier over the table.*
2. *preposition* More than: *My shoes cost over $50.*
3. *adjective* Finished or done with: *The meeting was over before we arrived.*
4. *preposition* Across or to the other side of something: *Take the bridge that goes over the stream.*
5. *adverb* Remaining or left: *There were two pieces of chicken left over.*
6. *adverb* Again: *I failed the test, but the teacher is letting me do it over.*
7. *adverb* Leaning, falling, or hanging downward: *The lamp fell over when Doug ran into it.*
8. If you **get over** something, it doesn't bother you anymore: *My sister was furious when I took her bike, but she got over it.*
o·ver (**oh**-vur)

overall *adverb* Taken as a whole, or considering everything: *Overall, I think the class did a great job on the bulletin board.* **o·ver·all** (oh-vur-**awl**)

oval

▷ *adjective* **overall** (oh-vur-*awl*)

overalls *noun, plural* Loose pants with a front flap over the chest held up by shoulder straps. **o·ver·alls** (**oh**-vur-*awlz*)

overboard *adverb*
1. Over the side of a boat and into the water: *Our hats fell overboard in the storm.*
2. If you **go overboard** with something, you are too enthusiastic or excited about it.
o·ver·board (**oh**-vur-*bord*)

overcast *adjective* Covered with clouds or mist: *The day started out sunny, but the sky was overcast by noon.* **o·ver·cast** (**oh**-vur-*kast*)

overcoat *noun* A long, heavy coat worn in cold weather. **o·ver·coat** (**oh**-vur-*kote*)

overcome *verb*
1. To defeat or get control of a problem: *She was eventually able to overcome her shyness.*
2. To strongly affect someone: *When Jake was punished instead of me, I was overcome by guilt.*
o·ver·come (**oh**-vur-**kuhm**)
▷ *verb* **overcoming, overcame, overcome**

overdo *verb* To do too much of something: *Don't overdo it on your first day at the gym.* **o·ver·do** (*oh*-vur-**doo**) ▷ *verb* **overdoes, overdoing, overdid, overdone** ▷ *adjective* **overdone**

overdose *noun* A large dose of a drug that can make you sick or kill you. **o·ver·dose** (**oh**-vur-*dohs*)
▷ *verb* **overdose** (**oh**-vur-**dohs**)

overdue *adjective* Past the time payment or arrival is due; late: *These bills are long overdue.* **o·ver·due** (*oh*-vur-**doo**)

overeat *verb* To eat more than you need. **o·ver·eat** (*oh*-vur-**eet**) ▷ *verb* **overeating, overate**

overflow *verb*
1. To flow over the brim or edges of something: *If you pour any more into that mug, it will overflow.*
2. To flood: *The river overflowed its bank during the storm.*
o·ver·flow (**oh**-vur-**floh**)
▷ *verb* **overflowing, overflowed**

overgrown *adjective* Covered with weeds or plants that have been allowed to grow wild: *The garden will get completely overgrown if you don't weed it.*
o·ver·grown (*oh*-vur-**grohn**)

overhand *adjective* Done with your arm raised above your shoulder, as in *an overhand serve.* **o·ver·hand** (**oh**-vur-*hand*)

overhaul *verb* To thoroughly examine equipment or machinery and make necessary repairs: *The mechanic said the engine needs to be overhauled.* **o·ver·haul** (**oh**-vur-**hawl**) ▷ *verb* **overhauling, overhauled** ▷ *noun* **overhaul** (**oh**-vur-*hawl*)

a
b
c
d
e
f
g
h
i
j
k
l
m
n
o
p
q
r
s
t
u
v
w
x
y
z

overhead

1. (*oh*-vur-**hed**) *adverb* Above your head; in the sky: *A helicopter flew overhead.* ▷ *adjective* **overhead** (*oh*-vur-*hed*)

2. (**oh**-vur-*hed*) *noun* The regular expenses involved in running a business, such as salaries, rent, and utilities. **o·ver·head**

overhear *verb* To hear something without meaning to or without the speaker's knowledge: *It was impossible not to overhear their argument.* **o·ver·hear** (*oh*-vur-**heer**) ▷ *verb* **overhearing, overheard**

overlap *verb*

1. To extend over or partly cover something: *The feathers of a bird overlap.*

2. To cover the same period of time or the same area of interest or responsibility: *Some of what we are learning in social studies overlaps with our history class.* **o·ver·lap** (*oh*-vur-**lap**) ▷ *verb* **overlapping, overlapped** ▷ *noun* **overlap** (*oh*-vur-*lap*)

overload *verb*

1. To give something or someone too much to carry or too much work or responsibility: *I can't go out—I'm too overloaded with homework.*

2. To put too much demand on an electrical system or device so that it burns out: *Don't overload the circuit.* **o·ver·load** (*oh*-vur-**lode**) ▷ *verb* **overloading, overloaded** ▷ *noun* **overload** (*oh*-vur-*lohd*)

overlook *verb*

1. To be able to look down on something from above: *Our cabin overlooked the lake.*

2. To fail to notice or consider something: *They thought of everything but overlooked the weather report.*

3. To excuse or choose to ignore something: *I overlooked Dylan's carelessness because he was my friend.* **o·ver·look** (*oh*-vur-**luk**) ▷ *verb* **overlooking, overlooked**

overly *adverb* Too or excessively: *You can't be overly cautious when it comes to investing your money.* **o·ver·ly** (*oh*-vur-lee)

overnight

1. (*oh*-vur-**nite**) *adverb* During or for the night: *It had snowed overnight.*

2. (*oh*-vur-**nite**) *adverb* Suddenly or very quickly: *They became celebrities overnight.*

3. (*oh*-vur-*nite*) *adjective* For one night: *I stayed overnight at my friend's house.*

4. (**oh**-vur-*nite*) *adjective* To be used for one night or for short trips, as in *an overnight bag.* **o·ver·night**

overpass *noun* A road or bridge that goes over another road or a railroad. **o·ver·pass** (**oh**-vur-*pas*) ▷ *noun, plural* **overpasses**

overpopulation *noun* The situation in which the number of humans or animals in an area is too large to be sustained by the natural resources available. **o·ver·pop·u·la·tion** (*oh*-vur-*pahp*-yuh-**lay**-shuhn)

overpower *verb*

1. To defeat someone because you have more strength: *The boxer won the match by overpowering his opponent.*

2. If something **overpowers** you, it overwhelms you or makes you helpless: *I was overpowered by the smell of freshly baked bread.* **o·ver·pow·er** (*oh*-vur-**pou**-ur) ▷ *verb* **overpowering, overpowered**

overrule *verb* If someone in authority **overrules** a decision, the person reverses that decision or does not allow it to stand. **o·ver·rule** (*oh*-vur-**rool**) ▷ *verb* **overruling, overruled**

overrun *verb*

1. To fill a place or spread out over it in large numbers: *The vegetable garden was overrun with snails.*

2. To flood over, or go beyond a boundary or limit: *The river overran its banks. The runner overran third base and was tagged out.* **o·ver·run** (*oh*-vur-**ruhn**) ▷ *verb* **overrunning, overran, overrun**

overseas

1. (*oh*-vur-**seez**) *adverb* To or in a foreign country, or across an ocean: *We traveled overseas to Greece.*

2. (**oh**-vur-*seez*) *adjective* Of or having to do with foreign countries or countries across an ocean, as in *overseas travel.* **o·ver·seas**

oversight *noun*

1. A mistake you make because you forget or do not notice something: *Leaving you off the list was an oversight.*

2. The responsibility for seeing that something is done correctly: *The department has oversight for all evening student activities.* **o·ver·sight** (**oh**-vur-*site*)

overtake *verb*

1. To catch up to and pass someone: *I overtook the other runners on the last turn.*

2. To happen suddenly or by surprise and strongly affect everything: *A flood overtook the town in 1977.* **o·ver·take** (*oh*-vur-**take**) ▷ *verb* **overtaking, overtook, overtaken**

over-the-counter *adjective* Available for purchase without a prescription: *Over-the-counter medicines are not strong enough for my allergies.*

Ozone Layer

A layer of ozone covers the earth, protecting it from the sun's damaging ultraviolet rays. Pollution may be causing it to get thinner. In 2006, scientists from the National Aeronautics and Space Administration (NASA) and the National Oceanic and Atmospheric Administration (NOAA) discovered that a hole in the ozone above Antarctica had reached a record-breaking size. The dark circle in the satellite image shows the hole over Antarctica, outlined in white. The ozone hole varies in size seasonally and has shrunk since 2006, indicating that the ozone layer in the Southern Hemisphere is improving.

overthrow *verb*

1. To put an end to something or to force someone from power: *The dictator was overthrown by the new government.*

2. To throw a ball past where it should go: *The pitcher overthrew the plate and hit the catcher.*

o·ver·throw (*oh*-vur-**throh**)

▷ *verb* **overthrowing, overthrew, overthrown** ▷ *noun* **overthrow**

overtime *noun*

1. Time you spend working after you have worked your normal number of hours: *We put in a lot of overtime during the holiday season.*

2. Extra time in a game or competition because the score was tied at the end of normal play.

o·ver·time (*oh*-vur-*time*)

▷ *adjective* **overtime** ▷ *adverb* **overtime**

overture *noun* A piece of music played at the beginning of an opera, a ballet, or a musical.

o·ver·ture (*oh*-vur-chur)

overturn *verb*

1. To turn something upside down or on its side: *The dog overturned the table and broke the vase.*

2. To reverse something, especially a decision: *The judge overturned the verdict.*

o·ver·turn (*oh*-vur-**turn**)

▷ *verb* **overturning, overturned**

overweight *adjective* Above a normal or desirable weight: *I was charged $25 for my overweight suitcase.*

o·ver·weight (*oh*-vur-**wate**)

overwhelm *verb*

1. To defeat someone or something completely: *The army was overwhelmed by enemy forces.*

2. To have a very strong emotional effect: *He was overwhelmed by the support he received from the community.*

o·ver·whelm (*oh*-vur-**welm**)

▷ *verb* **overwhelming, overwhelmed** ▷ *adjective* **overwhelming**

owe *verb*

1. To be responsible for giving money or goods to someone, especially if you have borrowed something from that person: *I owe my sister $50 for the tickets.*

2. To feel you should do or give something to someone, especially in return for something they have done: *She owes me a favor.*

3. To exist or be successful because of someone or something: *I owe my success to my parents.*

owe (oh)

Owe sounds like **oh**. ▷ *verb* **owing, owed**

owl *noun* A bird that has a round head, large eyes, and a hooked beak. Owls hunt at night and live mainly on mice and other small animals. **owl** (oul)

own

1. *adjective* Used to show that something belongs to or is connected with someone: *I'm using my own money.*

2. *verb* To possess or have something: *I own two cars.* ▷ *noun* **owner**

3. *verb* If you **own up** to something, you admit to having done something wrong.

4. on your own Alone or by your own efforts: *I made the cake on my own.*

own (ohn)

▷ *verb* **owning, owned**

ox *noun*

1. An adult male cow that is used as a work animal or for meat.

2. An animal that is related to cattle, such as a buffalo, bison, or yak.

ox (ahks)

▷ *noun, plural* **oxen** (**ahk**-suhn)

oxidize *verb* To undergo a chemical change by combining with oxygen. **ox·i·dize** (**ahk**-si-*dize*)

▷ *verb* **oxidizing, oxidized** ▷ *noun* **oxidizer** ▷ *noun* **oxidation** (*ahk*-si-**day**-shuhn)

oxygen *noun* A colorless gas found in the air and water. Humans and animals need oxygen to breathe, and fires need it to burn. **ox·y·gen** (**ahk**-si-juhn)

oyster *noun* A flat shellfish that has a hinged shell and lives in shallow waters. Some oysters can be eaten, and some produce pearls. **oy·ster** (**oi**-stur)

oz. Short for **ounce** or the plural form *ounces.*

ozone *noun*

1. A form of oxygen that has a pale blue color and a strong smell.

2. ozone layer A layer in the earth's upper atmosphere that contains ozone and blocks out some of the sun's harmful rays.

o·zone (**oh**-zone)

About P In its earliest version, the letter **P** faced to the left. The Romans turned the letter around and gave it the form we know today. In English, the letter is silent if it is followed by the consonants *s*, *t*, or *n* at the beginning of a word. Examples: psalm, pterodactyl, pneumatic. Combined with the letter *h*, it can sound like an *f*, as in *photograph*. In baseball, the letter is the abbreviation for the word *pitcher*.

pace

1. *noun* A step or a stride: *The treasure was buried ten paces from the tree.*

2. *noun* The average length of a step when you are walking, about two feet for an adult.

3. *verb* To measure distance in paces: *Pace off the length of the driveway.*

4. *noun* A rate of speed, as in *a rapid pace.*

5. *verb* To walk back and forth: *Jim paced the hall.*
pace (pase)
▷ *verb* **pacing, paced**

pacemaker *noun* An electronic device put into someone's body to help the heart beat more regularly. **pace·mak·er** (**pays**-*may*-kur)

Pacific Ocean *noun* The world's largest ocean. The Pacific Ocean is bordered by Asia and Australia on one side and by North and South America on the other. **Pa·cif·ic Ocean** (puh-**sif**-ik)

pacifist *noun* A person who believes very strongly that war and violence are wrong, and who refuses to fight or to enter the armed forces. **pac·i·fist** (**pas**-uh-fist) ▷ *noun* **pacifism**

pacify *verb*

1. To make a person feel calmer and more peaceful.

2. To settle an agitated situation.
pac·i·fy (**pas**-uh-*fye*)
▷ *verb* **pacifies, pacifying, pacified**

pack

1. *verb* To put objects into a box, case, bag, or other container, especially in order to move or store them: *We packed our books in boxes before we moved.* ▷ *noun* **packing**

2. *verb* To fill a space tightly: *A huge crowd packed the auditorium.*

3. *noun* A group of similar animals, people, or things, as in *a pack of dogs* or *a pack of cards.*

4. *noun* A bundle of things tied or wrapped together for carrying, as in *a pack of gum.*

5. *noun* A sturdy bag for carrying things on your back.

6. *noun* A large quantity or amount, as in *a pack of lies.*
pack (pak)
▷ *verb* **packing, packed**

package *noun*

1. A parcel, or a bundle of something that is packed, wrapped, or put into a box.

2. A carton, box, or case that can be packed with something: *The ingredients were listed on the package.*
pack·age (**pak**-ij)
▷ *verb* **package**

packaging *noun* The wrapping on something, especially something that you buy. **pack·ag·ing** (**pak**-uh-jing)

pack animal *noun* An animal, usually a horse or mule, that can carry heavy supplies.

packet *noun* A small container, package, or bundle, as in *a packet of sugar.* **pack·et** (**pak**-it)

pact *noun* A formal agreement between two individuals, groups, or countries, as in *a peace pact.* **pact** (pakt)

pad

1. *verb* To walk softly and steadily: *She padded down the hall in her bedroom slippers.*

2. *noun* A wad or cushion of soft material, usually used to absorb liquid, give comfort, or provide protection. ▷ *verb* **pad**

3. *noun* Sheets of paper fastened together along one edge, as in *a memo pad.*

4. *noun* The soft, cushioned parts on the bottom of the feet of dogs, cats, and many other animals.

5. *noun* A platform from which a rocket is fired, as in *a launching pad.*

6. *verb* To add words to a speech or piece of writing just to make it longer.

7. pad a bill *verb* To charge someone for more work than you really did.
pad (pad)
▷ *verb* **padding, padded**

padding *noun* Cotton, foam rubber, or any other material used to make or stuff a pad, or to protect items being packed into a container. **pad·ding** (**pad**-ing)

paddle

1. *noun* A short, wide oar used to move and steer some kinds of small boats. ▷ *verb* **paddle**

2. *noun* A small board with a short handle used to

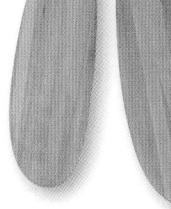
paddles

paddle wheel

strike a ball in table tennis and other games.

3. *noun* A flat, wooden tool used for stirring, mixing, or beating.

4. *verb* To walk or splash with your hands in shallow water.

5. *verb* To spank with a paddle or the hand.

pad·dle (**pad**-uhl)

▷ *verb* **paddling, paddled**

paddle wheel *noun* A large wheel with boards arranged around it, placed on the side or back of a ship to propel it through the water.

paddock *noun* An enclosed field or area where horses can graze or exercise. **pad·dock** (**pad**-uhk)

paddy *noun* A flooded field where rice is grown. **pad·dy** (**pad**-ee) ▷ *noun, plural* **paddies**

padlock *noun* A lock with a U-shaped metal bar that can be put through an opening or link and snapped shut. **pad·lock** (**pad**-*lahk*) ▷ *verb* **padlock**

pagan *noun* A person who is not a member of the Christian, Jewish, or Muslim religions. A pagan may worship many gods or have no religion at all. **pa·gan** (**pay**-guhn) ▷ *adjective* **pagan**

page

1. *noun* One side of a sheet of paper in a book, newspaper, or magazine: *Read page 156 silently.*

2. *noun* In the past, a **page** was a boy servant. Today, a **page** can be a person of any age who assists someone, such as a senator. A **page** can also be a boy attendant at a wedding.

3. *verb* To find someone by calling out or announcing the person's name or by using a pager: *Annaliese had her mother paged when they got separated in the department store.*

4. *verb* To turn pages in a book or other printed material: *Rashid paged through the newspaper until he found the baseball scores.*

page (payj)

▷ *verb* **paging, paged**

pageant *noun* A public entertainment where people walk in a procession, often in costume, or act out historical scenes, as in *a beauty pageant* or *a Thanksgiving pageant.* **pag·eant** (**paj**-uhnt)

pageantry *noun* Elaborate display or ceremony: *The coronation of a king involves a great deal of pageantry.* **pag·eant·ry** (**paj**-uhn-tree)

pager *noun* A small, electronic beeping device that doctors and other emergency personnel wear so that they can be contacted quickly. **pag·er** (**pay**-jur)

pagoda *noun* A shrine or temple in eastern religions. A pagoda is shaped like a tower with many roofs that curve upward. **pa·go·da** (puh-**goh**-duh)

paid

1. *verb* The past tense and the past participle of **pay**.

2. *adjective* Involving the exchange of money for something, as in *a paid newspaper ad.*

3. *adjective* Some jobs include **paid** vacations, which means that an employee continues to receive regular pay while away from work.

paid (payd)

pail *noun* A bucket, as in *a pail of water.* **pail** (payl) **Pail** sounds like **pale**.

pain *noun*

1. Physical or emotional suffering caused by injury, illness, or great unhappiness. ▷ *verb* **pain**

2. A nuisance, or an unpleasant experience: *Waiting around for the bus in the snow was a pain.*

3. pains *noun, plural* Great care or effort: *Marcie took pains to make sure that everyone was OK.*

pain (payn)

Pain sounds like **pane**.

painful *adjective* Causing physical or emotional distress. **pain·ful** (**payn**-fuhl) ▷ *adverb* **painfully**

painkiller *noun* Medicine taken to stop pain. **pain·kill·er** (**payn**-*kil*-ur)

painless *adjective* Free from pain: *Donatella's medical examination was painless.* **pain·less** (**payn**-lis) ▷ *adverb* **painlessly**

painstaking *adjective* Very thorough and careful, as in *painstaking research.* **pains·tak·ing** (**paynz**-*tay*-king) ▷ *adverb* **painstakingly**

paint

1. *noun* A liquid that you spread over a surface to color or decorate it, or to make a picture.

2. *verb* To cover something with paint, or to use paint to make a picture: *Trish painted her room orange.* ▷ *verb* **painting, painted**

paint (paynt)

paintbrush *noun* A brush for applying paint. **paint·brush** (**paynt**-*bruhsh*) ▷ *noun, plural* **paintbrushes**

a
b
c
d
e
f
g
h
i
j
k
l
m
n
o
p
q
r
s
t
u
v
w
x
y
z

palace: Neuschwanstein in Germany

painter *noun*
1. Someone whose job is to paint: *The painters are coming over on Tuesday to start painting the house.*
2. An artist: *Rembrandt is my favorite painter.*
paint·er (**payn**-tur)

painting *noun*
1. A work of art that has been created with paint.
2. The process of putting paint onto something: *We'll do the painting after sanding the shelves.*
3. The occupation of a painter.
paint·ing (**payn**-ting)

pair
1. *noun* A set of two things that are used together or make one unit, as in *a pair of socks.*
2. *noun* One thing that is made up of two parts, as in *a pair of scissors* or *a pair of glasses.*
3. *noun* Two persons or animals that are alike or that work together, as in *a pair of dancers* or *a pair of horses.*
4. *verb* To join or put together: *I wouldn't pair that sweater with those pants if I were you.*
5. **pair off** *verb* To form a pair or into pairs: *The students paired off for their dance lesson.*
pair (pair)
Pair sounds like **pare** and **pear.** ▷ *verb* **pairing, paired**

paisley
1. *noun* A colorful pattern made of curved teardrop shapes and leaves or flowers: *The fabric for the chair's upholstery was a beautiful green, blue, and orange paisley.*
2. *adjective* Having a paisley design, as in *a paisley curtain* or *a paisley skirt.*
pais·ley (**payz**-lee)

pajamas *noun, plural* A set of clothes to sleep in, consisting of a loose shirt and pants or shorts. **pa·ja·mas** (puh-**jah**-muhz *or* puh-**jam**-uhz)

Word History

Pajamas is a combination of two Persian words: *pae* or *pay,* which means "leg," and *jama,* the word for "clothing." The word *pajamas* was brought to India and passed into English during the United Kingdom's long rule over India. Originally referring to loose, lightweight trousers, *pajamas* came to be applied to any two-piece set of clothes for sleeping.

pal *noun* A good friend or a buddy. **pal** (pal)

palace *noun* A large, grand residence for a king, queen, or other ruler. **pal·ace** (**pal**-is)

Word History

The word **palace** can trace its origins to one of the seven great hills of Rome, the Palatine Hill. In ancient times, the emperors and leading citizens of Rome built their big and beautiful houses on this hill. The Latin word *palatium* became the French *palais,* and the English *palace.*

palate *noun*
1. The roof of the mouth.
2. A person's appreciation of taste, as in *a dish that delights the palate.*
pal·ate (**pal**-it)
Palate sounds like **palette.**

pale
1. *adjective* Having a light skin color, often because of an illness: *His face looked thin and pale.*
2. *adjective* Not bright in color: *Naomi's dress was pale green.*
3. *verb* To become pale: *Vincent's face paled with fright.* ▷ *verb* **paling, paled**
pale (payl)
Pale sounds like **pail.** ▷ *noun* **paleness** ▷ *adjective* **paler, palest**

paleontology *noun* The science that deals with fossils and other ancient life forms. A person who studies paleontology is called a *paleontologist.* **pa·le·on·tol·o·gy** (*pay*-lee-uhn-**tah**-luh-jee)

Paleozoic *noun* An era in the earth's history that began about 540 million years ago and ended about 250 million years ago. During this time, land plants, fish, amphibians, and reptiles began to appear. **Pa·le·o·zo·ic** (*pay*-lee-uh-**zoh**-ik) ▷ *adjective* **Paleozoic**

palette *noun* A flat board held in the hand, with a hole for the thumb. A palette is used for mixing paints. **pal·ette** (**pal**-it) **Palette** sounds like **palate**.

palindrome *noun* A word, sentence, or number that reads the same backward as forward: *"Anna," "Step on no pets," and the number 96769 are all palindromes.* **pal·in·drome** (**pal**-in-*drohm*)

palisade *noun* A line of steep cliffs, often bordering a river. **pal·i·sade** (*pal*-i-**sayd**)

pallid *adjective* Pale-looking, especially in the face or skin. **pal·lid** (**pal**-id) ▷ *noun* **pallor** (**pal**-ur)

palm
1. *noun* The flat inside surface of your hand.
2. *noun* A tall, tropical tree with large leaves shaped like feathers or fans at the top.
3. *verb* To hide something in your palm: *The magician palmed a quarter and made us think it had disappeared.* ▷ *verb* **palming, palmed**
palm (pahm)

palmetto *noun* A kind of palm tree with leaves shaped like fans. Palmettos grow in the southern United States. **pal·met·to** (pal-**met**-oh) ▷ *noun, plural* **palmettos** *or* **palmettoes**

palmistry *noun* The practice of telling people's fortunes by looking at the lines in the palms of their hands. **palm·ist·ry** (**pah**-mi-stree) ▷ *noun* **palmist**

palomino *noun* A golden-tan or cream horse with a white mane and tail. **pal·o·mi·no** (*pal*-uh-**mee**-noh) ▷ *noun, plural* **palominos**

pampas *noun, plural* Large, treeless plains in South America. The **pampas** are mainly in central Argentina and Uruguay. **pam·pas** (**pam**-puhz)

pamper *verb* To take very good care of yourself or someone else with food, kindness, or anything special: *Brenna loved and pampered her cat.* **pam·per** (**pam**-pur) ▷ *verb* **pampering, pampered**

pamphlet *noun* A small, thin booklet that usually contains an essay or information on one particular topic. **pam·phlet** (**pam**-flit)

pan
1. *noun* A wide, shallow metal container that is used for cooking.
2. *verb* To wash gravel in a pan or sieve, looking for gold: *Many people panned for gold in California during the late 1840s.*

panda

3. *verb* To move a movie or television camera over a wide area in order to display that area or to follow an action: *The camera panned the crowd before focusing on the president.*
4. *verb* (*informal*) To criticize someone or something harshly: *The drama critic panned both the play and the playwright.*
5. **pan out** *verb* (*informal*) To turn out well; to succeed: *Our plan to get together didn't pan out.*
pan (pan) ▷ *verb* **panning, panned**

pancake *noun* A thin, flat cake made from batter and cooked in a pan or on a griddle. **pan·cake** (**pan**-*kake*)

pancreas *noun* A gland near your stomach that makes a fluid that helps you digest food. The pancreas also makes insulin, a hormone that helps your body use glucose. **pan·cre·as** (**pan**-kree-uhs)

panda *noun*
1. An animal found in China that looks like a bear and has thick, black-and-white fur. It is also called a *giant panda*.
2. A small, reddish-brown animal that is found in Asia. It looks like a raccoon and has short legs, a long, bushy tail with rings, and a white face. It is also called a *lesser panda* or *red panda*.
pan·da (**pan**-duh)

pandemic *noun* An outbreak of a disease that affects a very large region or the whole world: *The flu pandemic in 1918 killed millions of people.* **pan·dem·ic** (pan-**dem**-ik)

pandemonium *noun* Noisy chaos or confusion. **pan·de·mo·ni·um** (*pan*-duh-**moh**-nee-uhm)

pane *noun* A sheet of glass or plastic in a window or door. **pane** (payn) **Pane** sounds like **pain**.

panel *noun*
1. A flat piece of wood or other material made to form part of a surface such as a wall. ▷ *noun* **paneling** ▷ *verb* **panel**
2. A board with instruments or controls on it, as in *a control panel in an airplane*.
3. A group of people chosen to do something such as judge a competition or discuss a topic. ▷ *noun* **panelist**
pan·el (**pan**-uhl)

a
b
c
d
e
f
g
h
i
j
k
l
m
n
o
p
q
r
s
t
u
v
w
x
y
z

panorama

pang *noun* A sudden, brief pain or emotion, as in *hunger pangs* or *a pang of guilt*. **pang** (pang)

panhandle

1. *verb* To ask for money from strangers passing by on the street: *Two homeless people were panhandling near the exit from the parking lot.* ▷ *verb* **panhandling, panhandled** ▷ *noun* **panhandler**

2. *noun* A long and narrow piece of land that sticks out from a broader area and looks like the handle of a pan. The word is often capitalized: *Tallahassee is the largest city in the Florida Panhandle.*
pan·han·dle (**pan**-*han*-duhl)

panic

1. *noun* A sudden feeling of terror or fright, often affecting many people at once, and so severe that people cannot act normally or make good decisions: *When the ship hit an iceberg, panic spread among the passengers.*

2. *verb* To feel sudden, overwhelming fear or anxiety: *Try not to panic when you hear the tornado sirens.* ▷ *verb* **panicking, panicked**

3. **panic-stricken** *adjective* Struck with sudden fear: *The panic-stricken villagers ran in all directions as the enemy tanks moved in.*
pan·ic (**pan**-ik)
▷ *adjective* **panicky**

panorama *noun* A wide or complete view of an area: *You can see a panorama of New York City from the top of the Empire State Building.* **pan·o·ram·a** (*pan*-uh-**ram**-uh) ▷ *adjective* **panoramic**

pansy *noun* A small garden flower with five rounded petals that are often purple, yellow, or white. **pan·sy** (**pan**-zee) ▷ *noun, plural* **pansies**

pant *verb* To breathe quickly and loudly because you are exhausted: *Josephine was panting by the time she caught up with us.* **pant** (pant) ▷ *verb* **panting, panted**

panther *noun* A general name for a large wildcat. The leopard, mountain lion, puma, cougar, and jaguar are all called panthers. **pan·ther** (**pan**-thur)

pantomime *noun*

1. The telling of a story with gestures, body movements, and facial expressions rather than words. ▷ *verb* **pantomime**

2. A play or scene acted out with gestures instead of words.
pan·to·mime (**pan**-tuh-*mime*)

pantry *noun* A small room or a closet in or near a kitchen where food and kitchen supplies are kept. **pan·try** (**pan**-tree) ▷ *noun, plural* **pantries**

pants *noun, plural* A piece of clothing with two legs that covers your body from the waist to the ankles. **pants** (pants)

panty hose *noun, plural* An undergarment, similar to tights, that covers the hips, legs, and feet and is often made of nylon. **pan·ty hose** (**pan**-tee)

paparazzi *noun, plural* Photographers who work for the entertainment media and spend a lot of time trying to get pictures of famous people: *The paparazzi swarmed around the actress as she stepped out of her car.* **pa·pa·raz·zi** (*pah*-puh-**raht**-see)

Word History

In the famous 1960 Italian film *La Dolce Vita*, the character of a news photographer was named Signor Paparazzo. Italian speakers began to call a photographer of celebrities a *paparazzo*. The Italian plural form, **paparazzi**, entered English by 1981, and is used to talk about one or more photographers. Federico Fellini, the movie's director, said the name Paparazzo made him think of a buzzing insect, which is as bothersome as an intrusive photographer. A word like this that comes from someone's name is called an eponym.

papaya *noun* The yellow or orange sweet fruit that grows on a tropical tree. It looks like a melon. **pa·pa·ya** (puh-**pah**-yuh)

paper

1. *noun* A thin piece or sheet of material made from wood pulp or rags. Paper is used for writing, printing, drawing, wrapping, and covering walls.

2. *noun* A single sheet of paper.

3. *noun* A document, or a sheet of paper with something printed or written on it: *Mr. Hernández*

keeps all of his important papers in a safe.

4. *noun* A written report or essay for school: *We write a paper every week for English class.*

5. *noun* A newspaper, as in *the morning paper.*

6. *verb* To put wallpaper up, or to cover something with paper. ▷ *verb* **papering, papered**
pa·per (**pay**-pur)

paperback *noun* A book with a paper cover.
pa·per·back (**pay**-pur-*bak*)

paper clip *noun* A bent piece of thin wire that is used to hold sheets of paper together.

paperweight *noun* A heavy, often decorative object used to hold down papers on a desk or other flat surface. **pa·per·weight** (**pay**-pur-*wayt*)

paperwork *noun* The part of a job or routine task that involves writing down information and keeping records: *DJ filled out a lot of paperwork at the emergency room.* **pa·per·work** (**pay**-pur-*wurk*)

papier-mâché *noun* Paper that has been soaked in glue, which hardens when it dries. Before hardening, this material can be molded into dolls, toys, furniture, and other shapes.
pa·pier-mâ·ché (**pay**-pur-muh-**shay**) ▷ *adjective* **papier-mâché**

paprika *noun* A reddish-orange spice made from sweet red peppers. **pap·ri·ka** (pa-**pree**-kuh)

papyrus *noun*

1. A tall water plant that grows in northern Africa and southern Europe.

2. Paper made from the stems of this plant. The ancient Egyptians wrote on papyrus.
pa·py·rus (puh-**pye**-ruhs)
▷ *noun, plural* **papyri** (puh-**pye**-ree) *or* **papyruses**

par *noun*

1. An equal level: *Her singing is on a par with yours.*

2. An accepted or normal level: *I have to get my grades up to par to stay on the football team.*

3. In golf, the number of strokes it should take a player to get the ball into the hole or finish a particular course.
par (pahr)

parable *noun* A story that illustrates a moral or religious lesson. **par·a·ble** (**par**-uh-buhl)

parachute *noun* A large piece of strong but lightweight fabric attached to thin ropes that spreads out in the air to slow the descent of whatever is attached to it. A parachute is used to drop people or loads safely from airplanes. **par·a·chute** (**pa**-ruh-*shoot*) ▷ *noun* **parachutist** ▷ *verb* **parachute**

parade

1. *noun* A procession of people and vehicles as part of a ceremony or festivity.

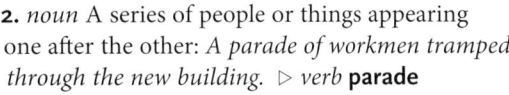

paper
clip

2. *noun* A series of people or things appearing one after the other: *A parade of workmen tramped through the new building.* ▷ *verb* **parade**

3. *verb* To show something off: *Gil paraded his new cowboy boots around the school.* ▷ *verb* **parading, paraded**
pa·rade (puh-**rade**)

paradise *noun*

1. A place that is considered extremely beautiful and that makes people feel happy and contented, as in *a vacation paradise.*

2. In some religions, **paradise** is another word for heaven.
par·a·dise (**par**-uh-*dise*)

paradox *noun*

1. A statement that seems to contradict itself but in fact may be true: *The phrase "a well-known secret agent" is an example of a paradox.*

2. A person or thing that seems to contradict itself: *My brother is a real paradox. Some days he's the nicest guy in the world; other times he's just plain mean to me.*
par·a·dox (**par**-uh-*dahks*)
▷ *noun, plural* **paradoxes** ▷ *adjective* **paradoxical**

paraffin *noun* A white, waxy substance used in making candles and for sealing jars. **par·af·fin** (**par**-uh-fin)

Papyrus

Papyrus was invented around 4000 B.C. in Egypt. It was made from a plant that grew along the Nile River. Papyrus was a very durable paper that was used until around A.D. 1000. It made writing and record keeping much easier. Boats, rope, and baskets were also made from this plant. The ancient Egyptians kept their production method secret, and exported papyrus to other areas.

Egyptian papyrus from 1100 B.C.

paragliding *noun* The sport of traveling long distances through the air using a specially designed canopy that looks like a long, narrow parachute. **par·a·glid·ing** (**par**-uh-*glye*-ding) ▷ *verb* **paraglide** ▷ *noun* **paraglider**

paragraph *noun* A section in a piece of writing that begins on a new line and often is indented. A paragraph is made up of one or more sentences about a single subject or idea. **par·a·graph** (**par**-uh-*graf*)

parakeet *noun* A small parrot with brightly colored feathers and a long, pointed tail. Parakeets often are kept as pets. **par·a·keet** (**par**-uh-*keet*)

paralegal *noun* A trained person who assists a lawyer. **par·a·le·gal** (*par*-uh-**lee**-guhl) ▷ *adjective* **paralegal**

parallel
1. *adjective* Staying the same distance from each other and never crossing or meeting, as in *parallel streets*.
2. *noun* A situation very similar to another one: *The detective noticed several parallels between the two crimes.* ▷ *verb* **parallel**
3. *noun* Any of the imaginary lines that circle the earth parallel to the equator. On a map, parallels represent degrees of latitude. **par·al·lel** (**par**-uh-*lel*)

parallel

parallel bars *noun, plural* A pair of horizontal wooden bars at the same or different heights used for doing exercises in gymnastics.

parallelogram *noun* A four-sided figure with opposite sides that are parallel and equal in length. **par·al·lel·o·gram** (*par*-uh-**lel**-uh-*gram*)

parallelogram

paralysis *noun*
1. A loss of the power to move or feel a part of the body.
2. An inability to act or function: *The budget crisis caused complete paralysis in the city government.* **pa·ral·y·sis** (puh-**ral**-i-sis)

paralyze *verb*
1. To cause paralysis in: *The accident paralyzed him.*
2. To make someone or something helpless or unable to function: *A blizzard paralyzed the airport.* **par·a·lyze** (**par**-uh-*lize*) ▷ *verb* **paralyzing, paralyzed**

paramecium *noun* A microscopic organism with only one cell that lives in freshwater. It is shaped like a

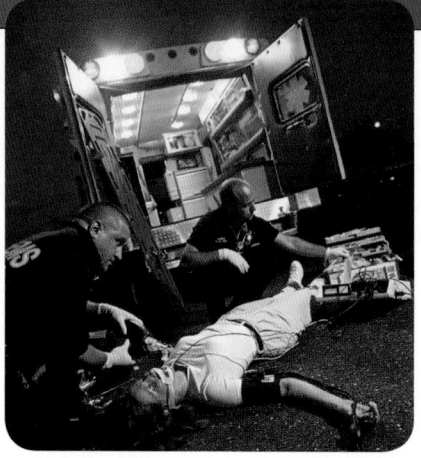
paramedic

slipper. **par·a·me·ci·um** (*par*-uh-**mee**-see-uhm) ▷ *noun, plural* **paramecia** (*par*-uh-**mee**-see-uh)

paramedic *noun* A person who is trained to give emergency medical treatment but who is not a doctor or a nurse. **par·a·med·ic** (*par*-uh-**med**-ik)

paramount *adjective* Above all others in rank, power, or importance: *A good education is of paramount importance in today's world.* **par·a·mount** (**par**-uh-*mount*)

paranoia *noun*
1. A mental illness that causes people to feel suspicious and believe strongly that others are trying to harm them or are plotting against them: *His paranoia led him to think the nurses were trying to poison his food.*
2. A state of suspicion, anxiety, and strong, often irrational, fear: *The city has been gripped by paranoia ever since the attack, even though the bomber was caught.* **par·a·noi·a** (*par*-uh-**noi**-uh)

paranoid *adjective*
1. Suffering from paranoia, as in *a paranoid schizophrenic*.
2. Having strong, irrational fears: *He was paranoid that his phone was bugged.*
3. (*informal*) Being overly anxious about something: *Stop being so paranoid! We'll be fine.* **par·a·noid** (**par**-uh-*noid*)

paraphernalia *noun* Numerous pieces of equipment, belongings, and other personal items, especially those needed for a particular activity: *Before the school year ended, I had to clean out all the paraphernalia from my desk.* **par·a·pher·na·lia** (*par*-uh-fur-**nayl**-yuh)

paraphrase *verb* To say or write something again in a different way. **par·a·phrase** (*par*-uh-*fraze*) ▷ *verb* **paraphrasing, paraphrased** ▷ *noun* **paraphrase**

paraplegic *noun* A person who has no feeling or movement in the lower part of his or her body, usually because of an injury or a disease of the spinal cord. **par·a·ple·gic** (*par*-uh-**plee**-jik) ▷ *adjective* **paraplegic**

parasite *noun*
1. An animal or plant that lives on or inside of another animal or plant.
2. A person who gets money, food, and shelter from another without doing anything in return. **par·a·site** (**par**-uh-*site*) ▷ *adjective* **parasitic** (*par*-uh-**sit**-ik)

paratroops

parasol *noun* A small, light umbrella that shades you from the sun. **par·a·sol** (**par**-uh-*sawl*)

paratroops *noun, plural* Soldiers who are trained to jump by parachute into battle. **par·a·troops** (**par**-uh-*troops*) ▷ *noun* **paratrooper**

parcel
1. *noun* A package, or something that is packed, wrapped, or put into a box.
2. *noun* A section or plot of land.
3. *verb* To divide into parts and give out: *The art teacher began the class by parceling out supplies.*
▷ *verb* **parceling, parceled**
par·cel (**pahr**-suhl)

parch *verb*
1. To make very dry: *The hot sun parched the soil.*
2. To make very thirsty.
parch (pahrch)
▷ *verb* **parches, parching, parched** ▷ *adjective* **parched**

parchment *noun* Heavy sheets of paper-like material made from the skin of sheep, goats, or other animals and used for writing on. **parch·ment** (**pahrch**-muhnt)

pardon
1. *verb* To forgive or excuse someone, or to cancel a person's punishment or other consequences: *The governor pardoned the prisoner.* ▷ *verb* **pardoning, pardoned** ▷ *noun* **pardon**
2. *interjection* You say **I beg your pardon** as a polite way of asking someone to repeat what he or she has said or asking someone for forgiveness.
par·don (**pahr**-duhn)

pare *verb*
1. To cut off the outer layer: *She pared the apple with a knife.*

2. To reduce or make less step by step, as if by cutting: *He pared down his book report until it was only one page long.*
pare (pair)
Pare sounds like **pair** and **pear**. ▷ *verb* **paring, pared**

parent *noun*
1. A mother or a father.
2. A plant or an animal that produces offspring.
par·ent (**pair**-uhnt)
▷ *noun* **parenthood** ▷ *verb* **parent**

parental *adjective* Of or having to do with being a parent, as in *parental supervision.* **pa·ren·tal** (puh-**ren**-tuhl)

parenthesis *noun* One of the curved lines ( ) used to enclose a word or phrase in a sentence or to enclose symbols or numbers in a mathematical expression. **pa·ren·the·sis** (puh-**ren**-thuh-sis) ▷ *noun, plural* **parentheses** (puh-**ren**-thuh-seez)

parenting *noun* The activities involved in being a parent and raising children: *New parents may need to learn some basic skills required for good parenting.* **par·ent·ing** (**pair**-uhn-ting)

parish *noun*
1. A particular church and the people who attend it.
2. In Louisiana, a county.
par·ish (**par**-ish)

parishioner *noun* A person who attends a particular church. **pa·rish·ion·er** (puh-**rish**-uh-nur)

park

park
1. *noun* An area of land with trees, benches, and sometimes playgrounds, used by the public for recreation.
2. *noun* An area of land set aside by the government so that it can be kept in its natural state.
3. *verb* To leave a car or other vehicle in a space in a garage or lot or at the curb of a street: *My mother parked the car near the library door.* ▷ *verb* **parking, parked**
park (pahrk)

parka *noun* A large, heavy jacket suitable for winter weather. It has a hood and is usually made of fur or a windproof material filled with down. **par·ka** (**pahr**-kuh)

Word History

The Nenets people of northern Russia wore very warm coats made from animal skin with the fur still on it. Their word for this type of coat was **parka**, which meant "a coat made from animal pelt."

parking meter *noun* A machine that you put money into in order to pay for parking. The meter allows you a certain amount of time for each coin you put into it.

parkway *noun* A wide highway or road that has grass, bushes, trees, and flowers planted down the middle or along the sides. **park·way** (**pahrk**-*way*)

parliament *noun* The group of people who have been elected to make the laws in some countries, such as Canada, the United Kingdom, and Israel. **par·lia·ment** (**pahr**-luh-muhnt) ▷ *adjective* **parliamentary**

Word History

A **parliament** is a place for "speaking." English speakers borrowed the term from the French word *parlement,* meaning "conversation"; at the root of *parlement* is the verb *parler,* meaning "to speak." In a 14th-century poem called "Parliament of Fowls," a group of birds gather to talk about choosing mates.

parlor *noun*
1. A formal living room, especially in an old house.
2. A room or rooms used for a business, as in *an ice-cream parlor.*
par·lor (**pahr**-lur)

Parmesan cheese *noun* A very hard cheese with a sharp flavor, usually grated and used especially with pasta dishes. Parmesan cheese was originally made in Parma, Italy. **Par·me·san cheese** (**pahr**-muh-*zahn*)

parochial *adjective*
1. Of or having to do with a church parish, as in *a parochial school.*
2. Having a narrow, shortsighted point of view: *Minnie's parochial views were old-fashioned.*
pa·ro·chi·al (puh-**roh**-kee-uhl)

parody *noun* An imitation of a serious piece of writing or a song that makes fun of the original work. **par·o·dy** (**par**-uh-dee) ▷ *noun, plural* **parodies** ▷ *verb* **parody**

parole *noun* The early release of a prisoner, usually for good behavior, on the condition that he or she continues to obey the law. **pa·role** (puh-**role**) ▷ *verb* **parole**

paroxysm *noun* A sudden outburst or fit, as in *a paroxysm of weeping.* **par·ox·ysm** (**par**-uhk-*siz*-uhm)

parrot
1. *noun* A brightly colored tropical bird with a curved beak and a rough voice. Some parrots can learn to repeat things that are said to them: *The scarlet macaw is one of the largest members of the parrot family.*
2. *noun* A person who repeats or imitates words without understanding what they mean.
3. *verb* To repeat something in a mechanical way: *My two-year-old sister parrots the way I say "hello" when answering the phone.* ▷ *verb* **parroting, parroted**
par·rot (**par**-uht)

Word History

Pierre is the French form of the name Peter, and the English word **parrot** may be based on this name. Several centuries ago, French speakers added an ending meaning "little" to the name Pierre, and the result was Pierrot, meaning "little Peter." Another form of this name was Perrot. People perhaps then applied this name to parrots, just as parrots are sometimes called Polly by English speakers. In the early 1500s, the word *parrot* appeared for the first time in English, and English speakers may have taken the term from the French name.

parse *verb* To identify the parts of speech and the grammatical structures of a sentence. **parse** (pahrs) ▷ *verb* **parsing, parsed**

parsley *noun* A leafy, green herb with small leaves, used to season or to decorate food. **pars·ley** (**pahr**-slee)

parsnip *noun* A plant with a pale yellow root eaten as a vegetable. Parsnips resemble carrots. **pars·nip** (**pahr**-snip)

parson *noun* A minister, especially a Protestant minister. **par·son** (**pahr**-suhn)

part
1. *noun* A portion or division of a whole: *I fell asleep during the last part of the movie.*
2. *noun* A piece in a machine or device: *Our television has a broken part.*
3. *noun* An expected share of responsibility or work: *If you all do your part, the school carnival will be a success.*
4. *noun* A character or role in a play or film.

parsley

5. *noun* A line in your hair where the hair is combed in two directions. ▷ *verb* **part**

6. *verb* To separate or to divide: *We parted at the entrance of the store.*

7. *adjective* Not completely or entirely: *My grandfather is part Cherokee.*

8. part with *verb* To give something away or give it up.

9. take part *verb* To join with others in an activity.

part (pahrt)

▷ *verb* **parting, parted**

Synonyms

A **part** is anything less than all of something. A part may be very small or very large, just as long as it is not the whole thing: *Part of the story takes place in Indiana. Part of Jaime's tooth broke off when he bit into the apple.*

- -

■ A **piece** is a fragment of something that is separated from the whole: *We found the last piece of the jigsaw puzzle under the couch.*

■ A **portion** is a share of something, usually one that is assigned or given to someone: *When Pierre finished his portion of roast beef, he asked if he could have some more.*

■ A **section** is a part that is often separate or distinct in some way: *Julia ate a section of grapefruit. My dad loves to read the sports section of the newspaper.*

■ A **component** is a part that is important in helping to complete the whole: *Math is one component of a good education.*

■ A **division** is one of the parts into which something large has been organized: *Sharice's mom works for the magazine division at the publishing company.*

partial *adjective*

1. Incomplete: *Our science fair project was only a partial success.*

2. Favoring one person or side over another.

3. partial to Especially fond of a particular thing: *I'm partial to a cold glass of iced tea on a hot day.*

par·tial (**pahr**-shuhl)

▷ *noun* **partiality** (pahr-shee-**al**-i-tee)

partially *adverb* To a degree; not entirely: *My skin was partially sunburned—where I hadn't kept it covered, it got burned.* **par·tial·ly** (**pahr**-shuh-lee)

participant *noun* Someone who takes part in something, as in *a participant in team sports.* **par·tic·i·pant** (pahr-**tis**-uh-puhnt)

participate *verb* To join with others in an activity or event: *To participate in the study, all I had to do was answer a few questions.* **par·tic·i·pate**

(pahr-**tis**-uh-*pate*) ▷ *verb* **participating, participated** ▷ *noun* **participation**

participle *noun* A form of a verb that is used with a helping verb or that can be used as an adjective. English has two kinds of participles: the **present participle**, ending in *-ing*, as in *walking* or *singing*, and the **past participle**, often but not always ending in *-ed* or *-en*, as in *finished* or *swollen*. **par·ti·ci·ple** (**pahr**-ti-*sip*-uhl)

particle *noun* An extremely small piece or amount of something. **par·ti·cle** (**pahr**-ti-kuhl)

particle physics *noun* The study of the behavior of the components of atoms.

particular

1. *adjective* Individual or special: *The cat always sits in this particular chair.*

2. *adjective* Very careful about details: *My teacher is particular about neat handwriting.*

3. *adjective* Special or unusual: *Pay particular attention to his instructions.*

4. *noun* A detail: *We can check the particulars of the movie schedule in the newspaper.*

5. in particular Especially: *I am interested in these two authors in particular.*

par·tic·u·lar (pur-**tik**-yuh-lur)

particularly *adverb* Especially: *I'm not feeling particularly well today.* **par·tic·u·lar·ly** (pur-**tik**-yuh-lur-lee)

parting

1. *noun* A departure or a separation, as in *a sad parting.*

2. *adjective* Of or having to do with a departure or separation, as in *a parting handshake.*

part·ing (**pahr**-ting)

partisan

1. *noun* A person who is completely loyal to a group or political party, without thinking about whether they are right or wrong.

2. *adjective* Based on loyalty to a group rather than genuine debate and examination of facts: *The speeches the Congressmen gave were mostly partisan bickering and neither of them gave good answers to our questions.* **par·ti·san** (**pahr**-ti-zuhn)

partition

1. *noun* A movable wall or panel used to divide an area or a room.

2. *verb* To section something off or to separate something: *We partitioned the dining room from the living room with a painted screen.*

3. *verb* To divide into sections or parts: *The town partitioned the land into lots for houses.* **par·ti·tion** (pahr-**tish**-uhn)

▷ *verb* **partitioning, partitioned**

a b c d e f g h i j k l m n o p q r s t u v w x y z

partly *adverb* In part or to some extent: *He was partly to blame for the accident.* **part·ly** (pahrt-lee)

partner *noun* A person who works or does some other activity with another person or persons, as in *trading partners* or *tennis partners*. **part·ner** (pahrt-nur)

partnership *noun*
1. The state of being a partner, as in *a business partnership* or *a romantic partnership*.
2. An association or business involving two or more people as partners: *The three brothers formed a partnership to build more low-income housing.* **part·ner·ship** (pahrt-nur-*ship*)

part of speech *noun* A grammatical class into which a word can be placed according to the way it is used in a phrase or sentence, such as **noun**, **verb**, or **adjective**. ▷ *noun, plural* **parts of speech**

partridge *noun* A plump game bird that has gray, brown, and white feathers. **par·tridge** (pahr-trij)

part-time *adjective* Done for only a few hours each day or a few days each week, as in *a part-time job.* ▷ *noun* **part-timer** ▷ *adverb* **part time**

party *noun*
1. An organized occasion when people enjoy themselves in a group, often to celebrate a special event. ▷ *verb* **party**
2. A group of people working together on a particular task: *The search party found the stranded hikers.*
3. An organized group of people with similar political beliefs who sponsor candidates in elections: *The Democratic and Republican parties are the largest political parties in the United States.* **par·ty** (pahr-tee)
▷ *noun, plural* **parties** ▷ *adjective* **party**

pass
1. *verb* To go by someone or something: *I always pass the library on my way to school.*
2. *verb* To give something to somebody who is farther away from it: *Yusef passed the salad to me.*
3. *verb* To kick, throw, or hit a ball to someone on your own team in a game or sport. ▷ *noun* **pass** ▷ *noun* **passer**
4. *verb* To succeed in a test or course: *My mom passed all her exams, and now she can practice law.* ▷ *noun* **pass**
5. *verb* To move on or to go by: *The days passed quickly.*
6. *verb* To approve or to make into law: *The Senate passed the gun control bill.*
7. *noun* A narrow passage in a mountain range.
8. *noun* Written permission, as in *a hall pass.*

9. *noun* A free ticket: *I won two passes to the game.*
10. **pass away** *verb* To die.
11. **pass out** *verb* To faint.
12. **pass up** *verb* To give up the opportunity to have or do something: *Ellen passed up a party in order to finish her report.*
pass (pas)
▷ *verb* **passes, passing, passed** ▷ *noun, plural* **passes**

passage *noun*
1. A hall or a corridor.
2. A short section of a book or piece of music.
3. A journey by ship or airplane: *The boat made a safe passage across the Atlantic Ocean.*
4. Approval of a bill into law by a legislature: *At this time, passage of the bill is uncertain.*
pas·sage (pas-ij)

passageway *noun* An alley, a hallway, a tunnel, or anything that allows you to pass from one place to another. **pas·sage·way** (pas-ij-*way*)

passenger *noun* Someone besides the driver who travels in a vehicle. **pas·sen·ger** (pas-uhn-jur)

passerby *noun* A person who happens to be passing. **pass·er·by** (pas-ur-*bye*) ▷ *noun, plural* **passersby**

passion *noun*
1. A very strong feeling, such as anger, love, or hatred.
2. Great devotion or enthusiasm: *He has a passion for football.*
pas·sion (pash-uhn)

passionate *adjective* Having or showing very strong feelings, as in *a passionate speech.* **pas·sion·ate** (pash-uh-nit)
▷ *adverb* **passionately**

passive *adjective*
1. Not inclined to fight back, react to, or resist things that happen. ▷ *adverb* **passively**
2. The subject of a **passive** verb has something done to it. It receives an action, while the subject of an active verb performs an action: *The verb in the sentence "He was dismissed from school" is passive, because the subject, "He," is receiving rather than performing the action.* See **active**.
pas·sive (pas-iv)

Passover *noun* An important Jewish holiday celebrated in the spring. It commemorates the Jews' escape from slavery in Egypt. **Pass·o·ver** (pas-oh-vur)

passport *noun* An official document that verifies that you are a citizen of a certain country and allows you to cross international borders. **pass·port** (pas-*port*)

passport

password *noun* A secret word, code, or phrase that you need to know to get into a guarded area or a computer system. **pass·word** (**pas**-*wurd*)

past

1. *noun* The period of time before the present: *In the past, people traveled by stagecoach.* ▷ *adjective* **past**

2. *adjective* Just finished or ended: *The past month was rainy.*

3. *preposition* To or on the far side of: *We went past the exit.* ▷ *adverb* **past**

4. *adjective* Former, as in *the past president of the club.*

5. past tense *noun* The form of a verb that shows that an action took place in the past.

past (past)

pasta *noun* A food made from dough that is formed into shapes and dried. It is boiled in a liquid and usually served with a sauce. **pas·ta** (**pah**-stuh)

paste

1. *noun* A soft, sticky mixture used to hold things together.

2. *noun* Any soft, creamy mixture, as in *tomato paste.*

3. *verb* To fasten with paste.

4. *verb* On a computer, to insert text or graphics copied or cut from another location.

paste (payst)

▷ *verb* **pasting, pasted**

pastel *noun*

1. A chalky crayon that is used in drawing.

2. A picture made with pastels.

3. A light, soft shade of a color.

pas·tel (pa-**stel**)

▷ *adjective* **pastel**

pasteurize *verb* To heat milk or another liquid to a temperature that is high enough to kill harmful bacteria. **pas·teur·ize** (**pas**-chuh-*rize*) ▷ *noun* **pasteurization** (*pas*-chur-i-**zay**-shuhn) ▷ *adjective* **pasteurized**

Word History

The first person to **pasteurize** milk was the French scientist and inventor Louis Pasteur (1822–1895). The process was named after him.

pastime *noun* A hobby, an activity, or an entertainment that makes the time pass in an enjoyable way: *Watching basketball is my favorite pastime.* **pas·time** (**pas**-*time*)

pasta

pastor *noun* A minister or priest in charge of a church or parish. **pas·tor** (**pas**-tur)

pastoral *adjective*

1. Of or having to do with rural areas: *Paintings of pastoral scenes make me want to live on a farm.*

2. Having to do with or coming from a pastor, as in *pastoral guidance.*

pas·tor·al (**pas**-tur-uhl)

past participle *noun* A form of a verb that often, but not always, ends in -*ed* or -*en* and can be used with a helping verb to show that an action or a condition is completed. In the sentence "I have wrapped his gift," the word *wrapped* is a past participle. A past participle is also used to help form a passive verb, such as *kicked* in the sentence "The ball was kicked." Past participles may also be used as adjectives, such as *swollen* in "a swollen ankle."

pastry *noun*

1. A dough that is used for pie crusts.

2. Pies, tarts, and other sweet baked goods.

pas·try (**pay**-stree)

▷ *noun, plural* **pastries**

past tense *noun* A form of a verb that shows that an action took place in the past, such as *went* in "She went to school late yesterday."

pasture *noun* Grazing land for animals. **pas·ture** (**pas**-chur)

pasty *adjective* Pale and sickly-looking, as in *a pasty complexion.* **pas·ty** (**pay**-stee) ▷ *adjective* **pastier, pastiest**

pat

1. *verb* To touch something gently with your hand: *Erika patted the frightened kitten to calm it down.* ▷ *verb* **patting, patted** ▷ *noun* **pat**

2. *noun* A small, flat piece, as in *a pat of butter.*

3. pat on the back *noun* Praise for a person who has done something well.

pat (pat)

patch

1. *verb* To repair a small hole or tear by covering it with the same or similar material, as in *to patch a shirt* or *to patch a street.* ▷ *noun* **patch**

2. *noun* A small part or area of something: *The pine tree was a patch of green against the snow.*

3. *noun* A small piece of ground: *We planted tomatoes in our vegetable patch.*

4. patch up *verb* To settle or to smooth over: *We patched up our quarrel.*

patch (pach)

▷ *verb* **patches, patching, patched** ▷ *noun, plural* **patches**

patchwork *noun* A type of needlework consisting of a pattern made by sewing small patches of different material together. Some quilts are patchwork. **patch·work** (**pach**-*wurk*)

patchy *adjective* Uneven; made up of or similar to patches, as in *patchy clouds*. **patch·y** (**pach**-ee)
▷ *adjective* **patchier, patchiest**

pâté *noun* A smooth spread made of meat, fish, or vegetables that is usually eaten on toast or crackers. **pâ·té** (pah-**tay** *or* pa-**tay**)

patent

1. (**pat**-uhnt) *noun* A legal document giving the inventor of an item the sole rights to manufacture or sell it: *My great-uncle took out a patent on a new kind of baseball bat.*

2. (**pat**-uhnt) **patent leather** *noun* Very shiny leather used for shoes, belts, handbags, and other accessories.

3. (**pay**-tuhnt *or* **pat**-uhnt) *verb* To obtain a patent for: *He should patent his invention before someone else comes up with the same idea.*

4. *adjective* Obvious or open: *Liam told a patent falsehood.*

pat·ent
▷ *verb* **patenting, patented** ▷ *adverb* **patently**

Word History

In medieval England, the phrase *letters patent* referred to a letter from the ruler of the country that gave someone something, such as land or rights. Anyone in the kingdom could read the *letters patent* because the sheets were not folded up and sealed on the outside as other letters from the ruler were. The word *patent* meant "open." It was based on the word part *patent-* in Latin, from the present participle of the verb *patere*, meaning "to be open." English speakers shortened *letters patent* to just *patent,* and today, we call the legal document that gives rights to an inventor a **patent**.

paternal *adjective*

1. Having to do with or like a father: *He has paternal concern for his young neighbor.*

2. Related through your father: *My paternal grandparents come from Cuba.*
pat·er·nal (puh-**tur**-nuhl)
▷ *adverb* **paternally**

path *noun*

1. A trail or track for walking.

2. The line or route along which a person or thing moves: *Scientists tracked the path of the hurricane.*
path (path)

pathetic *adjective*

1. Causing pity, sorrow, or sympathy: *The cold, hungry kitten was a pathetic sight.*

patchwork

2. Completely inadequate, as in *a pathetic attempt*. **pa·thet·ic** (puh-**thet**-ik)
▷ *adverb* **pathetically**

pathogen *noun* Something that causes a disease when it enters an organism. Viruses and bacteria are the most common pathogens. **path·o·gen** (**path**-uh-juhn)
▷ *adjective* **pathogenic** (path-uh-**jen**-ik)

patient

1. *adjective* Able to put up with problems and delays without getting angry or upset. ▷ *noun* **patience** (**pay**-shuhns) ▷ *adverb* **patiently**

2. *noun* A person who is receiving treatment from a doctor or other health care provider: *The doctor was ready to see his next patient.*
pa·tient (**pay**-shuhnt)

patio *noun* A paved area next to a house, used for relaxing or eating outdoors. **pat·i·o** (**pat**-ee-*oh*)
▷ *noun, plural* **patios**

patriarch *noun*

1. The male head of a family or tribe: *Grandpa is the patriarch of our family.*

2. An older man in a group, tribe, or village who is respected and who holds a place of honor.

3. the Patriarch The head of the Eastern Orthodox Church.
pa·tri·arch (**pay**-tree-*ahrk*)

patriot *noun* A person who loves his or her country and is ready to defend it. **pa·tri·ot** (**pay**-tree-uht)
▷ *noun* **patriotism**

patriotic *adjective* A person who is **patriotic** has a strong loyalty to his or her own country. **pa·tri·ot·ic** (*pay*-tree-**ah**-tik) ▷ *adverb* **patriotically**

patrol

1. *verb* To walk or travel around an area to watch or protect it or the people within it: *Police patrol the area regularly.* ▷ *verb* **patrolling, patrolled**

2. *noun* A group of people who watch and protect an

area, as in *a highway patrol*.

3. *noun* A group of soldiers, sometimes aboard ships or airplanes, sent out to find or learn about the enemy. **pa·trol** (puh-**trohl**)

patron *noun*

1. A customer, as in *a restaurant patron*.

2. A person who gives money to or helps another person, an activity, or a cause, as in *a patron of the arts*.

pa·tron (**pay**-truhn)

▷ *noun* **patronage** (**pay**-truh-nij)

patronize *verb*

1. To act or talk to someone as though you are better or more knowledgeable than he or she is.

2. To go to a store, restaurant, or other business regularly.

pa·tron·ize (**pay**-truh-*nize* or **pat**-ruh-*nize*)

▷ *verb* **patronizing, patronized**

patron saint *noun* A saint who is believed to look after an individual, a group of people, a particular activity, a city, or a country.

patter

1. *verb* To make light, quick sounds: *I love to hear the rain patter on the roof.* ▷ *verb* **pattering, pattered** ▷ *noun* **patter**

2. *noun* Continuous, fast talking, especially in order to distract someone: *The magician kept up a steady patter while he performed his tricks.*

pat·ter (**pat**-ur)

pattern *noun*

1. A repeating arrangement of colors, shapes, and figures: *The scarf has a pattern of flowers.* ▷ *adjective* **patterned**

2. A sample or model that you can follow as a guide: *I made my dress from a pattern.*

3. A repeated set of actions or characteristics: *There was a pattern to the crimes.*

pat·tern (**pat**-urn)

▷ *verb* **pattern**

patty *noun*

1. A round, flat piece of chopped or ground food, as in *a hamburger patty*.

2. A round, flat piece of candy, as in *a mint patty*.

pat·ty (**pat**-ee)

▷ *noun, plural* **patties**

pauper *noun* A very poor person. **pau·per** (**paw**-pur)

pause *verb* To stop briefly: *Gretchen paused in the middle of her walk to enjoy the scenery.* **pause** (pawz) ▷ *verb* **pausing, paused** ▷ *noun* **pause**

pave *verb*

1. To cover a road or other surface with a hard material such as concrete or asphalt.

2. pave the way To lead the way, or to make progress

easier: *Her experiments paved the way for future research.*

pave (payv)

▷ *verb* **paving, paved**

pavement *noun*

1. A hard material, such as concrete or asphalt, that is used to cover roads or sidewalks.

2. A paved road or a sidewalk.

pave·ment (**payv**-muhnt)

pavilion *noun*

1. An open building that is used for shelter or recreation or for a show or an exhibit, as in *an art pavilion*.

2. One of a group of buildings, especially a building that is part of a hospital.

pa·vil·ion (puh-**vil**-yuhn)

paw

1. *noun* The foot of an animal that has four feet and claws.

2. *verb* To touch with a paw: *The dog paws at the door when he wants to go out.*

3. *verb* To handle roughly or carelessly: *Jillian pawed through the lost-and-found box looking for her scarf.*

paw (paw)

▷ *verb* **pawing, pawed**

pawn

1. *verb* To leave a valuable item at a pawnbroker's in return for a loan. The item is returned to you if you repay the money, or it may be sold if you do not.

▷ *verb* **pawning, pawned**

2. *noun* The smallest piece in the game of chess, having the lowest value.

3. *noun* A person or thing that is used by someone else to get something or to gain an advantage.

pawn (pawn)

pawnbroker *noun* A person whose business is to make loans to people who leave valuable objects as security for the loans. **pawn·brok·er** (**pawn**-*broh*-kur)

pawn

pay

1. *verb* To give money for something.

2. *verb* To be worthwhile or advantageous: *It pays to arrive early.*

3. *verb* To give or offer: *Celeste paid me a compliment.*

4. *verb* To suffer consequences for an action: *O'Connor will pay for not following directions.*

5. *noun* Money earned from working, as in *overtime pay*.

pay (pay)

▷ *verb* **pays, paying, paid**

payable *adjective* Able to be paid or that must be paid: *Enclose a check payable to the Internal Revenue Service.* **pay·a·ble** (**pay**-uh-buhl)

payment *noun* Money given in return for something: *They always made their mortgage payments on time.* **pay·ment** (**pay**-mint)

payoff *noun*
1. An act of giving or receiving money for something that has happened before: *If that horse wins, the payoff would be $47 on a $2 bet.*
2. A benefit received from an effort or investment that came before: *It takes a long time to get good at playing chess, but when you do the payoff is worth it.* **pay·off** (**pay**-*awf*)

pay-per-view *noun* A service for cable television viewers in which customers order and view a single movie or televised event for a fee.

payroll *noun*
1. A list of workers who are paid by a company, along with the amount each is to be paid.
2. The total of all money paid to workers: *The guard picked up the payroll from the bank.* **pay·roll** (**pay**-*rohl*)

PC
1. *noun* Short for **personal computer**.
2. *adjective* (*informal*) A person who is **PC** makes a great effort to be sensitive to the needs and wishes of all groups, including minorities, women, and the disabled. PC is short for *politically correct*.

PDF *noun* A popular format for electronic documents, or a document formatted in this way. PDF is short for *portable document format*.

PE *noun* A period in school during which you play sports or do any kind of physical exercise. PE is short for *physical education*.

pea *noun* A small, round, green vegetable that grows as a seed in a pod. **pea** (pee)

Word History

The nursery rhyme called "Pease Porridge Hot" shows us what the old word for **pea** was. *Pease* meant "pea," so in this children's rhyme, *pease porridge* meant "pea porridge." Pease porridge was a dish made of cooked peas. English speakers began interpreting *pease* as a plural form, however, and thought that the singular was *pea*. Eventually, the spelling *pease* was dropped entirely, and now *pea* has the regular plural form of *peas*.

---

peace *noun*
1. A period without war or fighting. ▷ *noun* **peacetime**
2. Calmness of mind or environment: *I'd like some peace and quiet.*

peacock

3. Public security, or law and order: *In frontier times, a sheriff's job was to keep the peace.* **peace** (pees)
Peace sounds like **piece**.

peaceful *adjective*
1. Quiet and without any disturbance: *We enjoy the peaceful atmosphere of the lake on summer evenings.*
2. Tending to avoiding conflict: *"We're a peaceful nation, yet we are prepared to confront any danger,"* the president said. **peace·ful** (**pees**-fuhl)
▷ ad*verb* **peacefully**

peacekeeping *noun* A policy of keeping law and order; especially, an arrangement by which international troops who do not support either side in a conflict are sent to try to prevent war. **peace·keep·ing** (**pees**-*kee*-ping)

peach *noun*
1. A soft, round, sweet fruit with a fuzzy, reddish-yellow skin and a pit at the center. ▷ *noun, plural* **peaches**
2. A pink-yellow color. **peach** (peech)
▷ *adjective* **peach**

peacock *noun* A large bird that is related to the pheasant. The male peacock has brilliant blue-and-green feathers that spread out in a fan shape when it raises its tail. **pea·cock** (**pee**-*kahk*)

peak
1. *noun* The pointed top of a high mountain.
2. *noun* A mountain with a pointed top: *We hiked up the peak in two days.*
3. *noun* The highest or best point: *Becoming the president of the company was the peak of Justin's career.*
4. *verb* To reach the highest or best point: *The*

popularity of the waltz peaked in the 19th century.
▷ *verb* **peaking, peaked**
peak (peek)
Peak sounds like **peek**.

peal
1. *verb* To ring out loudly: *The bells pealed at midnight on Christmas Day.* ▷ *verb* **pealing, pealed**
2. *noun* A loud sound or series of sounds, as in *peals of laughter.*
peal (peel)
Peal sounds like **peel**.

peanut *noun* A nutlike seed that grows in underground pods. Peanuts are eaten roasted or made into peanut butter and cooking oil. **pea·nut** (**pee**-nuht)

peanut butter *noun* A thick, light brown spread made from ground, roasted peanuts.

pear *noun* A juicy, sweet, yellow, green, red, or brown fruit with a smooth skin. **pear** (pair) **Pear** sounds like **pair** and **pare**.

pearl *noun*
1. A small, round object that grows inside oysters and is used to make valuable jewelry.
2. A valuable person, thing, or idea, as in *pearls of wisdom.*
pearl (purl)

Word History

If a friend of yours told you about her beautiful new *margarite* ring, you would wonder what a *margarite* was. But if she said it was a **pearl** ring, you would understand. The old-fashioned word *margarite* was the usual word for a pearl a thousand years ago. The word *pearl* was introduced later, when English speakers heard the French word *perle* and adopted it. The origin of *perle* may be the Latin word *perna*, the ancient Romans' name for an animal with two shells, like a clam. The connection between *perle* and *perna* would be that oysters, where pearls grow, also have two shells.

peasant *noun* A person who owns a small farm or works on a farm, especially in Europe and some Asian nations. **peas·ant** (**pez**-uhnt)

peat *noun* Dark brown, partly decayed plant matter that is found in bogs and swamps. Peat can be used as fuel or compost. **peat** (peet)

pebble *noun* A small, round, smooth stone. **peb·ble** (**peb**-uhl) ▷ *adjective* **pebbly**

pecan *noun* A sweet nut with a thin, smooth shell. Pecans grow on large trees. **pe·can** (**pee**-kan *or* pi-**kahn**)

peck
1. *verb* To strike or pick up something with the beak: *The ducks pecked at the bread on the edge of the pond.*
2. *verb* To eat in small bites or without enthusiasm: *Natasha pecked at her lunch without eating much.* ▷ *noun* **peck**
3. *noun* (*informal*) A quick, light kiss: *Gabe's grandmother gave him a peck on the cheek.* ▷ *verb* **peck**
4. *noun* A unit of measure for dry things, such as produce or grain. A peck is equal to eight quarts, or one-fourth of a bushel.
peck (pek)
▷ *verb* **pecking, pecked**

peculiar *adjective*
1. Odd or unusual.
2. **peculiar to** Belonging to or having to do with a certain person, group, place, or thing: *This type of flower is peculiar to swamps.*
pe·cu·liar (pi-**kyool**-yur)
▷ *noun* **peculiarity** (pi-*kyoo*-lee-**ar**-i-tee) ▷ *adverb* **peculiarly**

pedal
1. *noun* A lever that you push with your foot, such as on a bicycle or a car.
2. *verb* To operate something by using a pedal or pedals. ▷ *verb* **pedaling, pedaled**
ped·al (**ped**-uhl)
Pedal sounds like **peddle**.

peddle *verb* To sell things by going from house to house or place to place: *When my grandfather was a boy, he used a horse and wagon to peddle fruits and vegetables.* **ped·dle** (**ped**-uhl) **Peddle** sounds like **pedal**. ▷ *verb* **peddling, peddled** ▷ *noun* **peddler**

pedestal *noun*
1. The base of a statue.
2. Any base or support, as for a large vase.
3. **put someone on a pedestal** To admire a person excessively: *Gwen put her drama teacher on a pedestal.*
ped·es·tal (**ped**-i-stuhl)

pedestrian *noun* A person who travels on foot. **pe·des·tri·an** (puh-**des**-tree-uhn)

pediatrician *noun* A doctor who specializes in the care and treatment of babies and children. **pe·di·a·tric·ian** (*pee*-dee-uh-**tri**-shuhn)

pediatrics *noun* The branch of medicine that is concerned with babies and children. **pe·di·at·rics** (*pee*-dee-**at**-riks) ▷ *adjective* **pediatric**

pedigree *noun* A line or list of ancestors, especially of an animal: *My dog's pedigree includes many champion show dogs.* **ped·i·gree** (**ped**-i-*gree*)

peek *verb*

1. To look at something secretly or quickly: *It was difficult not to peek at the package that arrived a few days before my birthday.* ▷ *noun* **peek**

2. To be barely visible: *The edge of a coat peeked from the closet door.*

peek (peek)

Peek sounds like **peak**. ▷ *verb* **peeking, peeked**

peel

1. *noun* The outer skin of a fruit.

2. *verb* To remove the skin of a vegetable or a fruit.

3. *verb* To remove or to pull off: *Before you paint this wall, you must peel off the wallpaper.*

4. *verb* To come off in pieces or strips: *The paint was peeling off the porch of the abandoned house.*

peel (peel)

Peel sounds like **peal**. ▷ *verb* **peeling, peeled**

peep

1. *verb* To peek or look secretly at something. ▷ *verb* **peeping, peeped** ▷ *noun* **peep**

2. *noun* The high, sharp sound that a young bird or chicken makes. ▷ *verb* **peep**

peep (peep)

peer

1. *verb* To look at something with difficulty: *He peered at the note but could not read it in the dim light.* ▷ *verb* **peering, peered**

2. *noun* An equal, or a person of the same age, rank, or standing as another, as in *a jury of one's peers.*

3. *noun* A member of the British nobility, such as a duke or an earl. ▷ *noun* **peerage**

peer (peer)

Peer sounds like **pier**.

peg *noun* A short, cylindrical piece of wood, metal, or plastic used to hold things together, hang things on, or mark a position. **peg** (peg) ▷ *verb* **peg**

Pekingese *noun* A breed of small dog originally from China. A Pekingese has a long, silky coat and a flat face. **Pe·king·ese** (*pee*-ki-**neez**) ▷ *noun, plural* **Pekingese**

pelican *noun* A large waterbird with a long bill and a pouch below the bill that can hold the fish it catches. **pel·i·can** (**pel**-i-kuhn)

pellet *noun* A small, hard ball of something, such as food or ice. **pel·let** (**pel**-it)

pell-mell *adverb* In a confused or disorderly way: *The frightened child rushed pell-mell into the crowd.* **pell-mell** (**pel**-mel)

pelt

1. *verb* To strike or beat again and again: *Hail pelted the windshield.* ▷ *verb* **pelting, pelted**

Pelicans

Pelicans live on coastal and inland waters of every continent except Antarctica. They have a long neck, short legs, and a very large bill with a pouch underneath. The pouch helps the pelicans catch the fish and other small animals that they eat. Their long wingspan lets them fly and glide as far as 100 miles to find food.

2. *noun* An animal's skin with the hair or fur still on it.

pelt (pelt)

pelvis *noun* A sturdy ring of bones that protects the organs in your lower abdomen. Your spine is attached at the top of it, and your legs at the bottom. **pel·vis** (**pel**-vis)

pen

1. *noun* An instrument used for writing or drawing with ink. ▷ *verb* **pen**

2. *noun* A small, enclosed area for sheep, cattle, pigs, or other animals.

3. *verb* To keep or shut up in a pen: *Zahra penned the pigs so they wouldn't destroy her garden.* ▷ *verb* **penning, penned**

pen (pen)

penalize *verb* To punish someone in some way, or to put someone at a disadvantage: *The referee penalized the basketball player for shoving.* **pe·nal·ize** (**pee**-nuh-lize) ▷ *verb* **penalizing, penalized**

penalty *noun*

1. A punishment: *In my town, the penalty for littering is a $100 fine.*

2. In sports, a disadvantage or punishment that a team or player suffers for breaking the rules: *The referee called a penalty of ten yards against our team.*

pen·al·ty (**pen**-uhl-tee)

pencil *noun*

1. An instrument used for drawing and writing, made of a stick of graphite in a wooden, metal, or plastic casing.

2. A similar instrument containing a cosmetic, medication, or other material, as in *a charcoal pencil.* **pen·cil** (**pen**-suhl)

▷ *verb* **pencil**

pendant *noun* A hanging ornament, especially one worn on a necklace. **pen·dant** (**pen**-duhnt)

pendulum *noun* A weight in a large clock that moves from side to side and keeps the clock's mechanism in regular motion. **pen·du·lum** (**pen**-juh-luhm *or* **pen**-dyuh-luhm)

penetrate *verb*

1. To go inside or through something: *The syrup penetrated the waffle.*

2. To understand or to solve, as in *to penetrate a mystery.* **pen·e·trate** (**pen**-i-*trate*)

▷ *verb* **penetrating, penetrated**

▷ *noun* **penetration**

penguin *noun* A waterbird of the Antarctic region that cannot fly. Instead, the penguin uses its wings as flippers for swimming underwater. **pen·guin** (**pen**-gwin *or* **peng**-gwin)

penicillin *noun* A drug made from a mold called *penicillium* that kills bacteria and helps fight some diseases. Penicillin was the first antibiotic. It was discovered in 1928 by Sir Alexander Fleming, a British scientist. **pen·i·cil·lin** (*pen*-i-**sil**-uhn)

peninsula *noun* A piece of land that sticks out from a larger landmass and is almost completely surrounded by water. **pen·in·su·la** (puh-**nin**-suh-luh) ▷ *adjective* **peninsular**

Word History

Peninsula comes from the Latin words *paene*, which means "almost," and *insula*, which means "island." A peninsula is indeed almost an island. All but one side is surrounded by water.

penis *noun* The male organ for urination or reproduction. **pe·nis** (**pee**-nis) ▷ *noun, plural* **penises** *or* **penes** (**pee**-neez)

penitent *adjective* Extremely sorry for what you have done wrong. **pen·i·tent** (**pen**-i-tuhnt) ▷ *noun* **penitent** ▷ *noun* **penitence**

penitentiary *noun* A state or federal prison for people found guilty of serious crimes. **pen·i·ten·tia·ry** (pen-i-**ten**-chur-ee) ▷ *noun, plural* **penitentiaries**

penknife *noun* A small knife with different kinds of blades that fold into a case. **pen·knife** (**pen**-*nife*) ▷ *noun, plural* **penknives**

penmanship *noun*

1. The art of writing with a pen.

2. The style or quality of handwriting: *His penmanship is so poor I can't read his note.* **pen·man·ship** (**pen**-muhn-*ship*)

pen name *noun* A made-up name used by an author instead of his or her real name; a pseudonym: *Mark Twain is the pen name of Samuel Langhorne Clemens.*

pennant *noun*

1. A long, triangular flag, often with the name of a school or team on it.

2. A championship, especially in professional baseball, symbolized by a flag: *My favorite team won the pennant last year.* **pen·nant** (**pen**-uhnt)

penniless *adjective* Having no money at all. **pen·ni·less** (**pen**-ee-lis)

penny *noun* The coin that is the smallest unit of money in the United States and Canada. A penny equals one cent. One hundred pennies equal one dollar. **pen·ny** (**pen**-ee) ▷ *noun, plural* **pennies**

pen pal *noun* Someone, often from another country, who exchanges letters with you.

pension *noun* A regular payment of money to a person who has retired from work, or who cannot work because of a disability. **pen·sion** (**pen**-shuhn) ▷ *noun* **pensioner**

pentagon *noun*

1. A shape with five sides. ▷ *adjective* **pentagonal** (pen-**tag**-uh-nuhl)

2. the Pentagon A building with five sides in Arlington, Virginia, that is the headquarters of the US Department of Defense. **pen·ta·gon** (**pen**-tuh-*gahn*)

penthouse *noun* An apartment located on the top floor of a tall building. **pent·house** (**pent**-*hous*)

peony *noun* A garden plant with large flowers that may be red, pink, or white. **pe·o·ny** (**pee**-uh-nee) ▷ *noun, plural* **peonies**

Word History

In ancient Greek legend, Ares, the god of war, was wounded in the Trojan War. Luckily, Ares knew he could get help from Paeon, the doctor of the gods, who healed him by treating his wounds with herbs. The Greeks thought that the **peony** had healing powers, so they named it *paionia* after the doctor. Its seeds were used to prevent nightmares.

penguin

a
b
c
d
e
f
g
h
i
j
k
l
m
n
o
p
q
r
s
t
u
v
w
x
y
z

people *noun*

1. Persons or human beings.

2. A collection of human beings who make up a nation, race, tribe, or group, as in *the American people.* ▷ *noun, plural* **peoples**

3. Family or relatives: *His people come from Korea.* **peo·ple** (**pee**-puhl)

pep

1. *noun* Great energy and high spirits: *She was full of pep.* ▷ *adjective* **pep**

2. pep up *verb* To fill someone with energy. ▷ *verb* **pepping, pepped**
pep (pep)

pepper

1. *noun* A spicy powder made from the dried berries of a tropical climbing plant. ▷ *adjective* **peppery**

2. *noun* A hollow vegetable that is usually red, green, or yellow, with a taste ranging from slightly sharp to extremely hot.

3. *verb* To season a food with pepper.

4. *verb* To hit repeatedly with small objects: *The attackers peppered the walls with stones.*

5. *verb* To overwhelm someone with suggestions or questions: *The reporters peppered the actor with questions about his next film.*
pep·per (**pep**-ur)
▷ *verb* **peppering, peppered**

peppers

peppermint *noun*

1. A kind of mint plant. The oil from peppermint leaves is used as a flavoring, especially in candy and toothpaste.

2. A candy flavored with peppermint oil.
pep·per·mint (**pep**-ur-*mint*)
▷ *adjective* **peppermint**

pepperoni *noun* A kind of hard Italian sausage made from beef or pork and seasoned with pepper.
pep·per·o·ni (*pep*-uh-**roh**-nee)

per *preposition* In each or for each: *His job pays $7 per hour.* **per** (pur) **Per** sounds like **purr**.

per capita *adjective, adverb* By or for each person in a population: *Some places in northern China use more water per capita than much of Europe.* **per cap·i·ta** (pur **kap**-i-tuh)

Word History

The ancient Roman word for "head" survives in the phrase **per capita**. This English term means "by or for each person in a population." In Latin, *per capita* meant "by heads." Latin speakers used the word *head* as an easy way of referring to an individual person. The word *per* meant "by," and *capita* was the plural of *caput*, meaning "head." Several other English words can also trace their origins to the Latin word *caput*, such as *capital*, *captain*, and *chapter*.

perceive *verb*

1. To become aware of through the senses, especially through sight or hearing: *I perceived a small, dark figure in the distance.*

2. To understand: *She perceived that I was angry.*
per·ceive (pur-**seev**)
▷ *verb* **perceiving, perceived**

percent *noun* A part that is one one-hundredth. A quarter is 25 percent of one dollar. Percent is also written using the symbol %. **per·cent** (pur-**sent**)

percentage *noun* A fraction or proportion of something, expressed as a number out of a hundred. **per·cent·age** (pur-**sen**-tij)

perceptible *adjective* Noticeable and clear: *There was a perceptible difference in Kareem's height after the summer.* **per·cep·ti·ble** (pur-**sep**-tuh-buhl)
▷ *adverb* **perceptibly**

perception *noun*

1. The act of noticing something with one of your senses or with your mind: *The perception of color varies widely from one species to another.*

2. An idea based on what you have seen, heard, or experienced: *The workshop is intended to change people's perception of electric cars.*
per·cep·tion (pur-**sep**-shuhn)

perceptive *adjective* Quick to notice or understand things. **per·cep·tive** (pur-**sep**-tiv)

perch

1. *noun* A bar or branch on which a bird can rest. ▷ *verb* **perch**

2. *noun* Any raised place where a person can sit or stand.

3. *verb* To sit or stand on the edge of something, often high up: *The robin perched on the highest tree branch.* ▷ *verb* **perches, perching, perched**

4. *noun* An edible freshwater fish.
perch (purch)
▷ *noun, plural* **perches** (for all senses) *or* **perch** (for sense 4)

percolate *verb*
1. When a liquid or gas **percolates**, it slowly passes through a porous material and gradually spreads: *The water from the rain percolated down through the soil.*
2. When coffee **percolates**, water is turning into coffee by being passed through the ground coffee beans in a percolator or coffee machine: *Once the coffee began to percolate, we could smell its rich aroma.*
3. When ideas or feelings **percolate**, they gradually spread and become known or felt by more people: *It took a few days for the management's decision to percolate down to the employees.*
per·co·late (**pur**-kuh-*layt*)
▷ *verb* **percolating, percolated**

percussion instrument *noun* A musical instrument, such as a drum, that is played by being hit or shaken. **per·cus·sion instrument** (pur-**kuhsh**-uhn) ▷ *noun* **percussionist**

perennial
1. *noun* A plant that lives and flowers for more than two years: *Roses are perennials.*
2. *adjective* Lasting for a long time, or never ending: *If you seem to have a perennial cold, your problem might be allergies.* ▷ *adverb* **perennially**
per·en·ni·al (puh-**ren**-ee-uhl)

perfect
1. (**pur**-fikt) *adjective* Without any flaws or mistakes, as in *a perfect copy.* ▷ *noun* **perfection** (pur-**fek**-shuhn)
2. (pur-**fekt**) *verb* To make something as flawless as possible: *Fatima spent many years perfecting her French.* ▷ *verb* **perfecting, perfected**
per·fect

perfectly *adverb*
1. In a way that couldn't be better or more perfect: *The wedding gown fit her perfectly.*
2. Completely: *I am perfectly happy to stay home tonight.*
per·fect·ly (**pur**-fikt-lee)

perforate *verb*
1. To make a hole or holes in something: *Ming's rib perforated his lung in the accident.*
2. To make a row of small holes through something, usually paper, so that a portion can be torn off easily.
per·fo·rate (**pur**-fuh-*rayt*)
▷ *verb* **perforating, perforated** ▷ *noun* **perforation** ▷ *adjective* **perforated**

perform *verb*
1. To do or accomplish something: *He performed many useful tasks around the house.*
2. To entertain an audience: *Our class will perform a play during the Spring Festival.*
per·form (pur-**form**)
▷ *verb* **performing, performed**

performance *noun*
1. The public presentation of a play, movie, or piece of music.
2. The way something works, compared to a standard: *Engineers tested the car's performance on slippery roads.*
per·form·ance (pur-**for**-muhns)

performer *noun* A person who entertains an audience in public. **per·form·er** (pur-**for**-mur)

perfume *noun*
1. A liquid you put on your skin to make yourself smell pleasant.
2. Any pleasing smell: *I love the perfume of springtime flowers.*
per·fume (**pur**-fyoom)
▷ *verb* **perfume** ▷ *adjective* **perfumed**

perhaps *adverb* Maybe or possibly: *Perhaps I'll join you later.* **per·haps** (pur-**haps**)

peril *noun*
1. Danger: *A police officer's life is often in peril.*
2. Something dangerous: *She feared the peril of global warming.*
per·il (**per**-uhl)
▷ *adjective* **perilous** ▷ *adverb* **perilously**

perimeter *noun*
1. The boundary of an area: *Keep the dog within the perimeter of the backyard.*
2. The distance around the edge of a shape or an area.
pe·rim·e·ter (puh-**rim**-i-tur)

percussion instruments

period *noun*
1. A length of time: *Eleni left the room for a short period.*
2. A part of a school day: *After lunch we have a free period.*
3. The punctuation mark (.) used to show that a sentence has ended or that a word has been abbreviated.
pe·ri·od (**peer**-ee-uhd)

periodic *adjective* Happening or repeating at regular intervals, as in *periodic immunizations.* **pe·ri·od·ic** (*peer*-ee-**ah**-dik) ▷ *adverb* **periodically**

periodical *noun* A journal or magazine that is published at regular intervals, most often once a week or once a month. **pe·ri·od·i·cal** (*peer*-ee-**ah**-di-kuhl)

periodic table *noun* A table that displays all of the chemical elements in a way that shows their relationships to each other.

peripheral
1. *adjective* Of or having to do with the outer part or edge of something, as in *peripheral vision.* ▷ *adverb* **peripherally**
2. *noun* An external device, such as a printer or modem, that is connected to and controlled by a computer.
pe·riph·er·al (puh-**rif**-ur-uhl)

periphery *noun* The outside edge of something. **pe·riph·er·y** (puh-**rif**-ur-ee) ▷ *noun, plural* **peripheries**

periscope

periscope *noun* A vertical tube containing a series of prisms or mirrors and lenses that allows you to see an object that is far above you or behind an obstacle. Periscopes are often used in submarines. **per·i·scope** (**per**-i-*skope*)

perish *verb* To die, or to be destroyed: *Many people perished in the fire.* **per·ish** (**per**-ish) ▷ *verb* **perishes, perishing, perished**

perishable *adjective* Likely to spoil or decay quickly:

Put the meat and other perishable food in the refrigerator. **per·ish·a·ble** (**per**-i-shuh-buhl) ▷ *noun* **perishable**

perjury *noun* The act of lying in a court of law while under oath to tell the truth. Perjury is a crime. **per·ju·ry** (**pur**-jur-ee) ▷ *noun, plural* **perjuries** ▷ *verb* **perjure**

perk
1. **perk up** *verb* To become more cheerful. ▷ *verb* **perking, perked** ▷ *adjective* **perky**
2. *noun* (*informal*) An extra advantage or benefit that comes with a particular job: *One of the perks of working in the theater is seeing movies for free.*
perk (purk)

perm *noun* (*informal*) A method of setting hair in waves or curls and treating it with chemicals to make the style last for a few months. Perm is short for *permanent wave.* **perm** (purm)

permanent *adjective* Lasting or meant to last for a long time, as in *a permanent job.* **per·ma·nent** (**pur**-muh-nuhnt) ▷ *noun* **permanence**

permanently *adverb* In a lasting or uninterrupted way: *The accident victim was permanently disabled.* **per·ma·nent·ly** (**pur**-muh-nuhnt-lee)

permeate *verb* To spread throughout something: *Louise's perfume permeated the room.* **per·me·ate** (**pur**-mee-*ate*) ▷ *verb* **permeating, permeated**

permissible *adjective* Allowed or permitted. **per·mis·si·ble** (pur-**mis**-uh-buhl)

permission *noun* Consent; an agreement to allow something to happen. **per·mis·sion** (pur-**mish**-uhn)

permissive *adjective* Not strict; allowing more freedom than others might allow in the same situation. **per·mis·sive** (pur-**mis**-iv) ▷ *noun* **permissiveness**

permit
1. (pur-**mit**) *verb* To allow or consent to something. ▷ **permitting, permitted**
2. (**pur**-mit) *noun* An official document giving someone permission to do something, as in *a hunting permit.*
per·mit

permutation *noun* One of several different ways in which a set of things can be ordered or arranged. **per·mu·ta·tion** (*pur*-myuh-**tay**-shuhn)

perp *noun* (*slang*) Short for **perpetrator**. **perp** (purp)

perpendicular
1. *noun* A line that is at right angles to another line or to a surface. ▷ *adjective* **perpendicular**
2. *adjective* Straight up and down or extremely steep, as in *the perpendicular face of a mountain.*
per·pen·dic·u·lar (*pur*-puhn-**dik**-yuh-lur)

perpetrator *noun* Someone who commits a crime. Often shortened to **perp**: *The police arrested the perpetrator of the robbery.* **per·pe·tra·tor** (**pur**-puh-*tray*-tur)

perpetual *adjective* Without ending or changing, as in *perpetual motion.* **per·pet·u·al** (pur-**pech**-oo-uhl) ▷ *adverb* **perpetually**

perpetuate *verb* To make something last or continue for a very long time: *The war memorial perpetuates the memory of the soldiers who died in combat.* **per·pet·u·ate** (pur-**pech**-oo-*ate*) ▷ *verb* **perpetuating, perpetuated** ▷ *noun* **perpetuation**

perplex *verb* To make someone puzzled or unsure: *Her sudden change in attitude perplexed us.* **per·plex** (pur-**pleks**) ▷ *verb* **perplexes, perplexing, perplexed** ▷ *noun* **perplexity** (pur-**pleks**-i-tee) ▷ *adjective* **perplexed**

persecute *verb* To continually treat someone cruelly and unfairly, especially because of that person's ideas or political beliefs. **per·se·cute** (**pur**-suh-*kyoot*) ▷ *verb* **persecuting, persecuted** ▷ *noun* **persecution** (*pur*-suh-**kyoo**-shuhn)

persevere *verb* To continue to do or try to do something, even if you have difficulties or are unlikely to succeed. **per·se·vere** (*pur*-suh-**veer**) ▷ *verb* **persevering, persevered** ▷ *noun* **perseverance**

Persian
1. *noun* The language that the people of Iran and some parts of Afghanistan speak. This language is also called **Farsi**.
2. *adjective* Of or having to do with Iran or made in Iran, as in *a Persian carpet.* **Per·sian** (**pur**-zhuhn)

persimmon *noun* An orange-red fruit that is shaped like a plum and is sweet and soft when ripe. **per·sim·mon** (pur-**sim**-uhn)

persist *verb*
1. To last or to continue steadily: *Her cold persisted all week.*
2. To keep on doing something in spite of obstacles or warnings: *If you persist in teasing your brother, you'll be sent to your room.* **per·sist** (pur-**sist**) ▷ *verb* **persisting, persisted** ▷ *noun* **persistence**

persistent *adjective*
1. Continuing to do something in spite of difficulty or obstacles: *Jana was persistent in her efforts to get on the volleyball team.*
2. Lasting or continuing over a long period of time, as in *persistent snowstorms.* **per·sist·ent** (pur-**sis**-tuhnt) ▷ *adverb* **persistently**

persimmons

person *noun*
1. An individual human being.
2. In grammar, the term *first person* means "I" or "we"; the *second person* means "you"; and the *third person* means "he," "she," "it," or "they."
3. **in person** Physically present: *The actor looked shorter in person than on TV.* **per·son** (**pur**-suhn)

Word History

If you were attending a play in ancient Rome, you would not be able to see the actors' faces because they wore masks. An actor's mask was usually made of clay, and it was called a *persona*. Latin speakers also used the word *persona* to mean "a character in a play," and from this, the meaning "a human being" evolved. The word **person** in English goes back to this Latin word, and in English, the phrase *dramatis personae*, a Latin term that means "persons of the drama," is still used in the theater and refers to the cast of characters in a play. But today the main meaning of *person* is of an individual human being.

personal *adjective*
1. Private, or having to do with one person only, as in *personal property.*
2. Done or made in person, as in *a personal appearance.* **per·son·al** (**pur**-suh-nuhl)

personal computer *noun* A desktop or portable computer that can be used at home, at school, or in an office. Abbreviated as *PC.*

personality *noun*
1. All of the qualities or traits that make one person different from others: *Meri has the perfect personality for this sales job—she is friendly and enthusiastic.*
2. A famous person, especially in entertainment or sports, as in *a radio personality.* **per·son·al·i·ty** (*pur*-suh-**nal**-i-tee) ▷ *noun, plural* **personalities**

personally *adverb*
1. Without assistance; directly: *I invited them personally.*
2. For oneself: *Don't take the remark personally.*
3. As an individual: *I don't like my boss personally, but I think he's good at his job.* **per·son·al·ly** (**pur**-suh-nuh-lee)

a b c d e f g h i j k l m n o **p** q r s t u v w x y z

personnel *noun* The group of people who work for a company or an organization. **per·son·nel** (*pur*-suh-**nel**) ▷ *noun, plural* **personnel** ▷ *adjective* **personnel**

perspective *noun*
1. A particular attitude toward or way of looking at something: *From my perspective, she's the best person for the job.*
2. The way things or events relate to each other in size or importance: *If you put your problems into perspective, you'll see that most of them are minor.*
3. in perspective Drawn or painted so as to give the illusion of depth and distance, with distant objects smaller than closer ones.
per·spec·tive (pur-**spek**-tiv)

perspire *verb* To sweat. **per·spire** (pur-**spire**) ▷ *verb* **perspiring, perspired** ▷ *noun* **perspiration**

persuade *verb* To succeed in making someone do or believe something by giving the person good reasons. **per·suade** (pur-**swade**) ▷ *verb* **persuading, persuaded** ▷ *noun* **persuasion** (pur-**sway**-zhuhn) ▷ *adjective* **persuasive**

pertain *verb* To be connected or related: *The president's speech pertained to the state of the US economy.* **per·tain** (pur-**tayn**) ▷ *verb* **pertaining, pertained**

pertinent *adjective* Having to do with what is being discussed or considered: *Your remarks are pertinent to the subject at hand.* **per·ti·nent** (**purt**-uh-nuhnt)

perturb *verb* To make someone uncomfortable or anxious: *Wilhelm's statements perturbed me.* **per·turb** (pur-**turb**) ▷ *verb* **perturbing, perturbed**

perverse *adjective* Deliberately stubborn and unreasonable: *His perverse logic caused him to get into a lot of arguments.* **per·verse** (pur-**vurs**) ▷ *noun* **perversity**

peso *noun* The main unit of money in Mexico, the Philippines, and several South and Central American countries. **pe·so** (**pay**-soh) ▷ *noun, plural* **pesos**

pessimistic *adjective* Always seeing the worst side of a situation or believing that the worst will happen. **pes·si·mis·tic** (*pes*-uh-**mis**-tik) ▷ *noun* **pessimism** (*pes*-uh-*miz*-uhm) ▷ *noun* **pessimist** ▷ *adverb* **pessimistically**

pest *noun*
1. An insect or other animal that destroys or damages crops, food, or livestock.
2. Any creature that interferes dangerously with human activity.

petunia

3. An annoying person or thing; a nuisance. **pest** (pest)

pester *verb* To annoy someone with frequent questions, interruptions, or reminders: *Stop pestering me about my homework.* **pes·ter** (**pes**-tur) ▷ *verb* **pestering, pestered**

pesticide *noun* A chemical used to kill pests, such as insects. **pes·ti·cide** (**pes**-ti-*side*)

pestle *noun* A short, heavy stick with a thick, rounded end, used to crush things such as herbs and medicine in a container called a mortar. **pes·tle** (**pes**-uhl *or* **pes**-tuhl)

pet
1. *noun* A tame animal kept for company or pleasure and treated with affection.
2. *noun* A person who is unfairly treated with special favor, as in *teacher's pet*.
3. *verb* To stroke or pat an animal affectionately. ▷ *verb* **petting, petted** ▷ *adjective* **pet**
pet (pet)

petal *noun* One of the colored outer parts of a flower. **pet·al** (**pet**-uhl)

petition *noun* A letter signed by many people asking those in power to change their policy or actions or telling them how the signers feel about a certain issue or situation. **pe·ti·tion** (puh-**tish**-uhn) ▷ *verb* **petition**

petrified
1. *adjective* So frightened that you are unable to move.
2. petrified wood *noun* Dead wood that has become hard like stone because minerals have seeped into its cells.
pet·ri·fied (**pet**-ruh-*fide*) ▷ *verb* **petrify**

petroleum *noun* A thick, oily liquid found below the earth's surface. It is used to make gasoline, kerosene, heating oil, and many other products. **pe·tro·le·um** (puh-**troh**-lee-uhm)

petticoat *noun* A light, loose undergarment that hangs from the shoulders or the waist and is worn underneath a dress or skirt. **pet·ti·coat** (**pet** ee-*kote*)

petty *adjective*
1. Small and unimportant, as in *petty complaints.*
2. Mean or spiteful, as in *petty gossip.*
pet·ty (**pet**-ee) ▷ *adjective* **pettier, pettiest**

petunia *noun* A garden plant with colorful flowers shaped like trumpets. **pe·tu·nia** (puh-**toon**-yuh)

pew *noun* A long, wooden bench with a high back that people sit on in a church. **pew** (pyoo)

pewter *noun*
1. A metal made of tin mixed with lead or copper. Pewter is used to make plates, pitchers, and other utensils.
2. Utensils made of pewter.
pew·ter (**pyoo**-tur)
▷ *adjective* **pewter**

pH *noun* A measure of how acidic or alkaline a substance is. The initials pH are short for *potential of hydrogen*. Acids have pH values less than 7, and alkalis have pH values greater than 7. If a substance has a pH value of 7, it is neutral. **pH** (**pee aych**)

phantom *noun* A ghost, or an imagined figure. **phan·tom** (**fan**-tuhm) ▷ *adjective* **phantom**

pharaoh *noun* The title given to kings in ancient Egypt. **phar·aoh** (**fair**-oh)

pharmaceutical *adjective* Of or having to do with medicines or drugs. A pharmaceutical company manufactures medicines and drugs. **phar·ma·ceu·ti·cal** (*fahr*-muh-**soo**-ti-kuhl)

pharaoh

pharmacist

pharmacist *noun* A person who is trained to prepare and dispense drugs and medicines. **phar·ma·cist** (**fahr**-muh-sist)

pharmacy *noun* A drugstore, or a special department of a larger store where medicines are sold. **phar·ma·cy** (**fahr**-muh-see) ▷ *noun, plural* **pharmacies**

phase
1. *noun* A stage in something or someone's growth or development: *My two-year-old sister is going through a crying phase.*
2. *noun* A stage of the moon's change in shape as it appears from earth.

3. *noun* One part or side of something: *Let's go over every phase of the problem.*
4. phase in *verb* To start something gradually.
5. phase out *verb* To stop something gradually: *I'm trying to phase out sugar from my diet.*
phase (faze)
▷ *verb* **phasing, phased**

pheasant *noun* A large, brightly colored bird with a long tail that is hunted for sport and for food. Peacocks, partridges, and quail are related to pheasants. **pheas·ant** (**fez**-uhnt)

phenomenal *adjective* Amazing, extraordinary: *The composer's new opera was a phenomenal success.* **phe·nom·e·nal** (fuh-**nah**-muh-nuhl) ▷ *adverb* **phenomenally**

phenomenon *noun*
1. An event or a fact that can be seen or felt: *An earthquake is a natural phenomenon.*
2. Something very unusual and remarkable: *This video clip is an internet phenomenon.*
phe·nom·e·non (fuh-**nah**-muh-*nahn*)
▷ *noun, plural* **phenomena** (fuh-**nah**-muh-*nuh*) or **phenomenons**

philanthropist *noun* A person who helps others by giving time or money to causes and charities. **phil·an·thro·pist** (fuh-**lan**-thruh-pist)

philodendron *noun* A tropical American climbing vine with leaves that are shaped like hearts. The philodendron is a popular indoor plant. **phil·o·den·dron** (*fil*-uh-**den**-druhn)

philosopher *noun* Someone who thinks deeply and writes about the basic problems and questions of human existence: *Philosophers have taken an interest in sense perception for centuries.* **phi·los·o·pher** (fuh-**lah**-suh-fur)

philosophical *adjective*
1. Of or having to do with philosophy.
2. Accepting difficulties and problems calmly, as in *a philosophical view of life.*
phil·o·soph·i·cal (*fil*-uh-**sah**-fi-kuhl)
▷ *adverb* **philosophically**

philosophy *noun*
1. The study of truth, wisdom, the nature of reality, and knowledge.
2. The systematic study of the basic ideas in any field, as in *the philosophy of science.*
3. A person's basic ideas and beliefs that guide his or her actions and decisions.
phi·los·o·phy (fuh-**lah**-suh-fee)

a b c d e f g h i j k l m n o **p** q r s t u v w x y z

phishing *noun* The activity of trying to steal someone's identity or credit information by lying about who you really are. Phishing usually involves sending emails that trick people into entering personal information at a fake website. **phish·ing** (**fish**-ing)

Word History

In the mid-20th century, long-distance telephone calls were expensive, so a group of people who called themselves phone phreaks invented machines that made the calls for free. They made the word *phreak* by spelling *freak* with the letters *ph* from *phone*. People who try **phishing** want to get something without paying, and phishing is also like "fishing" for information, so the word *phishing* might be a mix of the words *phreak* and *fishing*.

phlegm *noun* The thick substance, produced by the mucous membranes of the lungs, that you cough up when you have a cold. **phlegm** (flem)

phobia *noun* An extremely strong fear: *Johann has a phobia of spiders.* **pho·bi·a** (**foh**-bee-uh) ▷ *adjective* **phobic** (**foh**-bik)

Phoenician
1. *adjective* Of or having to do with an ancient Mediterranean civilization that had a major influence on ancient Greece and Rome.
2. *noun* The language of this ancient civilization, which is no longer spoken. Modern Arabic and Hebrew are related to Phoenician. **Phoe·ni·cian** (fuh-**nee**-shuhn)

phone *noun* Short for **telephone**. **phone** (fone) ▷ *verb* **phone**

phonetically *adverb* If something is spelled **phonetically**, it is spelled as it is pronounced, sometimes by using special symbols to represent sounds. The words in this dictionary are spelled phonetically in parentheses. **pho·net·i·cal·ly** (fuh-**net**-ik-lee)

phonetics *noun* The study of the sounds that are used in speaking. **pho·net·ics** (fuh-**net**-iks)

phonograph *noun* A machine that picks up and reproduces the sounds that have been recorded in the grooves cut into a record. **pho·no·graph** (**foh**-nuh-*graf*)

photobomb

phony
1. *adjective* Intended to deceive; not the real

thing, as in *a phony birth certificate.*
2. *noun* A person or thing that is not honest or genuine; a fraud: *The painting turned out to be a phony.* **pho·ny** (**foh**-nee) ▷ *noun, plural* **phonies**

phosphorescence *noun*
1. Light that is given off from a substance after the source of energy has been removed.
2. The light that is given off by a living thing, such as a fish or an insect. **phos·pho·res·cence** (*fahs*-fuh-**res**-uhns) ▷ *adjective* **phosphorescent**

phosphorus *noun* A chemical element that glows in the dark. It is used in making matches, fertilizers, glass, and steel. **phos·pho·rus** (**fahs**-fur-uhs)

photo *noun* Short for **photograph**. **pho·to** (**foh**-toh)

photobomb
1. *verb* To spoil a picture someone is taking by stepping into the frame and doing something silly: *I photobombed my sister at her wedding when they were cutting the cake.* ▷ *verb* **photobombing, photobombed**
2. *noun* A photograph that someone has photobombed: *Gerald has a scrapbook of celebrity photobombs.* **pho·to·bomb** (**foh**-toh-*bahm*)

photocopier *noun* A machine that copies documents using a special lens and ink called toner. **pho·to·cop·i·er** (**foh**-toh-*kah*-pee-ur)

photocopy *noun* A copy of a document made by a photocopier. **pho·to·cop·y** (**foh**-toh-*kah*-pee) ▷ *verb* **photocopy**

photo finish *noun* A very close end to a race, where the winner can be identified only by examining a photograph taken as the contestants crossed the finish line. ▷ *noun, plural* **photo finishes**

photogenic *adjective* Having a particularly good appearance in photographs: *Bill was so photogenic that his friends all encouraged him to become a model.* **pho·to·gen·ic** (*foh*-tuh-**jen**-ik)

photograph *noun*
1. A picture taken by a camera on film and developed on paper.
2. A picture taken with a digital camera and printed on paper or shown on a computer screen. **pho·to·graph** (**foh**-tuh-*graf*) ▷ *verb* **photograph**

photographer *noun* Someone who takes a picture with a camera, especially as a job. **pho·tog·ra·pher** (fuh-**tah**-gruh-fur)

photography *noun*
  1. The recording of visual images by exposing film inside a camera to light.
  2. The recording of visual images using a digital camera to make an image that can be reproduced by a computer.
  pho·tog·ra·phy (fuh-**tah**-gruh-fee)
  ▷ *adjective* **photographic**

photojournalist *noun* A photographer who takes photographs of news events and tells the story of what has happened through the photos.
  pho·to·jour·nal·ist (*foh*-toh-**jur**-nuh-list) ▷ *noun* **photojournalism**

photosynthesis *noun* A chemical process by which green plants and some other organisms make their food. Plants use energy from the sun to turn water and carbon dioxide into food, and they produce oxygen as a by-product. **pho·to·syn·the·sis** (*foh*-toh-**sin**-thi-sis)

phrase
  1. *noun* A group of words that have a meaning but do not form a sentence. *In the dark* is a phrase.
  2. *noun* In music, a group of notes that are played as a unit and which can be performed on a single breath by a singer or wind instrumentalist.
  3. *verb* To put into words in a particular way: *Phrase the question in different words.* ▷ *verb* **phrasing, phrased**
  phrase (fraze)

phylum *noun* A group of related plants or animals that is larger than a class but smaller than a kingdom. **phy·lum** (**fye**-luhm) ▷ *noun, plural* **phyla** (**fye**-luh)

physical
  1. *adjective* Of or having to do with the body, as in *a physical examination.* ▷ *adverb* **physically**
  2. *adjective* Of or having to do with matter and energy: *Chemistry is a physical science.*
  3. *adjective* Of or having to do with nature or natural objects: *The map shows the mountains, rivers, and other physical features of the United States.*
  4. *noun* A complete examination of a person's body, made by a doctor or nurse, to check the person's health: *I have to get a physical before I can go to camp.*
  phys·i·cal (**fiz**-i-kuhl)

physical fitness *noun* The state of being in good health as a result of exercising and eating nutritious foods.

physical therapy *noun* The treatment of diseased or injured muscles and joints by physical and mechanical means, such as exercise, massage, and heat. ▷ *noun* **physical therapist**

physician *noun* Someone with a medical degree who has been trained and licensed to treat injured and sick people; a doctor. Physicians are also authorized to write prescriptions for medicine. **phy·si·cian** (fi-**zish**-uhn)

physics *noun* The science that deals with matter and energy. It includes the study of light, heat, sound, electricity, motion, and force. **phys·ics** (**fiz**-iks) ▷ *noun* **physicist** (**fiz**-i-sist)

physique *noun* The shape of a person's body and how muscular or physically fit it is: *Even at 65, Wright still has an athletic physique.* **phy·sique** (fi-**zeek**)

pi *noun* In math, a symbol (π) for the ratio of the circumference of a circle to its diameter. Pi equals about 3.1416. **pi** (pye) **Pi** sounds like **pie**.

piano
  1. (pee-**an**-oh *or* **pyan**-oh) *noun* A large keyboard instrument that produces musical sounds when fingers strike the keys, causing padded hammers inside the piano to strike tuned metal strings.
  ▷ *noun* **pianist** (pee-**an**-ist) ▷ *noun, plural* **pianos**
  2. (**pyah**-noh) *adverb* Softly. This word is used in music.
  pi·an·o

Word History

In Italian, **piano** means "soft." The name for the instrument comes from the Italian phrase *piano e forte,* or "soft and loud." This refers to the fact that a piano's tones can vary from soft to loud.

piano

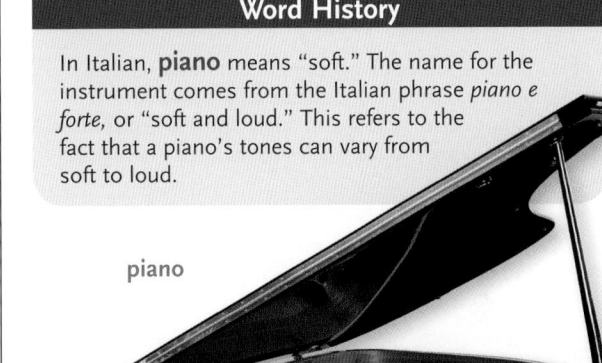

a b c d e f g h i j k l m n o **p** q r s t u v w x y z

piccolo *noun* An instrument that looks like a flute but is smaller and has a higher pitch. **pic·co·lo** (pik-uh-*loh*)

pick

1. *verb* To choose or select: *Galina picked an apple from the bowl of fruit.* ▷ *noun* **pick**

2. *verb* To collect or to gather, especially taking fruits or flowers from the plants on which they grow: *Have you picked any blueberries this season?* ▷ *noun* **picker**

3. *noun* A tool with pointed metal ends, used for breaking up soil or rocks.

4. *noun* A small piece of plastic or metal used to strum or pluck banjo or guitar strings. ▷ *verb* **pick**

5. *noun* The right to choose, or a turn to choose: *Beth was allowed to take her pick of the desserts.*

6. *noun* The best of a group: *The black puppy was the pick of the litter.*

7. *verb* To cause on purpose: *He's trying to pick a fight.*

8. pick on *verb* To tease someone or treat him or her in a mean way.

9. pick at *verb* To take bits off of something: *I wasn't hungry, so I just picked at my food.*

pick (pik)

▷ *verb* **picking, picked**

Synonyms

Pick means to decide on something from among a number of possibilities. You can pick something at random or because you've made a specific decision: *I picked a comedy at the video store because I needed a good laugh.*

- -

■ **Choose** means to decide on something after giving the matter some thought: *Ms. Chang will choose the best paper after she reads them all.*

■ **Select** means to pick something after carefully considering the choices: *After much thought, I think I selected the perfect gift for my mother's birthday.*

■ **Prefer** means that you have chosen something because you like it better or best: *Karle prefers books to magazines, football to baseball, and movies to TV.*

■ **Elect** means to choose someone for office by voting: *The town will elect a new mayor on June 8.*

pickax *or* **pickaxe** *noun* A tool with a long handle and a metal head. One end of the head is a sharp blade, and the other is a pick. A pickax can be used to cut through roots, loosen soil, and break up rocks. **pick·ax** *or* **pick·axe** (pik-aks) ▷ *noun, plural* **pickaxes**

pickerel *noun* A freshwater fish found in the waters of North America. The pickerel has a long, pointed head and is used for food. **pick·er·el** (pik-ur-uhl) ▷ *noun, plural* **pickerel** *or* **pickerels**

picket

1. *verb* To stand outside a place in protest. When a person or group pickets a location, they often carry signs and shout slogans to get attention and sometimes try to prevent others from entering. ▷ *verb* **picketing, picketed** ▷ *noun* **picket** ▷ *noun* **picketer**

2. *noun* A pointed stake that is driven into the ground to hold something in place or to build a fence. **pick·et** (pik-it)

pickle

1. *verb* To preserve food in vinegar or saltwater. ▷ *verb* **pickling, pickled**

2. *noun* Any food, such as a cucumber, that has been pickled.

3. *noun* (*informal*) A difficult or awkward situation: *Peter hadn't done his homework, and he was in a pickle because there was a surprise quiz.* **pick·le** (pik-uhl)

Word History

A **pickle** was originally a liquid for preserving food. Later, English speakers also began using the term for the food that was preserved in the liquid. They adopted the word from the Dutch term *pekel*, referring to a liquid for preserving food. *Pekel* is probably related to the Dutch verb *peken*, meaning "to prick." The liquid received its name from its sharp flavor, because it seemed to be "pricking" people's mouths.

pickpocket *noun* A person who steals from people's pockets or handbags. **pick·pock·et** (pik-*pah*-kit)

pickup *noun*

1. An increase in speed: *Our car has good pickup.*

2. A small truck with a driver's cab and an open back. **pick·up** (pik-*uhp*)

picky *adjective* (*informal*) Particular or choosy: *My brother is a picky eater.* **pick·y** (pik-ee) ▷ *adjective* **pickier, pickiest**

picnic *noun* A party or trip that includes a meal eaten out of doors. **pic·nic** (pik-nik) ▷ *noun* **picnicker** ▷ *verb* **picnic**

pictograph *noun*

1. A picture used as a symbol in ancient writing systems.

2. Another name for **picture graph**. **pic·to·graph** (pik-tuh-*graf*)

pictorial *adjective* Using pictures, or expressed in pictures: *My book about birds is a pictorial guide.* **pic·to·ri·al** (pik-tor-ee-uhl) ▷ *adverb* **pictorially**

picture

1. *noun* An image, such as a painting, photograph, or drawing. ▷ *verb* **picture**

2. *noun* An image on a television screen: *The TV picture keeps jumping up and down.*

3. *noun* A movie, as in *a horror picture.*

4. *verb* To imagine something: *Can you picture Sally as a cowgirl?*

5. *verb* To describe something vividly in words: *The writer pictured the horrors of the Civil War.* ▷ *noun* **picture**

pic·ture (**pik**-chur)

▷ *verb* **picturing, pictured**

picture graph *noun* A graph that shows information by means of picture symbols instead of lines or bars. Another name for picture graph is **pictograph**.

picturesque *adjective* Pretty or charming to look at. **pic·tur·esque** (*pik*-chuh-**resk**)

pie *noun* Pastry filled with fruit, custard, meat, or vegetables and baked in an oven. **pie** (pye) **Pie** sounds like **pi**.

piece *noun*

1. A part or section of something larger: *The novelist read a piece from her new book.*

2. A part that has been broken, torn, or cut from a whole, as in *a piece of broken glass* or *a piece of pie.*

3. An artistic creation, as in *a musical piece* or *a piece of pottery.*

4. A coin: *I put a 25-cent piece into the pay phone to make my call.*

5. A small object used in playing checkers, chess, and other board games.

6. An example of something, or one of a set, as in *a piece of silverware* or *a piece of luggage.*

7. a piece of cake Something that is easy to do: *Replacing the bicycle's chain was a piece of cake.*

piece (pees)

Piece sounds like **peace**.

piecework *noun* Work that is paid for by the amount completed, not by the time it takes to do it. **piece·work** (**pees**-*wurk*)

pie chart A chart in the shape of a circle that is divided into sections by lines coming from the center to show the size of different parts relative to the whole.

pier *noun*

1. A platform of metal, stone, concrete, or wood that extends over a body of water. A pier can be used as a landing place for ships and boats.

2. A pillar that supports a bridge.

pier (peer)

Pier sounds like **peer**.

pierce *verb*

1. To make a hole in something: *For my birthday, I got my ears pierced.*

2. To pass into or through, as if with a sharp instrument: *The coyote's cries pierced the stillness.*

pierce (peers)

▷ *verb* **piercing, pierced**

piercing

1. *adjective* Going through or seeming to go through something, as in *a piercing cry* or *a piercing wind.*

2. *noun* A small hole made in a part of the body for holding jewelry: *There is always a risk of infection with a new piercing.*

pierc·ing (**peer**-sing)

piety *noun* The quality of being religious or reverent; taking one's religion seriously. **pi·e·ty** (**pye**-i-tee)

pig

1. *noun* A farm animal with a blunt snout that is raised for its meat, which is called pork.

2. *noun* (*informal*) A greedy, messy, or disgusting person.

3. pig out *verb* To eat a lot, usually in a greedy or messy way.

pig (pig)

pigeon *noun* A plump bird sometimes used for racing or for carrying messages. Pigeons are often found in cities. They are related to doves. **pi·geon** (**pij**-uhn)

piggyback *adverb* Carried on the shoulders or back: *Lorenzo carried his little sister piggyback through the crowd.* **pig·gy·back** (**pig**-ee-*bak*)

piggy bank *noun* A small bank, often in the shape of a pig, used mainly by children for saving coins. **pig·gy bank** (**pig**-ee)

pigment *noun* A substance that gives color to something. Pigments can be natural, as in people's skin, or added to something, as in paint. **pig·ment** (**pig**-muhnt)

pigpen *noun* An enclosed area where pigs are kept. It is also called a **sty** or a **pigsty**. **pig·pen** (**pig**-*pen*)

pigpen

pigsty *noun*
1. A pigpen.
2. *(informal)* A very messy and often dirty place: *His room is a pigsty.*
pig·sty (**pig**-stye)
▷ *noun, plural* **pigsties**

pigtail *noun* A length of hair that has been divided into three sections and braided: *She always wore her hair in pigtails.* **pig·tail** (**pig**-tayl)

pike *noun*
1. A large, thin freshwater fish with a flat snout and very sharp teeth.
2. A type of dive in which the diver bends at the waist to touch the toes while in midair, then enters the water with the body fully extended.
3. A gymnastics movement in which a person's body bends at the waist to touch the toes and then is fully extended again.
4. A weapon used in the Middle Ages, consisting of a sharp metal head attached to a long pole.
pike (pike)

Pilates *noun* A type of exercise that strengthens your abdominal and lower back muscles: *She does Pilates and yoga every week.* **Pi·la·tes** (pi-**lah**-teez)

pile *noun*
1. A heap of something, as in *a pile of old newspapers.* ▷ *verb* **pile**
2. A very great amount of something: *I have a pile of homework to do.*
3. A heavy wood or steel beam that is driven into the ground to support a bridge or pier.
4. The raised loops or pieces of yarn that form the surface of a carpet: *The pile of the rug feels nice on my bare feet.*
pile (pile)

pilfer *verb* To steal small amounts of something or small things: *The store clerk was fired for pilfering merchandise.* **pil·fer** (**pil**-fur) ▷ *verb* **pilfering, pilfered** ▷ *noun* **pilferer** ▷ *noun* **pilferage**

pilgrim *noun*
1. A person who travels to a holy place to worship there. ▷ *noun* **pilgrimage**
2. **the Pilgrims** *noun, plural* The group of people who left England because of religious persecution, came to America, and founded Plymouth Colony in 1620.
pil·grim (**pil**-gruhm)

pill *noun* A small, solid tablet of medicine, such as aspirin: *I have trouble swallowing pills.* **pill** (pil)

pillage
1. *verb* To rob a place violently, especially during a war: *Vikings pillaged and burned the city and its cathedral in 858.* ▷ *verb* **pillaging, pillaged**
2. *noun* The act of robbing a place violently in wartime.
pil·lage (**pil**-ij)

pillar *noun*
1. A column that supports part of a building or that stands alone as a monument.
2. A person who is looked up to or relied upon in a particular way, as in *a pillar of the community* or *a pillar of strength.*
pil·lar (**pil**-ur)

pillow *noun* A large, soft cushion for your head when you are sleeping. Some pillows are used to support the back or to sit on. **pil·low** (**pil**-oh)

pillowcase *noun* A cloth cover that you put over a pillow to keep it clean. **pil·low·case** (**pil**-oh-*kase*)

pilot
1. *noun* A person who flies an aircraft: *The pilot landed the plane smoothly.*
2. *noun* A person who guides a ship in and out of port: *The harbor pilot steered the ship around the sandbars.*
3. *verb* To test or guide something: *I was asked to pilot a class project.* ▷ *verb* **piloting, piloted**
4. *adjective* Done as an experiment, as in *a pilot study.* ▷ *noun* **pilot**
pi·lot (**pye**-luht)

pimple *noun* A small, raised spot on the skin that is sometimes painful and filled with pus. **pim·ple** (**pim**-puhl) ▷ *adjective* **pimply**

pin
1. *noun* A thin, pointed piece of metal, usually used to fasten fabric together.
2. *noun* A piece of jewelry or a badge fastened to clothing with a pin or clasp: *I wore my favorite pin on the lapel of my blazer.*

Pilates

3. *verb* To fasten things together with a pin.

4. *verb* To hold something or someone firmly in position: *I pinned my brother to the floor and won our living room wrestling match.*

5. *noun* One of ten pieces of wood shaped like bottles that are knocked over in bowling.

6. *noun* In golf, the flag that indicates where the hole is on the green: *My mom's putt was inches from the pin.*

pin (pin)

▷ *verb* **pinning, pinned**

PIN *noun* A number used to identify a person who is using an automatic bank machine, a computer program, or other kinds of equipment. PIN is short for *personal identification number.* **PIN** (pin)

piñata *noun* A decorated container filled with candies and gifts. It is hung from the ceiling at parties to be broken with sticks by blindfolded children. Piñatas are traditionally Latin American in origin and now are common at all kinds of parties and celebrations. **pi·ña·ta** (peen-**yah**-tuh)

pinball *noun* A game in which you shoot small balls around a number of obstacles and targets on an enclosed, slanted table. **pin·ball** (**pin**-*bawl*)

pincer *noun* The pinching claw of a crustacean such as a crab. **pin·cer** (**pin**-sur)

pinch

1. *verb* To squeeze someone's skin sharply between the thumb and index finger: *My aunt pinches my cheeks every time I see her.* ▷ *noun* **pinch**

2. *noun* A small amount of something, as in *a pinch of cinnamon.*

3. *verb* To make thin or wrinkled: *His lips were pinched with rage.*

4. *noun* An emergency or time of need: *If you're in a pinch, I can lend you some money.*

5. pinch pennies *verb* To spend money only when absolutely necessary: *We'll have to pinch our pennies for months to be able to buy a new television.*

pinch (pinch)

▷ *verb* **pinches, pinching, pinched** ▷ *noun, plural* **pinches**

pincushion *noun* A small cushion used to stick pins in when they are not being used. **pin·cush·ion** (**pin**-*kush*-uhn)

pine

1. *noun* A tall evergreen tree that produces cones and leaves that look like needles.

2. pine for *verb* To feel very sad because someone has

pincushion

gone away and you miss him or her. ▷ *verb* **pining, pined**

pine (pine)

pineapple *noun* A large, tropical fruit with yellow flesh and a tough, prickly skin. Pineapples grow on plants with long, stiff leaves. **pine·ap·ple** (**pine**-*ap*-uhl)

ping

1. *verb* To contact someone, especially with text or email, to remind him or her of something or to get their attention: *Ping me when you're in town again and we can have lunch or something.*

2. *verb* If one computer **pings** another, it sends a signal to determine if the other computer is responding and how long it takes.

3. *noun* The electronic signal that one computer sends another to see whether it is responding.

ping (ping)

▷ *verb* **pinging, pinged**

Ping-Pong *noun* A trademark for table tennis: *We played a game of Ping-Pong. See **table tennis**.* **Ping-Pong** (**ping**-*pahng*)

pink *noun* A pale red color made by mixing red and white. **pink** (pingk) ▷ *adjective* **pink** ▷ *adjective* **pinkish**

pinkeye *or* **pink eye** *noun* A highly contagious disease that causes the surface of the eyeball and the inside of the eyelid to become red, sore, and itchy. **pink·eye** *or* **pink eye** (**pingk**-*eye*)

pinkie *or* **pinky** *noun* The smallest finger on a person's hand: *She wore a ring on her right pinkie.* **pink·ie** *or* **pink·y** (**ping**-kee)

pinpoint

1. *adjective* Very exact or precise: *The expert gunner fired with pinpoint accuracy.*

2. *verb* To locate something precisely: *The sailors used sonar to pinpoint the enemy submarine.* ▷ *verb* **pinpointing, pinpointed**

pin·point (**pin**-*point*)

pins and needles *noun, plural*

1. A prickly, tingling feeling that you get when some of the blood supply to part of your body has been temporarily cut off.

2. on pins and needles Very nervous or excited about something that is going to happen soon.

pinstripe *noun* A very narrow stripe woven into a fabric: *Bert's new suit is black with blue pinstripes.* **pin·stripe** (**pin**-*stripe*)

pint *noun* A unit of measure equal to half a quart or 16 fluid ounces. **pint** (pinte)

pinto *noun*

1. A horse or pony that has spots or patches of two or more colors.

2. A type of kidney bean that is spotted. It is grown mainly in the southwestern part of the United States and is used for food.

pin·to (**pin**-toh)

▷ *noun, plural* **pintos**

pinwheel *noun* A toy wheel that spins in the wind. It is made of colored paper or plastic that is pinned to a stick. **pin·wheel** (**pin**-*weel*)

pioneer

1. *noun* One of the first people to investigate or work in a new and unknown field of knowledge: *The Curies were pioneers in the study of radiation.*

2. *noun* A person who explores unknown territory and settles there: *The pioneers who settled the American West were brave and determined.*

3. *adjective* Referring to one of the first people or attempts to develop or study something, as in *a pioneer surgeon.*

4. *verb* To be the first to develop or use something: *The school pioneered a program that allowed students to earn college credits for high-school courses.*

pi·o·neer (*pye*-uh-**neer**)

▷ *verb* **pioneering, pioneered**

Word History

A **pioneer** used to be a soldier who went ahead of an army to prepare the land. These soldiers, called *pionniers* in French, had to dig trenches and repair roads. Speakers of Old French created this word from their word for "foot soldier," *peon.* It developed from the Latin word part *pedon-*, with the same meaning, and this was based on the root *ped-*, the ancient Roman word for "foot." Our current meaning for *pioneer*, referring to a person who is among the first to explore and settle in a new area, evolved from the duties of these foot soldiers.

pious *adjective* Practicing a religion faithfully and seriously. **pi·ous** (**pye**-uhs) ▷ *adverb* **piously**

pipe

1. *noun* A tube, usually used to carry a liquid or gas: *The pipes in the basement are dripping.*

2. *verb* To send something along pipes, tubes, or wires: *The reservoir pipes water to all the houses in town.*

3. *noun* A narrow tube with a bowl on the end of it, for smoking tobacco. Pipes are usually made of wood or clay.

4. *noun* A tube with holes along its length, played as a musical instrument or joined with other similar pipes to make a larger instrument.

5. *verb* To play music on pipes.

6. piped music *noun* Music that can be heard through speakers all over a building.

7. pipe up *verb* To speak suddenly, or more loudly than before.

8. pipe down *verb* To speak more quietly, or to make less noise.

pipe (pipe)

▷ *verb* **piping, piped**

pipeline *noun*

1. A line of large pipes that carry water, gas, or oil over long distances: *They're building a pipeline to transport gas throughout Europe.*

2. A direct route for sending information or supplies: *The senator has a direct pipeline to the president's office.*

pipe·line (**pipe**-*line*)

piping

1. *noun* A system of pipes.

2. *noun* A shrill sound or call, as in *the piping of tiny frogs.*

3. *noun* A thin line of decoration on a cake, piece of clothing, or furniture: *The coat was navy blue with white piping.*

4. piping hot *adjective* Very hot, usually describing food.

pip·ing (**pye**-ping)

piracy *noun*

1. The crime of attacking and robbing ships at sea.

2. Illegal copying or use of material such as computer software, a book, or music that has been created by someone else.

pi·ra·cy (**pye**-ruh-see)

▷ *noun, plural* **piracies**

pirate

1. *noun* A person who attacks and robs ships at sea.

2. *verb* To make unauthorized copies of music, film, a computer game, or other entertainment created by someone else and sell them illegally. ▷ *verb* **pirating, pirated** ▷ *adjective* **pirated**

pi·rate (**pye**-rit)

Word History

The verb for "to try" in ancient Greek, *peiran,* could also mean "to attack," and the English term **pirate** can trace its origins to this Greek word. Greek speakers created the word *peirates,* meaning a "pirate," from *peiran.* The word *peirates* ended up as *pirate* in English. A pirate, then, is a person who "attacks."

pistachio *noun*

1. A small, green nut with a hard shell that is sometimes dyed red.

pita sandwich

2. A light green color.
pis·ta·chi·o (pi-**stash**-ee-*oh*)
▷ *noun, plural* **pistachios**

pistil *noun* The female part of a flower that is shaped like a stalk. It is the place where the seeds are produced. The pistil includes the ovule, the style, and the stigma of a flower. **pis·til** (**pis**-tuhl) Pistil sounds like **pistol**.

pistol *noun* A small gun designed to be held in the hand. **pis·tol** (**pis**-tuhl) Pistol sounds like **pistil**.

piston *noun* A disk or cylinder that moves back and forth in a larger cylinder. Automobile engines have pistons. Their back-and-forth movement is converted to rotational motion. **pis·ton** (**pis**-tuhn)

pit
1. *noun* A hole in the ground, often one from which something is being dug out, as in *a coal pit.*
2. *noun* The large, hard seed in the middle of some fruits, such as peaches and plums.
3. the pit of one's stomach *noun* An indefinite place in your abdomen where you seem to feel fear, excitement, or anxiety: *The roller coaster gave me a nervous feeling in the pit of my stomach.*
4. pitted against *verb* Made to compete with someone or something else: *In this race, the fastest cars in the world are pitted against each other.* ▷ *verb* **pitting, pitted**
5. pit stop *noun* A short break when a race car stops

for fuel and repairs in a separate area called the pit.
pit (pit)

pita *noun* A thin, flat Middle Eastern bread that can be separated into two layers to form a pocket for meat, vegetables, or another filling: *I filled my pita with hummus and vegetables.* **pi·ta** (**pee**-tuh)

pitch
1. *verb* To throw or toss something, such as a baseball or horseshoe: *I pitched the baseball as fast as I could.* ▷ *noun* **pitch**
2. *verb* To fall or plunge forward: *The ship pitched in the heavy seas.*
3. *verb* To put up a tent.
4. *noun* A dark, sticky substance that is made from tar or petroleum. Pitch is used to waterproof roofs and pave streets.
5. *noun* A high point or degree, as in *a high pitch of excitement.*
6. *noun* The highness or lowness of a musical sound.
7. *noun (informal)* A talk meant to persuade you to do or buy something, as in *a sales pitch.*
8. pitch in *verb* To join in to help with a task: *If we all pitch in, we can weed the garden in an hour.*
pitch (pich)
▷ *verb* **pitches, pitching, pitched**
▷ *noun, plural* **pitches**

pitcher *noun*
1. A container with an open top for liquids. Pitchers usually have a handle and a lip or spout.
2. A baseball player who throws the ball to the batter.
pitc·her (**pich**-ur)

pitchfork *noun* A large fork with a long handle and two or three prongs, used for lifting and throwing hay. **pitch·fork** (**pich**-*fork*)

pitchfork

pitfall *noun* A hidden or unsuspected danger or difficulty: *There are many pitfalls in the video game's last level.* **pit·fall** (**pit**-*fawl*)

pitiful *adjective*
1. Deserving or causing pity: *The abandoned house was in pitiful condition.*
2. Inadequate: *The losing team made a pitiful attempt to score a few more points.*
pit·i·ful (**pit**-i-fuhl)
▷ *adverb* **pitifully**

pitiless *adjective* Showing no pity or sympathy for anyone. **pit·i·less** (**pit**-i-lis) ▷ *adverb* **pitilessly**

pity

1. *verb* To feel sorry for someone. ▷ *verb* **pities, pitying, pitied** ▷ *adverb* **pityingly**

2. *noun* A feeling of sorrow or sympathy for the suffering of someone else: *Sharon felt great pity for the hurricane victims.*

3. *noun* A sad or unfortunate situation: *It's a pity that he had to miss the party.*

pit·y (**pit**-ee)

▷ *noun, plural* **pities**

Word History

Religious people in ancient Rome were described as having *pietas,* which was the Latin word for "the quality of being reverent." The word developed into *pitié* in Old French, but by that time it had a second meaning: "a tendency to be forgiving or kind," perhaps because of good works by people who were religious. In English, the term **pity** now has the narrower sense of a feeling of sadness or sympathy for someone else's suffering.

pivot

1. *noun* A central point on which something turns or balances.

2. *verb* To turn suddenly as if on a pivot: *The ballet dancer pivoted on her toes.* ▷ *verb* **pivoting, pivoted**

piv·ot (**piv**-uht)

pivotal *adjective* Very important in determining the outcome of something: *Ursula played a pivotal role in the winning soccer game.* **piv·ot·al** (**piv**-uh-tuhl)

pixel *noun* One of the tiny dots on a video screen or computer monitor that make up the visual image. **pix·el** (**piks**-uhl)

pixie *or* **pixy** *noun* A small, mischievous elf or fairy in legends and fairy tales. **pix·ie** *or* **pix·y** (**pik**-see) ▷ *noun, plural* **pixies**

pizza *noun* A flat pie that is baked with toppings of tomato sauce, cheese, and various meats and vegetables, as in *pepperoni pizza.* **piz·za** (**peet**-suh)

pizzeria *noun* A place where pizza is made and sold. **piz·ze·ri·a** (*peet*-suh-**ree**-uh)

placard *noun* A poster, sign, or notice that is put up in a public place: *The concert was announced on placards around the city.* **plac·ard** (**plak**-ahrd)

placate *verb* To make someone calm or less angry, often by giving the person something that he or she wants: *The company tried to placate the angry strikers by agreeing to sit down and talk.* **pla·cate** (**play**-kate) ▷ *verb* **placating, placated**

place

1. *noun* A particular location: *We visited many interesting places on our trip.*

2. *noun* A particular position or rank: *My cake won first place in the baking contest.*

3. *noun* A space for a person or thing: *Please save me a place at the table.*

4. *verb* To put something in a particular location: *Sameerah placed the fishbowl out of the cat's reach.*

5. *verb* To identify by putting in context: *I've seen her before, but I can't place her.*

6. in place *phrase* In its proper spot or location: *There were already sandbags in place when the river began to overflow its banks.*

7. out of place *phrase* Not in its proper spot or location: *I was much younger than everybody else at the party and felt out of place.*

place (plase)

▷ *verb* **placing, placed**

placebo *noun* A pill that contains no medicine but that is given to patients because the doctor thinks they will feel better if they believe they are taking medicine. **pla·ce·bo** (pluh-**see**-boh) ▷ *noun, plural* **placebos**

Word History

Families in the Middle Ages sometimes paid unrelated people to go to a funeral in the place of family members. These substitutes would cry and sing loudly. A common funeral song began with the Latin word *placebo,* meaning "I shall please," and after a while, singing a placebo meant "trying to get things by acting nice." Beginning in the 1700s, doctors used the word **placebo** to mean a medicine they gave to please a patient even though it might not be necessary, and so was a substitute for a genuine and effective medical treatment.

place mat *noun* A mat for the dishes, glasses, and utensils for each person at a table. It protects the table and is often decorated and part of a set. **place mat** (**plase** *mat*)

placid *adjective* Calm or peaceful, as in *a placid disposition* or *a placid lake.* **plac·id** (**plas**-id) ▷ *adverb* **placidly**

plagiarize *verb* To steal the ideas or words of another and present them as your own. **pla·gia·rize** (**play**-juh-rize) ▷ *verb* **plagiarizing, plagiarized** ▷ *noun* **plagiarism** ▷ *noun* **plagiarist**

plague

1. *noun* A very serious disease that spreads quickly to many people and often causes death: *The plague killed nearly 200 million people.*

2. *noun* A large number of an annoying or destructive thing, as in *a plague of grasshoppers.*

3. *verb* To trouble and annoy someone severely:

The campers were plagued by mosquitoes. ▷ *verb* **plaguing, plagued**
plague (playg)

plaid *noun* A pattern of squares in cloth formed by weaving stripes of different widths and colors that cross each other. **plaid** (plad)

plain
1. *adjective* Easy to see or hear: *She was in plain view.*
2. *adjective* Easy to understand: *The meaning of his actions is perfectly plain.*
3. *adjective* Not decorated or elaborate, as in *plain food* or *plain dress.*
4. *adjective* Simple and honest: *The plain truth is that Jerry doesn't like it here.*
5. *adjective* Not beautiful or handsome, as in *a plain face.*
6. *noun* A large, flat area of land: *We drove through miles of prairies and plains.*
plain (playn)
Plain sounds like **plane**.
▷ *adjective* **plainer, plainest**

plaintive *adjective* Sounding sad and mournful: *The kitten let out a plaintive cry.* **plain·tive** (**playn**-tiv)
▷ *adverb* **plaintively**

plan
1. *verb* To figure out ahead of time what you will do or how you will do it, as in *to plan a trip.*
2. *noun* An idea about how you intend to do something, as in *plans for the future.*
3. *verb* To intend to do something: *I plan to exercise today.*
4. *noun* A diagram or drawing that shows how the parts of something are arranged or put together, as in *plans for a new building.*
plan (plan)
▷ *verb* **planning, planned**

plane *noun*
1. A machine with wings that flies through the air. Plane is short for **airplane**: *Our plane landed at the airport on time.*
2. A hand tool with a sharp blade used for smoothing wood: *We used a plane to smooth out the top of the table.* ▷ *verb* **plane**

plane

3. A level of difficulty or achievement: *The lecture was on such a high plane that few people could understand it.*
4. A more or less flat surface, either real or imaginary: *The sun and the planets all lie in the same plane.*
5. In geometry, a flat, two-dimensional surface.
plane (playn)
Plane sounds like **plain**.

planet *noun*
1. One of the eight large heavenly bodies circling the sun. ▷ *adjective* **planetary** (**plan**-i-*ter*-ee)
2. A large heavenly body orbiting a star.
plan·et (**plan**-it)

Word History

To the ancient Greeks, the earth was not a **planet**, because for them a planet was anything that "wandered" across the sky, as seen from the earth! They thought the earth was in the center, with the stars moving around it in a circular motion while the planets "wandered" around. The word *planetes* was a form of the Greek word for "wanderer" and was based on the verb *planasthai*, meaning "to wander."

planetarium *noun* A building with equipment for reproducing the positions and movements of the sun, moon, planets, and stars by projecting their images onto a curved ceiling. **plan·e·tar·i·um** (*plan*-i-**tair**-ee-uhm)

planets

Neptune

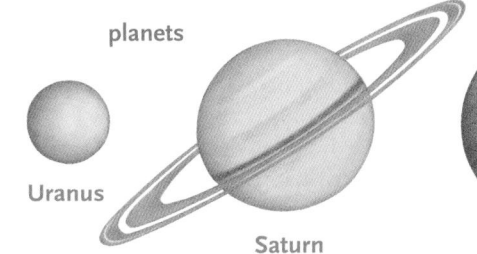
Uranus

Saturn

Jupiter

Mars

Earth

Venus

Mercury

plank *noun* A long, flat piece of wood used, for example, for flooring in a house. **plank** (plangk)

plankton *noun* Tiny animals and plants that drift or float in oceans and lakes. **plank·ton** (**plangk**-tuhn)

plant

1. *noun* A living organism with a green pigment called chlorophyll that allows the organism to make food from the energy of the sun. Many land plants have stems, roots, leaves, and flowers.

2. *verb* To put a plant or seed in the ground so that it can grow: *My grandpa plants herbs in his garden every year.*

3. *verb* To put something firmly in place: *My teacher planted the idea of becoming a doctor in my mind.*

4. *noun* The buildings and equipment used to make a product or carry out a process; a factory: *This power plant produces electricity for half the state.*

plant (plant)

▷ *verb* **planting, planted**

plantain *noun* A tropical fruit that looks like a banana but is eaten cooked. **plan·tain** (**plan**-tin)

plantation *noun* A large farm found in warm climates where crops such as coffee, rubber, and cotton are grown. **plan·ta·tion** (plan-**tay**-shuhn)

plaque *noun*

1. A metal plate with words inscribed on it, commemorating a person or an event, usually placed on a wall in a public place: *The plaque honored the school's football champions.*

2. A sticky deposit of food and bacteria that forms on your teeth and can cause tooth decay.

plaque (plak)

plasma

1. *noun* The clear, yellow, liquid part of the blood. Red and white blood cells float in the watery plasma.

2. *adjective* Of or having to do with a type of electronic display that uses small bits of plasma to emit light.

plas·ma (**plaz**-muh)

plaster

1. *noun* A soft mixture of lime, sand, and water that is spread on walls and ceilings and forms a smooth, hard surface when it dries. ▷ *noun* **plasterer** ▷ *verb* **plaster**

2. *verb* To cover or coat something as if you were using plaster: *The little boy plastered his bedroom walls with animal posters.* ▷ *verb* **plastering, plastered**

3. plaster cast *noun* A hard, white case that immobilizes broken bones so that they can heal properly.

plas·ter (**plas**-tur)

plastic *noun* A synthetic substance that is light and strong and can be molded into different shapes. Cellophane and vinyl are plastics. **plas·tic** (**plas**-tik)

plastic surgery *noun* Operations done to improve someone's appearance or to repair visible damage caused by injury or disease.

plate *noun*

1. A flat dish from which food is served or eaten.

2. A flat sheet of a hard substance, as in *a license plate* or *a plate of glass.*

3. A color illustration in a book.

4. Home base in baseball.

5. One of the flat, rigid, rocky pieces that make up the earth's outer crust.

plate (playt)

plateau *noun* An area of level ground that is higher than the surrounding area. **pla·teau** (pla-**toh**)

Word History

From an old French word meaning "flat," **plateau** is the name for a hill with a flat top. The same French word is the source for the modern English word *plate.* The word *platform* also comes from the same root.

platelet *noun* A disk-shaped body in the blood that helps the blood clot. **plate·let** (**plate**-lit)

plate tectonics *noun* The theory that the earth's crust is made up of huge rigid sections, or "plates," that move very slowly. **plate tec·ton·ics** (tek-**tah**-niks)

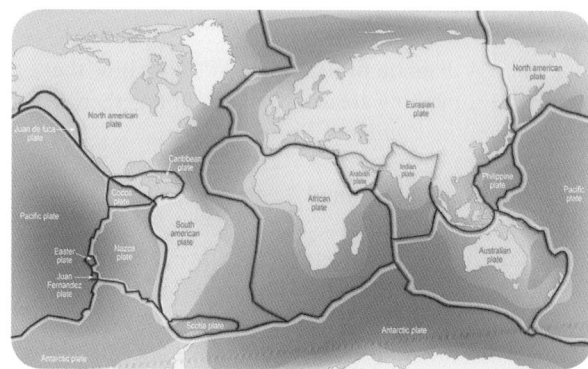

plate tectonics

platform *noun*

1. A flat, raised structure where people or objects can stand, as in *a train platform* or *a speaker's platform.*

2. A statement of beliefs of a group: *The political party's platform stressed tax cuts.*

3. The hardware or software of a computer that determines what programs will run on it and what devices can be connected to it: *The game was tested on various platforms before it was released.*

plat·form (**plat**-form)

plating *noun* A thin coating or layer of metal, usually gold or silver. **plat·ing** (**play**-ting)

platinum *noun* A very valuable silvery-white metal that is often used in jewelry. **plat·i·num** (**plat**-uh-nuhm)

platoon *noun* A group of soldiers made up of two or more squads. A platoon is usually commanded by a lieutenant. **pla·toon** (pluh-**toon**)

platter *noun* A large, shallow plate used to serve food. **plat·ter** (**plat**-ur)

platypus *noun* An Australian mammal with webbed feet, a broad bill, and dense fur. The platypus is one of the few mammals that lay eggs. **plat·y·pus** (**plat**-uh-pus) ▷ *noun, plural* **platypuses**

plausible *adjective* Believable or probable, as in *a plausible explanation.* **plau·si·ble** (**plaw**-zuh-buhl) ▷ *adverb* **plausibly**

play

1. *verb* To take part in a game or other recreation.
2. *noun* Fun or recreation: *The children spent hours at play.*
3. *noun* A story that is acted out on a stage: *I went to see my sister in the school play.*
4. *noun* A move, a turn, or an action in a game: *The goalie made a great play.*
5. *verb* To make music on: *Tia plays the viola.*
6. *verb* To take part in a sport or game: *Our team plays the Suns tomorrow.*
7. *verb* To act a part in a play: *I played the role of a knight.*
8. *verb* To act or to behave: *She is not playing fair.*
play (play) ▷ *verb* **playing, played**

playback *noun* The act of listening to or watching an audio or video recording, especially for the first time: *We paused the playback while Sasha got snacks from the kitchen.* **play·back** (**play**-bak) ▷ *verb* **play back**

player *noun*
1. Someone who participates in a game or sport: *Julio is one of the best tennis players I've ever seen.*
2. Someone who plays a musical instrument, as in *a piano player.*
3. An active or influential participant in an activity, as in *a major player in state politics.*
play·er (**play**-ur)

playful *adjective*
1. Frisky and willing to play: *My new puppy is very playful.*
2. Humorous, or meant to amuse or tease: *Tishawna's playful remark reminded me that I was taking the whole situation much too seriously.*
play·ful (**play**-fuhl)

playground *noun* An outdoor area, often with swings, slides, seesaws, and other equipment, where children can play. **play·ground** (**play**-ground)

playing card *noun* A card used in a game. The most common type of playing cards has 52 cards divided into four suits called spades, clubs, hearts, and diamonds.

playlist *noun* A list of songs or videos that you put together so that you can listen to or watch them one after the other. **play·list** (**play**-*list*)

playmate *noun* A child who plays with another child or children. **play·mate** (**play**-*mate*)

playoff *noun* One of a series of games after the regular season that determine which teams will compete for the championship. **play·off** (**play**-*awf*)

playpen *noun* A usually square folding structure that is a safe place for a baby to play in. **play·pen** (**play**-*pen*)

playroom *noun* A room intended for children to play in. **play·room** (**play**-*room*)

playwright *noun* A person who writes plays. **play·wright** (**play**-*rite*)

plaza *noun*
1. A public square.
2. An open area near large city buildings that often has walkways, trees, shrubs, and benches.
pla·za (**plaz**-uh *or* **plah**-zuh)

playpen

plea *noun*
  1. An emotional request, as in *a plea for forgiveness*.
  2. A defendant's answer to a charge in a court of law: *The defendant entered a plea of not guilty.*
  plea (plee)

plead *verb*
  1. To beg someone to do something.
  2. To say whether you are guilty or not guilty in a court of law: *He pleaded guilty to robbery.*
  plead (pleed)
  ▷ *verb* **pleading, pleaded** *or* **pled** (pled)

pleasant *adjective*
  1. Enjoyable or giving pleasure: *A pleasant breeze blew across the porch.*
  2. Likable or friendly, as in *a pleasant personality*.
  pleas·ant (**plez**-uhnt)
  ▷ *adverb* **pleasantly**

please
  1. *verb* To satisfy or to give pleasure: *The beautiful flowers pleased Grandma very much.* ▷ *adjective* **pleased** ▷ *adjective* **pleasing**
  2. *adverb* A polite word used when you ask for something. It means "be so kind as to": *Please be quiet.*
  3. *verb* To choose or to prefer: *They think they can do whatever they please.*
  please (pleez)
  ▷ *verb* **pleasing, pleased**

pleasure *noun*
  1. A feeling of satisfaction or enjoyment: *They smiled with pleasure.*
  2. Something that gives you a feeling of satisfaction or enjoyment: *Reading is one of my greatest pleasures.*
  pleas·ure (**plezh**-ur)
  ▷ *adjective* **pleasurable**

pleat *noun* One or more parallel folds in a piece of clothing such as a skirt, held in place by stitching at one end. **pleat** (pleet) ▷ *adjective* **pleated**

pledge *verb*
  1. To make a sincere promise: *I pledge never to betray your trust.*
  2. To promise to give an amount of money for a particular purpose: *The company pledged five thousand dollars to the library fund.*
  pledge (plej)
  ▷ *verb* **pledging, pledged** ▷ *noun* **pledge**

plentiful *adjective* Available in large amounts: *Bargains were plentiful at the sale.* **plen·ti·ful** (**plen**-ti-fuhl) ▷ *adverb* **plentifully**

plenty *noun* A great number or amount that is more than enough: *There are plenty of warm sweaters in the drawer.* **plen·ty** (**plen**-tee)

pliable *adjective*
  1. Easily bent or shaped, as in *pliable leather*.
  2. Easily influenced, as in *a pliable mind*.
  pli·a·ble (**plye**-uh-buhl)

pliers *noun, plural* A tool with two handles and jaws that can grip and bend objects or cut wire. **pli·ers** (**plye**-urz)

plight *noun* A dangerous, difficult, or unfortunate situation, as in *the terrible plight of the earthquake victims*. **plight** (plite)

plod *verb*
  1. To walk in a slow and heavy way: *We plodded through the snow.*
  2. To work in a dull, slow way: *Markus plodded through the long homework assignment.*
  plod (plahd)
  ▷ *verb* **plodding, plodded** ▷ *noun* **plodder**

plot
  1. *verb* To make a secret plan, usually to do something wrong or illegal: *The criminal plotted to rob the bank.* ▷ *noun* **plot**
  2. *noun* A small area of land, as in *a vegetable plot*.
  3. *noun* The main story of a novel, movie, play, or any work of fiction.
  4. *verb* To mark out something based on calculations, such as a graph or a route on a map: *My family plotted out our road trip on the map.*
  plot (plaht)
  ▷ *verb* **plotting, plotted**

plover *noun* A bird with long, pointed wings and a short bill that runs along the beach to find food. **plo·ver** (**pluhv**-ur *or* **ploh**-vur)

plow
  1. *noun* A piece of farm equipment pulled by an animal or a tractor and used to dig up soil and cut furrows before seeds are planted.
  2. *noun* A device used to remove or push aside matter, such as snow, from roads and sidewalks.
  3. *verb* To break up soil using a plow: *The farmer plows the field before planting.*
  4. plow through *verb* To work hard to complete a

plow

task: *Carmen plowed through two whole pages of math problems.*
plow (plou)
▷ *verb* **plowing, plowed**

pluck
1. *verb* To pull feathers out of a bird: *We have to pluck the chicken before we can cook it.*
2. *verb* To play notes on a stringed instrument by pulling on the strings with your fingers or by using a pick.
3. *noun* Courage and determination: *It took pluck to give the speech in front of that rowdy audience.* ▷ *adjective* **plucky** ▷ *adverb* **pluckily**
4. *verb* To pull something briskly from its place: *The workers plucked the apples from the trees.*
pluck (pluhk)
▷ *verb* **plucking, plucked** ▷ *adjective* **plucked**

plug
1. *noun* An object that blocks a hole or a pipeline: *Josh pulled the plug to let the dishwater drain from the sink.* ▷ *verb* **plug**
2. *noun* A device at the end of a wire that is put into an electrical outlet to make a connection with a source of electricity. Plugs have metal prongs.
3. *verb* (*informal*) To mention something in order to get publicity for it, often on radio or television: *The singer plugged her new CD on the talk show.*
4. *verb* To work in a steady way: *Mark plugged away at his term paper until he was finally done.*
plug (pluhg)
▷ *verb* **plugging, plugged**

plug and play *noun* A computer that has the essential software and programs already installed when you buy it. ▷ *adjective* **plug-and-play**

plug-in *noun* A small program that works with another program on a computer, usually to provide a specific function: *You can get a plug-in for your browser that will stop pop-up ads.*

plum *noun* A fruit that is soft when ripe and has purple, red, or yellow skin and a pit in the center.
plum (pluhm)

plumage *noun* A bird's feathers, considered all together: *The peacock's plumage is truly beautiful.*
plum·age (ploo-mij)

plumber *noun* A person who installs and repairs

plumber

water and sewage systems in buildings. **plumb·er** (pluhm-ur)

plumbing *noun* The system of water and drainage pipes in a building. **plumb·ing** (pluhm-ing)

plume *noun*
1. A long, fluffy feather often used as an ornament on clothing.
2. Something that has a feathery shape: *A plume of smoke rose from the chimney.*
plume (ploom)
▷ *verb* **plume**

plump *adjective*
1. Somewhat fat or round in shape, as in *a plump baby* or *a plump cushion.*
▷ *adjective* **plumper, plumpest**
2. *verb* To make a pillow or cushion fluffier by patting it.
3. *verb* To land, or to set something down, heavily: *Viktor plumped down on the sofa.*
plump (pluhmp)
▷ *verb* **plumping, plumped**

plunder *verb* To steal things by force, often during a battle: *The soldiers plundered supplies from the enemy camp.* **plun·der** (pluhn-dur) ▷ *verb* **plundering, plundered** ▷ *noun* **plunder** ▷ *noun* **plunderer**

plunge *verb*
1. To dive into water: *Tom plunged into the pool.*
2. To put or push something in suddenly or with force: *She plunged the knife into the watermelon.*
3. To fall steeply or sharply: *The waterfall plunged down the side of a cliff. The temperature plunged.*
4. To do something suddenly: *We plunged into action.*
5. take the plunge To decide to do something you've never done before and feel nervous about: *I've always wanted to learn how to dance and decided to take the plunge.*
plunge (pluhnj)
▷ *verb* **plunging, plunged**

Word History

Lead has been a useful substance for thousands of years. The Romans made pipes out of it, and in the Middle Ages, it held together the beautiful stained-glass windows of churches. Since lead is so heavy, builders used it to define a vertical line: They would attach a piece of lead to a string and throw the string down. It would then hang in a line straight down toward the earth. The Latin word for "lead" was *plumbum*, and we get the English word **plunge** from it, with the idea of falling down heavily like lead.

a
b
c
d
e
f
g
h
i
j
k
l
m
n
o
p
q
r
s
t
u
v
w
x
y
z

plural *noun* The form of a word used for two or more of something. The plural of *foot* is *feet*. The plural of *desk* is *desks*. **plu·ral** (**ploor**-uhl) ▷ *adjective* **plural**

plus

1. *noun* In math, a sign (+) used in addition that is also called a *plus sign*. ▷ *noun, plural* **pluses**

2. *preposition* Added to: *Three plus three equals six.*

3. *preposition* In addition to: *The dining room set consists of a table plus six chairs.*

4. *adjective* Slightly higher than, as in *a grade of B plus.*

5. *noun* An advantage: *The comfortable seats in this car are a definite plus.*

plus (pluhs)

Pluto *noun* A dwarf planet in our solar system. Pluto is farther from the sun than the planet Neptune and can be seen only through a telescope. Until 2006 Pluto was classified as a planet, and its designation is still under debate. **Plu·to** (**ploo**-toh)

plutonium *noun* A radioactive metallic element that is made artificially from uranium. Plutonium is used as a fuel in nuclear reactors and to make atomic bombs. **plu·to·ni·um** (ploo-**toh**-nee-uhm)

plywood *noun* Board made from several thin sheets of wood that have been glued together. Plywood is used for building and carpentry. **ply·wood** (**plye**-wud)

p.m. An abbreviation of the Latin phrase *post meridiem,* which means "after midday." It is used to indicate the time between noon and 11:59 at night: *School ends at 3 p.m.*

pneumatic *adjective*

1. Filled with air: *My bike has pneumatic tires.*

2. Operated by compressed air: *The workers used a pneumatic drill to break up the sidewalk.* **pneu·mat·ic** (noo-**mat**-ik)

pneumonia *noun* A serious disease that causes the lungs to become inflamed and filled with a thick fluid that makes breathing difficult. **pneu·mo·nia** (noo-**mohn**-yuh)

poach *verb*

1. To hunt or fish illegally on someone else's property.

2. To cook food, such as eggs or fish, by heating it in gently boiling liquid.

poach (pohch)

▷ *verb* **poaches, poaching, poached**

poacher *noun*

1. A person who hunts or fishes illegally on someone else's land: *The police are looking for the poacher who shot all my geese.*

2. A pot designed to poach eggs or fish.

poach·er (**poh**-chur)

pocket

1. *noun* A small cloth pouch that is sewn into clothing and used for carrying small items: *I keep my keys in the pocket of my pants.*

2. *noun* A compartment within a larger carrier: *My new backpack has lots of special pockets.*

3. *verb* To take something secretly, as in *to pocket the candy.* ▷ *verb* **pocketing, pocketed**

4. *noun* A small area or an isolated group: *A few pockets of wildlife remained after the forest fire.*

5. *adjective* Small enough to be carried in your pocket, as in *a pocket calculator.*

pock·et (**pah**-kit)

pocketbook *noun* A woman's purse or handbag that is used to carry personal items such as a wallet and keys. **pock·et·book** (**pah**-kit-*buk*)

pocketknife *noun* A small knife with a blade or blades that fold into the handle. **pock·et·knife** (**pah**-kit-*nife*) ▷ *noun, plural* **pocketknives**

pocket money *noun* Money for minor expenses, such as bus fare or snacks.

pod *noun*

1. A long, thin case that grows on certain plants and contains seeds, as in *a pea pod.*

2. A unit that is detachable from a larger vehicle and has a special function, as in *a landing pod.*

3. A group of certain kinds of sea animals, as in *a pod of whales.*

pod (pahd)

pea pod

podcast

1. *verb* To supply a program over the internet for people to listen to or watch on a mobile device or on a computer: *The school choir concert is going to be podcast.* ▷ *verb* **podcasting, podcast** or **podcasted**

2. *noun* A program for viewing or listening that is distributed in this way: *Download podcasts of our programs from our website.*

pod·cast (**pahd**-*kast*)

podium *noun*

1. A stand with a surface for holding things such as papers, for use by a person who is speaking to an audience.

2. A small platform, such as the one that an orchestra conductor stands on.

po·di·um (**poh**-dee-uhm)

▷ *noun, plural* **podiums** or **podia**

poem *noun* A piece of writing arranged in lines, often with a regular rhythm and some words that rhyme. Many poems are written to help the reader or listener share an experience or feel a strong emotion. In a poem, words are often chosen for their sounds as well as their meanings. **po·em** (**poh**-uhm)

poet *noun* A person who writes poetry. **po·et** (**poh**-it)

poetry *noun*
1. Literary work in the form of poems.
2. Anything that has the effect of a poem: *The dancer's graceful movements were poetry in motion.* **po·et·ry** (**poh**-i-tree)
▷ *adjective* **poetic**

poinsettia *noun* A decorative plant with large red, white, or pink leaves that look like flower petals. **poin·set·ti·a** (poin-**set**-uh *or* poin-**set**-ee-uh)

point
1. *verb* To show where something is by using your index finger or your arm: *She pointed in the direction I needed to walk.*
2. *noun* The sharp end of something, as in *the point of an arrow.* ▷ *adjective* **pointed**
3. *noun* A dot in writing, as in *a decimal point.*
4. *noun* A very small mark on a surface or in an area, as in *points of light.*
5. *noun* The main purpose or reason for saying or doing something: *The point of the new gate was to close off the parking lot at night.*
6. *noun* An idea presented in speech or writing: *The speaker made three important points.*
7. *noun* A specific place or location: *Visitors are not allowed past this point.*
8. *noun* A unit for scoring in a game: *The score was two points to one.*
9. *noun* In geometry, a location in space with no dimensions.
10. *noun* A particular time or moment: *At that point, a hush settled over the audience.*
11. *noun* A quality or a trait: *Her sense of humor is one of her best points.*
12. *verb* To aim at someone or something: *Don't point that gun at me!*
13. **point out** *verb* To draw attention to something: *Matt pointed out that the group would not all fit into one car.* **point** (point)
▷ *verb* **pointing, pointed**

point-blank *adjective*
1. Very close: *He fired the gun at point-blank range.*
2. Plain and blunt, as in *point-blank questions.*

pointless *adjective* Useless, or without purpose: *It's pointless to make lunch if there will be pizza at the cafeteria today.* **point·less** (**point**-lis) ▷ *adverb* **pointlessly**

point of view *noun* An attitude, a viewpoint, or a way of looking at or thinking about something: *From my point of view, it is better to make gifts than to buy them.*

poise
1. *verb* To balance: *Soledad's basketball was poised on her fingertip.* ▷ *verb* **poising, poised**
2. *noun* A confident and graceful manner. **poise** (poiz)

poised *adjective* Self-confident and graceful. **poised** (poizd)

poison *noun* A substance that can kill or harm a person, animal, or plant if it is swallowed, inhaled, absorbed, or sometimes even touched. **poi·son** (**poi**-zuhn) ▷ *verb* **poison**

poison ivy *noun* A shrub or climbing vine with clusters of three shiny, green leaves. Poison ivy causes an itchy rash on most people who touch it.

poison ivy

poisonous *adjective* Having a poison that can harm or kill. Some snakes, insects, and even plants are poisonous. **poi·son·ous** (**poi**-zuh-nuhs)

poison sumac *noun* A variety of sumac that can cause a rash similar to that from poison ivy.

poke *verb*
1. To jab sharply with a finger or pointed object: *It hurts when you poke me that hard.* ▷ *noun* **poke**
2. To stick out or thrust quickly: *The groundhog poked its head out of the hole.*
3. To move slowly: *My little brother poked along behind me.* **poke** (pohk)
▷ *verb* **poking, poked** ▷ *adjective* **poky** *or* **pokey**

poker *noun*
1. A long, metal tool used for stirring up a fire or arranging the burning wood.
2. A card game in which a player bets that the value of his or her cards is greater than that of the cards held by the other players. **pok·er** (**poh**-kur)

a b c d e f g h i j k l m n o **p** q r s t u v w x y z

polar *adjective* Near or having to do with the icy regions around the North or South Pole: *The polar icecaps are melting.* **po·lar** (**poh**-lur)

polar bear *noun* A large bear with thick, white fur that lives in Arctic regions.

pole *noun*
1. A long, smooth piece of wood, metal, or plastic, as in *a telephone pole.*
2. One of the two geographical points, the North Pole or the South Pole, that are farthest away from the equator.
3. One of the two opposite ends of a magnet.
4. **poles apart** Very different or having very different ideas: *Chris's and Seung's ideas on politics are poles apart.*
pole (pohl)
Pole sounds like **poll**.

polecat *noun*
1. A European animal of the weasel family that has brown or black fur. A polecat gives off a strong,

pole-vaulter

unpleasant odor when attacked or frightened.
2. Any of a group of North American skunks.
pole·cat (**pohl**-kat)

pole vault *noun* An athletic event that involves jumping over a very high bar with the help of a long, flexible pole. ▷ *noun* **pole-vaulter** ▷ *verb* **pole-vault**

police
1. *noun, plural* The people whose job is to keep order, make sure that the law is obeyed, stop crimes that are being committed, and investigate crimes that have occurred.
2. *verb* To guard or patrol an area and keep order: *Government agents policed the airport until the president's plane took off.* ▷ *verb* **policing, policed**
po·lice (puh-**lees**)

policeman *noun* A man who is a member of a police force. **po·lice·man** (puh-**lees**-muhn) ▷ *noun, plural* **policemen**

Polar Regions

The continent of Antarctica surrounds the South Pole. It is the coldest, windiest area on earth. Only a few insects and plants live on the land, but the ocean around it has seals, whales, and birds, including penguins. The only human inhabitants are scientists, who live in special research stations.

The Arctic region, around the North Pole, includes the ice-covered Arctic Ocean and northern Europe, Asia, and North America. Mammals such as polar bears and reindeer, as well as birds and fish, live there. Humans have also lived there for thousands of years.

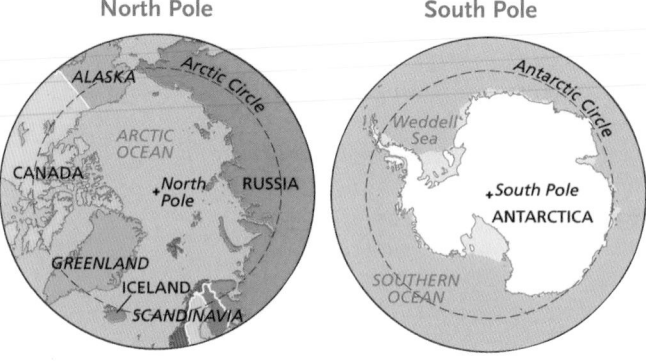

North Pole

ALASKA
Arctic Circle
ARCTIC OCEAN
CANADA
North Pole
RUSSIA
GREENLAND
ICELAND
SCANDINAVIA

South Pole

Antarctic Circle
Weddell Sea
South Pole
ANTARCTICA
SOUTHERN OCEAN

polar bear

penguins

police officer *noun* A man or woman who is a member of a police department.

policewoman *noun* A woman who is a member of a police force. **po·lice·wom·an** (puh-**lees**-*wum*-uhn) ▷ *noun, plural* **policewomen**

policy *noun*
1. A general plan or principle that people use to help them make decisions or take action, as in *a government policy.*
2. An insurance contract.
pol·i·cy (**pah**-li-see) ▷ *noun, plural* **policies**

polio *noun* An infectious viral disease that attacks the brain and spinal cord. Polio occurs mainly in children. In serious cases, it can cause paralysis. This disease is now easily prevented with a vaccine. Polio is short for *poliomyelitis.* **po·li·o** (**poh**-lee-*oh*)

polish
1. *verb* To rub something to make it shine, often using a special substance designed for that purpose, as in *to polish the furniture.* ▷ *noun* **polish**
2. *verb* To revise or prepare something to the best of your ability, as in *to polish an essay.*
3. *noun* A substance used to clean things and make them shine, as in *shoe polish.* ▷ *noun, plural* **polishes**
pol·ish (**pah**-lish) ▷ *verb* **polishes, polishing, polished**

polished *adjective*
1. Smooth and shiny: *He wore perfectly polished shoes.*
2. Well rehearsed and skillfully presented, as in *a polished performance.*
pol·ished (**pah**-lisht)

polite *adjective* Having good manners; being well behaved and courteous to others: *It is polite to let others get off the bus before you get on.* **po·lite** (puh-**lite**) ▷ *adjective* **politer, politest** ▷ *noun* **politeness** ▷ *adverb* **politely**

political *adjective*
1. Of or having to do with governments and how they are run, or with politicians, as in *lively political discussions around the dinner table.*
2. A **political party** is an organization that elects representatives to be candidates for government and creates or supports their policies.
po·lit·i·cal (puh-**lit**-i-kuhl) ▷ *adverb* **politically**

politician *noun* A person who runs for or holds a government office, such as a senator. **pol·i·ti·cian** (*pah*-li-**tish**-uhn)

politics *noun*
1. The activity and discussions involved in governing a country, state, or city, as in *local politics.*
2. *noun, plural* The activities of politicians and political parties: *What are the politics involved in switching from one party to another?*
3. *noun, plural* An individual's beliefs about how the government should be run: *Her politics are conservative.* ▷ *adjective* **political** ▷ *adverb* **politically** **pol·i·tics** (**pah**-li-tiks)

polka *noun* A fast dance in which couples swirl around the floor in a circular pattern. The polka came from central Europe. **pol·ka** (**pohl**-kuh *or* **poh**-kuh)

Word History

In 1830 and 1831, the Polish people fought for their freedom from Russia. To honor their struggle, other Europeans performed a dance called a **polka**. The word *polka* meant "a Polish woman" in the Czech language. The dance was not from Poland; it was from a region that is now in the Czech Republic.

polka dots *noun* Round, colored dots that form a regular pattern on fabric or other materials. ▷ *adjective* **polka-dot** *or* **polka-dotted**

poll *noun*
1. A survey of people's opinions or beliefs: *Students took a poll to decide the winner.* ▷ *verb* **poll**
2. **polls** *noun, plural* The place where votes are cast and recorded during an election.
poll (pohl)
Poll sounds like **pole.**

pollen *noun*
1. Tiny yellow grains produced in the anthers of flowers. Pollen grains are the male cells of flowering plants.
2. **pollen count** A measurement of the amount of pollen in the air, which indicates how badly people with pollen allergies will be affected.
pol·len (**pah**-luhn)

pollinate

pollinate *verb* To carry or transfer pollen from the stamen to the pistil of the same flower or another flower where female cells can be fertilized to produce seed: *Insects, birds, the wind, and some animals can help pollinate plants.* **pol·li·nate** (**pah**-luh-nate) ▷ *verb* **pollinating, pollinated** ▷ *noun* **pollination**

pollutant *noun* A substance that contaminates another substance: *Gasoline-powered vehicles release many pollutants into the air.* **pol·lut·ant** (puh-**loo**-tuhnt)

a
b
c
d
e
f
g
h
i
j
k
l
m
n
o
p
q
r
s
t
u
v
w
x
y
z

pollute *verb* To contaminate or make dirty or impure, especially with industrial waste or other products produced by humans: *Oil from the damaged tanker polluted the ocean.* **pol·lute** (puh-**loot**)
▷ *verb* **polluting, polluted**

pollution *noun*
1. Harmful materials that damage or contaminate the air, water, and soil, such as chemicals, gasoline exhaust, industrial waste, and excessive noise and light: *The government is trying to reduce the pollution in drinking water.*
2. The act of polluting or the state of being polluted. **pol·lu·tion** (puh-**loo**-shuhn)

pollution

polo *noun* A game played on horseback by two teams of four players. The players try to hit a small ball using long, wooden mallets. **po·lo** (**poh**-loh)

polyester *noun* A synthetic substance used to make plastic products and fabric. **pol·y·es·ter** (*pah*-lee-**es**-tur)

polygon *noun* A shape with three or more straight sides. Triangles, squares, pentagons, and hexagons are all polygons. **pol·y·gon** (**pah**-li-*gahn*)

Word History

A **polygon** has at least three straight sides and therefore at least three angles. This word comes from two Greek words meaning "many" and "angle." You can see the combining form *poly-* in other English words, such as *polyester* and *polystyrene*.

polymer *noun* A natural or synthetic compound made up of small, simple molecules linked together in long chains of repeating units. **pol·y·mer** (**pah**-luh-mur)

Polynesia A group of more than a thousand islands scattered in the central and southern Pacific Ocean, east of Australia. It includes Hawaii, Tonga, Samoa, Tuvalu, New Zealand, and other island groups. **Po·ly·ne·sia** (*pah*-luh-**nee**-zhuh) ▷ *adjective* **Polynesian**

polyp *noun*
1. A small sea animal with a tubular body and a round mouth surrounded by tentacles. Coral is an example of a polyp.
2. A tumor or mass on the lining of the nose, mouth, or other body passage open to the outside. **pol·yp** (**pah**-luhp)

polystyrene *noun* A light, firm plastic often used to make disposable cups, foams, and packing materials. Styrofoam is one form of polystyrene. **pol·y·sty·rene** (*pah*-lee-**stye**-reen)

polyunsaturates *noun, plural* Vegetable fats and oils thought to be healthier for you than other fats. **pol·y·un·sat·u·rates** (*pah*-lee-uhn-**sach**-ur-its) ▷ *adjective* **polyunsaturated** (*pah*-lee-uhn-**sach**-uh-*ray*-tid)

pomegranate *noun* A round fruit that has a tough, reddish-yellow skin and many seeds covered with juicy red flesh. Pomegranates have a tart flavor. **pome·gran·ate** (**pah**-muh-*gran*-it)

pomp *noun* An elaborate and stately ceremony or display: *The prince and princess were married with great pomp.* **pomp** (pahmp)

pompous *adjective* Self-important to a degree that irritates other people, as in *a pompous know-it-all.* **pomp·ous** (**pahm**-puhs) ▷ *adverb* **pompously**

poncho *noun*
1. A cloak that looks like a blanket with a hole in the center for the head. Ponchos were originally worn in South America.
2. A similar waterproof garment with a hood. **pon·cho** (**pahn**-choh)
▷ *noun, plural* **ponchos**

pond *noun* An enclosed body of freshwater that is smaller than a lake: *We went swimming in the small pond.* **pond** (pahnd)

ponder *verb* To think about something carefully: *Philosophers ponder the meaning of life.* **pon·der** (**pahn**-dur) ▷ *verb* **pondering, pondered**

ponderous *adjective*
1. Heavy and slow or clumsy: *Elephants are ponderous animals.*
2. Hard to understand and dull: *The politician gave a ponderous speech.*
pon·der·ous (**pahn**-dur-uhs)
▷ *adverb* **ponderously**

pony *noun*
1. A breed of horse that stays small when fully grown.

2. Any horse, especially a small one.
po·ny (**poh**-nee)
▷ *noun, plural* **ponies**

Pony Express *noun* A mail service in which a series of riders carried the mail on horseback from Missouri to California. Pony Express service started in April 1860 and ended in October 1861.

ponytail *noun* A hairstyle that looks like a pony's tail, in which the hair is pulled together and held with a band. **po·ny·tail** (**poh**-nee-*tayl*)

poodle *noun* A breed of dog with thick, curly hair that is usually cut in a fancy style. Poodles range in size from the fairly large standard poodle to the very small toy poodle. **poo·dle** (**poo**-duhl)

Word History

While we think of **poodles** as French, the breed's name actually comes from the German word *Pudelhund,* which means "splashing hound" or "dog that splashes in the water." These intelligent dogs are excellent at retrieving things in the water, even if it means getting a little wet.

pool
1. *noun* A small, shallow area of water or other liquid: *Try not to step in the pools of rainwater.*
2. *noun* A swimming pool: *Nina took swimming lessons at the pool every summer.*
3. *noun* A game in which players use a stick called a cue to hit wooden balls into pockets around the edges of a table.
4. *noun* A group of people who share something, as in *a typing pool* or *a car pool.*
5. *verb* To put things together to be shared, such as ideas or money: *We pooled our allowances and bought a new basketball.* ▷ *verb* **pooling, pooled**
pool (pool)

poor *adjective*
1. Having little or no money.
2. Worse than normal, or worse than what people might desire, as in *poor health* or *a poor crop.*
3. Deserving sympathy or pity: *Poor Alex had to walk home in the pouring rain.*
poor (poor)
▷ *adjective* **poorer, poorest**

poorly *adverb* Badly: *The new clothes fit poorly.* **poor·ly** (**poor**-lee)

pop
1. *verb* To explode with a small bang or bursting sound: *The balloon*

poppies

popped. ▷ *noun* **pop**
2. *noun* A sweet, carbonated soft drink. Also called **soda** or **soda pop.**
3. *verb* To move or appear quickly or unexpectedly.
4. *noun (informal)* Father.
5. pop out *verb* In baseball, to hit a fly ball that is caught by a player on the other team.
6. pop the question *verb* To propose marriage.
pop (pahp)
▷ *verb* **popping, popped**

popcorn *noun* Kernels of corn that are heated until they swell up and burst open into a fluffy mass with a popping sound. Popcorn is eaten as a snack. **pop·corn** (**pahp**-*korn*)

pope or **Pope** *noun* The head of the Roman Catholic Church. **pope** or **Pope** (pohp)

poplar *noun* A tall tree with wide leaves. The aspen and the cottonwood are both poplar trees. **pop·lar** (**pahp**-lur)

pop music *noun* Modern popular music with a strong, and usually fast, beat. ▷ *noun* **pop**

poppy *noun* A plant with large, brightly colored flowers. Some species are grown on a large scale to produce drugs or seeds. Poppy seeds are used as toppings or fillings for baked goods. **pop·py** (**pah**-pee)
▷ *noun, plural* **poppies**

populace *noun*
1. The people who live in a particular place, as in *the urban populace.*
2. The people who form a population; the general public: *The populace rose up against the dictator.*
pop·u·lace (**pahp**-yuh-luhs)

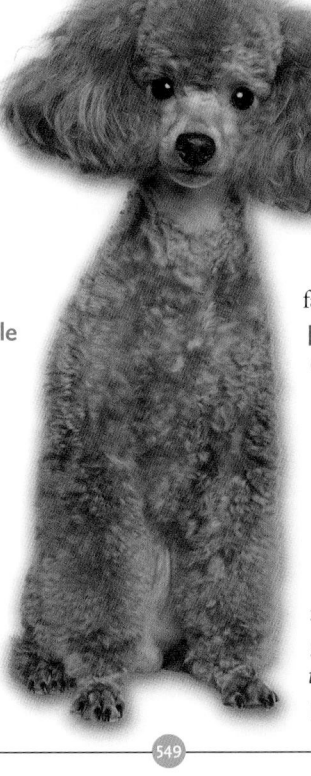
poodle

popular *adjective*

1. Liked or used by many people: *The park is a popular spot for picnics in the summer.* ▷ *adverb* **popularly**

2. Having many friends, or liked by many people: *Jana is the most popular girl in our class.*

3. Of or for the people: *In the United States, local officials are elected by popular vote.*
pop·u·lar (**pahp**-yuh-lur)

popularity *noun* The state of being liked or admired by many or by a particular group of people: *Susannah's popularity increased after she became a DJ.* **pop·u·lar·i·ty** (*pahp*-yuh-**lar**-i-tee)

populated *adjective* Having people living in it: *The summer resort is heavily populated in July and August.* **pop·u·lat·ed** (**pahp**-yuh-*lay*-tid)

population *noun*

1. The total number of people who live in a place: *The population of our town is 15,025.*

2. All of the people living in a certain place: *The entire population of the town was evacuated after the flood.*
pop·u·la·tion (*pahp*-yuh-**lay**-shuhn)

pop-up

1. *adjective* Appearing on a computer screen in front of another window: *When you move your cursor there, a pop-up menu appears.*

2. *adjective* Having a section that opens outward, as in *a pop-up camper.*

3. *noun* Something that pops up on a computer screen, especially an ad.

porcelain *noun* Very fine china, often used to make ornaments or cups and saucers or to cover bathroom fixtures. **por·ce·lain** (**por**-suh-lin)

porch *noun* A structure with a roof that is attached to the outside of a house, usually near a door: *Natasha sat outside on the porch.* **porch** (porch) ▷ *noun, plural* **porches**

porcupine *noun* A large rodent covered with long, sharp quills that are used for protection. **por·cu·pine** (**por**-kyuh-*pine*)

Word History

Because it looks like a tiny pig covered with spikes, the **porcupine** was given its name from the Latin words *porcus*, meaning "pig," and *spina*, meaning "thorn." The word *pork*, the name for the meat from a pig, comes from the same root.

pore

1. *noun* One of the tiny holes in your skin through which you sweat.

2. *verb* To read or study something carefully: *After poring over the directions, I began putting together the model airplane.* ▷ *verb* **poring, pored**
pore (por)
Pore sounds like **pour**.

pork *noun* The meat from a pig. **pork** (pork)

porous *adjective* Full of tiny holes that let liquid or gas pass through: *The porous cutting board stained easily.* **po·rous** (**por**-uhs)

porpoise *noun* An ocean mammal with a rounded head and a short, blunt snout. The porpoise is related to but is usually smaller than the dolphin and the whale. **por·poise** (**por**-puhs)

Word History

The **porpoise**'s name comes from a French word that in turn comes from the Latin words *porcus*, meaning "pig," and *piscis*, meaning "fish." The porpoise's nose is rounded like that of a pig.

porridge *noun* A kind of hot cereal made by boiling oats or other grains in milk or water until the mixture is thick. **por·ridge** (**por**-ij)

port *noun*

1. A harbor or place where boats and ships can dock or anchor safely.

2. A town or city with a harbor where ships can dock and load and unload cargo: *San Francisco and New Orleans are two important US ports.*

3. The left side of a ship or an aircraft as one faces forward. ▷ *adjective* **port**

4. A place on a computer that is designed for a particular kind of plug: *My laptop has four USB ports.*

5. A strong, sweet red wine.
port (port)

portable *adjective* Able to be carried or moved easily, as in *a portable radio.* **port·a·ble** (**por**-tuh-buhl)

portal *noun*

1. An entrance, especially a large or important one: *Enter through the arched portal.*

2. A website that provides links to many other websites.
por·tal (**por**-tuhl)

portcullis *noun* A strong, heavy grating that can be raised and lowered to defend the entrance to a castle. **port·cul·lis** (*port*-**kuhl**-is) ▷ *noun, plural* **portcullises**

portrait

porter *noun*
1. A person who carries luggage for people at a railroad station or hotel.
2. A person who waits on train passengers.
3. A person who carries equipment on an expedition.
por·ter (**por**-tur)

porthole *noun* A small, round window in the side of a ship or boat. **port·hole** (**port**-*hohl*)

portico *noun* A porch or walkway with a roof that is supported by columns. **por·ti·co** (**por**-ti-*koh*)
▷ *noun, plural* **porticos** *or* **porticoes**

portion *noun*
1. A part, section, or piece of something: *He spent a large portion of the evening doing his homework.*
2. An amount of food that is served to someone: *I'd like another portion of mashed potatoes, please.*
por·tion (**por**-shuhn)
▷ *verb* **portion**

portly *adjective* Heavy or stout: *His white beard and portly appearance make him look like Santa Claus.*
port·ly (**port**-lee) ▷ *noun* **portliness**

portrait *noun*
1. A drawing, painting, photograph, or engraving of a person, especially one that shows only the face, or the head and shoulders.
2. A description: *The author painted a glowing portrait of life in the city.*
por·trait (**por**-trit *or* **por**-trayt)

portray *verb*
1. To describe in words: *In the book, the villain is portrayed as a greedy ogre.*
2. To make a picture of something or someone: *Alice portrayed her mother in a drawing.*
3. To act a part in a play or movie: *In the movie, my favorite actress portrays a tough lawyer.*
por·tray (**por**-**tray**)
▷ *verb* **portraying, portrayed** ▷ *noun* **portrayal**

pose *verb*
1. To take a particular position and stay there so that you can be photographed, painted, or drawn: *The model posed in a ball gown.* ▷ *noun* **pose**
2. To pretend to be someone else in order to deceive people: *The police officers posed as drug buyers in order to arrest the dealers.*
3. **pose a question** To ask a question.
pose (pohz)
▷ *verb* **posing, posed**

posh *adjective (informal)* Very stylish or expensive: *After they won the lottery, they ate only at posh restaurants.* **posh** (pahsh) ▷ *adjective* **posher, poshest**

position
1. *noun* The place where someone or something is located: *We changed the position of our chairs so we could see better.*
2. *verb* To put someone or something in a particular place, or to arrange people or things in a particular order: *Paula positioned the flowerpots carefully on the windowsill.* ▷ *verb* **positioning, positioned**
3. *noun* A person's opinion or point of view on a particular issue or subject: *What is the governor's position on tax reform?*
4. *noun* The way in which someone or something is standing, sitting, or lying, as in *an upright position.*
5. *noun* The right place to be: *We got in position for the class picture.*
6. *noun* A particular job: *Reynaldo has a new position as a computer salesman.*
7. *noun* A set of circumstances: *After saving her money, Teri is in a position to buy a car.*
8. *noun* A particular role on a team: *Gary can play any of the infield positions.*
po·si·tion (puh-**zish**-uhn)

posing for a selfie

positive *adjective*

1. Certain, definite: *Grace is positive that this book is hers.*

2. Helpful or constructive: *He gave me some positive comments about my short story.*

3. Showing approval or acceptance: *I received many positive replies to my invitation.*

4. A **positive** number is more than zero.

5. Having one of two opposite kinds of electrical charge: *A magnet has a positive pole and a negative pole.*

6. Showing that a particular disease, condition, or organism is present: *If you get a positive result from this test, the doctor will give you antibiotics.*

pos·i·tive (**pah**-zi-tiv)

positively *adverb*

1. In a constructive or confident way, as in *think positively.*

2. Used to emphasize that something is the case or that someone means what they are saying: *Sharon is positively the nicest person you will ever meet.*

pos·i·tive·ly (**pah**-zi-tiv-lee)

posse *noun* A group of people with a common purpose, especially a group gathered together by a sheriff to help capture a criminal. **pos·se** (**pah**-see)

Word History

In England, when a sheriff needed to chase criminals or deal with troublemakers, he could gather up any men he found and have them help him. This group was known as a *posse comitatus*, a phrase from Latin that meant "a group of men of the county." The word *posse* meant "power" or "group of men," and the word *comitatus* meant "of the county." Eventually, people stopped saying the word *comitatus*, leaving just **posse.**

possess *verb*

1. To have or to own: *They possessed very few things of value.*

2. If you are **possessed by** someone or something, you are in its power: *She was possessed by evil spirits.*

pos·sess (puh-**zes**)

▷ *verb* **possessing, possessed**

possession *noun*

1. Something that belongs to you, as in *treasured possessions.*

2. in your possession Owned or held by you: *This jewelry came into my possession when my grandmother died.*

pos·ses·sion (puh-**zesh**-uhn)

possessive

1. *adjective* Wanting to keep someone or something for yourself and not wanting to share it.

2. *noun* The form of a noun or pronoun that shows that something belongs to the one referred to. In "This coat is yours" and "Carolina's hair," "yours" and "Carolina's" are possessives. ▷ *adjective* **possessive**

pos·ses·sive (puh-**zes**-iv)

possibility *noun*

1. An event that may happen: *There is a possibility that we could leave tomorrow.*

2. One thing among several that may be chosen: *If the weather improves, a picnic and a hike are both possibilities.*

pos·si·bil·i·ty (pah-suh-**bil**-i-tee)

▷ *noun, plural* **possibilities**

possible *adjective* Able to be done: *I'll let you know as soon as possible.* **pos·si·ble** (**pah**-suh-buhl)

possibly *adverb* Perhaps: *I could possibly come over tomorrow afternoon.* **pos·si·bly** (**pah**-suh-blee)

possum *noun*

1. An opossum.

2. play possum To pretend to be asleep or dead.

pos·sum (**pah**-suhm)

Prefix

The prefix **post-** adds one of the following meanings to a root word:

1. After, as in *postwar* (after the war).

2. Later, as in *postpone* (put off till later).

post

1. *noun* A long, thick piece of wood, concrete, or metal that is fixed in the ground to support or mark something, as in *a fence post.*

2. *verb* To put up a notice or an announcement of information: *The winners' names were posted on the bulletin board.*

3. *noun* A place where someone is on duty: *The guard never left his post.*

4. *noun* A military base where soldiers are stationed or trained, as in *an army post.*

5. *noun* A particular job that someone has: *Ms. Clugston has accepted a teaching post in South Carolina.*

6. *verb* To assign someone to a post.

7. keep posted *verb (informal)* To give someone information or the latest news: *Please keep me posted on how she's recovering from her illness.*

post (pohst)

▷ *verb* **posting, posted**

postage *noun* The cost of sending a letter or package by mail. **post·age** (**poh**-stij)

postage stamp *noun* A small printed piece of paper issued by a government and attached to mail to show that postage has been paid.

postage stamp

Postal Service *noun* The agency that is in charge of selling stamps and delivering the mail. Although the Postal Service is run by the US government, it is an independent agency. **Post·al Service (poh**-stuhl)

postcard *noun* A card, sometimes with a picture on one side, that you send by mail. A postcard does not require an envelope to be mailed. **post·card (pohst**-*kahrd*)

poster *noun* A large, printed sign that often has a picture. A poster can be put up as an advertisement, a notice, or a decoration. **post·er (poh**-stur)

posthumous *adjective* Coming or happening after death, as in *a posthumous tribute.* **post·hu·mous (pahs**-chuh-muhs) ▷ *adverb* **posthumously**

postman *noun* A mail carrier, if the person is a man. **post·man (pohst**-muhn) ▷ *noun, plural* **postmen**

postmark *noun* An official stamp on a piece of mail that marks, or cancels, the postage stamp and shows the place and date of mailing. **post·mark (pohst**-*mahrk*)

postmaster *noun* The head of a post office, if the person is a man. **post·mast·er (pohst**-*mas*-tur)

postmistress *noun* The head of a post office, if the person is a woman. **post·mis·tress (pohst**-*mis*-tris)

post office *noun* The place where people go to buy stamps and to send letters and packages.

postpone *verb* To put something off until later: *The coach postponed the game because of the approaching storm.* **post·pone (pohst**-pone) ▷ *verb* **postponing, postponed** ▷ *noun* **postponement**

postscript *noun* A short message beginning "PS" that is added to the end of a letter, after the writer's signature. **post·script (pohst**-*skript*)

posture *noun* The position of your body when you stand, sit, or walk: *The dancer had good posture.* **pos·ture (pahs**-chur)

postwar *adjective* After or later in time than a war, as in *the postwar period.* **post·war (pohst**-**wawr**)

pot *noun*
1. A deep, round container used for cooking or storing food, as in *a pot of soup.*
2. A container made of clay or plastic that is used for growing plants. ▷ *verb* **pot**
pot (paht)

potassium *noun* A silvery-white, metallic chemical element that is necessary for good nutrition. It is found in foods such as bananas and potatoes and is also used in making fertilizers, explosives, and soap. **po·tas·si·um** (puh-**tas**-ee-uhm)

plant pot

pothole

potato *noun* The thick underground tuber of a leafy plant, eaten as food. This vegetable was originally grown in South America. **po·ta·to** (puh-**tay**-toh) ▷ *noun, plural* **potatoes**

potent *adjective* Very strong, as in *a potent drug.* **po·tent (poh**-tuhnt) ▷ *noun* **potency (poh**-tuhn-see) ▷ *adverb* **potently**

potential
1. *noun* What a person is capable of achieving in the future: *Carina shows great potential as an artist.*
2. *noun* The possibility of being developed into something better: *I think Ron's ideas for promoting recycling have a lot of potential.*
3. *adjective* Possible but not yet actual or real, as in *a potential danger* or *a potential customer.* ▷ *adverb* **potentially**
po·ten·tial (puh-**ten**-shuhl)

pothole *noun* A large hole in the surface of a road. **pot·hole (paht**-*hohl*)

potion *noun* A liquid drunk as a medicine or poison or to bring about a magical or mysterious result: *In the story they drank a potion that made them fall in love.* **po·tion (poh**-shuhn)

potter *noun* A person who makes dishes, cups, and other objects out of clay. **pot·ter (pah**-tur)

pottery *noun*
1. Objects made of baked clay, such as bowls, plates, or vases. Pottery can be used for decorative or practical purposes.
2. A place where clay objects are made.
pot·ter·y (pah-tur-ee) ▷ *noun, plural* **potteries**

POTUS *noun* A name for the president of the United States. POTUS is short for *President of the United States.* **POTUS (poh**-tuhs)

pouch *noun*

1. A leather or fabric bag, as in *mail pouch*.

2. A pocket in the mother's body in which kangaroos and other marsupials carry their young. **pouch** (pouch)

▷ *noun, plural* **pouches**

poultry *noun* Farm birds raised for their eggs and meat. Chickens, turkeys, ducks, and geese are poultry. **poul·try (pohl**-tree)

pounce *verb* To jump forward and grab something suddenly: *The lion pounced on its prey.* **pounce** (pouns) ▷ *verb* **pouncing, pounced**

Word History

What is the favorite pastime of a kitten? Probably pouncing on a trailing strand of yarn pulled by its owner. The verb **pounce** makes us think of a short, sharp action, and this fits with the word's beginnings. In medieval England, a *pounce* was the claw of a bird of prey, and seizing prey with claws was called *pouncing*. Now creatures other than birds, such as kittens, are said to pounce.

pound

1. *noun* A unit of weight equal to 16 ounces. A soccer ball weighs about one pound. Pound is abbreviated as **lb**.

2. *noun* A unit of money used in the United Kingdom and several other countries.

3. *verb* To hit heavily and repeatedly: *Mike pounded on the door until we let him in.*

▷ *verb* **pounding, pounded**

4. *noun* A place where stray dogs and other animals are kept. **pound** (pound)

pour *verb*

1. To make something flow in a steady stream: *I'll pour the tea.*

2. To rain heavily: *It poured all night.*

3. To move in a steady stream and in large numbers: *The soccer fans poured onto the field at the end of the game.* **pour** (por)

Pour sounds like **pore**. ▷ *verb* **pouring, poured**

pout *verb* To push out your lips to express annoyance or disappointment: *My little brother pouts to get his way.* **pout** (pout)

▷ *verb* **pouting, pouted** ▷ *noun* **pout**

pout

poverty *noun* The state of being poor, as in *extreme poverty*. **pov·er·ty (pah**-vur-tee)

powder

1. *noun* Tiny particles made by grinding, crushing, or pounding a solid substance. ▷ *adjective* **powdery** ▷ *adjective* **powdered**

2. *noun* A cosmetic or other preparation made from powder: *She always put lipstick and powder on her face.*

3. *verb* To make or turn something into powder: *I powdered the nutmeg for the recipe.*

4. *verb* To cover something with powder: *Jay powdered the top of the cake with sugar.* **pow·der (pou**-dur)

▷ *verb* **powdering, powdered**

power *noun*

1. The strength or ability to do something: *It took all my power to move the heavy couch.*

2. The authority or right to command, control, or make decisions: *The president has the power to veto a bill.*

3. A person, group, or nation that has great strength, influence, or control over others: *The United States is a major world power.*

4. Electricity or other forms of energy.

5. In mathematics, the number of times you use a number as a factor in multiplication. Three to the fifth power means three multiplied by three five times, or $3 \times 3 \times 3 \times 3 \times 3$, equaling 243. **pow·er (pou**-ur)

powerful *adjective* Having great power, strength, or authority, as in *a powerful punch* or *a powerful king*. **pow·er·ful (pou**-ur-fuhl) ▷ *adverb* **powerfully**

powerless *adjective* Having no power, strength, or authority: *We were powerless to help them.* **pow·er·less (pou**-ur-lis)

powwow *noun*

1. A gathering of Native Americans or Native Canadians that is organized for social or ceremonial reasons or in order to discuss something. Powwows usually include traditional singing, dancing, and drumming.

2. *(informal)* Any meeting or conference: *We are going to have a powwow to plan the trip.* **pow·wow (pou**-*wou*)

practical *adjective*

1. Of or having to do with experience

or practice rather than theory and ideas: *This class will give you some practical experience in creating a spreadsheet.*

2. Useful: *Putting a boot rack next to the door is a practical idea.*

3. Sensible, or showing good judgment: *Moving those sandbags all by yourself just isn't practical.* **prac·ti·cal** (**prak**-ti-kuhl)

practical joke *noun* A mischievous trick often done to make someone look or feel foolish.

practically *adverb*

1. Almost or nearly: *The party decorations are practically finished.*

2. In a sensible way: *We could approach this job more practically by dividing it up.* **prac·ti·cal·ly** (**prak**-tik-lee)

practice

1. *noun* The repetition of an action regularly in order to improve a skill: *After school I have hockey practice.* ▷ *verb* **practice**

2. *noun* A custom or a habit: *It is Sofi's practice to read the newspaper every morning.*

3. *noun* The business of a doctor, lawyer, or other professional, as in *a medical practice.*

4. *verb* To work as a doctor, lawyer, or other professional: *Chiara practices law in Chicago.*

5. *verb* To follow the teachings of a religion and attend its services or ceremonies: *Many people in the Middle East practice Islam.*

6. *verb* To put something into action: *Kim practices kindness to animals.*

7. **in practice** *adverb* What actually occurs, rather than what someone thinks will happen: *The idea sounded good in theory but failed in practice.* **prac·tice** (**prak**-tis)

▷ *verb* **practicing, practiced**

prairie *noun* A large area of flat or rolling grassland with few or no trees. **prai·rie** (**prair**-ee)

Word History

Prairie was an Old World word for something that only existed in the New World: a huge, flat expanse of grass as far as the eye could see. The European explorers had never experienced anything like it. Still, they named it using the French word *prairie,* or "a large field of grass." *Prairie* evolved from the Latin word *pratum,* meaning "a meadow."

prairie dog *noun* A small burrowing mammal that is related to the squirrel. Prairie dogs live in large colonies mainly in the plains of west-central North America. Their call sounds like a dog's bark.

prairie dog

prairie schooner *noun* A large covered wagon used by pioneers to journey westward over the flat, grassy prairies of central North America.

praise

1. *noun* Words of approval or admiration: *The reviews were full of praise for the new show.*

2. *verb* To offer approval or admiration to someone or about something: *The teacher praised the class for its cooperation.*

3. *verb* To worship and express thanks to: *The preacher praised God.*

praise (praze)

▷ *verb* **praising, praised**

praiseworthy *adjective* Deserving praise: *Students made praiseworthy efforts to get everything out of the rain.* **praise·wor·thy** (**praze**-wur-THee)

prance *verb*

1. To walk or move in a lively or proud way: *She pranced around the room saying, "I have a new baby sister!"*

2. To spring forward on hind legs: *The show horse pranced across the arena.*

prance (prans)

▷ *verb* **prancing, pranced**

prank *noun* A playful or mischievous trick: *They played a silly prank on the new kid.* **prank** (prangk)

praying mantis

pray *verb*
  1. To talk to God to give thanks or ask for help.
  2. To hope very much that something happens: *Just pray that we get to the airport on time.*
  pray (pray)
  Pray sounds like **prey**. ▷ *verb* **praying, prayed**

prayer *noun*
  1. The act of praying.
  2. An expression of appeal or thanks to God: *The reverend's family says a prayer before meals.*
  3. A set of words used in praying.
  4. Something requested or prayed for: *The girl's prayers were answered when her dog was found.*
  prayer (prair)

praying mantis *noun* An insect that is related to the grasshopper. When it rests, the praying mantis folds its front legs, which then look like hands folded in prayer. **pray·ing man·tis** (**man**-tis)

Prefix

The prefix **pre-** adds the following meaning to a root word: Before, as in *precede* (to go before), *prewar* (before the war), or *prepare* (be ready before something happens).

preach *verb*
  1. To talk on a religious subject, especially during a worship service: *The minister preached about loving our neighbor.* ▷ *noun* **preacher**
  2. To tell other people what you think they should do, often in an annoying way: *He is always preaching to me about not wasting my money.*
  preach (preech)
  ▷ *verb* **preaches, preaching, preached**

precarious *adjective* Not in a secure position: *The dishes were stacked in a precarious pile on the counter.* **pre·car·i·ous** (pri-**kair**-ee-uhs) ▷ *adverb* **precariously**

precaution *noun* Something you do in advance in order to prevent a dangerous or unpleasant occurrence: *Angie took the precaution of removing all the breakable items before the toddler came to visit.* **pre·cau·tion** (pri-**kaw**-shuhn) ▷ *adjective* **precautionary** (pri-**kaw**-shuh-*ner*-ee)

precede *verb* To come before something else: *A short advertisement preceded the television show.* **pre·cede** (pree-**seed**) ▷ *verb* **preceding, preceded** ▷ *adjective* **preceding**

precedent *noun* Something done, said, or written that becomes an example to be followed in the future: *My parents' decision not to let my older sister go to rock concerts set a precedent for me and my brother.* **prec·e·dent** (**pres**-i-duhnt)

precinct *noun*
  1. An area or a district in a city or town, as in *a police precinct* or *an election precinct.*
  2. A police station in such a district.
  pre·cinct (**pree**-singkt)

precious *adjective*
  1. Very valuable, as in *a precious gem.*
  2. Very special or dear, as in *a precious child.*
  pre·cious (**presh**-uhs)

precipice *noun* A tall, steep cliff: *The cartoon character ran straight over the precipice and kept running in the air.* **prec·i·pice** (**pres**-uh-pis)

precipitate *verb*
  1. To rain, sleet, hail, or snow.
  2. To make something happen suddenly or sooner than expected: *The bombing of Pearl Harbor precipitated the United States' involvement in World War II.*
  pre·cip·i·tate (pri-**sip**-i-*tate*)
  ▷ *verb* **precipitating, precipitated**

precipice

precipitation *noun* The falling of water from the sky in the form of rain, sleet, hail, or snow. **pre·cip·i·ta·tion** (pri-*sip*-i-**tay**-shuhn)

precise *adjective*
1. Very accurate or exact: *The precise time is 9:04 p.m.*
2. Very neat and careful about details: *Brittany drew a cat with precise lines and shading.* **pre·cise** (pri-**sise**)

precisely *adverb* In exact or precise terms: *He refused to say precisely how much money he earned.* **pre·cise·ly** (pri-**sise**-lee)

precision *noun* Exactness. Something done with precision is done very carefully and accurately: *She made a drawing of the house, working quickly but with precision.* **pre·ci·sion** (pri-**sizh**-uhn)

precocious *adjective* Advanced in development or abilities beyond what is normal for your age: *Walter was a precocious math student, doing complex calculations at the age of eight.* **pre·co·cious** (pri-**koh**-shuhs)

precursor *noun*
1. A thing that comes before another and is either a cause or an indication of what is to come: *Government employees invented the precursor to the internet when they set up a group of computers to exchange messages with each other.*
2. A molecule, cell, or substance that is transformed into something else in a natural process: *Cholesterol is the precursor of all hormones.* **pre·cur·sor** (pri-**kur**-sur)

predator *noun* An animal that lives by hunting other animals for food. Lions, sharks, and hawks are predators. **pred·a·tor** (**pred**-uh-tur)

predatory *adjective*
1. Of or having to do with predators: *Lake Superior contains many predatory fish.*
2. A **predatory** person, organization, or action uses others unfairly: *The new legislation will stop some forms of predatory lending that hurt the poor most.* **pred·a·to·ry** (**pred**-uh-*tor*-ee)

predecessor *noun* A person who held an office or a job before another person: *Her predecessor gave her advice about how to be a good principal.* **pred·e·ces·sor** (**pred**-uh-*ses*-ur)

predicament *noun* A difficult or embarrassing situation: *My predicament is that my best friend is running against me for class president.* **pre·dic·a·ment** (pri-**dik**-uh-muhnt)

predicate *noun* The part of a sentence or clause that tells what the subject does or what is done to the subject. In the sentence "The kitten purred softly," the predicate is "purred softly." **pred·i·cate** (**pred**-i-kit)

predict *verb* To say what will happen in the future: *Can you predict tomorrow's weather?* **pre·dict** (pri-**dikt**) ▷ *verb* **predicting, predicted**

prediction *noun*
1. A statement about what will happen in the future: *She refused to make a prediction about the game.*
2. The action of predicting something. **pre·dic·tion** (pri-**dik**-shuhn)

predominant *adjective* More important, dominant, or obvious than all others: *The court ruled that race cannot be a predominant factor in determining district boundaries.* **pre·dom·i·nant** (pri-**dah**-muh-nuhnt) ▷ *noun* **predominance**

predominantly *adverb* For the most part; mainly: *We live in a predominantly middle-class suburb.* **pre·dom·i·nant·ly** (pri-**dah**-muh-nuhnt-lee)

predominate *verb* To be larger, stronger, or more numerous than others: *Cats predominate among the animals at the shelter.* **pre·dom·i·nate** (pri-**dah**-muh-*nate*) ▷ *verb* **predominating, predominated**

preen *verb*
1. When a bird **preens** its feathers, it is cleaning and arranging its feathers with its beak: *The robins preened their feathers before they flew off.*
2. To fuss over your appearance and then admire yourself: *The actors preened in the dressing-room mirrors.* **preen** (preen) ▷ *verb* **preening, preened**

preface *noun* An introduction to a book or speech: *The preface of the book explains how the author collected her information.* **pref·ace** (**pref**-is)

prefer *verb* To like one person or thing better than another: *Marianne prefers sledding to ice-skating.* **pre·fer** (pri-**fur**) ▷ *verb* **preferring, preferred**

preference *noun*
1. Something that you prefer over another thing: *My preference is to leave early in the morning.*
2. Something helpful that benefits a person or group: *As he picks the team, the soccer coach is giving preference to the players who have gone to soccer camp.* **pref·er·ence** (**pref**-ruhns)

prefix *noun* A word part added to the beginning of a word or root to change the meaning. *Sub-, un-,* and *re-* are all prefixes. The prefix *un-,* which means "not," is used in the words *unhappy* and *unusual.* **pre·fix** (**pree**-fiks) ▷ *noun, plural* **prefixes**

pregnant *adjective* Having a baby (for a woman) or young (for animals) growing inside the uterus. **preg·nant** (**preg**-nuhnt) ▷ *noun* **pregnancy**

a b c d e f g h i j k l m n o p q r s t u v w x y z

prehistoric *adjective* Belonging to a time before history was recorded in written form: *Dinosaurs are prehistoric animals.* **pre·his·tor·ic** (*pree*-hi-**stor**-ik)
▷ *noun* **prehistory**

prejudice

1. *noun* An opinion or a judgment formed unfairly or without knowing all the facts: *My prejudice against dogs is something I inherited from my mother.*

2. *noun* An immovable, unreasonable, or unfair opinion about someone based on the person's race, religion, or other characteristic: *It's a chance for us to put aside our prejudices and learn to get along.*

3. *noun* Hatred or unfair treatment that results from having fixed opinions about some group of people: *The event will raise awareness about racial prejudice in the workplace.*

4. *verb* To cause or create prejudice or bias: *The lawyer tried to prejudice the jury against the defendant.*

prej·u·dice (**prej**-uh-dis)
▷ *adjective* **prejudicial** (*prej*-uh-**dish**-uhl)

prejudiced *adjective* Disliking, mistreating, or mistrusting someone unfairly, because of prejudice: *The group claims that the company is prejudiced against older employees.* **prej·u·diced** (**prej**-uh-dist)

preliminary *adjective* Preparing the way for something more important or more complete that comes later: *The ballet class did some preliminary exercises before starting the rehearsal.* **pre·lim·i·nar·y** (pri-**lim**-uh-*ner*-ee) ▷ *noun* **preliminary**

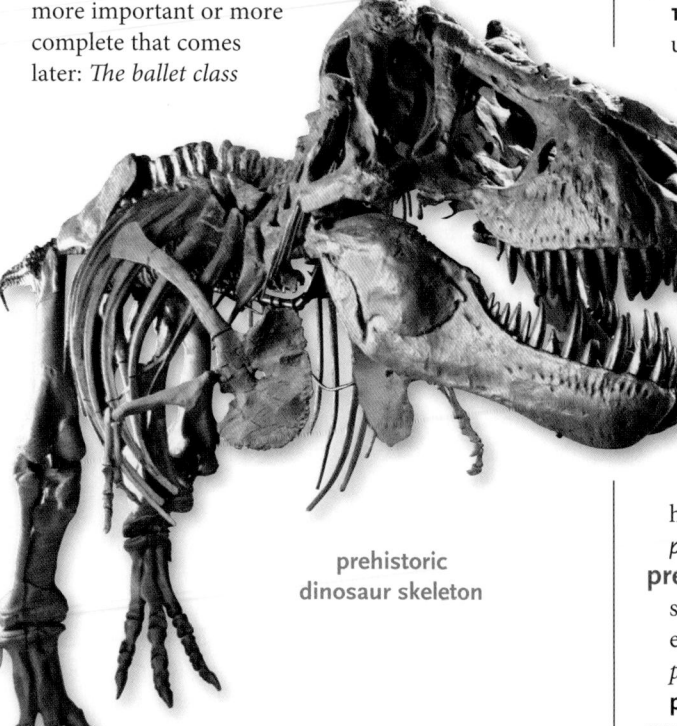

prehistoric
dinosaur skeleton

premature *adjective* Happening, appearing, or done too soon, as in *a premature birth* or *a premature decision.* **pre·ma·ture** (*pree*-muh-**choor** or *pree*-muh-**toor**) ▷ *adverb* **prematurely**

premeditated *adjective* Planned in advance, usually a crime or other wrong action, as in *premeditated murder.* **pre·med·i·tat·ed** (*pree*-**med**-i-*tay*-tid) ▷ *verb* **premeditate**

premier

1. *adjective* Leading or most important, as in *the city's premier theater group.*

2. *noun* A prime minister.

pre·mier (pri-**meer**)

premiere *noun* The first public performance of a film, play, dance, or work of music. **pre·miere** (pri-**meer** or prim-**yair**)

premise *noun*

1. A statement or principle that is accepted as true or taken for granted: *The author started his novel with the premise that human beings could survive a nuclear war.*

2. premises *noun, plural* Land and the buildings on it: *No pets are permitted on these premises.*

prem·ise (**prem**-is)

premium

1. *noun* Something that is free or less expensive than usual when you buy something else: *I got an MP3 player as a premium when I bought my computer.*

2. *noun* An amount added to the normal cost: *Some shoppers are willing to pay a premium for organic vegetables.*

3. *noun* Money that is paid to take out and maintain an insurance policy.

4. *adjective* Of better quality, and therefore sold at a higher price, as in *premium ice cream.*

5. at a premium Scarce and in demand: *Tickets for the concert were at a premium.*

pre·mi·um (**pree**-mee-uhm)

premonition *noun* A feeling that something is going to happen, especially something bad or harmful. **pre·mo·ni·tion** (*pree*-muh-**nish**-uhn or *prem*-uh-**nish**-uhn)

preoccupied *adjective* Thinking so much about something that you cannot pay attention to anything else: *She was preoccupied with ideas for her birthday party.* **pre·oc·cu·pied** (*pree*-**ahk**-yuh-*pide*) ▷ *noun* **preoccupation**

preparation *noun*

1. The act or process of getting ready: *The sequel to the* *film is in preparation.*

2. Something done in order to get ready for something else: *The party preparations were completed the day before the event.*

3. A substance that is made up for a specific purpose, such as food or medicine, as in *an herbal preparation* or *a cough preparation.*

prep·a·ra·tion (*prep*-uh-**ray**-shuhn)

prepare *verb*

1. To get ready: *I'm preparing for the test by studying every night.*

2. To put together various parts or ingredients: *Have you prepared lunch?*

3. be prepared to To be willing to do something: *I'm not prepared to spend my Saturday stuck in the house with nothing to do.*

pre·pare (pri-**pair**)

▷ *verb* **preparing, prepared**

preposition *noun* A word such as *with* or *on* that shows the relation of a noun or pronoun to other items in a sentence, as in the sentence "The book with the red cover is on the table." **prep·o·si·tion** (*prep*-uh-**zish**-uhn)

prepositional phrase *noun* A phrase that begins with a preposition. The phrase "in the secret garden" is a prepositional phrase because it begins with the word *in,* which is a preposition. **prep·o·si·tion·al phrase** (*prep*-uh-**zish**-uh-nuhl)

preposterous *adjective* Completely absurd, as in *a preposterous idea.* **pre·pos·ter·ous** (pri-**pah**-stur-uhs)

▷ *adverb* **preposterously**

prep school *noun* A private school that prepares students for college. Prep school is short for *preparatory school.* **prep school** (prep)

preschool

1. *adjective* Of or having to do with children who are younger than elementary-school age.

2. *noun* A school for children who are too young for elementary school, such as a child care center or a nursery school.

pre·school (**pree**-skool)

prescribe *verb*

1. To recommend strongly, or to order: *The football coach prescribed some tough rules for training.*

2. To write an order for a specific kind of medicine for a patient: *The doctor prescribed this cream for my poison ivy.*

pre·scribe (pri-**skribe**)

▷ *verb* **prescribing, prescribed**

prescription *noun* An order for drugs or medicine written by a doctor to a pharmacist. A prescription specifies what type and quantity of medicine to give. **pre·scrip·tion** (pri-**skrip**-shuhn)

preschool

presence *noun*

1. Being in a place at a certain time: *Santa Claus's presence at the party excited the children.*

2. The area immediately around a person or thing: *I'm shy in the presence of strangers.*

pres·ence (**prez**-uhns)

present

1. (pri-**zent**) *verb* To give someone a gift or a prize in a formal way: *I would like to present you with this medal.*

2. (**prez**-uhnt) *noun* Something that you give to somebody, as in *a birthday present.*

3. (**prez**-uhnt) *noun* The time that is happening now: *Few horse-drawn carriages exist in the present.*

4. (**prez**-uhnt) *noun* The **present tense**.

5. (**prez**-uhnt) *adjective* In a place: *All the students in the class are present today.*

6. (pri-**zent**) *verb* To introduce a person or thing: *I'd like to present my cousin.* ▷ *noun* **presenter**

pre·sent

▷ *verb* **presenting, presented**

presentation *noun*

1. The act of giving a prize or present, as in *the presentation of awards.*

2. A speech or other way of giving information: *Sarah gave an interesting presentation on frogs.*

3. The way that something is produced and the way it looks, as in *a colorful presentation.*

pres·en·ta·tion (*prez*-uhn-**tay**-shuhn)

presently *adverb* Now or at the present time: *We are presently studying the Middle Ages.* **pres·ent·ly** (**prez**-uhnt-lee)

present participle *noun* A form of a verb that ends in *-ing* and can be used with a helping verb to form certain tenses and to show that an action or condition is in progress. In the sentence "I am working," the word *working* is a present participle. Present participles may also be used as adjectives, for example, *thinking* in "a thinking man."

present tense *noun* A form of the verb that is used to indicate present time, as *likes* in "He likes cereal for breakfast."

preservation *noun* Keeping something from being damaged or destroyed, as in *the preservation of the wetlands.* **pres·er·va·tion** (*prez*-ur-**vay**-shuhn)

preservative *noun* Something used to preserve an item, especially a chemical used to keep food from spoiling. **pre·serv·a·tive** (pri-**zur**-vuh-tiv) ▷ *adjective* **preservative**

preserve
1. *verb* To protect something so that it stays in its original or current state: *Glass cases preserve artifacts in the museum.*
2. *noun* A place where plants and animals are protected in their natural environment, as in *a nature preserve.*
3. *verb* To treat food so that it does not become spoiled: *You can preserve fruit by drying it out.*
4. **preserves** *noun, plural* Jam that contains chunks of fruit.

pre·serve (pri-**zurv**) ▷ *verb* **preserving, preserved**

preserves

preside *verb* To be in authority over something: *The chairman presides over the meetings.* **pre·side** (pri-**zide**) ▷ *verb* **presiding, presided**

president *noun*
1. The elected leader or chief executive of a republic.
2. The head of a company, society, college, club, or organization: *The president of the school board is going to send a letter to every parent about the change to the school schedule.*

pres·i·dent (**prez**-i-duhnt) ▷ *noun* **presidency** ▷ *adjective* **presidential** (*prez*-i-**den**-shuhl)

president-elect *noun* The person who has won the election for president but has not yet been sworn into office.

Presidents' Day *noun* A holiday observed in most of the United States on the third Monday in February, celebrating the birthdays of George Washington and Abraham Lincoln.

press
1. *verb* To push firmly: *Press the button to ring the doorbell.*
2. *verb* To try hard to persuade someone to do something: *We pressed Erin to make up her mind quickly.*
3. *verb* To remove the wrinkles in clothes with an iron: *I pressed my blue shirt for the concert.* ▷ *noun* **presser**
4. *noun* A machine for printing: *This press produces thousands of newspapers every hour.*
5. **pressed for time** *adjective* In a big hurry: *I can't stay—I'm too pressed for time.*
6. **the press** *noun* The journalists and the organizations that collect, publish, and broadcast the news.

press (pres) ▷ *verb* **presses, pressing, pressed** ▷ *noun, plural* **presses**

pressing *adjective* Urgent and very important, as in *a pressing appointment.* **press·ing** (**pres**-ing)

pressure *noun*
1. The force produced by pressing on something, as in *blood pressure* or *water pressure.*
2. Strong influence, force, or persuasion: *Kathy is under a lot of pressure to get her project finished before the weekend.* ▷ *verb* **pressure**
3. A burden or a strain: *He could not handle the pressure of meeting deadlines.*

pres·sure (**presh**-ur)

pressurize *verb* To seal off an aircraft cabin, a spacecraft, or a diving chamber so that the air pressure inside is the same as the pressure at the earth's surface. **pres·sur·ize** (**presh**-uh-*rize*) ▷ *verb* **pressurizing, pressurized** ▷ *adjective* **pressurized**

prestige *noun* The great respect and high status that come from being successful, powerful, rich, or famous: *There's a lot of prestige that comes with winning a gold medal.* **pres·tige** (pre-**steezh**) ▷ *adjective* **prestigious** (pres-**tij**-uhs)

presto *interjection* A word used to indicate that something happens suddenly, as if by magic: *Just twist the balloons together like this, and—presto!—you have a bunny.* **pres·to** (**pres**-toh)

Word History

Magicians introduced the word **presto** into English by using it in their magic acts as a command. The Italian word *presto* means "quick" or "quickly." Magicians often direct the audience's attention to one place while they are secretly doing something in another place. Everything in a magic act has to happen "quickly" so that the audience does not have time to look carefully at everything onstage and figure out the magic tricks.

presumably *adverb* Probably: *If you have finished sixth grade, you presumably know how to read and write.* **pre·sum·a·bly** (pri-**zoo**-muh-blee)

presume *verb*
1. To think that something is true without being certain or having all the facts: *I presume that you like ice cream, so I brought some with me.*
2. To dare: *Don't presume to borrow my clothes without asking.*
pre·sume (pri-**zoom**)
▷ *verb* **presuming, presumed**

presumption *noun*
1. A belief that something is true without knowing for certain: *I brought these books over for you on the presumption that you enjoy mysteries.*
2. Behavior that others think is arrogant or inappropriate: *He had the presumption to call her his girlfriend after one date.*
pre·sump·tion (pri-**zuhmp**-shuhn)

preteen
1. *noun* A boy or girl who has not turned 13 yet: *He lived in Indonesia for four years as a preteen.*
2. *adjective* Made for or happening in the two or three years before a child's 13th birthday: *The preteen years are very smooth and easy for some kids.*
pre·teen (pree-**teen**)

pretend *verb*
1. To make believe: *The little girl pretended she was an astronaut.*
2. To claim falsely: *I do not pretend to be a computer expert.*
3. To give a false show in order to trick or deceive: *He pretended illness to get out of going to school.*
pre·tend (pri-**tend**)
▷ *verb* **pretending, pretended**

pretense *noun*
1. Dishonest behavior that is intended to make something false appear true: *He frowned, making no pretense at being friendly.*
2. A false excuse or justification for something: *Jarod left the table on the pretense of not feeling well, but I think he just wanted to check his email.*
pre·tense (**pree**-tens *or* pri-**tens**)

pretext *noun* A false reason or excuse given to hide a real reason: *Junshiro left the boring party on the pretext that he had to get up early the next morning.* **pre·text** (**pree**-tekst)

pretty
1. *adjective* Pleasant to look at: *I feel pretty when I'm dressed up.*
2. *adverb* Quite, as in *a pretty exciting game.*

pret·ty (**prit**-ee)
▷ *adjective* **prettier, prettiest** ▷ *noun* **prettiness**
▷ *adverb* **prettily**

Word History

If you played a trick on someone in the Middle Ages, it would be called a *prat*. A person good at *prats*, or clever at tricking people, would be called *pratty*, and this is the former spelling of **pretty**. After a while, it seemed clear that someone who was a good tricker would be a fairly clever person, and since we admire people who are smart, *pretty* came to mean "attractive and pleasing."

pretzel *noun* Dough that has been shaped into a stick or a knot and baked until it is crisp. Pretzels are usually salted on the outside. **pret·zel** (**pret**-suhl)

Word History

German speakers who settled in the United States introduced many words into English, including **pretzel** and *kindergarten*. *Brezel* was the German word for "pretzel"; in the Middle Ages it had been spelled *brezila*. Germans had adopted the Latin word for "arm," *brachium*, and named the bread roll "little thing with arms," because its shape looked like folded arms.

pretzel

prevail *verb*
1. To succeed in spite of difficulties: *Justice prevailed when the innocent woman was acquitted.*
2. To be common or usual in a particular area at a particular time: *Anxiety prevailed until the announcement that the plane had landed safely.*
pre·vail (pri-**vayl**)
▷ *verb* **prevailing, prevailed** ▷ *adjective* **prevalent** (**prev**-uh-luhnt)

prevent *verb*
1. To keep something from happening: *Brushing your teeth prevents tooth decay.*
2. To keep someone from doing something: *Our neighbor's loud party prevented us from sleeping.*
pre·vent (pri-**vent**)
▷ *verb* **preventing, prevented** ▷ *noun* **prevention** (pri-**ven**-shuhn)

preventive
1. *adjective* Meant to prevent or stop something, as in *preventive medicine.*
2. *noun* Something that prevents, especially something that prevents a disease: *The vaccine is a preventive against polio.*
pre·ven·tive (pri-**ven**-tiv)

a b c d e f g h i j k l m n o **p** q r s t u v w x y z

preview *noun* A limited performance of a play, a movie, or another kind of show before it is released to the general public. **pre·view** (**pree**-*vyoo*) ▷ *verb* **preview**

previous *adjective* Former, or happening before: *Molly ate the lunch she had packed the previous night.* **pre·vi·ous** (**pree**-vee-uhs)

previously *adverb* Before now: *Scientists announced the discovery of a previously unknown species of fish.* **pre·vi·ous·ly** (**pree**-vee-uhs-lee)

prey
1. *noun* An animal that is hunted by another animal for food: *The lion hunted its prey.*
2. prey on *verb* To hunt and eat another animal: *Hawks prey on chickens and other smaller birds.*
3. *verb* To rob, attack, or take advantage of someone who is helpless or unable to fight back: *The robber preyed on frail senior citizens.*
4. *noun* The victim of an attack or robbery: *The burglar waited for his prey to leave home.*
prey (pray)
Prey sounds like **pray**. ▷ *verb* **preying, preyed**

price
1. *noun* The amount that you pay for something: *What's the price of this hat?*
2. *verb* To assign a price to something: *She priced the books at two dollars each.* ▷ *verb* **pricing, priced**
3. *noun* The cost at which something is accomplished: *The battle was won at the price of many lives.*
price (prise)

priceless *adjective* Too precious for anyone to put a value on it, as in *a priceless antique.* **price·less** (**prise**-lis)

prick *verb*
1. To make a small hole in something with a sharp point. ▷ *noun* **prick**
2. To raise up: *The dog pricked up his ears when he heard the whistle.*
prick (prik)
▷ *verb* **pricking, pricked**

prickle *noun* A small, sharp point, such as a thorn. **prick·le** (**prik**-uhl) ▷ *adjective* **prickly**

prickly pear *noun* A cactus with yellow flowers and fruit shaped like a pear.

pride
1. *noun* Self-respect, or a sense of your own importance or worth: *The criticism hurt her pride.*
2. *noun* A feeling of satisfaction in something that you or someone else has achieved: *Moira takes pride in her work.*
3. pride oneself on *verb* To be proud of a specific quality or accomplishment: *Carmela prides herself on the neatness of her handwriting.* ▷ *verb* **priding, prided**

prickly pear

4. *noun* An exaggerated opinion of yourself or your own importance: *Talia's pride and arrogance make her very unpopular at school.*
pride (pride)

priest *noun* In certain Christian and other religions, a member of the clergy who can lead services and perform rites. **priest** (preest) ▷ *noun* **priesthood** (**preest**-hud) ▷ *adjective* **priestly**

prim *adjective* Stiffly formal and proper. **prim** (prim) ▷ *adjective* **primmer, primmest**

prima donna *noun*
1. A female opera or concert star.
2. *(informal)* A person who is demanding, selfish, or conceited.
pri·ma don·na (**pree**-muh **dah**-nuh) ▷ *noun, plural* **prima donnas**

primal *adjective*
1. Of or having to do with the most basic and important needs or instincts: *Most human beings have a primal fear of death.*
2. Original or coming before all others: *Happiness was not really an important trait for our primal ancestors.*
pri·mal (**prye**-muhl)

primarily *adverb* Mainly or chiefly: *Kenny was primarily interested in dinosaurs.* **pri·mar·i·ly** (prye-**mair**-uh-lee)

primary
1. *adjective* Biggest or most important, as in *a primary concern.*
2. *adjective* Earliest or most basic, as in *primary grades.*
3. *noun* An election to choose a party candidate who will run in the general election.
pri·mar·y (**prye**-mair-ee or **prye**-mur-ee)

primary colors *noun, plural* Red, yellow, and blue, which can be mixed to make all the other colors.

primary school *noun* A school that includes the first three or four grades and sometimes kindergarten.

primate *noun* Any member of the group of mammals that includes monkeys, apes, and humans. **pri·mate** (**prye**-mate)

prime
1. *adjective* Most important: *Getting a raise is Lena's prime reason for working hard.*
2. Of the best quality or kind, as in *prime meat* or *a prime example.*
3. *verb* To prepare a surface to be painted: *You have to prime the wood before applying the stain.*
4. *noun* The best part, as in *the prime of life.*
5. *verb* To pour water into a dry pump in order to start it working properly.
prime (prime)
▷ *verb* **priming, primed**

prime minister *noun* The person in charge of a government in many countries. Great Britain and Canada have prime ministers.

prime number *noun* A number that can be evenly divided only by itself or 1: *The numbers 2, 3, 5, 7, 11, 13, 17, and 19 are the first eight prime numbers.*

Word History

One of the great mathematicians of ancient Greece, Euclid, coined the phrase *protos arithmos,* referring to a "first," or prime, "number." Since a prime number can be divided only by itself and the number one, he considered it to be a basic and necessary number, so described it as "first." The ancient Romans translated the name as *primus numerus,* also meaning "first number," and the English used this phrase as a model for the term **prime number**.

primeval *adjective* Belonging to the earliest stages in the history of the world, as in *primeval forests.*
pri·me·val (prye-**mee**-vuhl)

primitive *adjective*
1. Very simple or crude: *Cave dwellers used primitive tools and weapons.*
2. Very basic and unrefined: *Conditions at the campsite were very primitive.*
3. Of or having to do with an early stage of development: *Baby talk is a primitive form of speech.*
prim·i·tive (**prim**-i-tiv)

primrose *noun* A small garden plant with clusters of brightly colored flowers. **prim·rose** (**prim**-roze)

prince *noun*
1. The son of a king or queen: *The crown prince would*

primrose

become king one day.
2. The husband of a queen.
3. A nobleman of high rank.
prince (prins)

princess *noun*
1. The daughter of a king or queen.
2. The wife of a prince: *Liza became a princess when she married the prince.*
3. A noblewoman of high rank.
prin·cess (**prin**-sis *or* **prin**-ses)
▷ *noun, plural* **princesses**

principal
1. *adjective* Main or most important: *She is a principal dancer with the ballet company.* ▷ *adverb* **principally**
2. *noun* The head of a school: *The principal called our teacher into her office to discuss the field trip.*
prin·ci·pal (**prin**-suh-puhl)
Principal sounds like **principle**.

principle
1. *noun* A basic truth, law, or belief: *Our government is based on the principle that all people are created equal.*
2. *noun* A basic rule that governs a person's behavior: *It's against Stephanie's principles to lie.*
3. in principle With regard to the general idea, but not the details or the way in which the idea will be carried out: *Kyra's plan was a good one in principle, but it was too expensive for us to follow.*
prin·ci·ple (**prin**-suh-puhl)
Principle sounds like **principal**.

print
1. *verb* To produce words or pictures on a page with a machine that uses ink or a special powder called toner. ▷ *noun* **printer**
2. *verb* To write using letters that are separate: *Print the address so it's easier to read.*
3. *noun* A photograph or a printed copy of a painting or drawing: *I have a print of my favorite painting on my wall.*
4. *verb* To publish: *The newspaper printed my letter to the editor.*
print (print)
▷ *verb* **printing, printed** ▷ *adjective* **printed**

printing press *noun* A large machine that prints words and designs by pressing sheets of paper against a surface, such as a metal plate, that has ink on it.

printout *noun* Information or pictures printed from a computer: *Look at the printout of the school rules.* **print·out** (**print**-out)

prior *adjective* Earlier, or existing before: *Peter can't come to the meeting because of a prior appointment.* **pri·or** (**prye**-ur)

prioritize *verb*

1. To put things in order from most important to least important, as in *to prioritize goals.*

2. To make something more important or most important: *Prioritize your homework so that it gets done on time.* **pri·or·i·tize** (prye-**or**-i-*tize*)

▷ *verb* **prioritizes, prioritizing, prioritized**

priority *noun* Something that is more important or more urgent than other things: *Finishing my paper on time is a priority for me.* **pri·or·i·ty** (prye-**or**-i-tee)

▷ *noun, plural* **priorities**

prism *noun* A clear, solid glass or plastic shape that breaks up light into the colors of the spectrum. Prisms usually have a triangular base. **prism** (**priz**-uhm)

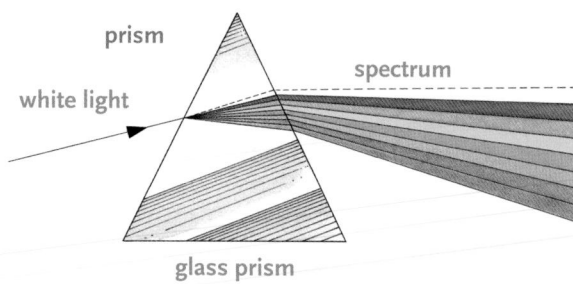

prism

spectrum

white light

glass prism

prison *noun* A building where people are confined as punishment for a crime: *The thief was sent to prison for two years.* **pris·on** (**priz**-uhn)

prisoner *noun*

1. A person who is in prison.

2. Any person who has been captured or is held by force, as in *a prisoner of war.* **pris·on·er** (**priz**-uh-nur)

privacy *noun* A state in which others do not disturb or interfere with your personal matters: *Students in the dorm often complain of a lack of privacy.* **pri·va·cy** (**prye**-vuh-see)

private

1. *adjective* Belonging to or concerning one person or group and no one else: *My diary is one of my private possessions.*

2. *adjective* Not meant to be shared, as in *a private conversation.* ▷ *adverb* **privately**

3. *adjective* Not holding a public office, as in *a private citizen.*

4. *adjective* Owned by one or more individuals or by a company, not by the government, as in *private property.*

5. *adjective* Unwilling to share thoughts and feelings with others: *Olivia is a very private person.*

6. *noun* A soldier of the lowest rank. **pri·vate** (**prye**-vit)

private school *noun* A school where parents pay for their children's education, as opposed to a public school, which is supported by tax dollars.

privilege *noun* A special right or advantage given to a person or a group of people. **priv·i·lege** (**priv**-uh-lij) ▷ *adjective* **privileged**

prize

1. *noun* A reward for winning a competition, as in *first prize.*

2. *adjective* Good enough to win a prize, or likely to win a prize, as in *a prize recipe.*

3. *verb* To value something very much, as in *to prize liberty.* ▷ *verb* **prizing, prized** ▷ *adjective* **prized** **prize** (prize)

pro

1. *preposition* In favor of something: *This newspaper article is strongly pro-union.*

2. *noun* A shortened form of **professional**, often used in sports, as in *a tennis pro.*

3. pros and cons (kahnz) Advantages and disadvantages: *We debated the pros and cons of the proposed law.* **pro** (proh)

probability *noun*

1. The likelihood that a particular thing will happen: *Lou's improved pitching increases the probability that his team will win their next game.*

2. The most probable thing: *The probability is that the car needs a new battery.* **prob·a·bil·i·ty** (*prah*-buh-**bil**-i-tee)

probable *adjective* Likely to happen or be true: *Thunderstorms are probable tomorrow.* **prob·a·ble** (**prah**-buh-buhl)

probably *adverb*

1. In all likelihood, with little doubt: *I'll probably arrive around 8 p.m.*

2. Approximately: *There were probably 50 people there, waving signs and shouting.* **prob·a·bly** (**prah**-buh-blee)

probation *noun*

1. A period of time for testing a person's behavior or job qualifications: *Sherry will be on probation in her new job for three months.*

2. A period of time during which a person who has committed a crime is not kept in prison but is allowed to go free under the close supervision of a probation officer. **pro·ba·tion** (proh-**bay**-shuhn)

probe *noun*
1. A thorough examination or investigation.
2. A tool or device used to explore or examine something, as in *a space probe.*
probe (prohb)
▷ *verb* **probe**

problem
1. *noun* A difficult situation that needs to be solved: *Dimitri's absence created a problem for the team.*
2. *noun* A puzzle or question that requires an answer, as in *a physics problem.*
3. *adjective* Being or creating a problem, as in *a problem child.*
prob·lem (**prah**-bluhm)

procedure *noun* A way of doing something, especially by a series of steps: *The procedure for printing files is posted next to the printer.* **pro·ce·dure** (pruh-**see**-jur)

proceed
1. (pruh-**seed**) *verb* To move forward or continue: *Proceed to the corner, then turn right.* ▷ **proceeding, proceeded**
2. **proceeds** (**proh**-seedz) *noun, plural* The sum of money that is raised by an event: *The proceeds from the book fair will buy a new set of encyclopedias.*
pro·ceed

process
1. *noun* A series of actions or steps that produces a particular result: *The process of moving into the new house took two days.* ▷ *noun, plural* **processes**
2. *verb* To prepare or change by a series of steps, as in *to process recycled newspapers.* ▷ *verb* **processes, processing, processed** ▷ *noun* **processing** ▷ *adjective* **processed**
proc·ess (**prah**-ses *or* **proh**-ses)

procession *noun*
1. A number of people walking or driving along a route in an orderly way as part of a public festival, a religious service, or a parade: *The holiday procession included bands, cars, and bicycles.*
2. A number of people, animals, or vehicles moving along as if they were in a parade: *A procession of wet, miserable students trooped onto the buses.*
pro·ces·sion (pruh-**sesh**-uhn)

processor *noun*
1. A person, machine, or company that processes something.
2. A computer's CPU.
proc·es·sor (**prah**-ses-ur)

proclaim *verb* To announce something publicly: *The announcer proclaimed the contest winners.* **pro·claim** (pruh-**klaym**) ▷ *verb* **proclaiming, proclaimed** ▷ *noun* **proclamation** (prah-kluh-**may**-shuhn)

procrastinate *verb* To put off or delay doing something that you really need to do: *If you procrastinate any longer, you won't have time to finish your homework.* **pro·cras·ti·nate** (proh-**kras**-tuh-*nate*) ▷ *verb* **procrastinating, procrastinated** ▷ *noun* **procrastination** ▷ *noun* **procrastinator**

procure *verb* To buy or obtain something, especially something that is difficult to get: *He was finally able to procure an immigration visa.* **pro·cure** (pruh-**kyoor**) ▷ *verb* **procuring, procured**

prod
1. *verb* To poke or jab something or someone: *Curt prodded me in the ribs to make me pay attention.*
2. *verb* To push or urge someone into action: *My parents had to prod me to study for my test.*
3. *noun* A poke or a jab, either physical or mental, to make or remind someone to do something: *Leon needs a prod to get started.*
4. *noun* A stick or other sharp or electrified instrument used to control animals, as in *a cattle prod.*
prod (prahd)
▷ *verb* **prodding, prodded**

prodigy *noun* A person, especially a young one, who has exceptional ability in a particular area, as in *a chess prodigy.* **prod·i·gy** (**prah**-di-jee) ▷ *noun, plural* **prodigies**

Word History

If the ancient Romans saw something amazing, they called it a *prodigium*. A *prodigium* was considered to be a sign of something that was going to happen. This was also the first meaning of the English word **prodigy**: "an unusual occurrence that is seen as an omen." Eventually, English speakers started using the word to mean only "a surprising thing." Today, a *prodigy* is a person, especially a child, with "surprising" abilities.

produce
1. (pruh-**doos**) *verb* To make or manufacture something: *This factory produces hundreds of shirts a day.*
2. (**prah**-doos *or* **proh**-doos) *noun* Things that are produced or grown for eating, especially fruits and vegetables, as in *to buy produce at the farmers' market.*
3. (pruh-**doos**) *verb* To bring something out for inspection or use: *Nick produced a pen from his backpack.*
4. (pruh-**doos**) *verb* To be in charge of putting on a play or making a movie or TV program. ▷ *noun* **producer**
pro·duce
▷ *verb* **producing, produced**

product *noun*
1. Something that is manufactured, or made by a natural process, as in *a dairy product*.
2. The result you get when you multiply two numbers: *The product of 6 times 4 is 24.*
prod·uct (**prah**-duhkt)

production *noun*
1. The process of creating, growing, or manufacturing something: *Fruit production is a major activity in this area.*
2. The total amount produced: *Production is down this year.*
3. Any form of entertainment that is presented to others, as in *a production of a play*.
4. production line A system of manufacturing in which the steps needed to make the product are carried out one at a time, in a specific order, as the product moves along slowly on a belt or track.
pro·duc·tion (pruh-**duhk**-shuhn)

productive *adjective* Making a lot of products, accomplishing a lot of work, or producing good results: *We had a productive meeting.* **pro·duc·tive** (pruh-**duhk**-tiv)

productivity *noun* The state of being productive, or the rate at which production happens: *The company has increased productivity by 20 percent in the past 12 months.* **pro·duc·tiv·i·ty** (proh-duhk-**tiv**-i-tee)

profess *verb*
1. To state openly or to make known: *I will profess my feelings for her at the Valentine's Day dance.*
2. To say something insincerely, or to pretend that something is true: *He professed to be a great player, but he couldn't make the basketball team.*
pro·fess (pruh-**fes**)
▷ *verb* **professes, professing, professed**

profession *noun*
1. An occupation for which you need special training or study: *Our school's career day showed us a lot of interesting professions.*
2. The whole group of people in an occupation that requires special training or study, as in *the medical profession*.
3. Something that you state openly, as in *a profession of loyalty*.
pro·fes·sion (pruh-**fesh**-uhn)

professional
1. *noun* A member of a profession, such as a doctor, teacher, nurse, or lawyer. ▷ *adjective* **professional**
2. *adjective* Making money for doing something others do for fun, as in *a professional athlete*. ▷ *noun* **professional**
pro·fes·sion·al (pruh-**fesh**-uh-nuhl)

professor *noun* A teacher of the highest teaching rank at a college or university, as in *a history professor*. **pro·fes·sor** (pruh-**fes**-ur)

proficient *adjective* Able to do something properly and skillfully, as in *a proficient mechanic*. **pro·fi·cient** (pruh-**fish**-uhnt) ▷ *noun* **proficiency** ▷ *adverb* **proficiently**

profile
1. *noun* A side view or drawing of someone's head: *Lou sketched a profile of Yvette.*
2. *noun* A brief account of someone's life or work: *The newspaper published a profile of a famous musician.*
3. *verb* To describe someone in a written article: *Steve will profile the new teacher for the magazine.* ▷ *verb* **profiling, profiled**
pro·file (**proh**-file)

profile

profit
1. *noun* The amount of money left after all the costs of running a business have been subtracted from the money earned: *We had a profit of $5,000.*
2. *noun* A gain or a benefit: *Hard work always yields a profit.*
3. *verb* To gain or benefit in some way: *You will profit by doing well in school.* ▷ *verb* **profiting, profited**
prof·it (**prah**-fit)
Profit sounds like **prophet**.

profitable *adjective* Producing a profit: *They have a profitable business.* **prof·it·a·ble** (**prah**-fi-tuh-buhl)

profound *adjective* Very deep or intense, as in *profound regret*. **pro·found** (pruh-**found**) ▷ *adverb* **profoundly**

profuse *adjective* Plentiful or more than enough, as in *profuse apologies*. **pro·fuse** (pruh-**fyoos**) ▷ *noun* **profusion** (pruh-**fyoo**-zhuhn) ▷ *noun* **profuseness**

progeny *noun*
1. Someone's child or descendant. Progeny can refer to a single person or to a group: *They are the progeny of Mormon settlers.*
2. The offspring of a plant or animal: *Bees build honeycombs to store honey and pollen and to protect the progeny of the queen bee.*
prog·e·ny (**prah**-juh-nee)

program
1. *noun* A television or radio show: *My favorite program comes on at seven.*
2. *noun* A booklet that gives you information about a performance or a sporting event.
3. *noun* A schedule or plan for doing something, as in *a new program to help the homeless*.

4. *noun* A series of instructions, written in a computer language, that controls the way a computer works: *This program creates maps.*
5. *verb* To give a computer or other machine instructions to make it work in a certain way. ▷ *verb* **programming, programmed**
pro·gram (**proh**-gram)

programmer *noun* A person whose job is to program a computer. **pro·gram·mer** (**proh**-gram-ur)

programming *noun*
1. The entire set of broadcasts or performances of a television station, a radio station, or a theater, as in *excellent children's programming.*
2. The process of creating programs for computers.
pro·gram·ming (**proh**-gram-ing)

progress
1. (pruh-**gres**) *verb* To move forward or to improve: *How are you progressing with your French lessons?* ▷ *verb* **progresses, progressing, progressed**
2. (**prah**-gres) *noun* A forward movement or improvement: *The teacher saw some progress in Mariah's work.*
3. in progress (**prah**-gres) *phrase* Happening: *Band camp is now in progress.*
prog·ress

progressive
1. *adjective* Moving forward or happening steadily, as in *progressive improvement.*
2. *adjective* In favor of improvement, progress, or reform, especially in political or social matters: *The liberal candidate had many progressive ideas for protecting the environment.*
3. *noun* A person who favors improvement or reform, especially in political, social, or educational matters.
pro·gress·ive (pruh-**gres**-iv)

prohibit *verb* To forbid or ban something officially, as in *to prohibit smoking.* **pro·hib·it** (proh-**hib**-it) ▷ *verb* **prohibiting, prohibited** ▷ *noun* **prohibition**

project
1. (**prah**-jekt) *noun* A plan or a proposal: *The Senate approved the highway project.*
2. (**prah**-jekt) *noun* A job or assignment worked on over a period of time: *Denise's latest project is a model for the science fair.*
3. (pruh-**jekt**) *verb* To stick out: *The roof projects far out over the porch.* ▷ *adjective* **projecting**

4. (pruh-**jekt**) *verb* To display an image or a movie on a screen.
5. (pruh-**jekt**) *verb* To predict or to forecast: *Economic growth is projected to be stable next year.*
6. (pruh-**jekt**) *verb* To make your voice carry very far: *The singer projected her voice to the very back of the auditorium.*
7. (**prah**-jekt) *noun* A group of apartment buildings planned and built as a unit.
proj·ect
▷ *verb* **projecting, projected**

projectile *noun* An object, such as a bullet or missile, that is thrown or shot through the air. **pro·jec·tile** (pruh-**jek**-tuhl)

projection *noun*
1. Something that sticks out, as in *a rocky projection along the coast.*
2. An estimate or a prediction: *The latest projection says that the number of cars will double.*
3. map projection A way of representing the globe on a flat page.
pro·jec·tion (pruh-**jek**-shuhn)

projector *noun* A machine that shows slides or movies on a screen: *Mark set up the projector to show a movie in class.* **pro·jec·tor** (pruh-**jek**-tur)

prolific *adjective* Producing a large quantity of something: *The prolific author has written more than 40 books.* **pro·li·fic** (pruh-**lif**-ik)

prologue *noun* The introductory section of a literary work or a musical composition: *The prologue introduces all the characters.*
pro·logue (**proh**-lawg)

prolong *verb* To make something last longer: *Debbie prolonged the suspense by not telling us who was coming until after dinner.* **pro·long** (pruh-**lawng**) ▷ *verb* **prolonging, prolonged**

prom *noun* A formal dance for high-school students that is usually held near the end of the school year. **prom** (prahm)

prom

promenade
1. *noun* A walk taken for pleasure.
2. *verb* To walk for pleasure: *We love to promenade along the upper deck of the ocean liner.* ▷ *verb* **promenading, promenaded**
3. *noun* A place for taking a leisurely walk: *There is a lovely promenade along the river.*
prom·e·nade (*prah*-muh-**nade** or *prah*-muh-**nahd**)

prominent *adjective*
1. Very noticeable, as in *a prominent building*.
2. Famous or important, as in *a prominent lawyer*.
prom·i·nent (**prah**-muh-nuhnt)
▷ *noun* **prominence**

promise
1. *verb* To declare that you will definitely do a particular thing, or that a particular thing will happen. ▷ *verb* **promising, promised**
2. *noun* A pledge given by someone that he or she will do something: *Sue made a promise to keep her room clean.*
3. *noun* The likelihood of doing well in the future: *Angelo shows great promise as a writer.* ▷ *adjective* **promising**
prom·ise (**prah**-mis)

promontory *noun* A high point of land or rock that sticks out into a body of water. **prom·on·tor·y** (**prah**-muhn-*tor*-ee)

promote *verb*
1. To move someone to a higher job or to a higher grade in school: *The boss promoted Maria to supervisor.*
2. To help with the growth or development of something: *Sugary foods promote tooth decay.*
3. To make the public aware of something or someone: *The city put up banners to promote its new sports arena.*
pro·mote (pruh-**mote**)
▷ *verb* **promoting, promoted**

promotion *noun*
1. Advancement to a higher job or a higher grade in school.
2. Encouragement or publicity: *The health department has a new program for the promotion of immunizations.*
pro·mo·tion (pruh-**moh**-shuhn)

prompt
1. *adjective* Immediate, without delay: *I received a prompt answer to my question.*
2. *adjective* On time: *Please be prompt for dinner.*
3. *noun* A reminder or encouragement to do something: *A prompt will appear on the computer screen, asking you to provide your password.*
4. *verb* To move someone to action: *The anger in her voice prompted me to drop the discussion.*
5. *verb* To remind actors of their lines when they have forgotten them during a play.* ▷ *noun* **prompter**
prompt (prahmpt)
▷ *verb* **prompting, prompted** ▷ *adjective* **prompter, promptest** ▷ *adverb* **promptly**

prone *adjective*
1. Likely to act, feel, or be a certain way: *She is prone to mischief.*

pronghorn

2. Lying with your face down, as in *a prone position*.
prone (prohn)

prong *noun* One of the sharp points of a fork or other tool. **prong** (prahng)

pronghorn *noun* A wild animal with horns that lives in western North America. Pronghorns look a little like antelopes, but they are not closely related to any other animals. **prong·horn** (**prahng**-*horn*) ▷ *noun, plural* **pronghorns** *or* **pronghorn**

pronoun *noun* A word that takes the place of a noun. The words *I, you, him,* and *it* are all pronouns.
pro·noun (**proh**-*noun*)

pronounce *verb*
1. To say words or sounds in a particular way: *You pronounce the word "present" two different ways, depending on the meaning you are using.*
2. To make a formal announcement: *The doctor pronounced him completely cured.*
pro·nounce (pruh-**nouns**)
▷ *verb* **pronouncing, pronounced** ▷ *noun* **pronouncement**

pronunciation *noun* The way a word is pronounced: *This dictionary shows pronunciations without using special symbols.* **pro·nun·ci·a·tion** (pruh-*nuhn*-see-**ay**-shuhn)

proof *noun* Facts or evidence that something is true: *The lawyer claimed to have proof of his client's innocence.* **proof** (proof)

proofread *verb* To read something carefully and correct any mistakes in spelling, punctuation, and grammar that you find. **proof·read** (**proof**-*reed*) ▷ *verb* **proofreading, proofread** (**proof**-*red*) ▷ *noun* **proofreader**

prop
1. *verb* To support something in order to keep it from

falling down: *We propped the sagging porch roof with planks.* ▷ *verb* **propping, propped**

2. *noun* Something used as a support: *The crumbling wall was held up by props.*

3. *noun* Any item other than costumes or furniture that appears on a stage or a movie set. Prop is short for *property.*
prop (prahp)

propaganda *noun* Information that is spread to influence the way people think, to gain supporters, or to damage an opposing group. Propaganda is often incomplete or biased information. **prop·a·gan·da** (*prah*-puh-**gan**-duh)

propel *verb* To push something forward: *A small engine propelled the boat across the lake.* **pro·pel** (pruh-**pel**) ▷ *verb* **propelling, propelled**

propellant *noun*
1. A chemical or fuel that propels something when it is burned: *An engine requires the proper propellant to run.*
2. A compressed gas or a liquid that releases the contents of an aerosol can.
pro·pel·lant (pruh-**pel**-uhnt)

propeller *noun* A set of rotating blades that provide force to move an object through air or water.
pro·pel·ler (pruh-**pel**-ur)

proper *adjective*
1. Right or suitable for a given purpose or occasion: *Do you have the proper tools for the job?*
2. Stiffly formal or respectable, as in *prim and proper.*
prop·er (**prah**-pur)

properly *adverb*
1. In a correct, appropriate, or suitable way: *Can he do the job properly?*
2. In an exact or strict sense: *Properly speaking, a tomato is a fruit, although people usually think of it as a vegetable.*
prop·er·ly (**prah**-pur-lee)

proper noun *noun* The name of a particular person, place, or thing, such as *Jane, New York,* and *Washington Monument.* A proper noun begins with a capital letter.

property *noun*
1. Anything that is owned by an individual: *That bicycle is Zack's property.*
2. Buildings and land belonging to a person or a company: *He put his property up for sale.*
3. A special quality or characteristic of something, as

in *the properties of a liquid.*
prop·er·ty (**prah**-pur-tee)
▷ *noun, plural* **properties**

prophecy *noun* A prediction: *Do you think that prophecy will come true?* **proph·e·cy** (**prah**-fuh-see)
▷ *noun, plural* **prophecies** ▷ *verb* **prophesy**
(**prah**-fuh-sye)

prophet *noun*
1. A person who speaks or claims to speak for God.
2. A person who predicts the future: *Like a prophet, he's always predicting the end of the world.*
proph·et (**prah**-fit)
Prophet sounds like **profit.**

proportion *noun*
1. A part of something: *Only a small proportion of the citizens voted in the last election.*
2. The size, number, or amount of something in relation to another thing: *The proportion of girls to boys in the school is two to one.*
3. In mathematics, a statement that two ratios are equal.
4. in proportion The correct size in relation to something else: *The huge porch was in proportion to the rest of the grand mansion.*
5. proportions *noun, plural* The measurements or size of something.
pro·por·tion (pruh-**por**-shuhn)
▷ *adjective* **proportional**
▷ *adverb* **proportionally**

proposal *noun*
1. A plan or suggestion for others to consider: *The teacher accepted the students' proposal to get a class pet.*
2. An offer of marriage: *He made his proposal on Valentine's Day.*
pro·pos·al (pruh-**poh**-zuhl)

propose *verb*
1. To suggest an idea or a course of action: *I propose that we walk over to the store.*
2. To ask someone to marry you: *Luke proposed to Sophia on Valentine's Day.*
pro·pose (pruh-**poze**)
▷ *verb* **proposing, proposed**

proposition *noun*
1. An offer, or a suggestion: *The neighbors considered my proposition to mow their lawn all summer.*
2. Anything brought up for discussion: *The proposition before the class is whether or not to put on a class play.*
pro·po·si·tion (*prah*-puh-**zish**-uhn)

propeller

a
b
c
d
e
f
g
h
i
j
k
l
m
n
o
p
q
r
s
t
u
v
w
x
y
z

propriety

1. *noun* The quality of being proper and consistent with widely accepted rules of behavior: *Her grandparents have a strict sense of propriety and don't approve of her wearing short skirts.*
2. *noun, plural* **the proprieties** The usual standards of proper behavior: *Our parents expect us to observe the proprieties when we are out at a restaurant.* **pro·pri·e·ty** (pruh-**prye**-i-tee)

propulsion *noun*

1. The force by which a vehicle or some other object is pushed along, as in *jet propulsion.*
2. The act of moving forward by means of some kind of force: *Ducks use their webbed feet for propulsion in the water.* **pro·pul·sion** (pruh-**puhl**-shuhn)

prose *noun* Ordinary written or spoken language, as opposed to verse or poetry. Short stories and essays are examples of prose. **prose** (proze)

prosecute *verb* To begin and carry out a legal action in a court of law against a person accused of a crime: *Stella plans to prosecute the people who damaged her fence.* **pros·e·cute** (**prah**-si-kyoot)

prosecution *noun* The side in a lawsuit that represents the person bringing a complaint or accusing someone of a crime: *The lawyer for the prosecution began by questioning witnesses.* **pros·e·cu·tion** (prah-si-**kyoo**-shuhn)

prosecutor *noun* A lawyer who represents the government in criminal trials. **pros·e·cu·tor** (**prah**-si-kyoo-tur)

prospect

1. *noun* Something that is looked forward to or expected: *I was excited by the prospect of getting my own dog.*
2. *noun* A wide view of a landscape: *The view from the hillside offered a pleasing prospect.*
3. *verb* To explore or search for something, especially gold or silver. ▷ *verb* **prospecting, prospected** ▷ *noun* **prospector**
4. *noun* A possible customer or a possible winner in a political or athletic contest: *New parents are good prospects for buying baby furniture.* **pros·pect** (**prahs**-pekt)

prospective *adjective*

1. Possible or likely: *I've calculated my prospective earnings from my weekend babysitting job.*
2. Future or likely to become, as in *a prospective buyer* or *a prospective bride.* **pro·spec·tive** (pruh-**spek**-tiv)

prospectus *noun* A brochure giving information about a company or any organization. **pro·spec·tus** (pruh-**spek**-tuhs) ▷ *noun, plural* **prospectuses**

prosper *verb* To succeed or thrive: *Al is prospering in his new career.* **pros·per** (**prahs**-pur) ▷ *verb* **prospering, prospered** ▷ *noun* **prosperity** (prah-**sper**-i-tee) ▷ *adjective* **prosperous**

prosthesis *noun* An artificial device that replaces a missing part of a body: *The accident victim's prosthesis looked and worked a lot like a real leg.* **pros·the·sis** (prahs-**thee**-sis) ▷ *noun, plural* **prostheses** (prahs-**thee**-seez)

prosthetic *adjective* Of or having to do with an artificial device that is worn to replace a missing leg, arm, foot, or other body part: *After his accident, he had to learn how to adapt to his new prosthetic hand.* **pros·thet·ic** (pruhs-**thet**-ik) ▷ *adverb* **prosthetically**

protect *verb* To guard or keep something safe from harm, attack, or injury: *Speed skaters wear helmets to protect their heads.* **pro·tect** (pruh-**tekt**) ▷ *verb* **protecting, protected** ▷ *noun* **protector**

protection *noun*

1. The act of protecting something: *This sunscreen offers extra protection from the sun.*
2. The state of being protected: *Once the tent blew down, we were completely without protection.* **pro·tec·tion** (pruh-**tek**-shuhn)

protective *adjective*

1. Intended to protect someone or something from harm, damage, or destruction: *Leslie wore protective gloves when gardening.*
2. Having a strong wish to keep someone or something safe from harm or injury: *I feel very protective toward my little sister.* **pro·tec·tive** (pruh-**tek**-tiv)

protein *noun* A type of chemical compound found in all living plant and animal cells. Foods such as meat, cheese, eggs, beans, and fish are sources of dietary protein. **pro·tein** (**proh**-teen)

protest

1. (pruh-**test**) *verb* To object strongly to something: *The students protested the increase in college tuition.* ▷ *verb* **protesting, protested**
2. (**proh**-test) *noun* A demonstration or statement against something, as in *a protest against war.*
3. (**proh**-test) *noun* An objection to something: *The team made an official protest against the referee's decision.* **pro·test**

Protestant *noun* A Christian who does not belong to either the Roman Catholic Church or the Eastern Orthodox Church. **Prot·es·tant** (**prah**-tuh-stuhnt) ▷ *adjective* **Protestant**

protist *noun* Any organism from the kingdom Protista. Protists include amoebas, paramecia, and some algae. **pro·tist** (**proh**-tist)

protocol *noun*

1. The correct and official rules for the way something should be done or arranged: *What's the protocol for seating governors and senators at the same table?*

2. An international agreement about a particular subject, as in *a new protocol on climate change.*

3. A set of rules about how data is moved between computers or over a network so that no information is lost. **pro·to·col** (**proh**-tuh-*kawl*)

proton *noun* One of the very small parts in the nucleus of an atom. A proton carries a positive electrical charge. **pro·ton** (**proh**-tahn)

protoplasm *noun* The colorless, jelly-like material that makes up the living part of all cells. **pro·to·plasm** (**proh**-tuh-*plaz*-uhm)

prototype *noun* The first version of an invention that tests an idea to see if it will work: *The test pilots tried out the prototype of the new plane.* **pro·to·type** (**proh**-tuh-*tipe*)

protozoan *noun* A microscopic animal with one cell that reproduces by dividing. Paramecia and amoebas are protozoans. **pro·to·zo·an** (*proh*-tuh-**zoh**-uhn) ▷ *noun, plural* **protozoans** *or* **protozoa** (*proh*-tuh-**zoh**-uh)

protractor *noun* A semicircular instrument used for measuring and drawing angles. Protractors are marked off in degrees. **pro·trac·tor** (proh-**trak**-tur)

protractor

protrude *verb* To extend beyond, above, or into something: *The tree branches protruded into the broken attic window.* **pro·trude** (proh-**trood**) ▷ *verb* **protruding, protruded** ▷ *noun* **protrusion** (proh-**troo**-zhuhn)

proud *adjective*

1. Pleased and satisfied with what you or someone else has achieved.

2. Having self-respect and a sense of your own worth.

3. Having too high an opinion of your own value or abilities: *Georgia was too proud to admit that she might have been wrong.* **proud** (proud) ▷ *adjective* **prouder, proudest** ▷ *adverb* **proudly**

prove *verb* To demonstrate definitely that something is true: *The lawyer tried to prove that her client was innocent.* **prove** (proov) ▷ *verb* **proving, proved**

proverb *noun* A familiar saying that tells a common truth. "A stitch in time saves nine" is a proverb. **prov·erb** (**prah**-vurb) ▷ *adjective* **proverbial**

provide

1. *verb* To make something available for use: *The art teacher provided paper and paint to the students.* ▷ *noun* **provider**

2. *verb* To set down as a rule or condition: *The Constitution provides that all adult citizens have the right to vote.*

3. **provided** *conjunction* On condition that; as long as: *We can go to the park provided that we're home by six.* **pro·vide** (pruh-**vide**) ▷ *verb* **providing, provided**

province *noun* A district or a region of some countries. Canada is made up of provinces. **prov·ince** (**prah**-vins)

provincial *adjective*

1. Of or having to do with a province, as in *a provincial government.*

2. Narrow-minded or having a limited or prejudiced point of view, as in *the provincial attitude that girls should never wear short skirts.* **pro·vin·cial** (pruh-**vin**-shuhl)

provision *noun*

1. The act of providing something: *We made provisions for a photographer to be at the wedding.*

2. Something that is named as a condition in an agreement, a law, or a document: *A provision of the treaty bans the production of new nuclear weapons.*

3. **provisions** *noun, plural* A supply of groceries or food. **pro·vi·sion** (pruh-**vizh**-uhn)

provisional *adjective* Temporary or not yet final, as in *a provisional government.* **pro·vi·sion·al** (pruh-**vizh**-uh-nuhl) ▷ *adverb* **provisionally**

provoke *verb*

1. To annoy someone and make the person angry: *Jay provoked his little brother by teasing him.*

2. To bring on or to arouse: *The editorial provoked a heated debate.* **pro·voke** (pruh-**voke**) ▷ *verb* **provoking, provoked** ▷ *noun* **provocation** (*prah*-vuh-**kay**-shuhn) ▷ *adjective* **provocative** (pruh-**vah**-kuh-tiv)

prow *noun* The bow or front part of a boat or ship. **prow** (prou)

prowess *noun* Skill or bravery, as in *her prowess as a swimmer.* **prow·ess** (**prou**-is)

prowl *verb* To move around quietly and secretly, like an animal looking for prey: *The cat prowls through the neighbors' backyards every night.* **prowl** (proul) ▷ *verb* **prowling, prowled** ▷ *noun* **prowler**

Word History

It is a mystery why **prowl** rhymes with *growl* instead of *roll*, since *prowl* used to be spelled *proll*. But an even bigger question is where the word *prowl* comes from, because it seems to have come out of nowhere. Did it come from another English word? Is it from another language? No one is sure. *Prowl* originally meant "to go around looking for something," but now it means "to move around stealthily."

proximity *noun* Nearness in space, time, or relationship: *The playground is in close proximity to the school.* **prox·im·i·ty** (prahk-**sim**-i-tee)

prudent *adjective* Cautious, giving thought to the future or to the consequences of your actions. **pru·dent** (**proo**-duhnt) ▷ *noun* **prudence** (**proo**-duhns) ▷ *adverb* **prudently**

prune
1. *noun* A dried plum.
2. *verb* To cut off branches from a tree or bush in order to increase its growth: *We need to prune these overgrown bushes.* ▷ *verb* **pruning, pruned**
prune (proon)

pruning

pry *verb*
1. To inquire too closely into someone else's business.
2. To remove, raise, or pull apart with force, as with a lever: *I pried the lid off the crate.*
3. To get with difficulty or much effort: *The police tried to pry a confession out of the suspect.*
pry (prye)
▷ *verb* **pries, prying, pried**

PS Short for **postscript** or **public school**.

psalm *noun* A religious song or poem, especially one from the Book of Psalms in the Bible. **psalm** (sahm)

pseudonym *noun* A false name, especially a pen name used by an author instead of his or her real name: *Lewis Carroll is the pseudonym of Charles L. Dodgson, who wrote "Alice's Adventures in Wonderland."* **pseu·do·nym** (**soo**-duh-nim)

psyched *adjective* (*informal*) Very excited to do or begin something: *The team is really psyched about the game tomorrow.* **psyched** (syekt)

psychiatrist *noun* A medical doctor who is trained to treat emotional and mental illness. **psy·chi·a·trist** (sye-**kye**-uh-trist) ▷ *noun* **psychiatry** ▷ *adjective* **psychiatric** (sye-kee-**at**-rik)

psychic *adjective* Seeming or claiming to be able to tell what people are thinking or to predict the future. **psy·chic** (**sye**-kik) ▷ *noun* **psychic**

psychological *adjective*
1. Of or having to do with psychology: *The counselor gave Dina some psychological tests.*
2. Having to do with or arising from the mind: *His problem is psychological, not physical.*
psy·cho·log·i·cal (sye-kuh-**lah**-ji-kuhl)

psychologist *noun* A person who studies people's minds and emotions and the ways that people behave. **psy·chol·o·gist** (sye-**kah**-luh-jist)

psychology *noun* The study of the mind, the emotions, and human behavior. **psy·chol·o·gy** (sye-**kah**-luh-jee)

psychopath *noun* A person who is mentally unbalanced, especially a person who is violent or dangerous. **psy·cho·path** (**sye**-kuh-*path*) ▷ *adjective* **psychopathic**

pt. Short for **pint** or the plural form *pints*.

pterodactyl *noun* A prehistoric flying reptile with wide wings supported by very large fourth fingers. **pter·o·dac·tyl** (*ter*-uh-**dak**-til)

PTSD *noun* A mental illness that is caused by living through an extremely difficult and traumatic experience. Sufferers of PTSD often have nightmares and may be paranoid and unable to concentrate. PTSD is short for *post-traumatic stress disorder.*

pub *noun* A bar where adults can go to drink alcohol. **pub** (puhb)

puberty *noun* The time when a person's body changes from a child's to an adult's: *Most people grow taller when they reach puberty.* **pu·ber·ty** (**pyoo**-bur-tee)

public
1. *adjective* Of or having to do with the people or the community, as in *public safety* or *public opinion.*
2. *adjective* Belonging or available to everybody, as in *public transportation* or *a public beach.*
3. *adjective* Working for the government of a town, city, or country, as in *a public official.*
4. **in public** *adverb* In front of or among other people: *Tony is nervous about speaking in public.*

5. the public *noun* People in general.
pub·lic (**puhb**-lik)
▷ *adverb* **publicly**

publication *noun*
1. A book, magazine, or newspaper, as in *a weekly publication.*
2. The production and distribution of a book, magazine, or newspaper: *The publication of the new book is scheduled for July.*
pub·li·ca·tion (*puhb*-li-**kay**-shuhn)

public domain *noun* The state of being unprotected by copyright and therefore available to everyone to use or copy: *A lot of old music is now in the public domain and can be downloaded from the internet.*

publicity *noun* Information about a person or an event that is given out to get the public's attention or approval: *The movie received a lot of publicity in the weeks before it was released.* **pub·lic·i·ty** (puh-**blis**-i-tee)

publicize *verb* To make something known to as many people as possible. **pub·li·cize** (**puhb**-li-*size*)
▷ *verb* **publicizing, publicized**

public opinion *noun* The views or beliefs of most of the people in a town, city, or country, usually found out through a public opinion poll.

public relations *noun, plural* The methods or activities an organization or a business uses to promote goodwill or a good image with the public.

public school *noun* A school supported by tax money, offering free education to students who live within a certain area.

publish *verb* To produce and distribute a book, magazine, newspaper, or any other material so that many people can read it: *The newspaper is published every day.* **pub·lish** (**puhb**-lish) ▷ *verb* **publishes, publishing, published** ▷ *noun* **publisher** ▷ *noun* **publishing**

puce *noun* A dark brownish-red color, like the color of dried blood. **puce** (pyoos) ▷ *adjective* **puce**

puck *noun* A hard, round, flat piece of rubber used in ice hockey. **puck** (puhk)

pucker *verb* To wrinkle, fold, or draw together: *Eating a lemon always makes my lips pucker.* **puck·er** (**puhk**-ur) ▷ *verb* **puckering, puckered** ▷ *noun* **pucker**

pudding *noun* A sweet, soft dessert, as in *rice pudding* or *chocolate pudding.* **pud·ding** (**pud**-ing)

puddle *noun* A small pool of water or other liquid, as in *a puddle of spilled milk.* **pud·dle** (**puhd**-uhl)

pueblo *noun*
1. A village consisting of stone and adobe buildings built next to and on top of each other. Pueblos were built by Native American tribes in the southwestern United States. ▷ *noun, plural* **pueblos**

2. Pueblo A member of a Native American tribe of New Mexico and Arizona. ▷ *noun, plural* **Pueblo** *or* **Pueblos**
pueb·lo (**pweb**-loh)

Word History

The Spanish explorers expected to find much gold and silver in the Native American **pueblos**, which they first visited in the 1500s. They called the villages *pueblos* because that was their word for "towns." It was based on the word *populus* in Latin, meaning "people"; you can see the same root in the word *people.* As it turned out, the explorers were very disappointed when they discovered that the pueblos had no gold or silver.

---

puff
1. *noun* A short, sudden burst of air, breath, or smoke.
2. *noun* Anything that looks soft, light, and fluffy, as in *puffs of clouds.*
3. *verb* To blow or come out in puffs: *Smoke puffed from the chimney.*
4. puff up *verb* To swell: *The mosquito bite caused my finger to puff up.*
puff (puhf)
▷ *verb* **puffing, puffed** ▷ *adjective* **puffy**

puffin *noun* A black-and-white seabird of northern regions that has a short neck, and a colorful beak.
puf·fin (**puhf**-in)

pug *noun* A dog with short hair, a flat nose, a wrinkled face, and a curled tail. **pug** (puhg)

pugnacious *adjective* Eager to pick fights: *That pugnacious bully scares everyone off the playground.*
pug·na·cious (puhg-**nay**-shuhs) ▷ *adverb* **pugnaciously**

pull
1. *verb* To move something forward or toward you: *An ox pulled the cart. He pulled the door open.*
2. *verb* To tug or pluck something, as in *to pull weeds.*
3. *noun* The act of pulling something, or the effort required to pull something: *Give the door a good pull when you open it.*
4. *noun* Attraction or influence, as in *the pull of a magnet.*
5. *verb* To stretch or strain a part of the body: *I pulled a muscle in my leg.*
6. pull off *verb* To do something with great success.
7. pull out *verb* To withdraw from an activity: *Arthur had to pull out of the race because he was injured.*
8. pull through *verb* To get through a hard, painful, or dangerous time.
pull (pul)
▷ *verb* **pulling, pulled**

pulley *noun*
1. A wheel with a grooved rim around which a rope or chain can run. A pulley is used to lift heavy loads more easily.
2. A lifting machine made from a rope or chain and a set of pulleys linked together.
pul·ley (**pul**-ee)

pullover *noun* A shirt or sweater that you can pull over your head: **pull·o·ver** (**pul**-*oh*-vur)

pulp *noun*
1. The soft, juicy, or fleshy part of fruits and vegetables: *Tom strained the pulp out of the orange juice.*
2. Any soft, wet mixture, as in *wood pulp.*
3. The soft inner part of a tooth.
pulp (puhlp)
▷ *verb* **pulp**

pulpit *noun* A raised, partially enclosed platform in a church where a minister stands to speak to a congregation. **pul·pit** (**puhl**-pit)

pulsate *verb* To beat, vibrate, or change in intensity regularly: *Rock music pulsated from the car.* **pul·sate** (**puhl**-sate) ▷ *verb* **pulsating, pulsated**

pulse *noun* A steady beat or throb, especially the feeling of the heart moving blood through your body. **pulse** (puhls) ▷ *verb* **pulse**

puma *noun* Another name for **mountain lion**. **pu·ma** (**pyoo**-muh *or* **poo**-muh)

pumice *noun* A light, grayish volcanic rock that is used for cleaning, smoothing, or polishing. **pum·ice** (**puhm**-is)

pummel
1. *verb* To punch someone or something repeatedly: *Jeremy pummeled his sister's doll.* ▷ *verb* **pummeling, pummeled**
2. *noun* The act of punching someone or something. **pum·mel** (**puhm**-uhl)

Word History

A round knob at the end of a sword's hilt looked like a tiny apple, so speakers of Old French called it a *pomel,* meaning "little apple." English speakers adopted the word as *pommel,* and hitting with the *pommel* of a sword (rather than hitting with the edge or end) was called *pommelling.* **Pummel** is a later spelling. The Latin word for "apple," *pomum,* was the source for the Old French *pomel.* You can see the same root in the English word *pomegranate.*

pump
1. *noun* A machine that forces liquids or gases from one place to another, as in *a gas pump.*
2. *verb* To empty or fill using a pump: *We pumped out*

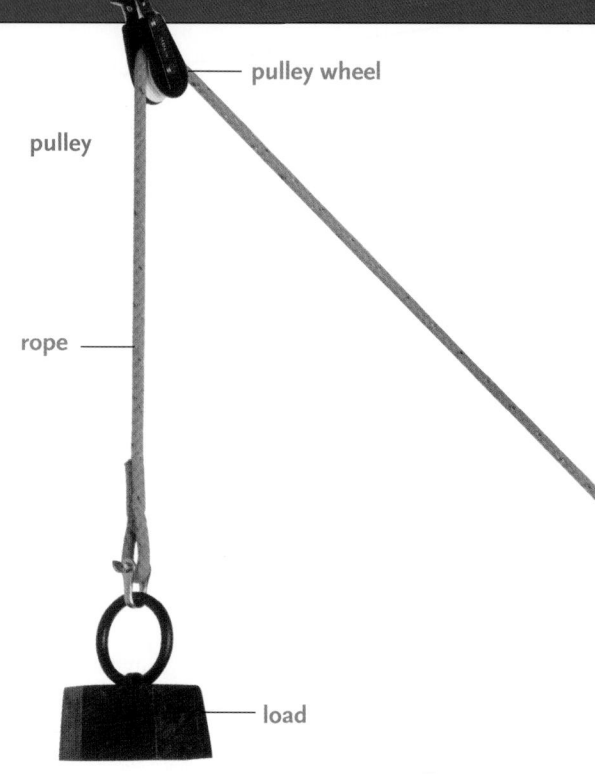

pulley wheel

pulley

rope

load

the water that had leaked into our basement.
3. pumps *noun, plural* Plain women's shoes with a medium to high heel.
4. *verb* To keep asking someone questions: *Callie was pumping me for information about the party plans.*
pump (puhmp)
▷ *verb* **pumping, pumped**

pumpkin *noun* A big, round, orange squash with a thick rind and many seeds that grows on a vine along the ground. People often carve faces in pumpkins at Halloween. **pump·kin** (**puhmp**-kin)

pumpkin

pun *noun* A joke based on one word that has two meanings or two words that sound the same but have different meanings. Here is an example of a pun: "People work as bakers because they knead (need) the dough (money)." **pun** (puhn) ▷ *verb* **pun**

punch
1. *verb* To hit someone or something with your fist. ▷ *noun* **punch** ▷ *noun* **puncher**
2. *noun* A drink made by mixing several ingredients, usually fruit juices and soda.
3. *noun* A metal tool for making holes.
4. *verb* To make a hole in something.

5. punch line *noun* The last line of a joke or story that makes it funny or surprising.
punch (puhnch)
▷ *verb* **punches, punching, punched**

punctual *adjective* Arriving or happening right on time. **punc·tu·al** (puhngk-choo-uhl) ▷ *noun* **punctuality** (*puhnk*-choo-**al**-i-tee) ▷ *adverb* **punctually**

punctuation *noun*
1. The use of periods, commas, and other marks to help make the meaning of written material clear. *See the Punctuation Guide in the* **Reference Section**.
▷ *verb* **punctuate**
2. One or more punctuation marks.
punc·tu·a·tion (*puhngk*-choo-**ay**-shuhn)

punctuation mark *noun* A written mark, such as a comma, period, colon, semicolon, question mark, or exclamation point, used in writing.

puncture *noun* A hole made by a sharp object: *The tire is flat because of a puncture.* **punc·ture** (**puhngk**-chur) ▷ *verb* **puncture**

pungent *adjective* Having a strong or sharp smell or taste, as in *a pungent odor.* **pun·gent** (**puhn**-juhnt)

punish *verb* To inflict a penalty for committing a crime or to make a person suffer for behaving badly: *Olivia was punished for teasing the cat.*
pun·ish (**puhn**-ish) ▷ *verb* **punishes, punishing, punished**

punishment *noun* The act of punishing someone, or the penalty imposed on someone who is punished: *The punishment for cheating on a test is detention for two weeks.* **pun·ish·ment** (**puhn**-ish-muhnt)

punk *noun*
1. *(slang)* A young person who is always getting into trouble: *Those punks grabbed my lunch.*
2. A style of music and dress that became popular in the late 1970s. People who dressed in this style wore black clothes, used safety pins for decoration, and had brightly colored hair.
3. punk rock Loud, hard rock music that became popular in the late 1970s.
punk (puhngk)

punt
1. *noun* A boat with a flat bottom that you push along with a long pole. ▷ *verb* **punt**
2. *verb* To drop and kick a football or soccer ball before it strikes the ground: *He punted the ball 40 yards down the field.* ▷ *verb* **punting, punted**

punk

▷ *noun* **punt** ▷ *noun* **punter**
punt (puhnt)

puny *adjective* Small and weak, or unimportant: *The puny tree did not bear any fruit* **pu·ny** (**pyoo**-nee)
▷ *adjective* **punier, puniest** ▷ *noun* **puniness**
▷ *adverb* **punily** (**pyoo**-nuh-lee)

Word History

In earlier times, calling someone **puny** was not an insult. Judges were even referred to as *puny* if they had not spent a long time on the court. The French words *puis né* meant "born later," so a *puny* person was "younger." Our meaning of *puny* as small and unimportant developed later.

pupa *noun* An insect in an inactive stage of development between a larva and an adult. **pu·pa** (**pyoo**-puh) ▷ *noun, plural* **pupas** *or* **pupae** (**pyoo**-pee)

pupil *noun*
1. A person who is being taught, especially in school: *There are 20 pupils in the third grade.*
2. The round, black center of your eye that lets light enter.
pu·pil (**pyoo**-puhl)

Word History

Have you ever looked into the **pupil** of someone's eye? If so, you probably saw a tiny reflection of whatever the person was looking at. This tiny image gave the pupil its name. It is based on the Latin word *pupilla,* or "tiny doll."

puppet *noun* A movable model in the shape of a person or an animal that you control by pulling strings that are attached to it or by moving your hand inside it: *The class acted out a fairy tale with puppets.* **pup·pet** (**puhp**-it)
▷ *noun* **puppetry**

puppy *noun* A dog that is not fully grown: *Our dog had four puppies yesterday.* **pup·py** (**puhp**-ee)
▷ *noun, plural* **puppies**

purchase
1. *verb* To buy something: *My parents purchased a new sofa for the living room.* ▷ *verb* **purchasing, purchased** ▷ *noun* **purchaser**
2. *noun* Something that has been bought: *We carried our purchases into the house.*
3. *noun* The act of purchasing: *We saved our money for the purchase of a new stereo.*
pur·chase (**pur**-chuhs)

pure *adjective*
1. Not mixed with anything else, as in *pure gold*.
2. Not dirty or not polluted, as in *pure water*.
3. Innocent or free from evil or guilt, as in *a pure heart* or *a pure mind*.
4. Complete or nothing but, as in *pure luck* or *pure nonsense*. **pure** (pyoor)
▷ *adjective* **purer, purest** ▷ *noun* **purity** (**pyoor**-i-tee)

purebred *adjective* Having ancestors of the same breed or kind of animal: *One of my dogs is a purebred poodle.* **pure·bred** (**pyoor**-bred)

puree *or* **purée** *noun* A thick paste made from food that has been put through a sieve or blender, as in *a tomato puree.* **pu·ree** *or* **pu·rée** (pyoo-**ray**) ▷ *verb* **puree** *or* **purée**

purge *verb* To clean thoroughly by getting rid of unwanted items: *We purged the house of all our old clothes.* **purge** (purj) ▷ *verb* **purging, purged** ▷ *noun* **purge**

purify *verb* To make something pure or clean: *We need a filter to purify our water.* **pu·ri·fy** (**pyoor**-uh-*fye*) ▷ *verb* **purifies, purifying, purified** ▷ *noun* **purification** (*pyoor*-uh-fi-*kay*-shuhn)

Puritan *noun* One of a group of Protestants in 16th- and 17th-century England who sought simple church services and a strict moral code. Many Puritans fled from England and settled in America. **Pur·i·tan** (**pyoor**-i-tuhn)

purple *noun* The color that is made by mixing red and blue. **pur·ple** (**pur**-puhl) ▷ *adjective* **purple**

purpose *noun*
1. A goal or an aim: *My purpose in getting a part-time job is to save money for college.*
2. The reason why something is made or done, or an object's function: *What's the purpose of this key on the computer?*
3. **on purpose** Deliberately rather than by accident: *She ripped her jeans on purpose because it was in fashion.* **pur·pose** (**pur**-puhs) ▷ *adjective* **purposeful**

purposely *adverb* With a particular effect in mind; on purpose: *You purposely stepped on my foot!* **pur·pose·ly** (**pur**-puhs-lee)

purr *verb*
1. To make a low, vibrating sound in the throat: *The cat purred contentedly on the chair.*

purse

2. To make a low, vibrating sound like a cat: *The new car purred when he turned the key in the ignition.* **purr** (pur)
Purr sounds like **per**. ▷ *verb* **purring, purred** ▷ *noun* **purr**

purse
1. *noun* A handbag or a pocketbook: *She carries her wallet in her purse.*
2. *noun* A small container for carrying money: *There were three quarters in the coin purse.*
3. *noun* A sum of money given as a prize in an athletic contest: *The boxer won a purse of five thousand dollars.*
4. **purse your lips** *verb* To press your lips together into wrinkles. ▷ *verb* **pursing, pursed**
purse (purs)

pursue *verb*
1. To follow or chase someone in order to catch him or her: *The police pursued the robber.* ▷ *noun* **pursuer**
2. To continue something: *We'll pursue this discussion later.*
3. To try to accomplish a goal: *Joyce is pursuing a degree in accounting.* **pur·sue** (pur-**soo**) ▷ *verb* **pursuing, pursued**

pursuit *noun*
1. A chase, in order to catch someone or something: *The dog shot off in pursuit of the rabbit.*
2. An activity, hobby, or interest: *Collecting baseball cards is one of my favorite pursuits.* **pur·suit** (pur-**soot**)

pus *noun* A thick, yellow liquid that comes out of an infected wound or sore. **pus** (puhs)

push
1. *verb* To make something move by pressing on or against it: *I pushed my bike up the hill.*
2. *verb* To shove or press roughly: *He pushed me off the sidewalk.*
3. *verb* To use your hands or arms to press past someone or something: *We pushed past all the people and headed for the exit.*

push

4. *noun* An act of pushing or shoving: *Give the sled a push to get it started.*
5. *verb* To try very hard to sell or do something:

Pyramids

In geometry, a pyramid is a three-dimensional figure with a square base and four triangular sides that meet in a point. The Great Pyramid, in Giza, Egypt, was built in about 2700 B.C. as a tomb for the pharaoh Khufu, also known as Cheops. This pyramid and the smaller pyramids nearby are made of huge stone slabs and are still standing today.

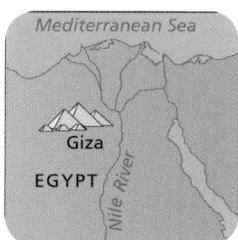

the Great Pyramid of Khufu in Giza, Egypt

The new cars are due in next week, so the dealer is pushing last year's models.

6. *verb* To try to make someone do something: *Troy's parents were pushing him to find a job.*

7. *noun* A great effort or drive, as in *a final push to victory.*

push (push)

▷ *verb* **pushes, pushing, pushed** ▷ *noun, plural* **pushes** ▷ *noun* **pusher**

push-up *noun* An exercise in which you raise your body off the floor from a facedown position by pushing with your arms.

pushy *adjective* Too forceful in trying to convince someone to do something: *Stop being so pushy—I need time to make up my own mind about it!* **push·y** (**push**-ee) ▷ *adjective* **pushier, pushiest** ▷ *noun* **pushiness** ▷ *adverb* **pushily**

pussy willow *noun* A shrub with gray, furry flowers on long, thin branches. **pus·sy willow** (**pus**-ee)

put *verb*

1. To place or lay something: *I put the book on the desk.*

2. To state in words, as in *to put it another way.*

3. To cause someone to undergo or experience

something: *Allie put me to a great deal of trouble.*

4. put off To delay doing something.

5. put someone up To let the person sleep overnight at your house.

6. put up with To tolerate something or allow it to continue.

7. put upon To feel excessively or unfairly burdened.

8. put down To insult or degrade.

put (put)

▷ *verb* **putting, put**

putt *verb* To hit a golf ball lightly into the hole on a green. **putt** (puht) ▷ *verb* **putting, putted** ▷ *noun* **putt** ▷ *noun* **putter**

putter *verb* To work aimlessly without getting much done: *Cassie puttered around the house all day.* **put·ter** (**puht**-ur) ▷ *verb* **puttering, puttered**

putty *noun* A kind of soft cement made of powdered chalk and linseed oil. It dries hard and is used to fasten windows into frames and to fill holes in wood. **put·ty** (**puht**-ee)

puzzle

1. *noun* A game or an activity that involves solving a mystery, a problem, or a complex task.

2. *noun* Someone or something that is hard to understand: *This complicated mystery is a real puzzle.*

3. *verb* To make someone confused or unsure: *His question puzzled me.* ▷ *verb* **puzzling, puzzled** ▷ *adjective* **puzzled** ▷ *adjective* **puzzling**

puz·zle (**puhz**-uhl)

Word History

In a 17th-century description of sailing, the ships were "jumbled together like so many baskets, and *puzzling* one another." How could a ship be *puzzled*? The writer meant that they were in each other's way and so couldn't move easily. This old meaning of the verb **puzzle** is lost, but it led to the idea of someone becoming confused. Eventually, a game in which you have to solve confusing problems was called a *puzzle.*

pylon *noun* A tall metal tower that supports electrical cables. **py·lon** (**pye**-lahn)

pyramid *noun*

1. A solid shape with a polygon as a base and triangular sides that meet at a point on top. Most pyramids have a square base and four sides.

2. An ancient Egyptian stone monument where pharaohs and their treasures were buried. **pyr·a·mid** (**pir**-uh-mid)

python *noun* A large, powerful snake that wraps itself around its prey and crushes it. **py·thon** (**pye**-thahn)

Qq

About Q The ancestor of the letter **Q** was called *ooph,* the Phoenician word for "monkey." The letter had a tail. By the time of the Romans, the tail slanted to the right, as does our present-day letter. *Q* is the second least used letter in English. It is usually followed by a *u* and rarely appears at the end of a word. Words that have been adopted from other languages are the main exceptions. Examples: Iraq, Iraqi.

qt. Short for **quart** or the plural form *quarts.*

quack
1. *verb* To make the sound that is typical of a duck. ▷ *verb* **quacking, quacked** ▷ *noun* **quack**
2. *noun* A dishonest person who pretends to be a doctor or have medical skills. ▷ *adjective* **quack** **quack** (kwak)

quad *noun* A rectangular yard with buildings around it, especially at a college. Quad is short for **quadrangle.** **quad** (kwahd)

quadrangle *noun*
1. A closed shape with four sides and four angles; a quadrilateral.
2. A quad, as at a college. **quad·ran·gle** (**kwahd**-*rang*-guhl)

quadrant *noun* A quarter of a circle, or a quarter of its circumference. **quad·rant** (**kwahd**-ruhnt)

quadrilateral *noun* A closed shape with four straight sides and four angles. Squares and rectangles are quadrilaterals. **quad·ri·lat·er·al** (*kwahd*-ruh-**lat**-ur-uhl) ▷ *adjective* **quadrilateral**

quadruped *noun* An animal with four feet. Horses are quadrupeds. **quad·ru·ped** (**kwahd**-ruh-*ped*)

quadruple
1. *verb* To multiply something by four. ▷ *verb* **quadrupling, quadrupled**
2. *adjective* Four times as many, or as big. **qua·dru·ple** (kwah-**droo**-puhl *or* **kwahd**-ruh-puhl)

quadruplet *noun* One of four babies born at the same time to one mother. **qua·dru·plet** (kwah-**droo**-plit)

quagmire *noun*
1. A wet and muddy area of ground.
2. A situation that is difficult to get out of. **quag·mire** (**kwag**-mire)

quail *noun* A small, fat bird with a short tail and gray or brown feathers. **quail** (kwayl)

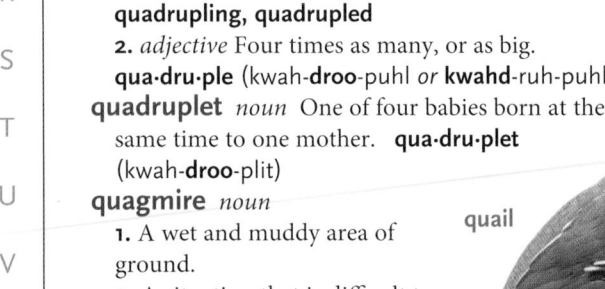

quail

quaint *adjective* Old-fashioned, charming, and attractive, as in *a quaint little cottage.* **quaint** (kwaynt) ▷ *adjective* **quainter, quaintest** ▷ *noun* **quaintness** ▷ *adverb* **quaintly**

quake
1. *verb* To shake or tremble, especially with fear: *I quaked when the monster appeared on the stage.*
2. *verb* To shake or to tremble: *The earth quaked.*
3. *noun* An earthquake, or a trembling of the ground.
4. *noun* Any trembling or shaking. **quake** (kwake) ▷ *verb* **quaking, quaked**

Quaker *noun* A member of the Society of Friends, a Christian group founded in the 17th century that prefers simple religious services and opposes war. **Quak·er** (**kway**-kur)

qualification *noun* A skill or an ability that makes you able to do a job or a task: *Teaching experience is a qualification for a job as a school principal.* **qual·i·fi·ca·tion** (*kwahl*-uh-fi-**kay**-shuhn)

qualify *verb*
1. To reach a standard or level that allows you to do something: *Her goal was to qualify for the Boston Marathon.* ▷ *adjective* **qualified**
2. To limit or restrict something you have just said in order to make it more specific or less severe: *She promised me an A in the class, then qualified that by saying "As long as you do well on the final exam."*
3. To limit or modify the meaning of a word or phrase: *Adjectives qualify nouns.* **qual·i·fy** (**kwah**-luh-*fye*) ▷ *verb* **qualifies, qualifying, qualified**

quality *noun*
1. The degree of excellence of something: *The company maintains a high level of quality for its products.*
2. A special characteristic of something or someone: *Heather has all the right qualities to be a good teacher.* **qual·i·ty** (**kwah**-li-tee) ▷ *noun, plural* **qualities**

qualm *noun* A feeling of concern or doubt over whether what you are doing is right or wrong: *I had serious qualms about* *criticizing my boss.* **qualm** (kwahm *or* kwahlm)

quandary *noun* If you are **in a quandary**, you are in a difficult situation and do not know what to do about it. **quan·da·ry** (**kwahn**-dur-ee) ▷ *noun, plural* **quandaries**

quantity *noun*
1. A number or amount.
2. A large number or amount: *Restaurants buy food in quantity.*
quan·ti·ty (**kwahn**-ti-tee)
▷ *noun, plural* **quantities**

quantum leap *noun* A sudden, extremely large change or improvement. **quan·tum leap** (**kwahn**-tuhm)

quantum theory *noun* A scientific method for describing matter and energy at a level smaller than atoms.

quarantine *noun* A situation in which a person, animal, or plant is kept away from others for a period of time to stop a disease from spreading. **quar·an·tine** (**kwor**-uhn-*teen*) ▷ *verb* **quarantine**

Word History

Quarantine comes from the Italian word *quaranta*, meaning "forty." The first quarantines date back to the Middle Ages, when sailors and other travelers were suspected of carrying diseases from one country to another. People who arrived by ship from countries with widespread disease had to wait 40 days before they were allowed onshore.

quark *noun* In physics, any of several particles that are believed to come in pairs. A quark is smaller than an atom. **quark** (kwork)

quarrel
1. *verb* To disagree or argue: *My younger brothers always quarrel over who gets the larger piece of cake.*
2. *noun* An argument, especially between people who know each other well.
3. *verb* To find fault: *I can't quarrel with your decision.*
quar·rel (**kwor**-uhl)
▷ *verb* **quarreling, quarreled**

quarrelsome *adjective* If you are **quarrelsome**, you tend to argue a lot with other people. **quar·rel·some** (**kwor**-uhl-suhm)

quarry *noun*
1. A place where stone, slate, or sand is dug from the ground. ▷ *verb* **quarry**
2. A person or an animal that is being hunted or chased: *The chipmunk was easy quarry for the cat.*
quar·ry (**kwor**-ee)
▷ *noun, plural* **quarries**

quarter

quart *noun* A unit of liquid measure equal to 32 ounces, or two pints, as in *a quart of milk.* **quart** (kwort)

quarter
1. *noun* One of four equal parts of something: *He cut the pie into quarters.* ▷ *verb* **quarter**
2. *noun* A coin of the United States and Canada equal to 25 cents.
3. *noun* One of four equal periods that make up a game such as football or basketball.
4. *noun* An area of a town: *The French Quarter in New Orleans is a great place to hear jazz.*
5. **quarters** *noun, plural* Rooms where people such as soldiers live, especially as part of their job: *The maid took me to my quarters in the boarding school.*
6. *verb* To provide people, usually soldiers, with food and a place to sleep. ▷ *verb* **quartering, quartered**
quar·ter (**kwor**-tur)

quarterback *noun* In football, the player who leads the offense by throwing the ball or handing it to a runner. **quar·ter·back** (**kwor**-tur-*bak*)

quarterly
1. *adjective* Happening once every three months, as in *quarterly interest on a savings account.*
2. *adverb* Once every three months: *Some magazines are published quarterly.*
quart·er·ly (**kwor**-tur-lee)

quartet *noun*
1. A piece of music that is written to be played or sung by four people.
2. Four people who play music or sing together.
quar·tet (kwor-**tet**)

quartz *noun* A hard mineral that is used to make very accurate clocks, watches, and electronic equipment. **quartz** (kworts)

quasar *noun* An object in space that is larger than a star but smaller than a galaxy. Quasars give off powerful radio waves and huge amounts of light and radioactivity. **qua·sar** (**kway**-zahr)

quash *verb*
1. To stop something from continuing, especially by force, as in *to quash a rebellion.*
2. To officially decide that a legal decision is no longer valid: *The Supreme Court quashed the prime minister's sentence.*
quash (kwahsh)
▷ *verb* **quashes, quashing, quashed**

quaver *verb* If your voice **quavers**, it sounds unsteady. **qua·ver** (**kway**-vur) ▷ *verb* **quavering, quavered** ▷ *noun* **quaver**

quay *noun* A place built on land near water where boats can stop to load or unload goods or passengers. **quay** (kee) **Quay** sounds like **key**.

queasy *adjective*

1. Sick to your stomach, or nauseated: *After eating the food at the carnival, she felt queasy all night.*

2. Uneasy or troubled: *I had a queasy feeling that I was lost.*

quea·sy (**kwee**-zee)

▷ *adjective* **queasier, queasiest** ▷ *noun* **queasiness**

queen *noun*

1. A female ruler of a country who comes from a royal family.

2. The wife of a king.

3. A playing card that has a picture of a queen on it.

4. The most powerful chess piece. It can move in any direction.

5. A female bee, wasp, or ant that can lay eggs.

queen (kween)

queer *adjective* Strange or odd: *Before the tornado, the sky turned a queer shade of purple.* **queer** (kweer) ▷ *adjective* **queerer, queerest** ▷ *adverb* **queerly**

quell *verb* To stop something happening, especially by force, as in *to quell a disturbance.* **quell** (kwel) ▷ *verb* **quelling, quelled**

quench *verb*

1. If you **quench** your thirst, you drink something until you are no longer thirsty.

2. If you **quench** a fire, you stop it from burning.

quench (kwench)

▷ *verb* **quenches, quenching, quenched**

query

1. *noun* A question or request for information, especially because you have a doubt about something. ▷ *noun, plural* **queries**

2. *verb* To ask a question to: *She queried the waiter about the menu.* ▷ *verb* **queries, querying, queried**

que·ry (**kweer**-ee)

quesadilla *noun* A folded, usually fried tortilla filled with a mixture of cheese and vegetables or meat. **que·sa·dil·la** (*kay*-suh-**dee**-yuh)

quesadillas

quest *noun*

1. A long and difficult search, as in *a quest for gold.* ▷ *verb* **quest**

2. A long journey made to do or to find something: *The knight embarked on a quest to save the princess.*

quest (kwest)

question

1. *noun* A sentence that asks for information: *Bernardo has a question about the assignment.*

2. *noun* A problem, or something that needs to be dealt with: *The government needs to address the question of poverty.*

3. *verb* To ask questions in order to get information, as in *to question a suspect.*

4. *verb* To have suspicions or doubt about something: *I question whether she's telling us the truth.*

5. *noun* Doubt: *Without question, Toby is the best person for the job.*

ques·tion (**kwes**-chuhn)

▷ *verb* **questioning, questioned**

question mark *noun* The punctuation mark (?) used in writing, that follows a question.

questionnaire *noun* A list of questions used to get information or to find out about people's opinions: *My bank sent me a questionnaire to determine which checking account I need.* **ques·tion·naire** (*kwes*-chuh-**nair**)

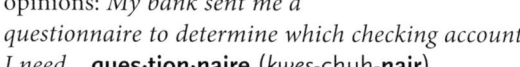

question mark

quetzal *noun* A bird of Mexico and Central America with red and green feathers. The male has long tail feathers. **quet·zal** (ket-**sahl**)

queue

1. *noun* A line of people who are waiting for something: *There was a long queue of people waiting for bagels in the morning.*

2. *noun* A list of items or jobs on a computer that are dealt with in order, as in *a print queue.*

3. *verb* To add an item or job to a queue on a computer.

4. *verb* To form or wait in a line of people.

queue (kyoo)

Queue sounds like **cue.** ▷ *verb* **queuing, queued**

quibble *verb* To argue about things that are not important: *Before their divorce, my parents quibbled about everything.* **quib·ble** (**kwib**-uhl) ▷ *verb* **quibbling, quibbled** ▷ *noun* **quibble**

quiche *noun* A food like a pie made with a pastry crust and filled with eggs, milk, cheese, vegetables, and sometimes meat. **quiche** (keesh)

quick *adjective*

1. Moving or doing something fast: *I chased Ira but he was too quick for me.* ▷ *verb* **quicken**

2. Done or happening in a short period of time, as in *a quick lunch.*

quilt

3. Able to understand things fast, as in *a quick learner.*
quick (kwik)
▷ *adjective* **quicker, quickest** ▷ *adverb* **quick**
▷ *adverb* **quickly**

quicksand *noun* Loose, wet sand that is dangerous because you can sink into it. **quick·sand** (**kwik**-*sand*)

quiet
1. *adjective* Not loud: *Please be quiet—my parents are sleeping.*
2. *adjective* Calm and peaceful: *We spent a quiet evening at home.*
3. *noun* The state of being quiet: *The teacher asked for quiet.*
qui·et (**kwye**-it)
▷ *adjective* **quieter, quietest** ▷ *adverb* **quietly**
▷ *noun* **quietness** ▷ *verb* **quiet**

quill *noun*
1. The long, hollow central part of a feather.
2. One of the hollow, sharp spines on a porcupine.
3. **quill pen** A pen made from a bird's feather, with the end of its quill carved to form a point.
quill (kwil)

quilt *noun* A warm, thick covering for a bed that usually has a decorative, stitched top layer of fabric. **quilt** (kwilt) ▷ *verb* **quilt**

quilted *adjective* If material is **quilted**, it is padded with soft material and sewn in lines or patterns. **quilt·ed** (**kwil**-tid)

quintet *noun*
1. A piece of music that is written to be played or sung by five people.
2. Five people who play music or sing together.
quin·tet (kwin-**tet**)

quintuplet *noun* One of five babies born at the same time to one mother. **quin·tup·let** (kwin-**tuhp**-lit)

quip *noun* A funny and clever remark. **quip** (kwip)
▷ *verb* **quip**

quirk *noun*
1. An odd trait or a strange way of acting. ▷ *noun* **quirkiness** ▷ *adjective* **quirky**
2. A sudden and strange thing that happens: *It was a quirk of fate that we were there at the same time.*
quirk (kwurk)

quit *verb*
1. To stop doing something: *I've been trying to quit eating junk food.*
2. To leave something, such as your job or school.
quit (kwit)
▷ *verb* **quitting, quit** *or* **quitted** ▷ *noun* **quitter**

quite *adverb*
1. Entirely: *I haven't quite finished my homework.*
2. Actually or really: *Winning the marathon was quite an achievement.*
3. Rather or very: *The movie was quite good.*
quite (kwite)

quiver
1. *verb* To shake slightly: *His eyes filled with tears and his lips quivered.* ▷ *verb* **quivering, quivered**
▷ *noun* **quiver**
2. *noun* A container for arrows.
quiv·er (**kwiv**-ur)

quiz
1. *noun* A short test. ▷ *noun, plural* **quizzes**
2. *verb* To ask someone a lot of questions about something: *The attorney quizzed the witness carefully.* ▷ *verb* **quizzes, quizzing, quizzed**
quiz (kwiz)

quota *noun* A limit on an amount or share of something: *He wants the government to set a quota on the number of cars that can be imported from overseas.* **quo·ta** (**kwoh**-tuh)

quotation *noun*
1. A sentence or short passage from something such as a book, play, or speech that is repeated by someone else, as in *a short quotation from a poem.*
2. The act of repeating another person's words.
quo·ta·tion (kwoh-**tay**-shuhn)

quotation mark *noun* One of the punctuation marks (", ", ', or ') used in writing to show where speech begins and ends.

quote
1. *verb* To repeat the exact words that someone else spoke or wrote: *Rebecca quoted Martin Luther King Jr. in her speech.* ▷ *verb* **quoting, quoted**
2. *noun* A quotation.
quote (kwote)

quotient *noun* The number that is the result when you divide one number by another: *In the problem 12 divided by 4, the quotient is 3.* **quo·tient** (**kwoh**-shuhnt)

Rr

About R The 14th consonant in the English alphabet, the letter **R** had its beginnings in an Egyptian hieroglyph that had the shape of a mouth and was called *ro*. Of the 100 most used words in English, not a single one begins with *r*. Nevertheless, it is a popular letter, ranking ninth in frequency in the language. Some words that begin with an *r* sound are spelled *rh* or *wr*. Examples: rhinoceros, rhubarb, rhythm, wrench, wristwatch, wrong.

rabbi *noun* A Jewish religious leader and teacher. **rab·bi** (**rab**-eye)

Word History

A Jewish religious leader who has studied the Hebrew Bible and the Talmud is called a **rabbi**. Commonly understood to mean "teacher," the Hebrew word *rabbi* originally meant "my master."

rabbit *noun* A small, furry mammal with long ears that lives in a hole that it digs in the ground. **rab·bit** (**rab**-it)

rabble *noun* A noisy crowd: *The rumor caused an unruly rabble to gather.* **rab·ble** (**rab**-uhl)

rabies *noun* An often fatal disease that can affect humans, dogs, bats, and other warm-blooded animals. **ra·bies** (**ray**-beez) ▷ *adjective* **rabid** (**rab**-id)

raccoon *noun* A mammal with rings on its tail and black and white face markings that look like a mask. **rac·coon** (ra-**koon**)

race

1. *noun* A competition to see which person, animal, or vehicle is the fastest: *Dale won the bicycle race.* ▷ *verb* **race**

2. *noun* One of the major groups into which human beings can be divided. People of the same race have similar physical characteristics, such as skin color, which are passed on from generation to generation: *Children of many races attend our school.*

3. *verb* To run, go, or move very fast: *Angela raced down the hall to get to her next class.* ▷ *verb* **racing, raced**

race (rase)

race car *noun* A car designed to race at very high speeds.

race relations *noun, plural* The way that people of different races get along with each other when they live in the same community.

racetrack *noun* A round or oval path that is used for racing. **race·track** (**rase**-trak)

racial *adjective*

1. Of or having to do with a person's race, as in *racial characteristics*.

2. Between or among races, as in *racial prejudice* or *racial equality*.

ra·cial (**ray**-shuhl)

racist *noun* A person who thinks that a particular race is better than others or treats people unfairly or cruelly because of their race. **rac·ist** (**ray**-sist) ▷ *noun* **racism** ▷ *adjective* **racist**

rack

1. *noun* A frame for holding or hanging things, as in *a clothing rack* or *a bike rack*.

2. the rack *noun* An instrument of torture used in the past to stretch the body of a victim.

3. *verb* To torture someone on the rack.

4. rack or **wrack** *verb* To cause someone to feel tortured or anguished, or to feel tortured or anguished: *After he stole the money, he was racked by guilt.*

5. *idiom* If you **rack your brain** or **rack your brains**, you try hard to remember something or to figure out something: *She racked her brain to remember where she had put the letter.*

rack (rak)

▷ *verb* **racking, racked**

racket *noun*

1. racket or **racquet** An oval stringed frame with a handle that you use in games such as tennis and badminton.

2. A lot of noise; a din: *The falling dishes*

race car

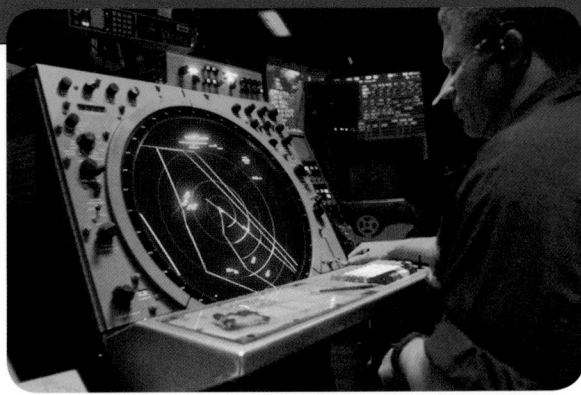

radar

made quite a racket.

3. A dishonest scheme or business activity: *The police exposed a gambling racket.*
rack·et (**rak**-it)

racquet *See* **racket**. **rac·quet** (**rak**-it)

racquetball *noun* A game played by two or four players who use short rackets to hit a small rubber ball against the walls, floor, and ceiling of an enclosed court. **rac·quet·ball** (**rak**-it-*bawl*)

radar *noun* A way that ships and planes find solid objects by reflecting radio waves off them and by receiving the reflected waves. Radar is short for *radio detection and ranging.* **ra·dar** (**ray**-dahr)

radial *adjective*
1. Spreading out from the center or arranged like rays: *The petals of a daisy are arranged in a radial pattern.*
2. Of or having to do with a kind of automobile or truck tire whose design makes it grip the road better than traditional tires.
ra·di·al (**ray**-dee-uhl)
▷ *noun* **radial**

radiant *adjective*
1. Shining brightly: *The full moon was radiant in the sky.*
2. If someone looks **radiant**, he or she looks very healthy and filled with happiness.
ra·di·ant (**ray**-dee-uhnt)
▷ *noun* **radiance**

radiate *verb*
1. To give off rays of light or heat: *The campfire radiated warmth.*
2. To spread out from the center: *Ripples radiated from the spot where the stone hit the water.*
3. To send out an emotion strongly: *The actress could radiate great joy or deep sadness at will.*
ra·di·ate (**ray**-dee-ate)
▷ *verb* **radiating, radiated**

radiation *noun*
1. The giving off of energy in the form of light or heat.
2. Atomic particles that are sent out from a

radioactive substance: *Nuclear radiation can be dangerous to health.*
ra·di·a·tion (*ray*-dee-**ay**-shuhn)

radiator *noun*
1. A series of pipes through which hot water or steam circulates, sending heat into a room. Some radiators use electricity: *The radiator heated the bedroom quickly.*
2. A metal device through which a liquid, usually water, circulates to cool a vehicle's engine.
ra·di·a·tor (*ray*-dee-**ay**-tur)

radical *adjective*
1. If a change is **radical**, it is thorough and has a wide range of important effects. ▷ *adverb* **radically**
2. If a person is **radical**, he or she is in favor of extreme political change.
rad·i·cal (**rad**-i-kuhl)
▷ *noun* **radical**

radio
1. *noun* A way of communicating using electromagnetic waves broadcast from a central antenna.
2. *noun* A device that sends or receives these broadcasts and converts them into sound, as in *a portable radio.*
3. *verb* To send a message using radio signals: *The stranded hikers radioed for help.* ▷ *verb* **radios, radioing, radioed**
ra·di·o (**ray**-dee-oh)
▷ *noun, plural* **radios**

Word History

The electromagnetic waves that are used in radio communication gave the **radio** its name. The waves can be thought of as rays or beams sent through the air, so *radio* was coined from *radius*, the Latin word for "ray." The *radius* of a circle in mathematics goes back to the same Latin word.

radioactive *adjective* **Radioactive** materials are made up of atoms whose nuclei break down, giving off harmful radiation. **ra·di·o·ac·tive** (*ray*-dee-oh-**ak**-tiv) ▷ *noun* **radioactivity**

radio button *noun* A small colored circle on a webpage that you can click to make something happen, such as choosing an option.

radiography *noun* The science and techniques of taking X-ray photographs of people's bones or organs. **ra·di·og·ra·phy** (*ray*-dee-**ah**-gruh-fee) ▷ *noun* **radiographer**

radish

radish *noun* A crisp, small root vegetable, usually white inside with red skin, that you eat raw in salads.
rad·ish (**rad**-ish) ▷ *noun, plural* **radishes**

radium *noun* A highly radioactive chemical element sometimes used to treat cancer. **ra·di·um** (**ray**-dee-uhm)

radius *noun*
1. A straight line segment drawn from the exact center of a circle to its edge: *The radius of the earth is about 4,000 miles.*
2. The outer bone in your lower arm.
3. The geographic area that makes a circle around a thing or a place: *There are six churches within a three-mile radius of my house.*
ra·di·us (**ray**-dee-uhs)
▷ *noun, plural* **radii** (**ray**-dee-*eye*)

radon *noun* An odorless, colorless, radioactive gas that can seep up from the earth and rocks. Radon is a chemical element produced by radium. **ra·don** (**ray**-dahn)

raffle *noun* A form of lottery to raise money by selling tickets and then giving small prizes to those holding winning tickets. **raf·fle** (**raf**-uhl) ▷ *verb* **raffle**

raft
1. *noun* A floating platform made of wood and used to carry people or things: *The explorers floated downstream on a raft.*
2. *verb* To travel on a raft: *We rafted down the Colorado River on our vacation.* ▷ *verb* **rafting, rafted** ▷ *noun* **rafting**
3. *noun* An inflatable rubber boat that is propelled by oars.
raft (raft)

Word History

Originally, a **raft** was only a single wooden beam. The word *raft* is related to the Norwegian word *raft,* meaning a "long piece of wood" or a "wooden beam." Later, English speakers started using *raft* to refer to many pieces of wood fastened together to make a floating platform.

rag
1. *noun* An old, worn piece of material, as in *a dusty rag.*
2. **rags** *noun, plural* Old, worn-out clothing, often ripped or torn.
rag (rag)

rage
1. *noun* Violent anger: *The frustrated girl flew into a rage.*
2. *verb* To happen with great force: *The storm raged across Lake Erie.* ▷ *verb* **raging, raged**
rage (rayj)

ragged *adjective* Old, torn, and worn-out, as in *ragged clothes.* **rag·ged** (**rag**-id) ▷ *adjective* **raggedy** ▷ *adverb* **raggedly**

ragtime *noun* An early style of jazz having a strong, syncopated rhythm. **rag·time** (**rag**-*time*)

ragweed *noun* A weed whose pollen is a cause of hay fever in the fall. **rag·weed** (**rag**-*weed*)

raid *noun*
1. A sudden, surprise attack on a place: *The knights made a raid on the castle.* ▷ *noun* **raider**
2. A surprise visit by the police, especially to search for criminals or seize illegal drugs or stolen goods, as in *a drug raid.*
raid (rayd)
▷ *verb* **raid**

rail *noun*
1. A fixed bar supported by posts.
2. Railroad: *Grandma prefers to travel by rail.*
rail (rayl)
▷ *adjective* **rail**

train track rails

railing *noun* A wooden or metal bar that is a part of a fence or a staircase, as in *the porch railing.* **rail·ing** (**ray**-ling)

railroad *noun*
1. A track of double rails for a train.
2. A system of transport using trains: *Most of the town's residents travel to work by railroad.*
rail·road (**rayl**-*rohd*)

railway *noun* A railroad, or the tracks of a railroad. **rail·way** (**rayl**-*way*)

rain
1. *noun* Water that falls in drops from clouds: *We stopped the game when the rain started to come down in sheets.*
2. *noun* A falling of rain: *Yesterday's rain was good for the garden.*
3. *verb* To fall in rain: *It's raining today.*
4. *verb* To fall or pour like rain: *Tears rained down their faces.*
rain (rayn)
Rain sounds like **reign** and **rein.** ▷ *verb* **raining, rained** ▷ *adjective* **rainy**

Rain Forests

Tropical rain forests grow near the equator, while temperate rain forests exist in cooler climates. A rain forest's emergent layer includes very tall trees that can withstand heat. In the tropics, the dense canopy is inhabited by animals such as monkeys and parrots. Large leaves in the understory absorb any sunlight that reaches them. The largest animals live on the forest floor, where fungi and insects also break down decaying matter. Rain forests (indicated in dark green on the map) contain more than half the world's plant and animal species and help balance the earth's climate. They are threatened, as they are cleared for lumber, farming, and housing.

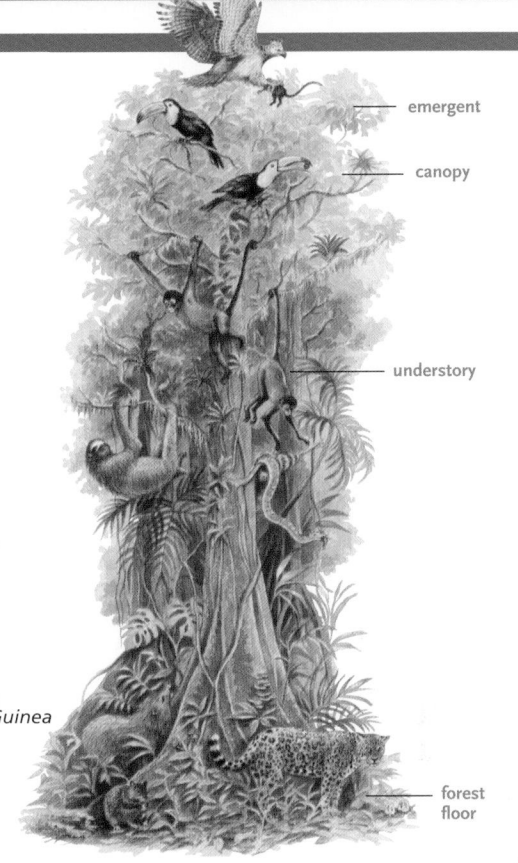

rainbow *noun* An arc of different colors caused by the bending of sunlight as it shines through water vapor. **rain·bow** (**rayn**-*boh*)

raincoat *noun* A waterproof coat that keeps you dry when it is raining. **rain·coat** (**rayn**-*koht*)

raindrop *noun* A drop of rain: *She woke to the sound of raindrops drumming against the window.* **rain·drop** (**rayn**-*drahp*)

rainfall *noun* The amount of rain that falls in a certain place during a period of time. **rain·fall** (**rayn**-*fawl*)

rain forest *noun* A dense, tropical forest where a lot of rain falls much of the year.

raise
1. *verb* To lift something to a higher position: *Raise your hand if you know the answer.*
2. *verb* To assemble or collect something, as in *to raise an army* or *to raise money.*
3. *verb* To take care of children or young animals until they are grown: *Timmy was raised by his grandmother after his parents died in the accident.*
4. *noun* An increase in salary: *I got a raise at the end of the year.* ▷ *verb* **raise**
5. *verb* To ask or to bring up, as in *to raise an objection.*
raise (rayz)
▷ *verb* **raising, raised**

raisin *noun* A sweet grape that has been dried. **rai·sin** (**ray**-zin)

rake
1. *noun* A garden tool with a row of teeth or prongs for working over soil or collecting leaves.
2. *verb* To use a rake to level soil, collect leaves, cut grass, or the like: *Sasha raked up the fallen leaves.*
3. *verb (informal)* If you **rake it in**, you make a lot of money, especially without working hard.
rake (rayk)
▷ *verb* **raking, raked**

rally
1. *verb* To bring together again: *The officer rallied his troops.*
2. *verb* To join together to help or support a person or thing: *My friends rallied to my defense.*
3. *verb* To regain strength, energy, or health: *The patient rallied overnight.*
4. *noun* A large meeting for a purpose, as in *a campaign rally.*
5. *noun* A long exchange of shots before a point is scored in a game such as tennis or badminton.
ral·ly (**ral**-ee)
▷ *verb* **rallies, rallying, rallied** ▷ *noun, plural* **rallies**

ram

1. *noun* A male sheep.

2. *verb* To crash into something with great force: *The car rammed into the pole.*

3. *verb* To force something into a space: *Sarah rammed the key into the lock.*

ram (ram)

▷ *verb* **ramming, rammed**

RAM *noun* The part of a computer's memory that is lost when you turn the computer off. RAM is short for *random access memory.* **RAM** (ram)

Ramadan *noun* The ninth month of the Muslim year, when Muslims fast each day from sunrise to sunset. **Ram·a·dan** (*rah*-muh-**dahn**)

Word History

Muslims fast from sunrise to sunset during the month of **Ramadan**, which is the ninth month of the Muslim calendar. The name *Ramadan* in Arabic originally meant "the hot month." The Muslim calendar is calculated according to the moon. As a result, the beginning of Ramadan is 11 days earlier every year, so over time this month occurs during all the seasons, one after the other. It is thought, however, that at the time the month of Ramadan received its name, it was one of the hot months.

ramble *verb*

1. To wander around without direction or purpose: *We rambled through town looking at the sights.*

2. To go on a long walk for pleasure: *Pat rambled along the path through the woods.*

3. To speak for a long time or write a lot without sticking to the point: *The speaker rambled until everyone was bored.*

ram·ble (**ram**-buhl)

▷ *verb* **rambling, rambled** ▷ *noun* **ramble**

▷ *noun* **rambler**

rambling *adjective* Going or growing in many directions, as in *a rambling conversation* or *a rambling rose.* **ram·bling** (**ram**-bling)

ramen *noun, plural* Curly noodles that cook very quickly, usually served in a broth and garnished with bits of meat and vegetables. **ra·men** (**rah**-muhn)

Word History

Japanese speakers took their term **ramen** from the Chinese word *lamian*, which received its name, "pull noodle," from how it was made. *Lamian* was based on the words *la*, meaning "to pull," and *mian*, meaning "noodle."

ramp *noun* A sloping passageway or roadway linking one level with another: *Greg pushed the wheelbarrow up the ramp.* **ramp** (ramp)

rampage *noun* If someone goes **on a rampage**, the person rushes around in a violent and excited way: *Pete went on a rampage when he found his papers scattered across the floor.* **ram·page** (**ram**-payj)

▷ *verb* **rampage, rampaging**

rampant *adjective* Wild and without restraint, as in *a rampant growth of weeds.* **ram·pant** (**ram**-puhnt)

rampart *noun* A wall or embankment surrounding a fort or castle, built to protect against attack. **ram·part** (**ram**-pahrt)

ramshackle *adjective* Rickety, poorly built, or likely to fall apart, as in *a ramshackle house.* **ram·shack·le** (**ram**-shak-uhl)

ran *verb* The past tense of **run**. **ran** (ran)

ranch *noun* A large farm for cattle, sheep, or horses. **ranch** (ranch) ▷ *noun, plural* **ranches** ▷ *noun* **rancher** ▷ *verb* **ranch**

rancid *adjective* Spoiled and not fit to eat, as in *rancid butter.* **ran·cid** (**ran**-sid)

random *adjective*

1. Without any order or purpose: *Beth took random courses in college before deciding to study history.*

▷ *adverb* **randomly**

2. If you make a **random** selection from a group of items, each item in the group has the same chance of being chosen.

3. If you do something **at random**, you do it without any order or method: *Alison pulled a book at random off the shelf.*

ran·dom (**ran**-duhm)

Word History

If you are in a big hurry, you may not be as careful as usual, and may not follow a plan very well. "Moving at great speed" is the idea behind the word **random**, which came from the Old French verb *randir*, meaning "run fast."

range

1. *verb* To vary within certain limits: *The dogs ranged in size from tiny terriers to medium-sized ones.*

▷ *noun* **range**

2. *noun* The distance that a bullet or rocket can travel or a person can see.

3. *noun* A place for shooting at targets or testing rockets, as in *an archery range.*

4. *noun* An area of open land used for grazing animals, as in *a bison range.*

5. *noun* A chain of mountains, as in *a mountain range.*

6. *verb* To roam over a large area: *Extinct relatives of* *the giant sloth ranged across all of South America.*

7. *noun* A stove with several burners and at least one oven. **range** (raynj)

▷ *verb* **ranging, ranged**

ranger *noun* A person in charge of a park or forest. **rang·er** (**rayn**-jur)

rank

1. *noun* An official job level or position: *Stephen rose to the rank of lieutenant commander in the US Navy.*

2. *verb* To assign a position to: *Our team is ranked first.* ▷ *verb* **ranking, ranked** ▷ *noun* **rank**

3. *adjective* Having a strong and unpleasant odor or taste: *The muddy clothes were rank.*

4. *adjective* Complete or absolute, as in *a rank amateur.* **rank** (rangk)

▷ *adjective* **ranker, rankest**

ransack *verb* To search a place violently, usually looking for things to steal: *The intruders ransacked the house.* **ran·sack** (**ran**-sak) ▷ *verb* **ransacking, ransacked**

ransom *noun* Money that is demanded before someone who is being held captive can be set free: *The kidnappers demanded a huge ransom.* **ran·som** (**ran**-suhm) ▷ *verb* **ransom**

rant *verb* To talk loudly and angrily: *Steve ranted about how he had been cheated.* **rant** (rant) ▷ *verb* **ranting, ranted**

rap

1. *verb* To hit something with a quick, sharp blow:

park ranger

rapids

Bettina rapped on the window. ▷ *noun* **rap**

2. *noun* A type of popular music in which the words are spoken rhythmically to a musical background. ▷ *noun* **rapper** ▷ *verb* **rap**

3. *verb* (*slang*) To talk: *The boys rapped for hours.* **rap** (rap)

Rap sounds like **wrap**. ▷ *verb* **rapping, rapped**

rapid *adjective* Very fast or quick, as in *a rapid heartbeat.* **rap·id** (**rap**-id) ▷ *noun* **rapidity** (ra-**pid**-i-tee)

rapidly *adverb* Quickly or within a short period of time: *The company grew rapidly from six employees to more than 3,000.* **rap·id·ly** (**rap**-id-lee)

rapids *noun, plural* A place in a river where the water flows very fast: *Our canoe nearly capsized in the rapids.* **rap·ids** (**rap**-idz)

rapier *noun* A long sword with two edges, often used in duels in the 16th and 17th centuries. **ra·pi·er** (**ray**-pee-ur)

rapture *noun* Great happiness, joy, or delight: *My brother stared in rapture at his new bicycle.* **rap·ture** (**rap**-chur)

rare *adjective*

1. Not often seen, found, or happening: *The musician made a rare appearance.* ▷ *noun* **rarity**

2. Not cooked very much, as in *a rare steak.*

3. Unusually good or excellent, as in *a rare beauty* or *a rare gift.* **rare** (rair)

▷ *adjective* **rarer, rarest**

rarely *adverb* Not very often: *This particular bird is rarely seen in the wild.* **rare·ly** (**rair**-lee)

rascal *noun*

1. Someone who is very mischievous.

2. A dishonest person. **ras·cal** (**ras**-kuhl)

Word History

If you were a **rascal** in the Middle Ages, you were one of the common people, or a common soldier. Hunters also referred to certain animals as rascals: These animals were young and small, and the hunters thought that killing them was not worth the trouble. *Rascal* may go back to *rasquer*, a verb in French meaning "to scrape." So a *rascal* is perhaps "something scraped off" that is not worth very much.

rash

1. *noun* An occurrence of small spots or blotchy red patches on the skin caused by an allergy or disease.
2. *noun* An occurrence of many events of the same type, as *a rash of burglaries.*
3. *adjective* Acting quickly, without thinking first: *It was rash to run into the street without looking both ways.* ▷ *adjective* **rasher, rashest** ▷ *adverb* **rashly**
rash (rash)
▷ *noun, plural* **rashes**

rasp

1. *verb* To speak in a harsh, grating voice: *The drill sergeant rasped an order to the troops.* ▷ *verb* **rasping, rasped**
2. *noun* A harsh, grating sound: *The rusty gate closed with a rasp.*
3. *noun* A coarse file with cone-shaped teeth, used to smooth wood or metal.
rasp (rasp)

raspberry *noun*

1. A small, sweet, black or red berry with very small seeds that grows on a prickly bush.
2. A dark purple-red color.
rasp·ber·ry (**raz**-ber-ee)
▷ *noun, plural* **raspberries**

raspberry

rat *noun*

1. A rodent that looks like a large mouse and has a long tail. Rats sometimes spread disease.
2. *(informal)* A disloyal person: *That rat told everyone my secret!*
3. **rat race** A very stressful routine or competition at work.
rat (rat)

rate

1. *noun* A degree of speed: *The train hurtled forward at an alarming rate.*
2. *noun* A fee or price, as in *a discount rate.*
3. *noun* A standard amount used to calculate a total: *The rate of the phone call was 15 cents for each minute.*
4. *verb* To judge the quality or worth of a person or thing: *The critic rated the restaurant as very good.*
5. *verb* To place in a particular position or rank: *Gwen rated the brands of ice cream according to price.*
rate (rayt)
▷ *noun* **rating** ▷ *verb* **rating, rated**

rather *adverb*

1. Fairly or quite; more than a little: *It's a rather long walk to school.*
2. More willingly: *I'd rather have a hamburger than a hot dog, thanks.*

3. More correctly: *That man is my father, or rather my stepfather.*
rath·er (**raTH**-ur)

ratify *verb* To agree to or approve officially: *Members of Congress ratified the treaty.* **rat·i·fy** (**rat**-uh-*fye*)
▷ *verb* **ratifies, ratifying, ratified** ▷ *noun* **ratification**

ratio *noun* A comparison of two quantities or numbers using division. Ratios are usually expressed as fractions, or using the word *to: The ratio of the number of a human being's fingers to eyes is 10 to 2; the ratio is also 5 to 1, five times as many fingers as eyes.* **ra·ti·o** (**ray**-shee-*oh* or **ray**-shoh)

Word History

The English word **ratio** goes back to a term in Latin meaning "calculation," *ratio.* Division is the type of "calculation" that a *ratio* uses. The verb for "to think" in Latin was *reri,* and its past participle was *ratus.* Latin speakers formed the word *ratio* from this past participle.

ration

1. *noun* A limited amount or share, especially of food: *Each person got the same small ration of bread.*
2. *verb* To give out in limited amounts: *During World War II, the government rationed gasoline.* ▷ *verb* **rationing, rationed** ▷ *noun* **rationing**
ra·tion (**rash**-uhn or **ray**-shuhn)

rational *adjective*

1. Logical and sensible and not emotional, as in *a rational argument.*
2. Reasonable and sane, as in *rational actions.*
ra·tion·al (**rash**-uh-nuhl)
▷ *adverb* **rationally**

rattle

1. *verb* To make a series of short, sharp noises: *The windows rattled in the wind.* ▷ *noun* **rattle**
2. **rattle off** *verb* To talk or say quickly: *The teacher rattled off the answers.*
3. *verb* To upset or embarrass: *Speaking in front of the group rattled Jim.*
4. *noun* A baby's toy that makes a rattling sound, as in *a wooden rattle.*
5. *noun* The end part of a rattlesnake's tail that produces a rattling sound.
rat·tle (**rat**-uhl)
▷ *verb* **rattling, rattled**

rattlesnake *noun* A poisonous snake of North and South America with a tail that makes a rattling noise as it shakes. **rat·tle·snake** (**rat**-uhl-*snayk*)

raucous *adjective*

1. Harsh or loud in a way that is unpleasant, as in *a raucous voice.*

2. Loud and rowdy, as in *a raucous party.*
rau·cous (**raw**-kuhs)
▷ *adverb* **raucously**

rave *verb*
  1. To talk wildly: *He raved like a lunatic.*
  2. *(informal)* To praise something enthusiastically: *We raved about the movie.*
  rave (rayv)
  ▷ *verb* **raving, raved**

ravel *verb* To fray, or separate into single loose threads; to unravel: *My sweater raveled at the sleeve when I caught a thread on a nail.* **ra·vel** (**rav**-uhl)
  ▷ *verb* **raveling, raveled**

raven *noun* A large bird with shiny black feathers, belonging to the crow family. **ra·ven** (**ray**-vuhn)

Word History

In ancient Scandinavian mythology, **ravens** were the creatures of the war god Odin, and in early English poetry, they were often mentioned in connection with battles. Speakers of Old English called this bird a *hraefn*, and *hraefn* developed into the modern word *raven. Raven* is related to the German name for the bird, *Rabe.*

ravenous *adjective* Extremely hungry: *We were ravenous after working all day.* **rav·en·ous** (**rav**-uh-nuhs)

ravine *noun* A steep, extremely narrow valley: *The scouts climbed down the ravine.* **ra·vine** (ruh-**veen**)

ravioli *noun, plural* Square pockets of pasta that can be filled with meat, vegetables, or cheese. **rav·i·o·li** (*rav*-ee-**oh**-lee)

raw *adjective*
  1. Not cooked, as in *raw vegetables.*
  2. Not treated, processed, or refined: *Milk is raw before it is pasteurized.*
  3. Not trained or inexperienced, as in *a raw recruit.*

ravine

4. Having the skin rubbed off, as in *a raw wound.*
5. Unpleasantly damp and chilly, as in *raw weather.*
raw (raw)
▷ *adjective* **rawer, rawest**

rawhide *noun* The skin of cattle or other animals before it has been soaked in a special solution and made into leather. **raw·hide** (**raw**-*hide*)

raw material *noun* A substance that is treated or processed and made into a useful finished product. Crude oil is the raw material from which we get gasoline.

ray *noun*
  1. A narrow beam of light or other radiation, as in *the rays of the sun.*
  2. A type of fish with a flat body, large winglike fins, and a thin, whiplike tail.
  3. A tiny amount, as in *a ray of hope.*
  4. Part of a line that extends on and on in one direction from a single point.
  ray (ray)

rayon *noun* A synthetic fabric made from cellulose that has the look and feel of silk. **ray·on** (**ray**-ahn)

razor *noun* A tool with a sharp blade used to shave hair from the skin. **ra·zor** (**ray**-zur)

re *preposition* Concerning. The word *re* is used to introduce the subject to be talked about: *His letter to the editor began, "I am writing to you re the traffic problems in my neighborhood."* **re** (ree)

Prefix

The prefix **re-** adds one of the following meanings to a root word:
1. Again, as in *reelect* (to elect again) or *rerun* (to run again).
2. Back or backward, as in *return* (to turn back) or *revoke* (to take back).

reach

  1. *verb* To stretch or hold out to something with your hand: *She reached for the salt.*
  2. *verb* To go as far as: *Our yard reaches right to the river.*
  3. *noun* The distance a person or thing can reach.
  4. *noun* An expanse, as in *vast reaches of the sea.*
  5. *verb* To get to or arrive somewhere: *We reached the top of the hill. Your letter reached me yesterday.*
  6. *verb* To contact: *Alison reached her mother by phone.*
  7. *noun* The act of reaching.
  reach (reech)
  ▷ *verb* **reaches, reaching, reached** ▷ *noun, plural* **reaches**

react *verb*

1. To behave in a particular way as a response to something that has happened: *The crowd reacted to the win with cheers.*

2. If a substance **reacts** with another, a chemical change occurs in one or both of the substances as they are mixed together.
re·act (ree-**akt**)
▷ *verb* **reacting, reacted**

reaction *noun* An action in response to something; a response: *Shawn's reaction to the joke was wild laughter.* **re·act·ion** (ree-**ak**-shuhn)

reactionary *adjective* Against change and wanting things to return to the way they were in the past. **re·ac·tion·ar·y** (ree-**ak**-shuh-*ner*-ee) ▷ *noun* **reactionary** ▷ *noun, plural* **reactionaries**

reactor *noun* A large device in which nuclear energy is produced by splitting atoms under controlled conditions. **re·ac·tor** (ree-**ak**-tur)

read *verb*

1. To look at and understand written or printed words: *I read a book about a girl who wanted to join the circus.*

2. To say aloud something that is written: *I read the book to Rachel.*

3. To learn by reading: *We're reading about life in the Middle Ages.*

4. To understand some form of communication, especially by observing someone's behavior: *I sometimes think my mother can read my mind.*

5. To show or to register: *The speedometer reads 55 miles per hour.*
read (reed)
▷ *verb* **reading, read** (red)

reader *noun*

1. A person who reads: *Sally is a fast reader.*

2. A book with passages to practice reading or to read about a particular subject; an anthology.
read·er (**ree**-dur)

readily *adverb*

1. Easily: *This product is readily available on the internet.*

2. Willingly and quickly: *Michael answered the teacher readily.*
read·i·ly (**red**-uh-lee)

reading *noun*

1. The activity of someone who reads: *Reading has helped me get through many rainy weekends.*

2. The spoken performance of a written work in front of an audience: *Sheila and I went to a poetry reading last night.*
read·ing (**ree**-ding)

ready *adjective*

1. Prepared: *When I finish studying, I'll be ready for the test.*

nuclear reactor

2. Willing: *She is ready to work hard.*

3. Likely or about to do something: *I was ready to scream.*

4. Quick, as in *a ready answer.*
read·y (**red**-ee)
▷ *adjective* **readier, readiest**

real *adjective*

1. True and not made up: *The real story about his scar had absolutely nothing to do with a duel at dawn.*

2. Genuine and not imitation or artificial: *I prefer real flowers to plastic ones.*
re·al (**ree**-uhl *or* reel)

real estate *noun* Land and the buildings that are on it.

realistic *adjective*

1. Very similar to the real thing, as in *a realistic painting.*

2. Seeing things as they really are: *Jamal was very realistic about his chances for a scholarship; he knew he would have to earn good grades.*
re·al·is·tic (*ree*-uh-**lis**-tik)
▷ *noun* **realism** ▷ *adverb* **realistically**

reality *noun*

1. Truth, or what actually happens, especially in contrast to what you want or expect: *Being a model looks glamorous, but the reality is that it's very hard work.*

2. The actual facts that must be dealt with: *After summer vacation, we returned to the reality of school and tons of homework.*
re·al·i·ty (ree-**al**-i-tee)
▷ *noun, plural* **realities**

realize *verb*

1. To come to understand something: *Jean realized she'd made a wrong turn.*

2. To make real or to achieve: *After years of study, Juan finally realized his dream of becoming a professional musician.*

re·al·ize (**ree**-uh-*lize*)

▷ *verb* **realizing, realized** ▷ *noun* **realization**

really *adverb*

1. Actually, or in fact: *Are the stories about the new teacher really true?*

2. Very: *That's a really cute little kitten.*

re·al·ly (**ree**-uh-lee *or* **ree**-lee)

realm *noun*

1. An area or field of knowledge or interest, as in *the realm of science.*

2. A kingdom: *He was king of the whole realm.*

realm (relm)

reap *verb*

1. To cut grain or to gather a crop by hand or machine. ▷ *noun* **reaper**

2. To get as a reward: *The actor reaped high praise for his fine performance.*

reap (reep)

▷ *verb* **reaping, reaped**

reappear *verb* To come into view again: *The moon reappeared from behind the cloud.* **re·ap·pear** (*ree*-uh-**peer**) ▷ *verb* **reappearing, reappeared** ▷ *noun* **reappearance**

rear

1. *verb* To give birth to and bring up young animals: *The tiger reared her cubs.*

2. *verb* To care for and raise: *My aunt reared seven children.*

3. *noun* The back part of something: *There was a locked room in the rear of the house.* ▷ *adjective* **rear**

4. *verb* If a horse **rears**, it stands on its hind legs.   **rearing**

5. *verb* To lift up: *The lion reared its head and roared.*

rear (reer)

▷ *verb* **rearing, reared**

rearrange *verb* To arrange things in a new way: *I rearranged the furniture in my room.* **re·ar·range** (*ree*-uh-**raynj**) ▷ *verb* **rearranging, rearranged**

rearview *adjective* Showing things that are behind you, as in *a rearview mirror in a car.* **rear·view** (**reer**-*vyoo*)

reason

1. *noun* The basis or cause of a belief, fact, or action: *There was no reason to doubt his honesty.*

2. *noun* An explanation or an excuse: *What is your reason for being late to class?*

3. *verb* To think logically: *Helen reasoned that she could earn enough money by babysitting several nights a week.* ▷ *noun* **reason**

4. *verb* To try to persuade someone that what you suggest is sensible.

rea·son (**ree**-zuhn)

▷ *verb* **reasoning, reasoned**

reasonable *adjective*

1. Fair or just: *The teacher's decision seemed reasonable to most of the students.*

2. Sensible and not foolish: *It can be hard to be reasonable when you're very upset.*

3. Costing a fair price: *The chair was reasonable.*

rea·son·a·ble (**ree**-zuh-nuh-buhl)

▷ *adverb* **reasonably**

reasoning *noun*

1. The process of thinking in an orderly fashion, drawing conclusions from facts: *Scientific thought is based on reasoning.*

2. The reasons used in this process: *I don't agree with your reasoning.*

rea·son·ing (**ree**-zuh-ning)

reassure *verb* To make someone feel calm and confident and give the person courage: *The doctor reassured the woman before the operation.* **re·as·sure** (*ree*-uh-**shoor**) ▷ *verb* **reassuring, reassured** ▷ *noun* **reassurance** ▷ *adjective* **reassuring**

rebate

1. *noun* Money that is given back to the purchaser of a product, as a sales promotion: *The company was offering a rebate of $50 on the $200 printer.*

2. *verb* To give back part of the price paid for something.

▷ *verb* **rebating, rebated**

re·bate (**ree**-bayt)

rebel *noun* Someone who fights against a government or against the people in charge of something. **re·bel** (**reb**-uhl)

▷ *verb* **rebel** (ri-**bel**)

rebellion *noun*

1. Armed fight against a government: *Two provinces joined the rebellion.*

2. Any struggle against the people in charge of something: *The employees' dissatisfaction turned into open rebellion.*

re·bel·lion (ri-**bel**-yuhn)

rebellious *adjective* Resistant to or disrespectful of authority: *Anya was a rebellious teenager, but she is coming to appreciate her parents' rules as she gets older.* **re·bel·lious** (ri-**bel**-yuhs)

reboot *verb* To start a computer again: *Jim rebooted the computer after installing the new software.* **re·boot** (ree-**boot**) ▷ *verb* **rebooting, rebooted**

rebound
1. (ree-**bound**) *verb* To bounce or spring back after hitting something: *The puck rebounded from the boards.*
2. (ree-**bound**) *verb* To recover from a defeat or an upset, as if bouncing back: *Their spirits rebounded when they heard that their puppy had been found.*
3. (**ree**-*bound*) *noun* The action of bouncing back.
4. (**ree**-*bound*) *noun* Something that bounces back, such as a basketball off the backboard.
5. (ree-**bound**) *verb* To get hold of a rebound in basketball.
6. (**ree**-*bound*) *noun* If you catch a ball that bounces off a wall, you can say that you caught it **on the rebound**.
re·bound
▷ *verb* **rebounding, rebounded**

rebuild *verb* To build something again after it has been damaged or destroyed: *Do you think the town will rebuild the library after the storm damage has been cleared?* **re·build** (ree-**bild**) ▷ *verb* **rebuilding, rebuilt**

rebuke *verb* To scold someone because he or she has done something wrong. **re·buke** (ri-**byook**) ▷ *verb* **rebuking, rebuked** ▷ *noun* **rebuke**

recall *verb*
1. To bring something to your mind; to remember: *I definitely recall your saying that you would help me.*
2. To call back a purchased product that has a defect: *The company recalled thousands of infant car seats that had defective buckles.* ▷ *noun* **recall** (ri-**kawl** or **ree**-kawl)
3. To summon someone to return: *The witness was recalled to the stand.*
re·call (ri-**kawl**)
▷ *verb* **recalling, recalled**

recap *verb* (*informal*) To repeat the main points of something that has already been said. Recap is short for *recapitulate*: *The announcer recaps the news every hour.* **re·cap** (ree-*kap*) ▷ *verb* **recapping, recapped** ▷ *noun* **recap**

recede *verb*
1. To move back: *After the flood, the water slowly receded.*
2. To fade little by little: *Hopes of rescue receded as night fell.*
re·cede (ri-**seed**)

receipt

▷ *verb* **receding, receded** ▷ *adjective* **receding**

receipt *noun* A piece of paper showing that money, goods, mail, or a service has been received: *Ask for a receipt when you buy the tickets.* **re·ceipt** (ri-**seet**)

receive *verb*
1. To get or accept something that has been sent or given: *I received a letter from my pen pal.*
2. To experience: *I received a shock when I heard the bad news.*
3. To greet or to welcome: *The hostess received her guests at the door.*
re·ceive (ri-**seev**)
▷ *verb* **receiving, received**

receiver *noun*
1. The part of a telephone that you hold in your hand next to your ear and mouth.
2. A piece of equipment that receives radio or television signals and changes them into sounds or pictures, as in *a radio receiver*.
3. A person who receives something.
4. A member of the offensive team in football who is expected to catch the ball.
re·ceiv·er (ri-**see**-vur)

recent *adjective* Done, made, or taking place a short time ago: *The city is still recovering from a recent storm.* **re·cent** (**ree**-suhnt)

recently *adverb* Not very long ago: *We recently visited Philadelphia.* **re·cent·ly** (**ree**-suhnt-lee)

receptacle *noun* A container, as in *a trash receptacle*. **re·cep·ta·cle** (ri-**cep**-tuh-kuhl)

reception *noun*
1. The way in which someone or something is received: *We gave our visitors a warm reception. I can't get any reception on my cell phone.*
2. A large formal party: *Many diplomats were invited to the reception at the governor's mansion.*
re·cep·tion (ri-**sep**-shuhn)

receptionist *noun* A person whose job is to greet people in an office, clinic, or other place of business, and sometimes to answer the telephone. **re·cep·tion·ist** (ri-**sep**-shuh-nist)

receptor *noun*
1. A nerve ending that is sensitive to a stimulus, such as pressure, touch, or heat.
2. A specific protein molecule on the surface of a cell that binds with a hormone, antibody, or other chemical messenger, as in *a receptor for insulin*.
re·cep·tor (ri-**sep**-tur)

recess

   1. *noun* A break from schoolwork during the morning or afternoon: *We played softball in the schoolyard at recess.*

   2. *verb* To halt activity for a set amount of time: *The court recessed for lunch. The committee recessed for the summer.* ▷ *verb* **recessing, recessed**

   3. *noun* A part of a wall set back farther than the rest of the wall: *The television sat in a small recess.*

   re·cess (**ree**-ses *or* ri-**ses**)

   ▷ *noun, plural* **recesses** ▷ *adjective* **recessed**

recession *noun* A time when business slows down and more workers than usual are unemployed.

   re·ces·sion (ri-**sesh**-uhn)

recipe *noun* Instructions for preparing food, as in *a cake recipe.* **rec·i·pe** (**res**-uh-pee)

Word History

Originally, **recipe** came from the Latin verb *recipere,* meaning "to receive." It was first used by doctors, who wrote it at the top of their instructions for making medicines. The word later also came to apply to instructions for making food.

recipient *noun* A person who receives something: *The recipients of the awards filed up onto the stage.*

   re·cip·i·ent (ri-**sip**-ee-uhnt)

recital *noun*

   1. A performance, usually given by a single performer or a small group, as in *a piano recital* or *a dance recital.*

   2. A detailed account or report: *The speaker gave a long recital of the events that led to the Civil War.*

   re·cit·al (ri-**sye**-tuhl)

recite *verb*

   1. To say aloud something that you memorized, in front of others: *Joelle recited the poem.*

recital

2. To tell about in detail: *He slowly recited the story of his life.*

   re·cite (ri-**site**)

   ▷ *verb* **reciting, recited** ▷ *noun* **recitation** (*res*-i-**tay**-shuhn)

reckless *adjective* Careless about your own or other people's safety, as in *a reckless driver.* **reck·less** (**rek**-lis) ▷ *adverb* **recklessly**

Word History

Sometimes words are commonly spoken for hundreds of years, then rarely heard again. The old verb *reck* is like this: Today, you mainly see it with the suffix *-less,* as **reckless**. *Reck* meant "pay attention," so *reckless* describes someone who does *not* pay attention or take care. Eventually, English speakers began describing a person who isn't careful about safety as *reckless.*

reckon *verb*

   1. To calculate or figure the value of: *I reckoned the bills and I owe you $10.*

   2. To have an opinion; to think: *She reckoned that her friends would get used to her new idea.*

   reck·on (**rek**-uhn)

   ▷ *verb* **reckoning, reckoned** ▷ *noun* **reckoning**

reclaim *verb*

   1. To get back something that belongs to you: *Stacy reclaimed her bag at the counter.*

   2. To make land suitable for building, farming, or grazing by clearing or draining it.

   re·claim (ri-**klaym**)

   ▷ *verb* **reclaiming, reclaimed** ▷ *noun* **reclamation** (*rek*-luh-**may**-shuhn)

recline *verb* To lean back or lie down: *I reclined on the couch.* **re·cline** (ri-**kline**) ▷ *verb* **reclining, reclined**

recognition *noun* Appreciation or acknowledgment of someone or something: *I believe our mayor hasn't received the recognition he deserves.* **rec·og·ni·tion** (*rek*-uhg-**nish**-uhn)

recognize *verb*

   1. To see someone and know who the person is:

   ▷ *adjective* **recognizable** ▷ *adverb* **recognizably**

   2. To understand a situation and accept it as true or right: *They recognized their duty to vote in the presidential election.*

   rec·og·nize (**rek**-uhg-*nize*)

   ▷ *verb* **recognizing, recognized**

recollect *verb* To remember or to recall something: *I tried to recollect the first time we met.* **rec·ol·lect** (*rek*-uh-**lekt**) ▷ *verb* **recollecting, recollected**

   ▷ *noun* **recollection**

recommend *verb*

1. To suggest as being good or worthy: *My dentist recommended this toothpaste.*

2. To advise: *I recommend that you forget your differences and make up.*

rec·om·mend (*rek*-uh-**mend**)

▷ *verb* **recommending, recommended**

recommendation *noun*

1. A suggestion or proposal: *It's my recommendation that we leave as early as possible to avoid traffic.*

2. A favorable statement about someone's character or qualifications for something: *As part of her college application, Marga included a letter of recommendation from her teacher.*

rec·om·men·da·tion (*rek*-uh-men-**day**-shuhn)

reconcile *verb*

1. To make up or become friendly again after a disagreement: *The couple reconciled after a short separation.* ▷ *noun* **reconciliation**

2. If you **reconcile yourself** to something, you decide to put up with it: *Lorene reconciled herself to having to miss the big game.*

rec·on·cile (**rek**-uhn-*sile*)

▷ *verb* **reconciling, reconciled**

reconsider *verb* To think again about a previous decision, especially with the idea of making a change: *The mayor reconsidered her opposition to raising taxes.* **re·con·sid·er** (*ree*-kuhn-**sid**-ur) ▷ *verb* **reconsidering, reconsidered**

reconstruct *verb*

1. To rebuild something that has been destroyed: *The workers reconstructed the fallen wall.*

2. To carefully piece together past events: *The police reconstructed the events leading to the robbery.*

re·con·struct (*ree*-kuhn-**struhkt**)

▷ *verb* **reconstructed, reconstructing** ▷ *noun* **reconstruction**

record

1. (ri-**kord**) *verb* To write something down so that it can be kept: *Record your thoughts in this diary.* ▷ *noun* **record** (**rek**-urd)

2. (**rek**-urd) *noun* The facts about what a person or group has done: *Because the prisoner had a good record, she was granted parole.*

3. (**rek**-urd) *noun* A disk with grooves on which sound, especially music, used to be recorded to be played by a phonograph. It is also known as a *phonograph record.*

4. (ri-**kord**) *verb* To put music or other sounds onto a tape, compact disk, or record: *The band recorded its best songs.*

5. (**rek**-urd) *noun* If you **set a record** in something

such as a sport, you do it faster, better, higher, or the like, than anyone has ever done it before: *Joe set a new record for home runs in a single game.*

rec·ord

▷ *verb* **recording, recorded**

recorder *noun*

1. A device for recording sounds on magnetic tape.

2. A woodwind musical instrument that you play by blowing into the mouthpiece and covering holes with your fingers to make different notes.

re·cord·er (ri-**kor**-dur)

recording *noun*

1. A tape, compact disk, or record, as in *a recording of bird songs.*

2. The sounds on a tape, compact disk, or record.

re·cord·ing (ri-**kor**-ding)

recount

1. (ri-**kount**) *verb* To narrate or tell about: *Maria recounted her adventures on the canoe trip.*

2. (ree-**kount**) *verb* To count again. Also spelled as *re-count*: *I was interrupted and now I have to recount all these pennies.*

3. (**ree**-*kount*) *noun* An instance of recounting. Also spelled as *re-count*: *The election was so close, both candidates demanded a recount of the votes.*

re·count

▷ *verb* **recounting, recounted**

recover *verb*

1. To get better after an illness, accident, or other difficulty: *It took six weeks to fully recover from the surgery.*

2. To get back something that has been lost, stolen, or taken away: *The police recovered a lot of stolen goods.*

3. To make up for: *In order to recover the time we had lost, we skipped lunch.*

re·cov·er (ri-**kuhv**-ur)

▷ *verb* **recovering, recovered**

re-cover *verb* To cover again: *We re-covered that old couch and it's as good as new.* **re·cov·er** (ree-**kuhv**-ur) ▷ *verb* **re-covering, re-covered**

recovery *noun*

1. A return to health or to a normal state or condition: *Kerry made a quick recovery from the flu.*

2. The process of regaining something that was lost or stolen: *The museum celebrated the recovery of the missing paintings.*

re·cov·er·y (ri-**kuhv**-ur-ee)

recreation *noun* The games, sports, and hobbies that you like to do in your spare time.

rec·re·a·tion (*rek*-ree-**ay**-shuhn) ▷ *adjective* **recreational**

recorder

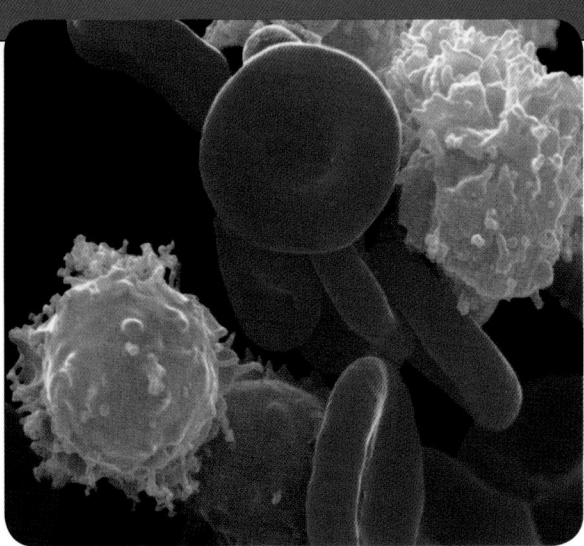

red blood cells

recruit

1. *noun* Someone who has recently joined the armed forces or any group or organization: *The new recruits report for duty today.*

2. *verb* To get a person to join: *The coach is recruiting new players for the basketball team.*

▷ *verb* **recruiting, recruited** ▷ *noun* **recruitment** **re·cruit** (ri-**kroot**)

rectangle *noun* A shape with four sides and four right angles. **rec·tan·gle** (**rek**-*tang*-guhl) ▷ *adjective* **rectangular**

rectify *verb* To make right or correct, as in *to rectify a mistake.* **rec·ti·fy** (**rek**-tuh-*fye*) ▷ *verb* **rectifies, rectifying, rectified**

rectum *noun* The lowest portion of the large intestine, ending at the anus. **rec·tum** (**rek**-tuhm) ▷ *adjective* **rectal** (**rek**-tuhl)

recuperate *verb* To recover from an illness or injury. **re·cu·per·ate** (ri-**koo**-puh-*rate*) ▷ *verb* **recuperating, recuperated** ▷ *noun* **recuperation**

recur *verb* To appear or happen again: *The same dream recurred over and over.* **re·cur** (ri-**kur**) ▷ *verb* **recurring, recurred** ▷ *noun* **recurrence** ▷ *adjective* **recurrent**

recycle *verb* To process old items such as glass, plastic, newspapers, and aluminum and tin cans so that they can be used to make new products: *Our town instituted a new program, where we all have to recycle our garbage.* **re·cy·cle** (ree-**sye**-kuhl) ▷ *verb* **recycling, recycled** ▷ *adjective* **recyclable**

red *noun* One of the three primary colors, along with blue and yellow. Red is the color of beets and blood. **red** (red) ▷ *adjective* **red, reddish**

red blood cell *noun* A cell in your blood that carries oxygen from your lungs to all the tissues and cells of your body.

redcoat *noun* A British soldier during the time of the Revolutionary War and later wars. These soldiers' uniforms included bright red coats. **red·coat** (**red**-koht)

Red Cross *noun* An international organization that helps victims of disasters of all kinds, from floods and earthquakes to war and famine.

redden *verb*

1. To make red or to become red: *They left camp very early that morning, just as the sky was beginning to redden.*

2. To blush: *He reddened with embarrassment.* **red·den** (**red**-uhn)

▷ *verb* **reddening, reddened**

redeem *verb*

1. To exchange something for money or merchandise: *Forty percent of the coupons were redeemed for lottery tickets.*

2. To save, or to make up for: *Sarah redeemed her reputation by pitching a two-hitter.* **re·deem** (ri-**deem**)

▷ *verb* **redeeming, redeemed** ▷ *noun* **redemption** (ri-**demp**-shuhn)

red-eye *noun*

1. A flight that leaves at night and reaches its destination in the morning, with tired passengers: *We took a red-eye from Los Angeles in order to be back for the first day of school.*

2. The appearance of redness in the eyes of people in a photograph because of the way that the camera captures light.

red-handed *adjective* If you catch someone **red-handed**, you catch the person in the act of doing something wrong: *The police caught the thief red-handed.* **red-hand·ed** (**han**-did)

red herring *noun* Something that distracts a person's attention from the real issue: *In the story, the discovery of a bloody knife was a red herring.*

red tape *noun* Excessive rules and regulations and detailed paperwork that make it hard to get things done: *I couldn't speak to the dean directly because of all of the school's red tape.*

reduce *verb* To decrease something in size, amount, or weight: *The store will reduce its prices during the sale.* **re·duce** (ri-**doos**) ▷ *verb* **reducing, reduced**

reduced *adjective* Smaller or less in size, amount, or degree: *Eating right and exercising lead to a reduced risk of heart disease.* **re·duced** (ri-**doost**)

reduction *noun* The act or process of making something smaller or less: *Over the last 20 years, we've had a gradual reduction in the amount of rainfall.* **re·duc·tion** (ri-**duhk**-shuhn)

redundant *adjective* Using repetitive words for what you mean to say or write: *Saying "three triplets" is redundant.* **re·dun·dant** (ri-**duhn**-duhnt) ▷ *noun* **redundancy**

redwood *noun* A very large evergreen tree found along the western coast of the United States, especially in northern California. The world's tallest redwood, found in Humboldt County, California, is nearly 380 feet tall. **red·wood** (**red**-wud)

reed *noun*
1. A tall grass with long, thin, hollow stems that grows in or near water.
2. A piece of thin wood, metal, or plastic in the mouthpieces of some musical instruments, such as the clarinet, oboe, and saxophone. When you blow over the reed the right way, it vibrates and makes a sound. **reed** (reed)

reef *noun* A strip of rock, sand, or coral close to the surface of the ocean or another body of water. **reef** (reef)

Word History

A coral reef would have been called a coral *riff* a few hundred years ago, because *riff* is the old form of the word **reef**. English speakers adopted *riff* from the ancient Dutch word *riffe*. The Dutch word was perhaps related to the English word *rib*, referring to one of the curved bones enclosing a person's chest. So *reefs* may be named after people's ribs because of their similar shape.

reek
1. *verb* To give off an unpleasant smell: *The dock reeked of old, dead fish.*
▷ *verb* **reeking, reeked**
2. *noun* A strong bad smell, as in *the reek of cigarette smoke.*
reek (reek)
Reek sounds like **wreak**.

reel
1. *verb* To stagger: *The drunken man reeled down the street.*
2. *noun* A cylinder on which something, such as thread, fishing line, or film, is wound.
▷ *verb* **reel**
3. *noun* A type of folk dance that is lively and spirited.
4. *verb* If you **reel** something **off**, you say it quickly, especially from memory: *Tim reeled off the names of the first ten presidents of the United States.*
reel (reel)
▷ *verb* **reeling, reeled**

reelect *verb* To elect for another term, as in *to reelect the president.* **re·e·lect** (ree-i-**lekt**) ▷ *verb* **reelecting, reelected** ▷ *noun* **reelection**

reenact *verb*
1. To enact again: *The law was repealed but then reenacted a decade later.*
2. To act or perform something again: *Teasing me, Chris reenacted how I'd screamed when I saw the cockroach.*
3. To re-create an event by acting it out: *The men wore Civil War uniforms and reenacted the Battle of New Market.*
re·en·act (ree-uh-**nakt**) ▷ *verb* **reenacting, reenacted** ▷ *noun* **reenactor** (ree-uh-**nak**-tur) ▷ *noun* **reenactment** (ree-uh-**nakt**-ment)

reentry *noun* The return of a spacecraft or missile to the earth's atmosphere: *The orbiting space station is scheduled for reentry next year.* **re·en·try** (ree-**en**-tree) ▷ *noun, plural* **reentries** ▷ *verb* **reenter**

refer *verb*
1. To look at something for information, as in *to refer to a book.*
2. To bring attention to something by mentioning it when you speak or write: *The newscaster referred to the recent flooding in her discussion of the National Guard.*
3. To send someone for additional or more detailed information or advice: *The doctor referred her patient to a foot specialist.*
re·fer (ri-**fur**) ▷ *verb* **referring, referred** ▷ *noun* **referral**

referee *or* **ref** *noun* An official who supervises a sports match or a game and makes sure that the players obey the rules. **ref·er·ee** (ref-uh-**ree**) *or* **ref** (ref) ▷ *verb* **referee**

football referee

reference *noun*
1. A mention of something or someone, or the act of mentioning something or someone: *There was a reference to the upcoming science fair in the principal's announcement.*
2. A statement about someone's personal qualities and abilities: *I asked my pastor for a reference for the job at summer camp.*
3. A book, magazine, website, or the like from which you get information that you use in an essay or other piece of work: *List your references at the end of your paper.*
ref·er·ence (**ref**-ur-uhns)

reference book *noun* A book that you use to find information quickly and easily. Encyclopedias, dictionaries, atlases, and almanacs are reference books.

referendum *noun* A vote by the people on a public measure: *The ballot included a referendum on building a new school.* **ref·er·en·dum** (*ref*-uh-**ren**-duhm) ▷ *noun, plural* **referendums** *or* **referenda** (*ref*-uh-**ren**-duh)

refill *verb* To fill a glass, cup, or container again: *The waitress refilled Meg's coffee cup.* **re·fill** (ree-**fil**) ▷ *verb* **refilling, refilled** ▷ *noun* **refill** (**ree**-*fil*)

refinance *verb* To change your agreement with a bank about how you will pay back a loan, usually for a house: *We can't decide whether we should refinance now or wait to see if rates come down further.* **re·fi·nance** (*ree*-fuh-**nans** *or* ree-**fye**-nans) ▷ *verb* **refinancing, refinanced**

refine *verb*
1. To purify, or to remove unwanted matter from a substance such as oil or sugar.
2. To improve or perfect something, especially by making minor changes: *I'd like to refine my essay before I turn it in.*
re·fine (ri-**fine**)
▷ *verb* **refining, refined**

refined *adjective*
1. A **refined** person is well educated and very polite, with good taste and elegant manners.
2. Purified or processed, as in *refined sugar*.
re·fined (ri-**fined**)

refinement *noun*
1. Good taste, elegance, and good manners: *The princess displayed grace and refinement.*
2. A slight change made to something in order to improve it: *Bob's latest refinements make his machine run more smoothly.*
re·fine·ment (ri-**fine**-muhnt)

refinery *noun* A factory where raw materials, such as crude oil or sugar, are purified and made into finished products, as in *an oil refinery.* **re·fin·er·y** (ri-**fye**-nur-ee) ▷ *noun, plural* **refineries**

refit *verb* To prepare something for additional use by replacing parts and equipment: *The old ship was refitted with a new mast.* **re·fit** (ree-**fit**) ▷ *verb* **refitting, refitted**

reflect *verb*
1. To show an image of something on a shiny surface, such as water or a mirror: *The sunset was reflected in the lake.*
2. To throw back heat, light, or sound from a surface: *Music from the town square was reflected by the buildings that surrounded it.*
3. To think carefully or seriously about something: *After reflecting on the day's events, Margot changed her mind.*
4. To bring about an impression of someone or

something, either good or bad: *His bad behavior reflects poorly on his parents.*
5. To show or to express: *Amanda's clothes reflect her good taste.*
re·flect (ri-**flekt**)
▷ *verb* **reflecting, reflected** ▷ *noun* **reflection**

reflective *adjective*
1. Able to reflect light, images, or sound waves: *The new office building is covered in reflective windows.*
2. Tending to think deeply and seriously about things: *I love talking to Erik because he's so reflective and intellectual.*
re·flec·tive (ri-**flek**-tiv)
▷ *adverb* **reflectively**

reflector *noun* A shiny surface or device that bounces back light or heat. **re·flec·tor** (ri-**flek**-tur)

reflex *noun* An automatic action or movement that happens without a person's control or effort. **re·flex** (**ree**-*fleks*) ▷ *noun, plural* **reflexes** ▷ *adjective* **reflex**

reflex angle *noun* An angle between 180 degrees and 360 degrees.

reforest *verb* To replant trees where all the original trees were cut down or destroyed by fire or disaster. **re·for·est** (ree-**for**-est) ▷ *verb* **reforesting, reforested** ▷ *noun* **reforestation**

reform
1. *verb* To make changes in something so that it is corrected or improved: *The candidate believes that tax laws need to be reformed.*
2. *verb* To change for the better, especially to abandon bad behavior: *The thief promised to reform and live an honest life.*
3. *noun* An improvement, or the correcting of something unsatisfactory, as in *health care reform.*
re·form (ri-**form**)
▷ *verb* **reforming, reformed**

reformatory *noun* A special school or institution for young people who have broken the law. **re·for·ma·to·ry** (ri-**for**-muh-*tor*-ee) ▷ *noun, plural* **reformatories**

refract *verb* When a ray of light is **refracted**, it bends because it has entered another medium, such as water or glass. **re·fract** (ri-**frakt**) ▷ *verb* **refracting, refracted** ▷ *noun* **refraction** (ri-**frak**-shuhn)

refrain
1. *verb* To hold yourself back from doing or saying something you want to do: *Mel was determined to refrain from eating any desserts.* ▷ *verb* **refraining, refrained**
2. *noun* A regularly repeated part of a song or poem: *No one remembered all the words of the song, but at least we could sing the refrain.*
re·frain (ri-**frayn**)

refresh *verb*

1. To bring someone new energy and strength: *A walk in the woods after lunch will refresh us.*

2. If a webpage **refreshes** or if you **refresh** it, you see the newest version of it.

3. If something **refreshes your memory**, it makes you remember something more clearly than you did before: *Reading those pages from my diary refreshed my memory about our trip to Norway.* **re·fresh** (ri-**fresh**)
▷ *verb* **refreshes, refreshing, refreshed** ▷ *adjective* **refreshing**

refreshments *noun, plural* Light snacks and drinks: *There were refreshments after the music school's annual recital.* **re·fresh·ments** (ri-**fresh**-muhnts)

refrigerator

refrigerator *noun* A cabinet, a room, or an appliance with a very cold interior, used for storing food and drink. **re·frig·er·a·tor** (ri-**frij**-uh-*ray*-tur) ▷ *noun* **refrigeration** ▷ *verb* **refrigerate**

refuel *verb* To supply or to take on more fuel: *The plane to Antarctica had to refuel in Brazil.* **re·fu·el** (ree-**fyoo**-uhl) ▷ *verb* **refueling, refueled**

refuge *noun*

1. Protection or shelter from danger or trouble: *The frightened kitten took refuge under the couch.*

2. A place that provides protection or shelter, as in *a wildlife refuge.* **ref·uge** (**ref**-yooj)

refugee *noun* A person who is forced to leave his or her home or country to escape war, religious persecution, or a natural disaster. **ref·u·gee** (*ref*-yoo-**jee**)

refund *verb* To return or repay money: *The store owner refunded what I paid for the stale loaf of bread.* **re·fund** (ri-**fuhnd**) ▷ *verb* **refunding, refunded** ▷ *noun* **refund** (**ree**-*fuhnd*)

refusal *noun* An instance or expression of unwillingness to do something: *His refusal to take responsibility for the crime angered the judge.* **re·fus·al** (ri-**fyoo**-zuhl)

refuse

1. (ri-**fyooz**) *verb* To say you will not do, accept, or allow something: *Alec refused to go on the amusement park ride by himself.* ▷ *verb* **refusing, refused**

2. (**ref**-yoos) *noun* Trash. **re·fuse**

regain *verb* To get something back, especially after you have lost control, possession, or use of it: *I was hoping that Terry would regain her health in time for the tournament.* **re·gain** (ree-**gayn**) ▷ *verb* **regaining, regained**

regal *adjective* Of or having to do with or suitable for a king or queen, as in *a regal manner.* **re·gal** (**ree**-guhl) ▷ *adverb* **regally**

regale *verb*

1. To give great pleasure, delight, or entertainment: *The old man regaled his grandchildren with stories about his adventures at sea.*

2. To entertain lavishly with a lot of food and drink: *The king regaled his guests with a feast.* **re·gale** (ri-**gale**) ▷ *verb* **regaling, regaled**

regard

1. *verb* To think of someone or something in a particular way or from a particular point of view: *Carl regards racists with contempt.*

2. *noun* A good opinion; esteem: *I have a high regard for volunteer workers.*

3. *verb* To look at closely: *The cats regarded each other with suspicion.*

4. *verb* To respect or show consideration for someone or something: *Melissa regards her sister's privacy even more highly than her own.*

5. *noun* Respect or consideration, as in *no regard for danger.*

6. regards *noun, plural* Good wishes: *Please give your parents my regards.* **re·gard** (ri-**gahrd**) ▷ *verb* **regarding, regarded**

refugees

regarding *preposition* About, in reference to, or concerning: *The teacher wrote a note regarding Maureen's lateness.* **re·gard·ing** (ri-**gahr**-ding)

regardless

1. *adjective* Without considering anyone or anything else; heedless: *Regardless of what happened in class, we are still friends.*

2. *adverb* In spite of everything: *I know the truth might hurt, but I'm going to tell it regardless.* **re·gard·less** (ri-**gahrd**-lis)

regatta *noun* A boat race, or a series of boat races. **re·gat·ta** (ri-**gat**-uh *or* ri-**gah**-tuh)

reggae *noun* A type of popular music with a strong beat that comes from Jamaica in the West Indies. **reg·gae** (**reg**-ay)

Word History

In **reggae** music, the accent is on the offbeat. Reggae started in Jamaica, an island country in the West Indies, in the 1960s. Around this time, a group of people in Jamaica wanted equal rights for all. These people were called Rastafari and included Bob Marley and other musicians who developed reggae. The first spelling of *reggae* was *reggay*, in the 1968 song "Do the Reggay." *Reggay* may be based on the word *rege-rege* in Jamaican English, meaning "clothing that looks like rags." Perhaps people thought that the beat sounded "ragged."

regime *noun* A government that rules a people during a specific period of time: *The new regime plans to focus on fighting crime and improving education.* **re·gime** (ri-**zheem** *or* ray-**zheem**)

regiment *noun* A military unit made up of two or more battalions. **reg·i·ment** (**rej**-uh-muhnt)

region *noun* A general area, or a specific district or territory: *In which region of the country do you live?* **re·gion** (**ree**-juhn) ▷ *adjective* **regional** ▷ *adverb* **regionally**

register

1. *noun* A formal list of names or items, or a book in which official records are kept.

2. *verb* To enter someone or something on an official list: *You must be registered before the first day of classes.*

3. *noun* The range of notes that a human voice or a musical instrument can produce.

4. *verb* To express or to show an emotion: *Ariel's face registered her disappointment.*

5. *noun* A machine that automatically records and counts, as in *a cash register.*

6. *verb* To show on a scale or other device: *His temperature registered 98.6 degrees Fahrenheit on the thermometer.*

reg·is·ter (**rej**-i-stur) ▷ *verb* **registering, registered**

registered nurse *noun* A nurse who has completed certain training and is licensed by the state in which he or she practices.

registration *noun*

1. The process of recording or registering someone or something: *Before I could join the gym, I had to complete the registration.*

2. A certificate stating that someone or something has been registered, as in *a car registration.* **reg·is·tra·tion** (*rej*-i-**stray**-shuhn)

registry *noun*

1. An official list of something, or a department that keeps such a list: *We put our home phone on the do-not-call registry.*

2. A system file on a computer that keeps track of all the hardware and software on it. **reg·is·try** (**rej**-i-stree)

regret *verb* To be sad, sorry, or disappointed about something: *I regretted losing my temper.* **re·gret** (ri-**gret**) ▷ *verb* **regretting, regretted** ▷ *noun* **regret** ▷ *adjective* **regretful** ▷ *adverb* **regretfully**

regrettable *adjective* Causing or deserving regret, as in *a regrettable incident.* **re·gret·ta·ble** (ri-**gret**-uh-buhl) ▷ *adverb* **regrettably**

regular *adjective*

1. Usual or customary: *My regular walking route is down Main Street and through the park.*

2. According to habit or usual behavior, as in *a regular customer.*

3. Always happening at the same time, as in *a regular weekly meeting.*

4. Occurring at normal or healthy intervals, as in *regular breathing.*

5. A **regular** verb is one whose main parts are formed according to a regular pattern. *Love* is a regular verb because its past tense is *loved.* **reg·u·lar** (**reg**-yuh-lur) ▷ *noun* **regularity** (*reg*-yuh-**lar**-i-tee)

regularly *adverb* At short and regular intervals: *All doctors agree that exercising regularly is vital for maintaining good health.* **reg·u·lar·ly** (**reg**-yuh-lur-lee)

regulate *verb*

1. To control or manage according to the rules: *Laws are passed to regulate behavior.*

2. To adjust or to keep at some standard: *A thermostat can be used to regulate the temperature in a room.* **reg·u·late** (**reg**-yuh-*late*) ▷ *verb* **regulating, regulated**

a b c d e f g h i j k l m n o p q **r** s t u v w x y z

regulation *noun*
1. An official rule or order, as in *the regulations of a sport.*
2. The state of being controlled, or the act of controlling or adjusting something, as in *government regulation of the banking industry.* **reg·u·la·tion** (*reg*-yuh-**lay**-shuhn)

regurgitate *verb* To bring food that has been swallowed back up to your mouth: *Baby birds eat food that has been regurgitated by their mothers.* **re·gur·gi·tate** (ri-**gur**-ji-*tate*) ▷ *verb* **regurgitating, regurgitated**

rehearsal *noun* A practice, especially for a performance. **re·hears·al** (ri-**hur**-suhl)

rehearse *verb*
1. To practice in preparation for a public performance: *The cast rehearsed the play.*
2. To review or recount something in order: *He rehearsed his plans for the trip.* **re·hearse** (ri-**hurs**)
▷ *verb* **rehearsing, rehearsed**

reign *verb*
1. To rule a country as a king or queen: *The queen reigned for 50 years.* ▷ *noun* **reign**
2. To be widespread or prevalent: *Peace and harmony reigned throughout the country.* **reign** (rayn)
Reign sounds like **rain** and **rein**.
▷ *verb* **reigning, reigned**

reimburse *verb* To pay back money spent on your behalf, or to be paid back for money that you have spent: *My parents promised to reimburse me for the bus fare home.* **re·im·burse** (*ree*-im-**burs**) ▷ *verb* **reimbursing, reimbursed** ▷ *noun* **reimbursement**

rein *noun*
1. reins *noun, plural* Straps attached to a bridle to control or guide a horse: *Leni took the horse's reins to lead it into the field.*
2. A controlling or restraining force: *The leader of our group kept a tight rein on us.* **rein** (rayn)
Rein sounds like **rain** and **reign**.

reincarnation *noun*
1. Being born on earth again in another body after dying. Reincarnation is part of the beliefs of some religions.
2. Something that is very similar to something from the past: *Fashion writers called the new style a reincarnation of the 1980s.* **re·in·car·na·tion** (*ree*-in-kahr-**nay**-shuhn)

reindeer *noun* A deer that lives in the earth's far north regions. Both male and female reindeer have large, branching antlers. **rein·deer** (**rayn**-*deer*) ▷ *noun, plural* **reindeer**

reinforce *verb* To make something stronger or more effective: *The wall was reinforced by stacks of sandbags.* **re·in·force** (*ree*-in-**fors**) ▷ *verb* **reinforcing, reinforced**

reinforcement *noun*
1. The act of making something stronger or more effective: *This writer's argument is interesting but needs reinforcement.*
2. reinforcements *noun, plural* Extra troops sent to strengthen an army or other fighting force: *Eli was called into service when the army began recruiting reinforcements.* **re·in·force·ment** (*ree*-in-**fors**-muhnt)

reject
1. (ri-**jekt**) *verb* To refuse to accept, consider, or agree to something: *We all tried to help Marcus, but he rejected our offers.* ▷ *verb* **rejecting, rejected**
2. (**ree**-jekt) *noun* Something that has been discarded: *Put the torn clothing over there with the other rejects.* **re·ject**

rejection *noun* An act of rejecting something: *She was surprised by the committee's rejection of her application.* **re·jec·tion** (ri-**jek**-shuhn)

rejoice *verb* To feel great joy or happiness: *We rejoiced at the wonderful news.* **re·joice** (ri-**jois**) ▷ *verb* **rejoicing, rejoiced**

relapse *noun* The act of falling back to a former condition, especially the return of an illness after you were feeling better: *Pat recovered from the flu, but now she's had a relapse.* **re·lapse** (ri-**laps** or **ree**-laps) ▷ *verb* **relapse** (ri-**laps**)

relate *verb*
1. To tell the story or to give an account of something: *The lawyer related how the crime occurred.*
2. To have a relationship or connection: *All the comments at the meeting related to the new schedule.*
3. To understand, to get along with, or to feel sympathy for someone or something: *The Millers really relate well to their kids.*

reindeer

re·late (ri-**late**)
▷ *verb* **relating, related**

related *adjective*

1. Belonging to the same family.

2. Having some connection, as in *related events*.
re·lat·ed (ri-**lay**-tid)

relation *noun*

1. A connection between two or more people or things: *There is a relation between exercise and health.*

2. A relative or member of your family: *I'll need to contact all of my relations about my engagement.*

3. **relations** *noun, plural* The way in which two or more persons, groups, or nations behave toward each other, as in *Japanese-American relations.*
re·la·tion (ri-**lay**-shuhn)

relationship *noun*

1. The way in which people feel about and behave toward each other: *Although they sometimes argue, my parents basically have a good relationship.*

2. The way in which two or more things are connected: *There is a relationship between how much you study and how well you do on a test.*
re·la·tion·ship (ri-**lay**-shuhn-*ship*)

relative

1. *noun* A family member or someone connected to you by marriage: *I only put up with Billy's attitude because he's a relative.*

2. *adjective* Compared with others or to something else: *We were living in relative comfort, but many of the campers were cold and wet.*
rel·a·tive (**rel**-uh-tiv)

relatively *adverb* In comparison with others or to something else; somewhat: *I am relatively old compared to you.* **rel·a·tive·ly** (**rel**-uh-tiv-lee)

relax *verb*

1. To take a rest from work or to do something enjoyable: *My father was finally able to relax on vacation.*

2. To become less tense, anxious, or strained: *Try to relax before taking the test.*

3. To make something less strict or intense, as in *to relax the rules.*
re·lax (ri-**laks**)
▷ *verb* **relaxes, relaxing, relaxed**

relaxation *noun*

1. A state of rest, recreation, or freedom from tension or worry: *Meg is looking forward to some relaxation at the end of the night.*

2. The action of making something looser, more relaxed, or less strict, as in *the relaxation of a rule* or *the relaxation of a muscle.*
re·lax·a·tion (*ree*-lak-**say**-shuhn)

relay

1. *noun* A team race, usually in running or swimming, in which each team member covers a portion of the total distance.

2. *verb* To pass along: *Yoko relayed the news to the others.* ▷ *verb* **relaying, relayed**
re·lay (**ree**-lay)

Word History

French hunters in the Middle Ages would release some dogs in the middle of a hunt so that the dogs who had been running in the chase could rest. The hunters referred to the group of fresh dogs as a *relais.* English speakers adopted the word and spelled it **relay**, and later applied the term to a group of workers who served as replacements for others. Today, a *relay* is a race in which each team member "replaces" the previous one.

release *verb*

1. To set someone or something free: *The boy released the trapped squirrel.*

2. If a CD, DVD, or movie is **released**, it is made available to the public for the first time.
re·lease (ri-**lees**)
▷ *verb* **releasing, released** ▷ *noun* **release**

relegate *verb*

1. To send to a place or position of less importance: *The old clothes were relegated to the garbage heap.*

2. To turn over or assign a task to another person: *I relegated the job of writing the story to the newest reporter on the school paper.*
rel·e·gate (**rel**-uh-*gate*)
▷ *verb* **relegating, relegated**

relent *verb*

1. To become less strict or more forgiving: *My mom was going to punish me, but at the last minute she relented.*

2. To become less intense: *It snowed all day, but by evening the storm had relented.*
re·lent (ri-**lent**)
▷ *verb* **relenting, relented**

Word History

If someone is determined to be strict, but then thinks better of it, we say that the person has *relented.* Some 600 years ago, this would have meant "melted," because the first meaning of the verb **relent** was "to melt." French speakers in England used the verb *relenter* to mean "to melt" or "to be slow." They formed *relenter* from the prefix *re-,* meaning "very," and the word *lent,* meaning "slow." So someone who relents is going slowly and can be said to be "slowing down."

relentless *adjective* Unlikely to stop or grow weaker: *Sheila was relentless in her efforts to catch up with her classmates.* **re·lent·less** (ri-**lent**-lis) ▷ *adverb* **relentlessly**

relevance *noun* The quality of being important or appropriate in relation to something else: *I'm using a search engine to find the topics that have the most relevance for my essay.* **rel·e·vance** (**rel**-uh-vuhns)

relevant *adjective* Concerned with or connected to what is being dealt with or discussed: *Whether the crime was committed before or after midnight is not relevant.* **rel·e·vant** (**rel**-uh-vuhnt)

reliable *adjective* Able to be relied upon or trusted: *Mika is so reliable: She always finds a solution to my problems.* **re·li·a·ble** (ri-**lye**-uh-buhl) ▷ *noun* **reliability** ▷ *adverb* **reliably**

relic *noun*
1. An object, belief, or custom that has survived from the past: *Deacon found a relic from the former tenants in his attic.*
2. An object that belonged to or is associated with a saint or other holy person.
rel·ic (**rel**-ik)

relief *noun*
1. A feeling of release from pain, anxiety, or distress: *It was a relief to find my cat waiting for me by the back door.*
2. Assistance given to people in need, as in *hurricane relief.*
3. Freedom from a job or duty, especially when one person takes over for another: *I'm waiting for relief so I can take a break and call home.*
4. A type of sculpture in which figures or details stand out from the surface: *The building was decorated with animals carved in relief.*
5. relief map A map that uses shading or a model that uses relief to show hills and valleys.
re·lief (ri-**leef**)

relieve *verb*
1. To ease someone's pain, trouble, or difficulty: *The medicine relieved my cough.*
2. To take over someone's post, station, or duty: *More foreign soldiers will be brought in to relieve American troops.*
re·lieve (ri-**leev**)
▷ *verb* **relieving, relieved**

religion *noun*
1. Belief in, devotion to, and worship of a God or gods.

2. A specific system of belief, faith, and worship. Some world religions are Buddhism, Christianity, Hinduism, Islam, and Judaism.
3. A principle, a cause, or a pursuit that is very important to someone: *My grandmother always said that family was her religion.*
re·lig·ion (ri-**lij**-uhn)

religious *adjective*
1. Of or about religion, as in *religious practices* or *a religious festival.*
2. A **religious** person is one who believes in a religion and follows its teachings.
re·li·gious (ri-**lij**-uhs)

relinquish *verb*
1. To give up a right or advantage, or to give up control of something: *He had to relinquish his boxing career when he was drafted into the military.*
2. To release something or let go of it: *The dog growled at me, at first refusing to relinquish its hold on the bone.*
re·lin·quish (ri-**ling**-kwish)
▷ *verb* **relinquishing, relinquished**
▷ *noun* **relinquishment**

relish
1. *verb* To take great pleasure in something: *Wesley relishes sleeping late on weekends.* ▷ *verb* **relishes, relishing, relished** ▷ *noun* **relish**
2. *noun* A mixture of spices and chopped vegetables, such as olives or pickles, used to flavor food.
▷ *noun, plural* **relishes**
rel·ish (**rel**-ish)

relief

reluctant *adjective* Hesitant or unwilling to do something: *I was reluctant to lend him money.* **re·luc·tant** (ri-**luhk**-tuhnt) ▷ *noun* **reluctance** ▷ *adverb* **reluctantly**

rely *verb* To have trust in or to be dependent on someone or something: *I relied on my experience to get me through the ordeal.* **re·ly** (ri-**lye**) ▷ *verb* **relies, relying, relied** ▷ *noun* **reliance** (ri-**lye**-uhns) ▷ *adjective* **reliant** (ri-**lye**-uhnt)

remain *verb*
1. To stay in the same place: *While we rode our bikes, my sister remained at home.*
2. To be left after others have been used up, removed, or destroyed: *Only three bananas remained in the fruit bowl.*
3. To continue being: *We remained loyal fans.*
re·main (ri-**mayn**)

▷ *verb* **remaining, remained**

remainder *noun*

1. The part or amount that is left over: *I'll put the remainder of my allowance into the bank.*

2. The number found when one number is subtracted from another: *If you subtract 5 from 20, the remainder is 15.*

3. The number left over when one number cannot be divided evenly by another: *If you divide 7 by 2, the quotient is 3 with a remainder of 1.* **re·main·der** (ri-**mayn**-dur)

remains *noun, plural*

1. All that is left over: *We threw the remains of our feast in the trash.*

2. Parts of something that was once alive: *The remains of my houseplant are still sticking out of the pot.*

3. A dead body: *Police identified the remains and notified the family.* **re·mains** (ri-**maynz**)

remark *verb*

1. To mention or make a comment about something: *My mother remarked that I looked nice.*

2. To notice or to observe: *I couldn't help but remark her nervousness.* **re·mark** (ri-**mahrk**) ▷ *verb* **remarking, remarked** ▷ *noun* **remark**

remarkable *adjective* Worth noticing; extraordinary: *The computer is a remarkable invention.* **re·mark·a·ble** (ri-**mahr**-kuh-buhl) ▷ *adverb* **remarkably**

remedial *adjective* Intended to help or correct something, as in *a remedial reading program.* **re·me·di·al** (ri-**mee**-dee-uhl)

remedy *noun* Something that relieves pain, cures a disease, or corrects a disorder: *Will there ever be a remedy for the common cold?* **rem·e·dy** (**rem**-i-dee) ▷ *noun, plural* **remedies** ▷ *verb* **remedy**

remember *verb*

1. To recall or to bring back to mind: *I'll always remember our family gatherings. Try to remember where you left your bag.*

2. To keep in mind carefully: *Please remember that you have a test tomorrow.* **re·mem·ber** (ri-**mem**-bur) ▷ *verb* **remembering, remembered**

remind *verb* To cause someone to remember something: *Please remind me to get up an hour earlier tomorrow.* **re·mind** (ri-**minde**) ▷ *verb* **reminding, reminded**

remote-controlled car

reminder *noun* Something that helps a person remember: *Elise left me a reminder to get the laundry from the cleaners.* **re·mind·er** (ri-**mine**-dur)

reminisce *verb* To think or talk about past events or experiences: *The couple reminisced about their first date.* **rem·i·nisce** (*rem*-uh-**nis**) ▷ *verb* **reminiscing, reminisced** ▷ *noun* **reminiscence**

remission *noun* If the symptoms of a disease start to disappear or become less severe, the disease is in **remission**. **re·mis·sion** (ri-**mish**-uhn)

remnant *noun* A small piece or amount of something that is left over, especially a piece of cloth: *My mother made matching pillows from the remnants of the quilt.* **rem·nant** (**rem**-nuhnt)

remodel *verb* To make a major change to the structure or design of something: *The owners remodeled their restaurant so that it would seat more people.* **re·mod·el** (ree-**mah**-duhl) ▷ *verb* **remodeling, remodeled**

remorse *noun* A strong feeling of guilt or distress over something wrong that you have done in the past: *The criminal felt no remorse for his horrible crime.* **re·morse** (ri-**mors**) ▷ *adjective* **remorseful** ▷ *adverb* **remorsefully**

remote

1. *adjective* Far away in time or space; secluded or isolated, as in *a remote island.*

2. *adjective* Aloof and unfriendly: *She is remote and prefers to keep her distance from other people.*

3. *adjective* Extremely small or slight, as in *a remote possibility.*

4. *noun* Short for **remote control**. **re·mote** (ri-**moht**) ▷ *noun* **remoteness** ▷ *adverb* **remotely**

Word History

A remote control can change a television channel from a distance, and the word **remote** means "far away." This adjective goes back to the Latin verb *movere*, meaning "to move." We also get our verb *move* from this same source. Latin speakers added the prefix *re-* to *movere*, creating *removere*, meaning "to move away." The past participle was *remotus*. Therefore, something that is *remote* has been "removed" or "moved away."

remote control *noun* A system or device for operating machines from a distance by means of radio signals or a beam of light. ▷ *adjective* **remote-controlled**

removable *adjective* Able to be easily removed, as in *a removable hard drive.* **re·mov·a·ble** (ri-**moo**-vuh-buhl)

removal *noun* The process or activity of taking something off or away: *The city spends a lot of money on snow removal.* **re·mov·al** (ri-**moo**-vuhl)

remove *verb*
1. To take something away from a place or position: *They removed the boxes from the garage.*
2. To take off: *Please remove your shoes before you enter the restaurant.*
re·move (ri-**moov**)
▷ *verb* **removing, removed**

Renaissance *noun* The revival of art and learning, inspired by the ancient Greeks and Romans, that took place in Europe between the 14th and 16th centuries. The Renaissance marked the transition from medieval to modern times. **Re·nais·sance** (**ren**-uh-*sahns*)

render *verb*
1. To make or cause to become: *She was rendered helpless by an injury to her spinal cord.*
2. To give or to deliver: *The jury rendered a guilty verdict.*
ren·der (**ren**-dur)
▷ *verb* **rendering, rendered**

rendezvous *noun*
1. An appointment to meet at a certain time or place.
2. The place chosen for a meeting: *The restaurant is a famous rendezvous for young couples.*
ren·dez·vous (**rahn**-duh-*voo* or **rahn**-day-*voo*)
▷ *verb* **rendezvous**

renew *verb*
1. To make something that is broken or worn look new again; to restore: *I renewed the finish on the table.*
2. To start something again after a break or interruption; to resume: *We renewed our efforts to complete the puzzle after dinner.*
3. To extend the period of a library loan, license, subscription, contract, or club membership, as in *to renew your gym membership.*
re·new (ri-**noo**)
▷ *verb* **renewing, renewed** ▷ *noun* **renewal** (ri-**noo**-uhl) ▷ *adjective* **renewable** ▷ *adjective* **renewed**

renewable energy *noun* Power from sources that can never be used up, such as wind, tides, sunlight, and geothermal heat.

renovate *verb* To modernize or restore something to good condition by cleaning, repairing, or remodeling, as in *to renovate an old house.* **ren·o·vate** (**ren**-uh-*vate*)
▷ *verb* **renovating, renovated** ▷ *noun* **renovation**

renovate

renowned *adjective* Famous and widely acclaimed: *Edgar Allan Poe is renowned for his scary stories.*
re·nowned (ri-**nound**) ▷ *noun* **renown**

rent
1. *noun* Money paid by a tenant to the owner of a building or other property in return for living in it or using it: *My older brother has just found an apartment and will start paying rent on it next week.*
2. *verb* To get or give the right to use something in return for payment: *Jack rented a car for his trip.*
▷ *verb* **renting, rented**
rent (rent)

rental *noun*
1. The amount paid to rent something: *The rental on our vacation cottage is quite low.*
2. Something that is hired or rented, such as a car or property: *My parents don't want to buy a house; they're looking for a rental.*
rent·al (**ren**-tuhl)
▷ *adjective* **rental**

repair *verb* To restore something that has been damaged or broken to good working condition; to fix: *The man repaired the watch.* **re·pair** (ri-**pair**)
▷ *verb* **repairing, repaired** ▷ *noun* **repair**

repatriation *noun* The return of someone to the country where he or she was born or where he or she is a citizen, as in *the repatriation of the prisoners of war.* **re·pa·tri·a·tion** (ree-*pay*-tree-**ay**-shuhn)
▷ *verb* **repatriate**

repay *verb*
1. To pay someone back: *I knew I would have to repay my father for the loan.*
2. To give or do something in return: *How can I repay you for your kindness?*
re·pay (ree-**pay**)

▷ *verb* **repaying, repaid** ▷ *noun* **repayment**

repeal *verb* To cancel or do away with something officially, such as a law: *The president will repeal the tax cuts.* **re·peal** (ri-**peel**) ▷ *verb* **repealing, repealed** ▷ *noun* **repeal**

repeat *verb* To say or do something again or more than once: *Jane repeated the message. I'll never repeat that mistake.* **re·peat** (ri-**peet**) ▷ *verb* **repeating, repeated** ▷ *noun* **repeat** (ri-**peet** *or* **ree**-peet)

repeatedly *adverb* More than once or at frequent intervals: *Todd's mother warned him repeatedly never to go out canoeing without his life jacket.* **re·peat·ed·ly** (ri-**pee**-tid-lee)

repel *verb*
1. To drive back or keep away: *This spray is supposed to repel insects.*
2. To cause disgust or horror: *His violence repelled me.*
re·pel (ri-**pel**)
▷ *verb* **repelling, repelled**

repellent
1. *noun* A chemical that wards off insects and other pests, as in *a mosquito repellent.*
2. *adjective* Repulsive or disgusting, as in *a repellent odor.*
re·pel·lent (ri-**pel**-uhnt)

repent *verb* To feel or to express regret for something that you have done: *She repented her terrible behavior.* **re·pent** (ri-**pent**) ▷ *verb* **repenting, repented** ▷ *noun* **repentance** ▷ *adjective* **repentant**

repertoire *noun* A collection of songs, jokes, plays, stories, or musical compositions that an individual or a company knows well and is prepared to perform in public. **rep·er·toire** (**rep**-ur-*twahr*)

repetition *noun* The act of repeating something: *Young children learn the alphabet by repetition.* **rep·e·ti·tion** (*rep*-i-**tish**-uhn) ▷ *adjective* **repetitive** (ri-**pet**-i-tiv)

replace *verb*
1. To take the place of or to substitute for someone or something: *Computers have replaced typewriters.*
2. To put something back in its former place or position: *I replaced the playing card in the deck.*
3. To put something new in the place of something that is worn or damaged: *We replaced the old tires.*
re·place (ri-**plase**)
▷ *verb* **replacing, replaced**

replacement *noun*
1. The activity or process of replacing someone or something: *The replacement of the damaged floor tiles will take about a week.*
2. Someone or something that takes the place of another: *They finally hired a replacement for the janitor who is retiring.*
re·place·ment (ri-**plase**-muhnt)

replay
1. (ree-**play**) *verb* To play a recording again: *Nora asked me to replay the Beastie Boys album.*
2. (**ree**-*play*) *noun* The playing of a recording.
3. (ree-**play**) *verb* To play a second contest or match between two teams or players because the first one ended in a tie: *Our team will replay the championship game on Friday.* ▷ *noun* **replay** (**ree**-*play*)
re·play
▷ *verb* **replaying, replayed**

replenish *verb* To provide or get more of something that has been partially used up: *Grandma will need to replenish her baking supplies when we finish making all these cookies.* **re·plen·ish** (ri-**plen**-ish) ▷ *verb* **replenishing, replenished**

replica *noun* An exact copy of something, especially a copy made on a smaller scale than the original, as in *a replica of an old sailing ship.* **rep·li·ca** (**rep**-li-kuh) ▷ *verb* **replicate** (**rep**-li-*kate*)

reply *verb* To answer or respond in speech or in writing: *Brad replied to the letter he had received.* **re·ply** (ri-**plye**) ▷ *verb* **replies, replying, replied** ▷ *noun* **reply**

report
1. *noun* A detailed written or spoken account of an event: *He gave me a thorough report of the meeting.*
2. *verb* To give a report or to make known: *Cynthia reported the fire to the fire department.*
3. *verb* To make a formal charge or complaint about someone.
4. *verb* To present yourself as ready to do something: *You'll have to report for work at nine every morning.*
5. *verb* If you **report to** someone, you work for him or her.
re·port (ri-**port**)
▷ *verb* **reporting, reported**

report card *noun* A listing of a student's grades that is compiled and sent home several times a year. A report card can also include comments from a teacher about a student's behavior.

replica

a
b
c
d
e
f
g
h
i
j
k
l
m
n
o
p
q
r
s
t
u
v
w
x
y
z

reporter *noun* Someone who gathers and reports the news for radio or television, or for a newspaper, magazine, or website, as in *a sports reporter.*
re·port·er (ri-**por**-tur)

represent *verb*
1. To speak or act for someone else: *My lawyer represented me.*
2. To be a sign or symbol of something: *The flag on the front of their house represents their support for the troops.*
rep·re·sent (*rep*-ri-**zent**)
▷ *verb* **representing, represented**

representation *noun*
1. An image or model that stands for something: *The painting was a beautiful representation of winter.*
2. The act of representing or being represented: *Each county received equal representation in the state senate.*
rep·re·sen·ta·tion
(*rep*-ri-zen-**tay**-shuhn)
▷ *adjective* **representational**

representative *noun*
1. Someone who is chosen to speak or act for others: *I wrote to my representative in Congress.*
2. A person or thing that is typical of a class or group: *This church is a good representative of Gothic architecture.*
rep·re·sen·ta·tive (*rep*-ri-**zen**-tuh-tiv)
▷ *adjective* **representative**

repress *verb*
1. If you **repress** an emotion, you try not to let it show.
2. To use force to keep someone or something under very strict control: *The dictator was able to repress the rebellion, but not for long.*
re·press (ri-**pres**)
▷ *verb* **represses, repressing, repressed** ▷ *noun* **repression** ▷ *adjective* **repressed** ▷ *adjective* **repressive**

reprieve *verb* To cancel or delay a punishment: *The prisoner was reprieved by the governor minutes before he was scheduled to be executed.* **re·prieve** (ri-**preev**)
▷ *verb* **reprieving, reprieved** ▷ *noun* **reprieve**

reprimand *verb* To criticize someone sharply or formally: *The teacher reprimanded the student.*
rep·ri·mand (**rep**-ruh-*mand*) ▷ *verb* **reprimanding, reprimanded** ▷ *noun* **reprimand**

reprisal *noun* An act of revenge or retaliation: *Fear of reprisal kept her from complaining about her boss.* **re·pri·sal** (ri-**prye**-zuhl)

reprimand

reproach *verb* To show that you disapprove of or are disappointed by what someone has done or said; to blame: *My mother reproached me for being late.* **re·proach** (ri-**prohch**) ▷ *verb* **reproaches, reproaching, reproached** ▷ *noun* **reproach**

reproduce *verb*
1. To make an image or copy of something: *This machine reproduces color photographs.*
2. To produce offspring or individuals of the same kind.
re·pro·duce (*ree*-pruh-**doos**)
▷ *verb* **reproducing, reproduced**

reproduction *noun*
1. An image or copy of something, such as a work of art: *I bought a reproduction of the painting at the museum shop.*
2. The act of producing offspring or individuals of the same kind.
re·pro·duc·tion
(*ree*-pruh-**duhk**-shuhn)

reptile *noun* A cold-blooded animal that crawls across the ground or creeps on short legs. Most reptiles have backbones and reproduce by laying eggs. **rep·tile** (**rep**-tile *or* **rep**-tuhl)
▷ *adjective* **reptilian** (rep-**til**-ee-uhn *or* rep-**til**-yuhn)

republic *noun*
1. A form of government in which the people have the power to elect representatives who manage the government. Republics often have presidents.
2. A country that has such a form of government. The United States is a republic.
re·pub·lic (ri-**puhb**-lik)

republican *adjective* Of or having to do with, typical of, or supporting a republic, as in *a republican government.* **re·pub·li·can** (ri-**puhb**-li-kuhn)

Republican Party *noun* One of the two main political parties in the United States. The other is the Democratic Party.

repugnant *adjective* Disgusting or offensive: *Miranda found cleaning the stable repugnant.* **re·pug·nant** (ri-**puhg**-nuhnt)

repulse *verb*
1. To drive back by using force: *Our army repulsed the enemy's attack.*
2. To refuse or reject something, as in *to repulse an offer.*
re·pulse (ri-**puhls**)
▷ *verb* **repulsing, repulsed**

repulsive *adjective* Very distasteful or disgusting: *This medicine smells repulsive.* **re·pul·sive** (ri-**puhl**-siv) ▷ *noun* **repulsion** ▷ *adverb* **repulsively**

reputable *adjective* Honorable and trustworthy; having a good reputation, as in *a reputable dealer.* **rep·u·ta·ble** (**rep**-yuh-tuh-buhl) ▷ *adverb* **reputably**

reputation *noun* Your worth or character, as judged by other people: *Mark has a reputation for honesty.* **rep·u·ta·tion** (*rep*-yuh-**tay**-shuhn)

repute *noun* The state of being highly esteemed; fame, as in *a poet of great repute.* **re·pute** (ri-**pyoot**)

reputed *adjective* Generally supposed or believed to be, as in *the reputed mobster.* **re·put·ed** (ri-**pyoo**-tid) ▷ *adverb* **reputedly**

request
1. *verb* To ask politely or formally for something, as in *to request a reservation.* ▷ *verb* **requesting, requested**
2. *noun* Something that you ask for politely or formally: *The band played our request.* **re·quest** (ri-**kwest**)

requiem *noun*
1. A church service, especially in the Roman Catholic Church, for the souls of the dead or for someone who has died.
2. A piece of music composed in memory of someone who has died, often a musical setting of the Mass for the dead. **re·qui·em** (**rek**-wee-uhm)

require *verb*
1. To need something: *All animals require food to survive.*
2. If you are **required** to do something, you are told or expected to do it: *I am required to pass a reading exam in French.* **re·quire** (ri-**kwire**) ▷ *verb* **requiring, required**

required *adjective* Necessary: *She sent the required documents by courier.* **re·quired** (ri-**kwired**)

requirement *noun* Something that you need to do or are required to have: *It is a requirement for graduation that you have at least two years of foreign language study.* **re·quire·ment** (ri-**kwire**-muhnt)

reread *verb* To read a passage or piece of writing again: *I love that book so much, I reread it every Christmas.* **re·read** (ree-**reed**) ▷ *verb* **rereading, reread** (ree-**red**)

Reptiles

Reptiles are most common in warm climates, but they also live in temperate areas. They are cold-blooded vertebrates with scaly, dry skin, and they use lungs to breathe. Reptiles originated more than 300 million years ago. Dinosaurs were reptiles that became extinct. Today, there are more than 8,000 species of reptiles.

lizard

turtle

chameleon

tortoise

snake

crocodile

rerun

1. (ree-**ruhn**) *verb* To run again: *After a tie was declared, we had to rerun the race.* ▷ **rerunning, reran**

2. (**ree**-*ruhn*) *noun* A television program that has been shown before.
re·run

rescind *verb* To officially cancel or end something such as an order, an offer, or a policy: *The college rescinded the scholarship offer because his grades had fallen so low in his final term.* **re·scind** (ri-**sind**) ▷ *verb* **rescinding, rescinded** ▷ *noun* **rescindment**

rescue *verb* To save someone who is in danger or in a difficult situation: *The lifeguard rescued the drowning swimmer.* **res·cue** (**res**-kyoo) ▷ *verb* **rescuing, rescued** ▷ *noun* **rescue** ▷ *noun* **rescuer**

Word History

We don't really think of rescuing as a rough, violent action, but the history of the word **rescue** involves the use of force. If you were *rescuing* someone in the 14th century, you were setting them free after their capture by enemies. The Latin verb *quatere* meant "to shake," and two prefixes were added to the beginning: *re-*, meaning "again," and *ex-*, meaning "out." So the meaning of *rescue* became "to shake out again," as though people were shaking an object to try to get something out of it.

research

1. *verb* To collect information about a subject through reading, investigating, or experimenting: *Ariel researched the Civil War for her project.* ▷ *verb* **researches, researching, researched**

2. *noun* A study or investigation in a particular field, usually to learn new facts or to solve a problem, as in *medical research.*
re·search (ri-**surch** or **ree**-*surch*)
▷ *noun* **researcher**

resemble *verb* To look like or be similar to something or someone: *Doesn't Anne resemble a poodle with that new hairdo of hers?* **re·sem·ble** (ri-**zem**-buhl) ▷ *verb* **resembling, resembled** ▷ *noun* **resemblance** (ri-**zem**-bluhns)

resent *verb* To feel anger or annoyance toward someone or about something: *I resent that you always interfere in my private affairs.* **re·sent** (ri-**zent**) ▷ *verb* **resenting, resented** ▷ *noun* **resentment** ▷ *adjective* **resentful**

reservation

1. *noun* An arrangement to save space or a seat for someone: *He showed up at the airport without a reservation.*

2. *noun* An area of land set aside by the government for a special purpose, as in *a tribal reservation.*

3. reservations *noun, plural* Doubts or fears about something: *I have reservations about rock climbing.*
res·er·va·tion (*rez*-ur-**vay**-shuhn)

reserve

1. *verb* To arrange for something to be kept for later or future use: *Would you reserve a seat for me when you get to the theater?*

2. *verb* To save for a special purpose or later use: *Let's reserve our strength for the trip home.*

3. *verb* To keep for oneself: *The defendant reserves the right to remain silent.*

4. *noun* A protected place where hunting is not allowed and where animals can live and breed safely, as in *a forest reserve.*

5. reserves *noun, plural* The part of the armed forces that is kept ready to serve in an emergency.
re·serve (ri-**zurv**)
▷ *verb* **reserving, reserved**

reserved *adjective*

1. Kept for someone to use later: *All of the restaurant's tables are reserved for tonight.*

2. A **reserved** person is reluctant to reveal his or her feelings or opinions: *Jonathan is quiet and reserved.*
re·served (ri-**zurvd**)

reservoir *noun* A natural or artificial lake in which water is collected and stored for use. **res·er·voir** (**rez**-ur-*vwahr*)

reset

1. (ree-**set**) *verb* To make a machine, program, or device start again from the beginning: *Reset the modem by turning it off and then on again.*

2. (ree-*set*) *verb* To change something from the setting it had before, as in *to reset a password.*

3. (ree-*set*) **reset button** *noun* A button that you push to reset a device or machine.
re·set
▷ *verb* **resetting, reset**

reside *verb* To live in a place: *Many young families reside in this part of town.* **re·side** (ri-**zide**) ▷ *verb* **residing, resided**

residence *noun* The place where someone lives; a home, as in *the Smith residence.* **res·i·dence** (**rez**-i-duhns) ▷ *noun* **residency**

resident *noun* Someone who lives in a particular place on a long-term basis, as in *the residents of a community.* **res·i·dent** (**rez**-i-duhnt)

residential *adjective* Of or having to do with a neighborhood or an area where people live, as in *a residential section of the city.* **res·i·den·tial** (rez-i-**den**-shuhl)

resort

residue *noun*

1. What is left after something burns up or evaporates: *The spilled soda left a sticky residue on the counter.*

2. Anything that remains after the main part has been taken away: *Katrina's art project left a residue of glitter on the kitchen floor.*
res·i·due (**rez**-i-*doo*)
▷ *adjective* **residual** (ri-**zij**-oo-uhl)

resign *verb*

1. To give up a job, a position, or an office voluntarily: *The coach resigned so that he could spend more time with his family.*

2. If you **resign yourself** to something, you accept it because you realize it cannot be avoided.
re·sign (ri-**zine**)
▷ *verb* **resigning, resigned** ▷ *adjective* **resigned**

resignation *noun*

1. The act of giving up a job or position: *The principal's resignation was a shock to everybody at school.*

2. A letter formally stating your intention to give up a job or position: *I handed in my resignation as soon as my boss returned from vacation.*

3. The acceptance of something undesirable that can't be avoided: *You could see the resignation in Alison's face as she watched her team lose.*
res·ig·na·tion (*rez*-ig-**nay**-shuhn)

resin *noun*
A yellow or brown, sticky substance that oozes from pine, balsam, and other trees and plants. Resin is used to make varnishes, lacquers, plastics, glue, and rubber. **res·in** (**rez**-in)

resist *verb*

1. To refuse to accept; to oppose: *Javier resisted his mother's attempts to make him clean his room.*

2. To fight back or to struggle against someone or something: *The townspeople resisted the idea of adding more parking lots.*

3. To stop yourself from having or doing something you want, as in *to resist temptation.*
re·sist (ri-**zist**)
▷ *verb* **resisting, resisted**

resistance *noun*

1. The act of resisting or fighting back: *Halfway through the argument, it became clear that resistance was useless.*

2. The ability to fight off or overcome something: *He developed a sore throat because his resistance was low.*

3. A force that opposes the motion of an object, as in *air resistance.*

4. The ability of a substance or a device to resist the passage of an electrical current.
re·sis·tance (ri-**zis**-tuhns)

resistant *adjective*
Able to withstand or fight off something: *The bacteria have become resistant to this antibiotic.* **re·sis·tant** (ri-**zis**-tuhnt)

resolute *adjective*
Strongly determined to do something: *Casey is resolute in his decision to go to law school.* **res·o·lute** (**rez**-uh-*loot*) ▷ *adverb* **resolutely**

resolution *noun*

1. A promise that you make to yourself, particularly at the start of a new year.

2. The state of being very determined: *She approached the difficult task with great resolution.*

3. A measure of the quality of an image, often measured in dots per inch.
res·o·lu·tion (*rez*-uh-**loo**-shuhn)

resolve *verb*

1. To make a firm decision about something: *Sue resolved to stop fighting with her mother.* ▷ *noun* **resolve**

2. To find a solution to a problem or to settle a difficulty: *We resolved the issue of how we would get home by calling a taxi.*
re·solve (ri-**zahlv**)
▷ *verb* **resolving, resolved**

resonant *adjective*

1. Having a full, deep sound: *The opera singer's voice is rich and resonant.*

2. Able to amplify sounds or make them last longer: *Guitars are made of resonant wood.*
res·o·nant (**rez**-uh-nuhnt)
▷ *noun* **resonance** ▷ *verb* **resonate** (**rez**-uh-*nayt*)

resort

1. *noun* A place where people go for rest and recreation, as in *a ski resort.*

2. *verb* If you **resort to** something, you do it because you have no other way of resolving a difficult situation: *When the child's pleas didn't work, he resorted to tears.* ▷ *verb* **resorting, resorted**

3. *noun* If you do something as **a last resort**, you do it because everything else you have tried has failed.
re·sort (ri-**zort**)

resound *verb*
1. To be filled with sound: *The theater resounded with cheers when the actors took their bows.*
2. To make a long, loud, echoing sound: *The chorus of voices resounded through the auditorium.*
re·sound (ri-**zound**)
▷ *verb* **resounding, resounded**

resource *noun*
1. Something that is of value or use, as in *natural resources.*
2. Something that you can go to for help or support: *The library is a good resource for anyone doing a research report.*
re·source (**ree**-sors *or* **ree**-zors)

resourceful *adjective* If you are **resourceful**, you are good at knowing what to do or where to get help in any situation. **re·source·ful** (ri-**sors**-fuhl *or* ri-**zors**-fuhl)

respect
1. *verb* To feel admiration and esteem for someone or something: *In our family, children are taught to respect their elders.* ▷ *verb* **respecting, respected**
2. *noun* A feeling of admiration or high regard for someone or something: *I felt great respect for Angie after reading her poetry.*
3. *noun* A particular feature or detail of something: *In many respects, your plan is the best one.*
4. respects *noun, plural* Regards or greetings: *Please give my respects to your parents.*
re·spect (ri-**spekt**)

respectable *adjective*
1. Behaving honestly and decently.
2. Acceptable or reasonably good: *Brian got a respectable grade on the test.*
re·spect·a·ble (ri-**spek**-tuh-buhl)
▷ *adverb* **respectably**

respectful *adjective* Showing proper respect, consideration, or courtesy: *I am respectful of my elders.* **re·spect·ful** (ri-**spekt**-fuhl) ▷ *adverb* **respectfully**

respective *adjective* Belonging to or having to do with each one: *After getting off the school bus, they went to their respective homes.* **re·spec·tive** (ri-**spek**-tiv)
▷ *adverb* **respectively**

respiration *noun* The act or process of breathing in and breathing out. **res·pi·ra·tion** (res-puh-**ray**-shuhn)
▷ *adjective* **respiratory** (**res**-pur-uh-*tor*-ee)

respond *verb*
1. To reply or to give an answer: *Please respond to the invitation in writing.*
2. To react to someone or something: *Try not to respond if they make fun of you.*
re·spond (ri-**spahnd**)
▷ *verb* **responding, responded**

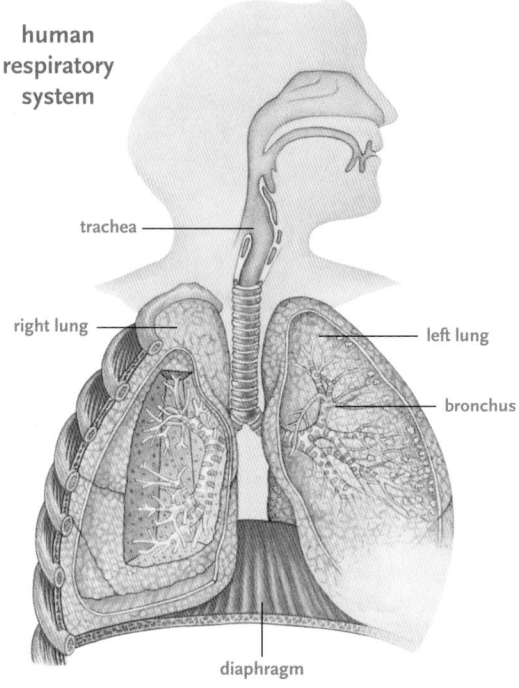

human respiratory system

trachea

right lung

left lung

bronchus

diaphragm

response *noun* A spoken or written reply; a reaction: *She left the room without waiting for a response.* **re·sponse** (ri-**spahns**)

responsibility *noun*
1. A duty or a job: *It's Billy's responsibility to make sure that everyone wears a life jacket.*
2. If you **take responsibility** for something that has happened, you agree that it is your burden or that you should take the blame for it.
re·spon·si·bil·i·ty (ri-*spahn*-suh-**bil**-i-tee)
▷ *noun, plural* **responsibilities**

responsible *adjective*
1. If someone is **responsible** for something, it is their duty to do it: *I am responsible for printing the programs for the concert.*
2. If a person is **responsible**, he or she can be trusted: *Greta is very responsible and makes a good babysitter.*
3. Being the cause: *Drunk driving is responsible for many accidents.*
4. Having or involving important duties, as in *a responsible job.*
re·spon·si·ble (ri-**spahn**-suh-buhl)
▷ *adverb* **responsibly**

rest
1. *verb* To stop doing something in order to relax or sleep: *We rested after lunch.*
2. *noun* A stopping of work or some activity: *I need a rest before I go back to studying.*

3. *noun* Sleep: *I need eight hours of rest at night.*

4. *noun* The others, or those that remain: *She wore her new earrings every day and left the rest in her jewelry box.*

5. *verb* To lean against something: *You can rest your bicycle against the stone wall.*

6. *verb* To sit, lie, or be supported in a specific position: *The small boat rested in the shallow water near the beach.*

7. *noun* The state or fact of not moving: *The horses slowed gradually and came to a rest.*

8. *noun* A pause or period of silence in a piece of music.

9. *verb* To finish presenting evidence in a court of law: *The prosecution rests.*

rest (rest)

Rest sounds like **wrest**. ▷ *verb* **resting, rested**

restaurant *noun* A place where meals can be purchased and eaten, as in *a Japanese restaurant.*
res·tau·rant (**res**-tur-uhnt *or* **res**-tuh-*rahnt*)

restless *adjective* Unable to relax or be still because of anxiety or boredom: *Carina gets restless if she has to stay indoors.* **rest·less** (**rest**-lis) ▷ *adverb* **restlessly**

restoration *noun*

1. The return of something to its former condition, place, or owner: *After being occupied for 20 years, the country is celebrating the restoration of its independence.*

2. The renovation or repair of a building or a work of art: *Colin is working for a company that specializes in the restoration of historic houses.*
res·to·ra·tion (*res*-tuh-**ray**-shuhn)

restore *verb*

1. To bring back or to establish again: *The judge tried to restore order in the court after the spectators cheered the verdict.*

2. To bring back to an original condition: *Catherine restored the old table.* ▷ *noun* **restorer**

3. To give something back or to put someone back in a former position: *The king was restored to the throne.*
re·store (ri-**stor**)
▷ *verb* **restoring, restored**

restrain *verb*

1. To prevent someone from doing what he or she wants to do: *We managed to restrain Jon from eating too much.*

2. To hold back or keep under control: *Please restrain your temper.*
re·strain (ri-**strayn**)
▷ *verb* **restraining, restrained**

restrained *adjective* Very reserved and unemotional: *Jay seems restrained, but he's really passionate about*

animals. **re·strained** (ri-**straynd**)

restraint *noun*

1. The act of limiting or controlling something: *I was tempted to buy another CD but exercised restraint.*

2. A force, device, or influence that limits or controls: *Because of the recession, the city is facing budgetary restraints.*
re·straint (ri-**straynt**)

restrict *verb* To confine or keep within limits: *The dog was restricted to a small, fenced-in yard.*
re·strict (ri-**strikt**) ▷ *verb* **restricting, restricted**
▷ *adjective* **restricted** ▷ *adjective* **restrictive**

restriction *noun*

1. The act of keeping or confining someone or something within limits: *The movie has no age restriction and is suitable for all viewers.*

2. A rule, measure, or condition that limits or controls: *To maintain discipline, the army puts a lot of restrictions on its soldiers.*
re·stric·tion (ri-**strik**-shuhn)

restroom *noun* A bathroom, especially in a public building. **rest·room** (**rest**-*room*)

result

1. *noun* Something that is produced or caused by something else: *I worked hard on this project, and I'm happy with the result.*

2. *verb* To be caused by or to happen because of something else: *His carelessness resulted in an accident.* ▷ *verb* **resulting, resulted**
re·sult (ri-**zuhlt**)

resume *verb* To start doing or to return to something after an interruption: *We resumed our studies after Christmas break.* **re·sume** (ri-**zoom**)
▷ *verb* **resuming, resumed**

résumé *or* **resume** *noun* A brief list or summary of a person's education, jobs, and achievements: *The company wants me to send a résumé along with my job application.* **ré·su·mé** (**rez**-uh-*may*)

resuscitate *verb* To make conscious again, or to bring back from a near-death condition: *The doctor resuscitated the accident victim.* **re·sus·ci·tate** (ri-**suhs**-i-*tate*) ▷ *verb* **resuscitating, resuscitated**
▷ *noun* **resuscitation** (ri-*suhs*-i-**tay**-shuhn)

retail

1. *adjective* Of or having to do with the sale of goods directly to customers, as in *a retail store.*
▷ *noun* **retail** ▷ *verb* **retail**

2. *noun* The **retail price** of something is the price at which it is sold in stores: *The suggested retail price is $14.95.*
re·tail (**ree**-tayl)

retailer *noun* Someone who sells goods to the public, usually in a store. **re·tail·er** (**ree**-tay-lur)

retain *verb*
1. To continue to have or to keep something: *Please retain your ticket if you want to leave the arena.*
2. To hold in or to contain: *Sponges retain water.* ▷ *noun* **retention** (ri-**ten**-shuhn)
3. If you **retain** a lawyer, you pay him or her a fee to represent you.
re·tain (ri-**tayn**)
▷ *verb* **retaining, retained**

retaliate *verb* To get revenge or to respond to an injury or attack with similar behavior: *Gerald retaliated when Les punched him.* **re·tal·i·ate** (ri-**tal**-ee-ate) ▷ *verb* **retaliating, retaliated** ▷ *noun* **retaliation** ▷ *adjective* **retaliatory**

retard *verb* To slow down or to hold back: *Lack of sunlight retarded the growth of our tomato plants.*
re·tard (ri-**tahrd**) ▷ *verb* **retarding, retarded**

retarded *adjective* Slow or limited in mental or emotional development. Many people find this word offensive and use the words *challenged* or *disabled* instead. **re·tard·ed** (ri-**tahr**-did) ▷ *noun* **retardation** (*ree*-tahr-**day**-shuhn)

retch *verb* To try to vomit or to start vomiting.
retch (rech) ▷ *verb* **retches, retching, retched** ▷ *noun* **retch**

reticent *adjective* Reluctant to tell people what you know, think, or feel: *I was too reticent to join the conversation when I first met Zuza and Carmen.*
ret·i·cent (**ret**-i-suhnt) ▷ *noun* **reticence**

retina *noun* The lining at the back of the eyeball. The retina is sensitive to light and sends images of the things you see to your brain. **ret·i·na** (**ret**-uh-nuh)

retire *verb*
1. To stop working, usually because you have reached a certain age: *My grandfather retired when he was 67.* ▷ *adjective* **retired**
2. To go to bed: *We retired at 10 p.m.*
3. To go to a quieter or more private place: *We retired to the living room.*
4. To put out in baseball: *The pitcher retired the batter, and the game was over.*
re·tire (ri-**tire**)
▷ *verb* **retiring, retired**

retirement *noun* The period in your life after you've stopped working: *Many people retire at 65, but my grandfather wants to delay his retirement until he is 70.* **re·tire·ment** (ri-**tire**-muhnt)

retiring *adjective* Shy and reserved; preferring to spend time alone rather than with other people: *Chris has a retiring personality, but that doesn't keep him from making friends.* **re·tir·ing** (re-**tire**-ing)

retort
1. (ri-**tort**) *verb* To respond in a quick, sharp, or witty manner: *When teased about my height, I always retort that tall people can see farther.* ▷ **retorting, retorted** ▷ *noun* **retort**
2. (ri-**tort** *or* ree-tort) *noun* A long-necked glass container used in laboratories.
re·tort

retrace *verb* To go back over the same route or path that you have just taken: *I retraced my steps to look for the lost button.* **re·trace** (ri-**trays**) ▷ *verb* **retracing, retraced**

retreat
1. *verb* To withdraw from an attack or move away from a difficult situation: *The enemy retreated into the woods.* ▷ *verb* **retreating, retreated** ▷ *noun* **retreat**
2. *noun* A quiet place where you can go to relax, to think, or to be alone; a refuge, as in *a yoga retreat.*
re·treat (ri-**treet**)

retrieve *verb*
1. To get or bring something back; to regain: *Felicia was able to retrieve her dog from the pound.*
2. To locate information in storage, especially by using a computer: *Erin asked me to retrieve the files on last summer's architectural projects.*
re·trieve (ri-**treev**)

golden retriever

▷ *verb* **retrieving, retrieved** ▷ *noun* **retrieval**

retriever *noun* Any of several popular breeds of large dogs. Retrievers can be trained to find and bring back game shot by hunters. **re·triev·er** (ri-**tree**-vur)

retrorocket *noun* A small rocket that slows down or turns a spacecraft. **re·tro·rock·et** (**ret**-roh-*rah*-kit)

retrovirus *noun* Any of a group of viruses that contain RNA instead of the usual DNA. When retroviruses enter the cells of their hosts, they make copies of themselves and attach themselves permanently to the chromosomes of the cells that they attack. **ret·ro·vi·rus** (**ret**-roh-*vye*-ruhs) ▷ *noun, plural* **retroviruses**

return
1. *verb* To come back or to go back: *My dog waits patiently for me to return from school.*

family reunion

2. *verb* To take, put, or send something back: *I have to return my library books this afternoon.*

3. *verb* To appear or happen again: *Autumn returns each year.*

4. *verb* To give back in the same way, as in *to return a compliment.*

5. *noun* The act of returning: *I'll be in touch after our return from Guatemala.*

6. *noun* Money made as a profit: *The returns from the book fair were excellent.*

7. *noun* An official form, as in *a tax return.*

8. *noun* A large key on a keyboard that you hit to end a line or to move to another place on your screen. It has that name because in some programs, hitting this key causes you to return to the left margin and start a new line. Also called **enter.**

9. in return *phrase* To give or to do something in exchange for or as a payment for something else: *I brought Kira cookies in return for her help on my term paper.*

10. return ticket *noun* A ticket that covers travel to and from a place. ▷ *verb* **returning, returned**
re·turn (ri-**turn**)

reunion *noun* A meeting or gathering of two or more people who have not seen each other for a long time, as in *a family reunion.* **re·un·ion** (ree-**yoon**-yuhn)

reusable *adjective* Capable of being used again rather than thrown away, as in *reusable glass containers.* **re·us·a·ble** (ree-**yoo**-zuh-buhl)

rev *verb* (informal) To increase the speed of an engine by pressing on the accelerator: *Mimi revved up the car's engine.* **rev** (rev) ▷ *verb* **revving, revved**

reveal *verb*

1. To make known: *The newspaper reporter would not reveal his sources.*

2. To show or bring into view: *The clouds parted to reveal a beautiful blue sky.*
re·veal (ri-**veel**)
▷ *verb* **revealing, revealed** ▷ *adjective* **revealing**

revel *verb* If you **revel in** something, you find great pleasure or enjoyment in it: *Peter reveled in his work.* **rev·el** (**rev**-uhl) ▷ *verb* **reveling, reveled**

revelation *noun* A very surprising and previously unknown fact that is made known: *It was a revelation to Janet that ducks can fly.* **rev·e·la·tion** (*rev*-uh-**lay**-shuhn)

revenge *noun* Something you do to get back at someone for the injury or harm that the person has done to you or to someone you care about: *The widow swore to get revenge on her husband's killer.* **re·venge** (ri-**venj**) ▷ *verb* **revenge**

revengeful *adjective* Seeking or driven by revenge: *Gary was hurt by what Malia said, but his prank to get back at her was petty and revengeful.* **re·venge·ful** (ri-**venj**-fuhl)

revenue *noun*

1. The money that a government gets from taxes and other sources: *The state's revenue is higher this year.*

2. The money that is made from property or other investments.
rev·e·nue (**rev**-uh-*noo*)

reverberate *verb* To echo or resound as if in a series of echoes: *The sounds of traffic reverberated in the long tunnel.* **re·ver·ber·ate** (ri-**vur**-buh-*rate*) ▷ *verb* **reverberating, reverberated** ▷ *noun* **reverberation**

reverence *noun* Honor and respect that is felt or shown: *Everyone expressed reverence for the retiring teacher.* **rev·er·ence** (**rev**-ur-uhns) ▷ *verb* **revere** (ri-**veer**) ▷ *adjective* **reverent** (**rev**-ur-uhnt) ▷ *adverb* **reverently**

reverse

1. *verb* To turn something around, upside down, or inside out: *I reversed the painting but still couldn't decide which side was the top.* ▷ *adjective* **reversible**

2. *noun* The opposite of something: *I thought the math test would be easy and the science test would be hard, but it turned out to be the reverse.*

3. *adjective* Opposite in position, order, or direction: *The answers are on the reverse side of the page.*

4. *noun* The back or rear side of something, as in *the reverse of a record album.*

5. *verb* To transfer telephone fees to someone receiving the call: *Liz reversed the charges.*

6. *verb* To cancel or change to the opposite position: *The verdict was reversed, and the prisoner was allowed to go free.*

7. *noun* A position of gears that allows a motor vehicle to move backward: *Stuart put the car in reverse and backed it into the garage.*
re·verse (ri-**vurs**)
▷ *verb* **reversing, reversed** ▷ *adjective* **reversal** (ri-**vur**-suhl)

revert *verb* To go back to a previous state or condition: *After the developers ran out of money, the neighborhood reverted to a ghost town.* **re·vert** (ri-**vurt**) ▷ *verb* **reverting, reverted** ▷ *noun* **reversion** (ri-**vur**-zhuhn)

review

1. *noun* A piece of writing that gives an opinion about a movie, a written work, or a performance: *The play received a good review.* ▷ *noun* **reviewer** ▷ *verb* **review**

2. *verb* To study something carefully and to make changes if necessary: *The committee's report will be reviewed before any action is taken.*

3. *verb* To study or go over again: *Yong reviewed her notes before the quiz.*

4. *verb* To make a formal inspection of: *The general reviewed the troops.*

re·view (ri-**vyoo**)

▷ *verb* **reviewing, reviewed** ▷ *noun* **review**

revise *verb*

1. To examine and change something, often to make it more up-to-date: *The local business directory hasn't been revised in years.*

2. To reconsider and change something in the light of new information: *I'm sure he'll revise his opinion when he hears the facts.*

re·vise (ri-**vize**)

▷ *verb* **revising, revised**

revision *noun*

1. The preparation of a new version of something: *Revision is my least favorite part of writing a story or poem.*

2. A new version or form of something, especially a piece of writing: *This is my third revision of the article.*

re·vi·sion (ri-**vizh**-uhn)

revival *noun*

1. The act of making something popular, known, or useful again: *The revival of the musical has met with great success.*

2. A return to good health or consciousness.

3. A reawakening of religious faith or a meeting intended to achieve this.

re·viv·al (ri-**vye**-vuhl)

revive *verb*

1. To bring someone back to life or consciousness: *The doctor revived the patient.*

2. To restore interest in something or to bring it back into use: *There is a group in town trying to revive the old Fourth of July parade.*

3. To give new strength or freshness to: *A good night's sleep revived the weary traveler.*

re·vive (ri-**vive**)

▷ *verb* **reviving, revived**

Revolutionary War

revoke *verb* To take away or to cancel: *His driver's license was revoked.* **re·voke** (ri-**voke**) ▷ *verb* **revoking, revoked** ▷ *noun* **revocation** (rev-uh-**kay**-shuhn)

revolt

1. *verb* To try to overthrow a ruler or a government: *The people revolted against the dictator.*

2. *noun* A rebellion against a government or an authority: *The revolt against the dictator resulted in massive casualties.*

3. *verb* If something **revolts** you, it fills you with disgust: *This wormy compost pile revolts me.*

re·volt (ri-**vohlt**)

▷ *verb* **revolting, revolted**

revolting *adjective* Very unpleasant or disgusting, as in *a revolting smell.* **re·volt·ing** (ri-**vohl**-ting)

revolution *noun*

1. A violent overthrow of a country's government or ruler by the people who live there: *There is talk on the streets of a possible revolution.*

2. A sudden, radical, or far-reaching change: *The invention of the airplane caused a revolution in travel.*

3. A complete movement of one object around another, such as of the earth around the sun.

rev·o·lu·tion (rev-uh-**loo**-shuhn)

revolutionary *adjective*

1. Involving or bringing about a dramatic change: *His innovations in musical structure were revolutionary.*

2. Of or having to do with a political or social revolution, as in *revolutionary forces.*

rev·o·lu·tion·ar·y (rev-uh-**loo**-shuh-*ner*-ee)

Revolutionary War *noun* The war in which the 13 American colonies won their independence from Great Britain. The war lasted from 1775 to 1783 and is also known as the *American Revolution.*

revolutionize *verb* To bring about a complete change in something: *The internet revolutionized*

how we communicate and gather information.
rev·o·lu·tion·ize (*rev*-uh-**loo**-shuh-*nize*) ▷ *verb*
revolutionizing, revolutionized

revolve *verb*
1. To keep turning in a circle or orbit around a central point or object: *The moon revolves around the earth.*
2. To spin around or to rotate: *The car's wheels revolved slowly.*
3. **revolve around** To center or focus on: *Jack's life revolves around his family.*
re·volve (ri-**vahlv**)
▷ *verb* **revolving, revolved**

revolver *noun* A small pistol with a revolving cylinder that enables it to be fired several times before it needs to be reloaded. **re·volv·er** (ri-**vahl**-vur)

reward *noun* Something that you receive in recognition of your efforts or achievements: *I was treated to dinner as a reward for helping my grandparents.* **re·ward** (ri-**word**) ▷ *verb* **reward**

Word History

A **reward** was, at first, just a "look." Soon, though, just "looking" changed to "looking at someone with a feeling of being thankful." Eventually, people used *reward* to mean "something you give to show your thanks." In the 14th century in England, there were many French speakers, and their word for a "look" was *regard*. But they sometimes pronounced it as *reward* instead. The spelling *reward* ended up as a separate word meaning "something you receive for doing something good."

rewarding *adjective* If something is **rewarding**, it offers or brings you satisfaction, as in *a rewarding career.* **re·ward·ing** (ri-**wor**-ding)

reword *verb* To say or write something using different words: *Erin reworded the sentence.* **re·word** (ree-**wurd**) ▷ *verb* **rewording, reworded**

Reye's syndrome *noun* A rare children's disease whose symptoms include high fever, vomiting, and swelling of the liver and brain. **Reye's syndrome** (rize *or* rayz)

rheumatic fever *noun* A serious disease, especially in children, that causes fever, joint pain, and possible heart damage. **rheu·mat·ic fever** (roo-**mat**-ik)

rheumatism *noun* A disease that causes pain, swelling, and stiffness in the joints and muscles. **rheu·ma·tism** (**roo**-muh-*tiz*-uhm) ▷ *adjective* **rheumatic** (roo-**mat**-ik)

rhinoceros *noun* A large mammal from Africa and Asia that has thick, folded skin and one or two upright horns on its nose. **rhi·noc·er·os** (rye-**nah**-sur-uhs) ▷ *noun, plural* **rhinoceroses**

Word History

Rhinoceros comes from a Greek word meaning "animal with a horn on its nose." It is based on *rhin,* "nose," and *keros,* "having a horn."

rhododendron *noun* A large evergreen shrub with showy clusters of bell-shaped flowers. **rho·do·den·dron** (roh-duh-**den**-druhn)

rhombus *noun* A parallelogram with four straight sides of equal length but often no right angles. **rhom·bus** (**rahm**-buhs) ▷ *noun, plural* **rhombuses** *or* **rhombi** (**rahm**-bye)

rhubarb *noun* A tall plant with reddish or greenish stems that can be cooked and eaten. Its leaves are poisonous: *For dessert, we had rhubarb pie.* **rhu·barb** (**roo**-bahrb)

rhyme
1. *verb* If words **rhyme**, they have the same ending sounds. The word *love* rhymes with *dove* and *above.* ▷ *verb* **rhyming, rhymed** ▷ *noun* **rhyme**
2. *noun* A short poem that rhymes: *I love reading his witty rhymes.*
rhyme (rime)

rhythm *noun* A repeated pattern of sound or movement in music, poetry, or dance. **rhythm** (**riTH**-uhm)

Word History

Rhyme and **rhythm** go back to the same Greek word: *rhuthmos,* meaning "rhythm." In the Middle Ages, a poem with a regular rhythm was called a *rithmus* in Latin. The word *rithmus* had come from *rhuthmos* in Greek. This type of poetry also rhymed, and eventually people started thinking of "rhyme," not "rhythm," as the meaning of the word *rithmus,* leading to the English word *rhyme.*

rhinoceros

rickshaw

rhythmic *adjective* Of, relating to, or having a rhythm, as in *rhythmic clapping.* **rhyth·mic** (**riTH**-mik) ▷ *adjective* **rhythmical** ▷ *adverb* **rhythmically**

rib *noun*
1. One of the curved bones that enclose your chest and protect your heart and lungs.
2. Something that looks or functions like a rib, as in *the ribs of an umbrella.*
rib (rib)

ribbon *noun*
1. A long, thin band of material, such as satin or velvet, that is used for tying something or for decoration, as in *a hair ribbon.*
2. A long, thin band of material used for something other than decoration, as in *a typewriter ribbon.*
rib·bon (**rib**-uhn)

rice *noun* The seeds of a grasslike cereal plant that is grown for food in flooded fields. **rice** (rise)

rich *adjective*
1. Having a great deal of money or many possessions: *A rich family donated generously to the local theater.*
2. Existing in large quantities or having an abundant supply of something: *Berries are rich in antioxidants.*
3. Containing a lot of fat or sugar: *The cake was so rich that I could only eat a bite.*
4. Fertile, as in *rich soil.*
5. **riches** *noun, plural* Material wealth or abundant natural resources. ▷ *adjective* **richer, richest** ▷ *adverb* **richly**
rich (rich)

rickety *adjective* Poorly made and likely to break or collapse, as in *rickety wooden steps.* **rick·et·y** (**rik**-i-tee)

Word History

In the 17th century in England, a disease affecting children suddenly appeared, in which the children's bones became soft and twisted. Much later, doctors discovered that the cause was a lack of vitamin D in the children's diet. People called the disease *rickets;* those who suffered from it often became bowlegged, and their spines became abnormally curved. After a while, anything that was weak and unsteady was called **rickety**, after the effects of the disease on people. English speakers possibly based the name *rickets* on the old verb *wrick,* meaning "to move jerkily from side to side."

rickshaw *or* **ricksha** *noun* A small carriage with two wheels and a cover that usually is pulled by one person. Rickshaws originally were used in Asia. **rick·shaw** *or* **rick·sha** (**rik**-*shaw*)

Word History

The name for a small, two-wheeled carriage pulled by one person, **rickshaw**, is short for the earlier term *jinricksha.* In Japanese, *jin-riki-sha* was formed from the words *jin,* meaning "human," *riki,* meaning "power," and *sha,* meaning "vehicle." So the name meant "human-powered vehicle." This vehicle was first used in Japan in the late 19th century.

ricochet *verb* To rebound off a hard surface: *Bullets ricocheted off the stone walls and the sides of the buildings.* **ric·o·chet** (**rik**-uh-*shay*) ▷ *verb* **ricocheting** (**rik**-uh-*shay*-ing), **ricocheted** (**rik**-uh-**shayd**)

rid
1. *verb* To remove an unwanted or annoying person or thing: *I must rid my house of mice.* ▷ *verb* **ridding, rid**
2. If you **get rid of** something, you free yourself of it by throwing it away or removing it.
3. If you **get rid of** a cold, you overcome it.
rid (rid)

riddle *noun* A statement or question that makes you think hard and that usually has a clever answer. For example: *What has four wheels and flies?* Answer: *A garbage truck.* **rid·dle** (**rid**-uhl)

ride
1. *verb* To travel on an animal or in a vehicle, as in *to ride a horse.*
2. *noun* A journey on an animal or in a vehicle: *We decided to go on a ride to the country this weekend.*
3. *noun* A device or machine such as a merry-go-round that people ride for fun: *The town carnival is full of rides and games.*
4. *verb* To be supported or carried along: *The surfers rode the waves.*

ride (ride)
▷ *verb* **riding, rode, ridden** (**rid**-uhn)

rider *noun*

1. Someone who rides a horse: *The riders gathered around the barn before starting the pony trek.*

2. Someone who rides a two-wheeled vehicle, or who is a passenger in a motor vehicle, as in *a motorcycle rider* or *a bus rider.*

3. An addition to a document that modifies or adds to information in the main part: *The rider to her car insurance provides towing in case her car breaks down.*
rid·er (**rye**-dur)

ridge *noun*

1. A narrow, raised strip on the surface of something.

2. A long, narrow chain of mountains or hills.
ridge (rij)
▷ *adjective* **ridged**

ridicule *verb* To make fun of someone or something in a mocking or unkind way: *Many people ridiculed the inventor's new idea.* **rid·i·cule** (**rid**-i-kyool) ▷ *verb* **ridiculing, ridiculed** ▷ *noun* **ridicule**

ridiculous *adjective* Absurd, silly, or foolish, as in *a ridiculous hat* or *a ridiculous idea.* **ri·dic·u·lous** (ri-**dik**-yuh-luhs) ▷ *adverb* **ridiculously**

rifle

1. *noun* A gun with a long barrel that is fired from the shoulder.

2. *verb* To search through and rob: *The burglar rifled the safe.* ▷ *verb* **rifling, rifled**
ri·fle (**rye**-fuhl)

rift *noun*

1. A split or crack in a rock or other hard substance.

2. A serious disagreement between people who used to have a close relationship: *The rift between the brothers was finally healed after many years.*
rift (rift)

rig

1. *verb* To provide or to equip: *The car is rigged with an alarm.*

2. *verb* To equip a ship with the necessary masts, sails, ropes, and other gear.

3. *noun* The arrangement of a boat's or ship's masts and sails: *Have you seen the rig on that boat that just pulled into the harbor?*

4. *noun* A structure specially designed to drill for oil or gas, as in *an offshore oil rig.*

5. *noun* A carriage led by a horse or horses that is used for moving people or goods.

6. *noun* A truck that has a small cab for the driver and a larger trailer in back, used for hauling commercial goods.

7. *noun* Equipment or gear used for a special purpose: *The drummer grabbed his rig and hauled it into the club.*

8. *verb* To manage, arrange, or control something in a dishonest way, as in *to rig an election.*

9. *verb* If you **rig up** something, you put it together in a casual or makeshift way, using whatever you can find: *We rigged up some curtains by using a broom handle and a beach towel.*
rig (rig)
▷ *verb* **rigging, rigged**

rigging *noun* The system of ropes, chains, and wires that support and control the sails on a boat or ship. **rig·ging** (**rig**-ing)

right

1. *adjective* On the side opposite the left. ▷ *noun* **right** ▷ *adverb* **right**

2. *adjective* Conforming to fact, reason, or truth; correct: *If you don't study, you'll never get the right answers on tomorrow's test.*

3. *adverb* Correctly: *I did it right.*

4. *adjective* Morally good, fair, or acceptable: *It's not right to make an animal stay outdoors in this cold.*

5. *adjective* Suitable: *He's just right for the job.*

6. *adverb* Exactly in a particular position or location: *She's waiting for me right outside the door.*

7. *adverb* Immediately: *We have to leave right now.*

8. *adverb* Toward the right-hand side or direction: *Turn right at the light.*

9. *adverb* In a straight line; directly: *Brenda walked right to the front of the line.*

10. *noun* If you have **the right** to do something, then you are legally or morally entitled to do it, as in *the right to remain silent.*

11. In politics, people **on the right** have conservative views.
right (rite)
Right sounds like **write**. ▷ *adverb* **rightly**

right angle *noun* An angle of 90 degrees, such as one of the corners of a square.

right angle

right-click *verb* To click the button on the right side of a computer mouse that has more than one button. **right-click** (rite-klik) ▷ *verb* **right-clicking, right-clicked**

righteous *adjective*

1. Without guilt or sin; morally good: *She's a very righteous woman who never has an unkind word to say about anyone.* ▷ *noun* **righteousness** ▷ *adverb* **righteously**

2. Justifiable: *The voters were filled with righteous anger over how the election had been handled.*
righ·teous (**rye**-chuhs)

right-handed *adjective* Using your right hand more easily than your left hand. **right-hand·ed** (**han**-did) ▷ *noun* **right-hander**

right triangle *noun* A triangle that includes one right angle.

rigid *adjective*
1. Stiff and difficult to bend or move: *The soldiers stood at rigid attention.*
2. Strict and not easily changed: *In some states there are rigid rules about using a cell phone while driving.*
rig·id (**rij**-id)
▷ *noun* **rigidity** (ri-**jid**-i-tee) ▷ *adverb* **rigidly**

rile *verb* To annoy or to irritate: *We really riled Mom when we knocked the lamp off the table.* **rile** (rile)
▷ *verb* **riling, riled** ▷ *adjective* **riled**

Word History

Water will become muddy-looking if it is mixed with some types of materials, and English speakers thought that making someone angry is like making water cloudy by stirring it. The verb *roil* meant "to stir up material with water," and people began using it to mean "to irritate someone." Some began to pronounce the word as *rile* instead, giving us the verb **rile**, meaning "to annoy."

rim *noun* The border or outside edge of something round: *Hand me that cup with the orange rim.* **rim** (rim)

rind *noun* The tough outer skin of some fruits, or the hard outer edge of some cheeses and bacon. **rind** (rinde)

ring
1. *noun* A small, circular band of metal or some other material, worn on your finger as a piece of jewelry, as in *a wedding ring.*
2. *noun* A circular form or arrangement: *Dance in a ring.*
3. *verb* To make or form a circle around: *Houses ringed the lake.*
4. *verb* To make or cause to make a clear, musical sound: *The phone rang. I'll ring the doorbell.* ▷ *noun* **ring**
5. *noun* (*informal*) A telephone call: *Give me a ring soon.*
6. *noun* The enclosed space in which a boxing or wrestling match is held.
7. *noun* A group of people working together for some unlawful purpose, as in *a smuggling ring.*
ring (ring)
Ring sounds like **wring.** ▷ *verb* **ringing, rang** (rang), **rung** (ruhng)

ringleader *noun* A person who leads others, especially those who commit crimes or cause trouble. **ring·lead·er** (**ring**-lee-dur)

ringlet *noun* A long, spiral curl of hair. **ring·let** (**ring**-lit)

rink *noun* An enclosed area with a smooth surface that is used for ice-skating, roller-skating, or hockey. **rink** (ringk)

rinse
1. *verb* To get rid of soap or dirt by washing something in clean water: *Rinse out your bathing suit.* ▷ *noun* **rinse**
2. *verb* To wash lightly: *Rinse the plates before you put them in the dishwasher.*
3. *noun* A special liquid that you can use to color or condition your hair, as in *a cream rinse.*
rinse (rins)
▷ *verb* **rinsing, rinsed**

riot
1. *verb* To take part in a noisy or violent public disturbance involving a lot of people. *The people rioted when they couldn't get enough food.* ▷ *verb* **rioting, rioted** ▷ *noun* **riot** ▷ *noun* **rioter** ▷ *noun* **rioting** ▷ *adjective* **riotous** (**rye**-uh-tuhs)
2. *noun* (*informal*) A person or thing that is extremely funny: *Jeff's jokes are a riot.*
ri·ot (**rye**-uht)

rip *verb*
1. To tear or pull something forcefully apart or away: *When he saw his grade, Jeremy ripped his exam paper in half.* ▷ *noun* **rip**
2. To copy music or sound files from one place to another, especially from a CD to your hard drive.
3. (*slang*) If someone **rips** you **off**, the person cheats, steals from, or takes advantage of you.
rip (rip)
▷ *verb* **ripping, ripped**

ripe *adjective* Fully developed or mature; ready to be harvested, picked, or eaten, as in *a ripe banana.* **ripe** (ripe) ▷ *adjective* **riper, ripest** ▷ *noun* **ripeness** ▷ *verb* **ripen**

rip-off *noun* (*slang*) Something that is a lot more expensive than it is worth: *Those baseball caps are a real rip-off.* **rip-off** (**rip**-awf)

ripple *noun*
1. A very small wave or series of waves on the surface of a body of water.
2. Anything that looks like a ripple: *The intense heat caused ripples in the pavement.*
3. A small wave of sound, or a feeling that moves through a place or a group of people, as in *a ripple of excitement.*
rip·ple (**rip**-uhl)
▷ *verb* **ripple**

rise
1. *verb* To move from a lower to a higher position: *The balloon rose slowly into the air.*
2. *verb* To stand up from a sitting, kneeling, or lying

Rivers

Rivers form when constantly flowing water carves a channel in the ground. The source, or beginning, of some rivers is in the mountains, where melted snow and rain collect. Most rivers end where they empty into another body of water. This area is known as the mouth, or delta, of the river. The Amazon and the Nile are the world's longest rivers.

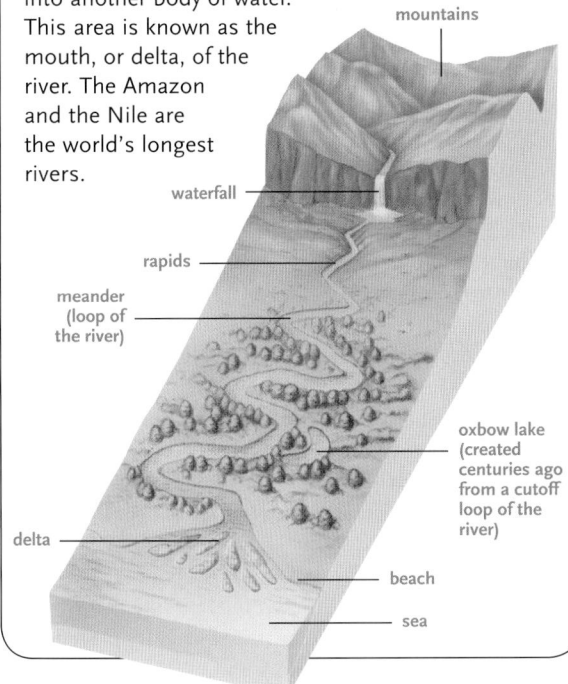

mountains

waterfall

rapids

meander (loop of the river)

delta

oxbow lake (created centuries ago from a cutoff loop of the river)

beach

sea

position: *The audience rose to its feet.*

3. *verb* To get out of bed: *Ruben rises at 7:00 every morning.*

4. *verb* To increase in value, number, amount, or intensity: *The cost of gasoline rose dramatically last summer.* ▷ *noun* **rise**

5. *verb* To move up in position, rank, or importance: *She rose to the position of company president.*

6. *verb* To rebel: *The people rose up against the cruel tyrant.*

7. *noun* An upward slope, as in *the rise of a hill.*

8. *noun* An increase in power, importance, influence, or the like: *The 18th century saw the rise of democracy in America.*

rise (rize)

▷ *verb* **rising, rose** (rohz), **risen** (riz-uhn)

risk

1. *noun* The possibility of loss or harm; danger: *Mountain climbing involves a lot of risk.* ▷ *adjective* **risky**

2. *verb* To expose to risk: *Joel risked his life to save the kitten.*

3. *verb* To take the risk or chance of: *Don't risk being late.*

risk (risk)

▷ *verb* **risking, risked**

ritual *noun*

1. An act or series of acts that are always performed in the same way, usually as part of a religious or social ceremony: *A bar mitzvah is a Jewish ritual.*

2. An action or set of actions that you repeat often: *Eating a good breakfast is part of my morning ritual.*

rit·u·al (**rich**-oo-uhl)

▷ *adjective* **ritual** ▷ *adverb* **ritually**

rival

1. *noun* One of two or more people who are competing against each other: *The two brothers had been rivals since they were young.* ▷ *noun* **rivalry** ▷ *adjective* **rival**

2. *verb* To be equal to or almost as good as something or someone else: *No team can rival us at ice hockey.* ▷ *verb* **rivaling, rivaled**

ri·val (**rye**-vuhl)

river *noun* A large, natural stream of freshwater that flows into a lake, an ocean, or another river. **riv·er** (**riv**-ur)

rivet

1. *noun* A short metal pin or bolt that is used to fasten pieces of metal together. Once the rivet is in place, the plain end is hammered down to form a second head. ▷ *noun* **riveter** ▷ *verb* **rivet**

2. *verb* If you are **riveted** by something, it holds your attention completely: *We were riveted by the earthquake coverage on TV.* ▷ *verb* **riveting, riveted** ▷ *adjective* **riveting**

riv·et (**riv**-it)

RNA *noun* The complex molecule produced by living cells and viruses that is responsible for manufacturing the protein in a cell. RNA is short for *ribonucleic acid.*

road *noun*

1. A wide path with a smooth, hard surface on which vehicles and people travel: *Many cars use this road every day.*

2. The route or path a person takes to achieve a goal, as in *the road to success.*

road (rohd)

Road sounds like **rode**.

road map *noun* A map for motorists that shows the streets and highways of a particular area.

road rage *noun* Dangerous and uncontrollable anger experienced by the driver of a car when another driver does something irritating or upsetting.

a
b
c
d
e
f
g
h
i
j
k
l
m
n
o
p
q
r
s
t
u
v
w
x
y
z

roadrunner *noun* A small bird with brown-black feathers and a long tail found mainly in the southwestern United States. It gets around by running very fast instead of flying. **road·run·ner** (**rohd**-*ruhn*-ur)

roadside *noun* The area beside a road. **road·side** (**rohd**-*side*) ▷ *adjective* **roadside**

roam *verb* To wander around without a purpose or plan: *Coyotes often roam the streets after dark.* **roam** (rohm) ▷ *verb* **roaming, roamed**

Word History

Religious pilgrims traveling to Rome probably gave us the verb **roam**. Rome is the capital of Italy, and many Christians in the Middle Ages journeyed there so that they could honor saints at their tombs. In those days, getting all the way from England to Rome took a long time, and English speakers most likely created the verb *roam*, meaning "to wander," from the destination of these pilgrims.

roar *verb*
1. To make a loud, deep, prolonged sound: *The tiger roared. The audience roared.*
2. To laugh very loudly: *We roared at the joke.* **roar** (ror)
▷ *verb* **roaring, roared** ▷ *noun* **roar**

roast
1. *verb* To cook meat or vegetables with dry heat, in a hot oven or over a fire: *Jamal roasted a chicken.*
2. *noun* A piece of meat that has been roasted or that is suitable for roasting, as in *a standing rib roast.*
3. *adjective* Roasted: *Do you like roast beef?*
4. *verb* To make or to be very hot: *We were roasting in the sun.* ▷ *verb* **roasting, roasted** ▷ *adjective* **roasted** ▷ *adjective* **roasting** **roast** (rohst)

rob *verb* To steal something from a person or place: *The police caught the men who robbed the store.* **rob** (rahb) ▷ *verb* **robbing, robbed** ▷ *noun* **robber**

robbery *noun* The act or crime of stealing from a person or place. **rob·ber·y** (**rah**-bur-ee) ▷ *noun, plural* **robberies**

robe *noun*
1. A long, loose outer garment: *The judge wore a long, black robe.*
2. A bathrobe. **robe** (rohb)

robin *noun* A songbird that has a reddish-orange chest. **rob·in** (**rah**-bin)

robot *noun* A machine that is programmed to perform complex human tasks and that sometimes resembles a human being. **ro·bot** (**roh**-baht) ▷ *adjective* **robotic** (roh-**bah**-tik)

robotic arm *noun* A mechanical arm that works like a human arm to control tools or operate machines.

robotics *noun* The science of designing, making, and using robots. **ro·bot·ics** (roh-**bah**-tiks)

robust *adjective*
1. Strong and healthy, as in *a robust young woman.*
2. Powerfully built, as in *a robust athlete.*
3. Rich; strong in flavor, as in *robust coffee.* **ro·bust** (roh-**buhst**)
▷ *adverb* **robustly**

rock
1. *noun* A stone of any size, especially one small enough to be picked up and thrown.
2. *noun* The hard mineral matter that forms an important part of the earth's crust.
3. *verb* To move backward and forward or from side to side, as if in a cradle: *The boat rocked gently on its mooring.*

rocket

4. *verb* To shake or move violently: *The bomb blast rocked the building.*
5. *noun* Popular music, usually played on electric guitars and other amplified instruments, with a strong beat and a simple, repetitive tune; rock 'n' roll. Also known as *rock music.* **rock** (rahk)
▷ *verb* **rocking, rocked** ▷ *adjective* **rocky** (**rah**-kee)

rock climbing *noun* The sport of climbing steep rock faces, usually with the help of ropes, harnesses, and other special equipment.

rocker *noun*
1. One of the curved pieces of wood or metal on which a rocking chair, cradle, or other item rocks.
2. Another name for a **rocking chair**.
3. A person who plays or likes rock 'n' roll music. **rock·er** (**rah**-kur)

rocket
1. *noun* A tube-shaped vehicle, propelled by a very powerful engine, that is designed for traveling through space or carrying missiles.
2. *verb* To increase very quickly and suddenly: *Housing prices rocketed last spring.* ▷ *verb* **rocketing, rocketed** **rock·et** (**rah**-kit)

the Rocky Mountains

Rockies *See* **Rocky Mountains.** **Rock·ies** (**rah**-keez)

rocking chair *noun* A chair mounted on curved runners that allow the sitter to rock back and forth.

rocking horse *noun* A toy horse mounted on curved runners so that it can rock back and forth.

rock 'n' roll *noun* A kind of popular music with a strong beat, a simple melody, and lyrics that often repeat. **rock 'n' roll** (**rahk** uhn **rohl**) ▷ *adjective* **rock 'n' roll**

Rocky Mountains *noun* A large mountain range in North America. The Rocky Mountains extend from western Canada to New Mexico in the United States. Also called the **Rockies**.

rod *noun*
1. A long, thin pole or stick.
2. A unit of length equal to 5.5 yards, or 16.5 feet. **rod** (rahd)

rode *verb* The past tense of **ride**. **rode** (rohd) **Rode** sounds like **road**.

rodent *noun* A mammal with large, sharp front teeth that are constantly growing and used for gnawing things. Rats, beavers, and squirrels are all rodents. **ro·dent** (**roh**-duhnt)

rodeo *noun* A contest in which cowboys and cowgirls compete at riding wild horses and bulls and catching cattle with lassos. **ro·de·o** (**roh**-dee-*oh* or roh-**day**-oh)

Word History

Rodeo was first used to mean rounding up and counting cattle. It comes from the Spanish word *rodear*, which means "to surround." Only recently has *rodeo* come to mean an exhibition of roping and riding skills.

roe *noun* The eggs of a fish, often eaten as food. **roe** (roh)

rogue *noun*
1. A worthless or dishonest person.
2. A person whose behavior you disapprove of but whom you still like.
3. A vicious and dangerous animal, especially an elephant, that lives apart from the herd. **rogue** (rohg)

role *noun*
1. An actor's part in a play or movie: *I was given the role of the pet dog in our school play.*
2. The job or purpose of someone or something in a particular situation: *Your diet plays a vital role in your overall health.* **role** (rohl) **Role** sounds like **roll**.

role model *noun* A person whose behavior in a particular area is imitated by others.

roll
1. *verb* To move by turning over and over: *We rolled the barrel down the street.*
2. *verb* To form the shape of a ball or cylinder: *I rolled myself into a tight ball and covered my ears.*
3. *noun* Something that is in the shape of a cylinder or tube, as in *a roll of film.*
4. *verb* To flatten something by pushing a roller or cylindrical object over it: *Roll out the pie dough.*
5. *noun* A small, round piece of baked bread dough, as in *a cinnamon roll.*
6. *noun* A list of names: *Check the class roll.*
7. *verb* To move in a side-to-side or up-and-down way: *The ship rolled in the heavy surf.*
8. *verb* To make a deep, loud sound: *The drums rolled.* **roll** (rohl) **Roll** sounds like **role**. ▷ *verb* **rolling, rolled**

roller *noun*
1. A cylinder or rod that has something rolled around it, such as a window shade: *Carl repaired the roller so the shade could be raised.*
2. A cylinder that is used to spread, squeeze, smooth, or crush something, as in *a paint roller.* **roll·er** (**roh**-lur)

Rollerblade *noun* A trademark for an in-line skate. **Roll·er·blade** (**roh**-lur-*blade*)

roller coaster *noun* An amusement park ride consisting of a train of open cars in which people ride at high speeds over a track with steep slopes and tight turns. **roller coast·er** (**koh**-stur)

roller-skating *noun* The sport of gliding across a smooth surface wearing shoes or boots with wheels attached. ▷ *noun* **roller skate** ▷ *verb* **roller-skate**

rolling pin *noun* A cylinder, often made of wood, that is used to flatten out dough.

Rom *noun* A member of a group of people who originated in India and who now live mainly in Europe and North America. **Rom** (rohm) ▷ *noun, plural* **Roma** (**roh**-muh) ▷ *adjective* **Romany** or **Romani** (**rah**-muh-nee *or* **roh**-muh-nee)

ROM *noun* Memory in a computer with data that can be used but not changed. ROM is short for *read-only memory*. **ROM** (rahm)

Roman
1. *noun* A person who lived in ancient Rome.
2. *noun* A person who was born or is living in modern Rome, Italy.
3. *adjective* Of or having to do with the people or culture of ancient or modern Rome, as in *the Roman army*.
4. roman *noun* A style of type with upright letters. This sentence is printed in roman.
Ro·man (**roh**-muhn)

Roman Catholic
1. *noun* A member of the Roman Catholic Church.
2. *adjective* Of or having to do with the Roman Catholic Church and its beliefs, as in *Roman Catholic saints*.

Roman Catholic Church *noun* A Christian church that has the pope as its leader.

romance *noun*
1. An affectionate relationship between people who are in love, as in *a teenage romance*.
2. A poem or story about the loves and adventures of heroes and heroines.
3. A quality of mystery, excitement, and adventure: *The faraway setting added to the novel's romance*.
ro·mance (roh-**mans**)

Romance language *noun* One of a group of languages that developed from Latin. The Romance languages include Spanish, Italian, French, Portuguese, and Romanian.

Roman numerals *noun, plural* Letters that represent numbers in the ancient Roman numbering system. The number 16, for example, is written XVI.

romantic *adjective*
1. Of or having to do with love or romance: *Sending roses to someone is a very romantic thing to do*.
2. Imaginative but not practical, as in *romantic ideas*.
ro·man·tic (roh-**man**-tik)

romp *verb* To run or play in a noisy, carefree, and energetic way: *The parents watched as their children romped in the surf*. **romp** (rahmp) ▷ *verb* **romping, romped** ▷ *noun* **romp**

roof *noun*
1. The covering on the top of a house, building, or vehicle.
2. The top inner surface of something, as in *the roof of your mouth*.
roof (roof *or* ruf)

rook
1. *noun* A chess piece, shaped like a battlement and also known as a castle, that can move across the board in straight lines but not diagonally.
2. *noun* A type of crow with black feathers and a bare face.
3. *verb* (*informal*) To cheat someone: *The gambler rooked the others in a card game*. ▷ *verb* **rooking, rooked**
rook (ruk)

rookie *noun*
1. Someone who has just joined a group and lacks experience and training, especially an inexperienced police officer.

Roman Empire

According to legend, Rome was founded by Romulus, the city's first king. It became a republic in 509 B.C. The Roman Forum was its government and community center. Around 48 B.C., Julius Caesar became dictator, and in 27 B.C. Augustus became emperor. The Romans built roads and aqueducts, introducing their culture as they conquered territories. At its largest, the Roman Empire spanned from Britain to western Asia, including part of North Africa. It lasted in the West until A.D. 476, and in the East until A.D. 1453.

the Roman Forum

2. An athlete who is in his or her first season with a professional sports team. **rook·ie (ruk**-ee)

room

1. *noun* One of the separate parts of a house or building that is enclosed by walls, a floor, and a ceiling: *We keep all our toys in this room.*

2. *noun* Empty space that can be occupied or used for something: *Is there room for two more people at the dinner table tonight?*

3. *noun* An opportunity or chance: *There's plenty of room for improvement in her work.*

4. *verb* To share a room or living space with one or more people: *I'm rooming with my sister.* ▷ *verb* **rooming, roomed**

room (room *or* rum)

roommate *noun* Someone who shares a room or living space with one or more people. **room·mate (room**-*mate*)

roomy *adjective* Large, or having a lot of space: *The house looked small, but it was quite roomy inside.* **room·y (roo**-mee) ▷ *adjective* **roomier, roomiest**

roost

1. *noun* A place where birds or other winged animals, such as chickens, gather to rest at night.

2. *verb* When birds **roost**, they settle somewhere to rest or sleep. ▷ *verb* **roosting, roosted**

roost (roost)

rooster *noun* An adult male chicken. **roost·er (roo**-stur)

root

1. *noun* The part of a plant or tree that grows under the ground, where it collects water and nutrients.

2. *verb* To grow roots: *I tried to plant a tree, but it didn't root.*

3. *noun* A part that functions like a root or resembles one, as in *the root of a tooth.*

4. *noun* The source, origin, or cause of something: *Let's get to the root of the problem.*

5. *noun* A word to which a prefix or suffix is added to make another word. *Hungry* is the root of *hungriest.*

6. *verb* To cheer: *I rooted for my sister's team.*

7. roots *noun, plural* If you have **roots** in a particular place, that place is where your family comes from or where you grew up. Many Americans have their roots in Europe, Africa, or Asia.

root (root *or* rut) ▷ *verb* **rooting, rooted**

rooster

root canal *noun*

1. A groove in a tooth's root through which the nerve passes.

2. A dental procedure to replace the pulp in a tooth's root with another substance in order to save the tooth.

rope

1. *noun* A strong, thick cord made from twisted or braided strands of hemp, nylon, or some other material: *We can tie the dog to the tree with this rope.*

2. *verb* To fasten with a cord: *Heather roped the cartons together.*

3. *verb* To catch with a lasso or rope: *The cowhand roped the steer.*

4. *verb* To separate an area or object with ropes: *The police roped off the scene of the crime before they started their investigation.*

rope (rohp) ▷ *verb* **roping, roped**

rose *noun*

1. A garden flower that grows on a prickly bush and usually has a sweet smell. Roses may be red, pink, yellow, or white.

2. A light red or warm pink color.

rose (roze) ▷ *adjective* **rose**

rosebud *noun* The bud from which the rose flower blooms. **rose·bud (roze**-*buhd*)

rosemary *noun* An evergreen plant of the mint family that has needlelike leaves used for adding flavor in cooking. **rose·mar·y (rohz**-*mair*-ee)

Rosh Hashana *noun* The Jewish New Year, occurring in September or October. **Rosh Ha·sha·na (rohsh** huh-**shah**-nuh)

roster *noun* A list of people, especially a list that shows duties or assignments: *He was relieved to find his name on the team roster.* **ros·ter (rah**-stur)

rosy *adjective*

1. Having a pinkish color, as in *rosy cheeks.*

2. Promising or hopeful, as in *a rosy future.*

ros·y (roh-zee) ▷ *adjective* **rosier, rosiest**

rot *verb* To make or become rotten; to decay: *Damp air rotted the magazines in the basement. Fruit rots if it is not refrigerated.* **rot** (raht) ▷ *verb* **rotting, rotted** ▷ *noun* **rot**

rotary *adjective* Having a part or parts that turn around and around or rotate, as in *a rotary telephone dial* or *a rotary engine.* **ro·ta·ry (roh**-tur-ee)

rotate *verb*

1. To move in a circle around a central point, like a wheel: *The earth rotates on its axis once a day.*

2. To take turns doing things in a regular, repeated order: *The teacher rotates the classroom jobs.*

3. To grow different crops, one after the other, on the same piece of land: *Farmers who rotate their crops avoid exhausting the soil.*

ro·tate (**roh**-tate)

▷ *verb* **rotating, rotated** ▷ *noun* **rotation**

▷ *adjective* **rotational**

rotator cuff *noun* The muscles and tendons that attach the upper arm to the shoulder and allow the arm to rotate in its socket. **ro·ta·tor cuff** (**roh**-*tay*-tur)

rotor *noun*

1. The part of an engine or other machine that turns or rotates.

2. The blades of a helicopter that turn and lift the helicopter into the air.

ro·tor (**roh**-tur)

rotten *adjective*

1. If food is **rotten**, it has gone bad or has started to decay from the action of bacteria or fungi.

2. If wood is **rotten**, it is weak and likely to crack, break, or give way.

3. *(informal)* Very bad or extremely unpleasant, as in *rotten weather.*

rot·ten (**rah**-tuhn)

Rottweiler *noun* One of a breed of powerful black-and-brown dogs with short hair and a short tail, often used as guard dogs. **Rott·wei·ler** (**raht**-*wye*-lur)

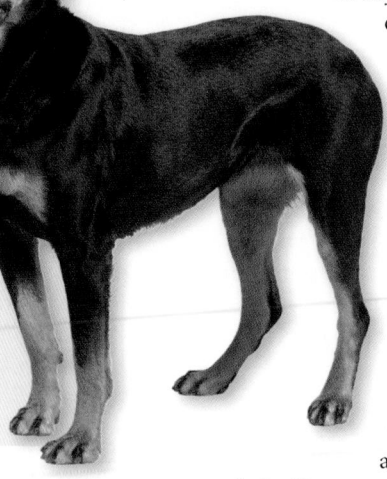

Word History

The **Rottweiler** dogs we know today are descendants of dogs that helped the Roman armies drive cattle and guard their camp in the town of Rottweil, Germany. In the Middle Ages, butchers used these fierce dogs to carry money for them in a neck pouch as the butchers went to markets in and around Rottweil. The dogs' place of origin is preserved in their name, even if many dogs of this breed live in areas other than Rottweil.

rouge *noun* Red or pink makeup put on the cheeks to make them look less pale. **rouge** (roozh)

rough

1. *adjective* Not smooth or level; having an irregular surface with many bumps or dents: *My dad's face feels rough when he forgets to shave.*

2. *adjective* Not gentle or polite and often loud or violent: *The men who hang around by the docks are pretty rough.*

3. *adjective (informal)* Difficult and unpleasant, as in *a rough time.*

4. *adjective* Not completely worked out or not exact: *The teacher gave us a rough idea of what our assignment would be.*

5. *adjective* Preliminary, hastily done, or unfinished, as in *a rough sketch.*

6. *verb (informal)* If you **rough it**, you manage with only the basic necessities or comforts. ▷ *verb* **roughing, roughed**

rough (ruhf)

Rough sounds like **ruff**. ▷ *adjective* **rougher, roughest**

roughage *noun* The fiber found in fruit, cereals, vegetables, and other foods, which cannot be digested but helps food move through the intestines. **rough·age** (**ruhf**-ij)

roughly *adverb*

1. In a rough, harsh, or violent way: *Andy interrupted his younger sister and spoke roughly to her, instead of listening to what she had to say.*

2. Approximately: *The island is roughly half the size of Connecticut.*

rough·ly (**ruhf**-lee)

roughneck *noun* A rough and rowdy person. **rough·neck** (**ruhf**-nek)

round

1. *adjective* Shaped like a circle, a sphere, or a cylinder: *The full moon is round.*

2. *adjective* Having a curved surface or outline: *The table had round corners.*

3. *noun* Something round in shape: *We cut the carrot into rounds.*

4. rounds *noun, plural* A regular route or course of action followed by someone such as a mail carrier, doctor, or guard: *The mailman uses a bicycle for his rounds.*

5. *noun* A long burst, as in *a round of applause.*

6. *noun* A series of repeated actions or events, as in *the latest round of talks.*

7. *noun* A period of play in a sport or contest: *The boxer was knocked out in the third round.*

8. *noun* A complete game, as in *a round of golf.*

9. *noun* A simple song for three or more voices in which people sing the same melody but start at

roundhouse

different times, one after the other.

10. *noun* One shot fired by a weapon or by each person in a military unit.

11. *verb* To make or become round: *I used sandpaper to round the corners of the table.*

12. *verb* To go around: *The bus rounded the corner.*

13. *preposition* Around: *The hikers gathered round the campfire.*

14. *adverb* Around: *The ballerina spun round and round.*

15. round off *verb* To make into a round number: *I rounded off 33.7 to 34.*

16. round up *verb* To gather together: *I rounded up the children for lunch.*

round (round)

▷ *verb* **rounding, rounded** ▷ *adjective* **rounder, roundest** ▷ *adjective* **rounded**

roundabout *adjective* Indirect in travel, thought, or conversation: *He told me the truth in a roundabout way.* **round·a·bout** (**roun**-duh-*bout*)

roundhouse *noun* A circular building with a large turntable in the center, used for storing, repairing, and switching locomotive engines. **round·house** (**round**-*hous*)

round number *noun* A number rounded off to the nearest whole number or to the nearest ten, hundred, thousand, and so on. Rounding off 158 to the nearest ten gives you a round number of 160. Rounding off 158 to the nearest hundred gives you a round number of 200.

round trip

1. *noun* A trip to a place and back again: *The round trip from my house to your house takes an hour.*

2. round-trip *adjective* Of or having to do with a round trip, as in *a round-trip ticket.*

roundup *noun*

1. The gathering together of cattle for branding or shipping to market.

2. A gathering together of people, things, or facts, as in *a news roundup.*

round·up (**round**-*uhp*)

rouse *verb*

1. To wake up or to awaken someone: *We were roused by the sound of a catfight in the yard.*

2. To make someone feel angry, interested, or excited; to stir up: *His fiery speech roused the crowd.*

rouse (rouz)

▷ *adjective* **rousing** ▷ *verb* **rousing, roused**

rout

1. *noun* A complete or overwhelming defeat: *The soccer game turned into a rout for the home team.*

2. *verb* To defeat or beat totally: *Our team routed their team by a score of 20–2.*

3. *verb* To drive or force out: *The fighting routed the civilians from their homes.*

rout (rout)

▷ *verb* **routing, routed**

route

1. *noun* The road, path, or course that you follow to get from one place to another: *Tell me the best route to Chicago.*

2. *noun* A series of places or customers visited regularly by a person who delivers or sells something, as in *a newspaper route.*

3. *verb* To send or direct someone or something along a particular course: *Our flight was routed through New York.* ▷ *verb* **routing, routed**

route (root *or* rout)

network router

router *noun*

1. A device that handles signals between computers or computer networks.

2. An electric tool used in woodworking that digs out holes or spaces in wood.

rout·er (**rou**-tur)

routine

1. *noun* A regular sequence of actions or way of doing things: *Taking out the garbage is part of my daily routine.*

2. *noun* A performance that has been thoroughly learned and that is repeated regularly and in the same way, as in *a comedy routine* or *an ice-skating routine.*

3. *adjective* Commonplace; done as part of a regular procedure, as in *routine chores* or *a routine checkup.*

rou·tine (roo-**teen**)

▷ *adverb* **routinely**

a
b
c
d
e
f
g
h
i
j
k
l
m
n
o
p
q
r
s
t
u
v
w
x
y
z

row

1. (roh) *noun* People or things arranged in a straight line, as in *a row of chairs.*

2. (roh) *verb* To move a boat through water by using oars: *Ruth rowed the boat across the lake.* ▷ **rowing, rowed** ▷ *noun* **rower**

3. (roh) *noun* A trip made by rowboat: *Do you want to go for a row with me tomorrow?*

4. (rou) *noun* A noisy fight or quarrel: *Our neighbors had a terrible row last night.*
row

rowboat *noun* A small boat that is moved through the water by using oars. **row·boat** (**roh**-*boht*)

rowdy *adjective* Noisy and wild or disorderly: *My mother doesn't like us to get too rowdy when we play indoors.* **row·dy** (**rou**-*dee*) ▷ *adjective* **rowdier, rowdiest** ▷ *noun* **rowdiness** ▷ *adverb* **rowdily**

royal *adjective*

1. Relating to or belonging to a king or queen or a member of his or her family, as in *the royal jewels.* ▷ *noun* **royalty**

2. Magnificent or fit for a king or queen, as in *a royal welcome.*
roy·al (**roi**-*uhl*)

RSS feed *noun* An electronic news service that sends new information to your computer whenever it is available. RSS is short for *really simple syndication.*

RSVP The initials of the French phrase *Répondez s'il vous plaît,* meaning "please reply," that is often written at the end of an invitation.

rub *verb*

1. To move one thing against the surface of another with firm pressure: *Josefina rubbed her hands in delight.*

2. To put on or spread something by using pressure: *Rub some sunscreen on your arms and legs.*

3. To clean, polish, or make smooth by pressing something against a surface and moving it back and forth: *I rubbed the table with a damp sponge.* ▷ *noun* **rub**

4. (*informal*) If you **rub it in**, you keep reminding someone about something unpleasant: *I know I was wrong—don't rub it in!*
rub (*ruhb*)
▷ *verb* **rubbing, rubbed**

rubber *noun*

1. A waterproof, elastic substance made from the milky sap of a tropical plant or produced artificially.

2. **rubbers** *noun, plural* Low boots that protect shoes from water.
rub·ber (**ruhb**-*ur*)

rubber band *noun* A loop of thin rubber that can be stretched and used to hold things together.

rubber stamp

1. *noun* A stamp with a rubber end. Raised letters or a design in the rubber can be covered with ink and used to print something.

2. **rubber-stamp** *verb* (*informal*) To approve or vote for without question: *The committee always rubber-stamps the president's decisions.*

rubbish *noun*

1. Things that you throw away; waste or worthless items: *Toss all the rubbish into that box.*

2. Nonsense or foolish talk: *I'm not talking rubbish—I'm serious!*
rub·bish (**ruhb**-*ish*)

rubble *noun* Broken fragments of stone, brick, and concrete that are left after a building is destroyed or falls down: *After the earthquake, the streets were blocked by rubble.* **rub·ble** (**ruhb**-*uhl*)

ruble *noun* The main unit of money in Russia. **ru·ble** (**roo**-*buhl*)

ruby *noun*

1. A precious stone of a deep red color. ▷ *noun, plural* **rubies**

2. A deep red color.
ru·by (**roo**-*bee*)
▷ *adjective* **ruby**

rudder *noun* A hinged piece of wood or metal attached to the back of a boat, ship, or airplane and used for steering. **rud·der** (**ruhd**-*ur*)

rude *adjective*

1. Bad-mannered or offensive, as in *rude behavior* or *a rude answer.*

2. Roughly or crudely made: *In some countries, farmers still use rude wooden plows.*
rude (*rood*)
▷ *adjective* **ruder, rudest** ▷ *adverb* **rudely**

rudeness *noun* Rude behavior or speech: *I apologized for my rudeness.* **rude·ness** (**rood**-*nis*)

ruff *noun*

1. A starched, ruffled collar worn by men and women in Western Europe from the mid-16th to the mid-17th century.

2. A collar of feathers or hair on certain birds or animals.
ruff (*ruhf*)
Ruff sounds like **rough.**

ruffian *noun* A rough or violent person, especially one who breaks the law. **ruf·fi·an** (**ruhf**-*ee-uhn*)

ruby

ruffle

1. *verb* To disturb the surface of something, or to make it uneven or messy: *The breeze ruffled the water. His mother ruffled his hair.*

2. *verb* To annoy, irritate, or upset someone: *That last question really ruffled the speaker.*

3. *noun* A strip of gathered material used as a decoration or trimming; a frill: *The curtains were decorated with ruffles.*

ruf·fle (**ruhf**-uhl)

▷ *verb* **ruffling, ruffled**

rug *noun* A thick mat made from wool or other fibers and used as a floor covering. **rug** (ruhg)

rugby *noun* A form of football played by two teams that kick, pass, or carry an oval ball. **rug·by** (**ruhg**-bee)

rugged *adjective*

1. Rough and uneven, or having a jagged outline, as in *rugged mountain peaks.*

2. Tough, strong, and able to withstand rough handling or conditions, as in *a rugged vehicle.*

3. Harsh or difficult; requiring determination and toughness: *Settlers of the frontier led a very rugged life.* **rug·ged** (**ruhg**-id)

ruin

1. *verb* To spoil or destroy something completely: *The storm ruined our picnic.*

2. *noun* The destruction of something: *Heavy rain resulted in the ruin of the outdoor art festival.*

3. *verb* To make someone lose all of his or her money: *Jeb was almost ruined by medical expenses.*

4. *noun* Loss of wealth or social position: *The story tells about the ruin of a wealthy family.*

5. ruins *noun, plural* The remains of something that has collapsed or been destroyed.

ru·in (**roo**-in)

▷ *verb* **ruining, ruined**

rule

1. *noun* An official instruction or principle that governs behavior or actions: *We play this game according to the rules.*

2. *verb* To govern or to have power and authority over something, usually a country: *The king ruled his country for 30 years.*

3. *noun* Control, or government: *The people were unhappy under the dictator's rule.*

4. *verb* To make an official decision or to state with authority that something is the case: *The judge ruled that the parents should share custody of their children.* ▷ *noun* **ruling**

5. *noun* The normal or usual state of things; what is usually done: *Jeans and sneakers are the rule among the kids in my town.*

6. If you do something **as a rule**, you do it most of the time, but not always: *As a rule, I'm up before 7 a.m. on weekdays.*

7. *verb* If you **rule** something **out**, you exclude or eliminate it as a possibility: *Arson was ruled out as the cause of the fire.*

rule (rool)

▷ *verb* **ruling, ruled**

ruler *noun*

1. A flat, smooth-edged strip of wood, plastic, or metal used to measure something or to draw straight lines.

2. Someone who rules a country or a group of people: *A king or queen is the ruler of Britain.*

rul·er (**roo**-lur)

ruling *noun* A decision or a statement made by someone in authority: *The Supreme Court's ruling that the law was unconstitutional led to its being struck down in every state.* **rul·ing** (**roo**-ling)

rum *noun* An alcoholic drink made from sugarcane. **rum** (ruhm)

rumble *verb* To make or move with a low, deep, continuous noise like the sound of thunder: *Traffic rumbled in the distance.* **rum·ble** (**ruhm**-buhl)

▷ *verb* **rumbling, rumbled** ▷ *noun* **rumble**

rummage *verb* To search for something in a haphazard or careless way: *Nathan rummaged through his desk drawer for a pen.* **rum·mage** (**ruhm**-ij) ▷ *verb* **rummaging, rummaged**

ruler

Word History

The verb **rummage** comes from sailing. It used to refer to stowing goods in the hold of a ship. English speakers then began using *rummage* to mean "to search a hold thoroughly." Today, the connection to sailing has been lost, and the word has changed its meaning. When we use the verb, we mean that we are searching for something in a disorganized way, without much planning or thought.

rumor *noun* A story or report that is spread by word of mouth but that may not be true: *There was a rumor going around that we would be let out of school early.* **ru·mor** (**roo**-mur) ▷ *verb* **rumor** ▷ *adjective* **rumored**

rump *noun* The hindquarters or buttocks of a mammal, or the lower back part of a bird. **rump** (ruhmp)

rumple *verb* To wrinkle or crease. **rum·ple** (**ruhm**-puhl) ▷ *verb* **rumpling, rumpled** ▷ *adjective* **rumpled**

run

1. *verb* To move at a speed faster than a walk, using your legs: *Blair ran to the corner to meet his friends.*
2. *noun* The act of running, as in *to take a run.*
3. *noun* A running pace: *We broke into a run.*
4. *verb* To function or to make something function: *Most heavy trucks run on diesel fuel.*
5. *verb* To manage or be in charge of people or an organization: *Olivia runs a hair salon.*
6. *verb* To travel a regular route: *A bus runs to the city every morning.*
7. *verb* To be a candidate in an election: *Alonzo is running for class president.*
8. *verb* To continue: *The fair runs for one week.*
9. *verb* To flow in a steady stream: *Melted wax ran down the candle.*
10. *verb* To organize, carry out, or proceed with something: *I have to run some errands.*
11. *verb* To operate a computer program: *Can you run that program again?*
12. *noun* A small enclosure for pets or other animals, as in *a dog run.*
13. *noun* Freedom to move about or use something: *Our dog has the run of the yard.*
14. *noun* A series of actions that continue to happen: *The team had a run of eight losses.*
15. *noun* A length of torn stitches: *I have a run in my stocking.* ▷ *verb* **run**
16. *noun* In baseball, a score made by touching home plate after touching the other three bases.
17. *verb* If you **run away**, you escape from a person, place, or situation.
18. *verb* If you have **run out of** something, you have used it all up.
19. *verb* If you **run into** or **run across** someone or something, you meet the person or find the thing by chance.

run (ruhn)
▷ *verb* **running, ran** (ran), **run**

Synonyms

Run means to move along steadily with springing steps at a speed faster than a walk: *Rob can walk a mile in 20 minutes, but he can run a mile in 8 minutes.*

- -

■ **Jog** means to run at a slow but steady pace: *My dog loves to prance around me as I jog.*

■ **Trot** means to go at a pace between a walk and a run. It is used mainly to describe the gait of horses: *The horse trotted to the fence.*

■ **Dash** means to move with sudden speed: *When the rain began, we dashed into the nearest store.*

■ **Race** means to run with great speed: *The nurse raced over to help the man who had collapsed.*

■ **Sprint** means to run at top speed for a short distance: *Toward the end of the one-mile race, the runners put on a burst of speed and sprinted across the finish line.*

runaway

1. *noun* A person, usually a young person, who has run away from home or an institution: *The police brought the runaway back home.*
2. *adjective* Happening quickly, easily, or uncontrollably, as in *a runaway success* or *a runaway car.*

run·a·way (**ruhn**-uh-*way*)

run-down *adjective*

1. Old and in need of repair, as in *a run-down house.*
2. Tired or weak: *I'm feeling a little run-down today.*

rung *noun* One of the horizontal bars on a ladder where you put your foot. **rung** (ruhng) **Rung** sounds like **wrung**.

runner *noun*

1. Someone who runs in a race or in a particular way: *The fastest runner will win a prize. He's an awkward runner, but he is determined to compete.*
2. The long, narrow part of an object that enables it to move or slide, as the blade on an ice skate or a sled.
3. A long, narrow carpet, often used on stairs.

run·ner (**ruhn**-ur)

runner-up *noun* The person or team that takes second place in a race or competition. ▷ *noun, plural* **runners-up**

running mate *noun* A person who runs for public office with another candidate in a less important

runners

position: *The person running for vice president is the presidential candidate's running mate.*

runny *adjective*

1. More like liquid than you expected, or tending to flow like a liquid, as in *runny custard.*

2. If you have a **runny** nose, it tends to drip mucus. **run·ny** (**ruhn**-ee)

▷ *adjective* **runnier, runniest**

runway *noun*

1. A strip of hard, level ground that aircraft use for taking off and landing.

2. A raised aisle that extends from a stage into the audience, used in fashion shows. **run·way** (**ruhn**-*way*)

rupture *verb* To break open or to burst: *His appendix ruptured. The steam pipe ruptured.* **rup·ture** (**ruhp**-chur) ▷ *verb* **rupturing, ruptured** ▷ *noun* **rupture**

rural *adjective* Of or having to do with the countryside, country life, or farming, as in *a rural area* or *a rural economy.* **ru·ral** (**roor**-uhl)

ruse *noun* A clever trick meant to confuse or mislead someone: *The magician's story was just a ruse to distract everyone from what he was really doing.* **ruse** (rooz *or* roos)

Word History

The term **ruse** originally referred to the movements of a hunted animal as it was escaping from dogs. So a ruse was a "dodge" or "escape." English speakers then started using *ruse* when they meant a "trick." The word *ruse* went back to the Old French verb *ruser*, meaning "to escape." We get the English verb *rush* from the same French word.

rush

1. *verb* To move or act quickly: *Debbie rushed into the station just as the train was leaving.* ▷ *verb* **rushes, rushing, rushed**

2. *noun* The act of rushing: *Jay was in a big rush to get out of the house.*

3. *noun* A sudden burst of speed or flurry of activity, as in *the Christmas rush.*

4. *adjective* Requiring or done with speed or urgency: *I placed a rush order for some flowers for my parents' anniversary.*

5. rushes *noun, plural* Tall, marshy plants with hollow stems, used for making baskets and chair seats. **rush** (ruhsh)

rush hour *noun* A period of time when traffic is at its heaviest, on weekday mornings and afternoons as workers go to or leave their jobs: *We were late because of all the rush hour traffic.* **rush hour** (**ruhsh** *our*)

rust

1. *noun* The flaky, reddish-brown coating that can form on iron and steel when they are exposed to moist air.

2. *noun* A reddish-brown color.

3. *verb* To form rust: *The wheel rims on my new bike have rusted already.* ▷ *verb* **rusting, rusted**

4. *noun* Red or brown disease spots on plants, caused by a fungus. **rust** (ruhst)

▷ *adjective* **rusty**

rustic *adjective* Of or having to do with life in the country; simple and unsophisticated, as in *a rustic cabin.* **rus·tic** (**ruhs**-tik)

rustle *verb*

1. To make a soft, fluttering sound like dry leaves or pieces of paper: *The pages rustled as they were turned.* ▷ *noun* **rustle**

2. To steal horses, cattle, or sheep. ▷ *noun* **rustler** **rus·tle** (**ruhs**-uhl)

▷ *verb* **rustling, rustled** ▷ *noun* **rustling**

rusty *adjective*

1. Covered with rust or having rust spots on it, as in *a rusty chain.*

2. Not as good as before, especially because of a lack of practice or use: *Jean's violin playing got rusty over the summer.* **rust·y** (**ruhs**-tee)

rut *noun*

1. A deep, narrow track in the ground made by the repeated passage of wheels or vehicles.

2. If someone is **in a rut**, he or she keeps doing things in the same dull, boring way: *She was in a rut and needed some change in her life.* **rut** (ruht)

ruthless *adjective* Someone who is **ruthless** has no pity or sympathy for other people: *He was a ruthless boss who exploited his workers.* **ruth·less** (**rooth**-lis)

▷ *noun* **ruthlessness** ▷ *adverb* **ruthlessly**

Word History

We might call a cruel person **ruthless**, but we don't say that a nice person has a lot of *ruth*. The old word *ruth* meant a feeling of pity for someone in trouble, but it survives only in the word *ruthless* today. So a *ruthless* person is someone who does not have any *ruth*, or pity.

rye *noun*

1. A cereal grass that looks like wheat and is used to make flour and whiskey.

2. A chewy, dark brown bread made from rye flour, usually with caraway seeds added. **rye** (rye)

S s

About S The Declaration of Independence uses a form of the letter **S** that looks like the lowercase *f* introduced by the Romans and used in some medieval alphabets. But this similarity made it confusing, so it was not much used after 1800. In English, more words begin with s than with any other letter of the alphabet. Some words that begin with a *sye* sound are spelled *ci, cy, psy,* or *sci.* Examples: cider, cyberspace, psychic, science.

Sabbath *noun* A day of the week that is supposed to be used for rest and religious activities. **Sab·bath** (**sab**-uhth)

saber *noun* A heavy sword with a curved blade and one cutting edge. **sa·ber** (**say**-bur)

saber-toothed tiger A prehistoric animal related to the lion and tiger that had long, curved teeth in its upper jaw. **saber-toothed tiger** (tootht)

sable *noun*
1. A small European animal with soft, dark brown fur that looks like a weasel. ▷ *noun, plural* **sable** or **sables**
2. The color of a sable, either black or dark brown. ▷ *adjective* **sable**
sa·ble (**say**-buhl)

sabotage *noun* The deliberate damage or destruction of property, especially to prevent or stop something: *Enemy agents use sabotage to stop or slow down a nation's war efforts.* **sab·o·tage** (**sab**-uh-*tahzh*)
▷ *verb* **sabotage**

saber-toothed tigers

Word History

The French word *sabotage* means "doing work fast and badly." Later, after railroad workers went on strike in 1910, refusing to work, it also came to mean "damage to equipment at a workplace." It is not clear how the first meaning arose. The word *sabot* in French means "a block" holding train rails in place. It also means "a wooden shoe," and **sabotage** perhaps originally meant workers making noise with their shoes or throwing them into machines.

sac *noun* A bag or pouchlike structure in a plant or animal that often contains a liquid: *Skunks store their foul-smelling spray in a pair of sacs under the tail.* **sac** (sak) **Sac** sounds like **sack**.

saccharin *noun* A sweet artificial compound with no calories that is used as a sugar substitute. **sac·cha·rin** (**sak**-ur-in)

sack
1. *noun* A large bag made of strong material that is used for storing and carrying things, as in *a sack of groceries.*
2. *verb* To fire a person from a job: *The boss sacked the lazy employee.*
3. *verb* To steal things from a place that has been captured in a war or battle; loot.
sack (sak)
Sack sounds like **sac**. ▷ *verb* **sacking, sacked**

sacred *adjective*
1. Holy, or having to do with religion, as in *sacred music* or *sacred ground.*
2. Very important and deserving great respect, as in *a sacred promise.*
sa·cred (**say**-krid)

sacrifice
1. *verb* To give up something you value or enjoy for the sake of something that is more important: *I sacrificed my free time to help my brother with his homework.* ▷ *verb* **sacrificing, sacrificed** ▷ *noun* **sacrifice**
2. *noun* The offering of something to God or a god.
▷ *adjective* **sacrificial** (*sak*-ruh-**fish**-uhl)
sac·ri·fice (**sak**-ruh-*fise*)

sacrilege *noun* Treating something that is holy or very important with disrespect: *Damaging a house of worship is a sacrilege.* **sac·ri·lege** (**sak**-ruh-lij)
▷ *adjective* **sacrilegious** (*sak*-ruh-**lij**-uhs) ▷ *adverb* **sacrilegiously**

sad *adjective*
1. Unhappy or sorrowful.
2. Causing you to feel sorrowful or gloomy, as in *sad news* or *a sad sight.* ▷ *noun* **sadness** ▷ *adverb* **sadly**

sad (sad)
▷ *adjective* **sadder, saddest**

sadden *verb* To cause someone to feel sad: *We were all saddened by the news of the plane crash.* **sad·den** (**sad**-uhn) ▷ *verb* **saddening, saddened**

saddle

1. *noun* A leather seat for a rider that is strapped to a horse's back. ▷ *verb* **saddle**

2. *noun* A seat on a bicycle or motorcycle.

3. *verb* To cause difficulty or hardship: *The family is saddled with debt.* ▷ *verb* **saddling, saddled** **sad·dle** (**sad**-uhl)

safari *noun* A trip taken, especially in Africa, to see or hunt large wild animals. **sa·fa·ri** (suh-**fahr**-ee)

Word History

Safari comes from the Arabic word *safara,* meaning "travel." Although safaris at one time were hunting expeditions into the African jungle, today they are often sightseeing trips, as the original word implies.

safe

1. *adjective* Protected from danger, injury, theft, or risk: *The money is safe in the bank.* ▷ *adverb* **safely**

2. *adjective* Unable or unlikely to cause trouble or harm; not dangerous, as in *safe stairs.*

3. *adjective* Careful, as in *a safe driver.*

4. *adjective* In baseball, a hitter is **safe** if he or she reaches a base without being tagged by an opposing player or called out by the umpire.

5. *noun* A fireproof box or container with a lock for storing money or valuables.
safe (sayf)
▷ *adjective* **safer, safest**

safeguard

1. *verb* To guard or protect someone or something: *A vaccination will safeguard you against smallpox.* ▷ *verb* **safeguarding, safeguarded**

2. *noun* Something that protects: *A healthy diet is a safeguard against disease.*
safe·guard (**sayf**-gahrd)

safe space *noun* A place where you or an identified group of people can feel comfortable because they know they will not be criticized, harassed, or bullied.

safety *noun* The condition of being protected from harm or danger: *Parents are always concerned about their children's safety.* **safe·ty** (**sayf**-tee)

safety pin *noun* A fastening pin with a guard at one end that covers and holds the point.

safety pin

sagebrush

sag *verb*

1. To sink, droop, bend, or settle as a result of weight or pressure: *The heavy snow made the roof sag.*

2. To lose strength: *His spirits sagged after he failed the test.*
sag (sag)
▷ *verb* **sagging, sagged**

sage

1. *noun* An herb with grayish-green leaves that are often used in cooking.

2. *adjective* Very wise, as in *sage advice.*

3. *noun* A person, especially an elderly man, who is widely respected for his judgment and wisdom: *The sage offered advice to the rulers.*
sage (sayj)

sagebrush *noun* A common shrub on the dry plains of the western United States. **sage·brush** (**sayj**-bruhsh)

Sahara *noun* The largest hot desert in the world. It stretches across northern Africa from the Red Sea to the Atlantic Ocean. **Sa·har·a** (suh-**har**-uh) ▷ *adjective* **Saharan**

said *verb* The past tense and the past participle of **say**. **said** (sed)

sail

1. *noun* A large piece of canvas or other strong material that is attached to the mast of a boat or ship and moves it forward by catching the wind.

2. *verb* To travel by water. ▷ *noun* **sailing**

3. *verb* When a boat or ship **sails**, it begins a voyage.

4. *verb* To glide or move smoothly: *The kite sailed across the sky.*

5. *noun* Something that resembles or works like a sail, such as the arm of a windmill.
sail (sayl)
Sail sounds like **sale**. ▷ *verb* **sailing, sailed**

sailboat *noun* A boat that is moved through the water by the wind blowing against its sail or sails. **sail·boat** (**sayl**-*boht*)

sailor *noun*
1. A person who works as a member of the crew on a ship or boat.
2. A member of a country's navy. **sail·or** (**say**-lur)

saint *noun*
1. In certain Christian churches, a person who has been officially recognized for having lived a very holy life. Abbreviated as *St.*
2. A very kind and patient person: *Ms. Price is a saint to put up with us every day.* **saint** (saynt) ▷ *adjective* **saintly** ▷ *adjective* **sainted**

Saint Bernard *noun* A very large, powerful dog with a big head and fur that is white and reddish brown. The Saint Bernard was originally used to locate lost travelers in the snowy mountains of Switzerland. **Saint Ber·nard** (bur-**nahrd**)

sake *noun*
1. A benefit or an advantage: *The Thomases moved to the new house for the sake of their children, who now have a big backyard to play in.*
2. A reason or a purpose: *I added many details to the story for the sake of being realistic.* **sake** (sayk)

salad *noun*
1. A combination of raw vegetables, usually served with a dressing.
2. A cold dish of chopped fruit, meat, eggs, fish, or some other food, mixed in with a dressing, as in *egg salad.* **sal·ad** (**sal**-uhd)

salamander *noun* An animal that looks like a small, brightly colored lizard. **sal·a·man·der** (**sal**-uh-*man*-dur)

salary *noun* The fixed amount of money someone is paid for his or her work: *Shirley earns a good salary as a banker.* **sal·a·ry** (**sal**-ur-ee) ▷ *noun, plural* **salaries**

sale *noun*
1. The act of exchanging property or services for money, as in *the sale of a house.*
2. A period of time when items are sold at lower than usual prices, as in *a shoe sale.*
3. sales *noun, plural* The number or amount of things sold: *Sales were high in June.*
4. for sale Available for purchase: *All of these bikes are for sale.*
5. on sale For sale at reduced prices: *Halloween decorations go on sale in November.* **sale** (sayl)

Sale sounds like **sail.**

salesman *noun* A man who sells goods or services. **sales·man** (**saylz**-muhn) ▷ *noun, plural* **salesmen**

salesperson *noun* A man or woman who sells goods or services. **sales·per·son** (**saylz**-*pur*-suhn) ▷ *noun, plural* **salespeople**

saliva *noun* The watery fluid in your mouth that keeps it moist and helps you soften and swallow food. **sa·li·va** (suh-**lye**-vuh)

salmon *noun*
1. A large fish with silvery skin and edible pink flesh. Most salmon live in saltwater but swim to freshwater to lay their eggs. ▷ *noun, plural* **salmon**
2. A yellowish-pink or light orange color. **salm·on** (**sam**-uhn)

salmonella *noun* Any of a group of bacteria that are shaped like rods and that can cause disease in humans and other warm-blooded animals. **sal·mo·nel·la** (*sal*-muh-**nel**-uh) ▷ *noun, plural* **salmonellas** *or* **salmonellae** (*sal*-muh-**nel**-ee)

salamander

Word History

Imagine a bacterium having your name. For Daniel E. Salmon, that is what happened. He was an American veterinarian who studied animal disease for the US government, and in 1885 he discovered one type of the **salmonella** bacteria. When a name becomes a word, it is called an eponym.

salon *noun*
1. A shop where people go to have someone work on their appearance. It is also called a **beauty salon, beauty shop,** or **beauty parlor.** If its main business is hair care, it may be called a **hair salon.** A salon that especially caters to nail care is called a **nail salon.**
2. A shop for clothes by a fashion designer or for specialty clothing, as in *a dress salon* or *a bridal salon.*
3. A drawing room in a large and elegant house; a parlor. **sa·lon** (suh-**lahn**)

salsa *noun*
1. A hot, spicy tomato sauce that can be flavored with onions and hot peppers and eaten with tortilla chips.
2. A popular style of music that originated in the Caribbean. It has been influenced by jazz and rock. **sal·sa** (**sahl**-suh)

salt *noun*
1. A white substance in the form of crystals, found in seawater and under the ground. Salt is used to season and preserve food. ▷ *noun* **saltiness** ▷ *verb* **salt** ▷ *adjective* **salt**

2. In chemistry, a compound formed from an acid and a base.

3. If you take something with **a grain of salt**, you are aware that it might be exaggerated or not absolutely true.

salt (sawlt)

Word History

Long ago, **salt** was the main way of keeping meat and some other foods from spoiling. In fact, it was so important that Roman soldiers were paid in salt. This "salt money" was called a *salary,* from the Latin root for "salt," *sal.* This same root is in the Latin word *salsa,* meaning "salted," and gives us the English words *salsa* and *sauce.*

saltwater *noun* Water that is very salty, such as that found in the oceans. **salt·wa·ter** (**sawlt**-*waw*-tur)

salty *adjective*

1. Containing salt, often too much salt: *Would you like sweet or salty snacks?*

2. A **salty** story or **salty** language is impolite or about sex.

salt·y (**sawl**-tee)

▷ *adjective* **saltier, saltiest**

salute *verb*

1. To show your respect by raising your hand to your forehead, as in *to salute an officer.*

2. To express admiration or respect for something someone has done: *I salute you for your courage in telling the truth.*

sa·lute (suh-**loot**)

▷ *verb* **saluting, saluted** ▷ *noun* **salute**

salvage *verb* To rescue property from a shipwreck, fire, flood, or other disaster: *Eve was able to salvage a few boxes from the flooded basement.* **sal·vage** (**sal**-vij) ▷ *verb* **salvaging, salvaged** ▷ *noun* **salvage** ▷ *noun* **salvager**

salvation *noun*

1. The state of being saved or protected from sin, evil, harm, or destruction: *Different religions have different ways of salvation.*

2. Someone or something that saves or protects: *On a hot day at the beach, sunscreen is my salvation.*

sal·va·tion (sal-**vay**-shuhn)

salve *noun* An ointment or a cream that relieves pain and helps heal wounds, burns, or sores. **salve** (sav)

same

1. *adjective* Exactly alike: *Two girls wore the same dress to the party.*

2. *adjective* Being the very one and not another: *This is the same seat I had yesterday.*

3. *adjective* Not changed or different: *She's the same thoughtful person she's always been.*

4. *pronoun* The identical person or thing: *Malcolm ordered a hamburger, and I asked for the same.*

5. the same In an identical manner: *He treats all his students the same.*

same (saym)

sample

1. *noun* A small part or quantity of something that shows what the whole of it is like, as in *free samples of cheese.*

2. *verb* To take a small amount of something to test its quality or to see if you like it, as in *to sample the snacks.* ▷ *verb* **sampling, sampled**

sam·ple (**sam**-puhl)

samurai *noun* A Japanese warrior who lived in medieval times. **sam·u·rai** (**sam**-u-*rye*) ▷ *noun, plural* **samurai** ▷ *adjective* **samurai**

sanction

1. *verb* To permit or to give approval: *The city sanctioned the use of the park for the demonstration.* ▷ *verb* **sanctioning, sanctioned**

2. *noun* Permission or approval: *The voters gave their sanction to the amendment.*

3. sanctions *noun, plural* A punishment, such as a blockade of shipping, that a nation or group of nations enforces against another, as in *trade sanctions against Cuba.*

sanc·tion (**sangk**-shuhn)

samurai

sanctuary *noun*

1. Safety or protection: *The outlaws found sanctuary in the deep, dark woods.*

2. A natural area where birds or animals are protected from hunters, as in *a nature sanctuary.*

3. A holy or sacred place, such as a church, temple, or mosque. **sanc·tu·ar·y** (sangk-choo-*er*-ee)

▷ *noun, plural* **sanctuaries**

sanctuary city *noun* A city that is friendly to immigrants who don't have all the necessary permissions to live in a country. Sanctuary cities make it easier for these immigrants to avoid being deported.

sand

1. *noun* The small, loose particles made of rock and shell that cover beaches and deserts. ▷ *adjective* **sandy**

2. *verb* To sprinkle or cover with sand: *People sand icy roads in winter.*

3. *verb* To smooth a surface with sandpaper or other abrasive substance, as in *to sand boards for shelves.* **sand** (sand)

▷ *verb* **sanding, sanded**

sandal *noun* A shoe that is partly open on top or has straps that attach the sole to the foot. **san·dal** (**san**-duhl)

sandbar *noun* A ridge of sand in a river or bay or along an ocean's shore. **sand·bar** (**sand**-*bahr*)

sandbox *noun* A large wooden box with low sides that is filled with sand for children to play in. **sand·box** (**sand**-*bahks*)

sandpaper *noun* Heavy paper coated with grains of sand and used for smoothing rough surfaces. **sand·pa·per** (**sand**-*pay*-pur)

sandpiper *noun* A small shorebird with a long bill, brown or gray feathers, and long, slender legs. **sand·pip·er** (**sand**-*pye*-pur)

sandstone *noun* A kind of rock made up mostly of sandlike grains of quartz cemented together by lime or other materials. **sand·stone** (**sand**-*stohn*)

sandwich *noun* Two or more slices of bread with cheese, meat, or some other filling between them, as in *a chicken sandwich.* **sand·wich** (**sand**-wich)

▷ *noun, plural* **sandwiches**

Word History

The popular food that we call a **sandwich** is named after a man who lived in the 18th century, the fourth Earl of Sandwich, John Montagu, an English diplomat. Since he did not like to take time away from the games he enjoyed playing, he ordered slices of bread with fillings to be brought to him at the game table.

sane *adjective*

1. Mentally healthy: *Alex says some strange things, but he's perfectly sane.*

2. Sensible, or showing good judgment: *Jill has a very sane approach to the problem.* **sane** (sayn)

▷ *adjective* **saner, sanest** ▷ *adverb* **sanely**

sang *verb* The past tense of **sing**. **sang** (sang)

sanitary *adjective* Clean, healthful, and free of germs, as in *a sanitary kitchen.* **san·i·tar·y** (**san**-i-*ter*-ee)

sanitation *noun* Systems for cleaning the water supply and disposing of sewage and garbage in a town or city. **san·i·ta·tion** (san-i-**tay**-shuhn)

sanity *noun* Good mental health: *He felt he needed a break from the constant noise and confusion to keep his sanity.* **san·i·ty** (**san**-i-tee)

sank *verb* The past tense of **sink**. **sank** (sangk)

sap

1. *noun* The liquid that flows through a plant, carrying water and food from one part of the plant to another.

2. *verb* To gradually weaken or to drain someone's strength or power: *The flu had completely sapped Paul's energy.* ▷ *verb* **sapping, sapped** **sap** (sap)

sapling *noun* A young, slender tree. **sap·ling** (**sap**-ling)

sapphire *noun* A transparent blue gemstone. **sap·phire** (**saf**-ire)

sarcastic *adjective* Using bitter or mocking words that are meant to hurt or make fun of someone or something. **sar·cas·tic** (sahr-**kas**-tik) ▷ *noun* **sarcasm** (**sahr**-*kaz*-uhm) ▷ *adverb* **sarcastically**

sardine *noun* A small, edible, saltwater fish, often packed tightly in cans. **sar·dine** (sahr-**deen**)

sari *noun* A long piece of light material worn wrapped around the body and over one shoulder. Saris are worn mainly by Indian and Pakistani women and girls. **sa·ri** (**sahr**-ee)

sarong *noun* A long piece of brightly colored cloth wrapped around the body and tucked in at the waist or under the armpits. Sarongs are worn by men and women in Malaysia, Indonesia, and the Pacific Islands. **sa·rong** (suh-**rahng**)

sash *noun*

1. A wide strip of material worn around the waist or over one shoulder as an ornament or as part of a uniform.

2. A frame that holds the glass in a window or door: *Lift the bottom sash to open the window.* **sash** (sash)

▷ *noun, plural* **sashes**

sassy *adjective*

1. Disrespectful and rude: *He gave the teacher a sassy answer.*

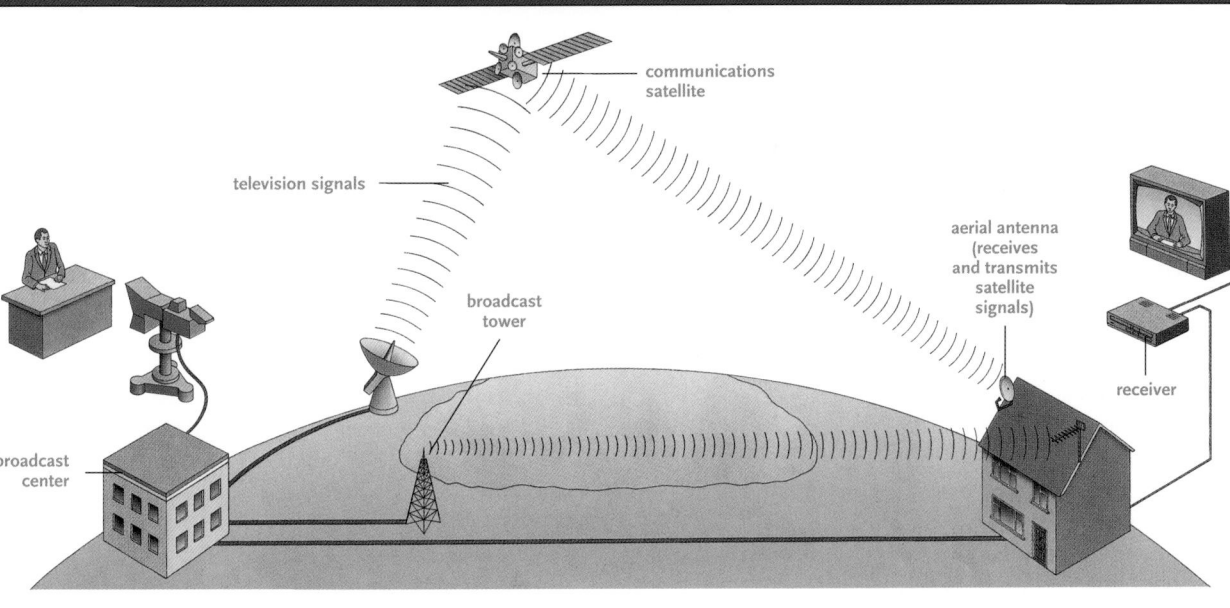

communications
satellite

television signals

broadcast
tower

aerial antenna
(receives
and transmits
satellite
signals)

receiver

broadcast
center

satellite

2. Bold and lively in an entertaining way: *Everyone got a kick out of her sassy new boyfriend.*

3. Smart and fashionable, with a distinctive and bold style, as in *a sassy haircut* or *a sassy dress.*
sas·sy (**sas**-ee)
▷ *adjective* **sassier, sassiest** ▷ *noun* **sassiness**
▷ *adverb* **sassily** (**sas**-uh-lee)

sat *verb* The past tense and the past participle of **sit**. **sat** (sat)

Satan *noun* The devil in the Old Testament. Satan is described as an evil spirit that was sent away from the presence of God and confined to hell. **Sa·tan** (**say**-tuhn)

satellite *noun*
1. A spacecraft that is sent into orbit around the earth, the moon, or another heavenly body.
2. A moon or other heavenly body that travels in an orbit around a larger heavenly body. *See* **moon**.
sat·el·lite (**sat**-uh-*lite*)

satin *noun* A very smooth fabric that is shiny on one side and dull on the other. **sat·in** (**sat**-in)

satire *noun* A type of mocking humor intended to show how foolish or misguided someone or something is: *My favorite television show is a satire of the evening news.* **sat·ire** (**sat**-ire) ▷ *noun* **satirist** ▷ *adjective* **satirical** (suh-**tir**-i-kuhl)

satisfaction *noun* A feeling of being pleased or content because you have achieved something or met certain needs: *Sarah felt great satisfaction about her math grade.* **sat·is·fac·tion** (*sat*-is-**fak**-shuhn)

satisfactory *adjective* Good enough but not outstanding, as in *satisfactory exam results.*
sat·is·fac·to·ry (*sat*-is-**fak**-tur-ee) ▷ *adverb* **satisfactorily**

satisfied *adjective* Happy because a need or want has been met: *Satisfied customers return again and again to Andy's Ribs.* **sat·is·fied** (**sat**-is-*fide*)

satisfy *verb*
1. To please someone by meeting his or her needs or desires: *The pizzas soon satisfied the hungry children.*
2. To convince or to free from doubt: *My mother was satisfied by my explanation of how the window broke.*
sat·is·fy (**sat**-is-*fye*)
▷ *verb* **satisfies, satisfying, satisfied**

saturate *verb* To soak thoroughly: *The rain saturated my shoes.* **sat·u·rate** (**sach**-uh-*rate*) ▷ *verb* **saturating, saturated** ▷ *noun* **saturation** ▷ *adjective* **saturated**

Saturday *noun* The seventh day of the week, after Friday and before Sunday. **Sat·ur·day** (**sat**-ur-day *or* **sat**-ur-*dee*)

Word History

Saturday, the seventh day of the week, and the planet **Saturn** share a common history. Both were named for Saturn, the Roman god of farming.

Saturn *noun* The sixth planet in distance from the sun and the second-largest planet in our solar system. Saturn has 62 moons and is surrounded by rings that are thought to be made of ice, rock, and frozen gases. **Sat·urn** (**sat**-urn)

sauce *noun* A thick liquid served with food to add flavor and make it more appealing, as in *mushroom sauce.* **sauce** (saws)

saucepan *noun* A deep metal or glass cooking pot with a long handle and a lid. **sauce·pan** (**saws**-*pan*)

a b c d e f g h i j k l m n o p q r **s** t u v w x y z

saucer *noun* A small, shallow plate designed to go under a cup and catch spills. **sau·cer** (**saw**-sur)

sauna *noun*
1. A bath using dry heat, or a steam bath in which the steam is made by throwing water on hot stones.
2. A room for such a bath.
sau·na (**saw**-nuh)

saunter *verb* To walk in a slow, leisurely, or casual way. **saun·ter** (**sawn**-tur) ▷ *verb* **sauntering, sauntered**

sausage *noun* Chopped and seasoned meat that is sometimes stuffed into a thin case shaped like a tube. **sau·sage** (**saw**-sij)

savage
1. *adjective* Not tamed, or not under human control, as in *a savage beast.*
2. *adjective* Fierce, dangerous, or violent, as in *a savage battle.* ▷ *adverb* **savagely**
3. *adjective* Not civilized, as in *a savage society.*
4. *noun* A person who lives in a way that is not civilized: *The explorers encountered savages who ate their meat raw.*
5. *noun* A fierce or violent person: *He's such a savage that no one goes near his house.*
sav·age (**sav**-ij)

savanna *or* **savannah** *noun* A flat, grassy plain with few or no trees. Savannas are found in tropical and subtropical areas. **sa·van·na** *or* **sa·van·nah** (suh-**van**-uh)

save *verb*
1. To rescue someone or something from danger or harm: *The firefighters saved the man from the burning house.*
2. To make the best use of something and not waste it, as in *to save time* or *to save energy.*
3. To store or keep something, especially money, for future use: *I save part of my allowance every week.*
4. To stop a ball or puck from going into a goal in soccer or hockey. ▷ *noun* **save**
5. To copy a file from a computer's RAM, or random access memory, onto a disk or other storage device.
save (sayv)
▷ *verb* **saving, saved** ▷ *noun* **saver**

savings *noun, plural* Money that has been saved or not spent: *Greg plans to use his savings to take a trip.* **sav·ings** (**say**-vingz)

savior *noun* A person or thing that saves someone from danger, difficulty, or death. **sav·ior** (**sayv**-yur)

savory *adjective* Pleasing to the taste or smell, as in *savory cooking odors.* **sa·vor·y** (**say**-vur-ee)

saw
1. *noun* A hand- or power-driven tool with sharp teeth on its blade, used for cutting wood: *We'll need a good saw to cut down these branches.*
2. *verb* To use a saw for cutting something: *Please saw these logs for the fireplace.* ▷ *verb* **sawing, sawed, sawn** (sawn)
3. *verb* The past tense of **see**.
saw (saw)

sawdust *noun* Tiny particles of wood that fall off when you saw wood: *The floor of the carpentry shop was covered with sawdust.* **saw·dust** (**saw**-*duhst*)

sawmill *noun* A place where people use machines to saw logs into lumber. **saw·mill** (**saw**-*mil*)

saxophone *noun* A wind instrument made of brass, with a mouthpiece that holds a reed, keys for the fingers, and a body that is usually curved. **sax·o·phone** (**sak**-suh-*fone*) ▷ *noun* **saxophonist**

say
1. *verb* To speak: *Did you say anything?*
2. *verb* To state, or to express in words: *The sign says this is a one-way street.*
3. *verb* To repeat or to recite, as in *to say one's prayers.*
4. *noun* The chance to speak, as in *to have your say.*
say (say)
▷ *verb* **saying, said** (sed)

Synonyms

Say means to express something out loud using words. *Said,* the past tense of *say,* is often used in writing about conversations. For example: "*My mom says that it's too late to go to the store now,*" said Tony. "*OK,*" said Eloise. "*How about tomorrow?*" Here are some other words that can sometimes take the place of *say.*

■ **State** means to announce or declare something in very straightforward terms: *The lawyer asked the witness to state his name, address, and occupation.*

■ **Report** means to give a detailed account of something that has happened: *My mom reported every word of her conversation with my teacher.*

■ **Remark** means to point out or offer a comment or an opinion on something: *After reading the article, Jed remarked that he thought the author didn't know what he was talking about.*

■ **Exclaim** means to cry out or say something with sudden emotion, such as surprise or anger: "*I can't believe you ate that entire cake!*" exclaimed Simon.

■ **Declare** means to say something formally or officially: *The mayor declared that next week will be Be Kind to Animals Week in our town.*

saying *noun* A well-known phrase or proverb that gives advice or expresses a truth. "Don't cry over spilled milk" is a saying. **say·ing** (**say**-ing)

scab *noun* The hard crust that forms over a sore or wound when it is healing. **scab** (skab)

scabbard *noun* A case that holds a sword, dagger, or bayonet when it is not in use. **scab·bard** (**skab**-urd)

scaffold *noun* A temporary, raised structure made of planks and poles. It serves as a platform for workers to stand on while doing construction or such jobs as painting or cleaning a building. **scaf·fold** (**skaf**-uhld)

scald *verb* To burn with very hot liquid or steam, as in *to scald yourself with boiling water*. **scald** (skawld) ▷ *verb* **scalding, scalded** ▷ *noun* **scald** ▷ *adjective* **scalding**

scale

1. *noun* One of the thin, flat, overlapping pieces of hard skin that cover the body of a fish, snake, or other reptile. ▷ *adjective* **scaly**

2. *verb* To remove all the scales from something.

3. *noun* Musical notes arranged in a series of rising or falling pitches, as in *practicing scales on the piano*.

4. *noun* A series of numbers, units, or values used to measure something, as in *the moment magnitude scale for earthquakes*.

5. *noun* The ratio between the measurements on a map, model, drawing, or plan and the actual measurements, as in *a scale of one inch to 100 miles*.

6. *noun* A device for weighing things.

7. *verb* To climb or go up something, as in *to scale a mountain*.

8. *noun* A series of stages or steps: *The pay scale ranged from $7 per hour to $15 per hour*. **scale** (skale) ▷ *verb* **scaling, scaled**

scalene triangle *noun* In geometry, a triangle with three sides of different lengths. **sca·lene triangle** (skay-**leen**)

scallion *noun* An onion with long, grasslike leaves and a small bulb. **scal·lion** (**skal**-yuhn)

scallop *noun*

1. A shellfish with two fan-shaped, hinged shells that swims by snapping its shells together and shooting out a jet of water.

2. One of a series of small curves in a decorative border that looks like the edge of a scallop shell. ▷ *verb* **scallop** ▷ *adjective* **scalloped** **scal·lop** (**skah**-luhp or **skal**-uhp)

scalp *noun* The skin covering the top and back of your head, usually covered with hair. **scalp** (skalp)

scalpel *noun* A small, straight knife with a very sharp blade, used in surgery. **scal·pel** (**skal**-puhl)

scale

scamper *verb* To run lightly and quickly: *The rabbit scampered away*. **scam·per** (**skam**-pur) ▷ *verb* **scampering, scampered**

Word History

Perhaps soldiers quickly packing up their army camp were the first people to **scamper**. The origin of the verb, which means "to run with light, quick steps," is not certain, but one of its first meanings was "to run away for safety." It may be based on the French verb *escamper*, meaning "to break up a camp." French speakers based this term on their word *camp*.

scan *verb*

1. To read quickly, without looking for details, as in *to scan the headlines*.

2. To examine in a searching way: *I scanned the audience for my parents*.

3. To move a beam of light over something to obtain or transmit an image: *I can scan these photos and send copies by email*. **scan** (skan) ▷ *verb* **scanning, scanned** ▷ *noun* **scan**

scandal *noun*

1. A dishonest or immoral act that shocks people and disgraces those involved, as in *a cheating scandal*.

2. Harmful gossip: *Those television shows seem to thrive on scandal*. **scan·dal** (**skan**-duhl) ▷ *verb* **scandalize** ▷ *adjective* **scandalous**

Scandinavian *noun* Someone who was born in or is a citizen of Norway, Denmark, or Sweden. Iceland and Finland also are sometimes considered Scandinavian countries. **Scan·di·na·vi·an** (skan-duh-**nay**-vee-uhn) ▷ *adjective* **Scandinavian**

scanner *noun* A machine that uses a beam of light to copy an image or read information. **scan·ner** (**skan**-ur)

scant *adjective*

1. Barely enough, or not enough, as in *a scant supply of water*.

2. Not quite the full amount, as in *a scant teaspoon of salt*. **scant** (skant)

Scantron *noun*

1. A trademark for a machine that reads prepared forms that contain the answers to multiple choice questions.

2. A trademark for a piece of paper that is designed to be read by a Scantron machine: *The teacher collected all of the Scantrons at the end of the test*. **Scan·tron** (**skan**-trahn)

scanty *adjective* Too little in size or amount, as in *scanty information.* **scant·y** (**skan**-tee) ▷ *adjective* **scantier, scantiest** ▷ *adverb* **scantily**

scapegoat *noun* A person who is made to take the blame for the mistakes or wrongdoings of others. **scape·goat** (**skape**-*goht*)

scar *noun* A mark left on your skin by an injury or wound that has healed, as in *a burn scar.* **scar** (skahr) ▷ *verb* **scar**

scarce *adjective* Hard to get or find, or available in quantities too small to meet the demand: *Fresh vegetables are scarce in the winter.* **scarce** (skairs) ▷ *noun* **scarcity** (**skair**-si-tee)

scarcely *adverb*
1. Hardly; almost not: *I've scarcely seen her since she got home.*
2. Probably not or certainly not: *After the way they treated us, I could scarcely forgive them.*
scarce·ly (**skairs**-lee)

scare
1. *verb* To frighten or be frightened by someone or something: *The thunder scared the cats.* ▷ *verb* **scaring, scared**
2. *noun* Widespread fear or panic, as in *a bomb scare.* ▷ *adjective* **scared**
scare (skair)

scarecrow *noun* A figure made of straw that is shaped and dressed to look like a person and put in a field to frighten birds away from crops. **scare·crow** (**skair**-*kroh*)

scarf *noun* A square or strip of material worn around the neck or head for decoration or warmth, as in *a woolen scarf.* **scarf** (skahrf) ▷ *noun, plural* **scarfs** or **scarves** (skahrvz)

scarlet *noun* A bright red color. **scar·let** (**skahr**-lit) ▷ *adjective* **scarlet**

scary *adjective* Causing feelings of fear, as in *a scary movie.* **scar·y** (**skair**-ee) ▷ *adjective* **scarier, scariest**

scatter *verb*
1. To throw things here and there: *Leaves were scattered all over the porch.*
2. To move off in different directions: *The insects scattered when I turned over the log.*
scat·ter (**skat**-ur) ▷ *verb* **scattering, scattered**

scavenge *verb* To search through garbage for something useful or edible: *The dogs scavenged for scraps in the trash cans.* **scav·enge** (**skav**-uhnj) ▷ *verb*

scavenging, scavenged ▷ *noun* **scavenger**

scenario *noun*
1. An outline of a movie, a play, or an opera that summarizes the story.
2. An outline of a series of events that might happen in a particular situation, as in *an emergency scenario.* **sce·nar·i·o** (suh-**nair**-ee-*oh*) ▷ *noun, plural* **scenarios**

scene *noun*
1. A view of people or places, as in *a restful country scene.*
2. A part of a story, play, or movie that shows what is happening in one particular place and time.
3. The place where something happens, as in *the scene of the crime.*
4. make a scene To show your anger or other emotion in a very public way.
scene (seen)

scenery *noun*
1. The natural features of a landscape, such as trees, lakes, and mountains: *The scenery along the river is especially beautiful.*
2. The painted screens and backdrops that are used on stage to represent the location of a scene in a play, an opera, or a ballet: *We spent all afternoon painting woodland scenery for the play.*
scen·er·y (**see**-nur-ee)

scenic *adjective* Having beautiful natural surroundings, as in *a scenic mountain.* **sce·nic** (**see**-nik)

scent
1. *noun* A distinctive smell, especially a pleasant one, as in *the scent of roses.* ▷ *adjective* **scented**
2. *noun* A pleasant-smelling liquid that you put on your skin; a perfume.
3. *noun* The odor or trail of a hunted animal or person, as in *a fox's scent.*
4. *verb* To feel that something exists or is about to happen. ▷ *verb* **scenting, scented**
scent (sent)
Scent sounds like **cent** and **sent.**

— scepter

scepter *noun* A rod or staff carried by a king or queen as a symbol of authority. **scep·ter** (**sep**-tur)

schedule
1. *noun* A plan, a list of events, or a timetable, as in *the daily schedule.*
2. *verb* To plan an event for a certain date or time. ▷ *verb* **scheduling, scheduled**
sched·ule (**skej**-ool or **skej**-ul)

scheme
1. *noun* A plan or plot for doing something, as in *a*

scheme for getting in through the back way.
2. *verb* To make plans for something in a secret or underhanded way: *The girls schemed all day to get even with the boys.* ▷ *verb* **scheming, schemed** ▷ *noun* **schemer** ▷ *adjective* **scheming**
scheme (skeem)

scholar *noun*
1. A person who has a great deal of knowledge in a particular field, as in *a scholar of American history.*
2. A serious student: *Meredith is a brilliant math scholar.*
schol·ar (**skah**-lur)
▷ *adjective* **scholarly**

scholarship *noun*
1. Money given to pay for you to go to college or to follow a course of study, as in *an engineering scholarship.*
2. Knowledge achieved by studying hard: *This report shows excellent scholarship.*
schol·ar·ship (**skah**-lur-*ship*)

scholastic *adjective* Of or having to do with school and learning: *He was proud of his sister's scholastic achievements.* **scho·las·tic** (skuh-**las**-tik)

school *noun*
1. A place where people go to be taught and to learn, as in *the neighborhood school.*
2. Learning that takes place in school: *Jeremy likes school.* ▷ *noun* **schooling** ▷ *verb* **school**
3. All the people in a school: *The whole school went on a field trip.*
4. A part of a university, as in *a medical school.*
5. A group of fish or sea creatures swimming or feeding together, as in *a school of dolphins.*
school (skool)

schoolchild *noun* A **schoolchild** is a boy or girl who goes to school. **school·child** (**skool**-*childe*) ▷ *noun, plural* **schoolchildren**

schooner *noun* A fast ship with two masts, a narrow hull, and sails that run lengthwise. **schoon·er** (**skoo**-nur)

schwa *noun* The sound of a short, unstressed vowel in English, such as the sound of the letter *a* in the word *ago,* or the sound of the *o* in *gallop.* Dictionaries represent the schwa by the symbol ə. **schwa** (shwah)

Word History

For such a little sound, a **schwa** has a complicated-looking name. The word in Hebrew was *shewa,* which was the name of a mark meaning "no vowel." Hebrew speakers based it on the word *shaw,* meaning "emptiness." The word *shewa* was later adapted by the Germans for their language. They capitalized it and spelled it as *Schwa,* dropping the letter *e* and changing the *sh* to *sch.* English speakers adopted the term from German.

science *noun*
1. The study of nature and the physical world through observation and experiment: *Science has improved our lives in many ways.*
2. Any of the branches or fields of scientific study, such as biology, physics, or geology.
sci·ence (**sye**-uhns)
▷ *noun* **scientist** (**sye**-uhn-tist) ▷ *adjective* **scientific** (sye-uhn-**tif**-ik) ▷ *adverb* **scientifically**

Word History

The word **science** comes from the Latin word *scientia,* which means "knowledge." Although the term *science* was used in English as early as 1340, the word *scientist* was not coined until 500 years later, by the English philosopher and historian William Whewell.

science fiction *noun* Fantasy stories that are set in the future and usually involve science and technology, space travel, or life on other planets.

scientific *adjective*
1. Of or having to do with science: *Matthew's class does a different scientific experiment each week.*
2. To use the **scientific method** when you do an experiment, you first collect and organize information about the problem you are trying to solve, and then you test your ideas about it very carefully.
sci·en·tif·ic (sye-uhn-**tif**-ik)
▷ *adverb* **scientifically**

scientist *noun* A person who is trained and works in science. Many scientists work in laboratories, doing experiments. **sci·en·tist** (**sye**-uhn-tist)

scissors *noun, plural* A sharp tool for cutting cloth and paper, with looped handles and two blades that press against each other. **scis·sors** (**siz**-urz)

scold *verb* To tell someone in an angry way that he or she has done something wrong or done a bad job: *Dad scolded the children for running in the house.* **scold** (skohld) ▷ *verb* **scolding, scolded**

scoliosis *noun* An abnormal curving of the spine to the side. **sco·li·o·sis** (*skoh*-lee-**oh**-sis)

scoop
1. *verb* To pick up or gather up something in a quick, smooth movement: *Jan scooped up the marbles in her hands.* ▷ *verb* **scooping, scooped**
2. *noun* A utensil shaped like a spoon with a short handle and a deep hollow, as in *an ice-cream scoop.*
3. *noun* A story reported in a newspaper before other papers have a chance to report it: *The story about the mayor's resignation was a scoop for our local paper.*
▷ *verb* **scoop**
scoop (skoop)

a
b
c
d
e
f
g
h
i
j
k
l
m
n
o
p
q
r
s
t
u
v
w
x
y
z

scooter *noun*

1. A child's vehicle with a handle, two wheels, and a board that you stand on with one foot while pushing against the ground with the other.

2. A small, light motorcycle.

scoot·er (**skoo**-tur)

Word History

Rush, whiz, zip. These are all ways to say "move fast." Another word like these is *scoot,* and from *scoot* we get the name for a popular child's vehicle, the **scooter.** Sailors were probably the first people to say *scoot,* because in the earliest written appearances of the word, ships are described as *scooting*—"moving fast." Beyond that, the history of the verb *scoot* is unknown. It's clear, though, that the name *scooter* means "the thing that moves fast."

scope *noun*

1. The opportunity or possibility: *Working as an illustrator gave Aunt Martha plenty of scope for her artistic talents.*

2. The area or range of operation, as in *the scope of an investigation.*

scope (skohp)

scorch

1. *verb* To burn something on the surface, as with an iron. ▷ *noun* **scorch**

2. *verb* To wither or dry up with intense heat: *The front lawn has been scorched by the sun.*

3. *adjective* If the weather is **scorching,** it is almost too hot to bear.

scorch (skorch)

▷ *verb* **scorches, scorching, scorched**

score

1. *verb* To make a point or points in a game, contest, or test: *Our team only scored six points.* ▷ *noun* **scorer**

2. *noun* The number of points made by each person or team in a game, contest, or test: *I evened the score by spelling my word correctly.*

3. *noun* A written piece of music, showing all the parts for voices or instruments.

4. *verb* To arrange a piece of music so that it can be played by different instruments: *The composer scored my favorite song for a five-piece band.*

5. *verb* To mark the surface of something with cuts, scratches, notches, or lines: *My father scored the soles of my new dress-up shoes so I wouldn't slip.*

6. *noun* Twenty: *The skyscraper was built four score years ago, so it is 80 years old.*

7. scores *noun, plural* A large number, as in *scores of letters.*

8. know the score *(informal)* To be well informed about the situation.

score (skor)

▷ *verb* **scoring, scored**

scorn

1. *noun* A feeling of contempt for someone or something you think of as worthless or bad: *Gerry is full of scorn for any new ideas.*

2. *verb* To treat with contempt: *Don't scorn the man's efforts to make a better life for himself.*

3. *verb* To refuse something because you think it is not worth your while.

scorn (skorn)

▷ *verb* **scorning, scorned** ▷ *adjective* **scornful**

scorpion *noun* An animal related to the spider with a long, jointed tail that ends in a poisonous stinger. **scor·pi·on** (**skor**-pee-uhn)

scoundrel *noun* Someone who deceives or takes advantage of others. **scoun·drel** (**skoun**-druhl)

scour *verb*

1. To clean or polish something by rubbing it hard with soap and water or something rough, as in *to scour a bathtub.* ▷ *noun* **scourer**

2. To search a place thoroughly: *We scoured the woods for our dog.*

scour (skour)

▷ *verb* **scouring, scoured**

scout

1. *noun* Someone sent to find out and bring back information: *The scout went ahead of the group in search of water.*

2. *verb* To search in the hope of discovering something: *We scouted the neighborhood for witnesses.* ▷ *verb* **scouting, scouted**

scout (skout)

scorpion

Word History

A **scout** used to be called a *scout-watch,* meaning someone who kept guard. For example, *scout-watches* kept a lookout for newcomers to a town. Soon English speakers started using the word *scout* on its own. At that point, a *scout* was a soldier sent on ahead of the main army to check on the enemy's position, and this led to our current meanings. The origins of the word *scout* lie in the Latin verb that meant "to listen," *auscultare,* because in order to keep guard, you must listen well.

scowl *verb* To make an angry frown: *Margaret scowled when she didn't know the answer.*

scowl (skoul) ▷ *verb* **scowling, scowled** ▷ *noun* **scowl**

scramble *verb*

1. To crawl or climb in a hurried way, using hands and feet: *The bear scrambled into the woods the minute he saw us.*

2. To rush or struggle to get somewhere or something: *Jessica scrambled to get to the front row.*

3. To mix up or throw together: *Scramble the letters and see how many words you can spell.*

4. To alter an electronic signal so that it requires a special receiver to decode the message: *The cable television company scrambled its signal so that only subscribers could receive it.* ▷ *noun* **scrambler**
scram·ble (skram-buhl)
▷ *verb* **scrambling, scrambled** ▷ *noun* **scramble**
▷ *adjective* **scrambled**

scrambled eggs *noun, plural* Egg yolks and whites mixed together and cooked in a frying pan.

scrap

1. *noun* A small piece or bit of something, as in *scraps of meat.*

2. *noun* Metal that is saved from old cars or machines for reuse.

3. *verb* To abandon or get rid of something: *When it started to rain, we scrapped our plans for the evening.*

4. *verb* (*informal*) To quarrel or to fight: *Three dogs scrapped over a single steak bone.* ▷ *noun* **scrap**
▷ *noun* **scrapper**
scrap (skrap)
▷ *verb* **scrapping, scrapped**

scrapbook *noun* A book with blank pages on which you mount pictures, newspaper clippings, and other items you wish to keep. **scrap·book** (skrap-buk)

scrape

1. *verb* To clean, smooth, or scratch something with a rough or sharp object, as in *to scrape a knee.*
▷ *noun* **scrape** ▷ *noun* **scraper**

2. *noun* (*informal*) An awkward or embarrassing situation.

3. scrape together *verb* To gather or collect with great difficulty, as in *to scrape a few dollars together.*

4. scrape by *verb* To manage or make your way with difficulty: *The man scraped by on his small salary.*
scrape (skrape)
▷ *verb* **scraping, scraped**

scratch *verb*

1. To scrape lightly with your fingernails a part of you that itches, as in *to scratch a mosquito bite.*

2. To mark or cut the surface of something, as in *to scratch furniture.*

3. To tear or dig at with fingernails or claws: *The*

dog scratched at the door until we let him in.

4. (*informal*) To erase or cancel something, as in *to scratch plans.*

5. from scratch (*informal*) Starting from fresh ingredients or from the very beginning: *We made cupcakes from scratch.*

6. up to scratch (*informal*) Acceptable, ready, or up to standard.
scratch (skrach)
▷ *verb* **scratches, scratching, scratched** ▷ *noun* **scratch**

scratchy *adjective*

1. Causing an itch, as in *a scratchy fabric.*

2. Rough and irritating, as in *a scratchy throat.*
scratch·y (skrach-ee)
▷ *adjective* **scratchier, scratchiest**

scrawl

1. *verb* To write in a hurried, careless way, as in *to scrawl a note.* ▷ *verb* **scrawling, scrawled**

2. *noun* Sloppy handwriting that is difficult to read.
scrawl (skrawl)

scream

1. *verb* To make a loud, shrill, piercing cry or sound, as in *to scream in fright.* ▷ *verb* **screaming, screamed** ▷ *noun* **scream**

2. *noun* (*informal*) Someone or something that is considered very funny: *Angie is a scream when she dances.*
scream (skreem)

screech *verb* To make a loud, high-pitched sound: *My brakes screech every time I use them.*
screech (skreech) ▷ *verb* **screeches, screeching, screeched** ▷ *noun* **screech**

screen

1. *noun* Wire or plastic netting in a frame, as in *a window screen.*

2. *noun* A light, movable partition used to hide or divide a room. ▷ *verb* **screen**

3. *noun* The flat front surface of a television or computer monitor.

4. *noun* The white surface on which movies or slides are projected.

5. *verb* To show on a screen, as in *to screen a movie.*

6. *verb* To test someone to find out whether or not they have a disease, as in *to screen for diabetes.*

7. *verb* To examine carefully in order to make a selection, or to separate into groups, as in *to screen phone calls.*
screen (skreen)
▷ *verb* **screening, screened**

screenplay *noun* A play written to be made into a movie, with all the actors' lines and their directions. **screen·play (skreen**-*play)*

screensaver *noun* A computer program that replaces the still image on a computer monitor with one that changes or that uses less light. **screen·sav·er (skreen**-*say*-vur)

screenshot *noun* An image of what appears on a computer monitor. Screenshots are often used to show people how different programs work. **screen·shot (skreen**-*shaht)*

screw
1. *noun* A device for fastening things together that looks like a nail with a spiral thread and a slotted head.
2. *verb* To fasten something with screws: *Screw those shelves in and finish the bookcase.*
3. *verb* To turn or twist something until it is tightly fastened, as in *to screw on a lid.*
4. *verb* To twist into an unnatural shape or position, as in *to screw up your face.*
5. screw up *verb* (*informal*) To make a really bad mistake.
screw (skroo)
▷ *verb* **screwing, screwed**

screwdriver *noun* A tool with a tip that fits into the slot in the head of a screw so that you can turn it. **screw·driv·er (skroo**-*drye*-vur)

scribble *verb*
1. To write or draw something carelessly or in a rush: *Dorothy scribbled the directions as I talked.*
2. To make or cover with meaningless marks: *I scribbled in the margins of my notebook.*
scrib·ble (skrib-uhl)
▷ *verb* **scribbling, scribbled** ▷ *noun* **scribble**

scribe *noun* A person who copied documents by hand before printing was invented. **scribe** (skribe)

script *noun*
1. The written text of a play, a movie, or a television or radio show. ▷ *verb* **script**
2. Writing in which the letters are joined together: *Faith's letter to her pen pal was written in beautiful script.*
script (skript)

scripture *noun* The sacred writings of a religion. **scrip·ture (skrip**-chur)

scroll
1. *noun* A piece of paper or parchment with writing on it that is rolled up into the shape of a tube.
2. *verb* To move text or graphics up or down on a computer screen: *If you scroll down a little farther, you will see the author's name.* ▷ *verb* **scrolling, scrolled**
scroll (skrohl)

scroll bar *noun* A horiziontal or vertical bar on a computer monitor that you can move with your mouse to see different parts of a document.

scroll wheel *noun* A small disk on a mouse that you turn in order to scroll through a document or zoom into or out of an image on your computer monitor.

scrotum *noun* A pouch of skin, lying outside the body, that contains the testicles in men and most male mammals. **scro·tum (skroh**-tuhm)

scrounge *verb*
1. To get things from people without paying: *She always hung around, trying to scrounge something to eat.*
2. To get or collect things with difficulty, as in *to scrounge up some money.*
scrounge (skrounj)
▷ *verb* **scrounging, scrounged** ▷ *noun* **scrounger**

scrub

screwdriver

1. *verb* To clean something by rubbing or brushing it hard, as in *to scrub a sink.* ▷ *verb* **scrubbing, scrubbed** ▷ *noun* **scrub**
2. *noun* Low bushes or short trees that grow thickly together and cover an area of land.
scrub (skruhb)

scruffy *adjective* Shabby and messy or dirty, as in *a scruffy dog.* **scruff·y (skruhf**-ee) ▷ *adjective* **scruffier, scruffiest** ▷ *adverb* **scruffily**

scruple *noun* A strong feeling about what is right that keeps you from doing something wrong: *Alonzo's scruples kept him from cheating on the test.* **scru·ple (skroo**-puhl)

scrupulous *adjective*
1. Having strict beliefs about what is right and proper: *Gwen is scrupulous when it comes to eating healthily.*
2. Very careful and exact, as in *scrupulous detail.*
scru·pu·lous (skroo-pyuh-luhs)
▷ *adverb* **scrupulously**

scrunchie *or* **scrunchy** *noun* A round, fabric-covered elastic band, used mostly by girls and women to gather and fasten their hair: *She chose a green scrunchie to hold her ponytail because it matched her top.* **scrunch·ie** *or* **scrunch·y (skruhn**-chee)

scrutinize *verb* To examine, observe, or inspect something closely: *The doctor scrutinized the X-ray.* **scru·ti·nize (skroo**-tuh-*nize)* ▷ *verb* **scrutinizing, scrutinized**

scrutiny *noun* The close and critical observation or inspection of someone or something: *The study's conclusions were solid and withstood scrutiny.* **scru·ti·ny (skroo**-tuh-nee)

scuba diving *noun* Underwater swimming with a tank of compressed air on your back that you can breathe through a hose. Scuba is short for *self-contained underwater breathing apparatus.* **scu·ba diving**

scythe

(**skoo**-buh) ▷ *noun* **scuba diver**

scuff *verb* To scratch or scrape something and leave a mark, as in *to scuff your shoes.* **scuff** (**skuhf**) ▷ *verb* **scuffing, scuffed**

scuffle *noun* A confused and disorderly struggle or fight: *When the foul ball landed in the stands, there was a scuffle over who would keep it.* **scuf·fle** (**skuhf**-uhl) ▷ *verb* **scuffle**

sculpture *noun*
1. Something carved or shaped out of stone, wood, marble, or clay or cast in bronze or another metal.
2. The art or practice of making sculpture.
sculp·ture (**skuhlp**-chur)
▷ *noun* **sculptor** (**skuhlp**-tuhr) ▷ *verb* **sculpt** (skulpt)

scum *noun* A filmy layer that forms on the surface of a liquid or body of water, especially stagnant water. **scum** (skuhm)

scurry *verb* To hurry, or to move with light, quick steps: *An army of ants scurried over the picnic plates.* **scur·ry** (**skur**-ee) ▷ *verb* **scurries, scurrying, scurried**

scythe *noun* A tool with a long handle and a large, curved blade used for cutting grass or crops by hand. **scythe** (siTHe)

Word History

The Old English word for **scythe** was *sithe,* so where did the letter *c* in the word come from? Since the *scythe* was an instrument for cutting, people connected it with *scissors,* and they ended up writing *sc* at the beginning of *scythe.* The old word *sithe* was related to the Latin verb meaning "to cut," *secare.* People can stand while using the scythe. But the sickle, a more ancient tool, has a short handle, which requires workers to stoop or squat.

sea *noun*
1. The body of saltwater that covers nearly three-fourths of the earth's surface; the ocean.
2. A body of saltwater that may be partly enclosed or mostly or fully enclosed by land, such as the Caribbean or Mediterranean Seas.

3. An overwhelming amount or number, as in *a sea of troubles.*
sea (see)
Sea sounds like **see.**

sea anemone *noun* A sea animal with a body shaped like a tube and a mouth opening that is surrounded by brightly colored tentacles.

seaboard *noun* The land along or near the ocean shore, as in *the Eastern Seaboard.* **sea·board** (**see**-bord)

seacoast *noun* The area of land along the edge of a sea or an ocean, as in *the New England seacoast.* **sea·coast** (**see**-kohst)

seafaring *adjective*
1. Earning your living by working at sea, as in *a seafaring merchant.*
2. Of or having to do with sailors or the sea, as in *a seafaring vessel* or *seafaring tales.*
sea·far·ing (**see**-*fair*-ing)

seafood *noun* Edible fish and shellfish: *The only seafood I like is shrimp.* **sea·food** (**see**-*food*)

seagull *noun* A gray-and-white bird that is commonly found near the seacoast. **sea·gull** (**see**-*guhl*)

seahorse *noun* A small ocean fish with a head shaped like that of a horse that swims through the water in an upright position. **sea·horse** (**see**-*hors*)

Seahorses

Unlike other fish, seahorses swim upright and have skin, not scales. Their tiny fins make them slow swimmers. To rest, they hook their tails in the sea grass. The female puts her eggs into a pouch on the front of the male. The male seahorse carries them there until the babies are born.

a
b
c
d
e
f
g
h
i
j
k
l
m
n
o
p
q
r
s
t
u
v
w
x
y
z

seal

1. *noun* A sea mammal that lives in coastal waters and has thick fur and flippers.

2. *verb* To shut, fasten, or close something up, as in *to seal a container.* ▷ *verb* **sealing, sealed** ▷ *noun* **seal** ▷ *noun* **sealant** (see-luhnt)

3. *noun* A design pressed into wax and made into a stamp. A seal is used to secure the contents of an envelope or to make a document official. ▷ *verb* **seal**
seal (seel)

sea level *noun* The average level of the ocean's surface, used as a starting point from which to measure the height or depth of a place: *Cities at sea level are at greater risk of flooding.*

sea lion *noun* A large marine mammal similar to a seal but with ear flaps and longer front flippers.

seam *noun*

1. A line of sewing that joins two pieces of material, as in *the side seam of a skirt.*

2. A band of mineral or metal in the earth, as in *a seam of coal.*
seam (seem)
Seam sounds like **seem.**

seamstress *noun* A woman who sews for a living. **seam·stress** (**seem**-stris) ▷ *noun, plural* **seamstresses**

search

1. *verb* To explore or examine something carefully and thoroughly in order to find someone or something: *Elise searched the cabinet for cookies.*

2. *verb* To look for something on the internet using a search engine: *Did you try searching "autumn flowering" instead of "fall flowering"?*

3. *noun* The activity of looking or searching for something or someone: *The search went on for days. You can save this search and then try it again on another day.*

4. search warrant *noun* An order from a court that allows the police to enter and search a place.

5. search engine *noun* A computer program that will search the World Wide Web for the words or data you request.
search (surch)
▷ *verb* **searches, searching, searched** ▷ *noun* **searcher**

searchlight *noun* A large lamp with a powerful beam of light that can be focused in any direction.
search·light (**surch**-lite)

seashell *noun* The shell of a sea animal such as an oyster or a clam. **sea·shell** (**see**-shel)

seashore *noun* The land along the seacoast: *We always go to the seashore for our vacations.*
sea·shore (**see**-shor)

seasick *adjective* Feeling nauseous and dizzy because of the rolling or tossing movement of a boat or ship. **sea·sick** (**see**-sik) ▷ *noun* **seasickness**

season

1. *noun* One of the four natural parts of the year. The four seasons are spring, summer, autumn or fall, and winter. ▷ *adjective* **seasonal** ▷ *adverb* **seasonally**

2. *noun* A part of the year when a certain activity or event takes place, as in *the rainy season* or *football season.*

3. *verb* To add flavor to food by adding herbs, salt, or spices, as in *to season a stew.* ▷ *verb* **seasoning, seasoned**

4. If a food is **in season**, it is available fresh for eating.

5. season ticket *noun* A ticket for a series of events in a season, such as to all the home games of a sports team or performances of a ballet or an opera company.
sea·son (**see**-zuhn)

seasoning *noun* Anything that is added to food to give it more flavor, such as salt, herbs, or spices: *Mom says her salad seasoning is a secret.*
sea·son·ing (**see**-zuh-ning)

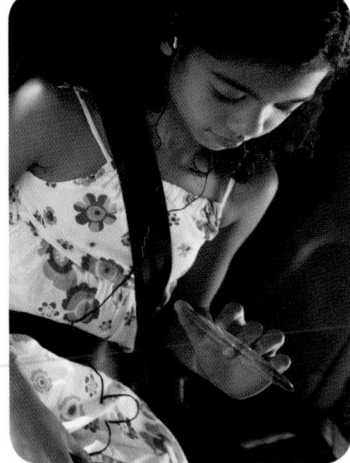

seat belt

seat

1. *noun* Something such as a chair or bench that you can sit on: *There were plenty of empty seats left in the theater.*

2. *noun* Anyplace where you can sit: *Take a seat whenever you get tired.*

3. *verb* To cause to sit: *Jack seated himself on the arm of the sofa.*

4. *noun* The part of the body you sit on, or the fabric that covers it, as in *the seat of your jeans.*

5. *noun* The central location of something: *Ottawa is the seat of the national government in Canada.*

6. *verb* To have enough seats for a certain number of people: *This table seats six.*
seat (seet)
▷ *verb* **seating, seated**

seat belt *noun* A strap or harness that holds a person securely in the seat of a car, a truck, or an airplane for protection in case of an accident: *I loosened the seat belt and took a nap.*

sea turtle *noun* A large turtle with paddle-like feet that lives in the sea, has a very long life span, and migrates across huge distances: *The seven species of living sea turtles are all endangered.*

sea urchin *noun* A sea creature with a hard, spiny shell. The spines are used for protection and also help the sea urchin move around. **sea ur·chin** (**ur**-chin)

seaweed *noun* Any of various types of algae that grow in the sea and need sunlight to make their own food. **sea·weed** (**see**-*weed*)

secede *verb* To formally withdraw from a group or an organization, often to form another organization: *By 1861, 11 Southern states had seceded from the Union to form the Confederate States of America.* **se·cede** (si-**seed**) ▷ *verb* **seceding, seceded** ▷ *noun* **secession** (si-**sesh**-uhn)

secluded *adjective* Quiet and private; not seen or visited by many people, as in *a secluded cabin.* **se·clud·ed** (si-**kloo**-did) ▷ *noun* **seclusion** (si-**kloo**-zhuhn)

second
1. *noun* A unit of time equal to one-sixtieth of a minute.
2. *noun* Any very short period of time: *Ivan couldn't wait another second.*
3. *adjective* Next after the first: *This hound is the second dog we found today.* ▷ *noun* **second** ▷ *adverb* **second** ▷ *adverb* **secondly**
4. seconds *noun, plural* Another, or a second, helping of food: *Ethan always asks for seconds.*
5. *verb* To support or approve a suggestion or idea. ▷ *verb* **seconding, seconded**
sec·ond (**sek**-uhnd)

secondary *adjective*
1. Coming after or less important than, as in *a secondary problem* or *a secondary cause.* ▷ *adverb* **secondarily** (**sek**-uhn-*der*-uh-lee)
2. Based on something that is not original: *He used secondary sources to do his research.*
3. Of or having to do with the second stage of something, as in *secondary symptoms of pneumonia.* **sec·on·dar·y** (**sek**-uhn-*der*-ee)

secondary school *noun* A school between elementary school and college; a high school, as in *a private secondary school.*

second-guess *verb* To think that your own opinion about a person or a decision is better or more accurate than someone else's: *I asked a couple of questions, and suddenly the doctor thought I was second-guessing him.*

secondhand *adjective*
1. Owned, worn, or used by someone else before you, as in *secondhand clothes.*
2. Selling used goods, as in *a secondhand furniture store.*
sec·ond·hand (**sek**-uhnd-*hand*)

secondhand smoke *noun* Smoke that a person inhales from cigarettes, cigars, or pipes that other people are smoking.

second-rate *adjective* Of poor quality, as in *second-rate merchandise.*

secrecy *noun*
1. The practice or habit of keeping things secret: *I can't tell you what he said because I have been sworn to secrecy.*
2. The condition of being secret: *We planned her surprise party in complete secrecy.*
se·cre·cy (**see**-kruh-see)

secret
1. *noun* Something that is kept hidden or that only a few people know: *The location of the treasure is a secret.*
2. *adjective* Not known or seen by many people, as in *a secret ambition.* ▷ *adverb* **secretly**
3. in secret Without anyone else knowing.
se·cret (**see**-krit)

secretary *noun*
1. A person who handles letters, telephone calls, appointments, and other office tasks for an employer, as in *a personal secretary.* ▷ *adjective* **secretarial**
2. A person in charge of a cabinet department in a government, as in *the secretary of defense.*
sec·re·tar·y (**sek**-ri-*ter*-ee) ▷ *noun, plural* **secretaries**

secrete *verb*
1. To produce and release a liquid: *The salivary glands secrete saliva.* ▷ *noun* **secretion**
2. To put in a secret place; to hide: *The pirate secreted his loot in a cave.*
se·crete (si-**kreet**) ▷ *verb* **secreting, secreted**

secretive *adjective* Tending to be silent about your thoughts, feelings, and activities, as in *secretive behavior.* **se·cre·tive** (**see**-kri-tiv)

sect *noun* A group whose members share the same beliefs and practices or follow the same leader. A sect is often a small group that has broken away from a larger religious group. **sect** (sekt)

section *noun*
1. One of the parts into which something is divided: *The sofa we ordered arrived in three sections.*
2. A part of a town, city, or country, as in *the old section of town.*
3. A **cross section**.
sec·tion (**sek**-shuhn)

a
b
c
d
e
f
g
h
i
j
k
l
m
n
o
p
q
r
s
t
u
v
w
x
y
z

sector *noun* A part or division of a city or group of people, as in *the public and private sectors.* **sec·tor** (**sek**-tur)

secular *adjective* Belonging to the physical world; not religious or sacred. **sec·u·lar** (**sek**-yuh-lur)

secure

1. *adjective* Safe, confident, and not worried or anxious: *Jasmine felt secure when she began the test.*
2. *adjective* Safely kept or firmly fastened so that it can't become loose or be lost: *The money is secure in the safe.*
3. *verb* To make something safe, especially by fastening, tying, or closing it tightly, as in *to secure a building.*
4. *adjective* Firm and steady, or strong, as in *a secure ladder* or *a secure lock.*
5. *adjective* Certain or guaranteed, as in *a secure job.*
6. *verb* To get: *Zena secured four tickets to the concert.*
se·cure (si-**kyoor**)
▷ *verb* **securing, secured** ▷ *adverb* **securely**

security *noun*

1. The state of being free from danger; safety: *The country has enjoyed peace and security for many years.*
2. Protection from danger or disruption: *Security at the president's speech was tight.*
3. A private service providing protection for a specific business, school, or area, as in *store security.*
se·cu·ri·ty (si-**kyoor**-i-tee)

sedan

sedan *noun* An enclosed car for four or more people with either two or four doors and a full-size rear seat. **se·dan** (si-**dan**)

sedative *noun* A drug that makes you calm or sleepy. **sed·a·tive** (**sed**-uh-tiv)

sediment *noun*

1. Material that settles at the bottom of a liquid: *The sediment at the bottom of the juice is pulp.* ▷ *noun* **sedimentation** (sed-uh-muhn-**tay**-shuhn)
2. Rock, sand, or dirt that has been carried to a place by water, wind, or a glacier: *That island was formed by sediment.*
sed·i·ment (**sed**-uh-muhnt)

sedimentary *adjective*

1. Of or having to do with sediment, as in *sedimentary fossils* or *sedimentary geology.*
2. Of or having to do with rock that is formed from layers of sediment that have been pressed together. Some rocks of this type have bands of color. Limestone, flint, and sandstone are examples of sedimentary rocks.
sed·i·men·tar·y (sed-uh-**men**-tur-ee)

see *verb*

1. To become aware of something or someone with your eyes.
2. To understand or to get a clear mental impression of something, as in *to see a point.*
3. To find out or to discover: *I need to see what the weather is going to be like.*
4. To visit and spend some time with someone, as in *to see a friend.*
5. To date someone regularly: *Are you seeing anyone?*
6. see about To investigate or look into something: *Mom went to see about getting a refund.*
7. see through To be able to recognize the true nature of someone or something: *I had the perfect excuse, but my mother saw through it.*
8. To **see** a job **through** is to finish a job.
see (see)
See sounds like **sea.** ▷ *verb* **seeing, saw** (saw), **seen** (seen)

seed

1. *noun* The part of a flowering plant from which a new plant can grow, especially a grain, nut, or kernel: *Eric planted a packet of seeds.*
2. *noun* The source or beginning of something, as in *the seeds of hope.*
3. *verb* To plant land with seeds: *We will seed the field in the fall for a spring crop.*
4. *verb* To remove seeds from: *I seeded the watermelon before eating it.*
seed (seed)
▷ *verb* **seeding, seeded**

seedling *noun* A young plant that has been grown from a seed rather than a cutting: *It's hard to believe this seedling will become a tree.* **seed·ling** (**seed**-ling)

seek *verb*

1. To try to find something, as in *to seek a solution* or *to seek recognition.* ▷ *noun* **seeker**
2. To try: *Joseph will seek to win the election.*
3. To ask for.
seek (seek)
▷ *verb* **seeking, sought** (sawt)

seem *verb*

1. To appear to be, or to give the impression of being: *They seem like a perfect match for each other.*

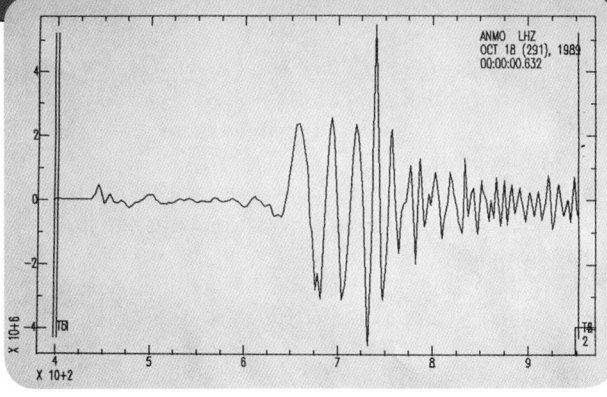

seismograph

2. To appear to oneself: *I seem to have forgotten my keys.*
seem (seem)
Seem sounds like **seam**. ▷ *verb* **seeming, seemed**

seemingly *adverb* In a way that appears to be real or true; apparently: *We looked out the car window at a seemingly endless stretch of desert.* **seem·ing·ly** (**see**-ming-lee)

seep *verb* To flow or leak slowly: *Water from the upstairs bathroom seeped through the ceiling.* **seep** (seep) ▷ *verb* **seeping, seeped** ▷ *noun* **seepage** (**see**-pij)

seesaw
1. *noun* A long board balanced on a support in the middle. When people sit on opposite sides, one end goes up as the other goes down.
2. *verb* To ride on a seesaw.
3. *verb* To move up and down or back and forth: *The price of gasoline has seesawed.*
see·saw (**see**-saw)
▷ *verb* **seesawing, seesawed**

seethe *verb*
1. To be very angry without expressing that anger, as in *to seethe with rage.*
2. To bubble or foam as if a liquid were boiling.
seethe (seeTH)
▷ *verb* **seething, seethed**
▷ *adjective* **seething**

segment *noun*
1. A part or section of something, as in *grapefruit segments.*
2. In geometry, the portion of a line between two points on the line.
seg·ment (**seg**-muhnt)
▷ *verb* **segment** (seg-**ment**)
▷ *adjective* **segmental** (seg-**men**-tuhl)

segregate *verb* To separate or keep people or things apart from the main group: *The warden segregated*

seesaw

the violent prisoners. **seg·re·gate** (**seg**-ri-gate) ▷ *verb* **segregating, segregated** ▷ *adjective* **segregated**

segregation *noun* The act or practice of keeping people or groups apart, as in *racial segregation.* **seg·re·ga·tion** (seg-ri-**gay**-shuhn)

seismograph *noun* An instrument that detects earthquakes and measures their power. **seis·mo·graph** (**size**-muh-*graf*) ▷ *noun* **seismography** (size-**mah**-gruh-fee)

seize *verb*
1. To grab or take hold of something suddenly: *I seized the rail to keep myself from falling down the steps.*
2. To arrest or capture someone or something: *Police seized the burglars as they came out of the building.*
seize (seez)
▷ *verb* **seizing, seized**

seizure *noun*
1. A sudden attack of illness, especially of a disease such as epilepsy: *We called for help when Tim had an unexpected seizure.*
2. The act of seizing something or someone: *The seizure of the stolen goods made headlines.*
sei·zure (**see**-zhur)

seldom *adverb* Rarely; not often: *We seldom see our friends now that they live so far away.* **sel·dom** (**sel**-duhm)

select
1. *verb* To choose someone or something carefully: *I selected the apples that would go into the pie.*
2. *verb* To mark text or an image on a computer screen in order to do something with it, as in *to select a paragraph.* ▷ *noun* **selector**
3. *adjective* Carefully chosen as the best, as in *a select group.*
se·lect (suh-**lekt**)
▷ *verb* **selecting, selected**

selection *noun*
1. The act of picking or choosing something: *I had a hard time making a selection from the desserts.*
2. A person or thing that has been chosen: *Emily questioned my selection of music for the party.*
3. A section of data on a computer screen that you have selected: *You have the option to print just your selection.*
4. A range of things from which you can choose, as in *a wide selection of colors.*
se·lec·tion (suh-**lek**-shuhn)

selective *adjective* Choosing carefully: *Irene is selective in her choice of friends.* **se·lec·tive** (suh-**lek**-tiv)

a
b
c
d
e
f
g
h
i
j
k
l
m
n
o
p
q
r
s
t
u
v
w
x
y
z

self *noun* One's individual nature or personality: *He was upset this morning and not like his usual self.* **self** (self) ▷ *noun, plural* **selves**

self-assurance Confidence in yourself and your abilities.

self-centered *adjective* Thinking only about your own feelings or needs; selfish: *Young children are typically self-centered.*

self-confident *adjective* Sure of one's own abilities or worth, as in *a self-confident performer.* ▷ *noun* **self-confidence** ▷ *adverb* **self-confidently**

self-conscious *adjective* Constantly worried about how you look to other people and what they are thinking. ▷ *adverb* **self-consciously**

self-control *noun* Control of your feelings and behavior: *By exercising great self-control, Nora managed to be polite to the rude customers.* ▷ *adjective* **self-controlled**

self-defense *noun* The act of protecting yourself against attacks or threats: *When Leonard punched the mugger, he was acting in self-defense.*

self-employed *adjective* Working as your own boss or running your own business, as in *a self-employed plumber.*

self-esteem *noun* A feeling of personal pride and of respect for yourself: *Winning the race really boosted Jenny's self-esteem.*

self-explanatory *adjective* Easily understood and requiring no further explanation: *The directions for the DVD player are self-explanatory.*

selfie *noun* A picture you take of yourself, especially on that you upload to a social media site. **self·ie** (sel-fee)

selfie stick *noun* A rod that you can attach to a smartphone in order to take a selfie with the camera farther away from you than your arm can reach.

selfie stick

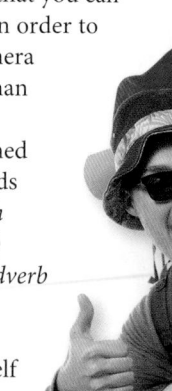

selfish *adjective* Concerned only with one's own needs and wishes, as in *a selfish desire.* **self·ish** (sel-fish) ▷ *noun* **selfishness** ▷ *adverb* **selfishly**

self-respect *noun* Pride and confidence in yourself and your abilities: *Telling the truth about the way she'd been treated was a matter of self-respect.* ▷ *adjective* **self-respecting**

self-righteous *adjective* Too confident that you are right and that others are wrong: *Carla has become so self-righteous about healthy eating that I feel I can't even eat a cheeseburger in front of her.* ▷ *noun* **self-righteousness** ▷ *adverb* **self-righteously**

self-service *adjective* If a store or gas station is **self-service**, you help yourself to what you want and then pay a cashier.

self-starter *noun* A person who has the ability or willingness to take a first step in doing or learning something.

sell *verb*
1. To exchange something for money: *Julie sold me her tickets to the baseball game.*
2. To offer for sale: *This store sells sports equipment.*
3. To be sold or to be on sale: *A rare baseball card can sell for $1,000.*
4. To help the sale of something: *TV commercials are used to sell new products.*
5. *(informal)* To persuade someone that he or she wants something: *The travel agent tried to sell us on the idea of a cruise to Antarctica.*
sell (sel)
Sell sounds like **cell**. ▷ *verb* **selling, sold** (sohld)

seller *noun* Someone who sells something or who has something for sale: *The seller has received four offers for the house so far but has not accepted any.* **sell·er** (sel-ur)

selves *noun, plural* The plural of **self**. **selves** (selvz)

semester *noun* One of two terms that make up a school year, as in *the fall semester.* **se·mes·ter** (suh-mes-tur)

semicircle *noun* A half of a circle. **sem·i·cir·cle** (sem-i-sur-kuhl) ▷ *adjective* **semicircular**

semicolon *noun* The punctuation mark (;) used to separate parts of a sentence. A semicolon shows a greater separation of thoughts or ideas than a comma does. **sem·i·co·lon** (sem-i-koh-luhn)

semicolon

semiconductor *noun* A substance, such as silicon, that doesn't conduct electricity well at low temperatures but whose conductivity improves at higher temperatures. **sem·i·con·duc·tor** (sem-ee-kuhn-duhk-tur)

semifinal *noun* A match or game to decide who will play in the final match or game of a series or tournament. **sem·i·fi·nal** (sem-ee-fye-nuhl) ▷ *noun* **semifinalist** ▷ *adjective* **semifinal**

seminar *noun*
1. A conference or meeting for the purpose of training or discussion, as in *a seminar on human rights.*
2. A college class with a small number of students who meet with a professor to discuss a particular topic: *My brother is an English major and is taking a seminar on 17th-century British literature.*
sem·i·nar (**sem**-uh-*nahr*)

seminary *noun* A school that trains students to become priests, ministers, or rabbis. **sem·i·nar·y** (**sem**-uh-*ner*-ee) ▷ *noun, plural* **seminaries**

Seminole *noun* A member of a group of Native Americans who originally lived in Florida. Today, the Seminoles mainly live in Oklahoma, but some still live in Florida. **Sem·i·nole** (**sem**-uh-*nole*) ▷ *noun, plural* **Seminoles** *or* **Seminole**

senate *noun*
1. A body of officials elected to make laws.
2. **Senate** One of the two houses of the US Congress that make laws. Each state has two senators. **sen·ate** (**sen**-it)
▷ *noun* **senator** (**sen**-uh-tuhr)

send *verb*
1. To make someone or something go or be taken somewhere, as in *to send a letter* or *to send someone on an errand.*
▷ *noun* **sender**
2. To write to ask for something: *We sent away for the free offer.*
3. **send for** To ask a person to come to you, or to ask for something to be brought to you: *While I waited nervously, the principal sent for my parents.*
send (send)
▷ *verb* **sending, sent**

send-off *noun* (*informal*) A gathering to say good-bye to someone and to wish him or her good luck: *I got a nice send-off before heading to summer camp.*

senile *adjective* Showing a loss of mental ability as a result of old age. **se·nile** (**see**-nile) ▷ *noun* **senility** (si-**nil**-i-tee)

senior
1. *adjective* When a father and son have identical names, **senior** is placed after the surname to indicate the father, as in *John Doe Senior.* Abbreviated as *Sr.*
2. *adjective* Older than someone else, or higher in rank or status, as in *a senior police officer.* ▷ *noun* **seniority**
3. *noun* A student in the fourth year of high school or college. ▷ *adjective* **senior**
sen·ior (**see**-nyur)

senior citizen *noun* An elderly person, especially someone who is older than 65 and has retired.

sensation *noun*
1. The ability to feel or be aware of something through one of the senses, as in *the sensation of touch.*
2. A feeling or an awareness, as in *the sensation of being followed.*
3. Someone or something that causes widespread excitement or interest: *The telephone caused a big sensation when it was first invented.*
sen·sa·tion (sen-**say**-shuhn)

sensational *adjective*
1. Very good, and so attracting a lot of positive attention: *The play was sensational and became a big hit.*
2. Attracting a lot of attention because people are shocked or disapprove: *The quiet, conservative community was bracing for the sensational kidnapping trial.*
sen·sa·tion·al (sen-**say**-shuh-nuhl)
▷ *adverb* **sensationally**

sense
1. *noun* One of the powers a living being uses to learn about its surroundings. Sight, hearing, touch, taste, and smell are the five senses.
2. *noun* A feeling, as in *a sense of pride* or *a sense of failure.*
3. *noun* An understanding or an appreciation, as in *a good sense of humor.*
4. *noun* Good judgment: *Have the sense to eat a healthy breakfast.*
5. *noun* Meaning, especially when there are several meanings available: *Frances is persistent, in the best sense of the word.*
6. *verb* To be or become aware of something: *I sensed that Gene had heard enough criticism.* ▷ *verb* **sensing, sensed**
7. **make sense** To be understandable or logical: *My homework makes more sense after my tutor works with me.*
sense (sens)

sense organ *noun* An organ in the body that receives information, or stimuli, from its surroundings. The human sense organs include the eyes, ears, nose, taste buds, and skin.

sensible *adjective* Showing common sense and sound judgment, as in *a sensible solution.* **sen·si·ble** (**sen**-suh-buhl) ▷ *adverb* **sensibly**

senior citizens

sensitive *adjective*
1. Easily offended or upset: *Max is sensitive to criticism.*
2. Painful: *The infected tooth was very sensitive.*
3. Aware of other people's attitudes, feelings, or circumstances: *The counselor was sensitive to Joelle's problems at home.*
4. Affected by even slight changes, as in *a sensitive measuring device.*
sen·si·tive (**sen**-si-tiv)
▷ *adverb* **sensitively**

sensitivity *noun* An awareness or appreciation of the feelings of others: *The teacher showed sensitivity to the needs of her students.* **sen·si·tiv·i·ty** (*sen*-si-**tiv**-i-tee)

sensor *noun* An instrument that can detect and measure changes and transmit the information to a controlling device, as in *a motion sensor.* **sen·sor** (**sen**-sur)

sent *verb* The past tense and the past participle of *send.* **sent** (sent) **Sent** sounds like **scent** and **cent**.

sentence *noun*
1. A group of words that has a subject and a verb and expresses a complete thought.
2. A punishment given to someone who has been found guilty in court, as in *a jail sentence.*
sen·tence (**sen**-tuhns)
▷ *verb* **sentence**

sentiment *noun*
1. An opinion about a specific matter: *Popular sentiment is against lowering the voting age.*
2. A thought or an attitude that is based on feeling or emotion instead of reason, as in *patriotic sentiments.*
3. Tender or sensitive feeling: *I tried to find a Valentine's Day card that would express my sentiment.*
sen·ti·ment (**sen**-tuh-muhnt)

sentimental *adjective*
1. Of or having to do with emotion rather than reason: *It's an old rug, but it has sentimental value because it belonged to my grandparents.*
2. Too emotional, or emotional in a superficial way, as in *a sentimental movie.*
sen·ti·men·tal (*sen*-tuh-**men**-tuhl)
▷ *noun* **sentimentality** (*sen*-tuh-men-**tal**-i-tee)
▷ *adverb* **sentimentally**

sentry *noun* A person who stands guard and warns others of danger: *The sentry would sound the bell if he saw any trouble.* **sen·try** (**sen**-tree) ▷ *noun, plural* **sentries**

sepal *noun* The green outer covering of a flower bud. The sepal opens to allow the flower to bloom and remains to protect the petals. **se·pal** (**see**-puhl)

separate
1. (**sep**-uh-*rate*) *verb* To set, put, or keep apart: *Separate the orange into sections. Separate those fighting boys.*
2. (**sep**-ur-it) *adjective* Different, individual, or not joined together, as in *separate rooms.* ▷ *adverb* **separately**
3. (**sep**-uh-*rate*) *verb* To stop living together as husband and wife: *Philippe cried when his mom and dad separated.*
sep·a·rate
▷ *verb* **separating, separated**

separately *adverb* Apart from others or from each other: *Wash the peaches separately or they may bruise.* **sep·a·rate·ly** (**sep**-ur-it-lee)

separation *noun*
1. The act or process of being moved or coming apart: *My sister is leaving for college, and my parents are dreading the separation.*
2. A situation in which a husband and wife are married but live apart: *My aunt and uncle have agreed to a trial separation.*
sep·a·ra·tion (*sep*-uh-**ray**-shuhn)

September *noun* The ninth month on the calendar, after August and before October. September has 30 days. **Sep·tem·ber** (sep-**tem**-bur)

sentry

Word History

In ancient Rome, the year began in March, making **September** the seventh month. That's why our ninth month, September, takes its name from the Latin word *septem,* which means "seven."

sequel *noun* A book or movie that continues the story of an earlier work: *I hope there's a sequel to my favorite book of the summer.* **se·quel** (**see**-kwuhl)

sequence *noun*
1. The following of one thing after another in a regular or fixed order, as in *numerical sequence*.
2. A series or collection of things that follow each other in a particular order: *This sequence of four photographs shows our house during the different seasons of the year.*
se·quence (**see**-kwuhns)
▷ *adjective* **sequential** (si-**kwen**-shuhl)

sequin *noun* A small, shiny disk, often in a bright color, that can be sewn onto clothing for decoration. **se·quin** (**see**-kwin)

Word History

In order to make a coin, a block with a carved design is pressed into metal, transferring the design. A **sequin** originally was one of these blocks: The Arabic word was *sikkah*. Then Italian speakers used the word *zecchino* to refer to one of their coins, and that was the first meaning of the word *sequin* in English: "an Italian gold coin." Eventually, people thought that small shiny decorations looked like coins, so they called them *sequins*.

sequoia *noun* A giant evergreen tree that can reach a height of over 300 feet. Redwoods are a type of sequoia. **se·quoi·a** (si-**kwoi**-uh)

Word History

The **sequoia**, among the largest and tallest of trees, was named in honor of the Cherokee scholar Sequoyah, who was born around 1770. Sequoyah spent 12 years developing a written alphabet for the spoken Cherokee language. The giant tree was named for him shortly after his death in 1843.

serene *adjective* Calm, peaceful, or untroubled, as in *a serene setting* or *a serene person*. **se·rene** (suh-**reen**) ▷ *noun* **serenity** (suh-**ren**-i-tee) ▷ *adverb* **serenely**

serf *noun* In medieval times, a farm worker who was owned by a lord and treated as a slave. **serf** (surf) **Serf** sounds like **surf**. ▷ *noun* **serfdom** (**surf**-duhm)

sergeant *noun* A military officer who ranks above a corporal and is in charge of troops. **ser·geant** (**sahr**-juhnt)

serial
1. *noun* A story or play that is published or broadcast in several parts, which are presented one at a time on television or radio or in a magazine.

sequoias

2. *adjective* Repeatedly committing the same criminal act or following the same behavior pattern, as in *a serial liar*.
se·ri·al (**seer**-ee-uhl)
Serial sounds like **cereal**. ▷ *noun* **serialization**
▷ *verb* **serialize**

series *noun*
1. A group of related things that come one after another, as in *a series of classes*.
2. A number of books or television or radio programs that deal with the same characters or are linked in some way, as in *a detective series*.
3. Electrical parts that are connected **in series** are arranged so that the current passes though each one of them in turn.
se·ries (**seer**-eez)
▷ *noun, plural* **series**

serious *adjective*
1. Solemn or caused by deep thought, as in *a serious voice*.
2. Meaning what you say or do; sincere: *Are you serious about leaving school?*
3. Dangerous, or giving cause for concern, as in *a serious illness*.
4. Important and requiring a lot of thought, as in *serious plans*.
se·ri·ous (**seer**-ee-uhs)
▷ *noun* **seriousness** ▷ *adverb* **seriously**

a b c d e f g h i j k l m n o p q r **s** t u v w x y z

sermon *noun*

1. A speech given during a religious service: *The preacher's sermon was about forgiveness.*

2. Any serious talk, especially one that deals with morals or correct behavior: *My parents gave me a sermon about the importance of studying.*

ser·mon (**sur**-muhn)

▷ *verb* **sermonize**

serpent *noun* A snake. **ser·pent** (**sur**-puhnt)

Word History

A 16th-century writer described "very hideous and terrible serpents called crocodiles." We no longer call crocodiles serpents, but the word **serpent** used to refer to any creature that crawled. The name meant "crawling thing" in Latin. The word part *serpent-* was from the present participle of the verb *serpere,* meaning "to crawl." When we say the word *serpent* today, though, we simply mean "snake."

serrated *adjective* Having a blade like that of a saw, as in *a serrated steak knife.* **ser·rat·ed** (**ser**-*ay*-tid)

serum *noun*

1. The clear, thin, liquid part of the blood. It separates from blood when a clot forms.

2. A liquid used to prevent or cure a disease. Serum is taken from the blood of an animal that has had the disease and is already immune to it. **se·rum** (**seer**-uhm)

▷ *noun, plural* **serums** or **sera** (**seer**-uh)

servant *noun* Someone who is employed to do housework, cooking, or other domestic chores in someone else's house: *There were several servants at the holiday party.* **serv·ant** (**sur**-vuhnt)

serve

1. *verb* To work for someone as a servant: *The housekeeper served our family for years.*

2. *verb* To give someone food or drink, or to help a customer in a store, as in *to serve a meal* or *to serve a customer.*

3. *verb* To do your duty in some form of service, as in *to serve on a jury.*

4. *verb* To supply: *The recipe serves four people.*

5. *verb* To spend: *The criminal served his full sentence in jail.*

6. *verb* In games such as tennis and volleyball, to begin play by hitting the ball.

7. *noun* The act of hitting a ball over a net to begin play in games such as tennis and volleyball: *That serve was out of bounds.*

serve (surv)

▷ *verb* **serving, served**

server *noun*

1. Someone who serves others, such as a waiter or waitress: *We asked our server for more bread.*

2. The player who serves the ball in tennis, volleyball, or other games.

3. A computer shared by two or more users in a network. This kind of computer is also known as a *file server.*

serv·er (**sur**-vur)

service *noun*

1. The way in which the staff in a store or restaurant helps and takes care of you: *The best thing about that new seafood restaurant is the service.*

2. Work that helps others, as in *service to the homeless* or *the services of a doctor.*

3. Employment as a servant: *Many people work in the service of the town's only millionaire.*

4. A system or way of providing something useful or necessary, as in *mail service.*

5. A branch of the armed forces: *After high school, my father spent four years in the service.*

6. A ceremony of religious worship, as in *a church service.*

7. A branch of the government, as in *the postal service* or *the foreign service.*

8. The repairing of a car or an appliance: *We brought the television in for service.*

9. A complete set of matched dishes, as in *a dinner service.*

10. A serve in tennis, volleyball, or any game in which a ball is hit over a net.

serv·ice (**sur**-vis)

▷ *verb* **service**

servile *adjective* Too eager to serve or please someone, as in *a servile manner.* **ser·vile** (**sur**-vile)

serving *noun* An amount of food for one person at a meal; a helping, as in *a serving of French fries.* **serv·ing** (**sur**-ving)

sesame *noun* A small oval seed, or the tropical plant from which this seed comes. Sesame seeds and their oil are used in cooking and baking. **ses·a·me** (**ses**-uh-mee)

session *noun*

1. A formal meeting, as in *a session of the Supreme Court.*

2. A series of meetings of a court or legislature: *This session of Congress ends next week.*

3. A period of time devoted to a certain activity, as in *a training session.*

ses·sion (**sesh**-uhn)

set

1. *noun* A group of people or things that go together, as in *a chess set* or *the under-21 set.*

2. *noun* The stage or scenery for a play or movie: *Jack helped build the set for the new school play.*

3. *adjective* Ready to do or begin something: *Are you all set for school tomorrow?*

4. *adjective* Fixed or established ahead of time, as in *a set schedule.*

5. *verb* To put or to place: *He set the book back on its shelf.*

6. *verb* To lay out, arrange, or put in order, as in *to set the table.*

7. *verb* To begin or to start, as in *to set to work.*

8. *verb* To decide on, as in *to set a date for a wedding.*

9. *verb* To establish or provide something as a model for other people to follow, as in *to set an example.*

10. *verb* To become firm or hardened: *That pudding will set in the refrigerator overnight.*

11. *verb* To go toward or below the horizon: *My little brother has to go to bed when the sun sets.*

12. *noun* A device for sending out or receiving electronic signals, as in *a television set.*

13. *noun* In math, a collection of items that are grouped together or have something in common.

14. set up To arrange something, especially for a particular use: *Carl set up enough chairs for all of his guests.*

15. set aside To save something for another time: *I set aside my allowance for three weeks so I could buy the new game.*

16. set out To begin a trip: *We set out before dawn to get to the airport on time.*

17. be set on To want something very much and to be determined to get or achieve it: *I'm set on going to the movie when it first comes out.*

set (set)

▷ *verb* **setting, set**

setback *noun* A problem that delays you or keeps you from making progress: *The builders promised that the house would be built by September, despite setbacks caused by the weather.* **set·back** (**set**-bak)

setting *noun*

1. Background or surroundings: *They found an ideal setting for their picnic, under a tree, with the broad valley before them.*

2. A set for a play or movie, or a background for a story.

3. The way in which a machine or appliance is set or adjusted, as in *the settings on a printer.*

4. The frame in which something, such as a jewel, sits. **set·ting** (**set**-ing)

sew

settle *verb*

1. To decide or agree on something, as in *to settle a fight.*

2. To sit or place comfortably: *Jessie settled down with a good book.*

3. To make a home or to live in a new place: *Pioneers settled in the West.* ▷ *noun* **settler**

4. To sink: *Our sidewalk has settled and cracked.*

5. To calm: *The medicine settled my stomach.*

6. settle in To get used to a new situation, as in *to settle into a new house.*

7. settle up To pay a bill or a debt. **set·tle** (**set**-uhl)

▷ *verb* **settling, settled**

settlement *noun*

1. An agreement or a decision about something that was in doubt: *The strike dragged on because the two sides could not reach a settlement.*

2. A small village or group of houses where people live: *Grandma grew up in a settlement just north of town.* **set·tle·ment** (**set**-uhl-muhnt)

setup *noun* The way that something is arranged: *The teacher changed the setup of our classroom while we were on vacation.* **set·up** (**set**-uhp)

sever *verb*

1. To cut off or apart, as in *to sever a limb.*

2. To end or to break off, as in *to sever relations.* **sev·er** (**sev**-ur)

▷ *verb* **severing, severed**

several

1. *adjective* More than two, but not many: *Several days passed before Tim returned our call.*

2. *noun* More than two, or a few, people or things: *Several of the guests were late.* **sev·er·al** (**sev**-ur-uhl)

severe *adjective*

1. Strict or harsh, as in *severe punishment* or *severe criticism.*

2. Extreme, intense, or dangerous, as in *a severe burn* or *a severe illness.*

3. Violent, or causing great discomfort or difficulty, as in *a severe storm.* **se·vere** (suh-**veer**)

▷ *adjective* **severer, severest** ▷ *noun* **severity** (suh-**ver**-i-tee) ▷ *adverb* **severely**

sew *verb* To make, repair, or fasten something with stitches made by a needle and thread. **sew** (soh) **Sew** sounds like **so.** ▷ *verb* **sewing, sewed, sewn** (sohn) ▷ *noun* **sewing**

sewage *noun* Liquid and solid waste that is carried off by sewers and drains: *The city's sewage is treated before it empties into the bay.* **sew·age** (**soo**-ij)

sewer *noun* An underground pipe that carries off drainage water and liquid and solid waste. **sew·er** (**soo**-ur)

Word History

The word **sewer** looks completely different from its source, the Latin word *aqua*. This term meant "water." From *aqua*, Latin speakers created a word meaning "channel for draining," *exaquaria*. The prefix *ex-* meant "out," so an *exaquaria* was a channel for "taking water out." This word developed into *sewiere* in Old French, meaning "a channel for draining a pond." Today, the English word is *sewer*.

sex *noun*
1. One of the two classes, male or female, into which people and most other living things are divided.
2. The fact or condition of being male or female: *The sex of the candidate should not be important in our decision.*
3. The activity that people or animals engage in to reproduce or for pleasure.
sex (seks)
▷ *noun, plural* **sexes**

sexist *adjective* Discriminating on the basis of a person's sex: *It is sexist to assume that girls can't learn to use power tools.* **sex·ist** (**sek**-sist) ▷ *noun* **sexism** ▷ *noun* **sexist**

sext *verb* To text a picture to someone that shows private parts of your body. Sexting is illegal for minors and it is illegal for an adult to sext to a minor. **sext** (sekst) ▷ *verb* **sexting, sexted** ▷ *noun* **sexting**

shabby *adjective*
1. Showing signs of wear and tear; worn out, as in *shabby clothes.* ▷ *noun* **shabbiness**
2. Mean or unfair, as in *a shabby trick.*
shab·by (**shab**-ee)
▷ *adjective* **shabbier,**

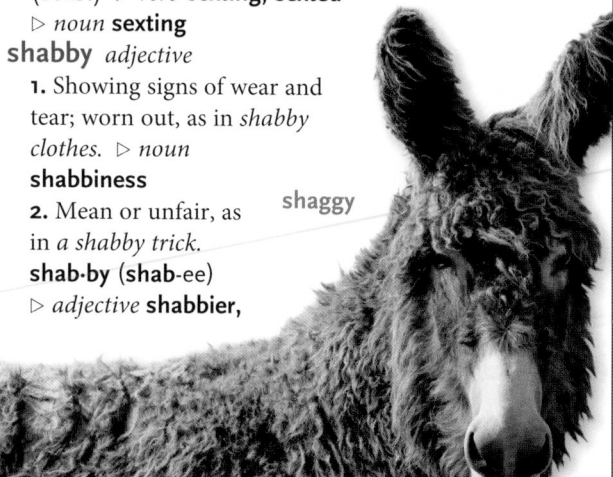

shaggy

shabbiest ▷ *adverb* **shabbily**

shack *noun* A small, roughly built hut or cabin: *The old shack was a perfect spot for our clubhouse.* **shack** (shak)

shade
1. *verb* To protect or screen someone or something from the light: *The huge trees shaded us while we ate.*
2. *verb* To make part of a drawing or picture darker by reproducing the effects of shade: *Shade in that area with your piece of charcoal.*
3. *noun* Most colors come in different **shades**, from dark to light: *That shade of blue looks great on you.*
4. *noun* A device that provides shelter or protection from light, as in *a window shade.*
5. *noun* A place that is protected from the heat and light of the sun, as in *sitting in the shade.*
6. *noun* The degree of darkness of a color, as in *different shades of green.*
7. *noun* A small amount or difference: *Randall is a shade shorter than his father.*
8. *noun* See also **throw shade.**
9. shades *noun, plural (slang)* Sunglasses: *Mom wears shades when she drives in the daytime.*
shade (shayd)
▷ *noun, plural* **shades** ▷ *verb* **shading, shaded** ▷ *noun* **shading**

shadow
1. *noun* An area of shade on a surface made by something blocking out the light: *The truck's shadow covers the entire sidewalk in front of my house.*
▷ *adjective* **shadowy** (**shad**-oh-ee)
2. *noun* A faint trace or suggestion, as in *a shadow of a doubt.*
3. *verb* To follow or stay close to someone, usually secretly, as in *to shadow a suspect.* ▷ *verb* **shadowing, shadowed**
shad·ow (**shad**-oh)

shady *adjective*
1. Out of the light or out of the sun, as in *a shady lawn.*
2. Dishonest or underhanded, as in *a shady deal.*
shad·y (**shay**-dee)

shaft *noun*
1. The long, narrow handle of a spear, an arrow, a paddle, or a tool: *We carved arrow shafts from tree branches.*
2. A rotating rod that transmits power in a machine or engine, as in *a drive shaft.*
3. A ray or beam, as in *a shaft of light.*
4. A long, narrow passage that goes straight down, as in *an elevator shaft.*
shaft (shaft)

shaggy *adjective* Having or covered with long, rough hair or wool, as in *a shaggy carpet.* **shag·gy** (**shag**-ee)

▷ *adjective* **shaggier, shaggiest**

shake *verb*

1. To move quickly up and down or back and forth: *Shake the bottle before you open it. The trees shook in the wind.*

2. To remove or scatter something by making short, quick movements: *I shook the rain from my umbrella.*

3. To tremble, or to cause to tremble: *I shook with cold. The earthquake shook our house.*

4. To upset: *The whole family was shaken by news of the accident.*

5. To clasp someone's hand as a way of greeting or agreeing with the person: *Now that we have a deal, let's shake on it.*

shake (shayk)

▷ *verb* **shaking, shook** (shuk), **shaken** (**shay**-kuhn) ▷ *noun* **shake**

shaky *adjective*

1. Not sturdy or reliable, as in *a shaky foundation.*

2. Trembling or quivering, as in *a shaky voice.*

3. Questionable or unpromising, as in *shaky evidence* or *a shaky start.*

shak·y (**shay**-kee)

▷ *adjective* **shakier, shakiest**

shale *noun* A rock that is formed from hardened clay or mud. It has many thin layers that separate easily. **shale** (shayl)

shall *verb* A helping verb that is used in the following ways:

1. To show an action that will take place in the future: *I shall arrive tomorrow.*

2. To show that an action is required: *You shall do what I say.*

3. To ask a question, or to offer a suggestion: *Shall we dance?*

shall (shal)

shallow *adjective*

1. Not deep, as in *a shallow lake.*

2. Lacking depth of thought, feeling, or knowledge, as in *a shallow mind.*

shal·low (**shal**-oh)

▷ *adjective* **shallower, shallowest**

sham *noun*

1. Something that is meant to deceive or is not what it seems to be: *The television offer seemed like a sham.* ▷ *adjective* **sham**

2. A decorative cover, as in *a pillow sham.*

sham (sham)

shaman *noun* A healer in some traditional societies who deals with beings in the spirit world. **sha·man** (**shah**-muhn)

Word History

The Russian emperor Peter the Great sent an ambassador to China in the 1600s, who visited the Evenk people in northern Russia on his way. He reported that if several Evenk families lived near each other, they would share a **shaman**, who was like a sorcerer or priest. Before that, the history of the word *shaman* is murky, but it might go back to an old language of India, where the word *sramana* (pronounced "shramana") meant "Buddhist monk."

shame

1. *noun* A feeling of embarrassment and upset that you get when you know you have done something wrong or foolish: *The shame I felt after getting caught was worse than the punishment.*

2. *noun* Something that is unfortunate or a pity: *It's a shame that the boys won't be able to come with us tonight.*

3. *noun* Dishonor or disgrace: *His arrest brought shame to his entire family.*

4. *verb* To make someone feel guilty or embarrassed about something: *Karl was shamed into returning the stolen books.* ▷ *verb* **shaming, shamed**

shame (shame)

shameful *adjective* A **shameful** act is one that should cause the person who did it to feel ashamed: *It was shameful, the way they left their dog out in the storm.* **shame·ful** (**shaym**-ful) ▷ *adverb* **shamefully**

shampoo *noun* A liquid soap used for washing hair, carpets, or upholstery, as in *dandruff shampoo.* **sham·poo** (sham-**poo**) ▷ *verb* **shampoo**

Word History

Shampoo, one of the very few English words that ends in *-oo*, comes from India. It developed from the Hindi word *champo*, meaning "massage" or "knead," which describes the action of working soap into your hair.

shamrock *noun* A small, cloverlike plant with three leaves. The shamrock is the national emblem of Ireland. **sham·rock** (**sham**-rahk)

shape

1. *noun* The form or outline of an object or a figure.

2. *verb* To mold or to determine how someone or something will develop: *The teacher hopes to shape us into good citizens.*

3. *noun* Good or fit condition: *Exercise helps keep you in shape.*

4. **shape up** *verb* (*informal*) To develop: *The new team is shaping up well.*

shape (shayp)

▷ *verb* **shaping, shaped**

shamrock

Sharks

Sharks date back 400 million years, before dinosaurs. Their skin is like sandpaper, and their giant liver, which takes up 30 percent of their body, helps them stay afloat. Instead of having bony skeletons like most fish, sharks have thick cartilage. Although sharks often lose teeth, their gums hold several rows of teeth that can replace them. Sharks can detect small amounts of electric current in the water, which allows them to sense and track the movement of prey. Most don't attack humans unless provoked, but several species of sharks, such as the great white shark and the tiger shark, mean danger.

great white shark

shark tooth

tiger shark

hammerhead shark

shark jaw

share

1. *verb* To divide something between two or more people: *Elaine shared her sandwich.*
2. *noun* The portion of something that someone receives or that belongs to someone: *I hope you do your share of the work.*
3. *verb* To use together: *My cousins share a house.*
4. *verb* To take part: *Jeff shared in the fun.*
5. *noun* One of many equal parts into which the ownership of a business is divided: *I own ten shares of stock in a computer company.*
share (shair)
▷ *verb* **sharing, shared**

shareware *noun* Computer software that has a copyright but is provided free on a trial basis. If a person decides to continue using the software, he or she is expected to pay a fee to the author. **share·ware** (**shair**-*wair*) ▷ *noun, plural* **shareware**

shark *noun*

1. A large and often fierce fish with a fin on its back, a torpedo-like body, and very sharp teeth.
2. Someone who is very skilled at a certain activity and uses that skill to cheat people, as in *a card shark.*
shark (shahrk)

sharp

1. *adjective* Having an edge or a point that cuts or pierces easily, as in *a sharp knife* or *a sharp needle.*
2. *adjective* Pointed, as in *a sharp mountain peak.*
3. *adjective* Able to think or notice things quickly, as in *a sharp mind* or *sharp eyes.*
4. *adjective* Abrupt or sudden, as in *a sharp curve.*
5. *adjective* Strong, biting, or harsh, as in *a sharp cheese, sharp words,* or *a sharp wind.*
6. *adjective* Distinct or clearly outlined, as in *a sharp photograph.*
7. *adverb* Exactly, as in *five o'clock sharp.*
8. *adjective* In music, a **sharp** note is one that is higher in pitch than the usual note: *C sharp is a half step higher than C.* ▷ *noun* **sharp**
9. *adjective* (*slang*) Very attractive or stylish, as in *a sharp outfit.*
sharp (shahrp)
▷ *adjective* **sharper, sharpest**

sharpen *verb* To make sharp: *He used a grindstone to sharpen the knives.* **sharp·en** (**shahr**-puhn)
▷ *verb* **sharpening, sharpened**

shatter *verb*

1. To break suddenly into many small pieces: *The mirror shattered when I dropped it.*
2. To destroy completely or to ruin: *His life was shattered by a tragic car accident.*

shat·ter (**shat**-ur)
▷ *verb* **shattering, shattered**

shave

1. *verb* To remove hair from the face or body with a razor or an electric shaver. ▷ *noun* **shave**

2. *verb* To cut off or slice in thin layers: *Mom is shaving chocolate for my birthday cake.*

3. close shave *(informal)* An occasion when you come very close to or barely manage to escape something: *I thought she was going to ask me if I would go in her place—that was a close shave!*
shave (shayv)
▷ *verb* **shaving, shaved**

shawl *noun* A piece of soft material that is worn over the shoulders or around the head. **shawl** (shawl)

Shawnee *noun* A member of a group of Native Americans who once lived in the central Ohio Valley. The Shawnee now live mainly in Oklahoma.
Shaw·nee (shaw-**nee**) ▷ *noun, plural* **Shawnee** or **Shawnees**

she *pronoun* The female person or animal mentioned before: *I like Sheila; she is my friend.* **she** (shee)

sheaf *noun* A bundle or collection of things gathered together, as in *a sheaf of papers.* **sheaf** (sheef)
▷ *noun, plural* **sheaves** (sheevz)

shear *verb*

1. To clip or cut with scissors or shears, as in *to shear a hedge.*

2. To cut the hair or wool off a sheep or other animal.
shear (sheer)
Shear sounds like **sheer**. ▷ *verb* **shearing, sheared** or **shorn** (shorn)

shears *noun, plural* A large cutting tool that resembles a pair of scissors. Shears are used in gardening and for cutting metal: *You'll need more than shears to trim that hedge.* **shears** (sheerz)

sheath *noun* A case for a knife, sword, or dagger: *Fernando admired the swordsman's leather sheath.*
sheath (sheeth)

shed

1. *noun* A small building, often attached to a larger one, used for storing things, as in *a garden shed.*

2. *verb* To lose, to get rid of, or to let something fall, as in *to shed hair* or *to shed tears.*

3. *verb* To give off or to supply: *The lamp didn't shed enough light for me to read.*
shed (shed)
▷ *verb* **shedding, shed**

she'd *contraction* A short form of *she had* or *she would*: *She'd never been to a big city before. She'd help you if she could.* **she'd** (sheed)

sheen *noun* A soft shine or luster: *Polish the counter until it has a sheen.* **sheen** (sheen)

sheepdog

sheep *noun* A grass-eating farm animal raised for its wool and meat. **sheep** (sheep) ▷ *noun, plural* **sheep**

sheepdog *noun* A dog that has been trained to guard and round up sheep. **sheep·dog** (**sheep**-dawg)

sheepish *adjective* Embarrassed because of having done something foolish, as in *a sheepish grin.* **sheep·ish** (**shee**-pish) ▷ *adverb* **sheepishly**

sheeple *noun* *(informal)* People, when they are considered to be followers of something popular rather than thinking for themselves: *I don't plan to join the hundreds of sheeple who are demonstrating against the proposed building development.* **shee·ple** (**shee**-puhl)

sheer *adjective*

1. So thin as to be almost transparent, as in *sheer curtains.*

2. Total; nothing but, as in *sheer nonsense* or *sheer exhaustion.*

3. Vertical or close to vertical, as in *a sheer cliff* or *a sheer drop.*
sheer (sheer)
Sheer sounds like **shear**. ▷ *adjective* **sheerer, sheerest**

sheet *noun*

1. A large, rectangular piece of cotton or other fabric used to cover a bed or to lie under.

2. A broad, thin piece of paper, glass, metal, or other material, as in *a sheet of newspaper.*
sheet (sheet)

sheik *noun* The head or chief of an Arab family, tribe, or village. **sheik** (sheek or shayk)

shelf *noun*

1. A length of wood or other rigid material, inside a cupboard or fastened to a wall, used for holding or storing things: *Get the cat food from the bottom shelf.*

2. Something flat that looks like a shelf, such as a ledge of rock.
shelf (shelf)
▷ *noun, plural* **shelves** (shelvz) ▷ *noun* **shelving** (**shel**-ving)

a b c d e f g h i j k l m n o p q r **s** t u v w x y z

shell

1. *noun* A hard outer covering or case. Nuts, tortoises, and eggs all have shells: *Out of all the eggs I collected, only one shell cracked.*

2. *noun* A type of small bomb that is fired from a cannon: *The crew member fired four shells at the pirate ship.*

3. *noun* A metal or paper case that holds a bullet and its explosive and is fired from a gun.

4. *verb* To remove something from its shell, as in *to shell nuts.*

5. *verb* To bombard or to attack with shells: *The small city was shelled all night by the enemy army.*
shell (shel)
▷ *verb* **shelling, shelled**

she'll *contraction* A short form of *she will* or *she shall*: *She'll arrive next week. She'll water my plants while I'm away.* **she'll** (sheel)

shellac *noun* A hard varnish used on wooden floors and furniture to protect them and give them a shiny finish. **shel·lac** (shuh-**lak**)

shellfish *noun* A creature with a shell that lives in water, such as a crab, oyster, or mussel. **shell·fish** (**shel**-fish) ▷ *noun, plural* **shellfish** or **shellfishes**

shelter *noun*

1. A place that offers protection from bad weather or danger, as in *a bus shelter* or *a bomb shelter.*

2. Protection from something unpleasant or dangerous: *During the tornado warning, they took shelter in their basement.*

3. A place where a homeless person, a victim of a disaster, or an animal that is not wanted can stay: *We got our new dog from the animal shelter.*
shel·ter (**shel**-tur)
▷ *verb* **shelter**

shelve *verb*

1. To cancel or decide not to continue with something, as in *to shelve a project.*

2. To place something on a shelf or shelves, as in *to shelve library books.*
shelve (shelv)
▷ *verb* **shelving, shelved**

shepherd

1. *noun* Someone whose job is to herd, guard, and take care of sheep: *The shepherd guided the flock of sheep safely down the hill.*

2. *verb* To watch over or to guide: *The ski patrol shepherded us out of the area hit by an avalanche.*
▷ *verb* **shepherding, shepherded**
shep·herd (**shep**-urd)

shell

sherbet *noun* A frozen dessert made of fruit juices, water, sugar, and milk, egg white, or gelatin. **sher·bet** (**shur**-bit)

sheriff *noun* The person in charge of enforcing the law in a county or town. **sher·iff** (**sher**-if)

Word History

Law officers in medieval England were called *shire-reeves*: A *shire* was a county, and a *reeve* was the person in charge of enforcing the law in the shire. Over time, people shortened this word to **sheriff**, so that it is now one word instead of two. It still means the main law enforcement officer in a county.

she's *contraction* A short form of *she is* or *she has*: *She's almost ready. She's been at the computer for hours.* **she's** (sheez)

Shetland pony *noun* A small horse with a long mane and tail and a rough coat, originally bred in Scotland's Shetland Islands. **Shet·land pony** (**shet**-luhnd)

shield

1. *noun* A piece of armor carried in front of the body to protect it from attack: *The knight held his shield on his left arm.*

2. *noun* Someone or something that provides protection, as in *a heat shield.*

3. *noun* A police officer's badge: *She had a police shield attached to her shirt.*

4. *verb* To protect someone or something from something that is risky, harmful, or unpleasant: *The porch roof shielded us from the rain.* ▷ *verb* **shielding, shielded**
shield (sheeld)

shift

1. *verb* To change or move something: *I used to respect the mayor, but my opinion of her has shifted. Abby shifted her books to her other arm.*

2. *noun* A movement or a change, as in *a shift in attitude.*

3. *noun* A period of several hours' continuous work, or the group of people who work those hours, as in *the night shift.*

4. *verb* To change the gears in a motor vehicle that does not have an automatic transmission: *Shift into second gear.* ▷ *noun* **shift**
shift (shift)
▷ *verb* **shifting, shifted**

shiitake *noun* A dark brown, edible Asian mushroom. **shii·ta·ke** (shee-**tah**-kee)

shimmer *verb* To shine with a faint, unsteady light: *The water shimmered in the sunset.* **shim·mer**

(**shim**-ur) ▷ *verb* **shimmering, shimmered**

shin

1. *noun* The front part of your leg, below your knee and above your ankle: *The soccer player wore shin guards to protect her legs.*

2. *verb* To climb by using your hands and legs to hold on and pull your weight, as in *to shin up a tree.* ▷ *verb* **shinning, shinned**

shin (shin)

shine *verb*

1. To give off or reflect light: *The lights from the mall shine all night.*

2. To aim light in a particular direction: *Don't shine your flashlight in my eyes.*

3. To be bright; to make bright or polish, as in *to shine shoes* or *to shine with joy.*

4. To do something very well: *When it comes to baking cookies, my grandma really shines.*

shine (shine)

▷ *verb* **shining, shone** (shohn) *or* **shined** ▷ *noun* **shine**

shingle *noun* A thin, flat piece of wood or other material used to cover roofs or outside walls. Shingles are put on in overlapping rows so that water runs off them. **shin·gle** (**shing**-guhl) ▷ *verb* **shingle**

Shinto *noun* The main religion of Japan, which involves the worship of nature and of ancestors and ancient heroes. **Shin·to** (**shin**-toh)

shipwreck

shiny *adjective* Reflecting a lot of light: *He polished the silver bowl until it was shiny.* **shin·y** (**shye**-nee) ▷ *adjective* **shinier, shiniest**

Suffix

The suffix **-ship** adds one of the following meanings to a root word:

1. The state or quality of being, as in *friendship* (the state of being a friend) and *leadership* (the quality of being a leader).

2. The art or skill of, as in *scholarship* (the skill of a scholar).

ship

1. *noun* A large boat that can travel across deep water.

2. *noun* An airplane, an airship, or a spacecraft.

3. *verb* To send on a ship, a truck, a train, or an airplane: *I will ship my clothes to camp in a trunk.*

4. *verb* To go on a ship, usually to work: *The sailor shipped as a crew member.*

ship (ship)

▷ *verb* **shipping, shipped**

shipment *noun*

1. A package or a group of packages that is sent from one place to another, as in *a shipment of supplies.*

2. The act of shipping: *The library bundled the books for shipment overseas.*

ship·ment (**ship**-muhnt)

shipshape *adjective* Neat, clean, and in good order: *I cleaned my room until it was shipshape.* **ship·shape** (**ship**-shayp)

shipwreck *noun*

1. The sinking or destruction of a ship at sea: *The storm caused the shipwreck.* ▷ *verb* **shipwreck**

2. The remains of a ship that has sunk or been destroyed at sea: *The divers found a shipwreck at the bottom of the ocean.*

ship·wreck (**ship**-rek)

▷ *adjective* **shipwrecked**

shipyard *noun* A place where ships are built or repaired: *The museum has a working shipyard where historic vessels are brought in for repairs.* **ship·yard** (**ship**-yahrd)

shirk *verb* To avoid doing something that should be done, as in *to shirk one's responsibilities.* **shirk** (shurk) ▷ *verb* **shirking, shirked** ▷ *noun* **shirker**

shirt *noun* A piece of clothing that covers the upper half of your body: *Tuck your shirt into your pants.* **shirt** (shurt)

shiver *verb* To shake with or as if with cold, as in *to shiver with fear.* **shiv·er** (**shiv**-ur) ▷ *verb* **shivering, shivered** ▷ *noun* **shiver** ▷ *adjective* **shivery**

a
b
c
d
e
f
g
h
i
j
k
l
m
n
o
p
q
r
s
t
u
v
w
x
y
z

shoal *noun*

1. An area of shallow water or a submerged sandbar that can be seen at low tide: *The speedboat hit a shoal and was stuck there for hours.*

2. A large number of fish swimming together, as in *a shoal of minnows.*
shoal (shole)

shoal of fish

shock

1. *noun* A sudden, violent event, such as an accident or a death, that upsets or disturbs you greatly: *Her decision to leave was a shock to everyone.*

2. *noun* The mental or emotional upset caused by such an event: *The accident left her in shock.*

3. *noun* A medical condition caused by a serious drop in blood pressure, sometimes causing loss of consciousness. Shock may be caused by severe injury or great emotional upset.

4. *noun* A sudden, violent impact: *The shock of the crash set off the airbag.*

5. *noun* Injury to the body caused by an electric current passing through it: *Don't touch that lamp; you'll get a shock.* ▷ *verb* **shock**

6. *noun* A thick, heavy mass of something, especially hair: *He had a shock of dark hair hanging down over his forehead.*

7. *verb* To surprise, horrify, or disgust someone: *The news of the murders shocked us all.* ▷ *verb* **shocking, shocked** ▷ *adjective* **shocking**
shock (shahk)

shoddy *adjective* Poorly made or made from cheap materials, as in *shoddy merchandise.* **shod·dy** (**shah**-dee) ▷ *adjective* **shoddier, shoddiest** ▷ *noun* **shoddiness**

shoe

1. *noun* An outer covering for the foot with a thick sole and a heel. Shoes are usually made of leather or vinyl: *Joe's heavy hiking shoes protect his feet from rocks.*

2. *noun* A horseshoe.

3. *noun* The part of a brake that presses against a wheel to slow or stop it.

4. *verb* To fit a shoe or shoes on a horse: *We watched experts shoe the horse.* ▷ *verb* **shoeing, shod** (shahd) or **shoed**
shoe (shoo)

shoehorn *noun* A narrow piece of plastic or metal that you put in the heel of your shoe to make it easier for your foot to slide in. **shoe·horn** (**shoo**-horn)

shoelace *noun* A cord or string used for fastening a shoe: *You'll trip if you don't tie your shoelaces!*
shoe·lace (**shoo**-lase)

shoestring

1. *noun* Another name for a **shoelace**.

2. *adjective* Having a long and narrow shape like a shoestring, as in *shoestring potatoes.*

3. *phrase* If a person starts a business **on a shoestring**, he or she has very little money to work with.

4. *adjective* Done with little or barely enough money, as in *a shoestring budget.*
shoe·string (**shoo**-string)

shone *verb* The past tense and past participle of **shine**. **shone** (shohn) **Shone** sounds like **shown**.

shook *verb* The past tense of **shake**. **shook** (shuk)

shoot

1. *verb* To wound or kill a person or an animal with a bullet or an arrow: *They shot the robber in the knee.*

2. *verb* To fire a gun: *Don't shoot until you are close enough to hit your target.*

3. *verb* To film a movie or video or to photograph someone or something: *The movie was shot in Italy.*

4. *verb* To move with great speed and sudden force: *The race car shot past.*

5. *noun* A new sprout or twig growing from the main trunk or stem of a plant or tree: *My uncle showed me the new shoots growing in the garden.*

6. *verb* To aim and kick, hit, or throw a ball or puck toward a goal or net, as in *to shoot a basketball.*

7. *verb* To strive for: *I'm shooting for an A on my paper.*
shoot (shoot)
Shoot sounds like **chute**. ▷ *verb* **shooting, shot**

shooting star *noun* A meteor that burns up as it enters the earth's atmosphere.

shop

1. *noun* A place where goods are offered for sale, as in *a pet shop.*

2. *noun* A place

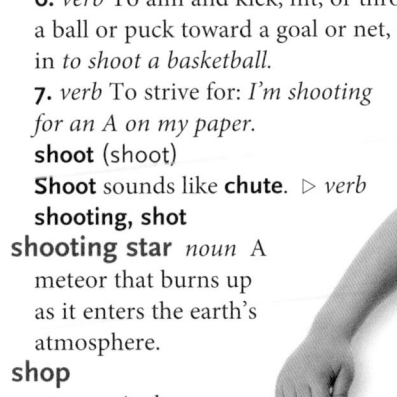

shoelace

where a particular kind of work is done, as in *a flower shop* or *a repair shop*.

3. *verb* To visit a store so that you can look at or buy goods, as in *to shop for groceries.* ▷ *verb* **shopping, shopped** ▷ *noun* **shopper** ▷ *noun* **shopping shop** (shahp)

shopaholic *noun* (*informal*) Someone who really enjoys shopping, or who cannot control the urge to shop: *The court documents described her as a shopaholic buried in debt.* **shop·a·hol·ic** (*shah*-puh-**haw**-lik)

shoplifter *noun* Someone who takes something from a store without paying for it: *Shoplifters will be arrested.* **shop·lift·er** (**shahp**-*lif*-tur) ▷ *noun* **shoplifting** ▷ *verb* **shoplift**

shopping channel *noun* A television channel whose only programs are commercials for products that you can buy using your telephone or the internet.

shore *noun* The land along the edge of an ocean, a river, or a lake: *It's nice to walk barefoot along the shore.* **shore** (shor)

shorebird *noun* A bird that lives or feeds mainly on the shores of lakes, rivers, or seas. **shore·bird** (**shor**-burd)

short

1. *adjective* Less than the average or expected length, height, distance, time, or scope, as in *a short book, a short girl, a short walk,* or *a short wait.* ▷ *adverb* **short**

2. short of or **short on** *adjective* Lacking the full amount that you need, as in *short of money*.

3. *adjective* Abrupt in a rude or unfriendly way; curt, as in *a short manner*.

4. *adverb* Suddenly: *The car stopped short at the red light.*

5. *noun* A **short circuit**.

6. short for *adjective* Shortened from something longer. For example, the word *dorm* is short for *dormitory*.

short (short)

▷ *adjective, adverb* **shorter, shortest**

shortage *noun* A situation where there is not enough of something that is needed or expected, as in *a water shortage*. **short·age** (**shor**-tij)

shortbread *noun* A rich cookie made with flour, sugar, and butter. **short·bread** (**short**-bred)

short circuit

1. *noun* An electric circuit that bypasses a device that was designed to be included in the circuit. Sometimes a short circuit can cause a fire or blow a fuse.

2. short-circuit *verb* To bypass: *I applied for the job in person to short-circuit the long hiring process.*

▷ *verb* **short-circuiting, short-circuited**

shoplifter

shortcoming *noun* A weakness or fault in something or someone: *One of Tim's shortcomings is that he doesn't handle criticism very well.* **short·com·ing** (**short**-*kuhm*-ing)

shortcut *noun*

1. A shorter route for getting somewhere, or a quicker way of doing something: *We took a shortcut on back roads.*

2. Short for **keyboard shortcut**. **short·cut** (**short**-*kuht*)

shorten *verb* To make short or shorter, as in *to shorten a pair of pants.* **short·en** (**shor**-tuhn) ▷ *verb* **shortening, shortened**

shortening *noun* Butter, lard, or other fat used in baking, especially to make pastry crisp or flaky. **short·en·ing** (**shor**-tuh-ning)

shortfall *noun* An amount or quantity that is the difference between what is needed or wanted, and what is available: *The heavy snow this winter resulted in a shortfall of $2 million in the county's budget.* **short·fall** (**short**-*fawl*)

shorthand *noun* Any system for writing quickly that uses symbols or abbreviations instead of words: *Use "gov" as shorthand for "government."* **short·hand** (**short**-*hand*)

short-handed *adjective* Not having enough or the usual number of people to do a job. **short·hand·ed** (**han**-did)

shortly *adverb* In a short time; very soon: *My ride should be here shortly.* **short·ly** (**short**-lee)

shortness *noun*

1. The state of being short: *Keith's shortness kept him off the basketball team.*

2. An insufficient amount, as in *shortness of breath*. **short·ness** (**short**-nis)

short-range *adjective* Not reaching far in time or distance, as in *a short-range weather forecast*.

shorts *noun, plural*

1. Pants that reach to or above the knees, as in *cutoff shorts.*

2. A man's or boy's underpants.

shorts (shorts)

shortsighted *adjective* Not thinking carefully about future consequences, as in *a shortsighted decision.* **short·sight·ed** (short-**sye**-tid)

▷ *noun* **shortsightedness**

shortstop *noun* In baseball or softball, the player whose position is between second and third base. **short·stop** (short-*stahp*)

shot

1. *verb* The past tense and the past participle of **shoot**.

2. *noun* The firing of a gun or cannon: *I think I heard a shot.*

3. *noun* A person who shoots: *She is a good shot.*

4. *noun* A single bullet fired from a gun: *He fired a shot at the sky.*

5. *noun* A single metal ball or pellet fired from a gun or cannon. ▷ *noun, plural* **shots** *or* **shot**

6. *noun* A throw or thrust of a ball or puck toward a net or other goal in various sports: *Lara won the game by getting three shots in a row.*

7. *noun* The distance or range over which something such as a missile or bullet can travel: *The cannon fired a very long shot.*

8. *noun* A photograph: *I like this shot of the dog the best.*

9. *noun* An injection, as in *a flu shot.*

10. *noun* A heavy metal ball thrown at a track-and-field event.

11. *noun (informal)* An attempt or a chance: *Tonya had a shot at beating the record.*

shot (shaht)

shotgun *noun*

1. A gun with a long barrel that fires cartridges filled with pellets, often used in hunting small game: *The hunter fired his shotgun.*

2. When you **ride shotgun**, you sit in the front passenger seat of a car, next to the driver. This expression comes from the days of the stagecoach, when a guard sat beside the driver with a shotgun.

shot·gun (**shaht**-*guhn*)

shot put *noun* A track-and-field event in which a heavy metal ball is thrown as far as possible. ▷ *noun* **shot-putter** ▷ *noun* **shot-putting**

should *verb* A helping verb that is used in the following ways:

1. To show a duty or an obligation: *You should be doing your homework right now.*

2. To show that something is likely or expected: *We*

shot-putter

should arrive at the station soon.

3. To make a suggestion or invite others' opinions: *Should we pitch our tent here?*

4. To show that something might happen: *If we should see a gas station, let's stop and ask for directions.*

should (shud)

shoulder

1. *noun* The joint or part of the body between your neck and your upper arm: *He held the phone between his ear and his shoulder.*

2. *noun* A similar part on an animal's body.

3. *noun* The sloping side or edge of a road or highway: *We pulled off the road and onto the shoulder to read the map.*

4. *verb* To push with your shoulder or shoulders: *I shouldered my way through the crowd.*

5. *verb* To take on a burden, as in *to shoulder the blame* or *to shoulder a responsibility.*

shoul·der (**shohl**-dur)

▷ *verb* **shouldering, shouldered**

shoulder blade *noun* One of two large, flat bones in the upper back, just below the shoulder.

shouldn't *contraction* A short form of *should not*: *We shouldn't stay up so late.* **should·n't** (**shud**-uhnt)

shout *verb* To speak or call out loudly: *You'll have to shout to be heard.* **shout** (shout) ▷ *verb* **shouting, shouted** ▷ *noun* **shout**

shove *verb* To push hard or roughly: *My sister shoved me out of her way.* **shove** (shuhv) ▷ *verb* **shoving, shoved** ▷ *noun* **shove**

shovel

1. *noun* A tool with a long handle and a flattened scoop, used for moving earth, snow, and other materials, as in *a garden shovel.*

2. *verb* To dig, clear, or make something with a shovel.

3. *verb* To move something with a shovel, as in *to shovel snow.*

4. *verb* To move, put, or throw something in large quantities, as if with a shovel, as in *to shovel food into your mouth.*

shov·el (**shuhv**-uhl)

▷ *verb* **shoveling, shoveled**

show

1. *verb* To let see or be seen: *Show me the book.*

2. *verb* To explain something to someone by doing it yourself: *Show me how to mix the paints.*

3. *verb* To make known or clear: *He showed his happiness by whistling on the way home from school.*

4. *verb* To guide or lead, as in *to show someone to a room.*

5. *verb* To be or to make visible: *Once you get your shoes on, that hole in your sock won't show.*

6. show up *verb* To arrive or make an appearance somewhere.

7. *noun* A public display, performance, or exhibition, as in *an art show.*

show (shoh)

▷ *verb* **showing, showed, shown** (shohn)

Synonyms

Show means to let someone see or examine something: *Brian showed his mother his art project before taking it to school.*

- -

■ **Display** means to show something in a careful way so others can see it: *The store displays all the new books on a table near the front.*

■ **Exhibit** means to display something in public so that it is easy for people to see: *After the judges choose the winners, we will exhibit all of the students' paintings in the library.*

■ **Present** can mean to offer something for viewing: *My class is going to present a play about the experiences of immigrant children.*

■ **Reveal** means to uncover or show something that previously had been hidden: *Moving the picture revealed a secret hiding place in the wall.*

■ **Parade** suggests that someone is showing off something: *The little girl paraded past her friends in her brand-new clothes.*

show business *noun* Popular entertainment such as music, television, and movies, and the industry that provides it: *The actress started out in show business at the age of six.*

showcase

1. *noun* A case or cabinet for displaying items, especially in a store.

2. *noun* A place for displaying something to advantage: *The TV show is a showcase for new talent.*

3. *verb* To display something or someone boldly and elaborately. ▷ *verb* **showcasing, showcased**

show·case (**shoh**-kase)

shower

1. *noun* A mounted device that sprays water over a person's body for washing.

2. *noun* A washing of the body by means of this device: *I couldn't wait to take a shower after our hike.*

3. *verb* To wash yourself under a shower: *I always shower and brush my teeth before bed.*

4. *noun* A brief rainfall: *Expect clouds and showers tomorrow afternoon.* ▷ *adjective* **showery**

5. *verb* To pour down on, to scatter over, or to cover, as in *to shower a parade with confetti.*

6. *verb* To give someone lots of things, as in *to shower someone with presents.*

7. *noun* A party at which a woman who is about to marry or give birth is honored and receives presents.

show·er (**shou**-er)

▷ *verb* **showering, showered**

shown *verb* The past participle of **show**. **shown** (shohn) **Shown** sounds like **shone**.

show-off *noun* Someone who behaves in a bragging way about his or her possessions or abilities: *He's such a show-off about his dancing.* ▷ *verb* **show off**

showroom *noun* A room used to display cars, furniture, or other items that are for sale, as in *a car showroom.* **show·room** (**shoh**-room)

showy *adjective*

1. Striking, or attracting attention because of color or size, as in *showy flowers.*

2. Flashy, or too bright and colorful, as in *a showy hat.* **show·y** (**shoh**-ee)

shrank *verb* The past tense of **shrink**. **shrank** (shrank)

shrapnel *noun* Small pieces of metal thrown out by an exploding shell or bomb. **shrap·nel** (**shrap**-nuhl)

shred *noun*

1. A long, thin strip of something made by tearing or cutting, as in *shreds of paper.* ▷ *verb* **shred**

2. A small amount; a bit, as in *a shred of truth.* **shred** (shred)

shredder *noun* A machine for cutting documents into thin strips or small pieces so that no one can read them. **shred·der** (**shred**-ur)

shrew *noun*

1. A small, insect-eating mammal that resembles a mouse, with a pointed nose and tiny eyes.

2. A nagging, scolding woman. **shrew** (shroo)

shrewd *adjective* Showing cleverness or sharp powers of judgment in practical situations, as in *a shrewd businessman* or *a shrewd shopper*. **shrewd** (shrood)
▷ *adjective* **shrewder, shrewdest** ▷ *adverb* **shrewdly**

Word History

The words **shrewd** and **shrew** are connected. An old meaning of *shrew* was "a wicked man." English speakers then started using *shrew* as a verb meaning "to curse." The past participle was *shrewed*, meaning "cursed." Later, people spelled *shrewed* as *shrewd*, and its meaning evolved into "good at tricking." Now *shrewd* has a positive meaning: "showing good judgment and cleverness."

shriek *verb* To make a shrill, piercing cry: *Tanya's nightmares made her shriek in her sleep.* **shriek** (shreek) ▷ *verb* **shrieking, shrieked** ▷ *noun* **shriek**

shrill *adjective* Having a high, sharp sound, as in *a shrill whistle.* **shrill** (shril) ▷ *adjective* **shriller, shrillest**

shrimp *noun* A small shellfish with a long tail that is highly valued as food. **shrimp** (shrimp)

shrine *noun* A building or small structure that contains objects associated with a holy person. **shrine** (shrine)

shrink
1. *verb* To make or to become smaller, often as a result of heat, cold, or moisture: *That blouse will shrink if you wash it in hot water.*
2. *verb* To draw back or turn away because you are frightened or disgusted: *The beautiful princess shrank from the hideous beast.*
3. *noun (slang)* A psychiatrist or a psychologist.
shrink (shringk)
▷ *verb* **shrinking, shrank** (shrangk) or **shrunk** (shruhngk), **shrunk** or **shrunken**

shrivel *verb* To shrink and become wrinkled, often after exposure to heat or sunlight: *If you stay in a hot bath long enough, your fingertips will shrivel.* **shriv·el** (shriv-uhl) ▷ *verb* **shriveling, shriveled** ▷ *adjective* **shriveled**

shroud
1. *noun* A cloth used to wrap a dead body for burial.
2. *noun* Something that covers or hides, as in *a shroud of mist.*
3. *verb* To cover or hide with a thin veil or haze: *Fog shrouded the highway.* ▷ *verb* **shrouding, shrouded** **shroud** (shroud)

shrub *noun* A plant or bush with woody stems that branch out at or near the ground: *My sister cut back the shrub in front of our house.* **shrub** (shruhb)

shrubbery *noun* A number of shrubs planted together: *The garden has beautiful shrubbery.* **shrub·ber·y** (shruhb-ur-ee)

shrug *verb* To raise your shoulders briefly to show that you don't know or don't care about someone or something: *When I asked if he was okay, he just shrugged.* **shrug** (shruhg) ▷ *verb* **shrugging, shrugged** ▷ *noun* **shrug**

shrunk *verb* The past participle of **shrink**. **shrunk** (shruhngk)

shrunken
1. *verb* A past participle of **shrink**.
2. *adjective* Made smaller, as in *a shrunken sweater.* **shrunk·en** (shruhng-kuhn)

shudder *verb* To shake or tremble violently from cold, fear, or disgust: *I shudder whenever I see a scary movie.* **shud·der** (shuhd-ur) ▷ *verb* **shuddering, shuddered** ▷ *noun* **shudder**

shuffle *verb*
1. To walk slowly, without lifting your feet completely off the floor or ground.
2. To mix playing cards so that they are in a random order.
3. To move something from one place to another, as in *to shuffle papers.* **shuf·fle** (shuhf-uhl) ▷ *verb* **shuffling, shuffled** ▷ *noun* **shuffle**

shun *verb* To avoid or ignore someone or something on purpose: *After their argument, Keith shunned Margaret.* **shun** (shuhn) ▷ *verb* **shunning, shunned**

shut *verb*
1. To close an opening or passage, or to fasten something securely, as in *to shut a window.* ▷ *adjective* **shut**
2. To confine or to enclose: *The animal was shut inside a cage.*
3. **shut down** To stop operating or to close: *The local newspaper has shut down.*
4. **shut out** To stop the opposing team from scoring any points.
5. **shut up** To stop talking or to make someone stop talking.
shut (shuht)
▷ *verb* **shutting, shut**

shrug

shutters

shutter *noun*
1. One of a pair of hinged panels attached to a window that can be closed to keep out weather or the light.
2. The part of a camera that opens and closes to expose the film to light when a picture is taken. **shut·ter** (**shuht**-ur)

shuttle *noun*
1. The part of a loom that carries the thread from side to side as a piece of cloth is being woven.
2. A bus, train, or aircraft that travels frequently between two places, as in *a shuttle from an airport to a parking lot. See also* **space shuttle.** **shut·tle** (**shuht**-uhl) ▷ *verb* **shuttle**

shuttlecock *noun* A small object, usually made of plastic, that is hit back and forth over the net in the game of badminton. **shut·tle·cock** (**shuht**-uhl-*kahk*)

shy
1. *adjective* Bashful and uncomfortable around people or with strangers. ▷ *noun* **shyness** ▷ *adverb* **shyly**
2. *adjective* Easily frightened or startled; timid: *Most wild deer are too shy to get close to people.*
3. *adjective* Lacking, or short: *I am $5 shy of the amount I need to buy a new basketball.*
4. *verb* If a horse **shies**, it moves suddenly backward or sideways because it has been frightened or startled. ▷ *verb* **shying, shied** **shy** (shye) ▷ *adjective* **shier, shiest**

sibling *noun* A brother or a sister: *Joan and her siblings were all born in this house.* **sib·ling** (**sib**-ling)

sick *adjective*
1. Suffering from a disease; ill: *She stayed home sick with the flu.*
2. Nauseated, or feeling as though you are going to vomit: *I ate too much, and now I feel sick.*
3. Tired, annoyed, bored by, or disgusted with someone or something: *I'm sick of your silly excuses.*
4. Upset or very unhappy: *Yolanda is sick about having to move away from her friends.* **sick** (sik) ▷ *adjective* **sicker, sickest** ▷ *noun* **sickness**

sicken *verb* To make someone feel nauseated or disgusted. **sick·en** (**sik**-uhn) ▷ *verb* **sickening, sickened** ▷ *adjective* **sickening** ▷ *adverb* **sickeningly**

sickle *noun* A tool with a short handle and a curved blade that is used for cutting grain, grass, or weeds. **sick·le** (**sik**-uhl)

sickle-cell disease *noun* A form of anemia in which many normal red blood cells take on a sickle shape and cannot carry oxygen. Sickle-cell disease is inherited and occurs mainly in people of African ancestry.

sickly *adjective*
1. In poor health and often ill, as in *a sickly child.*
2. Caused by or showing sickness, as in *a sickly complexion.* **sick·ly** (**sik**-lee) ▷ *adjective* **sicklier, sickliest**

side
1. *noun* One of the lines or surfaces that form the boundaries or limits of a shape or object: *A square has four equal sides. Write on both sides of the paper.*
2. *noun* An outer part of something that is not the top, bottom, front, or back, as in *the sides of a house.*
3. *noun* The right or left part of the body: *I fell and scraped my right side.*
4. *noun* One of two opposing individuals, groups, teams, or positions: *Our side won the game. I took Randall's side during the argument.*
5. *noun* The area next to someone: *When Emma heard the bad news, her parents were at her side.*
6. *noun* A line of ancestors: *She is my aunt on my mother's side.*
7. **side with** *verb* To agree with or support someone: *My mom always sides with my little sister when we fight.* ▷ *verb* **siding, sided**
8. *adjective* At or near one side, as in *a side door.* **side** (side)

sidebar *noun* A box containing text or graphics that appears in a book, newspaper, or magazine beside an article. Sidebars are ways of highlighting related information: *A sidebar in the article about the earthworm's habitat has maps showing the places where they are found.* **side·bar** (**side**-bahr)

sideburns *noun, plural* The hair that grows down the sides of a man's face, just in front of his ears. **side·burns** (**side**-burnz)

side effect *noun* A usually unpleasant or undesired effect of taking a medicine: *Internal bleeding is a possible side effect of taking too much aspirin.*

665

side-eye *noun* *(informal)* A look at someone from the corner of your eye, because you are suspicious, distrustful, or disapproving: *Mom gave me the side-eye when I came downstairs with blue hair.*

sidekick *noun* A person who is often by a more important person's side, helping them: *Batman is accompanied in his exploits by his sidekick, Robin.* **side·kick** (**side**-*kik*)

sideline *noun*
1. A line that marks the side boundary of the playing area in sports such as football, basketball, and soccer: *We watched the soccer game from the sideline.*
2. An activity or work done in addition to a regular job: *My mother's sideline is coaching the girls' soccer team.* **side·line** (**side**-*line*)

sidestep *verb*
1. To step to one side: *He was running right at me, so I sidestepped to avoid being hit.*
2. To avoid a problem or decision, as in *to sidestep a question.* **side·step** (**side**-*step*)
▷ *verb* **sidestepping, sidestepped**

sidetrack *verb* To distract or to be distracted from the main issue or something important: *I don't want to sidetrack you, but I have a few questions.* **side·track** (**side**-*trak*) ▷ *verb* **sidetracking, sidetracked**

sidewalk *noun* A paved path beside a street. **side·walk** (**side**-*wawk*)

sidewalk

sideways
1. *adjective* To or from one side: *Take three sideways steps.*
2. *adverb* With one side forward: *To get through this narrow tunnel, you'll have to walk sideways.*
3. *adjective* Moving or directed toward one side, as in

a sideways glance. **side·ways** (**side**-*wayz*)

siding *noun*
1. A short section of railroad track next to the main track, used for storing or shunting cars.
2. Material that covers the outside of a house, as in *aluminum siding.* **sid·ing** (**sye**-ding)

siege *noun* The surrounding of a place such as a castle or city to cut off supplies and then wait for those inside to surrender: *The siege of the city lasted three months.* **siege** (seej)

sierra *noun* A chain of hills or mountains with peaks that look like sharp, jagged teeth. **si·er·ra** (see-**er**-uh)

Word History

The word **sierra** was borrowed from a Spanish word that means "saw." From a distance, a sierra looks like the jagged teeth of a saw.

siesta *noun* An afternoon nap or rest, usually taken after a midday meal. **si·es·ta** (see-**es**-tuh)

sieve *noun* A container consisting of a wire or plastic mesh in a frame, used for separating large pieces from small pieces or liquids from solids: *Use the sieve to get the seeds out of the juice.* **sieve** (siv) ▷ *verb* **sieve**

sift *verb*
1. To pass a substance through a mesh to get rid of lumps or large chunks, as in *to sift flour.*
2. To examine something carefully to determine what is most important or useful, as in *to sift through evidence.* **sift** (sift)
▷ *verb* **sifting, sifted**

sigh *verb* To let out a long, deep breath, often to express sadness, weariness, or relief: *Marnie sighed in frustration.* **sigh** (sye) ▷ *verb* **sighing, sighed** ▷ *noun* **sigh**

sight
1. *noun* The ability to see; vision: *The infection caused a loss of sight in her left eye.*
2. *noun* The act of seeing: *It was love at first sight.*
3. *noun* The range or distance a person can see: *Don't let your little brother out of your sight.*
4. *noun* Something that is seen; a view: *The New York skyline is a marvelous sight.*
5. *verb* To see or to spot, as in *to sight land.* ▷ *verb* **sighting, sighted**
6. *noun* A small metal device on a rifle that helps you aim: *Use the sight to help you hit your target.* ▷ *verb* **sight**
7. *noun* Something funny or odd to look at: *Carl*

was a sight in his costume.
sight (site)
Sight sounds like **cite** and **site**.

sightseer *noun* A person who visits places of interest: *My cousin guides sightseers around the White House.*
sight·se·er (**site**-*see*-ur) ▷ *noun* **sightseeing**
▷ *verb* **sightsee**

sign
1. *noun* A symbol that has a specific meaning, as in *a dollar sign* or *a plus sign.*
2. *noun* A publicly displayed notice that gives information about or advertises something, as in *a road sign.*
3. *verb* To write your name as a signature on something, as in *to sign a letter.*
4. *verb* To communicate using sign language.
5. *noun* A trace, or evidence left by someone: *There was no sign of breaking and entering.*
6. *noun* Something that points out what is to come: *Blossoming trees are a sign of spring.*
sign (sine)
▷ *verb* **signing, signed**

signal *noun*
1. A sign or device that sends a message or warning, as in *a traffic signal.* ▷ *verb* **signal**
2. The electrical pulses transmitted for radio, television, or telephone communications: *All we're getting is static and no signal.*
sig·nal (**sig**-nuhl)

signature *noun* A person's name, written in his or her own individual way, usually in script. **sig·na·ture** (**sig**-nuh-chur)

significance *noun* Importance or meaning: *In my essay, I wrote about how rain plays a big role in this novel and explained its significance.* **sig·nif·i·cance** (sig-**nif**-i-kuhns)

significant *adjective* Important, meaningful, or likely to have a major effect, as in *a significant event.*
sig·nif·i·cant (sig-**nif**-i-kuhnt) ▷ *adverb* **significantly**

signify *verb*
1. To stand as a symbol or sign of something: *In math, a zero with a slash through it signifies an empty set.*
2. To express or show something: *We shook hands to signify that we both agreed to the terms of the deal.*
sig·ni·fy (**sig**-nuh-*fye*)
▷ *verb* **signifying, signified**

sign language *noun* A language in which hand gestures, in combination with facial expressions and larger body movements, are used instead of speech.

signpost *noun* A post with signs on it to direct travelers: *The signpost said we were heading toward Chicago.* **sign·post** (**sine**-*pohst*)

Sikh *noun* A member of a religious sect, founded in India in the 16th century, that believes in a single god. **Sikh** (seek) ▷ *noun* **Sikhism** (**see**-*kiz*-uhm)

silence *noun* Absence of sound; stillness and quiet: *I need to study in silence.* **si·lence** (**sye**-luhns)

silencer *noun* A device that reduces noise, especially from a gun: *They used a silencer so no one would hear the shots.* **si·lenc·er** (**sye**-luhn-sur)

silent *adjective* Making no sound; absolutely quiet: *It was silent in the room during the test.* **si·lent** (**sye**-luhnt) ▷ *adverb* **silently**

silhouette *noun*
1. A drawing made by filling in the outline of a figure with a solid color, usually black.
2. A dark outline of someone or something, visible against a light background: *Through the window shade we saw a silhouette of a man.*
sil·hou·ette (*sil*-oo-**et**)
▷ *verb* **silhouette**

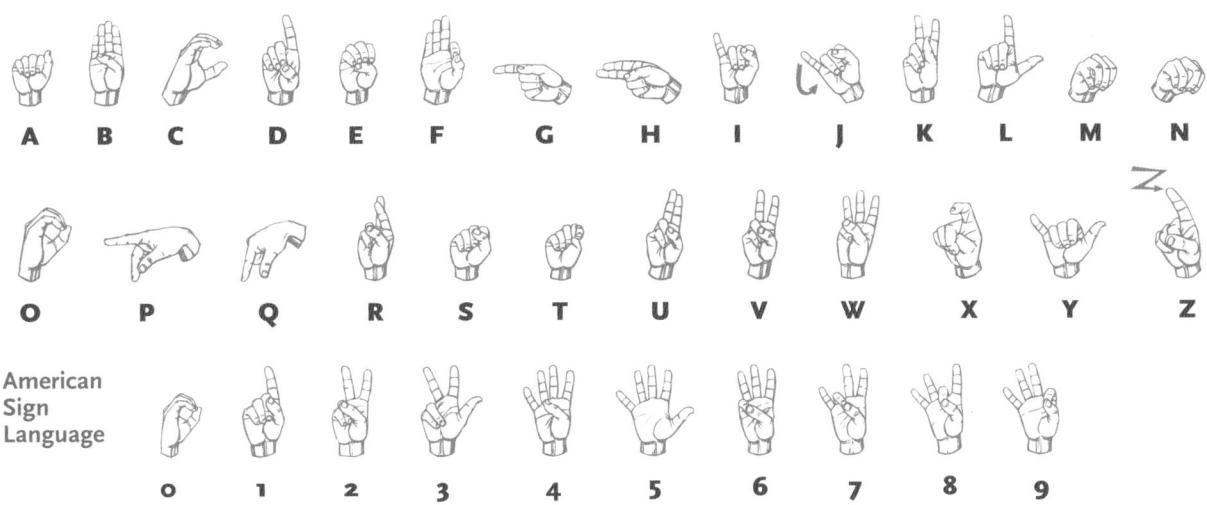

American Sign Language

silicon *noun* A chemical element found in sand and rocks and used to make glass, microchips, and transistors. **sil·i·con** (**sil**-i-kuhn *or* **sil**-i-*kahn*)

silicone *noun* A stable chemical compound containing silicon, used for making plastics, lubricants, and artificial body parts. **sil·i·cone** (**sil**-i-*kohn*)

silk *noun* A soft, shiny fiber produced by silkworms, or the thread or fabric made from this fiber: *In the days before nylon was invented, stockings were made out of silk.* **silk** (silk)

silkworm *noun* A caterpillar that spins a cocoon made of silk fibers. **silk·worm** (**silk**-*wurm*)

silky *adjective* Made of silk or like silk in texture; smooth, as in *silky hair.* **silk·y** (**sil**-kee)

sill *noun* A piece of wood or stone that runs across the bottom of a door or window: *Antoine leaned against the windowsill.* **sill** (sil)

silly *adjective*
1. Foolish or showing a lack of common sense, as in *a silly mistake.*
2. Ridiculous or laughable, as in *a silly nickname.*
sil·ly (**sil**-ee)
▷ *adjective* **sillier, silliest** ▷ *noun* **silliness**

silo *noun*
1. A tall, round tower used to store food for farm animals: *They were filling the silo with corn.*
2. An underground structure for storing and launching a guided missile.
si·lo (**sye**-loh)
▷ *noun, plural* **silos**

silt *noun* The fine particles of soil that are carried along by flowing water and that eventually settle to the bottom of a river or lake. **silt** (silt)

silver *noun*
1. A soft, shiny, white metal that is used to make jewelry, coins, bowls, and utensils: *Selma's watch is made of silver and gold.*
2. Coins made from silver or a metal that looks like silver: *The pirates found a treasure chest full of silver.*
3. Forks, spoons, and other items made of or coated with silver; silverware.
4. A grayish-white color: *My mom has a patch of silver in her hair.*
sil·ver (**sil**-vur)
▷ *adjective* **silver** ▷ *adjective* **silvery**

silverware *noun* Objects made of or coated with silver, especially forks, spoons, and knives. **sil·ver·ware** (**sil**-vur-*wair*)

similar *adjective* Nearly but not exactly alike: *The twins are very similar, but you can tell them apart.* **sim·i·lar** (**sim**-uh-lur)

Silk

Silkworms spin cocoons made of silk threads. More than 4,500 years ago, the Chinese discovered that they could unwind these threads and weave them into silk. China guarded the secret of how to make silk and established a profitable trade route to the West called the Silk Road. Eventually the secret became known, and now many countries produce silk.

silk fabric

silkworm

similarity *noun* The quality of being similar or alike: *One similarity is that both the missing notebooks are pink.* **sim·i·lar·i·ty** (*sim*-uh-**lar**-i-tee) ▷ *noun, plural* **similarities**

similarly *adverb* In a way that resembles but is not identical to someone or something else: *The rooms are similarly sized.* **sim·i·lar·ly** (**sim**-uh-lur-lee)

simile *noun* A way of describing something by comparing it to something quite different. A simile uses the word *like* or *as.* For example: *His smile is as warm as the sun.* **sim·i·le** (**sim**-uh-lee)

simmer *verb*
1. To stay at or just below the boiling point: *The sauce simmered on the stove.* ▷ *noun* **simmer**
2. simmer down (*informal*) To become calmer: *He asked the class to simmer down.*
sim·mer (**sim**-ur)
▷ *verb* **simmering, simmered**

simple *adjective*
1. Easily done or understood, as in *a simple test* or *a simple task.*
2. With nothing added, as in *the simple truth.*
3. Plain, or not fancy, as in *a simple white dress.*
sim·ple (**sim**-puhl)
▷ *adjective* **simpler, simplest** ▷ *noun* **simplicity** (sim-**plis**-i-tee)

simple sentence *noun* A sentence that consists of only one independent clause. "The lion roared" is a simple sentence.

simplify *verb* To make something less complicated or easier to understand, as in *to simplify a procedure.* **sim·pli·fy** (**sim**-pluh-*fye*) ▷ *verb* **simplifies, simplifying, simplified** ▷ *noun* **simplification** (*sim*-pluh-fi-**kay**-shuhn)

simply *adverb*
1. In a simple way, or plainly, as in *to dress simply.*
2. Merely, or just: *If you need help, simply ask me.*
3. Very: *You look simply wonderful.*
sim·ply (**sim**-plee)

simulation *noun*
1. A trial run to act out a real event: *Astronauts must train by doing simulations on land.*
2. A copy or an imitation: *Listen to the computer simulation of a piano.*
sim·u·la·tion (*sim*-yuh-**lay**-shuhn) ▷ *verb* **simulate** (**sim**-yuh-*layt*)

simulator *noun* A machine that allows you to experience or perform a complex task, such as flying a plane, by imitating the conditions and controls. **sim·u·la·tor** (**sim**-yuh-*lay*-tur)

simulator

simultaneous *adjective* Happening or done at the same time, as in *simultaneous attacks.* **si·mul·ta·ne·ous** (*sye*-muhl-**tay**-nee-uhs)

simultaneously *adverb* At the same time: *She learned English and French simultaneously.* **si·mul·ta·ne·ous·ly** (*sye*-muhl-**tay**-nee-uhs-lee)

sin *noun* An act that goes against moral or religious laws, especially when it is done on purpose: *Greed is a sin in most religions.* **sin** (sin) ▷ *noun* **sinner** ▷ *verb* **sin** ▷ *adjective* **sinful** ▷ *adverb* **sinfully**

since
1. *conjunction* During the period following the time when: *She has lived there since she was in fourth grade.*
2. *conjunction* As, or because: *Since you asked, I'll tell you how you can help.*
3. *adverb* Ago; before now: *I have long since forgotten our argument.*
4. *adverb* From then until now: *Tony left the party in a huff and hasn't been seen since.*
5. *preposition* From or during the time after: *I've been here since July.*
since (sins)

sincere *adjective* Straightforward and honest, as in *a sincere apology.* **sin·cere** (sin-**seer**) ▷ *adjective* **sincerer, sincerest** ▷ *noun* **sincerity** (sin-**ser**-i-tee)

sincerely *adverb* If you say something sincerely, you are saying what you truly feel or think: *I told him I was sorry that I'd hurt his feelings, and I meant it sincerely.* **sin·cere·ly** (sin-**seer**-lee)

sinew *noun* A band of tissue that connects a muscle to a bone; a tendon or ligament. **sin·ew** (**sin**-yoo)

sing *verb*
1. To produce words and musical sounds with your voice: *She loves to sing older songs.*
2. To perform by singing, as in *to sing a song.*
3. To produce musical sounds: *Not all birds sing.*
sing (sing) ▷ *verb* **singing, sang** (sang), **sung** (suhng)

singe *verb* To burn something slightly: *Crystal singed her dress while ironing it.* **singe** (sinj) ▷ *verb* **singeing, singed**

singer *noun* Someone who sings, especially who sings well or who sings professionally: *The local women's chorus is looking for experienced singers.* **sing·er** (**sing**-ur)

single
1. *adjective* One and no more than one: *A single rose remained on the bush.*
2. *adjective* Intended for one person or family, as in *a single room.*
3. *adjective* Not married: *The single mother raised her kids on her own.*
4. single out *verb* To choose out of a group: *The firefighter was singled out for a medal.* ▷ *verb* **singling, singled**
5. *noun* A recording that features one main song, as in *a hit single.*
6. *noun* A hit in baseball that allows the runner to get to first base. ▷ *verb* **single**
sin·gle (**sing**-guhl)

single-handed *adjective* Done alone or without help from others, as in *a single-handed rescue.* **single-hand·ed** (**han**-did) ▷ *adverb* **single-handedly**

single-minded *adjective* Focused on one main purpose or goal: *She was single-minded in her quest to get a dog.* **single-mind·ed** (**mine**-did)

singular *adjective* Of or having to do with the form of a word that refers to just one person or thing. *Chair* and *singer* are singular nouns. **sin·gu·lar** (**sing**-gyuh-lur)

sinister *adjective* Suggesting or threatening harm, evil, or misfortune, as in *a sinister laugh.* **sin·is·ter** (**sin**-i-stur)

Word History

Since there is a long tradition of thinking that anything on the left side is a bad omen, the word for "on the left" in Latin, *sinister,* took on a negative meaning that remains today in the English word **sinister**. Unlike the left side, the right side has positive connotations: *Dexter,* the Latin word for "on the right," is the source of an English word meaning "skill," *dexterity.*

sink
1. *noun* A basin used for washing, with faucets for hot and cold water and a drain, as in *a kitchen sink.*
2. *verb* To go down slowly or gradually, as in *to sink to your knees.*
3. *verb* To go or to make someone or something go beneath the surface, as in *to sink a ship.* ▷ *noun* **sinking**
4. *verb* To fall or drop into a certain state: *I sank into a deep sleep.*
5. *verb* To become lower in amount: *Our food supply sank to an all-time low.*
6. *verb* To fall in pitch or volume: *Their voices sank to a whisper.*
7. *verb* To penetrate or go through or into deeply: *The water sank into the earth.*
sink (singk)
Sink sounds like **sync**.
▷ *verb* **sinking, sank** (sangk), **sunk** (suhngk)

sinus *noun* One of four hollow channels in the skull around the eyes and nose, all leading to the nose: *My sinuses are blocked because of allergies.* **si·nus** (**sye**-nuhs) ▷ *noun, plural* **sinuses**

Sioux *noun* A member of a group of Native Americans who live in Minnesota and North and South Dakota. **Sioux** (soo) ▷ *noun, plural* **Sioux**

sip *verb* To drink slowly, a little at a time: *I sipped my hot chocolate.* **sip** (sip) ▷ *verb* **sipping, sipped** ▷ *noun* **sip**

siphon *noun* A bent tube through which liquid can drain upward and then down to a lower level,

using the difference in pressure at the two ends to keep the liquid flowing: *My dad used a siphon to drain the gas from the tank.* **si·phon** (**sye**-fuhn) ▷ *verb* **siphon**

sir *noun*
1. A polite way to address a man, used in speaking and writing: *Can I help you, sir?*
2. Sir The title of someone who has been made a knight, as in *Sir Lancelot.*
sir (sur)

siren *noun* A device that makes a loud, shrill sound. A siren is often used as a signal or warning, as in *a fire siren.* **si·ren** (**sye**-ruhn)

sister *noun*
1. A girl or woman who has the same parents as another person, as in *twin sisters.* ▷ *adjective* **sisterly**
2. A female member of a religious community, such as a nun: *She had wanted to be a sister and live in a convent since she was a little girl.*
3. A woman who shares an interest or cause with another: *My door is open to any sister willing to fight against violence.*
sis·ter (**sis**-tur)

sisterhood *noun*
1. The warm, close feeling between sisters or among women.
2. A group of women who share a common interest, aim, or cause: *My grandma was president of the sisterhood for four years.*
sis·ter·hood (**sis**-tur-*hud*)

sister-in-law *noun* The sister of a person's spouse or the wife of a person's brother. ▷ *noun, plural* **sisters-in-law**

sit *verb*
1. To rest your weight on your buttocks: *Sit down on the couch.*
2. To be in a place or on a surface: *Books sit on shelves.*
3. To pose, as in *to sit for a portrait.*
4. To take a place as an official member of a club or legislature, as in *to sit in Congress.*
5. To hold a session or meeting: *The Supreme Court will sit next month.*
6. To babysit: *I sit for the neighbors' children.*
7. sit in To take someone's place temporarily: *Aimee will sit in for Fran until she feels better.*
sit (sit)
▷ *verb* **sitting, sat** (sat)

sitcom *noun* (*informal*) A humorous television program that features the same group of characters each week.

sink

Sitcom is short for *situation comedy*.
sit·com (**sit**-*kahm*)

site *noun*
1. The place where something is located or taking place, as in *the site of the new firehouse*.
2. On site means at the same place where something is happening: *Transportation officials were on site this morning, trying to determine what caused the train wreck.*
3. Short for **website**: *I visited your site yesterday and really loved the pictures.*
4. site map A page that serves as an index for a website, showing you all the pages on the site and how they are connected with each other.
site (site)
Site sounds like **cite** and **sight**.

situate *verb* To place something in a particular spot or location: *The baseball stadium is situated near the train station.* **sit·u·ate** (**sich**-oo-*ate*)
▷ *verb* **situating, situated**

situation *noun* The circumstances that exist at a particular time and place, as in *a desperate situation*. **sit·u·a·tion** (*sich*-oo-**ay**-shuhn)

sit-up *noun* An exercise for stomach muscles that is done by lying down and then raising the body to a sitting position without lifting the feet or legs, or using the arms: *I did 50 sit-ups in gym today.*

sizable or **sizeable** *adjective* Fairly large, as in *a sizable donation*. **siz·a·ble** or **size·a·ble** (**sye**-zuh-buhl)

size *noun*
1. The measurements or extent of something: *What's the size of the table?*
2. One in a series of standard measurements for items of clothing or other articles, as in *a dress size*.
size (size)

sizzle *verb* To make a hissing, crackling noise, especially when frying food: *I heard the bacon sizzling in the pan.* **siz·zle** (**siz**-uhl) ▷ *verb* **sizzling, sizzled**

skate
1. *noun* A boot with a blade fastened to the sole. Skates are used for gliding over ice.
2. *noun* A roller skate.
3. *verb* To glide or move along on skates: *The kids can skate on the frozen lake in the winter.* ▷ *verb* **skating, skated**
4. *noun* A large, flat, saltwater fish with a long, narrow tail and a diamond-shaped body. Skates are related to sharks and rays.
skate (skayt)

skateboard *noun* A small board with four roller skate wheels on the bottom that you ride in a standing or crouching position. **skate·board**

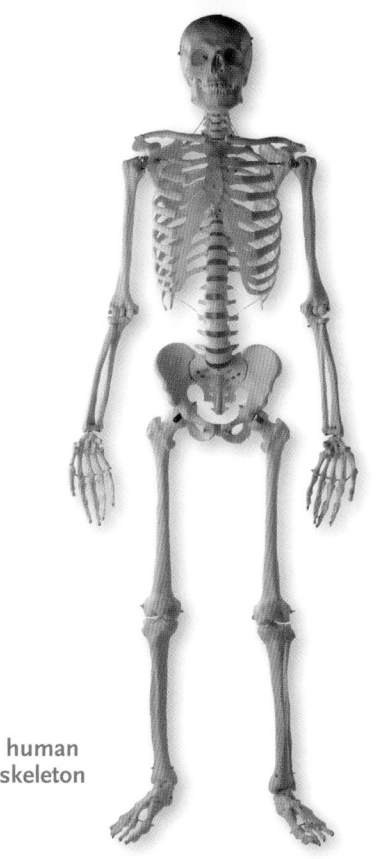

human
skeleton

(**skate**-*bord*) ▷ *verb* **skateboard** ▷ *noun* **skateboarding**

skedaddle *verb* (*informal*) To move along quickly or to run away from something that scares you: *I've got to skedaddle or I'll be late for class.* **ske·dad·dle** (ski-**dad**-uhl) ▷ *verb* **skedaddling, skedaddled**

skeleton *noun* The framework of bones that supports and protects the body of an animal with a backbone: *We saw a real skeleton in science class.* **skel·e·ton** (**skel**-uh-tuhn)

Word History

Skeleton comes from the Greek expression *soma skeleton*, or "dried-up body." The Greeks observed that buried bodies eventually became dry bones.

skeptic *noun* Someone who does not accept views or opinions readily from others: *He was one of the few scientists who remained a skeptic about climate change.* **skep·tic** (**skep**-tik) ▷ *noun* **skepticism** (**skep**-ti-*siz*-uhm)

skeptical *adjective* Doubting that something is really true: *When I said that I had already done my homework, my mother gave me a skeptical look.* **skep·ti·cal** (**skep**-ti-kuhl) ▷ *adverb* **skeptically**

sketch *noun*

1. A rough or unfinished drawing, done quickly and without much detail, as in *preliminary sketches.*
▷ *verb* **sketch**

2. A short essay or written description of someone or something: *He wrote a sketch of the principal for the school paper.*

3. A short play, skit, or story that is usually humorous.
sketch (skech)
▷ *noun, plural* **sketches**

sketchy *adjective*

1. Roughly drawn or done without detail, as in *a sketchy outline.*

2. Incomplete and not very clear, as in *a sketchy description.*
sketch·y (**skech**-ee)
▷ *adjective* **sketchier, sketchiest**

skewer *noun* A long metal or wooden pin for holding pieces of meat or vegetables together while they are being cooked: *Put the meat on the skewer, then give it to me to grill.* **skew·er** (**skyoo**-ur) ▷ *verb* **skewer**

ski *noun*

1. One of a pair of long, narrow runners that curve up in the front and are fastened to special boots, used for gliding over snow.

2. A water ski.
ski (skee)
▷ *noun* **skiing** ▷ *verb* **ski**

skid

1. *verb* To slide out of control on a slippery surface, as in *to skid on ice.* ▷ *verb* **skidding, skidded**
▷ *noun* **skid**

2. *noun* A runner on the bottom of a helicopter or other aircraft, used in place of wheels for landing.
skid (skid)

skiff *noun* A boat small enough to be sailed or rowed by one person. **skiff** (skif)

skill *noun* The ability to do something well, usually as a result of training or practice, as in *math skills.* **skill** (skil) ▷ *adjective* **skillful**

skilled *adjective* Having, showing, or requiring mastery or expertise: *My sister is a skilled musician.*
skilled (skild)

skillet *noun* A frying pan, as in *an iron skillet.*
skil·let (**skil**-it)

skim *verb*

1. To remove something that is floating on the top of a liquid: *My grandmother skimmed the fat from the soup.* ▷ *adjective* **skimmed**

2. To read through something quickly, just to get the main ideas: *Skim the first chapter of the book.*

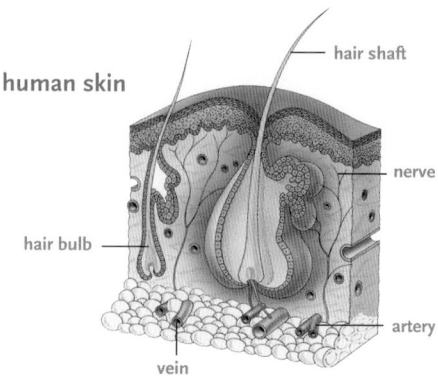

human skin — hair shaft — nerve — hair bulb — artery — vein

3. To glide across or pass quickly and lightly over something: *The bird skimmed over the surface of the water.*
skim (skim)
▷ *verb* **skimming, skimmed**

skim milk *noun* Milk from which the cream has been removed. It is also known as *skimmed milk.*

skin

1. *noun* The thin layer of tissue that forms the outer covering of human and animal bodies: *I rubbed the cream into my skin.*

2. *noun* The peel or outer layer of a fruit or vegetable, as in *an apple skin.*

3. *verb* To scrape your skin, as in *to skin your knees.*

4. *verb* To remove the skin from a killed animal, as in *to skin a deer.*
skin (skin)
▷ *verb* **skinning, skinned**

skinny *adjective*

1. Very thin: *She ate more food so she wouldn't be so skinny.*

2. Fitting very tightly, as in *skinny pants.*
skin·ny (**skin**-ee)
▷ *adjective* **skinnier, skinniest**

skewers

skip *verb*

1. To move along by hopping on one foot and then the other: *I skipped home from school.* ▷ *noun* **skip**

2. To jump over, as in *to skip rope.*

3. To leave something out or to pass over it

4. *(informal)* To leave a place quickly or secretly, as in *to skip town.* **skip** (skip)

▷ *verb* **skipping, skipped**

skirmish

1. *noun* A small battle, between a few soldiers or fighters, that is not part of a larger war or conflict. Skirmishes are usually short and not planned: *The troops along the border engaged in several small skirmishes with the enemy, but most of the fighting occurred near the capital.*

2. *noun* A minor or brief argument or dispute, especially in politics: *The Democrats and Republicans were again having a skirmish about whose tax plan was better.*

3. *verb* To take part in a skirmish: *The rioters vandalized some stores and skirmished with the police.* ▷ *verb* **skirmishing, skirmished** **skir·mish** (skur-mish)

▷ *noun* **skirmisher**

skirt

1. *noun* A piece of clothing traditionally worn by women and girls that hangs from the waist and covers all or part of the legs: *Taryn put on her best skirt and blouse for the party.*

2. *verb* To pass around a place or to lie around its border or edge: *A walking path skirts the lake.*

3. *verb* To avoid a question, a discussion, or an issue because it is difficult or because you are afraid that others might disagree with you: *Ken skirted the issue by changing the subject.* **skirt** (skurt)

▷ *verb* **skirting, skirted**

skit *noun* A short, usually funny play. **skit** (skit)

skittish *adjective* Excitable or easily frightened and therefore hard to control, as in *a skittish horse.* **skit·tish** (skit-ish)

skull *noun* The bony framework of the head that protects the brain. **skull** (skuhl)

skunk *noun*

1. A black-and-white mammal with a stripe down its back and a bushy tail. Skunks spray a foul-smelling liquid when they are frightened or in danger.

2. *(informal)* An obnoxious or offensive person: *He's a bully and a skunk.* **skunk** (skuhngk)

sky *noun* The upper atmosphere, or the area of space

skydiving

that seems to arch over the earth: *They watched clouds move across the sky.* **sky** (skye) ▷ *noun, plural* **skies**

skydiving *noun* The sport of jumping from an airplane and falling as far as safely possible before opening a parachute. Skydiving often involves stunts. **sky·div·ing** (skye-*dye*-ving) ▷ *noun* **skydiver** ▷ *verb* **skydive**

skylight *noun* A window in a roof or ceiling: *I get all the light I need from the skylight in my room.* **sky·light** (skye-*lite*)

skyline *noun*

1. The outline of buildings, mountains, or other objects seen against the sky from a distance, as in *the city skyline.*

2. The horizon, or the line at which the earth and sky seem to meet. **sky·line** (skye-*line*)

sky marshal *noun See* **air marshal**.

Skype

1. *noun* A trademark for a service that allows you to use your internet connection as a telephone.

2. *verb* To call someone or take part in a conversation using Skype. ▷ *verb* **Skyping, Skyped** **Skype** (skipe)

skyrocket

1. *noun* A type of firework that shoots into the air and explodes in a shower of many-colored sparks.

2. *verb* To rise suddenly and quickly: *Sales of the book skyrocketed after the author appeared on television.* ▷ *verb* **skyrocketing, skyrocketed** **sky·rock·et** (skye-*rah*-kit)

skyscraper *noun* A very tall building: *The Empire State Building is one of New York's tallest skyscrapers.* **sky·scrap·er** (skye-*skray*-pur)

a
b
c
d
e
f
g
h
i
j
k
l
m
n
o
p
q
r
s
t
u
v
w
x
y
z

slab *noun* A broad, flat, thick piece of something, as in *a slab of concrete* or *a slab of bread.* **slab** (slab)

slack *adjective*

1. Not tight or firm; loose: *When the breeze died down, the kite string went slack.*

2. Not busy or active: *The recession was a slack period for many stores.*

3. Careless or lazy in your work, as in *a slack office staff.*

slack (slak)

▷ *adjective* **slacker, slackest** ▷ *verb* **slacken**

slacks *noun, plural* Pants for casual wear, as in *corduroy slacks.* **slacks** (slaks)

slalom *noun* An athletic event in which competitors ski down a hill, zigzagging between poles. **sla·lom** (**slah**-luhm)

Word History

Skiing is a very popular sport in Norway, and the athletic event called the **slalom** owes its name to a word in Norwegian. *Slalåm* means "sloping track," and is a combination of the words *sla,* meaning "sloping," and *låm,* meaning "track." The slalom race was created by someone who was not from Norway, however. In 1922, the British skier Arnold Lunn invented the idea of paired poles that skiers must pass through.

---

slam *verb*

1. To close something loudly and forcefully, as in *to slam a door.*

2. To strike something with great force: *The truck slammed into a car. The batter slammed the ball into center field.*

slam (slam)

▷ *verb* **slamming, slammed** ▷ *noun* **slam**

slander *noun* An untrue statement about someone that damages that person's reputation: *Calling me a thief on TV is slander!* **slan·der** (**slan**-dur) ▷ *verb* **slander** ▷ *adjective* **slanderous**

slang *noun* Colorful or lively words and phrases used in ordinary conversation but not in formal speech or writing. Slang often gives new and different meanings to old words. **slang** (slang)

slant

1. *verb* To slope, lean, or be at an angle: *I love the way the afternoon light slants in the window.* ▷ *verb* **slanting, slanted** ▷ *noun* **slant**

2. *noun* An attitude, opinion, or point of view: *When Henry told the story, he gave it a very different slant.*

▷ *verb* **slant**

slant (slant)

slap *verb*

1. To hit someone or something with a flat object or the palm of your hand, as in *to slap someone's face.* ▷ *noun* **slap**

2. To throw down or put on with great force: *The officer slapped the handcuffs on the criminal.*

slap (slap)

▷ *verb* **slapping, slapped**

slapdash *adjective* Done carelessly and in a rush, as in *slapdash work.* **slap·dash** (**slap**-*dash*)

slapstick *noun* Comedy that stresses loud, rough action or horseplay and visual jokes. **slap·stick** (**slap**-*stik*)

slash

1. *verb* To cut or wound with a forceful, sweeping motion, as in *to slash tires.* ▷ *noun* **slash**

2. *verb* To reduce something drastically, as in *to slash prices.*

3. *noun* A symbol (/) that is used to separate choices, to indicate where lines of text should be broken, and in many computer commands. ▷ *noun, plural* **slashes**

slash (slash)

▷ *verb* **slashes, slashing, slashed**

slat *noun* A long, narrow strip of wood or metal, as in *fence slats.* **slat** (slat)

slate *noun*

1. A grayish-green or bluish-gray rock that can be split into thin, smooth layers.

2. A tile for roofs or floors made from slate.

3. A piece of slate or other material used for writing on.

4. A dark blue-gray color.

5. A complete list of candidates who are running for office, as in *a full slate of candidates.*

slate (slayt)

slaughter

1. *verb* To kill animals for food, as in *to slaughter a pig.* ▷ *verb* **slaughtering, slaughtered** ▷ *noun* **slaughter**

slalom

2. *noun* The killing of a large number of people in a brutal, violent way. ▷ *verb* **slaughter**
slaugh·ter (**slaw**-tur)

slave

1. *noun* A person who is owned by another person and thought of as property: *Ships brought Africans to the Americas to work as slaves.*

2. *noun* A person who is completely dominated by a habit or influence: *When I grow up, I don't want to be a slave to television.*

3. *noun* A person who works as hard as a slave: *Lately, Joe has been a slave to his job.*

4. *verb* To work very hard or like a slave: *She slaved all day over a hot stove.* ▷ *verb* **slaving, slaved**
slave (slayv)

slavery *noun* The condition of being a slave, or a system in which some people own slaves. For instance, slavery was legal in parts of the United States until 1863, ending after the Civil War. **slav·er·y** (**slay**-vur-ee)

slay *verb* To kill violently, as in *to slay one's enemies.* **slay** (slay) **Slay** sounds like **sleigh**. ▷ *verb* **slaying, slayed** *or* **slew** (sloo), **slain** (slayn)

sled *noun* A vehicle with wooden or metal runners that can be pushed, pulled, or allowed to slide over snow and ice, as in *a dog sled.* **sled** (sled) ▷ *verb* **sled**

sledgehammer *noun* A heavy hammer with a long handle. A sledgehammer is usually held with both hands: *Workers used sledgehammers to drive in the huge railroad spikes.* **sledge·ham·mer** (**slej**-ham-ur)

sleek *adjective* Smooth and glossy, as if polished: *After swimming, the dog's coat was sleek and wet.* **sleek** (sleek) ▷ *adjective* **sleeker, sleekest**

sleep *verb* To rest with the eyes closed, the muscles relaxed, and no conscious thought or movement. **sleep** (sleep) ▷ *verb* **sleeping, slept** (slept) ▷ *noun* **sleep**

sleeping bag *noun* A warm, zippered, padded bag in which you can sleep outdoors, especially while camping.

sleepwalker *noun* A person who gets out of bed and walks around while asleep. **sleep·walk·er** (**sleep**-waw-kur) ▷ *verb* **sleepwalk**

sleepy *adjective* Drowsy, or ready for sleep: *I'm going to keep reading because I'm not sleepy yet.* **sleep·y** (**slee**-pee) ▷ *adjective* **sleepier, sleepiest** ▷ *noun* **sleepiness**

sleet *noun* Frozen or partly frozen rain; a mixture of rain and snow: *A little sleet couldn't stop the bike racers.* **sleet** (sleet) ▷ *verb* **sleet**

sleeve *noun*

1. The part of a shirt, coat, or other garment that covers the upper or the entire arm.

2. up your sleeve Hidden or secret but ready to be used when needed: *I have a special surprise up my sleeve for Janie's party.*
sleeve (sleev)

sleigh *noun* A vehicle on runners with one or more seats, used in snow and usually pulled by horses or other animals. **sleigh** (slay) **Sleigh** sounds like **slay**.

slender *adjective*

1. Slim or thin in an attractive way, as in *a slender girl.*

2. Limited in amount, size, or extent; barely enough, as in *a slender margin.*
slen·der (**slen**-dur)
▷ *adjective* **slenderer, slenderest**

slept *verb* The past tense and the past participle of **sleep**. **slept** (slept)

sleuth *noun* A detective, or anyone good at finding out facts: *Mystery novels often feature a crime-fighting sleuth.* **sleuth** (slooth) ▷ *verb* **sleuth**

slice *noun* A thin, flat piece cut from something larger, as in *a slice of bread.* **slice** (slise) ▷ *verb* **slice**

slick

1. *adjective* Very smooth, wet, and slippery, as in *slick roads.* ▷ *verb* **slick**

2. *noun* A layer of oil on the surface of water or on a road: *Victor's car hit an oil slick, and he lost control.*

3. *adjective* Very clever, efficient, or professional, as in *a slick presentation.*
slick (slik)
▷ *adjective* **slicker, slickest**

slide

1. *verb* To move smoothly over a surface while never losing contact with it: *Those new patio doors slide so easily.*

2. *verb* To move or fall suddenly: *The car hit an icy patch and slid off the road.* ▷ *noun* **slide**

3. *noun* A smooth, slanted surface or chute down which people can slide: *There was a slide in the backyard, right next to the swings.*

4. *noun* A photographic transparency inside a frame that you view by projecting the image onto a screen.

5. *noun* One of a series of pictures or text that make up a computer presentation: *Can we go back to that last slide for a minute?*

6. *noun* A small piece of glass on which you put specimens that you want to examine under a microscope: *Dr. Li prepared a slide to view the bacteria.*

7. *noun* A large mass of snow, earth, or rock that falls down a slope from a great height: *The hikers narrowly avoided being caught in a slide.*
slide (slide)
▷ *verb* **sliding, slid** (slid)

slideshow *noun*
1. A series of photographic slides that tell a story, usually of an interesting place that someone visited.
2. A series of images or text arranged to be viewed as a single presentation, either on a computer or projected onto a screen: *I'll send you a link where you can look at all my India pictures as a slideshow.*
slide·show (**slide**-*shoh*)

slight
1. *adjective* Not very significant, as in *a slight change.*
2. *adjective* Slender: *The jockey has a slight build.*
3. *verb* To treat something as unimportant or to do something carelessly, as in *to slight your work.*
4. *verb* To insult someone or to treat a person coldly: *Irene was slighted by her visitors when they left without saying good-bye.* ▷ *noun* **slight**
slight (slite)
▷ *adjective* **slighter, slightest** ▷ *verb* **slighting, slighted**

slightly *adverb*
1. To a small degree or extent: *The box was slightly damaged.*
2. In a slender or delicate way: *She was a slightly built girl of 13.*
slight·ly (**slite**-lee)

slim
1. *adjective* Slender and graceful, as in *a slim model.*
2. *adjective* Small in quantity or amount; meager, as in *a slim possibility.*
3. *verb* To try to reduce your weight: *Slim down with a diet.* ▷ *verb* **slimming, slimmed**
slim (slim)
▷ *adjective* **slimmer, slimmest**

slime *noun* A moist, soft, and slippery substance usually thought of as unpleasant: *The bottom of the pond is coated with slime.* **slime** (slime) ▷ *adjective* **slimy**

Word History

It's not too surprising that the word **slime** is related to the German word for "mucus," *Schleim,* because mucus is a soft, slippery substance. A related word is *lime,* a white substance that people obtain from limestone. Mortar for building with bricks is made from lime. These meanings of the words *slime, mucus,* and *lime* all have to do with a soft substance that is slippery or sticky.

sling
1. *noun* A loop of cloth suspended from the neck and used to support an injured arm: *My dad will have to wear a sling until his wrist heals.*
2. *noun* A strap or loop of leather used for throwing stones.
3. *noun* A strong loop of cable, chain, or rope used to raise heavy objects: *Cargo was placed aboard the freighter with heavy slings.*
4. *verb* To hang or throw something loosely or in a rough way: *Dan slung his suitcase onto the bed.*
▷ *verb* **slinging, slung** (sluhng)
sling (sling)

slingshot *noun* A piece of metal or wood shaped like a Y with an elastic band attached. Slingshots are used for shooting small stones. **sling·shot** (**sling**-*shaht*)

slip
1. *verb* To lose your footing on a slippery surface, as in *to slip on ice.* ▷ *noun* **slip**
2. *verb* To move quickly and quietly, without attracting attention, as in *to slip out of the room.*
3. *verb* To put on or take off quickly and easily, as in *to slip off your shoes.*
4. *verb* To escape: *The task slipped my mind.*
5. *verb* To move or slide from a place: *The stool slipped out from under me.*
6. *noun* A small mistake, as in *a slip of the tongue.* ▷ *verb* **slip**
7. *noun* A light undergarment worn by girls and women under a skirt or dress.
8. *noun* A small piece, as in *a slip of paper.*
9. *noun* A small shoot or twig cut from a plant for grafting or planting.
10. *noun* A place where a boat or ship is docked.
slip (slip)
▷ *verb* **slipping, slipped**

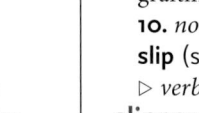
slippers

slipper *noun* A soft, lightweight shoe that you slip on and wear indoors, as in *bedroom slippers.* **slip·per** (**slip**-ur)

slippery *adjective* Smooth, oily, or wet and very hard to hold on to or stand on, as in *a slippery path.* **slip·per·y** (**slip**-ur-ee)

slipshod *adjective* Careless or sloppy in appearance or workmanship: *You did a slipshod job of cleaning your room.* **slip·shod** (**slip**-shahd)

slit *verb* To make a long, straight, narrow cut or opening in something: *Dad slit the potatoes in half and spread butter inside.* **slit** (slit) ▷ *verb* **slitting, slit** ▷ *noun* **slit**

slither *verb* To move along by sliding, like a snake: *The soldiers slithered quietly through the field on their bellies.* **slith·er** (**sliTH**-ur) ▷ *verb* **slithering, slithered**

sliver *noun* A very thin and sometimes pointed piece of something, as in *a sliver of cake* or *a sliver of wood.* **sliv·er** (**sliv**-ur)

slob *noun*

1. Someone who is not neat or clean in the way they dress or live, and who is often lazy as well: *My brother is such a slob—his room is too disgusting to go into.*

2. *(informal)* An ordinary person: *I'm just a poor slob trying to make a living like the next guy.* **slob** (slahb)

▷ *adjective* **slobbish** ▷ *adjective* **slobby**

slogan *noun* A phrase or motto used by a business, a group, or an individual to express a goal or belief: *The slogan of the Barnum & Bailey Circus was "The Greatest Show on Earth."* **slo·gan** (**sloh**-guhn)

Word History

Groups of related people in the Highlands of Scotland were called clans, and originally a **slogan** was the battle cry of a clan. The word *slogan*, or *sluagh-ghairm* as it was called in the Gaelic language, could also be used as a password if people had to pass by a guard in times of emergency or at night. *Sluagh-ghairm* was a combination of the words *sluagh*, meaning "army," and *gairm*, which meant a shout or cry.

sloop *noun* A sailboat with one mast and sails that are set from front to back. **sloop** (sloop)

slop *verb* To splash or spill a liquid over the edge of a container: *Water slopped from the pail.* **slop** (slahp) ▷ *verb* **slopping, slopped**

slope *verb* To slant or be at an angle: *The bookshelves slope toward the door.* **slope** (slohp) ▷ *verb* **sloping, sloped** ▷ *noun* **slope** ▷ *adjective* **sloping**

sloppy *adjective*

1. Messy and disorganized, as in *a sloppy room.*

2. Carelessly done, as in *sloppy work.*

3. Muddy or slushy, as in *sloppy weather* or *sloppy ground.* **slop·py** (**slah**-pee) ▷ *adjective* **sloppier, sloppiest** ▷ *noun* **sloppiness** ▷ *adverb* **sloppily**

slot *noun* A small, narrow opening or groove: *The piggy bank has a slot for pennies.* **slot** (slaht)

sloth *noun*

1. A tropical mammal with long arms and legs, curved claws, and a shaggy coat. Sloths move very slowly and hang upside down in trees.

2. A tendency to avoid exerting yourself or making much of an effort; laziness. **sloth** (slawth *or* slahth) ▷ *adjective* **slothful**

slouch

1. *verb* To sit, stand, or walk with your head and shoulders drooping or bent forward: *Don't slouch when you walk.* ▷ *verb* **slouches, slouching, slouched** ▷ *noun* **slouch**

2. *noun* An awkward, lazy, or incompetent person: *When it comes to public speaking, Darby is no slouch.* ▷ *noun, plural* **slouches** **slouch** (slouch)

slovenly *adjective* Careless, dirty, and untidy in dress, habits, or appearance: *I'm not a slovenly person, but I'm more comfortable in a cluttered room.* **slov·en·ly** (**sluhv**-uhn-lee) ▷ *noun* **slovenliness**

slow

1. *adjective* Moving at a low speed or taking a long time, as in *a slow train.* ▷ *noun* **slowness** ▷ *adverb* **slowly**

2. *adjective* Behind the correct time: *My watch is five minutes slow.*

3. *verb* To cut down your speed: *Slow down in a school zone.* ▷ *verb* **slowing, slowed**

4. *adjective* Not busy: *Business was slow all week.*

5. *adjective* Not able to learn or understand quickly: *He is slow in math.*

6. *adverb* In a slow way or at a slow speed: *Go slow as you approach the crosswalk.* **slow** (sloh) ▷ *adjective, adverb* **slower, slowest**

sloth

sludge *noun* Mud, ooze, or any heavy, slimy industrial waste: *They waded waist-deep through the sludge.* **sludge** (sluhj)

slug

1. *noun* A slimy creature that looks like a snail without a shell.

2. *noun* A bullet, as in *a lead slug.*

3. *noun* A metal disk that is used in place of a coin, often illegally: *Joel stole soda from the machine using a slug tied to a string.*

4. *verb* To hit with force, as in *to slug a baseball.* ▷ *verb* **slugging, slugged** ▷ *noun* **slug** **slug** (sluhg)

sluggish *adjective* Moving slowly and without energy or alertness: *I woke up this morning feeling sick and sluggish.* **slug·gish** (**sluhg**-ish) ▷ *noun* **sluggishness**

slum *noun* An overcrowded area in a town or city where poor people live in run-down buildings: *Living conditions in the slums are often inhuman and unsafe.* **slum** (sluhm)

slumber
1. *verb* To sleep: *We slumbered until dawn.* ▷ *verb* **slumbering, slumbered**
2. *noun* Sleep: *The noise disturbed our slumber.* **slum·ber** (**sluhm**-bur)

slump
1. *verb* To sink down heavily and suddenly: *Pat fainted and slumped to the ground.* ▷ *verb* **slumping, slumped**
2. *noun* A sudden drop or decline, as in *a slump in sales* or *a batting slump.* ▷ *verb* **slump** **slump** (sluhmp)

slur
1. *verb* To speak in an unclear way by running words together: *In her haste to tell the story, Kerry was slurring her speech.* ▷ *verb* **slurring, slurred**
2. *noun* An insult or accusation that hurts a person's reputation: *She took the man's comment as a deliberate slur on her character.* **slur** (slur)

slurp *verb* To drink or eat something noisily: *John displayed bad manners during dinner when he slurped his soup.* **slurp** (slurp) ▷ *verb* **slurping, slurped**

slush *noun* Partly melted snow or ice: *The day after the storm, the city streets were lined with slush.* **slush** (sluhsh) ▷ *adjective* **slushy**

sly *adjective* Crafty and cunning, or suggesting that you know something that could be embarrassing or damaging, as in *sly remarks* or *a sly smile.* **sly** (slye) ▷ *adjective* **slier, sliest** ▷ *adverb* **slyly** (**slye**-lee)

smack
1. *verb* To strike or hit someone or something with the palm of your hand or a flat object: *Riley smacked the fly with a folded-up magazine.*
2. *verb* To strike or hit something noisily and with force: *The car smacked into a tree.*
3. *verb* To close and open the lips quickly, making a sharp sound: *At the mention of pizza, Frank smacked his lips loudly.*
4. *noun* A loud kiss, as in *a smack on the cheek.* **smack** (smak) ▷ *verb* **smacking, smacked** ▷ *noun* **smack**

smackdown *noun*
1. *(informal)* A decisive defeat: *The team deserved the smackdown they got, with their lousy defense.*
2. *(informal)* A contest or competition between rivals: *The smackdown is expected to attract a record TV audience.* **smack·down** (**smak**-doun)

small
1. *adjective* Less than average in size, number, or amount; little: *A ferry is small compared to an oil tanker.*
2. *adjective* Not important, as in *a small problem.*
3. *adjective* Low, soft, or weak, as in *a small voice.*
4. **small talk** *noun* Casual conversation about unimportant things: *After some small talk, the women got down to business.* **small** (smawl) ▷ *adjective* **smaller, smallest**

small intestine *noun* The long, coiled part of the digestive system between the stomach and the large intestine, where most nutrients are removed from food and passed into the bloodstream.

smallpox *noun* A very contagious disease that causes a rash, high fever, and blisters that can leave permanent scars. **small·pox** (**smawl**-pahks)

smart
1. *adjective* Clever and quick-witted; bright: *Jamal is smart and is the best student in his class.*
2. *verb* To cause or to feel a sharp, stinging pain: *This burn really smarts.* ▷ *verb* **smarting, smarted**
3. *adjective* Nicely dressed, tidy, and clean: *You're certainly looking smart today.*
4. *adjective* Fashionable or stylish, as in *a smart new suit.* **smart** (smahrt) ▷ *adjective* **smarter, smartest** ▷ *noun* **smartness** ▷ *adverb* **smartly**

smartphone

Word History

If you've had a stinging pain, you know that it seems strong and fast, at least at first. When we get a pain like this, we sometimes say, "It smarts!" In a roundabout way, the adjective **smart** took on a new meaning because of these annoying pains. Since it was related to the verb *smart*, the adjective meant "painful" at first. Then people began saying *smart* to mean "quick," and now this word describes a clever person who thinks fast.

smartphone *noun* A cell phone that lets the user email and access the internet, as well as run programs and applications. **smart·phone** (**smahrt**-fone)

smash

1. *verb* To break something into many pieces suddenly and noisily, as in *to smash a mirror.*
2. *verb* To collide violently with something: *The runaway truck smashed into the telephone pole.*
3. *verb* To destroy or defeat completely: *The English fleet smashed the Spanish Armada in 1588.*
4. smash hit *noun* (*informal*) A recording, movie, or show that is a huge popular success.
smash (smash)
▷ *verb* **smashes, smashing, smashed**

smear *verb*

1. To spread a sticky or greasy substance over a surface: *Hannah smeared her face with sunscreen.*
2. To become messy or blurred: *The paint smeared on the canvas.*
3. To try to damage someone's reputation by accusing the person of things that aren't true, as in *to smear someone's reputation.*
smear (smeer)
▷ *verb* **smearing, smeared** ▷ *noun* **smear**

smell

1. *verb* To sense an odor with your nose, as in *to smell smoke.*
2. *verb* To give off a particular odor or scent: *Perfume smells nice.*
3. *verb* To give off a strong or unpleasant odor: *This garbage smells!*
4. *verb* To sniff, as in *to smell a flower.*
5. *noun* An odor or a scent: *A lovely smell wafted up from the kitchen.*
6. *noun* The ability to sense odors with the nose: *Dogs have an excellent sense of smell.*
smell (smel)
▷ *verb* **smelling, smelled** *or* **smelt**

smelly *adjective* Having a strong and usually unpleasant smell: *After wearing them for two days, his socks were pretty smelly.* **smell·y** (smel-ee) ▷ *adjective* **smellier, smelliest**

smelt

1. *verb* To melt ore so that the metal can be removed. ▷ *verb* **smelting, smelted**
2. *noun* A thin, silvery food fish that lives in cold ocean waters and swims up rivers to lay its eggs.
▷ *noun, plural* **smelts** *or* **smelt**
smelt (smelt)

smile *verb* To turn up the corners of your mouth and make a facial expression that shows you are pleased, happy, or amused: *He smiled at the happy thought.* **smile** (smile) ▷ *verb* **smiling, smiled** ▷ *noun* **smile**

smiley *noun* A simple image of a smiling face that people sometimes add to written messages to show that they are happy or laughing. **smil·ey** (smye-lee)

smirk *verb* To smile in a smug, knowing, or annoying way: *The boys were smirking at the new kid's funny clothes.* **smirk** (smurk) ▷ *verb* **smirking, smirked** ▷ *noun* **smirk**

smock *noun* A garment that looks like a long, loose shirt. Smocks are worn over other clothes to keep them from getting dirty, as in *a painter's smock.* **smock** (smahk)

smog *noun* Fog that has become mixed with smoke or other pollution and hangs in the air over a city or industrial area. **smog** (smahg)

smoke

1. *noun* The vapor that is produced when something burns, as in *wood smoke.* ▷ *adjective* **smoky**
2. *verb* To give off smoke: *Our campfire was still smoking this morning.*
3. *verb* To draw the smoke from a cigarette, pipe, or cigar into your mouth and lungs and blow it out again: *You're not allowed to smoke on airplanes.*
▷ *noun* **smoker** ▷ *noun* **smoking**
4. *verb* To preserve meat or fish by hanging it in smoke, as in *smoked ham.* ▷ *adjective* **smoked**
smoke (smohk)
▷ *verb* **smoking, smoked**

smoke alarm *noun* Another name for a **smoke detector**.

smoke detector *noun* A device that warns people of smoke or fire by letting out a loud, piercing sound.

smokestack *noun* A chimney that allows smoke or gases to escape from a factory, a ship, or a locomotive. **smoke·stack** (smoke-stak)

smolder *verb*

1. To burn slowly, with smoke but no flames: *After the fire was put out, the ashes smoldered for hours.*
2. To show hidden anger, hate, or jealousy: *His eyes smoldered with resentment when she took full credit for the project.*
3. To exist or continue in a hidden state: *Rage smoldered in the mind of the victim.*
smol·der (smohl-dur)
▷ *verb* **smoldering, smoldered**

smokestacks

smooth

1. *adjective* Having a regular or even surface, without roughness or bumps: *The lake looked as smooth as glass.*

2. *adjective* Happening without interruptions, problems, or difficulties, as in *a smooth landing.* ▷ *adverb* **smoothly**

3. *verb* To make things more level, even, or flat, as in *to smooth bedcovers.* ▷ *verb* **smoothing, smoothed**

4. *adjective* Able or skillful, as in *a smooth dancer.* **smooth** (smooTH)

▷ *noun* **smoothness** ▷ *adjective* **smoother, smoothest**

smorgasbord *noun*

1. A meal consisting of many different dishes displayed on a long table so that people can choose what they want.

2. A wide variety of something: *Online music stores offer a smorgasbord of choices.*

smor·gas·bord (**smor**-guhs-*bord*)

Word History

A traditional Swedish *smörgåsbord* is a table loaded with different hot and cold dishes: cold pickled fish, cheeses, bread, butter, and also hot foods such as sausages and Swedish meatballs. Its name means "bread-and-butter table": *Smörgås* means "a slice of bread and butter," and *bord* means "table." The "rich selection" led to the meaning of the English word **smorgasbord**.

smother *verb*

1. To keep someone from breathing by covering his or her nose and mouth: *Lying under the blankets, Ari felt smothered.*

2. To cover someone or something thickly or entirely, as in *to smother food with ketchup.*

3. To hide or to hold back, as in *to smother a yawn.* **smoth·er** (**smuTH**-ur)

▷ *verb* **smothering, smothered**

smudge *verb* To blur or smear by rubbing something, as in *to smudge a drawing.* **smudge** (smuhj) ▷ *verb* **smudging, smudged** ▷ *noun* **smudge** ▷ *adjective* **smudged**

smug *adjective* So pleased with yourself that you annoy other people, as in *a smug competitor.* **smug** (smuhg) ▷ *adjective* **smugger, smuggest** ▷ *noun* **smugness** ▷ *adverb* **smugly**

smuggle *verb*

1. To move goods into or out of a country illegally, as in *to smuggle drugs.* ▷ *noun* **smuggler**

2. To bring someone or something into or out of a place secretly: *We managed to smuggle my friend's*

dog into the classroom. **smug·gle** (**smuhg**-uhl)

▷ *verb* **smuggling, smuggled**

snack *noun* A light meal or small quantity of food: *Carrots and celery make a healthy snack.* **snack** (snak) ▷ *verb* **snack**

snag

1. *noun* An unexpected problem or drawback: *I've hit a snag on this research paper.*

2. *verb* To catch on something: *I snagged my sleeve on a nail.* ▷ *verb* **snagging, snagged**

▷ *noun* **snag**

snag (snag)

snail *noun*

1. A small animal with a soft, slimy body and a spiral shell on its back. Snails live on land or in water, and some are used as food.

2. A person who moves slowly.

snail (snayl)

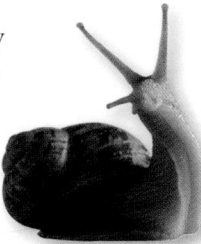

snail

snake *noun* A long, slender reptile without limbs that slithers along the ground. In the United States, only rattlesnakes, copperheads, water moccasins, and coral snakes have poisonous bites. **snake** (snayk)

snap

1. *verb* To break with a sudden, sharp cracking sound: *We snapped off some dry twigs and used them to start a fire.*

2. *noun* A sudden cracking sound: *The alligator's mouth closed with a snap.*

3. *verb* To bite suddenly or bring the jaws together as if to bite: *When I held out my hand, the dog snapped at me.*

4. *verb* To speak to someone quickly and sharply: *Don't snap at me; it's not my fault.*

5. *verb* To open or close with a click or snapping sound: *The lock snapped shut.*

6. cold snap *noun* A brief period of cold weather.

7. *noun* (*informal*) Another name for a **snapshot**. ▷ *verb* **snap**

8. *noun* The moment in a football game when the ball is put in play by the center, a lineman on the offense. ▷ *verb* **snap**

9. snap decision *noun* A decision that is made on the spur of the moment.

snap (snap

▷ *verb* **snapping, snapped** ▷ *noun* **snap**

snapdragon *noun* A garden plant with brightly colored flowers that grow on spikes. Each flower has two petals that look like lips. **snap·drag·on** (**snap**-*drag*-uhn)

snappy *adjective*
1. Short and clever, as in *a snappy slogan.*
2. Neat, stylish, and elegant, as in *a snappy dresser.*
3. Irritable and sharp, as in *a snappy reply.*
4. **make it snappy** To do something immediately: *Bring me a bowl of ice cream and make it snappy!* **snap·py** (**snap**-ee)

snapshot *noun* An informal photograph, especially one taken with a simple, handheld camera: *Lia took lots of snapshots on her vacation.* **snap·shot** (**snap**-shaht)

snare
1. *noun* A trap for catching birds or small animals, consisting of a loop of wire that pulls tight when a trigger is released.
2. *verb* To catch a bird or an animal in a trap or snare: *The hunters snared three rabbits today.* ▷ *verb* **snaring, snared**
snare (snair)

snare drum *noun* A double-headed drum with strings or wires stretched across the bottom head that produce a rattling sound.

snarl
1. *verb* To growl with bared teeth: *The dog snarled at all the passersby.* ▷ *noun* **snarl**
2. *verb* To say something angrily or theateningly: *"Get out!" Mr. Riley snarled.*
3. *noun* A tangle or knot, as in *a snarl of yarn.* ▷ *verb* **snarl**
snarl (snahrl)
▷ *verb* **snarling, snarled**

snarl

snatch
1. *verb* To take or grab something quickly or eagerly, as in *to snatch someone's purse.* ▷ *verb* **snatches, snatching, snatched** ▷ *noun* **snatch**
2. *noun* A fragment of something, as in *a snatch of conversation.* ▷ *noun, plural* **snatches**
snatch (snach)

sneak
1. *verb* To move in a quiet, secretive way, as in *to sneak into a room.* ▷ *adjective* **sneaky** ▷ *adverb* **sneakily**
2. *verb* To put, carry, or take someone or something secretly into or out of a place: *Jerry sneaked the turtle into the house without anyone noticing.*
3. *adjective* Done secretly or with no warning, as in *a sneak attack.*
4. *noun* Someone who is tricky and dishonest.
sneak (sneek)
▷ *verb* **sneaking, sneaked** *or* **snuck** (snuhk)

sneakers *noun, plural* Athletic shoes with rubber soles, as in *basketball sneakers.* **sneak·ers** (**snee**-kurz)

sneer *verb* To smile in a hateful or scornful way: *The drill sergeant sneered at the new soldiers.* **sneer** (sneer) ▷ *verb* **sneering, sneered** ▷ *noun* **sneer**

sneeze *verb* To push air out through your nose and mouth suddenly and explosively: *Whenever I go near a cat, I sneeze uncontrollably.* **sneeze** (sneez)
▷ *verb* **sneezing, sneezed** ▷ *noun* **sneeze**

Word History

Sneeze was originally spelled and pronounced "fnese" in Old English, but the *f* was mistaken for an *s* because the two letters looked very similar then. *Fnese* is related to the Greek word *pneuma*, meaning "breath." You see that root in the words *pneumatic* and *pneumonia.*

snicker
1. *noun* A mean or disrespectful little laugh.
2. *verb* To laugh in such a way: *The children snickered at her behind her back.* ▷ *verb* **snickering, snickered**
snick·er (**snik**-ur)

sniff *verb*
1. To breathe in through your nose with enough force to be heard: *The dogs sniffed the air for their dinner.*
2. To smell something: *Mara walked into the kitchen and immediately sniffed apple pie.*
sniff (snif)
▷ *verb* **sniffing, sniffed** ▷ *noun* **sniff**

sniffle *verb* To take short breaths noisily and repeatedly, usually because you are crying or have a cold: *Olivia sat in bed all day, sniffling and coughing.* **snif·fle** (**snif**-uhl) ▷ *verb* **sniffling, sniffled** ▷ *noun* **sniffle**

snip *verb* To cut, clip, or separate something using shears or scissors in short, quick strokes, as in *to snip a thread.* **snip** (snip) ▷ *verb* **snipping, snipped** ▷ *noun* **snip**

snipe

1. *verb* To shoot at a person or persons from a hidden place. ▷ *verb* **sniping, sniped** ▷ *noun* **sniper**

2. *noun* A marsh bird with a long bill and brown feathers spotted with black and white.

snipe (snipe)

snitch

1. *noun* **snitch** or **snitcher** A person who is a tattletale, especially a criminal who gives information to the authorities in order to help them catch other criminals.

2. *verb* To be a tattletale, or to give information that helps the police catch someone who is committing a crime: *His former partner snitched on him, telling the detective about the fraud and other crooked schemes.*

3. *verb* To secretly take something that you should not take: *Ryan snitched another piece of cake while Mom wasn't looking.*

snitch (snich)

▷ *verb* **snitches, snitching, snitched**

snob *noun*

1. Someone who looks down on people who are not rich, successful, or intelligent.

2. A person who thinks that he or she is better than or superior to others: *Julio is quite a music snob.*

snob (snahb)

▷ *noun* **snobbery**

snoop

1. *verb* (*informal*) To pry or look around in a sly or sneaky way, as in *to snoop around for clues.* ▷ *verb* **snooping, snooped**

2. *noun* A nosy person who pries into other people's business. ▷ *adjective* **snoopy**

snoop (snoop)

snooze *verb* (*informal*) To sleep lightly and briefly, usually during the day; to doze: *Thalia snoozed for ten minutes while waiting for her mom.* **snooze** (snooz) ▷ *verb* **snoozing, snoozed** ▷ *noun* **snooze**

snore *verb* To breathe with harsh snorting noises while you are asleep: *My grandpa snores really loudly.* **snore** (snor) ▷ *verb* **snoring, snored** ▷ *noun* **snore** ▷ *noun* **snorer**

snorkel *noun* A long tube that you hold in your mouth and use to breathe when you're swimming underwater. **snor·kel** (**snor**-kuhl) ▷ *noun* **snorkeling**

snort *verb*

1. To breathe out forcefully through your nose with a harsh sound: *The goat snorted and pawed the ground.*

2. To show scorn, anger, or disbelief by snorting: *"Give me a break," he snorted.*

snort (snort)

▷ *verb* **snorting, snorted**

▷ *noun* **snort**

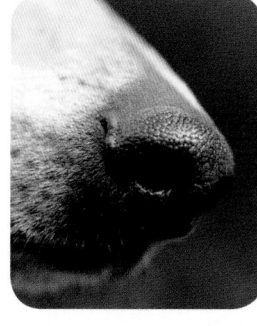

snout *noun* The long front part of an animal's head. It includes the nose, mouth, and jaws. **snout** (snout)

snout

snow

1. *noun* White crystals of ice that form when water vapor freezes in the air: *Playing in the snow is a great way to enjoy winter.*

2. *verb* To fall from the sky as snow: *Richard was surprised to see it snowing in May.* ▷ *verb* **snowing, snowed** ▷ *adjective* **snowy**

snow (snoh)

snowball

1. *noun* Snow that has been packed together into a ball: *Cam and his friends threw snowballs at each other.*

2. *verb* To grow quickly in size or importance: *The idea of holding a reunion snowballed among the old students.* ▷ *verb* **snowballing, snowballed**

snow·ball (**snoh**-*bawl*)

snowboard *noun* A board like a wide ski for riding downhill on snow. **snow·board** (**snoh**-*bord*) ▷ *verb* **snowboard** ▷ *noun* **snowboarding** ▷ *noun* **snowboarder**

snowfall *noun* The amount of snow that falls in one place in a given period of time, as in *above-average snowfall.* **snow·fall** (**snoh**-*fawl*)

snowflake *noun* A single flake or crystal of snow. **snow·flake** (**snoh**-*flake*)

snowman *noun* A figure made out of large, stacked balls of snow that resembles a person. **snow·man** (**snoh**-*man*) ▷ *noun, plural* **snowmen**

snowmobile *noun* A vehicle with an engine and skis or runners, used to travel over snow. **snow·mo·bile** (**snoh**-muh-*beel*) ▷ *verb* **snowmobile**

snowplow

1. *noun* A device or vehicle used to push snow off a road, sidewalk, or other surface.

2. *verb* In skiing, to spread your skis apart and turn the tips inward so that you can slow down or turn.

▷ *verb* **snowplowing, snowplowed**

▷ *noun* **snowplow**

snow·plow (**snoh**-*plou*)

snowshoe *noun* A webbed frame that is shaped like a racket and attached to a boot to keep the foot from

snowflake

sinking into the snow. **snow·shoe** (snoh-*shoo*)

snowstorm *noun* A storm with strong winds and heavy snow. **snow·storm** (**snoh**-*storm*)

snub *verb* To treat someone coldly or with disrespect; to ignore a person: *Our new neighbors snubbed us by pretending they didn't see us wave.* **snub** (snuhb) ▷ *verb* **snubbing, snubbed** ▷ *noun* **snub**

snuck *verb (informal)* A past tense and the past participle of **sneak**. **snuck** (snuhk)

snuff
1. *noun* Powdered tobacco that is sniffed up the nose, chewed, or rubbed into the gums.
2. **snuff out** *verb* To extinguish, as in *to snuff out a candle.* ▷ *verb* **snuffing, snuffed**
snuff (snuhf)

snug *adjective*
1. Cozy and comfortable: *We were warm and snug in our sleeping bags.*
2. Fitting closely or tightly: *The jacket was a little snug, so I gave it to my younger sister.*
snug (snuhg)
▷ *adjective* **snugger, snuggest** ▷ *adverb* **snugly**

snuggle *verb* To lie close to someone, or to hold something close for warmth or protection or to show affection, as in *to snuggle a teddy bear.* **snug·gle** (**snuhg**-uhl) ▷ *verb* **snuggling, snuggled** ▷ *adjective* **snuggly**

so
1. *adverb* In this or that way: *If you want to throw a sinking pitch, hold the baseball so.*
2. *adverb* To that extent: *I'm so hungry I could eat a horse.*
3. *adverb* Very: *The puppy is so cute.*
4. *adverb* Very much: *I miss her so.*
5. *conjunction* Therefore: *I was bored, so I left the party early.*
6. *adverb* Too or also: *I dance, and so does he.*
7. *adjective* True: *Say it isn't so.*
8. *conjunction* In order that: *Open the window so we can get some air.*
9. *pronoun* More or less: *Use a teaspoon or so.*
10. *pronoun* That way, or the same: *Our parents are strict and have always been so.*
11. *interjection* A word that shows surprise, shock, or annoyance: *So! This is where you've been hiding.*
so (soh)
So sounds like **sew**.

soak *verb*
1. To make something completely wet: *The rain soaked my clothes.*

2. To put something in water for a long period of time, as in *to soak dirty laundry.*
3. **soak up** To take in a liquid by absorbing it: *We soaked up the olive oil with pieces of bread.*
soak (sohk)
▷ *verb* **soaking, soaked**

soaking *adjective* Thoroughly wet: *By the time we got out of the rain, we were soaking.* **soak·ing** (**soh**-king)

soap *noun* A substance used for washing and cleaning. Soap is usually made from fat and lye. **soap** (sohp) ▷ *verb* **soap** ▷ *adjective* **soapy**

soap opera *noun* A television series about the difficult lives of a group of people. Soap operas stress suspense and exaggerated emotions.

Word History

The term **soap opera** dates back to 1939, when *Newsweek* magazine used it to describe the melodramatic 15-minute plays then featured on the radio. *Newsweek* used the word *opera* because the plays were similar to short operas. The word *soap* referred to soap manufacturers, the sponsors of many of these programs.

soar *verb*
1. To fly or to rise high in the air: *The hot-air balloon soared into the sky.*
2. To rise or increase quickly above the usual or normal level: *Gas prices are expected to soar this summer.*
soar (sor)
Soar sounds like **sore**. ▷ *verb* **soaring, soared**

sob *verb* To take short, gasping breaths because you have been crying: *Everyone at the funeral started sobbing.* **sob** (sahb) ▷ *verb* **sobbing, sobbed** ▷ *noun* **sob**

sober
1. *adjective* Not drunk: *The surest way to remain sober is to avoid alcohol.*
2. *adjective* Solemn, serious, and sensible, as in *a sober warning.*
3. *verb* To make someone more serious, solemn, or sober: *The injury to our teammate sobered us quickly.* ▷ *verb* **sobering, sobered**
4. *adjective* Dark in color, not bright or flashy, as in *sober earth tones.*
so·ber (**soh**-bur)
▷ *adjective* **soberer, soberest** ▷ *adverb* **soberly**

soccer *noun* A game played by two teams of 11 players who try to score by kicking a ball into goals at each end of a field. **soc·cer** (**sah**-kur)

soccer

sociable *adjective* Friendly, enjoying the company of other people, as in *a sociable group of friends.* **so·cia·ble** (**soh**-shuh-buhl) ▷ *noun* **sociability** ▷ *adverb* **sociably**

social

1. *adjective* Of or having to do with the way that people live together as a society, as in *social problems.*

2. *adjective* Of or having to do with people getting together in a friendly way or for companionship, as in *a social visit* or *a social club.*

3. *adjective* Friendly or sociable: *I'm a very social person.*

4. *adjective* Living in colonies or communities rather than on their own, as in *social animals.*

5. *noun* A party or a gathering of people, as in *an ice-cream social.*

so·cial (**soh**-shuhl)

▷ *adverb* **socially**

socialism *noun* An economic system in which the government, rather than private individuals, owns and operates the factories, businesses, and farms. **so·cial·ism** (**soh**-shuh-*liz*-uhm) ▷ *noun* **socialist** ▷ *adjective* **socialist**

social media *noun, plural* Websites and applications that let users create online communities in which they participate in social networking or share messages, videos, and other content.

social networking *noun*

1. The activity of using computer networks to communicate and form friendly relationships with other people.

2. social networking site A website that helps people to connect with each other in a friendly way.

Social Security *noun* A US government program that pays money to people who are elderly, retired, unemployed, or disabled. Sometimes also spelled "social security."

social studies *noun* A subject in school that includes geography, history, and government.

society *noun*

1. All people, or people as a group: *Laws are made to protect society.*

2. All the people who live in   **sock puppet**
the same country or region and share the same culture, customs, laws, and organizations, as in *American society.*

3. An organization or club for people who share the same interests or activities, as in *animal welfare society.*

4. The social group that often sets or follows current fashions and style, as in *high society.*

so·ci·e·ty (suh-**sye**-i-tee)

▷ *noun, plural* **societies**

sociology *noun* The study of human social behavior and the development of human society. **so·ci·ol·o·gy** (soh-see-**ah**-luh-jee) ▷ *noun* **sociologist** ▷ *adjective* **sociological** (*soh*-see-uh-**lah**-ji-kuhl)

sock

1. *noun* A knitted item of clothing that covers your foot and the lower part of your leg, as in *athletic socks.*

2. *verb (informal)* To hit someone hard, especially with your fist. ▷ *verb* **socking, socked**

sock (sahk)

socket *noun* A hole or hollow place where something fits in, as in *an electrical socket* or *an eye socket.*

sock·et (**sah**-kit)

sock puppet *noun*

1. A simple puppet made from a sock.

2. An online identity that someone uses to say flattering things about himself or herself.

sod

1. *noun* The top layer of soil and the grass that grows in it.

2. *noun* A piece of sod that is held together by matted roots and cut in a square or strip. Sod is often used to lay lawns instead of planting grass seed.

3. *verb* To cover with pieces of sod, as in *to sod a new lawn.* ▷ *verb* **sodding, sodded**

sod (sahd)

soda *noun*

1. A soft drink made with soda water. Also called **soda pop**: *I bought a can of orange soda.*

2. A drink made with soda water, flavoring, and ice cream, as in *a strawberry ice-cream soda.*

3. Soda water.

4. Baking soda.

so·da (**soh**-duh)

soda pop *noun See* **soda** (sense 1) and **pop** (sense 2).

soda water *noun* A drink with bubbles, made by mixing water with carbon dioxide gas.

sodium *noun* A silver-white metallic element found in salt. **so·di·um** (**soh**-dee-uhm)

sodium bicarbonate *noun* A white substance used in baking powder, fire extinguishers, and medicines. Also called **baking soda.** **sodium bi·car·bon·ate** (*bye*-**kahr**-buh-nit)

sock puppet

sofa *noun* A long, padded seat with a fixed back, arms, and room for two or more people; a couch. **so·fa** (**soh**-fuh)

soft *adjective*

1. Easy to press, bend, or mold into a different shape, as in *a soft pillow.* ▷ *noun* **softness**

2. Smooth or fine to the touch; not rough, as in *soft skin.*

3. Pleasantly mild or gentle, as in *a soft breeze.* ▷ *adverb* **softly**

4. Kind, as in *a soft heart.*

soft (sawft)

▷ *adjective* **softer, softest**

softball *noun* A sport, similar to baseball, that is played on a smaller field with a larger, softer ball that is pitched underhand: *Every Sunday my friends and I play softball.* **soft·ball** (**sawft**-*bawl*)

soft drink *noun* A beverage that contains no alcohol.

soften *verb*

1. To become soft or make something soft: *This lotion is supposed to soften your skin.*

2. To become softer and more agreeable: *She was angry with him, but her manner softened once she realized he hadn't meant to be rude.*

3. To become weaker or less intense: *Car sales have softened during the recession.*

soft·en (**saw**-fuhn)

▷ *verb* **softening, softened**

softhearted *adjective* Very kind, caring, and sympathetic: *My softhearted grandmother takes in lots of stray animals.* **soft·heart·ed** (**sawft**-*hahr*-tid)

software *noun* Computer programs that control the workings of the equipment, or hardware, and direct it to do specific tasks, as in *word processing software.* **soft·ware** (**sawft**-*wair*)

Word History

When we use a computer, we need both the actual hardware and the **software** programs that run on it. The word *software* was made to resemble the word *hardware*. *Software* refers to the procedures, and programming, rather than to the physical equipment. The people who created the word probably thought that "soft" things were more often and easily changed than "hard" things. English speakers built both terms using the word *ware*, meaning a thing that is made.

soggy *adjective* Very wet, heavy, and soft, as in *soggy ground.* **sog·gy** (**sah**-gee) ▷ *adjective* **soggier, soggiest**

soil

1. *noun* The top layer of earth in which plants grow, as in *fertile soil.*

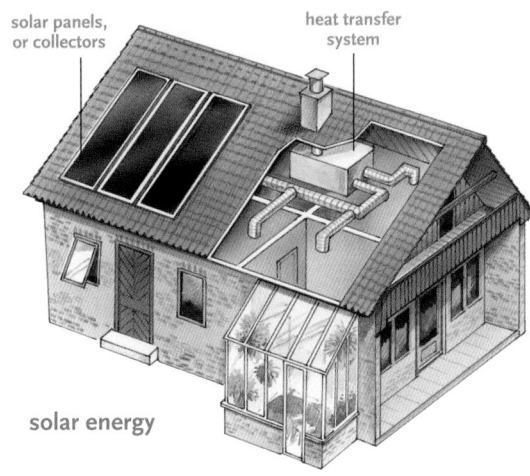

solar panels, or collectors

heat transfer system

solar energy

2. *noun* A land or a country, as in *German soil.*

3. *verb* To make something dirty or bring disgrace upon it, as in *to soil a shirt* or *to soil a reputation.*

▷ *verb* **soiling, soiled**

soil (soil)

solar *adjective*

1. Of or having to do with the sun, as in *a solar eclipse.*

2. Powered by energy from the sun, as in *solar lamps.* **so·lar** (**soh**-lur)

solar energy *noun* Energy from the sun that can be used for heating and generating electricity.

solar system *noun* The sun together with its orbiting bodies: the planets, circled by their moons, as well as asteroids, comets, and meteors.

sold *verb* The past tense and the past participle of **sell.** **sold** (sohld)

solder *verb* To join pieces of metal by putting a small amount of heated, melted alloy between them. As the alloy cools, it hardens: *He soldered the wires together.* **sol·der** (**sah**-dur) ▷ *verb* **soldering, soldered** ▷ *noun* **solder**

soldier *noun* A person serving in an army. **sol·dier** (**sohl**-jur)

sole

1. *noun* The bottom part of the foot: *The soles of my feet were dirty from walking barefoot in the yard.*

2. *noun* The bottom part of a shoe, boot, or sock: *These sneakers' soles are completely worn out.* ▷ *verb* **sole**

3. *noun* A kind of edible ocean flatfish.

4. *adjective* One and only, as in *a sole survivor.* ▷ *adverb* **solely**

sole (sole)

Sole sounds like **soul.**

solemn *adjective* Grave or very serious, as in *a solemn occasion* or *a solemn promise*. **sol·emn** (**sah**-luhm) ▷ *noun* **solemnness** ▷ *noun* **solemnity** (suh-**lem**-ni-tee) ▷ *adverb* **solemnly**

solid

1. *adjective* Hard and firm; not a liquid or gas: *The pond had frozen solid.* ▷ *adverb* **solidly** ▷ *noun* **solidity**

2. *adjective* Not mixed with anything else, as in *solid gold*.

3. *adjective* Having no spaces or gaps; not hollow, as in *a solid block of ice*.

4. *adjective* Dependable, as in *solid citizens*.

5. *adjective* Not interrupted; continuous: *I jogged for a solid hour.*

6. *noun* A three-dimensional object or geometric figure: *Cubes and pyramids are solids.* ▷ *adjective* **solid**

sol·id (**sah**-lid)

solidify *verb* To become solid, hard, and firm: *The surface of the lake began to solidify in the cold weather.* **so·lid·i·fy** (suh-**lid**-uh-*fye*) ▷ *verb* **solidifies, solidifying, solidified**

soliloquy *noun*

1. In a play, the act of talking to yourself and speaking your thoughts out loud, often when alone but also among others who do not hear or pay attention to what you are saying. This dramatic technique allows the audience to know the inner thoughts of the person who is giving the speech: *The actor was performing Hamlet's most famous soliloquy, "To be, or not to be."*

2. A part of a play that has a soliloquy, or a piece of writing that is in the style of a soliloquy.

3. The act of talking to yourself, normally when alone and usually about things that are deep, revealing, and very important to you: *She looked at the mountains and launched into a soliloquy on the value of being out in nature.*

so·lil·o·quy (suh-**lil**-uh-kwee) ▷ *noun* **soliloquist**

solitary *adjective*

1. Not requiring or without the companionship of others, as in *a solitary pastime*.

2. Single or only: *Not a solitary person volunteered to help.*

3. Isolated and remote, as in *a solitary cabin*.

sol·i·tar·y (**sah**-li-*ter*-ee)

solo

1. *noun* A song, dance, or piece of music that is performed by one person, with or without accompaniment, as in *a piano solo*. ▷ *noun, plural* **solos** ▷ *noun* **soloist**

2. *adjective* Done by one person: *Angela offered to help, but fixing the bookcase is a solo job.* ▷ *adverb* **solo**

3. *verb* To fly a plane alone, especially for the first time. ▷ *verb* **soloing, soloed**

so·lo (**soh**-loh)

solstice *noun* The moment of time during the year when the overhead sun reaches its farthest point north or south of the equator. In the Northern Hemisphere, the summer solstice occurs about June 22 and the winter solstice about December 22. **sol·stice** (**sahl**-stis *or* **sohl**-stis)

Word History

The height of the sun's arc across the sky changes throughout the year. The solstices are six months apart. In the Northern Hemisphere, the sun's arc is at its lowest point around Christmas, then begins to rise, reaching its highest point in late June. The Romans named the **solstice** days *solstitium*, meaning "sun standing still," because the sun's arc seemed to "stop." *Solstitium* was a combination of *sol*, meaning "sun," and the word part *-stitium*, from the past participle of the verb *sistere*, meaning "to stand still."

soluble *adjective* Easily dissolved in liquid, especially water, as in *soluble fiber*. **sol·u·ble** (**sahl**-yuh-buhl)

solution *noun*

1. The answer to or the means of solving a problem, as in *a simple solution*.

2. A mixture made up of a substance that has been dissolved in a liquid: *Saya carefully prepared the solution in chemistry lab.*

so·lu·tion (suh-**loo**-shuhn)

solve *verb* To find an answer to or a way of dealing with a problem, as in *to solve a mystery*. **solve** (sahlv) ▷ *verb* **solving, solved** ▷ *noun* **solver**

solvent

1. *noun* A substance, usually a liquid, that can make another substance dissolve: *Nail polish remover is*

solitary

a useful household solvent.

2. *adjective* Having enough money to pay one's debts: *After he found a good job, Gabriel was finally solvent.* **sol·vent** (**sahl**-vuhnt)

somber *adjective*

1. Dark, gloomy, and dull, as in *a rainy, chilly, somber day.*

2. Very sad or depressed, as in *a somber mood.* **som·ber** (**sahm**-bur)

sombrero *noun* A tall hat with a wide brim that is worn in Mexico and the southwestern United States. **som·bre·ro** (sahm-**brair**-oh) ▷ *noun, plural* **sombreros**

Word History

Sombrero is taken from a Spanish word that was formed from two Latin word parts meaning "under" and "shade." The wide brim of a sombrero casts a lot of shade.

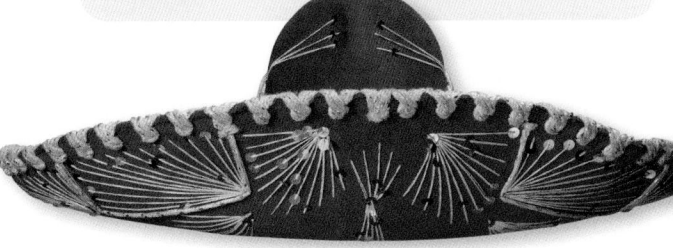

sombrero

some

1. *adjective* An unknown number or amount of something: *I'll have some of that coffee when it's ready.*

2. *pronoun* A certain small number of people or amount of something: *Some of us are getting together after the game.*

3. *adjective* (*informal*) Remarkable: *That was some soccer match!*

some (suhm)

Some sounds like **sum.**

somebody

1. *pronoun* A person who is not specified or known: *There is somebody on the phone asking for you.*

2. *noun* An important or famous person: *When I grow up, I'm going to be somebody.*

some·bod·y (**suhm**-bah-dee or **suhm**-buh-dee)

someday *adverb* At some future time: *I would like to live in California someday.* **some·day** (**suhm**-day)

somehow *adverb* In a way that is not known or understood: *Somehow the paint got spilled all over the floor.* **some·how** (**suhm**-hou)

someone *pronoun* Somebody; some person: *Someone has been using my computer.* **some·one** (**suhm**-wuhn)

somersault *noun* A gymnastic move in which you tuck your chin into your chest and roll in a complete circle forward or backward. **som·er·sault** (**suhm**-ur-*sawlt*) ▷ *verb* **somersault**

something

1. *pronoun* A thing that is not specified or known: *Something brushed against my arm.*

2. *adverb* A little bit: *My sister looks something like our cousin.*

some·thing (**suhm**-*thing*)

sometime *adverb* At a time that is not specified or known: *I'll call her back sometime next week.* **some·time** (**suhm**-*time*)

sometimes *adverb* Now and then; occasionally: *Sometimes I really enjoy going out to a restaurant with friends.* **some·times** (**suhm**-*timez*)

somewhat

1. *adverb* Rather: *My idea is somewhat like yours.*

2. *pronoun* Something: *The news was somewhat of a surprise.*

some·what (**suhm**-*waht*)

somewhere *adverb*

1. To, in, or at a place that is not specified or known: *They're somewhere over the Pacific Ocean right now.* ▷ *noun* **somewhere**

2. At some time, or in some amount: *We plan to arrive somewhere between seven and eight o'clock.* **some·where** (**suhm**-*wair*)

son *noun* Someone's male child; a boy or man in relation to his parents. **son** (suhn) **Son** sounds like **sun.**

sonar *noun* An instrument used on ships and submarines that sends out underwater sound waves to determine the location of objects and the distance to the bottom. Sonar is short for *sound navigation and ranging.* **so·nar** (**soh**-nahr)

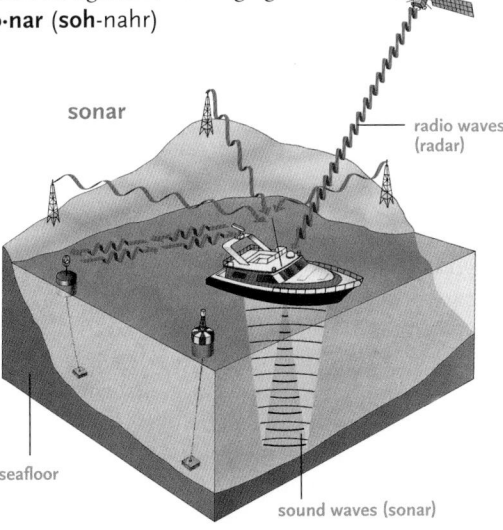

sonar

radio waves (radar)

seafloor

sound waves (sonar)

sonata *noun* A piece of classical music written for a solo instrument, often with a piano, and consisting of several movements or sections. **so·na·ta** (suh-**nah**-tuh)

song *noun*

1. A piece of music that has words and is meant to be sung, as in *a Christmas song*.

2. The musical sounds made by a whale, a bird, or an insect: *I am listening to an audio file of a nightingale's song.*

3. for a song At a very cheap price. **song** (sawng)

songbird *noun* A bird that has a musical call or song. Larks, finches, and cardinals are songbirds. **song·bird** (**sawng**-burd)

sonic *adjective*

1. Of or having to do with sound waves, as in *a sonic boom*.

2. Of or having to do with the speed of sound in air, or about 760 miles per hour at sea level. **son·ic** (**sah**-nik)

sonic boom *noun* The loud noise produced by a vehicle when it travels faster than the speed of sound and breaks through the sound barrier.

son-in-law *noun* The husband of a person's child. ▷ *noun, plural* **sons-in-law**

sonnet *noun* A poem with 14 lines that uses any of a number of fixed patterns of rhyme. **son·net** (**sah**-nit)

soon *adverb*

1. In or after a short time; shortly: *I'll call you soon, I promise.*

2. Before the usual time; early: *The alarm rang too soon this morning.*

3. Quickly; without delay: *Come back soon.*

4. sooner Would rather, or would prefer to: *She'd sooner die than admit she was wrong.* **soon** (soon) ▷ *adverb* **sooner, soonest**

soot *noun* Black powder that is produced when a fuel such as coal, wood, or oil is burned. **soot** (sut) ▷ *adjective* **sooty**

soothe *verb*

1. To gently calm someone who is angry or upset: *Rocking the baby seemed to soothe him.*

2. To relieve something that is painful or uncomfortable: *Do you have anything that would soothe my poison ivy rash?* **soothe** (sooTH) ▷ *verb* **soothing, soothed** ▷ *adjective* **soothing**

sophisticated *adjective*

1. Having a lot of knowledge about the world, especially when it comes to culture and fashion: *Raphael's sophisticated cousin is visiting from Tokyo.*

2. Very complicated or advanced; highly developed, as in *sophisticated technology*. **so·phis·ti·ca·ted** (suh-**fis**-tuh-*kay*-tid) ▷ *noun* **sophistication**

sophomore *noun* A student in the second year of high school or college. **soph·o·more** (**sahf**-*mor* or **sah**-fuh-*mor*)

sopping *adjective* Wet all the way through: *My clothes were sopping after the rainstorm.* **sop·ping** (**sah**-ping)

soprano *noun*

1. The highest singing voice. ▷ *adjective* **soprano**

2. A person who sings in a soprano voice. **so·pran·o** (suh-**pran**-oh) ▷ *noun, plural* **sopranos**

sorcerer *noun* A person who practices magic by controlling evil spirits; a wizard. **sor·cer·er** (**sor**-sur-er) ▷ *noun* **sorcery**

sore

1. *adjective* Aching or painful, as in *sore muscles*. ▷ *noun* **soreness**

2. *noun* An area of raw or painful skin, especially one that has become infected.

3. *adjective* Angry or upset: *Eric was sore at his friends.* **sore** (sor) **Sore** sounds like **soar**. ▷ *adjective* **sorer, sorest**

sorrow *noun* Great sadness, grief, or regret: *I hid my sorrow when my bunny died.* **sor·row** (**sahr**-oh) ▷ *adjective* **sorrowful** ▷ *adverb* **sorrowfully**

sorry *adjective*

1. Feeling sadness, sympathy, or regret because you have done something wrong or because someone is suffering: *I'm sorry I hurt your feelings. I'm sorry you are ill.*

2. Worthless, inferior, or poor, as in *a sorry excuse* or *a sorry state.* **sor·ry** (**sahr**-ee) ▷ *adjective* **sorrier, sorriest** ▷ *adverb* **sorrily**

Word History

The word **sorry** looks similar to the term **sorrow**, and they have similar meanings, but they have different origins. *Sorrow* derives from *sorg*, an Old English word that meant "sorrow" or "worry." *Sorry* comes from the Old English word *sarig*, meaning "full of sorrow." Speakers of Old English created *sarig* from their word for "pain" or "wound," *sar*. If you were *sarig*, it meant that you had a "pain" in your heart. The noun *sar* developed into our word **sore**, which means a place on the body that is painful. So the adjective *sorry* came from the noun *sore*.

sort

1. *noun* A group of people or things that have something in common; a type or a kind: *What sort of ice cream do you want?*

2. *verb* To arrange or separate things: *I will sort my socks into pairs.* ▷ *verb* **sorting, sorted**
sort (sort)

SOS *noun* An international signal of distress, sent out by ships or planes in need of urgent help: *The Coast Guard responded to an SOS from a ship in distress.*

sought *verb* The past tense and the past participle of **seek.** **sought** (sawt)

soul
1. *noun* The spiritual part of a person that is often thought to control the ability to think, feel, and act: *They prayed for the souls of the dead.*
2. *noun* A person: *We didn't see a soul in the park.*
3. *adjective* Of or having to do with African Americans or black culture, as in *soul music* and *soul food.*
soul (sole)
Soul sounds like **sole.**

sound
1. *noun* Something that you sense with your ears, as in *a loud sound.*
2. *noun* One of the noises that make up human speech. *Write begins with an r sound.*
3. *verb* To make a noise: *Everyone scrambled to leave the classroom when the bell sounded.*
4. *verb* To appear to be or to give an impression: *That sounds like a good idea.*
5. *verb* To be said or pronounced: *The word "sore" sounds like "soar."*
6. *adjective* Healthy or strong, as in *a sound mind* or *sound construction.*
7. *adjective* Sensible or reliable, as in *sound advice.*
8. *adjective* Deep and undisturbed, as in *a sound sleep.*
9. *noun* A long, narrow arm of water between two bodies of water or between the mainland and an island: *My uncle is taking us sailing on the sound this afternoon.*
sound (sound)
▷ *verb* **sounding, sounded**

sound barrier *noun* When an object breaks the **sound barrier**, it is going faster than the sound waves it produces. As a result, all of the sound waves get bunched together, resulting in a single loud boom.

sound bite *noun* A small portion of a political speech or interview that is recorded and played on a newscast or other program.

sound effects *noun, plural* Sounds, other than speech or music, that are used to make a play, a movie, or a radio or television program seem more realistic: *The horror movie was ruined by its silly sound effects.*

soundproof *adjective* Not allowing any sound to enter or escape, as in *a soundproof room.*
sound·proof (**sound**-*proof*) ▷ *verb* **soundproof**

sound track *noun*
1. A recording of music from a movie or play: *The movie is well-known for its sound track.*
2. The narrow strip on a motion picture film or videotape that carries the sound recording.

sound wave *noun* A wave or series of vibrations in the air, in a solid, or in a liquid that can be heard.

soup
1. *noun* A liquid food made by cooking vegetables, meat, or fish in broth, milk, or water, as in *lentil soup.* ▷ *adjective* **soupy**
2. soup up *verb* (*slang*) To increase the power of an engine or motor vehicle. ▷ *verb* **souping, souped**
soup (soop)

sour
1. *adjective* Having a sharp, acid taste, as in *a sour lemon.*
2. *adjective* Disagreeable, as in *a sour expression.*
3. *verb* To make acidic or to become acidic through spoiling: *We left the milk out and it soured.* ▷ *verb* **souring, soured** ▷ *noun* **sourness**
sour (sour)

source *noun*
1. The place, person, or thing from which something comes or develops, as in *the source of the problem* or *the source of an idea.*
2. The starting point of a stream or river.
3. A person, book, or document that provides information: *An encyclopedia is a useful reference source.*
source (sors)

south
1. *noun* One of the four main points of the compass. South is to your left when you face the direction where the sun sets. ▷ *adjective* **south** ▷ *adverb* **south**
2. South *noun* Any area or region that is lying in this direction.
3. *adjective* To do with or existing in the south, as in *the south side of the city.*
4. the South *noun* In the United States, the states lying south of Pennsylvania and the Ohio River and east of the Mississippi River.
south (south)

South America *noun* The southern continent of the Western Hemisphere. It lies south of North America and is surrounded by the Pacific Ocean, the Atlantic Ocean, and the Caribbean Sea. **South A·mer·i·ca** (**south** uh-**mer**-i-kuh)

South American

   1. *adjective* From South America or having to do with South America.

   2. *noun* Someone who was born in South America or whose parents come from there.

southern *adjective*

   1. In or toward the south, as in *a southern exposure.*

   2. Coming from the south, as in *a southern wind.*

   3. Southern Of or having to do with the part of the United States that is in the South.

   south·ern (suhTH-urn)

Southern Hemisphere *noun* The half of the earth that is south of the equator.

South Pole *noun* The most southern part of the earth, located at the bottom tip of the earth's axis.

southward *adverb* To or toward the south: *The weather grew warmer as we drove southward.*
   south·ward (south-wurd) ▷ *adjective* **southward**

souvenir *noun* An object that you keep to remind you of a place, a person, or something that happened, as in *a souvenir of a vacation.* **sou·ve·nir** (soo-vuh-**neer**)

sovereign

   1. *noun* A king or queen.

   2. *adjective* Having the highest power, as in *a sovereign ruler.*

   3. *adjective* Independent, as in *a sovereign nation.*
   sov·er·eign (sahv-ruhn-tee)

sovereignty *noun* Supreme authority or the power to rule: *The two countries fought for sovereignty of the island.* **sov·er·eign·ty (sahv-**rin-tee)

Soviet Union *noun* A former country of 15 republics that included Russia, Ukraine, and other nations of eastern Europe and northern Asia. Also known as the *Union of Soviet Socialist Republics.*
   So·vi·et Union (soh-vee-*et*)

sow

   1. (soh) *verb* To scatter seeds over the ground so that they will grow; to plant: *I sowed wildflower seeds in our garden this spring.* ▷ **sowing, sowed, sown** (sohn) *or* **sowed**

   2. (sou) *noun* An adult female pig.
   sow

soybean *noun* A seed that grows in pods on bushy plants. Soybeans are a good source of protein and oil. **soy·bean (soi-***been*)

soy sauce *noun* A dark liquid that is made from soaked and fermented soybeans. It is used as a sauce to flavor food. **soy sauce** (soi)

space

   1. *verb* To leave an empty area between things: *Space your lines evenly as you write.* ▷ *verb* **spacing, spaced**

   2. *noun* The physical universe beyond the earth's atmosphere. Also called **outer space**: *There are several ships in space, studying our galaxy.*

   3. *noun* An area that is unoccupied or available, as in *space in a suitcase* or *a parking space.*

   4. *noun* A period of time, usually of a specified length, as in *the space of 15 minutes.*

   5. *noun* The open area in which all objects are located. Space has height, width, and depth.
   space (spays)

space bar *noun* A bar at the bottom of a computer or typewriter keyboard that adds a space to the right of a character when pressed.

spacecraft *noun* A vehicle that travels or is used in space. **space·craft (spays-***kraft*)

spaceship *noun* A spacecraft designed and built to break free of the earth's atmosphere and travel into space. **space·ship (spays-***ship*)

space shuttle *noun* A spacecraft designed to make repeated journeys into space, carrying astronauts and equipment back and forth between the earth and a space station.

space station *noun* A spacecraft that stays in orbit and is large enough to house a crew for long periods of time.

spacesuit *noun* The sealed and pressurized suit that an astronaut wears in space. **space·suit (spays-***soot*)

space station

spacewalk *noun* A period of time during which an astronaut leaves his or her spacecraft and moves around in space. **space·walk (spays-***wawk*)
▷ *noun* **spacewalker** ▷ *verb* **spacewalk**

spacious *adjective* Having plenty of space, as in *a*

Space Shuttle

With 2.5 million separate parts, the space shuttle is an extremely complex machine. It began flying missions for the National Aeronautics and Space Administration (NASA) in 1982, and was the first space vehicle that could be used more than once for a mission. The spacecraft in the space shuttle fleet have moved astronauts, scientific equipment, and various support items for NASA's space program. Rocket boosters launch it into space. When it returns to earth, it lands on a runway, just like an airplane. Its payload—the equipment it moves to perform specific space missions—has been essential to building and maintaining space stations, conducting experiments in space, and launching probes of other planets.

NASA retired the fleet in 2011. A new spacecraft, *Orion,* will not only move people and cargo but also orbit Mars and the moon.

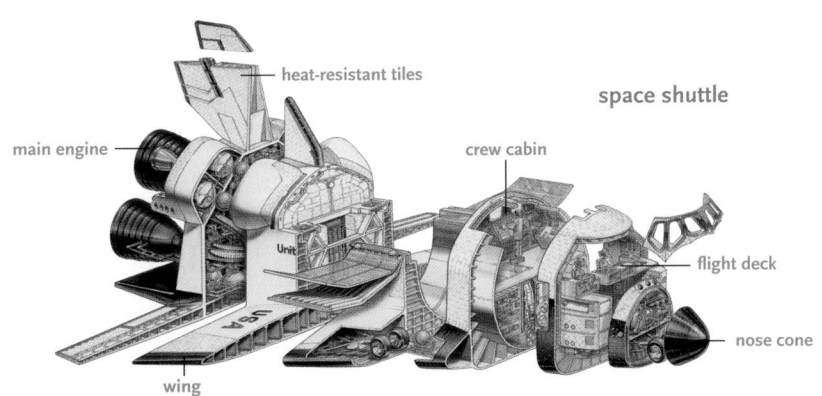

space shuttle

heat-resistant tiles — main engine — crew cabin — flight deck — nose cone — wing

shuttle on the launch pad

Discovery **astronauts in space**

---

spacious house. **spa·cious** (**spay**-shuhs)

spade *noun*

1. A tool used for digging, with a long, sturdy handle and a flat blade that you can push into the earth with your foot. ▷ *verb* **spade**

2. spades *noun, plural* One of the four suits in a deck of playing cards. Spades have a black symbol that looks like an upside-down heart with a stalk.

spade (spayd)

spaghetti *noun* Long, thin strands of pasta that are cooked by boiling and usually served with a sauce. **spa·ghet·ti** (spuh-**get**-ee)

spam

1. *noun* Messages or advertisements sent by email to people who did not ask for them: *I got spam about fake job opportunities again today.*

2. *verb* To send email messages to people who have not asked for them: *The company agreed to stop spamming its customers.* ▷ *verb* **spamming, spammed**

spam (spam)

Word History

A skit on a TV comedy show called "Monty Python's Flying Circus" showed a couple ordering food in a restaurant where every dish included Spam, a type of canned meat. Eventually, the characters began to say "spam" in the middle of sentences. A newscaster then appeared, and he also kept saying "spam," and the word appeared many times in the show's credits. When internet users began seeing unwanted messages in online bulletin boards, often repeated many times, they began calling the messages **spam**.

span

1. *noun* The distance between two points. The span of a bridge is its length from one end to the other.

2. *noun* The full reach or length of something, as in *the wingspan of an airplane* or *a person's life span.*

3. *noun* The length of time that something lasts: *In the span of a single heartbeat, everything changed.*

4. *verb* To reach over or stretch across something: *A bridge spans this river.* ▷ *verb* **spanning, spanned**

span (span)

spank *verb* To hit someone with an open hand or a flat object, especially on the buttocks, as a punishment. **spank** (spangk) ▷ *verb* **spanking, spanked**

spare

1. *adjective* Kept for use when needed; extra, as in *a spare tire.* ▷ *noun* **spare**

2. *adjective* Not taken up by work; free, as in *spare time.*

3. *adjective* With no excess fat; lean: *Abraham Lincoln was tall and spare.*

4. *verb* To give something that you have enough of or to make something available: *Can you spare an hour of your time tomorrow?*

5. *verb* To show mercy, or to not hurt someone, as in *to spare a life* or *to spare someone's feelings.*

6. *verb* To free from the need to do something: *She spared us from having to wash the dishes.*

7. *noun* In bowling, the knocking down of all ten pins with two rolls of the ball.

spare (spair)

▷ *verb* **sparing, spared**

spark

1. *noun* A small bit of burning material thrown off by a fire: *Sparks from the campfire twinkled in the dark.*

2. *noun* A quick flash of light, as in *an electrical spark.*

3. *noun* A small bit or trace, as in *a spark of enthusiasm.*

4. *verb* To make something happen or to stir something up: *The lecture sparked my interest in the environmental movement.* ▷ *verb* **sparking, sparked**

spark (spahrk)

▷ *verb* **spark**

sparkle *verb*

1. To shine with or to reflect flashes of light; to glitter, as in *to sparkle in the sun.*

2. To fizz or bubble: *Soda water sparkles.*

3. To accomplish something in a brilliant or lively way: *The pianist sparkled at last night's concert.*

spar·kle (**spahr**-kuhl)

▷ *verb* **sparkling, sparkled** ▷ *noun* **sparkle** ▷ *adjective* **sparkling**

spark plug *noun* A device in a gasoline engine that ignites the fuel-and-air mixture in a cylinder by producing an electrical spark.

sparrow *noun* A small, common songbird with brown, white, and gray feathers and a short bill. **spar·row** (**spar**-oh)

sparse *adjective* Thinly spread; not crowded or dense, as in *sparse vegetation.* **sparse** (spahrs) ▷ *adverb* **sparsely**

spark plug

spasm *noun* A sudden tightening of a muscle that cannot be controlled: *Jack was awakened by a muscle spasm in his leg.* **spasm** (**spaz**-uhm)

spat *noun* A short, unimportant argument or quarrel: *Our spat was resolved quickly, and we laughed about it later.* **spat** (spat)

spatter *verb* To scatter or splash in drops or small bits: *She spattered paint all over her clothes.* **spat·ter** (**spat**-ur) ▷ *verb* **spattering, spattered**

spatula *noun* A tool with a broad, flat blade that bends easily. It is used to mix, spread, or lift food or to mix plaster or paint: *Margot stood at the stove with a spatula, flipping pancakes.* **spat·u·la** (**spach**-uh-luh)

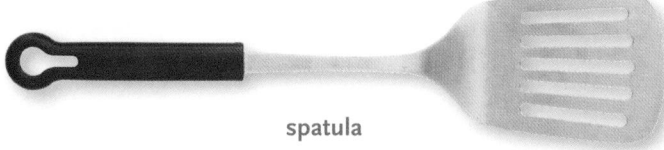

spatula

spawn

1. *noun* The large number of eggs produced by fish, mollusks, and amphibians.

2. *verb* To produce a large number of eggs: *Most salmon live in saltwater but swim to freshwater to spawn.* ▷ *verb* **spawning, spawned**

spawn (spawn)

speak *verb*

1. To talk, or to say words in an ordinary voice: *The baby is just learning how to speak.*

2. To tell or make known your ideas, opinions, or feelings: *Can I speak to you about a problem I'm having?*

3. To deliver a speech: *I have been asked to speak at the conference in Montreal.*

4. To talk in a certain language: *At home we speak English and Spanish.*

5. speak out or **speak up** To speak loudly, or to speak openly and honestly about what you really believe.

speak (speek)

▷ *verb* **speaking, spoke** (spohk), **spoken** (**spoh**-kin)

speaker *noun*

1. The one who is speaking: *Although Sam was the speaker, we all supported the issues he raised.*

2. Somebody who makes a speech: *The speaker at the meeting was really interesting.*

3. A loudspeaker, especially one attached to a sound system.

speak·er (**spee**-kur)

spear

1. *noun* A weapon with a long handle and a pointed head.

2. *noun* A long blade, shoot, or stalk of a plant, as in *a spear of asparagus.*

3. *verb* To pick up with something sharp: *I speared the piece of cheese with a toothpick.* ▷ *verb* **spearing, speared**

spear (speer)

spearhead

1. *verb* To take the lead in a project to make sure that it succeeds: *The family spearheaded an effort to build a new playground within the park.* ▷ *verb* **spearheading, spearheaded**

2. *noun* The point of a spear.

spear·head (**speer**-*hed*)

spearmint *noun* A fragrant mint plant with spear-shaped leaves that is used to flavor candy and food. **spear·mint** (**speer**-*mint*)

special

1. *adjective* Different or unusual, as in *a special occasion* or *a special request.* ▷ *adverb* **specially**

2. *adjective* For a particular purpose or occasion: *You need a special pass to get backstage.*

3. *noun* A television program intended as a single show rather than as one in a series: *I want to be home by nine to catch the special on PBS.*

spe·cial (**spesh**-uhl)

specialist *noun* An expert in a particular field of knowledge or kind of work, as in *a heart specialist.* **spe·cial·ist** (**spesh**-uh-list)

specialize *verb* To focus on one area of work, or to learn a lot about one subject: *Alice specializes in illustrating children's books.* **spe·cial·ize** (**spesh**-uh-*lize*) ▷ *verb* **specializing, specialized** ▷ *noun* **specialization** (*spesh*-uh-li-**zay**-shuhn)

specialty *noun*

1. The skill or area of study that you are particularly good at: *Susan's specialty is playing the harp.*

2. A particular product or service: *That store's specialty is greeting cards.*

spe·cial·ty (**spesh**-uhl-tee)
▷ *noun, plural* **specialties**

species *noun* One of the groups into which animals and plants of the same genus are divided. Members of the same species can mate and have offspring: *The lion and cheetah are two different species of cat.* **spe·cies** (**spee**-sheez *or* **spee**-seez) ▷ *noun, plural* **species**

Word History

The Latin word **species** meant "appearance" or "kind." This word was created by the ancient Romans from their verb *specere,* meaning "to look." You can see the same root in the English words *spy* and *spectacle.*

specific *adjective* Precise, definite, or of a particular kind, as in *a specific brand.* **spe·ci·fic** (spuh-**sif**-ik) ▷ *adverb* **specifically**

specifications *noun, plural* A detailed statement about the design, materials, and workmanship required for something that is to be built or made: *The architect drew up specifications for the house.* **spec·i·fi·ca·tions** (*spes*-uh-fi-**kay**-shuhnz)

specify *verb* To mention, describe, or define something in an exact or detailed way: *Please specify your sweater size on the catalog order form.* **spec·i·fy** (**spes**-uh-*fye*) ▷ *verb* **specifies, specifying, specified**

specimen *noun* A sample, or an example used to stand for a whole group, as in *a butterfly specimen* or *a blood specimen.* **spec·i·men** (**spes**-uh-muhn) ▷ *adjective* **specimen**

speck *noun*

1. A small spot or mark, as in *a speck of paint.*

2. A tiny particle or bit, as in *a speck of dust.*

speck (spek)

speckled *adjective* Covered with small, irregular spots or patches of color, as in *a speckled egg.* **speck·led** (**spek**-uhld)

spectacle *noun* A remarkable or impressive sight: *The opening ceremony of the Olympics was quite a spectacle.* **spec·ta·cle** (**spek**-tuh-kuhl)

spectacles *noun, plural* Eyeglasses: *He pushed his spectacles back up the bridge of his nose.* **spec·ta·cles** (**spek**-tuh-kuhlz)

spectacular *adjective* Remarkable or very impressive, as in *a spectacular sunset.* **spec·tac·u·lar** (spek-**tak**-yuh-lur) ▷ *adverb* **spectacularly**

spectator *noun* Someone who watches an event but does not participate in it: *I am a spectator at all of Ian's tennis matches.* **spec·ta·tor** (**spek**-*tay*-tur) ▷ *adjective* **spectator**

specter *noun* A ghost or phantom. **spec·ter** (**spek**-tur) ▷ *adjective* **spectral** (**spek**-truhl)

spectrum

spectrum *noun*

1. The bands of color that are revealed when light shines through a prism or through drops of water, as in a rainbow.

2. A wide range of activities, qualities, or ideas, as in *a broad spectrum of opinions.*

spec·trum (**spek**-truhm)
▷ *noun, plural* **spectrums** *or* **spectra** (**spek**-truh)

a b c d e f g h i j k l m n o p q r **s** t u v w x y z

speculate *verb*
1. To make a guess or form an opinion about something without knowing all the facts.
2. To invest in something that is risky, such as a business or a stock, as in *to speculate in the stock market.* **spec·u·late** (spek-yuh-*late*)
▷ *verb* **speculating, speculated** ▷ *noun* **speculator**

speculation *noun* Reasoning based on evidence that is insufficient or not firm: *Her speculation about the cause of the argument proved to be true.* **spec·u·la·tion** (spek-yuh-**lay**-shuhn)

sped *verb* The past tense and the past participle of **speed.** **sped** (sped)

speech *noun*
1. The ability to speak or the act of speaking: *She worked with children who had problems with their speech.*
2. A talk given to an audience, as in *the president's speech.* ▷ *noun, plural* **speeches**
3. The way in which someone speaks: *I can tell by your speech that you're from the South.* **speech** (speech)

speechless *adjective* Temporarily unable to speak, especially as a result of shock or emotion, as in *speechless with embarrassment.* **speech·less** (speech-lis)

speed
1. *noun* The rate at which someone or something moves, as in *walking speed.*
2. *noun* The rate of any action, as in *reading speed.*
3. *verb* To move or travel at a rate faster than what is safe or allowed: *Brianne was speeding on the highway and got caught.* ▷ *verb* **speeding, sped** (sped) *or* **speeded**
4. *noun* Swiftness of movement. **speed** (speed)

speed bump *noun* A ridge of asphalt or hard rubber that has been laid across a road or parking lot to make drivers slow down.

speedometer *noun* An instrument on a vehicle, such as a bike or a car, that tells you how fast you are traveling. **speed·om·e·ter** (spi-**dah**-mi-tur)

speed trap *noun* A stretch of road where drivers typically speed and police catch them using radar.

speedy *adjective* Done, happening, or moving quickly, as in *a speedy recovery.* **speed·y** (**spee**-dee) ▷ *adverb* **speedily**

spell
1. *verb* To name or write the letters that make up a word in their correct order, as in *to spell someone's name.*
2. *verb* To mean: *The captain's injury spelled trouble for the team.*

3. *verb* To take someone's place for a time: *During our cross-country car trip, my parents spelled each other at the wheel.*
4. *noun* A brief period of time, as in *a spell of rainy weather.*
5. *noun* Words or a formula believed to have magical powers: *The sorcerer cast a spell over the town and all its inhabitants.*
6. *noun* An irresistible charm or fascination: *From the moment I met her, I fell under the spell of Lydia's talented older sister.*
7. spell out *verb* To explain something clearly and in detail, as in *to spell out your plans.* **spell** (spel)
▷ *verb* **spelling, spelled**

spelling *noun*
1. The letters used to write a word: *Do you know the correct spelling of "pneumonia"?*
2. Writing or saying the correct letters to form a word or words: *Theresa has always been good at spelling.* **spell·ing** (spel-ing)

spelunking *noun* Exploring caves, especially as a hobby: *We like to go spelunking on weekends.* **spe·lunk·ing** (spi-**luhng**-king) ▷ *noun* **spelunker**

spelunking

spend *verb*
1. To use money to buy goods or services, as in *to spend your allowance.*
2. To pass time: *We will spend our vacation at the beach.*
3. To use up or to devote time, energy, or resources: *She spent most of her creativity on projects that no one ever saw.* **spend** (spend)
▷ *verb* **spending, spent** (spent)

sperm *noun* A male reproductive cell that is capable of fertilizing eggs in a female. **sperm** (spurm)
▷ *noun, plural* **sperm** *or* **sperms**

sphere *noun*

1. A solid form like that of a basketball or globe, with all points on the surface the same distance from the center. ▷ *adjective* **spherical** (**sfer**-i-kuhl *or* **sfeer**-i-kuhl)

2. An area of activity, interest, or knowledge, as in *a sphere of interest.*
sphere (sfeer)

sphinx *noun*

1. In Egyptian mythology, a creature with the body of a lion and the head of a man, ram, or hawk. ▷ *noun, plural* **sphinxes**

2. the Sphinx A large statue of this creature in Giza, Egypt.
sphinx (sfingks)

spice *noun*

1. A plant substance with a distinctive smell or taste, such as cinnamon or paprika, that is used to flavor food.

2. Anything that adds excitement or interest: *Variety is the spice of life.*
spice (spise)
▷ *verb* **spice**

spicy *adjective* Containing lots of spices; having a pungent taste, as in *a spicy dish.* **spi·cy** (**spye**-see)
▷ *adjective* **spicier, spiciest**

spider *noun* An insect-like creature with eight legs, a body divided into two parts, and no wings. Spiders spin webs to trap insects for food. **spi·der** (**spye**-dur)

Word History

In the Middle Ages, a **spider** was called a *spithre.* It's thought that English speakers originally formed this name as *spinthra,* from their verb meaning "to spin," *spinnan,* because they observed spiders spinning webs. But after a while, the letter *n* in the middle of the word was no longer pronounced. A later change occurred when people started using a *d* instead of the *th* sound, giving us the current spelling of *spider.* The German name for a spider, *Spinne,* is related to our word for this creature.

spigot *noun* A device used to control the flow of liquid in a pipe; a faucet. **spig·ot** (**spig**-uht)

spike

1. *noun* A large, heavy nail often used to fasten rails to railroad ties. ▷ *verb* **spike**

2. *noun* One of several pointed pieces of metal attached to the sole of a shoe to help athletes avoid slipping: *Some of the spikes in my old soccer cleats are coming loose.*

3. spike heel *noun* A very high, narrow heel on a woman's shoe.

spigot

4. *noun* An ear of wheat or grain, such as corn.

5. *noun* A long cluster of flowers on one stem, as in *a spike of gladiolas.*

6. *verb* To form something into sharp points, as in *to spike your hair.*

7. *verb* To hit a volleyball down and over the net with force so that it is difficult to return.
spike (spike)
▷ *verb* **spiking, spiked** ▷ *noun* **spike** ▷ *adjective* **spiked** ▷ *adjective* **spiky**

spill

1. *verb* To let the contents of a container flow or fall out, often accidentally, as in *to spill a cup of water.*

2. *verb* To shed, as in *to spill blood.*

3. *noun* A serious fall: *Mike took a bad spill off his motorcycle.*
spill (spil)
▷ *verb* **spilling, spilled** *or* **spilt** (spilt)

spin

1. *verb* To make thread by twisting fibers together.

2. *verb* To make a web or cocoon by giving off a liquid that hardens into thread: *Spiders spin webs.*

3. *verb* To rotate: *The earth spins around the sun.*

4. *verb* To whirl around, as in *to spin a top.*

5. *verb* To tell or to relate, as in *to spin a tale.*

6. *verb* To feel dizzy, or as if your head is whirling around: *The roller coaster made my head spin.*

7. *noun* A short ride: *We took the new car out for a spin around the block.*

8. *noun* A special interpretation or point of view: *The senator put a positive spin on the poll results.*
spin (spin)
▷ *verb* **spinning, spun** (spuhn)

spinach *noun* A vegetable with edible dark green leaves. **spin·ach** (**spin**-ich)

spinal column *noun* A series of connected bones in your back that support and protect the spinal cord; the backbone.

spinal cord *noun* A thick cord of nerve tissue that starts at the brain and runs through the center of the spinal column.

spindle *noun* The round stick or rod on a spinning wheel that holds and winds thread. **spin·dle** (**spin**-duhl)

spine *noun*

1. The backbone: *A chill traveled up and down her spine.* ▷ *adjective* **spinal**

2. A hard, sharp, pointed growth, such as a thorn or quill, on some plants and animals. ▷ *adjective* **spiny**

3. The central, vertical piece of a book's cover: *I ran my hand over the spines of the old books at the library.*
spine (spine)

spinning wheel *noun* A device worked by hand consisting of a large wheel and a spindle. A spinning wheel is used to spin fibers into thread or yarn.

spin-off *noun*

1. An unrelated benefit or product that comes from something used or developed earlier: *Teflon is a spin-off from the space program.*

2. A television show starring a character who had a popular but less important role on an earlier program.
▷ *verb* **spin off**

spinster *noun* A woman who has stayed single beyond the age at which most women marry. **spin·ster** (**spin**-stur)

spiral *adjective* Winding in a continuous curve around a fixed point or central axis, as in *a spiral staircase.* **spi·ral** (**spye**-ruhl) ▷ *noun* **spiral** ▷ *verb* **spiral**

spire *noun* A structure that comes to a point at the top. Spires are often built on top of church towers. **spire** (spire)

spirit

1. *noun* The invisible part of a person that is believed to control thoughts and feelings; the soul: *Even when he was an infant, his spirit shone through.*

2. *noun* The essential character, quality, or mood of a person or group of people, as in *a spirit of hope.*

3. *noun* Courage, enthusiasm, and determination: *Even though they had lost their homes, the people responded to the crisis with spirit.* ▷ *adjective* **spirited**

4. *noun* A ghost or supernatural being, as in *evil spirits.*

5. spirits *noun, plural* A person's mood or state of mind: *The patient is recovering nicely and is in good spirits.*

6. *noun* The real meaning or intent, as in *the spirit of the law.*

7. spirit away *verb* To carry off mysteriously or secretly: *Zoe spirited me away to a restaurant on the coast for my birthday.* ▷ *verb* **spiriting, spirited** **spir·it** (**spir**-it)

spiritual

1. *adjective* Of or having to do with the soul and not with material or physical things. ▷ *adverb* **spiritually**

2. *adjective* Of or having to do with religion, as in *spiritual advice.*

3. *noun* A type of religious folk song that was originated by African Americans in the South: *During Black History Month, the choir prepared a concert of spirituals.* **spir·i·tu·al** (**spir**-i-*choo*-uhl)

spit

1. *verb* To force food, liquid, or saliva out of your mouth: *He spit in the road to get the terrible taste out of his mouth.*

2. *noun* Saliva: *My baby niece got spit all over my shirt.*

3. *verb* To make an angry, hissing sound: *The cat was backed into a corner, spitting at the puppy.*

4. *noun* A long, pointed rod that holds meat over a fire for cooking.

5. *noun* A narrow point of land that sticks out into the water: *Let's walk all the way to the end of the spit this afternoon.*
spit (spit)
▷ *verb* **spitting, spat** (spat) *or* **spit**

spite

1. *noun* A deliberate wish to hurt, annoy, humiliate, or offend someone: *She hid my backpack out of spite.*
▷ *adjective* **spiteful** ▷ *adverb* **spitefully**

2. *verb* To be mean or nasty to someone: *Grace played that trick on Alan just to spite him.* ▷ *verb* **spiting, spited**

3. in spite of Without being hindered by; regardless, or in defiance of: *Dan ran the marathon in spite of his cold.*
spite (spite)

splash *verb*

1. To throw or scatter a liquid so that it falls in drops: *Jim splashed water on his face.*

2. To make wet by splashing: *My cousins splashed me when I sat down next to the pool.*
splash (splash)
▷ *verb* **splashes, splashing, splashed** ▷ *noun* **splash**

spinning wheel

splendid *adjective*
  1. Very beautiful or impressive; brilliant, as in *a splendid performance.*
  2. Very good; excellent, as in *a splendid idea.*
  splen·did (**splen**-did)
  ▷ *adverb* **splendidly**

splendor *noun* Great or magnificent beauty, as in *the splendor of nature.* **splen·dor** (**splen**-dur)

splint *noun* A strip of something rigid, used to support a broken or injured limb: *The ski patrol put a splint on his leg and brought him down the mountain.* **splint** (splint)

splinter
  1. *noun* A thin, sharp piece of wood, glass, bone, or metal that has broken off from a larger piece: *I got a splinter in my knee from the unfinished floorboards.*
  2. *verb* To break into thin, sharp pieces: *The tree splintered when it was struck by lightning.* ▷ *verb* **splintering, splintered**
  splin·ter (**splin**-tur)

split
  1. *verb* To break along the grain, as in *to split logs.*
  2. *verb* To divide, as in *to split the profits.*
  3. *verb* To burst or break apart by force: *The seam split. Scientists can split atoms.*
  4. *(slang)* To leave a place: *It was getting late, so we split.*
  5. *noun* A crack or a break: *There was a split in the center of the table.*
  split (split)
  ▷ *verb* **splitting, split**

splits *noun, plural* An acrobatic move in which you slide to the floor with your legs spread in opposite directions. **splits** (splits)

spoil
  1. *verb* To ruin or take the joy out of something: *Her bad mood spoiled our trip to the zoo.*
  2. *verb* To become rotten or unfit for eating: *No one ate the canteloupe, and it spoiled in the refrigerator.*
  3. *adjective* If children are **spoiled**, their parents have let them have their own way too often, and as a result they expect or demand too much.
  spoil (spoil)
  ▷ *verb* **spoiling, spoiled** *or* **spoilt** (spoilt)

spoiler *noun*
  1. Information about events in a movie, show, or book that you prefer not to know because you haven't seen or read it yet: *Tell me what you liked about the movie, but no spoilers, please!*
  2. A competitor who does not have a chance of winning but who spoils the chances of another to win.
  3. An aerodynamic device attached to a car or aircraft that makes it easier to handle.
  spoil·er (**spoi**-lur)

spoke
  1. *verb* The past tense of **speak**.
  2. *noun* One of the thin rods that connect the rim of a wheel to the hub.
  spoke (spoke)

spoken
  1. *verb* The past participle of **speak**.
  2. *adjective* Said out loud rather than written, as in *spoken commands.*
  spo·ken (**spoh**-kuhn)

sponge *noun*
  1. A sea animal that has a rubbery skeleton with many holes.
  2. A cleaning pad made of a sponge skeleton or artificial material that absorbs water.
  sponge (spuhnj)
  ▷ *verb* **sponge** ▷ *adjective* **spongy**

sponge

sponsor
  1. *verb* To give money and support to a worthwhile program or activity: *A pharmaceutical company is sponsoring our new arts program.* ▷ *noun* **sponsorship**
  2. *verb* To pay the costs of a radio or television broadcast in return for having your products advertised. ▷ *noun* **sponsor**
  3. *noun* A person who is responsible for someone or something: *Jim is the sponsor of his son's baseball team.*
  spon·sor (**spahn**-sur)
  ▷ *verb* **sponsoring, sponsored**

spontaneous *adjective*
  1. Done on impulse, without previous thought or planning, as in *spontaneous applause.*
  2. Happening by itself, without any apparent outside cause, as in *a spontaneous explosion.*
  spon·ta·ne·ous (spahn-**tay**-nee-uhs)
  ▷ *noun* **spontaneity** (*spahn*-tuh-**nee**-i-tee)
  ▷ *adverb* **spontaneously**

spool *noun* A cylinder or roller on which film, wire, thread, or string is wound. **spool** (spool)

spoon *noun* A utensil with a handle on one end and a surface shaped like a shallow bowl on the other. **spoon** (spoon) ▷ *verb* **spoon**

spore *noun* A plant cell that develops into a new plant. Spores are produced by plants that do not flower, such as mosses and ferns: *Mushrooms, toadstools, and other fungi have spores.* **spore** (spor)

a
b
c
d
e
f
g
h
i
j
k
l
m
n
o
p
q
r
s
t
u
v
w
x
y
z

sport *noun*

1. A game involving physical effort and skill: *Her favorite sport is hockey.*

2. A person judged by whether he or she plays fair and accepts losing with good grace, as in *a good sport.*

sport (sport)

sports jacket *noun* An informal jacket, similar to a suit jacket, that a man wears with slacks.

sportsmanship *noun* The way a person or team acts while playing a sport. Behaving in a fair and reasonable manner shows good sportsmanship.

sports·man·ship (**sports**-muhn-*ship*)

spot

1. *noun* A small mark or stain, as in *a spot of blood.*

2. *noun* An area on the skin or fur that is different from the area around it: *A dalmatian is white with black spots.* ▷ *adjective* **spotted**

3. *noun* A particular place or position: *I picked the best spot in the house for a nap.*

4. *verb* To notice something or someone: *I spotted my dog at the end of the street.* ▷ *verb* **spotting, spotted**

5. hit the spot *phrase* To be satisfying and exactly the right thing to have at that moment: *That lemonade really hit the spot after we biked all afternoon.*

6. in a tight spot *phrase* In a lot of trouble and unable to get out of it easily.

spot (spaht)

spotless *adjective*

1. Perfectly clean, as in *a spotless kitchen.*

2. Without a flaw or fault, as in *a spotless reputation.*

spot·less (**spaht**-lis)

▷ *adverb* **spotlessly**

spotlight *noun*

1. A powerful beam of light aimed at a particular person, thing, or area: *Spotlights played across the front of the building on the night of the grand opening.*

2. A lamp that sends a strong beam of light, used especially on a theater stage or in an exhibit to highlight items on display: *The spotlight illuminated the singer as she began her solo.*

3. in the spotlight In the news, or the focus of a lot of public attention.

spot·light (**spaht**-*lite*)

▷ *verb* **spotlight**

spouse *noun* A husband or a wife. **spouse** (spous)

spout

1. *noun* A pipe, a tube, or an opening through which liquid flows or is poured, as in *the spout of a teakettle.*

2. *verb* To shoot or pour out with force: *Volcanoes spout lava.* ▷ *verb* **spouting, spouted**

spout (spout)

sprain *verb* To injure a joint by twisting or tearing its

muscles or ligaments: *I sprained my ankle when I tried to run down the stairs.* **sprain** (sprayn) ▷ *verb* **spraining, sprained** ▷ *noun* **sprain**

sprang *verb* The past tense of **spring**. **sprang** (sprang)

sprawl *verb*

1. To sit, lie, or fall with your arms and legs spread out in a relaxed or awkward way, as in *to sprawl on the grass.*

2. To spread out unevenly over a large area: *The city sprawled for miles in every direction.*

sprawl (sprawl)

▷ *verb* **sprawling, sprawled** ▷ *noun* **sprawl**

spray *verb* To scatter liquid in fine droplets or a mist, as in *to spray water.* **spray** (spray) ▷ *verb* **spraying, sprayed** ▷ *noun* **spray**

spread

1. *verb* To open or stretch out, as in *to spread a blanket* or *to spread wings.*

2. *verb* To cover a surface with something, or to apply an even layer of something: *We spread mayonnaise on one slice of the bread and mustard on the other.*

▷ *noun* **spread**

3. *verb* To reach out or extend over an area: *The fire spread quickly.*

4. *verb* To distribute or to make something more widely known, as in *to spread news.*

5. *noun* (*informal*) An elaborate meal put on a table: *Grandma laid out a nice spread for Thanksgiving.*

spread (spred)

▷ *verb* **spreading, spread**

spreadsheet *noun*

1. A wide sheet of paper that is divided into rows and columns. Spreadsheets are used for organizing numerical data.

2. A computer program that allows you to keep track of and use numerical information in a table format.

spread·sheet (**spred**-*sheet*)

spree *noun* A period of excessive or unrestrained activity, as in *a shopping spree.* **spree** (spree)

spring

1. *noun* The season after winter and before summer, when the weather becomes warmer and plants and flowers begin to grow.

2. *verb* To move suddenly forward or upward from the ground; to leap: *My cat sprang into the air and nearly caught a bird.* ▷ *noun* **spring**

3. *verb* To appear suddenly: *Flowers are springing up everywhere.*

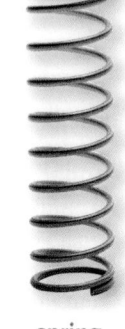

spring

4. *verb* To make known suddenly: *He is always springing surprises on us.*

5. *noun* A spiral coil of metal that returns to its original shape or position after being stretched or pressed down, as in *mattress springs.*

6. *noun* A place where water rises to the surface from an underground source.
spring (spring)
▷ *verb* **springing, sprang** (sprang), **sprung** (spruhng)

springboard *noun* A flexible board used in diving or gymnastics to help a person jump high in the air. **spring·board** (**spring**-bord)

spring fever *noun* A lazy or restless feeling that often is associated with the coming of spring.

sprinkle *verb*
1. To scatter something in small drops or bits: *Sprinkle grated chocolate over the ice cream.*
2. To rain in small amounts: *We thought it would pour, but it barely sprinkled.*
sprin·kle (**spring**-kuhl)
▷ *verb* **sprinkling, sprinkled**
▷ *noun* **sprinkle**

sprinkler *noun* A device that attaches to a hose and sprays water over a lawn or garden. **sprin·kler** (**spring**-klur)

sprint
1. *verb* To run fast for a short distance: *Marietta sprinted across the park so she wouldn't be late for school.* ▷ *verb* **sprinting, sprinted**
2. *noun* A short race, run at the fastest possible speed. ▷ *noun* **sprinter** ▷ *adjective* **sprint**
sprint (sprint)

sprocket *noun* A wheel with a rim made of toothlike points that fit into the holes of a chain. The chain then drives the wheel. **sprock·et** (**sprah**-kit)

sprout
1. *verb* To begin to grow and produce shoots or buds: *My basil plant is just beginning to sprout.*
2. *noun* A new or young plant growth, such as a bud or shoot: *The tree outside my window is covered in sprouts.*
3. sprouts *noun, plural* The young edible shoots of various plants that are often eaten raw, as in *alfalfa sprouts.*
4. *verb* To grow, appear, or develop suddenly or quickly: *Weeds have sprouted up all over the lawn.*
sprout (sprout)
▷ *verb* **sprouting, sprouted**

spruce *noun* An evergreen tree with short leaves shaped like needles, drooping cones, and wood that is often used in making pulp for paper. **spruce** (sproos)

sprung *verb* The past participle of **spring**. **sprung** (spruhng)

spry *adjective* Able to move quickly and easily; nimble: *She's a spry little thing and she crawled over the baby gate the first time it was put up.* **spry** (sprye)

spun *verb* The past tense and the past participle of **spin**. **spun** (spuhn)

spur
1. *noun* A pointed device, often a spiked wheel, on the heel of a rider's boot.
2. spur on *verb* To encourage someone to make more of an effort: *The teacher's compliments spurred me on to study harder.* ▷ *verb* **spurring, spurred** ▷ *noun* **spur**
spur (spur)

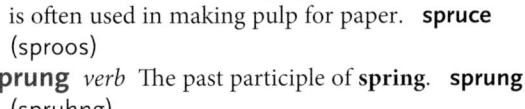

spurt
1. *verb* To come out suddenly in a stream or gush. ▷ *verb* **spurting, spurted** ▷ *noun* **spurt**
2. *noun* A sudden, brief burst of energy, growth, or activity, as in *a growth spurt.* ▷ *verb* **spurt**
spurt (spurt)

sputter *verb*
1. To make popping, spitting, or coughing noises: *The old car sputtered down the street.*
2. To speak quickly and in a confused way: *Sam sputtered in excitement when he found out he had won the contest.*
3. To spit out small bits of food or saliva, especially when you are talking in an excited way.
sput·ter (**spuht**-ur)
▷ *verb* **sputtering, sputtered**

spy
1. *verb* To watch someone or something closely and secretly, as in *to spy on the neighbors.*
2. *verb* To sight, as in *to spy land.*
3. *noun* Someone who secretly collects information about an enemy or a competitor. ▷ *noun, plural* **spies** ▷ *verb* **spy**
spy (spye)
▷ *verb* **spies, spying, spied**

spying *noun* The activity of observing someone or something secretly in order to get information: *An American journalist accused of spying in Iran has now been tried behind closed doors.* **spy·ing** (**spye**-ing)

spyware *noun* Software that is secretly installed on your computer in order to gather information about you and how you use your computer. **spy·ware** (**spye**-wair)

sprockets

squabble *noun* A noisy argument or quarrel, usually over something unimportant: *My friends had a brief squabble over what kind of pizza to order.* **squab·ble (skwah-buhl)** ▷ *verb* **squabble**

squad *noun* A small group of people who work together or are involved in the same activity, such as soldiers, football players, or police officers. **squad (skwahd)**

squadron *noun* A group of ships, cavalry troops, or other military units. **squad·ron (skwah-druhn)**

squalid *adjective* Dirty and miserable, usually because of neglect or poverty, as in *a squalid apartment.* **squal·id (skwah-lid)**

squall *noun* A sudden, violent wind that usually brings rain, snow, or sleet with it. **squall (skwawl)**

squalor *noun* The condition of being dirty, miserable, and very poor: *After the war, the refugees lived in squalor.* **squa·lor (skwah-lur)**

squander *verb* To spend money, time, or opportunity wastefully or foolishly: *Alec squandered his entire allowance on junk food.* **squan·der (skwahn-dur)** ▷ *verb* **squandering, squandered**

square
1. *noun* A shape with four straight, equal sides and four right angles. ▷ *adjective* **square**
2. *verb* To multiply a number by itself: *Five squared equals 25.* ▷ *verb* **squaring, squared**
3. *noun* A number is a **square** if it can be expressed as the product of the same two numbers. Four is the square of 2 because $2 \times 2 = 4$.
4. *noun* An open area in a town or city with streets on all four sides.
5. *adjective* Honest or fair, especially in business affairs, as in *a square deal.*
6. *adjective* Nutritious and filling, as in *a square meal.*
7. *adjective (slang)* Not cool or not hip; old-fashioned, as in *square ideas.* ▷ *noun* **square** ▷ *adjective* **squarer, squarest** **square (skwair)**

square dance *noun* A dance in which four couples form the sides of a square and move to spoken commands. ▷ *verb* **square-dance**

square root *noun* A number that, when multiplied by itself, produces a given number. The square root of 25 is 5, because $5 \times 5 = 25$. The symbol for a square root is √.

squash

squash
1. *verb* To crush or to squeeze someone or something into a soft, flat mass, as in *to squash a bug.* ▷ *verb* **squashes, squashing, squashed**
2. *noun* A game in which two players with rackets hit a small rubber ball against the walls of an enclosed court.
3. *noun* A fleshy fruit that grows on a vine in many shapes, sizes, and colors. Squash are related to pumpkins and gourds. ▷ *noun, plural* **squash** or **squashes** **squash (skwahsh)**

squat
1. *verb* To crouch, or to sit on your heels with your knees bent. ▷ *noun* **squat**
2. *verb* To settle on an area of land or to live in an empty house that does not belong to you. ▷ *noun* **squatter**
3. *adjective* Short and wide, as in *a squat building.* ▷ *adjective* **squatter, squattest** **squat (skwaht)** ▷ *verb* **squatting, squatted**

squawk
1. *noun* A loud, harsh screech like the sound made by a parrot or a chicken: *The bird house at the zoo was filled with birds squawking wildly.*
2. *verb* To make this sound: *Her pet bird squawked at me loudly.*
3. *verb (informal)* To complain loudly: *Stop squawking and do your chores.*
4. *noun (informal)* Any loud complaint or protest. ▷ *noun* **squawker** **squawk (skwawk)** ▷ *verb* **squawking, squawked**

squeak *verb* To make a short, sharp, high-pitched sound. **squeak (skweek)** ▷ *verb* **squeaking, squeaked** ▷ *noun* **squeak** ▷ *adjective* **squeaky**

squeal *verb*
1. To make a shrill, high sound or cry, as in *to squeal with delight.*
2. *(informal)* To betray a friend or secret; to inform on someone: *He planned to sneak out at night, but his brother squealed on him.* **squeal (skweel)** ▷ *verb* **squealing, squealed** ▷ *noun* **squeal**

squeamish *adjective* Easily shocked, disgusted, or nauseated, as in *squeamish about dead animals.* **squea·mish** (**skwee**-mish) ▷ *adverb* **squeamishly**

squeeze *verb*
1. To exert pressure on someone or something from two or more sides, as in *to squeeze a plastic bottle.* ▷ *noun* **squeezer**
2. To barely get into or through a space, as in *to squeeze into an elevator.*
3. To hug someone: *He squeezed me tightly when we met at the airport.*
squeeze (skweez)
▷ *verb* **squeezing, squeezed** ▷ *noun* **squeeze**

squid *noun* A sea creature with a long, soft body and ten arms or tentacles that swims by squirting out water with great force. **squid** (skwid) ▷ *noun, plural* **squid** or **squids**

squid

squint *verb* To look at something through partly closed eyes, especially when there is too much light: *The sun was so bright that I had to squint to see across the river.* **squint** (skwint) ▷ *verb* **squinting, squinted** ▷ *noun* **squint**

squire *noun*
1. In medieval times, a young nobleman who served as an attendant to a knight.
2. An English country gentleman who owns land.
squire (skwire)

squirm *verb*
1. To wriggle or twist about, especially because you are nervous or uncomfortable: *The children squirmed during the long, boring movie.*
2. To show or feel discomfort because you are embarrassed or ashamed: *The defendant squirmed in front of the judge.*
squirm (skwurm)
▷ *verb* **squirming, squirmed**

squirrel *noun* A rodent that climbs trees and has a long, bushy tail. **squir·rel** (skwurl)

squirt *verb* To force out a stream or jet of liquid, as in *to squirt water.* **squirt** (skwurt) ▷ *verb* **squirting, squirted** ▷ *noun* **squirt**

squishy *adjective (informal)* Soft and spongy, as in *squishy ground.* **squish·y** (**skwish**-ee)

stab
1. *verb* To thrust a knife or other sharp instrument into someone. ▷ *noun* **stab**
2. *verb* To stick or drive a pointed object into something: *The farmer stabbed the pitchfork into the bale of hay.*
3. *noun* A sharp, brief feeling or pang, as in *a stab of pain* or *a stab of guilt.*
4. take a stab at or **make a stab at** *(informal)* To attempt something: *I'm not much of a baker, but I'll take a stab at making the apple pie.*
stab (stab)
▷ *verb* **stabbing, stabbed**

squirt

stability *noun* The quality of being firm and steady: *He didn't trust the stability of the ladder, so he didn't climb it.* **sta·bil·i·ty** (stuh-**bil**-i-tee)

stable
1. *noun* A building or a part of a building where horses or cattle are fed and housed. ▷ *verb* **stable**
2. *adjective* Firmly fixed; not likely to fail or give way, as in *a stable ladder.* ▷ *verb* **stabilize** (**stay**-buh-*lize*)
3. *adjective* Mentally and emotionally steady or secure, as in *a stable home life.*
sta·ble (**stay**-buhl)
▷ *adjective* **stabler, stablest**

staccato *adverb* In music, when you play notes **staccato**, you play them abruptly and separately, so that each sound is distinct. **stac·ca·to** (stuh-**kah**-toh) ▷ *adjective* **staccato**

stack
1. *verb* To arrange things in a pile, as in *to stack bricks.* ▷ *verb* **stacking, stacked**
2. *noun* A large, neat pile of hay, straw, or grain.
3. *noun* A neat pile of something arranged in layers, as in *a stack of magazines.*
4. *noun* A chimney or a smokestack.
stack (stak)

stadium *noun* A large structure in which sports events and concerts are held. It usually has an open field surrounded by rows of rising seats. **sta·di·um** (**stay**-dee-uhm) ▷ *noun, plural* **stadiums** or **stadia** (**stay**-dee-uh)

a
b
c
d
e
f
g
h
i
j
k
l
m
n
o
p
q
r
s
t
u
v
w
x
y
z

staff

1. *noun* A group of people who work for a company, an institution, or a person, as in *a newspaper staff.* ▷ *noun, plural* **staffs**

2. *verb* To provide an organization with employees: *The supervisor staffed her office with young, creative workers.* ▷ *verb* **staffing, staffed**

3. *noun* A stick or pole used as a support in walking or as a weapon, as in *a shepherd's staff.*

4. *noun* A flagpole.

5. *noun* The set of lines and spaces on which music is written.
staff (staf)
▷ *noun, plural* **staffs** *or* **staves** (stayvz)

stag *noun* A fully grown male deer. **stag** (stag)

stage

1. *noun* A raised platform on which actors and other entertainers perform.

2. *noun* The profession of acting: *She left the stage because there were no good parts for older women.*

3. *noun* A step, level, or point in a process, as in *an early stage.*

4. *noun* A period of development, as in *the toddler stage.*

5. *verb* To present a public performance of a play or similar event: *The school is staging "Our Town" this year.* ▷ *verb* **staging, staged**
stage (stayj)

stagecoach

stagecoach *noun* A four-wheeled, horse-drawn coach, used in the past to carry mail and passengers on scheduled trips over regular routes. **stage·coach** (**stayj**-kohch) ▷ *noun, plural* **stagecoaches**

stagger *verb*

1. To walk or move unsteadily, as if you're about to collapse.

2. To feel amazed or deeply shocked: *The callousness of his remark staggered us.*

3. To arrange events so that they don't all occur at the same time: *The nurses staggered their lunch breaks so*

that someone was always on duty.
stag·ger (**stag**-ur)
▷ *adjective* **staggered** ▷ *verb* **staggering, staggered**

staggering *adjective* Causing great amazement or upset, as in *a staggering defeat.* **stag·ger·ing** (**stag**-ur-ing)

stagnant *adjective*

1. Not moving or not flowing; still, as in *a stagnant pond.*

2. Foul or polluted as a result of not moving.

3. Not active or not growing, as in *a stagnant economy.*
stag·nant (**stag**-nuhnt)

stagnate *verb*

1. When water **stagnates**, it becomes dirty or polluted, changes color, and often gives off a foul odor.

2. If situations or persons **stagnate**, they stop developing or progressing and remain the same.
stag·nate (**stag**-nate)
▷ *verb* **stagnating, stagnated** ▷ *noun* **stagnation**

staid *adjective* Proper, serious, and not very adventurous, as in *a staid old lady.* **staid** (stayd)
▷ *adjective* **staider, staidest** ▷ *noun* **staidness**
▷ *adverb* **staidly**

stain

1. *noun* A mark or spot that is hard to remove, as in *a grass stain.*

2. *verb* To mark or discolor something, as in *to stain a shirt.* ▷ *verb* **staining, stained**

3. *noun* A dye used to color wood: *We rubbed a dark cherry stain into the table.*
stain (stayn)

stained glass *noun* Colored pieces of glass, held in place by lead strips, that form a picture, pattern, or design. ▷ *adjective* **stained-glass**

stainless steel *noun* A type of steel that contains chromium and therefore does not rust or tarnish. **stain·less steel** (**stayn**-lis)

stair *noun*

1. One of a group of fixed steps that allow you to walk from the ground to the entrance of a building or from one level to another.

2. stairs *noun, plural* Another word for **stairway.**
stair (stair)
Stair sounds like **stare.**

stairway *noun* A flight of steps with a railing and a structure that supports it: *Take this stairway up to the library.* **stair·way** (**stair**-way)

stake

1. *noun* A post with a point at one end that can be driven into the ground to support something, such as a tree or a fence. ▷ *verb* **stake**

2. *verb* To risk or to gamble: *She staked her reputation on coaching a winning team.* ▷ *verb* **staking, staked**

3. *noun* Something, especially money, that is bet or risked, as in *high stakes.*

4. have a stake in *phrase* To have a personal interest or involvement in something: *We all have a stake in protecting the environment.*

5. at stake *phrase* At risk of being lost, ruined, injured, or damaged: *He installed the smoke alarms carefully because his family's safety was at stake.*

6. pull up stakes *phrase* To leave a place.
stake (stayk)
Stake sounds like **steak**.

stalactite *noun* An icicle-shaped mineral deposit that hangs from the roof of a cave. Stalactites form as dripping water, full of minerals, slowly evaporates. **sta·lac·tite** (stuh-**lak**-*tite*)

stalagmite *noun* A tapering column that sticks up from the floor of a cave. Stalagmites are formed when water containing minerals drips from the ceiling to the floor of the cave and slowly solidifies. **sta·lag·mite** (stuh-**lag**-*mite*)

stalactites
stalagmites

stalactites and stalagmites

stale *adjective*

1. No longer fresh, as in *stale bread* or *stale air.*

2. No longer new or interesting, as in *a stale joke* or *stale news.*
stale (stale)
▷ *adjective* **staler, stalest**

stalemate *noun*

1. A situation in a game of chess in which a player cannot make a move without placing his or her king in check.

2. Any position or situation that results in a deadlock, with no progress possible: *The two countries reached a stalemate over the border dispute.*

stale·mate (**stale**-*mate*)

stalk

1. *noun* The main stem of a plant from which the leaves and flowers grow.

2. *verb* To hunt or track a person or an animal in a quiet, secret way, as in *to stalk a suspect.* ▷ *noun* **stalker**

3. *verb* To walk in a proud, stiff, or angry way: *Maria slammed her book shut and stalked out of the classroom.*
stalk (stawk)
▷ *verb* **stalking, stalked**

stall

1. *verb* When a vehicle **stalls**, its engine stops running and it loses power: *The car stalled after it drove through a deep puddle.*

2. *noun* A counter or booth where things are displayed for sale at a market, as in *a pastry stall.*

3. *noun* An enclosed space for one animal in a stable or barn, as in *a horse stall.*

4. *verb* To deliberately put off doing something: *Stop stalling and make those phone calls!* ▷ *noun* **stall**
stall (stawl)
▷ *verb* **stalling, stalled**

stallion *noun* An adult male horse. **stal·lion** (**stal**-yuhn)

stalwart

1. *adjective* Very loyal in your support of someone or something: *The senator has been a stalwart ally of the groups that try to protect the environment, supporting every bill that strengthens their cause.*

2. *adjective* (*old-fashioned*) Physically or mentally very robust and vigorous. This sense of the word is used mainly in a literary way to describe someone who looks very strong: *The sailor had a stalwart build.*

3. *noun* Someone who strongly supports an idea, person, or group: *He is a Republican stalwart who has always contributed heavily to the party.*
stal·wart (**stawl**-wurt)
▷ *noun* **stalwartness** ▷ *adverb* **stalwartly**

stamen *noun* The part of a flower that produces pollen. It consists of a thin stalk, called the filament, and a tip, called the anther, that has pollen on it. **sta·men** (**stay**-muhn)

stamina *noun* The energy and strength to keep doing something, or to resist fatigue and illness: *Running or swimming requires a great deal of physical stamina.* **stam·i·na** (**stam**-uh-nuh)

stammer *verb* To speak in an unsure way, stopping often and repeating certain sounds. **stam·mer** (**stam**-ur) ▷ *verb* **stammering, stammered** ▷ *noun* **stammer**

a b c d e f g h i j k l m n o p q r **s** t u v w x y z

stamp

1. *noun* A small piece of gummed paper that you stick on a letter or package that is going to be mailed; a postage stamp.

2. *noun* An object used to transfer a mark, signature, or design to paper by pressing it against a pad of ink first.

3. *verb* To bring your foot down hard: *Stamp your feet to keep them from getting cold.* ▷ *verb* **stamping, stamped** ▷ *noun* **stamp**
stamp (stamp)

stampede
verb To make a sudden, wild rush in one direction, usually out of fear, as in *horses stampeding.* **stam·pede** (stam-**peed**) ▷ *verb* **stampeding, stampeded** ▷ *noun* **stampede**

Word History

The young Spanish explorer Francisco Vásquez de Coronado, who marched with his men all the way from Mexico to Kansas in the 1500s, observed what happened when his group frightened a herd of buffaloes: a **stampede**. These huge animals, which are also known as bison, roamed the western plains of America in herds of a hundred thousand or more. Spanish speakers based the word *stampede* on *estampar*, a verb meaning "to stamp." The people who chose this name probably felt the force of the animals' feet stamping in their wild rush forward.

stance
noun

1. The way someone stands; posture: *She took a defiant stance, with her feet apart and her hands on her hips.*

2. Attitude or point of view: *My parents don't agree with my antiwar stance.*
stance (stans)

stand

1. *verb* To be on your feet or to rise to an upright position, as in *to stand in line.*

2. *verb* To put something in an upright position: *Stand the cookbook on the counter.*

3. *verb* To be located: *My house stands on a hill.*

4. *verb* To be in a certain rank or order: *Maya stands first in her class.*

5. *verb* To have an opinion or to take a position: *Where do you stand on capital punishment?* ▷ *noun* **stand**

6. *verb* To continue without change or to remain valid: *My decision still stands, but you're welcome to argue against it.*

7. *noun* An object or piece of furniture for holding or displaying things, as in *a dictionary stand.*

8. stands *noun, plural* A covered area for spectators at a ballpark or stadium.

9. *noun* A small booth, counter, or stall where goods are sold, as in *a newspaper stand* or *a flower stand.*

10. stand for *verb* To represent: *NATO stands for "North Atlantic Treaty Organization."*

11. *verb* To tolerate or put up with something: *I can't stand cabbage.*

12. stand by *verb* To support and remain loyal to someone: *Ray stands by his friends no matter what.*

13. stand out *verb* To show up clearly or to be easily seen: *Carla's red jacket stands out in the photograph.*

14. take a stand To state your opinion on an issue in a clear and forceful way: *The principal took a strong stand about cheating on exams.*
stand (stand)
▷ *verb* **standing, stood** (stud)

standalone
adjective Available or able to operate by itself; not depending on another thing: *They market their monitors as standalone products, better than the ones that come with a computer.* **stand·a·lone** (**stand**-uh-*lohn*)

standard

1. *noun* A rule or model that is used to judge or measure how good something is: *New cars must meet safety and pollution standards.*

2. *noun* The flag or banner of a nation or military group.

3. *adjective* Normal or average, as in *the standard price.*

4. *adjective* Used or accepted as a standard, rule, or model: *The meter is a standard unit of length in the metric system.*

5. *adjective* Widely used or accepted as correct, as in *standard spelling* or *standard English.*
stan·dard (**stan**-durd)

standby
noun

1. Someone or something that is kept in reserve, to be used if needed: *We brought a second camera on our trip as a standby in case the first one broke.*

2. The state of being available if needed: *National Guard troops were put on standby when the river reached flood stage.*

3. A setting for an electrical device that takes less power, for times when it is not being used: *I usually put my computer in standby when I leave my desk.*

4. Someone who doesn't hold a ticket for a flight but will get a seat if there is one available.

5. Your favorite or most frequent choice: *When there's nothing else for dessert, vanilla ice cream is my standby.*
stand·by (**stand**-*bye*)

stand-in *noun* A person who takes the place of another person: *I was the stand-in for Rudy, who had the lead role in the play.* ▷ *verb* **stand in**

standing *noun*
1. Position, rank, or reputation: *Kelly's standing at work has improved as a result of her successful project.*
2. in good standing Respected and accepted within a group: *Martha is a member in good standing of the garden club.*
3. standings *noun, plural* The positions or rankings of all the teams within a sport during a regular season of play, as in *the baseball standings.* **stand·ing** (**stan**-ding)

standout *noun* A person or thing that is easy to distinguish, usually because they are better than others; one that stands out: *The standout of the afternoon was a guy from Wyoming who sang and played his guitar.* **stand·out** (**stand**-out)

standstill *noun* A complete halt: *An accident brought traffic to a standstill.* **stand·still** (**stand**-stil)

stand-up *adjective* A **stand-up** comic or comedian performs while standing alone on a stage or in front of a camera. ▷ *noun* **stand-up**

stank *verb* The past tense of **stink.** **stank** (stangk)

stanza *noun* One of the units, consisting of two or more lines, into which a poem or song is divided; a verse. **stan·za** (**stan**-zuh)

Word History

When you read a poem, you naturally rest at the end of one **stanza** before going on to the next group of lines. The word *stanza* got its name from this pause, or brief stop: The noun *stanza* in Italian was based on the Latin word *stantia,* meaning "a stopping place." Many English words about music, painting, and poetry come from Italian; *piano* and *opera* are two others.

staple *noun*
1. A thin piece of wire that is shaped like a U and punched through sheets of paper to fasten them together. ▷ *noun* **stapler** ▷ *verb* **staple**
2. Any food or product that is used regularly and kept in large amounts: *Flour, salt, and sugar are staples.*
3. A main product that is grown or produced in a country or region: *Timber is a staple of many economies.*
sta·ple (**stay**-puhl)

star
1. *noun* A mass of burning gas, seen in the sky at night as a glowing point of light. ▷ *adjective* **starry**
2. *noun* A shape with five or more points: *The picture frame was decorated with stars.*

3. *noun* A person who plays a leading role in a movie, television program, or play.
4. *noun* A person who is outstanding in some field, as in *a basketball star.*
5. *verb* To take the leading role in a movie, television program, or play: *My favorite actor stars in this new movie.* ▷ *verb* **starring, starred**
star (stahr)

starboard *noun* The right-hand side of a ship or an aircraft when you are facing forward. **star·board** (**stahr**-burd *or* **stahr**-bord) ▷ *adjective* **starboard**

starch *noun*
1. A tasteless, odorless white substance found in potatoes, rice, corn, wheat, and other plant foods that is considered an important part of the human diet.
2. A substance used in laundering for making fabric stiff.
starch (stahrch)
▷ *noun, plural* **starches** ▷ *verb* **starch**

starfish

stare *verb* To look at someone or something steadily with your eyes wide open: *The cat stared at the birds on the roof.* **stare** (stair) **Stare** sounds like **stair.** ▷ *verb* **staring, stared** ▷ *noun* **stare**

starfish *noun* A sea animal with a flattened, star-shaped body and five or more arms. **star·fish** (**stahr**-fish) ▷ *noun, plural* **starfish**

stark *adjective*
1. Bare and grim; having little or no plant life, as in *a stark landscape.*
2. Complete or extreme, as in *stark poverty.*
stark (stahrk)
▷ *adjective* **starker, starkest**

starling *noun* A songbird with a pointed yellow bill and dark, shiny feathers. Starlings are found in most parts of the world. **star·ling** (**stahr**-ling)

Stars and Stripes *noun* The flag of the United States. The red and white stripes represent the 13 original colonies. The white stars represent the 50 states.

Stars and Stripes

start

1. *verb* To begin to move, act, or happen: *Have you started your book report? The movie starts in ten minutes.*

2. *verb* To make something move, act, or happen: *Start the car. I didn't start the fight.*

3. *noun* A place where or time when something begins: *We arrived right at the start of the show.*

4. *verb* To jump or move suddenly: *Jeremy started at the loud noise.* ▷ *noun* **start**

5. *noun* An advantage at the beginning of a race or contest, as in *a ten-yard start.*

start (stahrt)

▷ *verb* **starting, started**

startle *verb* To surprise, frighten, or alarm someone, often causing a quick, involuntary movement: *You startled me! I thought no one was home.* **star·tle** (stahr-tuhl) ▷ *verb* **startling, startled** ▷ *adjective* **startled** ▷ *adjective* **startling**

start-up or **startup** *noun* A new company, formed by the people who are going to run it.

starve *verb*

1. To suffer or die from lack of food: *Many animals starved during the severe winter.* ▷ *noun* **starvation**

2. To need or want something very much, as in *starved for affection.*

starve (stahrv)

▷ *verb* **starving, starved**

starving *adjective*

1. Suffering or dying from lack of food: *The starving birds crowded around the feeder.*

2. *(informal)* Very hungry: *I'm starving—can we eat lunch?*

starv·ing (stahr-ving)

stash

1. *verb* To hide something away: *Mom stashed the cookies in the far back corner of the pantry, but I quickly found them.* ▷ *verb* **stashing, stashed**

2. *noun* Something, such as money or food, that has been hidden away: *I went to my drawer and counted my stash—yes! I had enough to buy the new video game.*

stash (stash)

state

1. *verb* To say something in words; to tell or explain: *Please state your reasons for being late.* ▷ *verb* **stating, stated**

2. *noun* A group of people united under one government; a nation.

3. *noun* Any of the political and geographical units that make up a country such as the United States. ▷ *noun* **statehood** (**state**-hud)

4. *noun* The condition that someone or something is in, as in *a state of chaos* or *a state of shock.*

state (state)

stately *adjective* Grand, dignified, or majestic, as in *a stately mansion.* **state·ly** (**state**-lee)

statement *noun*

1. Something that is said in words: *The mayor's statement made his opinion clear.*

2. A monthly report from a bank listing all the amounts paid into and out of an account. **state·ment** (**state**-muhnt)

state-of-the-art *adjective* At the highest level of development; very up-to-date, as in *state-of-the-art technology.*

statesman *noun* A person respected for great experience and leadership in government. **states·man** (**stayts**-muhn) ▷ *noun, plural* **statesmen**

stateswoman *noun* A woman respected for great experience and leadership in government. **states·wom·an** (**stayts**-*wum*-uhn) ▷ *noun, plural* **stateswomen**

static

1. *adjective* Not moving, changing, or growing, as in *a static situation* or *a static population.*

2. *noun* Electrical discharges in the air that interfere with radio or television signals and cause a hissing, crackling sound: *We could hardly hear the program because of the static.*

stat·ic (**stat**-ik)

static electricity *noun* Electricity that builds up in an object as a result of friction and is released in the form of sparks or a mild electric shock.

station *noun*

1. A place where tickets for trains, buses, or other vehicles are sold and where passengers are let on and off.

2. A building where a service is provided, as in *a fire station, a police station,* or *a gas station.*

3. A place with equipment to send out television or radio signals: *The show is broadcast from a station downtown.*

4. A place where a person or thing stands or is supposed to stand while carrying out a duty, as in *a*

fire station

guard station.
sta·tion (**stay**-shuhn)

stationary *adjective*
1. Not moving or not able to be moved, as in *a stationary bicycle.*
2. Not changing, as in *stationary prices.*
sta·tion·ar·y (**stay**-shuh-*ner*-ee)
Stationary sounds like **stationery**.

stationery *noun*
1. Materials used for writing, such as paper, pens, and notebooks; office supplies: *The store on the corner sells books and stationery.*
2. Paper and envelopes used to write letters: *I wrote to my grandmother on my best stationery.*
sta·tion·er·y (**stay**-shuh-*ner*-ee)
Stationery sounds like **stationary**.

statistic *noun* A fact or piece of information taken from a study that covers a much larger quantity of information: *The number of motorcycles versus cars was a surprising statistic.* **sta·tis·tic** (stuh-**tis**-tik)
▷ *adjective* **statistical** ▷ *adverb* **statistically**

statue *noun* A model of a person or an animal, especially one that is life-size or larger, made from metal, stone, wood, or any solid material. **stat·ue** (**stach**-oo)

stature *noun*
1. Height: *In spite of her small stature, she was an excellent basketball player.*
2. Good reputation: *Their donation to the hospital increased the family's stature in the community.*
stat·ure (**stach**-ur)

status *noun*
1. A person's rank or position in a group, an organization, or a society: *Her position as a judge gave her a higher status in the community.*
2. The condition of a person, situation, project, or event: *What's the status of the survivors who were found yesterday?*
sta·tus (**stay**-tuhs or **stat**-uhs)

status bar *noun* An area at the bottom of the screen in many computer programs and browsers that shows information about what is currently happening in the main display area.

statute *noun* A written rule or law, as in *local statutes.* **stat·ute** (**stach**-oot)

statutory *adjective* Required, permitted, or regulated by a

statute or law, as in *a statutory offense.* **stat·u·to·ry** (**stach**-uh-*tor*-ee)

staunch *adjective* Showing strong and long-lasting support for a person, group, or idea: *I have been a staunch supporter of the governor since he was first elected, and I have voted for him ever since.* **staunch** (stawnch) ▷ *noun* **staunchness** ▷ *adverb* **staunchly**)

stave
1. *noun* One of the long, thin strips of wood that form the sides of a barrel.
2. *noun* The set of lines and spaces on which musical notes are written; a staff.
3. stave in *verb* To break by forcing inward or to smash a hole in something: *The ocean liner's hull had been staved in by an iceberg.*
4. stave off *verb* To manage to prevent or delay something: *We staved off hunger by snacking.*
stave (stayv)
▷ *verb* **staving, staved** or **stove** (stohv)

stay
1. *verb* To remain in one place or condition: *Stay where you are. They stayed friends for many years.*
2. *verb* To live or spend time somewhere: *Harold stayed on the West Coast for five years. We stayed at the party until midnight.*
3. *noun* A period of time spent somewhere as a guest or visitor: *We had a wonderful stay in the Adirondack Mountains.*
stay (stay)
▷ *verb* **staying, stayed**

STD *noun* Any disease that you can catch by having sex with an infected person. STD is short for *sexually transmitted disease.*

steadfast *adjective* Firm and steady or not changing, as in *steadfast loyalty* or *a steadfast gaze.* **stead·fast** (**sted**-*fast*)

steady
1. *adjective* Uniform and continuous, as in *a steady rain.* ▷ *adverb* **steadily**
2. *adjective* Firm or stable; not shaky, as in *a steady hand* or *a steady chair.*
3. *verb* To stop something from shaking, trembling, or tottering: *I steadied my grandmother by giving her my arm.* ▷ *verb* **steadies, steadying, steadied**
4. *adjective* Sensible, reliable, or dependable, as in *a steady worker.*
5. *adjective* Regular, as in *a steady customer.*
stead·y (**sted**-ee)
▷ *adjective* **steadier, steadiest**

steak *noun* A thick slice of beef or some other meat or fish. **steak** (stayk) **Steak** sounds like **stake**.

Statue of Liberty

a
b
c
d
e
f
g
h
i
j
k
l
m
n
o
p
q
r
s
t
u
v
w
x
y
z

steam engine

steal

1. *verb* To take something that does not belong to you, without permission and with no thought of returning it: *Ben steals other people's lunches.*
2. *verb* To do something in a secret or tricky way, as in *to steal a look at something.*
3. *verb* To get to the next base in baseball without a hit or an error, as in *to steal second.* ▷ *noun* **steal**
4. *noun* Something bought at a very low price; a bargain: *My new sweater was a steal.*
steal (steel)
Steal sounds like **steel**. ▷ *verb* **stealing, stole** (stohl), **stolen** (stohl-in)

stealthy

adjective Acting with or characterized by silence, secrecy, and caution, as in *a stealthy approach.* **stealth·y** (**stel**-thee) ▷ *adjective* **stealthier, stealthiest** ▷ *noun* **stealth** ▷ *adverb* **stealthily**

steam

1. *noun* The vapor that water turns into when it boils. ▷ *verb* **steam**
2. *verb* To cook using steam, as in *to steam vegetables.*
3. *noun* The mist formed when water vapor condenses: *It was so cold that we could see steam coming out of our mouths and noses.*
4. steam up *verb* To become covered with condensed water vapor: *My glasses steamed up in the rain.*
5. let off steam or **blow off steam** (*informal*) To release the energy or angry feelings that you have stored up.
6. run out of steam (*informal*) To lose your energy or enthusiasm: *Pat ran out of steam before she finished painting the kitchen.*
steam (steem)
▷ *verb* **steaming, steamed**

steamboat

noun A boat powered by a steam engine. **steam·boat** (**steem**-boht)

steam engine

noun An engine that uses pressurized steam to drive pistons up and down in closed cylinders, which in turn creates the mechanical energy to move a ship, car, locomotive, or other vehicle forward.

steamer

noun
1. A boat powered by steam.
2. A pot or appliance used to cook foods with steam. **steam·er** (**stee**-mur)

steamroller

noun A heavy vehicle with a roller that is used to flatten road surfaces. **steam·roll·er** (**steem**-*roh*-lur)

steamship

noun A ship powered by a steam engine. **steam·ship** (**steem**-*ship*)

steel

1. *noun* A hard, strong metal made chiefly from iron and carbon, used in heavy construction.
2. *verb* To prepare oneself by becoming determined and hard, like steel: *I steeled myself for my parents' questions when I came home late.* ▷ *verb* **steeling, steeled**
steel (steel)
Steel sounds like **steal**.

steel wool

noun A mass of very fine threads of steel. Steel wool is used for cleaning, smoothing, and polishing things.

steep

1. *adjective* Having a sharp rise or slope, as in *a steep incline.* ▷ *adverb* **steeply**
2. *adjective* Very large or at a rapid rate: *There was a steep drop in attendance during the snowy months.*
3. *verb* To soak in a liquid for the purpose of cleaning, softening, or drawing the essence out of something, as in *to steep tea leaves.*
4. *verb* To be full of something: *Our family celebrations are steeped in tradition.*
5. *adjective* Very high, as in *steep cliffs.*
steep (steep)
▷ *adjective* **steeper, steepest**
▷ *verb* **steeping, steeped**

steeple

noun A high tower on a church or other building, often with a spire on top. **stee·ple** (**stee**-puhl)

steeple

a
b
c
d
e
f
g
h
i
j
k
l
m
n
o
p
q
r
s
t
u
v
w
x
y
z

steer

1. *verb* To make a vehicle go in a particular direction by using a wheel, rudder, or paddle: *She steered the boat into the harbor.*

2. *verb* To be guided: *This car steers easily.*

3. *verb* To guide or to direct: *The bodyguard steered the actor through the crowd of fans.*

4. *noun* A young male of the domestic cattle family, raised especially for its beef.
steer (steer)
▷ *verb* **steering, steered**

stegosaurus *noun* A dinosaur that fed on plants and had bony plates along its back, a small head, and a long tail with spikes. **steg·o·sau·rus** (*steg*-uh-**sor**-uhs)

stellar *adjective*

1. Associated with stars, as in *stellar dust.*

2. Outstanding and noticeably superior: *The company has a stellar reputation for putting its customers first.*
stel·lar (**stel**-ur)

Word History

Something described as **stellar** has the qualities of a star. *Stellar* became an English word in the 18th century. It is from the Latin word *stellaris,* meaning "starry," which comes from the Latin word for "star," *stella.* In English, outstanding leaders or performers have been called stars since the early 19th century. In the same way, we began to describe a person or thing that is especially good as stellar in the late 19th century.

stem

1. *noun* The main, upward-growing part of a plant from which the leaves and flowers grow; the stalk.

2. stem from *verb* To originate or come from: *The conflict stemmed from an argument that had taken place years ago.*

3. *verb* To stop or check the flow or progress of something, as in *to stem a flood.*
stem (stem)
▷ *verb* **stemming, stemmed**

STEM *noun* An educational program that prepares students to be competitive in science-related subjects. STEM is short for *science, technology, engineering, and math.* **STEM** (stem)

stem cell *noun* A cell in the body or in an embryo that can develop into different kinds of cells with special purposes.

stench *noun* An offensive odor, as in *the stench at the garbage dump.* **stench** (stench) ▷ *noun, plural* **stenches**

stencil

stencil *noun* A piece of paper, plastic, or metal with letters or a pattern cut out of it. Applying paint or ink over the holes transfers the design to a surface below. **sten·cil** (**sten**-suhl) ▷ *verb* **stencil**

step

1. *noun* One of the flat surfaces on a stairway where you put your foot: *There are 12 steps up to the second floor.*

2. steps *noun, plural* A set of stairs.

3. *verb* To move your foot forward and put it down in walking, climbing, or dancing. ▷ *verb* **stepping, stepped** ▷ *noun* **step**

4. *noun* The distance covered by a step: *We live just a few steps from the school.*

5. *noun* The sound of a footstep: *I heard rapid steps coming toward me.*

6. *noun* One of a series of actions taken to make or achieve something: *You can make brownies in three easy steps.*

7. *noun* The difference in pitch between notes in a musical scale. A half step is the difference between two adjacent keys on a piano, such as F and F sharp; a whole step is the difference between most of the notes in a major scale, such as between F and G.

8. step by step In a gradual and steady way: *We followed the directions step by step.*

9. watch your step Walk or act carefully: *Henry had better watch his step if he doesn't want to get Joe mad at him.*
step (step)
Step sounds like **steppe**.

stepbrother *noun* A person's **stepbrother** is that person's stepparent's son from a former marriage.
step·broth·er (**step**-*bruhTH*-ur)

stepchild *noun* A child that a person's husband or wife had by a former marriage. **step·child** (**step**-*childe*) ▷ *noun, plural* **stepchildren**

stepdaughter *noun* A female stepchild. **step·daugh·ter** (**step**-*daw*-tuhr)

stepfamily *noun* The family of your stepfather or stepmother. **step·fam·i·ly** (**step**-*fam*-uh-lee) ▷ *noun, plural* **stepfamilies**

stepfather *noun* The man who married a person's parent after the death or divorce of the person's father. **step·fa·ther** (**step**-*fah*-THur)

stepmother *noun* The woman who married a person's parent after the death or divorce of the person's mother. **step·moth·er** (**step**-*muhTH*-ur)

stepparent *noun* A stepfather or a stepmother. **step·par·ent** (**step**-*pair*-uhnt)

steppe *noun* Any of the wide, treeless plains found in southeastern Europe and Asia. **steppe** (step) **Steppe** sounds like **step**.

stepsister *noun* A person's **stepsister** is that person's stepparent's daughter from a former marriage. **step·sis·ter** (**step**-*sis*-tur)

stepson *noun* A male stepchild. **step·son** (**step**-*suhn*)

stereo *noun* A phonograph, radio, or other sound system that uses two or more channels of sound so that the listener hears sounds in a more natural way. **ste·re·o** (**ster**-ee-*oh*) ▷ *adjective* **stereo**

stereotype *noun* A widely held but overly simple idea, opinion, or image of a person, group, or thing: *It is a stereotype to say all old people are forgetful.* **ste·re·o·type** (**ster**-ee-oh-*tipe*) ▷ *verb* **stereotype** ▷ *adjective* **stereotypical** (*ster*-ee-oh-**tip**-i-kuhl)

sterile *adjective* Free from germs and dirt, as in *a sterile bandage.* **ster·ile** (**ster**-uhl)

sterilize *verb* To rid something of germs and dirt by exposing it to heat or chemicals: *You can sterilize baby bottles by boiling them in water.* **ster·i·lize** (**ster**-uh-*lize*) ▷ *verb* **sterilizing, sterilized** ▷ *noun* **sterilization** (*ster*-uh-li-**zay**-shuhn)

sterling *noun* The currency of the United Kingdom. **ster·ling** (**stur**-ling)

stern
1. *adjective* Strict or harsh, as in *a stern teacher* or *a stern lecture.* ▷ *adjective* **sterner, sternest**
2. *noun* The rear end of a ship or boat.
stern (sturn)

steroid *noun* A chemical substance found naturally in plants and animals, including humans. The use of steroids by athletes to improve their strength and performance is banned in most sports competitions. **ste·roid** (**ster**-oid)

stethoscope *noun* A medical instrument used by doctors and nurses to listen to the sounds from a patient's heart, lungs, and other parts of the body. **steth·o·scope** (**steth**-uh-*skope*)

Word History

In the 19th century, a French doctor wanted a way to listen to the chest sounds of his patients without putting his ear on their chests, so he invented the **stethoscope**. The doctor's name was René Théophile Hyacinthe Laënnec. His book about the new invention, and the different heart and lung sounds that doctors could hear through it, made him famous all over Europe. Laënnec based the name of his instrument, *stéthoscope*, on the ancient Greek words *stethos*, meaning "chest," and *skopein*, meaning "to look at."

stethoscope

stew
1. *noun* A dish made of meat or fish and vegetables, boiled or simmered slowly over a long period of time, as in *beef stew.*
2. *verb* To cook something for a long time over low heat: *Stew the chicken for an hour, then add potatoes.* ▷ *adjective* **stewed**
3. stew in your own juices To suffer as a result of your own actions.
4. *verb* To worry about something: *Rebecca stewed for days about whether or not she should go to the party.*
stew (stoo) ▷ *verb* **stewing, stewed**

steward *noun*
1. A man who serves passengers on an airplane or a ship.
2. A person who serves food and drink at a hotel, club, or restaurant, as in *a wine steward.*
stew·ard (**stoo**-urd)

stewardess *noun* A woman who serves passengers, especially on an airplane. **stew·ard·ess** (**stoo**-ur-dis) ▷ *noun, plural* **stewardesses**

stick
1. *noun* A long, thin piece of wood, especially one that has fallen off a tree.
2. *noun* Something shaped like a stick, as in *a stick of gum, a stick of dynamite,* or *carrot sticks.*
3. *verb* To fasten or attach one thing to another with something sticky, such as glue or tape: *I stuck the stamp on the envelope.*

4. *verb* To push a pointed object into or through something else: *I stuck my finger into the soup to see how hot it was.*

5. *verb* To remain attached, as if glued: *Peanut butter sticks to the roof of my mouth.*

6. *verb* To remain attached or become fixed in a particular position: *The porch door sticks; you'll have to push hard to open it.*

7. stick out *verb* To be prominent, often because the object is higher or longer than other things nearby: *The modern office building sticks out among the older houses on the street.*

8. stick up for *verb* (*informal*) To support or defend a person: *Melanie stuck up for her sister when the others accused her of stealing.*

9. stick to *verb* To continue doing or using something: *I'm going to stick to bottled water until the well clears up.*
stick (stik)
▷ *verb* **sticking, stuck** (stuhk)

sticker *noun* A paper or plastic label with glue on the back, as in *a parking sticker.* **stick·er** (**stik**-ur)

sticky

sticky *adjective*

1. Tending to stick to things when touched: *Yuck! Your hand is all sticky!*

2. Uncomfortably humid: *It feels too sticky outside for a walk.*

3. (*informal*) Likely to cause upset or hurt feelings, and so difficult to deal with: *Would you rather deal with a sticky situation via email, in a letter, on the telephone, or face-to-face?*
stick·y (**stik**-ee)
▷ *adjective* **stickier, stickiest**

stiff *adjective*

1. Difficult to bend, stretch, turn, or operate, as in *a stiff mechanism* or *stiff shoes.*

2. Difficult to move easily or without pain, as in *stiff legs.*

3. Not flowing easily; thick: *Beat the egg whites until they are stiff.*

4. Severe or difficult to deal with, as in *stiff competition* or *stiff punishment.*

5. Not natural or easy in manner; formal, as in *stiff conversation.*

6. Strong and steady; powerful, as in *a stiff wind.*
stiff (stif)
▷ *verb* **stiffen** ▷ *adjective* **stiffer, stiffest** ▷ *adverb* **stiffly**

stifle *verb*

1. To hold back or to stop, as in *to stifle a yawn* or *to stifle someone's creativity.*

2. To feel smothered because of a lack of fresh or cool air: *I'm stifling in this heat—can you open a window?*
sti·fle (**stye**-fuhl)
▷ *verb* **stifling, stifled** ▷ *adjective* **stifling**

stigma *noun*

1. A mark or sign of disgrace or embarrassment: *Frederick feels the stigma of dropping out of school before graduation.*

2. The tip of the pistil of a flower, where pollen is received.
stig·ma (**stig**-ma)
▷ *noun, plural* **stigmata** (stig-**mat**-uh) *or* **stigmas**

still

1. *adjective* Without sound; silent, as in *a still evening.*

2. *adjective* Without motion; quiet and calm, as in *a still lake.*

3. *noun* A state of quietness, as in *the still of the night.*

4. *verb* To calm or quiet, as in *to still a baby's cries.*

5. *adverb* Without moving, as in *to sit still.*

6. *adverb* Even now, or at a particular time: *Will you still be here tomorrow?*

7. *adverb* All the same; nevertheless: *You are late, but you may still participate.*

8. *adverb* Even; yet: *After three weeks of freezing weather, it became still colder.*
still (stil)
▷ *adjective* **stiller, stillest** ▷ *noun* **stillness**

stilt *noun*

1. One of two poles, each with a rest or strap for the foot, used to raise the wearer above the ground in walking.

2. One of the posts that holds a building, pier, or other structure above the ground or water level: *The beach house was built on stilts in case of high tides.*
stilt (stilt)

stimulant *noun* A substance that stimulates activity in a part of the body: *Coffee contains a stimulant.*
stim·u·lant (**stim**-yuh-luhnt) ▷ *adjective* **stimulant**

stimulate *verb*

1. To encourage something to grow, develop, or become more active: *Fertilizer stimulates the growth of plants.*

2. To make someone interested, excited, or enthusiastic: *The play stimulated us so much that we were up all night talking.*

stim·u·late (**stim**-yuh-*late*)
▷ *verb* **stimulating, stimulated** ▷ *noun* **stimulation**
▷ *adjective* **stimulating**

stimulus *noun*

1. Anything that excites or causes an action: *An electric shock is sometimes used as a stimulus in experiments.*

2. Something that causes or speeds up a reaction in a person, an animal, or a plant. Your eyes, ears, and nose receive stimuli from your surroundings.

stim·u·lus (**stim**-yuh-luhs)
▷ *noun, plural* **stimuli** (**stim**-yuh-*lye*)

sting

1. *verb* To pierce or wound with a small, sharp point: *Bees and wasps can sting you.*

2. *verb* To hurt with or as if with a sharp, pricking pain: *My eyes were stinging when I got out of the pool. That remark really stings.*

3. *noun* A stinger.

sting (sting)
▷ *verb* **stinging, stung** (stuhng) ▷ *noun* **sting**

stinger *noun* A sharp, pointed part of an insect or animal that can be used to sting. **sting·er** (**sting**-ur)

stingray *noun* A fish with a flat body; large, winglike fins; and a whiplike tail with poisonous spines that can cause a painful wound. **sting·ray** (**sting**-*ray*)

stingy *adjective* Not willing to give or spend money; not generous: *Fred is too stingy to buy his own snacks.* **stin·gy** (**stin**-jee) ▷ *adjective* **stingier, stingiest** ▷ *adverb* **stingily** (**stin**-juh-lee)

stink *verb*

1. To give off a strong, unpleasant smell: *That garbage can really stinks.* ▷ *noun* **stink**

2. *(slang)* To be very bad or worthless: *That idea stinks.*

stink (stingk)
▷ *verb* **stinking, stank** (stangk), **stunk** (stuhngk)
▷ *adjective* **stinky**

stir

1. *verb* To mix a liquid or soft substance thoroughly by moving a spoon or stick around and around in it, as in *to stir batter.*

2. *verb* To move slightly or to become active: *The air barely stirred. I was awake before anyone else was stirring.*

3. *verb* To excite or cause strong feelings in someone: *Her fiery speech stirred the crowd.*

4. *noun* A state of excitement or disturbance: *The new school uniforms caused quite a stir.*

stir (stur)
▷ *verb* **stirring, stirred**

stir-fry *verb* To fry food quickly over high heat in a lightly oiled pan or wok while stirring continuously, as in *to stir-fry vegetables.* ▷ *verb* **stir-fries, stir-frying, stir-fried**

stirrup *noun*

1. A ring or loop that hangs down from a saddle and holds a rider's foot.

2. One of the three small bones in the middle ear. It looks somewhat like a stirrup.

stir·rup (**stur**-uhp *or* **stir**-uhp)

Word History

Two Old English words, *stig*, which meant "a climbing up," and *rap*, or "rope," were used to make the word **stirrup**. At one time, a stirrup was a loop of rope that hung from a saddle.

stitch

1. *noun* A complete movement of a needle with thread on it, used in sewing and embroidery and to close wounds: *It will take just a few stitches to mend that tear.*

2. *noun* A loop of yarn produced in knitting or crocheting: *When I watch TV while knitting, I tend to drop stitches.*

3. *verb* To make stitches in sewing or knitting: *Susan stitched the sleeve onto the dress.*

4. *verb* To close up a wound with stitches: *The doctor stitched the cut in her forehead.*

5. *noun* A sudden, sharp pain in your side, usually caused by running: *The stitch in Al's side made him bend over double.*

stitch (stich)
▷ *verb* **stitches, stitching, stitched**
▷ *noun, plural* **stitches**

stock

1. *verb* To keep a supply of a product to sell: *That store doesn't stock my favorite shampoo anymore.*

2. *noun* The supply of merchandise or materials that a factory, warehouse, or store has to sell, as in *a truckload of new stock.*

3. *noun* Cattle, sheep, pigs, and other animals raised

stingray

on a ranch or farm; livestock: *The stock needs to be fed twice a day.*

4. *noun* Water in which meat, fish, or vegetables have been cooked slowly, as in *chicken stock.*

5. *noun* If you own **stock** in a company, you have invested money in it and own a part of the company: *Andrea purchased stock in a new computer company.*

6. *noun* Ancestors: *My family is from Irish stock.*

7. stock up *verb* To gather or store a large supply of something for sale or future use. **stock** (stahk)
▷ *verb* **stocking, stocked**

stockade *noun*

1. A fence or enclosure made of strong posts set firmly in the ground to protect against attacks.

2. A jail for people in the military. **stock·ade** (stah-**kade**)

stockbroker *noun* A person who buys and sells stocks and shares in companies on behalf of other people. **stock·bro·ker** (**stahk**-*broh*-kur)

stock car *noun* A car for racing, made from a regular model sold to the public.

stockholder *noun* A person who owns shares, or stock, in a company: *This company pays good dividends to its stockholders.* **stock·hold·er** (**stahk**-*hohl*-dur)

stocking *noun* A snug, knitted covering for the foot and leg, as in *silk stockings.* **stock·ing** (**stah**-king)

Word History

When you put on a **stocking**, you are covering your leg with a "stock." The main meaning of the word *stock* was "tree stump," and a *stock* was a covering for the legs, because without the main body, a person's legs would be like a "tree stump." Eventually, people divided the *stock* into two parts, upper and lower, and began to use the word *stock* just for the lower part. The upper stock became pants that ended at the knee, and the lower stock became the *stocking* that we know today.

stock market *or* **stock exchange** *noun* A place where stocks and shares in companies are bought and sold.

stockpile *verb* To gather a large supply of food or weapons in case you run out or face an emergency in the future: *The family stockpiled canned goods before the blizzard.* **stock·pile** (**stahk**-*pile*) ▷ *verb* **stockpiling, stockpiled** ▷ *noun* **stockpile**

stocks *noun, plural* A heavy wooden frame with holes for confining people by their ankles and sometimes wrists, used in the past to punish people publicly for minor offenses. **stocks** (stahks)

stocky *adjective* Having a short, sturdy build: *Ted is stocky, but his brother is tall and thin.* **stock·y** (**stah**-kee) ▷ *adjective* **stockier, stockiest**

stockyard *noun* An enclosed area where livestock is kept before being shipped or slaughtered. **stock·yard** (**stahk**-*yahrd*)

stole *verb* The past tense of **steal**. **stole** (stohl)

stolen

1. *verb* The past participle of **steal**.

2. *adjective* Taken away illegally from the owner, as in *a stolen car.* **stol·en** (**stoh**-luhn)

stomach

1. *noun* The muscular, pouchlike organ of your body where chewed food begins to be digested.

2. *noun* The front part of your body, between your chest and thighs, containing this organ; the belly or abdomen, as in *lying on your stomach.*

3. *verb* To accept or put up with something: *Caroline can't stomach cruelty to animals.* ▷ *verb* **stomaching, stomached** **stom·ach** (**stuhm**-uhk)

stomp *verb*

1. To walk heavily or loudly across a floor: *The tired skiers stomped in, covered with snow.*

2. To bang your foot down, especially in anger: *Adam stomped his foot and roared with fury.* **stomp** (stahmp) ▷ *verb* **stomping, stomped** ▷ *noun* **stomp**

stone

1. *noun* Naturally hardened mineral matter that is found in the earth; rock. ▷ *adjective* **stony**

2. *noun* A small piece of this material, as in *to throw stones.*

3. *verb* To hit with stones: *In the old days, people were stoned for committing crimes.* ▷ *verb* **stoning, stoned**

4. *noun* A valuable jewel or gem, as in *precious stones.*

5. *noun* The hard covering that encloses the seed in the middle of certain fruits, as in *cherry stones.* **stone** (stone)

stock market

Stone Age

Prehistoric humans probably used stones as simple tools for a broad period of time. By 9000 B.C., people had already begun to make tools out of such materials as wood and bone. They skinned animals with stone scrapers, which they chipped to create a sharp edge. To make their weapons more deadly, they chiseled arrowheads out of flint or other hard rocks. This era is called the New Stone Age, or Neolithic Period.

arrowheads

Stone Age *noun* A period in history when stone was commonly used to make tools and weapons. Different parts of the world experienced a Stone Age at different times.

stood *verb* The past tense and the past participle of **stand**. **stood** (stud)

stool *noun* A seat without a back or arms: *Several tall stools were lined up at the counter.* **stool** (stool)

stoop

1. *verb* To bend forward and down, often with the knees bent: *Ben stooped to pick up the book he had dropped.*

2. *verb* To carry your head and shoulders, or the upper part of your body, bent forward all the time: *She stooped to avoid hitting her head on the low door frame.*

3. *verb* To lower yourself to do something; to condescend or degrade yourself: *Don't stoop to his level if he starts an argument.*

4. *noun* A small porch with steps outside a doorway, as in *the front stoop.*

stoop (stoop)

▷ *verb* **stooping, stooped** ▷ *noun* **stoop**

stop

1. *verb* To come or bring something to an end: *You could stop this fight right now. The rain finally stopped.*

2. *verb* To prevent something from moving, continuing, or operating, as in *to stop people from fighting* or *to stop a car.*

3. *verb* To be no longer moving or operating: *My watch stopped two days ago.*

4. *verb* To close up or block an opening: *Hair stopped up the bathtub drain.*

5. *noun* The act of stopping, as in *a sudden stop.*

6. *noun* One of the regular places on a route where someone or something pauses, such as the place where a bus or train picks up and drops off passengers: *My bus stop is right in front of the park.*

7. *noun* A brief stay or visit: *We made a stop at the Grand Canyon.*

stop (stahp)

▷ *verb* **stopping, stopped**

Synonyms

Stop, the opposite of the word *start*, means to keep something from continuing or to bring an action to an end: *I wish my brother would stop bothering me! Ms. Morales stopped the car when she saw the dog run into the street.*

- -

■ **Cease** means to bring something to an end, usually with the idea that it will not start again: *The rioting ceased after the mayor appealed for calm.*

■ **Discontinue** means to give up or stop something that has been going on for a while: *The artist will discontinue issuing her music on CDs because most people now stream her music online.*

■ **Quit** means to stop or leave, often suddenly or for good: *Carolyn quit her job to go back to college.*

■ **Halt** means to stop some kind of movement, such as marching or traveling: *The police halted traffic so the ambulance could zoom up the street.*

stoplight *noun*

1. Another word for **traffic light**.

2. A light on the rear part of a motor vehicle that comes on when the driver steps on the brakes. **stop·light** (**stahp**-*lite*)

stopper *noun* Something that fits into the top of a container to keep the contents from escaping: *Phil pulled the stopper and poured soda for everyone.* **stop·per** (**stah**-pur)

stopwatch *noun* A watch that you can start and stop with buttons to see how long something takes. **stop·watch** (**stahp**-*wahch*)

storage *noun*

1. Space where you can keep something that you are not using: *We've got a lot of extra storage in the loft of the garage.*

2. in storage Put away until it is needed: *Our camping equipment is in storage for the winter.*

3. storage device A disk, tape, or drive that can be used to store computer files. **stor·age** (**stor**-ij)

store

1. *noun* A place where things are sold, as in *a grocery store, a toy store,* or *a department store.*

2. *noun* A supply or stock of something kept for future use, as in *a store of wood* or *a store of weapons.*

3. *verb* To put things away for future use, as in *to store food in a cupboard.*

4. *verb* To copy data into the memory of a computer or onto a floppy disk or other storage device, as in *to store files on a disk.* **store** (stor)

▷ *verb* **storing, stored**

storekeeper *noun* A person who owns or runs a store. **store·keep·er** (**stor**-*kee*-pur)

stork *noun* A large wading bird with long, thin legs; a long neck; and a long, straight bill. **stork** (stork)

storm

1. *noun* Heavy rain, snow, sleet, or hail accompanied by strong winds. Some storms also can have thunder and lightning: *We had to cancel our picnic because of the storm.* ▷ *verb* **storm**

2. *noun* A sudden, strong outburst, as in *a storm of applause* or *a storm of protest.*

3. *verb* To attack suddenly or violently, as in *to storm a fort.*

4. storm out *verb* To leave a place angrily or violently. **storm** (storm)

▷ *verb* **storming, stormed**

storm surge *noun* An extremely tall mound of water that sweeps across the coastline near the area where a hurricane passes or makes landfall. The term *storm surge* refers to the amount of water over and above the water from the tides: *Meteorologists are expecting the storm surge to reach up to 45 feet high as it hits the Jersey Shore.* **storm surge** (**storm** *surj*)

stormy *adjective* **Stormy** weather is weather that is turbulent, with strong winds and frequent periods of rain or snow, sometimes with thunder and lightning. **storm·y** (**stor**-mee) ▷ *adjective* **stormier, stormiest**

story *noun*

1. A spoken or written account of something that happened, as in *a news story* or *the story of the first Thanksgiving.*

2. A tale made up to entertain people, as in *a science fiction story.*

3. A lie: *Stop telling stories about me.*

4. A floor or level of a building: *Karen's apartment building is ten stories high.* **sto·ry** (**stor**-ee)

▷ *noun, plural* **stories**

stout *adjective*

1. Quite fat; large and heavily built: *Santa Claus is short and stout.*

2. Strong and sturdy, as in *a stout pair of boots.*

3. Brave or determined, as in *a stout heart.* **stout** (stout)

▷ *adjective* **stouter, stoutest**

stove *noun* A piece of equipment used for cooking or heating, fueled by gas, electricity, wood, or oil, as in *a kitchen stove.* **stove** (stohv)

stow *verb* To put away or to store, as in *to stow your gear* or *to stow trunks in the attic.* **stow** (stoh)

▷ *verb* **stowing, stowed** ▷ *noun* **stowage** (**stoh**-ij)

stowaway

stowaway *noun* A person who secretly boards a plane, ship, or other vehicle to avoid paying a fare or to escape unnoticed. **stow·a·way** (**stoh**-uh-*way*)

▷ *verb* **stow away**

straddle *verb*

1. To sit with one leg on each side of something: *She jumped up on the horse, straddling it easily, and rode away.*

2. To be on or touching both sides of something: *The bridge straddles the canal that divides Cape Cod from mainland Massachusetts.*

3. To include or involve more than one quality or feature: *The house is designed to straddle the divide between 19th-century and modern architecture, using elements of both styles.* **strad·dle** (**strad**-uhl)

▷ *verb* **straddling, straddled**

a b c d e f g h i j k l m n o p q r **s** t u v w x y z

straggle *verb* To trail slowly behind a group of people; to wander or stray: *The slower walkers straggled behind the rest of the group.* **strag·gle** (**strag**-uhl) ▷ *verb* **straggling, straggled** ▷ *noun* **straggler**

straight

1. *adjective* Without a curve or bend, as in *a straight line.*

2. *adjective* Not curly or wavy, as in *straight hair.*

3. *adjective* Not crooked or stooping, as in *straight posture.*

4. *adjective* Level or even, as in *a straight hem.*

5. *adjective* Honest, sincere, or correct, as in *a straight answer.*

6. *adjective* A **straight** person is attracted to people of the opposite sex.

7. *adverb* Immediately or directly: *Go straight home after school.*

straight (strayt)

Straight sounds like **strait**. ▷ *adjective* **straighter, straightest** ▷ *adverb* **straight**

straightaway *noun* A section of a road or racetrack that doesn't curve: *The driver sped up as he reached the straightaway.* **straight·a·way** (**strayt**-uh-**way**)

straighten *verb*

1. If you **straighten** something **out** or **up**, you put it in the proper order: *Anything you can do to help straighten out this situation would be greatly appreciated.*

2. To make something straight or to become straight. **straight·en** (**stray**-tuhn) ▷ *verb* **straightening, straightened**

straightforward *adjective*

1. Honest and open, as in *a straightforward answer.*

2. Easy to understand, as in *straightforward instructions.* **straight·for·ward** (*strayt*-**for**-wurd)

strain

1. *verb* To draw or pull tight; to stretch, as in *to strain at the leash.*

2. *noun* A state of tension or exhaustion: *Melissa has been under a terrible strain since her mother got sick.*

3. *verb* To pour a mostly liquid substance through a sieve or colander to separate out the solid pieces, as in *to strain orange juice.* ▷ *noun* **strainer**

4. *verb* To injure a muscle by making it work too hard, as in *to strain your back.*

5. *verb* To make as much of an effort as you possibly can to do something: *We strained to hear what was going on in the next room.* **strain** (strayn) ▷ *verb* **straining, strained** ▷ *adjective* **strained**

strait *noun*

1. A narrow strip of water that connects two larger bodies of water.

2. dire straits *noun, plural* A very difficult situation. **strait** (strayt)

Strait sounds like **straight**.

strand

1. *noun* One of the lengths of thread or wire that are twisted together to form a rope, string, or cable.

2. *noun* Something that looks like a thread, as in *a strand of hair* or *a strand of spaghetti.*

3. *noun* Something made up of objects strung or twisted together, as in *a strand of pearls.*

4. *verb* To force onto the shore; to drive onto a beach, reef, or sandbar: *The storm stranded several whales.*

5. *verb* To leave in a strange or unpleasant place, especially without any money or way to depart: *When our car broke down, we were stranded in the middle of a wasteland.* **strand** (strand) ▷ *verb* **stranding, stranded**

strange *adjective*

1. Different from the usual; odd or peculiar, as in *a strange noise.*

2. Not known, heard, or seen before; not familiar, as in *a strange voice.*

3. Ill at ease; not comfortable: *I felt strange wearing pajamas during the daytime.* **strange** (straynj) ▷ *adjective* **stranger, strangest** ▷ *noun* **strangeness** ▷ *adverb* **strangely**

stranger *noun*

1. Someone you do not recognize and have never met: *A stranger stood on the sidewalk.*

2. A newcomer or an outsider: *He was a stranger to American customs.* **strang·er** (**strayn**-jur)

strangle *verb*

1. To kill someone by squeezing the person's throat and cutting off his or her air supply: *The movie was about a criminal who strangled people.*

2. To be unable to breathe; to choke: *The firefighters strangled in the smoky building.* **stran·gle** (**strang**-guhl) ▷ *verb* **strangling, strangled** ▷ *noun* **strangler** ▷ *noun* **strangulation** (*strang*-gyuh-**lay**-shuhn)

strap

1. *noun* A strip of leather or some other flexible material used to fasten, carry, or hold on to someone or something: *Ernie fastened the boards together with a strap.*

strands of hair

2. *verb* To use a strap to fasten or to hold things in place: *We strapped the luggage onto the roof of the car.* ▷ *verb* **strapping, strapped**
strap (strap)

strategy *noun* A clever plan for winning a military battle or achieving a goal, as in *a game strategy.* **strat·e·gy** (**strat**-i-jee) ▷ *noun, plural* **strategies** ▷ *noun* **strategist** ▷ *adjective* **strategic** (struh-**tee**-jik) ▷ *adverb* **strategically**

Word History

When a new man assumed command as general in an ancient Greek army, he now held the *strategia,* meaning "the position of general." The word came from *stratos,* meaning "army," and *agein,* meaning "to lead." So the word **strategy** in English originally had only a military meaning.

stratosphere *noun* The layer of the earth's atmosphere that begins about 8 miles above the earth and ends about 31 miles above the earth. **strat·o·sphere** (**strat**-uh-*sfeer*)

straw *noun*
1. The dried stalks of wheat, barley, oats, or other cereal plants that are left after the grain has been removed.
2. A thin, hollow plastic or paper tube used to suck liquid from a container.
straw (straw)

strawberry *noun* The red, juicy fruit of a small, low plant of the rose family. **straw·ber·ry** (**straw**-ber-ee) ▷ *noun, plural* **strawberries**

stray
1. *verb* To wander off without a destination; to become lost, as in *to stray from a path.* ▷ *verb* **straying, strayed** ▷ *adjective* **stray**
2. *noun* A cat or dog that has wandered away from its home or that has no home.
stray (stray)

streak
1. *noun* A long, thin mark or stripe, as in *a streak of gray hair* or *a streak of lightning.* ▷ *adjective* **streaky**
2. *noun* A character trait, as in *a mean streak.*
3. *noun* A small series of events, as in *a winning streak.*
4. *verb* To move very fast: *The car streaked by so fast that we couldn't tell who was driving.* ▷ *verb* **streaking, streaked**
streak (streek)

stream
1. *noun* A body of flowing water, especially a brook or a small river.

streetcar

2. *noun* A steady flow of anything, as in *a stream of cars* or *a stream of light.*
3. *verb* To move or flow steadily: *Fans streamed out of the stadium.*
4. *verb* To float or to wave in the wind: *The flag streamed in the breeze.*
5. *verb* To watch or listen to video or music at the same time that it is being downloaded to your computer.
stream (streem) ▷ *verb* **streaming, streamed**

streamer *noun* A long, thin strip of cloth, ribbon, or colored paper used as a decoration: *We draped streamers from the corners of the room to the chandelier in the center.* **stream·er** (**stree**-mur)

streamlined *adjective*
1. Designed or shaped to minimize resistance to air or water, as in *a streamlined ship.*
2. Made simpler or more efficient, as in *a streamlined checkout lane.*
stream·lined (**streem**-*lined*)

street *noun*
1. A road in a city or town, often with sidewalks, houses, or other buildings along it.
2. Everyone who lives or works on a street: *The whole street heard about the new neighbors.*
street (street)

streetcar *noun* An electricity-powered vehicle that holds many passengers and runs on rails through city streets; a trolley. **street·car** (**street**-*kahr*)

streetlight *noun* A light mounted on a pole by the side of a street to help drivers and pedestrians see at night. **street·light** (**street**-*lite*)

strawberry

streetwise *adjective* Having the skills and experience needed to survive in a difficult or dangerous, usually urban, environment. **street·wise** (**street**-*wize*)

strength *noun*
1. The quality of being strong; force; power: *I'm building up my strength by lifting weights.*
2. The power to resist or hold up under strain or stress; toughness: *Test the strength of the rope before you climb it.*
3. A good quality or something at which you excel: *Jackie's strength is her ability to solve problems.* **strength** (strengkth *or* strength)

strengthen *verb* To make stronger: *They worked long hours to strengthen the dike against the rising flood waters.* **strength·en** (**streng**-thuhn) ▷ *verb* **strengthening, strengthened**

strenuous *adjective*
1. Requiring great energy or effort, as in *strenuous exercise.*
2. Very active or energetic, as in *strenuous opposition.* **stren·u·ous** (**stren**-yoo-uhs) ▷ *adverb* **strenuously**

stress
1. *noun* Mental or emotional strain or pressure: *My dad is under a lot of stress at work.* ▷ *noun, plural* **stresses** ▷ *adjective* **stressful**
2. *verb* To emphasize one or more syllables within a word.
3. *verb* To emphasize something because you think it's important: *Our doctor stresses good eating habits.* **stress** (stres) ▷ *verb* **stresses, stressing, stressed** ▷ *noun* **stress**

stretch
1. *verb* To spread out your arms, legs, or body to full length: *I always stretch when I first wake up.*
2. *verb* To extend or spread out over an area: *The oil spill stretches for miles along the coast.*
3. *verb* To make something reach or extend farther: *We shop carefully so we can stretch our dollars.*
4. *noun* (*slang*) An unbroken period of time: *We've had a long stretch of good weather.*
5. *noun* An unbroken length or distance, as in *a stretch of highway.*
6. stretch out *verb* To lie fully extended: *Cal stretched out on the sofa.* **stretch** (strech) ▷ *verb* **stretches, stretching, stretched** ▷ *noun* **stretch** ▷ *noun, plural* **stretches**

stretcher *noun* A piece of canvas attached to two poles, used for carrying an injured or sick person. **stretch·er** (**strech**-ur)

strict *adjective*
1. Demanding that the rules be followed exactly, as in *a strict teacher.*
2. Enforced all the time, as in *a strict rule.*
3. Complete or absolute, as in *strict concentration.* **strict** (strikt) ▷ *adjective* **stricter, strictest** ▷ *noun* **strictness** ▷ *adverb* **strictly**

stride *verb* To take long, energetic steps, as in *to stride down a hallway.* **stride** (stride) ▷ *verb* **striding, strode** (strode), **stridden** (**strid**-uhn) ▷ *noun* **stride**

strife *noun* A bitter conflict between enemies; a fight or a struggle: *The strife between the two countries eventually led to war.* **strife** (strife)

strike
1. *verb* To hit or attack suddenly and forcefully: *The branch struck the side of the house.*
2. *verb* To announce the time with a chime or other sound: *The clock strikes on the hour.*
3. *verb* To make an impression on someone or to seem to be something: *She didn't strike me as the courageous type.*
4. *verb* To find or discover suddenly, as in *to strike gold.*
5. *verb* To light a match by rubbing it quickly and forcefully against something rough.
6. *verb* To refuse to go to work until an employer meets certain demands: *The workers are striking for shorter hours.* ▷ *noun* **striker**
7. *noun* A situation in which workers refuse to work until their demands are met.
8. *noun* In baseball, a ball pitched over the plate between the batter's chest and knees, or any pitch that is swung at and missed.
9. *noun* In bowling, the act of knocking down all ten pins with the first ball. **strike** (strike) ▷ *verb* **striking, struck** (struhk), **stricken**

striking *adjective* Attracting attention or notice: *My grandmother looks very striking in her new dress.* **strik·ing** (**strye**-king) ▷ *adverb* **strikingly**

string
1. *noun* A thin cord or rope made of twisted fiber.
2. *noun* A thin cord of wire, gut, or nylon on a musical instrument such as a guitar or violin. ▷ *verb* **string** ▷ *adjective* **stringed**

stretch

3. *verb* To run a cord, thread, or piece of wire through a row of objects, as in *to string beads.* ▷ *verb* **stringing, strung** (struhng)

4. *noun* A number of things of the same or similar kind all in a row, as in *a string of thefts.*

5. strung out *adjective* Very tense or nervous about something: *I was so strung out before the exam that I couldn't sleep.*
string (string)

strip
1. *verb* To take off clothing; to undress.
2. *verb* To pull, tear, or take something off, as in *to strip wallpaper.*
3. *noun* A long, narrow piece of something, as in *a strip of paper* or *a strip of land.*
strip (strip)
▷ *verb* **stripping, stripped**

stripe *noun* A narrow band of color, as in *red and white stripes.* **stripe** (stripe) ▷ *verb* **stripe**
▷ *adjective* **striped**

strive *verb* To try very hard to achieve or prevent something, as in *to strive for perfection.* **strive** (strive)
▷ *verb* **striving, strove** (strohv), **striven** (striv-in)

strobe *noun* A device that produces very brief, high-intensity flashes of light. **strobe** (strohb)

stroke
1. *verb* To draw your hand gently over the surface of something, as in *to stroke a cat.* ▷ *verb* **stroking, stroked** ▷ *noun* **stroke**
2. *noun* An unexpected action or event that has a powerful effect, as in *a stroke of lightning* or *a stroke of good luck.*
3. *noun* A hit or a blow, as in *the stroke of an ax.*
4. *noun* A mark made by a pen, pencil, or brush: *Ruth drew a face with a few quick pencil strokes.*
5. *noun* A sudden lack of oxygen in part of the brain caused by the blocking or breaking of a blood vessel.
6. *noun* One of a series of repeated movements in swimming or rowing, or a method of hitting the ball in tennis.
stroke (strohk)

stroll *noun* A slow, relaxed walk, as in *a stroll through the park.* **stroll** (strohl) ▷ *verb* **stroll**

stroller *noun* A small, folding carriage for a baby or small child to sit in and be pushed around, as in *a collapsible stroller.* **strol·ler** (stroh-lur)

strong *adjective*
1. Physically powerful or exerting great force, as in *strong arms* or *a strong wind.*
2. Tough, firm, long-lasting, or hard to break, as in *a strong rope* or *strong beliefs.*
3. Having a sharp or bitter taste or odor, as in *a strong cheese* or *a strong smell.*

strong (strawng)
▷ *adjective* **stronger, strongest** ▷ *adverb* **strongly**

stronghold *noun* A place that is well protected against attack or danger: *Their stronghold was a former castle, surrounded by walls and a moat.* **strong·hold** (strawng-hohld)

structure *noun*
1. Something that has been built, such as a house, an office building, a bridge, or a dam.
2. How something is arranged, organized, or put together, as in *the structure of government* or *the structure of a cell.*
struc·ture (struhk-chur)
▷ *verb* **structure** ▷ *adjective* **structural**

struggle *verb*
1. To try very hard or make a great effort to do something: *George struggled to learn the capitals of all 50 states.*
2. To fight or compete with someone, as in *to struggle against an opponent.*
3. To fight against a problem or difficulty, as in *to struggle with dyslexia.*
strug·gle (struhg-uhl)
▷ *verb* **struggling, struggled** ▷ *noun* **struggle**

strum *verb* To play a musical instrument such as a guitar or harp by sweeping your thumb or fingers over the strings. **strum** (struhm) ▷ *verb* **strumming, strummed** ▷ *noun* **strum**

strut
1. *verb* To walk with a swagger or in a proud way.
▷ *verb* **strutting, strutted** ▷ *noun* **strut**
2. *noun* A wooden or metal bar designed to brace or stabilize a structure.
strut (struht)

stub
1. *noun* A short part of something that remains after the rest has been used or torn off, as in *a pencil stub* or *a check stub.* ▷ *adjective* **stubby**
2. *verb* To accidentally hit something with your toe or foot: *I stubbed my toe on the leg of the table.* ▷ *verb* **stubbing, stubbed**
stub (stuhb)

ticket stub

stubble *noun*
1. Short, spiky stalks of corn or grain that are left in the ground after harvesting.
2. The short, stiff hairs that grow on a man's face when he has not shaved for a while.
stub·ble (stuhb-uhl)
▷ *adjective* **stubbly**

stubborn *adjective*

1. Not willing to give in or change; set on having your own way: *I was too stubborn to admit that I was wrong.*

2. Hard to treat or deal with, as in *a stubborn cold.*

stub·born (**stuhb**-urn)

▷ *noun* **stubbornness** ▷ *adverb* **stubbornly**

stuck

1. *verb* The past tense and the past participle of **stick.**

2. *adjective* Firmly fixed in a position and not able to move or be moved: *The driver had to swerve into a ditch, and now his car is stuck there.*

3. *adjective* If you are **stuck in** a place, you are not able to leave it: *We got stuck in Denver on the way to Phoenix because of the blizzard.*

4. *adjective* If you are **stuck with** something or someone, you are not able to get rid of it or of him or her: *It's nice outside, but I'm stuck with chores today.*

stuck (stuhk)

student *noun*

1. A person who studies at a school, as in *an elementary school student.*

2. A person who studies or observes something on his or her own, as in *a student of human nature.*

stu·dent (**stoo**-duhnt)

studio *noun*

1. A room or building in which an artist, dancer, or photographer works or practices, as in *a painter's studio.*

2. A place where movies, television and radio shows, or recordings are made.

3. A place that transmits radio or television programs.

4. A one-room apartment.

stu·di·o (**stoo**-dee-*oh*)

studio

studious *adjective* Liking or tending to study very hard. **stu·di·ous** (**stoo**-dee-uhs) ▷ *noun* **studiousness** ▷ *adverb* **studiously**

study

1. *verb* To spend time learning a subject or skill by reading about it or by practicing it, as in *to study medicine.*

2. *noun* A room used for studying or reading. ▷ *noun, plural* **studies**

3. *verb* To look at something closely, as in *to study a map.* ▷ *noun* **study**

stud·y (**stuhd**-ee)

▷ *verb* **studies, studying, studied**

stuff

1. *noun* The substance, material, or ingredients out of which something is made: *What kind of stuff did you put in this stew?*

2. *noun* Personal belongings: *I put my stuff in my schoolbag.*

3. *noun* Useless or worthless things; junk: *The garage is full of old stuff.*

4. *verb* To cram something into a container; to fill a space tightly: *James stuffed a suitcase with his belongings.*

5. *verb* To fill the inside of something, as in *to stuff a turkey.*

6. *verb* To fill yourself with too much food.

7. **stuffed up** *adjective* Having a blocked nose because of a cold or an allergy.

stuff (stuhf)

▷ *verb* **stuffing, stuffed**

stuffing *noun*

1. Soft material used to fill pillows, cushions, and other articles made of or covered with cloth.

2. A mixture of chopped food that is cooked inside poultry or meat or a hollowed-out vegetable, as in *turkey stuffing.*

stuff·ing (**stuhf**-ing)

stuffy *adjective*

1. Hard to breathe in because it lacks fresh air, as in *a stuffy room.*

2. Dull, old-fashioned, and narrow-minded, as in *a stuffy lecturer.*

stuf·fy (**stuhf**-ee)

▷ *adjective* **stuffier, stuffiest** ▷ *noun* **stuffiness** ▷ *adverb* **stuffily**

stumble *verb*

1. To trip and lose your balance briefly; to walk unsteadily, as in *to stumble over a crack.*

2. To speak or act in a blundering or confused way: *Gwen stumbled when she read the poem aloud to the class.*

3. **stumble on** *or* **stumble upon** To come upon or discover something unexpectedly: *We stumbled on a valuable baseball card while cleaning out the attic.*

stum·ble (**stuhm**-buhl)

▷ *verb* **stumbling, stumbled**

tree stumps

stump

1. *noun* The part of a tree trunk that is left in the ground after a tree has been cut down.

2. *noun* A piece of something that remains after the rest of it has broken off or worn away, as in *a pencil stump.*

3. *verb (informal)* To puzzle or to confuse: *The math problem completely stumped me.* ▷ *verb* **stumping, stumped**

stump (stuhmp)

stun *verb* To shock, overwhelm, or knock unconscious: *We were stunned when we heard about the accident.* **stun** (stuhn) ▷ *verb* **stunning, stunned**

stung *verb* The past tense and the past participle of **sting.** **stung** (stuhng)

stunk *verb* The past participle of **stink.** **stunk** (stuhngk)

stunning *adjective*

1. *(informal)* Extremely beautiful or attractive, as in *a stunning gown.*

2. Amazing or remarkable, as in *a stunning victory.*

3. Hard enough to knock you out, as in *a stunning blow.*

stun·ning (**stuhn**-ing)
▷ *adverb* **stunningly**

stunt

1. *noun* An act that shows great skill or daring: *Joining hands as they fell was the skydivers' favorite stunt.*

2. *noun* Something that is done to show off or attract attention: *Henry's skateboard stunt drew looks from everyone.*

3. *verb* To stop the growth or development of something: *Not eating enough protein can stunt your growth.* ▷ *verb* **stunting, stunted** ▷ *adjective* **stunted**

4. stunt person *noun* A person who takes the place of an actress or actor in an action scene or when a special skill or great risk is involved. Also called a *stunt man, stunt woman,* or *stunt double.*

stunt (stuhnt)

stupid *adjective*

1. Slow to learn or understand; not intelligent: *It's never OK to call someone stupid.*

2. Lacking common sense; foolish or silly, as in *a stupid risk.*

stu·pid (**stoo**-pid)
▷ *adjective* **stupider, stupidest** ▷ *noun* **stupidity** (stoo-**pid**-i-tee) ▷ *adverb* **stupidly**

sturdy *adjective* Strong and solidly made or built, as in *a sturdy ladder* or *a sturdy build.* **stur·dy** (**stur**-dee) ▷ *adjective* **sturdier, sturdiest**

sturgeon *noun* A large food fish covered with rows of bony, pointed scales. Its eggs, called caviar, are also eaten. **stur·geon** (**stur**-juhn)

stutter *verb* To involuntarily repeat the first sound or syllable of a word before saying the whole word. **stut·ter** (**stuht**-ur) ▷ *verb* **stuttering, stuttered** ▷ *noun* **stutter** ▷ *noun* **stutterer**

sty *noun*

1. A pen or enclosed area where pigs live. ▷ *noun, plural* **sties**

2. A small, inflamed swelling on the rim of an eyelid. ▷ *noun, plural* **sties** *or* **styes**

sty (stye)

style

1. *noun* The way in which something is written, spoken, made, or done, as in *a literary style* or *a modern style.*

2. *noun* The way in which people act and dress in a particular time period, especially the most recent one; fashion: *She was dressed in the latest style.*

3. *noun* An elegant manner: *The French actor delivered his lines with style.*

4. *verb* To arrange or design something in a particular way, as in *to style hair.* ▷ *verb* **styling, styled** ▷ *noun* **style** ▷ *noun* **stylist**

5. *noun* The slender structure that joins the ovary of a flower to the stigma.

style (stile)

stylish *adjective* Displaying the latest style; fashionable, as in *a stylish outfit.* **sty·lish** (**stye**-lish) ▷ *adverb* **stylishly**

stylus *noun* A small stick that you use like a pen to input data to some devices. **sty·lus** (**stye**-luhs)

stymie *verb* To stop, slow down, or get in the way of the progress of someone or something: *The lack of money stymied the researchers' efforts to find a cure.* **sty·mie** (**stye**-mee) ▷ *verb* **stymieing, stymied**

Synonyms

Stymie To prevent or postpone something because of an obstacle: *The continuing bad weather stymied the relief efforts for flood victims.*

- -

■ **Impede** means to slow down the progress or success of something: *The poor soil results in bad root systems which impede the growth of the plants.*

■ **Hamper** means to hold back or interfere with a process or activity: *The rapid population growth is hampering the ability to bring electricity to new areas of the country.*

■ **Hinder** means to cause a delay or difficulty: *Joint pain in older people often hinders their movements.*

■ **Thwart** means to prevent from happening or succeeding: *A quick-thinking customer thwarted the robbery by tackling the suspect.*

Styrofoam *noun* The trademark for a very lightweight, rigid plastic that is used in many items, from building insulation to drinking cups. **Sty·ro·foam** (**stye**-ruh-*fohm*)

suave *adjective* Pleasant, charming, and attractive: *The fictional British spy James Bond is known for his suave, sophisticated manner.* **suave** (swahv) ▷ *adjective* **suaver, suavest**

subconscious *noun* The part of the mind where hidden thoughts are, as well as feelings of which you are not aware. **sub·con·scious** (suhb-**kahn**-shuhs) ▷ *adjective* **subconscious** ▷ *adverb* **subconsciously**

Styrofoam cups

subdivide *verb*
1. To divide something that has already been divided into even smaller parts, as in *to subdivide a room.*
2. To divide an area of land into lots for building homes: *The real-estate developer planned to subdivide the large field into home lots.*
sub·di·vide (*suhb*-duh-**vide**)
▷ *verb* **subdividing, subdivided** ▷ *noun* **subdivision** (**suhb**-duh-*vizh*-uhn)

subdue *verb*
1. To defeat in battle; to conquer: *The tribe was completely subdued by invaders from the east.*
2. To control, as in *to subdue your anger.*
sub·due (suhb-**doo**)
▷ *verb* **subduing, subdued**

subdued *adjective*
1. Unusually quiet and thoughtful: *Nicole seemed subdued after her outburst.*
2. Not harsh; muted, as in *subdued colors.*
sub·dued (suhb-**dood**)

subject
1. (**suhb**-jikt) *noun* The person or thing that is discussed, studied, dealt with, or written about, as in *the subject of the conversation.*
2. (**suhb**-jikt) *noun* An area of study in a school or college.
3. (**suhb**-jikt) *noun* A word or group of words in a sentence that tells who or what performs the action expressed by the verb. In the sentence "John likes milk," *John* is the subject.
4. (**suhb**-jikt) *noun* A person or thing that is studied or examined: *Scientists often use mice as subjects when they do experiments.*
5. (**suhb**-jikt) *noun* A person who lives in a kingdom or under the authority of a king or queen.
6. (**suhb**-jikt) **subject to** *adjective* Having a tendency to be affected by something, especially if it is something unpleasant: *I am subject to allergies.*
7. (suhb-**jekt**) *verb* To force someone to go through an unpleasant experience: *We were subjected to the noise of a jackhammer for several hours.* ▷ *verb* **subjecting, subjected**
sub·ject

subjective *adjective* Of or having to do with your feelings, tastes, or opinions rather than with facts, as in *a subjective report.* **sub·jec·tive** (suhb-**jek**-tiv) ▷ *adverb* **subjectively**

sublime *adjective* Extremely beautiful or magnificent in a way that makes you feel wonder and awe, as in *a sublime singing voice* or *sublime mountain scenery.* **sub·lime** (suh-**blime**) ▷ *noun* **sublimeness** *or* **sublimity** (suh-**blim**-uh-tee) ▷ *adverb* **sublimely**

submarine *noun* A ship that can travel both on the surface and under the water. **sub·ma·rine** (**suhb**-muh-*reen* or *suhb*-muh-**reen**)

submerge *verb*

1. To sink or plunge beneath the surface of a liquid, especially water: *I submerged my hands in soapy water.*

2. To cover with water or another liquid: *The flood submerged most of the town.*

sub·merge (suhb-**murj**)

▷ *verb* **submerging, submerged**

submission *noun*

1. Acceptance of or giving in to the will or authority of someone or something: *When the queen appeared, he bowed as a mark of respect and submission.*

2. A proposal, application, or some other document that is submitted for consideration or judgment: *I sent in my submission to the school literary magazine last week.*

sub·mis·sion (suhb-**mish**-uhn)

submit *verb*

1. To propose, offer, hand in, or present something, as in *to submit a contest entry.*

2. To give in to or to agree to obey someone or something, as in *to submit to a decision.*

sub·mit (suhb-**mit**)

▷ *verb* **submitting, submitted**

subordinate

1. *adjective* Less important; lower in rank: *Sergeants are subordinate to captains.*

2. *noun* A person who is under the authority or control of someone else and can therefore be told what to do: *The president of the company asked one of her subordinates to open the mail.* ▷ *verb*

subordinate (suh-**bor**-duh-*nate*)

sub·or·di·nate (suh-**bor**-duh-nit)

subscribe *verb*

1. To pay money regularly for a product or service such as a newspaper, magazine, or cable television, as in *to subscribe to a newsletter.* ▷ *noun* **subscriber** ▷ *noun* **subscription**

2. To agree with or go along with a belief or an idea: *I subscribe to the belief that people are basically good.*

sub·scribe (suhb-**skribe**)

▷ *verb* **subscribing, subscribed**

subsequent *adjective* Coming after something in time, place, or order: *We thought we had solved the problem, but subsequent events proved that we hadn't.* **sub·se·quent** (**suhb**-si-kwuhnt)

▷ *adverb* **subsequently**

subset *noun* A set of items that are all contained within a larger set. For example, the numbers 1 through 10 are a subset of the numbers 1 through 1,000. **sub·set** (**suhb**-*set*)

subside *verb*

1. To sink to a lower or more normal level: *It took several days for the floodwaters to subside.*

2. To become less intense or active: *Gradually, the noise subsided.*

sub·side (suhb-**side**)

▷ *verb* **subsiding, subsided**

subsidiary *adjective*

1. Related but not as important; secondary, as in *a subsidiary role.*

2. *noun* A company that is owned or controlled by a larger company: *The subsidiary was doing more business than its parent company.*

sub·sid·i·ar·y (suhb-**sid**-ee-*er*-ee)

subsidy *noun* Money that a government or person contributes to help a worthy enterprise or to keep the price of a product or service low, as in *a housing subsidy.* **sub·si·dy** (**suhb**-si-dee) ▷ *noun, plural* **subsidies** ▷ *verb* **subsidize** (*suhb*-si-*dize*)

substance *noun*

1. Something that has weight and takes up space; matter: *Solid objects, powders, and liquids are substances.*

2. The physical matter of which someone or something is made.

3. The most important or essential part of something; the gist, as in *the substance of a plan.*

sub·stance (**suhb**-stuhns)

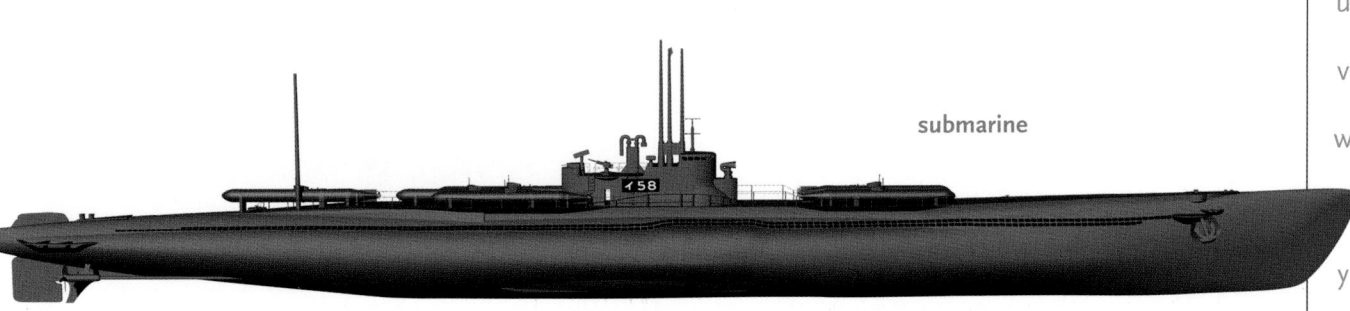

submarine

a
b
c
d
e
f
g
h
i
j
k
l
m
n
o
p
q
r
s
t
u
v
w
y
z

substantial *adjective*
  1. Of great size, value, or importance, as in *a substantial improvement*.
  2. Solidly built; strong or firm, as in *a substantial bridge*.
  3. Not imaginary; real: *The danger of fire was quite substantial*.
  sub·stan·tial (suhb-**stan**-shuhl)

substantially *adverb*
  1. To a significant extent: *Our new house is substantially larger than our old one*.
  2. For the most part: *I think my circle of friends will remain substantially the same until I graduate*.
  sub·stan·tial·ly (suhb-**stan**-shuh-lee)

substitute *noun* Something or someone acting or used in place of another, such as a teacher who takes over when another teacher is ill.
  sub·sti·tute (**suhb**-sti-*toot*) ▷ *noun* **substitution** (*suhb*-sti-**too**-shuhn) ▷ *verb* **substitute**

subtitle *noun*
  1. A second title that explains the main title of a book, movie, play, essay, or song.
  2. subtitles *noun, plural* The translated words that appear at the bottom of the screen when a foreign-language movie or television program is shown.
  sub·ti·tle (**suhb**-*tye*-tuhl)

subtle *adjective*
  1. Not strong; faint or delicate, as in *a subtle flavor*.
  2. Clever and not overly obvious, as in *a subtle hint*.
  sub·tle (**suht**-uhl)
  ▷ *adjective* **subtler, subtlest** ▷ *noun* **subtlety** (**suht**-uhl-tee) ▷ *noun* **subtleness** ▷ *adverb* **subtly** (**sut**-uh-lee)

subtract *verb* To take one number or amount away from another: *If you subtract 2 from 6, you get 4.* **sub·tract** (suhb-**trakt**) ▷ *verb* **subtracting, subtracted**

subtraction *noun* In math, **subtraction** is the taking away of one number from another to come up with a figure that shows the difference between them. **sub·trac·tion** (suhb-**trak**-shuhn)

subtrahend *noun* In math, a number that is subtracted from another number. In the equation 7 − 4 = 3, the subtrahend is 4. **sub·tra·hend** (**suhb**-truh-*hend*)

suburb *noun* An area or a district on or close to the outer edge of a city. A suburb is made up mostly of homes, with few businesses. **sub·urb** (**suhb**-urb) ▷ *noun* **suburbia** (suh-**bur**-bee-uh) ▷ *noun* **suburbanite** (suh-**bur**-buh-*nite*) ▷ *adjective* **suburban**

subway *noun* An electric train or a system of trains that runs underground in a city. **sub·way** (**suhb**-*way*)

succeed *verb*
  1. To achieve or accomplish something: *We didn't succeed in our efforts to win back the trophy*.
  2. To have or to enjoy success: *Carlotta succeeds at everything she does*.
  3. To come after and take the place left by someone else: *Kim succeeded her older brother as class president*.
  suc·ceed (suhk-**seed**)
  ▷ *verb* **succeeding, succeeded**

success *noun*
  1. A good or favorable outcome; desired results: *The success of the show is due mostly to the actors*.
  2. A person or thing that has achieved success: *The experiment was a success*.
  suc·cess (suhk-**ses**)
  ▷ *noun, plural* **successes**

successful *adjective*
  1. Producing a favorable and intended result: *My cousin's heart transplant operation was successful*.
  2. Able to do something well and make money at it: *The glass factory is the town's biggest employer and the most successful business in the area*.
  suc·cess·ful (suhk-**ses**-fuhl)
  ▷ *adverb* **successfully**

succession *noun*
  1. A number of persons or things that follow one after another in order; a series, as in *a succession of losses*.
  2. The coming of one person or thing after another: *The party guests arrived in quick succession*.
  3. The order in which one person after another takes over a title, a throne, or a political office.
  suc·ces·sion (suhk-**sesh**-uhn)

successive *adjective* Following in order or sequence, as in *successive wins*. **suc·cess·ive** (suhk-**ses**-iv)
  ▷ *adverb* **successively**

subway

724

successor *noun* One who follows another in a position or sequence: *She is my successor as president of the Drama Club.* **suc·ces·sor** (suhk-**ses**-ur)

succulent

1. *adjective* Full of juice, as in *a succulent peach.* ▷ *noun* **succulence**

2. *noun* A plant, such as a cactus, that has thick, fleshy leaves for storing moisture. **suc·cu·lent** (**suhk**-yuh-luhnt)

such

1. *adjective* Of the same or that kind: *I've never seen such a magic trick before.*

2. *adjective* Like, or similar: *I like skating, skiing, and other such winter sports.*

3. *adjective* So much, or so great: *We had such fun at the carnival.*

4. *pronoun* Others of that kind: *We'll buy flowers, streamers, balloons, and such to decorate the house.* **such** (suhch)

suck *verb*

1. To draw air or a liquid into your mouth by using your lungs, tongue, or lips.

2. To pull strongly or draw in, as in *to suck someone underwater* or *to suck someone into an argument.*

3. To hold something in your mouth as if you were sucking, as in *to suck your thumb.* **suck** (suhk)

▷ *verb* **sucking, sucked** ▷ *noun* **suck**

sucker *noun*

1. A body part of certain animals that is used to stick to surfaces: *An octopus uses its suckers to cling to underwater rocks.*

2. *(slang)* A person who is easily cheated or fooled: *I hope no one's enough of a sucker to buy that old piece of junk.*

3. A piece of candy, such as a lollipop, that is held in the mouth until it dissolves. **suck·er** (**suhk**-ur)

suction *noun* The act of drawing air out of a space to create a vacuum. This causes the surrounding air or liquid to be sucked into the empty space. **suc·tion** (**suhk**-shuhn)

sudden *adjective*

1. Happening without warning; unexpected, as in *a sudden storm.*

2. Quick, hasty, or abrupt, as in *a sudden decision* or *a sudden stop.* **sud·den** (**suhd**-uhn)

▷ *noun* **suddenness** ▷ *adverb* **suddenly**

sudden infant death syndrome *noun* The death, usually during sleep, of a seemingly healthy infant for no known cause. Also known as *SIDS.*

sudoku

sudoku *noun* A number puzzle on a grid of squares in which each row, column, or square must contain the numbers 1 through 9 only once. **su·do·ku** (soo-**doh**-koo)

Word History

If you have worked on a **sudoku**, you know that you can't have the same number twice in the same row, column, or square; the number can only appear once in each of these places. The original name of this puzzle was a Japanese phrase meaning "the numbers can only appear once" or "they can only have single status." Japanese speakers coined the word *sudoku* from this phrase, from the word for "number," *suji*, and *dokushin*, meaning "single status."

suds *noun, plural* The bubbles that form on top of a substance, such as water, that contains soap, as in *laundry suds.* **suds** (suhdz)

sue *verb* To start a suit or case against someone in a court of law: *The company might get sued for selling faulty toys.* **sue** (soo) ▷ *verb* **suing, sued**

suede *noun* Soft leather with a velvety finish on one side. **suede** (swayd)

suet *noun* A hard fat from cattle and sheep that is used in cooking. **su·et** (**soo**-it)

suffer *verb*

1. To have pain, discomfort, or sorrow.

2. To experience or undergo something unpleasant, as in *to suffer defeat.*

3. To be damaged, or to become worse: *If you don't study, your grades will suffer.* **suf·fer** (**suhf**-ur)

▷ *verb* **suffering, suffered** ▷ *noun* **suffering**

sufferer *noun* Someone who must endure a condition, illness, or something unpleasant: *James is a fellow sufferer of motion sickness.* **suf·fer·er** (**suhf**-ur-ur)

a b c d e f g h i j k l m n o p q r **s** t u v w x y z

suffice

1. *verb* To be enough, adequate, or sufficient: *The treaty has sufficed for more than 60 years, but is it relevant to the world we live in today?* ▷ *verb* **sufficing, sufficed**

2. *phrase* If you talk about something and use the phrase **suffice it to say**, you are indicating that what you say is enough to express what you mean but that you do not want to go into details, either because you are being discreet or because you wish to be brief: *"They didn't get along," she told me. "Suffice it to say, their friendship ended quickly."*
suf·fice (suh-**fise**)

sufficient *adjective* As much as is needed; adequate, as in *sufficient time*. **suf·fi·cient** (suh-**fish**-uhnt) ▷ *adverb* **sufficiently**

suffix *noun* A syllable or syllables added at the end of a word or root that changes its meaning. For example, in *sadness* the suffix is *-ness*. **suf·fix** (**suhf**-iks) ▷ *noun, plural* **suffixes**

Word History

Suffix comes from the Latin word parts *sub-*, meaning "below," and *figere,* meaning "to fasten." A suffix, like *-ship*, is fastened or attached to the end of a word or word root to form a new word.

suffocate *verb*

1. To kill by cutting off the supply of air or oxygen: *The mother cat accidentally suffocated one of her newborn kittens by lying on top of him.*

2. To die from lack of oxygen: *The gopher suffocated when I accidentally plugged its hole.*

3. To have difficulty breathing: *I'm suffocating in this hot room.*
suf·fo·cate (**suhf**-uh-**kate**) ▷ *verb* **suffocating, suffocated** ▷ *noun* **suffocation** (**suhf**-uh-**kay**-shuhn)

suffrage *noun* The right to vote, as in *women's suffrage*. **suf·frage** (**suhf**-rij)

sugar *noun* A sweet substance that comes from sugar beets and sugarcane and is used in foods and drinks: *My dentist warned me about eating too much sugar.*
sug·ar (**shug**-ur) ▷ *adjective* **sugary** (**shug**-ur-ee)

sugar beet *noun* A vegetable with fleshy white roots from which sugar is produced.

sugarcane *noun* A tropical grass whose tall, woody stems are used to make sugar. **sugar·cane** (**shug**-ur-kane)

sugarcane

campaigning for women's suffrage

suggest *verb*

1. To mention something as an idea, a plan, or a possibility, as in *to suggest a solution.*

2. To bring or call to mind: *Those soft, fluffy clouds suggest sheep to me.*

3. To hint or show indirectly: *This painter uses different colors to suggest his feelings.*
sug·gest (suhg-**jest** *or* suh-**jest**) ▷ *verb* **suggesting, suggested**

suggestion *noun*

1. Something that you suggest, such as an idea, a piece of advice, or a plan: *Has anyone got any suggestions for what we should do on Saturday?*

2. A small but noticeable amount: *There's just a suggestion of garlic in the salad dressing.*
sug·ges·tion (suhg-**jes**-chuhn *or* suh-**jes**-chuhn)

suicide *noun* The act of killing oneself on purpose. **su·i·cide** (**soo**-i-*side*) ▷ *adjective* **suicidal** (*soo*-i-**sye**-duhl) ▷ *adverb* **suicidally**

suit

1. *noun* A set of matching clothes, usually a man's jacket and pants or a woman's jacket and skirt.

2. *noun* One of the sets into which playing cards are divided. The four suits are clubs, diamonds, hearts, and spades.

3. *noun* A case that is brought before a court of law; a lawsuit.

4. *verb* To be acceptable or convenient; to be right or appropriate for someone or something: *I saw the apartment and knew it would suit my grandmother. The new curtains suited the room perfectly.*

5. *verb* To look good on someone: *That haircut suits you very well.*
suit (soot) ▷ *verb* **suiting, suited**

suitable *adjective* Right for a particular purpose, occasion or condition: *Megan's shoes were suitable for playing soccer.* **suit·a·ble** (**soo**-tuh-buhl) ▷ *noun* **suitability** (soo-tuh-**bil**-i-tee) ▷ *adverb* **suitably**

suitcase *noun* A flat case with a handle and a hinged lid, used for carrying clothes and belongings when you travel. **suit·case** (**soot**-*kase*)

suite *noun*
1. A group of rooms that are connected, as in *a hotel suite.*
2. A set of matching furniture or other items, as in *a bedroom suite.*
3. A piece of music made up of several parts. **suite** (sweet)

suitor *noun* A man who courts a woman. **suit·or** (**soo**-tur)

sulfur *noun* A yellow chemical element used in gunpowder, matches, and fertilizer. **sul·fur** (**suhl**-fur)

sulfur dioxide *noun* A poisonous gas found in some industrial waste. Sulfur dioxide causes air pollution. **sulfur di·ox·ide** (dye-**ahk**-side)

sulk *verb* To be angry, resentful, or disappointed but also very quiet and withdrawn: *Melissa sulked after she failed the exam.* **sulk** (suhlk) ▷ *verb* **sulking, sulked** ▷ *noun* **sulk** ▷ *adjective* **sulky**

sullen *adjective* Gloomy and silent because you feel angry, bitter, or hurt: *Deirdre was sullen when she wasn't picked to be on the team.* **sul·len** (**suhl**-uhn) ▷ *adverb* **sullenly**

sultan *noun* An emperor or ruler of some Muslim countries. **sul·tan** (**suhl**-tuhn)

sultry *adjective* Very hot and humid, as in *sultry weather.* **sul·try** (**suhl**-tree) ▷ *adjective* **sultrier, sultriest** ▷ *noun* **sultriness**

sum
1. *noun* A particular amount of money.
2. *noun* A number that you get from adding two or more numbers together: *In the equation 2 + 2 = 4, the sum is 4.*
3. sum up *verb* To briefly summarize the main points: *Brenda summed up the group's reasons for not wanting to make the trip.* ▷ *verb* **summing, summed**
4. sum *or* **sum total** *noun* The whole or final amount: *What is the sum total of the cost of this vacation?* **sum** (suhm)
Sum sounds like **some**.

sumac *noun* A bush or tree with pointed leaves and clusters of flowers or red berries. **su·mac** (**soo**-mak)

summary *noun* A brief statement that gives the main points or ideas of something that has been said or written. **sum·ma·ry** (**suhm**-ur-ee) ▷ *noun, plural* **summaries** ▷ *verb* **summarize**

summer *noun* The season after spring and before autumn, when the days are long and the weather is warm. **sum·mer** (**suhm**-ur) ▷ *adjective* **summery**

summit *noun*
1. The highest point; the top, as in *the summit of a mountain.*
2. A meeting of the heads of government or highest officials from different countries. **sum·mit** (**suhm**-it)

summit

summon *verb*
1. To request or to order that someone come or appear: *The detective was summoned to the crime scene.*
2. To make an effort to show a certain quality or response, as in *to summon courage.* **sum·mon** (**suhm**-uhn) ▷ *verb* **summoning, summoned**

summons *noun* An order to appear in a court of law. **sum·mons** (**suhm**-uhnz) ▷ *noun, plural* **summonses** ▷ *verb* **summons**

sun
1. *noun* The star that the earth and other planets revolve around and that gives us light and warmth. Sometimes capitalized as *Sun.*
2. *noun* Any star that is the center of a system of planets.
3. *noun* The light or warmth that comes from the sun, as in *lying in the sun.*
4. *verb* To sit or lie in the sun: *I try not to sun myself for more than ten minutes.* ▷ *verb* **sunning, sunned**
sun (suhn)
Sun sounds like **son**.

sunbathe *verb* To sit or lie in the sun so you can get a suntan. **sun·bathe** (suhn-*bayTH*) ▷ *verb* **sunbathing, sunbathed** ▷ *noun* **sunbath**

sunburn *noun* Redness or blistering of the skin caused by spending too much time in the sun. **sun·burn** (**suhn**-burn) ▷ *adjective* **sunburned** or **sunburnt** (**suhn**-*burnt*)

sundae *noun* Ice cream served with one or more toppings, such as syrup, whipped cream, nuts, or fruit, as in *a chocolate fudge sundae*. **sun·dae** (**suhn**-day *or* **suhn**-*dee*)

Sunday *noun* The first day of the week, after Saturday and before Monday. **Sun·day** (**suhn**-day *or* **suhn**-*dee*)

Word History

In ancient Rome, the first day of the week was dedicated to the sun. The Romans originally called the day *dies solis,* which meant "day of the sun." In Old English, the Roman phrase was translated as "sun's day," which later became **Sunday**.

sundial *noun* An instrument that shows the time with a pointer that casts a shadow on a flat dial similar to the face of a clock. **sun·di·al** (**suhn**-*dye*-uhl)

sunflower *noun* A large flower with yellow petals and a dark center, grown for its edible seeds and their oil. **sun·flow·er** (**suhn**-*flou*-ur)

sung *verb* The past participle of **sing**. **sung** (suhng)

sunglasses *noun, plural* Eyeglasses with a dark tint that protects your eyes from the glare of sunlight. **sun·glass·es** (**suhn**-*glas*-iz)

sunk *verb* The past participle of **sink**. **sunk** (suhngk)

sunken *adjective*
1. Below the surface, as in *sunken treasure*.
2. Below the other areas nearby, as in *a sunken living room*.
sunk·en (**suhng**-kuhn)

sunlight *noun* The light of the sun. **sun·light** (**suhn**-*lite*)

sunrise *noun* The event or the time of day when the sun first appears above the eastern horizon. **sun·rise** (**suhn**-*rize*)

sunscreen *noun* A lotion containing a chemical that protects the skin from the harmful rays of the sun. **sun·screen** (**suhn**-*skreen*)

sunset *noun* The event or the time in the evening when the sun sinks below the western horizon. **sun·set** (**suhn**-*set*)

sunshine *noun* The light from the sun or the sun's direct rays. **sun·shine** (**suhn**-*shine*)

sunstroke *noun* An illness caused by too much exposure to the sun. Symptoms of sunstroke include fever, dizziness, and headaches. **sun·stroke** (**suhn**-*strohk*)

superhero

super *adjective* Very good; excellent, as in *a super idea*. **su·per** (**soo**-pur)

superb *adjective* Excellent or outstanding, as in *a superb meal* or *a superb performance*. **su·perb** (soo-**purb**) ▷ *adverb* **superbly** (soo-**purb**-lee)

superficial *adjective*
1. Existing or happening on the surface, as in *a superficial wound*.
2. Concerned only with what is obvious and easy to understand; not deep or thorough, as in *superficial knowledge*.
su·per·fi·cial (*soo*-pur-**fish**-uhl)
▷ *adverb* **superficially**

superfood *noun* A food that is thought to be especially valuable for the nutrients it contains. This word is used mainly by advertisers and food sellers, not by scientists. **su·per·food** (**soo**-pur-*food*)

superhero *noun* A fictional character with superhuman powers such as extraordinary strength or the ability to fly. **su·per·her·o** (**soo**-pur-*heer*-oh) ▷ *noun, plural* **superheroes**

superhuman *adjective* Having or requiring characteristics or abilities beyond those of an ordinary human, as in *superhuman strength* or *a superhuman task*. **su·per·hu·man** (*soo*-pur-**hyoo**-muhn)

superintendent *noun*
1. An official who directs or manages an organization, as in *superintendent of schools*.
2. A person in charge of a building; a janitor or custodian.
su·per·in·ten·dent (*soo*-pur-in-**ten**-duhnt)

superior
1. *adjective* Higher in rank or position, as in *a superior officer*.
2. *adjective* Above average in quality or ability; excellent, as in *a superior piece of writing* or *a*

sundial

superior team.

3. *noun* A person who has a higher rank or position than others: *The privates listened because the captain was their superior.*

4. *adjective* Believing that or behaving as if you are better than other people, as in *a superior attitude.* ▷ *noun* **superiority** (su-*peer*-ee-**or**-i-tee) **su·pe·ri·or** (su-**peer**-ee-ur)

superlative *adjective*

1. Superlative adjectives and adverbs are used to describe the highest degree of a certain quality. *Largest* is the superlative form of *large,* and *most difficult* is the superlative form of *difficult.* ▷ *noun* **superlative**

2. The very best, as in *a superlative performance.* **su·per·la·tive** (suh-**pur**-luh-tiv) ▷ *adverb* **superlatively**

supermarket *noun* A large self-service store that sells food and household goods. **su·per·mar·ket** (**soo**-pur-*mahr*-kit)

supernatural *noun* Existing outside normal human experience or knowledge, as in *supernatural forces.* **su·per·nat·u·ral** (*soo*-pur-**nach**-ur-uhl) ▷ *adverb* **supernaturally**

supernova *noun* An extremely bright exploding star that can give off millions of times more light than the sun. **su·per·no·va** (*soo*-pur-**noh**-vuh) ▷ *noun, plural* **supernovas** or **supernovae** (*soo*-pur-**noh**-vee)

supersonic *adjective* At or having to do with a speed faster than that of sound, as in *supersonic planes.* **su·per·son·ic** (*soo*-pur-**sah**-nik)

superstition *noun* A belief that explains the cause of something in a magical way that cannot be tested or proven. **su·per·sti·tion** (*soo*-pur-**stish**-uhn)

superstitious *adjective*

1. More influenced by superstition than by reason or facts: *A superstitious man told me to avoid black cats.*

2. Based on or resulting from superstition: *That's an old superstitious belief that has no basis in fact.* **su·per·sti·tious** (*soo*-pur-**stish**-uhs)

supertanker *noun* A very large oil tanker used to transport large amounts of crude oil to refineries. **su·per·tank·er** (**soo**-pur-*tang*-kur)

supervise *verb* To watch over or direct a group of people; to be in charge of someone or something: *Aaron supervised the judges of the talent show.* **su·per·vise** (**soo**-pur-*vize*) ▷ *verb* **supervising, supervised**

supervision *noun* Direct oversight or management of someone or something, especially a person's work: *Despite having almost no supervision, the children behaved surprisingly well.* **su·per·vi·sion** (*soo*-pur-**vizh**-uhn)

supervisor *noun* Someone who watches over and directs the work of other people: *Ms. Jones will be your supervisor during your training period.* **su·per·vi·sor** (**soo**-pur-*vye*-zur)

supervision

supper *noun* A light evening meal or a dinner. **sup·per** (**suhp**-ur)

supple *adjective* Able to move or bend easily; limber or flexible, as in *supple limbs.* **sup·ple** (**suhp**-uhl) ▷ *adjective* **suppler, supplest** ▷ *noun* **suppleness**

supplement

1. *noun* Something added to complete another thing or to make up for what is missing, as in *a newspaper supplement.*

2. *verb* To add to something: *I try to supplement my exercise routine with a daily walk to the post office, which is about two miles away.* ▷ *verb* **supplementing, supplemented** ▷ *adjective* **supplementary** (*suhp*-luh-**men**-tur-ee) **sup·ple·ment** (**suhp**-luh-muhnt)

supplier *noun* Someone who provides something that is needed or who makes something available: *The bakery supplier dropped off the flour, milk, and butter.* **sup·pli·er** (suh-**plye**-ur)

supply

1. *verb* To provide something that is needed or wanted: *Forests supply trees for lumber. An encyclopedia supplies information.* ▷ *verb* **supplies, supplying, supplied**

2. *noun* An amount of something that is available for use, as in *a supply of firewood.* ▷ *noun, plural* **supplies**

3. supplies *noun, plural* Materials needed to do something, as in *school supplies.* **sup·ply** (suh-**plye**)

support *verb*

1. To bear the weight of someone or something: *The dock at the lake is supported by eight log pilings.*

2. To earn a living for; to provide for, as in *to support a family.*

3. To give help, comfort, or encouragement to someone or something: *My friends supported my efforts to find a job.* ▷ *adjective* **supportive**

4. To believe in someone or to be in favor of something, as in *to support environmentalism.*

5. To show to be true: *My findings support your theory.*

sup·port (suh-**port**)

▷ *verb* **supporting, supported** ▷ *noun* **support**

supporter *noun* Someone who promotes or encourages someone or something, such as a sports team or a political party: *Grace is a strong supporter of human rights.* **sup·port·er** (suh-**por**-tur)

suppose *verb*

1. To imagine or assume that something is true or possible: *Let's suppose that people were able to fly like birds.*

2. To believe or to guess: *I suppose she's right.*

3. To expect: *It is supposed to snow this week.*

sup·pose (suh-**poze**)

▷ *verb* **supposing, supposed** ▷ *adjective* **supposed**
▷ *adverb* **supposedly**

suppress *verb*

1. To put a stop to something, especially by using authority or force, as in *to suppress a rebellion.*

2. To hold back or to control the expression of something, as in *to suppress a yawn.*

sup·press (suh-**pres**)

▷ *verb* **suppresses, suppressing, suppressed**
▷ *noun* **suppression** (suh-**presh**-uhn)

supreme *adjective*

1. The highest in power, authority, or importance, as in *supreme leader.*

2. The greatest or most excellent: *The courthouse is a supreme example of colonial architecture.*

su·preme (su-**preem**)

▷ *noun* **supremacy** (su-**prem**-uh-see) ▷ *adverb* **supremely**

Supreme Court *noun*

1. The highest and most powerful court in the United States. It has the power to overturn decisions made in lower courts and also to declare laws unconstitutional.

2. The highest court in a state.

sure

1. *adjective* Having no doubt; certain; confident: *I'm sure he's right.*

2. *adjective* Certain to happen; impossible to avoid,

Supreme Court

The Supreme Court in Washington, DC, is the highest court in the United States. It is headed by a chief justice, and includes eight associate justices. Each takes two oaths of office: one, to uphold and defend the Constitution, the basis of the nation's democratic government; and two, to administer justice equally to all.

as in *a sure defeat.*

3. *adjective* Firm or steady, as in *sure footing* or *a sure grip.*

4. *adverb* Without a doubt; certainly: *Sure, I'll be there.* ▷ *adjective* **surer, surest**

sure (shoor)

surely *adverb* With certainty; absolutely; without a doubt: *Many people surely would have been stranded if the snowplows hadn't cleared the roads.* **sure·ly** (**shoor**-lee)

surf

1. *noun* Waves as they break on the shore: *Heavy surf pounded the shore during the storm.*

2. *verb* To balance on a surfboard and ride the crest of a breaking wave toward shore. ▷ *noun* **surfer**
▷ *noun* **surfing**

3. *verb* To look through pages or sites on the World Wide Web: *I was surfing the web and I found a link to our school's homepage.*

surf (surf)

Surf sounds like **serf**. ▷ *verb* **surfing, surfed**

surface

1. *noun* The outside or outermost layer of something,

as in *the surface of the earth.*

2. *noun* One of the sides of something that has several sides: *Dice have six surfaces.*

3. on the surface In its outward appearance: *He seemed like a nice enough guy on the surface.*

4. *verb* To rise to the surface: *The fish surfaced to catch insects.*

5. *verb* To appear, especially from a hidden location: *My sweatshirt surfaced when I cleaned out my gym bag.*

sur·face (**sur**-fis)

▷ *verb* **surfacing, surfaced**

surfboard *noun* A long, narrow board with rounded ends on which surfers stand as they ride breaking waves. **surf·board** (**surf**-bord)

surge

1. *verb* To rush or sweep forward with force, like a wave: *The fans surged forward as the band walked onto the stage.* ▷ *verb* **surging, surged**

2. *noun* A sudden, strong rush, as in *a storm surge.*

3. *noun* A sudden increase, as in *a surge in prices* or *a surge of interest.* ▷ *verb* **surge**

surge (surj)

surgeon *noun* A doctor who specializes in performing operations. **sur·geon** (**sur**-juhn)

surge protector *noun* A device that protects devices plugged into it from being damaged by a sudden increase in voltage.

surgery *noun*

1. Medical treatment that involves repairing, removing, or replacing injured or diseased parts of the body, usually by cutting. ▷ *adjective* **surgical** (**sur**-ji-kuhl)

2. The branch of medicine that deals with injury and disease in this way.

3. An operation performed by a surgeon, as in *knee surgery.*

sur·ger·y (**sur**-jur-ee)

surly *adjective* Mean, rude, and unfriendly, as in *a surly customer.* **sur·ly** (**sur**-lee)

▷ *adjective* **surlier, surliest**

surname *noun* A person's last name or family name: *The surname Smith is extremely common.* **sur·name** (**sur**-name)

surpass *verb*

1. To be better, greater, or stronger

surfboard

than another person or thing, as in *to surpass a record.*

2. To go beyond the limits or powers of something, as in *to surpass description.*

sur·pass (sur-**pas**)

▷ *verb* **surpasses, surpassing, surpassed**

surplus *noun* An amount greater than what is used or needed; excess, as in *a surplus of grain.* **sur·plus** (**sur**-pluhs) ▷ *adjective* **surplus**

surprise *verb*

1. To amaze or astonish someone by doing or saying something unexpected: *The whole family was surprised when Sunil announced that he was getting married.*

2. To come upon suddenly and without warning, as in *to surprise a thief.*

sur·prise (sur-**prize**)

▷ *verb* **surprising, surprised** ▷ *noun* **surprise**

▷ *adjective* **surprising**

surreal *adjective* Having an unreal or dreamlike quality that makes a situation seem hard to believe: *In a surreal scene in the movie, the monuments in Washington, DC, all lie in ruins.* **sur·re·al** (suh-**ree**-uhl)

▷ *adverb* **surreally**

surrender *verb*

1. To give up or to stop resisting someone or something, as in *to surrender to the police.*

2. To give something up or to hand something over, as in *to surrender a weapon.*

sur·ren·der (suh-**ren**-dur)

▷ *verb* **surrendering, surrendered** ▷ *noun* **surrender**

surreptitious *adjective* Done or collected without anyone knowing; secret: *The surreptitious recordings of the senator's conversations were leaked to the press.* **sur·rep·ti·tious** (sur-uhp-**tish**-uhs)

surround *verb* To be on all sides of someone or something; to encircle: *A fence surrounds the garden.* **sur·round** (suh-**round**)

▷ *verb* **surrounding, surrounded**

surroundings *noun, plural* The conditions or objects around a person or thing; the environment, as in *familiar surroundings.* **sur·round·ings** (suh-**roun**-dingz)

survey

1. (**sur**-vay) *noun* A study of the opinions or experiences of a group of people, based on their responses to questions, as in *a customer survey.*
▷ *verb* **survey** (sur-**vay**)

2. (sur-**vay**) *verb* To examine someone or something carefully and thoroughly, as in *to survey a scene.*

3. (sur-**vay**) *verb* To measure the lines and angles of a piece of land in order to make a map or plan, as in *to survey a building site.* ▷ *noun* **survey** (**sur**-vay)
▷ *noun* **surveyor**
sur·vey
▷ *verb* **surveying, surveyed**

survive *verb*

1. To continue to live after or in spite of an accident or dangerous event, as in *to survive a bombing.*

2. To continue to live or exist: *Humans need food and water to survive.*

3. To live longer than someone or something: *My grandmother survived my grandfather by five years.*
sur·vive (sur-**vive**)
▷ *verb* **surviving, survived** ▷ *noun* **survival** (sur-**vye**-vuhl)

survivor *noun* Someone who lives through a disaster or other horrible event: *The plane crash left only a dozen survivors.* **sur·vi·vor** (sur-**vye**-vur)

sushi *noun* A Japanese dish made of small cakes of cooked rice with raw fish or vegetables, wrapped in seaweed. **su·shi** (**soo**-shee)

suspect

1. (suh-**spekt**) *verb* To think that something may be true; to guess or suppose: *His mother suspected that James had more than a cold.* ▷ *adjective* **suspect** (**suhs**-pekt)

2. (suh-**spekt**) *verb* To think that someone is guilty with little or no proof: *When his favorite pen disappeared, Ben suspected Susan.*

3. (suh-**spekt**) *verb* To have doubts about; to distrust, as in *to suspect someone's motives.*

4. (**suhs**-pekt) *noun* Someone who is thought to have committed a crime: *Police say the suspect is six feet tall.*
sus·pect
▷ *verb* **suspecting, suspected**

suspend *verb*

1. To attach something to a support so that it hangs downward, as in *to suspend a flag from a pole.*

2. To keep from falling as if attached from above: *The hummingbird was suspended over the flower.*

3. To stop something for a brief period of time, as in *to suspend a search.*

4. To punish someone by not allowing him or her to participate, as in *to suspend someone from a team.*
sus·pend (suh-**spend**)

sushi

▷ *verb* **suspending, suspended**

suspenders *noun, plural* A pair of elastic straps worn over the shoulders and attached to pants or a skirt to hold up the garment. **sus·pend·ers** (suh-**spen**-durz)

suspense *noun* An anxious and uncertain feeling caused by not knowing what might happen next: *We were all in suspense as we waited to find out who won the contest.* **sus·pense** (suh-**spens**)

suspension *noun*

1. A period during which an activity is not allowed or does not take place. During a cease-fire, for example, there is a suspension of fighting.

2. The dismissal of someone from a place or position by an authority for a period of time: *He got a two-week suspension for fighting in class.*

3. The state of being suspended from something.

4. The part of a car that has springs to make the car stable, protecting it from the road and helping the driver maintain control of the vehicle.
sus·pen·sion (suh-**spen**-shuhn)

suspension bridge *noun* A bridge hung from cables or chains strung from towers.

suspicion *noun*

1. A thought, based more on feeling than on fact, that something is wrong or bad: *Robin left the house with a suspicion that she would never return.*

2. under suspicion Believed to have done something wrong: *Because of her sudden wealth, Harriet was under suspicion of burglary.*
sus·pi·cion (suh-**spish**-uhn)

suspicious *adjective*

1. Thinking that something is wrong or bad, but having little or no proof to back up your feelings: *The owner became suspicious when the boys kept hanging around after the store had closed.*

2. Giving an impression of being wrong, untrustworthy, or dangerous, as in *a suspicious package.*
sus·pi·cious (suh-**spish**-uhs)

sustain *verb*

1. To keep something going; to maintain, as in *to sustain a business.*

2. To encourage someone, or to give someone the energy and strength to keep going: *Although we were exhausted, we were sustained by the shouts and cheers of the crowd.*

3. To suffer or experience something unpleasant, as in *to sustain an injury.*

sus·tain (suh-**stayn**)

▷ *verb* **sustaining, sustained**

sustainability *noun* A method or plan to carry on with something in a way that does not harm the environment: *The council's job is to ensure the environmental sustainability of the seafood industry.*

sus·tain·a·bil·i·ty (suh-*stay*-nuh-**bil**-i-tee)

sustainable *adjective* Done in a way that can be continued and that doesn't use up natural resources, as in *sustainable agriculture.* **sus·tain·a·ble** (suh-**stay**-nuh-buhl)

sustenance *noun* The food and drink that someone requires to live; nourishment: *In some villages, corn, squash, and some roots provide the main sustenance.* **sus·te·nance** (**suhs**-tuh-nuhns)

SUV *noun* A large car that is built like a truck and that can be driven where there are no roads. SUV is short for *sport utility vehicle.*

swagger *verb* To walk or act in a bold, confident way: *Billy swaggered down the hall, trying to look important.* **swag·ger** (**swag**-ur) ▷ *verb* **swaggering, swaggered** ▷ *noun* **swagger**

swallow

1. *verb* To make food or drink go from your mouth down to your stomach. ▷ *noun* **swallow**

2. *verb* To cause to disappear as if by swallowing: *The raging flood swallowed the house.*

3. *verb* To suppress or hold back, as in *to swallow your pride.*

4. *noun* A migrating, insect-eating bird with long, pointed wings and a forked tail.

5. *verb (informal)* To accept or believe without question, as in *to swallow an explanation.* **swal·low** (**swah**-loh)

▷ *verb* **swallowing, swallowed**

swam *verb* The past tense of **swim.** **swam** (swam)

swamp

1. *noun* An area of wet, spongy ground; a marsh: *The swamp on the edge of town is a breeding ground for mosquitoes.* ▷ *adjective* **swampy**

2. *verb* To fill with or sink in water, as in *to swamp a boat.*

3. *verb* To overwhelm, as in *to swamp with homework.*

swamp (swahmp)

▷ *verb* **swamping, swamped**

swan *noun* A large, usually white waterbird with webbed feet and a long, graceful neck. **swan** (swahn)

swap *verb* To trade or exchange someone or something for another: *I'll swap you my CD for a video game.* **swap** (swahp) ▷ *verb* **swapping, swapped** ▷ *noun* **swap**

swarm

1. *noun* A group of people or insects that gather or move in large numbers, as in *a swarm of hornets.*

2. *verb* To fly closely together, forming a dense mass, as in *bees swarming.*

3. swarm with *verb* To be filled with: *In summer, the beaches swarm with tourists.*

swarm (sworm)

▷ *verb* **swarming, swarmed**

swastika *noun* An ancient symbol consisting of a cross with the arms bent at right angles. During the 20th century, the swastika was adopted as the emblem of the Nazi party in Germany. **swas·ti·ka** (**swah**-sti-kuh)

swat *verb* To hit with a quick, sharp blow, as in *to swat a bug.* **swat** (swaht) ▷ *verb* **swatting, swatted** ▷ *noun* **swat**

sway

1. *verb* To move or swing slowly backward and forward or from side to side, as in *flowers swaying in the wind.*

2. *verb* To change or influence the way someone thinks or acts: *The candidate's speech swayed the voters.*

3. *noun* A rhythmical movement from side to side, as in *the sway of the palm trees.*

4. *noun* Influence or control: *Britain held sway in India for centuries.*

sway (sway)

▷ *verb* **swaying, swayed**

swan

swear *verb*

1. To make a solemn promise; to vow: *I swear I'll be your friend forever.*

2. To use rude or bad language; to curse, as in *to swear at someone.*

swear (swair)

▷ *verb* **swearing, swore** (swor), **sworn** (sworn)

sweat *verb* To have salty drops of moisture come out through the pores in your skin; to perspire. **sweat** (swet)

▷ *verb* **sweating, sweat** *or* **sweated**

▷ *noun* **sweat**

sweater *noun* A knitted or crocheted piece of clothing that you wear on your upper body, as in *a turtleneck sweater.* **sweat·er** (**swet**-ur)

sweatshirt *noun* A casual, collarless, long-sleeved top made of cotton jersey with a fleece backing. **sweat·shirt** (**swet**-*shurt*)

sweep *verb*

1. To clean or clear away with a brush or broom, as in *to sweep the floor.*

2. To move or carry rapidly and forcefully: *The fire swept through the building.*

3. To touch or brush lightly: *A wisp of hair swept her face.*

4. To move or pass over a wide area quickly and steadily: *The searchlight swept the night sky.* **sweep** (sweep)

▷ *verb* **sweeping, swept** (swept) ▷ *noun* **sweep**

sweeping *adjective* Affecting many people or things; wide-ranging, as in *sweeping changes.* **sweep·ing** (**swee**-ping)

sweet

1. *adjective* Tasting like sugar or honey, as in *a sweet peach.*

2. *adjective* Pleasant in taste, smell, or sound, as in *the sweet smell of roses* or *sweet music.*

3. *adjective* Gentle and kind; good-natured, as in *a sweet disposition.*

4. sweets *noun, plural* Candy, cookies, or other sweet-tasting foods: *Too many sweets will damage your teeth.*

sweet (sweet)

▷ *adjective* **sweeter, sweetest** ▷ *adverb* **sweetly**

sweeten *verb* To make something sweet or sweeter, usually by adding sugar, as in *to sweeten tea.* **sweet·en** (**swee**-tuhn) ▷ *verb* **sweetening, sweetened**

sweetheart *noun*

1. Either person of a loving couple: *They've been sweethearts since high school.*

2. A lovable person: *She's a real sweetheart.* **sweet·heart** (**sweet**-*hahrt*)

sweet potato *noun* The thick, sweet, orange root of a vine, eaten as a vegetable. ▷ *noun, plural* **sweet potatoes**

sweet potatoes

swell

1. *verb* To grow larger, greater, or stronger: *I could see my knee swell after I twisted it. The fans' cheers swelled to a roar.* ▷ *verb* **swelling, swelled, swollen** ▷ *noun* **swelling**

2. *noun* A long, rolling wave or waves: *A boat rocked gently in the swell.*

3. *adjective* (slang) Wonderful: *We had a swell time today.*

swell (swel)

sweltering *adjective* Uncomfortably hot, as in *sweltering weather.* **swel·ter·ing** (**swel**-tur-ing) ▷ *verb* **swelter**

swerve *verb* To turn aside suddenly while moving forward, usually to avoid hitting something: *The car swerved to avoid the squirrel.* **swerve** (swurv) ▷ *verb* **swerving, swerved** ▷ *noun* **swerve**

swift

1. *adjective* Moving or able to move very fast, as in *a swift runner.* ▷ *noun* **swiftness** ▷ *adverb* **swiftly**

2. *adjective* Happening or done quickly, as in *a swift reply.* ▷ *adjective* **swifter, swiftest**

3. *noun* A migrating bird, similar to a swallow, with long, narrow wings.

swift (swift)

swig *verb* To drink a liquid in large gulps, usually from a bottle or other container. **swig** (swig) ▷ *verb* **swigging, swigged** ▷ *noun* **swig**

swim *verb*

1. To move through the water using the arms and legs or the fins, flippers, or tail. ▷ *noun* **swim** ▷ *noun* **swimmer**

2. To float on or be covered by liquid: *The potatoes were swimming in gravy.*

swim (swim)

▷ *verb* **swimming, swam** (swam), **swum** (swuhm)

swimsuit *noun* A piece of clothing worn for swimming. **swim·suit** (**swim**-*soot*)

swindle *verb* To cheat someone out of money, property, or possessions: *I was swindled out of my last dollar.* **swin·dle** (**swin**-duhl) ▷ *verb* **swindling, swindled** ▷ *noun* **swindle** ▷ *noun* **swindler** (**swind**-luhr)

swine *noun*

1. A pig or a hog.

2. A hateful, vicious, or greedy person.

swine (swine)

swipe

swine flu *noun* A form of flu that was first found in pigs and that can spread to humans.

swing
1. *verb* To move back and forth or from side to side while hanging from above.
2. *verb* To move on a hinge or pivot: *The door swung shut.*
3. *verb* To move or turn with a curved, sweeping motion: *The batter swung at the pitch.* ▷ *noun* **swing**
4. *noun* A piece of playground equipment, consisting of a seat hanging from ropes or chains on which you sit and move back and forth.
5. *noun* A style of lively jazz music originally played by large dance bands in the 1930s.
swing (swing)
▷ *verb* **swinging, swung** (swuhng)

swipe
1. *verb (informal)* To hit someone or something with a hard, sweeping blow or stroke: *The batter took a swipe at the ball, but he missed.*
2. *verb (slang)* To steal something, as in *to swipe candy.*
3. *verb* To run a card with a magnetic strip through a machine in order to do something, such as make a payment: *You have to swipe your ID card to get into the building.*
4. *noun* An instance of swiping something: *I got the jelly off the table with a quick swipe of a sponge.*
swipe (swipe)
▷ *verb* **swiping, swiped**

swirl *verb* To move with a twisting, spiraling, or whirling motion: *The tornado picked up the car and swirled it around.* **swirl** (swurl) ▷ *verb* **swirling, swirled** ▷ *noun* **swirl**

swish
1. *verb* To move with a soft, rustling sound: *My skirt swished along the floor as I walked.* ▷ *verb* **swishes, swishing, swished**
2. *noun* A soft, rustling sound, as in *the swish of branches.* ▷ *noun, plural* **swishes**
swish (swish)

switch
1. *verb* To trade one thing for something similar, as in *to switch seats.*
2. *verb* To shift, transfer, or change from one thing to another, as in *to switch from coffee to tea.*
3. *noun* A change or a trade, as in *a switch in the order of the program.*
4. *verb* To turn a piece of electrical equipment on or off, as in *to switch on the television.*
5. *noun* A device that interrupts the flow of electricity in a circuit, as in *a light switch.*
6. *noun* A long, thin stick or rod used for whipping.
7. *noun* A section of railroad track used to move a train from one track to another. ▷ *verb* **switch**
switch (swich)
▷ *verb* **switches, switching, switched** ▷ *noun, plural* **switches**

swivel *verb* To turn or rotate around a central point, as in *to swivel in your seat.* **swiv·el** (**swiv**-uhl) ▷ *verb* **swiveling, swiveled**

swollen
1. *verb* The past participle of **swell**.
2. *adjective* Made large by swelling, as in *a swollen gland.*
swol·len (**swoh**-luhn)

swoop *verb* To rush down or pounce upon suddenly: *The owl swooped down on its prey.* **swoop** (swoop) ▷ *verb* **swooping, swooped** ▷ *noun* **swoop**

sword *noun* A weapon with a handle and a long, pointed blade with a sharp edge on one or both sides. **sword** (sord)

sword

swordfish *noun* A large saltwater food fish with a swordlike bone sticking out from its upper jaw. **sword·fish** (**sord**-fish) ▷ *noun, plural* **swordfish**

swore *verb* The past tense of **swear**. **swore** (swor)

a b c d e f g h i j k l m n o p q r **s** t u w x y z

sworn *verb* The past participle of **swear.** **sworn** (sworn)

swum *verb* The past participle of **swim.** **swum** (swuhm)

sycamore *noun* A North American and European tree with smooth, brown bark that peels off in layers. **syc·a·more** (**sik**-uh-*mor*)

syllable *noun* A unit of sound in a word. A syllable contains a vowel and possibly one or more consonants: *The word "long" contains one syllable.* **syl·la·ble** (**sil**-uh-buhl)

syllabus *noun* An outline or a summary of work that must be covered for a particular course of study: *On the first day of class, the teacher handed out the syllabus.* **syl·la·bus** (**sil**-uh-buhs) ▷ *noun, plural* **syllabuses** *or* **syllabi** (**sil**-uh-*bye*)

symbol *noun* A design or an object that stands for, suggests, or represents something else: *On many maps, a small tree is the symbol for a forest.* **sym·bol** (**sim**-buhl) **Symbol** sounds like **cymbal.**

symbolic *adjective* Standing for something else: *The covered wagon is symbolic of the settlement of the American West.* **sym·bol·ic** (sim-**bah**-lik)

symbolize *verb* To stand for or represent something else: *The dove symbolizes peace.* **sym·bol·ize** (**sim**-buh-*lize*) ▷ *verb* **symbolizing, symbolized**

symmetrical *adjective* Having matching points, parts, or shapes on both sides of a dividing line. For example, the capital letters "M" and "X" are symmetrical because you can draw a line dividing them into two matching halves. **sym·met·ri·cal** (si-**met**-ri-kuhl) ▷ *adverb* **symmetrically**

symmetry *noun* A balanced arrangement of parts on either side of a line or around a central point: *The symmetry of that crystal vase adds to its beauty.* **sym·me·try** (**sim**-i-tree)

sympathetic *adjective* Feeling or showing sympathy toward someone or something: *Her mother gave her a sympathetic hug and told her not to worry.* **sym·pa·thet·ic** (*sim*-puh-**thet**-ik) ▷ *adverb* **sympathetically**

sympathize *verb*
1. To understand or appreciate other people's troubles, as in *to sympathize with someone's sorrow.*
2. To be in agreement, as in *to sympathize with someone's views.*
sym·pa·thize (**sim**-puh-*thize*) ▷ *verb* **sympathizing, sympathized**

sympathy *noun*
1. The ability to identify with and to share other people's feelings: *Our neighbors' sympathy got us through a very difficult Christmas.*

synagogue

2. **in sympathy** In agreement with someone or something: *We welcomed those who were in sympathy with our goals.*
sym·pa·thy (**sim**-puh-thee) ▷ *adjective* **sympathetic** (*sim*-puh-**thet**-ik) ▷ *adverb* **sympathetically**

symphony *noun*
1. A long piece of music written for a full orchestra, usually consisting of several parts called movements.
2. A large orchestra that usually plays classical music.
sym·pho·ny (**sim**-fuh-nee) ▷ *noun, plural* **symphonies** ▷ *adjective* **symphonic** (sim-**fah**-nik)

symptom *noun*
1. A sign of an illness, as in *flu symptoms.*
2. An indication of something: *Josh's failing grades were a symptom of his lack of interest in school.*
symp·tom (**simp**-tuhm)

synagogue *noun* A building for Jewish worship and religious study. **syn·a·gogue** (**sin**-uh-*gahg*)

sync
1. *verb* Short for **synchronize.**
2. *noun* If two things are **in sync**, they work well together. If two things are **out of sync**, there is a problem with the way they work together.
sync (singk)
Sync sounds like **sink.**

synchronize *verb*
1. To arrange events so that they happen at the same time or in a certain order, as in *to synchronize the film with the sound track.*
2. To set to the same time, as in *to synchronize watches.*
syn·chro·nize (**sing**-kruh-*nize*) ▷ *verb* **synchronizing, synchronized** ▷ *noun* **synchronization** (*sin*-kruh-ni-**zay**-shuhn)

syndrome *noun* A group of signs and symptoms that occur together and are characteristic of a particular disease or disorder. **syn·drome** (**sin**-*drohm*)

synonym *noun* A word that has the same or nearly the same meaning as another word in the same language. For example, the word *shut* is a synonym for the word *close*. **syn·o·nym** (**sin**-uh-nim)

synonymous *adjective*
1. Having the same or almost the same meaning: *The words "gigantic" and "huge" are synonymous.*
2. Implying or referring to the same thing: *For many people, the owl is synonymous with wisdom.*
syn·on·y·mous (si-**nah**-nuh-muhs)

synopsis *noun* A brief summary or outline, as in *a synopsis of an article.* **syn·op·sis** (si-**nahp**-sis) ▷ *noun, plural* **synopses** (si-**nahp**-seez)

syntax *noun*
1. The arrangement of words and phrases in a sentence: *Her syntax was poor because she didn't speak the language very well.*
2. The rules that govern a programming or command language and determine the way that letters, numbers, and symbols must be entered.
syn·tax (**sin**-taks)
▷ *adjective* **syntactic** (sin-**tak**-tik)

synthesizer *noun* An electronic keyboard instrument that can imitate the sound of various musical instruments or produce sounds that ordinary instruments cannot. **syn·the·siz·er** (**sin**-thuh-*sye*-zur)

synthetic *adjective* Manufactured or artificial rather than found in nature, as in *synthetic* sweeteners. **syn·thet·ic** (sin-**thet**-ik) ▷ *noun* **synthetic** ▷ *adverb* **synthetically**

syringe *noun* A tube with a plunger and a hollow needle, used for giving injections and drawing out blood or bodily fluids. **sy·ringe** (suh-**rinj**)

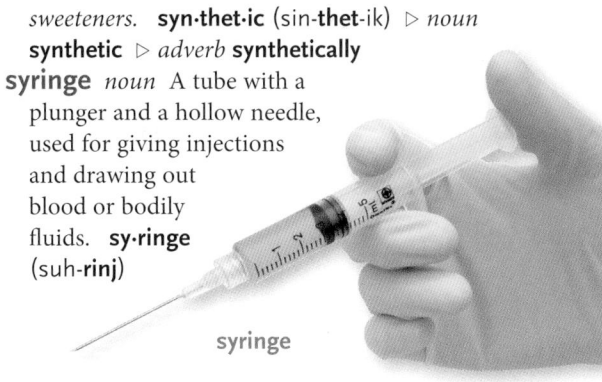

syringe

syrup *noun*
1. A sweet, thick liquid made by boiling sugar and water, usually with some flavoring, as in *chocolate syrup.*
2. A sweet, thick liquid made by boiling down the sap of a tree or plant, as in *maple syrup.*
syr·up (**sir**-uhp)
▷ *adjective* **syrupy** (**sir**-uh-pee)

system *noun*
1. A group of things or parts, related or connected so that they work together in an organized way, as in *the nervous system* or *a computer system.*
2. An organized and coordinated way of getting something done, as in *the educational system* or *a system of government.*
3. A method or procedure: *I need a better system for studying.*
sys·tem (**sis**-tuhm)
▷ *adjective* **systematic** (sis-tuh-**mat**-ik) ▷ *adverb* **systematically**

synthesizer

Tt

tab *noun*

1. A small flap or loop that is attached to something, such as a file folder or soda can. Tabs are used for labeling, pulling, or opening.

2. A key on a computer keyboard that you use to move around in tables.

3. The character that your keyboard sends to the computer when you hit the tab key.

4. One of a group of displays that you have open in a web browser, allowing you to have views of several webpages at once.

5. *(informal)* If you **keep tabs on** someone, you watch the person closely to see what he or she is doing.

6. *(informal)* If you **pick up the tab**, you pay for something for a group of people, such as the bill in a restaurant.
tab (tab)

tabby *noun*

1. A cat with a striped coat.

2. Any domestic cat, especially a female.
tab·by (**tab**-ee)   tabby

table *noun*

1. A piece of furniture that has a flat top resting on legs.

2. A chart that lists facts and figures, usually in columns: *Watch your savings grow each month by making a table.*

3. Food put on a table: *Grandma set a nice table.*

4. If you **turn the tables** on someone, you reverse the situation so that things are in your favor.

5. If something is done **under the table**, it is done in secret or illegally.
ta·ble (**tay**-buhl)

tablecloth *noun* A piece of material put over a table to protect or decorate it, as in *a linen tablecloth.*
ta·ble·cloth (**tay**-buhl-*klawth*)

table manners *noun, plural* Your behavior when you are eating a meal, especially with other people.

tablespoon *noun* A large spoon that you use to serve food or as a measure in cooking. A tablespoon is equal to three teaspoons. **ta·ble·spoon** (**tay**-buhl-*spoon*) ▷ *noun* **tablespoonful**

tablet *noun*

1. A pad of writing paper glued together at one end.

2. A small, hard piece of medicine that you swallow: *This antibiotic comes in a tablet.*

3. A piece of stone with writing carved into it.

4. A small, portable computer that you can use by touching the screen with your finger or a stylus, or by typing on a keyboard. Also known as a *tablet computer.*
tab·let (**tab**-lit)

table tennis *noun* A game for two or four players who use wooden paddles to hit a small, light ball over a low net on a table. Also called **Ping-Pong**.

tabloid *noun* A newspaper that contains brief articles and many pictures. The pictures and articles are often intended to stir up interest or excitement. **tab·loid** (**tab**-loid) ▷ *adjective* **tabloid**

taboo *adjective* If a subject is **taboo**, it may offend or upset people if you talk about it: *My friends and I try to avoid taboo topics like religion and politics.* **ta·boo** (tuh-**boo** *or* ta-**boo**) ▷ *noun* **taboo**

tabulate *verb* To arrange information into a table or chart: *We tabulated the student council votes by classroom.* ▷ *noun* **tabulation**

tacit *adjective* Agreed to or understood without being stated, as in *tacit approval.* **tac·it** (**tas**-it) ▷ *adverb* **tacitly**

taciturn *adjective* Quiet and shy and not saying much. **tac·i·turn** (**tas**-i-turn) ▷ *adverb* **taciturnly**

tack

1. *noun* A small nail with a sharp point and a large, flat head.

2. *noun* A way of doing something: *If you have trouble solving a problem one way, try a different tack.*

3. *verb* To add or attach something extra or different: *The teacher tacked five extra minutes onto recess.*

4. *verb* To sew material loosely before doing it neatly. ▷ *noun* **tack**

5. *verb* To turn a boat so that the wind blows into the sails from the opposite side.

6. *noun* Equipment that you need for riding a horse, such as a bridle and saddle.
tack (tak)
▷ *verb* **tacking, tacked**

tackle

1. *verb* In football, to knock or throw a player to the ground in order to stop him from moving forward. ▷ *noun* **tackle** ▷ *noun* **tackler**

2. *verb* To try to take the ball from another player in a sport such as soccer. ▷ *noun* **tackle** ▷ *noun* **tackler**

3. *verb* To attempt to deal with a difficult problem: *We must tackle the problem of vandalism.*

4. *noun* The equipment that you need for a particular activity, as in *fishing tackle.*

5. *noun* A system of ropes and pulleys used to raise, lower, or move heavy loads.
tack·le (**tak**-uhl)
▷ *verb* **tackling, tackled**

taco *noun* A Mexican food consisting of a fried or soft tortilla that is folded around one or more fillings such as beef, chicken, or cheese. **ta·co** (**tah**-koh) ▷ *noun, plural* **tacos**

taco

tact *noun* The ability to deal with a difficult situation or person without causing anyone to be upset or embarrassed. **tact** (takt) ▷ *adjective* **tactful** ▷ *adverb* **tactfully**

tactic *noun* An action or plan undertaken to achieve a specific goal: *He found that the best tactic to increase his vocabulary was to read more.* **tac·tic** (**tak**-tik) ▷ *adjective* **tactical** ▷ *adverb* **tactically**

tactics *noun, plural* Plans or methods to win a game or battle or achieve a goal. **tac·tics** (**tak**-tiks) ▷ *adjective* **tactical** ▷ *adverb* **tactically**

tadpole *noun* A young frog or toad that lives in water, breathes through gills, and has a long tail but no legs. **tad·pole** (**tad**-*pole*)

Word History

The **tadpole** gets its name from its shape. *Tad* is from the Middle English word for "toad," and *pole* is from the Middle English word for "head." Since a tadpole's head takes up most of its body, the name "toad-head" seems an appropriate one.

taffy *noun* A thick, chewy candy that is made of brown sugar or molasses and butter. The ingredients are boiled together, then stretched and folded over and over until the mixture holds its shape. **taf·fy** (**taf**-ee) ▷ *noun, plural* **taffies**

tag

1. *noun* A label that identifies or gives information, as in *a price tag* or *a name tag.* ▷ *verb* **tag**

2. *noun* A children's game in which the player called "It" has to chase the other players and touch one of them. ▷ *verb* **tag**

3. *noun* A code that tells a computer how it should deal with text or data. ▷ *verb* **tag**

4. *verb* In baseball, to put a runner out by touching him or her with the ball. ▷ *noun* **tag**

5. *verb* If you **tag along** with someone, you follow the person: *Marian's little brother tagged along wherever we went.*
tag (tag)
▷ *verb* **tagging, tagged**

tai chi *noun* An ancient Chinese martial art using slow, smooth, and flowing movements. It is now a popular form of exercise to relax the body and mind. **tai chi** (**tye chee**)

tail

1. *noun* A part that sticks out at the back end of an animal's body and is often long and thin, as in *a horse's tail.*

2. *noun* Something that is shaped like a **tail**, as in *the tail of a kite* or *the tail of a comet.*

3. *noun* The rear part or end of something: *We joined the tail of the procession.*

4. **tails** *noun* The side of a coin that doesn't have a head or face; the back of the coin.

5. *verb* (*informal*) If you **tail** someone, you follow the person closely. ▷ *verb* **tailing, tailed** ▷ *noun* **tail**
tail (tayl)
Tail sounds like **tale**.

tailgate

1. *noun* A board or gate at the rear of a vehicle that can be folded down or removed for loading and unloading.

2. *verb* To drive very closely behind another vehicle in a way that is considered dangerous.

3. *verb* To set up a picnic or barbecue on the tailgate of a vehicle, especially in the parking lot of a sports stadium. ▷ *noun* **tailgater**
tail·gate (**tale**-*gayt*)
▷ *verb* **tailgating, tailgated**

a
b
c
d
e
f
g
h
i
j
k
l
m
n
o
p
q
r
s
t
u
v
w
x
y
z

tailor

1. *noun* Someone who makes or alters clothes. ▷ *verb*
tailor

2. *verb* To design or change something for a
particular purpose: *The computer company has
promised to tailor its system to meet our needs.* ▷ *verb*
tailoring, tailored
tai·lor (**tay**-lur)

take *verb*

1. To get, seize, or capture something with the hands:
Steve took my notebook!

2. To move, carry, or remove something: *Take your
bag up to your room.*

3. To accept something: *Do you take fresh fruit for the
food drive?*

4. To use something: *This radio takes AA batteries.*

5. To receive or to accept something, especially
something bad: *Dolores took the news well.*

6. To do or perform an action: *Ed takes a shower
every night.*

7. To tolerate, or to permit something: *Our parents
won't take any rudeness from us.*

8. To win something: *Sandra took first place in the
race.*

9. To lead: *I take my dog for a walk twice a day.*

10. To understand or believe something: *I take it that
you are not hungry, because you haven't touched your
food.*

11. If you **take after** someone in your family, you look
or act like the person: *My cousins all say I take after
my uncle Ray.*

12. *(informal)* If you are **taken in** by someone, you
believe the lies that the person tells you: *We almost
got taken in by that man who wanted to trade cars
with us.*

13. If you **take off** something, you remove it: *Take off
those wet clothes before you come into the living room.*

14. If you **take up** something, you begin it, as in *I am
taking up French;* or you shorten it, as in *I will take
up the hem of my skirt before the party.*

15. If you **take to** something or someone, you like
the thing or person: *I am really taking to the idea of
learning to play the French horn.*
take (tayk)
▷ *verb* **taking, took** (tuk), **taken** (**tay**-kin)

takeoff *noun* The process of an aircraft leaving the
ground. **take·off** (**tayk**-*awf*) ▷ *verb* **take off**

takeout *noun*

1. A restaurant selling meals that you take and eat
somewhere else. ▷ *adjective* **take-out**

2. Food that you buy from a take-out restaurant: *We
ordered some Chinese takeout.*
take·out (**tayk**-*out*)

takeover *noun*

1. The action of one company taking control of
another company by buying lots of its stock.

2. If there is a **takeover** of a country, a new group
or individual seizes possession or control.
take·o·ver (**tayk**-*oh*-vur)
▷ *verb* **take over**

talc *noun* A soft mineral that is ground up to make
talcum powder, face powder, paint, and plastics.
talc (talk)

talcum powder *noun* A fine, white powder made
from talc. You can use talcum powder to dry your
body or to make it smell good. **tal·cum powder**
(**tal**-kuhm)

tale *noun*

1. A story about exciting and imaginary events, as
in *a tale of adventure.*

2. An interesting story about someone's
experiences that may not be completely true.
tale (tayl)
Tale sounds like **tail**.

talent *noun*

1. A natural ability or skill: *Don has a talent for
carpentry.*

2. A person with talent: *The director is always
looking for new talent.*
tal·ent (**tal**-uhnt)

talented *adjective* Good at a particular skill or
talent, especially without much training: *She is
a talented singer and is going to audition for the
music school.* **tal·ent·ed** (**tal**-uhn-tid)

talk

1. *verb* To say words; to speak: *The kids wouldn't
stop talking!* ▷ *noun* **talker**

2. *verb* To discuss something, especially
something important: *Let's talk about the
assignment.*

3. *verb* If you **talk** a person or group **into** doing
something, you persuade that person or group to
do something: *Lucy talked Charlie into going on
the roller coaster.*

4. *noun* A conversation: *We need to have a talk
about what happened this morning.*

5. *noun* A speech or a lecture: *My mom is giving a
talk to my class about her work as a lawyer.*
talk (tawk)
▷ *verb* **talking, talked**

talkative *adjective* Someone who is **talkative** talks
a lot: *A talkative roommate can make studying
impossible.* **talk·a·tive** (**taw**-kuh-tiv)

talk show *noun* A television or radio program in
which a host interviews or has discussions with
guests, audience members, or callers.

tall *adjective*
1. Higher than usual; not short or low, as in *a tall building.*
2. Having a certain height: *She is five feet tall.*
3. Incredible and therefore hard to believe, as in *a tall tale.*
tall (tawl)
▷ *adjective* **taller, tallest**

talisman *noun* An object someone keeps with him or her to bring good luck or to fend off evil: *He kept the old coin in his pocket as a talisman, because he had never had bad luck when it was with him.* **tal·is·man** (**tal**-is-muhn *or* **tal**-iz-muhn) ▷ *adjective* **talismanic** (*tal*-iz-**man**-ik)

tallow *noun* Fat from cattle and sheep that is used mainly to make candles and soap. **tal·low** (**tal**-oh)

tally
1. *noun* An account, a record, or a score: *Keep a tally of what I owe you.*
2. *verb* To add up an account, record, or score: *The waiter tallied our bill.*
3. *verb* To match, or to agree: *His account of the accident doesn't tally with mine.*
tal·ly (**tal**-ee)
▷ *verb* **tallies, tallying, tallied**

Talmud *noun* The collection of Jewish civil and religious laws. **Tal·mud** (**tal**-mud)

talon *noun* A sharp claw of a bird such as an eagle, hawk, or falcon. **tal·on** (**tal**-uhn)

tamale *noun* A Mexican dish made up of seasoned chopped meat rolled in cornmeal, then wrapped in husks of corn and steamed. **ta·ma·le** (tuh-**mah**-lee)

tamarind *noun* A tropical tree, or the soft, sticky fruit that grows on this tree. Tamarinds are sometimes used in Asian cooking. **tam·a·rind** (**tam**-ur-ind)

Word History

Arabic speakers called the **tamarind** the "date of India," *tamr-hindi.* Dates grow on date palms, and the Arabs probably thought it was the fruit of a palm tree like the date. But the tree that produces tamarinds is an evergreen, not a palm. The name entered Spanish as one word, *tamarindo,* from which we get the English word *tamarind.*

tambourine *noun* A small, round musical instrument that is similar to a drum. It has small, metal disks around the rim and is played by shaking or striking it with the hand. **tam·bou·rine** (*tam*-buh-**reen**)

talons

tambourine

tame *adjective*
1. Taken from a wild or natural state and trained to live with or be useful to people: *At the circus, we saw a tame elephant that could perform tricks.* ▷ *verb*
tame ▷ *noun* **tamer**
2. Gentle and not afraid around people: *The deer was so tame that it ate food from my hand.*
3. Not exciting or interesting enough: *The movie was supposed to be controversial, but I thought it was pretty tame.*
tame (taym)
▷ *adjective* **tamer, tamest** ▷ *adverb* **tamely**

tamper *verb* To interfere with something so that it becomes harmed or damaged: *It was clear that someone had tampered with the window lock.* **tam·per** (**tam**-pur)
▷ *verb* **tampering, tampered**

tan
1. *noun* A light yellow-brown color. ▷ *adjective* **tan**
2. *noun* If you have a **tan**, your skin has become darker because you have spent time in the sun. ▷ *verb* **tan**
3. *verb* To make animal skin into leather by soaking it in a chemical solution. ▷ *verb* **tanning, tanned** ▷ *noun* **tannery**
tan (tan)

tandem
1. *noun* A bicycle for two people, with one seat behind the other.
2. **in tandem** Together with or at the same time as someone or something else: *The CD was released in tandem with the book.*
3. **in tandem** One in front of another: *We were hooked together and could only move in tandem.*
tan·dem (**tan**-duhm)

tangent *noun*
1. In geometry, a straight line that touches a curve in one place.
2. If you **go off on a tangent**, you suddenly start talking about something that is not related to the main topic of discussion.
tan·gent (**tan**-juhnt)

tangerine *noun* A sweet, orange citrus fruit that is smaller than an orange and easier to peel. **tan·ger·ine** (*tan*-juh-**reen**)

tangle *verb* To twist together in a messy way and become difficult to separate: *Try not to tangle the cable wires.* **tan·gle** (**tang**-guhl)
▷ *verb* **tangling, tangled** ▷ *noun* **tangle**

tangram *noun* A Chinese puzzle made of a square cut into various shapes that you can put together to make a number of different patterns. **tan·gram** (**tang**-gram)

tangy *adjective* Having a strong, sharp flavor or odor: *I like the tangy taste of grapefruit.* **tang·y** (**tang**-ee)
▷ *adjective* **tangier, tangiest** ▷ *noun* **tang**

tank
1. *noun* A large container for gas or liquid, as in *a fuel tank*.
2. *noun* A military vehicle covered in heavy armor with a large gun at the front. Tanks have two metal belts with wheels inside them that allow them to move over rough ground.
3. *verb (informal)* To decrease sharply or fail suddenly: *The team's spirit really tanked after the loss.* ▷ *verb* **tanking, tanked**
tank (tangk)

tanker *noun* A ship, a truck, or an airplane that contains large tanks for carrying liquids or gas. **tank·er** (**tang**-kur)

tantrum *noun* A sudden outburst of uncontrolled anger or bad temper, considered to be typical of a child: *I haven't thrown a tantrum since I was eight years old.* **tan·trum** (**tan**-truhm)

tap
1. *verb* To hit something gently or lightly; *I tapped on the window.* ▷ *noun* **tap**
2. *noun* A small metal plate attached to the sole of a shoe for tap dancing.
3. *verb* To make or do by tapping again and again: *He tapped out a rhythm with his fingers.*
4. *verb* To make a

hole in order to draw off a liquid, as in *to tap a maple tree for its sap.*
5. *verb* To secretly listen in on a telephone conversation using a special device: *The police tapped the suspect's phone.* ▷ *noun* **tap**
6. *noun* A device used to control the flow of a liquid in a pipe; a faucet.
tap (tap)
▷ *verb* **tapping, tapped**

tap dancing *noun* Dancing in which shoes with taps are worn in order to make a clicking sound with the feet: *Dawn wants to learn tap dancing.* ▷ *noun* **tap dance** ▷ *noun* **tap dancer** ▷ *verb* **tap-dance**

tape
1. *noun* A thin strip of material, paper, or plastic, as in *adhesive tape*.
2. *verb* To fasten together, wrap, or bind with tape: *We taped the box closed and mailed it to her.*
3. *noun* A long piece of plastic covered with a magnetic substance and used to record sound or pictures. The tape is usually contained in a plastic case, or cassette.
4. *verb* To record sound or pictures on tape: *Tonight I'm taping my favorite TV show.*
tape (tayp)
▷ *verb* **taping, taped**

tape measure *noun* A long, thin piece of ribbon or steel marked in inches or centimeters so that you can measure things easily.

tape measure

taper
1. *verb* To make or become narrower at one end: *Wendy tapered the legs of her pants.*
2. **taper off** *verb* To gradually become smaller or less: *The storm finally tapered off.*
3. *noun* A slender candle.
ta·per (**tay**-pur)
Taper sounds like **tapir**. ▷ *verb* **tapering, tapered**

tape recorder *noun* A machine that you use to play back or record music and sound on magnetic tape.
▷ *noun* **tape recording** ▷ *verb* **tape-record**

tapestry *noun* A heavy piece of cloth with threads woven into it to make pictures or patterns.
tap·es·try (**tap**-i-stree) ▷ *noun, plural* **tapestries**

tapir *noun* A large animal that has hoofs and a long, flexible snout. The tapir looks like a pig. It is found in Central America, South America, and southern Asia, and is distantly related to the horse and rhinoceros.
ta·pir (**tay**-pur) **Tapir** sounds like **taper**.

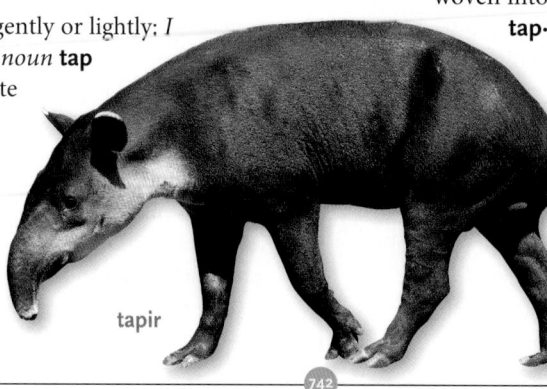
tapir

target

taps *noun* A song played on a bugle at the end of the day in military camps as a signal that all lights must be put out. Taps is also played at military funerals. **taps** (taps)

tar *noun* A thick, black, sticky substance used for making roads and patching roofs. Tar is made from coal or wood. **tar** (tahr) ▷ *verb* **tar**

tarantula *noun* A large, hairy spider found mainly in warm regions. Its bite is painful but not seriously poisonous to people. **ta·ran·tu·la** (tuh-**ran**-chuh-luh)

tardy *adjective* Not on time; late: *Several students were tardy this morning.* **tar·dy** (**tahr**-dee) ▷ *adjective* **tardier, tardiest** ▷ *noun* **tardiness**

target
1. *noun* A mark, a circle, or an object at which you aim and shoot. ▷ *verb* **target**
2. *noun* Someone or something that is criticized or made fun of: *My little brother is always the target of Gwen's jokes.*
3. *noun* A goal or an aim: *My target is to improve my science grade.*
4. *verb* If you **target** something, you direct your attention to it: *The movie is targeted at teenagers.* ▷ *verb* **targeting, targeted**
tar·get (**tahr**-git)

tariff *noun* A tax charged on goods that are imported or exported. **tar·iff** (**tar**-if)

Word History

Officials at the borders of a country have to follow a lot of complicated rules, so they have lists to help them. The English word **tariff** originally referred to a list like this: It was a list of taxes that customs officials were supposed to charge people for their goods. Then the meaning of the word changed to the tax itself. The word goes back to the Arabic term for "telling or making something known," *ta'rif*, because a list is a way of telling people something.

tarmac *noun* Pavement made from crushed stone and tar, especially on an airport runway or road. The word *tarmac* comes from *tarmacadam,* the substance that this pavement is made from: *The planes were lined up in a row on the tarmac, waiting to take off.* **tar·mac** (**tahr**-mak)

tarnish *verb* If something **tarnishes**, it becomes less bright. **tar·nish** (**tahr**-nish) ▷ *verb* **tarnishes, tarnishing, tarnished** ▷ *noun* **tarnish**

tarp *noun* Short for **tarpaulin**. **tarp** (tahrp)

tarpaulin *noun* A heavy, waterproof covering, usually made of canvas, that is used to protect playing fields, boats, or any outdoor item from wet weather. A tarpaulin is also known as a **tarp**. **tar·pau·lin** (**tahr**-puh-lin)

tart
1. *noun* A small pie or pastry that usually contains fruit, as in *an apricot tart.*
2. *adjective* Sour-tasting.
3. *adjective* A **tart** remark is mean, sharp, or bitter in tone. ▷ *adjective* **tarter, tartest** ▷ *adverb* **tartly** ▷ *noun* **tartness**
tart (tahrt)

tartan *noun* A type of plaid, or a woolen cloth with a plaid pattern. Tartan is used especially for Scottish kilts. **tar·tan** (**tahr**-tuhn)

tartar *noun* A yellow substance that forms on the teeth. Tartar consists of food particles, saliva, and calcium. If not removed, it becomes hard. **tar·tar** (**tahr**-tur)

tartar sauce *noun* A sauce made with mayonnaise and chopped pickles, often served with fish.

Taser *noun* A trademark for a weapon used especially by police that sends a very powerful and painful electric shock through a person's body. **Ta·ser** (**tay**-zur)

task *noun* A piece of work to be done, especially work assigned by another person: *No task is too great for my big brother.* **task** (task)

taskbar *noun* A horizontal bar at the bottom of your computer screen that shows which programs you have open. **task·bar** (**task**-bahr)

task force *noun* A group formed for a limited period of time to deal with a specific problem: *A task force was formed to study the water quality.*

tassel *noun*
1. A bunch of threads tied at one end and used as a decoration on shoes, clothing, graduation caps, furniture, or rugs.
2. Something that is like a tassel, such as the tassel of silk on an ear of corn.
tas·sel (**tas**-uhl) ▷ *adjective* **tasseled**

a b c d e f g h i j k l m n o p q r s t u v w x y z

taste

1. *noun* Your sense of **taste** allows you to identify a food by its flavor.

2. *noun* The **taste** of a food is its flavor, for example, sweet, sour, salty, or bitter. ▷ *adjective* **tasty**

3. *noun* If you have good **taste**, you choose clothes, furniture, and other things carefully and well: *Karen has good taste in music.* ▷ *adjective* **tasteful**

4. *verb* To have a certain flavor: *Sugar tastes sweet.*

5. *verb* To try a bit of food or drink to see if you like it: *Would you like to taste this soup that I made?* ▷ *noun* **taste**

taste (tayst) ▷ *verb* **tasting, tasted**

taste bud *noun* One of the groups of cells in the tongue that sense whether something is sweet, sour, salty, or bitter.

tasteless *adjective*

1. Having little or no flavor; bland: *This plain oatmeal is tasteless.*

2. Showing little sense of what is appropriate; rude, as in *a tasteless remark.* **taste·less** (tayst-lis)

tattered *adjective* Old and torn, as in *a tattered jacket.* **tat·tered** (tat-urd)

tattle *verb* To tell someone in authority that someone else is doing something wrong. This word is used especially by and about children: *I could have tattled on you when the teacher asked me what happened.* **tat·tle** (tat-uhl) ▷ *verb* **tattling, tattled** ▷ *noun* **tattler**

tattletale *noun* Someone who tells other people's secrets. This word is used especially by and about children. **tat·tle·tale** (tat-uhl-*tale*)

tattoo *noun* A picture or words that have been printed onto somebody's skin with needles and ink. **tat·too** (ta-**too**) ▷ *verb* **tattoo**

taught *verb* The past tense and the past participle of **teach**. **taught** (tawt)

taunt *verb* To try to make someone angry or upset by saying unkind things about him or her: *He wouldn't stop taunting her about her weight.* **taunt** (tawnt) ▷ *verb* **taunting, taunted** ▷ *noun* **taunt**

taut *adjective* Stretched tight, as in *a taut wire.* **taut** (tawt) ▷ *adjective* **tauter, tautest**

tavern *noun* A place where people can sit and drink alcoholic beverages; a bar. **tav·ern** (tav-urn)

tawny *adjective* Having a light, sandy-brown color, as in *a tawny lion.* **taw·ny** (taw-nee) ▷ *adjective* **tawnier, tawniest**

tax

1. *noun* Money that people and businesses must pay in order to support a government, as in *a sales tax* or *an income tax.* ▷ *noun, plural* **taxes** ▷ *verb* **tax**

2. *verb* To make heavy demands on; to strain: *His rude behavior taxed my patience.* ▷ *verb* **taxes, taxing, taxed** ▷ *adjective* **taxing**

tax (taks)

taxable *adjective* If something is **taxable**, you have to pay tax on it, as in *taxable income.* **tax·a·ble** (tak-suh-buhl)

taxation *noun*

1. The system a government uses to collect money from people and businesses.

2. The money a government collects from people and businesses: *The president promised to reduce taxation on the middle class.*

tax·a·tion (tak-**say**-shuhn)

taxi

1. *noun* A car with a driver whom you pay to take you somewhere.

2. *verb* When planes **taxi**, they move along the ground before taking off or after landing. ▷ *verb* **taxies, taxiing, taxied**

tax·i (tak-see)

taxonomy *noun* The system that scientists use for classifying and naming plants, animals, and microbes. **tax·on·o·my** (tak-**sah**-nuh-mee) ▷ *adjective* **taxonomic** (tak-suh-**nah**-mik)

teakettle

TB

1. Short for **terabyte**.

2. Short for **tuberculosis**.

tbsp. Short for **tablespoon** or the plural form *tablespoons.*

T cell *noun* Any of a group of cells found in the lymph glands that help protect the body against disease.

tea *noun*

1. A drink made from the leaves of a plant that is grown in China, Japan, and India: *We steeped the tea in hot water for five minutes.*

2. This plant or its dried leaves.

3. A similar drink made from the leaves of other plants, as in *herb tea.*

4. A late-afternoon social gathering at which tea and other refreshments are served: *Harrison would serve biscuits when neighbors came over for tea.*

tea (tee)

teach *verb* To tell or show someone how to do something: *Tim is going to teach me how to play the piano.* **teach** (teech) ▷ *verb* **teaches, teaching, taught** (tawt)

teakettle *noun* A kettle with a handle and a spout. A teakettle is used for boiling water. **tea·ket·tle** (tee-*ket*-uhl)

teammates

teal *noun*
1. A dark color between green and blue. ▷ *adjective* **teal**
2. Any of several small ducks with short necks. Teal live in rivers and marshes. The males often have brightly colored feathers.
teal (teel)
▷ *noun, plural* **teal** *or* **teals**

team
1. *noun* A group of people who work together or play a sport together against another group, as in *a team of doctors* or *a hockey team.*
2. *noun* Two or more animals that are fastened together to do work, as in *a team of horses.*
3. **team up** *verb* To join together to achieve something: *Mom and Dad teamed up to plant a tree in the yard.* ▷ *verb* **teaming, teamed**
team (teem)
Team sounds like **teem.**

teammate *noun* Someone who is a member of your team. **team·mate** (**teem**-*mate*)

tear
1. (teer) *noun* A drop of clear, salty liquid that comes from your eye. ▷ *adjective* **tearful** ▷ *adjective* **teary**
2. (tair) *noun* A rip in a piece of paper or other substance: *There was a tear in my dress.*
3. (tair) *verb* To pull or be pulled apart by force: *Tear the paper into strips. This material tears easily.*
4. (tair) *verb* To make a hole in something by pulling; to rip: *I tore my pants on a nail.*

5. (tair) *verb* To move very quickly: *Carlos tore down the road in his brand-new truck.*
tear
▷ *verb* **tearing, tore** (tor), **torn** (torn)

tease *verb* To say unkind things to someone in a way that is meant to be playful: *Morris was teasing Evan about his new shoes.* **tease** (teez) ▷ *verb* **teasing, teased** ▷ *noun* **tease** ▷ *noun* **teaser**

teaspoon *noun* A small spoon that you use as a measure in cooking or for stirring liquids. Three teaspoons equal one tablespoon. **tea·spoon** (**tee**-*spoon*) ▷ *noun* **teaspoonful**

techie *noun* (*informal*) Someone who is an expert in designing or fixing computers, software, and other technology: *Whenever we have a computer problem, we call the techies in the IT department to come fix it.* **tech·ie** (**tek**-ee)

technical *adjective*
1. Of or having to do with science, engineering, or the mechanical or industrial arts: *You can learn how to be an auto mechanic at a technical school.*
2. Using words that only experts in a particular field or subject understand: *I read the directions, but they're too technical.*
tech·ni·cal (**tek**-ni-kuhl)
▷ *adverb* **technically**

technician *noun* Someone who works with specialized equipment or does practical laboratory work, as in *a lighting technician* or *a dental technician.* **tech·ni·cian** (tek-**nish**-uhn)

technique *noun* A method or way of doing something that requires skill, as in the arts, sports, or the sciences: *Scientists have developed a new technique for growing brain tissue.* **tech·nique** (tek-**neek**)

technology *noun* The use of science and engineering to do practical things, such as make businesses and factories more efficient: *Improved technology is helping video games become more realistic.* **tech·nol·o·gy** (tek-**nah**-luh-jee) ▷ *noun, plural* **technologies** ▷ *adjective* **technological** (tek-nuh-**lah**-ji-kuhl)

teddy bear *noun* A soft, stuffed toy bear. **ted·dy bear** (**ted**-ee)

Word History

Morris Michtom, a candy store owner from Brooklyn, New York, made the first **teddy bear** in 1902 as a tribute to President Theodore "Teddy" Roosevelt. When he heard that Roosevelt had refused to shoot a small, helpless bear cub on one of his hunting trips, Michtom decided to name his brown stuffed bears after the president.

tedious *adjective* Tiring and boring: *Working on an assembly line is a tedious job.* **te·di·ous** (**tee**-dee-uhs or **tee**-juhs) ▷ *adverb* **tediously**

teem *verb* If a place is **teeming with** people or animals, there are many of them moving around: *The jungle was teeming with insects.* **teem** (teem) **Teem** sounds like **team**. ▷ *verb* **teeming, teemed**

teenager *noun* A person who is between the ages of 13 and 19. **teen·ag·er** (**teen**-ay-jur) ▷ *adjective* **teenage** or **teenaged**

teens *noun, plural* The years of a person's life between 13 and 19: *Emily is in her teens.* **teens** (teenz)

teeny *adjective* (*informal*) Tiny. **tee·ny** (**tee**-nee)

teepee Another spelling of **tepee**. **tee·pee** (**tee**-*pee*)

teeth *noun, plural* The white, bony parts of the mouth that are used for biting and chewing food. **teeth** (teeth)

teethe *verb* If a baby is **teething**, teeth are coming through his or her gums for the first time. **teethe** (teeTH) ▷ *verb* **teething, teethed**

Teflon *noun* The trademark for a type of plastic used especially on the insides of pans to prevent sticking. **Tef·lon** (**tef**-lahn)

Prefix

The prefix **tele-** means "far away" in Greek. You can see this form in many words, including *telegraph* (a device that lets you send messages far away), *telephone* (a machine that lets you talk to someone far away), and *telescope* (an instrument that allows you to see images that are far away).

telecast *noun* A program broadcast on television. **tel·e·cast** (**tel**-i-*kast*) ▷ *verb* **telecast**

telecom *noun* A company that provides phone numbers and telephone services. **tel·e·com** (**tel**-uh-*kahm*)

telecommunication *noun*
1. The science that deals with the sending of messages over long distances by telephone, satellite, radio, and other electronic means. Also known as *telecommunications.*
2. Any message sent this way. **tel·e·com·mu·ni·ca·tion** (*tel*-i-kuh-*myoo*-nih-**kay**-shuhn)

telecommute *verb* To do your work by staying at home and communicating with your office by means of a computer with a modem, a fax machine, or any other form of electronic communication. **tel·e·com·mute** (*tel*-i-kuh-**myoot**) ▷ *verb* **telecommuting, telecommuted** ▷ *noun* **telecommuter**

telegram *noun* A message that is sent by telegraph: *Uncle Shawn sent a telegram as soon as he arrived in Japan.* **tel·e·gram** (**tel**-i-*gram*) ▷ *verb* **telegram**

telegraph *noun* A device or system for sending messages over long distances using a code of electrical signals sent by wire or radio. **tel·e·graph** (**tel**-i-*graf*) ▷ *verb* **telegraph**

telemarketing *noun* The selling of goods and services by telephone. **tel·e·mar·ket·ing** (*tel*-uh-**mahr**-ki-ting) ▷ *noun* **telemarketer**

teleoperation *noun* Operating a machine, such as a mobile robot, from a distance using an electronic remote control device. **tel·e·op·er·a·tion** (*tel*-uh-*ah*-puh-**ray**-shuhn)

telepathy *noun* The ability to know other people's thoughts, or to communicate without speaking or gesturing. Also known as **mental telepathy**. **te·lep·a·thy** (tuh-**lep**-uh-thee) ▷ *adjective* **telepathic** (*tel*-uh-**path**-ik) ▷ *adverb* **telepathically**

telephone *noun*
1. A device for sending and receiving sounds, especially speech, by changing them into electrical signals. The signals are sent by wires or radio waves and then changed back into sounds.
2. A system for sending sounds over distances in this way.
tel·e·phone (**tel**-uh-*fone*) ▷ *verb* **telephone**

telephoto lens *noun* A camera lens that makes distant objects seem larger and closer. **tel·e·pho·to lens** (*tel*-uh-**foh**-toh)

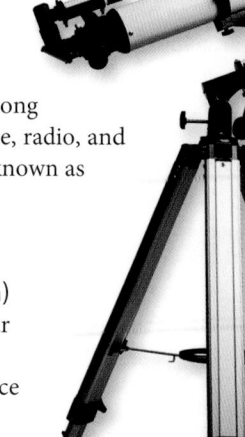
telescope

telescope *noun* An instrument that makes distant objects seem larger and closer. Telescopes are used especially for studying the stars and other heavenly bodies. **tel·e·scope** (**tel**-uh-*skope*) ▷ *adjective* **telescopic** (*tel*-uh-**skah**-pik)

televise *verb* To broadcast by television: *I heard they might televise the game.* **tel·e·vise** (**tel**-uh-*vize*) ▷ *verb* **televising, televised**

television *noun*
1. A piece of electrical equipment with a screen that receives and shows moving pictures with sound. Also known as a *television set* or *TV*: *We vowed to spend less time in front of the television.*
2. The system of sending sounds and moving pictures along radio waves to be picked up by a television set, as in *cable television.*
3. The programs that are broadcast on

Teleoperation

This term for the electronic remote control of machines is often used to describe robotics. However, it can refer to a wide variety of activities, from using a remote control to turn on the television to flying a drone, performing remote surgery, or sending commands from earth to a space probe. Teleoperated machines and vehicles are useful in hazardous places, such as minefields or contaminated environments. The first teleoperation systems were created in the late 1800s by Serbian-American inventor Nikola Tesla.

police-controlled bomb squad robot

television: *The average American watches more than four hours of television each day.*
tel·e·vi·sion (**tel**-uh-*vizh*-uhn)

tell *verb*

1. To put into words by speaking or writing: *Please tell the truth.*

2. To report information to someone: *Tell me what really happened.*

3. To show or indicate something: *The red light tells you that the engine is too hot.*

4. To order or to command: *The librarian told us to lower our voices.*

5. To recognize or to identify: *It was hard to tell who it was without my glasses.*

6. If you **tell** someone **off**, you speak to the person in an angry way because he or she has done something wrong: *I wish I had told off the man who cut in front of me in line.*

7. If you **tell on** someone, you report to someone else what that person has done: *Neither brother would ever tell on the other.*

tell (tel)
▷ *verb* **telling, told** (tohld)

teller *noun*

1. Someone who tells or relates stories.

2. A bank employee who gives out and receives money.
tel·ler (**tel**-ur)

temper

1. *noun* A tendency to suddenly get angry: *He has quite a temper.*

2. *noun* A person's usual attitude or mood: *Carl had his father's good temper.*

3. *noun* A calm state of mind: *She lost her temper and started screaming at everyone.*

4. *verb* To make something less severe: *Please temper your anger.*

5. *verb* To make something hard or strong, as in *to temper steel.*

tem·per (**tem**-pur)
▷ *verb* **tempering, tempered**

temperament *noun* Your nature or personality; the way you usually think, act, or respond to other people or to situations: *Lolly has a very sweet temperament.* **tem·per·a·ment** (**tem**-pur-uh-muhnt)

temperamental *adjective* Moody, unpredictable, or too sensitive: *Since his best friend moved away, Alex has been very temperamental.* **tem·per·a·men·tal** (*tem*-pur-uh-**men**-tuhl) ▷ *adverb* **temperamentally**

temperate *adjective* If an area has a **temperate** climate, the temperature is rarely very high or very low. **tem·per·ate** (**tem**-pur-it)

temperature *noun*

1. The degree of heat or cold in something, usually measured by a thermometer: *In the winter the temperature can drop below freezing.*

2. If you have a **temperature**, your body is hotter than normal. Normal human body temperature is around 98.6 degrees Fahrenheit, or 37 degrees Celsius.
tem·per·a·ture (**tem**-pur-uh-chur)

tempest *noun*

1. A violent storm with strong winds: *The tempest struck the southern coast with a fury.*

2. A violent or noisy commotion: *There was a tempest in the courtroom when the verdict was handed down.*
tem·pest (**tem**-pist)

Greek temple: the Parthenon

template *noun*

1. A shape or pattern that you draw or cut around to make the same shape in another material, such as paper or metal.

2. In computers, a document or pattern that is used to create similar documents. For example, a magazine designer could use a template for a page that follows the same general format from issue to issue.

tem·plate (**tem**-plit)

temple *noun*

1. The flat area on either side of the forehead, above the cheek and in front of the ear.

2. A building used for worshipping a god or gods.

tem·ple (**tem**-puhl)

tempo *noun* The speed or rhythm of a piece of music: *The jazz musician played an upbeat tempo.* **tem·po** (**tem**-poh) ▷ *noun, plural* **tempos** *or* **tempi** (**tem**-pee)

temporary *adjective* Lasting for only a short time: *The dentist said my braces will be temporary.* **tem·po·rar·y** (**tem**-puh-*rer*-ee) ▷ *adverb* **temporarily** (*tem*-puh-**rer**-uh-lee)

tempt *verb*

1. To try to get someone to do or want something that is wrong or foolish. ▷ *noun* **tempter** ▷ *adjective* **tempting**

2. To appeal strongly to someone: *His offer tempts me.* **tempt** (tempt)

▷ *verb* **tempting, tempted**

temptation *noun*

1. Something that you want to have or do, although you know you should not: *Ben resisted the temptation to go to bed and kept studying.*

2. The act of being tempted.

temp·ta·tion (temp-**tay**-shuhn)

tenacious *adjective*

1. Holding or clinging firmly to something, as in *a*

tenacious grip or *a tenacious barnacle.*

2. Holding on to an idea or goal and not giving up on it; persistent: *She is a tenacious prosecutor who is determined to get a conviction in the case.*

te·na·cious (tuh-**nay**-shuhs)

▷ *noun* **tenaciousness** ▷ *adverb* **tenaciously**

tenacity *noun* The quality or state of holding on to ideas or goals and not giving up on them: *Claudia showed a lot of tenacity in college, working extra jobs so that she could afford it.* **te·nac·i·ty** (tuh-**nas**-uh-tee)

tenant *noun* Someone who rents a room, a house, an apartment, an office, or land that belongs to someone else. **ten·ant** (**ten**-uhnt)

tend *verb*

1. If something **tends** to happen, it usually or often happens: *I tend to get up early.*

2. To take care of a person, an animal, or a plant: *I tended to the seedling and watched it grow.*

tend (tend)

▷ *verb* **tending, tended**

tendency *noun* If you have a **tendency** to do something, you usually or often do it: *I have a tendency to talk with my mouth full.* **ten·den·cy** (**ten**-duhn-see) ▷ *noun, plural* **tendencies**

tender *adjective*

1. Sore or painful: *He put an ice pack on his tender shoulder.*

2. Soft or easy to chew: *The steak was so tender, I was able to cut it with my fork.*

3. Kind and gentle: *She gave the new baby a tender kiss.*

ten·der (**ten**-dur)

▷ *adverb* **tenderly** ▷ *noun* **tenderness**

tendon *noun* A strong, thick cord or band of tissue that joins a muscle to a bone or other body part. **ten·don** (**ten**-duhn)

Word History

The ancient Greek word for "tendon" was *tenon*, but in the Middle Ages, people writing in Latin associated the name with the Latin verb *tendere*, meaning "to stretch." Perhaps because the words looked similar, and we are able to "stretch" our tendons, the writers inserted the letter *d* into the middle of the Greek word, forming words that were spelled as "tendon-." Their word part *tendon-* ended up as our English word **tendon**.

tendril *noun* A threadlike, curly part. Some climbing plants climb by means of tendrils that curl around supports. **ten·dril** (**ten**-druhl)

tenement *noun* A large building divided into apartments, especially one that is crowded and in a poor part of a city. **ten·e·ment (ten-**uh-muhnt)

tennis *noun* A game in which two or four players use rackets to hit a ball over a net on a court. **ten·nis (ten-**is)

tenor *noun* An adult male singing voice in the highest range, or a singer with a voice like this. **ten·or (ten-**ur) ▷ *adjective* **tenor**

tense
1. *adjective* Nervous or worried: *Maria is always tense before she gives a speech.* ▷ *adverb* **tensely**
2. *adjective* Stretched stiff and tight: *My muscles were still tense the day after the game.*
3. *noun* A form of a verb that indicates whether an action happened in the past, is happening in the present, or will happen in the future. *I was, I am, and I will be are examples of the past, present, and future tenses of the verb to be.* ▷ *noun* **tenseness** ▷ *verb* **tense**
tense (tens)
▷ *adjective* **tenser, tensest**

tension *noun*
1. A feeling of nervousness, stress, or suspense that makes it difficult to relax: *Tension mounted as the votes were counted.*
2. The stiffness or tightness of something such as a rope or wire: *The tension of a guitar string partly determines the sound that the string makes.*
3. If there is **tension** between two people, there is difficulty in their relationship and they may suddenly start arguing: *The tension between his sisters made Mitch uncomfortable.*
ten·sion (ten-shuhn)

tent *noun* A portable shelter made of nylon or canvas supported by poles and ropes: *We put up the tent and slept in the backyard.* **tent (**tent)

tentacle *noun* One of the long, flexible limbs of some animals, such as jellyfish, octopuses, squid, and sea anemones. They use their tentacles to move and to feel and grasp things. **ten·ta·cle (ten-**tuh-kuhl)

tentative *adjective*
1. Unsure or not confident: *I heard a tentative knock at the door.*
2. Not certain or definite, and may be changed: *We set a tentative date for the wedding.*
ten·ta·tive (ten-tuh-tiv)
▷ *adverb* **tentatively**

tenterhooks *noun, plural* If you are **on tenterhooks**, you are nervously waiting for something to happen. **ten·ter·hooks (ten-**tur-*huks*)

tenuous *adjective* Not very strong or certain: *His essay had only a tenuous connection to the topic.* **ten·u·ous (ten-**yoo-uhs) ▷ *adverb* **tenuously**

tepee *noun* A tent shaped like a cone and made from animal skins, formerly made by certain Native American tribes to use as homes. **te·pee (tee-***pee*)

tepid *adjective* Slightly warm, as in *tepid water.* **tep·id (tep-**id)

terabyte *noun* A unit used to measure large amounts of data. A terabyte is one thousand gigabytes. **ter·a·byte (ter-**uh-*bite*)

teriyaki *noun* A Japanese dish of chicken, meat, or fish that has been soaked in soy sauce and broiled or grilled. **ter·i·ya·ki (***ter*-ee-**yah**-kee)

Tennis

Tennis is played on a court divided by a net. Players on each side take turns serving and hitting the ball with rackets. Points are scored each time either side fails to return the ball within bounds. Unless there is a tie, a game is won with four points. A tennis match typically includes two parts, known as sets, made up of six games each.

racket

tennis court

term *noun*

1. A word with a specific meaning in some particular field, as in *musical terms* or *computer terms*.

2. A definite or limited period of time: *A president's term of office is four years.*

3. A part of the school year: *Javier finished the first term with straight As.*

4. terms *noun, plural* The conditions of an agreement, a contract, a will, or a sale: *The final terms of the sale were determined by lawyers.*

5. terms *noun, plural* A relationship between people: *After the argument, we were on good terms again.*

term (turm)

terminal

1. *noun* A station at either end of a transportation line, as in *an airport terminal.*

2. *noun* A computer keyboard and screen that are connected to a network.

3. *adjective* A **terminal** illness cannot be cured and causes death, often slowly. ▷ *adverb* **terminally**

4. terminal velocity *noun* The maximum speed an object can reach falling through the air.

ter·mi·nal (**tur**-muh-nuhl)

terminate *verb*

1. To stop or to end: *The train terminates here.*

2. To remove someone from a job: *My boss was terminated last week.*

ter·mi·nate (**tur**-muh-*nate*)

▷ *verb* **terminating, terminated**

terminology *noun* The special vocabulary of a particular field of knowledge. Each of the sciences has its own terminology. **ter·mi·nol·o·gy** (*tur*-muh-**nah**-luh-jee)

termite *noun* An insect like an ant that eats wood. Termites build large mounds, where they live together in colonies. **ter·mite** (**tur**-mite)

terrace *noun*

1. A paved, open area next to a building where you can sit.

2. A balcony of an apartment building.

3. A raised, flat platform of land with sloping sides.

ter·race (**ter**-is)

▷ *adjective* **terraced**

Word History

In the early history of the word **terrace**, we find that it meant "pile of earth." The Latin word *terra* meant "earth." Later, Latin speakers formed *terracea* from it. The ending *-acea* added the meaning of "big" to the word, so *terracea* meant "big earth," or a mound. English speakers first used the term *terrace* to refer to a raised platform or a balcony, and we also call a paved, open area a *terrace* now. You can see the same Latin root in the word *terrarium*.

terra-cotta *noun* A hard, waterproof clay used in making pottery and roofs. **ter·ra·cot·ta** (ter-uh **kah**-tuh) ▷ *adjective* **terra-cotta**

terrain *noun* An area of land: *The terrain was very rocky.* **ter·rain** (tuh-**rayn**)

terrapin *noun* A North American turtle that lives in or near freshwater or along seashores. **ter·ra·pin** (**ter**-uh-pin)

terrarium *noun* A glass or plastic container for growing small plants or raising small land animals. **ter·rar·i·um** (tuh-**rair**-ee-uhm) ▷ *noun, plural* **terrariums** or **terraria** (tuh-**rair**-ee-uh)

terrestrial *adjective* Of or having to do with the earth, or living on the earth. **ter·res·tri·al** (tuh-**res**-tree-uhl)

terrible *adjective*

1. Very great; extreme or severe, as in *terrible suffering* or *terrible heat.*

2. Very bad or unpleasant, as in *a terrible movie.*

3. Causing great fear or terror, as in *a terrible flood* or *a terrible roar.*

ter·ri·ble (**ter**-uh-buhl)

terribly *adverb*

1. Extremely: *I had a terribly embarrassing experience yesterday—I slipped on some ice right in front of the school.*

2. Very badly: *My best friend is away at camp, and I miss her terribly.*

ter·ri·bly (**ter**-uh-blee)

terrier *noun* Any of several breeds of small, lively dogs that were originally used for hunting small animals. **ter·ri·er** (**ter**-ee-ur)

Word History

The **terrier** got its name from *terra*, the Latin word for "earth." Terriers are common house pets today, but originally these dogs helped hunters by digging into burrows, or holes in the earth, to drive out the animals inside.

terrier

terrific *adjective*

1. Extremely good; excellent, as in *a terrific idea.*

2. Very large or great, in a way that is surprising: *We flew high across the sky at terrific speed.*

3. Causing great fear or terror: *All of a sudden we heard a terrific explosion.*

ter·ri·fic (tuh-**rif**-ik)

▷ *adverb* **terrifically**

terrify *verb* To frighten someone greatly: *Flying terrifies my brother.* **ter·ri·fy** (**ter**-uh-*fye*) ▷ *verb* **terrifies, terrifying, terrified** ▷ *adjective* **terrifying** ▷ *adverb* **terrifyingly**

territory *noun*

1. Any large area of land, as in *enemy territory.*

2. The land and waters under the control of a state, nation, or ruler.

3. An area connected with or owned by a country that is outside the country's main borders.

ter·ri·to·ry (**ter**-i-*tor*-ee)

▷ *noun, plural* **territories** ▷ *adjective* **territorial** (*ter*-i-**tor**-ee-uhl)

terror *noun*

1. Very great fear: *People ran out of the burning building in terror.*

2. A person or thing that causes very great fear: *My little brother can be a terror sometimes.*

ter·ror (**ter**-ur)

terrorist *noun* Someone who uses violence and threats in order to, for example, frighten people, obtain power, or force a government to do something. **ter·ror·ist** (**ter**-ur-ist) ▷ *noun* **terrorism** (**ter**-uh-**riz**-uhm)

terrorize *verb* To frighten someone a great deal: *Passengers were terrorized by the runaway train.* **ter·ror·ize** (**ter**-uh-*rize*) ▷ *verb* **terrorizing, terrorized**

terse *adjective* Brief and direct in a way that may be considered rude, as in *a terse response.* **terse** (turs) ▷ *adjective* **terser, tersest**

tessellate *verb* When shapes **tessellate**, they fit together exactly on a flat surface, without leaving gaps. **tes·sel·late** (**tes**-uh-*late*) ▷ *verb* **tessellating, tessellated** ▷ *noun* **tessellation** ▷ *adjective* **tessellated**

test *noun*

1. A set of questions, problems, or tasks used to measure your knowledge or skill: *I studied hard and passed the test.*

2. A way of studying something to find out what something is like, what it contains, or how good it is, as in *a road test, a blood test,* or *an eye test.*

3. An examination of a small amount of something to check if it works correctly or is finished, or to learn more information about it. ▷ *verb* **test**

test (test)

testament *noun*

1. Proof that something exists or is true: *The marriage license was a testament to their love.*

2. Testament Either of the two main divisions of the Christian Bible, the New Testament or the Old Testament.

tes·ta·ment (**tes**-tuh-muhnt)

testicle *noun* One of two oval organs that produces sperm and testosterone in men and male animals. In most mammals, the two testicles are enclosed in the scrotum. **tes·ti·cle** (**tes**-ti-kuhl) ▷ *adjective* **testicular** (tes-**tik**-yuh-lur)

testify *verb* To state what you have witnessed or what you know in a court of law: *You may be asked to testify in court about what you saw.* **tes·ti·fy** (**tes**-tuh-*fye*) ▷ *verb* **testifies, testifying, testified**

testimony *noun* A formal statement given by a witness or an expert in a court of law: *Her solid testimony was enough to convince the jury.* **tes·ti·mo·ny** (**tes**-tuh-*moh*-nee) ▷ *noun, plural* **testimonies**

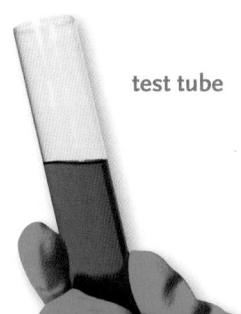

test tube

testosterone *noun* A hormone found in the human body, especially in males, that produces typically male physical and sexual characteristics. **tes·tos·ter·one** (tes-**tah**-stuh-*rohn*)

test pilot *noun* A pilot who flies new airplanes in order to test them for safety and strength.

test tube *noun* A narrow glass tube that is closed at one end. Test tubes are used in laboratory tests and experiments.

tetanus *noun* A serious, sometimes fatal disease caused by bacteria getting into a cut or wound. Tetanus makes your muscles, especially those in your jaw, become very stiff. It is also called **lockjaw. tet·a·nus** (**tet**-uh-nuhs)

tether *noun*

1. A rope or chain that is used to tie up an animal so that it cannot move far. ▷ *verb* **tether**

2. If you are **at the end of your tether**, you have run out of patience or energy and can no longer deal with a difficult situation.

teth·er (**teTH**-ur)

Tex-Mex *adjective* Of or having to do with a style of cooking or music that originated in southern Texas and combines Mexican and American culture. **Tex-Mex** (teks meks)

a
b
c
d
e
f
g
h
i
j
k
l
m
n
o
p
q
r
s
t
u
v
w
x
y
z

text

1. *noun* The main section of writing in a book, not including the pictures, notes, or index.

2. *noun* The original or exact words of a speaker or writer: *The text of the president's speech was printed in today's paper.*

3. *noun* The topic or theme of a piece of writing or a speech.

4. *noun* A textbook: *Please open your text to page 352.*

5. *noun* In a word processing program, words and sentences as opposed to such things as images, graphs, or other illustrations.

6. *noun* A written message sent by using the keys of a cell phone to spell words that will appear on the display screen of the phone receiving it: *Did you get my text?*

7. *verb* To send a text message by cellular telephone: *Steve texted his friend during the movie.* ▷ *verb* **texting, texted**
text (tekst)

Word History

The ancient Romans thought that writing was similar to weaving threads together to make cloth, so they used their word for "weave" to refer to the style of a literary work. *Textus* meant "style of writing," and originally was the past participle of the verb *texere,* meaning "to weave." The Latin word *textus* eventually led to the English word **text.**

textbook *noun* A book used to teach and study a subject. **text·book (tekst-**buk)

text editor *noun* A computer program that you can use to create and edit documents that contain text.

textile *noun* A woven or knitted fabric or cloth. **tex·tile (tek-**stuhl *or* **tek-**stile)

texture *noun* The way something feels, especially how rough or smooth it is: *The hotel towel had a soft texture.* **tex·ture (teks-**chur)

than *conjunction*

1. In comparison with: *She is taller than I am.*

2. Except; besides: *Can someone other than Ed offer to solve the equation?*
than (THan *or* THuhn)

thank

1. *verb* To tell someone that you are grateful for something: *The traveler thanked his host for the meal.*

2. *verb* To hold someone or something responsible for something, especially something bad or unpleasant: *We have her to thank for this terrible mess.*

3. thanks *interjection* An expression showing that you are grateful.

4. thanks *noun, plural* Gratitude: *We expressed our thanks.*
thank (thangk)
▷ *verb* **thanking, thanked**

thankful *adjective* Showing thanks; grateful: *Abby was thankful she didn't get caught in the rain.* **thank·ful (thangk-**fuhl) ▷ *adverb* **thankfully**

thankless *adjective*

1. Not appreciated: *Cleaning up after my dog is a thankless job.*

2. A **thankless** person is not likely to give thanks or show gratitude.
thank·less (thangk-lis)

Thanksgiving dinner

Thanksgiving Day *noun*

1. A holiday observed in the United States on the fourth Thursday in November in order to remember the first Pilgrims' harvest feast, which was held in 1621.

2. A similar holiday observed in Canada on the second Monday in October.
Thanks·giv·ing Day (*thangks-***giv-**ing)

that

1. *pronoun* A person or thing mentioned or indicated: *That was a delicious cake.*

2. *pronoun* A thing farther away than or contrasted with another thing: *This is a chocolate cake, and that is a carrot cake.*

3. *pronoun* Used to introduce a clause defining which person or thing you are referring to. In the sentence *I took a bite of the cake that he baked,* "that he baked" defines which cake is meant.

4. *adjective* Used to indicate a person, place, or thing present or already mentioned: *He made that cake yesterday.*

5. *adjective* Used to indicate a person or thing farther away than or contrasted with another thing: *This cake is his, and that one is mine.*

6. *conjunction* Used to show reason or cause: *I'm sorry that you can't try the chocolate cake.*

7. *conjunction* Used to introduce a clause in a

sentence: *She thinks that she will try every cake on the table.*

8. *conjunction* Used to indicate a result: *We ate so much cake that we couldn't think about dinner.*

9. *adverb* To the extent that is stated; so: *Was the cake really that good?*

that (THat)

▷ *pronoun, plural* **those** ▷ *adjective, plural* **those**

thatch *noun* Dried plants, such as straw or reeds, used to make a roof, or a roof made from these materials. **thatch** (thach) ▷ *noun, plural* **thatches** ▷ *verb* **thatch** ▷ *adjective* **thatched**

that's *contraction* A short form of *that is* or *that has.* **that's** (THats)

thaw

1. *verb* To melt: *Our boat was stuck until the ice on the river began to thaw.*

2. *verb* To become room temperature after being frozen: *Leave the turkey to thaw overnight.*

3. *noun* A time of year when snow and ice melt because the weather has become warmer, as in *January thaw.*

thaw (thaw)

▷ *verb* **thawing, thawed**

the

1. *definite article* Used before a noun or noun phrase that stands for a particular or previously mentioned person or thing: *The chair in the hall is an antique.*

2. *definite article* Used to show that a thing is the only one of it there is, as in *the Colosseum* or *the Mississippi River.*

3. *definite article* Used to show that a person or thing is thought of as the best, most important, or greatest, and therefore one of a kind: *It was the movie to see last year.*

4. *definite article* Used to make a singular noun general: *The hippopotamus lives in central and southern Africa.*

5. *adverb* To that degree; that much; by that much: *I'd like to see you—the sooner the better.*

the (THuh *or* THee)

theater *or* **theatre** *noun*

1. A building where plays or movies are shown.

2. The work of writing, producing, or acting in plays: *She plans to study theater in college.*

the·a·ter *or* **the·a·tre** (thee-uh-tur)

theatrical *adjective*

1. Of or having to do with the theater, as in *a theatrical production.*

2. Done in a way that is intended to create a dramatic effect: *Jonathan's theatrical entrance got the classroom's attention.*

the·at·ri·cal (thee-**at**-ri-kuhl)

thee *pronoun* An old word for **you**. **thee** (THee)

theft *noun* The act of stealing: *Keith is accused of theft.* **theft** (theft)

their *adjective* Belonging to or having to do with them: *Have the students brought their books?* **their** (THair) **Their** sounds like **there** and **they're**.

theirs *pronoun* The one or ones belonging to or having to do with them: *That idea was theirs.* **theirs** (THairz)

them *pronoun* The form of the word *they* that is used as the object of a verb or preposition. It refers to the things or people just mentioned: *Do you see them? The gift is from them.* **them** (THem)

theme *noun*

1. The main subject or idea of a piece of writing or a talk: *The theme of this book is that good triumphs over evil.*

2. A short essay or piece of writing on one subject: *His homework was to draft a theme on the life of Robert E. Lee.*

3. The main melody in a piece of music.

4. theme park A park with rides and attractions based on a particular subject, such as space travel.

theme (theem)

themselves *pronoun* Them and no one else; their own selves: *The children dressed themselves. They blamed themselves.* **them·selves** (THem-**selvz** *or* THuhm-**selvz**)

Theater

Theater is an art form in which performers act out stories before a live audience. Egyptian passion plays about the god Osiris date back to 2000 B.C. In Asia, theater also had its origins in religion. The ancient Greeks were the first to develop dramas and comedies as distinct types of theater. Plays by Greek playwrights, as well as by the great 16th-century dramatist William Shakespeare, are still performed today.

then

1. *adverb* At that time: *I didn't know Emily then.*

2. *adverb* After that; next: *Finish your homework, and then you can go outside.*

3. *adverb* In that case; therefore: *If you can't go, then give the ticket to me.*

4. *noun* That time: *Justine's family eats dinner at 6:30, so we have to get to her house by then.*
then (THen)

theology *noun* The study of religion and religious beliefs. **the·ol·o·gy** (thee-**ah**-luh-jee) ▷ *adjective* **theological** (*thee*-uh-**lah**-ji-kuhl)

theorem *noun* A statement, especially in mathematics, that can be proved to be true. **the·o·rem** (**thee**-ur-uhm *or* **theer**-uhm)

theoretical *adjective*

1. Existing only as a theory; not practically possible: *One day people may be able to travel to Jupiter, but for now, it's still only theoretical.*

2. Of or having to do with a theory: *The data helped us develop a theoretical framework to predict the city's growth over the next ten years.*
the·o·ret·i·cal (*thee*-uh-**ret**-i-kuhl)
▷ *adverb* **theoretically**

theory *noun*

1. An idea or a statement that explains how or why something happens, as in *the theory of evolution.*

2. An idea or opinion based on some facts or evidence but not proved: *The police have a theory about who robbed the bank.*

3. The rules and principles of an art or a science, rather than its practice: *I'm taking a class on music theory.*

4. If something is true or should happen **in theory**, it should be true or happen but it may not.
the·o·ry (**thee**-ur-ee *or* **theer**-ee)

therapist *noun* A person whose work is providing therapy for illnesses, injuries, or psychological problems. **ther·a·pist** (**ther**-uh-pist)

therapy *noun* A treatment for an illness, injury, disability, or psychological problem, as in *art therapy* or *speech therapy*. **ther·a·py** (**ther**-uh-pee) ▷ *noun, plural* **therapies** ▷ *noun* **therapist** (**ther** uh pist)

there

1. *adverb* At, to, or in a particular place: *I haven't been there in years.*

2. *pronoun* A word used to introduce a sentence in which the verb comes before the subject: *There is a man at the door.*

3. *noun* That place: *Let's meet at the diner and leave from there.*
there (THair)

There sounds like **their** and **they're**.

thereabouts *adverb* Near the place or near the time that is being talked about: *They should get back by five or thereabouts.* **there·a·bouts** (**thair**-uh-*bouts*)

thereafter *adverb* Afterward; from that time on: *It rained for 40 days, but it was sunny every day thereafter.* **there·af·ter** (THair-**af**-tur)

thereby *adverb* In that way; by that means: *We stopped watching TV, thereby giving ourselves more time to talk.* **there·by** (THair-*bye or* THair-**bye**)

therefore *adverb* As a result; for that reason: *I have to work late; therefore I won't be able to meet you for dinner.* **there·fore** (THair-*for*)

therm *noun* A unit for measuring heat. **therm** (thurm)

thermal

1. *adjective* Of or having to do with heat or holding in heat: *I wear thermal underwear when I go skiing.*

2. *noun* A rising current of warm air.
ther·mal (**thur**-muhl)

thermometer *noun* An instrument that is used to measure temperature. **ther·mom·e·ter** (thur-**mah**-mi-tur)

thermos *noun* A container that keeps liquids hot or cold for many hours. Also known as a *thermos bottle.* **ther·mos** (**thur**-muhs)

Word History

In 1892 Sir James Dewar, a Scottish chemist, made the first **thermos** to store liquid gases at low temperatures. This container was called a Dewar flask after its inventor until a German company, Thermos, began to sell a version of it. The bottle became known by the firm's name. It used to be capitalized as a trademark but is now a common word, set in lowercase.

thermostat *noun* A device that automatically controls the temperature of furnaces, refrigerators, air conditioners, and other heating and cooling systems. **ther·mo·stat** (**thur**-muh-*stat*)

thesaurus *noun* A book that groups together words that have similar and opposite meanings. *See the Thesaurus in the* **Reference Section**. **the·sau·rus** (thi-**sor**-uhs) ▷ *noun, plural* **thesauri** (thi-**sor**-eye) *or* **thesauruses**

these *pronoun, plural* The plural of **this**: *I'll buy these.* **these** (THeez) ▷ *adjective, plural* **these**

thesis *noun* An idea or argument that is to be debated or proved. **the·sis** (**thee**-sis) ▷ *noun, plural* **theses** (**thee**-seez)

they *pronoun*

1. The people, animals, or things mentioned before: *My parents said that they couldn't come.*

2. People in general: "*Well, you know what they say: 'A penny saved is a penny earned.'*"
they (THay)

they'd *contraction* A short form of *they had* or *they would.* **they'd** (THayd)

they'll *contraction* A short form of *they will* or *they shall.* **they'll** (THayl)

they're *contraction* A short form of *they are.* **they're** (THair) **They're** sounds like **their** and **there.**

they've *contraction* A short form of *they have*: *They've got a lot to learn about teamwork.* **they've** (THayv)

thick *adjective*
1. Great in width or depth; not thin, as in *a thick slice of bread.*
2. As measured from one side or surface to the other: *This wall is one foot thick.*
3. Growing, being, or having parts that are close together; dense, as in *thick hair* or *a thick forest.*
4. Not flowing or pouring easily, as in *thick soup.*
thick (thik)
▷ *adjective* **thicker, thickest** ▷ *noun* **thickness**
▷ *adverb* **thick** ▷ *adverb* **thickly**

thicken *verb* To make thick or to become thick: *You can thicken the sauce by adding flour.* **thick·en** (thik-uhn) ▷ *verb* **thickening, thickened** ▷ *noun* **thickener**

thicket *noun* An area of plants, bushes, or small trees growing very close together. **thick·et** (thik-it)

thief *noun* Someone who steals things from a person or place. **thief** (theef) ▷ *noun, plural* **thieves** (theevz) ▷ *verb* **thieve** (theev) ▷ *adjective* **thieving**

thigh *noun* The top part of your leg, between your knee and your hip. **thigh** (thye)

thimble *noun* A small cap worn on the finger to protect it while you are sewing. **thim·ble** (thim-buhl)

thin *adjective*
1. Small in width or depth; not thick, as in *a thin sheet of paper.*
2. Not fat; slender, as in *a thin waist.*
3. Not close together; not dense, as in *thin hair.*
4. Containing mostly water and so flowing or pouring easily, as in *thin soup.*
5. Not deep or firm; weak, as in *a thin voice.*
6. Not very effective, as in *a thin excuse.*
thin (thin)

deer in a thicket

thimble

▷ *adjective* **thinner, thinnest** ▷ *noun* **thinness** ▷ *verb* **thin** ▷ *adverb* **thinly**

thing *noun*
1. An object that is not alive: *He likes to make things out of wood.*
2. An object whose name you do not know or do not state: *Hand me that thing on the floor.*
3. An idea, action, or event: *We have a lot of things to talk about.*
4. things *noun, plural* Items that belong to someone: *Pick up your things and take them to your room.*
5. things *noun, plural* Life in general at a particular time: *How are things with you?*
thing (thing)

think *verb*
1. To use your mind in order to form an idea, solve a problem, or make a decision: *Think before you speak.* ▷ *noun* **thinker**
2. To have an opinion or believe that something is true: *I think she's a great teacher.*
3. To have as a thought; to imagine: *I was just thinking about you.*
4. To remember something: *Try to think about the good times you had with your grandmother.*
5. To consider someone and that person's particular situation or needs: *He always thinks of other people's feelings.*
think (thingk)
▷ *verb* **thinking, thought**

Synonyms

Think is a general term for the process of forming a thought or an idea in your mind: *I told my parents that I would think about what I want for my birthday.*

- -

■ **Imagine** describes the process of picturing something as you think about it: *Our teacher asked us to imagine that we were in another city and to write about what we saw.*

■ **Consider** means to think about all the possibilities of a situation before making a decision or taking action: *Heather considered three different musical instruments before she decided to learn to play the drums.*

■ **Reflect** describes the process of recalling a memory or an event in a calm, unhurried manner: *Hector reflected on the first summer he spent with his grandfather.*

■ **Ponder** means to weigh a problem in your mind carefully and quietly, often for a long time: *Celia pondered what to say to Jeff for weeks before she got up the nerve to speak to him.*

Third World *noun* The poorer, developing countries of the world.

thirst *noun*

1. A dry feeling in the mouth, caused by a need to drink liquids.

2. A need or desire for liquid.

3. The feeling of wanting something very much: *Nick has a great thirst for knowledge.*

thirst (thurst)

▷ *verb* **thirst**

thirsty *adjective* Needing or wanting to drink something. **thirst·y** (**thur**-stee) ▷ *adjective* **thirstier, thirstiest** ▷ *adverb* **thirstily** (**thur**-stuh-lee)

this

1. *pronoun* A person or thing present, nearby, or just mentioned: *This is my book.*

2. *pronoun* Something that is nearer than or is being compared to something else: *This is old, and that is new.*

3. *pronoun* Something about to be said: *This will make you change your mind.*

4. *adjective* Used to indicate a person or thing present, nearby, or just mentioned: *This book is the one I want.*

5. *adjective* Used to indicate a person or thing nearer than or contrasted with another thing: *This book is old, and that one is new.*

6. *adverb* To this extent: *Are they always this late?*

this (THis)

▷ *pronoun, plural* **these** ▷ *adjective, plural* **these**

thistle *noun* A wild plant that has leaves with sharp points and purple, pink, white, blue, or yellow flowers. **this·tle** (**this**-uhl)

thong *noun*

1. A narrow strip of leather used to fasten things together.

2. A sandal held to the foot with a piece of leather or plastic that goes between the first two toes.

thong (thawng)

thorax *noun*

1. The part of your body between your neck and your abdomen.

2. The part of an insect's body between its head and its abdomen.

tho·rax (**thor**-aks)

▷ *noun, plural* **thoraxes** or **thoraces** (**thor**-uh-seez)

thorax

thorn *noun* A sharp point that sticks out from a branch or stem of a plant such as a rose.

thorn (thorn)

market in a Third World country

thorny *adjective*

1. Covered with thorns, as in *a thorny bush.*

2. Causing difficulty, as in *a thorny issue.*

thorn·y (**thor**-nee)

▷ *adjective* **thornier, thorniest**

thorough *adjective* Done in a careful and complete way: *The police have promised a thorough investigation.* **thor·ough** (**thur**-oh)

▷ *noun* **thoroughness**

thoroughbred *noun*

1. Thoroughbred A breed of English horses developed especially for racing.

2. An animal whose parents are of the same breed.

thor·ough·bred (**thur**-uh-*bred*)

▷ *adjective* **thoroughbred**

thoroughfare *noun* A main road: *There was a traffic jam on the town's main thoroughfare.* **thor·ough·fare** (**thur**-uh-*fair*)

thoroughly *adverb* In a complete, detailed, or very careful manner: *Hank reviewed his report thoroughly before handing it in.* **thor·ough·ly** (**thur**-uh-lee)

those *pronoun, plural* The plural of **that**: *I like this painting much more than those.* **those** (THoze)

▷ *adjective, plural* **those**

thou *pronoun* An old word for **you**. **thou** (THou)

though

1. *conjunction* In spite of the fact that; although: *I kept on working though I was tired.*

2. *conjunction* Yet; but; however: *You wrote a good report, though you could have included more details.*

3. *adverb* However; nevertheless: *I hated the movie; I loved the music, though.*

though (THoh)

thistle

thought

1. *verb* The past tense and the past participle of **think**.

2. *noun* If you are **deep in thought** or **lost in thought**, you are thinking so hard that you do not notice what is going on around you.

3. *noun* An idea or an opinion: *Do you have any thoughts on what we should do next?*

4. *noun* Close attention to something: *Give some thought to your career plans.*

thought (thawt)

thoughtful *adjective*

1. Involving a lot of thought, as in *a thoughtful analysis*.

2. Kind and considering other people's feelings and needs: *How thoughtful of you to send me a card on my birthday.*

thought·ful (**thawt**-fuhl)

▷ *adverb* **thoughtfully**

thoughtless *adjective*

1. Not concerned about other people's feelings and needs.

2. Careless: *It was thoughtless of you to forget to turn off the iron.*

thought·less (**thawt**-lis)

▷ *adverb* **thoughtlessly**

thousand

1. *noun* The number that is equal to 10 times 100, written numerically as 1,000.

2. *adjective* Of or having to do with the number 1,000.

thou·sand (**thou**-zuhnd)

thrash *verb*

1. To beat someone severely: *He thrashed the man who had attacked him.*

2. To move wildly or violently: *A seizure can cause someone to thrash about uncontrollably.*

3. To beat someone thoroughly in a game.

4. If you **thrash out** an idea or a problem, you talk about it until you make a decision.

thrash (thrash)

▷ *verb* **thrashes, thrashing, thrashed** ▷ *noun* **thrashing**

thread

1. *noun* A strand of material such as cotton or silk that is used for sewing.

2. *verb* To pass something such as a thread or piece of string through a hole.

3. *verb* To move through a place by going between and around things or people that are in your way: *He threaded his way through the crowd.*

4. *noun* The theme or main idea that connects different ideas or events: *I can't follow the thread of this story.*

5. *noun* The raised line that winds continuously around a screw or nut.

thread (thred)

▷ *verb* **threading, threaded**

threadbare *adjective* If your clothes are **threadbare**, they are old and in bad condition. **thread·bare** (**thred**-*bair*)

threat *noun*

1. A warning that punishment or harm will follow if a certain thing is done or not done: *The criminal made threats against the judge and his family.*

2. A sign or possibility that something harmful or dangerous might happen: *There's a threat of snow this weekend.*

3. A person or thing regarded as a danger: *Cats can be a threat to the bird population.*

threat (thret)

threaten *verb* To say that you will hurt or cause trouble for someone if you do not get what you want: *The neighbors threatened to call the police if we didn't keep the noise down.* **threat·en** (**thret**-uhn) ▷ *verb* **threatening, threatened**

three-dimensional *or* 3-D *adjective*

1. Having or seeming to have the three dimensions of length, width, and height, as in a *three-dimensional shape.*

2. Having or seeming to have depth, as in a *three-dimensional drawing.*

three-di·men·sion·al (**three** duh-**men**-shuh-nuhl)

three-dimensional drawing

thresh *verb* To separate the grain or seed from a cereal plant such as wheat by beating. **thresh** (thresh) ▷ *verb* **threshes, threshing, threshed**

threshold *noun*

1. The bottom of a door frame, usually made of wood, metal, or stone.

2. The level at which something starts to happen or change: *Marvyn has a low threshold for boredom.*

3. The start of something new, especially something important: *We are on the threshold of an exciting scientific development.*

thresh·old (**thresh**-hohld)

threw *verb* The past tense of **throw**. **threw** (throo)

thrift *noun* Careful management of money or other resources: *Because of her thrift, she was able to save money for a nice vacation.* **thrift** (thrift)

thrifty *adjective* Careful not to waste money: *Julian saved money with his thrifty spending habits.* **thrift·y** (**thrif**-tee) ▷ *adjective* **thriftier, thriftiest**

thrill *noun* A strong feeling of excitement and pleasure: *The thrill of the evening was riding the roller coaster.* **thrill** (thril) ▷ *verb* **thrill** ▷ *adjective* **thrilling**

thriller *noun* An exciting story that is filled with action, mystery, or suspense. **thril·ler** (**thril**-ur)

thrive *verb* To become successful or healthy and strong: *Joann thrived at her new job. Until recently, koalas thrived in Australian forests.* **thrive** (thrive) ▷ *verb* **thriving, thrived** ▷ *adjective* **thriving**

throat *noun*
1. The front of your neck.
2. The tube inside the neck that runs from the mouth into the stomach or lungs.
throat (throht)

throb *verb*
1. If a part of your body **throbs**, you feel a pain there that stops and starts in a regular pattern.
2. If music or a sound **throbs**, it beats repeatedly with a strong regular rhythm: *The loud music throbbed in my ears.*
throb (thrahb)
▷ *verb* **throbbing, throbbed**
▷ *noun* **throb**

throne *noun*
1. A special chair for a king or queen to sit on during a ceremony.
2. The power or authority of a king or queen: *Rulers sometimes abuse the power of the throne.*
throne (throhn)

throng *noun* A large group of people, as in *throngs of tourists.* **throng** (thrawng) ▷ *verb* **throng**

throttle
1. *verb* To injure or kill someone by squeezing the person's throat so that he or she cannot breathe. ▷ *verb* **throttling, throttled** ▷ *noun* **throttle**
2. *noun* A piece of equipment that controls the amount of fuel that flows in a vehicle's engine. ▷ *verb* **throttle**
throt·tle (**thrah**-tuhl)

through
1. *preposition* In one side and out the other: *I walked through the hall and into the kitchen.*
2. *preposition* To many places in; around: *We traveled through Europe.*
3. *preposition* By way of; because of: *Peter got the job through a friend.*
4. *preposition* As a result of: *We lost the game through inexperience.*
5. *preposition* From the beginning to the end of: *School goes through June.*
6. *preposition* In the midst of; among or between: *A hiking path winds through the trees.*
7. *preposition* Finished with: *We are through the worst part of the storm now.*
8. *adverb* From one side or end to the other: *Many people were blocking the door, but Lily managed to squeeze through.*
9. *adverb* Completely: *When he came in from the storm, Jack was soaked through.*
10. *adverb* From beginning to end: *I read the book through again.*
11. *adjective* Allowing passage from one end or side to the other: *I live on a through street.*
12. *adjective* Finished: *Are you through with your homework?*
through (throo)

throughout
1. *preposition* All the way through; in every part: *The company has stores throughout the West Coast.*
2. *preposition* During the whole of a particular period of time: *The person sitting behind me coughed throughout the entire movie.*
3. *adverb* In every part; everywhere: *The book was scary throughout.*
through·out (throo-**out**)

throughway *noun* Another spelling of **thruway**. **through·way** (**throo**-way)

throw *verb*
1. To use your hand to send something through the air: *Alex threw the ball to Chris.* ▷ *noun* **throw**
2. To make someone or something fall to the ground: *The horse reared up and threw its rider.*
3. To put on or take off quickly or carelessly: *I threw on my coat and left.*
4. To put in a certain condition or place: *The fire alarm threw everyone into a panic.*
5. *(informal)* To make someone feel confused or surprised: *My mother's sudden appearance really threw me.*
6. throw away To get rid of something that you do not want: *Don't throw away what can be recycled.*

throne

7. throw up (*informal*) To vomit.
throw (throh)
▷ *verb* **throwing, threw** (throo), **thrown** (throhn)

throw shade *verb* (*slang*) To insult someone in a way that others think is deserved or very clever: *In her new song she throws shade at all of her old boyfriends.*

thrush *noun* A small songbird. Robins, bluebirds, and nightingales are types of thrushes. **thrush** (thruhsh) ▷ *noun, plural* **thrushes**

thrush

thrust
1. *verb* To push something suddenly and roughly: *Janet thrust coins into the pinball machine.* ▷ *verb* **thrusting, thrust** ▷ *noun* **thrust**
2. *noun* The forward force produced by the engine of a jet or rocket.
3. *noun* The main point of an argument.
thrust (thruhst)

thruway *noun* A wide highway used especially for traveling at high speeds over long distances. **thru·way** (**throo**-*way*)

thud *noun* The dull thump made when a heavy object falls to the ground or hits something else: *You could hear the thud of the boulder as it landed.* **thud** (thuhd) ▷ *verb* **thud**

thug *noun* A rough, violent person. **thug** (thuhg)

thumb
1. *noun* The short, thick finger that you have on the end of each hand.
2. thumb through *verb* To turn over the pages of a book: *Gabriella thumbed through her photo album.* ▷ *verb* **thumbing, thumbed**
3. If someone is **all thumbs,** the person is very clumsy.
thumb (thuhm)

thumb drive *noun* Another name for a **flash drive**.

thumbnail
1. *noun* The nail of your thumb.
2. *noun* A small representation of a larger image: *Click on the thumbnail to see the photo full-size.*
3. *adjective* Brief and concise, as in *a thumbnail biography.*
thumb·nail (**thuhm**-*nayl*)

thumbtack *noun* A small pin with a flat, round head, used for attaching paper to bulletin boards, walls, and other surfaces. **thumb·tack** (**thuhm**-*tak*)

thump
1. *noun* An act of hitting someone or something hard: *I gave Morris a thump on the back.*
2. *noun* A deep, heavy sound made when something heavy hits a surface: *The newspaper landed on the front porch with a thump.*
3. *verb* To beat heavily with a steady rhythm: *My heart thumped with excitement.* ▷ *verb* **thumping, thumped**
thump (thuhmp)

thunder
1. *noun* The loud sound that comes during a storm after a flash of lightning.
2. *verb* To make a very loud noise like thunder: *The train thundered past.* ▷ *verb* **thundering, thundered** ▷ *noun* **thunder**
thun·der (**thuhn**-dur)

thundercloud *noun* A large, dark cloud that produces lightning and thunder during a storm. **thun·der·cloud** (**thuhn**-dur-*kloud*)

thunderstorm *noun* A storm with heavy rain, thunder, and lightning. **thun·der·storm** (**thuhn**-dur-*storm*)

Thursday *noun* The fifth day of the week, after Wednesday and before Friday. **Thurs·day** (**thurz**-*day* or **thurz**-dee)

Word History

There's no proof that it thunders more on **Thursday** than on any other day, but it would be appropriate if that were the case. Thursday is named for Thor, the ancient god of thunder.

thus *adverb*
1. In this way: *Hold the tennis racket thus.*
2. As a result: *She got terrific grades and was thus able to get into a good college.*
thus (THuhs)

thwart *verb* To prevent a plan from happening or succeeding: *My plan to eat all the cookies was thwarted when relatives stopped by.* **thwart** (thwort) ▷ *verb* **thwarting, thwarted**

thy *pronoun* An old word for **your**. **thy** (THye)

thyme *noun* An herb related to mint. **thyme** (time) **Thyme** sounds like **time**.

thyme

thyroid *noun* A gland in the throat that produces a hormone that regulates the body's growth and the process by which food is changed into energy in the body. **thy·roid** (**thye**-roid)

tiara *noun* A piece of jewelry like a small crown, typically worn by women, as in *a diamond tiara*. **ti·ar·a** (tee-**ar**-uh or tee-**ahr**-uh)

tiara

tick

1. *noun* The light clicking sound that a clock or watch makes.

2. *verb* To make such a sound: *The clock was ticking.*

3. *verb* To mark time passing by ticking: *The clock ticked off the seconds.*

4. *noun* A mark that someone makes to show that an answer is correct or that something has been done.

5. *verb* To put a mark next to something on a list: *Hugh ticked off the chores on his list as he did them.*

6. *noun* A very small insect that looks like a spider. Ticks suck blood from under the skin of animals and people.

7. *verb* If you **tick** someone **off**, you make the person extremely angry.

tick (tik)

▷ *verb* **ticking, ticked**

ticket *noun*

1. A printed piece of paper or card that proves you have paid to do something, such as ride on a train or sit in a movie theater: *Kabir bought a ticket to the school play.*

2. A written order to pay a fine or appear in court for breaking a traffic law: *The traffic ticket was more expensive than she expected.*

3. A price tag or a label.

4. The list of candidates belonging to a particular political party to be voted on in an election.

tick·et (**tik**-it)

▷ *verb* **ticket**

tickle *verb*

1. To keep touching or poking someone gently in order to try to make the person laugh: *Sofia's little brother wriggled when she lightly tickled him.*

2. To have a slightly uncomfortable feeling on a part of your body: *The dust in the attic made my nose tickle.*

3. To please or amuse someone: *The children were tickled by the circus dog's tricks.*

tick·le (**tik**-uhl)

▷ *verb* **tickling, tickled** ▷ *noun* **tickle**

ticklish *adjective*

1. Easily tickled: *She was very ticklish just below her ribs.*

2. Requiring sensitivity or delicate treatment, as in *a ticklish situation.*

tick·lish (**tik**-lish)

tic-tac-toe *or* **tick-tack-toe** *noun* A game played on a grid of nine squares. Two players take turns putting an X or an O in an empty square. The winner is the first person to get three X's or O's in a row. **tic-tac-toe** *or* **tick-tack-toe** (*tik* tak **toh**)

tidal wave *noun* An extremely large and powerful ocean wave, often caused by an underwater earthquake.

tidbit *noun*

1. A small piece of food.

2. A small piece of interesting news or information, as in *tidbits of gossip.*

tid·bit (**tid**-bit)

tide *noun*

1. The constant change in sea level that is caused by the pull of the sun and the moon on the earth.

▷ *adjective* **tidal** (**tye**-duhl)

2. Something that changes like the tides of the sea: *The tide of public opinion turned against the candidate.*

tide (tide)

Word History

The words **tide** and **time** used to have the same meaning, and today *tide* still means "time" in some words. For example, *Yuletide* means "Yule time," or Christmas time. In its more common meaning, *tide* refers to the regular rise and fall of the oceans' surfaces, which take place at timely, usually predictable, intervals.

tidings *noun, plural* News or information, as in *good tidings.* **tid·ings** (**tye**-dingz)

tidy *adjective* Neat, clean, and organized: *Try to keep the place tidy while we're away.* **ti·dy** (**tye**-dee)

▷ *adjective* **tidier, tidiest** ▷ *noun* **tidiness** ▷ *verb* **tidy**

tie

1. *verb* To join two pieces of something such as string or rope together with a knot or bow: *Tie your shoelaces.* ▷ *verb* **ties, tying, tied** ▷ *noun* **tie**

2. *noun* A long narrow piece of fabric that is worn knotted around the collar of a shirt; a necktie.

3. *noun* Something that holds or bonds people together, as in *strong family ties.*

4. *noun* A situation in which two people or teams have exactly the same score in a competition: *There was a tie for third place.* ▷ *verb* **tie**

tie (tye)

tiebreaker *noun* A special or extra game played to decide the winner of a tie game. **tie·break·er** (**tye**-bray-kur)

tier *noun* One of several rows or layers placed one above the other, such as a row of seats in a stadium or layers on a wedding cake. **tier** (teer)

tiger *noun* A large, striped wildcat that lives in Asia. The tiger is the largest member of the cat family. **ti·ger** (**tye**-gur)

tiger lily *noun* A large flower that is shaped like a trumpet and has red or orange flowers and black spots.

tight *adjective*
1. Fitting closely, as in *tight shoes* or *a tight belt*.
2. Fastened or held firmly; secure, as in *a tight knot* or *a tight grip*.
3. Fully stretched; not loose, as in *a tight rope*.
4. Not letting water or air pass through, as in *a tight seal*.
5. *(informal)* Not generous with money; stingy.
6. Having little time to spare: *I am on a tight schedule today.*
7. Difficult: *Knowing what you've done puts me in a tight situation.*
8. Even or almost even in score; close, as in *a tight game.*
tight (tite)
▷ *adjective* **tighter, tightest** ▷ *adverb* **tightly**

tighten *verb* To make something tight or to become tight: *Please tighten those bolts so that the seat won't slide forward.* **tight·en** (**tye**-tuhn) ▷ *verb* **tightening, tightened**

tightrope *noun* A rope or wire stretched high above the ground on which circus performers walk. **tight·rope** (**tite**-rope)

tights *noun, plural* A piece of clothing that fits closely and covers the hips, legs, and feet. **tights** (tites)

tilde *noun* An accent that is used over the letter *n* in Spanish, and over other letters in other languages. For example, the English word *canyon* is spelled *cañon* in Spanish. **til·de** (**til**-duh)

tile *noun* A square made of stone, plastic, or baked clay, often used to make roofs or to cover floors or walls. **tile** (tile)

till
1. *preposition and conjunction* Another word for **until**.
2. *noun* A drawer or box in a store, used to hold money; part of a cash register.
3. *verb* To prepare land for growing crops: *A plow is used to till the soil.* ▷ *verb* **tilling, tilled** **till** (til)

tiller *noun* A handle attached to the rudder of a small boat. The tiller is used to steer the boat. **till·er** (**til**-ur)

tilt *verb* To lean or tip to one side: *The picture was tilted at a weird angle.* **tilt** (tilt) ▷ *verb* **tilting, tilted** ▷ *noun* **tilt**

timber *noun*
1. Cut wood used for building; lumber: *We bought enough timber to build a shed.*
2. A long, heavy piece of wood; a beam.
3. Trees; forest, as in *an acre of timber.*
tim·ber (**tim**-bur)

timberline *noun* The highest point at which trees can grow on a mountain, or the farthest northern point in the arctic regions where trees can grow. The **timberline** on a mountain is also known as the *tree line.* **tim·ber·line** (**tim**-bur-*line*)

time
1. *noun* The past, present, and future measured in seconds, minutes, hours, and so on: *Time seemed to pass quickly during our vacation.*
2. *noun* A particular moment shown on a clock or watch in hours and minutes: *What time is it?* ▷ *noun* **timer**
3. *noun* An amount of time: *You should have plenty of time to finish the test.*
4. *noun* A specific period in someone's life: *I really enjoyed my time as a teacher.*
5. *noun* A specific period in history: *The story takes place during the time of the Great Depression. The castle was built during medieval times.*
6. *verb* To measure how long it takes to do something: *Time how long it takes me to run to the end of the driveway.*
7. *verb* To arrange for something to happen at a particular time: *Julie timed her vacation so that she wouldn't miss any classes.* ▷ *adjective* **timely**
8. *noun* One in a series of repeated actions: *I just finished reading that book for the third time.*
9. *noun* The beat in a piece of music: *We kept time by clapping.*
time (time)
Time sounds like **thyme.** ▷ *verb* **timing, timed**

timberline

time-consuming *adjective* Taking a long time to do or complete: *Managing a website can be a very time-consuming process.*

timeless *adjective*
1. Not affected, changed, or weakened by time, as in *timeless beauty.*
2. Not referring to a particular time or date, as in *a timeless story of good versus evil.* **time·less** (**time**-lis) ▷ *adverb* **timelessly**

timeline *noun* A chart or graph of a period of time with important events noted at points where they happened or are supposed to happen: *Mrs. Wittle's class made up a timeline of the Civil War in Virginia.* **time·line** (**time**-*line*)

times
1. *noun, plural* A particular period of time: *The museum has a collection of tools from ancient times.*
2. *preposition* Multiplied by: *Seven times 6 is 42.* **times** (timez)

timetable *noun* A list of the times when buses, trains, planes, or boats arrive and depart; a schedule. **time·ta·ble** (**time**-*tay*-buhl)

time zone *noun* A region in which all the clocks are set to the same time. The earth is divided into 24 time zones.

timid *adjective* Shy and without courage: *At the beginning of the year, Rita was too timid to raise her hand in class.* **tim·id** (**tim**-id) ▷ *noun* **timidity** (ti-**mid**-i-tee) ▷ *adverb* **timidly**

tin *noun*
1. A soft, silvery metal that does not rust easily. Tin is used to coat steel cans.
2. A container that is made of or coated with tin: *Campers keep their matches in a waterproof tin.* **tin** (tin)

tinder *noun* Material that is dry and burns easily, such as paper or wood, used especially when starting a fire: *The kids were in the woods gathering dry leaves, twigs, and other tinder to light the campfire.* **tin·der** (**tin**-dur)

tinfoil *noun* A paper-thin, flexible sheet of tin or aluminum used for wrapping food. **tin·foil** (**tin**-*foil*)

tinge *noun* A very small amount of a color, quality, or emotion: *Her voice had a tinge of a German accent. The bird was black with a tinge of red.* **tinge** (tinj) ▷ *verb* **tinge**

tingle *verb* To sting or tickle slightly: *Their skin tingled from the cold.* **tin·gle** (**ting**-guhl) ▷ *verb* **tingling, tingled** ▷ *noun* **tingle**

tinker
1. *verb* To make small adjustments to something in a casual way, especially in order to repair it: *Fred tinkered with the engine.* ▷ *verb* **tinkering, tinkered**
2. *noun* A person in the past who traveled from place to place fixing metal objects such as pots and pans. **tin·ker** (**ting**-kur)

tinkle *verb* To make a light, ringing sound such as that made by a small bell: *The Christmas bells tinkled cheerily.* **tin·kle** (**ting**-kuhl) ▷ *verb* **tinkling, tinkled** ▷ *noun* **tinkle**

tint
1. *noun* A variety of a color, often one with white added.
2. *noun* A pale, delicate color.
3. *verb* To give a slight color to: *My mother tints her hair.* ▷ *verb* **tinting, tinted** ▷ *adjective* **tinted** **tint** (tint)

tiny *adjective* Very small: *Tiny flowers grew under the bush.* **ti·ny** (**tye**-nee) ▷ *adjective* **tinier, tiniest**

tip
1. *verb* To cause something to move into a slanted position or fall over: *Justin tipped his chair back.* ▷ *noun* **tip**
2. *verb* To move into a slanted position or fall over: *The cans of dog food tipped over because they were piled too high.*
3. *noun* The end part or point of something, as in *the tips of the fingers* or *the tip of a spear.*
4. *noun* A helpful piece of advice, as in *a sewing tip.*
5. *noun* An amount of extra money that you give to someone such as a taxi driver or waitress as thanks for good service. ▷ *verb* **tip**
6. *verb* To raise or touch your hat as a greeting to someone: *The gentleman tipped his hat at Mary.*
7. tip off *verb* To give information or a warning to someone: *Police were tipped off by one of the robbers.* **tip** (tip) ▷ *verb* **tipping, tipped**

tinder

tiptoe *verb* To walk very quietly on or as if you were on your toes: *Mom tiptoed into the room where the baby was sleeping.* **tip·toe** (**tip**-*toh*) ▷ *verb* **tiptoeing, tiptoed**

tire
1. *noun* A band of rubber that fits around the outside of a wheel and usually is filled with air.

2. *verb* To become weak or unable to continue because you need rest, or to make someone do this.
▷ *adjective* **tired**

3. *verb* To become bored: *I tired of all the talk about football.*
tire (tire)
▷ *verb* **tiring, tired** ▷ *noun* **tiredness**

tiresome *adjective* Making you feel annoyed or bored, as in *tiresome behavior.* **tire·some** (**tire**-suhm)

tissue *noun*

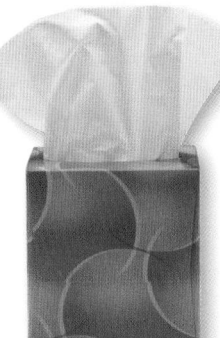

tissue

1. Soft, thin paper used as a handkerchief, or for cleaning or wrapping things.
2. A mass of similar cells that form a particular part or organ of an animal or a plant, as in *muscle tissue.*
tis·sue (**tish**-oo)

title *noun*
1. The name of a book, movie, song, painting, or other work: *The title of this book tells what the story is about.* ▷ *verb* **title**
2. A word used to show a person's status, rank, or occupation. *Ms., Dr., Lord,* and *Senator* are titles.
3. Legal ownership, or a document that shows legal ownership: *Mr. Robbins holds the title to his new car.*
4. A championship.
ti·tle (**tye**-tuhl)

title bar *noun* The horizontal bar that appears at the top of a computer program that you are using, with the name of the program in it.

Tlingit *noun* A member of a group of Native Americans who live on the islands and coast of southern Alaska. **Tlin·git** (**tling**-git) ▷ *noun, plural* **Tlingit** *or* **Tlingits**

tn. Short for **ton** or the plural form *tons.*

to *preposition*
1. Toward; in the direction of: *The kitten ran to me.*
2. As far as: *The astronauts went to the moon.*
3. On, against, or in contact with: *Nail the wreath to the door.*
4. In or for each: *There are four quarts to a gallon.*
5. Until: *Our booth is open from nine to eight.*
6. Compared with: *The score was nine to eight.*
7. For the attention, benefit, or purpose of: *Mom came to my rescue.*

toadstool

8. Concerning or regarding: *What do you say to that?*
9. Before: *It's five minutes to two.*
10. Used before a verb to form an infinitive: *I'd like to go now.*
11. Used to show the receiver of an action: *We gave the trophy to her.*
12. In agreement with: *Lunch was cooked to my liking.*
to (too *or* tuh)
To sounds like **too** and **two**.

toad *noun* An amphibian that looks like a frog but has rougher, drier skin. Toads live mainly on land. **toad** (tohd)

toadstool *noun* A mushroom, especially one that is poisonous. **toad·stool** (**tohd**-stool)

toast
1. *noun* Bread browned by heat. ▷ *verb* **toast**
2. *verb* To warm thoroughly: *We toasted our cold feet by the fire.*
3. *verb* To hold up your glass and drink something such as a glass of wine in honor of someone: *Let's toast the bride and groom.* ▷ *noun* **toast**
toast (tohst)
▷ *verb* **toasting, toasted**

toaster *noun* An electrical appliance that toasts bread. **toast·er** (**toh**-stur)

tobacco *noun* The chopped, dried leaves of the tobacco plant. Tobacco is used for smoking, as in cigarettes, or chewing. **to·bac·co** (tuh-**bak**-oh)
▷ *noun, plural* **tobaccos**

toboggan
1. *noun* A long, flat sled with a front edge that turns up.
2. *verb* To travel downhill on a toboggan. ▷ *verb* **tobogganing, tobogganed**
to·bog·gan (tuh-**bah**-guhn)

toboggan

today

1. *noun* This present day or time: *Today is my birthday.*

2. *adverb* On or during this day: *I'm going to the dentist today.*

3. *adverb* At the present time; nowadays: *Today many people spend more time watching sports than playing them.*

to·day (tuh-**day**)

toddler *noun* A very young child who has just learned to walk. **tod·dler** (**tahd**-lur)

toe *noun*

1. One of the five slender parts at the end of your foot.

2. The part of a shoe, boot, sock, or stocking that covers the toes.

toe (toh)

Toe sounds like **tow**.

toffee *noun* A hard, chewy candy made by boiling sugar and butter together, as in *butterscotch toffee.* **tof·fee** (**taw**-fee)

tofu *noun* A soft food with a texture like cheese that is made from soybeans. Tofu is also known as *bean curd.* **to·fu** (**toh**-foo)

Word History

Japanese speakers borrowed their word for bean curd, **tofu**, from Chinese. The name in Chinese for this food was *doufu.* Speakers of Chinese formed *doufu* from the words *dou,* meaning "beans," and *fu,* meaning "rotten." Tofu has been made in China for about two thousand years.

toga *noun* A piece of clothing worn by people in ancient Rome. It was wrapped around the body and draped over the left shoulder. **to·ga** (**toh**-guh)

together *adverb*

1. With each other: *The boys arrived together.*

2. Into one group, mass, or place: *Mix the cake ingredients together.*

3. At the same time: *All of the horses started the race together.*

4. In agreement or cooperation: *We completed the class project by working together.*

to·geth·er (tuh-**geTH**-ur)

toil

1. *verb* To work very hard for a long time: *The repair crew toiled in the summer heat.*

2. *verb* To move slowly with pain or effort: *The hikers toiled up the mountain.*

3. *noun* Hard, exhausting work. ▷ *noun* **toiler**

toil (toil)

▷ *verb* **toiling, toiled**

toilet *noun*

1. A device connected to plumbing in which people get rid of waste from their bodies.

2. A room containing a toilet; a bathroom.

toi·let (**toi**-lit)

token *noun*

1. Something that stands for something else; a sign or symbol: *Randy gave Sue a ring as a token of his love.*

2. A piece of stamped metal that can be used in place of money: *The machines at the penny arcade require tokens instead of coins.*

to·ken (**toh**-kuhn)

told *verb* The past tense and the past participle of **tell**. **told** (tohld)

tolerance *noun*

1. The willingness to respect or accept the customs, beliefs, or opinions of others: *In our classroom, we try to show tolerance for other people's ideas.*

2. The ability to put up with or endure something such as pain or hardship: *Mom's tolerance was tested when all the kids started screaming at once.*

tol·er·ance (**tah**-lur-uhns)

tolerant *adjective* Willing to put up with something or someone, such as a challenging situation or a person who is very different from you. **tol·er·ant** (**tah**-lur-uhnt) ▷ *adverb* **tolerantly**

tolerate *verb* To put up with or endure something or someone: *Jo doesn't tolerate cold weather very well.* **tol·er·ate** (**tah**-luh-*rate*) ▷ *verb* **tolerating, tolerated** ▷ *noun* **toleration**

toll

1. *verb* To ring a bell slowly and regularly: *The bell on the courthouse tolls at noon.* ▷ *verb* **tolling, tolled** ▷ *noun* **toll**

2. *noun* A charge or tax paid for using a highway, bridge, or tunnel: *We have to pay a toll to cross this bridge.*

3. *noun* The number of deaths or injuries as a result of something such as an accident, war, or illness, as in *death toll.*

4. *noun* A charge for a service such as a long-distance telephone call.

5. If something **takes its toll** on someone or something, it causes serious damage or suffering: *The hot weather took its toll on the athletes.*

toll (tohl)

toga

tomahawk *noun* A small ax once used by some Native Americans as a tool or weapon. **tom·a·hawk** (**tah**-muh-*hawk*)

tomato *noun* A red, juicy fruit eaten as a vegetable either raw or cooked. **to·ma·to** (tuh-**may**-toh *or* tuh-**mah**-toh) ▷ *noun, plural* **tomatoes**

tomb *noun* A grave, room, or building for holding a dead body. **tomb** (toom)

tomboy *noun* A girl who enjoys activities that were once associated with boys, such as climbing trees or playing sports. **tom·boy** (**tahm**-*boi*)

tombstone *noun* A carved block of stone that marks the place where someone is buried. It usually gives the dead person's name and dates of birth and death. **tomb·stone** (**toom**-*stone*)

tomcat *noun* A male cat. **tom·cat** (**tahm**-*kat*)

tomorrow *noun*
1. The day after today: *Tomorrow is New Year's Eve.*
2. The future, as in *the world of tomorrow.*
to·mor·row (tuh-**mor**-oh) ▷ *adverb* **tomorrow**

tom-tom *noun*
1. A small drum that is usually beaten with the hands.
2. A small to medium-sized drum in a drum set that makes a low, hollow sound.
tom-tom (**tahm**-*tahm*)

ton *noun* A unit of weight equal to 2,000 pounds in the United States and Canada, and 2,240 pounds in Great Britain. A small automobile weighs about one ton. **ton** (tuhn)

tone *noun*
1. A single sound, especially one that is musical, thought of in terms of its pitch, length, quality, or loudness, as in *the deep tones of an organ.*
2. A way of speaking or writing that shows a certain feeling or attitude: *Rosa's tone was gentle.*
3. The general quality, feeling, or style of something: *The tone of the speech was positive.*
4. In music, a **tone** is the difference in pitch between certain musical notes.
5. A tint or shade of a color.
6. The normal, healthy firmness of the muscles.
tone (tohn)

tongs *noun, plural* A tool with two connected arms used for picking up or holding things, as in *salad tongs.* **tongs** (tawngz)

tongue *noun*
1. The movable muscle in your mouth that is used for tasting, swallowing, and talking.

2. The tongue of an animal such as a cow, cooked and used as food.
3. A language: *The exchange student spoke to her friends in her native tongue.*
4. The ability to speak: *Have you lost your tongue?*
5. The flap of material under the laces of a shoe.
6. **hold your tongue** To stop yourself from saying something.
tongue (tuhng)

tongue twister *noun* A sentence or verse that is very hard to say or repeat quickly, such as "red leather, yellow leather."

tonic *noun* Something that makes you feel stronger or refreshed: *Spring sunshine is a tonic after a long winter.* **ton·ic** (**tah**-nik)

tonight *noun* This evening or night: *Tonight's weather report doesn't sound good.* **to·night** (tuh-**nite**) ▷ *adverb* **tonight**

tonsillitis *noun* An illness that makes your tonsils infected and painful. **ton·sil·li·tis** (*tahn*-suh-**lye**-tis)

tonsils *noun, plural* Two flaps of soft tissue that lie one on each side of the throat. **ton·sils** (**tahn**-suhlz)

too *adverb*
1. As well; also; in addition: *Is Emily coming, too?*
2. More than enough: *It's too hot in here.*
3. Very; extremely. Too is used in this way especially with negatives: *She wasn't too excited when I told her the news.*
too (too)

Too sounds like **to** and **two**.

took *verb* The past tense of **take**. **took** (tuk)

tool *noun*
1. A piece of equipment that you use to do a particular job, for example, to repair or make things: *A hammer is the right tool for hanging a picture.*
2. Anything that helps you accomplish something: *A thesaurus is a useful tool for writing.*
tool (tool)

toolbar *noun* A horizontal bar near the top of the screen in some computer programs that you click on to use various commands and features. **tool·bar** (**tool**-*bahr*)

toolbox *noun* A box designed for storing or carrying hand tools. **tool·box** (**tool**-*bahks*) ▷ *noun, plural* **toolboxes**

toon *noun* (*informal*) A cartoon. **toon** (toon)

toot *verb* To sound a horn or whistle in short blasts. **toot** (toot) ▷ *verb* **tooting, tooted** ▷ *noun* **toot**

tomato

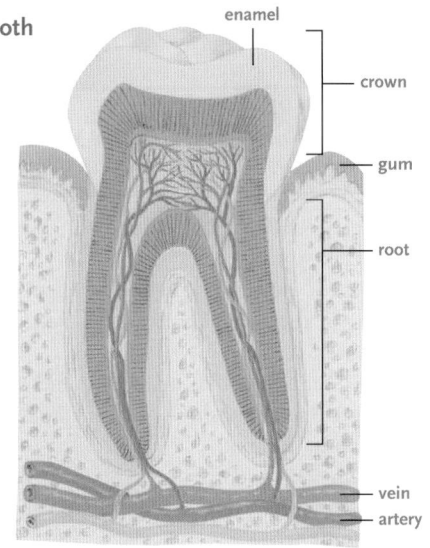

tooth

enamel

crown

gum

root

vein

artery

tooth *noun*

1. One of the white, bony parts of your mouth that you use for biting and chewing food.

2. One of a row of parts that stick out on a saw, comb, or gear.

tooth (tooth)

▷ *noun, plural* **teeth**

toothache *noun* A pain in or near a tooth.

tooth·ache (**tooth**-*ake*)

toothbrush *noun* A small brush that is used to clean the teeth. **tooth·brush** (**tooth**-*bruhsh*) ▷ *noun, plural* **toothbrushes**

toothpaste *noun* A paste that is put on a toothbrush and used to clean the teeth. **tooth·paste** (**tooth**-*payst*)

toothpick *noun* A small, thin piece of wood or plastic that is used to remove food from between the teeth. **tooth·pick** (**tooth**-*pik*)

top

1. *noun* The highest point or part of something, as in *the top of a hill* or *the top of a page*.

2. *noun* A cover or a lid, as in *a bottle top*.

3. *noun* The highest rank or position: *My sister is at the top of her class.*

▷ *adjective* **top**

4. *noun* A piece of clothing worn on the upper part of your body: *Pam wore a red top with her tan skirt.*

5. *noun* The highest or greatest degree or pitch: *He yelled at the top of his voice.*

6. *noun* A toy that is shaped like a cone and spins on a pointed end.

7. *verb* To do better than someone or something:

Bert's time in the 100-yard dash tops the old record.

▷ *verb* **topping, topped**

top (tahp)

topaz *noun* A clear mineral that is used as a gem. It is usually a color ranging from yellow to brown. **to·paz** (**toh**-paz)

topic *noun* The subject of a discussion, study, lesson, speech, or piece of writing: *The topic of my essay is soccer.* **top·ic** (**tah**-pik)

topical *adjective*

1. Of interest now; in the news at present: *The class gives students the opportunity to discuss topical issues.*

2. A **topical** medicine is applied directly to the skin. **top·i·cal** (**tah**-pi-kuhl)

topography *noun* The detailed description of the physical features of an area, including hills, valleys, mountains, plains, and rivers. **to·pog·ra·phy** (tuh-**pah**-gruh-fee) ▷ *noun* **topographer**

toponym *noun* The name of a place: *Many toponyms in this area are from Native American languages.* **top·o·nym** (**tah**-puh-nim)

topple *verb*

1. To become unsteady and fall over, usually from a height: *The tower of blocks toppled over.*

2. To make something fall. *He hit the table so hard he nearly toppled the glasses.*

3. To remove a leader or government from power, especially by force; overthrow: *Foreign troops invaded and toppled the government.*

top·ple (**tah**-puhl)

▷ *verb* **toppling, toppled**

topsoil *noun* The top layer of soil that contains the nutrients that plants need to grow. **top·soil** (**tahp**-*soil*)

topsy-turvy *adjective* Upside down, mixed-up, or confused: *The tornado left the house in a topsy-turvy mess.* **top·sy·tur·vy** (tahp-see **tur**-vee)

▷ *adverb* **topsy-turvy**

Torah

Torah *noun* The first five books of the Jewish Bible, which make up the traditional principles of Judaism. **To·rah** (**tor**-uh *or* **toh**-ruh)

torch

1. *noun* A flaming light that can be carried in the hand.

2. *noun* A tool that gives off a very hot flame used to weld or cut metals; a blowtorch.

3. *verb* To set fire to something: *Someone torched the abandoned house on Church Street.* ▷ *verb* **torches, torching, torched**

torch (torch)

▷ *noun, plural* **torches**

tore *verb* The past tense of **tear**. **tore** (tor)

toreador *noun* A bullfighter. **to·re·a·dor**
(**tor**-ee-uh-*dor*)

torment

  1. (tor-**ment**) *verb* To annoy or upset someone
deliberately: *Jed torments his younger brother.*
  ▷ **tormenting, tormented** ▷ *noun* **tormentor**

  2. (**tor**-ment) *noun* Great pain or suffering: *The years
of torment showed on the woman's wrinkled face.*
tor·ment

torn *verb* The past participle of **tear**. **torn** (torn)

tornado *noun* A violent and very destructive
windstorm that appears as a dark cloud shaped like
a funnel. **tor·na·do** (tor-**nay**-doh) ▷ *noun, plural*
tornadoes *or* **tornados**

Word History

"We had nothing but tornadoes, with such thunder,
lightning, and rain, that we could not keep our men
dry," wrote a 16th-century voyager. At that time, the
word **tornado** meant "a thunderstorm." *Tronada*, a
Spanish word, was the source of *tornado*. But English
speakers mixed up the spelling, confusing *tronada*
with the Spanish word *tornado*, meaning "turned"
or "twisted."

Tornado Alley *noun* The central part of the United
States where tornadoes are frequent, including some
or all of Kansas, Nebraska, Oklahoma, the Dakotas,
Missouri, and Iowa.

torpedo *noun* An underwater bomb shaped like
a tube that explodes when it hits a target, such as
a ship. **tor·pe·do** (tor-**pee**-doh) ▷ *noun, plural*
torpedoes ▷ *verb* **torpedo**

torrent *noun* A violent, quickly moving stream of
water or other liquid: *The boat was swept away in the
torrent.* **tor·rent** (**tor**-uhnt) ▷ *adjective* **torrential**
(tuh-**ren**-chuhl)

torrid *adjective* Extremely hot, as in *a torrid
climate.* **tor·rid** (**tor**-id) ▷ *noun* **torridness** ▷ *adverb*
torridly

torso *noun* The part of your body between your
neck and your waist, not including your arms; the
trunk. **tor·so** (**tor**-soh) ▷ *noun, plural* **torsos**

tortilla *noun* A round, flat bread made from cornmeal
or flour. Tortillas are often served with a topping or
filling. **tor·til·la** (tor-**tee**-yuh)

tortoise *noun* A turtle, especially one that lives on
land. **tor·toise** (**tor**-tuhs)

torture

  1. *verb* To deliberately cause someone extreme pain or
mental suffering as punishment or as a way to force
the person to do or say something: *They tortured*
the prisoner until he confessed to the crime. ▷ *verb*
torturing, tortured

  2. *noun* The act of causing extreme pain as a
punishment or as a way of forcing someone to do or
say something: *The spies tried to get information out
of their captive by torture.*

  3. *noun* Extreme pain or mental suffering: *Not
knowing whether the plane has arrived safely is
torture.*
tor·ture (**tor**-chur)

toss *verb*

  1. To throw something with little force: *Toss me that
pencil, will you?*

  2. To move, fling, or rock something back and forth:
The high waves tossed the boat.

  3. To mix a salad lightly.

  4. To throw a coin into the air to decide something
according to which side lands faceup.
toss (taws)
  ▷ *verb* **tosses, tossing, tossed** ▷ *noun* **toss**
  ▷ *adjective* **tossed**

tot *noun* (*informal*) A small child. **tot** (taht)

Tornadoes

Tornadoes occur mainly in the United States,
particularly in the middle part of the country known
as Tornado Alley. When warm, moist air in the lower
atmosphere meets cold, dry air above it, they create
an upward and a downward draft. If these two winds
speed up, their rotation produces a twister, another
name for a tornado.

total

1. *adjective* Making up the whole amount; entire: *What is the total amount of my bill?*

2. *adjective* Complete: *The party was a total disaster.*

3. *noun* A number gotten by adding; a sum: *The total comes to $29.72.* ▷ *verb* **total**

4. *verb (informal)* To damage a vehicle so badly that it cannot be repaired or is not worth repairing: *Bill totaled his car in an accident.* ▷ *verb* **totaling, totaled**

to·tal (**toh**-tuhl)

totally *adverb* Completely, entirely, or absolutely: *The beach was totally destroyed by the tsunami.* **to·tal·ly** (**toh**-tuh-lee)

tote *verb (informal)* To carry something: *I toted that umbrella everywhere, and it never rained.* **tote** (toht) ▷ *verb* **toting, toted**

totem pole *noun* A pole carved and painted with animals, plants, and other natural objects that represent a family or clan. Certain Native American tribes placed totem poles in front of their homes. **to·tem pole** (**toh**-tuhm)

totter *verb*

1. To walk in an unsteady way: *The baby tottered slowly across the yard.*

2. To tremble or rock as if about to fall; to sway: *Many buildings tottered during the earthquake.* **tot·ter** (**tah**-tur)

▷ *verb* **tottering, tottered**

toucan *noun* A brightly colored tropical American bird that has a very large beak. **tou·can** (**too**-kan)

touch

1. *verb* To make contact with your hand or finger, or another area of your body: *Penny touched the hot stove.*

2. *verb* To make light contact with another object: *The falling leaf touched his cheek.*

totem pole

3. *noun* The act of touching: *Her touch was soft.*

4. *verb* To affect emotionally: *I was touched by the tender story of the girl who found her birth mother.*

5. *noun* The sense that you use to feel things with your fingers or other parts of your body.

6. *noun* A very small amount: *The cook added a touch of salt to the stew.*

7. keep in touch To contact someone

touch pad

regularly, for example, by telephone or email. **touch** (tuhch)

▷ *verb* **touches, touching, touched** ▷ *noun, plural* **touches**

touchdown *noun*

1. In football, a play in which the ball is carried over the opponent's goal line, scoring six points.

2. The moment when an aircraft or a spacecraft lands after a flight.

touch·down (**tuhch**-*doun*)

touching *adjective* Making you feel an emotion such as compassion or sympathy, as in *a touching scene.* **touch·ing** (**tuhch**-ing) ▷ *adverb* **touchingly**

touch pad *noun*

1. A panel on an electronic device with options you can touch in order to use the machine. The touch pad of a microwave oven, for example, has settings for the number of minutes or seconds you can cook something.

2. A surface on a laptop or netbook that you touch to make the cursor move and point to things on the screen so that you can use the computer.

touch screen *noun* A screen on a computer or phone that lets you operate the device by touching the words or pictures on the screen instead of using a keyboard.

touchy *adjective*

1. Sensitive and easily annoyed: *Brian is touchy about his weight, so don't talk about it.*

2. Being of such a controversial nature that it requires tact to avoid offending people: *The issue of abortion is a touchy subject.*

touch·y (tuhch-ee)
▷ *adjective* **touchier, touchiest** ▷ *noun* **touchiness**

Word History

Judging from its spelling, the adjective **touchy**, meaning "irritable," seems to be from the word *touch*. However, this connection for the word doesn't quite fit. In fact, the source of the English word *touchy* was another adjective, *tetchy*, which also had the sense of "irritable." People probably thought that an irritable person was especially sensitive to being touched, so the word *touch* came to mind when people said the word *tetchy*. In the end, *tetchy* was changed to *touchy*.

tough *adjective*
1. Difficult to do: *I have a tough decision to make.*
2. Able to deal with pain or difficult situations; rugged: *Pioneer women had to be tough.*
3. Strong and difficult to damage, as in *a tough pair of boots.*
4. Hard to cut or chew, as in *tough meat.*
5. Difficult to deal with, as in *a tough stain.*
6. Rough or violent, as in *a tough neighborhood.*
7. Unhappy or unlucky, as in *a tough life.*
tough (tuhf)
▷ *adjective* **tougher, toughest**

toupee *noun* A wig used to cover a man's baldness.
tou·pee (too-**pay**)

tour *noun*
1. A trip around an area or place in order to see different parts of it and learn about it, as in *a tour of Italy* or *a tour of the art museum.* ▷ *verb* **tour**
2. When a band, team, or theater group goes **on tour**, it travels to different places to play or perform.
tour (toor)

tourist *noun* Someone who is traveling and visiting a place for pleasure: *New York is a popular destination for tourists.* **tour·ist** (**toor**-ist) ▷ *noun* **tourism**

tournament *noun* A series of contests in which a number of people or teams try to win the championship, as in *a tennis tournament* or *a chess tournament.* **tour·na·ment** (**toor**-nuh-muhnt)

tourniquet *noun* A bandage or band twisted tightly around a limb to prevent a wound or cut from bleeding too much. **tour·ni·quet** (**tur**-nuh-kit)

tout *verb* To praise or publicize someone or something in order to convince other people that the person or thing is important or good: *The baseball player was highly touted by the press.* **tout** (tout) ▷ *verb* **touting, touted**

tow *verb* To pull a vehicle by attaching it behind another vehicle, usually with a rope or chain: *We tow the motorboat on a special trailer.* **tow** (toh) **Tow**

sounds like **toe**. ▷ *verb* **towing, towed** ▷ *noun* **tow**

toward *or* **towards** *preposition*
1. In the direction of: *The crowd started moving toward the exit.*
2. With regard to; concerning: *The children showed great respect toward their grandparents.*
3. Just before; near: *It started to snow toward morning.*
4. In order to buy; for: *My parents are saving money toward a new car.*
to·ward (tord *or* tword) *or* **to·wards** (tordz *or* twordz)

towel *noun* A piece of thick, soft cloth or paper that is used for drying or wiping wet things. **tow·el** (**tou**-uhl) ▷ *verb* **towel**

tower
1. *noun* A tall and narrow structure that stands by itself or is part of a building, such as a castle or church.
2. *noun* The case of a desktop computer that contains the CPU and the hard drive, often shaped like a tall box. Tower is also used as a name for this kind of computer, as opposed to a laptop.
3. *verb* To be much taller than the people or things around someone or something: *The skyscraper towered over the other buildings.* ▷ *verb* **towering, towered** ▷ *adjective* **towering**
tow·er (**tou**-ur)

town *noun* A place where people live and work that has things such as houses, stores, offices, and schools. A town is larger than a village but smaller than a city. **town** (toun)

town hall *noun*
1. The building in a town that contains offices for local government.
2. A public meeting between an elected official and voters where the official can answer questions and address concerns: *The senator took questions about forest fire management at the most recent town hall.*

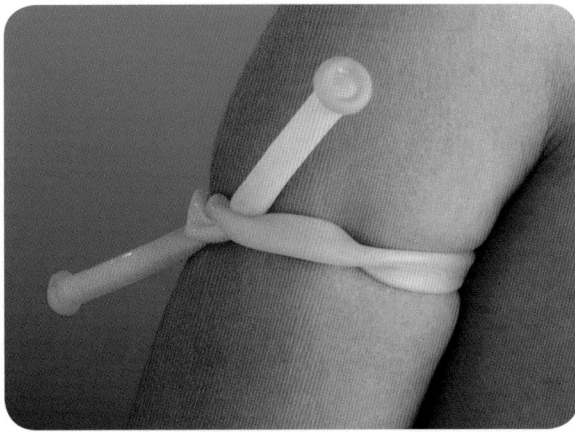

tourniquet

township *noun* A division of a county in some states. **town·ship** (**toun**-*ship*)

toxic *adjective* Poisonous, as in *toxic waste*. **tox·ic** (**tahk**-sik) ▷ *noun* **toxin** (**tahk**-sin) ▷ *noun* **toxicity** (tahk-**sis**-i-tee)

Word History

The word **toxic** comes from the Greek word *toxikon*, which referred to the poison in which an arrow was dipped. This word came from the Greek word *toxon*, meaning a bow for shooting arrows. Hunters used poison on the tips of their arrows to make sure their shots killed their prey.

toy
1. *noun* An object that children can play with.
2. *verb* If you **toy** with an idea or plan, you consider it but not in a serious way: *When I was younger, I toyed with the idea of going to law school.* ▷ *verb* **toying, toyed**
toy (toi)

trace
1. *verb* To find someone or something that has disappeared after looking carefully: *The police were able to trace the boy, who was lost in the nearby woods.*
2. *verb* To copy a picture or shape by following lines visible through a piece of thin paper. ▷ *noun* **tracing**
3. *verb* To follow, study, or describe the history or development of something: *We traced the history of my family back to Africa.*
4. *noun* A small, visible sign that something has happened or that someone has been somewhere: *He left without a trace.*
trace (trays)
▷ *verb* **tracing, traced**

track
1. *noun* The marks left behind by a moving animal, person, or vehicle: *Our boots left deep tracks in the snow.*
2. *noun* A path or a trail.
3. *noun* A prepared path or course for runners or racing animals: *The runners lined up at one end of the track.*
4. *noun* A rail or set of rails for vehicles to run on, as in *a train track.*
5. *verb* To look for someone or something by following marks left behind on the ground: *The hunters tracked the bear.* ▷ *verb* **tracking, tracked** ▷ *noun* **tracking** ▷ *noun* **tracker**
track (trak)

track and field *noun* A group of sports events that includes running, jumping, and throwing contests, such as the hurdles, pole vault, and shot put.
▷ *adjective* **track-and-field**

tract *noun*
1. A large area of land, as in *a tract of farmland.*
2. A group of parts or organs in the body that perform a specific function, as in *the digestive tract.*
3. A booklet or pamphlet, especially one on a religious or political subject.
tract (trakt)

traction *noun* The force that keeps a moving body from slipping on a surface: *The tires lost traction on the icy roads.* **trac·tion** (**trak**-shuhn)

tractor *noun*
1. A powerful vehicle used on farms to, for example, plow fields or pull heavy loads.
2. A truck that has a cab and no body. It is used for pulling a trailer.
trac·tor (**trak**-tur)

trade
1. *noun* The business of buying and selling goods; commerce. ▷ *verb* **trade**
2. *noun* A particular job or craft, especially one that requires working with the hands or with machines: *Dale is a carpenter by trade.*
3. *verb* To exchange something you have for something someone else has; swap: *My friends and I like to trade baseball cards.* ▷ *verb* **trading, traded** ▷ *noun* **trade**
trade (trade)

trademark *noun* A word, picture, or design that shows that a product is made by a particular company. A trademark is usually registered with the government so that it cannot be used by any other company. **trade·mark** (**trade**-*mahrk*) ▷ *verb* **trademark**

trader *noun*
1. A person whose business is buying and selling or bartering goods: *Arab traders brought silk from China.*

track and field

traffic circle

2. A person who buys and sells stocks in hopes of making short-term profits, as in *a day trader.*
trad·er (**tray**-dur)

trading post *noun* A store in a wilderness area where people can exchange local products such as furs or hides for food and supplies.

tradition *noun*
1. The handing down of customs, ideas, and beliefs from one generation to the next: *Following family tradition, he went to the same college as his father and grandfather.*
2. A custom, an idea, or a belief that is handed down in this way: *It's a tradition to hang stockings on Christmas Eve.*
tra·di·tion (truh-**dish**-uhn)

traditional *adjective* Of or having to do with customs, beliefs, or activities that are handed down from one generation to the next, or are long established, as in *a traditional costume* or *a traditional Fourth of July parade.* **tra·di·tion·al** (truh-**dish**-uh-nuhl)

traffic
1. *noun* All the moving vehicles on a particular road at a particular time: *We were stuck in heavy traffic.*
2. *verb* To buy and sell illegal goods, as in *to traffic in stolen property.* ▷ *verb* **trafficking, trafficked** ▷ *noun* **trafficking** ▷ *noun* **trafficker**
traf·fic (**traf**-ik)

traffic circle *noun* An intersection formed by a circle around which the traffic moves in only one direction. Each vehicle enters the circle from a street and continues around the circle until it arrives at the desired street to turn.

traffic light *noun* A set of lights that controls traffic. Traffic lights are usually placed where streets intersect.

traffic light

tragedy *noun*
1. A very sad and shocking event, especially one that involves death: *The plane crash was a terrible tragedy.*
2. A serious play, movie, or book with a sad ending, such as the death of the main character, or plays of this type in general.
trag·e·dy (**traj**-i-dee)
▷ *noun, plural* **tragedies**

Word History

In ancient Greece, a **tragedy** was a play with an unhappy ending. Greek speakers formed the word *tragoidia* by combining the words *tragos,* meaning "goat," and *oide,* meaning "song." The reason for the name is unclear. Perhaps a goat was the prize for the best play in a festival, or maybe the *tragoidia* originally involved the sacrifice of a goat. Today, a *tragedy* is still a serious play with a sad ending, and we also now call a very sad event a *tragedy.*

tragic *adjective*
1. Of or having to do with or in the style of a tragedy or sad story: *The book had a tragic ending.*
2. Causing great sadness, especially because someone has died or suffered in a shocking way, as in *a tragic accident.*
trag·ic (**traj**-ik)
▷ *adverb* **tragically**

trail
1. *noun* A track or path for people to follow, especially in the woods: *The mountain trail is marked with blue signs.*
2. *noun* A mark, scent, or path left behind by an animal or a person: *The dogs were able to pick up the lost hiker's trail.*
3. *noun* Something that follows along behind, as in *a trail of dust.*
4. *verb* To follow a scent or tracks in order to catch an animal or a person: *The hound kept its nose to the ground as it trailed the squirrel.*
5. *verb* To walk or move slowly behind others: *Jake trailed us as we hiked through the woods.*
trail (trayl)
▷ *verb* **trailing, trailed**

trail bike *noun* A light, strong motorcycle built for cross-country racing and riding.

trailer *noun*
1. A vehicle that is pulled by another vehicle, especially a car or truck, and used to carry things, as in *a horse trailer.*
2. A mobile home.
3. A group of scenes that are used to advertise a movie.
trail·er (**tray**-lur)

train

1. *noun* A group of railroad cars that are connected to each other and pulled along a railway by an engine.
2. *noun* A group of people, animals, or vehicles traveling in a line, as in *a mule train* or *a wagon train*.
3. *verb* To prepare yourself to be something or do something by practicing or learning: *Jocelyn trained as a doctor.*
4. *verb* To teach a person or an animal how to do something: *We trained the dog to get the newspaper.*
5. *verb* To bring up children a certain way: *My parents trained me to be polite.*
6. *verb* To make a plant grow in a certain direction or shape.
7. *noun* A long, trailing piece of fabric at the back of a gown, robe, or wedding dress.
train (trayn)
▷ *verb* **training, trained**

trainee *noun* Someone who is being trained, especially for a job: *My older sister is a trainee in the bank's management program.* **train·ee** (tray-**nee**)

trainer *noun*

1. A person who trains circus animals, show animals, or pets: *The dog trainer demonstrated the tricks the animals could do.*
2. Someone who helps people, especially athletes, get in the best possible physical condition: *The trainer gave the players exercises to strengthen their arms.*
train·er (**tray**-nur)

training *noun*

1. The activity of teaching a person or animal how to do something or how to behave in a certain way: *The employees got special training on the new software.*
2. The process of becoming physically fit for an activity through diet and exercise: *He's in training for the Boston Marathon.*
train·ing (**tray**-ning)

train wreck *noun*

1. An accident involving a train, especially one in which part of the train leaves the track.
2. A situation where something has gone terribly wrong, often because of mistakes, bad management, or poor decisions: *His first speech as governor was a train wreck and people lost confidence in his leadership abilities.*

traipse *verb* To walk or travel around without a plan or purpose: *We traipsed through the woods with our sketchbooks.* **traipse** (trayps) ▷ *verb* **traipsing, traipsed**

trait *noun* A quality or characteristic that makes one person or thing different from another: *Loyalty is an important trait for a friend to have.* **trait** (trayt)

traitor *noun*

1. Someone who helps the enemy of his or her country.
2. Someone who is unfaithful to a friend, cause, or trust.
trai·tor (**tray**-tur)

tramp

1. *verb* To walk with heavy steps: *We tramped up the hill.*
2. *verb* To go for a long walk or hike: *Lucy and I tramped through the hills outside of town.* ▷ *noun* **tramp**
3. *noun* Someone who wanders from place to place and does not have a permanent home.
4. *noun* The sound made by heavy steps.
tramp (tramp)
▷ *verb* **tramping, tramped**

trample *verb* To damage or crush something by walking heavily all over it: *The crowd trampled the lawn.* **tram·ple** (**tram**-puhl) ▷ *verb* **trampling, trampled**

trampoline *noun* A piece of equipment used for jumping up and down on, either as a sport or for pleasure. A trampoline consists of a sheet of canvas attached to a frame by elastic ropes or springs. **tram·po·line** (*tram*-puh-**leen**)

trance *noun* A mental state in which you are conscious but not really aware of what is happening around you. **trance** (trans)

tranquil *adjective* Peaceful and calm: *We sat on the porch and enjoyed the tranquil evening.* **tran·quil** (**trang**-kwuhl) ▷ *noun* **tranquillity** or **tranquility** (trang-**kwil**-i-tee)

trans *adjective* See **transgender.** **trans** (tranz or trans)

transaction *noun* An exchange of goods, services, or money: *At our bank, we can do many transactions via computer.* **trans·ac·tion** (tran-**sak**-shuhn) ▷ *verb* **transact**

trampoline

transatlantic *adjective*
1. Crossing the Atlantic Ocean, as in *a transatlantic flight.*
2. Involving countries or people on both sides of the Atlantic Ocean, as in *transatlantic trade.*
3. On or coming from the other side of the Atlantic Ocean. **trans·at·lan·tic** (*trans*-uht-**lan**-tik)

transcontinental *adjective* Crossing a continent: *We took a transcontinental trip from California to New York.* **trans·con·ti·nen·tal** (*trans*-kahn-tuh-**nen**-tuhl)

transfer
1. (trans-**fur** *or* **trans**-fur) *verb* To move someone or something from one person or place to another: *The prisoner was transferred to the Harris County Jail.* ▷ *noun* **transfer** (trans-**fur** *or* **trans**-fur)
2. (**trans**-fur) *verb* To change from one vehicle or method of transportation to another: *Dustin transferred from the bus to the train.*
3. (**trans**-fur) *noun* A printed ticket that permits you to change from one vehicle or route to another without paying more money.
trans·fer
▷ *verb* **transferring, transferred** ▷ *noun* **transferral** (trans-**fur**-uhl)

transform *verb* To completely change something: *Having children transformed my life.* **trans·form** (trans-**form**) ▷ *verb* **transforming, transformed**

transformation *noun* A complete or dramatic change in form, appearance, or character: *All of the recent construction has led to a major transformation of the city's skyline.* **trans·for·ma·tion** (*trans*-for-**may**-shuhn)

transformer *noun* A piece of equipment that reduces or increases the voltage of an electric current. **trans·form·er** (trans-**for**-mur)

transfusion *noun* The injection of blood from one person into the body of someone else who is injured or sick. **trans·fu·sion** (trans-**fyoo**-zhuhn)

transgender *adjective* Of or pertaining to a person who identifies with a gender that does not match the one they were born with. **trans·gen·der** (trans-**jen**-dur)

transient
1. *adjective* Lasting for only a short time, as in *a transient illness.*
2. *noun* A person without a permanent home who moves from place to place: *There is a shelter for transients on the corner.*
tran·sient (**tran**-shuhnt)

transistor *noun* A small electronic device that controls the flow of electric current in items such as radios, television sets, and computers. **tran·sis·tor** (tran-**zis**-tur)

transit *noun*
1. A system for carrying people or goods from one place to another on trains, buses, and other vehicles.
2. **in transit** In the process of going from one place to another.
tran·sit (**tran**-sit *or* **tran**-zit)

transition *noun* A change from one form, condition, or place to another: *Moving from the city to the country was a difficult transition for Hannah.* **tran·si·tion** (tran-**zish**-uhn)

transitive *adjective* If a verb is **transitive**, it needs an object in order to complete its meaning. For example, in the sentence "We called our friends and then visited them," the verbs *called* and *visited* depend on their objects (*our friends* and *them*) to be clear and meaningful. *See* **intransitive**. **tran·si·tive** (**tran**-si-tiv)

translate *verb* To change spoken or written words from one language into another: *Juanita translated the paragraph from English into Spanish.* **trans·late** (trans-**late**) ▷ *verb* **translating, translated** ▷ *noun* **translator**

translation *noun*
1. The activity of translating words or a text from one language into another: *He speaks English and Arabic, and was hired to provide translations at the conference.*
2. A text in a language other than the original, after it has been translated: *We read the Russian novel in an English translation.*
trans·la·tion (trans-**lay**-shuhn)

translucent *adjective* A **translucent** substance is not completely clear like glass but will let some light through. **trans·lu·cent** (trans-**loo**-suhnt) ▷ *noun* **translucence**

transmission *noun*
1. The act of transmitting or sending something from one person or place to another: *The radio transmission did not come through clearly.*
2. Something that is transmitted, such as a telegram.
3. In an automobile, a series of gears that send power from the engine to the wheels.
trans·mis·sion (trans-**mish**-uhn)

transmit *verb*
1. To send or pass something from one place or person to another, as in *to transmit a message* or *to transmit a disease.*
2. To send out radio or television signals: *The program was transmitted to more than 140 countries throughout the world.* ▷ *noun* **transmitter**
3. To cause or allow something such as light, heat, or sound to pass through a material or substance: *Water transmits light.*
trans·mit (trans-**mit**)
▷ *verb* **transmitting, transmitted**

transom *noun* A small window over a door or another window. **tran·som** (tran-suhm)

transparency *noun* A sheet of thin, clear plastic with writing or pictures on it that you can shine light through in order to view the writing or pictures on a screen. **trans·par·en·cy** (trans-**pair**-uhn-see or trans-**par**-uhn-see) ▷ *noun, plural* **transparencies**

transparent *adjective*
1. A **transparent** substance is clear like glass and lets light through so that objects on the other side can be seen clearly: *The lake water was so transparent we could see all the way to the bottom.*
2. Obvious, as in *a transparent lie.*
trans·par·ent (trans-**pair**-uhnt or trans-**par**-uhnt)

transpiration *noun* The process by which plants give off moisture. **tran·spi·ra·tion** (*tran*-spuh-**ray**-shuhn) ▷ *verb* **transpire** (tran-**spire**)

transplant
1. (**trans**-*plant*) *noun* A medical operation in which a damaged organ, such as a kidney, is replaced by a healthy one. ▷ *verb* **transplant** (trans-**plant**)
2. (**trans**-*plant*) *verb* To dig up a plant and plant it somewhere else: *Grace transplanted her tulips from the backyard to the front.* ▷ *verb* **transplanting, transplanted** ▷ *noun* **transplant** (**trans**-*plant*) **trans·plant**

transport
1. (trans-**port**) *verb* To move people or freight from one place to another: *The truck transported chickens.* ▷ *noun* **transport** (**trans**-port)
2. (**trans**-port) *noun* A vehicle that carries people or freight, such as a ship or plane.
3. (**trans**-port) *verb* To feel very strong emotions, such as happiness: *Rachel was transported by the beauty of the music.*
trans·port
▷ *verb* **transporting, transported**

transportation *noun* A means or system for moving people and freight from one place to another: *My bicycle is my main transportation.* **trans·por·ta·tion** (*trans*-pur-**tay**-shuhn)

trap
1. *noun* A device for capturing an animal: *I caught a mouse in a trap.*
2. *noun* Anything used to trick or catch someone: *The police set a trap at the jewelry store and caught the burglar the next night.*
3. *verb* To capture a person or an animal in a trap: *The hunter trapped two wolves.* ▷ *verb* **trapping, trapped**
trap (trap)

trapdoor *noun* A door in a floor, ceiling, or roof: *That trapdoor leads to the attic.* **trap·door** (**trap**-dor)

trapeze *noun* A horizontal bar hanging from two ropes used especially by circus performers and gymnasts. **tra·peze** (tra-**peez**)

trash

trapezium *noun* A shape with four sides, none of which is parallel to another. **tra·pe·zi·um** (truh-**pee**-zee-uhm) ▷ *noun, plural* **trapeziums** or **trapezia** (truh-**pee**-zee-uh)

trapezoid *noun* A shape with four sides of which only two are parallel. **trap·e·zoid** (**trap**-uh-*zoid*)

trapper *noun* Someone who makes a living by trapping wild animals, usually for their fur. **trap·per** (**trap**-ur)

trash
1. *noun* Things that you have thrown away because they are worthless; garbage: *Peggy filled a whole bag with trash from the yard.*
2. *noun* Nonsense: *There's nothing but trash on television.*
3. *noun* A place on some computers where you can move files that you don't need anymore.
4. *verb* (*informal*) To damage or destroy something, making a big mess: *Vandals trashed the empty theater over the weekend.*
5. *verb* (*informal*) To criticize something or someone in a very harsh way: *Critics trashed the actor's performance.*
trash (trash)
▷ *verb* **trashes, trashing, trashed**

trauma *noun*
1. A severe and painful emotional shock: *The old woman never recovered from the trauma of the fire.*
2. A severe physical wound or injury: *Emergency rooms deal with trauma from accidents.*
trau·ma (**trou**-muh or **traw**-muh)

traumatic *adjective* Shocking and very upsetting: *The loss of her dog was traumatic to Karen.* **trau·mat·ic** (traw-**mat**-ik)

traumatize *verb* If an experience **traumatizes** someone, it causes him or her to feel mental distress, fear, or shock, usually for a long time: *Many soldiers* *return from war traumatized by the horrors they have witnessed.* **trau·ma·tize** (**trou**-muh-*tize* or **traw**-muh-*tize*) ▷ *verb* **traumatizing, traumatized** ▷ *noun* **traumatization** (*trou*-muh-tuh-**zay**-shuhn or *traw*-muh-tuh-**zay**-shuhn)

travel *verb*
1. To go from one place to another, especially a place that is far away: *I have to travel to Salt Lake City for a conference.* ▷ *noun* **travel** ▷ *adjective* **traveling**
2. To move a particular distance, in a particular direction, or at a particular speed: *We traveled nearly 400 miles per day.*
3. To pass or to move; to be transmitted: *Sound travels through water.*
4. In basketball, to move illegally by failing to bounce the ball while walking or running. **trav·el** (**trav**-uhl) ▷ *verb* **traveling, traveled**

Word History

Travel comes from the Old French word *travailler,* meaning "to suffer; to be troubled; to be worn out." Going from place to place was a difficult experience hundreds of years ago, a fact that no doubt explains the origin of the word.

travel agent *noun* A person or company that arranges travel and vacations for its customers. ▷ *noun* **travel agency**

traveler *noun* Someone who travels: *My uncle is a world traveler.* **trav·el·er** (**trav**-uh-lur)

trawler *noun* A boat that drags a large net through the water to catch fish. **trawl·er** (**traw**-lur) ▷ *verb* **trawl**

tray *noun* A flat container made of metal, plastic, or wood with a low rim around the edges that is used for carrying things, as in *a tea tray.* **tray** (tray)

treacherous *adjective*
1. Disloyal and not to be trusted, as in *a treacherous spy.* ▷ *noun* **treachery**
2. Dangerous: *The icy roads were treacherous.* **treach·er·ous** (**trech**-ur-uhs) ▷ *adverb* **treacherously**

tread
1. *verb* To walk on, over, or along: *We trod the path toward the beach.*
2. *verb* To press or crush with the feet: *Be careful not to tread mud on the floor.*
3. *noun* The flat, horizontal part of a step.
4. *noun* The ridges on a car tire or the sole of a shoe that help prevent you from slipping.
5. **tread water** *verb* To swim in one place with your body in a vertical position. **tread** (tred) ▷ *verb* **treading, trod** (trahd), **trodden** (**trah**-duhn)

treadmill *noun*
1. An exercise machine with a large moving belt that you can walk or run on while staying in the same place.
2. A situation that is boring or tiring because you always do the same things without making any progress, as in *a career treadmill.* **tread·mill** (**tred**-*mil*)

treason *noun* The crime of being disloyal to your country by spying for another country or by helping an enemy during a war. **trea·son** (**tree**-zuhn)

treasure
1. *noun* Gold, jewels, money, or other valuable things that have been collected or hidden, as in *buried treasure.*
2. *verb* To consider something to be very valuable: *I treasure my relationship with my grandmother.* ▷ *verb* **treasuring, treasured** ▷ *noun* **treasure** ▷ *adjective* **treasured** **treas·ure** (**trezh**-ur)

treasurer *noun* The person in charge of the money of a government, company, or club. **treas·ur·er** (**trezh**-ur-ur)

treasure trove *noun*
1. A collection of valuable things, such as gold or jewels, that is found in the place where it was buried, hidden, or lost. The term is often shortened to **trove**: *The diving expedition discovered a treasure trove of 17th-century silver coins in the shipwreck.*
2. A collection of valuable things or information: *I found a treasure trove of books on prehistoric animals at the used bookstore.*

treasure

treasury *noun*
1. The funds of a government, company, or club: *The monthly dues are paid into the treasury.*
2. **Treasury** A government department that is in charge of collecting taxes and managing the public's money.
3. A place where money or treasure is stored. **treas·ur·y** (**trezh**-ur-ee) ▷ *noun, plural* **treasuries**

treat *verb*

1. To deal with or act toward people or things in a certain way: *All she wants is to be treated fairly.*

2. To try to cure or heal a sickness or injury; to give medical attention to someone: *The doctor treated the patient's burns.*

3. To use a chemical substance to clean, change, or protect something: *Many fruits and vegetables are treated with chemicals.*

4. To pay for something for someone, especially when you do not usually do this: *I'll treat you to dinner on your birthday.* ▷ *noun* **treat**
treat (treet)
▷ *verb* **treating, treated**

treatment *noun*

1. The way that you treat someone or something: *The Winthrops were very impressed by the courteous treatment they received from the hotel's staff.*

2. The actions of a medical professional to cure or treat patients: *What sorts of treatment are available for this type of cancer?*
treat·ment (**treet**-muhnt)

treaty *noun* A formal written agreement between two or more countries, as in *an international treaty.* **trea·ty** (**tree**-tee) ▷ *noun, plural* **treaties**

treble

1. *adjective* Three times as big or three times as many; triple.

2. *adjective* High in pitch or tone, as in *a treble voice.*

3. *verb* To increase to three times the original amount; to triple: *He expected to treble his original investment by the end of the year.* ▷ *verb* **trebling, trebled**

4. *noun* The highest musical part, voice, or instrument.
treb·le (**treb**-uhl)

tree

1. *noun* A large plant with a long trunk, roots, branches, and leaves, as in *an oak tree.*

2. *verb* To pursue and chase up a tree: *Hounds treed the raccoon.* ▷ *verb* **treeing, treed**

3. *noun* Something that looks like a tree, such as the diagram used to show family relationships or a pole for hanging up clothes.
tree (tree)

tree house *noun* A platform built in a tree, sometimes with walls, for children to play in.

trek *verb* To make a slow, difficult journey: *The hikers trekked up the mountain.* **trek** (trek) ▷ *verb* **trekking, trekked** ▷ *noun* **trek**

trellis *noun* A framework made up of thin strips of wood that cross each other. Trellises are used to support growing plants. **trel·lis** (**trel**-is) ▷ *noun, plural* **trellises**

tree house

tremble *verb*

1. To shake in a way that you are unable to control, especially from cold, fear, or excitement: *Carla's hands were trembling as she accepted the music award for the best song.*

2. To vibrate: *The earth trembled as the volcano erupted.*
trem·ble (**trem**-buhl)
▷ *verb* **trembling, trembled**

tremendous *adjective*

1. Very large: *A tremendous explosion shook the house.*

2. Excellent or very good: *We had a tremendous time skiing last weekend.*
tre·men·dous (truh-**men**-duhs)
▷ *adverb* **tremendously**

tremor *noun* A shaking movement: *Earth tremors are very common in places that often have earthquakes.*
trem·or (**trem**-ur)

trench *noun* A long, narrow ditch, especially one used to protect soldiers in battle. **trench** (trench) ▷ *noun, plural* **trenches**

trend *noun*

1. The general direction in which things are developing: *Lately there has been a trend toward improving school lunches.* ▷ *verb* **trend**

2. The newest fashion: *The trend this season is to wear shoes with very high heels.* ▷ *adjective* **trendy**
trend (trend)

trespass

1. *verb* To go on someone's private property

without permission: *He was accused of trespassing on state property.* ▷ *verb* **trespasses, trespassing, trespassed** ▷ *noun* **trespasser**
2. *noun* A sin. ▷ *noun, plural* **trespasses** ▷ *verb* **trespass**
tres·pass (**tres**-puhs *or* **tres**-pas)

tresses *noun, plural* A woman's or girl's hair, especially when it is worn long and loose: *Hilary's blonde tresses hung to her waist.* **tresses** (**tres**-iz)

trestle

trestle *noun* A frame shaped like the letter A that supports a bridge or railroad track. **tres·tle** (**tres**-uhl)

Prefix

The prefix **tri-** adds the following meaning to a root word: Having or involving three, as in *triangle* (a shape having three angles), *triathlon* (an athletic event having three parts), and *tricycle* (a vehicle having three wheels).

---

trial *noun*
1. The examination of evidence in a court of law to decide if a charge or claim is true: *The robber's trial lasted three days.*
2. The act of trying or testing something; a test: *We gave the new computer program a week's trial.*
3. A frustrating or difficult experience that reveals how strong or patient you are: *The first settlers faced a great many trials.*
tri·al (**trye**-uhl)

triangle *noun*
1. A shape with three straight sides and three angles. ▷ *adjective* **triangular** (trye-**ang**-gyuh-lur)
2. A steel percussion instrument in the shape of a triangle. You play it by striking it with a small metal rod.
tri·an·gle (**trye**-ang-guhl)

triathlon *noun* A long-distance race made up of three parts—usually swimming, bicycling, and

running. **tri·ath·lon** (trye-**ath**-lahn) ▷ *noun* **triathlete** (trye-**ath**-leet)

tribe *noun* A large group of related people who share the same language, customs, and laws, and who usually live in the same area. **tribe** (tribe) ▷ *adjective* **tribal** (**trye**-buhl)

tribulation *noun*
1. Unhappiness or suffering: *The earthquake resulted in severe tribulation for many people.*
2. A difficult experience: *The movie is about the tribulations of a poor farmer and his family.*
trib·u·la·tion (*trib*-yuh-**lay**-shuhn)

tribunal *noun* A court of law. **tri·bu·nal** (tri-**byoo**-nuhl)

tributary *noun* A stream that flows into a larger stream, river, or lake. **trib·u·tar·y** (**trib**-yuh-*ter*-ee) ▷ *noun, plural* **tributaries**

tribute *noun* Something done, given, or said to show thanks or respect: *The president's speech was a tribute to the soldiers who died in the war.* **trib·ute** (**trib**-yoot)

triceratops *noun* A large dinosaur that ate plants and had three horns and a bony collar in the shape of a fan at the back of its head. **tri·cer·a·tops** (trye-**ser**-uh-*tahps*) ▷ *noun, plural* **triceratops** *or* **triceratopses**

trichinosis *noun* A disease caused by tiny worms often found in pork that has not been fully cooked. **trich·i·no·sis** (*trik*-uh-**noh**-sis)

trick
1. *verb* To make someone believe something that is not true: *Amy was tricked into thinking there was no school on Monday.* ▷ *verb* **tricking, tricked** ▷ *noun* **trick** ▷ *noun* **trickery** ▷ *noun* **trickster**
2. *noun* A clever or skillful action that you do to entertain someone, as in *a card trick.*
3. *noun* A prank or a practical joke: *My sister and I played a trick on our little brother.*
trick (trik)

trickle *verb* To flow very slowly in a thin stream, or to fall in drops: *Water trickled constantly from the faucet.* **trick·le** (**trik**-uhl) ▷ *verb* **trickling, trickled** ▷ *noun* **trickle**

trick or treat *noun* The words that children say to ask for candy when they go from house to house on Halloween. ▷ *verb* **trick-or-treat**

tricky *adjective*
1. Someone who is **tricky** is clever and likely to try to deceive you.
2. Difficult in an unexpected way; requiring careful thought or handling, as in *a tricky question* or *a tricky situation.*
trick·y (**trik**-ee) ▷ *adjective* **trickier, trickiest**

a b c d e f g h i j k l m n o p q r s **t** u v w x y z

tricycle *noun* A children's vehicle that has three wheels. **tri·cy·cle** (**trye**-sik-uhl)

trifle

1. *noun* Something that is not very valuable or important: *Bob brought a few trifles as gifts for the children.* ▷ *adjective* **trifling**

2. *noun* A small amount; a bit: *Janine was a trifle annoyed because I was late.*

3. *verb* To play with or not take seriously: *Don't trifle with my feelings.* ▷ *verb* **trifling, trifled**
tri·fle (**trye**-fuhl)

trigger

1. *noun* The lever on a gun that you pull to fire the gun: *Dana aimed at the target and pulled the trigger.*

2. *verb* To cause something to happen immediately: *The fight was triggered when one of the men insulted the other.* ▷ *verb* **triggering, triggered**
trig·ger (**trig**-ur)

trilogy *noun* A group of three related works, such as plays, novels, or programs, that together make a series: *The second book of the trilogy is the best.* **tril·o·gy** (**tril**-uh-jee) ▷ *noun, plural* **trilogies**

trim

1. *verb* To cut small pieces off something in order to improve its shape or to get rid of what is not needed or wanted: *She trimmed our hair. The butcher trimmed the fat off the roast.*

2. *adjective* Neat, tidy, or in good condition: *The house sat in the middle of a trim little yard.* ▷ *adjective* **trimmer, trimmest**

3. *verb* To add ornaments or decorations to something, as in *to trim a tree* or *to trim a gown.* ▷ *noun* **trim**
trim (trim)
▷ *verb* **trimming, trimmed**

trimming

1. *noun* Something used to decorate something else: *Let's put the trimmings on the Christmas tree.*

2. trimmings *noun, plural* The things that are added to something or that go with it: *We had roast pork with all the trimmings.*
trim·ming (**trim**-ing)

trinket *noun* A small, cheap souvenir, decoration, or piece of jewelry: *All the shops on the boardwalk sell postcards and trinkets.* **trin·ket** (**tring**-kit)

trio *noun*

1. Three things or people together as a group: *The trio of friends went everywhere together.*

2. A piece of music for three musicians. **tri·o** (**tree**-oh)
▷ *noun, plural* **trios**

trip

1. *verb* To hit your foot on something by accident and fall or almost fall: *He tripped on the step.*

2. *verb* To catch someone's foot and cause the person to fall or almost fall: *Scott stuck his foot into the aisle and tripped me.*

3. *noun* A journey to a place, as in *a trip to the mall* or *a business trip.*

4. trip up *verb* To make a mistake or to cause another person to make a mistake: *Some of the interview questions were designed to trip her up.*
trip (trip)
▷ *verb* **tripping, tripped**

tripe *noun*

1. The lining of the stomach of an ox or a cow. Tripe is eaten as food.

2. *(informal)* Anything that is useless or worthless: *That television show is the most boring tripe.*
tripe (tripe)

triple

1. *adjective* Three times as big, or three times as many. ▷ *verb* **triple**

2. *adjective* Made up of three parts: *The skater fell while attempting a triple flip.*

3. *noun* In baseball, a hit that allows you to reach third base. ▷ *verb* **triple**
trip·le (**trip**-uhl)

triplet *noun* One of three children born to the same mother at the same birth. **trip·let** (**trip**-lit)

tripod *noun* A stand with three legs that is used to steady a camera or other piece of equipment. **tri·pod** (**trye**-pahd)

trite *adjective* If something is **trite**, it is not interesting because it is so common and overly used. A cliché is an example of something that is trite: *John made the trite remark that the early bird gets the worm.* **trite** (trite)

triumph *noun* A great victory, success, or achievement: *He considered winning a gold medal in the Olympics to be his greatest triumph.* **tri·umph** (**trye**-uhmf) ▷ *verb* **triumph** ▷ *adjective* **triumphant** (trye-**uhm**-fuhnt)

trivial *adjective* Not very important, as in *trivial details.* **triv·i·al** (**triv**-ee-uhl) ▷ *noun, plural* **trivia** (**triv**-ee-uh)

trio

Trojan horse *noun*
1. A person, action, or thing that seems harmless but that people believe will later prove to be harmful.
2. A kind of software that is advertised as something useful but that in fact damages your computer after you install it: *The hackers used a Trojan horse to steal from online bank accounts.*
Tro·jan horse (**troh**-juhn)

Word History

According to legend, the Greek army had been outside the ancient city of Troy for ten years, unable to enter and defeat the Trojans. So the Greeks built a huge wooden horse, and some warriors hid inside. The Trojans, thinking the horse was a gift, brought it inside the walls; the warriors came out and attacked, conquering Troy and bringing the Trojan War to an end. We still call anything that brings downfall from within a **Trojan horse**.

troll
1. *verb* To fish by pulling a line with bait behind a slowly moving boat.
2. *verb* To tease or harass someone online by posting humorous or rude comments: *Some people say the actress is using her Twitter account to troll her critics.*
3. *noun* In fairy tales, an ugly creature that is very large or very small and lives in a cave, in the hills, or under a bridge.
4. *noun* Someone who posts things online in order to make others angry or upset: *She doesn't allow comments on her blog because of all the trolls.*
troll (trohl)
▷ *verb* **trolling, trolled** ▷ *noun* **troller**

Word History

In early Scandinavia, the term for an evil, giant being with magic powers was *troll*. A *troll* turned to stone, or burst, if he or she was exposed to sunlight. The word *trolldómr* meant "witchcraft," so it's clear that the term *troll* was closely connected with magic. English speakers adopted the Old Norse word *troll*, but our ideas about trolls have changed. Now a **troll** can be either very big or very small, and the connection with magic has mostly been lost.

trolley *noun* An electric streetcar that runs on tracks and gets its power from an overhead wire. **trol·ley** (**trah**-lee)

trombone *noun* A brass musical instrument with a long, bent tube that the player slides back and forth to change the pitch of the tones. **trom·bone** (trahm-**bone**)

troop
1. *noun* An organized group of people, such as soldiers or scouts, as in *a Girl Scout troop*.
2. *verb* To walk somewhere in a group: *The boys trooped into the kitchen.* ▷ *verb* **trooping, trooped**
troop (troop)

trooper *noun* A state police officer: *The trooper pulled her over for speeding.* **troop·er** (**troo**-pur)

trophy *noun* A prize such as a large silver cup given to the winner of a competition, or to someone who has done something outstanding. **tro·phy** (**troh**-fee) ▷ *noun, plural* **trophies**

tropical *adjective* Of or having to do with the hot, rainy area of the tropics: *Plants grow quickly in a tropical climate.* **trop·i·cal** (**trah**-pi-kuhl)

tropical fish *noun* Any of various small or brightly colored fish that originally come from the tropics. Tropical fish are often kept as pets in aquariums. ▷ *noun, plural* **tropical fish** or **tropical fishes**

tropics *noun, plural* The extremely hot area of the earth near the equator: *Many kinds of plants live in the tropics.* **trop·ics** (**trah**-piks)

trot *verb*
1. When a horse **trots**, it moves at a pace that is faster than a walk but not as fast as a run. ▷ *noun* **trot** ▷ *noun* **trotter**
2. When a person **trots**, he or she runs slowly or jogs: *The players trotted onto the field.*
trot (traht)
▷ *verb* **trotting, trotted**

trouble
1. *noun* A difficult, dangerous, or upsetting situation: *You kids stay out of trouble, all right?* ▷ *adjective* **troublesome** (**truhb**-uhl-suhm)
2. *verb* To disturb or worry someone: *Ozzie's behavior troubled me.* ▷ *adjective* **troubling** ▷ *adjective* **troubled**
3. *noun* A cause of difficulty, worry, or annoyance: *The trouble with Bob is that he can never be serious.*
4. If you **take the trouble** to do something, you make a special effort to do it: *Thank you for taking the trouble to be here tonight.*
5. *verb* To ask someone for help, or to make an extra effort: *Can I trouble you for a glass of water?*
trou·ble (**truhb**-uhl)
▷ *verb* **troubling, troubled**

trough *noun*
1. A long, narrow container from which animals can eat or drink.
2. The lowest part of something: *Many analysts think that the trough of the recession is now past.*
trough (trawf)

trounce *verb* To beat soundly in a competition or game: *They really trounced us, with a final score of 12 to 0.* **trounce** (trouns) ▷ *verb* **trouncing, trounced**

trousers *noun, plural* Another word for **pants**. **trou·sers** (**trou**-zurz) ▷ *adjective* **trouser**

trout *noun* A freshwater fish, related to the salmon, that you can eat. **trout** (trout)

trove *noun* Short for **treasure trove**. **trove** (trohv)

trowel *noun*
1. A hand tool with a flat blade shaped like a diamond. Trowels are used for doing things such as laying cement or filling holes in plaster.
2. A hand tool with a small, curved blade, used for planting and other light garden work.
trow·el (**trou**-uhl)

truant *noun* A student who stays away from school without permission. **tru·ant** (**troo**-uhnt) ▷ *noun* **truancy** ▷ *adjective* **truant**

truce *noun* An agreement between enemies to stop fighting for a short time: *The armies called a truce to care for their wounded.* **truce** (troos)

truck *noun* A large motor vehicle with space in the back to carry loads. **truck** (truhk)

trudge *verb* To walk slowly and with effort; to plod: *We trudged through the snow on our way back to the house.* **trudge** (truhj) ▷ *verb* **trudging, trudged**

true *adjective*
1. Correct or agreeing with the facts, as in *a true story*.
2. Loyal or faithful, as in *a true friend*.
3. Real or genuine: *I have finally found true love.*
true (troo)
▷ *adjective* **truer, truest**

truly *adverb*
1. Really or actually: *If you truly want to learn a language, you have to practice every day.*
2. Used to emphasize that you really mean what you are saying: *I am truly sorry that I disturbed you.*
tru·ly (**troo**-lee)

trumpet *noun*
1. A brass musical instrument that consists of a long tube with a wide funnel shape at one end. You play it by blowing into it and pressing a combination of the three valves on top to change the tones.
2. A loud sound like that of a trumpet, such as the cry of an elephant.
trum·pet (**truhm**-pit)
▷ *verb* **trumpet**

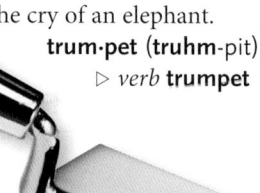

trowel

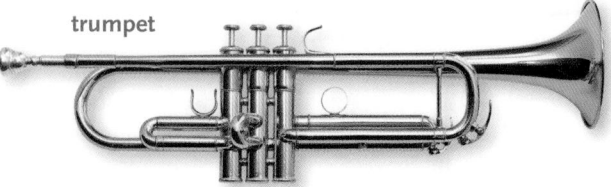

trumpet

trunk *noun*
1. The thick, main part of a tree.
2. A large case used for storing things or carrying things such as clothes on a long journey: *Lisa packed her winter clothes into a trunk.*
3. The upper part of your body, not including your arms and head.
4. The long nose of an elephant.
5. An enclosed compartment in a car, usually at the back, where things such as bags and a spare tire can be stored.
6. **trunks** *noun, plural* Shorts worn by men or boys for swimming or boxing.
trunk (truhngk)

trust *verb* To believe that someone is honest and reliable: *I don't trust that new guy.* **trust** (truhst) ▷ *verb* **trusting, trusted** ▷ *noun* **trust** ▷ *adjective* **trusting**

trustee *noun*
1. A person who has the legal authority to manage property for the benefit of another person or of other people.
2. A person who directs the funds and policies of an organization or institution: *My mother is a trustee for our local art museum.*
trust·ee (truh-**stee**)

trustworthy *adjective* Able to be trusted and relied on to do what is right, as in *a trustworthy friend*. **trust·wor·thy** (**truhst**-*wur*-THee)

trusty *adjective* Something that is **trusty** can be relied on, especially because you have had it for a long time: *My trusty old car will get us there!* **trust·y** (**truhs**-tee)

truth *noun*
1. The real facts about something, rather than what is false or not known: *Is he telling the truth?*
2. The quality of being true, real, honest, or accurate: *I doubt the truth of this witness's testimony.*
truth (trooth)
▷ *adjective* **truthful** ▷ *adverb* **truthfully**

try *verb*
1. To attempt to do something: *Try to behave.*
▷ *noun* **try**
2. To examine in a court of law someone accused of a criminal offense: *The person was tried for robbery.*
3. To test the quality, strength, or effect of something: *I decided to try a new chicken recipe.*

4. If someone or something **tries** your **patience**, that person or thing causes you to feel impatient. **try** (trye)

▷ *verb* **tries, trying, tried**

trying *adjective* Annoying or difficult to deal with: *My little sister can be very trying when she starts asking me a million questions.* **try·ing** (**trye**-ing)

tryout *noun* A trial or test to see if a person is qualified to do something such as perform a role in a play or play on a team; an audition. **try·out** (**trye**-out) ▷ *verb* **try out**

tsar *See* **czar**. **tsar** (zahr)

tsarina *See* **czarina**. **tsa·ri·na** (zah-**ree**-nuh)

T-shirt *or* **tee shirt** *noun* A light cotton shirt or undershirt with no collar and usually short sleeves. **T-shirt** *or* **tee shirt** (**tee**-*shurt*)

tsp. Short for **teaspoon** or the plural form *teaspoons*.

tsunami *noun* A very large, destructive wave caused by an underwater earthquake or volcano. **tsu·na·mi** (tsu-**nah**-mee)

tub *noun*

1. A bathtub: *Isabelle filled the tub with hot water.*

2. A round, open container used for packing or storing foods, as in *a tub of butter.*

3. A large, wide container used for washing clothes or bathing. **tub** (tuhb)

tuba *noun* A large, brass wind instrument with several valves. Tubas have a full, deep tone. **tu·ba** (**too**-buh)

tube *noun*

1. A long, hollow cylinder, especially one used to carry or hold liquids, as in *a test tube.*

2. A long container made of soft metal or plastic with a cap that screws on, as in *a tube of toothpaste.*

3. The hollow rubber ring that is put inside some bicycle tires and filled with air.

4. the tube (*informal*) Television. **tube** (toob)

tuber *noun* The thick underground stem of a plant such as a potato. **tu·ber** (**too**-bur)

tuberculosis *noun* A highly contagious disease caused by bacteria that usually affects the lungs. **tu·ber·cu·lo·sis** (tu-*bur*-kyuh-**loh**-sis)

tubular *adjective* In the shape of a tube: *A hot dog has a tubular shape.* **tu·bu·lar** (**too**-byuh-lur)

tuck

1. *verb* To fold or push the ends of something into place: *Don't forget to tuck in your shirt.*

2. tuck in *verb* To make someone warm and comfortable in bed by pulling up the blankets around him or her.

3. tuck away *verb* To hide something in a safe place.

4. *noun* A small fold sewn into clothing as a

tuba

decoration or to make the clothes fit better. **tuck** (tuhk)

▷ *verb* **tucking, tucked**

tucker out *verb* (*informal*) To make tired or exhausted: *Cleaning out the garage is tuckering me out.* **tuck·er out** (**tuk**-ur **out**) ▷ *verb* **tuckering out, tuckered out** ▷ *adjective* **tuckered out**

Tuesday *noun* The third day of the week, after Monday and before Wednesday. **Tues·day** (**tooz**-*day or* **tooz**-dee)

Word History

Tuesday was named for Tiw, the old English god of war. The name of the third day of the week was pronounced "Tiw's day," which eventually was spelled "Tuesday."

tuft *noun* A bunch of individual pieces of something such as hair, grass, or feathers that are attached together at the bottom. **tuft** (tuhft) ▷ *adjective* **tufted**

tug

1. *verb* To pull something hard with a short, quick movement: *The little boy tugged on his father's sleeve.* ▷ *verb* **tugging, tugged** ▷ *noun* **tug**

2. *noun* See **tugboat**. **tug** (tuhg)

tugboat *noun* A small, powerful boat that pulls or pushes large ships. **tug·boat** (**tuhg**-boht)

a
b
c
d
e
f
g
h
i
j
k
l
m
n
o
p
q
r
s
t
u
v
w
x
y
z

tug-of-war

tug-of-war *noun* A contest between two teams, each holding on to opposite ends of a rope, who try to pull each other over a center line.

tuition *noun* Money paid to a college or private school in order for a student to study there. **tu·i·tion** (too-**ish**-uhn)

tulip *noun* A plant with a tall stem and a colorful flower on top that is shaped like a cup. **tu·lip** (**too**-lip)

tumble *verb*
1. To fall down suddenly and hit the ground several times: *Chris slipped and tumbled down the stairs.*
2. To do somersaults or other acrobatic movements.
3. To roll or toss around: *The sheets and towels tumbled in the clothes dryer.*
4. To move in a quick and uncontrolled way: *The puppies tumbled out the door.*
tum·ble (**tuhm**-buhl)
▷ *verb* **tumbling, tumbled** ▷ *noun* **tumble**

tumbler *noun*
1. A tall drinking glass with straight sides.
2. Someone who does acrobatic movements, such as somersaults or handsprings.
tum·bler (**tuhm**-blur)

tumbleweed *noun* A bushy plant found in the deserts of western North America that breaks off from its roots and blows around in the wind. **tum·ble·weed** (**tum**-buhl-*weed*)

tummy *noun* (*informal*) The stomach. **tum·my** (**tuhm**-ee) ▷ *noun, plural* **tummies**

tumor *noun* An abnormal lump or mass of cells in the body. **tu·mor** (**too**-mur)

tumult *noun* A state of noisy confusion: *Marlena shouted above the tumult.* **tu·mult** (**too**-muhlt)
▷ *adjective* **tumultuous** (tuh-**muhl**-choo-uhs)
▷ *adverb* **tumultuously**

tuna *noun* A large fish that you can eat that is found in warm seas throughout the world. **tu·na** (**too**-nuh) ▷ *noun, plural* **tuna** *or* **tunas**

tundra *noun* A very cold area of northern Europe, Asia, and North America where there are no trees and the soil under the surface of the ground is always frozen. **tun·dra** (**tuhn**-druh)

tune
1. *noun* A series of musical notes arranged in a pattern; a simple melody that is easy to remember: *Let's see if the piano player will play us a tune.*
▷ *adjective* **tuneful**
2. *verb* To adjust the pitch of a musical instrument: *Mr. Nelson tuned our piano.* ▷ *noun* **tuner**
3. *noun* The condition of having the correct musical pitch: *The piano was out of tune.*
4. *noun* Agreement or understanding: *Some of my grandfather's ideas are not in tune with the times.*
5. *verb* If you **tune in** a radio or television program or station, you adjust the dial to receive it.
6. *verb* If you **tune** a car engine **up**, you put it in good working order by adjusting the parts.
tune (toon)
▷ *verb* **tuning, tuned**

tungsten *noun* A hard, gray metallic element that has a very high melting point and is used to make steel and the thin wire inside lightbulbs. **tung·sten** (**tung**-stuhn)

tunic *noun* A loose shirt without sleeves, as in *a wool tunic.* **tu·nic** (**too**-nik)

tuning fork *noun* A piece of metal with two long, thin parts joined together at one end, used for tuning musical instruments. When you hit it, it vibrates to produce a particular musical note.

tunnel *noun*
1. A passage built beneath the ground or water or through a mountain for cars, trains, or other vehicles to use.
2. An animal's underground passage.
tun·nel (**tuhn**-uhl)
▷ *verb* **tunnel**

tunnel vision *noun*
1. A tendency to only think about one part of a problem or situation and ignore other parts.
2. A condition in which the eye can only see things that are straight ahead, as if through a tunnel.

tuning fork

turban *noun* A long scarf wound around the head or around a cap. Turbans are worn especially by men in Arab countries and India. **tur·ban** (**tur**-buhn)

turban

turbine *noun* An engine powered by water, steam, wind, or gas passing through the blades of a wheel and making it spin. **tur·bine** (**tur**-buhn)

turbo *adjective* A **turbo** or **turbo-charged** engine has high-pressure air forced into it to create extra power. **tur·bo** (**tur**-boh)

turbofan *noun* A type of aircraft engine in which a large fan, powered by a turbine, pushes air into the hot exhaust at the rear of the engine, giving extra power. **tur·bo·fan** (**tur**-boh-*fan*)

turbulent *adjective* Wild, confused, or violent, as in *turbulent rapids* or *a turbulent time in history.* **tur·bu·lent** (**tur**-byuh-luhnt) ▷ *noun* **turbulence**

turf *noun* The top layer of grass and earth on a lawn or playing field. **turf** (turf)

turkey *noun*
1. A large North American bird with red-brown feathers and a tail that spreads out like a fan.
2. *(slang)* A silly or foolish person: *That turkey can't even put his hat on straight.*
tur·key (**tur**-kee)

Word History

The **turkey** got its name quite by accident. Although it's native to North America, it looks like an African bird that had been brought to Europe from Turkey. When the first European settlers saw this bird in America, they thought it was the African bird, which by then had been named "turkey." By the time the settlers realized the birds were different, they were all already calling the American bird a turkey.

turmoil *noun* Great confusion: *The city was in turmoil after the blizzard.* **tur·moil** (**tur**-moil)

turn
1. *verb* To go in a new direction: *Turn right at the church.*
2. *noun* A change in direction or position, or the point where such a change takes place: *He took a turn to the right.*
3. *verb* To rotate, or to make something rotate: *Turn the key to the left.*
4. *noun* The act of turning; a rotation, as in *one turn of the wheel.*
5. *verb* To change appearance or state, or to make something do this: *The caterpillar turns into a butterfly.*
6. *noun* A change in events or time, as in *a turn for the worse* or *the turn of the century.*
7. *verb* To become: *My skin turns darker in the sun. The milk turned sour.*
8. *verb* If something **turns** your **stomach**, it makes you feel sick.
9. *noun* A chance or duty to do something: *The pitcher had her turn at bat.*
10. *noun* A **good turn** is an action that helps someone: *You did a good turn by helping Mr. Hinton carry his groceries into the house.*
11. *verb* If you **turn** something or someone **down**, you refuse an opportunity or invitation: *Ron turned down the job because he didn't want to move to another city.*
12. **turn down** *verb* To move a switch on a piece of equipment so that you lower the amount of heat, sound, or light being produced: *Turn down the stereo—the neighbors are complaining.*
13. **turn in** *verb* To go to bed: *It's after midnight—I'm turning in.*
14. *verb* If you **turn** something **on**, you make it start to work by, for example, moving a switch: *She opened the door and turned on the lights.*
15. *verb* If you **turn** something **off**, you make it stop working by, for example, moving a switch: *Please turn off the television before you go to bed.*
16. **turn up** *verb* To appear, especially when you are not expected: *Marina turned up at my door just as I was leaving.*
17. **turn up** *verb* To move a switch on a piece of equipment so that you increase the amount of heat, sound, or light being produced: *Can you turn up the radio? I can't hear it.*
18. *verb (slang)* If something **turns** you **on**, it makes you interested or excited: *I love most sports but football doesn't turn me on.* ▷ *noun* **turn-on**
turn (turn)
▷ *verb* **turning, turned**

turnip *noun* A white or yellow root vegetable with a round shape. **tur·nip** (**tur**-nip)

turnout *noun* The number of people at a gathering or an event: *We expected a big turnout, but few came because of the rain.* **turn·out** (**turn**-out)

turnpike *noun* A highway that you have to pay money to drive on. **turn·pike** (**turn**-*pike*)

turnstile *noun* A metal bar inside an entrance or exit gate that moves forward in a circle when pushed so that only one person at a time can pass through. **turn·stile** (**turn**-*stile*)

turntable *noun* A flat, round surface that turns around and around in a circle. A turntable is used for playing phonograph records. **turn·ta·ble** (**turn**-*tay*-buhl)

turpentine *noun* A clear liquid made from the sap of certain pine trees. Turpentine is often used to thin paints. **tur·pen·tine** (**tur**-puhn-*tine*)

turquoise *noun*
1. A valuable, blue-green stone used in making jewelry.
2. A blue-green color.
tur·quoise (**tur**-koiz *or* **tur**-kwoiz)
▷ *adjective* **turquoise**

Word History

In the Middle Ages, a gem seller who wanted to buy **turquoise** went looking for it in the narrow streets of a Turkish bazaar because the gems passed through these centers on their way along the trade routes to Europe. French speakers named it "Turkish stone," *pierre turqueise,* after these Turkish bazaars. After a while they left out the word for "stone," *pierre,* and just called it *turqueise,* which speakers of English adopted as the name.

turret *noun*
1. A round or square tower on a building, usually on a corner. Many castles have turrets.
2. A structure on a tank, warship, or fighter plane that holds one or more guns. It usually rotates so that the gun can be fired in different directions.
tur·ret (**tur**-it)

turtle *noun* A reptile that can pull its head, legs, and tail into its hard shell for protection. Turtles live on land and in water. **tur·tle** (**tur**-tuhl)

turtleneck *noun*
1. A high collar that turns down and fits tightly around the neck.
2. A sweater or shirt with such a collar: *Amir wore a black turtleneck and jeans.*
tur·tle·neck (**tur**-tuhl-*nek*)

tusk *noun* One of the pair of long, curved, pointed teeth that stick out of the mouth of an animal such as an elephant, walrus, or wild boar. **tusk** (tuhsk)

tussle *noun* A short fight, argument, or struggle: *My brother got in a tussle with the bully.* **tus·sle** (**tuhs**-uhl) ▷ *verb* **tussle**

tutor *noun* A teacher who gives private lessons to only one student or a few students at a time, as in *a reading tutor.* **tu·tor** (**too**-tur) ▷ *verb* **tutor**

tutorial *noun* A short course in which you learn to do, or learn about, a particular thing. Many tutorials are designed so that people can do them alone on a computer. **tu·tor·i·al** (too-**tor**-ee-uhl)

tutu *noun* A short skirt made of several layers of stiff net, worn by a ballet dancer. **tu·tu** (**too**-too)

tuxedo *noun*
1. A man's jacket, usually black, worn with a bow tie for formal occasions.
2. A man's suit that includes this jacket.
tux·e·do (tuhk-**see**-doh)
▷ *noun, plural* **tuxedos**

TV *noun* Short for **television**.

tweed *noun* A rough wool cloth woven with yarns of two or more colors. **tweed** (tweed)

tween *noun* (*informal*) A child between 10 and 14; a pre-teenager or young teenager. **tween** (tween)

tweet
1. *noun* A short, high sound; a chirp.
2. *verb* If a bird **tweets**, it makes a short, high-pitched sound.
3. *noun* A short message that you send using the internet service Twitter: *Did you see Marcia's tweet this morning about her doctor visit?*
4. *verb* To send a message or messages using Twitter: *I usually tweet just about hockey and football.*
tweet (tweet)
▷ *verb* **tweeting, tweeted**

tweezers *noun, plural* A small metal tool with two long pieces joined at one end, used for pulling out hairs or for picking up very small objects. **twee·zers** (**twee**-zurz)

twice *adverb* Two times: *I've read that book twice.* **twice** (twise)

twig *noun* A small, thin branch of a tree or other woody plant. **twig** (twig)

twilight *noun* The time when the day is ending and the night is beginning, when the sun has just set and it is beginning to get dark. **twi·light** (**twye**-*lite*)

twin
1. *noun* One of two children born at the same birth to the same mother. ▷ *adjective* **twin**
2. *adjective* Belonging to a pair that are exactly the same, as in *twin engines.* ▷ *noun* **twin**
twin (twin)

twine
1. *noun* A very strong string made of two or more strands twisted together.
2. *verb* To wind or grow in a coil: *Ivy twined around the trellis.* ▷ *verb* **twining, twined**
twine (twine)

twinge *noun* A sudden slight pain or unpleasant feeling: *Ellen felt a twinge of sadness as she waved good-bye.* **twinge** (twinj)

twinkle
1. *verb* To shine with quick flashes of light; to sparkle: *The diamond twinkled in the light.* ▷ *verb* **twinkling, twinkled**

2. *noun* A flash of light: *Grandpa always has a twinkle in his eye.* **twin·kle** (**twing**-kuhl)

twirl *verb* To turn or spin around quickly: *Courtney felt dizzy from twirling around the room.* **twirl** (twurl) ▷ *verb* **twirling, twirled** ▷ *noun* **twirl**

twist *verb*

1. To turn, wind, or bend, or to do this to something: *Andy twisted the top off the jar. The river twisted through the forest.* ▷ *noun* **twist**

2. To wind two pieces of something like thread or wire together: *Rita twisted the strips of fabric together to make a bracelet.*

3. To turn a part of your body, such as your knee or wrist, suddenly in a way that is painful but does not cause a serious injury: *I twisted my ankle.*

4. When you **twist** someone's **words**, you purposely change the meaning of what he or she said. **twist** (twist) ▷ *verb* **twisting, twisted**

twister *noun* (*informal*) A tornado. **twis·ter** (**twis**-tur)

twitch *verb* To make small, sudden movements: *The animal's nose twitched.* **twitch** (twich) ▷ *verb* **twitches, twitching, twitched** ▷ *noun* **twitch** ▷ *adjective* **twitchy**

twitter *noun*

1. The short, high, chirping sounds that a bird makes. ▷ *verb* **twitter**

2. A state of nervous excitement: *The crowd was in a twitter before the concert started.*

3. **Twitter** A trademark for an online service that lets you post short messages for anyone to read. **twit·ter** (**twit**-ur)

tycoon *noun* A very wealthy, powerful businessperson, as in *an oil tycoon.* **ty·coon** (tye-**koon**)

Word History

Commodore Matthew Perry traveled to Japan in 1853, arriving with four ships in the harbor of Tokyo. His visit led to Japan trading with countries in the West. The military commander of Japan was called the "shogun," and when the Japanese were talking with foreigners, they referred to him as a *taikun,* meaning "a great lord." So English speakers called the shogun "the **tycoon** of Japan." Today, the word *tycoon* means "a wealthy, powerful businessperson."

type

1. *noun* A sort or a kind: *What type of bike do you have?*

typewriter

2. *noun* Small pieces of metal with raised letters, numbers, punctuation marks, or other symbols on their surfaces. Type is used in printing.

3. *verb* To write something with a typewriter or computer: *Have you finished typing your essay?* ▷ *verb* **typing, typed**

4. *noun* Printed numbers and letters. **type** (tipe)

typeface *noun* A particular style of type used in printing and desktop publishing. **type·face** (**tipe**-fase)

typeset *verb* To put a piece of writing into a typed form that can be used in printing. **type·set** (**tipe**-*set*) ▷ *verb* **typesetting, typeset** ▷ *noun* **typesetter** ▷ *adjective* **typeset**

typewriter *noun* A machine that prints letters, numbers, and punctuation marks when you press keys with your fingers. **type·writ·er** (**tipe**-*rye*-tur)

typhoid *noun* A serious infectious disease caused by germs in food or water. Typhoid's symptoms include high fever and diarrhea, and it sometimes leads to death. **ty·phoid** (**tye**-foid)

typhoon *noun* A violent tropical storm that occurs in the western Pacific Ocean. **ty·phoon** (tye-**foon**)

typical *adjective*

1. Having traits or qualities that are normal for a particular type or class: *My family lives in a typical small town.*

2. If someone does something that is **typical**, the person behaves in a way that is expected or not surprising: *It's typical of Nicholas to be late for a party.* **typ·i·cal** (**tip**-i-kuhl)

typically *adverb* In an expected or usual manner; normally: *I typically don't stay up this late.* **typ·i·cal·ly** (**tip**-ik-lee)

typist *noun* Someone who uses a computer or typewriter to write things, especially as a job. **typ·ist** (**tye**-pist)

tyrannosaur *noun* A huge dinosaur that ate meat and walked upright. **ty·ran·no·saur** (ti-**ran**-uh-*sor*)

tyranny *noun* A system of government in which a tyrant or a small group has all the power and unfair laws are harshly enforced: *The country's king was deposed, only to be replaced by a military tyranny.* **tyr·an·ny** (**tir**-uh-nee) ▷ *noun, plural* **tyrannies** ▷ *adjective* **tyrannical** (ti-**ran**-i-kuhl)

tyrant *noun* Someone who rules other people in a cruel or unjust way. **ty·rant** (**tye**-ruhnt) ▷ *adjective* **tyrannical** (ti-**ran**-i-kuhl)

a
b
c
d
e
f
g
h
i
j
k
l
m
n
o
p
q
r
s
t
u
v
w
x
y
z

Uu

About U Although it is a vowel in English, **U** was used by the Romans and the Greeks as both a vowel and a consonant. Until the 16th century, *u* and *v* were considered different forms of the same letter. Today, *u* is a shorthand way to say "you" in a text message. Words that begin with a *yoo* sound are spelled *u* or *eu*. Examples: ukulele, utility, eucalyptus, European.

udder *noun* The baglike part of a female cow, sheep, or other similar mammal that hangs down near its back legs. The udder contains the glands that produce milk. **ud·der** (**uhd**-ur)

UFO *noun* An object that is seen or is thought to be seen flying in the sky, and that some people believe to be a spaceship from another planet. UFO is short for *unidentified flying object.*

ugly *adjective*
1. Not attractive or pleasant to look at.
2. Disgusting or unpleasant, as in *an ugly rumor.*
3. Nasty or mean, as in *an ugly mood.*
ug·ly (**uhg**-lee)
▷ *adjective* **uglier, ugliest**

uh-oh *interjection* An expression of surprise at something bad: *Uh-oh! You were supposed to turn off the electricity first!*

ukulele *noun* A small, four-stringed guitar originally made popular in Hawaii. **u·ku·le·le** (*yoo*-kuh-**lay**-lee)

Word History

Ukulele is the Hawaiian name for the musical instrument that was first brought to Hawaii by the Portuguese in 1879. Generally made of wood, the "uke," as it is often called, was introduced to the US mainland around 1915, and quickly became popular with jazz musicians. In Hawaiian, *uku* means "flea" and *lele* means "jumping." This seemed an appropriate name because a ukulele player's fingers can seem to move around the strings like a jumping flea.

ulcer *noun* An open, painful sore on the skin or on the lining of the stomach. **ul·cer** (**uhl**-sur)

ultimate *adjective*
1. Final, or happening at the end of a process, as in *her ultimate career goal.*
2. Basic, original, or fundamental: *The king has the ultimate authority in the kingdom.*
3. Greatest or best: *Gavin's award is the ultimate accomplishment for someone in his profession.*
ul·ti·mate (**uhl**-tuh-mit)
▷ *noun* **ultimate** ▷ *adverb* **ultimately**

umbrella

ultimatum *noun* A final offer or demand, especially one that carries with it the threat of punishment or the use of force if rejected. **ul·ti·ma·tum** (*uhl*-tuh-**may**-tuhm) ▷ *noun, plural* **ultimatums** or **ultimata** (*uhl*-tuh-**may**-tuh)

ultralight *noun* A very light aircraft, usually for one person, which is powered by a small engine. **ul·tra·light** (**uhl**-truh-*lite*)

ultrasound *noun* Sound whose frequency is too high for the human ear to hear. Ultrasound waves are used in medical scans. **ul·tra·sound** (**uhl**-truh-*sound*) ▷ *adjective* **ultrasound**

ultraviolet light *noun* A type of light that cannot be seen by the human eye. It is given off by the sun and causes the skin to get darker. **ul·tra·vi·o·let light** (*uhl*-truh-**vye**-uh-lit)

umbilical cord *noun* The flexible tube containing blood vessels that connects an unborn baby to its mother's body. The baby receives food and oxygen through this cord, and it also lets the baby's body eliminate wastes. **um·bil·i·cal cord** (uhm-**bil**-i-kuhl)

umbrella *noun* A folding frame with a circular cloth stretched over it that you hold over your head to protect you from the rain. **um·brel·la** (uhm-**brel**-uh)

umpire *noun* An official who rules on plays in baseball, tennis, and certain other sports. **um·pire** (**uhm**-pire) ▷ *verb* **umpire**

Prefix

The prefix **un-** adds one of the following meanings to a root word:

1. Not, as in *unemployed* (not employed), *unbelievable* (not believable), and *unavoidable* (not avoidable).

2. The opposite of, as in *unlock* (to do the opposite of lock) and *undress* (to do the opposite of dress).

unable *adjective* Lacking the ability to do something: *With my wrist broken, I was unable to tie my shoes.* **un·a·ble** (uhn-**ay**-buhl)

unacceptable *adjective* Not good enough, or not allowable. **un·ac·cept·a·ble** (uhn-uhk-**sep**-tuh-buhl) ▷ *adverb* **unacceptably**

unaccustomed *adjective* Not used to something: *Gloria was unaccustomed to eating at fancy restaurants.* **un·ac·cus·tomed** (uhn-uh-**kuhs**-tuhmd)

unadulterated *adjective* Pure, with nothing extra or artificial added to it. **un·adul·ter·at·ed** (*uhn*-uh-**duhl**-tuh-*ray*-tid)

unaided *adjective* Without any help. **un·aid·ed** (uhn-**ay**-did)

unanimous *adjective* Agreed on by everyone, as in *a unanimous vote.* **u·nan·i·mous** (yoo-**nan**-uh-muhs) ▷ *adverb* **unanimously**

unapproachable *adjective*

1. Not easy to talk to or to get to know; unfriendly: *He was rude and unapproachable.*

2. Difficult or impossible to get to: *The mountain hut is unapproachable by road.* **un·ap·proach·a·ble** (*uhn*-uh-**proh**-chuh-buhl)

unarmed *adjective* Not carrying any weapons. **un·armed** (uhn-**ahrmd**)

unauthorized *adjective* Done without official permission. **un·au·tho·rized** (uhn-**aw**-thuh-*rized*)

unavoidable *adjective* Impossible to avoid or prevent. **un·a·void·a·ble** (*uhn*-uh-**voi**-duh-buhl) ▷ *adverb* **unavoidably**

unaware *adjective* Not knowing that something exists or is happening. **un·a·ware** (*uhn*-uh-**wair**)

unbearable *adjective* Too bad or unpleasant to tolerate. **un·bear·a·ble** (uhn-**bair**-uh-buhl) ▷ *adverb* **unbearably**

unbecoming *adjective*

1. Not attractive or not flattering, as in *an unbecoming outfit.*

2. Not in good taste; not proper, as in *unbecoming behavior.*

un·be·com·ing (*uhn*-bi-**kuhm**-ing)

unbelievable *adjective* Impossible to believe, or unlikely to be true. **un·be·liev·a·ble** (*uhn*-bi-**lee**-vuh-buhl)

unbending *adjective* Unwilling to change your mind. **un·bend·ing** (uhn-**ben**-ding)

unbreakable *adjective* Not able to be broken, or not likely to be broken, as in *unbreakable dishes.* **un·break·a·ble** (uhn-**bray**-kuh-buhl)

unbroken *adjective*

1. Not broken; whole.

2. Not interrupted; without a stop or break; continuous, as in *miles of unbroken forest.*

3. Not tamed or trained for use with a harness: *Only the best rider can manage an unbroken horse.*

4. Not bettered or topped, as in *an unbroken sports record.*

un·bro·ken (uhn-**broh**-kuhn)

unburden *verb* To relieve yourself of something that is causing worry or distress: *The remorseful thief finally unburdened himself to the detective.* **un·bur·den** (uhn-**bur**-duhn) ▷ *verb* **unburdening, unburdened**

uncanny *adjective*

1. Very strange and difficult to explain or understand; mysterious; eerie.

2. Remarkable or extraordinary, as in *an uncanny sense of direction.*

un·can·ny (uhn-**kan**-ee) ▷ *adverb* **uncannily**

uncomfortable

uncertain *adjective*

1. Not sure: *She was uncertain of the answer.*

2. Likely to change, as in *uncertain weather.*

un·cer·tain (uhn-**sur**-tuhn) ▷ *noun* **uncertainty** (uhn-**sur**-tuhn-tee)

uncivilized *adjective*

1. Considered to be less advanced socially or culturally, as in *an uncivilized people.*

2. Impolite or unruly, as in *uncivilized behavior.*

un·civ·i·lized (uhn-**siv**-uh-*lized*)

uncle *noun* The brother of your mother or father, or the husband of your aunt. **un·cle** (**uhng**-kuhl)

uncomfortable *adjective*

1. Not relaxed or at ease in your body or your mind. ▷ *adverb* **uncomfortably**

2. Causing worry or pain, as in *an uncomfortable situation* or *uncomfortable shoes.*

un·com·fort·a·ble (uhn-**kuhm**-fur-tuh-buhl)

uncommon *adjective* Rare or unusual; out of the ordinary: *Grizzly bears are uncommon in this area.* **un·com·mon** (uhn-**kah**-muhn) ▷ *adverb* **uncommonly**

uncomplimentary *adjective* Insulting, rude, or negative, as in *uncomplimentary remarks.* **un·com·pli·men·ta·ry** (*uhn*-kahm-pluh-**men**-tur-ee)

uncompromising *adjective* Refusing to give in, change your ideas, or accept something as it is: *My teacher is uncompromising in her strictness.* **un·com·pro·mis·ing** (uhn-**kahm**-pruh-*mye*-zing) ▷ *adverb* **uncompromisingly**

unconcerned *adjective*
1. Not interested; indifferent: *Dan is unconcerned with what other people think.*
2. Not worried, anxious, or upset: *Although the boy had a fever, the doctor remained unconcerned.* **un·con·cerned** (uhn-kuhn-**surnd**)

unconditional *adjective* Not limited by any conditions; without limitations, as in *unconditional surrender.* **un·con·di·tion·al** (uhn-kuhn-**dish**-uh-nuhl) ▷ *adverb* **unconditionally**

unconfirmed *adjective* Not yet known to be definitely true, as in *unconfirmed reports.* **un·con·firmed** (*uhn*-kuhn-**furmd**)

unconscious *adjective*
1. Not awake; not able to see, feel, or think.
2. Unaware: *Bill went on talking, unconscious of the fact that everyone was leaving.*
3. Done without realizing it: *It was an unconscious mistake.* **un·con·scious** (uhn-**kahn**-shuhs)

unconstitutional *adjective* Not in keeping with the basic principles or laws set forth in the constitution of a state or country, especially the Constitution of the United States. **un·con·sti·tu·tion·al** (*uhn*-kahn-sti-**too**-shuh-nuhl)

uncontrollable *adjective* Not able to be stopped, held in, or restrained, as in *uncontrollable laughter.* **un·con·trol·la·ble** (*uhn*-kuhn-**troh**-luh-buhl) ▷ *adverb* **uncontrollably**

uncooperative *adjective* Unwilling to help or work with others. **un·co·op·er·a·tive** (*uhn*-koh-**ah**-pur-uh-tiv)

uncouth *adjective* Lacking good manners or refinement: *We were surprised at their uncouth behavior.* **un·couth** (uhn-**kooth**)

uncover *verb*
1. To remove a cover from something.
2. To discover or reveal something; to make something known: *The investigation uncovered a major fraud.* **un·cov·er** (uhn-**kuhv**-ur)

▷ *verb* **uncovering, uncovered**

undaunted *adjective* Not discouraged or frightened by dangers or difficulties: *We were undaunted by the long drive ahead.* **un·daunt·ed** (uhn-**dawn**-tid)

undecided *adjective*
1. Not having made up your mind: *Nearly half of the voters are undecided.*
2. Not yet settled, as in *an undecided election.* **un·de·cid·ed** (*uhn*-di-**sye**-did)

undeniable *adjective* So clearly true that it cannot be denied: *Knowing Spanish is an undeniable advantage when you're traveling in Mexico.* **un·de·ni·a·ble** (*uhn*-di-**nye**-uh-buhl) ▷ *adverb* **undeniably**

under *preposition*
1. Below or beneath: *The suitcases are in a closet under the stairs.* ▷ *adverb* **under**
2. Less than a particular number or amount: *Use the express checkout if you have under 12 items in your cart.*
3. According to: *Under the rules, she can't reenter the game.*
4. Controlled or bound by, as in *under oath.*
5. Subordinate to or responsible for: *Jeff has 20 people working under him.*
6. Hidden by something: *Under his rough appearance, Blake is a polite and considerate person.* **un·der** (**uhn**-dur)

underarm
1. *adverb* Underhand; with your arm below shoulder level: *Helene pitched underarm.*
2. *noun* The armpit, or the part of the body that is under the arm. **un·der·arm** (**uhn**-dur-*ahrm*) ▷ *adjective* **underarm**

underbrush *noun* Bushes, shrubs, and other plants that grow beneath the large trees in the forest or woods. **un·der·brush** (**uhn**-dur-*bruhsh*)

underclothes *noun, plural* Underwear. **un·der·clothes** (**uhn**-dur-*kloze*)

undercover
1. *adjective* Working or done in secret, especially police work or espionage: *Three undercover police officers were assigned to watch the suspected burglars.*
2. *adverb* Secretly: *She worked undercover for several months on the fraud investigation.* **un·der·cov·er** (*uhn*-dur-**kuhv**-ur)

underdeveloped *adjective*
1. Not completely or normally developed, as in *underdeveloped film* or *underdeveloped muscles.*
2. Having an economy that is not very advanced compared to others, as in *an underdeveloped nation.* **un·der·de·vel·oped** (*uhn*-dur-di-**vel**-uhpt)

underdog *noun* A person, team, or group that is expected to lose a game, race, election, or other contest. **un·der·dog** (**uhn**-dur-*dawg*)

underestimate *verb*
1. To think that something is smaller, weaker, or less important than it really is: *Never underestimate your opponent's ability.*
2. To make a guess that is too low: *Karen underestimated the number of pies we would need.* **un·der·es·ti·mate** (*uhn*-dur-**es**-tuh-*mate*)
▷ *verb* **underestimating, underestimated**
▷ *noun* **underestimate** (*uhn*-dur-**es**-tuh-mit)
▷ *noun* **underestimation**

Underground Railroad

During the 1800s, the Underground Railroad enabled thousands of slaves who worked on the plantations in the South to escape to the North, where slavery was illegal. Organized by abolitionists, it included hiding places in several states.

To avoid slave catchers, the people who helped the slaves, such as Harriet Tubman, herself a former slave, were careful to keep their movements secret, or "underground."

Harriet Tubman

underfoot *adverb*
1. Under your feet; on the ground: *The fallen leaves crackled underfoot.*
2. In the way: *The kitten was always underfoot.* **un·der·foot** (*uhn*-der-**fut**)

undergarment *noun* A piece of clothing that you wear next to your skin, under other clothes, such as a T-shirt. **un·der·gar·ment** (*uhn*-dur-*gahr*-muhnt)

undergo *verb* To experience or have to go through something: *Heather had to undergo a serious operation.* **un·der·go** (*uhn*-dur-*goh*) ▷ *verb* **undergoes, undergoing, underwent** (*uhn*-dur-**went**), **undergone** (*uhn*-dur-**gawn**)

underground *adjective*
1. Below the ground, as in *an underground shelter.*
2. Secret or hidden, as in *an underground spy ring.* **un·der·ground** (**uhn**-dur-*ground*)
▷ *adverb* **underground** (**uhn**-dur-**ground**)

Underground Railroad *noun* A network of people who secretly helped slaves from the South escape to free states in the North or to Canada before the American Civil War.

undergrowth *noun* Saplings, seedlings, shrubs, and other plants, especially those that grow beneath the tall, mature trees in a forest. **un·der·growth** (**uhn**-dur-*grohth*)

underhand *adjective* Thrown or pitched with the hand below the shoulder or elbow level: *She used an underhand throw.* **un·der·hand** (*uhn*-dur-*hand*)
▷ *adverb* **underhand**

underhanded *adjective* Sneaky or dishonest; done in secret; unfair, as in *underhanded methods to defeat her opponent.* **un·der·hand·ed** (*uhn*-dur-**han**-did)

underline *verb*
1. To draw a line under something: *Paco underlined the word "please" five times in his note.*
2. To emphasize the importance of something: *The president underlined the significance of the treaty.*
un·der·line (**uhn**-dur-*line*)
▷ *verb* **underlining, underlined**

undermine *verb* To weaken or destroy something slowly and often secretly: *His constant criticism undermined my confidence.* **un·der·mine** (*uhn*-dur-*mine*) ▷ *verb* **undermining, undermined**

underneath *preposition* Under or below. **un·der·neath** (*uhn*-dur-**neeth**) ▷ *adverb* **underneath**

undernourished *adjective* Weak and unhealthy from lack of nutritious food. **un·der·nour·ished** (*uhn*-dur-**nur**-isht)

underpants *noun, plural* Short pants worn as underwear. **un·der·pants** (*uhn*-dur-*pants*)

underpass

underpass *noun* A road or passage that goes underneath another road or a bridge: *Turn left after the underpass.* **un·der·pass** (**uhn**-dur-*pas*)

underprivileged *adjective* Lacking the advantages or opportunities that other people have, usually because of poverty. **un·der·priv·i·leged** (*uhn*-dur-**priv**-uh-lijd)

undersea *adjective* Located, done, or used below the surface of the ocean, as in *undersea plants* or *undersea exploration.* **un·der·sea** (*uhn*-dur-**see**)

undershirt *noun* A shirt with short sleeves or no sleeves worn as underwear. **un·der·shirt** (**uhn**-dur-*shurt*)

underside *noun* The bottom side or surface of something, as in *the underside of a boat* or *the underside of a rock.* **un·der·side** (**uhn**-dur-*side*)

understand *verb*
1. To grasp the meaning of something or the way something works: *I don't understand your question.*
2. To know very well: *Do you understand Spanish?*
3. To have sympathy for someone: *The therapist understands teenagers.*
4. To believe that something is true; to gather from indirect information: *I understand that Jane's family is moving to New Jersey.*
un·der·stand (*uhn*-dur-**stand**) ▷ *verb* **understanding, understood** (*uhn*-dur-**stud**) ▷ *adjective* **understanding**

understandable *adjective*
1. Easy to understand.
2. Natural, to be expected: *The little boy's fear of big dogs is understandable.*

un·der·stand·a·ble (*uhn*-dur-**stan**-duh-buhl) ▷ *adverb* **understandably**

understanding *noun*
1. The ability to understand something.
2. Someone's perception of a fact or a situation: *It was my understanding that Kay would meet us here.*
3. Sympathy or tolerance: *A good friend offers understanding and encouragement.*
4. An informal agreement: *Jake and I have an understanding—we share his basketball.*
un·der·stand·ing (*uhn*-dur-**stan**-ding)

undertake *verb*
1. To agree to do a job or task; to accept a responsibility: *Benito undertook the care of the homeless puppy.*
2. To set about; to try or attempt: *We will undertake a long, difficult journey.*
un·der·take (*uhn*-dur-**take**)
▷ *verb* **undertaking, undertook, undertaken** ▷ *noun* **undertaking**

undertaker *noun* A person whose job is to prepare dead bodies for burial or cremation and to arrange funerals. **un·der·tak·er** (*uhn*-dur-*tay*-kur)

undertow *noun* A strong current below the surface of a body of water that can pull swimmers away from the shore. **un·der·tow** (*uhn*-dur-*toh*)

underwater *adjective* Located, used, or done under the surface of the water. **un·der·wa·ter** (*uhn*-dur-**waw**-tur) ▷ *adverb* **underwater**

under way *adverb, adjective* Already begun or happening now: *The parade was already under way and we couldn't drive across Main Street.*

underwear *noun* Clothes that you wear next to your skin, under your outer clothes; underclothes. **un·der·wear** (**uhn**-dur-*wair*)

underweight *adjective* Having less than the normal or required weight; weighing too little. **un·der·weight** (*uhn*-dur-**wayt**)

underworld *noun*
1. The part of society that is involved in organized crime.
2. In Greek and Roman mythology, the place under the ground where the spirits of dead people go.
un·der·world (**uhn**-dur-*wurld*)

underwear

undesirable *adjective* Not wanted or not pleasant. **un·de·sir·a·ble** (*uhn*-di-**zye**-ruh-buhl)

undisturbed *adjective* Not bothered, or not interrupted; peaceful and calm: *The baby slept undisturbed through the entire party.* **un·dis·turbed** (*uhn*-dis-**turbd**)

undo *verb*
1. To untie, unfasten, or open something.
2. To remove or reverse the effects of something: *I wish I could undo my mistake.*
un·do (uhn-**doo**)
▷ *verb* **undoes, undoing, undid, undone**

undone *adjective* Not finished or not completed, as in *to leave the last part of the mathematics test undone.* **un·done** (uhn-**duhn**)

undress *verb* To take clothes off: *Martha undressed the baby.* **un·dress** (uhn-**dres**) ▷ *verb* **undresses, undressing, undressed** ▷ *adjective* **undressed**

undying *adjective* Lasting forever: *You have my undying gratitude.* **un·dy·ing** (uhn-**dye**-ing)

unearth *verb*
1. To dig up something: *While gardening one day, my mother unearthed an old coin.*
2. To find, discover, or uncover something after searching for it, as in *to unearth more clues.*
un·earth (uhn-**urth**)
▷ *verb* **unearthing, unearthed**

uneasy *adjective*
1. Worried, nervous, or anxious.
2. Awkward, uncomfortable, or embarrassed: *An uneasy silence followed Dan's outburst in the classroom.*
un·eas·y (uhn-**ee**-zee)
▷ *noun* **uneasiness** ▷ *adverb* **uneasily**

unemployed *adjective* Without a job or paid work of any kind. **un·em·ployed** (*uhn*-em-**ploid**) ▷ *noun* **unemployment**

unequal *adjective*
1. Not the same in amount, size, or value, as in *an unequal division of property.*
2. Not well matched or not well balanced, as in *unequal teams.*
un·e·qual (uhn-**ee**-kwuhl)
▷ *adverb* **unequally**

unequivocal *adjective* Leaving no doubt or uncertainty: *Her answer was an unequivocal no.* **un·equiv·o·cal** (*uhn*-i-**kwiv**-uh-kuhl)

uneven *adjective*
1. Not flat, smooth, or straight, as in *uneven ground.*
2. Not regular, or not consistent: *The actor gave an uneven performance.*
un·e·ven (uhn-**ee**-vuhn)
▷ *adverb* **unevenly**

uneven number *noun* A number that cannot be divided exactly by 2: *Seven is an uneven number.*

uneventful *adjective* With nothing interesting or exciting happening, as in *an uneventful afternoon.* **un·e·vent·ful** (*uhn*-i-**vent**-fuhl) ▷ *adverb* **uneventfully**

unexpected *adjective* Surprising because you did not think it would happen: *The crowd went wild at the unexpected victory.* **un·ex·pect·ed** (*uhn*-ik-**spek**-tid) ▷ *adverb* **unexpectedly**

unfair *adjective* Not fair, right, or just, as in *unfair criticism.* **un·fair** (uhn-**fair**) ▷ *adjective* **unfairer, unfairest** ▷ *noun* **unfairness** ▷ *adverb* **unfairly**

unfamiliar *adjective*
1. Not well-known or not easily recognized; strange: *An unfamiliar face appeared at the door.*
2. Not knowing about something, or having no experience using it, as in *unfamiliar with art.*
un·fa·mil·iar (*uhn*-fuh-**mil**-yur)

unfasten *verb*
1. To release or to detach: *He unfastened the boat from its mooring.*
2. To open something that has been fastened.
un·fas·ten (uhn-**fas**-uhn)
▷ *verb* **unfastening, unfastened**

unfeeling *adjective* Without kindness or sympathy; cruel: *Only an unfeeling person would ignore this injured dog.* **un·feel·ing** (uhn-**fee**-ling)

unfit *adjective*
1. Not suitable or good enough for a particular purpose: *Polluted water is unfit to drink.*
2. Unhealthy or in poor physical condition.
un·fit (uhn-**fit**)

unfold *verb*
1. To open and spread out something that was folded: *Paul unfolded the map.*
2. To become known gradually: *As the story unfolds, we come to know the characters better.*
un·fold (uhn-**fohld**)
▷ *verb* **unfolding, unfolded**

unforeseen *adjective* Not expected or not planned: *I was late because of an unforeseen delay.* **un·fore·seen** (*uhn*-for-**seen**)

unforgettable *adjective* So special, in some way, that you cannot forget it, as in *an unforgettable experience.* **un·for·get·ta·ble** (*uhn*-fur-**get**-uh-buhl) ▷ *adverb* **unforgettably**

unforgivable *adjective* So bad that it cannot be forgiven. **un·for·giv·a·ble** (*uhn*-fur-**giv**-uh-buhl) ▷ *adverb* **unforgivably**

unfortunate *adjective*
1. Unlucky, as in *an unfortunate delay.* ▷ *adverb* **unfortunately**
2. Not wise, proper, or suitable: *Robert was an unfortunate choice for goalie.*
un·for·tu·nate (uhn-**for**-chuh-nit)

unfriend *verb* (*informal*) To remove someone from your list of friends on a social networking site. **un·friend** (*uhn*-**frend**)

unfriendly *adjective*
1. Not friendly; feeling or showing dislike: *Those girls are extremely mean and unfriendly.*
2. Not pleasant or not favorable: *This jungle has a hot, unfriendly climate.*
un·friend·ly (uhn-**frend**-lee)
▷ *adjective* **unfriendlier, unfriendliest**
▷ *noun* **unfriendliness**

ungrateful *adjective* Not thankful for or appreciative of something.
un·grate·ful (uhn-**grate**-fuhl)
▷ *adverb* **ungratefully**

unhappy

unhappy *adjective*
1. Without joy; sad, as in *an unhappy child.*
2. Not lucky or fortunate, as in *an unhappy incident.*
3. Not suitable, as in *an unhappy choice for president.*
un·hap·py (uhn-**hap**-ee)
▷ *adjective* **unhappier, unhappiest**
▷ *noun* **unhappiness** ▷ *adverb* **unhappily**

unhealthy *adjective*
1. Not healthy; in poor health; not well.
2. Resulting from poor health: *His unhealthy weight was due to his poor diet.*
3. Harmful to one's health: *Eating too much junk food is an unhealthy habit.*
un·health·y (uhn-**hel**-thee)

unheard-of *adjective* Not known or done before, as in *an unheard-of artist* or *an unheard-of athletic feat.* **un·heard-of** (uhn-**hurd** uhv)

unicorn *noun* An imaginary animal that looks like a horse with a single straight horn growing from its forehead. **u·ni·corn** (**yoo**-ni-korn)

Word History

The term **unicorn** comes from the Latin words *uni*, meaning "one," and *cornu*, meaning "horn." There were legends of these pure white beasts with one horn in many countries in ancient times, including India, China, Europe, and the Islamic nations. You can also find the Latin root *corn* in the English word *cornet*, which is a type of musical horn.

unidentified *adjective* Not identified; not known or recognized: *The witness saw an unidentified man leaving the scene of the crime.* **un·i·den·ti·fied** (uhn-eye-**den**-tuh-fide) ▷ *adjective* **unidentifiable**

uniform
1. *noun* A special set of clothes worn by all the members of a particular group or organization. Nurses, soldiers, police officers, and mail carriers wear uniforms. ▷ *adjective* **uniformed**

2. *adjective* Always the same; never changing.
3. *adjective* All alike; not different in any way, as in *a uniform row of houses.* ▷ *noun* **uniformity** (yoo-nuh-**for**-mi-tee) ▷ *adverb* **uniformly**
u·ni·form (**yoo**-nuh-form)

unify *verb* To bring or join together into a whole or a unit; to unite. **u·ni·fy** (**yoo**-nuh-fye) ▷ *verb* **unifies, unifying, unified** ▷ *noun* **unification** (yoo-nuh-fi-**kay**-shuhn)

unimportant *adjective* Not important; of no special value or interest; minor, as in *unimportant details.* **un·im·por·tant** (uhn-im-**por**-tuhnt)

uninhabited *adjective* Having no one living there. **un·in·hab·it·ed** (uhn-in-**hab**-i-tid)

unintelligible *adjective* Not able to be understood. **un·in·tel·li·gi·ble** (uhn-in-**tel**-i-juh-buhl) ▷ *adverb* **unintelligibly**

unintentional *adjective* Done by accident, not on purpose. **un·in·ten·tion·al** (uhn-in-**ten**-shuh-nuhl) ▷ *adverb* **unintentionally**

uninterested *adjective* Having no interest in something, or not wanting to know anything about it. **un·in·ter·est·ed** (uhn-**in**-tri-stid)

union *noun*
1. An organized group of workers set up to help improve such things as working conditions, wages, and health benefits.
2. The joining together of two or more things or people to form a larger group.
3. **the Union** The United States of America: *The president gave the State of the Union address.*
4. **the Union** The Northern states that remained loyal to the federal government during the Civil War.
un·ion (**yoon**-yuhn)

unique *adjective* Being the only one of its kind; unlike anything else. **u·nique** (yoo-**neek**) ▷ *adverb* **uniquely**

unisex *adjective* Able to be worn or used by both men and women, as in *unisex clothing.* **u·ni·sex** (**yoo**-ni-seks)

unison *noun* Saying, singing, or doing something together, as in *to stand in unison.* **u·ni·son** (**yoo**-ni-suhn)

unit *noun*
1. An individual thing or person, considered complete in itself: *Each household counts as a family unit.*
2. A single person, thing, or group that is part of a larger group or whole, as in *an apartment unit.*
3. An amount used as a standard of measurement: *An ounce is a unit of weight.*

Universe

Many scientists believe that the universe began in a huge explosion, the Big Bang, billions of years ago. The Milky Way, which contains our solar system, is only one of many galaxies that formed as a result.

Telescopes on earth make objects in space visible to human eyes. Other telescopes, in orbit above the earth, collect radiation, which is analyzed by computers. This tells us about stars and planets too far away to be seen.

observatory

telescope

astronaut

Milky Way galaxy

4. A machine or piece of equipment that has a special purpose, as in *an air-conditioning unit.*

5. The number one.

u·nit (**yoo**-nit)

unite *verb*

1. To join together or work together to achieve something: *Let's unite to fight poverty.*

2. To put or join together in order to make a whole: *The states united to form a single nation.*

u·nite (yoo-**nite**)

▷ *verb* **uniting, united** ▷ *noun* **unity** (**yoo**-ni-tee)

▷ *adjective* **united**

universal *adjective*

1. True of everyone or everything, or applying to everyone or everything, as in *a universal appeal.*

2. Found everywhere, as in *a universal problem.*

u·ni·ver·sal (*yoo*-nuh-**vur**-suhl)

▷ *adverb* **universally**

universe *noun* All existing matter and space.

u·ni·verse (**yoo**-nuh-*vurs*)

university *noun* A school for higher learning after high school where people can study for degrees, do research, or learn a profession such as law or medicine. **u·ni·ver·si·ty** (*yoo*-nuh-**vur**-si-tee)

▷ *noun, plural* **universities**

unjust *adjective* Not just, fair, or right, as in *an unjust rule.* **un·just** (uhn-**juhst**) ▷ *adverb* **unjustly**

unkempt *adjective*

1. Not combed, as in *unkempt hair.*

2. Not tidy or neat in appearance, as in *an unkempt room* or *an unkempt lawn.*

un·kempt (uhn-**kempt**)

unkind *adjective* Not kind; harsh or cruel, as in *unkind words.* **un·kind** (uhn-**kinde**) ▷ *adjective* **unkinder, unkindest** ▷ *adverb* **unkindly**

unknown *adjective* Not familiar or not known about, as in *unknown territory.* **un·known** (uhn-**nohn**)

▷ *noun* **unknown**

unless *conjunction* Except on the condition that: *I can't come unless I get a ride.* **un·less** (uhn-**les**)

unlike

1. *adjective* Not alike; different.

2. *preposition* Different from; not like: *Unlike Tina, I love music.*

3. *preposition* Not typical of: *It's unlike Doug to be late.*

4. *adjective* In a pair of magnets, **unlike** poles attract each other while like poles repel each other.

un·like (uhn-**like**)

unlikely *adjective*
1. Not probable: *It is unlikely to snow today.*
2. Not likely to be true or to succeed, as in *an unlikely story* or *an unlikely plan.*
un·like·ly (*uhn*-**like**-lee)

unlimited *adjective* Having no limits, bounds, or restrictions. **un·lim·it·ed** (uhn-**lim**-i-tid)

unload *verb*
1. To remove things from a container, ship, or vehicle: *Unload the groceries from the car.*
2. To remove ammunition from a gun.
un·load (uhn-**lohd**)
▷ *verb* **unloading, unloaded**

unlock *verb*
1. To open something with a key.
2. To solve, or to provide a key to, as in *to unlock a mystery.*
un·lock (uhn-**lahk**)
▷ *verb* **unlocking, unlocked**

unlucky *adjective*
1. Unfortunate; having bad luck.
2. Happening by chance and unfortunate, as in *an unlucky fall.* ▷ *adverb* **unluckily**
3. Bringing or believed to bring bad luck, as in *an unlucky number* or *an unlucky day.*
un·luck·y (uhn-**luhk**-ee)
▷ *adjective* **unluckier, unluckiest**

unmistakable *adjective* Very obvious and impossible to confuse with anything else: *The resemblance between the twins was unmistakable.* **un·mis·tak·a·ble** (*uhn*-mi-**stay**-kuh-buhl) ▷ *adverb* **unmistakably**

unnatural *adjective*
1. Not usual or not normal; not happening in nature: *It is unnatural for a fish to live on land.*
2. False or insincere: *Her voice sounded stiff and unnatural.*
un·nat·u·ral (uhn-**nach**-ur-uhl)
▷ *adverb* **unnaturally**

unnecessary *adjective* Not necessary or required, as in *unnecessary stops.* **un·nec·es·sar·y** (uhn-**nes**-uh-ser-ee) ▷ *adverb* **unnecessarily**

unobserved *adjective* Not seen or not noticed.
un·ob·served (*uhn*-uhb-**zurvd**)

unoccupied *adjective*
1. Having no occupants; vacant, as in *an unoccupied apartment.*
2. Not held by enemy forces, as in *unoccupied territory.*
3. Not busy or in use: *The workers are unoccupied all day because the factory is on strike.*
un·oc·cu·pied (uhn-**ahk**-yuh-*pide*)

unofficial *adjective*
1. Not issued or approved by someone in authority, as in *an unofficial document.*

2. Informal, as in *unofficial rules.*
un·of·fi·cial (*uhn*-uh-**fish**-uhl)
▷ *adverb* **unofficially**

unpack *verb* To take objects out of a box, suitcase, trunk, vehicle, or container of any kind. **un·pack** (uhn-**pak**) ▷ *verb* **unpacking, unpacked**

unpleasant *adjective* Not pleasing; offensive; disagreeable, as in *an unpleasant odor.* **un·pleas·ant** (uhn-**plez**-uhnt) ▷ *adverb* **unpleasantly**

unplug *verb*
1. To disconnect an electrical device by removing its plug from an electric socket.
2. To remove a stopper or something that blocks an opening: *She unplugged the drain.*
un·plug (uhn-**pluhg**)
▷ *verb* **unplugging, unplugged**

unpopular *adjective* Not liked or approved of by many people. **un·pop·u·lar** (uhn-**pahp**-yuh-lur)

unprecedented *adjective* Not known or done before; without a previous example. **un·prec·e·dent·ed** (un-**pres**-i-*den*-tid)

unpredictable *adjective*
1. Not able to be predicted, as in *unpredictable weather.*
2. Behaving in a way that cannot be predicted.
un·pre·dict·a·ble (*uhn*-pri-**dik**-tuh-buhl)
▷ *adverb* **unpredictably**

unprepared *adjective*
1. Not ready, as in *unprepared for the test.*
2. Unwilling: *Carla was unprepared to agree to everything that Jill suggested.*
un·pre·pared (*uhn*-pri-**paird**)

unprovoked *adjective* Not caused by anyone or anything: *Charlotte's tantrum was unprovoked.*
un·pro·voked (*uhn*-pruh-**vohkt**)

unravel *verb*
1. To unwind a tangled mass of string, yarn, or strands of any kind: *Unravel the headphone cords.*
2. To undo or pull apart a woven or knitted fabric.
3. To search for and discover the truth about a complex situation, as in *to unravel a mystery.*
un·rav·el (uhn-**rav**-uhl)
▷ *verb* **unraveling, unraveled**

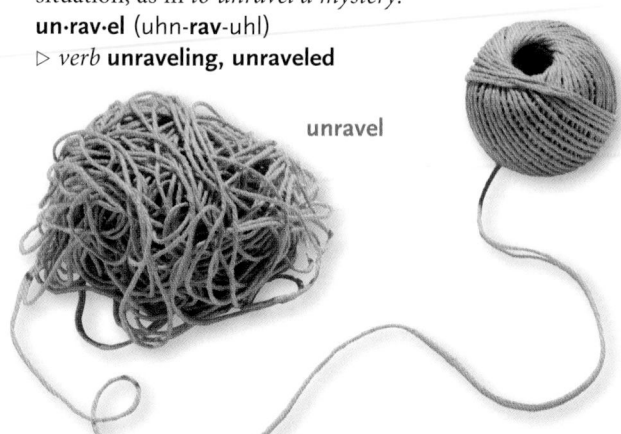
unravel

unreasonable *adjective*
1. Not showing reason or good sense: *Don't be so unreasonable; you can't always get your way.*
2. Unfair or unacceptable, as in *an unreasonable request.*
3. Too great; excessive, as in *an unreasonable price.* **un·rea·son·a·ble** (uhn-**ree**-zuh-nuh-buhl)
▷ *adverb* **unreasonably**

unrecognizable *adjective* Unable to be recognized. **un·rec·og·niz·a·ble** (uhn-**rek**-uhg-*nye*-zuh-buhl)

unreliable *adjective* Not dependable; not to be trusted: *My sister is unreliable and always late.* **un·re·li·a·ble** (uhn-ri-**lye**-uh-buhl)

unrest *noun* Disturbance and trouble; a lack of calm; dissatisfaction, as in *political unrest.* **un·rest** (uhn-**rest**)

unrestricted *adjective* Without limitations or restrictions, as in *an unrestricted airline ticket.* **un·re·strict·ed** (*uhn*-ri-**strik**-tid)

unripe *adjective* Not mature enough to be harvested or eaten, as in *unripe fruit.* **un·ripe** (uhn-**ripe**)

unrivaled *adjective* Better than anyone or anything of the same type; having no equal: *Leah's skill at chess is unrivaled.* **un·ri·valed** (uhn-**rye**-vuhld)

unripe tomatoes

unroll *verb* To open or spread out something that is rolled up: *We unrolled the new carpets onto the floor.* **un·roll** (uhn-**role**) ▷ *verb* **unrolling, unrolled**

unruffled *adjective* Completely calm, especially after a disturbing incident. **un·ruf·fled** (un-**ruhf**-uhld)

unruly *adjective* Hard to control or discipline, as in *unruly hair* or *an unruly mob.* **un·rul·y** (uhn-**roo**-lee) ▷ *adjective* **unrulier, unruliest**

unsatisfactory *adjective* Not good enough to meet a certain need or standard, as in *an unsatisfactory report.* **un·sat·is·fac·to·ry** (*uhn*-sat-is-**fak**-tur-ee) ▷ *adverb* **unsatisfactorily**

unscathed *adjective* Not hurt or damaged: *The tree fell over in the storm, but the house was unscathed.* **un·scathed** (uhn-**skayTHd**)

unscrupulous *adjective* Not guided by principles; not concerned about whether your actions are right or wrong. **un·scru·pu·lous** (uhn-**skroo**-pyuh-luhs) ▷ *adverb* **unscrupulously**

unseen *adjective* Not seen or noticed. **un·seen** (uhn-**seen**)

unsettle *verb* To upset or to disturb: *The horror movie unsettled me.* **un·set·tle** (uhn-**set**-uhl) ▷ *verb* **unsettling, unsettled** ▷ *adjective* **unsettling**

unsettled *adjective*
1. Not calm or not orderly; disturbed, as in *unsettled political conditions.*
2. Not decided or not determined, as in *an unsettled question.*
3. Not inhabited.
4. Likely to change; uncertain, as in *unsettled weather.*
5. Not paid, as in *an unsettled bill.* **un·set·tled** (uhn-**set**-uhld)

unsightly *adjective* Unattractive, not pleasant to look at, as in *an unsightly scar* or *unsightly litter.* **un·sight·ly** (uhn-**site**-lee)

unskilled *adjective* Having no particular skill, training, or experience. **un·skilled** (uhn-**skild**)

unsound *adjective*
1. Not strong or not solid; weak; unsafe, as in *an old, unsound bridge.*
2. Not based on good judgment or clear thinking; not sensible, as in *unsound advice.*
3. Not healthy, as in *an unsound mind.* **un·sound** (uhn-**sound**)

unstable *adjective*
1. Not firm; unsteady or shaky, as in *an unstable ladder.*
2. Likely to change, as in *an unstable government.*
3. Showing rapid changes of behavior and mood, as in *an unstable patient.* **un·sta·ble** (uhn-**stay**-buhl)

unsteady *adjective* Shaky or wobbly; not firm, as in *an unsteady voice.* **un·stead·y** (uhn-**sted**-ee) ▷ *adverb* **unsteadily**

unsuccessful *adjective* Unable to do something well or to get what you want. **un·suc·cess·ful** (*uhn*-suhk-**ses**-fuhl) ▷ *adverb* **unsuccessfully**

unsuitable *adjective* Not right for a particular purpose or occasion. **un·suit·a·ble** (uhn-**soo**-tuh-buhl) ▷ *noun* **unsuitability** ▷ *adverb* **unsuitably**

unsure *adjective*
1. Not definite or not certain: *I'm unsure if he will come.*
2. Lacking confidence and certainty: *Betty felt unsure of herself as she began to recite her poem.* **un·sure** (uhn-**shoor**)

untangle *verb*
1. To remove knots or tangles, as in *to untangle a necklace.*
2. To clear up or explain, as in *to untangle a mystery.* **un·tan·gle** (uhn-**tang**-guhl) ▷ *verb* **untangling, untangled**

unthinkable *adjective* So unlikely or undesirable that it cannot be considered or imagined. **un·think·a·ble** (uhn-**thing**-kuh-buhl)

untidy *adjective* Not neat; messy: *I'm sorry for my untidy room.* **un·ti·dy** (uhn-**tye**-dee) ▷ *noun* **untidiness** ▷ *adverb* **untidily**

untie *verb*
1. To loosen or undo something that has been tied: *I untied my shoelaces.*
2. To free from something that ties, fastens, or restrains: *The guard untied the prisoner's hands.* **un·tie** (uhn-**tye**)
▷ *verb* **untying, untied**

until
1. *preposition* Up to the time of: *Wait until tomorrow before you decide.*
2. *preposition* Before: *I won't be ready until Monday.*
3. *conjunction* Up to the time that: *I was enjoying the book until I got to the scary part.*
4. *conjunction* Before: *You can't watch television until you finish your homework.*
5. *conjunction* To the point, degree, or place that: *They ate until they were full.* **un·til** (uhn-**til**)

unto *preposition* An old word for **to**. **un·to** (**uhn**-too)

untold *adjective*
1. Too great to be counted or measured: *The hurricane caused untold suffering.*
2. Not told or not revealed: *The true story will remain untold.* **un·told** (uhn-**tohld**)

untouched *adjective*
1. Not handled or touched by anyone.
2. Ignored or undisturbed: *The thieves took the money but left the jewelry untouched.*
3. Not moved or not affected: *I cried at the end of the sad movie, but my friend was untouched.* **un·touched** (uhn-**tuhcht**)

untrue *adjective*
1. False or incorrect, as in *an untrue story.*
2. Not faithful or not loyal. **un·true** (uhn-**troo**)

unused *adjective*
1. (uhn-**yoozd**) Never used: *The unused glass was covered in dust.*
2. (uhn-**yoost**) Not accustomed: *I am unused to this cold weather.* **un·used**

unusual *adjective* Not usual, common, or ordinary; rare: *She has an unusual name.* **un·u·su·al** (uhn-**yoo**-zhoo-uhl) ▷ *adverb* **unusually**

unveil *verb* To uncover or show something that has been hidden or secret: *Tomorrow, the company will unveil the newest models in its line of hybrid cars.* **un·veil** (uhn-**vayl**) ▷ *verb* **unveiling, unveiled**

unwelcome *adjective* Not needed, wanted, or willingly received. **un·wel·come** (uhn-**wel**-kuhm)

unwell *adjective* Sick or ill. **un·well** (uhn-**wel**)

unwieldy *adjective* Difficult to hold or manage because of shape, size, weight, or complexity, as in *an unwieldy package.* **un·wield·y** (uhn-**weel**-dee)

unwilling *adjective* Not eager to do something. **un·will·ing** (uhn-**wil**-ing) ▷ *adverb* **unwillingly**

unwind *verb*
1. To undo something that has been rolled or wound up: *Unwind the yarn.*
2. To relax after being tense or worried. **un·wind** (uhn-**winde**)
▷ *verb* **unwinding, unwound** (uhn-**wound**)

unworthy *adjective*
1. Not deserving: *We felt unworthy of such praise.*
2. Not fitting, proper, or appropriate: *His rude behavior was unworthy of a gentleman.* **un·wor·thy** (uhn-**wur**-THee)
▷ *adverb* **unworthily**

unwrap *verb* To remove the packaging or outer layer from something. **un·wrap** (uhn-**rap**) ▷ *verb* **unwrapping, unwrapped**

unzip *verb*
1. To unfasten a zipper or garment.
2. To expand a computer file or set of files that has been compressed in zipped form. ▷ *verb* **unzipping, unzipped** **un·zip** (*uhn*-**zip**)

up
1. *adverb* From a lower to a higher place.
2. *adverb* In, at, or to a higher place or position: *I looked up at the roof.*
3. *adverb* To a higher point or degree: *Food prices have gone up.*
4. *adverb* On one's feet; in an upright position: *I got up from the chair.*
5. *adverb* Entirely: *I used up all the rice.*
6. *adverb* To a higher volume: *Please turn up the radio.*
7. *adjective* Moving upward, as in *an up escalator.*
8. *adverb* Out of bed: *Are you up yet?*
9. *adjective* Above the horizon: *The sun is up.*
10. *preposition* From a lower to a higher position or place in or on: *We hiked up the mountain.*
11. *preposition* At or to a farther point in or on: *They walked up the street.*
12. *preposition* Toward the source or inner part of: *We sailed up the river.*
13. **up against** Faced with: *We were up against a tough problem.*
14. **up for** Ready or eager to do something: *Are you guys up for a bike ride?*
15. **up to** Capable of performing or dealing with

something: *Are you up to helping me rake?*

16. up to Depending on a particular person, or being his or her responsibility: *Mom left it up to us where we should have dinner tonight.*

17. up to Doing or occupied with something: *Do you know what Bill is up to today?*

up (uhp)

upbeat *adjective* (*informal*) Cheerful and optimistic, as in *upbeat music.* **up·beat** (**uhp**-*beet*)

upbringing *noun* The care and training a person receives while growing up: *Brenda had a strict upbringing.* **up·bring·ing** (**uhp**-*bring*-ing)

update *verb*

1. To provide someone with the latest information, as in *to update on the train schedule.* ▷ *noun* **update** (**uhp**-*date*)

2. To make something more modern or up-to-date: *We're going to update the entire computer system.* **up·date** (**uhp**-*date* or *uhp*-**date**)

▷ *verb* **updating, updated**

up front

1. *adverb* Before anything else; at the very beginning: *Using solar energy costs more up front, but in the long run you'll save.*

2. up-front *adjective* Being or coming in first or at the front.

3. up-front *adjective* Open and willing to share information, as in *an up-front manner.*

upgrade

1. (*uhp*-**grade**) *verb* To promote someone to a better or more important job or status, as in *upgraded to manager.*

2. (*uhp*-**grade**) *verb* To improve something: *The restaurant upgraded its service.*

3. (*uhp*-**grade**) *verb* To replace a computer part or a piece of software with a better, more powerful, or more recently released version. ▷ *noun* **upgrade**

4. (**uhp**-*grade*) *noun* The upward slope of a hill or road.

up·grade

▷ *verb* **upgrading, upgraded**

upheaval *noun*

1. A sudden and violent upset or disturbance, as in *the emotional upheaval caused by war.*

2. A forceful lifting up of part of the earth's crust, especially during an earthquake. **up·heav·al** (*uhp*-**hee**-vuhl)

uphill

1. *adjective* Sloping upward: *The uphill path was difficult to walk.* ▷ *adverb* **uphill** (**uhp**-*hil*)

2. uphill battle Something that is very tiring or difficult to accomplish. **up·hill** (**uhp**-*hil*)

uphold *verb*

1. To support something: *The Girl Scouts uphold the values of honesty and citizenship.*

2. To confirm a claim or a decision: *The appeals court upheld the verdict of the lower court.* **up·hold** (*uhp*-**hohld**)

▷ *verb* **upholding, upheld**

upholster *verb* To put new upholstery on a piece of furniture. **up·hol·ster** (uhp-**hohl**-stur) ▷ *verb* **upholstering, upholstered** ▷ *noun* **upholsterer** ▷ *adjective* **upholstered**

upholstery *noun* The stuffing, springs, cushions, and covering that are put on furniture: *The couch was covered in blue plaid upholstery.* **up·hol·ster·y** (uhp-**hohl**-stur-ee) ▷ *noun, plural* **upholsteries**

upholstery

upkeep *noun* The work or cost of keeping something in good condition, as in *the upkeep of the museum.* **up·keep** (**uhp**-*keep*)

upload *verb* To send information to another computer over a network. **up·load** (**uhp**-*lohd*)

▷ *verb* **uploading, uploaded**

upon *preposition* On. **up·on** (uh-**pahn**)

upper *adjective* Higher in position or rank, as in *the upper house of a legislature.* **up·per** (**uhp**-ur)

uppercase *adjective* **Uppercase** letters are capital letters. **up·per·case** (**uhp**-ur-**kase**) ▷ *noun* **uppercase** ▷ *verb* **uppercase**

upper hand *noun* A position of advantage or control: *Her years of experience gave her the upper hand in the tennis match.*

uppermost

1. *adjective* Highest in place, rank, or importance: *Our apartment is on the uppermost floor.*

2. *adverb* In the highest or most important place or rank, as in *uppermost in my mind.* **up·per·most** (**uhp**-ur-*mohst*)

a
b
c
d
e
f
g
h
i
j
k
l
m
n
o
p
q
r
s
t
u
v
w
x
y
z

upright
   1. *adjective* Standing straight up; vertical: *Fence posts are upright.* ▷ *noun* **upright** ▷ *adverb* **upright**
   2. *adjective* Honorable and moral: *He is an upright citizen.*
   up·right (uhp-*rite*)

uprising *noun* A revolt or a rebellion. **up·ris·ing** (uhp-*rye*-zing)

uproar *noun* A confused, noisy disturbance: *The judge's decision caused an uproar.* **up·roar** (uhp-*ror*)

uproarious *adjective*
   1. Noisy or confused; full of uproar: *Karen's neighbors complained about her uproarious party.*
   2. Extremely funny, as in *an uproarious joke.*
   up·roar·i·ous (uhp-*ror*-ee-uhs)

uproot *verb*
   1. To tear or pull out by the roots.
   2. To force someone to leave: *The fire uprooted many families from their homes.*
   up·root (uhp-**root**)
   ▷ *verb* **uprooting, uprooted**

upset *verb*
   1. To make someone nervous or worried.
   2. To tip, turn, or knock something over: *Matt upset his can of soda.*
   3. To make someone feel ill.
   4. To interfere with: *The storm upset our plans.*
   5. To defeat unexpectedly: *Our team upset the state champions.*
   up·set (uhp-**set**)
   ▷ *verb* **upsetting, upset** ▷ *noun* **upset** (uhp-*set*)
   ▷ *adjective* **upset** (uhp-*set*)

upside down *adverb*
   1. With the top at the bottom: *Turn the hourglass upside down.* ▷ *adjective* **upside-down**
   2. In a confused or messy condition: *The children turned the room upside down looking for the doll.*
   up·side down (uhp-**side**)

upstairs
   1. *adverb* Up the stairs: *I ran upstairs to get a book.*
   2. *adverb* To or on a higher floor: *My bedroom is upstairs.*
   3. *adjective* On an upper floor: *You'll have more privacy if you use the upstairs phone.*
   4. *noun* The upper floor or floors of a building.
   up·stairs (uhp-**stairz**)

upstream *adverb* Toward the source of a stream or river; against the current, as in *to row upstream.*
   up·stream (uhp-**steem**) ▷ *adjective* **upstream**

uproot

uptight *adjective (slang)* Tense, nervous, or anxious.
   up·tight (uhp-**tite**)

up-to-date *adjective* Containing the most recent information or in the latest style: *Read my website to find all the up-to-date information.*

upward or **upwards**
   1. *adverb* Toward a higher place or position: *The wind took the balloon steadily upward.*
   2. *adjective* Moving or rising toward a higher place or position, as in *an upward slope.*
   up·ward (uhp-wurd) or **up·wards** (uhp-wurdz)

uranium *noun* A silver-white radioactive metal that is the main source of nuclear energy. Uranium is a chemical element. **ur·a·ni·um** (yu-**ray**-nee-uhm)

Uranus *noun* The seventh planet in distance from the sun. Uranus is the third-largest planet in our solar system. It has 27 known moons as well as nine rings circling its equator. **Ur·a·nus** (**yur**-uh-nuhs or yu-**ray**-nuhs)

urban *adjective* Having to do with or living in a city, as in *urban problems.* **ur·ban** (**ur**-buhn)

urge
   1. *verb* To try very hard to persuade someone to do something: *Cameron's friends urged him to try out for the basketball team.* ▷ *verb* **urging, urged**
   2. *noun* A strong desire to do something.
   urge (urj)

urgent *adjective* Requiring immediate action or attention. **ur·gent** (**ur**-juhnt)
   ▷ *noun* **urgency** (**ur**-juhn-see) ▷ *adverb* **urgently**

urgent care *noun* Medical treatment that needs to be done immediately.

urinary system *noun* The organs and body parts that produce, store, and release urine. In humans and other mammals, it includes the kidneys, bladder, and tubes that carry urine. **u·rin·ar·y system** (**yoor**-uh-*ner*-ee)

urinate *verb* To pass urine from the body. **u·ri·nate** (**yoor**-uh-*nate*) ▷ *verb* **urinating, urinated** ▷ *noun* **urination**

urine *noun* The yellowish liquid that people and animals pass out of their bodies. Urine consists of water and wastes taken out of the blood by the kidneys. It is stored in the bladder. **u·rine** (**yoor**-uhn)

URL *noun* The address of a file on the internet or the World Wide Web. URL is short for *uniform resource locator* or *universal resource locator*: *The URL for the White House's website is http://www.whitehouse.gov.*

urn *noun*
  1. A vase with a base or pedestal. An urn is used as an ornament or a container.
  2. A large metal container with a faucet used for making and serving coffee or tea.
  urn (urn)
  Urn sounds like **earn**.

us *pronoun* The form of the pronoun *we* that is used after a verb or preposition: *No one saw us.* **us** (uhs)

US *or* **U.S.** An abbreviation for *United States*.

usage *noun*
  1. The way that something is used: *This system keeps track of electricity usage in the building.*
  2. The way that words and phrases are used in a language.
  us·age (**yoo**-sij *or* **yoo**-zij)

USB *noun* A common type of computer connection used for many different devices. Computers usually have a number of USB ports where these devices can be plugged in. USB is short for *universal serial bus*.

use
  1. (yooz) *verb* To do a job with something: *I used a penknife to cut through the wrapping.*
  2. (yooz) *verb* To spend or consume by using: *Use your time wisely. He used up the mustard.*
  3. (yoos) *noun* The action of using something: *All the phones were in use.*
  4. (yoos) *noun* The right or ability to use something: *My sister has the use of the car today.*
  5. (yoos) *noun* A purpose for which something can be used: *This tool has several uses.*
  6. (yoos) *noun* Advantage or benefit: *There's no use in worrying about it.*
  7. (yooz) *verb* To take advantage of a person in order to get something that you want.
  use
  ▷ *verb* **using, used** ▷ *noun* **user**

used
  1. (yoozd) *adjective* Already made use of; secondhand, as in *used clothing.*
  2. (yoost) *adjective* Accustomed to something: *I'm used to getting up very early.*
  3. (yoost) *verb* Did something in the past: *I used to ice-skate until I broke my ankle.*
  used

useful *adjective* Helpful, or able to be used in a practical way: *You might find it useful to take notes*

USB cord

during class. **use·ful** (**yoos**-fuhl) ▷ *noun* **usefulness**

useless *adjective*
  1. Not helpful, or having no value.
  2. Hopeless; not capable of producing any result: *It's useless to ring that broken doorbell.*
  3. (informal) Not very good or not very skilled: *I'm useless in the kitchen.*
  use·less (**yoos**-lis)

user-friendly *adjective* Easy for people without experience to learn and operate.

username *noun* A name that you use to identify yourself to a computer, network, or website.
  us·er·name (**yoo**-zur-naym)

usher *noun* A person who shows people to their seats in a church, theater, or stadium. **ush·er** (**uhsh**-ur) ▷ *verb* **usher**

usual *adjective* Normal, common, or expected: *My usual breakfast is cereal with milk.* **u·su·al** (**yoo**-zhoo-uhl) ▷ *adverb* **usually**

utensil *noun* A tool or container, often used in the kitchen, that has a special purpose. **u·ten·sil** (yoo-**ten**-suhl)

uterus *noun* The hollow organ in women and other female mammals that holds and nourishes a fetus; the womb. **u·ter·us** (**yoo**-tur-uhs) ▷ *noun, plural* **uteri** (**yoo**-tuh-rye) *or* **uteruses**

utility *noun*
  1. A basic service supplied to a community, such as telephone, water, gas, or electricity.
  2. A company that supplies a basic utility.
  3. Usefulness: *Tools were invented for their utility.*
  4. utility program A computer program that performs a specific task that allows the computer to run more efficiently.
  u·til·i·ty (yoo-**til**-i-tee)
  ▷ *noun, plural* **utilities**

utmost *noun* The greatest or most extreme extent or amount, as in *doing his utmost to keep order on the school bus.* **ut·most** (**uht**-mohst) ▷ *adjective* **utmost**

utter
  1. *verb* To speak or to make a sound with your voice: *Ian uttered a few words under his breath.* ▷ *verb* **uttering, uttered** ▷ *noun* **utterance**
  2. *adjective* Complete or total: *Sharon's arrival was an utter surprise.* ▷ *adverb* **utterly** (**uht**-ur-lee)
  ut·ter (**uht**-ur)

U-turn *noun*
  1. A turn made by a vehicle in the shape of a U, in order to go in the opposite direction.
  2. A complete reversal of plan, policy, or attitude, as in *to make a U-turn in my thinking.*
  U-turn (**yoo**-turn)

V v

About V This letter is not used very frequently in English. For example, there are no words that begin with a **V** in the 100 most commonly used words in the language. The letter *v* didn't even have an identity of its own in English until a few centuries ago. Before then, it was used interchangeably with *u*. When you see a word that begins with a *v*, its history most likely can be traced to Latin.

vacant *adjective*
1. Unoccupied or empty, as in *a vacant building* or *a vacant lot.*
2. Not filled: *The job has been vacant since he retired.*
3. Unintelligent or uninterested, as in *a vacant look.*
va·cant (**vay**-kuhnt)
▷ *noun* **vacancy** (**vay**-kuhn-see)

vacate *verb* To leave, or to leave something empty: *Pat vacated his seat for the boy on crutches.* **va·cate** (**vay**-kate) ▷ *verb* **vacating, vacated**

vacation *noun* A time of rest from school, work, and other regular duties; especially a pleasure trip away from home. **va·ca·tion** (vay-**kay**-shuhn) ▷ *verb* **vacation**

vaccinate *verb* To protect someone against a disease by giving the person an injection or a dose of a vaccine. **vac·ci·nate** (**vak**-suh-*nate*) ▷ *verb* **vaccinating, vaccinated** ▷ *noun* **vaccination**

vaccine *noun* A substance containing dead, weakened, or living organisms that can be injected or taken orally. A vaccine causes a person to produce antibodies that protect him or her from the disease produced by the organisms. **vac·cine** (vak-**seen**)

vacuum *noun*
1. A sealed space or container from which all air or gas has been removed.
2. A vacuum cleaner.
vac·u·um (**vak**-yoom)
▷ *verb* **vacuum**

vacuum cleaner *noun* A machine that picks up dirt from carpets, furniture, and other surfaces. To work, a vacuum cleaner reduces the air pressure inside itself. Then dirt is carried into it by outside air rushing to fill the partial vacuum.

vagina *noun* The passage in women and other female mammals that leads from the uterus, through which babies are born. **va·gi·na** (vuh-**jye**-nuh)

vague *adjective* Indefinite or unclear: *Sherry has a vague idea of where Paul's office is.* **vague** (vayg) ▷ *adjective* **vaguer, vaguest**

valentine

vain *adjective*
1. Having too high an opinion of your appearance, your abilities, or your worth.
2. Unsuccessful or useless: *Ginny made a vain attempt to stop the quarrel.*
vain (vayn)
Vain sounds like **vane** and **vein**. ▷ *adjective* **vainer, vainest**

valedictorian *noun* The student who has the honor of giving the valedictory speech at a graduation and who usually has the highest grades in the graduating class: *The valedictorian's inspiring speech had all her classmates cheering.* **val·e·dic·to·ri·an** (*val*-uh-dik-**tor**-ee-uhn)

valentine *noun*
1. A gift or greeting card sent to a friend, relative, or loved one on Valentine's Day.
2. A sweetheart or loved one chosen on Valentine's Day: *Be my valentine.*
val·en·tine (**val**-uhn-*tine*)

Valentine's Day *noun* February 14, a day named in honor of Saint Valentine, a Christian martyr of the third century A.D. It is celebrated by sending valentines.

valiant *adjective* Showing courage or determination, as in *valiant soldiers* or *a valiant effort.* **val·iant** (**val**-yuhnt) ▷ *adverb* **valiantly**

valid *adjective*
1. Acceptable in support of a claim: *Illness is a valid reason for missing school.*
2. Legal or officially acceptable: *Your bus ticket is valid until midnight.*
val·id (**val**-id)
▷ *noun* **validity** (vuh-**lid**-i-tee)

validate *verb*
1. To affirm or support the truth or value of something: *Winning the art contest validated her talent.*
2. To make valid or legal: *You can validate your ticket by getting it stamped at the counter.*
val·i·date (**val**-i-*dayt*)

valley *noun*

1. A low area of land between two hills or mountains, often containing a river or stream.

2. An area of land drained by a river system.

val·ley (**val**-ee)

valor *noun* Great bravery or courage, especially in battle. **val·or** (**val**-ur)

valuable

1. *adjective* Worth a lot of money, or very important or useful in some other way, as in *a valuable necklace* or *valuable papers.*

2. valuables *noun, plural* Possessions that are very important or worth a lot of money: *My mother put her jewelry and other valuables in the hotel safe.*

val·u·a·ble (**val**-yoo-uh-buhl *or* **val**-yuh-buhl)

value

1. *noun* The amount of money that something is worth: *These paintings are of great value.*

2. *verb* To think that something is precious or important: *I value the time I spend reading.*

3. *verb* To estimate how much something is worth: *The art dealer valued the sculpture at $500.*

4. *noun* In mathematics, an assigned or calculated number or quantity: *Find the value of 33 ÷ 18.*

5. values *noun, plural* A person's principles of behavior and beliefs about what is most important in life.

val·ue (**val**-yoo)

▷ *verb* **valuing, valued**

valve *noun* A movable part that controls the flow of a liquid or gas through a pipe or other channel.

valve (valv)

vampire *noun* A dead person who rises from the grave at night to feed on the blood of humans, according to folktales and horror stories. **vam·pire** (**vam**-pire)

vampire bat *noun* Any of the bats of Central America and South America that feed on the blood of birds and mammals.

van *noun*

1. A large, enclosed truck used for moving animals or household goods from place to place: *We hired a moving van to take our furniture to our new house.*

2. A smaller motor vehicle that is shaped like a box and used for carrying passengers or cargo. A van has rear or side doors and side panels that often have windows.

van (van)

vandal *noun* A person who deliberately damages or destroys other people's property. **van·dal** (**van**-duhl)

vampire bat

▷ *noun* **vandalism** ▷ *verb* **vandalize**

vane *noun*

1. *See* **weather vane**.

2. The flat part on the shaft of a bird's feather.

vane (vayn)

Vane sounds like **vain** and **vein**.

vanilla *noun* A flavoring made from the seed pods of a tropical orchid. It is used in ice cream, candies, cookies, and other foods. **va·nil·la** (vuh-**nil**-uh)

vanish *verb*

1. To disappear suddenly and completely.

2. To cease to exist: *Dinosaurs vanished millions of years ago.*

van·ish (**van**-ish)

▷ *verb* **vanishes, vanishing, vanished**

vanity *noun* Excessive pride in your own appearance or achievements: *His long hair was his one vanity.* **van·i·ty** (**van**-i-tee)

▷ *noun, plural* **vanities**

vanity plate *noun* A motor vehicle license plate with letters or numbers selected by the owner.

vanilla

vanquish *verb*

1. To defeat or conquer an enemy in battle.

2. To defeat an opponent in a contest or competition: *This cake will vanquish all the other cakes at the county fair.*

3. To overcome an emotion or a fear: *She vanquished her demons in therapy.*

van·quish (**vang**-kwish)

▷ *verb* **vanquishes, vanquishing, vanquished**

vapor *noun*
1. Fine particles of mist, steam, or smoke that can be seen hanging in the air.
2. A gas formed from something that is usually a liquid or solid at normal temperatures: *Clouds are made of condensed water vapor.*
va·por (**vay**-pur)

variable
1. *adjective* Likely to change, as in *variable opinions.*
2. *noun* In mathematics, a symbol, such as *x, y,* or *z,* that stands for a number.
var·i·a·ble (**vair**-ee-uh-buhl)

variation *noun*
1. A change from the usual: *My hospital stay was boring because there was no variation in the routine.*
2. Something that is slightly different from another thing of the same type: *This story is a variation of a familiar fairy tale.*
var·i·a·tion (*vair*-ee-**ay**-shuhn)

variety *noun*
1. Difference, or change: *My little brother only eats burgers; there is no variety in his diet.*
2. A selection of different things in a particular category, as in *a variety of fruit.*
3. A different type of the same thing, as in *a healthier variety of rice.*
va·ri·e·ty (vuh-**rye**-i-tee)
▷ *noun, plural* **varieties**

various *adjective*
1. Of different kinds, as in *various colors.*
2. An indefinite number; several: *I have various ways of getting my dad to let me stay out late.*
var·i·ous (**vair**-ee-uhs)

varmint *noun* (*informal*)
1. An undesirable animal, such as one that kills a rancher's livestock.
2. A person who is undesirable, obnoxious, or troublesome.
var·mint (**vahr**-muhnt)

Word History

Varmint, a word often used in stories and movies about the American West, is an informal version of the word *vermin* and developed from the Latin word *vermis,* meaning "worm."

varnish *noun* A clear coating that you put on wood or other materials to protect it and make it shiny. **var·nish** (**vahr**-nish) ▷ *noun, plural* **varnishes** ▷ *verb* **varnish**

varsity *noun*
1. The team consisting of the best players at a school, college, or club in a particular sport: *She made varsity in soccer when she was only in tenth grade.*

bank vault

2. junior varsity The team consisting of the players who are usually younger and not as experienced as the players on a varsity team.
var·si·ty (**vahr**-suh-tee)

vary *verb*
1. To change or to be different in some way from other similar things: *Springtime weather can vary from cool and rainy to sunny and warm.*
2. To make changes to something: *I try to vary my diet by eating different foods each day.*
var·y (**vair**-ee)
▷ *verb* **varies, varying, varied** ▷ *noun* **variant**

vase *noun* A decorative container, usually made of glass, clay, or china, and often used for displaying flowers. **vase** (vays *or* vayz *or* vahz)

vassal *noun* In the Middle Ages, a person who was given land and protection by a lord in return for loyalty and military service. **vas·sal** (**vas**-uhl)

vast *adjective* Very large in extent or amount: *The vast prairie stretched to the horizon.* **vast** (vast) ▷ *adjective* **vaster, vastest** ▷ *noun* **vastness** ▷ *adverb* **vastly**

vat *noun* A large tank or container used for storing liquids, as in *a vat of water.* **vat** (vat)

vault
1. *verb* To jump over something using your hands or a pole for support: *Jonathan vaulted over the fence.*
▷ *verb* **vaulting, vaulted** ▷ *noun* **vault** ▷ *noun* **vaulter**
2. *noun* A room or compartment for keeping money and other valuables safe, as in *a bank vault.*
3. *noun* An underground burial chamber.
4. vaulted *adjective* In the form of an arch, as in *a vaulted roof.*
vault (vawlt)

V-chip *noun* A device that can be installed in a TV set to allow parents to block certain programs so that children cannot watch them.

VCR *noun* An electronic machine that is connected to a television set. It uses magnetic tape to record or play back movies and television programs. VCR is short for *videocassette recorder.*

veal *noun* The meat from a young calf. **veal** (veel)

veejay *noun* An announcer on a television program that features music videos. Veejay is short for *video jockey* and is abbreviated as *VJ.* **vee·jay** (**vee**-*jay*)

veer *verb* To change direction or turn suddenly: *The car veered to avoid hitting a dog.* **veer** (veer) ▷ *verb* **veering, veered**

vegan *noun* A person who does not eat or use any animal products. **veg·an** (**vee**-guhn) ▷ *noun* **veganism** ▷ *adjective* **vegan**

vegetable *noun* A plant or part of a plant used as food. Vegetables are usually eaten as side dishes or in salads. **veg·e·ta·ble** (**vej**-tuh-buhl *or* **vej**-i-tuh-buhl)

vegetarian *noun* A person who eats only plants and plant products and sometimes eggs or dairy products. **veg·e·tar·i·an** (*vej*-i-**tair**-ee-uhn) ▷ *noun* **vegetarianism** ▷ *adjective* **vegetarian**

vegetation *noun* Plant life or the plants that cover an area: *Jungles have thick vegetation.* **veg·e·ta·tion** (*vej*-i-**tay**-shuhn)

vehement *adjective* Showing strong feeling about something: *We are vehement about seat belts on buses.* **ve·he·ment** (**vee**-uh-muhnt) ▷ *noun* **vehemence** (**vee**-uh-muhns) ▷ *adverb* **vehemently**

vehicle *noun* A thing, such as a car or cart, that is used to transport people or goods. **ve·hi·cle** (**vee**-i-kuhl)

veil *noun*
1. A piece of material worn by women as a covering for the head or face.
2. Something that hides like a veil or curtain, as in *a veil of mist.*
veil (vayl)
▷ *verb* **veil**

vein *noun*
1. One of the vessels through which blood is sent back to the heart from other parts of the body.
2. One of the stiff, narrow tubes that form the framework of a leaf or an insect's wing.
3. A narrow band of mineral in rock: *A vein of silver ran through the mine.*
vein (vayn)
Vein sounds like **vain** and **vane**.

Velcro *noun* The trademark for a fastener that consists of two pieces of fabric. One piece is covered with tiny hooks that stick to the tiny loops on the second piece. **Vel·cro** (**vel**-kroh)

velocity *noun* Speed, especially in scientific work, as in *wind velocity.* **ve·loc·i·ty** (vuh-**lah**-si-tee) ▷ *noun, plural* **velocities**

velvet
1. *noun* A thick, soft fabric made from cotton, silk, or other materials, slightly fuzzy on one side.
2. *adjective* Made of velvet, or covered in velvet, as in *a velvet jacket.*
3. *adjective* Smooth and soft like velvet.
4. *noun* The soft skin that covers a deer's antlers while they are growing.
vel·vet (**vel**-vit)

vendetta *noun* A long-lasting feud between two families, gangs, or other groups. **ven·det·ta** (ven-**det**-uh)

vending machine *noun* A machine into which you insert money to buy food items, beverages, or other products. **vend·ing machine** (**ven**-ding)

vendor *noun* A person who sells something, as in *a fruit vendor.* **ven·dor** (**ven**-dur)

venetian blind *noun* An indoor window covering made from thin strips of metal or plastic that can be raised or tilted to vary the amount of light that comes in. **ve·ne·tian blind** (vuh-**nee**-shuhn)

vengeance *noun* Action that you take to pay someone back for harm that he or she has done to you or someone you care about: *In the comic book, the superhero took vengeance on the ring of smugglers.* **ven·geance** (**ven**-juhns)

wedding veil

venison *noun* The meat of a deer. **ven·i·son** (**ven**-i-suhn)

venom *noun*
1. Poison produced by some snakes and spiders. Venom is usually passed into a victim's body through a bite or sting.
2. Ill will; spite or malice: *The bully mocked them, speaking with venom in his voice.*
ven·om (**ven**-uhm)

vent
1. *noun* An opening through which smoke or fumes can escape: *Open the vent to get the smoke out.*
2. *noun* The opening in a volcano through which smoke and lava escape.
3. *verb* To express an emotion: *Tyrone vented his anger by slamming the door.* ▷ *verb* **venting, vented**
vent (vent)

ventilate *verb* To allow fresh air into a place and let stale air out. **ven·ti·late** (**ven**-tuh-*late*) ▷ *verb* **ventilating, ventilated** ▷ *noun* **ventilation** (*ven*-tuh-**lay**-shuhn) ▷ *noun* **ventilator** (**ven**-tuh-*lay*-tur)

ventricle *noun* Either one of the two lower chambers of the heart. The ventricles receive blood from the atria and pump it to the arteries. **ven·tri·cle** (**ven**-tri-kuhl)

ventriloquism *noun* The art of throwing your voice without opening your mouth, so that your words don't seem to be coming from you but from another source, such as a puppet. **ven·tril·o·quism** (ven-**tril**-uh-*kwiz*-uhm) ▷ *noun* **ventriloquist** (ven-**tril**-uh-*kwist*)

venture
1. *noun* A risky or daring journey or project, as in *a business venture.*
2. *verb* To go somewhere or do something daring, dangerous, or unpleasant, as in *to venture cautiously into the jungle.* ▷ *verb* **venturing, ventured** **ven·ture** (**ven**-chur)

venue *noun* The place where an event is held: *The lawyer asked for a change of venue for the trial.* **ven·ue** (**ven**-yoo)

Venus *noun* The second planet in distance from the sun. Venus is the sixth-largest planet in our solar system and is brighter in our sky than any other heavenly body except the sun and moon. **Ve·nus** (**vee**-nuhs)

veranda *or* **verandah** *noun* An open porch around the outside of a house, often with a roof. **ve·ran·da** *or* **ve·ran·dah** (vuh-**ran**-duh)

verb *noun* A word that expresses an action or a state of being. *Do, run, be, have,* and *think* are verbs. **verb** (vurb)

verbal *adjective*
1. Of or having to do with words, as in *a verbal aptitude test.*

veranda

2. Spoken, as in *a verbal agreement.* **ver·bal** (**vur**-buhl)

verdict *noun*
1. The decision of a jury on whether an accused person is guilty or not guilty.
2. An opinion or judgment.
ver·dict (**vur**-dikt)

verge
1. on the verge About to do something very soon: *Bert is on the verge of quitting his job.*
2. *verb* To be very near to something: *The man's odd behavior verged on insanity.* ▷ *verb* **verging, verged** **verge** (vurj)

verify *verb*
1. To prove that something is true: *Several witnesses verified Bonnie's account of the accident.*
2. To test or check the accuracy of something, as in *to verify scientific findings by doing more testing.* **ver·i·fy** (**ver**-uh-*fye*) ▷ *verb* **verifies, verifying, verified** ▷ *noun* **verification** (*ver*-uh-fi-**kay**-shuhn) ▷ *adjective* **verifiable**

vermin *noun*
1. Any of various small, common insects or animals that are harmful pests. Fleas, rats, and lice are vermin.
2. An offensive person, or a person who is regarded as bad or troublesome.
ver·min (**vur**-min) ▷ *noun, plural* **vermin**

Word History

Vermin were not always small. About 200 years ago, they could be badgers or wildcats, or "wild beasts" that preyed on sheep. The word *vermin* goes back to *vermis,* a Latin word meaning "worm." The first use in English was for any annoying creature that was difficult to control.

versatile *adjective* Able to function or to be used in many different ways, as in *a versatile singer* or *a versatile utensil.* **ver·sa·tile** (**vur**-suh-tuhl) ▷ *noun* **versatility** (*vur*-suh-**til**-i-tee)

verse *noun*
1. One section of a poem or song. A verse is made up of several lines.
2. Poetry: *She wrote her story in verse.*
verse (vurs)

version *noun*
1. One description or account given from a particular point of view: *If you believe Alexandra's version of the accident, her brother was not at fault.*
2. A different or changed form of something such as

Vertebrates

What do fish, reptiles, birds, amphibians, and people and other mammals have in common? They are all vertebrates, which means they have skeletons made of vertebrae, formed from either bone or cartilage. This backbone, or spinal column, protects their internal organs and nervous system. There are more than 53,000 vertebrate species.

fish

bird

snake

human being

frog

dog

a book or software, as in *a movie version of the novel.* **ver·sion** (**vur**-zhuhn)

versus *preposition* Against: *Today's game is the Baltimore Orioles versus the New York Yankees.* In general, versus is abbreviated *vs.* When referring to court cases, however, it is abbreviated *v.,* as in *Brown v. Board of Education.* **ver·sus** (**vur**-suhs)

vertebra *noun* One of the small bones that make up the backbone. **ver·te·bra** (**vur**-tuh-bruh) ▷ *noun, plural* **vertebrae** (**vur**-tuh-*bree* or **vur**-tuh-*bray*)

Word History

Vertebra comes from the Latin word *vertere,* meaning "to turn." Having separate vertebrae in the backbone rather than a single, solid bone allows the body to turn and bend easily.

vertebrate *noun* Any animal that has a backbone. Fish, amphibians, reptiles, birds, and mammals are all vertebrates. **ver·te·brate** (**vur**-tuh-brit or **vur**-tuh-*brate*) ▷ *adjective* **vertebrate**

vertex *noun*
1. The top or highest point of something, as in *the vertex of the mountain.*
2. The meeting point of two lines that form an angle.

ver·tex (**vur**-teks)
▷ *noun, plural* **vertices** (**vur**-tuh-*seez*)

vertical *adjective* Upright, or straight up and down: *Telephone poles and skyscrapers are in a vertical position.* **ver·ti·cal** (**vur**-ti-kuhl) ▷ *adverb* **vertically**

vertigo *noun* Dizziness and difficulty finding your balance, especially as the result of being in a high place. When you have vertigo, you often feel like you might fall: *She began experiencing vertigo while she was on top of the Empire State Building, so she stayed close to the wall in order to feel safe.* **ver·ti·go** (**vur**-ti-*goh*)

very
1. *adverb* To a great degree: *Shauna is very tall for her age.*
2. *adjective* Exact: *I've found the very coat I was looking for.*

ver·y (**ver**-ee)

vessel *noun*
1. A ship or a large boat, as in *a sailing vessel.*
2. A tube in the body that fluids pass through. Arteries and veins are blood vessels.
3. A hollow container for holding liquids, such as a bowl, vase, or jar.

ves·sel (**ves**-uhl)

vest
1. *noun* A short, sleeveless piece of clothing that is worn over a blouse or shirt: *Does the suit come with a vest?*
2. *verb* To give power or authority to some person or group: *The Constitution vests the president with the power to veto a bill.* ▷ *verb* **vesting, vested**
vest (vest)

vestige *noun*
1. A trace or sign of something that is hard to perceive or that no longer exists: *The explorer found the vestiges of an enormous dinosaur in the sedimentary rock.*
2. An organ or body part that remains a part of the body but that no longer works.
ves·tige (**ves**-tij)

vet *noun*
1. *(informal)* A veterinarian.
2. *(informal)* A veteran, as in *a Vietnam vet.*
vet (vet)

veteran *noun*
1. Someone with a lot of experience in a profession, a position, or an activity: *The candidate is a veteran of many political campaigns.*
2. A person who has served in the armed forces, especially during a war.
vet·er·an (**vet**-ur-uhn)
▷ *adjective* **veteran**

Veterans Day *noun*
November 11, a day honoring men and women who served in the armed services and fought in wars for the United States. Formerly known as Armistice Day, this national holiday was first observed to celebrate the armistice, or truce, that ended World War I on November 11, 1918.

veterinarian *noun*
A doctor who is trained to diagnose and treat sick or injured animals. **vet·er·i·nar·i·an** (*vet*-ur-uh-**nair**-ee-uhn)

veterinary *adjective*
Of or having to do with the treatment of animals, as in *veterinary studies.*
vet·er·i·nar·y (**vet**-ur-uh-*ner*-ee)

veto
1. *noun* The right or power of a president, a governor, or an official group to reject a bill that has been passed by a legislature and to keep it from becoming a law.
▷ *noun, plural* **vetoes**
2. *verb* To stop a bill from becoming a law.
3. *verb* To forbid, or to refuse to approve: *Mom vetoed my idea of watching a late movie on a school night.*
ve·to (**vee**-toh)
▷ *verb* **vetoes, vetoing, vetoed**

vex *verb*
To annoy or worry somebody: *That constant buzzing vexes me.* **vex** (veks) ▷ *verb* **vexes, vexing, vexed** ▷ *noun* **vexation** (vek-**say**-shuhn) ▷ *adjective* **vexatious** (vek-**say**-shuhs) ▷ *adjective* **vexed**

via *preposition*
By way of: *This train goes to Los Angeles*

veterinarian

via Denver. **vi·a** (**vye**-uh or **vee**-uh)

viable *adjective*
Capable of succeeding, as in *a viable project.* **vi·a·ble** (**vye**-uh-buhl) ▷ *noun* **viability** (*vye*-uh-**bil**-i-tee)

viaduct *noun*
A large bridge that carries a railroad track, road, or pipeline across a valley or over a city street. **vi·a·duct** (**vye**-uh-*duhkt*)

vibrant *adjective*
1. Full of energy or enthusiasm, as in *a vibrant city.*
2. Bright or lively, as in *vibrant colors.*
vi·brant (**vye**-bruhnt)
▷ *noun* **vibrancy** (**vye**-bruhn-see) ▷ *adverb* **vibrantly**

vibraphone *noun*
An electronic xylophone with two rows of metal keys. **vi·bra·phone** (**vye**-bruh-*fone*)

vibrate *verb*
To move back and forth rapidly: *The house vibrated during the earthquake.* **vi·brate** (**vye**-brate) ▷ *verb* **vibrating, vibrated** ▷ *noun* **vibration** (vye-**bray**-shuhn)

vice *noun*
Immoral or harmful behavior: *Lying and cheating are vices.* **vice** (vise) **Vice** sounds like **vise**.

vice president *noun*
An officer who ranks second to a president and acts for the president when necessary.

vice versa *adverb*
A Latin phrase meaning "the other way around": *You help me and vice versa.* **vice ver·sa** (**vye**-suh **vur**-suh or **vise vur**-suh)

vicinity *noun*
The area surrounding a particular place: *After the robbery, the police sealed off all roads in the vicinity.* **vi·cin·i·ty** (vi-**sin**-i-tee) ▷ *noun, plural* **vicinities**

vicious *adjective*
1. Cruel and mean, as in *vicious lies.*
2. Evil or wicked, as in *a vicious crime.*
3. Fierce or dangerous, as in *a vicious dog.*
vi·cious (**vish**-uhs)
▷ *noun* **viciousness** ▷ *adverb* **viciously**

victim *noun*
1. A person who is hurt, killed, or made to suffer, as in *an accident victim* or *a murder victim.*
2. A person who is cheated or tricked, as in *a swindler's victim.*
vic·tim (**vik**-tuhm)

victimize *verb* To single someone out for cruel or unfair treatment: *The gang victimized the new boy.* **vic·tim·ize** (**vik**-tuh-*mize*) ▷ *verb* **victimizing, victimized** ▷ *noun* **victimizer** ▷ *noun* **victimization** (*vik*-tuh-mi-**zay**-shuhn)

victor *noun* The winner in a battle, war, game, or contest. **vic·tor** (**vik**-tur)

victory *noun* A win in a battle, war, game, or contest. **vic·to·ry** (**vik**-tur-ee) ▷ *noun, plural* **victories** ▷ *adjective* **victorious** (vik-**tor**-ee-uhs) ▷ *adverb* **victoriously**

victuals *or* **vittles** *noun* (*old-fashioned*) Supplies of food; provisions. The word is used in an informal way. **vict·uals** *or* **vit·tles** (**vit**-uhlz)

video
1. *adjective* Of or having to do with the visual part of a television program or with a computer display.
2. *noun* The visual part of television.
3. *noun* A recording of a movie or television show that can be played on a VCR.
4. *noun* A videotaped performance of a song, as in *a rock video.*
vid·e·o (**vid**-ee-*oh*)
▷ *noun, plural* **videos**

videocassette *noun* A plastic case that contains videotape. It can be inserted into a VCR and used to record or play back movies and television programs. **vid·e·o·cas·sette** (*vid*-ee-*oh*-kuh-**set**)

video game *noun* An electronic or computerized game played by using buttons or levers to move images around on a television or computer screen. Video games often emphasize fast action.

videotape *noun*
1. Magnetic tape for recording and playing sound and pictures.
2. A recording on this kind of tape: *We watched a videotape of our third-grade play.*
vid·e·o·tape (**vid**-ee-oh-*tape*)
▷ *verb* **videotape**

vie *verb* To compete: *Jason vied with Eliza for their*

video game

mother's attention. **vie** (vye) ▷ *verb* **vying, vied**

view
1. *noun* What you can see from a certain place.
2. *noun* The range or field of sight: *The deer disappeared from view.*
3. *noun* What you think about something, or your opinion: *What are your views on gun control?*
4. *verb* To look at something: *Many people viewed the dinosaur exhibit.*
5. *verb* To consider something in a particular way: *Sue views the new bus route as a definite improvement.*
view (vyoo)
▷ *verb* **viewing, viewed**

viewpoint *noun*
1. The place or position from which a person views a situation or an event.
2. An attitude or a way of thinking: *I tried to understand her viewpoint, but I don't agree.*
view·point (**vyoo**-*point*)

vigilant *adjective* Keeping a careful watch: *The guard finds it hard to stay vigilant when he's tired.* **vig·i·lant** (**vij**-uh-luhnt) ▷ *noun* **vigilance** ▷ *adverb* **vigilantly**

vigor *noun*
1. Great force or energy: *The lawyer defended her client with vigor.*
2. Physical energy or strength.
vig·or (**vig**-ur)

vigorous *adjective* Involving physical effort, strength, or energy, as in *a vigorous workout.* **vig·or·ous** (**vig**-ur-uhs) ▷ *adverb* **vigorously**

Viking *noun* A member of one of the Scandinavian peoples who invaded the coasts of Europe and explored the North American coast between the 8th and 11th centuries. **Vi·king** (**vye**-king)

vile *adjective*
1. Evil or immoral, as in *a vile crime.*
2. Disgusting or repulsive, as in *vile language.*
vile (vile)
▷ *adjective* **viler, vilest** ▷ *noun* **vileness**

villa *noun* A large, luxurious house, especially one in the country. **vil·la** (**vil**-uh)

village *noun* A small group of houses that make up a community. A village is usually smaller than a town. **vil·lage** (**vil**-ij) ▷ *noun* **villager** ▷ *adjective* **village**

villain *noun* An evil person, often a character in a play, movie, or story. **vil·lain** (**vil**-uhn) ▷ *adjective* **villainous**

vindictive *adjective* Unforgiving and seeking revenge, as in *vindictive criticism*. **vin·dic·tive** (vin-**dik**-tiv) ▷ *noun* **vindictiveness** ▷ *adverb* **vindictively**

vine *noun* A plant with a long, twining stem that grows along the ground or climbs on trees, fences, or other supports. Melons, cucumbers, grapes, and pumpkins grow on vines. **vine** (vine)

vinegar *noun* A sour liquid made from fermented wine, cider, or other juices, and used to flavor and preserve food. **vin·e·gar** (**vin**-i-gur)

vineyard *noun* An area of land where grapes are grown. **vine·yard** (**vin**-yurd)

vintage
1. *noun* The wine or grapes of a particular season.
2. *adjective* Among the best of a person's work, as in *a vintage performance*.
3. *adjective* Old but in good condition and still valuable, as in *a vintage car*.
vin·tage (**vin**-tij)

vinyl *noun* A flexible, waterproof, shiny plastic that is used to make floor coverings, raincoats, and other products. **vi·nyl** (**vye**-nuhl)

viola *noun* A stringed musical instrument that looks like a violin but is slightly larger and has a deeper tone. **vi·o·la** (vee-**oh**-luh)

violate *verb*
1. To break or ignore a promise, a rule, or a law: *He violated my trust by lying.*
2. To treat a sacred place with disrespect.
3. To disturb rudely or without any right, as in *to violate someone's privacy*.
vi·o·late (**vye**-uh-*late*)
▷ *verb* **violating, violated** ▷ *noun* **violation** (*vye*-uh-**lay**-shuhn) ▷ *noun* **violator** (**vye**-uh-**lay**-tur)

violence *noun*
1. The use of physical force to cause harm: *I am worried about the crime and violence in our town.*
2. Great force or strength: *The violence of the hurricane destroyed many homes.*
vi·o·lence (**vye**-uh-luhns)

violent *adjective*
1. Showing or caused by great physical force, as in *a violent storm*.
2. Showing or caused by strong feeling or emotion, as in *a violent temper*.
vi·o·lent (**vye**-uh-luhnt)

violet *noun*
1. A plant that grows close to the ground, with small purple, yellow, or white flowers.
2. A blue-purple color.
vi·o·let (**vye**-uh-lit)
▷ *adjective* **violet**

violin *noun* A musical instrument with four strings,

vintage car

held under the chin and played with a bow. **vi·o·lin** (*vye*-uh-**lin**) ▷ *noun* **violinist**

VIP *noun* Short for *very important person*.

viper *noun* Any poisonous snake. **vi·per** (**vye**-pur)

viral *adjective*
1. Of or pertaining to a virus or viruses, as in *a viral infection*.
2. If a video, photo, or other item **goes viral**, it becomes immediately popular online and many people see it and know about it: *Videos that go viral are often funny or unexpected.*
vi·ral (**vye**-ruhl)

virgin *adjective* In its natural state; untouched, as in *virgin snow* or *virgin forests*. **vir·gin** (**vur**-jin)

virtual *adjective*
1. Almost, but not complete or exact: *Traffic was at a virtual standstill after a six-car pileup in thick fog.*
2. Made to seem like the real thing, but consisting mainly of sound and images: *Take a virtual tour of the building online.*
vir·tu·al (**vur**-choo-uhl)

virtually *adverb* Almost, nearly: *There are virtually no fish left in this polluted lake.* **vir·tu·al·ly** (**vur**-choo-uh-lee)

virtual reality *noun* An environment that looks three-dimensional but was created through a computer. Virtual reality seems real to the person who experiences it.

virtue *noun*
1. Moral goodness. ▷ *adjective* **virtuous** (**vur**-choo-uhs) ▷ *adverb* **virtuously**
2. An example of moral goodness: *Kindness is a virtue.*
3. Any good quality or trait.
vir·tue (**vur**-choo)

virtuoso *noun* A particularly skillful performer, especially a musician. **vir·tu·o·so** (*vur*-choo-**oh**-soh) ▷ *noun, plural* **virtuosos** *or* **virtuosi** (*vur*-choo-**oh**-see)

virulent *adjective*
1. Very severe, aggressive, or harmful, as in *a virulent illness*.

2. Bitter, spiteful, or full of hate, as in *virulent criticism* or *a virulent speech.*
vir·u·lent (**vir**-uh-luhnt)
▷ *noun* **virulence** (**vir**-uh-luhns) ▷ *adverb* **virulently**

virus *noun*
1. A very tiny organism that can reproduce and grow only when inside living cells. Viruses are smaller than bacteria. They cause diseases such as polio, measles, the common cold, and AIDS.
2. The illness caused by a virus.
3. A computer program, hidden within another, seemingly innocent program, that produces many copies of itself and is designed to destroy a computer system or damage data.
vi·rus (**vye**-ruhs)
▷ *noun, plural* **viruses**

visa *noun* A document, usually stamped in a passport, giving permission for someone to enter a foreign country or stay there for a certain period of time. **vi·sa** (**vee**-zuh)

vise *noun* A device with two jaws that open and close with a screw or lever. A vise is used to hold an object firmly in place while it is being worked on. **vise** (vise) **Vise** sounds like **vice.**

visible *adjective* Able to be seen: *The house was barely visible in the heavy snowstorm.* **vis·i·ble** (**viz**-uh-buhl) ▷ *noun* **visibility** (*viz*-uh-**bil**-i-tee) ▷ *adverb* **visibly** (**viz**-uh-blee)

vision *noun*
1. The sense of sight: *Many people wear glasses to improve their vision.*
2. A lovely or beautiful sight: *In her youth, my grandmother was a vision of loveliness.*
3. The ability to think ahead and plan, as in *a leader of great vision.* ▷ *noun* **visionary** (**vizh**-uh-*ner*-ee)
4. Something that you imagine or dream about: *Malcolm has visions of being a famous author.*
vi·sion (**vizh**-uhn)

visit *verb* To go to see people or places and spend a certain amount of time there. **vis·it** (**viz**-it) ▷ *verb* **visiting, visited** ▷ *noun* **visit** ▷ *noun* **visitor** (**viz**-i-tur)

visor *noun*
1. A brim that sticks out of the front of a cap to shade the eyes from the sun.
2. A movable shade inside a car, above the windshield, that protects the eyes from glare.

visor

3. The movable, see-through shield on the front of a helmet that protects the face.
vi·sor (**vye**-zur)

visual *adjective*
1. Of or having to do with seeing, as in *visual perception.* ▷ *adverb* **visually**
2. Designed or able to be seen: *Charts, films, and slides are visual aids used to improve learning.*
vis·u·al (**vizh**-oo-uhl)

visualize *verb* To imagine something; to see something in your mind: *I can't visualize myself driving a motorcycle.* **vi·su·al·ize** (**vizh**-oo-uh-*lize*) ▷ *verb* **visualizing, visualized** ▷ *noun* **visualization** (*vizh*-oo-uh-li-**zay**-shuhn)

vital *adjective*
1. Very important or essential: *A good education is vital.* ▷ *adverb* **vitally**
2. Of or having to do with life: *The doctor checked the accident victim's vital signs.*
3. Necessary for life, as in *vital organs.*
4. Full of life or energetic, as in *a vital personality.*
vi·tal (**vye**-tuhl)

vitality *noun* A state of being strong and lively: *Puppies are full of vitality.* **vi·tal·i·ty** (vye-**tal**-i-tee)

vitamin *noun* One of the substances in food that is essential for good health and nutrition: *Fruits and vegetables are excellent sources of vitamins.* **vi·ta·min** (**vye**-tuh-min)

vittles *noun, plural* See **victuals.** **vit·tles** (**vit**-uhlz)

vivacious *adjective* Having a lively and animated personality, as in *a vivacious girl.* **vi·va·cious** (vi-**vay**-shuhs) ▷ *noun* **vivacity** (vi-**vas**-i-tee) ▷ *adverb* **vivaciously**

vivid *adjective*
1. Bright and strong, as in *vivid colors.*
2. Lively or active, as in *a vivid imagination.*
3. Sharp and clear, as in *vivid memories.*
viv·id (**viv**-id) ▷ *noun* **vividness** ▷ *adverb* **vividly**

vivisection *noun* The practice of operating on live animals for scientific and medical research. **viv·i·sec·tion** (*viv*-i-**sek**-shuhn)

vocabulary *noun* All the words that a person can use and understand: *Charles impressed his teachers with his large vocabulary.* **vo·cab·u·lar·y** (voh-**kab**-yuh-*ler*-ee) ▷ *noun, plural* **vocabularies**

Volcanoes

Below the earth's surface is the crust, a layer of solid, dense rock. Underneath it are two layers, the mantle and the core, that are hot enough to melt rocks, producing magma. The earth's crust is made up of large formations called plates. When they move, they cause the crust to open, forming vents. Volcanoes erupt from these holes, releasing magma, ash clouds, and hot gases.

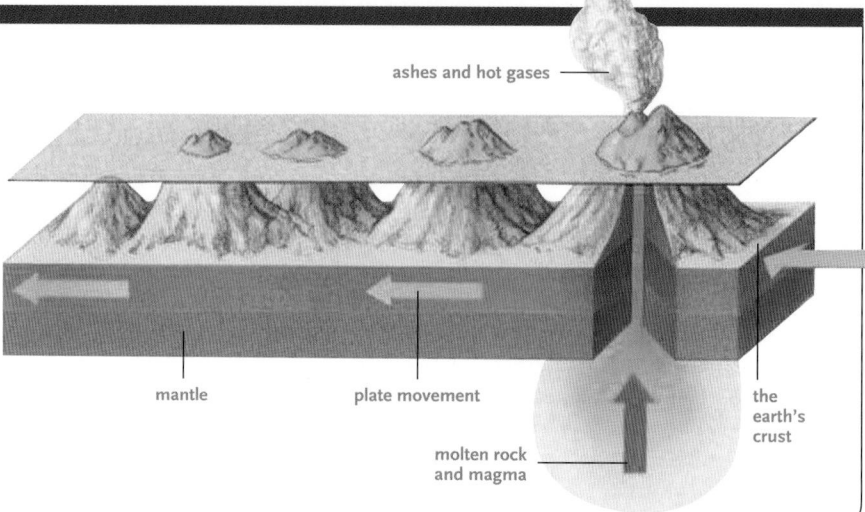

ashes and hot gases

mantle

plate movement

molten rock and magma

the earth's crust

vocal

1. *adjective* Of or having to do with the voice: *Singers and actors do a lot of vocal work.*

2. *adjective* Outspoken and unafraid to express opinions.

3. vocals *noun, plural* In music, the **vocals** are the parts that are sung.

vo·cal (**voh**-kuhl)

▷ *verb* **vocalize** ▷ *adverb* **vocally**

vocal cords

noun, plural Either of two pairs of bands or folds of membranes in the larynx. When air from the lungs passes through the lower pair, it causes them to vibrate and produce sound.

vocalist

noun A singer: *A good vocalist must master a wide range of tones.* **vo·cal·ist** (**voh**-kuh-list)

vocation

noun

1. A job, profession, or occupation. ▷ *adjective* **vocational** (voh-**kay**-shuh-nuhl)

2. A strong feeling for a particular job, especially a religious career.

vo·ca·tion (voh-**kay**-shuhn)

vociferous

adjective Noisy and vehement, as in *a vociferous argument.* **vo·cif·er·ous** (voh-**sif**-ur-uhs)

▷ *adverb* **vociferously**

vodka

noun A strong alcoholic drink that is clear in color and is made from grain or potatoes. **vod·ka** (**vahd**-kuh)

vogue

noun The fashion or style at a particular time: *Very short skirts were in vogue in the 1960s.* **vogue** (vohg)

voice

1. *noun* The sound produced by air passing through the larynx and out of the mouth.

2. *noun* The power to speak and sing: *My mother has lost her voice.*

3. *verb* To express in words, as in *to voice an opinion.*

▷ *verb* **voicing, voiced**

4. *noun* The right to express your opinion: *They had no voice in making the decision.*

voice (vois)

voice mail

noun A system that allows you to leave and play back spoken messages by telephone.

voiceprint

noun A graph that shows the special patterns and characteristics of an individual speaker's voice. **voice·print** (**vois**-print)

void

1. *noun* A completely empty space: *Clara felt a void in her life after her friend moved.* ▷ *adjective* **void**

2. *adjective* Not valid or legal: *The will was declared void by the court.* ▷ *verb* **void**

void (void)

volatile

adjective

1. Evaporating easily, or unstable in some other way.

2. Showing rapid changes of mood, as in *a volatile personality.*

vol·a·tile (**vah**-luh-tuhl)

▷ *noun* **volatility** (*vah*-luh-**til**-i-tee)

volcano

noun A mountain with openings through which molten lava, ash, and hot gases erupt, sometimes violently. Volcanoes are found along the boundaries of the earth's plates, where molten rock is forced upward from magma reservoirs in or below the earth's crust. **vol·ca·no** (vahl-**kay**-noh) ▷ *noun, plural* **volcanoes** or **volcanos**

volition

noun The power a person has to choose their actions; free will: *I was acting of my own volition when I resigned from the company—nobody forced me into it.* **vo·li·tion** (voh-**lish**-uhn) ▷ *adjective* **volitional**

volley

noun

1. In games such as tennis or soccer, a shot in which the ball is hit or kicked before it can bounce. ▷ *verb* **volley**

2. The firing of a number of bullets or missiles at the same time.

3. A burst or outburst of many things at the same time, as in *a volley of protests.*
vol·ley (**vah**-lee)

volleyball *noun*

1. A team game in which the players use their hands and forearms to hit a large ball over a net and try to make the ball land on the ground on their opponent's side. Volleyball can be played on a court or on a beach.

2. The ball used in this game.
vol·ley·ball (**vah**-lee-*bawl*)

volt *noun* A unit for measuring the force of an electrical current or the stored power of a battery. Volts are used to measure voltage. **volt** (vohlt)

Word History

The word **volt** can be traced back to Count Alessandro Giuseppe Antonio Anastasio Volta (1745–1827). This Italian scientist invented the first electric battery in 1800.

voltage *noun* The force of an electrical current, expressed in volts. **volt·age** (**vohl**-tij)

volume *noun*

1. A book: *Our library owns thousands of volumes.*

2. One book of a set: *This encyclopedia has 20 volumes.*

3. The amount of space taken up by a three-dimensional object, such as a box, or by a substance within a container. To figure out the volume of a rectangular object, you multiply its length by its height by its width.

4. The amount of something, especially a large amount, as in *a huge volume of homework.*

5. Loudness: *Please turn down the volume!*
vol·ume (**vahl**-yoom *or* **vahl**-yuhm)

voluntary *adjective*

1. Willing; not forced, as in *a voluntary donation.*

2. Controlled by the will, as in *voluntary muscles.*

3. Done on purpose and not by accident, as in *voluntary manslaughter.*
vol·un·tar·y (**vah**-luhn-*ter*-ee)

volunteer

1. *verb* To offer to do a job without pay:

vulture

I'll volunteer to clean up the living room. ▷ *verb*
volunteering, volunteered ▷ *noun* **volunteer**

2. *adjective* Formed or made up of volunteers, or done as a volunteer, as in *volunteer firefighters.*
vol·un·teer (*vah*-luhn-**teer**)

vomit *verb* To bring up food and other substances from your stomach and expel them from your mouth. **vom·it** (**vah**-mit) ▷ *verb* **vomiting, vomited** ▷ *noun* **vomit**

vote

1. *verb* To cast a ballot, making a choice in an election: *Kelly urged everyone in her class to vote for her.* ▷ *verb* **voting, voted**

2. *noun* A choice or opinion expressed in an election: *In a close contest, every vote counts.*

3. *noun* All of the ballots in an election, considered as a whole: *The losing candidate finished with 45 percent of the vote.*
vote (voht)
▷ *noun* **voter**

vouch *verb* To say that someone or something is true, honest, or reliable: *I can vouch for his honesty.* **vouch** (vouch) ▷ *verb* **vouching, vouched**

vow *verb* To make a solemn and important promise: *Paul vowed revenge on whoever had hurt his brother.* **vow** (vou) ▷ *verb* **vowing, vowed** ▷ *noun* **vow**

vowel *noun* A speech sound made with a free flow of air through the mouth. Vowels are represented by the letters *a, e, i, o, u,* and sometimes *y,* or combinations of these letters. **vow·el** (**vou**-uhl)

voyage *noun* A long journey by sea or in space, as in *an ocean voyage to the United States.* **voy·age** (**voi**-ij) ▷ *noun* **voyager** ▷ *verb* **voyage**

vulgar *adjective* Rude or in bad taste, as in *vulgar language* or *a vulgar joke.* **vul·gar** (**vuhl**-gur) ▷ *noun* **vulgarity** (vuhl-**gar**-i-tee)

vulnerable *adjective* In a position or condition where a person or thing could easily be damaged: *Roses are vulnerable to frost if they are not properly covered.* **vul·ner·a·ble** (**vuhl**-nur-uh-buhl) ▷ *noun* **vulnerability** (*vuhl*-nur-uh-**bil**-i-tee) ▷ *adverb* **vulnerably**

vulture *noun* A large bird of prey that has dark feathers and a bald head and neck. Vultures are related to hawks, eagles, and falcons. They feed mainly on the meat of dead animals. **vul·ture** (**vuhl**-chur)

a b c d e f g h i j k l m n o p q r s t u **v** w x y z

Ww

A B C D E F G H I J K L M N O P Q R S T U V W X Y Z

About W In many words that begin with a **W**, the letter is silent, as in the words *wrap*, *wreck*, *wrist*, and *wrong*. Some words that start with *w* are followed by a silent *h*. Examples: whack, wheel, whistle, whole. The three ws in a website address stand for the World Wide Web.

wacky *adjective (slang)* Odd or crazy in a silly or amusing way: *Holly learned some wacky songs at summer camp.* **wack·y** (**wak**-ee) ▷ *adjective* **wackier, wackiest** ▷ *noun* **wackiness** ▷ *adverb* **wackily**

wad
1. *noun* A small, tightly packed ball or piece of something soft, as in *a wad of cotton* or *a wad of chewing gum.*
2. *noun* A tight, thick roll, as in *a wad of dollar bills.*
3. *verb* To press or roll something into a wad: *Wad up the shirt and throw it in the laundry bag.* ▷ *verb* **wadding, wadded**
wad (wahd)

waddle *verb* To walk awkwardly, taking short steps and moving slightly from side to side: *The ducks waddled toward the pond.* **wad·dle** (**wah**-duhl) ▷ *verb* **waddling, waddled** ▷ *noun* **waddle**

wade *verb*
1. To walk through water or mud.
2. To move through something slowly and with difficulty, as in *to wade through a lot of technical material.*
wade (wayd)
▷ *verb* **wading, waded**

wader *noun*
1. A bird such as the crane or heron that wades in shallow water looking for food.
2. waders *noun, plural* High, waterproof boots used for fishing in deep water.
wad·er (**way**-dur)

wafer *noun*
1. A thin, light, crisp cookie or cracker, as in *a Communion wafer.*
2. A thin, flat piece of candy, as in *mint-chocolate wafers.*
wa·fer (**way**-fur)

waffle
1. *noun* A type of cake baked in an appliance that presses a crisscross pattern into it.
2. *verb (informal)* To avoid giving a direct answer to a question; to keep changing your mind or position: *The governor waffled on the question of raising taxes.*
▷ *verb* **waffling, waffled** ▷ *noun* **waffle** ▷ *noun* **waffler**
waf·fle (**wah**-fuhl)

Word History

The crisscross pattern of lines on a **waffle** makes it look like a woven piece of cloth, and this is how the waffle got its name. The word came from *wafel* in the Dutch language, and *wafel* is related to the English word *weave*. So a *waffle* is like a cloth that someone has "woven."

waffles

waft *verb* To float or be carried through the air, as if by a breeze: *As it grew colder, snowflakes started wafting to the ground.* **waft** (wahft) ▷ *verb* **wafting, wafted** ▷ *noun* **waft**

wag *verb* To move something quickly from side to side or up and down: *The dog wagged its tail.* **wag** (wag) ▷ *verb* **wagging, wagged** ▷ *noun* **wag**

wage
1. wage or **wages** *noun* The money someone is paid for the work he or she does.
2. *verb* If you **wage** a war or a campaign, you start it and continue it: *The mayor is waging a citywide recycling campaign.* ▷ *verb* **waging, waged**
wage (waje)

wager *noun* A bet: *The two boys made a wager on who could eat the most hot dogs.* **wa·ger** (**way**-jur) ▷ *verb* **wager**

wagon *noun*
1. A vehicle with four wheels that is used to carry heavy loads and is pulled by a horse or horses.
2. A child's toy vehicle or cart with four wheels and a long handle that is used for pulling and carrying things.
wag·on (**wag**-uhn)

wagon train *noun* In frontier times, a line or group of covered wagons that traveled west together for safety.

waif *noun*
1. Someone, especially a young child, who is small, pale, and thin and looks like he or she has no home.

2. A stray animal.
waif (wayf)

wail *verb* To make a long cry of pain or sadness: *The baby began to wail when her mother left the room.* **wail** (wayl) ▷ *verb* **wailing, wailed** ▷ *noun* **wail**

waist *noun*
1. The middle part of your body between your ribs and your hips.
2. The part of a piece of clothing that covers the body around the waist area.
waist (wayst)
Waist sounds like **waste**.

wait *verb*
1. To stay in a place or do nothing for a period of time until someone comes or something happens: *We waited an hour for the train.* ▷ *noun* **wait**
2. To look forward to something: *Nilda waited all week for her best friend to return from vacation.*
3. To be delayed or put off: *The picnic will have to wait until the weather clears.*
4. If you **wait on** someone, you serve as the person's waiter, waitress, salesperson, or servant.
wait (wate)
Wait sounds like **weight**. ▷ *verb* **waiting, waited**

waiter *noun* A man who serves people food and drinks in a restaurant. **wait·er** (**way**-tur)

waiting room *noun* A room or an area where people sit and wait for something such as a train or a doctor's appointment.

waitress *noun* A woman who serves people food and drinks in a restaurant. **wait·ress** (**way**-tris) ▷ *noun, plural* **waitresses**

waive *verb*
1. To give up something by choice: *The man waived his right to a lawyer and confessed everything to the police.*
2. To postpone or to set aside: *The speaker waived the presentation and instead answered questions from the audience.*
waive (wayv)
Waive sounds like **wave**. ▷ *verb* **waiving, waived**

waiver *noun*
1. A document that you can sign to say that you are choosing to give up your legal right to do or have something: *You have to sign a waiver before going skydiving.*
2. The act of choosing to give up your legal right to do or have something.
waiv·er (**way**-vur)
Waiver sounds like **waver**.

waiting room

wake
1. *verb* To stop sleeping and become fully conscious: *I wake up at 6 a.m. when my alarm goes off.*
2. *verb* To cause someone to stop sleeping: *Wake me at 5 a.m.*
3. *noun* An occasion before or after a funeral in which people meet to remember the dead person.
4. *noun* The trail in the water left by a boat as it moves away.
5. *noun* What is left behind by something or someone: *The tornado left destruction in its wake.*
wake (wayk)
▷ *verb* **waking, woke** (wohk) *or* **waked, waked** *or* **woken** (**woh**-kuhn)

walk
1. *verb* To move along by placing one foot on the ground before lifting the other: *It won't be long before the baby is able to walk.* ▷ *noun* **walker**
2. *noun* A trip that you make by walking: *It's just a short walk from our house to the theater.*
3. *noun* A way or style of walking, as in *a jaunty walk.*
4. *verb* To go with someone to a place: *I'll walk you to school.*
5. *noun* A path or other area that is set apart or designed for walking.
6. *verb* To make or help walk: *It's your turn to walk the dog.*
7. *noun* In baseball, the right of the batter to go to first base after the pitcher has thrown four pitches that are not swung at and are not called strikes by the umpire. ▷ *verb* **walk**
8. *(informal)* If you **walk all over** somebody, you treat the person badly and take advantage of him or her.
walk (wawk)
▷ *verb* **walking, walked**

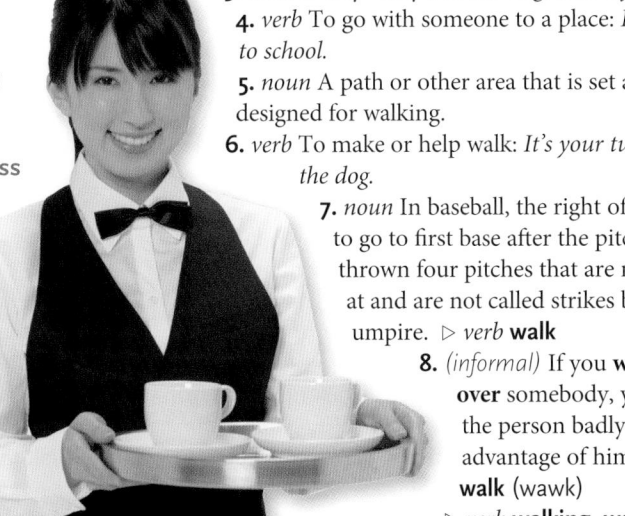
waitress

Great Wall of China

walk back *verb* To take back or lessen the force of something you said earlier: *At the press conference the president walked back his earlier threat to cancel the treaty.* ▷ *verb* **walking back, walked back**

walkie-talkie *noun* A radio that is held in the hand, powered by batteries, and is used to communicate over short distances. **walk·ie-talk·ie** (**waw**-kee-**taw**-kee)

walkway *noun* A path or passage for walking. **walk·way** (**wawk**-*way*)

wall *noun*
1. A vertical, solid structure, usually made of brick or stone, that surrounds an area or separates one area from another. ▷ *verb* **wall**
2. The vertical side of a room or building that supports a roof: *Erika hung some posters on the wall.*
3. Anything that divides one thing from another, shuts something in, or stops anything from getting past; a barrier, as in *a wall of marchers* or *a wall of fire.*
4. A situation in which no one will talk to you, help you, or give you information: *The investigator was met with a wall of resistance when he looked for witnesses to the crime.*
wall (wawl)

wallaby *noun* A small marsupial that is related to the kangaroo. Wallabies are found in Australia, New Zealand, and New Guinea. **wal·la·by** (**wah**-luh-*bee*) ▷ *noun, plural* **wallabies**

wallet *noun* A small, flat case, usually made of leather, for holding money, photographs, credit cards, and personal documents such as business cards and a driver's license. **wal·let** (**wah**-lit)

wallop *verb* (*informal*)
1. To hit someone or something very hard: *The batter walloped the ball over the fence.*
2. To defeat severely.
wal·lop (**wah**-luhp) ▷ *verb* **walloping, walloped** ▷ *noun* **wallop**

wallow *verb*
1. To roll around in mud or water: *The seals wallowed in the shallow pool.*
2. To enjoy something greatly, or to get completely involved in something: *Dan wallowed in self-pity after he lost the game.*
wal·low (**wah**-loh) ▷ *verb* **wallowing, wallowed**

wallpaper *noun*
1. Paper that is pasted in sections to a wall in order to decorate a room. ▷ *verb* **wallpaper**
2. A pattern or image that serves as the background of a computer desktop.
wall·pa·per (**wawl**-*pay*-pur)

walnut *noun* A sweet nut that grows on a tall tree and has a hard, wrinkled shell. The wood of the walnut tree is often used to make furniture. **wal·nut** (**wawl**-nuht)

walnut

walrus *noun* A large sea animal that lives in the Arctic. Walruses have tusks, flippers, tough skin, and a thick layer of blubber. **wal·rus** (**wawl**-ruhs) ▷ *noun, plural* **walruses** *or* **walrus**

Word History

Early hunters and explorers often used familiar words to name new and unusual animals that they came across. **Walrus** comes from two Dutch words, *walvis,* meaning "whale," and *ros,* meaning "horse." In Old English, the animal had been called a "horsewhale."

waltz *noun*
1. A ballroom dance in which a couple turns continuously in a regular series of three steps. ▷ *verb* **waltz** ▷ *noun* **waltzer**
2. A piece of music that is used with a waltz.
waltz (wawlts) ▷ *noun, plural* **waltzes**

wampum *noun* Beads made from polished shells

strung together or woven to make belts, collars, and necklaces. Wampum was used by some Native American tribes as money. **wam·pum** (**wahm**-puhm)

Word History

Wampum is the name that Native Americans in New England gave to the strings of polished shells they used as money. It is short for *wampumpeak*. Tribes in other parts of North America called their money by different names. In the Virginia area it was called *roanoke,* and in the northwest part of the United States it was called *hiaqua.*

wand *noun* A thin rod or stick, especially one used by magicians, as in *a magic wand.* **wand** (wahnd)

wander *verb*
1. To move around without a particular purpose or place to go; to roam: *She spent the afternoon wandering in the park.* ▷ *noun* **wanderer**
2. To walk away from where you ought to be; to stray: *The hikers wandered from the trail.*
3. If your mind or thoughts **wander,** you become distracted from something and start thinking about something else: *My mind wandered during the long car ride.*
wan·der (**wahn**-dur)
▷ *verb* **wandering, wandered**

wane *verb*
1. To become less or smaller in size, importance, or strength: *As the job progressed, Jewel's enthusiasm waned.*
2. When the moon **wanes,** it seems to get smaller.
wane (wayn)
▷ *verb* **waning, waned**

wangle *verb* (*informal*) To gain something by clever or dishonest methods: *I managed to wangle a seat near the stage.*
wan·gle (**wang**-guhl) ▷ *verb* **wangling, wangled**

want
1. *verb* To feel that you would like to have, do, or get something; to wish for; to desire: *I want an apple. I want to go on vacation.*
2. *verb* To need or require something: *What this story wants is some suspense.*
3. *noun* A lack of something: *In many poor countries, people are dying for want of food and medicine.*
4. *noun* Something that you need or desire: *My wants are few.*
want (wahnt)
▷ *verb* **wanting, wanted**

war *noun*
1. A long period of fighting between two or more opposing countries or groups.
2. A struggle over a long period of time to stop or control something harmful: *We are waging a war against hunger.*
war (wor)
War sounds like **wore**.

warbler *noun* Any of several small songbirds, many of which have brightly colored feathers. **war·bler** (**wahr**-blur)

ward
1. *noun* A large room or section in a hospital where many patients are taken care of, as in *the maternity ward.*
2. *noun* A person who is officially cared for by a guardian or the court: *The orphan was a ward of the state.*
3. *noun* For voting purposes, a district of a town or city.
4. ward off *verb* To do something to protect yourself from something attacking or hurting you: *He wore a cap to ward off the sun.* ▷ *verb* **warding, warded**
ward (word)

warden *noun*
1. Someone in charge of a prison.
2. An official who is responsible for making sure certain laws are obeyed, as in *a game warden.*
war·den (**wor**-duhn)

wardrobe

wardrobe *noun*
1. A collection of clothes, especially all the clothes belonging to one person: *Ted's wardrobe includes a lot of Hawaiian shirts.*
2. A tall piece of furniture or a closet used for storing clothes.
ward·robe (**wor**-drobe)

warehouse *noun* A large building used for storing goods or merchandise. **ware·house** (**wair**-hous) ▷ *verb* **warehouse**

wares *noun, plural* Things that are for sale; goods: *Many merchants displayed their wares at the fair.*
wares (wairz)

warfare *noun* The fighting of wars, especially using a particular method, as in *naval warfare.*
war·fare (**wor**-fair)

warlike *adjective* Aggressive and liking to fight, as in *warlike people*. **war·like** (**wor**-*like*)

warm

1. *adjective* Slightly hot: *It's a nice warm day, perfect for playing Frisbee.*

2. *verb* To raise the temperature of something: *Come in and warm your hands by the fire.*

3. *adjective* Holding in body heat, as in *a warm sweater.*

4. *adjective* Very friendly: *She greeted me with a warm smile.* ▷ *adverb* **warmly**

5. *verb* If you **warm up** before a sports match or athletic activity, you stretch or exercise lightly in preparation. ▷ *noun* **warm-up** ▷ *adjective* **warm-up**

6. *verb* If you **warm up** an engine, you turn it on and let it run until it is ready to be used.

warm (worm)

▷ *verb* **warming, warmed** ▷ *noun* **warmth**

▷ *adjective* **warmer, warmest**

warm-blooded *adjective* **Warm-blooded** animals have a warm body temperature that does not change, even if the temperature around them is very hot or very cold. **warm-blood·ed** (**bluhd**-id)

warn *verb*

1. To tell someone to do or not do something in order to avoid danger or something bad: *My mother is always warning me not to eat too much candy.*

2. To give someone advice about something bad that might happen: *The reports warned about the dangers of smoking.*

warn (worn)

Warn sounds like **worn**. ▷ *verb* **warning, warned** ▷ *noun* **warning**

warp *verb* If an object **warps**, it gets twisted, curved, or bent out of shape, especially because of dampness or heat. **warp** (worp) ▷ *verb* **warping, warped**

warrant

1. *noun* An official piece of paper that gives someone the right to do something, as in *an arrest warrant.*

2. *verb* To guarantee: *The manufacturer warrants all its products.*

3. *verb* To deserve: *Barbara's history report warrants an A.*

war·rant (**wor**-uhnt)

▷ *verb* **warranting, warranted**

warranty *noun* A written agreement in which a company agrees that it is responsible for repairing or replacing a product it has sold if it breaks within a specific period of time, as in *a two-year warranty.* **war·ran·ty** (**wor**-uhn-tee)

warren *noun* A system of underground holes and tunnels where rabbits live. **war·ren** (**wor**-uhn)

warrior *noun* A soldier, or someone who fights with courage and determination. **war·ri·or** (**wor**-ee-ur)

warship *noun* A ship with heavy guns that is used in war. **war·ship** (**wor**-*ship*)

wart *noun*

1. A small, hard lump on the skin that is caused by a virus.

2. A small lump or bump that grows on a plant.

wart (wort)

▷ *adjective* **warty**

wary *adjective* Nervous and cautious: *Danny is always very wary when a dog rushes up to him.* **war·y** (**wair**-ee) ▷ *adjective* **warier, wariest** ▷ *noun* **wariness** ▷ *adverb* **warily**

was *verb* The form of **be** used with *I, he, she,* or *it* or with singular nouns in the past tense: *I was at the restaurant before everyone else.* **was** (wuhz or wahz)

wash

1. *verb* To clean with water or soap and water: *Dad told us to wash our hands before dinner.* ▷ *noun* **wash** ▷ *noun* **washing**

2. *noun* Clothing that needs to be or has been washed: *Put the wash in the laundry room.*

3. *noun* A liquid containing soap that is used for cleaning, as in *body wash.*

4. *verb* To be carried by the movement of water: *Hundreds of shells washed ashore.*

5. wash up *verb* To clean your hands and face using soap and water: *I just need five minutes to wash up.*

6. *verb* If waves or the sea **washes** something **up**, it brings it to the shore.

wash (wahsh)

▷ *verb* **washes, washing, washed** ▷ *noun, plural* **washes**

washable *adjective* If a material is **washable**, you can wash it without causing any damage to it. **wash·a·ble** (**wah**-shuh-buhl)

washer *noun*

1. A washing machine.

2. A ring that fits between a nut and a bolt to give a tighter fit or prevent a leak.

wash·er (**wah**-shur)

Washington, DC *noun* The capital of the United States. It is the home of the federal government, which includes the White House, Congress, and the Supreme Court. It is also referred to as the District of Columbia, its legal name, or as DC. **Wash·ing·ton, DC** (**wah**-shing-tuhn)

wasn't *contraction* A short form of *was not*: *Today's weather wasn't great, but our picnic was fun anyway.* **was·n't** (**wuhz**-uhnt)

wasp *noun* A thin, flying insect with black and yellow stripes. Female wasps can sting. **wasp** (wahsp)

wasp

waste

1. *verb* To use or spend something foolishly or carelessly: *She wasted all her money on clothes she didn't need. Don't waste your time.* ▷ *noun* **waste**

2. *verb* If someone **wastes away**, the person gets thinner and weaker, especially because of sickness.

3. *noun* Garbage, or something left over and not needed, as in *industrial waste.*

4. *noun* What the body does not use or need after food has been digested. **waste** (wayst)

Waste sounds like **waist**. ▷ *verb* **wasting, wasted** ▷ *adjective* **waste**

wastebasket *noun* A small basket or open container used for scraps of paper or other small items of trash. **waste·bas·ket** (**wayst**-*bas*-kit)

wasteful *adjective* If you are **wasteful**, you use things up carelessly and do not think about saving them. **waste·ful** (**wayst**-fuhl) ▷ *noun* **wastefulness** ▷ *adverb* **wastefully**

wasteland *noun* An area of land that is barren or empty, and where few plants or animals can live. **waste·land** (**wayst**-*land*)

watch

1. *noun* A small clock that you can wear on your wrist.

2. *verb* To look at something or someone for a period of time: *Annie was watching the news on TV.*

3. *verb* To be alert or careful about something: *Why don't you watch where you're going?*

4. *verb* To keep guard over someone or something: *Will you watch my packages while I go get a soda?*

5. *noun* A person or group that guards someone or something, or the activity of doing this: *The sailor was on the night watch.*

6. *noun* The time that a guard is on duty: *His watch ends at midnight.* **watch** (wahch)

▷ *verb* **watches, watching, watched** ▷ *noun, plural* **watches**

watchdog *noun*

1. A dog trained to guard a house, property, or people.

2. A person or group of people who make sure companies or the government do not do anything illegal, as in *a government watchdog.* **watch·dog** (**wahch**-*dawg*)

watchful *adjective* Observing carefully; alert: *The dog kept a watchful eye on the door until the family came* home. **watch·ful** (**wahch**-fuhl) ▷ *noun* **watchfulness** ▷ *adverb* **watchfully**

water

1. *noun* The colorless liquid that falls as rain and fills oceans, rivers, and lakes.

2. waters *noun, plural* The water in an ocean, a river, or a lake.

3. *verb* To pour water on something: *You'll need to water the plants every morning.*

4. *verb* If your mouth **waters**, it produces saliva because you are hungry.

5. *verb* If your eyes **water**, they become full of tears.

6. water down *verb* To add water or another liquid to make something weaker.

7. water down *verb* To make something less effective, less difficult, or less offensive: *The law needs to be strengthened, not watered down.* **wa·ter** (**waw**-tur)

▷ *verb* **watering, watered**

waterbird *noun* A bird that lives near the water and can swim or wade. **wa·ter·bird** (**waw**-tur-*burd*)

water buffalo *noun* A black buffalo with long horns that curve upward and outward. Found in Asia, it is often used to pull or carry heavy loads.

watercolor *noun*

1. Paint that is mixed with water instead of oil.

2. A picture painted with watercolors: *Her favorite work of art is a watercolor by John Audubon.* **wa·ter·col·or** (**waw**-tur-*kuhl*-ur)

watercolor paints

watercress *noun* A plant that grows in wet soil or running water with sharp-tasting, edible leaves. **wa·ter·cress** (**waw**-tur-*kres*)

water cycle *noun* The constant movement of the earth's water. Plants give off moisture, and water from lakes, rivers, and oceans evaporates, making water vapor. This vapor rises, forms clouds, and eventually falls as rain, hail, or snow.

a b c d e f g h i j k l m n o p q r s t u v **w** x y z

waterfall *noun* Water from a stream or river that falls from a high place to a lower place. **wa·ter·fall** (**waw**-tur-*fawl*)

waterfront *noun* An area of a city or town that is located beside a body of water. **wa·ter·front** (**waw**-tur-*fruhnt*) ▷ *adjective* **waterfront**

water lily *noun* A plant with wide, flat leaves and colorful flowers that grows in freshwater ponds and lakes. ▷ *noun, plural* **water lilies**

waterlogged *adjective* If something is **waterlogged**, it is so filled or soaked with water that it becomes heavy or hard to manage: *My shoes became waterlogged from walking in puddles.* **wa·ter·logged** (**waw**-tur-*lawgd*)

watermark *noun*
1. A mark or design in paper that you can see when you hold the paper up to the light.
2. A mark on a wall or other surface left by water from a river, a lake, or an ocean during a flood. **wa·ter·mark** (**waw**-tur-*mahrk*)

watermelon *noun* A large, sweet, juicy fruit that grows on vines. It usually has a thick, green skin, many black seeds, and pink or red flesh. **wa·ter·mel·on** (**waw**-tur-*mel*-uhn)

water moccasin *noun* A poisonous snake that lives near water and in swamps in the southeastern part of the United States. It is also called a **cottonmouth**.

waterproof *adjective* If something is **waterproof**, it does not allow water to enter, as in *waterproof boots.* **wa·ter·proof** (**waw**-tur-*proof*) ▷ *verb* **waterproof**

watershed *noun*
1. A ridge or area of high land that separates two river basins.
2. The region or land area that drains into a river or lake.
3. An important factor; a turning point: *The Civil War was a watershed in US history.* **wa·ter·shed** (**waw**-tur-*shed*)

water-ski *verb* To travel on skis over water while being pulled by a boat. ▷ *verb* **water-skiing, water-skied** ▷ *noun* **water-skier** ▷ *noun* **waterskiing**

watertight *adjective*
1. Completely sealed so that water cannot enter or leave: *Make sure that the cover on the jar is watertight.*
2. If an argument is **watertight**, it has no mistakes or flaws. **wa·ter·tight** (**waw**-tur-*tite*)

waterwheel

waterway *noun* A river, canal, or other body of water on which ships and boats can travel. **wa·ter·way** (**waw**-tur-*way*)

waterwheel *noun* A large wheel that is turned by water flowing over or under it. **wa·ter·wheel** (**waw**-tur-*weel*)

waterworks *noun, plural* The system that provides water to a community or town, including reservoirs, pipes, machinery, and buildings. *Waterworks* can be used with a singular or a plural verb. **wa·ter·works** (**waw**-tur-*wurks*)

watt *noun* A unit for measuring electrical power. **watt** (waht) ▷ *noun* **wattage** (**wah**-tij)

wave
1. *verb* To move your hand back and forth to get someone's attention or to say hello or good-bye: *Sonya waved at me as she was leaving the basketball game.* ▷ *noun* **wave**
2. *verb* To move or sway back and forth or up and down, or to make something do this: *The trees waved in the breeze. Thousands of people waved flags as the parade marched past.*
3. *noun* A line of water that rises up and moves across the surface of an ocean or sea: *Waves were crashing against the side of the boat.*
4. *noun* A slight curl in your hair. ▷ *verb* **wave**
5. *noun* An amount of energy that travels through air or water in the shape of a wave, as in *sound waves* or *light waves.*
6. *noun* A period of time in which there is a sudden change or increase in something, as in *a heat wave* or *a crime wave.*
wave (wayv)

Wave sounds like **waive**. ▷ *verb* **waving, waved** ▷ *adjective* **wavy**

wavelength *noun*
1. The distance between one point on a wave of light or sound and the next.
2. (*informal*) The state of having similar thoughts or opinions as another person: *My sister and I have always been on the same wavelength.*
wave·length (**wayv**-*lengkth*)

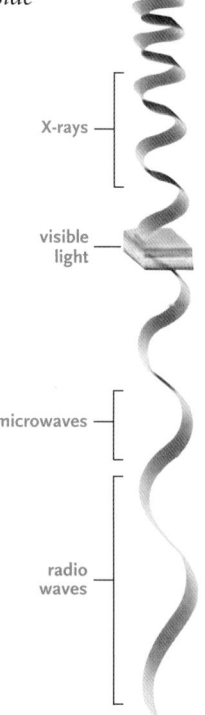

X-rays

visible light

microwaves

radio waves

wavelength

waver *verb*
1. To be uncertain about what you think or believe about someone or something: *Amanda never wavered in her belief that her book would be a success.*
2. To become weak or unsteady: *My voice wavered when I was asked to speak in front of the whole class.*
wa·ver (**way**-vur)
Waver sounds like **waiver**.
▷ *verb* **wavering, wavered**
▷ *noun* **waver**

wax
1. *noun* A hard substance made from oils or fats and used to make candles, crayons, and polish. Wax becomes soft when heated.
2. *noun* A substance like this produced by bees; beeswax.
3. *verb* To put wax or polish on something such as a car or furniture: *When Stephen finished waxing the table, he could see his own reflection in it.*
4. *verb* When the moon **waxes**, it appears to get bigger.
5. *verb* To grow, or to become: *They waxed enthusiastic about the party plans.*
wax (waks)
▷ *verb* **waxes, waxing, waxed** ▷ *adjective* **waxy**

sealing wax

way *noun*
1. A direction: *Which way is the exit?*
2. A road or a route to get to a place: *Do you know the way to the airport?*
3. A method or style that you use to do something: *What's the right way to hold chopsticks?*
4. A particular manner or a style: *She smiled in a way that warmed up the whole room.*
5. Distance: *I ran a long way before stopping to catch my breath.*
6. The opportunity to do or get what you wish: *My bossy sister always tries to get her way.*
7. A point or a detail: *In many ways, you are right.*
8. Space or a path: *Make way for the people coming through.*
9. ways *noun, plural* A group of people's typical habits or customs: *Although he grew up on a farm, it didn't take him long to adapt to the ways of the big city.*
way (way)
Way sounds like **weigh**.

wayback *noun* The area at the very back of a vehicle: *The wayback is full of groceries that you can bring in.*
way·back (**way**-bak)

waylay *verb*
1. To stop or delay someone who is trying to reach a goal or destination: *Our neighbor waylaid my mother as she was rushing to get to the bank.*

2. To hide and then attack someone on their way to a place: *The soldiers were waylaid by the enemy as they tried to get back to the fort.*
way·lay (**way**-lay)
▷ *verb* **waylaying, waylaid** ▷ *noun* **waylayer**

we *pronoun, plural* The people who are speaking or writing. **we** (wee) **We** sounds like **wee**.

weak *adjective*
1. Having little strength, force, or power, as in *a weak person, a weak argument,* or *a weak light.* ▷ *adverb* **weakly**
2. Likely to break, fall, or collapse: *The bracelet has a weak link near the clasp.*
3. Lacking flavor: *This is very weak tea.*
4. Lacking in skill or knowledge: *I am weak in spelling.*
5. Your **weak** points are the things that you are not very good at.
weak (week)
Weak sounds like **week**. ▷ *adjective* **weaker, weakest** ▷ *noun* **weakness** ▷ *verb* **weaken**

weakling *noun* A person without physical or moral strength. **weak·ling** (**week**-ling)

weak sauce *noun* *(informal)* Something that is not effective and needs to be improved: *Their scoring was good but their defense was weak sauce and they lost the game.*

wealth *noun*
1. A great amount of money, property, or valuable possessions: *For a man of wealth, he lived in such a simple house.*
2. A great amount of anything, as in *a wealth of ideas* or *a wealth of information.*
wealth (welth)

wealthy *adjective* Someone who is **wealthy** has a lot of money, property, or possessions: *The town is full of wealthy families.* **wealth·y** (**wel**-thee) ▷ *adjective* **wealthier, wealthiest**

wean *verb*
1. When you **wean** babies, you start giving them food other than their mothers' milk or formula.
2. If you **wean** someone **from** something, you help him or her stop doing it or give it up gradually.
wean (ween)
▷ *verb* **weaning, weaned**

weapon *noun*
1. Something that can be used in a fight to attack or defend, such as a sword, gun, knife, or bomb: *Surrounded, the robbers dropped their weapons.*
▷ *noun* **weaponry**
2. Anything that can be used to win a fight, struggle, or contest: *This team's best weapon is its quarterback.*
weap·on (**wep**-uhn)

wear

1. *verb* To be dressed in something, or to have something on your body: *Tara wore a black dress. Joe wore glasses for reading.* ▷ *noun* **wearer**

2. *verb* To have your hair in a particular style: *She wears her hair short.*

3. *verb* To show a particular expression on your face: *He wore an angry frown.*

4. *noun* Clothes worn by a particular group of people, or for a particular occasion: *Let's go to the boys' wear department.*

5. *noun* The gradual damage done to something that has been used a lot over a period of time: *After all these years, my jacket shows no signs of wear.*

6. *verb* To last a long time: *These boots have worn well.*

7. wear away *verb* To destroy something slowly and gradually: *Carlos wore away my patience.*

8. wear off *verb* To gradually decrease or stop: *After a few hours, the effects of the medication wore off.*

9. *verb* If an activity **wears** you **out**, it makes you extremely tired: *I'm worn out from running back and forth.*

10. *verb* If you **wear out** your clothes, you use them so much that they are damaged and no longer useful.

wear (wair)

▷ *verb* **wearing, wore** (wor), **worn**

wearable

1. *adjective* Capable of being worn, like clothing.

2. *noun* An article of clothing that contains some working technology: *The company is developing a line of wearables that monitor your health.*

wear·able (**wair**-uh-buhl)

weary *adjective*

1. Extremely tired: *We were weary after the long trip.*

2. Having little patience or interest; bored: *James grew weary of eating the same lunch every day.*

wea·ry (**weer**-ee)

▷ *adjective* **wearier,**

weather vane

weasel

weariest ▷ *noun* **weariness** ▷ *adverb* **wearily**

weasel

1. *noun* A small animal with a long, thin body, short legs, and soft, thick, reddish-brown fur. It eats other small animals.

2. *noun* (*informal*) A person who uses tricks and lies to get what he or she wants: *Did that little weasel get you to pay for lunch again?*

3. weasel out *verb* (*informal*) To use tricks and lies in order to avoid doing something: *This is the third time she's weaseled out of doing the dishes.*

wea·sel (**wee**-zuhl)

weather

1. *noun* The condition of the outside air or atmosphere at a particular time and place. Weather can be described, for example, as hot or cold, wet or dry, calm or windy, clear or cloudy.

2. *verb* If wood, stone, or another material **weathers**, it changes after being outside for a long time.

3. *verb* If you **weather** a difficult situation, such as a storm or crisis, you manage to get through it safely: *We decided to weather the hurricane in a shelter.*

4. If you are **under the weather**, you are sick.

weath·er (**weTH**-ur)

▷ *verb* **weathering, weathered**

weather vane *noun* A pointer that swings around on a pole to show which way the wind is blowing.

weave

1. *verb* To make cloth, baskets, or other objects by passing threads or strips over and under each other. ▷ *noun* **weaver**

2. *verb* To spin a web or cocoon: *The spider wove a web.*

3. *verb* To move from side to side or in and out in order to get through something: *The car wove its way through traffic.*

4. *noun* A method or pattern of weaving: *That basket has an open weave. This carpet has a tight weave.*

weave (weev)

Weave sounds like **we've**. ▷ *verb* **weaving, wove** (wohv) *or* **weaved, woven** (**woh**-vuhn) *or* **weaved**

web *noun*

1. A very thin net of sticky threads made by a spider to catch flies and other insects.

2. Short for the **World Wide Web**.

3. A pattern of related things put together in a careful or complicated way, as in *a web of city streets* or *a web of lies.*

4. The fold of skin or tissue that connects the toes of a duck, frog, or other animal that swims. **web** (web)

web browser *noun* The full form of **browser** (sense 1).

webcam *noun* A video camera that broadcasts directly to a website so that people online can watch it. **web·cam** (web-*kam*)

web-footed *adjective* Having toes that are connected by a web or fold of skin: *Ducks are web-footed.* **web·foot·ed** (**fut**-id)

web hosting *noun* The business of providing internet addresses and server storage space for people or companies who have websites.

webmaster *noun* Someone whose job or responsibility is to take care of a website and make sure that all its links and other functions are working properly. **web·mas·ter** (web-*mas*-tur)

webpage *noun* A single page on a website. **web·page** (web-*payj*)

website *noun* A group of linked computer files on the World Wide Web. **web·site** (web-*site*)

wed *verb*

1. To get married to someone: *Someday I hope to wed my sweetheart.*

2. To perform a marriage ceremony: *The judge wed the happy couple.* **wed** (wed)

▷ *verb* **wedding, wedded** or **wed**

we'd *contraction* A short form of *we had* or *we would*: *We'd like to go to Aunt Ruth's house.* **we'd** (weed) **We'd** sounds like **weed**.

wedding *noun* A marriage ceremony. **wed·ding** (**wed**-ing)

wedge

1. *noun* A piece of food, wood, metal, or plastic that is thin and pointed at one end and thick at the other, as in *a wedge of cake.*

2. *verb* To split, force apart, or hold in place with a wedge: *We had to wedge open the door with a pair of pliers.*

3. *verb* To squeeze or crowd into a limited space: *The six of us wedged ourselves into the tiny car.* **wedge** (wej)

▷ *verb* **wedging, wedged**

Wednesday *noun* The fourth day of the week, after Tuesday and before Thursday. **Wed·nes·day** (**wenz**-*day* or **wenz**-dee)

wee *adjective* Very small; tiny: *Aria has liked coffee*

webcam

since she was a wee child. **wee** (wee) **Wee** sounds like **we**.

weed

1. *noun* A plant that is seen as useless or harmful and growing where it is not wanted.

2. *verb* If you **weed** your garden, you pull unwanted plants out.

3. *verb* If you **weed** people or things **out**, you remove them from a group because they are useless, harmful, or not wanted: *The new coach promises to weed out the team's weaker players.* **weed** (weed)

Weed sounds like **we'd**. ▷ *verb* **weeding, weeded**

week *noun*

1. A period of seven days, usually measured from Sunday to Saturday.

2. The hours or days that a person works or spends in school each week: *My mother works a 40-hour week. The school week begins on Monday morning.* **week** (week)

Week sounds like **weak**.

weekday *noun* Any day of the week except Saturday or Sunday. **week·day** (**week**-*day*)

weekend *noun* The period of time from Friday night through Sunday night. **week·end** (**week**-*end*)

weekly

1. *adjective* Done, happening, or appearing once a week or every week, as in *a weekly visit* or *a weekly newspaper.*

2. *adverb* Once a week, or every week: *We do our grocery shopping weekly.*

3. *noun* A newspaper or magazine that is published once a week. ▷ *noun, plural* **weeklies** **week·ly** (**week**-lee)

weep *verb* To cry because you feel great sadness or emotion. **weep** (weep) ▷ *verb* **weeping, wept** (wept) ▷ *adjective* **weepy**

weevil *noun* A small beetle that is a pest to farmers because it eats and damages crops. **wee·vil** (**wee**-vuhl)

weigh *verb*

1. To measure how heavy or light someone or something is by using a scale.

2. To have a particular weight: *He weighs 75 pounds.*

3. To consider something carefully before deciding: *The jury weighed the evidence.*

4. If you are **weighed down**, you have too much to carry, do, or think about. **weigh** (way)

Weigh sounds like **way**. ▷ *verb* **weighing, weighed**

weight *noun*

1. A measurement that shows how heavy someone or something is: *Blue whales can be 100 tons in weight.*

2. The heaviness of someone or something: *You look like you've lost weight.*

3. A unit, such as the ounce, pound, or ton, that is used for measuring weight. *See the Measurements Tables in the* **Reference Section**.

4. A heavy object used to hold things down: *I used a stapler as a weight to keep the pages from blowing away.*

5. weights *noun, plural* Heavy objects that people lift as an exercise to make their muscles stronger: *Football players train by lifting weights.*

6. Something that causes you a lot of worry because you are responsible for it: *The weight of all this work is making me nervous and tense.*

7. Something that has the power to influence people: *His dad's opinion carries a lot of weight with him.*

weight (wate)

Weight sounds like **wait**.

weightless

weightless *adjective*

1. Having little or no weight: *Snowflakes are weightless.*

2. Free of the pull of gravity: *Astronauts are weightless in outer space.*

weight·less (wate-lis)

▷ *noun* **weightlessness** ▷ *adverb* **weightlessly**

weightlifter *noun* A person who lifts weights in competitions or for pleasure. **weight·lift·er** (wate-*lif*-tur) ▷ *noun* **weightlifting**

weird *adjective* Unusual or mysterious: *A weird thing happened to me the other day.* **weird** (weerd) ▷ *adjective* **weirder, weirdest** ▷ *noun* **weirdness** ▷ *adverb* **weirdly**

welcome

1. *verb* If you **welcome** someone, you greet the person in a warm and friendly way. ▷ *interjection* **welcome**

2. *adjective* If something is **welcome**, you are glad to have it because you need it: *After seven straight days of rain, the sun was very welcome.*

3. *verb* If you **welcome** something, you are glad to have it: *I would welcome a vacation right about now.*

4. *adjective* "You're **welcome**" is the polite response when someone says "Thank you."

wel·come (wel-kuhm)

▷ *verb* **welcoming, welcomed** ▷ *noun* **welcome**

▷ *adjective* **welcoming**

weld *verb* To join two pieces of metal or plastic by heating them until they are soft enough to be joined together. **weld** (weld) ▷ *verb* **welding, welded** ▷ *noun* **weld** ▷ *noun* **welder**

welfare *noun*

1. Someone's **welfare** is the person's health, happiness, and comfort: *For your own welfare, you should try to get more sleep.*

2. Money or other help given by a government to people who are in need.

wel·fare (wel-fair)

well

1. *adverb* If you do something **well**, you do it in a good, skillful, or satisfactory way: *Rino is doing well in school.*

2. *adverb* Completely and thoroughly: *Add a cup of milk and stir well.*

3. *adverb* Much; to a great extent: *It was well after midnight when the telephone rang.*

4. *adverb* In a close or familiar way: *I know them well.*

5. *adjective* Healthy: *Get well soon.*

6. *noun* A deep hole in the ground from which you can remove water, oil, or natural gas.

7. *interjection* You say **well** to show surprise or doubt: *Well, it's about time you showed up!*

well (wel)

we'll *contraction* A short form of *we will* or *we shall*: *We'll have to send Uncle Bill a birthday card tomorrow.* **we'll** (weel)

well-balanced *adjective*

1. Nicely or evenly balanced, as in *a well-balanced diet.*

2. A **well balanced** person is sensible and not easily upset.

well-behaved *adjective* Acting properly and with good manners, as in *well-behaved students.*

well-being *noun* A feeling of being healthy and happy: *A good diet gives you a sense of well-being.*

well-known *adjective* Known by many people; famous, as in *a well-known actor.*

well-off *adjective* If someone is **well-off**, he or she has a lot of money.

well-rounded *adjective* A **well-rounded** person has experience or interests in many different areas: *She* *is a well-rounded student, with excellent grades in all her classes.*

went *verb* A verb form that is used as the past tense of **go.** *Went* is actually the past tense of *wend,* an old-fashioned verb that is not used very much today. **went** (went)

wept *verb* The past tense and past participle of **weep.** **wept** (wept)

we're *contraction* A short form of *we are: We're about to begin a new chapter in our geography books.* **we're** (weer)

were *verb* The form of **be** used with *we, you,* or *they* or with plural nouns in the past tense: *We were thrilled to hear that our class won first prize in the recycling contest.* **were** (wur)

weren't *contraction* A short form of *were not: Weren't you at the party?* **weren't** (wurnt *or* **wur**-uhnt)

werewolf *noun* In stories and legends, a person, usually a man, who changes into a wolf when there is a full moon. **were·wolf** (**wair**-*wulf*)

Word History

Legends of human beings becoming wolves have existed for millennia, and stories of werewolves are told around the world. *Wer* is the Old English word for "man," and in the word **werewolf** it is combined with wolf. Other languages have combined words meaning "man" and "wolf" to form their own words or phrases for werewolves. An example is *hombre lobo* in Spanish.

west

1. *noun* One of the four main points of the compass. West is the direction in which the sun sets. ▷ *adverb* **west**

2. West *noun* Any area or region lying in this direction.

3. *adjective* Of or having to do with or existing in the west, as in *the west side of the street.* ▷ *adverb, adjective* **westerly** (**wes**-tur-lee)

west (west)

western

1. *adjective* In, of, toward, or from the west.

2. *adjective* Of or having to do with a western region, as in *western Canada.*

3. Western *adjective* Of or having to do with the West, as in *Western ranches.*

4. Western *or* **western** *noun* A cowboy movie or television show set in the western part of the United States, especially during the last half of the 19th century.

west·ern (**wes**-turn)

Western Hemisphere *noun* The half of the world west of the Atlantic Ocean. It includes North, Central, and South America and surrounding waters.

West Indies *noun, plural* A group of islands in the Western Hemisphere that separates the Caribbean Sea from the Atlantic Ocean. **West In·dies** (**in**-deez) ▷ *adjective* **West Indian**

westward *adverb* To or toward the west: *The afternoon sun shone in our faces as we drove westward.* **west·ward** (**west**-wurd) ▷ *adjective* **westward**

wet

1. *adjective* Covered with or full of liquid, especially water, as in *a wet cloth.*

2. *adjective* Not yet dry; still moist, as in *wet cement* or *wet paint.*

3. *adjective* Rainy: *This is the wet season.*

4. *verb* To make something wet: *Wet your hair before adding shampoo.* ▷ *verb* **wetting, wet** *or* **wetted** **wet** (wet)

▷ *adjective* **wetter, wettest**

wetland *or* **wetlands** *noun* Land where there is a lot of moisture in the soil. **wet·land** (**wet**-*land*) *or* **wet·lands** (**wet**-*landz*)

Wetlands

Swamps, bayous, and marshes are typical wetlands. Their soggy earth and shallow ponds house water-loving plants, as well as amphibians, fish, and reptiles. Many wetlands were destroyed by draining before their importance to the environment was understood. Wetlands help control floods by absorbing their waters. They buffer against soil erosion, lessen the effects of climate change, and provide a natural means of water purification. Several countries, including the United States, have now passed laws to protect them.

we've *contraction* A short form of *we have*: *We've finished the main course; now it's time for dessert.* **we've** (weev) **We've** sounds like **weave**.

whack

1. *noun (informal)* A hard, sharp hit or slap.

2. *noun (slang)* An attempt: *I'll take a whack at the math problem.*

3. *verb* To hit or slap something sharply: *Glen whacked the golf ball as hard as he could.* ▷ *verb* **whacking, whacked**

whack (wak)

whale

1. *noun* A large sea animal that looks like a fish but is actually a mammal that breathes air. Dolphins and porpoises are members of the whale family.

2. *verb* To hunt for whales. ▷ *verb* **whaling, whaled**

whale (wale)

whaler *noun*

1. Someone who hunts whales. ▷ *noun* **whaling**

2. A boat used for hunting whales.

whal·er (**way**-lur)

wharf *noun* A long platform, built along a shore, where boats and ships can load and unload. **wharf** (worf) ▷ *noun, plural* **wharves** (worvz) *or* **wharfs**

what

1. *pronoun* The word **what** is used in questions to get information about something or someone: *What is your favorite subject at school? What did you say?*

2. *pronoun* The thing or things that: *Show me what you got for your birthday.*

3. *adjective* The word **what** is used to stress a particular quality, such as how great, small, or strange something or someone is: *What a great song! What a jerk!*

4. *adverb* In which way; how: *What does it matter?*

5. *interjection* The word **what** is used to show surprise or anger: *What! That can't be true!*

what (waht *or* wuht)

whatever

1. *pronoun* Anything that: *Help yourself to whatever is in the fridge.*

2. *pronoun* No matter what: *Whatever you do, don't be late.*

3. *pronoun* Which thing or things; what: *Whatever made him think that I wouldn't mind if he took my notebook?*

4. *adjective* Any that: *Order whatever food you want.*

5. *adjective* Of any kind or type; at all: *I had nothing whatever to do with that.*

what·ev·er (waht-**ev**-ur *or* wuht-**ev**-ur)

what's *contraction* A short form of *what is* or *what has*: *What's the problem? What's happened to my dress?* **what's** (wahts *or* wuhts)

wheat *noun* A plant that produces grain that is used

killer whale

for making flour, pasta, and breakfast foods. **wheat** (weet)

wheatgrass *noun*

1. A kind of grass that is grown in the western United States for feeding animals.

2. Blades of grass from wheat, which are ground up very fine with water to make a healthy drink.

wheat·grass (**weet**-gras)

wheel

1. *noun* A round frame or object that turns on an axle. Wheels are used to move a vehicle or work machinery.

2. *noun* Anything that uses or is shaped like a wheel, as in *a spinning wheel* or *a steering wheel*.

3. *verb* To push something that has wheels: *He wheeled his shopping cart through the store.*

4. *verb* To turn: *The car wheeled and sped away.*

5. wheels *noun, plural (slang)* An automobile.

wheel (weel) ▷ *verb* **wheeling, wheeled**

wheelbarrow *noun* A small cart with one or two wheels at the front, often used to carry things around in yards or gardens. **wheel·bar·row** (**weel**-bar-oh)

wheelchair *noun* A chair on wheels for people who are not able to walk because they are sick, injured, or disabled. **wheel·chair** (**weel**-chair)

wheelie *noun (informal)* If you do a **wheelie** on a bicycle or motorcycle, you ride for a short time with the front wheel off the ground. **wheel·ie** (**wee**-lee)

wheelbarrow

wheeze *verb* To breathe with difficulty, making a whistling noise. People sometimes wheeze when they have asthma or a bad cold. **wheeze** (weez) ▷ *verb* **wheezing, wheezed** ▷ *noun* **wheeziness** ▷ *adjective* **wheezy**

whelk *noun* A large snail that lives in saltwater and has a spiral shell. **whelk** (welk)

when
  1. *adverb* The word **when** is used to ask about the time of an event: *When was Martin Luther King Jr. born?*
  2. *conjunction* At the time that: *My parents gave me a bicycle when I turned ten.*
  3. *conjunction* At any time; whenever: *When I swim, I get water in my ears.*
  4. *conjunction* Although; but: *I went out when I should have been studying.*
  5. *conjunction* Considering the fact that: *How can we meet the deadline when we have so much left to do?*
  when (wen)

whenever *conjunction* At any time: *Whenever we go out to eat, my brother always pays.* **when·ev·er** (*wen*-**ev**-ur)

where
  1. *adverb* The word **where** is used to ask about the position or place of someone or something: *Where are my keys?*
  2. *conjunction* In, at, or to the place that or in which: *She moved to New York, where she got a job as an editor. I'll go where you go.*
  3. *conjunction* In or at which place: *I went home, where I took a nap.*
  4. *pronoun* What place: *Where are you from?*
  where (wair)

whereabouts
  1. *adverb* Approximately where: *Whereabouts did you buy that hat?*
  2. *noun* The place where a person or thing is. **Whereabouts** can be used with a singular or plural verb: *Anyone with any information about Mr. Haag's whereabouts should contact the police.*
  where·a·bouts (**wair**-uh-*bouts*)

whereas *conjunction* On the other hand: *My wife likes the beach, whereas I like the mountains.* **where·as** (*wair*-**az**)

wherever *conjunction* In, at, or to any place or situation: *He carries an umbrella wherever he goes.* **wher·ev·er** (*wair*-**ev**-ur) ▷ *adverb* **wherever**

whether *conjunction*
  1. If: *I wonder whether we have enough money.*
  2. The word **whether** is used to indicate a choice between two things or possibilities: *Have you decided whether you'll go out or stay in?*

whelk

weth·er (we**TH**-ur)

whew *interjection* A word used to show relief, discomfort, or surprise: *Whew! Am I glad that my exams are finished.* **whew** (hwyoo)

whey *noun* The watery part of milk that separates when milk sours or when you make cheese. **whey** (way)

which
  1. *adjective* The word **which** is used to ask about a choice among a limited number of people or things: *Which game do you want to play?*
  2. *pronoun* What one or ones: *Which is yours?*
  3. *pronoun* The one or ones that: *I agree on which tastes best.*
  4. *conjunction* The one or ones mentioned; that: *Our car, which we bought several years ago, has never given us trouble.*
  which (wich)

whichever
  1. *pronoun, adjective* Any one or ones: *Buy whichever you want. Read whichever book interests you.*
  2. *pronoun, adjective* No matter which: *Whichever you buy is fine with me. Whichever book you read, you'll like it.*
  which·ev·er (*wich*-**ev**-ur)

whiff *noun*
  1. A light puff of air or smoke.
  2. A faint smell in the air: *Enrique caught a whiff of strawberries.*
  whiff (wif) ▷ *verb* **whiff**

while
  1. *noun* A period of time: *It was a long while before I spoke to him again.*
  2. *conjunction* During the time that: *Can you get me a glass of water while you're up?*
  3. *conjunction* Although: *While I usually do well in math, I think I failed this test.*
  4. *conjunction* Used to contrast two different people, things, or situations: *My brother likes dogs, while I prefer cats.*
  5. *verb* To pass or spend time in a pleasant or relaxed way: *We whiled away the morning reading the Sunday newspaper.* ▷ *verb* **whiling, whiled** **while** (wile)

whim *noun* A sudden wish to do or have something, especially when it seems unnecessary or silly: *I drove all the way to Florida on a whim.* **whim** (wim)

whimper *verb* To make quiet, crying noises: *The puppy whimpered when I stopped petting him.* **whim·per** (**wim**-pur) ▷ *verb* **whimpering, whimpered** ▷ *noun* **whimper**

whine *verb*

1. To complain about something in an annoying way: *Jerry whines when he doesn't get his way.* ▷ *noun* **whiner**

2. To make a long, high sound that is sad or unpleasant: *The wind whined in the chimney.* **whine** (wine)

▷ *verb* **whining, whined**

whinny *verb* If a horse **whinnies,** it makes a gentle, high-pitched sound. **whin·ny** (**win**-ee) ▷ *verb* **whinnied, whinnying** ▷ *noun* **whinny** ▷ *noun, plural* **whinnies**

whip

1. *noun* A long piece of rope or leather on a handle, used especially for hitting horses and cattle. ▷ *verb* **whip**

2. *verb* To move, pull, or take something suddenly: *The man whipped out one of his business cards and handed it to me.*

3. *verb* (*informal*) To defeat an opponent badly: *Our team whipped the Tigers last week.*

4. *verb* To beat something, such as eggs or cream, until it is stiff. **whip** (wip)

▷ *verb* **whipping, whipped**

whippoorwill *noun* A brown North American bird with brown, gray, and black spots. Its call sounds very much like its name. **whip·poor·will** (**wip**-uhr-*wil*)

whir

1. *verb* To move, fly, or operate with a buzzing or humming sound: *The dragonfly whirred around the room.* ▷ *verb* **whirring, whirred**

2. *noun* A buzzing or humming sound, as in *the whir of a helicopter.* **whir** (wur)

whirl

1. *verb* To move around quickly in a circle, or to make someone or something do this: *Snow whirled across the trail.*

2. *verb* To turn around quickly: *She whirled around, but there was no one there.*

3. *noun* Fast or confused activity and movement: *There was a whirl of activity just before the party.*

4. (*informal*) If you **give** something **a whirl,** you try it out to see if you like it. **whirl** (wurl)

▷ *verb* **whirling, whirled**

whirlpool *noun*

1. A powerful current of water that moves quickly in a circle and pulls floating objects toward its center.

2. A special bathtub in which strong currents of hot water move in circles around all or part of the body. Also known as a *whirlpool bath.* **whirl·pool** (**wurl**-*pool*)

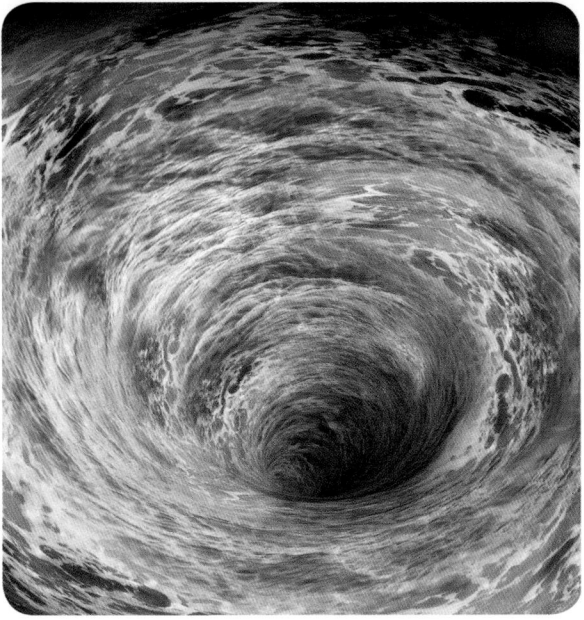

whirlpool

whirlwind

1. *noun* A wind that rotates in a tall column, smaller and less violent than a tornado.

2. *adjective* Happening very quickly, as in *a whirlwind romance.* **whirl·wind** (**wurl**-*wind*)

whisk

1. *noun* A kitchen tool consisting of loops of wire attached to a handle. ▷ *verb* **whisk**

2. *verb* To move something or someone quickly or suddenly: *The man was whisked away by security officials.*

3. *verb* To brush or remove something with a quick, sweeping motion: *He whisked the crumbs off the table.* **whisk** (wisk)

▷ *verb* **whisking, whisked**

whisker *noun*

1. One of the long, stiff hairs near the mouth of some animals, such as cats and rabbits.

2. One of the hairs that grows on a man's face, especially on the cheeks and jaw. **whisk·er** (**wis**-kur)

whiskey *or* **whisky** *noun* A strong alcoholic drink made from barley, corn, or rye. **whis·key** *or* **whis·ky** (**wis**-kee) ▷ *noun, plural* **whiskeys** *or* **whiskies**

whisper

1. *verb* To talk very quietly or softly: *I whispered a question to the girl in the next row.* ▷ *verb* **whispering, whispered** ▷ *noun* **whisper**

2. *noun* A soft rustling sound, as in *the whisper of leaves in the breeze.* ▷ *verb* **whisper** **whis·per** (**wis**-pur)

whistle

1. *verb* To make a high, loud sound by blowing air through your lips: *The dog came running when his master whistled.*

2. *verb* To make a whistling sound: *The kettle will whistle when the water is boiling.*

3. *verb* To cause a whistling sound by moving very fast: *The wind whistled through the trees.*

4. *noun* An instrument that makes a loud, shrill sound when you blow into it.

5. *noun* A whistling sound made by the lips or by a whistle: *I heard a whistle and looked up to see my friend.*

whis·tle (**wis**-uhl)

▷ *verb* **whistling, whistled**

whistle

white

1. *noun* The lightest color; the color of snow or milk. ▷ *adjective* **white**

2. *noun* The **white** of an egg is the clear part around the yolk.

3. *adjective* Light in color, as in *white meat of a chicken.*

4. *adjective* Belonging to or related to the race of people with light-colored skin.

5. *adjective* Looking pale, especially because you are sick or frightened: *Her face was white with fear.*

6. *adjective* Pale gray or silver: *My grandfather has white hair.* ▷ *adjective* **whiter, whitest**

white (wite)

white blood cell *noun* A colorless blood cell that helps to protect the body against infection.

whiteboard *noun* A white surface, similar to a blackboard, that can be written on with special markers and wiped clean afterward. **white·board** (wite-*bord*)

White House *noun*

1. The official home of the president of the United States, located at 1600 Pennsylvania Avenue in Washington, DC.

2. The office or power of the president of the United States: *The White House issued a statement about the president's health.*

whiten *verb* To make white or become white: *You should use bleach to whiten your shirt.* **whit·en** (**wye**-tuhn) ▷ *verb* **whitening, whitened**

white noise *noun*

1. A mixture of sound waves that creates a noise used to cover annoying or distracting sounds.

2. Background noise from appliances, such as air conditioners and fans.

whitewash

1. *noun* A mixture of white powder and water used for painting walls and wooden fences white.

2. *noun* Something that hides a crime or wrong action:

The report about the missing funds is a whitewash.

3. *verb* To hide or disguise wrongdoing: *One newspaper complained that the report whitewashed the governor's ethical mistakes.*

4. *verb* To make it seem as if white people behaved better than they did, ignoring their wrongdoing against others: *The plantation tour whitewashes the evils of slavery.*

white·wash (**wite**-*wahsh*)

▷ *verb* **whitewashing, whitewashed**

whittle *verb*

1. To cut or shave small pieces from wood or soap with a knife.

2. To make or carve something by doing this: *Grandpa whittled a ship out of a scrap of kindling.*

3. whittle away To reduce little by little: *Music downloads are whittling away at my allowance.*

whit·tle (**wit**-uhl)

▷ *verb* **whittling, whittled** ▷ *noun* **whittling**

whiz *or* whizz

1. *verb* To move very quickly, often with a buzzing sound: *Cars and trucks whizzed by.* ▷ *verb* **whizzes, whizzing, whizzed**

2. *noun* (*slang*) A person who has great skill or ability in a particular field or activity, as in *a math whiz.* ▷ *noun, plural* **whizzes**

whiz *or* **whizz** (wiz)

White House

The White House is the president's home. But it also has a symbolic meaning: Around the world, it stands for the president, the president's administration, and the United States.

The president heads the US government's executive branch, and serves as the country's head of state and the commander in chief of the nation's armed forces.

who *pronoun*

1. The word **who** is used to ask questions about people, for example, to find out a person's name: *Who is that woman talking on the telephone?*

2. The word **who** is used to show which person or people you are talking about or to give more information about a person or persons: *The woman who lives next door is our good friend.* **who** (hoo)

who'd *contraction* A short form of *who would* or *who had*: *I needed to talk to someone who'd help me.* **who'd** (hood)

whoever *pronoun*

1. Any person at all, or no matter which person: *Whoever took my bicycle better bring it back.*

2. Who: *Whoever would have guessed we would run into each other after all these years?* **who·ev·er** (*hoo*-ev-ur)

whole

1. *adjective* Entire or total; all of: *We don't have to go back to school for a whole week. The whole class applauded.*

2. *adjective* Complete, with nothing missing: *I have the whole series, all 25 books.*

3. *noun* The entire thing, including all of its parts: *Four quarters make a whole.*

4. on the whole In general: *On the whole I thought the book was good.*

5. as a whole Considering all the parts of something together: *The project should be done by the class as a whole.* **whole** (hole)

Whole sounds like **hole**.

whole number *noun* Any of the set of numbers beginning with 0 and continuing with each number being one more than the number before it. The whole numbers are 0, 1, 2, 3, 4 . . . They go on and on without end. Numbers with fractions are not whole numbers.

wholesale

1. *adverb* When storekeepers buy things **wholesale**, they buy them cheaply in large quantities in order to sell them at a profit. ▷ *adjective* **wholesale** ▷ *noun* **wholesaler**

2. *adjective* Affecting a large number of things or people: *The early 1900s saw the wholesale extinction of the passenger pigeon.* **whole·sale** (hole-*sale*)

wholesome *adjective*

1. Good for your health, as in *wholesome food.*

2. Considered to have a good moral influence: *It was a fun night of wholesome entertainment.* **whole·some** (hole-suhm)

whole wheat *adjective* Made from the entire grain of wheat, as in *whole wheat bread.*

who'll *contraction* A short form of *who will* or *who shall*: *Who'll go next?* **who'll** (hool)

wholly *adverb* Completely: *When Ira got back from the army, he was a wholly different person.* **whol·ly** (**hoh**-lee) **Wholly** sounds like **holy**.

whom *pronoun* What or which person or people. *Whom* is the form of the pronoun *who* when it is the object of a verb or preposition. It is often used in formal speech and writing: *To whom am I speaking? I don't know whom to call. For whom are you buying this gift?* **whom** (hoom)

whomever *pronoun* The form of **whoever** used as the object of a verb or preposition: *Give it to whomever you want.* **whom·ev·er** (hoom-ev-ur)

whoop *noun* A loud cry or shout, as in *a whoop of delight.* **whoop** (hoop *or* hup *or* wup) ▷ *verb* **whoop**

whooping cough *noun* An infectious disease, especially affecting children, that makes them cough violently and have trouble breathing. **whoop·ing cough** (**hoo**-ping)

whooping crane *noun* A large, white waterbird with a red face and black tips on its wings. Whooping cranes live in Canada and the United States. There are very few of them left.

who's *contraction* A short form of *who is* or *who has*: *Who's Matthew's favorite sports star?* **who's** (hooz) **Who's** sounds like **whose**.

whose *pronoun*

1. The word **whose** is used to ask which person or people something belongs to: *Whose coat is this?*

2. The word **whose** is used to indicate which person or thing you are talking about: *That's the man whose wife is my teacher.* **whose** (hooz)

Whose sounds like **who's**.

whooping cranes

why

1. *adverb* The word **why** is used to ask for the reason for something: *Why didn't you call me?*

2. *conjunction* The reason for which: *That is why I'm mad at him.*

3. *interjection* The word **why** is used to show mild surprise or to show that a person is pausing to think: *Why, I guess you're right.*

why (wye)

wick *noun* The twisted cord in a candle, an oil lamp, or a lighter that soaks up the fuel and burns when lit. **wick** (wik)

wicked *adjective* Evil or cruel: *The wicked witch cast a spell on the poor boy.* **wick·ed** (**wik**-id) ▷ *noun* **wickedness** ▷ *adverb* **wickedly**

wicker *noun* Thin twigs or branches, usually from a willow tree, that are bent and woven to make baskets and furniture. **wick·er** (**wik**-ur) ▷ *adjective* **wicker**

wicket *noun* One of several small wire arches through which balls are hit in croquet. **wick·et** (**wik**-it)

wide

1. *adjective* Large from side to side; broad: *Moscow is a city of wide streets.* ▷ *verb* **widen** (**wye**-duhn)

2. *adjective* Having a certain distance from one side to the other or from edge to edge: *The room is 14 feet wide.*

3. *adjective* Involving or including a large number of people or things: *In my garden I grow a wide variety of flowers.*

4. *adjective* Completely open, as in *wide eyes.*

5. *adverb* Not close to: *The batter swung wide of the ball.*

6. *adverb* Over a large area: *We traveled far and wide.*

7. *adverb* To the full extent: *The dentist told me to open my mouth wide.*

wide (wide)

▷ *adjective* **wider, widest** ▷ *adverb* **widely**

widespread *adjective*

1. Happening or existing in many places or among many people: *There is widespread support among parents for a shorter summer vacation.*

2. Fully open: *I greeted my aunt with widespread arms.*

wide·spread (**wide**-spred)

widow *noun* A woman whose husband has died and who has not married again. **wid·ow** (**wid**-oh) ▷ *adjective* **widowed**

widower *noun* A man whose wife has died and who has not married again. **wid·ow·er** (**wid**-oh-ur) ▷ *adjective* **widowed**

width *noun* The distance from one side of something to the other; breadth: *What is the width of this door?* **width** (width)

wiener *noun* A long, thin, pink sausage; the kind of sausage used to make a hot dog. **wie·ner** (**wee**-nur)

Word History

Wieners are named after the city in Austria where they were first made. German speakers based the word on Wien, the German name for Vienna. The letter *w* is pronounced like a *v* in German, so *Wiener* sounds like "veen-uhr" in German. Interestingly, another of America's favorite foods gets its name from a European city. Hamburgers get their name from Hamburg, Germany.

wife *noun* A female partner in a marriage, or any married woman. **wife** (wife) ▷ *noun, plural* **wives** (wivez)

Wi-Fi *noun* A trademark for the standard kind of wireless signal that allows computers and other devices to connect to the internet where there is a signal available. **Wi-Fi** (**wye**-**fye**)

wig *noun* A covering of real or artificial hair made to be worn on someone's head. **wig** (wig)

wiggle *verb* To make short, quick movements from side to side or up and down, or to move something in this way. **wig·gle** (**wig**-uhl) ▷ *verb* **wiggling, wiggled** ▷ *noun* **wiggle** ▷ *noun* **wiggler** ▷ *adjective* **wiggly**

wigwam *noun* A hut made of poles and covered with bark or animal skins. Some Native American tribes once lived in wigwams. **wig·wam** (**wig**-*wahm*)

wiki *noun* A website that grows by allowing users to change or add knowledge, information, and images. **wi·ki** (**wik**-ee)

wicker basket

Word History

The American inventor of the **wiki** named the program for its speed. Ward Cunningham, a computer scientist, put the wiki that he had created on a website in 1995, calling it WikiWikiWeb. He based the name on the Hawaiian term *wikiwiki,* meaning "very quick," from *wiki,* the Hawaiian word for "quick."

wild

1. *adjective* Living in natural conditions and not controlled or cared for by humans, as in *wild animals*.
2. *adjective* Not controlled, or not disciplined, as in *wild children*.
3. *adjective* Overcome with an emotion such as grief, anger, or happiness: *My dad went wild when we won the game.*
4. *adjective* Crazy, fantastic, or reckless: *He had a wild plan for how to get rich overnight.*
5. the wild *noun* An area that has been left in its natural state; wilderness: *Our cell phones stopped working once we were out in the wild.*
wild (wilde)
▷ *adjective* **wilder, wildest** ▷ *noun* **wildness**
▷ *adverb* **wildly**

wildcat *noun* Any of several wild members of the cat family that are small or medium in size, including the bobcat, ocelot, and lynx. **wild·cat** (**wilde**-*kat*)

wilderness *noun* An area of wild land where no people live, such as a forest or desert. **wil·der·ness** (**wil**-dur-nis) ▷ *noun, plural* **wildernesses**

wildflower *noun* Any flower of a plant that grows in a field, woods, or any wild area without the help of human beings. **wild·flow·er** (**wilde**-*flou*-ur)

wildflowers

wildlife *noun* Wild animals living in their natural environment. **wild·life** (**wilde**-*life*)

will¹ *verb* A helping verb that is used in the following ways:
1. To show that something is going to take place or exist in the future: *We will leave tonight.*
2. To show a possible action that depends on something that could happen in the future: *I will* give you a ride to school if you miss the bus.
3. To ask someone to do something: *Will you answer the phone, please?*
4. To give an order or say what must happen or not happen: *Students will report to the auditorium at 2 p.m.*
5. To say what is true or likely to happen in a particular situation: *This recipe will serve six people.*
will (wil)

will²
1. *noun* A legal document that contains instructions stating what should happen to someone's property and money when the person dies.
2. *verb* To leave money, property, or possessions to someone still living after you die: *Her father willed her some land in Hawaii.*
3. *noun* The power to choose or control what you will and will not do: *Do you have the will to go on a strict diet?*
4. *noun* Strong purpose; determination: *Andy has an incredible will to win.*
5. *verb* To make something happen by a very strong determination.
will (wil)
▷ *verb* **willing, willed**

willful *adjective*
1. Deliberate, as in *willful damage*. ▷ *adjective* **willfully**
2. Someone who is **willful** is determined to have his or her own way.
will·ful (**wil**-fuhl)
▷ *noun* **willfulness**

willing *adjective* Ready and eager to offer help or do what is asked: *Jed is willing to do whatever it takes to win.* **will·ing** (**wil**-ing) ▷ *noun* **willingness** ▷ *adverb* **willingly**

willow *noun* A tree with narrow leaves and thin branches that bend easily. Willows are often found near water. **wil·low** (**wil**-oh)

wilt *verb*
1. If a plant **wilts**, it begins to bend over because it is dying or needs water.
2. To become tired because you are hot, have no energy, or need food.
wilt (wilt)
▷ *verb* **wilting, wilted**

wimp *noun* (informal) A weak or cowardly person. **wimp** (wimp) ▷ *adjective* **wimpy**

win *verb*
1. To be the best or most successful in a competition, such as a game or an election: *If you want to win, you have to take chances. The Yankees won the World Series in 2009.* ▷ *noun* **win** ▷ *noun* **winner**
2. To get something as a prize: *Jim won a trophy in the spelling bee.*

wind farm

3. To gain something good that you want or deserve: *Liza is starting to win some recognition for her drawing skills.* **win** (win) ▷ *verb* **winning, won**

wince *verb* To make a sudden expression on your face because you are in pain, embarrassed, or disgusted: *Logan winced when the teacher corrected him in front of the whole class.* **wince** (wins) ▷ *verb* **wincing, winced** ▷ *noun* **wince**

winch *noun* A machine that lifts or pulls heavy objects. A winch is made up of cable wound around a rotating drum. **winch** (winch) ▷ *noun, plural* **winches** ▷ *verb* **winch**

wind
1. (wind) *noun* Moving air. ▷ *adjective* **windy**
2. (wind) *noun* Breath, or the ability to breathe: *That tackle really knocked the wind out of the quarterback.* ▷ *verb* **wind**
3. (winde) *verb* To wrap or twist something around something else: *Wind this scarf around your neck before you go outside.*
4. (winde) *verb* To have a series of turns and curves: *The river winds through a beautiful valley.*
5. (winde) *verb* To turn a knob or handle around several times in order to make a machine start working: *Be sure to wind the clock so that it keeps time correctly.*
6. wind up (winde) *verb* (*slang*) If you **wind** something **up**, you finish it: *It's time to start winding up this meeting.* ▷ *noun* **windup**
wind
▷ *verb* **winding, wound** (wound)

windbreaker *noun* A light jacket that protects you from the wind. **wind·break·er** (wind-*bray*-kur)

wind-chill factor *noun* A measurement given in degrees that reports the combined effect of low temperature and wind speed on the human body. Also known as the *chill factor* or the *wind-chill index.*

winded *adjective* If you are **winded**, you have difficulty breathing because of exercise or a sudden blow to the stomach: *Claire was winded after the ten-mile run.* **wind·ed** (**win**-did)

windfall *noun*
1. A sudden piece of good news or good luck that you get unexpectedly, especially an amount of money: *The company's hot new toy produced a windfall.*
2. Fruit that has fallen off a tree.
wind·fall (**wind**-*fawl*)

wind farm *noun* A windy place with a lot of wind turbines or windmills for generating electricity.

wind instrument *noun* A musical instrument, such as a flute, trumpet, or harmonica, played by blowing.

windmill *noun* A structure with long blades that turn in the wind. This produces power that is used to grind grain into flour, pump water, or generate electricity. **wind·mill** (**wind**-*mil*)

window *noun*
1. An opening, especially in the wall of a building or vehicle, that lets in air and light. Windows are usually covered with a sheet of glass.
2. A single sheet of glass in a window: *I hit a long fly ball that broke my neighbor's window.*
3. The viewing space on a computer screen in which you can see information and work with a program.
win·dow (**win**-doh)

Word History

Window is based on two old Norwegian words, *vindr,* meaning "wind," and *auga,* meaning "eye." Appropriately, a window is an "eye on the wind," allowing light and air into a room.

windowpane *noun* A single sheet or section of glass in a window. **win·dow·pane** (**win**-doh-*pane*)

window-shop *verb* To look at items in store windows but not buy anything: *Wilma and her mom liked to window-shop for expensive clothing.* ▷ *verb* **window-shopping, window-shopped**

windpipe *noun* The tube that connects the lungs with the throat and carries air for breathing. **wind·pipe** (**wind**-*pipe*)

wind shear *noun* A sudden change in wind speed and direction that is caused by a downward flow of cool air. **Wind shears** occur during thunderstorms. They can cause aircraft to lose altitude quickly.

a b c d e f g h i j k l m n o p q r s t u v **w** x y z

windshield *noun* The large window in the front of a motor vehicle that protects the driver and passengers from the wind. **wind·shield** (**wind**-*sheeld*)

windsurfing *noun* The sport of sailing across water by standing on a surfboard and holding and moving a large sail attached to the board. **wind·surf·ing** (**wind**-*sur*-fing) ▷ *noun* **windsurfer**

windswept *adjective* Exposed to strong winds or blown by the wind. **wind·swept** (**wind**-*swept*)

wine *noun* An alcoholic drink made from the juice of grapes that has been allowed to ferment. **wine** (wine)

wing *noun*
1. One of the parts of a bird's, insect's, or bat's body that it uses in order to fly.
2. A structure that sticks out of the side of an aircraft that makes it able to fly.
3. An outer part or extension of a building: *The museum's new wing will open next month.*
4. The far left or right side of a sports field, or a person who plays in that area in sports such as soccer or hockey: *Milner passed the ball to the left wing.*
5. wings *noun, plural* The sides of a theater stage that cannot be seen by the audience.
wing (wing)

wingspan *noun* The distance between one end of a wing of a bird or an aircraft and the other. **wing·span** (**wing**-*span*)

wink
1. *verb* To close one eye quickly as a signal or a friendly gesture: *I winked at Tania from across the room.* ▷ *verb* **winking, winked** ▷ *noun* **wink**
2. *noun* A very short time; an instant: *I'll be ready in a wink.*
3. If you **do not sleep a wink**, you do not sleep at all.
wink (wingk)

wingspan

winner *noun*
1. A person, a team, an animal, or a thing that wins a contest.
2. (*informal*) A person, an idea, or a plan that seems likely to succeed: *We think your new invention is a winner.*
win·ner (**win**-*ur*)

winning
1. *adjective* Successful or victorious: *Our softball team had its first winning season this year.*
2. *adjective* Pleasing, attractive, or charming: *You have a winning smile.*
3. winnings *noun, plural* Something that is won in a game or competition, especially money.
win·ning (**win**-*ing*)

winter *noun* The season between fall and spring, when the weather is coldest. **win·ter** (**win**-*tur*) ▷ *adjective* **wintry**

wintergreen *noun* A low evergreen plant with white flowers and red berries. Its leaves produce a minty oil used in medicines and flavorings. **win·ter·green** (**win**-*tur*-*green*) ▷ *adjective* **wintergreen**

wipe *verb*
1. To clean or dry something by rubbing: *Wipe the table with a sponge. Wipe your feet before you come in here.*
2. To clear or remove something by rubbing: *Wipe the lipstick off your cheek.*
3. wipe out To destroy something completely: *A hurricane wiped out the entire neighborhood.*
wipe (wipe)
▷ *verb* **wiping, wiped**

wire
1. *noun* A long, thin, flexible thread of metal. Wire can be used to pull or support things or to conduct an electrical current.
2. *verb* To fasten things together with a piece of wire.
3. *verb* To install or put in wires for electricity or data transfer: *The house was so old it had never been wired for electricity.*
wire (wire *or* **wye**-*ur*)
▷ *verb* **wiring, wired** ▷ *noun* **wiring**

wireless *adjective* Not requiring wires to send or receive data or to work properly, as in *wireless networking.* **wire·less** (**wire**-*lis*)

wiry *adjective*
1. Strong and stiff, as in *wiry hair.*
2. A **wiry** person is thin but strong.
wir·y (**wye**-*ree*)
▷ *adjective* **wirier, wiriest**

wisdom *noun* Knowledge, experience, and good judgment. **wis·dom** (**wiz**-*duhm*)

wisdom tooth *noun* Any of the four teeth at the back of your mouth that come in last, usually when you are a young adult. ▷ *noun, plural* **wisdom teeth**

wise *adjective* Having or showing good judgment and intelligence: *A wise old man gave me some excellent advice. You made a wise decision.* **wise** (wize)
▷ *adjective* **wiser, wisest** ▷ *adverb* **wisely**

wish
1. *verb* To want something very much: *I wish I could go home now.*
2. *verb* To hope for something for another person: *I wish you good luck in your game tomorrow.*
3. *noun* A strong desire for something: *The old man's dying wish was to see his son again.* ▷ *noun, plural* **wishes**
4. Something that you want or that you want to have

happen: *My wish is to one day visit Australia.*

5. The act of wanting something and hoping you will get it or that it will happen: *Blow out your candles and make a wish!*

wish (wish)

▷ *verb* **wishes, wishing, wished**

wishbone *noun* A bone shaped like a Y in front of the breastbone of most birds. **wish·bone** (**wish**-*bohn*)

wisp *noun* A long, thin piece or streak of something, as in *a wisp of fog.* **wisp** (wisp) ▷ *adjective* **wispy**

wisteria *noun* A climbing vine plant with bunches of blue, white, pink, or purple flowers that hang down. **wis·te·ri·a** (wi-**steer**-ee-uh)

wit *noun*

1. The ability to say things that are clever and funny: *Lisa is known for her wit.*

2. Someone who has the ability to say clever and funny things.

3. wits *noun, plural* The ability to think quickly and make good decisions: *The detective used his wits to solve crimes.* **wit** (wit)

witch *noun* A person, especially a woman, believed by some people to have magic powers. **witch** (wich) ▷ *noun, plural* **witches** ▷ *adjective* **witchy**

with *preposition*

1. In the company or care of: *Come with me. You can leave the package with me.*

2. Having: *I'm looking for someone with a good sense of humor.*

3. In a way that shows: *She dressed with care.*

4. In addition to: *We had chicken with rice.*

5. In the opinion of: *It's OK with me.*

6. By using: *You cut meat with a knife.*

7. In regard to: *Are you happy with your grades?*

8. Against: *The brothers fought with each other constantly.*

9. In support of: *Are you with me on this issue?* **with** (wiTH *or* with)

withdraw *verb*

1. To take away or remove something: *Yuko went to the bank to withdraw some money. The political party withdrew its support for the government.*

2. To go away or drop out of an event: *The soldiers withdrew from the town.* **with·draw** (wiTH-**draw** *or* with-**draw**) ▷ *verb* **withdrawing, withdrew, withdrawn** ▷ *noun* **withdrawal** (wiTH-**draw**-uhl)

withdrawn *adjective* Very shy and quiet. **with·drawn** (wiTH-**drawn** *or* with-**drawn**)

wither *verb* To dry up or become smaller and weaker: *In winter, some plants normally wither and die.* **with·er** (wiTH-ur) ▷ *verb* **withering, withered**

withhold *verb* To keep something back, or to refuse to give something to someone: *She tried to withhold her anger. She threatened to withhold the rent until the landlord fixed her sink.* **with·hold** (with-**hohld** *or* wiTH-**hohld**) ▷ *verb* **withholding, withheld**

within *preposition*

1. Inside: *I could hear a dog barking from within the house.* ▷ *adverb* **within**

2. Not beyond the limits of: *I want you back within the next ten minutes.* **with·in** (wiTH-**in** *or* with-**in**)

without *preposition*

1. Not having something: *I completed the project without help.*

2. Not being with someone or something: *My parents went on vacation without me.*

3. In a way that avoids something: *We ate dinner without speaking.* **with·out** (wiTH-**out** *or* with-**out**)

withstand *verb* To stand strongly against something: *The tent is able to withstand high winds.* **with·stand** (with-**stand** *or* wiTH-**stand**) ▷ *verb* **withstanding, withstood**

witness *noun*

1. A person who has seen or heard something: *I was a witness to the accident.*

2. A person who gives evidence in a court of law: *The lawyer called her next witness.*

3. A person who signs an official paper to prove that he or she watched a contract, will, or other legal document being signed. **wit·ness** (**wit**-nis) ▷ *noun, plural* **witnesses** ▷ *verb* **witness**

witty *adjective* Funny and clever, as in *a witty remark.* **wit·ty** (**wit**-ee) ▷ *adjective* **wittier, wittiest** ▷ *adverb* **wittily** (**wit**-uh-lee)

wives *noun, plural* The plural of **wife**. **wives** (wyvez)

wizard *noun*

1. A person, especially a man, believed to have magical powers.

2. Someone who is extremely good at doing something: *My dad is a wizard in the kitchen.*

3. A small computer program that takes you through a task step by step to make it easier. **wiz·ard** (**wiz**-urd)

wizened *adjective* Wrinkled or shriveled, especially from age: *The wizened old sorcerer waved his wand and disappeared.* **wiz·ened** (**wiz**-uhnd)

wishbone

wobble *verb* To move from side to side in an unsteady way, or to make something do this: *The boat wobbled dangerously.* **wob·ble** (**wah**-buhl) ▷ *verb* **wobbling, wobbled** ▷ *adjective* **wobbly**

woe *noun* Great sadness and suffering: *Illness can bring trouble and woe to families.* **woe** (woh) ▷ *adjective* **woeful** ▷ *adverb* **woefully**

wok *noun* A large pan shaped like a bowl that is used especially for cooking Asian food. **wok** (wahk)

woke *verb* The past tense of **wake.** **woke** (woke)

woken *verb* The past participle of **wake.** **woken** (**wo**-kin)

wolf
1. *noun* A wild mammal that is related to the dog and hunts for food in a group. ▷ *noun, plural* **wolves** (wulvz)
2. *verb* If you **wolf** something **down**, you eat it quickly: *The hungry child wolfed down his dinner.* ▷ *verb* **wolfing, wolfed**
wolf (wulf)

wolverine *noun* A powerfully built mammal, related to the weasel, with dark brown fur and a long, bushy tail. **wol·ver·ine** (**wul**-vuh-*reen*)

woman *noun* An adult female human being. **wom·an** (**wum**-uhn) ▷ *noun, plural* **women** (**wim**-in) ▷ *adverb* **womanly**

womanhood *noun*
1. The time or state of being a female adult: *My mom says that entering womanhood brings with it many responsibilities.*
2. Women as a group: *I stand before you representing all of American womanhood.*
wom·an·hood (**wum**-uhn-*hud*)

womb *noun* The organ in female mammals where babies grow before they are born; the uterus. **womb** (woom)

wombat *noun* An Australian animal that looks like a small bear. **wom·bat** (**wahm**-*bat*)

won *verb* The past tense and past participle of **win**: *We have won the game.* **won** (wuhn) **Won** sounds like **one.**

wonder
1. *verb* To want to know or learn more about something: *I wonder why they're late.*
2. *verb* To be surprised or impressed by something: *We wondered at Linda's ability to hit the bull's-eye every time.*

wolverine

3. *noun* Something so remarkable or impressive that it causes surprise or amazement: *The Grand Canyon is one of the natural wonders of the world.*
4. *noun* The feeling caused by something remarkable or impressive: *I listened in wonder as my grandmother told me about the day she met Martin Luther King Jr.*
won·der (**wuhn**-dur) ▷ *verb* **wondering, wondered**

wonderful *adjective*
1. Very good; excellent, as in *a wonderful teacher.*
2. Remarkable and making you feel admiration: *The porpoise is a wonderful and intelligent creature.*
won·der·ful (**wuhn**-dur-*fuhl*) ▷ *adverb* **wonderfully**

Synonyms

Wonderful originally described something that caused someone to be filled with awe or wonder. Now it also refers to anything that is unusually good: *That was a wonderful party. Tony is a wonderful human being.*

- -

■ **Interesting** describes something that is intriguing or captures someone's attention: *The short story had an interesting plot and unforgettable characters.*

■ **Fascinating** describes something so interesting that you want to know more about it: *Delia thinks the idea of space travel is fascinating.*

■ **Delightful** means highly pleasing: *My friend Jan has a delightful personality.*

■ **Spectacular** means dramatic and sensational: *After the ball game we watched a spectacular fireworks display.*

■ **Astonishing** describes something that causes great wonder or surprise: *We received the astonishing news that we won the contest!*

wondrous *adjective* Causing a feeling of wonder and amazement: *The universe is a wondrous place of physical processes that we are only just beginning to understand.* **won·drous** (**wuhn**-druhs) ▷ *noun* **wondrousness** ▷ *adverb* **wondrously**

won't *contraction* A short form of *will not*: *You won't be sorry if you vote for Joe for class president.* **won't** (wohnt)

wood *noun*
1. The hard substance that the trunk and branches of trees are made of, often used for construction or to

make furniture. ▷ *adjective* **wooden**

2. woods *noun, plural* An area of land with many trees growing close together; a forest. ▷ *adjective* **wooded**

wood (wud)

Wood sounds like **would**.

woodchuck *noun* A name used in some areas for a **groundhog**. **wood·chuck** (**wud**-*chuhk*)

Word History

In the 17th century, settlers in the American colonies learned a name for the **woodchuck** from the Native Americans. We do not know exactly what the word was, but it was probably related to the word *wuchak* in the Native American language called Cree. When people try to spell a new word, they sometimes think it sounds like one they already know. So the settlers spelled the name as "woodchuck," because they already knew the word *wood*.

woodland *noun* Land covered mainly by trees; a forest. **wood·land** (**wud**-*land*)

woodpecker *noun* Any of a number of birds that live in forests throughout the world. Woodpeckers have strong, pointed bills, which they use to drill holes in trees to get insects. **wood·peck·er** (**wud**-*pek*-ur)

woodwind *adjective* The **woodwind** section of an orchestra is made up of wind instruments that were originally made of wood, such as the flute, clarinet, and oboe. **wood·wind** (**wud**-*wind*) ▷ *noun* **woodwind**

woodwork *noun* Things made out of wood, especially wooden parts inside a house, such as window frames, doors, and moldings. **wood·work** (**wud**-*wurk*) ▷ *noun* **woodworker**

wool *noun*

1. The soft, thick, curly hair of sheep and certain other animals, such as the llama and alpaca. Wool is spun into yarn, which is used to make fabric.

2. Yarn or fabric made of wool: *Mary knitted me a wool hat.*

wool (wul)

▷ *adjective* **woolen** ▷ *adjective* **woolly**

woo-woo *adjective* (*informal*) Too accepting of unscientific or superstitious explanations: *He's very woo-woo about astrology and lives by the horoscope he reads in the paper.*

word

1. *noun* A unit of one or more spoken sounds or written letters that has a meaning in a particular language: *There are seven words in this sentence.*

2. *noun* A brief remark or comment: *Let me give you a word of advice.*

3. *noun* A short conversation: *May I have a word with you?*

4. *noun* A message or a piece of information: *I received word that my application had been accepted.*

5. If you **give your word**, you promise you will do something: *Now that you've given your word, you can't change your mind.*

6. *verb* To put into words: *Make sure you word your request so that everyone can understand it.* ▷ *verb* **wording, worded**

word (wurd)

wording *noun* The way in which words are chosen and arranged in something that is said or written: *Ben rewrote the letter several times to get the wording just right.* **word·ing** (**wur**-ding)

word processing *noun* The use of a computer or similar machine to type and print documents. Words can be seen on the screen and are easily changed, moved, copied, and stored. ▷ *noun* **word processor**

wordy *adjective* Having or using too many words: *The newspaper article criticized the politician's speech as being too wordy.* **word·y** (**wur**-dee) ▷ *adjective* **wordier, wordiest** ▷ *noun* **wordiness**

wore *verb* The past tense of **wear**. **wore** (wor) **Wore** sounds like **war**.

work

1. *noun* Effort or labor to get something done: *Solving problems is hard work.*

2. *verb* To have a job: *I work in the advertising department of a newspaper.*

3. *verb* To get something done by using your energy or ability: *Let's work together on the project.*

4. *verb* If a machine or device **works**, it operates in the proper way: *My cell phone isn't working.*

5. *verb* To bring about or to cause: *This medicine worked wonders on my cold.*

6. *noun* A person's job; what someone does to make money: *What kind of work do you do?*

7. *noun* A task: *We finished our work on the car today.*

8. *noun* Something produced by an artist, such as a piece of music, a painting, or a sculpture, as in *the complete works of Edgar Allan Poe.*

9. works *noun, plural* The moving parts of a watch or machine.

10. work out *verb* To solve a problem by thinking hard: *I can't work out this crossword puzzle.*

11. work out *verb* To do physical exercise, especially in a gym. ▷ *noun* **workout**

work (wurk)

▷ *verb* **working, worked**

workable *adjective* Practical and likely to be successful: *It's still possible to find a workable solution to the problem.* **work·a·ble** (**wur**-kuh-buhl)

workaholic *noun* Someone who chooses to work a lot and has little interest in anything else. **work·a·hol·ic** (*wur*-kuh-**haw**-lik)

workbench *noun* A strong table used by someone who works with tools, such as a carpenter or a mechanic. **work·bench** (**wurk**-bench)

workbook *noun* A book with problems and exercises to be done by students. **work·book** (**wurk**-*buk*)

worker *noun*
1. Someone who does a particular type of job in order to make money, as in *a factory worker.*
2. A female bee, ant, termite, or other insect that does all the work for the colony but does not reproduce. **work·er** (**wur**-kur)

workman *noun* A man who does manual work or who works with machines. **work·man** (**wurk**-muhn) ▷ *noun, plural* **workmen**

worksheet *noun* A paper that has problems, questions, or exercises on it, especially one assigned as homework. **work·sheet** (**wurk**-*sheet*)

workmanship *noun* The skill and care with which something is made, usually by hand. **work·man·ship** (**wurk**-muhn-*ship*)

workshop

workshop *noun*
1. A room or other building where things are made or fixed: *My dad lets me use his workshop to build stuff.*
2. A meeting where a group of people discuss, learn about, or practice a particular skill, as in *a theater workshop.* **work·shop** (**wurk**-*shahp*)

workstation *noun*
1. An area, usually for one person, with the equipment needed to do a specific job.
2. A computer that runs programs and allows people to gain access to a computer network. **work·sta·tion** (**wurk**-*stay*-shuhn)

world *noun*
1. The earth: *We took a trip around the world.*
2. A particular part of the earth, as in *the Western world.*

3. Everyone who lives on earth: *The world is threatened by pollution.*
4. An area of activity or interest and the people connected with it, as in *the world of art.*
5. A large amount: *Your advice did me a world of good.*
6. Living things, considered as a group, as in *the animal world.* **world** (wurld)

world-class *adjective* Of the highest rank or level in the world, as in *a world-class golfer.*

worldly *adjective*
1. Concerned with ordinary life and activities, rather than with spiritual or religious ideas, as in *worldly success.*
2. Having a lot of practical knowledge and life experience. *For someone who has never traveled much, Sarah is very worldly.* **world·ly** (**wurld**-lee)

World War I *noun* A war fought from 1914 to 1918, mainly in Europe. The United States, Great Britain, France, Russia, Italy, Japan, and other allied nations defeated Germany, Austria-Hungary, Turkey, and Bulgaria.

World War II *noun* A war fought from 1939 to 1945 in which the United States, France, Great Britain, the Soviet Union, and other allied nations defeated Germany, Italy, and Japan.

worldwide *adjective* Existing or known about throughout the world, as in *worldwide fame* or *worldwide concern.* **world·wide** (**wurld**-wide)

World Wide Web *noun* The system of websites connected on the internet. Also called the **web**. Abbreviated as *WWW.*

worm
1. *noun* A small animal that lives in the soil. Worms have long, thin, soft bodies and no backbones or legs.
2. *noun* A small, harmful computer program that makes copies of itself and then travels on the internet, causing damage to different computers.
3. *verb* If you **worm into** or **worm through** something, you move slowly like a worm by twisting and turning from side to side: *George wormed his way through the narrow tunnel.* ▷ *verb* **worming, wormed**
worm (wurm)

worn
1. *verb* The past participle of **wear**.
2. *adjective* Damaged by wear or use, as in *worn leather boots.*
worn (worn)
Worn sounds like **warn**.

worn-out *adjective*

1. No longer useful or in good condition, as in *a pair of worn-out jeans.*

2. Very tired: *The runner was worn-out after the marathon.*

worn-out sneaker

worry

1. *verb* To think about your problems or about bad things that could happen: *Workers are worried about losing their jobs.* ▷ *verb* **worries, worrying, worried**

2. *noun* Something that makes you anxious or concerned: *The sick child was a great worry to his parents.* ▷ *noun, plural* **worries**

3. *noun* The feeling of being anxious or nervous: *I was awake all night with worry.* ▷ *noun* **worrier** ▷ *adjective* **worrying** ▷ *adverb* **worriedly**

wor·ry (**wur**-ee)

worse

1. *adjective* More inferior; less good: *The traffic in Atlanta is worse than the traffic in Boston.*

2. *adjective* More evil or bad: *His next crime will be even worse.*

3. *adjective* More unpleasant, severe, or harmful: *The weather is supposed to be worse tomorrow.*

4. *adjective* More sick or in poorer health than before: *The patient is worse.*

5. *adverb* Less well: *We played worse than ever.*

6. *noun* Something that is worse: *You've heard the bad news, but I have worse to tell you.*

worse (wurs)

worship

1. *verb* To show love and devotion to God or a god, especially by praying or going to a church service. ▷ *noun* **worship**

2. *noun* The act of showing love and devotion to God or a god, especially by praying or singing in a religious building with others, as in *a place of worship.*

3. *verb* To admire and love someone or something very much: *We live in a society that worships celebrities.*

wor·ship (**wur**-ship)

▷ *verb* **worshiping** *or* **worshipping, worshiped** *or* **worshipped**

worst

1. *adjective* The most inferior, harmful, or unpleasant; worse than any other one: *That was the worst storm this town has had in ten years.*

2. *adverb* In the worst way: *She played worst in the final match.*

3. *noun* Someone or something that is the worst: *Of the three actors, he was the worst.*

worst (wurst)

worth

1. *adjective* Having a certain value in money: *He has a rare coin that's worth a fortune.* ▷ *noun* **worth**

2. *adjective* Deserving, or good enough for doing something: *It's worth going to the movie just to see the special effects.*

3. *noun* The quality that makes someone or something valuable or important: *Do you know the worth of a good education?*

worth (wurth)

worthless *adjective* Useless or having no value: *A penny is almost worthless.* **worth·less** (**wurth**-lis) ▷ *noun* **worthlessness**

worthwhile *adjective* Useful and important, as in *a worthwhile experience.* **worth·while** (**wurth**-wile)

worthy *adjective*

1. Having value; good or worthwhile, as in *a worthy goal.*

2. Good enough for something; deserving: *This candidate is worthy of our support.*

wor·thy (**wur**-THee)

▷ *adjective* **worthier, worthiest**

would *verb* A helping verb that is used in the following ways:

1. As the past tense of the helping verb **will**: *He said he would go.*

2. To express a possibility based on something that is not true right now: *It would snow if it were colder.*

3. To express action that happened often or regularly in the past: *I would go to the beach every summer when I was young.*

4. To make a request: *Would you please open the window?*

would (wud)

Would sounds like **wood.**

wouldn't *contraction* A short form of *would not*: *Wouldn't you rather play ball than watch television?*

would·n't (**wud**-uhnt)

wound

1. (woond) *noun* An injury in which the skin is cut, usually because of an accident or violence: *The nurse bandaged Samantha's wound.* ▷ *verb* **wound**

2. (woond) *verb* To hurt someone's feelings: *Your insult wounded me deeply.* ▷ *verb* **wounding, wounded** ▷ *noun* **wound**

3. (wound) *verb* The past tense and the past participle of **wind**: *He wound up the clock.*

wound

wove *verb* The past tense of **weave.** **wove** (wove)

woven *verb* The past participle of **weave.** **woven** (**wo**-vin)

wrap

1. *verb* To cover something completely by winding paper or another material around it: *Did you wrap the present?*

2. *verb* To wind something around someone or something else: *The baby wrapped her arms around her father's neck.*

3. *verb* To hide by covering: *The mountain was wrapped in fog.*

4. *noun* A piece of clothing worn around your upper body, such as a coat or shawl.

5. *noun* A sandwich consisting of a soft tortilla that has been rolled up with a filling inside.

6. If you are **wrapped up** in something, you are totally involved in it.

wrap (rap)

Wrap sounds like **rap.** ▷ *verb* **wrapping, wrapped**

wrapper *noun* The thin material that wraps and protects something, as in *a candy wrapper.* **wrap·per** (**rap**-ur)

wrath *noun* Great anger that is openly expressed. **wrath** (rath)

wreak *verb* To cause great problems or damage: *The snowstorm wreaked havoc all throughout New England.* **wreak** (reek) **Wreak** sounds like **reek.** ▷ *verb* **wreaking, wreaked**

wreath *noun* A group of flowers, leaves, or branches that are twisted together in the shape of a circle. **wreath** (reeth)

wreck

1. *verb* To destroy or ruin something: *My sister wrecked her car on the icy road.* ▷ *verb* **wrecking, wrecked**

2. *noun* The remains of a vehicle that has been destroyed or damaged: *The divers were searching for the wreck of an ancient ship.* **wreck** (rek)

wreckage *noun* The broken parts or pieces lying around at the site of a crash or an explosion: *Dogs sniffed around the wreckage for survivors.* **wreck·age** (**rek**-ij)

wren *noun* A small songbird with a long, thin bill, brown feathers, and a small tail that sticks up. **wren** (ren)

wrench

1. *noun* A tool used for tightening and loosening bolts and nuts. ▷ *noun, plural* **wrenches**

2. *verb* To pull something suddenly and with a lot of force: *He wrenched the book from her hands.*

3. *verb* To injure yourself by twisting a part of your body: *I wrenched my back.*

wrench (rench)

▷ *verb* **wrenches, wrenching, wrenched**

wrest *verb*

1. To twist, pull, or tear something away: *Enrique wrested the ball from his puppy's mouth.*

2. To take something by force or violence: *The soldiers wrested control of the town from the rebels.*

wrest (rest)

Wrest sounds like **rest.**

wrestle *verb*

1. To fight by gripping or holding your opponent and trying to push the person to the ground.

2. If you **wrestle** with a problem, you try to find a solution by thinking very hard.

wres·tle (**res**-uhl)

▷ *verb* **wrestling, wrestled**

wrestling *noun* A sport in which two opponents hold each other and try to force each other to the ground. **wres·tling** (**res**-ling) ▷ *noun* **wrestler**

wretched *adjective* Miserable or unfortunate: *I can't wait till I am over this wretched cold.* **wretch·ed** (**rech**-id)

wriggle *verb* To twist and turn your body: *Sarah wriggled in her seat.* **wrig·gle** (**rig**-uhl) ▷ *verb* **wriggling, wriggled**

wring *verb*

1. To remove most of the liquid out of wet material by twisting it with your hands: *Annie wrung out the soaked towel.* ▷ *noun* **wringer**

2. To get something from someone by using force or threats: *The government agents tried to wring a confession from the spy.*

wring (ring)

Wring sounds like **ring.** ▷ *verb* **wringing, wrung** (ruhng)

wrinkles *noun, plural*

1. Lines in your skin that appear as you get older.

2. Unwanted folds in clothes or paper: *Bill's shirt was full of wrinkles.*

wrin·kles (**ring**-kuhlz)

▷ *verb* **wrinkle**

wrist *noun* The joint that connects the hand and the arm. **wrist** (rist)

wristwatch *noun* A watch worn on a strap or band that fits around the wrist. **wrist·watch** (rist-*wahch*)

write *verb*

1. To produce letters, words, or numbers on a surface, such as paper, especially using a pen or pencil: *Please write your name at the top of the page.*

2. To create stories, poems, articles, or music: *I wrote my first novel when I was 23.*

3. To use words to create a letter or email and send it to someone: *Please write when you're away.*

write (rite)

Write sounds like **right.** ▷ *verb* **writing, wrote** (rote), **written** (**rit**-in) ▷ *noun* **writer**

wrench

writhe *verb* To twist and turn around, as in pain: *Sammy writhed in agony after breaking his ankle.* **writhe** (riTHe) ▷ *verb* **writhing, writhed**

writing *noun*
1. The act of putting letters on paper: *Writing gives me a chance to organize my thoughts.*
2. A written work such as a story, book, or poem.
3. Written form: *Put your request in writing.*
4. Handwriting: *I can't read your writing.*
writ·ing (**rye**-ting)

wrong
1. *adjective* Not correct or not true: *I'm sorry, but that's the wrong answer.*
2. *adjective* Bad or immoral: *It is wrong to cheat.*
3. *adjective* Not appropriate for a particular situation: *I'm always saying the wrong thing.*
4. *adjective* If something is **wrong** with a machine or vehicle, it is not working properly: *There's something wrong with my bicycle.*
5. *adverb* In a way that is not correct or does not produce the result you want: *Stop! You're doing it all wrong.*
6. *verb* To treat someone badly or in an unfair way: *She was convinced she had been wronged.* ▷ *verb* **wronging, wronged**
7. *noun* An act that is illegal or unfair: *The company admits that wrongs were committed.*
8. *noun* Behavior that is bad or immoral: *He doesn't understand the difference between right and wrong.*
wrong (rawng)
▷ *adverb* **wrongly**

wrongdoing *noun* Behavior that is wrong, evil, or illegal. **wrong·do·ing** (**rawng**-*doo*-ing)

About X Words with the letter **X** usually have a *ks* sound. Examples: ax, box, mix. When a word begins with an *x* followed by a hyphen, the *x* is pronounced eks, like the letter, as in *X-ray*. But most words that start with an *x* have a *z* sound, such as *xylophone*. At the end of an email or other message, the letter *X* is a symbol that represents a kiss.

Xerox *noun* Trademark name for a kind of photocopier. **Xe·rox** (**zeer**-ahks) ▷ *verb* **Xerox**

Xmas *noun* Christmas. **X·mas** (**kris**-muhs *or* **eks**-muhs)

Word History

The *X* in **Xmas** represents the Greek letter *chi*. *X* is the first letter of the Greek word for "Christ" and is often used alone to stand for the name of Christ.

XML *noun* The set of computer codes that is often used to make complicated webpages. XML is short for *extensible markup language.*

X-ray *noun*
1. An invisible and powerful beam of light that can pass through solid objects. X-rays are used to take pictures of teeth, bones, and organs inside the body.
2. A picture of the inside of a person's body, taken using X-rays.
X-ray (eks)
▷ *verb* **X-ray** ▷ *adjective*
X-ray

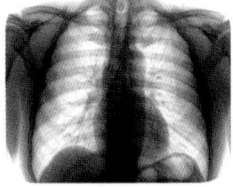

X-ray

xylophone

xylophone *noun* A musical instrument with wooden bars of different lengths that you hit with two small sticks to produce different notes. **xy·lo·phone** (**zye**-luh-*fone*)

Word History

The word **xylophone** literally means "the sound of wood." It combines two Greek words: *xylon*, meaning "wood," and *phone*, meaning "sound."

Yy

About Y The letter Y serves as either a vowel or a consonant. If *y* is the first letter of a word, it acts as a consonant, as in the words *yarn*, *year*, *yolk*, and *young*. If *y* is in the middle of a word, it acts as a vowel and sounds like an *i*, as in *myth*. When y is the last letter of a word that includes a vowel, the y sounds like a long *e*. Examples: happy, funny, silly. *Y* is often silent when it follows a vowel, as in the word *key*.

yacht *noun* A large boat or small ship with sails, used for pleasure or for racing. **yacht** (yaht)
▷ *noun* **yachting**

yak *noun* An ox of Tibet and central Asia that has long, shaggy hair. Yaks are used as work animals. **yak** (yak)

yam *noun*
1. The thick root of a tropical plant that is ground into flour or eaten as a vegetable.
2. A large sweet potato that has orange flesh.
yam (yam)

yank *verb* To suddenly pull something with force: *Joel yanked the ball out of my hands.* **yank** (yangk)
▷ *verb* **yanking, yanked** ▷ *noun* **yank**

Yankee *noun*
1. A person born or living in one of the northern states, especially a state in New England.
2. A person who fought for the Union during the Civil War.
3. Any person born or living in the United States.
Yan·kee (yang-kee)

yap *verb*
1. If a small dog **yaps**, it barks repeatedly with short, high sounds.
2. *(slang)* To talk in a noisy, irritating way.
yap (yap)
▷ *verb* **yapping, yapped**

yard *noun*
1. A unit of length equal to 3 feet or 36 inches.
2. An area of ground around or next to a house, school, or other building, as in *a front yard.*
3. An enclosed area used for a certain type of work or business, as in *a navy yard.*
4. An area next to a railroad station where trains are switched, repaired, or stored.
yard (yahrd)

yak

yarn

yardstick *noun*
1. A measuring stick that is one yard long.
2. A standard used to judge or compare things or people: *Success is a good yardstick.*
yard·stick (yahrd-*stik*)

yarmulke *noun* A small, round cap that Jewish men and boys wear on their heads, especially during religious services. **yar·mul·ke** (**yah**-muh-kuh *or* **yahr**-muhl-kuh)

yarn *noun*
1. Fibers such as wool or cotton that are twisted or spun into long strands for knitting or weaving.
2. *(informal)* If someone **spins a yarn**, he or she tells a long story that may not be completely true.
yarn (yahrn)

yawn *verb*
1. To open your mouth wide and breathe in deeply, especially because you are tired or bored: *Zia yawned with fatigue.* ▷ *noun* **yawn**
2. To open wide: *The cave entrance yawned before us.*
yawn (yawn)
▷ *verb* **yawning, yawned**

yd. Short for **yard** or the plural form *yards.*

year *noun*
1. The period of time in which the earth makes one trip around the sun, about 365 days and 6 hours.
2. On the calendar that we commonly use today, a **year** is a period of 365 days, or 366 in a leap year,

divided into 52 weeks or 12 months. The year begins January 1 and ends December 31.

3. Any period of 12 months.

4. A part of a year spent in a particular activity, as in *the school year*.

year (yeer)

yearly *adjective* Happening or done each year, as in *a yearly trip*. **year·ly** (**yeer**-lee) ▷ *adverb* **yearly**

yearn *verb* To wish for something very strongly, especially something that is difficult to get or achieve: *Deirdre yearned to be a doctor.* **yearn** (yurn) ▷ *verb* **yearning, yearned** ▷ *noun* **yearning**

year-round *adjective* Happening or operating through the entire year: *The town only has about 2,000 year-round residents.* ▷ *adverb* **year-round**

yeast *noun* A yellow fungus used to make bread dough rise and to make alcoholic drinks. **yeast** (yeest)

yell *verb* To shout, cry out, or scream loudly. **yell** (yel) ▷ *verb* **yelling, yelled** ▷ *noun* **yell**

yellow

1. *noun* One of the three primary colors, along with red and blue. Yellow is the color of lemons. ▷ *adjective* **yellow, yellowish**

2. *noun* The yolk of an egg.

3. *verb* To become or make yellow: *The old newspaper had yellowed with age.* ▷ *verb* **yellowing, yellowed**
yel·low (**yel**-oh)

yellow jacket *noun* A wasp that has black and bright yellow stripes. It usually builds its nest in or near the ground and has a painful sting.

yelp *verb* To make a sharp, high, crying sound, usually of pain. *One of the sled dogs yelped and stopped running.* **yelp** (yelp) ▷ *verb* **yelping, yelped** ▷ *noun* **yelp**

yen *noun*

1. The unit of money in Japan.

2. *(informal)* A strong desire: *My brother has always had a yen for a pet cat.*
yen (yen)

yes

1. *adverb* A word used to show that you agree or that something is true: *Yes, I think you are right.*

2. *noun* An answer that shows agreement, approval, or acceptance: *Everyone said yes to our invitation.*

3. *noun* A vote or voter in favor of something.
yes (yes) ▷ *noun, plural* **yeses** *or* **yesses**

yesterday

1. *noun* The day before today: *Yesterday was Monday.*

2. *noun* The recent past: *Many fashions of yesterday look silly today.*

Yoga

Yoga is a system of structured exercises and meditations begun in India 5,000 years ago. Yoga traditionally included mental and physical practices that had a religious significance. Today, yoga is popular in the United States and many other countries as a means to better health. Yoga exercises are done to tone the body, improve posture, reduce stress, and maintain a healthy weight.

3. *adverb* On the day before today: *I started my report yesterday.*
yes·ter·day (**yes**-tur-*day* or **yes**-tur-dee)

yet

1. *adverb* Up to now; so far: *She hasn't come yet.*

2. *adverb* At the present time; now: *You're not allowed out yet.*

3. *adverb* In addition; even, as in *yet another party.*

4. *adverb* At some future time; eventually: *I'll win her heart yet.*

5. *conjunction* But: *He practiced for weeks yet still didn't make the team.*
yet (yet)

yew *noun* An evergreen tree or shrub with poisonous, dark green needles and red berries. **yew** (yoo)
Yew sounds like **ewe** and **you**.

yield *verb*

1. To produce or provide something: *The recipe yields 20 biscuits.* ▷ *noun* **yield**

2. To allow an opponent to have something or to win a fight or an argument: *The troops yielded the town to the enemy.*
yield (yeeld) ▷ *verb* **yielding, yielded**

yo *interjection* *(slang)* A word used to get someone's attention, say hello, or acknowledge being called.
yo (yoh)

yodel *verb* To sing loudly in a voice that changes quickly between high and low sounds. Yodeling is traditionally done in the mountains of Switzerland. **yo·del** (**yoh**-duhl) ▷ *verb* **yodeling, yodeled** ▷ *noun* **yodeler**

yoga *noun* A system of exercises and meditation that helps people control their minds and bodies and become physically fit. Yoga came originally from Hindu teachings. **yo·ga** (**yoh**-guh)

yogurt *noun* A slightly sour food that is made by adding bacteria to milk. Yogurt is often mixed with fruit or sweetened with flavors such as vanilla. **yo·gurt** (**yoh**-gurt)

Word History

The word **yogurt** comes to us from Turkey and has been in our language for over 300 years. Making yogurt was a way of preserving milk before machines for refrigeration were invented.

yoke *noun*
1. A wooden frame attached to the necks of work animals, such as oxen, to connect them so they can plow or pull a heavy load. ▷ *verb* **yoke**
2. The part of a shirt, blouse, or dress that fits around the shoulders and neck.
yoke (yoke)
Yoke sounds like **yolk**.

yolk *noun* The yellow part of an egg. **yolk** (yoke)
Yolk sounds like **yoke**.

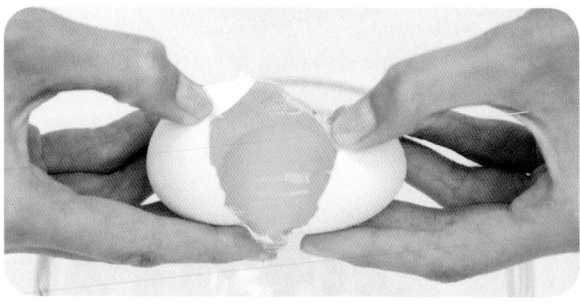

yolk

Yom Kippur *noun* A Jewish religious holiday that falls ten days after Rosh Hashanah during September or October. On Yom Kippur, Jewish people do not eat or drink and ask God to forgive the things they have done wrong. **Yom Kip·pur** (*yahm* **kip**-ur or *yohm* ki-**poor**)

yonder *adverb* Over there: *The lake is yonder, just over that hill.* **yon·der** (**yahn**-dur) ▷ *adjective* **yonder**

you *pronoun*
1. The person or people that someone is speaking or writing to: *Maria likes you a lot.*
2. People in general: *You need a license to drive a car in this country.*
you (yoo)
You sounds like **ewe** and **yew**.

you'd *contraction* A short form of *you had* or *you would*: *I thought you'd gone.* **you'd** (yood)

you'll *contraction* A short form of *you shall* or *you will*: *You'll be happy to know I got an A on my history report.* **you'll** (yool) **You'll** sounds like **Yule**.

young
1. *adjective* Having lived or existed for only a short

time: *A young sheep is called a lamb.*
2. *adjective* Having the qualities of people who are younger than you: *My aunt is young for her age.*
3. *noun* The young animals that belong to a particular mother, considered as a group. ▷ *noun, plural*
young
young (yuhng)
▷ *adjective* **younger, youngest**

youngster *noun* A young person, especially a child: *Back when I was a youngster, a soda cost five cents.* **young·ster** (**yuhng**-stur)

your *adjective* Belonging to or having to do with you: *Your homework is late.* **your** (yoor *or* yor)

you're *contraction* A short form of *you are*: *You're the first person I've spoken to about this problem.* **you're** (yoor *or* yur)

yours *pronoun* The one or ones belonging to or having to do with you: *I like my bike even though yours is newer.* **yours** (yoorz *or* yorz)

yourself *pronoun* Your own self: *Help yourself to a sandwich.* **your·self** (yoor-**self**) ▷ *pronoun, plural* **yourselves**

youth *noun*
1. The time of life when a person is no longer a child but is not yet an adult: *In their youth, they performed in one of the best jazz bands around.*
2. The quality or state of being young: *The rookie player has youth on his side.*
3. A young person, especially a young male between 13 and 18 years of age.
4. Young people in general: *The future of our nation lies in the hands of today's youth.*
youth (yooth)

you've *contraction* A short form of *you have*: *You've got to be kidding!* **you've** (yoov)

yowl *noun* A long, loud cry of pain or unhappiness. **yowl** (youl) ▷ *verb* **yowl**

yo-yo *noun* A toy that consists of a piece of string wound around a circular plastic or wooden object. You wrap the string around your finger and make the yo-yo go up and down by raising and lowering your hand. **yo-yo** (**yoh** yoh)

Yule *noun* Another word for **Christmas**. **Yule** (yool)
Yule sounds like **you'll**.

Yuletide *noun* The Christmas season. **Yule·tide** (**yool**-tide)

yuppie *noun* A young adult with an expensive lifestyle and a job that pays a lot of money. Yuppie comes from the phrase *young urban professional*. **yup·pie** (**yuhp**-ee) ▷ *noun, plural* **yuppies**

zany *adjective* Unusual or crazy in a way that is funny: *His stage act consisted of juggling and telling zany jokes.* **za·ny** (**zay**-nee) ▷ *adjective* **zanier, zaniest** ▷ *adverb* **zanily**

zap *verb (slang)*
1. To shoot or destroy with force, as in an electronic game.
2. To cook something in a microwave oven: *Dinner will be ready as soon as we zap the potatoes.*
3. To change channels on a television set with a remote control.
zap (zap)
▷ *verb* **zapping, zapped**

zeal *noun* A lot of energy and enthusiasm: *Wanda attacked the job with zeal.* **zeal** (zeel) ▷ *adjective* **zealous** (**zel**-uhs)

zealot *noun* Someone who has very strong beliefs about something, such as politics or religion, and tries to convince other people to share the same beliefs, especially if this is done in a way that is considered excessive. **zeal·ot** (**zel**-uht)

zebra *noun* A wild animal of southern and eastern Africa. A zebra is similar to a horse except that it is smaller and has black and white stripes on its body. **ze·bra** (**zee**-bruh)

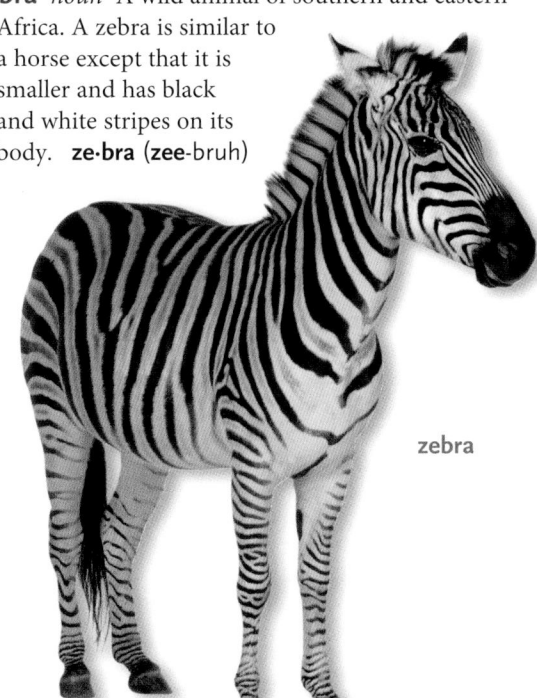

zebra

zenith *noun*
1. The period of time when something or someone is most effective or successful: *His new hit record puts him at the zenith of his career.*
2. The highest point in the sky reached by the sun or moon, directly overhead.
ze·nith (**zee**-nith)

zeppelin *noun* An airship with a rigid frame. A zeppelin is shaped like a cigar. **zep·pe·lin** (**zep**-uh-lin)

Word History

Count Ferdinand von Zeppelin of Germany was a soldier and adventurer with a keen interest in flight. After he retired from the German army, Zeppelin devoted his time to designing and building airships. In 1900, he completed his first rigid dirigible, which was named a **zeppelin** in his honor. By the time he died in 1917, the word *zeppelin* was being used to mean any dirigible.

zero
1. *noun* The number that indicates that there is no quantity of something, written numerically as 0.
2. *noun* A point on a thermometer or other scale at which numbering or measurement begins: *It was ten degrees below zero yesterday.*
3. *noun* Nothing: *All their hard work added up to zero when it snowed and the party was canceled.*
4. *adjective* Not any: *Paul has zero interest in politics.*
5. *verb* If you **zero in on** something or someone, you focus all of your attention on that thing or person: *The detectives have zeroed in on a suspect.*
▷ *verb* **zeroes, zeroing, zeroed**
ze·ro (**zeer**-oh)
▷ *noun, plural* **zeros** or **zeroes**

zest *noun* Enthusiasm and enjoyment, as in *a zest for life.* **zest** (zest)

zigzag *noun* A line or course that moves in short, sharp turns or angles from one side to the other. **zig·zag** (**zig**-zag) ▷ *verb* **zigzag**

zilch *noun (slang)* Absolutely nothing; zero: *I looked for the results of the ball game in the newspaper but found zilch.* **zilch** (zilch)

zinc *noun* A blue-white metal that is mixed with copper to make brass and used to coat other metals so that they will not rust. Zinc is a chemical element. **zinc** (zingk)

zinnia *noun* A garden plant with round, brightly colored flowers. **zin·ni·a** (**zin**-ee-uh)

zip

1. zip up *verb* To fasten clothes with a zipper: *This dress zips up in the back.*

2. *noun* A short hissing sound, as in *the zip of a bullet.*

3. *verb* To make a computer file or set of files smaller so that they will be easier to store or send to someone.

4. *verb (informal)* To move fast or to make something do this: *The car zipped around the corner.*

zip (zip)

▷ *verb* **zipping, zipped**

ZIP code *or* **zip code** *noun* A number given by the Postal Service to each delivery area in the United States in order to speed the sorting and delivery of mail.

zip file *noun* A computer file that contains one or more compressed files and that can only be opened with a special program that returns the files to their normal size.

zip line *noun* A pulley attached to a cable that is hung between two high places. People ride on a zip line by sitting in a sling that is attached to the pulley.

zipper *noun* A fastener for clothes or other objects. A zipper consists of two strips of metal or plastic teeth that link up when the strips are pulled together. **zip·per** (**zip**-ur)

Word History

The **zipper** can trace its roots to Whitcomb L. Judson, the American who invented it in 1890. Judson named his invention the Universal Fastener, but people kept trying to find a more clever term. An employee of the B. F. Goodrich Company came up with the name *zipper* after the company decided to use these fasteners on the sides of their new rain boots.

zither *noun* A musical instrument made up of a flat box with strings stretched across it. Instruments in the zither family can have up to 40 strings, which are plucked with a pick or with the fingers. **zith·er** (**zith**-ur *or* **ziTH**-ur)

zodiac *noun* An imaginary area in the sky in the shape of a circle that the sun, the moon, and the planets travel through. The zodiac is divided into 12 equal parts, each named for a different constellation. **zo·di·ac** (**zoh**-dee-*ak*)

zone *noun*

1. An area that is separate from other areas and used for a special purpose, as in *a "No Parking" zone* or *the end zone of a football field.*

2. Any of the five areas of the earth divided according to climate. There are two frigid zones, two temperate zones, and one torrid zone.

zone (zohn)

zoning *adjective* Of or pertaining to the activity of deciding where it is legal for certain things to be built, such as businesses, churches, houses, or roads: *The zoning board will have to decide if the old church can be converted to a nightclub.* **zon·ing** (**zoh**-ning)

zoo *noun* A place where many different animals are kept so that people can see or study them. **zoo** (zoo)

zoology *noun* The science that deals with the study of animal life. **zo·ol·o·gy** (zoh-**ah**-luh-jee) ▷ *noun* **zoologist** (zoh-**ah**-luh-jist) ▷ *adjective* **zoological** (*zoh*-uh-**lah**-ji-kuhl)

zoom *verb*

1. To move quickly with a loud humming sound: *The train zoomed by us.*

2. To increase or rise rapidly and suddenly: *The song zoomed to the top of the charts.*

3. zoom in To adjust a camera's lens so that the person or thing you are taking a picture of appears to be closer.

4. zoom out To adjust a camera's lens so that the person or thing you are taking a picture of appears to be farther away.

zoom (zoom)

▷ *verb* **zooming, zoomed**

zucchini *noun* A long squash that has green skin. **zuc·chi·ni** (zoo-**kee**-nee) ▷ *noun, plural* **zucchini** *or* **zucchinis**

Zuni *or* **Zuñi** *noun* A member of a group of Native Americans who now live in western New Mexico. **Zu·ni** (**zoo**-nee) *or* **Zu·ñi** (**zoon**-yee) ▷ *noun, plural* **Zuni** *or* **Zunis**, *or* **Zuñi** *or* **Zuñis**

Zoning

Governments regulate the way property is used and developed through this method of urban planning. Land is divided into areas, or zones, and reserved for purposes such as residential, commercial, or industrial use. These regulations can help protect the comfort and safety of a community—to prevent a factory from opening next to someone's home, for example. Zoning laws can also determine how tall buildings can be, or what noise level is allowed in a certain zone. Some zones are reserved for farms, or exist to preserve historic districts. Mixed-use zones blend more than one type of property, such as houses and businesses, in the same area.

Thesaurus

Each entry in this thesaurus is made up of a group of synonyms that share the same general meaning. The main entry word is highlighted in red. Each synonym has its own definition. In general, these synonyms progress from familiar terms to a less common and more sophisticated vocabulary.

In addition, the definition for each synonym contrasts with, or expands on, the main entry word and its definition. You can follow the progression of senses from one synonym to the next as you read through the entry. This allows you to see more clearly how the synonyms differ, so that you can make an informed selection and choose the best synonym for your writing.

Remember that your best guide on how to choose a synonym will be your own knowledge and sense of the language. First, pick the synonym that seems to you to be the right one. You may change your mind after thinking it over, but in many cases you will have made a good choice. Read your sentence aloud with the new synonym in it. Does the sentence sound correct and does it express your idea well? If you don't think it sounds quite right or says what you mean, trust your judgment. Check the thesaurus again and you may come up with a better choice.

A

■ **affect** *verb* To have an effect on, or to produce a reaction in, someone or something: *How has all this rain affected the tourism industry?*

influence To have an effect on someone or something so as to produce a change: *I am not going to let the weather influence my decision to go camping this weekend.*

impress To have an effect on someone's mind, especially to make people think highly of someone or something: *The whole group was impressed by the Statue of Liberty.*

■ **anger** *noun* The strong feeling of being very annoyed or wanting to argue or fight: *Rachel tried to hide her anger from her friends.*

rage Strong or violent anger, often out of control: *Tom lashed out in rage at anyone who spoke to him.*

fury Extreme anger or force: *The storm attacked with such fury that we ran into the house.*

wrath Very strong anger, especially when accompanied by a desire to punish or get revenge for some wrong: *I could not contain my wrath when I discovered that Leanne had copied answers from my test.*

indignation Strong anger, especially when caused by something you believe is mean or shameful: *We were filled with indignation when the mayor refused to meet with us.*

exasperation Strong irritation: *His dawdling made everyone late and caused a lot of exasperation.*

■ **appreciate** *verb* To think well of someone or to be grateful for something: *I appreciate your willingness to help me.*

value To think that something is important: *I value Anna's friendship greatly.*

prize To appreciate something very highly: *Juan prizes honesty above all else.*

cherish To care for someone or something in a kind and loving way: *Bradley cherishes the time he spends with his grandfather.*

treasure To love something that you have or own: *I treasure my independence.*

■ **ascend** *verb* To rise from a lower level: *The balloon slowly ascended toward the clouds.*

climb To move or go up: *The car slowly climbed the steep mountainside.*

rise To reach a higher level: *We watched the cake rise in the oven.*

mount To get onto something above ground level: *The mayor mounted the platform to give a speech.*

scale To climb up or over: *It took the climbers all day to scale the cliff.*

■ **avoid** *verb* To keep away or withdraw from a person or place: *I've been avoiding Elaine ever since she shouted at me.*

dodge To get out of the way of something quickly: *That bully tried to hit me, but I dodged the blow and walked away.*

evade To get away from something by being clever or skillful: *Roger always tries to evade his chores.*

duck To lower your head quickly, so as not to be seen or hit by something: *I ducked as the ball came right at me.*

sidestep To avoid or dodge a problem or decision as if by stepping around it: *I sidestepped my mother's question about my math homework by showing her the perfect grade on my spelling test.*

B

■ **bear** *verb* To take on the burden of or to put up with: *I can't bear the pain of losing my puppy.*

endure To hold up firmly against suffering, especially over a long time: *After the earthquake, the survivors had to endure hunger and thirst until help could arrive.*

stand To bear or put up with without flinching: *I can't stand loud music.*

tolerate To put up with something or someone: *I won't tolerate these constant interruptions.*

■ **boast** *verb* To talk proudly about yourself or someone or something connected with you: *Bryan loved to boast about his sister, who is a state champion swimmer.*

brag To boast too much, especially about yourself: *After a week everyone got tired of hearing Alicia brag about her trip to Australia.*

gloat To think or talk about something in a highly smug way: *He just sat in his room, gloating over his trophy.*

crow To boast too much and too loudly: *Henry crowed over his victory in the bicycle race.*

■ **broad** *adjective* Extending a great distance from side to side: *Richard is six feet tall and has broad shoulders.*

wide Having a certain distance from one side to the other; large from side to side: *The lake is nine miles long and two miles wide.*

tip

Broad and wide are close synonyms that both refer to the distance across something, as in *a broad street* or *a wide street*. However, **broad** suggests the whole area or expanse of the surface itself and **wide** stresses more the distance from one side to the other. If you want to give the actual distance, use **wide**: *three feet wide*.

C

■ **choose** *verb* To take or prefer something out of a larger number: *It is important to choose a career you will enjoy.*

select To choose carefully and thoughtfully: *The members of the all-star team were selected from all the players in the league.*

pick To choose carefully using your own preference: *I picked my favorite CDs to listen to during the trip.*

elect To choose by vote: *The class elected a president, secretary, and treasurer.*

tip

The phrase **pick and choose** means "to choose very carefully from a number of possibilities": *There are some subjects you must study in school; you can't just pick and choose the things you like. Beth must have a dozen outfits she can pick and choose from!*

■ **compare** *verb* To examine in order to discover similarities or differences: *They look alike, but if you compare these two violins carefully, you will notice that one has a sweeter tone than the other.*

contrast To identify the differences between things: *I want you to contrast the attitudes of the two main characters in this story.*

distinguish To tell the difference between things: *Can you distinguish between a fir tree and a pine tree?*

■ **contain** *verb* To have in it: *My purse contains $3, some change, and a broken pencil.*

hold To be able to contain: *This bottle holds a gallon, but right now it contains only about a pint.*

include To have as part of a whole: *This list includes the names and addresses of everyone in the school.*

D

■ **defeat** *verb* To win victory over: *My sister's basketball team defeated last year's champions and went on to win the tournament.*

conquer To get control of, as if by winning a war: *He conquered*

his fear of flying by taking several airplane trips.

beat To defeat in a game, contest, or struggle: *My little brother always beats my dad at chess.*

overcome To get the better of after a hard struggle: *Roger is determined to overcome his shyness.*

overpower To get the better of by using greater power or strength: *The mutineers overpowered the captain and took over the ship.*

subdue To bring completely under control or authority: *The cowboys subdued the startled cattle before they caused a stampede.*

E

■ **effect** *noun* The change that happens because of an act or action: *Exercising every day has had a positive effect on my health.*

result Something that happens because of something else: *Sarah studied hard and as a result she got an A on the test.*

outcome What happens at the end of an event or series of events: *Have you heard the outcome of the election yet?*

consequence The often bad or unfortunate effect of a particular action or series of actions: *I broke the rules and had to suffer the consequences.*

tip

Effect can also be used as a verb meaning "to bring about" or "to cause to happen": *The negotiators were able to effect a compromise to settle the strike. Do you think the new rules will effect any change in their behavior?* Be careful not to confuse the verb **effect** with the verb **affect**.

■ **ensure** *verb* To make sure or certain that something happens: *Please ensure that the door is locked when you leave.*

insure To make payments to a company that will give you the money you need if you have an accident, fire, illness, or other loss: *We insured the boat against fire and theft.*

assure To make certain of something: *I can assure you that we will be there on time.*

secure To make something safe, especially by closing it tightly: *Will you secure the latch on the gate, please?*

■ **exclude** *verb* To prohibit or leave out: *They were excluded from membership in the club.*

eliminate To get rid of or to remove from a competition by a defeat: *Our team was eliminated from the tournament in the semifinals.*

suspend To stop something for a short time: *The construction was suspended over the winter because of the fierce weather.*

expel To send or force something out: *His behavior was so bad he was expelled from school.*

F

■ **fair** *adjective* Reasonable and honest: *A referee has to be fair to both teams.*

just In accordance with the law or moral principles: *A just society will not tolerate prejudice.*

impartial Not favoring one person or one point of view over another: *The case was tried by an impartial jury.*

equal The same for each member of a group: *Everyone will have an equal opportunity to play during the game.*

■ **fault** *noun* A defect or lack of strength, especially in character or personality: *Jake's biggest fault is that he lies.*

failing A minor fault: *My brother is happy to point out that being late is the least of my failings.*

weakness A special desire for something that results in a lack of self-control: *Vasiliki has a weakness for ice cream.*

vice Immoral or harmful behavior: *Eating too much chocolate is unhealthy, but it's not exactly a vice.*

G

■ **game** *noun* An activity organized for diversion or amusement: *Let's play a game of capture the flag.*

sport A game involving physical activity: *Soccer is the only sport Marilyn likes to play.*

pastime A hobby, a sports activity, or an entertainment that passes the time in an enjoyable way: *His favorite pastimes are basketball, computer games, and playing the cello.*

competition The act or process of competing in business or in a game or sport: *The traditionally strong competition between the two military academies makes this football game more exciting than usual.*

contest A struggle for victory: *Angelo won the statewide essay writing contest.*

recreation The enjoyment of a game, sport, or hobby after working: *My mother's favorite recreation is waterskiing.*

govern *verb* To be in charge, usually of a country or an organization: *In a democracy, the people themselves decide who will govern them.*

rule To have power and authority, usually over a country: *The tyrant ruled the country for more than a decade.*

reign To rule as a monarch: *Queen Victoria reigned over England for 64 years.*

H

habit *noun* Something that you do regularly, often without thinking about it: *I'm trying to break myself of the habit of biting my nails.*

custom A tradition in a culture or society: *In this country, it is the custom to say "You're welcome" if someone says "Thank you" to you.*

practice An action that is repeated regularly, especially to improve a skill: *Catrina has band practice every day after school.*

routine A regular way or pattern of doing things: *Washing my hair is part of my daily routine.*

homonym *noun* A word that has the same pronunciation and sometimes the same spelling, but a different meaning as another word: *The nouns "bass" (meaning "a low voice") and "base" ("the bottom of something") are homonyms.*

homograph One of two or more words that have the same spelling but different meanings and possibly different pronunciations: *The nouns "bass" ("a low singing voice") and "bass" (the name for the fish) are homographs.*

homophone A word that has the same pronunciation but a different spelling and a different meaning from another word: *The words "site," "sight," and "cite" are homophones.*

tip

Homonyms: *broke* (past tense of *break*)—*broke* ("out of money"); a *lock* of hair—a *lock* on a door; *so* tired—*sew* a dress.

Homographs: the *bow* of a ship—to *bow* from the waist—to tie a *bow*; *fast* ("rapid")—*fast* ("to not eat"); *finish* ("to end")—*finish* ("to paint").

Homophones: *cell*—*sell*; *have*—*halve*; *key*—*quay*; *weigh*—*way*.

Note that homonyms can be either homographs or homophones, but homographs and homophones are different from each other.

humble *adjective* Not proud: *Even though he had won a great prize, he was humble and gave credit to the many people who had helped him.*

meek Quiet, humble, and obedient, sometimes too much so: *He was a meek little man who never spoke up to give his opinion.*

modest Not boastful about your abilities, possessions, or achievements: *She was a world-famous violinist, but she was very modest about her accomplishments.*

I

interesting *adjective* Attracting and holding your attention and interest: *She has led a very interesting life.*

fascinating Extremely interesting or attractive: *I think botany is a fascinating subject.*

exciting Producing a strong interest and excitement: *We watched an exciting film about the first trip to the moon.*

intriguing Arousing a strong interest and curiosity: *The discovery of ice on Mars raises some intriguing questions about the possibility of life on other planets.*

engrossing Taking up all your attention: *This book is so engrossing I didn't hear you come in.*

absorbing Taking up all your attention and drawing you in: *I found my task so absorbing that I completely lost track of time.*

irony *noun* A way of speaking or writing that means the opposite of what the words say: *"What a beautiful day!" said David with irony, as the blizzard raged around us.*

satire A type of clever, mocking humor that points out the faults in certain people or ideas: *Many of Mark Twain's writings are full of satire and make us realize how foolish people can be.*

parody An imitation of a serious piece of writing, film, or music that makes fun of the original work: *Most of the poems in "Alice's Adventures in Wonderland" are parodies of popular 19th-century poems for children.*

J

job *noun* Something you have to do, especially regularly or for pay: *It's my job to feed the guinea pig every morning.*

task A small job that you have been given to do: *Ms. Reyes* *gave us the task of decorating the classroom for the party.*

chore A small job that you must do regularly: *I have to do three chores before school: make my bed, pick up my room, and take out the garbage.*

errand A trip to do a small job, often for someone else: *We can go swimming as soon as I get back from running errands for my mother.*

work A regular job, often for pay: *My mother got work as a nurse at the hospital.*

■ **join** *verb* To put together or bring together; to come together: *The sides of a picture frame should join at a right angle.*

connect To join two things; to join or become joined to or with another: *If we connect these hoses, they will reach the pool.*

attach To join by tying, sticking, screwing, clipping, or in some other way: *The basketball hoop is attached to the wall above the garage door with three long bolts.*

link To join in a series like a chain: *The children linked hands to form a circle.*

fasten To join one thing firmly to another: *Fasten these posters to the bulletin board with thumbtacks.*

unite To join to make one: *All of these puzzle pieces can be united into a single picture.*

K

■ **knot** *noun* A fastening made by looping and twisting one or more pieces of string, rope, or thread: *It is handy to know several different kinds of knots if you go sailing.*

tangle String, rope, thread, or hair twisted together in a confused mass: *I spent all morning trying to get a big tangle out of my fishing line.*

snarl A knotted or tangled mass, especially in thread or hair: *Amy didn't like having to brush the snarls out of her hair every morning, so she got her hair cut short.*

■ **know** *verb* To be familiar with a person, place, or piece of information: *He knows the names of everyone in the school.*

understand To know what something means or how something works: *She understands automobile engines better than anyone else in the family.*

realize To be aware that something is true: *Do you realize how happy your letter makes me?*

recognize To see someone and know who the person is or to understand a situation: *Bessie recognized her best friend despite her Halloween costume.*

L

■ **laugh** *verb* To make sounds with the voice that express joy, amusement, or scorn: *The show was so funny I laughed for an hour.*

giggle To laugh in a quiet and silly or nervous way: *We all giggled when Michael pretended he was the principal.*

chuckle To laugh quietly in a low tone: *I chuckled quietly as I read the comics to myself.*

snicker To laugh in a sly way: *My new boots were so large, I just knew that everyone was snickering behind my back.*

roar To laugh loudly: *The crowd roared when the clowns kept tripping over each other's shoes.*

tip

All of these words can also be used as nouns: *I like the sound of my brother's* **laugh**. *Her* **giggle** *gave away the secret of her hiding place. Joe let out a* **chuckle** *when he heard the joke. She gave a* **snicker** *as I turned away. The audience reacted with a* **roar** *every time I got hit by a pie.*

M

■ **myth** *noun* A traditional story that tells about gods or goddesses, tries to explain something in nature, or provides an account of a country's history: *Most cultures have a creation myth that explains how the world began.*

legend A story handed down from earlier times that may have some basis in historical fact: *The legend of Santa Claus is based on Saint Nicholas of Myra.*

fable A story that teaches a lesson and often has animal characters that act like people: *The French fable is about a frog that wanted to be as big as an ox.*

epic A long poem, story, or film that tells the deeds of legendary or historical figures: *Melville's epic, Moby-Dick, is the tale of a hunt for a white whale.*

N

■ **normal** *adjective* Not different from what is usual or expected: *A person's normal body temperature is about 98.6 degrees Fahrenheit.*

typical Having traits or qualities that are normal for a type or class: *It is typical for home buyers to pay a mortgage.*

average About midway in value, rate, or size: *What is the average price of a gallon of gas in this state?*

O

■ **obvious** *adjective* Very easy to see or understand: *His frown was an obvious sign that he was unhappy.*

evident Easy to see or recognize: *It is evident from her success that she knows how to handle money wisely.*

apparent Easy to know or understand: *It soon became apparent that Tim is a much better tennis player than I am.*

clear Easy to understand, see through, or hear: *These instructions are clear and easy to follow.*

plain Easy to see or hear: *The book was sitting on the table in plain sight.*

P

■ **pamper** *verb* To take very good care of, with kindness, food, comfort, or anything special: *Grandparents love to pamper their grandchildren.*

spoil To pamper too much or too often: *She has been so spoiled by her parents that she has a tantrum if she doesn't immediately get her way.*

indulge To give in to a desire or craving: *Dennis rarely indulges his love of chocolate.*

humor To keep a person happy by agreeing with him or her or doing what he or she wants: *Let's humor him just so that he stops complaining.*

baby To pamper someone too much, as if the person were

younger than he or she really is: *Even though I am 19 years old, my mother still babies me whenever I get sick.*

■ **persuade** *verb* To lead to do or believe something by giving good reasons: *Alice persuaded everybody to participate in the charity drive.*

convince To overcome doubt by arguing or giving good reasons: *Jessica tried to convince me that she knew the way home, but I was sure that we were lost.*

influence To have an effect on: *My parents' encouragement influenced me to try out for the baseball team.*

■ **prejudice** *noun* A preconceived opinion based on race, religion, or other characteristics: *Racial prejudice has been the cause of great suffering for many centuries.*

intolerance A lack of willingness to respect or accept the customs, beliefs, or opinions of others: *The mutual intolerance of the two groups has kept them from ending the war.*

bigotry An intense and often open dislike or hatred of a group, based on prejudice and intolerance: *One of the goals of the struggle for civil rights has been to eliminate bigotry and hatred.*

bias A mental leaning, either for or against something, that may influence our judgment: *She has a strong bias against rock 'n' roll music.*

■ **prevent** *verb* To take action in order to stop something from happening: *We must do everything we can to prevent war.*

hinder To delay or make progress difficult: *Our first attempt to climb the mountain was hindered by rain and fog.*

block To put something in the way of: *The mayor tried to block our plan to march in the parade.*

stop To bring to an end: *I stopped the neighbor's dog from digging in our yard.*

check To slow down or bring to an end: *I checked the impulse to jump up and cheer when I won the final game in the chess match.*

restrain To hold back: *Amy restrained the little boy from running into the street.*

■ **pride** *noun* A sense of your own importance or worth: *George felt a sense of pride when he finished the job by himself.*

vanity A feeling of extreme pride and conceit and a desire to be admired by others: *His vanity was wounded when I criticized his clothes.*

self-respect Pride in yourself and your abilities: *He has too much self-respect to do anything that would embarrass his friends.*

self-esteem A feeling of pride and belief in yourself and your abilities: *Joanna's dignity and self-esteem helped her get through the interview successfully.*

Q

■ **quality** *noun* A special feature that helps to make something what it is: *Tasia is intelligent, patient, hardworking, and understanding—all qualities necessary for being a successful doctor.*

property A basic quality: *Two of the properties of a liquid are that it will flow downward and that it has no shape of its own.*

characteristic A typical quality or feature that helps to identify something: *The large loop on her letter "g" is a characteristic of her handwriting.*

character The main or essential nature: *The town's rapid population growth has greatly changed the character of our community.*

trait A quality or characteristic that helps to distinguish one thing from another: *Curiosity is said to be a trait of cats.*

R

■ **refuse** *verb* To say that you will not do something or accept something: *Donald refused to attend the party unless Jane could go with him.*

reject To refuse to accept: *Matthew proposed marriage, but Celeste rejected him.*

decline To turn down or refuse, especially politely: *He declined the reward for finding my wallet.*

■ **reveal** *verb* To uncover, show, or tell something hidden or unknown: *I didn't want to reveal my name.*

disclose To make known or make public: *The reporter refused to disclose the source of her information.*

divulge To make known, especially something secret: *My grandmother would never divulge her true age.*

expose To uncover something so it can be seen or understood: *I didn't want to expose my ignorance by asking a foolish question.*

S

■ **similar** *adjective* Having some features or characteristics in common: *Phil and I have similar ideas about how to train the puppy.*

alike Looking or acting the same: *The twins are alike in the way they look and how they dress, but not in how they behave!*

like The same or almost the same: *Tina and Stephanie were of like minds and opinions and thus they became close friends.*

tip

Alike is also frequently used as an adverb meaning "in the same manner": *All the students in her class were treated alike.*

■ **stubborn** *adjective* Not willing to give in or change: *Sam is too stubborn to admit that he made a mistake.*

obstinate Stubborn and not willing to give in to argument, reason, or persuasion: *Irene was obstinate in her belief that the store clerk had cheated her.*

willful Not yielding to the wishes of others: *He persisted in his willful refusal to ask for directions, and we ended up hopelessly lost.*

headstrong Determined to have your own way: *Jennifer was a headstrong girl, and she was determined to join the all-boy basketball team.*

■ **sudden** *adjective* Happening without warning: *Janie was caught in a sudden rainstorm.*

abrupt Happening quickly, without preparation or warning: *Paul made an abrupt decision to quit his job.*

impetuous Doing things suddenly, eagerly, or impatiently, without thinking first: *She made an impetuous decision to go to France.*

■ **surrender** *verb* To give up: *The troops surrendered when they realized they were greatly outnumbered.*

submit To agree to obey: *I submitted to my parents' rules.*

yield To give up or surrender under pressure of force or persuasion: *The band yielded to the enthusiastic cheers of the crowd and played an encore.*

concede To admit unwillingly: *The candidate conceded victory to his opponent.*

resign To give up a job, a position, or an office voluntarily: *Alisa told her boss that she had to resign because she had been offered a better job.*

quit To give up an activity: *My father quit smoking the day I was born.*

T

■ **tell** *verb* To put into words: *Can you tell us exactly what happened?*

report To give a detailed account of something that has happened: *My mom reported every word of her conversation with my teacher.*

declare To say something formally or officially: *The mayor declared that next week will be Be Kind to Animals Week in our town.*

inform To give knowledge or information to someone: *The police are required to inform suspects of their rights.*

disclose To reveal: *André promised not to disclose where his parents hid his brother's birthday present.*

notify To tell someone about something officially or formally: *The hospital notified us about the test results.*

convey To tell or communicate by speech or action: *His slumping posture conveyed his disappointment.*

■ **trash** *noun* Items that are judged to be worthless and are discarded: *We fill up a 30-gallon can with trash every week at our house alone.*

garbage Food waste or other things thrown away: *Once a week we take our garbage to the dump.*

tip

In the Middle Ages, **garbage** meant the heads, feet, and innards of chickens and other birds that were eaten. Several recipes from the 15th century tell how to cook these parts into a stew that was also called *garbage*. Here is an example: *"Take the garbage of young geese—heads, necks, wings, feet, gizzard, heart, and the liver—and boil them well and cut the wings, the feet, and the gizzards, the heart, the liver, and the lungs, and fry them in clean grease."* Sound good? Today we no longer eat all of these parts; instead we throw them away, and thus **garbage** primarily refers to food waste that we throw away.

rubbish Something worthless: *The basement is full of rubbish that we should just throw away.*

refuse Things or materials that are useless and thrown away: *Several tons of refuse are carted away from the factory every month.*

waste Something left over and not needed: *Chemical wastes from the paint factory used to be poured right into the river.*

debris The scattered pieces of something that has been broken or destroyed: *The debris caused by the hurricane was spread far and wide.*

rubble Broken fragments, as of bricks and stones: *All that was left of their house was a pile of rubble.*

U

■ **urge** *verb* To try to persuade, to recommend, or to present strongly: *Joni's father urged her to work a little harder.*

coax To influence, urge, or persuade gently: *We had to coax the parakeet back into its cage with its favorite treat.*

encourage To give confidence by praise or support: *The teacher encouraged us to do an extra presentation.*

goad To tease or urge into doing something: *Will was goaded into fighting by the constant taunts of the bully.*

prod To push or urge into action: *My parents had to prod me to clean my room.*

spur To urge or stimulate into action: *I was spurred to run faster by the cheering of the crowd.*

tip

Goad, **prod**, and **spur** all derive from the use of a sharp or pointed rod or spur to make animals, such as cattle or horses, move where you want them to go. Thus, these words have stronger connotations than the others in this list. **Goad**, **prod**, and, to a lesser extent, **spur** suggest an unwillingness on the part of the person being urged.

V

■ **valid** *adjective* Based on facts, evidence, or good sense: *You can leave early if you have a valid reason.*

sound Based on facts, logic, or evidence and free from mistakes: *He presented a sound argument in favor of completing our project early.*

convincing Having the power to convince or overcome doubt: *Your excuse for being late is not very convincing.*

W

■ **walk** *verb* To move yourself forward by taking footsteps: *I walk to school every morning.*

stroll To walk in a slow, relaxed way: *Saadja and I strolled around the park for an hour.*

march To walk somewhere quickly and in a determined way: *Elaine marched straight into her boss's office and demanded a raise.*

hike To walk vigorously, especially for a long distance through the countryside: *We hiked for six miles and camped by the river.*

stride To walk with long steps, especially in an active manner:

The team strode proudly across the field after winning the game.

trudge To walk slowly and with effort: *The losing team trudged wearily into the locker room.*

shuffle To walk slowly, hardly raising your feet from the floor or ground: *Angela shuffled through the piles of dry leaves.*

strut To walk with a swagger or in an arrogant manner: *The dancer strutted across the stage.*

■ **wisdom** *noun* The quality of being wise: *I rely on my grand-father's wisdom to help me make important decisions.*

judgment The ability to decide or to form opinions wisely: *They showed good judgment in deciding not to drink and drive.*

knowledge The things that someone knows: *We had to demonstrate our knowledge of physics for the project.*

reason The ability to think logically and clearly and to make sound decisions: *It is better to be guided by reason than by desire, greed, or envy.*

understanding The ability to know what something means or how something works: *Risa had a clear understanding of how her choices would affect her life.*

X

■ **xylophone** *noun* A musical instrument with bars of different lengths that are struck with small hammers to give different notes: *The notes on a xylophone are arranged like those on a piano.*

marimba A type of xylophone with long, hollow resonators

beneath the bars to increase the sound: *The marimba originated in Africa.*

vibraphone A type of marimba with electrically operated valves in the resonators to make the sound vibrate: *The vibraphone is a popular jazz instrument.*

glockenspiel A portable instrument like a xylophone, with metal bars in a frame: *Many marching bands include a glockenspiel because of the clear, bell-like sound it makes.*

Y

■ **yell** *verb* To cry out in a loud voice, as in surprise or anger, or to attract attention: *Mother yelled at us for tracking mud through the house.*

shout To cry out in a loud voice, especially to be heard a long distance or above other sounds: *Mason shouted "Timber!" as the tree began to fall.*

scream To cry out loudly in a high voice, especially out of fear, horror, or pain: *I screamed when I saw a large spider walking up my arm.*

shriek To cry out in a shrill, piercing way: *The whole audience shrieked when the*

tip

All of these words are also used as nouns: *Give a **yell** if you need help. Phil heard a **shout** coming from the barn. I gave a **scream** when the wind blew the door shut. There were **shrieks** of laughter coming from the children's bedroom. The cat gave a **screech** when I stepped on its tail. We could hear the coach's **bellow** from the other end of the field.*

monster suddenly appeared on the screen.

screech To make a high, unpleasant sound: *The car screeched to a halt.*

bellow To roar or cry out loudly with a powerful sound: *We heard a bull moose bellow across the lake.*

■ **young** *adjective* In an early stage of growth or development: *Sammy is too young to ride the bus by himself.*

immature Young and not fully developed: *The immature ducks all have brown feathers for camouflage.*

juvenile Childish or immature: *His juvenile behavior began to annoy his sister.*

Z

■ **zone** *noun* A space that is separate from others and used for a special purpose: *Dad got a ticket for parking in a No Parking zone.*

area A space on a surface, especially one that is marked by boundaries or is in some way different from others around it: *This whole area of the state is covered with forests.*

region A large area, especially one characterized by some specific feature: *What region of the brain controls your eyesight?*

district A locality with known boundaries or with some clearly defined feature: *We live in the 12th congressional district.*

belt An area or strip that is marked by some particular feature: *The city is surrounded by a wide belt of parkland.*

The Parts of Speech

All the words in English can be divided into eight groups called the parts of speech.

Nouns

Persons	Places	Things	Ideas
grandmother	*farm*	*pencil*	*freedom*
Margaret	*continent*	*window*	*happiness*
teacher	*city*	*banana*	*bravery*
kitten	*house*	*telephone*	*childhood*

Uses of Nouns

Subject: who or what performs the action of the verb	*The **dog** bit the man.*
Direct Object: who or what receives the action of the verb	*The dog bit the **man**.*
Indirect Object: shows *to* or *for* whom	*She baked the **girl** a cake and gave the **boy** a cookie.*
Object of a Preposition: comes after a preposition	*They went to a **restaurant** after the **movies**.*
Possession: shows ownership	*The **kid's** sneakers were new.*
Noun of Direct Address: the person spoken to	***David**, please help me fix my computer.*
Predicate Noun: comes after the verb of being, means the same thing as the subject	*My mother is the **mayor** of this town.*
Appositive: follows a noun, gives information about it	*Jen, my **neighbor**, has two cats.*

Verbs

A verb shows action (doing) or being.

Tense: Tells time. Verbs have six tenses:

Present	*Karen **writes** a poem.*
Past	*Karen **wrote** a poem.*
Future	*Karen **will write** a poem.*
Present Perfect	*Karen **has written** a poem.*
Past Perfect	*Karen **had written** a poem.*
Future Perfect	*Karen **will have written** a poem.*

The verb **to be** (of being) is
***am, are, is, was, were, be, being, been**.*

Adjectives

An adjective describes a noun or pronoun and answers these questions:

What kind of?	*It was a **beautiful** day.*
How many? How much?	*I'd like **three** apples and **some** grapes, please.*
Which one? Which ones?	***That** tie is mine; **those** socks are yours.*

Adverbs

An adverb describes a verb, adjective, or other adverb and answers four questions:

How?	*The cat howled **loudly**.*
When?	*The cat howled **today**.*
Where?	*The cat howled **there**.*
To what extent (by how much)?	*The cat howled **extremely** loudly.*

Prepositions

A preposition shows the relationship of one noun to another.

*The mouse is **in** the house.*
*The cow is **near** the plow.*
*The fish is **on** the dish.*
*The bug is **under** the rug.*
*The bee is **between** the tree and the sea.*

Pronouns

A pronoun takes the place of a noun.

Subject Pronouns	*I, you, he, she, it, we, they*
Object Pronouns	*me, you, him, her, it, us, them*
Possessive Pronouns	*my, mine, your, yours, his, her, hers, its, our, ours, their, theirs*

***Mary** told **Christopher** to wash **Christopher's** hands.*
***She** told **him** to wash **his** hands.*

Conjunctions

A conjunction joins words or parts of sentences together. Some common conjunctions:

and	*either/or*	*when*
so	*but*	*therefore*
if	*after*	*yet*
while	*though*	*because*
nor	*however*	*where*
or	*for*	*nevertheless*
since	*although*	*unless*

*The boy **and** the girl are related, **but** they don't look alike,*
***so** they must be in disguise, **or** my glasses are foggy.*

Interjections

An interjection is a word that expresses strong feelings or emotions.

***Wow**, it's great!*   ***Hurray**, it's raining!*
***Eek**, a snake!*   ***Ouch**, that hurts.*
***Hey**, don't do that!*   ***Well**, that's all, folks.*
***Gosh**, that's nice.*   ***Whoa**, slow down!*
***Yippee**, we won!*   ***Ugh**, how disgusting!*

Four Kinds of Sentences

Declarative: states a **fact**
The baseball game is tomorrow.

Interrogative: asks a **question**
How many feet are in a mile?

Imperative: gives an **order**
Please line up in single file.

Exclamatory: expresses **strong feelings**
The animals have escaped from their cages!

Glossary of Grammar Terms

Articles: *a, an, the*

Clause: a group of words with a subject and a verb

Paragraph: a group of sentences written together about the same thing

Phrase: a group of words

Sentence: a group of words with a subject and a verb that makes complete sense

Punctuation Guide

Punctuation marks are like little road signs that help you understand a sentence better.

Apostrophes '

Use an apostrophe in contractions to take the place of missing letters.
it is = it's   you are = you're   they will = they'll

Use an apostrophe in all possessive nouns.
the boy's jackets, the babies' toys

Colons :

Use a colon to introduce a list.
Take the following items: a blanket, food, and a first aid kit.

Put a colon after headings in a memo.
To: Mrs. Youngman
From: Ms. Stevens

Use a colon after the greeting of a business letter.
Dear Customer Service Department:

Commas ,

Use commas to separate three or more items in a series.
David, Jennifer, and Tim went to the movies.

Use a comma to separate the name of the person spoken to.
After you move, Lorraine, you'll be closer to work.

Use commas to set off a direct quotation.
I said, "Your dog needs a haircut," and Roslyn laughed.

Use a comma between clauses in a sentence.
Audrey baked the cake, and Irwin ate it.

Use a comma between adjectives describing the same noun.
Karen took beautiful, colorful, spectacular nature photos.

Dashes —

Use dashes when you interrupt a thought.
Abraham Lincoln—we celebrate his birthday in February—was our 16th president.

Ellipses . . .

Put ellipses where you leave words out.
She had many pets . . . when she lived in Chelsea.

Exclamation Points !

Put an exclamation point at the end of an exclamatory sentence.
A 95-pound chicken just escaped from the coop!

Hyphens -

Use a hyphen to connect parts of some compound words.
custom-made   well-known   mother-in-law

Use a hyphen to separate syllables in a word when a word can't fit at the end of a line.
In the 1990s, my grandparents lived in a very tall building in the heart of New York City.

Use hyphens in word numbers from twenty-one to ninety-nine.
sixty-seven   thirty-five   forty-two

Parentheses ( )

Put parentheses around extra words that give more facts.
Post Imaging (that's my brother's company) is on Madison Avenue.

Periods .

Put a period at the end of a sentence.
She was born on July 19, 2003.

Use periods after initials.
Franklin D. Roosevelt was president during World War II.

Use periods after abbreviations.
Shawmut St.   N.Y.   3 a.m.   Dr. Sen

Question Marks **?**

Put a question mark at the end of a question.
Are you a student at Columbia Prep School?

Quotation Marks **" "**

Put quotation marks around words you are quoting directly.
"My goose just laid a golden egg!" shouted the farmer.

Semicolons **;**

Use a semicolon to join two main clauses in a sentence.
She retouches photographs; he sings in a heavy metal band.

Use a semicolon before some conjunctions or phrases.
It had rained all morning; therefore, the picnic was called off.

Slashes **/**

Put a slash between words used in pairs.
either/or   neither/nor

Put slashes between parts of an internet address.
http://www.scholastic.com/kids

CAPITAL LETTERS

The following section shows you how to capitalize words. Abbreviations often include periods.

Capitalize the first word of a sentence.
My teacher's pet frog fell into a bucket of paint.

Capitalize the first word of a direct quote.
Abby said, "Mommy, I like alligators."

Capitalize the first word of each line of poetry.
A cow flew by
While chewing gum;
She ate a pie;
Do you want some?

Capitalize the pronoun *I*.
I couldn't stop laughing after I heard that joke.

Capitalize people's names.
Richard Soghoian, Sue Kilmer, Lorrie Gerson

Capitalize titles used with people's names.
Ms. Liz Pierce, Dr. William Brown, Mr. Doug Gibson

Capitalize the names of buildings and monuments.
Chrysler Building, Sears Tower, Lincoln Memorial

Capitalize the names of organizations.
Internet Society, American Medical Association

Capitalize the names of colleges and museums.
Tufts University, San Francisco Museum of Modern Art

Capitalize the names of sports teams.
Chicago Bears, Denver Nuggets

Capitalize proper adjectives (made from proper nouns).
French cooking, Italian opera, Japanese cars

Capitalize initials in a person's name.
John F. Kennedy, J. K. Rowling

Capitalize official titles used with people's names.
General Jones, President Freedman, Queen Rozzie

Capitalize the names of the days of the week.
Monday, Tuesday, Wednesday, etc.

Capitalize the names of the months of the year.
January, February, March, etc.

Capitalize the first word in the greeting and closing of a letter.
Dear Mr. Greenblatt,   Sincerely yours,

Capitalize the main words in the titles of books, movies, plays, and songs.
Island of the Blue Dolphins, The Sound of Music

Capitalize the names of college or school courses.
Introduction to Cartography, Advanced Physics

Capitalize geographic locations.
He lived in the East but moved to the Southwest.

Capitalize the names of religions, nationalities, and races.
Muslims, Christians, Canadians

Capitalize the names of holidays, festivals, and special events.
Thanksgiving, Rosh Hashana, Christmas, Fall Fair

Capitalize the names of languages.
Greek, Hebrew, Swahili, English

Capitalize the names of historical periods, documents, and events.
the Civil War, the Constitution, the Middle Ages

Capitalize the names of gods and deities.
Buddha, Allah, God, Jehovah

Capitalize the names of religious books and books of the Bible.
the Koran, the Torah, Genesis, Bible

Capitalize the names of the planets.
Mars, Venus, Saturn, Jupiter

Capitalize the abbreviations of titles after someone's name.
Herbert Wigglesworth Jr.   Anthony Smart, MD

Capitalize the postal abbreviations for states.
MA, TX, NY, FL, CA

Capitalize the names of products and companies.
Tylenol, Ford Motor Company, Adidas, Wikipedia

Capitalize CE and BCE.
I saw ancient statues from 230 CE and 51 BCE.

An idiom is an expression that has a special meaning that is different from what the individual words usually mean. For instance, "Keep a stiff upper lip" means "be brave." Here are some other well-known idioms and their meanings:

ants in your pants: extreme restlessness

apple of your eye: something or someone greatly loved

at the drop of a hat: immediately

baker's dozen: 13 for the price of 12

beat around the bush: avoid answering a question

between a rock and a hard place: in a difficult situation

bite the bullet: prepare for an unpleasant experience

blow your own horn: praise yourself

bolt from the blue: something unexpected and surprising

break a leg: good luck in a show

burn the candle at both ends: work late into the night

bury the hatchet: settle an argument

butter someone up: flatter someone

butterflies in your stomach: a feeling of nervousness

calm before the storm: a period of quiet before a crisis

climbing the walls: be restless and frustrated

cold feet: a fear of doing something

cool as a cucumber: very calm

cost an arm and a leg: very expensive

cry wolf: give a false alarm

dime a dozen: very common and cheap

drop in the bucket: a very small amount of something

eat your words: take back what you've said

elbow grease: hard work

eleventh hour: the last minute

face the music: accept the punishment you deserve

feather in your cap: a great achievement or honor

fight tooth and nail: fight fiercely

fish out of water: a person out of his or her usual place

fly off the handle: lose your temper; become angry

forty winks: a short nap

from soup to nuts: everything from beginning to end

get a kick out of something: really enjoy something

get under someone's skin: to bother or annoy someone

gift of gab: skill in talking

give me five: slap a person's hand as a greeting

go bananas: act in a crazy manner

green thumb: good at growing flowers and plants

head in the clouds: absent-minded; lost in thought

hit the books: do your homework or study harder

hit the jackpot: win a lot of money; be very lucky

in hot water: in big trouble

jump the gun: start too soon

keep your shirt on: remain calm; don't get angry

lend an ear: listen carefully; pay attention

like two peas in a pod: exactly alike in looks or behavior

make waves: cause trouble

needle in a haystack: something very hard to find

no dice: absolutely not!

on cloud nine: very happy

on top of the world: feeling joyously happy

open a can of worms: cause trouble

out like a light: fast asleep

pass the hat: ask for money

piece of cake: very easy to do

play with fire: do something dangerous

pull yourself together: get control of yourself

raining cats and dogs: raining very heavily

red-letter day: a very significant and happy day

ring a bell: sound familiar

scratch the surface: just begin to deal with a problem

shake a leg: speed up; go faster

skate on thin ice: take a big chance

spill the beans: give away a secret

throw in the towel: give up

tickled pink: very pleased or amused

tighten your belt: spend less money

two-faced: dishonest; false

under the weather: sick

walking on air: very happy, excited, joyful

wet blanket: a dull or sour person who spoils the fun

white elephant: something useless and unwanted

Initials, Acronyms, and Abbreviations Guide

An **initial** is a letter, usually followed by a period, that takes the place of a whole word.

An **acronym** is a group of initials that forms another word or phrase.

An **abbreviation** is a shortened form of a word, followed by a period.

AA = Alcoholics Anonymous

ACLU = American Civil Liberties Union

aka = also known as

AM = amplitude modulation

anon = anonymous

ASAP = as soon as possible

ASPCA = American Society for the Prevention of Cruelty to Animals

Aug. = August

AWOL = absent without leave

C = Celsius or centigrade

CEO = chief executive officer

CIA = Central Intelligence Agency

cm = centimeter

co. = company

COD = cash on delivery

corp. = corporation

dB = decibel

DC = District of Columbia

DDS = Doctor of Dental Science

Dec. = December

dept. = department

DOB = date of birth

e.g. = for example

EMT = emergency medical technician

EPA = Environmental Protection Agency

ERA = Equal Rights Amendment

ESL = English as a second language

F = Fahrenheit

FBI = Federal Bureau of Investigation

Feb. = February

FM = frequency modulation

Fri. = Friday

ft. = foot

FYI = for your information

g = gram

GCF = greatest common factor

GOP = Grand Old Party (Republican Party)

govt. = government

HDTV = high-definition television

HQ = headquarters

hr. = hour

ICU = intensive care unit

ID = identification

i.e. = that is

in. = inch

inc. = incorporated

IRS = Internal Revenue Service

Jan. = January

Jr. = junior

kg = kilogram

km = kilometer

l = liter

lb. = pound

LCD = lowest (or least) common denominator

LCM = lowest (or least) common multiple

m = meter

MADD = Mothers Against Drunk Driving

MC = master of ceremonies

MD = *medicinae doctor* (Latin for "doctor of medicine")

mi. = mile

min. = minute

misc. = miscellaneous

mm = millimeter

mo. = month

Mon. = Monday

NAACP = National Association for the Advancement of Colored People

NASA = National Aeronautics and Space Administration

NASCAR = National Association for Stock Car Auto Racing

NBA = National Basketball Association

NFL = National Football League

NHL = National Hockey League

no. = number

Nov. = November

NOW = National Organization for Women

Oct. = October

OPEC = Organization of the Petroleum Exporting Countries

oz. = ounce

PA = public address

PIN = personal identification number

P.O. = post office

POW = prisoner of war

PTA = Parent-Teacher Association

PTO = Parent-Teacher Organization

RN = registered nurse

RV = recreational vehicle

SADD = Students Against Drunk Driving

SASE = self-addressed stamped envelope

Sat. = Saturday

sec. = second

Sept. = September

SIDS = sudden infant death syndrome

sq. = square

Sr. = senior

Sun. = Sunday

tn. = ton

T or tbsp. = tablespoon

TBA = to be announced

Thurs. = Thursday

TM = trademark

tsp. = teaspoon

Tues. = Tuesday

UN = United Nations

UNICEF = United Nations Children's Fund

UPC = Universal Product Code

US = United States

U.S.A. = United States of America

VP = vice president

Wed. = Wednesday

w/o = without

WWW = World Wide Web

yd. = yard

yr. = year

Numbers

Cardinal numbers are used for counting. They tell you how many there are of something. Ordinal numbers show the position of something in a series. In the sentence "He was up at bat five times and on the fifth time, he hit a home run," the word *five* is a cardinal number and *fifth* is an ordinal number. Cardinal numbers can be nouns, adjectives, or pronouns; ordinal numbers may be nouns or adjectives. Each number in this table is listed by its cardinal symbol, then by its cardinal name and ordinal information. Zero does not have an ordinal number.

0 **zero**	11 **eleven**, 11th, eleventh	30 **thirty**, 30th, thirtieth
1 **one**, 1st, first	12 **twelve**, 12th, twelfth	40 **forty**, 40th, fortieth
2 **two**, 2nd, second	13 **thirteen**, 13th, thirteenth	50 **fifty**, 50th, fiftieth
3 **three**, 3rd, third	14 **fourteen**, 14th, fourteenth	60 **sixty**, 60th, sixtieth
4 **four**, 4th, fourth	15 **fifteen**, 15th, fifteenth	70 **seventy**, 70th, seventieth
5 **five**, 5th, fifth	16 **sixteen**, 16th, sixteenth	80 **eighty**, 80th, eightieth
6 **six**, 6th, sixth	17 **seventeen**, 17th, seventeenth	90 **ninety**, 90th, ninetieth
7 **seven**, 7th, seventh	18 **eighteen**, 18th, eighteenth	100 **hundred**, 100th, hundredth
8 **eight**, 8th, eighth	19 **nineteen**, 19th, nineteenth	1,000 **thousand**, 1,000th, thousandth
9 **nine**, 9th, ninth	20 **twenty**, 20th, twentieth	1,000,000 **million**, 1,000,000th, millionth
10 **ten**, 10th, tenth	21 **twenty-one**, 21st, twenty-first	1,000,000,000 **billion**, 1,000,000,000th, billionth

Measurements

	Length	Weight	Volume (liquids)	Area
US	1 foot = 12 inches 1 yard = 3 feet 1 mile = 5,280 feet = 1,760 yards	1 pound = 16 ounces 1 ton = 2,000 pounds	1 cup = 8 fluid ounces 1 pint = 2 cups 1 quart = 2 pints 1 gallon = 4 quarts	1 square foot = 144 square inches = 0.111 square yards 1 square yard = 9 square feet 1 acre = 4,840 square yards 1 square mile = 640 acres
Metric	1 centimeter = 10 millimeters 1 meter = 100 centimeters 1 kilometer = 1,000 meters	1 gram = 1,000 milligrams 1 kilogram = 1,000 grams 1 metric ton = 1,000 kilograms	1 centiliter = 10 milliliters 1 liter = 100 centiliters 1 kiloliter = 1,000 liters	1 square centimeter = 100 square millimeters 1 square meter = 10,000 square centimeters 1 square kilometer = 1,000,000 square meters
Conversion	1 inch = 2.54 centimeters 1 centimeter = 0.394 inches 1 foot = 30.48 centimeters 1 yard = 0.914 meters 1 meter = 1.094 yards 1 mile = 1.609 kilometers 1 kilometer = 0.621 miles	1 ounce = 28.350 grams 1 gram = 0.035 ounces 1 pound = 0.454 kilograms 1 kilogram = 2.205 pounds 1 ton = 0.907 metric tons 1 metric ton = 1.102 tons	1 fluid ounce = 29.57 milliliters 1 centiliter = 0.338 fluid ounces 1 cup = 0.237 liters 1 pint = 0.473 liters 1 quart = 0.946 liters 1 liter = 1.057 quarts 1 gallon = 3.785 liters 1 kiloliter = 264.172 gallons	1 square inch = 6.452 square centimeters 1 square centimeter = 0.155 square inches 1 square foot = 929.030 square centimeters 1 square yard = 0.836 square meters 1 square meter = 1.196 square yards 1 acre = 4,046.86 square meters 1 square mile = 2.590 square kilometers 1 square kilometer = 0.386 square miles

George Washington

Born: Feb. 22, 1732
Birthplace: Westmoreland Co., VA
Died: Dec. 14, 1799
Dates of terms:
April 30, 1789–March 4, 1793;
March 4, 1793–March 4, 1797
Party: Federalist

John Adams

Born: Oct. 30, 1735
Birthplace: Braintree, MA
Died: July 4, 1826
Dates of term:
March 4, 1797–March 4, 1801
Party: Federalist

Thomas Jefferson

Born: April 13, 1743
Birthplace: Shadwell, VA
Died: July 4, 1826
Dates of terms:
March 4, 1801–March 4, 1805;
March 4, 1805–March 4, 1809
Party: Democratic-Republican

James Madison

Born: March 16, 1751
Birthplace: Port Conway, VA
Died: June 28, 1836
Dates of terms:
March 4, 1809–March 4, 1813;
March 4, 1813–March 4, 1817
Party: Democratic-Republican

James Monroe

Born: April 28, 1758
Birthplace: Westmoreland Co., VA
Died: July 4, 1831
Dates of terms:
March 4, 1817–March 4, 1821;
March 5, 1821–March 4, 1825
Party: Democratic-Republican

John Quincy Adams

Born: July 11, 1767
Birthplace: Braintree, MA
Died: Feb. 23, 1848
Dates of term:
March 4, 1825–March 4, 1829
Party: Democratic-Republican

Andrew Jackson

Born: March 15, 1767
Birthplace: Waxhaws, NC/SC
Died: June 8, 1845
Dates of terms:
March 4, 1829–March 4, 1833;
March 4, 1833–March 4, 1837
Party: Democratic

Martin Van Buren

Born: Dec. 5, 1782
Birthplace: Kinderhook, NY
Died: July 24, 1862
Dates of term:
March 4, 1837–March 4, 1841
Party: Democratic

William Henry Harrison

Born: Feb. 9, 1773
Birthplace: Berkeley, VA
Died: April 4, 1841
Dates of term:
March 4, 1841–April 4, 1841*
Party: Whig

John Tyler

Born: March 29, 1790
Birthplace: Charles City Co., VA
Died: Jan. 18, 1862
Dates of term:
April 6, 1841–March 4, 1845
Party: Whig/Independent

James K. Polk

Born: Nov. 2, 1795
Birthplace: Mecklenburg Co., NC
Died: June 15, 1849
Dates of term:
March 4, 1845–March 4, 1849
Party: Democratic

Zachary Taylor

Born: Nov. 24, 1784
Birthplace: Orange Co., VA
Died: July 9, 1850
Dates of term:
March 5, 1849–July 9, 1850*
Party: Whig

Millard Fillmore

Born: Jan. 7, 1800
Birthplace: Cayuga Co., NY
Died: March 8, 1874
Dates of term:
July 10, 1850–March 4, 1853
Party: Whig

Franklin Pierce

Born: Nov. 23, 1804
Birthplace: Hillsboro, NH
Died: Oct. 8, 1869
Dates of term:
March 4, 1853–March 4, 1857
Party: Democratic

James Buchanan

Born: April 23, 1791
Birthplace: Franklin Co., PA
Died: June 1, 1868
Dates of term:
March 4, 1857–March 4, 1861
Party: Democratic

Abraham Lincoln

Born: Feb. 12, 1809
Birthplace: Hardin Co., KY
Died: April 15, 1865
Dates of terms:
March 4, 1861–March 4, 1865;
March 4, 1865–April 15, 1865*
Party: Republican

Andrew Johnson

Born: Dec. 29, 1808
Birthplace: Raleigh, NC
Died: July 31, 1875
Dates of term:
April 15, 1865–March 4, 1869
Party: Democratic

Ulysses S. Grant

Born: April 27, 1822
Birthplace: Point Pleasant, OH
Died: July 23, 1885
Dates of terms:
March 4, 1869–March 4, 1873;
March 4, 1873–March 4, 1877
Party: Republican

Rutherford B. Hayes

Born: Oct. 4, 1822
Birthplace: Delaware, OH
Died: Jan. 17, 1893
Dates of term:
March 5, 1877–March 4, 1881
Party: Republican

James Garfield

Born: Nov. 19, 1831
Birthplace: Orange, OH
Died: Sept. 19, 1881
Dates of term:
March 4, 1881–Sept. 19, 1881*
Party: Republican

Chester A. Arthur

Born: Oct. 5, 1829
Birthplace: Fairfield, VT
Died: Nov. 18, 1886
Dates of term:
Sept. 20, 1881–March 4, 1885
Party: Republican

Grover Cleveland

Born: March 18, 1837
Birthplace: Caldwell, NJ
Died: June 24, 1908
Dates of term:
March 4, 1885–March 4, 1889
Party: Democratic

Benjamin Harrison

Born: Aug. 20, 1833
Birthplace: North Bend, OH
Died: March 13, 1901
Dates of term:
March 4, 1889–March 4, 1893
Party: Republican

Grover Cleveland

Born: March 18, 1837
Birthplace: Caldwell, NJ
Died: June 24, 1908
Dates of term:
March 4, 1893–March 4, 1897**
Party: Democratic

William McKinley

Born: Jan. 29, 1843
Birthplace: Niles, OH
Died: Sept. 14, 1901
Dates of terms:
March 4, 1897–March 4, 1901;
March 4, 1901–Sept. 14, 1901*
Party: Republican

*Died while in office   **Second, non-consecutive, term of office   ***Resigned while in office

Theodore Roosevelt

Born: Oct. 27, 1858
Birthplace: New York, NY
Died: Jan. 6, 1919
Dates of terms:
Sept. 14, 1901–March 4, 1905;
March 4, 1905–March 4, 1909
Party: Republican

William Howard Taft

Born: Sept. 15, 1857
Birthplace: Cincinnati, OH
Died: March 8, 1930
Dates of term:
March 4, 1909–March 4, 1913
Party: Republican

Woodrow Wilson

Born: Dec. 28, 1856
Birthplace: Staunton, VA
Died: Feb. 3, 1924
Dates of terms:
March 4, 1913–March 4, 1917;
March 4, 1917–March 4, 1921
Party: Democratic

Warren G. Harding

Born: Nov. 2, 1865
Birthplace: Corsica, OH
Died: Aug. 2, 1923
Dates of term:
March 4, 1921–Aug. 2, 1923*
Party: Republican

Calvin Coolidge

Born: July 4, 1872
Birthplace: Plymouth Notch, VT
Died: Jan. 5, 1933
Dates of terms:
Aug. 3, 1923–March 4, 1925;
March 4, 1925–March 4, 1929
Party: Republican

Herbert Hoover

Born: Aug. 10, 1874
Birthplace: West Branch, IA
Died: Oct. 20, 1964
Dates of term:
March 4, 1929–March 4, 1933
Party: Republican

Franklin D. Roosevelt

Born: Jan. 30, 1882
Birthplace: Hyde Park, NY
Died: April 12, 1945
Dates of terms:
March 4, 1933–Jan. 20, 1937;
Jan. 20, 1937–Jan. 20, 1941;
Jan. 20, 1941– Jan. 20, 1945;
Jan. 20, 1945–April 12, 1945*
Party: Democratic

Harry S. Truman

Born: May 8, 1884
Birthplace: Lamar, MO
Died: Dec. 26, 1972
Dates of terms:
April 12, 1945–Jan. 20, 1949;
Jan. 20, 1949–Jan. 20, 1953
Party: Democratic

Dwight D. Eisenhower

Born: Oct. 14, 1890
Birthplace: Denison, TX
Died: March 28, 1969
Dates of terms:
Jan. 20, 1953–Jan. 20, 1957;
Jan. 21, 1957–Jan. 20, 1961
Party: Republican

John F. Kennedy

Born: May 29, 1917
Birthplace: Brookline, MA
Died: Nov. 22, 1963
Dates of term:
Jan. 20, 1961–Nov. 22, 1963*
Party: Democratic

Lyndon B. Johnson

Born: Aug. 27, 1908
Birthplace: Stonewall, TX
Died: Jan. 22, 1973
Dates of terms:
Nov. 22, 1963–Jan. 20, 1965;
Jan. 20, 1965–Jan. 20, 1969
Party: Democratic

Richard M. Nixon

Born: Jan. 9, 1913
Birthplace: Yorba Linda, CA
Died: April 22, 1994
Dates of terms:
Jan. 20, 1969–Jan. 20, 1973;
Jan. 20, 1973–Aug. 9, 1974***
Party: Republican

Gerald R. Ford

Born: July 14, 1913
Birthplace: Omaha, NE
Died: Dec. 26, 2006
Dates of term:
Aug. 9, 1974–Jan. 20, 1977
Party: Republican

James Carter

Born: Oct. 1, 1924
Birthplace: Plains, GA
Dates of term:
Jan. 20, 1977–Jan. 20, 1981
Party: Democratic

Ronald Reagan

Born: Feb. 6, 1911
Birthplace: Tampico, IL
Died: June 5, 2004
Dates of terms:
Jan 20, 1981–Jan. 20, 1985;
Jan. 21, 1985–Jan. 20, 1989
Party: Republican

George H. W. Bush

Born: June 12, 1924
Birthplace: Milton, MA
Died: Nov. 30, 2018
Dates of term:
Jan. 20, 1989–Jan. 20, 1993
Party: Republican

William J. Clinton

Born: Aug. 19, 1946
Birthplace: Hope, AR
Dates of terms:
Jan. 20, 1993–Jan. 20, 1997;
Jan. 20, 1997–Jan. 20, 2001
Party: Democratic

George W. Bush

Born: July 6, 1946
Birthplace: New Haven, CT
Dates of terms:
Jan. 20, 2001–Jan. 20, 2005;
Jan. 20, 2005–Jan. 20, 2009
Party: Republican

Barack Obama

Born: Aug. 4, 1961
Birthplace: Honolulu, HI
Dates of terms:
Jan. 20, 2009–Jan. 20, 2013;
Jan. 21, 2013–Jan. 20, 2017
Party: Democratic

Donald J. Trump

Born: June 14, 1946
Birthplace: New York, NY
Dates of terms:
Jan. 20, 2017–
Party: Republican

US STATES

Alabama
Al·a·bam·a (*al*-uh-**bam**-uh)

A state in the southeastern United States. It has a short border on the Gulf of Mexico and is in the Deep South, a region that was part of the Confederacy during the Civil War.

Postal abbreviation: AL
Nicknames: Yellowhammer State, Heart of Dixie
Population: 4,874,747
Demonym: Alabamian
Capital: Montgomery
Year of admission: 1819
Order of admission: 22

Alaska
A·las·ka (uh-**las**-kuh)

A state north of the mainland of the United States. The largest US state, it lies west of Canada on the northwestern tip of North America, just across from Russia. It is the home of such native Alaskan tribes as the Inuit, also known as Eskimos.

Postal abbreviation: AK
Nickname (unofficial): Last Frontier
Population: 739,795
Demonym: Alaskan
Capital: Juneau
Year of admission: 1959
Order of admission: 49

Arizona
Ar·i·zo·na (*ar*-i-**zoh**-nuh)

A state in the southwestern United States. Arizona borders Mexico and is to the east of California. It has a desert landscape, with a dry climate and giant cacti, and is best known for being the site of the Grand Canyon.

Postal abbreviation: AZ
Nicknames: Grand Canyon State, Copper State
Demonym: Arizonan
Population: 7,016,270
Capital: Phoenix
Year of admission: 1912
Order of admission: 48

Arkansas
Ar·kan·sas (**ahr**-kin-*saw*)

A state in the southern United States. The Mississippi River runs along its eastern border; the Ozarks, a mountain range in the northwestern part of the state, extend into Oklahoma, Missouri, and Kansas.

Postal abbreviation: AR
Nickname: Natural State
Population: 3,004,279
Demonyms: Arkansan, Arkansawyer
Capital: Little Rock
Year of admission: 1836
Order of admission: 25

California
Cal·i·for·nia (*kal*-uh-**forn**-yuh)

A state in the western United States. It is on the West Coast, bordering the Pacific Ocean. The most populated US state, California is the home of the Hollywood film industry and Silicon Valley, the center of the high-tech industry.

Postal abbreviation: CA
Nickname: Golden State
Population: 39,536,653
Demonym: Californian
Capital: Sacramento
Year of admission: 1850
Order of admission: 31

Colorado
Col·o·ra·do
(*kah*-luh-**rah**-doh *or* kah-luh-**rad**-oh)

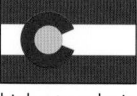

A state in the western United States. It is north of New Mexico and contains many of the highest peaks in the Rocky Mountains, including Pikes Peak, the most visited mountain in North America.

Postal abbreviation: CO
Nickname: Centennial State
Population: 5,607,154
Demonym: Coloradan
Capital: Denver
Year of admission: 1876
Order of admission: 38

Connecticut
Con·nect·i·cut (kuh-**net**-i-kuht)

A state in the northeastern United States. It is the southernmost state in New England and lies on Long Island Sound, an estuary of the Atlantic Ocean. Settled by the English in the 1630s, Connecticut was one of the 13 original colonies.

Postal abbreviation: CT
Nicknames: Nutmeg State, Constitution State
Population: 3,588,184
Demonyms: Connecticuter, Connecticutian, Nutmegger
Capital: Hartford
Year of admission: 1788
Order of admission: 5

Delaware
Del·a·ware (**del**-uh-*wair*)

A state in the eastern central United States. It is south of New Jersey, on the Atlantic Ocean. Delaware was one of the 13 original colonies. On December 7, 1787, it was the first colony to ratify the Constitution, thereby becoming the first state.

Postal abbreviation: DE
Nicknames: First State, Diamond State
Population: 961,939
Demonym: Delawarean
Capital: Dover
Year of admission: 1787
Order of admission: 1

Florida
Flor·i·da (**flor**-i-duh)

A state in the southeastern United States. A large peninsula surrounded by the Gulf of Mexico, the Atlantic Ocean, and the Caribbean Sea, Florida is known as the "Sunshine State" because of its warm climate.

Postal abbreviation: FL
Nickname: Sunshine State
Population: 20,984,400
Demonym: Floridian
Capital: Tallahassee
Year of admission: 1845
Order of admission: 27

Georgia

Geor·gia (**jor**-juh)

A state in the southeastern United States. Georgia is north of Florida, and its coast is on the Atlantic Ocean. One of the original 13 colonies, it was the only one to be named after a king, George II of England.

Postal abbreviation: GA
Nicknames: Peach State, Empire State of the South
Population: 10,429,379
Demonym: Georgian
Capital: Atlanta
Year of admission: 1788
Order of admission: 4

Hawaii

Ha·wa·ii (huh-**wye**-ee)

A state west of the mainland of the United States. Hawaii is in the Pacific Ocean and consists of eight main islands and many smaller ones. The newest of the 50 states, it is popular with tourists for its beaches and tropical climate.

Postal abbreviation: HI
Nicknames: Aloha State, Paradise
Population: 1,427,538
Demonym: Hawaiian
Capital: Honolulu
Year of admission: 1959
Order of admission: 50

Idaho

I·da·ho (**eye**-duh-*hoh*)

A state in the northwestern United States. It borders Canada on the north. Idaho is the largest producer of potatoes in the United States. Landlocked and mountainous, it is called the Gem State because of the wide variety of gems found there.

Postal abbreviation: ID
Nickname: Gem State
Population: 1,716,943
Demonym: Idahoan
Capital: Boise
Year of admission: 1890
Order of admission: 43

Illinois

Il·li·nois (*il*-uh-**noy**)

A state in the northern central United States. Its largest city is Chicago. Illinois is in the Midwest and has many museums devoted to Abraham Lincoln, who worked as a lawyer in the state's capital, Springfield, before becoming president.

Postal abbreviation: IL
Nicknames: Prairie State, Land of Lincoln
Population: 12,802,023
Demonym: Illinoisan
Capital: Springfield
Year of admission: 1818
Order of admission: 21

Indiana

In·di·an·a (*in*-dee-**an**-uh)

A state in the northern central United States. Indiana is in the Midwest, east of Illinois. Its inhabitants are known as Hoosiers, but the origin of the term is unknown. Some people say that it comes from "Who's there?" or is an old word meaning "roughneck."

Postal abbreviation: IN
Nickname: Hoosier State
Population: 6,666,818
Demonym: Hoosier
Capital: Indianapolis
Year of admission: 1816
Order of admission: 19

Iowa

I·o·wa (**eye**-uh-wuh)

A state in the northern central United States. Iowa is often referred to as the "Food Capital of the World." It is in the heart of the Corn Belt, a region in the Midwest that produces much of the corn grown in the United States.

Postal abbreviation: IA
Nickname: Hawkeye State
Population: 3,145,711
Demonym: Iowan
Capital: Des Moines
Year of admission: 1846
Order of admission: 29

Kansas

Kan·sas (**kan**-zuhs)

A state in the central United States. Located in almost the exact center of the US mainland, Kansas is in the Midwest and consists primarily of farmland. It grows the most wheat in the country and is known for its fields of sunflowers.

Postal abbreviation: KS
Nickname: Sunflower State
Population: 2,913,123
Demonym: Kansan
Capital: Topeka
Year of admission: 1861
Order of admission: 34

Kentucky

Ken·tuck·y (ken-**tuhk**-kee)

A state in the eastern central United States. It is north of Tennessee. Known for its fertile soil, bluegrass pastures, and Thoroughbreds, it is the home of the Kentucky Derby, one of the oldest Thoroughbred horse races in the country.

Postal abbreviation: KY
Nickname: Bluegrass State
Population: 4,454,189
Demonym: Kentuckian
Capital: Frankfort
Year of admission: 1792
Order of admission: 15

Louisiana

Lou·i·si·an·a (loo-*ee*-zee-**an**-uh)

A state in the southern United States. It is on the Gulf of Mexico. A former French colony, it was sold to the United States in 1803 in what became known as the Louisiana Purchase. Some of its residents still speak Cajun, a local French dialect.

Postal abbreviation: LA
Nicknames: Pelican State, Bayou State
Population: 4,684,333
Demonym: Louisianan
Capital: Baton Rouge
Year of admission: 1812
Order of admission: 18

Maine

Maine (mayn)

A state in the northeastern United States. It is the northernmost state in New England and the easternmost state in the country. Maine is known for its lobsters and scenic, rocky coastline on the Atlantic Ocean.

Postal abbreviation: ME
Nickname: Pine Tree State
Population: 1,335,907
Demonym: Mainer
Capital: Augusta
Year of admission: 1820
Order of admission: 23

Maryland

Mar·y·land (**mer**-uh-luhnd)

A state in the eastern central United States. It is in the Mid-Atlantic region, south of New England. The Chesapeake Bay, the largest estuary in the United States, runs through the state. Maryland is noted for seafood, especially crabs.

Postal abbreviation: MD
Nicknames: Free State, Old Line State
Population: 6,052,177
Demonym: Marylander
Capital: Annapolis
Year of admission: 1788
Order of admission: 7

Massachusetts

Mas·sa·chu·setts (*mas*-uh-**choo**-sits)

A state in the northeastern United States. Located in New England, it is where the Pilgrims landed in 1620 and established a colony near Cape Cod, on the state's Atlantic coast. It is the home of Harvard and other colleges and universities.

Postal abbreviation: MA
Nicknames: Bay State, Old Colony State
Population: 6,859,819
Demonyms: Bay Stater, Massachusite
Capital: Boston
Year of admission: 1788
Order of admission: 6

Michigan

Mich·i·gan (**mish**-i-guhn)

A state in the northern United States. It consists of two peninsulas and borders four of the five Great Lakes: Lakes Superior, Michigan, Huron, and Erie. Michigan also has almost 65,000 inland lakes and ponds.

Postal abbreviation: MI
Nicknames: Great Lakes State, Wolverine State
Population: 9,962,311
Demonyms: Michigander, Michiganian
Capital: Lansing
Year of admission: 1837
Order of admission: 26

Minnesota

Min·ne·so·ta (*min*-uh-**soh**-tuh)

A state in the northern United States. Minnesota is one of the border states with Canada and has a shoreline on Lake Superior, one of the Great Lakes. Known as the "Land of 10,000 Lakes," it also has more than 6,000 rivers and streams.

Postal abbreviation: MN
Nicknames: Gopher State, North Star State
Population: 5,576,606
Demonym: Minnesotan
Capital: St. Paul
Year of admission: 1858
Order of admission: 32

Mississippi

Mis·sis·sip·pi (*mis*-i-**sip**-ee)

A state in the southern United States. It is named for the Mississippi River, which forms its western boundary. The name Mississippi, in the Native American language of the Ojibwa, means "great river."

Postal abbreviation: MS
Nickname: Magnolia State
Population: 2,984,100
Demonym: Mississippian
Capital: Jackson
Year of admission: 1817
Order of admission: 20

Missouri

Mis·sour·i (mi-**zoor**-ee *or* mi-**zoor**-uh)

A state in the central United States. It is west of Illinois. The state used to be called the gateway to the West. In the 19th century, many explorers headed west from Missouri, including the Lewis and Clark expedition, which reached the Pacific.

Postal abbreviation: MO
Nickname: Show Me State
Population: 6,113,532
Demonym: Missourian
Capital: Jefferson City
Year of admission: 1821
Order of admission: 24

Montana

Mon·tan·a (mahn-**tan**-uh)

A state in the northern United States. It borders Canada and is west of North and South Dakota. Named after the Spanish word for mountain, it has numerous mountain ranges, including the Rockies, and is the home of Glacier National Park.

Postal abbreviation: MT
Nicknames: Treasure State, Big Sky Country
Population: 1,050,493
Demonym: Montanan
Capital: Helena
Year of admission: 1889
Order of admission: 41

Nebraska

Ne·bras·ka (nuh-**bras**-kuh)

A state in the central region of the United States. Nebraska is in the Midwest and is north of Kansas. It is largely prairie land, and its economy is based on farming and ranching.

Postal abbreviation: NE
Nickname: Cornhusker State
Population: 1,920,076
Demonym: Nebraskan
Capital: Lincoln
Year of admission: 1867
Order of admission: 37

Nevada

Ne·vad·a (nuh-**vad**-uh *or* nuh-**vah**-duh)

 A state in the western United States. It is east of California. A part of the Mojave Desert is in Nevada, the most arid state in the country. Its largest city, Las Vegas, is world-famous for its gambling resorts.

Postal abbreviation: NV
Nicknames: Silver State, Sagebrush State, Battle Born State
Population: 2,998,039
Demonym: Nevadan
Capital: Carson City
Year of admission: 1864
Order of admission: 36

New Hampshire

New Hamp·shire (noo **hamp**-shur)

 A state in the northeastern United States. It is in New England, south of Maine. The state has a small coastline on the Atlantic Ocean. Every four years, New Hampshire holds the first presidential primary in the United States.

Postal abbreviation: NH
Nickname: Granite State
Population: 1,342,795
Demonyms: Granite Stater, New Hampshirite
Capital: Concord
Year of admission: 1788
Order of admission: 9

New Jersey

New Jer·sey (noo **jur**-zee)

 A state in the northeastern United States. One of the original 13 colonies, it is south of New York. New Jersey is the most densely populated state in the United States and is known for its beaches on the Atlantic Ocean, called the Jersey Shore.

Postal abbreviation: NJ
Nickname: Garden State
Population: 9,005,644
Demonyms: New Jerseyan, New Jerseyite
Capital: Trenton
Year of admission: 1787
Order of admission: 3

New Mexico

New Mex·i·co (noo **mek**-si-*koh*)

 A state in the southwestern United States. It is east of Arizona. Various Native American tribes have lived in New Mexico for centuries, and it is still home to large Navajo and Pueblo populations, as well as to a large Hispanic population.

Postal abbreviation: NM
Nickname: Land of Enchantment
Population: 2,088,070
Demonym: New Mexican
Capital: Santa Fe
Year of admission: 1912
Order of admission: 47

New York

New York (noo **york**)

 A state in the northeastern United States. New York City is located in the southeastern part of the state. It is the most populated US city. Its skyline includes such famous skyscrapers as the Empire State Building and the Chrysler Building.

Postal abbreviation: NY
Nickname: Empire State
Population: 19,849,399
Demonym: New Yorker
Capital: Albany
Year of admission: 1788
Order of admission: 11

North Carolina

North Car·o·li·na (**north** *kar*-uh-**lye**-nuh)

 A state in the southeastern United States. Its eastern shore is on the Atlantic. The Appalachian range runs through western North Carolina and includes the Blue Ridge Mountains and the Great Smoky Mountains, which extend into Tennessee.

Postal abbreviation: NC
Nicknames: Tar Heel State, Old North State
Population: 10,273,419
Demonyms: North Carolinian, Tar Heel
Capital: Raleigh
Year of admission: 1789
Order of admission: 12

North Dakota

North Da·ko·ta (**north** duh-**koh**-tuh)

 A state in the northern central United States. It borders Canada and lies north of South Dakota. Most of it is covered in grassland. North Dakota has one of the largest Native American populations in the country.

Postal abbreviation: ND
Nickname: Peace Garden State
Population: 755,393
Demonym: North Dakotan
Capital: Bismarck
Year of admission: 1889
Order of admission: 39

Ohio

O·hi·o (oh-**hye**-oh)

 A state in the northern central United States. Ohio is in the Midwest. It has a shoreline on Lake Erie, one of the Great Lakes. Lake Erie is the fourth largest of the Great Lakes, which make up the biggest group of freshwater lakes in the world.

Postal abbreviation: OH
Nickname: Buckeye State
Population: 11,658,609
Demonyms: Ohioan, Buckeye
Capital: Columbus
Year of admission: 1803
Order of admission: 17

Oklahoma

O·kla·ho·ma (*oh*-kluh-**hoh**-muh)

 A state in the southern central United States. It is north of Texas and is one of the states in Tornado Alley, a region that has frequent tornadoes. Oklahoma is known for its production of natural gas and crude oil.

Postal abbreviation: OK
Nickname: Sooner State
Population: 3,930,864
Demonyms: Oklahoman, Okie
Capital: Oklahoma City
Year of admission: 1907
Order of admission: 46

Oregon

Or·e·gon (or-i-guhn *or* **or-i-***gahn***)**

 A state in the northwestern United States. It is in the Pacific Northwest, a region along the Pacific Ocean. The Cascades, a mountain range that extends from Northern California to Canada, run through Oregon and include volcanoes.

Postal abbreviation: OR
Nickname: Beaver State
Population: 4,142,776
Demonym: Oregonian
Capital: Salem
Year of admission: 1859
Order of admission: 33

Pennsylvania

Penn·syl·va·nia (*pen***-suhl-***vayn***-yuh)**

 A state in the eastern United States. It is south of New York. Pennsylvania was one of the original 13 colonies. Philadelphia, its largest city, has many historical landmarks. It was where the Declaration of Independence was signed.

Postal abbreviation: PA
Nickname: Keystone State
Population: 12,805,537
Demonym: Pennsylvanian
Capital: Harrisburg
Year of admission: 1787
Order of admission: 2

Rhode Island

Rhode Isl·and (*rohd* **eye-luhnd)**

 A state in the northeastern United States. It is the smallest US state. It is in New England and has a coast on the Atlantic. One of its cities, Newport, is famous for its 19th-century mansions, built when it was a summer resort for the wealthy.

Postal abbreviation: RI
Nickname: Ocean State
Population: 1,059,639
Demonym: Rhode Islander
Capital: Providence
Year of admission: 1790
Order of admission: 13

South Carolina

South Car·o·li·na (south *kar***-uh-***lye***-nuh)**

 A state in the southeastern United States. It is on the Atlantic Ocean, south of North Carolina. The Civil War began there on April 12, 1861, when the Confederates fired on the Union troops who held Fort Sumter, near the city of Charleston.

Postal abbreviation: SC
Nickname: Palmetto State
Population: 5,024,369
Demonym: South Carolinian
Capital: Columbia
Year of admission: 1788
Order of admission: 8

South Dakota

South Da·ko·ta (south duh-*koh***-tuh)**

 A state in the northern central United States. It is north of Nebraska. Mount Rushmore, in the Black Hills, is famed for its huge, carved faces of presidents George Washington, Thomas Jefferson, Theodore Roosevelt, and Abraham Lincoln.

Postal abbreviation: SD
Nicknames: Mount Rushmore State, Coyote State
Population: 869,666
Demonym: South Dakotan
Capital: Pierre
Year of admission: 1889
Order of admission: 40

Tennessee

Ten·nes·see (*ten***-uh-***see***)**

 A state in the southeastern United States. It is north of Georgia. Its largest city, Memphis, is considered the birthplace of the blues and was important to the growth of rock 'n' roll. Nashville, its capital, is the center of the country music industry.

Postal abbreviation: TN
Nickname: Volunteer State
Population: 6,715,984
Demonym: Tennessean
Capital: Nashville
Year of admission: 1796
Order of admission: 16

Texas

Tex·as (tek-suhs)

 A state in the southern central United States. It borders Mexico and is the second-largest US state, after Alaska. Before becoming a state, Texas belonged to Mexico, then was an independent republic for almost ten years.

Postal abbreviation: TX
Nickname: Lone Star State
Population: 28,304,596
Demonym: Texan
Capital: Austin
Year of admission: 1845
Order of admission: 28

Utah

U·tah (yoo-taw *or* **yoo-tah)**

 A state in the western United States. It is north of Arizona. Utah was founded by Mormon pioneers. More than half of its inhabitants are members of the Church of Jesus Christ of Latter-day Saints (Mormon Church). The church's headquarters is in Salt Lake City, the state's capital.

Postal abbreviation: UT
Nickname: Beehive State
Population: 3,101,833
Demonyms: Utahn, Utahan
Capital: Salt Lake City
Year of admission: 1896
Order of admission: 45

Vermont

Ver·mont (vur-*mahnt***)**

 A state in the northeastern United States. It borders Canada and is in New England, west of New Hampshire. Vermont is known for its Green Mountains, rural landscapes, and maple syrup production.

Postal abbreviation: VT
Nickname: Green Mountain State
Population: 623,657
Demonym: Vermonter
Capital: Montpelier
Year of admission: 1791
Order of admission: 14

Virginia
Vir·gin·ia (vur-**jin**-yuh)

 A state in the eastern central United States. It is a Mid-Atlantic state, lying south of Maryland on the Atlantic Ocean. Virginia was the site of the first permanent English colony in the New World, Jamestown, established in 1607.

Postal abbreviation: VA
Nickname: Old Dominion
Population: 8,470,020
Demonym: Virginian
Capital: Richmond
Year of admission: 1788
Order of admission: 10

Washington
Wash·ing·ton (**wah**-shing-tuhn)

 A state in the northwestern United States. It borders Canada and the Pacific Ocean. The state's Cascade Mountain Range has several active volcanoes, including Mount St. Helens and Mount Rainier, the highest mountain in the state.

Postal abbreviation: WA
Nickname: Evergreen State
Population: 7,405,743
Demonym: Washingtonian
Capital: Olympia
Year of admission: 1889
Order of admission: 42

West Virginia
West Vir·gin·ia (**west** vur-**jin**-yuh)

 A state in the eastern central United States. West Virginia became a state during the Civil War, when it joined the Union after separating from Virginia, a Confederate state. It is in the Appalachian mountain range and is heavily forested.

Postal abbreviation: WV
Nickname: Mountain State
Population: 1,815,857
Demonym: West Virginian
Capital: Charleston
Year of admission: 1863
Order of admission: 35

Wisconsin
Wis·con·sin (wis-**kahn**-sin)

 A state in the northern central United States. Wisconsin is north of Illinois and is bordered by two Great Lakes that separate it from Canada: Lake Superior and Lake Michigan. It is known for its production of cheese, milk, and butter.

Postal abbreviation: WI
Nicknames: Badger State, America's Dairyland
Population: 5,795,483
Demonym: Wisconsinite
Capital: Madison
Year of admission: 1848
Order of admission: 30

Wyoming
Wy·o·ming (wye-**oh**-ming)

 A state in the western United States. It is in the Rocky Mountains, south of Montana. Its Yellowstone National Park has the world's largest number of geysers. The state motto is "Equal Rights." It was the first US state to allow women to vote.

Postal abbreviation: WY
Nickname: Equality State
Population: 579,315
Demonym: Wyomingite
Capital: Cheyenne
Year of admission: 1890
Order of admission: 44

American Samoa

A·mer·i·can Sa·mo·a
(uh-**mer**-i-kuhn suh-**moh**-uh)

A US territory in the southern Pacific Ocean. Part of the Samoan Islands chain, American Samoa is a group of islands located about halfway between Hawaii and New Zealand. It lies southeast of the country of Samoa.

Postal abbreviation: AS
Population: 63,000
Demonym: American Samoan
Capital: Pago Pago
Year acquired by the US: 1899

Guam

Guam (gwahm)

A US territory in the western Pacific Ocean. Guam is the largest island in Micronesia and lies east of the Philippines. The most southern and largest of the Mariana Islands, it has one of the most important US military bases in the Pacific.

Postal abbreviation: GU
Population: 162,000
Demonym: Guamanian
Capital: Hagåtña
Year acquired by the US: 1898

Northern Mariana Islands

North·ern Mar·i·an·a Is·lands
(**nor**-THurn *mair*-ee-**an**-uh **eye**-luhdz)

A US commonwealth in the western Pacific Ocean. The Northern Mariana Islands are a group of 15 islands about three-quarters of the way from Hawaii to the Philippines, located north of Guam.

Postal abbreviation: MP
Population: 53,500
Demonym: Northern Mariana Islander
Capital: Saipan
Year acquired by the US: 1947

Puerto Rico

Puer·to Ri·co
(**pwer**-toh **ree**-koh *or* **por**-tuh **ree**-koh)

A US commonwealth in the northeastern Caribbean Sea. It lies east of the Dominican Republic and west of the US and British Virgin Islands. Puerto Rico consists of a main island and several smaller ones, and is a popular vacation destination.

Postal abbreviation: PR
Population: 3,337,177
Demonym: Puerto Rican
Capital: San Juan
Year acquired by the US: 1898

US Virgin Islands

US Vir·gin Is·lands
(**yoo** *es* **vur**-jin **eye**-luhndz)

A US territory in the northeastern Caribbean Sea. The main islands are Saint Croix, Saint John, and Saint Thomas. The US Virgin Islands lie south of Puerto Rico and west of the British Virgin Islands, a territory of the United Kingdom.

Postal abbreviation: VI
Population: 103,000
Demonym: US Virgin Islander
Capital: Charlotte Amalie
Year acquired by the US: 1917

Alberta

Al·ber·ta (al-**bur**-tuh)

A province in western Canada. It is the most populated and westernmost of Canada's three prairie provinces, which include Manitoba and Saskatchewan. Alberta and Saskatchewan are the only two Canadian provinces that are landlocked.

Postal abbreviation: AB
Population: 4,067,175
Demonym: Albertan
Capital: Edmonton
Year of admission: 1905

British Columbia

Brit·ish Co·lum·bi·a (*brit*-ish kuh-**luhm**-bee-uh)

A province in western Canada. British Columbia is the westernmost province in Canada and lies on the Pacific Ocean. It has 17,000 miles of rugged coastline and about 6,000 islands, most of which are uninhabited.

Postal abbreviation: DC
Population: 4,648,055
Demonym: British Columbian
Capital: Victoria
Year of admission: 1871

Manitoba

Man·i·to·ba (*man*-i-**toh**-buh)

A province in central Canada. It is south of Nunavut. The Manitoba town of Churchill, in the Canadian Arctic, is known as the polar bear capital of the world and attracts visitors who take expeditions across the tundra to see the area's polar bears.

Postal abbreviation: MB
Population: 1,278,365
Demonym: Manitoban
Capital: Winnipeg
Year of admission: 1870

New Brunswick

New Bruns·wick (noo **bruhnz**-wik)

A province in eastern Canada. New Brunswick, Nova Scotia, and Prince Edward Island are Canada's three maritime provinces, lying on the Atlantic. The Bay of Fundy, on New Brunswick's southern border, has the highest tides in the world.

Postal abbreviation: NB
Population: 747,101
Demonym: New Brunswicker
Capital: Fredericton
Year of admission: 1867

Newfoundland and Labrador
New·found·land and Lab·ra·dor
(**noo**-fuhnd-luhnd and **lab**-ruh-*dor*)

A province in eastern Canada. It is Canada's easternmost province and lies on the Atlantic Ocean. It consists of two parts: Labrador, on the mainland, and the island of Newfoundland, where most of its population lives.

Postal abbreviation: NL
Population: 519,716
Demonyms: Newfoundlander; Labradorian
Capital: St. John's
Year of admission: 1949

Northwest Territories
North·west Ter·ri·to·ries
(**north**-west **ter**-i-*tor*-eez)

A territory in northern Canada. It lies between Yukon and Nunavut, and has a coastline as well as islands on the Beaufort Sea, part of the Arctic Ocean. The Northwest Territories include Great Bear Lake, the largest lake entirely within Canada.

Postal abbreviation: NT
Population: 41,786
Demonym: Northwest Territorian
Capital: Yellowknife
Year of admission: 1870

Nova Scotia
No·va Sco·tia (**noh**-vuh **skoh**-shuh)

A province in eastern Canada. It is on the Atlantic Ocean, east of New Brunswick. Nova Scotia was named after Scotland, and people of Scottish descent constitute the largest ethnic group living there today.

Postal abbreviation: NS
Population: 923,598
Demonym: Nova Scotian
Capital: Halifax
Year of admission: 1867

Nunavut
Nu·na·vut (noo-nuh-*voot*)

A territory in northern Canada. It is Canada's largest and most northern territory, formed in 1999 after separating from the Northwest Territories. Most of its small population is Inuit, spread out over an area three times the size of Texas.

Postal abbreviation: NU
Population: 35,944
Demonyms: Nunavummiuq (singular), Nunavummiut (plural)
Capital: Iqaluit
Year of admission: 1999

Ontario
On·tar·i·o (ahn-**tair**-ee-oh)

A province in southeastern Canada. It is west of Quebec and borders the Great Lakes. Ontario is Canada's most populated province. Ottawa, Canada's capital, is in Ontario, as is Toronto, the province's capital and Canada's biggest city.

Postal abbreviation: ON
Population: 13,448,494
Demonym: Ontarian
Capital: Toronto
Year of admission: 1867

Prince Edward Island
Prince Ed·ward Is·land
(*prins* **ed**-wurd **eye**-luhnd)

A province in eastern Canada. Canada's smallest province, it is located north of Nova Scotia. Prince Edward Island is known for its lush, green landscapes and is the setting for the novel *Anne of Green Gables*.

Postal abbreviation: PE
Population: 142,907
Demonym: Prince Edward Islander
Capital: Charlottetown
Year of admission: 1873

Quebec
Que·bec *or* **Qué·bec** (kwuh-**bek** *or* kuh-**bek**)

A province in eastern Canada. It is south of Newfoundland and Labrador, and borders the Labrador Sea, an arm of the Atlantic between Greenland and Canada. Quebec is the only Canadian province whose sole official language is French.

Postal abbreviation: QC
Population: 8,164,361
Demonyms: Quebec *or* Quebecker; Québécois (male), Québécoise (female)
Capital: Quebec City *or* Québec City
Year of admission: 1867

Saskatchewan
Sas·katch·e·wan (sas-**kach**-uh-*wahn*)

A province in central Canada. It lies between Alberta and Manitoba, the two other prairie provinces. Saskatchewan produces much of the grain in Canada. Its flag includes a coat of arms with three wheat sheaves.

Postal abbreviation: SK
Population: 1,098,352
Demonyms: Saskatchewanian, Saskatchewaner
Capital: Regina
Year of admission: 1905

Yukon
Yu·kon (**yoo**-kahn)

A territory in northwestern Canada. It is the westernmost and smallest of Canada's three federal territories, which include Nunavut and the Northwest Territories. Sparsely populated, it borders the US state of Alaska on the west.

Postal abbreviation: YT
Population: 35,874
Demonym: Yukoner
Capital: Whitehorse
Year of admission: 1898

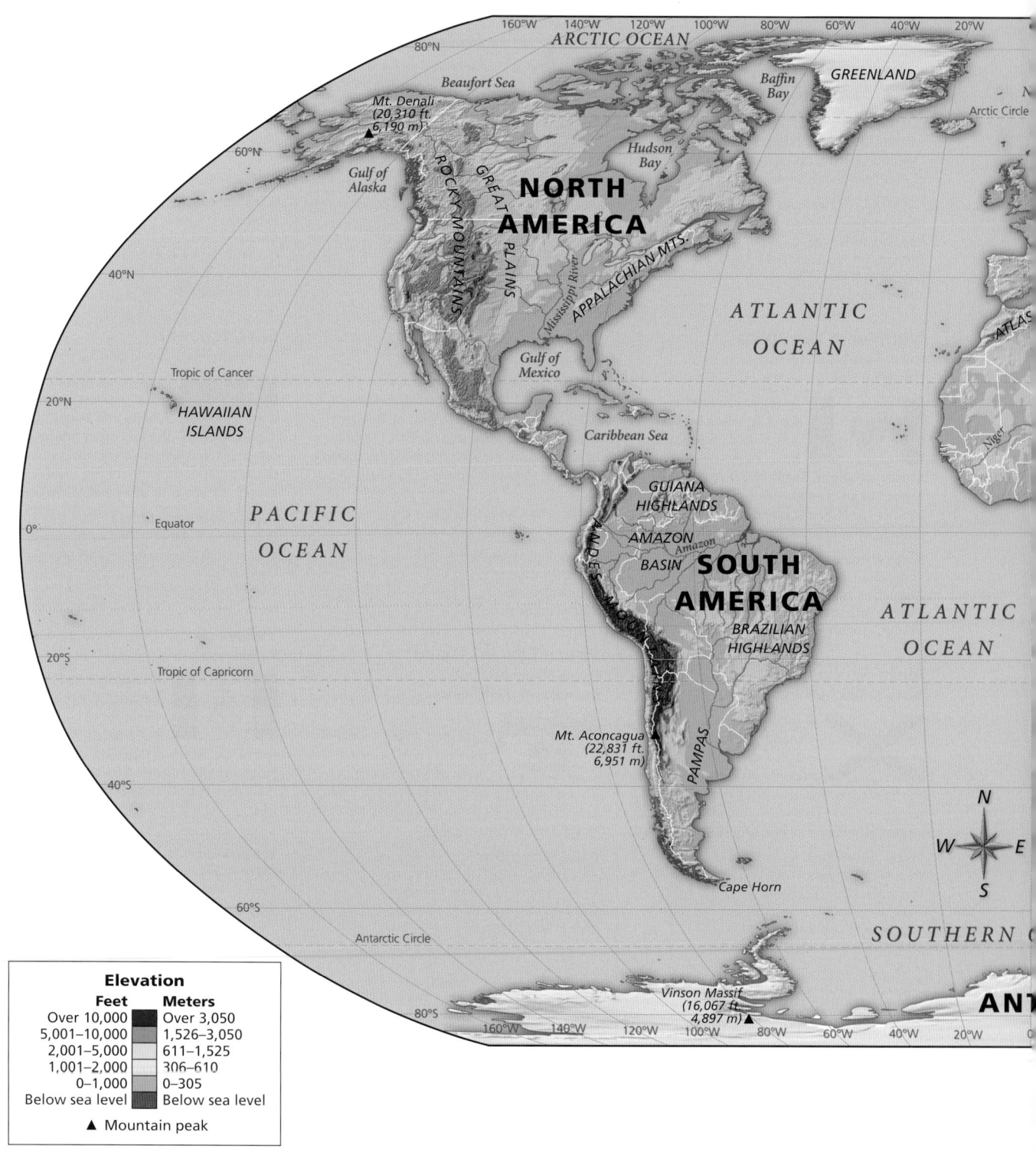

160°W 140°W 120°W 100°W 80°W 60°W 40°W 20°W

ARCTIC OCEAN

80°N

Beaufort Sea

Baffin Bay

GREENLAND

Arctic Circle

Mt. Denali
(20,310 ft.
6,190 m) ▲

60°N

*Gulf of
Alaska*

*Hudson
Bay*

ROCKY MOUNTAINS

GREAT PLAINS

**NORTH
AMERICA**

40°N

Mississippi River

APPALACHIAN MTS.

ATLANTIC

OCEAN

ATLAS

Tropic of Cancer

20°N

*HAWAIIAN
ISLANDS*

*Gulf of
Mexico*

Caribbean Sea

Niger

PACIFIC

Equator 0°

OCEAN

GUIANA
HIGHLANDS

AMAZON

Amazon

ANDES MOUNTAINS

BASIN

**SOUTH
AMERICA**

ATLANTIC

BRAZILIAN
HIGHLANDS

OCEAN

20°S

Tropic of Capricorn

Mt. Aconcagua ▲
(22,831 ft.
6,951 m)

PAMPAS

40°S

N

W   E

S

60°S

Cape Horn

Antarctic Circle

SOUTHERN O

Vinson Massif
(16,067 ft.
4,897 m) ▲

AN

80°S

160°W 140°W 120°W 100°W 80°W 60°W 40°W 20°W 0

Elevation

Feet	Meters
Over 10,000	Over 3,050
5,001–10,000	1,526–3,050
2,001–5,000	611–1,525
1,001–2,000	306–610
0–1,000	0–305
Below sea level	Below sea level

▲ Mountain peak

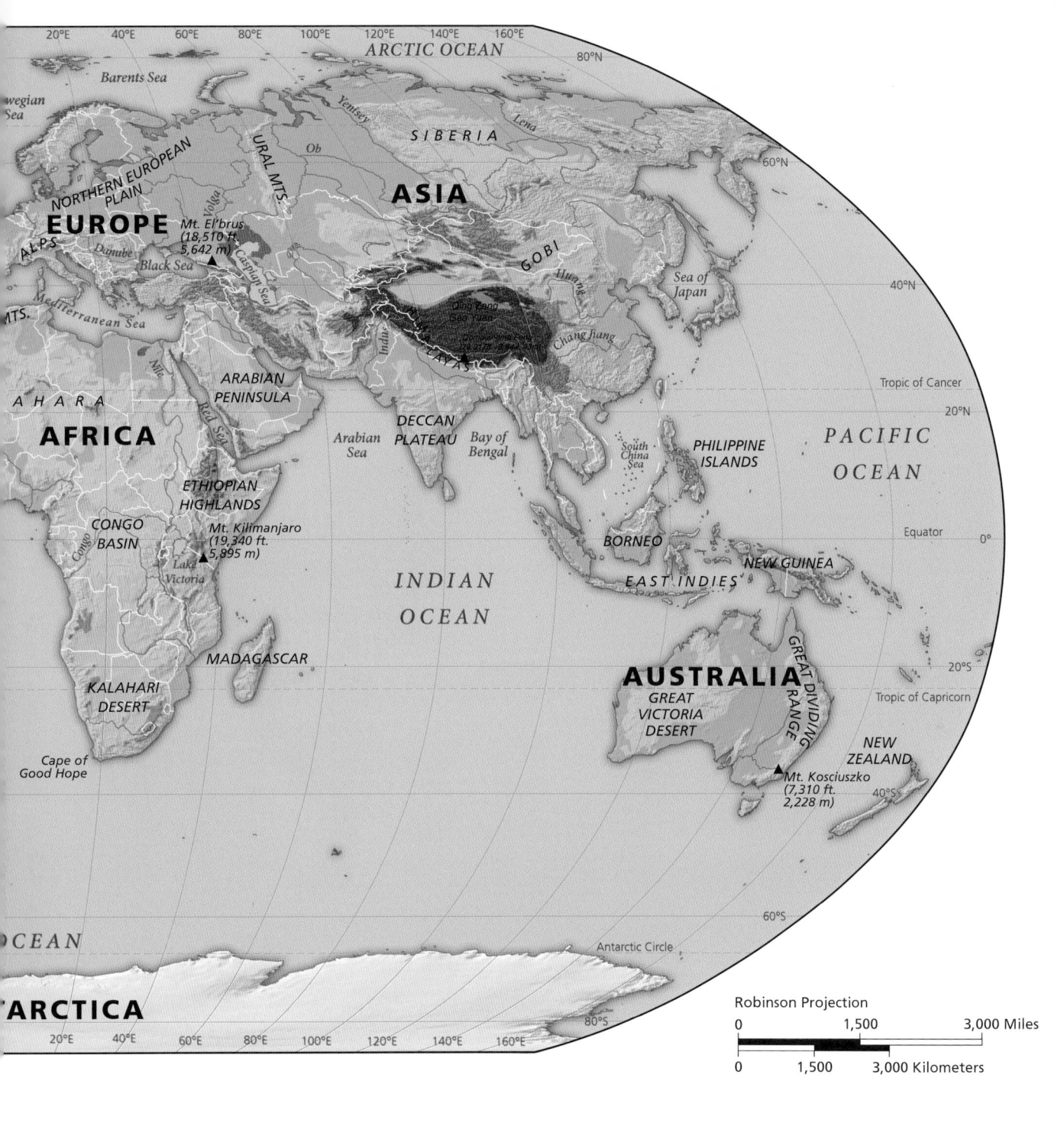

20°E 40°E 60°E 80°E 100°E 120°E 140°E 160°E 80°N

Barents Sea

wegian Sea

SIBERIA

Yenisey *Lena*

Ob

60°N

URAL MTS.

ASIA

NORTHERN EUROPEAN PLAIN

EUROPE

Volga

Mt. El'brus (18,510 ft. 5,642 m)

GOBI

ALPS

Danube

Black Sea

Caspian Sea

Huang

40°N

Sea of Japan

MTS.

Mediterranean Sea

Qing Zang Gao Yuan

Chang Jiang

Nile

Indus

ALAYAS

20°N

AHARA

ARABIAN PENINSULA

DECCAN PLATEAU

Tropic of Cancer

AFRICA

Red Sea

Arabian Sea

Bay of Bengal

South China Sea

PHILIPPINE ISLANDS

PACIFIC OCEAN

ETHIOPIAN HIGHLANDS

CONGO BASIN

Congo

Mt. Kilimanjaro (19,340 ft. 5,895 m)

Lake Victoria

BORNEO

EAST INDIES

NEW GUINEA

Equator 0°

INDIAN OCEAN

MADAGASCAR

20°S

KALAHARI DESERT

AUSTRALIA

GREAT VICTORIA DESERT

GREAT DIVIDING RANGE

Tropic of Capricorn

Cape of Good Hope

NEW ZEALAND

Mt. Kosciuszko (7,310 ft. 2,228 m)

40°S

60°S

OCEAN

Antarctic Circle

80°S

20°E 40°E 60°E 80°E 100°E 120°E 140°E 160°E

Robinson Projection

0 .... 1,500 .... 3,000 Miles

0 .... 1,500 .... 3,000 Kilometers

ARCTIC OCEAN

NORTH AMERICA

ATLANTIC OCEAN

PACIFIC OCEAN

Equator

SOUTH AMERICA

ATLANTIC OCEAN

EUROPE

ASIA

AFRICA

PACIFIC
OCEAN

INDIAN
OCEAN

AUSTRALIA

N
W E
S

SOUTHERN OCEAN

ANTARCTICA

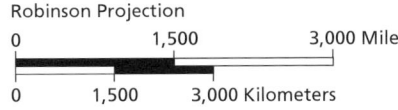

Robinson Projection

| 0 | 1,500 | 3,000 Miles |

| 0 | 1,500 | 3,000 Kilometers |

Map of the US Territories

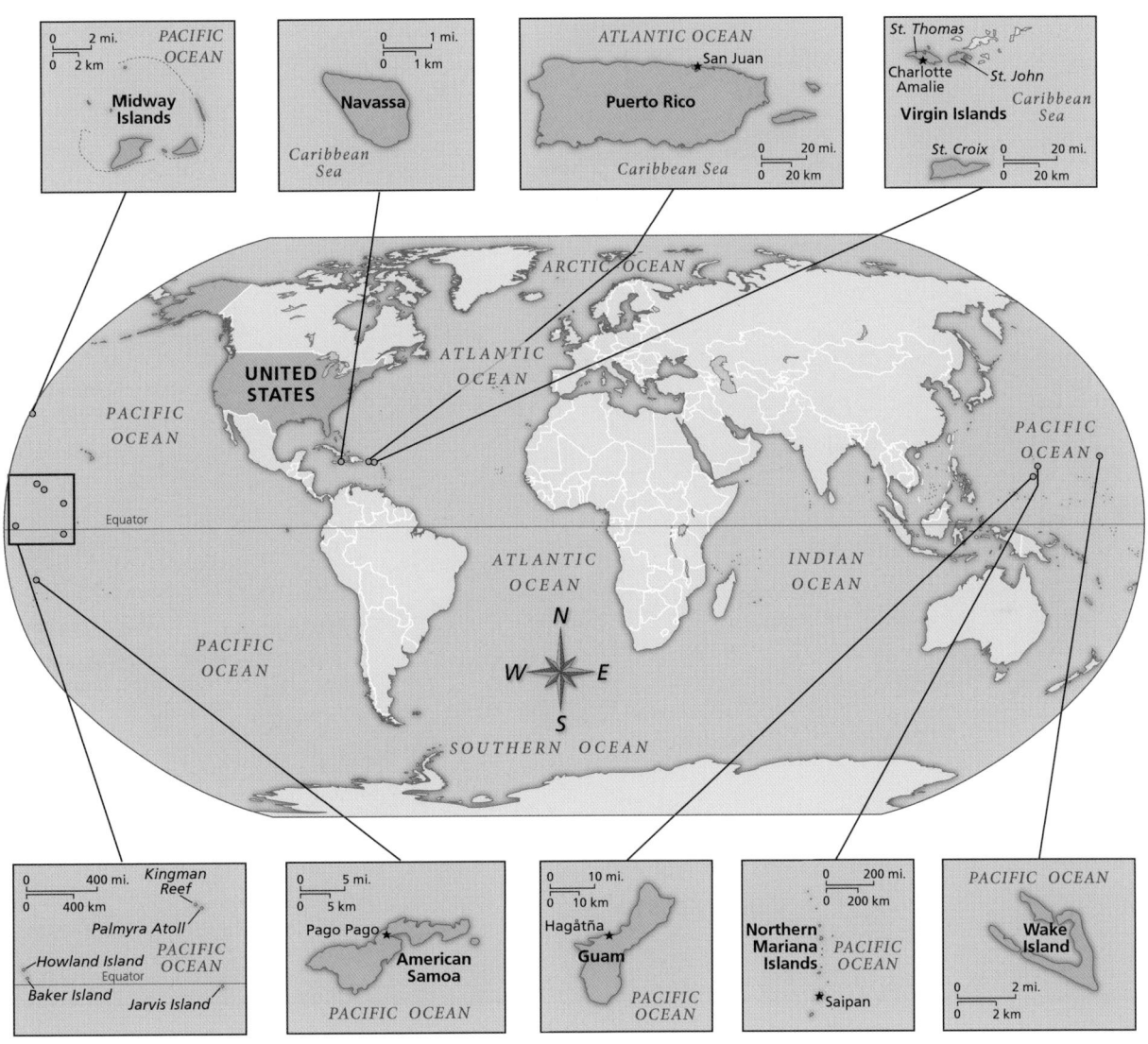

0 2 mi.
0 2 km
PACIFIC OCEAN
Midway Islands

0 1 mi.
0 1 km
Navassa
Caribbean Sea

ATLANTIC OCEAN
San Juan
Puerto Rico
0 20 mi.
0 20 km
Caribbean Sea

St. Thomas
Charlotte Amalie
St. John
Caribbean Sea
Virgin Islands
St. Croix
0 20 mi.
0 20 km

ARCTIC OCEAN
ATLANTIC OCEAN
UNITED STATES
PACIFIC OCEAN
Equator
ATLANTIC OCEAN
INDIAN OCEAN
PACIFIC OCEAN
N
W E
S
SOUTHERN OCEAN
PACIFIC OCEAN

0 400 mi.
0 400 km
Kingman Reef
Palmyra Atoll
Howland Island
Equator
Baker Island
Jarvis Island
PACIFIC OCEAN

0 5 mi.
0 5 km
Pago Pago
American Samoa
PACIFIC OCEAN

0 10 mi.
0 10 km
Hagåtña
Guam
PACIFIC OCEAN

0 200 mi.
0 200 km
Northern Mariana Islands
PACIFIC OCEAN
Saipan

PACIFIC OCEAN
Wake Island
0 2 mi.
0 2 km

ARCTIC
OCEAN

GREENLAND
(Kalaalit Nunaat)
(Denmark)

ICELAND

Baffin
Bay

Alaska
(US)

Beaufort
Sea

Davis Strait

Labrador
Sea

Iqaluit ★

Yukon

Whitehorse ★

*Great Bear
Lake*

Northwest
Territories

Nunavut

Newfoundland
& Labrador

Yellowknife
★

*Great Slave
Lake*

Hudson
Bay

St. John's
★

PACIFIC OCEAN

*Lake
Athabasca*

*Reindeer
Lake*

British
Columbia

Alberta

Saskatchewan

Manitoba

*Lake
Winnipeg*

Québec

Prince
Edward
Island

Charlottetown

Edmonton
★

Québec City
★

New
Brunswick

Nova
Scotia

Victoria
★

Ontario

Regina ★

*Lake
Manitoba*

Fredericton
★

Halifax
★

Winnipeg ★

ATLANTIC
OCEAN

Great Lakes

Ottawa ✪

N
W ✦ E
S

Toronto ★

UNITED STATES

0   250   500 Miles

0   250   500 Kilometers

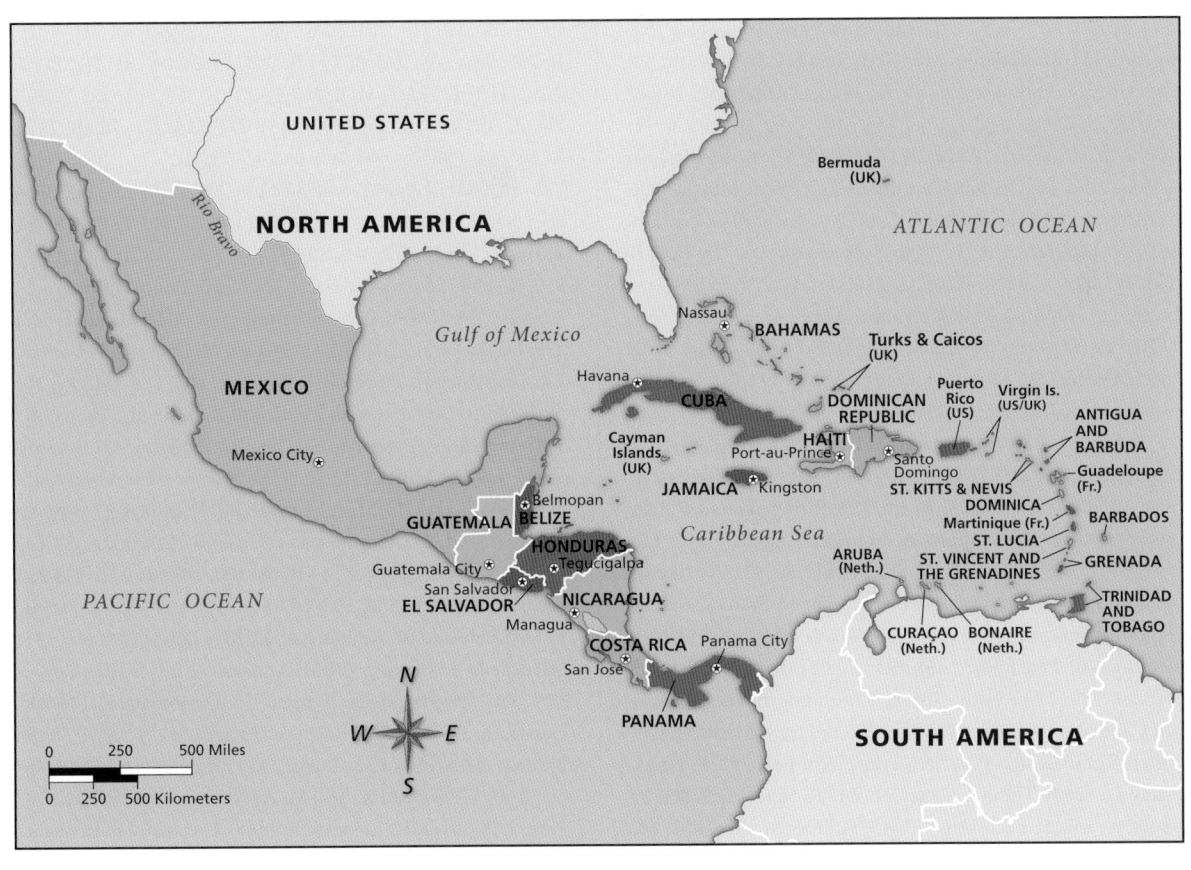

UNITED STATES

NORTH AMERICA

ATLANTIC OCEAN

Bermuda
(UK)

Rio Bravo

Gulf of Mexico

MEXICO

Mexico City

Nassau

BAHAMAS

Turks & Caicos
(UK)

Havana

CUBA

DOMINICAN
REPUBLIC

Puerto
Rico
(US)

Virgin Is.
(US/UK)

ANTIGUA
AND
BARBUDA

Cayman
Islands
(UK)

HAITI

Port-au-Prince

Santo
Domingo

Guadeloupe
(Fr.)

Belmopan

JAMAICA

Kingston

ST. KITTS & NEVIS

DOMINICA

GUATEMALA BELIZE

Caribbean Sea

Martinique (Fr.)

BARBADOS

HONDURAS

ST. LUCIA

Guatemala City

Tegucigalpa

ARUBA
(Neth.)

ST. VINCENT AND
THE GRENADINES

GRENADA

San Salvador

NICARAGUA

PACIFIC OCEAN

EL SALVADOR

TRINIDAD
AND
TOBAGO

Managua

CURAÇAO
(Neth.)

BONAIRE
(Neth.)

COSTA RICA

Panama City

San José

N

SOUTH AMERICA

W   E

PANAMA

S

| 0 | 250 | 500 Miles |

| 0 | 250 | 500 Kilometers |

162; Roxana Gonzalez, 166 B; Kevin Eaves, 167 T; Natalie Jean, 169; kurt_G, 172 B; Elizabeth O. Weller, 176; Ruth Black, 177; Kostyantyn Ivanyshen, 180; rdonar, 183; RCPPHOTO, 184; Janos Nemeth, 188; Tyler Olson, 189; Bojan Pavlukovic, 190; Kristian Sekulic, 193; David P. Smith, 194; Martin Maun, 195 B; Teekaygee, 197 B; Luther, 198; Atiketta Sangasaeng, 199 T; laviana, 199 B; Andreas Meyere, 203 BL; roadk, 207; Daboost, 208; Ocean Image, 212; Andrea Izzotti, 214; ifong, 217 B; fizkes, 218; aapsky, 222 T; Reddogs, 222 B; vchal, 224 T; Anyka, 224 B, ericlefrancais, 225 B; ungvar, 226 T; Coprid, 226 B; Photographee. eu, 227 T; Andrea Danti, 228 B; Four Oaks, 235 B; Richard Peterson, 235 B; Dusan Jankovic, 236; Angelina Dimitrova, 238 R; Hywit Dimyadi, 238 L; Nicholas Sutcliffe, 243; elnavegante, 245; Bob Denelzen, 249 T; Timur Kulgarin, 249 B; Serge75, 254; Rob Marmion, 256; Ivan Cholakov Gostock, 257; Marcin Perkowski, 259 B; AGCuesta, 270; friedhelm, 275 B; Le Do, 276, 655; IB Photography, 277 T; IrinaK, 279; Daniel Huebner, 282; stockcreations, 283 B; Nicholas Piccillo, 284 L; glo, 284 M; VajuAriel, 284 R; frantic00, 285; Prostock-studio, 286 L; Orhan Cam, 286 R; Irina Fischer, 287 B; Ihor Pasternak, 288; Abrilla, 289; cretolamna, 293 TM; Ronald Sumners, 294; Africa Studio, 297, 447 L, 521, 684, 711; Karin Hildenbrand Lau, 303; Madlen, 305 B; Edward Westmacott, 307 T; Petr Salinger, 307 B; S-F, 312 B; Dominic Dudley, 314 B; Aaron Kohr, 319 T; Awardimages, 323 B; Whiteandb, 327; Radu Bercan, 329; Cultura Motion, 332; Dmytro Kohut, 335; GUNDAM_Ai, 337 B; Suradech Prapairat, 340; Master1305, 345; Dionisvera, 349 B; irin-k, 351 T; Valentina Razumova, 352 B; Vadim Sadvoski, 354 B; lisegagne, 355 B; Sasa Prudkov, 363; doglikehorse, 367 B; forest71, 369 T; mark reinstein, 371 B; Lee Jorgensen, 385; dvs71, 399; mashe, 405 B; Lucky Team Studio, 406; Aumm graphixphoto, 408; Feng Yu, 410 T; Willyam Bradberry, 410 B; Brent Hofacker, 413; michelmond, 415; Doug Lemke, 419; napocka, 423; zhu difeng, 424 T; Ruth Black, 426; revers, 433 B; Dan Kosmayer, 436; Vereshchagin Dmitry, 437 B; sirtravelalot, 439; Kjuuurs, 441 B; Ljupco Smokovski, 442 B; Tom Wang, 446; urfin, 447 R; travellight, 451 B; Bjoern Wylezich, 454 T; Puffin's Pictures, 457; Silja R, 473; Denis Dryashkin, 474; whitehoune, 480; Dmytro Tkachuk, 491 B; yanikap, 510; Charles Taylor, 516; Alexei Logvinovich, 524; fulya atalay, 525; Aleksandar Karanov, 529 T; Petr Bonek, 529 T; SuperStockShots, 530; ESB Basic, 534; Vadym Zaitsev, 537 R; Sergey Ryzhov, 539 T; Designua, 540; Tim Mainiero, 545; CHAIUDON, 547; Volodymyr Tverdokhlib, 549 T; Jaogodka, 549 B; GaudiLab, 551 B; Flavia Molachetti, 552; Marc Bruxelle, 553 T; Karel Bartik, 556 T; Marco Ossino, 562; Lubava, 563; Jacques Durocher, 566; Iakov Filimonov, 575; Nasimi Babaev, 576 T; Ieven Panasiyk, 589; Thomas Koch, 598 B; Benoit Daoust, 604; Kostenyukova Nataliya, 607 TR; kyslynskahal, 607 BL; Vera Larina, 620; Marcos Mesa Sam Wordley, 648; UfaBizPhoto, 653; D.Pimborough, 657; Michael Negrao, 660 T; Andrey_Popov, 661; Protasov AN, 665; Mikhail Leonov, 669; Timolina, 672 B; Sky Antonio, 681; Matej Kastelic, 686; NikoNomad, 690; Mccallk69, 695; Prabhjit S. Kalsi, 699; By courtyard pix, 701 R; meunierd, 70; astudio, 706; Josef Hanus, 707; Oleinik Iuliia, 709; MsMaria, 716; Pam Walker, 722; tuthelens, 735 T; Fotografiecor.nl, 737; Digital Storm, 747; RonTech3000, 758; Cris Foto, 764; Rostislav_Sedlacek, 768 T; Mariusz Szczygiel, 771 T; frantic00, 772; GagliardImages, 777; furtseff, 780 T; Ranta Images, 783; Mega Pixel, 786 T; ChiccoDodiFC, 820 T; Richard Seeley, 828; Ondrej Prosicky, 834; rybart, 871 MBL. **Superstock:** De Agostini, 38 B; Food Collection, 46, BL; Busse Yankushev/Mauritius, 124 T; Masterton/age fotostock, 150; Blend Images, 156; Corbis, 202 T, 225 T; Photononstop, 216, 678; Blend Images, 220; FogStock LLC, 228 T; age fotostock, 252; Big Cheese Photo, 253 B, 649; Nick Garbutt, 342; Fotosearch, 352 T, 357; Stockbroker, 364 T; Philippe Michel/age fotostock, 616; Radius, 621, 715; imagebroker.net, 654; Roderick Chen, 713; Fancy Collection, 720, 725; Jiang Jin, 729. **US Navy:** Jay C. Pugh, 197 T.

Illustration Credits

Digital Wisdom: 862-869. ©**Dorling Kindersley Ltd:** 15; 24; 31 B; 50 T; 51; 59; 67; 92 B; 95; 116; 124 B; 131; 138; 170; 201; 203 ML, MR, BR; 213; 259 T; 280; 319 B; 337 T; 339; 393; 411; 431; 471; 479 B; 493 T; 498; 499; 539 B; 564; 585; 610; 619; 630; 633; 635; 672 T; 671; 672 T; 685; 687 B; 691 T; 723; 766 T; 810; 818 B; 832. **Mapping Specialists:** 246; 490; 546 MR; 577 TL; 585 TL; 870–877.

Cover Credits

Front: Getty Images: bracken BL. **Shutterstock:** ProstoSvet TL; Steven R Smith TC; AmyLv BC; Sascha Burkard TR and spine; Eric Isselee CR; Yellow Cat BR.
Back: Superstock: Photononstop 2149432 BL; **Shutterstock:** Eric Isselee BR

Thesaurus content adapted from the *Scholastic Children's Thesaurus* by Joseph K. Bollard. Copyright © 1998, 2006 by Scholastic Inc.

Grammar, Punctuation, and Idioms Guides by Marvin Terban.